Co

SC E®

Collins

SCRABBLE®

first edition 2005

HarperCollins Publishers
Westerhill Road, Bishopbriggs, Glasgow G64 2QT
Great Britain

www.collins.co.uk

ISBN 0-00-774870-1

A catalogue record for this book is available from the British Library

This book is set in CollinsFedra, a typeface specially created for Collins dictionaries by Peter Bil'ak.

Printed and bound in Germany by Bercker

Contributors

Editors
Sandra Anderson
Kay Cullen
Penny Hands
Andrew Holmes
Mike Munro

Project Manager
Justin Crozier

For the Publisher
Morven Dooner
Elaine Higgleton

Computing Support
Thomas Callan

Collins Corpus Programmer
Nigel Rochford

Typesetting
Wordcraft

Contents

Introduction

Collins Essential Scrabble Dictionary – Every Word Counts

The **Collins Essential Scrabble Dictionary** is the ideal reference book for people who play Scrabble for enjoyment, in the social or family setting. This dictionary doesn't include every word eligible for Scrabble, but does contain the most commonly used of the 260,000 words in Collins Scrabble Words 2005, the definitive Scrabble wordlist. The concise definitions in the **Essential Scrabble Dictionary** allow players to check the meaning of words, as well as using the book for settling arguments during games.

The **Collins Essential Scrabble Dictionary** contains only words of up to 15 letters in length, as longer words cannot be used in Scrabble. Because the dictionary is designed for family play, it does not include offensive terms. Such words are included in **Collins Scrabble Words 2005**, the complete wordlist for tournaments and club competitions.

Word Order

In the **Collins Essential Scrabble Dictionary**, words are listed in alphabetical order, rather than being grouped at the base form as in a conventional dictionary. Where words are inflections of a base form, they are listed alphabetically as individual entries for easy reference.

Special Scrabble Words

To help family players learn and use some of the rarer and higher-scoring words in the game, the **Collins Essential Scrabble Dictionary** includes a number of special panel entries. These list unusual words which are particularly useful in the game. There are also panel entries at the start of every letter section, which offer advice on useful words beginning with that letter.

Play Better Scrabble

A special section at the start of this book contains a wealth of hints and tips for improving your game, with lists of some of the most useful words for top scores.

The **Collins Essential Scrabble Dictionary** is designed to be useful to new players and Scrabble veterans alike – we hope you enjoy using it!

Play Better Scrabble

Contents

Introduction

While most people in the UK are familiar with Scrabble – with more than half of British homes containing a Scrabble set – not everyone is aware of just how complex and demanding the game can be. Even many regular players are content simply to put together the longest word they can see on their rack in each round, without thought of tactics or strategy.

There is much more to Scrabble than this, however. The game is as flexible and multi-faceted as the English language itself. A carefully deployed short word – perhaps of only two or three letters – can earn a higher score than a much longer word played without due tactical concern. As an example, there's little point in playing a six-letter word that allows your opponent to reach a triple-word square in the next round. Far better, in that situation, to play a short word and deny your opponent the opportunity – and thus preserving the premium square for a word of your own in a future round.

Awareness of your position on the board is one key factor in successful Scrabble; another is an understanding of the different ways in which words can be formed during play. The next section, Forming Words, explains techniques such as hooking and parallel play in detail, to help you improve your awareness of opportunities for high scores.

On pages 10–23, there is a complete list of all of the two-letter and three-letter words valid in the game – some of the most useful words for Scrabble. Definitions are provided for all of the two-letter words, to aid memorization of the more unusual terms.

Pages 24–34 contain sections on each of the 'power tiles' (J, Q, X, and Z), with lists of useful words containing these letters, and a special section on words that contain Q without U.

Please note that the diagrams in this section include words that are not in the *Collins Essential Scrabble Dictionary*. All of these words, however, are included in *Collins Scrabble Words* 2005, the complete wordlist for competitive players, and in the *Collins Official Scrabble Dictionary*.

Forming Words

The key to successful Scrabble is constant awareness of the various opportunities for forming words on the board. At the end of a game, the Scrabble board looks like a completed crossword – but always remember that it looks like an American crossword, with blocks of letters in which many short words are contained, rather than a British crossword where words intersect each other without overlap. Indeed, Scrabble was invented by a crossword enthusiast, Alfred Butts; as Mr Butts was American, the US type of crossword was the model for the game.

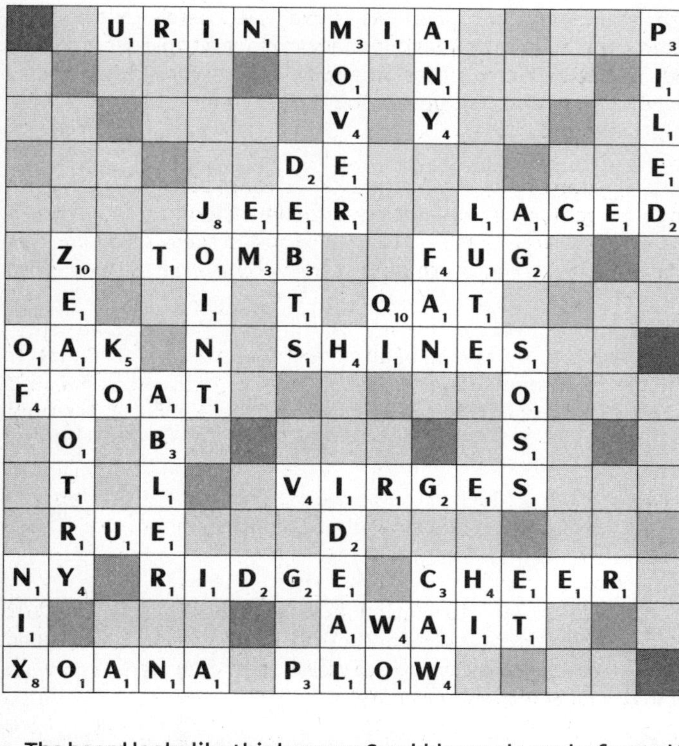

The board looks like this because Scrabble words can be formed in several ways other than by simply playing the new word so that it intersects a word already on the board through a common letter, or adding letters to an existing word. Scrabble veterans know this already, of course; if you are new to the game, however, you might want to read the rest of this chapter before moving onto the lists themselves.

When words are formed in ways other than simple intersection or expansion, more than one new word will be created in the process, giving a higher score. The two main ways of doing this are 'hooking' and 'tagging'.

Hooking

Hooking is a Scrabble term for the act of 'hanging' one word on another – the word already on the board acts as a 'hook' on which the other word can be hung – changing the first word in the process. When you form a word by hooking, you add a letter to the beginning or end of a word already on the board in the process, transforming it into a longer word as you do so, as in the following example:

In this situation, you get the points for COMETH (13) as well as for HETAIRA. COMET is thus an 'end-hook', allowing any word with an H or S to be 'hung' on it. S is a particularly useful letter when hooking, as most nouns have a plural formed by adding an S to the end of the singular form.

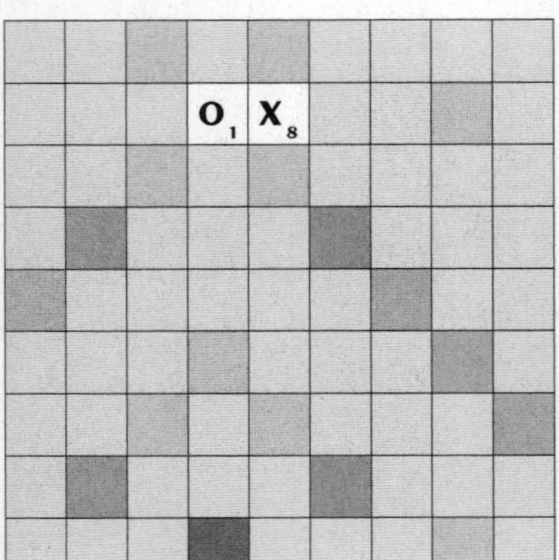

Here you get the 13 points for FOX as well as those for FICKLE. So you can see that hooking is generally a much more profitable method of word-formation than simply playing a word through, or adjacent to, one that is already on the board. In particular, hooking allows you to benefit from high-scoring 'power tiles' that your opponent has played, as with the X in FOX in the above example.

Obviously, only certain words can act as hooks. Those that cannot form other words by having a letter added to their front or back are known as *blockers*, as they prevent other players from adding words by hooking.

Parallel Play

Playing a word parallel to one already on the board, so that one or more tiles are in contact, is known as parallel play. Parallel play, or tagging, is more difficult than hooking because you need to form one additional word for each tile in contact with the word already on the board. In most circumstances, these will be two-letter words, which is why these short words are so vital to the game. The more two-letter words you know, the greater your opportunities for fitting words onto the board through tagging – and of running up some impressive scores!

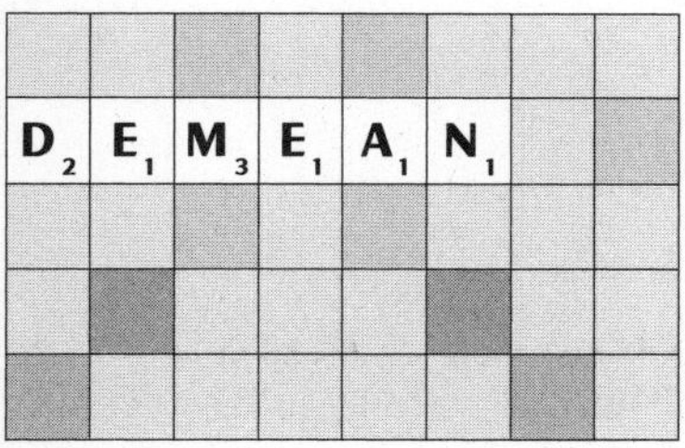

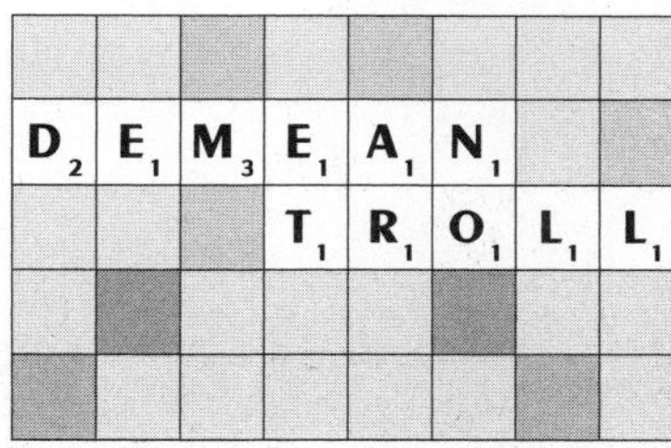

In the example above, playing TROLL thus forms ET, AR and NO (all valid two-letter words), adding the scores for these three words to the points you make from TROLL.

In theory, you could form eight words at once by tagging (though this is unlikely to happen very often!). Consider the following situation:

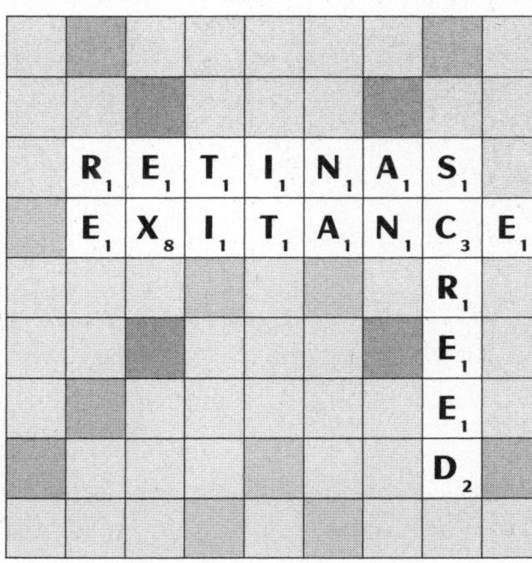

If you had the letters AEINRST, you could play RETINAS as shown above, earning the points for RETINAS, the 50-point bonus for using all your tiles, plus the points for RE, EX, TI, IT, NA and SCREED, giving you a very decent score indeed!

Short words

Two-letter words are essential for tagging: generally, you need one two-letter word for every 'point of contact'. Three-letter words are also very useful in Scrabble, as a crowded board will often prevent you from playing longer words late in the game. Moreover, some very respectable scores can be generated by tagging with three-letter words – creating more two-letter words in the process. See pages 10–23 for a complete list of valid two-letter words.

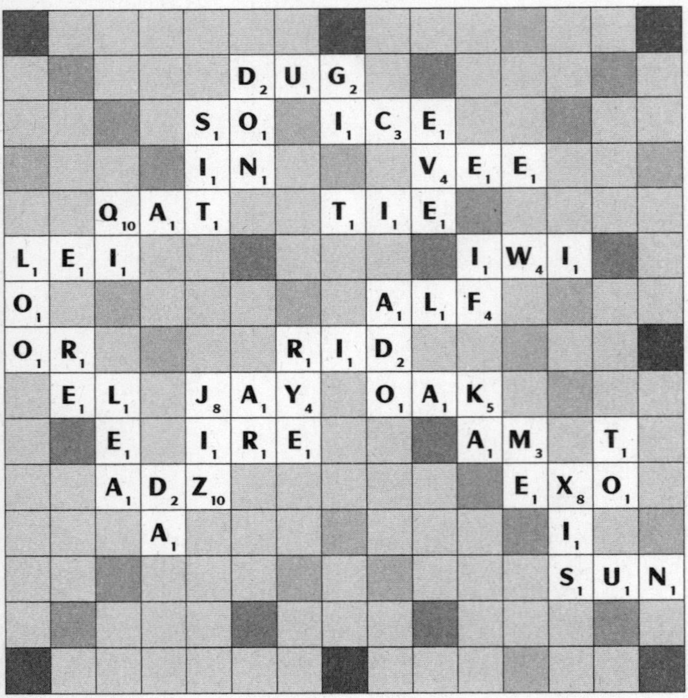

While many of these words will be familiar, it's a good idea to equip yourself with some of the less common ones, as knowing whether a given combination of two or three letters is a valid word can be vital when you are trying to get a high-scoring set of tiles onto the board through tagging or hooking.

Power tiles

It's important to use the 'power tiles' – J, Q, X and Z – wisely when they land on your rack. Pages 24–34 give lists of words that use these letters. Learning some of these words will help you to employ the power tiles judiciously when they appear on your rack. Of especial interest here are words that use Q but not U, as these allow you to avoid the problem of needing to find a U to play your high-scoring Q tile.

In the average two-player Scrabble game, you are likely to have two of the power tiles on your rack at some point during play. It's a very good idea, therefore, to give some thought to how best to use these tiles, as they are easily wasted on fairly mediocre plays. Learning 'power tile' words will help you to manoeuvre your power tiles onto premium squares for high scores.

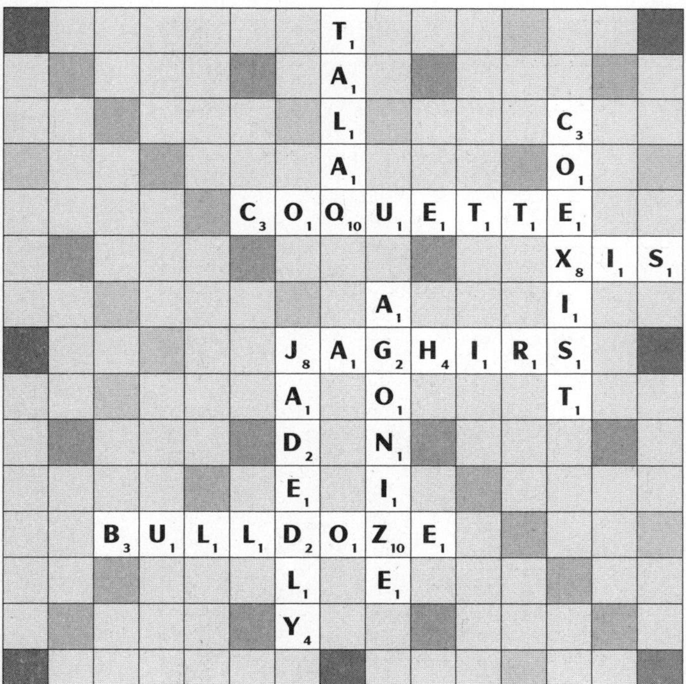

Bonus words

Always remember that no matter how many words you form, you are likely to achieve a higher score by playing all seven of your letters in one go, as this earns you a 50-point bonus. It takes a lot of power tiles or bonus squares to achieve 50 points, so playing a bonus word – or 'bingo', as they are known in the US – is the most reliable method of getting an impressive score.

A bonus play generally involves a word of seven or eight letters – either by tagging or hooking a complete seven-letter word onto a word already on the board, or by forming an eight-letter word intersecting an existing word by playing all seven tiles.

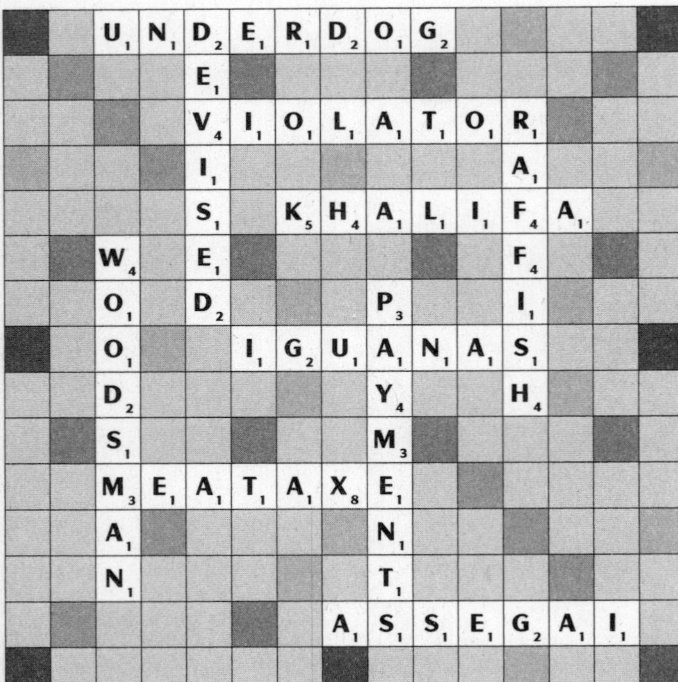

There are, of course, thousands of potential bonus words, but the list on the following page provides you with 69 of the most useful. The six letters A, E, I, N, R, and T are some of the most likely to appear on your rack; the list opposite shows the seven-letter words that can be formed by grouping these six letters with other letters of the alphabet. Those words grouped together are anagrams of each other.

RETINA

ATEBRIN

CANTIER
CERATIN
CERTAIN
CREATIN
CRINATE
NACRITE

ANTIRED
DETRAIN
TRAINED

ARENTIE
RETINAE
TRAINEE

FAINTER
FENITAR

GRANITE
GRATINE
INGRATE
TANGIER
TEARING

HAIRNET
INEARTH
THERIAN

INTERTIA

JANTIER
NARTJIE

KERATIN

ENTRAIL
LATRINE
RATLINE
RELIANT
RETINAL
TRENAIL

MERANTI
MINARET
RAIMENT

ENTRAIN
TRANNIE

OTARINE

PAINTER
PERTAIN
REPAINT

RETRAIN
TERRAIN
TRAINER

ANESTRI
ANTSIER
NASTIER
RATINES
RESIANT
RETAINS
RETINAS
RETSINA
STAINER
STARNIE
STEARIN

INTREAT
ITERANT
NATTIER
NITRATE
TARTINE
TERTIAN

RUINATE
TAURINE
URANITE
URINATE

TAWNIER
TINWARE

Short Words

Short words are vital for winning Scrabble, as they allow you to play several words at a time through parallel play. This section provides a complete list of all two- and three-letter words valid in Scrabble, with definitions for all of the two-letter words.

Two-letter words

This list contains every permissible two-letter words, along with its definition. Two-letter words are the building blocks of parallel play, and are thus some of the most useful words in the entire game. While a single two-letter word will only earn you between two and eleven points, when you play a longer word parallel to a word already on the board, you can form several two-letter words in the process, thus earning a mammoth score. You do, of course, need to be aware of what your two-letter options are to achieve this! Note that many three-letter words are simply the plural forms of two-letter nouns.

AA *determiner*	Scots variant of *all*. **AA** scores 2 points.
AB *noun* **ABS**	an abdominal muscle. **AB** scores 4 points.
AD *noun* **ADS**	short form of *advertisement*. **AD** scores 3 points.
AE *determiner*	Scots word meaning *one* or *a single*. **AE** scores 2 points.
AG *adjective*	relating to agriculture. **AG** scores 3 points.
AH *interjection*	an expression of pleasure, pain or sympathy. **AH** scores 5 points.
AI *noun* **AIS**	the three-toed sloth. **AI** scores 2 points.
AL *conjunction*	an obsolete word for *if* or *although*. **AL** scores 2 points.
AM *verb*	part of the verb *to be*. **AM** scores 4 points.
AN *determiner*	a form of *a* used before an initial vowel sound. **AN** scores 2 points.
AR *noun* **ARS**	the letter R. **AR** scores 2 points.
AS *conjunction*	while. **AS** scores 2 points.
AT *preposition*	used to indicate location or position. **AT** scores 2 points.

AW *interjection* an expression of disapproval, commiseration, or appeal. **AW** scores 5 points.

AX *noun* **AXES** a US spelling of *axe*. **AX** scores 9 points.

AY *adverb* an archaic word for *ever* or *always*. **AY** scores 5 points.

BA *noun* **BAS** in Egyptian myth, the soul represented as a bird with a human head. **BA** scores 4 points.

BE *verb* to exist. **BE** scores 4 points.

BI *adjective* short for *bisexual*. **BI** scores 4 points.

BO *interjection* an exclamation uttered to startle someone. **BO** scores 4 points.

BY *preposition* used to indicate the agent after a passive verb. **BY** scores 7 points.

CH *pronoun* an obsolete dialect form of *I*. **CH** scores 7 points.

DA *noun* **DAS** a Burmese knife. **DA** scores 3 points.

DE *preposition* of or from. **DE** scores 3 points.

DEUS *noun* **DI** a god. **DI** scores 3 points.

DO *verb* to perform or complete something. **DO** scores 3 points.

EA *noun* **EAS** a dialect word for *river*. **EA** scores 2 points.

ED *noun* **EDS** a short form of *education*. **ED** scores 3 points.

EE *noun* **EEN** a Scots word for *eye*. **EE** scores 2 points.

EF *noun* **EFS** the letter F. **EF** scores 5 points.

EH *interjection* an exclamation of questioning surprise. **EH** scores 5 points.

EL *noun* **ELS** a short form of *elevated railway*. **EL** scores 2 points.

EM *noun* **EMS** a unit of measurement in printing. **EM** scores 4 points.

EN *noun* **ENS** a unit of measurement in printing. **EN** scores 2 points.

ER *interjection*	a sound made when hesitating in speech. **ER** scores 2 points.
ES *noun* **ESES**	the letter S. **ES** scores 2 points.
ET *verb*	a dialect form of the past and past participle of *eat*. **ET** scores 2 points.
EX *noun* **EXES**	a person's former wife, husband etc. **EX** scores 9 points.
FA *noun* **FAS**	a variant spelling of *fah*. **FA** scores 5 points.
FY *interjection*	a variant spelling of *fie*. **FY** scores 8 points.
GI *noun* **GIS**	a suit worn by martial artist. **GI** scores 3 points.
GO *verb*	to move or proceed. **GO** scores 3 points.
GU *noun* **GUS**	a stringed musical instrument formerly used in Shetland. **GU** scores 3 points.
HA *interjection*	an exclamation expressing derision, triumph, surprise,etc. **HA** scores 5 points.
HE *pronoun*	refers to a male person or animal. **HE** scores 5 points.
HI *sentence substitute*	an informal word for *hello*. **HI** scores 5 points.
HM *interjection*	expressing thoughtful consideration. **HM** scores 5 points.
HO *interjection*	an exclamation used to attract attention. **HO** scores 5 points.
ID *noun* **IDS**	the mass of primitive instincts and energies in the unconscious mind. **ID** scores 3 points.
IF *conjunction*	in case that, or on condition that. **IF** scores 5 points.
IN *preposition*	inside, within. **IN** scores 2 points.
IO *interjection*	a cry of joy or grief. **IO** scores 2 points.
IS *verb*	part of the verb *to be*. **IS** scores 2 points.

IT *pronoun* refers to a nonhuman, animal, plant, or inanimate thing. **IT** scores 2 points.

JA *interjection* South African word for *yes*. **JA** scores 9 points.

JO *noun* **JOES** a Scots word for *sweetheart*. **JO** scores 9 points.

KA *noun* **KAS** an attendant spirit in ancient Egypt. **KA** scores 6 points.

KO *noun* **KOS** a Maori digging-stick. **KO** scores 6 points.

KY *noun* a Scots word for *cows*. **KY** scores 9 points.

LA *noun* **LAS** a variant spelling of *lah*. **LA** scores 2 points.

LI *noun* **LIS** a Chinese unit of length. **LI** scores 2 points.

LO *interjection* look! **LO** scores 2 points.

MA *noun* **MAS** an informal word for *mother*. **MA** scores 4 points.

ME *pronoun* refers to the speaker or writer. **ME** scores 4 points.

MI *noun* **MIS** the third degree of a major scale in music. **MI** scores 4 points.

MM *interjection* an expression of satisfaction. **MM** scores 6 points.

MO *noun* **MOS** a short form of *moment*. **MO** scores 4 points.

MU *noun* **MUS** the 12th letter in the Greek alphabet. **MU** scores 4 points.

MY *determiner* of or belonging to the writer or speaker. **MY** scores 7 points.

NA *interjection* a Scots word for *no* or *not*. **NA** scores 2 points.

NE *adverb* an obsolete word meaning *not*. **NE** scores 2 points.

NO *sentence substitute* used to express denial, disagreement, refusal, disapproval, disbelief, or acknowledgement of negative statements. **NO** scores 2 points.

NU *noun* **NUS** the 13th letter in the Greek alphabet. **NU** scores 2 points.

NY *adjective, adverb* an obsolete variant of *night*. **NY** scores 5 points.

OB *noun* **OBS** an objection. **OB** scores 4 points.

OD *noun* **ODS** a hypothetical force formerly thought to be responsible for many natural phenomena. **OD** scores 3 points.

OE *noun* **OES** a Scots word for *grandchild*. **OE** scores 2 points.

OF *preposition* belonging to or associated with. **OF** scores 5 points.

OH *interjection* an exclamation expressive of surprise, pain, pleasure, etc. **OH** scores 5 points.

OI *interjection* an exclamation to attract attention. **OI** scores 2 points.

OM *interjection* a word chanted as part of a mantra. **OM** scores 4 points.

ON *preposition* in contact with the surface of. **ON** scores 2 points.

OO *noun* **OOS** a Scots word for *wool*. **OO** scores two points.

OP *noun* **OPS** a short form of *operation*. **OP** scores 4 points.

OR *conjunction* used to join alternatives. **OR** scores 2 points.

OS *noun* **OSSA** the technical name for *bone*. **OS** scores 2 points.

OU *noun* **OUS** South African slang for *man*. **OU** scores 2 points.

OW *interjection* an exclamation of pain. **OW** scores 5 points.

OX *noun* **OXEN** an adult castrated male of any species of cattle. **OX** scores 9 points.

OY *noun* **OYS** a Scots word for *grandchild*. **OY** scores 5 points.

PA *noun* **PAS** an informal word for *father*. **PA** scores 4 points.

PE *noun* **PES** the 17th letter in the Hebrew alphabet. **PE** scores 4 points.

PH *noun* **PHS** a measure of acidity or alkalinity. **PH** scores 7 points.

PI *noun* **PIS** the 16th letter in the Greek alphabet. **PI** scores 4 points.

PO *noun* **POS** an informal word for *chamberpot*. **PO** scores 4 points.

QI *noun* **QIS** energy believed to circulate in the body. **QI** scores 11 points.

RE *noun* **RES** a variant spelling of *ray*, the second degree of any major scale. **RE** scores 2 points.

SH *interjection* an exclamation to request silence or quiet. **SH** scores 5 points.

SI *noun* **SIS** a variant of *te*. **SI** scores 2 points.

SO *adverb* to such an extent. **SO** scores 2 points.

ST *interjection* an exclamation to request silence or quiet. **ST** scores 2 points.

TA *interjection* thank you. **TA** scores 2 points.

TE *noun* **TES** the syllable used for the seventh note or subtonic of any scale. **TE** scores 2 points.

TI *noun* **TIS** a variant spelling of *te*. **TI** scores 2 points.

TO *preposition* used to indicate the destination of the subject or object of an action. **TO** scores 2 points.

UG *verb* to cause loathing in. **UG** scores 3 points.

UH *interjection* an expression of uncertainty. **UH** scores 5 points.

UM *interjection* a sound made when hesitating in speech. **UM** scores 4 points.

UN *pronoun* a dialect variant of *one*. **UN** scores 2 points.

UP *preposition* indicating movement from a lower to a higher position. **UP** scores 4 points.

UR *interjection* a sound made when hesitating in speech. **UR** scores 2 points.

US *pronoun* refers to the speaker or writer and another person or other people. **US** scores 2 points.

UT *noun* **UTS** the first note of a hexachord in medieval music. **UT** scores 2 points.

WE *pronoun* refers to the speaker or writer and another person or other people. **WE** scores 5 points.

WO *noun* **WOS** an archaic spelling of *woe*. **WO** scores 5 points.

XI *noun* **XIS** the 14th letter of the Greek alphabet. **XI** scores 9 points.

XU *noun* **XUS** a monetary unit ofVietnam. **XU** scores 9 points.

YA *adverb* an obsolete variant of *yea*. **YA** scores 5 points.

YE *pronoun* refers to more than one person including the person addressed but not including the speaker. **YE** scores 5 points.

YO *sentence substitute* an expression used as a greeting. **YO** scores 5 points.

YU *noun* **YUS** Chinese jade. **YU** scores 5 points.

ZO *noun* **ZOS** one of a Tibetan breed of cattle, developed by crossing the yak with common cattle. **ZO** scores 11 points.

Three-letter words

There are many more three-letter words than two-letter words in the English language, and thus in Scrabble. While two-letter words are absolutely vital for parallel play, three-letter words are not quite as crucial in the game. They are extremely useful, however, as they can often be fitted in when the board is cramped with tiles. This can be especially handy when you are trying to reach a premium square that is still unused in the late stages of the game.

Three-letter words are also useful in parallel play, as you only need to spot three consecutive opportunities for two-letter words in order to form four words at a single stroke. As an example, you might be able to play **BAT** so that **BE**, **AX**, and **TO** are formed at the same time, giving you an impressive total score of 20 aside from any premium squares that might be involved.

The next seven pages contain every three-letter word that can be played in Scrabble. For reasons of space, definitions are not provided here, although many of these words are contained in the main dictionary text. This section allows you to quickly check whether any given three-letter word is valid for play, and so build up a formidable arsenal of short words.

AAH
AAL
AAS
ABA
ABB
ABO
ABS
ABY
ACE
ACH
ACT
ADD
ADO
ADS
ADZ
AFF
AFT
AGA
AGE
AGO
AGS
AHA
AHI
AHS
AIA
AID
AIL
AIM
AIN
AIR
AIS
AIT
AKA
AKE
ALA
ALB
ALE
ALF
ALL
ALP
ALS
ALT
AMA
AMI
AMP
AMU
ANA
AND
ANE
ANI
ANN
ANT
ANY
APE
APO
APP
APT
ARB
ARC
ARD
ARE
ARF
ARK
ARM
ARS
ART
ARY
ASH
ASK
ASP
ASS
ATE
ATT
AUA
AUE
AUF
AUK
AVA
AVE
AVO
AWA
AWE
AWL
AWN
AXE
AYE
AYS
AYU
AZO
BAA
BAC
BAD
BAG
BAH
BAL
BAM
BAN
BAP
BAR
BAS
BAT
BAY
BED
BEE
BEG
BEL
BEN
BET
BEY
BEZ
BIB
BID
BIG
BIN
BIO
BIS
BIT
BIZ
BOA
BOB
BOD
BOG
BOH
BOK
BON
BOO
BOP
BOR
BOS
BOT
BOW
BOX
BOY
BRA
BRO
BRR
BUB
BUD
BUG
BUM
BUN
BUR
BUS
BUT
BUY
BYE
BYS
CAA
CAB
CAD
CAG
CAM
CAN
CAP
CAR
CAT
CAW
CAY
CAZ
CEE
CEL
CEP
CHA
CHE
CHI
CID
CIG
CIS
CIT
CLY
COB
COD
COG
COL
CON
COO
COP
COR
COS
COT
COW
COX
COY
COZ

CRU
CRY
CUB
CUD
CUE
CUM
CUP
CUR
CUT
CUZ
CWM
DAB
DAD
DAE
DAG
DAH
DAK
DAL
DAM
DAN
DAP
DAS
DAW
DAY
DEB
DEE
DEF
DEG
DEI
DEL
DEN
DEV
DEW
DEX
DEY
DIB
DID
DIE
DIG
DIM
DIN
DIP
DIS
DIT
DIV
DOB
DOC
DOD
DOE
DOG
DOH
DOL
DOM
DON
DOO
DOP
DOR
DOS
DOT
DOW
DOY
DRY
DSO
DUB
DUD
DUE
DUG
DUH
DUI
DUN
DUO
DUP
DUX
DYE
DZO
EAN
EAR
EAS
EAT
EAU
EBB
ECH
ECO
ECU
EDH
EDS
EEK
EEL
EEN
EFF
EFS
EFT
EGG
EGO
EHS
EIK
EKE
ELD
ELF
ELK
ELL
ELM
ELS
ELT
EME
EMF
EMS
EMU
END
ENE
ENG
ENS
EON
ERA
ERE
ERF
ERG
ERK
ERN
ERR
ERS
ESS
EST
ETA
ETH
EUK
EVE
EVO
EWE
EWK
EWT
EXO
EYE
FAA
FAB
FAD
FAE
FAG
FAH
FAN
FAP
FAR
FAS
FAT
FAW
FAX
FAY
FED
FEE
FEG
FEH
FEM
FEN
FER
FET
FEU
FEW
FEY
FEZ
FIB
FID
FIE
FIG
FIL
FIN
FIR
FIT
FIX
FIZ
FLU
FLY
FOB
FOE
FOG
FOH
FON
FOP
FOR
FOU
FOX
FOY
FRA
FRO
FRY

FUB
FUD
FUG
FUM
FUN
FUR
GAB
GAD
GAE
GAG
GAL
GAM
GAN
GAP
GAR
GAS
GAT
GAU
GAY
GED
GEE
GEL
GEM
GEN
GEO
GET
GEY
GHI
GIB
GID
GIE
GIF
GIG
GIN
GIO
GIP
GIS
GIT
GJU
GNU
GOA
GOB
GOD
GOE
GON
GOO
GOR
GOS
GOT
GOV
GOX
GOY
GUB
GUE
GUL
GUM
GUN
GUP
GUR
GUS
GUT
GUV
GUY
GYM
GYP
HAD
HAE
HAG
HAH
HAJ
HAM
HAN
HAO
HAP
HAS
HAT
HAW
HAY
HEH
HEM
HEN
HEP
HER
HES
HET
HEW
HEX
HEY
HIC
HID
HIE
HIM
HIN
HIP
HIS
HIT
HMM
HOA
HOB
HOC
HOD
HOE
HOG
HOH
HOI
HOM
HON
HOO
HOP
HOS
HOT
HOW
HOX
HOY
HUB
HUE
HUG
HUH
HUI
HUM
HUN
HUP
HUT
HYE
HYP
ICE
ICH
ICK
ICY
IDE
IDS
IFF
IFS
ILK
ILL
IMP
INK
INN
INS
ION
IOS
IRE
IRK
ISH
ISM
ISO
ITA
ITS
IVY
IWI
JAB
JAG
JAI
JAK
JAM
JAP
JAR
JAW
JAY
JEE
JET
JEU
JEW
JIB
JIG
JIN
JIZ
JOB
JOE
JOG
JOL
JOR
JOT
JOW
JOY
JUD
JUG
JUN
JUS
JUT
KAB
KAE
KAF
KAI

KAK
KAM
KAS
KAT
KAW
KAY
KEA
KEB
KED
KEF
KEG
KEN
KEP
KET
KEX
KEY
KHI
KID
KIF
KIN
KIP
KIR
KIT
KOA
KOB
KOI
KON
KOP
KOR
KOS
KOW
KUE
KYE
KYU
LAB
LAC
LAD
LAG
LAH
LAM
LAP
LAR
LAS
LAT
LAV
LAW
LAX
LAY
LEA
LED
LEE
LEG
LEI
LEK
LEP
LES
LET
LEU
LEV
LEW
LEX
LEY
LEZ
LIB
LID
LIE
LIG
LIN
LIP
LIS
LIT
LOB
LOD
LOG
LOO
LOP
LOR
LOS
LOT
LOU
LOW
LOX
LOY
LUD
LUG
LUM
LUR
LUV
LUX
LUZ
LYE
LYM
MAA
MAC
MAD
MAE
MAG
MAK
MAL
MAM
MAN
MAP
MAR
MAS
MAT
MAW
MAX
MAY
MED
MEG
MEL
MEM
MEN
MES
MET
MEU
MEW
MHO
MIB
MID
MIG
MIL
MIM
MIR
MIS
MIX
MIZ
MNA
MOA
MOB
MOC
MOD
MOE
MOG
MOI
MOL
MOM
MON
MOO
MOP
MOR
MOS
MOT
MOU
MOW
MOY
MOZ
MUD
MUG
MUM
MUN
MUS
MUT
MUX
NAB
NAE
NAG
NAH
NAM
NAN
NAP
NAS
NAT
NAW
NAY
NEB
NED
NEE
NEF
NEK
NEP
NET
NEW
NIB
NID
NIE
NIL
NIM
NIP
NIS
NIT
NIX
NOB
NOD

NOG
NOH
NOM
NON
NOO
NOR
NOS
NOT
NOW
NOX
NOY
NTH
NUB
NUN
NUR
NUS
NUT
NYE
NYS
OAF
OAK
OAR
OAT
OBA
OBE
OBI
OBO
OBS
OCA
OCH
ODA
ODD
ODE
ODS
OES
OFF
OFT
OHM
OHO
OHS
OIK
OIL
OKA
OKE
OLD
OLE
OLM
OMS
ONE
ONS
ONY
OOF
OOH
OOM
OON
OOP
OOR
OOS
OOT
OPE
OPS
OPT
ORA
ORB
ORC
ORD
ORE
ORF
ORS
ORT
OSE
OUD
OUK
OUP
OUR
OUT
OVA
OWE
OWL
OWN
OWT
OXO
OXY
OYE
OYS
PAC
PAD
PAH
PAL
PAM
PAN
PAP
PAR
PAS
PAT
PAV
PAW
PAX
PAY
PEA
PEC
PED
PEE
PEG
PEH
PEN
PEP
PER
PES
PET
PEW
PHI
PHO
PHS
PHT
PIA
PIC
PIE
PIG
PIN
PIP
PIR
PIS
PIT
PIU
PIX
PLU
PLY
POA
POD
POH
POI
POL
POM
POO
POP
POS
POT
POW
POX
POZ
PRE
PRO
PRY
PSI
PST
PUB
PUD
PUG
PUH
PUL
PUN
PUP
PUR
PUS
PUT
PUY
PYA
PYE
PYX
QAT
QIS
QUA
RAD
RAG
RAH
RAI
RAJ
RAM
RAN
RAP
RAS
RAT
RAW
RAX
RAY
REB
REC
RED
REE
REF
REG
REH
REI

REM
REN
REO
REP
RES
RET
REV
REW
REX
REZ
RHO
RHY
RIA
RIB
RID
RIF
RIG
RIM
RIN
RIP
RIT
RIZ
ROB
ROC
ROD
ROE
ROK
ROM
ROO
ROT
ROW
RUB
RUC
RUD
RUE
RUG
RUM
RUN
RUT
RYA
RYE
SAB
SAC
SAD
SAE
SAG
SAI
SAL
SAM
SAN
SAP
SAR
SAT
SAU
SAV
SAW
SAX
SAY
SAZ
SEA
SEC
SED
SEE
SEG
SEI
SEL
SEN
SER
SET
SEW
SEX
SEY
SEZ
SHA
SHE
SHH
SHY
SIB
SIC
SIK
SIM
SIN
SIP
SIR
SIS
SIT
SIX
SKA
SKI
SKY
SLY
SMA
SNY
SOB
SOC
SOD
SOG
SOH
SOL
SON
SOP
SOS
SOT
SOU
SOV
SOW
SOX
SOY
SPA
SPY
SRI
STY
SUB
SUD
SUE
SUI
SUK
SUM
SUN
SUP
SUQ
SUR
SUS
SWY
SYE
SYN
TAB
TAD
TAE
TAG
TAI
TAJ
TAK
TAM
TAN
TAO
TAP
TAR
TAS
TAT
TAU
TAV
TAW
TAX
TAY
TEA
TEC
TED
TEE
TEF
TEG
TEL
TEN
TES
TET
TEW
THE
THO
THY
TIC
TID
TIE
TIG
TIL
TIN
TIP
TIS
TIT
TIX
TOC
TOD
TOE
TOG
TOM
TON
TOO
TOP
TOR
TOT
TOW
TOY
TRY
TSK
TUB

TUG
TUI
TUM
TUN
TUP
TUT
TUX
TWA
TWO
TWP
TYE
TYG
UDO
UDS
UEY
UFO
UGH
UGS
UKE
ULE
ULU
UMM
UMP
UMU
UNI
UNS
UPO
UPS
URB
URD
URE
URN
USE
UTA
UTE
UTS
UTU
UVA
VAC
VAE
VAG
VAN
VAR
VAS
VAT
VAU
VAV
VAW
VEE
VEG
VET
VEX
VIA
VID
VIE
VIG
VIM
VIN
VIS
VLY
VOE
VOL
VOR
VOW
VOX
VUG
VUM
WAB
WAD
WAE
WAG
WAI
WAN
WAP
WAR
WAS
WAT
WAW
WAX
WAY
WEB
WED
WEE
WEM
WEN
WET
WEX
WEY
WHA
WHO
WHY
WIG
WIN
WIS
WIT
WIZ
WOE
WOF
WOG
WOK
WON
WOO
WOP
WOS
WOT
WOW
WOX
WRY
WUD
WUS
WYE
WYN
XIS
YAD
YAE
YAH
YAK
YAM
YAP
YAR
YAW
YAY
YEA
YEH
YEN
YEP
YES
YET
YEW
YEX
YGO
YID
YIN
YIP
YOB
YOD
YOK
YOM
YON
YOS
YOU
YOW
YUG
YUK
YUM
YUP
YUS
ZAG
ZAP
ZAX
ZEA
ZED
ZEE
ZEK
ZEL
ZEX
ZHO
ZIG
ZIN
ZIP
ZIT
ZIZ
ZOA
ZOO
ZOS
ZUZ

Power Tiles

The highest-scoring tiles in the game are J, Q, X and Z, with J and X scoring eight points each, while Q and Z are worth ten. These 'power tiles' are the most potent weapons in the Scrabble player's arsenal, but need to be carefully deployed. This isn't always a matter of using them in a long word – a carefully positioned short word can be just as good a move.

This section lists all of the power-tile words of two and three letters, with a brief definition for each. It's worth learning all of these words as they can be tremendously useful, combining the assets of all short words with the high scores afforded by the power tiles. Knowing the definitions of these words will help you commit them to memory.

In addition, the Q section contains a very useful list of words that use Q without U, as well as a list of words which can use either K or Q.

J

There is only one J tile in Scrabble, so for any word with two Js (eg HAJJ or HAJJAH) a blank is required. When you are trying to use a word with J for tagging, remember that there are only two two-letter words with J: JA and JO. Bearing this in mind will prevent you from wasting time looking for options that aren't there. If there is a Z on the board or on your rack when you have a J, remember that there are quite a few words that use both J and Z (JIZ and JAZY, for example, though you will need a blank tile to take advantage of the JAZZ family of words).

Two-letter words:

JA South African word for *yes*

JO Scots word for *sweetheart*

Three-letter words:

GJU stringed instrument from Shetland

HAJ pilgrimage a Muslim makes to Mecca

JAB poke sharply

JAG injection

JAI Indian word for victory
JAK Asian tree

JAM food made from fruit boiled with sugar

JAP lacquer with japan

JAR glass container

JAW one of the bones in which the teeth are set

JAY bird with pinkish body and blue-and-black wings

JEE exclamation to urge on horses

JET hard black mineral

JEU game

JEW outbargain

JIB triangular sail set in front of a mast

JIG type of lively dance

JIN a spirit in Muslim belief

JIZ wig

JOB occupation or paid employment

JOE man or fellow

JOG run at a gentle pace

JOL South African word for party

JOR part of an Indian musical pattern

JOT very small amount

JOW ring a bell

JOY great delight or pleasure

JUD block of coal

JUG container for liquids, with a handle and spout

JUN	North Korean coin
JUS	right, power or authority
JUT	project or stick out
RAJ	government; rule
TAJ	conical cap worn by Muslims

Q

Along with Z, Q is the highest-scoring letter in Scrabble. Unlike Z, Q can be tricky to use because the majority of words that contain Q also require a U. There are, however, a number of words that contain Q but no U; a complete list of these follows in this section. It's easy enough to learn all of these. There's only one two-letter word with Q, QI, which is very useful as it allows you to tag onto one of the most common tiles in the game. It's also worth committing all of the three-letter words that use Q to memory, as most of these words don't use U, and thus enable you to deploy your Q tile without hoping for a U to become available either on the board or on your rack.

Two-letter words

QI	vital energy in Chinese medicine

Three-letter words

QAT	shrub that grows in Africa and Asia
QIS	plural of qi
QUA	in the capacity of
SUQ	open-air marketplace

Q but not U

There are few things more infuriating than having a Q on your rack but no U with which to play it! But this situation needn't be disastrous: there is a surprisingly high number of words that have a Q but not U. A complete list of these words is included here. These have short definitions to help you remember them; it is well worth learning them all, as they can be extremely useful.

FAQIR *noun* **FAQIRS**	Muslim ascetic
INQILAB *noun* **INQILABS**	revolution
MBAQANGA *noun* **MBAQANGAS**	type of South African pop music
QABALAH *noun* **QABALAHS**	ancient Jewish mystical tradition
QADI *noun* **QADIS**	Muslim judge
QAID *noun* **QAIDS**	Muslim leader
QAIMAQAM *noun* **QAIMAQAMS**	Ottoman governor
QALAMDAN *noun* **QALAMDANS**	pen-case
QANAT *noun* **QANATS**	ancient water-supply system
QASIDA *noun* **QASIDAS**	Arabic poetry form
QAT *noun* **QATS**	evergreen shrub with narcotic properties
QAWWAL *noun* **QAWWALS**	qawwali singer
QAWWALI *noun* **QAWWALIS**	Islamic religious song
QI *noun* **QIS**	vital energy in Chinese medicine
QIBLA *noun* **QIBLAS**	direction of the Kaaba in Mecca
QIGONG *noun* **QIGONGS**	Chinese system of exercise
QINDAR noun **QINDARKA, QINDARS**	an Albanian monetary unit
QINTAR *noun* **QINTARS**	Albanian monetary unit
QOPH *noun* **QOPHS**	letter of the Hebrew alphabet
QORMA *noun* **QORMAS**	Indian dish
QWERTY *noun* **QWERTIES, QWERTYS**	standard English keyboard layout
SHEQEL *noun* **SHEQALIM**	Israeli currency unit

TALAQ *noun* **TALAQS**	Muslim divorce
TRANQ *noun* **TRANQS**	tranquilizer
TSADDIQ *noun* **TSADDIQIM, TSADDIQS**	Hasidic Jewish leader
TZADDIQ *noun* **TZADDIQIM, TZADDIQS**	Hasidic Jewish leader
WAQF *noun* **WAQFS**	charitable donation of land
YAQONA *noun* **YAQONAS**	Polynesian shrub

Q and K

Looking at the words that contain Q but not U, you may well notice that many are of Arabic or Hebrew origin. Of course, these languages aren't written using the Roman alphabet, so these words are transliterations from a different script. It's an interesting – and helpful – fact that the Arabic consonant that is represented as a Q in Roman script can also be transliterated as a K, which means that many of the Q-but-no-U words can also be spelt with a K. This is useful for two reasons. Firstly, looking at the list of K alternatives will help you remember the Q-only words. Secondly, K is a sort of 'semi-power' tile, scoring five points and being the most valuable letter after the power tiles. Thus it's quite useful to know these unusual words using K for their own sake.

FAQIR	**FAKIR**
FAQIRS	**FAKIRS**
QADI	**KADI**
QADIS	**KADIS**
QAID	**KAID**
QAIDS	**KAIDS**
QAIMAQAM	**KAIMAKAM**
QAIMAQAMS	**KAIMAKAMS**
QALAMDAN	**KALAMDAN**
QALAMDANS	**KALAMDANS**

QAT	KAT
QATS	KATS
QIBLA	KIBLA
QIBLAS	KIBLAS
QOPH	KOPH
QOPHS	KOPHS
QORMA	KORMA
QORMAS	KORMAS
SHEQEL	SHEKEL
TALAQ	TALAK
TALAQS	TALAKS
TRANQ	TRANK
TRANQS	TRANKS
TSADDIQ	TSADDIK
TSADDIQIM	TSADDIKIM
TSADDIQS	TSADDIKS
TZADDIQ	TZADDIK
TZADDIQIM	TZADDIKIM
TZADDIQS	TZADDIKS
WAQF	WAKF
WAQFS	WAKFS

X

X is perhaps the most versatile of the power tiles. It's useful for tagging as it forms a two-letter word with every vowel. This means that when you have X on your rack, you should look out for opportunities to tag your new word on to a word on the board so that you can harvest the eight points for X twice. Towards the end of a game, when the board is filling up, it's worth considering tagging with a two-letter word containing X; words like AX, EX, and XI are very easy to tag onto others to form four words, two of which will contain the eight-point power-tile. X also forms more three-letter words than J, Q or Z. It's well worth learning all of them, along with the two-letter words, so that you can make full use of the X tile, whether it's on your rack or on the board.

Two-letter words

AX alternative spelling of *axe*

EX former wife or husband

OX castrated bull

XI 14th letter of the Greek alphabet

XU Vietnamese unit of currency

Three-letter words

AXE tool for chopping wood or felling trees

BOX container with a firm flat base and sides

COX coxswain; helmsman of a boat

DEX dextroamphetamine

DUX top pupil in a class or school

EXO Australian word for excellent

FAX electronic system for sending facsimiles of documents

FIX repair

FOX bushy-tailed wild animal of the dog family

GOX gaseous

HEX curse

HOX cut a horse's hamstrings

KEX hollow-stemmed plant

LAX not strict

LEX system or body of laws

LOX smoked salmon

LUX unit of illumination

MAX highest, furthest, or greatest thing

MIX combine or blend into one mass

MUX muck

NIX water spirit

NOX short form of nitrogen oxide

OXO containing oxygen

OXY containing oxygen

PAX Christian greeting

PIX pictures

POX disease in which skin pustules form

PYX box in which coins are weighed

RAX stretch or extend

REX king

SAX saxophone

SEX either of male or female

SIX number between five and seven

SOX socks

TAX compulsory payment levied by a government

TIX tickets

TUX tuxedo

VEX frustrate, annoy

VOX voice or sound

WAX solid shiny fatty or oily substance

WEX old word for wax

WOX old form of waxed

XIS plural of *xi*

YEX hiccup or cough

ZAX small axe for cutting slates

ZEX another word for *zax*

Z

Z scores the same as Q (ten points) but is an easier letter to use – there is no need for a U as there is in the majority of Q words. The only two-letter word containing Z, ZO, is useful as it allows you to tag onto one of the most common tiles in the game. It's a good idea to learn the short Z words that use other power tiles, such as JIZ, JAZY, ZAX and ZEX, as these can provide high scores, especially if you can deploy them on bonus squares. Remember also that there are quite a few words with a double Z (BUZZ and FUZZ, for example); while these may appear useless for Scrabble, as there is only one Z in the game, a blank tile can be used for the other Z.

Two-letter words

ZO Tibetan animal bred from cows and yaks

Three-letter words

ADZ tool with an arched blade at right angles to the handle

AZO consisting of, or containing, the divalent group -N:N-

BEZ second spike of a deer's antler

BIZ business

CAZ casual

COZ archaic word for cousin

CUZ archaic word for cousin

DZO Tibetan animal bred from cows and yaks

FEZ brimless tasselled cap

FIZ fizz

JIZ wig

LEZ lesbian

LUZ indestructable bone in Jewish belief

MIZ misery

MOZ curse or hex

POZ positive

REZ reservation

RIZ risen

SAZ Turkish musical instrument

SEZ says

WIZ amphetamine

ZAG sharp turn

ZAP kill by shooting

ZAX small axe for cutting slates

ZEA type of grain

ZED the letter Z

ZEE the letter Z

ZEK Soviet prisoner

ZEL Moorish cymbal

ZEX another word for zax

ZHO Tibetan animal bred from cows and yaks

ZIG sharp turn

ZIN wine grape; zinfandel

ZIP fastener with two rows of teeth

ZIT pimple

ZIZ short sleep

ZOA independent animal bodies

ZOO place where live animals are kept for show

ZOS Tibetan animals bred from cows and yaks

ZUZ Biblican coin

Aa

A forms a two-letter word when followed by any one of A, B, D, E, G, H, I, M, N, R, S, T, W, X and Y – 15 letters out of 26 – so it's a really useful tile. There are also a number of short high-scoring words beginning with A. **Axe** (10 points) and **adze** (14 points) are good examples, but don't forget their US variants, **ax** (9 points) and **adz** (13 points). Also remember their plurals and the verb form **axed** (12 points). **Aye** (6) and **ay** (5) are handy for tight corners.

a *adj* indefinite article, used before a noun being mentioned for the first time

aa aa *n* (**aas**). Aa is a type of volcanic rock. Aa scores 2 points, and is a good way of getting rid of annoying multiples of A.
aah *interj*. Aah is a sound people make when they're pleased or amazed. Aah scores 6 points.
aal *adj* Aal is a Scots word for **all**. Aal scores 3 points.

aardvark *n* (*pl* **-s**) S African anteater with long ears and snout
aardvarks *n* ▷ **aardvark**
ab *n* (*pl* **-s**) (*Informal*) (usually plural) abdominal muscle

aba *noun* (**abas**). Cloth made from goat or camel hair. This is a useful word to remember for when you have more than one A on your rack. Aba scores 5 points.

aback *adv* startled or disconcerted
abacus (*pl* **-es**) *n* beads on a wire frame, used for doing calculations
abacuses *n* ▷ **abacus**
abalone (*pl* **-s**) [ab-a-**lone**-ee] *n* edible sea creature with a shell lined with mother of pearl
abalones *n* ▷ **abalone**
abandon *v* (**-s, -ing, -ed**) desert or leave (one's wife, children, etc.) ▶ *n* lack of inhibition > **abandonment** *n* (*pl* **-s**)
abandoned *adj* deserted ▶ *v* ▷ **abandon**
abandoning *v* ▷ **abandon**
abandonment *n* ▷ **abandon**
abandonments *n* ▷ **abandon**
abandons *v* ▷ **abandon**
abase *v* (**-ses, -sing, -sed**) humiliate or degrade (oneself) > **abasement** *n* (*pl* **-s**)
abased *v* ▷ **abase**
abasement *n* ▷ **abase**
abasements *n* ▷ **abase**
abases *v* ▷ **abase**
abashed *adj* embarrassed and ashamed
abasing *v* ▷ **abase**
abate *v* (**-tes, -ting, -ted**) make or become less strong > **abatement** *n* (*pl* **-s**)
abated *v* ▷ **abate**
abatement *n* ▷ **abate**
abatements *n* ▷ **abate**
abates *v* ▷ **abate**
abating *v* ▷ **abate**
abattoir [**ab**-a-twahr] *n* place where animals are killed for food (*pl* **-s**)
abattoirs *n* ▷ **abattoir**

abb *noun* (**abbs**). Abb is yarn used in weaving. Remember this word for when you have two Bs on your rack, as there will probably already be an A on the board that you can use. Abb scores 7 points.

abbess *n* (*pl* **-es**) nun in charge of a convent
abbesses *n* ▷ **abbess**
abbey *n* (*pl* **-s**) dwelling place of, or a church belonging to, a community of monks or nuns
abbeys *n* ▷ **abbey**
abbot *n* (*pl* **-s**) head of an abbey of monks
abbots *n* ▷ **abbot**
abbreviate *v* (**-tes, -ting, -ted**) shorten (a word) by leaving out some letters
abbreviated *v* ▷ **abbreviate**
abbreviates *v* ▷ **abbreviate**
abbreviating *v* ▷ **abbreviate**
abbreviation *n* (*pl* **-s**) shortened form of a word or words
abbreviations *n* ▷ **abbreviation**

abdicate *v* **(-tes, -ting, -ted)** give up (the throne or a responsibility) **> abdication** *n* (*pl* **-s**)
abdicated *v* ▷ **abdicate**
abdicates *v* ▷ **abdicate**
abdicating *v* ▷ **abdicate**
abdication *n* ▷ **abdicate**
abdications *n* ▷ **abdicate**
abdomen *n* (*pl* **-s**) part of the body containing the stomach and intestines **> abdominal** *adj*
abdomens *n* ▷ **abdomen**
abdominal *adj* ▷ **abdomen**
abduct *v* **(-s, -ing, -ed)** carry off, kidnap **> abduction** *n* (*pl* **-s**) **> abductor** *n* (*pl* **-s**)
abducted *v* ▷ **abduct**
abducting *v* ▷ **abduct**
abduction *n* ▷ **abduct**
abductions *n* ▷ **abduct**
abductor *n* ▷ **abduct**
abductors *n* ▷ **abduct**
abducts *v* ▷ **abduct**
aberrant *adj* showing aberration
aberration *n* (*pl* **-s**) sudden change from what is normal, accurate, or correct
aberrations *n* ▷ **aberration**
abet *v* **(-s, -ting, -ted)** help or encourage in wrongdoing **> abettor** *n* (*pl* **-s**)
abets *v* ▷ **abet**
abetted *v* ▷ **abet**
abetting *v* ▷ **abet**
abettor *n* ▷ **abet**
abettors *n* ▷ **abet**
abeyance *n* (*pl* **-s**) not in use
abeyances *n* ▷ **abeyance**
abhor *v* **(-s, -horring, -horred)** detest utterly **> abhorrence** *n* (*pl* **-s**)
abhorred *v* ▷ **abhor**
abhorrence *n* ▷ **abhor**
abhorrences *n* ▷ **abhor**
abhorrent *adj* hateful, loathsome
abhorring *v* ▷ **abhor**
abhors *v* ▷ **abhor**
abide *v* **(-des, -ding, -ded)** endure, put up with
abided *v* ▷ **abide**
abides *v* ▷ **abide**
abiding *adj* lasting ▶ *v* ▷ **abide**
abilities *n* ▷ **ability**
ability *n* (*pl* **-ties**) competence, power
abject *adj* utterly miserable **> abjectly** *adv*
abjectly *adv* ▷ **abject**
abjure *v* **(-res, -ring, -red)** deny or renounce on oath
abjured *v* ▷ **abjure**
abjures *v* ▷ **abjure**
abjuring *v* ▷ **abjure**
ablative *n* (*pl* **-s**) case of nouns in Latin and other languages, indicating source, agent, or instrument of action
ablatives *n* ▷ **ablative**
ablaze *adj* burning fiercely
able *adj* **(-r, -st)** capable, competent **> ably** *adv*
abler *adj* ▷ **able**
ablest *adj* ▷ **able**
ablution *n* (*pl* **-s**) (usually plural) act of washing
ablutions *n* ▷ **ablution**
ably *adv* ▷ **able**
abnormal *adj* not normal or usual **> abnormally** *adv* **> abnormality** *n* (*pl* **-ties**)
abnormalities *n* ▷ **abnormal**
abnormality *n* ▷ **abnormal**
abnormally *adv* ▷ **abnormal**
aboard *adv, prep* on, in, onto, or into (a ship, train, or plane)
abode *n* (*pl* **-s**) home, dwelling
abodes *n* ▷ **abode**
abolish *v* **(-shes, -shing, -shed)** do away with **> abolition** *n* (*pl* **-s**)
abolished *v* ▷ **abolish**
abolishes *v* ▷ **abolish**
abolishing *v* ▷ **abolish**
abolition *n* ▷ **abolish**
abolitionist *n* (*pl* **-s**) person who wishes to do away with something, esp. slavery
abolitionists *n* ▷ **abolitionist**
abolitions *n* ▷ **abolish**
abominable *adj* detestable, very bad **> abominably** *adv*
abominably *adv* ▷ **abominable**
abomination *n* (*pl* **-s**) someone or something that is detestable
abominations *n* ▷ **abomination**
aboriginal *n, adj* ▷ **aborigine**
aboriginals *n* ▷ **aborigine**
aborigine, aboriginal [ab-or-**rij**-in-ee] *n* (*pl* **-s**) original inhabitant of a country or region, esp. **(A-)** Australia **> aboriginal** *adj*
aborigines *n* ▷ **aborigine**
abort *v* **(-s, -ing, -ed)** have an abortion or perform an abortion on
aborted *v* ▷ **abort**
aborting *v* ▷ **abort**
abortion *n* (*pl* **-s**) operation to end a pregnancy
abortionist *n* (*pl* **-s**) person who performs abortions, esp. illegally
abortionists *n* ▷ **abortionist**
abortions *n* ▷ **abortion**
abortive *adj* unsuccessful
aborts *v* ▷ **abort**
abound *v* **(-s, -ing, -ed)** be plentiful

> **abounding** *adj*
abounded *v* ▷ **abound**
abounding *v, adj* ▷ **abound**
abounds *v* ▷ **abound**
about *prep* concerning, on the subject of ▶ *adv* nearly, approximately
above *adv, prep* over or higher (than)
abracadabra *n* (*pl* **-s**) supposedly magic word
abracadabras *n* ▷ **abracadabra**
abrasion *n* (*pl* **-s**) scraped area on the skin
abrasions *n* ▷ **abrasion**
abrasive *adj* harsh and unpleasant in manner ▶ *n* (*pl* **-s**) substance for cleaning or polishing by rubbing
abrasives *n* ▷ **abrasive**
abreast *adv, adj* side by side
abridge *v* (**-ges, -ging, -ged**) shorten by using fewer words > **abridgment, abridgement** *n* (*pl* **-s**)
abridged *v* ▷ **abridge**
abridgement *n* ▷ **abridge**
abridgements *n* ▷ **abridge**
abridges *v* ▷ **abridge**
abridging *v* ▷ **abridge**
abridgment *n* ▷ **abridge**
abridgments *n* ▷ **abridge**
abroad *adv* to or in a foreign country
abrogate *v* (**-tes, -ting, -ted**) cancel (a law or agreement) formally > **abrogation** *n* (*pl* **-s**)
abrogated *v* ▷ **abrogate**
abrogates *v* ▷ **abrogate**
abrogating *v* ▷ **abrogate**
abrogation *n* ▷ **abrogate**
abrogations *n* ▷ **abrogate**
abrupt *adj* (**-er, -est**) sudden, unexpected > **abruptly** *adv* > **abruptness** *n* (*pl* **-es**)
abrupter *adj* ▷ **abrupt**
abruptest *adj* ▷ **abrupt**
abruptly *adv* ▷ **abrupt**
abruptness *n* ▷ **abrupt**
abruptnesses *n* ▷ **abrupt**
abs *n* ▷ **ab**
abscess *n* (*pl* **abscesses**) inflamed swelling containing pus
abscesses *n* ▷ **abscess**
abscond *v* (**-s, -ing, -ed**) leave secretly
absconded *v* ▷ **abscond**
absconding *v* ▷ **abscond**
absconds *v* ▷ **abscond**
abseil [**ab**-sale] *v* (**-s, -ing, -ed**) go down a steep drop by a rope fastened at the top and tied around one's body
abseiled *v* ▷ **abseil**
abseiling *v* ▷ **abseil**
abseils *v* ▷ **abseil**
absence *n* (*pl* **-s**) being away
absences *n* ▷ **absence**
absent *adj* not present ▶ *v* (**-s, -ing, -ed**) stay away > **absently** *adv*
absented *v* ▷ **absent**
absentee *n* (*pl* **-s**) person who should be present but is not
absenteeism *n* (*pl* **-s**) persistent absence from work or school
absenteeisms *n* ▷ **absenteeism**
absentees *n* ▷ **absentee**
absenting *v* ▷ **absent**
absently *adv* ▷ **absent**
absents *v* ▷ **absent**
absinthe *n* (*pl* **-s**) strong green aniseed-flavoured liqueur
absinthes *n* ▷ **absinthe**
absolute *adj* complete, perfect
absolutely *adv* completely ▶ *interj* certainly, yes
absolution *n* ▷ **absolve**
absolutions *n* ▷ **absolve**
absolutism *n* (*pl* **-s**) government by a ruler with unrestricted power
absolutisms *n* ▷ **absolutism**
absolve *v* (**-ves, -ving, -ved**) declare to be free from blame or sin > **absolution** *n* (*pl* **-s**)
absolved *v* ▷ **absolve**
absolves *v* ▷ **absolve**
absolving *v* ▷ **absolve**
absorb *v* (**-s, -ing, -ed**) soak up (a liquid) > **absorption** *n* (*pl* **-s**) > **absorbency** *n* (*pl* **-s**)
absorbed *v* ▷ **absorb**
absorbencies *n* ▷ **absorb**
absorbency *n* ▷ **absorb**
absorbent *adj* able to absorb liquid
absorbing *v* ▷ **absorb**
absorbs *v* ▷ **absorb**
absorption *n* ▷ **absorb**
absorptions *n* ▷ **absorb**
abstain *v* (**-s, -ing, -ed**) choose not to do something > **abstainer** *n* (*pl* **-s**)
abstained *v* ▷ **abstain**
abstainer *n* ▷ **abstain**
abstainers *n* ▷ **abstain**
abstaining *v* ▷ **abstain**
abstains *v* ▷ **abstain**
abstemious *adj* taking very little alcohol or food > **abstemiousness** *n* (*pl* **-es**)
abstemiousness *n* ▷ **abstemious**
abstemiousnesses *n* ▷ **abstemious**
abstention *n* (*pl* **-s**) abstaining, esp. from voting
abstentions *n* ▷ **abstention**
abstinence *n* (*pl* **-s**) abstaining, esp. from

drinking alcohol > **abstinent** *adj*
abstinences *n* ▷ **abstinence**
abstinent *adj* ▷ **abstinence**
abstract *adj* (**-er, -est**) existing as a quality or idea rather than a material object ▶ *n* (*pl* **-s**) summary ▶ *v* (**-s, -ing, -ed**) summarize > **abstraction** *n* (*pl* **-s**)
abstracted *adj* lost in thought *v* ▷ **abstract**
abstracter *adj* ▷ **abstract**
abstractest *adj* ▷ **abstract**
abstracting *adj* ▷ **abstract**
abstraction *n* ▷ **abstract**
abstractions *n* ▷ **abstract**
abstracts *n, v* ▷ **abstract**
abstruse *adj* (**-er, -est**) not easy to understand
abstruser *adj* ▷ **abstruse**
abstrusest *adj* ▷ **abstruse**
absurd *adj* (**-er, -est**) incongruous or ridiculous > **absurdly** *adv* > **absurdity** *n* (*pl* **-ties**)
absurder *adj* ▷ **absurd**
absurdest *adj* ▷ **absurd**
absurdities *n* ▷ **absurd**
absurdity *n* ▷ **absurd**
absurdly *adv* ▷ **absurd**
abundance *n* ▷ **abundant**
abundances *n* ▷ **abundant**
abundant *adj* plentiful > **abundantly** *adv* > **abundance** *n* (*pl* **-s**)
abundantly *adv* ▷ **abundant**
abuse *v* (**-ses, -sing, -sed**) use wrongly ▶ *n* (*pl* **-s**) prolonged ill-treatment > **abuser** *n* (*pl* **-s**) > **abusive** *adj* > **abusively** *adv* > **abusiveness** *n* (*pl* **-es**)
abused *v* ▷ **abuse**
abuser *n* ▷ **abuse**
abusers *n* ▷ **abuse**
abuses *v, n* ▷ **abuse**
abusing *v* ▷ **abuse**
abusive *adj* ▷ **abuse**
abusively *adv* ▷ **abuse**
abusiveness *n* ▷ **abuse**
abusivenesses *n* ▷ **abuse**
abut *v* (**-s, abutting, abutted**) be next to or touching
abuts *v* ▷ **abut**
abutted *v* ▷ **abut**
abutting *v* ▷ **abut**

aby *verb* (**abys abying abought**). Aby is an old word meaning to pay a penalty. If someone plays this word, remember that it can be expanded to **baby**, **abysmal** or **abyss**. Aby scores 8 points.

abysmal *adj* (*Informal*) extremely bad, awful > **abysmally** *adv*
abysmally *adv* ▷ **abysmal**
abyss *n* (*pl* **-es**) very deep hole or chasm
abysses *n* ▷ **abyss**
acacia [a-**kay**-sha] *n* (*pl* **-s**) tree or shrub with yellow or white flowers
acacias *n* ▷ **acacia**
academic *adj* of an academy or university ▶ *n* (*pl* **-s**) lecturer or researcher at a university > **academically** *adv*
academically *adv* ▷ **academic**
academician *n* (*pl* **-s**) member of an academy
academicians *n* ▷ **academician**
academics *n* ▷ **academician**
academies *n* ▷ **academy**
academy *n* (*pl* **-mies**) society to advance arts or sciences
acanthus *n* (*pl* **-es**) prickly plant
acanthuses *n* ▷ **acanthus**
accede *v* (**-des, -ding, -ded**) consent or agree (to)
acceded *v* ▷ **accede**
accedes *v* ▷ **accede**
acceding *v* ▷ **accede**
accelerate *v* (**-tes, -ting, -ted**) (cause to) move faster > **acceleration** *n* (*pl* **-s**)
accelerated *v* ▷ **accelerate**
accelerates *v* ▷ **accelerate**
accelerating *v* ▷ **accelerate**
acceleration *n* ▷ **accelerate**
accelerations *n* ▷ **accelerate**
accelerator *n* (*pl* **-s**) pedal in a motor vehicle to increase speed
accelerators *n* ▷ **accelerator**
accent *n* (*pl* **-s**) distinctive style of pronunciation of a local, national, or social group ▶ *v* (**-s, -ing, -ed**) place emphasis on
accented *v* ▷ **accent**
accenting *v* ▷ **accent**
accents *n, v* ▷ **accent**
accentuate *v* (**-tes, -ting, -ted**) stress, emphasize > **accentuation** *n* (*pl* **-s**)
accentuated *v* ▷ **accentuate**
accentuates *v* ▷ **accentuate**
accentuating *v* ▷ **accentuate**
accentuation *n* ▷ **accentuate**
accentuations *n* ▷ **accentuate**
accept *v* (**-s, -ing, -ed**) receive willingly > **acceptance** *n* (*pl* **-s**)
acceptabilities *n* ▷ **acceptable**
acceptability *n* ▷ **acceptable**
acceptable *adj* tolerable > **acceptably** *adv* > **acceptability** *n* (*pl* **-ties**)
acceptably *adv* ▷ **acceptable**
acceptance *n* ▷ **accept**
acceptances *n* ▷ **accept**
accepted *v* ▷ **accept**

accepting *v* ▷ **accept**
accepts *v* ▷ **accept**
access *n* (*pl* **-es**) means of or right to approach or enter ▶ *v* (**-es, -ing, -ed**) obtain (data) from a computer
accessed *v* ▷ **access**
accesses *n, v* ▷ **access**
accessibilities *n* ▷ **accessible**
accessibility *n* ▷ **accessible**
accessible *adj* easy to reach > **accessibility** *n* (*pl* **-ties**)
accessing *v* ▷ **access**
accession *n* (*pl* **-s**) taking up of an office or position
accessions *n* ▷ **accession**
accessories *n* ▷ **accessory**
accessory *n* (*pl* **-ries**) supplementary part or object
accident *n* (*pl* **-s**) mishap, often causing injury
accidental *adj* happening by chance or unintentionally ▶ *n* (*pl* **-s**) (MUSIC) symbol indicating that a sharp, flat, or natural note is not a part of the key signature > **accidentally** *adv*
accidentally *adv* ▷ **accidental**
accidentals *n* ▷ **accidental**
accidents *n* ▷ **accident**
acclaim *v* (**-s, -ing, -ed**) applaud, praise ▶ *n* (*pl* **-s**) enthusiastic approval > **acclamation** *n* (*pl* **-s**)
acclaimed *v* ▷ **acclaim**
acclaiming *v* ▷ **acclaim**
acclaims *v, n* ▷ **acclaim**
acclamation *n* ▷ **acclaim**
acclamations *n* ▷ **acclaim**
acclimatization *n* ▷ **acclimatize**
acclimatizations *n* ▷ **acclimatize**
acclimatize *v* (**-zes, -zing, -zed**) adapt to a new climate or environment > **acclimatization** *n* (*pl* **-s**)
acclimatized *v* ▷ **acclimatize**
acclimatizes *v* ▷ **acclimatize**
acclimatizing *v* ▷ **acclimatize**
accolade *n* (*pl* **-s**) award, honour, or praise
accolades *n* ▷ **accolade**
accommodate *v* (**-tes, -ting, -ted**) provide with lodgings
accommodated *v* ▷ **accommodate**
accommodates *v* ▷ **accommodate**
accommodating *adj* obliging ▶ *v* ▷ **accommodate**
accommodation *n* (*pl* **-s**) house or room for living in
accommodations *n* ▷ **accommodation**
accompanied *v* ▷ **accompany**
accompanies *v* ▷ **accompany**
accompaniment *n* (*pl* **-s**) something that accompanies
accompaniments *n* ▷ **accompaniment**
accompanist *n* ▷ **accompany**
accompanists *n* ▷ **accompany**
accompany *v* (**-nies, -nying, -nied**) go along with > **accompanist** *n* (*pl* **-s**)
accompanying *v* ▷ **accompany**
accomplice *n* (*pl* **-s**) person who helps another to commit a crime
accomplices *n* ▷ **accomplice**
accomplish *v* (**-es, -ing, -ed**) manage to do
accomplished *adj* expert, proficient ▶ *v* ▷ **accomplish**
accomplishes *v* ▷ **accomplish**
accomplishing *v* ▷ **accomplish**
accomplishment *n* (*pl* **-s**) completion
accomplishments *n* ▷ **accomplishment**
accord *n* (*pl* **-s**) agreement, harmony ▶ *v* (**-s, -ing, -ed**) fit in with
accordance *n* (*pl* **-s**) conforming to or according to
accordances *n* ▷ **accordance**
accorded *v* ▷ **accord**
according *adv* as stated by ▶ *v* ▷ **accord**
accordingly *adv* in an appropriate manner
accordion *n* (*pl* **-s**) portable musical instrument played by moving the two sides apart and together, and pressing a keyboard or buttons to produce the notes > **accordionist** *n*
accordionist *n* (*pl* **-s**) ▷ **accordion**
accordionists *n* ▷ **accordion**
accordions *n* ▷ **accordion**
accords *v* ▷ **accord**
accost *v* (**-s, -ing, -ed**) approach and speak to, often aggressively
accosted *v* ▷ **accost**
accosting *v* ▷ **accost**
accosts *v* ▷ **accost**
account *n* (*pl* **-s**) report, description ▶ *v* (**-s, -ing, -ed**) judge to be
accountabilities *n* ▷ **accountable**
accountability *n* ▷ **accountable**
accountable *adj* responsible to someone or for something > **accountability** *n* (*pl* **-ties**)
accountancies *n* ▷ **accountant**
accountancy *n* ▷ **accountant**
accountant *n* (*pl* **-s**) person who maintains and audits business accounts > **accountancy** *n* (*pl* **-cies**)
accountants *n* ▷ **accountant**
accounted *v* ▷ **account**
accounting *n* (*pl* **-s**) skill or practice of

maintaining and auditing business accounts ▶ *v* ▷ **account**
accountings *n* ▷ **accounting**
accounts *n, v* ▷ **account**
accoutrement *n* (*pl* **-s**) an item of clothing and equipment for a particular activity
accoutrements *n* ▷ **accoutrement**
accredited *adj* authorized, officially recognized
accretion [ak-**kree**-shun] *n* (*pl* **-s**) gradual growth
accretions *n* ▷ **accretion**
accrual *n* ▷ **accrue**
accruals *n* ▷ **accrue**
accrue *v* (**-crues, -cruing, -crued**) increase gradually > **accrual** *n* (*pl* **-s**)
accrued *v* ▷ **accrue**
accrues *v* ▷ **accrue**
accruing *v* ▷ **accrue**
accumulate *v* (**-tes, -ting, -ted**) gather together in increasing quantity > **accumulation** *n* (*pl* **-s**) > **accumulative** *adj*
accumulated *v* ▷ **accumulate**
accumulates *v* ▷ **accumulate**
accumulating *v* ▷ **accumulate**
accumulation *n* ▷ **accumulate**
accumulations *v* ▷ **accumulate**
accumulative *adj* ▷ **accumulate**
accumulator *n* (*pl* **-s**) (BRIT & AUST) rechargeable electric battery
accumulators *n* ▷ **accumulator**
accuracies *n* ▷ **accurate**
accuracy *n* ▷ **accurate**
accurate *adj* exact, correct > **accurately** *adv* > **accuracy** *n* (*pl* **-cies**)
accurately *adv* ▷ **accurate**
accursed *adj* under a curse
accusation *n* ▷ **accuse**
accusations *n* ▷ **accuse**
accusative *n* (*pl* **-s**) grammatical case indicating the direct object
accusatives *n* ▷ **accusative**
accusatory *adj* ▷ **accuse**
accuse *v* (**-ses, -sing, -sed**) charge with wrongdoing > **accused** *n* > **accuser** *n* (*pl* **-s**) > **accusing** *adj* > **accusation** *n* (*pl* **-s**) > **accusatory** *adj*
accused *v* ▷ **accuse**
accused *n* ▷ **accuse**
accuser *n* ▷ **accuse**
accusers *n* ▷ **accuser**
accuses *v* ▷ **accuse**
accusing *v, adj* ▷ **accuse**
accusing *adj* ▷ **accuse**
accustom *v* (**-s, -ing, -ed**) make used to
accustomed *adj* usual *v* ▷ **accustom**
accustoming *v* ▷ **accustom**
accustoms *v* ▷ **accustom**
ace *n* (*pl* **-s**) playing card with one symbol on it ▶ *adj* (*Informal*) excellent
acerbic [ass-**sir**-bik] *adj* harsh or bitter > **acerbity** *n* (*pl* **-ties**)
acerbities *n* ▷ **acerbic**
acerbity *n* ▷ **acerbic**
aces *n* ▷ **ace**
acetate [**ass**-it-tate] *n* (*pl* **-s**) (CHEM) salt or ester of acetic acid
acetates *n* ▷ **acetate**
acetic [ass-**see**-tik] *adj* of or involving vinegar
acetone [**ass**-it-tone] *n* (*pl* **-s**) colourless liquid used as a solvent
acetones *n* ▷ **acetone**
acetylene [ass-**set**-ill-een] *n* (*pl* **-s**) colourless flammable gas used in welding metals
acetylenes *n* ▷ **acetylene**
ache *n* (*pl* **-s**) dull continuous pain ▶ *v* (**-ches, -ching, -ched**) be in or cause continuous dull pain
ached *n* ▷ **ache**
aches *v, n* ▷ **ache**
achieve *v* (**-ves, -ving, -ved**) gain by hard work or ability
achieved *v* ▷ **achieve**
achievement *n* (*pl* **-s**) something accomplished
achievements *n* ▷ **achievement**
achieves *v* ▷ **achieve**
achieving *v* ▷ **achieve**
aching *v* ▷ **ache**
achromatic *adj* colourless
acid *n* (*pl* **-s**) (CHEM) one of a class of compounds, corrosive and sour when dissolved in water, that combine with a base to form a salt ▶ *adj* containing acid > **acidic** *adj* > **acidify** *v* > **acidity** *n* (*pl* **-ties**)
acidic *adj* ▷ **acid**
acidify *v* ▷ **acid**
acidities *n* ▷ **acid**
acidity *n* ▷ **acid**
acids *n* ▷ **acid**
acknowledge *v* (**-ges, -ging, -ged**) admit, recognize > **acknowledgment, acknowledgement** *n* (*pl* **-s**)
acknowledged *v* ▷ **acknowledge**
acknowledgement *n* ▷ **acknowledge**
acknowledgements *n* ▷ **acknowledge**
acknowledges *v* ▷ **acknowledge**
acknowledging *v* ▷ **acknowledge**
acknowledgment *n* ▷ **acknowledge**
acknowledgments *n* ▷ **acknowledge**

acme [**ak**-mee] *n* (*pl* **-s**) highest point of achievement or excellence
acmes *n* ▷ **acme**
acne [**ak**-nee] *n* (*pl* **-s**) pimply skin disease
acnes *n* ▷ **acne**
acolyte *n* (*pl* **-s**) follower or attendant
acolytes *n* ▷ **acolyte**
aconite *n* (*pl* **-s**) poisonous plant with hoodlike flowers
aconites *n* ▷ **aconite**
acorn *n* (*pl* **-s**) nut of the oak tree
acorns *n* ▷ **acorn**
acoustic *adj* of sound and hearing > **acoustically** *adv*
acoustically *adv* ▷ **acoustic**
acoustics *n* science of sounds
acquaint *v* (**-s, -ing, -ed**) make familiar, inform > **acquainted** *adj*
acquaintance *n* (*pl* **-s**) person known
acquaintances *n* ▷ **acquaintance**
acquainted *v, adj* ▷ **acquaint**
acquainting *v* ▷ **acquaint**
acquaints *v* ▷ **acquaint**
acquiesce [ak-wee-**ess**] *v* (**-sces, -scing, -sced**) agree to what someone wants > **acquiescence** *n* (*pl* **-s**) > **acquiescent** *adj*
acquiesced *v* ▷ **acquiesce**
acquiescence *n* ▷ **acquiesce**
acquiescences *n* ▷ **acquiesce**
acquiescent *adj* ▷ **acquiesce**
acquiesces *v* ▷ **acquiesce**
acquiescing *v* ▷ **acquiesce**
acquire *v* (**-res, -ring, -red**) gain, get
acquired *v* ▷ **acquire**
acquires *v* ▷ **acquire**
acquiring *v* ▷ **acquire**
acquisition *n* (*pl* **-s**) thing acquired
acquisitions *n* ▷ **acquisition**
acquisitive *adj* eager to gain material possessions > **acquisitiveness** *n* (*pl* **-es**)
acquisitiveness *n* ▷ **acquisitive**
acquisitivenesses *n* ▷ **acquisitive**
acquit *v* (**-s, -quitting, -quitted**) pronounce (someone) innocent > **acquittal** *n* (*pl* **-s**)
acquits *v* ▷ **acquit**
acquittal *n* ▷ **acquit**
acquittals *n* ▷ **acquit**
acquitted *v* ▷ **acquit**
acquitting *v* ▷ **acquit**
acre *n* (*pl* **-s**) measure of land, 4840 square yards (4046.86 square metres)
acreage [**ake**-er-rij] *n* (*pl* **-s**) land area in acres
acreages *n* ▷ **acreage**
acres *n* ▷ **acre**
acrid [**ak**-rid] *adj* (**-er, -est**) pungent, bitter
acrider *adj* ▷ **acrid**
acridest *adj* ▷ **acrid**
acrimonies *n* ▷ **acrimonious**
acrimonious *adj* bitter in speech or manner > **acrimony** *n* (*pl* **-ies**)
acrimony *n* ▷ **acrimonious**
acrobat *n* (*pl* **-s**) person skilled in gymnastic feats requiring agility and balance > **acrobatic** *adj*
acrobatic *adj* ▷ **acrobatic**
acrobatics *pl n* acrobatic feats
acrobats *n* ▷ **acrobat**
acronym *n* (*pl* **-s**) word formed from the initial letters of other words, such as NASA
acronyms *n* ▷ **acronym**
across *adv, prep* from side to side (of)
acrostic *n* (*pl* **-s**) lines of writing in which the first or last letters of each line spell a word or saying
acrostics *n* ▷ **acrostic**
acrylic *n* (*pl* **-s**) ▶ *adj* (synthetic fibre, paint, etc.) made from acrylic acid
acrylics *n* ▷ **acrylic**
act *n* (*pl* **-s**) thing done ▶ *v* (**-s, -ing, -ed**) do something
acted *v* ▷ **act**
acting *n* (*pl* **-s**) art of an actor ▶ *adj* temporarily performing the duties of ▶ *v* ▷ **act**
actings *n* ▷ **acting**
actinium *n* (*pl* **-s**) (CHEM) radioactive chemical element
actiniums *n* ▷ **actinium**
action *n* (*pl* **-s**) process of doing something
actionable *adj* giving grounds for a lawsuit
actions *n* ▷ **action**
activate *v* (**-tes, -ting, -ted**) make active > **activation** *n* (*pl* **-s**) > **activator** *n* (*pl* **-s**)
activated *v* ▷ **activate**
activates *v* ▷ **activate**
activating *v* ▷ **activate**
activation *n* ▷ **activate**
activations *n* ▷ **activate**
activator *n* ▷ **activate**
activators *n* ▷ **activate**
active *adj* moving, working > **actively** *adv*
actively *adv* ▷ **active**
activism *n* ▷ **activist**
activisms *n* ▷ **activist**
activist *n* (*pl* **-s**) person who works energetically to achieve political or social goals > **activism** *n* (*pl* **-s**)
activists *n* ▷ **activist**
activities *n* ▷ **activity**
activity *n* (*pl* **-ties**) state of being active
actor *n* (*pl* **-s**) person who acts in a play, film,

etc.

actors *n* ▷ **actor**

actress *n* (*pl* **-es**) woman who acts in a play, film, etc.

actresses *n* ▷ **actress**

acts *n, v* ▷ **act**

actual *adj* existing in reality > **actuality** *n* (*pl* **-ties**)

actualities *n* ▷ **actual**

actuality *n* ▷ **actual**

actually *adv* really, indeed

actuarial *adj* ▷ **actuary**

actuaries *n* ▷ **actuary**

actuary *n* (*pl* **-ries**) statistician who calculates insurance risks > **actuarial** *adj*

actuate *v* (**-tes, -ting, -ted**) start up (a device)

actuated *v* ▷ **actuate**

actuates *v* ▷ **actuate**

actuating *v* ▷ **actuate**

acuities *n* ▷ **acuity**

acuity [ak-**kew**-it-ee] *n* (*pl* **-ties**) keenness of vision or thought

acumen [**ak**-yew-men] *n* (*pl* **-s**) ability to make good judgments

acumens *n* ▷ **acumen**

acupuncture *n* (*pl* **-s**) medical treatment involving the insertion of needles at various points on the body > **acupuncturist** *n* (*pl* **-s**)

acupunctures *n* ▷ **acupuncture**

acupuncturist *n* ▷ **acupuncture**

acupuncturists *n* ▷ **acupuncture**

acute *adj* (**-r, -st**) severe ▶ *n* (*pl* **-s**) accent (´) over a letter to indicate the quality or length of its sound, as in café > **acutely** *adv* > **acuteness** *n*

acutely *adv* ▷ **acute**

acuteness *n* ▷ **acute**

acuter *adj* ▷ **acute**

acutes *n* ▷ **acute**

acutest *adj* ▷ **acute**

ad *n* (*pl* **-s**) (*Informal*) advertisement

adage *n* (*pl* **-s**) wise saying, proverb

adages *n* ▷ **adage**

adagio *n* (*pl* **-gios**) ▶ *adv* (MUSIC) (piece to be played) slowly and gracefully

adagios *n* ▷ **adagio**

adamant *adj* unshakable in determination or purpose > **adamantly** *adv*

adamantly *adv* ▷ **adamant**

adapt *v* (**-s, -ing, -ed**) alter for new use or new conditions > **adaptable** *adj* > **adaptability** *n* (*pl* **-ties**)

adaptabilities *n* ▷ **adapt**

adaptability *n* ▷ **adapt**

adaptable *adj* ▷ **adapt**

adaptation *n* (*pl* **-s**) thing produced by adapting something

adaptations *n* ▷ **adaptation**

adapted *v* ▷ **adapt**

adapter *n* ▷ **adaptor**

adapters *n* ▷ **adaptor**

adapting *v* ▷ **adapt**

adaptor, adapter *n* (*pl* **-s**) device for connecting several electrical appliances to a single socket

adaptors *n* ▷ **adaptor**

adapts *v* ▷ **adapt**

add *v* (**-s, -ing, -ed**) combine (numbers or quantities)

added *v* ▷ **add**

addenda *n* ▷ **addendum**

addendum *n* (*pl* **-da**) addition

adder *n* (*pl* **-s**) small poisonous snake

adders *n* ▷ **adder**

addict *n* (*pl* **-s**) person who is unable to stop taking drugs > **addicted** *adj* > **addiction** *n* (*pl* **-s**)

addicted *adj* ▷ **addict**

addiction *n* ▷ **addict**

addictions *n* ▷ **addict**

addictive *adj* causing addiction

addicts *n* ▷ **addict**

adding *v* ▷ **add**

addition *n* (*pl* **-s**) adding > **additional** *adj* > **additionally** *adv*

additional *adj* ▷ **addition**

additionally *adv* ▷ **addition**

additions *n* ▷ **addition**

additive *n* (*pl* **-s**) something added, esp. to a foodstuff, to improve it or prevent deterioration

additives *n* ▷ **additive**

addled *adj* confused or unable to think clearly

address *n* (*pl* **-es**) place where a person lives ▶ *v* (**-es, -ing, -ed**) mark the destination, as on an envelope

addressed *v* ▷ **address**

addressee *n* (*pl* **-s**) person addressed

addressees *n* ▷ **addressee**

addresses *n, v* ▷ **address**

addressing *v* ▷ **address**

adds *v* ▷ **add**

adduce *v* (**-ces, -cing, -uced**) mention something as evidence or proof

adduced *v* ▷ **adduce**

adduces *v* ▷ **adduce**

adducing *v* ▷ **adduce**

adenoid [**ad**-in-oid] *n* (*pl* **-s**) (usually plural) mass of tissue at the back of the throat

adenoidal *adj* having a nasal voice caused by

swollen adenoids
adenoids *n* ▷ **adenoid**
adept *adj* (**-er, -est**) ▶ *n* (*pl* **-s**) very skilful (person)
adepter *adj* ▷ **adept**
adeptest *adj* ▷ **adept**
adepts *n* ▷ **adept**
adequacies *n* ▷ **adequate**
adequacy *n* ▷ **adequate**
adequate *adj* sufficient, enough > **adequately** *adv* > **adequacy** *n* (*pl* **-ies**)
adequately *adv* ▷ **adequate**
adhere *v* (**-res, -ring, -red**) stick (to) > **adherence** *n* (*pl* **-ces**)
adhered *v* ▷ **adhere**
adherence *n* ▷ **adhere**
adherences *n* ▷ **adhere**
adherent *n* (*pl* **-s**) devotee, follower
adherents *n* ▷ **adherent**
adheres *v* ▷ **adhere**
adhering *v* ▷ **adhere**
adhesion *n* (*pl* **-s**) sticking (to)
adhesions *n* ▷ **adhesion**
adhesive *n* (*pl* **-s**) substance used to stick things together ▶ *adj* able to stick to things
adhesives *n* ▷ **adhesive**
adieu [a-**dew**] *interj* (*Lit*) farewell, goodbye
adipose *adj* of or containing fat
adjacent *adj* near or next (to)
adjectival *adj* ▷ **adjective**
adjective *n* (*pl* **-es**) word that adds information about a noun or pronoun > **adjectival** *adj*
adjectives *n* ▷ **adjective**
adjoin *v* (**-s, -ing, -ed**) be next to > **adjoining** *adj*
adjoined *v* ▷ **adjoin**
adjoining *v, adj* ▷ **adjoin**
adjoins *v* ▷ **adjoin**
adjourn *v* (**-s, -ing, -ed**) close (a court) at the end of a session > **adjournment** *n* (*pl* **-s**)
adjourned *v* ▷ **adjourn**
adjourning *v* ▷ **adjourn**
adjournment *n* ▷ **adjourn**
adjournments *n* ▷ **adjourn**
adjourns *v* ▷ **adjourn**
adjudge *v* (**-ges, -ging, -ged**) declare (to be)
adjudged *v* ▷ **adjudge**
adjudges *v* ▷ **adjudge**
adjudging *v* ▷ **adjudge**
adjudicate *v* (**-tes, -ting, -ted**) give a formal decision on (a dispute) > **adjudication** *n* (*pl* **-s**) > **adjudicator** *n* (*pl* **-s**)
adjudicated *v* ▷ **adjudicate**
adjudicates *v* ▷ **adjudicate**
adjudicating *v* ▷ **adjudicate**
adjudication *n* ▷ **adjudicate**
adjudications *n* ▷ **adjudicate**
adjudicator *n* ▷ **adjudicate**
adjudicators *n* ▷ **adjudicate**
adjunct *n* (*pl* **-s**) subordinate or additional person or thing
adjuncts *n* ▷ **adjunct**
adjure *v* (**-res, -ring, -red**) command (to do)
adjured *v* ▷ **adjure**
adjures *v* ▷ **adjure**
adjuring *v* ▷ **adjure**
adjust *v* (**-s, -ing, -ted**) adapt to new conditions > **adjustable** *adj* > **adjuster** *n* (*pl* **-s**) > **adjustment** *n* (*pl* **-s**)
adjustable *adj* ▷ **adjust**
adjusted *v* ▷ **adjust**
adjuster *n* ▷ **adjust**
adjusters *n* ▷ **adjust**
adjustment *n* ▷ **adjust**
adjustments *n* ▷ **adjust**
adjusts *v* ▷ **adjust**
adjutant [**aj**-oo-tant] *n* (*pl* **-s**) army officer in charge of routine administration
adjutants *n* ▷ **adjutant**
admin *n* (*pl* **-s**) (*Informal*) administration
administer *v* (**-s, -ing, -ed**) manage (business affairs)
administered *v* ▷ **administer**
administering *v* ▷ **administer**
administers *v* ▷ **administer**
administrate *v* (**-tes, -ting, -ated**) manage (an organization) > **administrator** *n* (*pl* **-s**)
administrated *v* ▷ **administrate**
administrates *v* ▷ **administrate**
administrating *v* ▷ **administrate**
administration *n* (*pl* **-s**) management of an organization
administrations *n* ▷ **administration**
administrative *adj* of the management of an organization
administrator *n* ▷ **administrate**
administrators *n* ▷ **administrate**
admins *n* ▷ **admin**
admirable *adj* ▷ **admire**
admirably *adv* ▷ **admire**
admiral *n* (*pl* **-s**) highest naval rank
admirals *n* ▷ **admiral**
admiralties *n* ▷ **admiralty**
admiralty *n* (*pl* **-ties**) the office or jurisdiction of an admiral
admiration *n* ▷ **admire**
admirations *n* ▷ **admire**
admire *v* (**-res, -ring, -red**) regard with esteem and approval > **admirable** *adj* > **admirably** *adv* > **admiration** *n* (*pl* **-s**) > **admirer** *n* (*pl* **-s**) > **admiring** *adj* > **admiringly** *adv*

admired *v* ▷ **admire**

admirer *n* ▷ **admire**

admirers *n* ▷ **admire**

admires *v* ▷ **admire**

admiring *v, adj* ▷ **admire**

admiringly *adv* ▷ **admire**

admissibilities *n* ▷ **admissible**

admissibility *n* ▷ **admissible**

admissible *adj* allowed to be brought in as evidence in court > **admissibility** *n* (*pl* **-ties**)

admission *n* (*pl* **-s**) permission to enter

admissions *n* ▷ **admission**

admit *v* (**-mits, -mitting, -mitted**) confess, acknowledge

admits *v* ▷ **admit**

admittance *n* (*pl* **-s**) permission to enter

admittances *n* ▷ **admittance**

admitted *v* ▷ **admit**

admittedly *adv* it must be agreed

admitting *v* ▷ **admit**

admixture *n* (*pl* **-s**) mixture

admixtures *n* ▷ **admixture**

admonish *v* (**-es, -ing, -ed**) reprove sternly > **admonition** *n* (*pl* **-s**)

admonished *v* ▷ **admonish**

admonishes *v* ▷ **admonish**

admonishing *v* ▷ **admonish**

admonition *n* ▷ **admonish**

admonitions *n* ▷ **admonish**

ado *n* (*pl* **-s**) (*Lit*) fuss, trouble

adobe [ad-**oh**-bee] *n* (*pl* **-s**) sun-dried brick

adobes *n* ▷ **adobe**

adolescence *n* (*pl* **-s**) period between puberty and adulthood

adolescences *n* ▷ **adolescence**

adolescent *n* (*pl* **-s**), *adj* (person) between puberty and adulthood

adolescents *n* ▷ **adolescent**

adopt *v* (**-s, -ing, -ed**) take (someone else's child) as one's own > **adoption** *n* (*pl* **-s**)

adopted *v* ▷ **adopt**

adopting *v* ▷ **adopt**

adoption *n* ▷ **adopt**

adoptions *n* ▷ **adopt**

adoptive *adj* related by adoption

adopts *v* ▷ **adopt**

adorable *adj* ▷ **adore**

adoration *n* ▷ **adore**

adorations *n* ▷ **adore**

adore *v* (**-res, -ring, -red**) love intensely > **adorable** *adj* > **adoration** *n* (*pl* **-s**) > **adoring** *adj* > **adoringly** *adv*

adored *v* ▷ **adore**

adores *v* ▷ **adore**

adoring *v, adj* ▷ **adore**

adoringly *adv* ▷ **adore**

adorn *v* (**-s, -ing, -ed**) decorate, embellish > **adornment** *n* (*pl* **-s**)

adorned *v* ▷ **adorn**

adorning *v* ▷ **adorn**

adornment *n* ▷ **adorn**

adornments *n* ▷ **adorn**

adorns *v* ▷ **adorn**

ados *n* ▷ **ado**

adrenal [ad-**reen**-al] *adj* near the kidneys

adrenalin, adrenaline *n* (*pl* **-s**) hormone secreted by the adrenal glands in response to stress

adrenaline *n* ▷ **adrenalin**

adrenalines *n* ▷ **adrenalin**

adrenalins *n* ▷ **adrenalin**

adrift *adj, adv* drifting

adroit *adj* quick and skilful > **adroitly** *adv* > **adroitness** *n*

adroitly *adv* ▷ **adroit**

adroitness *n* ▷ **adroit**

ads *n* ▷ **ad**

adsorb *v* (**-s, -ing, -ed**) (of a gas or vapour) condense and form a thin film on a surface > **adsorption** *n* (*pl* **-s**)

adsorbed *v* ▷ **adsorb**

adsorbing *v* ▷ **adsorb**

adsorbs *v* ▷ **adsorb**

adsorption *n* ▷ **adsorb**

adsorptions *n* ▷ **adsorb**

adulation *n* (*pl* **-s**) uncritical admiration

adulations *n* ▷ **adulation**

adult *adj* fully grown, mature ▶ *n* (*pl* **-s**) adult person or animal > **adulthood** *n* (*pl* **-s**)

adulterate *v* (**-tes, -ting, -ted**) spoil something by adding inferior material > **adulteration** *n* (*pl* **-s**)

adulterated *v* ▷ **adulterate**

adulterates *v* ▷ **adulterate**

adulterating *v* ▷ **adulterate**

adulteration *n* ▷ **adulterate**

adulterations *n* ▷ **adulterate**

adulterer *n* ▷ **adultery**

adulterers *n* ▷ **adultery**

adulteress *n* ▷ **adultery**

adulteresses *n* ▷ **adultery**

adulteries *n* ▷ **adultery**

adulterous *adj* ▷ **adultery**

adultery *n* (*pl* **-teries**) sexual unfaithfulness of a husband or wife > **adulterer** *n* (*pl* **-s**) > **adulteress** *n* (*pl* **-es**) > **adulterous** *adj*

adulthood *n* ▷ **adult**

adulthoods *n* ▷ **adult**

adults *n* ▷ **adult**

advance *v* (**-ces, -cing, -ced**) go or bring

forward ▶ *n* (*pl* **-s**) forward movement ▶ *adj* done or happening before an event
advanced *adj* at a late stage in development ▶ *v* ▷ **advance**
advancement *n* (*pl* **advancements**) promotion
advancements *n* ▷ **advancement**
advances *v, n* ▷ **advance**
advancing *v* ▷ **advance**
advantage *n* (*pl* **-s**) more favourable position or state > **advantageous** *adj* > **advantageously** *adv*
advantageous *adj* ▷ **advantage**
advantageously *adv* ▷ **advantage**
advantages *n* ▷ **advantage**
advent *n* (*pl* **-s**) arrival
adventitious *adj* added or appearing accidentally
advents *n* ▷ **advent**
adventure *n* (*pl* **-s**) exciting and risky undertaking or exploit > **adventurous** *adj*
adventurer *n* (*pl* **-s**) person who unscrupulously seeks money or power
adventurers *n* ▷ **adventurer**
adventures *n* ▷ **adventure**
adventuress *n* (*pl* **-es**) woman who unscrupulously seeks money or power
adventuresses *n* ▷ **adventuress**
adventurous *adj* ▷ **adventure**
adverb *n* (*pl* **-s**) word that adds information about a verb, adjective, or other adverb > **adverbial** *adj*
adverbial *adj* ▷ **adverb**
adverbs *n* ▷ **adverb**
adversaries *n* ▷ **adversary**
adversary [**ad**-verse-er-ree] *n* (*pl* **-ries**) opponent or enemy
adverse *adj* unfavourable > **adversely** *adv*
adversely *adv* ▷ **adverse**
adversities *n* ▷ **adversity**
adversity *n* (*pl* **-ties**) very difficult or hard circumstances
advert *n* (*pl* **-s**) (*Informal*) advertisement
advertise *v* (**-ses, -sing, -sed**) present or praise (goods or services) to the public in order to encourage sales > **advertiser** *n* (*pl* **-s**) > **advertising** *adj, n* (*pl* **-s**)
advertised *v* ▷ **advertise**
advertisement *n* (*pl* **-s**) public announcement to sell goods or publicize an event
advertisements *n* ▷ **advertisement**
advertiser *n* ▷ **advertise**
advertises *v* ▷ **advertise**
advertising *v, adj n* ▷ **advertise**
advertisings *n* ▷ **advertise**
adverts *n* ▷ **advert**
advice *n* (*pl* **-s**) recommendation as to what to do
advices *n* ▷ **advice**
advisabilities *n* ▷ **advisable**
advisability *n* ▷ **advisable**
advisable *adj* prudent, sensible > **advisability** *n* (*pl* **-ties**)
advise *v* (**-ses, -sing, -sed**) offer advice to
advised *adj* considered, thought-out ▶ *v* ▷ **advise**
advisedly *adv* deliberately
adviser, advisor *n* (*pl* **-s**) person who offers advice, e.g. on careers to students or school pupils
advisers *n* ▷ **adviser**
advises *v* ▷ **advise**
advising *v* ▷ **advise**
advisor *n* ▷ **adviser**
advisors *n* ▷ **adviser**
advisory *adj* giving advice
advocaat *n* (*pl* **-s**) liqueur with a raw egg base
advocaats *n* ▷ **advocaat**
advocacies *n* ▷ **advocate**
advocacy *n* ▷ **advocate**
advocate *v* (**-tes, -ting, -ted**) propose or recommend ▶ *n* (*pl* **-s**) person who publicly supports a cause > **advocacy** *n* (*pl* **-cies**)
advocated *v* ▷ **advocate**
advocates *v, n* ▷ **advocate**
advocating *v* ▷ **advocate**
adz *n* ▷ **adze**
adze, adz *n* (*pl* **adzes**) tool with an arched blade at right angles to the handle
adzes *n* ▷ **adze**

ae *adj*. Ae is a Scots word that means **one**. This is a useful word to remember when you want to form words in two directions at once. Ae scores 2 points.

aegis [**ee**-jiss] *n* (*pl* **-es**) sponsorship, protection
aegises *n* ▷ **aegis**
aeon [**ee**-on] *n* (*pl* **-s**) immeasurably long period of time
aeons *n* ▷ **aeon**
aerate *v* (**-tes, -ting, -ted**) put gas into (a liquid), as when making a fizzy drink > **aeration** *n* (*pl* **-s**)
aerated *v* ▷ **aerate**
aerates *v* ▷ **aerate**
aerating *v* ▷ **aerate**
aeration *n* ▷ **aerate**
aerations *n* ▷ **aerate**
aerial *adj* in, from, or operating in the air ▶ *n* (*pl* **-ls**) metal pole, wire, etc., for receiving or transmitting radio or TV signals

aerials *n* ▷ **aerial**
aerobatic *adj* ▷ **aerobatics**
aerobatics *pl n* stunt flying > **aerobatic** *adj*
aerobic *adj* ▷ **aerobics**
aerobics *n* exercises designed to increase the amount of oxygen in the blood > **aerobic** *adj*
aerodrome *n* (*pl* **-s**) small airport
aerodromes *n* ▷ **aerodrome**
aerodynamic *adj* ▷ **aerodynamics**
aerodynamics *n* study of how air flows around moving solid objects > **aerodynamic** *adj*
aerofoil *n* (*pl* **-s**) part of an aircraft, such as the wing, designed to give lift
aerofoils *n* ▷ **aerofoil**
aerogram *n* (*pl* **-s**) airmail letter on a single sheet of paper that seals to form an envelope
aerograms *n* ▷ **aerogram**
aeronautical *adj* ▷ **aeronautics**
aeronautics *n* study or practice of aircraft flight > **aeronautical** *adj*
aeroplane *n* (*pl* **-s**) powered flying vehicle with fixed wings
aeroplanes *n* ▷ **aeroplane**
aerosol *n* (*pl* **-s**) pressurized can from which a substance can be dispensed as a fine spray
aerosols *n* ▷ **aerosol**
aerospace *n* (*pl* **-s**) earth's atmosphere and space beyond
aerospaces *n* ▷ **aerospace**
aesthete [**eess**-theet] *n* (*pl* **-s**) person who has or affects an extravagant love of art > **aestheticism** *n* (*pl* **-s**)
aesthetes *n* ▷ **aesthete**
aesthetic [iss-**thet**-ik] *adj* relating to the appreciation of art and beauty > **aesthetically** *adv*
aesthetically *adv* ▷ **aesthetic**
aestheticism *n* ▷ **aesthete**
aestheticisms *n* ▷ **aesthete**
aesthetics *n* study of art, beauty, and good taste
aether *n* (*pl* **-s**) ▷ **ether**
aethers *n* ▷ **aether**
aetiologies *n* ▷ **aetiology**
aetiology [ee-tee-**ol**-a-jee] *n* (*pl* **-gies**) ▷ **etiology**
afar *adv* from or at a great distance
affabilities *n* ▷ **affable**
affability *n* ▷ **affable**
affable *adj* friendly and easy to talk to > **affably** *adv* > **affability** *n* (*pl* **-ties**)
affably *adv* ▷ **affable**
affair *n* (*pl* **-s**) event or happening
affairs *n* ▷ **affair**
affect[1] *v* (**-s, -ing, -ed**) act on, influence
affect[2] *v* (**-s, -ing, -ed**) put on a show of
affectation *n* (*pl* **-s**) attitude or manner put on to impress
affectations *n* ▷ **affectation**
affected *adj* displaying affectation ▶ *v* ▷ **affect**[1, 2]
affecting *v* ▷ **affect**[1, 2]
affection *n* (*pl* **-s**) fondness or love
affectionate *adj* loving > **affectionately** *adv*
affectionately *adv* ▷ **affectionate**
affections *n* ▷ **affection**
affects *v* ▷ **affect**[1, 2]
affianced [af-**fie**-anst] *adj* (*Old-fashioned*) engaged to be married
affidavit [af-fid-**dave**-it] *n* (*pl* **-s**) written statement made on oath
affidavits *n* ▷ **affidavit**
affiliate *v* (**-tes, -ting, -ted**) (of a group) link up with a larger group > **affiliation** *n* (*pl* **-s**)
affiliated *v* ▷ **affiliate**
affiliates *v* ▷ **affiliate**
affiliating *v* ▷ **affiliate**
affiliation *n* ▷ **affiliate**
affiliations *n* ▷ **affiliate**
affinities *n* ▷ **affinity**
affinity *n* (*pl* **-ties**) close connection or liking
affirm *v* (**-s, -ing, -ed**) declare to be true > **affirmation** *n* (*pl* **-s**)
affirmation *n* ▷ **affirm**
affirmations *n* ▷ **affirm**
affirmative *n* (*pl* **-s**), *adj* (word or phrase) indicating agreement
affirmatives *n* ▷ **affirmative**
affirmed *v* ▷ **affirm**
affirming *v* ▷ **affirm**
affirms *v* ▷ **affirm**
affix *v* (**-fixes, -fixing, -fixed**) attach or fasten ▶ *n* (*pl* **-fixes**) word or syllable added to a word to change its meaning
affixed *v* ▷ **affix**
affixes *v, n* ▷ **affix**
affixing *v* ▷ **affix**
afflict *v* (**-s, -ing, -ed**) give pain or grief to > **affliction** *n* (*pl* **-s**)
afflicted *v* ▷ **afflict**
afflicting *v* ▷ **afflict**
affliction *n* ▷ **afflict**
afflictions *n* ▷ **afflict**
afflicts *v* ▷ **afflict**
affluence *n* (*pl* **-s**) wealth
affluences *n* ▷ **affluence**
affluent *adj* having plenty of money
afford *v* (**-s, -ing, -ed**) have enough money to buy > **affordable** *adj*
affordable *adj* ▷ **afford**

afforded *v* ▷ **afford**
affording *v* ▷ **afford**
affords *v* ▷ **afford**
afforest *v* (**-s, -ing, -ed**) plant trees on > **afforestation** *n* (*pl* **-s**)
afforestation *n* ▷ **afforest**
afforestations *n* ▷ **afforest**
afforested *v* ▷ **afforest**
afforesting *v* ▷ **afforest**
afforests *v* ▷ **afforest**
affray *n* (*pl* **-s**) (BRIT, AUST & NZ) (LAW) noisy fight, brawl
affrays *n* ▷ **affray**
affront *v* (**-s, -ing, -ed**), *n* (*pl* **-s**) insult
affronted *v* ▷ **affront**
affronting *v* ▷ **affront**
affronts *v, n* ▷ **affront**
afghan *adj* of Afghanistan or its language
aficionado [af-fish-yo-**nah**-do] *n* (*pl* **-dos**) enthusiastic fan of something or someone
aficionados *n* ▷ **aficionado**
afield *adv* far away
aflame *adj* burning
afloat *adv, adj* floating
afoot *adv, adj* happening, in operation
aforementioned *adj* referred to previously
aforesaid *adj* referred to previously
aforethought *adj* premeditated
afraid *adj* frightened
afresh *adv* again, anew
aft *adv* at or towards the rear of a ship or aircraft
after *prep* following in time or place ▶ *conj* at a later time than ▶ *adv* at a later time
afterbirth *n* (*pl* **-s**) material expelled from the womb after childbirth
afterbirths *n* ▷ **afterbirth**
aftercare *n* (*pl* **-s**) support given to a person discharged from a hospital or prison
aftercares *n* ▷ **aftercare**
aftereffect *n* (*pl* **-s**) result occurring some time after its cause
aftereffects *n* ▷ **aftereffect**
afterglow *n* (*pl* **-s**) glow left after a source of light has gone
afterglows *n* ▷ **afterglow**
afterlife *n* (*pl* **-lives**) life after death
afterlives *n* ▷ **afterlife**
aftermath *n* (*pl* **-s**) results of an event considered together
aftermaths *n* ▷ **aftermath**
afternoon *n* (*pl* **-s**) time between noon and evening
afternoons *n* ▷ **afternoon**
afters *pl n* (BRIT) (*Informal*) dessert
aftershave *n* (*pl* **-s**) lotion applied to the face after shaving
aftershaves *n* ▷ **aftershave**
afterthought *n* (*pl* **-s**) idea occurring later
afterthoughts *n* ▷ **afterthought**
afterward *adv* ▷ **afterwards**
afterwards, afterward *adv* later

> **ag** *adj*. Ag means to do with **agriculture**. This is a good short word to remember, as it can come in handy when you need to form words in more than one direction. Ag scores 3 points.

again *adv* once more
against *prep* in opposition or contrast to
agape *adj* (of the mouth) wide open
agaric *n* (*pl* **-s**) fungus with gills on the underside of the cap, such as a mushroom
agarics *n* ▷ **agaric**
agate [**ag**-git] *n* (*pl* **-s**) semiprecious form of quartz with striped colouring
agates *n* ▷ **agate**
age *n* (*pl* **-s**) length of time a person or thing has existed ▶ *v* (**-s, ageing** *or* **aging, -d**) make or grow old > **ageing, aging** *n, adj*
aged *adj* [**ay**-jid] old ▷ **age**
ageing *v, n, adj* ▷ **age**
ageless *adj* apparently never growing old
agencies *n* ▷ **agency**
agency *n* (*pl* **-cies**) organization providing a service
agenda *n* (*pl* **-s**) list of things to be dealt with, esp. at a meeting
agendas *n* ▷ **agenda**
agent *n* (*pl* **-s**) person acting on behalf of another
agents *n* ▷ **agent**
ages *n, v* ▷ **age**
agglomeration *n* (*pl* **-s**) confused mass or cluster
agglomerations *n* ▷ **agglomeration**
aggrandize *v* (**-zes, -zing, -zed**) make greater in size, power, or rank > **aggrandizement** *n* (*pl* **-s**)
aggrandized *v* ▷ **aggrandize**
aggrandizement *n* ▷ **aggrandize**
aggrandizements *n* ▷ **aggrandize**
aggrandizes *v* ▷ **aggrandize**
aggrandizing *v* ▷ **aggrandize**
aggravate *v* (**-tes, -ting, -ted**) make worse > **aggravating** *adj* > **aggravation** *n* (*pl* **-s**)
aggravated *v* ▷ **aggravate**
aggravates *v* ▷ **aggravate**
aggravating *v, adj* ▷ **aggravate**
aggravation *n* ▷ **aggravate**
aggravations *n* ▷ **aggravate**

aggregate *n* (*pl* **-s**) total ▶ *adj* gathered into a mass ▶ *v* (**-tes, -ting, -ted**) combine into a whole > **aggregation** *n* (*pl* **-s**)
aggregated *v* ▷ **aggregate**
aggregates *n, v* ▷ **aggregate**
aggregating *v* ▷ **aggregate**
aggregation *n* ▷ **aggregate**
aggregations *n* ▷ **aggregate**
aggression *n* (*pl* **-s**) hostile behaviour > **aggressor** *n* (*pl* **-s**)
aggressions *n* ▷ **aggression**
aggressive *adj* showing aggression > **aggressively** *adv* > **aggressiveness** *n*
aggressively *adv* ▷ **aggressive**
aggressiveness *n* ▷ **aggressive**
aggressor *n* ▷ **aggression**
aggressors *n* ▷ **aggression**
aggrieved *adj* upset and angry
aggro *n* (*pl* **-s**) (BRIT, AUST & NZ) (*Slang*) aggressive behaviour
aggros *n* ▷ **aggro**
aghast *adj* overcome with amazement or horror
agile *adj* (**-r, -st**) nimble, quick-moving > **agility** *n* (*pl* **-ties**)
agiler *adj* ▷ **agile**
agilest *adj* ▷ **agile**
agilities *n* ▷ **agile**
agility *n* ▷ **agile**
aging *v, n, adj* ▷ **age**
agitate *v* (**-tes, -ting, -ted**) disturb or excite > **agitation** *n* (*pl* **-s**) > **agitator** *n* (*pl* **-s**)
agitated *v* ▷ **agitate**
agitates *v* ▷ **agitate**
agitating *v* ▷ **agitate**
agitation *n* ▷ **agitate**
agitations *n* ▷ **agitate**
agitator *n* ▷ **agitate**
agitators *n* ▷ **agitate**
aglow *adj* glowing
agnostic *n* (*pl* **-s**) person who believes that it is impossible to know whether God exists ▶ *adj* of agnostics > **agnosticism** *n* (*pl* **-s**)
agnosticism *n* ▷ **agnostic**
agnosticisms *n* ▷ **agnostic**
agnostics *n* ▷ **agnostic**
ago *adv* in the past
agog *adj* eager or curious
agonies *n* ▷ **agony**
agonize *v* (**-zes, -zing, -zed**) worry greatly > **agonizing** *adj*
agonized *v* ▷ **agonize**
agonizes *v* ▷ **agonize**
agonizing *v, adj* ▷ **agonize**
agony *n* (*pl* **-nies**) extreme physical or mental pain
agoraphobia *n* (*pl* **-s**) fear of open spaces > **agoraphobic** *n* (*pl* **-s**), *adj*
agoraphobias *n* ▷ **agoraphobia**
agoraphobic *n, adj* ▷ **agoraphobia**
agoraphobics *n* ▷ **agoraphobic**
agrarian *adj* of land or agriculture
agree *v* (**-s, -ing, -d**) be of the same opinion
agreeable *adj* pleasant and enjoyable > **agreeably** *adv*
agreeably *adv* ▷ **agreeable**
agreed *v* ▷ **agree**
agreeing *v* ▷ **agree**
agreement *n* (*pl* **agreements**) agreeing
agreements *n* ▷ **agreement**
agrees *v* ▷ **agree**
agricultural *adj* ▷ **agriculture**
agriculturalist *n* ▷ **agriculture**
agriculturalists *n* ▷ **agriculture**
agriculture *n* (*pl* **-s**) raising of crops and livestock > **agricultural** *adj* > **agriculturalist** *n* (*pl* **-s**)
agricultures *n* ▷ **agriculture**
agronomies *n* ▷ **agronomy**
agronomist *n* ▷ **agronomy**
agronomists *n* ▷ **agronomy**
agronomy [ag-**ron**-om-mee] *n* (*pl* **-mies**) science of soil management and crop production > **agronomist** *n* (*pl* **-s**)
aground *adv* onto the bottom of shallow water
ague [**aig**-yew] *n* (*pl* **-s**) (*Old-fashioned*) periodic fever with shivering
agues *n* ▷ **ague**

ah *interj*. Ah is a sound people make to show pleasure or pain. Ah scores 5 points, and is a good word to form as a result of playing a longer word.

ahead *adv* in front
ahoy *interj* shout used at sea to attract attention

ai *n* (**ais**). An ai is a three-toed sloth. Although ai only scores 2 points, it's a useful word to remember when you're trying to form several words at once.

aid *v* (**-s, -ing, -ed**) ▶ *n* (*pl* **-s**) (give) assistance or support
aide *n* (*pl* **-s**) assistant
aided *v* ▷ **aid**
aides *n* ▷ **aide**
aiding *v* ▷ **aid**
aids *v, n* ▷ **aid**
ail *v* (**-s, -ing, -ed**) trouble, afflict
ailed *v* ▷ **ail**
aileron *n* (*pl* **-s**) movable flap on an aircraft

wing which controls rolling
ailerons *n* ▷ **aileron**
ailing *adj* sickly ▶ *v* ▷ **ail**
ailment *n* (*pl* **-s**) illness
ailments *n* ▷ **ailment**
ails *v* ▷ **ail**
aim *v* (**-s, -ing, -ed**) point (a weapon or missile) or direct (a blow or remark) at a target ▶ *n* (*pl* **-s**) aiming
aimed *v* ▷ **aim**
aiming *v* ▷ **aim**
aimless *adj* having no purpose > **aimlessly** *adv*
aimlessly *adv* ▷ **aimless**
aims *v, n* ▷ **aim**
air *n* (*pl* **-s**) mixture of gases forming the earth's atmosphere ▶ *v* (**-s, -ing, -ed**) make known publicly
airborne *adj* carried by air
airbrush *n* (*pl* **-es**) atomizer spraying paint by compressed air
airbrushes *n* ▷ **airbrush**
aircraft *n* any machine that flies, such as an aeroplane
aired *v* ▷ **air**
airfield *n* (*pl* **-s**) place where aircraft can land and take off
airfields *n* ▷ **airfield**
airier *adj* ▷ **airy**
airiest *adj* ▷ **airy**
airily *adv* ▷ **airy**
airing *n* (*pl* **-s**) exposure to air for drying or ventilation ▶ *v* ▷ **air**
airings *n* ▷ **airing**
airless *adj* stuffy
airlift *n* (*pl* **-s**) transport of troops or cargo by aircraft when other routes are blocked ▶ *v* (**-s, -ing, -ed**) transport by airlift
airlifted *v* ▷ **airlift**
airlifting *v* ▷ **airlift**
airlifts *n, v* ▷ **airlift**
airline *n* (*pl* **-s**) company providing scheduled flights for passengers and cargo
airliner *n* (*pl* **-s**) large passenger aircraft
airliners *n* ▷ **airliner**
airlines *n* ▷ **airline**
airlock *n* (*pl* **-s**) air bubble blocking the flow of liquid in a pipe
airlocks *n* ▷ **airlock**
airmail *n* system of sending mail by aircraft
airman *n* (*pl* **-men**) member of the air force
airmen *n* ▷ **airman**
airplay *n* (*pl* **-s**) broadcast performances of a record on radio
airplays *n* ▷ **airplay**
airport *n* (*pl* **-s**) airfield for civilian aircraft, with facilities for aircraft maintenance and passengers
airports *n* ▷ **airport**
airs *n, v* ▷ **air**
airship *n* (*pl* **-s**) lighter-than-air self-propelled aircraft
airships *n* ▷ **airship**
airspace *n* (*pl* **-s**) atmosphere above a country, regarded as its territory
airspaces *n* ▷ **airspace**
airstrip *n* (*pl* **-s**) cleared area where aircraft can take off and land
airstrips *n* ▷ **airstrip**
airtight *adj* sealed so that air cannot enter
airworthiness *n* ▷ **airworthy**
airworthinesses *n* ▷ **airworthy**
airworthy *adj* (of aircraft) fit to fly > **airworthiness** *n* (*pl* **-es**)
airy *adj* (**-rier, -riest**) well-ventilated > **airily** *adv*
aisle [rhymes with **mile**] *n* (*pl* **-s**) passageway separating seating areas in a church, theatre, etc., or row of shelves in a supermarket
aisles *n* ▷ **aisle**
ajar *adj, adv* (of a door) partly open
akimbo *adv* with hands on hips and elbows outwards
akin *adj* similar, related
al *conj*. Al is an old word for **if** or **although**. Al scores 2 points.
alabaster *n* (*pl* **-s**) soft white translucent stone
alabasters *n* ▷ **alabaster**
alacrities *n* ▷ **alacrity**
alacrity *n* (*pl* **-ies**) speed, eagerness
alarm *n* (*pl* **-s**) sudden fear caused by awareness of danger ▶ *v* (**-s, -ing, -med**) fill with fear > **alarming** *adj*
alarmed *v* ▷ **alarm**
alarming *v, adj* ▷ **alarm**
alarmist *n* (*pl* **-s**) person who alarms others needlessly
alarmists *n* ▷ **alarmist**
alarms *n, v* ▷ **alarm**
alas *adv* unfortunately, regrettably
albatross *n* (*pl* **-es**) large sea bird with very long wings
albatrosses *n* ▷ **albatross**
albeit *conj* even though
albino *n* (*pl* **-nos**) person or animal with white skin and hair and pink eyes
albinos *n* ▷ **albino**
album *n* (*pl* **-s**) book with blank pages for keeping photographs or stamps in
albumen *n* (*pl* **-s**) egg white
albumens *n* ▷ **albumen**
albumin *n* (*pl* **-s**) protein found in blood

plasma, egg white, milk, and muscle
albumins *n* ▷ **albumin**
albums *n* ▷ **album**
alchemies *n* ▷ **alchemy**
alchemist *n* ▷ **alchemy**
alchemists *n* ▷ **alchemy**
alchemy *n* (*pl* **-ies**) medieval form of chemistry concerned with trying to turn base metals into gold and to find the elixir of life > **alchemist** *n* (*pl* **-s**)
alcohol *n* (*pl* **-s**) colourless flammable liquid present in intoxicating drinks
alcoholic *adj* of alcohol ▶ *n* (*pl* **-s**) person addicted to alcohol
alcoholics *n* ▷ **alcoholic**
alcoholism *n* (*pl* **-s**) addiction to alcohol
alcoholisms *n* ▷ **alcoholism**
alcohols *n* ▷ **alcohol**
alcopop *n* (*pl* **-s**) (BRIT, AUST & S AFR) (*Informal*) alcoholic drink that tastes like a soft drink
alcopops *n* ▷ **alcopop**
alcove *n* (*pl* **-s**) recess in the wall of a room
alcoves *n* ▷ **alcove**
aldehyde *n* (*pl* **-s**) one of a group of chemical compounds derived from alcohol by oxidation
aldehydes *n* ▷ **aldehyde**
alder *n* (*pl* **-s**) tree related to the birch
alderman *n* (*pl* **-men**) formerly, senior member of a local council
aldermen *n* ▷ **alderman**
alders *n* ▷ **alder**
ale *n* (*pl* **-s**) kind of beer
alert *adj* (**-er, -est**) watchful, attentive ▶ *n* (*pl* **-s**) warning of danger ▶ *v* (**-s, -ing, -ed**) warn of danger > **alertness** *n* (*pl* **-es**)
alerted *v* ▷ **alert**
alerter *adj* ▷ **alert**
alertest *adj* ▷ **alert**
alerting *v* ▷ **alert**
alertness *n* ▷ **alert**
alertnesses *n* ▷ **alert**
alerts *n, v* ▷ **alert**
ales *n* ▷ **ale**
alfalfa *n* (*pl* **-s**) kind of plant used to feed livestock
alfalfas *n* ▷ **alfalfa**
alfresco *adv, adj* in the open air
alga *n* (*pl* **-e**) (usually plural) plant which lives in or near water and has no true stems, leaves, or roots
algae [**al**-jee] *n* ▷ **alga**
algebra *n* (*pl* **-s**) branch of mathematics using symbols to represent numbers > **algebraic** *adj*
algebraic *adj* ▷ **algebra**
algebras *n* ▷ **algebra**
algorithm *n* (*pl* **-s**) logical arithmetical or computational procedure for solving a problem
algorithms *n* ▷ **algorithm**
alias *adv* also known as ▶ *n* (*pl* **-ses**) false name
aliases *n* ▷ **alias**
alibi *n* (*pl* **-s**) plea of being somewhere else when a crime was committed
alibis *n* ▷ **alibi**
alien *adj* foreign ▶ *n* (*pl* **-s**) foreigner
alienate *v* (**-tes, -ting, -ted**) cause to become hostile > **alienation** *n* (*pl* **-s**)
alienated *v* ▷ **alienate**
alienates *v* ▷ **alienate**
alienating *v* ▷ **alienate**
alienation *n* ▷ **alienate**
alienations *n* ▷ **alienate**
aliens *n* ▷ **alien**
alight[1] *v* (**-s, -ing, -ed**) step out of (a vehicle)
alight[2] *adj* on fire
alighted *v* ▷ **alight[1]**
alighting *v* ▷ **alight[1]**
alights *v* ▷ **alight[1]**
align [a-**line**] *v* (**-s, -ing, -ed**) bring (a person or group) into agreement with the policy of another > **alignment** *n* (*pl* **-s**)
aligned *v* ▷ **align**
aligning *v* ▷ **align**
alignment *n* ▷ **align**
alignments *n* ▷ **align**
aligns *v* ▷ **align**
alike *adj* like, similar ▶ *adv* in the same way
alimentary *adj* of nutrition
alimonies *n* ▷ **alimony**
alimony *n* (*pl* **-nies**) allowance paid under a court order to a separated or divorced spouse
aliquot (MATHS) *adj* of or denoting an exact divisor of a number ▶ *n* (*pl* **-s**) exact divisor
aliquots *n* ▷ **aliquot**
alive *adj* living, in existence
alkali [**alk**-a-lie] *n* (*pl* **-s**) substance which combines with acid and neutralizes it to form a salt > **alkaline** *adj* > **alkalinity** *n* (*pl* **-ties**)
alkaline *adj* ▷ **alkali**
alkalinities *n* ▷ **alkali**
alkalinity *n* ▷ **alkali**
alkalis *n* ▷ **alkali**
alkaloid *n* (*pl* **-s**) any of a group of organic compounds containing nitrogen
alkaloids *n* ▷ **alkaloid**
all *adj* whole quantity or number (of) ▶ *adv* wholly, entirely
allay *v* (**-s, -ing, -ed**) reduce (fear or anger)
allayed *v* ▷ **allay**

allaying *v* ▷ **allay**
allays *v* ▷ **allay**
allegation *n* (*pl* **-s**) unproved accusation
allegations *n* ▷ **allegation**
allege *v* (**-ges, -ging, -ged**) state without proof > **alleged** *adj* > **allegedly** *adv*
alleged *v, adj* ▷ **allege**
allegedly *adv* ▷ **allege**
alleges *v* ▷ **allege**
allegiance *n* (*pl* **-s**) loyalty to a person, country, or cause
allegiances *n* ▷ **allegiance**
alleging *v* ▷ **allege**
allegorical *adj* ▷ **allegory**
allegories *n* ▷ **allegory**
allegory *n* (*pl* **-ries**) story with an underlying meaning as well as the literal one > **allegorical** *adj*
allegretto *n* (*pl* **-s**) ▶ *adv* (MUSIC) (piece to be played) fairly quickly or briskly
allegrettos *n* ▷ **allegretto**
allegro *n* (*pl* **-s**) ▶ *adv* (MUSIC) (piece to be played) in a brisk lively manner
allegros *n* ▷ **allegro**
alleluia *interj* ▷ **hallelujah**
allergen *n* (*pl* **-s**) substance capable of causing an allergic reaction
allergens *n* ▷ **allergen**
allergic *adj* having or caused by an allergy
allergies *n* ▷ **allergy**
allergy *n* (*pl* **-gies**) extreme sensitivity to a substance, which causes the body to react to it
alleviate *v* (**-tes, -ting, -ted**) lessen (pain or suffering) > **alleviation** *n* (*pl* **-s**)
alleviated *v* ▷ **alleviate**
alleviates *v* ▷ **alleviate**
alleviating *v* ▷ **alleviate**
alleviation *n* ▷ **alleviate**
alleviations *n* ▷ **alleviate**
alley *n* (*pl* **-s**) narrow street or path
alleys *n* ▷ **alley**
alliance *n* (*pl* **-s**) state of being allied
alliances *n* ▷ **alliance**
allied *v, adj* ▷ **ally**
allies *n, v* ▷ **ally**
alligator *n* (*pl* **-s**) reptile of the crocodile family, found in the southern US and China
alligators *n* ▷ **alligator**
alliteration *n* (*pl* **-s**) use of the same sound at the start of words occurring together, e.g. *moody music* > **alliterative** *adj*
alliterations *n* ▷ **alliteration**
alliterative *adj* ▷ **alliteration**
allocate *v* (**-tes, -ting, -ted**) assign to someone or for a particular purpose > **allocation** *n* (*pl* **-s**)
allocated *v* ▷ **allocate**
allocates *v* ▷ **allocate**
allocating *v* ▷ **allocate**
allocation *n* ▷ **allocate**
allocations *n* ▷ **allocate**
allot *v* (**-lots, -lotting, -lotted**) assign as a share or for a particular purpose
allotment *n* (*pl* **-s**) distribution
allotments *n* ▷ **allotment**
allotrope *n* (*pl* **-s**) any of two or more physical forms in which an element can exist
allotropes *n* ▷ **allotrope**
allots *v* ▷ **allot**
allotted *v* ▷ **allot**
allotting *v* ▷ **allot**
allow *v* (**-s, -ing, -ed**) permit > **allowable** *adj*
allowable *adj* ▷ **allow**
allowance *n* (*pl* **-s**) amount of money given at regular intervals
allowances *n* ▷ **allowance**
allowed *v* ▷ **allow**
allowing *v* ▷ **allow**
allows *v* ▷ **allow**
alloy *n* (*pl* **-s**) mixture of two or more metals ▶ *v* (**-s, -ing, -ed**) mix (metals)
alloyed *v* ▷ **alloy**
alloying *v* ▷ **alloy**
alloys *n, v* ▷ **alloy**
allspice *n* (*pl* **-s**) spice made from the berries of a tropical American tree
allspices *n* ▷ **allspice**
allude *v* (**-des, -ding, -ded**) (*foll. by* **to**) refer indirectly to
alluded *v* ▷ **allude**
alludes *v* ▷ **allude**
alluding *v* ▷ **allude**
allure *n* (*pl* **-s**) attractiveness ▶ *v* (**-s, -ing, -ed**) entice or attract > **alluring** *adj*
allured *v* ▷ **allure**
allures *n, v* ▷ **allure**
alluring *v, adj* ▷ **allure**
allusion *n* (*pl* **-s**) indirect reference > **allusive** *adj*
allusions *n* ▷ **allusion**
allusive *adj* ▷ **allusion**
alluvial *adj* ▷ **alluvium**
alluvium *n* (*pl* **-s**) fertile soil deposited by flowing water > **alluvial** *adj*
alluviums *n* ▷ **alluvium**
ally *n* (*pl* **-lies**) country, person, or group with an agreement to support another ▶ *v* (**-lies, -lying, -lied**) > **allied** *adj*
allying *v* ▷ **ally**

almanac *n* (*pl* **-s**) yearly calendar with detailed information on anniversaries, phases of the moon, etc.
almanacs *n* ▷ **almanac**
almighty *adj* having absolute power
almond *n* (*pl* **-s**) edible oval-shaped nut which grows on a small tree
almonds *n* ▷ **almond**
almoner *n* (*pl* **-s**) (BRIT) formerly, a hospital social worker
almoners *n* ▷ **almoner**
almost *adv* very nearly
alms [**ahmz**] *pl n* (*Old-fashioned*) gifts to the poor
aloe *n* (*pl* **-s**) plant with fleshy spiny leaves
aloes *n* ▷ **aloe**
aloft *adv* in the air
alone *adj*, *adv* without anyone or anything else
along *prep* over part or all the length of ▶ *adv* forward
alongside *prep*, *adv* beside (something)
aloof *adj* distant or haughty in manner > **aloofness** *n* (*pl* **-es**)
aloofness *n* ▷ **aloof**
aloofnesses *n* ▷ **aloof**
alopecia [al-loh-**pee**-sha] *n* (*pl* **-s**) loss of hair
alopecias *n* ▷ **alopecia**
aloud *adv* in an audible voice
alpaca *n* (*pl* **-s**) Peruvian llama
alpacas *n* ▷ **alpaca**
alpenstock *n* (*pl* **-s**) iron-tipped stick used by climbers
alpenstocks *n* ▷ **alpenstock**
alpha *n* (*pl* **-s**) first letter in the Greek alphabet
alphabet *n* (*pl* **-s**) set of letters used in writing a language
alphabetical *adj* in the conventional order of the letters of an alphabet > **alphabetically** *adv*
alphabetically *adv* ▷ **alphabetical**
alphabetize *v* (**-zes, -zing, -zed**) put in alphabetical order
alphabetized *v* ▷ **alphabetize**
alphabetizes *v* ▷ **alphabetize**
alphabetizing *v* ▷ **alphabetize**
alphabets *n* ▷ **alphabet**
alphas *n* ▷ **alpha**
alpine *adj* of high mountains ▶ *n* (*pl* **-s**) mountain plant
alpines *n* ▷ **alpine**
already *adv* before the present time
alright *adj*, *interj* all right
also *adv* in addition, too
altar *n* (*pl* **-s**) table used for Communion in Christian churches
altarpiece *n* (*pl* **-s**) work of art above and behind the altar in some Christian churches
altarpieces *n* ▷ **altarpiece**
altars *n* ▷ **altar**
alter *v* (**-s, -ing, -ed**) make or become different > **alteration** *n* (*pl* **-s**)
alteration *n* ▷ **alter**
alterations *n* ▷ **alter**
altercation *n* (*pl* **-s**) heated argument
altercations *n* ▷ **altercation**
altered *v* ▷ **alter**
altering *v* ▷ **alter**
alternate *v* (**-tes, -ting, -ted**) (cause to) occur by turns ▶ *adj* occurring by turns > **alternately** *adv* > **alternation** *n* (*pl* **-s**)
alternated *v* ▷ **alternate**
alternately *adv* ▷ **alternate**
alternates *v* ▷ **alternate**
alternating *v* ▷ **alternate**
alternation *n* ▷ **alternate**
alternations *n* ▷ **alternate**
alternative *n* (*pl* **-s**) one of two choices ▶ *adj* able to be done or used instead of something else > **alternatively** *adv*
alternatively *adv* ▷ **alternative**
alternatives *n* ▷ **alternative**
alternator *n* (*pl* **-s**) electric generator for producing alternating current
alternators *n* ▷ **alternator**
alters *v* ▷ **alter**
although *conj* despite the fact that
altimeter [al-**tim**-it-er] *n* (*pl* **-s**) instrument that measures altitude
altimeters *n* ▷ **altimeter**
altitude *n* (*pl* **-s**) height above sea level
altitudes *n* ▷ **altitude**
alto *n* (*pl* **-s**) (MUSIC) (singer with) the highest adult male voice
altogether *adv* entirely
altos *n* ▷ **alto**
altruism *n* (*pl* **-s**) unselfish concern for the welfare of others > **altruist** *n* (*pl* **-s**) > **altruistic** *adj* > **altruistically** *adv*
altruisms *n* ▷ **altruism**
altruist *n* ▷ **altruism**
altruists *n* ▷ **altruism**
altruistic *adj* ▷ **altruism**
altruistically *adv* ▷ **altruism**
aluminium *n* (*pl* **-s**) (CHEM) light silvery-white metal that does not rust
aluminiums *n* ▷ **aluminium**
alumna *n* ▷ **alumnus**
alumnae *n* ▷ **alumnus**
alumni *n* ▷ **alumnus**
alumnus [al-**lumm**-nuss] *n* (*pl* **-ni**) [-nie] graduate of a college > **alumna** [al-**lumm**-na]

▶ *n fem* (*pl* **-nae**) [-nee]
always *adv* at all times
alyssum *n* (*pl* **-s**) garden plant with small yellow or white flowers
alyssums *n* ▷ **alyssum**
am *v* ▷ **be**
amalgam *n* (*pl* **-s**) blend or combination
amalgamate *v* (**-tes, -ting, -ted**) combine or unite > **amalgamation** *n* (*pl* **-s**)
amalgamated *v* ▷ **amalgamate**
amalgamates *v* ▷ **amalgamate**
amalgamating *v* ▷ **amalgamate**
amalgamation *n* ▷ **amalgamate**
amalgamations *n* ▷ **amalgamate**
amalgams *n* ▷ **amalgam**
amandla [ah-**mand**-lah] *n* (S AFR) political slogan calling for power to the Black population
amanuenses *n* ▷ **amanuensis**
amanuensis [am-man-yew-**en**-siss] *n* (*pl* **-ses**) [-seez] person who writes from dictation
amaranth *n* (*pl* **-s**) imaginary flower that never fades
amaranths *n* ▷ **amaranth**
amaryllis *n* (*pl* **-ses**) lily-like plant with large red, pink, or white flowers
amaryllises *n* ▷ **amaryllis**
amass *v* (**-ses, -sing, -sed**) collect or accumulate
amassed *v* ▷ **amass**
amasses *v* ▷ **amass**
amassing *v* ▷ **amass**
amateur *n* (*pl* **-s**) person who engages in a sport or activity as a pastime rather than as a profession
amateurish *adj* lacking skill > **amateurishly** *adv*
amateurishly *adv* ▷ **amateurish**
amateurs *n* ▷ **amateur**
amatory *adj* relating to romantic or sexual love
amaze *v* (**-zes, -zing, -zed**) surprise greatly, astound > **amazing** *adj* > **amazingly** *adv* > **amazement** *n* (*pl* **-s**)
amazed *v* ▷ **amaze**
amazement *n* ▷ **amaze**
amazements *n* ▷ **amaze**
amazes *v* ▷ **amaze**
amazing *v, adj* ▷ **amaze**
amazingly *adv* ▷ **amaze**
amazon *n* (*pl* **-s**) strong and powerful woman > **amazonian** *adj*
amazonian *adj* ▷ **amazon**
amazons *n* ▷ **amazon**
ambassador *n* (*pl* **-s**) senior diplomat who represents his or her country in another country > **ambassadorial** *adj*
ambassadorial *adj* ▷ **ambassador**
ambassadors *n* ▷ **ambassador**
amber *n* (*pl* **-s**) clear yellowish fossil resin ▶ *adj* brownish-yellow
ambergris [**am**-ber-greece] *n* (*pl* **-es**) waxy substance secreted by the sperm whale, used in making perfumes
ambergrises *n* ▷ **ambergris**
ambers *n* ▷ **amber**
ambidextrous *adj* able to use both hands with equal ease
ambience *n* (*pl* **-s**) atmosphere of a place
ambiences *n* ▷ **ambience**
ambient *adj* surrounding
ambiguities *n* ▷ **ambiguous**
ambiguity *n* ▷ **ambiguous**
ambiguous *adj* having more than one possible meaning > **ambiguously** *adv* > **ambiguity** *n* (*pl* **-ties**)
ambiguously *adv* ▷ **ambiguous**
ambit *n* (*pl* **-s**) limits or boundary
ambition *n* (*pl* **-s**) desire for success > **ambitious** *adj* > **ambitiously** *adv*
ambitions *n* ▷ **ambition**
ambitious *adj* ▷ **ambition**
ambitiously *adv* ▷ **ambition**
ambits *n* ▷ **ambit**
ambivalence *n* (*pl* **-s**) state of feeling two conflicting emotions at the same time > **ambivalent** *adj* > **ambivalently** *adv*
ambivalences *n* ▷ **ambivalence**
ambivalent *adj* ▷ **ambivalence**
ambivalently *adv* ▷ **ambivalence**
amble *v* (**-les, -ling, -led**) walk at a leisurely pace ▶ *n* (*pl* **-s**) leisurely walk or pace
ambled *v* ▷ **amble**
ambles *v, n* ▷ **amble**
ambling *v* ▷ **amble**
ambrosia *n* (*pl* **-s**) (MYTH) food of the gods > **ambrosial** *adj*
ambrosial *adj* ▷ **ambrosia**
ambrosias *n* ▷ **ambrosia**
ambulance *n* (*pl* **-s**) motor vehicle designed to carry sick or injured people
ambulances *n* ▷ **ambulance**
ambush *n* (*pl* **-es**) act of waiting in a concealed position to make a surprise attack ▶ *v* (**-shes, -shing, -shed**) attack from a concealed position
ambushed *v* ▷ **ambush**
ambushes *n, v* ▷ **ambush**
ambushing *v* ▷ **ambush**
ameliorate [am-**meal**-yor-rate] *v* (**-tes,**

-ting, -ted) make (something) better **> amelioration** *n* (*pl* **-s**)
ameliorated *v* ▷ **ameliorate**
ameliorates *v* ▷ **ameliorate**
ameliorating *v* ▷ **ameliorate**
amelioration *n* ▷ **ameliorate**
ameliorations *n* ▷ **ameliorate**
amen *interj* so be it: used at the end of a prayer
amenable *adj* likely or willing to cooperate
amend *v* (**-s, -ing, -ed**) make small changes to correct or improve (something) **> amendment** *n* (*pl* **-s**)
amended *v* ▷ **amend**
amending *v* ▷ **amend**
amendment *n* ▷ **amend**
amends *pl n* compensation for ▶ *v* ▷ **amend**
amenities *n* ▷ **amenity**
amenity *n* (*pl* **-ties**) useful or enjoyable feature
amethyst [**am**-myth-ist] *n* (*pl* **-s**) bluish-violet variety of quartz used as a gemstone
amethysts *n* ▷ **amethyst**
amiabilities *n* ▷ **amiable**
amiability *n* ▷ **amiable**
amiable *adj* friendly, pleasant-natured **> amiably** *adv* **> amiability** *n* (*pl* **-ties**)
amiably *adv* ▷ **amiable**
amicable *adj* friendly **> amicably** *adv*
amicably *adv* ▷ **amicable**
amid, amidst *prep* in the middle of, among
amidships *adv* at or towards the middle of a ship
amidst *prep* ▷ **amid**
amiss *adv* wrongly, badly ▶ *adj* wrong, faulty
amities *n* ▷ **amity**
amity *n* (*pl* **-ties**) friendship
ammeter *n* (*pl* **-s**) instrument for measuring electric current
ammeters *n* ▷ **ammeter**
ammonia *n* (*pl* **-s**) strong-smelling alkaline gas containing hydrogen and nitrogen
ammonias *n* ▷ **ammonia**
ammonite *n* (*pl* **-s**) fossilized spiral shell of an extinct sea creature
ammonites *n* ▷ **ammonite**
ammunition *n* (*pl* **-s**) bullets, bombs, and shells that can be fired from or as a weapon
ammunitions *n* ▷ **ammunition**
amnesia *n* (*pl* **-s**) loss of memory **> amnesiac** *adj, n* (*pl* **-s**)
amnesiac *adj, n* ▷ **amnesia**
amnesiacs *n* ▷ **amnesia**
amnesias *n* ▷ **amnesia**
amnesties *n* ▷ **amnesty**
amnesty *n* (*pl* **-ties**) general pardon for offences against a government
amniocenteses *n* ▷ **amniocentesis**
amniocentesis *n* (*pl* **-ses**) removal of some amniotic fluid to test for possible abnormalities in a fetus
amoeba [am-**mee**-ba] *n* (*pl* **-bae, -bas**) microscopic single-celled animal able to change its shape
amoebae *n* ▷ **amoeba**
amoebas *n* ▷ **amoeba**
amok [a-**muck**, a-**mock**] *adv* in a violent frenzy
among, amongst *prep* in the midst of
amongst *prep* ▷ **among**
amoral [aim-**mor**-ral] *adj* without moral standards **> amorality** *n* (*pl* **-ties**)
amoralities *n* ▷ **amoral**
amorality *n* ▷ **amoral**
amorous *adj* feeling, showing, or relating to sexual love **> amorously** *adv*
amorously *adv* ▷ **amorous**
amorphous *adj* without distinct shape
amortize *v* (**-zes, -zing, -zed**) pay off (a debt) gradually by periodic transfers to a sinking fund
amortized *v* ▷ **amortize**
amortizes *v* ▷ **amortize**
amortizing *v* ▷ **amortize**
amount *n* (*pl* **-s**) extent or quantity ▶ *v* (**-s, -ing, -ed**) (*foll. by* **to**) be equal or add up to
amounted *v* ▷ **amount**
amounting *v* ▷ **amount**
amounts *n, v* ▷ **amount**
amour *n* (*pl* **-s**) (secret) love affair
amours *n* ▷ **amour**
amp *n* (*pl* **-s**) ampere
ampere [**am**-pair] *n* (*pl* **-s**) basic unit of electric current
amperes *n* ▷ **ampere**
ampersand *n* (*pl* **-s**) the character (&) meaning *and*
ampersands *n* ▷ **ampersand**
amphetamine [am-**fet**-am-mean] *n* (*pl* **-s**) drug used as a stimulant
amphetamines *n* ▷ **amphetamine**
amphibian *n* (*pl* **-s**) animal that lives on land but breeds in water
amphibians *n* ▷ **amphibian**
amphibious *adj* living or operating both on land and in water
amphitheatre *n* (*pl* **-s**) open oval or circular building with tiers of seats rising round an arena
amphitheatres *n* ▷ **amphitheatre**
amphora [**am**-for-ra] *n* (*pl* **-phorae**) two-handled ancient Greek or Roman jar
amphorae *n* ▷ **amphora**

ample *adj* (**-r, -st**) more than sufficient > **amply** *adv*
ampler *adj* ▷ **ample**
amplest *adj* ▷ **ample**
amplification *n* ▷ **amplify**
amplifications *n* ▷ **amplify**
amplified *v* ▷ **amplify**
amplifier *n* (*pl* **-s**) device used to amplify a current or sound signal
amplifiers *n* ▷ **amplifier**
amplifies *v* ▷ **amplifly**
amplify *v* (**-fies, -fying, -fied**) increase the strength of (a current or sound signal)of > **amplification** *n* (*pl* **-s**)
amplifying *v* ▷ **amplify**
amplitude *n* (*pl* **-s**) greatness of extent
amplitudes *n* ▷ **amplitude**
amply *adv* ▷ **ample**
ampoule *n* (*pl* **-s**) small sealed glass vessel containing liquid for injection
ampoules *n* ▷ **ampoule**
amps *n* ▷ **amp**
amputate *v* (**-tes, -ting, -ted**) cut off (a limb or part of a limb) for medical reasons > **amputation** *n* (*pl* **-s**)
amputated *v* ▷ **amputate**
amputates *v* ▷ **amputate**
amputating *v* ▷ **amputate**
amputation *n* ▷ **amputate**
amputations *n* ▷ **amputate**
amuck *adv* ▷ **amok**
amulet *n* (*pl* **-s**) something carried or worn as a protection against evil
amulets *n* ▷ **amulet**
amuse *v* (**-ses, -sing, -sed**) cause to laugh or smile > **amusing** *adj*
amused *v* ▷ **amuse**
amusement *n* (*pl* **-s**) state of being amused
amusements *n* ▷ **amusement**
amuses *v* ▷ **amuse**
amusing *v, adj* ▷ **amuse**
an *adj* form of **a** used before vowels, and sometimes before *h*
anachronism [an-**nak**-kron-iz-zum] *n* (*pl* **-s**) person or thing placed in the wrong historical period or seeming to belong to another time > **anachronistic** *adj*
anachronisms *n* ▷ **anachronism**
anachronistic *adj* ▷ **anachronism**
anaconda *n* (*pl* **-s**) large S American snake which kills by constriction
anacondas *n* ▷ **anaconda**
anaemia [an-**neem**-ee-a] *n* (*pl* **-s**) deficiency in the number of red blood cells
anaemias *n* ▷ **anaemia**
anaemic *adj* having anaemia
anaesthesia [an-niss-**theez**-ee-a] *n* (*pl* **-s**) loss of bodily feeling
anaesthesias *n* ▷ **anaesthesia**
anaesthetic [an-niss-**thet**-ik] *n* (*pl* **-s**), *adj* (substance) causing loss of bodily feeling
anaesthetics *n* ▷ **anaesthetic**
anaesthetist [an-**neess**-thet-ist] *n* (*pl* **-s**) doctor trained to administer anaesthetics > **anaesthetize** *v* (**-zes, -zing, -zed**)
anaesthetists *n* ▷ **anaesthetist**
anaesthetize *v* ▷ **anaesthetist**
anaesthetized *v* ▷ **anaesthetist**
anaesthetizes *v* ▷ **anaesthetist**
anaesthetizing *v* ▷ **anaesthetist**
anagram *n* (*pl* **-s**) word or phrase made by rearranging the letters of another word or phrase
anagrams *n* ▷ **anagram**
anal [**ain**-al] *adj* of the anus
analgesia *n* (*pl* **-s**) absence of pain
analgesias *n* ▷ **analgesia**
analgesic [an-nal-**jeez**-ik] *n* (*pl* **-s**) ▶ *adj* (drug) relieving pain
analgesics *n* ▷ **analgesic**
analogical *adj* ▷ **analogy**
analogies *n* ▷ **analogy**
analogous *adj* similar in some respects
analogue *n* (*pl* **-s**) something that is similar in some respects to something else ▶ *adj* displaying information by means of a dial
analogues *n* ▷ **analogue**
analogy *n* (*pl* **-gies**) similarity in some respects > **analogical** *adj*
analyse *v* (**-ses, -sing, -sed**) make an analysis of (something)
analysed *v* ▷ **analyse**
analyses *v* ▷ **analyse** ▶ *n* ▷ **analysis**
analysing *v* ▷ **analyse**
analysis *n* (*pl* **-ses**) separation of a whole into its parts for study and interpretation > **analytical, analytic** *adj* > **analytically** *adv*
analyst *n* (*pl* **-s**) person skilled in analysis
analysts *n* ▷ **analyst**
analytic *adj* ▷ **analysis**
analytical *adj* ▷ **analysis**
analytically *adv* ▷ **analysis**
anarchic *adj* ▷ **anarchy**
anarchies *n* ▷ **anarchy**
anarchism *n* (*pl* **-s**) doctrine advocating the abolition of government
anarchisms *n* ▷ **anarchism**
anarchist *n* (*pl* **-s**) person who advocates the abolition of government > **anarchistic** *adj*
anarchistic *adj* ▷ **anarchist**

anarchists *n* ▷ **anarchist**
anarchy [**an**-ark-ee] *n* (*pl* **-ies**) lawlessness and disorder > **anarchic** *adj*
anathema [an-**nath**-im-a] *n* (*pl* **-s**) detested person or thing
anathemas *n* ▷ **anathema**
anatomical *adj* ▷ **anatomy**
anatomically *adv* ▷ **anatomy**
anatomies *n* ▷ **anatomy**
anatomist *n* (*pl* **-s**) expert in anatomy
anatomists *n* ▷ **anatomist**
anatomy *n* (*pl* **-mies**) science of the structure of the body > **anatomical** *adj* > **anatomically** *adv*
ancestor *n* (*pl* **-s**) person from whom one is descended > **ancestral** *adj*
ancestors *n* ▷ **ancestor**
ancestral *adj* ▷ **ancestor**
ancestries *n* ▷ **ancestry**
ancestry *n* (*pl* **-ries**) lineage or descent
anchor *n* (*pl* **-s**) heavy hooked device attached to a boat by a cable and dropped overboard to fasten the ship to the sea bottom ▶ *v* (**-s, -ing, -ed**) fasten with or as if with an anchor
anchorage *n* (*pl* **-s**) place where boats can be anchored
anchorages *n* ▷ **anchorage**
anchored *v* ▷ **anchor**
anchoring *v* ▷ **anchor**
anchorite *n* (*pl* **-s**) religious recluse
anchorites *n* ▷ **anchorite**
anchorman *n* (*pl* **-men**) broadcaster in a central studio who links up and presents items from outside camera units and other studios
anchormen *n* ▷ **anchorman**
anchors *n, v* ▷ **anchor**
anchorwoman *n* (*pl* **-women**) female broadcaster in a central studio who links up and presents items from outside camera units and other studios
anchorwomen *n* ▷ **anchorwoman**
anchovies *n* ▷ **anchovy**
anchovy [**an**-chov-ee] *n* (*pl* **-vies**) small strong-tasting fish
ancient *adj* dating from very long ago
ancients *pl n* people who lived very long ago
ancillary *adj* supporting the main work of an organization
and *conj* in addition to
andante [an-**dan**-tay] *n* (*pl* **-s**) ▶ *adv* (MUSIC) (piece to be played) moderately slowly
andantes *n* ▷ **andante**
andiron *n* (*pl* **-s**) iron stand for supporting logs in a fireplace
andirons *n* ▷ **andiron**
androgynous *adj* having both male and female characteristics
android *n* (*pl* **-s**) robot resembling a human
androids *n* ▷ **android**
anecdotal *adj* ▷ **anecdote**
anecdote *n* (*pl* **-s**) short amusing account of an incident > **anecdotal** *adj*
anecdotes *n* ▷ **anecdote**
anemometer *n* (*pl* **-s**) instrument for recording wind speed
anemometers *n* ▷ **anemometer**
anemone [an-**nem**-on-ee] *n* (*pl* **-s**) plant with white, purple, or red flowers
anemones *n* ▷ **anemone**
aneurism *n* ▷ **aneurysm**
aneurisms *n* ▷ **aneurysm**
aneurysm, aneurism [**an**-new-riz-zum] *n* (*pl* **-s**) permanent swelling of a blood vessel
aneurysms *n* ▷ **aneurysm**
anew *adv* once more
angel *n* (*pl* **-s**) spiritual being believed to be an attendant or messenger of God > **angelic** *adj* > **angelically** *adv*
angelic *adj* ▷ **angel**
angelica *n* (*pl* **-s**) aromatic plant
angelically *adv* ▷ **angel**
angelicas *n* ▷ **angelica**
angels *n* ▷ **angel**
angelus [**an**-jell-uss] *n* (*pl* **-es**) (in the Roman Catholic Church) prayers recited in the morning, at midday, and in the evening
angeluses *n* ▷ **angelus**
anger *n* (*pl* **-s**) fierce displeasure or extreme annoyance ▶ *v* (**-s, -ing, -ed**) make (someone) angry
angered *v* ▷ **anger**
angering *v* ▷ **anger**
angers *n, v* ▷ **anger**
angina [an-**jine**-a] *n* (*pl* **-s**) heart disorder causing sudden severe chest pains
anginas *n* ▷ **angina**
angle[1] *n* (*pl* **-s**) space between or shape formed by two lines or surfaces that meet ▶ *v* (**-s, -ing, -ed**) bend or place (something) at an angle
angle[2] *v* (**-s, -ing, -ed**) fish with a hook and line > **angling** *n* (*pl* **-s**)
angled *v* ▷ **angle**[1, 2]
angler *n* (*pl* **-s**) person who fishes with a hook and line
anglers *n* ▷ **angler**
angles *n* ▷ **angle**[1] ▶ *v* ▷ **angle**[1, 2]
anglicize *v* (**-zes, -zing, -zed**) make or become English in outlook, form, etc.
anglicized *v* ▷ **anglicize**

anglicizes *v* ▷ **anglicize**
anglicizing *v* ▷ **anglicize**
angling *n* ▷ **angle[2]** ▶ *v* ▷[1, 2]
anglings *n* ▷ **angle[2]**
angophora *n* (*pl* **-s**) Australian tree related to the eucalyptus
angophoras *n* ▷ **angophora**
angora *n* (*pl* **-s**) variety of goat, cat, or rabbit with long silky hair
angoras *n* ▷ **angora**
angrier *adj* ▷ **angry**
angriest *adj* ▷ **angry**
angrily *adv* ▷ **angry**
angry *adj* (**-grier, -griest**) full of anger > **angrily** *adv*
angst *n* feeling of anxiety
angstrom *n* (*pl* **angstroms**) unit of length used to measure wavelengths
angstroms *n* ▷ **angstrom**
anguish *n* (*pl* **-es**) great mental pain > **anguished** *adj*
anguished *adj* ▷ **anguish**
anguishes *n* ▷ **anguish**
angular *adj* (of a person) lean and bony > **angularity** *n* (*pl* **-ties**)
angularities *n* ▷ **angular**
angularity *n* ▷ **angular**
anhydrous *adj* (CHEM) containing no water
aniline *n* (*pl* **-s**) colourless oily liquid obtained from coal tar and used for making dyes, plastics, and explosives
anilines *n* ▷ **aniline**
animal *n* (*pl* **-s**) living creature with specialized sense organs and capable of voluntary motion, esp. one other than a human being ▶ *adj* of animals
animals *n* ▷ **animal**
animate *v* (**-tes, -ting, -ted**) give life to ▶ *adj* having life > **animated** *adj* > **animator** *n* (*pl* **-s**)
animated *v, adj* ▷ **animate**
animates *v* ▷ **animate**
animating *v* ▷ **animate**
animation *n* (*pl* **-s**) technique of making cartoon films
animations *n* ▷ **animation**
animator *n* ▷ **animate**
animators *n* ▷ **animate**
animism *n* (*pl* **-s**) belief that natural objects possess souls > **animist** *n* (*pl* **-s**) *adj* > **animistic** *adj*
animisms *n* ▷ **animism**
animist *n, adj* ▷ **animism**
animistic *adj* ▷ **animism**
animists *n* ▷ **animism**
animosities *n* ▷ **animosity**
animosity *n* (*pl* **-ties**) hostility, hatred
animus *n* (*pl* **-es**) hatred, animosity
animuses *n* ▷ **animus**
anion [**an**-eye-on] *n* (*pl* **-s**) ion with negative charge
anions *n* ▷ **anion**
anise [**an**-niss] *n* (*pl* **-s**) plant with liquorice-flavoured seeds
aniseed *n* (*pl* **-s**) liquorice-flavoured seeds of the anise plant
aniseeds *n* ▷ **aniseed**
anises *n* ▷ **anise**
ankle *n* (*pl* **-s**) joint between the foot and leg
ankles *n* ▷ **ankle**
anklet *n* (*pl* **-s**) ornamental chain worn round the ankle
anklets *n* ▷ **anklet**
annal *n* (usually plural) yearly record of events
annals *n* ▷ **annal**
anneal *v* (**-s, -ing, -ed**) toughen (metal or glass) by heating and slow cooling
annealed *v* ▷ **anneal**
annealing *v* ▷ **anneal**
anneals *v* ▷ **anneal**
annelid *n* (*pl* **-s**) worm with a segmented body, such as an earthworm
annelids *n* ▷ **annelid**
annex *v* (**-es, -ing, -ed**) seize (territory) > **annexation** *n* (*pl* **-s**)
annexation *n* ▷ **annex**
annexations *n* ▷ **annex**
annexe *n* (*pl* **-s**) extension to a building
annexed *v* ▷ **annex**
annexes *v* ▷ **annex** ▶ *n* ▷ **annexe**
annexing *v* ▷ **annex**
annihilate *v* (**-tes, -ting, -ted**) destroy utterly > **annihilation** *n* (*pl* **-s**)
annihilated *v* ▷ **annihilate**
annihilates *v* ▷ **annihilate**
annihilating *v* ▷ **annihilate**
annihilation *n* ▷ **annihilate**
annihilations *n* ▷ **annihilate**
anniversaries *n* ▷ **anniversary**
anniversary *n* (*pl* **-ries**) date on which something occurred in a previous year
annotate *v* (**-tes, -ting, -ted**) add notes to (a written work) > **annotation** *n* (*pl* **-s**)
annotated *v* ▷ **annotate**
annotates *v* ▷ **annotate**
annotating *v* ▷ **annotate**
annotation *n* ▷ **annotate**
annotations *n* ▷ **annotate**
announce *v* (**-ces, -cing, -ced**) make known publicly > **announcement** *n* (*pl* **-s**)
announced *v* ▷ **announce**

announcement *n* ▷ **announce**
announcements *n* ▷ **announce**
announcer *n* (*pl* **-s**) person who introduces radio or television programmes
announcers *n* ▷ **announcer**
announces *v* ▷ **announce**
announcing *v* ▷ **announce**
annoy *v* (**-s, -ing, -ed**) irritate or displease > **annoyance** *n* (*pl* **-s**)
annoyance *n* ▷ **annoy**
annoyances *n* ▷ **annoy**
annoyed *v* ▷ **annoy**
annoying *v* ▷ **annoy**
annoys *v* ▷ **annoy**
annual *adj* happening once a year ▶ *n* (*pl* **-s**) plant that completes its life cycle in a year > **annually** *adv*
annually *adv* ▷ **annual**
annuals *n* ▷ **annual**
annuities *n* ▷ **annuity**
annuity *n* (*pl* **-ties**) fixed sum paid every year
annul *v* (**-ls, -lling, -lled**) declare (something, esp. a marriage) invalid > **annulment** *n* (*pl* **-s**)
annular [an-new-lar] *adj* ring-shaped
annulled *v* ▷ **annul**
annulling *v* ▷ **annul**
annulment *n* ▷ **annul**
annulments *n* ▷ **annul**
annuls *v* ▷ **annul**
anode *n* (*pl* **-s**) (ELECTRICITY) positive electrode in a battery, valve, etc.
anodes *n* ▷ **anode**
anodize *v* (**-zes, -zing, -zed**) coat (metal) with a protective oxide film by electrolysis
anodized *v* ▷ **anodize**
anodizes *v* ▷ **anodize**
anodizing *v* ▷ **anodize**
anodyne *n* (*pl* **-s**) something that relieves pain or distress ▶ *adj* relieving pain or distress
anodynes *n* ▷ **anodyne**
anoint *v* (**-s, -ing, -ed**) smear with oil as a sign of consecration
anointed *v* ▷ **anoint**
anointing *v* ▷ **anoint**
anoints *v* ▷ **anoint**
anomalies *n* ▷ **anomaly**
anomalous *adj* ▷ **anomaly**
anomaly [an-**nom**-a-lee] *n* (*pl* **-lies**) something that deviates from the normal, irregularity > **anomalous** *adj*
anon *adv* (*Obs*) in a short time, soon
anonymity *n* ▷ **anonymous**
anonymous *adj* by someone whose name is unknown or withheld > **anonymously** *adv* > **anonymity** *n*
anonymously *adv* ▷ **anonymous**
anorak *n* (*pl* **-s**) light waterproof hooded jacket
anoraks *n* ▷ **anorak**
anorexia *n* (*pl* **-s**) psychological disorder characterized by fear of becoming fat and refusal to eat > **anorexic** *adj, n*
anorexias *n* ▷ **anorexia**
anorexic *adj, n* ▷ **anorexia**
another *adj, pron* one more
answer *n* (*pl* **-s**) reply to a question, request, letter, etc. ▶ *v* (**-s, -ing, -ed**) give an answer (to)
answerable *adj* (*foll. by* **for** *or* **to**) responsible for or accountable to
answered *v* ▷ **answer**
answering *v* ▷ **answer**
answers *n, v* ▷ **answer**
ant *n* (*pl* **-s**) small insect living in highly organized colonies
antacid *n* (*pl* **-s**) substance that counteracts acidity, esp. in the stomach
antacids *n* ▷ **antacid**
antagonism *n* (*pl* **-s**) open opposition or hostility
antagonisms *n* ▷ **antagonism**
antagonist *n* (*pl* **-s**) opponent or adversary > **antagonistic** *adj*
antagonistic *adj* ▷ **antagonist**
antagonists *n* ▷ **antagonist**
antagonize *v* (**-zes, -zing, -zed**) arouse hostility in, annoy
antagonized *v* ▷ **antagonize**
antagonizes *v* ▷ **antagonize**
antagonizing *v* ▷ **antagonize**
antarctic *n* area around the South Pole ▶ *adj* of this region
ante *n* (*pl* **-s**) player's stake in poker ▶ *v* (**-tes, -teing, -ted** *or* **-teed**) place (one's stake) in poker
anteater *n* (*pl* **-s**) mammal which feeds on ants by means of a long snout
anteaters *n* ▷ **anteater**
antecedent *n* (*pl* **-s**) event or circumstance happening or existing before another ▶ *adj* preceding, prior
antecedents *n* ▷ **antecedent**
anted *v* ▷ **ante**
antedate *v* (**-tes, -ting, -ted**) precede in time
antedated *v* ▷ **antedate**
antedates *v* ▷ **antedate**
antedating *v* ▷ **antedate**
antediluvian *adj* of the time before the biblical Flood
anteed *v* ▷ **ante**
anteing *v* ▷ **ante**
antelope *n* (*pl* **-s**) deerlike mammal with long

legs and horns
antelopes *n* ▷ **antelope**
antenatal *adj* during pregnancy, before birth
antenna *n* (*pl* **-e**) insect's feeler; (*pl* **-s**) aerial
antennae *n* ▷ **antenna**
antennas *n* ▷ **antenna**
anterior *adj* to the front
anteroom *n* (*pl* **-s**) small room leading into a larger one, often used as a waiting room
anterooms *n* ▷ **anteroom**
antes *n, v* ▷ **ante**
anthem *n* (*pl* **-s**) song of loyalty, esp. to a country
anthems *n* ▷ **anthem**
anther *n* (*pl* **-s**) part of a flower's stamen containing pollen
anthers *n* ▷ **anther**
anthologies *n* ▷ **anthology**
anthologist *n* ▷ **anthology**
anthologists *n* ▷ **anthology**
anthology *n* (*pl* **-gies**) collection of poems or other literary pieces by various authors > **anthologist** *n* (*pl* **-s**)
anthraces *n* ▷ **anthrax**
anthracite *n* (*pl* **-s**) hard coal burning slowly with little smoke or flame but intense heat
anthracites *n* ▷ **anthracite**
anthrax *n* (*pl* **-thraces**) dangerous disease of cattle and sheep, communicable to humans
anthropoid *adj* like a human ▶ *n* (*pl* **-s**) ape, such as a chimpanzee, that resembles a human
anthropoids *n* ▷ **anthropoid**
anthropological *adj* ▷ **anthropology**
anthropologies *n* ▷ **anthropology**
anthropologist *n* ▷ **anthropology**
anthropologists *n* ▷ **anthropology**
anthropology *n* (*pl* **-ies**) study of human origins, institutions, and beliefs > **anthropological** *adj* > **anthropologist** *n* (*pl* **-s**)
anthropomorphic *adj* attributing human form or personality to a god, animal, or object > **anthropomorphism** *n* (*pl* **-s**)
anthropomorphism *n* ▷ **anthropomorphic**
anthropomorphisms *n* ▷ **anthropomorphic**
antibiotic *n* (*pl* **-s**) chemical substance capable of destroying bacteria ▶ *adj* of antibiotics
antibiotics *n* ▷ **antibiotic**
antibodies *n* ▷ **antibody**
antibody *n* (*pl* **-dies**) protein produced in the blood, which destroys bacteria
anticipate *v* (**-tes, -ting, -ted**) foresee and act in advance of > **anticipation** *n* (*pl* **-s**) > **anticipatory** *adj*
anticipated *v* ▷ **anticipate**
anticipates *v* ▷ **anticipate**
anticipating *v* ▷ **anticipate**
anticipation *n* ▷ **anticipate**
anticipations *n* ▷ **anticipate**
anticipatory *adj* ▷ **anticipate**
anticlimax *n* (*pl* **-es**) disappointing conclusion to a series of events
anticlimaxes *n* ▷ **anticlimax**
anticlockwise *adv, adj* in the opposite direction to the rotation of the hands of a clock
antics *pl n* absurd acts or postures
anticyclone *n* (*pl* **-s**) area of moving air of high pressure in which the winds rotate outwards
anticyclones *n* ▷ **anticyclone**
antidote *n* (*pl* **-s**) substance that counteracts a poison
antidotes *n* ▷ **antidote**
antifreeze *n* (*pl* **-s**) liquid added to water to lower its freezing point, used esp. in car radiators
antifreezes *n* ▷ **antifreeze**
antigen [**an**-tee-jen] *n* (*pl* **-s**) substance, usu. a toxin, causing the blood to produce antibodies
antigens *n* ▷ **antigen**
antihero *n* (*pl* **-roes**) central character in a book, film, etc., who lacks the traditional heroic virtues
antiheroes *n* ▷ **antihero**
antihistamine *n* (*pl* **-s**) drug used to treat allergies
antihistamines *n* ▷ **antihistamine**
antimacassar *n* (*pl* **-s**) cloth put over a chair-back to prevent soiling
antimacassars *n* ▷ **antimacassar**
antimonies *n* ▷ **antimony**
antimony *n* (*pl* **-ies**) (CHEM) brittle silvery-white metallic element
antipathetic *adj* ▷ **antipathy**
antipathies *n* ▷ **antipathy**
antipathy [an-**tip**-a-thee] *n* (*pl* **-thies**) dislike, hostility > **antipathetic** *adj*
antiperspirant *n* (*pl* **-s**) substance used to reduce or prevent sweating
antiperspirants *n* ▷ **antiperspirant**
antiphon *n* (*pl* **-s**) hymn sung in alternate parts by two groups of singers > **antiphonal** *adj*
antiphonal *adj* ▷ **antiphon**
antiphons *n* ▷ **antiphon**
antipodean *adj* ▷ **antipodes**
antipodes [an-**tip**-pod-deez] *pl n* any two places diametrically opposite one another on the earth's surface > **antipodean** *adj*

antipyretic *adj* reducing fever ▶ *n* (*pl* **-s**) drug that reduces fever
antipyretics *n* ▷ **antipyretic**
antiquarian *adj* of or relating to antiquities or rare books ▶ *n* (*pl* **-s**) antiquary
antiquarians *n* ▷ **antiquarian**
antiquaries *n* ▷ **antiquary**
antiquary *n* (*pl* **-ries**) student or collector of antiques or ancient works of art
antiquated *adj* out-of-date
antique *n* (*pl* **-s**) object of an earlier period, valued for its beauty, workmanship, or age ▶ *adj* made in an earlier period
antiques *n* ▷ **antique**
antiquities *pl n* objects dating from ancient times ▶ *n* ▷ **antiquity**
antiquity *n* (*pl* **-ties**) great age
antiracism *n* (*pl* **-s**) policy of challenging racism and promoting racial tolerance
antiracisms *n* ▷ **antiracism**
antirrhinum *n* (*pl* **-s**) two-lipped flower of various colours
antirrhinums *n* ▷ **antirrhinum**
antiseptic *adj* preventing infection by killing germs ▶ *n* (*pl* **-s**) antiseptic substance
antiseptics *n* ▷ **antiseptic**
antisocial *adj* avoiding the company of other people
antistatic *adj* reducing the effects of static electricity
antitheses *n* ▷ **antithesis**
antithesis [an-**tith**-iss-iss] *n* (*pl* **-ses**) [-seez] exact opposite > **antithetical** *adj*
antithetical *adj* ▷ **antithesis**
antitoxin *n* (*pl* **-s**) (serum containing) an antibody that acts against a toxin
antitoxins *n* ▷ **antitoxin**
antitrust *adj* (AUST & S AFR) (of laws) opposing business monopolies
antler *n* (*pl* **-s**) branched horn of male deer
antlers *n* ▷ **antler**
antonym *n* (*pl* **-s**) word that means the opposite of another
antonyms *n* ▷ **antonym**
ants *n* ▷ **ant**
anus [**ain**-uss] *n* (*pl* **-es**) opening at the end of the alimentary canal, through which faeces are discharged
anuses *n* ▷ **anus**
anvil *n* (*pl* **-s**) heavy iron block on which metals are hammered into particular shapes
anvils *n* ▷ **anvil**
anxieties *n* ▷ **anxiety**
anxiety *n* (*pl* **-ties**) state of being anxious
anxious *adj* worried and tense > **anxiously** *adv*
anxiously *adv* ▷ **anxious**
any *adj, pron* one or some, no matter which ▶ *adv* at all > **anything** *pron*
anybody *pron* anyone
anyhow *adv* anyway
anyone *pron* any person
anything *pron* ▷ **any**
anyway *adv* at any rate, nevertheless
anywhere *adv* in, at, or to any place
aorta [eh-**or**-ta] *n* (*pl* **-s**) main artery of the body, carrying oxygen-rich blood from the heart
aortas *n* ▷ **aorta**
apace *adv* (*Lit*) swiftly
apalled *v* ▷ **appal**
apart *adv* to or in pieces
apartheid *n* (*pl* **-s**) former official government policy of racial segregation in S Africa
apartheids *n* ▷ **apartheid**
apartment *n* (*pl* **-s**) room in a building
apartments *n* ▷ **apartment**
apathetic *adj* ▷ **apathy**
apathy *n* (*pl* **-thies**) lack of interest or enthusiasm > **apathetic** *adj*
apethies *n* ▷ **apathy**
ape *n* (*pl* **-s**) tailless monkey such as the chimpanzee or gorilla ▶ *v* (**apes, aping, aped**) imitate
aped *v* ▷ **ape**
aperient [ap-**peer**-ee-ent] *adj* having a mild laxative effect ▶ *n* (*pl* **-s**) mild laxative
aperients *n* ▷ **aperient**
aperitif [ap-per-rit-**teef**] *n* (*pl* **-s**) alcoholic drink taken before a meal
aperitifs *n* ▷ **aperitif**
aperture *n* (*pl* **-s**) opening or hole
apertures *n* ▷ **aperture**
apes *n, v* ▷ **ape**
apex *n* (*pl* **-es**) highest point
apexes *n* ▷ **apex**
aphasia *n* disorder of the central nervous system that affects the ability to speak and understand words
aphid [**eh**-fid], **aphis** [**eh**-fiss] *n* (*pl* **aphids**) small insect which sucks the sap from plants
aphids *n* ▷ **aphid**
aphis *n* ▷ **aphid**
aphorism *n* (*pl* **-s**) short clever saying expressing a general truth
aphorisms *n* ▷ **aphorism**
aphrodisiac [af-roh-**diz**-zee-ak] *n* (*pl* **-s**) substance that arouses sexual desire ▶ *adj* arousing sexual desire
aphrodisiacs *n* ▷ **aphrodisiac**
apiaries *n* ▷ **apiary**
apiary *n* (*pl* **-ries**) place where bees are kept

apiculture *n* (*pl* **-s**) breeding and care of bees
apicultures *n* ▷ **apiculture**
apiece *adv* each
aping *v* ▷ **ape**
aplomb *n* (*pl* **-s**) calm self-possession
aplombs *n* ▷ **aplomb**
apocalypse *n* (*pl* **-s**) end of the world > **apocalyptic** *adj*
apocalypses *n* ▷ **apocalypse**
apocalyptic *adj* ▷ **apocalypse**
apocryphal [ap-**pok**-rif-al] *adj* (of a story) of questionable authenticity
apogee [**ap**-oh-jee] *n* (*pl* **-s**) point of the moon's or a satellite's orbit that is farthest from the earth
apogees *n* ▷ **apogee**
apologetic *adj* showing or expressing regret > **apologetically** *adv*
apologetically *adv* ▷ **apologetic**
apologetics *n* branch of theology concerned with the reasoned defence of Christianity
apologies *n* ▷ **apology**
apologist *n* (*pl* **-s**) person who formally defends a cause
apologists *n* ▷ **apologist**
apologize *v* (**-zes, -zing, -zed**) make an apology
apologized *v* ▷ **apologize**
apologizes *v* ▷ **apologize**
apologizing *v* ▷ **apologize**
apology *n* (*pl* **-gies**) expression of regret for wrongdoing
apoplectic *adj* of apoplexy
apoplexies *n* ▷ **apoplexy**
apoplexy *n* (*pl* **-xies**) (MED) stroke
apostasies *n* ▷ **apostasy**
apostasy [ap-**poss**-stass-ee] *n* (*pl* **-sies**) abandonment of one's religious faith or other belief > **apostate** *n* (*pl* **-s**) *adj*
apostate *n, adj* ▷ **apostasy**
apostates *n* ▷ **apostasy**
apostle *n* (*pl* **-s**) ardent supporter of a cause or movement > **apostolic** *adj*
apostles *n* ▷ **apostle**
apostolic *adj* ▷ **apostle**
apostrophe [ap-**poss**-trof-fee] *n* (*pl* **-s**) punctuation mark (') showing the omission of a letter or letters in a word, e.g. *don't*, or forming the possessive, e.g. *Jill's car*
apostrophes *n* ▷ **apostrophe**
apothecaries *n* ▷ **apothecary**
apothecary *n* (*pl* **-ries**) (*Obs*) chemist
apotheoses *n* ▷ **apotheosis**
apotheosis [ap-poth-ee-**oh**-siss] *n* (*pl* **-ses**) [-seez] perfect example
appal *v* (**-s, -lling, -lled**) dismay, terrify
appalled *v* ▷ **appal**
appalling *adj* dreadful, terrible ▶ *v* ▷ **appal**
appals *v* ▷ **appal**
apparatus *n* (*pl* **-es**) equipment for a particular purpose
apparatuses *n* ▷ **apparatus**
apparel *n* (*pl* **-s**) (*Old-fashioned*) clothing
apparels *n* ▷ **apparel**
apparent *adj* readily seen, obvious > **apparently** *adv*
apparently *adv* ▷ **apparent**
apparition *n* (*pl* **-s**) ghost or ghostlike figure
apparitions *n* ▷ **apparition**
appeal *v* (**-s, -ing, -ed**) make an earnest request ▶ *n* (*pl* **-s**) earnest request > **appealing** *adj*
appealed *v* ▷ **appeal**
appealing *v, adj* ▷ **appeal**
appeals *v, n* ▷ **appeal**
appear *v* (**-s, -ing, -ed**) become visible or present
appearance *n* (*pl* **-s**) appearing
appearances *n* ▷ **appearance**
appeared *v* ▷ **appear**
appearing *v* ▷ **appear**
appears *v* ▷ **appear**
appease *v* (**-s, -ing, -ed**) pacify (a person) by yielding to his or her demands > **appeasement** *n* (*pl* **-s**)
appeased *v* ▷ **appease**
appeasement *n* ▷ **appeal**
appeasements *n* ▷ **appeal**
appeases *v* ▷ **appease**
appeasing *v* ▷ **appease**
appellant *n* (*pl* **-s**) person who makes an appeal to a higher court
appellants *n* ▷ **appellant**
appellation *n* (*pl* **-s**) (*Formal*) name, title
appellations *n* ▷ **appellation**
append *v* (**-s, -ing, -ed**) join on, add
appendage *n* (*pl* **-s**) thing joined on or added
appendages *n* ▷ **appendage**
appended *v* ▷ **append**
appendices *n* ▷ **appendix**
appendicitis *n* (*pl* **-es**) inflammation of the appendix
appendicitises *n* ▷ **appendicitis**
appending *v* ▷ **append**
appendix *n* (*pl* **-dices, -dixes**) separate additional material at the end of a book
appendixes *n* ▷ **appendix**
appends *v* ▷ **append**
appertain *v* (**-s, -ing, -ed**) (*foll. by* **to**) belong to
appertained *v* ▷ **appertain**
appertaining *v* ▷ **appertain**
appertains *v* ▷ **appertain**

appetite *n* (*pl* **-s**) desire for food or drink
appetites *n* ▷ **appetite**
appetizer *n* (*pl* **-s**) thing eaten or drunk to stimulate the appetite > **appetizing** *adj* stimulating the appetite
appetizers *n* ▷ **appetizer**
appetizing *adj* ▷ **appetizer**
applaud *v* (**-s, -ing, -ed**) show approval of by clapping one's hands
applauded *v* ▷ **applaud**
applauding *v* ▷ **applaud**
applauds *v* ▷ **applaud**
applause *n* (*pl* **-s**) approval shown by clapping one's hands
applauses *n* ▷ **applause**
apple *n* (*pl* **-s**) round firm fleshy fruit that grows on trees
apples *n* ▷ **apple**
appliance *n* (*pl* **-s**) device with a specific function
appliances *n* ▷ **appliance**
applicabilities *n* ▷ **applicable**
applicability *n* ▷ **applicable**
applicable *adj* relevant, appropriate > **applicability** *n* (*pl* **-ties**)
applicant *n* (*pl* **-s**) person who applies for something
applicants *n* ▷ **applicant**
application *n* (*pl* **-s**) formal request
applications *n* ▷ **application**
applied *adj* (of a skill, science, etc.) put to practical use ▶ *v* ▷ **apply**
applies *v* ▷ **apply**
appliqué [ap-**plee**-kay] *n* (*pl* **-s**) kind of decoration in which one material is cut out and attached to another
appliqués *n* ▷ **appliqué**
apply *v* (**-plies, -plying, -plied**) make a formal request
applying *v* ▷ **apply**
appoint *v* (**-s, -ing, -ed**) assign to a job or position
appointed *v* ▷ **appoint**
appointing *v* ▷ **appoint**
appointment *n* (*pl* **-s**) arrangement to meet a person
appointments *n* ▷ **appointment**
appoints *v* ▷ **appoint**
apportion *v* (**-s, -ing, -ed**) divide out in shares
apportioned *v* ▷ **apportion**
apportioning *v* ▷ **apportion**
apportions *v* ▷ **apportion**
apposite *adj* suitable, apt
apposition *n* (*pl* **-s**) grammatical construction in which two nouns or phrases referring to the same thing are placed one after another without a conjunction
appositions *n* ▷ **apposition**
appraisal *n* ▷ **appraise**
appraisals *n* ▷ **appraise**
appraise *v* (**-ses, -sing, -sed**) estimate the value or quality of > **appraisal** *n* (*pl* **-s**)
appraised *v* ▷ **appraise**
appraises *v* ▷ **appraise**
appraising *v* ▷ **appraise**
appreciable *adj* enough to be noticed > **appreciably** *adv*
appreciably *adv* ▷ **appreciable**
appreciate *v* (**-tes, -ting, -ted**) value highly > **appreciation** *n* (*pl* **-s**)
appreciated *v* ▷ **appreciate**
appreciates *v* ▷ **appreciate**
appreciating *v* ▷ **appreciate**
appreciation *n* ▷ **appreciate**
appreciations *n* ▷ **appreciate**
appreciative *adj* feeling or showing appreciation
apprehend *v* (**-s, -ing, -ed**) arrest and take into custody
apprehended *v* ▷ **apprehend**
apprehending *v* ▷ **apprehend**
apprehends *v* ▷ **apprehend**
apprehension *n* (*pl* **-s**) dread, anxiety
apprehensions *n* ▷ **apprehension**
apprehensive *adj* fearful or anxious
apprentice *n* (*pl* **-s**) someone working for a skilled person for a fixed period in order to learn his or her trade ▶ *v* (**-ces, -cing, -ced**) take or place (someone) as an apprentice > **apprenticeship** *n* (*pl* **-s**)
apprenticed *v* ▷ **apprentice**
apprentices *n, v* ▷ **apprentice**
apprenticing *v* ▷ **apprentice**
apprise *v* (**-ses, -sing, -sed**) make aware (of)
apprised *v* ▷ **apprise**
apprises *v* ▷ **apprise**
apprising *v* ▷ **apprise**
appro *n* (*pl* **-s**) (BRIT, AUST, NZ & S AFR) (*Informal*) on approval
approach *v* (**-ches, -ching, -ched**) come near or nearer (to) ▶ *n* (*pl* **-es**) approaching or means of approaching > **approachable** *adj*
approachable *adj* ▷ **approach**
approached *v* ▷ **approach**
approaches *v, n* ▷ **approach**
approaching *v* ▷ **approach**
approbation *n* (*pl* **-s**) approval
approbations *n* ▷ **approbation**
appropriate *adj* suitable, fitting ▶ *v* (**-tes, -ting, -ted**) take for oneself > **appropriately**

adv > **appropriateness** *n* > **appropriation** *n* (*pl* **-s**)
appropriated *v* ▷ **appropriate**
appropriately *adv* ▷ **appropriate**
appropriateness *n* ▷ **appropriate**
appropriates *v* ▷ **appropriate**
appropriating *v* ▷ **appropriate**
appropriation *n* ▷ **appropriate**
appropriations *n* ▷ **appropriate**
appros *n* ▷ **appro**
approval *n* (*pl* **-s**) consent
approvals *n* ▷ **approval**
approve *v* (**-ves, -ving, -ved**) consider good or right
approved *v* ▷ **approve**
approves *v* ▷ **approve**
approving *v* ▷ **approve**
approximate *adj* almost but not quite exact ▶ *v* (**-tes, -ting, -ted**) (*foll. by* **to**) come close to > **approximately** *adv* > **approximation** *n* (*pl* **-s**)
approximated *v* ▷ **approximate**
approximately *adv* ▷ **approximate**
approximates *v* ▷ **approximate**
approximating *v* ▷ **approximate**
approximation *n* ▷ **approximate**
approximations *n* ▷ **approximate**
appurtenance *n* (*pl* **-s**) a minor or additional feature
appurtenances *n* ▷ **appurtenance**
apricot *n* (*pl* **-s**) yellowish-orange juicy fruit like a small peach ▶ *adj* yellowish-orange
apricots *n* ▷ **apricot**
apron *n* (*pl* **-s**) garment worn over the front of the body to protect the clothes
aprons *n* ▷ **apron**
apropos [ap-prop-**poh**] *adj, adv* appropriate(ly)
apse *n* (*pl* **-s**) arched or domed recess, esp. in a church
apses *n* ▷ **apse**
apt *adj* having a specified tendency > **aptly** *adv* > **aptness** *n* (*pl* **-es**)
aptitude *n* (*pl* **-s**) natural ability
aptitudes *n* ▷ **aptitude**
aptly *adv* ▷ **apt**
aptness *n* ▷ **apt**
aptnesses *n* ▷ **apt**
aqualung *n* (*pl* **-s**) mouthpiece attached to air cylinders, worn for underwater swimming
aqualungs *n* ▷ **aqualung**
aquamarine *n* (*pl* **-s**) greenish-blue gemstone ▶ *adj* greenish-blue
aquamarines *n* ▷ **aquamarine**
aquaplane *n* (*pl* **-s**) board on which a person stands to be towed by a motorboat ▶ *v* (**-nes, -ning, -ned**) ride on an aquaplane
aquaplaned *v* ▷ **aquaplane**
aquaplanes *n, v* ▷ **aquaplane**
aquaplaning *v* ▷ **aquaplane**
aquaria *n* ▷ **aquarium**
aquarium *n* (*pl* **-s, -ria**) tank in which fish and other underwater creatures are kept
aquariums *n* ▷ **aquarium**
aquatic *adj* living in or near water
aquatics *pl n* water sports
aquatint *n* (*pl* **-s**) print like a watercolour, produced by etching copper
aquatints *n* ▷ **aquatint**
aqueduct *n* (*pl* **-s**) structure carrying water across a valley or river
aqueducts *n* ▷ **aqueduct**
aqueous *adj* of, like, or containing water
aquiline *adj* (of a nose) curved like an eagle's beak

ar *n* (**ars**). Ar is the letter R. This is a good two-letter word to remember because it uses two very common tiles, and so is easy to fit on the board. Ar scores 2 points.

arabesque [ar-ab-**besk**] *n* (*pl* **-s**) ballet position in which one leg is raised behind and the arms are extended
arabesques *n* ▷ **arabesque**
arable *adj* suitable for growing crops on
arachnid [ar-**rak**-nid] *n* (*pl* **-s**) eight-legged invertebrate, such as a spider, scorpion, tick, or mite
arachnids *n* ▷ **arachnid**
arbiter *n* (*pl* **-s**) person empowered to judge in a dispute
arbiters *n* ▷ **arbiter**
arbitrarily *adv* ▷ **arbitrary**
arbitrary *adj* based on personal choice or chance, rather than reason > **arbitrarily** *adv*
arbitrate *v* ▷ **arbitration**
arbitrated *v* ▷ **arbitration**
arbitrates *v* ▷ **arbitration**
arbitrating *v* ▷ **arbitration**
arbitration *n* (*pl* **-s**) hearing and settling of a dispute by an impartial referee chosen by both sides > **arbitrate** *v* (**-tes, -ting, -ted**) > **arbitrator** *n* (*pl* **-s**)
arbitrations *n* ▷ **arbitration**
arbitrator *n* ▷ **arbitration**
arbitrators *n* ▷ **arbitration**
arboreal *adj* of or living in trees
arboreta *n* ▷ **arboretum**
arboretum [ahr-bore-**ee**-tum] *n* (*pl* **-ta**) place where rare trees or shrubs are cultivated
arboriculture *n* (*pl* **-s**) cultivation of trees or shrubs

arboricultures *n* ▷ **arboriculture**
arbour *n* (*pl* **-s**) glade sheltered by trees
arbours *n* ▷ **arbour**
arc *n* (*pl* **-s**) part of a circle or other curve ▶ *v* (**-s, -ing, -ed**) form an arc
arcade *n* (*pl* **-s**) covered passageway lined with shops
arcades *n* ▷ **arcade**
arcane *adj* mysterious and secret
arced *v* ▷ **arc**
arch[1] *n* (*pl* **-es**) curved structure supporting a bridge or roof ▶ *v* (**-es, -ing, -ed**) (cause to) form an arch
arch[2] *adj* (**-er, -est**) superior, knowing > **archly** *adv* > **archness** *n* (*pl* **-es**)
archaeological *adj* ▷ **archaeology**
archaeologies *n* ▷ **archaeology**
archaeologist *n* ▷ **archaeology**
archaeologists *n* ▷ **archaeology**
archaeology *n* (*pl* **-ies**) study of ancient cultures from their physical remains > **archaeological** *adj* > **archaeologist** *n* (*pl* **-s**)
archaic [ark-**kay**-ik] *adj* ancient > **archaism** [**ark**-kay-iz-zum] ▶ *n* (*pl* **-s**) archaic word or phrase
archaism *n* ▷ **archaic**
archaisms *n* ▷ **archaic**
archangel [**ark**-ain-jell] *n* (*pl* **-s**) chief angel
archangels *n* ▷ **archangel**
archbishop *n* (*pl* **-s**) chief bishop
archbishops *n* ▷ **archbishop**
archdeacon *n* (*pl* **-s**) priest ranking just below a bishop
archdeacons *n* ▷ **archdeacon**
archdiocese *n* (*pl* **-es**) diocese of an archbishop
archdioceses *n* ▷ **archdiocese**
arched *v* ▷ **arch**[1]
archer *n* (*pl* **-s**) person who shoots with a bow and arrow ▶ *adj* ▷ **arch**[2] > **archery** *n* (*pl* **-ries**)
archeries *n* ▷ **archer**
archers *n* ▷ **archer**
archery *n* ▷ **archer**
arches *n, v* ▷ **arch**[1]
archest *adj* ▷ **arch**[2]
archetypal *adj* ▷ **archetype**
archetype [**ark**-ee-type] *n* (*pl* **-s**) perfect specimen > **archetypal** *adj*
archetypes *n* ▷ **archetype**
arching *v* ▷ **arch**[1]
archipelago [ark-ee-**pel**-a-go] *n* (*pl* **-gos**) group of islands
archipelagos *n* ▷ **archipelago**
architect *n* (*pl* **-s**) person qualified to design and supervise the construction of buildings
architects *n* ▷ **architect**
architectural *adj* ▷ **architecture**
architecture *n* (*pl* **-s**) style in which a building is designed and built > **architectural** *adj*
architectures *n* ▷ **architecture**
architrave *n* (*pl* **-s**) (ARCHIT) beam that rests on columns
architraves *n* ▷ **architrave**
archival *adj* ▷ **archive**
archive [**ark**-ive] *n* (*pl* **-s**) (*often pl* collection of records or documents > **archival** *adj*
archives *n* ▷ **archive**
archivist [**ark**-iv-ist] *n* (*pl* **-s**) person in charge of archives
archivists *n* ▷ **archivist**
archly *adv* ▷ **arch**[2]
archness *n* ▷ **arch**[2]
archnesses *n* ▷ **arch**[2]
archway *n* (*pl* **-s**) passageway under an arch
archways *n* ▷ **archway**
arcing *v* ▷ **arc**
arcs *n, v* ▷ **arc**
arctic *n* (*pl* **-s**) area around the North Pole ▶ *adj* of this region
arctics *n* ▷ **arctic**
ardent *adj* passionate > **ardently** *adv*
ardently *adv* ▷ **ardent**
ardour *n* (*pl* **-s**) passion
ardours *n* ▷ **ardour**
arduous *adj* hard to accomplish, strenuous > **arduously** *adv*
arduously *adv* ▷ **arduous**
are[1] *v* ▷ **be**
are[2] *n* (*pl* **-s**) unit of measure, 100 square metres
area *n* (*pl* **-s**) part or region
areas *n* ▷ **area**
arena *n* (*pl* **-s**) seated enclosure for sports events
arenas *n* ▷ **arena**
areola *n* (*pl* **-lae, -las**) small circular area, such as the coloured ring around the human nipple
areolae *n* ▷ **areola**
areolas *n* ▷ **areola**
ares *n* ▷ **are**[2]
argon *n* (*pl* **-s**) (CHEM) inert gas found in the air
argons *n* ▷ **argon**
argot [**ahr**-go] *n* (*pl* **-s**) slang or jargon
argots *n* ▷ **argot**
arguable *adj* ▷ **argue**
arguably *adv* ▷ **argue**
argue *v* (**-gues, -guing, -gued**) try to prove by giving reasons > **arguable** *adj* > **arguably** *adv*
argued *v* ▷ **argue**
argues *v* ▷ **argue**

arguing *v* ▷ **argue**
argument *n* (*pl* **-s**) quarrel
argumentation *n* (*pl* **-s**) process of reasoning methodically
argumentations *n* ▷ **argumentation**
argumentative *adj* given to arguing
arguments *n* ▷ **argument**
aria [**ah**-ree-a] *n* (*pl* **-s**) elaborate song for solo voice, esp. one from an opera
arias *n* ▷ **aria**
arid *adj* parched, dry > **aridity** *n* (*pl* **-ties**)
aridities *n* ▷ **arid**
aridity *n* ▷ **arid**
aright *adv* rightly
arise *v* (**arises, arising, arose, arisen**) come about
arisen *v* ▷ **arise**
arises *v* ▷ **arise**
arising *v* ▷ **arise**
aristocracies *n* ▷ **aristocracy**
aristocracy *n* (*pl* **-cies**) highest social class
aristocrat *n* (*pl* **-s**) member of the aristocracy > **aristocratic** *adj*
aristocratic *adj* ▷ **aristocrat**
aristocrats *n* ▷ **aristocrat**
arithmetic *n* (*pl* **-s**) calculation by or of numbers ▶ *adj* of arithmetic > **arithmetical** *adj* > **arithmetically** *adv*
arithmetical *adj* ▷ **arithmetic**
arithmetically *adv* ▷ **arithmetic**
arithmetics *n* ▷ **arithmetic**
ark *n* (*pl* **-s**) (OLD TESTAMENT) boat built by Noah, which survived the Flood
arks *n* ▷ **ark**
arm[1] *n* (*pl* **-s**) either of the upper limbs from the shoulder to the wrist
arm[2] *v* (**-s, -ing, -ed**) supply with weapons
armada *n* (*pl* **-s**) large number of warships
armadas *n* ▷ **armada**
armadillo *n* (*pl* **-s**) small S American mammal covered in strong bony plates
armadillos *n* ▷ **armadillo**
armament *n* (*pl* **-s**) military weapons
armaments *n* ▷ **armament**
armature *n* (*pl* **-s**) revolving structure in an electric motor or generator, wound with coils carrying the current
armatures *n* ▷ **armature**
armchair *n* (*pl* **-s**) upholstered chair with side supports for the arms
armchairs *n* ▷ **armchair**
armed *v* ▷ **arm**[2]
armful *n* (*pl* **-s**) as much as can be held in the arms
armfuls *n* ▷ **armful**
armhole *n* (*pl* **-s**) opening in a garment through which the arm passes
armholes *n* ▷ **armhole**
armies *n* ▷ **army**
arming *v* ▷ **arm**[2]
armistice [**arm**-miss-stiss] *n* (*pl* **-s**) agreed suspension of fighting
armistices *n* ▷ **armistice**
armour *n* (*pl* **-s**) metal clothing formerly worn to protect the body in battle
armourer *n* (*pl* **-s**) maker, repairer, or keeper of arms or armour
armourers *n* ▷ **armourer**
armouries *n* ▷ **armoury**
armours *n* ▷ **armour**
armoury *n* (*pl* **-ries**) place where weapons are stored
armpit *n* (*pl* **-s**) hollow under the arm at the shoulder
armpits *n* ▷ **armpit**
arms *pl n* weapons ▶ *n* ▷ **arm**[1] ▶ *v* ▷ **arm**[2]
army *n* (*pl* **-mies**) military land forces of a nation
aroma *n* (*pl* **-s**) pleasant smell > **aromatic** *adj*
aromas *n* ▷ **aroma**
aromatherapies *n* ▷ **aromatherapy**
aromatherapy *n* (*pl* **-pies**) massage with fragrant oils to relieve tension
aromatic *adj* ▷ **aroma**
arose *v* ▷ **arise**
around *prep, adv* on all sides (of)
arouse *v* (**-ses, -sing, -sed**) stimulate, make active
aroused *v* ▷ **arouse**
arouses *v* ▷ **arouse**
arousing *v* ▷ **arouse**
arpeggio [arp-**pej**-ee-oh] *n* (*pl* **-s**) (MUSIC) notes of a chord played or sung in quick succession
arpeggios *n* ▷ **arpeggio**
arraign [ar-**rain**] *v* (**-s, -ing, -ed**) bring (a prisoner) before a court to answer a charge > **arraignment** *n* (*pl* **-s**)
arraigned *v* ▷ **arraign**
arraigning *v* ▷ **arraign**
arraignment *n* ▷ **arraign**
arraignments *n* ▷ **arraign**
arraigns *v* ▷ **arraign**
arrange *v* (**-ges, -ging, -ged**) plan > **arrangement** *n* (*pl* **-s**)
arranged *v* ▷ **arrange**
arrangement *n* ▷ **arrange**
arrangements *n* ▷ **arrange**
arranges *v* ▷ **arrange**
arranging *v* ▷ **arrange**
arrant *adj* utter, downright
arras *n* (*pl* **-es**) tapestry wall-hanging
arrases *n* ▷ **arras**
array *n* (*pl* **-s**) impressive display or collection

(*Poetic*) ▶ *v* (**-s, -ing, -ed**) arrange in order
arrayed *v* ▷ **array**
arraying *v* ▷ **array**
arrays *n, v* ▷ **array**
arrear *n* (*p* **-s**) (usually plural) money owed
arrears *n* ▷ **arrear**
arrest *v* (**-s, -ing, -ed**) take (a person) into custody ▶ *n* (*pl* **-s**) act of taking a person into custody
arrested *v* ▷ **arrest**
arresting *adj* attracting attention, striking ▶ *v* ▷ **arrest**
arrests *v, n* ▷ **arrest**
arrival *n* (*pl* **-s**) arriving
arrivals *n* ▷ **arrival**
arrive *v* (**-ves, -ving, -ved**) reach a place or destination
arrived *v* ▷ **arrive**
arrives *v* ▷ **arrive**
arriving *v* ▷ **arrive**
arrogance *n* ▷ **arrogant**
arrogances *n* ▷ **arrogant**
arrogant *adj* proud and overbearing > **arrogantly** *adv* > **arrogance** *n* (*pl* **-s**)
arrogantly *adv* ▷ **arrogant**
arrogate *v* (**-tes, -ting, -ted**) claim or seize without justification
arrogated *v* ▷ **arrogate**
arrogates *v* ▷ **arrogate**
arrogating *v* ▷ **arrogate**
arrow *n* (*pl* **-s**) pointed shaft shot from a bow
arrowhead *n* (*pl* **-s**) pointed tip of an arrow
arrowheads *n* ▷ **arrowhead**
arrowroot *n* (*pl* **-s**) nutritious starch obtained from the root of a W Indian plant
arrowroots *n* ▷ **arrowroot**
arrows *n* ▷ **arrow**
arsenal *n* (*pl* **-s**) place where arms and ammunition are made or stored
arsenals *n* ▷ **arsenal**
arsenic *n* (*pl* **-s**) toxic grey element > **arsenical** *adj*
arsenical *adj* ▷ **arsenic**
arsenics *n* ▷ **arsenic**
arson *n* (*pl* **-s**) crime of intentionally setting property on fire > **arsonist** *n* (*pl* **-s**)
arsonist *n* ▷ **arson**
arsonists *n* ▷ **arson**
arsons *n* ▷ **arson**
art *n* (*pl* **-s**) creation of works of beauty, esp. paintings or sculpture
artefact *n* (*pl* **-s**) something made by human beings
artefacts *n* ▷ **artefact**
arterial *adj* of an artery
arteries *n* ▷ **artery**
artery *n* (*pl* **-ries**) one of the tubes carrying blood from the heart
artful *adj* cunning, wily > **artfully** *adv* > **artfulness** *n* (*pl* **-es**)
artfully *adv* ▷ **artful**
artfulness *n* ▷ **artful**
artfulnesses *n* ▷ **artful**
arthritic *adj, n* ▷ **arthritis**
arthritics *n* ▷ **arthritis**
arthritis *n* (*pl* **-es**) painful inflammation of a joint or joints > **arthritic** *adj, n* (*pl* **-s**)
arthritises *n* ▷ **arthritis**
arthropod *n* (*pl* **-s**) animal, such as a spider or insect, with jointed limbs and a segmented body
arthropods *n* ▷ **arthropod**
artichoke *n* (*pl* **-s**) flower head of a thistle-like plant, cooked as a vegetable
artichokes *n* ▷ **artichoke**
article *n* (*pl* **-s**) written piece in a magazine or newspaper
articled *adj* bound (as an apprentice) by a written contract
articles *n* ▷ **article**
articulate *adj* able to express oneself clearly and coherently ▶ *v* (**-tes, -ting, -ted**) speak or say clearly and coherently > **articulately** *adv* > **articulation** *n* (*pl* **-s**)
articulated *adj* jointed ▶ *v* ▷ **articulate**
articulates *v* ▷ **articulate**
articulating *v* ▷ **articulate**
articulation *n* ▷ **articulate**
articulations *n* ▷ **articulate**
artier *adj* ▷ **arty**
artiest *adj* ▷ **arty**
artifice *n* (*pl* **-s**) clever trick
artificer [art-tiff-iss-er] *n* (*pl* **-s**) craftsman
artificers *n* ▷ **artificer**
artifices *n* ▷ **artifice**
artificial *adj* man-made, not occurring naturally > **artificially** *adv* > **artificiality** *n* (*pl* **-ties**)
artificialities *n* ▷ **artificial**
artificiality *n* ▷ **artificial**
artificially *adv* ▷ **artificial**
artilleries *n* ▷ **artillery**
artillery *n* (*pl* **-ies**) large-calibre guns
artisan *n* (*pl* **-s**) skilled worker, craftsman
artisans *n* ▷ **artisan**
artist *n* (*pl* **-s**) person who produces works of art, esp. paintings or sculpture > **artistic** *adj* > **artistically** *adv*
artiste *n* (*pl* **-s**) professional entertainer such as a singer or dancer

artistes *n* ▷ **artiste**
artistic *adj* ▷ **artist**
artistically *adv* ▷ **artist**
artistries *n* ▷ **artistry**
artistry *n* (*pl* **-ries**) artistic skill
artists *n* ▷ **artist**
artless *adj* free from deceit or cunning > **artlessly** *adv*
artlessly *adv* ▷ **artless**
arts *n* ▷ **art**
arty *adj* (**-tier, -tiest**) (*Informal*) having an affected interest in art
arvie *n* (*pl* **-s**) (S AFR) (*Informal*) afternoon
arvies *n* ▷ **arvie**
as *conj* while, when ▶ *adv, conj* used to indicate amount or extent in comparisons ▶ *prep* in the role of, being
asafoetida *n* (*pl* **-s**) strong-smelling plant resin used as a spice in Eastern cookery
asafoetidas *n* ▷ **asafoetida**
asbestos *n* (*pl* **-es**) fibrous mineral which does not burn
asbestoses *n* ▷ **asbestos, asbestosis**
asbestosis *n* (*pl* **-ses**) lung disease caused by inhalation of asbestos fibre
ascend *v* (**-s, -ing, -ed**) go or move up
ascendancies *n* ▷ **ascendancy**
ascendancy *n* (*pl* **-cies**) condition of being dominant
ascendant *adj* dominant or influential
ascended *v* ▷ **ascend**
ascending *v* ▷ **ascend**
ascends *v* ▷ **ascend**
ascent *n* (*pl* **-s**) ascending
ascents *n* ▷ **ascent**
ascertain *v* (**-s, -ing, -ed**) find out definitely > **ascertainable** *adj* > **ascertainment** *n* (*pl* **-s**)
ascertainable *adj* ▷ **ascertain**
ascertained *v* ▷ **ascertain**
ascertaining *v* ▷ **ascertain**
ascertainment *n* ▷ **ascertain**
ascertainments *n* ▷ **ascertain**
ascertains *v* ▷ **ascertain**
ascetic [ass-**set**-tik] *n* (*pl* **-s**) ▶ *adj* (person) abstaining from worldly pleasures and comforts > **asceticism** *n* (*pl* **-s**)
asceticism *n* ▷ **ascetic**
asceticisms *n* ▷ **ascetic**
ascetics *n* ▷ **ascetic**
ascribe *v* (**-bes, -bing, -bed**) attribute, as to a particular origin > **ascription** *n* (*pl* **-s**)
ascribed *v* ▷ **ascribe**
ascribes *v* ▷ **ascribe**
ascribing *v* ▷ **ascribe**
ascription *n* ▷ **ascribe**
ascriptions *n* ▷ **ascribe**
aseptic [eh-**sep**-tik] *adj* free from harmful bacteria
asexual [eh-**sex**-yew-al] *adj* without sex > **asexually** *adv*
asexually *adv* ▷ **asexual**
ash¹ *n* (*pl* **-es**) powdery substance left when something is burnt
ash² *n* (*pl* **-es**) tree with grey bark
ashamed *adj* feeling shame
ashen *adj* pale with shock
ashes *n* ▷ **ash¹, ²**
ashlar *n* (*pl* **-s**) square block of hewn stone used in building
ashlars *n* ▷ **ashlar**
ashore *adv* towards or on land
ashram *n* (*pl* **-s**) religious retreat where a Hindu holy man lives
ashrams *n* ▷ **ashram**
ashtray *n* (*pl* **-s**) receptacle for tobacco ash and cigarette butts
ashtrays *n* ▷ **ashtray**
aside *adv* to one side ▶ *n* (*pl* **-s**) remark not meant to be heard by everyone present
asides *n* ▷ **aside**
asinine *adj* stupid, idiotic
ask *v* (**-s, -ing, -ed**) say or write (something) in a form that requires an answer
askance [ass-**kanss**] *adv* with an oblique glance
asked *v* ▷ **ask**
askew *adv, adj* to one side, crooked
asking *v* ▷ **ask**
asks *v* ▷ **ask**
aslant *adv, prep* at a slant (to), slanting (across)
asleep *adj* sleeping
asp *n* (*pl* **-s**) small poisonous snake
asparagus *n* (*pl* **-es**) plant whose shoots are cooked as a vegetable
asparaguses *n* ▷ **asparagus**
aspect *n* (*pl* **-s**) feature or element
aspects *n* ▷ **aspect**
aspen *n* (*pl* **-s**) kind of poplar tree
aspens *n* ▷ **aspen**
asperities *n* ▷ **asperity**
asperity *n* (*pl* **-ties**) roughness of temper
aspersion *n* (*pl* **-s**) derogatory remark
aspersions *n* ▷ **aspersion**
asphalt *n* (*pl* **-s**) black hard tarlike substance used for road surfaces etc.
asphalts *n* ▷ **asphalt**
asphodel *n* (*pl* **-s**) plant with clusters of yellow or white flowers
asphodels *n* ▷ **asphodel**
asphyxia [ass-**fix**-ee-a] *n* (*pl* **-s**) suffocation
asphyxiate *v* (**-tes, -ting, -ted**) suffocate

> **asphyxiation** *n* (*pl* **-s**)
asphyxiated *v* ▷ **asphyxiate**
asphyxiates *v* ▷ **asphyxiate**
asphyxiating *v* ▷ **asphyxiate**
asphyxiation *n* ▷ **asphyxiate**
asphyxiations *n* ▷ **asphyxiate**
aspic *n* (*pl* **-s**) savoury jelly used to coat meat, eggs, fish, etc.
aspics *n* ▷ **aspic**
aspidistra *n* (*pl* **-s**) plant with long tapered leaves
aspidistras *n* ▷ **aspidistra**
aspirant *n* (*pl* **-s**) person who aspires
aspirants *n* ▷ **aspirant**
aspirate (PHONETICS) *v* (**-tes, -ting, -ted**) pronounce with an *h* sound ▶ *n* (*pl* **-s**) *h* sound
aspirated *v* ▷ **aspirate**
aspirates *v, n* ▷ **aspirate**
aspirating *v* ▷ **aspirate**
aspiration *n* (*pl* **-s**) strong desire or aim
aspirations *n* ▷ **aspiration**
aspire *v* (**-res, -ring, -red**) (*foll. by* **to**) yearn (for), hope (to do or be)
aspired *v* ▷ **aspire**
aspires *v* ▷ **aspire**
aspirin *n* (*pl* **-s**) drug used to relieve pain and fever
aspiring *v* ▷ **aspire**
aspirins *n* ▷ **aspirin**
asps *n* ▷ **asp**
ass *n* (*pl* **-es**) donkey
assail *v* (**-s, -ing, -ed**) attack violently > **assailant** *n* (*pl* **-s**)
assailant *n* ▷ **assail**
assailants *n* ▷ **assail**
assailed *v* ▷ **assail**
assailing *v* ▷ **assail**
assails *v* ▷ **assail**
assassin *n* (*pl* **-s**) person who murders a prominent person
assassinate *v* (**-tes, -ting, -ted**) murder (a prominent person) > **assassination** *n* (*pl* **-s**)
assassinated *v* ▷ **assassinate**
assassinates *v* ▷ **assassinate**
assassinating *v* ▷ **assassinate**
assassination *n* ▷ **assassinate**
assassinations *n* ▷ **assassinate**
assassins *n* ▷ **assassin**
assault *n* (*pl* **-ts**) violent attack ▶ *v* (**-s, -ing, -ed**) attack violently
assaulted *v* ▷ **assault**
assaulting *v* ▷ **assault**
assaults *n, v* ▷ **assault**
assay *n* (*pl* **-s**) analysis of a substance, esp. a metal, to ascertain its purity ▶ *v* (**-s, -ing, -ed**)
assayed *v* ▷ **assay**
assaying *v* ▷ **assay**
assays *n, v* ▷ **assay**
assegai [ass-a-guy] *n* (*pl* **-s**) slender spear used in S Africa
assegais *n* ▷ **assegai**
assemblage *n* (*pl* **-s**) collection or group
assemblages *n* ▷ **assemblage**
assemble *v* (**-bles, -bling, -bled**) collect or congregate
assembled *v* ▷ **assemble**
assembles *v* ▷ **assemble**
assemblies *n* ▷ **assembly**
assembling *v* ▷ **assemble**
assembly *n* (*pl* **-blies**) assembled group
assent *n* (*pl* **-s**) agreement or consent ▶ *v* (**-s, -ing, -ed**) agree or consent
assented *v* ▷ **assent**
assenting *v* ▷ **assent**
assents *n, v* ▷ **assent**
assert *v* (**-s, -ing, -ed**) declare forcefully > **assertion** *n* (*pl* **-s**) > **assertive** *adj* > **assertively** *adv*
asserted *v* ▷ **assert**
asserting *v* ▷ **assert**
assertion *n* ▷ **assert**
assertions *n* ▷ **assert**
assertive *adj* ▷ **assert**
assertively *adv* ▷ **assert**
asserts *v* ▷ **assert**
asses *n* ▷ **ass**
assess *v* (**-es, -ing, -ed**) judge the worth or importance of > **assessment** *n* (*pl* **-s**) > **assessor** *n* (*pl* **-s**)
assessed *v* ▷ **assess**
assesses *v* ▷ **assess**
assessing *v* ▷ **assess**
assessment *n* ▷ **assess**
assessments *n* ▷ **assess**
assessor *n* ▷ **assess**
assessors *n* ▷ **assess**
asset *n* (*pl* **-s**) valuable or useful person or thing
assets *n* ▷ **asset**
asseverate *v* (**-tes, -ting, -ted**) declare solemnly
asseverated *v* ▷ **asseverate**
asseverates *v* ▷ **asseverate**
asseverating *v* ▷ **asseverate**
assiduities *n* ▷ **assiduous**
assiduity *n* ▷ **assiduous**
assiduous *adj* hard-working > **assiduously** *adv* > **assiduity** *n* (*pl* **-ties**)
assiduously *adv* ▷ **assiduous**
assign *v* (**-s, -ing, -ed**) appoint (someone) to a job or task

assignation *n* (*pl* **-s**) assigning
assignations *n* ▷ **assignation**
assigned *v* ▷ **assign**
assigning *v* ▷ **assign**
assignment *n* (*pl* **-s**) task assigned
assignments *n* ▷ **assignment**
assigns *v* ▷ **assign**
assimilable *adj* ▷ **assimilate**
assimilate *v* (**-tes, -ting, -ted**) learn and understand (information) > **assimilable** *adj* > **assimilation** *n* (*pl* **-s**)
assimilated *v* ▷ **assimilate**
assimilates *v* ▷ **assimilate**
assimilating *v* ▷ **assimilate**
assimilation *n* ▷ **assimilate**
assimilations *n* ▷ **assimilate**
assist *v* (**-s, -ing, -ed**) give help or support > **assistance** *n* (*pl* **-s**)
assistance *n* ▷ **assist**
assistances *n* ▷ **assist**
assistant *n* (*pl* **-s**) helper ▶ *adj* junior or deputy
assistants *n* ▷ **assistant**
assisted *v* ▷ **assist**
assisting *v* ▷ **assist**
assists *v* ▷ **assist**
assizes *pl n* (BRIT) court sessions formerly held in each county of England and Wales
associate *v* (**-tes, -ting, -ted**) connect in the mind ▶ *n* (*pl* **-s**) partner in business ▶ *adj* having partial rights or subordinate status
associated *v* ▷ **associate**
associates *v, n* ▷ **associate**
associating *v* ▷ **associate**
association *n* (*pl* **-s**) society or club
associations *n* ▷ **association**
assonance *n* (*pl* **-s**) rhyming of vowel sounds but not consonants, as in *time* and *light*
assonances *n* ▷ **assonance**
assorted *adj* consisting of various types mixed together
assortment *n* (*pl* **-s**) assorted mixture
assortments *n* ▷ **assortment**
assuage [ass-**wage**] *v* (**-ges, -ging, -ged**) relieve (pain, grief, thirst, etc.)
assuaged *v* ▷ **assuage**
assuages *v* ▷ **assuage**
assuaging *v* ▷ **assuage**
assume *v* (**-mes, -ming, -med**) take to be true without proof
assumed *v* ▷ **assume**
assumes *v* ▷ **assume**
assuming *v* ▷ **assume**
assumption *n* (*pl* **-s**) thing assumed
assumptions *n* ▷ **assumption**
assurance *n* (*pl* **-s**) assuring or being assured
assurances *n* ▷ **assurance**
assure *v* (**-res, -ring, -red**) promise or guarantee
assured *adj* confident ▶ *v* ▷ **assure**
assuredly *adv* definitely
assures *v* ▷ **assure**
assuring *v* ▷ **assure**
astatine *n* (*pl* **-s**) (CHEM) radioactive nonmetallic element
astatines *n* ▷ **astatine**
aster *n* (*pl* **-s**) plant with daisy-like flowers
asterisk *n* (*pl* **-s**) star-shaped symbol (*) used in printing or writing to indicate a footnote etc. ▶ *v* (**-s, -ing, -ed**) mark with an asterisk
asterisked *v* ▷ **asterisk**
asterisking *v* ▷ **asterisk**
asterisks *n, v* ▷ **asterisk**
astern *adv* at or towards the stern of a ship
asteroid *n* (*pl* **-s**) any of the small planets that orbit the sun between Mars and Jupiter
asteroids *n* ▷ **asteroid**
asters *n* ▷ **aster**
asthma [**ass**-ma] *n* (*pl* **-s**) illness causing difficulty in breathing > **asthmatic** *adj, n* (*pl* **-s**)
asthmas *n* ▷ **asthma**
asthmatic *adj, n* ▷ **asthma**
asthmatics *n* ▷ **asthma**
astigmatism [eh-**stig**-mat-tiz-zum] *n* (*pl* **-s**) inability of a lens, esp. of the eye, to focus properly
astigmatisms *n* ▷ **astigmatism**
astir *adj* (*Old-fashioned*) out of bed
astonish *v* (**-es, -ing, -ed**) surprise greatly > **astonishment** *n* (*pl* **-s**)
astonished *v* ▷ **astonish**
astonishes *v* ▷ **astonish**
astonishing *v* ▷ **astonish**
astonishment *n* ▷ **astonish**
astonishments *n* ▷ **astonish**
astound *v* (**-s, -ing, -ed**) overwhelm with amazement > **astounding** *adj*
astounded *v* ▷ **astound**
astounding *v, adj* ▷ **astound**
astounds *v* ▷ **astound**
astrakhan *n* (*pl* **-s**) dark curly fleece of lambs from Astrakhan in Russia
astrakhans *n* ▷ **astrakhan**
astral *adj* of stars
astray *adv* off the right path
astride *adv, prep* with a leg on either side (of)
astringencies *n* ▷ **astringent**
astringency *n* ▷ **astringent**
astringent *adj* causing contraction of body tissue ▶ *n* (*pl* **-s**) astringent substance

> **astringency** *n* (*pl* **-cies**)
astringents *n* ▷ **astringent**
astrolabe *n* (*pl* **-s**) instrument formerly used to measure the altitude of stars and planets
astrolabes *n* ▷ **astrolabe**
astrologer *n* ▷ **astrology**
astrologers *n* ▷ **astrology**
astrological *adj* ▷ **astrology**
astrologies *n* ▷ **astrology**
astrology *n* (*pl* **-gies**) study of the alleged influence of the stars, planets, and moon on human affairs > **astrologer** *n* (*pl* **-s**) > **astrological** *adj*
astronaut *n* (*pl* **-s**) person trained for travelling in space
astronautical *adj* ▷ **astronautics**
astronautics *n* science and technology of space flight > **astronautical** *adj*
astronauts *n* ▷ **astronaut**
astronomer *n* ▷ **astronomy**
astronomers *n* ▷ **astronomy**
astronomical *adj* very large > **astronomically** *adv*
astronomically *adv* ▷ **astronomical**
astronomies *n* ▷ **astronomy**
astronomy *n* (*pl* **-mies**) scientific study of heavenly bodies > **astronomer** *n* (*pl* **-s**)
astrophysical *adj* ▷ **astrophysics**
astrophysicist *n* ▷ **astrophysics**
astrophysicists *n* ▷ **astrophysics**
astrophysics *n* science of the physical and chemical properties of stars, planets, etc. > **astrophysical** *adj* > **astrophysicist** *n* (*pl* **-s**)
astute *adj* perceptive or shrewd > **astutely** *adv* > **astuteness** *n* (*pl* **-es**)
astutely *adv* ▷ **astute**
astuteness *n* ▷ **astute**
astutenesses *n* ▷ **astute**
asunder *adv* (*Obs or poetic*) into parts or pieces
asylum *n* (*pl* **-s**) refuge or sanctuary
asylums *n* ▷ **asylum**
asymmetric *adj* ▷ **asymmetry**
asymmetrical *adj* ▷ **asymmetry**
asymmetries *n* ▷ **asymmetry**
asymmetry *n* (*pl* **-tries**) lack of symmetry > **asymmetrical, asymmetric** *adj*
asymptote [**ass**-im-tote] *n* (*pl* **-s**) straight line closely approached but never met by a curve
asymptotes *n* ▷ **asymptote**
at *prep* indicating position in space or time, movement towards an object, etc.
atavism [**at**-a-viz-zum] *n* (*pl* **-s**) recurrence of a trait present in distant ancestors > **atavistic** *adj*
atavisms *n* ▷ **atavism**
atavistic *adj* ▷ **atavism**
ate *v* ▷ **eat**
atheism [**aith**-ee-iz-zum] *n* (*pl* **-s**) belief that there is no God > **atheist** *n* (*pl* **-s**) > **atheistic** *adj*
atheisms *n* ▷ **atheism**
atheist *n* ▷ **atheism**
atheistic *adj* ▷ **atheism**
atheists *n* ▷ **atheism**
atherosclerosis *n* disease in which deposits of fat cause the walls of the arteries to thicken
athlete *n* (*pl* **-s**) person trained in or good at athletics
athletes *n* ▷ **athlete**
athletic *adj* physically fit or strong > **athletically** *adv* > **athleticism** *n* (*pl* **-s**)
athletically *adv* ▷ **athletic**
athleticism *n* ▷ **athletic**
athleticisms *n* ▷ **athletic**
athletics *pl n* track-and-field sports such as running, jumping, throwing, etc.
athwart *prep* across ▶ *adv* transversely
atlas *n* (*pl* **-es**) book of maps
atlases *n* ▷ **atlas**
atmosphere *n* (*pl* **-s**) mass of gases surrounding a heavenly body, esp. the earth > **atmospheric** *adj*
atmospheres *n* ▷ **atmosphere**
atmospheric *adj* ▷ **atmosphere**
atmospherics *pl n* radio interference due to electrical disturbance in the atmosphere
atoll *n* (*pl* **-s**) ring-shaped coral reef enclosing a lagoon
atolls *n* ▷ **atoll**
atom *n* (*pl* **-s**) smallest unit of matter which can take part in a chemical reaction
atomic *adj* of or using atomic bombs or atomic energy
atomize *v* (**-zes, -zing, -zed**) reduce to atoms or small particles
atomized *v* ▷ **atomize**
atomizer *n* (*pl* **-s**) device for discharging a liquid in a fine spray
atomizers *n* ▷ **atomizer**
atomizes *v* ▷ **atomize**
atomizing *v* ▷ **atomize**
atoms *n* ▷ **atom**
atonal [eh-**tone**-al] *adj* (of music) not written in an established key
atone *v* (**-nes, -ning, -ned**) make amends (for sin or wrongdoing) > **atonement** *n* (*pl* **-s**)
atoned *v* ▷ **atone**
atonement *n* ▷ **atone**
atonements *n* ▷ **atone**
atones *v* ▷ **atone**
atoning *v* ▷ **atone**

atop *prep* (*Lit*) on top of
atria *n* ▷ **atrium**
atrium *n* (*pl* **atria**) upper chamber of either half of the heart
atrocious *adj* extremely cruel or wicked > **atrociously** *adv*
atrociously *adv* ▷ **atrocious**
atrocities *n* ▷ **atrocity**
atrocity *n* (*pl* **-ties**) wickedness
atrophied *v* ▷ **atrophy**
atrophies *n, v* ▷ **atrophy**
atrophy [at-trof-fee] *n* (*pl* **-phies**) wasting away of an organ or part ▶ *v* (**-phies, -phying, -phied**) (cause to) waste away
atrophying *v* ▷ **atrophy**
attach *v* (**-es, -ing, -ed**) join, fasten, or connect > **attached** *adj* (*foll. by* **to**) fond of > **attachment** *n* (*pl* **-s**)
attaché [at-**tash**-shay] *n* (*pl* **-s**) specialist attached to a diplomatic mission
attached *v, adj* ▷ **attach**
attaches *v* ▷ **attach**
attachés *n* ▷ **attaché**
attaching *v* ▷ **attach**
attack *v* (**-s, -ing, -ed**) launch a physical assault (against) ▶ *n* (*pl* **-s**) act of attacking > **attacker** *n* (*pl* **-s**)
attacked *v* ▷ **attack**
attacker *n* ▷ **attack**
attackers *n* ▷ **attack**
attacking *v* ▷ **attack**
attacks *v, n* ▷ **attack**
attain *v* (**-s, -ing, -ed**) achieve or accomplish (a task or aim) > **attainable** *adj*
attainable *adj* ▷ **attain**
attained *v* ▷ **attain**
attaining *v* ▷ **attain**
attainment *n* (*pl* **-s**) accomplishment
attainments *n* ▷ **attainment**
attains *v* ▷ **attain**
attar *n* (*pl* **-s**) fragrant oil made from roses
attars *n* ▷ **attar**
attempt *v* (**-s, -ing, -ed**) try, make an effort ▶ *n* (*pl* **-s**) effort or endeavour
attempted *v* ▷ **attempt**
attempting *v* ▷ **attempt**
attempts *v, n* ▷ **attempt**
attend *v* (**-s, -ing, -ed**) be present at
attendance *n* (*pl* **-s**) attending
attendances *n* ▷ **attendance**
attendant *n* (*pl* **-s**) person who assists, guides, or provides a service ▶ *adj* accompanying
attendants *n* ▷ **attendant**
attended *v* ▷ **attend**
attending *v* ▷ **attend**
attends *v* ▷ **attend**
attention *n* (*pl* **-s**) concentrated direction of the mind
attentions *n* ▷ **attention**
attentive *adj* giving attention > **attentively** *adv* > **attentiveness** *n* (*pl* **-es**)
attentively *adv* ▷ **attentive**
attentiveness *n* ▷ **attentive**
attentivenesses *n* ▷ **attentive**
attenuated *adj* weakened > **attenuation** *n* (*pl* **-s**)
attenuation *n* ▷ **attenuated**
attenuations *n* ▷ **attenuated**
attest *v* (**-s, -ing, -ed**) affirm the truth of, be proof of > **attestation** *n* (*pl* **-s**)
attestation *n* ▷ **attest**
attestations *n* ▷ **attest**
attested *v* ▷ **attest**
attesting *v* ▷ **attest**
attests *v* ▷ **attest**
attic *n* (*pl* **-s**) space or room within the roof of a house
attics *n* ▷ **attic**
attire *n* (*pl* **-s**) (*Formal*) fine or formal clothes
attired *adj* dressed in a specified way
attires *n* ▷ **attire**
attitude *n* (*pl* **-s**) way of thinking and behaving
attitudes *n* ▷ **attitude**
attorney *n* (*pl* **-s**) person legally appointed to act for another (US & S AFR)
attorneys *n* ▷ **attorney**
attract *v* (**-s, -ing, -ed**) arouse the interest or admiration of
attracted *v* ▷ **attract**
attracting *v* ▷ **attract**
attraction *n* (*pl* **-s**) power to attract > **attractive** *adj* > **attractively** *adv* > **attractiveness** *n*
attractions *n* ▷ **attraction**
attractive *adj* ▷ **attraction**
attractively *adv* ▷ **attraction**
attractiveness *n* ▷ **attraction**
attracts *v* ▷ **attract**
attributable *adj* ▷ **attribute**
attribute *v* (**-tes, -ting, -ted**) (*usu. foll. by* **to**) regard as belonging to or produced by ▶ *n* (*pl* **-s**) quality or feature representative of a person or thing > **attributable** *adj* > **attribution** *n* (*pl* **-s**)
attributed *v* ▷ **attribute**
attributes *v, n* ▷ **attribute**
attributing *v* ▷ **attribute**
attributive *adj* (GRAMMAR) (of an adjective) preceding the noun modified
attrition *n* (*pl* **-s**) constant wearing down to weaken or destroy

attritions *n* ▷ **attrition**
attune *v* (**-nes, -ning, -ned**) adjust or accustom (a person or thing)
attuned *v* ▷ **attune**
attunes *v* ▷ **attune**
attuning *v* ▷ **attune**
atypical [eh-**tip**-ik-al] *adj* not typical
aubergine [**oh**-bur-zheen] *n* (*pl* **-s**) (BRIT) dark purple tropical fruit, cooked and eaten as a vegetable
aubergines *n* ▷ **aubergine**
aubrietia [aw-**bree**-sha] *n* (*pl* **-s**) trailing plant with purple flowers
aubrietias *n* ▷ **aubrietia**
auburn *adj* (of hair) reddish-brown
auction *n* (*pl* **-s**) public sale in which articles are sold to the highest bidder ▶ *v* (**-s, -ing, -ed**) sell by auction
auctioned *v* ▷ **auction**
auctioneer *n* (*pl* **-s**) person who conducts an auction
auctioneers *n* ▷ **auctioneer**
auctioning *v* ▷ **auction**
auctions *n, v* ▷ **auction**
audacious *adj* recklessly bold or daring > **audaciously** *adv* > **audacity** *n* (*pl* **-ties**)
audaciously *adv* ▷ **audacious**
audacities *n* ▷ **audacious**
audacity *n* ▷ **audacious**
audibilities *n* ▷ **audible**
audibility *n* ▷ **audible**
audible *adj* loud enough to be heard > **audibly** *adv* > **audibility** *n* (*pl* **-ties**)
audibly *adv* ▷ **audible**
audience *n* (*pl* **-s**) group of spectators or listeners
audiences *n* ▷ **audience**
audio *adj* of sound or hearing > **audiovisual** *adj* (esp. of teaching aids) involving both sight and hearing
audiovisual *adj* ▷ **audio**
audit *n* (*pl* **-s**) official examination of business accounts ▶ *v* (**-s, -ing, -ted**) examine (business accounts) officially > **auditor** *n* (*pl* **-s**)
audited *v* ▷ **audit**
auditing *v* ▷ **audit**
audition *n* (*pl* **-s**) test of a performer's ability for a particular role or job ▶ *v* (**-s, -ing, -ed**) test or be tested in an audition
auditioned *v* ▷ **audition**
auditioning *v* ▷ **audition**
auditions *n, v* ▷ **audition**
auditor *n* ▷ **audit**
auditoria *n* ▷ **auditorium**
auditorium *n* (*pl* **-riums, -ria**) area of a concert hall or theatre where the audience sits
auditoriums *n* ▷ **auditorium**
auditors *n* ▷ **audit**
auditory *adj* of or relating to hearing
audits *n, v* ▷ **audit**

auf *n* (**aufs**). An auf is an elf-child left in place of a human baby. Auf scores 6 points.

auger *n* (*pl* **-s**) tool for boring holes
augers *n* ▷ **auger**
aught *pron* (*Obs*) anything whatever
augment *v* (**-s, -ing, -ed**) increase or enlarge > **augmentation** *n* (*pl* **-s**)
augmentation *n* ▷ **augment**
augmentations *n* ▷ **augment**
augmented *v* ▷ **augment**
augmenting *v* ▷ **augment**
augments *v* ▷ **augment**
augur *v* (**-s, -ing, -ed**) be a sign of (future events)
augured *v* ▷ **augur**
auguries *n* ▷ **augury**
auguring *v* ▷ **augur**
augurs *v* ▷ **augur**
augury *n* (*pl* **-ries**) foretelling of the future
august [aw-**gust**] *adj* dignified and imposing
auk *n* (*pl* **-s**) northern sea bird with short wings and black-and-white plumage
auks *n* ▷ **auk**
aunt *n* (*pl* **-s**) father's or mother's sister
auntie, aunty *n* (*pl* **-ties**) (*Informal*) aunt
aunties *n* ▷ **auntie**
aunts *n* ▷ **aunt**
aunty *n* ▷ **auntie**
aura *n* (*pl* **-s**) distinctive air or quality of a person or thing
aural *adj* of or using the ears or hearing
auras *n* ▷ **aura**
aureola *n* ▷ **aureole**
aureolas *n* ▷ **aureole**
aureole, aureola *n* (*pl* **-s**) halo
aureoles *n* ▷ **aureole**
auricle *n* (*pl* **-s**) upper chamber of the heart > **auricular** *adj*
auricles *n* ▷ **auricle**
auricular *adj* ▷ **auricle**
aurochs *n* (*pl* **aurochs**) recently extinct European wild ox
aurora *n* (*pl* **-ras, -rae**) bands of light sometimes seen in the sky in polar regions
aurorae *n* ▷ **aurora**
auroras *n* ▷ **aurora**
auscultation *n* (*pl* **-s**) listening to the internal sounds of the body, usu. with a stethoscope, to help with diagnosis
auscultations *n* ▷ **auscultation**

auspice [**aw**-spiss] *n* (*pl* **-s**) (usually plural) patronage or guidance
auspices *n* ▷ **auspice**
auspicious *adj* showing signs of future success, favourable > **auspiciously** *adv*
auspiciously *adv* ▷ **auspicious**
austere *adj* (**-r, -st**) stern or severe > **austerely** *adv* > **austerity** *n* (*pl* **-ties**)
austerely *adv* ▷ **austere**
austerer *adj* ▷ **austere**
austerest *adj* ▷ **austere**
austerities *n* ▷ **austere**
austerity *n* ▷ **austere**
autarchies *n* ▷ **autarchy**
autarchy [**aw**-tar-kee] *n* (*pl* **-chies**) absolute power or autocracy
autarkies *n* ▷ **autarky**
autarky [**aw**-tar-kee] *n* (*pl* **-kies**) policy of economic self-sufficiency
authentic *adj* known to be real, genuine > **authentically** *adv* > **authenticity** *n* (*pl* **-ties**)
authentically *adv* ▷ **authentic**
authenticate *v* (**-tes, -ting, -ted**) establish as genuine > **authentication** *n* (*pl* **-s**)
authenticated *v* ▷ **authenticate**
authenticates *v* ▷ **authenticate**
authenticating *n* ▷ **authenticate**
authentication *n* ▷ **authenticate**
authentications *n* ▷ **authenticate**
authenticities *n* ▷ **authentic**
authenticity *n* ▷ **authentic**
author *n* (*pl* **-s**) writer of a book etc. > **authorship** *n* (*pl* **-s**)
authoritarian *n* (*pl* **-s**) ▸ *adj* (person) insisting on strict obedience to authority
authoritarians *n* ▷ **authoritarian**
authoritative *adj* recognized as being reliable > **authoritatively** *adv*
authoritatively *adv* ▷ **authoritative**
authorities *n* ▷ **authority**
authority *n* (*pl* **-ties**) power to command or control others
authorization *n* ▷ **authorize**
authorizations *n* ▷ **authorize**
authorize *v* (**-zes, -zing, -zed**) give authority to > **authorization** *n* (*pl* **-s**)
authorized *v* ▷ **authorize**
authorizes *v* ▷ **authorize**
authorizing *v* ▷ **authorize**
authors *n* ▷ **author**
authorship *n* ▷ **author**
authorships *n* ▷ **author**
autism *n* (*pl* **-s**) (PSYCHIATRY) disorder, usu. of children, characterized by lack of response to people and limited ability to communicate > **autistic** *adj*
autisms *n* ▷ **autism**
autistic *adj* ▷ **autism**
autobiographical *adj* ▷ **autobiography**
autobiographically *adv* ▷ **autobiography**
autobiographies *n* ▷ **autobiography**
autobiography *n* (*pl* **-phies**) account of a person's life written by that person > **autobiographical** *adj* > **autobiographically** *adv*
autocracies *n* ▷ **autocracy**
autocracy *n* (*pl* **-cies**) government by an autocrat
autocrat *n* (*pl* **-s**) ruler with absolute authority > **autocratic** *adj* > **autocratically** *adv*
autocratic *adj* ▷ **autocrat**
autocratically *adv* ▷ **autocrat**
autocrats *n* ▷ **autocrat**
autocross *n* (*pl* **-es**) motor-racing over a rough course
autocrosses *n* ▷ **autocross**
autocue *n* (*pl* **autocues**)® electronic television prompting device displaying a speaker's script, unseen by the audience
autocues *n* ▷ **autocue**
autogiro, autogyro *n* (*pl* **-ros**) self-propelled aircraft resembling a helicopter but with an unpowered rotor
autogiros *n* ▷ **autogiro**
autograph *n* (*pl* **-s**) handwritten signature of a (famous) person ▸ *v* (**-s, -ing, -ed**) write one's signature on or in
autographed *v* ▷ **autograph**
autographing *v* ▷ **autograph**
autographs *n, v* ▷ **autograph**
autogyro *n* ▷ **autogiro**
autogyros *n* ▷ **autogiro**
automat *n* (*pl* **-s**) (US) vending machine
automate *v* (**-tes, -ting, -ted**) make (a manufacturing process) automatic > **automation** *n* (*pl* **-s**)
automated *v* ▷ **automate**
automates *v* ▷ **automate**
automatic *adj* (of a device) operating mechanically by itself ▸ *n* (*pl* **-s**) self-loading firearm > **automatically** *adv*
automatically *adv* ▷ **automatic**
automatics *n* ▷ **automatic**
automating *v* ▷ **automate**
automation *n* ▷ **automate**
automations *n* ▷ **automate**
automaton *n* (*pl* **-s**) robot
automatons *n* ▷ **automaton**
automats *n* ▷ **automat**
automobile *n* (*pl* **-s**) (US) motor car

automobiles *n* ▷ **automobile**
autonomies *n* ▷ **autonomy**
autonomous *adj* ▷ **autonomy**
autonomy *n* (*pl* **-mies**) self-government > **autonomous** *adj*
autopsies *n* ▷ **autopsy**
autopsy *n* (*pl* **-sies**) examination of a corpse to determine the cause of death
autosuggestion *n* (*pl* **-s**) process in which a person unconsciously influences his or her own behaviour or beliefs
autosuggestions *n* ▷ **autosuggestion**
autumn *n* (*pl* **-s**) season between summer and winter > **autumnal** *adj*
autumnal *adj* ▷ **autumn**
autumns *n* ▷ **autumn**
auxiliaries *n* ▷ **auxiliary**
auxiliary *adj* secondary or supplementary ▶ *n* (*pl* **-ries**) person or thing that supplements or supports
avail *v* (**-s, -ing, -ed**) be of use or advantage (to) ▶ *n* (*pl* **-s**) use or advantage
availabilities *n* ▷ **available**
availability *n* ▷ **available**
available *adj* obtainable or accessible > **availability** *n* (*pl* **-ties**)
availed *v* ▷ **avail**
availing *v* ▷ **avail**
avails *v, n* ▷ **avail**
avalanche *n* (*pl* **-s**) mass of snow or ice falling down a mountain
avalanches *n* ▷ **avalanche**
avarice [av-a-riss] *n* (*pl* **-s**) greed for wealth > **avaricious** *adj*
avarices *n* ▷ **avarice**
avaricious *adj* ▷ **avarice**
avast *interj* (NAUT) stop
avatar *n* (*pl* **-s**) (HINDUISM) appearance of a god in animal or human form
avatars *n* ▷ **avatar**
avenge *v* (**-ges, -ging, -ged**) take revenge in retaliation for (harm done) or on behalf of (a person harmed) > **avenger** *n* (*pl* **-s**)
avenged *v* ▷ **avenge**
avenger *n* ▷ **avenge**
avengers *n* ▷ **avenge**
avenges *v* ▷ **avenge**
avenging *v* ▷ **avenge**
avenue *n* (*pl* **-s**) wide street
avenues *n* ▷ **avenue**
aver [av-vur] *v* (**avers, averring, averred**) state to be true
average *n* (*pl* **-s**) typical or normal amount or quality ▶ *adj* usual or typical ▶ *v* (**-ges, -ging, -ged**) calculate the average of
averaged *v* ▷ **average**
averages *n, v* ▷ **average**
averred *v* ▷ **aver**
averring *v* ▷ **aver**
avers *v* ▷ **aver**
averages *n, v* ▷ **average**
averse *adj* (*usu. foll. by* **to**) disinclined or unwilling
aversion *n* (*pl* **-s**) strong dislike
aversions *n* ▷ **aversion**
avert *v* (**-s, -ing, -ed**) turn away
averted *v* ▷ **avert**
averting *v* ▷ **avert**
averts *v* ▷ **avert**
aviaries *n* ▷ **aviary**
aviary *n* (*pl* **-ries**) large cage or enclosure for birds
aviation *n* (*pl* **-s**) art of flying aircraft > **aviator** *n* (*pl* **-s**)
aviations *n* ▷ **aviation**
aviator *n* ▷ **aviation**
aviators *n* ▷ **aviation**
avid *adj* (**-er, -est**) keen or enthusiastic > **avidly** *adv* > **avidity** *n* (*pl* **-ties**)
avider *adj* ▷ **avid**
avidest *adj* ▷ **avid**
avidities *n* ▷ **avid**
avidity *n* ▷ **avid**
avidly *adv* ▷ **avid**
avocado *n* (*pl* **-dos**) pear-shaped tropical fruit with a leathery green skin and yellowish-green flesh
avocados *n* ▷ **avocado**
avocation *n* (*pl* **-s**) (*Old-fashioned*) occupation
avocations *n* ▷ **avocation**
avocet *n* (*pl* **-s**) long-legged wading bird with a long slender upward-curving bill
avocets *n* ▷ **avocet**
avoid *v* (**-s, -ing, -ed**) prevent from happening > **avoidable** *adj* > **avoidance** *n* (*pl* **-s**)
avoidable *adj* ▷ **avoid**
avoidance *n* ▷ **avoid**
avoidances *n* ▷ **avoid**
avoided *v* ▷ **avoid**
avoiding *v* ▷ **avoid**
avoids *v* ▷ **avoid**
avoirdupois [av-er-de-**poise**] *n* (*pl* **-es**) system of weights based on pounds and ounces
avoirdupoises *n* ▷ **avoirdupois**
avow *v* (**-s, -ing, -ed**) state or affirm > **avowal** *n* (*pl* **-s**) > **avowed** *adj* > **avowedly** *adv*
avowal *n* ▷ **avow**
avowals *n* ▷ **avow**
avowed *v, adj* ▷ **avow**
avowedly *adv* ▷ **avow**

avowing *v* ▷ **avow**
avows *v* ▷ **avow**
avuncular *adj* (of a man) friendly, helpful, and caring towards someone younger

aw *interj*. A sound people make when they're feeling sorry for someone. Aw scores 5 points.

await *v* (**-s, -ing, -ed**) wait for
awaited *v* ▷ **await**
awaiting *v* ▷ **await**
awaits *v* ▷ **await**
awake *v* (**awakes, awaking, awoke, awoken**) emerge or rouse from sleep ▶ *adj* not sleeping
awaken *v* (**-s, -ing, -ed**) awake
awakened *v* ▷ **awaken**
awakening *v* ▷ **awaken**
awakens *v* ▷ **awaken**
awakes *v* ▷ **awake**
awaking *v* ▷ **awake**
award *v* (**-s, -ing, -ed**) give (something, such as a prize) formally ▶ *n* (*pl* **-s**) something awarded, such as a prize
awarded *v* ▷ **award**
awarding *v* ▷ **award**
awards *v, n* ▷ **award**
aware *adj* having knowledge, informed > **awareness** *n* (*pl* **-es**)
awareness *n* ▷ **aware**
awarenesses *n* ▷ **aware**
awash *adv* washed over by water
away *adv* from a place ▶ *adj* not present
awe *n* (*pl* **-s**) wonder and respect mixed with dread ▶ *v* (**awes, awing, awed**) fill with awe
awed *v* ▷ **awe**
awes *n, v* ▷ **awe**
awesome *adj* inspiring awe
awestruck *adj* filled with awe
awful *adj* (**-ller, -llest**) very bad or unpleasant
awfuller *adj* ▷ **awful**
awfullest *adj* ▷ **awful**
awfully *adv* in an unpleasant way
awhile *adv* for a brief time
awing *v* ▷ **awe**
awkward *adj* (**-er, -est**) clumsy or ungainly > **awkwardly** *adv* > **awkwardness** *n* (*pl* **-es**)
awkwarder *adj* ▷ **awkward**
awkwardest *adj* ▷ **awkward**
awkwardly *adv* ▷ **awkward**
awkwardness *n* ▷ **awkward**
awkwardnesses *n* ▷ **awkward**
awl *n* (*pl* **-s**) pointed tool for piercing wood, leather, etc.
awls *n* ▷ **awl**
awning *n* (*pl* **-s**) canvas roof supported by a frame to give protection against the weather
awnings *n* ▷ **awning**
awoke *v* ▷ **awake**
awoken *v* ▷ **awake**
awry [a-**rye**] *adv, adj* with a twist to one side, askew
ax *n* ▷ **axe**
axe, ax *n* (*pl* **axes**) tool with a sharp blade for felling trees or chopping wood (*Informal*) ▶ *v* (**axes, axing, axed**) (*Informal*) dismiss (employees), restrict (expenditure), or terminate (a project)
axed *v* ▷ **axe**
axes *n, v* ▷ **axe, axis**
axial *adj* ▷ **axis**
axil *n* (*pl* **-s**) angle where the stalk of a leaf joins a stem
axils *n* ▷ **axil**
axing *v* ▷ **axe**
axiom *n* (*pl* **-s**) generally accepted principle
axiomatic *adj* self-evident
axioms *n* ▷ **axiom**
axis *n* (*pl* **axes**) (imaginary) line round which a body can rotate or about which an object or geometrical figure is symmetrical > **axial** *adj*
axle *n* (*pl* **-s**) shaft on which a wheel or pair of wheels turns
axles *n* ▷ **axle**
axolotl *n* (*pl* **-s**) aquatic salamander of central America
axolotls *n* ▷ **axolotl**
ay *interj* ▷ **aye**
ayatollah *n* (*pl* **-s**) Islamic religious leader in Iran
ayatollahs *n* ▷ **ayatollah**
aye, ay *interj* yes ▶ *n* (*pl* **-s**) affirmative vote or voter
ayes *n* ▷ **aye**
azalea [az-**zale**-ya] *n* (*pl* **-s**) garden shrub grown for its showy flowers
azaleas *n* ▷ **azalea**
azimuth *n* (*pl* **-s**) arc of the sky between the zenith and the horizon
azimuths *n* ▷ **azimuth**

azo *adj*. Azo describes a kind of chemical. Azo scores 12 points, and so is a very high-scoring word for only three letters.

azulejo *n* (**azulejos**). An azulejo is a painted and glazed tile. Azulejo scores 23 points, and if you are lucky enough to have all seven letters needed for it, you'll get the 50-point bonus for using all of your tiles.

azure *adj, n* (*pl* **-s**) (of) the colour of a clear blue sky
azures *n* ▷ **azure**

Bb

B forms a two-letter word with every vowel except U – and with Y as well. With a B in your rack, you can play lots of short everyday words that will give you relatively high scores. The best of these is **box** (12 points), but don't forget **bay** (8), **by** (7), **bow** (8), **boy** (8), **buy** (8) and **bye** (8).

ba *n* (**bas**). A ba is the human soul in Egyptian mythology, shown in paintings as a bird with a human head. Ba scores 4 points.

baa *v* (**-s, -ing, -ed**) make the characteristic bleating sound of a sheep ▶ *n* (*pl* **-s**) cry made by a sheep
baaed *v* ▷ **baa**
baaing *v* ▷ **baa**
baas *v, n* ▷ **baa**
babble *v* (**-les, -ling, -led**) talk excitedly or foolishly ▶ *n* (*pl* **-s**) muddled or foolish speech
babbled *v* ▷ **babble**
babbles *v, n* ▷ **babble**
babbling *v* ▷ **babble**
babe *n* (*pl* **-s**) baby
babel *n* (*pl* **-s**) confused mixture of noises or voices
babels *n* ▷ **babel**
babes *n* ▷ **babe**
babies *n* ▷ **baby**
baboon *n* (*pl* **-s**) large monkey with a pointed face and a long tail
baboons *n* ▷ **baboon**
baby *n* (*pl* **-bies**) very young child or animal ▶ *adj* comparatively small of its type > **babyish** *adj*
babyish *adj* ▷ **baby**
babysitter *n* (*pl* **-s**) someone who looks after children when the parents are out
babysitters *n* ▷ **babysitter**
baccarat [**back**-a-rah] *n* (*pl* **-s**) card game involving gambling
baccarats *n* ▷ **baccarat**
bacchanalia [back-a-**nail**-ee-a] *n* (*pl* **-s**) wild drunken party or orgy
bacchanalias *n* ▷ **bacchanalia**
bach [**batch**] (NZ) *n* (*pl* **-es**) small holiday cottage ▶ *v* (**-es, -ing, -ed**) look after oneself when one's spouse is away
bached *v* ▷ **bach**
bachelor *n* (*pl* **-s**) unmarried man
bachelors *n* ▷ **bachelor**
baches *n, v* ▷ **bach**
baching *v* ▷ **bach**
bacilli *n* ▷ **bacillus**
bacillus [bass-**ill**-luss] *n* (*pl* **-li**) [-lie] rod-shaped bacterium
back *n* (*pl* **-s**) rear part of the human body, from the neck to the pelvis ▶ *v* (**-s, -ing, -ed**) (cause to) move backwards ▶ *adv* at, to, or towards the rear
backbencher *n* (*pl* **-s**) Member of Parliament who does not hold office in the government or opposition
backbenchers *n* ▷ **backbencher**
backbiting *n* (*pl* **-s**) spiteful talk about an absent person
backbitings *n* ▷ **backbiting**
backbone *n* (*pl* **-s**) spinal column
backbones *n* ▷ **backbone**
backchat *n* (*pl* **-s**) (*Informal*) impudent replies
backchats *n* ▷ **backchat**
backcloth *n* (*pl* **-s**) painted curtain at the back of a stage set
backcloths *n* ▷ **backcloth**
backdate *v* (**-tes, -ting, -ted**) make (a document) effective from a date earlier than its completion
backdated *v* ▷ **backdate**
backdates *v* ▷ **backdate**
backdating *v* ▷ **backdate**
backdrop *n* (*pl* **-s**) painted curtain at the back of a stage set
backdrops *n* ▷ **backdrop**
backed *v* ▷ **back**
backer *n* (*pl* **-s**) person who gives financial support
backers *n* ▷ **backer**
backfire *v* (**-res, -ring, -red**) (of a plan) fail to

have the desired effect
backfired *v* ▷ **backfire**
backfires *v* ▷ **backfire**
backfiring *v* ▷ **backfire**
backgammon *n* (*pl* **-s**) game played with counters and dice
backgammons *n* ▷ **backgammon**
background *n* (*pl* **-s**) events or circumstances that help to explain something
backgrounds *n* ▷ **background**
backhand *n* (*pl* **-s**) (TENNIS ETC.) stroke played with the back of the hand facing the direction of the stroke
backhanded *adj* ambiguous or implying criticism
backhander *n* (*pl* **-s**) (*Slang*) bribe
backhanders *n* ▷ **backhander**
backhands *n* ▷ **backhand**
backing *n* (*pl* **-s**) support ▶ *v* ▷ **back**
backings *n* ▷ **backing**
backlash *n* (*pl* **-es**) sudden and adverse reaction
backlashes *n* ▷ **backlash**
backlog *n* (*pl* **-s**) accumulation of things to be dealt with
backlogs *n* ▷ **backlog**
backpack *n* (*pl* **-s**) large pack carried on the back
backpacks *n* ▷ **backpack**
backs *n, v* ▷ **back**
backside *n* (*pl* **-s**) (*Informal*) buttocks
backsides *n* ▷ **backside**
backslid *v* ▷ **backslide**
backslide *v* (**-slides, -sliding, -slid**) relapse into former bad habits > **backslider** *n* (*pl* **-s**)
backslider *n* ▷ **backslide**
backsliders *n* ▷ **backslide**
backslides *v* ▷ **backslide**
backsliding *v* ▷ **backslide**
backstage *adv, adj* behind the stage in a theatre
backstroke *n* (*pl* **-s**) swimming stroke performed on the back
backstrokes *n* ▷ **backstroke**
backtrack *v* (**-s, -ing, -ed**) return by the same route by which one has come
backtracked *v* ▷ **backtrack**
backtracking *v* ▷ **backtrack**
backtracks *v* ▷ **backtrack**
backup *n* (*pl* **-s**) support or reinforcement
backups *n* ▷ **backup**
backward *adj* directed towards the rear > **backwardness** *n* (*pl* **-es**)
backwardness *n* ▷ **backward**
backwardnesses *n* ▷ **backwardness**
backwards *adv* towards the rear
backwash *n* (*pl* **-es**) water washed backwards by the motion of a boat
backwashes *n* ▷ **backwash**
backwater *n* (*pl* **-s**) isolated or backward place or condition
backwaters *n* ▷ **backwater**
backwood *n* (*pl* **-s**) (usually plural) remote sparsely populated area
backwoods *n* ▷ **backwood**
bacon *n* (*pl* **-s**) salted or smoked pig meat
bacons *n* ▷ **bacon**
bacteria *pl n* (*sing* **-rium**) large group of microorganisms, many of which cause disease > **bacterial** *adj*
bacterial *adj* ▷ **bacteria**
bacteriologist *n* ▷ **bacteriology**
bacteriologists *n* ▷ **bacteriology**
bacteriology *n* study of bacteria > **bacteriologist** *n* (*pl* **-s**)
bacterium *n* ▷ **bacteria**
bad *adj* (**worse, worst**) of poor quality > **badly** *adv* > **badness** *n* (*pl* **-es**)
bade *v* ▷ **bid**
badge *n* (*pl* **-s**) emblem worn to show membership, rank, etc.
badger *n* (*pl* **-s**) nocturnal burrowing mammal of Europe, Asia, and N America with a black and white head ▶ *v* (**-s, -ing, -ed**) pester or harass
badgered *v* ▷ **badger**
badgering *v* ▷ **badger**
badgers *n, v* ▷ **badger**
badges *n* ▷ **badge**
badinage [**bad**-in-nahzh] *n* (*pl* **-s**) playful and witty conversation
badinages *n* ▷ **badinage**
badly *adv* ▷ **bad**
badminton *n* (*pl* **-s**) game played with rackets and a shuttlecock, which is hit back and forth over a high net
badmintons *n* ▷ **badminton**
badness *n* ▷ **bad**
badnesses *n* ▷ **bad**
baffle *v* (**-les, -ling, -led**) perplex or puzzle ▶ *n* (*pl* **-s**) device to limit or regulate the flow of fluid, light, or sound > **bafflement** *n*
baffled *v* ▷ **baffle**
bafflement *n* ▷ **baffle**
baffles *v, n* ▷ **baffle**
baffling *v* ▷ **baffle**
bag *n* (*pl* **-s**) flexible container with an opening at one end ▶ *v* (**bags, bagging, bagged**) put into a bag
bagatelle *n* (*pl* **-s**) something of little value

bagatelles *n* ▷ **bagatelle**

bagel *n* (*pl* **-s**) hard ring-shaped bread roll

bagels *n* ▷ **bagel**

baggage *n* (*pl* **-s**) suitcases packed for a journey

baggages *n* ▷ **baggage**

bagged *n* ▷ **bag**

baggier *adj* ▷ **baggy**

baggiest *adj* ▷ **baggy**

bagging *n* ▷ **bag**

baggy *adj* **(-ggier, -ggiest)** (of clothes) hanging loosely

bagpipes *pl n* musical wind instrument with reed pipes and an inflatable bag

bags *n, v* ▷ **bag**

bah *interj*. Bah is something people say when they are annoyed or disgusted. Bah scores 8 points.

bail[1] *n* (*pl* **-s**) (LAW) money deposited with a court as security for a person's reappearance in court ▶ *v* **(-s, -ing, -ed)** pay bail for (a person)

bail[2], bale *v* **(-s, -ing, -ed)** (*foll. by* **out**) remove (water) from (a boat) (*Informal*)

bail[3] *n* (*pl* **-s**) (CRICKET) either of two wooden bars across the tops of the stumps

bailed *v* ▷ **bail[1, 2]**

bailey *n* (*pl* **-s**) outermost wall or court of a castle

baileys *n* ▷ **bailey**

bailiff *n* (*pl* **-s**) sheriff's officer who serves writs and summonses

bailiffs *n* ▷ **bailiff**

bailing *v* ▷ **bail[1, 2]**

bails *n* ▷ **bail[1, 3]** ▶ *v* ▷ **bail[1, 2]**

bairn *n* (*pl* **-s**) (SCOT) child

bairns *n* ▷ **bairn**

bait *n* (*pl* **-s**) piece of food on a hook or in a trap to attract fish or animals ▶ *v* **(-s, -ing, -ed)** put a piece of food on or in (a hook or trap)

baited *v* ▷ **bait**

baiting *v* ▷ **bait**

baits *n, v* ▷ **bait**

baize *n* (*pl* **-s**) woollen fabric used to cover billiard and card tables

baizes *n* ▷ **bait**

bake *v* **(-kes, -king, -ked)** cook by dry heat as in an oven

baked *v* ▷ **bake**

baker *n* (*pl* **-s**) person whose business is to make or sell bread, cakes, etc.

bakeries *n* ▷ **bakery**

bakers *n* ▷ **baker**

bakery *n* (*pl* **-eries**) place where bread, cakes, etc. are baked or sold

bakes *v* ▷ **bake**

baking *v* ▷ **bake**

bakkie *n* (*pl* **-s**) (S AFR) small truck

bakkies *n* ▷ **bakkie**

balaclava *n* (*pl* **-s**) close-fitting woollen hood that covers the ears and neck

balaclavas *n* ▷ **balaclava**

balalaika *n* (*pl* **-s**) guitar-like musical instrument with a triangular body

balalaikas *n* ▷ **balalaika**

balance *n* (*pl* **-s**) state in which a weight or amount is evenly distributed ▶ *v* **(-ces, -cing, -ced)** weigh in a balance

balanced *v* ▷ **balance**

balances *n, v* ▷ **balance**

balancing *v* ▷ **balance**

balconies *n* ▷ **balcony**

balcony *n* (*pl* **-nies**) platform on the outside of a building with a rail along the outer edge

bald *adj* **(-er, -est)** having little or no hair on the scalp > **baldness** *n* (*pl* **-es**)

balder *adj* ▷ **bald**

balderdash *n* (*pl* **-es**) stupid talk

balderdashes *n* ▷ **balderdash**

baldest *adj* ▷ **bald**

balding *adj* becoming bald

baldness *n* ▷ **bald**

baldnesses *n* ▷ **bald**

bale[1] *n* (*pl* **-s**) large bundle of hay or goods tightly bound together ▶ *v* **(-les, -ling, -led)** make or put into bales

bale[2] *v* ▷ **bail[2]**

baled *v* ▷ **bale[1, 2]**

baleful *adj* vindictive or menacing > **balefully** *adv*

balefully *adv* ▷ **baleful**

bales *n, v* ▷ **bale[1, 2]**

baling *v* ▷ **bale[1, 2]**

balk, baulk *v* **(-s, -ing, -ed)** be reluctant to (do something)

balked *v* ▷ **balk**

balking *v* ▷ **balk**

balks *v* ▷ **balk**

ball[1] *n* (*pl* **-s**) round or nearly round object, esp. one used in games ▶ *v* **(-lls, -lling, -lled)** form into a ball

ball[2] *n* (*pl* **-s**) formal social function for dancing > **ballroom** *n* (*pl* **-s**)

ballad *n* (*pl* **-s**) narrative poem or song

ballads *n* ▷ **ballad**

ballast *n* (*pl* **-s**) substance, such as sand, used to stabilize a ship when it is not carrying cargo

ballasts *n* ▷ **ballast**

balled *v* ▷ **ball[1]**

ballerina *n* (*pl* **-s**) female ballet dancer
ballerinas *n* ▷ **ballerina**
ballet *n* (*pl* **-s**) classical style of expressive dancing based on conventional steps
ballets *n* ▷ **ballet**
balling *v* ▷ **ball**[1]
ballistic *adj* ▷ **ballistics**
ballistics *n* study of the flight of projectiles, such as bullets > **ballistic** *adj*
balloon *n* (*pl* **-s**) inflatable rubber bag used as a plaything or decoration ▶ *v* (**-s, -ing, -ed**) fly in a balloon > **balloonist** *n* (*pl* **-s**)
ballooned *v* ▷ **balloon**
ballooning *v* ▷ **balloon**
balloonist *n* ▷ **balloon**
balloonists *n* ▷ **balloonist**
balloons *n, v* ▷ **balloon**
ballot *n* (*pl* **-s**) method of voting ▶ *v* (**-lots, -loting, -loted**) vote or ask for a vote from
balloted *v* ▷ **ballot**
balloting *v* ▷ **ballot**
ballots *n, v* ▷ **ballot**
ballpoint *n* (*pl* **-s**) pen with a tiny ball bearing as a writing point
ballpoints *n* ▷ **ballpoint**
ballroom *n* ▷ **ball**[2]
ballrooms *n* ▷ **ball**[2]
balls *n* ▷ **ball**[1, 2] ▶ *v* ▷ **ball**[1]
ballyhoo *n* (*pl* **-s**) exaggerated fuss
ballyhoos *n* ▷ **ballyhoo**
balm *n* (*pl* **-s**) aromatic substance used for healing and soothing
balmier *adj* ▷ **balmy**
balmiest *adj* ▷ **balmy**
balms *n* ▷ **balm**
balmy *adj* (**-mier, -miest**) (of weather) mild and pleasant
baloney, boloney *n* (*pl* **-s**) (*Informal*) nonsense
baloneys *n* ▷ **baloney**
balsa [**bawl**-sa] *n* (*pl* **-s**) very light wood from a tropical American tree
balsam *n* (*pl* **-s**) soothing ointment
balsams *n* ▷ **balsam**
balsas *n* ▷ **balsa**
baluster *n* (*pl* **-s**) set of posts supporting a rail
balusters *n* ▷ **baluster**
balustrade *n* (*pl* **-s**) ornamental rail supported by balusters
balustrades *n* ▷ **balustrade**
bamboo *n* (*pl* **-s**) tall treelike tropical grass with hollow stems
bamboos *n* ▷ **bamboo**
bamboozle *v* (**-zles, -zling, -zled**) (*Informal*) cheat or mislead
bamboozled *v* ▷ **bamboozle**
bamboozles *v* ▷ **bamboozle**
bamboozling *v* ▷ **bamboozle**
ban *v* (**-s, -nning, -nned**) prohibit or forbid officially ▶ *n* (*pl* **-s**) official prohibition
banal [ban-**nahl**] *adj* (**-er, -est**) ordinary and unoriginal > **banality** *n* (*pl* **-ties**)
banaler *adj* ▷ **banal**
banalest *adj* ▷ **banal**
banalities *n* ▷ **banal**
banality *n* ▷ **banal**
banana *n* (*pl* **-s**) yellow crescent-shaped fruit
bananas *n* ▷ **banana**
band[1] *n* (*pl* **-s**) group of musicians playing together > **bandsman** *n* (*pl* **-men**)
band[2] *n* (*pl* **-s**) strip of some material, used to hold objects
bandage *n* (*pl* **-s**) piece of material used to cover a wound or wrap an injured limb ▶ *v* (**-ges, -ging, -ged**) cover with a bandage
bandaged *v* ▷ **bandage**
bandages *n, v* ▷ **bandage**
bandaging *v* ▷ **bandage**
bandana *n* ▷ **bandanna**
bandanas *n* ▷ **bandanna**
bandanna, bandana *n* (*pl* **-s**) large brightly coloured handkerchief or neckerchief
bandannas *n* ▷ **bandanna**
bandicoot *n* (*pl* **-s**) ratlike Australian marsupial
bandicoots *n* ▷ **bandicoot**
bandied *v* ▷ **bandy**
bandier *adj* ▷ **bandy**
bandies *v* ▷ **bandy**
bandiest *n* ▷ **bandy**
bandit *n* (*pl* **-s**) robber, esp. a member of an armed gang > **banditry** *n*
banditry *n* ▷ **bandit**
bandits *n* ▷ **bandit**
bandolier *n* (*pl* **-s**) shoulder belt for holding cartridges
bandoliers *n* ▷ **bandolier**
bands *n* ▷ **band**[1, 2]
bandsman *n* ▷ **band**[1]
bandsmen *n* ▷ **band**[1]
bandstand *n* (*pl* **-s**) roofed outdoor platform for a band
bandstands *n* ▷ **bandstand**
bandwagon *n* (*pl* **-s**) a party or movement that seems assured of success
bandwagons *n* ▷ **bandwagon**
bandy *adj* (**-dier, -diest**) ▶ *v* (**-dies, -dying, -died**) exchange (words) in a heated manner
bandying *v* ▷ **bandy**
bane *n* (*pl* **-s**) person or thing that causes misery or distress > **baneful** *adj*

baneful *adj* ▷ **bane**
banes *n* ▷ **bane**
bang *n* (*pl* **-s**) short loud explosive noise ▸ *v* (**-s, -ging, -ged**) hit or knock, esp. with a loud noise ▸ *adv* precisely
banged *v* ▷ **bang**
banger *n* (*pl* **-s**) (*Informal*) (BRIT & AUST) old decrepit car
bangers *n* ▷ **banger**
banging *v* ▷ **bang**
bangle *n* (*pl* **-s**) bracelet worn round the arm or the ankle
bangles *n* ▷ **bangle**
bangs *n*, *v* ▷ **bang**
banish *v* (**-es, -ing, -ed**) send (someone) into exile > **banishment** *n* (*pl* **-s**)
banished *v* ▷ **banish**
banishes *v* ▷ **banish**
banishing *v* ▷ **banish**
banishment *n* ▷ **banish**
banishments *n* ▷ **banish**
banisters, bannisters *pl n* railing supported by posts on a staircase

> **banjax** *v* (**banjaxes, banjaxing, banjaxed**). If you banjax something, you wreck or ruin it. This is a great word to remember, with its high-scoring combination of J and X. Look out for chances to form it from either **ban** or **ax**. Banjax scores 22 points.

banjo *n* (*pl* **-jos, -joes**) guitar-like musical instrument with a circular body
banjoes *n* ▷ **banjo**
banjos *n* ▷ **banjo**
bank[1] *n* (*pl* **-s**) institution offering services such as the safekeeping and lending of money ▸ *v* (**-s, -ing, -ed**) deposit (cash or cheques) in a bank > **banking** *n*
bank[2] *n* (*pl* **-s**) raised mass, esp. of earth ▸ *v* (**-s, -ing, -ed**) form into a bank
bank[3] *n* (*pl* **-s**) arrangement of switches, keys, oars, etc. in a row or in tiers
banked *v* ▷ **bank**[1, 2]
banker *n* (*pl* **-s**) manager or owner of a bank
bankers *n* ▷ **banker**
banking *v* ▷ **bank**[1, 2] ▸ *n* ▷ **bank**[1]
banknote *n* (*pl* **-s**) piece of paper money
banknotes *n* ▷ **banknote**
bankrupt *n* (*pl* **-s**) person declared by a court to be unable to pay his or her debts ▸ *adj* financially ruined ▸ *v* (**-s, -ing, -ed**) make bankrupt > **bankruptcy** *n* (*pl* **-cies**)
bankruptcies *n* ▷ **bankrupt**
bankruptcy *n* ▷ **bankrupt**
bankrupted *v* ▷ **bankrupt**
bankrupting *v* ▷ **bankrupt**
bankrupts *n*, *v* ▷ **bankrupt**
banks *n* ▷ **bank**[1, 2, 3] ▸ *v* ▷ **bank**[1, 2]
banksia *n* (*pl* **-s**) Australian evergreen tree or shrub
banksias *n* ▷ **banksia**
banned *v* ▷ **ban**
banner *n* (*pl* **-s**) long strip of cloth displaying a slogan, advertisement, etc.
banners *n* ▷ **banner**
banning *v* ▷ **ban**
bannisters *pl n* ▷ **banisters**
banns *pl n* public declaration, esp. in a church, of an intended marriage
banquet *n* (*pl* **-s**) elaborate formal dinner
banquets *n* ▷ **banquet**
bans *v*, *n* ▷ **ban**
banshee *n* (*pl* **-s**) (in Irish folklore) female spirit whose wailing warns of a coming death
banshees *n* ▷ **banshee**
bantam *n* (*pl* **-s**) small breed of chicken
bantams *n* ▷ **bantam**
bantamweight *n* (*pl* **-s**) boxer weighing up to 118lb (professional) or 54kg (amateur)
bantamweights *n* ▷ **bantamweight**
banter *v* (**-s, -ing, -ed**) tease jokingly ▸ *n* (*pl* **-s**) teasing or joking conversation
bantered *v* ▷ **banter**
bantering *v* ▷ **banter**
banters *v*, *n* ▷ **banter**
baobab [**bay**-oh-bab] *n* (*pl* **-s**) African tree with a thick trunk and angular branches
baobabs *n* ▷ **baobab**
baptism *n* (*pl* **-s**) Christian religious ceremony in which a person is immersed in or sprinkled with water as a sign of being cleansed from sin and accepted into the Church > **baptismal** *adj*
baptismal *adj* ▷ **baptism**
baptisms *n* ▷ **baptism**
baptist *n* (*pl* **-s**) member of a Protestant denomination that believes in adult baptism by immersion
baptists *n* ▷ **baptist**
baptize *v* (**-zes, -zing, -zed**) perform baptism on
baptized *v* ▷ **baptize**
baptizes *v* ▷ **baptize**
baptizing *v* ▷ **baptize**
bar[1] *n* (*pl* **-s**) rigid length of metal, wood, etc. ▸ *v* (**bars, barring, barred**) secure with a bar > **barman** (*pl* **-men**), **barmaid** (*pl* **-s**) ▸ *n*
bar[2] *n* (*pl* **-s**) unit of atmospheric pressure
barb *n* (*pl* **-s**) cutting remark > **barbed** *adj*
barbarian *n* (*pl* **-s**) member of a primitive or

uncivilized people
barbarians *n* ▷ **barbarian**
barbaric *adj* cruel or brutal
barbarism *n* (*pl* **-s**) condition of being backward or ignorant
barbarisms *n* ▷ **barbarism**
barbarities *n* ▷ **barbarity**
barbarity *n* (*pl* **-ties**) state of being barbaric or barbarous
barbarous *adj* uncivilized
barbecue *n* (*pl* **-s**) grill on which food is cooked over hot charcoal, usu. outdoors ▶ *v* (**-cues, -cuing, -cued**) cook (food) on a barbecue
barbecued *v* ▷ **barbecue**
barbecues *n, v* ▷ **barbecue**
barbecuing *v* ▷ **barbecue**
barbed *adj* ▷ **barb**
barber *n* (*pl* **-s**) person who cuts men's hair and shaves beards
barbers *n* ▷ **barber**
barbiturate *n* (*pl* **-s**) drug used as a sedative
barbiturates *n* ▷ **barbiturate**
barbs *n* ▷ **barb**
bard *n* (*pl* **-s**) (*Lit*) poet
bards *n* ▷ **bard**
bare *adj* (**-r, -st**) unclothed, naked ▶ *v* (**-res, -ring, -red**) uncover > **bareness** *n* (*pl* **-es**)
bareback *adj, adv* (of horse-riding) without a saddle
bared *v* ▷ **bare**
barefaced *adj* shameless or obvious
barely *adv* only just
bareness *n* ▷ **bare**
barenesses *n* ▷ **bare**
barer *adj* ▷ **bare**
bares *v* ▷ **bare**
barest *adj* ▷ **bare**
bargain *n* (*pl* **-s**) agreement establishing what each party will give, receive, or perform in a transaction ▶ *v* (**-s, -ing, -ed**) negotiate the terms of an agreement
bargained *v* ▷ **bargain**
bargaining *v* ▷ **bargain**
bargains *n, v* ▷ **bargain**
barge *n* (*pl* **-s**) flat-bottomed boat used to transport freight ▶ *v* (**-ges, -ging, -ged**) (*Informal*) push violently
barged *v* ▷ **barge**
barges *n, v* ▷ **barge**
barging *v* ▷ **barge**
baring *v* ▷ **bare**
barista [bar-**ee**-sta] *n* (*pl* **-s**) person who makes and sells coffee in a coffee bar
baristas *n* ▷ **barista**
baritone *n* (*pl* **-s**) (singer with) the second lowest adult male voice
baritones *n* ▷ **baritone**
barium *n* (*pl* **-s**) (CHEM) soft white metallic element
bariums *n* ▷ **barium**
bark[1] *n* (*pl* **-s**) loud harsh cry of a dog ▶ *v* (**-s, -ing, -ed**) (of a dog) make its typical cry
bark[2] *n* (*pl* **-s**) tough outer layer of a tree
barked *v* ▷ **bark[1]**
barking *v* ▷ **bark[1]**
barks *n, v* ▷ **bark[1]** ▶ *n* ▷ **bark[2]**
barley *n* (*pl* **-s**) tall grasslike plant cultivated for grain
barleys *n* ▷ **barley**
barmaid *n* ▷ **bar[1]**
barmaids *n* ▷ **bar[1]**
barman *n* ▷ **bar[1]**
barmen *n* ▷ **bar[1]**
barmier *adj* ▷ **barmy**
barmiest *adj* ▷ **barmy**
barmy *adj* (**-mier, -miest**) (*Slang*) insane
barn *n* (*pl* **-s**) large building on a farm used for storing grain
barnacle *n* (*pl* **-s**) shellfish that lives attached to rocks, ship bottoms, etc.
barnacles *n* ▷ **barnacle**
barney *n* (*pl* **-s**) (*Informal*) noisy fight or argument
barneys *n* ▷ **barney**
barns *n* ▷ **barn**
barometer *n* (*pl* **-s**) instrument for measuring atmospheric pressure > **barometric** *adj*
barometers *n* ▷ **barometer**
barometric *adj* ▷ **barometer**
baron *n* (*pl* **-s**) member of the lowest rank of nobility > **baroness** *n* (*pl* **-es**) > **baronial** *adj*
baroness *n* ▷ **baron**
baronesses *n* ▷ **baron**
baronet *n* (*pl* **baronets**) commoner who holds the lowest hereditary British title
baronets *n* ▷ **baronet**
baronial *adj* ▷ **baron**
barons *n* ▷ **baron**
baroque [bar-**rock**] *n* (*pl* **-s**) highly ornate style of art, architecture, or music from the late 16th to the early 18th century ▶ *adj* ornate in style
baroques *n* ▷ **baroque**
barque [**bark**] *n* (*pl* **-s**) sailing ship, esp. one with three masts
barques *n* ▷ **barque**
barra *n* (*pl* **-s**) (AUST) (*Informal*) ▷ **barramundi**
barrack *v* (**-s, -ing, -ed**) criticize loudly or shout against (a team or speaker)
barracked *v* ▷ **barrack**

barracking *v* ▷ **barrack**
barracks *v* ▷ **barrack** ▶ *pl n* building used to accommodate military personnel
barracouta *n* (*pl* **-s**) large Pacific fish with a protruding lower jaw and strong teeth
barracoutas *n* ▷ **barracouta**
barracuda *n* (*pl* **barracuda**) tropical sea fish
barrage [bar-rahzh] *n* (*pl* **-s**) continuous delivery of questions, complaints, etc.
barrages *n* ▷ **barrage**
barramundi *n* (*pl* **-s**) edible Australian fish
barramundis *n* ▷ **barramundi**
barras *n* ▷ **barra**
barred *v* ▷ **bar**[1]
barrel *n* (*pl* **-s**) cylindrical container with rounded sides and flat ends
barrels *n* ▷ **barrel**
barren *adj* (**-er, -est**) (of a woman or female animal) incapable of producing offspring > **barrenness** *n* (*pl* **-es**)
barrener *adj* ▷ **barren**
barrenest *adj* ▷ **barren**
barrenness *n* ▷ **barren**
barrennesses *n* ▷ **barren**
barricade *n* (*pl* **-s**) barrier, esp. one erected hastily for defence ▶ *v* (**-des, -ding, -ded**) erect a barricade across (an entrance)
barricaded *v* ▷ **barricade**
barricades *n, v* ▷ **barricade**
barricading *v* ▷ **barricade**
barrier *n* (*pl* **-s**) anything that prevents access, progress, or union
barriers *n* ▷ **barrier**
barring *v* ▷ **bar**[1] ▶ *prep* except for
barrister *n* (*pl* **-s**) (BRIT, AUST & NZ) lawyer qualified to plead in a higher court
barristers *n* ▷ **barrister**
barrow[1] *n* (*pl* **-s**) wheelbarrow
barrow[2] *n* (*pl* **-s**) mound of earth over a prehistoric tomb
barrows *n* ▷ **barrow**[1, 2]
bars *n* ▷ **bar**[1, 2] ▶ *v* ▷ **bar**[1]
barter *v* (**-s, -ing, -ed**) trade (goods) in exchange for other goods ▶ *n* (*pl* **-s**) trade by the exchange of goods
bartered *v* ▷ **barter**
bartering *v* ▷ **barter**
barters *v, n* ▷ **barter**
basalt [bass-awlt] *n* (*pl* **-s**) dark volcanic rock > **basaltic** *adj*
basaltic *adj* ▷ **basalt**
basalts *n* ▷ **basalt**
base[1] *n* (*pl* **-s**) bottom or supporting part of anything ▶ *v* (**bases, basing, based**) (*foll. by* **on** *or* **upon**) use as a basis (for) > **baseless** *adj*
base[2] *adj* (**-r, -st**) dishonourable or immoral > **baseness** *n*
baseball *n* (*pl* **-s**) team game in which runs are scored by hitting a ball with a bat then running round four bases
baseballs *n* ▷ **baseball**
based *v* ▷ **base**[1]
baseless *adj* ▷ **base**[1]
basement *n* (*pl* **-s**) partly or wholly underground storey of a building
basements *n* ▷ **basement**
baseness *n* ▷ **base**[2]
baser *adj* ▷ **base**[2]
bases *n* ▷ **base**[1], **basis** ▶ *v* ▷ **base**[1]
basest *adj* ▷ **base**[2]
bash (*Informal*) *v* (**-es, -ing, -ed**) hit violently or forcefully ▶ *n* (*pl* **bashes**) heavy blow
bashed *v* ▷ **bash**
bashes *v, n* ▷ **bash**
bashful *adj* shy or modest > **bashfully** *adv* > **bashfulness** *n*
bashfully *adv* ▷ **bash**
bashfulness *n* ▷ **bash**
bashing *v* ▷ **bash**
basic *adj* of or forming a base or basis > **basically** *adv*
basically *adv* ▷ **basic**
basics *pl n* fundamental principles, facts, etc.
basil *n* (*pl* **-s**) aromatic herb used in cooking
basilica *n* (*pl* **-s**) rectangular church with a rounded end and two aisles
basilicas *n* ▷ **basilica**
basilisk *n* (*pl* **-s**) legendary serpent said to kill by its breath or glance
basilisks *n* ▷ **basilisk**
basils *n* ▷ **basil**
basin *n* (*pl* **-s**) round open container
basing *v* ▷ **base**[1]
basins *n* ▷ **basin**
basis *n* (*pl* **-ses**) fundamental principles etc. from which something is started or developed
bask *v* (**-s, -ing, -ed**) lie in or be exposed to something, esp. pleasant warmth
basked *v* ▷ **bask**
basket *n* (*pl* **-s**) container made of interwoven strips of wood or cane > **basketwork** *n* (*pl* **-s**)
basketball *n* (*pl* **-s**) team game in which points are scored by throwing the ball through a high horizontal hoop
basketballs *n* ▷ **basketball**
baskets *n* ▷ **basket**
basketwork *n* ▷ **basket**
basketworks *n* ▷ **basket**
basking *v* ▷ **bask**

basks *v* ▷ **bask**
bass¹ [**base**] *n* (*pl* **-es**) (singer with) the lowest adult male voice ▶ *adj* of the lowest range of musical notes
bass² *n* (*pl* **bass**) edible sea fish
basses *n* ▷ **bass¹**
bassoon *n* (*pl* **-s**) low-pitched woodwind instrument
bassoons *n* ▷ **bassoon**
bastard *n* (*pl* **-s**) (*Offens*) obnoxious or despicable person
bastards *n* ▷ **bastard**
baste¹ *v* (**bastes, basting, basted**) moisten (meat) during cooking with hot fat
baste² *v* (**bastes, basting, basted**) sew with loose temporary stitches
basted *v* ▷ **baste¹, ²**
bastes *v* ▷ **baste¹, ²**
basting *v* ▷ **baste¹, ²**
bastion *n* (*pl* **-s**) projecting part of a fortification
bastions *n* ▷ **bastion**
bat¹ *n* (*pl* **-s**) any of various types of club used to hit the ball in certain sports ▶ *v* (**bats, batting, batted**) strike with or as if with a bat
bat² *n* (*pl* **-s**) nocturnal mouselike flying animal
batch *n* (*pl* **-es**) group of people or things dealt with at the same time
batches *n* ▷ **batch**
bath *n* (*pl* **-s**) large container in which to wash the body ▶ *pl* public swimming pool ▶ *v* (**-s, -ing, -ed**) wash in a bath
bathe *v* (**-thes, -thing, -thed**) swim in open water for pleasure > **bather** *n* (*pl* **-s**)
bathed *v* ▷ **bath** ▷ **bathe**
bather *n* ▷ **bathe**
bathers *n* ▷ **bathe**
bathes *v* ▷ **bath** ▷ **bathe**
bathing *v* ▷ **bath** ▷ **bathe**
bathos [**bay**-thoss] *n* (*pl* **-es**) sudden ludicrous change in speech or writing from a serious subject to a trivial one
bathoses *n* ▷ **bathos**
bathroom *n* (*pl* **-s**) room with a bath, sink, and usu. a toilet
bathrooms *n* ▷ **bathe**
baths *n, v* ▷ **bath**
batik [bat-**teek**] *n* (*pl* **-s**) process of printing fabric using wax to cover areas not to be dyed
batiks *n* ▷ **batik**
batman *n* (*pl* **-men**) officer's servant in the armed forces
batmen *n* ▷ **batman**
baton *n* (*pl* **-s**) thin stick used by the conductor of an orchestra
batons *n* ▷ **baton**
bats *n* ▷ **bat¹, ²** ▶ *v* ▷ **bat¹**
batsman *n* (*pl* **-men**) (CRICKET) person who bats or specializes in batting
batsmen *n* ▷ **batsman**
battalion *n* (*pl* **-s**) army unit consisting of three or more companies
battalions *n* ▷ **battalion**
batted *v* ▷ **bat¹**
batten *n* (*pl* **-s**) strip of wood fixed to something, esp. to hold it in place
battens *n* ▷ **batten**
batter¹ *v* (**-s, -ing, -ed**) hit repeatedly
batter² *n* (*pl* **-s**) mixture of flour, eggs, and milk, used in cooking
battered *v* ▷ **batter¹**
batteries *n* ▷ **battery**
battering *v* ▷ **batter¹**
batters *v, n* ▷ **batter¹, ²**
battery *n* (*pl* **-teries**) device that produces electricity in a torch, radio, etc. ▶ *adj* kept in series of cages for intensive rearing
battier *adj* ▷ **batty**
battiest *adj* ▷ **batty**
batting *adj* ▷ **bat¹**
battle *n* (*pl* **-s**) fight between large armed forces ▶ *v* (**battles, battling, battled**) struggle
battled *v* ▷ **battle**
battlement *n* (*pl* **-s**) wall with gaps along the top for firing through
battlements *n* ▷ **battlement**
battles *n, v* ▷ **battle**
battleship *n* (*pl* **-s**) large heavily armoured warship
battleships *n* ▷ **battleship**
battling *v* ▷ **battle**
batty *adj* (**-tier, -tiest**) (*Slang*) eccentric or crazy
bauble *n* (*pl* **-s**) trinket of little value
baubles *n* ▷ **bauble**
bauera *n* (*pl* **-s**) small evergreen Australian shrub
baueras *n* ▷ **bauera**
baulk *v* (**-s, -ing, -ed**) ▷ **balk**
baulked *v* ▷ **baulk**
baulking *v* ▷ **baulk**
baulks *v* ▷ **baulk**
bauxite *n* (*pl* **-s**) claylike substance that is the chief source of aluminium
bauxites *n* ▷ **bauxite**
bawdier *adj* ▷ **bawdy**
bawdiest *adj* ▷ **bawdy**
bawdy *adj* (**-ier, -iest**) (of writing etc.) containing humorous references to sex
bawl *v* (**-s, -ing, -ed**) shout or weep noisily
bawled *v* ▷ **bawl**

bawling *v* ▷ **bawl**
bawls *v* ▷ **bawl**
bay¹ *n* (*pl* **-s**) stretch of coastline that curves inwards
bay² *n* (*pl* **-s**) recess in a wall
bay³ *v* (**-s, -ing, -ed**) howl in deep prolonged tones
bay⁴ *n* (*pl* **-s**) Mediterranean laurel tree
bay⁵ *adj, n* (*pl* **-s**) reddish-brown (horse)
bayed *v* ▷ **bay³**
baying *v* ▷ **bay³**
bayonet *n* (*pl* **-s**) sharp blade that can be fixed to the end of a rifle ▶ *v* (**-nets, -neting, -neted**) stab with a bayonet
bayoneted *v* ▷ **bayonet**
bayoneting *v* ▷ **bayonet**
bayonets *n, v* ▷ **bayonet**
bays *n* ▷ **bay¹, ², ⁴, ⁵** ▶ *v*³
bazaar *n* (*pl* **-s**) sale in aid of charity
bazaars *n* ▷ **bazaar**
bazooka *n* (*pl* **-s**) portable rocket launcher that fires an armour-piercing projectile
bazookas *n* ▷ **bazooka**
be *v* (*present sing* (*1st person* **am**) (*2nd person* **are**) (*3rd person* **is**) (*present pl* **are**) (*past sing* (*1st person* **was**) (*2nd person* **were**) (*3rd person* **was**) (*past pl* **were**) (*present participle* **being**) (*past participle* **been**) exist or live
beach *n* (*pl* **-es**) area of sand or pebbles on a shore ▶ *v* (**-es, -ing, -ed**) run or haul (a boat) onto a beach
beached *v* ▷ **beach**
beaches *n, v* ▷ **beach**
beachhead *n* (*pl* **-s**) beach captured by an attacking army on which troops can be landed
beachheads *v* ▷ **beachhead**
beaching *v* ▷ **beach**
beacon *n* (*pl* **-s**) fire or light on a hill or tower, used as a warning
beacons *n* ▷ **beacon**
bead *n* (*pl* **-s**) small piece of plastic, wood, etc., pierced for threading on a string to form a necklace etc. > **beaded** *adj*
beaded *n* ▷ **bead**
beadier *adj* ▷ **beady**
beadiest *adj* ▷ **beady**
beading *n* strip of moulding used for edging furniture
beads *n* ▷ **bead**
beady *adj* (**-ier, -iest**) small, round, and glittering
beagle *n* (*pl* **-s**) small hound with short legs and drooping ears
beagles *n* ▷ **beagle**
beak¹ *n* (*pl* **-s**) projecting horny jaws of a bird > **beaky** *adj* (**-ier, -iest**)
beak² *n* (*pl* **-s**) (BRIT, AUST & NZ) (*Slang*) judge, magistrate, or headmaster
beaker *n* (*pl* **-s**) large drinking cup
beakers *n* ▷ **beaker**
beakier *adj* ▷ **beak¹**
beakiest *adj* ▷ **beak¹**
beaks *n* ▷ **beak¹, ²**
beaky *adj* ▷ **beak¹**
beam *n* (*pl* **-s**) broad smile ▶ *v* (**-s, -ing, -ed**) smile broadly
beamed *v* ▷ **beam**
beaming *v* ▷ **beam**
beams *n, v* ▷ **beam**
bean *n* (*pl* **-s**) seed or pod of various plants, eaten as a vegetable or used to make coffee etc.
beanie *n* (*pl* **-s**) close-fitting woollen hat
beanies *n* ▷ **beanie**
beans *n* ▷ **bean**
bear¹ *v* (**bears, bearing, bore, borne**) support or hold up (*passive* **born**) > **bearable** *adj*
bear² *n* (*pl* **-s**) large heavy mammal with a shaggy coat
bearable *adj* ▷ **bear¹**
beard *n* (*pl* **-s**) hair growing on the lower parts of a man's face > **bearded** *adj*
bearded *adj* ▷ **beard**
beards *n* ▷ **beard**
bearer *n* (*pl* **-s**) person who carries, presents, or upholds something
bearers *n* ▷ **bearer**
bearing *n* (*pl* **-s**) relevance (to) ▶ *pl* sense of one's own relative position ▶ *v* ▷ **bear¹**
bearings *n* ▷ **bearing**
bears *v* ▷ **bear¹** ▶ *n* ▷ **bear²**
bearskin *n* (*pl* **-s**) tall fur helmet worn by some British soldiers
bearskins *n* ▷ **bearskin**
beast *n* (*pl* **-s**) large wild animal
beastliness *n* ▷ **beastly**
beastly *adj* unpleasant or disagreeable > **beastliness** *n*
beasts *n* ▷ **beast**
beat *v* (**beats, beating, beat, beaten** *or* **beat**) hit hard and repeatedly ▶ *n* (*pl* **beats**) regular throb
beaten *v* ▷ **beat**
beatific *adj* displaying great happiness
beatification *n* ▷ **beatify**
beatifications *n* ▷ **beatify**
beatified *v* ▷ **beatify**
beatifies *v* ▷ **beatify**
beatify [bee-at-if-fie] *v* (**-fies, -fying, -fied**) (RC

CHURCH) declare (a dead person) to be among the blessed in heaven: the first step towards canonization > **beatification** *n* (*pl* **-s**)
beatifying *v* ▷ **beatify**
beating *v* ▷ **beat**
beatitude *n* (*pl* **-s**) (CHRISTIANITY) any of the blessings on the poor, meek, etc., in the Sermon on the Mount
beatitudes *n* ▷ **beatitude**
beats *v*, *n* ▷ **beat**
beau [**boh**] *n* (*pl* **beaux, beaus**) boyfriend or admirer
beaus *n* ▷ **beau**
beautician *n* (*pl* **-s**) person who gives beauty treatments professionally
beauticians *n* ▷ **beautician**
beauties *n* ▷ **beauty**
beautification *n* ▷ **beautify**
beautified *v* ▷ **beautify**
beautifies *v* ▷ **beautify**
beautiful *adj* very attractive to look at > **beautifully** *adv*
beautifully *adv* ▷ **beautiful**
beautify *v* (**-fies, -fying, -fied**) make beautiful > **beautification** *n*
beautifying *v* ▷ **beautify**
beauty *n* (*pl* **-ties**) combination of all the qualities of a person or thing that delight the senses and mind
beaux *n* ▷ **beau**
beaver *n* (*pl* **-s**) amphibious rodent with a big flat tail
beavers *n* ▷ **beaver**
becalmed *adj* (of a sailing ship) motionless through lack of wind
became *v* ▷ **become**
because *conj* on account of the fact that
beck *n* (*pl* **-s**) (N ENGLISH) stream
beckon *v* (**-s, -ing, -ed**) summon with a gesture
beckoned *v* ▷ **beckon**
beckoning *v* ▷ **beckon**
beckons *v* ▷ **beckon**
becks *n* ▷ **beck**
become *v* (**-coming, -came, -come**) come to be
becoming *adj* attractive or pleasing
bed *n* (*pl* **-s**) piece of furniture on which to sleep > **bedroom** *n* (*pl* **-s**)
bedding *n* (*pl* **-s**) sheets and covers that are used on a bed
beddings *n* ▷ **bedding**
bedevil *v* (**-s, -illing, -illed**) harass, confuse, or torment
bedevilled *v* ▷ **bedevil**
bedevilling *v* ▷ **bedevil**
bedevils *v* ▷ **bedevil**
bedlam *n* (*pl* **-s**) noisy confused situation
bedlams *n* ▷ **bedlam**
bedpan *n* (*pl* **-s**) shallow bowl used as a toilet by bedridden people
bedpans *n* ▷ **bedpan**
bedraggled *adj* untidy, wet, or dirty
bedridden *adj* confined to bed because of illness or old age
bedrock *n* (*pl* **-s**) solid rock beneath the surface soil
bedrocks *n* ▷ **bedrock**
bedroom *n* ▷ **bed**
bedrooms *n* ▷ **bed**
beds *n* ▷ **bed**
bedsit, bedsitter *n* (*pl* **-s**) furnished sitting room with a bed
bedsits *n* ▷ **bedsit**
bedsitters *n* ▷ **bedsit**
bee *n* (*pl* **-s**) insect that makes wax and honey
beech *n* (*pl* **-es**) tree with a smooth greyish bark
beeches *n* ▷ **beech**
beef *n* (*pl* **beeves**) flesh of a cow, bull, or ox
beefburger *n* (*pl* **-s**) flat grilled or fried cake of minced beef
beefburgers *n* ▷ **beefburger**
beefeater *n* (*pl* **-s**) yeoman warder at the Tower of London
beefeaters *n* ▷ **beefeater**
beefier *adj* ▷ **beefy**
beefiest *adj* ▷ **beefy**
beefy *adj* (**-fier, -fiest**) like beef
beehive *n* (*pl* **-s**) structure in which bees live
beehives *n* ▷ **beehive**
been *v* ▷ **be**
beep *n* (*pl* **-s**) high-pitched sound, like that of a car horn ▶ *v* (**-s, -ing, -ed**) (cause to) make this noise
beeped *v* ▷ **beep**
beeping *v* ▷ **beep**
beeps *n*, *v* ▷ **beep**
beer *n* (*pl* **-s**) alcoholic drink brewed from malt and hops > **beery** (**-ier, -iest**) ▶ *adj*
beerier *adj* ▷ **beer**
beeriest *adj* ▷ **beer**
beers *n* ▷ **beer**
beery *adj* ▷ **beer**
bees *n* ▷ **bee**
beeswax *n* (*pl* **-es**) wax secreted by bees, used in polishes etc.
beeswaxes *n* ▷ **beeswax**
beet *n* (*pl* **-s**) plant with an edible root and leaves
beetle *n* (*pl* **-s**) insect with a hard wing cover on its back

beetles *n* ▷ **beetle**
beetroot *n* (*pl* **-s**) type of beet plant with a dark red root
beetroots *n* ▷ **beetroot**
beets *n* ▷ **beet**
beeves *n* ▷ **beef**
befall *v* (**-falls, -falling, -fell, -fallen**) (*Old-fashioned*) happen to (someone)
befallen *v* ▷ **befall**
befalling *v* ▷ **befall**
befalls *v* ▷ **befall**
befell *v* ▷ **befall**
befit *v* (**-fits, -fitting, -fitted**) be appropriate or suitable for > **befitting** *adj*
befits *v* ▷ **befit**
befitted *v* ▷ **befit**
befitting *v, adj* ▷ **befit**
before *conj, prep adv* indicating something earlier in time, in front of, or preferred to
beforehand *adv* in advance
befriend *v* (**-s, -ing, -ed**) become friends with
befriended *v* ▷ **befriend**
befriending *v* ▷ **befriend**
befriends *v* ▷ **befriend**
beg *v* (**begs, begging, begged**) solicit (for money or food), esp. in the street
began *v* ▷ **begin**
begat *v* ▷ **beget**
beget *v* (**-gets, -getting, -got** *or* **-gat; -gotten** *or* **-got**) (*Old-fashioned*) cause or create
begets *v* ▷ **beget**
begetting *v* ▷ **beget**
beggar *n* (*pl* **s**) person who lives by begging > **beggarly** *adj* > **beggarliness** *n*
beggarliness *n* ▷ **beggar**
beggarly *adj* ▷ **beggar**
beggars *n* ▷ **beggar**
begged *v* ▷ **beg**
begging *v* ▷ **beg**
begin *v* (**-gins, -ginning, -gan, -gun**) start > **beginning** *n* (*pl* **-s**)
beginner *n* (*pl* **-s**) person who has just started learning to do something
beginners *n* ▷ **begin**
beginning *v, n* ▷ **begin**
begins *v* ▷ **begin**
begonia *n* (*pl* **-s**) tropical plant with waxy flowers
begonias *n* ▷ **begonia**
begot *v* ▷ **beget**
begotten *v* ▷ **beget**
begrudge *v* (**-grudges, -grudging, -grudged**) envy (someone) the possession of something
begrudged *v* ▷ **begrudge**
begrudges *v* ▷ **begrudge**
begrudging *v* ▷ **begrudge**
begs *v* ▷ **beg**
beguile [big-**gile**] *v* (**-guiles, -guiling, -guiled**) cheat or mislead > **beguiling** *adj*
beguiled *v* ▷ **beguile**
beguiles *v* ▷ **beguile**
beguiling *v, adj* ▷ **beguile**
begun *v* ▷ **begin**
behalf *n* in the interest of or for the benefit of
behave *v* (**-haves, -having, -haved**) act or function in a particular way
behaved *v* ▷ **behave**
behaves *v* ▷ **behave**
behaving *v* ▷ **behave**
behaviour *n* (*pl* **-s**) manner of behaving
behaviours *n* ▷ **behaviour**
behead *v* (**-s, -ing, -ed**) remove the head from
beheaded *v* ▷ **behead**
beheading *v* ▷ **behead**
beheads *v* ▷ **behead**
beheld *v* ▷ **behold**
behest *n* (*pl* **-s**) order or earnest request
behests *n* ▷ **behest**
behind *prep, adv* indicating position to the rear, lateness, responsibility, etc. ▶ *n* (*pl* **-s**) (*Informal*) buttocks
behinds *n* ▷ **behind**
behold *v* (**-holds, -holding, -held**) (*Old-fashioned*) look (at) > **beholder** *n* (*pl* **-s**)
beholden *adj* indebted or obliged
beholder *n* ▷ **behold**
beholders *n* ▷ **behold**
beholding *v* ▷ **behold**
beholds *v* ▷ **behold**
behove *v* (**-hoves, -hoving, -hoved**) (*Old-fashioned*) be necessary or fitting for
behoved *v* ▷ **behove**
behoves *v* ▷ **behove**
behoving *v* ▷ **behove**
beige *adj* pale brown
being *n* (*pl* **-s**) state or fact of existing ▶ *v* ▷ **be**
beings *n* ▷ **being**
belabour *v* (**-s, -ing, -ed**) attack verbally or physically
belaboured *v* ▷ **belabour**
belabouring *v* ▷ **belabour**
belabours *v* ▷ **belabour**
belated *adj* late or too late > **belatedly** *adv*
belatedly *adv* ▷ **belated**
belch *v* (**-es, -ing, -ed**) expel wind from the stomach noisily through the mouth ▶ *n* (*pl* **belches**) act of belching
belched *v* ▷ **belch**
belches *v, n* ▷ **belch**
belching *v* ▷ **belch**

beleaguered *adj* struggling against difficulties or criticism
belfries *n* ▷ **belfry**
belfry *n* (*pl* **-fries**) part of a tower where bells are hung
belie *v* (**belies, belying, belied**) show to be untrue
belied *v* ▷ **belie**
belief *n* (*pl* **-s**) faith or confidence
beliefs *n* ▷ **belief**
belies *v* ▷ **belie**
believable *adj* ▷ **believe**
believe *v* (**-lieves, -lieving, -lieved**) accept as true or real > **believable** *adj* > **believer** *n* (*pl* **-s**)
believed *v* ▷ **believe**
believer *n* ▷ **believe**
believers *n* ▷ **believe**
believes *v* ▷ **believe**
believing *v* ▷ **believe**
belittle *v* (**-ttles, -ttling, -ttled**) treat as having little value or importance
belittled *v* ▷ **belittle**
belittles *v* ▷ **belittle**
belittling *v* ▷ **belittle**
bell *n* (*pl* **-s**) hollow, usu. metal, cup-shaped instrument that emits a ringing sound when struck
belladonna *n* (*pl* **-s**) (drug obtained from) deadly nightshade
belladonnas *n* ▷ **belladonna**
bellbird *n* (*pl* **-s**) Australasian bird with bell-like call
bellbirds *n* ▷ **bellbird**
belle *n* (*pl* **-s**) beautiful woman, esp. the most attractive woman at a function
belles *n* ▷ **belle**
bellicose *adj* warlike and aggressive
bellied *v* ▷ **belly**
bellies *n, v* ▷ **belly**
belligerence *n* ▷ **belligerent**
belligerent *adj* hostile and aggressive ▶ *n* (*pl* **-s**) person or country engaged in war > **belligerence** *n*
belligerents *n* ▷ **belligerent**
bellow *v* (**-s, -ing, -ed**) make a low deep cry like that of a bull ▶ *n* (*pl* **-s**) loud deep roar
bellowed *v* ▷ **bellow**
bellowing *v* ▷ **bellow**
bellows *v, n* ▷ **bellow** ▶ *pl n* instrument for pumping a stream of air into something
bells *n* ▷ **bell**
belly *n* (*pl* **-lies**) part of the body of a vertebrate which contains the intestines ▶ *v* (**-lies, -lying, -lied**) (cause to) swell out
bellyful *n* (*pl* **-s**) (*Slang*) more than one can tolerate
bellyfuls *n* ▷ **bellyful**
bellying *v* ▷ **belly**
belong *v* (**-s, -ing, -ed**) (*foll. by* **to**) be the property of
belonged *v* ▷ **belong**
belonging *v* ▷ **belong**
belongings *pl n* personal possessions
belongs *v* ▷ **belong**
beloved *adj* dearly loved ▶ *n* (*pl* **-s**) person dearly loved
beloveds *n* ▷ **beloved**
below *prep, adv* at or to a position lower than, under
belt *n* (*pl* **-s**) band of cloth, leather, etc., worn usu. around the waist ▶ *v* (**-s, -ing, -ed**) fasten with a belt
belted *v* ▷ **belt**
belting *v* ▷ **belt**
belts *n, v* ▷ **belt**
belying *v* ▷ **belie**
bemoan *v* (**-s, -ing, -ed**) express sorrow or dissatisfaction about
bemoaned *v* ▷ **bemoan**
bemoaning *v* ▷ **bemoan**
bemoans *v* ▷ **bemoan**
bemused *adj* puzzled or confused
bench *n* (*pl* **-es**) long seat
benches *n* ▷ **bench**
benchmark *n* (*pl* **-s**) criterion by which to measure something
benchmarks *n* ▷ **benchmark**
bend *v* (**-s, -ing, bent**) (cause to) form a curve ▶ *n* curved part > **bendy** *adj* (**-dier, -diest**) > **bendiness** *n* (*pl* **-es**)
bendier *adj* ▷ **bend**
bendiest *adj* ▷ **bend**
bendiness *n* ▷ **bend**
bendinesses *n* ▷ **bend**
bending *v* ▷ **bend**
bends *v* ▷ **bend** ▶ *pl n* (*Informal*) decompression sickness
bendy *adj* ▷ **bend**
beneath *adv, prep* below
benediction *n* (*pl* **-s**) prayer for divine blessing
benedictions *n* ▷ **benediction**
benefaction *n* ▷ **benefactor**
benefactions *n* ▷ **benefactor**
benefactor, benefactress *n* (*pl* **-s, -esses**) someone who supports a person or institution by giving money > **benefaction** *n* (*pl* **-s**)
benefactors *n* ▷ **benefactor**
benefactress *n* ▷ **benefactor**
benefactresses *n* ▷ **benefactor**

beneficence *n* ▷ **beneficent**
beneficent [bin-**eff**-iss-ent] *adj* charitable or generous > **beneficence** *n*
beneficial *adj* helpful or advantageous
beneficiaries *n* ▷ **beneficiary**
beneficiary *n* (*pl* **-ciaries**) person who gains or benefits
benefit *n* (*pl* **-s**) something that improves or promotes ▶ *v* (**-s, -fiting, -fited**) do or receive good
benefited *v* ▷ **benefit**
benefiting *v* ▷ **benefit**
benefits *n, v* ▷ **benefit**
benevolence *n* (*pl* **-s**) inclination to do good > **benevolent** *adj* > **benevolently** *adv*
benevolences *n* ▷ **benevolence**
benevolent *adj* ▷ **benevolence**
benevolently *adv* ▷ **benevolence**
benighted *adj* ignorant or uncultured
benign [bin-**nine**] *adj* showing kindliness > **benignly** *adv*
benignly *adv* ▷ **benign**
bent *v* ▷ **bend** ▶ *adj* curved ▶ *n* (*pl* **-s**) personal inclination or aptitude
bento *n* (*pl* **-s**) thin lightweight box divided into compartments, which contain small separate dishes comprising a Japanese meal
bentos *n* ▷ **bento**
bents *n* ▷ **bent**
benzene *n* (*pl* **-s**) flammable poisonous liquid used as a solvent, insecticide, etc.
benzenes *n* ▷ **benzene**
bequeath *v* (**-s, -ing, -ed**) dispose of (property) as in a will
bequeathed *v* ▷ **bequeath**
bequeathing *v* ▷ **bequeath**
bequeaths *v* ▷ **bequeath**
bequest *n* (*pl* **-s**) legal gift of money or property by someone who has died
bequests *v* ▷ **bequest**
berate *v* (**-ates, -ating, -ated**) scold harshly
berated *v* ▷ **berate**
berates *v* ▷ **berate**
berating *v* ▷ **berate**
bereaved *adj* having recently lost a close friend or relative through death > **bereavement** *n* (*pl* **-s**)
bereavements *n* ▷ **bereavement**
bereft *adj* (*foll. by* **of**) deprived
beret [**ber**-ray] *n* (*pl* **-s**) round flat close-fitting brimless cap
berets *n* ▷ **beret**
berg[1] *n* (*pl* **-s**) iceberg
berg[2] *n* (*pl* **-s**) (S AFR) mountain
bergamot *n* (*pl* **-s**) small Asian tree, the fruit of which yields an oil used in perfumery
bergamots *n* ▷ **bergamot**
bergs *n* ▷ **berg**[1, 2]
beriberi *n* (*pl* **-s**) disease caused by vitamin B deficiency
beriberis *n* ▷ **beriberi**
berk *n* (*pl* **-s**) (BRIT, AUST & NZ) (*Slang*) stupid person
berks *n* ▷ **berk**
berm *n* (*pl* **-s**) (NZ) narrow grass strip between the road and the footpath in a residential area
berms *n* ▷ **berm**
berries *n* ▷ **berry**
berry *n* (*pl* **-ries**) small soft stoneless fruit
berserk *adj* violent or destructive
berth *n* (*pl* **-s**) bunk in a ship or train ▶ *v* (**-s, -ing, -ed**) dock (a ship)
berthed *v* ▷ **berth**
berthing *v* ▷ **berth**
berths *n, v* ▷ **berth**
beryl *n* (*pl* **-s**) hard transparent mineral
beryllium *n* (*pl* **-s**) (CHEM) toxic silvery-white metallic element
berylliums *n* ▷ **beryllium**
beryls *n* ▷ **beryl**
beseech *v* (**-seeches, -seeching, -sought** *or* **-seeched**) ask earnestly; beg
beseeched *v* ▷ **beseech**
beseeches *v* ▷ **beseech**
beseeching *v* ▷ **beseech**
beset *v* (**-sets, -setting, -set**) trouble or harass constantly
besets *v* ▷ **beset**
besetting *v* ▷ **beset**
beside *prep* at, by, or to the side of
besides *adv, prep* in addition
besiege *v* (**-sieges, -sieging, -sieged**) surround with military forces
besieged *v* ▷ **besiege**
besieges *v* ▷ **besiege**
besieging *v* ▷ **besiege**
besotted *adj* infatuated
besought *v* ▷ **beseech**
bespeak *v* (**-speaks, -speaking, -spoke, -spoken**) indicate or suggest
bespeaking *v* ▷ **bespeak**
bespeaks *v* ▷ **bespeak**
bespoke *v* ▷ **bespeak** ▶ *adj* (esp. of a suit) made to the customer's specifications
bespoken *v* ▷ **bespeak**
best *adj* most excellent of a particular group etc. ▶ *adv* in a manner surpassing all others ▶ *n* (*pl* **-s**) most outstanding or excellent person, thing, or group in a category

bestial *adj* brutal or savage > **bestiality** *n* (*pl* **-ities**)
bestialities *n* ▷ **bestial**
bestiality *n* ▷ **bestial**
bestir *v* (**-stirs, -stirring, -stirred**) cause (oneself) to become active
bestirred *v* ▷ **bestir**
bestirring *v* ▷ **bestir**
bestirs *v* ▷ **bestir**
bestow *v* (**-s, -ing, -ed**) present (a gift) or confer (an honour) > **bestowal** *n* (*pl* **-s**)
bestowal *n* ▷ **bestow**
bestowals *n* ▷ **bestow**
bestowed *v* ▷ **bestow**
bestowing *v* ▷ **bestow**
bestows *v* ▷ **bestow**
bestridden *v* ▷ **bestride**
bestride *v* (**-strides, -striding, -strode, -stridden**) have or put a leg on either side of
bestrides *v* ▷ **bestride**
bestriding *v* ▷ **bestride**
bestrode *v* ▷ **bestride**
bests *n* ▷ **best**
bestseller *n* (*pl* **-s**) book or other product that has sold in great numbers
bestsellers *n* ▷ **bestseller**
bet *n* (*pl* **-s**) the act of staking a sum of money or other stake on the outcome of an event ▶ *v* (**bets, betting, bet** *or* **betted**) make or place (a bet)
betel [**bee**-tl] *n* (*pl* **-s**) Asian climbing plant, the leaves and nuts of which can be chewed
betels *n* ▷ **betels**
betide *v* (**-tides, -tiding, -tided**) happen (to)
betided *v* ▷ **betide**
betides *v* ▷ **betide**
betiding *v* ▷ **betide**
betoken *v* (**-s, -ing, -ed**) indicate or signify
betokened *v* ▷ **betoken**
betokening *v* ▷ **betoken**
betokens *v* ▷ **betoken**
betray *v* (**-s, -ing, -ed**) hand over or expose (one's nation, friend, etc.) treacherously to an enemy > **betrayal** *n* (*pl* **-s**) > **betrayer** *n* (*pl* **-s**)
betrayal *n* ▷ **betray**
betrayals *n* ▷ **betray**
betrayed *v* ▷ **betray**
betrayer *n* ▷ **betray**
betrayers *n* ▷ **betray**
betraying *v* ▷ **betray**
betrays *v* ▷ **betray**
betrothal *n* ▷ **betrothed**
betrothals *n* ▷ **betrothed**
betrothed *adj* engaged to be married > **betrothal** *n* (*pl* **-s**)
bets *n, v* ▷ **bet**
betted *v* ▷ **bet**
better *adj* more excellent than others ▶ *adv* in a more excellent manner ▶ *pl n* one's superiors ▶ *v* (**-s, -ing, -ed**) improve upon
bettered *v* ▷ **better**
bettering *v* ▷ **better**
betters *n, v* ▷ **better**
betting *v* ▷ **bet**
bettong *n* (*pl* **-s**) short-nosed rat kangaroo
bettongs *n* ▷ **bettong**
between *prep, adv* indicating position in the middle, alternatives, etc.
betwixt *prep, adv* (*Old-fashioned*) between
bevel *n* (*pl* **-s**) slanting edge ▶ *v* (**-els, -elling, -elled**) cut a bevel on (a piece of timber etc.)
bevelled *v* ▷ **bevel**
bevelling *v* ▷ **bevel**
bevels *n, v* ▷ **bevel**
beverage *n* (*pl* **-s**) drink
beverages *n* ▷ **beverage**
bevies *n* ▷ **bevy**
bevy *n* (*pl* **bevies**) flock or group
bewail *v* (**-s, -ing, -ed**) express great sorrow over
bewailed *v* ▷ **bewail**
bewailing *v* ▷ **bewail**
bewails *v* ▷ **bewail**
beware *v* (**-wares, -waring, -wared**) be on one's guard (against)
bewared *v* ▷ **beware**
bewares *v* ▷ **beware**
bewaring *v* ▷ **beware**
bewilder *v* (**-s, -ing, -ed**) confuse utterly > **bewildering** *adj* > **bewilderment** *n* (*pl* **-s**)
bewildered *v* ▷ **bewilder**
bewildering *v, adj* ▷ **bewilder**
bewilderment *n* ▷ **bewilder**
bewilderments *n* ▷ **bewilder**
bewilders *v* ▷ **bewilder**
bewitch *v* (**-es, -ing, -ed**) attract and fascinate > **bewitching** *adj*
bewitched *v* ▷ **bewitch**
bewitches *v* ▷ **bewitch**
bewitching *v, adj* ▷ **bewitch**

bey *n* (**beys**). A bey was an official in the Ottoman empire, and scores 8 points

beyond *prep* at or to a point on the other side of ▶ *adv* at or to the far side of something

bez *n* (**bezes**). A bez is the second spike of a deer's antler. This is a really handy word when you have Z on your rack. Bez scores 14 points.

bezique *n* (**beziques**). Bezique is a card game; if you're lucky enough to be able to play it, you'll score 27 points.

bi *adj, n* (*pl* **-s**) short for bisexual

biannual *adj* occurring twice a year > **biannually** *adv*

biannually *adv* ▷ **biannual**

bias *n* (*pl* **-es**) mental tendency, esp. prejudice ▶ *v* (**-ases, -asing, -ased** *or* **-asses** *or* **-assing** *or* **-assed**) cause to have a bias > **biased, biassed** *adj*

biased *v* ▷ **bias**

biases *n, v* ▷ **bias**

biasing *v* ▷ **bias**

biassed *v* ▷ **bias**

biasses *n, v* ▷ **bias**

biassing *v* ▷ **bias**

bib *n* (*pl* **-s**) piece of cloth or plastic worn to protect a young child's clothes when eating

bible *n* (*pl* **-s**) book regarded as authoritative > **biblical** *adj*

bibles *n* ▷ **bible**

biblical *n* ▷ **bible**

bibliographer *n* ▷ **bibliography**

bibliographers *n* ▷ **bibliography**

bibliographies *n* ▷ **bibliography**

bibliography *n* (*pl* **-phies**) list of books on a subject > **bibliographer** *n* (*pl* **-s**)

bibliophile *n* (*pl* **-s**) person who collects or is fond of books

bibliophiles *n* ▷ **bibliophile**

bibs *n* ▷ **bib**

bibulous *adj* addicted to alcohol

bicarbonate *n* (*pl* **-s**) salt of carbonic acid

bicarbonates *n* ▷ **bicarbonate**

bicentenaries *n* ▷ **bicentenary**

bicentenary *n* (*pl* **-naries**) 200th anniversary

biceps *n* (*pl* **-es**) muscle with two origins, esp. the muscle that flexes the forearm

bicker *v* (**-s, -ing, -ed**) argue over petty matters

bickered *v* ▷ **bicker**

bickering *v* ▷ **bicker**

bickers *v* ▷ **bicker**

bicycle *n* (*pl* **-s**) vehicle with two wheels, one behind the other, pedalled by the rider

bicycles *n* ▷ **bicycle**

bid *v* (**bids, bidding, bade, bidden**) say (a greeting) (*past* **bid**) ▶ *n* (*pl* **-s**) offer of a specified amount > **bidder** *n* (*pl* **-s**)

biddable *adj* obedient

bidden *v* ▷ **bid**

bidder *n* ▷ **bid**

bidders *n* ▷ **bid**

bidding *n* (*pl* **-s**) command ▶ *v* ▷ **bid**

bide *v* (**bides, biding, bided**) wait patiently for an opportunity

bided *v* ▷ **bide**

bides *v* ▷ **bide**

bidet [**bee**-day] *n* (*pl* **-s**) low basin for washing the genital area

bidets *n* ▷ **bidet**

biding *v* ▷ **bide**

bids *v, n* ▷ **bid**

biennial *adj* occurring every two years ▶ *n* (*pl* **-s**) plant that completes its life cycle in two years

biennials *n* ▷ **biennial**

bier *n* (*pl* **-s**) stand on which a corpse or coffin rests before burial

biers *n* ▷ **bier**

bifocals *pl n* spectacles with lenses permitting near and distant vision

big *adj* (**bigger, biggest**) of considerable size, height, number, or capacity ▶ *adv* on a grand scale

bigamies *n* ▷ **bigamy**

bigamist *n* ▷ **bigamy**

bigamists *n* ▷ **bigamy**

bigamous *adj* ▷ **bigamy**

bigamously *adv* ▷ **bigamy**

bigamy *n* (*pl* **-mies**) crime of marrying a person while still legally married to someone else > **bigamist** *n* (*pl* **-s**) > **bigamous** *adj* > **bigamously** *adv*

bigger *adj* ▷ **big**

biggest *adj* ▷ **big**

bighead *n* (*pl* **-s**) (*Informal*) conceited person > **bigheaded** *adj*

bigheaded *n* ▷ **bighead**

bigheads *n* ▷ **bighead**

bigot *n* (*pl* **-s**) person who is intolerant, esp. regarding religion or race > **bigoted** *adj* > **bigotry** *n* (*pl* **-tries**)

bigoted *adj* ▷ **bigot**

bigotries *n* ▷ **bigot**

bigotry *n* ▷ **bigot**

bigots *n* ▷ **bigot**

bigwig *n* (*pl* **-s**) (*Informal*) important person

bigwigs *n* ▷ **bigwig**

bijou *n* (**bijoux**). A bijou is an intricate trinket. The plural form, bijoux, uses an X and allows you to score 22 points.

bike *n* (*pl* **-s**) (*Informal*) bicycle or motorcycle

bikes *n* ▷ **bike**

bikini *n* (*pl* **-s**) woman's brief two-piece swimming costume

bikinis *n* ▷ **bikini**

bilateral *adj* affecting or undertaken by two parties > **bilaterally** *adv*

bilaterally *adv* ▷ **bilateral**

bilberries *n* ▷ **bilberry**

bilberry *n* (*pl* **-berries**) bluish-black edible berry

bilbies *n* ▷ **bilby**
bilby *n* (*pl* **-bies**) Australian marsupial with long pointed ears and grey fur
bile *n* (*pl* **-s**) bitter yellow fluid secreted by the liver
biles *n* ▷ **bile**
bilge *n* (*pl* **-s**) (*Informal*) nonsense
bilges *n* ▷ **bilge**
bilingual *adj* involving or using two languages
bilious *adj* sick, nauseous > **biliousness** *n*
biliousness *n* ▷ **bilious**
bill[1] *n* (*pl* **-s**) statement of money owed for goods or services supplied ▶ *v* (**-s, -ing, -ed**) send or present a bill to
bill[2] *n* (*pl* **-s**) bird's beak
billabong *n* (*pl* **-s**) (AUST) stagnant pool in an intermittent stream
billabongs *n* ▷ **billabong**
billed *v* ▷ **bill**[1]
billet *v* (**-lets, -leting, -leted**) assign a lodging to (a soldier) ▶ *n* (*pl* **-s**) accommodation for a soldier in civil lodgings
billeted *v* ▷ **billet**
billeting *v* ▷ **billet**
billets *v*, *n* ▷ **billet**
billhook *n* (*pl* **-s**) tool with a hooked blade, used for chopping etc.
billhooks *n* ▷ **billhook**
billiards *n* game played on a table with balls and a cue
billies *n* ▷ **billy**
billing *v* ▷ **bill**[1]
billion *n* (*pl* **-s**) one thousand million > **billionth** *adj*
billions *n* ▷ **billion**
billionth *adj* ▷ **billion**
billow *n* (*pl* **-s**) large sea wave ▶ *v* (**-s, -ing, -ed**) rise up or swell out > **billowy, billowing** *adj*
billowed *v* ▷ **billow**
billowing *v*, *adj* ▷ **billow**
billows *n*, *v* ▷ **billow**
billowy *adj* ▷ **billow**
bills *n* ▷ **bill**[1, 2] ▶ *v* ▷ **bill**[1]
billy, billycan *n* (*pl* **-lies, -s**) metal can or pot for cooking on a camp fire
billycan *n* ▷ **billy**
billycans *n* ▷ **billy**
biltong *n* (*pl* **-s**) (S AFR) strips of dried meat
biltongs *n* ▷ **biltong**
bimbo *n* (*pl* **-s**) (*Slang*) attractive but empty-headed young person, esp. a woman
bimbos *n* ▷ **bimbo**
bin *n* (*pl* **-s**) container for rubbish or for storing grain, coal, etc.
binary *adj* composed of two parts (MATHS) (COMPUTERS)
bind *v* (**binds, binding, bound**) make secure with or as if with a rope ▶ *n* (*pl* **-s**) (*Informal*) annoying situation
binder *n* (*pl* **-s**) firm cover for holding loose sheets of paper together
binders *n* ▷ **binder**
binding *n* (*pl* **-s**) anything that binds or fastens ▶ *n* ▷ **bind**
bindings *n* ▷ **binding**
bindweed *n* (*pl* **-s**) plant that twines around a support
bindweeds *n* ▷ **bindweed**
binge *n* (*pl* **-s**) (*Informal*) bout of excessive indulgence, esp. in drink
binges *n* ▷ **binge**
bingo *n* (*pl* **-s**) gambling game in which numbers are called out and covered by the players on their individual cards
bingos *n* ▷ **bingo**
binoculars *pl n* optical instrument consisting of two small telescopes joined together
binomial *n* (*pl* **-s**), *adj* (mathematical expression) consisting of two terms
binomials *n* ▷ **binomial**
bins *n* ▷ **bin**
biochemistries *n* ▷ **biochemistry**
biochemistry *n* (*pl* **-ries**) study of the chemistry of living things > **biochemist** *n* (*pl* **-s**)
biochemists *n* ▷ **biochemistry**
biodegradable *adj* capable of being decomposed by natural means
biodiversities *n* ▷ **biodiversity**
biodiversity *n* (*pl* **-ities**) existence of a wide variety of species in their natural environment
biographer *n* (*pl* **-s**) person who writes an account of another person's life
biographers *n* ▷ **biographer**
biographical *n* ▷ **biography**
biographies *n* ▷ **biography**
biography *n* (*pl* **-phies**) account of a person's life by another person > **biographical** *adj*
biological *adj* of or relating to biology > **biologically** *adv*
biologically *adv* ▷ **biological**
biologies *n* ▷ **biology**
biologist *n* ▷ **biology**
biologists *n* ▷ **biology**
biology *n* (*pl* **-ogies**) study of living organisms > **biologist** *n* (*pl* **-s**)
biometric *adj* of any automated system using physiological or behavioural traits as a means of identification.

bionic *adj* having a part of the body that is operated electronically
biopsies *n* ▷ **biopsy**
biopsy *n* (*pl* **-sies**) examination of tissue from a living body
biotechnologies *n* ▷ **biotechnology**
biotechnology *n* (*pl* **-ologies**) use of microorganisms, such as cells or bacteria, in industry and technology
bioterrorism *n* (*pl* **-s**) use of viruses, bacteria, etc., by terrorists > **bioterrorist** *n* (*pl* **-s**)
bioterrorisms *n* ▷ **bioterrorism**
bioterrorists *n* ▷ **bioterrorism**
biped [**bye**-ped] *n* (*pl* **-s**) animal with two feet
bipeds *n* ▷ **biped**
biplane *n* (*pl* **-s**) aeroplane with two sets of wings, one above the other
biplanes *n* ▷ **biplane**
birch *n* (*pl* **-es**) tree with thin peeling bark
birches *n* ▷ **birch**
bird *n* (*pl* **-s**) creature with feathers and wings, most types of which can fly
birdie *n* (*pl* **-s**) (GOLF) score of one stroke under par for a hole
birdies *n* ▷ **birdie**
birds *n* ▷ **bird**
biretta *n* (*pl* **-s**) stiff square cap worn by the Catholic clergy
birettas *n* ▷ **biretta**
birth *n* (*pl* **-s**) process of bearing young; childbirth
birthday *n* (*pl* **-s**) anniversary of the day of one's birth
birthdays *n* ▷ **birthday**
birthmark *n* (*pl* **-s**) blemish on the skin formed before birth
birthmarks *n* ▷ **birthmark**
birthright *n* (*pl* **-s**) privileges or possessions that someone is entitled to as soon as he or she is born
birthrights *n* ▷ **birthright**
births *n* ▷ **birth**
bis *n* ▷ **bi**
biscuit *n* (*pl* **-s**) small flat dry sweet or plain cake
biscuits *n* ▷ **biscuit**
bisect *v* (**-s, -ing, -ed**) divide into two equal parts
bisected *v* ▷ **bisect**
bisecting *v* ▷ **bisect**
bisects *v* ▷ **bisect**
bisexual *adj* sexually attracted to both men and women > **bisexuality** *n* (*pl* **-ties**)
bisexualities *n* ▷ **bisexual**
bisexuality *n* ▷ **bisexual**
bishop *n* (*pl* **-s**) clergyman who governs a diocese
bishopric *n* (*pl* **-s**) diocese or office of a bishop
bishoprics *n* ▷ **bishopric**
bishops *n* ▷ **bishop**
bismuth *n* (*pl* **-s**) (CHEM) pinkish-white metallic element
bismuths *n* ▷ **bismuth**
bison *n* (*pl* **-bison**) large hairy animal of the cattle family, native to N America and Europe
bistro *n* (*pl* **-s**) small restaurant
bistros *n* ▷ **bistro**
bit[1] *n* (*pl* **-s**) small piece, portion, or quantity
bit[2] *n* (*pl* **-s**) metal mouthpiece on a bridle
bit3 *v* ▷ **bite**
bit[3] *n* (*pl* **-s**) (MATHS) (COMPUTERS) single digit of binary notation, either 0 or 1
bitch *n* (*pl* **-es**) female dog, fox, or wolf ▶ *v* (**-es, -ing, -ed**) (*Informal*) complain or grumble > **bitchy** *adj* (**-ier, -iest**) > **bitchiness** *n*
bitched *v* ▷ **bitch**
bitches *n, v* ▷ **bitch**
bitchier *adj* ▷ **bitch**
bitchiest *adj* ▷ **bitch**
bitching *v* ▷ **bitch**
bitchy *adj* ▷ **bitch**
bite *v* (**bites, biting, bit, bitten**) grip, tear, or puncture the skin, as with the teeth or jaws ▶ *n* (*pl* **-s**) act of biting > **biter** *n* (*pl* **-s**)
biter *n* ▷ **bite**
biters *n* ▷ **bite**
bites *v, n* ▷ **bite**
biting *adj* piercing or keen ▶ *v* ▷ **bite**
bits *n* ▷ **bit**[1, 2, 4]
bitten *v* ▷ **bite**
bitter *adj* (**-er, -est**) having a sharp unpleasant taste ▶ *n* (*pl* **-s**) beer with a slightly bitter taste ▶ *pl* bitter-tasting alcoholic drink > **bitterly** *adv* > **bitterness** *n* (*pl* **-es**)
bitterer *adj* ▷ **bitter**
bitterest *adj* ▷ **bitter**
bitterly *adv* ▷ **bitter**
bittern *n* (*pl* **-s**) wading marsh bird with a booming call
bitterness *n* ▷ **bitter**
bitternesses *n* ▷ **bitter**
bitterns *n* ▷ **bittern**
bitters *n* ▷ **bitter**
bitumen *n* (*pl* **-s**) black sticky substance obtained from tar or petrol
bitumens *n* ▷ **bitumen**
bivalve *n* (*pl* **-s**) ▶ *adj* (marine mollusc) with two hinged segments to its shell
bivalves *n* ▷ **bivalve**
bivouac *n* (*pl* **-s**) temporary camp in the

open air ▶ *v* (**-acs, -acking, -acked**) camp in a bivouac
bivouacked *v* ▷ **bivouac**
bivouacking *v* ▷ **bivouac**
bivouacs *n, v* ▷ **bivouac**
bizarre *adj* odd or unusual > **bizarrely** *adv* > **bizarreness** *n*
bizarrely *adv* ▷ **bizarre**
bizarreness *n* ▷ **bizarre**
blab *v* (**blabs, blabbing, blabbed**) reveal (secrets) indiscreetly
blabbed *v* ▷ **blab**
blabbing *v* ▷ **blab**
blabs *v* ▷ **blab**
black *adj* (**-er, -est**) of the darkest colour, like coal ▶ *n* (*pl* **-s**) darkest colour ▶ *v* (**-s, -ing, -ed**) make black > **blackness** *n*
blackball *v* (**-balls, -balling, -balled**) exclude from a group ▶ *n* (*pl* **-balls**) (NZ) hard boiled sweet with black-and-white stripes
blackballed *v* ▷ **blackball**
blackballing *v* ▷ **blackball**
blackballs *v, n* ▷ **blackball**
blackberries *n* ▷ **blackberry**
blackberry *n* (*pl* **-rries**) small blackish edible fruit
blackbird *n* (*pl* **-s**) common European thrush
blackbirds *n* ▷ **blackbird**
blackboard *n* (*pl* **-s**) hard black surface used for writing on with chalk
blackboards *n* ▷ **blackboard**
blackboy *n* (*pl* **-s**) Australian plant with grasslike leaves and a spike of small white flowers
blackboys *n* ▷ **blackboy**
blackbutt *n* (*pl* **-s**) Australian eucalyptus tree with hard wood used as timber
blackbutts *n* ▷ **blackbutt**
blackcurrant *n* (*pl* **-s**) very small blackish edible fruit that grows in bunches
blackcurrants *n* ▷ **blackcurrant**
blacked *v* ▷ **black**
blacken *v* (**-s, -ing, -ed**) make or become black
blackened *v* ▷ **blacken**
blackening *v* ▷ **blacken**
blackens *v* ▷ **blacken**
blacker *adj* ▷ **black**
blackest *adj* ▷ **black**
blackfish *n* (*pl* **blackfish**) small dark Australian estuary fish
blackguard [**blag**-gard] *n* (*pl* **-s**) unprincipled person
blackguards *n* ▷ **blackguard**
blackhead *n* (*pl* **-s**) black-tipped plug of fatty matter clogging a skin pore
blackheads *n* ▷ **blackhead**
blacking *v* ▷ **black**
blackleg *n* (*pl* **-s**) person who continues to work during a strike
blacklegs *n* ▷ **blackleg**
blacklist *n* (*pl* **-s**) list of people or organizations considered untrustworthy etc.
blacklists *n* ▷ **blacklist**
blackmail *n* (*pl* **-s**) act of attempting to extort money by threats ▶ *v* (**-s, -ing, -ed**) (attempt to) obtain money by blackmail
blackmailed *v* ▷ **blackmail**
blackmailing *v* ▷ **blackmail**
blackmails *n, v* ▷ **blackmail**
blackness *n* ▷ **black**
blackout *n* (*pl* **-s**) extinguishing of all light as a precaution against an air attack
blackouts *n* ▷ **blackout**
blacks *n, v* ▷ **black**
blacksmith *n* (*pl* **-s**) person who works iron with a furnace, anvil, etc.
blacksmiths *n* ▷ **blacksmith**
bladder *n* (*pl* **-s**) sac in the body where urine is held
bladders *n* ▷ **bladder**
blade *n* (*pl* **-s**) cutting edge of a weapon or tool
blades *n* ▷ **blade**
blame *v* (**-mes, -ming, -med**) consider (someone) responsible for ▶ *n* (*pl* **-s**) responsibility for something that is wrong > **blameless** *adj*
blamed *v* ▷ **blame**
blameless *adj* ▷ **blame**
blames *v, n* ▷ **blame**
blameworthy *adj* deserving blame
blaming *v* ▷ **blame**
blanch *v* (**-es, -ing, -ed**) become white or pale
blanched *v* ▷ **blanch**
blanches *v* ▷ **blanch**
blanching *v* ▷ **blanch**
blancmange [blam-**monzh**] *n* (*pl* **-s**) jelly-like dessert made with milk
blancmanges *n* ▷ **blancmange**
bland *adj* (**-er, -est**) dull and uninteresting > **blandly** *adv*
blander *adj* ▷ **bland**
blandest *adj* ▷ **bland**
blandishments *pl n* flattery intended to coax or persuade
blandly *adj* ▷ **bland**
blank *adj* not written on ▶ *n* (*pl* **-s**) empty space > **blankly** *adv*
blanket *n* (*pl* **-s**) large thick cloth used as covering for a bed ▶ *v* (**-s, -ing, -ed**) cover as with a blanket

blanketed *v* ▷ **blanket**
blanketing *v* ▷ **blanket**
blankets *n, v* ▷ **blanket**
blankly *adv* ▷ **blank**
blanks *n* ▷ **blank**
blare *v* (**blares, blaring, blared**) sound loudly and harshly ▶ *n* (*pl* **-s**) loud harsh noise
blared *v* ▷ **blare**
blares *v, n* ▷ **blare**
blaring *v* ▷ **blare**
blarney *n* (*pl* **-s**) flattering talk
blarneys *n* ▷ **blarney**
blasé [**blah**-zay] *adj* indifferent or bored through familiarity
blaspheme *v* (**-phemes, -pheming, -phemed**) speak disrespectfully of (God or sacred things) > **blasphemy** *n* (*pl* **-phemies**) > **blasphemous** *adj* > **blasphemously** *adv* > **blasphemer** *n* (*pl* **-s**)
blasphemed *v* ▷ **blaspheme**
blasphemer *n* ▷ **blaspheme**
blasphemers *n* ▷ **blaspheme**
blasphemes *v* ▷ **blaspheme**
blasphemies *n* ▷ **blaspheme**
blaspheming *v* ▷ **blaspheme**
blasphemous *v* ▷ **blaspheme**
blasphemously *v* ▷ **blaspheme**
blast *n* (*pl* **-s**) explosion ▶ *v* (**-s, -ing, -ed**) blow up (a rock etc.) with explosives
blasted *v* ▷ **blast**
blasting *v* ▷ **blast**
blastoff *n* (*pl* **-s**) launching of a rocket
blastoffs *n* ▷ **blastoff**
blasts *n, v* ▷ **blast**
blatant *adj* glaringly obvious > **blatantly** *adv*
blatantly *adv* ▷ **blatant**
blaze[1] *n* (*pl* **-s**) strong fire or flame ▶ *v* (**-s, -ing, -d**) burn or shine brightly
blaze[2] *n* (*pl* **-s**) mark made on a tree to indicate a route
blazed *v* ▷ **blaze**[1]
blazer *n* (*pl* **-s**) lightweight jacket, often in the colours of a school etc.
blazers *n* ▷ **blazer**
blazes *n* ▷ **blaze**[1, 2] ▶ *v* ▷ **blaze**[1]
blazing *v* ▷ **blaze**[1]
blazon *v* (**-s, -ing, -ed**) proclaim publicly
blazoned *v* ▷ **blazon**
blazoning *v* ▷ **blazon**
blazons *v* ▷ **blazon**
bleach *v* (**-es, -ing, -ed**) make or become white or colourless ▶ *n* (*pl* **-es**) bleaching agent
bleached *v* ▷ **bleach**
bleaches *v, n* ▷ **bleach**
bleaching *v* ▷ **bleach**
bleak *adj* (**-er, -est**) exposed and barren > **bleakly** *adv* > **bleakness** *n* (*pl* **-es**)
bleaker *adj* ▷ **bleak**
bleakest *adj* ▷ **bleak**
bleakly *adv* ▷ **bleak**
bleakness *n* ▷ **bleak**
bleaknesses *n* ▷ **bleak**
blearier *adj* ▷ **bleary**
bleariest *adj* ▷ **bleary**
blearily *adv* ▷ **bleary**
bleariness *n* ▷ **bleary**
blearinesses *n* ▷ **bleary**
bleary *adj* (**-rier, -riest**) with eyes dimmed, as by tears or tiredness > **blearily** *adv* > **bleariness** *n* (*pl* **-es**)
bleat *v* (**-s, -ing, -ed**) (of a sheep, goat, or calf) utter its plaintive cry ▶ *n* (*pl* **-s**) cry of sheep, goats, and calves
bleated *v* ▷ **bleat**
bleating *v* ▷ **bleat**
bleats *v, n* ▷ **bleat**
bled *v* ▷ **bleed**
bleed *v* (**-s, -ing, bled**) lose or emit blood
bleeding *v* ▷ **bleed**
bleeds *v* ▷ **bleed**
bleep *n* (*pl* **-s**) short high-pitched sound made by an electrical device ▶ *v* (**-s, -ing, -ed**) make a bleeping sound
bleeped *v* ▷ **bleep**
bleeper *n* (*pl* **-s**) small portable radio receiver that makes a bleeping signal
bleepers *n* ▷ **bleeper**
bleeping *v* ▷ **bleep**
bleeps *n, v* ▷ **bleep**
blemish *n* (*pl* **-es**) defect or stain ▶ *v* (**-es, -ing, -ed**) spoil or tarnish
blemished *v* ▷ **blemish**
blemishes *n, v* ▷ **blemish**
blemishing *v* ▷ **blemish**
blench *v* (**-es, -ing, -ed**) shy away, as in fear
blenched *v* ▷ **blench**
blenches *v* ▷ **blench**
blenching *v* ▷ **blench**
blend *v* (**-s, -ing, -ed**) mix or mingle (components or ingredients) ▶ *n* (*pl* **-s**) mixture
blended *v* ▷ **blend**
blender *n* (*pl* **-s**) electrical appliance for puréeing vegetables etc.
blenders *n* ▷ **blender**
blending *v* ▷ **blend**
blends *v, n* ▷ **blend**
bless *v* (**-es, -ing, -ed**) make holy by means of a religious rite
blessed *adj* holy ▶ *v* ▷ **blessed** > **blessedness** *n*

blessedness *n* ▷ **blessed**
blesses *v* ▷ **bless**
blessing *n* (*pl* **-s**) invoking of divine aid ▶ *v* ▷ **bless**
blessings *n* ▷ **blessing**
blether (Scot) *v* (**-s, -ing, -ed**) talk, esp. foolishly or at length ▶ *n* (*pl* **-s**) conversation
blethered *v* ▷ **blether**
blethering *v* ▷ **blether**
blethers *v, n* ▷ **blether**
blew *v* ▷ **blow**[1]
blight *n* (*pl* **-s**) person or thing that spoils or prevents growth ▶ *v* (**-s, -ing, -ed**) frustrate or disappoint
blighted *v* ▷ **blight**
blighter *n* (*pl* **-s**) (*Informal*) irritating person
blighters *n* ▷ **blighter**
blighting *v* ▷ **blight**
blights *n, v* ▷ **blight**
blimp *n* (*pl* **-s**) small airship
blimps *n* ▷ **blimp**
blind *adj* (**-er, -est**) unable to see ▶ *v* (**-s, -ing, -ed**) deprive of sight ▶ *n* (*pl* **-s**) covering for a window > **blindly** *adv* > **blindness** *n* (*pl* **-es**)
blinded *v* ▷ **blind**
blinder *adj* ▷ **blind**
blindest *adj* ▷ **blind**
blindfold *v* (**-s, -ing, -ed**) prevent (a person) from seeing by covering the eyes ▶ *n* (*pl* **-s**) piece of cloth used to cover the eyes
blindfolded *v* ▷ **blindfold**
blindfolding *v* ▷ **blindfold**
blindfolds *v, n* ▷ **blindfold**
blinding *adj, v* ▷ **blind**
blindly *adv* ▷ **blind**
blindness *n* ▷ **blind**
blindnesses *n* ▷ **blind**
blinds *v, n* ▷ **blind**
blink *v* (**-s, -ing, -ed**) close and immediately reopen (the eyes) ▶ *n* (*pl* **-s**) act of blinking
blinked *v* ▷ **blink**
blinkers *pl n* leather flaps on a horse's bridle to prevent sideways vision
blinking *v* ▷ **blink**
blinks *v, n* ▷ **blink**
blip *n* (*pl* **-s**) spot of light on a radar screen indicating the position of an object
blips *n* ▷ **blip**
bliss *n* (*pl* **-es**) perfect happiness > **blissful** *adj* > **blissfully** *adv*
blisses *n* ▷ **bliss**
blissful *adj* ▷ **bliss**
blissfully *adv* ▷ **bliss**
blister *n* (*pl* **-s**) small bubble on the skin ▶ *v* (**-s, -ing, -ed**) (cause to) have blisters
blistered *v* ▷ **blister**
blistering *adj* (of weather) very hot ▶ *v* ▷ **blister** > **blisteringly** *adv*
blisteringly *adv* ▷ **blistering**
blisters *n, v* ▷ **blister**
blithe *adj* (**-r, -st**) casual and indifferent > **blithely** *adv* > **blitheness** *n* (*pl* **-es**)
blithely *adv* ▷ **blithe**
blitheness *n* ▷ **blithe**
blithenesses *n* ▷ **blithe**
blither *adj* ▷ **blithe**
blithest *adj* ▷ **blithe**
blitz *n* (*pl* **-es**) violent and sustained attack by aircraft ▶ *v* (**-es, -ing, -ed**) attack suddenly and intensively
blitzed *v* ▷ **blitz**
blitzes *n, v* ▷ **blitz**
blitzing *v* ▷ **blitz**
blizzard *n* (*pl* **-s**) blinding storm of wind and snow
blizzards *n* ▷ **blizzard**
bloat *v* (**-s, -ing, -ed**) cause to swell, as with liquid or air
bloated *v* ▷ **bloat**
bloater *n* (*pl* **-s**) (Brit) salted smoked herring
bloaters *n* ▷ **bloater**
bloating *v* ▷ **bloat**
bloats *v* ▷ **bloat**
blob *n* (*pl* **-s**) soft mass or drop
blobs *n* ▷ **blob**
bloc *n* (*pl* **-s**) people or countries combined by a common interest
block *n* (*pl* **-s**) large solid piece of wood, stone, etc. ▶ *v* (**-s, -ing, -ed**) obstruct or impede by introducing an obstacle > **blockage** *n* (*pl* **-s**)
blockade *n* (*pl* **-s**) sealing off of a place to prevent the passage of goods ▶ *v* (**-ades, -ading, -aded**) impose a blockade on
blockaded *n* ▷ **blockade**
blockades *n, v* ▷ **blockade**
blockading *v* ▷ **blockade**
blockage *n* ▷ **block**
blockages *n* ▷ **block**
blocked *v* ▷ **block**
blockhead *n* (*pl* **-s**) stupid person
blockheads *n* ▷ **blockhead**
blockie *n* (*pl* **-s**) (Aust) owner of a small property, esp. a farm
blockies *n* ▷ **blockie**
blocking *v* ▷ **block**
blocks *n, v* ▷ **block**
blocs *n* ▷ **bloc**
blog *n* (*pl* **-s**) ▷ **weblog**
blogs *n* ▷ **blog**
bloke *n* (*pl* **-s**) (*Informal*) man

blokes *n* ▷ **bloke**
blonde, *masc* **blond** *adj, n* (*pl* **-es, -s**) fair-haired (person)
blondes *n* ▷ **blonde**
blonds *n* ▷ **blonde**
blood *n* (*pl* **-s**) red fluid that flows around the body > **bloodless** *adj* > **bloodlessness** *n*
bloodhound *n* (*pl* **-s**) large dog formerly used for tracking
bloodhounds *n* ▷ **bloodhound**
bloodied *v* ▷ **bloody**
bloodies *v* ▷ **bloody**
bloodily *adv* ▷ **bloody**
bloodiness *n* ▷ **bloody**
bloodless *adj* ▷ **blood**
bloodlessness *n* ▷ **blood**
bloods *n* ▷ **blood**
bloodshed *n* (*pl* **-s**) slaughter or killing
bloodsheds *n* ▷ **bloodshed**
bloodshot *adj* (of an eye) inflamed
bloodstream *n* (*pl* **-s**) flow of blood round the body
bloodstreams *n* ▷ **bloodstream**
bloodsucker *n* (*pl* **-s**) animal that sucks blood
bloodsuckers *n* ▷ **bloodsucker**
bloodthirstily *adv* ▷ **bloodthirsty**
bloodthirstiness *n* ▷ **bloodthirsty**
bloodthirsty *adj* taking pleasure in violence > **bloodthirstily** *adv* > **bloodthirstiness** *n*
bloody *adj* covered with blood ▶ *adj, adv* (*Slang*) extreme or extremely ▶ *v* (**-dies, -dying, -died**) stain with blood > **bloodily** *adv* > **bloodiness** *n*
bloodying *v* ▷ **bloody**
bloom *n* (*pl* **-s**) blossom on a flowering plant ▶ *v* (**-s, -ing, -ed**) bear flowers
bloomed *v* ▷ **bloom**
bloomer *n* (*pl* **-s**) (BRIT) (*Informal*) stupid mistake
bloomers *n* ▷ **bloomer** ▶ *pl n* woman's baggy knickers
blooming *v* ▷ **bloom**
blooms *n, v* ▷ **bloom**
blooper *n* (*pl* **-s**) (CHIEFLY US) (*Informal*) stupid mistake
bloopers *n* ▷ **blooper**
blossom *n* (*pl* **-s**) flowers of a plant ▶ *v* (**-s, -ing, -ed**) (of plants) flower
blossomed *v* ▷ **blossom**
blossoming *v* ▷ **blossom**
blossoms *n, v* ▷ **blossom**
blot *n* (*pl* **-s**) spot or stain ▶ *v* (**-s, -tting, -tted**) cause a blemish in or on > **blotter** *n* (*pl* **-s**)
blotch *n* (*pl* **-es**) discoloured area or stain > **blotchy** *adj*
blotches *n* ▷ **blotch**
blotchy *adj* ▷ **blotch**
blots *n, v* ▷ **blot**
blotted *v* ▷ **blot**
blotter *n* ▷ **blot**
blotters *n* ▷ **blot**
blotting *v* ▷ **blot**
blotto *adj* (BRIT, AUST & NZ) (*Slang*) extremely drunk
blouse *n* (*pl* **-s**) woman's shirtlike garment
blouses *n* ▷ **blouse**
blow¹ *v* (**-s, -ing, blew, blown**) (of air, the wind, etc.) move > **blower** *n* (*pl* **-s**)
blow² *n* (*pl* **-s**) hard hit
blower *n* ▷ **blow¹**
blowers *n* ▷ **blow¹**
blowie *n* (*pl* **blowies**) (AUST) (*Informal*) bluebottle
blowier *n* ▷ **blowy**
blowies *n* ▷ **blowie**
blowiest *n* ▷ **blowy**
blowing *v* ▷ **blow¹**
blown *v* ▷ **blow¹**
blowout *n* (*pl* **-s**) sudden loss of air in a tyre
blowouts *n* ▷ **blowout**
blows *v* ▷ **blow¹** ▶ *n* ▷ **blow²**
blowsier *n* ▷ **blowsy**
blowsiest *n* ▷ **blowsy**
blowsy *adj* (**-sier, -siest**) fat, untidy, and red-faced
blowy *adj* (**-wier, -wiest**) windy
blubber *n* (*pl* **-s**) fat of whales, seals, etc. ▶ *v* (**-s, -ing, -ed**) sob without restraint
blubbered *v* ▷ **blubber**
blubbering *v* ▷ **blubber**
blubbers *n, v* ▷ **blubber**
bludge (*Informal*) *v* (**-s, -ging, -d**) (AUST & NZ) evade work (AUST & NZ) ▶ *n* (*pl* **-s**) (AUST) easy task
bludged *v* ▷ **bludge**
bludgeon *n* (*pl* **-s**) short thick club ▶ *v* (**-s, -ing, -ed**) hit with a bludgeon
bludgeoned *v* ▷ **bludgeon**
bludgeoning *v* ▷ **bludgeon**
bludgeons *n, v* ▷ **bludgeon**
bludger *n* (*pl* **-s**) person who scrounges
bludgers *n* ▷ **bludger**
bludges *v, n* ▷ **bludge**
bludging *v* ▷ **bludge**
blue *n* (*pl* **-s**) colour of a clear unclouded sky ▶ *pl* feeling of depression ▶ *adj* (**bluer, bluest**) of the colour blue > **bluish** *adj*
bluebell *n* (*pl* **-s**) flower with blue bell-shaped flowers
bluebells *n* ▷ **bluebell**
bluebottle *n* (*pl* **-s**) large fly with a dark-blue body
bluebottles *n* ▷ **bluebottle**

blueprint *n* (*pl* **-s**) photographic print of a plan
blueprints *n* ▷ **blueprint**
bluer *adj* ▷ **blue**
blues *n* ▷ **blue**
bluest *adj* ▷ **blue**
bluetongue *n* (*pl* **-s**) Australian lizard with a blue tongue
bluetongues *n* ▷ **bluetongue**
bluff[1] *v* (**-s, -ing, -ed**) pretend to be confident in order to influence (someone) ▶ *n* (*pl* **-s**) act of bluffing
bluff[2] *n* (*pl* **-s**) steep cliff or bank ▶ *adj* good-naturedly frank and hearty
bluffed *v* ▷ **bluff**[1]
bluffing *v* ▷ **bluff**[1]
bluffs *v, n* ▷ **bluff**[1, 2]
bluish *adj* ▷ **blue**
blunder *n* (*pl* **-s**) clumsy mistake ▶ *v* (**-s, -ing, -ed**) make a blunder
blunderbuss *n* (*pl* **-es**) obsolete gun with a wide flared muzzle
blunderbusses *n* ▷ **blunderbuss**
blundered *v* ▷ **blunder**
blundering *v* ▷ **blunder**
blunders *n, v* ▷ **blunder**
blunt *adj* (**blunter, bluntest**) not having a sharp edge or point ▶ *v* (**-s, -ing, -ed**) make less sharp > **bluntly** *adv* > **bluntness** *n*
blunted *v* ▷ **blunt**
blunter *adj* ▷ **blunt**
bluntest *adj* ▷ **blunt**
blunting *v* ▷ **blunt**
bluntly *adv* ▷ **blunt**
bluntness *n* ▷ **blunt**
blunts *v* ▷ **blunt**
blur *v* (**-s, -rring, -rred**) make or become vague or less distinct ▶ *n* (*pl* **-s**) something vague, hazy, or indistinct > **blurry** *adj* (**-rrier, -rriest**)
blurb *n* (*pl* **-s**) promotional description, as on the jacket of a book
blurbs *n* ▷ **blurb**
blurred *v* ▷ **blur**
blurrier *adj* ▷ **blur**
blurriest *adj* ▷ **blur**
blurring *v* ▷ **blur**
blurry *adj* ▷ **blur**
blurs *v, n* ▷ **blur**
blurt *v* (**-s, -ing, -ed**) (*foll. by* **out**) utter suddenly and involuntarily
blurted *v* ▷ **blurt**
blurting *v* ▷ **blurt**
blurts *v* ▷ **blurt**
blush *v* (**-es, -ing, -ed**) become red in the face, esp. from embarrassment or shame ▶ *n* (*pl* **-es**) reddening of the face
blushed *v* ▷ **blush**
blushes *v, n* ▷ **blush**
blushing *v* ▷ **blush**
bluster *v* (**-s, -ing, -ed**) speak loudly or in a bullying way ▶ *n* (*pl* **-s**) empty threats or protests
blustered *v* ▷ **bluster**
blusteriness *n* ▷ **blustery**
blustering *v* ▷ **bluster**
blusters *v, n* ▷ **bluster**
blustery *adj* (of weather) rough and windy > **blusteriness** *n*

bo or **boh** interjection. Bo is an exclamation used to startle someone. Bo scores 4 points, while boh scores 8.

boa *n* (*pl* **-s**) large nonvenomous snake
boab [boh-ab] *n* (*pl* **-s**) (AUST) (*Informal*) ▷ **baobab**
boabs *n* ▷ **boab**
boar *n* (*pl* **-s**) uncastrated male pig
board *n* (*pl* **-s**) long flat piece of sawn timber ▶ *v* (**-s, -ing, -ed**) go aboard (a train, aeroplane, etc.)
boarded *v* ▷ **board**
boarder *n* (*pl* **-s**) person who pays rent in return for accommodation in someone else's home
boarders *n* ▷ **boarder**
boarding *v* ▷ **board**
boardroom *n* (*pl* **-s**) room where the board of a company meets
boardrooms *n* ▷ **boardroom**
boards *n, v* ▷ **board**
boars *n* ▷ **boar**
boas *n* ▷ **boa**
boast *v* (**-s, -ing, -ed**) speak too proudly about one's talents etc. ▶ *n* (*pl* **-s**) bragging statement > **boastful** *adj* > **boastfully** *adv* > **boastfulness** *n*
boasted *v* ▷ **boast**
boastful *adj* ▷ **boast**
boastfully *adv* ▷ **boast**
boastfulness *n* ▷ **boast**
boasting *v* ▷ **boast**
boasts *v, n* ▷ **boast**
boat *n* (*pl* **-s**) small vehicle for travelling across water > **boating** *n*
boater *n* (*pl* **-s**) flat straw hat
boaters *n* ▷ **boater**
boating *n* ▷ **boat**
boats *n* ▷ **boat**
boatswain *n* (*pl* **-s**) ▷ **bosun**
boatswains *n* ▷ **boatswain**
bob[1] *v* (**bobs, bobbing, bobbed**) move up and down repeatedly ▶ *n* (*pl* **-s**) short abrupt movement
bob[2] *n* (*pl* **-s**) hairstyle in which the hair is cut

short evenly all round the head ▶ *v* (**bobs, bobbing, bobbed**) cut (the hair) in a bob

bobbed *v* ▷ **bob**[1,2]

bobbies *n* ▷ **bobby**

bobbin *n* (*pl* **-s**) reel on which thread is wound

bobbing *v* ▷ **bob**[1,2]

bobbins *n* ▷ **bobbin**

bobble *n* (*pl* **-s**) small ball of material, usu. for decoration

bobbles *n* ▷ **bobble**

bobby *n* (*pl* **-bies**) (BRIT) (*Informal*) policeman

bobotie [ba-**boot**-ee] *n* (*pl* **-s**) (S AFR) dish of curried mince

boboties *n* ▷ **bobotie**

bobs *v* ▷ **bob**[1,2] ▶ *n*[1,2]

bobsleigh *n* (*pl* **-s**) sledge for racing down an icy track ▶ *v* (**-s, -ing, -ed**) ride on a bobsleigh

bobsleighed *v* ▷ **bobsleigh**

bobsleighing *v* ▷ **bobsleigh**

bobsleighs *n, v* ▷ **bobsleigh**

bode *v* (**-s, -ding, -ed**) be an omen of (good or ill)

boded *v* ▷ **bode**

bodes *v* ▷ **bode**

bodice *n* (*pl* **-s**) upper part of a dress

bodices *n* ▷ **bodice**

bodies *n* ▷ **body**

bodily *adj* relating to the body ▶ *adv* by taking hold of the body

boding *v* ▷ **bode**

bodkin *n* (*pl* **-s**) blunt large-eyed needle

bodkins *n* ▷ **bodkin**

body *n* (*pl* **-dies**) entire physical structure of an animal or human

bodyboard *n* (*pl* **-s**) small polystyrene surfboard

bodyboards *n* ▷ **bodyboard**

bodyguard *n* (*pl* **-s**) person or group of people employed to protect someone

bodyguards *n* ▷ **bodyguard**

bodywork *n* (*pl* **-s**) outer shell of a motor vehicle

bodyworks *n* ▷ **bodywork**

boerewors *n* (S AFR) spiced sausage

boffin *n* (*pl* **-s**) (BRIT, AUST, NZ & S AFR) (*Informal*) scientist or expert

boffins *n* ▷ **boffin**

bog *n* (*pl* **-s**) wet spongy ground > **boggy** *adj* (**boggier, boggiest**)

bogan *n* (*pl* **-s**) (AUST DATED & NZ) (*Slang*) youth who dresses and behaves rebelliously

bogans *n* ▷ **bogan**

bogey, bogy *n* (*pl* **bogeys, bogies**) something that worries or annoys

bogeys *n* ▷ **bogey**

boggier *adj* ▷ **bog**

boggiest *adj* ▷ **bog**

boggle *v* (**boggles, boggling, boggled**) be surprised, confused, or alarmed

boggled *v* ▷ **boggle**

boggles *v* ▷ **boggle**

boggling *v* ▷ **boggle**

boggy *adj* ▷ **bog**

bogies *n* ▷ **bogey**

bogong, bugong *n* (*pl* **-s, -s**) large nocturnal Australian moth

bogongs *n* ▷ **bogong**

bogs *n* ▷ **bog**

bogus *adj* not genuine

bogy *n* (*pl* **-gies**) ▷ **bogey**

bohemian *n* (*pl* **-s**) ▶ *adj* (person) leading an unconventional life

bohemians *n* ▷ **bohemian**

boil[1] *v* (**-s, -ing, -ed**) (cause to) change from a liquid to a vapour so quickly that bubbles are formed ▶ *n* (*pl* **-s**) state or action of boiling

boil[2] *n* (*pl* **-s**) red pus-filled swelling on the skin

boiled *v* ▷ **boil**[1]

boiler *n* (*pl* **-s**) piece of equipment which provides hot water

boilers *n* ▷ **boiler**

boiling *v* ▷ **boil**[1]

boils *v, n* ▷ **boil**[1,2]

boisterous *adj* noisy and lively > **boisterously** *adv* > **boisterousness** *n*

boisterously *adv* ▷ **boisterous**

boisterousness *n* ▷ **boisterous**

bok *n* (**boks**). A bok is a goat or antelope. Bok scores 9 points.

bold *adj* (**-er, -est**) confident and fearless > **boldly** *adv* > **boldness** *n* (*pl* **-es**)

bolder *adj* ▷ **bold**

boldest *adj* ▷ **bold**

boldly *adv* ▷ **bold**

boldness *n* ▷ **bold**

boldnesses *n* ▷ **bold**

bole *n* (*pl* **-s**) tree trunk

bolero *n* (*pl* **-s**) (music for) traditional Spanish dance

boleros *n* ▷ **bolero**

boles *n* ▷ **bole**

bollard *n* (*pl* **-s**) short thick post used to prevent the passage of motor vehicles

bollards *n* ▷ **bollard**

boloney *n* (*pl* **-s**) ▷ **baloney**

boloneys *n* ▷ **boloney**

bolshie, bolshy *adj* (*Informal*) difficult or rebellious

bolshy *n* ▷ **bolshie**

bolster *v* (**-s, -ing, -ed**) support or strengthen

▸ *n* (*pl* **-s**) long narrow pillow
bolstered *v* ▹ **bolster**
bolstering *v* ▹ **bolster**
bolsters *v, n* ▹ **bolster**
bolt *n* (*pl* **-s**) sliding metal bar for fastening a door etc. ▸ *v* (**-s, -ing, -ed**) run away suddenly
bolted *v* ▹ **bolt**
bolting *v* ▹ **bolt**
bolts *n, v* ▹ **bolt**
bomb *n* (*pl* **-s**) container fitted with explosive material ▸ *v* (**-s, -ing, -ed**) attack with bombs
bombard *v* (**-s, -ing, -ed**) attack with heavy gunfire or bombs > **bombardment** *n* (*pl* **-s**)
bombarded *v* ▹ **bombard**
bombarding *v* ▹ **bombard**
bombardment *n* ▹ **bombard**
bombardments *n* ▹ **bombard**
bombards *n* ▹ **bombard**
bombast *n* (*pl* **-s**) pompous language > **bombastic** *adj*
bombastic *adj* ▹ **bombast**
bombasts *n* ▹ **bombast**
bombed *v* ▹ **bomb**
bomber *n* (*pl* **-s**) aircraft that drops bombs
bombers *n* ▹ **bomber**
bombing *v* ▹ **bomb**
bombs *n, v* ▹ **bomb**
bombshell *n* (*pl* **-s**) shocking or unwelcome surprise
bombshells *n* ▹ **bombshell**
bonanza *n* (*pl* **-s**) sudden good luck or wealth
bonanzas *n* ▹ **bonanza**
bond *n* (*pl* **-s**) something that binds, fastens or holds together ▸ *pl* something that restrains or imprisons ▸ *v* (**-s, -ing, -ed**) bind > **bonded** *adj*
bondage *n* (*pl* **-s**) slavery
bondages *n* ▹ **bondage**
bonded *v, adj* ▹ **bond**
bonding *v* ▹ **bond**
bonds *n, v* ▹ **bond**
bone *n* (*pl* **-s**) any of the hard parts in the body that form the skeleton ▸ *v* (**-s, -ing, -d**) remove the bones from (meat for cooking etc.) > **boneless** *adj*
boned *v* ▹ **bone**
boneless *adj* ▹ **bone**
bones *n, v* ▹ **bone**
bonfire *n* (*pl* **-s**) large outdoor fire
bonfires *n* ▹ **bonfire**
bongo *n* (*pl* **-gos, -goes**) small drum played with the fingers
bongoes *n* ▹ **bongo**
bongos *n* ▹ **bongo**
bonhomie [**bon**-om-ee] *n* (*pl* **-s**) cheerful friendliness
bonhomies *n* ▹ **bonhomie**
boning *v* ▹ **bone**
bonito [ba-**nee**-toh] *n* (*pl* **-s**) small tunny-like marine food fish
bonitos *n* ▹ **bonito**
bonnet *n* (*pl* **-s**) metal cover over a vehicle's engine
bonnets *n* ▹ **bonnet**
bonnier *adj* ▹ **bonny**
bonniest *adj* ▹ **bonny**
bonnily *adv* ▹ **bonny**
bonny *adj* (**-nier, -niest**) (Scot) beautiful > **bonnily** *adv*
bonsai *n* (*pl* **bonsai**) ornamental miniature tree or shrub
bonus *n* (*pl* **-es**) something given, paid, or received above what is due or expected
bonuses *n* ▹ **bonus**
bony *adj* having many bones
boo *interj* shout of disapproval ▸ *v* (**-s, -ing, -ed**) shout 'boo' to show disapproval
boob (*Slang*) *n* (*pl* **-s**) foolish mistake
boobies *n* ▹ **booby**
boobook [**boo**-book] *n* (*pl* **-s**) small spotted Australian brown owl
boobooks *n* ▹ **boobook**
boobs *n* ▹ **boob**
booby *n* (*pl* **-bies**) foolish person
booed *v* ▹ **boo**
boogie *v* (**-s, -ing, -ied**) (*Informal*) dance to fast pop music
boogied *v* ▹ **boogie**
boogieing *v* ▹ **boogie**
boogies *v* ▹ **boogie**
booing *v* ▹ **boo**
book *n* (*pl* **-s**) number of pages bound together between covers ▸ *pl* record of transactions of a business or society ▸ *v* (**-s, -ing, -ed**) reserve (a place, passage, etc.) in advance
booked *n* ▹ **book**
booking *v* ▹ **book**
booklet *n* (*pl* **-s**) thin book with paper covers
booklets *v* ▹ **booklet**
bookmaker *n* (*pl* **-s**) person whose occupation is taking bets
bookmakers *n* ▹ **bookmaker**
bookmark *n* (*pl* **-s**) strip of material used to mark a place in a book ▸ *v* (**-s, -ing, -ed**) (COMPUTERS) identify and store (a website) so that one can return to it quickly and easily
bookmarked *v* ▹ **bookmark**
bookmarking *v* ▹ **bookmark**
bookmarks *n, v* ▹ **bookmark**
books *n, v* ▹ **book**

bookworm *n* (*pl* **-s**) person devoted to reading
bookworms *n* ▷ **bookworm**
boom[1] *v* (**-s, -ing, -ed**) make a loud deep echoing sound ▶ *n* (*pl* **-s**) loud deep echoing sound
boom[2] *n* (*pl* **-s**) pole to which the foot of a sail is attached
boomed *v* ▷ **boom**[1]
boomer *n* (*pl* **-s**) (AUST) large male kangaroo
boomerang *n* (*pl* **-s**) curved wooden missile which can be made to return to the thrower ▶ *v* (**-s, -ing, -ed**) (of a plan) recoil unexpectedly
boomeranged *n* ▷ **boomerang**
boomeranging *v* ▷ **boomerang**
boomerangs *n, v* ▷ **boomerang**
boomers *n* ▷ **boomer**
booming *v* ▷ **boom**[1]
booms *v, n* ▷ **boom**[1, 2]
boon *n* (*pl* **-s**) something helpful or beneficial
boongaries *n* ▷ **boongary**
boongary [**boong**-gar-ree] *n* (*pl* **-garies**) tree kangaroo of NE Queensland, Australia
boons *n* ▷ **boon**
boor *n* (*pl* **-s**) rude or insensitive person > **boorish** *adj* > **boorishly** *adv* > **boorishness** *n*
boorishly *adv* ▷ **boor**
boorishness *n* ▷ **boor**
boors *n* ▷ **boor**
boos *v* ▷ **boo**
boost *n* (*pl* **-s**) encouragement or help ▶ *v* (**-s, -ing, -ed**) improve
boosted *v* ▷ **boost**
booster *n* (*pl* **-s**) small additional injection of a vaccine
boosters *n* ▷ **booster**
boosting *v* ▷ **boost**
boosts *n, v* ▷ **boost**
boot *n* (*pl* **-s**) outer covering for the foot that extends above the ankle ▶ *v* (**-s, -ing, -ed**) (*Informal*) kick
booted *v* ▷ **boot**
bootee *n* (*pl* **-s**) baby's soft shoe
bootees *n* ▷ **bootee**
booth *n* (*pl* **-s**) small partly enclosed cubicle
booths *n* ▷ **booth**
booties *n* ▷ **booty**
booting *v* ▷ **boot**[1]
bootleg *adj* produced, distributed, or sold illicitly ▶ *v* (**-legs, -legging, -legged**) make, carry, or sell (illicit goods) > **bootlegger** *n* (*pl* **-s**)
bootlegged *v* ▷ **bootleg**
bootlegger *n* ▷ **bootleg**
bootleggers *n* ▷ **bootleg**
bootlegging *v* ▷ **bootleg**
bootlegs *v* ▷ **bootleg**
boots *n* ▶ *v* ▷ **boot**
booty *n* (*pl* **-ties**) valuable articles obtained as plunder
booze *v* (**-zes, -zing, -zed**) ▶ *n* (*pl* **-s**) (*Informal*) (consume) alcoholic drink > **boozy** *adj* (**-zier, -ziest**) > **boozily** *adv*
boozed *v* ▷ **booze**
boozer *n* (*pl* **-s**) (*Informal*) person who is fond of drinking
boozers *n* ▷ **booze**
boozes *v, n* ▷ **booze**
boozier *adj* ▷ **booze**
booziest *adj* ▷ **booze**
boozily *adv* ▷ **booze**
boozing *v* ▷ **booze**
boozy *adj* ▷ **booze**
bop *v* (**-s, -pping, -pped**) (*Informal*) dance to pop music
bopped *v* ▷ **bop**
bopping *v* ▷ **bop**
bops *v* ▷ **bop**
bora *n* (*pl* **-s**) (AUST) Aboriginal ceremony
boras *n* ▷ **bora**
borax *n* (*pl* **-es**) white mineral used in making glass
boraxes *n* ▷ **borax**
border *n* (*pl* **-s**) dividing line between political or geographical regions ▶ *v* (**-s, -ing, -ed**) provide with a border
bordered *v* ▷ **border**
bordering *v* ▷ **border**
borders *n, v* ▷ **border**
bore[1] *v* (**-s, -ring, -d**) make (a hole) with a drill etc. ▶ *n* (*pl* **-s**) (diameter of) the hollow of a gun barrel or other tube
bore[2] *v* (**-s, -ring, -d**) make weary by being dull or repetitious ▶ *n* dull or repetitious person or thing > **bored** *adj* > **boredom** *n*
bore[3] *n* (*pl* **-s**) high wave in a narrow estuary, caused by the tide
bore[4] *v* ▷ **bear**[1]
bored *v, n* ▷ **bore**[1, 2]
boree [**baw**-ree] *n* (*pl* **-s**) (AUST) ▷ **myall**
borees *n* ▷ **boree**
bores *n* ▷ **bore**[1, 2, 3] ▶ *v* ▷ **bore**[1, 2]
boring *v* ▷ **bore**[1, 2]
born *v* ▷ **bear**[1] ▶ *adj* possessing certain qualities from birth
borne *v* ▷ **bear**[1]
boron *n* (*pl* **-s**) (CHEM) element used in hardening steel
boronia *n* (*pl* **-s**) Australian aromatic flowering shrub

boronias *n* ▷ **boronia**
borons *n* ▷ **boron**
borough *n* (*pl* **-s**) (CHIEFLY BRIT) town or district with its own council
boroughs *n* ▷ **borough**
borrow *v* (**-s, -ing, -ed**) obtain (something) temporarily > **borrower** *n* (*pl* **-s**)
borrowed *v* ▷ **borrow**
borrower *n* ▷ **borrow**
borrowers *n* ▷ **borrow**
borrowing *v* ▷ **borrow**
borrows *v* ▷ **borrow**
borstal *n* (*pl* **-s**) (formerly in Britain) prison for young criminals
borstals *n* ▷ **borstal**
borzoi *n* (*pl* **-s**) tall dog with a long silky coat
borzois *n* ▷ **borzoi**
bosh *n* (*pl* **-es**) (BRIT, AUST & NZ) (*Informal*) empty talk, nonsense
boshes *n* ▷ **bosh**
bosom *n* (*pl* **-s**) chest of a person, esp. the female breasts ▶ *adj* very dear
bosoms *n* ▷ **bosom**
boss[1] *n* (*pl* **-es**) person in charge of or employing others ▶ *v* (**-es, -ing, -ed**) be domineering towards > **bossy** *adj* > **bossiness** *n*
boss[2] *n* (*pl* **-es**) raised knob or stud
bossed *v* ▷ **boss[1]**
bosses *n* ▷ **boss[1, 2]** ▶ *v* ▷ **boss[1]**
bossiness *n* ▷ **boss[1]**
bossing *v* ▷ **boss[1]**
bossy *adj* ▷ **boss[1]**
bosun *n* (*pl* **-s**) officer responsible for the maintenance of a ship
bosuns *n* ▷ **bosun**
botanic *adj* ▷ **botany**
botanical *adj* ▷ **botany**
botanies *n* ▷ **botany**
botanist *n* ▷ **botany**
botanists *n* ▷ **botany**
botany *n* (*pl* **-ies**) study of plants > **botanical, botanic** *adj* > **botanist** *n* (*pl* **-s**)
botch *v* (**-es, -ing, -ed**) spoil through clumsiness ▶ *n* (*pl* **-es**) (*also* **botch-up**) (*pl* **-s**) badly done piece of work or repair
botched *v* ▷ **botch**
botches *v, n* ▷ **botch**
botching *v* ▷ **botch**
both *adj, pron* two considered together
bother *v* (**-s, -ing, -ed**) take the time or trouble ▶ *n* (*pl* **-s**) trouble, fuss, or difficulty > **bothersome** *adj*
bothered *v* ▷ **bother**
bothering *v* ▷ **bother**
bothers *v, n* ▷ **bother**
bothersome *adj* ▷ **bother**
bottle *n* (*pl* **-s**) container for holding liquids ▶ *v* (**-s, -ttling, -d**) put in a bottle
bottled *v* ▷ **bottle**
bottleneck *n* (*pl* **-s**) narrow stretch of road where traffic is held up
bottlenecks *n* ▷ **bottleneck**
bottles *n, v* ▷ **bottle**
bottling *v* ▷ **bottle**
bottom *n* (*pl* **-s**) lowest, deepest, or farthest removed part of a thing ▶ *adj* lowest or last > **bottomless** *adj*
bottomless *adj* ▷ **bottom**
bottoms *n* ▷ **bottom**
botulism *n* (*pl* **-s**) severe food poisoning
botulisms *n* ▷ **botulism**
boudoir [**boo**-dwahr] *n* (*pl* **-s**) woman's bedroom or private sitting room
boudoirs *n* ▷ **boudoir**
bougainvillea *n* (*pl* **-s**) climbing plant with red or purple flowers
bougainvilleas *n* ▷ **bougainvillea**
bough *n* (*pl* **-s**) large branch of a tree
boughs *n* ▷ **bough**
bought *v* ▷ **buy**
boulder *n* (*pl* **-s**) large rounded rock
boulders *n* ▷ **boulder**
boulevard *n* (*pl* **-s**) wide, usu. tree-lined, street
boulevards *n* ▷ **boulevard**
bounce *v* (**-s, -cing, -d**) (of a ball etc.) rebound from an impact (*Slang*) ▶ *n* (*pl* **-s**) act of rebounding
bounced *v* ▷ **bounce**
bouncer *n* (*pl* **-s**) person employed at a disco etc. to remove unwanted people
bouncers *n* ▷ **bouncer**
bounces *v, n* ▷ **bounce**
bouncing *v* ▷ **bounce** ▶ *adj* vigorous and robust
bound[1] *v* (**-s, -ing, -ed**) ▷ **bind** ▶ *adj* destined or certain
bound[2] *v* (**-s, -ing, -ed**) move forwards by jumps ▶ *n* (*pl* **-s**) jump upwards or forwards
bound[3] *v* (**-s, -ing, -ed**) form a boundary of ▶ *pl n* limit
bound[4] *adj* going or intending to go towards
boundaries *n* ▷ **boundary**
boundary *n* (*pl* **-aries**) dividing line that indicates the farthest limit
bounded *v* ▷ **bound[2, 3]**
bounding *v* ▷ **bound[2, 3]**
bounds *v, n* ▷ **bound[2, 3]**
bounteous *adj* ▷ **bounty**
bounties *n* ▷ **bounty**

bountiful *adj* ▷ **bounty**

bounty *n* (*pl* **-ties**) generosity > **bountiful, bounteous** *adj*

bouquet *n* (*pl* **-s**) bunch of flowers

bouquets *n* ▷ **bouquet**

bourbon [**bur**-bn] *n* (*pl* **-s**) whiskey made from maize

bourbons *n* ▷ **bourbon**

bourgeois [**boor**-zhwah] *adj, n* (*pl* **bourgeois**) middle-class (person)

bout *n* (*pl* **-s**) period of activity or illness

boutique *n* (*pl* **-s**) small clothes shop

boutiques *n* ▷ **boutique**

bouts *n* ▷ **bout**

bovine *adj* relating to cattle

bow[1] [rhymes with **now**] *v* (**-s, -ing, -ed**) lower (one's head) or bend (one's knee or body) as a sign of respect or shame ▶ *n* (*pl* **-s**) movement made when bowing

bow[2] [rhymes with **go**] *n* (*pl* **-s**) knot with two loops and loose ends

bow[3] [rhymes with **now**] *n* (*pl* **-s**) front end of a ship

bowdlerize *v* (**-zes, -zing, -zed**) remove words regarded as indecent from (a play, novel, etc.)

bowdlerized *v* ▷ **bowdlerize**

bowdlerizes *v* ▷ **bowdlerize**

bowdlerizing *v* ▷ **bowdlerize**

bowed *v* ▷ **bow[1]**

bowel *n* (*pl* **-s**) intestine, esp. the large intestine ▶ *pl* innermost part

bowels *n* ▷ **bowel**

bower *n* (*pl* **-s**) shady leafy shelter

bowerbird *n* (*pl* **-s**) songbird of Australia and New Guinea, the males of which build bower-like display grounds to attract females

bowerbirds *n* ▷ **bowerbird**

bowers *n* ▷ **bower**

bowing *v* ▷ **bow[1]**

bowl[1] *n* (*pl* **-s**) round container with an open top

bowl[2] *n* (*pl* **-s**) large heavy ball ▶ *pl* game played on smooth grass with wooden bowls ▶ *v* (**-s, -ing, -ed**) (CRICKET) send (a ball) towards the batsman

bowled *v* ▷ **bowl[2]**

bowlegged *adj* having legs that curve outwards at the knees

bowler[1] *n* (*pl* **-s**) (CRICKET) player who sends (a ball) towards the batsman

bowler[2] *n* (*pl* **-s**) stiff felt hat with a rounded crown

bowlers *n* ▷ **bowler[1, 2]**

bowling *n* game in which bowls are rolled at a group of pins ▶ *v* ▷ **bowl[2]**

bowls *n* ▷ **bowl[1, 2]** ▶ *v* ▷ **bowl[2]**

bows *v* ▷ **bow[1]** ▶ *n* ▷ **bow[1, 2, 3]**

box[1] *n* (*pl* **-es**) container with a firm flat base and sides ▶ *v* (**-es, -ing, -ed**) put into a box

box[2] *v* (**-es, -ing, -ed**) fight (an opponent) in a boxing match

box[3] *n* (*pl* **-es**) evergreen tree with shiny leaves bark

boxed *v* ▷ **box[1, 2]**

boxer *n* (*pl* **-s**) person who participates in the sport of boxing

boxers *n* ▷ **boxer**

boxes *v* ▷ **box[1, 2]** ▶ *n* ▷ **box[1, 2, 3]**

boxing *n* sport of fighting with the fists ▶ *v* ▷ **box[1, 2]**

boy *n* (*pl* **-s**) male child > **boyish** *adj* > **boyhood** *n* (*pl* **-s**)

boycott *v* (**-cotts, -cotting, -cotted**) refuse to deal with (an organization or country) ▶ *n* (*pl* **-s**) instance of boycotting

boycotted *v* ▷ **boycott**

boycotting *v* ▷ **boycott**

boycotts *v, n* ▷ **boycott**

boyfriend *n* (*pl* **-s**) male friend with whom a person is romantically or sexually involved

boyfriends *n* ▷ **boyfriend**

boyhood *n* ▷ **boy**

boyhoods *n* ▷ **boy**

boyish *n* ▷ **boy**

boys *n* ▷ **boy**

bra *n* (*pl* **-s**) woman's undergarment for supporting the breasts

braai *n* ▷ **braaivlies**

braaied *v* ▷ **braaivlies**

braaiing *v* ▷ **braaivlies**

braais *n, v* ▷ **braaivlies**

braaivlies [**brye**-flayss], **braai** (S AFR) *n* (*pl* **braais**) grill on which food is cooked over hot charcoal, usu. outdoors ▶ *v* (**braais, braaiing, braaied**) cook (food) on in this way

brace *n* (*pl* **-s**) object fastened to something to straighten or support it ▶ *pl* straps worn over the shoulders to hold up trousers ▶ *v* (**-ces, -cing, -ced**) steady or prepare (oneself) for something unpleasant

braced *n, v* ▷ **brace**

bracelet *n* (*pl* **-s**) ornamental chain or band for the wrist

bracelets *n* ▷ **bracelet**

braces *n, v* ▷ **brace**

bracing *adj* refreshing and invigorating ▶ *v* ▷ **brace**

bracken *n* (*pl* **-s**) large fern

brackens *n* ▷ **bracken**

bracket *n* (*pl* **-s**) either of a pair of characters

used to enclose a section of writing ▶ *v* (**-ets, -eting, -eted**) put in brackets
bracketed *v* ▷ **bracket**
bracketing *v* ▷ **bracket**
brackets *n, v* ▷ **bracket**
brackish *adj* (of water) slightly salty > **brackishness** *n*
brackishness *n* ▷ **bracket**
bract *n* (*pl* **-s**) leaf at the base of a flower
bracts *n* ▷ **bract**
brag *v* (**-s, -gging, -gged**) speak arrogantly and boastfully > **braggart** *n* (*pl* **-s**)
braggart *n* ▷ **brag**
braggarts *n* ▷ **brag**
bragged *v* ▷ **brag**
bragging *v* ▷ **brag**
brags *v* ▷ **brag**
braid *v* (**-s, -ing, -ed**) interweave (hair, thread, etc.) ▶ *n* (*pl* **-s**) length of hair etc. that has been braided
braided *v* ▷ **braid**
braiding *v* ▷ **braid**
braids *v, n* ▷ **braid**
braille *n* (*pl* **-s**) system of writing for the blind, consisting of raised dots interpreted by touch
brailles *n* ▷ **braille**
brain *n* (*pl* **-s**) soft mass of nervous tissue in the head ▶ *v* (**-s, -ing, -ed**) hit (someone) hard on the head
brainchild *n* (*pl* **-children**) idea produced by creative thought
brainchildren *n* ▷ **brainchild**
brained *v* ▷ **brain**
brainier *adj* ▷ **brainy**
brainiest *adj* ▷ **brainy**
braininess *n* ▷ **brainy**
braininesses *n* ▷ **brainy**
braining *v* ▷ **brain**
brainless *adj* stupid
brains *n, v* ▷ **brain**
brainwash *v* (**-es, -ing, -ed**) cause (a person) to alter his or her beliefs, esp. by methods based on isolation, sleeplessness, etc.
brainwashed *v* ▷ **brainwash**
brainwashes *v* ▷ **brainwash**
brainwashing *v* ▷ **brainwash**
brainwave *n* (*pl* **-s**) sudden idea
brainwaves *v* ▷ **brainwave**
brainy *adj* (**-nier, -niest**) (*Informal*) clever > **braininess** *n* (*pl* **-es**)
braise *v* (**-ses, -sing, -sed**) cook slowly in a covered pan with a little liquid
braised *v* ▷ **braise**
braises *v* ▷ **braise**
braising *v* ▷ **braise**
brake *n* (*pl* **-s**) device for slowing or stopping a vehicle ▶ *v* (**-kes, -king, -ked**) slow down or stop by using a brake
braked *v* ▷ **brake**
brakes *n, v* ▷ **brake**
braking *v* ▷ **brake**
bramble *n* (*pl* **-s**) prickly shrub that produces blackberries
brambles *n* ▷ **bramble**
bran *n* (*pl* **-s**) husks of cereal grain
branch *n* (*pl* **-es**) secondary stem of a tree ▶ *v* (**-es, -ing, -ed**) (of stems, roots, etc.) divide, then develop in different directions
branched *n* ▷ **branch**
branches *n, v* ▷ **branch**
branching *v* ▷ **branch**
brand *n* (*pl* **-s**) particular product ▶ *v* (**-s, -ing, -ed**) mark with a brand
branded *v* ▷ **brand**
brandies *n* ▷ **brandy**
branding *v* ▷ **brand**
brandish *v* (**-es, -ing, -ed**) wave (a weapon etc.) in a threatening way
brandished *v* ▷ **brandish**
brandishes *v* ▷ **brandish**
brandishing *v* ▷ **brandish**
brands *n, v* ▷ **brand**
brandy *n* (*pl* **-dies**) alcoholic spirit distilled from wine
brans *n* ▷ **bran**
bras *n* ▷ **bra**
brash *adj* offensively loud, showy, or self-confident > **brashness** *n*
brashness *n* ▷ **brash**
brass *n* (*pl* **-es**) alloy of copper and zinc
brasses *n* ▷ **brass**
brassier *adj* ▷ **brassy**
brassiere *n* (*pl* **-s**) bra
brassieres *n* ▷ **brassiere**
brassiest *adj* ▷ **brassy**
brassiness *adj* ▷ **brassy**
brassinesses *adj* ▷ **brassy**
brassy *adj* (**-ssier, -ssiest**) brazen or flashy > **brassiness** *n* (*pl* **-es**)
brat *n* (*pl* **-s**) unruly child
brats *n* ▷ **brat**
bravado *n* (*pl* **-oes**) showy display of self-confidence
bravadoes *n* ▷ **bravado**
brave *adj* (**-r, -st**) having or showing courage, resolution, and daring ▶ *n* (*pl* **-s**) Native American warrior ▶ *v* (**-ves, -ving, -ved**) confront with resolution or courage > **bravery** *n* (*pl* **-ies**)

braved *v* ▷ **brave**
braver *adj* ▷ **brave**
braveries *n* ▷ **brave**
bravery *n* ▷ **brave**
braves *n, v* ▷ **brave**
bravest *adj* ▷ **brave**
braving *v* ▷ **brave**
bravo *interj* well done!
brawl *n* (*pl* **-s**) noisy fight ▸ *v* (**-s, -ing, -ed**) fight noisily
brawled *v* ▷ **brawl**
brawling *v* ▷ **brawl**
brawls *n, v* ▷ **brawl**
brawn *n* (*pl* **-s**) physical strength > **brawny** (**-nier, -niest**) *adj*
brawnier *adj* ▷ **brawn**
brawniest *adj* ▷ **brawn**
brawns *n* ▷ **brawn**
brawny *adj* ▷ **brawn**
bray *v* (**-s, -ing, -ed**) (of a donkey) utter its loud harsh sound ▸ *n* (*pl* **-s**) donkey's loud harsh sound
brayed *v* ▷ **bray**
braying *v* ▷ **bray**
brays *v, n* ▷ **bray**
brazen *adj* shameless and bold ▸ *v* (**-s, -ing, -ed**) > **brazenly** *adv* > **brazenness** *n*
brazened *v* ▷ **brazen**
brazening *v* ▷ **brazen**
brazenly *adv* ▷ **brazen**
brazenness *n* ▷ **brazen**
brazens *v* ▷ **brazen**
brazier [**bray**-zee-er] *n* (*pl* **-s**) portable container for burning charcoal or coal
braziers *n* ▷ **brazier**
breach *n* (*pl* **-es**) breaking of a promise, obligation, etc. ▸ *v* (**-es, -ing, -ed**) break (a promise, law, etc.)
breached *v* ▷ **breach**
breaches *n, v* ▷ **breach**
breaching *v* ▷ **breach**
bread *n* (*pl* **-s**) food made by baking a mixture of flour and water or milk
breads *n* ▷ **bread**
breadth *n* (*pl* **-s**) extent of something from side to side
breadths *n* ▷ **breadth**
breadwinner *n* (*pl* **-s**) person whose earnings support a family
breadwinners *n* ▷ **breadwinner**
break *v* (**breaks, breaking, broke, broken**) separate or become separated into two or more pieces ▸ *n* (*pl* **-s**) act or result of breaking > **breakable** *adj* > **breakage** *n* (*pl* **-s**)
breakable *adj* ▷ **break**
breakage *n* ▷ **break**
breakages *n* ▷ **break**
breakdown *n* (*pl* **-s**) act or instance of breaking down
breakdowns *n* ▷ **breakdown**
breaker *n* (*pl* **-s**) large wave
breakers *n* ▷ **breaker**
breakfast *v* (**-s, -ing, -ed**) ▸ *n* (*pl* **-s**) (eat) the first meal of the day
breakfasted *v* ▷ **breakfast**
breakfasting *v* ▷ **breakfast**
breakfasts *v, n* ▷ **breakfast**
breaking *v* ▷ **break**
breakneck *adj* fast and dangerous
breaks *v, n* ▷ **break**
breakthrough *n* (*pl* **-s**) important development or discovery
breakthroughs *n* ▷ **breakthrough**
breakwater *n* (*pl* **-s**) wall that extends into the sea to protect a harbour or beach from the force of waves
breakwaters *n* ▷ **breakwater**
bream *n* (*pl* **bream**) freshwater fish with silvery scales
breast *n* (*pl* **-s**) either of the two soft fleshy milk-secreting glands on a woman's chest
breastbone *n* (*pl* **-s**) long flat bone in the front of the body, to which most of the ribs are attached
breastbones *n* ▷ **breastbone**
breasts *n* ▷ **breast**
breaststroke *n* (*pl* **-s**) swimming stroke in which the arms are extended in front of the head and swept back on either side
breaststrokes *n* ▷ **breaststroke**
breath *n* (*pl* **-s**) taking in and letting out of air during breathing > **breathless** *adj* > **breathlessly** *adv* > **breathlessness** *n*
breathalysed *v* ▷ **breathalyser**
breathalyser *n* (*pl* **-s**)® device for estimating the amount of alcohol in the breath > **breathalyse** *v* (**-ses, -sing, -sed**)
breathalysers *n* ▷ **breathalyser**
breathalyses *v* ▷ **breathalyser**
breathalysing *v* ▷ **breathalyser**
breathe *v* (**-thes, -thing, -thed**) take in oxygen and give out carbon dioxide > **breathing** *n*
breathed *v* ▷ **breathe**
breather *n* (*pl* **-s**) (*Informal*) short rest
breathers *n* ▷ **breather**
breathes *v* ▷ **breathe**
breathing *v, n* ▷ **breathe**
breathless *adj* ▷ **breath**
breathlessly *adv* ▷ **breath**
breathlessness *n* ▷ **breath**

breaths *n* ▷ **breath**
breathtaking *adj* causing awe or excitement
bred *v* ▷ **breed**
breech *n* (*pl* **-es**) buttocks
breeches *pl n* trousers extending to just below the knee ▶ *n* ▷ **breech**
breed *v* (**-s, -ding, bred**) produce new or improved strains of (domestic animals or plants) ▶ *n* (*pl* **-s**) group of animals etc. within a species that have certain clearly defined characteristics > **breeder** *n* (*pl* **-s**)
breeder *n* ▷ **breed**
breeders *n* ▷ **breed**
breeding *n* (*pl* **-s**) result of good upbringing or training ▶ *v* ▷ **breed**
breedings *n* ▷ **breeding**
breeds *v, n* ▷ **breed**
breeze *n* (*pl* **-s**) gentle wind ▶ *v* (**-zes, -zing, -zed**) move quickly or casually
breezed *v* ▷ **breeze**
breezes *n, v* ▷ **breeze**
breezier *adj* ▷ **breezy**
breeziest *adj* ▷ **breezy**
breezily *adj* ▷ **breezy**
breezing *v* ▷ **breeze**
breezy *adj* (**-zier, -ziest**) windy > **breezily** *adv*
brethren *pl n* (*Old-fashioned*) (used in religious contexts) brothers
brevities *n* ▷ **brevity**
brevity *n* (*pl* **-ities**) shortness
brew *v* (**-s, -ing, -ed**) make (beer etc.) by steeping, boiling, and fermentation ▶ *n* (*pl* **-s**) beverage produced by brewing
brewed *v* ▷ **brew**
brewer *n* (*pl* **-s**) person or company that brews beer
breweries *n* ▷ **brewery**
brewers *n* ▷ **brewer**
brewery *n* (*pl* **-eries**) place where beer etc. is brewed
brewing *v* ▷ **brew**
brews *v, n* ▷ **brew**
briar[1], **brier** *n* (*pl* **-s**) European shrub with a hard woody root
briar2 *n* (*pl* **-s**) ▷ **brier**[1]
briars *n* ▷ **briar**[1, 2]
bribe *v* (**bribes, bribing, bribed**) offer or give something to someone to gain favour, influence, etc. ▶ *n* (*pl* **-s**) something given or offered as a bribe > **bribery** *n*
bribed *v* ▷ **bribe**
bribes *v, n* ▷ **bribe**
bribing *v* ▷ **bribe**
brick *n* (*pl* **-s**) (rectangular block of) baked clay used in building ▶ *v* (**-s, -ing, -ed**) (*foll. by* **up** *or* **over**) build, enclose, or fill with bricks
bricked *v* ▷ **brick**
bricking *v* ▷ **brick**
bricklayer *n* (*pl* **-s**) person who builds with bricks
bricklayers *n* ▷ **bricklayer**
bricks *n, v* ▷ **brick**
bridal *adj* ▷ **bride**
bride *n* (*pl* **-s**) woman who has just been or is about to be married > **bridal** *adj*
bridegroom *n* (*pl* **-s**) man who has just been or is about to be married
bridegrooms *n* ▷ **bridegroom**
brides *n* ▷ **bride**
bridesmaid *n* (*pl* **-s**) girl or woman who attends a bride at her wedding
bridesmaids *n* ▷ **bridesmaid**
bridge[1] *n* (*pl* **-s**) structure for crossing a river etc. ▶ *v* (**-dges, -dging, -dged**) build a bridge over (something)
bridge[2] *n* (*pl* **-s**) card game based on whist, played between two pairs
bridged *v* ▷ **bridge**[1]
bridgehead *n* (*pl* **-s**) fortified position at the end of a bridge nearest the enemy
bridgeheads *n* ▷ **bridgehead**
bridges *n* ▷ **bridge**[1, 2] ▶ *v* ▷ **bridge**[1]
bridging *v* ▷ **bridge**[1]
bridle *n* (*pl* **-s**) headgear for controlling a horse ▶ *v* (**-dles, -dling, -dled**) show anger or indignation
bridled *v* ▷ **bridle**
bridles *n, v* ▷ **bridle**
bridling *v* ▷ **bridle**
brief *adj* (**-er, -est**) short in duration ▶ *n* (*pl* **-s**) condensed statement or written synopsis (*also* **briefing**) (*pl* **-s**) ▶ *pl* men's or women's underpants ▶ *v* (**-s, -ing, -ed**) give information and instructions to (a person) > **briefly** *adv*
briefcase *n* (*pl* **-s**) small flat case for carrying papers, books, etc.
briefcases *n* ▷ **briefcase**
briefed *v* ▷ **brief**
briefer *adj* ▷ **brief**
briefest *adj* ▷ **brief**
briefing *v, n* ▷ **brief**
briefings *n* ▷ **brief**
briefly *adv* ▷ **brief**
briefs *n, v* ▷ **brief**
brier[1], **briar** *n* (*pl* **-s**) wild rose with long thorny stems
brier[2] *n* (*pl* **-s**) ▷ **briar**[1]
briers *n* ▷ **brier**[1, 2]
brig *n* (*pl* **-s**) two-masted square-rigged ship
brigade *n* (*pl* **-s**) army unit smaller than a

division
brigades *n* ▷ **brigade**
brigadier *n* (*pl* **-s**) high-ranking army officer
brigadiers *n* ▷ **brigadier**
brigalow *n* (*pl* **-s**) (AUST) type of acacia tree
brigalows *n* ▷ **brigalow**
brigand *n* (*pl* **-s**) (*Lit*) bandit
brigands *n* ▷ **brigand**
brigantine *n* (*pl* **-s**) two-masted sailing ship
brigantines *n* ▷ **brigantine**
bright *adj* (**-er, -est**) emitting or reflecting much light > **brightly** *adv* > **brightness** *n* > **brighten** *v* (**-s, -ing, -ed**)
brighten *v* ▷ **bright**
brightened *v* ▷ **bright**
brightening *v* ▷ **bright**
brightens *v* ▷ **bright**
brighter *adj* ▷ **bright**
brightest *adj* ▷ **bright**
brightly *adj* ▷ **bright**
brigs *n* ▷ **brig**
brilliance *n* ▷ **brilliant**
brilliancy *n* ▷ **brilliant**
brilliant *adj* shining with light > **brilliance, brilliancy** *n* > **brilliantly** *adv*
brilliantly *adv* ▷ **brilliant**
brim *n* (*pl* **-s**) upper rim of a cup etc. ▶ *v* (**brims, brimming, brimmed**) be full to the brim
brimmed *v* ▷ **brim**
brimming *v* ▷ **brim**
brims *n, v* ▷ **brim**
brimstone *n* (*pl* **-s**) (*Obs*) sulphur
brimstones *n* ▷ **brimstone**
brine *n* (*pl* **-s**) salt water
brines *n* ▷ **brine**
bring *v* (**-s, -ing, brought**) carry, convey, or take to a designated place or person
bringing *v* ▷ **bring**
brings *v* ▷ **bring**
brinier *adj* ▷ **briny**
briniest *adj* ▷ **briny**
brinjal *n* (*pl* **-s**) (S AFR) aubergine
brinjals *n* ▷ **brinjal**
brink *n* (*pl* **-s**) edge of a steep place
brinks *n* ▷ **brink**
briny (**brinier, briniest**) *adj* very salty
brisk *adj* (**-er, -est**) lively and quick > **briskly** *adv*
brisker *adj* ▷ **brisk**
briskest *adj* ▷ **brisk**
brisket *n* (*pl* **-s**) beef from the breast of a cow
briskets *n* ▷ **brisket**
briskly *adv* ▷ **brisk**
bristle *n* (*pl* **-s**) short stiff hair ▶ *v* (**-les, -ling, -led**) (cause to) stand up like bristles > **bristly** *adj* (**-lier, -liest**)
bristled *v* ▷ **bristle**
bristles *n, v* ▷ **bristle**
bristlier *adj* ▷ **bristle**
bristliest *adj* ▷ **bristle**
bristling *v* ▷ **bristle**
bristly *adj* ▷ **bristle**
brit *n* (*pl* **-s**) (*Informal*) British person
brits *n* ▷ **brit**
brittle *adj* (**-r, -st**) hard but easily broken > **brittleness** *n* (*pl* **-es**)
brittleness *n* ▷ **brittle**
brittlenesses *n* ▷ **brittle**
brittler *adj* ▷ **brittle**
brittlest *adj* ▷ **brittle**
broach *v* (**-es, -ing, -ed**) introduce (a topic) for discussion
broached *v* ▷ **broach**
broaches *v* ▷ **broach**
broaching *v* ▷ **broach**
broad *adj* (**-er, -est**) having great breadth or width > **broadly** *adv* > **broaden** *v* (**-s, -ing, -ed**)
broadband *n* (*pl* **-s**) telecommunication transmission technique using a wide range of frequencies
broadbands *n* ▷ **broadband**
broadcast *n* (*pl* **-s**) programme or announcement on radio or television ▶ *v* (**-s, -ing, broadcast**) transmit (a programme or announcement) on radio or television > **broadcaster** *n* (*pl* **-s**) > **broadcasting** *n*
broadcaster *n* ▷ **broadcast**
broadcasters *n* ▷ **broadcast**
broadcasting *v, n* ▷ **broadcast**
broadcasts *n, v* ▷ **broadcast**
broaden *v* ▷ **broad**
broadened *v* ▷ **broad**
broadening *v* ▷ **broad**
broadens *v* ▷ **broad**
broader *adj* ▷ **broad**
broadest *adj* ▷ **broad**
broadly *adv* ▷ **broad**
broadminded *adj* tolerant
broadside *n* (*pl* **-s**) strong verbal or written attack
broadsides *n* ▷ **broadside**
brocade *n* (*pl* **-s**) rich fabric woven with a raised design
brocades *n* ▷ **brocade**
broccoli *n* (*pl* **-s**) type of cabbage with greenish flower heads
broccolis *n* ▷ **broccoli**
brochure *n* (*pl* **-s**) booklet that contains information about a product or service
brochures *n* ▷ **brochure**
broekies [**brook**-eez] *pl n* (S AFR) (*Informal*)

underpants
brogue[1] *n* (*pl* **-s**) sturdy walking shoe
brogue[2] *n* (*pl* **-s**) strong accent, esp. Irish
brogues *n* ▷ **brogue[1, 2]**
broil *v* (**-s, -ing, -ed**) (AUST, NZ, US & CANADIAN) cook by direct heat under a grill
broiled *v* ▷ **broil**
broiling *v* ▷ **broil**
broils *v* ▷ **broil**
broke *v* ▷ **break** ▶ *adj* (*Informal*) having no money
broken *v* ▷ **break** ▶ *adj* fractured or smashed
brokenhearted *adj* overwhelmed by grief
broker *n* (*pl* **-s**) agent who buys or sells goods, securities, etc.
brokers *n* ▷ **broker**
brolga *n* (*pl* **-s**) large grey Australian crane with a trumpeting call
brolgas *n* ▷ **brolga**
brollies *n* ▷ **brolly**
brolly *n* (*pl* **-lies**) (*Informal*) umbrella
bromide *n* (*pl* **-s**) chemical compound used in medicine and photography
bromides *n* ▷ **bromide**
bromine *n* (*pl* **-s**) (CHEM) dark red liquid element that gives off a pungent vapour
bromines *n* ▷ **bromine**
bronchi *n* ▷ **bronchus**
bronchial [**bronk**-ee-al] *adj* of the bronchi
bronchitis [bronk-**eye**-tiss] *n* inflammation of the bronchi
bronchus [**bronk**-uss] *n* (*pl* **bronchi**) [**bronk**-eye] either of the two branches of the windpipe
bronco *n* (*pl* **-s**) (in the US) wild or partially tamed pony
broncos *n* ▷ **bronco**
brontosaurus *n* (*pl* **-es**) very large plant-eating four-footed dinosaur
brontosauruses *n* ▷ **brontosaurus**
bronze *n* (*pl* **-s**) alloy of copper and tin ▶ *adj* made of, or coloured like, bronze ▶ *v* (**-zes, -zing, -zed**) (esp. of the skin) make or become brown
bronzed *v* ▷ **bronze**
bronzes *n, v* ▷ **bronze**
bronzing *v* ▷ **bronze**
brooch *n* (*pl* **-es**) ornament with a pin, worn fastened to clothes
brooches *n* ▷ **brooch**
brood *n* (*pl* **-s**) number of birds produced at one hatching ▶ *v* (**-s, -ing, -ed**) think long and unhappily > **broody** *adj* moody and sullen (*Informal*)
brooded *v* ▷ **brood**
brooding *v* ▷ **brood**
broods *n, v* ▷ **brood**
broody *adj* ▷ **brood**
brook[1] *n* (*pl* **-s**) small stream
brook[2] *v* (**-s, -ing, -ed**) bear or tolerate
brooked *v* ▷ **brook[2]**
brooking *v* ▷ **brook[2]**
brooks *n* ▷ **brook[1]** ▶ *v* ▷ **brook[2]**
broom *n* (*pl* **-s**) long-handled sweeping brush
brooms *n* ▷ **broom**
broomstick *n* (*pl* **-s**) handle of a broom
broomsticks *n* ▷ **broomstick**
broth *n* (*pl* **-s**) soup, usu. containing vegetables
brothel *n* (*pl* **-s**) house where men pay to have sex with prostitutes
brothels *n* ▷ **brothel**
brother *n* (*pl* **-s**) boy or man with the same parents as another person > **brotherly** *adj*
brotherhood *n* (*pl* **-s**) fellowship
brotherhoods *n* ▷ **brotherhood**
brotherly *adj* ▷ **brother**
brothers *n* ▷ **brother**
broths *n* ▷ **broth**
brought *v* ▷ **bring**
brow *n* (*pl* **-s**) part of the face from the eyes to the hairline
browbeat *v* (**-s, -ing, browbeat, -en**) frighten (someone) with threats
browbeaten *v* ▷ **browbeat**
browbeating *v* ▷ **browbeat**
browbeats *v* ▷ **browbeat**
brown *n* (*pl* **-s**) colour of earth or wood ▶ *adj* (**-er, -est**) of the colour brown ▶ *v* (**-s, -ing, -ed**) make or become brown > **brownish** *adj*
browned *v* ▷ **brown**
browner *adj* ▷ **brown**
brownest *adj* ▷ **brown**
browning *v* ▷ **brown**
brownish *adj* ▷ **brown**
browns *n, v* ▷ **brown**
brows *n* ▷ **brow**
browse *v* (**-ses, -sing, -sed**) look through (a book or articles for sale) in a casual manner ▶ *n* (*pl* **-s**) instance of browsing
browsed *v* ▷ **browse**
browser *n* (*pl* **-s**) (COMPUTERS) software package that enables a user to read hypertext, esp. on the Internet
browsers *n* ▷ **browser**
browses *v, n* ▷ **browse**
browsing *v* ▷ **browse**
bruise *n* (*pl* **-s**) discoloured area on the skin caused by an injury ▶ *v* (**-ses, -sing, -sed**) cause a bruise on
bruised *v* ▷ **bruise**
bruiser *n* (*pl* **-s**) strong tough person

bruisers *n* ▷ **bruiser**
bruises *n, v* ▷ **bruise**
bruising *v* ▷ **bruise**
brumbies *n* ▷ **brumby**
brumby *n* (*pl* **-bies**) (AUST) wild horse
brunch *n* (*pl* **-es**) (*Informal*) breakfast and lunch combined
brunches *n* ▷ **brunch**
brunette *n* (*pl* **-s**) girl or woman with dark brown hair
brunettes *n* ▷ **brunette**
brunt *n* (*pl* **-s**) main force or shock of a blow, attack, etc.
brunts *n* ▷ **brunt**
brush[1] *n* (*pl* **-es**) device made of bristles, wires, etc. used for cleaning, painting, etc. ▶ *v* (**-es, -ing, -ed**) clean, scrub, or paint with a brush
brush[2] *n* (*pl* **-es**) thick growth of shrubs
brushed *v* ▷ **brush**[1]
brushes *v* ▷ **brush**[1] ▶ *n* ▷ **brush**[1, 2]
brushing *v* ▷ **brush**[1]
brusque *adj* (**-r, -st**) blunt or curt in manner or speech > **brusquely** *adv* > **brusqueness** *n* (*pl* **-es**)
brusquely *adv* ▷ **brusque**
brusqueness *n* ▷ **brusque**
brusquenesses *n* ▷ **brusque**
brusquer *adj* ▷ **brusque**
brusquest *adj* ▷ **brusque**
brutal *adj* cruel and vicious > **brutally** *adv* > **brutality** *n* (*pl* **-alities**) > **brutalize** *v* (**-lizes, -lizing, -lized**)
brutalities *n* ▷ **brutal**
brutality *n* ▷ **brutal**
brutalized *v* ▷ **brutal**
brutalizes *v* ▷ **brutal**
brutalizing *v* ▷ **brutal**
brutally *adv* ▷ **brutal**
brute *n* (*pl* **-s**) brutal person ▶ *adj* wholly instinctive or physical, like an animal
brutes *n* ▷ **brute**
brutish *adj* of or like an animal > **brutishly** *adv* > **brutishness** *n*
brutishly *adv* ▷ **brutish**
brutishness *n* ▷ **brutish**
bubble *n* (*pl* **-s**) ball of air in a liquid or solid ▶ *v* (**-les, -ling, -led**) form bubbles
bubbled *v* ▷ **bubble**
bubbles *n, v* ▷ **bubble**
bubblier *adj* ▷ **bubbly**
bubbliest *adj* ▷ **bubbly**
bubbling *v* ▷ **bubble**
bubbly *adj* (**-lier, -liest**) excited and lively
buccaneer *n* (*pl* **-s**) (HIST) pirate
buccaneers *n* ▷ **buccaneer**
buck[1] *n* (*pl* **-s**) male of the goat, hare, kangaroo, rabbit, and reindeer ▶ *v* (**-s, -ing, -ed**) (of a horse etc.) jump with legs stiff and back arched
buck[2] *n* (*pl* **-s**) (US, CANADIAN, AUST & NZ) (*Slang*) dollar
bucked *v* ▷ **buck**[1]
bucket *n* (*pl* **-s**) open-topped round container with a handle ▶ *v* (**-ets, -eting, -eted**) rain heavily > **bucketful** *n* (*pl* **-s**)
bucketed *v* ▷ **bucket**
bucketful *n* ▷ **bucket**
bucketfuls *n* ▷ **bucket**
bucketing *v* ▷ **bucket**
buckets *n, v* ▷ **bucket**
bucking *v* ▷ **buck**[1]
buckle *n* (*pl* **-s**) clasp for fastening a belt or strap ▶ *v* (**-les, -ling, -led**) fasten or be fastened with a buckle
buckled *v* ▷ **buckle**
buckles *n, v* ▷ **buckle**
buckling *v* ▷ **buckle**
bucks *v* ▷ **buck**[1] ▶ *n* ▷ **buck**[1, 2]
buckshee *adj* (*Slang*) free
buckteeth *pl n* projecting upper front teeth > **buck-toothed** *adj*
buck-toothed *adj* ▷ **buckteeth**
buckwheat *n* (*pl* **-s**) small black grain used for making flour
buckwheats *n* ▷ **buckwheat**
bucolic [bew-**koll**-ik] *adj* of the countryside or country life
bud *n* (*pl* **-s**) swelling on a tree or plant that develops into a leaf or flower ▶ *v* (**buds, budding, budded**) produce buds
budded *v* ▷ **bud**
buddies *n* ▷ **buddy**
budding *adj* beginning to develop or grow ▶ *v* ▷ **bud**
buddleia *n* (*pl* **-s**) shrub with long spikes of purple flowers
buddleias *n* ▷ **buddleia**
buddy *n* (*pl* **-dies**) (*Informal*) friend
budge *v* (**budges, budging, budged**) move slightly
budged *v* ▷ **budge**
budgerigar *n* (*pl* **-s**) small cage bird bred in many different-coloured varieties
budgerigars *n* ▷ **budgerigar**
budges *v* ▷ **budge**
budget *n* (*pl* **-s**) financial plan for a period of time ▶ *v* (**-ets, -eting, -eted**) plan the expenditure of (money or time) ▶ *adj* cheap > **budgetary** *adj*
budgeted *v* ▷ **budget**

budgeting *v* ▷ **budget**
budgets *n, v* ▷ **budget**
budgie *n* (*pl* **-s**) (*Informal*) ▷ **budgerigar**
budgies *n* ▷ **budgie**
budging *v* ▷ **budge**
buds *n, v* ▷ **bud**
buff[1] *adj* dull yellowish-brown ▶ *v* (**-s, -ing, -ed**) clean or polish with soft material
buff[2] *n* (*pl* **-s**) (*Informal*) expert on or devotee of a given subject
buffalo *n* (*pl* **-oes**) type of cattle (US)
buffaloes *n* ▷ **buffalo**
buffed *v* ▷ **buff**[1]
buffer *n* (*pl* **-s**) something that lessens shock or protects from damaging impact, circumstances, etc.
buffers *n* ▷ **buffer**
buffet[1] [**boof**-ay, **buff**-ay] *n* (*pl* **-s**) counter where drinks and snacks are served
buffet[2] [**buff**-it] *v* (**-s, -feting, -feted**) knock against or about
buffeted *v* ▷ **buffet**[2]
buffeting *v* ▷ **buffet**[2]
buffets *n* ▷ **buffet**[1] ▶ *v* ▷ **buffet**[2]
buffing *v* ▷ **buff**[1]
buffoon *n* (*pl* **-s**) clown or fool > **buffoonery** *n* (*pl* **-ries**)
buffooneries *n* ▷ **buffoon**
buffoonery *n* ▷ **buffoon**
buffoons *n* ▷ **buffoon**
buffs *v* ▷ **buff**[1] ▶ *n* ▷ **buff**[2]
bug *n* (*pl* **-s**) small insect ▶ *v* (**bugs, bugging, bugged**) (*Informal*) irritate (someone)
bugbear *n* (*pl* **-s**) thing that causes obsessive anxiety
bugbears *n* ▷ **bugbear**
bugged *v* ▷ **bug**
bugging *v* ▷ **bug**
bugle *n* (*pl* **-s**) instrument like a small trumpet > **bugler** *n* (*pl* **-s**)
bugler *n* ▷ **bugle**
buglers *n* ▷ **bugle**
bugles *n* ▷ **bugle**
bugong *n* ▷ **bogong**
bugongs *n* ▷ **bogong**
bugs *n, v* ▷ **bug**
build *v* (**builds, building, built**) make, construct, or form by joining parts or materials ▶ *n* (*pl* **-s**) shape of the body > **builder** *n* (*pl* **-s**)
builder *n* ▷ **build**
builders *n* ▷ **build**
building *v* ▷ **build** ▶ *n* (*pl* **-s**) structure with walls and a roof
buildings *n* ▷ **building**
builds *v, n* ▷ **build**
built *v* ▷ **build**
bulb *n* (*pl* **-s**) onion-shaped root which grows into a flower or plant
bulbous *adj* round and fat
bulbs *n* ▷ **bulb**
bulge *n* (*pl* **-s**) swelling on a normally flat surface ▶ *v* (**bulges, bulging, bulged**) swell outwards > **bulging** *adj*
bulged *v* ▷ **bulge**
bulges *n, v* ▷ **bulge**
bulging *v, adj* ▷ **bulge**
bulimia *n* (*pl* **-s**) disorder characterized by compulsive overeating followed by vomiting > **bulimic** *adj, n* (*pl* **-s**)
bulimias *n* ▷ **bulimia**
bulimic *adj, n* ▷ **bulimia**
bulimics *n* ▷ **bulimia**
bulk *n* (*pl* **-s**) size or volume, esp. when great > **bulky** *adj* (**-ier, -iest**)
bulkhead *n* (*pl* **-s**) partition in a ship or aeroplane
bulkheads *n* ▷ **bulkhead**
bulkier *adj* ▷ **bulk**
bulkiest *adj* ▷ **bulk**
bulks *n* ▷ **bulk**
bulky *adj* ▷ **bulk**
bull[1] *n* (*pl* **-s**) male of some animals, such as cattle, elephants, and whales
bull[2] *n* (*pl* **-s**) (*Informal*) complete nonsense
bull[3] *n* (*pl* **-s**) papal decree
bulldog *n* (*pl* **-s**) thickset dog with a broad head and a muscular body
bulldogs *n* ▷ **bulldog**
bulldoze *v* ▷ **bulldozer**
bulldozed *v* ▷ **bulldozer**
bulldozer *n* (*pl* **-s**) powerful tractor for moving earth > **bulldoze** *v* (**-zes, -zing, -zed**)
bulldozers *n* ▷ **bulldozer**
bulldozes *v* ▷ **bulldozer**
bulldozing *v* ▷ **bulldozer**
bullet *n* (*pl* **-s**) small piece of metal fired from a gun
bulletin *n* (*pl* **-s**) short official report or announcement
bulletins *n* ▷ **bulletin**
bullets *n* ▷ **bullet**
bullfight *n* (*pl* **-s**) public show in which a matador kills a bull > **bullfighter** *n* (*pl* **-s**)
bullfighter *n* ▷ **bullfight**
bullfighters *n* ▷ **bullfight**
bullfights *n* ▷ **bullfight**
bullied *v* ▷ **bully**
bullies *n, v* ▷ **bully**

bullion *n* (*pl* **-s**) gold or silver in the form of bars
bullions *n* ▷ **bullion**
bullock *n* (*pl* **-s**) castrated bull
bullocks *n* ▷ **bullock**
bulls *n* ▷ **bull**[1,2,3]
bullswool *n* (AUST DATED & NZ) (*Slang*) nonsense
bully *n* (*pl* **-lies**) person who hurts, persecutes, or intimidates a weaker person ▶ *v* (**-lies, -lying, -lied**) hurt, intimidate, or persecute (a weaker person)
bullying *v* ▷ **bully**
bulrush *n* (*pl* **-es**) tall stiff reed
bulrushes *n* ▷ **bulrush**
bulwark *n* (*pl* **-s**) wall used as a fortification
bulwarks *n* ▷ **bulwark**
bum[1] *n* (*pl* **-s**) (*Slang*) buttocks or anus
bum[2] (*Informal*) *n* (*pl* **-s**) disreputable idler ▶ *adj* of poor quality
bumble *v* (**-bles, -bling, -bled**) speak, do, or move in a clumsy way > **bumbling** *adj, n*
bumblebee *n* (*pl* **-s**) large hairy bee
bumblebees *n* ▷ **bumblebee**
bumbled *v* ▷ **bumble**
bumbles *v* ▷ **bumble**
bumbling *v, adj n* ▷ **bumble**
bumf, bumph *n* (*pl* **-s**) (*Informal*) official documents or forms
bumfs *n* ▷ **bumf**
bump *v* (**-s, -ing, -ed**) knock or strike with a jolt ▶ *n* (*pl* **-s**) dull thud from an impact or collision > **bumpy** *adj* (**-ier, -iest**)
bumped *v* ▷ **bump**
bumper[1] *n* (*pl* **-s**) bar on the front and back of a vehicle to protect against damage
bumper[2] *adj* unusually large or abundant
bumpers *n* ▷ **bumper**[1]
bumph *n* ▷ **bumf**
bumphs *n* ▷ **bumf**
bumpier *adj* ▷ **bump**
bumpiest *adj* ▷ **bump**
bumping *v* ▷ **bump**
bumpkin *n* (*pl* **-s**) awkward simple country person
bumpkins *n* ▷ **bumpkin**
bumps *v, n* ▷ **bump**
bumptious *adj* offensively self-assertive > **bumptiously** *adv* > **bumptiousness** *n*
bumptiously *adj* ▷ **bumptious**
bumptiousness *adj* ▷ **bumptious**
bumpy *adj* ▷ **bump**
bums *n* ▷ **bum**[1,2]
bun *n* (*pl* **-s**) small sweet bread roll or cake
bunch *n* (*pl* **-es**) number of things growing, fastened, or grouped together ▶ *v* (**-es, -ing, -ed**) group or be grouped together in a bunch
bunched *v* ▷ **bunch**
bunches *n, v* ▷ **bunch**
bunching *v* ▷ **bunch**
bundle *n* (*pl* **-s**) number of things gathered loosely together ▶ *v* (**-dles, -dling, -dled**) cause to go roughly or unceremoniously
bundled *v* ▷ **bundle**
bundles *n, v* ▷ **bundle**
bundling *v* ▷ **bundle**
bung *n* (*pl* **-s**) stopper for a cask etc. ▶ *v* (**-s, -ing, -ed**) (*foll. by* **up**) (*Informal*) close with a bung
bungalow *n* (*pl* **-s**) one-storey house
bungalows *n* ▷ **bungalow**
bunged *v* ▷ **bung**
bunging *v* ▷ **bung**
bungle *v* (**-gles, -gling, -gled**) spoil through incompetence > **bungler** *n* (*pl* **-s**) > **bungling** *adj, n*
bungled *v* ▷ **bungle**
bungler *n* ▷ **bungle**
bunglers *n* ▷ **bungle**
bungles *v* ▷ **bungle**
bungling *v, adj n* ▷ **bungle**
bungs *n, v* ▷ **bung**
bunion *n* (*pl* **-s**) inflamed swelling on the big toe
bunions *n* ▷ **bunion**
bunk[1] *n* (*pl* **-s**) narrow shelflike bed
bunk[2] *n* (*pl* **-s**) ▷ **bunkum**
bunk[3] (*Slang*) *n* (*pl* **-s**) (BRIT) make a hurried and secret departure ▶ *v* (**-s, -ing, -ed**) (BRIT, NZ & S AFR) be absent without permission
bunked *v* ▷ **bunk**[3]
bunker *n* (*pl* **-s**) sand-filled hollow forming an obstacle on a golf course
bunkers *n* ▷ **bunker**
bunking *v* ▷ **bunk**[3]
bunks *n* ▷ **bunk**[1,2,3] ▶ *v* ▷ **bunk**[3]
bunkum *n* (*pl* **-s**) nonsense
bunkums *n* ▷ **bunkum**
bunnies *n* ▷ **bunny**
bunny *n* (*pl* **-nies**) child's word for a rabbit
buns *n* ▷ **bun**
bunting *n* (*pl* **-s**) decorative flags
buntings *n* ▷ **bunting**
bunya *n* (*pl* **-s**) tall dome-shaped Australian coniferous tree
bunyas *n* ▷ **bunya**
bunyip *n* (*pl* **-s**) (AUST) legendary monster said to live in swamps and lakes
bunyips *n* ▷ **bunyip**
buoy *n* (*pl* **-s**) floating marker anchored in the sea ▶ *v* (**-s, -ing, -ed**) prevent from sinking
buoyancy *n* ▷ **buoyant**
buoyant *adj* able to float > **buoyancy** *n*

buoyed *v* ▷ **buoy**
buoying *v* ▷ **buoy**
buoys *n, v* ▷ **buoy**
bur *n* (*pl* **-s**) ▷ **burr**[1]
burble *v* (**-bles, -bling, -bled**) make a bubbling sound
burbled *v* ▷ **burble**
burbles *v* ▷ **burble**
burbling *v* ▷ **burble**
burden[1] *n* (*pl* **-s**) heavy load ▶ *v* (**-s, -ing, -ed**) put a burden on > **burdensome** *adj*
burden[2] *n* (*pl* **-s**) theme of a speech etc.
burdened *v* ▷ **burden**[1]
burdening *v* ▷ **burden**[1]
burdens *v* ▷ **burden**[1] ▶ *n* ▷ **burden**[1, 2]
burdensome *adj* ▷ **burden**[1]
bureau *n* (*pl* **-reaus, -reaux**) office that provides a service
bureaucracies *n* ▷ **bureaucracy**
bureaucracy *n* (*pl* **-cies**) administrative system based on complex rules and procedures > **bureaucrat** *n* (*pl* **-s**) > **bureaucratic** *adj*
bureaucrat *n* ▷ **bureaucracy**
bureaucratic *adj* ▷ **bureaucracy**
bureaucrats *n* ▷ **bureaucracy**
bureaus *n* ▷ **bureau**
bureaux *n* ▷ **bureau**
burgeon *v* (**-s, -ing, -ed**) develop or grow rapidly
burgeoned *v* ▷ **burgeon**
burgeoning *v* ▷ **burgeon**
burgeons *v* ▷ **burgeon**
burgh *n* (*pl* **-s**) Scottish borough
burghs *n* ▷ **burgh**
burglar *n* (*pl* **-s**) person who enters a building to commit a crime, esp. theft > **burglary** *n* (*pl* **-glaries**) > **burgle** *v* (**burgles, burgling, burgled**)
burglaries *n* ▷ **burglar**
burglars *n* ▷ **burglar**
burglary *n* ▷ **burglar**
burgled *v* ▷ **burglar**
burgles *v* ▷ **burglar**
burgling *v* ▷ **burglar**
burgundy *adj* dark-purplish red
burial *n* (*pl* **-s**) burying of a dead body
burials *n* ▷ **burial**
buried *v* ▷ **bury**
buries *v* ▷ **bury**
burlesque *n* (*pl* **-s**) artistic work which satirizes a subject by caricature
burlesques *n* ▷ **burlesque**
burlier *adj* ▷ **burly**
burliest *adj* ▷ **burly**
burly *adj* (**-lier, -liest**) (of a person) broad and strong
burn[1] *v* (**-s, -ing, -t** *or* **-ed**) be or set on fire ▶ *n* (*pl* **burns**) injury or mark caused by fire or exposure to heat
burn[2] *n* (*pl* **-s**) (Scot) small stream
burned *v* ▷ **burn**[1]
burning *adj* intense ▶ *v* ▷ **burn**[1]
burnish *v* (**-es, -ing, -ed**) make smooth and shiny by rubbing
burnished *v* ▷ **burnish**
burnishes *v* ▷ **burnish**
burnishing *v* ▷ **burnish**
burns *n* ▷ **burn**[1, 2] ▶ *v* ▷ **burn**[1]
burnt *v* ▷ **burn**[1]
burp *v* (**-s, -ing, -ed**) ▶ *n* (*pl* **-s**) (*Informal*) belch
burped *v* ▷ **burp**
burping *v* ▷ **burp**
burps *v, n* ▷ **burp**
burr[1], **bur** *n* (*pl* **-s**) head of a plant with prickles or hooks
burr[2] *n* (*pl* **-s**) soft trilling sound given to the letter *r* in some dialects
burrawang *n* (*pl* **-s**) Australian plant with fernlike leaves and an edible nut
burrawangs *n* ▷ **burrawang**
burrow *n* (*pl* **-s**) hole dug in the ground by a rabbit etc. ▶ *v* (**-s, -ing, -ed**) dig holes in the ground
burrowed *v* ▷ **burrow**
burrowing *v* ▷ **burrow**
burrows *n, v* ▷ **burrow**
burrs *n* ▷ **burr**[1, 2]
burs *n* ▷ **bur**
bursar *n* (*pl* **-s**) treasurer of a school, college, or university
bursaries *n* ▷ **bursary**
bursars *n* ▷ **bursar**
bursary *n* (*pl* **-ries**) scholarship
burst *v* (**-s, -ing, burst**) (cause to) break open or apart noisily and suddenly ▶ *n* (*pl* **-s**) instance of breaking open suddenly
bursting *v* ▷ **burst**
bursts *v, n* ▷ **burst**
bury *v* (**buries, burying, buried**) place in a grave
burying *v* ▷ **bury**
bus *n* (*pl* **buses**) large motor vehicle for carrying passengers ▶ *v* (**busses, bussing, bussed**) travel or transport by bus
busbies *n* ▷ **busby**
busby *n* (*pl* **-bies**) tall fur hat worn by some soldiers
buses *n* ▷ **bus**
bush *n* (*pl* **-es**) dense woody plant, smaller than a tree
bushbabies *n* ▷ **bushbaby**

bushbaby *n* (*pl* **-babies**) small African tree-living mammal with large eyes
bushel *n* (*pl* **-s**) obsolete unit of measure equal to 8 gallons (36.4 litres)
bushels *n* ▷ **bushel**
bushes *n* ▷ **bush**
bushier *adj* ▷ **bushy**
bushiest *adj* ▷ **bushy**
bushy *adj* (**-shier, -shiest**) (of hair) thick and shaggy
busied *v* ▷ **busy**
busier *adj* ▷ **busy**
busies *v* ▷ **busy**
busiest *adj* ▷ **busy**
business *n* (*pl* **-es**) purchase and sale of goods and services > **businessman** *n* (*pl* **-men**), **businesswoman** (*pl* **-women**)
businesses *n* ▷ **business**
businesslike *adj* efficient and methodical
businessman *n* ▷ **business**
businessmen *n* ▷ **business**
businesswoman *n* ▷ **business**
businesswomen *n* ▷ **business**
busk *v* (**-s, -ing, -ed**) act as a busker
busked *v* ▷ **busk**
busker *n* (*pl* **-s**) street entertainer
buskers *n* ▷ **busker**
busking *v* ▷ **busk**
busks *v* ▷ **busk**
bussed *v* ▷ **bus**
busses *v* ▷ **bus**
bussing *v* ▷ **bus**
bust[1] *n* (*pl* **-s**) woman's bosom
bust[2] (*Informal*) *v* (**busts, busting, bust** *or* **busted**) burst or break ▶ *adj* broken
bustard *n* (*pl* **-s**) bird with long strong legs, a heavy body, a long neck, and speckled plumage
bustards *n* ▷ **bustard**
busted *v* ▷ **bust**[2]
busting *v* ▷ **bust**[2]
bustle[1] *v* (**-les, -ling, -led**) hurry with a show of activity or energy ▶ *n* (*pl* **-s**) energetic and noisy activity > **bustling** *adj*
bustle[2] *n* (*pl* **-s**) cushion or framework formerly worn under the back of a woman's skirt to hold it out
bustled *v* ▷ **bustle**[1]
bustles *v* ▷ **bustle**[1] ▶ *n* ▷ **bustle**[1, 2]
bustling *v, adj* ▷ **bustle**[1]
busts *n* ▷ **bust**[1] ▶ *v* ▷ **bust**[2]
busy *adj* (**busier, busiest**) actively employed ▶ *v* (**busies, busying, busied**) keep (someone, esp. oneself) busy > **busily** *adv*
busybodies *n* ▷ **busybody**
busybody *n* (*pl* **-bodies**) meddlesome or nosy person
busying *v* ▷ **busy**
but *conj* contrary to expectation ▶ *prep* except ▶ *adv* only
butane *n* (*pl* **-s**) gas used for fuel
butanes *n* ▷ **butane**
butch *adj* (**-er, -est**) (*Slang*) markedly or aggressively masculine
butcher *n* (*pl* **-s**) person who slaughters animals or sells their meat ▶ *v* (**-s, -ing, -ed**) kill and prepare (animals) for meat > **butchery** *n* (*pl* **-ries**) *adj* ▷ **butch**
butcherbird *n* (*pl* **-s**) Australian magpie that impales its prey on thorns
butcherbirds *n* ▷ **butcherbird**
butchered *v* ▷ **butcher**
butcheries *n* ▷ **butcher**
butchering *v* ▷ **butcher**
butchers *n, v* ▷ **butcher**
butchery *n* ▷ **butcher**
butchest *adj* ▷ **butch**
butler *n* (*pl* **-s**) chief male servant
butlers *n* ▷ **butler**
butt[1] *n* (*pl* **-s**) thicker end of something
butt[2] *n* (*pl* **-s**) person or thing that is the target of ridicule
butt[3] *v* (**-s, -ing, -ed**) strike with the head or horns
butt[4] *n* (*pl* **-s**) large cask
butted *v* ▷ **butt**[3]
butter *n* (*pl* **-s**) edible fatty solid made by churning cream ▶ *v* (**-s, -ing, -ed**) put butter on > **buttery** *adj*
buttercup *n* (*pl* **-s**) small yellow flower
buttercups *n* ▷ **buttercup**
buttered *v* ▷ **butter**
butterfingers *n* (*pl* **-s**) (*Informal*) person who drops things by mistake
butterflies *n* ▷ **butterfly**
butterfly *n* (*pl* **-flies**) insect with brightly coloured wings
buttering *v* ▷ **butter**
buttermilk *n* (*pl* **-s**) sourish milk that remains after the butter has been separated from milk
buttermilks *n* ▷ **buttermilks**
butters *n, v* ▷ **butter**
butterscotch *n* (*pl* **-es**) kind of hard brittle toffee
butterscotches *n* ▷ **butterscotch**
buttery *adj* ▷ **butter**
butting *v* ▷ **butt**[3]
buttock *n* (*pl* **-s**) either of the two fleshy masses that form the human rump
buttocks *n* ▷ **buttock**

button *n* (*pl* **-s**) small disc or knob sewn to clothing, which can be passed through a slit in another piece of fabric to fasten them ▶ *v* (**-s, -ing, -ed**) fasten with buttons
buttoned *v* ▷ **button**
buttonhole *n* (*pl* **-s**) slit in a garment through which a button is passed ▶ *v* (**-holes, -holing, -holed**) detain (someone) in conversation
buttonholed *v* ▷ **buttonhole**
buttonholes *n, v* ▷ **buttonhole**
buttonholing *v* ▷ **buttonhole**
buttoning *v* ▷ **button**
buttons *n, v* ▷ **button**
buttress *n* (*pl* **-es**) structure to support a wall ▶ *v* (**-es, -ing, -ed**) support with, or as if with, a buttress
buttressed *v* ▷ **buttress**
buttresses *n, v* ▷ **buttress**
buttressing *v* ▷ **buttress**
butts *n* ▷ **butt**^{1,2,4} ▶ *v* ▷ **butt**^{3}
buxom *adj* (**-er, -est**) (of a woman) healthily plump and full-bosomed
buxomer *adj* ▷ **buxom**
buxomest *adj* ▷ **buxom**
buy *v* (**-s, -ing, bought**) acquire by paying money for ▶ *n* (*pl* **-s**) thing acquired through payment
buyer *n* (*pl* **-s**) customer
buyers *n* ▷ **buyer**
buying *v* ▷ **buy**
buys *v, n* ▷ **buy**
buzz *n* (*pl* **-es**) rapidly vibrating humming sound (*Informal*) ▶ *v* (**-es, -ing, -ed**) make a humming sound > **buzzer** *n* (*pl* **-s**)
buzzard *n* (*pl* **-s**) bird of prey of the hawk family
buzzards *n* ▷ **buzzard**
buzzed *v* ▷ **buzz**
buzzer *n* ▷ **buzz**
buzzers *n* ▷ **buzz**
buzzes *n, v* ▷ **buzz**
buzzing *v* ▷ **buzz**
by *prep* indicating the doer of an action, nearness, movement past, time before or during which, etc. ▶ *adv* near
bye *interj* (*Informal*) goodbye
byelaw *n* ▷ **bylaw**
byelaws *n* ▷ **bylaw**
bygone *adj* past or former
bylaw, byelaw *n* (*pl* **-s**) rule made by a local authority
bylaws *n* ▷ **bylaw**
bypass *n* (*pl* **-es**) main road built to avoid a city ▶ *v* (**-es, -ing, -ed**) go round or avoid
bypassed *v* ▷ **bypass**
bypasses *n, v* ▷ **bypass**
bypassing *v* ▷ **bypass**
byre *n* (*pl* **-s**) (BRIT) shelter for cows
byres *n* ▷ **byre**
bystander *n* (*pl* **-s**) person present but not involved
bystanders *n* ▷ **bystander**
byte *n* (*pl* **-s**) (COMPUTERS) group of bits processed as one unit of data
bytes *n* ▷ **byte**
byway *n* (*pl* **-s**) minor road
byways *n* ▷ **byway**
byword *n* (*pl* **-s**) person or thing regarded as a perfect example of something
bywords *n* ▷ **byword**

Cc

C can be a tricky letter to use, especially as it only forms a single two-letter word **ch**. But if you remember this, you won't waste time racking your brains for two-letter words. There are, however, plenty of good three-letter words beginning with C. **Cox** scores 12 points, while **caw, cow** and **coy** are each worth 8. It's also a good idea to remember the short words starting with C that don't contain any vowels: **cly** and **cwm** as well as **ch**.

cab *n* (*pl* **-s**) taxi
cabal [kab-**bal**] *n* (*pl* **-s**) small group of political plotters
cabals *n* ▷ **cabal**
cabaret [**kab**-a-ray] *n* (*pl* **-s**) dancing and singing show in a nightclub
cabarets *n* ▷ **cabaret**
cabbage *n* (*pl* **-s**) vegetable with a large head of green leaves
cabbages *n* ▷ **cabbage**
cabbie, cabby *n* (*pl* **-bies**) (*Informal*) taxi driver
cabbies *n* ▷ **cabbie**
cabby *n* ▷ **cabbie**
caber *n* (*pl* **-s**) tree trunk tossed in competition at Highland games
cabers *n* ▷ **caber**
cabin *n* (*pl* **-s**) compartment in a ship or aircraft
cabinet *n* (*pl* **-s**) piece of furniture with drawers or shelves
cabinetmaker *n* (*pl* **-s**) person who makes fine furniture
cabinetmakers *n* ▷ **cabinetmaker**
cabinets *n* ▷ **cabinet**
cabins *n* ▷ **cabin**
cable *n* (*pl* **-s**) strong thick rope ▶ *v* (**-les, -ling, -led**) send (someone) a message by cable
cabled *v* ▷ **cable**
cables *n, v* ▷ **cable**
cabling *v* ▷ **cable**
caboodle *n* (*Informal*) the whole lot
cabriolet [kab-ree-oh-**lay**] *n* (*pl* **-s**) small horse-drawn carriage with a folding hood
cabriolets *n* ▷ **cabriolet**
cabs *n* ▷ **cab**
cacao [kak-**kah**-oh] *n* (*pl* **-s**) tropical tree with seed pods from which chocolate and cocoa are made
cacaos *n* ▷ **cacao**
cache [**kash**] *n* (*pl* **-s**) hidden store of weapons or treasure
caches *n* ▷ **cache**
cachet [**kash**-shay] *n* (*pl* **-s**) prestige, distinction
cachets *n* ▷ **cachet**
cackle *v* (**-les, -ling, -led**) laugh shrilly ▶ *n* (*pl* **-s**) cackling noise
cackled *v* ▷ **cackle**
cackles *v, n* ▷ **cackle**
cackling *v* ▷ **cackle**
cacophonies *n* ▷ **cacophony**
cacophonous *adj* ▷ **cacophony**
cacophony [kak-**koff**-on-ee] *n* (*pl* **-phonies**) harsh discordant sound > **cacophonous** *adj*
cacti *n* ▷ **cactus**
cactus *n* (*pl* **-tuses, -ti**) fleshy desert plant with spines but no leaves
cactuses *n* ▷ **cactus**
cad *n* (*pl* **-s**) (*Old-fashioned*) dishonourable man > **caddish** *adj*
cadaver [kad-**dav**-ver] *n* (*pl* **-s**) corpse
cadaverous *adj* pale, thin, and haggard
cadavers *n* ▷ **cadaver**
caddie, caddy *n* (*pl* **-dies**) person who carries a golfer's clubs ▶ *v* (**-dies, -dying, -died**) act as a caddie
caddies *n* ▷ **caddie, caddy** ▶ *v* ▷ **caddie**
caddish *adj* ▷ **cad**
caddy *n* (*pl* **-dies**) small container for tea ▷ **caddie**
cadence [**kade**-enss] *n* (*pl* **-s**) rise and fall in the pitch of the voice
cadences *n* ▷ **cadence**
cadenza *n* (*pl* **-s**) complex solo passage in a piece of music
cadenzas *n* ▷ **cadenza**
cadet *n* (*pl* **-s**) young person training for the armed forces or police

cadets *n* ▷ **cadet**
cadge *v* **(cadges, cadging, cadged)** (*Informal*) get (something) by taking advantage of someone's generosity > **cadger** *n* (*pl* **-s**)
cadged *v* ▷ **cadge**
cadger *n* ▷ **cadge**
cadgers *n* ▷ **cadge**
cadges *v* ▷ **cadge**
cadging *v* ▷ **cadge**
cadmium *n* (*pl* **-s**) (CHEM) bluish-white metallic element used in alloys
cadmiums *n* ▷ **cadmium**
cadre [**kah**-der] *n* (*pl* **-s**) small group of people selected and trained to form the core of a political organization or military unit
cadres *n* ▷ **cadre**
cads *n* ▷ **cad**
caeca *n* ▷ **caecum**
caecum [**seek**-um] *n* (*pl* **-ca**) [-ka] pouch at the beginning of the large intestine
caesium *n* (*pl* **-s**) (CHEM) silvery-white metallic element used in photocells
caesiums *n* ▷ **caesium**
café *n* (*pl* **-s**) small or inexpensive restaurant serving light refreshments
cafés *n* ▷ **café**
cafeteria *n* (*pl* **-s**) self-service restaurant
cafeterias *n* ▷ **cafeteria**
caffeine *n* (*pl* **-s**) stimulant found in tea and coffee
caffeines *n* ▷ **caffeine**
caftan *n* (*pl* **-s**) ▷ **kaftan**
caftans *n* ▷ **caftan**
cage *n* (*pl* **-s**) enclosure of bars or wires, for keeping animals or birds
caged *adj* kept in a cage
cages *n* ▷ **cage**
cagey *adj* **(cagier, cagiest)** (*Informal*) reluctant to go into details
cagier *adj* ▷ **cagey**
cagiest *adj* ▷ **cagey**
cagoule *n* (*pl* **-s**) (BRIT) lightweight hooded waterproof jacket
cagoules *n* ▷ **cagoule**
cahoots *pl n* (*Informal*) conspiring together
cairn *n* (*pl* **-s**) mound of stones erected as a memorial or marker
cairns *n* ▷ **cairn**
cajole *v* **(-les, -ling, -led)** persuade by flattery > **cajolery** *n*
cajoled *v* ▷ **cajole**
cajolery *n* ▷ **cajole**
cajoles *v* ▷ **cajole**
cajoling *v* ▷ **cajole**
cake *n* (*pl* **-s**) sweet food baked from a mixture of flour, eggs, etc. ▶ *v* **(cakes, caking, caked)** form into a hardened mass or crust
caked *v* ▷ **cake**
cakes *n, v* ▷ **cake**
caking *v* ▷ **cake**
calamine *n* (*pl* **-s**) pink powder consisting chiefly of zinc oxide, used in skin lotions and ointments
calamines *n* ▷ **calamine**
calamities *n* ▷ **calamity**
calamitous *adj* ▷ **calamity**
calamity *n* (*pl* **-ties**) disaster > **calamitous** *adj*
calcification *v* ▷ **calcify**
calcified *v* ▷ **calcify**
calcifies *v* ▷ **calcify**
calcify *v* **(-fies, -fying, -fied)** harden by the depositing of calcium salts > **calcification** *n*
calcifying *v* ▷ **calcify**
calcium *n* (*pl* **-s**) (CHEM) silvery-white metallic element found in bones, teeth, limestone, and chalk
calciums *n* ▷ **calcium**
calculable *adj* ▷ **calculate**
calculate *v* **(-lates, -lating, -lated)** solve or find out by a mathematical procedure or by reasoning > **calculable** *adj* > **calculation** *n* (*pl* **-s**)
calculated *v* ▷ **calculate**
calculates *v* ▷ **calculate**
calculating *adj* selfishly scheming ▶ *v* ▷ **calculate**
calculation *n* ▷ **calculate**
calculations *n* ▷ **calculate**
calculator *n* (*pl* **-s**) small electronic device for making calculations
calculators *n* ▷ **calculator**
calculus *n* (*pl* **-es**) branch of mathematics dealing with infinitesimal changes to a variable number or quantity
calculuses *n* ▷ **calculus**
calendar *n* (*pl* **-s**) chart showing a year divided up into months, weeks, and days
calendars *n* ▷ **calendar**
calendula *n* (*pl* **-s**) marigold
calendulas *n* ▷ **calendula**
calf[1] *n* (*pl* **calves**) young cow, bull, elephant, whale, or seal
calf[2] *n* (*pl* **calves**) back of the leg between the ankle and knee
calibrate *v* **(-brates, -brating, -brated)** mark the scale or check the accuracy of (a measuring instrument) > **calibration** *n* (*pl* **-s**)
calibrated *v* ▷ **calibrate**
calibrates *v* ▷ **calibrate**
calibrating *v* ▷ **calibrate**

calibration *n* ▷ **calibrate**
calibrations *n* ▷ **calibrate**
calibre *n* (*pl* **-s**) person's ability or worth
calibres *n* ▷ **calibre**
calico *n* (*pl* **-coes**) white cotton fabric
calicoes *n* ▷ **calico**
caliph *n* (*pl* **-s**) (HIST) Muslim ruler
caliphs *n* ▷ **caliph**
call *v* (**-s, -ing, -ed**) name ▶ *n* (*pl* **-s**) cry, shout > **caller** *n* (*pl* **-s**)
called *v* ▷ **call**
caller *n* ▷ **call**
callers *n* ▷ **call**
calligrapher *n* ▷ **calligraphy**
calligraphers *n* ▷ **calligraphy**
calligraphies *n* ▷ **calligraphy**
calligraphy *n* (*pl* **-phies**) (art of) beautiful handwriting > **calligrapher** *n* (*pl* **-s**)
calling *n* (*pl* **-s**) vocation, profession ▶ *v* ▷ **call**
callings *n* ▷ **calling**
calliper *n* (*pl* **-s**) metal splint for supporting the leg
callipers *n* ▷ **calliper**
callisthenics *pl n* light keep-fit exercises
callous *adj* showing no concern for other people's feelings > **callously** *adv* > **callousness** *n*
calloused *adj* (of skin) thickened and hardened
callously *adv* ▷ **callous**
callousness *adv* ▷ **callous**
callow *adj* (**-er, -est**) young and inexperienced > **callowness** *n* (*pl* **-es**)
callower *adj* ▷ **callow**
callowest *adj* ▷ **callow**
callowness *adv* ▷ **callow**
callownesses *adv* ▷ **callow**
calls *v, n* ▷ **call**
callus *n* (*pl* **-es**) area of thick hardened skin
calluses *n* ▷ **callus**
calm *adj* (**-er, -est**) not agitated or excited ▶ *n* (*pl* **-s**) peaceful state ▶ *v* (**-s, -ing, -ed**) (*often foll. by* **down**) make or become calm > **calmly** *adv* > **calmness** *n* (*pl* **-es**)
calmed *v* ▷ **calm**
calmer *adj* ▷ **calm**
calmest *adj* ▷ **calm**
calming *v* ▷ **calm**
calmly *adv* ▷ **calm**
calmness *adv* ▷ **calm**
calmnesses *adv* ▷ **calm**
calms *n, v* ▷ **calm**
calorie *n* (*pl* **-s**) unit of measurement for the energy value of food
calories *n* ▷ **calorie**
calorific *adj* of calories or heat
calumnies *n* ▷ **calumny**
calumny *n* (*pl* **-nies**) false or malicious statement
calve *v* (**calves, calving, calved**) give birth to a calf
calved *v* ▷ **calve**
calves *v* ▷ **calve** ▶ *n* ▷ **calf**[1, 2]
calving *v* ▷ **calve**
calyces *n* ▷ **calyx**
calypso *n* (*pl* **-s**) West Indian song with improvised topical lyrics
calypsos *n* ▷ **calypso**
calyx *n* (*pl* **calyxes, calyces**) outer leaves that protect a flower bud
calyxes *n* ▷ **calyx**
cam *n* (*pl* **-s**) device that converts a circular motion to a to-and-fro motion
camaraderie *n* (*pl* **-s**) comradeship
camaraderies *n* ▷ **camaraderie**
camber *n* (*pl* **-s**) slight upward curve to the centre of a surface
cambers *n* ▷ **camber**
cambric *n* (*pl* **-s**) fine white linen fabric
cambrics *n* ▷ **cambric**
camcorder *n* (*pl* **-s**) combined portable video camera and recorder
camcorders *n* ▷ **camcorder**
came *v* ▷ **come**
camel *n* (*pl* **-s**) humped mammal that can survive long periods without food or water in desert regions
camellia [kam-**meal**-ya] *n* (*pl* **-s**) evergreen ornamental shrub with white, pink, or red flowers
camellias *n* ▷ **camellia**
camels *n* ▷ **camel**
cameo *n* (*pl* **-s**) brooch or ring with a profile head carved in relief
cameos *n* ▷ **cameo**
camera *n* (*pl* **-s**) apparatus used for taking photographs or pictures for television or cinema
cameraman *n* (*pl* **-men**) man who operates a camera for television or cinema
cameramen *n* ▷ **cameraman**
cameras *n* ▷ **camera**
camiknickers *pl n* (BRIT) woman's undergarment consisting of knickers attached to a camisole
camisole *n* (*pl* **-s**) woman's bodice-like garment
camisoles *n* ▷ **camisole**
camomile *n* (*pl* **-s**) aromatic plant, used to make herbal tea
camomiles *n* ▷ **camomile**

camouflage [**kam**-moo-flahzh] *n* (*pl* **-s**) use of natural surroundings or artificial aids to conceal or disguise something ▶ *v* (**-lages, -flaging, -flaged**) conceal by camouflage
camouflaged *v* ▷ **camouflage**
camouflages *n, v* ▷ **camouflage**
camouflaging *v* ▷ **camouflage**
camp¹ *n* (*pl* **-s**) (place for) temporary lodgings consisting of tents, huts, or cabins ▶ *v* (**-s, -ing, -ed**) stay in a camp > **camper** *n* (*pl* **-s**)
camp² *adj* (**-er, -est**) (*Informal*) effeminate or homosexual
campaign *n* (*pl* **-s**) series of coordinated activities designed to achieve a goal ▶ *v* (**-s, -ing, -ed**) take part in a campaign
campaigned *v* ▷ **campaign**
campaigning *v* ▷ **campaign**
campaigns *n, v* ▷ **campaign**
campanologies *n* ▷ **campanology**
campanology *n* (*pl* **-gies**) art of ringing bells
campanula *n* (*pl* **-s**) plant with blue or white bell-shaped flowers
campanulas *n* ▷ **campanula**
camped *v* ▷ **camp¹**
camper *n* ▷ **camp¹** ▶ *adj* ▷ **camp²**
campers *n* ▷ **camp¹**
campest *adj* ▷ **camp²**
camphor *n* (*pl* **-s**) aromatic crystalline substance used medicinally and in mothballs
camphors *n* ▷ **camphor**
camping *v* ▷ **camp¹**
campion *n* (*pl* **-s**) red, pink, or white wild flower
campions *n* ▷ **campion**
camps *n, v* ▷ **camp¹**
campus *n* (*pl* **-es**) grounds of a university or college
campuses *n* ▷ **campus**
cams *n* ▷ **cam**
camshaft *n* (*pl* **-s**) part of an engine consisting of a rod to which cams are fixed
camshafts *n* ▷ **camshaft**
can¹ *v* (*past* **could**) be able to
can² *n* (*pl* **-s**) metal container for food or liquids ▶ *v* (**cans, canning, canned**) put (something) into a can
canal *n* (*pl* **-s**) artificial waterway
canals *n* ▷ **canal**
canapé [**kan**-nap-pay] *n* (*pl* **-s**) small piece of bread or toast with a savoury topping
canapés *n* ▷ **canapé**
canaries *n* ▷ **canary**
canary *n* (*pl* **-ries**) small yellow songbird often kept as a pet
canasta *n* (*pl* **-s**) card game like rummy, played with two packs
canastas *n* ▷ **canasta**
cancan *n* (*pl* **-s**) lively high-kicking dance performed by a female group
cancans *n* ▷ **cancan**
cancel *v* (**-cels, -celling, -celled**) stop (something that has been arranged) from taking place > **cancellation** *n* (*pl* **-s**)
cancellation *n* ▷ **cancel**
cancellations *n* ▷ **cancel**
cancelled *v* ▷ **cancel**
cancelling *v* ▷ **cancel**
cancels *v* ▷ **cancel**
cancer *n* (*pl* **-s**) serious disease resulting from a malignant growth or tumour > **cancerous** *adj*
cancerous *adj* ▷ **cancer**
cancers *n* ▷ **cancer**
candela [kan-**dee**-la] *n* (*pl* **-s**) unit of luminous intensity
candelabra *n* ▷ **candelabrum**
candelabrum *n* (*pl* **-bra**) large branched candle holder
candelas *n* ▷ **candela**
candid *adj* (**-er, -est**) honest and straightforward > **candidly** *adv* > **candidness** *n* (*pl* **-es**)
candidacies *n* ▷ **candidate**
candidacy *n* ▷ **candidate**
candidate *n* (*pl* **-s**) person seeking a job or position > **candidacy** (*pl* **-acies**), **candidature** *n* (*pl* **-s**)
candidates *n* ▷ **candidate**
candidature *n* ▷ **candidate**
candidatures *n* ▷ **candidate**
candider *adj* ▷ **candid**
candidest *adj* ▷ **candid**
candidly *adv* ▷ **candid**
candidness *n* ▷ **candid**
candidnesses *n* ▷ **candid**
candied *adj* coated with sugar
candies *n* ▷ **candy**
candle *n* (*pl* **-s**) stick of wax enclosing a wick, which is burned to produce light
candles *n* ▷ **candle**
candlestick *n* (*pl* **-s**) holder for a candle
candlesticks *n* ▷ **candlestick**
candlewick *n* (*pl* **-s**) cotton fabric with a tufted surface
candlewicks *n* ▷ **candlewick**
candour *n* (*pl* **-s**) honesty and straightforwardness
candours *n* ▷ **candour**
candy *n* (*pl* **-dies**) (US) sweet or sweets
candyfloss *n* (*pl* **-es**) light fluffy mass of spun sugar on a stick

candyflosses *n* ▷ **candyfloss**
cane *n* (*pl* **-s**) stem of the bamboo or similar plant ▶ *v* (**canes, caning, caned**) beat with a cane
caned *v* ▷ **cane**
canes *n, v* ▷ **cane**
canine *adj* of or like a dog ▶ *n* (*pl* **-s**) sharp pointed tooth between the incisors and the molars
canines *n* ▷ **canine**
caning *v* ▷ **cane**
canister *n* (*pl* **-s**) metal container
canisters *n* ▷ **canister**
canker *n* (*pl* **-s**) ulceration, ulcerous disease
cankers *n* ▷ **canker**
cannabis *n* (*pl* **-es**) Asian plant with tough fibres
cannabises *n* ▷ **cannabis**
canned *adj* preserved in a can ▶ *v* ▷ **can²**
cannelloni *pl n* tubular pieces of pasta filled with meat etc.
canneries *n* ▷ **cannery**
cannery *n* (*pl* **-ries**) factory where food is canned
cannibal *n* (*pl* **-s**) person who eats human flesh > **cannibalism** *n*
cannibalize *v* (**-lizes, -lizing, -lized**) use parts from (one machine) to repair another
cannibalized *v* ▷ **cannibalize**
cannibalizes *v* ▷ **cannibalize**
cannibalizing *v* ▷ **cannibalize**
cannibals *n* ▷ **cannibal**
cannier *adj* ▷ **canny**
canniest *adj* ▷ **canny**
cannily *adv* ▷ **canny**
canning *v* ▷ **can²**
cannon *n* (*pl* **-s**) large gun on wheels
cannonade *n* (*pl* **-s**) continuous heavy gunfire
cannonades *n* ▷ **cannonade**
cannonball *n* (*pl* **-s**) heavy metal ball fired from a cannon
cannonballs *n* ▷ **cannonball**
cannons *n* ▷ **cannon**
cannot *v* can not
canny *adj* (**-nier, -niest**) shrewd, cautious > **cannily** *adv*
canoe *n* (*pl* **-s**) light narrow open boat propelled by a paddle or paddles > **canoeist** *n* (*pl* **-s**)
canoeing *n* sport of rowing in a canoe
canoeist *n* ▷ **canoe**
canoeists *n* ▷ **canoe**
canoes *n* ▷ **canoe**
canon¹ *n* (*pl* **-s**) priest serving in a cathedral
canon² *n* (*pl* **-s**) Church decree regulating morals or religious practices > **canonical** *adj*
canonical *adj* ▷ **canon²**
canonization *n* ▷ **canonize**
canonizations *n* ▷ **canonize**
canonize *v* (**-izes, -izing, -ized**) declare (a person) officially to be a saint > **canonization** *n* (*pl* **-s**)
canonized *v* ▷ **canonize**
canonizes *v* ▷ **canonize**
canonizing *v* ▷ **canonize**
canons *n* ▷ **canon¹, ²**
canoodle *v* (**-les, -ling, -led**) (*Slang*) kiss and cuddle
canoodled *v* ▷ **canoodle**
canoodles *v* ▷ **canoodle**
canoodling *v* ▷ **canoodle**
canopied *adj* covered with a canopy
canopies *n* ▷ **canopy**
canopy *n* (*pl* **-pies**) covering above a bed, door, etc
cans *n, v* ▷ **can²**
cant¹ *n* (*pl* **-s**) insincere talk
cant² *n* (*pl* **-s**) tilted position ▶ *v* (**-s, -ing, -ed**) tilt, overturn
cantaloupe, cantaloup *n* (*pl* **-s**) kind of melon with sweet orange flesh
cantaloupes *n* ▷ **cantaloupe**
cantaloups *n* ▷ **cantaloupe**
cantankerous *adj* quarrelsome, bad-tempered
cantata *n* (*pl* **-s**) musical work consisting of arias, duets, and choruses
cantatas *n* ▷ **cantata**
canted *v* ▷ **cant²**
canteen *n* (*pl* **-s**) restaurant attached to a workplace or school
canteens *n* ▷ **canteen**
canter *n* (*pl* **-s**) horse's gait between a trot and a gallop ▶ *v* (**-s, -ing, -ed**) move at a canter
cantered *v* ▷ **canter**
cantering *v* ▷ **canter**
canters *n, v* ▷ **canter**
canticle *n* (*pl* **-s**) short hymn with words from the Bible
canticles *n* ▷ **canticle**
cantilever *n* (*pl* **-s**) beam or girder fixed at one end only
cantilevers *n* ▷ **cantilever**
canting *v* ▷ **cant²**
canto *n* (*pl* **-s**) main division of a long poem
canton *n* (*pl* **-s**) political division of a country, esp. Switzerland
cantons *n* ▷ **canton**
cantor *n* (*pl* **-s**) man employed to lead services in a synagogue

cantors *n* ▷ **cantor**
cantos *n* ▷ **canto**
cants *n* ▷ **cant**[1,2] ▶ *v* ▷ **cant**[2]
canvas *n* (*pl* **-es**) heavy coarse cloth used for sails and tents, and for oil painting
canvases *n* ▷ **canvas**
canvass *v* (**-es, -ing, -ed**) try to get votes or support (from) ▶ *n* (*pl* **-es**) canvassing
canvassed *v* ▷ **canvass**
canvasses *v, n* ▷ **canvass**
canvassing *v* ▷ **canvass**
canyon *n* (*pl* **-s**) deep narrow valley
canyons *n* ▷ **canyon**
cap *n* (*pl* **-s**) soft close-fitting covering for the head ▶ *v* (**caps, capping, capped**) cover or top with something
capabilities *n* ▷ **capable**
capability *n* ▷ **capable**
capable *adj* (*foll. by* **of**) having the ability (for) > **capably** *adv* > **capability** *n* (*pl* **-ties**)
capably *adv* ▷ **capable**
capacious *adj* roomy
capacitance *n* (*pl* **-s**) (measure of) the ability of a system to store electrical charge
capacitances *n* ▷ **capacit**
capacities *n* ▷ **capacity**
capacitor *n* (*pl* **-s**) device for storing electrical charge
capacitors *n* ▷ **capacitor**
capacity *n* (*pl* **-ties**) ability to contain, absorb, or hold
caparisoned *adj* magnificently decorated
cape[1] *n* (*pl* **-s**) short cloak
cape[2] *n* (*pl* **-s**) large piece of land that juts out into the sea
caper *n* (*pl* **-s**) high-spirited prank ▶ *v* (**-s, -ing, -ed**) skip about
capercaillie, capercailzie [kap-per-**kale**-yee] *n* (*pl* **-s**) large black European grouse
capercaillies *n* ▷ **capercaillie**
capercailzie *n* ▷ **capercaillie**
capercailzies *n* ▷ **capercaillie**
capered *v* ▷ **caper**
capering *v* ▷ **caper**
capers *pl n* pickled flower buds of a Mediterranean shrub used in sauces ▶ *n* ▷ **caper** ▶ *v* ▷ **caper**
capes *n* ▷ **cape**[1,2]
capillaries *n* ▷ **capillary**
capillary *n* (*pl* **-laries**) very fine blood vessel
capital[1] *n* (*pl* **-s**) chief city of a country ▶ *adj* involving or punishable by death
capital[2] *n* (*pl* **-s**) top part of a pillar
capitalism *n* (*pl* **-s**) economic system based on the private ownership of industry
capitalisms *n* ▷ **capitalism**
capitalist *adj* of capitalists or capitalism ▶ *n* (*pl* **-s**) supporter of capitalism > **capitalistic** *adj*
capitalistic *adj* ▷ **capitalist**
capitalists *n* ▷ **capitalist**
capitalize *v* (**-lizes, -lizing, -lized**) write or print (words) in capitals
capitalized *v* ▷ **capitalize**
capitalizes *v* ▷ **capitalize**
capitalizing *v* ▷ **capitalize**
capitals *n* ▷ **capital**[1,2]
capitation *n* (*pl* **-s**) tax of a fixed amount per person
capitations *n* ▷ **capitation**
capitulate *v* (**-lates, -lating, -lated**) surrender on agreed terms > **capitulation** *n* (*pl* **-s**)
capitulated *v* ▷ **capitulate**
capitulates *v* ▷ **capitulate**
capitulating *v* ▷ **capitulate**
capitulation *n* ▷ **capitulate**
capitulations *n* ▷ **capitulate**
capon *n* (*pl* **-s**) castrated cock fowl fattened for eating
capons *n* ▷ **capon**
capped *v* ▷ **cap**
capping *v* ▷ **cap**
cappuccino [kap-poo-**cheen**-oh] *n* (*pl* **-s**) coffee with steamed milk, sprinkled with powdered chocolate
cappuccinos *n* ▷ **cappuccino**
caprice [kap-**reess**] *n* (*pl* **-s**) sudden change of attitude
caprices *n* ▷ **caprice**
capricious *adj* tending to have sudden changes of attitude > **capriciously** *adv*
capriciously *adv* ▷ **capricious**
caps *n, v* ▷ **cap**
capsicum *n* (*pl* **-s**) kind of pepper used as a vegetable or as a spice
capsicums *n* ▷ **capsicum**
capsize *v* (**-sizes, -sizing, -sized**) (of a boat) overturn accidentally
capsized *v* ▷ **capsize**
capsizes *v* ▷ **capsize**
capsizing *v* ▷ **capsize**
capstan *n* (*pl* **-s**) rotating cylinder round which a ship's rope is wound
capstans *n* ▷ **capstan**
capsule *n* (*pl* **-s**) soluble gelatine case containing a dose of medicine
capsules *n* ▷ **capsule**
captain *n* (*pl* **-s**) commander of a ship or civil aircraft ▶ *v* (**-s, -ing, -ed**) be captain of > **captaincy** *n* (*pl* **-cies**)
captaincies *n* ▷ **captain**

captaincy *n* ▷ **captain**
captained *v* ▷ **captain**
captaining *v* ▷ **captain**
captains *n, v* ▷ **captain**
caption *n* (*pl* **-s**) title or explanation accompanying an illustration ▶ *v* (**-s, -ing, -ed**) provide with a caption
captioned *v* ▷ **caption**
captioning *v* ▷ **caption**
captions *n, v* ▷ **caption**
captious *adj* tending to make trivial criticisms > **captiously** *adv* > **captiousness** *n*
captiously *adv* ▷ **captious**
captiousness *n* ▷ **captious**
captivate *v* (**-ates, -ating, -ated**) attract and hold the attention of > **captivating** *adj*
captivated *v* ▷ **captivate**
captivates *v* ▷ **captivate**
captivating *adj, v* ▷ **captivate**
captive *n* (*pl* **-s**) person kept in confinement ▶ *adj* kept in confinement > **captivity** *n*
captives *n* ▷ **captive**
captivity *n* ▷ **captive**
captor *n* (*pl* **-s**) person who captures a person or animal
captors *n* ▷ **captor**
capture *v* (**-tures, -turing, -tured**) take by force ▶ *n* (*pl* **-s**) capturing
captured *v* ▷ **capture**
captures *v, n* ▷ **capture**
capturing *v* ▷ **capture**
car *n* (*pl* **-s**) motor vehicle designed to carry a small number of people
carafe [kar-**raff**] *n* (*pl* **-s**) glass bottle for serving water or wine
carafes *n* ▷ **carafe**
caramel *n* (*pl* **-s**) chewy sweet made from sugar and milk
caramelize *v* (**-izes, -izing, -ized**) turn into caramel
caramelized *v* ▷ **caramelize**
caramelizes *v* ▷ **caramelize**
caramelizing *v* ▷ **caramelize**
caramels *n* ▷ **caramel**
carapace *n* (*pl* **-s**) hard upper shell of tortoises and crustaceans
carapaces *n* ▷ **carapace**
carat *n* (*pl* **-s**) unit of weight of precious stones
carats *n* ▷ **carat**
caravan *n* (*pl* **-s**) large enclosed vehicle for living in, designed to be towed by a car or horse
caravans *n* ▷ **caravan**
caraway *n* (*pl* **-s**) plant whose seeds are used as a spice
caraways *n* ▷ **caraway**
carbide *n* (*pl* **-s**) compound of carbon with a metal
carbides *n* ▷ **carbide**
carbine *n* (*pl* **-s**) light automatic rifle
carbines *n* ▷ **carbine**
carbohydrate *n* (*pl* **-s**) any of a large group of energy-producing compounds in food, such as sugars and starches
carbohydrates *n* ▷ **carbohydrate**
carbon *n* (*pl* **-s**) nonmetallic element occurring as charcoal, graphite, and diamond, found in all organic matter
carbonate *n* (*pl* **-s**) salt or ester of carbonic acid
carbonated *adj* (of a drink) containing carbon dioxide
carbonates *n* ▷ **carbonate**
carbonize *v* (**-izes, -izing, -ized**) turn into carbon as a result of heating
carbonized *v* ▷ **carbonize**
carbonizes *v* ▷ **carbonize**
carbonizing *v* ▷ **carbonize**
carbons *n* ▷ **carbon**
carbuncle *n* (*pl* **-s**) inflamed boil
carbuncles *n* ▷ **carbuncle**
carburettor *n* (*pl* **-s**) device which mixes petrol and air in an internal-combustion engine
carburettors *n* ▷ **carburettor**
carcase *n* ▷ **carcass**
carcases *n* ▷ **carcass**
carcass, carcase *n* (*pl* **-es, -es**) dead body of an animal
carcasses *n* ▷ **carcass**
carcinogen *n* (*pl* **-s**) substance that produces cancer > **carcinogenic** *adj*
carcinogenic *adj* ▷ **carcinogen**
carcinogens *n* ▷ **carcinogen**
carcinoma *n* (*pl* **-s**) malignant tumour
carcinomas *n* ▷ **carcinoma**
card *n* (*pl* **-s**) piece of thick stiff paper or cardboard used for identification, reference, or sending greetings or messages ▶ *pl* any card game, or card games in general
cardboard *n* (*pl* **-s**) thin stiff board made from paper pulp
cardboards *n* ▷ **cardboard**
cardiac *adj* of the heart
cardigan *n* (*pl* **-s**) knitted jacket
cardigans *n* ▷ **cardigan**
cardinal *n* (*pl* **-s**) any of the high-ranking clergymen of the RC Church who elect the Pope and act as his counsellors ▶ *adj* fundamentally important
cardinals *n* ▷ **cardinal**
cardiogram *n* (*pl* **-s**) electrocardiogram

cardiograms *n* ▷ **cardiogram**
cardiograph *n* (*pl* **-s**) electrocardiograph
cardiographs *n* ▷ **cardiograph**
cardiologist *n* ▷ **cardiology**
cardiologists *n* ▷ **cardiology**
cardiology *n* study of the heart and its diseases > **cardiologist** *n* (*pl* **-s**)
cardiovascular *adj* of the heart and the blood vessels
cards *n* ▷ **card**
cardsharp *n* (*pl* **-s**) professional card player who cheats
cardsharps *n* ▷ **cardsharp**
care *v* (**cares, caring, cared**) be concerned ▶ *n* (*pl* **-s**) careful attention, caution > **careful** *adj* (**-ller, -llest**) > **carefully** *adv* > **carefulness** *n* (*pl* **-es**) > **careless** *adj* > **carelessly** *adv* > **carelessness** *n*
cared *v* ▷ **care**
careen *v* (**-s, -ing, -ed**) tilt over to one side
careened *v* ▷ **careen**
careening *v* ▷ **careen**
careens *v* ▷ **careen**
career *n* (*pl* **-s**) series of jobs in a profession or occupation that a person has through their life ▶ *v* (**-s, -ing, -ed**) rush in an uncontrolled way
careered *v* ▷ **career**
careering *v* ▷ **career**
careerist *n* (*pl* **-s**) person who seeks advancement by any possible means
careerists *n* ▷ **careerist**
careers *n, v* ▷ **career**
carefree *adj* without worry or responsibility
careful *adj* ▷ **care**
carefuller *adj* ▷ **care**
carefullest *adj* ▷ **care**
carefully *adv* ▷ **care**
carefulness *n* ▷ **care**
carefulnesses *n* ▷ **care**
careless *adj* ▷ **care**
carelessly *adv* ▷ **care**
carelessness *adv* ▷ **care**
cares *v, n* ▷ **care**
caress *n* (*pl* **-es**) gentle affectionate touch or embrace ▶ *v* (**-es, -ing, -ed**) touch gently and affectionately
caressed *v* ▷ **caress**
caresses *n, v* ▷ **caress**
caressing *v* ▷ **caress**
caret [**kar**-rett] *n* (*pl* **-s**) symbol (‸) indicating a place in written or printed matter where something is to be inserted
caretaker *n* (*pl* **-s**) person employed to look after a place
caretakers *n* ▷ **caretaker**
carets *n* ▷ **caret**
careworn *adj* showing signs of worry
cargo *n* (*pl* **-es**) goods carried by a ship, aircraft, etc.
cargoes *n* ▷ **cargo**
caribou *n* (*pl* **-bou** *or* **-bous**) large N American reindeer
caribous *n* ▷ **caribou**
caricature *n* (*pl* **-s**) drawing or description of a person that exaggerates features for comic effect ▶ *v* (**-tures, -turing, -tured**) make a caricature of
caricatured *v* ▷ **caricature**
caricatures *n, v* ▷ **caricature**
caricaturing *v* ▷ **caricature**
caries [**care**-reez] *n* (*pl* **caries**) tooth decay
carillon [kar-**rill**-yon] *n* (*pl* **-s**) set of bells played by keyboard or mechanically
carillons *n* ▷ **carillon**
caring *v* ▷ **care**
cark *v* (**-s, -ing, -ed**) (AUST & NZ) (*Slang*) die
carked *v* ▷ **cark**
carking *v* ▷ **cark**
carks *v* ▷ **cark**
carmine *adj* vivid red
carnage *n* (*pl* **-s**) extensive slaughter of people
carnages *n* ▷ **carnage**
carnal *adj* of a sexual or sensual nature > **carnally** *adv*
carnally *adv* ▷ **carnal**
carnation *n* (*pl* **-s**) cultivated plant with fragrant white, pink, or red flowers
carnations *n* ▷ **carnation**
carnival *n* (*pl* **-s**) festive period with processions, music, and dancing in the street
carnivals *n* ▷ **carnival**
carnivore *n* (*pl* **-s**) meat-eating animal > **carnivorous** *adj*
carnivores *n* ▷ **carnivore**
carnivorous *adj* ▷ **carnivore**
carob *n* (*pl* **-s**) pod of a Mediterranean tree, used as a chocolate substitute
carobs *n* ▷ **carob**
carol *n* (*pl* **-s**) joyful Christmas hymn ▶ *v* (**-ls, -lling, -lled**) sing carols
carolled *v* ▷ **carol**
carolling *v* ▷ **carol**
carols *n, v* ▷ **carol**
carotid *adj, n* (*pl* **-s**) (of) either of the two arteries supplying blood to the head
carotids *n* ▷ **carotid**
carouse *v* (**-ouses, -ousing, -oused**) have a merry drinking party
caroused *v* ▷ **carouse**

carousel [kar-roo-**sell**] *n* (*pl* **-s**) revolving conveyor belt for luggage or photographic slides
carousels *n* ▷ **carousel**
carouses *v* ▷ **carouse**
carousing *v* ▷ **carouse**
carp[1] *n* (*pl* **carp**) large freshwater fish
carp[2] *v* (**-s, -ing, -ed**) complain, find fault
carped *v* ▷ **carp**[2]
carpel *n* (*pl* **-s**) female reproductive organ of a flowering plant
carpels *n* ▷ **carpel**
carpenter *n* (*pl* **-s**) person who makes or repairs wooden structures > **carpentry** *n*
carpenters *n* ▷ **carpenter**
carpentry *n* ▷ **carpenter**
carpet *n* (*pl* **-s**) heavy fabric for covering floors ▶ *v* (**-s, -ing, -ed**) cover with a carpet
carpeted *v* ▷ **carpet**
carpeting *v* ▷ **carpet**
carpets *n, v* ▷ **carpet**
carpi *n* ▷ **carpus**
carping *v* ▷ **carp**[2]
carps *v* ▷ **carp**[2]
carpus *n* (*pl* **-pi**) set of eight bones of the wrist
carriage *n* (*pl* **-s**) one of the sections of a train for passengers
carriages *n* ▷ **carriage**
carriageway *n* (*pl* **-s**) (BRIT) part of a road along which traffic passes in one direction
carriageways *n* ▷ **carriageway**
carried *v* ▷ **carry**
carrier *n* (*pl* **-s**) person or thing that carries something
carriers *n* ▷ **carrier**
carries *v* ▷ **carry**
carrion *n* (*pl* **-s**) dead and rotting flesh
carrions *n* ▷ **carrion**
carrot *n* (*pl* **-s**) long tapering orange root vegetable
carrots *n* ▷ **carrot**
carroty *adj* (of hair) reddish-orange
carry *v* (**-ries, -rying, -ried**) take from one place to another
carrying *v* ▷ **carry**
cars *n* ▷ **car**
cart *n* (*pl* **-s**) open two-wheeled horse-drawn vehicle for carrying goods or passengers ▶ *v* (**-s, -ing, -ed**) carry, usu. with some effort
carted *v* ▷ **cart**
cartel *n* (*pl* **-s**) association of competing firms formed to fix prices
cartels *n* ▷ **cartel**
carthorse *n* (*pl* **-s**) large heavily built horse
carthorses *n* ▷ **carthorse**
cartilage *n* (*pl* **-s**) strong flexible tissue forming part of the skeleton > **cartilaginous** *adj*
cartilages *n* ▷ **cartilage**
cartilaginous *n* ▷ **cartilage**
carting *v* ▷ **cart**
cartographer *n* ▷ **cartography**
cartographers *n* ▷ **cartography**
cartographic *adj* ▷ **cartography**
cartographically *adj* ▷ **cartography**
cartographies *n* ▷ **cartography**
cartography *n* (*pl* **-ies**) map making > **cartographer** *n* (*pl* **-s**) > **cartographic** *adj* > **cartographically** *adv*
carton *n* (*pl* **-s**) container made of cardboard or waxed paper
cartons *n* ▷ **carton**
cartoon *n* (*pl* **-s**) humorous or satirical drawing > **cartoonist** *n* (*pl* **-s**)
cartoonist *n* ▷ **cartoon**
cartoonists *n* ▷ **cartoon**
cartoons *n* ▷ **cartoon**
cartridge *n* (*pl* **-s**) casing containing an explosive charge and bullet for a gun
cartridges *n* ▷ **cartridge**
carts *n, v* ▷ **cart**
cartwheel *n* (*pl* **-s**) sideways somersault supported by the hands with legs outstretched
cartwheels *n* ▷ **cartwheel**
carve *v* (**carves, carving, carved**) cut to form an object > **carving** *n* (*pl* **-s**)
carved *v* ▷ **carve**
carves *v* ▷ **carve**
carving *v, n* ▷ **carve**
carvings *n* ▷ **carve**
caryatid [kar-ree-**at**-id] *n* (*pl* **-s**) supporting column in the shape of a female figure
caryatids *n* ▷ **caryatid**
casbah *n* (*pl* **-s**) citadel of a N African city
casbahs *n* ▷ **casbah**
cascade *n* (*pl* **-s**) waterfall ▶ *v* (**-cades, -cading, -caded**) flow or fall in a cascade
cascaded *v* ▷ **cascade**
cascades *n, v* ▷ **cascade**
cascading *v* ▷ **cascade**
case[1] *n* (*pl* **-s**) instance, example
case[2] *n* (*pl* **-s**) container, protective covering ▶ *v* (**cases, casing, cased**) (*Slang*) inspect (a building) with the intention of burgling it
cased *v* ▷ **case**[2]
casement *n* (*pl* **-s**) window that is hinged on one side
casements *n* ▷ **casement**
cases *n* ▷ **case**[1, 2] ▶ *v* ▷ **case**[2]

cash *n* banknotes and coins ▶ *v* (**-es, -ing, -ed**) obtain cash for
cashed *v* ▷ **cash**
cashes *v* ▷ **cash**
cashew *n* (*pl* **-s**) edible kidney-shaped nut
cashews *n* ▷ **cashew**
cashier[1] *n* (*pl* **-s**) person responsible for handling cash in a bank, shop, etc.
cashier[2] *v* (**-s, -ing, -ed**) dismiss with dishonour from the armed forces
cashiered *v* ▷ **cashier**[2]
cashiering *v* ▷ **cashier**[2]
cashiers *n* ▷ **cashier**[1] ▶ *v* ▷ **cashier**[2]
cashing *v* ▷ **cash**
cashmere *n* (*pl* **-s**) fine soft wool obtained from goats
cashmeres *n* ▷ **cashmere**
casing *n* (*pl* **-s**) protective case, covering ▶ *v* ▷ **case**[2]
casings *n* ▷ **casing**
casino *n* (*pl* **-s**) public building or room where gambling games are played
casinos *n* ▷ **casino**
cask *n* (*pl* **-s**) barrel used to hold alcoholic drink
casket *n* (*pl* **-s**) small box for valuables
caskets *n* ▷ **casket**
casks *n* ▷ **cask**
cassava *n* (*pl* **-s**) starch obtained from the roots of a tropical American plant, used to make tapioca
cassavas *n* ▷ **cassava**
casserole *n* (*pl* **-s**) covered dish in which food is cooked slowly, usu. in an oven ▶ *v* (**-oles, -oling, -oled**) cook in a casserole
casseroled *v* ▷ **casserole**
casseroles *n, v* ▷ **casserole**
casseroling *v* ▷ **casserole**
cassette *n* (*pl* **-s**) plastic case containing a reel of film or magnetic tape
cassettes *n* ▷ **cassette**
cassock *n* (*pl* **-s**) long tunic, usu. black, worn by priests
cassocks *n* ▷ **cassock**
cassowaries *n* ▷ **cassowary**
cassowary *n* (*pl* **-waries**) large flightless bird of Australia and New Guinea
cast *n* (*pl* **-s**) actors in a play or film collectively ▶ *v* (**casts, casting, cast**) select (an actor) to play a part in a play or film
castanets *pl n* musical instrument, used by Spanish dancers, consisting of curved pieces of hollow wood clicked together in the hand
castaway *n* (*pl* **-s**) shipwrecked person
castaways *n* ▷ **castaway**
caste *n* (*pl* **-s**) any of the hereditary classes into which Hindu society is divided
castellated *adj* having battlements
castes *n* ▷ **caste**
castigate *v* (**-gates, -gating, -gated**) reprimand severely > **castigation** *n*
castigated *v* ▷ **castigate**
castigates *v* ▷ **castigate**
castigating *v* ▷ **castigate**
castigation *v* ▷ **castigate**
casting *v* ▷ **cast**
castle *n* (*pl* **-s**) large fortified building, often built as a ruler's residence
castles *n* ▷ **castle**
castoff *adj, n* (*pl* **-s**) discarded (person or thing)
castoffs *n* ▷ **castoff**
castor *n* (*pl* **-s**) small swivelling wheel fixed to the bottom of a piece of furniture for easy moving
castors *n* ▷ **castor**
castrate *v* (**-tes, -ting, -ted**) remove the testicles of > **castration** *n* (*pl* **-s**)
castrated *v* ▷ **castrate**
castrates *v* ▷ **castrate**
castrating *v* ▷ **castrate**
castration *n* ▷ **castrate**
castrations *n* ▷ **castrate**
casts *n, v* ▷ **cast**
casual *adj* careless, nonchalant > **casually** *adv*
casually *adv* ▷ **casual**
casualties *n* ▷ **casualty**
casualty *n* (*pl* **-ties**) person killed or injured in an accident or war
casuarina [kass-yew-a-**reen**-a] *n* (*pl* **-s**) Australian tree with jointed green branches
casuarinas *n* ▷ **casuarina**
casuistries *n* ▷ **casuistry**
casuistry *n* (*pl* **-ries**) reasoning that is misleading or oversubtle
cat *n* (*pl* **-s**) small domesticated furry mammal
cataclysm [**kat**-a-kliz-zum] *n* (*pl* **-s**) violent upheaval > **cataclysmic** *adj*
cataclysmic *adj* ▷ **cataclysm**
cataclysms *n* ▷ **cataclysm**
catacombs [**kat**-a-koomz] *pl n* underground burial place consisting of tunnels with recesses for tombs
catafalque [**kat**-a-falk] *n* (*pl* **-s**) raised platform on which a body lies in state before or during a funeral
catafalques *n* ▷ **catafalque**
catalepsies *n* ▷ **catalepsy**
catalepsy *n* (*pl* **-sies**) trancelike state in which the body is rigid > **cataleptic** *adj*
cataleptic *adj* ▷ **catalepsy**
catalogue *n* (*pl* **-s**) book containing details of

items for sale ▶ *v* (**-logues, -loguing, -logued**) make a systematic list of
catalogued *v* ▷ **catalogue**
catalogues *n, v* ▷ **catalogue**
cataloguing *v* ▷ **catalogue**
catalyse *v* (**-lyses, -lysing, -lysed**) speed up (a chemical reaction) by a catalyst
catalysed *v* ▷ **catalyse**
catalyses *v* ▷ **catalyse**
catalysing *v* ▷ **catalyse**
catalysis *n* ▷ **catalyst**
catalyst *n* (*pl* **-s**) substance that speeds up a chemical reaction without itself changing > **catalysis** *n* > **catalytic** *adj* > **catalytically** *adv*
catalysts *n* ▷ **catalyst**
catalytic *adj* ▷ **catalyst**
catalytically *adv* ▷ **catalyst**
catamaran *n* (*pl* **-s**) boat with twin parallel hulls
catamarans *n* ▷ **catamaran**
catapult *n* (*pl* **-s**) Y-shaped device with a loop of elastic, used by children for firing stones ▶ *v* (**-s, -ing, -ed**) shoot forwards or upwards violently
catapulted *v* ▷ **catapult**
catapulting *v* ▷ **catapult**
catapults *n, v* ▷ **catapult**
cataract *n* (*pl* **-s**) eye disease in which the lens becomes opaque
cataracts *n* ▷ **cataract**
catarrh [kat-**tar**] *n* (*pl* **-s**) excessive mucus in the nose and throat, during or following a cold > **catarrhal** *adj*
catarrhal *adj* ▷ **catarrh**
catarrhs *n* ▷ **catarrh**
catastrophe [kat-**ass**-trof-fee] *n* (*pl* **-s**) great and sudden disaster > **catastrophic** *adj* > **catastrophically** *adv*
catastrophes *n* ▷ **catastrophe**
catastrophic *adj* ▷ **catastrophe**
catastrophically *adv* ▷ **catastrophe**
catcall *n* (*pl* **-s**) derisive whistle or cry
catcalls *n* ▷ **catcall**
catch *v* (**catches, catching, caught**) seize, capture ▶ *n* (*pl* **-es**) device for fastening a door, window, etc.
catches *v, n* ▷ **catch**
catchier *adj* ▷ **catchy**
catchiest *adj* ▷ **catchy**
catchily *adv* ▷ **catchy**
catchiness *n* ▷ **catchy**
catchinesses *n* ▷ **catchy**
catching *adj* infectious ▶ *v* ▷ **catch**
catchword *n* (*pl* **-s**) well-known and frequently used phrase
catchwords *n* ▷ **catchword**
catchy *adj* (**-chier, -chiest**) (of a tune) pleasant and easily remembered > **catchily** *adv* > **catchiness** *n* (*pl* **-es**)
catechism [**kat**-ti-kiz-zum] *n* (*pl* **-s**) instruction on the doctrine of a Christian Church in a series of questions and answers
catechisms *n* ▷ **catechism**
categorical *adj* absolutely clear and certain > **categorically** *adv*
categorically *adv* ▷ **categorical**
categories *n* ▷ **category**
categorization *n* ▷ **categorize**
categorizations *n* ▷ **categorize**
categorize *v* (**-izes, -izing, -ized**) put in a category > **categorization** *n* (*pl* **-s**)
categorized *v* ▷ **categorize**
categorizes *v* ▷ **categorize**
categorizing *v* ▷ **categorize**
category *n* (*pl* **-ries**) class, group
cater *v* (**-s, -ing, -ed**) provide what is needed or wanted, esp. food or services > **caterer** *n* (*pl* **-s**)
catered *v* ▷ **cater**
caterer *n* ▷ **cater**
caterers *n* ▷ **cater**
catering *v* ▷ **cater**
caterpillar *n* (*pl* **-s**) wormlike larva of a moth or butterfly
caterpillars *n* ▷ **caterpillar**
caters *v* ▷ **cater**
caterwaul *v* (**-s, -ing, -ed**) wail, yowl
caterwauled *v* ▷ **caterwaul**
caterwauling *v* ▷ **caterwaul**
caterwauls *v* ▷ **caterwaul**
catfish *n* (*pl* **catfish, catfishes**) fish with whisker-like barbels round the mouth
catfishes *n* ▷ **catfish**
catgut *n* (*pl* **-s**) strong cord used to string musical instruments and sports rackets
catguts *n* ▷ **catgut**
catharses *n* ▷ **catharsis**
catharsis [kath-**thar**-siss] *n* (*pl* **-ses**) relief of strong suppressed emotions > **cathartic** *adj*
cathartic *adj* ▷ **catharsis**
cathedral *n* (*pl* **-s**) principal church of a diocese
cathedrals *n* ▷ **cathedral**
catheter [**kath**-it-er] *n* (*pl* **-s**) tube inserted into a body cavity to drain fluid
catheters *n* ▷ **catheter**
cathode *n* (*pl* **-s**) negative electrode, by which electrons leave a circuit
cathodes *n* ▷ **cathode**
catholic *adj* (of tastes or interests) covering a wide range > **catholicism** *n* (*pl* **-s**)
catholicism *n* ▷ **catholic**

catholicisms *n* ▷ **catholic**
cation [**kat**-eye-on] *n* (*pl* **-s**) positively charged ion
cations *n* ▷ **cation**
catkin *n* (*pl* **-s**) drooping flower spike of certain trees
catkins *n* ▷ **catkin**
catnap *n* (*pl* **-s**) ▶ *v* (**-naps, -napping, -napped**) doze
catnapped *v* ▷ **catnap**
catnapping *v* ▷ **catnap**
catnaps *n, v* ▷ **catnap**
cats *n* ▷ **cat**
cattier *adj* ▷ **catty**
cattiest *adj* ▷ **catty**
cattily *adv* ▷ **catty**
cattiness *n* ▷ **catty**
cattle *pl n* domesticated cows and bulls
catty *adj* (**cattier, cattiest**) (*Informal*) spiteful > **cattily** *adv* > **cattiness** *n*
catwalk *n* (*pl* **-s**) narrow pathway or platform
catwalks *n* ▷ **catwalk**
caucus *n* (*pl* **-es**) local committee or faction of a political party
caught *v* ▷ **catch**
cauldron *n* (*pl* **-s**) large pot used for boiling
cauldrons *n* ▷ **cauldron**
cauliflower *n* (*pl* **-s**) vegetable with a large head of white flower buds surrounded by green leaves
cauliflowers *n* ▷ **cauliflower**
caulk *v* (**-s, -ing, -ed**) fill in (cracks) with paste etc.
caulked *v* ▷ **caulk**
caulking *v* ▷ **caulk**
caulks *v* ▷ **caulk**
causal *adj* of or being a cause > **causally** *adv*
causality *n* ▷ **causation**
causally *adv* ▷ **causal**
causation, causality *n* relationship of cause and effect
cause *n* (*pl* **-s**) something that produces a particular effect ▶ *v* (**causes, causing, caused**) be the cause of
caused *v* ▷ **cause**
causes *n, v* ▷ **cause**
causeway *n* (*pl* **-s**) raised path or road across water or marshland
causeways *n* ▷ **causeway**
causing *v* ▷ **cause**
caustic *adj* capable of burning by chemical action > **caustically** *adv*
caustically *adv* ▷ **caustic**
cauterize *v* (**-izes, -izing, -ized**) burn (a wound) with heat or a caustic agent to prevent infection
cauterized *v* ▷ **cauterize**
cauterizes *v* ▷ **cauterize**
cauterizing *v* ▷ **cauterize**
caution *n* (*pl* **-s**) care, esp. in the face of danger ▶ *v* (**-s, -ing, -ed**) warn, advise
cautionary *adj* warning
cautioned *v* ▷ **caution**
cautioning *v* ▷ **caution**
cautions *n, v* ▷ **caution**
cautious *adj* showing caution > **cautiously** *adv*
cautiously *adv* ▷ **cautious**
cavalcade *n* (*pl* **-s**) procession of people on horseback or in cars
cavalcades *n* ▷ **cavalcade**
cavalier *adj* showing haughty disregard ▶ *n* (*pl* **-s**) (**C-**) supporter of Charles I in the English Civil War > **cavalierly** *adv*
cavalierly *adv* ▷ **cavalier**
cavaliers *n* ▷ **cavalier**
cavalries *n* ▷ **cavalry**
cavalry *n* (*pl* **-ries**) part of the army orig. on horseback, but now often using fast armoured vehicles
cave *n* (*pl* **-s**) hollow in the side of a hill or cliff
caveat [**kav**-vee-at] *n* (*pl* **-s**) warning
caveats *n* ▷ **caveat**
caveman *n* (*pl* **-men**) prehistoric cave dweller
cavemen *n* ▷ **caveman**
cavern *n* (*pl* **-s**) large cave > **cavernous** *adj*
cavernous *adj* ▷ **cavern**
caverns *n* ▷ **cavern**
caves *n* ▷ **cave**
caviar, caviare *n* (*pl* **-s**) salted sturgeon roe, regarded as a delicacy
caviare *n* ▷ **caviar**
caviares *n* ▷ **caviar**
caviars *n* ▷ **caviar**
cavil *v* (**-ils, -illing, -illed**) make petty objections ▶ *n* (*pl* **-s**) petty objection
cavilled *v* ▷ **cavil**
cavilling *v* ▷ **cavil**
cavils *v, n* ▷ **cavil**
caving *n* sport of exploring caves
cavities *v* ▷ **cavity**
cavity *n* (*pl* **-ties**) hollow space
cavort *v* (**-s, -ing, -ed**) skip about
cavorted *v* ▷ **cavort**
cavorting *v* ▷ **cavort**
cavorts *v* ▷ **cavort**
caw *n* (*pl* **-s**) cry of a crow, rook, or raven ▶ *v* (**-s, -ing, -ed**) make this cry
cawed *v* ▷ **caw**
cawing *v* ▷ **caw**

caws *n, v* ▷ **caw**

cay *n* **(cays)**. A cay is a small low island. Cay scores 8 points.

cayman *n* (*pl* **-s**) S American reptile similar to an alligator

caymans *n* ▷ **cayman**

caz *adj*. Caz is a slang word for **casual**. It's a great word to have up your sleeve as it scores 14 points.

cazique *n* **(caziques)**. A cazique is a chief among certain American Indian tribes. Cazique scores 27 points, and will earn you a 50-point bonus if you manage to use all of your tiles to form it.

cease *v* **(ceases, ceasing, ceased)** bring or come to an end > **ceaseless** *adj* > **ceaselessly** *adv*

ceased *v* ▷ **cease**

ceasefire *n* (*pl* **-s**) temporary truce

ceasefires *n* ▷ **ceasefire**

ceaseless *adj* ▷ **cease**

ceaselessly *adv* ▷ **cease**

ceases *v* ▷ **cease**

ceasing *v* ▷ **cease**

cedar *n* (*pl* **-s**) evergreen coniferous tree

cedars *n* ▷ **cedar**

cede *v* **(cedes, ceding, ceded)** surrender (territory or legal rights)

ceded *v* ▷ **cede**

cedes *v* ▷ **cede**

cedilla *n* (*pl* **-s**) character (¸) placed under a *c* in some languages, to show that it is pronounced *s*, not *k*

cedillas *n* ▷ **cedilla**

ceding *v* ▷ **cede**

ceilidh [**kay**-lee] *n* (*pl* **-s**) informal social gathering for singing and dancing, esp. in Scotland

ceilidhs *n* ▷ **ceilidh**

ceiling *n* (*pl* **-s**) inner upper surface of a room

ceilings *n* ▷ **ceiling**

celandine *n* (*pl* **-s**) wild plant with yellow flowers

celandines *n* ▷ **celandine**

celebrant *n* (*pl* **-s**) person who performs a religious ceremony

celebrants *n* ▷ **celebrant**

celebrate *v* **(-rates, -rating, -rated)** hold festivities to mark (a happy event, anniversary, etc.) > **celebration** *n* (*pl* **-s**)

celebrated *adj* well known ▶ *v* ▷ **celebrate**

celebrates *v* ▷ **celebrate**

celebrating *v* ▷ **celebrate**

celebration *n* ▷ **celebrate**

celebrations *n* ▷ **celebrate**

celebrities *n* ▷ **celebrity**

celebrity *n* (*pl* **-rities**) famous person

celeriac [sill-**ler**-ee-ak] *n* (*pl* **-s**) variety of celery with a large turnip-like root

celeriacs *n* ▷ **celeriac**

celeries *n* ▷ **celery**

celerities *n* ▷ **celerity**

celerity [sill-**ler**-rit-tee] *n* (*pl* **-ties**) swiftness

celery *n* (*pl* **-ries**) vegetable with long green crisp edible stalks

celestial *adj* heavenly, divine > **celestially** *adv*

celestially *adv* ▷ **celestial**

celibacy *n* ▷ **celibate**

celibate *adj* unmarried or abstaining from sex, esp. because of a religious vow of chastity ▶ *n* (*pl* **-s**) celibate person > **celibacy** *n*

celibates *n* ▷ **celibate**

cell *n* (*pl* **-s**) smallest unit of an organism that is able to function independently

cellar *n* (*pl* **-s**) underground room for storage

cellars *n* ▷ **cellar**

cellist *n* ▷ **cello**

cellists *n* ▷ **cello**

cello [**chell**-oh] *n* (*pl* **-s**) large low-pitched instrument of the violin family > **cellist** *n* (*pl* **-s**)

cellophane *n* (*pl* **-s**)® thin transparent cellulose sheeting used as wrapping

cellophanes *n* ▷ **cellophane**

cellos *n* ▷ **cello**

cells *n* ▷ **cell**

cellular *adj* of or consisting of cells

celluloid *n* (*pl* **-s**) kind of plastic used to make toys and, formerly, photographic film

celluloids *n* ▷ **celluloid**

cellulose *n* (*pl* **-s**) main constituent of plant cell walls, used in making paper, plastics, etc.

celluloses *n* ▷ **cellulose**

cement *n* (*pl* **-s**) fine grey powder mixed with water and sand to make mortar or concrete ▶ *v* **(-s, -ing, -ed)** join, bind, or cover with cement

cemented *v* ▷ **cement**

cementing *v* ▷ **cement**

cements *n, v* ▷ **cement**

cemeteries *n* ▷ **cemetery**

cemetery *n* (*pl* **-ries**) place where dead people are buried

cenotaph *n* (*pl* **-s**) monument honouring soldiers who died in a war

cenotaphs *n* ▷ **cenotaph**

censer *n* (*pl* **-s**) container for burning incense

censers *n* ▷ **censer**

censor *n* (*pl* **-s**) person authorized to examine

films, books, etc., to ban or cut anything considered obscene or objectionable ▶ *v* (**-s, -ing, -ed**) ban or cut parts of (a film, book, etc.) > **censorship** *n*
censored *v* ▷ **censor**
censoring *v* ▷ **censor**
censorious *adj* harshly critical > **censoriously** *adv*
censoriously *adv* ▷ **censorious**
censors *n, v* ▷ **censor**
censorship *n* ▷ **censor**
censure *n* (*pl* **-s**) severe disapproval ▶ *v* (**-sures, -suring, -sured**) criticize severely
censured *v* ▷ **censure**
censures *n, v* ▷ **censure**
censuring *v* ▷ **censure**
census *n* (*pl* **-es**) official count of a population
censuses *n* ▷ **census**
cent *n* (*pl* **-s**) hundredth part of a monetary unit such as the dollar or euro
centaur *n* (*pl* **-s**) mythical creature with the head, arms, and torso of a man, and the lower body and legs of a horse
centaurs *n* ▷ **centaur**
centenarian *n* (*pl* **-s**) person at least 100 years old
centenarians *n* ▷ **centenarian**
centenaries *n* ▷ **centenary**
centenary [sen-**teen**-a-ree] *n* (CHIEFLY BRIT) (*pl* **-naries**) 100th anniversary or its celebration
centennial *n* (*pl* **-s**) 100th anniversary or its celebration
centennials *n* ▷ **centennial**
centigrade *adj* of the temperature in which water freezes at 0° and boils at 100°
centigram, centigramme *n* (*pl* **-s**) one hundredth of a gram
centigramme *n* ▷ **centigram**
centigrammes *n* ▷ **centigram**
centigrams *n* ▷ **centigram**
centilitre *n* (*pl* **-s**) one hundredth of a litre
centilitres *n* ▷ **centilitre**
centimetre *n* (*pl* **-s**) one hundredth of a metre
centimetres *n* ▷ **centimetre**
centipede *n* (*pl* **-s**) small wormlike creature with many legs
centipedes *n* ▷ **centipede**
central *adj* of, at, or forming the centre > **centrally** *adv* > **centrality** *n*
centralism *n* principle of central control of a country or organization > **centralist** *n* (*pl* **-s**)
centralist *n* ▷ **centralism**
centralists *n* ▷ **centralism**
centrality *n* ▷ **central**
centralization *n* ▷ **centralize**
centralizations *n* ▷ **centralize**
centralize *v* (**-izes, -izing, -ized**) bring under central control > **centralization** *n* (*pl* **-s**)
centralized *v* ▷ **centralize**
centralizes *v* ▷ **centralize**
centralizing *v* ▷ **centralize**
centrally *adv* ▷ **central**
centre *n* (*pl* **-s**) middle point or part (SPORT) ▶ *v* (**centres, centring, centred**) put in the centre of something
centred *v* ▷ **centre**
centres *n, v* ▷ **centre**
centrifugal *adj* moving away from a centre > **centrifugally** *adv*
centrifugally *adv* ▷ **centrifugal**
centrifuge *n* (*pl* **-s**) machine that separates substances by centrifugal force
centrifuges *n* ▷ **centrifuge**
centring *v* ▷ **centre**
centripetal *adj* moving towards a centre > **centripetally** *adv*
centripetally *adv* ▷ **centripetal**
centrist *n* (*pl* **-s**) person favouring political moderation
centrists *n* ▷ **centrist**
cents *n* ▷ **cent**
centuries *n* ▷ **century**
centurion *n* (*pl* **-s**) (in ancient Rome) officer commanding 100 men
centurions *n* ▷ **centurion**
century *n* (*pl* **-ries**) period of 100 years
cep *n* (**ceps**). A cep is an edible fungus. Cep scores 7 points.
cephalopod [**seff**-a-loh-pod] *n* (*pl* **-s**) sea mollusc with a head and tentacles, such as the octopus
cephalopods *n* ▷ **cephalopod**
ceramic *n* (*pl* **-s**) hard brittle material made by heating clay to a very high temperature ▶ *pl* art of producing ceramic objects ▶ *adj* made of ceramic
ceramics *n* ▷ **ceramic**
cereal *n* (*pl* **-s**) grass plant with edible grain, such as oat or wheat
cereals *n* ▷ **cereal**
cerebra *n* ▷ **cerebrum**
cerebral [**ser**-rib-ral, ser-**reeb**-ral] *adj* of the brain
cerebrum [**serr**-rib-rum] *n* (*pl* **-brums, -bra**) [-bra] main part of the brain
cerebrums *n* ▷ **cerebrum**
ceremonial *adj* ▷ **ceremony**
ceremonially *adv* ▷ **ceremony**
ceremonials *n* ▷ **ceremony**
ceremonies *n* ▷ **ceremony**
ceremonious *adj* excessively polite or formal

> **ceremoniously** *adv*
ceremoniously *adv* ▷ **ceremonious**
ceremony *n* (*pl* **-nies**) formal act or ritual
> **ceremonial** *adj, n* (*pl* **-s**) > **ceremonially** *adv*
cerise [ser-**reess**] *adj* cherry-red
certain *adj* (**-er, -est**) positive and confident
> **certainly** *adv*
certainer *adj* ▷ **certain**
certainest *adj* ▷ **certain**
certainly *adv* ▷ **certain**
certainties *n* ▷ **certainty**
certainty *n* (*pl* **-ties**) state of being sure
certifiable *adj* considered legally insane
> **certifiably** *adv*
certifiably *n* ▷ **certifiable**
certificate *n* (*pl* **-s**) official document stating the details of a birth, academic course, etc.
certificates *n* ▷ **certificate**
certification *n* ▷ **certify**
certifications *n* ▷ **certify**
certified *v* ▷ **certify**
certifies *v* ▷ **certify**
certify *v* (**-fies, -fying, -fied**) confirm, attest to
> **certification** *n* (*pl* **-s**)
certifying *v* ▷ **certify**
certitude *n* (*pl* **-s**) confidence, certainty
certitudes *n* ▷ **certitude**
cervical *adj* ▷ **cervix**
cervices *n* ▷ **cervix**
cervix *n* (*pl* **cervixes, cervices**) narrow entrance of the womb > **cervical** *adj*
cervixes *n* ▷ **cervix**
cessation *n* (*pl* **-s**) ceasing
cessations *n* ▷ **cessation**
cesspit, cesspool *n* (*pl* **-s**) covered tank or pit for sewage
cesspits *n* ▷ **cesspit**
cesspool *n* ▷ **cesspit**
cesspools *n* ▷ **cesspit**
cetacean [sit-**tay**-shun] *n* (*pl* **-s**) fish-shaped sea mammal such as a whale or dolphin
cetaceans *n* ▷ **cetacean**

ch *pron*. This is an old dialect form of **I**. It's the only two-letter word that can be formed with the letter C, and it's a good word to remember because it doesn't use any vowels. Ch scores 7 points.
cha *n* (**chas**). Cha is a slang word for **tea**. Cha scores 8 points.

chafe *v* (**chafes, chafing, chafed**) make sore or worn by rubbing
chafed *v* ▷ **chafe**
chafes *v* ▷ **chafe**
chaff[1] *n* (*pl* **-s**) grain husks
chaff[2] *v* (**-s, -ing, -ed**) (*Old-fashioned*) tease good-naturedly
chaffed *v* ▷ **chaff**[2]
chaffinch *n* (*pl* **-es**) small European songbird
chaffinches *n* ▷ **chaffinch**
chaffing *v* ▷ **chaff**[2]
chaffs *n* ▷ **chaff**[1] ▶ *v* ▷ **chaff**[2]
chafing *v* ▷ **chafe**
chagrin [**shag**-grin] *n* (*pl* **-s**) annoyance and disappointment
chagrined *adj* annoyed and disappointed
chagrins *n* ▷ **chagrin**
chain *n* (*pl* **-s**) flexible length of connected metal links ▶ *v* (**-s, -ing, -ed**) restrict or fasten with or as if with a chain
chained *v* ▷ **chain**
chaining *v* ▷ **chain**
chains *n, v* ▷ **chain**
chair *n* (*pl* **-s**) seat with a back, for one person ▶ *v* (**-s, -ing, -ed**) preside over (a meeting)
chaired *v* ▷ **chair**
chairing *v* ▷ **chair**
chairlift (*pl* **-s**) series of chairs suspended from a moving cable for carrying people up a slope
chairlifts *n* ▷ **chairlift**
chairman, chairwoman *n* (*pl* **-men, -women**) person in charge of a company's board of directors or a meeting (*also* **chairperson**) (*pl* **-s**)
chairmen *n* ▷ **chairman**
chairperson *n* ▷ **chairman**
chairpersons *n* ▷ **chairman**
chairs *n, v* ▷ **chair**
chairwoman *n* ▷ **chairman**
chairwomen *n* ▷ **chairman**
chaise [**shaze**] *n* (*pl* **-s**) (HIST) light horse-drawn carriage
chaises *n* ▷ **chaise**
chalcedonies *n* ▷ **chalcedony**
chalcedony [kal-**sed**-don-ee] *n* (*pl* **-nies**) variety of quartz
chalet *n* (*pl* **-s**) kind of Swiss wooden house with a steeply sloping roof
chalets *n* ▷ **chalet**
chalice *n* (*pl* **-s**) large goblet
chalices *n* ▷ **chalice**
chalk *n* (*pl* **-s**) soft white rock consisting of calcium carbonate ▶ *v* (**-s, -ing, -ed**) draw or mark with chalk > **chalky** *adj* (**-kier, -kiest**)
chalked *v* ▷ **chalk**
chalkier *adj* ▷ **chalk**
chalkiest *adj* ▷ **chalk**
chalking *v* ▷ **chalk**
chalks *n, v* ▷ **chalk**
chalky *adj* ▷ **chalk**

challenge *n* (*pl* **-s**) demanding or stimulating situation ▶ *v* (**-ges, -ging, -ged**) issue a challenge to > **challenger** *n* (*pl* **-s**)
challenged *adj* disabled as specified ▶ *v* ▷ **challenge**
challenger *n* ▷ **challenge**
challengers *n* ▷ **challenge**
challenges *n*, *v* ▷ **challenge**
challenging *v* ▷ **challenge**
chamber *n* (*pl* **-s**) hall used for formal meetings (*Old-fashioned*) ▶ *pl* set of rooms used as offices by a barrister
chamberlain *n* (*pl* **-s**) (HIST) officer who managed the household of a king or nobleman
chamberlains *n* ▷ **chamberlain**
chambermaid *n* (*pl* **-s**) woman employed to clean bedrooms in a hotel
chambermaids *n* ▷ **chambermaid**
chambers *n* ▷ **chamber**
chameleon [kam-**meal**-yon] *n* (*pl* **-s**) small lizard that changes colour to blend in with its surroundings
chameleons *n* ▷ **chameleon**
chamfer [**cham**-fer] *v* (**-s, -ing, -ed**) bevel the edge of
chamfered *v* ▷ **chamfer**
chamfering *v* ▷ **chamfer**
chamfers *v* ▷ **chamfer**
chamois [**sham**-wah] *n* (*pl* **-ois**) small mountain antelope
chamomile [**kam**-mo-mile] *n* (*pl* **-s**) ▷ **camomile**
chamomiles *n* ▷ **chamomile**
champ¹ *v* (**-s, -ing, -ed**) chew noisily
champ² *n* (*pl* **-s**) ▷ **champion**
champagne *n* (*pl* **-s**) sparkling white French wine
champagnes *n* ▷ **champagne**
champed *v* ▷ **champ¹**
champing *v* ▷ **champ¹**
champion *n* (*pl* **-s**) overall winner of a competition (*foll. by* **of**) ▶ *v* (**-s, -ing, -ed**) support ▶ *adj* (*Dialect*) excellent > **championship** *n* (*pl* **-s**)
championed *v* ▷ **champion**
championing *v* ▷ **champion**
champions *n*, *v* ▷ **champion**
championship *n* ▷ **champion**
championships *n* ▷ **champion**
champs *v* ▷ **champ¹** ▶ *n* ▷ **champ²**
chance *n* (*pl* **-s**) likelihood, probability ▶ *v* (**chances, chancing, chanced**) risk, hazard
chanced *v* ▷ **chance**
chancel *n* (*pl* **-s**) part of a church containing the altar and choir
chancellor *n* (*pl* **-s**) head of government in some European countries > **chancellorship** *n* (*pl* **-s**)
chancellors *n* ▷ **chancellor**
chancellorship *n* ▷ **chancellor**
chancellorships *n* ▷ **chancellor**
chancels *n* ▷ **chancel**
chances *n*, *v* ▷ **chance**
chancier *adj* ▷ **chancy**
chanciest *adj* ▷ **chancy**
chancing *v* ▷ **chance**
chancy *adj* (**-cier, -ciest**) uncertain, risky
chandelier [shan-dill-**eer**] *n* (*pl* **-s**) ornamental light with branches and holders for several candles or bulbs
chandeliers *n* ▷ **chandelier**
chandler *n* (*pl* **-s**) dealer, esp. in ships' supplies
chandlers *n* ▷ **chandler**
change *n* (*pl* **-s**) becoming different ▶ *v* (**changes, changing, changed**) make or become different
changeable *adj* changing often
changed *v* ▷ **change**
changeling *n* (*pl* **-s**) child believed to have been exchanged by fairies for another
changelings *n* ▷ **changeling**
changes *n*, *v* ▷ **change**
changing *v* ▷ **change**
channel *n* (*pl* **-s**) band of broadcasting frequencies ▶ *v* (**-nels, -nelling, -nelled**) direct or convey through a channel
channelled *v* ▷ **channel**
channelling *v* ▷ **channel**
channels *n*, *v* ▷ **channel**
chant *v* (**-s, -ing, -ed**) utter or sing (a slogan or psalm) ▶ *n* (*pl* **-s**) rhythmic or repetitious slogan
chanted *v* ▷ **chant**
chanter *n* (*pl* **-s**) (on bagpipes) pipe on which the melody is played
chanters *n* ▷ **chanter**
chanting *v* ▷ **chant**
chants *v*, *n* ▷ **chant**
chaos *n* complete disorder or confusion > **chaotic** *adj* > **chaotically** *adv*
chaotic *adj* ▷ **chaos**
chaotically *adv* ▷ **chaos**
chap *n* (*pl* **-s**) (*Informal*) man or boy
chapati, chapatti *n* (*pl* **-s**) (in Indian cookery) flat thin unleavened bread
chapatis *n* ▷ **chapati**
chapatti *n* ▷ **chapati**
chapattis *n* ▷ **chapati**
chapel *n* (*pl* **-s**) place of worship with its own altar, within a church

chapels *n* ▷ **chapel**
chaperone [**shap**-per-rone] *n* (*pl* **-s**) older person who accompanies and supervises a young person or young people on a social occasion ▸ *v* (**-ones, -oning, -oned**) act as a chaperone to
chaperoned *v* ▷ **chaperone**
chaperones *n, v* ▷ **chaperone**
chaperoning *v* ▷ **chaperone**
chaplain *n* (*pl* **-s**) clergyman attached to a chapel, military body, or institution > **chaplaincy** *n* (*pl* **-cies**)
chaplaincies *n* ▷ **chaplain**
chaplaincy *n* ▷ **chaplain**
chaplains *n* ▷ **chaplain**
chaplet *n* (*pl* **-s**) garland for the head
chaplets *n* ▷ **chaplet**
chapped *adj* (of the skin) raw and cracked, through exposure to cold
chaps *n* ▷ **chap**
chapter *n* (*pl* **-s**) division of a book
chapters *n* ▷ **chapter**
char[1] *v* (**chars, charring, charred**) blacken by partial burning
char[2] (BRIT) (*Informal*) *n* (*pl* **-s**) charwoman ▸ *v* (**chars, charring, charred**) clean other people's houses as a job
char[3] *n* (BRIT) (*Old-fashioned slang*) tea
charabanc [**shar**-rab-bang] *n* (*pl* **-s**) (*Old-fashioned*) coach for sightseeing
charabancs *n* ▷ **charabanc**
character *n* (*pl* **-s**) combination of qualities distinguishing a person, group, or place
characteristic *n* (*pl* **-s**) distinguishing feature or quality ▸ *adj* typical > **characteristically** *adv*
characteristically *n* ▷ **characteristic**
characteristics *n* ▷ **characteristic**
characterization *n* ▷ **characterize**
characterizations *n* ▷ **characterize**
characterize *v* (**-rizes, -rizing, -rized**) be a characteristic of (*foll. by* **as**) > **characterization** *n* (*pl* **-s**)
characterized *v* ▷ **characterize**
characterizes *v* ▷ **characterize**
characterizing *v* ▷ **characterize**
characters *n* ▷ **character**
charade [shar-**rahd**] *n* (*pl* **-s**) absurd pretence ▸ *pl* game in which one team acts out a word or phrase, which the other team has to guess
charades *n* ▷ **charade**
charcoal *n* (*pl* **-s**) black substance formed by partially burning wood
charcoals *n* ▷ **charcoal**
charge *v* (**charges, charging, charged**) ask as a price ▸ *n* (*pl* **-s**) price charged > **chargeable** *adj*
chargeable *adj* ▷ **charge**
charged *v* ▷ **charge**
charger *n* (*pl* **-s**) device for charging an accumulator
chargers *n* ▷ **charger**
charges *v, n* ▷ **charge**
charging *v* ▷ **charge**
charier *adj* ▷ **chary**
chariest *adj* ▷ **chary**
chariot *n* (*pl* **-s**) two-wheeled horse-drawn vehicle used in ancient times in wars and races
charioteer *n* (*pl* **-s**) chariot driver
charioteers *n* ▷ **charioteer**
chariots *n* ▷ **chariot**
charisma [kar-**rizz**-ma] *n* (*pl* **-s**) person's power to attract or influence people > **charismatic** [kar-rizz-**mat**-ik] ▸ *adj*
charismas *n* ▷ **charisma**
charismatic *adj* ▷ **charisma**
charitable *adj* ▷ **charity**
charitably *adv* ▷ **charity**
charities *n* ▷ **charity**
charity *n* (*pl* **-ties**) organization that gives help, such as money or food, to those in need > **charitable** *adj* > **charitably** *adv*
charladies *n* ▷ **charlady**
charlady *n* (*pl* **-ladies**) (BRIT) (*Informal*) ▷ **charwoman**
charlatan [**shar**-lat-tan] *n* (*pl* **-s**) person who claims expertise that he or she does not have
charlatans *n* ▷ **charlatan**
charleston *n* (*pl* **-s**) lively dance of the 1920s
charlestons *n* ▷ **charleston**
charm *n* (*pl* **-s**) attractive quality ▸ *v* (**-s, -ing, -ed**) attract, delight > **charmer** *n* (*pl* **-s**)
charmed *v* ▷ **charm**
charmer *n* ▷ **charm**
charmers *n* ▷ **charm**
charming *adj* attractive ▸ *v* ▷ **charm**
charms *n, v* ▷ **charm**
charred *v* ▷ **char**[1, 2]
charring *v* ▷ **char**[1, 2]
chars *v* ▷ **char**[1, 2] ▸ *n* ▷ **char**[2]
chart *n* (*pl* **-s**) graph, table, or diagram showing information ▸ *v* (**-s, -ing, -ed**) plot the course of
charted *v* ▷ **chart**
charter *n* (*pl* **-s**) document granting or demanding certain rights ▸ *v* (**-s, -ing, -ed**) hire by charter
chartered *adj* officially qualified to practise a profession ▸ *v* ▷ **charter**
chartering *v* ▷ **charter**

charters *n, v* ▷ **charter**
charting *v* ▷ **chart**
chartreuse [shar-**trerz**] *n* (*pl* **-s**) sweet-smelling green or yellow liqueur
chartreuses *n* ▷ **chartreuse**
charts *n, v* ▷ **chart**
charwoman *n* (*pl* **charwomen**) woman whose job is to clean other people's homes
charwomen *n* ▷ **charwoman**
chary [**chair**-ee] *adj* (**-rier, -riest**) wary, careful
chase[1] *v* (**chases, chasing, chased**) run after quickly in order to catch or drive away ▶ *n* (*pl* **-s**) chasing, pursuit
chase[2] *v* (**chases, chasing, chased**) engrave or emboss (metal)
chased *v* ▷ **chase**[1, 2]
chaser *n* (*pl* **-s**) milder drink drunk after another stronger one
chasers *n* ▷ **chaser**
chases *v* ▷ **chase**[1, 2] ▶ *n* ▷ **chase**[1]
chasing *v* ▷ **chase**[1, 2]
chasm [**kaz**-zum] *n* (*pl* **-s**) deep crack in the earth
chasms *n* ▷ **chasm**
chassis [**shass**-ee] *n* (*pl* **-sis**) frame, wheels, and mechanical parts of a vehicle
chaste *adj* (**-r, -st**) abstaining from sex outside marriage or altogether > **chastely** *adv* > **chasteness** *n* (*pl* **-es**) > **chastity** *n* (*pl* **-ties**)
chastely *adv* ▷ **chaste**
chasten [**chase**-en] *v* (**-s, -ing, -ed**) subdue by criticism
chastened *v* ▷ **chasten**
chasteness *n* ▷ **chaste**
chastenesses *n* ▷ **chaste**
chastening *v* ▷ **chasten**
chastens *v* ▷ **chasten**
chaster *adj* ▷ **chaste**
chastest *adj* ▷ **chaste**
chastise *v* (**-ises, -ising, -ised**) scold severely > **chastisement** *n* (*pl* **-s**)
chastised *v* ▷ **chastise**
chastisement *n* ▷ **chastise**
chastisements *n* ▷ **chastise**
chastises *v* ▷ **chastise**
chastising *v* ▷ **chastise**
chastities *n* ▷ **chaste**
chastity *n* ▷ **chaste**
chat *n* (*pl* **-s**) informal conversation ▶ *v* (**chats, chatting, chatted**) have an informal conversation > **chatty** *adj* (**-ttier, -ttiest**) > **chattily** *adv* > **chattiness** *n* (*pl* **-es**)
chateau [**shat**-toe] *n* (*pl* **-teaux, -teaus**) French castle
chateaus *n* ▷ **chateau**
chateaux *n* ▷ **chateau**
chatelaine [**shat**-tell-lane] *n* (*pl* **-s**) (formerly) mistress of a large house or castle
chatelaines *n* ▷ **chatelaine**
chatroom *n* (*pl* **-s**) site on the Internet where users have group discussions by e-mail
chatrooms *n* ▷ **chatroom**
chats *n, v* ▷ **chat**
chatted *v* ▷ **chat**
chattel *n* (*pl* **-s**) (usually plural) possessions
chattels *n* ▷ **chattel**
chatter *v* (**-s, -ing, -ed**) speak quickly and continuously about unimportant things ▶ *n* (*pl* **-s**) idle talk
chatterbox *n* (*pl* **-es**) person who chatters a lot
chatterboxes *n* ▷ **chatterbox**
chattered *v* ▷ **chatter**
chattering *v* ▷ **chatter**
chatters *v, n* ▷ **chatter**
chattier *adj* ▷ **chat**
chattiest *adj* ▷ **chat**
chattily *adv* ▷ **chat**
chattiness *n* ▷ **chat**
chattinesses *n* ▷ **chat**
chatting *v* ▷ **chat**
chatty *adj* ▷ **chat**
chauffeur *n* (*pl* **-s**) person employed to drive a car for someone
chauffeurs *n* ▷ **chauffeur**
chauvinism [**show**-vin-iz-zum] *n* (*pl* **-s**) irrational belief that one's own country, race, group, or sex is superior > **chauvinist** *n* (*pl* **-s**) *adj* > **chauvinistic** *adj* > **chauvinistically** *adv*
chauvinisms *n* ▷ **chauvinism**
chauvinist *n* ▷ **chauvinism**
chauvinistic *adj* ▷ **chauvinism**
chauvinistically *adv* ▷ **chauvinism**
chauvinists *n* ▷ **chauvinism**

che *pron*. Like **ch**, che is an old dialect form of **I**. Che scores 8 points.

cheap *adj* (**-er, -est**) costing relatively little > **cheaply** *adv*
cheapen *v* (**-s, -ing, -ed**) lower the reputation of
cheapened *v* ▷ **cheapen**
cheapening *v* ▷ **cheapen**
cheapens *v* ▷ **cheapen**
cheaper *adj* ▷ **cheap**
cheapest *adj* ▷ **cheap**
cheaply *adv* ▷ **cheap**
cheapskate *n* (*pl* **-s**) (*Informal*) miserly person
cheapskates *n* ▷ **cheapskate**
cheat *v* (**-s, -ing, -ed**) act dishonestly to gain profit or advantage ▶ *n* (*pl* **-s**) person who cheats

cheated *v* ▷ **cheat**
cheating *v* ▷ **cheat**
cheats *v, n* ▷ **cheat**
check *v* (**-s, -ing, -ed**) examine, investigate ▶ *n* (*pl* **-s**) test to ensure accuracy or progress
checked *v* ▷ **check**
checking *v* ▷ **check**
checkmate *n* (*pl* **-s**) (CHESS) winning position in which an opponent's king is under attack and unable to escape ▶ *v* (**-mates, -mating, -mated**) (CHESS) place the king of (one's opponent) in checkmate
checkmated *v* ▷ **checkmate**
checkmates *n, v* ▷ **checkmate**
checkmating *v* ▷ **checkmate**
checkout *n* (*pl* **-s**) counter in a supermarket, where customers pay
checkouts *n* ▷ **checkout**
checks *v, n* ▷ **check**
checkup *n* (*pl* **-s**) thorough medical examination
checkups *n* ▷ **checkup**
cheddar *n* (*pl* **-s**) firm orange or yellowy-white cheese
cheddars *n* ▷ **cheddar**
cheek *n* (*pl* **-s**) either side of the face below the eye (*Informal*) ▶ *v* (**-s, -ing, -ed**) (BRIT, AUST & NZ) (*Informal*) speak impudently to
cheeked *v* ▷ **cheek**
cheekier *adj* ▷ **cheeky**
cheekiest *adj* ▷ **cheeky**
cheekily *adv* ▷ **cheeky**
cheekiness *n* ▷ **cheeky**
cheekinesses *n* ▷ **cheeky**
cheeking *v* ▷ **cheek**
cheeks *n, v* ▷ **cheek**
cheeky *adj* (**-kier, -kiest**) impudent, disrespectful > **cheekily** *adv* > **cheekiness** *n* (*pl* **-es**)
cheep *n* (*pl* **-s**) young bird's high-pitched cry ▶ *v* (**-s, -ing, -ed**) utter a cheep
cheeped *v* ▷ **cheep**
cheeping *v* ▷ **cheep**
cheeps *n, v* ▷ **cheep**
cheer *v* (**-s, -ing, -ed**) applaud or encourage with shouts ▶ *n* (*pl* **-s**) shout of applause or encouragement > **cheerful** *adj* (**-ller, -llest**) > **cheerfully** *adv* > **cheerfulness** *n* > **cheery** *adj* (**-rier, -riest**) > **cheerily** *adv*
cheered *v* ▷ **cheer**
cheerful *adj* ▷ **cheer**
cheerfuller *adj* ▷ **cheer**
cheerfullest *adj* ▷ **cheer**
cheerfully *adv* ▷ **cheer**
cheerfulness *n* ▷ **cheer**
cheerier *adj* ▷ **cheer**
cheeriest *adj* ▷ **cheer**
cheerily *adv* ▷ **cheer**
cheering *v* ▷ **cheer**
cheerio *interj* (*Informal*) goodbye ▶ *n* (*pl* **-s**) (AUST & NZ) small red cocktail sausage
cheerios *n* ▷ **cheerio**
cheerless *adj* dreary, gloomy > **cheerlessly** *adv* > **cheerlessness** *n*
cheerlessly *adv* ▷ **cheerless**
cheerlessness *n* ▷ **cheerless**
cheers *v, n* ▷ **cheer**
cheery *adj* ▷ **cheer**
cheese *n* (*pl* **-s**) food made from coagulated milk curd > **cheesy** *adj* (*pl* **-sier, -siest**) > **cheesily** *adv* > **cheesiness** *n*
cheeseburger *n* (*pl* **-s**) hamburger topped with melted cheese
cheeseburgers *n* ▷ **cheeseburger**
cheesecake *n* (*pl* **-s**) dessert with a biscuit-crumb base covered with a sweet cream-cheese mixture
cheesecakes *n* ▷ **cheesecake**
cheesecloth *n* (*pl* **-s**) light cotton cloth
cheesecloths *n* ▷ **cheesecloth**
cheeses *n* ▷ **cheese**
cheesier *adj* ▷ **cheese**
cheesiest *adj* ▷ **cheese**
cheesily *adv* ▷ **cheese**
cheesiness *n* ▷ **cheese**
cheesy *adj* ▷ **cheese**
cheetah *n* (*pl* **-s**) large fast-running spotted African wild cat
cheetahs *n* ▷ **cheetah**
chef *n* (*pl* **-s**) cook in a restaurant
chefs *n* ▷ **chef**
chemical *n* (*pl* **-s**) substance used in or resulting from a reaction involving changes to atoms or molecules ▶ *adj* of chemistry or chemicals > **chemically** *adv*
chemically *adv* ▷ **chemical**
chemicals *n* ▷ **chemical**
chemise [shem-**meez**] *n* (*pl* **-s**) (*Old-fashioned*) woman's loose-fitting slip
chemises *n* ▷ **chemise**
chemist *n* (*pl* **-s**) shop selling medicines and cosmetics
chemistries *n* ▷ **chemistry**
chemistry *n* (*pl* **-ries**) science of the composition, properties, and reactions of substances
chemists *n* ▷ **chemist**
chemotherapies *n* ▷ **chemotherapy**
chemotherapy *n* (*pl* **-apies**) treatment of disease, often cancer, using chemicals

chenille [shen-**neel**] *n* (*pl* **-s**) (fabric of) thick tufty yarn
chenilles *n* ▷ **chenille**
cheque *n* (*pl* **-s**) written order to one's bank to pay money from one's account
chequer *n* (*pl* **chequers**) piece used in Chinese chequers ▶ *pl* game of draughts
chequered *adj* marked by varied fortunes
chequers *n* ▷ **chequer**
cheques *n* ▷ **cheque**
cherish *v* (**-es, -ing, -ed**) cling to (an idea or feeling)
cherished *v* ▷ **cherish**
cherishes *v* ▷ **cherish**
cherishing *v* ▷ **cherish**
cheroot [sher-**root**] *n* (*pl* **-s**) cigar with both ends cut flat
cheroots *n* ▷ **cheroot**
cherries *n* ▷ **cherry**
cherry *n* (*pl* **-ries**) small red or black fruit with a stone ▶ *adj* deep red
cherub *n* (*pl* **-s, -ubim**) angel, often represented as a winged child > **cherubic** [cher-**rew**-bik] ▶ *adj*
cherubic *adj* ▷ **cherub**
cherubim *n* ▷ **cherub**
cherubs *n* ▷ **cherub**
chervil *n* (*pl* **-s**) aniseed-flavoured herb
chervils *n* ▷ **chervil**
chess *n* (*pl* **-es**) game for two players with 16 pieces each, played on a chequered board of 64 squares
chesses *n* ▷ **chess**
chessman *n* (*pl* **-men**) piece used in chess
chessmen *n* ▷ **chessman**
chest *n* (*pl* **-s**) front of the body, from neck to waist
chesterfield *n* (*pl* **-s**) couch with high padded sides and back
chesterfields *n* ▷ **chesterfield**
chestnut *n* (*pl* **-s**) reddish-brown edible nut (*Informal*) ▶ *adj* (of hair or a horse) reddish-brown
chestnuts *n* ▷ **chestnut**
chests *n* ▷ **chest**
chevron [**shev**-ron] *n* (*pl* **-s**) V-shaped pattern, esp. on the sleeve of a military uniform to indicate rank
chevrons *n* ▷ **chevron**
chew *v* (**-s, -ing, -ed**) grind (food) between the teeth
chewed *v* ▷ **chew**
chewier *adj* ▷ **chewy**
chewiest *adj* ▷ **chewy**
chewiness *n* ▷ **chewy**
chewinesses *n* ▷ **chewy**
chewing *v* ▷ **chew**
chews *v* ▷ **chew**
chewy *adj* (**-ier, -iest**) requiring a lot of chewing > **chewiness** *n* (*pl* **-es**)
chi *n* (**chis**). Chi is a letter of the Greek alphabet, and is worth 8 points.
chianti [kee-**ant**-ee] *n* (*pl* **-s**) dry red Italian wine
chiantis *n* ▷ **chianti**
chiaroscuro [kee-ah-roh-**skew**-roh] *n* (*pl* **-s**) distribution of light and shade in a picture
chiaroscuros *n* ▷ **chiaroscuro**
chic [**sheek**] *adj* (**-er, -est**) stylish, elegant ▶ *n* (*pl* **-s**) stylishness, elegance
chicane [shik-**kane**] *n* (*pl* **-s**) obstacle in a motor-racing circuit
chicaneries *n* ▷ **chicanery**
chicanery *n* (*pl* **-eries**) trickery, deception
chicanes *n* ▷ **chicane**
chicer *adj* ▷ **chic**
chicest *adj* ▷ **chic**
chick *n* (*pl* **-s**) baby bird
chicken *n* (*pl* **-s**) domestic fowl ▶ *adj* (*Slang*) cowardly
chickenpox *n* (*pl* **-es**) infectious disease with an itchy rash
chickenpoxes *n* ▷ **chickenpox**
chickens *n* ▷ **chicken**
chickpea *n* (*pl* **-s**) edible yellow pealike seed
chickpeas *n* ▷ **chickpea**
chicks *n* ▷ **chick**
chickweed *n* (*pl* **-s**) weed with small white flowers
chickweeds *n* ▷ **chickweed**
chicories *n* ▷ **chicory**
chicory *n* (*pl* **-ries**) plant whose leaves are used in salads
chics *n* ▷ **chic**
chid *v* ▷ **chide**
chidden *v* ▷ **chide**
chide *v* (**chiding, chided** *or* **chid**) (**chid** *or* **chidden**) rebuke, scold
chided *v* ▷ **chide**
chiding *v* ▷ **chide**
chief *n* (*pl* **-s**) head of a group of people ▶ *adj* most important
chiefly *adv* especially
chiefs *n* ▷ **chief**
chieftain *n* (*pl* **-s**) leader of a tribe
chieftains *n* ▷ **chieftain**
chiffon [**shif**-fon] *n* (*pl* **-s**) fine see-through fabric
chiffons *n* ▷ **chiffon**
chignon [**sheen**-yon] *n* (*pl* **-s**) knot of hair pinned up at the back of the head

chignons *n* ▷ **chignon**
chihuahua [chee-**wah**-wah] *n* (*pl* **-s**) tiny short-haired dog
chihuahuas *n* ▷ **chihuahua**
chilblain *n* (*pl* **-s**) inflammation of the fingers or toes, caused by exposure to cold
chilblains *n* ▷ **chilblain**
child *n* (*pl* **children**) young human being, boy or girl > **childhood** *n* (*pl* **-s**) > **childless** *adj* > **childlessness** *n*
childbirth *n* (*pl* **-s**) giving birth to a child
childbirths *n* ▷ **childbirth**
childhood *n* ▷ **child**
childhoods *n* ▷ **child**
childish *adj* immature, silly > **childishly** *adv* > **childishness** *n*
childishly *adv* ▷ **childish**
childishness *n* ▷ **childish**
childless *adj* ▷ **child**
childlessness *n* ▷ **child**
childlike *adj* innocent, trustful
children *n* ▷ **child**
chili *n* ▷ **chilli**
chilies *n* ▷ **chilli**
chill *n* (*pl* **-s**) feverish cold ▶ *v* (**-s, -ing, -ed**) make (something) cool or cold ▶ *adj* unpleasantly cold
chilled *v* ▷ **chill**
chilli, chili *n* (*pl* **-es**) small red or green hot-tasting capsicum pod, used in cooking
chillier *adj* ▷ **chilly**
chillies *n* ▷ **chilli**
chilliest *adj* ▷ **chilly**
chilliness *n* ▷ **chilly**
chillinesses *n* ▷ **chilly**
chilling *v* ▷ **chill**
chills *n, v* ▷ **chill**
chilly *adj* (**-llier, -lliest**) moderately cold > **chilliness** *n* (*pl* **-es**)
chime *n* (*pl* **-s**) musical ringing sound of a bell or clock ▶ *v* (**-mes, -ming, -med**) make a musical ringing sound
chimed *v* ▷ **chime**
chimera [kime-**meer**-a] *n* (*pl* **-s**) unrealistic hope or idea
chimeras *n* ▷ **chimera**
chimes *n, v* ▷ **chime**
chiming *v* ▷ **chime**
chimney *n* (*pl* **-s**) hollow vertical structure for carrying away smoke from a fire
chimneys *n* ▷ **chimney**
chimp *n* (*pl* **-s**) (*Informal*) ▷ **chimpanzee**
chimpanzee *n* (*pl* **-s**) intelligent black African ape
chimpanzees *n* ▷ **chimpanzee**
chimps *n* ▷ **chimp**
chin *n* (*pl* **-s**) part of the face below the mouth
china *n* (*pl* **-s**) fine earthenware or porcelain
chinas *n* ▷ **china**
chinchilla *n* (*pl* **-s**) S American rodent bred for its soft grey fur
chinchillas *n* ▷ **chinchilla**
chine *n* (*pl* **-s**) cut of meat including part of the backbone
chines *n* ▷ **chine**
chink[1] *n* (*pl* **-s**) small narrow opening
chink[2] *v* (**-s, -ing, -ed**) ▶ *n* (*pl* **-s**) (make) a light ringing sound
chinked *v* ▷ **chink**[2]
chinking *v* ▷ **chink**[2]
chinks *n* ▷ **chink**[1, 2] ▶ *v* ▷ **chink**[2]
chins *n* ▷ **chin**
chintz *n* (*pl* **-es**) printed cotton fabric with a glazed finish
chintzes *n* ▷ **chintz**
chinwag *n* (*pl* **-s**) (BRIT, AUST & NZ) (*Informal*) chat
chinwags *n* ▷ **chinwag**
chip *n* (*pl* **-s**) strip of potato, fried in deep fat ▶ *v* (**chips, chipping, chipped**) break small pieces from
chipboard *n* (*pl* **-s**) thin board made of compressed wood particles
chipboards *n* ▷ **chipboard**
chipmunk *n* (*pl* **-s**) small squirrel-like N American rodent with a striped back
chipmunks *n* ▷ **chipmunk**
chipped *v* ▷ **chip**
chippie *n* (*pl* **-s**) (BRIT, AUST & NZ) (*Informal*) carpenter
chippies *n* ▷ **chippie**
chipping *v* ▷ **chip**
chips *n, v* ▷ **chip**
chiropodist [kir-**rop**-pod-ist] *n* (*pl* **-s**) person who treats minor foot complaints > **chiropody** *n*
chiropodists *n* ▷ **chiropodist**
chiropody *n* ▷ **chiropodist**
chiropractic [kire-oh-**prak**-tik] *n* (*pl* **-s**) system of treating bodily disorders by manipulation of the spine > **chiropractor** *n* (*pl* **-s**)
chiropractics *n* ▷ **chiropractic**
chiropractor *n* ▷ **chiropractic**
chiropractors *n* ▷ **chiropractic**
chirp *v* (**-s, -ing, -ed**) (of a bird or insect) make a short high-pitched sound ▶ *n* (*pl* **-s**) chirping sound
chirped *v* ▷ **chirp**
chirpier *adj* ▷ **chirpy**
chirpiest *adj* ▷ **chirpy**
chirpily *adv* ▷ **chirpy**

chirpiness *n* ▷ **chirpy**
chirping *v* ▷ **chirp**
chirps *v, n* ▷ **chirp**
chirpy *adj* (**-pier, -piest**) (*Informal*) lively and cheerful > **chirpily** *adv* > **chirpiness** *n*
chisel *n* (*pl* **-s**) metal tool with a sharp end for shaping wood or stone ▶ *v* (**-els, -elling, -elled**) carve or form with a chisel
chiselled *v* ▷ **chisel**
chiselling *v* ▷ **chisel**
chisels *n, v* ▷ **chisel**
chit[1] *n* (*pl* **-s**) short official note, such as a receipt
chit[2] *n* (*pl* **-s**) (BRIT, AUST & NZ) (*old-fashioned*) pert or impudent girl
chitchat *n* (*pl* **-s**) chat, gossip
chitchats *n* ▷ **chitchat**
chits *n* ▷ **chit**[1, 2]
chitterlings *pl n* pig's intestines cooked as food
chivalries *n* ▷ **chivalry**
chivalrous *adj* ▷ **chivalry**
chivalrously *adv* ▷ **chivalry**
chivalry *n* (*pl* **-ries**) courteous behaviour, esp. by men towards women > **chivalrous** *adj* > **chivalrously** *adv*
chives *pl n* herb with a mild onion flavour
chivvied *v* ▷ **chivvy**
chivvies *v* ▷ **chivvy**
chivvy *v* (**-vies, -vying, -vied**) (*Informal*) harass, nag
chivvying *v* ▷ **chivvy**
chloride *n* (*pl* **-s**) compound of chlorine and another substance
chlorides *n* ▷ **chloride**
chlorinate *v* (**-ates, -ating, -ated**) disinfect (water) with chlorine > **chlorination** *n*
chlorinated *v* ▷ **chlorinate**
chlorinates *v* ▷ **chlorinate**
chlorinating *v* ▷ **chlorinate**
chlorination *n* ▷ **chlorinate**
chlorine *n* (*pl* **-s**) strong-smelling greenish-yellow gaseous element, used to disinfect water
chlorines *n* ▷ **chlorine**
chlorofluorocarbon *n* (*pl* **-s**) any of various gaseous compounds of carbon, hydrogen, chlorine, and fluorine, used in refrigerators and aerosol propellants, some of which break down the ozone in the atmosphere
chlorofluorocarbons *n* ▷ **chlorofluorocarbon**
chloroform *n* (*pl* **-s**) strong-smelling liquid formerly used as an anaesthetic
chloroforms *n* ▷ **chloroform**
chlorophyll *n* (*pl* **-s**) green colouring matter of plants, which enables them to convert sunlight into energy
chlorophylls *n* ▷ **chlorophyll**
chock *n* (*pl* **-s**) block or wedge used to prevent a heavy object from moving
chockablock *adj* completely full
chocks *n* ▷ **chock**
chocolate *n* (*pl* **-s**) sweet food made from cacao seeds ▶ *adj* dark brown
chocolates *n* ▷ **chocolate**
choice *n* (*pl* **-s**) choosing ▶ *adj* (**choicer, choicest**) of high quality
choicer *adj* ▷ **choice**
choices *n* ▷ **choice**
choicest *adj* ▷ **choice**
choir *n* (*pl* **-s**) organized group of singers, esp. in church
choirs *n* ▷ **choir**
choke *v* (**chokes, choking, choked**) hinder or stop the breathing of (a person) by strangling or smothering ▶ *n* (*pl* **-s**) device controlling the amount of air that is mixed with the fuel in a petrol engine
choked *v* ▷ **choke**
choker *n* (*pl* **-s**) tight-fitting necklace
chokers *n* ▷ **choker**
chokes *v, n* ▷ **choke**
choking *v* ▷ **choke**
cholera [**kol**-ler-a] *n* (*pl* **-s**) serious infectious disease causing severe vomiting and diarrhoea
choleras *n* ▷ **cholera**
choleric [**kol**-ler-ik] *adj* bad-tempered
cholesterol [kol-**lest**-er-oll] *n* (*pl* **-s**) fatty substance found in animal tissue, an excess of which can cause heart disease
cholesterols *n* ▷ **cholesterol**
chomp *v* (**-s, -ing, -ed**) chew noisily
chomped *v* ▷ **chomp**
chomping *v* ▷ **chomp**
chomps *v* ▷ **chomp**
chook *n* (*pl* **-s**) (AUST & NZ) hen or chicken
chooks *n* ▷ **chook**
choose *v* (**chooses, choosing, chose, chosen**) select from a number of alternatives
chooses *v* ▷ **choose**
choosier *adj* ▷ **choosy**
choosiest *adj* ▷ **choosy**
choosing *v* ▷ **choose**
choosy *adj* (**-sier, -siest**) (*Informal*) fussy, hard to please
chop[1] *v* (**chops, chopping, chopped**) cut with a blow from an axe or knife (BOXING) (KARATE) ▶ *n* (*pl* **-s**) cutting or sharp blow
chop[2] *v* (**chops, chopping, chopped**) change

one's mind repeatedly
chopped *v* ▷ **chop[1, 2]**
chopper *n* (*pl* **-s**) (*Informal*) helicopter
choppers *n* ▷ **chopper**
choppier *adj* ▷ **choppy**
choppiest *adj* ▷ **choppy**
choppiness *n* ▷ **choppy**
choppinesses *n* ▷ **choppy**
chopping *v* ▷ **chop[1, 2]**
choppy *adj* (**-ppier, -ppiest**) (of the sea) fairly rough > **choppiness** *n* (*pl* **-es**)
chops *pl n* (BRIT, AUST & NZ) (*Informal*) jaws, cheeks ▶ *v* ▷ **chop[1, 2]** ▶ *n* ▷ **chop[1]**
chopsticks *pl n* pair of thin sticks used to eat Chinese food
choral *adj* of a choir
chorale [kor-**rahl**] *n* (*pl* **-s**) slow stately hymn tune
chorales *n* ▷ **chorale**
chord[1] *n* (*pl* **-s**) (MATHS) straight line joining two points on a curve
chord[2] *n* (*pl* **-s**) simultaneous sounding of three or more musical notes
chords *n* ▷ **chord[1, 2]**
chore *n* (*pl* **-s**) routine task
choreographer *n* ▷ **choreography**
choreographers *n* ▷ **choreography**
choreographic *adj* ▷ **choreography**
choreographies *n* ▷ **choreography**
choreography *n* (*pl* **-phies**) composition of steps and movements for dancing > **choreographer** *n* (*pl* **-s**) > **choreographic** *adj*
chores *n* ▷ **chore**
chorister *n* (*pl* **-s**) singer in a choir
choristers *n* ▷ **chorister**
chortle *v* (**-tles, -tling, -tled**) chuckle in amusement ▶ *n* (*pl* **-s**) amused chuckle
chortled *v* ▷ **chortle**
chortles *v, n* ▷ **chortle**
chortling *v* ▷ **chortle**
chorus *n* (*pl* **-es**) large choir ▶ *v* (**-es, -ing, -ed**) sing or say together
chorused *v* ▷ **chorus**
choruses *n, v* ▷ **chorus**
chorusing *v* ▷ **chorus**
chose *v* ▷ **choose**
chosen *v* ▷ **choose**
chow *n* (*pl* **-s**) thick-coated dog with a curled tail, orig. from China
chowder *n* (*pl* **-s**) thick soup containing clams or fish
chowders *n* ▷ **chowder**
chows *n* ▷ **chow**
christen *v* (**-s, -ing, -ed**) baptize > **christening** *n* (*pl* **-s**)
christened *v* ▷ **christen**
christening *v, n* ▷ **christen**
christenings *n* ▷ **christen**
christens *v* ▷ **christen**
chromatic *adj* of colour or colours > **chromatically** *adv*
chromatically *adv* ▷ **chromatic**
chromatographies *n* ▷ **chromatic**
chromatography *n* (*pl* **-phies**) separation and analysis of the components of a substance by slowly passing it through an adsorbing material
chrome *n* ▷ **chromium**
chromes *n* ▷ **chromium**
chromium, chrome *n* (*pl* **-s**) (CHEM) grey metallic element used in steel alloys and for electroplating
chromiums *n* ▷ **chromium**
chromosome *n* (*pl* **-s**) microscopic gene-carrying body in the nucleus of a cell
chromosomes *n* ▷ **chromosome**
chronic *adj* (of an illness) lasting a long time > **chronically** *adv*
chronically *adv* ▷ **chronic**
chronicle *n* (*pl* **-s**) record of events in order of occurrence ▶ *v* (**-les, -ing, -led**) record in or as if in a chronicle > **chronicler** *n* (*pl* **-s**)
chronicled *v* ▷ **chronicle**
chronicler *n* ▷ **chronicle**
chroniclers *n* ▷ **chronicle**
chronicles *v* ▷ **chronicle**
chronicling *v* ▷ **chronicle**
chronological *adj* ▷ **chronology**
chronologically *adv* ▷ **chronology**
chronologies *n* ▷ **chronology**
chronology *n* (*pl* **-gies**) arrangement or list of events in order of occurrence > **chronological** *adj* > **chronologically** *adv*
chronometer *n* (*pl* **-s**) timepiece designed to be accurate in all conditions
chronometers *n* ▷ **chronometer**
chrysalis [**kriss**-a-liss] *n* (*pl* **-es**) insect in the stage between larva and adult, when it is in a cocoon
chrysalises *n* ▷ **chrysalis**
chrysanthemum *n* (*pl* **-s**) garden flower with a large head made up of thin petals
chrysanthemums *n* ▷ **chrysanthemum**
chub *n* (*pl* **chub**) European freshwater fish of the carp family
chubbier *adj* ▷ **chubby**
chubbiest *adj* ▷ **chubby**
chubbiness *n* ▷ **chubby**
chubby *adj* (**-bier, -biest**) plump and round > **chubbiness** *n*

chuck[1] *v* (**-s, -ing, -ed**) (*Informal*) throw
chuck[2] *n* (*pl* **-s**) cut of beef from the neck to the shoulder
chucked *v* ▷ **chuck[1]**
chucking *v* ▷ **chuck[1]**
chuckle *v* (**-les, -ling, -led**) laugh softly ▶ *n* (*pl* **-s**) soft laugh
chuckled *v* ▷ **chuckle**
chuckles *v, n* ▷ **chuckle**
chuckling *v* ▷ **chuckle**
chucks *v* ▷ **chuck[1]** ▶ *n* ▷ **chuck[2]**
chuffed *adj* (*Informal*) very pleased
chug *n* (*pl* **-s**) short dull sound like the noise of an engine ▶ *v* (**chugs, chugging, chugged**) operate or move with this sound
chugged *v* ▷ **chug**
chugging *v* ▷ **chug**
chugs *n, v* ▷ **chug**
chukka *n* (*pl* **-s**) period of play in polo
chukkas *n* ▷ **chukka**
chum (*Informal*) *n* (*pl* **-s**) close friend ▶ *v* (**chums, chumming, chummed**) form a close friendship with > **chummy** *adj* (**-mmier, -mmiest**) > **chumminess** *n* (*pl* **-es**)
chummed *v* ▷ **chum**
chummier *adj* ▷ **chum**
chummiest *adj* ▷ **chum**
chumminess *n* ▷ **chum**
chumminesses *n* ▷ **chum**
chumming *v* ▷ **chum**
chummy *adj* ▷ **chum**
chump *n* (*pl* **-s**) (*Informal*) stupid person
chumps *n* ▷ **chump**
chums *n, v* ▷ **chum**
chunk *n* (*pl* **-s**) thick solid piece
chunkier *adj* ▷ **chunky**
chunkiest *adj* ▷ **chunky**
chunkiness *n* ▷ **chunky**
chunkinesses *n* ▷ **chunky**
chunks *n* ▷ **chunk**
chunky *adj* (**-kier, -kiest**) (of a person) broad and heavy > **chunkiness** *n* (*pl* **-es**)
church *n* (*pl* **-s**) building for public Christian worship
churches *n* ▷ **church**
churchgoer *n* (*pl* **-s**) person who attends church regularly
churchgoers *n* ▷ **churchgoer**
churchwarden *n* (*pl* **-s**) member of a congregation who assists the vicar
churchwardens *n* ▷ **churchwarden**
churchyard *n* (*pl* **-s**) grounds round a church, used as a graveyard
churchyards *n* ▷ **churchyard**
churlish *adj* surly and rude > **churlishly** *adv* > **churlishness** *n*
churlishly *adv* ▷ **churlish**
churlishness *n* ▷ **churlish**
churn *n* (*pl* **-s**) machine in which cream is shaken to make butter ▶ *v* (**-s, -ing, -ed**) stir (cream) vigorously to make butter
churned *v* ▷ **churn**
churning *v* ▷ **churn**
churns *n, v* ▷ **churn**
chute[1] [**shoot**] *n* (*pl* **-s**) steep slope down which things may be slid
chute[2] *n* (*pl* **-s**) (*Informal*) ▷ **parachute**
chutes *n* ▷ **chute[1, 2]**
chutney *n* (*pl* **-s**) pickle made from fruit, vinegar, spices, and sugar
chutneys *n* ▷ **chutney**
cicada [sik-**kah**-da] *n* (*pl* **-s**) large insect that makes a high-pitched drone
cicadas *n* ▷ **cicada**
cicatrices *n* ▷ **cicatrix**
cicatrix [**sik**-a-trix] *n* (*pl* **-trices**) scar

cid *n* (**cids**). A cid is a hero or commander. Cid scores 6 points.

cider *n* (*pl* **-s**) alcoholic drink made from fermented apple juice
ciders *n* ▷ **cider**
cigar *n* (*pl* **-s**) roll of cured tobacco leaves for smoking
cigarette *n* (*pl* **-s**) thin roll of shredded tobacco in thin paper, for smoking
cigarettes *n* ▷ **cigarette**
cigars *n* ▷ **cigar**
cinch [**sinch**] *n* (*pl* **-es**) (*Informal*) easy task
cinches *n* ▷ **cinch**
cinder *n* (*pl* **-s**) piece of material that will not burn, left after burning coal
cinders *n* ▷ **cinder**
cinema *n* (*pl* **-s**) place for showing films > **cinematic** *adj*
cinemas *n* ▷ **cinema**
cinematic *adj* ▷ **cinema**
cinematographer *n* ▷ **cinematography**
cinematographers *n* ▷ **cinematography**
cinematography *n* technique of making films > **cinematographer** *n* (*pl* **-s**)
cineraria *n* (*pl* **-s**) garden plant with daisy-like flowers
cinerarias *n* ▷ **cineraria**
cinnamon *n* (*pl* **-s**) spice obtained from the bark of an Asian tree
cinnamons *n* ▷ **cinnamon**
cipher, cypher [**sife**-er] *n* (*pl* **-s**) system of secret writing
ciphers *n* ▷ **cipher**
circa [**sir**-ka] *prep* (LATIN) approximately, about

circle *n* (*pl* **-s**) perfectly round geometric figure, line, or shape ▶ *v* (**circles, circling, circled**) move in a circle (round)
circled *v* ▷ **circle**
circles *n*, *v* ▷ **circle**
circlet *n* (*pl* **-s**) circular ornament worn on the head
circlets *n* ▷ **circlet**
circling *v* ▷ **circle**
circuit *n* (*pl* **-s**) complete route or course, esp. a circular one
circuitous [sir-**kew**-it-uss] *adj* indirect and lengthy > **circuitously** *adv*
circuitously *adv* ▷ **circuitous**
circuitry [**sir**-kit-tree] *n* electrical circuit(s)
circuits *n* ▷ **circuit**
circular *adj* in the shape of a circle ▶ *n* (*pl* **-s**) letter for general distribution > **circularity** *n*
circularity *n* ▷ **circular**
circulars *n* ▷ **circular**
circulate *v* (**-lates, -lating, -lated**) send, go, or pass from place to place or person to person > **circulatory** *adj*
circulated *v* ▷ **circulate**
circulates *v* ▷ **circulate**
circulating *v* ▷ **circulate**
circulation *n* flow of blood around the body
circulatory *adj* ▷ **circulate**
circumcise *v* (**-cises, -cising, -cised**) remove the foreskin of > **circumcision** *n* (*pl* **-s**)
circumcised *v* ▷ **circumcise**
circumcises *v* ▷ **circumcise**
circumcising *v* ▷ **circumcise**
circumcision *n* ▷ **circumcise**
circumcisions *n* ▷ **circumcise**
circumference *n* (*pl* **-s**) boundary of a specified area or shape, esp. of a circle
circumferences *n* ▷ **circumference**
circumflex *n* (*pl* **-es**) mark (^) over a vowel to show that it is pronounced in a particular way
circumflexes *n* ▷ **circumflex**
circumlocution *n* (*pl* **-s**) indirect way of saying something
circumlocutions *n* ▷ **circumlocution**
circumnavigate *v* (**-gates, -gating, -gated**) sail right round > **circumnavigation** *n* (*pl* **-s**)
circumnavigated *v* ▷ **circumnavigate**
circumnavigates *v* ▷ **circumnavigate**
circumnavigating *v* ▷ **circumnavigate**
circumnavigation *n* ▷ **circumnavigate**
circumnavigations *n* ▷ **circumnavigate**
circumscribe *v* (**-scribes, -scribing, -scribed**) limit, restrict > **circumscription** *n* (*pl* **-s**)
circumscribed *v* ▷ **circumscribe**
circumscribes *v* ▷ **circumscribe**
circumscribing *v* ▷ **circumscribe**
circumscription *n* ▷ **circumscribe**
circumscriptions *n* ▷ **circumscribe**
circumspect *adj* cautious and careful not to take risks > **circumspectly** *adv* > **circumspection** *n*
circumspection *n* ▷ **circumspect**
circumspectly *adv* ▷ **circumspect**
circumstance *n* (*pl* **-s**) (*usu. pl* occurrence or condition that accompanies or influences a person or event
circumstances *n* ▷ **circumstance**
circumstantial *adj* (of evidence) strongly suggesting something but not proving it
circumvent *v* (**-s, -ing, -ed**) avoid or get round (a rule etc.) > **circumvention** *n* (*pl* **-s**)
circumvented *v* ▷ **circumvent**
circumventing *v* ▷ **circumvent**
circumvention *n* ▷ **circumvent**
circumventions *n* ▷ **circumvent**
circumvents *v* ▷ **circumvent**
circus *n* (*pl* **-es**) (performance given by) a travelling company of acrobats, clowns, performing animals, etc.
circuses *n* ▷ **circus**
cirrhosis [sir-**roh**-siss] *n* serious liver disease, often caused by drinking too much alcohol > **cirrhotic** *adj*
cirrhotic *adj* ▷ **cirrhosis**
cirri *n* ▷ **cirrus**
cirrus *n* (*pl* **-ri**) high wispy cloud
cistern *n* (*pl* **-s**) water tank, esp. one that holds water for flushing a toilet
cisterns *n* ▷ **cistern**
citadel *n* (*pl* **-s**) fortress in a city
citadels *n* ▷ **citadel**
citation *n* ▷ **cite**
citations *n* ▷ **cite**
cite *v* (**cites, citing, cited**) quote, refer to > **citation** *n* (*pl* **-s**)
cited *v* ▷ **cite**
cites *v* ▷ **cite**
cities *n* ▷ **city**
citing *v* ▷ **cite**
citizen *n* (*pl* **-s**) native or naturalized member of a state or nation > **citizenship** *n* (*pl* **-s**)
citizens *n* ▷ **citizen**
citizenship *n* ▷ **citizen**
citizenships *n* ▷ **citizen**
city *n* (*pl* **-ties**) large or important town
civet [siv-vit] *n* (*pl* **-s**) spotted catlike African mammal
civets *n* ▷ **civet**
civic *adj* of a city or citizens

civics *n* study of the rights and responsibilities of citizenship
civil *adj* relating to the citizens of a state as opposed to the armed forces or the Church **> civilly** *adv*
civilian *n* (*pl* **-s**) ▸ *adj* (person) not belonging to the armed forces
civilians *n* ▷ **civilian**
civilities *n* ▷ **civility**
civility *n* (*pl* **-ities**) polite or courteous behaviour
civilization *n* (*pl* **-s**) high level of human cultural and social development
civilizations *n* ▷ **civilization**
civilize *v* (**-izes, -izing, -ized**) refine or educate (a person)
civilized *v* ▷ **civilize**
civilizes *v* ▷ **civilize**
civilizing *v* ▷ **civilize**
civilly *adv* ▷ **civil**
civvies *pl n* (BRIT, AUST & NZ) (*Slang*) ordinary clothes that are not part of a uniform
clack *n* (*pl* **-s**) sound made by two hard objects striking each other ▸ *v* (**-s, -ing, -ed**) make this sound
clacked *v* ▷ **clack**
clacking *v* ▷ **clack**
clacks *n, v* ▷ **clack**
clad *v* (**clads, cladding, clad**) ▷ **clothe**
cladding *n* (*pl* **-s**) material used to cover the outside of a building ▸ *v* ▷ **clad**
claddings *n* ▷ **cladding**
clads *v* ▷ **clad**
claim *v* (**-s, -ing, -ed**) assert as a fact ▸ *n* (*pl* **-s**) assertion that something is true **> claimant** *n* (*pl* **-s**)
claimant *n* ▷ **claim**
claimants *n* ▷ **claim**
claimed *v* ▷ **claim**
claiming *v* ▷ **claim**
claims *v, n* ▷ **claim**
clairvoyance *n* (*pl* **-s**) power of perceiving things beyond the natural range of the senses **> clairvoyant** *n* (*pl* **-s**) *adj*
clairvoyances *n* ▷ **clairvoyance**
clairvoyant *n, adj* ▷ **clairvoyance**
clairvoyants *n* ▷ **clairvoyance**
clam *n* (*pl* **-s**) edible shellfish with a hinged shell ▸ *v* (**clams, clamming, clammed**) (*Informal*) stop talking, esp. through nervousness
clamber *v* (**-s, -ing, -ed**) climb awkwardly
clambered *v* ▷ **clamber**
clambering *v* ▷ **clamber**
clambers *v* ▷ **clamber**
clammed *v* ▷ **clam**
clammier *adj* ▷ **clammy**
clammiest *adj* ▷ **clammy**
clamming *v* ▷ **clam**
clammy *adj* (**-mier, -miest**) unpleasantly moist and sticky
clamour *n* (*pl* **-s**) loud protest ▸ *v* (**-s, -ing, -ed**) make a loud noise or outcry **> clamorous** *adj* **> clamorously** *adv* **> clamorousness** *n*
clamoured *v* ▷ **clamour**
clamouring *v* ▷ **clamour**
clamourous *adj* ▷ **clamour**
clamourously *adj* ▷ **clamour**
clamourousness *n* ▷ **clamour**
clamours *n, v* ▷ **clamour**
clamp *n* (*pl* **-s**) tool with movable jaws for holding things together tightly ▸ *v* (**-s, -ing, -ed**) fasten with a clamp
clamped *v* ▷ **clamp**
clamping *v* ▷ **clamp**
clamps *n, v* ▷ **clamp**
clams *v, n* ▷ **clam**
clan *n* (*pl* **-s**) group of families with a common ancestor, esp. among Scottish Highlanders
clandestine *adj* secret and concealed **> clandestinely** *adv*
clandestinely *adv* ▷ **clandestine**
clang *v* (**-s, -ing, -ed**) make a loud ringing metallic sound ▸ *n* (*pl* **-s**) ringing metallic sound
clanged *v* ▷ **clang**
clanger *n* (*pl* **-s**) (*Informal*) obvious mistake
clangers *n* ▷ **clanger**
clanging *v* ▷ **clang**
clangour *n* (*pl* **-s**) loud continuous clanging sound
clangours *n* ▷ **clangour**
clangs *v, n* ▷ **clang**
clank *n* (*pl* **-s**) harsh metallic sound ▸ *v* (**-s, -ing, -ed**) make such a sound
clanked *v* ▷ **clank**
clanking *v* ▷ **clank**
clanks *n, v* ▷ **clank**
clannish *adj* (of a group) tending to exclude outsiders **> clannishness** *n*
clannishness *n* ▷ **clannish**
clans *n* ▷ **clan**
clap *v* (**claps, clapping, clapped**) applaud by hitting the palms of one's hands sharply together ▸ *n* (*pl* **-s**) act or sound of clapping
clapped *v* ▷ **clap**
clapper *n* (*pl* **-s**) piece of metal inside a bell, which causes it to sound when struck against the side
clapperboard *n* (*pl* **-s**) pair of hinged boards

clapped together during filming to help in synchronizing sound and picture
clapperboards *n* ▷ **clapperboard**
clappers *n* ▷ **clapper**
clapping *v* ▷ **clap**
claps *v, n* ▷ **clap**
claptrap *n* (*pl* **-s**) (*Informal*) foolish or pretentious talk
claptraps *n* ▷ **claptrap**
claret [**klar**-rit] *n* (*pl* **-s**) dry red wine from Bordeaux
clarets *n* ▷ **claret**
clarification *n* ▷ **clarify**
clarifications *n* ▷ **clarify**
clarified *v* ▷ **clarify**
clarifies *v* ▷ **clarify**
clarify *v* (**-fies, -fying, -fied**) make (a matter) clear and unambiguous > **clarification** *n* (*pl* **-s**)
clarifying *v* ▷ **clarify**
clarinet *n* (*pl* **-s**) keyed woodwind instrument with a single reed > **clarinettist** *n* (*pl* **-s**)
clarinets *n* ▷ **clarinet**
clarinettist *n* ▷ **clarinet**
clarinettists *n* ▷ **clarinet**
clarion *n* (*pl* **-s**) obsolete high-pitched trumpet
clarions *n* ▷ **clarion**
clarities *n* ▷ **clarity**
clarity *n* (*pl* **-ities**) clearness
clash *v* (**-es, -ing, -ed**) come into conflict ▶ *n* (*pl* **-es**) fight, argument
clashed *v* ▷ **clash**
clashes *v, n* ▷ **clash**
clashing *v* ▷ **clash**
clasp *n* (*pl* **-s**) device for fastening things ▶ *v* (**-s, -ing, -ed**) grasp or embrace firmly
clasped *v* ▷ **clasp**
clasping *v* ▷ **clasp**
clasps *n, v* ▷ **clasp**
class *n* (*pl* **-es**) group of people sharing a similar social position ▶ *v* (**-es, -ing, -ed**) place in a class
classed *v* ▷ **class**
classes *n, v* ▷ **class**
classic *adj* being a typical example of something ▶ *n* (*pl* **-s**) author, artist, or work of art of recognized excellence ▶ *pl* study of ancient Greek and Roman literature and culture
classical *adj* of or in a restrained conservative style > **classically** *adv*
classically *adv* ▷ **classical**
classicism *n* artistic style showing emotional restraint and regularity of form > **classicist** *n* (*pl* **-s**)
classicist *n* ▷ **classicism**
classicists *n* ▷ **classicism**
classics *n* ▷ **classic**
classier *adj* ▷ **classy**
classiest *adj* ▷ **classy**
classifiable *adj* ▷ **classify**
classification *n* ▷ **classify**
classifications *n* ▷ **classify**
classified *v* ▷ **classify**
classifies *v* ▷ **classify**
classify *v* (**-fies, -fying, -fied**) divide into groups with similar characteristics > **classifiable** *adj* > **classification** *n* (*pl* **-s**)
classifying *v* ▷ **classify**
classing *v* ▷ **class**
classy *adj* (**classier, classiest**) (*Informal*) stylish and elegant
clatter *v* (**-s, -ing, -ed**) ▶ *n* (*pl* **-s**) (make) a rattling noise
clattered *v* ▷ **clatter**
clattering *v* ▷ **clatter**
clatters *v, n* ▷ **clatter**
clause *n* (*pl* **-s**) section of a legal document
clauses *n* ▷ **clause**
claustrophobia *n* (*pl* **-s**) abnormal fear of confined spaces > **claustrophobic** *adj*
claustrophobia *n* ▷ **claustrophobia**
claustrophobias *n* ▷ **claustrophobia**
claustrophobic *adj* ▷ **claustrophobia**
clavichord *n* (*pl* **-s**) early keyboard instrument
clavichords *n* ▷ **clavichord**
clavicle *n* (*pl* **-s**) ▷ **collarbone**
clavicles *n* ▷ **clavicle**
claw *n* (*pl* **-s**) sharp hooked nail of a bird or beast ▶ *v* (**-s, -ing, -ed**) tear with claws or nails
clawed *v* ▷ **claw**
clawing *v* ▷ **claw**
claws *n, v* ▷ **claw**
clay *n* (*pl* **-s**) fine-grained earth, soft when moist and hardening when baked, used to make bricks and pottery > **clayey** *adj*
clayey *adj* ▷ **clay**
claymore *n* (*pl* **-s**) large two-edged sword formerly used by Scottish Highlanders
claymores *n* ▷ **claymore**
clays *n* ▷ **clay**
clean *adj* (**-er, -est**) free from dirt or impurities ▶ *v* (**-s, -ing, -ed**) make (something) free from dirt ▶ *adv* (*Not standard*) completely > **cleaner** *n* (*pl* **-s**) > **cleanly** *adv* > **cleanliness** *n* (*pl* **-es**)
cleaned *v* ▷ **clean**
cleaner *n, adj* ▷ **clean**
cleaners *n* ▷ **clean**
cleanest *adj* ▷ **clean**
cleaning *v* ▷ **clean**

cleanliness *n* ▷ **clean**
cleanlinesses *n* ▷ **clean**
cleanly *adv* ▷ **clean**
cleans *v* ▷ **clean**
cleanse *v* (**-ses, -sing, -sed**) make clean > **cleanser** *n* (*pl* **-s**)
cleansed *v* ▷ **cleanse**
cleanser *n* ▷ **cleanse**
cleansers *n* ▷ **cleanse**
cleanses *v* ▷ **cleanse**
cleansing *v* ▷ **cleanse**
clear *adj* (**-er, -est**) free from doubt or confusion ▶ *adv* out of the way ▶ *v* (**-s, -ing, -ed**) make or become clear > **clearly** *adv*
clearance *n* (*pl* **-s**) clearing
clearances *n* ▷ **clear**
cleared *v* ▷ **clear**
clearer *adj* ▷ **clear**
clearest *adj* ▷ **clear**
clearing *n* (*pl* **-s**) treeless area in a wood ▶ *v* ▷ **clear**
clearings *n* ▷ **clearing**
clearly *adv* ▷ **clear**
clears *v* ▷ **clear**
clearway *n* (*pl* **-s**) stretch of road on which motorists may stop in an emergency
clearways *n* ▷ **clearway**
cleat *n* (*pl* **-s**) wedge
cleats *n* ▷ **cleat**
cleavage *n* (*pl* **-s**) space between a woman's breasts, as revealed by a low-cut dress
cleavages *n* ▷ **cleavage**
cleave[1] *v* (**-ves, -ving, cleft, -ved** *or* **clove**) (**cleft, cleaved** *or* **cloven**) split apart
cleave[2] *v* (**-ves, -ving, cleft, cleft**) cling or stick
cleaved *v* ▷ **cleave**[1]
cleaver *n* (*pl* **-s**) butcher's heavy knife with a square blade
cleavers *n* ▷ **cleaver**
cleaves *v* ▷ **cleave**[1, 2]
cleaving *v* ▷ **cleave**[1, 2]
clef *n* (*pl* **-s**) (MUSIC) symbol at the beginning of a stave to show the pitch
clefs *n* ▷ **clef**
cleft *n* (*pl* **-s**) narrow opening or crack ▶ *v* ▷ **cleave**[1, 2]
clefted *v* ▷ **cleft**
clefting *v* ▷ **cleft**
clefts *n, v* ▷ **cleft**
clematis *n* climbing plant with large colourful flowers
clemencies *n* ▷ **clemency**
clemency *n* (*pl* **-cies**) kind or lenient treatment
clement *adj* (of weather) mild
clementine *n* (*pl* **-s**) small orange citrus fruit
clementines *n* ▷ **clementine**
clench *v* (**-es, -ing, -ed**) close or squeeze (one's teeth or fist) tightly
clenched *v* ▷ **clench**
clenches *v* ▷ **clench**
clenching *v* ▷ **clench**
clerestories *n* ▷ **clerestory**
clerestory [**clear**-store-ee] *n* (*pl* **-ries**) row of windows at the top of a wall above an adjoining roof
clergies *n* ▷ **clergy**
clergy *n* (*pl* **clergies**) priests and ministers as a group > **clergyman** *n* (*pl* **-men**)
clergyman *n* ▷ **clergy**
clergymen *n* ▷ **clergy**
cleric *n* (*pl* **-s**) member of the clergy
clerical *adj* of clerks or office work
clerics *n* ▷ **cleric**
clerk *n* (*pl* **-s**) employee in an office, bank, or court who keeps records, files, and accounts
clerks *n* ▷ **clerk**
clever *adj* (**-er, -est**) intelligent, quick at learning > **cleverly** *adv* > **cleverness** *n* (*pl* **-es**)
cleverer *adj* ▷ **clever**
cleverest *adj* ▷ **clever**
cleverly *adv* ▷ **clever**
cleverness *n* ▷ **clever**
clevernesses *n* ▷ **clever**
clianthus [klee-**anth**-us] *n* (*pl* **-es**) Australian or NZ plant with slender scarlet flowers
clianthuses *n* ▷ **clianthus**
cliché [**klee**-shay] *n* (*pl* **-s**) expression or idea that is no longer effective because of overuse > **clichéd** *adj*
clichéd *n* ▷ **cliché**
clichés *n* ▷ **cliché**
click *n* (*pl* **-s**) short sharp sound ▶ *v* (**-s, -ing, -ed**) make this sound
clicked *v* ▷ **click**
clicking *v* ▷ **click**
clicks *n, v* ▷ **click**
client *n* (*pl* **-s**) person who uses the services of a professional person or company
clientele [klee-on-**tell**] *n* (*pl* **-s**) clients collectively
clienteles *n* ▷ **clientele**
clients *n* ▷ **client**
cliff *n* (*pl* **-s**) steep rock face, esp. along the sea shore
cliffhanger *n* (*pl* **-s**) film, game, etc., that is tense and exciting because its outcome is uncertain
cliffhangers *n* ▷ **cliffhanger**
cliffs *n* ▷ **cliff**
climactic *adj* ▷ **climax**

climate *n* (*pl* **-s**) typical weather conditions of an area > **climatic** *adj*
climates *n* ▷ **climate**
climatic *adj* ▷ **climate**
climax *n* (*pl* **-es**) most intense point of an experience, series of events, or story > **climactic** *adj*
climaxes *n* ▷ **climax**
climb *v* (**-s, -ing, -ed**) go up, ascend ▶ *n* (*pl* **-s**) climbing > **climber** *n* (*pl* **-s**)
climbed *v* ▷ **climb**
climber *n* ▷ **climb**
climbers *n* ▷ **climb**
climbing *v* ▷ **climb**
climbs *v, n* ▷ **climb**
clime *n* (*pl* **-s**) (*Poetic*) place or its climate
climes *n* ▷ **clime**
clinch *v* (**-es, -ing, -ed**) settle (an argument or agreement) decisively
clinched *v* ▷ **clinch**
clincher *n* (*pl* **-s**) (*Informal*) something decisive
clinchers *n* ▷ **clincher**
clinches *v* ▷ **clinch**
clinching *v* ▷ **clinch**
cling *v* (**clings, clinging, clung**) hold tightly or stick closely
clingfilm *n* (*pl* **-s**) thin polythene material for wrapping food
clingfilms *n* ▷ **clingfilm**
clinging *v* ▷ **cling**
clings *v* ▷ **cling**
clinic *n* (*pl* **-s**) building where outpatients receive medical treatment or advice
clinical *adj* of a clinic > **clinically** *adv*
clinically *adv* ▷ **clinic**
clinics *n* ▷ **clinic**
clink[1] *v* (**-s, -ing, -ed**) ▶ *n* (*pl* **-s**) (make) a light sharp metallic sound
clink[2] *n* (*pl* **-s**) (BRIT, AUST & NZ) (*Slang*) prison
clinked *v* ▷ **clink**[1]
clinker *n* (*pl* **-s**) fused coal left over in a fire or furnace
clinkers *n* ▷ **clinker**
clinking *v* ▷ **clink**[1]
clinks *n* ▷ **clink**[1, 2] ▶ *v* ▷ **clink**[1]
clip[1] *v* (**clips, clipping, clipped**) cut with shears or scissors ▶ *n* (**-s**) short extract of a film
clip[2] *n* device for attaching or holding things together ▶ *v* (**clips, clipping, clipped**) attach or hold together with a clip
clipped *v* ▷ **clip**[1, 2]
clipper *n* (*pl* **-s**) fast commercial sailing ship
clippers *pl n* tool for clipping ▶ *n* ▷ **clipper**
clipping *n* (**-s**) something cut out, esp. an article from a newspaper ▶ *v* ▷ **clip**[1, 2]
clippings *n* ▷ **clipping**
clips *n, v* ▷ **clip**[1, 2]
clique [**kleek**] *n* (*pl* **-s**) small exclusive group
cliques *n* ▷ **clique**
clitoral *adj* ▷ **clitoris**
clitoris [**klit**-or-iss] *n* (*pl* **-es**) small sexually sensitive organ at the front of the vulva > **clitoral** *adj*
clitorises *n* ▷ **clitoris**
cloak *n* (*pl* **-s**) loose sleeveless outer garment ▶ *v* (**-s, -ing, -ed**) cover or conceal
cloaked *v* ▷ **cloak**
cloaking *v* ▷ **cloak**
cloakroom *n* (*pl* **-s**) room where coats may be left temporarily
cloakrooms *n* ▷ **cloakroom**
cloaks *n, v* ▷ **cloak**
clobber[1] *v* (**-s, -ing, -ed**) (*Informal*) hit
clobber[2] *n* (*pl* **-s**) (BRIT, AUST & NZ) (*Informal*) belongings, esp. clothes
clobbered *v* ▷ **clobber**[1]
clobbering *v* ▷ **clobber**[1]
clobbers *v* ▷ **clobber**[1] ▶ *n* ▷ **clobber**[2]
cloche [**klosh**] *n* (*pl* **-s**) cover to protect young plants
cloches *n* ▷ **cloche**
clock *n* (*pl* **-s**) instrument for showing the time
clocks *n* ▷ **clock**
clockwise *adv, adj* in the direction in which the hands of a clock rotate
clockwork *n* mechanism similar to the kind in a clock, used in wind-up toys
clod *n* (*pl* **-s**) lump of earth
clods *n* ▷ **clod**
clog *v* (**clogs, clogging, clogged**) obstruct ▶ *n* (*pl* **-s**) wooden or wooden-soled shoe
clogged *v* ▷ **clog**
clogging *v* ▷ **clog**
clogs *v, n* ▷ **clog**
cloister *n* (*pl* **-s**) covered pillared arcade, usu. in a monastery
cloistered *adj* sheltered
cloisters *n* ▷ **cloister**
clone *n* (*pl* **-s**) animal or plant produced artificially from the cells of another animal or plant, and identical to the original (*Informal*) ▶ *v* (**clones, cloning, cloned**) produce as a clone
cloned *v* ▷ **clone**
clones *n, v* ▷ **clone**
cloning *v* ▷ **clone**
close[1] *v* (**-ses, -sing, -sed**) [rhymes with **nose**] shut ▶ *n* (*pl* **-s**) end, conclusion
close[2] *adj* (**-r, -st**) [rhymes with **dose**] near ▶ *adv* closely, tightly > **closely** *adv* > **closeness** *n*

(*pl* **-es**)
closed *v* ▷ **close**[1]
closely *adv* ▷ **close**[2]
closeness *n* ▷ **close**[2]
closenesses *n* ▷ **close**[2]
closer *adj* ▷ **close**[2]
closes *v, n* ▷ **close**[1]
closest *adj* ▷ **close**[2]
closet *n* (*pl* **-s**) (US) cupboard ▶ *adj* private, secret ▶ *v* (**-s, -ing, -ed**) shut (oneself) away in private
closeted *v* ▷ **closet**
closeting *v* ▷ **closet**
closets *n, v* ▷ **closet**
closing *v* ▷ **close**[1]
closure *n* (*pl* **-s**) closing
closures *n* ▷ **closure**
clot *n* (*pl* **-s**) soft thick lump formed from liquid ▶ *v* (**-s, -tting, -tted**) form soft thick lumps
cloth *n* (*pl* **-s**) (piece of) woven fabric
clothe *v* (**clothes, clothing, clothed** *or* **clad**) put clothes on
clothed *v* ▷ **clothe**
clothes *pl n* articles of dress ▶ *v* ▷ **clothe**
clothing *n* clothes collectively ▶ *v* ▷ **clothe**
cloths *n* ▷ **cloth**
clots *n, v* ▷ **clot**
clotted *v* ▷ **clot**
clotting *v* ▷ **clot**
cloud *n* (*pl* **-s**) mass of condensed water vapour floating in the sky ▶ *v* (**-s, -ing, -ed**) (*foll. by* **over**) become cloudy > **cloudless** *adj*
cloudburst *n* (*pl* **-s**) heavy fall of rain
cloudbursts *n* ▷ **cloudburst**
clouded *v* ▷ **cloud**
cloudier *adj* ▷ **cloud**
cloudiest *adj* ▷ **cloud**
cloudiness *n* ▷ **cloudy**
clouding *v* ▷ **cloud**
cloudless *adj* ▷ **cloud**
clouds *n, v* ▷ **cloud**
cloudy *adj* (**-dier, -diest**) having a lot of clouds > **cloudiness** *n*
clout (*Informal*) *n* (*pl* **-s**) hard blow ▶ *v* (**-s, -ed, -ing**) hit hard
clouted *v* ▷ **clout**
clouting *v* ▷ **clout**
clouts *n, v* ▷ **clout**
clove[1] *n* (*pl* **-s**) dried flower bud of a tropical tree, used as a spice
clove[2] *n* (*pl* **-s**) segment of a bulb of garlic
clove[3] *v* ▷ **cleave**[1]
cloven *v* ▷ **cleave**[1]
clover *n* (*pl* **-s**) plant with three-lobed leaves
clovers *n* ▷ **clover**
cloves *n* ▷ **clove**[1, 2]
clown *n* (*pl* **-s**) comic entertainer in a circus ▶ *v* (**-s, -ing, -ed**) behave foolishly > **clownish** *adj* > **clownishly** *adv* > **clownishness** *n*
clowned *v* ▷ **clown**
clowning *v* ▷ **clown**
clownish *adj* ▷ **clown**
clownishly *adv* ▷ **clown**
clownishness *n* ▷ **clown**
clowns *n, v* ▷ **clown**
club *n* (*pl* **-s**) association of people with common interests ▶ *v* (**clubs, clubbing, clubbed**) hit with a club
clubbed *v* ▷ **club**
clubbing *v* ▷ **club**
clubs *n, v* ▷ **club**
cluck *n* (*pl* **-s**) low clicking noise made by a hen ▶ *v* (**-s, -ing, -ed**) make this noise
clucked *v* ▷ **cluck**
clucking *v* ▷ **cluck**
clucks *n, v* ▷ **cluck**
clue *n* (*pl* **-s**) something that helps to solve a mystery or puzzle
clueless *adj* stupid > **cluelessly** *adv* > **cluelessness** *n*
cluelessly *adv* ▷ **clueless**
cluelessness *n* ▷ **clueless**
clues *n* ▷ **clue**
clump *n* (*pl* **-s**) small group of things or people ▶ *v* (**-s, -ing, -ed**) walk heavily
clumped *v* ▷ **clump**
clumping *v* ▷ **clump**
clumps *n, v* ▷ **clump**
clumsier *adj* ▷ **clumsy**
clumsiest *adj* ▷ **clumsy**
clumsily *adv* ▷ **clumsy**
clumsiness *n* ▷ **clumsy**
clumsy *adj* (**-sier, -siest**) lacking skill or physical coordination > **clumsily** *adv* > **clumsiness** *n*
clung *v* ▷ **cling**
clunk *n* (*pl* **-s**) dull metallic sound ▶ *v* (**-s, -ing, -ed**) make such a sound
clunked *v* ▷ **clunk**
clunking *v* ▷ **clunk**
clunks *n, v* ▷ **clunk**
cluster *n* (*pl* **-s**) small close group ▶ *v* (**-s, -ing, -ed**) gather in clusters
clustered *v* ▷ **cluster**
clustering *v* ▷ **cluster**
clusters *n, v* ▷ **cluster**
clutch[1] *v* (**-es, -ing, -ed**) grasp tightly (*foll. by* **at**) ▶ *n* (*pl* **-es**) device enabling two revolving shafts to be connected and disconnected, esp. in a motor vehicle

clutch[2] *n* (*pl* **-es**) set of eggs laid at the same time
clutched *v* ▷ **clutch**[1]
clutches *v* ▷ **clutch**[1] ▶ *n* ▷ **clutch**[1, 2]
clutching *v* ▷ **clutch**[1]
clutter *v* (**-s, -ing, -ed**) scatter objects about (a place) untidily ▶ *n* (*pl* **-s**) untidy mess
cluttered *v* ▷ **clutter**
cluttering *v* ▷ **clutter**
clutters *v, n* ▷ **clutter**

> **cly** verb (**clys, clying, clyed**). Cly is an old word meaning steal. The various forms of this word can be useful when you are short of vowels. Cly scores 8 points.

coach *n* (*pl* **-es**) long-distance bus ▶ *v* (**-es, -ing, -ed**) train, teach
coached *v* ▷ **coach**
coaches *n, v* ▷ **coach**
coaching *v* ▷ **coach**
coagulant *n* (*pl* **-s**) substance causing coagulation
coagulants *n* ▷ **coagulant**
coagulate [koh-**ag**-yew-late] *v* (**-lates, -lating, -lated**) change from a liquid to a semisolid mass > **coagulation** *n* (*pl* **-s**)
coagulated *v* ▷ **coagulate**
coagulates *v* ▷ **coagulate**
coagulating *v* ▷ **coagulate**
coagulation *n* ▷ **coagulate**
coagulations *n* ▷ **coagulate**
coal *n* (*pl* **-s**) black rock consisting mainly of carbon, used as fuel
coalesce [koh-a-**less**] *v* (**-lesces, -lescing, -lesced**) come together, merge > **coalescence** *n* (*pl* **-s**)
coalesced *v* ▷ **coalesce**
coalescence *n* ▷ **coalesce**
coalescences *n* ▷ **coalesce**
coalesces *v* ▷ **coalesce**
coalescing *v* ▷ **coalesce**
coalfield *n* (*pl* **-s**) area with coal under the ground
coalfields *n* ▷ **coalfield**
coalition [koh-a-**lish**-un] *n* (*pl* **-s**) temporary alliance, esp. between political parties
coalitions *n* ▷ **coalition**
coals *n* ▷ **coal**
coarse *adj* (**-r, -st**) rough in texture > **coarsely** *adv* > **coarseness** *n* (*pl* **-es**) > **coarsen** *v* (**-s, -ing, -ed**)
coarsely *adv* ▷ **coarse**
coarsen *v* ▷ **coarse**
coarsened *v* ▷ **coarse**
coarseness *n* ▷ **coarse**
coarsenesses *n* ▷ **coarse**
coarsening *v* ▷ **coarse**
coarsens *v* ▷ **coarse**
coarser *adj* ▷ **coarse**
coarsest *adj* ▷ **coarse**
coast *n* (*pl* **-s**) place where the land meets the sea ▶ *v* (**-s, -ing, -ed**) move by momentum, without the use of power > **coastal** *adj*
coastal *adj* ▷ **coast**
coasted *v* ▷ **coast**
coaster *n* (*pl* **-s**) small mat placed under a glass
coasters *n* ▷ **coaster**
coastguard *n* (*pl* **-s**) organization that aids ships and swimmers in trouble and prevents smuggling
coastguards *n* ▷ **coastguard**
coasting *v* ▷ **coast**
coastline *n* (*pl* **-s**) outline of a coast
coastlines *n* ▷ **coastline**
coasts *n, v* ▷ **coast**
coat *n* (*pl* **-s**) outer garment with long sleeves ▶ *v* (**-s, -ing, -ed**) cover with a layer
coated *v* ▷ **coat**
coating *n* (*pl* **-s**) covering layer ▶ *v* ▷ **coat**
coatings *n* ▷ **coating**
coats *n, v* ▷ **coat**
coax *v* (**-es, -ing, -ed**) persuade gently
coaxed *v* ▷ **coax**
coaxes *v* ▷ **coax**
coaxial [koh-**ax**-ee-al] *adj* (of a cable) transmitting by means of two concentric conductors separated by an insulator
coaxing *v* ▷ **coax**
cob *n* (*pl* **-s**) stalk of an ear of maize
cobalt *n* (*pl* **-s**) (CHEM) brittle silvery-white metallic element
cobalts *n* ▷ **cobalt**
cobber *n* (*pl* **-s**) (AUST & OLD-FASHIONED NZ) (*Informal*) friend
cobbers *n* ▷ **cobber**
cobble *n* (*pl* **-s**) cobblestone
cobbler *n* (*pl* **-s**) shoe mender
cobblers *n* ▷ **cobbler**
cobbles *n* ▷ **cobble**
cobblestone *n* (*pl* **-s**) rounded stone used for paving
cobblestones *n* ▷ **cobblestone**
cobia [**koh**-bee-a] *n* (*pl* **-s**) large dark-striped game fish of tropical and subtropical seas
cobias *n* ▷ **cobia**
cobra *n* (*pl* **-s**) venomous hooded snake of Asia and Africa
cobras *n* ▷ **cobra**
cobs *n* ▷ **cob**
cobweb *n* (*pl* **-s**) spider's web
cobwebs *n* ▷ **cobweb**

cocaine *n* (*pl* **-s**) addictive drug used as a narcotic and as an anaesthetic
cocaines *n* ▷ **cocaine**
coccyges *n* ▷ **coccyx**
coccyx [**kok**-six] *n* (*pl* **coccyges**) [kok-**sije**-eez] bone at the base of the spinal column
cochineal *n* (*pl* **-s**) red dye obtained from a Mexican insect, used for food colouring
cochineals *n* ▷ **cochineal**
cock *n* (*pl* **-s**) male bird, esp. of domestic fowl ▶ *v* (**-s, -ing, -ed**) draw back (the hammer of a gun) to firing position
cockade *n* (*pl* **-s**) feather or rosette worn on a hat as a badge
cockades *n* ▷ **cockade**
cockateel *n* ▷ **cockatiel**
cockateels *n* ▷ **cockatiel**
cockatiel, cockateel *n* (*pl* **-s**) crested Australian parrot with a greyish-brown and yellow plumage
cockatiels *n* ▷ **cockatiel**
cockatoo *n* (*pl* **-s**) crested parrot of Australia or the East Indies
cockatoos *n* ▷ **cockatoo**
cocked *v* ▷ **cock**
cockerel *n* (*pl* **-s**) young domestic cock
cockerels *n* ▷ **cockerel**
cockeyed *adj* (*Informal*) crooked, askew
cockie, cocky *n* (*pl* **-kies**) (AUST & NZ) (*Informal*) farmer
cockier *adj* ▷ **cocky**
cockies *n* ▷ **cockie**
cockiest *adj* ▷ **cocky**
cockily *adv* ▷ **cocky**
cockiness *n* ▷ **cocky**
cocking *v* ▷ **cock**
cockle *n* (*pl* **-s**) edible shellfish
cockles *n* ▷ **cockle**
cockney *n* (*pl* **-s**) native of the East End of London
cockneys *n* ▷ **cockney**
cockpit *n* (*pl* **-s**) pilot's compartment in an aircraft
cockpits *n* ▷ **cockpit**
cockroach *n* (*pl* **-es**) beetle-like insect which is a household pest
cockroaches *n* ▷ **cockroach**
cocks *n, v* ▷ **cock**
cocksure *adj* overconfident, arrogant
cocktail *n* (*pl* **-s**) mixed alcoholic drink
cocktails *n* ▷ **cocktail**
cocky *adj* (**cockier, cockiest**) conceited and overconfident ▶ *n* ▷ **cockie** > **cockily** *adv* > **cockiness** *n*
cocoa *n* (*pl* **-s**) powder made from the seed of the cacao tree
cocoas *n* ▷ **cocoa**
coconut *n* (*pl* **-s**) large hard fruit of a type of palm tree
coconuts *n* ▷ **coconut**
cocoon *n* (*pl* **-s**) silky protective covering of a silkworm ▶ *v* (**-s, -ing, -ed**) wrap up tightly for protection
cocooned *v* ▷ **cocoon**
cocooning *v* ▷ **cocoon**
cocoons *n, v* ▷ **cocoon**
cod *n* (*pl* **cod**) large food fish of the North Atlantic
coda *n* (*pl* **-s**) final part of a musical composition
codas *n* ▷ **coda**
coddle *v* (**coddles, coddling, coddled**) pamper, overprotect
coddled *v* ▷ **coddle**
coddles *v* ▷ **coddle**
coddling *v* ▷ **coddle**
code *n* (*pl* **-s**) system of letters, symbols, or prearranged signals by which messages can be communicated secretly or briefly ▶ *v* (**codes, coding, coded**) put into code
coded *v* ▷ **code**
codeine [**kode**-een] *n* (*pl* **-s**) drug used as a painkiller
codeines *v* ▷ **codeine**
codes *n, v* ▷ **code**
codex *n* (*pl* **codices**) volume of manuscripts of an ancient text
codger *n* (*pl* **-s**) (BRIT, AUST & NZ) (*Informal*) old man
codgers *n* ▷ **codger**
codices *n* ▷ **codex**
codicil [**kode**-iss-ill] *n* (*pl* **-s**) addition to a will
codicils *n* ▷ **codicil**
codification *n* ▷ **codify**
codifications *n* ▷ **codify**
codified *v* ▷ **codify**
codifies *v* ▷ **codify**
codify *v* (**-fies, -fying, -fied**) organize (rules or procedures) systematically > **codification** *n* (*pl* **-s**)
codifying *v* ▷ **codify**
coding *v* ▷ **code**
coeducation *n* education of boys and girls together > **coeducational** *adj*
coeducational *adj* ▷ **coeducation**
coefficient *n* (*pl* **-s**) (MATHS) number or constant placed before and multiplying a quantity
coefficients *n* ▷ **coefficient**
coelacanth [**seel**-a-kanth] *n* (*pl* **-s**) primitive marine fish

coelacanths *n* ▷ **coelacanth**
coerce [koh-**urss**] *v* (**-ces, -cing, -ced**) compel, force > **coercion** *n* > **coercive** *adj*
coerced *v* ▷ **coerce**
coerces *v* ▷ **coerce**
coercing *v* ▷ **coerce**
coercion *n* ▷ **coerce**
coercive *adj* ▷ **coerce**
coeval [koh-**eev**-al] *adj, n* (*pl* **-s**) contemporary
coevals *n* ▷ **coeval**
coexist *v* (**-s, -ing, -ed**) exist together, esp. peacefully despite differences > **coexistence** *n*
coexisted *v* ▷ **coexist**
coexistence *n* ▷ **coexist**
coexisting *v* ▷ **coexist**
coexists *v* ▷ **coexist**
coffee *n* (*pl* **-s**) drink made from the roasted and ground seeds of a tropical shrub ▶ *adj* medium-brown
coffees *n* ▷ **coffee**
coffer *n* (*pl* **-s**) chest for valuables ▶ *pl* store of money
coffers *n* ▷ **coffer**
coffin *n* (*pl* **-s**) box in which a corpse is buried or cremated
coffins *n* ▷ **coffin**
cog *n* (*pl* **-s**) one of the teeth on the rim of a gearwheel
cogency *n* ▷ **cogent**
cogent [**koh**-jent] *adj* forcefully convincing > **cogency** *n* > **cogently** *adv*
cogently *n* ▷ **cogent**
cogitate [**koj**-it-tate] *v* (**-tates, -tating, -tated**) think deeply about > **cogitation** *n* (*pl* **-s**)
cogitated *v* ▷ **cogitate**
cogitates *v* ▷ **cogitate**
cogitating *v* ▷ **cogitate**
cogitation *n* ▷ **cogitate**
cogitations *n* ▷ **cogitate**
cognac [**kon**-yak] *n* (*pl* **-s**) French brandy
cognacs *n* ▷ **cognac**
cognate *adj* derived from a common original form
cognition *n* (*pl* **-s**) act or experience of knowing or acquiring knowledge > **cognitive** *adj*
cognitions *n* ▷ **cognition**
cognitive *adj* ▷ **cognition**
cognizance *n* (*pl* **-s**) knowledge, understanding > **cognizant** *adj*
cognizances *n* ▷ **cognizance**
cognizant *adj* ▷ **cognizance**
cognoscenti [kon-yo-**shen**-tee] *pl n* connoisseurs
cogs *n* ▷ **cog**
cohabit *v* (**-s, -ing, -ed**) live together as husband and wife without being married > **cohabitation** *n* (*pl* **-s**)
cohabitation *n* ▷ **cohabit**
cohabitations *n* ▷ **cohabit**
cohabited *v* ▷ **cohabit**
cohabiting *v* ▷ **cohabit**
cohabits *v* ▷ **cohabit**
cohere *v* (**-heres, -hering, -hered**) hold or stick together
cohered *v* ▷ **cohere**
coherence *n* ▷ **coherent**
coherent *adj* logical and consistent > **coherence** *n* > **coherently** *adv*
coherently *n* ▷ **coherent**
coheres *v* ▷ **cohere**
cohering *v* ▷ **cohere**
cohesion *n* sticking together
cohesive *adj* sticking together to form a whole
cohort *n* (*pl* **-s**) band of associates
cohorts *n* ▷ **cohort**
coiffeur *n* ▷ **coiffure**
coiffeurs *n* ▷ **coiffure**
coiffeuse *n* ▷ **coiffure**
coiffeuses *n* ▷ **coiffure**
coiffure *n* (*pl* **-s**) hairstyle > **coiffeur, coiffeuse** *n* (*pl* **-s**) hairdresser
coiffures *n* ▷ **coiffure**
coil *v* (**-s, -ing, -ed**) wind in loops ▶ *n* (*pl* **-s**) something coiled
coiled *v* ▷ **coil**
coiling *v* ▷ **coil**
coils *v, n* ▷ **coil**
coin *n* (*pl* **-s**) piece of metal money ▶ *v* (**-s, -ing, -ed**) invent (a word or phrase)
coinage *n* (*pl* **-s**) coins collectively
coinages *n* ▷ **coinage**
coincide *v* (**-cides, -ciding, -cided**) happen at the same time
coincided *v* ▷ **coincide**
coincidence *n* (*pl* **-s**) occurrence of simultaneous or apparently connected events
coincidences *n* ▷ **coincidence**
coincident *adj* in agreement
coincidental *adj* resulting from coincidence > **coincidentally** *adv*
coincidentally *adv* ▷ **coincidental**
coincides *v* ▷ **coincide**
coinciding *v* ▷ **coincide**
coined *v* ▷ **coin**
coining *v* ▷ **coin**
coins *n, v* ▷ **coin**
coir *n* (*pl* **-s**) coconut fibre, used for matting

coirs *n* ▷ **coir**
coital *adj* ▷ **coitus**
coition *n* ▷ **coitus**
coitions *n* ▷ **coitus**
coitus [**koh**-it-uss], **coition** [koh-**ish**-un] *n* (*pl* **-s**) sexual intercourse > **coital** *adj*
coke[1] *n* (*pl* **-s**) solid fuel left after gas has been distilled from coal
coke[2] *n* (*pl* **-s**) (*Slang*) cocaine
cokes *n* ▷ **coke**[1, 2]
col *n* (*pl* **-s**) high mountain pass
cola *n* (*pl* **-s**) dark brown fizzy soft drink
colander *n* (*pl* **-s**) perforated bowl for straining or rinsing foods
colanders *n* ▷ **colander**
colas *n* ▷ **cola**
cold *adj* (**-er, -est**) lacking heat ▶ *n* (*pl* **-s**) lack of heat > **coldly** *adv* > **coldness** *n* (*pl* **-es**)
colder *adj* ▷ **cold**
coldest *adj* ▷ **cold**
coldly *adv* ▷ **cold**
coldness *n* ▷ **cold**
coldnesses *n* ▷ **cold**
colds *n* ▷ **cold**
coleslaw *n* (*pl* **-s**) salad dish of shredded raw cabbage in a dressing
coleslaws *n* ▷ **coleslaw**
coley *n* (*pl* **-s**) codlike food fish of the N Atlantic
coleys *n* ▷ **coley**
colic *n* (*pl* **-s**) severe pains in the stomach and bowels > **colicky** *adj* (**-ckier, -ckiest**)
colickier *adj* ▷ **colic**
colickiest *adj* ▷ **colic**
colicky *adj* ▷ **colic**
colics *n* ▷ **colic**
colitis [koh-**lie**-tiss] *n* inflammation of the colon
collaborate *v* (**-ates, -ating, -ated**) work with another on a project > **collaboration** *n* (*pl* **-s**) > **collaborative** *adj* > **collaboratively** *adv* > **collaborator** *n* (*pl* **-s**)
collaborated *v* ▷ **collaborate**
collaborates *v* ▷ **collaborate**
collaborating *v* ▷ **collaborate**
collaboration *n* ▷ **collaborate**
collaborations *n* ▷ **collaborate**
collaborative *adj* ▷ **collaborate**
collaboratively *adv* ▷ **collaborate**
collaborator *n* ▷ **collaborate**
collaborators *n* ▷ **collaborate**
collage [kol-**lahzh**] *n* (*pl* **-s**) art form in which various materials or objects are glued onto a surface
collages *n* ▷ **collage**
collapse *v* (**-lapses, -lapsing, -lapsed**) fall down suddenly ▶ *n* (*pl* **-s**) collapsing > **collapsible** *adj*
collapsed *v* ▷ **collapse**
collapses *v*, *n* ▷ **collapse**
collapsible *adj* ▷ **collapse**
collapsing *v* ▷ **collapse**
collar *n* (*pl* **-s**) part of a garment round the neck ▶ *v* (**-s, -ing, -ed**) (BRIT, AUST & NZ) (*Informal*) seize, arrest
collarbone *n* (*pl* **-s**) bone joining the shoulder blade to the breastbone
collarbones *n* ▷ **collarbone**
collared *v* ▷ **collar**
collaring *v* ▷ **collar**
collars *n*, *v* ▷ **collar**
collate *v* (**-lates, -lating, -lated**) gather together, examine, and put in order
collated *v* ▷ **collate**
collateral *n* (*pl* **-s**) security pledged for the repayment of a loan
collaterals *n* ▷ **collateral**
collates *v* ▷ **collate**
collating *v* ▷ **collate**
collation *n* (*pl* **-s**) collating
collations *n* ▷ **collation**
colleague *n* (*pl* **-s**) fellow worker, esp. in a profession
colleagues *n* ▷ **colleague**
collect[1] *v* (**-s, -ing, -ed**) gather together > **collector** *n* (*pl* **-s**)
collect[2] *n* (*pl* **-s**) short prayer
collected *adj* calm and controlled ▶ *v* ▷ **collect**[1] > **collectedly** *adv* > **collectedness** *n*
collectedly *adv* ▷ **collected**
collectedness *n* ▷ **collected**
collecting *v* ▷ **collect**[1]
collection *n* (*pl* **-s**) things collected
collections *n* ▷ **collection**
collective *adj* of or done by a group ▶ *n* (*pl* **-s**) group of people working together on an enterprise and sharing the benefits from it > **collectively** *adv*
collectively *adv* ▷ **collective**
collectives *n* ▷ **collective**
collects *v* ▷ **collect**[1] ▶ *n* ▷ **collect**[2]
colleen *n* (*pl* **-s**) (IRISH) girl
colleens *n* ▷ **colleen**
college *n* (*pl* **-s**) place of higher education > **collegiate** *adj*
colleges *n* ▷ **college**
collegiate *adj* ▷ **college**
collide *v* (**-lides, -liding, -lided**) crash together violently > **collision** *n* (*pl* **-s**)
collided *v* ▷ **collide**
collides *v* ▷ **collide**
colliding *v* ▷ **collide**

collie *n* (*pl* **-s**) silky-haired sheepdog
collier *n* (*pl* **-s**) coal miner
collieries *n* ▷ **colliery**
colliers *n* ▷ **collier**
colliery *n* (*pl* **-lieries**) coal mine
collies *n* ▷ **collie**
collision *n* ▷ **collide**
collisions *n* ▷ **collide**
collocate *v* (**-cates, -cating, -cated**) (of words) occur together regularly > **collocation** *n* (*pl* **-s**)
collocated *v* ▷ **collocate**
collocates *v* ▷ **collocate**
collocating *v* ▷ **collocate**
collocation *n* ▷ **collocate**
collocations *n* ▷ **collocate**
colloid *n* (*pl* **-s**) suspension of particles in a solution
colloids *n* ▷ **colloid**
colloquial *adj* suitable for informal speech or writing > **colloquially** *adv*
colloquialism *n* (*pl* **-s**) colloquial word or phrase
colloquialisms *n* ▷ **colloquialism**
colloquially *adv* ▷ **colloquial**
collude *v* (**-ludes, -luding, -luded**) act in collusion
colluded *v* ▷ **collude**
colludes *v* ▷ **collude**
colluding *v* ▷ **collude**
collusion *n* (*pl* **-s**) secret or illegal cooperation
collusions *n* ▷ **collusion**
collywobbles *pl n* (*Slang*) nervousness
cologne *n* (*pl* **-s**) mild perfume
colognes *n* ▷ **cologne**
colon[1] *n* (*pl* **-s**) punctuation mark (:)
colon[2] *n* (*pl* **-s**) part of the large intestine connected to the rectum
colonel *n* (*pl* **-s**) senior commissioned army or air-force officer
colonels *n* ▷ **colonel**
colonial *adj*, *n* (*pl* **-s**) (inhabitant) of a colony
colonialism *n* policy of acquiring and maintaining colonies
colonials *n* ▷ **colonial**
colonies *n* ▷ **colony**
colonist *n* (*pl* **-s**) settler in a colony
colonists *n* ▷ **colonist**
colonization *n* ▷ **colonize**
colonizations *n* ▷ **colonize**
colonize *v* (**-izes, -izing, -ized**) make into a colony > **colonization** *n* (*pl* **-s**)
colonized *v* ▷ **colonize**
colonizes *v* ▷ **colonize**
colonizing *v* ▷ **colonize**
colonnade *n* (*pl* **-s**) row of columns
colonnades *n* ▷ **colonnade**
colons *n* ▷ **colon**[1, 2]
colony *n* (*pl* **-nies**) group of people who settle in a new country but remain under the rule of their homeland
coloration *n* (*pl* **-s**) arrangement of colours
colorations *n* ▷ **coloration**
colosally *adv* ▷ **colossal**
colossal *adj* very large > **colossally** *adv*
colossi *n* ▷ **colossus**
colossus *n* (*pl* **-si, -suses**) huge statue
colossuses *n* ▷ **colossus**
colostomies *n* ▷ **colostomy**
colostomy *n* (*pl* **-mies**) operation to form an opening from the colon onto the surface of the body, for emptying the bowel
colour *n* (*pl* **-s**) appearance of things as a result of reflecting light ▶ *pl* flag of a country or regiment (SPORT) ▶ *v* (**-s, -ing, -ed**) apply colour to > **colourless** *adj* > **colourlessly** *adv*
coloured *adj* having colour ▶ *v* ▷ **colour**
colourful *adj* with bright or varied colours > **colourfully** *adv*
colourfully *adv* ▷ **colourful**
colouring *v* ▷ **colour**
colourless *adj* ▷ **colour**
colourlessly *adv* ▷ **colour**
colours *n*, *v* ▷ **colour**
cols *n* ▷ **col**
colt *n* (*pl* **-s**) young male horse
colts *n* ▷ **colt**
columbine *n* (*pl* **-s**) garden flower with five petals
columbines *n* ▷ **columbine**
column *n* (*pl* **-s**) pillar
columnist *n* (*pl* **-s**) journalist who writes a regular feature in a newspaper
columnists *n* ▷ **columnist**
columns *n* ▷ **column**
coma *n* (*pl* **-s**) state of deep unconsciousness
comas *n* ▷ **coma**
comatose *adj* in a coma
comb *n* (*pl* **-s**) toothed implement for arranging the hair ▶ *v* (**-s, -ing, -ed**) use a comb on
combat *n* (*pl* **-s**) ▶ *v* (**-s, -ing, -ed**) fight, struggle > **combatant** *n* (*pl* **-s**) > **combative** *adj* > **combativeness** *n*
combatant *n* ▷ **combat**
combatants *n* ▷ **combat**
combated *v* ▷ **combat**
combating *v* ▷ **combat**
combats *n*, *v* ▷ **combat**
combed *v* ▷ **comb**
combination *n* (*pl* **-s**) combining ▶ *pl* (BRIT) old-

fashioned undergarment with long sleeves and long legs
combinations *n* ▷ **combination**
combine *v* (**-bines, -bining, -bined**) join together ▶ *n* (*pl* **-s**) association of people or firms for a common purpose
combined *v* ▷ **combine**
combines *v, n* ▷ **combine**
combing *v* ▷ **comb**
combining *v* ▷ **combine**
combs *n, v* ▷ **comb**
combustible *adj* burning easily
combustion *n* (*pl* **-s**) process of burning
combustions *n* ▷ **combustion**
come *v* (**comes, coming, came, come**) move towards a place, arrive
comeback *n* (*pl* **-s**) (*Informal*) return to a former position
comebacks *n* ▷ **comeback**
comedian, comedienne *n* (*pl* **-s**) entertainer who tells jokes
comedians *n* ▷ **comedian**
comedienne *n* ▷ **comedian**
comediennes *n* ▷ **comedian**
comedies *n* ▷ **comedy**
comedown *n* (*pl* **-s**) decline in status
comedowns *n* ▷ **comedown**
comedy *n* (*pl* **-dies**) humorous play, film, or programme
comelier *adj* ▷ **comely**
comeliest *adj* ▷ **comely**
comeliness *n* ▷ **comely**
comely *adj* (**-lier, -liest**) (*Old-fashioned*) nice-looking > **comeliness** *n*
comes *v* ▷ **come**
comestibles *pl n* (*Formal*) food
comet *n* (*pl* **-s**) heavenly body with a long luminous tail
comets *n* ▷ **comet**
comeuppance *n* (*Informal*) deserved punishment
comfier *adj* ▷ **comfy**
comfiest *adj* ▷ **comfy**
comfit *n* (*pl* **-s**) (*Old-fashioned*) sugar-coated sweet
comfits *n* ▷ **comfit**
comfort *n* (*pl* **-s**) physical ease or wellbeing ▶ *v* (**-s, -ing, -ed**) soothe, console > **comforter** *n* (*pl* **-s**)
comfortable *adj* giving comfort > **comfortably** *adv*
comfortably *adv* ▷ **comfortable**
comforted *v* ▷ **comfort**
comforter *n* ▷ **comfort**
comforters *n* ▷ **comfort**
comforting *v* ▷ **comfort**
comforts *n, v* ▷ **comfort**
comfrey *n* (*pl* **-s**) tall plant with bell-shaped flowers
comfreys *n* ▷ **comfrey**
comfy *adj* (**-fier, -fiest**) (*Informal*) comfortable
comic *adj* humorous, funny ▶ *n* (*pl* **-s**) comedian
comical *adj* amusing > **comically** *adv*
comically *adv* ▷ **comical**
comics *n* ▷ **comic**
coming *v* ▷ **come**
comma *n* (*pl* **-s**) punctuation mark (,)
command *v* (**-s, -ing, -ed**) order ▶ *n* (*pl* **-s**) authoritative instruction that something must be done
commandant *n* (*pl* **-s**) officer commanding a military group
commandants *n* ▷ **commandant**
commanded *v* ▷ **command**
commandeer *v* (**-s, -ing, -ed**) seize for military use
commandeered *v* ▷ **commandeer**
commandeering *v* ▷ **commandeer**
commandeers *v* ▷ **commandeer**
commander *n* (*pl* **-s**) military officer in command of a group or operation
commanders *n* ▷ **commander**
commanding *v* ▷ **command**
commandment *n* (*pl* **-s**) command from God
commandments *n* ▷ **commandment**
commando *n* (*pl* **-dos, -does**) (member of) a military unit trained for swift raids in enemy territory
commandoes *n* ▷ **commando**
commandos *n* ▷ **commando**
commands *v, n* ▷ **command**
commas *n* ▷ **comma**
commemorate *v* (**-rates, -rating, -rated**) honour the memory of > **commemoration** *n* (*pl* **-s**) > **commemorative** *adj*
commemorated *v* ▷ **commemorate**
commemorates *v* ▷ **commemorate**
commemorating *v* ▷ **commemorate**
commemoration *n* ▷ **commemorate**
commemorations *n* ▷ **commemorate**
commemorative *adj* ▷ **commemorate**
commence *v* (**-mences, -mencing, -menced**) begin > **commencement** *n* (*pl* **-s**)
commenced *v* ▷ **commence**
commencement *n* ▷ **commence**
commencements *n* ▷ **commence**
commences *v* ▷ **commence**
commencing *v* ▷ **commence**
commend *v* (**-s, -ing, -ed**) praise

> **commendable** *adj* > **commendably** *adv* > **commendation** *n* (*pl* **-s**)
commendable *adj* ▷ **commend**
commendably *adv* ▷ **commend**
commendation *n* ▷ **commend**
commendations *n* ▷ **commend**
commended *v* ▷ **commend**
commending *v* ▷ **commend**
commends *v* ▷ **commend**
commensurable *adj* measurable by the same standards
commensurate *adj* corresponding in degree, size, or value
comment *n* (*pl* **-s**) remark ▶ *v* (**-s, -ing, -ed**) make a comment
commentaries *n* ▷ **commentary**
commentary *n* (*pl* **-taries**) spoken accompaniment to a broadcast or film
commentate *v* (**-tates, -tating, -tated**) provide a commentary > **commentator** *n* (*pl* **-s**)
commentated *v* ▷ **commentate**
commentates *v* ▷ **commentate**
commentating *v* ▷ **commentate**
commentator *n* ▷ **commentate**
commentators *n* ▷ **commentate**
commented *v* ▷ **comment**
commenting *v* ▷ **comment**
comments *n, v* ▷ **comment**
commerce *n* (*pl* **-s**) buying and selling, trade
commerces *n* ▷ **commerce**
commercial *adj* of commerce ▶ *n* (*pl* **-s**) television or radio advertisement
commercialization *n* ▷ **commercialize**
commercialize *v* (**-izes, -izing, -ized**) make commercial > **commercialization** *n*
commercialized *v* ▷ **commercialize**
commercializes *v* ▷ **commercialize**
commercializing *v* ▷ **commercialize**
commercials *n* ▷ **commercial**
commiserate *v* (**-rates, -rating, -rated**) (*foll. by* **with**) express sympathy (for) > **commiseration** *n* (*pl* **-s**)
commiserated *v* ▷ **commiserate**
commiserates *v* ▷ **commiserate**
commiserating *v* ▷ **commiserate**
commiseration *n* ▷ **commiserate**
commiserations *n* ▷ **commiserate**
commissar *n* (*pl* **-s**) (formerly) official responsible for political education in Communist countries
commissariat *n* (*pl* **-s**) (BRIT, AUST & NZ) military department in charge of food supplies
commissariats *n* ▷ **commissariat**
commissars *n* ▷ **commissar**
commission *n* (*pl* **-s**) piece of work that an artist is asked to do (MIL) ▶ *v* (**-s, -ing, -ed**) place an order for
commissionaire *n* (*pl* **-s**) uniformed doorman at a hotel, theatre, etc.
commissionaires *n* ▷ **commissionaire**
commissioned *v* ▷ **commission**
commissioner *n* (*pl* **-s**) appointed official in a government department
commissioners *n* ▷ **commissioner**
commissioning *v* ▷ **commission**
commissions *n, v* ▷ **commission**
commit *v* (**-mits, -mitting, -mitted**) perform (a crime or error)
commitment *n* (*pl* **-s**) dedication to a cause
commitments *n* ▷ **commitment**
commits *v* ▷ **commit**
committal *n* (*pl* **-s**) sending someone to prison or hospital
committals *n* ▷ **committal**
committed *v* ▷ **commit**
committee *n* (*pl* **-s**) group of people appointed to perform a specified service or function
committees *n* ▷ **committee**
committing *v* ▷ **commit**
commode *n* (*pl* **-s**) seat with a hinged flap concealing a chamber pot
commodes *n* ▷ **commode**
commodious *adj* roomy
commodities *n* ▷ **commodity**
commodity *n* (*pl* **-ities**) something that can be bought or sold
commodore *n* (*pl* **-s**) senior commissioned officer in the navy
commodores *n* ▷ **commodore**
common *adj* (**-er, -est**) occurring often ▶ *n* (*pl* **-s**) area of grassy land belonging to a community > **commonly** *adv*
commoner *n* (*pl* **-s**) person who does not belong to the nobility ▶ *adj* ▷ **common**
commoners *n* ▷ **commoner**
commonest *adj* ▷ **common**
commonly *adv* ▷ **common**
commonplace *adj* ordinary, everyday ▶ *n* (*pl* **-s**) trite remark
commonplaces *n* ▷ **commonplace**
commons *n* ▷ **common**
commonwealth *n* (*pl* **-s**) state or nation viewed politically
commonwealths *n* ▷ **commonwealth**
commotion *n* (*pl* **-s**) noisy disturbance
commotions *n* ▷ **commotion**
communal *adj* shared > **communally** *adv*
communally *n* ▷ **communal**
commune[1] *n* (*pl* **-s**) group of people who live

together and share everything
commune² *v* (**-munes, -muning, -muned**) (*foll. by* **with**) feel very close (to)
communed *v* ▷ **commune²**
communes *n* ▷ **commune¹** ▶ *v* ▷ **commune²**
communicable *adj* (of a disease) able to be passed on
communicant *n* (*pl* **-s**) person who receives Communion
communicants *n* ▷ **communicant**
communicate *v* (**-cates, -cating, -cated**) make known or share (information, thoughts, or feelings)
communicated *v* ▷ **communicate**
communicates *v* ▷ **communicate**
communicating *adj* (of a door) joining two rooms ▶ *v* ▷ **communicate**
communication *n* communicating ▶ *pl* (**-s**) means of travelling or sending messages
communications *n* ▷ **communication**
communicative *adj* talking freely
communing *v* ▷ **commune²**
communion *n* (*pl* **-s**) sharing of thoughts or feelings
communions *n* ▷ **communion**
communiqué [kom-**mune**-ik-kay] *n* (*pl* **-s**) official announcement
communiqués *n* ▷ **communiqué**
communism *n* belief that all property and means of production should be shared by the community > **communist** *n* (*pl* **-s**) *adj*
communists *n* ▷ **communism**
communities *n* ▷ **community**
community *n* (*pl* **-ties**) all the people living in one district
commutator *n* (*pl* **-s**) device used to change alternating electric current into direct current
commutators *n* ▷ **commutator**
commute *v* (**-mutes, -muting, -muted**) travel daily to and from work
commuted *v* ▷ **commute**
commuter *n* (*pl* **-s**) person who commutes to and from work
commuters *n* ▷ **commuter**
commutes *v* ▷ **commute**
commuting *v* ▷ **commute**
compact¹ *adj* (**-er, -est**) closely packed ▶ *n* (*pl* **-s**) small flat case containing a mirror and face powder ▶ *v* (**-s, -ing, -ed**) pack closely together > **compactly** *adv* > **compactness** *n*
compact² *n* (*pl* **-s**) contract, agreement
compacted *v* ▷ **compact¹**
compacter *adj* ▷ **compact¹**
compactest *adj* ▷ **compact¹**
compacting *v* ▷ **compact¹**
compactly *adv* ▷ **compact¹**
compactness *n* ▷ **compact¹**
compacts *n* ▷ **compact¹, ²** ▶ *v* ▷ **compact¹**
companies *n* ▷ **company**
companion *n* (*pl* **-s**) person who associates with or accompanies someone > **companionship** *n* (*pl* **-s**)
companionable *adj* friendly > **companionably** *adv*
companionably *adv* ▷ **companionable**
companions *n* ▷ **companion**
companionship *n* ▷ **companion**
companionships *n* ▷ **companion**
companionway *n* (*pl* **-s**) ladder linking the decks of a ship
companionways *n* ▷ **companionway**
company *n* (*pl* **-nies**) business organization
comparability *n* ▷ **compare**
comparable *adj* ▷ **compare**
comparative *adj* relative ▶ *n* (*pl* **-s**) (GRAMMAR) comparative form of a word > **comparatively** *adv*
comparatively *adv* ▷ **comparative**
comparatives *n* ▷ **comparative**
compare *v* (**-pares, -paring, -pared**) examine (things) and point out the resemblances or differences (*foll. by* **to**) (*foll. by* **with**) > **comparable** *adj* > **comparability** *n*
compared *v* ▷ **compare**
compares *v* ▷ **compare**
comparing *v* ▷ **compare**
comparison *n* (*pl* **-s**) comparing
comparisons *n* ▷ **comparison**
compartment *n* (*pl* **-s**) section of a railway carriage
compartments *n* ▷ **compartment**
compass *n* (*pl* **-es**) instrument for showing direction, with a needle that points north ▶ *pl* hinged instrument for drawing circles
compasses *n* ▷ **compass**
compassion *n* pity, sympathy > **compassionate** *adj* > **compassionately** *adv*
compassionate *adj* ▷ **compassion**
compassionately *adj* ▷ **compassion**
compatibility *n* ▷ **compatible**
compatible *adj* able to exist, work, or be used together > **compatibility** *n*
compatriot *n* (*pl* **-s**) fellow countryman or countrywoman
compatriots *n* ▷ **compatriot**
compel *v* (**-pels, -pelling, -pelled**) force (to be or do)
compelled *v* ▷ **compel**
compelling *v* ▷ **compel**

compels *v* ▷ **compel**
compendia *n* ▷ **compendium**
compendious *adj* brief but comprehensive
compendium *n* (*pl* **-diums, -dia**) selection of board games in one box
compendiums *n* ▷ **compendium**
compensate *v* (**-sates, -sating, -sated**) make amends to (someone), esp. for injury or loss (*foll. by* **for**) > **compensatory** *adj*
compensated *v* ▷ **compensate**
compensates *v* ▷ **compensate**
compensating *v* ▷ **compensate**
compensation *n* (*pl* **-s**) payment to make up for loss or injury
compensations *n* ▷ **compensation**
compensatory *adj* ▷ **compensate**
compere *n* (*pl* **-s**) person who presents a stage, radio, or television show ▶ *v* (**-peres, -pering, -pered**) be the compere of
compered *v* ▷ **compere**
comperes *n, v* ▷ **compere**
compering *v* ▷ **compere**
compete *v* (**-petes, -peting, -peted**) try to win or achieve (a prize, profit, etc.) > **competitive** *adj* > **competitively** *adv* > **competitiveness** *n* > **competitor** *n* (*pl* **-s**)
competed *v* ▷ **compete**
competence *n* ▷ **competent**
competent *adj* having the skill or knowledge to do something well > **competently** *adv* > **competence** *n*
competently *adv* ▷ **competent**
competes *v* ▷ **compete**
competing *v* ▷ **compete**
competition *n* (*pl* **-s**) competing
competitions *n* ▷ **competition**
competitive *adj* ▷ **compete**
competitively *adv* ▷ **compete**
competitiveness *n* ▷ **compete**
competitor *n* ▷ **compete**
competitors *n* ▷ **compete**
compilation *n* ▷ **compile**
compilations *n* ▷ **compile**
compile *v* (**-piles, -piling, -piled**) collect and arrange (information), esp. to make a book > **compilation** *n* (*pl* **-s**) > **compiler** *n* (*pl* **-s**)
compiled *v* ▷ **compile**
compiler *n* ▷ **compile**
compilers *n* ▷ **compile**
compiles *v* ▷ **compile**
compiling *v* ▷ **compile**
complacencies *n* ▷ **complacent**
complacency *n* ▷ **complacent**
complacent *adj* self-satisfied > **complacently** (*pl* **-cies**) *adv* > **complacency** *n*
complacently *adv* ▷ **complacent**
complain *v* (**-s, -ing, -ed**) express resentment or displeasure
complainant *n* (*pl* **-s**) (LAW) plaintiff
complainants *n* ▷ **complainant**
complained *v* ▷ **complain**
complaining *v* ▷ **complain**
complains *v* ▷ **complain**
complaint *n* (*pl* **-s**) complaining
complaints *n* ▷ **complaint**
complaisance *n* ▷ **complaisant**
complaisant [kom-**play**-zant] *adj* willing to please > **complaisance** *n*
complement *n* (*pl* **-s**) thing that completes something (GRAMMAR) ▶ *v* (**-s, -ing, -ed**) make complete > **complementary** *adj*
complementary *adj* ▷ **complement**
complemented *v* ▷ **complement**
complementing *v* ▷ **complement**
complements *n, v* ▷ **complement**
complete *adj* thorough, absolute ▶ *v* (**-pletes, -pleting, -pleted**) finish > **completely** *adv* > **completeness** *n*
completed *v* ▷ **complete**
completely *adv* ▷ **complete**
completeness *n* ▷ **complete**
completes *v* ▷ **complete**
completing *v* ▷ **complete**
completion *n* finishing
complex *adj* (**-er, -est**) made up of parts ▶ *n* (*pl* **-es**) whole made up of parts > **complexity** *n* (*pl* **-ities**)
complexer *adj* ▷ **complex**
complexes *n* ▷ **complex**
complexest *adj* ▷ **complex**
complexion *n* (*pl* **-s**) skin of the face
complexions *n* ▷ **complexion**
complexities *n* ▷ **complex**
complexity *n* ▷ **complex**
compliance *n* (*pl* **-s**) complying > **compliant** *adj*
compliances *n* ▷ **compliance**
compliant *adj* ▷ **compliance**
complicate *v* (**-cates, -cating, -cated**) make or become complex or difficult to deal with > **complication** *n* (*pl* **-s**)
complicated *v* ▷ **complicate**
complicates *v* ▷ **complicate**
complicating *v* ▷ **complicate**
complication *n* ▷ **complicate**
complications *n* ▷ **complicate**
complicities *n* ▷ **complicity**
complicity *n* (*pl* **-ities**) fact of being an accomplice in a crime
complied *v* ▷ **comply**

complies *v* ▷ **comply**
compliment *n* (*pl* **-s**) expression of praise ▶ *pl* formal greetings ▶ *v* (**-s, -ing, -ed**) praise
complimentary *adj* expressing praise
complimented *v* ▷ **compliment**
complimenting *v* ▷ **compliment**
compliments *n, v* ▷ **compliment**
compline *n* (*pl* **-s**) last service of the day in the Roman Catholic Church
complines *n* ▷ **compline**
comply *v* (**-plies, -plying, -plied**) (*foll. by* **with**) act in accordance (with)
complying *v* ▷ **comply**
component *n* (*pl* **-s**) ▶ *adj* (being) part of a whole
components *n* ▷ **component**
comport *v* (**-s, -ing, -ed**) (*Formal*) behave (oneself) in a specified way
comported *v* ▷ **comport**
comporting *v* ▷ **comport**
comports *v* ▷ **comport**
compose *v* (**-poses, -posing, -posed**) put together
composed *v* ▷ **compose**
composer *n* (*pl* **-s**) person who writes music
composers *n* ▷ **composer**
composes *v* ▷ **compose**
composing *v* ▷ **compose**
composite *n* (*pl* **-s**) ▶ *adj* (something) made up of separate parts
composites *n* ▷ **composite**
composition *n* (*pl* **-s**) way that something is put together or arranged
compositions *n* ▷ **composition**
compositor *n* (*pl* **-s**) person who arranges type for printing
compositors *n* ▷ **compositor**
compost *n* (*pl* **-s**) decayed plants used as a fertilizer
composts *n* ▷ **compost**
composure *n* calmness
compote *n* (*pl* **-s**) fruit stewed with sugar
compotes *n* ▷ **compote**
compound[1] *n* (*pl* **-s**) ▶ *adj* (thing, esp. chemical) made up of two or more combined parts or elements ▶ *v* (**-s, -ing, -ed**) combine or make by combining
compound[2] *n* (*pl* **-s**) fenced enclosure containing buildings
compounded *v* ▷ **compound[1]**
compounding *v* ▷ **compound[1]**
compounds *v* ▷ **compound[1]** ▶ *n* ▷ **compound[1, 2]**
comprehend *v* (**-s, -ing, -ed**) understand > **comprehensible** *adj* > **comprehensibly** *adv* > **comprehension** *n* (*pl* **-s**)
comprehended *v* ▷ **comprehend**
comprehending *v* ▷ **comprehend**
comprehends *v* ▷ **comprehend**
comprehensible *adj* ▷ **comprehend**
comprehensibly *adv* ▷ **comprehend**
comprehension *n* ▷ **comprehend**
comprehensions *n* ▷ **comprehend**
comprehensive *adj* of broad scope, fully inclusive ▶ *n* (*pl* **-s**) (BRIT) comprehensive school > **comprehensively** *adv* > **comprehensiveness** *n*
comprehensively *adv* ▷ **comprehensive**
comprehensiveness *n* ▷ **comprehensive**
comprehensives *n* ▷ **comprehensive**
compress *v* (**-es, -ing, -ed**) [kum-**press**] squeeze together ▶ *n* (*pl* **-es**) [**kom**-press] pad applied to stop bleeding or cool inflammation > **compression** *n* (*pl* **-s**)
compressed *v* ▷ **compress**
compresses *v, n* ▷ **compress**
compressing *v* ▷ **compress**
compression *n* ▷ **compress**
compressions *n* ▷ **compress**
compressor *n* (*pl* **-s**) machine that compresses gas or air
compressors *n* ▷ **compressor**
comprise *v* (**-ises, -ising, -ised**) be made up of or make up
comprised *v* ▷ **comprise**
comprises *v* ▷ **comprise**
comprising *v* ▷ **comprise**
compromise [**kom**-prom-mize] *n* (*pl* **-s**) settlement reached by concessions on each side ▶ *v* (**-ises, -ising, -ised**) settle a dispute by making concessions
compromised *v* ▷ **compromise**
compromises *n, v* ▷ **compromise**
compromising *v* ▷ **compromise**
comptroller *n* (*pl* **-s**) (in titles) financial controller
comptrollers *n* ▷ **comptroller**
compulsion *n* (*pl* **-s**) irresistible urge > **compulsive** *adj* > **compulsively** *adv*
compulsions *n* ▷ **compulsion**
compulsive *adj* ▷ **compulsion**
compulsively *adv* ▷ **compulsion**
compulsorily *adv* ▷ **compulsory**
compulsoriness *n* ▷ **compulsory**
compulsory *adj* required by rules or laws > **compulsorily** *adv* > **compulsoriness** *n*
compunction *n* (*pl* **-s**) feeling of guilt or shame
compunctions *n* ▷ **compunction**
computation *n* ▷ **compute**
computations *n* ▷ **compute**
compute *v* (**-putes, -puting, -puted**) calculate,

esp. using a computer > **computation** *n* (*pl* **-s**)
computed *v* ▷ **compute**
computer *n* (*pl* **-s**) electronic machine that stores and processes data > **computerize** *v* (**-izes, -izing, -ized**) adapt (a system) to be handled by computer > **computerization** *n* (*pl* **-s**)
computerization *n* ▷ **computerize**
computerizations *v* ▷ **computerize**
computerized *v* ▷ **computerize**
computerizes *v* ▷ **computerize**
computerizing *v* ▷ **computerize**
computers *n* ▷ **computer**
computes *v* ▷ **compute**
computing *v* ▷ **compute**
comrade *n* (*pl* **-s**) fellow member of a union or socialist political party > **comradeship** *n*
comrades *n* ▷ **comrade**
comradeship *n* ▷ **comrade**
con[1] (*Informal*) *n* (*pl* **-s**) ▷ **confidence trick** ▶ *v* (**cons, conning, conned**) deceive, swindle
con[2] *n* (*pl* **-s**) ▷ **pro**[1]
concatenation *n* (*pl* **-s**) series of linked events
concatenations *n* ▷ **concatenation**
concave *adj* curving inwards
conceal *v* (**-s, -ing, -ed**) cover and hide > **concealment** *n*
concealed *v* ▷ **conceal**
concealing *v* ▷ **conceal**
concealment *n* ▷ **conceal**
conceals *v* ▷ **conceal**
concede *v* (**-cedes, -ceding, -ceded**) admit to be true
conceded *v* ▷ **concede**
concedes *v* ▷ **concede**
conceding *v* ▷ **concede**
conceit *n* (*pl* **-s**) too high an opinion of oneself > **conceited** *adj* > **conceitedly** *adv* > **conceitedness** *n*
conceited *adj* ▷ **conceit**
conceitedly *adv* ▷ **conceit**
conceitedness *adv* ▷ **conceit**
conceits *n* ▷ **conceit**
conceivable *adj* imaginable, possible > **conceivably** *adv*
conceivably *adv* ▷ **conceivable**
conceive *v* (**-ceives, -ceiving, -ceived**) imagine, think
conceived *v* ▷ **conceive**
conceives *v* ▷ **conceive**
conceiving *v* ▷ **conceive**
concentrate *v* (**-rates, -rating, -rated**) fix one's attention or efforts on something ▶ *n* (*pl* **-s**) concentrated liquid
concentrated *v* ▷ **concentrate**
concentrates *v, n* ▷ **concentrate**
concentrating *v* ▷ **concentrate**
concentration *n* (*pl* **-s**) concentrating
concentrations *n* ▷ **concentration**
concentric *adj* having the same centre
concept *n* (*pl* **-s**) abstract or general idea
conception *n* (*pl* **-s**) general idea
conceptions *n* ▷ **conception**
concepts *n* ▷ **concept**
conceptual *adj* of or based on concepts > **conceptually** *adv*
conceptualize *v* (**-izes, -izing, -ized**) form a concept of
conceptualized *v* ▷ **conceptualize**
conceptualizes *v* ▷ **conceptualize**
conceptualizing *v* ▷ **conceptualize**
conceptually *adv* ▷ **conceptual**
concern *n* (*pl* **-s**) anxiety, worry ▶ *v* (**-s, -ing, -ed**) worry (someone)
concerned *adj* interested, involved ▶ *v* ▷ **concern**
concerning *prep* about, regarding ▶ *v* ▷ **concern**
concerns *n, v* ▷ **concern**
concert *n* (*pl* **-s**) musical entertainment
concerted *adj* done together
concerti *n* ▷ **concerto**
concertina *n* (*pl* **-s**) small musical instrument similar to an accordion ▶ *v* (**-nas, -naing, -naed**) collapse or fold up like a concertina
concertinaed *v* ▷ **concertina**
concertinaing *v* ▷ **concertina**
concertinas *n, v* ▷ **concertina**
concerto [kon-**chair**-toe] *n* (*pl* **-tos, -ti**) large-scale composition for a solo instrument and orchestra
concertos *n* ▷ **concerto**
concerts *n* ▷ **concert**
concession *n* (*pl* **-s**) grant of rights, land, or property > **concessionary** *adj*
concessionary *adj* ▷ **concession**
concessions *n* ▷ **concession**
conch *n* (*pl* **-s**) shellfish with a large spiral shell
conchs *n* ▷ **conch**
concierge [kon-see-**airzh**] *n* (*pl* **-s**) (in France) caretaker in a block of flats
concierges *n* ▷ **concierge**
conciliate *v* (**-ates, -ating, -ated**) try to end a disagreement (with) > **conciliation** *n* > **conciliator** *n* (*pl* **-s**)
conciliated *v* ▷ **conciliate**
conciliates *v* ▷ **conciliate**
conciliating *v* ▷ **conciliate**
conciliation *n* ▷ **conciliate**
conciliator *n* ▷ **conciliate**

conciliators *n* ▷ **conciliate**
conciliatory *adj* intended to end a disagreement
concise *adj* (**-r, -st**) brief and to the point > **concisely** *adv* > **concision, conciseness** *n* (*pl* **-s, -es**)
concisely *adv* ▷ **concise**
conciseness *n* ▷ **concise**
concisenesses *n* ▷ **concise**
conciser *adj* ▷ **concise**
concisest *adj* ▷ **concise**
concision *n* ▷ **concise**
concisions *n* ▷ **concise**
conclave *n* (*pl* **-s**) secret meeting
conclaves *n* ▷ **conclave**
conclude *v* (**-cludes, -cluding, -cluded**) decide by reasoning
concluded *v* ▷ **conclude**
concludes *v* ▷ **conclude**
concluding *v* ▷ **conclude**
conclusion *n* (*pl* **-s**) decision based on reasoning
conclusions *n* ▷ **conclusion**
conclusive *adj* ending doubt, convincing > **conclusively** *adv*
conclusively *adv* ▷ **conclusive**
concoct *v* (**-s, -ing, -ed**) make up (a story or plan) > **concoction** *n* (*pl* **-s**)
concocted *v* ▷ **concoct**
concocting *v* ▷ **concoct**
concoction *n* ▷ **concoct**
concoctions *n* ▷ **concoct**
concocts *v* ▷ **concoct**
concomitant *adj* existing along with something else
concord *n* (*pl* **-s**) state of peaceful agreement, harmony
concordance *n* (*pl* **-s**) similarity or consistency
concordances *n* ▷ **concordance**
concordant *adj* agreeing > **concordantly** *adv*
concordantly *adv* ▷ **concordant**
concords *n* ▷ **concord**
concourse *n* (*pl* **-s**) large open public place where people can gather
concourses *n* ▷ **concourse**
concrete *n* (*pl* **-s**) mixture of cement, sand, stone, and water, used in building ▶ *adj* made of concrete
concretes *n* ▷ **concrete**
concubine [**kon**-kew-bine] *n* (*pl* **-s**) (HIST) woman living in a man's house but not married to him and kept for his sexual pleasure
concubines *n* ▷ **concubine**
concupiscence [kon-**kew**-piss-enss] *n* (*Formal*) lust
concur *v* (**-curs, -curring, -curred**) agree > **concurrence** *n* (*pl* **-s**)
concurred *v* ▷ **concur**
concurrence *n* ▷ **concur**
concurrent *adj* happening at the same time or place
concurrently *adv* at the same time
concurring *v* ▷ **concur**
concurs *v* ▷ **concur**
concussed *adj* having concussion
concussion *n* (*pl* **-s**) period of unconsciousness caused by a blow to the head
concussions *n* ▷ **concussion**
condemn *v* (**-s, -ing, -ed**) express disapproval of > **condemnation** *n* (*pl* **-s**) > **condemnatory** *adj*
condemnation *n* ▷ **condemn**
condemnations *n* ▷ **condemn**
condemnatory *adj* ▷ **condemn**
condemned *v* ▷ **condemn**
condemning *v* ▷ **condemn**
condemns *v* ▷ **condemn**
condensation *n* ▷ **condense**
condense *v* (**-denses, -densing, -densed**) make shorter > **condensation** *n*
condensed *v* ▷ **condense**
condenser *n* (*pl* **-s**) (ELECTRICITY) capacitor
condensers *n* ▷ **condenser**
condenses *v* ▷ **condense**
condensing *v* ▷ **condense**
condescend *v* (**-s, -ing, -ed**) behave patronizingly towards someone > **condescension** *n*
condescended *v* ▷ **condescend**
condescending *v* ▷ **condescend**
condescends *v* ▷ **condescend**
condescension *n* ▷ **condescend**
condiment *n* (*pl* **-s**) seasoning for food, such as salt or pepper
condiments *n* ▷ **condiment**
condition *n* (*pl* **-s**) particular state of being ▶ *pl* circumstances ▶ *v* (**-s, -ed, -ing**) train or influence to behave in a particular way
conditional *adj* depending on circumstances > **conditionally** *adv*
conditionally *adv* ▷ **conditional**
conditioned *v* ▷ **condition**
conditioner *n* (*pl* **-s**) thick liquid used when washing to make hair or clothes feel softer
conditioning *v* ▷ **condition**
conditioners *n* ▷ **condition**
conditions *n, v* ▷ **condition**
condolence *n* (*pl* **-s**) sympathy ▶ *pl* expression of sympathy

condolences *n* ▷ **condolence**
condom *n* (*pl* **-s**) rubber sheath worn on the penis or in the vagina during sexual intercourse to prevent conception or infection
condominium *n* (*pl* **-s**) (AUST, US & CANADIAN) block of flats in which each flat is owned by the occupant
condominiums *n* ▷ **condominium**
condoms *n* ▷ **condom**
condone *v* (**-dones, -doning, -doned**) overlook or forgive (wrongdoing)
condoned *v* ▷ **condone**
condones *v* ▷ **condone**
condoning *v* ▷ **condone**
condor *n* (*pl* **-s**) large vulture of S America
condors *n* ▷ **condor**
conducive *adj* (*foll. by* **to**) likely to lead (to)
conduct *n* (*pl* **-s**) management of an activity ▶ *v* (**-s, -ing, -ed**) carry out (a task)
conducted *v* ▷ **conduct**
conducting *v* ▷ **conduct**
conduction *n* transmission of heat or electricity
conductive *adj* ▷ **conductivity**
conductivities *n* ▷ **conductivity**
conductivity *n* (*pl* **-vities**) ability to transmit heat or electricity > **conductive** *adj*
conductor *n* (*pl* **-s**) person who conducts musicians, *fem* **conductress** ▶ *n* (*pl* **-es**)
conductors *n* ▷ **conductor**
conductress *n* ▷ **conductor**
conductresses *n* ▷ **conductor**
conducts *n, v* ▷ **conduct**
conduit [**kon**-dew-it] *n* (*pl* **-s**) channel or tube for fluid or cables
conduits *n* ▷ **conduit**
cone *n* (*pl* **-s**) object with a circular base, tapering to a point
cones *n* ▷ **cone**
coney *n* (*pl* **-s**) ▷ **cony**
coneys *n* ▷ **coney**
confab *n* (*pl* **-s**) (*Informal*) conversation (*also* **confabulation**)
confabs *n* ▷ **confab**
confabulation *n* ▷ **confab**
confabulations *n* ▷ **confab**
confection *n* (*pl* **-s**) any sweet food (*Old-fashioned*)
confectioner *n* (*pl* **-s**) maker or seller of confectionery
confectioneries *n* ▷ **confectionery**
confectioners *n* ▷ **confectioner**
confectionery *n* (*pl* **-eries**) sweets
confections *n* ▷ **confection**
confederacies *n* ▷ **confederacy**
confederacy *n* (*pl* **-cies**) union of states or people for a common purpose
confederate *n* (*pl* **-s**) member of a confederacy ▶ *adj* united, allied ▶ *v* (**-rates, -rating, -rated**) unite in a confederacy
confederated *v* ▷ **confederate**
confederates *n, v* ▷ **confederate**
confederating *v* ▷ **confederate**
confederation *n* (*pl* **-s**) alliance of political units
confederations *n* ▷ **confederation**
confer *v* (**-fers, -ferring, -ferred**) discuss together
conference *n* (*pl* **-s**) meeting for discussion
conferences *n* ▷ **conference**
conferment *n* (*pl* **-s**) granting, giving
conferments *n* ▷ **conferment**
conferred *v* ▷ **confer**
conferring *v* ▷ **confer**
confers *v* ▷ **confer**
confess *v* (**-es, -ing, -ed**) admit (a fault or crime)
confessed *v* ▷ **confess**
confesses *v* ▷ **confess**
confessing *v* ▷ **confess**
confession *n* (*pl* **-s**) something confessed
confessional *n* (*pl* **-s**) small stall in which a priest hears confessions
confessionals *n* ▷ **confessional**
confessions *n* ▷ **confession**
confessor *n* (*pl* **-s**) priest who hears confessions
confessors *n* ▷ **confessor**
confetti *n* (*pl* **-s**) small pieces of coloured paper thrown at weddings
confettis *n* ▷ **confetti**
confidant *n* (*pl* **-s**) person confided in > **confidante** *n fem* (*pl* **-s**)
confidante *n* ▷ **confidant**
confidantes *n* ▷ **confidant**
confidants *n* ▷ **confidant**
confide *v* (**-fides, -fiding, -fided**) tell someone (a secret)
confided *v* ▷ **confide**
confidence *n* (*pl* **-s**) trust
confidences *n* ▷ **confidence**
confident *adj* sure, esp. of oneself > **confidently** *adv*
confidential *adj* private, secret > **confidentially** *adv* > **confidentiality** *n*
confidentiality *n* ▷ **confidential**
confidentially *adv* ▷ **confidential**
confidently *adv* ▷ **confident**
confides *v* ▷ **confide**

confiding *v* ▷ **confide**
configuration *n* (*pl* **-s**) arrangement of parts
configurations *n* ▷ **configuration**
confine *v* (**-fines, -fining, -fined**) keep within bounds
confined *v* ▷ **confine**
confinement *n* (*pl* **-s**) being confined
confines *pl n* boundaries, limits ▶ *v* ▷ **confine**
confining *v* ▷ **confine**
confirm *v* (**-s, -ing, -ed**) prove to be true
confirmation *n* (*pl* **-s**) confirming
confirmations *n* ▷ **confirmation**
confirmed *adj* firmly established in a habit or condition ▶ *v* ▷ **confirm**
confirming *v* ▷ **confirm**
confirms *v* ▷ **confirm**
confiscate *v* (**-cates, -cating, -cated**) seize (property) by authority > **confiscation** *n* (*pl* **-s**)
confiscated *v* ▷ **confiscate**
confiscates *v* ▷ **confiscate**
confiscating *v* ▷ **confiscate**
confiscation *n* ▷ **confiscate**
confiscations *n* ▷ **confiscate**
conflagration *n* (*pl* **-s**) large destructive fire
conflagrations *n* ▷ **conflagration**
conflate *v* (**-ates, -ating, -ated**) combine or blend into a whole > **conflation** *n* (*pl* **-s**)
conflated *v* ▷ **conflate**
conflates *v* ▷ **conflate**
conflating *v* ▷ **conflate**
conflation *n* ▷ **conflate**
conflations *n* ▷ **conflate**
conflict *n* (*pl* **-s**) disagreement ▶ *v* (**-s, -ing, -ed**) be incompatible
conflicted *v* ▷ **conflict**
conflicting *v* ▷ **conflict**
conflicts *n, v* ▷ **conflict**
confluence *n* (*pl* **-s**) place where two rivers join
confluences *n* ▷ **confluence**
conform *v* (**-s, -ing, -ed**) comply with accepted standards or customs (*foll. by* **to** *or* **with**)
conformed *v* ▷ **conform**
conforming *v* ▷ **conform**
conformist *n* (*pl* **-s**) ▶ *adj* (person) complying with accepted standards or customs
conformists *n* ▷ **conformist**
conformities *n* ▷ **conformity**
conformity *n* (*pl* **-ities**) compliance with accepted standards or customs
conforms *v* ▷ **conform**
confound *v* (**-s, -ing, -ed**) astound, bewilder
confounded *adj* (*Old-fashioned*) damned ▶ *v* ▷ **confound** > **confoundedly** *adv*
confoundedly *adv* ▷ **confounded**
confounding *v* ▷ **confound**
confounds *v* ▷ **confound**
confront *v* (**-s, -ing, -ed**) come face to face with
confrontation *n* (*pl* **-s**) serious argument > **confrontational** *adj*
confrontational *adj* ▷ **confrontation**
confrontations *n* ▷ **confrontation**
confronted *v* ▷ **confront**
confronting *v* ▷ **confront**
confronts *v* ▷ **confront**
confuse *v* (**-fuses, -fusing, -fused**) mix up > **confusion** *n* (*pl* **-s**)
confused *v* ▷ **confuse**
confuses *v* ▷ **confuse**
confusing *v* ▷ **confuse**
confusion *n* ▷ **confuse**
confusions *n* ▷ **confuse**
confute *v* (**-futes, -futing, -futed**) prove wrong
confuted *v* ▷ **confute**
confutes *v* ▷ **confute**
confuting *v* ▷ **confute**
conga *n* (*pl* **-s**) dance performed by a number of people in single file
congas *n* ▷ **conga**
congeal *v* (**-s, -ing, -ed**) (of a liquid) become thick and sticky
congealed *v* ▷ **congeal**
congealing *v* ▷ **congeal**
congeals *v* ▷ **congeal**
congenial *adj* pleasant, agreeable > **congeniality** *n* > **congenially** *adv*
congeniality *n* ▷ **congenial**
congenially *adv* ▷ **congenial**
congenital *adj* (of a condition) existing from birth > **congenitally** *adv*
congenitally *adv* ▷ **congenital**
conger *n* (*pl* **-s**) large sea eel
congers *n* ▷ **conger**
congested *adj* crowded to excess > **congestion** *n*
congestion *n* ▷ **congested**
conglomerate *n* (*pl* **-s**) large corporation made up of many companies ▶ *v* (**-rates, -rating, -rated**) form into a mass ▶ *adj* made up of several different elements > **conglomeration** *n* (*pl* **-s**)
conglomerated *v* ▷ **conglomerate**
conglomerates *n, v* ▷ **conglomerate**
conglomerating *v* ▷ **conglomerate**
conglomeration *n* ▷ **conglomerate**
conglomerations *n* ▷ **conglomerate**
congratulate *v* (**-lates, -lating, -lated**) express one's pleasure to (someone) at his or her good fortune or success > **congratulations** *pl n, interj* > **congratulatory** *adj*
congratulated *v* ▷ **congratulate**

congratulates *v* ▷ **congratulate**
congratulating *v* ▷ **congratulate**
congratulations *n* ▷ **congratulate**
congratulatory *adj* ▷ **congratulate**
congregate *v* (**-gates, -gating, -gated**) gather together in a crowd
congregated *v* ▷ **congregate**
congregates *v* ▷ **congregate**
congregating *v* ▷ **congregate**
congregation *n* (*pl* **-s**) people who attend a church > **congregational** *adj*
congregational *adj* ▷ **congregation**
congregations *n* ▷ **congregation**
congress *n* (*pl* **congresses**) formal meeting for discussion > **congressional** *adj*
congresses *n* ▷ **congress**
congressional *n* ▷ **congress**
congressman, congresswoman *n* (*pl* **-men, -women**) member of Congress
congressmen *n* ▷ **congressman**
congresswoman *n* ▷ **congressman**
congresswomen *n* ▷ **congressman**
congruence *n* ▷ **congruent**
congruent *adj* similar, corresponding > **congruence** *n*
conical *adj* cone-shaped
conies *n* ▷ **cony**
conifer *n* (*pl* **-s**) cone-bearing tree, such as the fir or pine > **coniferous** *adj*
coniferous *adj* ▷ **conifer**
conifers *n* ▷ **conifer**
conjectural *adj* ▷ **conjecture**
conjecture *n* (*pl* **-s**) ▶ *v* (**-tures, -turing, -tured**) guess > **conjectural** *adj*
conjectured *v* ▷ **conjecture**
conjectures *n, v* ▷ **conjecture**
conjecturing *v* ▷ **conjecture**
conjugal *adj* of marriage > **conjugally** *adv*
conjugally *adv* ▷ **conjugal**
conjugate *v* (**-gates, -gating, -gated**) give the inflections of (a verb)
conjugated *v* ▷ **conjugate**
conjugates *v* ▷ **conjugate**
conjugating *v* ▷ **conjugate**
conjugation *n* (*pl* **-s**) complete set of inflections of a verb
conjugations *n* ▷ **conjugation**
conjunction *n* (*pl* **-s**) combination
conjunctions *n* ▷ **conjunction**
conjunctiva *n* (*pl* **-s**) the membrane covering the eyeball and inner eyelid
conjunctivas *n* ▷ **conjunctiva**
conjunctivitis *n* inflammation of the conjunctiva
conjure *v* (**-jures, -juring, -jured**) perform tricks that appear to be magic > **conjuror** *n* (*pl* **-s**)
conjured *v* ▷ **conjure**
conjures *v* ▷ **conjure**
conjuring *v* ▷ **conjure**
conjuror *n* ▷ **conjure**
conjurors *n* ▷ **conjure**
conk *n* (*pl* **-s**) (BRIT, AUST & NZ) (*Slang*) nose
conker *n* (*pl* **-s**) (*Informal*) nut of the horse chestnut
conkers *n* ▷ **conker**
conks *n* ▷ **conk**
connect *v* (**-s, -ing, -ed**) join together > **connection, connexion** *n* (*pl* **-s**) relationship, association > **connective** *adj*
connected *v* ▷ **connect**
connecting *v* ▷ **connect**
connection *n* ▷ **connect**
connections *n* ▷ **connect**
connective *n* ▷ **connect**
connects *v* ▷ **connect**
conned *v* ▷ **con**[1]
connexion *n* ▷ **connect**
connexions *n* ▷ **connect**
conning *v* ▷ **con**[1]
connivance *n* ▷ **connive**
connivances *n* ▷ **connive**
connive *v* (**-nives, -niving, -nived**) (*foll. by* **at**) allow (wrongdoing) by ignoring it > **connivance** *n* (*pl* **-s**)
connived *v* ▷ **connive**
connives *v* ▷ **connive**
conniving *v* ▷ **connive**
connoisseur [kon-noss-**sir**] *n* (*pl* **-s**) person with special knowledge of the arts, food, or drink
connoisseurs *n* ▷ **connoisseur**
connotation *n* (*pl* **-s**) associated idea conveyed by a word > **connote** *v* (**-notes, -noting, -noted**)
connotations *n* ▷ **connotation**
connoted *v* ▷ **connotation**
connotes *v* ▷ **connotation**
connoting *v* ▷ **connotation**
connubial *adj* (*Formal*) of marriage
conquer *v* (**-s, -ing, -ed**) defeat > **conqueror** *n* (*pl* **-s**)
conquered *v* ▷ **conquer**
conquering *v* ▷ **conquer**
conqueror *n* ▷ **conquer**
conquerors *n* ▷ **conquer**
conquers *v* ▷ **conquer**
conquest *n* (*pl* **-s**) conquering
conquests *n* ▷ **conquest**
cons *n* ▷ **con**[1, 2]
conscience *n* (*pl* **-s**) sense of right or wrong as

regards thoughts and actions
consciences *n* ▷ **conscience**
conscientious *adj* painstaking
> **conscientiously** *adv*
conscientiously *adv* ▷ **conscientious**
conscious *adj* alert and awake > **consciously** *adv* > **consciousness** *n*
consciously *adv* ▷ **conscious**
consciousness *n* ▷ **conscious**
conscript *n* (*pl* **-s**) person enrolled for compulsory military service ▶ *v* (**-s, -ing, -ed**) enrol (someone) for compulsory military service > **conscription** *n* (*pl* **-s**)
conscripted *v* ▷ **conscript**
conscripting *v* ▷ **conscript**
conscription *n* ▷ **conscript**
conscriptions *n* ▷ **conscript**
conscripts *n, v* ▷ **conscript**
consecrate *v* (**-rates, -rating, -rated**) make sacred > **consecration** *n* (*pl* **-s**)
consecrated *v* ▷ **consecrate**
consecrates *v* ▷ **consecrate**
consecrating *v* ▷ **consecrate**
consecration *n* ▷ **consecrate**
consecrations *n* ▷ **consecrate**
consecutive *adj* in unbroken succession
> **consecutively** *adv*
consecutively *adv* ▷ **consecutive**
consensus *n* general agreement
consent *n* (*pl* **-s**) agreement, permission ▶ *v* (**-s, -ing, -ed**) (*foll. by* **to**) permit, agree to
consented *v* ▷ **consent**
consenting *v* ▷ **consent**
consents *v, n* ▷ **consent**
consequence *n* (*pl* **-s**) result, effect
consequences *n* ▷ **consequence**
consequent *adj* resulting
consequential *adj* important
consequently *adv* as a result, therefore
conservancies *n* ▷ **conservancy**
conservancy *n* (*pl* **-cies**) environmental conservation
conservation *n* (*pl* **-s**) protection of natural resources and the environment
> **conservationist** *n* (*pl* **-s**)
conservationist *n* ▷ **conservation**
conservationists *n* ▷ **conservation**
conservations *n* ▷ **conservation**
conservatism *adv* ▷ **conservative**
conservative *adj* opposing change ▶ *n* (*pl* **-s**) conservative person > **conservatively** *adv*
> **conservatism** *n*
conservatively *adv* ▷ **conservative**
conservatives *n* ▷ **conservative**
conservatoire [kon-serv-a-twahr] *n* (*pl* **-s**) school of music
conservatoires *n* ▷ **conservatoire**
conservatories *n* ▷ **conservatory**
conservatory *n* (*pl* **-ries**) room with glass walls and a glass roof, attached to a house
conserve *v* (**-serves, -serving, -served**) protect from harm, decay, or loss ▶ *n* (*pl* **-s**) jam containing large pieces of fruit
conserved *v* ▷ **conserve**
conserves *v, n* ▷ **conserve**
conserving *v* ▷ **conserve**
consider *v* (**-s, -ing, -ed**) regard as
considerable *adj* large in amount or degree
> **considerably** *adv*
considerably *adv* ▷ **considerable**
considerate *adj* thoughtful towards others
> **considerately** *adv*
considerately *adv* ▷ **considerate**
consideration *n* (*pl* **-s**) careful thought
considerations *n* ▷ **consideration**
considered *v* ▷ **consider**
considering *prep* taking (a specified fact) into account ▶ *v* ▷ **consider**
considers *v* ▷ **consider**
consign *v* (**-s, -ing, -ed**) put somewhere
consigned *v* ▷ **consign**
consigning *v* ▷ **consign**
consignment *n* (*pl* **-s**) shipment of goods
consignments *n* ▷ **consignment**
consigns *v* ▷ **consign**
consist *v* (**-s, -ing, -ed**) be made up of
consisted *v* ▷ **consist**
consistencies *n* ▷ **consistency**
consistency *n* (*pl* **-cies**) being consistent
consistent *adj* unchanging, constant (*foll. by* **with**) > **consistently** *adv*
consistently *adv* ▷ **consistent**
consisting *v* ▷ **consist**
consists *v* ▷ **consist**
consolation *n* (*pl* **-s**) consoling
consolations *n* ▷ **consolation**
console[1] *v* (**-soles, -soling, -soled**) comfort in distress
console[2] *n* (*pl* **-s**) panel of controls for electronic equipment
consoled *v* ▷ **console**[1]
consoles *v* ▷ **console**[1] ▶ *n* ▷ **console**[2]
consolidate *v* (**-dates, -dating, -dated**) make or become stronger or more stable
> **consolidation** *n* (*pl* **-s**)
consolidated *v* ▷ **consolidate**
consolidates *v* ▷ **consolidate**
consolidating *v* ▷ **consolidate**
consolidation *n* ▷ **consolidate**
consolidations *n* ▷ **consolidate**

consoling *v* ▷ **console**[1]
consommé [kon-**som**-may] *n* (*pl* **-s**) thin clear meat soup
consommés *n* ▷ **consommé**
consonance *n* agreement, harmony
consonant *n* (*pl* **-s**) speech sound made by partially or completely blocking the breath stream, such as *b* or *f* ▶ *adj* (*foll. by* **with**) agreeing (with) > **consonantly** *adv*
consonantly *adv* ▷ **consonant**
consonants *n* ▷ **consonant**
consort *v* (**-s, -ing, -ed**) (*foll. by* **with**) keep company (with) ▶ *n* (*pl* **-s**) husband or wife of a monarch
consorted *v* ▷ **consort**
consortia *n* ▷ **consortium**
consorting *v* ▷ **consort**
consortium *n* (*pl* **-tia**) association of business firms
consorts *v, n* ▷ **consort**
conspectus *n* (*pl* **-es**) (*Formal*) survey or summary
conspectuses *n* ▷ **conspectus**
conspicuous *adj* clearly visible > **conspicuously** *adv* > **conspicuousness** *n*
conspicuously *adv* ▷ **conspectus**
conspicuousness *n* ▷ **conspectus**
conspiracies *n* ▷ **conspiracy**
conspiracy *n* (*pl* **-cies**) conspiring > **conspirator** *n* (*pl* **-s**) > **conspiratorial** *adj*
conspirator *n* ▷ **conspiracy**
conspiratorial *adj* ▷ **conspiracy**
conspirators *n* ▷ **conspiracy**
conspire *v* (**-spires, -spiring, -spired**) plan a crime together in secret
conspired *v* ▷ **conspire**
conspires *v* ▷ **conspire**
conspiring *v* ▷ **conspire**
constable *n* (*pl* **-s**) police officer of the lowest rank
constables *n* ▷ **constable**
constabularies *n* ▷ **constabulary**
constabulary *n* (*pl* **-laries**) police force of an area
constancy *n* ▷ **constant**
constant *adj* continuous ▶ *n* (*pl* **-s**) unvarying quantity > **constantly** *adv* > **constancy** *n*
constantly *adv* ▷ **constant**
constants *n* ▷ **constant**
constellation *n* (*pl* **-s**) group of stars
constellations *n* ▷ **constellation**
consternation *n* anxiety or dismay
constipated *adj* having constipation
constipation *n* difficulty in defecating
constituencies *n* ▷ **constituency**
constituency *n* (*pl* **-cies**) area represented by a Member of Parliament
constituent *n* (*pl* **-s**) member of a constituency ▶ *adj* forming part of a whole
constituents *n* ▷ **constituent**
constitute *v* (**-tutes, -tuting, -tuted**) form, make up
constituted *v* ▷ **constitute**
constitutes *v* ▷ **constitute**
constituting *v* ▷ **constitute**
constitution *n* (*pl* **-s**) principles on which a state is governed
constitutional *adj* of a constitution ▶ *n* (*pl* **-s**) walk taken for exercise > **constitutionally** *adv*
constitutionally *adv* ▷ **constitutional**
constitutionals *n* ▷ **constitutional**
constitutions *n* ▷ **constitution**
constrain *v* (**-s, -ing, -ed**) compel, force > **constraint** *n* (*pl* **-s**)
constrained *v* ▷ **constrain**
constraining *v* ▷ **constrain**
constrains *v* ▷ **constrain**
constraint *n* ▷ **constrain**
constraints *n* ▷ **constrain**
constrict *v* (**-s, -ing, -ed**) make narrower by squeezing > **constriction** *n* (*pl* **-s**) > **constrictive** *adj*
constricted *v* ▷ **constrict**
constricting *v* ▷ **constrict**
constriction *n* ▷ **constrict**
constrictions *n* ▷ **constrict**
constrictive *adj* ▷ **constrict**
constrictor *n* (*pl* **-s**) large snake that squeezes its prey to death
constrictors *n* ▷ **constrictor**
constricts *v* ▷ **constrict**
construct *v* (**-s, -ing, -ed**) build or put together
constructed *v* ▷ **construct**
constructing *v* ▷ **construct**
construction *n* (*pl* **-s**) constructing
constructions *n* ▷ **construction**
constructive *adj* (of advice, criticism, etc.) useful and helpful > **constructively** *adv*
constructively *adv* ▷ **constructive**
constructs *v* ▷ **construct**
construe *v* (**-strues, -struing, -strued**) interpret
construed *v* ▷ **construe**
construes *v* ▷ **construe**
construing *v* ▷ **construe**
consul *n* (*pl* **-s**) official representing a state in a foreign country > **consular** *adj* > **consulship** *n* (*pl* **-s**)
consular *adj* ▷ **consul**
consulate *n* (*pl* **-s**) workplace or position of

a consul
consulates *n* ▷ **consulate**
consuls *n* ▷ **consul**
consulship *n* ▷ **consul**
consulships *n* ▷ **consul**
consult *v* (**-s, -ing, -ed**) go to for advice or information
consultancies *n* ▷ **consultancy**
consultancy *n* (*pl* **-cies**) work or position of a consultant
consultant *n* (*pl* **-s**) specialist doctor with a senior position in a hospital
consultants *n* ▷ **consultant**
consultation *n* (*pl* **-s**) (meeting for) consulting
consultations *n* ▷ **consultation**
consultative *adj* giving advice
consulted *v* ▷ **consult**
consulting *v* ▷ **consult**
consults *v* ▷ **consult**
consume *v* (**-sumes, -suming, -sumed**) eat or drink
consumed *v* ▷ **consume**
consumer *n* (*pl* **-s**) person who buys goods or uses services
consumers *n* ▷ **consumer**
consumes *v* ▷ **consume**
consuming *v* ▷ **consume**
consummate [**kon**-sum-mate] *v* (**-mates, -mating, -mated**) make (a marriage) legal by sexual intercourse ▶ *adj* [kon-**sum**-mit] supremely skilled > **consummately** *adv* > **consummation** *n* (*pl* **-s**)
consummated *v* ▷ **consummate**
consummately *adv* ▷ **consummate**
consummates *v* ▷ **consummate**
consummating *v* ▷ **consummate**
consummation *n* ▷ **consummate**
consummations *n* ▷ **consummate**
consumption *n* (*pl* **-s**) amount consumed
consumptions *n* ▷ **consumption**
consumptive *n* (*pl* **-s**) ▶ *adj* (*Old-fashioned*) (person) having tuberculosis
consumptives *n* ▷ **consumptive**
contact *n* (*pl* **-s**) communicating ▶ *v* (**-s, -ing, -ed**) get in touch with
contacted *v* ▷ **contact**
contacting *v* ▷ **contact**
contacts *n, v* ▷ **contact**
contagion *n* (*pl* **-s**) passing on of disease by contact
contagions *n* ▷ **contagion**
contagious *adj* spreading by contact, catching
contain *v* (**-s, -ing, -ed**) hold or be capable of holding
contained *v* ▷ **contain**
container *n* (*pl* **-s**) object used to hold or store things in
containers *n* ▷ **container**
containing *v* ▷ **contain**
containment *n* prevention of the spread of something harmful
contains *v* ▷ **contain**
contaminant *n* (*pl* **-s**) contaminating substance
contaminants *n* ▷ **contaminant**
contaminate *v* (**-nates, -nating, -nated**) make impure, pollute > **contamination** *n* (*pl* **-s**)
contaminated *v* ▷ **contaminate**
contaminates *v* ▷ **contaminate**
contaminating *v* ▷ **contaminate**
contamination *n* ▷ **contaminate**
contaminations *n* ▷ **contaminate**
contemplate *v* (**-lates, -lating, -lated**) think deeply > **contemplation** *n* (*pl* **-s**) > **contemplative** *adj*
contemplated *v* ▷ **contemplate**
contemplates *v* ▷ **contemplate**
contemplating *v* ▷ **contemplate**
contemplation *n* ▷ **contemplate**
contemplations *n* ▷ **contemplate**
contemplative *adj* ▷ **contemplate**
contemporaneous *adj* happening at the same time
contemporaries *n* ▷ **contemporary**
contemporary *adj* present-day, modern ▶ *n* (*pl* **-raries**) person or thing living or occurring at the same time as another
contempt *n* (*pl* **-s**) dislike and disregard
contemptible *adj* deserving contempt > **contemptibly** *adv*
contemptibly *adv* ▷ **contemptible**
contempts *n* ▷ **contempt**
contemptuous *adj* showing contempt > **contemptuously** *adv*
contemptuously *adv* ▷ **contemptuous**
contend *v* (**-s, -ing, -ed**) (*foll. by* **with**) deal with
contended *v* ▷ **contend**
contender *n* (*pl* **-s**) competitor, esp. a strong one
contenders *n* ▷ **contender**
contending *v* ▷ **contend**
contends *v* ▷ **contend**
content¹ *n* (*pl* **-s**) meaning or substance of a piece of writing ▶ *pl* what something contains
content² *adj* satisfied with things as they are ▶ *v* (**-s, -ing, -ed**) make (someone) content ▶ *n* happiness and satisfaction > **contented** *adj* > **contentedly** *adv* > **contentment** *n*

contented *v, adj* ▷ **content[2]**

contentedly *adv* ▷ **content[2]**

contenting *v* ▷ **content[2]**

contention *n* (*pl* **-s**) disagreement or dispute

contentions *n* ▷ **contention**

contentious *adj* causing disagreement > **contentiously** *adv* > **contentiousness** *n*

contentiously *adv* ▷ **contentious**

contentiousness *n* ▷ **contentious**

contentment *n* ▷ **content[2]**

contents *n* ▷ **content[1]** ▶ *v* ▷ **content[2]**

contest *n* (*pl* **-s**) competition or struggle ▶ *v* (**-s, -ing, -ed**) dispute, object to > **contestant** *n* (*pl* **-s**)

contestant *n* ▷ **contest**

contestants *n* ▷ **contest**

contested *v* ▷ **contest**

contesting *v* ▷ **contest**

contests *n, v* ▷ **contest**

context *n* (*pl* **-s**) circumstances of an event or fact > **contextual** *adj*

contexts *n* ▷ **context**

contextual *adj* ▷ **context**

contiguous *adj* very near or touching > **contiguously** *adv*

contiguously *adv* ▷ **contiguous**

continence *n* ▷ **continent[2]**

continent[1] *n* (*pl* **-s**) one of the earth's large masses of land > **continental** *adj* > **continentally** *adv*

continent[2] *adj* able to control one's bladder and bowels > **continence** *n*

continental *adj* ▷ **continent[1]**

continentally *adv* ▷ **continent[1]**

continents *n* ▷ **continent[1]**

contingencies *n* ▷ **contingency**

contingency *n* (*pl* **-cies**) something that may happen

contingent *n* (*pl* **-s**) group of people that represents or is part of a larger group ▶ *adj* (*foll. by* **on**) dependent on (something uncertain)

contingents *n* ▷ **contingent**

continua *n* ▷ **continuum**

continual *adj* constant > **continually** *adv*

continually *adv* ▷ **continual**

continuance *n* continuing

continuation *n* (*pl* **-s**) continuing

continuations *n* ▷ **continuation**

continue *v* (**-tinues, -tinuing, -tinued**) (cause to) remain in a condition or place

continued *v* ▷ **continue**

continues *v* ▷ **continue**

continuing *v* ▷ **continue**

continuities *n* ▷ **continuity**

continuity *n* (*pl* **-ities**) smooth development or sequence

continuo *n* (*pl* **-s**) (MUSIC) continuous bass part, usu. played on a keyboard instrument

continuos *n* ▷ **continuo**

continuous *adj* continuing uninterrupted > **continuously** *adv*

continuously *adv* ▷ **continuous**

continuum *n* (*pl* **-tinua, -tinuums**) continuous series

continuums *n* ▷ **continuum**

contort *v* (**-s, -ing, -ed**) twist out of shape > **contortion** *n* (*pl* **-s**)

contorted *v* ▷ **contort**

contorting *v* ▷ **contort**

contortion *n* ▷ **contort**

contortionist *n* (*pl* **-s**) performer who contorts his or her body to entertain

contortionists *n* ▷ **contortionist**

contortions *n* ▷ **contort**

contorts *v* ▷ **contort**

contour *n* (*pl* **-s**) outline

contours *n* ▷ **contour**

contraband *n, adj* smuggled (goods)

contraception *n* (*pl* **-s**) prevention of pregnancy by artificial means

contraceptions *n* ▷ **contraception**

contraceptive *n* (*pl* **-s**) device used or pill taken to prevent pregnancy ▶ *adj* preventing pregnancy

contraceptives *n* ▷ **contraceptive**

contract *n* (*pl* **-s**) (document setting out) a formal agreement ▶ *v* (**-s, -ing, -ed**) make a formal agreement (to do something) > **contraction** *n* (*pl* **-s**) > **contractual** *adj* > **contractually** *adv*

contracted *v* ▷ **contract**

contracting *v* ▷ **contract**

contraction *n* ▷ **contract**

contractions *n* ▷ **contract**

contractor *n* (*pl* **-s**) firm that supplies materials or labour

contractors *n* ▷ **contractor**

contracts *n, v* ▷ **contract**

contractual *adj* ▷ **contract**

contractually *adv* ▷ **contract**

contradict *v* (**-s, -ing, -ed**) declare the opposite of (a statement) to be true > **contradiction** *n* (*pl* **-s**) > **contradictory** *adj*

contradicted *v* ▷ **contradict**

contradicting *v* ▷ **contradict**

contradiction *n* ▷ **contradict**

contradictions *n* ▷ **contradict**

contradictory *adj* ▷ **contradict**

contradicts *v* ▷ **contradict**

contraflow *n* (*pl* **-s**) flow of traffic going alongside but in an opposite direction to the usual flow

contraflows *n* ▷ **contraflow**

contralto *n* (*pl* **-s**) (singer with) the lowest female voice

contraltos *n* ▷ **contralto**

contraption *n* (*pl* **-s**) strange-looking device

contraptions *n* ▷ **contraption**

contrapuntal *adj* (MUSIC) of or in counterpoint > **contrapuntally** *adv*

contrapuntally *adv* ▷ **contrapuntal**

contraries *n* ▷ **contrary**

contrarily *adv* ▷ **contrary**

contrariness *n* ▷ **contrary**

contrariwise *adv* ▷ **contrary**

contrary *n* (*pl* **-aries**) complete opposite ▶ *adj* opposed, completely different ▶ *adv* in opposition > **contrarily** *adv* > **contrariness** *n* > **contrariwise** *adv*

contrast *n* (*pl* **-s**) obvious difference ▶ *v* (**-s, -ing, -ed**) compare in order to show differences (*foll. by* **with**)

contrasted *v* ▷ **contrast**

contrasting *v* ▷ **contrast**

contrasts *n, v* ▷ **contrast**

contravene *v* (**-venes, -vening, -vened**) break (a rule or law) > **contravention** *n* (*pl* **-s**)

contravened *v* ▷ **contravene**

contravenes *v* ▷ **contravene**

contravening *v* ▷ **contravene**

contravention *n* ▷ **contravene**

contraventions *n* ▷ **contravene**

contretemps [**kon**-tra-tahn] *n* (*pl* **-temps**) embarrassing minor disagreement

contribute *v* (**-butes, -buting, -buted**) give for a common purpose or fund (*foll. by* **to**) > **contribution** *n* (*pl* **-s**) > **contributor** *n* (*pl* **-s**) > **contributory** *adj*

contributed *v* ▷ **contribute**

contributes *v* ▷ **contribute**

contributing *v* ▷ **contribute**

contribution *n* ▷ **contribute**

contributions *n* ▷ **contribute**

contributor *n* ▷ **contribute**

contributors *n* ▷ **contribute**

contributory *adj* ▷ **contribute**

contrite *adj* sorry and apologetic > **contritely** *adv* > **contrition** *n*

contritely *adv* ▷ **contrite**

contrition *n* ▷ **contrite**

contrivance *n* (*pl* **-s**) device

contrivances *n* ▷ **contrivance**

contrive *v* (**-trives, -triving, -trived**) make happen

contrived *adj* planned or artificial ▶ *v* ▷ **contrive**

contrives *v* ▷ **contrive**

contriving *v* ▷ **contrive**

control *n* (*pl* **-s**) power to direct something ▶ *pl* instruments used to operate a machine ▶ *v* (**-trols, -trolling, -trolled**) have power over > **controllable** *adj* > **controller** *n* (*pl* **-s**)

controllable *adj* ▷ **control**

controlled *v* ▷ **control**

controller *n* ▷ **control**

controllers *n* ▷ **control**

controlling *v* ▷ **control**

controls *n, v* ▷ **control**

controversial *adj* causing controversy > **controversially** *adv*

controversially *adv* ▷ **controversial**

controversies *adv* ▷ **controversy**

controversy *n* (*pl* **-sies**) fierce argument or debate

contumelies *n* ▷ **contumely**

contumely [**kon**-tume-mill-ee] *n* (*pl* **-melies**) (*Lit*) scornful or insulting treatment

contusion *n* (*pl* **-s**) (*Formal*) bruise

contusions *n* ▷ **contusion**

conundrum *n* (*pl* **-s**) riddle

conundrums *n* ▷ **conundrum**

conurbation *n* (*pl* **-s**) large urban area formed by the growth and merging of towns

conurbations *n* ▷ **conurbation**

convalesce *v* (**-lesces, -lescing, -lesced**) recover after an illness or operation > **convalescence** *n* (*pl* **-s**) > **convalescent** *n* (*pl* **-s**) *adj*

convalesced *v* ▷ **convalesce**

convalescence *n* ▷ **convalesce**

convalescences *n* ▷ **convalesce**

convalescent *n* ▷ **convalesce**

convalescents *n* ▷ **convalesce**

convalesces *v* ▷ **convalesce**

convalescing *v* ▷ **convalesce**

convection *n* (*pl* **-s**) transmission of heat in liquids or gases by the circulation of currents

convections *n* ▷ **convection**

convector *n* (*pl* **-s**) heater that gives out hot air

convectors *n* ▷ **convector**

convene *v* (**-venes, -vening, -vened**) gather or summon for a formal meeting

convened *v* ▷ **convene**

convener, convenor *n* (*pl* **-s**) person who calls a meeting

conveners *n* ▷ **convener**

convenes *v* ▷ **convene**

convenience *n* (*pl* **-s**) quality of being convenient

conveniences *n* ▷ **convenience**
convenient *adj* suitable or opportune > **conveniently** *adv*
conveniently *adv* ▷ **convenient**
convening *v* ▷ **convene**
convenor *n* ▷ **convener**
convenors *n* ▷ **convener**
convent *n* (*pl* **-s**) building where nuns live
convention *n* (*pl* **-s**) widely accepted view of proper behaviour
conventional *adj* (unthinkingly) following the accepted customs > **conventionally** *adv* > **conventionality** *n*
conventionality *n* ▷ **conventional**
conventionally *adv* ▷ **conventional**
conventions *n* ▷ **convention**
convents *n* ▷ **convent**
converge *v* (**-verges, -verging, -verged**) meet or join > **convergence** *n*
converged *v* ▷ **converge**
converges *v* ▷ **converge**
converging *v* ▷ **converge**
conversant *adj* having knowledge or experience of
conversation *n* (*pl* **-s**) informal talk > **conversational** *adj*
conversational *adj* ▷ **conversation**
conversationalist *n* (*pl* **-s**) person with a specified ability at conversation
conversationalists *n* ▷ **conversationalist**
conversations *n* ▷ **conversation**
converse[1] *v* (**-verses, -versing, versed**) have a conversation
converse[2] *adj*, *n* (*pl* **-s**) opposite or contrary > **conversely** *adv*
conversed *v* ▷ **converse**[1]
conversely *adv* ▷ **converse**[2]
converses *v* ▷ **converse**[1] ▶ *n* ▷ **converse**[2]
conversing *v* ▷ **converse**[1]
conversion *n* (*pl* **-s**) (thing resulting from) converting
conversions *n* ▷ **conversion**
convert *v* (**-s, -ing, ed**) change in form, character, or function ▶ *n* (*pl* **-s**) person who has converted to a different belief or religion
converted *v* ▷ **convert**
convertible *adj* capable of being converted ▶ *n* (*pl* **-s**) car with a folding or removable roof
convertibles *n* ▷ **convertible**
converting *v* ▷ **convert**
converts *v*, *n* ▷ **convert**
convex *adj* curving outwards
convey *v* (**-s, -ing, -ed**) communicate (information)
conveyance *n* (*pl* **-s**) (*Old-fashioned*) vehicle
conveyances *n* ▷ **conveyance**
conveyancing *n* branch of law dealing with the transfer of ownership of property
conveyed *v* ▷ **convey**
conveying *v* ▷ **convey**
conveys *v* ▷ **convey**
convict *v* (**-s, -ing, -ed**) declare guilty ▶ *n* (*pl* **-s**) person serving a prison sentence
convicted *v* ▷ **convict**
convicting *v* ▷ **convict**
conviction *n* (*pl* **-s**) firm belief
convictions *n* ▷ **conviction**
convicts *v*, *n* ▷ **convict**
convince *v* (**-vinces, -vincing, -vinced**) persuade by argument or evidence > **convincing** *adj* > **convincingly** *adv*
convinced *v* ▷ **convince**
convinces *v* ▷ **convince**
convincing *v*, *adj* ▷ **convince**
convincingly *adv* ▷ **convince**
convivial *adj* sociable, lively > **conviviality** *n* > **convivially** *adv*
conviviality *n* ▷ **convivial**
convivially *adv* ▷ **convivial**
convocation *n* (*pl* **-s**) calling together
convocations *n* ▷ **convocation**
convoke *v* (**-vokes, -voking, -voked**) call together
convoked *v* ▷ **convoke**
convokes *v* ▷ **convoke**
convoking *v* ▷ **convoke**
convoluted *adj* coiled, twisted > **convolution** *n* (*pl* **-s**)
convolution *n* ▷ **convoluted**
convolutions *n* ▷ **convoluted**
convolvulus *n* (*pl* **-es**) twining plant with funnel-shaped flowers
convolvuluses *n* ▷ **convolvulus**
convoy *n* (*pl* **-s**) group of vehicles or ships travelling together
convoys *n* ▷ **convoy**
convulse *v* (**-vulses, -vulsing, -vulsed**) (of part of the body) undergo violent spasms (*Informal*) > **convulsive** *adj* > **convulsively** *adv*
convulsed *v* ▷ **convulse**
convulses *v* ▷ **convulse**
convulsing *v* ▷ **convulse**
convulsion *n* (*pl* **-s**) violent muscular spasm ▶ *pl* uncontrollable laughter
convulsions *n* ▷ **convulsion**
convulsive *adj* ▷ **convulse**
convulsively *adv* ▷ **convulse**
cony, coney *n* (*pl* **conies, -s**) (BRIT) rabbit
coo *v* (**coos, cooing, cooed**) (of a dove or pigeon) make a soft murmuring sound

cooed *v* ▷ **coo**
cooee *interj* (BRIT, AUST & NZ) call to attract attention
cooing *v* ▷ **coo**
cook *v* **(-s, -ing, -ed)** prepare (food) by heating ▶ *n* (*pl* **-s**) person who cooks food
cooked *v* ▷ **cook**
cooker *n* (*pl* **-s**) (CHIEFLY BRIT) apparatus for cooking heated by gas or electricity
cookers *n* ▷ **cooker**
cookery *n* art of cooking
cookie *n* (*pl* **-s**) (US) biscuit
cookies *n* ▷ **cookie**
cooking *v* ▷ **cook**
cooks *v, n* ▷ **cook**
cool *adj* **(-er, -est)** moderately cold (*Informal*) ▶ *v* **(-s, -ing, -ed)** make or become cool ▶ *n* (*pl* **-s**) coolness > **coolly** *adv* > **coolness** *n* (*pl* **-es**)
coolant *n* (*pl* **-s**) fluid used to cool machinery while it is working
coolants *n* ▷ **coolant**
cooled *v* ▷ **cool**
cooler *n* (*pl* **-s**) container for making or keeping things cool ▶ *adj* ▷ **cool**
coolers *n* ▷ **cooler**
coolest *adj* ▷ **cool**
coolibah *n* (*pl* **-s**) Australian eucalypt that grows beside rivers
coolibahs *n* ▷ **coolibah**
cooling *v* ▷ **cool**
coolly *adv* ▷ **cool**
coolness *n* ▷ **cool**
coolnesses *n* ▷ **cool**
cools *v, n* ▷ **cool**
coomb, coombe *n* (*pl* **-s**) (S ENGLISH) short valley or deep hollow
coombe *n* ▷ **coomb**
coombes *n* ▷ **coomb**
coombs *n* ▷ **coomb**
coop[1] *n* (*pl* **-s**) cage or pen for poultry
coop[2] [**koh**-op] *n* (*pl* **-s**) (BRIT, US & AUST) (shop run by) a cooperative society
cooper *n* (*pl* **-s**) person who makes or repairs barrels
cooperate *v* **(-rates, -rating, -rated)** work or act together > **cooperation** *n*
cooperated *v* ▷ **cooperate**
cooperates *v* ▷ **cooperate**
cooperating *v* ▷ **cooperate**
cooperation *n* ▷ **cooperate**
cooperative *adj* willing to cooperate ▶ *n* (*pl* **-s**) cooperative organization
cooperatives *n* ▷ **cooperative**
coopers *n* ▷ **cooper**
coops *n* ▷ **coop**[1, 2]
coopt [koh-**opt**] *v* **(-s, -ing, -ed)** add (someone) to a group by the agreement of the existing members
coopted *v* ▷ **coopt**
coopting *v* ▷ **coopt**
coopts *v* ▷ **coopt**
coordinate *v* **(-nates, -nating, -nated)** bring together and cause to work together efficiently ▶ *n* (*pl* **-s**) (MATHS) any of a set of numbers defining the location of a point ▶ *pl* clothes designed to be worn together > **coordination** *n* > **coordinator** *n* (*pl* **-s**)
coordinated *v* ▷ **coordinate**
coordinates *v, n* ▷ **coordinate**
coordinating *v* ▷ **coordinate**
coordination *n* ▷ **coordinate**
coordinator *n* ▷ **coordinate**
coordinators *n* ▷ **coordinate**
coos *v* ▷ **coo**
coot *n* (*pl* **-s**) small black water bird
coots *n* ▷ **coot**
cop (*Slang*) *n* (*pl* **-s**) policeman ▶ *v* **(cops, copping, copped)** take or seize
cope[1] *v* **(copes, coping, coped)** (*often foll. by* **with**) deal successfully (with)
cope[2] *n* (*pl* **-s**) large ceremonial cloak worn by some Christian priests
coped *v* ▷ **cope**[1]
copes *v* ▷ **cope**[1] ▶ *n* ▷ **cope**[2]
copied *v* ▷ **copy**
copies *n, v* ▷ **copy**
coping *v* ▷ **cope**[1] ▶ *n* (*pl* **-s**) sloping top row of a wall
copings *n* ▷ **coping**
copious [**kope**-ee-uss] *adj* abundant, plentiful > **copiously** *adv*
copiously *adv* ▷ **copious**
copped *v* ▷ **cop**
copper[1] *n* (*pl* **-s**) soft reddish-brown metal
copper[2] *n* (*pl* **-s**) (BRIT) (*Slang*) policeman
copperplate *n* (*pl* **-s**) fine handwriting style
copperplates *n* ▷ **copperplate**
coppers *n* ▷ **copper**[1, 2]
coppice, copse *n* (*pl* **-s**) small group of trees growing close together
coppices *n* ▷ **coppice**
copping *v* ▷ **cop**
copra *n* (*pl* **-s**) dried oil-yielding kernel of the coconut
copras *n* ▷ **copra**
cops *n, v* ▷ **cop**
copse *n* ▷ **coppice**
copses *n* ▷ **coppice**
copulate *v* **(-lates, -lating, -lated)** have sexual intercourse > **copulation** *n* (*pl* **-s**)

copulated *v* ▷ **copulate**
copulates *v* ▷ **copulate**
copulating *v* ▷ **copulate**
copulation *n* ▷ **copulate**
copulations *n* ▷ **copulate**
copy *n* (*pl* **copies**) thing made to look exactly like another ▶ *v* (**copies, copying, copied**) make a copy of
copying *v* ▷ **copy**
copyright *n* (*pl* **-s**) exclusive legal right to reproduce and control a book, work of art, etc. ▶ *v* (**-s, -ing, -ed**) take out a copyright on ▶ *adj* protected by copyright
copyrighted *v* ▷ **copyright**
copyrighting *v* ▷ **copyright**
copyrights *n, v* ▷ **copyright**
copywriter *n* (*pl* **-s**) person who writes advertising copy
copywriters *n* ▷ **copywriter**
coquette *n* (*pl* **-s**) woman who flirts > **coquettish** *adj*
coquettes *n* ▷ **coquette**
coquettish *adj* ▷ **coquette**
coracle *n* (*pl* **-s**) small round boat of wicker covered with skins
coracles *n* ▷ **coracle**
coral *n* (*pl* **-s**) hard substance formed from the skeletons of very small sea animals ▶ *adj* orange-pink
corals *n* ▷ **coral**
cord *n* (*pl* **-s**) thin rope or thick string ▶ *pl* corduroy trousers
cordial *adj* warm and friendly ▶ *n* (*pl* **-s**) drink with a fruit base > **cordially** *adv* > **cordiality** *n*
cordiality *n* ▷ **cordial**
cordially *adv* ▷ **cordial**
cordials *n* ▷ **cordial**
cordite *n* (*pl* **-s**) explosive used in guns and bombs
cordites *n* ▷ **cordite**
cordon *n* (*pl* **-s**) chain of police, soldiers, etc., guarding an area
cordons *n* ▷ **cordon**
cords *n* ▷ **cord**
corduroy *n* (*pl* **-s**) cotton fabric with a velvety ribbed surface
corduroys *n* ▷ **corduroy**
core *n* (*pl* **-s**) central part of certain fruits, containing the seeds ▶ *v* (**cores, coring, cored**) remove the core from
cored *v* ▷ **core**
corella *n* (*pl* **-s**) white Australian cockatoo
corellas *n* ▷ **corella**
cores *n, v* ▷ **core**
corgi *n* (*pl* **-s**) short-legged sturdy dog
corgis *n* ▷ **corgi**
coriander *n* (*pl* **-s**) plant grown for its aromatic seeds and leaves
corianders *n* ▷ **coriander**
coring *v* ▷ **core**
cork *n* (*pl* **-s**) thick light bark of a Mediterranean oak ▶ *v* (**-s, -ing, -ed**) seal with a cork
corkage *n* (*pl* **-s**) restaurant's charge for serving wine bought elsewhere
corkages *n* ▷ **corkage**
corked *v* ▷ **cork**
corking *v* ▷ **cork**
corks *n, v* ▷ **cork**
corkscrew *n* (*pl* **-s**) spiral metal tool for pulling corks from bottles
corkscrews *n* ▷ **corkscrew**
corm *n* (*pl* **-s**) bulblike underground stem of certain plants
cormorant *n* (*pl* **-s**) large dark-coloured long-necked sea bird
cormorants *n* ▷ **cormorant**
corms *n* ▷ **corm**
corn[1] *n* (*pl* **-s**) cereal plant such as wheat or oats
corn[2] *n* (*pl* **-s**) painful hard skin on the toe
cornea [**korn**-ee-a] *n* (*pl* **-neas, -neae**) transparent membrane covering the eyeball > **corneal** *adj*
corneae *n* ▷ **cornea**
corneal *adj* ▷ **cornea**
corneas *n* ▷ **cornea**
corner *n* (*pl* **-s**) area or angle where two converging lines or surfaces meet (SPORT) ▶ *v* (**-s, -ing, -ed**) force into a difficult or inescapable position
cornered *v* ▷ **corner**
cornering *v* ▷ **corner**
corners *n, v* ▷ **corner**
cornerstone *n* (*pl* **-s**) indispensable part or basis
cornerstones *n* ▷ **cornerstone**
cornet *n* (*pl* **-s**) brass instrument similar to the trumpet
cornets *n* ▷ **cornet**
cornflakes *pl n* breakfast cereal made from toasted maize
cornflour *n* (*pl* **-s**) (CHIEFLY BRIT) fine maize flour
cornflours *n* ▷ **cornflour**
cornflower *n* (*pl* **-s**) plant with blue flowers
cornflowers *n* ▷ **cornflower**
cornice *n* (*pl* **-s**) decorative moulding round the top of a wall
cornices *n* ▷ **cornice**
cornier *adj* ▷ **corny**
corniest *adj* ▷ **corny**

corns *n* ▷ **corn**[1, 2]
cornucopia [korn-yew-**kope**-ee-a] *n* (*pl* **-s**) great abundance
cornucopias *n* ▷ **cornucopia**
corny (**-nier, -niest**) *adj* (*Slang*) unoriginal or oversentimental
corolla *n* (*pl* **-s**) petals of a flower collectively
corollaries *n* ▷ **corollary**
corollary *n* (*pl* **-laries**) idea, fact, or proposition which is the natural result of something else
corollas *n* ▷ **corolla**
corona *n* (*pl* **-nas, -nae**) ring of light round the moon or sun
coronae *n* ▷ **corona**
coronaries *n* ▷ **coronary**
coronary [**kor**-ron-a-ree] *adj* of the arteries surrounding the heart ▶ *n* (*pl* **-naries**)
coronas *n* ▷ **corona**
coronation *n* (*pl* **-s**) ceremony of crowning a monarch
coronations *n* ▷ **coronation**
coroner *n* (*pl* **-s**) (BRIT, AUST & NZ) official responsible for the investigation of violent, sudden, or suspicious deaths
coroners *n* ▷ **coroner**
coronet *n* (*pl* **-s**) small crown
coronets *n* ▷ **coronet**
corpora *n* ▷ **corpus**
corporal[1] *n* (*pl* **-s**) noncommissioned officer in an army
corporal[2] *adj* of the body > **corporally** *adv*
corporally *adv* ▷ **corporal**[2]
corporals *n* ▷ **corporal**[1]
corporate *adj* of business corporations
corporation *n* (*pl* **-s**) large business or company
corporations *n* ▷ **corporation**
corporeal [kore-**pore**-ee-al] *adj* physical or tangible
corps [**kore**] *n* (*pl* **corps**) military unit with a specific function
corpse *n* (*pl* **-s**) dead body
corpses *n* ▷ **corpse**
corpulence *n* ▷ **corpulent**
corpulent *adj* fat or plump > **corpulence** *n*
corpus *n* (*pl* **corpora**) collection of writings, esp. by a single author
corpuscle *n* (*pl* **-s**) red or white blood cell
corpuscles *n* ▷ **corpuscle**
corral (US) *n* (*pl* **-s**) enclosure for cattle or horses ▶ *v* (**-rals, -ralling, -ralled**) put in a corral
corralled *v* ▷ **corral**
corralling *v* ▷ **corral**
corrals *n, v* ▷ **corral**
correct *adj* free from error, true ▶ *v* (**-s, -ing, -ed**) put right > **correctly** *adv* > **correctness** *n*
corrected *v* ▷ **correct**
correcting *v* ▷ **correct**
correction *n* (*pl* **-s**) correcting
corrections *n* ▷ **correction**
corrective *adj* intended to put right something wrong
correctly *adv* ▷ **correct**
correctness *n* ▷ **correct**
corrects *v* ▷ **correct**
correlate *v* (**-lates, -lating, -lated**) place or be placed in a mutual relationship > **correlation** *n* (*pl* **-s**)
correlated *v* ▷ **correlate**
correlates *v* ▷ **correlate**
correlating *v* ▷ **correlate**
correlation *n* ▷ **correlate**
correlations *n* ▷ **correlate**
correspond *v* (**-s, -ing, -ed**) be consistent or compatible (with) > **corresponding** *adj* > **correspondingly** *adv*
corresponded *v* ▷ **correspond**
correspondence *n* communication by letters
correspondent *n* (*pl* **-s**) person employed by a newspaper etc. to report on a special subject or from a foreign country
correspondents *n* ▷ **correspondent**
corresponding *v, adj* ▷ **correspond**
correspondingly *adv* ▷ **correspond**
corresponds *v* ▷ **correspond**
corridor *n* (*pl* **-s**) passage in a building or train
corridors *n* ▷ **corridor**
corrigenda *n* ▷ **corrigendum**
corrigendum [kor-rij-**end**-um] *n* (*pl* **-da**) error to be corrected
corroborate *v* (**-rates, -rating, -rated**) support (a fact or opinion) by giving proof > **corroboration** *n* (*pl* **-s**) > **corroborative** *adj*
corroborated *v* ▷ **corroborate**
corroborates *v* ▷ **corroborate**
corroborating *v* ▷ **corroborate**
corroboration *n* ▷ **corroborate**
corroborations *n* ▷ **corroborate**
corroborative *adj* ▷ **corroborate**
corroboree *n* (*pl* **-s**) (AUST) Aboriginal gathering or dance
corroborees *n* ▷ **corroboree**
corrode *v* (**-rodes, -roding, -roded**) eat or be eaten away by chemical action or rust > **corrosion** *n* > **corrosive** *adj* > **corrosively** *adv* > **corrosiveness** *n*
corroded *v* ▷ **corrode**
corrodes *v* ▷ **corrode**
corroding *v* ▷ **corrode**
corrosion *n* ▷ **corrode**

corrosive *v* ▷ **corrode**
corrosively *adv* ▷ **corrode**
corrosiveness *n* ▷ **corrode**
corrugated *adj* folded into alternate grooves and ridges
corrupt *adj* (**-er, -est**) open to or involving bribery ▶ *v* (**-s, -ing, -ed**) make corrupt > **corruptly** *adv* > **corruption** *n* > **corruptible** *adj*
corrupted *v* ▷ **corrupt**
corrupter *adj* ▷ **corrupt**
corruptest *adj* ▷ **corrupt**
corruptible *adj* ▷ **corrupt**
corrupting *v* ▷ **corrupt**
corruption *n* ▷ **corrupt**
corruptly *adv* ▷ **corrupt**
corrupts *v* ▷ **corrupt**
corsage [kor-**sahzh**] *n* (*pl* **-s**) small bouquet worn on the bodice of a dress
corsages *n* ▷ **corsage**
corsair *n* (*pl* **-s**) pirate
corsairs *n* ▷ **corsair**
corset *n* (*pl* **-s**) women's close-fitting undergarment worn to shape the torso
corsets *n* ▷ **corset**
cortege [kor-**tayzh**] *n* (*pl* **-s**) funeral procession
corteges *n* ▷ **cortege**
cortex *n* (*pl* **-tices**) (ANAT) outer layer of the brain or other internal organ > **cortical** *adj*
cortical *adj* ▷ **cortex**
cortices *n* ▷ **cortex**
cortisone *n* (*pl* **-s**) steroid hormone used to treat various diseases
cortisones *n* ▷ **cortisone**
corundum *n* (*pl* **-s**) hard mineral used as an abrasive
corundums *n* ▷ **corundum**
coruscate *v* (**-cates, -cating, -cated**) (*Formal*) sparkle
coruscated *v* ▷ **coruscate**
coruscates *v* ▷ **coruscate**
coruscating *v* ▷ **coruscate**
corvette *n* (*pl* **-s**) lightly armed escort warship
corvettes *n* ▷ **corvette**
cosh *n* (*pl* **-es**) (BRIT) heavy blunt weapon ▶ *v* (**-es, -ing, -ed**) hit with a cosh
coshed *v, n* ▷ **cosh**
coshes *v* ▷ **cosh**
coshing *v* ▷ **cosh**
cosier *adj* ▷ **cosy**
cosies *adj* ▷ **cosy**
cosiest *adj* ▷ **cosy**
cosily *adv* ▷ **cosy**
cosine [**koh**-sine] *n* (*pl* **-s**) (in trigonometry) ratio of the length of the adjacent side to that of the hypotenuse in a right-angled triangle
cosines *n* ▷ **cosine**
cosiness *n* ▷ **cosy**
cosmetic *n* (*pl* **-s**) preparation used to improve the appearance of a person's skin ▶ *adj* improving the appearance only
cosmetics *n* ▷ **cosmetic**
cosmic *adj* of the whole universe > **cosmically** *adv*
cosmically *adv* ▷ **cosmic**
cosmological *adj* ▷ **cosmology**
cosmologist *n* ▷ **cosmology**
cosmologists *n* ▷ **cosmology**
cosmology *n* study of the origin and nature of the universe > **cosmological** *adj* > **cosmologist** *n* (*pl* **-s**)
cosmonaut *n* (*pl* **-s**) Russian name for an astronaut
cosmonauts *n* ▷ **cosmonaut**
cosmopolitan *adj* composed of people or elements from many countries ▶ *n* (*pl* **-s**) cosmopolitan person > **cosmopolitanism** *n*
cosmopolitanism *n* ▷ **cosmopolitan**
cosmopolitans *n* ▷ **cosmopolitan**
cosmos *n* (*pl* **cosmos**) the universe
cossack *n* (*pl* **-s**) member of a S Russian people famous as horsemen and dancers
cossacks *n* ▷ **cossack**
cosset *v* (**-s, -ing, -ed**) pamper
cosseted *v* ▷ **cosset**
cosseting *v* ▷ **cosset**
cossets *v* ▷ **cosset**
cost *n* (*pl* **-s**) amount of money, time, labour, etc., required for something ▶ *pl* expenses of a lawsuit ▶ *v* (**costs, costing, cost**) have as its cost
costermonger *n* (*pl* **-s**) (BRIT) person who sells fruit and vegetables from a street barrow
costermongers *n* ▷ **costermonger**
costing *v* ▷ **cost**
costlier *adj* ▷ **costly**
costliest *adj* ▷ **costly**
costliness *n* ▷ **costly**
costlinesses *n* ▷ **costly**
costly *adj* (**-lier, -liest**) expensive > **costliness** *n* (*pl* **-es**)
costs *n, v* ▷ **cost**
costume *n* (*pl* **-s**) style of dress of a particular place or time, or for a particular activity
costumes *n* ▷ **costume**
costumier *n* (*pl* **-s**) maker or seller of costumes
costumiers *n* ▷ **costumier**
cosy *adj* (**-sier, -siest**) warm and snug ▶ *n* (*pl* **-sies**) cover for keeping things warm > **cosily** *adv* > **cosiness** *n*

cot *n* (*pl* **-s**) baby's bed with high sides
cote *n* (*pl* **-s**) shelter for birds or animals
coterie [**kote**-er-ee] *n* (*pl* **-s**) exclusive group, clique
coteries *n* ▷ **coterie**
cotes *n* ▷ **cote**
cotoneaster [kot-tone-ee-**ass**-ter] *n* (*pl* **-s**) garden shrub with red berries
cotoneasters *n* ▷ **cotoneaster**
cots *n* ▷ **cot**
cottage *n* (*pl* **-s**) small house in the country
cottages *n* ▷ **cottage**
cotter *n* (*pl* **-s**) pin or wedge used to secure machine parts
cotters *n* ▷ **cotter**
cotton *n* (*pl* **-s**) white downy fibre covering the seeds of a tropical plant > **cottony** *adj*
cottons *n* ▷ **cotton**
cottony *adj* ▷ **cotton**
cotyledon [kot-ill-**ee**-don] *n* (*pl* **-s**) first leaf of a plant embryo
cotyledons *n* ▷ **cotyledon**
couch *n* (*pl* **couches**) piece of upholstered furniture for seating more than one person ▶ *v* (**-es, -ing, -ed**) express in a particular way
couched *v* ▷ **couch**
couches *n, v* ▷ **couch**
couchette [koo-**shett**] *n* (*pl* **-s**) bed converted from seats on a train or ship
couchettes *n* ▷ **couchette**
couching *v* ▷ **couch**
cougan *n* (*pl* **-s**) (AUST) (*Slang*) drunk and rowdy person
cougans *n* ▷ **cougan**
cougar *n* (*pl* **-s**) puma
cougars *n* ▷ **cougar**
cough *v* (**-s, -ing, -ed**) expel air from the lungs abruptly and noisily ▶ *n* (*pl* **-s**) act or sound of coughing
coughed *v* ▷ **cough**
coughing *v* ▷ **cough**
coughs *v, n* ▷ **cough**
could *v* ▷ **can**[1]
coulomb [**koo**-lom] *n* (*pl* **-s**) SI unit of electric charge
coulombs *n* ▷ **coulomb**
coulter *n* (*pl* **-s**) blade at the front of a ploughshare
coulters *n* ▷ **coulter**
council *n* (*pl* **-s**) group meeting for discussion or consultation ▶ *adj* of or by a council
councillor *n* (*pl* **-s**) member of a council
councillors *n* ▷ **councillor**
councils *n* ▷ **council**
counsel *n* (*pl* **-s**) advice or guidance ▶ *v* (**-sels, -selling, -selled**) give guidance to > **counsellor** *n* (*pl* **-s**)
counselled *v* ▷ **counsel**
counselling *v* ▷ **counsel**
counsellor *n* ▷ **counsel**
counsellors *n* ▷ **counsel**
counsels *n, v* ▷ **counsel**
count[1] *v* (**-s, -ing, -ed**) say numbers in order ▶ *n* (*pl* **-s**) counting
count[2] *n* (*pl* **-s**) European nobleman
countdown *n* (*pl* **-s**) counting backwards to zero of the seconds before an event
countdowns *n* ▷ **countdown**
counted *v* ▷ **count**[1]
countenance *n* (*pl* **-s**) (expression of) the face ▶ *v* (**-nances, -nancing, -nanced**) allow or tolerate
countenanced *v* ▷ **countenance**
countenances *n, v* ▷ **countenance**
countenancing *v* ▷ **countenance**
counter[1] *n* (*pl* **-s**) long flat surface in a bank or shop, on which business is transacted
counter[2] *v* (**-s, -ing, -ed**) oppose, retaliate against ▶ *adv* in the opposite direction ▶ *n* (*pl* **-s**) opposing or retaliatory action
counteract *v* (**-s, -ing, -ed**) act against or neutralize > **counteraction** *n*
counteracted *v* ▷ **counteract**
counteracting *v* ▷ **counteract**
counteraction *n* ▷ **counteract**
counteracts *v* ▷ **counteract**
counterattack *n* (*pl* **-s**) ▶ *v* (**-s, -ing, -ed**) attack in response to an attack
counterattacked *v* ▷ **counterattack**
counterattacking *v* ▷ **counterattack**
counterattacks *n, v* ▷ **counterattack**
counterbalance *n* (*pl* **-s**) weight or force balancing or neutralizing another ▶ *v* (**-ces, -cing, -ced**) act as a counterbalance to
counterbalanced *v* ▷ **counterbalance**
counterbalances *n, v* ▷ **counterbalance**
counterbalancing *v* ▷ **counterbalance**
counterblast *n* (*pl* **-s**) aggressive response to a verbal attack
counterblasts *n* ▷ **counterblast**
countered *v* ▷ **counter**
counterfeit *adj* fake, forged ▶ *n* (*pl* **-s**) fake, forgery ▶ *v* (**-s, -ing, -ed**) fake, forge
counterfeited *v* ▷ **counterfeit**
counterfeiting *v* ▷ **counterfeit**
counterfeits *n, v* ▷ **counterfeit**
counterfoil *n* (*pl* **-s**) part of a cheque or receipt kept as a record
counterfoils *n* ▷ **counterfoil**
countering *v* ▷ **counter**

countermand *v* (**-s, -ing, -ed**) cancel (a previous order)
countermanded *v* ▷ **countermand**
countermanding *v* ▷ **countermand**
countermands *v* ▷ **countermand**
counterpane *n* (*pl* **-s**) bed covering
counterpanes *n* ▷ **counterpane**
counterpart *n* (*pl* **-s**) person or thing complementary to or corresponding to another
counterparts *n* ▷ **counterpart**
counterpoint *n* (*pl* **-s**) (MUSIC) technique of combining melodies
counterpoints *n* ▷ **counterpoint**
counterpoise *n* (*pl* **-s**) ▶ *v* (**-ses, -sing, -sed**) counterbalance
counterpoised *v* ▷ **counterpoise**
counterpoises *n, v* ▷ **counterpoise**
counterpoising *v* ▷ **counterpoise**
counterproductive *adj* having an effect opposite to the one intended
counters *n* ▷ **counter[1, 2]** ▶ *v* ▷ **counter[2]**
countersank *v* ▷ **countersink**
countersign *v* (**-s, -ing, -ed**) sign (a document already signed by someone) as confirmation
countersigned *v* ▷ **countersign**
countersigning *v* ▷ **countersign**
countersigns *v* ▷ **countersign**
countersink *v* (**-sinks, -sinking, -sank, -sunk**) drive (a screw) into a shaped hole so that its head is below the surface
countersinking *v* ▷ **countersink**
countersinks *v* ▷ **countersink**
countersunk *v* ▷ **countersink**
countertenor *n* (*pl* **-s**) male alto
countertenors *n* ▷ **countertenor**
counterterrorism *n* measures to prevent terrorist attacks or eradicate terrorist groups
countess *n* (*pl* **-es**) woman holding the rank of count or earl
countesses *n* ▷ **countess**
counties *n* ▷ **county**
counting *v* ▷ **count[1]**
countless *adj* too many to count
countries *n* ▷ **country**
countrified *adj* rustic in manner or appearance
country *n* (*pl* **-tries**) nation
countryman, countrywoman *n* (*pl* **-men, -women**) person from one's native land
countrymen *n* ▷ **countryman**
countryside *n* land away from cities
countrywoman *n* ▷ **countryman**
countrywomen *n* ▷ **countryman**
counts *v* ▷ **count[1]** ▶ *n* ▷ **count[1, 2]**
county *n* (*pl* **-ties**) (in some countries) division of a country
coup [**koo**] *n* (*pl* **-s**) successful action
coupé [**koo**-pay] *n* (*pl* **-s**) sports car with two doors and a sloping fixed roof
coupés *n* ▷ **coupé**
couple *n* (*pl* **-s**) two people who are married or romantically involved ▶ *v* (**-ples, -pling, -pled**) connect, associate
coupled *v* ▷ **couple**
couples *n, v* ▷ **couple**
couplet *n* (*pl* **-s**) two consecutive lines of verse, usu. rhyming and of the same metre
couplets *n* ▷ **couplet**
coupling *n* (*pl* **-s**) device for connecting things, such as railway carriages ▶ *v* ▷ **couple**
couplings *n* ▷ **coupling**
coupon *n* (*pl* **-s**) piece of paper entitling the holder to a discount or gift
coupons *n* ▷ **coupon**
coups *n* ▷ **coup**
courage *n* ability to face danger or pain without fear > **courageous** *adj* > **courageously** *adv*
courageous *adj* ▷ **courage**
courageously *adv* ▷ **courage**
courgette *n* (*pl* **-s**) type of small vegetable marrow
courgettes *n* ▷ **courgette**
courier *n* (*pl* **-s**) person employed to look after holiday-makers
couriers *n* ▷ **courier**
course *n* (*pl* **-s**) series of lessons or medical treatment ▶ *v* (**-ses, -sing, -sed**) (of liquid) run swiftly
coursed *v* ▷ **course**
courses *n, v* ▷ **course**
coursing *v* ▷ **course**
court *n* (*pl* **-s**) body which decides legal cases ▶ *v* (**-s, -ing, -ed**) (*Old-fashioned*) try to gain the love of
courted *v* ▷ **court**
courteous *adj* polite > **courteously** *adv*
courteously *adv* ▷ **courteous**
courtesan [kor-tiz-**zan**] *n* (*pl* **-s**) (HIST) mistress or high-class prostitute
courtesans *n* ▷ **courtesan**
courtesies *n* ▷ **courtesy**
courtesy *n* (*pl* **-sies**) politeness, good manners
courtier *n* (*pl* **-s**) attendant at a royal court
courtiers *n* ▷ **courtier**
courting *v* ▷ **court**
courtlier *adj* ▷ **courtly**
courtliest *adj* ▷ **courtly**
courtliness *n* ▷ **courtly**

courtlinesses *n* ▷ **courtly**
courtly *adj* (**-lier, -liest**) ceremoniously polite > **courtliness** *n* (*pl* **-es**)
courts *n, v* ▷ **court**
courtship *n* (*pl* **-s**) courting of an intended spouse or mate
courtships *n* ▷ **courtship**
courtyard *n* (*pl* **-s**) paved space enclosed by buildings or walls
courtyards *n* ▷ **courtyard**
cousin *n* (*pl* **-s**) child of one's uncle or aunt
cousins *n* ▷ **cousin**
couture [koo-**toor**] *n* (*pl* **-s**) high-fashion designing and dressmaking
coutures *n* ▷ **couture**
couturier *n* (*pl* **-s**) person who designs women's fashion clothes
couturiers *n* ▷ **couturier**
cove *n* (*pl* **-s**) small bay or inlet
coven [**kuv**-ven] *n* (*pl* **-s**) meeting of witches
covenant [**kuv**-ven-ant] *n* (*pl* **-s**) contract ▶ *v* (**-s, -ing, -ed**) agree by a covenant
covenanted *v* ▷ **covenant**
covenanting *v* ▷ **covenant**
covenants *n, v* ▷ **covenant**
covens *n* ▷ **coven**
cover *v* (**-s, -ing, -ed**) place something over, to protect or conceal ▶ *n* (*pl* **-s**) anything that covers
coverage *n* amount or extent covered
covered *v* ▷ **cover**
covering *v* ▷ **cover**
coverlet *n* (*pl* **-s**) bed cover
coverlets *v* ▷ **coverlet**
covers *v, n* ▷ **cover**
covert *adj* concealed, secret ▶ *n* (*pl* **-s**) thicket giving shelter to game birds or animals > **covertly** *adv*
covertly *adv* ▷ **covert**
coverts *n* ▷ **covert**
coves *n* ▷ **cove**
covet *v* (**-s, -ing, -ed**) long to possess (what belongs to someone else) > **covetous** *adj* > **covetousness** *n*
coveted *v* ▷ **covet**
coveting *v* ▷ **covet**
covetous *adj* ▷ **covet**
covetousness *n* ▷ **covet**
covets *v* ▷ **covet**
covey [**kuv**-vee] *n* (*pl* **-s**) small flock of grouse or partridge
coveys *n* ▷ **covey**
cow[1] *n* (*pl* **-s**) mature female of cattle and of certain other mammals, such as the elephant or seal
cow[2] *v* (**-s, -ing, -ed**) intimidate, subdue
coward *n* (*pl* **-s**) person who lacks courage > **cowardly** *adj* > **cowardliness** *n*
cowardice *n* lack of courage
cowardliness *n* ▷ **coward**
cowardly *adj* ▷ **coward**
cowards *n* ▷ **coward**
cowboy *n* (*pl* **-s**) (in the US) ranch worker who herds and tends cattle, usu. on horseback
cowboys *n* ▷ **cowboy**
cowed *v* ▷ **cow**[2]
cower *v* (**-s, -ing, -ed**) cringe in fear
cowered *v* ▷ **cower**
cowering *v* ▷ **cower**
cowers *v* ▷ **cower**
cowing *v* ▷ **cow**[2]
cowl *n* (*pl* **-s**) loose hood
cowling *n* (*pl* **-s**) cover on an engine
cowlings *n* ▷ **cowling**
cowls *n* ▷ **cowl**
cowrie *n* (*pl* **-s**) brightly-marked sea shell
cowries *n* ▷ **cowrie**
cows *n* ▷ **cow**[1] ▶ *v* ▷ **cow**[2]
cowslip *n* (*pl* **-s**) small yellow wild European flower
cowslips *n* ▷ **cowslip**
cox *n* (*pl* **-es**) coxswain ▶ *v* (**-es, -ing, -ed**) act as cox of (a boat)
coxed *v* ▷ **cox**
coxes *n, v* ▷ **cox**
coxing *v* ▷ **cox**
coxswain [**kok**-sn] *n* (*pl* **-s**) person who steers a rowing boat
coxswains *n* ▷ **coxswain**
coy *adj* (**-er, -est**) affectedly shy or modest > **coyly** *adv* > **coyness** *n* (*pl* **-es**)
coyer *adj* ▷ **coy**
coyest *adj* ▷ **coy**
coyly *adv* ▷ **coy**
coyness *n* ▷ **coy**
coynesses *n* ▷ **coy**
coyote [koy-**ote**-ee] *n* (*pl* **-s**) prairie wolf of N America
coyotes *n* ▷ **coyote**
coypu *n* (*pl* **-s**) beaver-like aquatic rodent native to S America, bred for its fur
coypus *n* ▷ **coypu**

> **coz** *n* (**cozes**). Coz is an old word for **cousin**, and a good one to know as it scores 14 points.

cozen *v* (**-s, -ing, -ed**) (*Lit*) cheat, trick
cozened *v* ▷ **cozen**
cozening *v* ▷ **cozen**
cozens *v* ▷ **cozen**
crab *n* (*pl* **-s**) edible shellfish with ten legs, the

first pair modified into pincers
crabbed *adj* (of handwriting) hard to read (*also* **crabby**) (**crabbier, crabbiest**)
crabbier *adj* ▷ **crabbed**
crabbiest *adj* ▷ **crabbed**
crabby *adj* ▷ **crabbed**
crabs *n* ▷ **crab**
crack *v* (**-s, -ing, -ed**) break or split partially ▶ *n* (*pl* **-s**) sudden sharp noise ▶ *adj* (*Informal*) first-rate, excellent
crackdown *n* (*pl* **-s**) severe disciplinary measures
crackdowns *n* ▷ **crackdown**
cracked *v* ▷ **crack**
cracker *n* (*pl* **-s**) thin dry biscuit
crackers *n* ▷ **cracker** ▶ *adj* (*Slang*) insane
cracking *adj* very good ▶ *v* ▷ **crack**
crackle *v* (**-ckles, -ckling, -ckled**) make small sharp popping noises ▶ *n* (*pl* **-ckles**) crackling sound
crackled *v* ▷ **crackle**
crackles *v, n* ▷ **crackle**
crackling *n* crackle ▶ *v* ▷ **crackle**
crackpot *n* (*pl* **-s**) ▶ *adj* (*Informal*) eccentric (person)
crackpots *n* ▷ **crackpot**
cracks *v, n* ▷ **crack**
cradle *n* (*pl* **-s**) baby's bed on rockers ▶ *v* (**-dles, -dling, -dled**) hold gently as if in a cradle
cradled *v* ▷ **cradle**
cradles *n, v* ▷ **cradle**
cradling *v* ▷ **cradle**
craft *n* (*pl* **-s**) occupation requiring skill with the hands
craftier *adj* ▷ **crafty**
craftiest *adj* ▷ **crafty**
craftily *adv* ▷ **crafty**
craftiness *n* ▷ **crafty**
craftinesses *n* ▷ **crafty**
crafts *n* ▷ **craft**
craftsman, craftswoman *n* (*pl* **-men, -women**) skilled worker > **craftsmanship** *n* (*pl* **-s**)
craftsmanship *n* ▷ **craftsman**
craftsmanships *n* ▷ **craftsman**
craftsmen *n* ▷ **craftsman**
craftswoman *n* ▷ **craftsman**
craftswomen *n* ▷ **craftsman**
crafty *adj* (**-tier, -tiest**) skilled in deception > **craftily** *adv* > **craftiness** *n* (*pl* **-es**)
crag *n* (*pl* **-s**) steep rugged rock > **craggy** *adj* (**-ggier, -ggiest**)
craggier *adj* ▷ **crag**
craggiest *adj* ▷ **crag**
craggy *adj* ▷ **crag**
crags *n* ▷ **crag**
cram *v* (**-s, -mming, -mmed**) force into too small a space
crammed *v* ▷ **cram**
cramming *v* ▷ **cram**
cramp[1] *n* (*pl* **-s**) painful muscular contraction
cramp[2] *v* (**-s, -ing, -ed**) confine, restrict
cramped *v* ▷ **cramp**[2]
cramping *v* ▷ **cramp**[2]
crampon *n* (*pl* **-s**) spiked plate strapped to a boot for climbing on ice
crampons *n* ▷ **crampon**
cramps *n* ▷ **cramp**[1] ▶ *v* ▷ **cramp**[2]
crams *v* ▷ **cram**
cranberries *n* ▷ **cranberry**
cranberry *n* (*pl* **-berries**) sour edible red berry
crane *n* (*pl* **-s**) machine for lifting and moving heavy weights ▶ *v* (**cranes, craning, craned**) stretch (one's neck) to see something
craned *v* ▷ **crane**
cranes *n, v* ▷ **crane**
crania *n* ▷ **cranium**
cranial *adj* ▷ **cranium**
craning *v* ▷ **crane**
cranium *n* (*pl* **-niums, -nia**) (ANAT) skull > **cranial** *adj*
craniums *n* ▷ **cranium**
crank *n* (*pl* **-s**) arm projecting at right angles from a shaft, for transmitting or converting motion (*Informal*) ▶ *v* (**-s, -ing, -ed**) start (an engine) with a crank
cranked *v* ▷ **crank**
crankier *adj* ▷ **cranky**
crankiest *adj* ▷ **cranky**
cranking *v* ▷ **crank**
cranks *n, v* ▷ **crank**
crankshaft *n* (*pl* **-s**) shaft driven by a crank
crankshafts *n* ▷ **crankshaft**
cranky *adj* (**-kier, -kiest**) (*Informal*) eccentric
crannies *n* ▷ **cranny**
cranny *n* (*pl* **-nies**) narrow opening
crape *n* (*pl* **-s**) ▷ **crepe**
crapes *n* ▷ **crape**
craps *n* gambling game played with two dice
crash *n* (*pl* **-es**) collision involving a vehicle or vehicles ▶ *v* (**-es, -ing, -ed**) (cause to) collide violently with a vehicle, a stationary object, or the ground
crashed *v* ▷ **crash**
crashes *n, v* ▷ **crash**
crashing *v* ▷ **crash**
crass *adj* (**-er, -est**) stupid and insensitive > **crassly** *adv* > **crassness** *n* (*pl* **-es**)
crasser *adj* ▷ **crass**
crassest *adj* ▷ **crass**

crassly *adv* ▷ **crass**
crassness *n* ▷ **crass**
crassnesses *n* ▷ **crass**
crate *n* (*pl* **-s**) large wooden container for packing goods
crater *n* (*pl* **-s**) very large hole in the ground or in the surface of the moon
craters *n* ▷ **crater**
crates *n* ▷ **crate**
cravat *n* (*pl* **-s**) man's scarf worn like a tie
cravats *n* ▷ **cravat**
crave *v* (**craves, craving, craved**) desire intensely > **craving** *n* (*pl* **-s**)
craved *v* ▷ **crave**
craven *adj* cowardly
craves *v* ▷ **crave**
craving *n, v* ▷ **crave**
cravings *n* ▷ **crave**
crawfish *n* (*pl* **crawfish**) ▷ **crayfish**
crawl *v* (**-s, -ing, -ed**) move on one's hands and knees ▶ *n* (*pl* **-s**) crawling motion or pace > **crawler** *n* (*pl* **-s**)
crawled *v* ▷ **crawl**
crawler *n* ▷ **crawl**
crawlers *n* ▷ **crawl**
crawling *v* ▷ **crawl**
crawls *v, n* ▷ **crawl**
crayfish *n* (*pl* **crayfish**) edible shellfish like a lobster
crayon *v* (**-s, -ing, -ed**), *n* (*pl* **-s**) (draw or colour with) a stick or pencil of coloured wax or clay
crayoned *v* ▷ **crayon**
crayoning *v* ▷ **crayon**
crayons *v, n* ▷ **crayon**
craze *n* (*pl* **-s**) short-lived fashion or enthusiasm
crazed *adj* wild and uncontrolled
crazes *n* ▷ **craze**
crazier *adj* ▷ **crazy**
craziest *adj* ▷ **crazy**
crazily *adv* ▷ **crazy**
craziness *n* ▷ **crazy**
crazinesses *n* ▷ **crazy**
crazy *adj* (**-zier, -ziest**) ridiculous > **crazily** *adv* > **craziness** *n* (*pl* **-es**)
creak *v, n* (*pl* **-s**) (make) a harsh squeaking sound > **creaky** *adj* (**-kier, -kiest**)
creakier *adj* ▷ **creak**
creakiest *adj* ▷ **creak**
creaks *n* ▷ **creak**
creaky *adj* ▷ **creak**
cream *n* (*pl* **-s**) fatty part of milk ▶ *adj* yellowish-white ▶ *v* (**-s, -ing, -ed**) beat to a creamy consistency > **creamy** *adj* > **creaminess** *n*
creamed *v* ▷ **cream**
creaminess *n* ▷ **cream**
creaming *v* ▷ **cream**
creams *n, v* ▷ **cream**
creamy *adj* ▷ **cream**
crease *n* (*pl* **-s**) line made by folding or pressing ▶ *v* (**creases, creasing, creased**) crush or line
creased *v* ▷ **crease**
creases *n, v* ▷ **crease**
creasing *v* ▷ **crease**
create *v* (**creates, creating, created**) make, cause to exist > **creation** *n* (*pl* **-s**) > **creator** *n* (*pl* **-s**)
created *v* ▷ **create**
creates *v* ▷ **create**
creating *v* ▷ **create**
creation *n* ▷ **create**
creations *n* ▷ **create**
creative *adj* imaginative or inventive > **creatively** *adv* > **creativity** *n*
creatively *adv* ▷ **creative**
creativity *n* ▷ **creative**
creator *n* ▷ **create**
creators *n* ▷ **create**
creature *n* (*pl* **-s**) animal, person, or other being
creatures *n* ▷ **creature**
crèche *n* (*pl* **-s**) place where small children are looked after while their parents are working, shopping, etc.
crèches *n* ▷ **crèche**
credence *n* (*pl* **-s**) belief in the truth or accuracy of a statement
credences *n* ▷ **credence**
credentials *pl n* document giving evidence of a person's identity or qualifications
credibility *n* ▷ **credible**
credible *adj* believable > **credibly** *adv* > **credibility** *n*
credibly *adv* ▷ **credible**
credit *n* (*pl* **-s**) system of allowing customers to receive goods and pay later ▶ *v* (**-s, -ing, -ed**) enter as a credit in an account
creditable *adj* praiseworthy > **creditably** *adv*
creditably *adv* ▷ **creditable**
credited *v* ▷ **credit**
crediting *v* ▷ **credit**
creditor *n* (*pl* **-s**) person to whom money is owed
creditors *n* ▷ **creditor**
credits *n, v* ▷ **credit**
credulity *n* ▷ **credulous**
credulous *adj* too willing to believe > **credulity** *n* > **credulously** *adv*
credulously *adv* ▷ **credulous**

creed *n* (*pl* **-s**) statement or system of (Christian) beliefs or principles
creeds *n* ▷ **creed**
creek *n* (*pl* **-s**) narrow inlet or bay (AUST, NZ, US & CANADIAN)
creeks *n* ▷ **creek**
creel *n* (*pl* **-s**) wicker basket used by anglers
creels *n* ▷ **creel**
creep *v* (**creeps, creeping, crept**) move quietly and cautiously ▶ *n* (*pl* **-s**) (*Slang*) obnoxious or servile person
creeper *n* (*pl* **-s**) creeping plant
creepers *n* ▷ **creeper**
creepier *adj* ▷ **creepy**
creepiest *adj* ▷ **creepy**
creepily *adv* ▷ **creepy**
creepiness *n* ▷ **creepy**
creepinesses *n* ▷ **creepy**
creeping *v* ▷ **creep**
creeps *v*, *n* ▷ **creep**
creepy *adj* (**-pier, -piest**) (*Informal*) causing a feeling of fear or disgust > **creepily** *adv* > **creepiness** *n* (*pl* **-es**)
cremate *v* (**-mates, -mating, -mated**) burn (a corpse) to ash > **cremation** *n* (*pl* **-s**)
cremated *v* ▷ **cremate**
cremates *v* ▷ **cremate**
cremating *v* ▷ **cremate**
cremation *n* ▷ **cremate**
cremations *n* ▷ **cremate**
crematoria *n* ▷ **crematorium**
crematorium *n* (*pl* **-iums, -ia**) building where corpses are cremated
crematoriums *n* ▷ **crematorium**
crenellated *adj* having battlements
creole *n* (*pl* **-s**) language developed from a mixture of languages
creoles *n* ▷ **creole**
creosote *n* (*pl* **-s**) dark oily liquid made from coal tar and used for preserving wood ▶ *v* (**-sotes, -soting, -soted**) treat with creosote
creosoted *v* ▷ **creosote**
creosotes *n*, *v* ▷ **creosote**
creosoting *v* ▷ **creosote**
crepe, crape [krayp] *n* (*pl* **-s**) fabric or rubber with a crinkled texture
crepes *n* ▷ **crepe**
crept *v* ▷ **creep**
crepuscular *adj* (*Lit*) of or like twilight
crescendo [krish-**end**-oh] *n* (*pl* **-s**) gradual increase in loudness, esp. in music
crescendos *n* ▷ **creep**
crescent *n* (*pl* **-s**) (curved shape of) the moon as seen in its first or last quarter
crescents *n* ▷ **crescent**
cress *n* (*pl* **-es**) plant with strong-tasting leaves, used in salads
cresses *n* ▷ **cress**
crest *n* (*pl* **-s**) top of a mountain, hill, or wave > **crested** *adj*
crested *adj* ▷ **crest**
crestfallen *adj* disheartened
crests *n* ▷ **crest**
cretin *n* (*pl* **-s**) (*Informal*) stupid person > **cretinous** *adj*
cretinous *adj* ▷ **cretin**
cretins *n* ▷ **cretin**
crevasse *n* (*pl* **-s**) deep open crack in a glacier
crevasses *n* ▷ **crevasse**
crevice *n* (*pl* **-s**) narrow crack or gap in rock
crevices *n* ▷ **crevice**
crew *n* (*pl* **-s**) people who work on a ship or aircraft (*Informal*) ▶ *v* (**-s, -ing, -ed**) serve as a crew member (on)
crewed *v* ▷ **crew**
crewel *n* (*pl* **-s**) fine worsted yarn used in embroidery
crewels *n* ▷ **crewel**
crewing *v* ▷ **crew**
crews *n*, *v* ▷ **crew**
crib *n* (*pl* **-s**) piece of writing stolen from elsewhere ▶ *v* (**cribs, cribbing, cribbed**) copy (someone's work) dishonestly
cribbage *n* card game for two to four players
cribbed *v* ▷ **crib**
cribbing *v* ▷ **crib**
cribs *n*, *v* ▷ **crib**
crick *n* (*pl* **-s**) muscle spasm or cramp in the back or neck ▶ *v* (**-s, -ing, -ed**) cause a crick in
cricked *v* ▷ **crick**
cricket[1] *n* (*pl* **-s**) outdoor game played with bats, a ball, and wickets by two teams of eleven > **cricketer** *n* (*pl* **-s**)
cricket[2] *n* (*pl* **-s**) chirping insect like a grasshopper
cricketer *n* ▷ **cricket**[1]
cricketers *n* ▷ **cricket**[1]
crickets *n* ▷ **cricket**[1, 2]
cricking *v* ▷ **crick**
cricks *n*, *v* ▷ **crick**
cried *v* ▷ **cry**
cries *v* ▷ **cry**
crime *n* (*pl* **-s**) unlawful act
crimes *n* ▷ **crime**
criminal *n* (*pl* **-s**) person guilty of a crime ▶ *adj* of crime > **criminally** *adv* > **criminality** *n*
criminality *n* ▷ **criminal**
criminally *adv* ▷ **criminal**
criminals *n* ▷ **criminal**
criminologist *n* ▷ **criminology**

criminologists *n* ▷ **criminology**
criminology *n* study of crime > **criminologist** *n* (*pl* **-s**)
crimp *v* (**-s, -ing, -ed**) fold or press into ridges
crimped *v* ▷ **crimp**
crimping *v* ▷ **crimp**
crimps *v* ▷ **crimp**
crimson *adj* deep purplish-red
cringe *v* (**cringes, cringing, cringed**) flinch in fear
cringed *v* ▷ **cringe**
cringes *v* ▷ **cringe**
cringing *v* ▷ **cringe**
crinkle *v* (**-kles, -kling, -kled**) ▶ *n* (*pl* **-s**) wrinkle, crease, or fold
crinkled *v* ▷ **crinkle**
crinkles *v, n* ▷ **crinkle**
crinkling *v* ▷ **crinkle**
crinoline *n* (*pl* **-s**) hooped petticoat
crinolines *n* ▷ **crinoline**
cripple *n* (*pl* **-s**) person who is lame or disabled ▶ *v* (**-pples, -ppling, -ppled**) make lame or disabled
crippled *v* ▷ **cripple**
cripples *n, v* ▷ **cripple**
crippling *v* ▷ **cripple**
crises *n* ▷ **crisis**
crisis *n* (*pl* **-ses**) crucial stage, turning point
crisp *adj* (**-er, -est**) fresh and firm ▶ *n* (*pl* **-s**) (BRIT) very thin slice of potato fried till crunchy > **crisply** *adv* > **crispness** *n* (*pl* **-es**)
crispbread *n* (*pl* **-s**) thin dry biscuit
crispbreads *n* ▷ **crispbread**
crisper *adj* ▷ **crisp**
crispest *adj* ▷ **crisp**
crispier *adj* ▷ **crisp**
crispiest *adj* ▷ **crisp**
crisply *adv* ▷ **crisp**
crispness *adv* ▷ **crisp**
crispnesses *adv* ▷ **crisp**
crisps *n* ▷ **crisp**
crispy *adj* (**-pier, -piest**) hard and crunchy
crisscross *v* (**-es, -ing, -ed**) move in or mark with a crosswise pattern ▶ *adj* (of lines) crossing in different directions
crisscrossed *v* ▷ **crisscross**
crisscrosses *v* ▷ **crisscross**
crisscrossing *v* ▷ **crisscross**
criteria *n* ▷ **criterion**
criterion *n* (*pl* **-ria**) standard of judgment
critic *n* (*pl* **-s**) professional judge of any of the arts
critical *adj* very important or dangerous > **critically** *adv*
critically *adv* ▷ **critical**
criticism *n* (*pl* **-s**) fault-finding
criticisms *n* ▷ **criticism**
criticize *v* (**-cizes, -cizing, -cized**) find fault with
criticized *v* ▷ **criticize**
criticizes *v* ▷ **criticize**
criticizing *v* ▷ **criticize**
critics *n* ▷ **critic**
critique *n* (*pl* **-s**) critical essay
critiques *n* ▷ **critique**
croak *v* (**-s, -ing, -ed**) (of a frog or crow) give a low hoarse cry ▶ *n* (*pl* **-s**) low hoarse sound
croaked *v* ▷ **croak**
croakiness *n* ▷ **croaky**
croaking *v* ▷ **croak**
croaks *v, n* ▷ **croak**
croaky *adj* hoarse > **croakiness** *n*
crochet [**kroh**-shay] *v* (**-chets, -cheting, -cheted**) make by looping and intertwining yarn with a hooked needle ▶ *n* (*pl* **-s**) work made in this way
crocheted *v* ▷ **crochet**
crocheting *v* ▷ **crochet**
crochets *v, n* ▷ **crochet**
crock[1] *n* (*pl* **-s**) earthenware pot or jar
crock[2] *n* (*pl* **-s**) (BRIT, AUST & NZ) (*Informal*) old or decrepit person or thing
crockery *n* dishes
crocks *n* ▷ **crock[1, 2]**
crocodile *n* (*pl* **-s**) large amphibious tropical reptile
crocodiles *n* ▷ **crocodile**
crocus *n* (*pl* **-cuses**) small plant with yellow, white, or purple flowers in spring
crocuses *n* ▷ **crocus**
croft *n* (*pl* **-s**) small farm worked by one family in Scotland > **crofter** *n* (*pl* **-s**)
crofter *n* ▷ **croft**
crofters *n* ▷ **croft**
crofts *n* ▷ **croft**
croissant [**krwah**-son] *n* (*pl* **-s**) rich flaky crescent-shaped roll
croissants *n* ▷ **croissant**
cromlech *n* (*pl* **-s**) (BRIT) circle of prehistoric standing stones
cromlechs *n* ▷ **cromlech**
crone *n* (*pl* **-s**) witchlike old woman
crones *n* ▷ **crone**
cronies *n* ▷ **crony**
crony *n* (*pl* **-nies**) close friend
crook *n* (*pl* **-s**) (*Informal*) criminal ▶ *adj* (AUST & NZ) (*Slang*) unwell, injured
crooked *adj* bent or twisted > **crookedly** *adv* > **crookedness** *n*
crookedly *adv* ▷ **crooked**

crookedness *n* ▷ **crooked**
crooks *n* ▷ **crook**
croon *v* (**-s, -ing, -ed**) sing, hum, or speak in a soft low tone
crooned *v* ▷ **croon**
crooner *n* (*pl* **-s**) male singer of sentimental ballads
crooners *n* ▷ **crooner**
crooning *v* ▷ **croon**
croons *v* ▷ **croon**
crop *n* (*pl* **-s**) cultivated plant ▶ *v* (**crops, cropping, cropped**) cut very short > **cropper** *n* (*pl* **-s**)
cropped *v* ▷ **crop**
cropper *n* ▷ **crop**
croppers *n* ▷ **crop**
cropping *v* ▷ **crop**
crops *n, v* ▷ **crop**
croquet [**kroh**-kay] *n* (*pl* **-s**) game played on a lawn in which balls are hit through hoops
croquets *n* ▷ **croquet**
croquette [kroh-**kett**] *n* (*pl* **-s**) fried cake of potato, meat, or fish
croquettes *n* ▷ **croquette**
crosier *n* (*pl* **-s**) ▷ **crozier**
crosiers *n* ▷ **crosier**
cross *v* (**-es, -ing, -ed**) move or go across (something) ▶ *n* (*pl* **-es**) structure, symbol, or mark of two intersecting lines ▶ *adj* (**-er, -est**) angry, annoyed > **crossly** *adv* > **crossness** *n* (*pl* **-es**)
crossbar *n* (*pl* **-s**) horizontal bar across goalposts or on a bicycle
crossbars *n* ▷ **crossbar**
crossbow *n* (*pl* **-s**) weapon consisting of a bow fixed across a wooden stock
crossbows *n* ▷ **crossbow**
crossbred *adj* bred from two different types of animal or plant
crossbreed *n* (*pl* **-s**) crossbred animal or plant
crossbreeds *n* ▷ **crossbreed**
crossed *v* ▷ **cross**
crosser *adj* ▷ **cross**
crosses *v, n* ▷ **cross**
crossest *adj* ▷ **cross**
crossfire *n* (*pl* **-s**) gunfire crossing another line of fire
crossfires *n* ▷ **crossfire**
crossing *n* (*pl* **-s**) place where a street may be crossed safely ▶ *v* ▷ **cross**
crossings *n* ▷ **crossing**
crossly *adv* ▷ **cross**
crossness *n* ▷ **cross**
crossnesses *n* ▷ **cross**
crossroads *n* place where roads intersect
crosswise *adj, adv* across
crossword *n* (*pl* **-s**) puzzle in which words suggested by clues are written into a grid of squares
crosswords *n* ▷ **crossword**
crotch *n* (*pl* **-es**) part of the body between the tops of the legs
crotches *n* ▷ **crotch**
crotchet *n* (*pl* **-s**) musical note half the length of a minim
crotchetier *adj* ▷ **crotchety**
crotchetiest *adj* ▷ **crotchety**
crotchets *n* ▷ **crotchet**
crotchety *adj* (**-tier, -tiest**) (*Informal*) bad-tempered
crouch *v* (**-es, -ing, -ed**) bend low with the legs and body close ▶ *n* (*pl* **-es**) this position
crouched *v* ▷ **crouch**
crouches *v, n* ▷ **crouch**
crouching *v* ▷ **crouch**
croup¹ [**kroop**] *n* (*pl* **-s**) throat disease of children, with a cough
croup² [**kroop**] *n* (*pl* **-s**) hind quarters of a horse
croupier [**kroop**-ee-ay] *n* (*pl* **-s**) person who collects bets and pays out winnings at a gambling table in a casino
croupiers *n* ▷ **croupier**
croups *n* ▷ **croup¹, ²**
crouton *n* (*pl* **-s**) small piece of fried or toasted bread served in soup
croutons *n* ▷ **crouton**
crow¹ *n* (*pl* **-s**) large black bird with a harsh call
crow² *v* (**-s, -ing, -ed**) (of a cock) make a shrill squawking sound
crowbar *n* (*pl* **-s**) iron bar used as a lever
crowbars *n* ▷ **crowbar**
crowd *n* (*pl* **-s**) large group of people or things ▶ *v* (**-s, -ing, -ed**) gather together in large numbers
crowded *v* ▷ **crowd**
crowding *v* ▷ **crowd**
crowds *n, v* ▷ **crowd**
crowed *v* ▷ **crow²**
crowing *v* ▷ **crow²**
crown *n* (*pl* **-s**) monarch's headdress of gold and jewels ▶ *v* (**-s, -ing, -ed**) put a crown on the head of (someone) to proclaim him or her monarch
crowned *v* ▷ **crown**
crowning *v* ▷ **crown**
crowns *n, v* ▷ **crown**
crows *n* ▷ **crow¹** ▶ *v* ▷ **crow²**
crozier, crosier *n* (*pl* **-s**) bishop's hooked staff
croziers *n* ▷ **crozier**
crucial *adj* very important > **crucially** *adv*

crucially *adv* ▷ **crucial**
crucible *n* (*pl* **-s**) pot in which metals are melted
crucibles *n* ▷ **crucible**
crucified *v* ▷ **crucify**
crucifies *v* ▷ **crucify**
crucifix *n* (*pl* **-es**) model of Christ on the Cross
crucifixes *n* ▷ **crucify**
crucifixion *n* (*pl* **-s**) crucifying
crucifixions *n* ▷ **crucifixion**
cruciform *adj* cross-shaped
crucify *v* (**-fies, -fying, -fied**) put to death by fastening to a cross
crucifying *v* ▷ **crucify**
crude *adj* (**-r, -st**) rough and simple > **crudely** *adv* > **crudeness** *n* (*pl* **-es**) > **crudity** *n* (*pl* **-ties**)
crudely *adv* ▷ **crude**
crudeness *n* ▷ **crude**
crudenesses *n* ▷ **crude**
cruder *adj* ▷ **crude**
crudest *adj* ▷ **crude**
crudities *n* ▷ **crude**
crudity *n* ▷ **crude**
cruel *adj* (**-ller, -llest**) delighting in others' pain > **cruelly** *adv* > **cruelty** *n* (*pl* **-ties**)
crueller *adj* ▷ **cruel**
cruellest *adj* ▷ **cruel**
cruelly *adv* ▷ **cruel**
cruelties *n* ▷ **cruel**
cruelty *n* ▷ **cruel**
cruet *n* (*pl* **-s**) small container for salt, pepper, etc., at table
cruets *n* ▷ **cruet**
cruise *n* (*pl* **-s**) sail for pleasure ▶ *v* (**cruises, cruising, cruised**) sail from place to place for pleasure
cruised *n* ▷ **cruise**
cruiser *n* (*pl* **-s**) fast warship
cruisers *n* ▷ **cruiser**
cruises *n, v* ▷ **cruise**
cruising *v* ▷ **cruise**
crumb *n* (*pl* **-s**) small fragment of bread or other dry food
crumble *v* (**-bles, -bling, -bled**) break into fragments ▶ *n* (*pl* **-s**) pudding of stewed fruit with a crumbly topping > **crumbly** *adj* (**-blier, -bliest**)
crumbled *v* ▷ **crumble**
crumbles *v, n* ▷ **crumble**
crumblier *adj* ▷ **crumble**
crumbliest *adj* ▷ **crumble**
crumbling *v* ▷ **crumble**
crumbly *adj* ▷ **crumble**
crumbs *n* ▷ **crumb**
crummier *adj* ▷ **crummy**
crummiest *adj* ▷ **crummy**
crummy *adj* (**-mier, -miest**) (*Slang*) of poor quality
crumpet *n* (*pl* **-s**) round soft yeast cake, eaten buttered
crumpets *n* ▷ **crumpet**
crumple *v* (**-ples, -pling, -pled**) crush, crease > **crumpled** *adj*
crumpled *v, adj* ▷ **crumple**
crumples *v* ▷ **crumple**
crumpling *v* ▷ **crumple**
crunch *v* (**-es, -ing, -ed**) bite or chew with a noisy crushing sound ▶ *n* (*pl* **-es**) crunching sound (*Informal*) > **crunchy** *adj* (**-chier, -chiest**)
crunched *v* ▷ **crunch**
crunches *v, n* ▷ **crunch**
crunchier *adj* ▷ **crunch**
crunchiest *adj* ▷ **crunch**
crunching *v* ▷ **crunch**
crunchy *adj* ▷ **crunch**
crupper *n* (*pl* **-s**) strap that passes from the back of a saddle under a horse's tail
cruppers *n* ▷ **crupper**
crusade *n* (*pl* **-s**) medieval Christian war to recover the Holy Land from the Muslims ▶ *v* (**-sades, -sading, -saded**) take part in a crusade
crusaded *v* ▷ **crusade**
crusader *n* (*pl* **-s**) person who took part in the medieval Christian war to recover the Holy Land from the Muslims
crusaders *n* ▷ **crusader**
crusades *n, v* ▷ **crusade**
crusading *v* ▷ **crusade**
crush *v* (**-es, -ing, -ed**) compress so as to injure, break, or crumple ▶ *n* (*pl* **-es**) dense crowd
crushed *v* ▷ **crush**
crushes *v, n* ▷ **crush**
crushing *v* ▷ **crush**
crust *n* (*pl* **-s**) hard outer part of something, esp. bread ▶ *v* (**-s, -ing, -ed**) cover with or form a crust
crustacean *n* (*pl* **-s**) hard-shelled, usu. aquatic animal with several pairs of legs, such as the crab or lobster
crustaceans *n* ▷ **crustacean**
crusted *v* ▷ **crust**
crustier *adj* ▷ **crusty**
crustiest *adj* ▷ **crusty**
crusting *v* ▷ **crust**
crusts *n, v* ▷ **crust**
crusty *adj* (**-tier, -tiest**) having a crust
crutch *n* (*pl* **-es**) long sticklike support with a rest for the armpit, used by a lame person
crutches *n* ▷ **crutch**

crux *n* (*pl* **-es**) crucial or decisive point
cruxes *n* ▷ **crux**
cry *v* (**cries, crying, cried**) shed tears ▶ *n* (*pl* **cries**) fit of weeping
crybabies *n* ▷ **crybaby**
crybaby *n* (*pl* **-babies**) person, esp. a child, who cries too readily
crying *v* ▷ **cry**
cryogenic *adj* ▷ **cryogenics**
cryogenics *n* branch of physics concerned with very low temperatures > **cryogenic** *adj*
crypt *n* (*pl* **-s**) vault under a church, esp. one used as a burial place
cryptic *adj* obscure in meaning, secret > **cryptically** *adv*
cryptographer *n* ▷ **cryptography**
cryptographers *n* ▷ **cryptography**
cryptography *n* art of writing in and deciphering codes > **cryptographer** *n* (*pl* **-s**)
crypts *n* ▷ **crypt**
crystal *n* (*pl* **-s**) (single grain of) a symmetrically shaped solid formed naturally by some substances ▶ *adj* bright and clear
crystalline *adj* of or like crystal or crystals
crystallization *n* ▷ **crystallize**
crystallizations *n* ▷ **crystallize**
crystallize *v* (**-lizes, -lizing, -lized**) make or become definite > **crystallization** *n* (*pl* **-s**)
crystallized *v* ▷ **crystallize**
crystallizes *v* ▷ **crystallize**
crystallizing *v* ▷ **crystallize**
crystals *n* ▷ **crystal**
cub *n* (*pl* **-s**) young wild animal such as a bear or fox ▶ *v* (**cubs, cubbing, cubbed**) give birth to cubs
cubbed *v* ▷ **cub**
cubbing *v* ▷ **cub**
cubbyhole *n* (*pl* **-s**) small enclosed space or room
cubbyholes *n* ▷ **cubbyhole**
cube *n* (*pl* **-s**) object with six equal square sides ▶ *v* (**cubes, cubing, cubed**) cut into cubes
cubed *v* ▷ **cube**
cubes *n, v* ▷ **cube**
cubic *adj* having three dimensions
cubicle *n* (*pl* **-s**) enclosed part of a large room, screened for privacy
cubicles *n* ▷ **cubicle**
cubing *v* ▷ **cube**
cubism *n* style of art in which objects are represented by geometrical shapes > **cubist** *adj, n* (*pl* **-s**)
cubists *n* ▷ **cubist**
cubs *n, v* ▷ **cub**
cuckold *n* (*pl* **-s**) man whose wife has been unfaithful ▶ *v* (**-s, -ing, -ed**) be unfaithful to (one's husband)
cuckolded *v* ▷ **cuckold**
cuckolding *v* ▷ **cuckold**
cuckolds *n, v* ▷ **cuckold**
cuckoo *n* (*pl* **-s**) migratory bird with a characteristic two-note call, which lays its eggs in the nests of other birds ▶ *adj* (*Informal*) insane or foolish
cuckoos *n* ▷ **cuckoo**
cucumber *n* (*pl* **-s**) long green-skinned fleshy fruit used in salads
cucumbers *n* ▷ **cucumber**
cud *n* (*pl* **-s**) partially digested food which a ruminant brings back into its mouth to chew again
cuddle *v* (**cuddles, cuddling, cuddled**) ▶ *n* (*pl* **-s**) hug > **cuddly** *adj* (**-lier, -liest**)
cuddled *v* ▷ **cuddle**
cuddles *v, n* ▷ **cuddle**
cuddlier *adj* ▷ **cuddle**
cuddliest *adj* ▷ **cuddle**
cuddling *v* ▷ **cuddle**
cuddly *adj* ▷ **cuddle**
cudgel *n* (*pl* **-s**) short thick stick used as a weapon
cudgels *n* ▷ **cudgel**
cuds *n* ▷ **cud**
cue[1] *n* (*pl* **-s**) signal to an actor or musician to begin speaking or playing ▶ *v* (**cues, cueing, cued**) give a cue to
cue[2] *n* long tapering stick used in billiards, snooker, or pool ▶ *v* (**cues, cueing, cued**) hit (a ball) with a cue
cued *v* ▷ **cue**[1, 2]
cueing *v* ▷ **cue**[1, 2]
cues *n, v* ▷ **cue**[1, 2]
cuff[1] *n* (*pl* **-s**) end of a sleeve
cuff[2] (BRIT, AUST & NZ) *v* (**-s, -ing, -ed**) hit with an open hand ▶ *n* (*pl* **-s**) blow with an open hand
cuffed *v* ▷ **cuff**[2]
cuffing *v* ▷ **cuff**[2]
cuffs *n* ▷ **cuff**[1, 2] ▶ *v* ▷ **cuff**[2]
cuisine [quiz-**zeen**] *n* (*pl* **-s**) style of cooking
cuisines *n* ▷ **cuisine**
culinary *adj* of kitchens or cookery
cull *v* (**-s, -ing, -ed**) choose, gather ▶ *n* (*pl* **-s**) culling
culled *v* ▷ **cull**
culling *v* ▷ **cull**
culls *v, n* ▷ **cull**
culminate *v* (**-nates, -nating, -nated**) reach the highest point or climax > **culmination** *n* (*pl* **-s**)
culminated *v* ▷ **culminate**

culminates *v* ▷ **culminate**
culminating *v* ▷ **culminate**
culmination *n* ▷ **culminate**
culminations *n* ▷ **culminate**
culottes *pl n* women's knee-length trousers cut to look like a skirt
culpabilities *n* ▷ **culpable**
culpability *n* ▷ **culpable**
culpable *adj* deserving blame > **culpability** *n* (*pl* **-ties**)> **culpably** *adv*
culpably *adv* ▷ **culpable**
culprit *n* (*pl* **-s**) person guilty of an offence or misdeed
culprits *n* ▷ **culprit**
cult *n* (*pl* **-s**) specific system of worship
cultivate *v* (**-vates, -vating, -vated**) prepare (land) to grow crops > **cultivation** *n*
cultivated *adj* well-educated ▶ *v* ▷ **cultivate**
cultivates *v* ▷ **cultivate**
cultivating *v* ▷ **cultivate**
cultivation *n* ▷ **cultivate**
cults *n* ▷ **cult**
cultural *adj* ▷ **culture**
culturally *adv* ▷ **culture**
culture *n* (*pl* **-s**) ideas, customs, and art of a particular society > **cultural** *adj* > **culturally** *adv*
cultured *adj* showing good taste or manners
cultures *n* ▷ **culture**
culvert *n* (*pl* **-s**) drain under a road or railway
culverts *n* ▷ **culvert**
cumbersome *adj* awkward because of size or shape
cumin, cummin *n* (*pl* **-s**) sweet-smelling seeds of a Mediterranean plant, used in cooking
cumins *n* ▷ **cumin**
cummerbund *n* (*pl* **-s**) wide sash worn round the waist
cummerbunds *n* ▷ **cummerbund**
cummin *n* ▷ **cumin**
cummins *n* ▷ **cumin**
cumulative *adj* increasing steadily > **cumulatively** *adv*
cumulatively *adv* ▷ **cumulative**
cumuli *n* ▷ **cumulus**
cumulus [**kew**-myew-luss] *n* (*pl* **-li**) thick white or dark grey cloud
cuneiform [**kew**-nif-form] *n, adj* (written in) an ancient system of writing using wedge-shaped characters
cunjevoi *n* (*pl* **-s**) (AUST) plant of tropical Asia and Australia with small flowers, cultivated for its edible rhizome
cunjevois *n* ▷ **cunjevoi**
cunning *adj* clever at deceiving ▶ *n* cleverness at deceiving > **cunningly** *adv*
cunningly *adv* ▷ **cunning**
cup *n* (*pl* **-s**) small bowl-shaped drinking container with a handle ▶ *v* (**cups, cupping, cupped**) form (one's hands) into the shape of a cup > **cupful** *n* (*pl* **-s**)
cupboard *n* (*pl* **-s**) piece of furniture or alcove with a door, for storage
cupboards *n* ▷ **cupboard**
cupful *n* ▷ **cup**
cupfuls *n* ▷ **cup**
cupidity [kew-**pid**-it-ee] *n* greed for money or possessions
cupola [**kew**-pol-la] *n* (*pl* **-s**) domed roof or ceiling
cupolas *n* ▷ **cupola**
cupped *v* ▷ **cup**
cupping *v* ▷ **cup**
cups *n, v* ▷ **cup**
cur *n* (*pl* **-s**) (*Lit*) mongrel dog
curable *adj* ▷ **cure**
curaçao [**kew**-rah-so] *n* orange-flavoured liqueur
curacies *n* ▷ **curacy**
curacy [**kew**-rah-see] *n* (*pl* **-cies**) work or position of a curate
curare [kew-**rah**-ree] *n* (*pl* **-s**) poisonous resin of a S American tree, used as a muscle relaxant in medicine
curares *n* ▷ **curare**
curate *n* (*pl* **-s**) clergyman who assists a parish priest
curates *n* ▷ **curate**
curative *adj, n* (*pl* **-s**) (something) able to cure
curatives *n* ▷ **curative**
curator *n* (*pl* **-s**) person in charge of a museum or art gallery > **curatorship** *n* (*pl* **-s**)
curators *n* ▷ **curator**
curatorship *n* ▷ **curator**
curatorships *n* ▷ **curator**
curb *n* (*pl* **-s**) something that restrains ▶ *v* (**-s, -ing, -ed**) control, restrain
curbed *v* ▷ **curb**
curbing *v* ▷ **curb**
curbs *n, v* ▷ **curb**
curd *n* (*pl* **-s**) coagulated milk, used to make cheese
curdle *v* (**-dles, -dling, -dled**) turn into curd, coagulate
curdled *v* ▷ **curdle**
curdles *v* ▷ **curdle**
curdling *v* ▷ **curdle**
curds *n* ▷ **curd**
cure *v* (**cures, curing, cured**) get rid of (an illness or problem) ▶ *n* (*pl* **-s**) (treatment

causing) curing of an illness or person
> **curable** *adj*
cured *v* ▷ **cure**
cures *v*, *n* ▷ **cure**
curettage *n* ▷ **curette**
curettages *n* ▷ **curette**
curette *n* (*pl* **-s**) surgical instrument for scraping tissue from body cavities ▶ *v* (**curettes, curetting, curetted**) scrape with a curette > **curettage** *n* (*pl* **-s**)
curetted *v* ▷ **curette**
curettes *n*, *v* ▷ **curette**
curetting *v* ▷ **curette**
curfew *n* (*pl* **-s**) law ordering people to stay inside their homes after a specific time at night
curfews *n* ▷ **curfew**
curie *n* (*pl* **-s**) standard unit of radioactivity
curies *n* ▷ **curie**
curing *v* ▷ **cure**
curio *n* (*pl* **-s**) rare or unusual object valued as a collector's item
curios *n* ▷ **curio**
curiosities *n* ▷ **curiosity**
curiosity *n* eagerness to know or find out (*pl* **-ties**)
curiously *adv* ▷ **curious**
curious *adj* eager to learn or know > **curiously** *adv*
curl *n* (*pl* **-s**) curved piece of hair ▶ *v* (**-s, -ing, -ed**) make (hair) into curls or (of hair) grow in curls > **curler** *n* (*pl* **-s**) > **curly** *adj* (**-lier, -liest**)
curled *v* ▷ **curl**
curler *n* ▷ **curl**
curlers *n* ▷ **curl**
curlew *n* (*pl* **-s**) long-billed wading bird
curlews *n* ▷ **curlew**
curlier *adj* ▷ **curl**
curliest *adj* ▷ **curl**
curling *n* game like bowls, played with heavy stones on ice ▶ *v* ▷ **curl**
curls *n*, *v* ▷ **curl**
curly *adj* ▷ **curl**
curmudgeon *n* (*pl* **-s**) bad-tempered person > **curmudgeonly** *adj*
curmudgeonly *adj* ▷ **curmudgeon**
curmudgeons *n* ▷ **curmudgeon**
currajong *n* (*pl* **-s**) ▷ **kurrajong**
currajongs *n* ▷ **currajong**
currant *n* (*pl* **-s**) small dried grape
currants *n* ▷ **currant**
currawong *n* (*pl* **-s**) Australian songbird
currawongs *n* ▷ **currawong**
currencies *n* ▷ **currency**
currency *n* (*pl* **-cies**) money in use in a particular country
current *adj* of the immediate present ▶ *n* (*pl* **-s**) flow of water or air in one direction > **currently** *adv*
currently *adv* ▷ **current**
currents *n* ▷ **current**
curricula *n* ▷ **curriculum**
curriculum *n* (*pl* **-la, -lums**) all the courses of study offered by a school or college
curriculums *n* ▷ **curriculum**
curried *v* ▷ **curry**[1, 2]
curries *n* ▷ **curry**[1] ▶ *v* ▷ **curry**[1, 2]
curry[1] *n* (*pl* **-ries**) Indian dish of meat or vegetables in a hot spicy sauce ▶ *v* (**-ries, -rying, -ried**) prepare (food) with curry powder
curry[2] *v* (**-ries, -rying, -ried**) groom (a horse)
currying *v* ▷ **curry**[1, 2]
curs *n* ▷ **cur**
curse *v* (**curses, cursing, cursed**) swear (at) ▶ *n* (*pl* **-s**) swearword > **cursed** *adj*
cursed *adj*, *v* ▷ **curse**
curses *v*, *n* ▷ **curse**
cursing *v* ▷ **curse**
cursive *adj*, *n* (*pl* **-s**) (handwriting) done with joined letters > **cursively** *adv*
cursively *adv* ▷ **cursive**
cursives *n* ▷ **cursive**
cursor *n* (*pl* **-s**) movable point of light that shows a specific position on a visual display unit
cursorily *adv* ▷ **cursory**
cursoriness *n* ▷ **cursory**
cursors *n* ▷ **cursor**
cursory *adj* quick and superficial > **cursorily** *adv* > **cursoriness** *n*
curt *adj* (**-er, -est**) brief and rather rude > **curtly** *adv* > **curtness** *n* (*pl* **-es**)
curtail *v* (**-s, -ing, -ed**) cut short > **curtailment** *n* (*pl* **-s**)
curtailed *v* ▷ **curtail**
curtailing *v* ▷ **curtail**
curtailment *n* ▷ **curtail**
curtailments *n* ▷ **curtail**
curtails *v* ▷ **curtail**
curtain *n* (*pl* **-s**) piece of cloth hung at a window or opening as a screen ▶ *v* (**-s, -ing, -ed**) provide with curtains
curtained *v* ▷ **curtain**
curtaining *v* ▷ **curtain**
curtains *n*, *v* ▷ **curtain**
curter *adj* ▷ **curt**
curtest *adj* ▷ **curt**
curtly *adv* ▷ **curt**
curtness *n* ▷ **curt**

curtnesses *n* ▷ **curt**
curtsey *n* ▷ **curtsy**
curtseyed *v* ▷ **curtsy**
curtseying *v* ▷ **curtsy**
curtseys *n*, *v* ▷ **curtsy**
curtsied *v* ▷ **curtsy**
curtsies *n*, *v* ▷ **curtsy**
curtsy, curtsey *n* (*pl* **-sies, -seys**) woman's gesture of respect made by bending the knees and bowing the head ▶ *v* (**-sies, -seys, -sying, -sied** *or* **-seying**) (**-seyed**) make a curtsy
curtsying *v* ▷ **curtsy**
curvaceous *adj* (*Informal*) (of a woman) having a shapely body
curvature *n* (*pl* **-s**) curved shape
curvatures *n* ▷ **curvature**
curve *n* (*pl* **-s**) continuously bending line with no straight parts ▶ *v* (**curves, curving, curved**) form or move in a curve > **curvy** *adj* (**-vier, -viest**)
curved *v* ▷ **curve**
curves *n*, *v* ▷ **curve**
curvier *adj* ▷ **curve**
curviest *adj* ▷ **curve**
curvilinear *adj* consisting of or bounded by a curve
curving *v* ▷ **curve**
curvy *adj* ▷ **curve**
cuscus *n* (*pl* **-ses**) large Australian nocturnal possum
cuscuses *n* ▷ **cuscus**
cushier *adj* ▷ **cushy**
cushiest *adj* ▷ **cushy**
cushion *n* (*pl* **-s**) bag filled with soft material, to make a seat more comfortable ▶ *v* (**-s, -ing, -ed**) lessen the effects of
cushioned *v* ▷ **cushion**
cushioning *v* ▷ **cushion**
cushions *n*, *v* ▷ **cushion**
cushy *adj* (**cushier, cushiest**) (*Informal*) easy
cusp *n* (*pl* **-s**) pointed end, esp. on a tooth
cusps *n* ▷ **cusp**
cuss (*Informal*) *n* (*pl* **-es**) curse, oath ▶ *v* (**-es, -ing, -ed**) swear (at)
cussed [**kuss**-id] *adj* (*Informal*) obstinate ▶ *v* ▷ **cuss** > **cussedly** *adv* > **cussedness** *n*
cussedly *adv* ▷ **cussed**
cussedness *n* ▷ **cussed**
cusses *n*, *v* ▷ **cuss**
cussing *v* ▷ **cuss**
custard *n* (*pl* **-s**) sweet yellow sauce made from milk and eggs
custards *n* ▷ **custard**
custodial *adj* ▷ **custody**
custodian *n* (*pl* **-s**) person in charge of a public building
custodians *n* ▷ **custodian**
custodies *n* ▷ **custody**
custody *n* (*pl* **-dies**) protective care > **custodial** *adj*
custom *n* (*pl* **-s**) long-established activity or action ▶ *pl* duty charged on imports or exports
customarily *adv* ▷ **customary**
customary *adj* usual > **customarily** *adv*
customer *n* (*pl* **s**) person who buys goods or services
customers *n* ▷ **customer**
customs *n* ▷ **custom**
cut *v* (**cuts, cutting, cut**) open up, penetrate, wound, or divide with a sharp instrument ▶ *n* (*pl* **-s**) stroke or incision made by cutting
cutaneous [kew-**tane**-ee-uss] *adj* of the skin
cute *adj* (**cuter, cutest**) appealing or attractive > **cutely** *adv* > **cuteness** *n*
cutely *adv* ▷ **cute**
cuteness *n* ▷ **cute**
cuter *adj* ▷ **cute**
cutest *adj* ▷ **cute**
cuticle *n* (*pl* **-s**) skin at the base of a fingernail or toenail
cuticles *n* ▷ **cuticle**
cutlass *n* (*pl* **-es**) curved one-edged sword formerly used by sailors
cutlasses *n* ▷ **cutlass**
cutler *n* (*pl* **-s**) maker of cutlery
cutlers *n* ▷ **cutler**
cutlery *n* knives, forks, and spoons
cutlet *n* (*pl* **-s**) small piece of meat like a chop
cutlets *n* ▷ **cutlet**
cuts *v*, *n* ▷ **cut**
cutter *n* (*pl* **-s**) person or tool that cuts
cutters *n* ▷ **cutter**
cutting *n* (*pl* **-s**) article cut from a newspaper or magazine ▶ *adj* (of a remark) hurtful ▶ *v* ▷ **cut** > **cuttingly** *adv*
cuttingly *adv* ▷ **cutting**
cuttings *n* ▷ **cutting**
cuttlefish *n* (*pl* **cuttlefish**) squidlike sea mollusc

> **cuz** *n* (**cuzzes**). Like **coz**, cuz is an old word for **cousin**. You need a blank tile for the second Z if you're going to play the plural. Cuz scores 14 points.
> **cwm** *n* (**cwms**). Cwm is a Welsh word for a valley. It's a useful one to remember because it doesn't contain any vowels. Cwm scores 10 points.

cyanide *n* (*pl* **-s**) extremely poisonous chemical

compound
cyanides *n* ▷ **cyanide**
cybernetics *n* branch of science in which electronic and mechanical systems are studied and compared to biological systems
cyberspace *n* place said to contain all the data stored in computers
cyclamen [**sik**-la-men] *n* (*pl* **-s**) plant with red, pink, or white flowers
cyclamens *n* ▷ **cyclamen**
cycle *v* (**cycles, cycling, cycled**) ride a bicycle ▶ *n* (*pl* **-s**) (BRIT, AUST & NZ) bicycle
cycled *v* ▷ **cycle**
cycles *v, n* ▷ **cycle**
cyclic *adj* ▷ **cyclical**
cyclical, cyclic *adj* occurring in cycles > **cyclically** *adv*
cyclically *adv* ▷ **cyclical**
cycling *v* ▷ **cycle**
cyclist *n* (*pl* **-s**) person who rides a bicycle
cyclists *n* ▷ **cyclist**
cyclone *n* (*pl* **-s**) violent wind moving round a central area
cyclones *n* ▷ **cyclone**
cyclotron *n* (*pl* **-s**) apparatus that accelerates charged particles by means of a strong vertical magnetic field
cyclotrons *n* ▷ **cyclotron**
cygnet *n* (*pl* **-s**) young swan
cygnets *n* ▷ **cygnet**
cylinder *n* (*pl* **-s**) solid or hollow body with straight sides and circular ends > **cylindrical** *adj*
cylinders *n* ▷ **cylinder**
cylindrical *adj* ▷ **cylinder**
cymbal *n* (*pl* **-s**) percussion instrument consisting of a brass plate which is struck against another or hit with a stick
cymbals *n* ▷ **cymbal**
cynic [**sin**-ik] *n* (*pl* **-s**) person who believes that people always act selfishly > **cynical** *adj* > **cynically** *adv* > **cynicism** *n*
cynical *adj* ▷ **cynic**
cynically *adv* ▷ **cynic**
cynicism *n* ▷ **cynic**
cynics *n* ▷ **cynic**
cynosure [**sin**-oh-zyure] *n* (*pl* **-s**) centre of attention
cynosures *n* ▷ **cynosure**
cypher *n* (*pl* **-s**) ▷ **cipher**
cyphers *n* ▷ **cypher**
cypress *n* (*pl* **-es**) evergreen tree with dark green leaves
cypresses *n* ▷ **cypress**
cyst [**sist**] *n* (*pl* **-s**) (abnormal) sac in the body containing fluid or soft matter > **cystic** *adj*
cystic *adj* ▷ **cyst**
cystitis [siss-**tite**-iss] *n* inflammation of the bladder
cysts *n* ▷ **cyst**
cytological *adj* ▷ **cytology**
cytologically *adv* ▷ **cytology**
cytologies *n* ▷ **cytology**
cytologist *n* ▷ **cytology**
cytologists *n* ▷ **cytology**
cytology [site-**ol**-a-jee] *n* (*pl* **-logies**) study of plant and animal cells > **cytological** *adj* > **cytologically** *adv* > **cytologist** *n* (*pl* **-s**)
czar [**zahr**] *n* (*pl* **-s**) ▷ **tsar** > **czarism** *n* > **czarist** *adj, n* (*pl* **-s**)
czarism *n* ▷ **czar**
czarist *n* ▷ **czar**
czarists *n* ▷ **czar**
czars *n* ▷ **czar**

Dd

D only starts a handful of two-letter words, but it does form a two-letter word before every vowel except U. There are plenty of good three-letter words beginning with D, particularly those with a Y or W: **day, dye** and **dew** are worth 7 points each, for example.

da *n* (**das**). A da is a Burmese knife. Da scores 3 points.

dab[1] *v* (**-s, -bbing, -bbed**) pat lightly ▶ *n* (*pl* **-s**) small amount of something soft or moist
dab[2] *n* (*pl* **-s**) small European flatfish with rough scales
dabbed *v* ▷ **dab[1]**
dabbing *v* ▷ **dab[1]**
dabble *v* (**-les, -ling, -led**) be involved in something superficially > **dabbler** *n* (*pl* **-s**)
dabbled *v* ▷ **dabble**
dabbler *n* ▷ **dabble**
dabblers *n* ▷ **dabble**
dabbles *v* ▷ **dabble**
dabbling *v* ▷ **dabble**
dabs *n* ▷ **dab[1, 2]** ▶ *v* ▷ **dab[1]**
dace *n* (*pl* **dace**) small European freshwater fish
dachshund *n* (*pl* **-s**) dog with a long body and short legs
dachshunds *n* ▷ **dachshund**
dad *n* (*pl* **-s**) (*Informal*) father
daddies *n* ▷ **daddy**
daddy *n* (*pl* **-dies**) (*Informal*) father
dado [**day**-doe] *n* (*pl* **-does, -dos**) lower part of an interior wall, below a rail, decorated differently from the upper part
dadoes *n* ▷ **dado**
dados *n* ▷ **dado**
dads *n* ▷ **dad**
daffodil *n* (*pl* **-s**) yellow trumpet-shaped flower that blooms in spring
daffodils *n* ▷ **daffodil**
daft *adj* (**-er, -est**) (*Informal*) foolish or crazy > **daftness** *n* (*pl* **-es**)
dafter *adj* ▷ **daft**
daftest *adj* ▷ **daft**
daftness *n* ▷ **daft**
daftnesses *n* ▷ **daft**
dag (NZ) *n* (*pl* **-s**) dried dung on a sheep's rear (*Informal*) ▶ *v* (**-s, -gging, -gged**) remove the dags from a sheep
dagga *n* (*pl* **-s**) (S AFR) (*Informal*) cannabis
daggas *n* ▷ **dagga**
dagged *v* ▷ **dag**
dagger *n* (*pl* **-s**) short knifelike weapon with a pointed blade
daggers *n* ▷ **dagger**
daggier *adj* ▷ **daggy**
daggiest *adj* ▷ **daggy**
dagging *v* ▷ **dag**
daggy *adj* (**-ggier, -ggiest**) (NZ) (*Informal*) amusing
dags *n, v* ▷ **dag**
daguerreotype [dag-**gair**-oh-type] *n* (*pl* **-s**) type of early photograph produced on chemically treated silver
daguerreotypes *n* ▷ **daguerreotype**
dahlia [**day**-lya] *n* (*pl* **-s**) brightly coloured garden flower
dahlias *n* ▷ **dahlia**
dailies *n* ▷ **daily**
daily *adj* occurring every day or every weekday ▶ *adv* every day ▶ *n* (*pl* **-lies**) daily newspaper
daintier *adj* ▷ **dainty**
daintiest *adj* ▷ **dainty**
daintily *adv* ▷ **dainty**
dainty *adj* (**-tier, -tiest**) delicate or elegant > **daintily** *adv*
daiquiri [**dak**-eer-ee] *n* (*pl* **-s**) iced drink containing rum, lime juice, and sugar
daiquiris *n* ▷ **daiquiri**
dairies *n* ▷ **dairy**
dairy *n* (*pl* **-ies**) place for the processing or sale of milk and its products ▶ *adj* of milk or its products
dais [**day**-iss, **dayss**] *n* (*pl* **-es**) raised platform in a hall, used by a speaker
daises *n* ▷ **dais**
daisies *n* ▷ **daisy**
daisy *n* (*pl* **-sies**) small wild flower with a

yellow centre and white petals

dak *n* (**daks**). A dak is an old Indian mail or transport system. This is a good word to know if you have a K on your rack but can't think of a longer word in which to use it. Dak scores 8 points.

dale *n* (*pl* **-s**) (esp. in N England) valley
dales *n* ▷ **dale**
dalliance *n* (*pl* **-s**) flirtation
dalliances *n* ▷ **dalliance**
dallied *v* ▷ **dally**
dallies *v* ▷ **dally**
dally *v* (**-lies, -lying, -lied**) waste time
dallying *v* ▷ **dally**
dalmatian *n* (*pl* **-s**) large dog with a white coat and black spots
dalmatians *n* ▷ **dalmatian**
dam¹ *n* (*pl* **-s**) barrier built across a river to create a lake ▶ *v* (**dams, damming, dammed**) build a dam across (a river)
dam² *n* (*pl* **-s**) mother of an animal such as a sheep or horse
damage *v* (**-ages, -aging, -aged**) harm, spoil ▶ *n* (*pl* **-s**) harm to a person or thing ▶ *pl* money awarded as compensation for injury or loss
damaged *v* ▷ **damage**
damages *v, n* ▷ **damage**
damaging *v* ▷ **damage**
damask *n* (*pl* **-s**) fabric with a pattern woven into it, used for tablecloths etc.
damasks *n* ▷ **damask**
dame *n* (*pl* **-s**) (CHIEFLY US & CANADIAN) (*Slang*) woman
dames *n* ▷ **dame**
dammed *v* ▷ **dam¹**
damming *v* ▷ **dam¹**
damn *interj* (*Slang*) exclamation of annoyance ▶ *adv, adj* (*also* **damned**) (*Slang*) extreme(ly) ▶ *v* (**-s, -ing, -ed**) condemn as bad or worthless > **damnation** *interj, n* (*pl* **-s**)
damnable *adj* annoying > **damnably** *adv*
damnably *adv* ▷ **damnable**
damnation *interj, n* ▷ **damn**
damnations *n* ▷ **damn**
damned *v* ▷ **damn**
damning *adj* proving or suggesting guilt ▶ *v* ▷ **damn**
damns *v* ▷ **damn**
damp *adj* (**-er, -est**) slightly wet ▶ *n* (*pl* **-s**) slight wetness, moisture ▶ *v* (**-s, -ing, -ed**) (*also* **dampen**) (**-s, -ing, -ed**) make damp (*foll. by* **down**) > **damply** *adv* > **dampness** *n*
damped *v* ▷ **damp**
dampen *v* ▷ **dampen**
dampened *v* ▷ **dampen**
dampening *v* ▷ **dampen**
dampens *v* ▷ **dampen**
damper *n* (*pl* **-s**) movable plate to regulate the draught in a fire ▶ *adj* ▷ **damp**
dampers *n* ▷ **damper**
dampest *adj* ▷ **damp**
damping *v* ▷ **damp**
damply *adv* ▷ **damp**
dampness *n* ▷ **damp**
damps *v, n* ▷ **damp**
dams *n* ▷ **dam¹, ²** ▶ *v* ▷ **dam¹**
damsel *n* (*pl* **-s**) (*Old-fashioned*) young woman
damsels *n* ▷ **damsel**
damson *n* (*pl* **-s**) small blue-black plumlike fruit
damsons *n* ▷ **damson**
dance *v* (**dances, dancing, danced**) move the feet and body rhythmically in time to music ▶ *n* (*pl* **-s**) series of steps and movements in time to music > **dancer** *n* (*pl* **-s**)
danced *v* ▷ **dance**
dancer *n* ▷ **dance**
dancers *n* ▷ **dance**
dances *v, n* ▷ **dance**
dancing *v* ▷ **dance**
dandelion *n* (*pl* **-s**) yellow-flowered wild plant
dandelions *n* ▷ **dandelion**
dander *n* (*pl* **-s**) (*Slang*) anger
danders *n* ▷ **dander**
dandier *adj* ▷ **dandy**
dandies *n* ▷ **dandy**
dandiest *adj* ▷ **dandy**
dandified *adj* ▷ **dandy**
dandle *v* (**-dles, -dling, -dled**) move (a child) up and down on one's knee
dandled *v* ▷ **dandle**
dandles *v* ▷ **dandle**
dandling *v* ▷ **dandle**
dandruff *n* (*pl* **-s**) loose scales of dry dead skin shed from the scalp
dandruffs *n* ▷ **dandruff**
dandy *n* (*pl* **-dies**) man who is overconcerned with the elegance of his appearance ▶ *adj* (**-dier, -diest**) (*Informal*) very good > **dandified** *adj*
danger *n* (*pl* **-s**) possibility of being injured or killed > **dangerous** *adj* > **dangerously** *adv*
dangerous *adj* ▷ **danger**
dangerously *adv* ▷ **danger**
dangers *n* ▷ **danger**
dangle *v* (**-gles, -gling, -gled**) hang loosely
dangled *v* ▷ **dangle**
dangles *v* ▷ **dangle**
dangling *v* ▷ **dangle**
dank *adj* (**-er, -est**) unpleasantly damp and

chilly > **dankly** *adv* > **dankness** *n* (*pl* **-es**)
danker *adj* ▷ **dank**
dankest *adj* ▷ **dank**
dankly *adv* ▷ **dank**
dankness *n* ▷ **dank**
danknesses *n* ▷ **dank**
dapper *adj* (**-er, -est**) (of a man) neat in appearance > **dapperly** *adv* > **dapperness** *n* (*pl* **-es**)
dapperer *adj* ▷ **dapper**
dapperest *adj* ▷ **dapper**
dapperly *adv* ▷ **dapper**
dapperness *n* ▷ **dapper**
dappernesses *n* ▷ **dapper**
dappled *adj* marked with spots of a different colour
dare *v* (**dares, daring, dared**) be courageous enough to try (to do something) ▶ *n* (*pl* **-s**) challenge to do something risky
dared *v* ▷ **dare**
daredevil *adj, n* (*pl* **-s**) recklessly bold (person)
daredevils *n* ▷ **daredevil**
dares *v, n* ▷ **dare**
daring *adj* willing to take risks ▶ *n* courage to do dangerous things ▶ *v* ▷ **dare** > **daringly** *adv*
daringly *adv* ▷ **daring**
dark *adj* (**-er, -est**) having little or no light ▶ *n* (*pl* **-s**) absence of light > **darkly** *adv* > **darkness** *n* (*pl* **-es**) > **darken** *v* (**-s, -ing, -ed**)
darken *v* ▷ **dark**
darkened *v* ▷ **dark**
darkening *v* ▷ **dark**
darkens *v* ▷ **dark**
darker *adj* ▷ **dark**
darkest *adj* ▷ **dark**
darkly *adv* ▷ **dark**
darkness *n* ▷ **dark**
darknesses *n* ▷ **dark**
darkroom *n* (*pl* **-s**) darkened room for processing photographic film
darkrooms *n* ▷ **darkroom**
darks *n* ▷ **dark**
darling *n* (*pl* **-s**) much-loved person ▶ *adj* much-loved
darlings *n* ▷ **darling**
darn[1] *v* (**-s, -ing, -ed**) mend (a garment) with a series of interwoven stitches ▶ *n* (*pl* **-s**) patch of darned work
darn[2] *interj, adv, adj, v* (**-s, -ing, -ed**) (*Euphemistic*) damn
darned *v* ▷ **darn**[1, 2]
darning *v* ▷ **darn**[1, 2]
darns *v* ▷ **darn**[1, 2] ▶ *n* ▷ **darn**[1]
dart *n* (*pl* **-s**) small narrow pointed missile that is thrown or shot, esp. in the game of darts ▶ *pl* game in which darts are thrown at a circular numbered board ▶ *v* (**-s, -ing, -ed**) move or direct quickly and suddenly
darted *v* ▷ **dart**
darting *v* ▷ **dart**
darts *n, v* ▷ **dart**
dash *v* (**-es, -ing, -ed**) move quickly ▶ *n* (*pl* **-es**) sudden quick movement
dashboard *n* (*pl* **-s**) instrument panel in a vehicle
dashboards *n* ▷ **dashboard**
dashed *v* ▷ **dash**
dashes *v, n* ▷ **dash**
dashing *adj* stylish and attractive ▶ *v* ▷ **dash** > **dashingly** *adv*
dashingly *adv* ▷ **dashing**
dassie *n* (*pl* **-s**) (S AFR) type of hoofed rodent-like animal (*also* **hyrax**)
dassies *n* ▷ **dassie**
dastardliness *n* ▷ **dastardly**
dastardly *adj* wicked and cowardly > **dastardliness** *n*
dasyure [dass-ee-your] *n* (*pl* **-s**) small marsupial of Australia, New Guinea, and adjacent islands
dasyures *n* ▷ **dasyure**
data *n* information consisting of observations, measurements, or facts
date[1] *n* (*pl* **-s**) specified day of the month ▶ *v* (**dates, dating, dated**) mark with the date
date[2] *n* (*pl* **-s**) dark-brown sweet-tasting fruit of the date palm
dated *adj* old-fashioned ▶ *v* ▷ **date**[1]
dates *n* ▷ **date**[1, 2] ▶ *v* ▷ **date**[1]
dating *v* ▷ **date**[1]
dative *n* (*pl* **-s**) (in certain languages) the form of the noun that expresses the indirect object
datives *n* ▷ **dative**
datum *n* (*pl* **data**) single piece of information in the form of a fact or statistic
daub *v* (**-s, -ing, -ed**) smear or spread quickly or clumsily
daubed *v* ▷ **daub**
daubing *v* ▷ **daub**
daubs *v* ▷ **daub**
daughter *n* (*pl* **-s**) female child > **daughterly** *adj*
daughterly *adj* ▷ **daughter**
daughters *n* ▷ **daughter**
daunting *adj* intimidating or worrying > **dauntingly** *adv*
dauntingly *adv* ▷ **daunting**
dauntless *adj* fearless > **dauntlessly** *adv* > **dauntlessness** *n*
dauntlessly *adv* ▷ **dauntless**
dauntlessness *n* ▷ **dauntless**

dauphin [**doe**-fan] *n* (*pl* **-s**) (formerly) eldest son of the king of France
dauphins *n* ▷ **dauphin**
davenport *n* (*pl* **-s**) (CHIEFLY BRIT) small writing table with drawers
davenports *n* ▷ **davenport**
davit [**dav**-vit] *n* (*pl* **-s**) crane, usu. one of a pair, at a ship's side, for lowering and hoisting a lifeboat
davits *n* ▷ **davit**

daw *n* (**daws**). A daw is another name for a **jackdaw.** Daw scores 7 points.

dawdle *v* (**-dles, -dling, -dled**) walk slowly, lag behind
dawdled *v* ▷ **dawdle**
dawdles *v* ▷ **dawdle**
dawdling *v* ▷ **dawdle**
dawn *n* (*pl* **-s**) daybreak ▶ *v* (**-s, -ing, -ed**) begin to grow light
dawned *v* ▷ **dawn**
dawning *v* ▷ **dawn**
dawns *n, v* ▷ **dawn**
day *n* (*pl* **-s**) period of 24 hours
daybreak *n* time in the morning when light first appears
daydream *n* (*pl* **-s**) pleasant fantasy indulged in while awake ▶ *v* (**-s, -ing, -ed**) indulge in idle fantasy > **daydreamer** *n* (*pl* **-s**)
daydreamed *v* ▷ **daydream**
daydreamer *n* ▷ **daydream**
daydreamers *n* ▷ **daydream**
daydreaming *v* ▷ **daydream**
daydreams *n, v* ▷ **daydream**
daylight *n* light from the sun
days *n* ▷ **day**
daze *v* (**dazes, dazing, dazed**) stun, by a blow or shock ▶ *n* (*pl* **-s**) state of confusion or shock
dazed *v* ▷ **daze**
dazes *v, n* ▷ **daze**
dazing *v* ▷ **daze**
dazzle *v* (**-zles, -zling, -zled**) impress greatly ▶ *n* (*pl* **-s**) bright light that dazzles > **dazzling** *adj* > **dazzlingly** *adv*
dazzled *v* ▷ **dazzle**
dazzles *v, n* ▷ **dazzle**
dazzling *v, adj* ▷ **dazzle**
dazzlingly *adv* ▷ **dazzle**

de *prep*. De means of or from. This is a useful little word to fit in when trying to form several words at once. De scores 3 points.

deacon *n* (*pl* **-s**) (CHRISTIANITY) ordained minister ranking immediately below a priest
deacons *n* ▷ **deacon**
dead *adj* (**-er, -est**) no longer alive ▶ *n* (*pl* **-s**) period during which coldness or darkness is most intense ▶ *adv* extremely
deadbeat *n* (*pl* **-s**) (*Informal*) lazy useless person
deadbeats *n* ▷ **deadbeat**
deaden *v* (**-s, -ing, -ed**) make less intense
deadened *v* ▷ **deaden**
deadening *v* ▷ **deaden**
deadens *v* ▷ **deaden**
deader *adj* ▷ **dead**
deadest *adj* ▷ **dead**
deadlier *adj* ▷ **deadly**
deadliest *adj* ▷ **deadly**
deadline *n* (*pl* **-s**) time limit
deadlines *n* ▷ **deadline**
deadliness *n* ▷ **deadly**
deadlock *n* (*pl* **-s**) point in a dispute at which no agreement can be reached > **deadlocked** *adj*
deadlocked *adj* ▷ **deadlock**
deadlocks *n* ▷ **deadlock**
deadly *adj* (**-lier, -liest**) likely to cause death ▶ *adv* extremely > **deadliness** *n*
deadpan *adj, adv* showing no emotion or expression
deads *n* ▷ **dead**
deaf *adj* (**-er, -est**) unable to hear > **deafness** *n* (*pl* **-es**)
deafen *v* (**-s, -ing, -ed**) make deaf, esp. temporarily
deafened *v* ▷ **deafen**
deafening *v* ▷ **deafen**
deafens *v* ▷ **deafen**
deafer *adj* ▷ **deaf**
deafest *adj* ▷ **deaf**
deafness *n* ▷ **deaf**
deafnesses *n* ▷ **deaf**
deal[1] *n* (*pl* **-s**) agreement or transaction ▶ *v* (**deals, dealing, dealt**) inflict (a blow) on > **dealer** *n* (*pl* **-s**)
deal[2] *n* (*pl* **-s**) plank of fir or pine wood
dealer *n* ▷ **deal**[1]
dealers *n* ▷ **deal**[1]
dealing *v* ▷ **deal**[1]
dealings *pl n* transactions or business relations
deals *v* ▷ **deal**[1] ▶ *n* ▷ **deal**[1, 2]
dealt *v* ▷ **deal**[1]
dean *n* (*pl* **-s**) chief administrative official of a college or university faculty
deaneries *n* ▷ **deanery**
deanery *n* (*pl* **-eries**) office or residence of a dean
deans *n* ▷ **dean**
dear *n* (*pl* **-s**) someone regarded with affection ▶ *adj* (**-er, -est**) much-loved > **dearly** *adv*

>dearness *n* (*pl* **-es**)
dearer *adj* ▷ **dear**
dearest *adj* ▷ **dear**
dearly *adv* ▷ **dear**
dearness *n* ▷ **dear**
dearnesses *n* ▷ **dear**
dears *n* ▷ **dear**
dearth [**dirth**] *n* (*pl* **-s**) inadequate amount, scarcity
dearths *n* ▷ **dearth**
death *n* (*pl* **-s**) permanent end of life in a person or animal
deathly *adj*, *adv* like death
deaths *n* ▷ **death**
deb *n* (*pl* **-s**) (*Informal*) debutante
debacle [day-**bah**-kl] *n* (*pl* **-s**) disastrous failure
debacles *n* ▷ **debacle**
debar *v* (**-bars, -barring, -barred**) prevent, bar
debarred *v* ▷ **debar**
debarring *v* ▷ **debar**
debars *v* ▷ **debar**
debase *v* (**-bases, -basing, -based**) lower in value, quality, or character **>debasement** *n* (*pl* **-s**)
debased *v* ▷ **debase**
debasement *n* ▷ **debase**
debasements *n* ▷ **debase**
debases *v* ▷ **debase**
debasing *v* ▷ **debase**
debatable *adj* not absolutely certain **>debatably** *adv*
debate *n* (*pl* **-s**) discussion ▶ *v* (**-bates, -bating, -bated**) discuss formally
debated *v* ▷ **debate**
debates *n*, *v* ▷ **debate**
debating *v* ▷ **debate**
debauch [dib-**bawch**] *v* (**-es, -ing, -ed**) make (someone) bad or corrupt, esp. sexually **>debauchery** *n* (*pl* **-eries**)
debauched *adj* immoral, sexually corrupt ▶ *v* ▷ **debauch**
debaucheries *n* ▷ **debauch**
debauchery *n* ▷ **debauch**
debauches *v* ▷ **debauch**
debauching *v* ▷ **debauch**
debenture *n* (*pl* **-s**) long-term bond bearing fixed interest, issued by a company or a government agency
debentures *n* ▷ **debenture**
debilitate *v* (**-tates, -tating, -tated**) weaken, make feeble **>debilitation** *n*
debilitated *v* ▷ **debilitate**
debilitates *v* ▷ **debilitate**
debilitating *v* ▷ **debilitate**
debilitation *n* ▷ **debilitate**
debilities *n* ▷ **debility**
debility *n* (*pl* **-ities**) weakness, infirmity
debit *n* (*pl* **-s**) acknowledgment of a sum owing by entry on the left side of an account ▶ *v* (**-s, -ing, -ed**) charge (an account) with a debt
debited *v* ▷ **debit**
debiting *v* ▷ **debit**
debits *n*, *v* ▷ **debit**
debonair *adj* (of a man) charming and refined
debouch *v* (**-es, -ing, -ed**) move out from a narrow place to a wider one
debouched *v* ▷ **debouch**
debouches *v* ▷ **debouch**
debouching *v* ▷ **debouch**
debrief *v* (**-s, -ing, -ed**) receive a report from (a soldier, diplomat, etc.) after an event **>debriefing** *n* (*pl* **-s**)
debriefed *v* ▷ **debrief**
debriefing *v*, *n* ▷ **debrief**
debriefings *n* ▷ **debrief**
debriefs *v* ▷ **debrief**
debris [**deb**-ree] *n* fragments of something destroyed
debs *n* ▷ **deb**
debt *n* (*pl* **-s**) something owed, esp. money **>debtor** *n* (*pl* **-s**)
debtor *n* ▷ **debt**
debtors *n* ▷ **debt**
debts *n* ▷ **debt**
debunk *v* (**-s, -ing, -ed**) (*Informal*) expose the falseness of
debunked *v* ▷ **debunk**
debunking *v* ▷ **debunk**
debunks *v* ▷ **debunk**
debut [**day**-byoo] *n* (*pl* **-s**) first public appearance of a performer
debutante [**day**-byoo-tont] *n* (*pl* **-s**) young upper-class woman being formally presented to society
debutantes *n* ▷ **debutante**
debuts *n* ▷ **debut**
decade *n* (*pl* **-s**) period of ten years
decadence *n* (*pl* **-s**) deterioration in morality or culture **>decadent** *adj* **>decadently** *adv*
decadences *n* ▷ **decadence**
decadent *adj* ▷ **decadence**
decadently *adv* ▷ **decadence**
decades *n* ▷ **decade**
decaffeinated [dee-**kaf**-fin-ate-id] *adj* (of coffee, tea, or cola) with caffeine removed
decagon *n* (*pl* **-s**) geometric figure with ten faces **>decagonal** *adj*
decagonal *adj* ▷ **decagon**
decagons *n* ▷ **decagon**
decahedral *adj* ▷ **decahedron**

decahedron [deck-a-**heed**-ron] *n* (*pl* **-s**) solid figure with ten sides > **decahedral** *adj*
decahedrons *n* ▷ **decahedron**
decamp *v* (**-s, -ing, -ed**) depart secretly or suddenly
decamped *v* ▷ **decamp**
decamping *v* ▷ **decamp**
decamps *v* ▷ **decamp**
decant *v* (**-s, -ing, -ed**) pour (a liquid) from one container to another
decanted *v* ▷ **decant**
decanter *n* (*pl* **-s**) stoppered bottle for wine or spirits
decanters *n* ▷ **decanter**
decanting *v* ▷ **decant**
decants *v* ▷ **decant**
decapitate *v* (**-tates, -tating, -tated**) behead > **decapitation** *n* (*pl* **-s**)
decapitated *v* ▷ **decapitate**
decapitates *v* ▷ **decapitate**
decapitating *v* ▷ **decapitate**
decapitation *n* ▷ **decapitate**
decapitations *n* ▷ **decapitate**
decathlete *n* ▷ **decathlon**
decathletes *n* ▷ **decathlon**
decathlon *n* (*pl* **-s**) athletic contest with ten events > **decathlete** *n* (*pl* **-s**)
decathlons *n* ▷ **decathlon**
decay *v* (**-s, -ing, -ed**) become weaker or more corrupt ▶ *n* (*pl* **-s**) process of decaying
decayed *v* ▷ **decay**
decaying *v* ▷ **decay**
decays *v, n* ▷ **decay**
decease *n* (*pl* **-s**) (*Formal*) death
deceases *n* ▷ **decease**
deceased *adj* (*Formal*) dead
deceit *n* (*pl* **-s**) behaviour intended to deceive > **deceitful** *adj* > **deceitfully** *adv*
deceitful *adj* ▷ **deceit**
deceitfully *adv* ▷ **deceit**
deceits *n* ▷ **deceit**
deceive *v* (**-ceives, -ceiving, -ceived**) mislead by lying > **deceiver** *n* (*pl* **-s**)
deceived *v* ▷ **deceive**
deceiver *n* ▷ **deceive**
deceivers *n* ▷ **deceive**
deceives *v* ▷ **deceive**
deceiving *v* ▷ **deceive**
decelerate *v* (**-rates, -rating, -rated**) slow down > **deceleration** *n* (*pl* **-s**)
decelerated *v* ▷ **decelerate**
decelerates *v* ▷ **decelerate**
decelerating *v* ▷ **decelerate**
deceleration *n* ▷ **decelerate**
decelerations *n* ▷ **decelerate**
decencies *n* ▷ **decent**
decency *n* ▷ **decent**
decent *adj* (**-er, -est**) (of a person) polite and morally acceptable > **decently** *adv* > **decency** *n* (*pl* **-cies**)
decenter *adj* ▷ **decent**
decentest *adj* ▷ **decent**
decently *adv* ▷ **decent**
decentralization *n* ▷ **decentralize**
decentralize *v* (**-lizes, -lizing, -lized**) reorganize into smaller local units > **decentralization** *n*
decentralized *v* ▷ **decentralize**
decentralizes *v* ▷ **decentralize**
decentralizing *v* ▷ **decentralize**
deception *n* (*pl* **-s**) deceiving
deceptions *n* ▷ **deception**
deceptive *adj* likely or designed to deceive > **deceptively** *adv* > **deceptiveness** *n*
deceptively *adv* ▷ **deceptive**
deceptiveness *n* ▷ **deceptive**
decibel *n* (*pl* **-s**) unit for measuring the intensity of sound
decibels *n* ▷ **decibel**
decide *v* (**-cides, -ciding, -cided**) (cause to) reach a decision
decided *adj* unmistakable ▶ *v* ▷ **decide** > **decidedly** *adv*
decidedly *adv* ▷ **decided**
decides *v* ▷ **decide**
deciding *v* ▷ **decide**
deciduous *adj* (of a tree) shedding its leaves annually
decimal *n* (*pl* **-s**) fraction written in the form of a dot followed by one or more numbers ▶ *adj* relating to or using powers of ten > **decimalization** *n* > **decimally** *adv*
decimalization *n* ▷ **decimal**
decimally *adv* ▷ **decimal**
decimals *n* ▷ **decimal**
decimate *v* (**-mates, -mating, -mated**) destroy or kill a large proportion of > **decimation** *n* (*pl* **-s**)
decimated *v* ▷ **decimate**
decimates *v* ▷ **decimate**
decimating *v* ▷ **decimate**
decimation *n* ▷ **decimate**
decimations *n* ▷ **decimate**
decipher *v* (**-s, -ing, -ed**) work out the meaning of (something illegible or in code) > **decipherable** *adj*
decipherable *adj* ▷ **decipher**
deciphered *v* ▷ **decipher**
deciphering *v* ▷ **decipher**
deciphers *v* ▷ **decipher**

decision *n* (*pl* **-s**) judgment, conclusion, or resolution
decisions *n* ▷ **decision**
decisive *adj* having a definite influence > **decisively** *adv* > **decisiveness** *n*
decisively *adv* ▷ **decisive**
decisiveness *n* ▷ **decisive**
deck *n* (*pl* **-s**) area of a ship that forms a floor
decking *n* wooden platform in a garden
decks *n* ▷ **deck**
declaim *v* (**-s, -ing, -ed**) speak loudly and dramatically > **declamation** *n* (*pl* **-s**) > **declamatory** *adj*
declaimed *v* ▷ **declaim**
declaiming *v* ▷ **declaim**
declaims *v* ▷ **declaim**
declamation *n* ▷ **declaim**
declamations *n* ▷ **declaim**
declamatory *adj* ▷ **declaim**
declaration *n* ▷ **declare**
declarations *n* ▷ **declare**
declaratory *adj* ▷ **declare**
declare *v* (**-clares, -claring, -clared**) state firmly and forcefully > **declaration** *n* (*pl* **-s**) > **declaratory** *adj*
declared *v* ▷ **declare**
declares *v* ▷ **declare**
declaring *v* ▷ **declare**
declension *n* (*pl* **-s**) (GRAMMAR) changes in the form of nouns, pronouns, or adjectives to show case, number, and gender
declensions *n* ▷ **declension**
decline *v* (**-clines, -clining, -clined**) become smaller, weaker, or less important ▶ *n* (*pl* **-s**) gradual weakening or loss
declined *v* ▷ **decline**
declines *v, n* ▷ **decline**
declining *v* ▷ **decline**
declivities *n* ▷ **declivity**
declivity *n* (*pl* **-ties**) downward slope
declutch *v* (**-es, -ing, -ed**) disengage the clutch of a motor vehicle
declutched *v* ▷ **declutch**
declutches *v* ▷ **declutch**
declutching *v* ▷ **declutch**
decoct *v* (**-s, -ing, -ed**) extract the essence from (a substance) by boiling > **decoction** *n* (*pl* **-s**)
decocted *v* ▷ **decoct**
decocting *v* ▷ **decoct**
decoction *n* ▷ **decoct**
decoctions *n* ▷ **decoct**
decocts *v* ▷ **decoct**
decode *v* (**-codes, -coding, -coded**) convert from code into ordinary language > **decoder** *n* (*pl* **-s**)
decoded *v* ▷ **decode**
decoder *n* ▷ **decode**
decoders *n* ▷ **decode**
decodes *v* ▷ **decode**
decoding *v* ▷ **decode**
décolleté [day-**kol**-tay] *adj* (of a woman's garment) low-cut
decommission *v* (**-s, -ing, -ed**) dismantle (a nuclear reactor, weapon, etc.) which is no longer needed
decommissioned *v* ▷ **decommission**
decommissioning *v* ▷ **decommission**
decommissions *v* ▷ **decommission**
decompose *v* (**-poses, -posing, -posed**) be broken down through chemical or bacterial action > **decomposition** *n* (*pl* **-s**)
decomposed *v* ▷ **decompose**
decomposes *v* ▷ **decompose**
decomposing *v* ▷ **decompose**
decomposition *n* ▷ **decompose**
decompositions *n* ▷ **decompose**
decompress *v* (**-presses, -pressing, -pressed**) free from pressure > **decompression** *n* (*pl* **-s**)
decompressed *v* ▷ **decompress**
decompresses *v* ▷ **decompress**
decompressing *v* ▷ **decompress**
decompression *n* ▷ **decompress**
decompressions *n* ▷ **decompress**
decongestant *n* (*pl* **-s**) medicine that relieves nasal congestion
decongestants *n* ▷ **decongestant**
decontaminate *v* (**-nates, -nating, -nated**) make safe by removing poisons, radioactivity, etc. > **decontamination** *n* (*pl* **-s**)
decontaminated *v* ▷ **decontaminate**
decontaminates *v* ▷ **decontaminate**
decontaminating *v* ▷ **decontaminate**
decontamination *n* ▷ **decontaminate**
decontaminations *n* ▷ **decontaminate**
decor [**day**-core] *n* (*pl* **-s**) style in which a room or house is decorated
decorate *v* (**-rates, -rating, -rated**) make more attractive by adding something ornamental > **decoration** *n* (*pl* **-s**) > **decorative** *adj* > **decorator** *n* (*pl* **-s**)
decorated *v* ▷ **decorate**
decorates *v* ▷ **decorate**
decorating *v* ▷ **decorate**
decoration *n* ▷ **decorate**
decorations *n* ▷ **decorate**
decorator *n* ▷ **decorate**
decorators *n* ▷ **decorate**
decorous [**dek**-a-russ] *adj* polite, calm, and sensible in behaviour > **decorously** *adv* > **decorousness** *n*

decorously *adv* ▷ **decorous**
decorousness *n* ▷ **decorous**
decors *n* ▷ **decor**
decorum [dik-**core**-um] *n* (*pl* **-s**) polite and socially correct behaviour
decorums *n* ▷ **decorum**
decoy *n* (*pl* **-s**) person or thing used to lure someone into danger ▶ *v* (**-s, -ing, -ed**) lure away by means of a trick
decoyed *v* ▷ **decoy**
decoying *v* ▷ **decoy**
decoys *n, v* ▷ **decoy**
decrease *v* (**-creases, -creasing, -creased**) make or become less ▶ *n* (*pl* **-s**) lessening, reduction
decreased *v* ▷ **decrease**
decreases *v, n* ▷ **decrease**
decreasing *v* ▷ **decrease**
decree *n* (*pl* **-s**) law made by someone in authority ▶ *v* (**-crees, -creeing, -creed**) order by decree
decreed *v* ▷ **decree**
decreeing *v* ▷ **decree**
decrees *n, v* ▷ **decree**
decrepit *adj* weakened or worn out by age or long use > **decrepitude** *n* (*pl* **-s**)
decrepitude *n* ▷ **decrepit**
decrepitudes *n* ▷ **decrepit**
decried *v* ▷ **decry**
decries *v* ▷ **decry**
decry *v* (**-cries, -crying, -cried**) express disapproval of
decrying *v* ▷ **decry**
dedicate *v* (**-cates, -cating, -cated**) commit (oneself or one's time) wholly to a special purpose or cause > **dedication** *n* (*pl* **-s**)
dedicated *adj* devoted to a particular purpose or cause ▶ *v* ▷ **dedicate**
dedicates *v* ▷ **dedicate**
dedicating *v* ▷ **dedicate**
dedication *n* ▷ **dedicate**
dedications *n* ▷ **dedicate**
deduce *v* (**-duces, -ducing, -duced**) reach (a conclusion) by reasoning from evidence > **deducible** *adj*
deduced *v* ▷ **deduce**
deduces *v* ▷ **deduce**
deducible *adj* ▷ **deduce**
deducing *v* ▷ **deduce**
deduct *v* (**-s, -ing, -ed**) subtract
deducted *v* ▷ **deduct**
deducting *v* ▷ **deduct**
deduction *n* (*pl* **-s**) deducting > **deductive** *adj*
deductions *n* ▷ **deduction**
deductive *adj* ▷ **deduction**
deducts *v* ▷ **deduct**
deed *n* (*pl* **-s**) something that is done
deeds *n* ▷ **deed**
deem *v* (**-s, -ing, -ed**) consider, judge
deemed *v* ▷ **deem**
deeming *v* ▷ **deem**
deems *v* ▷ **deem**
deep *adj* (**-er, -est**) extending or situated far down, inwards, backwards, or sideways > **deepen** *v* (**-s, -ing, -ed**)
deepen *v* ▷ **deep**
deepened *v* ▷ **deep**
deepening *v* ▷ **deep**
deepens *v* ▷ **deep**
deeper *adj* ▷ **deep**
deepest *adj* ▷ **deep**
deepfreeze *n* (*pl* **-s**) ▷ **freezer**
deepfreezes *n* ▷ **deepfreeze**
deeply *adv* profoundly or intensely
deer *n* (*pl* **deer**) large wild animal, the male of which has antlers
deerstalker *n* (*pl* **-s**) cloth hat with peaks at the back and front and earflaps
deerstalkers *n* ▷ **deerstalker**
deface *v* (**-faces, -facing, -faced**) deliberately spoil the appearance of > **defacement** *n* (*pl* **-s**)
defaced *v* ▷ **deface**
defacement *n* ▷ **deface**
defacements *n* ▷ **deface**
defaces *v* ▷ **deface**
defacing *v* ▷ **deface**
defamation *n* ▷ **defame**
defamations *n* ▷ **defame**
defamatory *adj* ▷ **defame**
defame *v* (**-fames, -faming, -famed**) attack the good reputation of > **defamation** *n* (*pl* **-s**) > **defamatory** [dif-**fam**-a-tree] *adj*
defamed *v* ▷ **defame**
defames *v* ▷ **defame**
defaming *v* ▷ **defame**
default *n* (*pl* **-s**) failure to do something ▶ *v* (**-s, -ing, -ed**) fail to fulfil an obligation > **defaulter** *n* (*pl* **-s**)
defaulted *v* ▷ **default**
defaulter *n* ▷ **default**
defaulters *n* ▷ **default**
defaulting *v* ▷ **default**
defaults *n, v* ▷ **default**
defeat *v* (**-s, -ing, -ed**) win a victory over ▶ *n* (*pl* **-s**) defeating
defeated *v* ▷ **defeat**
defeating *v* ▷ **defeat**
defeatism *n* ready acceptance or expectation of defeat > **defeatist** *adj, n* (*pl* **-s**)
defeatist *n, adj* ▷ **defeatism**

defeatists *n* ▷ **defeatism**
defeats *v, n* ▷ **defeat**
defecate *v* (**-cates, -cating, -cated**) discharge waste from the body through the anus > **defecation** *n* (*pl* **-s**)
defecated *v* ▷ **defecate**
defecates *v* ▷ **defecate**
defecating *v* ▷ **defecate**
defecation *n* ▷ **defecate**
defecations *n* ▷ **defecate**
defect *n* (*pl* **-s**) imperfection, blemish ▶ *v* (**-s, -ing, -ed**) desert one's cause or country to join the opposing forces > **defection** *n* (*pl* **-s**) > **defector** *n* (*pl* **-s**)
defected *v* ▷ **defect**
defecting *v* ▷ **defect**
defection *n* ▷ **defect**
defections *n* ▷ **defect**
defective *adj* imperfect, faulty > **defectiveness** *n*
defectiveness *n* ▷ **defective**
defector *n* ▷ **defect**
defectors *n* ▷ **defect**
defects *n, v* ▷ **defect**
defence *n* (*pl* **-s**) resistance against attack > **defenceless** *adj*
defenceless *adj* ▷ **defence**
defences *n* ▷ **defence**
defend *v* (**-s, -ing, -ed**) protect from harm or danger
defendant *n* (*pl* **-s**) person accused of a crime
defendants *n* ▷ **defendant**
defended *v* ▷ **defend**
defender *n* (*pl* **-s**) person who supports someone or something in the face of criticism
defenders *n* ▷ **defender**
defending *v* ▷ **defend**
defends *v* ▷ **defend**
defensibilities *n* ▷ **defensible**
defensibility *n* ▷ **defensible**
defensible *adj* capable of being defended because believed to be right > **defensibility** *n* (*pl* **-ities**)
defensive *adj* intended for defence > **defensively** *adv*
defensively *adv* ▷ **defensive**
defer[1] *v* (**-fers, -ferring, -ferred**) delay (something) until a future time > **deferment, deferral** *n* (*pl* **-s**)
defer[2] *v* (**-fers, -ferring, -ferred**) (*foll. by* **to**) comply with the wishes (of)
deference *n* polite and respectful behaviour > **deferential** *adj* > **deferentially** *adv*
deferential *adj* ▷ **deference**
deferentially *adv* ▷ **deference**
deferment *n* ▷ **defer**[1]
deferments *n* ▷ **defer**[1]
deferral *n* ▷ **defer**[1]
deferrals *n* ▷ **defer**[1]
deferred *v* ▷ **defer**[1, 2]
deferring *v* ▷ **defer**[1, 2]
defers *v* ▷ **defer**[1, 2]
defiance *n* ▷ **defy**
defiances *n* ▷ **defy**
defiant *adj* ▷ **defy**
defiantly *adv* ▷ **defy**
deficiencies *n* ▷ **deficiency**
deficiency *n* (*pl* **-cies**) state of being deficient
deficient *adj* lacking some essential thing or quality > **deficiently** *adv*
deficiently *adv* ▷ **deficient**
deficit *n* (*pl* **-s**) amount by which a sum of money is too small
deficits *n* ▷ **deficit**
defied *v* ▷ **defy**
defies *v* ▷ **defy**
defile[1] *v* (**-files, -filing, -filed**) treat (something sacred or important) without respect > **defilement** *n* (*pl* **-s**)
defile[2] *n* (*pl* **-s**) narrow valley or pass
defiled *v* ▷ **defile**[1]
defilement *n* ▷ **defile**[1]
defilements *n* ▷ **defile**[1]
defiles *v* ▷ **defile**[1] ▶ *n* ▷ **defile**[1, 2]
defiling *v* ▷ **defile**[1]
definable *adj* ▷ **define**
define *v* (**-fines, -fining, -fined**) state precisely the meaning of > **definable** *adj*
defined *v* ▷ **define**
defines *v* ▷ **define**
defining *v* ▷ **define**
definite *adj* firm, clear, and precise > **definitely** *adv*
definitely *adv* ▷ **definite**
definition *n* (*pl* **-s**) statement of the meaning of a word or phrase
definitions *n* ▷ **definition**
definitive *adj* providing an unquestionable conclusion > **definitively** *adv*
definitively *adv* ▷ **definitive**
deflate *v* (**-flates, -flating, -flated**) (cause to) collapse through the release of air
deflated *v* ▷ **deflate**
deflates *v* ▷ **deflate**
deflating *v* ▷ **deflate**
deflation *n* (*pl* **-s**) (ECONOMICS) reduction in economic activity resulting in lower output and investment > **deflationary** *adj*
deflationary *adj* ▷ **deflation**

deflations *n* ▷ **deflation**
deflect *v* (**-flects, -flecting, -flected**) (cause to) turn aside from a course > **deflection** *n* (*pl* **-s**) > **deflector** *n* (*pl* **-s**)
deflected *v* ▷ **deflect**
deflecting *v* ▷ **deflect**
deflection *n* ▷ **deflect**
deflections *n* ▷ **deflect**
deflector *n* ▷ **deflect**
deflectors *n* ▷ **deflect**
deflects *v* ▷ **deflect**
deflower *v* (**-flowers, -flowering, -flowered**) (*Lit*) deprive (a woman) of her virginity
deflowered *v* ▷ **deflower**
deflowering *v* ▷ **deflower**
deflowers *v* ▷ **deflower**
defoliant *n* ▷ **defoliate**
defoliants *n* ▷ **defoliate**
defoliate *v* (**-ates, -ating, -ated**) deprive (a plant) of its leaves > **defoliant** *n* (*pl* **-s**) > **defoliation** *n* (*pl* **-s**)
defoliated *v* ▷ **defoliate**
defoliates *v* ▷ **defoliate**
defoliating *v* ▷ **defoliate**
defoliation *n* ▷ **defoliate**
defoliations *n* ▷ **defoliate**
deforestation *n* (*pl* **-s**) destruction of all the trees in an area
deforestations *n* ▷ **deforestation**
deform *v* (**-s, -ing, -ed**) put out of shape or spoil the appearance of > **deformation** *n* (*pl* **-s**) > **deformity** *n* (*pl* **-ties**)
deformation *n* ▷ **deform**
deformations *n* ▷ **deform**
deformed *v* ▷ **deform**
deforming *v* ▷ **deform**
deformities *n* ▷ **deform**
deformity *n* ▷ **deform**
deforms *v* ▷ **deform**
defraud *v* (**-s, -ing, -ed**) cheat out of money, property, etc.
defrauded *v* ▷ **defraud**
defrauding *v* ▷ **defraud**
defrauds *v* ▷ **defraud**
defray *v* (**-s, -ing, -ed**) provide money for (costs or expenses)
defrayed *v* ▷ **defray**
defraying *v* ▷ **defray**
defrays *v* ▷ **defray**
defrock *v* (**-s, -ing, -ed**) deprive (a priest) of priestly status
defrocked *v* ▷ **defrock**
defrocking *v* ▷ **defrock**
defrocks *v* ▷ **defrock**
defrost *v* (**-s, -ing, -ed**) make or become free of ice
defrosted *v* ▷ **defrost**
defrosting *v* ▷ **defrost**
defrosts *v* ▷ **defrost**
deft *adj* quick and skilful in movement > **deftly** *adv* > **deftness** *n* (*pl* **-es**)
deftly *adv* ▷ **deft**
deftness *n* ▷ **deft**
deftnesses *n* ▷ **deft**
defunct *adj* no longer existing or operative
defuse *v* (**-fuses, -fusing, -fused**) remove the fuse of (an explosive device)
defused *v* ▷ **defuse**
defuses *v* ▷ **defuse**
defusing *v* ▷ **defuse**
defy *v* (**-fies, -fying, -fied**) resist openly and boldly > **defiance** *n* (*pl* **-s**) > **defiant** *adj* > **defiantly** *adv*
defying *v* ▷ **defy**
degeneracies *n* ▷ **degeneracy**
degeneracy *n* (*pl* **-acies**) degenerate behaviour
degenerate *adj* having deteriorated to a lower mental, moral, or physical level ▶ *n* (*pl* **-s**) degenerate person ▶ *v* (**-ates, -ating, -ated**) become degenerate > **degeneration** *n* (*pl* **-s**)
degenerated *v* ▷ **degenerate**
degenerates *n, v* ▷ **degenerate**
degenerating *v* ▷ **degenerate**
degeneration *n* ▷ **degenerate**
degenerations *n* ▷ **degenerate**
degradation *n* ▷ **degrade**
degradations *n* ▷ **degrade**
degrade *v* (**-grades, -grading, -graded**) reduce to dishonour or disgrace (CHEM) > **degradation** *n* (*pl* **-s**)
degraded *v* ▷ **degrade**
degrades *v* ▷ **degrade**
degrading *v* ▷ **degrade**
degree *n* (*pl* **-s**) stage in a scale of relative amount or intensity
degrees *n* ▷ **degree**
dehumanization *n* ▷ **dehumanize**
dehumanizations *n* ▷ **dehumanize**
dehumanize *v* (**-izes, -izing, -ized**) deprive of human qualities > **dehumanization** *n* (*pl* **-s**)
dehumanized *v* ▷ **dehumanize**
dehumanizes *v* ▷ **dehumanize**
dehumanizing *v* ▷ **dehumanize**
dehydrate *v* (**-ates, -ating, -ated**) remove water from (food) to preserve it > **dehydration** *n* (*pl* **-s**)
dehydrated *v* ▷ **dehydrate**
dehydrates *v* ▷ **dehydrate**
dehydrating *v* ▷ **dehydrate**
dehydration *n* ▷ **dehydrate**

dehydrations *n* ▷ **dehydrate**
deification *n* ▷ **deify**
deifications *n* ▷ **deify**
deified *v* ▷ **deify**
deifies *v* ▷ **deify**
deify [day-if-fie] *v* (**-fies, -fying, -fied**) treat or worship as a god > **deification** *n* (*pl* **-s**)
deifying *v* ▷ **deify**
deign [dane] *v* (**-s, -ing, -ed**) agree (to do something), but as if doing someone a favour
deigned *v* ▷ **deign**
deigning *v* ▷ **deign**
deigns *v* ▷ **deign**
deities *n* ▷ **deity**
deity [dee-it-ee, day-it-ee] *n* (*pl* **-ties**) god or goddess
dejected *adj* unhappy > **dejectedly** *adv* > **dejection** *n* (*pl* **-s**)
dejectedly *adv* ▷ **dejected**
dejection *n* ▷ **dejected**
dejections *n* ▷ **dejected**
dekko *n* (*pl* **-s**) (BRIT, AUST & NZ) (*Slang*) look
dekkos *n* ▷ **dekko**
delay *v* (**-s, -ing, -ed**) put off to a later time ▶ *n* (*pl* **-s**) act of delaying
delayed *v* ▷ **delay**
delaying *v* ▷ **delay**
delays *v*, *n* ▷ **delay**
delectable *adj* delightful, very attractive
delectation *n* (*pl* **-s**) (*Formal*) great pleasure
delectations *n* ▷ **delectation**
delegate *n* (*pl* **-s**) person chosen to represent others, esp. at a meeting ▶ *v* (**-gates, -gating, -gated**) entrust (duties or powers) to someone
delegated *v* ▷ **delegate**
delegates *n*, *v* ▷ **delegate**
delegating *v* ▷ **delegate**
delegation *n* (*pl* **-s**) group chosen to represent others
delegations *n* ▷ **delegation**
delete *v* (**-letes, -leting, -leted**) remove (something written or printed) > **deletion** *n* (*pl* **-s**)
deleted *v* ▷ **delete**
deleterious [del-lit-eer-ee-uss] *adj* harmful, injurious
deletes *v* ▷ **delete**
deleting *v* ▷ **delete**
deletion *n* ▷ **deletion**
deletions *n* ▷ **deletion**
deliberate *adj* planned in advance, intentional ▶ *v* (**-ates, -ating, -ated**) think something over > **deliberately** *adv* > **deliberation** *n* (*pl* **-s**) > **deliberative** *adj*
deliberated *v* ▷ **deliberate**
deliberately *adv* ▷ **deliberate**
deliberates *v* ▷ **deliberate**
deliberating *v* ▷ **deliberate**
deliberation *n* ▷ **deliberate**
deliberations *n* ▷ **deliberate**
deliberative *adj* ▷ **deliberate**
delicacies *n* ▷ **delicacy**
delicacy *n* (*pl* **-cies**) being delicate
delicate *adj* fine or subtle in quality or workmanship > **delicately** *adv*
delicately *adv* ▷ **delicate**
delicatessen *n* (*pl* **-s**) shop selling imported or unusual foods, often already cooked or prepared
delicatessens *n* ▷ **delicatessen**
delicious *adj* very appealing to taste or smell > **deliciously** *adv* > **deliciousness** *n*
deliciously *adv* ▷ **delicious**
deliciousness *n* ▷ **delicious**
delight *n* (*pl* **-s**) (source of) great pleasure ▶ *v* (**-s, -ing, -ed**) please greatly > **delightful** *adj* > **delightfully** *adv*
delighted *v* ▷ **delight**
delightful *adj* ▷ **delight**
delightfully *adv* ▷ **delight**
delighting *v* ▷ **delight**
delights *n*, *v* ▷ **delight**
delimit *v* (**-s, -ing, -ed**) mark or lay down the limits of > **delimitation** *n* (*pl* **-s**)
delimitation *n* ▷ **delimit**
delimitations *n* ▷ **delimit**
delimited *v* ▷ **delimit**
delimiting *v* ▷ **delimit**
delimits *v* ▷ **delimit**
delineate [dill-lin-ee-ate] *v* (**-ates, -ating, -ated**) show by drawing > **delineation** *n* (*pl* **-s**)
delineated *v* ▷ **delineate**
delineates *v* ▷ **delineate**
delineating *v* ▷ **delineate**
delineation *n* ▷ **delineate**
delineations *n* ▷ **delineate**
delinquencies *n* ▷ **delinquent**
delinquency *n* ▷ **delinquent**
delinquent *n* (*pl* **-s**) someone, esp. a young person, who repeatedly breaks the law ▶ *adj* repeatedly breaking the law > **delinquency** *n* (*pl* **-cies**)
delinquents *n* ▷ **delinquent**
delirious *adj* ▷ **delirium**
deliriously *adv* ▷ **delirium**
delirium *n* (*pl* **-s**) state of excitement and mental confusion, often with hallucinations > **delirious** *adj* > **deliriously** *adv*
deliriums *n* ▷ **delirium**

deliver *v* (**-s, -ing, -ed**) carry (goods etc.) to a destination
deliverance *n* (*pl* **-s**) rescue from captivity or evil
deliverances *n* ▷ **deliverance**
delivered *v* ▷ **deliver**
deliveries *n* ▷ **delivery**
delivering *v* ▷ **deliver**
delivers *v* ▷ **deliver**
delivery *n* (*pl* **-eries**) delivering
dell *n* (*pl* **-s**) (CHIEFLY BRIT) small wooded hollow
dells *n* ▷ **dell**
delphinium *n* (*pl* **-s**) large garden plant with blue flowers
delphiniums *n* ▷ **delphinium**
delta *n* (*pl* **-s**) fourth letter in the Greek alphabet
deltas *n* ▷ **delta**
delude *v* (**-ludes, -luding, -luded**) deceive
deluded *v* ▷ **delude**
deludes *v* ▷ **delude**
deluding *v* ▷ **delude**
deluge [**del**-lyooj] *n* (*pl* **-s**) great flood ▶ *v* (**-luges, -luging, -luged**) flood
deluged *v* ▷ **deluge**
deluges *n, v* ▷ **deluge**
deluging *v* ▷ **deluge**
delusion *n* (*pl* **-s**) mistaken idea or belief > **delusive** *adj*
delusions *n* ▷ **delusion**
delusive *adj* ▷ **delusion**
delve *v* (**delves, delving, delved**) research deeply (for information)
delved *v* ▷ **delve**
delves *v* ▷ **delve**
delving *v* ▷ **delve**
demagogic *adj* ▷ **demagogue**
demagogies *v* ▷ **demagogue**
demagogue *n* (*pl* **-s**) political agitator who appeals to the prejudice and passions of the mob > **demagogic** *adj* > **demagogy** *n* (*pl* **-gies**)
demagogues *n* ▷ **demagogue**
demagogy *n* ▷ **demagogue**
demand *v* (**-s, -ing, -ed**) request forcefully ▶ *n* (*pl* **-s**) forceful request
demanded *v* ▷ **demand**
demanding *adj* requiring a lot of time or effort ▶ *v* ▷ **demand**
demands *v, n* ▷ **demand**
demarcation *n* (*pl* **-s**) (*Formal*) establishing limits or boundaries, esp. between the work performed by different trade unions
demarcations *n* ▷ **demarcation**
demean *v* (**-s, -ing, -ed**) do something unworthy of one's status or character
demeaned *v* ▷ **demean**
demeaning *v* ▷ **demean**
demeanour *n* (*pl* **-s**) way a person behaves
demeanours *n* ▷ **demeanour**
demeans *v* ▷ **demean**
demented *adj* mad > **dementedly** *adv*
dementedly *adv* ▷ **demented**
dementia [dim-**men**-sha] *n* (*pl* **-s**) state of serious mental deterioration
dementias *n* ▷ **dementia**
demerit *n* (*pl* **-s**) fault, disadvantage
demerits *n* ▷ **demerit**
demesne [dim-**mane**] *n* (*pl* **-s**) land surrounding a house
demesnes *n* ▷ **demesne**
demijohn *n* (*pl* **-s**) large bottle with a short neck, often encased in wicker
demijohns *n* ▷ **demijohn**
demilitarization *n* ▷ **demilitarize**
demilitarizations *n* ▷ **demilitarize**
demilitarize *v* (**-izes, -izing, -ized**) remove the military forces from > **demilitarization** *n* (*pl* **-s**)
demilitarized *v* ▷ **demilitarize**
demilitarizes *v* ▷ **demilitarize**
demilitarizing *v* ▷ **demilitarize**
demimonde *n* (*pl* **-s**) (esp. in the 19th century) class of women considered to be outside respectable society because of promiscuity
demimondes *n* ▷ **demimonde**
demise *n* (*pl* **-s**) eventual failure (of something successful)
demises *n* ▷ **demise**
demo *n* (*pl* **-s**) (*Informal*) demonstration, organized expression of public opinion
demob *v* (**-mobs, -mobbing, -mobbed**) (BRIT, AUST & NZ) (*Informal*) demobilize
demobbed *v* ▷ **demob**
demobbing *v* ▷ **demob**
demobilization *n* ▷ **demobilize**
demobilizations *n* ▷ **demobilize**
demobilize *v* (**-lizes, -lizing, -lized**) release from the armed forces > **demobilization** *n* (*pl* **-s**)
demobilized *v* ▷ **demobilize**
demobilizes *v* ▷ **demobilize**
demobilizing *v* ▷ **demobilize**
demobs *v* ▷ **demob**
democracies *n* ▷ **democracy**
democracy *n* (*pl* **-cies**) government by the people or their elected representatives
democrat *n* (*pl* **-s**) advocate of democracy
democratic *adj* of democracy > **democratically** *adv*
democratically *adv* ▷ **democratic**

democrats *n* ▷ **democrat**
demographer *n* ▷ **demography**
demographers *n* ▷ **demography**
demographic *adj* ▷ **demography**
demographies *n* ▷ **demography**
demography *n* (*pl* **-phies**) study of population statistics, such as births and deaths > **demographer** *n* (*pl* **-s**) > **demographic** *adj*
demolish *v* (**-es, -ing, -ed**) knock down or destroy (a building) > **demolition** *n* (*pl* **-s**)
demolished *v* ▷ **demolish**
demolishes *v* ▷ **demolish**
demolishing *v* ▷ **demolish**
demolition *n* ▷ **demolish**
demolitions *n* ▷ **demolish**
demon *n* (*pl* **-s**) evil spirit
demoniac *adj* ▷ **demonic**
demoniacal *adj* ▷ **demonic**
demoniacally *adv* ▷ **demonic**
demonic *adj* evil > **demoniac, demoniacal** *adj* appearing to be possessed by a devil > **demoniacally** *adv*
demonologies *n* ▷ **demonology**
demonologist *n* ▷ **demonology**
demonologists *n* ▷ **demonology**
demonology *n* (*pl* **-logies**) study of demons > **demonologist** *n* (*pl* **-s**)
demons *n* ▷ **demon**
demonstrable *adj* able to be proved > **demonstrably** *adv*
demonstrably *adv* ▷ **demonstrable**
demonstrate *v* (**-rates, -rating, -rated**) show or prove by reasoning or evidence
demonstrated *v* ▷ **demonstrate**
demonstrates *v* ▷ **demonstrate**
demonstrating *v* ▷ **demonstrate**
demonstration *n* (*pl* **-s**) organized expression of public opinion
demonstrations *n* ▷ **demonstration**
demonstrative *adj* tending to show one's feelings unreservedly > **demonstratively** *adv*
demonstratively *adv* ▷ **demonstrative**
demonstrator *n* (*pl* **-s**) person who demonstrates how a device or machine works
demonstrators *n* ▷ **demonstrator**
demoralization *n* ▷ **demoralize**
demoralizations *n* ▷ **demoralize**
demoralize *v* (**-lizes, -lizing, -lized**) undermine the morale of > **demoralization** *n* (*pl* **-s**)
demoralized *v* ▷ **demoralize**
demoralizes *v* ▷ **demoralize**
demoralizing *v* ▷ **demoralize**
demos *n* ▷ **demo**
demote *v* (**-motes, -moting, -moted**) reduce in status or rank > **demotion** *n* (*pl* **-s**)
demoted *v* ▷ **demote**
demotes *v* ▷ **demote**
demoting *v* ▷ **demote**
demotion *n* ▷ **demote**
demotions *n* ▷ **demote**
demur *v* (**-murs, -murring, -murred**) show reluctance
demure *adj* (**-r, -st**) quiet, reserved, and rather shy > **demurely** *adv*
demurely *adv* ▷ **demure**
demurer *adj* ▷ **demure**
demurest *adj* ▷ **demure**
demurred *v* ▷ **demur**
demurring *v* ▷ **demur**
demurs *v* ▷ **demur**
den *n* (*pl* **-s**) home of a wild animal
denationalization *n* ▷ **denationalize**
denationalizations *n* ▷ **denationalize**
denationalize *v* (**-lizes, -lizing, -lized**) transfer (an industry) from public to private ownership > **denationalization** *n* (*pl* **-s**)
denationalized *v* ▷ **denationalize**
denationalizes *v* ▷ **denationalize**
denationalizing *v* ▷ **denationalize**
denature *v* (**-tures, -turing, -tured**) change the nature of
denatured *v* ▷ **denature**
denatures *v* ▷ **denature**
denaturing *v* ▷ **denature**
deniable *adj* ▷ **deny**
deniably *adv* ▷ **deny**
denial *n* (*pl* **-s**) statement that something is not true
denials *n* ▷ **denial**
denied *v* ▷ **deny**
denier [**den**-yer] *n* (*pl* **-s**) unit of weight used to measure the fineness of nylon or silk
deniers *n* ▷ **denier**
denies *v* ▷ **deny**
denigrate *v* (**-grates, -grating, -grated**) criticize unfairly > **denigration** *n* (*pl* **-s**)
denigrated *v* ▷ **denigrate**
denigrates *v* ▷ **denigrate**
denigrating *v* ▷ **denigrate**
denigration *n* ▷ **denigrate**
denigrations *n* ▷ **denigrate**
denim *n* (*pl* **-s**) hard-wearing cotton fabric, usu. blue ▶ *pl* jeans made of denim
denims *n* ▷ **denim**
denizen *n* (*pl* **-s**) inhabitant
denizens *n* ▷ **denizen**
denominate *v* (**-nates, -nating, -nated**) give a specific name to
denominated *v* ▷ **denominate**

denominates *v* ▷ **denominate**
denominating *v* ▷ **denominate**
denomination *n* (*pl* **-s**) group having a distinctive interpretation of a religious faith > **denominational** *adj*
denominational *adj* ▷ **denomination**
denominations *n* ▷ **denomination**
denominator *n* (*pl* **-s**) number below the line in a fraction
denominators *n* ▷ **denominator**
denotation *n* ▷ **denote**
denotations *n* ▷ **denote**
denote *v* (**-notes, -noting, -noted**) be a sign of > **denotation** *n* (*pl* **-s**)
denoted *v* ▷ **denote**
denotes *v* ▷ **denote**
denoting *v* ▷ **denote**
denouement [day-**noo**-mon] *n* (*pl* **-s**) final outcome or solution in a play or book
denouements *n* ▷ **denouement**
denounce *v* (**-ces, -cing, -ced**) speak vehemently against
denounced *v* ▷ **denounce**
denounces *v* ▷ **denounce**
denouncing *v* ▷ **denounce**
dens *n* ▷ **den**
dense *adj* (**-r, -st**) closely packed > **densely** *adv*
densely *adv* ▷ **dense**
denser *adj* ▷ **dense**
densest *adj* ▷ **dense**
densities *n* ▷ **density**
density *n* (*pl* **-ties**) degree to which something is filled or occupied
dent *n* (*pl* **-s**) hollow in the surface of something, made by hitting it ▶ *v* (**-s, -ing, -ed**) make a dent in
dental *adj* of teeth or dentistry
dented *v* ▷ **dent**
dentine [**den**-teen] *n* (*pl* **-s**) hard dense tissue forming the bulk of a tooth
dentines *n* ▷ **dentine**
denting *v* ▷ **dent**
dentist *n* (*pl* **-s**) person qualified to practise dentistry
dentistries *n* ▷ **dentistry**
dentistry *n* (*pl* **-ries**) branch of medicine concerned with the teeth and gums
dentists *n* ▷ **dentist**
dents *n, v* ▷ **dent**
denture *n* (*pl* **-s**) false tooth
dentures *n* ▷ **denture**
denude *v* (**-nudes, -nuding, -nuded**) remove the covering or protection from
denuded *v* ▷ **denude**
denudes *v* ▷ **denude**
denuding *v* ▷ **denude**
denunciation *n* (*pl* **-s**) open condemnation
denunciations *n* ▷ **denunciation**
deny *v* (**-nies, -nying, -nied**) declare to be untrue > **deniable** *adj* > **deniably** *adv*
denying *v* ▷ **deny**
deodorant *n* (*pl* **-s**) substance applied to the body to mask the smell of perspiration
deodorants *n* ▷ **deodorant**
deodorize *v* (**-izes, -izing, -ized**) remove or disguise the smell of
deodorized *v* ▷ **deodorize**
deodorizes *v* ▷ **deodorize**
deodorizing *v* ▷ **deodorize**
depart *v* (**-s, -ing, -ed**) leave > **departed** > **departure** *n* (*pl* **-s**)
departed *adj* (*Euphemistic*) dead ▶ *v* ▷ **depart**
departing *v* ▷ **depart**
department *n* (*pl* **-s**) specialized division of a large organization > **departmental** *adj*
departmental *adj* ▷ **department**
departments *n* ▷ **department**
departs *v* ▷ **depart**
departure *n* ▷ **depart**
departures *n* ▷ **depart**
depend *v* (**-s, -ing, -ed**) (*foll. by* **on**) put trust (in) > **dependable** *adj* > **dependably** *adv* > **dependability** *n* (*pl* **-ities**)
dependabilities *n* ▷ **depend**
dependability *n* ▷ **depend**
dependable *adj* ▷ **depend**
dependably *adv* ▷ **depend**
dependant *n* (*pl* **-s**) person who depends on another for financial support
dependants *n* ▷ **dependant**
depended *v* ▷ **depend**
dependence *n* (*pl* **-s**) state of being dependent
dependences *n* ▷ **dependence**
dependencies *n* ▷ **dependency**
dependency *n* (*pl* **-cies**) country controlled by another country
dependent *adj* depending on someone or something > **dependently** *adv*
dependently *adv* ▷ **dependent**
depending *v* ▷ **depend**
depends *v* ▷ **depend**
depict *v* (**-s, -ing, -ed**) produce a picture of > **depiction** *n* (*pl* **-s**)
depicted *v* ▷ **depict**
depicting *v* ▷ **depict**
depiction *n* ▷ **depict**
depictions *n* ▷ **depict**
depicts *v* ▷ **depict**
depilatories *n* ▷ **depilatory**
depilatory [dip-**pill**-a-tree] *n* (*pl* **-tories**) ▶ *adj*

(substance) designed to remove unwanted hair

deplete *v* (**-letes, -leting, -leted**) use up

> depletion *n* (*pl* **-s**)

depleted *v* ▷ **deplete**

depletes *v* ▷ **deplete**

depleting *v* ▷ **deplete**

depletion *n* ▷ **deplete**

depletions *n* ▷ **deplete**

deplorable *adj* very bad or unpleasant

> deplorably *adv*

deplorably *adv* ▷ **deplorable**

deplore *v* (**-lores, -loring, -lored**) condemn strongly

deplored *v* ▷ **deplore**

deplores *v* ▷ **deplore**

deploring *v* ▷ **deplore**

deploy *v* (**-s, -ing, -ed**) organize (troops or resources) into a position ready for immediate action **> deployment** *n* (*pl* **-s**)

deployed *v* ▷ **deploy**

deploying *v* ▷ **deploy**

deployment *n* ▷ **deploy**

deployments *n* ▷ **deploy**

deploys *v* ▷ **deploy**

depopulate *v* (**-lates, -lating, -lated**) reduce the population of **> depopulation** *n* (*pl* **-s**)

depopulated *v* ▷ **depopulate**

depopulates *v* ▷ **depopulate**

depopulating *v* ▷ **depopulate**

depopulation *n* ▷ **depopulate**

depopulations *n* ▷ **depopulate**

deport *v* (**-s, -ing, -ed**) remove forcibly from a country **> deportation** *n* (*pl* **-s**) **> deportee** *n* (*pl* **-s**)

deportation *n* ▷ **deport**

deportations *n* ▷ **deport**

deported *v* ▷ **deport**

deportee *n* ▷ **deport**

deportees *n* ▷ **deport**

deporting *v* ▷ **deport**

deportment *n* (*pl* **-s**) way in which a person moves or stands

deportments *n* ▷ **deportment**

deports *v* ▷ **deport**

depose *v* (**-poses, -posing, -posed**) remove from an office or position of power

deposed *v* ▷ **depose**

deposes *v* ▷ **depose**

deposing *v* ▷ **depose**

deposit *v* (**-s, -ing, -ed**) put down ▸ *n* (*pl* **-s**) sum of money paid into a bank account

> depositor *n* (*pl* **-s**)

depositaries *n* ▷ **depositary**

depositary *n* (*pl* **-aries**) person to whom something is entrusted for safety

deposited *v* ▷ **deposit**

depositing *v* ▷ **deposit**

deposition *n* (*pl* **-s**) (LAW) sworn statement of a witness used in court in his or her absence

depositions *n* ▷ **deposition**

depositor *n* ▷ **deposit**

depositories *n* ▷ **deposit**

depositors *n* ▷ **deposit**

depository *n* (*pl* **-ories**) store for furniture etc.

deposits *v, n* ▷ **deposit**

depot [**dep**-oh] *n* (*pl* **-s**) building where goods or vehicles are kept when not in use

depots *n* ▷ **depot**

depraved *adj* morally bad **> depravity** *n* (*pl* **-ities**)

depravities *n* ▷ **depraved**

depravity *n* ▷ **depraved**

deprecate *v* (**-cates, -cating, -cated**) express disapproval of **> deprecation** *n* (*pl* **-s**)

> deprecatory *adj*

deprecated *v* ▷ **deprecate**

deprecates *v* ▷ **deprecate**

deprecating *v* ▷ **deprecate**

deprecation *n* ▷ **deprecate**

deprecations *n* ▷ **deprecate**

deprecatory *adj* ▷ **deprecate**

depreciate *v* (**-ates, -ating, -ated**) decline in value or price **> depreciation** *n* (*pl* **-s**)

depreciated *v* ▷ **depreciate**

depreciates *v* ▷ **depreciate**

depreciating *v* ▷ **depreciate**

depreciation *n* ▷ **depreciate**

depreciations *n* ▷ **depreciate**

depredation *n* (*pl* **-s**) plundering

depredations *n* ▷ **depredation**

depress *v* (**-es, -ing, -ed**) make sad

> depressing *adj* **> depressingly** *adv*

depressant *n* (*pl* **-s**) ▸ *adj* (drug) able to reduce nervous activity

depressants *n* ▷ **depressant**

depressed *v* ▷ **depress**

depresses *v* ▷ **depress**

depressing *v, adj* ▷ **depress**

depressingly *adv* ▷ **depress**

depression *n* (*pl* **-s**) mental state in which a person has feelings of gloom and inadequacy

depressions *n* ▷ **depression**

depressive *adj* tending to cause depression ▸ *n* (*pl* **-s**) person who suffers from depression

> depressively *adv*

depressively *adv* ▷ **depressive**

depressives *n* ▷ **depressive**

deprivation *n* ▷ **deprive**

deprivations *n* ▷ **deprive**

deprive *v* (**-rives, -riving, -rived**) (*foll. by* **of**) prevent from (having or enjoying) > **deprivation** *n* (*pl* **-s**)
deprived *adj* lacking adequate living conditions, education, etc. ▶ *v* ▷ **deprive**
deprives *v* ▷ **deprive**
depriving *v* ▷ **deprive**
depth *n* (*pl* **-s**) distance downwards, backwards, or inwards
depths *n* ▷ **depth**
deputation *n* (*pl* **-s**) body of people appointed to represent others
deputations *n* ▷ **deputation**
depute *v* (**-putes, -puting, -puted**) appoint (someone) to act on one's behalf
deputed *v* ▷ **depute**
deputes *v* ▷ **depute**
deputies *n* ▷ **deputy**
deputing *v* ▷ **depute**
deputize *v* (**-izes, -izing, -ized**) act as deputy
deputized *v* ▷ **deputize**
deputizes *v* ▷ **deputize**
deputizing *v* ▷ **deputize**
deputy *n* (*pl* **-ties**) person appointed to act on behalf of another
derail *v* (**-s, -ing, -ed**) cause (a train) to go off the rails > **derailment** *n* (*pl* **-s**)
derailed *v* ▷ **derail**
derailing *v* ▷ **derail**
derailment *n* ▷ **derail**
derailments *n* ▷ **derail**
derails *v* ▷ **derail**
deranged *adj* insane or uncontrolled > **derangement** *n* (*pl* **-s**)
derangement *n* ▷ **derange**
derangements *n* ▷ **derange**
derbies *n* ▷ **derby**
derby [**dah**-bee] *n* (*pl* **-bies**) sporting event between teams from the same area ▶ *n* any of various horse races
deregulate *v* (**-ates, -ating, -ated**) remove regulations or controls from > **deregulation** *n* (*pl* **-s**)
deregulated *v* ▷ **deregulate**
deregulates *v* ▷ **deregulate**
deregulating *v* ▷ **deregulate**
deregulation *n* ▷ **deregulate**
deregulations *n* ▷ **deregulate**
derelict *adj* unused and falling into ruins ▶ *n* (*pl* **-s**) social outcast, vagrant
dereliction *n* (*pl* **-s**) state of being abandoned
derelictions *n* ▷ **dereliction**
derelicts *n* ▷ **derelict**
deride *v* (**-rides, -riding, -rided**) treat with contempt or ridicule > **derision** *n* (*pl* **-s**)
derided *v* ▷ **deride**
derides *v* ▷ **deride**
deriding *v* ▷ **deride**
derision *n* ▷ **deride**
derisions *n* ▷ **deride**
derisive *adj* mocking, scornful > **derisively** *adv* > **derisiveness** *n*
derisively *adv* ▷ **derisive**
derisiveness *n* ▷ **derisive**
derisory *adj* too small or inadequate to be considered seriously
derivation *n* ▷ **derive**
derivations *n* ▷ **derive**
derivative *adj* word, idea, etc., derived from another > **derivatively** *adv*
derivatively *adv* ▷ **derivative**
derive *v* (**-rives, -riving, -rived**) (*foll. by* **from**) take or develop (from) > **derivation** *n* (*pl* **-s**)
derived *v* ▷ **derive**
derives *v* ▷ **derive**
deriving *v* ▷ **derive**
dermatitis *n* inflammation of the skin
dermatologies *n* ▷ **dermatology**
dermatologist *n* ▷ **dermatology**
dermatologists *n* ▷ **dermatology**
dermatology *n* (*pl* **-ogies**) branch of medicine concerned with the skin > **dermatologist** *n* (*pl* **-s**)
derogatorily *adv* ▷ **derogatory**
derogatory [dir-**rog**-a-tree] *adj* intentionally offensive > **derogatorily** *adv*
derrick *n* (*pl* **-s**) simple crane
derricks *n* ▷ **derrick**
derv *n* (*pl* **-s**) (BRIT) diesel oil, when used for road transport
dervish *n* (*pl* **-es**) member of a Muslim religious order noted for a frenzied whirling dance
dervishes *n* ▷ **dervish**
dervs *n* ▷ **derv**
descant *n* (*pl* **-s**) (MUSIC) tune played or sung above a basic melody
descants *n* ▷ **descant**
descend *v* (**-s, -ing, -ed**) move down (a slope etc.)
descendant *n* (*pl* **-s**) person or animal descended from an individual, race, or species
descendants *n* ▷ **descendant**
descended *v* ▷ **descend**
descendent *adj* descending
descending *v* ▷ **descend**
descends *v* ▷ **descend**
descent *n* (*pl* **-s**) descending
descents *v* ▷ **descent**

describe *v* (**-ribes, -ribing, -ribed**) give an account of (something or someone) in words
described *v* ▷ **describe**
describes *v* ▷ **describe**
describing *v* ▷ **describe**
descried *v* ▷ **descry**
descries *v* ▷ **descry**
description *n* (*pl* **-s**) statement that describes something or someone > **descriptive** *adj* > **descriptively** *adv* > **descriptiveness** *n*
descriptions *n* ▷ **description**
descriptive *adj* ▷ **description**
descriptively *adv* ▷ **description**
descriptiveness *n* ▷ **description**
descry *v* (**-scries, -scrying, -scried**) catch sight of
descrying *v* ▷ **descry**
desecrate *v* (**-rates, -rating, -rated**) damage or insult (something sacred) > **desecration** *n* (*pl* **-s**)
desecrated *v* ▷ **desecrate**
desecrates *v* ▷ **desecrate**
desecrating *v* ▷ **desecrate**
desecration *n* ▷ **desecrate**
desecrations *n* ▷ **desecrate**
desegregate *v* (**-gates, -gating, -gated**) end racial segregation in > **desegregation** *n* (*pl* **-s**)
desegregated *v* ▷ **desegregate**
desegregates *v* ▷ **desegregate**
desegregating *v* ▷ **desegregate**
desegregation *n* ▷ **desegregate**
desegregations *n* ▷ **desegregate**
deselect *v* (**-s, -ing, -ed**) (BRIT) (POLITICS) refuse to select (an MP) for re-election > **deselection** *n* (*pl* **-s**)
deselected *v* ▷ **deselect**
deselecting *v* ▷ **deselect**
deselection *n* ▷ **deselect**
deselections *n* ▷ **deselect**
deselects *v* ▷ **deselect**
desert¹ *n* (*pl* **-s**) region with little or no vegetation because of low rainfall
desert² *v* (**-s, -ing, -ed**) abandon (a person or place) without intending to return > **deserter** *n* (*pl* **-s**) > **desertion** *n* (*pl* **-s**)
deserted *v* ▷ **desert²**
deserter *n* ▷ **desert²**
deserters *n* ▷ **desert²**
deserting *v* ▷ **desert²**
desertion *n* ▷ **desert²**
desertions *n* ▷ **desert²**
deserts *n* ▷ **desert¹** ▶ *pl n* the punishment one deserves ▶ *v* ▷ **desert²**
deserve *v* (**-serves, -serving, -served**) be entitled to or worthy of
deserved *adj* rightfully earned ▶ *v* ▷ **deserve** > **deservedly** *adv*
deservedly *adv* ▷ **deserved**
deserves *v* ▷ **deserve**
deserving *adj* worthy of help, praise, or reward ▶ *v* ▷ **deserve**
deshabille [day-zab-**beel**] *n* (*pl* **-s**) state of being partly dressed
deshabilles *n* ▷ **deshabille**
desiccate *v* (**-siccates, -siccating, -siccated**) remove most of the water from > **desiccation** *n* (*pl* **-s**)
desiccated *v* ▷ **desiccate**
desiccates *v* ▷ **desiccate**
desiccating *v* ▷ **desiccate**
desiccation *n* ▷ **desiccate**
desiccations *n* ▷ **desiccate**
design *v* (**-s, -ing, -ed**) work out the structure or form of (something), by making a sketch or plans ▶ *n* (*pl* **-s**) preliminary drawing
designate [**dez**-zig-nate] *v* (**-nates, -nating, -nated**) give a name to ▶ *adj* appointed but not yet in office
designated *v* ▷ **designate**
designates *v* ▷ **designate**
designating *v* ▷ **designate**
designation *n* (*pl* **-s**) name
designations *v* ▷ **designation**
designed *v* ▷ **design**
designedly [dee-**zine**-id-lee] *adv* intentionally
designer *n* (*pl* **-s**) person who draws up original sketches or plans from which things are made ▶ *adj* designed by a well-known designer
designers *n* ▷ **designer**
designing *adj* cunning and scheming ▶ *v* ▷ **design**
designs *v, n* ▷ **design**
desirabilities *n* ▷ **desirable**
desirability *n* ▷ **desirable**
desirable *adj* worth having > **desirability** *n* (*pl* **-ities**) > **desirably** *adv*
desirably *adv* ▷ **desirable**
desire *v* (**-sires, -siring, -sired**) want very much ▶ *n* (*pl* **-s**) wish, longing
desired *v* ▷ **desire**
desires *v, n* ▷ **desire**
desiring *v* ▷ **desire**
desist *v* (**-s, -ing, -ed**) (*foll. by* **from**) stop (doing something)
desisted *v* ▷ **desist**
desisting *v* ▷ **desist**
desists *v* ▷ **desist**
desk *n* (*pl* **-s**) piece of furniture with a writing surface and drawers

desks *n* ▷ **desk**
desktop *adj* (of a computer) small enough to use at a desk
desolate *adj* uninhabited and bleak ▸ *v* (**-lates, -lating, -lated**) deprive of inhabitants > **desolately** *adv* > **desolateness** *n* > **desolation** *n* (*pl* **-s**)
desolated *v* ▷ **desolate**
desolately *adv* ▷ **desolate**
desolateness *n* ▷ **desolate**
desolates *v* ▷ **desolate**
desolating *v* ▷ **desolate**
desolation *n* ▷ **desolate**
desolations *n* ▷ **desolate**
despair *n* (*pl* **-s**) total loss of hope ▸ *v* (**-s, -ing, -ed**) lose hope > **despairingly** *adv*
despaired *v* ▷ **despair**
despairing *v* ▷ **despair**
despairingly *adv* ▷ **despair**
despairs *n, v* ▷ **despair**
despatch *v* (**-es, -ing, -ed**) ▸ *n* (*pl* **-es**) ▷ **dispatch**
despatched *v* ▷ **despatch**
despatches *v, n* ▷ **despatch**
despatching *v* ▷ **despatch**
desperado *n* (*pl* **-does, -dos**) reckless person ready to commit any violent illegal act
desperadoes *v* ▷ **desperado**
desperados *v* ▷ **desperado**
desperate *adj* in despair and reckless > **desperately** *adv* > **desperateness** *n* > **desperation** *n* (*pl* **-s**)
desperately *adv* ▷ **desperate**
desperateness *n* ▷ **desperate**
desperation *n* ▷ **desperate**
desperations *n* ▷ **desperate**
despicable *adj* deserving contempt > **despicably** *adv*
despicably *adv* ▷ **despicable**
despise *v* (**-pises, -pising, -pised**) regard with contempt
despised *v* ▷ **despise**
despises *v* ▷ **despise**
despising *v* ▷ **despise**
despite *prep* in spite of
despoil *v* (**-s, -ing, -ed**) (*Formal*) plunder > **despoliation** *n* (*pl* **-s**)
despoiled *v* ▷ **despoil**
despoiling *v* ▷ **despoil**
despoils *v* ▷ **despoil**
despoliation *n* ▷ **despoil**
despoliations *n* ▷ **despoil**
despondencies *n* ▷ **despondent**
despondency *n* ▷ **despondent**
despondent *adj* unhappy > **despondently** *adv* > **despondency** *n* (*pl* **-cies**)
despondently *adv* ▷ **despondent**
despot *n* (*pl* **-s**) person in power who acts unfairly or cruelly > **despotic** *adj* > **despotically** *adv*
despotic *adj* ▷ **despot**
despotically *adv* ▷ **despot**
despotism *n* (*pl* **-s**) unfair or cruel government or behaviour
despotisms *n* ▷ **despotism**
despots *n* ▷ **despot**
dessert *n* (*pl* **-s**) sweet course served at the end of a meal
desserts *n* ▷ **dessert**
dessertspoon *n* (*pl* **-s**) spoon between a tablespoon and a teaspoon in size
dessertspoons *n* ▷ **dessertspoon**
destination *n* (*pl* **-s**) place to which someone or something is going
destinations *n* ▷ **destination**
destined *adj* certain to be or to do something
destinies *n* ▷ **destiny**
destiny *n* (*pl* **-nies**) future marked out for a person or thing
destitute *adj* having no money or possessions > **destitution** *n*
destitution *n* ▷ **destitute**
destroy *v* (**-s, -ing, -ed**) ruin, demolish
destroyed *v* ▷ **destroy**
destroyer *n* (*pl* **-s**) small heavily armed warship
destroyers *n* ▷ **destroyer**
destroying *v* ▷ **destroy**
destroys *v* ▷ **destroy**
destruction *n* (*pl* **-s**) destroying
destructions *n* ▷ **destruction**
destructive *adj* (capable of) causing destruction > **destructively** *adv* > **destructiveness** *n*
destructively *adv* ▷ **destructive**
destructiveness *n* ▷ **destructive**
desuetude [diss-**syoo**-it-tude] *n* (*pl* **-s**) condition of not being in use
desuetudes *n* ▷ **desuetude**
desultorily *adv* ▷ **desultory**
desultoriness *n* ▷ **desultory**
desultory [**dez**-zl-tree] *adj* jumping from one thing to another, disconnected > **desultorily** *adv* > **desultoriness** *n*
detach *v* (**-es, -ing, -ed**) disengage and separate > **detachable** *adj*
detachable *adj* ▷ **detach**
detached *adj* (BRIT, AUST & S AFR) (of a house) not joined to another house ▸ *v* ▷ **detach**
detaches *v* ▷ **detach**
detaching *v* ▷ **detach**
detachment *n* (*pl* **-s**) lack of emotional

involvement
detachments *n* ▷ **detachment**
detail *n* (*pl* **-s**) individual piece of information ▶ *v* (**-s, -ing, -ed**) list fully
detailed *v* ▷ **detail**
detailing *v* ▷ **detail**
details *n, v* ▷ **detail**
detain *v* (**-s, -ing, -ed**) delay (someone) > **detainee** *n* (*pl* **-s**)
detained *v* ▷ **detain**
detainee *n* ▷ **detain**
detainees *n* ▷ **detain**
detaining *v* ▷ **detain**
detains *v* ▷ **detain**
detect *v* (**-s, -ing, -ed**) notice > **detectable** *adj* > **detection** *n* (*pl* **-s**)
detectable *adj* ▷ **detect**
detected *v* ▷ **detect**
detecting *v* ▷ **detect**
detection *n* ▷ **detect**
detections *n* ▷ **detect**
detective *n* (*pl* **-s**) policeman or private agent who investigates crime
detectives *n* ▷ **detective**
detector *n* (*pl* **-s**) instrument used to find something
detectors *n* ▷ **detector**
detects *v* ▷ **detect**
detente [day-**tont**] *n* (*pl* **-s**) easing of tension between nations
detentes *n* ▷ **detente**
detention *n* (*pl* **-s**) imprisonment
detentions *n* ▷ **detention**
deter *v* (**-ters, -terring, -terred**) discourage (someone) from doing something by instilling fear or doubt
detergent *n* (*pl* **-s**) chemical substance for washing clothes or dishes
detergents *n* ▷ **detergent**
deteriorate *v* (**-rates, -rating, -rated**) become worse > **deterioration** *n* (*pl* **-s**)
deteriorated *v* ▷ **deteriorate**
deteriorates *v* ▷ **deteriorate**
deteriorating *v* ▷ **deteriorate**
deterioration *n* ▷ **deteriorate**
deteriorations *n* ▷ **deteriorate**
determinant *n* (*pl* **-s**) factor that determines
determinants *n* ▷ **determinant**
determinate *adj* definitely limited or fixed > **determinateness** *n*
determinateness *n* ▷ **determinate**
determination *n* (*pl* **-s**) being determined or resolute
determinations *n* ▷ **determination**
determine *v* (**-mines, -mining, -mined**) settle (an argument or a question) conclusively
determined *adj* firmly decided, unable to be dissuaded ▶ *v* ▷ **determine** > **determinedly** *adv*
determiner *n* (*pl* **-s**) (GRAMMAR) word that determines the object to which a noun phrase refers
determiners *n* ▷ **determiner**
determines *v* ▷ **determine**
determining *v* ▷ **determine**
determinism *n* theory that human choice is not free, but decided by past events > **determinist** *n* (*pl* **-s**) *adj*
determinist *n* ▷ **determinism**
determinists *n* ▷ **determinism**
deterred *v* ▷ **deter**
deterrent *n* (*pl* **-s**) something that deters ▶ *adj* tending to deter
deterrents *n* ▷ **deterrent**
deterring *v* ▷ **deter**
deters *v* ▷ **deter**
detest *v* (**-s, -ing, -ed**) dislike intensely > **detestable** *adj* > **detestably** *adv* > **detestation** *n* (*pl* **-s**)
detestable *adj* ▷ **detest**
detestably *adv* ▷ **detest**
detestation *n* ▷ **detest**
detestations *n* ▷ **detest**
detested *v* ▷ **detest**
detesting *v* ▷ **detest**
detests *v* ▷ **detest**
dethrone *v* (**-rones, -roning, -roned**) remove from a throne or position of power
dethroned *v* ▷ **dethrone**
dethrones *v* ▷ **dethrone**
dethroning *v* ▷ **dethrone**
detonate *v* (**-nates, -nating, -nated**) explode > **detonation** *n* (*pl* **-s**)
detonated *v* ▷ **detonate**
detonates *v* ▷ **detonate**
detonating *v* ▷ **detonate**
detonation *n* ▷ **detonate**
detonations *n* ▷ **detonate**
detonator *n* (*pl* **-s**) small amount of explosive, or a device, used to set off an explosion
detonators *n* ▷ **detonator**
detour *n* (*pl* **-s**) route that is not the most direct one
detours *n* ▷ **detour**
detract *v* (**-s, -ing, -ed**) (*foll. by* **from**) make (something) seem less good > **detractor** *n* (*pl* **-s**)
detracted *v* ▷ **detract**
detracting *v* ▷ **detract**
detractor *n* ▷ **detract**

detractors *n* ▷ **detract**
detracts *v* ▷ **detract**
detriment *n* (*pl* **-s**) disadvantage or damage > **detrimental** *adj* > **detrimentally** *adv*
detrimental *adj* ▷ **detract**
detrimentally *adv* ▷ **detract**
detriments *n* ▷ **detract**
detritus [dit-**trite**-uss] *n* loose mass of stones and silt worn away from rocks
deuce [**dyewss**] *n* (*pl* **-s**) (TENNIS) score of forty all
deuces *n* ▷ **deuce**

> **deus** *n* (**di**). Deus is a Latin word for a god. Its plural, di, is a very handy word to know when trying to form several words at once. Di scores 3 points.

deuterium *n* (*pl* **-s**) isotope of hydrogen twice as heavy as the normal atom
deuteriums *n* ▷ **deuterium**

> **dev** *n* (**devs**). A dev is a Hindu god. Dev scores 7 points.

devaluation *n* ▷ **devalue**
devaluations *n* ▷ **devalue**
devalue *v* (**-lues, -luing, -lued**) reduce the exchange value of (a currency) > **devaluation** *n* (*pl* **-s**)
devalued *v* ▷ **devalue**
devalues *v* ▷ **devalue**
devaluing *v* ▷ **devalue**
devastate *v* (**-tates, -tating, -tated**) destroy > **devastation** *n* (*pl* **-s**)
devastated *adj* shocked and extremely upset ▶ *v* ▷ **devastate**
devastates *v* ▷ **devastate**
devastating *v* ▷ **devastate**
devastation *n* ▷ **devastate**
devastations *n* ▷ **devastate**
develop *v* (**-s, -ing, -ed**) grow or bring to a later, more elaborate, or more advanced stage > **development** *n* (*pl* **-s**)
developed *v* ▷ **develop**
developer *n* (*pl* **-s**) person who develops property
developers *n* ▷ **developer**
developing *v* ▷ **develop**
development *n* ▷ **develop**
developments *n* ▷ **develop**
develops *v* ▷ **develop**
deviance *n* ▷ **deviant**
deviances *n* ▷ **deviant**
deviant *n* (*pl* **-s**) ▶ *adj* (person) deviating from what is considered acceptable behaviour > **deviance** *n* (*pl* **-s**)
deviants *n* ▷ **deviant**
deviate *v* (**-ates, -ating, -ated**) differ from others in belief or thought > **deviation** *n* (*pl* **-s**)
deviated *v* ▷ **deviate**
deviates *v* ▷ **deviate**
deviating *v* ▷ **deviate**
deviation *n* ▷ **deviate**
deviations *n* ▷ **deviate**
device *n* (*pl* **-s**) machine or tool used for a specific task
devices *n* ▷ **device**
devil *n* (*pl* **-s**) evil spirit (*Informal*) ▶ *v* (**-ils, -illing, -illed**) prepare (food) with a highly flavoured spiced mixture
devilish *adj* cruel or unpleasant ▶ *adv* (*also* **devilishly**) (*Informal*) extremely
devilishly *adv* ▷ **devilish**
devilled *v* ▷ **devil**
devilling *v* ▷ **devil**
devil-may-care *adj* carefree and cheerful
devilment *n* (*pl* **-s**) mischievous conduct
devilments *n* ▷ **devilment**
devilries *n* ▷ **devilry**
devilry *n* (*pl* **-ries**) mischievousness
devils *n*, *v* ▷ **devil**
devious *adj* insincere and dishonest > **deviously** *adv* > **deviousness** *n*
deviously *adv* ▷ **devious**
deviousness *n* ▷ **devious**
devise *v* (**-vises, -vising, -vised**) work out (something) in one's mind
devised *v* ▷ **devise**
devises *v* ▷ **devise**
devising *v* ▷ **devise**
devoid *adj* (*foll. by* **of**) completely lacking (in)
devolution *n* (*pl* **-s**) transfer of authority from a central government to regional governments
devolutions *n* ▷ **devolution**
devolve *v* (**-volves, -volving, -volved**) (*foll. by* **on** *or* **to**) pass (power or duties) or (of power or duties) be passed to a successor or substitute
devolved *v* ▷ **devolve**
devolves *v* ▷ **devolve**
devolving *v* ▷ **devolve**
devote *v* (**-votes, -voting, -voted**) apply or dedicate to a particular purpose
devoted *adj* showing loyalty or devotion ▶ *v* ▷ **devote** > **devotedly** *adv*
devotedly *adv* ▷ **devoted**
devotee *n* (*pl* **-s**) person who is very enthusiastic about something
devotees *n* ▷ **devotee**
devotes *v* ▷ **devote**
devoting *v* ▷ **devote**
devotion *n* (*pl* **-s**) strong affection for or loyalty to someone or something ▶ *pl* prayers > **devotional** *adj*

devotional *adj* ▷ **devotion**
devotions *adj* ▷ **devotion**
devour *v* (**-s, -ing, -ed**) eat greedily
devoured *v* ▷ **devour**
devouring *v* ▷ **devour**
devours *v* ▷ **devour**
devout *adj* deeply religious > **devoutly** *adv* > **devoutness** *n*
devoutly *adv* ▷ **devout**
devoutness *n* ▷ **devout**
dew *n* (*pl* **-s**) drops of water that form on the ground at night from vapour in the air > **dewy** *adj* (**-wier, -wiest**)
dewier *adj* ▷ **dew**
dewiest *adj* ▷ **dew**
dewlap *n* (*pl* **-s**) loose fold of skin hanging under the throat in dogs, cattle, etc.
dewlaps *n* ▷ **dewlap**
dews *n* ▷ **dew**
dewy *adj* ▷ **dew**

dex *n* (**dexes**). Dex is a slang word for a kind of amphetamine. This is an easy way to pick up a some points after another player has used an X. Dex scores 11 points.

dexterities *n* ▷ **dexterity**
dexterity *n* (*pl* **-ities**) skill in using one's hands > **dexterous** *adj* > **dexterously** *adv*
dexterous *adj* ▷ **dexterity**
dexterously *adv* ▷ **dexterity**
dextrose *n* (*pl* **-s**) glucose occurring in fruit, honey, and the blood of animals
dextroses *n* ▷ **dextrose**

dey *n* (**deys**). A dey is an Ottoman governor. Dey scores 7 points.

diabetes [die-a-**beet**-eez] *n* disorder in which an abnormal amount of urine containing an excess of sugar is excreted > **diabetic** *n* (*pl* **-s**) *adj*
diabetic *n* ▷ **diabetes**
diabetics *n* ▷ **diabetes**
diabolic *adj* of the Devil
diabolical *adj* (*Informal*) extremely bad > **diabolically** *adv* > **diabolicalness** *n*
diabolically *adv* ▷ **diabolical**
diabolicalness *n* ▷ **diabolical**
diabolism *n* witchcraft, devil worship > **diabolist** *n* (*pl* **-s**)
diabolist *n* ▷ **diabolism**
diabolists *n* ▷ **diabolism**
diaconate *n* (*pl* **-s**) position or period of office of a deacon
diaconates *n* ▷ **diaconate**
diacritic *n* (*pl* **-s**) sign above or below a character to indicate phonetic value or stress
diacritics *n* ▷ **diacritic**
diadem *n* (*pl* **-s**) (*Old-fashioned*) crown
diadems *n* ▷ **diadem**
diaereses *n* ▷ **diaeresis**
diaeresis *n* (*pl* **-ses**) mark (¨) placed over a vowel to show that it is pronounced separately from the preceding one, for example in *Noël*
diagnosed *v* ▷ **diagnosis**
diagnoses *n, v* ▷ **diagnosis**
diagnosing *v* ▷ **diagnosis**
diagnosis [die-ag-**no**-siss] *n* (*pl* **-ses**) [-seez] discovery and identification of diseases from the examination of symptoms > **diagnose** *v* (**-noses, -nosing, -nosed**) > **diagnostic** *adj*
diagnostic *adj* ▷ **diagnosis**
diagonal *adj* from corner to corner ▶ *n* (*pl* **-s**) diagonal line > **diagonally** *adv*
diagonally *adv* ▷ **diagonal**
diagonals *n* ▷ **diagonal**
diagram *n* (*pl* **-s**) sketch showing the form or workings of something > **diagrammatic** *adj*
diagrammatic *adj* ▷ **diagram**
diagrams *n* ▷ **diagram**
dial *n* (*pl* **-s**) face of a clock or watch ▶ *v* (**dials, dialling, dialled**) operate the dial or buttons on a telephone in order to contact (a number)
dialect *n* (*pl* **-s**) form of a language spoken in a particular area > **dialectal** *adj* > **dialectally** *adv*
dialectal *adj* ▷ **dialect**
dialectally *adv* ▷ **dialect**
dialectic *n* (*pl* **-s**) logical debate by question and answer to resolve differences between two views > **dialectical** *adj* > **dialectically** *adv*
dialectical *adj* ▷ **dialectic**
dialectically *adv* ▷ **dialectic**
dialectics *n* ▷ **dialectic**
dialects *n* ▷ **dialect**
dialled *v* ▷ **dial**
dialling *v* ▷ **dial**
dialogue *n* (*pl* **-s**) conversation between two people, esp. in a book, film, or play
dialogues *n* ▷ **dialogue**
dials *n, v* ▷ **dial**
dialyses *n* ▷ **dialysis**
dialysis [die-**al**-iss-iss] *n* (*pl* **-ses**) (MED) filtering of blood through a membrane to remove waste products
diamanté [die-a-**man**-tee] *adj* decorated with artificial jewels or sequins
diameter *n* (*pl* **-s**) (length of) a straight line through the centre of a circle or sphere
diameters *n* ▷ **diameter**
diametric, diametrical *adj* of a diameter

> **diametrically** *adv*
diametrical *adj* ▷ **diametric**
diametrically *adv* ▷ **diametric**
diamond *n* (*pl* **-s**) exceptionally hard, usu. colourless, precious stone
diamonds *n* ▷ **diamond**
diaper *n* (*pl* **-s**) (US) nappy
diapers *n* ▷ **diaper**
diaphanous [die-**af**-fan-ous] *adj* fine and almost transparent > **diaphanously** *adv*
diaphanously *adv* ▷ **diaphanous**
diaphragm [**die**-a-fram] *n* (*pl* **-s**) muscular partition that separates the abdominal cavity and chest cavity
diaphragms *n* ▷ **diaphragm**
diaries *n* ▷ **diary**
diarist *n* ▷ **diary**
diarists *n* ▷ **diary**
diarrhoea [die-a-**ree**-a] *n* (*pl* **-s**) frequent discharge of abnormally liquid faeces
diarrhoeas *n* ▷ **diarrhoea**
diary *n* (*pl* **-ries**) (book for) a record of daily events, appointments, or observations > **diarist** *n* (*pl* **-s**)
diatribe *n* (*pl* **-s**) bitter critical attack
diatribes *n* ▷ **diatribe**
dibble *n* (*pl* **-s**) small hand tool used to make holes in the ground for seeds or plants
dibbles *n* ▷ **dibble**
dice *n* (*pl* **dice**) small cube each of whose sides has a different number of spots (1 to 6), used in games of chance ▶ *v* (**dices, dicing, diced**) cut (food) into small cubes
diced *v* ▷ **dice**
dices *v* ▷ **dice**
dicey *adj* (**dicier, diciest**) (*Informal*) dangerous or risky
dichotomies *n* ▷ **dichotomy**
dichotomy [die-**kot**-a-mee] *n* (*pl* **-mies**) division into two opposed groups or parts
dicier *adj* ▷ **dice**
diciest *adj* ▷ **dice**
dicing *v* ▷ **dice**
dickier *adj* ▷ **dicky**[2]
dickies *n* ▷ **dicky**[1]
dickiest *adj* ▷ **dicky**[2]
dicky[1] *n* (*pl* **dickies**) false shirt front
dicky[2] *adj* (**dickier, dickiest**) (*Informal*) shaky or weak
dickybird *n* (*pl* **-s**) child's word for a bird
dickybirds *n* ▷ **dickybird**
dicta *n* ▷ **dictum**
dictate *v* (**-tes, -ting, -ted**) say aloud for someone else to write down (*foll. by* **to**) ▶ *n* (*pl* **-s**) authoritative command > **dictation** *n* (*pl* **-s**)
dictated *v* ▷ **dictate**
dictates *v, n* ▷ **dictate**
dictating *v* ▷ **dictate**
dictation *n* ▷ **dictate**
dictations *n* ▷ **dictate**
dictator *n* (*pl* **-s**) ruler who has complete power > **dictatorship** *n* (*pl* **-s**)
dictatorial *adj* like a dictator > **dictatorially** *adv*
dictatorially *adv* ▷ **dictatorial**
dictators *n* ▷ **dictator**
dictatorship *n* ▷ **dictator**
dictatorships *n* ▷ **dictator**
diction *n* (*pl* **-s**) manner of pronouncing words and sounds
dictionaries *n* ▷ **dictionary**
dictionary *n* (*pl* **-aries**) book consisting of an alphabetical list of words with their meanings
dictions *n* ▷ **diction**
dictum *n* (*pl* **-tums, -ta**) formal statement
dictums *n* ▷ **dictum**
did *v* ▷ **do**
didactic *adj* intended to instruct > **didactically** *adv*
didactically *adv* ▷ **didactic**
diddle *v* (**-dles, -dling, -dled**) (*Informal*) swindle
diddled *v* ▷ **diddle**
diddles *v* ▷ **diddle**
diddling *v* ▷ **diddle**
didgeridoo *n* (*pl* **-s**) Australian musical instrument made from a long hollow piece of wood
didgeridoos *n* ▷ **didgeridoo**
didn't did not
die[1] *v* (**dies, dying, died**) (of a person, animal, or plant) cease all biological activity permanently
die[2] *n* (*pl* **-s**) shaped block used to cut or form metal
died *v* ▷ **die**[1]
diehard *n* (*pl* **-s**) person who resists change
diehards *n* ▷ **diehard**
diereses *n* ▷ **dieresis**
dieresis [die-**air**-iss-iss] *n* (*pl* **-ses**) [-seez] ▷ **diaeresis**
dies *v* ▷ **die**[1] ▶ *n* ▷ **die**[2]
diesel *n* (*pl* **-s**) diesel engine
diesels *n* ▷ **diesel**
diet[1] *n* (*pl* **-s**) food that a person or animal regularly eats ▶ *v* (**-s, -ing, -ed**) follow a special diet so as to lose weight ▶ *adj* (of food) suitable for a weight-reduction diet > **dietary** *adj* > **dieter** *n* (*pl* **-s**)

diet² *n* (*pl* **-s**) parliament of some countries
dietary *adj* ▷ **diet**
dieted *v* ▷ **diet**
dieter *n* ▷ **diet**
dieters *n* ▷ **diet**
dietetic *adj* prepared for special dietary requirements
dietetics *n* study of diet and nutrition
dietician *n* (*pl* **-s**) person who specializes in dietetics
dieticians *n* ▷ **dietician**
dieting *v* ▷ **diet**
diets *v* ▷ **diet¹** ▶ *n* ▷ **diet¹, ²**
differ *v* (**-s, -ing, -ed**) be unlike
differed *v* ▷ **differ**
difference *n* (*pl* **-s**) state of being unlike
differences *n* ▷ **difference**
different *adj* unlike > **differently** *adv*
differential *adj* of or using a difference ▶ *n* (*pl* **-s**) factor that differentiates between two comparable things > **differentially** *adv*
differentially *adv* ▷ **differential**
differentials *n* ▷ **differential**
differentiate *v*, *v* (**-te, -ting, -ted**) perceive or show the difference (between) > **differentiation** *n* (*pl* **-s**)
differentiated *v* ▷ **differentiate**
differentiates *v* ▷ **differentiate**
differentiating *v* ▷ **differentiate**
differentiation *n* ▷ **differentiate**
differentiations *n* ▷ **differentiate**
differently *n* ▷ **different**
differing *v* ▷ **differ**
differs *v* ▷ **differ**
difficult *adj* requiring effort or skill to do or understand > **difficultly** *adv* > **difficulty** *n* (*pl* **-ties**)
difficulties *n* ▷ **difficult**
difficultly *adv* ▷ **difficult**
difficulty *n* ▷ **difficult**
diffidence *n* ▷ **diffident**
diffidences *n* ▷ **diffident**
diffident *adj* lacking self-confidence > **diffidence** *n* (*pl* **-s**) > **diffidently** *adv*
diffidently *adv* ▷ **diffident**
diffraction *n* (*pl* **-s**) (PHYSICS) deviation in the direction of a wave at the edge of an obstacle in its path
diffractions *n* ▷ **diffraction**
diffuse *v* (**-fuses, -fusing, -fused**) spread over a wide area ▶ *adj* widely spread > **diffusely** *adv* > **diffuseness** *n* > **diffusion** *n* (*pl* **-s**)
diffused *v* ▷ **diffuse**
diffusely *adv* ▷ **diffuse**
diffuseness *n* ▷ **diffuse**
diffuses *v* ▷ **diffuse**
diffusing *v* ▷ **diffuse**
diffusion *n* ▷ **diffuse**
diffusions *n* ▷ **diffuse**
dig *v* (**digs, digging, dug**) cut into, break up, and turn over or remove (earth), esp. with a spade ▶ *n* (*pl* **-s**) digging ▶ *pl* (*pl* **-s**) (BRIT, AUST & S AFR) (*Informal*) lodgings
digest *v* (**-s, -ing, -ed**) subject to a process of digestion ▶ *n* (*pl* **-s**) shortened version of a book, report, or article > **digestible** *adj* > **digestibility** *n* > **digestive** *adj* > **digestively** *adv*
digested *v* ▷ **digest**
digestibility *n* ▷ **digest**
digestible *adj* ▷ **digest**
digesting *v* ▷ **digest**
digestion *n* (*pl* **-s**) (body's system for) breaking down food into easily absorbed substances
digestions *n* ▷ **digestion**
digestive *adj* ▷ **digest**
digestively *adv* ▷ **digest**
digests *v*, *n* ▷ **digest**
digger *n* (*pl* **-s**) machine used for digging
diggers *n* ▷ **digger**
digging *v* ▷ **dig**
diggings *n* ▷ **dig**
digit [dij-it] *n* (*pl* **-s**) finger or toe
digital *adj* displaying information as numbers rather than with hands and a dial > **digitally** *adv*
digitalis *n* drug made from foxglove leaves, used as a heart stimulant
digitally *adv* ▷ **digital**
digits *n* ▷ **digit**
dignified *n* ▷ **dignify**
dignifies *n* ▷ **dignify**
dignify *v* (**-s, -ing, -ed**) add distinction to
dignifying *v* ▷ **dignify**
dignitaries *n* ▷ **dignitary**
dignitary *n* (*pl* **-aries**) person of high official position
dignities *n* ▷ **dignity**
dignity *n* (*pl* **-ties**) serious, calm, and controlled behaviour or manner
digress *v* (**-es, -ing, -ed**) depart from the main subject in speech or writing > **digression** *n* (*pl* **-s**)
digressed *v* ▷ **digress**
digresses *v* ▷ **digress**
digressing *v* ▷ **digress**
digression *n* ▷ **digress**
digressions *n* ▷ **digress**
digs *v*, *n* ▷ **dig**
dike *n* (*pl* **-s**) ▷ **dyke**

dikes *n* ▷ **dike**
dilapidated *adj* (of a building) having fallen into ruin > **dilapidation** *n* (*pl* **-s**)
dilapidation *n* ▷ **dilapidated**
dilapidations *n* ▷ **dilapidated**
dilatation *n* ▷ **dilate**
dilatations *n* ▷ **dilate**
dilate *v* (**-lates, -lating, -lated**) make or become wider or larger > **dilation, dilatation** *n* (*pl* **-s**)
dilated *v* ▷ **dilate**
dilates *v* ▷ **dilate**
dilating *v* ▷ **dilate**
dilation *n* ▷ **dilate**
dilations *n* ▷ **dilate**
dilatorily *adv* ▷ **dilatory**
dilatoriness *n* ▷ **dilatory**
dilatory [**dill**-a-tree] *adj* tending or intended to waste time > **dilatorily** *adv* > **dilatoriness** *n*
dilemma *n* (*pl* **-s**) situation offering a choice between two equally undesirable alternatives
dilemmas *n* ▷ **dilemma**
dilettante [dill-it-**tan**-tee] *n* (*pl* **-tantes, -tanti**) person whose interest in a subject is superficial rather than serious > **dilettantism** *n*
dilettantes *n* ▷ **dilettante**
dilettanti *n* ▷ **dilettante**
dilettantism *n* ▷ **dilettante**
diligence *n* ▷ **diligent**
diligent *adj* careful and persevering in carrying out duties > **diligently** *adv* > **diligence** *n*
diligently *adv* ▷ **diligent**
dill *n* (*pl* **-s**) sweet-smelling herb
dills *n* ▷ **dill**
dilute *v* (**-lutes, -luting, -luted**) make (a liquid) less concentrated, esp. by adding water > **dilution** *n* (*pl* **-s**)
diluted *v* ▷ **dilute**
dilutes *v* ▷ **dilute**
diluting *v* ▷ **dilute**
dilution *n* ▷ **dilute**
dilutions *n* ▷ **dilute**
diluvial, diluvian *adj* of a flood, esp. the great Flood described in the Old Testament
diluvian *adj* ▷ **diluvial**
dim *adj* (**dimmer, dimmest**) badly lit ▶ *v* (**dims, dimming, dimmed**) make or become dim > **dimly** *adv* > **dimness** *n*
dime *n* (*pl* **-s**) coin of the US and Canada, worth ten cents
dimension *n* (*pl* **-s**) measurement of the size of something in a particular direction
dimensions *n* ▷ **dimension**
dimes *n* ▷ **dime**
diminish *v* (**-es, -ing, -ed**) make or become smaller, fewer, or less > **diminution** *n* (*pl* **-s**)
diminished *v* ▷ **diminish**
diminishes *v* ▷ **diminish**
diminishing *v* ▷ **diminish**
diminuendo *n* (*pl* **-s**) (MUSIC) gradual decrease in loudness
diminuendos *n* ▷ **diminuendo**
diminution *n* ▷ **diminish**
diminutions *n* ▷ **diminish**
diminutive *adj* very small ▶ *n* (*pl* **-s**) word or affix which implies smallness or unimportance > **diminutively** *adv* > **diminutiveness** *n*
diminutively *adv* ▷ **diminutive**
diminutiveness *n* ▷ **diminutive**
diminutives *n* ▷ **diminutive**
dimly *adv* ▷ **dim**
dimmed *v* ▷ **dim**
dimmer *n* (*pl* **-s**) device for dimming an electric light ▶ *adj* ▷ **dim**
dimmers *n* ▷ **dimmer**
dimmest *adj* ▷ **dim**
dimming *v* ▷ **dim**
dimness *n* ▷ **dim**
dimple *n* (*pl* **-s**) small natural dent, esp. in the cheeks or chin ▶ *v* (**-ples, -pling, -pled**) produce dimples by smiling
dimpled *v* ▷ **dimple**
dimples *n, v* ▷ **dimple**
dimpling *v* ▷ **dimple**
dims *v* ▷ **dim**
din *n* (*pl* **-s**) loud unpleasant confused noise ▶ *v* (**dins, dinning, dinned**) (*foll. by* **into**) instil (something) into someone by constant repetition
dinar [**dee**-nahr] *n* (*pl* **-s**) monetary unit of various Balkan, Middle Eastern, and North African countries
dinars *n* ▷ **dinar**
dine *v* (**dines, dining, dined**) eat dinner
dined *v* ▷ **dine**
diner *n* (*pl* **-s**) person eating a meal
diners *n* ▷ **diner**
dines *v* ▷ **dine**
ding *n* (*pl* **-s**) (AUST DATED & NZ) (*Informal*) small dent in a vehicle
dinghies *n* ▷ **dinghy**
dinghy [**ding**-ee] *n* (*pl* **-ghies**) small boat, powered by sails, oars, or a motor
dingier *adj* ▷ **dingy**
dingiest *adj* ▷ **dingy**
dinginess *n* ▷ **dingy**
dingo *n* (*pl* **-goes**) Australian wild dog

dingoes *n* ▷ **dingo**
dings *n* ▷ **ding**
dingy [**din**-jee] *adj* (**-gier, -giest**) (BRIT, AUST & NZ) dull and drab > **dinginess** *n*
dining *v* ▷ **dine**
dinkier *adj* ▷ **dinky**
dinkiest *adj* ▷ **dinky**
dinkum *adj* (AUST & NZ) (*Informal*) genuine or right
dinky *adj* (**-kier, -kiest**) (BRIT, AUST & NZ) (*Informal*) small and neat
dinned *v* ▷ **din**
dinner *n* (*pl* **-s**) main meal of the day, eaten either in the evening or at midday
dinners *n* ▷ **dinner**
dinning *v* ▷ **din**
dinosaur *n* (*pl* **-s**) type of extinct prehistoric reptile, many of which were of gigantic size
dinosaurs *n* ▷ **dinosaur**
dins *n, v* ▷ **din**
dint *n* (*pl* **-s**) means
dints *n* ▷ **dint**
diocesan *adj* ▷ **diocese**
diocese [**die**-a-siss] *n* (*pl* **-s**) district over which a bishop has control > **diocesan** *adj*
dioceses *n* ▷ **diocese**
diode *n* (*pl* **-s**) semiconductor device for converting alternating current to direct current
diodes *n* ▷ **diode**
dioptre [die-**op**-ter] *n* (*pl* **-s**) unit for measuring the refractive power of a lens
dioptres *n* ▷ **dioptre**
dioxide *n* (*pl* **-s**) oxide containing two oxygen atoms per molecule
dioxides *n* ▷ **dioxide**
dip *v* (**dips, dipping, dipped**) plunge quickly or briefly into a liquid ▶ *n* (*pl* **-s**) dipping
diphtheria [dif-**theer**-ya] *n* (*pl* **-s**) contagious disease producing fever and difficulty in breathing and swallowing
diphtherias *n* ▷ **diphtheria**
diphthong *n* (*pl* **-s**) union of two vowel sounds in a single compound sound
diphthongs *n* ▷ **diphthong**
diploma *n* (*pl* **-s**) qualification awarded by a college on successful completion of a course
diplomacies *n* ▷ **diplomacy**
diplomacy *n* (*pl* **-macies**) conduct of the relations between nations by peaceful means
diplomas *n* ▷ **diploma**
diplomat *n* (*pl* **-s**) official engaged in diplomacy
diplomatic *adj* of diplomacy > **diplomatically** *adv*
diplomatically *adv* ▷ **diplomatic**
diplomats *n* ▷ **diplomat**
dipped *v* ▷ **dip**
dipper *n* (*pl* **-s**) ladle used for dipping
dippers *n* ▷ **dipper**
dipping *v* ▷ **dip**
diprotodont [die-**pro**-toe-dont] *n* (*pl* **-s**) marsupial with fewer than three upper incisor teeth on each side of the jaw
diprotodonts *n* ▷ **diprotodont**
dips *v, n* ▷ **dip**
dipsomania *n* (*pl* **-s**) compulsive craving for alcohol > **dipsomaniac** *n* (*pl* **-s**) *adj*
dipsomaniac *n, adj* ▷ **dipsomania**
dipsomaniacs *n* ▷ **dipsomania**
dipsomanias *n* ▷ **dipsomania**
diptych [**dip**-tik] *n* (*pl* **-s**) painting on two hinged panels
diptychs *n* ▷ **diptych**
dire *adj* (**-er, -est**) disastrous, urgent, or terrible > **direly** *adv* > **direness** *n* (*pl* **-es**)
direct *adj* (of a route) shortest, straight ▶ *adv* in a direct manner ▶ *v* (**-s, -ing, -ed**) lead and organize > **directness** *n*
directed *v* ▷ **direct**
directing *v* ▷ **direct**
direction *n* (*pl* **-s**) course or line along which a person or thing moves, points, or lies ▶ *pl* instructions for doing something or for reaching a place > **directional** *adj*
directional *adj* ▷ **direction**
directions *n* ▷ **direction**
directive *n* (*pl* **-s**) instruction, order
directives *n* ▷ **directive**
directly *adv* in a direct manner ▶ *conj* as soon as
directness *n* ▷ **direct**
director *n* (*pl* **-s**) person or thing that directs or controls > **directorial** *adj* > **directorship** *n* (*pl* **-s**)
directorate *n* (*pl* **-s**) board of directors
directorates *n* ▷ **directorate**
directorial *adj* ▷ **director**
directories *n* ▷ **directory**
directors *n* ▷ **director**
directorship *n* ▷ **director**
directorships *n* ▷ **director**
directory *n* (*pl* **-ries**) book listing names, addresses, and telephone numbers
directs *v* ▷ **direct**
direly *adv* ▷ **dire**
direness *n* ▷ **dire**
direnesses *n* ▷ **dire**
direr *adj* ▷ **dire**
direst *adj* ▷ **dire**

dirge *n* (*pl* **-s**) slow sad song of mourning
dirges *n* ▷ **dirge**
dirigible [**dir**-rij-jib-bl] *adj* able to be steered ▶ *n* (*pl* **-s**) airship
dirigibles *n* ▷ **dirigible**
dirk *n* (*pl* **-s**) dagger, formerly worn by Scottish Highlanders
dirks *n* ▷ **dirk**
dirndl *n* (*pl* **-s**) full gathered skirt originating from Tyrolean peasant wear
dirndls *n* ▷ **dirndl**
dirt *n* (*pl* **-s**) unclean substance, filth
dirtied *v* ▷ **dirty**
dirtier *adj* ▷ **dirty**
dirties *v* ▷ **dirty**
dirtiest *adj* ▷ **dirty**
dirtily *adv* ▷ **dirty**
dirtiness *n* ▷ **dirty**
dirts *n* ▷ **dirt**
dirty *adj* (**dirtier, dirtiest**) covered or marked with dirt ▶ *v* (**dirties, dirtying, dirtied**) make dirty > **dirtily** *adv* > **dirtiness** *n*
dirtying *v* ▷ **dirty**
disabilities *n* ▷ **disability**
disability *n* (*pl* **-ties**) condition of being disabled
disable *v* (**-bles, -bling, -bled**) make ineffective, unfit, or incapable > **disablement** *n*
disabled *adj* lacking a physical power, such as the ability to walk ▶ *v* ▷ **disable**
disablement *n* ▷ **disable**
disables *v* ▷ **disable**
disabling *v* ▷ **disable**
disabuse *v* (**-buses, -busing, -bused**) (*foll. by* **of**) rid (someone) of a mistaken idea
disabused *v* ▷ **disabuse**
disabuses *v* ▷ **disabuse**
disabusing *v* ▷ **disabuse**
disadvantage *n* (*pl* **-s**) unfavourable or harmful circumstance > **disadvantageous** *adj* > **disadvantageously** *adv* > **disadvantageousness** *n*
disadvantaged *adj* socially or economically deprived
disadvantageous *adj* ▷ **disadvantage**
disadvantageously *adv* ▷ **disadvantage**
disadvantageousness *n* ▷ **disadvantage**
disadvantages *n* ▷ **disadvantage**
disaffected *adj* having lost loyalty to or affection for someone or something > **disaffectedly** *adv* > **disaffection** *n* (*pl* **-s**)
disaffectedly *adv* ▷ **disaffected**
disaffection *n* ▷ **disaffected**
disaffections *n* ▷ **disaffected**
disagree *v* (**-grees, -greeing, -greed**) argue or have different opinions > **disagreement** *n* (*pl* **-s**)
disagreeable *adj* unpleasant > **disagreeableness** *n* > **disagreeably** *adv*
disagreeableness *n* ▷ **disagreeable**
disagreeably *adv* ▷ **disagreeable**
disagreed *v* ▷ **disagree**
disagreeing *v* ▷ **disagree**
disagreement *n* ▷ **disagree**
disagreements *n* ▷ **disagree**
disagrees *v* ▷ **disagree**
disallow *v* (**-s, -ing, -ed**) reject as untrue or invalid
disallowed *v* ▷ **disallow**
disallowing *v* ▷ **disallow**
disallows *v* ▷ **disallow**
disappear *v* (**-s, -ing, -ed**) cease to be visible > **disappearance** *n* (*pl* **-s**)
disappearance *n* ▷ **disappear**
disappearances *n* ▷ **disappear**
disappeared *v* ▷ **disappear**
disappearing *v* ▷ **disappear**
disappears *v* ▷ **disappear**
disappoint *v* (**-s, -ing, -ed**) fail to meet the expectations or hopes of > **disappointingly** *adv*
disappointed *v* ▷ **disappoint**
disappointing *v* ▷ **disappoint**
disappointingly *adv* ▷ **disappoint**
disappointment *n* (*pl* **-s**) feeling of being disappointed
disappointments *n* ▷ **disappointment**
disappoints *v* ▷ **disappoint**
disapprobation *n* (*pl* **-s**) disapproval
disapprobations *n* ▷ **disapprobation**
disapproval *n* ▷ **disapprove**
disapprovals *n* ▷ **disapprove**
disapprove *v* (**-proves, -proving, -proved**) (*foll. by* **of**) consider wrong or bad > **disapproval** *n* (*pl* **-s**)
disapproved *v* ▷ **disapprove**
disapproves *v* ▷ **disapprove**
disapproving *v* ▷ **disapprove**
disarm *v* (**-s, -ing, -ed**) deprive of weapons > **disarmament** *n* (*pl* **-s**)
disarmament *n* ▷ **disarm**
disarmaments *n* ▷ **disarm**
disarmed *v* ▷ **disarm**
disarming *adj* removing hostility or suspicion ▶ *v* ▷ **disarm** > **disarmingly** *adv*
disarmingly *adv* ▷ **disarming**
disarms *v* ▷ **disarm**
disarrange *v* (**-ranges, -ranging, -ranged**) throw into disorder
disarranged *v* ▷ **disarrange**

disarranges *v* ▷ **disarrange**
disarranging *v* ▷ **disarrange**
disarray *n* (*pl* **-s**) confusion and lack of discipline
disarrays *n* ▷ **disarray**
disaster *n* (*pl* **-s**) occurrence that causes great distress or destruction > **disastrous** *adj* > **disastrously** *adv*
disasters *n* ▷ **disaster**
disastrous *adj* ▷ **disaster**
disastrously *adv* ▷ **disaster**
disavow *v* (**-s, -ing, -ed**) deny connection with or responsibility for > **disavowal** *n* (*pl* **-s**)
disavowal *n* ▷ **disavow**
disavowals *n* ▷ **disavow**
disavowed *v* ▷ **disavow**
disavowing *v* ▷ **disavow**
disavows *v* ▷ **disavow**
disband *v* (**-s, -ing, -ed**) (cause to) cease to function as a group
disbanded *v* ▷ **disband**
disbanding *v* ▷ **disband**
disbands *v* ▷ **disband**
disbelief *n* ▷ **disbelieve**
disbelieve *v* (**-lieves, -lieving, -lieved**) reject as false (*foll. by* **in**) > **disbelief** *n*
disbelieved *v* ▷ **disbelieve**
disbelieves *v* ▷ **disbelieve**
disbelieving *v* ▷ **disbelieve**
disburse *v* (**-burses, -bursing, -bursed**) pay out > **disbursement** *n* (*pl* **-s**)
disbursed *v* ▷ **disburse**
disbursement *n* ▷ **disburse**
disbursements *n* ▷ **disburse**
disburses *v* ▷ **disburse**
disbursing *v* ▷ **disburse**
disc *n* (*pl* **-s**) flat circular object ▷ **disk**
discard *v* (**-s, -ing, -ed**) get rid of (something or someone) as useless or undesirable
discarded *v* ▷ **discard**
discarding *v* ▷ **discard**
discards *v* ▷ **discard**
discern *v* (**-s, -ing, -ed**) see or be aware of (something) clearly > **discernible** *adj* > **discernibly** *adv* > **discernment** *n* (*pl* **-s**)
discerned *v* ▷ **discern**
discernible *adj* ▷ **discern**
discernibly *adv* ▷ **discern**
discerning *adj* having good judgment ▶ *v* ▷ **discern**
discernment *n* ▷ **discern**
discernments *n* ▷ **discern**
discerns *v* ▷ **discern**
discharge *v* (**-charges, -charging, -charged**) release, allow to go ▶ *n* (*pl* **-s**) substance that comes out from a place
discharged *v* ▷ **discharge**
discharges *v, n* ▷ **discharge**
discharging *v* ▷ **discharge**
disciple [diss-**sipe**-pl] *n* (*pl* **-s**) follower of the doctrines of a teacher, esp. Jesus Christ
disciples *n* ▷ **disciple**
disciplinarian *n* (*pl* **-s**) person who practises strict discipline
disciplinarians *n* ▷ **disciplinarian**
disciplinary *adj* ▷ **discipline**
discipline *n* (*pl* **-s**) practice of imposing strict rules of behaviour ▶ *v* (**-plines, -plining, -plined**) attempt to improve the behaviour of (oneself or another) by training or rules > **disciplinary** *adj*
disciplined *adj* able to behave and work in a controlled way ▶ *v* ▷ **discipline**
disciplines *n, v* ▷ **discipline**
disciplining *v* ▷ **discipline**
disclaimed *v* ▷ **disclaimer**
disclaimer *n* (*pl* **-s**) statement denying responsibility > **disclaim** *v* (**-s, -ing, -ed**)
disclaimers *n* ▷ **disclaimer**
disclaiming *v* ▷ **disclaimer**
disclaims *v* ▷ **disclaimer**
disclose *v* (**-closes, -closing, -closed**) make known > **disclosure** *n* (*pl* **-s**)
disclosed *v* ▷ **disclose**
discloses *v* ▷ **disclose**
disclosing *v* ▷ **disclose**
disclosure *n* ▷ **disclose**
disclosures *n* ▷ **disclose**
disco *n* (*pl* **-s**) nightclub where people dance to amplified pop records
discoloration *n* ▷ **discolour**
discolorations *n* ▷ **discolour**
discolour *v* (**-s, -ing, -ed**) change in colour, fade > **discoloration** *n* (*pl* **-s**)
discoloured *v* ▷ **discolour**
discolouring *v* ▷ **discolour**
discolours *v* ▷ **discolour**
discomfit *v* (**-s, -ing, -ed**) make uneasy or confused > **discomfiture** *n* (*pl* **-s**)
discomfited *v* ▷ **discomfit**
discomfiting *v* ▷ **discomfit**
discomfits *v* ▷ **discomfit**
discomfiture *n* ▷ **discomfit**
discomfitures *n* ▷ **discomfit**
discomfort *n* (*pl* **-s**) inconvenience, distress, or mild pain
discomforts *n* ▷ **discomfort**
discommode *v* (**-modes, -moding, -moded**) cause inconvenience to
discommoded *v* ▷ **discommode**

discommodes *v* ▷ **discommode**
discommoding *v* ▷ **discommode**
disconcert *v* (**-s, -ing, -ed**) embarrass or upset
disconcerted *v* ▷ **disconcert**
disconcerting *v* ▷ **disconcert**
disconcerts *v* ▷ **disconcert**
disconnect *v* (**-s, -ing, -ed**) undo or break the connection between (two things) > **disconnection** *n* (*pl* **-s**)
disconnected *adj* (of speech or ideas) not logically connected ▸ *v* ▷ **disconnect**
disconnecting *v* ▷ **disconnect**
disconnection *n* ▷ **disconnect**
disconnections *n* ▷ **disconnect**
disconnects *v* ▷ **disconnect**
disconsolate *adj* sad beyond comfort > **disconsolately** *adv*
disconsolately *adv* ▷ **disconsolate**
discontent *n* (*pl* **-s**) lack of contentment > **discontented** *adj* > **discontentedly** *adv*
discontented *adj* ▷ **discontent**
discontentedly *adv* ▷ **discontent**
discontents *n* ▷ **discontent**
discontinue *v* (**-nues, -nuing, -nued**) come or bring to an end
discontinued *v* ▷ **discontinue**
discontinues *v* ▷ **discontinue**
discontinuing *v* ▷ **discontinue**
discontinuities *n* ▷ **discontinuous**
discontinuity *n* ▷ **discontinuous**
discontinuous *adj* characterized by interruptions > **discontinuity** *n* (*pl* **-nuities**)
discord *n* (*pl* **-s**) lack of agreement or harmony between people > **discordant** *adj* > **discordantly** *adv* > **discordance** *n* (*pl* **-s**)
discordance *n* ▷ **discord**
discordances *n* ▷ **discord**
discordant *adj* ▷ **discord**
discordantly *adv* ▷ **discord**
discords *n* ▷ **discord**
discos *n* ▷ **disco**
discotheque *n* (*pl* **-s**) ▷ **disco**
discotheques *n* ▷ **discotheque**
discount *v* (**-s, -ing, -ed**) take no account of (something) because it is considered to be unreliable, prejudiced, or irrelevant ▸ *n* (*pl* **-s**) deduction from the full price of something
discounted *v* ▷ **discount**
discounting *v* ▷ **discount**
discounts *v, n* ▷ **discount**
discourage *v* (**-rages, -raging, -raged**) deprive of the will to persist in something > **discouragement** *n* (*pl* **-s**)
discouraged *v* ▷ **discourage**
discouragement *n* ▷ **discourage**
discouragements *n* ▷ **discourage**
discourages *v* ▷ **discourage**
discouraging *v* ▷ **discourage**
discourse *n* (*pl* **-s**) conversation ▸ *v* (**-ses, -sing, -sed**) (*foll. by* **on**) speak or write (about) at length
discoursed *v* ▷ **discourse**
discourses *n, v* ▷ **discourse**
discoursing *v* ▷ **discourse**
discourteous *adj* showing bad manners > **discourteously** *adv* > **discourtesy** *n* (*pl* **-esies**)
discourteously *adv* ▷ **discourteous**
discourtesies *n* ▷ **discourteous**
discourtesy *n* ▷ **discourteous**
discover *v* (**-s, -ing, -ed**) be the first to find or to find out about > **discoverer** *n* (*pl* **-s**)
discovered *v* ▷ **discover**
discoverer *n* ▷ **discover**
discoverers *n* ▷ **discover**
discoveries *n* ▷ **discovery**
discovering *v* ▷ **discover**
discovers *v* ▷ **discover**
discovery *n* (*pl* **-eries**) discovering
discredit *v* (**-s, -ing, -ed**) damage the reputation of ▸ *n* (*pl* **-s**) damage to someone's reputation
discreditable *adj* bringing shame
discredited *v* ▷ **discredit**
discrediting *v* ▷ **discredit**
discredits *v, n* ▷ **discredit**
discreet *adj* (**-er, -est**) careful to avoid embarrassment, esp. by keeping confidences secret > **discreetly** *adv* > **discreetness** *n* (*pl* **-es**)
discreeter *adj* ▷ **discreet**
discreetest *adj* ▷ **discreet**
discreetly *adv* ▷ **discreet**
discreetness *n* ▷ **discreet**
discreetnesses *n* ▷ **discreet**
discrepancies *n* ▷ **discrepancy**
discrepancy *n* (*pl* **-cies**) conflict or variation between facts, figures, or claims
discrete *adj* (**-r, -st**) separate, distinct > **discretely** *adv* > **discreteness** *n* (*pl* **-es**)
discretely *adv* ▷ **discrete**
discreteness *n* ▷ **discrete**
discretenesses *n* ▷ **discrete**
discreter *adj* ▷ **discrete**
discretest *adj* ▷ **discrete**
discretion *n* (*pl* **-s**) quality of behaving in a discreet way > **discretionary** *adj*
discretionary *adj* ▷ **discretion**
discretions *n* ▷ **discretion**
discriminate *v* (**-nates, -nating, -nated**) (*foll. by* **against** *or* **in favour of**) single

out (a particular person or group) for worse or better treatment than others > **discrimination** *n* (*pl* **-s**)
discriminated *v* ▷ **discriminate**
discriminates *v* ▷ **discriminate**
discriminating *adj* showing good taste and judgment ▶ *v* ▷ **discriminate**
discrimination *n* ▷ **discriminate**
discriminations *n* ▷ **discriminate**
discriminatory *adj* based on prejudice
discs *n* ▷ **disc**
discursive *adj* passing from one topic to another > **discursively** *adv* > **discursiveness** *n*
discursively *adv* ▷ **discursive**
discursiveness *n* ▷ **discursive**
discus *n* (*pl* **-es**) heavy disc-shaped object thrown in sports competitions
discuses *n* ▷ **discus**
discuss *v* (**-es, -ing, -ed**) consider (something) by talking it over > **discussion** *n* (*pl* **-s**)
discussed *v* ▷ **discuss**
discusses *v* ▷ **discuss**
discussing *v* ▷ **discuss**
discussion *n* ▷ **discuss**
discussions *n* ▷ **discuss**
disdain *n* feeling of superiority and dislike ▶ *v* (**-s, -ing, -ed**) refuse with disdain > **disdainful** *adj* > **disdainfully** *adv*
disdained *v* ▷ **disdain**
disdainful *adj* ▷ **disdain**
disdainfully *adv* ▷ **disdain**
disdaining *v* ▷ **disdain**
disdains *v* ▷ **disdain**
disease *n* (*pl* **-s**) illness, sickness > **diseased** *adj*
diseased *n* ▷ **disease**
diseases *n* ▷ **disease**
disembark *v* (**-s, -ing, -ed**) get off a ship, aircraft, or bus > **disembarkation** *n* (*pl* **-s**)
disembarkation *n* ▷ **disembark**
disembarkations *n* ▷ **disembark**
disembarked *v* ▷ **disembark**
disembarking *v* ▷ **disembark**
disembarks *v* ▷ **disembark**
disembodied *adj* lacking a body
disembowel *v* (**-els, -elling, -elled**) remove the entrails of
disembowelled *v* ▷ **disembowel**
disembowelling *v* ▷ **disembowel**
disembowels *v* ▷ **disembowel**
disenchanted *adj* disappointed and disillusioned > **disenchantment** *n* (*pl* **-s**)
disenchantment *n* ▷ **disenchant**
disenchantments *n* ▷ **disenchant**
disenfranchise, disfranchise *v* (**-ises, -ising, -ised**) deprive (someone) of the right to vote or of other rights of citizenship > **disenfranchisement** *n* (*pl* **-s**)
disenfranchised *v* ▷ **disenfranchise**
disenfranchisement *n* ▷ **disenfranchise**
disenfranchisements *n* ▷ **disenfranchise**
disenfranchises *v* ▷ **disenfranchise**
disenfranchising *v* ▷ **disenfranchise**
disengage *v* (**-gages, -gaging, -gaged**) release from a connection > **disengagement** *n* (*pl* **-s**)
disengaged *v* ▷ **disengage**
disengagement *n* ▷ **disengage**
disengagements *n* ▷ **disengage**
disengages *v* ▷ **disengage**
disengaging *v* ▷ **disengage**
disentangle *v* (**-tangles, -tangling, -tangled**) release from entanglement or confusion
disentangled *v* ▷ **disentangle**
disentangles *v* ▷ **disentangle**
disentangling *v* ▷ **disentangle**
disfavour *n* (*pl* **-s**) disapproval or dislike
disfavours *n* ▷ **disfavour**
disfigure *v* (**-gures, -guring, -gured**) spoil the appearance of > **disfigurement** *n* (*pl* **-s**)
disfigured *v* ▷ **disfigure**
disfigurement *n* ▷ **disfigure**
disfigurements *n* ▷ **disfigure**
disfigures *v* ▷ **disfigure**
disfiguring *v* ▷ **disfigure**
disfranchise *v* (**-ises, -ising, -ised**) ▷ **disenfranchise**
disfranchised *v* ▷ **disfranchise**
disfranchises *v* ▷ **disfranchise**
disfranchising *v* ▷ **disfranchise**
disgorge *v* (**-gorges, -gorging, -gorged**) empty out, discharge
disgorged *v* ▷ **disgorge**
disgorges *v* ▷ **disgorge**
disgorging *v* ▷ **disgorge**
disgrace *n* (*pl* **-s**) condition of shame, loss of reputation, or dishonour ▶ *v* (**-graces, -gracing, -graced**) bring shame upon (oneself or others) > **disgraceful** *adj* > **disgracefully** *adv*
disgraced *v* ▷ **disgrace**
disgraceful *adj* ▷ **disgrace**
disgracefully *adv* ▷ **disgrace**
disgraces *n, v* ▷ **disgrace**
disgracing *v* ▷ **disgrace**
disgruntled *adj* sulky or discontented > **disgruntlement** *n*
disgruntlement *n* ▷ **disgruntled**
disguise *v* (**-guises, -guising, -guised**) change the appearance or manner in order to conceal the identity of (someone or something) ▶ *n* (*pl* **-s**) mask, costume, or manner that

disguises
disguised *v* ▷ **disguise**
disguises *v, n* ▷ **disguise**
disguising *v* ▷ **disguise**
disgust *n* (*pl* **-s**) great loathing or distaste ▶ *v* (**-s, -ing, -ed**) sicken, fill with loathing
disgusted *v* ▷ **disgust**
disgusting *v* ▷ **disgust**
disgusts *v* ▷ **disgust**
dish *n* (*pl* **-es**) shallow container used for holding or serving food
dishabille [diss-a-**beel**] *n* (*pl* **-s**) ▷ **deshabille**
dishabilles *n* ▷ **dishabille**
dishcloth *n* (*pl* **-s**) cloth for washing dishes
dishcloths *n* ▷ **dishcloth**
dishearten *v* (**-s, -ing, -ed**) weaken or destroy the hope, courage, or enthusiasm of
disheartened *v* ▷ **dishearten**
disheartening *v* ▷ **dishearten**
disheartens *v* ▷ **dishearten**
dishes *n* ▷ **dish**
dishevelled *adj* (of a person's hair, clothes, or general appearance) disordered and untidy
dishonest *adj* not honest or fair > **dishonestly** *adv* > **dishonesty** *n* (*pl* **-ties**)
dishonesties *n* ▷ **dishonest**
dishonestly *adv* ▷ **dishonest**
dishonesty *n* ▷ **dishonest**
dishonour *v* (**-s, -ing, -ed**) treat with disrespect ▶ *n* (*pl* **-s**) lack of respect > **dishonourable** *adj* > **dishonourably** *adv*
dishonourable *adj* ▷ **dishonour**
dishonourably *adv* ▷ **dishonour**
dishonoured *v* ▷ **dishonour**
dishonouring *v* ▷ **dishonour**
dishonours *v, n* ▷ **dishonour**
disillusion *v* (**-s, -ing, -ed**) destroy the illusions or false ideas of (*also* **disillusionment**) ▶ *n* (*pl* **-s**) state of being disillusioned
disillusioned *v* ▷ **disillusion**
disillusioning *v* ▷ **disillusion**
disillusionment *n* ▷ **disillusion**
disillusionments *n* ▷ **disillusion**
disillusions *v, n* ▷ **disillusion**
disincentive *n* (*pl* **-s**) something that acts as a deterrent
disincentives *n* ▷ **disincentive**
disinclination *n* ▷ **disinclined**
disinclinations *n* ▷ **disinclined**
disinclined *adj* unwilling, reluctant > **disinclination** *n* (*pl* **-s**)
disinfect *v* (**-s, -ing, -ed**) rid of harmful germs, chemically > **disinfection** *n* (*pl* **-s**)
disinfectant *n* (*pl* **-s**) substance that destroys harmful germs
disinfectants *n* ▷ **disinfectant**
disinfected *v* ▷ **disinfect**
disinfecting *v* ▷ **disinfect**
disinfection *n* ▷ **disinfect**
disinfections *n* ▷ **disinfect**
disinfects *v* ▷ **disinfect**
disinformation *n* false information intended to mislead
disingenuous *adj* not sincere > **disingenuously** *adv* > **disingenuousness** *n*
disingenuously *adv* ▷ **disingenuous**
disingenuousness *n* ▷ **disingenuous**
disinherit *v* (**-s, -ing, -ed**) (LAW) deprive (an heir) of inheritance > **disinheritance** *n* (*pl* **-s**)
disinheritance *n* ▷ **disinherit**
disinheritances *n* ▷ **disinherit**
disinherited *v* ▷ **disinherit**
disinheriting *v* ▷ **disinherit**
disinherits *v* ▷ **disinherit**
disintegrate *v* (**-rates, -rating, -rated**) break up > **disintegration** *n* (*pl* **-s**)
disintegrated *v* ▷ **disintegrate**
disintegrates *v* ▷ **disintegrate**
disintegrating *v* ▷ **disintegrate**
disintegration *n* ▷ **disintegrate**
disintegrations *n* ▷ **disintegrate**
disinter *v* (**-ters, -terring, -terred**) dig up
disinterest *n* ▷ **disinterested**
disinterested *adj* free from bias or involvement > **disinterest** *n* > **disinterestedly** *adv* > **disinterestedness** *n*
disinterestedly *adv* ▷ **disinterested**
disinterestedness *n* ▷ **disinterested**
disinterred *v* ▷ **disinter**
disinterring *v* ▷ **disinter**
disinters *v* ▷ **disinter**
disjointed *adj* having no coherence, disconnected > **disjointedly** *adv*
disjointedly *adv* ▷ **disjointed**
disk *n* (*pl* **-s**) (COMPUTERS) storage device, consisting of a stack of plates coated with a magnetic layer, which rotates rapidly as a single unit
disks *n* ▷ **disk**
dislike *v* (**-likes, -liking, -liked**) consider unpleasant or disagreeable ▶ *n* (*pl* **-s**) feeling of not liking something or someone
disliked *v* ▷ **dislike**
dislikes *v, n* ▷ **dislike**
disliking *v* ▷ **dislike**
dislocate *v* (**-cates, -cating, -cated**) displace (a bone or joint) from its normal position > **dislocation** *n* (*pl* **-s**)
dislocated *v* ▷ **dislocate**
dislocates *v* ▷ **dislocate**

dislocating *v* ▷ **dislocate**
dislocation *n* ▷ **dislocate**
dislocations *n* ▷ **dislocate**
dislodge *v* (**-lodges, -lodging, -lodged**) remove (something) from a previously fixed position
dislodged *v* ▷ **dislodge**
dislodges *v* ▷ **dislodge**
dislodging *v* ▷ **dislodge**
disloyal *adj* not loyal, deserting one's allegiance > **disloyalty** *n* (*pl* **-ties**)
disloyalties *n* ▷ **disloyalty**
dismal *adj* gloomy and depressing > **dismally** *adv* > **dismalness** *n*
dismally *adv* ▷ **dismal**
dismalness *n* ▷ **dismal**
dismantle *v* (**-mantles, -mantling, -mantled**) take apart piece by piece
dismantled *v* ▷ **dismantle**
dismantles *v* ▷ **dismantle**
dismantling *v* ▷ **dismantle**
dismay *v* (**-s, -ing, -ed**) fill with alarm or depression ▶ *n* (*pl* **-s**) alarm mixed with sadness
dismayed *v* ▷ **dismay**
dismaying *v* ▷ **dismay**
dismays *v, n* ▷ **dismay**
dismember *v* (**-s, -ing, -ed**) remove the limbs of > **dismemberment** *n* (*pl* **-s**)
dismembered *v* ▷ **dismember**
dismembering *v* ▷ **dismember**
dismemberment *n* ▷ **dismember**
dismemberments *n* ▷ **dismember**
dismembers *v* ▷ **dismember**
dismiss *v* (**-es, -ing, -ed**) remove (an employee) from a job > **dismissal** *n* (*pl* **-s**)
dismissal *n* ▷ **dismiss**
dismissals *n* ▷ **dismiss**
dismissed *v* ▷ **dismiss**
dismisses *v* ▷ **dismiss**
dismissing *v* ▷ **dismiss**
dismissive *adj* scornful, contemptuous
dismount *v* (**-s, -ing, -ed**) get off a horse or bicycle
dismounted *v* ▷ **dismount**
dismounting *v* ▷ **dismount**
dismounts *v* ▷ **dismount**
disobedience *n* ▷ **disobey**
disobedient *adj* ▷ **disobey**
disobediently *adv* ▷ **disobey**
disobey *v* (**-s, -ing, -ed**) neglect or refuse to obey > **disobedient** *adj* > **disobediently** *adv* > **disobedience** *n*
disobeyed *v* ▷ **disobey**
disobeying *v* ▷ **disobey**
disobeys *v* ▷ **disobey**
disobliging *adj* unwilling to help
disorder *n* (*pl* **-s**) state of untidiness and disorganization
disordered *adj* untidy
disorderliness *n* ▷ **disorderly**
disorderly *adj* untidy and disorganized > **disorderliness** *n*
disorders *n* ▷ **disorder**
disorganization *n* ▷ **disorganize**
disorganizations *n* ▷ **disorganize**
disorganize *v* (**-nizes, -nizing, -nized**) disrupt the arrangement or system of > **disorganization** *n* (*pl* **-s**)
disorganized *v* ▷ **disorganize**
disorganizes *v* ▷ **disorganize**
disorganizing *v* ▷ **disorganize**
disorientate, disorient *v* (**-tates, -tating, -tated, -s, -ing, -ed**) cause (someone) to lose his or her bearings > **disorientation** *n* (*pl* **-s**)
disorientated *v* ▷ **disorientate**
disorientates *v* ▷ **disorientate**
disorientating *v* ▷ **disorientate**
disorientation *n* ▷ **disorientate**
disorientations *n* ▷ **disorientate**
disoriented *v* ▷ **disorientate**
disorienting *v* ▷ **disorientate**
disorients *v* ▷ **disorientate**
disown *v* (**-s, -ing, -ed**) deny any connection with (someone)
disowned *v* ▷ **disown**
disowning *v* ▷ **disown**
disowns *v* ▷ **disown**
disparage *v* (**-rages, -raging, -raged**) speak contemptuously of > **disparagement** *n* (*pl* **-s**)
disparaged *v* ▷ **disparage**
disparagement *n* ▷ **disparage**
disparagements *n* ▷ **disparage**
disparages *v* ▷ **disparage**
disparaging *v* ▷ **disparage**
disparate *adj* completely different > **disparately** *adv* > **disparateness** *n* > **disparity** *n* (*pl* **-ities**)
disparately *adv* ▷ **disparate**
disparateness *n* ▷ **disparate**
disparities *n* ▷ **disparate**
disparity *n* ▷ **disparate**
dispassionate *adj* not influenced by emotion > **dispassionately** *adv*
dispassionately *adv* ▷ **dispassionate**
dispatch *v* (**-es, -ing, -ed**) send off to a destination or to perform a task ▶ *n* (*pl* **-es**) official communication or report, sent in haste
dispatched *v* ▷ **dispatch**
dispatches *v, n* ▷ **dispatch**

dispatching *v* ▷ **dispatch**
dispel *v* (**-pels, -pelling, -pelled**) destroy or remove
dispelled *v* ▷ **dispel**
dispelling *v* ▷ **dispel**
dispels *v* ▷ **dispel**
dispensability *n* ▷ **dispensable**
dispensable *adj* not essential > **dispensability** *n*
dispensaries *n* ▷ **dispensary**
dispensary *n* (*pl* **-saries**) place where medicine is dispensed
dispensation *n* (*pl* **-s**) dispensing
dispensations *n* ▷ **dispensation**
dispense *v* (**-penses, -pensing, -pensed**) distribute in portions > **dispenser** *n* (*pl* **-s**)
dispensed *v* ▷ **dispense**
dispenser *n* ▷ **dispense**
dispensers *n* ▷ **dispense**
dispenses *v* ▷ **dispense**
dispensing *v* ▷ **dispense**
dispersal *n* ▷ **disperse**
dispersals *n* ▷ **disperse**
disperse *v* (**-perses, -persing, -persed**) scatter over a wide area > **dispersal, dispersion** *n* (*pl* **-s**)
dispersed *v* ▷ **disperse**
disperses *v* ▷ **disperse**
dispersing *v* ▷ **disperse**
dispersion *n* ▷ **disperse**
dispersions *n* ▷ **disperse**
dispirit *v* (**-s, -ing, -ed**) make downhearted
dispirited *v* ▷ **dispirit**
dispiriting *v* ▷ **dispirit**
dispirits *v* ▷ **dispirit**
displace *v* (**-places, -placing, -placed**) move from the usual location > **displacement** *n* (*pl* **-s**)
displaced *v* ▷ **displace**
displacement *n* ▷ **displace**
displacements *n* ▷ **displace**
displaces *v* ▷ **displace**
displacing *v* ▷ **displace**
display *v* (**-s, -ing, -ed**) make visible or noticeable ▶ *n* (*pl* **-s**) displaying
displayed *v* ▷ **display**
displaying *v* ▷ **display**
displays *v, n* ▷ **display**
displease *v* (**-ses, -sing, -sed**) annoy or upset > **displeasure** *n* (*pl* **-s**)
displeased *v* ▷ **displease**
displeases *v* ▷ **displease**
displeasing *v* ▷ **displease**
displeasure *n* ▷ **displease**
displeasures *n* ▷ **displease**
disport *v* (**-s, -ing, -ed**) indulge oneself in pleasure
disported *v* ▷ **disport**
disporting *v* ▷ **disport**
disports *v* ▷ **disport**
disposability *n* ▷ **disposable**
disposable *adj* designed to be thrown away after use > **disposability** *n*
disposal *n* (*pl* **-s**) getting rid of something
disposals *n* ▷ **disposal**
dispose *v* (**-poses, -posing, -posed**) place in a certain order
disposed *adj* willing or eager ▶ *v* ▷ **dispose**
disposes *v* ▷ **dispose**
disposing *v* ▷ **dispose**
disposition *n* (*pl* **-s**) person's usual temperament
dispositions *n* ▷ **disposition**
dispossess *v* (**-es, -ing, -ed**) (*foll. by* **of**) deprive (someone) of (a possession) > **dispossession** *n* (*pl* **-s**)
dispossessed *v* ▷ **dispossess**
dispossesses *v* ▷ **dispossess**
dispossessing *v* ▷ **dispossess**
dispossession *n* ▷ **dispossess**
dispossessions *n* ▷ **dispossess**
disproportion *n* (*pl* **-s**) lack of proportion or equality
disproportionate *adj* out of proportion > **disproportionately** *adv*
disproportionately *adv* ▷ **disproportionate**
disproportions *n* ▷ **disproportion**
disprove *v* (**-proves, -proving, -proved**) show (an assertion or claim) to be incorrect
disproved *v* ▷ **disprove**
disproves *v* ▷ **disprove**
disproving *v* ▷ **disprove**
dispute *n* (*pl* **-s**) disagreement, argument ▶ *v* (**-putes, -puting, -puted**) argue about (something)
disputed *v* ▷ **dispute**
disputes *n, v* ▷ **dispute**
disputing *v* ▷ **dispute**
disqualification *n* ▷ **disqualify**
disqualifications *n* ▷ **disqualify**
disqualified *v* ▷ **disqualify**
disqualifies *v* ▷ **disqualify**
disqualify *v* (**-fies, -fying, -fied**) stop (someone) officially from taking part in something for wrongdoing > **disqualification** *n* (*pl* **-s**)
disqualifying *v* ▷ **disqualify**
disquiet *n* (*pl* **-s**) feeling of anxiety ▶ *v* (**-s, -ing, -ed**) make (someone) anxious > **disquietude** *n* (*pl* **-s**)

disquieted *v* ▷ **disquiet**
disquieting *v* ▷ **disquiet**
disquiets *v, n* ▷ **disquiet**
disquietude *n* ▷ **disquiet**
disquietudes *n* ▷ **disquiet**
disregard *v* (**-s, -ing, -ed**) give little or no attention to ▶ *n* (*pl* **-s**) lack of attention or respect
disregarded *v* ▷ **disregard**
disregarding *v* ▷ **disregard**
disregards *v, n* ▷ **disregard**
disrepair *n* (*pl* **-s**) condition of being worn out or in poor working order
disrepairs *n* ▷ **disrepair**
disreputable *adj* having or causing a bad reputation > **disreputably** *adv*
disreputably *adv* ▷ **disreputable**
disrepute *n* (*pl* **-s**) loss or lack of good reputation
disreputes *n* ▷ **disrepute**
disrespect *n* (*pl* **-s**) lack of respect > **disrespectful** *adj* > **disrespectfully** *adv*
disrespectful *adj* ▷ **disrespect**
disrespectfully *adv* ▷ **disrespect**
disrespects *n* ▷ **disrespect**
disrobe *v* (**-robes, -robing, -robed**) undress
disrobed *v* ▷ **disrobe**
disrobes *v* ▷ **disrobe**
disrobing *v* ▷ **disrobe**
disrupt *v* (**-s, -ing, -ed**) interrupt the progress of > **disruption** *n* (*pl* **-s**) > **disruptive** *adj*
disrupted *v* ▷ **disrupt**
disrupting *v* ▷ **disrupt**
disruption *n* ▷ **disrupt**
disruptions *n* ▷ **disrupt**
disruptive *adj* ▷ **disrupt**
disrupts *v* ▷ **disrupt**
dissatisfaction *n* ▷ **dissatisfied**
dissatisfactions *n* ▷ **dissatisfied**
dissatisfied *adj* not pleased or contented > **dissatisfaction** *n* (*pl* **-s**)
dissect *v* (**-s, -ing, -ed**) cut open (a corpse) to examine it > **dissection** *n* (*pl* **-s**)
dissected *v* ▷ **dissect**
dissecting *v* ▷ **dissect**
dissection *n* ▷ **dissect**
dissections *n* ▷ **dissect**
dissects *v* ▷ **dissect**
dissemble *v* (**-bles, -bling, -bled**) conceal one's real motives or emotions by pretence
dissembled *v* ▷ **dissemble**
dissembles *v* ▷ **dissemble**
dissembling *v* ▷ **dissemble**
disseminate *v* (**-nates, -nating, -nated**) spread (information) > **dissemination** *n* (*pl* **-s**)
disseminated *v* ▷ **disseminate**
disseminates *v* ▷ **disseminate**
disseminating *v* ▷ **disseminate**
dissemination *n* ▷ **disseminate**
disseminations *n* ▷ **disseminate**
dissension *n* ▷ **dissent**
dissensions *n* ▷ **dissent**
dissent *v* (**-s, -ing, -ed**) disagree ▶ *n* (*pl* **-s**) disagreement > **dissension** *n* (*pl* **-s**) > **dissenter** *n* (*pl* **-s**)
dissented *v* ▷ **dissent**
dissenter *n* ▷ **dissent**
dissenters *n* ▷ **dissent**
dissenting *v* ▷ **dissent**
dissents *v* ▷ **dissent**
dissertation *n* (*pl* **-s**) written thesis, usu. required for a higher university degree
dissertations *n* ▷ **dissertation**
disservice *n* (*pl* **-s**) harmful action
disservices *n* ▷ **disservice**
dissidence *n* ▷ **dissident**
dissidences *n* ▷ **dissident**
dissident *n* (*pl* **-s**) person who disagrees with and criticizes the government ▶ *adj* disagreeing with the government > **dissidence** *n* (*pl* **-s**)
dissidents *n* ▷ **dissident**
dissimilar *adj* not alike, different > **dissimilarity** *n* (*pl* **-ities**)
dissimilarities *n* ▷ **dissimilar**
dissimilarity *n* ▷ **dissimilar**
dissimulate *v* (**-lates, -lating, -lated**) conceal one's real feelings by pretence > **dissimulation** *n* (*pl* **-s**)
dissimulated *v* ▷ **dissimulate**
dissimulates *v* ▷ **dissimulate**
dissimulating *v* ▷ **dissimulate**
dissimulation *n* ▷ **dissimulate**
dissimulations *n* ▷ **dissimulate**
dissipate *v* (**-pates, -pating, -pated**) waste or squander > **dissipation** *n* (*pl* **-s**)
dissipated *adj* showing signs of overindulgence in alcohol and other physical pleasures ▶ *v* ▷ **dissipate**
dissipates *v* ▷ **dissipate**
dissipating *v* ▷ **dissipate**
dissipation *n* ▷ **dissipate**
dissipations *n* ▷ **dissipate**
dissociate *v* (**-ciates, -ciating, -ciated**) regard or treat as separate > **dissociation** *n* (*pl* **-s**)
dissociated *v* ▷ **dissociate**
dissociates *v* ▷ **dissociate**
dissociating *v* ▷ **dissociate**
dissociation *n* ▷ **dissociate**
dissociations *n* ▷ **dissociate**

dissolute *adj* leading an immoral life **> dissolutely** *adv* **> dissoluteness** *n*
dissolutely *adv* ▷ **dissolute**
dissoluteness *n* ▷ **dissolute**
dissolution *n* (*pl* **-s**) official breaking up of an organization or institution, such as Parliament
dissolutions *n* ▷ **dissolution**
dissolve *v* (**-solves, -solving, -solved**) (cause to) become liquid
dissolved *v* ▷ **dissolve**
dissolves *v* ▷ **dissolve**
dissolving *v* ▷ **dissolve**
dissonance *n* (*pl* **-s**) lack of agreement or harmony **> dissonant** *adj*
dissonances *n* ▷ **dissonance**
dissonant *adj* ▷ **dissonance**
dissuade *v* (**-suades, -suading, -suaded**) deter (someone) by persuasion from doing something **> dissuasion** *n* (*pl* **-s**)
dissuaded *v* ▷ **dissuade**
dissuades *v* ▷ **dissuade**
dissuading *v* ▷ **dissuade**
dissuasion *n* ▷ **dissuade**
dissuasions *n* ▷ **dissuade**
distaff *n* (*pl* **-s**) rod on which wool etc. is wound for spinning
distaffs *n* ▷ **distaff**
distance *n* (*pl* **-s**) space between two points
distances *n* ▷ **distance**
distant *adj* far apart **> distantly** *adv*
distantly *adv* ▷ **distant**
distaste *n* (*pl* **-s**) dislike, disgust
distasteful *adj* unpleasant, offensive **> distastefulness** *n*
distastefulness *n* ▷ **distasteful**
distastes *n* ▷ **distaste**
distemper[1] *n* (*pl* **-s**) highly contagious viral disease of dogs
distemper[2] *n* (*pl* **-s**) paint mixed with water, glue, etc., used for painting walls
distempers *n* ▷ **distemper**[1, 2]
distend *v* (**-s, -ing, -ed**) (of part of the body) swell **> distension** *n* (*pl* **-s**)
distended *v* ▷ **distend**
distending *v* ▷ **distend**
distends *v* ▷ **distend**
distension *n* ▷ **distend**
distensions *n* ▷ **distend**
distil *v* (**-tils, -tilling, -tilled**) subject to or obtain by distillation
distillate *n* ▷ **distillation**
distillates *n* ▷ **distillation**
distillation *n* (*pl* **-s**) process of evaporating a liquid and condensing its vapour (*also* **distillate**) (*pl* **-s**)
distillations *n* ▷ **distillation**
distilled *v* ▷ **distil**
distiller *n* (*pl* **-s**) person or company that makes strong alcoholic drink, esp. whisky
distilleries *n* ▷ **distillery**
distillers *n* ▷ **distiller**
distillery *n* (*pl* **-leries**) place where a strong alcoholic drink, esp. whisky, is made
distilling *v* ▷ **distil**
distils *v* ▷ **distil**
distinct *adj* (**-er, -est**) not the same **> distinctly** *adv* **> distinctness** *n* (*pl* **-es**)
distincter *adj* ▷ **distinct**
distinctest *adj* ▷ **distinct**
distinction *n* (*pl* **-s**) act of distinguishing
distinctions *n* ▷ **distinction**
distinctive *adj* easily recognizable **> distinctively** *adv* **> distinctiveness** *n*
distinctively *adv* ▷ **distinctive**
distinctiveness *n* ▷ **distinctive**
distinctly *adv* ▷ **distinct**
distinctness *n* ▷ **distinct**
distinctnesses *n* ▷ **distinct**
distinguish *v* (**-es, -ing, -ed**) (*usu. foll. by* **between**) make, show, or recognize a difference (between) **> distinguishable** *adj*
distinguishable *adj* ▷ **distinguish**
distinguished *adj* dignified in appearance ▶ *v* ▷ **distinguish**
distinguishes *v* ▷ **distinguish**
distinguishing *v* ▷ **distinguish**
distort *v* (**-s, -ing, -ed**) misrepresent (the truth or facts) **> distortion** *n* (*pl* **-s**)
distorted *v* ▷ **distort**
distorting *v* ▷ **distort**
distortion *n* ▷ **distort**
distortions *n* ▷ **distort**
distorts *v* ▷ **distort**
distract *v* (**-s, -ing, -ed**) draw the attention of (a person) away from something **> distraction** *n* (*pl* **-s**)
distracted *adj* unable to concentrate, preoccupied ▶ *v* ▷ **distract > distractedly** *adv*
distractedly *adv* ▷ **distracted**
distracting *v* ▷ **distract**
distraction *n* ▷ **distract**
distractions *n* ▷ **distract**
distracts *v* ▷ **distract**
distrait [diss-**tray**] *adj* absent-minded or preoccupied
distraught [diss-**trawt**] *adj* extremely anxious or agitated
distress *n* (*pl* **-es**) extreme unhappiness ▶ *v* (**-es, -ing, -ed**) upset badly **> distressing** *adj*

> **distressingly** *adv*

distressed *adj* extremely upset ▶ *v* ▷ **distress**

distresses *n, v* ▷ **distress**

distressing *v, adj* ▷ **distress**

distressingly *adv* ▷ **distress**

distribute *v* (**-butes, -buting, -buted**) hand out or deliver > **distributive** *adj* > **distributively** *adv*

distributed *v* ▷ **distribute**

distributes *v* ▷ **distribute**

distributing *v* ▷ **distribute**

distribution *n* (*pl* **-s**) distributing

distributions *n* ▷ **distribution**

distributive *adj* ▷ **distribute**

distributively *adv* ▷ **distribute**

distributor *n* (*pl* **-s**) wholesaler who distributes goods to retailers in a specific area

distributors *n* ▷ **distributor**

district *n* (*pl* **-s**) area of land regarded as an administrative or geographical unit

districts *n* ▷ **district**

distrust *v* (**-s, -ing, -ed**) regard as untrustworthy ▶ *n* (*pl* **-s**) feeling of suspicion or doubt > **distrustful** *adj*

distrusted *v* ▷ **distrust**

distrustful *adj* ▷ **distrust**

distrusting *v* ▷ **distrust**

distrusts *v, n* ▷ **distrust**

disturb *v* (**-s, -ing, -ed**) intrude on > **disturbance** *n* (*pl* **-s**) > **disturbing** *adj* > **disturbingly** *adv*

disturbance *n* ▷ **disturb**

disturbances *n* ▷ **disturb**

disturbed *adj* (PSYCHIATRY) emotionally upset or maladjusted ▶ *v* ▷ **disturb**

disturbing *v, adj* ▷ **disturb**

disturbingly *adv* ▷ **disturb**

disturbs *v* ▷ **disturb**

disunite *v* (**-nites, -niting, -nited**) cause disagreement among > **disunity** *n* (*pl* **-ities**)

disunited *v* ▷ **disunite**

disunites *v* ▷ **disunite**

disunities *n* ▷ **disunite**

disuniting *v* ▷ **disunite**

disunity *n* ▷ **disunite**

disuse *n* (*pl* **-s**) state of being no longer used > **disused** *adj*

disused *adj* ▷ **disuse**

disuses *n* ▷ **disuse**

ditch *n* (*pl* **-es**) narrow channel dug in the earth for drainage or irrigation ▶ *v* (**-es, -ing, -ed**) (*Slang*) abandon

ditched *v* ▷ **ditch**

ditches *n, v* ▷ **ditch**

ditching *v* ▷ **ditch**

dither *v* (**-s, -ing, -ed**) be uncertain or indecisive ▶ *n* (*pl* **-s**) state of indecision or agitation > **ditherer** *n* (*pl* **-s**) > **dithery** *adj* > **ditheriness** *n*

dithered *v* ▷ **dither**

ditheriness *n* ▷ **dither**

dithering *v* ▷ **dither**

dithers *v, n* ▷ **dither**

dithery *adj* ▷ **dither**

ditties *n* ▷ **ditty**

ditto *n* (*pl* **-tos**) the same ▶ *adv* in the same way

dittos *n* ▷ **ditto**

ditty *n* (*pl* **-ties**) short simple poem or song

diuretic [die-yoor-**et**-ik] *n* (*pl* **-s**) drug that increases the flow of urine

diuretics *n* ▷ **diuretic**

diurnal [die-**urn**-al] *adj* happening during the day or daily > **diurnally** *adv*

diurnally *adv* ▷ **diurnal**

diva *n* (*pl* **-s**) distinguished female singer

divan *n* (*pl* **-s**) low backless bed

divans *n* ▷ **divan**

divas *n* ▷ **diva**

dive *v* (**dives, diving, dived**) plunge headfirst into water (*foll. by* **in** *or* **into**) ▶ *n* (*pl* **-s**) diving

dived *v* ▷ **dive**

diver *n* (*pl* **-s**) person who works or explores underwater

diverge *v* (**-verges, -verging, -verged**) separate and go in different directions > **divergence** *n* (*pl* **-s**) > **divergent** *adj*

diverged *v* ▷ **diverge**

divergence *n* ▷ **diverge**

divergences *n* ▷ **diverge**

divergent *adj* ▷ **diverge**

diverges *v* ▷ **diverge**

diverging *v* ▷ **diverge**

divers *adj* (*Old-fashioned*) various ▶ *n* ▷ **diver**

diverse *adj* having variety, assorted > **diversely** *adv* > **diversify** *v* (**-fies, -fying, -fied**) > **diversification** *n* (*pl* **-s**)

diversely *adv* ▷ **diverse**

diversification *n* ▷ **diverse**

diversifications *n* ▷ **diverse**

diversified *v* ▷ **diverse**

diversifies *v* ▷ **diverse**

diversify *v* ▷ **diverse**

diversifying *v* ▷ **diverse**

diversion *n* (*pl* **-s**) official detour used by traffic when a main route is closed > **diversionary** *adj*

diversionary *adj* ▷ **diversion**

diversions *n* ▷ **diversion**

diversities *n* ▷ **diversity**

diversity *n* (*pl* **-ties**) quality of being different or varied
divert *v* (**-s, -ing, -ed**) change the direction of
diverted *v* ▷ **divert**
diverting *v* ▷ **divert**
diverts *v* ▷ **divert**
dives *v, n* ▷ **dive**
divest *v* (**-s, -ing, -ed**) strip (of clothes)
divested *v* ▷ **divest**
divesting *v* ▷ **divest**
divests *v* ▷ **divest**
divide *v* (**-vides, -viding, -vided**) separate into parts ▶ *n* (*pl* **-s**) division, split
divided *v* ▷ **divide**
dividend *n* (*pl* **-s**) sum of money representing part of the profit made, paid by a company to its shareholders
dividends *n* ▷ **dividend**
divider *n* (*pl* **-s**) screen used to divide a room into separate areas ▶ *pl* compasses with two pointed arms, used for measuring or dividing lines
dividers *n* ▷ **divider**
divides *v, n* ▷ **divide**
dividing *v* ▷ **divide**
divination *n* (*pl* **-s**) art of discovering future events, as though by supernatural powers
divinations *n* ▷ **divine**
divine *adj* (**-r, -st**) of God or a god ▶ *v* (**-nes, -ning, -ned**) discover (something) by intuition or guessing > **divinely** *adv*
divined *v* ▷ **divine**
divinely *adv* ▷ **divine**
diviner *adj* ▷ **divine**
divines *v* ▷ **divine**
divinest *adj* ▷ **divine**
diving *v* ▷ **dive**
divining *v* ▷ **divine**
divinities *n* ▷ **divinity**
divinity *n* study of religion (*pl* **-ties**)
divisibility *n* ▷ **divisible**
divisible *adj* > **divisibility** *n*
division *n* (*pl* **-s**) dividing, sharing out
divisional *adj* of a division in an organization > **divisionally** *adv*
divisionally *adv* ▷ **divisional**
divisions *n* ▷ **division**
divisive *adj* tending to cause disagreement > **divisively** *adv* > **divisiveness** *n*
divisively *adv* ▷ **divisive**
divisiveness *n* ▷ **divisive**
divisor *n* (*pl* **-s**) number to be divided into another number
divisors *n* ▷ **divisor**
divorce *n* (*pl* **-s**) legal ending of a marriage ▶ *v* (**-ces, -cing, -ced**) legally end one's marriage (to)
divorcé *n* ▷ **divorcée**
divorced *v* ▷ **divorce**
divorcée, *masc* **divorcé** *n* (*pl* **-s**) person who is divorced
divorcées *n* ▷ **divorcée**
divorces *n, v* ▷ **divorce**
divorcés *n* ▷ **divorcée**
divorcing *v* ▷ **divorce**
divulge *v* (**-ges, -ging, -ged**) make known, disclose > **divulgence** *n* (*pl* **-s**)
divulged *v* ▷ **divulge**
divulgence *n* ▷ **divulge**
divulgences *n* ▷ **divulge**
divulges *v* ▷ **divulge**
divulging *v* ▷ **divulge**
dizzied *v* ▷ **dizzy**
dizzier *adj* ▷ **dizzy**
dizzies *v* ▷ **dizzy**
dizziest *adj* ▷ **dizzy**
dizzily *adv* ▷ **dizzy**
dizziness *n* ▷ **dizzy**
dizzy *adj* (**-zier, -ziest**) having or causing a whirling sensation ▶ *v* (**-zies, -zying, -zied**) make dizzy > **dizzily** *adv* > **dizziness** *n*
dizzying *v* ▷ **dizzy**
do *v* (**does, doing, did, done**) perform or complete (a deed or action) ▶ *n* (*pl* **dos, do's**) (*Informal*) party, celebration
docile *adj* (**-r, -st**) (of a person or animal) easily controlled > **docilely** *adv* > **docility** *n* (*pl* **-ties**)
docilely *adv* ▷ **docile**
dociler *adj* ▷ **docile**
docilest *adj* ▷ **docile**
docilities *n* ▷ **docile**
docility *n* ▷ **docile**
dock¹ *n* (*pl* **-s**) enclosed area of water where ships are loaded, unloaded, or repaired ▶ *v* (**-s, -ing, -ed**) bring or be brought into dock
dock² *v* (**docks, docking, docked**) deduct money from (a person's wages)
dock³ *n* (*pl* **-s**) enclosed space in a court of law where the accused person sits or stands
dock⁴ *n* (*pl* **-s**) weed with broad leaves
docked *v* ▷ **dock**
docker *n* (*pl* **-s**) (BRIT) person employed to load and unload ships
dockers *n* ▷ **docker**
docket *n* (*pl* **dockets**) label on a package or other delivery, stating contents, delivery instructions, etc.
dockets *n* ▷ **docket**
docking *v* ▷ **dock**
docks *n* ▷ **dock¹, ³, ⁴** ▶ *v* ▷ **dock¹, ²**

dockyard *n* (*pl* **-s**) place where ships are built or repaired
dockyards *n* ▷ **dockyard**
doctor *n* (*pl* **-s**) person licensed to practise medicine ▶ *v* (**-s, -ing, -ed**) alter in order to deceive > **doctoral** *adj*
doctoral *adj* ▷ **doctor**
doctorate *n* (*pl* **-s**) highest academic degree in any field of knowledge
doctorates *n* ▷ **doctorate**
doctored *v* ▷ **doctor**
doctoring *v* ▷ **doctor**
doctors *n*, *v* ▷ **doctor**
doctrinaire *adj* stubbornly insistent on the application of a theory without regard to practicality
doctrinal *adj* of doctrines > **doctrinally** *adv*
doctrinally *adv* ▷ **doctrinal**
doctrine *n* (*pl* **-s**) body of teachings of a religious, political, or philosophical group
doctrines *n* ▷ **doctrine**
document *n* (*pl* **-s**) piece of paper providing an official record of something ▶ *v* (**-s, -ing, -ed**) record or report (something) in detail > **documentation** *n* (*pl* **-s**)
documentaries *n* ▷ **documentary**
documentary *n* (*pl* **-ries**) film or television programme presenting the facts about a particular subject ▶ *adj* (of evidence) based on documents
documentation *n* ▷ **document**
documentations *n* ▷ **document**
documented *v* ▷ **document**
documenting *v* ▷ **document**
documents *n*, *v* ▷ **document**
dodder *v* (**-s, -ing, -ed**) move unsteadily > **doddery** *adj* (**-rier, -riest**)
doddered *v* ▷ **dodder**
dodderier *adj* ▷ **dodder**
dodderiest *adj* ▷ **dodder**
doddering *v* ▷ **dodder**
dodders *v* ▷ **dodder**
doddery *adj* ▷ **dodder**
dodecagon [doe-**deck**-a-gon] *n* (*pl* **-s**) geometric figure with twelve sides
dodecagons *n* ▷ **dodecagon**
dodge *v* (**dodges, dodging, dodged**) avoid (a blow, being seen, etc.) by moving suddenly ▶ *n* (*pl* **-s**) cunning or deceitful trick
dodged *v* ▷ **dodge**
dodger *n* (*pl* **-s**) person who evades a responsibility or duty
dodgers *n* ▷ **dodger**
dodges *v*, *n* ▷ **dodge**
dodgier *adj* ▷ **dodgy**
dodgiest *adj* ▷ **dodgy**
dodging *v* ▷ **dodge**
dodgy *adj* (**-gier, -giest**) (*Informal*) dangerous, risky
dodo *n* (*pl* **-s, -es**) large flightless extinct bird
dodoes *n* ▷ **dodo**
dodos *n* ▷ **dodo**
doe *n* (*pl* **-s**) female deer, hare, or rabbit
does *n* ▷ **doe** ▶ *v* ▷ **do**
doesn't does not
doff *v* (**-s, -ing, -ed**) take off or lift (one's hat) in polite greeting
doffed *v* ▷ **doff**
doffing *v* ▷ **doff**
doffs *v* ▷ **doff**
dog *n* (*pl* **-s**) domesticated four-legged mammal of many different breeds ▶ *v* (**dogs, dogging, dogged**) follow (someone) closely
dogcart *n* (*pl* **-s**) light horse-drawn two-wheeled cart
dogcarts *n* ▷ **dogcart**
doge [**doje**] *n* (*pl* **-s**) (formerly) chief magistrate of Venice or Genoa
dogeared *adj* (of a book) having pages folded down at the corner
doges *n* ▷ **doge**
dogfight *n* (*pl* **-s**) close-quarters combat between fighter aircraft
dogfights *n* ▷ **dogfight**
dogfish *n* (*pl* **-es**) small shark
dogfishes *n* ▷ **dogfish**
dogged [**dog**-gid] *adj* obstinately determined ▶ *v* ▷ **dog** > **doggedly** *adv* > **doggedness** *n* (*pl* **-es**)
doggedly *adv* ▷ **dogged**
doggedness *n* ▷ **dogged**
doggednesses *n* ▷ **dogged**
doggerel *n* (*pl* **-s**) poorly written poetry, usu. comic
doggerels *n* ▷ **doggerel**
doggie *n* ▷ **doggy**
doggies *n* ▷ **doggy**
dogging *v* ▷ **dog**
doggo *adv* (*Informal*) in hiding and keeping quiet
doggy, doggie *n* (*pl* **-gies**) child's word for a dog
doghouse *n* (*pl* **-s**) (US) kennel
doghouses *n* ▷ **doghouse**
dogleg *n* (*pl* **-s**) sharp bend
doglegs *n* ▷ **dogleg**
dogma *n* (*pl* **-s**) doctrine or system of doctrines proclaimed by authority as true > **dogmatic** *adj* habitually stating one's opinions forcefully or arrogantly > **dogmatically** *adv*

> **dogmatism** *n*
dogmas *n* ▷ **dogma**
dogs *n*, *v* ▷ **dog**
dogsbodies *n* ▷ **dogsbody**
dogsbody *n* (*pl* **-bodies**) (*Informal*) person who carries out boring tasks for others

doh *interj*. Doh is a sound people make when things go wrong. Doh scores 7 points.

doilies *n* ▷ **doily**
doily *n* (*pl* **-lies**) decorative lacy paper mat, laid on a plate
doing *v* ▷ **do**
doldrums *pl n* depressed state of mind
dole *n* (*pl* **-s**) (BRIT, AUST & NZ) (*Informal*) money received from the state while unemployed ▶ *v* (**doles, doling, doled**) (*foll. by* **out**) distribute in small quantities
doled *v* ▷ **dole**
doleful *adj* dreary, unhappy > **dolefully** *adv* > **dolefulness** *n*
dolefully *adv* ▷ **doleful**
dolefulness *n* ▷ **doleful**
doles *v*, *n* ▷ **dole**
doling *v* ▷ **dole**
doll *n* (*pl* **-s**) small model of a human being, used as a toy
dollar *n* (*pl* **-s**) standard monetary unit of many countries
dollars *n* ▷ **dollar**
dollies *n* ▷ **dolly**
dollop *n* (*pl* **-s**) (*Informal*) lump (of food)
dollops *n* ▷ **dollop**
dolls *n* ▷ **doll**
dolly *n* (*pl* **-lies**) child's word for a doll
dolmen *n* (*pl* **-s**) prehistoric monument consisting of a horizontal stone supported by vertical stones
dolmens *n* ▷ **dolmen**
dolomite *n* (*pl* **-s**) mineral consisting of calcium magnesium carbonate
dolomites *n* ▷ **dolomite**
dolorous *adj* sad, mournful > **dolorously** *adv*
dolorously *adv* ▷ **dolorous**
dolphin *n* (*pl* **-s**) sea mammal of the whale family, with a beaklike snout
dolphinaria *n* ▷ **dolphinarium**
dolphinarium *n* (*pl* **-ariums, -aria**) aquarium for dolphins
dolphinariums *n* ▷ **dolphinarium**
dolphins *n* ▷ **dolphin**
dolt *n* (*pl* **-s**) stupid person > **doltish** *adj* > **doltishness** *n*
doltish *adj* ▷ **dolt**
doltishness *n* ▷ **dolt**
dolts *n* ▷ **dolt**
domain *n* (*pl* **-s**) field of knowledge or activity
domains *n* ▷ **domain**
dome *n* (*pl* **-s**) rounded roof built on a circular base > **domed** *adj*
domes *n* ▷ **dome**
domestic *adj* of one's own country or a specific country ▶ *n* (*pl* **-s**) person whose job is to do housework in someone else's house > **domestically** *adv* > **domesticity** *n*
domestically *adv* ▷ **domestic**
domesticate *v* (**-cates, -cating, -cated**) bring or keep (a wild animal or plant) under control or cultivation > **domestication** *n* (*pl* **-s**)
domesticated *v* ▷ **domesticate**
domesticates *v* ▷ **domesticate**
domesticating *v* ▷ **domesticate**
domestication *n* ▷ **domesticate**
domestications *n* ▷ **domesticate**
domesticity *n* ▷ **domestic**
domestics *n* ▷ **domestic**
domicile [**dom**-miss-ile] *n* (*pl* **-s**) place where one lives
domiciles *n* ▷ **domicile**
dominance *n* ▷ **dominant**
dominances *n* ▷ **dominant**
dominant *adj* having authority or influence > **dominance** *n* (*pl* **-s**)
dominate *v* (**-nates, -nating, -nated**) control or govern > **domination** *n* (*pl* **-s**)
dominated *v* ▷ **dominate**
dominates *v* ▷ **dominate**
dominating *v* ▷ **dominate**
domination *n* ▷ **dominate**
dominations *n* ▷ **dominate**
domineering *adj* forceful and arrogant
dominion *n* (*pl* **-s**) control or authority
dominions *n* ▷ **dominion**
domino *n* (*pl* **-noes**) small rectangular block marked with dots, used in dominoes ▶ *pl* game in which dominoes with matching halves are laid together
dominoes *n* ▷ **domino**
don[1] *v* (**dons, donning, donned**) put on (clothing)
don[2] *n* (*pl* **-s**) (BRIT) member of the teaching staff at a university or college
donate *v* (**-nates, -nating, -nated**) give, esp. to a charity or organization
donated *v* ▷ **donate**
donates *v* ▷ **donate**
donating *v* ▷ **donate**
donation *n* (*pl* **-s**) donating
donations *n* ▷ **donation**
done *v* ▷ **do**

donga [**dong**-ga] *n* (*pl* **-s**) (S AFR, AUST & NZ) steep-sided gully created by soil erosion
dongas *n* ▷ **donga**
donkey *n* (*pl* **-s**) long-eared member of the horse family
donkeys *n* ▷ **donkey**
donkeywork *n* (*pl* **-s**) tedious hard work
donkeyworks *n* ▷ **donkeywork**
donned *v* ▷ **don¹**
donning *v* ▷ **don¹**
donnish *adj* serious and academic > **donnishness** *n* (*pl* **-es**)
donnishness *n* ▷ **donnish**
donnishnesses *n* ▷ **donnish**
donor *n* (*pl* **-s**) (MED) person who gives blood or organs for use in the treatment of another person
donors *n* ▷ **donor**
dons *v* ▷ **don¹** ▶ *n* ▷ **don²**
doodle *v* (**-dles, -dling, -dled**) scribble or draw aimlessly ▶ *n* (*pl* **-s**) shape or picture drawn aimlessly
doodled *v* ▷ **doodle**
doodles *v, n* ▷ **doodle**
doodling *v* ▷ **doodle**
doom *n* (*pl* **-s**) death or a terrible fate ▶ *v* (**-s, -ing, -ed**) destine or condemn to death or a terrible fate
doomed *v* ▷ **doom**
dooming *v* ▷ **doom**
dooms *n, v* ▷ **doom**
doomsday *n* (*pl* **-s**) (CHRISTIANITY) day on which the Last Judgment will occur
doomsdays *n* ▷ **doomday**
door *n* (*pl* **-s**) hinged or sliding panel for closing the entrance to a building, room, etc.
doormat *n* (*pl* **-s**) mat for wiping dirt from shoes before going indoors
doormats *n* ▷ **doormat**
doors *n* ▷ **door**
doorway *n* (*pl* **-s**) opening into a building or room
doorways *n* ▷ **doorway**
dope *n* (*pl* **-s**) (*Slang*) illegal drug, usu. cannabis ▶ *v* (**dopes, doping, doped**) give a drug to, esp. in order to improve performance in a race
doped *v* ▷ **dope**
dopes *n, v* ▷ **dope**
dopey, dopy (**dopier, dopiest**) *adj* half-asleep, drowsy
dopier *adj* ▷ **dopey**
dopiest *adj* ▷ **dopey**
doping *v* ▷ **dope**
dopy *adj* ▷ **dopey**
dorb *n* ▷ **dorba**
dorba *n* (*pl* **-s**) (AUST) (*Slang*) stupid, inept, or clumsy person (*also* **dorb**) (*pl* **-s**)
dorbas *n* ▷ **dorba**
dorbs *n* ▷ **dorba**
dories *n* ▷ **dory**
dork *n* (*pl* **-s**) (*Slang*) stupid person
dorks *n* ▷ **dork**
dormancy *n* ▷ **dormant**
dormant *adj* temporarily quiet, inactive, or not being used > **dormancy** *n*
dormer *n* (*pl* **-s**) window that sticks out from a sloping roof
dormers *n* ▷ **dormer**
dormice *n* ▷ **dormouse**
dormitories *n* ▷ **dormitory**
dormitory *n* (*pl* **-ries**) large room, esp. at a school, containing several beds
dormouse *n* (*pl* **-mice**) small mouselike rodent with a furry tail
dorp *n* (*pl* **-s**) (S AFR) small town
dorps *n* ▷ **dorp**
dorsal *adj* of or on the back
dory *n* (*pl* **-ries**) spiny-finned edible sea fish
dos *n* ▷ **do**
do's *n* ▷ **do**
dosage *n* (*pl* **-s**) size of a dose
dosages *n* ▷ **dosage**
dose *n* (*pl* **-s**) specific quantity of a medicine taken at one time ▶ *v* (**doses, dosing, dosed**) give a dose to
dosed *v* ▷ **dose**
doses *n, v* ▷ **dose**
dosing *v* ▷ **dose**
doss *v* (**-es, -ing, -ed**) (*Slang*) sleep in an uncomfortable place
dossed *v* ▷ **doss**
dosses *v* ▷ **doss**
dosshouse *n* (*pl* **-s**) (BRIT & S AFR) (*Slang*) cheap lodging house for homeless people
dosshouses *n* ▷ **dosshouse**
dossier [**doss**-ee-ay] *n* (*pl* **-s**) collection of documents about a subject or person
dossiers *n* ▷ **dossier**
dossing *v* ▷ **doss**
dot *n* (*pl* **-s**) small round mark ▶ *v* (**dots, dotting, dotted**) mark with a dot
dotage *n* (*pl* **-s**) weakness as a result of old age
dotages *n* ▷ **dotage**
dotcom *n* (*pl* **-s**) company that does most of its business on the Internet
dotcoms *n* ▷ **dotcom**
dote *v* (**dotes, doting, doted**) love to an excessive degree
doted *v* ▷ **dote**
dotes *v* ▷ **dote**

doting *v* ▷ **dote**
dots *n, v* ▷ **dot**
dotted *v* ▷ **dot**
dottier *adj* ▷ **dotty**
dottiest *adj* ▷ **dotty**
dottily *adv* ▷ **dotty**
dottiness *n* ▷ **dotty**
dottinesses *n* ▷ **dotty**
dotting *v* ▷ **dot**
dotty *adj* (**-ttier, -ttiest**) (*Slang*) rather eccentric > **dottily** *adv* > **dottiness** *n* (*pl* **-es**)
double *adj* as much again in number, amount, size, etc. ▶ *adv* twice over ▶ *n* (*pl* **-s**) twice the number, amount, size, etc. ▶ *pl* game between two pairs of players ▶ *v* (**-bles, -bling, -bled**) make or become twice as much or as many > **doubly** *adv*
doubled *v* ▷ **double**
doubles *n, v* ▷ **double**
doublet [**dub**-lit] *n* (*pl* **-s**) (HIST) man's close-fitting jacket, with or without sleeves
doublets *n* ▷ **doublet**
doubling *v* ▷ **double**
doubloon *n* (*pl* **-s**) former Spanish gold coin
doubloons *n* ▷ **doubloon**
doubly *adv* ▷ **double**
doubt *n* (*pl* **-s**) uncertainty about the truth, facts, or existence of something ▶ *v* (**-s, -ing, -ed**) question the truth of > **doubter** *n* (*pl* **-s**)
doubted *v* ▷ **doubt**
doubter *n* ▷ **doubt**
doubters *n* ▷ **doubt**
doubtful *adj* unlikely > **doubtfully** *adv*
doubtfully *adv* ▷ **doubtful**
doubting *v* ▷ **doubt**
doubtless *adv* probably or certainly > **doubtlessly** *adv*
doubtlessly *adv* ▷ **doubtless**
doubts *n, v* ▷ **doubt**
douche [**doosh**] *n* (*pl* **-s**) (instrument for applying) a stream of water directed onto or into the body for cleansing or medical purposes ▶ *v* (**-es, -ing, -ed**) cleanse or treat by means of a douche
douched *v* ▷ **douche**
douches *n, v* ▷ **douche**
douching *v* ▷ **douche**
dough *n* (*pl* **-s**) thick mixture of flour and water or milk, used for making bread etc.
doughnut *n* (*pl* **-s**) small cake of sweetened dough fried in deep fat
doughnuts *n* ▷ **doughnut**
doughs *n* ▷ **dough**
doughtier *adj* ▷ **doughty**
doughtiest *adj* ▷ **doughty**
doughtily *adv* ▷ **doughty**
doughtiness *n* ▷ **doughty**
doughtinesses *n* ▷ **doughty**
doughty [**dowt**-ee] *adj* (**-tier, -tiest**) (*Old-fashioned*) brave and determined > **doughtily** *adv* > **doughtiness** *n* (*pl* **-es**)
dour [**doo**-er] *adj* (**-er, -est**) sullen and unfriendly > **dourly** *adv* > **dourness** *n* (*pl* **-es**)
dourer *adj* ▷ **dour**
dourest *adj* ▷ **dour**
dourly *adv* ▷ **dour**
dourness *n* ▷ **dour**
dournesses *n* ▷ **dour**
douse [rhymes with **mouse**] *v* (**-ses, -sing, -sed**) drench with water or other liquid
doused *v* ▷ **douse**
douses *v* ▷ **douse**
dousing *v* ▷ **douse**
dove *n* (*pl* **-s**) bird with a heavy body, small head, and short legs
dovecot *n* ▷ **dovecote**
dovecote, dovecot *n* (*pl* **-s**) structure for housing pigeons
dovecotes *n* ▷ **dovecote**
dovecots *n* ▷ **dovecote**
doves *n* ▷ **dove**
dovetail *n* (*pl* **-s**) joint containing wedge-shaped tenons ▶ *v* (**-s, -ing, -ed**) fit together neatly
dovetailed *v* ▷ **dovetail**
dovetailing *v* ▷ **dovetail**
dovetails *v* ▷ **dovetail**

dow *n* (**dows**). A dow is an Arab ship. Dow scores 7 points.

dowager *n* (*pl* **-s**) widow possessing property or a title obtained from her husband
dowagers *n* ▷ **dowager**
dowdier *adj* ▷ **dowdy**
dowdiest *adj* ▷ **dowdy**
dowdily *adv* ▷ **dowdy**
dowdiness *n* ▷ **dowdy**
dowdy *adj* (**-dier, -diest**) dull and old-fashioned > **dowdily** *adv* > **dowdiness** *n*
dowel *n* (*pl* **-s**) wooden or metal peg that fits into two corresponding holes to join two adjacent parts
dowels *n* ▷ **dowel**
dower *n* (*pl* **-s**) life interest in a part of her husband's estate allotted to a widow by law
dowers *n* ▷ **dower**
down[1] *prep, adv* indicating movement to or position in a lower place ▶ *adv* indicating completion of an action, lessening of intensity, etc. ▶ *adj* depressed, unhappy ▶ *v* (**-s, -ing, -ed**) (*Informal*) drink quickly

down[2] *n* (*pl* **-s**) soft fine feathers > **downiness** *n* > **downy** *adj* (**-nier, -niest**)
downbeat *adj* (*Informal*) gloomy
downcast *adj* sad, dejected
downed *v* ▷ **down[1]**
downfall *n* (*pl* **-s**) (cause of) a sudden loss of position or reputation
downfalls *n* ▷ **downfall**
downgrade *v* (**-grades, -grading, -graded**) reduce in importance or value
downgraded *v* ▷ **downgrade**
downgrades *v* ▷ **downgrade**
downgrading *v* ▷ **downgrade**
downhearted *adj* sad and discouraged > **downheartedly** *adv*
downheartedly *adv* ▷ **downhearted**
downhill *adj* going or sloping down ▶ *adv* towards the bottom of a hill
downier *adj* ▷ **down[2]**
downiest *adj* ▷ **down[2]**
downiness *n* ▷ **down[2]**
downing *v* ▷ **down[1]**
download *v* (**-s, -ing, -ed**) transfer (data) from the memory of one computer to that of another, especially over the Internet ▶ *n* (*pl* **-s**) file transferred in such a way
downloaded *v* ▷ **download**
downloading *v* ▷ **download**
downloads *v, n* ▷ **download**
downpour *n* (*pl* **-s**) heavy fall of rain
downpours *n* ▷ **downpour**
downright *adj, adv* extreme(ly)
downs *pl n* low grassy hills, esp. in S England ▶ *v* ▷ **down[1]** ▶ *n* ▷ **down[2]**
downstairs *adv* to or on a lower floor ▶ *n* lower or ground floor
downtrodden *adj* oppressed and lacking the will to resist
downward *adj, adv* (descending) from a higher to a lower level, condition, or position
downwards *adv* from a higher to a lower level, condition, or position
downy *adj* ▷ **down[2]**
dowries *n* ▷ **dowry**
dowry *n* (*pl* **-ries**) property brought by a woman to her husband at marriage
dowse [rhymes with **cows**] *v* (**-ses, -sing, -sed**) search for underground water or minerals using a divining rod
dowsed *v* ▷ **dowse**
dowses *v* ▷ **dowse**
dowsing *v* ▷ **dowse**
doxologies *n* ▷ **doxology**
doxology *n* (*pl* **-gies**) short hymn of praise to God

doy *n* (**doys**). Doy is a dialect word for a beloved person. Doy scores 7 points.
doyen [**doy**-en] *n* (*pl* **-s**) senior member of a group, profession, or society > **doyenne** [doy-**en**] ▶ *n fem*
doyenne *n* ▷ **doyen**
doyennes *n* ▷ **doyen**
doyens *n* ▷ **doyen**
doze *v* (**dozes, dozing, dozed**) sleep lightly or briefly ▶ *n* (*pl* **-s**) short sleep
dozed *v* ▷ **doze**
dozen *adj, n* (*pl* **-s**) twelve > **dozenth** *adj*
dozens *n* ▷ **dozen**
dozenth *adj* ▷ **dozen**
dozes *v, n* ▷ **doze**
dozier *adj* ▷ **dozy**
doziest *adj* ▷ **dozy**
dozily *adv* ▷ **dozy**
doziness *n* ▷ **dozy**
dozing *v* ▷ **doze**
dozy *adj* (**dozier, doziest**) feeling sleepy > **dozily** *adv* > **doziness** *adv*
drab *adj* (**drabber, drabbest**) dull and dreary > **drably** *adv* > **drabness** *n* (*pl* **-es**)
drabber *adj* ▷ **drab**
drabbest *adj* ▷ **drab**
drably *adv* ▷ **drab**
drabness *n* ▷ **drab**
drabnesses *n* ▷ **drab**
drachm [**dram**] *n* (*pl* **-s**) (BRIT) one eighth of a fluid ounce
drachma *n* (*pl* **-mas, -mae**) former monetary unit of Greece
drachmae *n* ▷ **drachma**
drachmas *n* ▷ **drachma**
drachms *n* ▷ **drachm**
draconian *adj* severe, harsh
draft *n* (*pl* **-s**) plan, sketch, or drawing of something (US & AUST) ▶ *v* (**-s, -ing, -ed**) draw up an outline or plan of
drafted *v* ▷ **draft**
drafting *v* ▷ **draft**
drafts *n, v* ▷ **draft**
drag *v* (**-s, -gging, -gged**) pull with force, esp. along the ground (*foll. by* **on** *or* **out**) ▶ *n* (*pl* **-s**) person or thing that slows up progress
dragged *v* ▷ **drag**
dragging *v* ▷ **drag**
dragnet *n* (*pl* **-s**) net used to scour the bottom of a pond or river to search for something
dragnets *n* ▷ **dragnet**
dragon *n* (*pl* **-s**) mythical fire-breathing monster like a huge lizard
dragonflies *n* ▷ **dragonfly**
dragonfly *n* (*pl* **-flies**) brightly coloured insect

with a long slender body and two pairs of wings
dragons *n* ▷ **dragon**
dragoon *n* (*pl* **-s**) heavily armed cavalryman ▶ *v* (**-s, -ing, -ed**) coerce, force
dragooned *v* ▷ **dragoon**
dragooning *v* ▷ **dragoon**
dragoons *n, v* ▷ **dragoon**
drags *v, n* ▷ **drag**
drain *n* (*pl* **-s**) pipe or channel that carries off water or sewage ▶ *v* (**-s, -ing, -ed**) draw off or remove liquid from
drainage *n* (*pl* **-s**) system of drains
drainages *n* ▷ **drainage**
drained *v* ▷ **drain**
draining *v* ▷ **drain**
drains *n, v* ▷ **drain**
drake *n* (*pl* **-s**) male duck
drakes *n* ▷ **drake**
dram *n* (*pl* **-s**) small amount of a strong alcoholic drink, esp. whisky
drama *n* (*pl* **-s**) serious play for theatre, television, or radio
dramas *n* ▷ **drama**
dramatic *adj* of or like drama > **dramatically** *adv*
dramatically *adv* ▷ **dramatic**
dramatist *n* (*pl* **-s**) person who writes plays
dramatists *n* ▷ **dramatist**
dramatization *n* ▷ **dramatize**
dramatizations *n* ▷ **dramatize**
dramatize *v* (**-tizes, -tizing, -tized**) rewrite (a book) in the form of a play > **dramatization** *n* (*pl* **-s**)
dramatized *v* ▷ **dramatize**
dramatizes *v* ▷ **dramatize**
dramatizing *v* ▷ **dramatize**
drams *n* ▷ **dram**
drank *v* ▷ **drink**
drape *v* (**drapes, draping, draped**) cover with material, usu. in folds ▶ *n* (*pl* **-s**) (AUST, US & CANADIAN) piece of cloth hung at a window or opening as a screen
draped *v* ▷ **drape**
draper *n* (*pl* **-s**) (BRIT) person who sells fabrics and sewing materials
draperies *n* ▷ **drapery**
drapers *n* ▷ **draper**
drapery *n* (*pl* **-peries**) fabric or clothing arranged and draped
drapes *v, n* ▷ **drape**
draping *v* ▷ **drape**
drastic *adj* strong and severe > **drastically** *adv*
drastically *adv* ▷ **drastic**
draught *n* (*pl* **-s**) current of cold air, esp. in an enclosed space ▶ *pl* game for two players using a chessboard and twelve draughts each ▶ *adj* (of an animal) used for pulling heavy loads
draughtier *adj* ▷ **draughty**
draughtiest *adj* ▷ **draughty**
draughtiness *n* ▷ **draughty**
draughts *n* ▷ **draught**
draughtsman *n* (*pl* **-men**) person employed to prepare detailed scale drawings of machinery, buildings, etc. > **draughtsmanship** *n*
draughtsmanship *n* ▷ **draughtsman**
draughtsmen *n* ▷ **draughtsman**
draughty *adj* (**-tier, -tiest**) exposed to draughts of air > **draughtiness** *n*
draw *v* (**draws, drawing, drew, drawn**) sketch (a figure, picture, etc.) with a pencil or pen ▶ *n* (*pl* **-s**) raffle or lottery
drawback *n* (*pl* **-s**) disadvantage
drawbacks *n* ▷ **drawback**
drawbridge *n* (*pl* **-s**) bridge that may be raised to prevent access or to enable vessels to pass
drawbridges *n* ▷ **drawbridge**
drawer *n* (*pl* **-s**) sliding box-shaped part of a piece of furniture, used for storage ▶ *pl* (*Old-fashioned*) undergarment worn on the lower part of the body
drawers *n* ▷ **drawer**
drawing *n* (*pl* **-s**) picture or plan made by means of lines on a surface ▶ *v* ▷ **draw**
drawl *v* (**-s, -ing, -ed**) speak slowly, with long vowel sounds ▶ *n* (*pl* **drawls**) drawling manner of speech
drawled *v* ▷ **drawl**
drawling *v* ▷ **drawl**
drawls *v* ▷ **drawl**
drawls *n* ▷ **drawl**
drawn *v* ▷ **draw** ▶ *adj* haggard, tired, or tense in appearance
draws *n, v* ▷ **draw**
drawstring *n* (*pl* **-s**) cord run through a hem around an opening, so that when it is pulled tighter, the opening closes
drawstrings *n* ▷ **drawstring**
dray *n* (*pl* **-s**) low cart used for carrying heavy loads
drays *n* ▷ **dray**
dread *v* (**-s, -ing, -ed**) anticipate with apprehension or fear ▶ *n* (*pl* **-s**) great fear
dreaded *v* ▷ **dread**
dreadful *adj* very disagreeable or shocking > **dreadfully** *adv*
dreadfully *adv* ▷ **dreadful**
dreading *v* ▷ **dread**

dreadlocks *pl n* hair worn in the Rastafarian style of tightly twisted strands

dreads *v, n* ▷ **dread**

dream *n* (*pl* **-s**) imagined series of events experienced in the mind while asleep (*Informal*) ▶ *v* (**-s, -ing, -ed** *or* **-t**) see imaginary pictures in the mind while asleep (*often foll. by* **of** *or* **about**) (*foll. by* **of**) ▶ *adj* ideal > **dreamer** *n* (*pl* **-s**)

dreamed *v* ▷ **dream**

dreamer *n* ▷ **dream**

dreamers *n* ▷ **dream**

dreamier *adj* ▷ **dreamy**

dreamiest *adj* ▷ **dreamy**

dreamily *adv* ▷ **dreamy**

dreaminess *n* ▷ **dreamy**

dreaminesses *n* ▷ **dreamy**

dreaming *v* ▷ **dream**

dreams *n, v* ▷ **dream**

dreamt *v* ▷ **dream**

dreamy *adj* (**-mier, -miest**) vague or impractical > **dreamily** *adv* > **dreaminess** *n* (*pl* **-es**)

drearier *adj* ▷ **dreary**

dreariest *adj* ▷ **dreary**

drearily *adv* ▷ **dreary**

dreariness *n* ▷ **dreary**

dreary *adj* (**drearier, dreariest**) dull, boring > **drearily** *adv* > **dreariness** *n*

dredge[1] *v* (**dredges, dredging, dredged**) clear or search (a river bed or harbour) by removing silt or mud

dredge[2] *v* (**dredges, dredging, dredged**) sprinkle (food) with flour etc.

dredged *v* ▷ **dredge[1, 2]**

dredger *n* (*pl* **-s**) boat fitted with machinery for dredging

dredgers *n* ▷ **dredger**

dredges *v* ▷ **dredge[1, 2]**

dredging *v* ▷ **dredge[1, 2]**

dregs *pl n* solid particles that settle at the bottom of some liquids

drench *v* (**-es, -ing, -ed**) make completely wet

drenched *v* ▷ **drench**

drenches *v* ▷ **drench**

drenching *v* ▷ **drench**

dress *n* (*pl* **-es**) one-piece garment for a woman or girl, consisting of a skirt and bodice and sometimes sleeves ▶ *v* (**-es, -ing, -ed**) put clothes on

dressage [**dress**-ahzh] *n* (*pl* **-s**) training of a horse to perform manoeuvres in response to the rider's body signals

dressages *n* ▷ **dressage**

dressed *v* ▷ **dress**

dresser[1] *n* (*pl* **-s**) piece of furniture with shelves and with cupboards, for storing or displaying dishes

dresser[2] *n* (*pl* **-s**) (THEATRE) person employed to assist actors with their costumes

dressers *n* ▷ **dresser[1, 2]**

dresses *n, v* ▷ **dress**

dressier *adj* ▷ **dressy**

dressiest *adj* ▷ **dressy**

dressiness *n* ▷ **dressy**

dressinesses *n* ▷ **dressy**

dressing *n* (*pl* **-s**) sauce for salad ▶ *v* ▷ **dress**

dressings *n* ▷ **dressing**

dressmaker *n* (*pl* **-s**) person who makes women's clothes > **dressmaking** *n*

dressmakers *n* ▷ **dressmaker**

dressmaking *n* ▷ **dressmaker**

dressy *adj* (**-ssier, -ssiest**) (of clothes) elegant > **dressiness** *n* (*pl* **-es**)

drew *v* ▷ **draw**

drey *n* (*pl* **-s**) squirrel's nest

dreys *n* ▷ **drey**

dribble *v* (**-les, -ling, -led**) (allow to) flow in drops ▶ *n* (*pl* **-s**) small quantity of liquid falling in drops > **dribbler** *n* (*pl* **-s**)

dribbled *v* ▷ **dribble**

dribbler *n* ▷ **dribble**

dribblers *n* ▷ **dribble**

dribbles *v, n* ▷ **dribble**

dribbling *v* ▷ **dribble**

dried *v* ▷ **dry**

drier[1] *adj* ▷ **dry**

drier[2] *n* (*pl* **-s**) ▷ **dryer**

driers *n* ▷ **drier[2]**

dries *v* ▷ **dry**

driest *adj* ▷ **dry**

drift *v* (**-s, -ing, -ed**) be carried along by currents of air or water ▶ *n* (*pl* **-s**) something piled up by the wind or current, such as a snowdrift

drifted *v* ▷ **drift**

drifter *n* (*pl* **-s**) person who moves aimlessly from place to place or job to job

drifters *n* ▷ **drifter**

drifting *v* ▷ **drift**

drifts *v, n* ▷ **drift**

driftwood *n* (*pl* **-s**) wood floating on or washed ashore by the sea

driftwoods *n* ▷ **driftwood**

drill[1] *n* (*pl* **-s**) tool or machine for boring holes ▶ *v* (**-s, -ing, -ed**) bore a hole in (something) with or as if with a drill

drill[2] *n* (*pl* **-s**) machine for sowing seed in rows

drill[3] *n* (*pl* **-s**) hard-wearing cotton cloth

drilled *v* ▷ **drill[1]**

drilling *v* ▷ **drill**[1]
drills *n* ▷ **drill**[1, 2, 3] ▶ *v* ▷ **drill**[1]
drily *adv* ▷ **dry**
drink *v* (**drinks, drinking, drank, drunk**) swallow (a liquid) ▶ *n* (*pl* **-s**) (portion of) a liquid suitable for drinking > **drinkable** *adj* > **drinker** *n* (*pl* **-s**)
drinkable *adj* ▷ **drink**
drinker *n* ▷ **drink**
drinkers *n* ▷ **drink**
drinking *v* ▷ **drink**
drinks *v, n* ▷ **drink**
drip *v* (**drips, dripping, dripped**) (let) fall in drops ▶ *n* (*pl* **-s**) falling of drops of liquid
dripped *v* ▷ **drip**
dripping *n* (*pl* **-s**) fat that comes from meat while it is being roasted or fried ▶ *v* ▷ **drip**
drippings *n* ▷ **dripping**
drips *v, n* ▷ **drip**
drive *v* (**drives, driving, drove, driven**) guide the movement of (a vehicle) ▶ *n* (*pl* **-s**) journey by car, van, etc.; path for vehicles (*also* **driveway**) (*pl* **-s**)
drivel *n* (*pl* **-s**) foolish talk ▶ *v* (**-els, -elling, -elled**) speak foolishly
drivelled *v* ▷ **drivel**
drivelling *v* ▷ **drivel**
drivels *v, n* ▷ **drivel**
driven *v* ▷ **drive**
driver *n* (*pl* **-s**) person who drives a vehicle
drivers *n* ▷ **driver**
drives *v, n* ▷ **drive**
driveway *n* ▷ **drive**
driveways *n* ▷ **drive**
driving *v* ▷ **drive**
drizzle *n* (*pl* **-s**) very light rain ▶ *v* (**-zles, -zling, -zled**) rain lightly > **drizzly** *adj*
drizzled *v* ▷ **drizzle**
drizzles *n, v* ▷ **drizzle**
drizzling *v* ▷ **drizzle**
drizzly *adj* ▷ **drizzle**
droll *adj* (**-er, -est**) quaintly amusing > **drolly** *adv* > **drollery** *n* (*pl* **-ries**) > **drollness** *n* (*pl* **-es**)
droller *adj* ▷ **droll**
drolleries *n* ▷ **droll**
drollery *n* ▷ **droll**
drollest *adj* ▷ **droll**
drollness *n* ▷ **droll**
drollnesses *n* ▷ **droll**
drolly *adv* ▷ **droll**
dromedaries *n* ▷ **dromedary**
dromedary [**drom**-mid-er-ee] *n* (*pl* **-daries**) camel with a single hump
drone[1] *n* (*pl* **-s**) male bee
drone[2] *v* (**drones, droned, droning**) ▶ *n* (*pl* **-s**) (make) a monotonous low dull sound
droned *v* ▷ **drone**[2]
drones *n* ▷ **drone**[1, 2] ▶ *v* ▷ **drone**[2]
drongo *n* (*pl* **-gos**) tropical songbird with a glossy black plumage, a forked tail, and a stout bill
drongos *n* ▷ **drongo**
droning *v* ▷ **drone**[2]
drool *v* (**-s, -ing, -ed**) (*foll. by* **over**) show excessive enthusiasm (for)
drooled *v* ▷ **drool**
drooling *v* ▷ **drool**
drools *v* ▷ **drool**
droop *v* (**-s, -ing, -ed**) hang downwards loosely > **droopy** *adj* (**-pier, -piest**)
drooped *v* ▷ **droop**
droopier *adj* ▷ **droop**
droopiest *adj* ▷ **droop**
drooping *v* ▷ **droop**
droops *v* ▷ **droop**
droopy *adj* ▷ **droop**
drop *v* (**-s, -pping, -pped**) (allow to) fall vertically ▶ *n* (*pl* **-s**) small quantity of liquid forming a round shape ▶ *pl* liquid medication applied in small drops > **droplet** *n* (*pl* **-s**)
droplet *n* ▷ **drop**
droplets *n* ▷ **drop**
dropout *n* (*pl* **-s**) person who rejects conventional society
dropouts *n* ▷ **dropout**
dropped *v* ▷ **drop**
dropping *v* ▷ **drop**
droppings *pl n* faeces of certain animals, such as rabbits or birds
drops *v, n* ▷ **drop**
dropsical *adj* ▷ **dropsy**
dropsies *n* ▷ **dropsy**
dropsy *n* (*pl* **-sies**) illness in which watery fluid collects in the body > **dropsical** *adj*
dross *n* (*pl* **-es**) scum formed on the surfaces of molten metals
drosses *n* ▷ **dross**
drought *n* (*pl* **-s**) prolonged shortage of rainfall
droughts *n* ▷ **drought**
drove[1] *v* ▷ **drive**
drove[2] *n* (*pl* **-s**) very large group, esp. of people
drover *n* (*pl* **-s**) person who drives sheep or cattle
drovers *n* ▷ **drover**
droves *n* ▷ **drove**[2]
drown *v* (**-s, -ing, -ed**) die or kill by immersion in liquid
drowned *v* ▷ **drown**
drowning *v* ▷ **drown**
drowns *v* ▷ **drown**

drowse *v* (**-ses, -sing, -sed**) be sleepy, dull, or sluggish > **drowsy** *adj* (**-sier, -siest**) > **drowsily** *adv* > **drowsiness** *n* (*pl* **-es**)
drowsed *v* ▷ **drowse**
drowses *v* ▷ **drowse**
drowsier *adj* ▷ **drowse**
drowsiest *adj* ▷ **drowse**
drowsily *adv* ▷ **drowse**
drowsiness *n* ▷ **drowse**
drowsinesses *n* ▷ **drowse**
drowsing *v* ▷ **drowse**
drowsy *adj* ▷ **drowse**
drubbing *n* (*pl* **-s**) utter defeat in a contest etc.
drubbings *n* ▷ **drubbing**
drudge *n* (*pl* **-s**) person who works hard at uninteresting tasks > **drudgery** *n* (*pl* **-eries**)
drudgeries *n* ▷ **drudge**
drudgery *n* ▷ **drudge**
drudges *n* ▷ **drudge**
drug *n* (*pl* **-s**) substance used in the treatment or prevention of disease ▶ *v* (**drugs, drugging, drugged**) give a drug to (a person or animal) to cause sleepiness or unconsciousness
drugged *v* ▷ **drug**
drugging *v* ▷ **drug**
drugs *v, n* ▷ **drug**
drugstore *n* (*pl* **-s**) (US) pharmacy where a wide range of goods are available
drugstores *n* ▷ **drugstore**
druid *n* (*pl* **-s**) member of an ancient order of Celtic priests > **druidic, druidical** *adj*
druidic *adj* ▷ **druid**
druidical *adj* ▷ **druid**
druids *adj* ▷ **druid**
drum *n* (*pl* **-s**) percussion instrument sounded by striking a membrane stretched across the opening of a hollow cylinder ▶ *v* (**drums, drumming, drummed**) play (music) on a drum
drummed *v* ▷ **drum**
drummer *n* (*pl* **-s**) person who plays a drum or drums
drummers *n* ▷ **drummer**
drumming *v* ▷ **drum**
drums *n, v* ▷ **drum**
drumstick *n* (*pl* **-s**) stick used for playing a drum
drumsticks *n* ▷ **drumstick**
drunk *v* ▷ **drink** ▶ *adj* (**-er, -est**) intoxicated with alcohol to the extent of losing control over normal functions ▶ *n* (*pl* **-s**) person who is drunk or who frequently gets drunk
drunkard *n* (*pl* **-s**) person who frequently gets drunk
drunkards *n* ▷ **drunkard**
drunken *adj* drunk or frequently drunk > **drunkenly** *adv* > **drunkenness** *n* (*pl* **-es**)
drunkenly *adv* ▷ **drunken**
drunkenness *n* ▷ **drunken**
drunkennesses *n* ▷ **drunken**
drunker *adj* ▷ **drunk**
drunkest *adj* ▷ **drunk**
drunks *n* ▷ **drunk**
dry *adj* (**drier, driest** *or* **dryer, dryest**) lacking moisture ▶ *v* (**dries, drying, dried**) make or become dry > **drily, dryly** *adv* > **dryness** *n* (*pl* **-es**)
dryad *n* (*pl* **-s**) wood nymph
dryads *n* ▷ **dryad**
dryer, drier *n* (*pl* **-s**) apparatus for removing moisture
dryer *adj* ▷ **dry**
dryers *n* ▷ **dryer**
dryest *adj* ▷ **dry**
drying *v* ▷ **dry**
dryly *adv* ▷ **dry**
dryness *n* ▷ **dry**
drynesses *n* ▷ **dry**

> **dso** *n* (**dsos**). Dso is one of several spelling for a Tibetan animal bred from yaks and cattle. The other forms are **dzo, zho** and **zo,** and it's worth remembering all of them. Dso scores 4 points.

dual *adj* having two parts, functions, or aspects > **duality** *n* (*pl* **-ities**) > **dually** *adv*
dualities *n* ▷ **dual**
duality *n* ▷ **dual**
dually *adv* ▷ **dual**
dub¹ *v* (**dubs, dubbing, dubbed**) give (a person or place) a name or nickname
dub² *v* (**dubs, dubbing, dubbed**) provide (a film) with a new soundtrack, esp. in a different language
dubbed *v* ▷ **dub¹, ²**
dubbin *n* (*pl* **-s**) (BRIT) thick grease applied to leather to soften and waterproof it
dubbing *v* ▷ **dub¹, ²**
dubbins *n* ▷ **dubbin**
dubieties *n* ▷ **dubious**
dubiety *n* ▷ **dubious**
dubious [**dew**-bee-uss] *adj* feeling or causing doubt > **dubiously** *adv* > **dubiousness** *n* > **dubiety** [dew-**by**-it-ee] *n* (*pl* **-ities**)
dubiously *adv* ▷ **dubious**
dubiousness *n* ▷ **dubious**
dubs *v* ▷ **dub¹, ²**
ducal [**duke**-al] *adj* of a duke
ducat [**duck**-it] *n* (*pl* **-s**) former European gold or silver coin

ducats *n* ▷ **ducat**
duchess *n* (*pl* **-es**) woman who holds the rank of duke
duchesse *n* (*pl* **-s**) (NZ) dressing table with a mirror
duchesses *n* ▷ **duchess, duchesse**
duchies *n* ▷ **duchy**
duchy *n* (*pl* **duchies**) territory of a duke or duchess
duck¹ *n* (*pl* **-s**) water bird with short legs, webbed feet, and a broad blunt bill
duck² *v* (**-s, -ing, -ed**) move (the head or body) quickly downwards, to avoid being seen or to dodge a blow
ducked *v* ▷ **duck²**
ducking *v* ▷ **duck²**
duckling *n* (*pl* **-s**) baby duck
ducklings *n* ▷ **duckling**
ducks *n* ▷ **duck¹** ▸ *v* ▷ **duck²**
duct *n* (*pl* **-s**) tube, pipe, or channel through which liquid or gas is conveyed
ductile *adj* (of a metal) able to be shaped into sheets or wires
ducts *n* ▷ **duct**
dud (*Informal*) *n* (*pl* **-s**) ineffectual person or thing ▸ *adj* bad or useless
dude *n* (*pl* **-s**) (US) (*Informal*) man
dudes *n* ▷ **dude**
dudgeon *n* (*pl* **-s**) anger, resentment
dudgeons *n* ▷ **dudgeon**
duds *n* ▷ **dud**
due *adj* expected or scheduled to be present or arrive ▸ *n* (*pl* **-s**) something that is owed or required ▸ *pl* charges for membership of a club or organization ▸ *adv* directly or exactly
duel *n* (*pl* **-s**) formal fight with deadly weapons between two people, to settle a quarrel ▸ *v* (**-s, -lling, -lled**) fight in a duel > **duellist** *n* (*pl* **-s**)
duelled *v* ▷ **duel**
duelling *v* ▷ **duel**
duellist *n* ▷ **duel**
duellists *n* ▷ **duel**
duels *n, v* ▷ **duel**
dues *n* ▷ **due**
duet *n* (*pl* **-s**) piece of music for two performers
duets *n* ▷ **duet**
duff *adj* (**-er, -est**) (CHIEFLY BRIT) broken or useless
duffel, duffle *n* (*pl* **-s**) heavy woollen cloth
duffels *n* ▷ **duffel**
duffer *n* (*pl* **-s**) (*Informal*) dull or incompetent person ▸ *adj* ▷ **duff**
duffers *n* ▷ **duffer**
duffest *adj* ▷ **duff**
duffle *n* ▷ **duffel**
duffles *n* ▷ **duffel**
dug¹ *v* ▷ **dig**
dug² *n* (*pl* **-s**) teat or udder
dugite [**doo**-gyte] *n* (*pl* **-s**) medium-sized Australian venomous snake
dugites *n* ▷ **dugite**
dugong *n* (*pl* **-s**) whalelike mammal of tropical waters
dugongs *n* ▷ **dugong**
dugout *n* (*pl* **-s**) (BRIT) (at a sports ground) covered bench where managers and substitutes sit
dugouts *n* ▷ **dugout**
dugs *n* ▷ **dug²**
duke *n* (*pl* **-s**) nobleman of the highest rank > **dukedom** *n* (*pl* **-s**)
dukedom *n* ▷ **duke**
dukedoms *n* ▷ **duke**
dukes *n* ▷ **duke**
dulcet [**dull**-sit] *adj* (of a sound) soothing or pleasant
dulcimer *n* (*pl* **-s**) tuned percussion instrument consisting of a set of strings stretched over a sounding board and struck with hammers
dulcimers *n* ▷ **dulcimer**
dull *adj* (**-er, -est**) not interesting ▸ *v* (**-s, -ing, -ed**) make or become dull > **dullness** *n* (*pl* **-es**) > **dully** *adv*
dullard *n* (*pl* **-s**) dull or stupid person
dullards *n* ▷ **dullard**
dulled *v* ▷ **dull**
duller *adj* ▷ **dull**
dullest *adj* ▷ **dull**
dulling *v* ▷ **dull**
dullness *n* ▷ **dull**
dullnesses *n* ▷ **dull**
dulls *v* ▷ **dull**
dully *adv* ▷ **dull**
duly *adv* in a proper manner
dumb *adj* (**dumber, dumbest**) lacking the power to speak > **dumbly** *adv* > **dumbness** *n*
dumbbell *n* (*pl* **-s**) short bar with a heavy ball or disc at each end, used for physical exercise
dumbbells *n* ▷ **dumbbell**
dumber *adj* ▷ **dumb**
dumbest *adj* ▷ **dumb**
dumbfounded *adj* speechless with astonishment
dumbly *adv* ▷ **dumb**
dumbness *n* ▷ **dumb**
dumdum *n* (*pl* **-s**) soft-nosed bullet that expands on impact and causes serious wounds
dumdums *n* ▷ **dumdum**
dummies *n* ▷ **dummy**

dummy *n* (*pl* **-mies**) figure representing the human form, used for displaying clothes etc. ▶ *adj* imitation, substitute
dump *v* (**-s, -ing, -ed**) drop or let fall in a careless manner ▶ *n* (*pl* **-s**) place where waste materials are left
dumped *v* ▷ **dump**
dumpier *adj* ▷ **dumpy**
dumpiest *adj* ▷ **dumpy**
dumpily *adv* ▷ **dumpy**
dumpiness *n* ▷ **dumpy**
dumping *v* ▷ **dump**
dumpling *n* (*pl* **-s**) small ball of dough cooked and served with stew
dumplings *n* ▷ **dumpling**
dumps *v, n* ▷ **dump**
dumpy *adj* (**dumpier, dumpiest**) short and plump > **dumpily** *adv* > **dumpiness** *n*
dun (**dunner, dunnest**) *adj* brownish-grey
dunce *n* (*pl* **-s**) person who is stupid or slow to learn
dunces *n* ▷ **dunce**
dunderhead *n* (*pl* **-s**) slow-witted person
dunderheads *n* ▷ **dunderhead**
dune *n* (*pl* **-s**) mound or ridge of drifted sand
dunes *n* ▷ **dune**
dung *n* (*pl* **-s**) faeces from animals such as cattle
dungarees *pl n* trousers with a bib attached
dungeon *n* (*pl* **-s**) underground prison cell
dungeons *n* ▷ **dungeon**
dungs *n* ▷ **dung**
dunk *v* (**-s, -ing, -ed**) dip (a biscuit or bread) in a drink or soup before eating it
dunked *v* ▷ **dunk**
dunking *v* ▷ **dunk**
dunks *v* ▷ **dunk**
dunner *adj* ▷ **dun**
dunnest *adj* ▷ **dun**
dunnies *n* ▷ **dunny**
dunny *n* (*pl* **-nies**) (AUST & OLD-FASHIONED NZ) (*Informal*) toilet
duo *n* (*pl* **-s**) pair of performers
duodena *n* ▷ **duodenum**
duodenal *adj* ▷ **duodenum**
duodenum [dew-oh-**deen**-um] *n* (*pl* **-na, -nums**) first part of the small intestine, just below the stomach > **duodenal** *adj*
duodenums *n* ▷ **duodenum**
duos *n* ▷ **duo**
dupe *v* (**dupes, duping, duped**) deceive or cheat ▶ *n* (*pl* **-s**) person who is easily deceived
duped *v* ▷ **dupe**
dupes *v, n* ▷ **dupe**
duping *v* ▷ **dupe**
duple *adj* (MUSIC) having two beats in a bar
duplex *n* (*pl* **-es**) (CHIEFLY US) apartment on two floors
duplexes *n* ▷ **duplex**
duplicate *adj* copied exactly from an original ▶ *n* (*pl* **-s**) exact copy ▶ *v* (**-cates, -cating, -cated**) make an exact copy of > **duplication** *n* (*pl* **-s**) > **duplicator** *n* (*pl* **-s**)
duplicated *v* ▷ **duplicate**
duplicates *n, v* ▷ **duplicate**
duplicating *v* ▷ **duplicate**
duplication *n* ▷ **duplicate**
duplications *n* ▷ **duplicate**
duplicator *n* ▷ **duplicate**
duplicators *n* ▷ **duplicate**
duplicities *n* ▷ **duplicity**
duplicity *n* (*pl* **-ities**) deceitful behaviour
durability *n* ▷ **durable**
durable *adj* long-lasting > **durability** *n* > **durably** *adv*
durables *pl n* goods that require infrequent replacement
durably *adv* ▷ **durable**
duration *n* (*pl* **-s**) length of time that something lasts
durations *n* ▷ **duration**
duress *n* compulsion by use of force or threats
during *prep* throughout or within the limit of (a period of time)
dusk *n* (*pl* **-s**) time just before nightfall, when it is almost dark
duskier *adj* ▷ **dusky**
duskiest *adj* ▷ **dusky**
duskily *adv* ▷ **dusky**
duskiness *n* ▷ **dusky**
dusks *n* ▷ **dusk**
dusky *adj* (**duskier, duskiest**) dark in colour > **duskily** *adv* > **duskiness** *n*
dust *n* (*pl* **-s**) small dry particles of earth, sand, or dirt ▶ *v* (**-s, -ing, -ed**) remove dust from (furniture) by wiping
dustbin *n* (*pl* **-s**) large container for household rubbish
dustbins *n* ▷ **dustbin**
dusted *v* ▷ **dust**
duster *n* (*pl* **-s**) cloth used for dusting
dusters *n* ▷ **duster**
dustier *adj* ▷ **dusty**
dustiest *adj* ▷ **dusty**
dusting *v* ▷ **dust**
dustman *n* (*pl* **-men**) (BRIT) man whose job is to collect household rubbish
dustmen *n* ▷ **dustman**
dustpan *n* (*pl* **-s**) short-handled shovel into which dust is swept from floors

dustpans *n* ▷ **dustpan**
dusts *n, v* ▷ **dust**
dusty *adj* (**dustier, dustiest**) covered with dust
dutiability *n* ▷ **dutiable**
dutiable *adj* (of goods) requiring payment of duty > **dutiability** *n*
duties *n* ▷ **duty**
dutiful *adj* doing what is expected > **dutifully** *adv*
dutifully *adv* ▷ **dutiful**
duty *n* (*pl* **-ties**) work or a task performed as part of one's job
duvet [**doo**-vay] *n* (*pl* **-s**) kind of quilt used in bed instead of a top sheet and blankets
duvets *n* ▷ **duvet**

> **dux** *n* (**duces**). A dux is the top pupil in a school. This is a handy word to have ready if someone else has played a word containing X. Dux scores 11 points.

dwang *n* (*pl* **-s**) (NZ & S AFR) short piece of wood inserted in a timber-framed wall
dwangs *n* ▷ **dwang**
dwarf *n* (*pl* **dwarfs, dwarves**) person who is smaller than average ▶ *adj* (of an animal or plant) much smaller than the usual size for the species ▶ *v* (**dwarfs, dwarfing** *or* **dwarfed**) cause (someone or something) to seem small by being much larger
dwarfed *v* ▷ **dwarf**
dwarfing *v* ▷ **dwarf**
dwarfs *n, v* ▷ **dwarf**
dwarves *n* ▷ **dwarf**
dwell *v* (**dwells, dwelling, dwelt** *or* **dwelled**) live, reside
dwelled *v* ▷ **dwell**
dweller *n* (*pl* **-s**) person who lives in a specified place
dwellers *n* ▷ **dweller**
dwelling *n* (*pl* **-s**) place of residence ▶ *v* ▷ **dwell**
dwellings *n* ▷ **dwelling**
dwells *v* ▷ **dwell**
dwelt *v* ▷ **dwell**
dwindle *v* (**-dles, -dling, -dled**) grow less in size, strength, or number
dwindled *v* ▷ **dwindle**
dwindles *v* ▷ **dwindle**
dwindling *v* ▷ **dwindle**
dye *n* (*pl* **-s**) colouring substance ▶ *v* (**dyes, dyeing, dyed**) colour (hair or fabric) by applying a dye > **dyer** *n* (*pl* **-s**)
dyed *v* ▷ **dye**
dyeing *v* ▷ **dye**
dyer *n* ▷ **dye**
dyers *n* ▷ **dye**
dyes *n, v* ▷ **dye**
dying *v* ▷ **die**[1]
dyke *n* (*pl* **-s**) wall built to prevent flooding
dykes *n* ▷ **dyke**
dynamic *adj* full of energy, ambition, and new ideas > **dynamically** *adv*
dynamically *adv* ▷ **dynamic**
dynamics *n* branch of mechanics concerned with the forces that change or produce the motions of bodies ▶ *pl* forces that produce change in a system
dynamism *n* great energy and enthusiasm
dynamite *n* (*pl* **-s**) explosive made of nitroglycerine ▶ *v* (**-mites, -miting, -mited**) blow (something) up with dynamite
dynamited *v* ▷ **dynamite**
dynamites *n, v* ▷ **dynamite**
dynamiting *v* ▷ **dynamite**
dynamo *n* (*pl* **-s**) device for converting mechanical energy into electrical energy
dynamos *n* ▷ **dynamo**
dynastic *adj* ▷ **dynasty**
dynasties *n* ▷ **dynasty**
dynasty *n* (*pl* **-ties**) sequence of hereditary rulers > **dynastic** *adj*
dysenteries *n* ▷ **dysentery**
dysentery *n* (*pl* **-teries**) infection of the intestine causing severe diarrhoea
dysfunction *n* (*pl* **-s**) (MED) disturbance or abnormality in the function of an organ or part > **dysfunctional** *adj* > **dysfunctionally** *adv*
dysfunctional *adj* ▷ **dysfunction**
dysfunctionally *adv* ▷ **dysfunction**
dysfunctions *n* ▷ **dysfunction**
dyslexia *n* (*pl* **-s**) disorder causing impaired ability to read > **dyslexic** *adj*
dyslexias *n* ▷ **dyslexia**
dyslexic *adj* ▷ **dyslexia**
dysmenorrhoea *n* (*pl* **-s**) painful menstruation
dysmenorrhoeas *n* ▷ **dysmenorrhoea**
dyspepsia *n* (*pl* **-s**) indigestion > **dyspeptic** *adj*
dyspepsias *n* ▷ **dyspepsia**
dyspeptic *adj* ▷ **dyspepsia**
dystrophic *adj* ▷ **dystrophy**
dystrophies *n* ▷ **dystrophy**
dystrophy [**diss**-trof-fee] *n* (*pl* **-phies**) wasting disorder > **dystrophic** *adj*

dzho *n* (**dzhos**). A dzho is one of several ways of spelling the name of a Tibetan animal bred from yaks and cattle. This spelling is less useful than the others (**dso, dzo, zho** and **zo**) because it has four letters rather than two or three. It is, however, a very useful word to know when someone else has played zho, as you can use D to hook another word onto zho, or just to take advantage of the Z already on the board. Dzho scores 17 points.

dzo *n* (**dzos**). Dzo is one of several spelling for a Tibetan animal bred from yaks and cattle. The other forms are **dso, dzho, zho** and **zo,** and it's worth remembering all of them. Dzo scores 13 points.

Ee

E is the most common tile in the game and, while it is only worth one point, as the most frequent letter in English it is extremely useful. Many words contain two or more Es, so, unlike many tiles, it's good to have several Es on your rack. Keep in mind three-letter words formed by two Es either side of a consonant, like **eye, ewe** and **eve** (6 points each), and **eke** (7). E can also be handy for getting rid of double consonants: think of words like **egg** or **ebb** (each 5 points). E also combines well with K: as well as **eke,** we have **elk** and **eek** (both 7), and **ewk** (10). If you have an X on your rack, E offers you all kinds of options: just think of all the words that begin with ex-, like **exhaust** (17), which will give you a 50-point bonus if you use all of your tiles to form it. And don't forget **ex** itself, a nice little word that earns you 9 points.

ea *n* (**eas**). Ea is a dialect word for a river. This word won't earn you many points, but it does provide many opportunities to play longer words that form ea in the process. Ea scores 2 points.

each *adj, pron* every (one) taken separately
eager *adj* (**-er, -est**) showing or feeling great desire, keen > **eagerly** *adv* > **eagerness** *n* (*pl* **-es**)
eagerer *adj* ▷ **eager**
eagerest *adj* ▷ **eager**
eagerly *adv* ▷ **eager**
eagerness *n* ▷ **eager**
eagernesses *n* ▷ **eager**
eagle *n* (*pl* **-s**) large bird of prey with keen eyesight
eagles *n* ▷ **eagle**
eaglet *n* (*pl* **-s**) young eagle
eaglets *n* ▷ **eaglet**
ear[1] *n* (*pl* **-s**) organ of hearing, esp. the external part of it
ear[2] *n* (*pl* **-s**) head of corn
earache *n* (*pl* **-s**) pain in the ear
earaches *n* ▷ **earache**
earbash *v* (**-es, -ing, -ed**) (AUST & NZ) (*Informal*) talk incessantly > **earbashing** *n* (*pl* **-s**)
earbashed *n* ▷ **earbash**
earbashes *n* ▷ **earbash**
earbashing *v, n* ▷ **earbash**
earbashings *n* ▷ **earbash**
eardrum *n* (*pl* **-s**) thin piece of skin inside the ear which enables one to hear sounds
eardrums *n* ▷ **eardrum**
earl *n* (*pl* **-s**) British nobleman ranking next below a marquess > **earldom** *n* (*pl* **-s**)
earldom *n* ▷ **earl**
earldoms *n* ▷ **earl**
earlier *adj, adv* ▷ **early**
earliest *adj, adv* ▷ **early**
earls *n* ▷ **earl**
early *adj, adv* (**-ier, -iest**) before the expected or usual time
earmark *v* (**-s, -ing, -ed**) set (something) aside for a specific purpose
earmarked *v* ▷ **earmark**
earmarking *v* ▷ **earmark**
earmarks *v* ▷ **earmark**
earn *v* (**-s, -ing, -ed**) obtain by work or merit
earned *v* ▷ **earn**
earnest[1] *adj* serious and sincere > **earnestly** *adv*
earnest[2] *n* (*pl* **-s**) part payment given in advance, esp. to confirm a contract
earnests *n* ▷ **earnest**[2]
earning *v* ▷ **earn**
earnings *pl n* money earned
earns *v* ▷ **earn**
earphone *n* (*pl* **-s**) receiver for a radio etc., held to or put in the ear
earphones *n* ▷ **earphone**
earring *n* (*pl* **-s**) ornament for the lobe of the ear
earrings *n* ▷ **earring**
ears *n* ▷ **ear**[1, 2]
earshot *n* (*pl* **-s**) hearing range
earshots *n* ▷ **earshot**
earth *n* (*pl* **-s**) land, the ground ▶ *v* (**-s, -ing, -ed**)

connect (a circuit) to earth
earthed *v* ▷ **earth**
earthen *adj* made of baked clay or earth
earthenware *n* (*pl* **-s**) pottery made of baked clay
earthenwares *n* ▷ **earthenwares**
earthier *adj* ▷ **earthy**
earthiest *adj* ▷ **earthy**
earthing *v* ▷ **earth**
earthly *adj* conceivable or possible
earthquake *n* (*pl* **-s**) violent vibration of the earth's surface
earthquakes *n* ▷ **earthquake**
earths *n, v* ▷ **earth**
earthwork *n* (*pl* **-s**) fortification made of earth
earthworks *n* ▷ **earthwork**
earthworm *n* (*pl* **-s**) worm which burrows in the soil
earthworms *n* ▷ **earthworm**
earthy *adj* (**-thier, -thiest**) coarse or crude
earwig *n* (*pl* **-s**) small insect with a pincer-like tail
earwigs *n* ▷ **earwig**
ease *n* (*pl* **-ses**) freedom from difficulty, discomfort, or worry ▶ *v* (**-ses, -sing, -sed**) give bodily or mental ease to
eased *v* ▷ **ease**
easel *n* (*pl* **-s**) frame to support an artist's canvas or a blackboard
easels *n* ▷ **easel**
eases *n, v* ▷ **ease**
easier *adj* ▷ **easy**
easily *adv* ▷ **easy**
easiest *adj* ▷ **easy**
easiness *n* ▷ **easy**
easinesses *n* ▷ **easy**
easing *v* ▷ **ease**
east *n* (*pl* **-s**) (direction towards) the part of the horizon where the sun rises ▶ *adj* to or in the east ▶ *adv* in, to, or towards the east > **easterly** *adj* > **eastern** *adj* > **eastward** *adj, adv* > **eastwards** *adv*
easterly *adj* ▷ **east**
eastern *adj* ▷ **east**
easts *n* ▷ **east**
eastward *adj, adv* ▷ **east**
eastwards *adv* ▷ **east**
easy *adj* (**-ier, -iest**) not needing much work or effort > **easily** *adv* > **easiness** *n* (*pl* **-s**)
eat *v* (**eats, eating, ate, eaten**) take (food) into the mouth and swallow it
eatable *adj* fit or suitable for eating
eaten *v* ▷ **eat**
eating *v* ▷ **eat**
eats *v* ▷ **eat**
eaves *pl n* overhanging edges of a roof
eavesdrop *v* (**-s, -pping, -pped**) listen secretly to a private conversation > **eavesdropper** *n* (*pl* **-s**) > **eavesdropping** *n* (*pl* **-s**)
eavesdropped *v* ▷ **eavesdrop**
eavesdropper *n* ▷ **eavesdrop**
eavesdroppers *n* ▷ **eavesdrop**
eavesdropping *v, n* ▷ **eavesdrop**
eavesdroppings *n* ▷ **eavesdrop**
eavesdrops *v* ▷ **eavesdrop**
ebb *v* (**-s, -ing, -ed**) (of tide water) flow back ▶ *n* (*pl* **-s**) flowing back of the tide
ebbed *v* ▷ **ebb**
ebbing *v* ▷ **ebb**
ebbs *v, n* ▷ **ebb**
ebonies *n* ▷ **ebony**
ebony *n* (*pl* **-ies**) hard black wood ▶ *adj* deep black
ebullience *n* ▷ **ebullient**
ebulliences *n* ▷ **ebullient**
ebullient *adj* full of enthusiasm or excitement > **ebullience** *n* (*pl* **-s**)
eccentric *adj* odd or unconventional ▶ *n* (*pl* **-s**) eccentric person > **eccentrically** *adv* > **eccentricity** *n* (*pl* -ies)
eccentrically *adv* ▷ **eccentric**
eccentricities *n* ▷ **eccentric**
eccentricity *n* ▷ **eccentric**
eccentrics *n* ▷ **eccentric**
ecclesiastic *n* (*pl* **-s**) member of the clergy ▶ *adj* (*also* **ecclesiastical**) of the Christian Church or clergy
ecclesiastical *adj* ▷ **ecclesiastic**
ecclesiastics *n* ▷ **ecclesiastic**

ech *v* (**echs, eching, eched**). Ech is an old word that Shakespeare uses, and means **eke.** It's a good one to have ready if you have C and H but no obvious place to play them. Ech scores 8 points.

echelon [**esh**-a-lon] *n* (*pl* **-s**) level of power or responsibility
echelons *n* ▷ **echelon**
echidna [ik-**kid**-na] *n* (*pl* **-nas, -nae**) [-nee] Australian spiny egg-laying mammal
echidnae *n* ▷ **echidna**
echidnas *n* ▷ **echidna**
echo *n* (*pl* **-es**) repetition of sounds by reflection of sound waves off a surface ▶ *v* (**-es, -ing, -ed**) repeat or be repeated as an echo
echoed *v* ▷ **echo**
echoes *v, n* ▷ **echo**
echoing *v* ▷ **echo**
éclair *n* (*pl* **-s**) finger-shaped pastry filled with

cream and covered with chocolate
éclairs *n* ▷ **éclair**
éclat [ake-**lah**] *n* brilliant success
eclectic *adj* selecting from various styles, ideas, or sources > **eclecticism** *n* (*pl* **-s**)
eclecticism *n* ▷ **eclectic**
eclecticisms *n* ▷ **eclectic**
eclipse *n* (*pl* **-es**) temporary obscuring of one star or planet by another ▶ *v* (**-ses, -sing, -sed**) surpass or outclass
eclipsed *v* ▷ **eclipse**
eclipses *v* ▷ **eclipse**
eclipsing *v* ▷ **eclipse**
ecliptic *n* (*pl* **-s**) apparent path of the sun
ecliptics *n* ▷ **ecliptic**
ecological *adj* of ecology > **ecologically** *adv*
ecologically *adv* ▷ **ecological**
ecologist *n* ▷ **ecology**
ecologists *n* ▷ **ecology**
ecology *n* study of the relationships between living things and their environment > **ecologist** *n* (*pl* **-s**)
economic *adj* of economics
economical *adj* not wasteful, thrifty > **economically** *adv*
economically *adv* ▷ **economical**
economics *n* social science concerned with the production and consumption of goods and services
economies *n* ▷ **economy**
economist *n* (*pl* **-s**) specialist in economics
economists *n* ▷ **economist**
economize *v* (**-izes, -izing, -ized**) reduce expense or waste
economized *v* ▷ **economize**
economizes *v* ▷ **economize**
economizing *v* ▷ **economize**
economy *n* (*pl* **-ies**) system of interrelationship of money, industry, and employment in a country
ecosystem *n* (*pl* **-s**) system involving interactions between a community and its environment
ecosystems *n* ▷ **ecosystem**
ecru *adj* pale creamy-brown
ecstasies *n* ▷ **ecstasy**
ecstasy *n* (*pl* **-ies**) state of intense delight > **ecstatic** *adj* > **ecstatically** *adv*
ecstatic *adj* ▷ **ecstasy**
ecstatically *adv* ▷ **ecstasy**
ectoplasm *n* (*pl* **-s**) (SPIRITUALISM) substance that supposedly is emitted from the body of a medium during a trance
ectoplasms *n* ▷ **ectoplasm**
ecumenical *adj* of the Christian Church throughout the world, esp. with regard to its unity
eczema [**ek**-sim-a] *n* (*pl* **s**) skin disease causing intense itching
eczemas *n* ▷ **eczema**
eddied *v* ▷ **eddy**
eddies *n, v* ▷ **eddy**
eddy *n* (*pl* **eddies**) circular movement of air, water, etc. ▶ *v* (**eddies, eddying, eddied**) move with a circular motion
eddying *v* ▷ **eddy**
edelweiss [**ade**-el-vice] *n* (*pl* **-es**) alpine plant with white flowers
edelweisses *n* ▷ **edelweiss**
edge *n* (*pl* **-s**) border or line where something ends or begins ▶ *v* (**edges, edging, edged**) provide an edge or border for
edged *v* ▷ **edge**
edges *n, v* ▷ **edge**
edgeways *adv* with the edge forwards or uppermost
edgier *adj* ▷ **edgy**
edgiest *adj* ▷ **edgy**
edging *v* ▷ **edge** ▶ *n* (*pl* **-s**) anything placed along an edge to finish it
edgings *n* ▷ **edging**
edgy *adj* (**edgier, edgiest**) nervous or irritable
edibilities *n* ▷ **edible**
edibility *n* ▷ **edible**
edible *adj* fit to be eaten > **edibility** *n* (*pl* **-ties**)
edict [**ee**-dikt] *n* (*pl* **-s**) order issued by an authority
edicts *n* ▷ **edict**
edification *n* ▷ **edify**
edifications *n* ▷ **edify**
edifice [**ed**-if-iss] *n* (*pl* **-s**) large building
edifices *n* ▷ **edifice**
edified *v* ▷ **edify**
edifies *v* ▷ **edify**
edify [**ed**-if-fie] *v* (**-fies, -fying, -fied**) improve morally by instruction > **edification** *n* (*pl* **-s**)
edifying *v* ▷ **edify**
edit *v* (**-s, -ing, -ed**) prepare (a book, film, etc.) for publication or broadcast
edited *v* ▷ **edit**
editing *v* ▷ **edit**
edition *n* (*pl* **-s**) number of copies of a new publication printed at one time
editions *n* ▷ **edition**
editor *n* (*pl* **-s**) person who edits
editorial *n* (*pl* **-s**) newspaper article stating the opinion of the editor ▶ *adj* of editing or editors
editorials *n* ▷ **editorial**
editors *n* ▷ **editor**

edits *v* ▷ **edit**
educate *v* (**-tes, -ting, -ted**) teach > **education** *n* (*pl* **-s**) > **educational** *adj* > **educationally** *adv*
educated *v* ▷ **educate**
educates *v* ▷ **educate**
educating *v* ▷ **educate**
educational *adj* ▷ **educate**
educationalist *n* (*pl* **-s**) expert in the theory of education
educationalists *n* ▷ **educationalist**
educationally *adv* ▷ **educate**
educations *n* ▷ **educate**
educative *adj* educating

ee *n* (**een**). Ee is a Scots word for eye. While this word won't earn you a big score on its own, it can be very useful when you're trying to form several words at once. Ee scores 2 points.
eek *interj*. Eek is a noise that people make when they are startled or frightened. Eek scores 7 points.

eel *n* (*pl* **-s**) snakelike fish
eels *n* ▷ **eel**
eerie *adj* (**-ier, -iest**) uncannily frightening or disturbing > **eerily** *adv*
eerier *adj* ▷ **eerie**
eeriest *adj* ▷ **eerie**
eerily *adv* ▷ **eerie**

ef *n* (**efs**). Ef is the letter F, and is a handy word to know when you want to play a longer word parallel to a word that's already on the board. Ef scores 5 points.

efface *v* (**-ces, -cing, -ced**) remove by rubbing > **effacement** *n* (*pl* **-s**)
effaced *v* ▷ **efface**
effacement *n* ▷ **efface**
effacements *n* ▷ **efface**
effaces *v* ▷ **efface**
effacing *v* ▷ **efface**
effect *n* (*pl* **-s**) change or result caused by someone or something ▶ *pl* personal belongings ▶ *v* (**-s, -ing, -ed**) cause to happen, accomplish
effected *v* ▷ **effect**
effecting *v* ▷ **effect**
effective *adj* producing a desired result > **effectively** *adv*
effectively *adv* ▷ **effective**
effects *n, v* ▷ **effect**
effectual *adj* producing the intended result > **effectually** *adv*
effectually *adv* ▷ **effectual**
effeminacies *n* ▷ **effeminate**
effeminacy *n* ▷ **effeminate**
effeminate *adj* (of a man) displaying characteristics thought to be typical of a woman > **effeminacy** *n* (*pl* **-ies**)
effervescence *n* ▷ **effervescent**
effervescences *n* ▷ **effervescent**
effervescent *adj* (of a liquid) giving off bubbles of gas > **effervescence** *n* (*pl* **-s**)
effete [if-**feet**] *adj* powerless, feeble
efficacies *n* ▷ **efficacious**
efficacious *adj* producing the intended result > **efficacy** *n* (*pl* **-ies**)
efficacy *n* ▷ **efficacious**
efficiencies *n* ▷ **efficient**
efficiency *n* ▷ **efficient**
efficient *adj* functioning effectively with little waste of effort > **efficiently** *adv* > **efficiency** *n* (*pl* **-ies**)
efficiently *adv* ▷ **efficient**
effigies *n* ▷ **effigy**
effigy [**ef**-fij-ee] *n* (*pl* **-ies**) image or likeness of a person
efflorescence *n* (*pl* **-s**) flowering
efflorescences *n* ▷ **efflorescence**
effluent *n* (*pl* **-s**) liquid discharged as waste
effluents *n* ▷ **effluent**
effluvia *n* ▷ **effluvium**
effluvium *n* (*pl* **-via**) unpleasant smell, as of decaying matter or gaseous waste
effort *n* (*pl* **-s**) physical or mental exertion > **effortless** *adj*
effortless *adj* ▷ **effort**
efforts *n* ▷ **effort**
effronteries *n* ▷ **effrontery**
effrontery *n* (*pl* **-ies**) brazen impudence
effusion *n* (*pl* **-s**) unrestrained outburst
effusions *n* ▷ **effusion**
effusive *adj* openly emotional, demonstrative > **effusively** *adv*
effusively *adv* ▷ **effusive**
egalitarian *adj* upholding the equality of all people ▶ *n* (*pl* **-s**) person who holds egalitarian beliefs > **egalitarianism** *n* (*pl* **-s**)
egalitarianism *n* ▷ **egalitarian**
egalitarianisms *n* ▷ **egalitarian**
egalitarians *n* ▷ **egalitarian**
egg¹ *n* (*pl* **-s**) oval or round object laid by the females of birds and other creatures, containing a developing embryo
egg² *v* (**-s, -ing, -ed**) encourage or incite, esp. to do wrong
egged *v* ▷ **egg²**
egghead *n* (*pl* **-s**) (*Informal*) intellectual person
eggheads *n* ▷ **egghead**
egging *v* ▷ **egg²**
eggplant *n* (*pl* **-s**) (US, CANADIAN, AUST & NZ) aubergine

eggplants *n* ▷ **eggplant**
eggs *n, v* ▷ **egg**[1,2]
ego *n* (*pl* **-s**) the conscious mind of an individual
egocentric *adj* self-centred
egoism, egotism *n* excessive concern for one's own interests > **egoist, egotist** *n* (*pl* **-s**) > **egoistic, egotistic** *adj*
egoist *n* ▷ **egoism**
egoistic *adj* ▷ **egoism**
egoists *n* ▷ **egoism**
egos *n* ▷ **ego**
egotist *n* ▷ **egoism**
egotistic *adj* ▷ **egoism**
egotists *n* ▷ **egoism**
egregious [ig-**greej**-uss] *adj* outstandingly bad
egress [**ee**-gress] *n* (*pl* **-es**) departure
egresses *n* ▷ **egress**
egret [**ee**-grit] *n* (*pl* **-s**) lesser white heron
egrets *n* ▷ **egret**
eider *n* (*pl* **-s**) Arctic duck
eiderdown *n* (*pl* **-s**) quilt (orig. stuffed with eider feathers)
eiderdowns *n* ▷ **eiderdown**
eiders *n* ▷ **eider**
eight *adj, n* (*pl* **-s**) one more than seven
eighteen *adj, n* (*pl* **-s**) eight and ten > **eighteenth** *adj, n* (*pl* **-s**)
eighteens *n* ▷ **eighteen**
eighteenth *adj, n* ▷ **eighteen**
eighteenths *n* ▷ **eighteen**
eighth *adj, n* (*pl* **-s**) (of) number eight in a series
eighths *n* ▷ **eighth**
eighties *n* ▷ **eighty**
eightieth *n* ▷ **eighty**
eightieths *n* ▷ **eighty**
eights *n* ▷ **eight**
eighty *adj, n* (*pl* **-ies**) eight times ten > **eightieth** *adj, n* (*pl* **-s**)
eisteddfod [ice-**sted**-fod] *n* (*pl* **-s**) Welsh festival with competitions in music and other performing arts
eisteddfods *n* ▷ **eisteddfod**
either *adj, pron* one or the other (of two) ► *conj* used preceding two or more possibilities joined by *or* ► *adv* likewise
ejaculate *v* (**-tes, -ting, -ted**) eject (semen) > **ejaculation** *n* (*pl* **-s**)
ejaculated *v* ▷ **ejaculate**
ejaculates *v* ▷ **ejaculate**
ejaculating *v* ▷ **ejaculate**
ejaculation *n* ▷ **ejaculate**
ejaculations *n* ▷ **ejaculate**
eject *v* (**-s, -ing, -ed**) force out, expel > **ejection** *n* (*pl* **-s**) > **ejector** *n* (*pl* **-s**)
ejected *v* ▷ **eject**
ejecting *v* ▷ **eject**
ejection *n* ▷ **eject**
ejections *n* ▷ **eject**
ejector *n* ▷ **eject**
ejectors *n* ▷ **eject**
ejects *v* ▷ **eject**
eke *v* (**ekes, eking, eked**) (*usu. foll. by* **out**) make (a living) with difficulty
eked *v* ▷ **eke**
ekes *v* ▷ **eke**
eking *v* ▷ **eke**
elaborate *adj* with a lot of fine detail ► *v* (**-tes, -ting, -ted**) expand upon > **elaboration** *n* (*pl* **-s**)
elaborated *v* ▷ **elaborate**
elaborates *v* ▷ **elaborate**
elaborating *v* ▷ **elaborate**
elaboration *n* ▷ **elaborate**
elaborations *n* ▷ **elaborate**
élan [ale-**an**] *n* (*pl* **-s**) style and vigour
eland [**eel**-and] *n* (*pl* **-s**) large antelope of southern Africa
elands *n* ▷ **eland**
élans *n* ▷ **élan**
elapse *v* (**-ses, -sing, -sed**) (of time) pass by
elapsed *v* ▷ **elapse**
elapses *v* ▷ **elapse**
elapsing *v* ▷ **elapse**
elastic *adj* resuming normal shape after distortion ► *n* (*pl* **-s**) tape or fabric containing interwoven strands of flexible rubber > **elasticity** *n* (*pl* **-ies**)
elasticities *n* ▷ **elastic**
elasticity *n* ▷ **elastic**
elastics *n* ▷ **elastic**
elate *v* (**-tes, -ting, -ted**) make extremely happy and excited > **elation** *n* (*pl* **-s**)
elated *v* ▷ **elate**
elates *v* ▷ **elate**
elating *v* ▷ **elate**
elation *n* ▷ **elate**
elations *n* ▷ **elate**
elbow *n* (*pl* **-s**) joint between the upper arm and the forearm ► *v* (**-s, -ing, -ed**) shove or strike with the elbow
elbowed *v* ▷ **elbow**
elbowing *v* ▷ **elbow**
elbows *n, v* ▷ **elbow**
elder[1] *adj* older ► *n* (*pl* **-s**) older person
elder[2] *n* (*pl* **-s**) small tree with white flowers and black berries
elderly *adj* (fairly) old
elders *n* ▷ **elder**[1,2]
eldest *adj* oldest

eldritch *adj* (SCOT) weird, uncanny
elect *v* (**-s, -ing, -ed**) choose by voting ▶ *adj* appointed but not yet in office
elected *v* ▷ **elect**
electing *v* ▷ **elect**
election *n* (*pl* **-s**) choosing of representatives by voting
electioneering *n* (*pl* **-s**) active participation in a political campaign
electioneerings *n* ▷ **electioneering**
elections *n* ▷ **election**
elective *adj* chosen by election
elector *n* (*pl* **-s**) someone who has the right to vote in an election > **electoral** *adj*
electoral *adj* ▷ **elector**
electorate *n* (*pl* **-s**) people who have the right to vote
electorates *n* ▷ **electorate**
electors *n* ▷ **elector**
electric *adj* produced by, transmitting, or powered by electricity
electrical *adj* using or concerning electricity
electrician *n* (*pl* **-s**) person trained to install and repair electrical equipment
electricians *n* ▷ **electrician**
electricities *n* ▷ **electricity**
electricity *n* (*pl* **-ies**) form of energy associated with stationary or moving electrons or other charged particles
electrics *pl n* (BRIT) electric appliances
electrification *n* ▷ **electify**
electrifications *n* ▷ **electrify**
electrified *v* ▷ **electrify**
electrifies *v* ▷ **electrify**
electrify *v* (**-fies, -fying, -fied**) adapt for operation by electric power > **electrification** *n*
electrifying *v* ▷ **electrify**
electrocute *v* (**-tes, -ting, -ted**) kill or injure by electricity > **electrocution** *n* (*pl* **-s**)
electrocuted *v* ▷ **electrocute**
electrocutes *v* ▷ **electrocute**
electrocuting *v* ▷ **electrocute**
electrocution *n* ▷ **electrocute**
electrocutions *n* ▷ **electrocute**
electrode *n* (*pl* **-s**) conductor through which an electric current enters or leaves a battery, vacuum tube, etc
electrodes *n* ▷ **electrode**
electrodynamics *n* branch of physics concerned with the interactions between electrical and mechanical forces
electrolyses *n* ▷ **electrolysis**
electrolysis [ill-lek-**troll**-iss-iss] *n* (*pl* **-ses**) conduction of electricity by an electrolyte, esp. to induce chemical change
electrolyte *n* (*pl* **-s**) solution or molten substance that conducts electricity > **electrolytic** *adj*
electrolytes *n* ▷ **electrolyte**
electrolytic *adj* ▷ **electrolyte**
electromagnet *n* (*pl* **-s**) magnet containing a coil of wire through which an electric current is passed
electromagnetic *adj* of or operated by an electomagnet
electromagnets *n* ▷ **electromagnet**
electron *n* (*pl* **-s**) elementary particle in all atoms that has a negative electrical charge
electronic *adj* (of a device) dependent on the action of electrons
electronics *n* technology concerned with the development of electronic devices and circuits
electrons *n* ▷ **electron**
electronvolt *n* (*pl* **-s**) unit of energy used in nuclear physics
electronvolts *n* ▷ **electronvolt**
electroplate *v* (**-tes, -ting, -ted**) coat with silver etc. by electrolysis
electroplated *v* ▷ **electroplate**
electroplates *v* ▷ **electroplate**
electroplating *v* ▷ **electroplate**
elects *v* ▷ **elect**
elegance *n* ▷ **elegant**
elegances *n* ▷ **elegant**
elegant *adj* pleasing or graceful in dress, style, or design > **elegance** *n* (*pl* **-s**)
elegiac *adj* mournful or plaintive
elegies *n* ▷ **elegy**
elegy [**el**-lij-ee] *n* (*pl* **-ies**) mournful poem, esp. a lament for the dead
element *n* (*pl* **-s**) component part ▶ *pl* basic principles of something
elemental *adj* of primitive natural forces or passions
elementary *adj* simple and straightforward
elements *n* ▷ **element**
elephant *n* (*pl* **-s**) huge four-footed thick-skinned animal with ivory tusks and a long trunk
elephantiasis [el-lee-fan-**tie**-a-siss] *n* disease with hardening of the skin and enlargement of the legs etc.
elephantine *adj* unwieldy, clumsy
elephants *n* ▷ **elephant**
elevate *v* (**-ates, -ating, -ated**) raise in rank or status
elevated *v* ▷ **elevate**
elevates *v* ▷ **elevate**

elevating *v* ▷ **elevate**
elevation *n* (*pl* **-s**) raising
elevator *n* (*pl* **-s**) (AUST, US & CANADIAN) lift for carrying people
elevators *n* ▷ **elevator**
eleven *adj, n* (*pl* **-s**) one more than ten
elevens *n* ▷ **eleven**
elevenses *n* (BRIT & S AFR) (*Informal*) mid-morning snack
eleventh *adj, n* (*pl* **-s**) (of) number eleven in a series
elevenths *n* ▷ **eleventh**
elf *n* (*pl* **elves**) (in folklore) small mischievous fairy
elfin *adj* small and delicate
elicit *v* (**-s, -ing, -ed**) bring about (a response or reaction)
elicited *v* ▷ **elicit**
eliciting *v* ▷ **elicit**
elicits *v* ▷ **elicit**
elide *v* (**-des, -ding, -ded**) omit (a vowel or syllable) from a spoken word > **elision** *n* (*pl* **-s**)
elided *v* ▷ **elide**
elides *v* ▷ **elide**
eliding *v* ▷ **elide**
eligibilities *n* ▷ **eligible**
eligibility *n* ▷ **eligible**
eligible *adj* meeting the requirements or qualifications needed > **eligibility** *n* (*pl* **-ties**)
eliminate *v* (**-tes, -ting, -ted**) get rid of > **elimination** *n* (*pl* **-s**)
eliminated *v* ▷ **eliminate**
eliminates *v* ▷ **eliminate**
eliminating *v* ▷ **eliminate**
elimination *n* ▷ **eliminate**
eliminations *n* ▷ **eliminate**
elision *n* ▷ **elide**
elisions *n* ▷ **elide**
elite [ill-**eet**] *n* (*pl* **-s**) most powerful, rich, or gifted members of a group
elites *n* ▷ **elite**
elitism *n* (*pl* **-s**) belief that society should be governed by a small group of superior people > **elitist** *n, adj* (*pl* **-s**)
elitisms *n* ▷ **elitism**
elitists *n* ▷ **elitist**
elixir [ill-**ix**-er] *n* (*pl* **-s**) imaginary liquid that can prolong life or turn base metals into gold
elixirs *n* ▷ **elixir**
elk *n* (*pl* **-s**) large deer of N Europe and Asia
elks *n* ▷ **elk**
ellipse *n* (*pl* **-ses**) oval shape
ellipses *n* ▷ **ellipse, ellipsis**
ellipsis *n* (*pl* **-ses**) omission of letters or words in a sentence
elliptical *adj* oval-shaped
elm *n* (*pl* **-s**) tree with serrated leaves
elms *n* ▷ **elm**
elocution *n* (*pl* **-s**) art of speaking clearly in public
elocutions *n* ▷ **elocution**
elongate [**eel**-long-gate] *v* (**-tes, -ting, -ted**) make or become longer > **elongation** *n* (*pl* **-s**)
elongated *v* ▷ **elongate**
elongates *v* ▷ **elongate**
elongating *v* ▷ **elongate**
elongation *n* ▷ **elongate**
elongations *n* ▷ **elongate**
elope *v* (**-s, -ing, -ed**) (of two people) run away secretly to get married > **elopement** *n* (*pl* **-s**)
eloped *v* ▷ **elope**
elopement *n* ▷ **elope**
elopements *n* ▷ **elope**
elopes *v* ▷ **elope**
eloping *v* ▷ **elope**
eloquence *n* (*pl* **-s**) fluent powerful use of language > **eloquent** *adj* > **eloquently** *adv*
eloquencies *n* ▷ **eloquence**
eloquent *adj* ▷ **eloquence**
eloquently *adv* ▷ **eloquence**
else *adv* in addition or more
elsewhere *adv* in or to another place
elucidate *v* (**-tes, -ting, -ted**) make (something difficult) clear > **elucidation** *n* (*pl* **-s**)
elucidated *v* ▷ **elucidate**
elucidates *v* ▷ **elucidate**
elucidating *v* ▷ **elucidate**
elucidation *n* ▷ **elucidate**
elucidations *n* ▷ **elucidate**
elude *v* (**-s, -ing, -ed**) escape from by cleverness or quickness
eluded *v* ▷ **elude**
eludes *v* ▷ **elude**
eluding *v* ▷ **elude**
elusive *adj* difficult to catch or remember
elver *n* (*pl* **-s**) young eel
elvers *n* ▷ **elver**
elves *n* ▷ **elf**
emaciated [im-**mace**-ee-ate-id] *adj* abnormally thin > **emaciation** *n* (*pl* **-s**)
emaciation *n* ▷ **emaciated**
emaciations *n* ▷ **emaciated**
emanate [**em**-a-nate] *v* (**-tes, -ting, -ted**) issue, proceed from a source > **emanation** *n* (*pl* **-s**)
emanated *v* ▷ **emanate**
emanates *v* ▷ **emanate**
emanating *v* ▷ **emanate**
emanation *n* ▷ **emanate**
emanations *n* ▷ **emanate**
emancipate *v* (**-tes, -ting, -ted**) free

from social, political, or legal restraints **>emancipation** *n* (*pl* **-s**)
emancipated *v* ▷ **emancipate**
emancipates *v* ▷ **emancipate**
emancipating *v* ▷ **emancipate**
emancipation *n* ▷ **emancipate**
emancipations *n* ▷ **emancipate**
emasculate *v* (**-tes, -ting, -ted**) deprive of power **>emasculation** *n* (*pl* **-s**)
emasculated *v* ▷ **emasculate**
emasculates *v* ▷ **emasculate**
emasculating *v* ▷ **emasculate**
emasculation *n* ▷ **emasculate**
emasculations *n* ▷ **emasculate**
embalm *v* (**-s, -ing, -ed**) preserve (a corpse) from decay by the use of chemicals etc.
embalmed *v* ▷ **embalm**
embalming *v* ▷ **embalm**
embalms *v* ▷ **embalm**
embankment *n* (*pl* **-s**) man-made ridge that carries a road or railway or holds back water
embankments *n* ▷ **embankment**
embargo *n* (*pl* **-oes**) order by a government prohibiting trade with a country ▶ *v* (**-oes, -oing, -oed**) put an embargo on
embargoed *v* ▷ **embargo**
embargoes *n, v* ▷ **embargo**
embargoing *v* ▷ **embargo**
embark *v* (**-s, -ing, -ed**) board a ship or aircraft (*foll. by* **on**) **>embarkation** *n* (**-s**)
embarkation *n* ▷ **embark**
embarkations *n* ▷ **embark**
embarked *v* ▷ **embark**
embarking *v* ▷ **embark**
embarks *v* ▷ **embark**
embarrass *v* (**-es, -ing, -ed**) cause to feel self-conscious or ashamed **>embarrassed** *adj* **>embarrassing** *adj* **>embarrassment** *n* (*pl* **-s**)
embarrassed *v, adj* ▷ **embarrass**
embarrasses *v* ▷ **embarrass**
embarrassing *v, adj* ▷ **embarrass**
embarrassment *n* ▷ **embarrass**
embarrassments *n* ▷ **embarrass**
embassies *n* ▷ **embassy**
embassy *n* (*pl* **-ies**) offices or official residence of an ambassador
embattled *adj* having a lot of difficulties
embed *v* (**-s, -dding, -dded**) fix firmly in something solid
embedded *adj* (of a journalist) assigned to accompany an active military unit ▶ *v* ▷ **embed**
embedding *v* ▷ **embed**
embeds *v* ▷ **embed**
embellish *v* (**-es, -ing, -ed**) decorate **>embellishment** *n* (*pl* **-s**)
embellished *v* ▷ **embellish**
embellishes *v* ▷ **embellish**
embellishing *v* ▷ **embellish**
embellishment *n* ▷ **embellish**
embellishments *n* ▷ **embellish**
ember *n* (*pl* **-s**) glowing piece of wood or coal in a dying fire
embers *n* ▷ **ember**
embezzle *v* (**-s, -ing, -ed**) steal money that has been entrusted to one **>embezzlement** *n* (*pl* **-s**) **>embezzler** *n* (*pl* **-s**)
embezzled *v* ▷ **embezzle**
embezzlement *n* ▷ **embezzle**
embezzlements *n* ▷ **embezzle**
embezzler *n* ▷ **embezzle**
embezzlers *n* ▷ **embezzle**
embezzles *v* ▷ **embezzle**
embezzling *v* ▷ **embezzle**
embittered *adj* feeling anger as a result of misfortune
emblazon *v* (**-s, -ing, -ed**) decorate with bright colours
emblazoned *v* ▷ **emblazon**
emblazoning *v* ▷ **emblazon**
emblazons *v* ▷ **emblazon**
emblem *n* (*pl* **-s**) object or design that symbolizes a quality, type, or group **>emblematic** *adj*
emblematic *adj* ▷ **emblem**
emblems *n* ▷ **emblem**
embodied *v* ▷ **embody**
embodies *v* ▷ **embody**
embodiment *n* ▷ **embody**
embodiments *n* ▷ **embody**
embody *v* (**-dies, -dying, -died**) be an example or expression of **>embodiment** *n* (*pl* **-s**)
embodying *v* ▷ **embody**
embolden *v* (**-s, -ing, -ed**) encourage (someone)
emboldened *v* ▷ **embolden**
emboldening *v* ▷ **embolden**
emboldens *v* ▷ **embolden**
embolism *n* (*pl* **-s**) blocking of a blood vessel by a blood clot or air bubble
embolisms *n* ▷ **embolism**
embossed *adj* (of a design or pattern) standing out from a surface
embrace *v* (**-ces, -cing, -ced**) clasp in the arms, hug ▶ *n* (*pl* **-s**) act of embracing
embraced *v* ▷ **embrace**
embraces *v, n* ▷ **embrace**
embracing *v* ▷ **embrace**
embrasure *n* (*pl* **-s**) door or window having splayed sides so that the opening is larger

on the inside
embrasures *n* ▷ **embrasure**
embrocation *n* (*pl* **-s**) lotion for rubbing into the skin to relieve pain
embrocations *n* ▷ **embrocation**
embroider *v* (**-s, -ing, -ed**) decorate with needlework > **embroidery** *n* (*pl* **-ies**)
embroidered *v* ▷ **embroider**
embroideries *n* ▷ **embroider**
embroidering *v* ▷ **embroider**
embroiders *v* ▷ **embroider**
embroidery *n* ▷ **embroider**
embroil *v* (**-s, -ing, -ed**) involve (a person) in problems
embroiled *v* ▷ **embroil**
embroiling *v* ▷ **embroil**
embroils *v* ▷ **embroil**
embryo [**em**-bree-oh] *n* (*pl* **-s**) unborn creature in the early stages of development > **embryology** *n* (*pl* **-ies**)
embryologies *n* ▷ **embryo**
embryology *n* ▷ **embryo**
embryonic *adj* at an early stage
embryos *n* ▷ **embryo**
emend *v* (**-s, -ing, -ed**) remove errors from > **emendation** *n* (*pl* **emendations**)
emendation *n* ▷ **emend**
emendations *n* ▷ **emend**
emended *v* ▷ **emend**
emending *v* ▷ **emend**
emends *v* ▷ **emend**
emerald *n* (*pl* **-s**) bright green precious stone ▶ *adj* bright green
emeralds *n* ▷ **emerald**
emerge *v* (**-ges, -ging, -ged**) come into view > **emergence** *n* (*pl* **-s**) > **emergent** *adj*
emerged *v* ▷ **emerge**
emergence *n* ▷ **emerge**
emergences *n* ▷ **emerge**
emergencies *n* ▷ **emergency**
emergency *n* (*pl* **-ies**) sudden unforeseen occurrence needing immediate action
emergent *adj* ▷ **emerge**
emerges *v* ▷ **emerge**
emerging *v* ▷ **emerge**
emeries *n* ▷ **emery**
emeritus [im-**mer**-rit-uss] *adj* retired, but retaining an honorary title
emery *n* (*pl* **-ies**) hard mineral used for smoothing and polishing
emetic [im-**met**-ik] *n* (*pl* **-s**) substance that causes vomiting ▶ *adj* causing vomiting
emetics *n* ▷ **emetic**
emigrant *n* ▷ **emigrate**
emigrants *n* ▷ **emigrate**
emigrate *v* (**-tes, -ting, -ted**) go and settle in another country > **emigrant** *n* (*pl* **-s**) > **emigration** *n* (*pl* **-s**)
emigrated *v* ▷ **emigrate**
emigrates *v* ▷ **emigrate**
emigrating *v* ▷ **emigrate**
emigration *n* ▷ **emigrate**
emigrations *n* ▷ **emigrate**
émigré [**em**-mig-gray] *n* (*pl* **-s**) someone who has left his native country for political reasons
émigrés *n* ▷ **émigré**
eminence *n* (*pl* **-s**) position of superiority or fame
eminences *n* ▷ **eminence**
eminent *adj* distinguished, well-known > **eminently** *adv*
eminently *adv* ▷ **eminent**
emir [em-**meer**] *n* (*pl* **-s**) Muslim ruler
emirate *n* (*pl* **-s**) country ruled by an emir
emirates *n* ▷ **emirate**
emirs *n* ▷ **emir**
emissaries *n* ▷ **emissary**
emissary *n* (*pl* **-ies**) agent sent on a mission by a government
emission *n* ▷ **emit**
emissions ▷ **emit**
emit *v* (**-s, -tting, -tted**) give out (heat, light, or a smell) > **emission** *n* (*pl* **-s**)
emits *v* ▷ **emit**
emitted *v* ▷ **emit**
emitting *v* ▷ **emit**
emollient *adj* softening, soothing ▶ *n* (*pl* **-s**) substance which softens or soothes the skin
emollients *n* ▷ **emollient**
emolument *n* (*pl* **-s**) (*formal*) fees or wages from employment
emoluments *n* ▷ **emolument**
emoticon [i-**mote**-i-kon] *n* (*pl* **-s**) (COMPUTERS) ▷ **smiley**
emoticons *n* ▷ **emoticon**
emotion *n* (*pl* **-s**) strong feeling
emotional *adj* readily affected by or appealing to the emotions > **emotionally** *adv*
emotionally *adv* ▷ **emotional**
emotions *n* ▷ **emotion**
emotive *adj* tending to arouse emotion
empathies *n* ▷ **empathy**
empathy *n* (*pl* **-ies**) ability to understand someone else's feelings as if they were one's own
emperor *n* (*pl* **-s**) ruler of an empire > **empress** *n fem* (*pl* **-es**)
emperors *n* ▷ **emperor**
emphases *n* ▷ **emphasis**

emphasis *n* (*pl* **-ses**) special importance or significance > **emphasize** *v* (**-s, -ing, -ed**)
emphasize *v* ▷ **emphasis**
emphasized *v* ▷ **emphasis**
emphasizes *v* ▷ **emphasis**
emphasizing *v* ▷ **emphasis**
emphatic *adj* showing emphasis > **emphatically** *adv*
emphatically *adv* ▷ **emphatic**
emphysema [em-fiss-**see**-ma] *n* (*pl* **-s**) condition in which the air sacs of the lungs are grossly enlarged, causing breathlessness
emphysemas *n* ▷ **emphysema**
empire *n* (*pl* **-s**) group of territories under the rule of one state or person
empires *n* ▷ **empire**
empirical *adj* relying on experiment or experience, not on theory > **empirically** *adv*
empirically *adv* ▷ **empirical**
empiricism *n* (*pl* **-s**) doctrine that all knowledge derives from experience > **empiricist** *n* (*pl* **-s**)
empiricisms *n* ▷ **empiricism**
empiricist *n* ▷ **empiricism**
empiricists *n* ▷ **empiricism**
emplacement *n* (*pl* **-s**) prepared position for a gun
emplacements *n* ▷ **emplacement**
employ *v* (**-s, -ing, -ed**) hire (a person) ▶ *n* (*pl* **-s**) state of being employed > **employee** *n* (*pl* **-s**)
employed *v* ▷ **employ**
employee *n* ▷ **employ**
employees *n* ▷ **employ**
employer *n* (*pl* **-s**) person or organization that employs someone
employers *n* ▷ **employer**
employing *v* ▷ **employ**
employment *n* (*pl* **-s**) state of being employed
employments *n* ▷ **employment**
employs *v, n* ▷ **employ**
emporia *n* ▷ **emporium**
emporium *n* (*pl* **-riums, -ria**) (*Old-fashioned*) large general shop
emporiums *n* ▷ **emporia**
empower *v* (**-s, -ing, -ed**) enable, authorize
empowered *v* ▷ **empower**
empowering *v* ▷ **empower**
empowers *v* ▷ **empower**
empress *n* ▷ **emperor**
empresses *n* ▷ **emperor**
emptied *v* ▷ **empty**
emptier *adj* ▷ **empty**
empties *pl n* empty boxes, bottles, etc. ▶ *v* ▷ **empty**
emptiest *adj* ▷ **empty**
emptiness *n* ▷ **empty**
emptinesses *n* ▷ **empty**
empty *adj* (**-ier, -iest**) containing nothing ▶ *v* (**-ies, -ying, -ied**) make or become empty > **emptiness** *n* (*pl* **-es**)
emptying *v* ▷ **empty**
emu *n* (*pl* **-s**) large Australian flightless bird with long legs
emulate *v* (**-tes, -ting, -ted**) attempt to equal or surpass by imitating > **emulation** *n* (*pl* **-s**)
emulated *v* ▷ **emulate**
emulates *v* ▷ **emulate**
emulating *v* ▷ **emulate**
emulation *n* ▷ **emulate**
emulations *n* ▷ **emulate**
emulsified *v* ▷ **emulsify**
emulsifier *n* ▷ **emulsify**
emulsifiers *n* ▷ **emulsify**
emulsifies *v* ▷ **emulsify**
emulsify *v* (**-fies, -fying, -fied**) (of two liquids) join together or join (two liquids) together > **emulsifier** *n* (*pl* **-s**)
emulsifying *v* ▷ **emulsify**
emulsion *n* (*pl* **-s**) light-sensitive coating on photographic film ▶ *v* (**-s, -ing, -ed**) paint with emulsion paint
emulsioned *v* ▷ **emulsion**
emulsioning *v* ▷ **emulsion**
emulsions *n, v* ▷ **emulsion**
emus *n* ▷ **emu**
enable *v* (**-les, -ling, -led**) provide (a person) with the means, opportunity, or authority (to do something)
enabled *v* ▷ **enable**
enables *v* ▷ **enable**
enabling *v* ▷ **enable**
enact *v* (**-s, -ing, -ed**) establish by law > **enactment** *n* (*pl* **-s**)
enacted *v* ▷ **enact**
enacting *v* ▷ **enact**
enactment *n* ▷ **enact**
enactments *n* ▷ **enact**
enacts *v* ▷ **enact**
enamel *n* (*pl* **-s**) glasslike coating applied to metal etc. to preserve the surface ▶ *v* (**-s, -lling, -lled**) cover with enamel
enamelled *v* ▷ **enamel**
enamelling *v* ▷ **enamel**
enamels *n, v* ▷ **enamel**
enamoured *adj* inspired with love
encamp *v* (**-s, -ing, -ed**) set up in a camp > **encampment** *n* (*pl* **-s**)
encamped *v* ▷ **encamp**
encamping *v* ▷ **encamp**
encampment *n* ▷ **encamp**

encampments *n* ▷ **encamp**
encamps *v* ▷ **encamp**
encapsulate *v* (**-tes, -ting, -ted**) summarize
encapsulated *v* ▷ **encapsulate**
encapsulates *v* ▷ **encapsulate**
encapsulating *v* ▷ **encapsulate**
encephalitis [en-sef-a-**lite**-iss] *n* (*pl* **-es**) inflammation of the brain
encephalitises *n* ▷ **encephalitis**
enchant *v* (**-s, -ing, -ed**) delight and fascinate > **enchantment** *n* (*pl* **-s**) > **enchanter** *n* (*pl* **-s**) > **enchantress** *n fem* (*pl* **-es**)
enchanted *v* ▷ **enchant**
enchanter *n* ▷ **enchant**
enchanters *n* ▷ **enchant**
enchanting *v* ▷ **enchant**
enchantment *n* ▷ **enchant**
enchantments *n* ▷ **enchant**
enchantress *n* ▷ **enchant**
enchantresses *n* ▷ **enchant**
enchants *v* ▷ **enchant**
encircle *v* (**-s, -ling, -led**) form a circle around > **encirclement** *n* (*pl* **-s**)
encircled *v* ▷ **encircle**
encirclement *n* ▷ **encircle**
encirclements *n* ▷ **encircle**
encircles *v* ▷ **encircle**
encircling *v* ▷ **encircle**
enclave *n* (*pl* **-s**) part of a country entirely surrounded by foreign territory
enclaves *n* ▷ **enclave**
enclose *v* (**-s, -sing, -sed**) surround completely > **enclosure** *n* (*pl* **-s**)
enclosed *v* ▷ **enclose**
encloses *v* ▷ **enclose**
enclosing *v* ▷ **enclose**
enclosure *n* ▷ **enclose**
enclosures *n* ▷ **enclose**
encomia *n* ▷ **encomium**
encomium *n* (*pl* **-miums, -mia**) formal expression of praise
encomiums *n* ▷ **encomiums**
encompass *v* (**-es, -ing, -ed**) surround
encompassed *v* ▷ **encompass**
encompasses *v* ▷ **encompass**
encompassing *v* ▷ **encompass**
encore *interj* again, once more ▶ *n* (*pl* **-s**) extra performance due to enthusiastic demand
encores *n* ▷ **encore**
encounter *v* (**-s, -ing, -ed**) meet unexpectedly ▶ *n* (*pl* **-s**) unexpected meeting
encountered *v* ▷ **encounter**
encountering *v* ▷ **encounter**
encounters *v, n* ▷ **encounter**
encourage *v* (**-ges, -ging, -ged**) inspire with confidence > **encouragement** *n* (*pl* **-s**)
encouraged *v* ▷ **encourage**
encouragement *n* ▷ **encourage**
encouragements *n* ▷ **encourage**
encourages *v* ▷ **encourage**
encouraging *v* ▷ **encourage**
encroach *v* (**-es, -ing, -ed**) intrude gradually on a person's rights or land > **encroachment** *n* (*pl* **-s**)
encroached *v* ▷ **encroach**
encroaches *v* ▷ **encroach**
encroaching *v* ▷ **encroach**
encroachment *n* ▷ **encroach**
encroachments *n* ▷ **encroach**
encrust *v* (**-s, -ing, -ed**) cover with a layer of something
encrusted *v* ▷ **encrust**
encrusting *v* ▷ **encrust**
encrusts *v* ▷ **encrust**
encumber *v* (**-s, -ing, -ed**) hinder or impede
encumbered *v* ▷ **encumber**
encumbering *v* ▷ **encumber**
encumbers *v* ▷ **encumber**
encumbrance *n* (*pl* **-s**) something that impedes or is burdensome
encumbrances *n* ▷ **encumbrance**
encyclical [en-**sik**-lik-kl] *n* (*pl* **-s**) letter sent by the Pope to all bishops
encyclicals *n* ▷ **encyclical**
encyclopaedia *n* ▷ **encyclopedia**
encyclopaedias *n* ▷ **encyclopedia**
encyclopaedic *adj* ▷ **encyclopedia**
encyclopedia, encyclopaedia *n* (*pl* **-s**) book or set of books containing facts about many subjects, usu. in alphabetical order > **encyclopedic, encyclopaedic** *adj*
encyclopedias *n* ▷ **encyclopedia**
encyclopedic *adj* ▷ **encyclopedia**
end *n* (*pl* **-s**) furthest point or part ▶ *v* (**-s, -ing, -ed**) bring or come to a finish > **ending** *n* (*pl* **-s**) > **endless** *adj*
endanger *v* (**-s, -ing, -ed**) put in danger
endangered *v* ▷ **endanger**
endangering *v* ▷ **endanger**
endangers *v* ▷ **endanger**
endear *v* (**-s, -ing, -ed**) cause to be liked > **endearing** *adj*
endeared *v* ▷ **endear**
endearing *v, adj* ▷ **endear**
endearment *n* (*pl* **-s**) affectionate word or phrase
endearments *n* ▷ **endearment**
endears *v* ▷ **endear**
endeavour *v* (**-s, -ing, -ed**) try ▶ *n* (*pl* **-s**) effort
endeavoured *v* ▷ **endeavour**

endeavouring *v* ▷ **endeavour**
endeavours *v, n* ▷ **endeavour**
ended *v* ▷ **end**
endemic *adj* present within a localized area or peculiar to a particular group of people
ending *v, n* ▷ **end**
endings *n* ▷ **end**
endive *n* (*pl* **-s**) curly-leaved plant used in salads
endives *n* ▷ **endive**
endless *adj* ▷ **end**
endocrine *adj* relating to the glands which secrete hormones directly into the bloodstream
endogenous [en-**dodge**-in-uss] *adj* originating from within
endorse *v* (**-ses, -sing, -sed**) give approval to > **endorsement** *n* (*pl* **-s**)
endorsed *v* ▷ **endorse**
endorsement *n* ▷ **endorse**
endorsements *n* ▷ **endorse**
endorses *v* ▷ **endorse**
endorsing *v* ▷ **endorse**
endow *v* (**-s, -ing, -ed**) provide permanent income for > **endowment** *n* (*pl* **-s**)
endowed *v* ▷ **endow**
endowing *v* ▷ **endow**
endowment *v* ▷ **endow**
endowments *v* ▷ **endow**
endows *v* ▷ **endow**
ends *n, v* ▷ **end**
endurable *adj* ▷ **endure**
endurance *n* (*pl* **-s**) act or power of enduring
endurances *n* ▷ **endurance**
endure *v* (**-res, -ring, -red**) bear (hardship) patiently > **endurable** *adj*
endured *v* ▷ **endure**
endures *v* ▷ **endure**
enduring *v* ▷ **endure**
endways *adv* having the end forwards or upwards
enema [**en**-im-a] *n* (*pl* **-s**) medicine injected into the rectum to empty the bowels
enemas *n* ▷ **enema**
enemies *n* ▷ **enemy**
enemy *n* (*pl* **-ies**) hostile person or nation, opponent
energetic *adj* ▷ **energy**
energetically *adv* ▷ **energy**
energies *n* ▷ **energy**
energize *v* (**-izes, -izing, -ized**) give vigour to
energized *v* ▷ **energize**
energizes *v* ▷ **energize**
energizing *v* ▷ **energize**
energy *n* (*pl* **-ies**) capacity for intense activity > **energetic** *adj* > **energetically** *adv*
enervate *v* (**-tes, -ting, -ted**) deprive of strength or vitality > **enervation** *n* (*pl* **-s**)
enervated *v* ▷ **enervate**
enervates *v* ▷ **enervate**
enervating *v* ▷ **enervate**
enervation *n* ▷ **enervate**
enervations *n* ▷ **enervate**
enfeeble *v* (**-les, -ling, -led**) weaken
enfeebled *v* ▷ **enfeeble**
enfeebles *v* ▷ **enfeeble**
enfeebling *v* ▷ **enfeeble**
enfold *v* (**-s, -ing, -ed**) cover by wrapping something around
enfolded *v* ▷ **enfold**
enfolding *v* ▷ **enfold**
enfolds *v* ▷ **enfold**
enforce *v* (**-ces, -cing, -ced**) impose obedience (to a law etc.) > **enforceable** *adj* > **enforcement** *n* (*pl* **-s**)
enforced *v* ▷ **enforce**
enforcement *n* ▷ **enforce**
enforcements *n* ▷ **enforce**
enforces *v* ▷ **enforce**
enforcing *v* ▷ **enforce**
enfranchise *v* (**-ses, -sing, -sed**) grant (a person) the right to vote > **enfranchisement** *n* (*pl* **-s**)
enfranchised *v* ▷ **enfranchise**
enfranchisement *n* ▷ **enfranchise**
enfranchisements *n* ▷ **enfranchise**
enfranchises *v* ▷ **enfranchise**
enfranchising *v* ▷ **enfranchise**
engage *v* (**-ges, -ging, -ged**) take part, participate > **engagement** *n* (*pl* **-s**)
engaged *adj* pledged to be married ▶ *v* ▷ **engage**
engagement *n* ▷ **engage**
engagements *n* ▷ **engage**
engages *v* ▷ **engage**
engaging *adj* charming ▶ *v* ▷ **engage**
engender *v* (**-s, -ing, -ed**) produce, cause to occur
engendered *v* ▷ **engender**
engendering *v* ▷ **engender**
engenders *v* ▷ **engender**
engine *n* (*pl* **-s**) any machine which converts energy into mechanical work
engineer *n* (*pl* **-s**) person trained in any branch of engineering ▶ *v* (**-s, -ing, -ed**) plan in a clever manner
engineered *v* ▷ **engineer**
engineering *v* ▷ **engineer** ▶ *n* (*pl* **-s**) profession of applying scientific principles to the design and construction of engines, cars, buildings,

or machines
engineerings *n* ▷ **engineering**
engineers *n, v* ▷ **engineer**
engines *n* ▷ **engine**
English *n* (*pl* **-es**) official language of Britain, Ireland, Australia, New Zealand, South Africa, Canada, the US, and several other countries ▶ *adj* relating to England
Englishes *n* ▷ **English**
engrave *v* (**-ves, -ving, -ved**) carve (a design) onto a hard surface > **engraver** *n* (*pl* **-s**)
engraved *v* ▷ **engrave**
engraver *n* ▷ **engrave**
engravers *n* ▷ **engrave**
engraves *v* ▷ **engrave**
engraving *v* ▷ **engrave** ▶ *n* (*pl* **-s**) print made from an engraved plate
engravings *n* ▷ **engraving**
engross [en-**groce**] *v* (**-es, -ing, -ed**) occupy the attention of (a person) completely
engrossed *v* ▷ **engross**
engrosses *v* ▷ **engross**
engrossing *v* ▷ **engross**
engulf *v* (**-s, -ing, -ed**) cover or surround completely
engulfed *v* ▷ **engulf**
engulfing *v* ▷ **engulf**
engulfs *v* ▷ **engulf**
enhance *v* (**-s, -ing, -ed**) increase in quality, value, or attractiveness > **enhancement** *n* (*pl* **-s**)
enhanced *v* ▷ **enhance**
enhancement *n* ▷ **enhance**
enhancements *n* ▷ **enhance**
enhances *v* ▷ **enhance**
enhancing *v* ▷ **enhance**
enigma *n* (*pl* **-s**) puzzling thing or person > **enigmatic** *adj* > **enigmatically** *adv*
enigmas *n* ▷ **enigma**
enigmatic *adj* ▷ **enigma**
enigmatically *adv* ▷ **enigma**
enjoin *v* (**-s, -ing, -ed**) order (someone) to do something
enjoined *v* ▷ **enjoin**
enjoining *v* ▷ **enjoin**
enjoins *v* ▷ **enjoin**
enjoy *v* (**-s, -ing, -ed**) take joy in > **enjoyable** *adj* > **enjoyment** *n* (*pl* **-s**)
enjoyable *adj* ▷ **enjoy**
enjoyed *v* ▷ **enjoy**
enjoying *v* ▷ **enjoy**
enjoyment *n* ▷ **enjoy**
enjoyments *n* ▷ **enjoy**
enjoys *v* ▷ **enjoy**
enlarge *v* (**-ges, -ging, -ged**) make or grow larger (*foll. by* **on**) > **enlargement** *n* (*pl* **-s**)
enlarged *v* ▷ **enlarge**
enlargement *n* ▷ **enlarge**
enlargements *n* ▷ **enlarge**
enlarges *v* ▷ **enlarge**
enlarging *v* ▷ **enlarge**
enlighten *v* (**-s, -ing, -ed**) give information to > **enlightenment** *n* (*pl* **-s**)
enlightened *v* ▷ **enlighten**
enlightening *v* ▷ **enlighten**
enlightenment *n* ▷ **enlighten**
enlightenments *n* ▷ **enlighten**
enlightens *v* ▷ **enlighten**
enlist *v* (**-s, -ing, -ed**) enter the armed forces > **enlistment** *n* (*pl* **-s**)
enlisted *v* ▷ **enlist**
enlisting *v* ▷ **enlist**
enlistment *n* ▷ **enlist**
enlistments *n* ▷ **enlist**
enlists *v* ▷ **enlist**
enliven *v* (**-s, -ing, -ed**) make lively or cheerful
enlivened *v* ▷ **enliven**
enlivening *v* ▷ **enliven**
enlivens *v* ▷ **enliven**
enmeshed *adj* deeply involved
enmities *n* ▷ **enmity**
enmity *n* (*pl* **-ies**) ill will, hatred
ennoble *v* (**-s, -ing, -ed**) make noble, elevate
ennobled *v* ▷ **ennoble**
ennobles *v* ▷ **ennoble**
ennobling *v* ▷ **ennoble**
ennui [on-**nwee**] *n* (*pl* **-s**) boredom, dissatisfaction
ennuis *n* ▷ **ennui**
enormities *n* ▷ **enormity**
enormity *n* (*pl* **-ies**) great wickedness
enormous *adj* very big, vast
enough *adj* as much or as many as necessary ▶ *pron* sufficient quantity ▶ *adv* sufficiently
enquire *v* (**-res, -ring, -red**) ▷ **inquire** > **enquiry** *n* (*pl* **-ies**)
enquired *v* ▷ **enquire**
enquires *v* ▷ **enquire**
enquiries *n* ▷ **enquire**
enquiring *v* ▷ **enquire**
enquiry *n* ▷ **enquire**
enraptured *adj* filled with delight and fascination
enrich *v* (**-es, -ing, -ed**) improve in quality
enriched *v* ▷ **enrich**
enriches *v* ▷ **enrich**
enriching *v* ▷ **enrich**
enrol *v* (**-s, -lling, -lled**) (cause to) become a member > **enrolment** *n* (*pl* **-s**)

enrolled *v* ▷ **enrol**
enrolling *v* ▷ **enrol**
enrolment *n* ▷ **enrol**
enrolments *n* ▷ **enrol**
enrols *v* ▷ **enrol**
ensconce *v* (**-ces, -cing, -ced**) settle firmly or comfortably
ensconced *v* ▷ **ensconce**
ensconces *v* ▷ **ensconce**
ensconcing *v* ▷ **ensconce**
ensemble [on-**som**-bl] *n* (*pl* **-s**) all the parts of something taken together
ensembles *n* ▷ **ensemble**
enshrine *v* (**-nes, -ning, -ned**) cherish or treasure
enshrined *v* ▷ **enshrine**
enshrines *v* ▷ **enshrine**
enshrining *v* ▷ **enshrine**
ensign *n* (*pl* **-s**) naval flag
ensigns *n* ▷ **ensign**
enslave *v* (**-ves, -ving, -ved**) make a slave of (someone) > **enslavement** *n* (*pl* **-s**)
enslaved *v* ▷ **enslave**
enslavement *n* ▷ **enslave**
enslavements *n* ▷ **enslave**
enslaves *v* ▷ **enslave**
enslaving *v* ▷ **enslave**
ensnare *v* (**-res, -ring, -red**) catch in or as if in a snare
ensnared *v* ▷ **ensnare**
ensnares *v* ▷ **ensnare**
ensnaring *v* ▷ **ensnare**
ensue *v* (**-sues, -suing, -sued**) come next, result
ensued *v* ▷ **ensue**
ensues *v* ▷ **ensue**
ensuing *v* ▷ **ensue**
ensure *v* (**-re, -ring, -red**) make certain or sure
ensured *v* ▷ **ensure**
ensures *v* ▷ **ensure**
ensuring *v* ▷ **ensure**
entail *v* (**-s, -ing, -ed**) bring about or impose inevitably
entailed *v* ▷ **entail**
entailing *v* ▷ **entail**
entails *v* ▷ **entail**
entangle *v* (**-les, -ling, -led**) catch or involve in or as if in a tangle > **entanglement** *n* (*pl* **-s**)
entangled *v* ▷ **entangle**
entanglement *n* ▷ **entangle**
entanglements *n* ▷ **entangle**
entangles *v* ▷ **entangle**
entangling *v* ▷ **entangle**
entente [on-**tont**] *n* (*pl* **-s**) friendly understanding between nations
ententes *n* ▷ **entente**
enter *v* (**-s, -ing, -ed**) come or go in
entered *v* ▷ **enter**
enteric [en-**ter**-ik] *adj* intestinal
entering *v* ▷ **enter**
enteritis [en-ter-**rite**-iss] *n* (*pl* **-es**) inflammation of the intestine, causing diarrhoea
enteritises *n* ▷ **enteritis**
enterprise *n* (*pl* **-s**) company or firm
enterprises *n* ▷ **enterprise**
enterprising *adj* full of boldness and initiative
enters *v* ▷ **enter**
entertain *v* (**-s, -ing, -ed**) amuse > **entertainer** *n* (*pl* **-s**) > **entertainment** *n* (*pl* **-s**)
entertained *v* ▷ **entertain**
entertainer *n* ▷ **entertain**
entertainers *n* ▷ **entertain**
entertaining *v* ▷ **entertain**
entertainment *n* ▷ **entertain**
entertainments *n* ▷ **entertain**
entertains *v* ▷ **entertain**
enthral [en-**thrawl**] *v* (**-s, -lling, -lled**) hold the attention of > **enthralling** *adj*
enthralled *v* ▷ **enthral**
enthralling *v, adj* ▷ **enthral**
enthrals *v* ▷ **enthral**
enthuse *v* (**-s, -ing, -ed**) (cause to) show enthusiasm
enthused *v* ▷ **enthuse**
enthuses *v* ▷ **enthuse**
enthusiasm *n* (*pl* **-s**) ardent interest, eagerness
enthusiasms *n* ▷ **enthusiasm**
enthusiast *n* (*pl* **-s**) ardent supporter of something > **enthusiastic** *adj* > **enthusiastically** *adv*
enthusiastic *adj* ▷ **enthusiast**
enthusiastically *adv* ▷ **enthusiast**
enthusiasts *n* ▷ **enthusiast**
enthusing *v* ▷ **enthuse**
entice *v* (**-ces, -cing, -ced**) attract by exciting hope or desire, tempt > **enticement** *n* (*pl* **-s**)
enticed *v* ▷ **entice**
enticement *n* ▷ **entice**
enticements *n* ▷ **entice**
entices *v* ▷ **entice**
enticing *v* ▷ **entice**
entire *adj* including every detail, part, or aspect of something > **entirely** *adv* > **entirety** *n* (*pl* **-ties**)
entirely *adv* ▷ **entire**
entireties *n* ▷ **entire**
entirety *n* ▷ **entire**
entities *n* ▷ **entity**
entitle *v* (**-les, -ling, -led**) give a right to > **entitlement** *n* (*pl* **-s**)

entitled *v* ▷ **entitle**
entitlement *n* ▷ **entitle**
entitlements *n* ▷ **entitle**
entitles *v* ▷ **entitle**
entitling *v* ▷ **entitle**
entity *n* (*pl* **-ties**) separate distinct thing
entomological *adj* ▷ **entomology**
entomologies *n* ▷ **entomology**
entomologist *n* ▷ **entomology**
entomologists *n* ▷ **entomology**
entomology *n* (*pl* **-ies**) study of insects **> entomological** *adj* **> entomologist** *n* (*pl* **-s**)
entourage [**on**-toor-ahzh] *n* (*pl* **-s**) group of people who assist an important person
entourages *n* ▷ **entourage**
entrails *pl n* intestines
entrance¹ *n* (*pl* **-s**) way into a place
entrance² *v* (**-s, -ing, -ed**) delight
entranced *v* ▷ **entrance²**
entrances *n* ▷ **entrance¹** ▶ *v* ▷ **entrance²**
entrancing *v* ▷ **entrance²**
entrant *n* (*pl* **-s**) person who enters a university, contest, etc.
entrants *n* ▷ **entrant**
entreat *v* (**-s, -ing, -ed**) ask earnestly
entreated *v* ▷ **entreat**
entreaties *n* ▷ **entreaty**
entreating *v* ▷ **entreat**
entreats *v* ▷ **entreat**
entreaty *n* (*pl* **-ties**) earnest request
entrée [**on**-tray] *n* (*pl* **-s**) dish served before a main course
entrées *n* ▷ **entrée**
entrench *v* (**-es, -ing, -ed**) establish firmly **> entrenchment** *n* (*pl* **-s**)
entrenched *v* ▷ **entrench**
entrenches *v* ▷ **entrench**
entrenching *v* ▷ **entrench**
entrenchment *n* ▷ **entrench**
entrenchments *n* ▷ **entrench**
entrepreneur *n* (*pl* **-s**) business person who attempts to make a profit by risk and initiative
entrepreneurs *n* ▷ **entrepreneur**
entries *n* ▷ **entry**
entropies *n* ▷ **entropy**
entropy [**en**-trop-ee] *n* (*pl* **-ies**) lack of organization
entrust *v* (**-s, -ing, -ed**) put into the care or protection of
entrusted *v* ▷ **entrust**
entrusting *v* ▷ **entrust**
entrusts *v* ▷ **entrust**
entry *n* (*pl* **-ies**) entrance
entwine *v* (**-s, -ing, -ed**) twist together or around
entwined *v* ▷ **entwine**
entwines *v* ▷ **entwine**
entwining *v* ▷ **entwine**
enumerate *v* (**-tes, -ting, -ted**) name one by one **> enumeration** *n* (*pl* **-s**)
enumerated *v* ▷ **enumerate**
enumerates *v* ▷ **enumerate**
enumerating *v* ▷ **enumerate**
enumeration *n* ▷ **enumerate**
enumerations *n* ▷ **enumerate**
enuncation *n* ▷ **enunciate**
enunciate *v* (**-tes, -ting, -ted**) pronounce clearly **> enunciation** *n* (*pl* **-s**)
enunciated *v* ▷ **enunciate**
enunciates *v* ▷ **enunciate**
enunciating *v* ▷ **enunciate**
enunciation *n* ▷ **enunciate**
enunciations *n* ▷ **enunciate**
envelop *v* (**-s, -ing, -ed**) wrap up, enclose **> envelopment** *n* (*pl* **-s**)
envelope *n* (*pl* **-s**) folded gummed paper cover for a letter
enveloped *v* ▷ **envelop**
envelopes *n* ▷ **envelope**
enveloping *v* ▷ **envelop**
envelopment *n* ▷ **envelop**
envelopments *n* ▷ **envelop**
envelops *v* ▷ **envelop**
enviable *adj* arousing envy, fortunate
envied *v* ▷ **envy**
envies *n, v* ▷ **envy**
envious *adj* full of envy
environment [en-**vire**-on-ment] *n* (*pl* **-s**) external conditions and surroundings in which people, animals, or plants live **> environmental** *adj*
environmental *adj* ▷ **environment**
environmentalist *n* (*pl* **-s**) person concerned with the protection of the natural environment
environmentalists *n* ▷ **environmentalist**
environments *n* ▷ **environment**
environs *pl n* surrounding area, esp. of a town
envisage *v* (**-ges, -ging, -ged**) conceive of as a possibility
envisaged *v* ▷ **envisage**
envisages *v* ▷ **envisage**
envisaging *v* ▷ **envisage**
envoy *n* (*pl* **-s**) messenger
envoys *n* ▷ **envoy**
envy *n* (*pl* **-ies**) feeling of discontent aroused by another's good fortune ▶ *v* (**-ies, -ying, -ied**) grudge (another's good fortune, success, or qualities)

envying *v* ▷ **envy**
enzyme *n* (*pl* **-s**) any of a group of complex proteins that act as catalysts in specific biochemical reactions
enzymes *n* ▷ **enzyme**
eolithic *adj* of the early part of the Stone Age
epaulette *n* (*pl* **-s**) shoulder ornament on a uniform
epaulettes *n* ▷ **epaulette**
ephemeral *adj* short-lived
epic *n* (*pl* **-s**) long poem, book, or film about heroic events or actions ▸ *adj* very impressive or ambitious
epicentre *n* (*pl* **-s**) point on the earth's surface immediately above the origin of an earthquake
epicentres *n* ▷ **epicentre**
epics *n* ▷ **epic**
epicure *n* (*pl* **-s**) person who enjoys good food and drink
epicurean *adj* devoted to sensual pleasures, esp. food and drink ▸ *n* (*pl* **-s**) epicure
epicureans *n* ▷ **epicurean**
epicures *n* ▷ **epicure**
epidemic *n* (*pl* **-s**) widespread occurrence of a disease
epidemics *n* ▷ **epidemic**
epidermis *n* (*pl* **-ses**) outer layer of the skin
epidermises *n* ▷ **epidermis**
epidural [ep-pid-**dure**-al] *adj*, *n* (*pl* **-s**) (of) spinal anaesthetic injected to relieve pain during childbirth
epidurals *n* ▷ **epidural**
epiglottis *n* (*pl* **-ses**) thin flap that covers the opening of the larynx during swallowing
epiglottises *n* ▷ **epiglottis**
epigram *n* (*pl* **-s**) short witty remark or poem > **epigrammatic** *adj*
epigrammatic *adj* ▷ **epigram**
epigrams *n* ▷ **epigram**
epigraph *n* (*pl* **-s**) quotation at the start of a book
epigraphs *n* ▷ **epigraph**
epilepsies *n* ▷ **epilepsy**
epilepsy *n* (*pl* **-ies**) disorder of the nervous system causing loss of consciousness and sometimes convulsions
epileptic *adj* of or having epilepsy ▸ *n* (*pl* **-s**) person who has epilepsy
epileptics *n* ▷ **epileptic**
epilogue *n* (*pl* **-s**) short speech or poem at the end of a literary work, esp. a play
epilogues *n* ▷ **epilogue**
epiphanies *n* ▷ **epiphany**
epiphany *n* (*pl* **-ies**) a moment of great or sudden realization
episcopal [ip-**piss**-kop-al] *adj* of or governed by bishops
episcopalian *adj* advocating Church government by bishops ▸ *n* (*pl* **-s**) advocate of such Church government
episcopalians *n* ▷ **episcopalian**
episode *n* (*pl* **-s**) incident in a series of incidents
episodes *n* ▷ **episode**
episodic *adj* occurring at irregular intervals
epistemological *adj* ▷ **epistemology**
epistemologies *n* ▷ **epistemology**
epistemology [ip-iss-stem-**ol**-a-jee] *n* (*pl* **-ies**) study of the source, nature, and limitations of knowledge > **epistemological** *adj*
epistle *n* (*pl* **-s**) letter, esp. of an apostle > **epistolary** *adj*
epistles *n* ▷ **epistle**
epistolary *adj* ▷ **epistle**
epitaph *n* (*pl* **-s**) commemorative inscription on a tomb
epitaphs *n* ▷ **epitaph**
epithet *n* (*pl* **-s**) descriptive word or name
epithets *n* ▷ **epithet**
epitome [ip-**pit**-a-mee] *n* (*pl* **-s**) typical example
epitomes *n* ▷ **epitome**
epitomize *v* (**-izes, -izing, -ized**) be the epitome of
epitomized *v* ▷ **epitomize**
epitomizes *v* ▷ **epitomize**
epitomizing *v* ▷ **epitomize**
epoch [**ee**-pok] *n* (*pl* **-s**) period of notable events
epochs *n* ▷ **epoch**
eponymous [ip-**pon**-im-uss] *adj* after whom a book, play, etc. is named
equable [**ek**-wab-bl] *adj* even-tempered > **equably** *adv*
equably *adv* ▷ **equable**
equal *adj* identical in size, quantity, degree, etc. ▸ *n* (*pl* **-s**) person or thing equal to another ▸ *v* (**-s, -lling, -lled**) be equal to > **equally** *adv*
equalities *n* ▷ **equality**
equality *n* (*pl* **-ies**) state of being equal
equalization *n* ▷ **equalize**
equalizations *n* ▷ **equalize**
equalize *v* (**-lizes, -lizing, -lized**) make or become equal > **equalization** *n* (*pl* **-s**)
equalized *v* ▷ **equalize**
equalizes *v* ▷ **equalize**
equalizing *v* ▷ **equalize**
equalled *v* ▷ **equal**
equalling *v* ▷ **equal**
equally *adv* ▷ **equal**
equals *n*, *v* ▷ **equal**

equanimities *n* ▷ **equanimity**
equanimity *n* (*pl* **-ies**) calmness of mind
equate *v* (**-tes, -ting, -ted**) make or regard as equivalent
equated *v* ▷ **equate**
equates *v* ▷ **equate**
equating *v* ▷ **equate**
equation *n* (*pl* **-s**) mathematical statement that two expressions are equal
equations *n* ▷ **equation**
equator *n* (*pl* **-s**) imaginary circle round the earth, equidistant from the poles > **equatorial** *adj*
equatorial *adj* ▷ **equator**
equators *n* ▷ **equator**
equerries *n* ▷ **equerry**
equerry [**ek**-kwer-ee] *n* (*pl* **-ies**) (BRIT) officer who acts as an attendant to a member of a royal family
equestrian *adj* of horses and riding
equidistant *adj* equally distant
equilateral *adj* having equal sides
equilibria *n* ▷ **equilibriums**
equilibrium *n* (*pl* **-ria**) steadiness or stability
equine *adj* of or like a horse
equinoctial *adj* ▷ **equinox**
equinox *n* (*pl* **-es**) time of year when day and night are of equal length > **equinoctial** *adj*
equinoxes *n* ▷ **equinox**
equip *v* (**-s, -pping, -pped**) provide with supplies, components, etc.
equipment *n* (*pl* **-s**) set of tools or devices used for a particular purpose
equipments *n* ▷ **equipment**
equipoise *n* (*pl* **-s**) perfect balance
equipoises *n* ▷ **equipoise**
equipped *v* ▷ **equip**
equipping *v* ▷ **equip**
equips *v* ▷ **equips**
equitable *adj* fair and reasonable > **equitably** *adv*
equitably *adv* ▷ **equitable**
equities *n* ▷ **equity**
equity *n* (*pl* **-ties**) fairness ▶ *pl* interest of ordinary shareholders in a company
equivalence *n* ▷ **equivalent**
equivalences *n* ▷ **equivalent**
equivalent *adj* equal in value ▶ *n* (*pl* **-s**) something that is equivalent > **equivalence** *n* (*pl* **-s**)
equivalents *n* ▷ **equivalent**
equivocal *adj* ambiguous > **equivocally** *adv*
equivocally *adv* ▷ **equivocal**
equivocate *v* (**-tes, -ting, -ted**) use vague or ambiguous language to mislead people > **equivocation** *n* (*pl* **-s**)
equivocated *v* ▷ **equivocate**
equivocates *v* ▷ **equivocate**
equivocating *v* ▷ **equivocate**
equivocation *n* ▷ **equivocate**
equivocations *n* ▷ **equivocate**
era *n* (*pl* **-s**) period of time considered as distinctive
eradicate *v* (**-tes, -ting, -ted**) destroy completely > **eradication** *n* (*pl* **-s**)
eradicated *v* ▷ **eradicate**
eradicates *v* ▷ **eradicate**
eradicating *v* ▷ **eradicate**
eradication *n* ▷ **eradicate**
eradications *n* ▷ **eradicate**
eras *n* ▷ **era**
erase *v* (**-ses, -sing, -sed**) rub out
erased *v* ▷ **erase**
eraser *n* (*pl* **-s**) object for erasing something written
erasers *n* ▷ **eraser**
erases *v* ▷ **erase**
erasing *v* ▷ **erase**
erasure *n* (*pl* **-s**) erasing
erasures *n* ▷ **erasure**
ere *prep, conj* (*Poetic*) before
erect *v* (**-s, -ing, -ed**) build ▶ *adj* upright > **erection** *n* (*pl* **-s**)
erected *v* ▷ **erect**
erectile *adj* capable of becoming erect from sexual excitement
erecting *v* ▷ **erect**
erection *n* ▷ **erect**
erections *n* ▷ **erect**
erects *v* ▷ **erect**
erg *n* (*pl* **-s**) unit of work or energy
ergonomic *adj* ▷ **ergonomics**
ergonomics *n* (*pl* study of the relationship between workers and their environment > **ergonomic** *adj*
ergot *n* (*pl* **-s**) fungal disease of cereal
ergots *n* ▷ **ergot**
ergs *n* ▷ **erg**
ermine *n* (*pl* **-s**) stoat in northern regions
ermines *n* ▷ **ermine**
erode *v* (**-s, -ing, -ed**) wear away > **erosion** *n* (*pl* **-s**)
eroded *v* ▷ **erode**
erodes *v* ▷ **erode**
eroding *v* ▷ **erode**
erogenous [ir-**roj**-in-uss] *adj* sensitive to sexual stimulation
erosion *n* ▷ **erode**
erosions *n* ▷ **erode**
erotic *adj* relating to sexual pleasure or desire

> eroticism *n* (*pl* **-s**)
erotica *n* sexual literature or art
eroticism *n* ▷ **erotic**
eroticisms *n* ▷ **erotic**
err *v* (**-s, -ing, -ed**) make a mistake
errand *n* (*pl* **-s**) short trip to do something for someone
errands *n* ▷ **errand**
errant *adj* behaving in a manner considered to be unacceptable
errata *n* ▷ **erratum**
erratic *adj* irregular or unpredictable **> erratically** *adv*
erratically *adv* ▷ **erratic**
erratum *n* (*pl* **-ta**) error in writing or printing
erred *v* ▷ **err**
erring *v* ▷ **err**
erroneous *adj* incorrect, mistaken
error *n* (*pl* **-s**) mistake, inaccuracy, or misjudgment
errors *n* ▷ **error**
errs *v* ▷ **err**
ersatz [**air**-zats] *adj* made in imitation
erstwhile *adj* former
erudite *adj* having great academic knowledge **> erudition** *n* (*pl* **-s**)
erudition *v* ▷ **erudite**
eruditions *n* ▷ **erudite**
erupt *v* (**-s, -ing, -ed**) eject (steam, water, or volcanic material) violently **> eruption** *n* (*pl* **-s**)
erupted *v* ▷ **erupt**
erupting *v* ▷ **erupt**
eruption *n* ▷ **erupt**
eruptions *n* ▷ **erupt**
erupts *v* ▷ **erupt**
erysipelas [err-riss-**sip**-pel-ass] *n* (*pl* **-es**) acute skin infection causing purplish patches
erysipelases *n* ▷ **erysipelas**

es *n* (**eses**). Es is the letter S. This is a useful word when you want to play a high-scoring word that will touch words already on the board. Es scores 2 points.

escalate *v* (**-tes, -ting, -ted**) increase in extent or intensity **> escalation** *n* (*pl* **-s**)
escalated *v* ▷ **escalate**
escalates *v* ▷ **escalate**
escalating *v* ▷ **escalate**
escalation *n* ▷ **escalate**
escalations *n* ▷ **escalate**
escalator *n* (*pl* **-s**) moving staircase
escalators *n* ▷ **escalator**
escalope [**ess**-kal-lop] *n* (*pl* **-s**) thin slice of meat, esp. veal
escalopes *n* ▷ **escalope**
escapade *n* (*pl* **-s**) mischievous adventure
escapades *n* ▷ **escapade**
escape *v* (**-pes, -ping, -ped**) get free (of) ▶ *n* (*pl* **-s**) act of escaping
escaped *v* ▷ **escape**
escapee *n* (*pl* **-s**) person who has escaped
escapees *n* ▷ **escapee**
escapes *v, n* ▷ **escape**
escaping *v* ▷ **escape**
escapism *n* (*pl* **-s**) taking refuge in fantasy to avoid unpleasant reality
escapisms *n* ▷ **escapism**
escapologies *n* ▷ **escapologist**
escapologist *n* (*pl* **-s**) entertainer who specializes in freeing himself from confinement **> escapology** *n* (*pl* **-ies**)
escapologists *n* ▷ **escapologist**
escapology *n* ▷ **escapologist**
escarpment *n* (*pl* **-s**) steep face of a ridge or mountain
escarpments *n* ▷ **escarpment**
eschew [iss-**chew**] *v* (**-s, -ing, -ed**) abstain from, avoid
eschewed *v* ▷ **eschew**
eschewing *v* ▷ **eschew**
eschews *v* ▷ **eschew**
escort *n* (*pl* **-s**) people or vehicles accompanying another person for protection or as an honour ▶ *v* (**-s, -ing, -ed**) act as an escort to
escorted *v* ▷ **escort**
escorting *v* ▷ **escort**
escorts *n, v* ▷ **escort**
escudo [ess-**kyoo**-doe] *n* (*pl* **-dos**) former monetary unit of Portugal
escudos *n* ▷ **escudo**
escutcheon *n* (*pl* **-s**) shield with a coat of arms
escutcheons *n* ▷ **escutcheon**
esoteric [ee-so-**ter**-rik] *adj* understood by only a small number of people with special knowledge
espadrille [**ess**-pad-drill] *n* (*pl* **-s**) light canvas shoe with a braided cord sole
espadrilles *n* ▷ **espadrille**
espalier [ess-**pal**-yer] *n* (*pl* **-s**) shrub or fruit tree trained to grow flat
espaliers *n* ▷ **espalier**
esparto *n* (*pl* **-s**) grass of S Europe and N Africa used for making rope etc.
espartos *n* ▷ **esparto**
especial *adj* (*Formal*) special
especially *adv* particularly
espied *v* ▷ **espy**
espies *v* ▷ **espy**

espionage [ess-pyon-ahzh] *n* (*pl* **-s**) spying
espionages *n* ▷ **espionage**
esplanade *n* (*pl* **-s**) wide open road used as a public promenade
esplanades *n* ▷ **esplanade**
espousal *n* ▷ **espouse**
espousals *n* ▷ **espouse**
espouse *v* (**-ses, -sing, -sed**) adopt or give support to (a cause etc.) > **espousal** *n* (*pl* **-s**)
espoused *v* ▷ **espouse**
espouses *v* ▷ **espouse**
espousing *v* ▷ **espouse**
espresso *n* (*pl* **-s**) strong coffee made by forcing steam or boiling water through ground coffee beans
espressos *n* ▷ **espresso**
esprit [ess-**pree**] *n* (*pl* **-s**) spirit, liveliness, or wit
esprits *n* ▷ **esprit**
espy *v* (**-ies, -ying, -ied**) catch sight of
espying *v* ▷ **espy**
esquire *n* (*pl* **-s**) courtesy title placed after a man's name
esquires *n* ▷ **esquire**
essay *n* (*pl* **-s**) short literary composition ▶ *v* (**-s, -ing, -ed**) attempt > **essayist** *n* (*pl* **-s**)
essayed *v* ▷ **essay**
essaying *v* ▷ **essay**
essayist *n* ▷ **essay**
essayists *n* ▷ **essay**
essays *n, v* ▷ **essay**
essence *n* (*pl* **-s**) most important feature of a thing which determines its identity
essences *n* ▷ **essence**
essential *adj* vitally important ▶ *n* (*pl* **-s**) something fundamental or indispensable > **essentially** *adv*
essentially *adv* ▷ **essential**
essentials *n* ▷ **essential**
establish *v* (**-es, -ing, -ed**) set up on a permanent basis
established *v* ▷ **establish**
establishes *v* ▷ **establish**
establishing *v* ▷ **establish**
establishment *n* (*pl* **-s**) act of establishing
establishments *n* ▷ **establishment**
estate *n* (*pl* **-s**) landed property
estates *n* ▷ **estate**
esteem *n* (*pl* **-s**) high regard ▶ *v* (**-s, -ing, -ed**) think highly of
esteemed *v* ▷ **esteem**
esteeming *v* ▷ **esteem**
esteems *n, v* ▷ **esteem**
ester *n* (*pl* **-s**) (CHEM) compound produced by the reaction between an acid and an alcohol
esters *n* ▷ **ester**
estimable *adj* worthy of respect
estimate *v* (**-tes, -ting, -ted**) calculate roughly ▶ *n* (*pl* **-s**) approximate calculation
estimated *v* ▷ **estimate**
estimates *v, n* ▷ **estimate**
estimating *v* ▷ **estimate**
estimation *n* (*pl* **-s**) considered opinion
estimations *n* ▷ **estimation**
estranged *adj* no longer living with one's spouse > **estrangement** *n* (*pl* **-s**)
estrangement *n* ▷ **estranged**
estrangements *n* ▷ **estranged**
estuaries *n* ▷ **estuary**
estuary *n* (*pl* **--ies**) mouth of a river
etch *v* (**-es, -ing, -ed**) wear away or cut the surface of (metal, glass, etc.) with acid > **etching** *n* (*pl* **-s**)
etched *v* ▷ **etch**
etches *v* ▷ **etch**
etching *v, n* ▷ **etch**
eternal *adj* without beginning or end > **eternally** *adv*
eternally *adv* ▷ **eternal**
eternities *n* ▷ **eternity**
eternity *n* (*pl* **-ies**) infinite time
ether *n* (*pl* **-s**) colourless sweet-smelling liquid used as an anaesthetic
ethereal [eth-**eer**-ee-al] *adj* extremely delicate
ethers *n* ▷ **ether**
ethic *n* (*pl* **-s**) moral principle > **ethical** *adj* > **ethically** *adv*
ethical *adj* ▷ **ethic**
ethically *adv* ▷ **ethic**
ethics *n* ▷ **ethic**
ethnic *adj* relating to a people or group that shares a culture, religion, or language
ethnological *adj* ▷ **ethnology**
ethnologies *n* ▷ **ethnology**
ethnologist *n* ▷ **ethnology**
ethnologists *n* ▷ **ethnology**
ethnology *n* (*pl* **-ies**) study of human races > **ethnological** *adj* > **ethnologist** *n* (*pl* **-s**)
ethos [**eeth**-oss] *n* (*pl* **-es**) distinctive spirit and attitudes of a people, culture, etc.
ethoses *n* ▷ **ethos**
ethyl [**eeth**-ile] *adj* of, consisting of, or containing the hydrocarbon group C_2H_5
ethylene *n* (*pl* **-s**) poisonous gas used as an anaesthetic and as fuel
ethylenes *n* ▷ **ethylene**
etiolate [ee-tee-oh-late] *v* (**-tes, -ting, -ted**) become pale and weak (BOTANY)
etiolated *v* ▷ **etiolate**
etiolates *v* ▷ **etiolate**
etiolating *v* ▷ **etiolate**

etiologies *n* ▷ **etiology**
etiology *n* (*pl* **-ies**) study of the causes of diseases
etiquette *n* (*pl* **-s**) conventional code of conduct
etiquettes *n* ▷ **etiquette**
étude [**ay**-tewd] *n* (*pl* **-s**) short musical composition for a solo instrument, esp. intended as a technical exercise
études *n* ▷ **étude**
etymological *adj* ▷ **etymology**
etymologies *n* ▷ **etymology**
etymology *n* (*pl* **-gies**) study of the sources and development of words > **etymological** *adj*
eucalypt *n* ▷ **eucalyptus**
eucalypts *n* ▷ **eucalyptus**
eucalyptus, eucalypt *n* (*pl* **-ses, -s**) tree, mainly grown in Australia, that provides timber, gum, and medicinal oil from the leaves
eucalyptuses *n* ▷ **eucalyptus**
eugenics [yew-**jen**-iks] *n* (*pl* study of methods of improving the human race
eulogies *n* ▷ **eulogy**
eulogistic *adj* ▷ **euology**
eulogize *v* (**-s, -ing, -ed**) praise (a person or thing) highly in speech or writing
eulogized *v* ▷ **eulogize**
eulogizes *v* ▷ **eulogize**
eulogizing *v* ▷ **eulogize**
eulogy *n* (*pl* **-ies**) speech or writing in praise of a person > **eulogistic** *adj*
eunuch *n* (*pl* **-s**) castrated man, esp. (formerly) a guard in a harem
eunuchs *n* ▷ **eunuch**
euphemism *n* (*pl* **-s**) inoffensive word or phrase substituted for one considered offensive or upsetting > **euphemistic** *adj* > **euphemistically** *adv*
euphemisms *n* ▷ **euphemism**
euphemistic ▷ **euphemism**
euphemistically ▷ **euphemism**
euphonies *n* ▷ **euphony**
euphonious *adj* pleasing to the ear
euphonium *n* (*pl* **-s**) brass musical instrument, tenor tuba
euphoniums *n* ▷ **euphonium**
euphony *n* (*pl* **-nies**) pleasing sound
euphoria *n* (*pl* **-s**) sense of elation > **euphoric** *adj*
euphorias *n* ▷ **euphoria**
euphoric *adj* ▷ **euphoria**
eureka [yew-**reek**-a] *interj* exclamation of triumph at finding something
euro *n* (*pl* **-s**) unit of the single currency of the European Union
euros *n* ▷ **euro**
euthanasia *n* (*pl* **-s**) act of killing someone painlessly, esp. to relieve his or her suffering
euthanasias *n* ▷ **euthanasia**
evacuate *v* (**-tes, -ting, -ted**) send (someone) away from a place of danger > **evacuation** *n* (*pl* **-s**) > **evacuee** *n* (*pl* **-s**)
evacuated *v* ▷ **evacuate**
evacuates *v* ▷ **evacuate**
evacuating *v* ▷ **evacuate**
evacuation *n* ▷ **evacuate**
evacuations *n* ▷ **evacuate**
evacuee *n* ▷ **evacuate**
evacuees *n* ▷ **evacuate**
evade *v* (**-des, -ding, -ded**) get away from or avoid > **evasion** *n* (*pl* **-s**)
evaded *v* ▷ **evade**
evades *v* ▷ **evade**
evading *v* ▷ **evade**
evaluate *v* (**-tes, -ting, -ted**) find or judge the value of > **evaluation** *n* (*pl* **-s**)
evaluated *v* ▷ **evaluate**
evaluates *v* ▷ **evaluate**
evaluating *v* ▷ **evaluate**
evaluation *n* ▷ **evaluate**
evaluations *n* ▷ **evaluate**
evanescence *n* ▷ **evanescent**
evanescences *n* ▷ **evanescent**
evanescent *adj* quickly fading away > **evanescence** *n* (*pl* **-s**)
evangelical *adj* of or according to gospel teaching ▸ *n* (*pl* **-s**) member of an evangelical sect > **evangelicalism** *n* (*pl* **-s**)
evangelicalism *n* ▷ **evangelical**
evangelicalisms *n* ▷ **evangelical**
evangelicals *n* ▷ **evangelical**
evangelism *n* (*pl* **-s**) teaching and spreading of the Christian gospel
evangelisms *n* ▷ **evangelism**
evangelist *n* (*pl* **-s**) writer of one of the four gospels
evangelists *n* ▷ **evangelist**
evangelization *n* ▷ **evangelize**
evangelizations *n* ▷ **evangelize**
evangelize *v* (**-zes, -zing, -zed**) preach the gospel > **evangelization** *n* (*pl* **-s**)
evangelized *v* ▷ **evangelize**
evangelizes *v* ▷ **evangelize**
evangelizing *v* ▷ **evangelize**
evaporate *v* (**-tes, -ing, -ted**) change from a liquid or solid to a vapour > **evaporation** *n* (*pl* **-s**)
evaporated *v* ▷ **evaporate**
evaporates *v* ▷ **evaporate**

evaporating *v* ▷ **evaporate**
evaporation *n* ▷ **evaporate**
evaporations *n* ▷ **evaporate**
evasion *n* ▷ **evade**
evasions *n* ▷ **evade**
evasive *adj* not straightforward > **evasively** *adv*
evasively *adv* ▷ **evasive**
evasiveness *n* ▷ **evasive**
eve *n* (*pl* **-s**) evening or day before some special event
even (**-er, -est**) *adj* flat or smooth (*foll. by* **with**) ▶ *adv* equally ▶ *v* (**-s, -ing, -ed**) make even
evened *v* ▷ **even**
evener *adj* ▷ **even**
evenest *adj* ▷ **even**
evening *n* (*pl* **-s**) end of the day or early part of the night ▶ *adj* of or in the evening ▶ *v* ▷ **even**
evenings *n* ▷ **evening**
evens *v* ▷ **even**
evensong *n* (*pl* **-s**) evening prayer
evensongs *n* ▷ **evensong**
event *n* (*pl* **-s**) anything that takes place
eventful *adj* full of exciting incidents
eventing *n* (*pl* **-s**) (BRIT, AUST & NZ) riding competitions, usu. involving cross-country, jumping, and dressage
eventings *n* ▷ **eventing**
events *n* ▷ **event**
eventual *adj* ultimate
eventualities *n* ▷ **eventuality**
eventuality *n* (*pl* **-ies**) possible event
eventually *adv* at the end of a situation or process
ever *adv* at any time > **everlasting** *adj*
evergreen *adj*, *n* (*pl* **-s**) (tree or shrub) having leaves throughout the year
evergreens *n* ▷ **evergreen**
everlasting *adj* ▷ **ever**
evermore *adv* for all time to come
every *adj* each without exception
everybody *pron* every person
everyday *adj* usual or ordinary
everyone *pron* every person
everything *pron* all things
everywhere *adv* in all places
eves *n* ▷ **eve**
evict *v* (**-s, -ing, -ed**) legally expel (someone) from his or her home > **eviction** *n* (*pl* **-s**)
evicted *v* ▷ **evict**
evicting *v* ▷ **evict**
eviction *n* ▷ **evict**
evictions *n* ▷ **evict**
evicts *v* ▷ **evict**
evidence *n* (*pl* **-s**) ground for belief ▶ *v* (**-ces, -cing, -ced**) demonstrate, prove
evidenced *v* ▷ **evidence**
evidences *n*, *v* ▷ **evidence**
evidencing *v* ▷ **evidence**
evident *adj* easily seen or understood > **evidently** *adv*
evidential *adj* of, serving as, or based on evidence
evidently *adv* ▷ **evident**
evil *n* (*pl* **-s**) wickedness ▶ *adj* (**-ller, -llest**) harmful > **evilly** *adv*
evildoer *n* (*pl* **-s**) wicked person
evildoers *n* ▷ **evildoer**
eviller *adj* ▷ **evil**
evillest *adj* ▷ **evil**
evilly *adv* ▷ **evil**
evils *n* ▷ **evil**
evince *v* (**-s, -ing, -ed**) make evident
evinced *v* ▷ **evince**
evinces *v* ▷ **evince**
evincing *v* ▷ **evince**
eviscerate *v* (**-tes, -ting, -ted**) disembowel > **evisceration** *n* (*pl* **-s**)
eviscerated *v* ▷ **eviscerate**
eviscerates *v* ▷ **eviscerate**
eviscerating *v* ▷ **eviscerate**
evisceration *n* ▷ **eviscerate**
eviscerations *n* ▷ **eviscerate**
evocation *n* ▷ **evoke**
evocations *n* ▷ **evoke**
evocative *adj* ▷ **evoke**
evoke *v* (**-s, -ing, -ed**) call or summon up (a memory, feeling, etc.) > **evocation** *n* (*pl* **-s**) > **evocative** *adj*
evoked *v* ▷ **evoke**
evokes *v* ▷ **evoke**
evoking *v* ▷ **evoke**
evolution *n* (*pl* **-s**) gradual change in the characteristics of living things over successive generations, esp. to a more complex form > **evolutionary** *adj*
evolutionary *n* ▷ **evolution**
evolutions *n* ▷ **evolution**
evolve *v* (**-kes, -king, -ked**) develop gradually
evolved *v* ▷ **evolve**
evolves *v* ▷ **evolve**
evolving *v* ▷ **evolve**
ewe *n* (*pl* **-s**) female sheep
ewer *n* (*pl* **-s**) large jug with a wide mouth
ewers *n* ▷ **ewer**
ewes *n* ▷ **ewe**

ewk *n* (**ewks**). Ewk is a dialect word for **itch.** It's a handy little word and a good one to remember in case you end up with both K and W, as you're very likely to be able to play it from an E already on the board. Ewk scores 10 points.

ex *n* (*pl* **-es**) (*Informal*) former wife or husband

exacerbate [ig-zass-er-bate] *v* (**-tes, -ting, -ted**) make (pain, emotion, or a situation) worse > **exacerbation** *n* (*pl* **-s**)

exacerbated *v* ▷ **exacerbate**

exacerbates *v* ▷ **exacerbate**

exacerbating *v* ▷ **exacerbate**

exacerbation *n* ▷ **exacerbate**

exacerbations *n* ▷ **exacerbate**

exact *adj* (**-er, -est**) correct and complete in every detail ▶ *v* (**-s, -ing, -ed**) demand (payment or obedience) > **exactness** *n* (*pl* **-es**) > **exactitude** *n* (*pl* **-s**)

exacted *v* ▷ **exact**

exacter *adj* ▷ **exact**

exactest *adj* ▷ **exact**

exacting *adj* making rigorous or excessive demands ▶ *v* ▷ **exact**

exactitude *n* ▷ **exact**

exactitudes *n* ▷ **exact**

exactly *adv* precisely, in every respect

exactness *n* ▷ **exact**

exactnesses *n* ▷ **exact**

exacts *v* ▷ **exact**

exaggerate *v* (**-tes, -ting, -ted**) regard or represent as greater than is true > **exaggeratedly** *adv* > **exaggeration** *n* (*pl* **-s**)

exaggerated *v* ▷ **exaggerate**

exaggeratedly *adv* ▷ **exaggerate**

exaggerates *v* ▷ **exaggerate**

exaggerating *v* ▷ **exaggerate**

exaggeration *n* ▷ **exaggerate**

exaggerations *n* ▷ **exaggerate**

exalt *v* (**-s, -ing, -ed**) praise highly > **exalted** *adj* > **exaltation** *n* (*pl* **-s**)

exaltation *n* ▷ **exalt**

exaltations *n* ▷ **exalt**

exalted *v, adj* ▷ **exalt**

exalting *v* ▷ **exalt**

exalts *v* ▷ **exalt**

exam *n* (*pl* **-s**) ▷ **examination**

examination *n* (*pl* **-s**) examining

examinations *n* ▷ **examination**

examine *v* (**-nes, -ning, -ned**) look at closely > **examinee** *n* (*pl* **-s**) > **examiner** *n* (*pl* **-s**)

examined *v* ▷ **examine**

examinee *n* ▷ **examine**

examinees *n* ▷ **examine**

examiner *n* ▷ **examine**

examiners *n* ▷ **examine**

examines *v* ▷ **examine**

examining *v* ▷ **examine**

example *n* (*pl* **-s**) specimen typical of its group

examples *n* ▷ **example**

exams *n* ▷ **exam**

exasperate *v* (**-tes, -ting, -ted**) cause great irritation to > **exasperation** *n* (*pl* **-s**)

exasperated *v* ▷ **exasperate**

exasperates *v* ▷ **exasperate**

exasperating *v* ▷ **exasperate**

exasperation *v* ▷ **exasperate**

exasperations *v* ▷ **exasperate**

excavate *v* (**-tes, -ting, -ted**) unearth buried objects from (a piece of land) methodically to learn about the past > **excavation** *n* (*pl* **-s**)

excavated *v* ▷ **excavate**

excavates *v* ▷ **excavate**

excavating *v* ▷ **excavate**

excavation *n* ▷ **excavate**

excavations *n* ▷ **excavate**

excavator *n* (*pl* **-s**) large machine used for digging

excavators *n* ▷ **excavator**

exceed *v* (**-s, -ing, -ed**) be greater than

exceeded *v* ▷ **exceed**

exceeding *v* ▷ **exceed**

exceedingly *adv* very

exceeds *v* ▷ **exceed**

excel *v* (**-s, -lling, -lled**) be superior to

excelled *v* ▷ **excel**

excellence *n* ▷ **excellent**

excellences *n* ▷ **excellent**

excellent *adj* exceptionally good > **excellence** *n* (*pl* **-s**)

excelling *v* ▷ **excel**

excels *v* ▷ **excel**

except *prep* (*sometimes foll. by* **for**) other than, not including ▶ *v* (**-s, -ing, -ed**) not include

excepted *v* ▷ **except**

excepting *prep* except ▶ *v* ▷ **except**

exception *n* (*pl* **-s**) excepting

exceptional *adj* not ordinary

exceptions *n* ▷ **exception**

excepts *v* ▷ **except**

excerpt *n* (*pl* **-s**) passage taken from a book, speech, etc.

excerpts *n* ▷ **excerpt**

excess *n* (*pl* **-es**) state or act of exceeding the permitted limits > **excessive** *adj* > **excessively** *adv*

excesses *n* ▷ **excess**

excessive *adj* ▷ **excess**

excessively *adv* ▷ **excess**

exchange *v* (**-ges, -ging, -ged**) give or receive (something) in return for something else ▶ *n* (*pl* **-s**) act of exchanging > **exchangeable** *adj*

exchangeable *adj* ▷ **exchange**

exchanged *v* ▷ **exchange**

exchanges *v, n* ▷ **exchange**
exchanging *v* ▷ **exchange**
exchequer *n* (*pl* **-s**) (BRIT) government department in charge of state money
exchequers *n* ▷ **exchequer**
excise *v* (**-ses, -sing, -sed**) cut out or away > **excision** *n* (*pl* **-s**)
excised *v* ▷ **excise**
excises *v* ▷ **excise**
excising *v* ▷ **excise**
excision *n* ▷ **excise**
excisions *n* ▷ **excise**
excitabilities *n* ▷ **excitable**
excitability *n* ▷ **excitable**
excitable *adj* easily excited > **excitability** *n* (*pl* **-s**)
excite *v* (**-s, -ing, -ed**) arouse to strong emotion > **excitement** *n* (*pl* **-s**)
excited *v* ▷ **excite**
excitement *n* ▷ **excite**
excitements *n* ▷ **excite**
excites *v* ▷ **excite**
exciting *v* ▷ **excite**
exclaim *v* (**-s, -ing, -ed**) speak suddenly, cry out > **exclamation** *n* > **exclamatory** *adj*
exclaimed *v* ▷ **exclaim**
exclaiming *v* ▷ **exclaim**
exclaims *v* ▷ **exclaim**
exclamation *n* ▷ **exclaim**
exclamations *n* ▷ **exclaim**
exclamatory *adj* ▷ **exclaim**
exclude *v* (**-s, -ing, -ed**) keep out, leave out > **exclusion** *n* (*pl* **-s**)
excluded *v* ▷ **exclude**
excludes *v* ▷ **exclude**
excluding *v* ▷ **exclude**
exclusion *n* ▷ **exclude**
exclusions *n* ▷ **exclude**
exclusive *adj* excluding everything else ▶ *n* (*pl* **-s**) story reported in only one newspaper > **exclusively** *adv* > **exclusivity** *n* (*pl* **-ies**) > **exclusiveness** *n* (*pl* **-es**)
exclusively *adv* ▷ **exclusive**
exclusiveness *n* ▷ **exclusive**
exclusivenesses *n* ▷ **exclusive**
exclusives *n* ▷ **exclusive**
exclusivities *n* ▷ **exclusive**
exclusivity *n* ▷ **exclusive**
excommunicate *v* (**-tes, -ting, -ted**) exclude from membership and the sacraments of the Church > **excommunication** *n* (*pl* **-s**)
excommunicated *v* ▷ **excommunicate**
excommunicates *v* ▷ **excommunicate**
excommunicating *v* ▷ **excommunicate**
excommunication *n* ▷ **excommunicate**
excommunications *n* ▷ **excommunicate**
excoriate *v* (**-tes, -ting, -ted**) censure severely > **excoriation** *n* (*pl* **-s**)
excoriated *v* ▷ **excoriate**
excoriates *v* ▷ **excoriate**
excoriating *v* ▷ **excoriate**
excoriation *n* ▷ **excoriate**
excoriations *n* ▷ **excoriate**
excrement *n* (*pl* **-s**) waste matter discharged from the body
excrements *n* ▷ **excrement**
excrescence *n* (*pl* **-s**) lump or growth on the surface of an animal or plant
excrescences *n* ▷ **excrescence**
excreta [ik-**skree**-ta] *n* excrement
excrete *v* (**-tes, -ting, -ted**) discharge (waste matter) from the body > **excretion** *n* (*pl* **-s**) > **excretory** *adj*
excreted *v* ▷ **excrete**
excretes *v* ▷ **excrete**
excreting *v* ▷ **excrete**
excretion *n* ▷ **excrete**
excretions *n* ▷ **excrete**
excretory *adj* ▷ **excrete**
excruciating *adj* agonizing > **excruciatingly** *adv*
excruciatingly *adv* ▷ **excruciating**
exculpate *v* (**-tes, -ting, -ted**) free from blame or guilt
exculpated *v* ▷ **exculpate**
exculpates *v* ▷ **exculpate**
exculpating *v* ▷ **exculpate**
excursion *n* (*pl* **-s**) short journey, esp. for pleasure
excursions *n* ▷ **excursion**
excusable *adj* ▷ **excuse**
excuse *n* (*pl* **-s**) explanation offered to justify (a fault etc.) ▶ *v* (**-ses, -sing, -sed**) put forward a reason or justification for (a fault etc.) > **excusable** *adj*
excused *v* ▷ **excuse**
excuses *n, v* ▷ **excuse**
excusing *v* ▷ **excuse**
execrable [**eks**-sik-rab-bl] *adj* of very poor quality
execute *v* (**-tes, -ting, -ted**) put (a condemned person) to death > **execution** *n* (*pl* **-s**) > **executioner** *n* (*pl* **-s**)
executed *v* ▷ **execute**
executes *v* ▷ **execute**
executing *v* ▷ **execute**
execution *n* ▷ **execute**
executioner *n* ▷ **execute**
executioners *n* ▷ **execute**
executions *n* ▷ **execute**

executive *n* (*pl* **-s**) person or group in an administrative position ▶ *adj* having the function of carrying out plans, orders, laws, etc.
executives *n* ▷ **executive**
executor *n* (*pl* **-s**) person appointed to perform the instructions of a will
executors *n* ▷ **executor**
executrices *n* ▷ **executrix**
executrix *n* (*pl* **-ixes, -ices**) woman appointed to perform the instructions of a will
executrixes *n* ▷ **executrix**
exegeses *n* ▷ **exegesis**
exegesis [eks-sij-**jee**-siss] *n* (*pl* **-ses**) [-seez] explanation of a text, esp. of the Bible
exemplar *n* (*pl* **-s**) person or thing to be copied, model
exemplars *n* ▷ **exemplar**
exemplary *adj* being a good example
exemplification *n* ▷ **exemplify**
exemplifications *n* ▷ **exemplify**
exemplified *v* ▷ **exemplify**
exemplifies *v* ▷ **exemplify**
exemplify *v* (**-ies, -fying, -ied**) show an example of > **exemplification** *n* (*pl* **-s**)
exemplifying *v* ▷ **exemplify**
exempt *adj* not subject to an obligation etc. ▶ *v* (**-s, -ing, -ed**) release from an obligation etc. > **exemption** *n* (*pl* **-s**)
exempted *v* ▷ **exempt**
exempting *v* ▷ **exempt**
exemption *n* ▷ **exempt**
exemptions *n* ▷ **exempt**
exempts *v* ▷ **exempt**

exequy *n* (**exequies**). An exequy is a funeral rite. This is a great word if you have the tiles for it, combining X and Q. Even better, if you have all the letters for the plural, exequies, and can play it, you'll score an extra 50 points for using all your tiles. Exequy scores 25 points.

exercise *n* (*pl* **-s**) activity to train the body or mind ▶ *v* (**-ses, -sing, -sed**) make use of
exercised *v* ▷ **exercise**
exercises *n, v* ▷ **exercise**
exercising *v* ▷ **exercise**
exert *v* (**-s, -ing, -ed**) use (influence, authority, etc.) forcefully or effectively > **exertion** *n* (*pl* **-s**)
exerted *v* ▷ **exert**
exerting *v* ▷ **exert**
exertion *n* ▷ **exert**
exertions *n* ▷ **exert**
exerts *v* ▷ **exert**
exes *n* ▷ **ex**
exeunt [**eks**-see-unt] (LATIN) they go out: used as a stage direction
exhalation *n* ▷ **exhale**
exhalations *n* ▷ **exhale**
exhale *v* (**-les, -ling, -led**) breathe out > **exhalation** *n* (*pl* **-s**)
exhaled *v* ▷ **exhale**
exhales *v* ▷ **exhale**
exhaling *v* ▷ **exhale**
exhaust *v* (**-s, -ing, -ed**) tire out ▶ *n* (*pl* **-s**) gases ejected from an engine as waste products
exhausted *v* ▷ **exhaust**
exhausting *v* ▷ **exhaust**
exhaustion *n* (*pl* **-s**) extreme tiredness
exhaustions *n* ▷ **exhaustion**
exhaustive *adj* comprehensive > **exhaustively** *adv*
exhaustively *adv* ▷ **exhaustive**
exhausts *v, n* ▷ **exhaust**
exhibit *v* (**-s, -ing, -ed**) display to the public ▶ *n* (*pl* **-s**) object exhibited to the public (LAW) > **exhibitor** *n* (*pl* **-s**)
exhibited *v* ▷ **exhibit**
exhibiting *v* ▷ **exhibit**
exhibition *n* (*pl* **-s**) public display of art, skills, etc.
exhibitionism *n* (*pl* **-s**) compulsive desire to draw attention to oneself > **exhibitionist** *n* (*pl* **-s**)
exhibitionisms *n* ▷ **exhibitionism**
exhibitionist *n* ▷ **exhibitionism**
exhibitionists *n* ▷ **exhibitionism**
exhibitions *n* ▷ **exhibition**
exhibitor *n* ▷ **exhibit**
exhibitors *n* ▷ **exhibit**
exhibits *v, n* ▷ **exhibit**
exhilarate *v* (**-tes, -ting, -ted**) make lively and cheerful > **exhilaration** *n* (*pl* **-s**)
exhilarated *v* ▷ **exhilarate**
exhilarates *v* ▷ **exhilarate**
exhilarating *v* ▷ **exhilarate**
exhilaration *n* ▷ **exhilarate**
exhilarations *n* ▷ **exhilarate**
exhort *v* (**-s, -ing, -ed**) urge earnestly > **exhortation** *n* (*pl* **-s**)
exhortation *n* ▷ **exhort**
exhortations *n* ▷ **exhort**
exhorted *v* ▷ **exhort**
exhorting *v* ▷ **exhort**
exhorts *v* ▷ **exhort**
exhumation *n* ▷ **exhume**
exhumations *n* ▷ **exhume**
exhume [ig-**zyume**] *v* (**-mes, -ming, -med**) dig up (something buried, esp. a corpse) > **exhumation** *n* (*pl* **-s**)

exhumed *v* ▷ **exhume**
exhumes *v* ▷ **exhume**
exhuming *v* ▷ **exhume**
exigencies *n* ▷ **exigency**
exigency *n* (*pl* **-cies**) urgent demand or need > **exigent** *adj*
exigent *adj* ▷ **exigency**
exiguous *adj* scanty or meagre
exile *n* (*pl* **-s**) prolonged, usu. enforced, absence from one's country ▶ *v* (**-les, -ling, -led**) expel from one's country
exiled *v* ▷ **exile**
exiles *n* ▷ **exile**
exiles *n, v* ▷ **exile**
exiling *v* ▷ **exile**
exist *v* (**-s, -ing, -ed**) have being or reality > **existence** *n* (*pl* **-s**) > **existent** *adj*
existed *v* ▷ **exist**
existence *n* ▷ **exist**
existences *n* ▷ **exist**
existent *adj* ▷ **exist**
existential *adj* of or relating to existence, esp. human existence
existentialism *n* (*pl* **-s**) philosophical movement stressing the personal experience and responsibility of the individual, who is seen as a free agent > **existentialist** *adj*, *n* (*pl* **-s**)
existentialisms *n* ▷ **existentialism**
existentialist *adj, n* ▷ **existentialism**
existentialists *n* ▷ **existentialism**
existing *v* ▷ **exist**
exists *v* ▷ **exist**
exit *n* (*pl* **-s**) way out ▶ *v* (**-s, -ing, -ed**) go out
exited *v* ▷ **exit**
exiting *v* ▷ **exit**
exits *n, v* ▷ **exit**

exo *adj*. Exo is an informal Australian way of saying excellent. This is a great little word as it allows you to combine X with two of the most common tiles in the game, E and O. Exo scores 10 points.

exocrine *adj* relating to a gland, such as the sweat gland, that secretes externally through a duct
exodus [**eks**-so-duss] *n* (*pl* **-es**) departure of a large number of people
exoduses *n* ▷ **exodus**
exonerate *v* (**-tes, -ting, -ted**) free from blame or a criminal charge > **exoneration** *n* (*pl* **-s**)
exonerates *v* ▷ **exonerate**
exonerated *v* ▷ **exonerate**
exonerating *v* ▷ **exonerate**
exoneration *v* ▷ **exonerate**
exonerations *v* ▷ **exonerate**
exorbitant *adj* (of prices, demands, etc.) excessive, immoderate > **exorbitantly** *adv*
exorbitantly *adv* ▷ **exorbitant**
exorcism *n* ▷ **exorcize**
exorcisms *n* ▷ **exorcize**
exorcist *n* ▷ **exorcize**
exorcists *n* ▷ **exorcize**
exorcize *v* (**-zes, -zing, -zed**) expel (evil spirits) by prayers and religious rites > **exorcism** *n* (*pl* **-s**) > **exorcist** *n* (*pl* **-s**)
exorcized *v* ▷ **exorcize**
exorcizes *v* ▷ **exorcize**
exorcizing *v* ▷ **exorcize**
exotic *adj* having a strange allure or beauty ▶ *n* (*pl* **-s**) non-native plant > **exotically** *adv*
exotica *pl n* (collection of) exotic objects
exotically *adv* ▷ **exotic**
exotics *n* ▷ **exotic**
expand *v* (**-s, -ing, -ed**) make or become larger (*foll. by* **on**) > **expansion** *n* (*pl* **-s**)
expanded *v* ▷ **expand**
expanding *v* ▷ **expand**
expands *v* ▷ **expand**
expanse *n* (*pl* **-s**) uninterrupted wide area
expanses *n* ▷ **expanse**
expansion *n* ▷ **expand**
expansions *n* ▷ **expand**
expansive *adj* wide or extensive
expat *adj, n* (*pl* **-s**) short for **expatriate**
expatiate [iks-**pay**-shee-ate] *v* (**-tes, -ting, -ted**) (*foll. by* **on**) speak or write at great length (on)
expatiated *v* ▷ **expatiate**
expatiates *v* ▷ **expatiate**
expatiating *v* ▷ **expatiate**
expatriate [eks-**pat**-ree-it] *adj* living outside one's native country ▶ *n* (*pl* **-s**) person living outside his or her native country > **expatriation** *n* (*pl* **-s**)
expatriates *n* ▷ **expatriate**
expatriation *n* ▷ **expatriate**
expatriations *n* ▷ **expatriate**
expats *n* ▷ **expat**
expect *v* (**-s, -ing, -ed**) regard as probable
expectancies *n* ▷ **expectancy**
expectancy *n* (*pl* **-ies**) something expected on the basis of an average
expectant *adj* expecting or hopeful > **expectantly** *adv*
expectantly *adv* ▷ **expectant**
expectation *n* (*pl* **-s**) act or state of expecting
expectations *n* ▷ **expectation**
expected *v* ▷ **expect**
expecting *v* ▷ **expect**
expectorant *n* (*pl* **-s**) medicine that helps

to bring up phlegm from the respiratory passages
expectorants *n* ▷ **expectorant**
expectorate *v* (**-tes, -ting, -ted**) spit out (phlegm etc.) > **expectoration** *n* (*pl* **-s**)
expectorated *v* ▷ **expectorate**
expectorates *v* ▷ **expectorate**
expectorating *v* ▷ **expectorate**
expectoration *n* ▷ **expectorate**
expectorations *n* ▷ **expectorate**
expects *v* ▷ **expect**
expediencies *n* ▷ **expedient**
expediency *n* ▷ **expedient**
expedient *n* (*pl* **-s**) something that achieves a particular purpose ▶ *adj* suitable to the circumstances, appropriate > **expediency** *n* (*pl* **-ies**)
expedients *n* ▷ **expedient**
expedite *v* (**-s, -ing, -ed**) hasten the progress of
expedited *v* ▷ **expedite**
expedites *v* ▷ **expedite**
expediting *v* ▷ **expedite**
expedition *n* (*pl* **-s**) organized journey, esp. for exploration
expeditionary *adj* relating to an expedition, esp. a military one
expeditions *n* ▷ **expedition**
expeditious *adj* done quickly and efficiently
expel *v* (**-s, -lling, -lled**) drive out with force > **expulsion** *n* (*pl* **-s**)
expelled *v* ▷ **expel**
expelling *v* ▷ **expel**
expels *v* ▷ **expel**
expend *v* (**-s, -ing, -ed**) spend, use up
expendable *adj* able to be sacrificed to achieve an objective
expended *v* ▷ **expend**
expending *v* ▷ **expend**
expenditure *n* (*pl* **-s**) something expended, esp. money
expenditures *n* ▷ **expenditure**
expends *v* ▷ **expend**
expense *n* (*pl* **-s**) cost ▶ *pl* charges, outlay incurred
expenses *n* ▷ **expense**
expensive *adj* high-priced
experience *n* (*pl* **-s**) direct personal participation ▶ *v* (**-ces, -cing, -ced**) participate in
experienced *v* ▷ **experience** ▶ *adj* skilful from extensive participation
experiences *n*, *v* ▷ **experience**
experiencing *v* ▷ **experience**
experiment *n* (*pl* **experiments**) test to provide evidence to prove or disprove a theory ▶ *v* (**-s, -ing, -ed**) carry out an experiment > **experimental** *adj* > **experimentally** *adv* > **experimentation** *n* (*pl* **-s**)
experimental *adj* ▷ **experiment**
experimentally *adv* ▷ **experiment**
experimentation *n* ▷ **experiment**
experimentations *n* ▷ **experiment**
experimented *v* ▷ **experiment**
experimenting *v* ▷ **experiment**
experiments *n*, *v* ▷ **experiment**
expert *n* (*pl* **-s**) person with extensive skill or knowledge in a particular field ▶ *adj* skilful or knowledgeable
expertise [eks-per-**teez**] *n* (*pl* **-s**) special skill or knowledge
expertises *n* ▷ **expertise**
experts *n* ▷ **expert**
expiate *v* (**-tes, -ting, -ted**) make amends for > **expiation** *n* (*pl* **-s**)
expiated *v* ▷ **expiate**
expiates *v* ▷ **expiate**
expiating *v* ▷ **expiate**
expiation *n* ▷ **expiate**
expiations *n* ▷ **expiate**
expiration *n* ▷ **expire**
expirations *n* ▷ **expire**
expire *v* (**-res, -ring, -red**) finish or run out (*Lit*) > **expiration** *n* (*pl* **-s**)
expired *v* ▷ **expire**
expires *v* ▷ **expire**
expiries *n* ▷ **expiry**
expiring *v* ▷ **expire**
expiry *n* (*pl* **-ies**) end, esp. of a contract period
explain *v* (**-s, -ing, -ed**) make clear and intelligible > **explanation** *n* (*pl* **-s**) > **explanatory** *adj*
explained *v* ▷ **explain**
explaining *v* ▷ **explain**
explains *v* ▷ **explain**
explanation *n* ▷ **explain**
explanations *n* ▷ **explain**
explanatory *adj* ▷ **explain**
expletive *n* (*pl* **-s**) swearword
expletives *n* ▷ **expletive**
explicable *adj* able to be explained
explicate *v* (**-tes, -ting, -ted**) (*Formal*) explain > **explication** *n* (*pl* **-s**)
explicated *v* ▷ **explicate**
explicates *v* ▷ **explicate**
explicating *v* ▷ **explicate**
explication *n* ▷ **explicate**
explications *n* ▷ **explicate**
explicit *adj* precisely and clearly expressed > **explicitly** *adv*
explicitly *adv* ▷ **explicit**

explode *v* (**-des, -ding, -ded**) burst with great violence, blow up > **explosion** *n* (*pl* **-s**)
exploded *v* ▷ **explode**
explodes *v* ▷ **explode**
exploding *v* ▷ **explode**
exploit *v* (*pl* **-s**) take advantage of for one's own purposes ▶ *n* (*pl* **-s**) notable feat or deed > **exploitation** *n* (*pl* **-s**) > **exploiter** *n* (*pl* **-s**)
exploitation *n* ▷ **exploit**
exploitations *n* ▷ **exploit**
exploited *v* ▷ **exploit**
exploiter *n* ▷ **exploit**
exploiters *n* ▷ **exploit**
exploiting *v* ▷ **exploit**
exploits *v*, *n* ▷ **exploit**
exploration *n* ▷ **explore**
explorations *n* ▷ **explore**
exploratory *adj* ▷ **explore**
explore *v* (**-res, -ring, -red**) investigate > **exploration** *n* (*pl* **-s**) > **exploratory** *adj* > **explorer** *n* (*pl* **-s**)
explored *v* ▷ **explore**
explorer *n* ▷ **explore**
explorers *n* ▷ **explore**
explores *v* ▷ **explore**
exploring *v* ▷ **explore**
explosion *n* ▷ **explode**
explosions *n* ▷ **explode**
explosive *adj* tending to explode ▶ *n* (*pl* **-s**) substance that causes explosions
explosives *n* ▷ **explosive**
expo *n* (*pl* **-s**) (*Informal*) exposition, large public exhibition
exponent *n* (*pl* **-s**) person who advocates an idea, cause, etc.
exponential *adj* (*Informal*) very rapid > **exponentially** *adv*
exponentially *adv* ▷ **exponential**
exponents *n* ▷ **exponent**
export *n* (*pl* **-s**) selling or shipping of goods to a foreign country ▶ *v* (**-s, -ing, -ed**) sell or ship (goods) to a foreign country > **exporter** *n* (*pl* **-s**)
exported *v* ▷ **export**
exporter *n* ▷ **export**
exporters *n* ▷ **export**
exporting *v* ▷ **export**
exports *n*, *v* ▷ **export**
expos *n* ▷ **expo**
expose *v* (**-ses, -sing, -sed**) uncover or reveal > **exposure** *n* (*pl* **-s**) exposing
exposé [iks-**pose**-ay] *n* (*pl* **-s**) bringing of a crime, scandal, etc. to public notice
exposed *v* ▷ **expose**
exposes *v* ▷ **expose**
exposés *n* ▷ **exposé**
exposing *v* ▷ **expose**
exposition *n* ▷ **expound**
expositions *n* ▷ **expound**
expostulate *v* (**-tes, -ting, -ted**) (*foll. by* **with**) reason (with), esp. to dissuade
expostulated *v* ▷ **expostulate**
expostulates *v* ▷ **expostulate**
expostulating *v* ▷ **expostulate**
exposure *n* ▷ **expose**
exposures *n* ▷ **expose**
expound *v* (**-s, -ing, -ed**) explain in detail > **exposition** *n* (*pl* **-s**) explanation
expounded *v* ▷ **expound**
expounding *v* ▷ **expound**
expounds *v* ▷ **expound**
express *v* (**-es, -ing, -ed**) put into words ▶ *adj* explicitly stated ▶ *n* (*pl* **-es**) fast train or bus stopping at only a few stations ▶ *adv* by express delivery
expressed *v* ▷ **express**
expresses *v*, *n* ▷ **express**
expressing *v* ▷ **express**
expression *n* (*pl* **-s**) expressing > **expressionless** *adj* > **expressive** *adj*
expressionism *n* (*pl* **-s**) early 20th-century artistic movement which sought to express emotions rather than represent the physical world > **expressionist** *adj*, *n* (*pl* **-s**)
expressionisms *n* ▷ **expressionism**
expressionist *adj*, *n* ▷ **expressionism**
expressionists *n* ▷ **expressionism**
expressionless *adj* ▷ **expression**
expressions *n* ▷ **expression**
expressive *adj* ▷ **expression**
expropriate *v* (**-tes, -ting, -ted**) deprive an owner of (property) > **expropriation** *n* (*pl* **-s**)
expropriated *v* ▷ **expropriate**
expropriates *v* ▷ **expropriate**
expropriating *v* ▷ **expropriate**
expropriation *n* ▷ **expropriate**
expropriations *n* ▷ **expropriate**
expulsion *n* ▷ **expel**
expulsions *n* ▷ **expel**
expunge *v* (**-ges, -ging, -ged**) delete, erase, blot out
expunged *v* ▷ **expunge**
expunges *v* ▷ **expunge**
expunging *v* ▷ **expunge**
expurgate *v* (**-tes, -ting, -ted**) remove objectionable parts from (a book etc.)
expurgated *v* ▷ **expurgate**
expurgates *v* ▷ **expurgate**
expurgating *v* ▷ **expurgate**
exquisite *adj* of extreme beauty or delicacy

>**exquisitely** *adv*
exquisitely *adv* ▷ **exquisite**
extant *adj* still existing
extemporize *v* (**-zes, -zing, -zed**) speak, perform, or compose without preparation
extemporized *v* ▷ **extemporize**
extemporizes *v* ▷ **extemporize**
extemporizing *v* ▷ **extemporize**
extend *v* (**-s, -ing, -ed**) draw out or be drawn out, stretch (*foll. by* **to**) >**extendable** *adj*
extendable *adj* ▷ **extend**
extended *v* ▷ **extend**
extending *v* ▷ **extend**
extends *v* ▷ **extend**
extension *n* (*pl* **-s**) room or rooms added to an existing building
extensions *n* ▷ **extension**
extensive *adj* having a large extent, widespread
extensor *n* (*pl* **-s**) muscle that extends a part of the body
extensors *n* ▷ **extensor**
extent *n* (*pl* **-s**) range over which something extends, area
extents *n* ▷ **extent**
extenuate *v* (**-tes, -ting, -ted**) make (an offence or fault) less blameworthy >**extenuation** *n* (*pl* **-s**)
extenuated *v* ▷ **extenuate**
extenuates *v* ▷ **extenuate**
extenuating *v* ▷ **extenuate**
extenuation *n* ▷ **extenuate**
extenuations *n* ▷ **extenuate**
exterior *n* (*pl* **-s**) part or surface on the outside ▶ *adj* of, on, or coming from the outside
exteriors *n* ▷ **exterior**
exterminate *v* (**-tes, -ting, -ted**) destroy (animals or people) completely >**extermination** *n* (*pl* **-s**) >**exterminator** *n* (*pl* **-s**)
exterminated *v* ▷ **exterminate**
exterminates *v* ▷ **exterminate**
exterminating *v* ▷ **exterminate**
extermination *n* ▷ **exterminate**
exterminations *n* ▷ **exterminate**
exterminator *n* ▷ **exterminate**
exterminators *n* ▷ **exterminate**
external *adj* of, situated on, or coming from the outside >**externally** *adv*
externally *adv* ▷ **external**
extinct *adj* having died out >**extinction** *n* (*pl* **-s**)
extinction *n* ▷ **extinct**
extinctions *n* ▷ **extinct**
extinguish *v* (**-es, -ing, -ed**) put out (a fire or light)
extinguished *v* ▷ **extinguish**
extinguisher *n* (*pl* **-s**) device for extinguishing a fire or light
extinguishers *n* ▷ **extinguisher**
extinguishes *v* ▷ **extinguish**
extinguishing *v* ▷ **extinguish**
extirpate *v* (**-tes, -ting, -ted**) destroy utterly
extirpated *v* ▷ **extirpate**
extirpates *v* ▷ **extirpate**
extirpating *v* ▷ **extirpate**
extol *v* (**-s, -lling, -lled**) praise highly
extolled *v* ▷ **extol**
extolling *v* ▷ **extol**
extols *v* ▷ **extol**
extort *v* (**-s, -ing, -ed**) get (something) by force or threats >**extortion** *n* (*pl* **-s**)
extorted *v* ▷ **extort**
extorting *v* ▷ **extort**
extortion *n* ▷ **extort**
extortionate *adj* (of prices) excessive
extortions *n* ▷ **extort**
extorts *v* ▷ **extort**
extra *adj* more than is usual, expected or needed ▶ *n* (*pl* **-s**) additional person or thing ▶ *adv* unusually or exceptionally
extract *v* (**-s, -ing, -ed**) pull out by force ▶ *n* (*pl* **-s**) something extracted, such as a passage from a book etc. >**extraction** *n* (*pl* **-s**) >**extractor** (*pl* **-s**) *n*
extracted *v* ▷ **extract**
extracting *v* ▷ **extract**
extraction *n* ▷ **extract**
extractions *n* ▷ **extract**
extractor *n* ▷ **extract**
extractors *n* ▷ **extract**
extracts *n, v* ▷ **extract**
extradite *v* (**-tes, -ting, -ted**) send (an accused person) back to his or her own country for trial >**extradition** *n* (*pl* **-s**)
extradited *v* ▷ **extradite**
extradites *v* ▷ **extradite**
extraditing *v* ▷ **extradite**
extradition *n* ▷ **extradite**
extraditions *n* ▷ **extradite**
extramural *adj* connected with but outside the normal courses of a university or college
extraneous [iks-**train**-ee-uss] *adj* irrelevant
extraordinarily *adv* ▷ **extraordinary**
extraordinary *adj* very unusual >**extraordinarily** *adv*
extrapolate *v* (**-tes, -ting, -ted**) infer (something not known) from the known facts (MATHS) >**extrapolation** *n* (*pl* **-s**)
extrapolated *v* ▷ **extrapolate**

extrapolates *v* ▷ **extrapolate**
extrapolating *v* ▷ **extrapolate**
extrapolation *n* ▷ **extrapolate**
extrapolations *n* ▷ **extrapolate**
extras *n* ▷ **extra**
extrasensory *adj* beyond the normal range of the senses
extravagance *n* ▷ **extravagant**
extravagances *n* ▷ **extravagant**
extravagant *adj* spending money excessively > **extravagance** *n* (*pl* **-s**)
extravaganza *n* (*pl* **-s**) elaborate and lavish entertainment, display, etc.
extravaganzas *n* ▷ **extravaganza**
extreme *adj* of a high or the highest degree or intensity ▶ *n* (*pl* **-s**) either of the two limits of a scale or range > **extremely** *adv*
extremely *adv* ▷ **extreme**
extremes *n* ▷ **extreme**
extremist *n* (*pl* **-s**) person who favours immoderate methods ▶ *adj* holding extreme opinions
extremists *n* ▷ **extremist**
extremities *n* ▷ **extremity**
extremity *n* (*pl* **-ies**) farthest point
extricate *v* (**-tes, -ting, -ted**) free from complication or difficulty > **extrication** *n* (*pl* **-s**)
extricated *v* ▷ **extricate**
extricates *v* ▷ **extricate**
extricating *v* ▷ **extricate**
extrication *n* ▷ **extricate**
extrications *n* ▷ **extricate**
extrovert *adj* lively and outgoing ▶ *n* (*pl* **-s**) extrovert person
extroverts *n* ▷ **extrovert**
extrude *v* (**-des, -ding, -ded**) squeeze or force out > **extrusion** *n* (*pl* **-s**)
extruded *v* ▷ **extrude**
extrudes *v* ▷ **extrude**
extruding *v* ▷ **extrude**
extrusion *n* ▷ **extrude**
extrusions *n* ▷ **extrude**
exuberance *n* ▷ **exuberant**
exuberances *n* ▷ **exuberant**
exuberant *adj* high-spirited > **exuberance** *n* (*pl* **-s**)
exude *v* (**-s, -ing, -ed**) (of a liquid or smell) seep or flow out slowly and steadily
exuded *v* ▷ **exude**
exudes *v* ▷ **exude**
exuding *v* ▷ **exude**
exult *v* (**-s, -ing, -ed**) be joyful or jubilant > **exultation** *n* (*pl* **-s**) > **exultant** *adj*
exultant *adj* ▷ **exult**
exultation *n* ▷ **exult**
exultations *n* ▷ **exult**
exulted *v* ▷ **exult**
exulting *v* ▷ **exult**
exults *v* ▷ **exult**
eye *n* (*pl* **-s**) organ of sight ▶ *v* (**-s, eyeing** *or* **eying, eyed**) look at carefully or warily > **eyeless** *adj*
eyeball *n* (*pl* **-s**) ball-shaped part of the eye
eyeballs *n* ▷ **eyeball**
eyebrow *n* (*pl* **-s**) line of hair on the bony ridge above the eye
eyebrows *n* ▷ **eyebrow**
eyed *v* ▷ **eye**
eyeglass *n* (*pl* **-es**) lens for aiding defective vision
eyeglasses *n* ▷ **eyeglass**
eyeing *v* ▷ **eye**
eyelash *n* (*pl* **-es**) short hair that grows out from the eyelid
eyelashes *n* ▷ **eyelash**
eyeless *adj* ▷ **eye**
eyelet *n* (*pl* **-s**) small hole for a lace or cord to be passed through
eyelets *n* ▷ **eyelet**
eyelid *n* (*pl* **-s**) fold of skin that covers the eye when it is closed
eyelids *n* ▷ **eyelid**
eyeliner *n* (*pl* **-s**) cosmetic used to outline the eyes
eyeliners *n* ▷ **eyeliner**
eyes *n, v* ▷ **eye**
eyesight *n* (*pl* **-s**) ability to see
eyesights *n* ▷ **eyesight**
eyesore *n* (*pl* **-s**) ugly object
eyesores *n* ▷ **eyesore**
eyewitness *n* (*pl* **-es**) person who was present at an event and can describe what happened
eyewitnesses *n* ▷ **eyewitness**
eying *v* ▷ **eye**
eyrie *n* (*pl* **-s**) nest of an eagle
eyries *n* ▷ **eyrie**

Ff

F can be an awkward letter in Scrabble: there are only two two-letter words beginning with F, for example (**fa** and **fy**). But if you're aware of this, you won't waste time trying to think of other two-letter words. There are also quite a few words that combine F with X or Z, allowing high scores particularly if you can hit a bonus square with them. **Fax, fix** and **fox** are good examples (13 points each), and don't forgets **fez** (15). If you have a blank tile, you can use it for the second Z in **fuzz** (15) or **fuzzy** (19). **Fey, fly** and **fry** can also be useful (9 each).

fa *n* (**fas**). Fa is the musical note F. This word isn't going to win you a game on its own, but it's useful when you're trying to form several words at once. Fa scores 5 points.

fab *adj* Fab is a short form of **fabulous.** Fab scores 8 points.

fable *n* (*pl* **-s**) story with a moral
fabled *adj* made famous in legend
fables *n* ▷ **fable**
fabric *n* (*pl* **-s**) knitted or woven cloth
fabricate *v* (**-tes, -ting, -ted**) make up (a story or lie) > **fabrication** *n* (*pl* **-s**)
fabricated *v* ▷ **fabricate**
fabricates *v* ▷ **fabricate**
fabricating *v* ▷ **fabricate**
fabrication *n* ▷ **fabricate**
fabrications *n* ▷ **fabricate**
fabrics *n* ▷ **fabric**
fabulous *adj* (*Informal*) excellent > **fabulously** *adv*
fabulously *adv* ▷ **fabulous**
facade [fas-**sahd**] *n* (*pl* **-s**) front of a building
facades *n* ▷ **facade**
face *n* (*pl* **-s**) front of the head ▸ *v* (**-ces, -cing, -ced**) look or turn towards
faced *v* ▷ **face**
faceless *adj* impersonal, anonymous
faces *n, v* ▷ **face**
facet *n* (*pl* **-s**) aspect
facetious [fas-**see**-shuss] *adj* funny or trying to be funny, esp. at inappropriate times
facets *n* ▷ **facet**
facia *n* (*pl* **-ciae**) ▷ **fascia**
faciae *n* ▷ **fascia**
facial *adj* of the face ▸ *n* (*pl* **-s**) beauty treatment for the face
facials *n* ▷ **facial**
facile [**fas**-sile] *adj* (of a remark, argument, etc.) superficial and showing lack of real thought
facilitate *v* (**-tes, -ting, -ted**) make easy > **facilitation** *n* (*pl* **-s**)
facilitated *v* ▷ **facilitate**
facilitates *v* ▷ **facilitate**
facilitating *v* ▷ **facilitate**
facilitation *n* ▷ **facilitate**
facilitations *n* ▷ **facilitate**
facilities *n* ▷ **facility**
facility *n* (*pl* **-ties**) skill ▸ *pl* means or equipment for an activity
facing *v* ▷ **face**
facing *n* (*pl* **-s**) lining or covering for decoration or reinforcement ▸ *pl* contrasting collar and cuffs on a jacket
facings *n* ▷ **facing**
facsimile [fak-**sim**-ill-ee] *n* (*pl* **-s**) exact copy
facsimiles *n* ▷ **facsimile**
fact *n* (*pl* **-s**) event or thing known to have happened or existed > **factual** *adj*
faction *n* (*pl* **-s**) (dissenting) minority group within a larger body
factions *n* ▷ **faction**
factious *adj* of or producing factions
factitious *adj* artificial
factor *n* (*pl* **-s**) element contributing to a result
factorial *n* (*pl* **-s**) product of all the integers from one to a given number
factorials *n* ▷ **factorial**
factories *n* ▷ **factory**
factorize *v* (**-zes, -zing, -zed**) calculate the factors of (a number)
factorized *v* ▷ **factorize**
factorizes *v* ▷ **factorize**
factorizing *v* ▷ **factorize**

factors *n* ▷ **factor**
factory *n* (*pl* **-ies**) building where goods are manufactured
factotum *n* (*pl* **-s**) person employed to do all sorts of work
factotums *n* ▷ **factotum**
facts *n* ▷ **fact**
factual *adj* ▷ **fact**
faculties *n* ▷ **faculty**
faculty *n* (*pl* **-ties**) physical or mental ability
fad *n* (*pl* **-s**) short-lived fashion > **faddy** (**-ddier, -ddiest**), **faddish** *adj*
faddier *adj* ▷ **fad**
faddiest *adj* ▷ **fad**
faddish *adj* ▷ **fad**
faddy *adj* ▷ **fad**
fade *v* (**-des, -ding, -ded**) (cause to) lose brightness, colour, or strength
faded *v* ▷ **fade**
fades *v* ▷ **fade**
fading *v* ▷ **fade**
fads *n* ▷ **fad**
faecal *adj* ▷ **faeces**
faeces [**fee**-seez] *pl n* waste matter discharged from the anus > **faecal** [**fee**-kl] ▶ *adj*
fag[1] *n* (*pl* **-s**) (*Informal*) boring task (BRIT) ▶ *v* (**-gs, -gging, -gged**) (BRIT) do menial chores in a public school
fag[2] *n* (BRIT) (*Slang*) cigarette
fagged *v* ▷ **fag**[1]
fagging *v* ▷ **fag**[1]
faggot *n* (*pl* **-s**) (BRIT, AUST & NZ) ball of chopped liver, herbs, and bread
faggots *n* ▷ **faggot**
fags *n, v* ▷ **fag**[1, 2]
faïence [**fie**-ence] *n* (*pl* **-s**) tin-glazed earthenware
faïences *n* ▷ **faïence**
fail *v* (**-s, -ing, -ed**) be unsuccessful ▶ *n* (*pl* **-s**) instance of not passing an exam or test
failed *v* ▷ **fail**
failing *n* (*pl* **-s**) weak point ▶ *prep* in the absence of ▶ *v* ▷ **fail**
failings *n* ▷ **failing**
fails *v, n* ▷ **fail**
failure *n* (*pl* **-s**) act or instance of failing
failures *n* ▷ **failure**
fain *adv* (*Obs*) gladly
faint *adj* lacking clarity, brightness, or volume ▶ *v* (**-s, -ing, -ed**) lose consciousness temporarily ▶ *n* (*pl* **-s**) temporary loss of consciousness
fainted *v* ▷ **faint**
fainting *v* ▷ **faint**
faints *v, n* ▷ **faint**
fair[1] *adj* (**-er, -est**) unbiased and reasonable ▶ *adv* fairly > **fairness** *n* (*pl* **-s**)
fair[2] *n* (*pl* **-s**) travelling entertainment with sideshows, rides, and amusements
fairer *adj* ▷ **fair**[1]
fairest *adj* ▷ **fair**[1]
fairground *n* (*pl* **-s**) open space used for a fair
fairgrounds *n* ▷ **fairground**
fairies *n* ▷ **fairy**
fairly *adv* moderately
fairness *n* ▷ **fair**[1]
fairnesses *n* ▷ **fair**[1]
fairs *n* ▷ **fair**[1, 2]
fairway *n* (*pl* **-s**) (GOLF) smooth area between the tee and the green
fairways *n* ▷ **fairway**
fairy *n* (*pl* **-ries**) imaginary small creature with magic powers > **fairyland** *n* (*pl* **-s**)
fairyland *n* ▷ **fairy**
fairylands *n* ▷ **fairy**
faith *n* (*pl* **-s**) strong belief, esp. without proof
faithful *adj* loyal > **faithfully** *adv*
faithfully *adv* ▷ **faithful**
faithless *adj* disloyal or dishonest
faiths *n* ▷ **faith**
fake *v* (**-kes, -king, -ked**) cause something not genuine to appear real or more valuable by fraud ▶ *n* (*pl* **-s**) person, thing, or act that is not genuine ▶ *adj* not genuine
faked *v* ▷ **fake**
fakes *v, n* ▷ **fake**
faking *v* ▷ **fake**
fakir [**fay**-keer] *n* (*pl* **-s**) Muslim who spurns worldly possessions
fakirs *n* ▷ **fakir**
falcon *n* (*pl* **-s**) small bird of prey
falconer *n* ▷ **falconry**
falconers *n* ▷ **falconry**
falconries *n* ▷ **falconry**
falconry *n* (*pl* **-ries**) art of training falcons > **falconer** *n* (*pl* **-s**)
falcons *n* ▷ **falcon**
fall *v* (**-s, -ing, fell, fallen**) drop from a higher to a lower place through the force of gravity ▶ *n* (*pl* **-s**) falling
fallacies *n* ▷ **fallacy**
fallacious *adj* ▷ **fallacy**
fallacy *n* (*pl* **-cies**) false belief > **fallacious** *adj*
fallen *v* ▷ **fall**
fallibilities *n* ▷ **fallible**
fallibility *n* ▷ **fallible**
fallible *adj* (of a person) liable to make mistakes > **fallibility** *n* (*pl* **-ties**)
falling *v* ▷ **fall**
fallout *n* (*pl* **-s**) radioactive particles spread as

a result of a nuclear explosion
fallouts *n* ▷ **fallout**
fallow *adj* (of land) ploughed but left unseeded to regain fertility
falls *v, n* ▷ **fall**
false *adj* (**-r, -st**) not true or correct > **falsely** *adv* > **falseness** *n* (*pl* **-es**) > **falsity** *n* (*pl* **-ties**)
falsehood *n* (*pl* **-s**) quality of being untrue
falsehoods *n* ▷ **falsehood**
falsely *adv* ▷ **false**
falseness *n* ▷ **false**
falsenesses *n* ▷ **false**
falser *adj* ▷ **false**
falsest *adj* ▷ **false**
falsetto *n* (*pl* **-tos**) voice pitched higher than one's natural range
falsettos *n* ▷ **falsetto**
falsification *n* ▷ **falsify**
falsifications *n* ▷ **falsify**
falsified *v* ▷ **falsify**
falsifies *v* ▷ **falsify**
falsify *v* (**-fies, -fying, -fied**) alter fraudulently > **falsification** *n* (*pl* **-s**)
falsifying *v* ▷ **falsify**
falsities *n* ▷ **false**
falsity *n* ▷ **false**
falter *v* (**-s, -ing, -ed**) be hesitant, weak, or unsure
faltered *v* ▷ **falter**
faltering *v* ▷ **falter**
falters *v* ▷ **falter**
fame *n* (*pl* **-s**) state of being widely known or recognized
famed *adj* famous
famed *adj* ▷ **fame**
fames *n* ▷ **fame**
familial *adj* ▷ **family**
familiar *adj* well-known ▶ *n* (*pl* **-s**) demon supposed to attend a witch > **familiarly** *adv* > **familiarity** *n* (*pl* **-ties**)
familiarities *n* ▷ **familiarity**
familiarity *n* ▷ **familiarity**
familiarize (**-zes, -zing, -zed**) *v* acquaint fully with a particular subject > **familiarization** *n* (*pl* **-s**)
familiarization *n* ▷ **familiarize**
familiarizations *n* ▷ **familiarize**
familiarized *v* ▷ **familiarize**
familiarizes *v* ▷ **familiarize**
familiarizing *v* ▷ **familiarize**
familiarly *adv* ▷ **familiar**
familiars *n* ▷ **familiar**
families *n* ▷ **family**
family *n* (*pl* **-lies**) group of parents and their children ▶ *adj* suitable for parents and children together > **familial** *adj*
famine *n* (*pl* **-s**) severe shortage of food
famines *n* ▷ **famine**
famished *adj* very hungry
famous *adj* very well-known
famously *adv* (*Informal*) excellently
fan¹ *n* (*pl* **-s**) hand-held or mechanical object used to create a current of air for ventilation or cooling ▶ *v* (**-s, -nning, -nned**) blow or cool with a fan
fan² *n* (*pl* **-s**) (*Informal*) devotee of a pop star, sport, or hobby
fanatic *n* (*pl* **-s**) person who is excessively enthusiastic about something > **fanatical** *adj* > **fanatically** *adv* > **fanaticism** *n* (*pl* **-s**)
fanatical *adj* ▷ **fanatic**
fanatically *adv* ▷ **fanatic**
fanaticism *n* ▷ **fanatic**
fanaticisms *n* ▷ **fanatic**
fanatics *n* ▷ **fanatic**
fanbase *n* (*pl* **-s**) body of admirers of a particular pop singer, sports team, etc
fanbases *n* ▷ **fanbase**
fancied *v* ▷ **fancy**
fancier *adj* ▷ **fancy**
fancies *n, v* ▷ **fancy**
fanciest *adj* ▷ **fancy**
fanciful *adj* not based on fact > **fancifully** *adv*
fancifully *adv* ▷ **fanciful**
fancy *adj* (**-cier, -ciest**) elaborate, not plain ▶ *n* (*pl* **-cies**) sudden irrational liking or desire ▶ *v* (**-cies, -cying, -cied**) (*Informal*) be sexually attracted to
fancy-free *adj* not in love
fancying *v* ▷ **fancy**
fandango *n* (*pl* **-os**) lively Spanish dance
fandangos *n* ▷ **fandango**
fanfare *n* (*pl* **-s**) short loud tune played on brass instruments
fanfares *n* ▷ **fanfare**
fang *n* (*pl* **-s**) snake's tooth which injects poison
fangs *n* ▷ **fang**
fanned *n* ▷ **fan**
fanning *n* ▷ **fan**
fans *n, v* ▷ **fan**
fantail *n* (*pl* **-s**) small New Zealand bird with a tail like a fan
fantails *n* ▷ **fantail**
fantasia *n* (*pl* **-s**) musical composition of an improvised nature
fantasias *n* ▷ **fantasia**
fantasies *n* ▷ **fantasy**
fantasize *v* (**-zes, -zing, -zed**) indulge in daydreams

fantasized *v* ▷ **fantasize**
fantasizes *v* ▷ **fantasize**
fantasizing *v* ▷ **fantasize**
fantastic *adj* (*Informal*) very good > **fantastically** *adv*
fantastically *adv* ▷ **fantastic**
fantasy *n* (*pl* **-sies**) far-fetched notion
far *adv* (**farther** *or* **further, farthest** *or* **furthest**) at, to, or from a great distance ▸ *adj* remote in space or time
farad *n* (*pl* **-s**) unit of electrical capacitance
farads *n* ▷ **farad**
farce *n* (*pl* **-s**) boisterous comedy
farces *n* ▷ **farce**
farcical *adj* ludicrous > **farcically** *adv*
farcically *adv* ▷ **farcical**
fare *n* (*pl* **-s**) charge for a passenger's journey ▸ *v* (**-res, -ring, -red**) get on (as specified)
fared *v* ▷ **fare**
fares *n, v* ▷ **fare**
farewell *interj* goodbye ▸ *n* (*pl* **-s**) act of saying goodbye and leaving ▸ *v* (**-s, -ing, -ed**) (NZ) say goodbye
farewelled *v* ▷ **farewell**
farewelling *v* ▷ **farewell**
farewells *n, v* ▷ **farewell**
farinaceous *adj* containing starch or having a starchy texture
faring *v* ▷ **fare**
farm *n* (*pl* **-s**) area of land for growing crops or rearing livestock ▸ *v* (**-s, -ing, -ed**) cultivate (land) > **farmhouse** *n* (*pl* **-s**) > **farmyard** *n* (*pl* **-s**)
farmed *v* ▷ **farm**
farmer *n* (*pl* **-s**) person who owns or runs a farm
farmers *n* ▷ **farmer**
farmhouse *n* ▷ **farm**
farmhouses *n* ▷ **farm**
farming *v* ▷ **farm**
farms *n, v* ▷ **farm**
farmstead *n* (*pl* **-s**) farm and its buildings
farmsteads *n* ▷ **farmstead**
farmyard *n* ▷ **farm**
farmyards *n* ▷ **farm**
farrago [far-**rah**-go] *n* (*pl* **-gos, -goes**) jumbled mixture of things
farragoes *n* ▷ **farrago**
farragos *n* ▷ **farrago**
farrier *n* (*pl* **-s**) person who shoes horses
farriers *n* ▷ **farrier**
farrow *n* (*pl* **-s**) litter of piglets ▸ *v* (**-s, -ing, -ed**) (of a sow) give birth
farrowed *v* ▷ **farrow**
farrowing *v* ▷ **farrow**
farrows *n, v* ▷ **farrow**
farther, farthest *adv, adj* ▷ **far**
farthing *n* (*pl* **-s**) former British coin equivalent to a quarter of a penny
farthings *n* ▷ **farthing**
fascia [**fay**-shya] *n* (*pl* **-ciae, -cias**) outer surface of a dashboard
fasciae *n* ▷ **fascia**
fascias *n* ▷ **fascia**
fascinate *v* (**-tes, -ting, -ted**) attract and interest strongly > **fascinating** *adj* > **fascination** *n* (*pl* **-s**)
fascinated *v* ▷ **fascinate**
fascinates *v* ▷ **fascinate**
fascinating *v, adj* ▷ **fascinate**
fascination *n* ▷ **fascinate**
fascinations *n* ▷ **fascinate**
fascism [**fash**-iz-zum] *n* (*pl* **-s**) right-wing totalitarian political system characterized by state control and extreme nationalism > **fascist** *adj, n* (*pl* **-s**)
fascisms *n* ▷ **fascism**
fascist *n* ▷ **fascism**
fascists *n* ▷ **fascist**
fashion *n* (*pl* **-s**) style in clothes, hairstyle, etc., popular at a particular time ▸ *v* (**-s, -ing, -ed**) form or make into a particular shape
fashionable *adj* currently popular > **fashionably** *adv*
fashionably *adv* ▷ **fashionable**
fashioned *v* ▷ **fashion**
fashioning *v* ▷ **fashion**
fashions *n, v* ▷ **fashion**
fast[1] *adj* (**-er, -est**) (capable of) acting or moving quickly ▸ *adv* quickly
fast[2] *v* (**-s, -ing, -ed**) go without food, esp. for religious reasons ▸ *n* (*pl* **-s**) period of fasting
fasted *v* ▷ **fast**[2]
fasten *v* (**-s, -ing, -ed**) make or become firmly fixed or joined
fastened *v* ▷ **fasten**
fastener *n* (*pl* **-s**) device that fastens
fasteners *n* ▷ **fastener**
fastening *v* ▷ **fasten** ▸ *n* (*pl* **-s**) device that fastens
fastenings *n* ▷ **fastening**
fastens *v* ▷ **fasten**
faster *adj* ▷ **fast**[1]
fastest *adj* ▷ **fast**[1]
fastidious *adj* very fussy about details > **fastidiously** *adv* > **fastidiousness** *n*
fastidiously *adv* ▷ **fastidious**
fastidiousness *n* ▷ **fastidious**
fastidiousnesses *n* ▷ **fastidious**
fasting *v* ▷ **fast**[2]
fastness *n* (*pl* **-es**) fortress, safe place

fastnesses *n* ▷ **fastness**

fasts *v, n* ▷ **fast**[2]

fat *adj* (**-er, -est**) having excess flesh on the body ▶ *n* (*pl* **-s**) extra flesh on the body > **fatness** *n* (*pl* **-es**)

fatal *adj* causing death or ruin > **fatally** *adv*

fatalism *n* (*pl* **-s**) belief that all events are predetermined and people are powerless to change their destinies > **fatalist** *n* (*pl* **-s**) > **fatalistic** *adj*

fatalisms *n* ▷ **fatalism**

fatalist *n* ▷ **fatalism**

fatalistic *adj* ▷ **fatalism**

fatalists *n* ▷ **fatalism**

fatalities *n* ▷ **fatality**

fatality *n* (*pl* **-ties**) death caused by an accident or disaster

fatally *adv* ▷ **fatal**

fate *n* (*pl* **-s**) power supposed to predetermine events

fated *adj* destined

fateful *adj* having important, usu. disastrous, consequences

fates *n* ▷ **fate**

fathead *n* (*pl* **-s**) (*Informal*) stupid person > **fat-headed** *adj*

fatheaded *adj* ▷ **fathead**

fatheads *n* ▷ **fathead**

father *n* (*pl* **-s**) male parent ▶ *v* (**-s, -ing, -ed**) be the father of (offspring) > **fatherhood** *n* (*pl* **-s**) > **fatherless** *adj* > **fatherly** *adj*

fathered *v* ▷ **father**

fatherhood *n* ▷ **father**

fatherhoods *n* ▷ **fatherhood**

fathering *v* ▷ **father**

fatherland *n* one's native country

fatherlands *n* ▷ **fatherland**

fatherless *adj* ▷ **father**

fatherly *adj* ▷ **father**

fathers *n, v* ▷ **father**

fathom *n* (*pl* **-s**) unit of length, used in navigation, equal to six feet (1.83 metres) ▶ *v* (**-s, -ing, -ed**) understand > **fathomable** *adj*

fathomable *adj* ▷ **fathom**

fathomed *v* ▷ **fathom**

fathoming *v* ▷ **fathom**

fathomless *adj* too deep or difficult to fathom

fathoms *n, v* ▷ **fathom**

fatigue [fat-**eeg**] *n* (*pl* **-s**) extreme physical or mental tiredness ▶ *v* (**-gues, -guing, -gued**) tire out

fatigued *v* ▷ **fatigue**

fatigues *v, n* ▷ **fatigue**

fatiguing *v* ▷ **fatigue**

fatness *n* ▷ **fat**

fatnesses *n* ▷ **fat**

fats *n* ▷ **fat**

fatten *v* (**-s, -ing, -ed**) (cause to) become fat

fattened *v* ▷ **fatten**

fattening *v* ▷ **fatten**

fattens *v* ▷ **fatten**

fattier *adj* ▷ **fatty**

fattiest *adj* ▷ **fatty**

fatty *adj* (**-ier, -iest**) containing fat

fatuities *n* ▷ **fatuous**

fatuity *n* ▷ **fatuous**

fatuous *adj* foolish > **fatuously** *adv* > **fatuity** *n* (*pl* **-s**)

fatuously *adv* ▷ **fatuous**

faucet [**faw**-set] *n* (*pl* **-s**) (US) tap

faucets *n* ▷ **faucet**

fault *n* (*pl* **-s**) responsibility for something wrong ▶ *v* (**-s, -ing, -ed**) criticize or blame > **faulty** *adj* (**-tier, -tiest**) > **faultless** *adj* > **faultlessly** *adv*

faulted *v* ▷ **fault**

faultier *adj* ▷ **fault**

faultiest *adj* ▷ **fault**

faulting *v* ▷ **fault**

faultless *adj* ▷ **fault**

faultlessly *adv* ▷ **fault**

faults *v* ▷ **fault**

faulty *n* ▷ **fault**

faun *n* (*pl* **-s**) (in Roman legend) creature with a human face and torso and a goat's horns and legs

fauna *n* (*pl* **-as, -ae**) animals of a given place or time

faunae *n* ▷ **fauna**

faunas *n* ▷ **fauna**

fauns *n* ▷ **faun**

favour *n* (*pl* **-s**) approving attitude ▶ *v* (**-s, -ing, -ed**) prefer

favourable *adj* encouraging or advantageous > **favourably** *adv*

favourably *adv* ▷ **favourable**

favoured *v* ▷ **favour**

favouring *v* ▷ **favour**

favourite *adj* most liked ▶ *n* (*pl* **-s**) preferred person or thing

favourites *n* ▷ **favourite**

favouritism *n* (*pl* **-s**) practice of giving special treatment to a person or group

favouritisms *n* ▷ **favouritism**

favours *n, v* ▷ **favour**

faw *n* (**faws**). A faw is a gypsy. This is a good word for taking advantage of a nearby bonus square. Faw scores 9 points.

fawn[1] *n* (*pl* **-s**) young deer ▶ *adj* light yellowish-

brown
fawn² *v* (**-s, -ing, -ed**) (*foll. by* **on**) seek attention from (someone) by insincere flattery
fawned *v* ▷ **fawn²**
fawning *v* ▷ **fawn²**
fawns *n, v* ▷ **fawn¹, ²**
fax *n* (*pl* **-es**) electronic system for sending facsimiles of documents by telephone ▶ *v* (**-xes, -xing, -xed**) send (a document) by this system
faxed *n* ▷ **fax**
faxes *n, v* ▷ **fax**
faxing *v* ▷ **fax**

fay *n* (**fays**). A fay is a fairy. This is a fairly high-scoring short word that can be helpful in a tight game. Fay scores 9 points.

fealties *n* ▷ **fealty**
fealty *n* (*pl* **-ies**) (in feudal society) subordinate's loyalty to his ruler or lord
fear *n* (*pl* **-s**) distress or alarm caused by impending danger or pain ▶ *v* (**-s, -ing, -ed**) be afraid of (something or someone) > **fearless** *adj* > **fearlessly** *adv*
feared *v* ▷ **fear**
fearful *adj* feeling fear (*Informal*) > **fearfully** *adv*
fearfully *adv* ▷ **fearful**
fearing *v* ▷ **fear**
fearless *n* ▷ **fear**
fearlessly *adv* ▷ **fear**
fears *n, v* ▷ **fear**
fearsome *adj* terrifying
feasibilities *n* ▷ **feasible**
feasibility *n* ▷ **feasible**
feasible *adj* able to be done, possible > **feasibly** *adv* > **feasibility** *n* (*pl* **-s**)
feasibly *adv* ▷ **feasible**
feast *n* (*pl* **-s**) lavish meal ▶ *v* (**-s, -ing, -ed**) eat a feast
feasted *v* ▷ **feast**
feasting *v* ▷ **feast**
feasts *n, v* ▷ **feast**
feat *n* (*pl* **-s**) remarkable, skilful, or daring action
feather *n* (*pl* **-s**) one of the barbed shafts forming the plumage of birds ▶ *v* (**-s, -ing, -ed**) fit or cover with feathers > **feathered** *adj* > **feathery** *adj* (**-rier, -riest**)
feathered *v, adj* ▷ **feather**
featherier *adj* ▷ **feather**
featheriest *adj* ▷ **feather**
feathering *v* ▷ **feather**
feathers *n, v* ▷ **feather**
featherweight *n* (*pl* **-s**) boxer weighing up to 126lb (professional) or 57kg (amateur)
featherweights *n* ▷ **featherweight**
feathery *adj* ▷ **feather**
feats *n* ▷ **feat**
feature *n* (*pl* **-s**) part of the face, such as the eyes ▶ *v* (**-res, -ring, -red**) have as a feature or be a feature in > **featureless** *adj*
featured *v* ▷ **feature**
featureless *adj* ▷ **feature**
features *n, v* ▷ **feature**
featuring *v* ▷ **feature**
febrile [**fee**-brile] *adj* feverish
feckless *adj* ineffectual or irresponsible
fecund *adj* fertile > **fecundity** *n* (*pl* **-ties**)
fecundities *n* ▷ **fecund**
fecundity *n* ▷ **fecund**
fed *v* ▷ **feed**
federal *adj* of a system in which power is divided between one central government and several regional governments > **federalism** *n* (*pl* **-s**) > **federalist** *n* (*pl* **-s**)
federalism *n* ▷ **federal**
federalisms *n* ▷ **federal**
federalist *n* ▷ **federal**
federalists *n* ▷ **federal**
federate *v* (**-tes, -ting, -ted**) unite in a federation
federated *v* ▷ **federate**
federates *v* ▷ **federate**
federating *v* ▷ **federate**
federation *n* (*pl* **-s**) union of several states, provinces, etc.
federations *n* ▷ **federation**
fedora [fid-**or**-a] *n* (*pl* **-s**) man's soft hat with a brim
fedoras *n* ▷ **fedora**
fee *n* (*pl* **-s**) charge paid to be allowed to do something
feeble *adj* (**-r, -st**) lacking physical or mental power > **feebleness** *n* (*pl* **-es**) > **feebly** *adv*
feebleminded *adj* unable to think or understand effectively
feebleness *n* ▷ **feeble**
feeblenesses *n* ▷ **feeble**
feebler *adj* ▷ **feeble**
feeblest *adj* ▷ **feeble**
feebly *adv* ▷ **feeble**
feed *v* (**-s, -ing, fed**) give food to ▶ *n* (*pl* **-s**) act of feeding
feedback *n* (*pl* **-s**) information received in response to something done
feedbacks *n* ▷ **feedback**
feeder *n* (*pl* **-s**) road or railway line linking outlying areas to the main traffic network
feeders *n* ▷ **feeder**

feeding *v* ▷ **feed**
feeds *v, n* ▷ **feed**
feel *v* (**-s, -ing, felt**) have a physical or emotional sensation of ▶ *n* (*pl* **-s**) act of feeling
feeler *n* (*pl* **-s**) organ of touch in some animals
feelers *n* ▷ **feeler**
feeling *n* (*pl* **-s**) emotional reaction
feelings *n* ▷ **feeling** ▶ *v* ▷ **feel**
feels *v, n* ▷ **feel**
fees *n* ▷ **fee**
feet *n* ▷ **foot**
feign [**fane**] *v* (**-s, -ing, -ed**) pretend
feigned *v* ▷ **feign**
feigning *v* ▷ **feign**
feigns *v* ▷ **feign**
feint¹ [**faint**] *n* (*pl* **-s**) sham attack or blow meant to distract an opponent ▶ *v* (**-s, -ing, -ed**) make a feint
feint² [**faint**] *n* (*pl* **-s**) narrow lines on ruled paper
feinted *v* ▷ **feint¹**
feinting *v* ▷ **feint¹**
feints *n, v* ▷ **feint¹, ²**
feldspar *n* (*pl* **-s**) hard mineral that is the main constituent of igneous rocks
feldspars *n* ▷ **feldspar**
felicitations *pl n* congratulations
felicities *n* ▷ **felicity**
felicitous *adj* ▷ **felicity**
felicity *n* (*pl* **-ties**) happiness > **felicitous** *adj*
feline *adj* of cats ▶ *n* (*pl* **-s**) member of the cat family
felines *n* ▷ **feline**
fell¹ *v* ▷ **fall**
fell² *v* (**-s, -ing, -ed**) cut down (a tree)
fell³ *adj* (**-er, -est**) deadly
fell⁴ *n* (*pl* **-s**) (SCOT & N ENGLISH) mountain, hill, or moor
felled *v* ▷ **fell²**
feller *adj* ▷ **fell³**
fellest *adj* ▷ **fell³**
felling *v* ▷ **fell²**
felloe *n* (*pl* **-oes**) (segment of) the rim of a wheel
felloes *n* ▷ **felloe**
fellow *n* (*pl* **-s**) man or boy ▶ *adj* in the same group or condition
fellows *n* ▷ **fellow**
fellowship *n* (*pl* **-s**) sharing of aims or interests
fellowships *n* ▷ **fellowship**
fells *v, n* ▷ **fell², ⁴**
felon *n* (*pl* **-s**) (CRIMINAL LAW) (formerly) person guilty of a felony
felonies *n* ▷ **felony**
felonious *adj* ▷ **felony**
felons *n* ▷ **felon**
felony *n* (*pl* **-nies**) serious crime > **felonious** *adj*
felspar *n* (*pl* **-s**) ▷ **feldspar**
felspars *n* ▷ **felspar**
felt¹ *v* ▷ **feel**
felt² *n* (*pl* **-s**) matted fabric made by bonding fibres by pressure
felts *n* ▷ **felt²**
female *adj* of the sex which bears offspring ▶ *n* (*pl* **-s**) female person or animal
females *n* ▷ **female**
feminine *adj* having qualities traditionally regarded as suitable for, or typical of, women > **femininity** *n* (*pl* **-ties**)
femininities *n* ▷ **feminine**
femininity *n* ▷ **feminine**
feminism *n* (*pl* **-s**) advocacy of equal rights for women > **feminist** *adj, n* (*pl* **-s**)
feminisms *n* ▷ **feminism**
feminist *n* ▷ **feminism**
feminists *n* ▷ **feminism**
femoral *adj* of the thigh
femur [**fee**-mer] *n* (*pl* **-s**) thighbone
femurs *n* ▷ **femur**
fen *n* (*pl* **-s**) (BRIT) low-lying flat marshy land
fence *n* (*pl* **-s**) barrier of posts linked by wire or wood, enclosing an area ▶ *v* (**-ces, -cing, -ced**) enclose with or as if with a fence
fenced *v* ▷ **fence**
fencer *n* ▷ **fencing**
fencers *n* ▷ **fencing**
fences *n, v* ▷ **fence**
fencing *n* (*pl* **-s**) sport of fighting with swords ▶ *v* ▷ **fence** > **fencer** *n* (*pl* **-s**)
fencings *n* ▷ **fencing**
fend *v* (**-s, -ing, -ed**) provide (for oneself)
fended *v* ▷ **fend**
fender *n* (*pl* **-s**) low metal frame in front of a fireplace
fenders *n* ▷ **fender**
fending *v* ▷ **fend**
fends *v* ▷ **fend**
fennel *n* (*pl* **-s**) fragrant plant whose seeds, leaves, and root are used in cookery
fennels *n* ▷ **fennel**
fens *n* ▷ **fen**
fenugreek *n* (*pl* **-s**) Mediterranean plant grown for its heavily scented seeds
fenugreeks *n* ▷ **fenugreek**
feral *adj* wild
ferment *n* (*pl* **-s**) commotion, unrest ▶ *v* (**-s, -ing, -ed**) undergo or cause to undergo fermentation
fermentation *n* (*pl* **-s**) reaction in which

an organic molecule splits into simpler substances, esp. the conversion of sugar to alcohol
fermentations *n* ▷ **fermentation**
fermented *n* ▷ **ferment**
fermenting *v* ▷ **ferment**
ferments *n, v* ▷ **ferment**
fern *n* (*pl* **-s**) flowerless plant with fine fronds
ferns *n* ▷ **fern**
ferocious *adj* savagely fierce or cruel > **ferocity** *n* (*pl* **-ties**)
ferocities *n* ▷ **ferocious**
ferocity *n* ▷ **ferocious**
ferret *n* (*pl* **-s**) tamed polecat used to catch rabbits or rats ▶ *v* (**-s, -ing, -ed**) hunt with ferrets
ferreted *v* ▷ **ferret**
ferreting *v* ▷ **ferret**
ferrets *n, v* ▷ **ferret**
ferric, ferrous *adj* of or containing iron
ferried *v* ▷ **ferry**
ferries *n, v* ▷ **ferry**
ferrous *adj* ▷ **ferric**
ferry *n* (*pl* **-rries**) boat for transporting people and vehicles ▶ *v* (**-rries, -rrying, -rried**) carry by ferry > **ferryman** *n* (*pl* **-men**)
ferrying *v* ▷ **ferry**
ferryman *n* ▷ **ferry**
ferrymen *n* ▷ **ferry**
fertile *adj* capable of producing young, crops, or vegetation > **fertility** *n* (*pl* **-ties**)
fertilities *n* ▷ **fertile**
fertility *n* ▷ **fertile**
fertilization *n* ▷ **fertilize**
fertilizations *n* ▷ **fertilize**
fertilize *v* (**-zes, -zing, -zed**) provide (an animal or plant) with sperm or pollen to bring about fertilization > **fertilization** *n* (*pl* **-s**)
fertilized *v* ▷ **fertilize**
fertilizer *n* (*pl* **-s**) substance added to the soil to increase its productivity
fertilizers *n* ▷ **fertilizer**
fertilizes *v* ▷ **fertilize**
fertilizing *v* ▷ **fertilize**
fervent, fervid *adj* intensely passionate and sincere > **fervently** *adv*
fervently *adv* ▷ **fervent**
fervid *adj* ▷ **fervent**
fervour *n* (*pl* **-s**) intensity of feeling
fervours *n* ▷ **fervour**
fescue *n* (*pl* **-s**) pasture and lawn grass with stiff narrow leaves
fescues *n* ▷ **fescue**
fester *v* (**-s, -ing, -ed**) grow worse and increasingly hostile
festered *v* ▷ **fester**
festering *v* ▷ **fester**
festers *v* ▷ **fester**
festival *n* (*pl* **-s**) organized series of special events or performances
festivals *n* ▷ **festival**
festive *adj* of or like a celebration
festivities *n* ▷ **festivity**
festivity *n* (*pl* **-ties**) happy celebration ▶ *pl* celebrations
festoon *v* (**-s, -ing, -ed**) hang decorations in loops
festooned *v* ▷ **festoon**
festooning *v* ▷ **festoon**
festoons *v* ▷ **festoon**
feta *n* (*pl* **-as**) white salty Greek cheese
fetal *adj* ▷ **fetus**
fetas *n* ▷ **feta**
fetch *v* (**-es, -ing, -ed**) go after and bring back (*Informal*)
fetched *v* ▷ **fetch**
fetches *v* ▷ **fetch**
fetching *v* ▷ **fetch** ▶ *adj* attractive
fete [**fate**] *n* (*pl* **-s**) gala, bazaar, etc., usu. held outdoors ▶ *v* (**-tes, -ting, -ted**) honour or entertain regally
feted *v* ▷ **fete**
fetes *n, v* ▷ **fete**
fetid *adj* (**-er, -est**) stinking
fetider *adj* ▷ **fetid**
fetidest *adj* ▷ **fetid**
feting *v* ▷ **fete**
fetish *n* (*pl* **-es**) form of behaviour in which sexual pleasure is derived from looking at or handling an inanimate object > **fetishism** *n* (*pl* **-s**) > **fetishist** (*pl* **-s**) *n*
fetishes *n* ▷ **fetish**
fetishism *n* ▷ **fetish**
fetishisms *n* ▷ **fetish**
fetishist *n* ▷ **fetish**
fetishists *n* ▷ **fetish**
fetlock *n* (*pl* **-s**) projection behind and above a horse's hoof
fetlocks *n* ▷ **fetlock**
fetter *n* (*pl* **-s**) chain or shackle for the foot ▶ *pl* restrictions ▶ *v* (**-s, -ing, -ed**) restrict
fettered *v* ▷ **fetter**
fettering *v* ▷ **fetter**
fetters *n, v* ▷ **fetter**
fettle *n* (*pl* **-s**) state of health or spirits
fettles *n* ▷ **fettle**
fetus [**fee**-tuss] *n* (*pl* **-tuses**) embryo of a mammal in the later stages of development > **fetal** *adj*
fetuses *n* ▷ **fetus**

feu *n* (*pl* **-s**) (in Scotland) right of use of land in return for a fixed annual payment
feud *n* (*pl* **-s**) long bitter hostility between two people or groups ▶ *v* (**-s, -ing, -ed**) carry on a feud
feudal *adj* of or like feudalism
feudalism *n* (*pl* **-s**) medieval system in which people held land from a lord, and in return worked and fought for him
feudalisms *n* ▷ **feudalism**
feuded *v* ▷ **feud**
feuding *v* ▷ **feud**
feuds *n, v* ▷ **feud**
feus *n* ▷ **feu**
fever *n* (*pl* **-s**) (illness causing) high body temperature > **fevered** *adj*
fevered *adj* ▷ **fever**
feverish *adj* suffering from fever > **feverishly** *adv*
feverishly *adv* ▷ **feverish**
fevers *n* ▷ **fever**
few *adj* (**-er, -est**) not many
fewer *adj* ▷ **few**
fewest *adj* ▷ **few**
fey *adj* (**-er, -est**) whimsically strange
feyer *adj* ▷ **fey**
feyest *adj* ▷ **fey**
fez *n* (*pl* **fezzes**) brimless tasselled cap, orig. from Turkey
fezzes *n* ▷ **fez**
fiancé [fee-**on**-say] *n* (*pl* **-cés**) man engaged to be married > **fiancée** *n fem* (*pl* **-cées**)
fiancée *n* ▷ **fiancé**
fiancées *n* ▷ **fiancé**
fiancés *n* ▷ **fiancé**
fiasco *n* (*pl* **-cos, -coes**) ridiculous or humiliating failure
fiascoes *n* ▷ **fiasco**
fiascos *n* ▷ **fiasco**
fiat [**fee**-at] *n* (*pl* **-s**) arbitrary order
fiats *n* ▷ **fiat**
fib *n* (*pl* **-s**) trivial lie ▶ *v* (**-s, -bbing, -bbed**) tell a lie > **fibber** *n* (*pl* **-s**)
fibbed *v* ▷ **fib**
fibber *n* ▷ **fib**
fibbers *n* ▷ **fib**
fibbing *v* ▷ **fib**
fibre *n* (*pl* **-s**) thread that can be spun into yarn > **fibrous** *adj*
fibreglass *n* (*pl* **-es**) material made of fine glass fibres
fibreglasses *n* ▷ **fibreglass**
fibres *n* ▷ **fibre**
fibro *n* (*pl* **-ros**) (AUST) mixture of cement and asbestos fibre, used in sheets for building (*also* **fibrocement**)
fibroid [**fibe**-royd] *n* (*pl* **-s**) benign tumour composed of fibrous connective tissue
fibroids *n* ▷ **fibroid**
fibros *n* ▷ **fibro**
fibrosites *n* ▷ **fibrositis**
fibrositis [fibe-roh-**site**-iss] *n* (*pl* **-es**) inflammation of the tissues of muscle sheaths
fibrous *adj* ▷ **fibre**
fibs *n, v* ▷ **fib**
fibula *n* (*pl* **-lae, -las**) slender outer bone of the lower leg
fibulae *n* ▷ **fibula**
fibulas *n* ▷ **fibula**
fiche [**feesh**] *n* (*pl* **-s**) sheet of film for storing publications in miniaturized form
fiches *n* ▷ **fiche**
fickle *adj* changeable, inconstant > **fickleness** *n* (*pl* **-ess**)
fickleness *n* ▷ **fickle**
ficklenesses *n* ▷ **fickle**
fiction *n* (*pl* **-s**) literary works of the imagination, such as novels > **fictional** *adj*
fictional *adj* ▷ **fiction**
fictionalize *v* (**-zes, -zing, -zed**) turn into fiction
fictionalized *v* ▷ **fictionalize**
fictionalizes *v* ▷ **fictionalize**
fictionalizing *v* ▷ **fictionalize**
fictions *n* ▷ **fiction**
fictitious *adj* not genuine
fiddle *n* (*pl* **-s**) violin (*Informal*) ▶ *v* (**-les, -ling, -led**) play the violin
fiddled *v* ▷ **fiddle**
fiddles *n, v* ▷ **fiddle**
fiddlesticks *interj* expression of annoyance or disagreement
fiddlier *adj* ▷ **fiddly**
fiddliest *adj* ▷ **fiddly**
fiddling *v* ▷ **fiddle** ▶ *adj* trivial
fiddly *adj* (**-lier, -liest**) awkward to do or use
fidelities *n* ▷ **fidelity**
fidelity *n* (*pl* **-ies**) faithfulness
fidget *v* (**-s, -ing, -ed**) move about restlessly ▶ *n* (*pl* **-s**) person who fidgets ▶ *pl* restlessness > **fidgety** *adj* (**-tier, -tiest**)
fidgeted *v* ▷ **fidget**
fidgetier *adj* ▷ **fidget**
fidgetiest *adj* ▷ **fidget**
fidgeting *v* ▷ **fidget**
fidgets *v, n* ▷ **fidget**
fidgety *adj* ▷ **fidget**
fiduciaries *n* ▷ **fiduciary**
fiduciary [fid-**yew**-she-er-ee] (LAW) *n* (*pl* **-ies**)

person bound to act for someone else's benefit, as a trustee ▶ *adj* of a trust or trustee
fief [**feef**] *n* (*pl* **-s**) (HIST) land granted by a lord in return for war service
fiefs *n* ▷ **fief**
field *n* (*pl* **-s**) enclosed piece of agricultural land ▶ *v* (**-s, -ing, -ed**) (SPORT) catch and return (a ball)
fielded *v* ▷ **field**
fielder *n* (*pl* **-s**) (SPORT) player whose task is to field the ball
fielders *n* ▷ **fielder**
fieldfare *n* (*pl* **-s**) type of large Old World thrush
fieldfares *n* ▷ **fieldfare**
fielding *v* ▷ **field**
fields *n, v* ▷ **field**
fieldwork *n* (*pl* **-s**) investigation made in the field as opposed to the classroom or the laboratory
fieldworks *n* ▷ **fieldwork**
fiend [**feend**] *n* (*pl* **-s**) evil spirit (*Informal*) > **fiendish** *adj* > **fiendishly** *adv*
fiendish *adj* ▷ **fiend**
fiendishly *adv* ▷ **fiend**
fiends *n* ▷ **fiend**
fierce *adj* (**-r, -st**) wild or aggressive > **fiercely** *adv* > **fierceness** *n* (*pl* **-es**)
fiercely *adv* ▷ **fierce**
fierceness *n* ▷ **fierce**
fiercenesses *n* ▷ **fierce**
fiercer *adj* ▷ **fierce**
fiercest *adj* ▷ **fierce**
fierier *adj* ▷ **fiery**
fieriest *adj* ▷ **fiery**
fiery *adj* (**-rier, -riest**) consisting of or like fire
fiesta *n* (*pl* **-s**) religious festival, carnival
fiestas *n* ▷ **fiesta**
fife *n* (*pl* **-s**) small high-pitched flute
fifes *n* ▷ **fife**
fifteen *adj, n* (*pl* **-s**) five and ten > **fifteenth** *adj, n* (*pl* **-s**)
fifteens *n* ▷ **fifteen**
fifteenth *adj, n* ▷ **fifteen**
fifteenths *n* ▷ **fifteenth**
fifth *adj, n* (*pl* **-s**) (of) number five in a series
fifths *n* ▷ **fifth**
fifties *n* ▷ **fifty**
fiftieth *adj, n* ▷ **fifty**
fiftieths *n* ▷ **fifty**
fifty *adj, n* (*pl* **-ties**) five times ten > **fiftieth** *adj, n* (*pl* **-s**)
fig *n* (*pl* **-s**) soft pear-shaped fruit
fight *v* (**-s, -ing, fought**) struggle (against) in battle or physical combat ▶ *n* (*pl* **-s**) aggressive conflict between two (groups of) people
fighter *n* (*pl* **-s**) boxer
fighters *n* ▷ **fighter**
fighting *v* ▷ **fight**
fights *n, v* ▷ **fight**
figment *n* (*pl* **-s**) something imagined
figments *n* ▷ **figment**
figs *n* ▷ **fig**
figurative *adj* (of language) abstract, imaginative, or symbolic > **figuratively** *adv*
figuratively *adv* ▷ **figurative**
figure *n* (*pl* **-s**) numerical symbol (MATHS) ▶ *v* (**-res, -ring, -red**) consider, conclude
figured *v* ▷ **figure**
figurehead *n* (*pl* **-s**) nominal leader
figureheads *n* ▷ **figurehead**
figures *n, v* ▷ **figure**
figurine *n* (*pl* **-s**) statuette
figurines *n* ▷ **figurine**
figuring *v* ▷ **figure**
filament *n* (*pl* **-s**) fine wire in a light bulb that gives out light
filaments *n* ▷ **filament**
filbert *n* (*pl* **-s**) hazelnut
filberts *n* ▷ **filbert**
filch *v* (**-es, -ing, -ed**) steal (small amounts)
filched *v* ▷ **filch**
filches *v* ▷ **filch**
filching *v* ▷ **filch**
file[1] *n* (*pl* **-s**) box or folder used to keep documents in order ▶ *v* (**-les, -ling, -led**) place (a document) in a file
file[2] *n* (*pl* **-s**) tool with a roughened blade for smoothing or shaping ▶ *v* (**-les, -ling, -led**) shape or smooth with a file
filed *v* ▷ **file**[1, 2]
files *n, v* ▷ **file**[1, 2]
filial *adj* of or befitting a son or daughter
filibuster *n* (*pl* **-s**) obstruction of legislation by making long speeches ▶ *v* (**-s, -ing, -ed**) obstruct (legislation) with such delaying tactics
filibustered *v* ▷ **filibuster**
filibustering *v* ▷ **filibuster**
filibusters *n, v* ▷ **filibuster**
filigree *n* (*pl* **-s**) delicate ornamental work of gold or silver wire ▶ *adj* made of filigree
filigrees *n* ▷ **filigree**
filing *v* ▷ **file**[1, 2]
filings *pl n* shavings removed by a file
fill *v* (**-s, -ing, -ed**) make or become full
filled *v* ▷ **fill**
filler *n* (*pl* **-s**) substance that fills a gap or increases bulk
fillers *n* ▷ **filler**
fillet *n* (*pl* **-s**) boneless piece of meat or fish ▶ *v*

(**-s, -ing, -ed**) remove the bones from
filleted *v* ▷ **fillet**
filleting *v* ▷ **fillet**
fillets *n, v* ▷ **fillet**
fillies *n* ▷ **filly**
filling *n* (*pl* **-s**) substance that fills a gap or cavity, esp. in a tooth ▶ *adj* (of food) substantial and satisfying ▶ *v* ▷ **fill**
fillings *n* ▷ **filling**
fillip *n* (*pl* **-s**) something that adds stimulation or enjoyment
fillips *n* ▷ **fillip**
fills *v* ▷ **fill**
filly *n* (*pl* **-lies**) young female horse
film *n* (*pl* **-s**) sequence of images projected on a screen, creating the illusion of movement ▶ *v* (**-s, -ing, -ed**) photograph with a movie or video camera ▶ *adj* connected with films or the cinema
filmed *v* ▷ **film**
filmier *adj* ▷ **filmy**
filmiest *adj* ▷ **filmy**
filming *v* ▷ **film**
films *n, v* ▷ **film**
filmy *adj* (**-mier, -miest**) very thin, delicate
filter *n* (*pl* **-s**) material or device permitting fluid to pass but retaining solid particles ▶ *v* (**-s, -ing, -ed**) remove impurities from (a substance) with a filter
filtered *v* ▷ **filter**
filtering *v* ▷ **filter**
filters *n, v* ▷ **filter**
filth *n* (*pl* **-s**) disgusting dirt > **filthy** *adj* (**-thier, -thiest**) > **filthiness** *n* (*pl* **-es**)
filthier *adj* ▷ **filth**
filthiest *adj* ▷ **filth**
filthiness *n* ▷ **filth**
filthinesses *n* ▷ **filth**
filths *n* ▷ **filth**
filthy *adj* ▷ **filth**
filtrate *n* (*pl* **-s**) filtered gas or liquid ▶ *v* (**-tes, -ting, -ted**) remove impurities with a filter > **filtration** *n* (*pl* **-s**)
filtrated *v* ▷ **filtrate**
filtrates *n, v* ▷ **filtrate**
filtrating *v* ▷ **filtrate**
filtration *n* ▷ **filtrate**
filtrations *n* ▷ **filtrate**
fin *n* (*pl* **-s**) projection from a fish's body enabling it to balance and swim
finagle [fin-**nay**-gl] *v* (**-les, -ling, -led**) get or achieve by craftiness or trickery
finagled *v* ▷ **finagle**
finagles *v* ▷ **finagle**
finagling *v* ▷ **finagle**
final *adj* at the end ▶ *n* (*pl* **-s**) deciding contest between winners of previous rounds in a competition ▶ *pl* (BRIT & S AFR) last examinations in an educational course > **finally** *adv* > **finality** *n* (*pl* **-ties**)
finale [fin-**nah**-lee] (*pl* **-s**) *n* concluding part of a dramatic performance or musical work
finales *n* ▷ **finale**
finalist *n* (*pl* **-s**) competitor in a final
finalists *n* ▷ **finalist**
finalities *n* ▷ **final**
finality *n* ▷ **final**
finalize *v* (**-zes, -zing, -zed**) put into final form
finalized *v* ▷ **finalize**
finalizes *v* ▷ **finalize**
finalizing *v* ▷ **finalize**
finally *adv* ▷ **final**
finals *n* ▷ **final**
finance *v* (**-ces, -cing, -ced**) provide or obtain funds for ▶ *n* (*pl* **-s**) management of money, loans, or credits ▶ *pl* money resources > **financial** *adj* > **financially** *adv*
financed *v* ▷ **finance**
finances *v, n* ▷ **finance**
financial *adj* ▷ **finance**
financially *adv* ▷ **finance**
financier *n* (*pl* **-s**) person involved in large-scale financial business
financiers *n* ▷ **financier**
financing *v* ▷ **finance**
finch *n* (*pl* **-es**) small songbird with a short strong beak
finches *n* ▷ **finch**
find *v* (**-s, -ing, found**) discover by chance ▶ *n* (*pl* **-s**) person or thing found, esp. when valuable > **finder** *n* (*pl* **-s**)
finder *n* ▷ **find**
finders *n* ▷ **find**
finding *n* (*pl* **-s**) conclusion from an investigation ▶ *v* ▷ **find**
findings *n* ▷ **finding**
finds *v, n* ▷ **find**
fine[1] *adj* (**-r, -st**) very good > **finely** *adv* > **fineness** *n* (*pl* **-es**)
fine[2] *n* (*pl* **-s**) payment imposed as a penalty ▶ *v* (**-nes, -ning, -ned**) impose a fine on
fined *v* ▷ **fine**[2]
finely *adv* ▷ **fine**[1]
fineness *n* ▷ **fine**[1]
finenesses *n* ▷ **fine**[1]
finer *adj* ▷ **fine**[1]
fineries *n* ▷ **finery**
finery *n* (*pl* **-ries**) showy clothing
fines *n, v* ▷ **fine**[1, 2]
finesse [fin-**ness**] *n* (*pl* **-s**) delicate skill

finesses *n* ▷ **finesse**
finest *adj* ▷ **fine**[1]
finger *n* (*pl* **-s**) one of the four long jointed parts of the hand ▶ *v* (**-s, -ing, -ed**) touch or handle with the fingers
fingerboard *n* part of a stringed instrument against which the strings are pressed
fingerboards *n* ▷ **fingerboard**
fingered *v* ▷ **finger**
fingering *n* technique of using the fingers in playing a musical instrument ▶ *v* ▷ **finger**
fingerprint *n* (*pl* **-s**) impression of the ridges on the tip of the finger ▶ *v* take the fingerprints of (someone)
fingerprints *n* ▷ **fingerprint**
fingers *n, v* ▷ **finger**
finickier *adj* ▷ **finicky**
finickiest *adj* ▷ **finicky**
finicky *adj* (**-ckier, -ckiest**) excessively particular, fussy
fining *v* ▷ **fine**
finish *v* (**-es, -ing, -ed**) bring to an end, stop ▶ *n* (*pl* **-es**) end, last part
finished *v* ▷ **finish**
finishes *v, n* ▷ **finish**
finishing *v* ▷ **finish**
finite *adj* having limits in space, time, or size
fins *n* ▷ **fin**
fiord *n* (*pl* **-s**) ▷ **fjord**
fiords *n* ▷ **fiord**
fir *n* (*pl* **-s**) pyramid-shaped tree with needle-like leaves and erect cones
fire *n* (*pl* **-s**) state of combustion producing heat, flames, and smoke ▶ *v* (**-res, -ring, -red**) operate (a weapon) so that a bullet or missile is released
firearm *n* (*pl* **-s**) rifle, pistol, or shotgun
firearms *n* ▷ **firearms**
firebrand *n* (*pl* **-s**) person who causes unrest
firebrands *n* ▷ **firebrand**
firebreak *n* strip of cleared land to stop the advance of a fire
firebreaks *n* ▷ **firebreak**
fired *v* ▷ **fire**
firedamp *n* (*pl* **-s**) explosive gas, composed mainly of methane, formed in mines
firedamps *n* ▷ **firedamp**
firefighter *n* (*pl* **-s**) member of a fire brigade
firefighters *n* ▷ **firefighter**
fireflies *n* ▷ **firefly**
firefly *n* (*pl* **-flies**) beetle that glows in the dark
fireguard *n* (*pl* **-s**) protective grating in front of a fire
fireguards *n* ▷ **fireguard**
fireplace *n* (*pl* **-s**) recess in a room for a fire
fireplaces *n* ▷ **fireplace**
fires *n, v* ▷ **fire**
firewall *n* (*pl* **-s**) (COMPUTERS) computer that prevents unauthorized access to a computer network from the Internet
firewalls *n* ▷ **firewall**
firework *n* (*pl* **-s**) device containing chemicals that is ignited to produce spectacular explosions and coloured sparks ▶ *pl* show of fireworks
fireworks *n* ▷ **firework**
firing *v* ▷ **fire**
firm[1] *adj* (**-er, -est**) not soft or yielding ▶ *adv* in an unyielding manner ▶ *v* (**-s, -ing, -ed**) make or become firm > **firmly** *adv* > **firmness** *n* (*pl* **-es**)
firm[2] *n* (*pl* **-s**) business company
firmament *n* (*pl* **-s**) (*Lit*) sky or the heavens
firmaments *n* ▷ **firmament**
firmed *v* ▷ **firm**[1]
firmer *adj* ▷ **firm**[1]
firmest *adj* ▷ **firm**[1]
firming *v* ▷ **firm**[1]
firmly *adv* ▷ **firm**[1]
firmness *n* ▷ **firm**[1]
firmnesses *n* ▷ **firm**[1]
firms *v, n* ▷ **firm**[1, 2]
firs *n* ▷ **fir**
first *adj* earliest in time or order ▶ *n* (*pl* **-s**) person or thing coming before all others ▶ *adv* before anything else > **firstly** *adv*
firsthand *adj, adv* (obtained) directly from the original source
firstly *adv* ▷ **first**
firsts *n* ▷ **first**
firth *n* (*pl* **-s**) narrow inlet of the sea, esp. in Scotland
firths *n* ▷ **firth**
fiscal *adj* of government finances, esp. taxes
fish *n* (*pl* **fish, fishes**) cold-blooded vertebrate with gills, that lives in water ▶ *v* (**-es, -ing, -ed**) try to catch fish
fished *v* ▷ **fish**
fisheries *n* ▷ **fishery**
fisherman *n* (*pl* **-men**) person who catches fish for a living or for pleasure
fishermen *n* ▷ **fisherman**
fishery *n* (*pl* **-ries**) area of the sea used for fishing
fishes *n, v* ▷ **fish**
fishfinger *n* (*pl* **-s**) oblong piece of fish covered in breadcrumbs
fishfingers *n* ▷ **fishfinger**
fishier *adj* ▷ **fishy**
fishiest *adj* ▷ **fishy**

fishing *v* ▷ **fish**
fishmeal *n* (*pl* **-s**) dried ground fish used as animal feed or fertilizer
fishmeals *n* ▷ **fishmeal**
fishmonger *n* (*pl* **-s**) seller of fish
fishmongers *n* ▷ **fishmonger**
fishnet *n* (*pl* **-s**) open mesh fabric resembling netting
fishnets *n* ▷ **fishnet**
fishplate *n* (*pl* **-s**) metal plate holding rails together
fishplates *n* ▷ **fishplate**
fishwife *n* (*pl* **-wives**) coarse scolding woman
fishwives *n* ▷ **fishwife**
fishy *adj* (**-shier, -shiest**) of or like fish
fissile *adj* capable of undergoing nuclear fission
fission *n* (*pl* **-s**) splitting > **fissionable** *adj*
fissionable *adj* ▷ **fission**
fissions *n* ▷ **fission**
fissure [**fish**-er] *n* (*pl* **-s**) long narrow cleft or crack
fissures *n* ▷ **fissure**
fist *n* (*pl* **-s**) clenched hand
fisticuffs *pl n* fighting with the fists
fists *n* ▷ **fist**
fit[1] *v* (**-s, -tting, -tted**) be appropriate or suitable for ▶ *adj* appropriate ▶ *n* (**-tter, -ttest**) (*pl* **-s**) way in which something fits > **fitness** *n* (*pl* **-es**)
fit[2] *n* (*pl* **-s**) sudden attack or convulsion, such as an epileptic seizure
fitful *adj* occurring in irregular spells > **fitfully** *adv*
fitfully *adv* ▷ **fitful**
fitment *n* (*pl* **-s**) detachable part of the furnishings of a room
fitments *n* ▷ **fitment**
fitness *n* ▷ **fit**[1]
fitnesses *n* ▷ **fit**[1]
fits *v, n* ▷ **fit**[1, 2]
fitted *v* ▷ **fit**[1]
fitter *n* (*pl* **-s**) person skilled in the installation and adjustment of machinery ▶ *adj* ▷ **fit**[1]
fitters *n* ▷ **fitter**
fittest *adj* ▷ **fit**[1]
fitting *adj* appropriate, suitable ▶ *n* (*pl* **-s**) accessory or part ▶ *pl* furnishings and accessories in a building ▶ *v* ▷ **fit**
fittings *n* ▷ **fitting**
five *adj, n* (*pl* **-s**) one more than four
fiver *n* (*pl* **-s**) (*Informal*) five-pound note
fivers *n* ▷ **fiver**
fives *n* ball game resembling squash but played with bats or the hands ▶ *n* ▷ **five**
fix *v* (**-xes, -xing, -xed**) make or become firm, stable, or secure ▶ *n* (*pl* **-es**) (*Informal*) difficult situation > **fixed** *adj* > **fixedly** *adv* steadily
fixated *adj* obsessed
fixation *n* (*pl* **-s**) obsessive interest in something
fixations *n* ▷ **fixation**
fixative *n* (*pl* **-s**) liquid used to preserve or hold things in place
fixatives *n* ▷ **fixative**
fixed *v, adj* ▷ **fix**
fixedly *adv* ▷ **fix**
fixer *n* (*pl* **-s**) solution used to make a photographic image permanent
fixers *n* ▷ **fixer**
fixes *v, n* ▷ **fix**
fixing *v* ▷ **fix**
fixture *n* (*pl* **-s**) permanently fitted piece of household equipment
fixtures *n* ▷ **fixture**
fizz *v* (**-es, -ing, -ed**) make a hissing or bubbling noise ▶ *n* (*pl* **-es**) hissing or bubbling noise > **fizzy** *adj* (**-zzier, -zziest**)
fizzed *v* ▷ **fizz**
fizzes *v* ▷ **fizz**
fizzier *adj* ▷ **fizz**
fizziest *adj* ▷ **fizz**
fizzing *v* ▷ **fizz**
fizzle *v* (**-les, -ling, -led**) make a weak hissing or bubbling sound
fizzled *v* ▷ **fizzle**
fizzles *v* ▷ **fizzle**
fizzling *v* ▷ **fizzle**
fizzy *adj* ▷ **fizz**
fjord [fee-**ord**] *n* (*pl* **-s**) long narrow inlet of the sea between cliffs, esp. in Norway
fjords *n* ▷ **fjord**
flab *n* (*pl* **-s**) (*Informal*) unsightly body fat
flabbergasted *adj* completely astonished
flabbier *adj* ▷ **flabby**
flabbiest *adj* ▷ **flabby**
flabby *adj* (**-bbier, -bbiest**) having flabby flesh
flabs *n* ▷ **flab**
flaccid [**flas**-sid] *adj* (**-er, -est**) soft and limp > **flaccidity** *n* (*pl* **-ties**)
flaccider *adj* ▷ **flaccid**
flaccidest *adj* ▷ **flaccid**
flaccidities *n* ▷ **flaccid**
flaccidity *n* ▷ **flaccid**
flag[1] *n* (*pl* **-s**) piece of cloth attached to a pole as an emblem or signal ▶ *v* (**-s, -gging, -gged**) mark with a flag or sticker
flag[2] *v* (**-s, -gging, -gged**) lose enthusiasm or vigour
flag[3], **flagstone** (*pl* **-s**) *n* flat paving-stone

flagellant *n* (*pl* **-s**) person who whips himself or herself
flagellants *n* ▷ **flagellant**
flagellate [**flaj**-a-late] *v* (**-tes, -ting, -ted**) whip, esp. in religious penance or for sexual pleasure > **flagellation** *n* (*pl* **-s**)
flagellated *v* ▷ **flagellate**
flagellates *v* ▷ **flagellate**
flagellating *v* ▷ **flagellate**
flagellation *n* ▷ **flagellate**
flagellations *n* ▷ **flagellate**
flageolet [flaj-a-**let**] *n* (*pl* **-s**) small instrument like a recorder
flageolets *n* ▷ **flageolet**
flagged *adj* paved with flagstones ▶ *v* ▷ **flag**[1, 2]
flagged *v* ▷ **flag**[1, 2]
flagging *v* ▷ **flag**[1, 2]
flagon *n* (*pl* **-s**) wide bottle for wine or cider
flagons *n* ▷ **flagon**
flagpole, flagstaff (*pl* **-s**) *n* pole for a flag
flagpoles *n* ▷ **flagpole**
flagrant [**flayg**-rant] *adj* openly outrageous > **flagrantly** *adv*
flagrantly *adv* ▷ **flagrant**
flags *v, n* ▷ **flag**[1, 2, 3]
flagship *n* (*pl* **-s**) admiral's ship
flagships *n* ▷ **flagship**
flagstaff *n* ▷ **flagpole**
flagstaffs *n* ▷ **flagpole**
flagstone *n* ▷ **flag**[3]
flagstones *n* ▷ **flag**[3]
flail *v* (**-s, -ing, -ed**) wave about wildly ▶ *n* (*pl* **-s**) tool formerly used for threshing grain by hand
flailed *v* ▷ **flail**
flailing *v* ▷ **flail**
flails *v, n* ▷ **flail**
flair *n* (*pl* **-s**) natural ability
flairs *n* ▷ **flair**
flak *n* (*pl* **-s**) anti-aircraft fire
flake[1] *n* (*pl* **-s**) small thin piece, esp. chipped off something ▶ *v* (**-kes, -king, -ked**) peel off in flakes > **flaky** *adj* (**-kier, -kiest**)
flake[2] *n* (*pl* **-s**) (in Australia) the commercial name for the meat of the gummy shark
flaked *v* ▷ **flake**
flakes *v, n* ▷ **flake**[1, 2]
flakier *adj* ▷ **flaky**
flakiest *adj* ▷ **flaky**
flaking *v* ▷ **flake**
flaks *n* ▷ **flak**
flaky *adj* ▷ **flake**[1]
flambé [**flahm**-bay] *v* (**-bés, -béing, -béed**) cook or serve (food) in flaming brandy
flambéed *v* ▷ **flambé**
flambéing *v* ▷ **flambé**
flambés *v* ▷ **flambé**
flamboyances *n* ▷ **flamboyant**
flamboyant *adj* behaving in a very noticeable, extravagant way > **flamboyance** *n* (*pl* **-s**)
flamboyance *n* ▷ **flamboyant**
flame *n* (*pl* **-s**) luminous burning gas coming from burning material ▶ *v* (**-mes, -ming, -med**) burn brightly
flamed *v* ▷ **flame**
flamenco *n* (*pl* **-cos**) rhythmical Spanish dance accompanied by a guitar and vocalist
flamencos *n* ▷ **flamenco**
flames *n, v* ▷ **flame**
flaming *v* ▷ **flame**
flamingo *n* (*pl* **-gos, -goes**) large pink wading bird with a long neck and legs
flamingoes *n* ▷ **flamingo**
flamingos *n* ▷ **flamingo**
flammabilities *n* ▷ **flammable**
flammability *n* ▷ **flammable**
flammable *adj* easily set on fire > **flammability** *n* (*pl* **-ties**)
flan *n* (*pl* **-s**) open sweet or savoury tart
flange *n* (*pl* **-s**) projecting rim or collar
flanges *n* ▷ **flange**
flank *n* (*pl* **-s**) part of the side between the hips and ribs ▶ *v* (**-s, -ing, -ed**) be at or move along the side of
flanked *v* ▷ **flank**
flanking *v* ▷ **flank**
flanks *n, v* ▷ **flank**
flannel *n* (*pl* **-s**) (BRIT) small piece of cloth for washing the face ▶ *pl* trousers made of flannel ▶ *v* (**-s, -nelling, -nelled**) (*Informal*) talk evasively
flannelette *n* (*pl* **-s**) cotton imitation of flannel
flannelettes *n* ▷ **flannelette**
flannelled *v* ▷ **flannel**
flannelling *v* ▷ **flannel**
flannels *n, v* ▷ **flannel**
flans *n* ▷ **flan**
flap *v* (**-s, -pping, -pped**) move back and forwards or up and down ▶ *n* (*pl* **-s**) action or sound of flapping
flapjack *n* (*pl* **-s**) chewy biscuit made with oats
flapjacks *n* ▷ **flapjack**
flapped *v* ▷ **flap**
flapping *v* ▷ **flap**
flaps *v, n* ▷ **flap**
flare *v* (**-res, -ring, -red**) blaze with a sudden unsteady flame ▶ *n* (*pl* **-s**) sudden unsteady flame ▶ *pl* flared trousers
flared *adj* (of a skirt or trousers) becoming wider towards the hem ▶ *v* ▷ **flare**

flares *v, n* ▷ **flare**
flaring *v* ▷ **flare**
flash *n* (*pl* **-es**) sudden burst of light or flame ▶ *v* (**-es, -ing, -ed**) (cause to) burst into flame
flashback *n* (*pl* **-s**) scene in a book, play, or film, that shows earlier events
flashbacks *n* ▷ **flashback**
flashed *v* ▷ **flash**
flasher *n* (*pl* **-s**) (*Slang*) man who exposes himself indecently
flashers *n* ▷ **flasher**
flashes *n, v* ▷ **flash**
flashier *adj* ▷ **flashy**
flashiest *adj* ▷ **flashy**
flashing *n* (*pl* **-s**) watertight material used to cover joins in a roof ▶ *v* ▷ **flash**
flashings *n* ▷ **flashing**
flashlight *n* (*pl* **-s**) (US) torch
flashlights *n* ▷ **flashlight**
flashy *adj* (**-shier, -shiest**) vulgarly showy
flask *n* (*pl* **-s**) ▷ **vacuum flask** flat bottle for carrying alcoholic drink in the pocket
flasks *n* ▷ **flask**
flat[1] *adj* (**-tter, -ttest**) level and horizontal ▶ *adv* in or into a flat position ▶ *n* (*pl* **-s**) (MUSIC) symbol lowering the pitch of a note by a semitone > **flatly** *adv* > **flatness** *n* (*pl* **-es**) > **flatten** *v* (**-s, -ing, -ed**)
flat[2] *n* (*pl* **-s**) set of rooms for living in which are part of a larger building ▶ *v* (**-s, -tting, -tted**) (AUST & NZ) live in a flat
flatfish *n* (*pl* **-fish, -fishes**) sea fish, such as the sole, which has a flat body
flatfishes *n* ▷ **flatfish**
flatlet *n* (*pl* **-s**) (BRIT, AUST & S AFR) small flat
flatlets *n* ▷ **flatlet**
flatly *adv* ▷ **flat**[1]
flatmate *n* (*pl* **-s**) person with whom one shares a flat
flatmates *n* ▷ **flatmate**
flatness *n* ▷ **flat**[1]
flatnesses *n* ▷ **flat**[1]
flat-pack *adj* (of furniture, etc.) supplied in pieces in a flat box for assembly by the buyer
flats *n, v* ▷ **flat**[1, 2]
flatted *v* ▷ **flat**[2]
flatten *v* ▷ **flat**[1]
flattened *v* ▷ **flat**[1]
flattening *v* ▷ **flat**[1]
flatter[1] *v* (**-s, -ing, -ed**) praise insincerely > **flatterer** *n* (*pl* **-s**) > **flattery** *n* (*pl* **-ries**)
flatter[2] *adj* ▷ **flat**[1]
flattered *v* ▷ **flatter**[1]
flatterer *n* ▷ **flatter**
flatterers *n* ▷ **flatter**
flatteries *n* ▷ **flatter**
flattering *v* ▷ **flatter**[1]
flatters *v* ▷ **flatter**[1]
flattery *n* ▷ **flatter**
flattest *adj* ▷ **flat**[1]
flattie *n* (*pl* **-s**) (NZ & S AFR) (*Informal*) flat tyre
flatties *n* ▷ **flattie**
flatting *v* ▷ **flat**[2]
flatulence *n* ▷ **flatulent**
flatulences *n* ▷ **flatulent**
flatulent *adj* suffering from or caused by too much gas in the intestines > **flatulence** *n* (*pl* **-s**)
flaunt *v* (**-s, -ing, -ed**) display (oneself or one's possessions) arrogantly
flaunted *v* ▷ **flaunt**
flaunting *v* ▷ **flaunt**
flaunts *v* ▷ **flaunt**
flautist *n* (*pl* **-s**) flute player
flautists *n* ▷ **flautist**
flavour *n* (*pl* **-s**) distinctive taste ▶ *v* (**-s, -ing, -ed**) give flavour to > **flavourless** *adj*
flavoured *v* ▷ **flavour**
flavouring *n* (*pl* **-s**) substance used to flavour food ▶ *v* ▷ **flavour**
flavourings *n* ▷ **flavouring**
flavourless *adj* ▷ **flavour**
flavours *n, v* ▷ **flavour**
flaw *n* (*pl* **-s**) imperfection or blemish > **flawed** *adj* > **flawless** *adj*
flawed *adj* ▷ **flaw**
flawless *adj* ▷ **flaw**
flaws *n* ▷ **flaw**
flax *n* (*pl* **-es**) plant grown for its stem fibres and seeds
flaxen *adj* (of hair) pale yellow
flaxes *n* ▷ **flax**
flay *v* (**-s, -ing, -ed**) strip the skin off
flayed *v* ▷ **flay**
flaying *v* ▷ **flay**
flays *v* ▷ **flay**
flea *n* (*pl* **-s**) small wingless jumping bloodsucking insect
fleapit *n* (*pl* **-s**) (*Informal*) shabby cinema or theatre
fleapits *n* ▷ **fleapit**
fleas *n* ▷ **flea**
fleck *n* (*pl* **-s**) small mark, streak, or speck ▶ *v* (**-s, -ing, -ed**) speckle
flecked *n* ▷ **fleck**
flecking *v* ▷ **fleck**
flecks *n, v* ▷ **fleck**
fled *v* ▷ **flee**
fledged *adj* (of young birds) able to fly
fledgelings *n* ▷ **fledgling**

fledgling, fledgeling (*pl* **-s**) *n* young bird ▶ *adj* new or inexperienced
fledglings *n* ▷ **fledgling**
flee *v* (**-lees, -leeing, fled**) run away (from)
fleece *n* (*pl* **-s**) sheep's coat of wool ▶ *v* (**-ces, -cing, -ced**) defraud or overcharge
fleeced *v* ▷ **fleece**
fleeces *n, v* ▷ **fleece**
fleecier *adj* ▷ **fleecy**
fleeciest *adj* ▷ **fleecy**
fleecing *v* ▷ **fleece**
fleecy *adj* (**-cier, -ciest**) made of or like fleece
fleeing *v* ▷ **flee**
flees *v* ▷ **flee**
fleet[1] *n* (*pl* **-s**) number of warships organized as a unit
fleet[2] *adj* swift in movement
fleeting *adj* rapid and soon passing > **fleetingly** *adv*
fleetingly *adv* ▷ **fleeting**
fleets *n* ▷ **fleet**
flesh *n* (*pl* **-es**) soft part of a human or animal body (*Informal*)
fleshes *n* ▷ **flesh**
fleshier *adj* ▷ **fleshy**
fleshiest *adj* ▷ **fleshy**
fleshly *adj* carnal
fleshy *adj* (**-shier, -shiest**) plump
flew *v* ▷ **fly**[1]
flex *n* (*pl* **-xes**) flexible insulated electric cable ▶ *v* (**-xes, -xing, -xed**) bend
flexed *v* ▷ **flex**
flexes *n, v* ▷ **flex**
flexibility *n* ▷ **flexible**
flexible *adj* easily bent > **flexibly** *adv* > **flexibility** *n* (*pl* **-ties**)
flexibilities *n* ▷ **flexible**
flexibly *adv* ▷ **flexible**
flexing *v* ▷ **flex**
flexitime, flextime *n* (*pl* **-s**) system permitting variation in starting and finishing times of work
flexitimes *n* ▷ **flexitime**
flextimes *n* ▷ **flexitime**
flick *v* (**-s, -ing, -ed**) touch or move with the finger or hand in a quick movement ▶ *n* (*pl* **-s**) tap or quick stroke ▶ *pl* (*Slang*) the cinema
flicked *v* ▷ **flick**
flicker *v* (**-s, -ing, -ed**) shine unsteadily or intermittently ▶ *n* (*pl* **-s**) unsteady brief light
flickered *v* ▷ **flicker**
flickering *v* ▷ **flicker**
flickers *v, n* ▷ **flicker**
flicking *v* ▷ **flick**
flicks *v, n* ▷ **flick**
flier[1] *adj* ▷ **fly**[3]
flier[2] *n* ▷ **flyer**
fliers *n* ▷ **flyer**
flies *v, n* ▷ **fly**[1,2]
fliest *adj* ▷ **fly**[3]
flight[1] *n* (*pl* **-s**) journey by air
flight[2] *n* (*pl* **-s**) act of running away
flightier *adj* ▷ **flighty**
flightiest *adj* ▷ **flighty**
flightless *adj* (of certain birds or insects) unable to fly
flights *n* ▷ **flight**[1,2]
flighty *adj* (**-tier, -tiest**) frivolous and fickle
flimsier *adj* ▷ **flimsy**
flimsiest *adj* ▷ **flimsy**
flimsily *adv* ▷ **flimsy**
flimsiness *n* ▷ **flimsy**
flimsinesses *n* ▷ **flimsy**
flimsy *adj* (**-sier, -siest**) not strong or substantial > **flimsily** *adv* > **flimsiness** *n* (*pl* **-es**)
flinch *v* (**-es, -ing, -ed**) draw back or wince, as from pain
flinched *v* ▷ **flinch**
flinches *v* ▷ **flinch**
flinching *v* ▷ **flinch**
fling *v* (**-s, -ing, flung**) throw, send, or move forcefully or hurriedly ▶ *n* (*pl* **-s**) spell of self-indulgent enjoyment
flinging *v* ▷ **fling**
flings *v, n* ▷ **fling**
flint *n* (*pl* **-s**) hard grey stone
flintier *adj* ▷ **flinty**
flintiest *adj* ▷ **flinty**
flints *n* ▷ **flint**
flinty (**-tier, -tiest**) *adj* cruel
flip *v* (**-s, -pping, -pped**) throw (something small or light) carelessly ▶ *adj* (*Informal*) flippant
flippancies *n* ▷ **flippant**
flippancy *n* ▷ **flippant**
flippant *adj* treating serious things lightly > **flippancy** *n* (*pl* **-cies**)
flipped *v* ▷ **flip**
flipper (*pl* **-s**) *n* limb of a sea animal adapted for swimming
flippers *n* ▷ **flipper**
flipping *v* ▷ **flip**
flips *v* ▷ **flip**
flirt *v* (**-s, -ing, -ed**) behave as if sexually attracted to someone ▶ *n* (*pl* **-s**) person who flirts > **flirtation** *n* (*pl* **-s**) > **flirtatious** *adj*
flirtation *n* ▷ **flirt**
flirtations *n* ▷ **flirt**
flirtatious *adj* ▷ **flirt**

flirted *v* ▷ **flirt**
flirting *v* ▷ **flirt**
flirts *v, n* ▷ **flirt**
flit *v* (**-s, -tting, -tted**) move lightly and rapidly ▶ *n* (*pl* **-s**) act of flitting
flits *v, n* ▷ **flit**
flitted *v* ▷ **flit**
flitting *v* ▷ **flit**
float *v* (**-s, -ing, -ed**) rest on the surface of a liquid ▶ *n* (*pl* **-s**) light object used to help someone or something float
floated *v* ▷ **float**
floating *adj* moving about, changing ▶ *v* ▷ **float**
floats *v, n* ▷ **float**
flock[1] *n* (*pl* **-s**) number of animals of one kind together ▶ *v* (**-s, -ing, -ed**) gather in a crowd
flock[2] *n* (*pl* **-s**) wool or cotton waste used as stuffing ▶ *adj* (of wallpaper) with a velvety raised pattern
flocked *v* ▷ **flock**[1]
flocking *v* ▷ **flock**[1]
flocks *n, v* ▷ **flock**[1, 2]
floe *n* (*pl* **-s**) sheet of floating ice
floes *n* ▷ **floe**
flog *v* (**-s, -gging, -gged**) beat with a whip or stick > **flogging** *n* (*pl* **-s**)
flogged *v* ▷ **flog**
flogging *v, n* ▷ **flog**
floggings *n* ▷ **flog**
flogs *v* ▷ **flog**
flood *n* (*pl* **-s**) overflow of water onto a normally dry area ▶ *v* (**-s, -ing, -ed**) cover or become covered with water
flooded *v* ▷ **flood**
floodgate *n* (*pl* **-s**) gate used to control the flow of water
floodgates *n* ▷ **floodgate**
flooding *v* ▷ **flood**
floodlight *n* (*pl* **-s**) lamp that casts a broad intense beam of light ▶ *v* (**-lights, -lighting, -lit**) illuminate by floodlight
floodlighting *v* ▷ **floodlight**
floodlights *n, v* ▷ **floodlight**
floodlit *v* ▷ **floodlight**
floods *n, v* ▷ **flood**
floor *n* (*pl* **-s**) lower surface of a room ▶ *v* (**-s, -ing, -ed**) knock down
floored *adj* covered with a floor ▶ *v* ▷ **floor**
flooring *n* (*pl* **-s**) material for floors ▶ *v* ▷ **floor**
floorings *n* ▷ **flooring**
floors *n, v* ▷ **floor**
floozies *n* ▷ **floozy**
floozy *n* (*pl* **-zies**) (*Old-fashioned slang*) disreputable woman
flop *v* (**-s, -pping, -pped**) bend, fall, or collapse loosely or carelessly ▶ *n* (*pl* **-s**) failure
flopped *v* ▷ **flop**
floppier *adj* ▷ **floppy**
floppies *n* ▷ **floppy**
floppiest *adj* ▷ **floppy**
flopping *v* ▷ **flop**
floppy *adj* (**-ppier, -ppiest**) hanging downwards, loose ▶ *n* (*pl* **-ppies**) (COMPUTERS) a flexible magnetic disk that stores information
flops *v, n* ▷ **flop**
flora *n* (*pl* **-s**) plants of a given place or time
floral *adj* consisting of or decorated with flowers
floras *n* ▷ **flora**
floret *n* (*pl* **-s**) small flower forming part of a composite flower head
florets *n* ▷ **floret**
floribunda *n* (*pl* **-s**) type of rose whose flowers grow in large clusters
floribundas *n* ▷ **floribunda**
florid *adj* (**-er, -est**) with a red or flushed complexion
florider *adj* ▷ **florid**
floridest *adj* ▷ **florid**
florin *n* (*pl* **-s**) former British and Australian coin
florins *n* ▷ **florin**
florist *n* (*pl* **-s**) seller of flowers
florists *n* ▷ **florist**
floss *n* (*pl* **-es**) fine silky fibres
flosses *n* ▷ **floss**
flotation *n* (*pl* **-s**) launching or financing of a business enterprise
flotations *n* ▷ **flotation**
flotilla *n* (*pl* **-s**) small fleet or fleet of small ships
flotillas *n* ▷ **flotilla**
flotsam *n* (*pl* **-s**) floating wreckage
flotsams *n* ▷ **flotsam**
flounce[1] *v* (**-ces, -cing, -ced**) go with emphatic movements ▶ *n* (*pl* **-s**) flouncing movement
flounce[2] *n* (*pl* **-s**) ornamental frill on a garment
flounced *v* ▷ **flounce**
flounces *v, n* ▷ **flounce**[1, 2]
flouncing *v* ▷ **flounce**
flounder[1] *v* (**-s, -ing, -ed**) move with difficulty, as in mud
flounder[2] *n* (*pl* **-s**) edible flatfish
floundered *v* ▷ **flounder**
floundering *v* ▷ **flounder**
flounders *v, n* ▷ **flounder**[1, 2]
flour *n* (*pl* **-s**) powder made by grinding grain, esp. wheat ▶ *v* (**-s, -ing, -ed**) sprinkle with flour > **floury** *adj* (**-rier, -riest**)

floured *v* ▷ **flour**
flourier *adj* ▷ **flour**
flouriest *adj* ▷ **flour**
flouring *v* ▷ **flour**
flourish *v* (**-es, -ing, -ed**) be active, successful, or widespread ▶ *n* (*pl* **-es**) dramatic waving motion > **flourishing** *adj*
flourished *v* ▷ **flourish**
flourishes *v, n* ▷ **flourish**
flourishing *n, adj* ▷ **flourish**
flours *n, v* ▷ **flour**
floury *adj* ▷ **flour**
flout *v* (**-s, -ing, -ed**) deliberately disobey (a rule, law, etc.)
flouted *v* ▷ **flout**
flouting *v* ▷ **flout**
flouts *v* ▷ **flout**
flow *v* (**-s, -ing, -ed**) (of liquid) move in a stream ▶ *n* (*pl* **-s**) act, rate, or manner of flowing
flowed *v* ▷ **flow**
flower *n* (*pl* **-s**) part of a plant that produces seeds ▶ *v* (**-s, -ing, -ed**) produce flowers, bloom
flowerbed *n* (*pl* **-s**) piece of ground for growing flowers
flowerbeds *n* ▷ **flowerbed**
flowered *adj* decorated with a floral design ▶ *v* ▷ **flower**
flowerier *adj* ▷ **flowery**
floweriest *adj* ▷ **flowery**
flowering *v* ▷ **flower**
flowers *n, v* ▷ **flower**
flowery *adj* (**-rier, -riest**) decorated with a floral design
flowing *v* ▷ **flow**
flown *v* ▷ **fly**[1]
flows *v, n* ▷ **flow**
flu *n* (*pl* **flus**) ▷ **influenza**
fluctuate *v* (**-tes, -ting, -ted**) change frequently and erratically > **fluctuation** *n* (*pl* **-s**)
fluctuated *v* ▷ **fluctuate**
fluctuates *v* ▷ **fluctuate**
fluctuating *v* ▷ **fluctuate**
fluctuation *n* ▷ **fluctuate**
fluctuations *n* ▷ **fluctuate**
flue *n* (*pl* **-s**) passage or pipe for smoke or hot air
fluencies *n* ▷ **fluent**
fluency *n* ▷ **fluent**
fluent *adj* able to speak or write with ease > **fluently** *adv* > **fluency** *n* (*pl* **-cies**)
fluently *adv* ▷ **fluent**
flues *n* ▷ **flue**
fluff *n* (*pl* **-s**) soft fibres ▶ *v* (**-s, -ing, -ed**) make or become soft and puffy > **fluffy** *adj* (**-ffier, -ffiest**)
fluffed *v* ▷ **fluff**
fluffier *adj* ▷ **fluff**
fluffiest *adj* ▷ **fluff**
fluffing *v* ▷ **fluff**
fluffs *n, v* ▷ **fluff**
fluffy *adj* ▷ **fluff**
fluid *n* (*pl* **-s**) substance able to flow and change its shape; a liquid or a gas ▶ *adj* able to flow or change shape easily > **fluidity** *n* (*pl* **-ies**)
fluidities *n* ▷ **fluid**
fluidity *n* ▷ **fluid**
fluids *n* ▷ **fluid**
fluke[1] *n* (*pl* **-s**) accidental stroke of luck
fluke[2] (*pl* **-s**) *n* flat triangular point of an anchor
fluke[3] (*pl* **-s**) *n* parasitic worm
flukes *n* ▷ **fluke**[1, 2, 3]
flume *n* (*pl* **-s**) narrow sloping channel for water
flumes *n* ▷ **flume**
flummox *v* (**-xes, -xing, -xed**) puzzle or confuse
flummoxed *v* ▷ **flummox**
flummoxes *v* ▷ **flummox**
flummoxing *v* ▷ **flummox**
flung *v* ▷ **fling**
flunk *v* (**flunks, flunking, flunked**) (US, AUST, NZ & S AFR) (*Informal*) fail
flunked *v* ▷ **flunk**
flunkey *n* ▷ **flunky**
flunkeys *n* ▷ **flunky**
flunkies *n* ▷ **flunky**
flunking *v* ▷ **flunk**
flunks *v* ▷ **flunk**
flunky, flunkey *n* (*pl* **-kies, -keys**) servile person
fluoresce *v* (**-ces, -cing, -ced**) exhibit fluorescence
fluoresced *v* ▷ **fluoresce**
fluorescence *n* (*pl* **-s**) emission of light from a substance bombarded by particles, such as electrons, or by radiation
fluorescences *n* ▷ **fluorescence**
fluorescent *adj* of or resembling fluorescence
fluoresces *v* ▷ **fluoresce**
fluorescing *v* ▷ **fluoresce**
fluoridate *v* (**-tes, -ting, -ted**) add fluoride to (water) as protection against tooth decay > **fluoridation** *n* (*pl* **-s**)
fluoridated *v* ▷ **fluoridate**
fluoridates *v* ▷ **fluoridate**
fluoridating *v* ▷ **fluoridate**
fluoridation *n* ▷ **fluoridate**
fluoridations *n* ▷ **fluoridate**

fluoride *n* (*pl* **-s**) compound containing fluorine
fluorides *n* ▷ **fluoride**
fluorine *n* (*pl* **-s**) (CHEM) toxic yellow gas, most reactive of all the elements
fluorines *n* ▷ **fluorine**
flurried *v* ▷ **flurry**
flurries *n, v* ▷ **flurry**
flurry *n* (*pl* **-rries**) sudden commotion ▶ *v* (**-rries, -rrying, -rried**) confuse
flus *n* ▷ **flu**
flush[1] *v* (**-es, -ing, -ed**) blush or cause to blush ▶ *n* (*pl* **-es**) blush
flush[2] *adj* level with the surrounding surface
flush[3] *v* (**-es, -ing, -ed**) drive out of a hiding place
flush[4] *n* (*pl* **-es**) (in card games) hand all of one suit
flushed *v* ▷ **flush**[1, 3]
flushes *v, n* ▷ **flush**[1, 3, 4]
flushing *v* ▷ **flush**[1, 3]
fluster *v* (**-s, -ing, -ed**) make nervous or upset ▶ *n* (*pl* **-s**) nervous or upset state
flustered *v* ▷ **fluster**
flustering *v* ▷ **fluster**
flusters *v, n* ▷ **fluster**
flute *n* (*pl* **-s**) wind instrument consisting of a tube with sound holes and a mouth hole in the side
fluted *adj* having decorative grooves
flutes *n* ▷ **flute**
flutter *v* (**-s, -ing, -ed**) wave rapidly ▶ *n* (*pl* **-s**) flapping movement
fluttered *v* ▷ **flutter**
fluttering *v* ▷ **flutter**
flutters *v, n* ▷ **flutter**
fluvial *adj* of rivers
flux *n* (*pl* **-es**) constant change or instability
fluxes *n* ▷ **flux**
fly[1] *v* (**flying, flew, flown**) move through the air on wings or in an aircraft ▶ *n* (*pl* **flies**) (*often pl* (BRIT) fastening at the front of trousers ▶ *pl* space above a stage, used for storage
fly[2] *n* (*pl* **flies**) two-winged insect
fly[3] *adj* (**flier, fliest**) (*Slang*) sharp and cunning
flycatcher *n* (*pl* **-s**) small insect-eating songbird
flycatchers *n* ▷ **flycatcher**
flyer, flier (*pl* **-s**) *n* small advertising leaflet
flyers *n* ▷ **flyer**
flying *adj* hurried and brief ▶ *v* ▷ **fly**
flyleaf *n* (*pl* **-leaves**) blank leaf at the beginning or end of a book
flyleaves *n* ▷ **flyleaf**
flyover *n* (*pl* **-s**) road passing over another by a bridge
flyovers *n* ▷ **flyover**
flypaper *n* (*pl* **-s**) paper with a sticky poisonous coating, used to kill flies
flypapers *n* ▷ **flypaper**
flyweight *n* (*pl* **-s**) boxer weighing up to 112lb (professional) or 51kg (amateur)
flyweights *n* ▷ **flyweight**
flywheel (*pl* **-s**) *n* heavy wheel regulating the speed of a machine
flywheels *n* ▷ **flywheel**
foal *n* (*pl* **-s**) young of a horse or related animal ▶ *v* (**-s, -ing, -ed**) give birth to a foal
foaled *v* ▷ **foal**
foaling *v* ▷ **foal**
foals *n, v* ▷ **foal**
foam *n* (*pl* **-s**) mass of small bubbles on a liquid ▶ *v* (**-s, -ing, -ed**) produce foam > **foamy** *adj* (**-ier, -iest**)
foamed *v* ▷ **foam**
foamier *adj* ▷ **foam**
foamiest *adj* ▷ **foam**
foaming *v* ▷ **foam**
foams *n, v* ▷ **foam**
foamy *adj* ▷ **foam**
fob *n* (*pl* **-s**) short watch chain
fobs *n* ▷ **fob**
focal *adj* of or at a focus
foci *n* ▷ **focus**
fo'c's'le *n* (*pl* **fo'c's'les**) ▷ **forecastle**
fo'c's'les *n* ▷ **fo'c's'le**
focus *n* (*pl* **-cuses, -ci**) [-sye] point at which light or sound waves converge ▶ *v* (**-cuses, -cusing, -cused** *or* **-cusses, -cussing, -cussed**) bring or come into focus
focused *v* ▷ **focus**
focuses *n, v* ▷ **focus**
focusing *v* ▷ **focus**
focussed *v* ▷ **focus**
focussing ▷ **focus**
fodder *n* (*pl* **-s**) feed for livestock
fodders *n* ▷ **fodder**
foe *n* (*pl* **foes**) enemy, opponent
foes *n* ▷ **foe**
foetid *adj* (**-er, -est**) ▷ **fetid**
foetider *adj* ▷ **foetid**
foetidest *adj* ▷ **foetid**
foetus *n* (*pl* **-tuses**) ▷ **fetus**
foetuses *n* ▷ **foetus**
fog *n* (*pl* **-s**) mass of condensed water vapour in the lower air, often greatly reducing visibility ▶ *v* (**-s, fogging, fogged**) cover with steam > **foggy** *adj* (**-ggier, -ggiest**)
fogey, fogy *n* (*pl* **-geys, -gies**) old-fashioned person

fogeys *n* ▷ **fogey**
fogged *v* ▷ **fog**
foggier *adj* ▷ **fog**
foggiest *adj* ▷ **fog**
fogging *v* ▷ **fog**
foggy *adj* ▷ **fog**
foghorn *n* (*pl* **-s**) large horn sounded to warn ships in fog
foghorns *n* ▷ **foghorn**
fogies *n* ▷ **fogey**
fogs *n* ▷ **fog**
fogy *n* ▷ **fogey**
foible *n* (*pl* **-s**) minor weakness or slight peculiarity
foibles *n* ▷ **foible**
foil[1] *v* (**-s, -ing, -ed**) ruin (someone's plan)
foil[2] *n* (*pl* **-s**) metal in a thin sheet, esp. for wrapping food
foil[3] *n* (*pl* **-s**) light slender flexible sword tipped with a button
foiled *v* ▷ **foil**
foiling *v* ▷ **foil**
foils *v, n* ▷ **foil**[1, 2, 3]
foist *v* (**-s, -ing, -ed**) (*foll. by* **on** *or* **upon**) force or impose on
foisted *v* ▷ **foist**
foisting *v* ▷ **foist**
foists *v* ▷ **foist**
fold[1] *v* (**-s, -ing, -ed**) bend so that one part covers another ▶ *n* (*pl* **-s**) folded piece or part
fold[2] *n* (*pl* **-s**) (BRIT, AUST & S AFR) enclosure for sheep
folded *v* ▷ **fold**
folder *n* (*pl* **-s**) piece of folded cardboard for holding loose papers
folders *n* ▷ **folder**
folding *v* ▷ **fold**
folds *v, n* ▷ **fold**[1, 2]
foliage *n* (*pl* **-s**) leaves
foliages *n* ▷ **foliage**
foliation *n* (*pl* **-s**) process of producing leaves
foliations *n* ▷ **foliation**
folio *n* (*pl* **-lios**) sheet of paper folded in half to make two leaves of a book
folios *n* ▷ **folio**
folk *n* (*pl* **-s**) people in general ▶ *pl* relatives
folklore *n* (*pl* **-s**) traditional beliefs and stories of a people
folklores *n* ▷ **folklore**
folks *n* ▷ **folk**
folksier *adj* ▷ **folksy**
folksiest *adj* ▷ **folksy**
folksy *adj* (**-sier, -siest**) simple and unpretentious
follicle *n* (*pl* **-s**) small cavity in the body, esp. one from which a hair grows
follicles *n* ▷ **follicle**
follies *n* ▷ **folly**
follow *v* (**-s, -ing, -ed**) go or come after
followed *v* ▷ **follow**
follower *n* (*pl* **-s**) disciple or supporter
followers *n* ▷ **follower**
following *adj* about to be mentioned ▶ *n* (*pl* **-s**) group of supporters ▶ *prep* as a result of ▶ *v* ▷ **follow**
followings *n* ▷ **following**
follows *v* ▷ **follow**
folly *n* (*pl* **-llies**) foolishness
foment [foam-**ent**] *v* (**-s, -ing, -ed**) encourage or stir up (trouble)
fomented *v* ▷ **foment**
fomenting *v* ▷ **foment**
foments *v* ▷ **foment**
fond *adj* (**-er, -est**) tender, loving > **fondly** *adv* > **fondness** *n* (*pl* **-es**)
fondant *n* (*pl* **-s**) (sweet made from) flavoured paste of sugar and water
fondants *n* ▷ **fondant**
fonder *adj* ▷ **fond**
fondest *adj* ▷ **fond**
fondle *v* (**-les, -ling, -led**) caress
fondled *v* ▷ **fondle**
fondles *v* ▷ **fondle**
fondling *v* ▷ **fondle**
fondly *adv* ▷ **fond**
fondness *n* ▷ **fond**
fondnesses *n* ▷ **fond**
fondue *n* (*pl* **-dues**) Swiss dish of a hot melted cheese sauce into which pieces of bread are dipped
fondues *n* ▷ **fondue**
font[1] *n* (*pl* **-s**) bowl in a church for baptismal water
font[2] (*pl* **-s**) *n* set of printing type of one style and size
fontanelle *n* (*pl* **-s**) soft membranous gap between the bones of a baby's skull
fontanelles *n* ▷ **fontanelle**
fonts *n* ▷ **font**[1, 2]
food *n* (*pl* **-dies**) what one eats, solid nourishment
foodie *n* (*pl* **-s**) (*Informal*) gourmet
foodies *n* ▷ **foodie**
foods *n* ▷ **food**
foodstuff *n* (*pl* **-s**) substance used as food
foodstuffs *n* ▷ **foodstuff**
fool[1] *n* (*pl* **-s**) person lacking sense or judgment (HIST) ▶ *v* (**-s, -ing, -ed**) deceive (someone)
fool[2] (*pl* **-s**) *n* dessert of puréed fruit mixed with cream

fooled *v* ▷ **fool**
fooleries *n* ▷ **foolery**
foolery *n* (*pl* **-ries**) foolish behaviour
foolhardiness *n* ▷ **foolhardy**
foolhardinesses *n* ▷ **foolhardy**
foolhardy *adj* recklessly adventurous > **foolhardiness** *n* (*pl* **-es**)
fooling *v* ▷ **fool**
foolish *adj* (**-er, -est**) unwise, silly, or absurd > **foolishly** *adv* > **foolishness** *n* (*pl* **-es**)
foolisher *adj* ▷ **foolish**
foolishest *adj* ▷ **foolish**
foolishly *adv* ▷ **foolish**
foolishness *n* ▷ **foolish**
foolishnesses *n* ▷ **foolish**
foolproof *adj* unable to fail
fools *n, v* ▷ **fool**[1, 2]
foolscap *n* (*pl* **-s**) size of paper, 34.3 × 43.2 centimetres
foolscaps *n* ▷ **foolscap**
foot *n* (*pl* **feet**) part of the leg below the ankle
footage *n* (*pl* **-s**) amount of film used
footages *n* ▷ **footage**
football *n* (*pl* **-s**) game played by two teams of eleven players kicking a ball in an attempt to score goals > **footballer** *n* (*pl* **-s**)
footballer *n* ▷ **football**
footballers *n* ▷ **footballs**
footballs *n* ▷ **football**
footbridge *n* (*pl* **-s**) bridge for pedestrians
footbridges *n* ▷ **footbridge**
footfall *n* (*pl* **-s**) sound of a footstep
footfalls *n* ▷ **footfall**
foothills *pl n* hills at the foot of a mountain
foothold *n* (*pl* **-s**) secure position from which progress may be made
footholds *n* ▷ **foothold**
footing *n* (*pl* **-s**) basis or foundation
footings *n* ▷ **footing**
footlight *n* light at the front of a stage
footlights *pl n* ▷ **footlight**
footling *adj* (CHIEFLY BRIT) (*Informal*) trivial
footloose *adj* free from ties
footman *n* (*pl* **-men**) male servant in uniform
footmen *n* ▷ **footman**
footnote *n* note printed at the foot of a page
footnotes *n* ▷ **footnote**
footpath *n* (*pl* **-s**) narrow path for walkers only
footpaths *n* ▷ **footpath**
footplate *n* (*pl* **-s**) platform in the cab of a locomotive for the driver
footplates *n* ▷ **footplate**
footprint *n* (*pl* **-s**) mark left by a foot
footprints *n* ▷ **footprint**
footsie *n* (*pl* **-s**) (*Informal*) flirtation involving the touching together of feet
footsies *n* ▷ **footsie**
footstep *n* step in walking
footsteps *n* ▷ **footstep**
footstool *n* (*pl* **-s**) low stool used to rest the feet on while sitting
footstools *n* ▷ **footstool**
footwear *n* (*pl* **-s**) anything worn to cover the feet
footwears *n* ▷ **footwear**
footwork *n* (*pl* **-s**) skilful use of the feet, as in sport or dancing
footworks *n* ▷ **footwork**
fop *n* (*pl* **-s**) man excessively concerned with fashion > **foppery** *n* (*pl* **-ies**) > **foppish** *adj*
fopperies *n* ▷ **fop**
foppery *n* ▷ **fop**
foppish *n* ▷ **fop**
fops *n* ▷ **fop**
for *prep* indicating a person intended to benefit from or receive something, span of time or distance, person or thing represented by someone, etc. ▶ *conj* because
forage *v* (**-ges, -ging, -ged**) search about (for) ▶ *n* (*pl* **-s**) food for cattle or horses
foraged *v* ▷ **forage**
forages *v, n* ▷ **forage**
foraging *v* ▷ **forage**
foray *n* (*pl* **-s**) brief raid or attack
forays *n* ▷ **foray**
forbade *v* ▷ **forbid**
forbear *v* (**-s, -ing, forbore, forborne**) cease or refrain (from doing something)
forbearance *n* (*pl* **-s**) tolerance, patience
forbearances *n* ▷ **forbearance**
forbearing *v* ▷ **forbear**
forbears *v* ▷ **forbear**
forbid *v* (**-s, -dding, forbade, forbidden**) prohibit, refuse to allow > **forbidden** *adj*
forbidden *v, adj* ▷ **forbid**
forbidding *adj* severe, threatening ▶ *v* ▷ **forbid**
forbids *v* ▷ **forbid**
forbore *v* ▷ **forbear**
forborne *v* ▷ **forbear**
force *n* (*pl* **-s**) strength or power ▶ *v* (**-ces, -cing, -ced**) compel, make (someone) do something
forced *adj* compulsory ▶ *v* ▷ **force**
forceful *adj* emphatic and confident > **forcefully** *adv*
forceps *pl n* surgical pincers
forces *n, v* ▷ **force**
forcible *adj* involving physical force or violence > **forcibly** *adv*
forcibly *adv* ▷ **forcible**

forcing *v* ▷ **force**
ford *n* (*pl* **-s**) shallow place where a river may be crossed ▶ *v* (**-s, -ing, -ed**) cross (a river) at a ford
forded *v* ▷ **ford**
fording *v* ▷ **ford**
fords *n, v* ▷ **ford**
fore *adj* in, at, or towards the front ▶ *n* (*pl* **-s**) front part
forearm[1] *n* (*pl* **-s**) arm from the wrist to the elbow
forearm[2] *v* (**-s, -ing, -ed**) prepare beforehand
forearmed *v* ▷ **forearm**[2]
forearming *v* ▷ **forearm**[2]
forearms *n, v* ▷ **forearm**[1, 2]
forebear *n* (*pl* **-s**) ancestor
forebears *n* ▷ **forebear**
foreboding *n* (*pl* **-s**) feeling that something bad is about to happen
forebodings *n* ▷ **foreboding**
forecast *v* (**-casts, -casting, -cast** *or* **-casted**) predict (weather, events, etc.) ▶ *n* (*pl* **-s**) prediction
forecasted *v* ▷ **forecast**
forecasting *v* ▷ **forecast**
forecastle [**foke**-sl] *n* (*pl* **-s**) raised front part of a ship
forecastles *n* ▷ **forecastle**
forecasts *v, n* ▷ **forecast**
foreclose *v* (**-ses, -sing, -sed**) take possession of (property bought with borrowed money which has not been repaid) > **foreclosure** *n* (*pl* **-s**)
foreclosed *v* ▷ **foreclose**
forecloses *v* ▷ **foreclose**
foreclosing *v* ▷ **foreclose**
foreclosure *n* ▷ **foreclose**
foreclosures *n* ▷ **foreclose**
forecourt *n* (*pl* **-s**) courtyard or open space in front of a building
forecourts *n* ▷ **forecourt**
forefather *n* (*pl* **-s**) ancestor
forefathers *n* ▷ **forefather**
forefinger *n* (*pl* **-s**) finger next to the thumb
forefingers *n* ▷ **forefinger**
forefront *n* (*pl* **-s**) most active or prominent position
forefronts *n* ▷ **forefront**
foregather *v* (**-s, -ing, -ed**) meet together or assemble
foregathered *v* ▷ **foregather**
foregathering *v* ▷ **foregather**
foregathers *v* ▷ **foregather**
forego *v* (**-goes, -going, -went, -gone**) ▷ **forgo**
foregoes *v* ▷ **forego**
foregoing *adj* going before, preceding ▶ *v* ▷ **forego**
foregone *v* ▷ **forego**
foreground *n* (*pl* **-s**) part of a view, esp. in a picture, nearest the observer
foregrounds *n* ▷ **foreground**
forehand *n* (*pl* **-s**) (TENNIS ETC.) stroke played with the palm of the hand facing forward
forehands *n* ▷ **forehand**
forehead *n* (*pl* **-s**) part of the face above the eyebrows
foreheads *n* ▷ **forehead**
foreign *adj* not of, or in, one's own country > **foreigner** *n* (*pl* **-s**)
foreigner *n* ▷ **foreign**
foreigners *n* ▷ **foreign**
foreleg *n* (*pl* **-s**) either of the front legs of an animal
forelegs *n* ▷ **foreleg**
forelock *n* (*pl* **-s**) lock of hair over the forehead
forelocks *n* ▷ **forelock**
foreman *n* (*pl* **-men**) person in charge of a group of workers
foremast *n* (*pl* **-s**) mast nearest the bow of a ship
foremasts *n* ▷ **foremast**
foremen *n* ▷ **foreman**
foremost *adj, adv* first in time, place, or importance
forename *n* (*pl* **-s**) first name
forenames *n* ▷ **forename**
forenoon *n* (*pl* **-s**) (CHIEFLY US & CANADIAN) morning
forenoons *n* ▷ **forenoon**
forensic *adj* used in or connected with courts of law
foreplay *n* (*pl* **-s**) sexual stimulation before intercourse
foreplays *n* ▷ **foreplay**
forerunner *n* (*pl* **-s**) person or thing that goes before, precursor
forerunners *n* ▷ **forerunner**
fores *n* ▷ **fore**
foresail *n* (*pl* **-s**) main sail on the foremast of a ship
foresails *n* ▷ **foresail**
foresaw *v* ▷ **foresee**
foresee *v* (**-sees, -seeing, -saw, -seen**) see or know beforehand > **foreseeable** *adj*
foreseeable *adj* ▷ **foresee**
foreseeing *v* ▷ **foresee**
foreseen *v* ▷ **foresee**
foresees *v* ▷ **foresee**
foreshadow *v* (**-s, -ing, -ed**) show or indicate beforehand

foreshadowed *v* ▷ **foreshadow**
foreshadowing *v* ▷ **foreshadow**
foreshadows *v* ▷ **foreshadow**
foreshore *n* (*pl* **-s**) part of the shore between high- and low-tide marks
foreshores *n* ▷ **foreshore**
foreshorten *v* (**-s, -ing, -ed**) represent (an object) in a picture as shorter than it really is, in accordance with perspective
foreshortened *v* ▷ **foreshorten**
foreshortening *v* ▷ **foreshorten**
foreshortens *v* ▷ **foreshorten**
foresight *n* (*pl* **-s**) ability to anticipate and provide for future needs
foresights *n* ▷ **foresight**
foreskin *n* (*pl* **-s**) fold of skin covering the tip of the penis
foreskins *n* ▷ **foreskin**
forest *n* (*pl* **-s**) large area with a thick growth of trees > **forested** *adj*
forestall *v* (**-s, -ing, -ed**) prevent or guard against in advance
forestalled *v* ▷ **forestall**
forestalling *v* ▷ **forestall**
forestalls *v* ▷ **forestall**
forested *adj* ▷ **forest**
forester *n* (*pl* **-s**) person skilled in forestry
forester *n* ▷ **foresters**
forestries *n* ▷ **forestry**
forestry *n* (*pl* **-ries**) science of planting and caring for trees
forests *n* ▷ **forest**
foretaste *n* (*pl* **-s**) early limited experience of something to come
foretastes *n* ▷ **foretaste**
foretell *v* (**-s, f -ing, -told**) tell or indicate beforehand
foretelling *v* ▷ **foretell**
foretells *v* ▷ **foretell**
forethought *n* (*pl* **-s**) thoughtful planning for future events
forethoughts *n* ▷ **forethought**
foretold *v* ▷ **foretell**
forever *adv* without end
forewarn *v* (**-s, -ing, -ed**) warn beforehand
forewarned *v* ▷ **forewarn**
forewarning *v* ▷ **forewarn**
forewarns *v* ▷ **forewarn**
forewent *v* ▷ **forego**
foreword *n* (*pl* **-s**) introduction to a book
forewords *n* ▷ **foreword**
forfeit [**for**-fit] *n* (*pl* **-s**) thing lost or given up as a penalty for a fault or mistake ▸ *v* (**-s, -ing, -ed**) lose as a forfeit ▸ *adj* lost as a forfeit > **forfeiture** *n* (*pl* **-s**)
forfeited *v* ▷ **forfeit**
forfeiting *v* ▷ **forfeit**
forfeits *n, v* ▷ **forfeit**
forfeiture *n* ▷ **forfeit**
forfeitures *n* ▷ **forfeit**
forgave *v* ▷ **forgive**
forge[1] *n* (*pl* **-s**) place where metal is worked, smithy ▸ *v* (**-ges, -ging, -ged**) make a fraudulent imitation of (something)
forge[2] *v* (**-ges, -ging, -ged**) advance steadily
forged *n* ▷ **forge**[1, 2]
forger *n* (*pl* **-s**) person who makes an illegal copy of something
forgeries *n* ▷ **forgery**
forgers *n* ▷ **forger**
forgery *n* (*pl* **-ries**) illegal copy of something
forges *v, n* ▷ **forge**[1, 2]
forget *v* (**-s, -getting, -got, -gotten**) fail to remember
forgetful *adj* tending to forget > **forgetfulness** *n* (*pl* **-es**)
forgetfulness *n* ▷ **forgetful**
forgetfulnesses *n* ▷ **forgetful**
forgets *v* ▷ **forget**
forgetting *v* ▷ **forget**
forging *v* ▷ **forge**[1, 2]
forgive *v* (**-giving, -gave, -given**) cease to blame or hold resentment against, pardon > **forgiveness** *n* (*pl* **-es**)
forgiven *v* ▷ **forgive**
forgiveness *n* ▷ **forgive**
forgivenesses *n* ▷ **forgive**
forgiving *v* ▷ **forgive**
forgo *v* (**-goes, -going, -went, -gone**) do without or give up
forgoes *v* ▷ **forgo**
forgoing *v* ▷ **forgo**
forgone *v* ▷ **forgo**
forgot *v* ▷ **forget**
forgotten *v* ▷ **forget**
fork *n* (*pl* **-s**) tool for eating food, with prongs and a handle ▸ *v* (**-s, -ing, -ed**) pick up, dig, etc. with a fork > **forked** *adj*
forked *v, adj* ▷ **fork**
forking *v* ▷ **fork**
forks *n, v* ▷ **fork**
forlorn *adj* lonely and unhappy > **forlornly** *adv*
forlornly *adv* ▷ **forlorn**
form *n* (*pl* **-s**) shape or appearance ▸ *v* (**-s, -ing, -ed**) give a (particular) shape to or take a (particular) shape > **formless** *adj*
formal *adj* of or characterized by established conventions of ceremony and behaviour > **formally** *adv*
formaldehyde [for-**mal**-de-hide] *n* (*pl* **-s**)

colourless pungent gas used to make formalin
formaldehydes *n* ▷ **formaldehyde**
formalin *n* (*pl* **-s**) solution of formaldehyde in water, used as a disinfectant or a preservative for biological specimens
formalins *n* ▷ **formalin**
formalities *n* ▷ **formality**
formality *n* (*pl* **-ties**) requirement of custom or etiquette
formalize *v* (**-zes, -zing, -zed**) make official or formal
formalized *v* ▷ **formalize**
formalizes *v* ▷ **formalize**
formalizing *v* ▷ **formalize**
formally *adv* ▷ **formal**
format *n* (*pl* **-s**) style in which something is arranged ▶ *v* (**-s, -matting, -matted**) arrange in a format
formation *n* (*pl* **-s**) forming
formations *n* ▷ **formation**
formative *adj* of or relating to development
formats *n, v* ▷ **format**
formatted *v* ▷ **format**
formatting *v* ▷ **format**
formed *v* ▷ **form**
former *adj* of an earlier time, previous > **formerly** *adv*
formerly *adv* ▷ **former**
formidable *adj* frightening because difficult to overcome or manage > **formidably** *adv*
formidably *adv* ▷ **formidable**
forming *v* ▷ **form**
formless *adj* ▷ **form**
forms *n, v* ▷ **form**
formula *n* (*pl* **-las, -lae**) group of numbers, letters, or symbols expressing a scientific or mathematical rule > **formulaic** *adj*
formulae *n* ▷ **formula**
formulaic *adj* ▷ **formula**
formulas *n* ▷ **formula**
formulate *v* (**-tes, -ting, -ted**) plan or describe precisely and clearly > **formulation** *n* (*pl* **-s**)
formulated *v* ▷ **formulate**
formulates *v* ▷ **formulate**
formulating *v* ▷ **formulates**
formulation *n* ▷ **formulate**
formulations *n* ▷ **formulate**
fornicate *v* (**-tes, -ting, -ted**) have sexual intercourse without being married > **fornication** *n* (*pl* **-s**) > **fornicator** *n* (*pl* **-s**)
fornicated *v* ▷ **fornicate**
fornicates *v* ▷ **fornicate**
fornicating *v* ▷ **fornicate**
fornication *n* ▷ **fornicate**
fornications *n* ▷ **fornicate**
fornicator *n* ▷ **fornicate**
fornicators *n* ▷ **fornicate**
forsake *v* (**-sakes, -saking, -sook, -saken**) withdraw support or friendship from
forsaken *v* ▷ **forsake**
forsakes *v* ▷ **forsake**
forsaking *v* ▷ **forsake**
forsook *v* ▷ **forsake**
forsooth *adv* (*Obs*) indeed
forswear *v* (**-s, -swearing, -swore, -sworn**) renounce or reject
forswearing *v* ▷ **forswear**
forswears *v* ▷ **forswear**
forswore *v* ▷ **forswear**
forsworn *v* ▷ **forswear**
forsythia [for-**syth**-ee-a] *n* (*pl* **-as**) shrub with yellow flowers in spring
forsythias *n* ▷ **forsythia**
fort *n* (*pl* **-s**) fortified building or place
forte¹ [**for**-tay] *n* (*pl* **-s**) thing at which a person excels
forte² [**for**-tay] *adv* (MUSIC) loudly
fortes *n* ▷ **forte**
forth *adv* forwards, out, or away
forthcoming *adj* about to appear or happen
forthright *adj* direct and outspoken
forthwith *adv* at once
forties *n* ▷ **forty**
fortieth *adj, n* ▷ **forty**
fortieths *n* ▷ **forty**
fortifications *n* ▷ **fortify**
fortified *v* ▷ **fortify**
fortifies *v* ▷ **fortify**
fortify *v* (**-fies, -fying, -fied**) make (a place) defensible, as by building walls > **fortification** *n* (*pl* **-s**)
fortification *n* ▷ **fortify**
fortifying *v* ▷ **fortify**
fortissimo *adv* (MUSIC) very loudly
fortitude *n* (*pl* **-s**) courage in adversity or pain
fortitudes *n* ▷ **fortitude**
fortnight *n* (*pl* **-s**) two weeks > **fortnightly** *adv, adj*
fortnightly *adv, adj* ▷ **fortnight**
fortnights *n* ▷ **fortnight**
fortress *n* (*pl* **-es**) large fort or fortified town
fortresses *n* ▷ **fortress**
forts *n* ▷ **fort**
fortuitous [for-**tyew**-it-uss] *adj* happening by (lucky) chance > **fortuitously** *adv*
fortuitously *adv* ▷ **fortuitous**
fortunate *adj* having good luck > **fortunately** *adv*
fortunately *adv* ▷ **fortunate**

fortune *n* (*pl* **-s**) luck, esp. when favourable ▶ *pl* person's destiny
fortunes *n* ▷ **fortune**
forty *adj, n* (*pl* **-ties**) four times ten > **fortieth** *adj, n* (*pl* **-s**)
forum *n* (*pl* **-ums**) meeting or medium for open discussion or debate
forums *n* ▷ **forum**
forward *adj* directed or moving ahead ▶ *n* (*pl* **-s**) attacking player in various team games, such as soccer or hockey ▶ *adv* forwards ▶ *v* (**-s, -ing, -ed**) send (a letter etc.) on to an ultimate destination
forwarded *v* ▷ **forward**
forwarding *v* ▷ **forward**
forwards *adv* towards or at a place further ahead in space or time ▶ *n, v* ▷ **forward**
fossick *v* (**-s, -ing, -ed**) (AUST & NZ) search, esp. for gold or precious stones
fossicked *v* ▷ **fossick**
fossicking *v* ▷ **fossick**
fossicks *v* ▷ **fossick**
fossil *n* (*pl* **-s**) hardened remains of a prehistoric animal or plant preserved in rock
fossilize *v* (**-zes, -zing, -zed**) turn into a fossil
fossilized *v* ▷ **fossilize**
fossilizes *v* ▷ **fossilize**
fossilizing *v* ▷ **fossilize**
fossils *n* ▷ **fossil**
foster *v* (**-s, -ing, -ed**) promote the growth or development of ▶ *adj* of or involved in fostering a child
fostered *v* ▷ **foster**
fostering *v* ▷ **foster**
fosters *v* ▷ **foster**
fought *v* ▷ **fight**
foul *adj* (**-er, -est**) loathsome or offensive ▶ *n* (*pl* **-s**) (SPORT) violation of the rules ▶ *v* (**-s, -ing, -ed**) make dirty or polluted
fouled *v* ▷ **foul**
fouler *adj* ▷ **foul**
foulest *adj* ▷ **foul**
fouling *v* ▷ **foul**
foulmouthed *adj* habitually using foul language
fouls *n, v* ▷ **foul**
found[1] *v* ▷ **find**
found[2] *v* (**-s, -ing, -ed**) establish or bring into being (*foll. by* **on** *or* **upon**) > **founder** *n* (*pl* **-s**)
found[3] *v* (**-s, -ing, -ed**) cast (metal or glass) by melting and setting in a mould
foundation *n* (*pl* **-s**) basis or base
foundations *n* ▷ **foundation**
founded *v* ▷ **found**[2,3]
founder[1] *n* ▷ **found**[2]
founder[2] *v* (**-s, -ing, -ed**) break down or fail
foundered *v* ▷ **founder**
foundering *v* ▷ **founder**
founders[1] *n* ▷ **found**[2]
founders[2] *v* ▷ **founder**
founding *v* ▷ **found**[2,3]
foundling *n* (*pl* **-s**) (CHIEFLY BRIT) abandoned baby
foundlings *n* ▷ **foundling**
foundries *n* ▷ **foundry**
foundry *n* (*pl* **-dries**) place where metal is melted and cast
founds *v* ▷ **found**[2,3]
fount[1] *n* (*pl* **-s**) (*Lit*) fountain
fount[2] (*pl* **-s**) *n* set of printing type of one style and size
fountain *n* (*pl* **-s**) jet of water
fountainhead *n* (*pl* **-s**) original source
fountainheads *n* ▷ **fountainhead**
fountains *n* ▷ **fountain**
founts *n* ▷ **fount**[1,2]
four *adj, n* (*pl* **-s**) one more than three
fours *n* ▷ **four**
foursome *n* group of four people
foursomes *n* (*pl* **-s**) ▷ **foursome**
fourteen *adj, n* (*pl* **-s**) four and ten > **fourteenth** *adj, n* (*pl* **-s**)
fourteens *n* ▷ **fourteen**
fourteenth *adj, n* ▷ **fourteen**
fourteenths *n* ▷ **fourteen**
fourth *adj, n* (*pl* **-s**) (of) number four in a series ▶ *n* quarter
fourths *n* ▷ **fourth**
fowl *n* (*pl* **-s**) domestic cock or hen
fowls *n* ▷ **fowl**
fox *n* (*pl* **-es**) reddish-brown bushy-tailed animal of the dog family ▶ *v* (**-s, -ing, -ed**) (*Informal*) perplex or deceive
foxed *v* ▷ **fox**
foxes *n, v* ▷ **fox**
foxglove *n* (*pl* **-s**) tall plant with purple or white flowers
foxgloves *n* ▷ **foxglove**
foxhole *n* (*pl* **-s**) (MIL) small pit dug for protection
foxholes *n* ▷ **foxhole**
foxhound *n* (*pl* **-s**) dog bred for hunting foxes
foxhounds *n* ▷ **foxhound**
foxier *adj* ▷ **foxy**
foxiest *adj* ▷ **foxy**
foxing *v* ▷ **fox**
foxtrot *n* (*pl* **-s**) ballroom dance with slow and quick steps
foxtrots *n* ▷ **foxtrot**
foxy *adj* (**-xier, -xiest**) of or like a fox, esp. in

craftiness

> **foy** *n* (**foys**). Foy is an old dialect word meaning a farewell meal or gift. This unusual word can be useful when there is little space to form longer words. Foy scores 9 points.

foyer [**foy**-ay] *n* (*pl* **-s**) entrance hall in a theatre, cinema, or hotel
foyers *n* ▷ **foyer**
fracas [**frak**-ah] *n* (*pl* **-es**) noisy quarrel
fracases *n* ▷ **fracas**
fraction *n* (*pl* **-s**) numerical quantity that is not a whole number > **fractional** *adj* > **fractionally** *adv*
fractional *adj* ▷ **fraction**
fractionally *adv* ▷ **fraction**
fractions *n* ▷ **fraction**
fractious *adj* easily upset and angered
fracture *n* (*pl* **-s**) breaking, esp. of a bone ▶ *v* (**-res, -ring, -red**) break
fractured *v* ▷ **fracture**
fractures *n, v* ▷ **fracture**
fracturing *v* ▷ **fracture**
fragile *adj* easily broken or damaged > **fragility** *n* (*pl* **-lities**)
fragilities *n* ▷ **fragile**
fragility *n* ▷ **fragile**
fragment *n* (*pl* **-s**) piece broken off ▶ *v* (**-s, -ing, -ed**) break into pieces > **fragmentary** *adj* > **fragmentation** *n* (*pl* **-s**)
fragmentary *adj* ▷ **fragment**
fragmentation *n* ▷ **fragment**
fragmentations *n* ▷ **fragment**
fragmented *v* ▷ **fragment**
fragmenting *v* ▷ **fragment**
fragments *n, v* ▷ **fragment**
fragrance *n* (*pl* **-s**) pleasant smell
fragrances *n* ▷ **fragrance**
fragrant *adj* sweet-smelling
frail *adj* (**-er, -est**) physically weak
frailer *adj* ▷ **frail**
frailest *adj* ▷ **frail**
frailities *n* ▷ **frailty**
frailty *n* (*pl* **-ties**) physical or moral weakness
frame *n* (*pl* **-s**) structure giving shape or support ▶ *v* (**-mes, -ming, -med**) put together, construct
framed *v* ▷ **frame**
frames *n, v* ▷ **frame**
framework *n* (*pl* **-s**) supporting structure
frameworks *n* ▷ **framework**
framing *v* ▷ **frame**
franc *n* (*pl* **-s**) monetary unit of Switzerland, various African countries, and formerly of France and Belgium
franchise *n* (*pl* **-s**) right to vote
franchises *n* ▷ **franchise**
francium *n* (*pl* **-s**) (CHEM) radioactive metallic element
franciums *n* ▷ **francium**
francs *n* ▷ **franc**
frangipani [fran-jee-**pah**-nee] *n* (*pl* **-nis**) Australian evergreen tree with large yellow fragrant flowers
frangipanis *n* ▷ **frangipani**
frank *adj* (**-er, -est**) honest and straightforward in speech or attitude ▶ *n* (*pl* **-s**) official mark on a letter permitting delivery ▶ *v* (**-s, -ing, -ed**) put such a mark on (a letter) > **frankly** *adv* > **frankness** *n* (*pl* **-es**)
franked *v* ▷ **frank**
franker *adj* ▷ **frank**
frankest *adj* ▷ **frank**
frankfurter *n* (*pl* **-s**) smoked sausage
frankfurters *n* ▷ **frankfurter**
frankincense *n* (*pl* **-es**) aromatic gum resin burned as incense
frankincenses *n* ▷ **frankincense**
franking *v* ▷ **frank**
frankly *adv* ▷ **frank**
frankness *n* ▷ **frank**
franknesses *n* ▷ **frank**
franks *n, v* ▷ **frank**
frantic *adj* distracted with rage, grief, joy, etc. > **frantically** *adv*
frantically *adv* ▷ **frantic**
fraternal *adj* of a brother, brotherly > **fraternally** *adv*
fraternity *n* (*pl* **-ties**) group of people with shared interests, aims, etc. (US)
fraternize *v* associate on friendly terms > **fraternization** *n*
fratricide *n* (*pl* **-s**) crime of killing one's brother
fratricides *n* ▷ **fratricide**
frau [rhymes with **how**] *n* (*pl* **fraus, frauen**) married German woman
fraud *n* (*pl* **-s**) (criminal) deception, swindle > **fraudulent** *adj* > **fraudulence** *n* (*pl* **-s**)
frauds *n* ▷ **fraud**
fraudulence *n* ▷ **fraud**
fraudulences *n* ▷ **fraud**
fraudulent *adj* ▷ **fraud**
frauen *n* ▷ **frau**
fraught [**frawt**] *adj* (**-er, -est**) tense or anxious
fraughter *adj* ▷ **fraught**
fraughtest *adj* ▷ **fraught**
fräulein [**froy**-line] *n* (*pl* **-leins, -lein**) unmarried German woman
fräuleins *n* ▷ **fräulein**
fraus *n* ▷ **frau**

fray[1] *n* (*pl* **-s**) (BRIT, AUST & NZ) noisy quarrel or conflict
fray[2] *v* (**-s, -ing, -ed**) make or become ragged at the edge
frayed *v* ▷ **fray**[2]
fraying *v* ▷ **fray**[2]
frays *n, v* ▷ **fray**[1, 2]
frazzle *n* (*pl* **-s**) (*Informal*) exhausted state
frazzles *n* ▷ **frazzle**
freak *n* (*pl* **-s**) abnormal person or thing ▶ *adj* abnormal > **freakish** *adj*
freakish *adj* ▷ **freak**
freaks *n* ▷ **freak**
freckle *n* (*pl* **-s**) small brown spot on the skin
freckled *adj* marked with freckles
freckles *n* ▷ **freckle**
free *adj* (**freer, freest**) able to act at will, not compelled or restrained ▶ *v* (**frees, freeing, freed**) release, liberate > **freely** *adv*
freed *v* ▷ **free**
freedom *n* (*pl* **-s**) being free
freedoms *n* ▷ **freedom**
freehand *adj* drawn without guiding instruments
freehold *n* (*pl* **-s**) tenure of land for life without restrictions > **freeholder** *n* (*pl* **-s**)
freeholder *n* ▷ **freehold**
freeholders *n* ▷ **freehold**
freeholds *n* ▷ **freehold**
freeing *v* ▷ **free**
freelance *adj, n* (*pl* **-s**) (of) a self-employed person doing specific pieces of work for various employers
freelances *n* ▷ **freelance**
freeloader *n* (*pl* **-s**) (*Slang*) habitual scrounger
freeloaders *n* ▷ **freeloader**
freely *adv* ▷ **free**
freemason *n* (*pl* **-s**) member of a secret fraternity pledged to help each other
freemasons *n* ▷ **freemason**
freer *adj* ▷ **free**
frees *v* ▷ **free**
freesia *n* (*pl* **-s**) plant with fragrant tubular flowers
freesias *n* ▷ **freesia**
freest *adj* ▷ **free**
freeway *n* (*pl* **-s**) (US & AUST) motorway
freeways *n* ▷ **freeway**
freewheel *v* (**-s, -ing, -ed**) travel downhill on a bicycle without pedalling
freewheeled *v* ▷ **freewheel**
freewheeling *v* ▷ **freewheel**
freewheels *v* ▷ **freewheel**
freeze *v* (**-zes, -zing, froze, frozen**) change from a liquid to a solid by the reduction of temperature, as water to ice ▶ *n* period of very cold weather
freezer *n* (*pl* **-s**) insulated cabinet for cold-storage of perishable foods
freezers *n* ▷ **freezer**
freezes *v* ▷ **freeze**
freezing *adj* (*Informal*) very cold ▶ *v* ▷ **freeze**
freight [**frate**] *n* (*pl* **-s**) commercial transport of goods ▶ *v* (**-s, -ing, -ed**) send by freight
freighted *v* ▷ **freight**
freighter *n* (*pl* **-s**) ship or aircraft for transporting goods
freighters *n* ▷ **freighter**
freighting *v* ▷ **freight**
freights *n, v* ▷ **freight**
frenetic [frin-**net**-ik] *adj* uncontrolled, excited > **frenetically** *adv*
frenetically *adv* ▷ **frenetic**
frenzied *adj* ▷ **frenzy**
frenziedly *adv* ▷ **frenzy**
frenzies *n* ▷ **frenzy**
frenzy *n* (*pl* **-zies**) violent mental derangement > **frenzied** *adj* > **frenziedly** *adv*
frequencies *n* ▷ **frequency**
frequency *n* (*pl* **-cies**) rate of occurrence
frequent *adj* happening often ▶ *v* (**-s, -ing, -ed**) visit habitually > **frequently** *adv*
frequented *v* ▷ **frequent**
frequenting *v* ▷ **frequent**
frequently *adv* ▷ **frequent**
frequents *v* ▷ **frequent**
fresco *n* (*pl* **-coes, -cos**) watercolour painting done on wet plaster on a wall
frescoes *n* ▷ **fresco**
frescos *n* ▷ **fresco**
fresh *adj* (**-er, -est**) newly made, acquired, etc. > **freshly** *adv* > **freshness** *n* (*pl* **-es**)
freshen *v* (**-s, -ing, -ed**) make or become fresh or fresher
freshened *v* ▷ **freshen**
freshening *v* ▷ **freshen**
freshens *v* ▷ **freshen**
fresher *n* (*pl* **-s**) first-year student ▶ *adj* ▷ **fresh**
freshers *n* ▷ **fresher**
freshest *adj* ▷ **fresh**
freshly *adv* ▷ **fresh**
freshman *n* (*pl* **-men**) (BRIT & US) first-year student
freshmen *n* ▷ **freshman**
freshness *n* ▷ **fresh**
freshnesses *n* ▷ **fresh**
fret[1] *v* (**-s, -tting, -tted**) be worried
fret[2] *n* (*pl* **-s**) small bar on the fingerboard of a guitar etc.
fretful *adj* irritable

frets *n* ▷ **fret**[1, 2]
fretsaw *n* (*pl* **-s**) fine saw with a narrow blade, used for fretwork
fretsaws *n* ▷ **fretsaw**
fretted *v* ▷ **fret**[1]
fretting *v* ▷ **fret**[1]
fretwork *n* (*pl* **-s**) decorative carving in wood
fretworks *n* ▷ **fretwork**
friable *adj* easily crumbled
friar *n* (*pl* **-s**) member of a male Roman Catholic religious order
friaries *n* ▷ **friary**
friars *n* ▷ **friar**
friary *n* (*pl* **-ries**) house of friars
fricassee *n* (*pl* **-s**) stewed meat served in a thick white sauce
fricassees *n* ▷ **fricassee**
friction *n* (*pl* **-s**) resistance met with by a body moving over another > **frictional** *adj*
frictional *adj* ▷ **friction**
frictions *n* ▷ **friction**
fridge *n* (*pl* **-s**) apparatus in which food and drinks are kept cool
fridges *n* ▷ **fridge**
fried *v* ▷ **fry**[1]
friend *n* (*pl* **-s**) person whom one knows well and likes > **friendless** *adj* > **friendship** *n* (*pl* **-s**)
friendless *adj* ▷ **friend**
friendlier *adj* ▷ **friendly**
friendlies *n* ▷ **friendly**
friendliest *adj* ▷ **friendly**
friendliness *n* ▷ **friendly**
friendlinesses *n* ▷ **friendly**
friendly *adj* (**-lier, -liest**) showing or expressing liking ▶ *n* (*pl* **-lies**) (SPORT) match played for its own sake and not as part of a competition > **friendliness** *n* (*pl* **-es**)
friends *n* ▷ **friend**
friendship *n* ▷ **friend**
friendships *n* ▷ **friend**
fries *v, n* ▷ **fry**[1]
Friesian [**free**-zhan] *n* (*pl* **-s**) breed of black-and-white dairy cattle
Friesians *n* ▷ **Friesian**
frieze [**freeze**] *n* (*pl* **-s**) ornamental band on a wall
friezes *n* ▷ **frieze**
frigate [**frig**-it] *n* (*pl* **-s**) medium-sized fast warship
frigates *n* ▷ **frigate**
fright *n* (*pl* **-s**) sudden fear or alarm
frighten *v* (**-s, -ing, -ed**) scare or terrify > **frightening** *adj*
frightened *v* ▷ **frighten**
frightened *v* ▷ **frighten**
frightening *v, adj* ▷ **frighten**
frightful *adj* horrifying (*Informal*) > **frightfully** *adv*
frightfully *adv* ▷ **frightful**
frights *n* ▷ **fright**
frigid [**frij**-id] *adj* (of a woman) sexually unresponsive > **frigidity** *n* (*pl* **-ties**)
frigidities *n* ▷ **frigid**
frigidity *n* ▷ **frigid**
frill *n* (*pl* **-s**) gathered strip of fabric attached at one edge ▶ *pl* superfluous decorations or details > **frilled** *adj* > **frilly** *adj* (**-ier, -iest**)
frilled *adj* ▷ **frill**
frillier *adj* ▷ **frill**
frilliest *adj* ▷ **frill**
frills *n* ▷ **frill**
frilly *adj* ▷ **frill**
fringe *n* (*pl* **-es**) hair cut short and hanging over the forehead ▶ *v* (**-ges, -ging, -ged**) decorate with a fringe ▶ *adj* (of theatre) unofficial or unconventional > **fringed** *adj*
fringed *v, adj* ▷ **fringe**
fringes *n, v* ▷ **fringe**
fringing *v* ▷ **fringe**
fripperies *n* ▷ **frippery**
frippery *n* (*pl* **-ries**) useless ornamentation
frisk *v* (**-s, -ing, -ed**) move or leap playfully
frisked *v* ▷ **frisk**
friskier *adj* ▷ **frisky**
friskiest *adj* ▷ **frisky**
frisking *v* ▷ **frisk**
frisks *v* ▷ **frisk**
frisky *adj* (**-kier, -kiest**) lively or high-spirited
frisson [**frees**-sonn] *n* (*pl* **-s**) shiver of fear or excitement
frissons *n* ▷ **frisson**
fritter *n* (*pl* **-s**) piece of food fried in batter
fritters *n* ▷ **fritter**
frivolities *n* ▷ **frivolous**
frivolity *n* ▷ **frivolous**
frivolous *adj* not serious or sensible > **frivolity** *n* (*pl* **-ties**)
frizz *v* (**-es, -ing, -ed**) form (hair) into stiff wiry curls > **frizzy** *adj* (**-zzier, -zziest**)
frizzed *v* ▷ **frizz**
frizzes *v* ▷ **frizz**
frizzier *adj* ▷ **frizz**
frizziest *adj* ▷ **frizz**
frizzing *v* ▷ **frizz**
frizzle *v* (**-les, -ling, -led**) cook or heat until crisp and shrivelled
frizzled *v* ▷ **frizzle**
frizzles *v* ▷ **frizzle**
frizzling *v* ▷ **frizzle**
frizzy *adj* ▷ **frizz**

frock *n* (*pl* **-s**) dress
frocks *n* ▷ **frock**
frog *n* (*pl* **-s**) smooth-skinned tailless amphibian with long back legs used for jumping
frogman *n* (*pl* **-men**) swimmer with a rubber suit and breathing equipment for working underwater
frogmen *n* ▷ **frogman**
frogs *n* ▷ **frog**
frogspawn *n* (*pl* **-s**) jelly-like substance containing frog's eggs
frogspawns *n* ▷ **frogspawn**
frolic *v* (**-lics, -licking, -licked**) run and play in a lively way ▶ *n* (*pl* **-s**) lively and merry behaviour
frolicked *v* ▷ **frolic**
frolicking *v* ▷ **frolic**
frolics *v, n* ▷ **frolic**
frolicsome *adj* playful
from *prep* indicating the point of departure, source, distance, cause, change of state, etc.
frond *n* (*pl* **-s**) long leaf or leaflike part of a fern, palm, or seaweed
fronds *n* ▷ **frond**
front *n* (*pl* **-s**) fore part ▶ *adj* of or at the front ▶ *v* (**-s, -ing, -ed**) face (onto) > **frontal** *adj*
frontage *n* (*pl* **-s**) facade of a building
frontages *n* ▷ **frontage**
frontal *adj* ▷ **front**
fronted *v* ▷ **front**
frontier *n* (*pl* **-s**) area of a country bordering on another
frontiers *n* ▷ **frontier**
fronting *v* ▷ **front**
frontispiece *n* (*pl* **-s**) illustration facing the title page of a book
frontispieces *n* ▷ **frontispiece**
frontrunner (*pl* **-s**) *n* (*Informal*) person regarded as most likely to win a race, election, etc.
frontrunners *n* ▷ **frontrunner**
fronts *n, v* ▷ **front**
frost *n* (*pl* **-s**) white frozen dew or mist ▶ *v* (**-s, -ing, -ed**) become covered with frost
frostbite *n* destruction of tissue, esp. of the fingers or ears, by cold (*pl* **-s**) > **frostbitten** *adj*
frostbites *n* ▷ **frostbite**
frostbitten *adj* ▷ **frostbite**
frosted *v* ▷ **frost** ▶ *adj* (of glass) having a rough surface to make it opaque
frostier *adj* ▷ **frosty**
frostiest *adj* ▷ **frosty**
frostily *adv* ▷ **frosty**
frostiness *n* ▷ **frosty**
frostinesses *n* ▷ **frosty**
frosting *v* ▷ **frost** ▶ *n* (*pl* **-s**) (CHIEFLY US) sugar icing
frostings *n* ▷ **frosting**
frosts *n, v* ▷ **frost**
frosty *adj* (**-tier, -tiest**) characterized or covered by frost > **frostily** *adv* > **frostiness** *n* (*pl* **-es**)
froth *n* (*pl* **-s**) mass of small bubbles ▶ *v* (**-s, -ing, -ed**) foam > **frothy** *adj* (**-thier, -thiest**)
frothed *v* ▷ **froth**
frothier *adj* ▷ **froth**
frothiest *adj* ▷ **froth**
frothing *v* ▷ **froth**
froths *n, v* ▷ **froth**
frothy *adj* ▷ **froth**
frowiest *adj* ▷ **frowzy**
frown *v* (**-s, -ing, -ed**) wrinkle one's brows in worry, anger, or thought ▶ *n* (*pl* **-s**) frowning expression
frowned *v* ▷ **frown**
frowning *v* ▷ **frown**
frowns *v, n* ▷ **frown**
frowsier *adj* ▷ **frowzy**
frowsiest *adj* ▷ **frowzy**
frowstier *adj* ▷ **frowsty**
frowstiest *adj* ▷ **frowsty**
frowsty *adj* (**-ier, -iest**) (BRIT) stale or musty
frowzier *adj* ▷ **frowzy**
frowzy, frowsy *adj* (**-zier, -ziest**) dirty or unkempt
froze *v* ▷ **freeze**
frozen *v* ▷ **freeze**
frugal *adj* thrifty, sparing > **frugally** *adv* > **frugality** *n* (*pl* **-ties**)
frugalities *n* ▷ **frugal**
frugality *n* ▷ **frugal**
frugally *adv* ▷ **frugal**
fruit *n* (*pl* **-s**) part of a plant containing seeds, esp. if edible ▶ *v* (**-s, -ing, -ed**) bear fruit
fruited *v* ▷ **fruit**
fruiterer *n* (*pl* **-s**) person who sells fruit
fruiterers *n* ▷ **fruiterer**
fruitful *adj* useful or productive > **fruitfully** *adv*
fruitfully *adv* ▷ **fruitful**
fruitier *adj* ▷ **fruity**
fruitiest *adj* ▷ **fruity**
fruiting *v* ▷ **fruit**
fruition [froo-**ish**-on] *n* (*pl* **-s**) fulfilment of something worked for or desired
fruitions *n* ▷ **fruition**
fruitless *adj* useless or unproductive > **fruitlessly** *adv*
fruitlessly *adv* ▷ **fruitless**
fruits *n, v* ▷ **fruit**
fruity *adj* (**-tier, -tiest**) of or like fruit

frump *n* (*pl* **-s**) dowdy woman > **frumpy** *adj* (**-pier, -piest**)
frumpier *adj* ▷ **frump**
frumpiest *adj* ▷ **frump**
frumps *n* ▷ **frump**
frumpy *adj* ▷ **frump**
frustrate *v* (**-tes, -ting, -ted**) upset or anger > **frustrated** *adj* > **frustrating** *adj* > **frustration** *n* (*pl* **-s**)
frustrated *v, adj* ▷ **frustrate**
frustrates *v* ▷ **frustrate**
frustrating *v, adj* ▷ **frustrate**
frustration *n* ▷ **frustrate**
frustrations *n* ▷ **frustrate**
fry[1] *v* (**-ries, -rying, -ried**) cook or be cooked in fat or oil ▶ *n* (*pl* **fries**) potato chip
fry[2] *pl n* young fishes
frying *v* ▷ **fry**
fuchsia [**fyew**-sha] *n* (*pl* **-s**) ornamental shrub with hanging flowers
fuchsias *n* ▷ **fuchsia**
fuddle *v* (**-les, -ling, -led**) cause to be intoxicated or confused > **fuddled** *adj*
fuddled *v, adj* ▷ **fuddle**
fuddles *v* ▷ **fuddle**
fuddling *v* ▷ **fuddle**
fudge[1] *n* (*pl* **-s**) soft caramel-like sweet
fudge[2] *v* (**-ges, -ging, -ged**) avoid making a firm statement or decision
fudged *v* ▷ **fudge**[2]
fudges *n, v* ▷ **fudge**[1, 2]
fudging *v* ▷ **fudge**[2]
fuel *n* (*pl* **-s**) substance burned or treated to produce heat or power ▶ *v* (**-s, -lling, -lled**) provide with fuel
fuelled *v* ▷ **fuel**
fuelling *v* ▷ **fuel**
fuels *n, v* ▷ **fuel**
fug *n* (*pl* **-s**) hot stale atmosphere > **fuggy** *adj* (**-ggier, -ggiest**)
fuggier *adj* ▷ **fug**
fuggiest *adj* ▷ **fug**
fuggy *adj* ▷ **fug**
fugitive [**fyew**-jit-iv] *n* (*pl* **-s**) person who flees, esp. from arrest or pursuit ▶ *adj* fleeing
fugitives *n* ▷ **fugitive**
fugs *n* ▷ **fug**
fugue [**fyewg**] *n* (*pl* **-s**) musical composition in which a theme is repeated in different parts
fugues *n* ▷ **fugue**
fulcra *n* ▷ **fulcrum**
fulcrum *n* (*pl* **-crums, -cra**) pivot about which a lever turns
fulcrums *n* ▷ **fulcrum**
fulfil *v* (**-s, -lling, -lled**) bring about the achievement of (a desire or promise) > **fulfilment** *n* (*pl* **-s**)
fulfilled *n* ▷ **fulfil**
fulfilling *v* ▷ **fulfil**
fulfilment *n* ▷ **fulfil**
fulfilments *n* ▷ **fulfil**
fulfils *v* ▷ **fulfil**
full *adj* (**-er, -est**) containing as much or as many as possible ▶ *adv* completely > **fully** *adv* > **fullness** *n* (*pl* **-es**)
fuller *adj* ▷ **full**
fullest *adj* ▷ **full**
fullness *n* ▷ **full**
fullnesses *n* ▷ **full**
fully *adv* ▷ **full**
fulmar *n* (*pl* **-s**) Arctic sea bird
fulmars *n* ▷ **fulmar**
fulminate *v* (**-tes, -ting, -ted**) (*foll. by* **against**) criticize or denounce angrily
fulminated *v* ▷ **fulminate**
fulminates *v* ▷ **fulminate**
fulminating *v* ▷ **fulminate**
fulsome *adj* distastefully excessive or insincere
fumble *v* (**-les, -ling, -led**) handle awkwardly ▶ *n* (*pl* **-s**) act of fumbling
fumbled *v* ▷ **fumble**
fumbles *n, v* ▷ **fumble**
fumbling *v* ▷ **fumble**
fume *v* (**-s, -ing, -ed**) be very angry ▶ *pl n* pungent smoke or vapour
fumed *v* ▷ **fume**
fumes *v, n* ▷ **fume**
fumigate [**fyew**-mig-gate] *v* (**-tes, -ting, -ted**) disinfect with fumes > **fumigation** *n* (*pl* **-s**)
fumigated *v* ▷ **fumigate**
fumigates *v* ▷ **fumigate**
fumigating *v* ▷ **fumigate**
fumigation *n* ▷ **fumigate**
fumigations *n* ▷ **fuminate**
fuming *v* ▷ **fume**
fun *n* (*pl* **-s**) enjoyment or amusement
function *n* (*pl* **-s**) purpose something exists for ▶ *v* (**-s, -ing, -ed**) operate or work (*foll. by* **as**)
functional *adj* of or as a function > **functionally** *adv*
functionally *adv* ▷ **functional**
functionaries *n* ▷ **functionary**
functionary *n* (*pl* **-ries**) official
functioned *v* ▷ **function**
functioning *v* ▷ **function**
functions *n, v* ▷ **function**
fund *n* (*pl* **-s**) stock of money for a special purpose ▶ *pl* money resources ▶ *v* (**-s, -ing, -ed**) provide money to > **funding** *n* (*pl* **-s**)

fundamental *adj* essential or primary ▶ *n* (*pl* **-s**) basic rule or fact > **fundamentally** *adv*
fundamentalism *n* (*pl* **-s**) literal or strict interpretation of a religion > **fundamentalist** *adj*, *n* (*pl* **-s**)
fundamentalisms *n* ▷ **fundamentalism**
fundamentalist *adj*, *n* ▷ **fundamentalism**
fundamentalists *n* ▷ **fundamentalism**
fundamentally *adv* ▷ **fundamental**
fundamentals *n* ▷ **fundamental**
funded *v* ▷ **fund**
fundi *n* (*pl* **-dis**) (S AFR) expert or boffin
funding *v*, *n* ▷ **fund**
fundings *n* ▷ **fund**
fundis *n* ▷ **fundi**
funds *n*, *v* ▷ **fund**
funeral *n* (*pl* **-s**) ceremony of burying or cremating a dead person
funerals *n* ▷ **funeral**
funerary *adj* of or for a funeral
funereal [fyew-**neer**-ee-al] *adj* gloomy or sombre
funfair *n* (*pl* **-s**) entertainment with machines to ride on and stalls
funfairs *n* ▷ **funfair**
fungal *adj* ▷ **fungus**
fungi *n* ▷ **fungus**
fungicide *n* (*pl* **-s**) substance that destroys fungi
fungicides *n* ▷ **fungicides**
fungous *adj* ▷ **fungus**
fungus *n* (*pl* **-gi, -guses**) plant without leaves, flowers, or roots, such as a mushroom or mould > **fungal, fungous** *adj*
funguses *n* ▷ **fungus**
funicular *n* (*pl* **-s**) cable railway on a mountainside or cliff
funiculars *n* ▷ **funicular**
funk[1] *n* (*pl* **-s**) style of dance music with a strong beat
funk[2] (*Informal*) *n* nervous or fearful state ▶ *v* (**-s, -ing, -ed**) avoid (doing something) through fear
funked *v* ▷ **funk**
funkier *adj* ▷ **funky**
funkiest *adj* ▷ **funky**
funking *v* ▷ **funk**
funks *n*, *v* ▷ **funk**[1, 2]
funky *adj* (**-kier, -kiest**) (of music) having a strong beat
funnel *n* (*pl* **-s**) cone-shaped tube for pouring liquids into a narrow opening ▶ *v* (**-s, -lling, -lled**) (cause to) move through or as if through a funnel
funnelled *v* ▷ **funnel**
funnelling *v* ▷ **funnel**
funnels *n*, *v* ▷ **funnel**
funnier *adj* ▷ **funny**
funniest *adj* ▷ **funny**
funnily *adv* ▷ **funny**
funny *adj* (**-nnier, -nniest**) comical, humorous > **funnily** *adv*
funs *n* ▷ **fun**
fur *n* (*pl* **-s**) soft hair of a mammal ▶ *v* (**-s, -rring, -rred**) cover or become covered with fur > **furry** (**-rrier, -rriest**) ▶ *adj*
furbish *v* (**-es, -ing, -ed**) smarten up
furbished *v* ▷ **furbish**
furbishes *v* ▷ **furbish**
furbishing *v* ▷ **furbish**
furies *n* ▷ **fury**
furious *adj* very angry > **furiously** *adv*
furiously *adv* ▷ **furious**
furl *v* (**-s, -ing, -ed**) roll up and fasten (a sail, umbrella, or flag)
furled *v* ▷ **furl**
furling *v* ▷ **furl**
furlong *n* (*pl* **-s**) unit of length equal to 220 yards (201.168 metres)
furlongs *n* ▷ **furlongs**
furlough [**fur**-loh] *n* (*pl* **-s**) leave of absence
furloughs *n* ▷ **furlough**
furls *v* ▷ **furl**
furnace *n* (*pl* **-s**) enclosed chamber containing a very hot fire
furnaces *n* ▷ **furnace**
furnish *v* (**-es, -ing, -ed**) provide (a house or room) with furniture
furnished *v* ▷ **furnish**
furnishes *v* ▷ **furnish**
furnishing *v* ▷ **furnish**
furnishings *pl n* furniture, carpets, and fittings
furniture *n* (*pl* **-s**) large movable articles such as chairs and wardrobes
furnitures *n* ▷ **furniture**
furore [fyew-**ror**-ee] *n* (*pl* **-s**) very excited or angry reaction
furores *n* ▷ **furore**
furred *v* ▷ **fur**
furrier *n* (*pl* **-s**) dealer in furs ▶ *adj* ▷ **fur**
furriers *n* ▷ **furrier**
furriest *adj* ▷ **fur**
furring *v* ▷ **fur**
furrow *n* (*pl* **-s**) trench made by a plough ▶ *v* (**-s, -ing, -ed**) make or become wrinkled
furrowed *v* ▷ **furrow**
furrowing *v* ▷ **furrow**
furrows *n*, *v* ▷ **furrow**
furry *adj* ▷ **fur**

furrying *v* ▷ **flurry**
furs *n, v* ▷ **fur**
further *adv* in addition ▶ *adj* additional ▶ *v* (**-s, -ing, -ed**) assist the progress of > **furtherance** *n* (*pl* **-s**)
furtherance *n* ▷ **further**
furtherances *n* ▷ **further**
furthered *v* ▷ **further**
furthering *v* ▷ **further**
furthermore *adv* besides
furthermost *adj* most distant
furthers *v* ▷ **further**
furthest *adv* to the greatest distance or extent ▶ *adj* most distant
furtive *adj* sly and secretive > **furtively** *adv*
furtively *adv* ▷ **furtive**
fury *n* (*pl* **-ries**) wild anger
furze *n* (*pl* **-s**) gorse
furzes *n* ▷ **furze**
fuse[1] *n* (*pl* **-s**) cord containing an explosive for detonating a bomb
fuse[2] *n* (*pl* **-s**) safety device for electric circuits, containing a wire that melts and breaks the connection when the circuit is overloaded ▶ *v* (**-ses, -sing, -sed**) (cause to) fail as a result of a blown fuse
fused *v* ▷ **fuse**
fuselage [**fyew**-zill-lahzh] *n* (*pl* **-s**) body of an aircraft
fuselages *n* ▷ **fuselage**
fuses *v, n* ▷ **fuse**
fusilier [fyew-zill-**leer**] *n* (*pl* **-s**) soldier of certain regiments
fusiliers *n* ▷ **fusilier**
fusillade [fyew-zill-**lade**] *n* (*pl* **-s**) continuous discharge of firearms
fusillades *n* ▷ **fusillade**
fusing *v* ▷ **fuse**
fusion *n* (*pl* **-s**) melting ▶ *adj* of a style of cooking that combines traditional Western techniques and ingredients with those used in Eastern cuisine
fusions *n* ▷ **fusion**
fuss *n* (*pl* **-es**) needless activity or worry ▶ *v* (**-es, -ing, -ed**) make a fuss
fussed *v* ▷ **fuss**
fusses *n, v* ▷ **fuss**
fussier *adj* ▷ **fussy**
fussiest *adj* ▷ **fussy**
fussily *adv* ▷ **fussy**
fussiness *n* ▷ **fussy**
fussinesses *n* ▷ **fussy**
fussing *v* ▷ **fuss**
fussy *adj* (**-ssier, -ssiest**) inclined to fuss > **fussily** *adv* > **fussiness** *n* (*pl* **-es**)
fustier *adj* ▷ **fusty**
fustiest *adj* ▷ **fusty**
fustiness *n* ▷ **fusty**
fustinesses *n* ▷ **fusty**
fusty *adj* (**-tier, -tiest**) stale-smelling > **fustiness** *n* (*pl* **-es**)
futile *adj* unsuccessful or useless > **futility** *n* (*pl* **-ties**)
futilities *n* ▷ **futile**
futility *n* ▷ **futile**
futon [**foo**-tonn] *n* (*pl* **-s**) Japanese-style bed
futons *n* ▷ **futon**
future *n* (*pl* **-s**) time to come ▶ *adj* yet to come or be
futures *n* ▷ **future**
futuristic *adj* of a design appearing to belong to some future time
fuzz[1] *n* (*pl* **-es**) mass of fine or curly hairs or fibres
fuzz[2] *n* (*Slang*) police
fuzzes *n* ▷ **fuzz**[1]
fuzzier *adj* ▷ **fuzzy**
fuzziest *adj* ▷ **fuzzy**
fuzzily *adv* ▷ **fuzzy**
fuzziness *n* ▷ **fuzzy**
fuzzinesses *n* ▷ **fuzzy**
fuzzy *adj* (**-zzier, -zziest**) of, like, or covered with fuzz > **fuzzily** *adv* > **fuzziness** *n* (*pl* **-es**)

fy *interj*. Fy is an old word that people said when they were disgusted or dismayed. This very unusual word can be really useful when you're trying to form words in more than one direction. Fy scores 8 points.

Gg

Only three two-letter words begin with G (**gi, go** and **gu**). Knowing these will save you worrying about other possibilities. There are quite a few short words beginning with G that use Y, which can prove very useful. These include **gay, gey, goy** and **guy** (7 points each), as well as **gym** and **gyp** (9 points each).

gab *n* (*pl* **-s**) ▶ *v* (**-s, -ing, -ed**) (*Informal*) talk or chatter
gababouts *n* ▷ **gadabout**
gabardine, gaberdine *n* (*pl* **-s**) strong twill cloth used esp. for raincoats
gabardines *n* ▷ **gabardine**
gabbed *v* ▷ **gab**
gabbier *adj* ▷ **gabby**
gabbiest *adj* ▷ **gabby**
gabbing *v* ▷ **gab**
gabble *v* (**-s, -ing, -ed**) speak rapidly and indistinctly ▶ *n* (*pl* **-s**) rapid indistinct speech
gabbled *v* ▷ **gabble**
gabbles *v, n* ▷ **gabble**
gabbling *v* ▷ **gabble**
gabby *adj* (**-bbier, -bbiest**) (*Informal*) talkative
gable *n* (*pl* **-s**) triangular upper part of a wall between sloping roofs > **gabled** *adj*
gabled *adj* ▷ **gable**
gables *n* ▷ **gable**
gabs *n, v* ▷ **gab**
gad *v* (**-s, -dding, -dded**) go around in search of pleasure
gadabout *n* (*pl* **-s**) pleasure-seeker
gadded *v* ▷ **gad**
gadding *v* ▷ **gad**
gadflies *n* ▷ **gadfly**
gadfly *n* (*pl* **-flies**) fly that bites cattle
gadget *n* (*pl* **-s**) small mechanical device or appliance
gadgetries *n* ▷ **gadgetry**
gadgetry *n* (*pl* **-ries**) gadgets
gadgets *n* ▷ **gadget**
gads *v* ▷ **gad**
gaff *n* (*pl* **-s**) stick with an iron hook for landing large fish
gaffe *n* (*pl* **-s**) social blunder
gaffer *n* (*pl* **-s**) (BRIT) (*Informal*) foreman or boss
gaffers *n* ▷ **gaffer**
gaffes *n* ▷ **gaffe**
gaffs *n* ▷ **gaff**
gag[1] *v* (**-s, -gging, -gged**) choke or retch ▶ *n* (*pl* **-s**) cloth etc. put into or tied across the mouth
gag[2] *n* (*pl* **-s**) (*Informal*) joke
gaga [**gah**-gah] *adj* (*Slang*) senile
gagged *v* ▷ **gag**[1]
gagging *v* ▷ **gag**[1]
gaggle *n* (*pl* **-s**) (*Informal*) disorderly crowd
gaggles *n* ▷ **gaggle**
gags *v, n* ▷ **gag**[1, 2]
gaieties *n* ▷ **gaiety**
gaiety *n* (*pl* **-ties**) cheerfulness
gaily *adv* merrily
gain *v* (**-s, -ing, -ed**) acquire or obtain ▶ *n* (*pl* **-s**) profit or advantage
gained *v* ▷ **gain**
gainful *adj* useful or profitable > **gainfully** *adv*
gainfully *adv* ▷ **gainful**
gaining *v* ▷ **gain**
gains *v, n* ▷ **gain**
gainsaid *v* ▷ **gainsay**
gainsay *v* (**-s, -ing, -said**) deny or contradict
gainsaying *v* ▷ **gainsay**
gainsays *v* ▷ **gainsay**
gait *n* (*pl* **-s**) manner of walking
gaiter *n* (*pl* **-s**) cloth or leather covering for the lower leg
gaiters *n* ▷ **gaiter**
gaits *n* ▷ **gait**
gala [**gah**-la] *n* (*pl* **-s**) festival
galactic *adj* ▷ **galaxy**
galas *n* ▷ **gala**
galaxies *n* ▷ **galaxy**
galaxy *n* (*pl* **-xies**) system of stars > **galactic** *adj*
gale *n* (*pl* **-s**) strong wind
gales *n* ▷ **gale**

gall[1] [**gawl**] *n* (*pl* **-s**) (*Informal*) impudence
gall[2] [**gawl**] *v* (**-s, -ing, -ed**) annoy
gall[3] [**gawl**] *n* (*pl* **-s**) abnormal outgrowth on a tree or plant
gallant *adj* (**-er, -est**) brave and noble > **gallantly** *adv*
gallanter *adj* ▷ **gallant**
gallantest *adj* ▷ **gallant**
gallantly *adv* ▷ **gallant**
gallantries *n* ▷ **gallantry**
gallantry *n* (*pl* **-tries**) showy, attentive treatment of women
galled *v* ▷ **gall**[2]
galleon *n* (*pl* **-s**) large three-masted sailing ship of the 15th-17th centuries
galleons *n* ▷ **galleon**
galleries *n* ▷ **gallery**
gallery *n* (*pl* **-ries**) room or building for displaying works of art
galley *n* (*pl* **-s**) kitchen of a ship or aircraft
galleys *n* ▷ **galley**
galling *v* ▷ **gall**[2]
gallium *n* (*pl* **-iums**) (CHEM) soft grey metallic element used in semiconductors
galliums *n* ▷ **gallium**
gallivant *v* (**-s, -ing, -ed**) go about in search of pleasure
gallivanted *v* ▷ **gallivant**
gallivanting *v* ▷ **gallivant**
gallivants *v* ▷ **gallivant**
gallon *n* (*pl* **-s**) liquid measure of eight pints, equal to 4.55 litres
gallons *n* ▷ **gallon**
gallop *n* (*pl* **-s**) horse's fastest pace ▸ *v* (**-s, -ing, -ed**) go or ride at a gallop
galloped *v* ▷ **gallop**
galloping *v* ▷ **gallop**
gallops *n, v* ▷ **gallop**
gallows *n* (*pl* **-ses**) wooden structure used for hanging criminals
gallowses *n* ▷ **gallows**
galls *v, n* ▷ **gall**[1, 2, 3]
gallstone *n* (*pl* **-s**) hard mass formed in the gall bladder or its ducts
gallstones *n* ▷ **gallstone**
galore *adv* in abundance
galoshes *pl n* (BRIT, AUST & NZ) waterproof overshoes
galumph *v* (**-s, -ing, -ed**) (BRIT, AUST & NZ) (*Informal*) leap or move about clumsily
galumphed *v* ▷ **galumph**
galumphing *v* ▷ **galumph**
galumphs *v* ▷ **galumph**
galvanic *adj* of or producing an electric current generated by chemical means
galvanize *v* (**-zes, -zing, -zed**) stimulate into action
galvanized *v* ▷ **galvanize**
galvanizes *v* ▷ **galvanize**
galvanizing *v* ▷ **galvanize**
gambit *n* (*pl* **-s**) opening line or move intended to secure an advantage (CHESS)
gambits *n* ▷ **gambit**
gamble *v* (**-les, -ling, -led**) play games of chance to win money ▸ *n* (*pl* **-s**) risky undertaking > **gambler** *n* (*pl* **-s**) > **gambling** *n* (*pl* **-s**)
gambled *v* ▷ **gamble**
gambler *n* ▷ **gamble**
gamblers *n* ▷ **gamble**
gambles *v, n* ▷ **gamble**
gambling *v, n* ▷ **gamble**
gamblings *n* ▷ **gamble**
gamboge [gam-**boje**] *n* (*pl* **-s**) gum resin used as a yellow pigment and purgative
gamboges *n* ▷ **gamboge**
gambol *v* (**-s, -bolling, -bolled**) jump about playfully, frolic ▸ *n* (*pl* **-s**) frolic
gambolled *v* ▷ **gambol**
gambolling *v* ▷ **gambol**
gambols *v, n* ▷ **gambol**
game[1] *n* (*pl* **-s**) amusement or pastime ▸ *v* (**-mes, -ming, -med**) gamble ▸ *adj* (**-er, -est**) brave > **gamely** *adv*
game[2] *adj* (**-er, -est**) (BRIT, AUST & NZ) lame, crippled
gamed *v* ▷ **game**[1]
gamekeeper *n* (*pl* **-s**) (BRIT, AUST & S AFR) person employed to breed game and prevent poaching
gamekeepers *n* ▷ **gamekeeper**
gamely *adv* ▷ **game**[1]
gamer *n* person who plays computer games ▸ *adj* ▷ **game**[1, 2]
gamers *n* ▷ **gamer**
games *n, v* ▷ **game**[1]
gamesmanship *n* (**-s**) art of winning by cunning practices without actually cheating
gamesmanships *n* ▷ **gamesmanship**
gamest *adj* ▷ **game**[1, 2]
gamete *n* (*pl* **-s**) (BIOL) reproductive cell
gametes *n* ▷ **gamete**
gamine [**gam**-een] *n* (*pl* **-s**) slim boyish young woman
gamines *n* ▷ **gamine**
gaming *n* gambling ▸ *v* ▷ **game**[1]
gamma *n* (*pl* **-s**) third letter of the Greek alphabet
gammas *n* ▷ **gamma**
gammier *adj* ▷ **gammy**

gammiest *adj* ▷ **gammy**
gammon *n* (*pl* **-s**) cured or smoked ham
gammons *n* ▷ **gammon**
gammy *adj* (**-mier, -miest**) ▷ **game²**
gamut *n* (*pl* **-s**) whole range or scale (of music, emotions, etc.)
gamuts *n* ▷ **gamut**
gander *n* (*pl* **-s**) male goose
ganders *n* ▷ **gander**
gang *n* (*pl* **-s**) (criminal) group
gangland *n* (*pl* **-s**) criminal underworld
ganglands *n* ▷ **gangland**
gangling *adj* lanky and awkward
ganglion *n* (*pl* **-s**) group of nerve cells
ganglions *n* ▷ **ganglion**
gangplank *n* (*pl* **-s**) portable bridge for boarding or leaving a ship
gangplanks *n* ▷ **gangplank**
gangrene *n* (*pl* **-s**) decay of body tissue as a result of disease or injury > **gangrenous** *adj*
gangrenes *n* ▷ **gangrene**
gangs *n* ▷ **gang**
gangster *n* (*pl* **-s**) member of a criminal gang
gangsters *n* ▷ **gangster**
gangway *n* (*pl* **-s**) passage between rows of seats
gangways *n* ▷ **gangway**
gannet *n* (*pl* **-s**) large sea bird
gannets *n* ▷ **gannet**
gantries *n* ▷ **gantry**
gantry *n* (*pl* **-ries**) structure supporting something such as a crane or rocket
gaol [**jayl**] *n* (*pl* **-s**) ▷ **jail**
gaols *n* ▷ **gaol**
gap *n* (*pl* **-s**) break or opening > **gappy** *adj* (**-ppier, -ppiest**)
gape *v* (**-pes, -ping, -ped**) stare in wonder > **gaping** *adj*
gaped *v* ▷ **gape**
gapes *v* ▷ **gape**
gaping *v, adj* ▷ **gape**
gappier *adj* ▷ **gap**
gappiest *adj* ▷ **gap**
gappy *adj* ▷ **gap**
gaps *n* ▷ **gap**
garage *n* (*pl* **-s**) building used to house cars ▶ *v* (**-ges, -ging, -ged**) put or keep a car in a garage
garaged *v* ▷ **garage**
garages *n, v* ▷ **garage**
garaging *v* ▷ **garage**
garb *n* (*pl* **-s**) clothes ▶ *v* (**-s, -ing, -ed**) clothe
garbage *n* (*pl* **-s**) rubbish
garbages *n* ▷ **garbage**
garbed *v* ▷ **garb**
garbing *v* ▷ **garb**
garbled *adj* (of a story etc.) jumbled and confused
garbs *n, v* ▷ **garb**
garden *n* (*pl* **-s**) piece of land for growing flowers, fruit, or vegetables ▶ *pl* ornamental park ▶ *v* (**-s, -ing, -ed**) cultivate a garden > **gardener** *n* (*pl* **-s**) > **gardening** *n* (*pl* **-s**)
gardened *v* ▷ **garden**
gardenia [gar-**deen**-ya] *n* (*pl* **-s**) large fragrant white waxy flower
gardenias *n* ▷ **gardenia**
gardening *v* ▷ **garden**
gardens *n, v* ▷ **garden**
garfish *n* (*pl* **-fishes**) freshwater fish with a long body and very long toothed jaws
garfishes *n* ▷ **garfish**
gargantuan *adj* huge
gargle *v* (**-les, -ling, -led**) wash the throat with (a liquid) by breathing out slowly through the liquid ▶ *n* (*pl* **-s**) liquid used for gargling
gargled *v* ▷ **gargle**
gargles *v, n* ▷ **gargle**
gargling *v* ▷ **gargle**
gargoyle *n* (*pl* **-s**) waterspout carved in the form of a grotesque face, esp. on a church
gargoyles *n* ▷ **gargoyle**
garish *adj* crudely bright or colourful > **garishly** *adv* > **garishness** *n* (*pl* **-es**)
garishly *adv* ▷ **garish**
garishness *n* ▷ **garish**
garishnesses *n* ▷ **garish**
garland *n* (*pl* **-s**) wreath of flowers worn or hung as a decoration ▶ *v* (**-s, -ing, -ed**) decorate with garlands
garlanded *v* ▷ **garland**
garlanding *v* ▷ **garland**
garlands *n, v* ▷ **garland**
garlic *n* (*pl* **-s**) pungent bulb of a plant of the onion family, used in cooking
garlics *n* ▷ **garlic**
garment *n* (*pl* **-s**) article of clothing ▶ *pl* clothes
garments *n* ▷ **garment**
garner *v* (**-s, -ing, -ed**) collect or store
garnered *v* ▷ **garner**
garnering *v* ▷ **garner**
garners *v* ▷ **garner**
garnet *n* (*pl* **-s**) red semiprecious stone
garnets *n* ▷ **garnet**
garnish *v* (**-es, -ing, -ed**) decorate (food) ▶ *n* (*pl* **-es**) decoration for food
garnished *v* ▷ **garnish**
garnishes *v, n* ▷ **garnish**
garnishing *v* ▷ **garnish**
garotte *n* ▷ **garrotte**
garotted *v* ▷ **garrotte**

garottes *n, v* ▷ **garrotte**
garotting *v* ▷ **garrotte**
garret *n* (*pl* **-s**) attic in a house
garrets *n* ▷ **garret**
garrison *n* (*pl* **-s**) troops stationed in a town or fort ▶ *v* (**-s, -ing, -ed**) station troops in
garrisoned *v* ▷ **garrison**
garrisoning *v* ▷ **garrison**
garrisons *n, v* ▷ **garrison**
garrotte, garotte *n* (*pl* **-s**) Spanish method of execution by strangling ▶ *v* (**-tes, -ting, -ted**) kill by this method
garrotted *v* ▷ **garrotte**
garrottes *n, v* ▷ **garrotte**
garrotting *v* ▷ **garrotte**
garrulous *adj* talkative
garter *n* (*pl* **-s**) band worn round the leg to hold up a sock or stocking
garters *n* ▷ **garter**
gas *n* (*pl* **gases, gasses**) airlike substance that is not liquid or solid ▶ *v* (**gases, gasses, gassing, gassed**) poison or render unconscious with gas
gasbag *n* (*pl* **-s**) (*Informal*) person who talks too much
gasbags *n* ▷ **gasbag**
gaseous *adj* of or like gas
gases *n, v* ▷ **gas**
gash *v* (**-es, -ing, -ed**) make a long deep cut in ▶ *n* (*pl* **-es**) long deep cut
gashed *v* ▷ **gash**
gashes *v, n* ▷ **gash**
gashing *v* ▷ **gash**
gasholder, gasometer [gas-**som**-it-er] (*pl* **-s**) *n* large tank for storing gas
gasholders *n* ▷ **gasholder**
gasket *n* (*pl* **-s**) piece of rubber etc. placed between the faces of a metal joint to act as a seal
gaskets *n* ▷ **gasket**
gasoline *n* (*pl* **-s**) (US) petrol
gasolines *n* ▷ **gasoline**
gasometers *n* ▷ **gasholder**
gasp *v* (**-s, -ing, -ed**) draw in breath sharply or with difficulty ▶ *n* (*pl* **-s**) convulsive intake of breath
gasped *v* ▷ **gasp**
gasping *v* ▷ **gasp**
gasps *v, n* ▷ **gasp**
gassed *v* ▷ **gas**
gasses *n, v* ▷ **gas**
gassier *adj* ▷ **gassy**
gassiest *adj* ▷ **gassy**
gassing *v* ▷ **gas**
gassy *adj* (**-ssier, -ssiest**) filled with gas
gastric *adj* of the stomach
gastritis *n* (*pl* **-tes**) inflammation of the stomach lining
gastritises *n* ▷ **gastritis**
gastroenteritis *n* inflammation of the stomach and intestines
gastronomies *n* ▷ **gastronomy**
gastronomy *n* (*pl* **-mies**) art of good eating > **gastronomic** *adj*
gastropod *n* (*pl* **-s**) mollusc, such as a snail, with a single flattened muscular foot
gastropods *n* ▷ **gastropod**
gate *n* (*pl* **-s**) movable barrier, usu. hinged, in a wall or fence
gâteau [**gat**-toe] *n* (*pl* **-teaux**) [-toes] rich elaborate cake
gâteaux *n* ▷ **gâteau**
gatecrash *v* (**-es, -ing, -ed**) enter (a party) uninvited
gatecrashed *v* ▷ **gatecrash**
gatecrashes *v* ▷ **gatecrash**
gatecrashing *v* ▷ **gatecrash**
gatehouse *n* (*pl* **-s**) building at or above a gateway
gatehouses *n* ▷ **gatehouse**
gates *n* ▷ **gate**
gateway *n* (*pl* **-s**) entrance with a gate
gateways *n* ▷ **gateway**
gather *v* (**-s, -ing, -ed**) assemble
gathered *v* ▷ **gather**
gathering *n* (*pl* **-s**) assembly ▶ *v* ▷ **gather**
gatherings *n* ▷ **gathering**
gathers *pl n* gathered folds in material ▶ *v* ▷ **gather**
gauche [**gohsh**] *adj* (**-r, -st**) socially awkward > **gaucheness** *n* (*pl* **-es**)
gaucheness *n* ▷ **gauche**
gauchenesses *n* ▷ **gauche**
gaucher *adj* ▷ **gauche**
gauchest *adj* ▷ **gauche**
gaucho [**gow**-choh] *n* (*pl* **-hos**) S American cowboy
gauchos *n* ▷ **gaucho**
gaudier *adj* ▷ **gaudy**
gaudiest *adj* ▷ **gaudy**
gaudily *adv* ▷ **gaudy**
gaudiness *n* ▷ **gaudy**
gaudinesses *n* ▷ **gaudy**
gaudy *adj* (**-dier, -diest**) vulgarly bright or colourful > **gaudily** *adv* > **gaudiness** *n* (*pl* **-es**)
gauge [**gayj**] *v* (**-ges, -ging, -ged**) estimate or judge ▶ *n* (*pl* **-s**) measuring instrument
gauged *v* ▷ **gauge**
gauges *v, n* ▷ **gauge**
gauging *v* ▷ **gauge**

gaunt *adj* (**-er, -est**) lean and haggard
> **gauntness** *n* (*pl* **-es**)
gaunter *adj* ▷ **gaunt**
gauntest *adj* ▷ **gaunt**
gauntlet *n* (*pl* **-s**) heavy glove with a long cuff
gauntlets *n* ▷ **gauntlet**
gauntness *n* ▷ **gaunt**
gauntnesses *n* ▷ **gaunt**
gauze *n* (*pl* **-s**) transparent loosely-woven fabric, often used for surgical dressings
> **gauzy** *adj* (**-zier, -ziest**)
gauzes *n* ▷ **gauze**
gauzier *adj* ▷ **gauze**
gauziest *adj* ▷ **gauze**
gauzy *adj* ▷ **gauze**
gave *v* ▷ **give**
gavel [**gav**-el] *n* (*pl* **-s**) small hammer banged on a table by a judge, auctioneer, or chairman to call for attention
gavels *n* ▷ **gavel**
gavotte *n* (*pl* **-s**) old formal dance
gavottes *n* ▷ **gavotte**
gawk *v* (**-s, -ing, -ed**) stare stupidly
gawked *v* ▷ **gawk**
gawkier *adj* ▷ **gawky**
gawkiest *adj* ▷ **gawky**
gawkiness *n* ▷ **gawky**
gawkinesses *n* ▷ **gawky**
gawking *v* ▷ **gawk**
gawks *v* ▷ **gawk**
gawky *adj* (**-kier, -kiest**) clumsy or awkward
> **gawkiness** *n* (*pl* **-es**)
gawp *v* (**-s, -ing, -ed**) (*Slang*) stare stupidly
gawped *v* ▷ **gawp**
gawping *v* ▷ **gawp**
gawps *v* ▷ **gawp**
gay *adj* (**-er, -est**) homosexual ▶ *n* (*pl* **-s**) homosexual
gayer *adj* ▷ **gay**
gayest *adj* ▷ **gay**
gayness *n* (*pl* **-es**) homosexuality
gaynesses *n* ▷ **gayness**
gays *n* ▷ **gay**
gaze *v* (**-zes, -zing, -zed**) look fixedly ▶ *n* (*pl* **-s**) fixed look
gazebo [gaz-**zee**-boh] *n* (*pl* **-bos, -boes**) summerhouse with a good view
gazeboes *n* ▷ **gazebo**
gazebos *n* ▷ **gazebo**
gazed *v* ▷ **gaze**
gazelle *n* (*pl* **-s**) small graceful antelope
gazelles *n* ▷ **gazelle**
gazes *v, n* ▷ **gaze**
gazette *n* (*pl* **-s**) official publication containing announcements
gazetteer *n* (part of) a book that lists and describes places
gazetteers *n* ▷ **gazetteer**
gazettes *n* ▷ **gazette**
gazillion *n* (*pl* **-s**) (*Informal*) extremely large, unspecified amount
gazillionaire *n* (*Informal*) enormously rich person
gazillionaires *n* ▷ **gazillionaire**
gazillions *n* ▷ **gazillion**
gazing *v* ▷ **gaze**
gazump *v* (**-s, -ing, -ed**) (BRIT & AUST) raise the price of a property after verbally agreeing it with (a prospective buyer)
gazumped *v* ▷ **gazump**
gazumping *v* ▷ **gazump**
gazumps *v* ▷ **gazump**
gear *n* (*pl* **-s**) set of toothed wheels connecting with another or with a rack to change the direction or speed of transmitted motion ▶ *v* (**-s, -ing, -ed**) prepare or organize for something
gearbox *n* (*pl* **-es**) case enclosing a set of gears in a motor vehicle
gearboxes *n* ▷ **gearbox**
geared *v* ▷ **gear**
gearing *v* ▷ **gear**
gears *n, v* ▷ **gear**
gecko *n* (*pl* **-kos, -koes**) small tropical lizard
geckoes *n* ▷ **gecko**
geckos *n* ▷ **gecko**
geebung [**gee**-bung] *n* (*pl* **-s**) Australian tree or shrub with an edible but tasteless fruit
geebungs *n* ▷ **geebung**
geek *n* (*pl* **-s**) (*Informal*) boring, unattractive person > **geeky** *adj* (**-kier, -kiest**)
geekier *adj* ▷ **geek**
geekiest *adj* ▷ **geek**
geeks *n* ▷ **geek**
geeky *adj* ▷ **geek**
geelbek *n* (*pl* **-s**) (S AFR) edible marine fish
geelbeks *n* ▷ **geelbek**
geese *n* ▷ **goose**
geezer *n* (*pl* **-s**) (BRIT, AUST & NZ) (*Informal*) man
geezers *n* ▷ **geezer**
geisha [**gay**-sha] *n* (*pl* **-sha, -shas**) (in Japan) professional female companion for men
geishas *n* ▷ **geisha**
gel [**jell**] *n* (*pl* **-s**) jelly-like substance, esp. one used to secure a hairstyle ▶ *v* (**-s, gelling, gelled**) form a gel
gelatine [**jel**-at-teen]**, gelatin** *n* (*pl* **-s**) substance made by boiling animal bones
gelatines *n* ▷ **gelatine**
gelatinous [jel-**at**-in-uss] *adj* of or like jelly

geld *v* (**gelds, gelding, gelded**) castrate
gelded *v* ▷ **geld**
gelding *n* (*pl* **-s**) castrated horse ▶ *v* ▷ **geld**
geldings *n* ▷ **gelding**
gelds *v* ▷ **geld**
gelignite *n* (*pl* **-s**) type of dynamite used for blasting
gelignites *v* ▷ **gelignite**
gelled *v* ▷ **gell**
gelling *v* ▷ **gell**
gels *n, v* ▷ **gel**
gem *n* (*pl* **-s**) precious stone or jewel
gemfish (*pl* **-fishes**) *n* Australian food fish with a delicate flavour
gemfishes *n* ▷ **gemfish**
gems *n* ▷ **gem**
gen *n* (*pl* **-s**) (*Informal*) information
gendarme [**zhohn**-darm] *n* (*pl* **-s**) member of the French police force
gendarmes *n* ▷ **gendarme**
gender *n* (*pl* **-s**) state of being male or female
genders *n* ▷ **gender**
gene [**jean**] *n* (*pl* **-s**) part of a cell which determines inherited characteristics
genealogical *adj* ▷ **genealogy**
genealogies *n* ▷ **genealogy**
genealogist *n* ▷ **genealogy**
genealogists *n* ▷ **genealogy**
genealogy [jean-ee-**al**-a-gee] *n* (*pl* **-gies**) (study of) the history and descent of a family or families > **genealogical** *adj* > **genealogist** *n* (*pl* **-s**)
genera [**jen**-er-a] ▷ **genus**
general *adj* common or widespread ▶ *n* (*pl* **-s**) very senior army officer > **generally** *adv*
generalities *n* ▷ **generality**
generality *n* (*pl* **-ties**) general principle
generalization *n* ▷ **generalize**
generalizations *n* ▷ **generalize**
generalize *v* (**-zes, -zing, -zed**) draw general conclusions > **generalization** *n* (*pl* **-s**)
generalized *v* ▷ **generalize**
generalizes *v* ▷ **generalize**
generalizing *v* ▷ **generalize**
generally *adv* ▷ **general**
generals *n* ▷ **general**
generate *v* (**-tes, -ting, -ted**) produce or bring into being
generated *v* ▷ **generate**
generates *v* ▷ **generate**
generating *v* ▷ **generate**
generation *n* (*pl* **-s**) all the people born about the same time
generations *n* ▷ **generation**
generative *adj* capable of producing
generator *n* (*pl* **-s**) machine for converting mechanical energy into electrical energy
generators *n* ▷ **generator**
generic [jin-**ner**-ik] *adj* of a class, group, or genus > **generically** *adv*
generically *adv* ▷ **generic**
generosities *n* ▷ **generous**
generosity *n* ▷ **generous**
generous *adj* free in giving > **generously** *adv* > **generosity** *n* (*pl* **-ties**)
generously *adv* ▷ **generous**
genes *n* ▷ **gene**
geneses *n* ▷ **genesis**
genesis [**jen**-iss-iss] *n* (*pl* **-ses**) [-iss-eez] beginning or origin
genetic [jin-**net**-tik] *adj* of genes or genetics
geneticist *n* ▷ **genetics**
geneticists *n* ▷ **genetics**
genetics *n* study of heredity and variation in organisms > **geneticist** *n* (*pl* **-s**)
genial [**jean**-ee-al] *adj* cheerful and friendly > **genially** *adv* > **geniality** *n* (*pl* **-ties**)
genialities *n* ▷ **genial**
geniality *n* ▷ **genial**
genially *adv* ▷ **genial**
genie [**jean**-ee] *n* (*pl* **-s**) (in fairy tales) servant who appears by magic and grants wishes
genies *n* ▷ **genie**
genital *adj* of the sexual organs or reproduction
genitalia *n* ▷ **genitals**
genitals, genitalia [jen-it-**ail**-ya] *pl n* external sexual organs
genitive *n* (*pl* **-s**) grammatical case indicating possession or association
genitives *n* ▷ **genitive**
genius [**jean**-yuss] *n* (*pl* **-es**) (person with) exceptional ability in a particular field
geniuses *n* ▷ **genius**
genocide [**jen**-no-side] *n* (*pl* **-s**) murder of a race of people
genocides *n* ▷ **genocide**
genre [**zhohn**-ra] *n* (*pl* **-s**) style of literary, musical, or artistic work
genres *n* ▷ **genre**
gens *n* ▷ **gen**
gent *n* (*pl* **-s**) (BRIT, AUST & NZ) (*Informal*) gentleman
genteel *adj* (**-er, -est**) affectedly proper and polite > **genteelly** *adv*
genteeler *adj* ▷ **genteel**
genteelest *adj* ▷ **genteel**
genteelly *adv* ▷ **genteel**
gentian [**jen**-shun] *n* (*pl* **-s**) mountain plant with deep blue flowers

gentians *n* ▷ **gentian**
gentile *adj, n* (*pl* **-s**) non-Jewish (person)
gentiles *n* ▷ **gentile**
gentle *adj* (**-r, -st**) mild or kindly > **gentleness** *n* (*pl* **-es**) > **gently** *adv*
gentleman *n* (*pl* **-men**) polite well-bred man > **gentlemanly** *adj* > **gentlewoman** *n fem* (*pl* **-women**)
gentlemanly *adj* ▷ **gentleman**
gentlemen *n* ▷ **gentleman**
gentleness *n* ▷ **gentle**
gentlenesses *n* ▷ **gentle**
gentler *adj* ▷ **gentle**
gentlest *adj* ▷ **gentle**
gentlewoman *n* ▷ **gentleman**
gentlewomen *n* ▷ **gentleman**
gently *adv* ▷ **gentle**
gentries *n* ▷ **gentry**
gentries *n* ▷ **gentry**
gentrification *n* (*pl* **-s**) taking-over of a traditionally working-class area by middle-class incomers > **gentrify** *v* (**-fies, -fying, -fied**)
gentrifications *n* ▷ **gentrification**
gentrified *v* ▷ **gentrification**
gentrifies *v* ▷ **gentrification**
gentrifying *v* ▷ **gentrification**
gentry *n* (*pl* **-ies**) people just below the nobility in social rank
gents *n* men's public toilet ▶ *n* ▷ **gent**
genuflect *v* (**-s, -ing, -ed**) bend the knee as a sign of reverence or deference > **genuflection, genuflexion** *n* (*pl* **-s**)
genuflected *v* ▷ **genuflect**
genuflecting *v* ▷ **genuflect**
genuflection *n* ▷ **genuflect**
genuflections *n* ▷ **genuflect**
genuflects *v* ▷ **genuflect**
genuflexion *n* ▷ **genuflect**
genuflexions *n* ▷ **genuflect**
genuine *adj* not fake, authentic > **genuinely** *adv* > **genuineness** *n* (**-es**)
genuinely *adv* ▷ **genuine**
genuineness *n* ▷ **genuine**
genuinenesses *n* ▷ **genuine**
genus [**jean**-uss] *n* (*pl* **genera**) group into which a family of animals or plants is divided
geocentric *adj* having the earth as a centre
geographer *n* ▷ **geography**
geographers *n* ▷ **geography**
geographic *adj* ▷ **geography**
geographical *adj* ▷ **geography**
geographically *adv* ▷ **geography**
geographies *n* ▷ **geography**
geography *n* (*pl* **-phies**) study of the earth's physical features, climate, population, etc. > **geographer** *n* (*pl* **-s**) > **geographical, geographic** *adj* > **geographically** *adv*
geological *adj* ▷ **geology**
geologically *adv* ▷ **geology**
geologies *n* ▷ **geology**
geologist *n* ▷ **geology**
geologists *n* ▷ **geology**
geology *n* (*pl* **-gies**) study of the earth's origin, structure, and composition > **geological** *adj* > **geologically** *adv* > **geologist** *n* (*pl* **-s**)
geometric *adj* ▷ **geometry**
geometrical *adj* ▷ **geometry**
geometrically *adv* ▷ **geometry**
geometries *n* ▷ **geometry**
geometry *n* (*pl* **-tries**) branch of mathematics dealing with points, lines, curves, and surfaces > **geometric, geometrical** *adj* > **geometrically** *adv*
geostationary *adj* (of a satellite) orbiting so as to remain over the same point of the earth's surface
geothermal *adj* of or using the heat in the earth's interior
geranium *n* (*pl* **-s**) cultivated plant with red, pink, or white flowers
geraniums *n* ▷ **geranium**
gerbil [**jer**-bill] *n* (*pl* **-s**) burrowing desert rodent of Asia and Africa
gerbils *n* ▷ **gerbil**
geriatric *adj, n* (*pl* **-s**) old (person)
geriatrics *n* (*pl* branch of medicine dealing with old age and its diseases ▶ *n* ▷ **geriatric**
germ *n* (*pl* **-s**) microbe, esp. one causing disease
germane *adj* relevant to
germanium *n* (*pl* **-s**) (CHEM) brittle grey element that is a semiconductor
germaniums *n* ▷ **germanium**
germinal *adj* of or in the earliest stage of development
germinate *v* (**-tes, -ting, -ted**) (cause to) sprout or begin to grow > **germination** *n* (*pl* **-s**)
germinated *v* ▷ **germinate**
germinates *v* ▷ **germinate**
germinating *v* ▷ **germinate**
germination *n* ▷ **germinate**
germinations *n* ▷ **germinate**
germs *n* ▷ **germ**
gerrymandering *n* (*pl* **-s**) alteration of voting constituencies in order to give an unfair advantage to one party

gerrymanderings *n* ▷ **gerrymandering**
gerund [**jer**-rund] *n* (*pl* **-s**) noun formed from a verb
gerunds *n* ▷ **gerund**
gestation *n* (*pl* **-s**) (period of) carrying of young in the womb between conception and birth
gestations *n* ▷ **gestation**
gesticulate *v* (**-tes, -ting, -ted**) make expressive movements with the hands and arms > **gesticulation** *n* (*pl* **-s**)
gesticulated *v* ▷ **gesticulate**
gesticulates *v* ▷ **gesticulate**
gesticulating *v* ▷ **gesticulate**
gesticulation *n* ▷ **gesticulate**
gesticulations *n* ▷ **gesticulate**
gesture *n* (*pl* **-s**) movement to convey meaning ▶ *v* (**-res, -ring, -red**) gesticulate
gestured *v* ▷ **gesture**
gestures *n, v* ▷ **gesture**
gesturing *v* ▷ **gesture**
get *v* (**-s, -tting, got**) obtain or receive
getaway *adj, n* (*pl* **-s**) (used in) escape
getaways *n* ▷ **getaway**
gets *v* ▷ **get**
getting *v* ▷ **get**

> **gey** *adv*. Gey is a Scots word meaning **very.** If you have a G and a Y, it's highly likley that there will be an E you can use somewhere on the board. Gey scores 7 points.

geyser [**geez**-er] *n* (*pl* **-s**) spring that discharges steam and hot water (BRIT & S AFR)
geysers *n* ▷ **geyser**
ghastlier *adj* ▷ **ghastly**
ghastliest *adj* ▷ **ghastly**
ghastliness *n* ▷ **ghastly**
ghastlinesses *n* ▷ **ghastly**
ghastly *adj* (**-lier, -liest**) (*Informal*) unpleasant > **ghastliness** *n* (*pl* **-es**)
ghat *n* (*pl* **-s**) (in India) steps leading down to a river
ghats *n* ▷ **ghat**
ghee [**gee**] *n* (*pl* **-s**) (in Indian cookery) clarified butter
ghees *n* ▷ **ghee**
gherkin *n* (*pl* **-s**) small pickled cucumber
gherkins *n* ▷ **gherkin**
ghetto *n* (*pl* **-ttos, -ttoes**) slum area inhabited by a deprived minority
ghettoblaster *n* (*Informal*) large portable cassette recorder or CD player
ghettoblasters *n* ▷ **ghettoblaster**
ghettoes *n* ▷ **ghetto**
ghettos *n* ▷ **ghetto**
ghillie *n* (*pl* **-s**) ▷ **gillie**
ghillies *n* ▷ **ghillie**
ghost *n* (*pl* **-s**) disembodied spirit of a dead person ▶ *v* (**-s, -ing, -ed**) ghostwrite > **ghostly** *adj* (**-ier, -iest**)
ghosted *v* ▷ **ghost**
ghosting *v* ▷ **ghost**
ghostlier *adj* ▷ **ghost**
ghostliest *adj* ▷ **ghost**
ghostly *adj* ▷ **ghost**
ghosts *n, v* ▷ **ghost**
ghostwriter *n* (*pl* **-s**) writer of a book or article on behalf of another person who is credited as the author
ghostwriters *n* ▷ **ghostwriter**
ghoul [**gool**] *n* (*pl* **-s**) person with morbid interests > **ghoulish** *adj*
ghoulish *adj* ▷ **ghoul**
ghouls *n* ▷ **ghoul**

> **gi** *n*. A gi is a suit worn by judo or karate practitioners. Gi is one of only three two-letter words beginning with G, and so is worth knowing. Gi scores 3 points.

giant *n* (*pl* **-s**) mythical being of superhuman size ▶ *adj* huge
giants *n* ▷ **giant**
gibber[1] [**jib**-ber] *v* (**-s, -ing, -ed**) speak or utter rapidly and unintelligibly
gibber[2] [**gib**-ber] *n* (*pl* **-s**) (AUST) boulder
gibbered *v* ▷ **gibber**[1]
gibbering *v* ▷ **gibber**[1]
gibberish *n* rapid unintelligible talk
gibbers *n, v* ▷ **gibber**[1, 2]
gibbet [**jib**-bit] *n* (*pl* **-s**) gallows for displaying executed criminals
gibbets *n* ▷ **gibbet**
gibbon [**gib**-bon] *n* (*pl* **-s**) agile tree-dwelling ape of S Asia
gibbons *n* ▷ **gibbon**
gibbous *adj* (of the moon) more than half but less than fully illuminated
gibe [**jibe**] *v, n* (*pl* **-s**) ▷ **jibe**[1]
gibes *n* ▷ **gibe**
giblets [**jib**-lets] *pl n* gizzard, liver, heart, and neck of a fowl
gidday, g'day *interj* (AUST & NZ) expression of greeting
giddier *adj* ▷ **giddy**
giddiest *adj* ▷ **giddy**
giddily *adv* ▷ **giddy**
giddiness *n* ▷ **giddy**
giddinesses *n* ▷ **giddy**
giddy *adj* (**-ddier, -ddiest**) having or causing a feeling of dizziness > **giddily** *adv* > **giddiness**

n (*pl* **-es**)
gift *n* (*pl* **-s**) present ▶ *v* (**-s, -ing, -ed**) make a present of
gifted *adj* talented ▶ *v* ▷ **gift**
gifting *v* ▷ **gift**
gifts *n, v* ▷ **gift**
gig[1] *n* (*pl* **-s**) single performance by pop or jazz musicians ▶ *v* (**-s, -gging, -gged**) play a gig or gigs
gig[2] (*pl* **-s**) *n* light two-wheeled horse-drawn carriage
gigantic *adj* enormous
gigged *v* ▷ **gig**[1]
gigging *v* ▷ **gig**[1]
giggle *v* (**-les, -ling, -led**) laugh nervously or foolishly ▶ *n* (*pl* **-s**) such a laugh > **giggly** *adj* (**-lier, -liest**)
giggled *v* ▷ **giggle**
giggles *v, n* ▷ **giggle**
gigglier *adj* ▷ **giggle**
giggliest *adj* ▷ **giggle**
giggling *v* ▷ **giggle**
giggly *adj* ▷ **giggle**
gigolo [**jig**-a-lo] *n* (*pl* **-los**) man paid by an older woman to be her escort or lover
gigolos *n* ▷ **gigolo**
gigot *n* (*pl* **-s**) (CHIEFLY BRIT) leg of lamb or mutton
gigots *n* ▷ **gigot**
gigs *n, v* ▷ **gig**[1, 2]
gild *v* (**-s, -ing, -ed** *or* **gilt**) put a thin layer of gold on
gilded *v* ▷ **gild**
gilding *v* ▷ **gild**
gilds *v* ▷ **gild**
gill [**jill**] *n* (*pl* **-s**) liquid measure of quarter of a pint, equal to 0.142 litres
gillie *n* (*pl* **-s**) (in Scotland) attendant for hunting or fishing
gillies *n* ▷ **gillie**
gills [**gillz**] *pl n* breathing organs in fish and other water creatures ▶ *n* ▷ **gill**
gilt *adj* covered with a thin layer of gold ▶ *n* (*pl* **-s**) thin layer of gold used as decoration ▶ *v* ▷ **gild**
gilts *n* ▷ **gilt**
gimbals *pl n* set of pivoted rings which allow nautical instruments to remain horizontal at sea
gimcrack [**jim**-krak] *adj* showy but cheap
gimlet [**gim**-let] *n* (*pl* **-s**) small tool with a screwlike tip for boring holes in wood
gimlets *n* ▷ **gimlet**
gimmick *n* (*pl* **-s**) something designed to attract attention or publicity > **gimmickry** *n* (*pl* **-ries**) > **gimmicky** *adj* (**-ier, -iest**)
gimmickier *adj* ▷ **gimmick**
gimmickiest *adj* ▷ **gimmick**
gimmickries *n* ▷ **gimmick**
gimmickry *n* ▷ **gimmick**
gimmicks *n* ▷ **gimmick**
gimmicky *adj* ▷ **gimmick**
gin[1] *n* (*pl* **-s**) spirit flavoured with juniper berries
gin[2] *n* (*pl* **-s**) wire noose used to trap small animals
gin[3] *n* (*pl* **-s**) (AUST) (*Offens*) Aboriginal woman
ginger *n* (*pl* **-s**) root of a tropical plant, used as a spice > **gingery** *adj*
gingerbread *n* (*pl* **-s**) moist cake flavoured with ginger
gingerbreads *n* ▷ **gingerbread**
gingerly *adv* cautiously
gingers *n* ▷ **ginger**
gingery *adj* ▷ **ginger**
gingham *n* (*pl* **-s**) cotton cloth, usu. checked or striped
ginghams *n* ▷ **gingham**
gingivitis [jin-jiv-**vite**-iss] *n* (*pl* **-tes**) inflammation of the gums
gingivitises *n* ▷ **gingivitis**
ginkgo [**gink**-go] *n* (*pl* **-goes**) ornamental Chinese tree
ginkgoes *n* ▷ **ginkgo**
gins *n* ▷ **gin**[1, 2, 3]
ginseng [**jin**-seng] *n* (*pl* **-s**) (root of) a plant believed to have tonic and energy-giving properties
ginsengs *n* ▷ **ginseng**
gipsies *n* ▷ **gipsy**
gipsy *n* (*pl* **-sies**) ▷ **gypsy**
giraffe *n* (*pl* **-s**) African ruminant mammal with a spotted yellow skin and long neck and legs
giraffes *n* ▷ **giraffe**
gird *v* (**-s, girding, girded** *or* **girt**) put a belt round
girded *v* ▷ **gird**
girder *n* (*pl* **-s**) large metal beam
girders *n* ▷ **girder**
girding *v* ▷ **gird**
girdle[1] *n* (*pl* **-s**) woman's elastic corset ▶ *v* (**-les, -ling, -led**) surround or encircle
girdle[2] *n* (*pl* **-s**) (SCOT) griddle
girdled *v* ▷ **girdle**[1]
girdles *v, n* ▷ **girdle**[1, 2]
girdling *v* ▷ **girdle**[1]
girds *v* ▷ **gird**
girl *n* (*pl* **-s**) female child (*Informal*) > **girlhood** *n* > **girlish** *adj*

girlfriend *n* (*pl* **-s**) girl or woman with whom a person is romantically or sexually involved
girlfriends *n* ▷ **girlfriend**
girlhood *n* ▷ **girl**
girlhoods *n* ▷ **girl**
girlie, girly *adj* (*Informal*) featuring photographs of naked or scantily clad women
girlish *adj* ▷ **girl**
girls *n* ▷ **girl**
girly *n* ▷ **girlie**
giro [**jire**-oh] *n* (*pl* **-os**) (in some countries) system of transferring money within a post office or bank directly from one account to another
giros *n* ▷ **giro**
girt *v* ▷ **gird**
girth *n* (*pl* **-s**) measurement round something
girths *n* ▷ **girth**
gist [**jist**] *n* (*pl* **-s**) substance or main point of a matter
gists *n* ▷ **gist**
give *v* (**-s, giving, gave, given**) present (something) to another person ▶ *n* (*pl* **-s**) resilience or elasticity
giveaway *n* (*pl* **-s**) something that reveals hidden feelings or intentions ▶ *adj* very cheap or free
giveaways *n* ▷ **giveaway**
given *v* ▷ **give**
gives *v, n* ▷ **give**
giving *v* ▷ **give**
gizzard *n* (*pl* **-s**) part of a bird's stomach
gizzards *n* ▷ **gizzard**

> **gju** *n* (**gjus**). A gju (also spelt **gu**) is a kind of violin from Shetland. This unusual term is a great little word, especially when there's not much space on the board. Gju scores 11 points.

glacé [**glass**-say] *adj* preserved in a thick sugary syrup
glacial *adj* of ice or glaciers
glaciated *adj* covered with or affected by glaciers > **glaciation** *n* (*pl* **-s**)
glaciation *n* ▷ **glaciated**
glaciations *n* ▷ **glaciated**
glacier *n* (*pl* **-s**) slow-moving mass of ice formed by accumulated snow
glaciers *n* ▷ **glacier**
glad *adj* (**-dder, -ddest**) pleased and happy > **gladly** *adv* > **gladness** *n* (*pl* **-es**)
gladden *v* (**-s, -ing, -ed**) make glad
gladdened *v* ▷ **gladden**
gladdening *v* ▷ **gladden**
gladdens *v* ▷ **gladden**
gladder *adj* ▷ **glad**
gladdest *adj* ▷ **glad**
glade *n* (*pl* **-s**) open space in a forest
glades *n* ▷ **glade**
gladiator *n* (*pl* **-s**) (in ancient Rome) man trained to fight in arenas to provide entertainment
gladiators *n* ▷ **gladiator**
gladioli *n* ▷ **gladiolus**
gladiolus *n* (*pl* **-lus, -li, -luses**) garden plant with sword-shaped leaves
gladioluses *n* ▷ **gladiolus**
gladly *adv* ▷ **glad**
gladness *n* ▷ **glad**
gladnesses *n* ▷ **glad**
gladwrap ® (AUST, NZ & S AFR) *n* (*pl* **-wraps**) thin polythene material for wrapping food ▶ *v* (**-wraps, -wrapping, -wrapped**) wrap in gladwrap
gladwrapped *v* ▷ **gladwrap**
gladwrapping *v* ▷ **gladwrap**
gladwraps *n, v* ▷ **gladwrap**
glamorize *v* ▷ **glamorous**
glamorized *v* ▷ **glamorous**
glamorizes *v* ▷ **glamorous**
glamorizing *v* ▷ **glamorous**
glamorous *adj* alluring > **glamorize** *v* (**-zes, -zing, -zed**)
glamour *n* (*pl* **-s**) alluring charm or fascination
glamours *n* ▷ **glamour**
glance *v* (**-ces, -cing, -ced**) look rapidly or briefly ▶ *n* (*pl* **-s**) brief look
glanced *v* ▷ **glance**
glances *v, n* ▷ **glance**
glancing *adj* hitting at an oblique angle ▶ *v* ▷ **glance**
gland *n* (*pl* **-s**) organ that produces and secretes substances in the body > **glandular** *adj*
glands *n* ▷ **gland**
glandular *adj* ▷ **gland**
glare *v* (**-res, -ring, -red**) stare angrily ▶ *n* (*pl* **-s**) angry stare
glared *v* ▷ **glare**
glares *v, n* ▷ **glare**
glaring *adj* conspicuous ▶ *v* ▷ **glare** > **glaringly** *adv*
glaringly *adv* ▷ **glaring**
glass *n* (*pl* **-es**) hard brittle, usu. transparent substance consisting of metal silicates or similar compounds ▶ *pl* spectacles
glasses *n* ▷ **glass**
glasshouse *n* greenhouse
glasshouses *n* ▷ **glasshouse**

glassier *adj* ▷ **glassy**
glassiest *adj* ▷ **glassy**
glassy *adj* (**-ssier, -ssiest**) like glass
glaucoma *n* (*pl* **-s**) eye disease
glaucomas *n* ▷ **glaucoma**
glaze *v* (**-zes, -zing, -zed**) fit or cover with glass ▶ *n* (*pl* **-s**) transparent coating
glazed *v* ▷ **glaze**
glazes *v, n* ▷ **glaze**
glazier (*pl* **-s**) *n* person who fits windows with glass
glaziers *n* ▷ **glazier**
glazing *v* ▷ **glaze**
gleam *n* (*pl* **-s**) small beam or glow of light ▶ *v* (**-s, -ing, -ed**) emit a gleam > **gleaming** *adj*
gleamed *v* ▷ **gleam**
gleaming *v, adj* ▷ **gleam**
gleams *n, v* ▷ **gleam**
glean *v* (**-s, -ing, -ed**) gather (facts etc.) bit by bit > **gleaner** *n* (*pl* **-s**)
gleaned *v* ▷ **glean**
gleaner *n* ▷ **glean**
gleaners *n* ▷ **glean**
gleaning *v* ▷ **glean**
gleans *v* ▷ **glean**
glee *n* (*pl* **-s**) triumph and delight > **gleeful** *adj* > **gleefully** *adv*
gleeful *adj* ▷ **glee**
gleefully *adv* ▷ **glee**
glees *n* ▷ **glee**
glen *n* (*pl* **-s**) deep narrow valley, esp. in Scotland
glens *n* ▷ **glen**
glib *adj* (**-bber, -bbest**) fluent but insincere or superficial > **glibly** *adv* > **glibness** *n* (*pl* **-es**)
glibber *adj* ▷ **glib**
glibbest *adj* ▷ **glib**
glibly *adv* ▷ **glib**
glibness *n* ▷ **glib**
glibnesses *n* ▷ **glib**
glide *v* (**-des, -ding, -ded**) move easily and smoothly ▶ *n* (*pl* **-s**) smooth easy movement
glided *v* ▷ **glide**
glider *n* (AUST) flying phalanger
gliders *n* ▷ **glider**
glides *n* ▷ **glide**
gliding *n* sport of flying gliders ▶ *v* ▷ **glide**
glimmer *v* (**-s, -ing, -ed**) shine faintly, flicker ▶ *n* (*pl* **-s**) faint gleam
glimmered *v* ▷ **glimmer**
glimmering *v* ▷ **glimmer**
glimmers *v, n* ▷ **glimmer**
glimpse *n* (*pl* **-s**) brief or incomplete view ▶ *v* (**-ses, -sing, -sed**) catch a glimpse of
glimpsed *v* ▷ **glimpse**
glimpses *n, v* ▷ **glimpse**
glimpsing *v* ▷ **glimpse**
glint *v* (**-s, -ing, -ed**) gleam brightly ▶ *n* (*pl* **-s**) bright gleam
glinted *v* ▷ **glint**
glinting *v* ▷ **glint**
glints *v, n* ▷ **glint**
glissando *n* (*pl* **-dos**) (MUSIC) slide between two notes in which all intermediate notes are played
glissandos *n* ▷ **glissando**
glisten *v* (**-s, -ing, -ed**) gleam by reflecting light
glistened *v* ▷ **glisten**
glistening *v* ▷ **glisten**
glistens *v* ▷ **glisten**
glitch *n* (*pl* **-es**) small problem that stops something from working properly
glitches *n* ▷ **glitch**
glitter *v* (**-s, -ing, -ed**) shine with bright flashes ▶ *n* (*pl* **-s**) sparkle or brilliance
glittered *v* ▷ **glitter**
glittering *v* ▷ **glitter**
glitters *v, n* ▷ **glitter**
gloaming *n* (*pl* **-s**) (SCOT) (*poetic*) twilight
gloamings *n* ▷ **gloaming**
gloat *v* (**-s, -ing, -ed**) regard one's own good fortune or the misfortune of others with smug or malicious pleasure
gloated *v* ▷ **gloat**
gloating *v* ▷ **gloat**
gloats *v* ▷ **gloat**
glob *n* (*pl* **-s**) rounded mass of thick fluid
global *adj* worldwide > **globally** *adv*
globalization *n* (*pl* **-s**) process by which a company, etc., expands to operate internationally
globalizations *n* ▷ **globalization**
globally *adv* ▷ **global**
globe *n* (*pl* **globes**) sphere with a map of the earth on it
globes *n* ▷ **globe**
globetrotter *n* habitual worldwide traveller > **globetrotting** *adj, n* (*pl* **-s**)
globetrotters *n* ▷ **globetrotter**
globetrotting *n* ▷ **globetrotter**
globetrottings *n* ▷ **globetrotter**
globs *n* ▷ **glob**
globular *adj* ▷ **globule**
globule *n* (*pl* **-s**) small round drop > **globular** *adj*
globules *n* ▷ **globule**
glockenspiel *n* (*pl* **-s**) percussion instrument consisting of small metal bars played with hammers
glockenspiels *n* ▷ **glockenspiel**
gloom *n* (*pl* **glooms**) melancholy or depression

> **gloomy** *adj* (**-mier, -miest**) > **gloomily** *adv*
gloomier *adj* ▷ **gloom**
gloomiest *adj* ▷ **gloom**
gloomily *adv* ▷ **gloom**
glooms *n* ▷ **gloom**
gloomy *adj* ▷ **gloom**
gloried *v* ▷ **glory**
glories *n, v* ▷ **glory**
glorification *n* ▷ **glorify**
glorifications *n* ▷ **glorify**
glorified *v* ▷ **glorify**
glorifies *v* ▷ **glorify**

glorify *v* (**-fies, -fying, -fied**) make (something) seem more worthy than it is > **glorification** *n* (*pl* **-s**)
glorifying *v* ▷ **glorify**

glorious *adj* brilliantly beautiful > **gloriously** *adv*
gloriously *adv* ▷ **glorious**

glory *n* (*pl* **-ries**) praise or honour ▶ *v* (**-ries, -rying, -ried**) (*foll. by* **in**) triumph or exalt
glorying *v* ▷ **glory**

gloss[1] *n* (*pl* **-es**) surface shine or lustre

gloss[2] *n* (*pl* **-es**) explanatory comment added to the text of a book ▶ *v* (**-es, -ing, -ed**) add glosses to
glossaries *n* ▷ **glossary**

glossary *n* (*pl* **-ries**) list of special or technical words with definitions
glossed *v* ▷ **gloss**[2]
glosses *n, v* ▷ **gloss**[1, 2]
glossier *adj* ▷ **glossy**
glossiest *adj* ▷ **glossy**
glossily *adv* ▷ **glossy**
glossiness *n* ▷ **glossy**
glossinesses *n* ▷ **glossy**
glossing *v* ▷ **gloss**[2]

glossy *adj* (**-ssier, -ssiest**) smooth and shiny > **glossily** *adv* > **glossiness** *n* (*pl* **-es**)

glottal *adj* of the glottis
glottides *n* ▷ **glottis**

glottis *n* (*pl* **-tises, -tides**) vocal cords and the space between them
glottises *n* ▷ **glottis**

glove *n* (*pl* **-s**) covering for the hand with individual sheaths for each finger and the thumb

gloved *adj* covered by a glove or gloves
gloves *n* ▷ **glove**

glow *v* (**-s, -ing, -ed**) emit light and heat without flames ▶ *n* (*pl* **-s**) glowing light
glowed *v* ▷ **glow**

glower [rhymes with **power**] *v* (**-s, -ing, -ed**) ▶ *n* (*pl* **-s**) scowl
glowered *v* ▷ **glower**
glowering *v* ▷ **glower**
glowers *v, n* ▷ **glower**
glowing *v* ▷ **glow**
glows *v, n* ▷ **glow**

glowworm *n* (*pl* **-s**) insect giving out a green light
glowworms *n* ▷ **glowworm**

gloxinia *n* (*pl* **-s**) tropical plant with large bell-shaped flowers
gloxinias *n* ▷ **gloxinia**

glucose *n* (*pl* **-s**) kind of sugar found in fruit
glucoses *n* ▷ **glucose**

glue *n* (*pl* **glues**) natural or synthetic sticky substance used as an adhesive ▶ *v* (**glues, gluing** *or* **glueing, glued**) fasten with glue > **gluey** *adj*
glued *v* ▷ **glue**
glueing *v* ▷ **glue**
glues *n, v* ▷ **glue**
gluey *adj* ▷ **glue**
gluier *adj* ▷ **glue**
gluiest *adj* ▷ **glue**
gluing *v* ▷ **glue**

glum *adj* (**-mmer, -mmest**) sullen or gloomy > **glumly** *adv*
glumly *adv* ▷ **glum**
glummer *adj* ▷ **glum**
glummest *adj* ▷ **glum**

glut *n* (*pl* **-s**) excessive supply ▶ *v* (**-s, -tting, -tted**) oversupply

gluten [gloo-ten] *n* (*pl* **-s**) protein found in cereal grain
glutens *n* ▷ **gluten**

glutinous [gloo-tin-uss] *adj* sticky or gluey
gluts *n, v* ▷ **glut**
glutted *v* ▷ **glut**
glutting *v* ▷ **glut**

glutton *n* (*pl* **-s**) greedy person > **gluttonous** *adj* > **gluttony** *n* (*pl* **-nies**)
gluttonies *n* ▷ **glutton**
gluttonous *adj* ▷ **glutton**
gluttons *n* ▷ **glutton**
gluttony *n* ▷ **glutton**

glycerine, glycerin *n* (*pl* **-s**) colourless sweet liquid used widely in chemistry and industry
glycerines *n* ▷ **glycerine**
glycerins *n* ▷ **glycerine**

glycerol [gliss-ser-ol] *n* (*pl* **-s**) ▷ **glycerine**
glycerols *n* ▷ **glycerol**

gnarled *adj* rough, twisted, and knobbly

gnash *v* (**-es, -ing, -ed**) grind (the teeth) together in anger or pain
gnashed *v* ▷ **gnash**
gnashes *v* ▷ **gnash**
gnashing *v* ▷ **gnash**

gnat *n* (*pl* **-s**) small biting two-winged fly
gnats *n* ▷ **gnat**
gnaw *v* (**-s, -ing, -ed** *or* **gnawn**) bite or chew steadily
gnawed *v* ▷ **gnaw**
gnaws *v* ▷ **gnaw**
gneiss *n* (*pl* **-es**) coarse-grained metamorphic rock
gneisses *n* ▷ **gneiss**
gnome *n* (*pl* **-s**) imaginary creature like a little old man
gnomes *n* ▷ **gnome**
gnomic [**no**-mik] *adj* of pithy sayings
gnu [**noo**] *n* (*pl* **-s**) oxlike S African antelope
gnus *n* ▷ **gnu**
go *v* (**going, went, gone**) move to or from a place (*pl* **gos**) ▶ *n* attempt
goad *v* (**-s, -ing, -ed**) provoke (someone) to take some kind of action, usu. in anger ▶ *n* (*pl* **-s**) spur or provocation
goaded *v* ▷ **goad**
goading *v* ▷ **goad**
goads *v, n* ▷ **goad**
goal *n* (*pl* **-s**) (SPORT) posts through which the ball or puck has to be propelled to score
goalie *n* (*pl* **-s**) (*Informal*) goalkeeper
goalies *n* ▷ **goalie**
goalkeeper *n* (*pl* **-s**) player whose task is to stop shots entering the goal
goalkeepers *n* ▷ **goalkeeper**
goalpost (*pl* **-s**) *n* one of the two posts marking the limit of a goal
goalposts *n* ▷ **goalpost**
goals *n* ▷ **goal**
goanna *n* (*pl* **-s**) large Australian lizard
goannas *n* ▷ **goanna**
goat *n* (*pl* **-s**) sure-footed ruminant animal with horns
goatee *n* (*pl* **-s**) pointed tuftlike beard
goatees *n* ▷ **goatee**
goats *n* ▷ **goat**
gob *n* (*pl* **-s**) lump of a soft substance (BRIT, AUST & NZ)
gobbet *n* (*pl* **-s**) lump, esp. of food
gobbets *n* ▷ **gobbet**
gobble[1] *v* (**-les, -ling, -led**) eat hastily and greedily
gobble[2] *n* (*pl* **-s**) rapid gurgling cry of the male turkey ▶ *v* (**-les, -ling, -led**) make this noise
gobbled *v* ▷ **gobble**[1, 2]
gobbledegooks *n* ▷ **gobbledegook**
gobbledygooks *n* ▷ **gobbledegook**
gobbles *v, n* ▷ **gobble**[1, 2]
gobbledegook, gobbledygook *n* (*pl* **-s**) unintelligible (official) language or jargon
gobbling *v* ▷ **gobble**[1, 2]
gobies *n* ▷ **goby**
goblet *n* (*pl* **-s**) drinking cup without handles
goblets *n* ▷ **goblet**
goblin *n* (*pl* **-s**) (in folklore) small malevolent creature
goblins *n* ▷ **goblin**
gobs *n* ▷ **gob**
goby *n* (*pl* **-by, -bies**) small spiny-finned fish
god *n* (*pl* **-s**) spirit or being worshipped as having supernatural power
> **godlike** *adj*
godchild *n* (*pl* **-s**) child for whom a person stands as godparent
> **goddaughter** *n* (*pl* **-s**)
> **godson** *n* (*pl* **-s**)
goddaughter *n* ▷ **godchild**
goddaughters *n* ▷ **godchild**
goddess *n fem* (*pl* **-es**) female god
goddesses *n* ▷ **goddess**
godetia *n* (*pl* **-s**) plant with showy flowers
godetias *n* ▷ **godetia**
godfather *n* (*pl* **-s**) male godparent
> **godmother** *n* (*pl* **-s**)
godfathers *n* ▷ **godfather**
godforsaken *adj* desolate or dismal
godlier *adj* ▷ **godly**
godliest *adj* ▷ **godly**
godlike *adj* ▷ **god**
godliness *n* ▷ **godly**
godlinesses *n* ▷ **godly**
godly *adj* (**-lier, -liest**) devout or pious
> **godliness** *n* (*pl* **-es**)
godmother *n* ▷ **godfather**
godmothers *n* ▷ **godfather**
godparent *n* (*pl* **-s**) person who promises at a child's baptism to bring the child up as a Christian
godparents *n* ▷ **godparent**
gods *n* ▷ **god**
godsend *n* (*pl* **-s**) something unexpected but welcome
godsends *n* ▷ **godsend**
godson *n* ▷ **godchild**
godsons *n* ▷ **godchild**
gogga *n* (*pl* **-s**) (S AFR) (*Informal*) any small insect
goggas *n* ▷ **gogga**
goggle *v* (**-les, -ling, -led**) (of the eyes) bulge
goggled *v* ▷ **goggle**
goggles *pl n* protective spectacles ▶ *v* ▷ **goggle**
goggling *v* ▷ **goggle**
going *n* (*pl* **-s**) condition of the ground for

walking or riding over ▶ *adj* thriving ▶ *v* ▷ **go**
goings *n* ▷ **going**
goitre [**goy**-ter] *n* (*pl* **-s**) swelling of the thyroid gland in the neck
goitres *n* ▷ **goitre**
gold *n* (*pl* **-s**) yellow precious metal ▶ *adj* made of gold
goldcrest *n* (*pl* **-s**) small bird with a yellow crown
goldcrests *n* ▷ **goldcrest**
golden *adj* made of gold
goldfinch *n* (*pl* **-es**) kind of finch, the male of which has yellow-and-black wings
goldfinches *n* ▷ **goldfinch**
goldfish *n* (*pl* **-es**) orange fish kept in ponds or aquariums
goldfishes *n* ▷ **goldfish**
golds *n* ▷ **gold**
golf *n* (*pl* **-s**) outdoor game in which a ball is struck with clubs into a series of holes ▶ *v* (**-s, -ing, -ed**) play golf > **golfer** *n* (*pl* **-s**)
golfed *v* ▷ **golf**
golfer *n* ▷ **golf**
golfers *n* ▷ **golf**
golfing *v* ▷ **golf**
golfs *n, v* ▷ **golf**
golliwog *n* (*pl* **-s**) soft black-faced doll
golliwogs *n* ▷ **golliwog**
gonad *n* (*pl* **-s**) organ producing reproductive cells, such as a testicle or ovary
gonads *n* ▷ **gonad**
gondola *n* (*pl* **-s**) long narrow boat used in Venice
gondolas *n* ▷ **gondola**
gondolier *n* (*pl* **-s**) person who propels a gondola
gondoliers *n* ▷ **gondoliers**
gone *v* ▷ **go**
goner *n* (*pl* **-s**) (*Informal*) person or thing beyond help or recovery
goners *n* ▷ **goner**
gong *n* (*pl* **-s**) rimmed metal disc that produces a note when struck
gongs *n* ▷ **gong**
gonorrhoea [gon-or-**ree**-a] *n* (*pl* **-s**) venereal disease with a discharge from the genitals
gonorrhoeas *n* ▷ **gonorrhoea**
good *adj* (**better, best**) giving pleasure ▶ *n* benefit ▶ *pl* merchandise > **goodness** *n* (*pl* **-es**)
goodbye *interj, n* (*pl* **-s**) expression used on parting
goodbyes *n* ▷ **goodbye**
goodies *n* ▷ **goody**
goodly *adj* considerable
goodness *n* ▷ **good**
goodnesses *n* ▷ **good**
goodwill *n* (*pl* **-s**) kindly feeling
goodwills *n* ▷ **goodwill**
goody *n* (*pl* **-dies**) (*Informal*) hero in a book or film
gooey *adj* (**gooier, gooiest**) (*Informal*) sticky and soft
goof (*Informal*) *n* (*pl* **-s**) mistake ▶ *v* (**-s, -ing, -ed**) make a mistake
goofed *v* ▷ **goof**
goofing *v* ▷ **goof**
goofs *n, v* ▷ **goof**
googlies *n* ▷ **googly**
googly *n* (*pl* **-lies**) (CRICKET) ball that spins unexpectedly from off to leg on the bounce
gooier *adj* ▷ **gooey**
gooiest *adj* ▷ **gooey**
goon *n* (*pl* **-s**) (*Informal*) stupid person
goons *n* ▷ **goon**
goose *n* (*pl* **geese**) web-footed bird like a large duck
gooseberries *n* ▷ **gooseberry**
gooseberry *n* (*pl* **-ries**) edible yellowy-green berry
gopher [**go**-fer] *n* (*pl* **-s**) American burrowing rodent
gophers *n* ▷ **gopher**
gore[1] *n* (*pl* **-s**) blood from a wound
gore[2] *v* (**-res, -ring, -red**) pierce with horns
gored *v* ▷ **gore**[2]
gores *n, v* ▷ **gore**[1, 2]
gorge *n* (*pl* **-s**) deep narrow valley ▶ *v* (**-ges, -ging, -ged**) eat greedily
gorged *v* ▷ **gorge**
gorgeous *adj* strikingly beautiful or attractive (*Informal*) > **gorgeously** *adv*
gorgeously *adv* ▷ **gorgeous**
gorges *n, v* ▷ **gorge**
gorging *v* ▷ **gorge**
gorgon *n* (*pl* **-s**) terrifying or repulsive woman
gorgons *n* ▷ **gorgon**
gorier *adj* ▷ **gory**
goriest *adj* ▷ **gory**
gorilla *n* (*pl* **-s**) largest of the apes, found in Africa
gorillas *n* ▷ **gorilla**
goring *v* ▷ **gore**[2]
gormless *adj* (*Informal*) stupid
gorse *n* (*pl* **-s**) prickly yellow-flowered shrub
gorses *n* ▷ **gorse**
gory *adj* (**-rier, -riest**) horrific or bloodthirsty
gos *n* ▷ **go**
goshawk *n* (*pl* **-s**) large hawk
goshawks *n* ▷ **goshawk**
gosling *n* (*pl* **-s**) young goose

goslings *n* ▷ **gosling**
gospel *n* (*pl* **-s**) any of the first four books of the New Testament
gospels *n* ▷ **gospel**
gossamer *n* (*pl* **-s**) very fine fabric
gossamers *n* ▷ **gossamer**
gossip *n* (*pl* **-s**) idle talk, esp. about other people ▶ *v* (**-s, -ing, -ed**) engage in gossip > **gossipy** *adj* (**-ier, -iest**)
gossiped *v* ▷ **gossip**
gossipier *adj* ▷ **gossip**
gossipiest *adj* ▷ **gossip**
gossiping *v* ▷ **gossip**
gossips *n, v* ▷ **gossip**
gossipy *adj* ▷ **gossip**
got *v* ▷ **get**
gouache *n* (*pl* **-s**) (painting using) watercolours mixed with glue
gouaches *n* ▷ **gouache**
gouge [**gowj**] *v* (**-ges, -ging, -ged**) scoop or force out ▶ *n* (*pl* **-s**) hole or groove
gouged *v* ▷ **gouge**
gouges *v, n* ▷ **gouge**
gouging *v* ▷ **gouge**
goulash [**goo**-lash] *n* (*pl* **-es**) rich stew seasoned with paprika
goulashes *n* ▷ **goulash**
gourd [**goord**] *n* (*pl* **-s**) fleshy fruit of a climbing plant
gourds *n* ▷ **gourd**
gourmand [**goor**-mand] *n* (*pl* **-s**) person who is very keen on food and drink
gourmands *n* ▷ **gourmand**
gourmet [**goor**-may] *n* (*pl* **-s**) connoisseur of food and drink
gourmets *n* ▷ **gourmet**
gout [**gowt**] *n* (*pl* **-s**) disease causing inflammation of the joints
gouts *n* ▷ **gout**
govern *v* (**-s, -ing, -ed**) rule, direct, or control > **governable** *adj*
governable *adj* ▷ **govern**
governance *n* (*pl* **-s**) governing
governances *n* ▷ **governance**
governed *v* ▷ **govern**
governess *n* (*pl* **-es**) woman teacher in a private household
governesses *n* ▷ **governess**
governing *v* ▷ **govern**
government *n* (*pl* **-s**) executive policy-making body of a state
> **governmental** *adj*
governmental *adj* ▷ **government**
governments *n* ▷ **government**
governor *n* (*pl* **-s**) official governing a province or state
governors *n* ▷ **governor**
governs *v* ▷ **govern**
gown *n* (*pl* **-s**) woman's long formal dress
gowns *n* ▷ **gown**
goy *n* (*pl* **-yim, -ys**) (*Slang*) Jewish word for a non-Jew
goyim *n* ▷ **goy**
goys *n* ▷ **goy**

> **gox** *n* (**goxes**). Gox is a short word meaning gaseous oxygen. This unusual word can come in very useful, especially if you can use it to hit a bonus square. Gox scores 11 points.
> **goy** *n* (**goyim**) or (**goys**). Goy is a Yiddish word for someone who isn't Jewish. For a short word, this earns you a reasonable number of points, and the two plural forms can come in useful too. Goy scores 7 points.

grab *v* (**-s, -bbing, -bbed**) grasp suddenly, snatch ▶ *n* sudden snatch
grabbed *v* ▷ **grab**
grabbing *v* ▷ **grab**
grabs *v* ▷ **grab**
grace *n* (*pl* **-s**) beauty and elegance ▶ *v* (**-ces, -cing, -ced**) add grace to > **graceful** *adj*
> **gracefully** *adv*
> **graceless** *adj*
graced *v* ▷ **grace**
graceful *adj* ▷ **grace**
gracefully *adv* ▷ **grace**
graceless *adj* ▷ **grace**
graces *n, v* ▷ **grace**
gracing *v* ▷ **grace**
gracious *adj* kind and courteous > **graciously** *adv*
graciously *adv* ▷ **gracious**
gradation *n* (*pl* **-s**) (stage in) a series of degrees or steps
gradations *n* ▷ **gradation**
grade *n* (*pl* **-s**) place on a scale of quality, rank, or size ▶ *v* (**-des, -ding, -ded**) arrange in grades
graded *v* ▷ **grade**
grades *n, v* ▷ **grade**
gradient *n* (*pl* **-s**) (degree of) slope
gradients *n* ▷ **gradient**
grading *v* ▷ **grade**
gradual *adj* occurring, developing, or moving in small stages
> **gradually** *adv*
gradually *adv* ▷ **gradual**
graduate *v* (**-tes, -ting, -ted**) receive a degree or diploma ▶ *n* (*pl* **-s**) holder of a degree
> **graduation** *n* (*pl* **-s**)

graduated *v* ▷ **graduate**
graduates *v, n* ▷ **graduate**
graduating *v* ▷ **graduate**
graduation *n* ▷ **graduate**
graduations *n* ▷ **graduate**
graffiti [graf-**fee**-tee] *pl n* words or drawings scribbled or sprayed on walls etc.
graft[1] *n* (*pl* **-s**) surgical transplant of skin or tissue ▶ *v* (**-s, -ing, -ed**) transplant (living tissue) surgically
graft[2] (BRIT) (*Informal*) *n* hard work ▶ *v* work hard > **grafter** *n* (*pl* **-s**)
grafted *v* ▷ **graft**[1, 2]
grafter *n* ▷ **graft**
grafters *n* ▷ **graft**
grafting *v* ▷ **graft**[1, 2]
grafts *n, v* ▷ **graft**[1, 2]
grain *n* (*pl* **-s**) seedlike fruit of a cereal plant > **grainy** *adj* (**-ier, -iest**)
grainier *adj* ▷ **grain**
grainiest *adj* ▷ **grain**
grains *n* ▷ **grain**
grainy *adj* ▷ **grain**
gram, gramme *n* (*pl* **-s**) metric unit of mass equal to one thousandth of a kilogram
grammar *n* (*pl* **-s**) branch of linguistics dealing with the form, function, and order of words > **grammarian** *n* (*pl* **-s**)
grammarian *n* ▷ **grammar**
grammarians *n* ▷ **grammar**
grammars *n* ▷ **grammar**
grammatical *adj* according to the rules of grammar > **grammatically** *adv*
grammatically *adv* ▷ **grammatical**
gramophone *n* (*pl* **-s**) old-fashioned type of record player
gramophones *n* ▷ **gramophone**
grampus *n* (*pl* **-es**) dolphin-like mammal
grampuses *n* ▷ **grampus**
grams *n* ▷ **gram**
gran *n* (*pl* **-s**) (BRIT, AUST & NZ) (*Informal*) grandmother
granaries *n* ▷ **granary**
granary *n* (*pl* **-ries**) storehouse for grain
grand *adj* large or impressive, imposing ▶ *n* (*pl* **-s**) (*Slang*) thousand pounds or dollars
grandchild *n* (*pl* **-children**) child of one's child
grandchildren *n* ▷ **grandchild**
granddaughter *n* (*pl* **-s**) female grandchild
granddaughters *n* ▷ **granddaughter**
grandee *n* (*pl* **-s**) person of high station
grandees *n* ▷ **grandee**
grandeur *n* (*pl* **-s**) magnificence
grandeurs *n* ▷ **grandeur**
grandfather *n* (*pl* **-s**) male grandparent
grandfathers *n* ▷ **grandfather**
grandiloquences *n* ▷ **grandiloquent**
grandiloquent *adj* using pompous language > **grandiloquence** *n* (*pl* **-s**)
grandiloquence *n* ▷ **grandiloquent**
grandiose *adj* imposing > **grandiosity** *n* (*pl* **-ties**)
grandiosities *n* ▷ **grandiose**
grandiosity *n* ▷ **grandiose**
grandmother *n* (*pl* **-s**) female grandparent
grandmothers *n* ▷ **grandmother**
grandparent *n* (*pl* **-s**) parent of one's parent
grandparents *n* ▷ **grandparent**
grands *n* ▷ **grand**
grandson *n* (*pl* **-s**) male grandchild
grandsons *n* ▷ **grandson**
grandstand *n* (*pl* **-s**) terraced block of seats giving the best view at a sports ground
grandstands *n* ▷ **grandstand**
grange *n* (*pl* **-s**) (BRIT) country house with farm buildings
granges *n* ▷ **grange**
granite [**gran**-nit] *n* (*pl* **-s**) very hard igneous rock often used in building
granites *n* ▷ **granite**
grannies *n* ▷ **granny**
granny, grannie *n* (*pl* **-nies**) (*Informal*) grandmother
grans *n* ▷ **gran**
grant *v* (**-s, -ing, -ed**) consent to fulfil (a request) ▶ *n* (*pl* **-s**) sum of money provided by a government for a specific purpose, such as education
granted *v* ▷ **grant**
granting *v* ▷ **grant**
grants *v, n* ▷ **grant**
granular *adj* of or like grains
granulated *adj* (of sugar) in the form of coarse grains
granule *n* (*pl* **-s**) small grain
granules *n* ▷ **granule**
grape *n* (*pl* **-s**) small juicy green or purple berry, eaten raw or used to produce wine, raisins, currants, or sultanas
grapefruit *n* (*pl* **-s**) large round yellow citrus fruit
grapefruits *n* ▷ **grapefruit**
grapes *n* ▷ **grape**
grapevine *n* (*pl* **-s**) grape-bearing vine
grapevines *n* ▷ **grapevine**
graph *n* (*pl* **-s**) drawing showing the relation of different numbers or quantities plotted against a set of axes
graphic *adj* vividly descriptive > **graphically** *adv*

graphically *adv* ▷ **graphic**
graphics *pl n* diagrams, graphs, etc., esp. as used on a television programme or computer screen
graphite *n* (*pl* **-s**) soft black form of carbon, used in pencil leads
graphites *n* ▷ **graphite**
graphologies *n* ▷ **graphology**
graphologist *n* ▷ **graphology**
graphologists *n* ▷ **graphology**
graphology *n* (*pl* **-gies**) study of handwriting > **graphologist** *n* (*pl* **-s**)
graphs *n* ▷ **graph**
grapnel *n* (*pl* **-s**) device with several hooks, used to grasp or secure things
grapnels *n* ▷ **grapnel**
grapple *v* (**-les, -ling, -led**) try to cope with (something difficult)
grappled *v* ▷ **grapple**
grapples *v* ▷ **grapple**
grappling *v* ▷ **grapple**
grasp *v* (**-s, -ing, -ed**) grip something firmly ▶ *n* (*pl* **-s**) grip or clasp
grasped *v* ▷ **grasp**
grasping *adj* greedy or avaricious ▶ *v* ▷ **grasp**
grasps *v, n* ▷ **grasp**
grass *n* (*pl* **-es**) common type of plant with jointed stems and long narrow leaves, including cereals and bamboo ▶ *v* (**-es, -ing, -ed**) cover with grass > **grassy** *adj* (**-ssier, -ssiest**)
grassed *v* ▷ **grass**
grasses *n, v* ▷ **grass**
grasshopper *n* (*pl* **-s**) jumping insect with long hind legs
grasshoppers *n* ▷ **grasshopper**
grassier *adj* ▷ **grass**
grassiest *adj* ▷ **grass**
grassing *v* ▷ **grass**
grassroots *adj* of the ordinary members of a group, rather than its leaders
grassy *adj* ▷ **grass**
grate¹ *v* (**-tes, -ting, -ted**) rub into small bits on a rough surface > **grater** *n* (*pl* **-s**)
grate² *n* (*pl* **-s**) framework of metal bars for holding fuel in a fireplace
grated *v* ▷ **grate¹**
grateful *adj* feeling or showing gratitude > **gratefully** *adv*
gratefully *adv* ▷ **grateful**
grater *n* ▷ **grate¹**
graters *n* ▷ **grate¹**
grates *v, n* ▷ **grate¹, ²**
gratification *n* ▷ **gratify**
gratifications *n* ▷ **gratify**
gratified *v* ▷ **gratify**
gratifies *v* ▷ **gratify**
gratify *v* (**-fies, -fying, -fied**) satisfy or please > **gratification** *n* (*pl* **-s**)
gratifying *v* ▷ **gratify**
grating *n* (*pl* **-s**) framework of metal bars covering an opening ▶ *adj* harsh or rasping ▶ *v* ▷ **grate¹**
gratings *n* ▷ **grating**
gratis *adv, adj* free, for nothing
gratitude *n* (*pl* **-s**) feeling of being thankful for a favour or gift
gratitudes *n* ▷ **gratitude**
gratuities *n* ▷ **gratuity**
gratuitous *adj* unjustified > **gratuitously** *adv*
gratuitously *adv* ▷ **gratuitous**
gratuity *n* (*pl* **-ies**) money given for services rendered, tip
grave¹ *n* (*pl* **-s**) hole for burying a corpse
grave² *adj* causing concern > **gravely** *adv*
grave³ [rhymes with **halve**] *n* (*pl* **-s**) accent (`) over a vowel to indicate a special pronunciation
gravel *n* (*pl* **-s**) mixture of small stones and coarse sand
gravelled *adj* covered with gravel
gravellier *adj* ▷ **gravelly**
gravelliest *adj* ▷ **gravelly**
gravelly *adj* (**-llier, -lliest**) covered with gravel
gravels *n* ▷ **gravel**
gravely *adv* ▷ **grave²**
graven *adj* carved or engraved
graves *n* ▷ **grave¹, ³**
gravestone *n* (*pl* **-s**) stone marking a grave
gravestones *n* ▷ **gravestone**
graveyard *n* (*pl* **-s**) cemetery
graveyards *n* ▷ **graveyard**
gravid [grav-id] *adj* (MED) pregnant
gravies *n* ▷ **gravy**
gravitate *v* (**-tes, -ting, -ted**) be influenced or drawn towards > **gravitation** *n* (*pl* **-s**) > **gravitational** *adj*
gravitated *v* ▷ **gravitate**
gravitates *v* ▷ **gravitate**
gravitating *v* ▷ **gravitate**
gravitation *n* ▷ **gravitate**
gravitational *adj* ▷ **gravitate**
gravitations *n* ▷ **gravitate**
gravities *n* ▷ **gravity**
gravity *n* (*pl* **-ties**) force of attraction of one object for another, esp. of objects to the earth
gravy *n* (*pl* **-vies**) juices from meat in cooking
grawing *v* ▷ **gnaw**
grawn *v* ▷ **gnaw**
gray *adj* (**-er, -est**) (CHIEFLY US) grey

grayer *adj* ▷ **gray**
grayest *adj* ▷ **gray**
grayling *n* (*pl* **-s**) fish of the salmon family
graylings *n* ▷ **grayling**
graze¹ *v* (**-zes, -zing, -zed**) feed on grass
graze² *v* (**-zes, -zing, -zed**) scratch or scrape the skin ▶ *n* (*pl* **-s**) slight scratch or scrape
grazed *v* ▷ **graze¹, ²**
grazes *v, n* ▷ **graze¹, ²**
grazing *v* ▷ **graze¹, ²**
grease *n* (*pl* **-s**) soft melted animal fat ▶ *v* (**-ses, -sing, -sed**) apply grease to
greased *v* ▷ **grease**
greasepaint *n* (*pl* **-s**) theatrical make-up
greasepaints *n* ▷ **greasepaint**
greases *n, v* ▷ **grease**
greasier *adj* ▷ **greasy**
greasiest *adj* ▷ **greasy**
greasiness *n* ▷ **greasy**
greasinesses *n* ▷ **greasy**
greasing *v* ▷ **grease**
greasy *adj* (**-sier, -siest**) covered with or containing grease > **greasiness** *n* (*pl* **-s**)
great *adj* (**-er, -est**) large in size or number (*Informal*) > **greatly** *adv* > **greatness** *n* (*pl* **-es**)
greatcoat *n* (*pl* **-s**) heavy overcoat
greatcoats *n* ▷ **greatcoat**
greater *adj* ▷ **great**
greatest *adj* ▷ **great**
greatly *adv* ▷ **great**
greatness *n* ▷ **great**
greatnesses *n* ▷ **great**
greave *n* (*pl* **-s**) piece of armour for the shin
greaves *n* ▷ **greave**
grebe *n* (*pl* **-s**) diving water bird
grebes *n* ▷ **grebe**
greed *n* (*pl* **-s**) excessive desire for food, wealth, etc. > **greedy** *adj* (**-dier, -diest**) > **greedily** *adv* > **greediness** *n* (*pl* **-es**)
greedier *adj* ▷ **greed**
greediest *adj* ▷ **greed**
greedily *adv* ▷ **greed**
greediness *n* ▷ **greed**
greedinesses *n* ▷ **greed**
greeds *n* ▷ **greed**
greedy *adj* ▷ **greed**
green *adj* (**-er, -est**) of a colour between blue and yellow ▶ *n* (*pl* **-s**) colour between blue and yellow ▶ *pl* green vegetables ▶ *v* (**-s, -ing, -ed**) make or become green > **greenness** *n* (*pl* **-es**) > **greenish, greeny** *adj*
greened *v* ▷ **green**
greener *adj* ▷ **green**
greeneries *n* ▷ **greenery**
greenery *n* (*pl* **-ries**) vegetation
greenest *adj* ▷ **green**
greenfinch *n* (*pl* **-es**) European finch with dull green plumage in the male
greenfinches *n* ▷ **greenfinch**
greenflies *n* ▷ **greenfly**
greenfly *n* (*pl* **-flies**) green aphid, a common garden pest
greengage *n* (*pl* **-s**) sweet green plum
greengages *n* ▷ **greengage**
greengrocer *n* (*pl* **-s**) (BRIT) shopkeeper selling vegetables and fruit
greengrocer *n* ▷ **greengrocers**
greenhorn *n* (*pl* **-s**) (CHIEFLY US) novice
greenhorns *n* ▷ **greenhorn**
greenhouse *n* (*pl* **-s**) glass building for rearing plants
greenhouses *n* ▷ **greenhouse**
greening *v* ▷ **green**
greenish *adj* ▷ **green**
greenness *n* ▷ **green**
greennesses *n* ▷ **green**
greens *n, v* ▷ **green**
greenshank (*pl* **-s**) *n* large European sandpiper
greenshanks *n* ▷ **greenshanks**
greenstone *n* (*pl* **-s**) (NZ) type of green jade used for Maori ornaments
greenstones *n* ▷ **greenstone**
greeny *adj* ▷ **green**
greet *v* (**-s, -ing, -ed**) meet with expressions of welcome > **greeting** *n* (*pl* **-s**)
greeted *v* ▷ **greet**
greeting *v, n* ▷ **greet**
greetings *n* ▷ **greet**
greets *v* ▷ **greet**
gregarious *adj* fond of company
gremlin *n* (*pl* **-s**) imaginary being blamed for mechanical malfunctions
gremlins *n* ▷ **gremlin**
grenade *n* (*pl* **-s**) small bomb thrown by hand or fired from a rifle
grenades *n* ▷ **grenade**
grenadier *n* (*pl* **-s**) soldier of a regiment formerly trained to throw grenades
grenadiers *n* ▷ **grenadier**
grenadine [gren-a-**deen**] *n* (*pl* **-s**) syrup made from pomegranates
grenadines *n* ▷ **grenadine**
grevillea *n* (*pl* **-s**) any of various Australian evergreen trees and shrubs
grevilleas *n* ▷ **grevillea**
grew *v* ▷ **grow**
grey *adj* (**-er, -est**) of a colour between black and white ▶ *n* (*pl* **-s**) grey colour
greyer *adj* ▷ **grey**
greyest *adj* ▷ **grey**

greyhound *n* (*pl* **-s**) swift slender dog used in racing
greyhounds *n* ▷ **greyhound**
greying *adj* (of hair) turning grey > **greyish** *adj* > **greyness** *n* (*pl* **-es**)
greyish *adj* ▷ **grey**
greyness *n* ▷ **grey**
greynesses *n* ▷ **grey**
greys *n* ▷ **grey**
grid *n* (*pl* **-s**) network of horizontal and vertical lines, bars, etc.
griddle *n* (*pl* **-s**) flat iron plate for cooking
griddles *n* ▷ **griddle**
gridiron *n* (*pl* **-s**) frame of metal bars for grilling food
gridirons *n* ▷ **gridiron**
gridlock *n* (*pl* **-s**) situation where traffic is not moving > **gridlocked** *adj*
gridlocked *adj* ▷ **gridlock**
gridlocks *n* ▷ **gridlock**
grids *n* ▷ **grid**
grief *n* (*pl* **-s**) deep sadness
griefs *n* ▷ **grief**
grievance (*pl* **-s**) *n* real or imaginary cause for complaint
grievances *n* ▷ **grievances**
grieve *v* (**-ves, -ving, -ved**) (cause to) feel grief
grieved *v* ▷ **grieve**
grieves *v* ▷ **grieve**
grieving *adj* ▷ **grieve**
grievous *adj* very severe or painful
griffin *n* (*pl* **-s**) mythical monster with an eagle's head and wings and a lion's body
griffins *n* ▷ **griffin**
grill *n* (*pl* **-s**) device on a cooker that radiates heat downwards ▶ *v* (**-s, -ing, -ed**) cook under a grill
grille, grill *n* (*pl* **-s**) grating over an opening
grilled *v* ▷ **grill**
grilles *n* ▷ **grille**
grilling *n* (*pl* **-s**) relentless questioning ▶ *v* ▷ **grill**
grillings *n* ▷ **grilling**
grills[1] *n, v* ▷ **grill**
grills[2] *n* ▷ **grille**
grilse [**grillss**] *n* (*pl* **-s**) salmon on its first return from the sea to fresh water
grilses *n* ▷ **grilse**
grim *adj* (**-mmer, -mmest**) stern > **grimly** *adv* > **grimness** *n* (*pl* **-es**)
grimace *n* (*pl* **-s**) ugly or distorted facial expression of pain, disgust, etc. ▶ *v* (**-ces, -cing, -ced**) make a grimace
grimaced *v* ▷ **grimace**
grimaces *n, v* ▷ **grimace**
grimacing *v* ▷ **grimace**
grime *n* (*pl* **-s**) ingrained dirt ▶ *v* (**-mes, -ming, -med**) make very dirty > **grimy** *adj* (**-mier, -miest**)
grimed *v* ▷ **grime**
grimes *n, v* ▷ **grime**
grimier *adj* ▷ **grime**
grimiest *adj* ▷ **grime**
griming *v* ▷ **grime**
grimly *adv* ▷ **grim**
grimmer *adj* ▷ **grim**
grimmest *adj* ▷ **grim**
grimness *n* ▷ **grim**
grimnesses *n* ▷ **grim**
grimy *adj* ▷ **grime**
grin *v* (**-s, -nning, -nned**) smile broadly, showing the teeth ▶ *n* (**-s**) broad smile
grind *v* (**-s, -ing, ground**) crush or rub to a powder ▶ *n* (*pl* **-s**) (*Informal*) hard work
grinding *v* ▷ **grind**
grinds *v, n* ▷ **grind**
grindstone *n* (*pl* **-s**) stone used for grinding
grindstones *n* ▷ **grindstone**
grinned *v* ▷ **grin**
grinning *v* ▷ **grin**
grins *v, n* ▷ **grin**
grip *n* (*pl* **-s**) firm hold or grasp (US) ▶ *v* (**-s, -pping, -pped**) grasp or hold tightly > **gripping** *adj*
gripe *v* (**-pes, -ping, -ped**) (*Informal*) complain persistently ▶ *n* (*pl* **-s**) (*Informal*) complaint
griped *v* ▷ **gripe**
gripes *v, n* ▷ **gripe**
griping *v* ▷ **gripe**
gripped *v* ▷ **grip**
gripping *v, adj* ▷ **grip**
grips *n, v* ▷ **grip**
grislier *adj* ▷ **grisly**
grisliest *adj* ▷ **grisly**
grisly *adj* (**-lier, -liest**) horrifying or ghastly
grist *n* (*pl* **-s**) grain for grinding
gristle *n* (*pl* **-s**) tough stringy animal tissue found in meat > **gristly** *adj* (**-lier, -liest**)
gristles *n* ▷ **gristle**
gristlier *adj* ▷ **gristle**
gristliest *adj* ▷ **gristle**
gristly *adj* ▷ **gristle**
grists *n* ▷ **grist**
grit *n* (*pl* **-s**) rough particles of sand ▶ *pl* coarsely ground grain ▶ *v* (**-s, -tting, -tted**) spread grit on (an icy road etc.) > **gritty** *adj* (**-ttier, -ttiest**) > **grittiness** *n* (*pl* **-es**)
grits *v* ▷ **grit**
gritted *v* ▷ **grit**
grittier *adj* ▷ **grit**

grittiest *adj* ▷ **grit**
grittiness *n* ▷ **grit**
grittinesses *n* ▷ **grit**
gritting *v* ▷ **grit**
gritty *adj* ▷ **grit**
grizzle *v* (**-les, -ling, -led**) (BRIT, AUST & NZ) (*Informal*) whine or complain
grizzled *adj* grey-haired ▶ *v* ▷ **grizzle**
grizzles *v* ▷ **grizzle**
grizzlies *n* ▷ **grizzly**
grizzling *v* ▷ **grizzle**
grizzly *n* (*pl* **-lies**) large American bear
groan *n* (*pl* **-s**) deep sound of grief or pain ▶ *v* (**-s, -ing, -ed**) utter a groan
groaned *v* ▷ **groan**
groaning *v* ▷ **groan**
groans *n, v* ▷ **groan**
groat *n* (*pl* **-s**) (HIST) fourpenny piece
groats *n* ▷ **groat**
grocer *n* (*pl* **-s**) shopkeeper selling foodstuffs
groceries *n* ▷ **grocery**
grocers *n* ▷ **grocer**
grocery *n* (*pl* **-ceries**) business or premises of a grocer ▶ *pl* goods sold by a grocer
grog *n* (*pl* **-s**) (BRIT, AUST & NZ) spirit, usu. rum, and water
groggier *adj* ▷ **groggy**
groggiest *adj* ▷ **groggy**
groggy *adj* (**-ggier, -ggiest**) (*Informal*) faint, shaky, or dizzy
grogs *n* ▷ **grog**
groin *n* (*pl* **-s**) place where the legs join the abdomen
groins *n* ▷ **groin**
grommet *n* (*pl* **-s**) ring or eyelet
grommets *n* ▷ **grommet**
groom *n* (*pl* **-s**) person who looks after horses ▶ *v* (**-s, -ing, -ed**) make or keep one's clothes and appearance neat and tidy
groomed *v* ▷ **groom**
grooming *v* ▷ **groom**
grooms *n, v* ▷ **groom**
groove *n* (*pl* **-s**) long narrow channel in a surface
grooves *n* ▷ **groove**
grope *v* (**-pes, -ping, -ped**) feel about or search uncertainly > **groping** *n* (*pl* **-s**)
groped *v* ▷ **grope**
gropes *v* ▷ **grope**
groping *v, n* ▷ **grope**
gropings *n* ▷ **grope**
gross *adj* flagrant ▶ *n* (*pl* **-es**) twelve dozen ▶ *v* (**-es, -ing, -ed**) make as total revenue before deductions > **grossly** *adv* > **grossness** *n* (*pl* **-es**)
grossed *v* ▷ **gross**
grosses *n, v* ▷ **gross**
grossing *v* ▷ **gross**
grossly *adv* ▷ **gross**
grossness *n* ▷ **gross**
grossnesses *n* ▷ **gross**
grotesque [grow-**tesk**] *adj* (**-quer, -quest**) strangely distorted ▶ *n* (*pl* **-s**) grotesque person or thing > **grotesquely** *adv*
grotesquely *adv* ▷ **grotesque**
grotesquer *adj* ▷ **grotesque**
grotesques *n* ▷ **grotesque**
grotesquest *adj* ▷ **grotesque**
grottier *adj* ▷ **grotty**
grottiest *adj* ▷ **grotty**
grotto *n* (*pl* **-ttoes, -ttos**) small picturesque cave
grottoes *n* ▷ **grotto**
grottos *n* ▷ **grotto**
grotty *adj* (**-ttier, -ttiest**) (*Informal*) nasty or in bad condition
grouch (*Informal*) *v* (**-es, -ing, -ed**) grumble or complain ▶ *n* (*pl* **-es**) person who is always complaining > **grouchy** *adj* (**-chier, -chiest**)
grouched *v* ▷ **grouch**
grouches *v, n* ▷ **grouch**
grouchier *adj* ▷ **grouch**
grouchiest *adj* ▷ **grouch**
grouching *v* ▷ **grouch**
grouchy *adj* ▷ **grouch**
ground[1] *n* (*pl* **-s**) surface of the earth ▶ *pl* enclosed land round a house ▶ *v* (**-s, -ing, -ed**) base or establish
ground[2] *v* ▷ **grind**
groundbreaking *adj* innovative
grounded *v* ▷ **ground**[1]
grounding *n* (*pl* **-s**) basic knowledge of a subject ▶ *v* ▷ **ground**[1]
groundings *n* ▷ **grounding**
groundless *adj* without reason
groundnut *n* (*pl* **-s**) peanut
groundnuts *n* ▷ **groundnut**
grounds *n, v* ▷ **ground**[1]
groundsheet *n* (*pl* **-s**) waterproof sheet put on the ground under a tent
groundsheets *n* ▷ **groundsheet**
groundsman *n* (*pl* **-men**) person employed to maintain a sports ground or park
groundsmen *n* ▷ **groundsman**
groundswell *n* (*pl* **-s**) rapidly developing general feeling or opinion
groundswells *n* ▷ **groundswell**
groundwork *n* (*pl* **-s**) preliminary work
groundworks *n* ▷ **groundwork**
group *n* (*pl* **-s**) number of people or things regarded as a unit ▶ *v* (**-s, -ing, -ed**) place or

form into a group
grouped *v* ▷ **group**
grouping *v* ▷ **group**
groups *n, v* ▷ **group**
grouse[1] *n* (*pl* **-s**) stocky game bird
grouse[2] *v* (**-ses, -sing, -sed**) grumble or complain ▶ *n* (*pl* **-s**) complaint
groused *v* ▷ **grouse**[2]
grouses *n, v* ▷ **grouse**[1, 2]
grousing *v* ▷ **grouse**[2]
grout *n* (*pl* **-s**) thin mortar ▶ *v* (**-s, -ing, -ed**) fill up with grout
grouted *v* ▷ **grout**
grouting *v* ▷ **grout**
grouts *n, v* ▷ **grout**
grove *n* (*pl* **-s**) small group of trees
grovel [**grov**-el] *v* (**-s, -elling, -elled**) behave humbly in order to win a superior's favour
grovelled *v* ▷ **grovel**
grovelling *v* ▷ **grovel**
grovels *v* ▷ **grovel**
groves *n* ▷ **grove**
grow *v* (**-s, growing, grew, grown**) develop physically
growing *v* ▷ **grow**
growl *v* (**-s, -ing, -ed**) make a low rumbling sound ▶ *n* (*pl* **-s**) growling sound
growled *v* ▷ **growl**
growling *v* ▷ **growl**
growls *v, n* ▷ **growl**
grown *v* ▷ **grow**
grownup *adj, n* (*pl* **-s**) adult
grownups *n* ▷ **grownup**
grows *v* ▷ **grow**
growth *n* (*pl* **-s**) growing
growths *n* ▷ **growth**
groyne *n* (*pl* **-s**) wall built out from the shore to control erosion
groynes *n* ▷ **groyne**
grub *n* (*pl* **-s**) legless insect larva ▶ *v* (**-s, -bbing, -bbed**) search carefully for something by digging or by moving things about
grubbed *v* ▷ **grub**
grubbier *adj* ▷ **grubby**
grubbiest *adj* ▷ **grubby**
grubbiness *n* ▷ **grubby**
grubbinesses *n* ▷ **grubby**
grubbing *v* ▷ **grub**
grubby *adj* (**-bbier, -bbiest**) dirty > **grubbiness** *n* (*pl* **-es**)
grubs *n, v* ▷ **grub**
grudge *v* (**-ges, -ging, -ged**) be unwilling to give or allow ▶ *n* (*pl* **-s**) resentment
grudged *v* ▷ **grudge**
grudges *v, n* ▷ **grudge**
grudging *v* ▷ **grudge**
gruel *n* (*pl* **-s**) thin porridge
gruelling *adj* exhausting or severe
gruels *n* ▷ **gruel**
gruesome *adj* (**-er, -est**) causing horror and disgust
gruesomer *adj* ▷ **gruesome**
gruesomest *adj* ▷ **gruesome**
gruff *adj* (**-er, -est**) rough or surly in manner or voice > **gruffly** *adv* > **gruffness** *n* (*pl* **-es**)
gruffer *adj* ▷ **gruff**
gruffest *adj* ▷ **gruff**
gruffly *adv* ▷ **gruff**
gruffness *n* ▷ **gruff**
gruffnesses *n* ▷ **gruff**
grumble *v* (**-les, -ling, -led**) complain ▶ *n* (*pl* **-s**) complaint > **grumbler** *n* (*pl* **-s**) > **grumbling** *adj, n* (*pl* **-s**)
grumbled *v* ▷ **grumble**
grumbler *n* ▷ **grumble**
grumblers *n* ▷ **grumble**
grumbles *v, n* ▷ **grumble**
grumbling *v, n* ▷ **grumble**
grumblings *n* ▷ **grumble**
grumpier *adj* ▷ **grumpy**
grumpiest *adj* ▷ **grumpy**
grumpily *adv* ▷ **grumpy**
grumpiness *n* ▷ **grumpy**
grumpinesses *n* ▷ **grumpy**
grumpy *adj* (**-pier, -piest**) bad-tempered > **grumpily** *adv* > **grumpiness** *n* (*pl* **-es**)
grunge *n* (*pl* **-s**) style of rock music with a fuzzy guitar sound
grunges *n* ▷ **grunge**
grunt *v* (**-s, -ing, -ed**) make a low short gruff sound, like a pig ▶ *n* (*pl* **-s**) pig's sound
grunted *v* ▷ **grunt**
grunting *v* ▷ **grunt**
grunts *v, n* ▷ **grunt**
gryphon *n* (*pl* **-s**) ▷ **griffin**
gryphons *n* ▷ **gryphon**

> **gu** *n* (**gus**). A gu (also spelt **gju**) is a kind of violin from Shetland. This is one of only three two-letter words beginning with G, and so is a good one to remember. Gu scores 3 points.

guano [**gwah**-no] *n* (*pl* **-nos**) dried sea-bird manure, used as fertilizer
guanos *n* ▷ **guano**
guarantee *n* (*pl* **-s**) formal assurance, esp. in writing, that a product will meet certain standards ▶ *v* (**-s, -teeing, -teed**) give a guarantee
guaranteed *v* ▷ **guarantee**
guaranteeing *v* ▷ **guarantee**

guarantees *n, v* ▷ **guarantee**
guarantor *n* (*pl* **-s**) person who gives or is bound by a guarantee
guarantors *n* ▷ **guarantor**
guard *v* (**-s, -ing, -ed**) watch over to protect or to prevent escape ▶ *n* (*pl* **-s**) person or group that guards ▶ (**G-**) *pl* regiment with ceremonial duties
guarded *adj* cautious or noncommittal ▶ *v* ▷ **guard** > **guardedly** *adv*
guardedly *adv* ▷ **guarded**
guardian *n* (*pl* **-s**) keeper or protector > **guardianship** *n* (*pl* **-s**)
guardians *n* ▷ **guardian**
guardianship *n* ▷ **guardian**
guardianships *n* ▷ **guardian**
guarding *v* ▷ **guard**
guards *v, n* ▷ **guard**
guardsman *n* (*pl* **-s**) member of the Guards
guardsmen *n* ▷ **guardsman**
guava [**gwah**-va] *n* (*pl* **-s**) yellow-skinned tropical American fruit
guavas *n* ▷ **guava**
gudgeon *n* (*pl* **-s**) small freshwater fish
gudgeons *n* ▷ **gudgeon**
guerillas *n* ▷ **guerrilla**
guerrilla, guerilla *n* (*pl* **-s**) member of an unofficial armed force fighting regular forces
guerrillas *n* ▷ **guerrilla**
guess *v* (**-es, -ing, -ed**) estimate or draw a conclusion without proper knowledge ▶ *n* (*pl* **-es**) estimate or conclusion reached by guessing
guessed *v* ▷ **guess**
guesses *v, n* ▷ **guess**
guessing *v* ▷ **guess**
guesswork *n* (*pl* **-s**) process or results of guessing
guessworks *n* ▷ **guesswork**
guest *n* (*pl* **-s**) person entertained at another's house or at another's expense ▶ *v* (**-s, -ing, -ed**) appear as a visiting player or performer
guested *v* ▷ **guest**
guesthouse *n* (*pl* **-s**) boarding house
guesthouses *n* ▷ **guesthouse**
guesting *v* ▷ **guest**
guests *n, v* ▷ **guest**
guff *n* (*pl* **-s**) (BRIT, AUST & NZ) (*Slang*) nonsense
guffaw *n* (*pl* **-s**) crude noisy laugh ▶ *v* (**-s, -ing, -ed**) laugh in this way
guffawed *v* ▷ **guffaw**
guffawing *v* ▷ **guffaw**
guffaws *n, v* ▷ **guffaw**
guffs *n* ▷ **guff**
guidance *n* (*pl* **-s**) leadership, instruction, or advice
guidances *n* ▷ **guidance**
guide *n* (*pl* **-s**) person who conducts tour expeditions ▶ *v* (**-s, -ing, -ed**) act as a guide for
guided *v* ▷ **guide**
guideline *n* set principle for doing something
guidelines *n* ▷ **guideline**
guides *n, v* ▷ **guide**
guiding *v* ▷ **guide**
guild *n* (*pl* **-s**) organization or club
guilder *n* (*pl* **-s**) former monetary unit of the Netherlands
guilders *n* ▷ **guilder**
guilds *n* ▷ **guild**
guile [**gile**] *n* (*pl* **-s**) cunning or deceit > **guileful** *adj* > **guileless** *adj*
guileful *adj* ▷ **guile**
guileless *adj* ▷ **guile**
guiles *n* ▷ **guile**
guillemot [**gil**-lee-mot] *n* (*pl* **-s**) black-and-white diving sea bird of N hemisphere
guillemots *n* ▷ **guillemot**
guillotine *n* (*pl* **-s**) machine for beheading people ▶ *v* (**-s, -ing, -ed**) behead by guillotine
guillotined *v* ▷ **guillotine**
guillotines *n, v* ▷ **guillotine**
guillotining *v* ▷ **guillotine**
guilt *n* (*pl* **-s**) fact or state of having done wrong
guiltier *adj* ▷ **guilty**
guiltiest *adj* ▷ **guilty**
guiltily *adv* ▷ **guilty**
guiltless *adj* innocent
guilts *n* ▷ **guilt**
guilty *adj* (**-tier, -tiest**) responsible for an offence or misdeed > **guiltily** *adv*
guinea *n* (*pl* **-s**) former British monetary unit worth 21 shillings (1.05 pounds)
guineas *n* ▷ **guinea**
guise [rhymes with **size**] *n* (*pl* **-s**) false appearance
guises *n* ▷ **guise**
guitar *n* (*pl* **-s**) stringed instrument with a flat back and a long neck, played by plucking or strumming > **guitarist** *n*
guitarist *n* ▷ **guitar**
guitarists *n* ▷ **guitar**
guitars *n* ▷ **guitar**
gulch *n* (*pl* **-es**) (US) deep narrow valley
gulches *n* ▷ **gulch**
gulf *n* (*pl* **-s**) large deep bay
gulfs *n* ▷ **gulf**
gull *n* (*pl* **-s**) long-winged sea bird
gullet *n* (*pl* **-s**) muscular tube through which food passes from the mouth to the stomach
gullets *n* ▷ **gullet**

gullibilities *n* ▷ **gullible**
gullibility *n* ▷ **gullible**
gullible *adj* easily tricked > **gullibility** *n* (*pl* **-ties**)
gullies *n* ▷ **gully**
gulls *n* ▷ **gull**
gully *n* (*pl* **-llies**) channel cut by running water
gulp *v* (**-s, -ing, -ed**) swallow hastily ▶ *n* (*pl* **-s**) gulping
gulped *v* ▷ **gulp**
gulping *v* ▷ **gulp**
gulps *v, n* ▷ **gulp**
gum¹ *n* (*pl* **-s**) firm flesh in which the teeth are set
gum² *n* (*pl* **-s**) sticky substance obtained from certain trees ▶ *v* (**-s, -mming, -mmed**) stick with gum
gumboot *n* (*pl* **-s**) (CHIEFLY BRIT) Wellington boot
gumboots *n* ▷ **gumboot**
gumdrop *n* (*pl* **-s**) hard jelly-like sweet
gumdrops *n* ▷ **gumdrop**
gummed *v* ▷ **gum²**
gummier *adj* ▷ **gummy¹, ²**
gummiest *adj* ▷ **gummy¹, ²**
gumming *v* ▷ **gum²**
gummy¹ *adj* (**-mmier, -mmiest**) toothless
gummy² *adj* (**-mmier, -mmiest**) sticky
gumption *n* (*pl* **-s**) (*Informal*) resourcefulness
gumptions *n* ▷ **gumption**
gums *n* ▷ **gum¹, ²**
gun *n* (*pl* **-s**) weapon with a metal tube from which missiles are fired by explosion ▶ *v* (**-s, -nning, -nned**) cause (an engine) to run at high speed
gunboat *n* (*pl* **-s**) small warship
gunboats *n* ▷ **gunboat**
gunge *n* (*pl* **-s**) (*Informal*) sticky unpleasant substance > **gungy** *adj* (**-gier, -giest**)
gunges *n* ▷ **gunge**
gungier *adj* ▷ **gung**
gungiest *adj* ▷ **gung**
gungy *adj* ▷ **gung**
gunman *n* (*pl* **-men**) armed criminal
gunmen *n* ▷ **gunman**
gunmetal *n* (*pl* **-s**) alloy of copper, tin, and zinc ▶ *adj* dark grey
gunmetals *n* ▷ **gunmetal**
gunned *v* ▷ **gun**
gunnel *n* ▷ **gunwale**
gunnels *n* ▷ **gunwale**
gunner *n* (*pl* **-s**) artillery soldier
gunneries *n* ▷ **gunnery**
gunners *n* ▷ **gunner**
gunnery *n* (*pl* **-ries**) use or science of large guns
gunnies *n* ▷ **gunny**
gunning *v* ▷ **gun**
gunny *n* (*pl* **-ies**) strong coarse fabric used for sacks
gunpowder *n* (*pl* **-s**) explosive mixture of potassium nitrate, sulphur, and charcoal
gunpowders *n* ▷ **gunpowder**
gunrunner *n* ▷ **gunrunning**
gunrunners *n* ▷ **gunrunning**
gunrunning *n* (*pl* **-s**) smuggling of guns and ammunition > **gunrunner** *n* (*pl* **-s**)
gunrunnings *n* ▷ **gunrunning**
guns *n, v* ▷ **gun**
gunshot *n* (*pl* **-s**) shot or range of a gun
gunshots *n* ▷ **gunshot**
gunwale, gunnel [**gun**-nel] *n* (*pl* **-s**) top of a ship's side
gunwales *n* ▷ **gunwale**
gunyah *n* (*pl* **-s**) (AUST) hut or shelter in the bush
gunyahs *n* ▷ **gunyah**
guppies *n* ▷ **guppy**
guppy *n* (*pl* **-ppies**) small colourful aquarium fish
gurgle *v* (**-les, -ling, -led**) ▶ *n* (*pl* **-s**) (make) a bubbling noise
gurgled *v* ▷ **gurgle**
gurgles *v, n* ▷ **gurgle**
gurgling *v* ▷ **gurgle**
guru *n* (*pl* **-s**) Hindu or Sikh religious teacher or leader
gurus *n* ▷ **guru**
gush *v* (**-es, -ing, -ed**) flow out suddenly and profusely ▶ *n* (*pl* **-es**) sudden copious flow
gushed *v* ▷ **gush**
gusher *n* (*pl* **-s**) spurting oil well
gushers *n* ▷ **gusher**
gushes *v, n* ▷ **gush**
gushing *v* ▷ **gush**
gusset *n* (*pl* **-s**) piece of material sewn into a garment to strengthen it
gussets *n* ▷ **gusset**
gust *n* (*pl* **-s**) sudden blast of wind ▶ *v* (**-s, -ing, -ed**) blow in gusts > **gusty** *adj* (**-tier, -tiest**)
gusted *v* ▷ **gust**
gustier *adj* ▷ **gust**
gustiest *adj* ▷ **gust**
gusting *v* ▷ **gust**
gusto *n* (*pl* **-tos**) enjoyment or zest
gustos *n* ▷ **gusto**
gusts *n, v* ▷ **gust**
gusty *adj* ▷ **gust**
gut *n* (*pl* **-s**) intestine (*Informal*) ▷ **catgut** ▶ *pl* internal organs ▶ *v* (**-s, -tting, -tted**) remove the guts from ▶ *adj* basic or instinctive
guts *n* ▷ **gut**
gutsier *adj* ▷ **gutsy**

gutsiest *adj* ▷ **gutsy**
gutsy *adj* (**-sier, -siest**) (*Informal*) courageous
gutted *adj* (BRIT, AUST & NZ) (*Informal*) disappointed and upset ▶ *v* ▷ **gut**
gutter *n* (*pl* **-s**) shallow channel for carrying away water from a roof or roadside ▶ *v* (**-s, -ing, -ed**) (of a candle) burn unsteadily, with wax running down the sides
guttered *v* ▷ **gutter**
guttering *n* material for gutters ▶ *v* ▷ **gutter**
gutters *n, v* ▷ **gutter**
guttersnipe *n* (*pl* **-s**) (BRIT) neglected slum child
guttersnipes *n* ▷ **guttersnipe**
gutting *v* ▷ **gut**
guttural *adj* (of a sound) produced at the back of the throat
guy[1] *n* (*pl* **-s**) (*Informal*) man or boy
guy[2] *n* (*pl* **-s**) rope or chain to steady or secure something
guys *n* ▷ **guy[1, 2]**
guzzle *v* (**-les, -ling, -led**) eat or drink greedily
guzzled *v* ▷ **guzzle**
guzzles *v* ▷ **guzzle**
guzzling *v* ▷ **guzzle**
gybe [jibe] *v* (**-bes, -bing, -bed**) (of a fore-and-aft sail) swing suddenly from one side to the other
gybed *v* ▷ **gybe**
gybes *v* ▷ **gybe**
gybing *v* ▷ **gybe**
gym *n* (*pl* **-s**) gymnasium
gymkhana [jim-**kah**-na] *n* (*pl* **-s**) horse-riding competition
gymkhanas *n* ▷ **gymkhana**
gymnasium *n* (*pl* **-s**) large room with equipment for physical training
gymnasiums *n* ▷ **gymnasium**
gymnast *n* (*pl* **-s**) expert in gymnastics
gymnastic *n* ▷ **gymnastics**
gymnastics *pl n* exercises to develop strength and agility > **gymnastic** *adj*
gymnasts *n* ▷ **gymnast**
gyms *n* ▷ **gym**
gynaecological *adj* ▷ **gynaecology**
gynaecologies *n* ▷ **gynaecology**
gynaecologist *n* ▷ **gynaecology**
gynaecologists *n* ▷ **gynaecology**
gynaecology [guy-nee-**kol**-la-jee] *n* (*pl* **-ies**) branch of medicine dealing with diseases and conditions specific to women > **gynaecological** *adj* > **gynaecologist** *n* (*pl* **-s**)

> **gyp** *n* (**gyps, gypping, gyped**). Gyp is a slang word meaning to cheat or swindle. This word and its inflections can be very useful when there is a word ending in Y on the board. Gyp scores 9 points.

gypsies *n* ▷ **gypsy**
gypsophila *n* (*pl* **-s**) garden plant with small white flowers
gypsophilas *n* ▷ **gypsophila**
gypsum *n* (*pl* **-s**) chalklike mineral used to make plaster of Paris
gypsums *n* ▷ **gypsum**
gypsy *n* (*pl* **-sies**) member of a travelling people found throughout Europe
gyrate [jire-**rate**] *v* (**-tes, -ting, -ted**) rotate or spiral about a point or axis > **gyration** *n* (*pl* **-s**)
gyrated *v* ▷ **gyrate**
gyrates *v* ▷ **gyrate**
gyrating *v* ▷ **gyrate**
gyration *n* ▷ **gyrate**
gyrations *n* ▷ **gyrate**
gyratory *adj* gyrating
gyrocompass *n* (*pl* **-es**) compass using a gyroscope
gyrocompasses *n* ▷ **gyrocompass**
gyroscope [**jire**-oh-skohp] *n* (*pl* **-s**) disc rotating on an axis that can turn in any direction, so the disc maintains the same position regardless of the movement of the surrounding structure > **gyroscopic** *adj*
gyroscopes *n* ▷ **gyroscope**
gyroscopic *adj* ▷ **gyroscope**

Hh

H forms a two-letter word in front of every vowel except U (and you can make **uh** with U), making it a versatile tile when you want to form words in more than one direction. As H is worth 4 points on its own, you can earn some very high scores by doing this: even **ha, he, hi** and **ho** will give 5 points each. There are lots of good short words beginning with H, like **haw, hew, how, hay, hey** and **hoy** (9 each).

ha *interj*. Ha is a sound people make to express triumph or surprise. This gives a reasonable score for a two-letter word, and is a good one to form when making a longer word in another direction at the same time. Ha scores 5 points.

haberdasher *n* (*pl* **-s**) (BRIT, AUST & NZ) dealer in small articles used for sewing **> haberdashery** *n* (*pl* **-ries**)
haberdasheries *n* ▷ **haberdasher**
haberdashers *n* ▷ **haberdasher**
haberdashery *n* ▷ **haberdasher**
habit *n* (*pl* **-s**) established way of behaving
habitable *adj* fit to be lived in
habitat *n* (*pl* **-s**) natural home of an animal or plant
habitation *n* (*pl* **-s**) (occupation of) a dwelling place
habitations *n* ▷ **habitation**
habitats *n* ▷ **habitat**
habits *n* ▷ **habit**
habitual *adj* done regularly and repeatedly **> habitually** *adv*
habitually *adv* ▷ **habitual**
habituate *v* (**-tes, -ting, -ted**) accustom **> habituation** *n* (*pl* **-s**)
habituated *v* ▷ **habituate**
habituates *v* ▷ **habituate**
habituating *v* ▷ **habituate**
habituation *n* ▷ **habituate**
habituations *n* ▷ **habituate**
habitué [hab-**it**-yew-ay] *n* (*pl* **-s**) frequent visitor to a place
habitués *n* ▷ **habitué**
hacienda [hass-ee-**end**-a] *n* (*pl* **-s**) ranch or large estate in Latin America
haciendas *n* ▷ **hacienda**
hack¹ *v* (**-s, -ing, -ed**) cut or chop violently (BRIT & NZ) (*Informal*)
hack² *n* (*pl* **-s**) (inferior) writer or journalist
hacked *v* ▷ **hack¹**
hacker *n* (*pl* **-s**) (*Slang*) computer enthusiast, esp. one who breaks into the computer system of a company or government
hackers *n* ▷ **hacker**
hacking *v* ▷ **hack¹**
hackles *pl n* hairs on the neck and back of an animal
hackney *n* (*pl* **-s**) (BRIT) taxi
hackneyed *adj* (of a word or phrase) unoriginal and overused
hackneys *n* ▷ **hackney**
hacks *v* ▷ **hack¹** ▶ *n* ▷ **hack²**
hacksaw *n* (*pl* **-s**) small saw for cutting metal
hacksaws *n* ▷ **hacksaw**
had *v* ▷ **have**
haddock *n* (*pl* **-s**) edible sea fish of N Atlantic
haddocks *n* ▷ **haddock**
hadj *n* (*pl* **-es**) ▷ **hajj**
hadjes *n* ▷ **hadj**
haematologies *n* ▷ **haematology**
haematology *n* (*pl* **-gies**) study of blood and its diseases
haemoglobin [hee-moh-**globe**-in] *n* (*pl* **-s**) protein found in red blood cells which carries oxygen
haemoglobins *n* ▷ **haemoglobin**
haemophilia [hee-moh-**fill**-lee-a] *n* (*pl* **-s**) hereditary illness in which the blood does not clot **> haemophiliac** *n* (*pl* **-s**)
haemophiliac *n* ▷ **haemophilia**
haemophiliacs *n* ▷ **haemophilia**
haemophilias *n* ▷ **haemophilia**
haemorrhage [**hem**-or-ij] *n* (*pl* **-ges**) heavy bleeding ▶ *v* (**-ges, -ging, -ged**) bleed heavily
haemorrhaged *v* ▷ **haemorrhage**
haemorrhages *n, v* ▷ **haemorrhage**

haemorrhaging *v* ▷ **haemorrhage**
haemorrhoids [**hem**-or-oydz] *pl n* swollen veins in the anus (*also* **piles**)
hafnium *n* (*pl* **-s**) (CHEM) metallic element found in zirconium ores
hafniums *n* ▷ **hafnium**
haft *n* (*pl* **-s**) handle of an axe, knife, or dagger
hafts *n* ▷ **haft**
hag *n* (*pl* **-s**) ugly old woman
haggard *adj* looking tired and ill
haggis *n* (*pl* **-es**) Scottish dish made from sheep's offal, oatmeal, suet, and seasonings, boiled in a bag made from the sheep's stomach
haggises *n* ▷ **haggis**
haggle *v* (**-les, -ling, -led**) bargain or wrangle over a price
haggled *v* ▷ **haggle**
haggles *v* ▷ **haggle**
haggling *v* ▷ **haggle**
hagiographies *n* ▷ **hagiography**
hagiography *n* (*pl* **-phies**) writing about the lives of the saints
hags *n* ▷ **hag**
hail[1] *n* (*pl* **-s**) (shower of) small pellets of ice ▶ *v* (**-s, -ing, -ed**) fall as or like hail > **hailstone** *n* (*pl* **-s**)
hail[2] *v* (**-s, -ing, -ed**) call out to, greet
hailed *v* ▷ **hail**[1, 2]
hailing *v* ▷ **hail**[1, 2]
hails *v* ▷ **hail**[1, 2] ▶ *n* ▷ **hail**[1]
hailstone *n* ▷ **hail**[1]
hailstones *n* ▷ **hail**[1]
hair *n* (*pl* **hairs**) threadlike growth on the skin
hairclip *n* (*pl* **-s**) small bent metal hairpin
hairclips *n* ▷ **hairclip**
hairdo *n* (*pl* **-s**) (*Informal*) hairstyle
hairdos *n* ▷ **hairdo**
hairdresser *n* (*pl* **-s**) person who cuts and styles hair
hairdressers *n* ▷ **hairdresser**
hairgrip *n* (BRIT) (*pl* **-s**) ▷ **hairclip**
hairgrips *n* ▷ **hairgrip**
hairier *adj* ▷ **hairy**
hairiest *adj* ▷ **hairy**
hairiness *n* ▷ **hairy**
hairinesses *n* ▷ **hairy**
hairline *n* (*pl* **-s**) edge of hair at the top of the forehead ▶ *adj* very fine or narrow
hairlines *n* ▷ **hairline**
hairpin *n* (*pl* **-s**) U-shaped wire used to hold the hair in place
hairpins *n* ▷ **hairpin**
hairs *n* ▷ **hair**
hairsplitting *n* (*pl* **-s**) ▶ *adj* making petty distinctions
hairsplittings *n* ▷ **hairsplitting**
hairstyle *n* (*pl* **-s**) cut and arrangement of a person's hair
hairstyles *n* ▷ **hairstyle**
hairy *adj* (**-rier, -riest**) covered with hair > **hairiness** *n* (*pl* **-es**)

> **haj** *n*. Haj is the same as **hajj.** This is a very useful word, especially when there isn't much space on the board. Remember that this spelling doesn't have a plural form. Haj scores 13 points.

hajj *n* (*pl* **-es**) pilgrimage a Muslim makes to Mecca
hajjes *n* ▷ **hajj**
haka *n* (*pl* **-s**) (NZ) ceremonial Maori dance with chanting
hakas *n* ▷ **haka**
hake *n* (*pl* **hakes**) edible sea fish of N hemisphere (AUST) ▷ **barracouta**
hakea [**hah**-kee-a] *n* (*pl* **-s**) Australian tree or shrub with hard woody fruit
hakeas *n* ▷ **hakea**
hakes *n* ▷ **hake**
halal *n* (*pl* **-s**) meat from animals slaughtered according to Muslim law
halals *n* ▷ **halal**
halberd *n* (*pl* **-s**) (HIST) spear with an axe blade
halberds *n* ▷ **halberd**
halcyon [**hal**-see-on] *adj* peaceful and happy
hale *adj* (**-ler, -lest**) healthy, robust
haler *adj* ▷ **hale**
halest *adj* ▷ **hale**
half *n* (*pl* **-lves**) either of two equal parts ▶ *adj* denoting one of two equal parts ▶ *adv* to the extent of half
halfhearted *adj* unenthusiastic
halflife *n* (*pl* **-ves**) time taken for half the atoms in radioactive material to decay
halflives *n* ▷ **halflife**
halfpennies *n* ▷ **halfpenny**
halfpenny [**hayp**-nee] *n* (*pl* **-nnies**) former British coin worth half an old penny
halftime *n* (*pl* **-s**) (SPORT) short rest period between two halves of a game
halftimes *n* ▷ **halftime**
halftone *n* (*pl* **-s**) illustration showing lights and shadows by means of very small dots
halftones *n* ▷ **halftone**
halfway *adv, adj* at or to half the distance
halfwit *n* (*pl* **-s**) foolish or stupid person
halfwits *n* ▷ **halfwit**
halibut *n* (*pl* **halibuts**) large edible flatfish of N Atlantic
halibuts *n* ▷ **halibut**

halitosis *n* (*pl* **-ises**) unpleasant-smelling breath
halitosises *n* ▷ **halitosis**
hall *n* (*pl* **-s**) (*also* **hallway**) entrance passage
hallelujah [hal-ee-**loo**-ya] *interj* exclamation of praise to God
hallmark *n* (*pl* **-s**) typical feature ▶ *v* (**-s, -ing, -ed**) stamp with a hallmark
hallmarked *v* ▷ **hallmark**
hallmarking *v* ▷ **hallmark**
hallmarks *n, v* ▷ **hallmark**
hallo *interj* ▷ **hello**
hallowed *adj* regarded as holy
Halloween, Hallowe'en *n* (*pl* **-s**) October 31, celebrated by children by dressing up as ghosts, witches, etc.
Halloweens *n* ▷ **Halloween**
halls *n* ▷ **hall**
hallucinate *v* (**-tes, -ting, -ted**) seem to see something that is not really there > **hallucination** *n* (*pl* **-s**) > **hallucinatory** *adj*
hallucinated *v* ▷ **hallucinate**
hallucinates *v* ▷ **hallucinate**
hallucinating *v* ▷ **hallucinate**
hallucination *n* ▷ **hallucinate**
hallucinations *n* ▷ **hallucinate**
hallucinatory *adj* ▷ **hallucinate**
hallucinogen *n* (*pl* **-s**) drug that causes hallucinations > **hallucinogenic** *adj*
hallucinogenic *adj* ▷ **hallucinogen**
hallucinogens *n* ▷ **hallucinogen**
halo [**hay**-loh] *n* (*pl* **-loes, -los**) ring of light round the head of a sacred figure
haloes *n* ▷ **halo**
halogen [**hal**-oh-jen] *n* (*pl* **-s**) (CHEM) any of a group of nonmetallic elements including chlorine and iodine
halogens *n* ▷ **halogen**
halos *n* ▷ **halo**
halt *v* (**-s, -ing, -ed**) come or bring to a stop ▶ *n* (*pl* **-s**) temporary stop
halted *v* ▷ **halt**
halter *n* (*pl* **-s**) strap round a horse's head with a rope to lead it with
halterneck *n* (*pl* **-s**) woman's top or dress with a strap fastened at the back of the neck
halternecks *n* ▷ **halterneck**
halters *n* ▷ **halter**
halting *adj* hesitant, uncertain ▶ *v* ▷ **halt**
halts *v, n* ▷ **halt**
halve *v* (**-ves, -ving, -ved**) divide in half
halved *v* ▷ **halve**
halves *v* ▷ **halve** ▶ *n* ▷ **half**
halving *v* ▷ **halve**
halyard *n* (*pl* **-s**) rope for raising a ship's sail or flag
halyards *n* ▷ **halyard**
ham[1] *n* (*pl* **-s**) smoked or salted meat from a pig's thigh
ham[2] (*Informal*) *n* (*pl* **-s**) amateur radio operator ▶ *v* (**-s, -mming, -mmed**) overact
hamburger *n* (*pl* **-s**) minced beef shaped into a flat disc, cooked and usu. served in a bread roll
hamburgers *n* ▷ **hamburger**
hamlet *n* (*pl* **-s**) small village
hamlets *n* ▷ **hamlet**
hammed *v* ▷ **ham**[2]
hammer *n* (*pl* **-s**) tool with a heavy metal head and a wooden handle, used to drive in nails etc. ▶ *v* (**-s, -ing, -ed**) hit (as if) with a hammer
hammered *v* ▷ **hammer**
hammerhead *n* (*pl* **-s**) shark with a wide flattened head
hammerheads *n* ▷ **hammerhead**
hammering *v* ▷ **hammer**
hammers *n, v* ▷ **hammer**
hamming *v* ▷ **ham**[2]
hammock *n* (*pl* **-s**) hanging bed made of canvas or net
hammocks *n* ▷ **hammock**
hamper[1] *v* (**-s, -ing, -ed**) make it difficult for (someone or something) to move or progress
hamper[2] *n* (*pl* **-s**) large basket with a lid
hampered *v* ▷ **hamper**[1]
hampering *v* ▷ **hamper**[1]
hampers *v, n* ▷ **hamper**[1, 2]
hams *n, v* ▷ **ham**[1, 2]
hamster *n* (*pl* **-s**) small rodent with a short tail and cheek pouches
hamsters *n* ▷ **hamster**
hamstring *n* (*pl* **-s**) tendon at the back of the knee ▶ *v* (**-s, -ing, -rung**) make it difficult for (someone) to take any action
hamstringing *v* ▷ **hamstring**
hamstrings *n, v* ▷ **hamstring**
hamstrung *v* ▷ **hamstring**
hand *n* (*pl* **-s**) part of the body at the end of the arm, consisting of a palm, four fingers, and a thumb ▶ *v* (**-s, -ing, -ed**) pass, give
handbag *n* (*pl* **-s**) woman's small bag for carrying personal articles in
handbags *n* ▷ **handbag**
handbill *n* (*pl* **-s**) small printed notice
handbills *n* ▷ **handbill**
handbook *n* (*pl* **-s**) small reference or instruction book
handbooks *n* ▷ **handbook**
handcuff *n* (*pl* **-s**) one of a linked pair of metal rings designed to be locked round a

prisoner's wrists by the police ▶ *v* (**-s, -ing, -ed**) put handcuffs on
handcuffed *v* ▷ **handcuff**
handcuffing *v* ▷ **handcuff**
handcuffs *n, v* ▷ **handcuff**
handed *v* ▷ **hand**
handful *n* (*pl* **-s**) amount that can be held in the hand
handfuls *n* ▷ **handful**
handheld *adj* (*of a film camera*) held rather than mounted, as in close-up action shots ▶ *n* (*pl* **-s**) computer that can be held in the hand
handhelds *n* ▷ **handheld**
handicap *n* (*pl* **-s**) physical or mental disability ▶ *v* (**-s, -pping, -pped**) make it difficult for (someone) to do something
handicapped *v* ▷ **handicap**
handicapping *v* ▷ **handicap**
handicaps *n, v* ▷ **handicap**
handicraft *n* (*pl* **-s**) objects made by hand
handicrafts *n* ▷ **handicraft**
handier *adj* ▷ **handy**
handiest *adj* ▷ **handy**
handily *adv* ▷ **handy**
handing *v* ▷ **hand**
handiwork *n* (*pl* **-s**) result of someone's work or activity
handiworks *n* ▷ **handiwork**
handkerchief *n* (*pl* **-s**) small square of fabric used to wipe the nose
handkerchiefs *n* ▷ **handkerchief**
handle *n* (*pl* **-s**) part of an object that is held so that it can be used ▶ *v* (**-les, -ling, -led**) hold, feel, or move with the hands
handlebars *pl n* curved metal bar used to steer a cycle
handled *v* ▷ **handle**
handler *n* (*pl* **-s**) person who controls an animal
handlers *n* ▷ **handler**
handles *n, v* ▷ **handle**
handling *v* ▷ **handle**
handout *n* (*pl* **-s**) clothing, food, or money given to a needy person
handouts *n* ▷ **handout**
hands *n, v* ▷ **hand**
handsome *adj* (esp. of a man) good-looking
handstand *n* (*pl* **-s**) act of supporting the body on the hands in an upside-down position
handstands *n* ▷ **handstand**
handwriting *n* (*pl* **-s**) (style of) writing by hand
handwritings *n* ▷ **handwriting**
handy *adj* (**-dier, -diest**) convenient, useful > **handily** *adv*
handyman *n* (*pl* **-men**) man who is good at making or repairing things
handymen *n* ▷ **handyman**
hang *v* (**-s, -ing, hung** *or* **hanged**) attach or be attached at the top with the lower part free
hangar *n* (*pl* **-s**) large shed for storing aircraft
hangars *n* ▷ **hangar**
hangdog *adj* guilty, ashamed
hanged *v* ▷ **hang**
hanger *n* (*pl* **-s**) curved piece of wood, wire, or plastic, with a hook, for hanging up clothes (*also* **coat hanger**)
hangers *n* ▷ **hanger**
hangi *n* (*pl* **-gi, -gis**) (NZ) Maori oven consisting of a hole in the ground filled with hot stones
hanging *v* ▷ **hang**
hangis *n* ▷ **hangi**
hangman *n* (*pl* **-men**) man who executes people by hanging
hangmen *n* ▷ **hangman**
hangover *n* (*pl* **-s**) headache and nausea as a result of drinking too much alcohol
hangovers *n* ▷ **hangover**
hangs *v* ▷ **hang**
hangup *n* (*pl* **-s**) (*Informal*) emotional or psychological problem
hangups *n* ▷ **hangup**
hank *n* (*pl* **-s**) coil, esp. of yarn
hanker *v* (**-s, -ing, -ed**) (*foll. by* **after** *or* **for**) desire intensely
hankered *v* ▷ **hanker**
hankering *v* ▷ **hanker**
hankers *v* ▷ **hanker**
hankie *n* ▷ **hanky**
hankies *n* ▷ **hanky**
hanks *n* ▷ **hank**
hanky, hankie *n* (*pl* **hankies**) (*Informal*) handkerchief
haphazard *adj* not organized or planned > **haphazardly** *adv*
haphazardly *adv* ▷ **haphazard**
hapless *adj* unlucky
happen *v* (**-s, -ing, -ed**) take place, occur
happened *v* ▷ **happen**
happening *n* (*pl* **-s**) event, occurrence ▶ *v* ▷ **happen**
happenings *n* ▷ **happening**
happens *v* ▷ **happen**
happier *adj* ▷ **happy**
happiest *adj* ▷ **happy**
happily *adv* ▷ **happy**
happiness *n* ▷ **happy**
happinesses *n* ▷ **happiness**
happy *adj* (**-ppier, -ppiest**) feeling or causing joy > **happily** *adv* > **happiness** *n* (*pl* **-es**)
harangue *v* (**-gues, -guing, -gued**) address

angrily or forcefully ▶ *n* (*pl* **-gues**) angry or forceful speech
harangued *v* ▷ **harangue**
harangues *v, n* ▷ **harangue**
haranguing *v* ▷ **harangue**
harass *v* (**-es, -ing, -ssed**) annoy or trouble constantly > **harassed** *adj* > **harassment** *n* (*pl* **-s**)
harassed *v, adj* ▷ **harass**
harasses *v* ▷ **harass**
harassing *v* ▷ **harass**
harassment *n* ▷ **harrass**
harassments *n* ▷ **harassment**
harbinger [**har**-binj-a] *n* (*pl* **-s**) someone or something that announces the approach of something
harbingers *n* ▷ **harbinger**
harbour *n* (*pl* **-s**) sheltered port ▶ *v* (**-s, -ing, -ed**) maintain secretly in the mind
harboured *v* ▷ **harbour**
harbouring *v* ▷ **harbour**
harbours *n, v* ▷ **harbour**
hard *adj* firm, solid, or rigid ▶ *adv* with great energy or effort > **harden** *v* (**-s, -ing, -ed**) > **hardness** *n* (*pl* **-es**)
hardboard *n* (*pl* ▷ **-s**) thin stiff board made of compressed sawdust and wood chips
hardboards *n* ▷ **hardboard**
harden *v* ▷ **hard**
hardened *v* ▷ **hard**
hardening *v* ▷ **hard**
hardens *v* ▷ **hard**
hardfill *n* (*pl* **-s**) (NZ & S AFR) stone waste material used for landscaping
hardfills *n* ▷ **hardfill**
hardheaded *adj* shrewd, practical
hardhearted *adj* unsympathetic, uncaring
hardier *adj* ▷ **hardy**
hardiest *adj* ▷ **hardy**
hardiness *n* ▷ **hardy**
hardinesses *n* ▷ **hardy**
hardly *adv* scarcely or not at all
hardness *n* ▷ **hard**
hardnesses *n* ▷ **hard**
hardship *n* (*pl* **-s**) suffering
hardships *n* ▷ **hardship**
hardware *n* (*pl* **-s**) metal tools or implements
hardwares *n* ▷ **hardware**
hardwood *n* (*pl* **-s**) wood of a broadleaved tree such as oak or ash
hardwoods *n* ▷ **hardwood**
hardy *adj* (**-dier, -diest**) able to stand difficult conditions > **hardiness** *n* (*pl* **-es**)
hare *n* (*pl* **-s**) animal like a large rabbit, with longer ears and legs ▶ *v* (**-res, -ring, -red**) (*usu. foll. by* **off**) run (away) quickly
harebell *n* (*pl* **-s**) blue bell-shaped flower
harebells *n* ▷ **harebell**
harebrained *adj* foolish or impractical
hared *v* ▷ **hare**
harelip *n* (*pl* **-s**) slight split in the upper lip
harelips *n* ▷ **harelip**
harem *n* (*pl* **-s**) (apartments of) a Muslim man's wives and concubines
harems *n* ▷ **harem**
hares *v, n* ▷ **hare**
haring *v* ▷ **hare**
hark *v* (**-s, -ing, -ed**) (*Old-fashioned*) listen
harked *v* ▷ **hark**
harking *v* ▷ **hark**
harks *v* ▷ **hark**
harlequin *n* (*pl* **-s**) stock comic character with a diamond-patterned costume and mask ▶ *adj* in many colours
harlequins *n* ▷ **harlequin**
harlot *n* (*pl* **-s**) (*Lit*) prostitute
harlots *n* ▷ **harlot**
harm *v* (**-s, -ing, -ed**) injure physically, mentally, or morally ▶ *n* (*pl* **-s**) physical, mental, or moral injury > **harmful** *adj* > **harmless** *adj*
harmed *v* ▷ **harm**
harmful *adj* ▷ **harm**
harming *v* ▷ **harm**
harmless *adj* ▷ **harm**
harmonic *adj* of harmony
harmonica *n* (*pl* **-s**) small wind instrument played by sucking and blowing
harmonicas *n* ▷ **harmonica**
harmonics *n* science of musical sounds
harmonies *n* ▷ **harmony**
harmonious *adj* ▷ **harmony**
harmoniously *adv* ▷ **harmony**
harmonium *n* (*pl* **-s**) keyboard instrument like a small organ
harmoniums *n* ▷ **harmonium**
harmonization *v* ▷ **harmonize**
harmonizations *v* ▷ **harmonize**
harmonize *v* (**-zes, -zing, -zed**) blend well together > **harmonization** *n* (*pl* **-s**)
harmonized *v* ▷ **harmonize**
harmonizes *v* ▷ **harmonize**
harmonizing *v* ▷ **harmonize**
harmony *n* (*pl* **-nies**) peaceful agreement and cooperation > **harmonious** *adj* > **harmoniously** *adv*
harms *v, n* ▷ **harm**
harness *n* (*pl* **-es**) arrangement of straps for attaching a horse to a cart or plough ▶ *v* (**-es, -ing, -ed**) put a harness on

harnessed *v* ▷ **harness**
harnesses *n, v* ▷ **harness**
harnessing *v* ▷ **harness**
harp *n* (*pl* **-s**) large triangular stringed instrument played with the fingers > **harpist** *n* (*pl* **-s**)
harpies *n* ▷ **harpy**
harpist *n* ▷ **harp**
harpists *n* ▷ **harp**
harpoon *n* (*pl* **-s**) barbed spear attached to a rope used for hunting whales ▶ *v* (**-s, -ing, -ed**) spear with a harpoon
harpooned *v* ▷ **harpoon**
harpooning *v* ▷ **harpoon**
harpoons *n, v* ▷ **harpoon**
harps *n* ▷ **harp**
harpsichord *n* (*pl* **-s**) stringed keyboard instrument
harpsichords *n* ▷ **harpsichord**
harpy *n* (*pl* **-pies**) nasty or bad-tempered woman
harridan *n* (*pl* **-s**) nagging or vicious woman
harridans *n* ▷ **harridan**
harried *v* ▷ **harry**
harrier *n* (*pl* **-s**) cross-country runner
harriers *n* ▷ **harrier**
harries *v* ▷ **harry**
harrow *n* (*pl* **-s**) implement used to break up lumps of soil ▶ *v* (**-s, -ing, -ed**) draw a harrow over
harrowed *v* ▷ **harrow**
harrowing *adj* very distressing ▶ *v* ▷ **harrow**
harrows *n, v* ▷ **harrow**
harry *v* (**-rries, -rrying, -rried**) keep asking (someone) to do something, pester
harrying *v* ▷ **harry**
harsh *adj* severe and difficult to cope with > **harshly** *adv* > **harshness** *n* (*pl* **-es**)
harshly *adv* ▷ **harsh**
harshness *n* ▷ **harsh**
harshnesses *n* ▷ **harsh**
hart *n* (*pl* **-s**) adult male deer
harts *n* ▷ **hart**
harvest *n* (*pl* **-s**) (season for) the gathering of crops ▶ *v* (**-s, -ing, -ed**) gather (a ripened crop) > **harvester** *n* (*pl* **-s**)
harvested *v* ▷ **harvest**
harvester *n* ▷ **harvest**
harvesters *n* ▷ **harvest**
harvesting *v* ▷ **harvest**
harvests *n, v* ▷ **harvest**
has *v* ▷ **have**
hash[1] *n* (*pl* **-es**) dish of diced cooked meat and vegetables reheated
hash[2] *n* (*pl* **-es**) (*Informal*) hashish
hashes *n* ▷ **hash**[1, 2]
hashish [**hash**-eesh] *n* (*pl* **-es**) drug made from the cannabis plant, smoked for its intoxicating effects
hashishes *n* ▷ **hashish**
hasp *n* (*pl* **-s**) clasp that fits over a staple and is secured by a bolt or padlock, used as a fastening
hasps *n* ▷ **hasp**
hassle (*Informal*) *n* (*pl* **-s**) trouble, bother ▶ *v* (**-les, -ling, -led**) bother or annoy
hassled *v* ▷ **hassle**
hassles *n, v* ▷ **hassle**
hassling *v* ▷ **hassle**
hassock *n* (*pl* **-s**) cushion for kneeling on in church
hassocks *n* ▷ **hassock**
haste *n* (*pl* **-s**) (excessive) quickness
hasten *v* (**-s, -ing, -ed**) (cause to) hurry
hastened *v* ▷ **hasten**
hastening *n* ▷ **hasten**
hastens *n* ▷ **hasten**
hastes *n* ▷ **haste**
hastier *adj* ▷ **hasty**
hastiest *adj* ▷ **hasty**
hastily *adv* ▷ **hasty**
hasty *adj* (**-tier, -tiest**) (too) quick > **hastily** *adv*
hat *n* (*pl* **-s**) covering for the head, often with a brim, usu. worn to give protection from the weather
hatch[1] *v* (**-es, -ing, -ed**) (cause to) emerge from an egg
hatch[2] *n* (*pl* **-es**) hinged door covering an opening in a floor or wall
hatchback *n* (*pl* **-s**) car with a lifting door at the back
hatchbacks *n* ▷ **hatchback**
hatched *v* ▷ **hatch**[1]
hatches *v* ▷ **hatch**[1] ▶ *n* ▷ **hatch**[2]
hatchet *n* (*pl* **-s**) small axe
hatchets *n* ▷ **hatchet**
hatching *v* ▷ **hatch**[1]
hatchway *n* (*pl* **-s**) opening in the deck of a ship
hatchways *n* ▷ **hatchway**
hate *v* (**-tes, -ting, -ted**) dislike intensely ▶ *n* (*pl* **-s**) intense dislike > **hater** *n* (*pl* **-s**)
hated *v* ▷ **hate**
hateful *adj* causing or deserving hate
hater *n* ▷ **hate**
haters *n* ▷ **hate**
hates *v, n* ▷ **hate**
hating *v* ▷ **hate**
hatred *n* (*pl* **-s**) intense dislike
hatreds *n* ▷ **hatred**

hats *n* ▷ **hat**
haughtier *adj* ▷ **haughty**
haughtiest *adj* ▷ **haughty**
haughtily *adv* ▷ **haughty**
haughtiness *n* ▷ **haughty**
haughtinesses *n* ▷ **haughty**
haughty *adj* (**-tier, -tiest**) proud, arrogant > **haughtily** *adv* > **haughtiness** *n* (*pl* **-es**)
haul *v* (**-s, -ing, -ed**) pull or drag with effort ▶ *n* (*pl* **-s**) amount gained by effort or theft
haulage *n* (*pl* **-s**) (charge for) transporting goods
haulages *n* ▷ **haulage**
hauled *v* ▷ **haul**
haulier *n* (*pl* **-s**) firm or person that transports goods by road
hauliers *n* ▷ **haulier**
hauling *v* ▷ **haul**
hauls *v, n* ▷ **haul**
haunch *n* (*pl* **-es**) human hip or fleshy hindquarter of an animal
haunches *n* ▷ **haunch**
haunt *v* (**-s, -ing, -ed**) visit in the form of a ghost ▶ *n* (*pl* **-s**) place visited frequently
haunted *adj* frequented by ghosts ▶ *v* ▷ **haunt**
haunting *adj* memorably beautiful or sad ▶ *v* ▷ **haunt**
haunts *v, n* ▷ **haunt**
hauteur [oat-**ur**] *n* (*pl* **-s**) haughtiness
hauteurs *n* ▷ **hauteur**
have *v* (**has, having, had**) possess, hold
haven *n* (*pl* **-s**) place of safety
havens *n* ▷ **haven**
haversack *n* (*pl* **-s**) canvas bag carried on the back or shoulder
haversacks *n* ▷ **haversack**
having *v* ▷ **have**
havoc *n* (*pl* **-s**) disorder and confusion
havocs *n* ▷ **havoc**
haw *n* (*pl* **-s**) hawthorn berry
hawk[1] *n* (*pl* **-s**) bird of prey with a short hooked bill and very good eyesight > **hawkish, hawklike** *adj*
hawk[2] *v* (**-s, -ing, -ed**) offer (goods) for sale in the street or door-to-door > **hawker** *n* (*pl* **-s**)
hawk[3] *v* (**-s, -ing, -ed**) cough noisily
hawked *v* ▷ **hawk**[2,3]
hawker *n* ▷ **hawk**[2]
hawkers *n* ▷ **hawk**[2]
hawk-eyed *adj* having very good eyesight
hawking *v* ▷ **hawk**[2,3]
hawkish *adj* ▷ **hawk**[1]
hawks *n* ▷ **hawk**[1] ▶ *v* ▷ **hawk**[2,3]
hawlike *adj* ▷ **hawk**[1]
haws *n* ▷ **haw**
hawser *n* (*pl* **-s**) large rope used on a ship
hawsers *n* ▷ **hawser**
hawthorn *n* (*pl* **-s**) thorny shrub or tree
hawthorns *n* ▷ **hawthorn**
hay *n* (*pl* **hays**) grass cut and dried as fodder
hays *n* ▷ **hay**
haystack *n* (*pl* **-s**) large pile of stored hay
haystacks *n* ▷ **haystack**
haywire *adj* (*Informal*) not functioning properly
hazard *n* (*pl* **-s**) something that could be dangerous ▶ *v* (**-s, -ing, -ed**) put in danger > **hazardous** *adj*
hazarded *v* ▷ **hazard**
hazarding *v* ▷ **hazard**
hazardous *adj* ▷ **hazard**
hazards *n, v* ▷ **hazard**
haze *n* (*pl* **-s**) mist, often caused by heat
hazel *n* (*pl* **-s**) small tree producing edible nuts ▶ *adj* (of eyes) greenish-brown > **hazelnut** *n* (*pl* **-s**)
hazelnut *n* ▷ **hazel**
hazelnuts *n* ▷ **hazel**
hazels *n* ▷ **hazel**
hazes *n* ▷ **haze**
hazier *adj* ▷ **hazy**
haziest *adj* ▷ **hazy**
hazy *adj* (**-zier, -ziest**) not clear, misty
he *pron* refers to: male person or animal ▶ *n* (*pl* **-s**) male person or animal
head *n* (*pl* **-s**) upper or front part of the body, containing the sense organs and the brain ▶ *adj* chief, principal ▶ *v* (**-s, -ing, -ed**) be at the top or front of
headache *n* (*pl* **-s**) continuous pain in the head
headaches *n* ▷ **headache**
headboard *n* (*pl* **-s**) vertical board at the top end of a bed
headboards *n* ▷ **headboard**
headdress *n* (*pl* **-s**) decorative head covering
headdresses *n* ▷ **headdress**
headed *v* ▷ **head**
header *n* (*pl* **-s**) striking a ball with the head
headers *n* ▷ **header**
headhunt *v* (**-s, -ing, -ed**) (of a company) approach and offer a job to (a person working for a rival company) > **headhunter** *n* (*pl* **-s**)
headhunted *v* ▷ **headhunt**
headhunter *n* ▷ **headhunt**
headhunters *n* ▷ **headhunt**
headhunting *v* ▷ **headhunt**
headhunts *v* ▷ **headhunt**
headier *adj* ▷ **heady**
headiest *adj* ▷ **heady**
heading *n* (*pl* **-s**) title written or printed at the top of a page ▶ *v* ▷ **head**

headings *n* ▷ **heading**
headland *n* (*pl* **-s**) area of land jutting out into the sea
headlands *n* ▷ **headland**
headlight *n* (*pl* **-s**) powerful light on the front of a vehicle
headlights *n* ▷ **headlight**
headline *n* (*pl* **-s**) title at the top of a newspaper article, esp. on the front page
headlines *n* ▷ **headline** ▶ *pl n* main points of a news broadcast
headlong *adv, adj* with the head first
headphones *pl n* two small loudspeakers held against the ears
headquarters *pl n* centre from which operations are directed
heads *adv* (*Informal*) with the side of a coin which has a portrait of a head on it uppermost ▶ *n, v* ▷ **head**
headstone *n* (*pl* **-s**) memorial stone on a grave
headstones *n* ▷ **headstone**
headstrong *adj* self-willed, obstinate
headway *n* (*pl* **-s**) progress
headways *n* ▷ **headway**
headwind *n* (*pl* **-s**) wind blowing against the course of an aircraft or ship
headwinds *n* ▷ **headwind**
heady *adj* (**-dier, -diest**) intoxicating or exciting
heal *v* (**-s, -ing, -ed**) make or become well > **healer** *n* (*pl* **-s**)
healed *v* ▷ **heal**
healer *n* ▷ **heal**
healers *n* ▷ **heal**
healing *v* ▷ **heal**
heals *v* ▷ **heal**
health *n* (*pl* **-s**) normal (good) condition of someone's body
healthier *adj* ▷ **healthy**
healthiest *adj* ▷ **healthy**
healthily *adv* ▷ **healthy**
healths *n* ▷ **health**
healthy *adj* (**-thier, -thiest**) having good health > **healthily** *adv*
heap *n* (*pl* **-s**) pile of things one on top of another ▶ *v* (**-s, -ing, -ed**) gather into a pile
heaped *v* ▷ **heap**
heaping *v* ▷ **heap**
heaps *n, v* ▷ **heap**
hear *v* (**-s, -ing, heard**) perceive (a sound) by ear > **hearer** *n* (*pl* **-s**)
heard *v* ▷ **hear**
hearer *n* ▷ **hear**
hearers *n* ▷ **hear**
hearing *n* (*pl* **-s**) ability to hear ▶ *v* ▷ **hear**
hearings *n* ▷ **hearing**
hears *v* ▷ **hear**
hearsay *n* (*pl* **-s**) gossip, rumour
hearsays *n* ▷ **hearsay**
hearse *n* (*pl* **-s**) funeral car used to carry a coffin
hearses *n* ▷ **hearse**
heart *n* (*pl* **-s**) organ that pumps blood round the body
heartache *n* (*pl* **-s**) intense anguish
heartaches *n* ▷ **heartache**
heartbeat *n* (*pl* **-s**) one complete pulsation of the heart
heartbeats *n* ▷ **heartbeat**
heartbreak *n* (*pl* **-s**) intense grief
heartbreaks *n* ▷ **heartbreak**
heartburn *n* (*pl* **-s**) burning sensation in the chest caused by indigestion
heartburns *n* ▷ **heartburn**
hearten *v* (**-s, -ing, -ed**) encourage, make cheerful
heartened *v* ▷ **hearten**
heartening *v* ▷ **hearten**
heartens *v* ▷ **hearten**
heartfelt *adj* felt sincerely or strongly
hearth *n* (*pl* **-s**) floor of a fireplace
hearths *n* ▷ **hearth**
heartier *adj* ▷ **hearty**
heartiest *adj* ▷ **hearty**
heartily *adv* ▷ **hearty**
heartless *adj* cruel, unkind
heartrending *adj* causing great sorrow
hearts *n* ▷ **heart**
heartthrob *n* (*pl* **-s**) (*Slang*) very attractive man, esp. a film or pop star
heartthrobs *n* ▷ **heartthrob**
hearty *adj* (**-tier, -tiest**) substantial, nourishing > **heartily** *adv*
heat *v* (**-s, -ing, -ed**) make or become hot ▶ *n* (*pl* **-s**) state of being hot > **heater** *n* (*pl* **-s**)
heated *v* ▷ **heat** ▶ *adj* angry and excited > **heatedly** *adv*
heatedly *adv* ▷ **heated**
heater *n* ▷ **heat**
heaters *n* ▷ **heat**
heath *n* (*pl* **-s**) (BRIT) area of open uncultivated land
heathen *adj, n* (*pl* **-s**) (of) a person who does not believe in an established religion
heathens *n* ▷ **heathen**
heather *n* (*pl* **-s**) low-growing plant with small purple, pinkish, or white flowers, growing on heaths and mountains
heathers *n* ▷ **heather**
heaths *n* ▷ **heath**
heating *v* ▷ **heat**

heats *v, n* ▷ **heat**
heave *v* (**-ves, -ving, -ved**) lift with effort ▶ *n* (*pl* **-s**) heaving
heaved *v* ▷ **heave**
heaven *n* (*pl* **-s**) place believed to be the home of God, where good people go when they die
heavenly *adj* of or like heaven
heavens *n* ▷ **heaven**
heaves *v, n* ▷ **heave**
heavier *adj* ▷ **heavy**
heaviest *adj* ▷ **heavy**
heavily *adv* ▷ **heavy**
heaviness *n* ▷ **heavy**
heavinesses *n* ▷ **heavy**
heaving *v* ▷ **heave**
heavy *adj* (**-vier, -viest**) of great weight > **heavily** *adv* > **heaviness** *n* (*pl* **-es**)
heavyweight *n* (*pl* **-s**) boxer weighing over 175lb (professional) or 81kg (amateur)
heavyweights *n* ▷ **heavyweight**
heckle *v* (**-les, -ling, -led**) interrupt (a public speaker) with comments, questions, or taunts > **heckler** *n* (*pl* **-s**)
heckled *v* ▷ **heckle**
heckler *n* ▷ **heckle**
hecklers *n* ▷ **heckle**
heckles *v* ▷ **heckle**
heckling *v* ▷ **heckle**
hectare *n* (*pl* **-s**) one hundred ares or 10 000 square metres (2.471 acres)
hectares *n* ▷ **hectare**
hectic *adj* rushed or busy
hector *v* (**-s, -ing, -ed**) bully
hectored *v* ▷ **hector**
hectoring *v* ▷ **hector**
hectors *v* ▷ **hector**
hedge *n* (*pl* **-s**) row of bushes forming a barrier or boundary ▶ *v* (**-ges, -ging, -ged**) be evasive or noncommittal
hedged *v* ▷ **hedge**
hedgehog *n* (*pl* **-s**) small mammal with a protective covering of spines
hedgehogs *n* ▷ **hedgehog**
hedgerow *n* (*pl* **-s**) bushes forming a hedge
hedgerows *n* ▷ **hedgerow**
hedges *n, v* ▷ **hedge**
hedging *v* ▷ **hedge**
hedonism *n* (*pl* **-s**) doctrine that pleasure is the most important thing in life > **hedonist** *n* (*pl* **-s**) > **hedonistic** *adj*
hedonisms *n* ▷ **hedonism**
hedonist *n* ▷ **hedonism**
hedonistic *n* ▷ **hedonism**
hedonists *n* ▷ **hedonism**
heed *n* (*pl* **-s**) careful attention ▶ *v* (**-s, -ing, -ed**) pay careful attention to
heeded *v* ▷ **heed**
heeding *v* ▷ **heed**
heedless *adj* taking no notice of
heeds *v, n* ▷ **heed**
heel[1] *n* (*pl* **-s**) back part of the foot ▶ *v* (**-s, -ing, -ed**) repair the heel of (a shoe)
heel[2] *v* (**-s, -ing, -ed**) (*foll. by* **over**) lean to one side
heeled *v* ▷ **heel**[1, 2]
heeler *n* (*pl* **-s**) (AUST & NZ) dog that herds cattle by biting at their heels
heelers *n* ▷ **heeler**
heeling *v* ▷ **heel**[1, 2]
heels *n* ▷ **heel**[1] ▶ *v* ▷ **heel**[1, 2]
heftier *adj* ▷ **hefty**
heftiest *adj* ▷ **hefty**
hefty *adj* (**-tier, -tiest**) large, heavy, or strong
hegemonies *n* ▷ **hegemony**
hegemony [hig-**em**-on-ee] *n* (*pl* **-nies**) political domination
hegira *n* (*pl* **-s**) Mohammed's flight from Mecca to Medina in 622 AD
hegiras *n* ▷ **hegira**
heifer [**hef**-fer] *n* (*pl* **-s**) young cow
heifers *n* ▷ **heifer**
height *n* (*pl* **-s**) distance from base to top
heighten *v* (**-s, -ing, -ed**) make or become higher or more intense
heightened *v* ▷ **heighten**
heightening *v* ▷ **heighten**
heightens *v* ▷ **heighten**
heights *n* ▷ **height**
heinous *adj* evil and shocking
heir *n* (*pl* **-s**) person entitled to inherit property or rank > **heiress** *n fem* (*pl* **-es**)
heiresses *n* ▷ **heiress**
heirloom *n* (*pl* **-s**) object that has belonged to a family for generations
heirlooms *n* ▷ **heirloom**
heirs *n* ▷ **heir**
held *v* ▷ **hold**[1]
helical *adj* spiral
helices *n* ▷ **helix**
helicopter *n* (*pl* **-s**) aircraft lifted and propelled by rotating overhead blades
helicopters *n* ▷ **helicopter**
heliotrope *n* (*pl* **-s**) plant with purple flowers ▶ *adj* light purple
heliotropes *n* ▷ **heliotrope**
heliport *n* (*pl* **-s**) airport for helicopters
heliports *n* ▷ **heliport**
helium [**heel**-ee-um] *n* (*pl* **-s**) (CHEM) very light colourless odourless gas
heliums *n* ▷ **helium**

helix [**heel**-iks] *n* (*pl* **-ices, -ixes**) spiral
helixes *n* ▷ **helix**
hell *n* (*pl* **-s**) place believed to be where wicked people go when they die > **hellish** *adj*
hellbent *adj* (*foll. by* **on**) intent
hellish *adj* ▷ **hell**
hello *interj* expression of greeting or surprise
hells *n* ▷ **hell**
helm *n* (*pl* **-s**) tiller or wheel for steering a ship
helmet *n* (*pl* **-s**) hard hat worn for protection
helmets *n* ▷ **helmet**
helms *n* ▷ **helm**
help *v* (**-s, -ing, -ed**) make something easier, better, or quicker for (someone) ▶ *n* (*pl* **-s**) assistance or support > **helper** *n* (*pl* **-s**) > **helpful** *adj*
helped *v* ▷ **help**
helper *n* ▷ **help**
helpers *n* ▷ **help**
helpful *adj* ▷ **help**
helping *n* (*pl* **-s**) single portion of food ▶ *v* ▷ **help**
helpings *n* ▷ **helping**
helpless *adj* weak or incapable > **helplessly** *adv*
helplessly *adv* ▷ **helpless**
helpline *n* (*pl* **-s**) telephone line set aside for callers to contact an organization for help with a problem
helplines *n* ▷ **helpline**
helpmate *n* (*pl* **-s**) companion and helper, esp. a husband or wife
helpmates *n* ▷ **helpmate**
helps *v, n* ▷ **help**
hem *n* (*pl* **-s**) bottom edge of a garment, folded under and stitched down ▶ *v* (**-s, -mming, -mmed**) provide with a hem
hemisphere *n* (*pl* **-s**) half of a sphere, esp. the earth > **hemispherical** *adj*
hemispheres *n* ▷ **hemisphere**
hemline *n* (*pl* **-s**) level to which the hem of a skirt hangs
hemlines *n* ▷ **hemline**
hemlock *n* (*pl* **-s**) poison made from a plant with spotted stems and small white flowers
hemlocks *n* ▷ **hemlock**
hemmed *v* ▷ **hem**
hemming *v* ▷ **hem**
hemp *n* (*pl* **-s**) (*also* **cannabis**) Asian plant with tough fibres
hemps *n* ▷ **hemp**
hems *n, v* ▷ **hem**
hen *n* (*pl* **-s**) female domestic fowl
hence *conj* for this reason ▶ *adv* from this time
henceforth *adv* from now on
henchman *n* (*pl* **-men**) person employed by someone powerful to carry out orders
henchmen *n* ▷ **henchman**
henna *n* (*pl* **-s**) reddish dye made from a shrub or tree ▶ *v* (**-s, -ing, -ed**) dye (the hair) with henna
hennaed *v* ▷ **henna**
hennaing *v* ▷ **henna**
hennas *n, v* ▷ **henna**
henpecked *adj* (of a man) dominated by his wife
henries *n* ▷ **henry**
henry *n* (*pl* **-ries, -rys**) unit of electrical inductance
henrys *n* ▷ **henry**
hens *n* ▷ **hen**
hepatitis *n* (*pl* **-es**) inflammation of the liver
hepatitises *n* ▷ **hepatitis**
heptagon *n* (*pl* **-s**) geometric figure with seven sides
heptagons *n* ▷ **heptagon**
heptathlon *n* (*pl* **-s**) athletic contest for women, involving seven events
heptathlons *n* ▷ **heptathlon**
her *pron* refers to a female person or animal or anything personified as feminine when the object of a sentence or clause ▶ *adj* belonging to her
herald *n* (*pl* **-s**) person who announces important news ▶ *v* (**-s, -ing, -ed**) signal the approach of
heralded *v* ▷ **herald**
heraldic *adj* ▷ **heraldry**
heralding *v* ▷ **herald**
heraldries *n* ▷ **heraldry**
heraldry *n* (*pl* **-ries**) study of coats of arms and family trees > **heraldic** *adj*
heralds *n, v* ▷ **herald**
herb *n* (*pl* **-s**) plant used for flavouring in cookery, and in medicine > **herbal** *adj*
herbaceous *adj* (of a plant) soft-stemmed
herbal *adj* ▷ **herb**
herbalist *n* (*pl* **-s**) person who grows or specializes in the use of medicinal herbs
herbalists *n* ▷ **herbalist**
herbicide *n* (*pl* **-s**) chemical used to destroy plants, esp. weeds
herbicides *n* ▷ **herbicide**
herbivore *n* (*pl* **-s**) animal that eats only plants > **herbivorous** [her-**biv**-or-uss] ▶ *adj*
herbivores *n* ▷ **herbivore**
herbivorous *adj* ▷ **herbivore**
herbs *n* ▷ **herb**
herculean [her-kew-**lee**-an] *adj* requiring great strength or effort
herd *n* (*pl* **-s**) group of animals feeding and

living together ▶ *v* (**-s, -ing, -ed**) collect into a herd
herded *v* ▷ **herd**
herding *v* ▷ **herd**
herds *n, v* ▷ **herd**
herdsman *n* (*pl* **-men**) man who looks after a herd of animals
herdsmen *n* ▷ **herd**
here *adv* in, at, or to this place or point
hereabouts *adv* near here
hereafter *adv* after this point or time
hereby *adv* by means of or as a result of this
hereditary *adj* passed on genetically from one generation to another
heredities *n* ▷ **heredity**
heredity [hir-**red**-it-ee] *n* (*pl* **-ties**) passing on of characteristics from one generation to another
herein *adv* in this place, matter, or document
heresies *n* ▷ **heresy**
heresy [**herr**-iss-ee] *n* (*pl* **-sies**) opinion contrary to accepted opinion or belief
heretic [**herr**-it-ik] *n* (*pl* **-s**) person who holds unorthodox opinions > **heretical** [hir-**ret**-ik-al] ▶ *adj*
heretical *n* ▷ **heretic**
heretics *n* ▷ **heretic**
herewith *adv* with this
heritage *n* (*pl* **-s**) something inherited
heritages *n* ▷ **heritage**
hermaphrodite [her-**maf**-roe-dite] *n* (*pl* **-s**) animal, plant, or person with both male and female reproductive organs
hermaphrodites *n* ▷ **hermaphrodite**
hermetic *adj* sealed so as to be airtight > **hermetically** *adv*
hermetically *adv* ▷ **hermetic**
hermit *n* (*pl* **-s**) person living in solitude, esp. for religious reasons
hermitage *n* (*pl* **-s**) home of a hermit
hermitages *n* ▷ **hermitage**
hermits *n* ▷ **hermit**
hernia *n* (*pl* **-s**) protrusion of an organ or part through the lining of the surrounding body cavity
hernias *n* ▷ **hernia**
hero *n* (*pl* **-es**) principal character in a film, book, etc. > **heroine** *n fem* (*pl* **-s**) > **heroism** [**herr**-oh-izz-um] *n* (*pl* **-s**)
heroes *n* ▷ **hero**
heroic *adj* courageous > **heroically** *adv*
heroically *adv* ▷ **heroic**
heroics *pl n* extravagant behaviour
heroin *n* (*pl* **-s**) highly addictive drug derived from morphine
heroine *n* ▷ **hero**
heroines *n* ▷ **hero**
heroins *n* ▷ **heroin**
heroism *n* ▷ **hero**
heroisms *n* ▷ **hero**
heron *n* (*pl* **-s**) long-legged wading bird
herons *n* ▷ **heron**
herpes [**her**-peez] *n* (*pl* **-es**) any of several inflammatory skin diseases, including shingles and cold sores
herpeses *n* ▷ **herpes**
herring *n* (*pl* **-s**) important food fish of northern seas
herringbone *n* (*pl* **-s**) pattern of zigzag lines
herringbones *n* ▷ **herringbone**
herrings *n* ▷ **herring**
hertz *n* (*pl* **-es**) (PHYSICS) unit of frequency
hertzes *n* ▷ **hertz**
hes *n* ▷ **he**
hesitancies *n* ▷ **hesitant**
hesitancy *n* ▷ **hesitant**
hesitant *adj* undecided or wavering > **hesitantly** *adv* > **hesitancy** *n* (*pl* **-cies**)
hesitantly *adv* ▷ **hesitant**
hesitate *v* (**-tes, -ting, -ted**) be slow or uncertain in doing something > **hesitation** *n* (*pl* **-s**)
hesitated *v* ▷ **hesitate**
hesitates *v* ▷ **hesitate**
hesitating *v* ▷ **hesitate**
hesitation *n* ▷ **hesitate**
hesitations *n* ▷ **hesitate**
hessian *n* (*pl* **-s**) coarse jute fabric
hessians *n* ▷ **hessian**
heterodox *adj* differing from accepted doctrines or beliefs > **heterodoxy** *n* (*pl* **-xies**)
heterodoxies *n* ▷ **heterodox**
heterodoxy *n* ▷ **heterodox**
heterogeneities *n* ▷ **heterogeneous**
heterogeneity *n* ▷ **heterogeneous**
heterogeneous [het-er-oh-**jean**-ee-uss] *adj* composed of diverse elements > **heterogeneity** *n* (*pl* **-ties**)
heterosexual *n* (*pl* **-s**) person sexually attracted to members of the opposite sex ▶ *adj* > **heterosexuality** *n* (*pl* **-ties**)
heterosexualities *n* ▷ **heterosexual**
heterosexuality *n* ▷ **heterosexual**
heterosexuals *n* ▷ **heterosexual**
heuristic [**hew**-rist-ik] *adj* involving learning by investigation
hew *v* (**-s, -ing, -ed** *or* **hewn**) cut with an axe
hewed *v* ▷ **hew**
hewing *v* ▷ **hew**
hewn *v* ▷ **hew**

hews *v* ▷ **hew**

> **hex** *n* hexes. A hex is a curse or spell. This is a really useful word to remember when you have an X, as there is likely to be an E or H on the board already.

hexagon *n* (*pl* **-s**) geometrical figure with six sides > **hexagonal** *adj*
hexagonal *adj* ▷ **hexagon**
hexagons *n* ▷ **hexagon**
hey *interj* expression of surprise or for catching attention
heyday *n* (*pl* **-s**) time of greatest success, prime
heydays *n* ▷ **heyday**

> **hi** *interj*. Hi is an informal word for **hello.** This everyday word is worth keeping in mind when you want to form a word adjacent to a parallel word below or above. Hi scores 5 points.

hiatus [hie-**ay**-tuss] *n* (*pl* **-tuses, -tus**) pause or interruption in continuity
hiatuses *n* ▷ **hiatus**
hibernate *v* (**-tes, -ting, -ted**) (of an animal) pass the winter as if in a deep sleep > **hibernation** *n* (*pl* **-s**)
hibernated *v* ▷ **hibernate**
hibernates *v* ▷ **hibernate**
hibernating *v* ▷ **hibernate**
hibernation *n* ▷ **hibernate**
hibernations *n* ▷ **hibernate**
hibiscus *n* (*pl* **-cuses**) tropical plant with large brightly coloured flowers
hibiscuses *n* ▷ **hibiscus**
hiccough *n*, *v* ▷ **hiccup**
hiccoughed *v* ▷ **hiccup**
hiccoughing *v* ▷ **hiccup**
hiccoughs *n*, *v* ▷ **hiccup**
hiccup, hiccough *n* (*pl* **-s**) spasm of the breathing organs with a sharp coughlike sound (*Informal*) ▶ *v* (**-s, -pping, -pped**) make a hiccup
hiccupped *v* ▷ **hiccup**
hiccupping *v* ▷ **hiccup**
hiccups *n*, *v* ▷ **hiccup**
hick *n* (*pl* **-s**) (US, AUST & NZ) (*Informal*) unsophisticated country person
hickories *n* ▷ **hickory**
hickory *n* (*pl* **-ries**) N American nut-bearing tree
hicks *n* ▷ **hick**
hid *v* ▷ **hide**[1]
hidden *v* ▷ **hide**[1]
hide[1] *v* (**-des, -ding, hid, hidden**) put (oneself or an object) somewhere difficult to see or find ▶ *n* (*pl* **-s**) place of concealment, esp. for a bird-watcher
hide[2] *n* (*pl* **-s**) skin of an animal
hidebound *adj* unwilling to accept new ideas
hideous [**hid**-ee-uss] *adj* ugly, revolting > **hideously** *adv*
hideously *adv* ▷ **hideous**
hideout *n* (*pl* **-s**) place to hide in
hideouts *n* ▷ **hideout**
hides *v* ▷ **hide**[1] ▶ *n* ▷ **hide**[1, 2]
hiding *n* (*pl* **-s**) (*Slang*) severe beating ▶ *v* ▷ **hide**[1]
hidings *n* ▷ **hiding**
hierarchical *adj* ▷ **hierarchy**
hierarchies *n* ▷ **hierarchy**
hierarchy [**hire**-ark-ee] *n* (*pl* **-chies**) system of people or things arranged in a graded order > **hierarchical** *adj*
hieroglyphic [hire-oh-**gliff**-ik] *adj* of a form of writing using picture symbols, as used in ancient Egypt ▶ *n* (*pl* **-s**) symbol that is difficult to decipher (*also* **hieroglyph**)
hieroglyphics *n* ▷ **hieroglyphic**
high *adj* (**-er, -est**) of a great height ▶ *adv* at or to a high level > **highly** *adv*
highbrow *adj*, *n* (*pl* **-s**) intellectual and serious (person)
highbrows *n* ▷ **highbrow**
higher *adj* ▷ **high**
highest *adj* ▷ **high**
highlands *pl n* area of high ground
highlight *n* (*pl* **-s**) outstanding part or feature ▶ *v* (**-s, -ing, -ed**) give emphasis to
highlighted *v* ▷ **highlight**
highlighting *v* ▷ **highlight**
highlights *n*, *v* ▷ **highlight**
highly *adv* ▷ **high**
highway *n* (*pl* **-s**) (US, AUST & NZ) main road
highwayman *n* (*pl* **-men**) (formerly) robber, usu. on horseback, who robbed travellers at gunpoint
highwaymen *n* ▷ **highwayman**
highways *n* ▷ **highway**
hijack *v* (**-s, -ing, -ed**) seize control of (an aircraft or other vehicle) while travelling > **hijacker** *n* (*pl* **-s**)
hijacked *v* ▷ **hijack**
hijacker *n* ▷ **hijack**
hijackers *n* ▷ **hijack**
hijacking *v* ▷ **hijack**
hijacks *v* ▷ **hijack**
hike *n* (*pl* **-s**) long walk in the country, esp. for pleasure ▶ *v* (**-kes, -king, -ked**) go for a long walk > **hiker** *n* (*pl* **-s**)
hiked *v* ▷ **hike**
hiker *n* ▷ **hike**
hikers *n* ▷ **hike**

hikes *n, v* ▷ **hike**
hiking *v* ▷ **hike**
hilarious *adj* very funny > **hilariously** *adv* > **hilarity** *n* (*pl* **-ties**)
hilariously *adv* ▷ **hilarious**
hilarities *n* ▷ **hilarious**
hilarity *n* ▷ **hilarious**
hill *n* (*pl* **-s**) raised part of the earth's surface, less high than a mountain > **hilly** *adj* (**-llier, -lliest**)
hillbillies *n* ▷ **hillbilly**
hillbilly *n* (*pl* **-llies**) (US) unsophisticated country person
hillier *adj* ▷ **hill**
hilliest *adj* ▷ **hill**
hillock *n* (*pl* **-s**) small hill
hillocks *n* ▷ **hillock**
hills *n* ▷ **hill**
hilly *adj* ▷ **hill**
hilt *n* (*pl* **-s**) handle of a sword or knife
hilts *n* ▷ **hilt**
him *pron* refers to a male person or animal when the object of a sentence or clause
hind[1] *adj* (**-er, -most**) situated at the back
hind[2] *n* (*pl* **-s**) female deer
hinder *adj* ▷ **hind**[1] ▶ *v* (**-s, -ing, -ed**) get in the way of > **hindrance** *n* (*pl* **-s**)
hindered *v* ▷ **hinder**
hindering *v* ▷ **hinder**
hinders *v* ▷ **hinder**
hindmost *adj* ▷ **hind**[1]
hindrance *n* ▷ **hinder**
hindrances *n* ▷ **hinder**
hinds *n* ▷ **hind**[2]
hinge *n* (*pl* **-s**) device for holding together two parts so that one can swing freely ▶ *v* (**-ges, -ging, -ged**) (*foll. by* **on**) depend (on)
hinged *v* ▷ **hinge**
hinges *n, v* ▷ **hinge**
hinging *v* ▷ **hinge**
hint *n* (*pl* **-s**) indirect suggestion ▶ *v* (**-s, -ing, -ed**) suggest indirectly
hinted *v* ▷ **hint**
hinterland *n* (*pl* **-s**) land lying behind a coast or near a city, esp. a port
hinterlands *n* ▷ **hinterland**
hinting *v* ▷ **hint**
hints *n, v* ▷ **hint**
hip[1] *n* (*pl* **-s**) either side of the body between the pelvis and the thigh
hip[2] *n* (*pl* **-s**) rosehip
hippie *adj, n* (*pl* **-s**) ▷ **hippy**
hippies *n* ▷ **hippie**
hippo *n* (*pl* **-ppos**) (*Informal*) hippopotamus
hippodrome *n* (*pl* **-s**) music hall, variety theatre, or circus
hippodromes *n* ▷ **hippodrome**
hippopotami *n* ▷ **hippopotamus**
hippopotamus *n* (*pl* **-muses, -mi**) large African mammal with thick wrinkled skin, living near rivers
hippopotamuses *n* ▷ **hippopotamus**
hippos *n* ▷ **hippo**
hippy *adj, n* (*pl* **-ppies**) (esp. in the 1960s) (of) a person whose behaviour and dress imply a rejection of conventional values
hips *n* ▷ **hip**[1, 2]
hire *v* (**-res, -ring, -red**) pay to have temporary use of ▶ *n* (*pl* **-s**) hiring
hired *v* ▷ **hire**
hireling *n* (*pl* **-s**) person who works only for wages
hirelings *n* ▷ **hireling**
hires *v, n* ▷ **hire**
hiring *v* ▷ **hire**
hirsute [**her**-suit] *adj* hairy
his *pron, adj* (something) belonging to him
hiss *n* (*pl* **-es**) sound like that of a long *s* (as an expression of contempt) ▶ *v* (**-es, -ing, -ed**) utter a hiss
hissed *v* ▷ **hiss**
hisses *n, v* ▷ **hiss**
hissing *v* ▷ **hiss**
histamine [**hiss**-ta-meen] *n* (*pl* **-s**) substance released by the body tissues in allergic reactions
histamines *n* ▷ **histamine**
histogram *n* (*pl* **-s**) statistical graph in which the frequency of values is represented by vertical bars of varying heights and widths
histograms *n* ▷ **histogram**
histologies *n* ▷ **histology**
histology *n* (*pl* **-gies**) study of the tissues of an animal or plant
historian *n* (*pl* **-s**) writer of history
historians *n* ▷ **historian**
historic *adj* famous or significant in history
historical *adj* occurring in the past > **historically** *adv*
historically *adv* ▷ **historical**
histories *n* ▷ **history**
history *n* (*pl* **-ries**) (record or account of) past events and developments
histrionic *adj* excessively dramatic
histrionics *pl n* excessively dramatic behaviour
hit *v* (**-s, -tting, hit**) strike, touch forcefully ▶ *n* (*pl* **-s**) hitting ▶ *adj* sometimes successful and sometimes not
hitch *n* (*pl* **-es**) minor problem ▶ *v* (**-es, -ing, -ed**)

(*Informal*) obtain (a lift) by hitchhiking
hitched *v* ▷ **hitch**
hitches *n, v* ▷ **hitch**
hitchhike *v* (**-kes, -king, -ked**) travel by obtaining free lifts > **hitchhiker** *n* (*pl* **-s**)
hitchhiked *n* ▷ **hitchhike**
hitchhiker *n* ▷ **hitchhike**
hitchhikers *n* ▷ **hitchhike**
hitchhikes *n* ▷ **hitchhike**
hitchhiking *n* ▷ **hitchhike**
hitching *v* ▷ **hitch**
hither *adv* (*Old-fashioned*) to or towards this place
hitherto *adv* until this time
hits *n, v* ▷ **hit**
hitting *v* ▷ **hit**
hive *n* (*pl* **-s**) ▷ **beehive**
hives *n* ▷ **hive**

> **hm** or **hmm** *interj*. This is a noise that people make when they are thinking or considering something. Both forms of this word are useful because neither contains a vowel, which is great if you have no vowels on your rack. Hm scores 5 points, while hmm scores 8.
> **ho** *interj*. Ho is a noise people make when they laugh. This little word is useful when you want to go in two directions at once. It's also worth remembering that ho is oh backwards: if you can't use one, you might be able to use the other. Ho scores 5 points.

hoard *n* (*pl* **-s**) store hidden away for future use ▶ *v* (**-s, -ing, -ed**) save or store > **hoarder** *n* (*pl* **-s**)
hoarded *v* ▷ **hoard**
hoarder *n* ▷ **hoard**
hoarders *n* ▷ **hoard**
hoarding *n* (*pl* **-s**) large board for displaying advertisements ▶ *v* ▷ **hoard**
hoardings *n* ▷ **hoarding**
hoards *n, v* ▷ **hoard**
hoarfrost *n* (*pl* **-s**) white ground frost
hoarfrosts *n* ▷ **hoarfrost**
hoarier *adj* ▷ **hoary**
hoariest *adj* ▷ **hoary**
hoarse *adj* (**-ser, -sest**) (of a voice) rough and unclear > **hoarsely** *adv* > **hoarseness** *n* (*pl* **-es**)
hoarsely *adv* ▷ **hoarse**
hoarseness *n* ▷ **hoarse**
hoarsenesses *n* ▷ **hoarse**
hoarsest *adj* ▷ **hoarse**
hoarsest *adj* ▷ **hoarse**
hoary *adj* (**-rier, -riest**) grey or white(-haired)
hoax *n* (*pl* **-es**) deception or trick ▶ *v* (**-es, -ing, -ed**) deceive or play a trick upon > **hoaxer** *n*
hoaxed *v* ▷ **hoax**
hoaxer *n* ▷ **hoax**
hoaxers *n* ▷ **hoax**
hoaxes *n, v* ▷ **hoax**
hoaxing *v* ▷ **hoax**
hob *n* (*pl* **-s**) (BRIT) flat top part of a cooker, or a separate flat surface, containing gas or electric rings for cooking on
hobbies *n* ▷ **hobby**
hobble *v* (**-les, -ling, -led**) walk lamely
hobbled *v* ▷ **hobble**
hobbles *v* ▷ **hobble**
hobbling *v* ▷ **hobble**
hobby *n* (*pl* **-bbies**) activity pursued in one's spare time
hobbyhorse *n* (*pl* **-s**) favourite topic
hobbyhorses *n* ▷ **hobbyhorse**
hobgoblin *n* (*pl* **-s**) mischievous goblin
hobgoblins *n* ▷ **hobgoblin**
hobnob *v* (**-s, -nobbing, -nobbed**) (*foll. by* **with**) be on friendly terms (with)
hobnobbed *v* ▷ **hobnob**
hobnobbing *v* ▷ **hobnob**
hobnobs *v* ▷ **hobnob**
hobo *n* (*pl* **-s**) (US, AUST & NZ) tramp or vagrant
hobos *n* ▷ **hobo**
hobs *n* ▷ **hob**
hock[1] *n* (*pl* **-s**) joint in the back leg of an animal such as a horse that corresponds to the human ankle
hock[2] *n* (*pl* **-s**) white German wine
hock[3] *v* (**-s, -ing, -ed**) (*Informal*) pawn
hocked *v* ▷ **hock**
hockey *n* (*pl* **-s**) team game played on a field with a ball and curved sticks
hockeys *n* ▷ **hockey**
hocking *v* ▷ **hock**
hocks *n* ▷ **hock**[1, 2] ▶ *v* ▷ **hock**[3]
hod *n* (*pl* **-s**) open wooden box attached to a pole, for carrying bricks or mortar
hods *n* ▷ **hod**
hoe *n* (*pl* **-s**) long-handled tool used for loosening soil or weeding ▶ *v* (**-oes, -oeing, -oed**) scrape or weed with a hoe
hoed *v* ▷ **hoe**
hoeing *v* ▷ **hoe**
hoes *n, v* ▷ **hoe**
hog *n* (*pl* **-s**) castrated male pig (*Informal*) ▶ *v* (**-s, -gging, -gged**) (*Informal*) take more than one's share of
hogged *v* ▷ **hog**
hogging *v* ▷ **hog**
hogmanay *n* (*pl* **-s**) (in Scotland) New Year's Eve

hogmanays *n* ▷ **hogmanay**
hogs *n, v* ▷ **hog**
hogshead *n* (*pl* **-s**) large cask
hogsheads *n* ▷ **hogshead**
hogwash *n* (*pl* **-es**) (*Informal*) nonsense
hogwashes *n* ▷ **hogwash**
hoick *v* (**-s, -ing, -ed**) raise abruptly and sharply
hoicked *v* ▷ **hoick**
hoicking *v* ▷ **hoick**
hoicks *v* ▷ **hoick**
hoist *v* (**-s, -ing, -ed**) raise or lift up ▶ *n* (*pl* **-s**) device for lifting things
hoisted *v* ▷ **hoist**
hoisting *v* ▷ **hoist**
hoists *v, n* ▷ **hoist**
hold¹ *v* (**-s, -ing, held**) keep or support in or with the hands or arms ▶ *n* (*pl* **-s**) act or way of holding > **holder** *n* (*pl* **-s**)
hold² *n* (*pl* **-s**) cargo compartment in a ship or aircraft
holdall *n* (*pl* **-s**) large strong travelling bag
holdalls *n* ▷ **holdall**
holder *n* ▷ **hold¹**
holders *n* ▷ **hold¹**
holding *n* (*pl* **-s**) property, such as land or stocks and shares ▶ *v* ▷ **hold¹**
holds *n* ▷ **hold¹, ²** ▶ *v* ▷ **hold¹**
holdup *n* (*pl* **-s**) armed robbery
holdups *n* ▷ **holdup**
hole *n* (*pl* **-s**) area hollowed out in a solid ▶ *v* (**-les, -ling, -led**) make holes in
holed *v* ▷ **hole**
holes *n, v* ▷ **hole**
holiday *n* (*pl* **-s**) time spent away from home for rest or recreation
holidays *n* ▷ **holiday**
holier *adj* ▷ **holy**
holiest *adj* ▷ **holy**
holiness *n* (*pl* **-es**) state of being holy
holinesses *n* ▷ **holiness**
holing *v* ▷ **hole**
holisms *n* ▷ **holism**
holistic *adj* considering the complete person, physically and mentally, in the treatment of an illness > **holism** *n* (*pl* **-s**)
hollies *n* ▷ **holly**
holloganism *n* ▷ **hooligan**
hollow *adj* having a hole or space inside ▶ *n* (*pl* **-s**) cavity or space ▶ *v* (**-s, -ing, -ed**) form a hollow in
hollowed *v* ▷ **hollow**
hollowing *v* ▷ **hollow**
hollows *n, v* ▷ **hollow**
holly *n* (*pl* **-llies**) evergreen tree with prickly leaves and red berries
hollyhock *n* (*pl* **-s**) tall garden plant with spikes of colourful flowers
hollyhocks *n* ▷ **hollyhock**
holocaust *n* (*pl* **-s**) destruction or loss of life on a massive scale
holocausts *n* ▷ **holocaust**
hologram *n* (*pl* **-s**) three-dimensional photographic image
holograms *n* ▷ **hologram**
holograph *n* (*pl* **-s**) document handwritten by the author
holographs *n* ▷ **holograph**
holster *n* (*pl* **-s**) leather case for a pistol, hung from a belt
holsters *n* ▷ **holster**
holy *adj* (**-lier, -liest**) of God or a god
homage *n* (*pl* **-s**) show of respect or honour towards someone or something
homages *n* ▷ **homage**
home *n* (*pl* **-s**) place where one lives ▶ *adj* of one's home, birthplace, or native country (SPORT) ▶ *adv* to or at home ▶ *v* (**-mes, -ming, -med**) (*foll. by* **in** *or* **in on**) direct towards (a point or target) > **homeward** *adj, adv* > **homewards** *adv*
homed *v* ▷ **home**
homeland *n* (*pl* **-s**) country from which a person's ancestors came
homelands *n* ▷ **homeland**
homeless *adj* having nowhere to live ▶ *pl n* people who have nowhere to live > **homelessness** *n* (*pl* **-es**)
homelessness *n* ▷ **homeless**
homelessnesses *n* ▷ **homeless**
homelier *adj* ▷ **homely**
homeliest *adj* ▷ **homely**
homely *adj* (**-lier, -liest**) simple, ordinary, and comfortable
homemade *adj* made at home or on the premises
homeopath *n* (*pl* **-s**) person who practises homeopathy > **homeopathic** *adj*
homeopathic *adj* ▷ **homeopath**
homeopathies *n* ▷ **homeopathy**
homeopaths *n* ▷ **homeopath**
homeopathy [home-ee-**op**-ath-ee] *n* (*pl* **-thies**) treatment of disease by small doses of a drug that produces symptoms of the disease in healthy people
homes *n, v* ▷ **home**
homesick *adj* sad because missing one's home and family > **homesickness** *n* (*pl* **-es**)
homesickness *n* ▷ **homesick**
homesicknesses *n* ▷ **homesick**
homeward *adj, adv* ▷ **home**

homewards *adv* ▷ **home**
homework *n* (*pl* **-s**) school work done at home
homeworks *n* ▷ **homework**
homicidal *adj* ▷ **homicide**
homicide *n* (*pl* **-s**) killing of a human being > **homicidal** *adj*
homicides *n* ▷ **homicide**
homilies *n* ▷ **homliy**
homily *n* (*pl* **-lies**) speech telling people how they should behave
homing *v* ▷ **home**
hominid *n* (*pl* **-s**) man or any extinct forerunner of man
hominids *n* ▷ **hominid**
homogeneities *n* ▷ **homogeneous**
homogeneity *n* ▷ **homogeneous**
homogeneous [home-oh-**jean**-ee-uss] *adj* formed of similar parts > **homogeneity** *n* (*pl* **-ties**)
homogenize *v* (**-zes, -zing, -zed**) break up fat globules in (milk or cream) to distribute them evenly
homogenized *v* ▷ **homogenize**
homogenizes *v* ▷ **homogenize**
homogenizing *v* ▷ **homogenize**
homograph *n* (*pl* **-s**) word spelt the same as another, but with a different meaning
homographs *n* ▷ **homograph**
homologous [hom-**ol**-log-uss] *adj* having a related or similar position or structure
homonym *n* (*pl* **-s**) word spelt or pronounced the same as another, but with a different meaning
homonyms *n* ▷ **homonym**
homophobia *n* (*pl* **-s**) hatred or fear of homosexuals > **homophobic** *adj*
homophobias *n* ▷ **homophobia**
homophobic *adj* ▷ **homophobia**
homophone *n* (*pl* **-s**) word pronounced the same as another, but with a different meaning or spelling
homophones *n* ▷ **homophone**
homosexual *n* (*pl* **-s**) ▶ *adj* (person) sexually attracted to members of the same sex > **homosexuality** *n* (*pl* **-ties**)
homosexualities *n* ▷ **homosexual**
homosexuality *n* ▷ **homosexual**
homosexuals *n* ▷ **homosexual**
hone *v* (**-nes, -ning, -ned**) sharpen
honed *v* ▷ **hone**
hones *v* ▷ **hone**
honest *adj* (**-er, -est**) truthful and moral > **honestly** *adv*
honester *adj* ▷ **honest**
honestest *adj* ▷ **honest**
honesties *n* ▷ **honesty**
honestly *adv* ▷ **honest**
honesty *n* (*pl* **-ties**) quality of being honest
honey *n* (*pl* **-s**) sweet edible sticky substance made by bees from nectar
honeycomb *n* (*pl* **-s**) waxy structure of six-sided cells in which honey is stored by bees in a beehive
honeycombs *n* ▷ **honeycomb**
honeymoon *n* (*pl* **-s**) holiday taken by a newly married couple
honeymoons *n* ▷ **honeymoon**
honeys *n* ▷ **honey**
honeysuckle *n* (*pl* **-s**) climbing shrub with sweet-smelling flowers
honeysuckles *n* ▷ **honeysuckle**
hongi [**hong**-jee] *n* (*pl* **-s**) (NZ) Maori greeting in which people touch noses
hongis *n* ▷ **hongi**
honing *v* ▷ **hone**
honk *n* (*pl* **-s**) sound made by a car horn ▶ *v* (**-s, -ing, -ed**) (cause to) make this sound
honked *v* ▷ **honk**
honking *v* ▷ **honk**
honks *n, v* ▷ **honk**
honorary *adj* held or given only as an honour
honorific *adj* showing respect
honour *n* (*pl* **-s**) sense of honesty and fairness ▶ *v* (**-s, -ing, -ed**) give praise and attention to
honourable *adj* worthy of respect or esteem > **honourably** *adv*
honourably *adv* ▷ **honourable**
honoured *v* ▷ **honour**
honouring *v* ▷ **honour**
honours *n, v* ▷ **honour** ▶ *pl n* university degree of a higher standard than an ordinary degree
hood[1] *n* (*pl* **-s**) head covering, often attached to a coat or jacket
hood[2] *n* (*pl* **-s**) (CHIEFLY US) (*Slang*) hoodlum
hooded *adj* (of a garment) having a hood
hoodlum *n* (*pl* **-s**) (*Slang*) violent criminal, gangster
hoodlums *n* ▷ **hoodlum**
hoodoo *n* (*pl* **-s**) (cause of) bad luck
hoodoos *n* ▷ **hoodoo**
hoods *n* ▷ **hood**[1, 2]
hoodwink *v* (**-s, -ing, -ed**) trick, deceive
hoodwinked *v* ▷ **hoodwink**
hoodwinking *v* ▷ **hoodwink**
hoodwinks *v* ▷ **hoodwink**
hoof *n* (*pl* **hooves, hoofs**) horny covering of the foot of a horse, deer, etc.
hoofs *n* ▷ **hoof**
hook *n* (*pl* **-s**) curved piece of metal, plastic, etc., used to hang, hold, or pull something

▶ *v* (**-s, -ing, -ed**) fasten or catch (as if) with a hook

hookah *n* (*pl* **-s**) oriental pipe in which smoke is drawn through water and a long tube

hookahs *n* ▷ **hookah**

hooked *adj* bent like a hook ▶ *v* ▷ **hook**

hooker *n* (*pl* **-s**) (CHIEFLY US) (*Slang*) prostitute

hookers *n* ▷ **hooher**

hooking *v* ▷ **hook**

hooks *n, v* ▷ **hook**

hookup *n* (*pl* **-s**) linking of radio or television stations

hookups *n* ▷ **hookup**

hookworm *n* (*pl* **-s**) blood-sucking worm with hooked mouthparts

hookworms *n* ▷ **hookworm**

hooligan *n* (*pl* **-s**) rowdy young person > **hooliganism** *n* (*pl* **-s**)

hooliganisms *n* ▷ **hooligan**

hooligans *n* ▷ **hooligan**

hoon *n* (*pl* **-s**) (AUST & NZ) (*Slang*) loutish youth who drives irresponsibly

hoons *n* ▷ **hoon**

hoop *n* (*pl* **-s**) rigid circular band, used esp. as a child's toy or for animals to jump through in the circus

hoopla *n* (*pl* **-s**) fairground game in which hoops are thrown over objects in an attempt to win them

hooplas *n* ▷ **hoopla**

hoops *n* ▷ **hoop**

hooray *interj* ▷ **hurrah**

hoot *n* (*pl* **-s**) sound of a car horn ▶ *v* (**-s, -ing, -ed**) sound (a car horn)

hooted *v* ▷ **hoot**

hooter *n* (*pl* **-s**) device that hoots

hooters *n* ▷ **hooter**

hooting *v* ▷ **hoot**

hoots *n, v* ▷ **hoot**

hoover *n* ® (*pl* **-s**) vacuum cleaner ▶ *v* (**-s, -ing, -ed**) clean with a vacuum cleaner

hoovered *v* ▷ **hoover**

hoovering *v* ▷ **hoover**

hoovers *n, v* ▷ **hoover**

hooves *n* ▷ **hoof**

hop¹ *v* (**-s, -pping, -pped**) jump on one foot ▶ *n* (*pl* **-s**) instance of hopping

hop² *n* (*pl* **-s**) (*often pl*) climbing plant, the dried flowers of which are used to make beer

hope *v* (**-pes, -ping, -ped**) want (something) to happen or be true ▶ *n* (*pl* **-s**) expectation of something desired > **hopeless** *adj*

hoped *v* ▷ **hope**

hopeful *adj* having, expressing, or inspiring hope ▶ *n* (*pl* **-s**) person considered to be on the brink of success

hopefully *adv* in a hopeful manner

hopefully *adj* ▷ **hopeful**

hopefuls *n* ▷ **hopeful**

hopeless *adj* ▷ **hope**

hopes *v, n* ▷ **hope**

hoping *v* ▷ **hope**

hopped *v* ▷ **hop¹**

hopper *n* (*pl* **-s**) container for storing substances such as grain or sand

hoppers *n* ▷ **hopper**

hopping *v* ▷ **hop¹**

hops *n* ▷ **hop¹, ²** ▶ *v* ▷ **hop¹**

hopscotch *n* (*pl* **-es**) children's game of hopping in a pattern drawn on the ground

hopscotches *n* ▷ **hopscotch**

horde *n* (*pl* **-s**) large crowd

hordes *n* ▷ **horde**

horizon *n* (*pl* **-s**) apparent line that divides the earth and the sky

horizons *n* ▷ **horizon** ▶ *pl n* limits of scope, interest, or knowledge

horizontal *adj* parallel to the horizon, level, flat > **horizontally** *adv*

horizontally *adv* ▷ **horizontal**

hormonal *adj* ▷ **hormone**

hormone *n* (*pl* **-s**) substance secreted by certain glands which stimulates certain organs of the body > **hormonal** *adj*

hormones *n* ▷ **hormone**

horn *n* (*pl* **-s**) one of a pair of bony growths sticking out of the heads of cattle, sheep, etc. > **horned** *adj*

hornbeam *n* (*pl* **-s**) tree with smooth grey bark

hornbeams *n* ▷ **hornbeam**

hornbill *n* (*pl* **-s**) bird with a bony growth on its large beak

hornbills *n* ▷ **hornbill**

hornblende *n* (*pl* **-s**) mineral containing aluminium, calcium, sodium, magnesium, and iron

hornblendes *n* ▷ **hornblende**

horned *adj* ▷ **horn**

hornet *n* (*pl* **-s**) large wasp with a severe sting

hornets *n* ▷ **hornet**

hornpipe *n* (*pl* **-s**) (music for) a solo dance, traditionally performed by sailors

hornpipes *n* ▷ **hornpipe**

horns *n* ▷ **horn**

horny *adj* (**-nier, -niest**) of or like horn

horoscope *n* (*pl* **-s**) prediction of a person's future based on the positions of the planets, sun, and moon at his or her birth

horoscopes *n* ▷ **horoscope**

horrendous *adj* very unpleasant and shocking

horrible *adj* disagreeable, unpleasant
> **horribly** *adv*
horribly *adv* ▷ **horrible**
horrid *adj* disagreeable, unpleasant
horrific *adj* causing horror
horrified *v* ▷ **horrify**
horrifies *v* ▷ **horrify**
horrify *v* (**-fies, -fying, -fied**) cause to feel horror or shock
horrifying *v* ▷ **horrify**
horror *n* (*pl* **-s**) (thing or person causing) terror or hatred
horrors *n* ▷ **horror**
horse *n* (*pl* **-s**) large animal with hooves, a mane, and a tail, used for riding and pulling carts etc.
horseflies *n* ▷ **horsefly**
horsefly *n* (*pl* **-flies**) large bloodsucking fly
horsehair *n* (*pl* **-s**) hair from the tail or mane of a horse
horsehairs *n* ▷ **horsehair**
horseman *n* (*pl* **-men**) person riding a horse
horsemen *n* ▷ **horseman**
horseplay *n* (*pl* **-s**) rough or rowdy play
horseplays *n* ▷ **horseplay**
horsepower *n* (*pl* **-s**) unit of power (equivalent to 745.7 watts), used to measure the power of an engine
horsepowers *n* ▷ **horsepower**
horseradish *n* (*pl* **-es**) strong-tasting root of a plant, usu. made into a sauce
horseradishes *n* ▷ **horseradish**
horses *n* ▷ **horse**
horseshoe *n* (*pl* **-s**) protective U-shaped piece of iron nailed to a horse's hoof, regarded as a symbol of good luck
horseshoes *n* ▷ **horseshoe**
horsewoman *n* (*pl* **-men**) woman riding a horse
horsewomen *n* ▷ **horsewoman**
horsey, horsy *adj* (**-sier, -siest**) very keen on horses
horsier *adj* ▷ **horsey**
horsiest *adj* ▷ **horsey**
horsy *adj* ▷ **horsey**
horticultural *adj* ▷ **horticulture**
horticulturalist *n* ▷ **horticulture**
horticulturalists *n* ▷ **horticulture**
horticulture *n* (*pl* **-s**) art or science of cultivating gardens > **horticultural** *adj* > **horticulturalist, horticulturist** *n* (*pl* **-s**)
horticultures *n* ▷ **horticulture**
horticulturist *n* ▷ **horticulture**
horticulturists *n* ▷ **horticulture**
hosanna *interj* exclamation of praise to God
hose[1] *n* (*pl* **-s**) flexible pipe for conveying liquid ▶ *v* (**-ses, -sing, -sed**) water with a hose
hose[2] *n* (*pl* **-s**) stockings, socks, and tights
hosed *v* ▷ **hose**[1]
hoses *n, v* ▷ **hose**[1, 2] ▶ *v* ▷ **hose**[1]
hosieries *n* ▷ **hosiery**
hosiery *n* (*pl* **-ries**) stockings, socks, and tights collectively
hosing *v* ▷ **hose**[1]
hospice [**hoss**-piss] *n* (*pl* **-s**) nursing home for the terminally ill
hospices *n* ▷ **hospice**
hospitable *adj* welcoming to strangers or guests
hospital *n* (*pl* **-s**) place where people who are ill are looked after and treated
hospitalities *n* ▷ **hospitality**
hospitalities *n* ▷ **hospitality**
hospitality *n* (*pl* **-ties**) kindness in welcoming strangers or guests
hospitalization *n* ▷ **hospitalize**
hospitalizations *n* ▷ **hospitalize**
hospitalize *v* (**-izes, -izing, -ized**) send or admit to hospital > **hospitalization** *n* (*pl* **-s**)
hospitalized *v* ▷ **hospitalize**
hospitalizes *v* ▷ **hospitalize**
hospitalizing *v* ▷ **hospitalize**
hospitals *n* ▷ **hospital**
host[1] *n* (*pl* **-s**) man who entertains guests, esp. in his own home ▶ *v* (**-s, -ing, -ed**) be the host of
host[2] *n* (*pl* **-s**) large number
hostage *n* (*pl* **-s**) person who is illegally held prisoner until certain demands are met by other people
hostages *n* ▷ **hostage**
hosted *v* ▷ **host**[1]
hostel *n* (*pl* **-s**) building providing accommodation at a low cost for a specific group of people such as students, travellers, homeless people, etc.
hostelries *n* ▷ **hostelry**
hostelry *n* (*pl* **-ries**) (*Old-fashioned or facetious*) inn, pub
hostels *n* ▷ **hostel**
hostess *n* (*pl* **-es**) woman who entertains guests, esp. in her own home
hostesses *n* ▷ **hostess**
hostile *adj* unfriendly
hostilities *n* ▷ **hostility** ▶ *pl n* acts of warfare
hostility *n* (*pl* **-ties**) unfriendly and aggressive feelings or behaviour
hosting *v* ▷ **host**[1]
hosts *n* ▷ **host**[1, 2] ▶ *v* ▷ **host**[1]
hot *adj* (**-tter, -ttest**) having a high

temperature in trouble > **hotly** *adv*
hotbed *n* (*pl* **-s**) any place encouraging a particular activity
hotbeds *n* ▷ **hotbed**
hotchpotch *n* (*pl* **-es**) jumbled mixture
hotchpotches *n* ▷ **hotchpotch**
hotel *n* (*pl* **-s**) commercial establishment providing lodging and meals
hotelier *n* (*pl* **-s**) owner or manager of a hotel
hoteliers *n* ▷ **hotelier**
hotels *n* ▷ **hotel**
hotfoot *adv* (*Informal*) quickly and eagerly
hotheaded *adj* rash, having a hot temper
hothouse *n* (*pl* **-s**) greenhouse
hothouses *n* ▷ **hothouse**
hotline *n* (*pl* **-s**) direct telephone link for emergency use
hotlines *n* ▷ **hotline**
hotly *adv* ▷ **hot**
hotplate *n* (*pl* **-s**) heated metal surface on an electric cooker
hotplates *n* ▷ **hotplate**
hotter *adj* ▷ **hot**
hottest *adj* ▷ **hot**
hound *n* (*pl* **-s**) hunting dog ▶ *v* (**-s, -ing, -ed**) pursue relentlessly
hounded *v* ▷ **hound**
hounding *v* ▷ **hound**
hounds *n, v* ▷ **hound**
hour *n* (*pl* **-s**) twenty-fourth part of a day, sixty minutes
hourglass *n* (*pl* **-es**) device with two glass compartments, containing a quantity of sand that takes an hour to trickle from the top section to the bottom one
hourglasses *n* ▷ **hourglass**
houri *n* (*pl* **-s**) (ISLAM) any of the nymphs of paradise
houris *n* ▷ **houri**
hourly *adj, adv* (happening) every hour
hours *pl n* period regularly appointed for work or business ▶ *n* ▷ **hour**
house *n* (*pl* **-s**) building used as a home ▶ *v* (**-ses, -sing, -sed**) give accommodation to
houseboat *n* (*pl* **-s**) stationary boat used as a home
houseboats *n* ▷ **houseboat**
housebreaker *n* (*pl* **-s**) burglar
housebreakers *n* ▷ **housebreaker**
housecoat *n* (*pl* **-s**) woman's long loose coat-shaped garment for wearing at home
housecoats *n* ▷ **housecoat**
housed *v* ▷ **house**
household *n* (*pl* **-s**) all the people living in a house
householder *n* (*pl* **-s**) person who owns or rents a house
householders *n* ▷ **householder**
households *n* ▷ **household**
housekeeper *n* (*pl* **-s**) person employed to run someone else's household
housekeepers *n* ▷ **housekeeper**
housekeeping *n* (*pl* **-s**) (money for) running a household
housekeepings *n* ▷ **housekeeping**
housemaid *n* (*pl* **-s**) female servant employed to do housework
housemaids *n* ▷ **housemaid**
houses *n, v* ▷ **house**
housewarming *n* (*pl* **-s**) party to celebrate moving into a new home
housewarmings *n* ▷ **housewarming**
housewife *n* (*pl* **-wives**) woman who runs her own household and does not have a job
housewives *n* ▷ **housewife**
housework *n* (*pl* **-s**) work of running a home, such as cleaning, cooking, and shopping
houseworks *n* ▷ **housework**
housing *n* (*pl* **-s**) (providing of) houses ▶ *v* ▷ **house**
housings *n* ▷ **housing**
hovea *n* (*pl* **-s**) Australian plant with purple flowers
hoveas *n* ▷ **hovea**
hovel *n* (*pl* **-s**) small dirty house or hut
hovels *n* ▷ **hovel**
hover *v* (**-s, -ing, -red**) (of a bird etc.) remain suspended in one place in the air
hovercraft *n* (*pl* **-s**) vehicle which can travel over both land and sea on a cushion of air
hovercrafts *n* ▷ **hovercraft**
hovered *v* ▷ **hover**
hovering *v* ▷ **hover**
hovers *v* ▷ **hover**
how *adv* in what way, by what means
howdah *n* (*pl* **-s**) canopied seat on an elephant's back
howdahs *n* ▷ **howdah**
however *adv* nevertheless
howitzer *n* (*pl* **-s**) large gun firing shells at a steep angle
howitzers *n* ▷ **howitzer**
howl *n* (*pl* **-s**) loud wailing cry ▶ *v* (**-s, -ing, -ed**) utter a howl
howled *v* ▷ **howl**
howler *n* (*pl* **-s**) (*Informal*) stupid mistake
howlers *n* ▷ **howler**
howling *v* ▷ **howl**
howls *n, v* ▷ **howl**
hoyden *n* (*pl* **-s**) (*Old-fashioned*) wild or

boisterous girl
hoydens *n* ▷ **hoyden**

> **hox** *v* (**hoxes, hoxing, hoxed**). This is a word found in Shakespeare's plays, and means to cut a horse's hamstring. This unusual word is a handy one to remember if you draw an X. Hox scores 12 points.

hub *n* (*pl* **-s**) centre of a wheel, through which the axle passes
hubbies *n* ▷ **hubby**
hubbub *n* (*pl* **-s**) confused noise of many voices
hubbubs *n* ▷ **hubbub**
hubby *n* (*pl* **-bbies**) (*Informal*) husband
hubris [**hew**-briss] *n* (*pl* **-es**) (*Formal*) pride, arrogance
hubrises ▷ **hubris**
hubs *n* ▷ **hub**
huckster *n* (*pl* **-s**) person using aggressive methods of selling
hucksters *n* ▷ **huckster**
huddle *v* (**-les, -ling, -led**) hunch (oneself) through cold or fear ▶ *n* (*pl* **-s**) small group
huddled *v* ▷ **huddle**
huddles *n, v* ▷ **huddle**
huddling *v* ▷ **huddle**
hue *n* (*pl* **-s**) colour, shade
hues *n* ▷ **hue**
huff *n* (*pl* **-s**) passing mood of anger or resentment ▶ *v* (**-s, -ing, -ed**) blow or puff heavily > **huffy** *adj* (**-ffier, -ffiest**) > **huffily** *adv*
huffed *v* ▷ **huff**
huffier *adj* ▷ **huff**
huffiest *adj* ▷ **huff**
huffily *adv* ▷ **huff**
huffing *v* ▷ **huff**
huffs *n, v* ▷ **huff**
huffy *adj* ▷ **huff**
hug *v* (**-s, -gging, -gged**) clasp tightly in the arms, usu. with affection ▶ *n* (*pl* **-s**) tight or fond embrace
huge *adj* (**-r, -st**) very big > **hugely** *adv*
huger *adj* ▷ **huge**
hugest *adj* ▷ **huge**
hugged *v* ▷ **hug**
hugging *v* ▷ **hug**
hugs *n, v* ▷ **hug**
huh *interj* exclamation of derision, bewilderment, or inquiry
hui [**hoo**-ee] *n* (*pl* **huies**) (NZ) meeting of Maori people
huies *n* ▷ **hui**
hula *n* (*pl* **-s**) swaying Hawaiian dance
hulas *n* ▷ **hula**
hulk *n* (*pl* **-s**) body of an abandoned ship
hulking *adj* bulky, unwieldy
hulks *n* ▷ **hulk**
hull *n* (*pl* **-s**) main body of a boat ▶ *v* (**-s, -ing, -ed**) remove the hulls from
hullabaloo *n* (*pl* **-loos**) loud confused noise or clamour
hullabaloos *n* ▷ **hullabaloo**
hulled *v* ▷ **hull**
hulling *v* ▷ **hull**
hulls *n, v* ▷ **hull**
hum *v* (**-s, -mming, -mmed**) make a low continuous vibrating sound ▶ *n* (*pl* **-s**) humming sound
human *adj* of or typical of people ▶ *n* (*pl* **-s**) human being
humane *adj* (**-r, -st**) kind or merciful > **humanely** *adv*
humanely *adv* ▷ **humane**
humaner *adj* ▷ **humane**
humanest *adj* ▷ **humane**
humanism *n* (*pl* **-s**) belief in human effort rather than religion > **humanist** *n* (*pl* **-s**)
humanisms *n* ▷ **humanism**
humanist *n* ▷ **humanism**
humanists *n* ▷ **humanism**
humanitarian *adj, n* (*pl* **-s**) (person) having the interests of humankind at heart
humanitarians *n* ▷ **humanitarian**
humanities *n* ▷ **humanity** ▶ *pl n* study of literature, philosophy, and the arts
humanity *n* (*pl* **-ties**) human race
humanize *v* (**-zes, -zing, -zed**) make human or humane
humanized *v* ▷ **humanize**
humanizes *v* ▷ **humanize**
humanizing *v* ▷ **humanize**
humankind *n* (*pl* **-s**) human race
humankinds *n* ▷ **humankind**
humanly *adv* by human powers or means
humans *n* ▷ **human**
humble *adj* (**-r, -st**) conscious of one's failings ▶ *v* (**-les, -ling, -led**) cause to feel humble, humiliate > **humbly** *adv*
humbled *v* ▷ **humble**
humbler *adj* ▷ **humble**
humbles *v* ▷ **humble**
humblest *adj* ▷ **humble**
humbling *v* ▷ **humble**
humbly *adv* ▷ **humble**
humbug *n* (*pl* **-s**) (BRIT) hard striped peppermint sweet
humbugs *n* ▷ **humbug**
humdinger *n* (*pl* **-s**) (*Slang*) excellent person or thing
humdingers *n* ▷ **humdinger**

humdrum *adj* ordinary, dull
humeri *n* ▷ **humerus**
humerus [**hew**-mer-uss] *n* (*pl* **-meri**) [-mer-rye] bone from the shoulder to the elbow
humid *adj* (**-er, -est**) damp and hot > **humidity** *n* (*pl* **-ties**) > **humidify** *v* (**-fies, -fying, -fied**)
humider *adj* ▷ **humid**
humidest *adj* ▷ **humid**
humidified *v* ▷ **humid**
humidifier *n* (*pl* **-s**) device for increasing the amount of water vapour in the air in a room
humidifiers *n* ▷ **humidifier**
humidifies *v* ▷ **humid**
humidifying *v* ▷ **humidify**
humidities *n* ▷ **humid**
humidity *n* ▷ **humid**
humiliate *v* (**-tes, -ting, -ted**) lower the dignity or hurt the pride of > **humiliating** *adj* > **humiliation** *n* (*pl* **-s**)
humiliated *v* ▷ **humiliate**
humiliates *v* ▷ **humiliate**
humiliating *v, adj* ▷ **humiliate**
humiliation *n* ▷ **humiliate**
humiliations *n* ▷ **humiliate**
humilities *n* ▷ **humility**
humility *n* (*pl* **humilities**) quality of being humble
hummed *v* ▷ **hum**
humming *v* ▷ **hum**
hummingbird *n* (*pl* **-s**) very small American bird whose powerful wings make a humming noise as they vibrate
hummingbirds *n* ▷ **hummingbird**
hummock *n* (*pl* **-s**) very small hill
hummocks *n* ▷ **hummock**
humorist *n* (*pl* **-s**) writer or entertainer who uses humour in his or her work
humorists *n* ▷ **humorist**
humorous *adj* ▷ **humour**
humorously *adj* ▷ **humour**
humour *n* (*pl* **-s**) ability to say or perceive things that are amusing ▶ *v* (**-s, -ing, -ed**) be kind and indulgent to > **humorous** *adj* > **humorously** *adv*
humoured *v* ▷ **humour**
humouring *v* ▷ **humour**
humours *n, v* ▷ **humour**
hump *n* (*pl* **-s**) raised piece of ground ▶ *v* (**-s, -ing, -ed**) (*Slang*) carry or heave
humped *v* ▷ **hump**
humping *v* ▷ **hump**
humps *n, v* ▷ **hump**
hums *v, n* ▷ **hum**
humus [**hew**-muss] *n* (*pl* **-es**) decomposing vegetable and animal mould in the soil
humuses *n* ▷ **humus**
hunch *n* (*pl* **-es**) feeling or suspicion not based on facts ▶ *v* (**-es, -ing, -ed**) draw (one's shoulders) up or together
hunchback *n* (*pl* **-s**) (*Offens*) person with an abnormal curvature of the spine
hunchbacks *n* ▷ **hunchback**
hunched *v* ▷ **hunch**
hunches *n, v* ▷ **hunch**
hunching *v* ▷ **hunch**
hundred *adj* ten times ten ▶ *n* (*pl* **-s**) (*often pl*) large but unspecified number > **hundredth** *adj, n* (*pl* **-s**)
hundreds *n* ▷ **hundred**
hundredth *n* ▷ **hundred**
hundredths *n* ▷ **hundred**
hundredweight *n* (*pl* **-s**) (BRIT) unit of weight of 112 pounds (50.8 kilograms)
hundredweights *n* ▷ **hundredweight**
hung *v* ▷ **hang** ▶ *adj* (of a parliament or jury) with no side having a clear majority
hunger *n* (*pl* **-s**) discomfort or weakness from lack of food ▶ *v* (**-s, -ing, -ed**) (*foll. by* **for**) want very much
hungered *v* ▷ **hunger**
hungering *v* ▷ **hunger**
hungers *n, v* ▷ **hunger**
hungrier *adj* ▷ **hungry**
hungriest *adj* ▷ **hungry**
hungrily *adv* ▷ **hungry**
hungry *adj* (**-rier, -riest**) desiring food (*foll. by* **for**) > **hungrily** *adv*
hunk *n* (*pl* **-s**) large piece
hunks *n* ▷ **hunk**
hunt *v* (**-s, -ing, -ed**) seek out and kill (wild animals) for food or sport ▶ *n* (*pl* **-s**) hunting
huntaway *n* (*pl* **-s**) (NZ) sheepdog trained to drive sheep by barking
huntaways *n* ▷ **huntaway**
hunted *v* ▷ **hunt**
hunter *n* (*pl* **-s**) person or animal that hunts wild animals for food or sport
hunters *n* ▷ **hunter**
hunting *v* ▷ **hunt**
hunts *v, n* ▷ **hunt**
huntsman *n* (*pl* **-men**) man who hunts wild animals, esp. foxes
huntsmen *n* ▷ **huntsman**
hurdle *n* (*pl* **-s**) (SPORT) light barrier for jumping over in some races ▶ *v* (**-les, -ling, -led**) jump over (something) > **hurdler** *n* (*pl* **-s**)
hurdled *v* ▷ **hurdle**
hurdler *n* ▷ **hurdle**
hurdlers *n* ▷ **hurdle**
hurdles *n, v* ▷ **hurdle** ▶ *pl n* race involving

hurdles
hurdling *v* ▷ **hurdle**
hurl *v* (**-s, -ing, -ed**) throw or utter forcefully
hurled *v* ▷ **hurl**
hurley *n* ▷ **hurling**
hurleys *n* ▷ **hurling**
hurling, hurley *n* (*pl* **-s**) Irish game like hockey ▶ *v* ▷ **hurl**
hurlings *n* ▷ **hurling**
hurls *v* ▷ **hurl**
hurrah, hurray *interj* exclamation of joy or applause
hurricane *n* (*pl* **-s**) very strong, often destructive, wind or storm
hurricanes *n* ▷ **hurricane**
hurried *v* ▷ **hurry**
hurriedly *adv* ▷ **hurry**
hurries *v, n* ▷ **hurry**
hurry *v* (**-ries, -rying, -ried**) (cause to) move or act very quickly ▶ *n* (*pl* **-ries**) doing something quickly or the need to do something quickly > **hurriedly** *adv*
hurrying *v* ▷ **hurry**
hurt *v* (**-s, -ing, hurt**) cause physical or mental pain to ▶ *n* (*pl* **-s**) physical or mental pain
hurtful *adj* unkind
hurting *v* ▷ **hurt**
hurtle *v* (**-les, -ling, -led**) move quickly or violently
hurtled *v* ▷ **hurtle**
hurtles *v* ▷ **hurtle**
hurtling *v* ▷ **hurtle**
hurts *v, n* ▷ **hurt**
husband *n* (*pl* **-s**) woman's partner in marriage ▶ *v* (**-s, -ing, -ed**) use economically
husbanded *v* ▷ **husband**
husbanding *v* ▷ **husband**
husbandries *n* ▷ **husbandry**
husbandry *n* (*pl* **-ries**) farming
husbands *n, v* ▷ **husband**
hush *v* (**-es, -ing, -ed**) make or be silent ▶ *n* (*pl* **-es**) stillness or silence
hushed *v* ▷ **hush**
hushes *v, n* ▷ **hush**
hushing *v* ▷ **hush**
husk *n* (*pl* **-s**) outer covering of certain seeds and fruits ▶ *v* (**-s, -ing, -ed**) remove the husk from
husked *v* ▷ **husk**
huskier *adj* ▷ **husky¹**
huskies *n* ▷ **husky²**
huskiest *adj* ▷ **husky¹**
huskily *adv* ▷ **husky¹**
husking *v* ▷ **husk**
husks *n, v* ▷ **husk**
husky¹ *adj* (**-kier, -kiest**) slightly hoarse > **huskily** *adv*
husky² *n* (*pl* **-kies**) Arctic sledge dog with thick hair and a curled tail
hussar [hoo-**zar**] *n* (*pl* **-s**) (HIST) lightly armed cavalry soldier
hussars *n* ▷ **hussar**
hussies *n* ▷ **hussy**
hussy *n* (*pl* **-sies**) immodest or promiscuous woman
hustings *pl n* political campaigns and speeches before an election
hustle *v* (**-les, -ling, -led**) push about, jostle ▶ *n* (*pl* **-les**) lively activity or bustle
hustled *v* ▷ **hustle**
hustles *v, n* ▷ **hustle**
hustling *v* ▷ **hustle**
hut *n* (*pl* **-s**) small house, shelter, or shed
hutch *n* (*pl* **-es**) cage for pet rabbits etc.
hutches *n* ▷ **hutch**
huts *n* ▷ **hut**
hyacinth *n* (*pl* **-s**) sweet-smelling spring flower that grows from a bulb
hyacinths *n* ▷ **hyacinth**
hyaena *n* (*pl* **-s**) ▷ **hyena**
hyaenas *n* ▷ **hyaena**
hybrid *n* (*pl* **-s**) offspring of two plants or animals of different species ▶ *adj* of mixed origin
hybrids *n* ▷ **hybrid**
hydra *n* (*pl* **-s**) mythical many-headed water serpent
hydrangea *n* (*pl* **-s**) ornamental shrub with clusters of pink, blue, or white flowers
hydrangeas *n* ▷ **hydrangea**
hydrant *n* (*pl* **-s**) outlet from a water main with a nozzle for a hose
hydrants *n* ▷ **hydrant**
hydras *n* ▷ **hydra**
hydrate *n* (*pl* **-tes**) chemical compound of water with another substance
hydrates *n* ▷ **hydrate**
hydraulic *adj* operated by pressure forced through a pipe by a liquid such as water or oil
hydraulically *adv* ▷ **hydraulics**
hydraulics *n* study of the mechanical properties of fluids as they apply to practical engineering > **hydraulically** *adv*
hydro¹ *n* (*pl* **-s**) hotel offering facilities for hydropathy
hydro² *adj* ▷ **hydroelectric**
hydrocarbon *n* (*pl* **-s**) compound of hydrogen and carbon
hydrocarbons *n* ▷ **hydrocarbon**

hydroelectric *adj* of the generation of electricity by water pressure
hydrofoil *n* (*pl* **-s**) fast light boat with its hull raised out of the water on one or more pairs of fins
hydrofoils *n* ▷ **hydrofoil**
hydrogen *n* (*pl* **-s**) (CHEM) light flammable colourless gas that combines with oxygen to form water
hydrogens *n* ▷ **hydrogen**
hydrolyses *n* ▷ **hydrolysis**
hydrolysis [hie-**drol**-iss-iss] *n* (*pl* **-yses**) decomposition of a chemical compound reacting with water
hydrometer [hie-**drom**-it-er] *n* (*pl* **-s**) instrument for measuring the density of a liquid
hydrometers *n* ▷ **hydrometer**
hydropathies *n* ▷ **hydropathy**
hydropathy *n* (*pl* **-thies**) method of treating disease by the use of large quantities of water both internally and externally
hydrophobia *n* (*pl* **-s**) rabies
hydrophobias *n* ▷ **hydrophobia**
hydroplane *n* (*pl* **-s**) light motorboat that skims the water
hydroplanes *n* ▷ **hydroplane**
hydroponics *n* method of growing plants in water rather than soil
hydros *n* ▷ **hydro**[1]
hydrotherapies *n* ▷ **hydrotherapy**
hydrotherapy *n* (*pl* **-pies**) (MED) treatment of certain diseases by exercise in water
hyena *n* (*pl* **-s**) scavenging doglike mammal of Africa and S Asia
hyenas *n* ▷ **hyena**
hygiene *n* (*pl* **-s**) principles and practice of health and cleanliness > **hygienic** *adj* > **hygienically** *adv*
hygienic *adj* ▷ **hygiene**
hygienically *adj* ▷ **hygiene**
hymen *n* (*pl* **-s**) membrane partly covering the opening of a girl's vagina, which breaks before puberty or at the first occurrence of sexual intercourse
hymens *n* ▷ **hymen**
hymn *n* (*pl* **-s**) Christian song of praise sung to God or a saint
hymnal *n* (*pl* **-s**) book of hymns (*also* **hymn book**)
hymnals *n* ▷ **hymnal**
hymns *n* ▷ **hymn**
hype *n* (*pl* **-s**) intensive or exaggerated publicity or sales promotion ▶ *v* (**-pes, -ping, -ped**) promote (a product) using intensive or exaggerated publicity
hyped *v* ▷ **hype**
hyper *adj* (*Informal*) overactive or overexcited
hyperbola [hie-**per**-bol-a] *n* (*pl* **-s**) (GEOM) curve produced when a cone is cut by a plane at a steeper angle to its base than its side
hyperbolas *n* ▷ **hyperbola**
hyperbole [hie-**per**-bol-ee] *n* (*pl* **-s**) deliberate exaggeration for effect > **hyperbolic** *adj*
hyperboles *n* ▷ **hyperbole**
hyperbolic *adj* ▷ **hyperbole**
hyperlink (COMPUTERS) *n* (*pl* **-s**) link from a hypertext file that gives users instant access to related material in another file ▶ *v* (**-s, -ing, -ed**) link (files) in this way
hyperlinked *v* ▷ **hyperlink**
hyperlinking *v* ▷ **hyperlink**
hyperlinks *v, n* ▷ **hyperlink**
hypermarket *n* (*pl* **-s**) huge self-service store
hypermarkets *n* ▷ **hypermarket**
hypersensitive *adj* extremely sensitive to certain drugs, extremes of temperature, etc.
hypersonic *adj* having a speed of at least five times the speed of sound
hypertension *n* (*pl* **-s**) very high blood pressure
hypertensions *n* ▷ **hypertension**
hypertensions *n* ▷ **hypertension**
hypertext *n* (*pl* **-s**) computer software and hardware that allows users to store and view text and move between related items easily
hypertexts *n* ▷ **hypertext**
hypes *n, v* ▷ **hype**
hyphen *n* (*pl* **-s**) punctuation mark (-) indicating that two words or syllables are connected
hyphenated *adj* (of two words or syllables) having a hyphen between them > **hyphenation** *n* (*pl* **-s**)
hyphenation *n* ▷ **hyphenated**
hyphenations *n* ▷ **hyphenated**
hyphens *n* ▷ **hyphen**
hyping *v* ▷ **hype**
hypnoses *n* ▷ **hypnosis**
hypnosis *n* (*pl* **-noses**) artificially induced state of relaxation in which the mind is more than usually receptive to suggestion
hypnotic *adj* of or (as if) producing hypnosis
hypnotism *n* (*pl* **-s**) inducing hypnosis in someone > **hypnotist** *n* (*pl* **-s**) > **hypnotize** *v* (**-tizes, -tizing, -tized**)
hypnotisms *n* ▷ **hypnotism**
hypnotist *n* ▷ **hypnotism**
hypnotists *n* ▷ **hypnotism**
hypnotize *v* ▷ **hypnotism**

hypnotized *v* ▷ **hypnotism**
hypnotizes *v* ▷ **hypnotism**
hypnotizing *v* ▷ **hypnotism**
hypoallergenic *adj* (of cosmetics) not likely to cause an allergic reaction
hypochondria *n* (*pl* **-s**) undue preoccupation with one's health > **hypochondriac** *n* (*pl* **-s**)
hypochondriac *n* ▷ **hypochondria**
hypochondriacs *n* ▷ **hypochondria**
hypochondrias *n* ▷ **hypochondria**
hypocrisies *n* ▷ **hypocrisy**
hypocrisy [hip-**ok**-rass-ee] *n* (*pl* **-sies**) (instance of) pretence of having standards or beliefs that are contrary to one's real character or actual behaviour
hypocrite [**hip**-oh-krit] *n* (*pl* **-s**) person who pretends to be what he or she is not > **hypocritical** *adj* > **hypocritically** *adv*
hypocrites *n* ▷ **hypocrite**
hypocritical *adj* ▷ **hypocrite**
hypocritically *adv* ▷ **hypocrite**
hypodermic *adj, n* (*pl* **-s**) (denoting) a syringe or needle used to inject a drug beneath the skin
hypodermics *n* ▷ **hypodermic**
hypotension *n* (*pl* **-s**) very low blood pressure
hypotenuse [hie-**pot**-a-news] *n* (*pl* **-s**) side of a right-angled triangle opposite the right angle
hypotenuses *n* ▷ **hypotenuse**
hypothermia *n* (*pl* **-s**) condition in which a person's body temperature is dangerously low as a result of prolonged exposure to severe cold
hypothermias *n* ▷ **hypothermia**
hypotheses *n* ▷ **hypothesis**
hypothesis [hie-**poth**-iss-iss] *n* (*pl* **-ses**) [-seez] suggested but unproved explanation of something
hypothetical *adj* based on assumption rather than fact or reality > **hypothetically** *adv*
hypothetically *adj* ▷ **hypothetical**
hyraces *n* ▷ **hyrax**
hyrax *n* (*pl* **-raxes** *or* **-races**) type of hoofed rodent-like animal of Africa and Asia
hyraxes *n* ▷ **hyrax**
hysterectomies *n* ▷ **hysterectomy**
hysterectomy *n* (*pl* **-mies**) surgical removal of the womb
hysteria *n* (*pl* **-s**) state of uncontrolled excitement, anger, or panic > **hysterical** *adj* > **hysterically** *adv*
hysterias *n* ▷ **hysteria**
hysterical *adj* ▷ **hysteria**
hysterically *adj* ▷ **hysteria**
hysterics *pl n* attack of hysteria

Ii

The letter I can prove a difficult tile to use effectively in Scrabble. It's one of the most common tiles in the game, so you often end up with two or more on your rack, but it can be hard to get rid of. Where I does come in very useful, though, is in the number of everyday short words that can be formed from it, which are very helpful when you need to form short words in addition to the main word that you want to play. These words include **in, is, it** (2 points each), **id** (3) and **if** (5). Other handy words are **icy** (8), **ivy** (9) and **imp** (7). Don't forget the three-letter words that use K: **ilk, ink** and **irk** (7 each).

ibex [**ibe**-eks] *n* (*pl* **-es**) wild goat of N with large backward-curving horns
ibexes *n* ▷ **ibex**
ibis [**ibe**-iss] *n* (*pl* **-es**) large wading bird with long legs
ibises *n* ▷ **ibis**
ice *n* (*pl* **-s**) frozen water ▶ *v* (**-ces, -cing, -ced**) (*foll. by* **up** *or* **over**) become covered with ice
iceberg *n* (*pl* **-s**) large floating mass of ice
icebergs *n* ▷ **iceberg**
icebox *n* (*pl* **-es**) (US) refrigerator
iceboxes *n* ▷ **icebox**
icecap *n* (*pl* **-s**) mass of ice permanently covering an area
icecaps *n* ▷ **icecap**
iced *adj* covered with icing ▶ *v* ▷ **ice**
ices *v, n* ▷ **ice**

ich *pron*. Ich is an old dialect form of I. This is a useful little word that is worth remembering because of its unusual combination of letters and relatively high score. Ich scores 8 points.

ichthyologies *n* ▷ **ichthyology**
ichthyology [ik-thi-**ol**-a-jee] *n* (*pl* **-gies**) scientific study of fish
icicle *n* (*pl* **-s**) tapering spike of ice hanging where water has dripped
icicles *n* ▷ **icicle**
icier *adj* ▷ **icy**
iciest *adj* ▷ **icy**
icily *adv* ▷ **icy**
iciness *n* ▷ **icy**
icinesses *n* ▷ **icy**
icing *v* ▷ **ice** ▶ *n* (*pl* **-s**) mixture of sugar and water etc., used to cover and decorate cakes
icings *n* ▷ **icing**

ick *interj*. Ick is something that people say when they encounter something unpleasant or disgusting. Ick is a good word to remember because, in addition to being useful when there's little space, it's one of the highest-scoring three-letter word beginning with I. Ick scores 9 points.

icon *n* (*pl* **-s**) picture of Christ or another religious figure, regarded as holy in the Orthodox Church
iconoclast *n* (*pl* **-s**) person who attacks established ideas or principles > **iconoclastic** *adj*
iconoclastic *adj* ▷ **iconoclastic**
iconoclasts *n* ▷ **iconoclast**
icons *n* ▷ **icon**
icy *adj* (**-cier, -ciest**) very cold > **icily** *adv* > **iciness** *n* (*pl* **-es**)
id *n* (*pl* **-s**) (PSYCHOANALYSIS) the mind's instinctive unconscious energies

ide *n* (**ides**). An ide is a kind of fish. This combination of letters is a good one to keep in mind because it is both a suffix that can be added to words already on the board and a word in its own right. Ide scores 4 points.

idea *n* (*pl* **-s**) plan or thought formed in the mind
ideal *adj* most suitable ▶ *n* (*pl* **-s**) conception of something that is perfect > **idealist** *n* (*pl* **-s**) > **idealistic** *adj* > **ideally** *adv*
idealism *n* (*pl* **-s**) tendency to seek perfection in everything
idealisms *n* ▷ **idealism**
idealist *n* ▷ **ideal**
idealistic *adj* ▷ **ideal**
idealists *n* ▷ **ideal**

idealization *n* ▷ **idealize**
idealizations *n* ▷ **idealize**
idealize *v* (**-izes, -izing, -ized**) regard or portray as perfect or nearly perfect > **idealization** *n* (*pl* **-s**)
idealized *n* ▷ **idealize**
idealizes *n* ▷ **idealize**
idealizing *n* ▷ **idealize**
ideally *adv* ▷ **ideal**
ideals *n* ▷ **ideal**
ideas *n* ▷ **idea**
idem *pron, adj* (LATIN) the same: used to refer to an article, chapter, or book already quoted
identical *adj* exactly the same > **identically** *adv*
identically *adv* ▷ **identical**
identifiable *adj* ▷ **identify**
identification *n* ▷ **identify**
identifications *n* ▷ **identify**
identified *v* ▷ **identify**
identifies *v* ▷ **identify**
identify *v* (**-fies, -fying, -fied**) prove or recognize as being a certain person or thing > **identifiable** *adj* > **identification** *n* (*pl* **-s**)
identifying *v* ▷ **identify**
identities *n* ▷ **identity**
identity *n* (*pl* **-ties**) state of being a specified person or thing
ideological *adj* ▷ **ideology**
ideologies *n* ▷ **ideology**
ideologist *n* ▷ **ideology**
ideologists *n* ▷ **ideology**
ideology *n* (*pl* **-gies**) body of ideas and beliefs of a group, nation, etc. > **ideological** *adj* > **ideologist** *n* (*pl* **-s**)
idiocies *n* ▷ **idiocy**
idiocy *n* (*pl* **-cies**) utter stupidity
idiom *n* (*pl* **-s**) group of words which when used together have a different meaning from the words individually > **idiomatic** *adj* > **idiomatically** *adv*
idiomatic *adj* ▷ **idiom**
idiomatically *adv* ▷ **idiom**
idioms *n* ▷ **idiom**
idiosyncrasies *n* ▷ **idiosyncrasy**
idiosyncrasy *n* (*pl* **-sies**) personal peculiarity of mind, habit, or behaviour
idiot *n* (*pl* **-s**) foolish or stupid person > **idiotic** *adj* > **idiotically** *adv*
idiotic *adj* ▷ **idiot**
idiotically *adv* ▷ **idiot**
idiots *n* ▷ **idiot**
idle *adj* not doing anything ▶ *v* (**-les, -ling, -led**) (*usu. foll. by* **away**) spend (time) doing very little > **idleness** *n* (*pl* **-s**) > **idler** *n* (*pl* **-s**) > **idly** *adv*
idled *v* ▷ **idle**
idleness *n* ▷ **idle**
idlenesses *n* ▷ **idle**
idler *n* ▷ **idle**
idlers *n* ▷ **idle**
idles *v* ▷ **idle**
idling *v* ▷ **idle**
idly *adj* ▷ **idle**
idol *n* (*pl* **-s**) object of excessive devotion
idolatries *n* ▷ **idolatry**
idolatrous *adj* ▷ **idolatry**
idolatry *n* (*pl* **-ries**) worship of idols > **idolatrous** *adj*
idolize *v* (**-izes, -izing, -ized**) love or admire excessively
idolized *v* ▷ **idolize**
idolizes *v* ▷ **idolize**
idolizing *v* ▷ **idolize**
idols *n* ▷ **idol**
ids *n* ▷ **id**
idyll [**id**-ill] *n* (*pl* **-s**) scene or time of great peace and happiness > **idyllic** *adj* > **idyllically** *adv*
idyllic *adj* ▷ **idyll**
idyllically *adj* ▷ **idyll**
idylls *n* ▷ **idyll**
if *conj* on the condition or supposition that ▶ *n* (*pl* **-s**) uncertainty or doubt

> **iff** *conj*. Iff is a word used in logic to mean if and only if. This word is worth remembering: not only can it come in handy when there isn't much space on the board, but it's also one of the highest-scoring three-letter word beginning with I. Iff scores 9 points.

iffy *adj* (*Informal*) doubtful, uncertain
ifs *n* ▷ **if**
igloo *n* (*pl* **-loos**) dome-shaped Inuit house made of snow and ice
igloos *n* ▷ **igloo**
igneous [**ig**-nee-uss] *adj* (of rock) formed as molten rock cools and hardens
ignite *v* (**-tes, -ting, -ted**) catch fire or set fire to
ignited *v* ▷ **ignite**
ignites *v* ▷ **ignite**
igniting *v* ▷ **ignite**
ignition *n* (*pl* **-s**) system that ignites the fuel-and-air mixture to start an engine
ignitions *n* ▷ **ignition**
ignoble *adj* dishonourable
ignominies *n* ▷ **ignominy**
ignominious *adj* ▷ **ignominy**
ignominiously *adj* ▷ **ignominy**
ignominy [**ig**-nom-in-ee] *n* (*pl* **-nies**) humiliating disgrace > **ignominious** *adj* > **ignominiously** *adv*

ignoramus *n* (*pl* **-muses**) ignorant person
ignoramuses *n* ▷ **ignoramus**
ignorance *n* ▷ **ignorant**
ignorances *n* ▷ **ignorance**
ignorant *adj* lacking knowledge > **ignorance** *n* (*pl* **-s**)
ignore *v* (**-res, -ring, -red**) refuse to notice, disregard deliberately
ignored *v* ▷ **ignore**
ignores *v* ▷ **ignore**
ignoring *v* ▷ **ignore**
iguana *n* (*pl* **-s**) large tropical American lizard
iguanas *n* ▷ **iguana**
ileum *n* (*pl* **-s**) lowest part of the small intestine
ileums *n* ▷ **ileum**
ilk *n* (*pl* **-s**) type
ilks *n* ▷ **ilk**
ill *adj* not in good health ▶ *n* (*pl* **-s**) evil, harm ▶ *adv* badly > **illness** *n* (*pl* **-s**)
illegal *adj* against the law > **illegally** *adv* > **illegality** *n* (*pl* **-ties**)
illegalities *n* ▷ **illegal**
illegality *n* ▷ **illegal**
illegally *adv* ▷ **illegal**
illegible *adj* unable to be read or deciphered
illegitimacies *n* ▷ **illegitimate**
illegitimacy *n* ▷ **illegitimate**
illegitimate *adj* born of parents not married to each other > **illegitimacy** *n* (*pl* **-s**)
illicit *adj* illegal
illiteracies *n* ▷ **illiterate**
illiteracy *n* ▷ **illiterate**
illiterate *n* (*pl* **-s**) ▶ *adj* (person) unable to read or write > **illiteracy** *n* (*pl* **-s**)
illiterates *n* ▷ **illiterate**
illness *n* ▷ **ill**
illnesses *n* ▷ **ill**
illogical *adj* unreasonable > **illogicality** *n* (*pl* **-lities**)
illogicalities *adj* ▷ **illogical**
illogicality *adj* ▷ **illogical**
ills *n* ▷ **ill**
illuminate *v* (**-tes, -ting, -ted**) light up > **illumination** *n* (*pl* **-s**) > **illuminating** *adj*
illuminated *v* ▷ **illuminate**
illuminates *v* ▷ **illuminate**
illuminating *adj, v* ▷ **illuminate**
illumination *n* ▷ **illuminate**
illuminations *n* ▷ **illuminate**
illusion *n* (*pl* **-s**) deceptive appearance or belief
illusionist *n* (*pl* **-s**) conjuror
illusionists *n* ▷ **illusionist**
illusions *n* ▷ **illusion**
illusory *adj* seeming to be true, but actually false
illustrate *v* (**-tes, -ting, -ted**) explain by use of examples > **illustrative** *adj* > **illustrator** *n* (*pl* **-s**)
illustrated *v* ▷ **illustrate**
illustrates *v* ▷ **illustrate**
illustrating *v* ▷ **illustrate**
illustration *n* (*pl* **-s**) picture or diagram
illustrations *n* ▷ **illustrate**
illustrative *adj* ▷ **illustrate**
illustrator *n* ▷ **illustrate**
illustrators *n* ▷ **illustrate**
illustrious *adj* famous and distinguished
image *n* (*pl* **-s**) mental picture of someone or something
imageries *n* ▷ **imagery**
imagery *n* (*pl* **-ries**) images collectively, esp. in the arts
images *n* ▷ **image**
imaginable *adj* ▷ **imagine**
imaginary *adj* existing only in the imagination
imagination *n* (*pl* **-s**) ability to make mental images of things that may not exist in real life
imaginations *n* ▷ **imagination**
imaginative *adj* having or showing a lot of creative mental ability > **imaginatively** *adv*
imaginatively *adv* ▷ **imaginative**
imagine *v* (**-nes, -ning, -ned**) form a mental image of > **imaginable** *adj*
imagined *v* ▷ **imagine**
imagines *v* ▷ **imagine** ▶ *n* ▷ **imago**
imagining *v* ▷ **imagine**
imago [im-**may**-go] *n* (*pl* **-goes, -gines**) [im-**maj**-in-ees] sexually mature adult insect
imagoes *n* ▷ **imago**
imam *n* (*pl* **-s**) leader of prayers in a mosque
imams *n* ▷ **imam**
imbalance *n* (*pl* **-s**) lack of balance or proportion
imbalances *n* ▷ **imbalance**
imbecile [**imb**-ess-eel] *n* (*pl* **-s**) stupid person ▶ *adj* (*also* **imbecilic**) stupid or senseless > **imbecility** *n* (*pl* **-ties**)
imbeciles *n* ▷ **imbecile**
imbecilic *adj* ▷ **imbecile**
imbecilities *n* ▷ **imbecile**
imbecility *n* ▷ **imbecile**
imbibe *v* (**-bes, -bing, -bed**) drink (alcoholic drinks)
imbibed *v* ▷ **imbibe**
imbibes *v* ▷ **imbibe**
imbibing *v* ▷ **imbibe**
imbroglio [imb-**role**-ee-oh] *n* (*pl* **-ios**) confusing and complicated situation

imbroglios *n* ▷ **imbroglio**
imbue *v* (**-ues, -uing, -ued**) (*usu. foll. by* **with**) fill or inspire with (ideals or principles)
imbued *v* ▷ **imbue**
imbues *v* ▷ **imbue**
imbuing *v* ▷ **imbue**
imitate *v* (**-tes, -ting, -ted**) take as a model > **imitative** *adj* > **imitator** *n* (*pl* **-s**)
imitated *v* ▷ **imitate**
imitates *v* ▷ **imitate**
imitating *v* ▷ **imitate**
imitation *n* (*pl* **-s**) copy of an original
imitations *n* ▷ **imitation**
imitative *adj* ▷ **imitate**
imitator *n* ▷ **imitate**
imitators *n* ▷ **imitate**
immaculate *adj* completely clean or tidy > **immaculately** *adv*
immaculately *adv* ▷ **immaculate**
immanence *n* ▷ **immanent**
immanences *n* ▷ **immanent**
immanent *adj* present within and throughout something > **immanence** *n* (*pl* **-s**)
immaterial *adj* not important, not relevant
immature *adj* not fully developed > **immaturity** *n* (*pl* **-ties**)
immaturities *n* ▷ **immature**
immaturity *n* ▷ **immature**
immediacies *n* ▷ **immediate**
immediacy *n* ▷ **immediate**
immediate *adj* occurring at once > **immediately** *adv* > **immediacy** *n* (*pl* **-cies**)
immediately *adv* ▷ **immediate**
immemorial *adj* longer than anyone can remember
immense *adj* extremely large > **immensity** *n* (*pl* **-ties**)
immensely *adv* to a very great degree
immensities *n* ▷ **immense**
immensity *n* ▷ **immense**
immerse *v* (**-ses, -sing, -sed**) involve deeply, engross > **immersion** *n* (*pl* **-s**)
immersed *v* ▷ **immerse**
immerses *v* ▷ **immerse**
immersing *v* ▷ **immerse**
immersion *n* ▷ **immerse**
immersions *n* ▷ **immerse**
immigrant *n* ▷ **immigration**
immigrants *n* ▷ **immigration**
immigration *n* (*pl* **-s**) coming to a foreign country in order to settle there > **immigrant** *n* (*pl* **-s**)
immigrations *n* ▷ **immigration**
imminence *n* ▷ **imminent**
imminences *n* ▷ **imminent**
imminent *adj* about to happen > **imminently** *adv* > **imminence** *n* (*pl* **-s**)
imminently *adv* ▷ **imminent**
immobile *adj* not moving > **immobility** *n* (*pl* **-ties**)
immobilities *adj* ▷ **immobile**
immobility *adj* ▷ **immobile**
immobilize *v* (**-izes, -izing, -ized**) make unable to move or work
immobilized *v* ▷ **immobilize**
immobilizes *v* ▷ **immobilize**
immobilizing *v* ▷ **immobilize**
immoderate *adj* excessive or unreasonable
immolate *v* (**-tes, -ting, -ted**) kill as a sacrifice > **immolation** *n* (*pl* **-s**)
immolated *v* ▷ **immolate**
immolates *v* ▷ **immolate**
immolating *v* ▷ **immolate**
immolation *n* ▷ **immolate**
immolations *n* ▷ **immolate**
immoral *adj* morally wrong, corrupt > **immorality** *n* (*pl* **-ties**)
immoralities *n* ▷ **immoral**
immorality *n* ▷ **immoral**
immortal *adj* living forever ▶ *n* (*pl* **-s**) person whose fame will last for all time > **immortality** *n* (*pl* **-s**) > **immortalize** *v* (**-lizes, -lizing, -lized**)
immortalities *n* ▷ **immortal**
immortality *n* ▷ **immortal**
immortalized *v* ▷ **immortal**
immortalizes *v* ▷ **immortal**
immortalizing *v* ▷ **immortal**
immortals *n* ▷ **immortal**
immune *adj* protected against a specific disease
immunities *n* ▷ **immunity**
immunity *n* (*pl* **-ties**) ability to resist disease
immunization *n* ▷ **immunize**
immunizations *n* ▷ **immunize**
immunize *v* (**-izes, -izing, -ized**) make immune to a disease > **immunization** *n* (*pl* **-s**)
immunized *v* ▷ **immunize**
immunizes *v* ▷ **immunize**
immunizing *v* ▷ **immunize**
immunodeficiencies *n* ▷ **immunodeficiency**
immunodeficiency *n* (*pl* **-cies**) deficiency in or breakdown of a person's ability to fight diseases
immunological *adj* ▷ **immunology**
immunologies *n* ▷ **immunology**
immunologist *n* ▷ **immunology**
immunologists *n* ▷ **immunology**
immunology *n* (*pl* **-gies**) branch of medicine concerned with the study of immunity

> immunological *adj* **> immunologist** *n* (*pl* **-s**)
immutabilities *n* ▷ **immutable**
immutability *n* ▷ **immutable**
immutable [im-**mute**-a-bl] *adj* unchangeable **> immutability** *n* (*pl* **-ties**)
imp *n* (*pl* **-s**) (in folklore) mischievous small creature with magical powers
impact *n* (*pl* **-s**) strong effect ▶ *v* (**-s, -ing, -ed**) press firmly into something
impacted *v* ▷ **impact**
impacting *v* ▷ **impact**
impacts *n, v* ▷ **impact**
impair *v* (**-s, -ing, -ed**) weaken or damage **> impairment** *n* (*pl* **-s**)
impaired *v* ▷ **impair**
impairing *v* ▷ **impair**
impairment *n* ▷ **impair**
impairments *n* ▷ **impair**
impairs *v* ▷ **impair**
impala [imp-**ah**-la] *n* (*pl* **-s**) southern African antelope
impalas *n* ▷ **impala**
impale *v* (**-les, -ling, -led**) pierce with a sharp object
impaled *v* ▷ **impale**
impales *v* ▷ **impale**
impaling *v* ▷ **impale**
impalpable *adj* difficult to define or understand
impart *v* (**-s, -ing, -ed**) communicate (information)
imparted *v* ▷ **impart**
impartial *adj* not favouring one side or the other **> impartially** *adv* **> impartiality** *n* (*pl* **-ties**)
impartialities *n* ▷ **impartial**
impartiality *n* ▷ **impartial**
impartially *adv* ▷ **impartial**
imparting *v* ▷ **impart**
imparts *v* ▷ **impart**
impassable *adj* (of a road etc.) impossible to travel through or over
impasse [**am**-pass] *n* (*pl* **-s**) situation in which progress is impossible
impasses *n* ▷ **impasse**
impassioned *adj* full of emotion
impassive *adj* showing no emotion, calm
impatience *n* ▷ **impatient**
impatiences *n* ▷ **impatient**
impatient *adj* irritable at any delay or difficulty **> impatiently** *adv* **> impatience** *n* (*pl* **-s**)
impatiently *adv* ▷ **impatient**
impeach *v* (**-es, -ing, -ed**) charge with a serious crime against the state **> impeachment** *n* (*pl* **-s**)
impeached *v* ▷ **impeach**
impeaches *v* ▷ **impeach**
impeaching *v* ▷ **impeach**
impeachment *n* ▷ **impeach**
impeachments *n* ▷ **impeach**
impeccable *adj* without fault, excellent **> impeccably** *adv*
impeccably *adv* ▷ **impeccable**
impecunious *adj* penniless, poor
impedance [imp-**eed**-anss] *n* (*pl* **-s**) (ELECTRICITY) measure of the opposition to the flow of an alternating current
impedances *n* ▷ **impedance**
impede *v* (**-des, -ding, -ded**) hinder in action or progress
impeded *v* ▷ **impede**
impedes *v* ▷ **impede**
impediment *n* (*pl* **-s**) something that makes action, speech, or progress difficult
impedimenta *pl n* objects impeding progress, esp. baggage or equipment
impediments *n* ▷ **impediment**
impeding *v* ▷ **impede**
impel *v* (**-s, -lling, -lled**) push or force (someone) to do something
impelled *v* ▷ **impel**
impelling *v* ▷ **impel**
impels *v* ▷ **impel**
impending *adj* (esp. of something bad) about to happen
impenetrable *adj* impossible to get through
imperative *adj* extremely urgent, vital ▶ *n* (*pl* **-s**) (GRAMMAR) imperative mood
imperatives *n* ▷ **imperative**
imperceptible *adj* too slight or gradual to be noticed **> imperceptibly** *adv*
imperceptibly *adv* ▷ **imperceptible**
imperfect *adj* having faults or mistakes ▶ *n* (*pl* **-s**) (GRAMMAR) imperfect tense **> imperfection** *n* (*pl* **-s**)
imperfection *n* ▷ **imperfect**
imperfections *n* ▷ **imperfect**
imperfects *n* ▷ **imperfect**
imperial *adj* of or like an empire or emperor
imperialism *n* (*pl* **-s**) rule by one country over many others **> imperialist** *adj, n* (*pl* **-s**)
imperialisms *n* ▷ **imperialism**
imperialist *adj, n* ▷ **imperial**
imperialists *n* ▷ **imperialist**
imperil *v* (**-s, -lling, -lled**) put in danger
imperilled *v* ▷ **imperil**
imperilling *v* ▷ **imperil**
imperils *v* ▷ **imperil**
imperious *adj* proud and domineering

impersonal *adj* not relating to any particular person, objective > **impersonality** *n* (*pl* **-ties**)
impersonalities *n* ▷ **impersonal**
impersonality *n* ▷ **impersonal**
impersonate *v* (**-tes, -ting, -ted**) pretend to be (another person) > **impersonation** *n* (*pl* **-s**) > **impersonator** *n* (*pl* **-s**)
impersonated *v* ▷ **impersonate**
impersonates *v* ▷ **impersonate**
impersonating *v* ▷ **impersonate**
impersonation *n* ▷ **impersonate**
impersonations *n* ▷ **impersonate**
impersonator *n* ▷ **impersonate**
impersonators *n* ▷ **impersonate**
impertinence *n* ▷ **impertinent**
impertinences *n* ▷ **impertinent**
impertinent *adj* disrespectful or rude > **impertinently** *adv* > **impertinence** *n* (*pl* **-s**)
impertinently *adv* ▷ **impertinent**
imperturbable *adj* calm, not excitable
impervious *adj* (*foll. by* **to**) not letting (water etc.) through
impetigo [imp-it-**tie**-go] *n* (*pl* **-s**) contagious skin disease
impetigos *n* ▷ **impetigo**
impetuosities *n* ▷ **impetuous**
impetuosity *n* ▷ **impetuous**
impetuous *adj* done or acting without thought, rash > **impetuously** *adv* > **impetuosity** *n* (*pl* **-ties**)
impetuously *adv* ▷ **impetuous**
impetus [**imp**-it-uss] *n* (*pl* **-es**) incentive, impulse
impetuses *n* ▷ **impetus**
impinge *v* (**-ges, -ging, -ged**) (*foll. by* **on**) affect or restrict
impinged *v* ▷ **impinge**
impinges *v* ▷ **impinge**
impinging *v* ▷ **impinge**
impious [**imp**-ee-uss] *adj* showing a lack of respect or reverence
impish *adj* mischievous
implacabilities *n* ▷ **implacable**
implacability *n* ▷ **implacable**
implacable *adj* not prepared to be appeased, unyielding > **implacably** *adv* > **implacability** *n* (*pl* **-ties**)
implacably *adv* ▷ **implacably**
implant *n* (*pl* **-s**) (MED) something put into someone's body, usu. by surgical operation ▸ *v* (**-s, -ing, -ed**) put (something) into someone's body, usu. by surgical operation > **implantation** *n* (*pl* **-s**)
implantation *n* ▷ **implant**
implantations *n* ▷ **implant**
implanted *v* ▷ **implant**
implanting *v* ▷ **implant**
implants *n, v* ▷ **implant**
implement *v* (**-s, -ing, -ed**) carry out (instructions etc.) ▸ *n* (*pl* **-s**) tool, instrument > **implementation** *n* (*pl* **-s**)
implementation *n* ▷ **implement**
implementations *n* ▷ **implement**
implemented *v* ▷ **implement**
implementing *v* ▷ **implement**
implements *v, n* ▷ **implement**
implicate *v* (**-tes, -ting, -ted**) show to be involved, esp. in a crime
implicated *v* ▷ **implicate**
implicates *v* ▷ **implicate**
implicating *v* ▷ **implicate**
implication *n* (*pl* **-s**) something implied
implications *n* ▷ **implication**
implicit *adj* expressed indirectly > **implicitly** *adv*
implicitly *adv* ▷ **implicit**
implied *v* ▷ **imply**
implies *v* ▷ **imply**
implore *v* (**-res, -ring, -red**) beg earnestly
implored *v* ▷ **implore**
implores *v* ▷ **implore**
imploring *v* ▷ **implore**
imply *v* (**-lies, -lying, -lied**) indicate by hinting, suggest
implying *v* ▷ **imply**
impolitic *adj* unwise or inadvisable
imponderable *n* (*pl* **-s**) ▸ *adj* (something) impossible to assess
imponderables *n* ▷ **imponderable**
import *v* (**-s, -ing, -ed**) bring in (goods) from another country ▸ *n* (*pl* **-s**) something imported > **importation** *n* (*pl* **-s**) > **importer** *n* (*pl* **-s**)
importance *n* ▷ **important**
importances *n* ▷ **important**
important *adj* of great significance or value > **importance** *n* (*pl* **-s**)
importation *n* ▷ **import**
importations *n* ▷ **import**
imported *v* ▷ **import**
importer *n* ▷ **import**
importers *n* ▷ **import**
importing *v* ▷ **import**
imports *v, n* ▷ **import**
importunate *adj* persistent or demanding
importune *v* (**-nes, -ning, -ned**) harass with persistent requests > **importunity** *n* (*pl* **-ties**)
importuned *v* ▷ **importune**
importunes *v* ▷ **importune**
importuning *v* ▷ **importune**

importunities *n* ▷ **importune**
importunity *n* ▷ **importune**
impose *v* (**-ses, -sing, -sed**) force the acceptance of
imposed *v* ▷ **impose**
imposes *v* ▷ **impose**
imposing *adj* grand, impressive ▶ *v* ▷ **impose**
imposition *n* (*pl* **-s**) unreasonable demand
impositions *n* ▷ **imposition**
impossibilities *n* ▷ **impossible**
impossibility *n* ▷ **impossible**
impossible *adj* not able to be done or to happen > **impossibly** *adv* > **impossibility** *n* (*pl* **-ties**)
impossibly *adv* ▷ **impossible**
imposter, impostor *n* (*pl* **-s**) person who cheats or swindles by pretending to be someone else
imposters *n* ▷ **imposter**
impostor *n* ▷ **imposter**
impostors *n* ▷ **imposter**
impotence *n* ▷ **impotent**
impotences *n* ▷ **impotent**
impotent [**imp**-a-tent] *adj* powerless > **impotence** *n* (*pl* **-s**) > **impotently** *adv*
impotently *adv* ▷ **impotent**
impound *v* (**-s, -ing, -ed**) take legal possession of, confiscate
impounded *v* ▷ **impound**
impounding *v* ▷ **impound**
impounds *v* ▷ **impound**
impoverish *v* (**-es, -ing, -ed**) make poor or weak > **impoverishment** *n* (*pl* **-s**)
impoverished *v* ▷ **impoverish**
impoverishes *v* ▷ **impoverish**
impoverishing *v* ▷ **impoverish**
impoverishment *n* ▷ **impoverish**
impoverishments *n* ▷ **impoverish**
impracticable *adj* incapable of being put into practice
impractical *adj* not sensible
imprecation *n* (*pl* **-s**) curse
imprecations *n* ▷ **imprecation**
impregnabilities *n* ▷ **impregnable**
impregnability *n* ▷ **impregnable**
impregnable *adj* impossible to break into > **impregnability** *n* (*pl* **-ties**)
impregnate *v* (**-tes, -ting, -ted**) saturate, spread all through > **impregnation** *n* (*pl* **-s**)
impregnated *v* ▷ **impregnate**
impregnates *v* ▷ **impregnate**
impregnating *v* ▷ **impregnate**
impregnation *n* ▷ **impregnate**
impregnations *n* ▷ **impregnate**
impresario *n* (*pl* **-s**) person who runs theatre performances, concerts, etc.
impresarios *n* ▷ **impresario**
impress *v* (**-es, -ing, -ed**) affect strongly, usu. favourably
impressed *v* ▷ **impress**
impresses *v* ▷ **impress**
impressing *v* ▷ **impress**
impression *n* (*pl* **-s**) effect, esp. a strong or favourable one
impressionable *adj* easily impressed or influenced
impressionism *n* (*pl* **-s**) art style that gives a general effect or mood rather than form or structure > **impressionist** *n* (*pl* **-s**) > **impressionistic** *adj*
impressionisms *n* ▷ **impressionism**
impressionist *n* ▷ **impressionism**
impressionistic *adj* ▷ **impressionism**
impressionists *n* ▷ **impressionism**
impressions *n* ▷ **impression**
impressive *adj* making a strong impression, esp. through size, importance, or quality
imprimatur [imp-rim-**ah**-ter] *n* (*pl* **-s**) official approval to print a book
imprimaturs *n* ▷ **imprimatur**
imprint *n* (*pl* **-s**) mark made by printing or stamping ▶ *v* (**-s, -ing, -ed**) produce (a mark) by printing or stamping
imprinted *v* ▷ **imprint**
imprinting *v* ▷ **imprint**
imprints *n, v* ▷ **imprint**
imprison *v* (**-s, -ing, -ed**) put in prison > **imprisonment** *n* (*pl* **-s**)
imprisoned *v* ▷ **imprison**
imprisoning *v* ▷ **imprison**
imprisonment *n* ▷ **imprison**
imprisonments *n* ▷ **imprisonment**
imprisons *v* ▷ **imprison**
improbabilities *n* ▷ **improbable**
improbability *n* ▷ **improbable**
improbable *adj* not likely to be true or to happen > **improbability** *n* (*pl* **-ties**)
impromptu *adj* without planning or preparation
improper *adj* indecent
improprieties *n* ▷ **impropriety**
impropriety [imp-roe-**pry**-a-tee] *n* (*pl* **-ties**) unsuitable or slightly improper behaviour
improve *v* (**-ves, -ving, -ved**) make or become better > **improvement** *n* (*pl* **-s**)
improved *v* ▷ **improve**
improvement *n* ▷ **improvement**
improvements *n* ▷ **improvement**
improves *v* ▷ **improve**
improvidence *n* ▷ **improvident**

improvidences *n* ▷ **improvident**
improvident *adj* not planning for future needs > **improvidence** *n* (*pl* **-s**)
improving *v* ▷ **improve**
improvisation *n* ▷ **improvise**
improvisations *n* ▷ **improvise**
improvise *v* (**-ises, -sing, -sed**) make use of whatever materials are available > **improvisation** *n* (*pl* **-s**)
improvised *v* ▷ **improvise**
improvises *v* ▷ **improvise**
improvising *v* ▷ **improvise**
imps *n* ▷ **imp**
impudence *n* ▷ **impudent**
impudences *n* ▷ **impudent**
impudent *adj* cheeky, disrespectful > **impudently** *adv* > **impudence** *n* (*pl* **-s**)
impudently *adv* ▷ **impudently**
impugn [imp-**yoon**] *v* (**-s, -ing, -ed**) challenge the truth or validity of
impugned *v* ▷ **impugn**
impugning *v* ▷ **impugn**
impugns *v* ▷ **impugn**
impulse *n* (*pl* **-s**) sudden urge to do something > **impulsive** *adj* acting or done without careful consideration > **impulsively** *adv*
impulses *n* ▷ **impulse**
impulsive *adj* ▷ **impulse**
impulsively *adv* ▷ **impulse**
impunities *n* ▷ **impunity**
impunity [imp-**yoon**-it-ee] *n* (*pl* **-ties**) without punishment
impure *adj* having dirty or unwanted substances mixed in > **impurity** *n* (*pl* **-ties**)
impurities *n* ▷ **impure**
impurity *n* ▷ **impure**
imputation *n* ▷ **impute**
imputations *n* ▷ **impute**
impute *v* (**-tes, -ting, -ted**) attribute responsibility to > **imputation** *n* (*pl* **-s**)
imputed *v* ▷ **impute**
imputes *v* ▷ **impute**
imputing *v* ▷ **impute**
in *prep* indicating position inside, state or situation, etc. ▶ *adv* indicating position inside, entry into, etc. ▶ *adj* fashionable
inabilities *n* ▷ **inability**
inability *n* (*pl* **-ties**) lack of means or skill to do something
inaccuracies *n* ▷ **inaccurate**
inaccuracy *n* ▷ **inaccurate**
inaccurate *adj* not correct > **inaccuracy** *n* (*pl* **-cies**)
inadequacies *n* ▷ **inadequate**
inadequacy *n* ▷ **inadequate**
inadequate *adj* not enough > **inadequacy** *n* (*pl* **-cies**)
inadvertent *adj* unintentional > **inadvertently** *adv*
inadvertently *adv* ▷ **inadvertent**
inalienable *adj* not able to be taken away
inane *adj* senseless, silly > **inanity** *n* (*pl* **-ties**)
inanimate *adj* not living
inanities *n* ▷ **inane**
inanity *n* ▷ **inane**
inappropriate *adj* not suitable
inarticulate *adj* unable to express oneself clearly or well
inaugural *adj* ▷ **inaugurate**
inaugurate *v* (**-tes, -ting, -ted**) open or begin the use of, esp. with ceremony > **inaugural** *adj* > **inauguration** *n* (*pl* **-s**)
inaugurated *v* ▷ **inaugurate**
inaugurates *v* ▷ **inaugurate**
inaugurating *v* ▷ **inaugurate**
inauguration *n* ▷ **inaugurate**
inaugurations *n* ▷ **inaugurate**
inauspicious *adj* unlucky, likely to have an unfavourable outcome
inboard *adj* (of a boat's engine) inside the hull
inborn *adj* existing from birth, natural
inbred *adj* produced as a result of inbreeding
inbreeding *n* (*pl* **-s**) breeding of animals or people that are closely related
inbreedings *n* ▷ **inbreeding**
inbuilt *adj* present from the start
incalculable *adj* too great to be estimated
incandescence *n* ▷ **incandescent**
incandescences *n* ▷ **incandescent**
incandescent *adj* glowing with heat > **incandescence** *n* (*pl* **-s**)
incantation *n* (*pl* **-s**) ritual chanting of magic words or sounds
incantations *n* ▷ **incantation**
incapable *adj* (*foll. by* **of**) unable (to do something)
incapacitate *v* (**-tates, -tating, -tated**) deprive of strength or ability > **incapacity** *n* (*pl* **-ties**)
incapacitated *v* ▷ **incapacitate**
incapacitates *v* ▷ **incapacitate**
incapacitating *v* ▷ **incapacitate**
incapacities *n* ▷ **incapacitate**
incapacity *n* ▷ **incapacitate**
incarcerate *v* (**-tes, -ting, -ted**) imprison > **incarceration** *n* (*pl* **-s**)
incarcerated *v* ▷ **incarcerate**
incarcerates *v* ▷ **incarcerate**
incarcerating *v* ▷ **incarcerate**
incarceration *n* ▷ **incarcerate**
incarcerations *n* ▷ **incarcerate**

incarnate *adj* in human form > **incarnation** *n* (*pl* **-s**)
incarnation *n* ▷ **incarnate**
incarnations *n* ▷ **incarnate**
incendiaries *n* ▷ **incendiary**
incendiary [in-**send**-ya-ree] *adj* (of a bomb, attack, etc.) designed to cause fires ▶ *n* (*pl* **-ries**) bomb designed to cause fires
incense¹ *v* (**-ses, -sing, -sed**) make very angry
incense² *n* (*pl* **incenses**) substance that gives off a sweet perfume when burned
incensed *v* ▷ **incense¹**
incenses *v* ▷ **incense¹** ▶ *n* ▷ **incense²**
incensing *v* ▷ **incense¹**
incentive *n* (*pl* **-s**) something that encourages effort or action
incentives *n* ▷ **incentive**
inception *n* (*pl* **-s**) beginning
inceptions *n* ▷ **inception**
incessant *adj* never stopping > **incessantly** *adv*
incessantly *adv* ▷ **incessant**
incest *n* (*pl* **-s**) sexual intercourse between two people too closely related to marry > **incestuous** *adj*
incests *n* ▷ **incest**
incestuous *adj* ▷ **incest**
inch *n* (*pl* **-es**) unit of length equal to one twelfth of a foot or 2.54 centimetres ▶ *v* (**-ches, -ching, -ched**) move slowly and gradually
inched *v* ▷ **inch**
inches *v, n* ▷ **inch**
inching *v* ▷ **inch**
inchoate [in-**koe**-ate] *adj* just begun and not yet properly developed
incidence *n* (*pl* **-s**) extent or frequency of occurrence
incidences *n* ▷ **incidence**
incident *n* (*pl* **-s**) something that happens
incidental *adj* occurring in connection with or resulting from something more important > **incidentally** *adv*
incidentally *adv* ▷ **incidental**
incidents *n* ▷ **incident**
incinerate *v* (**-tes, -ting, -ted**) burn to ashes > **incineration** *n* (*pl* **-s**)
incinerated *v* ▷ **incinerate**
incinerates *v* ▷ **incinerate**
incinerating *v* ▷ **incinerate**
incineration *n* ▷ **incinerate**
incinerations *n* ▷ **incineration**
incinerator *n* (*pl* **-s**) furnace for burning rubbish
incinerators *n* ▷ **incinerator**
incipient *adj* just starting to appear or happen
incise *v* (**-ses, -sing, -sed**) cut into with a sharp tool > **incision** *n* (*pl* **-s**)
incised *v* ▷ **incise**
incises *v* ▷ **incise**
incising *v* ▷ **incise**
incision *n* ▷ **incise**
incisions *n* ▷ **incise**
incisive *adj* direct and forceful
incisor *n* (*pl* **-s**) front tooth, used for biting into food
incisors *n* ▷ **incisor**
incite *v* (**-tes, -ting, -ted**) stir up, provoke > **incitement** *n* (*pl* **-s**)
incited *v* ▷ **incite**
incitement *n* ▷ **incite**
incitements *n* ▷ **incite**
incites *v* ▷ **incite**
inciting *v* ▷ **incite**
incivilities *n* ▷ **incivility**
incivility *n* (*pl* **-ties**) rudeness or a rude remark
inclement *adj* (of weather) stormy or severe
inclination *n* (*pl* **-s**) liking, tendency, or preference
inclinations *n* ▷ **inclination**
incline *v* (**-nes, -ning, -ned**) lean, slope ▶ *n* (*pl* **-s**) slope
inclined *v* ▷ **incline**
inclines *v, n* ▷ **incline**
inclining *v* ▷ **incline**
include *v* (**-des, -ding, -ded**) have as part of the whole > **inclusion** *n* (*pl* **-s**)
included *v* ▷ **include**
includes *v* ▷ **include**
including *v* ▷ **include**
inclusion *n* ▷ **include**
inclusions *n* ▷ **include**
inclusive *adj* including everything (specified) > **inclusively** *adv*
inclusively *adv* ▷ **inclusive**
incognito [in-kog-**nee**-toe] *adj, adv* having adopted a false identity ▶ *n* (*pl* **-tos**) false identity
incognitos *n* ▷ **incognito**
incoherence *n* ▷ **incoherent**
incoherences *n* ▷ **incoherent**
incoherent *adj* unclear and impossible to understand > **incoherence** *n* (*pl* **-s**) > **incoherently** *adv*
incoherently *adv* ▷ **incoherent**
income *n* (*pl* **-s**) amount of money earned from work, investments, etc.
incomes *n* ▷ **income**
incoming *adj* coming in
incommode *v* (**-des, -ding, -ded**) cause inconvenience to

incommoded *v* ▷ **incommode**
incommodes *v* ▷ **incommode**
incommoding *v* ▷ **incommode**
incommunicado *adj, adv* deprived of communication with other people
incomparable *adj* beyond comparison, unequalled > **incomparably** *adv*
incomparably *adv* ▷ **incomparable**
incompatibilities *n* ▷ **incompatible**
incompatibility *n* ▷ **incompatible**
incompatible *adj* inconsistent or conflicting > **incompatibility** *n* (*pl* **-ties**)
incompetence *n* ▷ **incompetent**
incompetences *n* ▷ **incompetent**
incompetent *adj* not having the necessary ability or skill to do something > **incompetence** *n* (*pl* **-s**)
inconceivable *adj* extremely unlikely, unimaginable
inconclusive *adj* not giving a final decision or result
incongruities *n* ▷ **incongruous**
incongruity *n* ▷ **incongruous**
incongruous *adj* inappropriate or out of place > **incongruously** *adv* > **incongruity** *n* (*pl* **-ties**)
incongruously *adv* ▷ **incongruous**
inconsequential *adj* unimportant, insignificant
inconsiderable *adj* fairly large
inconstant *adj* liable to change one's loyalties or opinions
incontinence *n* ▷ **incontinent**
incontinences *n* ▷ **incontinent**
incontinent *adj* unable to control one's bladder or bowels > **incontinence** *n* (*pl* **-s**)
incontrovertible *adj* impossible to deny or disprove
inconvenience *n* (*pl* **-s**) trouble or difficulty ▶ *v* (**-ces, -ncing, -nced**) cause trouble or difficulty to > **inconvenient** *adj*
inconvenienced *v* ▷ **inconvenience**
inconveniences *n, v* ▷ **inconvenience**
inconveniencing *v* ▷ **inconvenience**
inconvenient *adj* ▷ **inconvenience**
incorporate *v* (**-tes, -ting, -ted**) include or be included as part of a larger unit
incorporated *v* ▷ **incorporate**
incorporates *v* ▷ **incorporate**
incorporating *v* ▷ **incorporate**
incorporeal *adj* without material form
incorrigible *adj* beyond correction or reform
incorruptible *adj* too honest to be bribed or corrupted
increase *v* (**-ses, -sing, -sed**) make or become greater in size, number, etc. ▶ *n* (*pl* **-s**) rise in number, size, etc. > **increasingly** *adv*
increased *v* ▷ **increase**
increases *v, n* ▷ **increase**
increasing *v* ▷ **increase**
increasingly *adv* ▷ **increase**
incredible *adj* hard to believe or imagine > **incredibly** *adv*
incredibly *adv* ▷ **incredible**
incredulities *n* ▷ **incredulous**
incredulity *n* ▷ **incredulous**
incredulous *adj* not willing to believe something > **incredulity** *n* (*pl* **-ties**)
increment *n* (*pl* **-s**) increase in money or value, esp. a regular salary increase > **incremental** *adj*
incremental *adj* ▷ **increment**
increments *n* ▷ **increment**
incriminate *v* (**-tes, -ting, -ted**) make (someone) seem guilty of a crime > **incriminating** *adj*
incriminated *v* ▷ **incriminate**
incriminates *v* ▷ **incriminate**
incriminating *v, adj* ▷ **incriminate**
incubate [in-cube-ate] *v* (**-tes, -ting, -ted**) (of a bird) hatch (eggs) by sitting on them > **incubation** *n* (*pl* **-s**)
incubated *v* ▷ **incubate**
incubates *v* ▷ **incubate**
incubating *v* ▷ **incubate**
incubation *n* ▷ **incubate**
incubations *n* ▷ **incubate**
incubator *n* (*pl* **-s**) heated enclosed apparatus for rearing premature babies
incubators *n* ▷ **incubator**
incubi *n* ▷ **incubus**
incubus [in-cube-uss] *n* (*pl* **-bi, -buses**) (in folklore) demon believed to have sex with sleeping women
incubuses *n* ▷ **incubus**
inculcate *v* (**-tes, -ting, -ted**) fix in someone's mind by constant repetition > **inculcation** *n* (*pl* **-s**)
inculcated *v* ▷ **inculcate**
inculcates *v* ▷ **inculcate**
inculcating *v* ▷ **inculcate**
inculcation *n* ▷ **inculcate**
inculcations *n* ▷ **inculcate**
incumbencies *n* ▷ **incumbent**
incumbency *n* ▷ **incumbent**
incumbent *n* (*pl* **-s**) person holding a particular office or position ▶ *adj* it is the duty of > **incumbency** *n* (*pl* **-cies**)
incumbents *n* ▷ **incumbent**
incur *v* (**-s, -rring, -rred**) cause (something unpleasant) to happen

incurable *adj* not able to be cured > **incurably** *adv*
incurably *adv* ▷ **incurable**
incurious *adj* showing no curiosity or interest
incurred *v* ▷ **incur**
incurring *v* ▷ **incur**
incurs *v* ▷ **incur**
incursion *n* (*pl* **-s**) sudden brief invasion
incursions *n* ▷ **incursion**
indebted *adj* owing gratitude for help or favours > **indebtedness** *n* (*pl* **-es**)
indebtedness *n* ▷ **indebted**
indebtednesses *n* ▷ **indebted**
indecencies *n* ▷ **indecent**
indecency *n* ▷ **indecent**
indecent *adj* morally or sexually offensive > **indecently** *adv* > **indecency** *n* (*pl* **-cies**)
indecently *adv* ▷ **indecent**
indecipherable *adj* impossible to read
indeed *adv* really, certainly ▶ *interj* expression of indignation or surprise
indefatigable *adj* never getting tired > **indefatigably** *adv*
indefatigably *adv* ▷ **indefatigable**
indefensible *adj* unable to be justified
indefinite *adj* without exact limits > **indefinitely** *adv*
indefinitely *adv* ▷ **indefinite**
indelible *adj* impossible to erase or remove > **indelibly** *adv*
indelibly *adv* ▷ **indelible**
indelicate *adj* offensive or embarrassing
indemnified *v* ▷ **indemnify**
indemnifies *v* ▷ **indemnify**
indemnify *v* (**-fies, -fying, -fied**) secure against loss, damage, or liability
indemnifying *v* ▷ **indemnify**
indemnities *v* ▷ **indemnity**
indemnity *n* (*pl* **-ties**) insurance against loss or damage
indent *v* (**-s, -ing, -ed**) start (a line of writing) further from the margin than the other lines
indentation *n* (*pl* **-s**) dent in a surface or edge
indentations *n* ▷ **indentation**
indented *v* ▷ **indent**
indenting *v* ▷ **indent**
indents *v* ▷ **indent**
indenture *n* (*pl* **-s**) contract, esp. one binding an apprentice to his or her employer
indentures *n* ▷ **indenture**
independence *n* ▷ **independent**
independences *n* ▷ **independent**
independent *adj* free from the control or influence of others ▶ *n* (*pl* **-s**) politician who does not represent any political party > **independently** *adv* > **independence** *n* (*pl* **-s**)
independently *adsv* ▷ **independent**
independents *n* ▷ **independent**
indescribable *adj* too intense or extreme for words > **indescribably** *adv*
indescribably *adv* ▷ **indescribable**
indeterminacies *n* ▷ **indeterminate**
indeterminacy *n* ▷ **indeterminate**
indeterminate *adj* uncertain in extent, amount, or nature > **indeterminacy** *n* (*pl* **-cies**)
index *n* (*pl* **-dices**) [**in**-diss-eez] alphabetical list of names or subjects dealt with in a book ▶ *v* (**-dexes, -dexing, -dexed**) provide (a book) with an index
indexed *v* ▷ **index**
indexes *v* ▷ **index**
indexing *v* ▷ **index**
indicate *v* (**-tes, -ting, -ted**) be a sign or symptom of > **indication** *n* (*pl* **-s**)
indicated *v* ▷ **indicate**
indicates *v* ▷ **indicate**
indicating *v* ▷ **indicate**
indication *n* ▷ **indicate**
indications *n* ▷ **indicate**
indicative *adj* (*foll. by* **of**) suggesting ▶ *n* (*pl* **-s**) (GRAMMAR) indicative mood
indicatives *n* ▷ **indicative**
indicator *n* (*pl* **-s**) something acting as a sign or indication
indicators *n* ▷ **indicator**
indices *n* ▷ **index**
indict [in-**dite**] *v* (**-s, -ing, -ed**) formally charge with a crime > **indictable** *adj* > **indictment** *n* (*pl* **-s**)
indictable *adj* ▷ **indict**
indicted *v* ▷ **indict**
indicting *v* ▷ **indict**
indictment *n* ▷ **indict**
indictments *n* ▷ **indict**
indicts *v* ▷ **indict**
indie *adj* (*Informal*) (of rock music) released by an independent record company
indifference *n* ▷ **indifferent**
indifferences *n* ▷ **indifferent**
indifferent *adj* showing no interest or concern > **indifference** *n* (*pl* **-s**) > **indifferently** *adv*
indifferently *adv* ▷ **indifferent**
indigence *n* ▷ **indigent**
indigences *n* ▷ **indigent**
indigenous [in-**dij**-in-uss] *adj* born in or natural to a country
indigent *adj* extremely poor > **indigence** *n* (*pl* **-s**)
indigestible *adj* ▷ **indigestion**
indigestion *n* (*pl* **-s**) (discomfort or pain

caused by) difficulty in digesting food
> **indigestible** *adj*
indigestions *n* ▷ **indigestion**
indignant *adj* feeling or showing indignation
> **indignantly** *adv*
indignantly *adv* ▷ **indignant**
indignation *n* (*pl* **-s**) anger at something unfair or wrong
indignations *n* ▷ **indignation**
indignities *n* ▷ **indignity**
indignity *n* (*pl* **-ties**) embarrassing or humiliating treatment
indigo *adj* deep violet-blue ▶ *n* (*pl* **-s**) dye of this colour
indigos *n* ▷ **indigo**
indirect *adj* done or caused by someone or something else
indiscreet *adj* incautious or tactless in revealing secrets > **indiscreetly** *adv*
> **indiscretion** *n* (*pl* **-s**)
indiscreetly *adv* ▷ **indiscreet**
indiscretion *n* ▷ **indiscreet**
indiscretions *n* ▷ **indiscreet**
indiscriminate *adj* showing lack of careful thought
indispensable *adj* absolutely essential
indisposed *adj* unwell, ill > **indisposition** *n* (*pl* **-s**)
indisposition *n* ▷ **indisposed**
indispositions *n* ▷ **indisposed**
indisputable *adj* beyond doubt > **indisputably** *adv*
indisputably *adv* ▷ **indisputable**
indissoluble *adj* permanent
indium *n* (*pl* **-s**) (CHEM) soft silvery-white metallic element
indiums *n* ▷ **indium**
individual *adj* characteristic of or meant for a single person or thing ▶ *n* (*pl* **-s**) single person or thing > **individually** *adv* > **individuality** *n* (*pl* **-ties**)
individualism *n* (*pl* **-s**) principle of living one's life in one's own way > **individualist** *n* (*pl* **-s**)
> **individualistic** *adj*
individualisms *n* ▷ **individualism**
individualist *n* ▷ **individualism**
individualistic *adj* ▷ **individualism**
individualists *n* ▷ **individualism**
individualities *n* ▷ **individual**
individuality *n* ▷ **individual**
individually *adv* ▷ **individual**
individuals *n* ▷ **individual**
indoctrinate *v* (**-tes, -ting, -ted**) teach (someone) to accept a doctrine or belief uncritically > **indoctrination** *n* (*pl* **-s**)
indoctrinated *v* ▷ **indoctrinate**
indoctrinates *v* ▷ **indoctrinate**
indoctrinating *v* ▷ **indoctrinate**
indoctrination *n* ▷ **indoctrinate**
indoctrinations *n* ▷ **indoctrinate**
indolence *n* ▷ **indolent**
indolences *n* ▷ **indolent**
indolent *adj* lazy > **indolence** *n* (*pl* **-s**)
indomitable *adj* too strong to be defeated or discouraged > **indomitably** *adv*
indomitably *adv* ▷ **indomitable**
indoor *adj* inside a building > **indoors** *adv*
indoors *adv* ▷ **indoor**
indubitable *adj* beyond doubt, certain
> **indubitably** *adv*
indubitably *adv* ▷ **indubitable**
induce *v* (**-ces, -cing, -ced**) persuade or influence
induced *v* ▷ **induce**
inducement *n* (*pl* **-s**) something used to persuade someone to do something
inducements *n* ▷ **inducement**
induces *v* ▷ **induce**
inducing *v* ▷ **induce**
induct *v* (**-s, -ing, -ed**) formally install (someone, esp. a clergyman) in office
inductance *n* (*pl* **-s**) property of an electric circuit creating voltage by a change of current
inductances *n* ▷ **inductance**
inducted *v* ▷ **induct**
inducting *v* ▷ **induct**
induction *n* (*pl* **-s**) reasoning process by which general conclusions are drawn from particular instances > **inductive** *adj*
inductions *n* ▷ **induction**
inductive *adj* ▷ **induction**
inducts *v* ▷ **induct**
indulge *v* (**-ges, -ging, -ged**) allow oneself pleasure > **indulgent** *adj* > **indulgently** *adv*
indulged *v* ▷ **indulge**
indulgence *n* (*pl* **-s**) something allowed because it gives pleasure
indulgences *n* ▷ **indulgence**
indulgent *adj* ▷ **indulge**
indulgently *adj* ▷ **indulge**
indulges *v* ▷ **indulge**
indulging *v* ▷ **indulge**
industrial *adj* of, used in, or employed in industry
industrialization *n* ▷ **industrialize**
industrializations *n* ▷ **industrialize**
industrialize *v* (**-izes, -izing, -ized**) develop large-scale industry in (a country or region)
> **industrialization** *n* (*pl* **-s**)

industrialized *v* ▷ **industrialize**

industrializes *v* ▷ **industrialize**

industrializing *v* ▷ **industrialize**

industries *n* ▷ **industry**

industrious *adj* ▷ **industry**

industry *n* (*pl* **-tries**) manufacture of goods > **industrious** *adj* hard-working

inebriate *n* (*pl* **-s**) ▶ *adj* (person who is) habitually drunk

inebriated *adj* drunk > **inebriation** *n* (*pl* **-s**)

inebriates *n* ▷ **inebriate**

inebriation *n* ▷ **inebriated**

inebriations *n* ▷ **inebriated**

inedible *adj* not fit to be eaten

ineffable *adj* too great for words > **ineffably** *adv*

ineffably *adv* ▷ **ineffable**

ineffectual *adj* having very little effect

ineligible *adj* not qualified for or entitled to something

ineluctable *adj* impossible to avoid

inept *adj* clumsy, lacking skill > **ineptitude** *n* (*pl* **-s**)

ineptitude *n* ▷ **inept**

ineptitudes *n* ▷ **inept**

inequitable *adj* unfair

ineradicable *adj* impossible to remove

inert *adj* without the power of motion or resistance > **inertness** *n* (*pl* **-es**)

inertia *n* (*pl* **-s**) feeling of unwillingness to do anything

inertias *n* ▷ **inertia**

inertness *n* ▷ **inert**

inertnesses *n* ▷ **inert**

inescapable *adj* unavoidable

inestimable *adj* too great to be estimated > **inestimably** *adv*

inestimably *adv* ▷ **inestimable**

inevitabilities *n* ▷ **inevitable**

inevitability *n* ▷ **inevitable**

inevitable *adj* unavoidable, sure to happen > **inevitably** *adv* > **inevitability** *n* (*pl* **-ties**)

inevitably *adv* ▷ **inevitable**

inexorable *adj* unable to be prevented from continuing or progressing > **inexorably** *adv*

inexorably *adv* ▷ **inexorable**

inexpert *adj* lacking skill

inexplicable *adj* impossible to explain > **inexplicably** *adv*

inexplicably *adv* ▷ **inexplicable**

inextricable *adj* impossible to escape from

infallibilities *adv* ▷ **infallible**

infallibility *adv* ▷ **infallible**

infallible *adj* never wrong > **infallibly** *adv* > **infallibility** *n* (*pl* **-ties**)

infallibly *adv* ▷ **infallible**

infamies *n* ▷ **infamous**

infamous [**in**-fam-uss] *adj* well-known for something bad > **infamously** *adv* > **infamy** *n* (*pl* **-mies**)

infamously *adv* ▷ **infamous**

infamy *n* ▷ **infamous**

infancies *n* ▷ **infancy**

infancy *n* (*pl* **-cies**) early childhood

infant *n* (*pl* **-s**) very young child

infanticide *n* (*pl* **-s**) murder of an infant

infanticides *n* ▷ **infanticide**

infantile *adj* childish

infantries *n* ▷ **infantry**

infantry *n* (*pl* **-ries**) soldiers who fight on foot

infants *n* ▷ **infant**

infatuated *adj* feeling intense unreasoning passion

infatuation *n* (*pl* **-s**) intense unreasoning passion

infatuations *n* ▷ **infatuation**

infect *v* (**-s, -ing, -ed**) affect with a disease > **infection** *n* (*pl* **-s**)

infected *v* ▷ **infect**

infecting *v* ▷ **infect**

infection *n* ▷ **infect**

infections *n* ▷ **infect**

infectious *adj* (of a disease) spreading without actual contact

infects *v* ▷ **infect**

infer *v* (**-s, -rring, -rred**) work out from evidence > **inference** *n* (*pl* **-s**)

inference *n* ▷ **infer**

inferences *n* ▷ **infer**

inferior *adj* lower in quality, position, or status ▶ *n* (*pl* **-s**) person of lower position or status > **inferiority** *n* (*pl* **-ties**)

inferiorities *n* ▷ **inferior**

inferiority *n* ▷ **inferior**

inferiors *n* ▷ **inferior**

infernal *adj* of hell (*Informal*) > **infernally** *adv*

infernally *adv* ▷ **infernal**

inferno *n* (*pl* **-s**) intense raging fire

infernos *n* ▷ **inferno**

inferred *v* ▷ **infer**

inferring *v* ▷ **infer**

infers *v* ▷ **infer**

infertile *adj* unable to produce offspring > **infertility** *n* (*pl* **-ties**)

infertilities *n* ▷ **infertile**

infertility *n* ▷ **infertile**

infest *v* (**-s, -ing, -ed**) inhabit or overrun in unpleasantly large numbers > **infestation** *n* (*pl* **-s**)

infestation *n* ▷ **infest**

infestations *n* ▷ **infest**
infested *v* ▷ **infest**
infesting *v* ▷ **infest**
infests *v* ▷ **infest**
infidel *n* (*pl* **-s**) person with no religion
infidelities *n* ▷ **infidelity**
infidelity *n* (*pl* **-ties**) (act of) sexual unfaithfulness to one's husband, wife, or lover
infidels *n* ▷ **infidel**
infighting *n* (*pl* **-s**) quarrelling within a group
infightings *n* ▷ **infighting**
infiltrate *v* (**-tes, -ting, -ted**) enter gradually and secretly > **infiltration** *n* (*pl* **-s**) > **infiltrator** *n* (*pl* **-s**)
infiltrated *v* ▷ **infiltrate**
infiltrates *v* ▷ **infiltrate**
infiltrating *v* ▷ **infiltrate**
infiltration *n* ▷ **infiltrate**
infiltrations *n* ▷ **infiltrate**
infiltrator *n* ▷ **infiltrate**
infiltrators *n* ▷ **infiltrate**
infinite [**in**-fin-it] *adj* without any limit or end > **infinitely** *adv*
infinitely *adv* ▷ **infinite**
infinitesimal *adj* extremely small
infinities *n* ▷ **infinity**
infinitive *n* (*pl* **-s**) (GRAMMAR) form of a verb not showing tense, person, or number
infinitives *n* ▷ **infinitive**
infinity *n* (*pl* **-ties**) endless space, time, or number
infirm *adj* physically or mentally weak > **infirmity** *n* (*pl* **-ties**)
infirmaries *n* ▷ **infirmary**
infirmary *n* (*pl* **-ries**) hospital
infirmities *n* ▷ **infirm**
infirmity *n* ▷ **infirm**
inflame *v* (**-mes, -ming, -med**) make angry or excited
inflamed *adj* (of part of the body) red, swollen, and painful because of infection ▶ *v* ▷ **inflame** > **inflammation** *n* (*pl* **-s**)
inflames *v* ▷ **inflame**
inflaming *v* ▷ **inflame**
inflammable *adj* easily set on fire
inflammation *n* ▷ **inflamed**
inflammations *n* ▷ **inflamed**
inflammatory *adj* likely to provoke anger
inflatable *adj* able to be inflated ▶ *n* (*pl* **-s**) plastic or rubber object which can be inflated
inflatables *n* ▷ **inflatable**
inflate *v* (**-tes, -ting, -ted**) expand by filling with air or gas
inflated *v* ▷ **inflate**
inflates *v* ▷ **inflate**
inflating *v* ▷ **inflate**
inflation *n* (*pl* **-s**) inflating > **inflationary** *adj*
inflationary *adj* ▷ **inflationary**
inflations *n* ▷ **inflation**
inflection, inflexion *n* (*pl* **-s**) change in the pitch of the voice
inflections *n* ▷ **inflection**
inflexibilities *n* ▷ **inflexible**
inflexibility *n* ▷ **inflexible**
inflexible *adj* unwilling to be persuaded, obstinate > **inflexibly** *adv* > **inflexibility** *n* (*pl* **-ties**)
inflexibly *n* ▷ **inflexibly**
inflexion *n* ▷ **inflection**
inflexions *n* ▷ **inflection**
inflict *v* (**-s, -ing, -ed**) impose (something unpleasant) on > **infliction** *n* (*pl* **-s**)
inflicted *v* ▷ **inflict**
inflicting *v* ▷ **inflict**
infliction *n* ▷ **inflict**
inflictions *n* ▷ **inflict**
inflicts *v* ▷ **inflict**
inflorescence *n* (*pl* **-s**) (BOTANY) arrangement of flowers on a stem
inflorescences *n* ▷ **inflorescence**
influence *n* (*pl* **-s**) effect of one person or thing on another ▶ *v* (**-ces, -cing, -ced**) have an effect on > **influential** *adj*
influenced *v* ▷ **influence**
influences *n, v* ▷ **influence**
influencing *v* ▷ **influence**
influential *adj* ▷ **influence**
influenza *n* (*pl* **-s**) contagious viral disease causing headaches, muscle pains, and fever
influenzas *n* ▷ **influenza**
influx *n* (*pl* **-es**) arrival or entry of many people or things
influxes *n* ▷ **influx**
info *n* (*pl* **-s**) (*Informal*) information
inform *v* (**-s, -ing, -ed**) tell
informal *adj* relaxed and friendly > **informally** *adv* > **informality** *n* (*pl* **-s**)
informalities *n* ▷ **informal**
informality *n* ▷ **informal**
informally *adv* ▷ **informal**
informant *n* (*pl* **-s**) person who gives information
informants *n* ▷ **informant**
information *n* (*pl* **-s**) knowledge or facts
informations *n* ▷ **information**
informative *adj* giving useful information
informed *v* ▷ **inform**
informer *n* (*pl* **-s**) person who informs to the police
informers *n* ▷ **informer**

informing *v* ▷ **inform**
informs *v* ▷ **inform**
infos *n* ▷ **info**
infrared *adj* of or using rays below the red end of the visible spectrum
infrastructure *n* (*pl* **-s**) basic facilities, services, and equipment needed for a country or organization to function properly
infrastructures *n* ▷ **infrastructure**
infringe *v* (**-ges, -ging, -ged**) break (a law or agreement) > **infringement** *n* (*pl* **-s**)
infringed *v* ▷ **infringe**
infringement *n* ▷ **infringe**
infringements *n* ▷ **infringe**
infringes *v* ▷ **infringe**
infringing *v* ▷ **infringe**
infuriate *v* (**-tes, -ting, -ted**) make very angry
infuriated *v* ▷ **infuriate**
infuriates *v* ▷ **infuriate**
infuriating *v* ▷ **infuriate**
infuse *v* (**-ses, -sing, -sed**) fill (with an emotion or quality) > **infusion** *n* (*pl* **-s**) infusing
infused *v* ▷ **infuse**
infuses *v* ▷ **infuse**
infusing *v* ▷ **infuse**
infusion *n* ▷ **infuse**
infusions *n* ▷ **infuse**
ingenious [in-**jean**-ee-uss] *adj* showing cleverness and originality > **ingeniously** *adv* > **ingenuity** [in-jen-**new**-it-ee] *n* (*pl* **-ties**)
ingeniously *adv* ▷ **ingenious**
ingénue [**an**-jay-new] *n* (*pl* **-s**) naive young woman, esp. as a role played by an actress
ingénues *n* ▷ **ingénue**
ingenuities *n* ▷ **ingenious**
ingenuity *n* ▷ **ingenious**
ingenuous [in-**jen**-new-uss] *adj* unsophisticated and trusting > **ingenuously** *adv*
ingenuously *adv* ▷ **ingenuously**
ingest *v* (**-s, -ing, -ed**) take (food or liquid) into the body > **ingestion** *n* (*pl* **-s**)
ingested *v* ▷ **ingest**
ingesting *v* ▷ **ingest**
ingestion *n* ▷ **ingest**
ingestions *n* ▷ **ingest**
ingests *v* ▷ **ingest**
inglorious *adj* dishonourable, shameful
ingot *n* (*pl* **-s**) oblong block of cast metal
ingots *n* ▷ **ingot**
ingrained *adj* firmly fixed
ingratiate *v* (**-iates, -iating, -iated**) try to make (oneself) popular with someone > **ingratiating** *adj* > **ingratiatingly** *adv*
ingratiated *v* ▷ **ingratiate**
ingratiates *v* ▷ **ingratiate**
ingratiating *v, adj* ▷ **ingratiate**
ingratiatingly *adv* ▷ **ingratiatingly**
ingredient *n* (*pl* **-s**) component of a mixture or compound
ingredients *n* ▷ **ingredient**
ingress *n* (*pl* **-es**) act or right of entering
ingresses *n* ▷ **ingress**
ingrowing *adj* (of a toenail) growing abnormally into the flesh
inhabit *v* (**-s, -ing, -ed**) live in > **inhabitable** *adj* > **inhabitant** *n* (*pl* **-s**)
inhabitable *adj* ▷ **inhabitable**
inhabitant *n* ▷ **inhabit**
inhabitants *n* ▷ **inhabit**
inhabited *v* ▷ **inhabit**
inhabiting *v* ▷ **inhabit**
inhabits *v* ▷ **inhabit**
inhalant *n* (*pl* **-s**) medical preparation inhaled to help breathing problems
inhalants *n* ▷ **inhalant**
inhalations *n* ▷ **inhalation**
inhale *v* (**-les, -ling, -led**) breathe in (air, smoke, etc.) > **inhalation** *n* (*pl* **-s**)
inhaled *v* ▷ **inhale**
inhaler *n* (*pl* **-s**) container for an inhalant
inhalers *n* ▷ **inhaler**
inhales *v* ▷ **inhale**
inhaling *v* ▷ **inhale**
inherent *adj* existing as an inseparable part > **inherently** *adv*
inherently *adv* ▷ **inherent**
inherit *v* (**-s, -ing, -ed**) receive (money etc.) from someone who has died > **inheritance** *n* (*pl* **-s**) > **inheritor** *n* (*pl* **-s**)
inheritance *n* ▷ **inherit**
inheritances *n* ▷ **inherit**
inherited *v* ▷ **inherit**
inheriting *v* ▷ **inherit**
inheritor *n* ▷ **inherit**
inheritors *n* ▷ **inherit**
inherits *v* ▷ **inherit**
inhibit *v* (**-s, -ing, -ed**) restrain (an impulse or desire) > **inhibited** *adj*
inhibited *v, adj* ▷ **inhibit**
inhibiting *v* ▷ **inhibit**
inhibition *n* (*pl* **-s**) feeling of fear or embarrassment that stops one from behaving naturally
inhibitions *n* ▷ **inhibition**
inhibits *v* ▷ **inhibit**
inhospitable *adj* not welcoming, unfriendly
inhuman *adj* cruel or brutal
inhumane *adj* cruel or brutal > **inhumanity** *n* (*pl* **-ties**)
inhumanities *n* ▷ **inhumane**

inhumanity *n* ▷ **inhumane**
inimical *adj* unfavourable or hostile
inimitable *adj* impossible to imitate, unique
iniquities *n* ▷ **iniquity**
iniquitous *adj* ▷ **iniquity**
iniquity *n* (*pl* **-ties**) injustice or wickedness > **iniquitous** *adj*
initial *adj* first, at the beginning ▶ *n* (*pl* **-s**) first letter, esp. of a person's name ▶ *v* (**-s, -lling, -lled**) sign with one's initials > **initially** *adv*
initialled *v* ▷ **initial**
initialling *v* ▷ **initial**
initially *adv* ▷ **initial**
initials *n, v* ▷ **initial**
initiate *v* (**-tes, -ting, -ted**) begin or set going ▶ *n* (*pl* **-s**) recently initiated person > **initiation** *n* (*pl* **-s**) > **initiator** *n* (*pl* **-s**)
initiated *v* ▷ **initiate**
initiates *v, n* ▷ **initiate**
initiating *v* ▷ **initiate**
initiation *n* ▷ **initiation**
initiations *n* ▷ **initiation**
initiative *n* (*pl* **-ves**) first step, commencing move
initiatives *n* ▷ **initiative**
initiator *n* ▷ **initiation**
initiators *n* ▷ **initiation**
inject *v* (**-s, -ing, -ed**) put (a fluid) into the body with a syringe > **injection** *n* (*pl* **-s**)
injected *v* ▷ **inject**
injecting *v* ▷ **inject**
injection *n* ▷ **inject**
injections *n* ▷ **inject**
injects *v* ▷ **inject**
injudicious *adj* showing poor judgment, unwise
injunction *n* (*pl* **-s**) court order not to do something
injunctions *n* ▷ **injunction**
injure *v* (**-res, -ring, -red**) hurt physically or mentally > **injury** *n* (*pl* **-ries**) > **injurious** *adj*
injured *v* ▷ **injure**
injures *v* ▷ **injure**
injuries *n* ▷ **injure**
injuring *v* ▷ **injure**
injurious *adj* ▷ **injure**
injury *n* ▷ **injure**
injustice *n* (*pl* **-s**) unfairness
injustices *n* ▷ **injustice**
ink *n* (*pl* **-s**) coloured liquid used for writing or printing ▶ *v* (**-s, -ing, -ed**) (*foll. by* **in**) mark in ink (something already marked in pencil)
inked *v* ▷ **ink**
inking *v* ▷ **ink**
inkling *n* (*pl* **-s**) slight idea or suspicion
inklings *n* ▷ **inkling**
inks *v, n* ▷ **ink**
inky *adj* dark or black
inlaid *adj* set in another material so that the surface is smooth
inland *adj, adv* in or towards the interior of a country, away from the sea
inlay *n* (*pl* **-s**) inlaid substance or pattern
inlays *n* ▷ **inlay**
inlet *n* (*pl* **-s**) narrow strip of water extending from the sea into the land
inlets *n* ▷ **inlet**
inmate *n* (*pl* **-s**) person living in an institution such as a prison
inmates *n* ▷ **inmate**
inmost *adj* innermost
inn *n* (*pl* **-s**) pub or small hotel, esp. in the country > **innkeeper** *n* (*pl* **-s**)
innards *pl n* (*Informal*) internal organs
innate *adj* being part of someone's nature, inborn
inner *adj* happening or located inside
innermost *adj* furthest inside
innings *n* (SPORT) player's or side's turn of batting
innkeeper *n* ▷ **inn**
innkeepers *n* ▷ **inn**
innocence *n* ▷ **innocent**
innocences *n* ▷ **innocent**
innocent *adj* not guilty of a crime ▶ *n* (*pl* **-s**) innocent person, esp. a child > **innocently** *adv* > **innocence** *n* (*pl* **-s**)
innocently *adv* ▷ **innocent**
innocents *n* ▷ **innocent**
innocuous *adj* not harmful > **innocuously** *adv*
innocuously *adv* ▷ **innocuous**
innovated *v* ▷ **innovation**
innovates *v* ▷ **innovation**
innovating *v* ▷ **innovation**
innovation *n* (*pl* **-s**) new idea or method > **innovate** *v* (**-tes, -ting, -ted**) > **innovative** *adj* > **innovator** *n* (*pl* **-s**)
innovations *n* ▷ **innovation**
innovative *adj* ▷ **innovation**
innovator *n* ▷ **innovation**
innovators *n* ▷ **innovation**
inns *n* ▷ **inn**
innuendo *n* (*pl* **-does**) (remark making) an indirect reference to something rude or unpleasant
innuendoes *n* ▷ **innuendo**
innumerable *adj* too many to be counted
innumeracies *n* ▷ **innumerate**
innumeracy *n* ▷ **innumerate**
innumerate *adj* having no understanding

of mathematics or science > **innumeracy** *n* (*pl* **-cies**)
inoculate *v* (**-tes, -ting, -ted**) protect against disease by injecting with a vaccine > **inoculation** *n* (*pl* **-s**)
inoculated *v* ▷ **inoculate**
inoculates *v* ▷ **inoculate**
inoculating *v* ▷ **inoculate**
inoculation *n* ▷ **inoculate**
inoculations *n* ▷ **inoculate**
inoperable *adj* (of a tumour or cancer) unable to be surgically removed
inopportune *adj* badly timed, unsuitable
inordinate *adj* excessive
inorganic *adj* not having the characteristics of living organisms
inpatient *n* (*pl* **-s**) patient who stays in a hospital for treatment
inpatients *n* ▷ **inpatient**
input *n* (*pl* **-s**) resources put into a project etc. ▶ *v* (**-s, -tting, -put**) enter (data) in a computer
inputs *v, n* ▷ **input**
inputting *v, n* ▷ **input**
inquest *n* (*pl* **-s**) official inquiry into a sudden death
inquests *n* ▷ **inquest**
inquire *v* (**-res, -ring, -red**) seek information or ask (about) > **inquirer** *n* (*pl* **-s**)
inquired *v* ▷ **inquire**
inquirer *n* ▷ **inquire**
inquirers *n* ▷ **inquire**
inquires *v* ▷ **inquire**
inquiries *n* ▷ **inquiry**
inquiring *v* ▷ **inquire**
inquiry *n* (*pl* **-ries**) question
inquisition *n* (*pl* **-s**) thorough investigation > **inquisitor** *n* (*pl* **-s**) > **inquisitorial** *adj*
inquisitions *n* ▷ **inquisition**
inquisitive *adj* excessively curious about other people's affairs > **inquisitively** *adv*
inquisitively *adv* ▷ **inquisitive**
inquisitor *n* ▷ **inquisition**
inquisitorial *adj* ▷ **inquisition**
inquisitors *n* ▷ **inquisition**
inquorate *adj* without enough people present to make a quorum
inroads *pl n* start affecting or reducing
insalubrious *adj* unpleasant, unhealthy, or sordid
insane *adj* mentally ill > **insanely** *adv* > **insanity** *n* (*pl* **-ties**)
insanely *adv* ▷ **insane**
insanitary *adj* dirty or unhealthy
insanities *n* ▷ **insane**
insanity *n* ▷ **insane**
insatiable [in-**saysh**-a-bl] *adj* unable to be satisfied
inscribe *v* (**-bes, -bing, -bed**) write or carve words on
inscribed *v* ▷ **inscribe**
inscribes *v* ▷ **inscribe**
inscribing *v* ▷ **inscribe**
inscription *n* (*pl* **-s**) words inscribed
inscriptions *n* ▷ **inscription**
inscrutable *adj* mysterious, enigmatic > **inscrutably** *adv*
inscrutably *adv* ▷ **inscrutable**
insect *n* (*pl* **-s**) small animal with six legs and usu. wings, such as an ant or fly
insecticide *n* (*pl* **-s**) substance for killing insects
insecticides *n* ▷ **insecticide**
insectivorous *adj* insect-eating
insects *n* ▷ **insect**
insecure *adj* anxious, not confident
inseminated *v* ▷ **insemination**
inseminates *v* ▷ **insemination**
inseminating *v* ▷ **insemination**
insemination *n* (*pl* **-s**) putting semen into a woman's or female animal's body to try to make her pregnant > **inseminate** *v* (**-tes, -ting, -ted**)
inseminations *n* ▷ **insemination**
insensate *adj* without sensation, unconscious
insensible *adj* unconscious, without feeling
insensitive *adj* unaware of or ignoring other people's feelings > **insensitivity** *n* (*pl* **-ties**)
insensitivities *n* ▷ **insensitive**
insensitivity *n* ▷ **insensitive**
inseparable *adj* (of two people) spending most of the time together
insert *v* (**-s, -ing, -ed**) put inside or include ▶ *n* (*pl* **-s**) something inserted > **insertion** *n* (*pl* **-s**)
inserted *v* ▷ **insert**
inserting *v* ▷ **insert**
insertion *n* ▷ **insert**
insertions *n* ▷ **insert**
inserts *v, n* ▷ **insert**
inset *n* (*pl* **-s**) small picture inserted within a larger one
insets *n* ▷ **inset**
inshore *adj* close to the shore ▶ *adj, adv* towards the shore
inside *prep* in or to the interior of ▶ *adj* on or of the inside ▶ *adv* on, in, or to the inside, indoors ▶ *n* (*pl* **-s**) inner side, surface, or part
insider *n* (*pl* **-s**) member of a group who has privileged knowledge about it
insiders *n* ▷ **insider**
insides *n* ▷ **inside** ▶ *pl n* (*Informal*) stomach

and bowels
insidious *adj* subtle or unseen but dangerous
> **insidiously** *adv*
insidiously *adv* ▷ **insidious**
insight *n* (*pl* **-s**) deep understanding
insights *n* ▷ **insight**
insignia *n* (*pl* **-s**) badge or emblem of honour or office
insignias *n* ▷ **insignia**
insignificance *n* ▷ **insignificant**
insignificances *n* ▷ **insignificant**
insignificant *adj* not important
> **insignificance** *n* (*pl* **-s**)
insincere *adj* showing false feelings, not genuine > **insincerely** *adv* > **insincerity** *n* (*pl* **-ties**)
insincerely *adv* ▷ **insincerely**
insincerities *n* ▷ **insincere**
insincerity *n* ▷ **insincere**
insinuate *v* (**-tes, -ting, -ted**) suggest indirectly > **insinuation** *n* (*pl* **-s**)
insinuated *v* ▷ **insinuate**
insinuates *v* ▷ **insinuate**
insinuating *v* ▷ **insinuate**
insinuation *n* ▷ **insinuate**
insinuations *n* ▷ **insinuate**
insipid *adj* lacking interest, spirit, or flavour
insist *v* (**-s, -ing, -ed**) demand or state firmly
> **insistent** *adj* making persistent demands
> **insistently** *adv* > **insistence** *n* (*pl* **-s**)
insisted *v* ▷ **insist**
insistence *n* ▷ **insist**
insistences *n* ▷ **insist**
insistent *adj* ▷ **insist**
insistently *adv* ▷ **insist**
insisting *v* ▷ **insist**
insists *v* ▷ **insist**
insole *n* (*pl* **-s**) inner sole of a shoe or boot
insolence *n* ▷ **insolent**
insolences *n* ▷ **insolent**
insolent *adj* rude and disrespectful
> **insolence** *n* (*pl* **-s**) > **insolently** *adv*
insolently *adv* ▷ **insolent**
insoles *n* ▷ **insole**
insoluble *adj* incapable of being solved
insolvencies *n* ▷ **insolvent**
insolvency *n* ▷ **insolvent**
insolvent *adj* unable to pay one's debts
> **insolvency** *n* (*pl* **-cies**)
insomnia *n* (*pl* **-s**) inability to sleep
> **insomniac** *n* (*pl* **-s**)
insomniac *n* ▷ **insomnia**
insomniacs *n* ▷ **insomnia**
insomnias *n* ▷ **insomnia**
insouciance *n* ▷ **insouciant**
insouciances *n* ▷ **insouciant**
insouciant *adj* carefree and unconcerned
> **insouciance** *n* (*pl* **-s**)
inspect *v* (**-s, -ing, -ed**) check closely or officially > **inspection** *n* (*pl* **-s**)
inspected *v* ▷ **inspect**
inspecting *v* ▷ **inspect**
inspection *n* ▷ **inspect**
inspections *n* ▷ **inspect**
inspector *n* (*pl* **-s**) person who inspects
inspectors *n* ▷ **inspector**
inspects *v* ▷ **inspect**
inspiration *n* (*pl* **-s**) creative influence or stimulus > **inspirational** *adj*
inspirational *adj* ▷ **inspiration**
inspirations *n* ▷ **inspiration**
inspire *v* (**-res, -ring, -red**) fill with enthusiasm, stimulate
inspired *v* ▷ **inspire**
inspires *v* ▷ **inspire**
inspiring *v* ▷ **inspire**
instabilities *n* ▷ **instability**
instability *n* (*pl* **-ties**) lack of steadiness or reliability
install *v* (**-lls, -lling, -lled**) put in and prepare (equipment) for use
installation *n* (*pl* **-s**) installing
installations *n* ▷ **installation**
installed *v* ▷ **install**
installing *v* ▷ **install**
installs *v* ▷ **install**
instalment *n* (*pl* **-s**) any of the portions of a thing presented or a debt paid in successive parts
instalments *n* ▷ **instalment**
instance *n* (*pl* **-s**) particular example ▶ *v* (**-ces, -cing, -ced**) mention as an example
instanced *v* ▷ **instance**
instances *n, v* ▷ **instance**
instancing *v* ▷ **instance**
instant *n* (*pl* **-s**) very brief time ▶ *adj* happening at once > **instantly** *adv*
instantaneous *adj* happening at once
> **instantaneously** *adv*
instantaneously *adv* ▷ **instantaneous**
instantly *adv* ▷ **instant**
instants *n* ▷ **instant**
instead *adv* as a replacement or substitute
instep *n* (*pl* **-s**) part of the foot forming the arch between the ankle and toes
insteps *n* ▷ **instep**
instigate *v* (**-tes, -ting, -ted**) cause to happen
> **instigation** *n* (*pl* **-s**) > **instigator** *n* (*pl* **-s**)
instigated *v* ▷ **instigate**
instigates *v* ▷ **instigate**

instigating *v* ▷ **instigate**
instigation *n* ▷ **instigate**
instigations *n* ▷ **instigate**
instigator *n* ▷ **instigate**
instigators *n* ▷ **instigate**
instil *v* (**-s, -lling, -lled**) introduce (an idea etc.) gradually into someone's mind
instilled *v* ▷ **instil**
instilling *v* ▷ **instil**
instils *v* ▷ **instil**
instinct *n* (*pl* **-s**) inborn tendency to behave in a certain way > **instinctive** *adj* > **instinctively** *adv*
instinctive *adj* ▷ **instinct**
instinctively *adv* ▷ **instinct**
instincts *n* ▷ **instinct**
institute *n* (*pl* **-s**) organization set up for a specific purpose, esp. research or teaching ▶ *v* (**-tutes, -tuting, -tuted**) start or establish
instituted *v* ▷ **institute**
institutes *n, v* ▷ **institute**
instituting *v* ▷ **institute**
institution *n* (*pl* **-s**) large important organization such as a university or bank > **institutional** *adj* > **institutionalize** *v* (**-izes, -izing, -ized**)
institutional *adj* ▷ **institution**
institutionalize *v* ▷ **institution**
institutionalized *v* ▷ **institution**
institutionalizes *v* ▷ **institution**
institutionalizing *n* ▷ **institution**
institutions *n* ▷ **institution**
instruct *v* (**-s, -ing, -ed**) order to do something > **instructor** *n* (*pl* **-s**)
instructed *v* ▷ **instruct**
instructing *v* ▷ **instruct**
instruction *n* (*pl* **-s**) order to do something
instructions *n* ▷ **instruction** ▶ *pl n* information on how to do or use something
instructive *adj* informative or helpful
instructor *n* ▷ **instruct**
instructors *n* ▷ **instruct**
instructs *v* ▷ **instruct**
instrument *n* (*pl* **-s**) tool used for particular work
instrumental *adj* (*foll. by* **in**) having an important function (in)
instrumentalist *n* (*pl* **-s**) player of a musical instrument
instrumentalists *n* ▷ **instrumentalist**
instrumentation *n* (*pl* **-s**) set of instruments in a car etc.
instrumentations *n* ▷ **instrumentation**
instruments *n* ▷ **instrument**
insubordinate *adj* not submissive to authority > **insubordination** *n* (*pl* **-s**)
insubordination *n* ▷ **insubordinate**
insubordinations *n* ▷ **insubordinate**
insufferable *adj* unbearable
insular *adj* not open to new ideas, narrow-minded > **insularity** *n* (*pl* **-ties**)
insularities *n* ▷ **insular**
insularity *n* ▷ **insular**
insulate *v* (**-tes, -ting, -ted**) prevent or reduce the transfer of electricity, heat, or sound by surrounding or lining with a nonconducting material > **insulation** *n* (*pl* **-s**) > **insulator** *n* (*pl* **-s**)
insulated *v* ▷ **insulate**
insulates *v* ▷ **insulate**
insulating *v* ▷ **insulate**
insulation *n* ▷ **insulate**
insulations *n* ▷ **insulate**
insulator *n* ▷ **insulate**
insulators *n* ▷ **insulate**
insulin *n* (*pl* **-s**) hormone produced in the pancreas that controls the amount of sugar in the blood
insulins *n* ▷ **insulin**
insult *v* (**-s, -ing, -ed**) behave rudely to, offend ▶ *n* (*pl* **-s**) insulting remark or action > **insulting** *adj*
insulted *v* ▷ **insult**
insulting *v, adj* ▷ **insult**
insults *v, n* ▷ **insult**
insuperable *adj* impossible to overcome
insupportable *adj* impossible to tolerate
insurance *n* (*pl* **-ces**) agreement by which one makes regular payments to a company who pay an agreed sum if damage, loss, or death occurs
insurances *n* ▷ **insurance**
insure *v* (**-res, -ring, -red**) protect by insurance
insured *v* ▷ **insure**
insures *v* ▷ **insure**
insurgent *n* (*pl* **-s**) ▶ *adj* (person) in revolt against an established authority
insurgents *n* ▷ **insurgent**
insuring *v* ▷ **insure**
insurrection *n* (*pl* **-s**) rebellion
insurrections *n* ▷ **insurrection**
intact *adj* not changed or damaged in any way
intaglio [in-**tah**-lee-oh] *n* (*pl* **-s**) (gem carved with) an engraved design
intaglios *n* ▷ **intaglio**
intake *n* (*pl* **-kes**) amount or number taken in
intakes *n* ▷ **intake**
integer *n* (*pl* **-s**) positive or negative whole number or zero
integers *n* ▷ **integer**

integral *adj* being an essential part of a whole ▶ *n* (*pl* **-s**) (MATHS) sum of a large number of very small quantities
integrals *n* ▷ **integral**
integrate *v* (**-tes, -ting, -ted**) combine into a whole > **integration** *n* (*pl* **-s**)
integrated *v* ▷ **integrate**
integrates *v* ▷ **integrate**
integrating *v* ▷ **integrate**
integration *n* ▷ **integrate**
integrations *n* ▷ **integrate**
integrities *n* ▷ **integrity**
integrity *n* (*pl* **-ties**) quality of having high moral principles
intellect *n* (*pl* **-s**) power of thinking and reasoning
intellects *n* ▷ **intellect**
intellectual *adj* of or appealing to the intellect ▶ *n* (*pl* **-s**) intellectual person > **intellectually** *adv*
intellectually *adv* ▷ **intellectual**
intellectuals *n* ▷ **intellectual**
intelligence *n* (*pl* **-s**) quality of being intelligent
intelligences *n* ▷ **intelligence**
intelligent *adj* able to understand, learn, and think things out quickly > **intelligently** *adv*
intelligently *adv* ▷ **intelligent**
intelligentsia *n* (*pl* **-s**) intellectual or cultured people in a society
intelligentsias *n* ▷ **intelligentsia**
intelligibilities *n* ▷ **intelligibile**
intelligibility *n* ▷ **intelligibile**
intelligible *adj* able to be understood > **intelligibility** *n* (*pl* **-ties**)
intemperance *n* ▷ **intemperate**
intemperances *n* ▷ **intemperate**
intemperate *adj* unrestrained, uncontrolled > **intemperance** *n* (*pl* **-s**)
intend *v* (**-s, -ing, -ed**) propose or plan (to do something)
intended *v* ▷ **intend**
intending *v* ▷ **intend**
intends *v* ▷ **intend**
intense *adj* of great strength or degree > **intensity** *n* (*pl* **-ties**)
intensification *n* ▷ **intensify**
intensifications *n* ▷ **intensify**
intensified *v* ▷ **intensify**
intensifies *v* ▷ **intensify**
intensify *v* (**-fies, -fying, -fied**) make or become more intense > **intensification** *n* (*pl* **-s**)
intensifying *v* ▷ **intensify**
intensities *n* ▷ **intense**
intensity *n* ▷ **intense**
intensive *adj* using or needing concentrated effort or resources > **intensively** *adv*
intensively *adv* ▷ **intensive**
intent *n* (*pl* **-s**) intention ▶ *adj* paying close attention > **intently** *adv* > **intentness** *n* (*pl* **-s**)
intention *n* (*pl* **-s**) something intended
intentional *adj* planned in advance, deliberate > **intentionally** *adv*
intentionally *adv* ▷ **intentional**
intentions *n* ▷ **intention**
intently *adv* ▷ **intent**
intentness *n* ▷ **intent**
intentnesses *n* ▷ **intent**
intents *n* ▷ **intent**
inter [in-**ter**] *v* (**-s, -rring, -rred**) bury (a corpse) > **interment** *n* (*pl* **-s**)
interact *v* (**-s, -ing, -ed**) act on or in close relation with each other > **interaction** *n* (*pl* **-s**) > **interactive** *adj*
interacted *v* ▷ **interact**
interacting *v* ▷ **interact**
interaction *n* ▷ **interact**
interactions *n* ▷ **interact**
interactive *adj* ▷ **interact**
interacts *v* ▷ **interact**
interbred *v* ▷ **interbreed**
interbreed *v* (**-s, -ing, -bred**) breed within a related group
interbreeding *v* ▷ **interbreed**
interbreeds *v* ▷ **interbreed**
intercede *v* (**-des, -ding, -ded**) try to end a dispute between two people or groups > **intercession** *n* (*pl* **-s**)
interceded *v* ▷ **intercede**
intercedes *v* ▷ **intercede**
interceding *v* ▷ **intercede**
intercept *v* (**-s, -ing, -ed**) seize or stop in transit > **interception** *n* (*pl* **-s**)
intercepted *v* ▷ **intercept**
intercepting *v* ▷ **intercept**
interception *n* ▷ **intercept**
interceptions *n* ▷ **intercept**
intercepts *v* ▷ **intercept**
intercession *n* ▷ **intercede**
intercessions *n* ▷ **intercede**
interchange *v* (**-ges, -ging, -ged**) (cause to) exchange places ▶ *n* (*pl* **-ges**) motorway junction > **interchangeable** *adj*
interchangeable *adj* ▷ **interchange**
interchanged *v* ▷ **interchange**
interchanges *v, n* ▷ **interchange**
interchanging *v* ▷ **interchange**
intercom *n* (*pl* **-s**) internal communication system with loudspeakers
intercoms *n* ▷ **intercom**

intercontinental *adj* travelling between or linking continents
intercourse *n* (*pl* **-s**) sexual intercourse
intercourses *n* ▷ **intercourse**
interdict *n* ▷ **interdiction**
interdiction, interdict *n* (*pl* **-s**) formal order forbidding something
interdictions *n* ▷ **interdiction**
interdicts *n* ▷ **interdiction**
interdisciplinary *adj* involving more than one branch of learning
interest *n* (*pl* **-s**) desire to know or hear more about something ▸ *v* (**-s, -ing, -ed**) arouse the interest of > **interesting** *adj* > **interestingly** *adv*
interested *adj* feeling or showing interest ▸ *v* ▷ **interest**
interesting *v, adj* ▷ **interest**
interestingly *adv* ▷ **interest**
interests *n, v* ▷ **interest**
interface *n* (*pl* **-s**) area where two things interact or link
interfaces *n* ▷ **interface**
interfere *v* (**-res, -ring, -red**) try to influence other people's affairs where one is not involved or wanted > **interfering** *adj* > **interference** *n* (*pl* **-s**) interfering
interfered *v* ▷ **interfere**
interference *n* ▷ **interfere**
interference *n* ▷ **interfere**
interferes *v* ▷ **interfere**
interfering *v, adj* ▷ **interfere**
interferon *n* (*pl* **-s**) protein that stops the development of an invading virus
interferons *n* ▷ **interferon**
interim *adj* temporary or provisional
interior *n* (*pl* **-s**) inside ▸ *adj* inside, inner
interiors *n* ▷ **interior**
interject *v* (**-s, -ing, -ed**) make (a remark) suddenly or as an interruption > **interjection** *n* (*pl* **-s**)
interjected *v* ▷ **interject**
interjecting *v* ▷ **interject**
interjection *n* ▷ **interject**
interjections *n* ▷ **interject**
interjects *v* ▷ **interject**
interlace *v* (**-ces, -cing, -ced**) join together as if by weaving
interlaced *v* ▷ **interlace**
interlaces *v* ▷ **interlace**
interlacing *v* ▷ **interlace**
interlink *v* (**-s, -ing, -ed**) connect together
interlinked *v* ▷ **interlink**
interlinking *v* ▷ **interlink**
interlinks *v* ▷ **interlink**
interlock *v* (**-s, -ing, -ed**) join firmly together
interlocked *v* ▷ **interlock**
interlocking *v* ▷ **interlock**
interlocks *v* ▷ **interlock**
interlocutor [in-ter-**lok**-yew-ter] *n* (*pl* **-s**) person who takes part in a conversation
interlocutors *n* ▷ **interlocutor**
interloper [**in**-ter-lope-er] *n* (*pl* **-s**) person in a place or situation where he or she has no right to be
interlopers *n* ▷ **interloper**
interlude *n* (*pl* **-s**) short rest or break in an activity or event
interludes *n* ▷ **interlude**
intermarriage *n* ▷ **intermarry**
intermarriages *n* ▷ **intermarry**
intermarried *v* ▷ **intermarry**
intermarries *v* ▷ **intermarry**
intermarry *v* (**-rries, -rrying, -rried**) (of families, races, or religions) become linked by marriage > **intermarriage** *n* (*pl* **-s**)
intermarrying *v* ▷ **intermarry**
intermediaries *n* ▷ **intermediary**
intermediary *n* (*pl* **-ries**) person trying to create agreement between others
intermediate *adj* coming between two points or extremes
interment *n* ▷ **inter**
interments *n* ▷ **inter**
intermezzo [in-ter-**met**-so] *n* (*pl* **-s**) short piece of music, esp. one performed between the acts of an opera
intermezzos *n* ▷ **intermezzo**
interminable *adj* seemingly endless because boring > **interminably** *adv*
interminably *adv* ▷ **interminable**
intermingle *v* (**-les, -ling, -led**) mix together
intermingled *v* ▷ **intermingle**
intermingles *v* ▷ **intermingle**
intermingling *v* ▷ **intermingle**
intermission *n* (*pl* **-s**) interval between parts of a play, film, etc.
intermissions *n* ▷ **intermission**
intermittent *adj* occurring at intervals > **intermittently** *adv*
intermittently *adv* ▷ **intermittent**
intern *v* (**-s, -ing, -ed**) imprison, esp. during a war ▸ *n* (*pl* **-s**) trainee doctor in a hospital > **internment** *n* (*pl* **-s**)
internal *adj* of or on the inside > **internally** *adv*
internally *adv* ▷ **internal**
international *adj* of or involving two or more countries ▸ *n* (*pl* **-s**) game or match between teams of different countries > **internationally** *adv*

internationally *adv* ▷ **international**
internationals *n* ▷ **international**
internecine *adj* mutually destructive
interned *v* ▷ **intern**
internee *n* (*pl* **-s**) person who is interned
internees *n* ▷ **internee**
interning *v* ▷ **intern**
internment *n* ▷ **intern**
internments *n* ▷ **intern**
interns *v, n* ▷ **intern**
interplanetary *adj* of or linking planets
interplay *n* (*pl* **-s**) action and reaction of two things upon each other
interplays *n* ▷ **interplay**
interpolate [in-**ter**-pole-ate] *v* (**-tes, -ting, -ted**) insert (a comment or passage) into (a conversation or text) > **interpolation** *n* (*pl* **-s**)
interpolated *v* ▷ **interpolate**
interpolates *v* ▷ **interpolate**
interpolating *v* ▷ **interpolate**
interpolation *n* ▷ **interpolate**
interpolations *n* ▷ **interpolate**
interpose *v* (**-ses, -sing, -sed**) insert between or among things
interposed *v* ▷ **interpose**
interposes *v* ▷ **interpose**
interposing *v* ▷ **interpose**
interpret *v* (**-s, -ing, -ed**) explain the meaning of > **interpretation** *n* (*pl* **-s**)
interpretation *n* ▷ **interpret**
interpretations *n* ▷ **interpret**
interpreted *v* ▷ **interpret**
interpreter *n* (*pl* **-s**) person who translates orally from one language into another
interpreters *n* ▷ **interpreter**
interpreting *v* ▷ **interpret**
interprets *v* ▷ **interpret**
interred *v* ▷ **inter**
interregna *n* ▷ **interregnum**
interregnum *n* (*pl* **-nums, -na**) interval between reigns
interregnums *n* ▷ **interregnum**
interring *v* ▷ **inter**
interrogate *v* (**-tes, -ting, -ted**) question closely > **interrogation** *n* (*pl* **-s**)
interrogated *v* ▷ **interrogate**
interrogates *v* ▷ **interrogate**
interrogating *v* ▷ **interrogate**
interrogation *n* ▷ **interrogate**
interrogations *n* ▷ **interrogate**
interrogative *adj* questioning ▶ *n* (*pl* **-s**) word used in asking a question, such as *how* or *why* > **interrogator** *n* (*pl* **-s**)
interrogatives *n* ▷ **interrogative**
interrogator *n* ▷ **interrogative**
interrogators *n* ▷ **interrogative**
interrupt *v* (**-s, -ing, -ed**) break into (a conversation etc.) > **interruption** *n* (*pl* **-s**)
interrupted *v* ▷ **interrupt**
interrupting *v* ▷ **interrupt**
interruption *n* ▷ **interrupt**
interruptions *n* ▷ **interrupt**
interrupts *v* ▷ **interrupt**
inters *v* ▷ **inter**
intersect *v* (**-s, -ing, -ed**) (of roads) meet and cross > **intersection** *n* (*pl* **-s**)
intersected *v* ▷ **intersect**
intersecting *v* ▷ **intersect**
intersection *n* ▷ **intersect**
intersections *n* ▷ **intersect**
intersects *v* ▷ **intersect**
interspersed *adj* scattered (among, between, or on)
interstellar *adj* between or among stars
interstice [in-**ter**-stiss] *n* (*pl* **-ces**) small crack or gap between things
interstices *n* ▷ **interstice**
intertwine *v* (**-nes, -ning, -ned**) twist together
intertwined *v* ▷ **intertwine**
intertwines *v* ▷ **intertwine**
intertwining *v* ▷ **intertwine**
interval *n* (*pl* **-s**) time between two particular moments or events
intervals *n* ▷ **interval**
intervene *v* (**-nes, -ning, -ned**) involve oneself in a situation, esp. to prevent conflict > **intervention** *n* (*pl* **-s**)
intervened *v* ▷ **intervene**
intervenes *v* ▷ **intervene**
intervening *v* ▷ **intervene**
intervention *n* ▷ **intervene**
interventions *n* ▷ **intervene**
interview *n* (*pl* **-s**) formal discussion, esp. between a job-seeker and an employer ▶ *v* (**-s, -ing, -ed**) conduct an interview with > **interviewee** *n* (*pl* **-s**) > **interviewer** *n* (*pl* **-s**)
interviewed *v* ▷ **interview**
interviewee *n* ▷ **interview**
interviewees *n* ▷ **interview**
interviewer *n* ▷ **interview**
interviewers *n* ▷ **interview**
interviewing *v* ▷ **interview**
interviews *n, v* ▷ **interview**
interweave *v* (**-ves, -ving, -wove, -woven**) weave together
interweaves *v* ▷ **interweave**
interweaving *v* ▷ **interweave**
interwove *v* ▷ **interweave**
interwoven *v* ▷ **interweave**
intestacies *n* ▷ **intestate**

intestacy *n* ▷ **intestate**
intestate *adj* not having made a will > **intestacy** *n* (*pl* **-cies**)
intestinal *adj* ▷ **intestine**
intestinally *adv* ▷ **intestine**
intestine *n* (*pl* **-s**) (*often pl* lower part of the alimentary canal between the stomach and the anus > **intestinal** *adj* > **intestinally** *adv*
intestines *n* ▷ **intestine**
intimacies *n* ▷ **intimate¹**
intimacy *n* ▷ **intimate¹**
intimate¹ *adj* having a close personal relationship ▶ *n* (*pl* **-s**) close friend > **intimately** *adv* > **intimacy** *n* (*pl* **-cies**)
intimate² *v* (**-tes, -ting, -ted**) hint at or suggest > **intimation** *n* (*pl* **-s**)
intimated *v* ▷ **intimate²**
intimately *adv* ▷ **intimate¹**
intimates *n* ▷ **intimate¹** ▶ *v* ▷ **intimate²**
intimating *v* ▷ **intimate²**
intimation *n* ▷ **intimate²**
intimations *n* ▷ **intimate²**
intimidate *v* (**-tes, -ting, -ted**) subdue or influence by fear > **intimidating** *adj* > **intimidation** *n* (*pl* **-s**)
intimidated *v* ▷ **intimidate**
intimidates *v* ▷ **intimidate**
intimidating *v, adj* ▷ **intimidate**
intimidation *n* ▷ **intimidate**
intimidations *n* ▷ **intimidate**
into *prep* indicating motion towards the centre, result of a change, division, etc.
intolerable *adj* more than can be endured > **intolerably** *adv*
intolerably *adv* ▷ **intolerable**
intolerance *n* ▷ **intolerant**
intolerances *n* ▷ **intolerant**
intolerant *adj* refusing to accept practices and beliefs different from one's own > **intolerance** *n* (*pl* **-s**)
intonation *n* (*pl* **-s**) sound pattern produced by variations in the voice
intonations *n* ▷ **intonation**
intone *v* (**-nes, -ning, -ned**) speak or recite in an unvarying tone of voice
intoned *v* ▷ **intone**
intones *v* ▷ **intone**
intoning *v* ▷ **intone**
intoxicant *n* (*pl* **-s**) intoxicating drink
intoxicants *n* ▷ **intoxicant**
intoxicate *v* (**-tes, -ting, -ted**) make drunk
intoxicated *v* ▷ **intoxicate**
intoxicates *v* ▷ **intoxicate**
intoxicating *v* ▷ **intoxicate**
intoxication *n* (*pl* **-s**) state of being drunk
intoxications *n* ▷ **intoxication**
intractable *adj* (of a person) difficult to control
intranet *n* (*pl* **-s**) (COMPUTERS) internal network that makes use of Internet technology
intranets *n* ▷ **intranet**
intransigence *n* ▷ **intransigent**
intransigences *n* ▷ **intransigent**
intransigent *adj* refusing to change one's attitude > **intransigence** *n* (*pl* **-s**)
intransitive *adj* (of a verb) not taking a direct object
intrauterine *adj* within the womb
intravenous [in-tra-**vee**-nuss] *adj* into a vein > **intravenously** *adv*
intravenously *adv* ▷ **intravenously**
intrepid *adj* fearless, bold > **intrepidity** *n* (*pl* **-ties**)
intrepidities *n* ▷ **intrepid**
intrepidity *n* ▷ **intrepid**
intricacies *n* ▷ **intricate**
intricacy *n* ▷ **intricate**
intricate *adj* involved or complicated > **intricately** *adv* > **intricacy** *n* (*pl* **-cies**)
intricately *adv* ▷ **intricate**
intrigue *v* (**-gues, -guing, -gued**) make interested or curious ▶ *n* (*pl* **-gues**) secret plotting > **intriguing** *adj*
intrigued *v* ▷ **intrigue**
intrigues *v, n* ▷ **intrigue**
intriguing *v, adj* ▷ **intrigue**
intrinsic *adj* essential to the basic nature of something > **intrinsically** *adv*
intrinsically *adv* ▷ **intrinsic**
introduce *v* (**-ces, -cing, -ced**) present (someone) by name (to another person)
introduced *v* ▷ **introduce**
introduces *v* ▷ **introduce**
introducing *v* ▷ **introduce**
introduction *n* (*pl* **-s**) presentation of one person to another > **introductory** *adj*
introductions *n* ▷ **introduction**
introductory *adj* ▷ **introduction**
introspection *n* (*pl* **-s**) examination of one's own thoughts and feelings > **introspective** *adj*
introspections *n* ▷ **introspection**
introspective *adj* ▷ **introspection**
introversion *n* ▷ **introvert**
introversions *n* ▷ **introvert**
introvert *n* (*pl* **-s**) person concerned more with his or her thoughts and feelings than with the outside world > **introverted** *adj* > **introversion** *n* (*pl* **-s**)
introverted *adj* ▷ **introvert**
introverts *n* ▷ **introvert**
intrude *v* (**-des, -ding, -ded**) come in or join

in without being invited > **intrusion** *n* (*pl* **-s**) > **intrusive** *adj*
intruded *v* ▷ **intrude**
intruder *n* (*pl* **-s**) person who enters a place without permission
intruders *n* ▷ **intruder**
intrudes *v* ▷ **intrude**
intruding *v* ▷ **intrude**
intrusion *n* ▷ **intrude**
intrusions *n* ▷ **intrude**
intrusive *adj* ▷ **intrude**
intuition *n* (*pl* **-s**) instinctive knowledge or insight without conscious reasoning > **intuitive** *adj* > **intuitively** *adv*
intuitions *n* ▷ **intuition**
intuitive *adj* ▷ **intuition**
intuitively *adv* ▷ **intuition**
inundate *v* (**-tes, -ting, -ted**) flood > **inundation** *n* (*pl* **-s**)
inundated *v* ▷ **inundate**
inundates *v* ▷ **inundate**
inundating *v* ▷ **inundate**
inundation *n* ▷ **inundate**
inundations *n* ▷ **inundate**
inured *adj* accustomed, esp. to hardship or danger
invade *v* (**-des, -ding, -ded**) enter (a country) by military force > **invader** *n* (*pl* **-s**)
invaded *v* ▷ **invade**
invader *n* ▷ **invade**
invaders *n* ▷ **invade**
invades *v* ▷ **invade**
invading *v* ▷ **invade**
invalid[1] *adj, n* (*pl* **-s**) disabled or chronically ill (person) ▶ *v* (**-s, -ing, -ed**) (*often foll. by* **out**) dismiss from active service because of illness or injury > **invalidity** *n* (*pl* **-ties**)
invalid[2] *adj* having no legal force
invalidate *v* (**-tes, -ting, -ted**) make or show to be invalid
invalidated *v* ▷ **invalidate**
invalidates *v* ▷ **invalidate**
invalidating *v* ▷ **invalidate**
invalided *v* ▷ **invalid**[1]
invaliding *v* ▷ **invalid**[1]
invalidities *n* ▷ **invalid**[1]
invalidity *n* ▷ **invalid**[1]
invalids *n, v* ▷ **invalid**[1]
invaluable *adj* of very great value or worth
invasion *n* (*pl* **-s**) invading
invasions *n* ▷ **invasion**
invective *n* (*pl* **-s**) abusive speech or writing
invectives *n* ▷ **invective**
inveigh [in-vay] *v* (**-s, -ing, -ed**) (*foll. by* **against**) criticize strongly
inveighed *v* ▷ **inveigh**
inveighing *v* ▷ **inveigh**
inveighs *v* ▷ **inveigh**
inveigle *v* (**-les, -ling, -led**) coax by cunning or trickery
inveigled *v* ▷ **inveigle**
inveigles *v* ▷ **inveigle**
inveigling *v* ▷ **inveigle**
invent *v* (**-s, -ing, -ed**) think up or create (something new)
invented *v* ▷ **invent**
inventing *v* ▷ **invent**
invention *n* (*pl* **-s**) something invented
inventive *adj* creative and resourceful > **inventiveness** *n* (*pl* **-s**) > **inventor** *n* (*pl* **-s**)
inventiveness *n* ▷ **inventive**
inventivenesses *n* ▷ **inventive**
inventor *n* ▷ **inventive**
inventories *v* ▷ **inventory**
inventors *n* ▷ **inventive**
inventory *n* (*pl* **-ries**) detailed list of goods or furnishings
invents *v* ▷ **invent**
inverse *adj* reversed in effect, sequence, direction, etc. > **inversely** *adv*
inversely *adv* ▷ **inverse**
inversion *n* ▷ **invert**
inversions *n* ▷ **invert**
invert *v* (**-s, -ing, -ed**) turn upside down or inside out > **inversion** *n* (*pl* **-s**)
invertebrate *n* (*pl* **-s**) animal with no backbone
invertebrates *n* ▷ **invertebrate**
inverted *v* ▷ **invert**
inverting *v* ▷ **invert**
inverts *v* ▷ **invert**
invest *v* (**-s, -ing, -ed**) spend (money, time, etc.) on something with the expectation of profit
invested *v* ▷ **invest**
investigate *v* (**-tes, -ting, -ted**) inquire into, examine > **investigation** *n* (*pl* **-s**) > **investigative** *adj* > **investigator** *n* (*pl* **-s**)
investigated *v* ▷ **investigate**
investigates *v* ▷ **investigate**
investigating *v* ▷ **investigate**
investigation *n* ▷ **investigate**
investigations *n* ▷ **investigate**
investigative *adj* ▷ **investigate**
investigator *n* ▷ **investigate**
investigators *n* ▷ **investigate**
investing *v* ▷ **invest**
investiture *n* (*pl* **-s**) formal installation of a person in an office or rank
investitures *n* ▷ **investiture**
investment *n* (*pl* **-s**) money invested

> **investor** *n* (*pl* **-s**)
investments *n* ▷ **investment**
investor *n* ▷ **investment**
investors *n* ▷ **investment**
invests *v* ▷ **invest**
inveterate *adj* firmly established in a habit or condition
invidious *adj* likely to cause resentment
invigilate *v* (**-tes, -ting, -ted**) supervise people sitting an examination > **invigilator** *n* (*pl* **-s**)
invigilated *v* ▷ **invigilate**
invigilates *v* ▷ **invigilate**
invigilating *v* ▷ **invigilate**
invigilation *n* ▷ **invigilate**
invigilations *n* ▷ **invigilate**
invigilator *n* ▷ **invigilate**
invigilators *n* ▷ **invigilate**
invigorate *v* (**-tes, -ting, -ted**) give energy to, refresh
invigorated *v* ▷ **invigorate**
invigorates *v* ▷ **invigorate**
invigorating *v* ▷ **invigorate**
invincibilities *n* ▷ **invincibile**
invincibility *n* ▷ **invincibile**
invincible *adj* impossible to defeat > **invincibility** *n* (*pl* **-ties**)
inviolable *adj* unable to be broken or violated
inviolate *adj* unharmed, unaffected
invisibilities *n* ▷ **invisible**
invisibility *adv* ▷ **invisible**
invisible *adj* not able to be seen > **invisibly** *adv* > **invisibility** *n* (*pl* **-ties**)
invisibly *adv* ▷ **invisible**
invitation *n* ▷ **invite**
invitations *n* ▷ **invite**
invite *v* (**-tes, -ting, -ted**) request the company of ▶ *n* (*pl* **-s**) (*Informal*) invitation > **invitation** *n* (*pl* **-s**)
invited *v* ▷ **invite**
invites *v, n* ▷ **invite**
inviting *adj* tempting, attractive ▶ *v* ▷ **invite**
invocation *n* ▷ **invoke**
invocations *n* ▷ **invoke**
invoice *v* (**-ces, -cing, -ced**) ▶ *n* (*pl* **-s**) (present with) a bill for goods or services supplied
invoiced *v* ▷ **invoice**
invoices *n, v* ▷ **invoice**
invoicing *v* ▷ **invoice**
invoke *v* (**-kes, -king, -ked**) put (a law or penalty) into operation > **invocation** *n* (*pl* **-s**)
invoked *v* ▷ **invoke**
invokes *v* ▷ **invoke**
invoking *v* ▷ **invoke**
involuntarily *adv* ▷ **involuntary**
involuntary *adj* not done consciously, unintentional > **involuntarily** *adv*
involve *v* (**-lves, -lving, -lved**) include as a necessary part > **involved** *adj* complicated > **involvement** *n* (*pl* **-s**)
involved *v, adj* ▷ **involve**
involvement *n* ▷ **involve**
involvements *n* ▷ **involve**
involves *v* ▷ **involve**
involving *v* ▷ **involve**
invulnerable *adj* not able to be wounded or harmed
inward *adj* directed towards the middle ▶ *adv* (*also* **inwards**) towards the inside or middle > **inwardly** *adv*
inwardly *adv* ▷ **inward**
inwards *adv* ▷ **inward**

io *n* (**ios**). An io a cry of joy or grief. While io doesn't earn many points, it's useful when you want to form words in more than one direction: I and O are two of the most common tiles in the game, so there's a good chance that you'll be able to use io when forming a word in another direction. Io scores 2 points.

iodine *n* (*pl* **-s**) (CHEM) bluish-black element used in medicine and photography
iodines *n* ▷ **iodine**
iodize *v* (**-izes, -izing, -ized**) treat with iodine
iodized *n* ▷ **iodize**
iodizes *n* ▷ **iodize**
iodizing *n* ▷ **iodize**
ion *n* (*pl* **-s**) electrically charged atom > **ionic** *adj*
ionic *adj* ▷ **ion**
ionization *n* ▷ **ionize**
ionizations *n* ▷ **ionize**
ionize *v* (**-izes, -izing, -ized**) change into ions > **ionization** *n* (*pl* **-s**)
ionized *v* ▷ **ionize**
ionizes *v* ▷ **ionize**
ionizing *v* ▷ **ionize**
ionosphere *n* (*pl* **-s**) region of ionized air in the upper atmosphere that reflects radio waves
ionospheres *n* ▷ **ionosphere**
ions *n* ▷ **ion**
iota *n* (*pl* **-s**) very small amount
iotas *n* ▷ **iota**
irascibilities *n* ▷ **irascible**
irascibility *n* ▷ **irascible**
irascible *adj* easily angered > **irascibility** *n* (*pl* **-ties**)
irate *adj* very angry
ire *n* (*pl* **-s**) (*Lit*) anger
ires *n* ▷ **ire**
iridescence *n* ▷ **iridescent**

iridescences *n* ▷ **iridescent**
iridescent *adj* having shimmering changing colours like a rainbow > **iridescence** *n* (*pl* **-s**)
iridium *n* (*pl* **-s**) (CHEM) very hard corrosion-resistant metal
iridiums *n* ▷ **iridium**
iris *n* (*pl* **-ses**) coloured circular membrane of the eye containing the pupil
irises *n* ▷ **iris**
irk *v* (**-s, -ing, -ed**) irritate, annoy
irked *v* ▷ **irk**
irking *v* ▷ **irk**
irks *v* ▷ **irk**
irksome *adj* irritating, annoying
iron *n* (*pl* **-s**) strong silvery-white metallic element, widely used for structural and engineering purposes ▶ *adj* made of iron ▶ *v* (**-s, -ing, -ed**) smooth (clothes or fabric) with an iron
ironbark *n* (*pl* **-s**) Australian eucalyptus with hard rough bark
ironbarks *n* ▷ **ironbark**
ironed *v* ▷ **iron**
ironic, ironical *adj* using irony > **ironically** *adv*
ironical *adj* ▷ **ironic**
ironically *adv* ▷ **ironic**
ironies *n* ▷ **irony**
ironing *n* (*pl* **-s**) clothes to be ironed ▶ *v* ▷ **iron**
ironings *n* ▷ **ironing**
ironmonger *n* (*pl* **-s**) shopkeeper or shop dealing in hardware > **ironmongery** *n* (*pl* **-ries**)
ironmongeries *n* ▷ **ironmonger**
ironmongers *n* ▷ **ironmonger**
ironmongery *n* ▷ **ironmonger**
irons *n, v* ▷ **iron** ▶ *pl n* chains, restraints
ironstone *n* (*pl* **-s**) rock consisting mainly of iron ore
ironstones *n* ▷ **ironstone**
irony *n* (*pl* **-nies**) mildly sarcastic use of words to imply the opposite of what is said
irradiate *v* (**-tes, -ting, -ted**) subject to or treat with radiation > **irradiation** *n* (*pl* **-s**)
irradiated *v* ▷ **irradiate**
irradiates *v* ▷ **irradiate**
irradiating *v* ▷ **irradiate**
irradiation *n* ▷ **irradiate**
irradiations *n* ▷ **irradiate**
irrational *adj* not based on or not using logical reasoning
irredeemable *adj* not able to be reformed or corrected
irreducible *adj* impossible to put in a simpler form
irrefutable *adj* impossible to deny or disprove
irregular *adj* not regular or even > **irregularly** *adv* > **irregularity** *n* (*pl* **-ties**)
irregularities *n* ▷ **irregular**
irregularity *n* ▷ **irregular**
irregularly *adv* ▷ **irregular**
irrelevance *n* ▷ **irrelevant**
irrelevances *n* ▷ **irrelevant**
irrelevant *adj* not connected with the matter in hand > **irrelevantly** *adv* > **irrelevance** *n* (*pl* **-s**)
irrelevantly *adv* ▷ **irrelevant**
irreparable *adj* not able to be repaired or put right > **irreparably** *adv*
irreparably *adv* ▷ **irreparable**
irreplaceable *adj* impossible to replace
irreproachable *adj* blameless, faultless
irresistible *adj* too attractive or strong to resist > **irresistibly** *adv*
irresistibly *adv* ▷ **irresistible**
irresponsibilities *n* ▷ **irresponsible**
irresponsibility *n* ▷ **irresponsible**
irresponsible *adj* not showing or not done with due care for the consequences of one's actions or attitudes > **irresponsibility** *n* (*pl* **-ties**)
irreverence *n* ▷ **irreverent**
irreverences *n* ▷ **irreverent**
irreverent *adj* not showing due respect > **irreverence** *n* (*pl* **-s**)
irreversible *adj* not able to be reversed or put right again > **irreversibly** *adv*
irreversibly *adv* ▷ **irreversible**
irrevocable *adj* not possible to change or undo > **irrevocably** *adv*
irrevocably *adv* ▷ **irrevocable**
irrigate *v* (**-tes, -ting, -ted**) supply (land) with water by artificial channels or pipes > **irrigation** *n* (*pl* **-s**)
irrigated *v* ▷ **irrigate**
irrigates *v* ▷ **irrigate**
irrigating *v* ▷ **irrigate**
irrigation *n* ▷ **irrigate**
irrigations *n* ▷ **irrigate**
irritable *adj* easily annoyed > **irritably** *adv*
irritably *adv* ▷ **irritable**
irritant *n* (*pl* **-s**) ▶ *adj* (person or thing) causing irritation
irritants *n* ▷ **irritant**
irritate *v* (**-tes, -ting, -ted**) annoy, anger > **irritation** *n* (*pl* **-s**)
irritated *v* ▷ **irritate**
irritates *v* ▷ **irritate**
irritating *v* ▷ **irritate**
irritation *n* ▷ **irritate**
irritations *n* ▷ **irritate**

is *v* ▷ **be**

ish *n* (**ishes**). An ish is a word for an issue in Scots law. If you have I, S and H on your rack, remember that as well as adding **ish** to the end of many words, you can also play those letters as a word in its own right. Ish scores 6 points.

isinglass [**ize**-ing-glass] *n* (*pl* **-es**) kind of gelatine obtained from some freshwater fish
isinglasses *n* ▷ **isinglass**
island *n* (*pl* **-s**) piece of land surrounded by water
islander *n* (*pl* **-s**) person who lives on an island
islanders *n* ▷ **islander**
islands *n* ▷ **island**
isle *n* (*pl* **-s**) (*Poetic*) island
isles *n* ▷ **isle**
islet *n* small island
islets *n* ▷ **islet**

ism *n* (**isms**). An ism is an informal word for a belief or doctrine. While **ism** can be added to the ends of many words as a suffix, it's worth remembering as a word in its own right. Ism scores 5 points.

isobar [**ice**-oh-bar] *n* (*pl* **-s**) line on a map connecting places of equal atmospheric pressure
isobars *n* ▷ **isobar**
isolate *v* (**-tes, -ting, -ted**) place apart or alone > **isolation** *n* (*pl* **-s**)
isolated *v* ▷ **isolate**
isolates *v* ▷ **isolate**
isolating *v* ▷ **isolate**
isolation *n* ▷ **isolate**
isolationism *n* (*pl* **-s**) policy of not participating in international affairs > **isolationist** *n* (*pl* **-s**) *adj*
isolationisms *n* ▷ **isolationism**
isolationist *n, adj* ▷ **isolationism**
isolationists *n* ▷ **isolationsim**
isolations *n* ▷ **isolate**
isomer [**ice**-oh-mer] *n* (*pl* **-s**) substance whose molecules contain the same atoms as another but in a different arrangement
isomers *n* ▷ **isomer**
isometric *adj* relating to muscular contraction without shortening of the muscle
isometrics *pl n* isometric exercises
isotherm [**ice**-oh-therm] *n* (*pl* **-s**) line on a map connecting points of equal temperature
isotherms *n* ▷ **isotherm**
isotope [**ice**-oh-tope] *n* (*pl* **-s**) one of two or more atoms with the same number of protons in the nucleus but a different number of neutrons
isotopes *n* ▷ **isotope**
issue *n* (*pl* **-s**) topic of interest or discussion ▶ *v* (**-ssues, -ssuing, -ssued**) make (a statement etc.) publicly
issued *v* ▷ **issue**
issues *n, v* ▷ **issue**
issuing *v* ▷ **issue**
isthmus [**iss**-muss] *n* (*pl* **-muses**) narrow strip of land connecting two areas of land
isthmuses *n* ▷ **isthmus**
it *pron* refers to a nonhuman, animal, plant, or inanimate object > **its** *adj, pron* belonging to it
italic *adj* (of printing type) sloping to the right
italicize *v* (**-izes, -izing, -ized**) put in italics
italicized *v* ▷ **italicize**
italicizes *v* ▷ **italicize**
italicizing *v* ▷ **italicize**
italics *pl n* this type, used for emphasis
itch *n* (*pl* **-es**) skin irritation causing a desire to scratch ▶ *v* (**-es, -ing, -ed**) have an itch > **itchy** *adj*
itched *v* ▷ **itch**
itches *n, v* ▷ **itch**
itching *v* ▷ **itch**
itchy *adj* ▷ **itch**
item *n* (*pl* **-s**) single thing in a list or collection > **itemize** *v* (**-izes, -izing, -ized**) make a list of
itemized *n* ▷ **item**
itemizes *n* ▷ **item**
itemizing *n* ▷ **item**
items *n* ▷ **item**
iterate *v* (**-tes, -ting, -ted**) repeat > **iteration** *n* (*pl* **-s**)
iterated *v* ▷ **iterate**
iterates *v* ▷ **iterate**
iterating *v* ▷ **iterate**
iteration *n* ▷ **iterate**
iterations *n* ▷ **iterate**
itinerant *adj* travelling from place to place
itineraries *n* ▷ **itinerary**
itinerary *n* (*pl* **-aries**) detailed plan of a journey
itself *pron* ▷ **it**
ivies *n* ▷ **ivy**
ivories *n* ▷ **ivory**
ivory *n* (*pl* **-ries**) hard white bony substance forming the tusks of elephants ▶ *adj* yellowish-white
ivy *n* (*pl* **-vies**) evergreen climbing plant
iwi [**ee**-wee] *n* (*pl* **-s**) (NZ) Maori tribe
iwis *n* ▷ **iwi**

Jj

J is one of the best tiles to have in Scrabble, as it is worth 8 points on its own. J also forms a number of words with X and Z, allowing you to earn some huge scores if you get the right tiles to go with it. Even better, some of these words are seven letters in length, so the right combination of tiles will give you a 50-point bonus if you are lucky enough to have it on your rack. On the other hand, J isn't the easiest tile to use when forming words in different directions. There's only one two-letter word that begins with J **jo.** If you remember this, however, you won't waste time trying to think of others. As J has such a high value, look out for double- and triple-letter squares when playing it. There are plenty of good three-letter words starting with J: **jab** (12 points), **jam** (12), **jar** (10), **jaw** (13), **jay** (13), **jet** (10), **jib** (12), **jig** (11), **job** (12), **jog** (11), **jot** (10), **joy** (13), **jug** (11) and **jut** (10). In addition to these, there are other fantastic words beginning with J. **Jazz** (19) is very useful – you'll need a blank tile for the second Z, but if you can form it, you may also be able to play **jazzes** (21) or **jazzy** (23). **Jinx** (18) is also handy, and don't forget **jukebox** (27), which can be formed from **box** or **ox** if someone has played those.

jab *v* (**-s, -bbing, -bbed**) poke sharply ▸ *n* (*pl* **-s**)
jabbed *v* ▷ **jab**
jabber *v* (**-s, -ing, -ed**) talk rapidly or incoherently
jabbered *v* ▷ **jabber**
jabbering *v* ▷ **jabber**
jabbers *v* ▷ **jabber**
jabbing *v* ▷ **jab**
jabiru *n* (*pl* **-s**) large white-and-black Australian stork
jabirus *n* ▷ **jabiru**
jabs *v*, *n* ▷ **jab**
jacaranda *n* (*pl* **-s**) tropical tree with sweet-smelling wood
jacarandas *n* ▷ **jacaranda**
jack *n* (*pl* **-s**) device for raising a motor vehicle or other heavy object
jacks *n* ▷ **jack**
jackal *n* (*pl* **-s**) doglike wild animal of Africa and Asia
jackals *n* ▷ **jackal**
jackaroo, jackeroo *n* (*pl* **-roos**) (AUST) trainee on a sheep station
jackaroos *n* ▷ **jackaroo**
jackass *n* (*pl* **-es**) fool
jackasses *n* ▷ **jackass**
jackboot *n* (*pl* **-s**) high military boot
jackboots *n* ▷ **jackboot**
jackdaw *n* (*pl* **-s**) black-and-grey Eurasian bird of the crow family
jackdaws *n* ▷ **jackdaw**
jackeroo *n* ▷ **jackaroo**
jackeroos *n* ▷ **jackaroo**
jacket *n* (*pl* **-s**) short coat
jackets *n* ▷ **jacket**
jackknife *v* (**-s, -fing, -fed**) (of an articulated truck) go out of control so that the trailer swings round at a sharp angle to the cab ▸ *n* (*pl* **-knives**) large clasp knife
jackknifed *v* ▷ **jackknife**
jackknifes *v* ▷ **jackknife**
jackknifing *v* ▷ **jackknife**
jackknives *n* ▷ **jackknife**
jackpot *n* (*pl* **-s**) largest prize that may be won in a game
jackpots *n* ▷ **jackpot**
jacuzzi [jak-**oo**-zee] *n* ® (*pl* **-s**) circular bath with a device that swirls the water
jacuzzis *n* ▷ **jacuzzi**
jade *n* (*pl* **-s**) ornamental semiprecious stone, usu. dark green ▸ *adj* bluish-green
jaded *adj* tired and unenthusiastic
jades *n* ▷ **jade**
jagged [**jag**-gid] *adj* having an uneven edge

with sharp points
jaguar *n* (*pl* **-s**) large S American spotted cat
jaguars *n* ▷ **jaguar**
jail *n* (*pl* **-s**) prison ▶ *v* (**-s, -ing, -ed**) send to prison > **jailer** *n* (*pl* **-s**)
jailbird *n* (*pl* **-s**) (*Informal*) person who has often been in prison
jailbirds *n* ▷ **jailbird**
jailed *v* ▷ **jail**
jailer *n* ▷ **jail**
jailers *n* ▷ **jail**
jailing *v* ▷ **jail**
jails *n, v* ▷ **jail**
jalopies *n* ▷ **jalopy**
jalopy [jal-**lop**-ee] *n* (*pl* **-pies**) (*Informal*) old car
jam[1] *v* (**-s, -mming, -mmed**) pack tightly into a place ▶ *n* (*pl* **-s**) hold-up of traffic
jam[2] *n* (*pl* **-s**) food made from fruit boiled with sugar
jamb *n* (*pl* **-s**) side post of a door or window frame
jamboree *n* (*pl* **-s**) large gathering or celebration
jamborees *n* ▷ **jamboree**
jambs *n* ▷ **jamb**
jammed *v* ▷ **jam**[1]
jamming *v* ▷ **jam**[1]
jams *v* ▷ **jam**[1] ▶ *n* ▷ **jam**[1, 2]
jandal *n* (*pl* **-s**) (NZ) sandal with a strap between the toes
jandals *n* ▷ **jandal**
jangle *v* (**-les, -ling, -led**) (cause to) make a harsh ringing noise
jangled *v* ▷ **jangle**
jangles *v* ▷ **jangle**
jangling *v* ▷ **jangle**
janitor *n* (*pl* **-s**) caretaker of a school or other building
janitors *n* ▷ **janitor**

> **janizar** or **janizary** *n* (**janizars, janizaries**). A janizar was an elite soldier in the armies of the Ottoman Empire. This is a very useful word, and will earn you a 50-point bonus if you are able to use all your letters in playing it. Also, if janizar is already on the board, you have an opportunity to earn a good score by adding an S, Y or IES. Janizar scores 23 points.

japan *n* (*pl* **-s**) very hard varnish, usu. black ▶ *v* (**-s, -nning, -nned**) cover with this varnish
japanned *v* ▷ **japan**
japanning *v* ▷ **japan**
japans *n, v* ▷ **japan**
jape *n* (*pl* **-s**) (*Old-fashioned*) joke or prank
japes *n* ▷ **jape**
japonica *n* (*pl* **-s**) shrub with red flowers
japonicas *n* ▷ **japonica**
jar[1] *n* (*pl* **-s**) wide-mouthed container, usu. round and made of glass
jar[2] *v* (**-s, -rring, -rred**) have a disturbing or unpleasant effect ▶ *n* (*pl* **-s**) jolt or shock
jargon *n* (*pl* **-s**) specialized technical language of a particular subject
jargons *n* ▷ **jargon**
jarrah *n* (*pl* **-s**) Australian eucalypt yielding valuable timber
jarrahs *n* ▷ **jarrah**
jarred *v* ▷ **jar**[2]
jarring *v* ▷ **jar**[2]
jars *v* ▷ **jar**[2] ▶ *n* ▷ **jar**[1, 2]
jasmine *n* (*pl* **-s**) shrub with sweet-smelling yellow or white flowers
jasmines *n* ▷ **jasmine**
jasper *n* (*pl* **-s**) red, yellow, dark green, or brown variety of quartz
jaspers *n* ▷ **jasper**
jaundice *n* (*pl* **-s**) disease marked by yellowness of the skin
jaundiced *adj* (of an attitude or opinion) bitter or cynical
jaundices *n* ▷ **jaundice**
jaunt *n* (*pl* **-s**) short journey for pleasure
jauntier *adj* ▷ **jaunty**
jauntiest *adj* ▷ **jaunty**
jauntily *adv* ▷ **jaunty**
jaunts *n* ▷ **jaunt**
jaunty *adj* (**-tier, -tiest**) sprightly and cheerful > **jauntily** *adv*
javelin *n* (*pl* **-s**) light spear thrown in sports competitions
javelins *n* ▷ **javelin**
jaw *n* (*pl* **-s**) one of the bones in which the teeth are set ▶ *v* (**-s, -ing, -ed**) (*Slang*) talk lengthily

> **jawbox** *n* (**jawboxes**). Jawbox is a Scots word for a sink. Watch out for opportunities to form this if someone else has played either jaw or box, and if jawbox itself is on the board, you can earn 27 points just by making it plural with es. Jawbox scores 25 points.

jawed *v* ▷ **jaw**
jawing *v* ▷ **jaw**
jaws *n, v* ▷ **jaw** ▶ *pl n* mouth
jay *n* (*pl* **-s**) bird with a pinkish body and blue-and-black wings
jays *n* ▷ **jay**
jaywalker *n* (*pl* **-s**) person who crosses the road in a careless or dangerous manner > **jaywalking** *n* (*pl* **-s**)

jaywalkers *n* ▷ **jaywalker**
jaywalking *n* ▷ **jaywalker**
jaywalkings *n* ▷ **jaywalker**

jazy *n* **(jazies)**. Jazy is an old word for a wig. This is a marvellous word, combining J and Z. If you get this combination and have either an A or a Y, look for the missing letter on the board, as it's highly likely to be there. Jazy scores 23 points.

jazz *n* (*pl* **-es**) kind of music with an exciting rhythm, usu. involving improvisation
jazzes *n* ▷ **jazz**
jazzier *adj* ▷ **jazzy**
jazziest *adj* ▷ **jazzy**
jazzy *adj* **(-zier, -ziest)** flashy or showy
jealous *adj* fearful of losing a partner or possession to a rival > **jealously** *adv* > **jealousy** *n* (*pl* **-sies**)
jealousies *n* ▷ **jealous**
jealously *adv* ▷ **jealous**
jealousy *n* ▷ **jealous**
jeans *pl n* casual denim trousers
jeer *v* **(-s, -ing, -ed)** scoff or deride ▶ *n* (*pl* **-s**) cry of derision
jeered *v* ▷ **jeer**
jeering *v* ▷ **jeer**
jeers *v, n* ▷ **jeer**
jejune *adj* simple or naive
jell *v* **(-s, -ing, -ed)** form into a jelly-like substance
jelled *v* ▷ **jell**
jellied *adj* prepared in a jelly
jelling *v* ▷ **jell**
jells *v* ▷ **jell**
jellies *n* ▷ **jelly**
jelly *n* (*pl* **-llies**) soft food made of liquid set with gelatine
jellyfish *n* (*pl* **jellyfish**) small jelly-like sea animal
jemmies *n* ▷ **jemmy**
jemmy *n* (*pl* **-mmies**) short steel crowbar used by burglars
jennies *n* ▷ **jenny**
jenny *n* (*pl* **-nnies**) female ass or wren
jeopardies *n* ▷ **jeopardy**
jeopardize *v* **(-izes, -izing, -ized)** place in danger
jeopardized *n* ▷ **jeopardy**
jeopardizes *n* ▷ **jeopardy**
jeopardizing *n* ▷ **jeopardy**
jeopardy *n* (*pl* **-dies**) danger
jerboa *n* (*pl* **-s**) small mouselike rodent with long hind legs
jerboas *n* ▷ **jerboa**
jerk *v* **(-s, -ing, -ed)** move or throw abruptly ▶ *n* (*pl* **-s**) sharp or abruptly stopped movement
jerked *v* ▷ **jerk**
jerkily *adv* ▷ **jerky**
jerkin *n* (*pl* **-s**) sleeveless jacket
jerkiness *n* ▷ **jerky**
jerkinesses *n* ▷ **jerky**
jerking *v* ▷ **jerk**
jerkins *n* ▷ **jerkin**
jerks *v, n* ▷ **jerk**
jerky *adj* sudden or abrupt > **jerkily** *adv* > **jerkiness** *n* (*pl* **-s**)

jerque *v* **(jerques, jerquing, jerqued)**, *n* **(jerquer, jerquers, jerquing, jerquings)**. Jerque means to search a ship for smuggled goods. If you have all the tiles for jerques, jerquer or jerqued, you'll get a 50-point bonus for using all your letters, which will give you a fantastic score. Jerque scores 22 points.

jersey *n* (*pl* **-s**) knitted jumper
jerseys *n* ▷ **jersey**
jest *n* (*pl* **-s**) ▶ *v* **(-s, -ing, -ed)** joke
jested *v* ▷ **jest**
jester *n* (*pl* **-s**) (HIST) professional clown at court
jesters *n* ▷ **jester**
jesting *v* ▷ **jest**
jests *n, v* ▷ **jest**
jet[1] *n* (*pl* **-s**) aircraft driven by jet propulsion ▶ *v* **(-s, jetting, jetted)** fly by jet aircraft
jet[2] *n* (*pl* **-s**) hard black mineral
jetboat *n* (*pl* **-s**) motorboat propelled by a jet of water
jetboats *n* ▷ **jetboat**
jets *n* ▷ **jet**[1, 2] ▶ *v* ▷ **jet**[1]
jetsam *n* (*pl* **-s**) goods thrown overboard to lighten a ship
jetsams *n* ▷ **jetsam**
jetted *v* ▷ **jet**[1]
jetties *n* ▷ **jetty**
jetting *v* ▷ **jet**[1]
jettison *v* **(-s, -ing, -ed)** abandon
jettisoned *v* ▷ **jettison**
jettisoning *v* ▷ **jettison**
jettisons *v* ▷ **jettison**
jetty *n* (*pl* **-ties**) small pier

jeu *n* **(jeux)**. Jeu is the French word for **game** or **play.** The plural form, jeux, is a great little word, using both J and X particularly if you can play it on a double- or triple-word square. Jeux scores 18 points.

jewel *n* (*pl* **-s**) precious stone
jeweller *n* (*pl* **-s**) dealer in jewels
jewelleries *n* ▷ **jewellery**

jewellers *n* ▷ **jeweller**
jewellery *n* (*pl* **-s**) objects decorated with precious stones
jewels *n* ▷ **jewel**
jewfish *n* (*pl* **jewfish**) (AUST) freshwater catfish

jezail *n* (**jezails**). A jezail is a kind of heavy Afghan musket. This word is potentially a very high scorer, as its plural uses seven tiles. If you can play all of these at once, you'll earn the 50-point bonus for a total of 73 points! Jezail scores 22 points.

jib[1] *n* (*pl* **-s**) triangular sail set in front of a mast
jib[2] *v* (**-s, -bbing, -bbed**) (of a horse, person, etc.) stop and refuse to go on
jib[3] *n* (*pl* **-s**) projecting arm of a crane or derrick
jibbed *v* ▷ **jib**[2]
jibbing *v* ▷ **jib**[2]
jibe[1] *n* (*pl* **-s**) ▸ *v* (**-jibes, -jibing, -jibed**) taunt or jeer
jibed *v* ▷ **jibe**[1]
jibes *n, v* ▷ **jibe**[1]
jibing *v* ▷ **jibe**[1]
jibs *n* ▷ **jib**[1, 3] ▸ *v* ▷ **jib**[2]
jiffies *n* ▷ **jiffy**
jiffy *n* (*pl* **-ffies**) (*Informal*) very short period of time
jig *n* (*pl* **-s**) type of lively dance ▸ *v* (**-s, -gging, -gged**) make jerky up-and-down movements
jigged *v* ▷ **jig**
jigging *v* ▷ **jig**
jiggle *v* (**-ggles, -ggling, -ggled**) move up and down with short jerky movements
jiggled *v* ▷ **jiggle**
jiggles *v* ▷ **jiggle**
jiggling *v* ▷ **jiggle**
jigs *n, v* ▷ **jig**
jigsaw *n* (*pl* **-s**) (*also* **jigsaw puzzle**) picture cut into interlocking pieces, which the user tries to fit together again
jigsaws *n* ▷ **jigsaw**
jihad *n* (*pl* **-s**) Islamic holy war against unbelievers
jihads *n* ▷ **jihad**
jilt *v* (**-s, -ing, -ed**) leave or reject (one's lover)
jilted *v* ▷ **jilt**
jilting *v* ▷ **jilt**
jilts *v* ▷ **jilt**
jingle *n* (*pl* **-s**) catchy verse or song used in a radio or television advert ▸ *v* (**-les, -ling, -led**) (cause to) make a gentle ringing sound
jingled *v* ▷ **jingle**
jingles *n, v* ▷ **jingle**
jingling *v* ▷ **jingle**
jingoism *n* (*pl* **-s**) aggressive nationalism **>jingoistic** *adj*
jingoisms *n* ▷ **jingoism**
jingoistic *adj* ▷ **jingoism**
jinks *pl n* boisterous merrymaking
jinn *n* ▷ **jinni**
jinni *n* (*pl* **jinn**) spirit in Muslim mythology
jinx *n* (*pl* **-es**) person or thing bringing bad luck ▸ *v* (**-xes, -xing, -xed**) be or put a jinx on
jinxed *v* ▷ **jinx**
jinxes *n, v* ▷ **jinx**
jinxing *v* ▷ **jinx**
jitters *pl n* worried nervousness
jittery *adj* nervous
jive *n* (*pl* **-s**) lively dance of the 1940s and '50s ▸ *v* (**-ves, -ving, -ved**) dance the jive
jived *v* ▷ **jive**
jives *n, v* ▷ **jive**
jiving *v* ▷ **jive**

jiz *n* (**jizes**). Jiz is an old word for a wig. This is a very useful word for when you find yourself with J and Z but nothing else that looks promising: there will almost certainly be an I on the board around which you can form jiz. Jiz scores 19 points.

jizz *n* (**jizzes**). A jizz is the combination of characteristics used to identify a bird or plant species. A blank tile is required to form jizz because it contains two Zs. If **jiz** is already on the board, a blank or a blank and ES will earn you 19 or 21 points. Jizz scores 19 points.

jo *n* (**joes**). Jo is a Scots word for a sweetheart. This is the only two-letter word that starts with J, and is worth remembering for that reason. It's also a good word to form when playing in more than one direction at once. Jo scores 9 points.

job *n* (*pl* **-s**) occupation or paid employment
jobbing *adj* doing individual jobs for payment
jobless *adj, pl n* unemployed (people)
jobs *n* ▷ **job**
jockey *n* (*pl* **-s**) (professional) rider of racehorses ▸ *v* (**-ys, -ying, -yed**) manoeuvre to obtain an advantage
jockeyed *v* ▷ **jockey**
jockeying *v* ▷ **jockey**
jockeys *n, v* ▷ **jockey**
jockstrap *n* (*pl* **-s**) belt with a pouch to support the genitals, worn by male athletes
jockstraps *n* ▷ **jockstrap**
jocose [joke-**kohss**] *adj* playful or humorous
jocular *adj* fond of joking **>jocularity** *n* (*pl*

-ties) > **jocularly** *adv*
jocularities *n* ▷ **jocular**
jocularity *n* ▷ **jocular**
jocularly *adv* ▷ **jocular**
jocund [**jok**-kund] *adj* (*Lit*) merry or cheerful
jodhpurs *pl n* riding trousers, loose-fitting above the knee but tight below
joey *n* (*pl* **-ys**) (AUST) young kangaroo
joeys *n* ▷ **joey**
jog *v* (**-s, -gging, -gged**) run at a gentle pace, esp. for exercise ▶ *n* (*pl* **-s**) slow run > **jogger** *n* (*pl* **-s**) > **jogging** *n* (*pl* **-s**)
jogged *v* ▷ **jog**
jogger *n* ▷ **jog**
joggers *n* ▷ **jog**
jogging *n, v* ▷ **jog**
joggings *n* ▷ **jog**
joggle *v* (**-les, -ling, -led**) shake or move jerkily
joggled *v* ▷ **joggle**
joggles *v* ▷ **joggle**
joggling *v* ▷ **joggle**
jogs *n, v* ▷ **jog**
join *v* (**-s, -ing, -ed**) become a member (of) ▶ *n* (*pl* **-s**) place where two things are joined
joined *v* ▷ **join**
joiner *n* (*pl* **-s**) maker of finished woodwork
joineries *n* ▷ **joinery**
joiners *n* ▷ **joiner**
joinery *n* (*pl* **-ries**) joiner's work
joining *v* ▷ **join**
joins *n, v* ▷ **join**
joint *adj* shared by two or more ▶ *n* (*pl* **-s**) place where bones meet but can move ▶ *v* (**-s, -ing, -ed**) divide meat into joints > **jointed** *adj* > **jointly** *adv*
jointed *v, adj* ▷ **joint**
jointing *v* ▷ **joint**
jointly *adv* ▷ **joint**
joints *n, v* ▷ **joint**
joist *n* (*pl* **-s**) horizontal beam that helps support a floor or ceiling
joists *n* ▷ **joist**
jojoba [hoe-**hoe**-ba] *n* (*pl* **-s**) shrub of SW North America whose seeds yield oil used in cosmetics
jojobas *n* ▷ **jojoba**
joke *n* (*pl* **-s**) thing said or done to cause laughter ▶ *v* (**-kes, -king, -ked**) make jokes > **jokey** *adj* > **jokingly** *adv*
joked *v* ▷ **joke**
joker *n* (*pl* **-s**) person who jokes
jokers *n* ▷ **joker**
jokes *n, v* ▷ **joke**
jokey *adj* ▷ **joke**
joking *v* ▷ **joke**
jokingly *adv* ▷ **joke**
jollied *v* ▷ **jolly**
jollier *adj* ▷ **jolly**
jollies *v* ▷ **jolly**
jolliest *adj* ▷ **jolly**
jollities *n* ▷ **jolly**
jollity *n* ▷ **jolly**
jolly *adj* (**-llier, -lliest**) (of a person) happy and cheerful ▶ *v* (**-lies, -lying, -lied**) try to keep (someone) cheerful by flattery or coaxing > **jollity** *n* (*pl* **-ties**)
jollification *n* (*pl* **-s**) merrymaking
jollifications *n* ▷ **jolly**
jollying *v* ▷ **jolly**
jolt *n* (*pl* **-s**) unpleasant surprise or shock ▶ *v* (**-s, -ing, -ed**) surprise or shock
jolted *v* ▷ **jolt**
jolting *v* ▷ **jolt**
jolts *n, v* ▷ **jolt**
jonquil *n* (*pl* **-s**) fragrant narcissus
jonquils *n* ▷ **jonquil**
josh *v* (**-es, -ing, -ed**) (CHIEFLY US) (*Slang*) tease
joshed *v* ▷ **josh**
joshes *v* ▷ **josh**
joshing *v* ▷ **josh**
jostle *v* (**-les, -ling, -led**) knock or push against
jostled *v* ▷ **jostle**
jostles *v* ▷ **jostle**
jostling *v* ▷ **jostle**
jot *v* (**-s, -tting, -tted**) write briefly ▶ *n* (*pl* **-s**) very small amount
jotted *v* ▷ **jot**
jotting *v* ▷ **jot**
jotter *n* (*pl* **-s**) notebook
jotters *n* ▷ **jotter**
jottings *pl n* notes jotted down
jots *v, n* ▷ **jot**
joule [**jool**] *n* (*pl* **-s**) (PHYSICS) unit of work or energy
joules *n* ▷ **joule**
journal *n* (*pl* **-s**) daily newspaper or magazine
journalese *n* (*pl* **-s**) superficial style of writing, found in some newspapers
journaleses *n* ▷ **journalese**
journalism *n* (*pl* **-s**) writing in or editing of newspapers and magazines > **journalist** *n* (*pl* **-s**) > **journalistic** *adj*
journalisms *n* ▷ **journalism**
journalist *n* ▷ **journalism**
journalistic *adj* ▷ **journalism**
journalists *n* ▷ **journalism**
journals *n* ▷ **journal**
journey *n* (*pl* **-s**) act or process of travelling from one place to another ▶ *v* (**-s, -ing, -ed**) travel

journeyed *v* ▷ **journey**
journeying *v* ▷ **journey**
journeyman *n* (*pl* **-men**) qualified craftsman employed by another
journeymen *n* ▷ **journeyman**
journeys *n, v* ▷ **journey**
joust (HIST) *n* (*pl* **-s**) combat with lances between two mounted knights ▶ *v* (**-s, -ing, -ed**) fight on horseback using lances
jousted *v* ▷ **joust**
jousting *v* ▷ **joust**
jousts *n, v* ▷ **joust**
jovial *adj* happy and cheerful > **jovially** *adv* > **joviality** *n* (*pl* **-ties**)
jovialities *n* ▷ **jovial**
joviality *n* ▷ **jovial**
jovially *adv* ▷ **jovial**
jowl¹ *n* (*pl* **-s**) lower jaw
jowl² *n* (*pl* **-s**) fatty flesh hanging from the lower jaw
jowls *n* ▷ **jowl¹, ²** ▶ *pl n* cheeks
joy *n* (*pl* **-s**) feeling of great delight or pleasure > **joyful** *adj* > **joyless** *adj*
joyful *adj* ▷ **joy**
joyless *adj* ▷ **joy**
joyous *adj* extremely happy and enthusiastic
joyride *n* ▷ **joyriding**
joyrider *n* ▷ **joyriding**
joyriders *n* ▷ **joyriding**
joyrides *n* ▷ **joyriding**
joyriding *n* (*pl* **-s**) driving for pleasure, esp. in a stolen car > **joyride** *n* (*pl* **-s**) > **joyrider** *n* (*pl* **-s**)
joyridings *n* ▷ **joyriding**
joystick *n* (*pl* **-s**) control device for an aircraft or computer
joysticks *n* ▷ **joystick**
joys *n* ▷ **joy**
jubilant *adj* feeling or expressing great joy > **jubilantly** *adv* > **jubilation** *n* (*pl* **-s**)
jubilantly *adv* ▷ **jubilant**
jubilation *n* ▷ **jubilant**
jubilations *n* ▷ **jubilant**
jubilee *n* (*pl* **-s**) special anniversary, esp. 25th (**silver jubilee**) or 50th (**golden jubilee**)
jubilees *n* ▷ **jubilee**
judder *v* (**-s, -ing, -ed**) vibrate violently ▶ *n* (*pl* **-s**) violent vibration
juddered *v* ▷ **judder**
juddering *v* ▷ **judder**
judders *v, n* ▷ **judder**
judge *n* (*pl* **-s**) public official who tries cases and passes sentence in a court of law ▶ *v* (**-dges, -dging, -dged**) act as a judge
judged *v* ▷ **judge**
judgement *n* ▷ **judgment**
judgements *n* ▷ **judgment**
judgemental *adj* ▷ **judgment**
judges *n, v* ▷ **judge**
judging *v* ▷ **judge**
judgment, judgement *n* (*pl* **-s**) opinion reached after careful thought > **judgmental, judgemental** *adj*
judgmental *adj* ▷ **judgment**
judgments *n* ▷ **judgment**
judicial *adj* of or by a court or judge > **judicially** *adv*
judicially *adv* ▷ **judicial**
judiciary *n* (*pl* **-ries**) system of courts and judges
judiciaries *n* ▷ **judiciary**
judicious *adj* well-judged and sensible > **judiciously** *adv*
judiciously *adv* ▷ **judicious**
judo *n* sport in which two opponents try to throw each other to the ground
jug *n* (*pl* **-s**) container for liquids, with a handle and small spout
juggernaut *n* (*pl* **-s**) (BRIT) large heavy truck
juggernauts *n* ▷ **juggernaut**
juggle *v* (**-les, -ling, -led**) throw and catch (several objects) so that most are in the air at the same time > **juggler** *n* (*pl* **-s**)
juggled *v* ▷ **juggle**
juggler *n* ▷ **juggle**
jugglers *n* ▷ **juggle**
juggles *v* ▷ **juggle**
juggling *v* ▷ **juggle**
jugs *n* ▷ **jug**
jugular *n* (*pl* **-s**) one of three large veins of the neck that return blood from the head to the heart
jugulars *n* ▷ **jugular**
juice *n* (*pl* **-s**) liquid part of vegetables, fruit, or meat
juices *n* ▷ **juice**
juicier *adj* ▷ **juicy**
juiciest *adj* ▷ **juicy**
juicy *adj* (**-cier, -ciest**) full of juice
jujitsu *n* (*pl* **-s**) Japanese art of wrestling and self-defence
jujitsus *n* ▷ **jujitsu**
juju *n* (*pl* **-s**) W African magic charm or fetish
jujus *n* ▷ **juju**
jukebox *n* (*pl* **-es**) coin-operated machine on which records, CDs, or videos can be played
jukeboxes *n* ▷ **jukebox**
julep *n* (*pl* **-s**) sweet alcoholic drink
juleps *n* ▷ **julep**
jumble *n* (*pl* **-s**) confused heap or state ▶ *v* (**-les, -ling, -led**) mix in a disordered way

jumbled *v* ▷ **jumble**
jumbles *n, v* ▷ **jumble**
jumbling *v* ▷ **jumble**
jumbo *adj* (*Informal*) very large ▶ *n* (*pl* **-s**) (*also* **jumbo jet**) large jet airliner
jumbos *n* ▷ **jumbo**
jumbuck *n* (*pl* **-s**) (AUST) (*Old-fashioned slang*) sheep
jumbucks *n* ▷ **jumbuck**
jump *v* (**-s, -ing, -ed**) leap or spring into the air using the leg muscles ▶ *n* (*pl* **-s**) act of jumping
jumped *v* ▷ **jump**
jumper *n* (*pl* **-s**) sweater or pullover
jumpers *n* ▷ **jumper**
jumpier *adj* ▷ **jumpy**
jumpiest *adj* ▷ **jumpy**
jumping *v* ▷ **jump**
jumps *v, n* ▷ **jump**
jumpy *adj* (**-pier, -piest**) nervous
junction *n* (*pl* **-s**) place where routes, railway lines, or roads meet
junctions *n* ▷ **junction**
juncture *n* (*pl* **-s**) point in time, esp. a critical one
junctures *n* ▷ **juncture**
jungle *n* (*pl* **-s**) tropical forest of dense tangled vegetation
jungles *n* ▷ **jungle**
junior *adj* of lower standing ▶ *n* (*pl* **-s**) junior person
juniors *n* ▷ **junior**
juniper *n* (*pl* **-s**) evergreen shrub with purple berries
junipers *n* ▷ **juniper**
junk[1] *n* (*pl* **-s**) discarded or useless objects
junk[2] *n* (*pl* **-s**) flat-bottomed Chinese sailing boat
junket *n* (*pl* **-s**) excursion by public officials paid for from public funds
junkets *n* ▷ **junket**
junkie, junky *n* (*pl* **-kies**) (*Slang*) drug addict
junkies *n* ▷ **junkie**
junks *n* ▷ **junk**[1, 2]
junky *n* ▷ **junkie**
junta *n* (*pl* **-s**) group of military officers holding power in a country, esp. after a coup
juntas *n* ▷ **junta**
juridical *adj* of law or the administration of justice
juries *n* ▷ **jury**
jurisdiction *n* (*pl* **-s**) right or power to administer justice and apply laws
jurisdictions *n* ▷ **jurisdiction**
jurisprudence *n* (*pl* **-s**) science or philosophy of law
jurisprudences *n* ▷ **jurisprudence**
jurist *n* (*pl* **-s**) expert in law
jurists *n* ▷ **jurist**
juror *n* (*pl* **-s**) member of a jury
jurors *n* ▷ **juror**
jury *n* (*pl* **-ries**) group of people sworn to deliver a verdict in a court of law
just *adv* very recently ▶ *adj* fair or impartial in action or judgment > **justly** *adv* > **justness** *n* (*pl* **-s**)
justice *n* (*pl* **-s**) quality of being just
justices *n* ▷ **justice**
justifiable *adj* ▷ **justify**
justifiably *adv* ▷ **justify**
justification *n* ▷ **justify**
justifications *n* ▷ **justify**
justified *v* ▷ **justify**
justifies *v* ▷ **justify**
justify *v* (**-fies, -fying, -fied**) prove right or reasonable > **justifiable** *adj* > **justifiably** *adv* > **justification** *n* (*pl* **-s**)
justifying *v* ▷ **justify**
justly *adv* ▷ **just**
justness *n* ▷ **just**
justnesses *n* ▷ **just**
jut *v* (**-s, -tting, -tted**) project or stick out
jute *n* (*pl* **-s**) plant fibre, used for rope, canvas, etc.
jutes *n* ▷ **jute**
juts *v* ▷ **jut**
jutted *v* ▷ **jut**
jutting *v* ▷ **jut**
juvenilia *pl n* works produced in an author's youth
juvenile *adj* young ▶ *n* (*pl* **-s**) young person or child
juveniles *n* ▷ **juvenile**
juxtapose *v* (**-ses, -sing, -sed**) put side by side > **juxtaposition** *n* (*pl* **-s**)
juxtaposed *v* ▷ **juxtapose**
juxtaposes *v* ▷ **juxtapose**
juxtaposing *v* ▷ **juxtapose**
juxtaposition *n* ▷ **juxtapose**
juxtapositions *n* ▷ **juxtapose**

jynx *n* (**jynxes**). A jynx is a kind of woodpecker. This unusual word is unique in combining J, Y and Z without using any vowels. Jynx scores 21 points.

Kk

Worth 5 points, K is a valuable tile to have in your rack. However, it's not the most useful tile for the short words that you need when forming words in different directions at the same time. There are only three two-letter words beginning with K: **ka, ko** and **ky.** Remembering these will stop you wasting time trying to think of others. There aren't very many three-letter words either, but remember **kak** (11 points), **keg** (8), **ken** (7), **key** (10), **kid** (8), **kin** (7), **kip** (9) and **kit (7).**

ka *n* (**kas**). A ka is a supernatural being in ancient Egyptian mythology. This is worth remembering as, along with **ko** and **ky,** it's one of only three two-letter words starting with K. Ka scores 6 points.

kaftan *n* (*pl* **-s**) long loose Eastern garment
kaftans *n* ▷ **kaftan**
kaiser [**kize**-er] *n* (*pl* **-s**) (HIST) German or Austro-Hungarian emperor
kaisers *n* ▷ **kaiser**
kak *n* (*pl* (S AFR) (*Slang*) faeces
kalashnikov *n* (*pl* **-s**) Russian-made automatic rifle
kalashnikovs *n* ▷ **kalashnikov**
kale *n* (*pl* **-s**) cabbage with crinkled leaves
kales *n* ▷ **kale**
kaleidoscope *n* (*pl* **-s**) tube-shaped toy containing loose coloured pieces reflected by mirrors so that intricate patterns form when the tube is twisted > **kaleidoscopic** *adj*
kaleidoscopes *n* ▷ **kaleidoscope**
kaleidoscopic *adj* ▷ **kaleidoscope**
kamikaze [kam-mee-**kah**-zee] *n* (*pl* **-s**) (in World War II) Japanese pilot who performed a suicide mission ▶ *adj* (of an action) undertaken in the knowledge that it will kill or injure the person performing it
kamikazes *n* ▷ **kamikaze**
kangaroo *n* (*pl* **-s**) Australian marsupial which moves by jumping with its powerful hind legs
kangaroos *n* ▷ **kangaroo**
kaolin *n* (*pl* **-s**) fine white clay used to make porcelain and in some medicines
kaolins *n* ▷ **kaolin**
kapok *n* (*pl* **-s**) fluffy fibre from a tropical tree, used to stuff cushions etc.
kapoks *n* ▷ **kapok**
kaput [kap-**poot**] *adj* (*Informal*) ruined or broken
karaoke *n* (*pl* **-s**) form of entertainment in which people sing over a prerecorded backing tape
karaokes *n* ▷ **karaoke**
karate *n* (*pl* **-s**) Japanese system of unarmed combat using blows with the feet, hands, elbows, and legs
karates *n* ▷ **karate**
karma *n* (*pl* **-s**) (BUDDHISM, HINDUISM) person's actions affecting his or her fate in the next reincarnation
karmas *n* ▷ **karma**
karri *n* (*pl* **-s**) Australian eucalypt
karris *n* ▷ **karri**
katipo *n* (*pl* **-s**) small poisonous New Zealand spider
katipos *n* ▷ **katipo**
kayak *n* (*pl* **-s**) Inuit canoe made of sealskins stretched over a frame
kayaks *n* ▷ **kayak**
kebab *n* (*pl* **-s**) dish of small pieces of meat grilled on skewers
kebabs *n* ▷ **kebab**
kedgeree *n* (*pl* **-s**) dish of fish with rice and eggs
kedgerees *n* ▷ **kedgeree**
keel *n* (*pl* **-s**) main lengthways timber or steel support along the base of a ship
keels *n* ▷ **keel**
keen[1] *adj* (**-er, -est**) eager or enthusiastic > **keenly** *adv* > **keenness** *n*
keen[2] *v* (**-s, -ing, -ed**) wail over the dead
keened *v* ▷ **keen**[2]
keener *adj* ▷ **keen**[1]
keenest *adj* ▷ **keen**[1]
keening *v* ▷ **keen**[2]

keenly *adv* ▷ **keen**[1]
keenness *n* ▷ **keen**[1]
keens *v* ▷ **keen**[2]
keep *v* (**-s, -ing, kept**) have or retain possession of ▶ *n* (**-s**) cost of food and everyday expenses
keeper *n* (**-s**) person who looks after animals in a zoo ▶ *n* ▷ **keeper**
keeping *v* ▷ **keep** ▶ *n* (**-s**) care or charge ▶ *n* ▷ **keeping** ▶ *v* ▷ **keep** ▶ *n* ▷ **keep** > **keepsake** *n* (**-s**) gift treasured for the sake of the giver
keepsakes *n* ▷ **keepsake**
keg *n* (*pl* **-s**) small metal beer barrel
kegs *n* ▷ **keg**
kelp *n* (*pl* **-s**) large brown seaweed
kelpie *n* (*pl* **-s**) Australian sheepdog with a smooth coat and upright ears
kelpies *n* ▷ **kelpie**
kelps *n* ▷ **kelp**
kelvin *n* (*pl* **-s**) SI unit of temperature
kelvins *n* ▷ **kelvin**
ken *v* (**-s, -nning, -nned** *or* **kent**) (SCOT) know
kenning *v* ▷ **ken**
kenned *v* ▷ **ken**
kendo *n* (*pl* **-s**) Japanese sport of fencing using wooden staves
kendos *n* ▷ **kendo**
kennel *n* (*pl* **-s**) hutlike shelter for a dog
kennels *n* ▷ **kennel**
kens *v* ▷ **ken**
kent *v* ▷ **ken**
kept *v* ▷ **keep**
keratin *n* (*pl* **-s**) fibrous protein found in the hair and nails
keratins *n* ▷ **keratin**
kerb *n* (*pl* **-s**) edging to a footpath
kerbs *n* ▷ **kerb**
kerchief *n* (*pl* **-s**) piece of cloth worn over the head or round the neck
kerchiefs *n* ▷ **kerchief**
kerfuffle *n* (*pl* **-s**) (*Informal*) commotion or disorder
kerfuffles *n* ▷ **kerfuffle**
kernel *n* (*pl* **-s**) seed of a nut, cereal, or fruit stone
kernels *n* ▷ **kernel**
kerosene *n* (*pl* **-s**) (US, CANADIAN, AUST & NZ) liquid mixture distilled from petroleum and used as a fuel or solvent
kerosenes *n* ▷ **kerosene**
kestrel *n* (*pl* **-s**) type of small falcon
kestrels *n* ▷ **kestrel**
ketch *n* (*pl* **-es**) two-masted sailing ship
ketches *n* ▷ **ketch**
ketchup *n* (*pl* **-s**) thick cold sauce, usu. made of tomatoes
ketchups *n* ▷ **ketchup**
kettle *n* (*pl* **-s**) container with a spout and handle used for boiling water
kettledrum *n* (*pl* **-s**) large bowl-shaped metal drum
kettledrums *n* ▷ **kettledrum**
kettles *n* ▷ **kettle**
key *n* (*pl* **-s**) device for operating a lock by moving a bolt ▶ *adj* of great importance ▶ *v* (**-s, -ing, -ed**) enter (text) using a keyboard
keyboard *n* (*pl* **-s**) set of keys on a piano, computer, etc. ▶ *v* (**-s, -ing, -ed**) enter (text) using a keyboard
keyboarded *v* ▷ **keyboard**
keyboarding *v* ▷ **keyboard**
keyboards *n, v* ▷ **keyboard**
keyed *v* ▷ **key**
keyhole *n* (*pl* **-s**) opening for inserting a key into a lock
keyholes *n* ▷ **keyhole**
keying *v* ▷ **key**
keynote *n* (*pl* **-s**) dominant idea of a speech etc.
keynotes *n* ▷ **keynote**
keys *n, v* ▷ **key**
keystone *n* (*pl* **-s**) most important part of a process, organization, etc.
keystones *n* ▷ **keystone**

> **kex** *n* (**kexes**). A kex is a hollow-stemmed plant. This is a great three-letter word, combining K with X. If you have these letters on your rack, you can be confident that there will be, or will soon be, an E on the board, around which you can form kex. Kex scores 14 points.

khaki *adj* dull yellowish-brown ▶ *n* (*pl* **-s**) hard-wearing fabric of this colour used for military uniforms
khakis *n* ▷ **khaki**

> **khi** *n* (**khis**). Khi is a letter of the Greek alphabet, also spelt **chi.** This is one of the higher-scoring three-letter words starting with K, and so is worth remembering. Khi scores 10 points.

kibbutz *n* (*pl* **-im**) communal farm or factory in Israel
kibbutzim *n* ▷ **kibbutz**
kick *v* (**-s, -ing, -ed**) drive, push, or strike with the foot ▶ *n* (*pl* **kicks**) thrust or blow with the foot
kickback (*Informal*) *n* (*pl* **-s**) money paid illegally for favours done
kickbacks *n* ▷ **kickback**
kicked *v* ▷ **kick**

kicking *n, v* ▷ **kick**
kicks *n, v* ▷ **kick**
kid[1] *n* (*pl* **-s**) (*Informal*) child
kid[2] *v* (**-s, -dding, -dded**) (*Informal*) tease or deceive (someone)
kidded *v* ▷ **kid**[2]
kidding *v* ▷ **kid**[2]
kidnap *v* (**-s, -pping, -pped**) seize and hold (a person) to ransom > **kidnapper** *n* (*pl* **-s**)
kidnapped *n* ▷ **kidnap**
kidnapper *n* ▷ **kidnap**
kidnappers *n* ▷ **kidnap**
kidnapping *n* ▷ **kidnap**
kidnaps *n* ▷ **kidnap**
kidney *n* (*pl* **kidneys**) either of the pair of organs that filter waste products from the blood to produce urine
kidneys *n* ▷ **kidney**
kids *n* ▷ **kid**[1] ▶ *v* ▷ **kid**[2]
kill *v* (**-s, -ing, -ed**) cause the death of (*Informal*) ▶ *n* (*pl* **-s**) act of killing > **killer** *n* (*pl* **killers**)
killed *v* ▷ **kill**
killer *n* ▷ **kill**
killers *n* ▷ **kill**
killing (*Informal*) *adj* very tiring ▶ *n* (*pl* **-s**) sudden financial success ▶ *v* ▷ **kill**
killings *n* ▷ **killing**
killjoy *n* (*pl* **-s**) person who spoils others' pleasure
killjoys *n* ▷ **killjoy**
kills *v, n* ▷ **kill**
kiln *n* (*pl* **-s**) oven for baking, drying, or processing pottery, bricks, etc.
kilns *n* ▷ **kiln**
kilobyte *n* (*pl* **-s**) (COMPUTERS) 1024 units of information
kilobytes *n* ▷ **kilobyte**
kilogram, kilogramme *n* (*pl* **-s**) one thousand grams
kilogrammes *n* ▷ **kilogram**
kilograms *n* ▷ **kilogram**
kilohertz *n* (*pl* **-es**) one thousand hertz
kilohertzes *n* ▷ **kilohertz**
kilometre *n* (*pl* **-s**) one thousand metres
kilometres *n* ▷ **kilometre**
kilowatt *n* (*pl* **-s**) (ELECTRICITY) one thousand watts
kilowatts *n* ▷ **kilowatt**
kilt *n* (*pl* **-s**) knee-length pleated tartan skirt worn orig. by Scottish Highlanders > **kilted** *adj*
kilted *n* ▷ **kilt**
kilts *n* ▷ **kilt**
kimono *n* (*pl* **-s**) loose wide-sleeved Japanese robe, fastened with a sash
kimonos *n* ▷ **kimono**
kin, kinsfolk *n* person's relatives collectively > **kinship** (*pl* **-s**) ▶ *n*
kind[1] *adj* (**-er, -est**) considerate, friendly, and helpful > **kindness** *n* (*pl* **-es**) > **kindliness** *n* (*pl* **-es**) > **kind-hearted** *adj*
kind[2] *n* (*pl* **-s**) class or group with common characteristics
kinder *adj* ▷ **kind**[1]
kindergarten *n* (*pl* **-s**) class or school for children under six years old
kindergartens *n* ▷ **kindergarten**
kindest *adj* ▷ **kind**[1]
kindhearted *adj* ▷ **kind**[1]
kindies *n* ▷ **kindy**
kindliness *n* (*pl* **-es**) ▷ **kind**[1]
kindlinesses *n* ▷ **kind**[1]
kindle *v* (**-les, -ling, -led**) set (a fire) alight
kindled *v* ▷ **kindle**
kindles *v* ▷ **kindle**
kindling *n* (*pl* **-s**) dry wood or straw for starting fires ▶ *v* ▷ **kindle**
kindly *adj* having a warm-hearted nature ▶ *adv* in a considerate way
kindness *n* (*pl* **-es**) ▷ **kind**[1]
kindnesses *n* ▷ **kind**[1]
kinds *n* ▷ **kind**[2]
kindred *adj* having similar qualities ▶ *n* (*pl* **-s**) ▷ **kin**
kindy, kindie *n* (*pl* **-dies**) (AUST & NZ) (*Informal*) kindergarten
kinetic [kin-**net**-ik] *adj* relating to or caused by motion
king *n* (*pl* **kings**) male ruler of a monarchy > **kingship** *n* (*pl* **-s**)
kingdom *n* (*pl* **-s**) state ruled by a king or queen
kingdoms *n* ▷ **kingdom**
kings *n* ▷ **king**
kingship *n* (*pl* **-s**) ▷ **king**
kingships *n* ▷ **king**
kingfisher *n* (*pl* **-s**) small bird, often with a bright-coloured plumage, that dives for fish
kingfishers *n* ▷ **kingfisher**
kingpin *n* (*pl* **-s**) most important person in an organization
kingpins *n* ▷ **kingpin**
kink *n* (*pl* **-s**) twist or bend in rope, wire, hair, etc.
kinks *n* ▷ **kink**
kinky *adj* (*Slang*) given to unusual sexual practices
kinships *n* ▷ **kinship**
kiosk *n* (*pl* **-s**) small booth selling drinks, cigarettes, newspapers, etc.
kiosks *n* ▷ **kiosk**

kip (*Informal*) *n* (*pl* **-s**) sleep ▸ *v* (**-s, -pping, -pped**) sleep
kipped *v* ▷ **kip**
kipper *n* (*pl* **-s**) cleaned, salted, and smoked herring
kippers *n* ▷ **kipper**
kipping *v* ▷ **kip**
kips *v* ▷ **kip**
kirk *n* (*pl* **-s**) (SCOT) church
kirks *n* ▷ **kirk**
kismet *n* (*pl* **-s**) fate or destiny
kismets *n* ▷ **kismet**
kiss *v* (**-es, -ing, -ed**) touch with the lips in affection or greeting ▸ *n* (*pl* **-es**) touch with the lips
kissagram *n* (*pl* **-s**) greetings service in which a messenger kisses the person celebrating
kissagrams *n* ▷ **kissagram**
kissed *v* ▷ **kiss**
kisser *n* (*pl* **-s**) (*Slang*) mouth or face
kissers *n* ▷ **kisser**
kisses *v, n* ▷ **kiss**
kissing *v* ▷ **kiss**
kist *n* (*pl* **-s**) (S AFR) large wooden chest
kists *n* ▷ **kist**
kit *n* (*pl* **-s**) outfit or equipment for a specific purpose
kitbag *n* (*pl* **-s**) bag for a soldier's or traveller's belongings
kitbags *n* ▷ **kitbag**
kits *n* ▷ **kit**
kitset *n* (*pl* **-s**) (NZ) unassembled pieces for constructing a piece of furniture
kitchen *n* (*pl* **-s**) room used for cooking
kitchenette *n* (*pl* **-s**) small kitchen
kitchenettes *n* ▷ **kitchetenette**
kitchens *n* ▷ **kitchen**
kitches *n* ▷ **kitch**
kite *n* (*pl* **-s**) light frame covered with a thin material flown on a string in the wind
kites *n* ▷ **kite**
kith *n* (*pl* **-s**) friends and relatives
kiths *n* ▷ **kith**
kitsch *n* (*pl* **-es**) art or literature with popular sentimental appeal
kitten *n* (*pl* **-s**) young cat
kittenish *adj* lively and flirtatious
kittens *n* ▷ **kitten**
kitties *n* ▷ **kitty**
kittiwake *n* (*pl* **-s**) type of seagull
kittiwakes *n* ▷ **kittiwake**
kitty *n* (*pl* **-ties**) communal fund
kiwi *n* (*pl* **-s**) New Zealand flightless bird with a long beak and no tail
kiwis *n* ▷ **kiwi**
klaxon *n* (*pl* **-s**) loud horn used on emergency vehicles as a warning signal
klaxons *n* ▷ **klaxon**
kleptomania *n* (*pl* **-s**) compulsive tendency to steal > **kleptomaniac** *n* (*pl* **-s**)
kleptomaniac *n* (*pl* **-s**) ▷ **kleptomania**
kleptomaniacs *n* ▷ **kleptomania**
kloof *n* (*pl* **kloofs**) (S AFR) mountain pass or gorge
kloofs *n* ▷ **kloof**
knack *n* (*pl* **knacks**) skilful way of doing something
knacks *n* ▷ **knack**
knacker *n* (*pl* **-s**) (BRIT) buyer of old horses for killing
knackered *adj* (*Slang*) extremely tired
knackers *n* ▷ **knacker**
knapsack *n* (*pl* **-s**) soldier's or traveller's bag worn strapped on the back
knapsacks *n* ▷ **knapsack**
knave *n* (*pl* **-s**) jack at cards (*Obs*)
knaves *n* ▷ **knave**
knead *v* (**-s, -ing, -ed**) work (dough) into a smooth mixture with the hands
kneaded *v* ▷ **knead**
kneading *v* ▷ **knead**
kneads *v* ▷ **knead**
knee *n* (*pl* **knees**) joint between thigh and lower leg ▸ *v* (**-s, -ing, -d**) strike or push with the knee
kneecap *n* (*pl* **kneecaps**) bone in front of the knee ▸ *v* (**-pping, -pped**) shoot in the kneecap
kneed *v* ▷ **knee**
kneeing *v* ▷ **knee**
kneejerk *adj* (of a reply or reaction) automatic and predictable
kneel *v* (**-s, -ing, -ed** *or* **knelt**) fall or rest on one's knees
kneeled, knelt *v* ▷ **kneel**
kneeling *v* ▷ **kneel**
kneels *v* ▷ **kneel**
knees *n, v* ▷ **knee**
knell *n* (*pl* **-s**) sound of a bell, esp. at a funeral or death
knells *n* ▷ **knell**
knelt *v* ▷ **kneel**
knew *v* ▷ **know**
knickerbockers *pl n* loose-fitting short trousers gathered in at the knee
knickers *pl n* woman's or girl's undergarment covering the lower trunk and having legs or legholes
knife *n* (*pl* **knives**) cutting tool or weapon consisting of a sharp-edged blade with a handle ▸ *v* (**-s, -ing, -ed**) cut or stab with a

knife
knifed *v* ▷ **knife**
knifes *v* ▷ **knife**
knifing *v* ▷ **knife**
knight *n* (*pl* **-s**) man who has been given a knighthood ▶ *v* (**-s, -ing, -ed**) award a knighthood to > **knightly** *adj* > **knighthood** *n* (*pl* **-s**) honorary title given to a man by the British sovereign
knighted *v* ▷ **knight**
knighthoods *n* ▷ **knighthood**
knighting *v* ▷ **knight**
knights *n*, *v* ▷ **knight**
knit *v* (**-s, -tting, -tted** *or* **knit**) make (a garment) by interlocking a series of loops in wool or other yarn > **knitting** *n* (*pl* **-s**)
knits *v* ▷ **knit**
knitted *v* ▷ **knit**
knitting *v* ▷ **knit**
knittings *n* ▷ **knit**
knitwear *n* (*pl* **-s**) knitted clothes, such as sweaters
knitwears *n* ▷ **knitwear**
knives *n* ▷ **knife**
knob *n* (*pl* **-s**) rounded projection, such as a switch on a radio
knobblier *adj* ▷ **knobbly**
knobbliest *adj* ▷ **knobbly**
knobbly *adj* (**-lier, -liest**) covered with small bumps
knobkerrie *n* (*pl* **-s**) (S AFR) club with a rounded end
knobkerries *n* ▷ **knobkerrie**
knobs *n* ▷ **knob**
knock *v* (**-s, -ing, -ed**) give a blow or push to ▶ *n* (*pl* **-s**) blow or rap
knockabout *adj* (of comedy) boisterous
knockdown *adj* (of a price) very low
knocked *v* ▷ **knock**
knocker *n* (*pl* **-s**) metal fitting for knocking on a door
knockers *n* ▷ **knocker**
knocking *v* ▷ **knock**
knockout *n* (*pl* **-s**) blow that renders an opponent unconscious
knockouts *n* ▷ **knockout**
knocks *v*, *n* ▷ **knock**
knoll *n* (*pl* **-s**) small rounded hill
knolls *n* ▷ **knoll**
knot *n* (*pl* **-s**) fastening made by looping and pulling tight strands of string, cord, or rope ▶ *v* (**-s, -tting, -tted**) tie with or into a knot
knots *n* ▷ **knot**
knotted *n* ▷ **knot**
knotting *n* ▷ **knot**
knotty *adj* full of knots
know *v* (**-s, -ing, knew, known**) be or feel certain of the truth of (information etc.) > **knowable** *adj*
knowing *v* ▷ **know** ▶ *adj* suggesting secret knowledge
knowingly *adv* deliberately
knowhow *n* (*pl* **-s**) (*Informal*) ingenuity, aptitude, or skill
knowhows *n* ▷ **know-how**
knowledgable *n* ▷ **knowledgeable**
knowledge *n* (*pl* **-s**) facts or experiences known by a person
knowledgeable, knowledgable *adj* intelligent or well-informed
knowledges *n* ▷ **knowledge**
known *v* ▷ **know**
knows *v* ▷ **know**
knuckle *n* (*pl* **-s**) bone at the finger joint
knuckles *n* ▷ **knuckle**

> **ko** *n* (**kos**). A ko is a Maori digging-stick. This is worth remembering as, along with ka and ky, it's one of only three two-letter words starting with K. Ko scores 6 points.

koala *n* (*pl* **-s**) tree-dwelling Australian marsupial with dense grey fur
koalas *n* ▷ **koala**
kohl *n* (*pl* **-s**) cosmetic powder used to darken the edges of the eyelids
kohls *n* ▷ **kohls**
kookaburra *n* (*pl* **-s**) large Australian kingfisher with a cackling cry
kookaburras *n* ▷ **kookaburra**
koori *n* (*pl* **-s**) Australian Aborigine
kooris *n* ▷ **koori**
kopje, koppie *n* (*pl* **-s**) (S AFR) small hill
kopjes *n* ▷ **kopje**
kosher [**koh**-sher] *adj* conforming to Jewish religious law, esp. (of food) to Jewish dietary law ▶ *n* (*pl* **-s**) kosher food
koshers *n* ▷ **kosher**
kowhai *n* (*pl* **-s**) New Zealand tree with clusters of yellow flowers
kowhais *n* ▷ **kowhai**

> **kow** *n* (**kows**). A kow is a Scots word for a bunch of twigs. Kow is relatively high-scoring for a three-letter word, and so can be a good one to form when playing in more than one direction. Kow scores 10 points.

kowtow *v* (**-s, -ing, -ed**) be servile (towards)
kowtowed *v* ▷ **kowtow**

kowtowing *v* ▷ **kowtow**
kowtows *v* ▷ **kowtow**
kraal *n* (*pl* **-s**) S African village surrounded by a strong fence
kraals *n* ▷ **kraal**
krill *n* small shrimplike sea creature(s)
krypton *n* (*pl* **-s**) (CHEM) colourless gas present in the atmosphere and used in fluorescent lights
kryptons *n* ▷ **krypton**
kudos *n* (*pl* **-es**) fame or credit
kudoses *n* ▷ **kudoses**
kugel [**koog**-el] *n* (*pl* **-s**) (S AFR) rich, fashion-conscious, materialistic young woman
kugels *n* ▷ **kugel**
kumara *n* (*pl* **-s**) (NZ) tropical root vegetable with yellow flesh
kumaras *n* ▷ **kumara**
kumquat [**kumm**-kwott] *n* (*pl* **-s**) citrus fruit resembling a tiny orange
kumquats *n* ▷ **kumquat**
kurrajong *n* (*pl* **-s**) Australian tree or shrub with tough fibrous bark
kurrajongs *n* ▷ **kurrajong**

ky or **kye** *n*. Ky is a Scots word for **cows.** If you are playing a longer word beginning with K, you may be able to use ky to tag onto a word on the board that ends in Y. Ky scores 9 points.

kyu *n* (**kyus**). A kyu is a beginner's grade in judo. The unusual combination of letters makes this a useful word to have when you have an unpromising set of letters on your rack. Kyu scores 10 points.

Ll

L can be a difficult letter to use well, especially when you need to play short words. Just three two-letter words begin with L: **la, li** and **lo.** Knowing this will save you valuable time in a game, especially when you are trying to fit words into a crowded board. There aren't a great number of three-letter words either, but don't forget common words like **lab** (5 points), **law** (6), **lay** (6), **low** (6) and **lye** (6). Try to remember the three-letter words that combine L with X: **lax, lex, lox** and **lux** (10 points each). These are particularly useful towards the end of a game if you have an X but little opportunity to play it.

la *n* (**las**). In music, la is the sixth note of a major scale. La is also spelt **lah**. La scores 2 points.

label *n* (*pl* **-s**) piece of card or other material fixed to an object to show its ownership, destination, etc. ▶ *v* (**-s, -lling, -lled**) give a label to

labels *n* ▷ **label**

labia *pl n* (*sing* **-bium**) four liplike folds of skin forming part of the female genitals

labial [**lay**-bee-al] *adj* of the lips

labium *n* ▷ **labia**

labor *n* (*pl* **-s**) (US & AUST) ▷ **labour**

laboratories *n* ▷ **laboratory**

laboratory *n* (*pl* **-ies**) building or room designed for scientific research or for the teaching of practical science

laborious *adj* involving great prolonged effort > **laboriously** *adv*

laboriously *adv* ▷ **laborious**

labors *n* ▷ **labor**

labour, (US & AUST) **labor** *n* (*pl* **-s**) physical work or exertion ▶ *v* (**-s, -ing, -ed**) work hard

laboured *adj* uttered or done with difficulty ▶ *v* ▷ **labour**

labourer *n* (*pl* **-s**) person who labours, esp. someone doing manual work for wages

labourers *n* ▷ **labourer**

labouring *v* ▷ **labour**

labours *n, v* ▷ **labour**

labrador *n* (*pl* **-s**) large retriever dog with a usu. gold or black coat

labradors *n* ▷ **labrador**

laburnum *n* (*pl* **-s**) ornamental tree with yellow hanging flowers

laburnums *n* ▷ **laburnum**

labyrinth [**lab**-er-inth] *n* (*pl* **-s**) complicated network of passages > **labyrinthine** *adj*

labyrinthine *adj* ▷ **labyrinth**

labyrinths *n* ▷ **labyrinth**

lace *n* (*pl* **-s**) delicate decorative fabric made from threads woven into an open weblike pattern ▶ *v* (**-ces, -cing, -ced**) fasten with laces

laced *v* ▷ **lace**

laces *n, v* ▷ **lace**

lacing *v* ▷ **lace**

lacerate [**lass**-er-rate] *v* (**-tes, -ting, -ted**) tear (flesh) > **laceration** *n* (*pl* **-s**)

lacerated *v* ▷ **lacerate**

lacerates *v* ▷ **lacerate**

lacerating *v* ▷ **lacerate**

lacerations *v* ▷ **lacerate**

lachrymose *adj* tearful

lack *n* (*pl* **-s**) shortage or absence of something needed or wanted ▶ *v* (**-s, -ing, -ed**) need or be short of (something)

lackadaisical *adj* lazy and careless in a dreamy way

lacked *v* ▷ **lack**

lackey *n* (*pl* **-s**) servile follower

lackeys *n* ▷ **lackey**

lacking *v* ▷ **lack**

lacklustre *adj* lacking brilliance or vitality

laconic *adj* using only a few words, terse > **laconically** *adv*

laconically *adv* ▷ **laconic**

lacquer *n* (*pl* **-s**) hard varnish for wood or metal

lacquers *n* ▷ **lacquer**

lacrimal *adj* of tears or the glands which produce them

lacrosse *n* (*pl* **-s**) sport in which teams catch

and throw a ball using long sticks with a pouched net at the end, in an attempt to score goals

lacks *n, v* ▷ **lack**

lactation *n* (*pl* **-s**) secretion of milk by female mammals to feed young

lactations *n* ▷ **lactation**

lactic *adj* of or derived from milk

lactose *n* (*pl* **-s**) white crystalline sugar found in milk

lactoses *n* ▷ **lactose**

lacuna [lak-**kew**-na] *n* (*pl* **-e**) gap or missing part, esp. in a document or series

lacy *adj* fine, like lace

lad *n* (*pl* **-s**) boy or young man

lads *n* ▷ **lad**

ladder *n* (*pl* **-s**) frame of two poles connected by horizontal steps used for climbing ▶ *v* (**-s, -ing, -ed**) have or cause to have such a line of undone stitches

laddered *v* ▷ **ladder**

laddering *v* ▷ **ladder**

ladders *n, v* ▷ **ladder**

laden *adj* loaded

ladle *n* (*pl* **-s**) spoon with a long handle and a large bowl, used for serving soup etc. ▶ *v* (**-les, -ling, -led**) serve out

ladled *v* ▷ **ladle**

ladles *n, v* ▷ **ladle**

ladling *v* ▷ **ladle**

lady *n* (*pl* **-dies**) woman regarded as having characteristics of good breeding or high rank

ladybird *n* (*pl* **-s**) small red beetle with black spots

ladybirds *n* ▷ **ladybird**

ladykiller *n* (*pl* **-s**) (*Informal*) man who is or thinks he is irresistible to women

ladykillers *n* ▷ **ladykiller**

ladylike *adj* polite and dignified

lag¹ *v* (**-s, -gging, -gged**) go too slowly, fall behind ▶ *n* (*pl* **-s**) delay between events

lag² *v* (**-s, -gging, -gged**) wrap (a boiler, pipes, etc.) with insulating material

lag³ *n* (*pl* **-s**) (BRIT, AUST & NZ) (*Slang*) convict

laggard *n* (*pl* **-s**) person who lags behind

laggards *n* ▷ **laggard**

lagging *n* (*pl* **-s**) insulating material ▶ *v* ▷ **lag¹,²**

laggings *n* ▷ **lagging**

lager *n* (*pl* **-s**) light-bodied beer

lagers *n* ▷ **lager**

lagoon *n* (*pl* **-s**) body of water cut off from the open sea by coral reefs or sand bars

lagoons *n* ▷ **lagoon**

lags *n* ▷ **lag¹,³**

laid *v* ▷ **lay¹**

lain *v* ▷ **lie²**

lair *n* (*pl* **-s**) resting place of an animal

lairs *n* ▷ **lair**

laird *n* (*pl* **-s**) Scottish landowner

lairds *n* ▷ **laird**

laity [**lay**-it-ee] *n* (*pl* **-ties**) people who are not members of the clergy

laities *n* ▷ **laity**

lake¹ *n* (*pl* **-s**) expanse of water entirely surrounded by land > **lakeside** *n* (*pl* **-s**)

lake² *n* (*pl* **-s**) red pigment

lakes *n* ▷ **lake¹,²**

lakesides *n* ▷ **lake¹**

lama *n* (*pl* **-s**) Buddhist priest in Tibet or Mongolia

lamas *n* ▷ **lama**

lamb *n* (*pl* **-s**) young sheep ▶ *v* (**-s, -ing, -ed**) (of sheep) give birth to a lamb or lambs > **lambskin** *n* (*pl* **-s**) > **lambswool** *n* (*pl* **-s**)

lambast, lambaste *v* (**-s, -ing, -ed**) beat or thrash

lambasted *v* ▷ **lambast**

lambasting *v* ▷ **lambast**

lambasts *v* ▷ **lambast**

lambed *v* ▷ **lamb**

lambent *adj* (*Lit*) (of a flame) flickering softly

lambing *v* ▷ **lamb**

lambs *n, v* ▷ **lamb**

lambskin *v* ▷ **lamb**

lambswool *v* ▷ **lamb**

lame *adj* (**-er, -est**) having an injured or disabled leg or foot ▶ *v* (**-mes, -ming, -med**) make lame > **lamely** *adv* > **lameness** *n* (*pl* **-s**)

lamé [**lah**-may] *n* (*pl* **-s**) ▶ *adj* (fabric) interwoven with gold or silver thread

lamed *v* ▷ **lame**

lamely *adv* ▷ **lame**

lamenesses *n* ▷ **lame**

lament *v* (**-s, -ing, -ed**) feel or express sorrow (for) ▶ *n* (*pl* **-s**) passionate expression of grief > **lamentation** *n* (*pl* **-s**)

lamentable *adj* very disappointing

lamentations *v* ▷ **lament**

lamented *adj* grieved for ▶ *v* ▷ **lament**

lamenting *v* ▷ **lament**

laments *v, n* ▷ **lament**

lamer *adj* ▷ **lame**

lames *v* ▷ **lame**

lamés *n* ▷ **lamé**

lamest *adj* ▷ **lame**

laminate *v* (**-tes, -ting, -ted**) make (a sheet of material) by sticking together thin sheets ▶ *n* (*pl* **-s**) laminated sheet > **laminated** *adj*

laminated *v, adj* ▷ **laminate**

laminates *v, n* ▷ **laminate**

laminating *v* ▷ **laminate**
laming *v* ▷ **lame**
lamington *n* (*pl* **-s**) (AUST & NZ) sponge cake coated with a sweet coating
lamingtons *n* ▷ **lamington**
lamp *n* (*pl* **-s**) device which produces light from electricity, oil, or gas > **lampshade** (*pl* **-s**) ▶ *n*
lamppost *n* (*pl* **-s**) post supporting a lamp in the street
lampposts *n* ▷ **lamppost**
lamps *n* ▷ **lamp**
lampoon *n* (*pl* **-s**) humorous satire ridiculing someone ▶ *v* (**-s, -ing, -ed**) satirize or ridicule
lampooned *v* ▷ **lampoon**
lampooning *v* ▷ **lampoon**
lampoons *n, v* ▷ **lampoon**
lamprey *n* (*pl* **-s**) eel-like fish with a round sucking mouth
lampreys *n* ▷ **lamprey**
lampshades *n* ▷ **lamp**
lance *n* (*pl* **-s**) long spear used by a mounted soldier ▶ *v* (**-ces, -cing, -ced**) pierce (a boil or abscess) with a lancet
lanced *v* ▷ **lance**
lancer *n* (*pl* **-s**) formerly, cavalry soldier armed with a lance
lancers *n* ▷ **lancer**
lances *n, v* ▷ **lance**
lancing *v* ▷ **lance**
lancet *n* (*pl* **-s**) pointed two-edged surgical knife
lancets *n* ▷ **lancet**
land *n* (*pl* **-s**) solid part of the earth's surface ▶ *v* (**-s, -ing, -ed**) come or bring to earth after a flight, jump, or fall > **landless** *adj*
landau [**lan**-daw] *n* (*pl* **-s**) four-wheeled carriage with two folding hoods
landaus *n* ▷ **landau**
landed *adj* possessing or consisting of lands ▶ *v* ▷ **land**
landfall *n* (*pl* **-s**) ship's first landing after a voyage
landfalls *n* ▷ **landfall**
landing *n* (*pl* **-s**) floor area at the top of a flight of stairs ▶ *v* ▷ **land**
landings *n* ▷ **landing**
landlocked *adj* completely surrounded by land
lands *n, v* ▷ **land**
landlady *n* (*pl* **-dies**) woman who rents out land, houses, etc.
landladies *n* ▷ **landlady**
landless *v* ▷ **land**
landlord *n* (*pl* **-s**) man who rents out land, houses, etc.
landlords *n* ▷ **landlord**
landlubber *n* (*pl* **-s**) person who is not experienced at sea
landlubbers *n* ▷ **landlubber**
landmark *n* (*pl* **-s**) prominent object in or feature of a landscape
landmarks *n* ▷ **landmark**
landscape *n* (*pl* **-s**) extensive piece of inland scenery seen from one place ▶ *v* (**-pes, -ping, -ped**) improve natural features of (a piece of land)
landscaped *v* ▷ **landscape**
landscapes *n, v* ▷ **landscape**
landscaping *v* ▷ **landscape**
landslide (*also* **landslip**) *n* (*pl* **-s**) falling of soil, rock, etc. down the side of a mountain
landslides *n* ▷ **landslide**
landslip *n* ▷ **landslide**
landslips *n* ▷ **landslide** ▶ *adj* nearest to or facing the land ▶ *adv* (*also* **landwards**) towards land
landwards *adv* ▷ **landward**
lane *n* (*pl* **-s**) narrow road
lanes *n* ▷ **lane**
language *n* (*pl* **-s**) system of sounds, symbols, etc. for communicating thought
languages *n* ▷ **language**
languid *adj* lacking energy or enthusiasm > **languidly** *adv*
languidly *adv* ▷ **languid**
languish *v* (**-es, -ing, -ed**) suffer neglect or hardship
languished *v* ▷ **languish**
languishes *v* ▷ **languish**
languishing *v* ▷ **languish**
languor [**lang**-ger] *n* (*pl* **-s**) state of dreamy relaxation > **languorous** *adj*
languorous *n* ▷ **languor**
languors *n* ▷ **languor**
lank *adj* (**-er, -est**) (of hair) straight and limp
lanker *adj* ▷ **lank**
lankest *adj* ▷ **lank**
lankier *adj* ▷ **lanky**
lankiest *adj* ▷ **lanky**
lanky *adj* (**-kier, -kiest**) ungracefully tall and thin
lanolin *n* (*pl* **-s**) grease from sheep's wool used in ointments etc.
lanolins *n* ▷ **lanolin**
lantana [lan-**tay**-na] *n* (*pl* **-s**) shrub with orange or yellow flowers, considered a weed in Australia
lantanas *n* ▷ **lantana**
lantern *n* (*pl* **-s**) light in a transparent protective case
lanterns *n* ▷ **lantern**

lanthanum *n* (*pl* **-s**) (CHEM) silvery-white metallic element
lanthanums *n* ▷ **lanthanum**
lanyard *n* (*pl* **-s**) cord worn round the neck to hold a knife or whistle
lanyards *n* ▷ **lanyard**
lap[1] *n* (*pl* **-s**) part between the waist and knees of a person when sitting
lap[2] *n* (*pl* **-s**) single circuit of a racecourse or track ▶ *v* (**-s, -pping, -pped**) overtake an opponent so as to be one or more circuits ahead
lap[3] *v* (**-s, -pping, -pped**) (of waves) beat softly against (a shore etc.)
lapel [lap-**pel**] *n* (*pl* **-s**) part of the front of a coat or jacket folded back towards the shoulders
lapels *n* ▷ **lapel**
lapidary *adj* of or relating to stones
lapped *v* ▷ **lap[2,3]**
lapping *v* ▷ **lap[2,3]**
laps *n* ▷ **lap[1,2]** ▶ *v* ▷ **lap[2,3]**
lapse *n* (*pl* **-s**) temporary drop in a standard, esp. through forgetfulness or carelessness ▶ *v* (**-ses, -sing, -sed**) drop in standard > **lapsed** *adj*
lapsed *v* ▷ **lapse**
lapses *n, v* ▷ **lapse**
lapsing *v* ▷ **lapse**
laptop *adj* (*of a computer*) small enough to fit on a user's lap ▶ *n* (*pl* **-s**) computer small enough to fit on a user's lap
laptops *n* ▷ **laptop**
lapwing *n* (*pl* **-s**) plover with a tuft of feathers on the head
lapwings *n* ▷ **lapwing**
larboard *adj, n* (*pl* **-s**) (*Old-fashioned*) port (side of a ship)
larboards *n* ▷ **larboard**
larcenies *n* ▷ **larceny**
larceny *n* (*pl* **-nies**) (LAW) theft
larch *n* (*pl* **-es**) deciduous coniferous tree
larches *n* ▷ **larch**
lard *n* (*pl* **-s**) soft white fat obtained from a pig ▶ *v* (**-s, -ing, -ed**) insert strips of bacon in (meat) before cooking
larded *v* ▷ **lard**
larder *n* (*pl* **-s**) storeroom for food
larders *n* ▷ **larder**
larding *v* ▷ **lard**
lards *n, v* ▷ **lard**
large *adj* (**-r, -st**) great in size, number, or extent > **largely** *adv* > **largish** *adj*
largely *adv* ▷ **large**
larger *adj* ▷ **large**
largess *n* (*pl* **-es**) ▷ **largesse**
largesse, largess [lar-**jess**] *n* (*pl* **-(es)** generous giving, esp. of money
largesses *n* ▷ **largesse**
largest *adj* ▷ **large**
largish *adj* ▷ **large**
largo *n* (*pl* **-s**) ▶ *adv* (MUSIC) (piece to be played) in a slow and dignified manner
largos *n* ▷ **largo**
lariat *n* (*pl* **-s**) lasso
lariats *n* ▷ **lariat**
lark[1] *n* (*pl* **-s**) small brown songbird, skylark
lark[2] *n* (*pl* **-s**) (*Informal*) harmless piece of mischief or fun
larks *n* ▷ **lark[1,2]**
larkspur *n* (*pl* **-s**) plant with spikes of blue, pink, or white flowers with spurs
larkspurs *n* ▷ **larkspur**
larrikin *n* (*pl* **-s**) (AUST & NZ) (*Old-fashioned slang*) mischievous or unruly person
larrikins *n* ▷ **larrikin**
larva *n* (*pl* **-e**) insect in an immature stage, often resembling a worm > **larval** *adj*
larval *adj* ▷ **larva**
larynges *n* ▷ **larynx**
laryngeal *adj* ▷ **larynx**
laryngitis *n* (*pl* **-ses**) inflammation of the larynx
laryngitises *n* ▷ **laryngitis**
larynx *n* (*pl* **-nges**) part of the throat containing the vocal cords > **laryngeal** *adj*
lasagne, lasagna [laz-**zan**-ya] *n* (*pl* **-s**) pasta in wide flat sheets
lasagnas *n* ▷ **lasagne**
lasagnes *n* ▷ **lasagne**
lascivious [lass-**iv**-ee-uss] *adj* showing or producing sexual desire > **lasciviously** *adv*
lasciviously *adv* ▷ **lascivious**
laser [**lay**-zer] *n* (*pl* **-s**) device that produces a very narrow intense beam of light, used for cutting very hard materials and in surgery etc.
lasers *n* ▷ **laser**
lash[1] *n* (*pl* **-es**) eyelash ▶ *v* (**-es, -ing, -ed**) hit with a whip
lash[2] *v* (**-es, -ing, -ed**) fasten or bind tightly with cord etc.
lashed *v* ▷ **lash[1,2]**
lashes *n* ▷ **lash[1]** ▶ *v* ▷ **lash[1,2]**
lashing *v* ▷ **lash[1,2]**
lashings *pl n* (*Old-fashioned*) large amounts
lass, lassie *n* (*pl* **-es, -s**) (SCOT & N ENGLISH) girl
lasses *n* ▷ **lass**
lassies *n* ▷ **lass**
lassitude *n* (*pl* **-s**) physical or mental weariness
lassitudes *n* ▷ **lassitude**
lasso [lass-**oo**] *n* (*pl* **-s, -es**) rope with a noose for

catching cattle and horses ▶ *v* (**-s, -ing, -ed**) catch with a lasso
lassoed *v* ▷ **lasso**
lassoes *n* ▷ **lasso**
lassoing *v* ▷ **lasso**
lassos *n, v* ▷ **lasso**
last[1] *adj, adv* coming at the end or after all others ▶ *adj* only remaining ▶ *n* (*pl* **-s**) last person or thing > **lastly** *adv*
last[2] *v* (**-s, -ing, -ed**) continue > **lasting** *adj*
last[3] *n* (*pl* **-s**) model of a foot on which shoes and boots are made or repaired
lasted *v* ▷ **last**[2]
lasting *v, adj* ▷ **last**[2]
lastly *adv* ▷ **last**[1]
lasts *n* ▷ **last**[1,3] ▶ *v* ▷ **last**[2]
latch *n* (*pl* **-es**) fastening for a door with a bar and lever ▶ *v* (**-es, -ing, -ed**) fasten with a latch
latched *v* ▷ **latch**
latches *n, v* ▷ **latch**
latching *v* ▷ **latch**
late *adj* (**-r, -st**) after the normal or expected time ▶ *adv* after the normal or expected time > **lateness** *n* (*pl* **-es**)
lately *adv* in recent times
latencies *n* ▷ **latent**
lateness *n* ▷ **late**
latenesses *n* ▷ **late**
latent *adj* hidden and not yet developed > **latency** *n* (*pl* **-cies**)
later *adj* ▷ **late**
lateral [**lat**-ter-al] *adj* of or relating to the side or sides > **laterally** *adv*
latest *adj* ▷ **late**
latex *n* (*pl* **-es**) milky fluid found in some plants, esp. the rubber tree, used in making rubber
latexes *n* ▷ **latex**
lath *n* (*pl* **-s**) thin strip of wood used to support plaster, tiles, etc.
laths *n* ▷ **lath**
lathe *n* (*pl* **-s**) machine for turning wood or metal while it is being shaped
lathes *n* ▷ **lathe**
lather *n* (*pl* **-s**) froth of soap and water ▶ *v* (**-s, -ing, -ed**) make frothy
lathered *v* ▷ **lather**
lathering *v* ▷ **lather**
lathers *n, v* ▷ **lather**
lathery *adj* (**-rier, -riest**) frothy
latherier *adj* ▷ **lathery**
latheriest *adj* ▷ **lathery**
latitude *n* (*pl* **-s**) angular distance measured in degrees N or S of the equator
latitudes *n* ▷ **latitude**
latrine *n* (*pl* **-s**) toilet in a barracks or camp
latrines *n* ▷ **latrine**
latter *adj* second of two > **latterly** *adv*
latter-day *adj* modern
latterly *adv* ▷ **latter**
lattice [**lat**-iss] *n* (*pl* **-s**) framework of intersecting strips of wood, metal, etc. > **latticed** *adj*
latticed *adj* ▷ **lattice**
lattices *n* ▷ **lattice**
laud *v* (**-s, -ing, -ed**) praise or glorify > **laudably** *adv*
laudable *adj* praiseworthy
laudably *adv* ▷ **laudable**
laudanum [**lawd**-a-num] *n* (*pl* **-s**) opium-based sedative
laudanums *n* ▷ **laudanum**
laudatory *adj* praising or glorifying
lauded *v* ▷ **laud**
lauding *v* ▷ **laud**
lauds *v* ▷ **laud**
laugh *v* (**-s, -ing, -ed**) make inarticulate sounds with the voice expressing amusement, merriment, or scorn ▶ *n* (*pl* **-s**) act or instance of laughing
laughable *adj* ▷ **laugh**
laughed *v* ▷ **laugh**
laughing *v* ▷ **laugh**
laughs *v, n* ▷ **laugh**
laughter *n* (*pl* **-s**) sound or action of laughing
laughters *n* ▷ **laughter**
launch[1] *v* (**-es, -ing, -ed**) put (a ship or boat) into the water, esp. for the first time ▶ *n* (*pl* **-es**) launching > **launcher** *n* (*pl* **-s**)
launch[2] *n* (*pl* **-s**) open motorboat
launched *v* ▷ **launch**[1]
launchers *n* ▷ **launch**[1]
launches *v* ▷ **launch**[1] ▶ *n* ▷ **launch**[1,2]
launches *n* ▷ **launch**[1]
launching *v* ▷ **launch**[1]
launder *v* (**-s, -ing, -ed**) wash and iron (clothes and linen)
launderette *n* ® (*pl* **-s**) shop with coin-operated washing and drying machines
laundered *v* ▷ **launder**
launderettes *n* ▷ **launderette**
laundering *v* ▷ **launder**
launders *v* ▷ **launder**
laundry *n* (*pl* **-ries**) clothes etc. for washing or which have recently been washed
laundries *n* ▷ **laundry**
laureate [**lor**-ee-at] *adj* (of a poet) appointed to the court of Britain
laurel *n* (*pl* **-s**) glossy-leaved shrub, bay tree ▶ *pl* wreath of laurel, an emblem of victory or merit

laurels *n* ▷ **laurel**
lava *n* (*pl* **-e**) molten rock thrown out by volcanoes, which hardens as it cools
lavae *n* ▷ **lava**
lavatory *n* (*pl* **-ries**) toilet
lavatories *n* ▷ **lavatory**
lavender *n* (*pl* **-s**) shrub with fragrant flowers ▶ *adj* bluish-purple
lavenders *n* ▷ **lavender**
lavish *adj* great in quantity or richness ▶ *v* (**-es, -ing, -ed**) give or spend generously > **lavishly** *adv*
lavished *v* ▷ **lavish**
lavishes *v* ▷ **lavish**
lavishing *v* ▷ **lavish**
lavishly *adv* ▷ **lavish**
law *n* (*pl* **-s**) rule binding on a community > **lawfully** *adv* > **lawlessness** *n* (*pl* **-es**) > **law-breaker** *n* (*pl* **-s**)
lawful *adj* allowed by law
lawfully *adv* ▷ **law**
lawless *adj* breaking the law, esp. in a violent way
lawlessness *n* ▷ **law**
lawlessnesses *n* ▷ **law**
lawn[1] *n* (*pl* **-s**) area of tended and mown grass
lawn[2] *n* (*pl* **-s**) fine linen or cotton fabric
lawns *n* ▷ **lawn**[1,2]
laws *n* ▷ **law**
lawsuit *n* (*pl* **-s**) court case brought by one person or group against another
lawsuits *n* ▷ **lawsuit**
lawyer *n* (*pl* **-s**) professionally qualified legal expert
lawyers *n* ▷ **lawyer**
lax *adj* not strict > **laxity** *n* (*pl* **-ties**)
laxative *n* (*pl* **-s**) ▶ *adj* (medicine) inducing the emptying of the bowels
laxatives *n* ▷ **laxative**
laxities *n* ▷ **lax**
laxity *n* ▷ **lax**
lay[1] *v* (**-s, -ing, laid**) cause to lie
lay[2] *v* ▷ **lie**[2]
lay[3] *adj* of or involving people who are not clergymen
lay[4] *n* (*pl* **-s**) short narrative poem designed to be sung
layabout *n* (*pl* **-s**) lazy person
layabouts *n* ▷ **layabout**
layer *n* (*pl* **-s**) single thickness of some substance, as a cover or coating on a surface ▶ *v* (**-s, -ing, -ed**) form a layer > **layered** *adj*
layered *v, adj* ▷ **layer**
layering *v* ▷ **layer**
layers *n, v* ▷ **layer**
layette *n* (*pl* **-s**) clothes for a newborn baby
layettes *n* ▷ **layette**
laying *v* ▷ **lay**[1]
layman *n* (*pl* **-men**) person who is not a member of the clergy
laymen *n* ▷ **layman**
layout *n* (*pl* **-s**) arrangement, esp. of matter for printing or of a building
layouts *n* ▷ **layout**
lays *v* ▷ **lay**[1] ▶ *n* ▷ **lay**[4]
laze *v* (**-s, -ing, -ed**) be idle or lazy ▶ *n* (*pl* **-s**) time spent lazing
lazed *v* ▷ **laze**
lazes *v, n* ▷ **laze**
lazily *adv* ▷ **lazy**
laziness *adv* ▷ **lazy**
lazinesses *adv* ▷ **lazy**
lazing *v* ▷ **laze**
lazy *adj* (**-zier, -ziest**) not inclined to work or exert oneself > **lazily** *adv* > **laziness** *n* (*pl* **-s**)
lea *n* (*pl* **-s**) (*Poetic*) meadow
leas *n* ▷ **lea**
leach *v* (**-es, -ing, -ed**) remove or be removed from a substance by a liquid passing through it
leached *v* ▷ **leach**
leaches *v* ▷ **leach**
leaching *v* ▷ **leach**
lead[1] *v* (**-s, -ing, led**) guide or conduct ▶ *n* (*pl* **-s**) first or most prominent place ▶ *adj* acting as a leader or lead
lead[2] *n* (*pl* **-s**) soft heavy grey metal
leaded *adj* (of windows) made from many small panes of glass held together by lead strips
leaden *adj* heavy or sluggish
leader *n* (*pl* **-s**) person who leads > **leadership** *n* (*pl* **-s**)
leaders *n* ▷ **leader**
leaderships *n* ▷ **leader**
leading *adj* principal
leads *n* ▷ **lead**[1,2] ▶ *v* ▷ **lead**[1]
leaf *n* (*pl* **leaves**) flat usu. green blade attached to the stem of a plant > **leafy** (**-fier, -fiest**) ▶ *adj* > **leafless** *adj*
leafier *adj* ▷ **leaf**
leafiest *adj* ▷ **leaf**
leafless *adj* ▷ **leaf**
leaflet *n* (*pl* **-s**) sheet of printed matter for distribution
leaflets *n* ▷ **leaflet**
leafy *adj* ▷ **leaf**
league[1] *n* (*pl* **-s**) association promoting the interests of its members
league[2] *n* (*Obs*) measure of distance, about

three miles
leagues *n* ▷ **league**[1,2]
leak *n* (*pl* **-s**) hole or defect that allows the escape or entrance of liquid, gas, radiation, etc. ▶ *v* (**-s, -ing, -ed**) let liquid etc. in or out > **leaky** (**-kier, -kiest**) ▶ *adj*
leakage *n* (*pl* **-s**) act or instance of leaking
leakages *n* ▷ **leakage**
leaked *v* ▷ **leak**
leakier *adj* ▷ **leak**
leakiest *adj* ▷ **leak**
leaking *v* ▷ **leak**
leaks *n*, *v* ▷ **leak**
leaky *adj* (**-kier, -kiest**) ▷ **leak**
lean[1] *v* (**-ing, -ed** *or* **leant**) rest against
lean[2] *adj* (**-er, -est**) thin but healthy-looking ▶ *n* (*pl* **-s**) lean part of meat > **leanness** *n* (*pl* **-es**)
leaner *adj* ▷ **lean**
leanest *adj* ▷ **lean**
leaning *n* (*pl* **-s**) tendency ▶ *v* ▷ **lean**[1]
leanings *n* ▷ **leaning**
leanness *n* ▷ **lean**[2]
leannesses *n* ▷ **lean**[2]
leans *v*, *n* ▷ **lean**[1]
leant *n* ▷ **lean**[1]
leap *v* (**-s, -ing, leapt** *or* **-ed**) make a sudden powerful jump ▶ *n* (*pl* **-s**) sudden powerful jump
leaped *v* ▷ **leap**
leapfrog *n* (*pl* **-s**) game in which a player vaults over another bending down
leapfrogs *n* ▷ **leapfrog**
leaping *v* ▷ **leap**
leaps *v*, *n* ▷ **leap**
leapt *v* ▷ **leap**
learn *v* (**-s, -ing, -ed** *or* **learnt**) gain skill or knowledge by study, practice, or teaching > **learner** *n* (*pl* **-s**)
learned *adj* erudite, deeply read
learner *n* ▷ **learn**
learners *n* ▷ **learn**
learning *n* (*pl* **-s**) knowledge got by study ▶ *v* ▷ **learn**
learnings *n* ▷ **learning**
lease *n* (*pl* **-s**) contract by which land or property is rented for a stated time by the owner to a tenant ▶ *v* (**-ses, -sing, -sed**) let or rent by lease > **leaseholder** *n* (*pl* **-s**)
leasehold *n*, *adj* (land or property) held on lease
leaseholder *n* ▷ **lease**
leaseholders *n* ▷ **lease**
leaseholds *n* ▷ **leasehold**
leased *v* ▷ **lease**
leases *n*, *v* ▷ **lease**
leash *n* (*pl* **-es**) lead for a dog
leashes *n* ▷ **leash**
leasing *v* ▷ **lease**
least *adj* ▷ **little** smallest ▶ *n* smallest one ▶ *adv* in the smallest degree
leather *n* (*pl* **-s**) material made from specially treated animal skins ▶ *adj* made of leather ▶ *v* (**-s, -ing, -ed**) beat or thrash
leathered *v* ▷ **leather**
leatherier *adj* ▷ **leathery**
leatheriest *adj* ▷ **leathery**
leathering *v* ▷ **leather**
leathers *n*, *v* ▷ **leather**
leathery *adj* (**-rier, -riest**) like leather, tough
leave[1] *v* (**-s, -ing, left**) go away from
leave[2] *n* (*pl* **-s**) permission to be absent from work or duty
leaven [**lev**-ven] *n* substance that causes dough to rise ▶ *v* (**-s, -ing, -ed**) raise with leaven
leavens *v* ▷ **leaven**
leavening *v* ▷ **leaven**
leavened *v* ▷ **leaven**
leaves *v* ▷ **leave**
leaving *v* ▷ **leave**
lecher *n* (*pl* **-s**) man who has or shows excessive sexual desire > **lechery** *n* (*pl* **-ries**)
lecheries *n* ▷ **lechery**
lecherous [**letch**-er-uss] *adj* (of a man) having or showing excessive sexual desire
lechers *n* ▷ **lecher**
lectern *n* (*pl* **-s**) sloping reading desk, esp. in a church
lecterns *n* ▷ **lectern**
lecture *n* (*pl* **-s**) informative talk to an audience on a subject ▶ *v* (**-s, -ing, -ed**) give a talk
lectured *v* ▷ **lecture**
lecturer *n* (*pl* **-s**) person who lectures, esp. in a university or college
lecturers *n* ▷ **lecturer**
lectures *n*, *v* ▷ **lecture**
lectureship *n* (*pl* **-s**) appointment as a lecturer
lectureships *n* ▷ **lectureship**
lecturing *v* ▷ **lecture**
ledge *n* (*pl* **-s**) narrow shelf sticking out from a wall
ledger *n* (*pl* **-s**) book of debit and credit accounts of a firm
ledgers *n* ▷ **ledger**
ledges *n* ▷ **ledge**
lee *n* (*pl* **-s**) sheltered part or side ▶ *adv* towards this side
leech *n* (*pl* **-es**) species of bloodsucking worm
leeches *n* ▷ **leech**
leek *n* (*pl* **-s**) vegetable of the onion family with

a long bulb and thick stem
leeks *n* ▷ **leek**
leer *v* (**-s, -ing, -ed**) look or grin at in a sneering or suggestive manner ▶ *n* (*pl* **-s**) sneering or suggestive look or grin
leered *v* ▷ **leer**
leerier *adj* ▷ **leery**
leeriest *adj* ▷ **leery**
leering *v* ▷ **leer**
leers *v*, *n* ▷ **leer**
leery *adj* (*Informal*) (**-rier, -riest**) suspicious or wary (of)
lees *pl n* sediment of wine ▶ *n* ▷ **lee**
leeward *adj*, *n* (*pl* **-s**) (on) the lee side
leewards *n* ▷ **leeward**
leeway *n* (*pl* **-s**) room for free movement within limits
leeways *n* ▷ **leeway**
left¹ *adj* of the side that faces west when the front faces north ▶ *adv* on or towards the left ▶ *n* (*pl* **-s**) left hand or part
left² *v* ▷ **leave¹**
leftist *n* (*pl* **-s**) ▶ *adj* (person) of the political left
leftists *n* ▷ **leftist**
leftover *n* (*pl* **-s**) unused portion of food or material
leftovers *n* ▷ **leftover**
lefts *n* ▷ **left¹**
leg *n* (*pl* **-s**) one of the limbs on which a person or animal walks, runs, or stands
legacies *n* ▷ **legacy**
legacy *n* (*pl* **-cies**) thing left in a will
legal *adj* established or permitted by law > **legally** *adv* > **legality** *n* (*pl* **-ties**) > **legalization** *n* (*pl* **-s**)
legalities *n* ▷ **legal**
legality *n* ▷ **legal**
legalization *n* ▷ **legal**
legalizations *n* ▷ **legal**
legalize *v* (**-zes, -zing, -zed**) make legal
legalized *adv* ▷ **legalize**
legalizes *adv* ▷ **legalize**
legalizing *adv* ▷ **legalize**
legally *adv* ▷ **legal**
legate *n* (*pl* **-s**) messenger or representative, esp. from the Pope
legatee *n* (*pl* **-s**) recipient of a legacy
legatees *n* ▷ **legatee**
legates *n* ▷ **legate**
legation *n* (*pl* **-s**) diplomatic minister and his staff
legations *n* ▷ **legation**
legato [leg-**ah**-toe] *n* (*pl* **-s**), *adv* (MUSIC) (piece to be played) smoothly
legatos *n* ▷ **legato**
legend *n* (*pl* **-s**) traditional story or myth
legendary *adj* famous
legends *n* ▷ **legend**
legerdemain [lej-er-de-**main**] *n* (*pl* **-s**) sleight of hand
legerdemains *n* ▷ **legerdemain**
leggier *adj* ▷ **leggy**
leggiest *adj* ▷ **leggy**
leggings *pl n* covering of leather or other material for the legs
leggy *adj* (**-gier, -giest**) having long legs
legibilities *n* ▷ **legible**
legibility *n* ▷ **legible**
legible *adj* easily read > **legibility** *n* (*pl* **-ties**) > **legibly** *adv*
legibly *adv* ▷ **legible**
legion *n* (*pl* **-s**) large military force > **legionary** *adj*, *n* (*pl* **-ries**)
legionaries *n* ▷ **legion**
legionary *adj*, *n* ▷ **legion**
legionnaire *n* (*pl* **-s**) member of a legion
legionnaires *n* ▷ **legionnaire**
legions *n* ▷ **legion**
legislate *v* (**-tes, -ting, -ted**) make laws > **legislative** *adj*
legislated *v* ▷ **legislate**
legislates *v* ▷ **legislate**
legislating *v* ▷ **legislate**
legislation *n* (*pl* **-s**) legislating
legislations *n* ▷ **legislation**
legislative *v* ▷ **legislate**
legislator *n* (*pl* **-s**) maker of laws
legislators *n* ▷ **legislator**
legislature *n* (*pl* **-s**) body of people that makes, amends, or repeals laws
legislatures *n* ▷ **legislature**
legitimacies *n* ▷ **legitimate**
legitimacy *n* ▷ **legitimate**
legitimate *adj* authorized by or in accordance with law ▶ *v* (**-tes, -ting, -ted**) make legitimate > **legitimacy** *n* (*pl* **-cies**) > **legitimately** *adv*
legitimated *v* ▷ **legitimate**
legitimately *adv* ▷ **legitimate**
legitimates *v* ▷ **legitimate**
legitimating *v* ▷ **legitimate**
legitimize *v* (**-zes, -zing, -zed**) make legitimate, legalize > **legitimization** *n* (*pl* **-s**)
legitimization *n* ▷ **legitimize**
legitimizations *n* ▷ **legitimize**
legitimized *v* ▷ **legitimize**
legitimizes *v* ▷ **legitimize**
legitimizing *v* ▷ **legitimize**
legless *adj* without legs
legs *n* ▷ **leg**

leguaan [**leg**-oo-ahn] *n* (*pl* **-s**) large S African lizard
leguaans *n* ▷ **leguaan**
legume *n* (*pl* **-s**) pod of a plant of the pea or bean family ▶ *pl* peas or beans
legumes *n* ▷ **legume**
leguminous *adj* (of plants) pod-bearing
lei *n* (*pl* **-s**) (in Hawaii) garland of flowers
leis *n* ▷ **lei**
leisure *n* (*pl* **-s**) time for relaxation or hobbies
leisured *adj* with plenty of spare time
leisurely *adj* deliberate, unhurried ▶ *adv* slowly
leisures *n* ▷ **leisure**
leitmotif [**lite**-mote-eef] *n* (*pl* **-s**) (MUSIC) recurring theme associated with a person, situation, or thought
leitmotifs *n* ▷ **leitmotif**
lekker *adj* (S AFR) (*Slang*) attractive or nice
lemming *n* (*pl* **-s**) rodent of arctic regions, reputed to run into the sea and drown during mass migrations
lemmings *n* ▷ **lemming**
lemon *n* (*pl* **-s**) yellow oval fruit that grows on trees ▶ *adj* pale-yellow
lemonade *n* (*pl* **-s**) lemon-flavoured soft drink, often fizzy
lemonades *n* ▷ **lemonade**
lemons *n* ▷ **lemon**
lemur *n* (*pl* **-s**) nocturnal animal like a small monkey, found in Madagascar
lemurs *n* ▷ **lemur**
lend *v* (**-s, -ing, lent**) give the temporary use of > **lender** *n* (*pl* **-s**)
lending *v* ▷ **lend**
lender *n* ▷ **lend**
lenders *n* ▷ **lend**
lends *v* ▷ **lend**
length *n* (*pl* **-s**) extent or measurement from end to end > **lengthily** *adv* > **lengthways, lengthwise** *adj, adv*
lengthen *v* (**-s, -ing, -ed**) make or become longer
lengthened *v* ▷ **lengthen**
lengthening *v* ▷ **lengthen**
lengthens *v* ▷ **lengthen**
lengthier *adj* ▷ **length**
lengthiest *adj* ▷ **length**
lengthily *adv* ▷ **length**
lengths *n* ▷ **length**
lengthways *adj, adv* ▷ **length**
lengthwise *adj, adv* ▷ **lengthen**
lengthy *adj* (**-thier, -thiest**) very long or tiresome
leniencies *n* ▷ **lenient**
leniency *n* ▷ **lenient**
lenient [**lee**-nee-ent] *adj* tolerant, not strict or severe > **leniency** *n* (*pl* **-cies**) > **leniently** *adv*
leniently *adv* ▷ **lenient**
lens *n* (*pl* **-es**) piece of glass or similar material with one or both sides curved, used to bring together or spread light rays in cameras, spectacles, telescopes, etc.
lenses *n* ▷ **lens**
lent *v* ▷ **lend**
lentil *n* (*pl* **-s**) edible seed of a leguminous Asian plant
lentils *n* ▷ **lentil**
lento *n* (*pl* **-tos**), *adv* (MUSIC) (piece to be played) slowly
lentos *n* ▷ **lento**
Lents *n* ▷ **Lent**
leonine *adj* like a lion
leopard *n* (*pl* **-s**) large spotted carnivorous animal of the cat family
leopards *n* ▷ **leopard**
leotard *n* (*pl* **-s**) tight-fitting garment covering the upper body, worn for dancing or exercise
leotards *n* ▷ **leotard**
leper *n* (*pl* **-s**) person suffering from leprosy
lepers *n* ▷ **leper**
lepidoptera *pl n* order of insects with four wings covered with fine gossamer scales, as moths and butterflies
lepidopterist *n* (*pl* **-s**) person who studies or collects butterflies or moths
lepidopterists *n* ▷ **lepidopterist**
leprechaun *n* (*pl* **-s**) mischievous elf of Irish folklore
leprechauns *n* ▷ **leprechaun**
leprosy *n* (*pl* **-sies**) disease attacking the nerves and skin, resulting in loss of feeling in the affected parts > **leprous** *adj*
leprosies *n* ▷ **leprosy**
leprous *adj* ▷ **leprosy**
lesbian *n* (*pl* **-s**) homosexual woman ▶ *adj* of homosexual women > **lesbianism** *n* (*pl* **-s**)
lesbians *n* ▷ **lesbian**
lesbianisms *n* ▷ **lesbian**
lesion *n* (*pl* **-s**) structural change in an organ of the body caused by illness or injury
lesions *n* ▷ **lesion**
less *adj* smaller in extent, degree, or duration ▷ **little** ▶ *pron* smaller part or quantity ▶ *adv* to a smaller extent or degree ▶ *prep* after deducting, minus
lessee *n* (*pl* **-s**) person to whom a lease is granted
lessees *n* ▷ **lessee**
lessen *v* (**-s, -ing, -ed**) make or become smaller or not as much

lessened *v* ▷ **lessen**
lessening *v* ▷ **lessen**
lessens *v* ▷ **lessen**
lesser *adj* not as great in quantity, size, or worth
lesson *n* (*pl* **-s**) single period of instruction in a subject
lessons *n* ▷ **lesson**
lest *conj* so as to prevent any possibility that
let[1] *v* (**-s, -tting, let**) allow, enable, or cause
let[2] *n* (*pl* **-s**) (TENNIS) minor infringement or obstruction of the ball requiring a replay of the point
letdown *n* (*pl* **-s**) disappointment
letdowns *n* ▷ **letdown**
lets *v* ▷ **let**[1] ▶ *n* ▷ **let**[2]
lethal *adj* deadly
lethargic *adj* ▷ **lethargy**
lethargically *adv* ▷ **lethargy**
lethargies *n* ▷ **lethargy**
lethargy *n* (*pl* **-gies**) sluggishness or dullness > **lethargic** *adj* > **lethargically** *adv*
letter *n* (*pl* **-s**) written message, usu. sent by post ▶ *pl* literary knowledge or ability > **lettering** *n* (*pl* **-s**)
lettered *adj* learned
letterhead *n* (*pl* **-s**) printed heading on stationery giving the sender's name and address
letterheads *n* ▷ **letterhead**
lettering *n* ▷ **letter**
letterings *n* ▷ **letter**
letters *n* ▷ **letter**
letting *v* ▷ **let**[1]
lettuce *n* (*pl* **-s**) plant with large green leaves used in salads
lettuces *n* ▷ **lettuce**
leucocyte [**loo**-koh-site] *n* (*pl* **-s**) white blood cell
leucocytes *n* ▷ **leucocyte**
leukaemia [loo-**kee**-mee-a] *n* (*pl* **-s**) disease caused by uncontrolled overproduction of white blood cells
leukaemias *n* ▷ **leukaemia**
levee *n* (*pl* **-s**) (US) natural or artificial river embankment
levees *n* ▷ **levee**
level *adj* (**-llest, -ller**) horizontal ▶ *v* (**-s, -lling, -lled, -ller**) make even or horizontal ▶ *n* (*pl* **-s**) horizontal line or surface
levelled *v* ▷ **level**
leveller *v* ▷ **level**
levellest *adj* ▷ **level**
levelling *v* ▷ **level**
levels *v, n* ▷ **level**
lever *n* (*pl* **-s**) handle used to operate machinery ▶ *v* (**-s, -ing, -ed**) prise or move with a lever
leverage *n* (*pl* **-s**) action or power of a lever
leverages *n* ▷ **leverage**
levered *v* ▷ **lever**
levering *v* ▷ **lever**
levers *n, v* ▷ **lever**
leveret [**lev**-ver-it] *n* (*pl* **-s**) young hare
leverets *n* ▷ **leveret**
leviathan [lev-**vie**-ath-an] *n* (*pl* **-s**) sea monster
leviathans *n* ▷ **leviathan**
levitate *v* (**-tes, -ting, -ted**) rise or cause to rise into the air
levitated *v* ▷ **levitate**
levitates *v* ▷ **levitate**
levitating *v* ▷ **levitate**
levitation *n* (*pl* **-s**) raising of a solid body into the air supernaturally
levitations *n* ▷ **levitation**
levities *n* ▷ **levity**
levity *n* (*pl* **-ties**) inclination to make a joke of serious matters
levy [**lev**-vee] *v* (**-vies, -ing, -vied**) impose and collect (a tax) ▶ *n* (*pl* **-vies**) imposition or collection of taxes
levied *v* ▷ **levy**
levies *v, n* ▷ **levy**
levying *v* ▷ **levy**
lewd *adj* (**-er, -est**) lustful or indecent > **lewdly** *adv* > **lewdness** *n* (*pl* **-es**)
lewder *adj* ▷ **lewd**
lewdest *adj* ▷ **lewd**
lewdly *adv* ▷ **lewd**
lewdness *n* ▷ **lewd**
lewdnesses *n* ▷ **lewd**

lex *n* (**leges**). A lex is a system or body of laws. This is a really handy word when you have L and X, as there is likely to be an E available on the board. Lex scores 10 points.

lexical *adj* relating to the vocabulary of a language
lexicographer *n* (*pl* **-s**) writer of dictionaries
lexicographers *n* ▷ **lexicographer**
lexicography *n* ▷ **lexicon**
lexicographies *n* ▷ **lexicon**
lexicon *n* (*pl* **-s**) dictionary > **lexicography** *n* (*pl* **-phies**)
lexicons *n* ▷ **lexicon**

li *n* (**lis**). The li is a Chinese unit of length. This low-scoring word is worth knowing for when you want to form words in more than one direction at the same time. Li scores 2 points.

liability *n* (*pl* **-ties**) hindrance or disadvantage

liable *adj* legally obliged or responsible
liaise *v* (**-ses, -sing, -sed**) establish and maintain communication (with)
liaised *v* ▷ **liaise**
liaises *v* ▷ **liaise**
liaising *v* ▷ **liaise**
liaison *n* (*pl* **-s**) communication and contact between groups
liaisons *n* ▷ **liaison**
liana *n* (*pl* **-s**) climbing plant in tropical forests
lianas *n* ▷ **liana**
liar *n* (*pl* **-s**) person who tells lies
liars *n* ▷ **liar**
libation [lie-**bay**-shun] *n* (*pl* **-s**) drink poured as an offering to the gods
libations *n* ▷ **libation**
libel *n* (*pl* **-s**) published statement falsely damaging a person's reputation ▶ *v* (**-s, -lling, -lled**) falsely damage the reputation of (someone) > **libellous** *adj*
libelled *v* ▷ **libel**
libelling *v* ▷ **libel**
libellous *adj* ▷ **libel**
libels *n, v* ▷ **libel**
liberal *adj* having social and political views that favour progress and reform ▶ *n* (*pl* **-s**) person who has liberal ideas or opinions > **liberally** *adv* > **liberalization** *n* (*pl* **-s**)
liberalism *n* (*pl* **-s**) belief in democratic reforms and individual freedom
liberalisms *n* ▷ **liberalism**
liberalities *n* ▷ **liberality**
liberality *n* (*pl* **-ties**) generosity
liberalization *n* ▷ **liberal**
liberalizations *n* ▷ **liberal**
liberalize *v* (**-zes, -zing, -zed**) make (laws, a country, etc.) less restrictive
liberalized *v* ▷ **liberalize**
liberalizes *v* ▷ **liberalize**
liberalizing *v* ▷ **liberalize**
liberally *adv* ▷ **liberal**
liberals *n* ▷ **liberal**
liberate *v* (**-tes, -ting, -ted**) set free > **liberation** *n* (*pl* **-s**) > **liberator** *n* (*pl* **-s**)
liberated *v* ▷ **liberate**
liberates *v* ▷ **liberate**
liberating *v* ▷ **liberate**
liberation *n* ▷ **liberate**
liberations *n* ▷ **liberate**
liberator *n* ▷ **liberate**
liberators *n* ▷ **liberate**
libertarian *n* (*pl* **-s**) believer in freedom of thought and action ▶ *adj* having such a belief
libertarians *n* ▷ **libertarian**
libertine [**lib**-er-teen] *n* (*pl* **-s**) morally dissolute person
libertines *n* ▷ **libertine**
liberties *n* ▷ **liberty**
liberty *n* (*pl* **-ties**) freedom
libidinous *adj* lustful
libido [lib-**ee**-doe] *n* (*pl* **-s**) psychic energy
libidos *n* ▷ **libido**
librarian *n* (*pl* **-s**) keeper of or worker in a library > **librarianship** *n* (*pl* **-s**)
librarians *n* ▷ **librarian**
librarianship *n* ▷ **librarian**
librarianships *n* ▷ **librarian**
libraries *n* ▷ **library**
library *n* (*pl* **-ries**) room or building where books are kept
libretti *n* ▷ **libretto**
librettist *n* ▷ **libretto**
librettists *n* ▷ **libretto**
libretto *n* (*pl* **-ttos, -tti**) words of an opera > **librettist** *n* (*pl* **-s**)
librettos *n* ▷ **libretto**
lice *n* ▷ **louse**
licence *n* (*pl* **-s**) document giving official permission to do something
licences *n* ▷ **licence**
license *v* (**-ses, -sing, -sed**) grant a licence to > **licensed** *adj*
licensed *v, adj* ▷ **license**
licensee *n* (*pl* **-s**) holder of a licence, esp. to sell alcohol
licensees *n* ▷ **licensee**
licenses *v* ▷ **license**
licensing *v* ▷ **license**
licentiate *n* (*pl* **-s**) person licensed as competent to practise a profession
licentiates *n* ▷ **licentiate**
licentious *adj* sexually unrestrained or promiscuous
lichen *n* (*pl* **-s**) small flowerless plant forming a crust on rocks, trees, etc.
lichens *n* ▷ **lichen**
licit *adj* lawful, permitted
lick *v* (**-s, -ing, -ed**) pass the tongue over ▶ *n* (*pl* **-s**) licking
licked *v* ▷ **lick**
licking *v* ▷ **lick**
licks *v, n* ▷ **lick**
licorice *n* (*pl* **-s**) ▷ **liquorice**
licorices *n* ▷ **licorice**
lid *n* (*pl* **-s**) movable cover
lids *n* ▷ **lid**
lido [**lee**-doe] *n* (*pl* **-s**) open-air centre for swimming and water sports
lidos *n* ▷ **lido**
lie[1] *v* (**-s, lying, lied**) make a deliberately false

statement ▶ *n* (*pl* **-s**) deliberate falsehood
lie² *v* (**-s, lying, lay, lain**) place oneself or be in a horizontal position ▶ *n* (*pl* **-s**) way something lies
lied¹ *v* ▷ **lie¹**
lied² [**leed**] *n* (*pl* **lieder**) (MUSIC) setting for voice and piano of a romantic poem
liege [**leej**] *adj* bound to give or receive feudal service ▶ *n* (*pl* **-s**) lord
lieges *n* ▷ **liege**
lien *n* (*pl* **-s**) (LAW) right to hold another's property until a debt is paid
liens *n* ▷ **lien**
lies *v, n* ▷ **lie¹,²**
lieutenant [lef-**ten**-ant] *n* (*pl* **-s**) junior officer in the army or navy
lieutenants *n* ▷ **lieutenant**
life *n* (*pl* **lives**) state of living beings, characterized by growth, reproduction, and response to stimuli > **lifelike** *adj*
lifeboat *n* (*pl* **-s**) boat used for rescuing people at sea
lifeboats *adj* ▷ **lifeboat**
lifeless *adj* dead
lifelike *adj* ▷ **life**
lifeline *n* (*pl* **-s**) means of contact or support
lifelines *n* ▷ **lifeline**
lifelong *adj* lasting all of a person's life
lifestyle *n* (*pl* **-s**) particular attitudes, habits, etc.
lifestyles *n* ▷ **lifestyle**
lifetime *n* (*pl* **-s**) length of time a person is alive
lifetimes *n* ▷ **lifetime**
lift *v* (**lifts, lifting, lifted**) move upwards in position, status, volume, etc. ▶ *n* (*pl* **lifts**) cage raised and lowered in a vertical shaft to transport people or goods
liftoff *n* moment a rocket leaves the ground
lifts *v* ▷ **lift**
lifting *v* ▷ **lift**
lifted *v* ▷ **lift**
lifts *n* ▷ **lift**
ligament *n* (*pl* **-s**) band of tissue joining bones
ligaments *n* ▷ **ligament**
ligature *n* (*pl* **-s**) link, bond, or tie
ligatures *n* ▷ **ligature**
light¹ *n* (*pl* **-s**) electromagnetic radiation by which things are visible ▶ *pl* traffic lights ▶ *adj* bright ▶ *v* (**-s, -ing, lit**) ignite
light² *adj* (**-er, -est**) not heavy, weighing relatively little ▶ *adv* with little equipment or luggage ▶ *v* (**-s, -ing, -ed, lit**) (esp. of birds) settle after flight > **lightly** *adv* > **lightness** *n* (*pl* **-s**)
lighted *v* ▷ **light²**
lighten¹ *v* (**-s, -ing, -ed**) make less dark
lighten² *v* (**-s, -ing, -ed**) make less heavy or burdensome
lightened *v* ▷ **lighten¹,²**
lightening *v* ▷ **lighten¹,²**
lightens *v* ▷ **lighten¹,²**
lighter *adj* ▷ **light²**
lightest *adj* ▷ **light²**
lighthouse *n* (*pl* **-s**) tower with a light to guide ships
lighthouses *n* ▷ **lighthouse**
lighting *n* (*pl* **-s**) apparatus for and use of artificial light in theatres, films, etc. ▶ *v* ▷ **light¹,²**
lightings *n* ▷ **lighting**
lighter¹ *n* (*pl* **-s**) device for lighting cigarettes etc.
lighter² *n* (*pl* **-s**) flat-bottomed boat for unloading ships
lighters *n* ▷ **lighter¹,²**
lightly *adv* ▷ **light²**
lightness *n* ▷ **light²**
lightnesses *n* ▷ **light²**
lightning *n* (*pl* **-s**) visible discharge of electricity in the atmosphere ▶ *adj* fast and sudden
lightnings *n* ▷ **lightning**
lights *pl n* lungs of animals as animal food ▶ *n* ▷ **light¹** ▶ *v* ▷ **light¹,²**
lightweight *n* (*pl* **-s**) ▶ *adj* (person) of little importance
lightweights *n* ▷ **lightweight**
ligneous *adj* of or like wood
lignite [**lig**-nite] *n* (*pl* **-s**) woody textured rock used as fuel
lignites *n* ▷ **lignite**
like¹ *prep, conj adj, pron* indicating similarity, comparison, etc.
like² *v* (**-s, -ing, -ed**) find enjoyable > **likeable, likable** *adj* > **liking** *n* fondness
liked *v* ▷ **like**
liken *v* (**-s, -ing, -ed**) compare
likelier *adj* ▷ **likely**
likeliest *adj* ▷ **likely**
likelihood *n* (*pl* **-s**) probability
likelihoods *n* ▷ **likelihood**
likely *adj* (**-lier, -liest**) tending or inclined ▶ *adv* probably
likened *v* ▷ **liken**
likeness *n* resemblance
likening *v* ▷ **liken**
likens *v* ▷ **liken**
likes *v* ▷ **like**
likewise *adv* similarly
liking *v* ▷ **like**

lilac *n* (*pl* **-s**) shrub with pale mauve or white flowers ▶ *adj* light-purple
lilacs *n* ▷ **lilac**
lilt *n* (*pl* **-s**) pleasing musical quality in speaking > **lilting** *adj*
lilting *adj* ▷ **lilt**
lilts *n* ▷ **lilt**
lily *n* (*pl* **-lies**) plant which grows from a bulb and has large, often white, flowers
limb *n* (*pl* **-s**) arm, leg, or wing
limbs *n* ▷ **limb**
limber *adj* pliant or supple
limbo *n* (*pl* **-s**) West Indian dance in which dancers lean backwards to pass under a bar
limbos *n* ▷ **limbo**
lime[1] *n* (*pl* **-s**) calcium compound used as a fertilizer or in making cement
lime[2] *n* (*pl* **-s**) small green citrus fruit
lime[3] *n* (*pl* **-s**) deciduous tree with heart-shaped leaves and fragrant flowers
limelight *n* (*pl* **-s**) glare of publicity
limelights *n* ▷ **lime**
limerick [**lim**-mer-ik] *n* (*pl* **-s**) humorous verse of five lines
limericks *n* ▷ **limerick**
limes *n* ▷ **lime[1,2,3]**
limestone *n* (*pl* **-s**) sedimentary rock used in building
limestones *n* ▷ **limestone**
limey *n* (*pl* **-s**) (US) (*Slang*) British person
limeys *n* ▷ **limey**
limit *n* (*pl* **-s**) ultimate extent, degree, or amount of something ▶ *v* (**-s, -ing, -ed**) restrict or confine > **limitation** *n* (*pl* **-s**) > **limitless** *adj*
limitation *n* ▷ **limit**
limitations *n* ▷ **limit**
limited *v* ▷ **limit**
limiting *v* ▷ **limit**
limitless *v* ▷ **limit**
limits *n, v* ▷ **limit**
limousine *n* (*pl* **-s**) large luxurious car
limousines *n* ▷ **limousine**
limp[1] *v* (**-s, -ing, -ed**) walk with an uneven step ▶ *n* (*pl* **-s**) limping walk
limp[2] (**-er, -est**) *adj* without firmness or stiffness > **limply** *adv*
limped *v* ▷ **limp[1]**
limper *adj* ▷ **limp[2]**
limpest *adj* ▷ **limp[2]**
limping *v* ▷ **limp[1]**
limply *adv* ▷ **limp[2]**
limps *v, n* ▷ **limp[1]**
limpet *n* (*pl* **-s**) shellfish which sticks tightly to rocks
limpets *n* ▷ **limpet**
limpid *adj* clear or transparent > **limpidity** *n* (*pl* **-ties**)
limpidities *n* ▷ **limpid**
limpidity *n* ▷ **limpid**
linchpin, lynchpin *n* (*pl* **-s**) pin to hold a wheel on its axle
linchpins *n* ▷ **linchpin**
linctus *n* (*pl* **-es**) syrupy cough medicine
linctuses *n* ▷ **linctus**
linden *n* (*pl* **-s**) ▷ **lime[3]**
lindens *n* ▷ **linden**
line[1] *n* (*pl* **-s**) long narrow mark ▶ *pl* words of a theatrical part ▶ *v* (**-s, -ing, -ed**) mark with lines
line[2] *v* (**-s, -ning, -ned**) give a lining to
lined *v* ▷ **line[1,2]**
lines *n, v* ▷ **line[1,2]**
lining *v* ▷ **line[1,2]**
lineage [**lin**-ee-ij] *n* (*pl* **-s**) descent from an ancestor
lineages *n* ▷ **lineage**
lineament *n* (*pl* **-s**) facial feature
lineaments *n* ▷ **lineament**
linear [**lin**-ee-er] *adj* of or in lines
linen *n* (*pl* **-s**) cloth or thread made from flax
linens *n* ▷ **linen**
liner[1] *n* (*pl* **-s**) large passenger ship or aircraft
liner[2] *n* something used as a lining
liners *n* ▷ **liner[1,2]**
linesman *n* (*pl* **-men**) (in some sports) an official who helps the referee or umpire
linesmen *n* ▷ **linesman**
ling[1] *n* slender food fish
ling[2] *n* (*pl* **lings**) heather
linger *v* (**-s, -ing, -ed**) delay or prolong departure
lingered *v* ▷ **linger**
lingerie [**lan**-zher-ee] *n* (*pl* **-s**) women's underwear or nightwear
lingeries *n* ▷ **lingerie**
lingering *v* ▷ **linger**
lingers *v* ▷ **linger**
lingo *n* (*pl* **-s**) (*Informal*) foreign or unfamiliar language or jargon
lingos *n* ▷ **lingo**
lings *n* ▷ **ling[2]**
lingual *adj* of the tongue
linguist *n* (*pl* **-s**) person skilled in foreign languages
linguistic *adj* of languages
linguistics *n* (*pl* **-s**) scientific study of language
linguists *n* ▷ **linguist**
liniment *n* (*pl* **-s**) medicated liquid rubbed on the skin to relieve pain or stiffness

liniments *n* ▷ **liniment**
lining *n* (*pl* **-s**) layer of cloth attached to the inside of a garment etc.
linings *n* ▷ **lining**
link *n* (*pl* **-s**) any of the rings forming a chain ▶ *v* (**-s, -ing, -ed**) connect with or as if with links > **linkage** *n* (*pl* **-s**)
linkage *n* ▷ **link**
linkages *n* ▷ **link**
linked *v* ▷ **link**
linking *v* ▷ **link**
links *pl n* golf course, esp. one by the sea
links *n, v* ▷ **link**
linnet *n* (*pl* **-s**) songbird of the finch family
linnets *n* ▷ **linnet**
linoleum *n* (*pl* **-s**) floor covering of hessian or jute with a smooth decorative coating of powdered cork
linoleums *n* ▷ **linoleum**
linseed *n* (*pl* **-s**) seed of the flax plant
linseeds *n* ▷ **linseeds**
lint *n* (*pl* **-s**) soft material for dressing a wound
lintel *n* (*pl* **-s**) horizontal beam at the top of a door or window
lintels *n* ▷ **lintel**
lints *n* ▷ **lint**
lion *n* (*pl* **-s**) large animal of the cat family, the male of which has a shaggy mane > **lioness** *n fem*
lioness *n* ▷ **lion**
lions *n* ▷ **lion**
lip *n* (*pl* **-s**) either of the fleshy edges of the mouth
lips *n* ▷ **lip**
lipstick *n* (*pl* **-s**) cosmetic in stick form, for colouring the lips
liquefy *v* (**-fies, -fying, -fied**) make or become liquid > **liquefaction** *n* (*pl* **-s**)
liquefaction *n* ▷ **liquefy**
liquefactions *n* ▷ **liquefy**
liquefied *v* ▷ **liquefy**
liquefies *v* ▷ **liquefy**
liquefying *v* ▷ **liquefy**
liqueur [lik-**cure**] *n* (*pl* **-s**) flavoured and sweetened alcoholic spirit
liqueurs *n* ▷ **liqueur**
liquid *n* (*pl* **-s**) substance in a physical state which can change shape but not size ▶ *adj* of or being a liquid
liquidate *v* (**-tes, -ting, -ted**) pay (a debt) > **liquidation** *n* (*pl* **-s**)
liquidated *v* ▷ **liquidate**
liquidates *v* ▷ **liquidate**
liquidating *v* ▷ **liquidate**
liquidation *n* ▷ **liquidate**
liquidations *n* ▷ **liquidate**
liquidities *n* ▷ **liquidity**
liquidator *n* (*pl* **-s**) official appointed to liquidate a business
liquidators *n* ▷ **liquidator**
liquidity *n* (*pl* **-ties**) state of being able to meet financial obligations ▶ *v* (**-zes, -zing, -zed**) make or become liquid
liquidized *v* ▷ **liquidize**
liquidizer *n* (*pl* **-s**) kitchen appliance that liquidizes food
liquidizers *v* ▷ **liquidizer**
liquidizes *v* ▷ **liquidize**
liquidizing *v* ▷ **liquidize**
liquids *n* ▷ **liquid**
liquor *n* (*pl* **-s**) alcoholic drink, esp. spirits
liquors *n* ▷ **liquor**
liquorice [**lik**-ker-iss] *n* (*pl* **-s**) black substance used in medicine and as a sweet
liquorices *n* ▷ **liquorice**
lira *n* (*pl* **-re, -ras**) monetary unit of Turkey and formerly of Italy
liras *n* ▷ **lira**
lire *n* ▷ **lira**
lisle [rhymes with **mile**] *n* (*pl* **-s**) strong fine cotton thread or fabric
lisles *n* ▷ **lisle**
lisp *n* (*pl* **-s**) speech defect in which *s* and *z* are pronounced *th* ▶ *v* (**-s, -ing, -ed**) speak or utter with a lisp
lisped *v* ▷ **lisp**
lisping *v* ▷ **lisp**
lisps *n, v* ▷ **lisp**
lissom, lissome *adj* supple, agile
lissome *adj* ▷ **lissom**
list[1] *n* (*pl* **-s**) item-by-item record of names or things, usu. written one below another ▶ *v* (**-s, -ing, -ed**) make a list of
list[2] *v* (**-s, -ing, -ed**) (of a ship) lean to one side ▶ *n* (*pl* **-s**) leaning to one side
listed *v* ▷ **list**[1,2]
listing *v* ▷ **list**[1,2]
lists *n, v* ▷ **list**[1,2]
listen *v* (**-s, -ing, -ed**) concentrate on hearing something > **listener** *n* (*pl* **-s**)
listened *v* ▷ **listen**
listener *n* ▷ **listen**
listeners *n* ▷ **listen**
listening *v* ▷ **listen**
listens *v* ▷ **listen**
listeriosis *n* (*pl* **-ses**) dangerous form of food poisoning
listerioses *n* ▷ **listeriosis**
listless *adj* lacking interest or energy > **listlessly** *adv*

listlessly *adv* ▷ **listless**
lit *v* ▷ **light**[1,2]
litanies *n* ▷ **litany**
litany *n* (*pl* **-nies**) prayer with responses from the congregation
literacies *n* ▷ **literacy**
literacy *n* (*pl* **-cies**) ability to read and write
literal *adj* according to the explicit meaning of a word or text, not figurative > **literally** *adv*
literally *adv* ▷ **literal**
literary *adj* of or knowledgeable about literature
literate *adj* able to read and write
literati *pl n* literary people
literature *n* (*pl* **-s**) written works such as novels, plays, and poetry
literatures *n* ▷ **literature**
lithe *adj* (**-ther, -thest**) flexible or supple, pliant
lither *adj* ▷ **lithe**
lithest *adj* ▷ **lithe**
lithium *n* (*pl* **-s**) (CHEM) chemical element, the lightest known metal
lithograph *n* (*pl* **-s**) print made by lithography
lithographer *n* ▷ **lithography**
lithographers *n* ▷ **lithography**
lithographic *adj* ▷ **lithography**
lithographied *v* ▷ **lithography**
lithographies *n, v* ▷ **lithography**
lithographs *n* ▷ **lithograph**
lithography [lith-**og**-ra-fee] *n* (*pl* **-phies**) method of printing from a metal or stone surface in which the printing areas are made receptive to ink ▶ *v* (**-phies, -ying, -phied**) reproduce by lithography > **lithographer** *n* (*pl* **-s**) > **lithographic** *adj*
lithographying *v* ▷ **lithography**
litigant *n* (*pl* **-s**) person involved in a lawsuit
litigants *n* ▷ **litigant**
litigate *v* (**-tes, -ting, -ted**) bring or contest a law suit
litigated *v* ▷ **litigate**
litigates *v* ▷ **litigate**
litigating *v* ▷ **litigate**
litigation *n* (*pl* **-s**) legal action
litigations *n* ▷ **litigation**
litigious [lit-**ij**-uss] *adj* frequently going to law
litmus *n* (*pl* **-es**) blue dye turned red by acids and restored to blue by alkalis
litmuses *n* ▷ **litmus**
litotes [lie-**toe**-teez] *n* ironical understatement used for effect
litre *n* (*pl* **-s**) unit of liquid measure equal to 1000 cubic centimetres or 1.76 pints
litres *n* ▷ **litre**
litter *n* (*pl* **-s**) untidy rubbish dropped in public places ▶ *v* (**-s, -ing, -ed**) strew with litter
littered *v* ▷ **litter**
littering *v* ▷ **litter**
litters *n, v* ▷ **litter**
little *adj* small or smaller than average ▶ *adv* not a lot ▶ *n* small amount, extent, or duration
littoral *adj* of or by the seashore ▶ *n* (*pl* **-s**) coastal district
littorals *n* ▷ **littoral**
liturgical *n* ▷ **liturgy**
liturgies *n* ▷ **liturgy**
liturgy *n* (*pl* **-gies**) prescribed form of public worship > **liturgical** *adj*
live[1] *v* (**-s, -ing, -ed**) be alive
live[2] *adj* living, alive ▶ *adv* in the form of a live performance > **liveliness** *n* (*pl* **-es**)
lived *v* ▷ **live**[1]
liveliness *n* ▷ **live**[2]
livelinesses *n* ▷ **live**[2]
lively *adj* full of life or vigour
livelihood *n* (*pl* **livelihoods**) occupation or employment
livelihoods *n* ▷ **livelihood**
lively *adj* full of life or vigour
liver[1] *n* (*pl* **-s**) organ secreting bile
liver[2] *n* (*pl* **-s**) person who lives in a specified way
liveried *adj* ▷ **livery**
liverish *adj* having a disorder of the liver
livers *n* ▷ **liver**[1,2]
livery *n* (*pl* **-ries**) distinctive dress, esp. of a servant or servants > **liveried** *adj*
lives *v* ▷ **live**[1] ▶ *n* ▷ **life**
livestock *n* (*pl* **-s**) farm animals
livestocks *n* ▷ **livestock**
livid *adj* (*Informal*) (**-er, -est**) angry or furious
livider *adj* ▷ **livid**
lividest *adj* ▷ **livid**
living *adj* possessing life, not dead or inanimate ▶ *n* (*pl* **-s**) condition of being alive ▶ *v* ▷ **live**
livings *n* ▷ **living**
lizard *n* (*pl* **-s**) four-footed reptile with a long body and tail
lizards *n* ▷ **lizard**
llama *n* (*pl* **-s**) woolly animal of the camel family used as a beast of burden in S America
llamas *n* ▷ **llama**

> **lo** *interj*. Lo is a command that means look! Along with **la** and **li**, lo is one of just three two-letter words that begin with L. Lo scores 2 points.

loach *n* (*pl* **-es**) carplike freshwater fish
loaches *n* ▷ **loach**

load *n* (*pl* **-s**) burden or weight ▶ *pl* (*Informal*) lots ▶ *v* (**-s, -ing, -ed**) put a load on or into
loaded *adj* (of a question) containing a hidden trap or implication
loaded *v, adj* ▷ **load**
loads *n, v* ▷ **load**
loading *v* ▷ **load**
loaf[1] *n* (*pl* **loaves**) shaped mass of baked bread
loaf[2] *v* (**-s, -ing, -ed**) idle, loiter > **loafer** *n* (*pl* **-s**)
loafed *v* ▷ **loaf**[2]
loafer *n* ▷ **loaf**[2]
loafers *n* ▷ **loaf**[2]
loafing *v* ▷ **loaf**[2]
loafs *v* ▷ **loaf**[2]
loam *n* (*pl* **-s**) fertile soil
loams *n* ▷ **loam**
loan *n* (*pl* **-s**) money lent at interest ▶ *v* (**-s, -ing, -ed**) lend
loaned *v* ▷ **loan**
loaning *v* ▷ **loan**
loans *n, v* ▷ **loan**
loath, loth [rhymes with **both**] *adj* unwilling or reluctant (to)
loathe *v* (**-s, -thing, -thed**) hate, be disgusted by > **loathing** *n* (*pl* **-s**) > **loathsome** *adj*
loathed *v* ▷ **loathe**
loathes *v* ▷ **loathe**
loathing *v, n* ▷ **loathe**
loathings *n* ▷ **loathe**
loathsome *adj* ▷ **loathe**
loaves *n* ▷ **loaf**[1]
lob (SPORT) *n* (*pl* **-s**) ball struck or thrown in a high arc ▶ *v* (**-s, -bbing, -bbed**) strike or throw (a ball) in a high arc
lobbed *v* ▷ **lob**
lobbied *v* ▷ **lobby**
lobbies *n, v* ▷ **lobby**
lobbing *v* ▷ **lob**
lobby *n* (*pl* **-bies**) corridor into which rooms open ▶ *v* (**-bies, -ing, -bied**) try to influence (legislators) in the formulation of policy > **lobbyist** *n*
lobbying *v* ▷ **lobby**
lobe *n* (*pl* **-s**) rounded projection > **lobed** *adj*
lobed *n* ▷ **lobe**
lobelia *n* (*pl* **-s**) garden plant with blue, red, or white flowers
lobelias *n* ▷ **lobelia**
lobes *n* ▷ **lobe**
lobola [law-**bawl**-a] *n* (*pl* **-s**) (S AFR) (in African custom) price paid by a bridegroom's family to his bride's family
lobolas *n* ▷ **lobola**
lobotomy *n* (*pl* **-mies**) surgical incision into a lobe of the brain to treat mental disorders
lobotomies *n* ▷ **lobotomy**
lobs *n, v* ▷ **lob**
lobster *n* (*pl* **-s**) shellfish with a long tail and claws, which turns red when boiled
lobsters *n* ▷ **lobster**
local *adj* of or existing in a particular place ▶ *n* (*pl* **-s**) person belonging to a particular district > **locally** *adv*
locale [loh-**kahl**] *n* (*pl* **-s**) scene of an event
localities *n* ▷ **locality**
locality *n* (*pl* **-ties**) neighbourhood or area
localize *v* (**-zes, -zing, -zed**) restrict to a particular place
localized *v* ▷ **localize**
localizes *v* ▷ **localize**
localizing *v* ▷ **localize**
locally *adv* ▷ **local**
locals *n* ▷ **local**
locate *v* (**-s, -ing, -ed**) discover the whereabouts of
located *v* ▷ **locate**
locates *v* ▷ **locate**
locating *v* ▷ **locate**
location *n* (*pl* **-s**) site or position
locations *n* ▷ **location**
loch *n* (*pl* **-s**) (SCOT) lake
lochs *n* ▷ **loch**
loci *n* ▷ **locus**
lock[1] *n* (*pl* **-s**) appliance for fastening a door, case, etc. ▶ *v* (**-s, -ing, -ed**) fasten or become fastened securely
lock[2] *n* (*pl* **-s**) strand of hair
locked *v* ▷ **lock**[1]
locker *n* (*pl* **-s**) small cupboard with a lock
lockers *n* ▷ **locker**
locket *n* (*pl* **-s**) small hinged pendant for a portrait etc.
lockets *n* ▷ **locket**
locking *v* ▷ **lock**[1]
lockjaw *n* (*pl* **-s**) tetanus
lockjaws *n* ▷ **lockjaw**
locomotion *n* (*pl* **-s**) action or power of moving
locomotions *n* ▷ **locomotion**
locomotive *n* (*pl* **-s**) self-propelled engine for pulling trains ▶ *adj* of locomotion
locomotives *n* ▷ **locomotive**
lockout *n* (*pl* **-s**) closing of a workplace by an employer to force workers to accept terms
lockouts *n* ▷ **lockout**
locks *n* ▷ **lock**[1,2] ▶ *v* ▷ **lock**[1]
locksmith *n* (*pl* **-s**) person who makes and mends locks
locksmiths *n* ▷ **locksmith**
lockup *n* (*pl* **-s**) prison
lockups *n* ▷ **lockup**

locum *n* (*pl* **-s**) temporary stand-in for a doctor or clergyman
locums *n* ▷ **locum**
locus [**loh**-kuss] *n* (*pl* **-ci**) [**loh**-sigh] area or place where something happens
locust *n* (*pl* **-s**) destructive African insect that flies in swarms and eats crops
locusts *n* ▷ **locust**
lode *n* (*pl* **-s**) vein of ore
lodes *n* ▷ **lode**
lodestar *n* (*pl* **-s**) star used in navigation or astronomy as a point of reference
lodestars *n* ▷ **lodestar**
lodestone *n* (*pl* **-s**) magnetic iron ore
lodestones *n* ▷ **lodestone**
lodge *n* (*pl* **-s**) (CHIEFLY BRIT) gatekeeper's house ▶ *v* (**-dges, -dging, -dged**) live in another's house at a fixed charge > **lodger** *n* (*pl* **-s**)
lodged *v* ▷ **lodge**
lodger *n* ▷ **lodge**
lodgers *n* ▷ **lodge**
lodges *n, v* ▷ **lodge**
lodging *n* (*pl* **-s**) temporary residence ▶ *pl* rented room or rooms in another person's house ▶ *v* ▷ **lodge**
lodgings *n* ▷ **lodging**
loft *n* (*pl* **-s**) space between the top storey and roof of a building ▶ *v* (**-s, -ing, -ed**) (SPORT) strike, throw, or kick (a ball) high into the air
lofted *v* ▷ **loft**
loftier *adj* ▷ **lofty**
loftiest *adj* ▷ **lofty**
loftily *adv* haughtily
lofting *v* ▷ **loft**
lofts *n, v* ▷ **loft**
lofty *adj* (**-tier, -tiest**) of great height
log¹ *n* (*pl* **-s**) portion of a felled tree stripped of branches ▶ *v* (**-s, -gging, -gged**) saw logs from a tree
log² *n* ▷ **logarithm**
loganberry *n* (*pl* **-rries**) purplish-red fruit, similar to a raspberry
loganberries *n* ▷ **loganberry**
logarithm *n* (*pl* **-s**) one of a series of arithmetical functions used to make certain calculations easier
logarithms *n* ▷ **logarithm**
logbook *n* (*pl* **-s**) book recording the details about a car or a ship's journeys
logbooks *n* ▷ **logbook**
logged *v* ▷ **log¹**
loggerheads *pl n* quarrelling, disputing
loggia [**loj**-ya] *n* (*pl* **-s**) covered gallery at the side of a building
loggias *n* ▷ **loggia**
logging *n* (*pl* **-s**) work of cutting and transporting logs ▶ *v* ▷ **log¹**
loggings *n* ▷ **logging**
logic *n* (*pl* **-s**) philosophy of reasoning > **logically** *adv* > **logician** *n* (*pl* **-s**)
logical *adj* of logic
logically *adv* ▷ **logic**
logician *n* ▷ **logic**
logicians *n* ▷ **logic**
logics *n* ▷ **logic**
logistical *adj* ▷ **logistics**
logistics *n* detailed planning and organization of a large, esp. military, operation > **logistical, logistic** *adj*
logo [**loh**-go] *n* (*pl* **-s**) emblem used by a company or other organization
logos *n* ▷ **logo**
logs *n* ▷ **log¹**
loin *n* (*pl* **-s**) part of the body between the ribs and the hips
loincloth *n* (*pl* **-s**) piece of cloth covering the loins only
loincloths *n* ▷ **loincloth**
loins *n* ▷ **loin**
loiter *v* (**-s, -ing, -ed**) stand or wait aimlessly or idly
loitered *v* ▷ **loiter**
loitering *v* ▷ **loiter**
loiters *v* ▷ **loiter**
loll *v* (**-s, -ing, -ed**) lounge lazily
lolled *v* ▷ **loll**
lollies *n* ▷ **lolly**
lolling *v* ▷ **loll**
lollipop *n* (*pl* **-s**) boiled sweet on a small wooden stick
lollipops *n* ▷ **lollipop**
lolls *v* ▷ **loll**
lolly *n* (*pl* **-llies**) (*Informal*) lollipop or ice lolly
lone *adj* solitary > **lonesome** *adj* lonely
loneliness *n* ▷ **lonely**
lonelinesses *n* ▷ **lonely**
lonely *adj* sad because alone > **loneliness** *n* (*pl* **-s**)
loner *n* (*pl* **-s**) (*Informal*) person who prefers to be alone
loners *n* ▷ **-s**
lonesome *adj* ▷ **lone**
long¹ *adj* (**-er, -est**) having length, esp. great length, in space or time ▶ *adv* for an extensive period
long² *v* (**-s, -ing, -ed**) have a strong desire (for)
longed *v* ▷ **long²**
longer *adj* ▷ **long¹**
longest *adj* ▷ **long¹**
longevities *n* ▷ **longevity**

longevity [lon-**jev**-it-ee] *n* (*pl* **-ties**) long life
longhand *n* (*pl* **-s**) ordinary writing, not shorthand or typing
longhands *n* ▷ **longhand**
longing *n* (*pl* **-s**) yearning ▶ *v* ▷ **long²** > **longingly** *adv*
longingly *adv* ▷ **longing**
longings *n* ▷ **longing**
longitude *n* (*pl* **-s**) distance east or west from a standard meridian
longitudes *n* ▷ **longitude**
longitudinal *adj* of length or longitude
longs *v* ▷ **long²**
longshoreman *n* (*pl* **-men**) (US) docker
longshoremen *n* ▷ **longshoreman**
loo *n* (*pl* **-s**) (*Informal*) toilet
loos *n* ▷ **loo**
loofah *n* (*pl* **-s**) sponge made from the dried pod of a gourd
loofahs *n* ▷ **loofah**
look *v* (**-s, -ing, -ed**) direct the eyes or attention (towards) ▶ *n* (*pl* **-s**) instance of looking
lookalike *n* (*pl* **-s**) person who is the double of another
lookalikes *n* ▷ **lookalike**
looked *v* ▷ **look**
looking *v* ▷ **look**
lookout *n* (*pl* **-s**) guard
lookouts *n* ▷ **lookout**
looks *v, n* ▷ **look**
loom¹ *n* (*pl* **-s**) machine for weaving cloth
loom² *v* (**-s, -ing, -ed**) appear dimly
loomed *v* ▷ **loom²**
looming *v* ▷ **loom²**
looms *n* ▷ **loom¹** ▶ *v* **loom²**
loonies *n* ▷ **loony**
loony (*Slang*) *adj* (**-nier, -niest**) foolish or insane ▶ *n* (*pl* **-nies**) foolish or insane person
loop *n* (*pl* **-s**) rounded shape made by a curved line or rope crossing itself ▶ *v* (**-s, -ing, -ed**) form or fasten with a loop
looped *v* ▷ **loop**
loophole *n* (*pl* **-s**) means of evading a rule without breaking it
loopholes *n* ▷ **loophole**
looping *v* ▷ **loop**
loops *n, v* ▷ **loop**
loose *adj* (**-r, -est**) not tight, fastened, fixed, or tense ▶ *adv* in a loose manner ▶ *v* (**-s, -sing, -sed**) free > **loosely** *adv* > **looseness** *n* (*pl* **-s**)
loosed *v* ▷ **loose**
loosely *adv* ▷ **loose**
loosen *v* (**-s, -ing, -ed**) make loose
loosened *v* ▷ **loosen**
looseness *n* ▷ **loose**
loosenesses *n* ▷ **loose**
loosening *v* ▷ **loosen**
loosens *v* ▷ **loosen**
looser *adj* ▷ **loose**
looses *v* ▷ **loose**
loosest *adj* ▷ **loose**
loosing *v* ▷ **loose**
loot *n, v* (**-s, -ing, -ed**) plunder ▶ *n* (*pl* **-s**) (*Informal*) money > **looter** *n* (*pl* **-s**) > **looting** *n* (*pl* **-s**)
looted *v* ▷ **loot**
looter *n* ▷ **loot**
looters *n* ▷ **loot**
looting *v, n* ▷ **loot**
lootings *n* ▷ **loot**
loots *v, n* ▷ **loot**
lop *v* (**-s, -pping, -pped**) cut away twigs and branches
lope *v* (**-s, -ing, -ed**) run with long easy strides
loped *v* ▷ **lope**
lopes *v* ▷ **lope**
loping *v* ▷ **lope**
lopsided *adj* greater in height, weight, or size on one side
loquacious *adj* talkative > **loquacity** *n* (*pl* **-ties**)
loquacities *n* ▷ **loquacity**
lord *n* (*pl* **-s**) person with power over others, such as a monarch or master
lordlier *adj* ▷ **lordly**
lordliest *adj* ▷ **lordly**
lordly *adj* (**-lier, -liest**) imperious, proud
lords *n* ▷ **lord**
lore *n* (*pl* **-s**) body of traditions on a subject
lores *n* ▷ **lore**
lorgnette [lor-**nyet**] *n* (*pl* **-s**) pair of spectacles mounted on a long handle
lorgnettes *n* ▷ **lorgnette**
lorries *n* ▷ **lorry**
lorikeet *n* (*pl* **-s**) small brightly coloured Australian parrot
lorikeets *n* ▷ **lorikeet**
lorry *n* (*pl* **-rries**) (BRIT & S AFR) large vehicle for transporting loads by road
lose *v* (**-s, -sing, lost**) come to be without, esp. by accident or carelessness
loser *n* (*pl* **-s**) person or thing that loses
losers *n* ▷ **loser**
loses *v* ▷ **lose**
losing *v* ▷ **lose**
loss *n* (*pl* **-es**) losing
losses *n* ▷ **loss**
lost *v* ▷ **lose** ▶ *adj* unable to find one's way
lot *pron* great number ▶ *n* (*pl* **-s**) collection of people or things
lots *n* ▷ **lot**

loth *adj* ▷ **loath**

lotion *n* (*pl* **-s**) medical or cosmetic liquid for use on the skin

lotions *n* ▷ **lotion**

lottery *n* (*pl* **-ries**) method of raising money by selling tickets that win prizes by chance

lotto *n* (*pl* **-s**) game of chance like bingo

lottos *n* ▷ **lotto**

lotus *n* (*pl* **-es**) legendary plant whose fruit induces forgetfulness

lotuses *n* ▷ **lotus**

loud *adj* (**-er, -est**) relatively great in volume > **loudly** *adv* > **loudness** *n* (*pl* **-es**)

louder *adj* ▷ **loud**

loudest *adj* ▷ **loud**

loudly *adv* ▷ **loud**

loudness *n* ▷ **loud**

loudnesses *n* ▷ **loud**

loudspeaker *n* (*pl* **-s**) instrument for converting electrical signals into sound

loudspeakers *n* ▷ **loudspeaker**

lough *n* (*pl* **-s**) (IRISH) loch

loughs *n* ▷ **lough**

lounge *n* (*pl* **-s**) living room in a private house ▶ *v* (**-s, -ging, -ged**) sit, lie, or stand in a relaxed manner

lounged *v* ▷ **lounge**

lounges *n, v* ▷ **lounge**

lounging *v* ▷ **lounge**

lour *v* (**-s, -ing, -ed**) ▷ **lower[2]**

loured *v* ▷ **lour**

louring *v* ▷ **lour**

lours *v* ▷ **lour**

louse *n* (*pl* **lice, louses**) wingless parasitic insect

louses *n* ▷ **louse**

lousier *adj* ▷ **lousy**

lousiest *adj* ▷ **lousy**

lousy *adj* (**-sier, -siest**) (*Slang*) mean or unpleasant

lout *n* (*pl* **-s**) crude, oafish, or aggressive person > **loutish** *adj*

loutish *adj* ▷ **lout**

louts *n* ▷ **lout**

louvre [**loo**-ver] *n* (*pl* **-s**) one of a set of parallel slats slanted to admit air but not rain > **louvred** *adj*

louvred *adj* ▷ **louvre**

louvres *n* ▷ **louvre**

love *v* (**-s, -ving, -ved**) have a great affection for ▶ *n* (*pl* **-s**) great affection > **lovable, loveable** *adj* > **loveless** *adj* > **lovemaking** *n* (*pl* **-s**)

lovable *adj* ▷ **love**

loveable *adj* ▷ **love**

lovebird *n* (*pl* **-s**) small parrot

lovebirds *n* ▷ **lovebird**

loved *v* ▷ **love**

loveless *adj* ▷ **love**

lovelier *adj* ▷ **lovely**

loveliest *adj* ▷ **lovely**

lovelorn *adj* miserable because of unhappiness in love

lovely *adj* (**-lier, -liest**) very attractive

lovemaking *n* ▷ **love**

lovemakings *n* ▷ **love**

lover *n* (*pl* **-s**) person having a sexual relationship outside marriage

lovers *n* ▷ **lover**

loves *v, n* ▷ **love**

loving *adj* affectionate, tender ▶ *v* ▷ **love** > **lovingly** *adv*

lovingly *adv* ▷ **loving**

low[1] *adj* not tall, high, or elevated ▶ *adv* in or to a low position, level, or degree ▶ *n* (*pl* **-s**) low position, level, or degree > **lowland** *n* (*pl* **-s**)

low[2] *n* (*pl* **-s**) cry of cattle, moo ▶ *v* (**-s, -ing, -ed**) moo

lowbrow *n* (*pl* **-s**) ▶ *adj* (person) with nonintellectual tastes and interests

lowbrows *n* ▷ **lowbrow**

lowdown *n* (*pl* **-s**) (*Informal*) inside information

lowdowns *n* ▷ **lowdown**

lowed *v* ▷ **low[2]**

lower[1] *adj* (**-est**) below one or more other things ▶ *v* (**-s, -ing, -ed**) cause or allow to move down

lower[2], lour *v* (of the sky or weather) look gloomy or threatening

lowered *v* ▷ **lower[1,2]**

lowering *v* ▷ **lower[1,2]**

lowers *v* ▷ **lower[1,2]**

lowest *adj* ▷ **lower**

lowing *v* ▷ **low[2]**

lowland *n* (*pl* **-s**) low-lying country

lowlands *n* ▷ **lowland**

lowlier *adj* ▷ **lowly**

lowliest *adj* ▷ **lowly**

lowliness *n* ▷ **lowly**

lowlinesses *n* ▷ **lowly**

lowly *adj* (**-lier, -liest**) modest, humble > **lowliness** *n* (*pl* **-s**)

lows *n* ▷ **low[1,2]** ▶ *v* ▷ **low[2]**

> **lox** *n* (**loxes**). Lox is a kind of smoked salmon. This is a good word if you get have an X and L in the late stages of the game: there's likely to be a usable O on the board already. Lox scores 10 points.

loyal *adj* (**-ler, -lest**) faithful to one's friends, country, or government > **loyally** *adv* > **loyalty** *n* (*pl* **-ties**) > **loyalist** *n* (*pl* **-s**)

loyalist *n* ▷ **loyal**
loyalists *n* ▷ **loyal**
loyaller *adj* ▷ **loyal**
loyallest *adj* ▷ **loyal**
loyally *adv* ▷ **loyal**
loyalties *n* ▷ **loyal**
loyalty *n* ▷ **loyal**
lozenge *n* (*pl* **-s**) medicated tablet held in the mouth until it dissolves
lozenges *n* ▷ **lozenge**
lubricate [loo-brik-ate] *v* (**-tes, -ting, -ted**) oil or grease to lessen friction > **lubrication** *n* (*pl* **-s**)
lubricant *n* (*pl* **-s**) lubricating substance, such as oil
lubricants *n* ▷ **lubricant**
lubricated *v* ▷ **lubricate**
lubricates *v* ▷ **lubricate**
lubricating *v* ▷ **lubricate**
lubrication *n* ▷ **lubricate**
lubrications *n* ▷ **lubricate**
lubricious *adj* (*Lit*) lewd
lucerne *n* (*pl* **-s**) fodder plant like clover, alfalfa
lucernes *n* ▷ **lucerne**
lucid *adj* clear and easily understood > **lucidly** *adv* > **lucidity** *n* (*pl* **-ties**)
lucidities *n* ▷ **lucid**
lucidity *n* ▷ **lucid**
lucidly *adv* ▷ **lucid**
luck *n* (*pl* **-s**) fortune, good or bad
luckily *adv* fortunately
luckless *adj* having bad luck
lucrative *adj* very profitable
lucre [loo-ker] *n* (*pl* **-s**) (*Facetious*) money
lucks *n* having bad luck
lucky *adj* having or bringing good luck
luderick *n* (*pl* **-s**) Australian fish, usu. black or dark brown in colour
ludericks *n* ▷ **luderick**
ludicrous *adj* absurd or ridiculous > **ludicrously** *adv*
ludicrously *adv* ▷ **ludicrous**
ludo *n* (*pl* **-s**) game played with dice and counters on a board
lug¹ *v* (**-s, -gging, -gged**) carry or drag with great effort
lug² *n* (*pl* **-s**) projection serving as a handle
luggage *n* (*pl* **-s**) traveller's cases, bags, etc.
luggages *n* projection serving as a handle ▷ **luggage**
lugs *v* ▷ **lug¹** ▶ *n* ▷ **lug²**
lugubrious *adj* mournful, gloomy > **lugubriously** *adv*
lugubriously *adv* ▷ **lugubrious**
lugworm *n* (*pl* **-s**) large worm used as bait
lugworms *n* ▷ **lugworm**
lukewarm *adj* moderately warm, tepid
lull *v* (**-s, -ing, -ed**) soothe (someone) by soft sounds or motions ▶ *n* (*pl* **-s**) brief time of quiet in a storm etc.
lullabies *n* ▷ **lullaby**
lullaby *n* (*pl* **-bies**) quiet song to send a child to sleep
lulled *v* ▷ **lull**
lulling *v* ▷ **lull**
lulls *v, n* ▷ **lull**
lumbago [lum-**bay**-go] *n* (*pl* **-s**) pain in the lower back
lumbagos *n* ▷ **lumbago**
lumbar *adj* relating to the lower back
lumber¹ *n* (*pl* **-s**) (BRIT) unwanted disused household articles ▶ *v* (**-s, -ing, -ed**) (*Informal*) burden with something unpleasant
lumber² *v* move heavily and awkwardly > **lumbering** *adj*
lumbered *v* ▷ **lumber¹,²**
lumbering *v* ▷ **lumber¹,²** ▶ *adj* ▷ **lumber²**
lumberjack *n* (*pl* **-s**) (US) man who fells trees and prepares logs for transport
lumberjacks *n* ▷ **lumberjack**
lumbers *n¹* ▶ *v* ▷ **lumber¹,²**
luminary *n* (*pl* **-s**) famous person
luminescence *n* (*pl* **-s**) emission of light at low temperatures by any process other than burning
luminescences *n* ▷ **luminescence**
luminescent *adj* ▷ **luminous**
luminosities *n* ▷ **luminous**
luminosity *n* ▷ **luminous**
luminous *adj* reflecting or giving off light > **luminosity** *n* (*pl* **-s**) > **luminescent** *adj*
lump¹ *n* (*pl* **-s**) shapeless piece or mass ▶ *v* (**-s, -ing, -ed**) consider as a single group > **lumpy** *adj* (**-pier, -piest**)
lump² *v* (*Informal*) tolerate or put up with it
lumped *v* ▷ **lump¹,²**
lumpier *adj* ▷ **lump¹**
lumpiest *adj* ▷ **lump¹**
lumping *v* ▷ **lump¹,²**
lumps *n, v* ▷ **lump¹,²**
lumpy *adj* ▷ **lump¹**
lunar *adj* relating to the moon
lunacies *n* ▷ **lunacy**
lunatic *adj* foolish and irresponsible ▶ *n* (*pl* **-s**) foolish or annoying person > **lunacy** *n* (*pl* **-cies**)
lunatics *n* ▷ **lunatic**
lunch *n* (*pl* **lunches**) meal taken in the middle of the day ▶ *v* (**-es, -ing, -ed**) eat lunch
lunched *v* ▷ **lunch**
luncheon *n* (*pl* **-s**) formal lunch

luncheons *n* ▷ **luncheon**
lunches *n, v* ▷ **lunch**
lunching *v* ▷ **lunch**
lung *n* (*pl* **-s**) organ that allows an animal or bird to breathe air: humans have two lungs in the chest
lungfish *n* freshwater bony fish with an air-breathing lung of South America and Australia
lungs *n* ▷ **lung**
lunge *n* (*pl* **-s**) sudden forward motion ▶ *v* (**-s, -ging, -ged**) move with or make a lunge
lunged *v* ▷ **lunge**
lunges *n, v* ▷ **lunge**
lunging *v* ▷ **lunge**
lupin *n* (*pl* **-s**) garden plant with tall spikes of flowers
lupins *n* ▷ **lupin**
lupine *adj* like a wolf
lurch *v* (**-es, -ing, -ed**) tilt or lean suddenly to one side ▶ *n* (*pl* **-es**) lurching movement
lurched *v* ▷ **lurch**
lurcher *n* (*pl* **-s**) crossbred dog trained to hunt silently
lurchers *n* ▷ **lurcher**
lurches *v, n* ▷ **lurch**
lurching *v* ▷ **lurch**
lure *v* (**-s, -red, -ring**) tempt or attract by the promise of reward ▶ *n* (*pl* **-s**) person or thing that lures
lured *v* ▷ **lure**
lures *v, n* ▷ **lure**
luring *v* ▷ **lure**
lurid *adj* (**-er, -est**) vivid in shocking detail, sensational > **luridly** *adv*
lurider *adj* ▷ **lurid**
luridest *adj* ▷ **lurid**
luridly *adv* ▷ **lurid**
luring *v* ▷ **lure**
lurk *v* (**-s, -ing, -ed**) lie hidden or move stealthily, esp. for sinister purposes
lurked *v* ▷ **lurk**
lurking *v* ▷ **lurk**
lurks *v* ▷ **lurk**
luscious [**lush**-uss] *adj* extremely pleasurable to taste or smell
lush[1] *adj* (**-er, -est**) (of grass etc.) growing thickly and healthily
lush[2] *n* (*pl* **-es**) (*Slang*) alcoholic
lusher *adj* ▷ **lush**[1]
lushes *n* ▷ **lush**[2]
lushest *adj* ▷ **lush**[1]
lust *n* (*pl* **-s**) strong sexual desire ▶ *v* (**-s, -ing, -ed**) have passionate desire (for) > **lustful** *adj* > **lusty** *adj* vigorous, healthy > **lustily** *adv*
lusted *v* ▷ **lust**
lustful *adj* ▷ **lust**
lustier *adj* ▷ **lusty**
lustiest *adj* ▷ **lusty**
lustily *adv* ▷ **lust**
lusting *v* ▷ **lust**
lustre *n* (*pl* **-s**) gloss, sheen
lustres *n* ▷ **lustre**
lustrous *adj* shining, luminous
lusts *n, v* ▷ **lust**
lusty *adj* (**-tier, -tiest**) vigorous, healthy
lute *n* (*pl* **-s**) ancient guitar-like musical instrument with a body shaped like a half pear
lutes *n* ▷ **lute**

> **lux** *n* (**lux**). A lux is a unit of illumination. This is a great word to know when you have an X but little opportunity to play it. Lux scores 10 points.

luxuriant *adj* rich and abundant > **luxuriance** *n* (*pl* **-ces**) > **luxuriantly** *adv*
luxuriance *n* ▷ **luxuriant**
luxuriances *n* ▷ **luxuriant**
luxuriantly *adv* ▷ **luxuriant**
luxuriate *v* (**-tes, -ting, -ted**) take self-indulgent pleasure (in)
luxuriated *v* ▷ **luxuriate**
luxuriates *v* ▷ **luxuriate**
luxuriating *v* ▷ **luxuriate**
luxurious *adj* full of luxury, sumptuous > **luxuriously** *adv*
luxuriously *adv* ▷ **luxurious**
luxury *n* (*pl* **-ries**) enjoyment of rich, very comfortable living ▶ *adj* of or providing luxury

> **luz** *n* (**luzzes**). In traditional Jewish writings, the luz was a bone that was supposed to be indestructible. This very unusual word is very useful, especially if you have a Z at the end of a game when there is little opportunity to use it in a longer word. Luz scores 12 points.

lychee [lie-**chee**] *n* (*pl* **-s**) Chinese fruit with a whitish juicy pulp
lychees *n* ▷ **lychee**
lye *n* (*pl* **-s**) caustic solution obtained by leaching wood ash
lyes *n* ▷ **lye**
lying *v* ▷ **lie**[1,2]
lymph *n* (*pl* **-s**) colourless bodily fluid consisting mainly of white blood cells > **lymphatic** *adj*
lymphatic *adj* ▷ **lymph**
lymphocyte *n* (*pl* **-s**) type of white blood cell
lymphocytes *n* ▷ **lymphocyte**

lymphs *n* ▷ **lymph**
lynch *v* (**-es, -ing, -ed**) put to death without a trial
lynched *v* ▷ **lynch**
lynches *v* ▷ **lynch**
lynching *v* ▷ **lynch**
lynchpin *n* ▷ **lynchpin**
lynchpins *n* ▷ **lynchpin**
lynx *n* (*pl* **-es**) animal of the cat family with tufted ears and a short tail
lynxes *n* ▷ **lynx**
lyre *n* (*pl* **-s**) ancient musical instrument like a U-shaped harp
lyres *n* ▷ **lyre**
lyric *adj* (of poetry) expressing personal emotion in songlike style ▶ *n* (*pl* **-s**) short poem in a songlike style > **lyrical** *adj* lyric
lyrical *n* ▷ **lyric**
lyricist *n* (*pl* **-s**) person who writes the words of songs or musicals
lyricists *n* ▷ **lyricist**
lyrics *n* ▷ **lyric**

Mm

M is a very useful letter when you need to form short words as it starts a two-letter word with every vowel, as well as with Y and with another M. Remembering this allows you to use M effectively when you're forming a word parallel to, and in contact with, a word that is already on the board. M also combines well with X and Z, so there is a lot of potential for high-scoring words. Keep **max, mix** and **mux** (12 points each) in mind, as well as **miz** and **muz** (14 each). It's also worth remembering the three-letter words ending in W: **maw, mew** and **mow** (8 points each).

ma *n* (*pl* **-s**) (*Informal*) mother
mas *n* ▷ **ma**
mac *n* (*pl* **-s**) (BRIT) (*Informal*) mackintosh
macs *n* ▷ **mac**
macabre [mak-**kahb**-ra] *adj* strange and horrible, gruesome
macadam *n* (*pl* **-s**) road surface of pressed layers of small broken stones
macadams *n* ▷ **macadam**
macadamia *n* (*pl* **-s**) Australian tree with edible nuts
macadamias *n* ▷ **macadamia**
macaroni *n* (*pl* **-s**) pasta in short tube shapes
macaronis *n* ▷ **macaroni**
macaroon *n* (*pl* **-s**) small biscuit or cake made with ground almonds
macaroons *n* ▷ **macaroon**
macaw *n* (*pl* **-s**) large tropical American parrot
macaws *n* ▷ **macaw**
mace[1] *n* (*pl* **-s**) ceremonial staff of office
mace[2] *n* (*pl* **-s**) spice made from the dried husk of the nutmeg
maces *n* ▷ **mace**[1,2]
macerate [**mass**-er-ate] *v* (**-tes, -ting, -ted**) soften by soaking > **maceration** *n* (*pl* **-s**)
macerated *v* ▷ **macerate**
macerates *v* ▷ **macerate**
macerating *v* ▷ **macerate**
maceration *n* ▷ **macerate**
macerations *n* ▷ **macerate**
machete [mash-**ett**-ee] *n* (*pl* **-s**) broad heavy knife used for cutting or as a weapon
machetes *n* ▷ **machete**
machinations [mak-in-**nay**-shunz] *pl n* cunning plots and ploys
machine *n* (*pl* **-s**) apparatus, usu. powered by electricity, designed to perform a particular task ▶ *v* (**-nes, -ning, -ned**) make or produce by machine
machined *v* ▷ **machine**
machinegun *v* (**-s, -nning, -nned**) fire at with such a gun
machinegunned *v* ▷ **machinegun**
machinegunning *v* ▷ **machinegun**
machineguns *v* ▷ **machinegun**
machineries *n* ▷ **machinery**
machinery *n* (*pl* **-ries**) machines or machine parts collectively
machines *n, v* ▷ **machine**
machining *v* ▷ **machine**
machinist *n* (*pl* **-s**) person who operates a machine
machinists *n* ▷ **machinist**
machismo [mak-**izz**-moh] *n* (*pl* **-s**) exaggerated or strong masculinity
machismos *n* ▷ **machismo**
macho [**match**-oh] *adj* strongly or exaggeratedly masculine
mackerel *n* edible sea fish
mackintosh *n* (*pl* **-es**) waterproof raincoat of rubberized cloth
mackintoshes *n* ▷ **mackintosh**
macramé [mak-**rah**-mee] *n* (*pl* **-s**) ornamental work of knotted cord
macramés *n* ▷ **macramé**
macrobiotics *n* dietary system advocating whole grains and vegetables grown without chemical additives > **macrobiotic** *adj*
macrobiotic *adj* ▷ **macrobiotics**
macrocosm *n* (*pl* **-s**) the universe
macrocosms *n* ▷ **macrocosm**
mad *adj* (**madder, maddest**) mentally deranged, insane > **madly** *adv* > **madness** *n* (*pl* **-es**) > **madman** *n* (*pl* **-men**) > **madwoman**

n (*pl* **-women**)
madam *n* (*pl* **madams**) polite form of address to a woman
madams *n* ▷ **madam**
madame [mad-**dam**] *n* (*pl* **mesdames**) [may-**dam**] French title equivalent to *Mrs*
madcap *adj* foolish or reckless
madden *v* (**-s, -ed, -ing**) infuriate or irritate > **maddening** *adj*
maddened *v* ▷ **madden**
maddening *v* ▷ **madden** ▶ *adj* ▷ **madden**
maddens *v* ▷ **madden**
madder *n* (*pl* **-s**) climbing plant ▶ *adj* ▷ **mad**
maddest *adj* ▷ **mad**
made *v* ▷ **make**
madeira [mad-**deer**-a] *n* (*pl* **-s**) fortified white wine
madeiras *n* ▷ **madeira**
mademoiselle [mad-mwah-**zel**, maid-mwah-**zel**] *n* (*pl* **-s**) French title equivalent to *Miss*
mademoiselles *n* ▷ **mademoiselle**
madonna *n* (*pl* **-s**) the Virgin Mary
madly *adv* ▷ **mad**
madman *n* ▷ **mad**
madmen *n* ▷ **mad**
madness *n* ▷ **mad**
madnesses *n* ▷ **madness**
madonnas *n* ▷ **madonna**
madrigal *n* (*pl* **-s**) 16th–17th-century part song for unaccompanied voices
madrigals *n* ▷ **madrigal**
madwoman *n* ▷ **mad**
madwomen *n* ▷ **mad**
maelstrom [**male**-strom] *n* (*pl* **-s**) great whirlpool
maelstroms *n* ▷ **maelstrom**
maestri *n* ▷ **maestro**
maestro [**my**-stroh] *n* (*pl* **-tri, -tros**) outstanding musician or conductor
maestros *n* ▷ **maestro**
mafia *n* (*pl* **-s**) international secret criminal organization
mafias *n* ▷ **mafia**
mafiosi *n* ▷ **mafioso**
mafioso *n* (*pl* **-sos, -si**) member of the Mafia
mafiosos *n* ▷ **mafioso**
magazine *n* (*pl* **-s**) periodical publication with articles by different writers
magazines *n* ▷ **magazine**
magenta [maj-**jen**-ta] *adj* deep purplish-red
maggot *n* (*pl* **-s**) larva of an insect > **maggoty** *adj*
maggots *n* ▷ **maggot**
maggoty *adj* ▷ **maggot**
magi [**maje**-eye] *pl n* wise men from the East who came to worship the infant Jesus
magic *n* (*pl* **-s**) supposed art of invoking supernatural powers to influence events ▶ *adj* (*also* **magical**) of, using, or like magic > **magically** *adv*
magical *adj* ▷ **magic**
magically *adv* ▷ **magic**
magician *n* (*pl* **-s**) conjuror
magicians *n* ▷ **magician**
magics *n* ▷ **magic**
magisterial *adj* commanding or authoritative
magistrate *n* (*pl* **-s**) public officer administering the law
magistrates *n* ▷ **magistrate**
magma *n* (*pl* **-s**) molten rock inside the earth's crust
magmas *n* ▷ **magma**
magnanimous *adj* noble and generous > **magnanimously** *adv* > **magnanimity** *n* (*pl* **-ties**)
magnanimities *n* ▷ **magnanimous**
magnanimity *n* ▷ **magnanimous**
magnanimously *n* ▷ **magnanimous**
magnate *n* (*pl* **-s**) influential or wealthy person, esp. in industry
magnates *n* ▷ **magnate**
magnesia *n* (*pl* **-s**) white tasteless substance used as an antacid and a laxative; magnesium oxide
magnesias *n* ▷ **magnesia**
magnesium *n* (*pl* **-s**) (CHEM) silvery-white metallic element
magnesiums *n* ▷ **magnesium**
magnet *n* (*pl* **-s**) piece of iron or steel capable of attracting iron and pointing north when suspended
magnetic *adj* having the properties of a magnet > **magnetically** *adv*
magnetically *adv* ▷ **magnetic**
magnetism *n* (*pl* **-s**) magnetic property
magnetisms *n* ▷ **magnetism**
magnetize *v* (**-zes, -zed, -zing**) make into a magnet
magnetized *v* ▷ **magnetize**
magnetizes *v* ▷ **magnetize**
magnetizing *v* ▷ **magnetize**
magnets *n* ▷ **magnet**
magneto [mag-**nee**-toe] *n* (*pl* **-s**) apparatus for ignition in an internal-combustion engine
magnificent *adj* splendid or impressive > **magnificently** *adv* > **magnificence** *n* (*pl* **-s**)
magnificence *n* ▷ **magnificent**
magnificences *n* ▷ **magnificent**
magnificently *adv* ▷ **magnificent**
magnify *v* (**-fies, -ing, -fied**) increase in

apparent size, as with a lens > **magnification** *n* (*pl* **-s**)
magnification *n* ▷ **magnify**
magnifications *n* ▷ **magnify**
magnified *v* ▷ **magnify**
magnifies *v* ▷ **magnify**
magnifying *v* ▷ **magnify**
magnitude *n* (*pl* **-s**) relative importance or size
magnitudes *n* ▷ **magnitude**
magnolia *n* (*pl* **-s**) shrub or tree with showy white or pink flowers
magnolias *n* ▷ **magnolia**
magnum *n* (*pl* **s**) large wine bottle holding about 1.5 litres
magnums *n* ▷ **magnum**
magpie *n* (*pl* **-s**) black-and-white bird
magpies *n* ▷ **magpie**
maharajah *n* (*pl* **-s**) former title of some Indian princes > **maharani** *n fem* (*pl* **-s**)
maharajahs *n* ▷ **maharajah**
maharani *n* ▷ **maharajah**
maharanis *n* ▷ **maharajah**
mahogany *n* (*pl* **-nies**) hard reddish-brown wood of several tropical trees
mahoganies *n* ▷ **mahogany**
mahout [ma-**howt**] *n* (*pl* **s**) (in India and the East Indies) elephant driver or keeper
mahouts *n* ▷ **mahout**
maid (*also* **maidservant**) *n* (*pl* **-s**) female servant
maiden *n* (*pl* **-s**) (*Lit*) young unmarried woman ▶ *adj* unmarried
maidenhair *n* (*pl* **-s**) fern with delicate fronds
maidenhairs *n* ▷ **maidenhair**
maidenhead *n* (*pl* **-s**) virginity
maidenheads *n* ▷ **maidenhead**
maidenly *adj* modest
maidens *n* ▷ **maiden**
maids *n* ▷ **maid**
maidservant *n* ▷ **maid**
maidservants *n* ▷ **maid**
mail¹ *n* (*pl* **-s**) letters and packages transported and delivered by the post office ▶ *v* (**-s, -ing, -ed**) send by mail
mail² *n* (*pl* **-s**) flexible armour of interlaced rings or links
mailbox *n* (*pl* **-es**) (US, CANADIAN & AUST) box into which letters and parcels are delivered
mailboxes *n* ▷ **mailbox**
mailed *v* ▷ **mail¹**
mailing *v* ▷ **mail¹**
mails *n* ▷ **mail¹,²** ▶ *v* ▷ **mail²**
mailshot *n* (*pl* **-s**) (BRIT) posting of advertising material to many selected people at once
mailshots *n* ▷ **mailshot**
maim *v* (**-s, -ing, -ed**) cripple or mutilate
maimed *v* ▷ **maim**
maiming *v* ▷ **maim**
maims *v* ▷ **maim**
main *adj* chief or principal ▶ *n* (*pl* **-s**) principal pipe or line carrying water, gas, or electricity
mainframe *n* (*pl* **-s**) ▶ *adj* (COMPUTERS) (denoting) a high-speed general-purpose computer
mainframes *n* ▷ **mainframe**
mainland *n* (*pl* **-s**) stretch of land which forms the main part of a country
mainlands *n* ▷ **mainland**
mainly *adv* for the most part, chiefly
mainmast *n* (*pl* **-s**) chief mast of a ship
mainmasts *n* ▷ **mainmast**
mains *n* ▷ **main**
mainsail *n* (*pl* **-s**) largest sail on a mainmast
mainsails *n* ▷ **mainsail**
mainspring *n* (*pl* **-s**) chief cause or motive
mainsprings *n* ▷ **mainspring**
mainstay *n* (*pl* **-s**) chief support
mainstays *n* ▷ **mainstay**
mainstream *adj* (of) a prevailing cultural trend
maintain *v* (**-s, -ing, -ed**) continue or keep in existence
maintained *v* ▷ **maintain**
maintaining *v* ▷ **maintain**
maintains *v* ▷ **maintain**
maintenance *n* (*pl* **-s**) maintaining
maintenances *n* ▷ **maintenance**
maisonette *n* (*pl* **-s**) (BRIT) flat with more than one floor
maisonettes *n* ▷ **maisonette**
maize *n* (*pl* **-s**) type of corn with spikes of yellow grains
maizes *n* ▷ **maize**
majesty *n* (*pl* **-ties**) stateliness or grandeur > **majestic** *adj* > **majestically** *adv*
majestic *adj* ▷ **majesty**
majestically *adv* ▷ **majesty**
majesties *n* ▷ **majesty**
major *adj* greater in number, quality, or extent ▶ *n* (*pl* **-s**) middle-ranking army officer ▶ *v* (**-s, -ing, -ed**) (*foll. by* **in**) (US, CANADIAN, S AFR, AUST & NZ) do one's principal study in (a particular subject)
majordomo *n* (*pl* **-s**) chief steward of a great household
majordomos *n* ▷ **majordomo**
majored *v* ▷ **major**
majoring *v* ▷ **major**
majorities *n* ▷ **majority**
majority *n* (*pl* **-ties**) greater number

majors *n, v* ▷ **major**
make *v* (**-kes, -king, made**) create, construct, or establish ▶ *n* (*pl* **-s**) brand, type, or style
maker *n* (*pl* **-s**) > **makeweight** *n* (*pl* **-s**) something unimportant added to make up a lack
maker *n* ▷ **make**
makers *n* ▷ **make**
makes *n, v* ▷ **make**
makeshift *adj* serving as a temporary substitute
makeup *n* (*pl* **-s**) cosmetics
makeups *n* ▷ **makeup**
making *v* ▷ **make** ▶ *n* (*pl* **-s**) creation or production
makings *n* ▷ **making**
malachite [**mal**-a-kite] *n* (*pl* **-s**) green mineral
malachites *n* ▷ **malachite**
maladjusted *adj* (PSYCHOL) unable to meet the demands of society > **maladjustment** *n* (*pl* **-s**)
maladjustment *n* ▷ **maladjusted**
maladjustments *n* ▷ **maladjusted**
maladministration *n* (*pl* **-s**) inefficient or dishonest administration
maladministrations *n* ▷ **maladministration**
maladroit *adj* clumsy or awkward
malady *n* (*pl* **-dies**) disease or illness
maladies *n* ▷ **malady**
malaise [mal-**laze**] *n* (*pl* **-s**) vague feeling of unease, illness, or depression
malaises *n* ▷ **malaise**
malapropism *n* (*pl* **-s**) comical misuse of a word by confusion with one which sounds similar, e.g. *I am not under the affluence of alcohol*
malapropisms *n* ▷ **malapropism**
malaria *n* (*pl* **-s**) infectious disease caused by the bite of some mosquitoes > **malarial** *adj*
malarias *n* ▷ **malaria**
malarial *adj* ▷ **malaria**
malcontent *n* (*pl* **-s**) discontented person
malcontents *n* ▷ **malcontent**
male *adj* of the sex which can fertilize female reproductive cells ▶ *n* (*pl* **males**) male person or animal
males *n* ▷ **male**
malediction [mal-lid-**dik**-shun] *n* (*pl* **-s**) curse
maledictions *n* ▷ **malediction**
malefactor [**mal**-if-act-or] *n* (*pl* **-s**) criminal or wrongdoer
malefactors *n* ▷ **malefactor**
malevolent [mal-**lev**-a-lent] *adj* wishing evil to others > **malevolently** *adv* > **malevolence** *n* (*pl* **-s**)
malevolence *n* ▷ **malevolent**
malevolences *n* ▷ **malevolent**
malevolently *adv* ▷ **malevolent**
malfeasance [mal-**fee**-zanss] *n* (*pl* **-s**) misconduct, esp. by a public official
malfeasances *n* ▷ **malfeasance**
malformed *adj* misshapen or deformed > **malformation** *n* (*pl* **-s**)
malformation *n* ▷ **malformed**
malformations *n* ▷ **malformed**
malfunction *v* (**-s, -ing, -ed**) function imperfectly or fail to function ▶ *n* (*pl* **-s**) defective functioning or failure to function
malfunctioned *v* ▷ **malfunction**
malfunctioning *v* ▷ **malfunction**
malfunctions *v, n* ▷ **malfunction**
malice [**mal**-iss] *n* (*pl* **-s**) desire to cause harm to others > **malicious** *adj* > **maliciously** *adv*
malices *n* ▷ **malice**
malicious *adj* ▷ **malice**
maliciously *adj* ▷ **malice**
malign [mal-**line**] *v* (**-s, -ing, -ed**) slander or defame ▶ *adj* evil in influence or effect > **malignity** *n* (*pl* **-nities**) evil disposition
malignancies *n* ▷ **malignant**
malignancy *n* ▷ **malignant**
malignant [mal-**lig**-nant] *adj* seeking to harm others > **malignancy** *n* (*pl* **-cies**)
maligned *v* ▷ **malign**
maligning *v* ▷ **malign**
malignities *n* ▷ **malign**
malignity *n* ▷ **malign**
maligns *v* ▷ **malign**
malinger *v* (**-s, -ing, -ed**) feign illness to avoid work > **malingerer** *n* (*pl* **-s**)
malingered *v* ▷ **malinger**
malingerer *n* ▷ **malinger**
malingering *v* ▷ **malinger**
malingerers *n* ▷ **malinger**
malingers *v* ▷ **malinger**
mall [**mawl**] *n* (*pl* **-s**) street or shopping area closed to vehicles
mallard *n* wild duck
malleable [**mal**-lee-a-bl] *adj* capable of being hammered or pressed into shape > **malleability** *n* (*pl* **-ties**)
malleability *n* ▷ **malleable**
malleabilities *n* ▷ **malleable**
mallee *n* (*pl* **-s**) (AUST) low-growing eucalypt in dry regions
mallees *n* ▷ **mallee**
mallet *n* (*pl* **-s**) (wooden) hammer
mallets *n* ▷ **mallet**
mallow *n* (*pl* **-s**) plant with pink or purple flowers
mallows *n* ▷ **mallow**

malls *n* ▷ **mall**
malnutrition *n* (*pl* **-s**) inadequate nutrition
malnutritions *n* ▷ **malnutrition**
malodorous [mal-**lode**-or-uss] *adj* bad-smelling
malpractice *n* (*pl* **-s**) immoral, illegal, or unethical professional conduct
malpractices *n* ▷ **malpractice**
malt *n* (*pl* **-s**) grain, such as barley, prepared for use in making beer or whisky
malts *n* ▷ **malt**
maltreat *v* (**-s, -ing, -ed**) treat badly > **maltreatment** *n* (*pl* **-s**)
maltreated *v* ▷ **maltreat**
maltreating *v* ▷ **maltreat**
maltreatment *n* ▷ **maltreat**
maltreatments *n* ▷ **maltreat**
maltreats *v* ▷ **maltreat**
mama *n* (*pl* **-s**) (*Old-fashioned*) mother
mamas *n* ▷ **mama**
mamba *n* (*pl* **-s**) deadly S African snake
mambas *n* ▷ **mamba**
mamma *n* (*pl* **-s**) ▷ **mama**
mammas *n* ▷ **mamma**
mammal *n* (*pl* **-s**) animal of the type that suckles its young > **mammalian** *adj*
mammalian *adj* ▷ **mammal**
mammals *n* ▷ **mammal**
mammary *adj* of the breasts or milk-producing glands
mammon *n* (*pl* **-s**) wealth regarded as a source of evil
mammons *n* ▷ **mammon**
mammoth *n* (*pl* **-s**) extinct elephant-like mammal ▶ *adj* colossal
mammoths *n* ▷ **mammoth**
man *n* (*pl* **men**) adult male ▶ *v* (**-s, -nning, -nned**) supply with sufficient people for operation or defence > **manhood** *n* (*pl* **-s**)
mana *n* (*pl* **-s**) (NZ) authority, influence
manacle [**man**-a-kl] *n* (*pl* **-s**) handcuff or fetter ▶ *v* (**-les, -ling, -led**) handcuff or fetter
manacled *v* ▷ **manacle**
manacling *v* ▷ **manacle**
manacles *n, v* ▷ **manacle**
manage *v* (**-ges, -ging, -ged**) succeed in doing > **manageable** *adj* > **management** *n* (*pl* **-s**) managers collectively
manageable *adj* ▷ **manage**
managed *v* ▷ **manage**
managing *v* ▷ **manage**
management *n* ▷ **manage**
managements *n* ▷ **manage**
manages *v* ▷ **manage**
manager *n* (*pl* **-s**) person in charge of a business, institution, actor, sports team, etc. > **managerial** *adj*
manageress *n* (*pl* **-es**) woman in charge of a business, institution, actor, sports team, etc.
manageresses *n* ▷ **manager**
managerial *adj* ▷ **manager**
managers *n* ▷ **manager**
manas *n* ▷ **mana**
manatee *n* (*pl* **-s**) large tropical plant-eating aquatic mammal
manatees *n* ▷ **manatee**
mandarin *n* (*pl* **-s**) high-ranking government official
mandarins *n* ▷ **mandarin**
mandate *n* (*pl* **-s**) official or authoritative command ▶ *v* (**-tes, -ting, -ted**) give authority to
mandated *v* ▷ **mandate**
mandates *n, v* ▷ **mandate**
mandating *v* ▷ **mandate**
mandatory *adj* compulsory
mandible *n* (*pl* **-s**) lower jawbone or jawlike part
mandibles *n* ▷ **mandible**
mandolin *n* (*pl* **s**) musical instrument with four pairs of strings
mandolins *n* ▷ **mandolin**
mandrake *n* (*pl* **-s**) plant with a forked root, formerly used as a narcotic
mandrakes *n* ▷ **mandrake**
mandrel *n* (*pl* **-s**) shaft on which work is held in a lathe
mandrels *n* ▷ **mandrel**
mandrill *n* (*pl* **-s**) large blue-faced baboon
mandrills *n* ▷ **mandrill**
mane *n* (*pl* **-s**) long hair on the neck of a horse, lion, etc.
manes *n* ▷ **mane**
manful *adj* determined and brave > **manfully** *adv*
manfully *adv* ▷ **manful**
manganese *n* (*pl* **-s**) (CHEM) brittle greyish-white metallic element
manganeses *n* ▷ **manganese**
mange *n* (*pl* **-s**) skin disease of domestic animals
manges *n* ▷ **mange**
mangelwurzel *n* (*pl* **-s**) variety of beet used as cattle food
mangelwurzels *n* ▷ **mangelwurzel**
manger *n* (*pl* **-s**) eating trough in a stable or barn
mangers *n* ▷ **manger**
mangetout [**mawnzh**-too] *n* (*pl* **-s**) variety of pea with an edible pod
mangetouts *n* ▷ **mangetout**

mangier *adj* ▷ **mangy**
mangiest *adj* ▷ **mangy**
mangle[1] *v* (**-les, -ling, -led**) destroy by crushing and twisting
mangle[2] *n* (*pl* **-s**) machine with rollers for squeezing water from washed clothes ▶ *v* (**-les, -ling, -led**) put through a mangle
mangled *v* ▷ **mangle**[1,2]
mangling *v* ▷ **mangle**[1,2]
mangles *v* ▷ **mangle**[1,2] ▶ *n* ▷ **mangle**[2]
mango *n* (*pl* **-goes, -gos**) tropical fruit with sweet juicy yellow flesh
mangoes *n* ▷ **mango**
mangos *n* ▷ **mango**
mangrove *n* (*pl* **-s**) tropical tree with exposed roots, which grows beside water
mangroves *n* ▷ **mangrove**
mangy *adj* (**-gier, -giest**) having mange
manhandle *v* (**-les, -ling, -led**) treat roughly
manhandled *v* ▷ **manhandle**
manhandling *v* ▷ **manhandle**
manhandles *v* ▷ **manhandle**
manhole *n* (*pl* **-s**) hole with a cover, through which a person can enter a drain or sewer
manholes *n* ▷ **manhole**
manhood *n* ▷ **man**
manhoods *n* ▷ **man**
mania *n* (*pl* **-s**) extreme enthusiasm > **maniacal** [man-**eye**-a-kl] ▶ *adj*
maniac *n* (*pl* **-s**) mad person
maniacal *adj* ▷ **mania**
maniacs *n* ▷ **mania**
manias *n* ▷ **mania**
manic *adj* affected by mania
manicure *n* (*pl* **-s**) cosmetic care of the fingernails and hands ▶ *v* (**-res, -ring, -red**) care for (the fingernails and hands) in this way > **manicurist** *n* (*pl* **-s**)
manicured *v* ▷ **manicure**
manicures *n, v* ▷ **manicure**
manicuring *v* ▷ **manicure**
manicurist *n* ▷ **manicure**
manicurists *n* ▷ **manicure**
manifest *adj* easily noticed, obvious ▶ *v* (**-s, -ing, -ed**) show plainly ▶ *n* (*pl* **-s**) list of cargo or passengers for customs > **manifestation** *n* (*pl* **-s**)
manifestation *n* ▷ **manifest**
manifestations *n* ▷ **manifest**
manifested *v* ▷ **manifest**
manifesting *v, n* ▷ **manifest**
manifesto *n* (*pl* **-tos, -toes**) declaration of policy as issued by a political party
manifestoes *n* ▷ **manifesto**
manifestos *n* ▷ **manifesto**
manifests *v* ▷ **manifest**
manifold *adj* numerous and varied ▶ *n* (*pl* **-s**) pipe with several outlets, esp. in an internal-combustion engine
manifolds *n* ▷ **manifold**
manikin *n* (*pl* **-s**) little man or dwarf
manikins *n* ▷ **manikin**
manila, manilla *n* (*pl* **-s**) strong brown paper used for envelopes
manilas *n* ▷ **manila**
manillas *n* ▷ **manila**
manipulate *v* (**-tes, -ting, -ted**) handle skilfully > **manipulation** *n* (*pl* **-s**) > **manipulative** *adj* > **manipulator** *n* (*pl* **-s**)
manipulated *v* ▷ **manipulate**
manipulates *v* ▷ **manipulate**
manipulating *v* ▷ **manipulate**
manipulation *n* ▷ **manipulate**
manipulations *n* ▷ **manipulate**
manipulative *adj* ▷ **manipulate**
manipulator *n* ▷ **manipulate**
manipulators *n* ▷ **manipulate**
mankind *n* (*pl* **-s**) human beings collectively
mankinds *n* ▷ **mankind**
manlier *adj* ▷ **manly**
manliest *adj* ▷ **manly**
manliness *n* ▷ **manly**
manlinesses *n* ▷ **manly**
manly *adj* (**-lier, -liest**) (possessing qualities) appropriate to a man > **manliness** *n* (*pl* **-s**)
manna *n* (*pl* **-s**) (BIBLE) miraculous food which sustained the Israelites in the wilderness
mannas *n* ▷ **manna**
manned *v* ▷ **man**
mannequin *n* (*pl* **-s**) woman who models clothes at a fashion show
mannequins *n* ▷ **mannequin**
manner *n* (*pl* **-s**) way a thing happens or is done > **mannered** *adj* affected
mannered *adj* ▷ **manner**
mannerism *n* (*pl* **-s**) person's distinctive habit or trait
mannerisms *n* ▷ **manner**
manners *n* ▷ **manner**
mannikin *n* (*pl* **-s**) ▷ **manikin**
mannikins *n* ▷ **mannikin**
manning *v* ▷ **man**
mannish *adj* (of a woman) like a man
manoeuvre [man-**noo**-ver] *n* (*pl* **-s**) skilful movement military or naval exercises ▶ *v* (**-res, -ring, -red**) manipulate or contrive skilfully or cunningly > **manoeuvrable** *adj*
manoeuvred *v* ▷ **manoeuvre**
manoeuvres *n, v* ▷ **manoeuvre**
manoeuvring *v* ▷ **manoeuvre**

manor *n* (*pl* **-s**) (BRIT) large country house and its lands > **manorial** *adj*
manorial *adj* ▷ **manor**
manors *n* ▷ **manor**
manpower *n* (*pl* **-s**) available number of workers
manpowers *n* ▷ **manpower**
manqué [**mong**-kay] *adj* would-be
mans *v* ▷ **man**
manse *n* (*pl* **-s**) house provided for a minister in some religious denominations
manses *n* ▷ **manse**
manservant *n* (*pl* **menservants**) male servant, esp. a valet
mansion *n* (*pl* **-s**) large house
mansions *n* ▷ **mansion**
manslaughter *n* (*pl* **-s**) unlawful but unintentional killing of a person
manslaughters *n* ▷ **manslaughter**
mantel *n* (*pl* **-s**) structure round a fireplace
mantelpiece *n* (*pl* **-es**) shelf above a fireplace
mantelpieces *n* ▷ **mantelpiece**
mantels *n* ▷ **mantel**
mantilla *n* (*pl* **-s**) (in Spain) a lace scarf covering a woman's head and shoulders
mantillas *n* ▷ **mantilla**
mantis *n* (*pl* **-ses, -tes**) carnivorous insect like a grasshopper
mantes *n* ▷ **mantis**
mantises *n* ▷ **mantis**
mantle *n* (*pl* **-s**) loose cloak
mantles *n* ▷ **mantle**
mantra *n* (*pl* **-s**) (HINDUISM, BUDDHISM) any sacred word or syllable used as an object of concentration
mantras *n* ▷ **mantra**
manual *adj* of or done with the hands ▶ *n* (*pl* **-s**) handbook > **manually** *adv*
manually *adv* ▷ **manual**
manuals *n* ▷ **manual**
manufacture *v* (**-res, -ring, -red**) process or make (goods) on a large scale using machinery ▶ *n* (*pl* **-s**) process of manufacturing goods
manufactured *v* ▷ **manufacture**
manufacturer *n* (*pl* **-s**) company that manufactures goods
manufacturers *n* ▷ **manufacturer**
manufactures *v*, *n* ▷ **manufacture**
manufacturing *v* ▷ **manufacture**
manure *n* (*pl* **-s**) animal excrement used as a fertilizer
manures *n* ▷ **manure**
manuscript *n* (*pl* **-s**) book or document, orig. one written by hand
manuscripts *n* ▷ **manuscript**
many *adj* (**more, most**) numerous ▶ *n* large number
map *n* (*pl* **-s**) representation of the earth's surface or some part of it, showing geographical features ▶ *v* (**-s, -pping, -pped**) make a map of
maple *n* (*pl* **-s**) tree with broad leaves, a variety of which (**sugar maple**) yields sugar
maples *n* ▷ **maple**
mapped *v* ▷ **map**
mapping *v* ▷ **map**
maps *n*, *v* ▷ **map**
mar *v* (**-s, -rring, -rred**) spoil or impair
marabou *n* (*pl* **-s**) large black-and-white African stork
marabous *n* ▷ **marabou**
maraca [mar-**rak**-a] *n* (*pl* **-s**) shaken percussion instrument made from a gourd containing dried seeds etc.
maracas *n* ▷ **maraca**
marae *n* (*pl* **-s**) (NZ) enclosed space in front of a Maori meeting house
maraes *n* ▷ **marae**
marathon *n* (*pl* **-s**) long-distance race of 26 miles 385 yards (42.195 kilometres)
marathons *n* ▷ **marathon**
marauder *n* ▷ **marauding**
marauders *n* ▷ **marauder**
marauding *adj* wandering or raiding in search of plunder > **marauder** *n* (*pl* **-s**)
marble *n* (*pl* **-s**) kind of limestone with a mottled appearance, which can be highly polished > **marbled** *adj* having a mottled appearance like marble
marbled *n* ▷ **marble**
marbles *n* ▷ **marble**
march¹ *v* (**-es, -ing, -ed**) walk with a military step ▶ *n* (*pl* **-es**) action of marching > **marcher** *n* (*pl* **-s**)
march² *n* (*pl* **-s**) border or frontier
marched *v* ▷ **march¹**
marches *v* ▷ **march¹** ▶ *n* ▷ **march¹,²**
marching *v* ▷ **march¹**
marchioness [marsh-on-**ness**] *n* (*pl* **-es**) woman holding the rank of marquis
marchionesses *n* ▷ **marchioness**
mare *n* (*pl* **-s**) female horse or zebra
mares *n* ▷ **mare**
margarine *n* (*pl* **-s**) butter substitute made from animal or vegetable fats
margarines *n* ▷ **margarine**
marge *n* (*pl* **-s**) (*Informal*) margarine
marges *n* ▷ **marge**
margin *n* (*pl* **-s**) edge or border > **marginal** *adj*

insignificant, unimportant > **marginally** *adv*

marginal *adj* ▷ **margin**

marginalize *v* (**-zes, -zing, -zed**) make or treat as insignificant

marginalized *v* ▷ **marginalize**

marginalizes *v* ▷ **marginalize**

marginalizing *v* ▷ **marginalize**

margins *n* ▷ **margin**

marguerite *n* (*pl* **-s**) large daisy

marguerites *n* ▷ **marguerite**

marigold *n* (*pl* **-s**) plant with yellow or orange flowers

marigolds *n* ▷ **marigold**

marijuana [mar-ree-**wah**-na] *n* (*pl* **-s**) dried flowers and leaves of the cannabis plant, used as a drug, esp. in cigarettes

marijuanas *n* ▷ **marijuana**

marina *n* (*pl* **-s**) harbour for yachts and other pleasure boats

marinas *n* ▷ **marina**

marinade *n* (*pl* **-s**) seasoned liquid in which fish or meat is soaked before cooking ▶ *v* (**-des, -ding, -ded**) ▷ **marinate**

marinaded *v* ▷ **marinade**

marinades *n, v* ▷ **marinade**

marinading *v* ▷ **marinade**

marinate *v* (**-tes, -ting, -ted**) soak in marinade

marinated *v* ▷ **marinate**

marinates *v* ▷ **marinate**

marinating *v* ▷ **marinate**

marine *adj* of the sea or shipping ▶ *n* (*pl* **-s**) (esp. in Britain and the US) soldier trained for land and sea combat

mariner *n* (*pl* **-s**) sailor

mariners *n* ▷ **mariner**

marines *n* ▷ **marine**

marionette *n* (*pl* **-s**) puppet worked with strings

marionettes *n* ▷ **marionette**

marital *adj* relating to marriage

maritime *adj* relating to shipping

marjoram *n* (*pl* **-s**) aromatic herb used for seasoning food and in salads

marjorams *n* ▷ **marjoram**

mark[1] *n* (*pl* **-s**) line, dot, scar, etc. visible on a surface ▶ *v* (**-s, -ing, -ed**) make a mark on > **marked** *adj* noticeable > **markedly** *adv* > **marker** *n* (*pl* **-s**)

mark[2] *n* ▷ **Deutschmark**

marked *v, adj* ▷ **mark**[1]

markedly *adv* ▷ **mark**[1]

marker *n* ▷ **mark**[1]

markers *n* ▷ **mark**

marking *v* ▷ **mark**[1]

marks *n* ▷ **mark**[1,2] ▶ *v* ▷ **mark**[1]

market *n* (*pl* **-s**) assembly or place for buying and selling ▶ *v* (**-s, -ing, -ed**) offer or produce for sale > **marketable** *adj*

marketable *adj* ▷ **market**

marketing *n* (*pl* **-s**) part of a business that controls the way that goods or services are sold

marketings *n* ▷ **marketing**

marketplace *n* (*pl* **-s**) market

marketplaces *n* ▷ **marketplace**

markets *n, v* ▷ **market**

marksman *n* (*pl* **-men**) person skilled at shooting > **marksmanship** *n* (*pl* **-s**)

marksmanship *n* ▷ **marksman**

marksmanships *n* ▷ **marksman**

marksmen *n* ▷ **marksman**

marl *n* (*pl* **-s**) soil formed of clay and lime, used as fertilizer

marls *n* ▷ **marl**

marlin *n* large food and game fish of warm and tropical seas, with a very long upper jaw

marlinespike, marlinspike *n* (*pl* **-s**) pointed hook used to separate strands of rope

marlinespikes *n* ▷ **marlinespike**

marlinspikes *n* ▷ **marlinespike**

marmalade *n* (*pl* **-s**) jam made from citrus fruits

marmalades *n* ▷ **marmalade**

marmoreal *adj* of or like marble

marmoset *n* (*pl* **-s**) small bushy-tailed monkey

marmosets *n* ▷ **marmoset**

marmot *n* (*pl* **-s**) burrowing rodent

marmots *n* ▷ **marmot**

maroon[1] *adj* reddish-purple

maroon[2] *v* (**-s, -ing, -ed**) abandon ashore, esp. on an island

marooned *v* ▷ **maroon**

marooning *v* ▷ **maroon**

maroons *v* ▷ **maroon**

marquee *n* (*pl* **-s**) large tent used for a party or exhibition

marquees *n* ▷ **marquee**

marquess [**mar**-kwiss] *n* (*pl* **-es**) (BRIT) nobleman of the rank below a duke

marquesses *n* ▷ **marquess**

marquetry *n* (*pl* **-ries**) ornamental inlaid work of wood

marquetries *n* ▷ **marquetry**

marquis *n* (*pl* **-es**) (in some European countries) nobleman of the rank above a count

marquises *n* ▷ **marquis**

marred *v* ▷ **mar**

marriage *n* (*pl* **-s**) state of being married > **marriageable** *adj*

marriageable *adj* ▷ **marriage**
marriages *n* ▷ **marriage**
married *v* ▷ **marry**
marries *v* ▷ **marry**
marring *v* ▷ **mar**
marrow *n* (*pl* **-s**) fatty substance inside bones
marrows *n* ▷ **marrow**
marry *v* (**-ries, -ing, -ried**) take as a husband or wife
marrying *v* ▷ **marry**
mars *v* ▷ **mar**
marsala [mar-**sah**-la] *n* (*pl* **-s**) dark sweet wine
marsh *n* (*pl* **-es**) low-lying wet land > **marshy** *adj* (**-shier, -shiest**)
marshal *n* (*pl* **-s**) officer of the highest rank ▶ *v* (**-s, -shalling, -shalled**) arrange in order
marshalled *v* ▷ **marshal**
marshalling *v* ▷ **marshal**
marshals *n, v* ▷ **marshal**
marshes *n* ▷ **marsh**
marshier *adj* ▷ **marsh**
marshiest *adj* ▷ **marsh**
marshmallow *n* (*pl* **-s**) spongy pink or white sweet
marshmallows *n* ▷ **marshmallow**
marshy *n* ▷ **marsh**
marsupial [mar-**soop**-ee-al] *n* (*pl* **-s**) animal that carries its young in a pouch, such as a kangaroo
marsupials *n* ▷ **marsupial**
mart *n* (*pl* **-s**) market
marts *n* ▷ **mart**
marten *n* (*pl* **-s**) weasel-like animal
martens *n* ▷ **marten**
martial *adj* of war, warlike
martian [**marsh**-an] *adj* of Mars ▶ *n* (*pl* **-s**) supposed inhabitant of Mars
martians *n* ▷ **martian**
martin *n* (*pl* **-s**) bird with a slightly forked tail
martins *n* ▷ **martin**
martinet *n* (*pl* **-s**) person who maintains strict discipline
martinets *n* ▷ **martinet**
martini *n* (*pl* **-s**) cocktail of vermouth and gin
martinis *n* ▷ **martini**
martyr *n* (*pl* **-s**) person who dies or suffers for his or her beliefs ▶ *v* (**-s, -ing, -ed**) make a martyr of > **martyrdom** *n* (*pl* **-s**)
martyrdom *n* ▷ **martyr**
martyrdoms *n* ▷ **martyr**
martyred *v* ▷ **martyr**
martyring *v* ▷ **martyr**
martyrs *n, v* ▷ **martyr**
marvel *v* (**-s, -velling, -velled**) be filled with wonder ▶ *n* wonderful thing
marvelled *v* ▷ **marvel**
marvelling *v* ▷ **marvel**
marvellous *adj* amazing
marvels *v* ▷ **marvel**
marzipan *n* (*pl* **-s**) paste of ground almonds, sugar, and egg whites
marzipans *n* ▷ **marzipan**
mascara *n* (*pl* **-s**) cosmetic for darkening the eyelashes
mascaras *n* ▷ **mascara**
mascot *n* (*pl* **-s**) person, animal, or thing supposed to bring good luck
mascots *n* ▷ **mascot**
masculine *adj* relating to males > **masculinity** *n* (*pl* **-ties**)
masculinities *n* ▷ **masculine**
masculinity *n* ▷ **masculine**
mash *n* (*pl* **-es**) (*Informal*) mashed potatoes ▶ *v* (**-es, -ing, -ed**) crush into a soft mass
mashed *v* ▷ **mash**
mashes *n, v* ▷ **mash**
mashing *v* ▷ **mash**
mask *n* (*pl* **-s**) covering for the face, as a disguise or protection ▶ *v* (**-s, -ing, -ed**) cover with a mask
masked *v* ▷ **mask**
masking *v* ▷ **mask**
masks *n, v* ▷ **mask**
masochism [**mass**-oh-kiz-zum] *n* (*pl* **-s**) condition in which (sexual) pleasure is obtained from feeling pain or from being humiliated > **masochist** *n* (*pl* **-s**) > **masochistic** *adj*
masochist *n* ▷ **masochism**
masochistic *n* ▷ **masochism**
masochists *n* ▷ **masochism**
mason *n* (*pl* **-s**) person who works with stone
masonic *adj* of Freemasonry
masonry *n* (*pl* **-ries**) stonework
masonries *n* (*pl* **-ries**) stonework
masons *n* ▷ **mason**
masque [**mask**] *n* (*pl* **-s**) (HIST) 16th–17th-century form of dramatic entertainment
masques *n* ▷ **masque**
masquerade [mask-er-**aid**] *n* (*pl* **-s**) deceptive show or pretence ▶ *v* (**-des, -ding, -ded**) pretend to be someone or something else
masqueraded *v* ▷ **masquerade**
masquerades *n, v* ▷ **masquerade**
masquerading *v* ▷ **masquerade**
mass *n* (*pl* **-es**) coherent body of matter ▶ *adj* large-scale ▶ *v* (**-es, -ing, -ed**) form into a mass
massacre [**mass**-a-ker] *n* (*pl* **-s**) indiscriminate killing of large numbers of people ▶ *v* (**-res, -ring, -red**) kill in large numbers

massacred *v* ▷ **massacre**
massacres *n, v* ▷ **massacre**
massacring *v* ▷ **massacre**
massage [**mass**-ahzh] *n* (*pl* **-s**) rubbing and kneading of parts of the body to reduce pain or stiffness ▶ *v* (**-ges, -ging, -ged**) give a massage to
massaged *v* ▷ **massage**
massages *n, v* ▷ **massage**
massaging *v* ▷ **massage**
massed *v* ▷ **mass**
masses *n, v* ▷ **mass**
masseur, *fem* **masseuse** *n* (*pl* **-s**) person who gives massages
masseurs *n* ▷ **masseur**
masseuse *n* ▷ **masseuses**
massing *v* ▷ **mass**
massive *adj* large and heavy
massif [**mass**-seef] *n* (*pl* **-s**) connected group of mountains
massifs *n* ▷ **massif**
mast[1] *n* (*pl* **-s**) tall pole for supporting something, esp. a ship's sails
mast[2] *n* (*pl* **-s**) fruit of the beech, oak, etc., used as pig fodder
masts *n* ▷ **mast**[1,2]
mastectomies *n* ▷ **mastectomy**
mastectomy [mass-**tek**-tom-ee] *n* (*pl* **-mies**) surgical removal of a breast
master *n* (*pl* **-s**) person in control, such as an employer or an owner of slaves or animals ▶ *adj* overall or controlling ▶ *v* (**-s, -ing, -ed**) acquire knowledge of or skill in
mastered *v* ▷ **master**
masterful *adj* domineering
masteries *n* ▷ **mastery**
mastering *v* ▷ **master**
masterly *adj* showing great skill
mastermind *v* plan and direct (a complex task) *n* person who plans and directs a complex task
masterpiece *n* outstanding work of art
masters *n, v* ▷ **master**
mastery *n* (*pl* **-ries**) expertise
mastic *n* (*pl* **-s**) gum obtained from certain trees
mastics *n* ▷ **mastic**
masticate *v* (**-tes, -ting, -ted**) chew > **mastication** *n* (*pl* **-s**)
masticated *v* ▷ **masticate**
masticates *v* ▷ **masticate**
masticating *v* ▷ **masticate**
mastication *n* ▷ **masticate**
mastications *n* ▷ **masticate**
mastiff *n* (*pl* **-s**) large dog
mastiffs *n* ▷ **mastiff**
mastitis *n* (*pl* **-tises**) inflammation of a breast or udder
mastitises *n* ▷ **mastitis**
mastodon *n* (*pl* **-s**) extinct elephant-like mammal
mastodons *n* ▷ **mastodon**
mastoid *n* (*pl* **-s**) projection of the bone behind the ear
mastoids *n* ▷ **mastoid**
masturbate *v* (**-tes, -ting, -ted**) fondle the genitals (of) > **masturbation** *n* (*pl* **-s**)
masturbated *v* ▷ **masturbate**
masturbates *v* ▷ **masturbate**
masturbating *v* ▷ **masturbate**
masturbation *n* ▷ **masturbate**
masturbations *n* ▷ **masturbate**
mat *n* (*pl* **-s**) piece of fabric used as a floor covering or to protect a surface ▶ *v* (**-s, -tting, -tted**) tangle or become tangled into a dense mass
matador *n* (*pl* **-s**) man who kills the bull in bullfights
matadors *n* ▷ **matador**
match[1] *n* (*pl* **-es**) contest in a game or sport ▶ *v* (**-es, -ing, -ed**) be exactly like, equal to, or in harmony with
match[2] *n* small stick with a tip which ignites when scraped on a rough surface > **matchbox** *n* (*pl* **-es**)
matchbox *n* ▷ **match**[2]
matchboxes *n* ▷ **match**[2]
matched *v* ▷ **match**[1]
matches *v* ▷ **match**[1] ▶ *n* ▷ **match**[1,2]
matching *v* ▷ **match**[1]
matchless *adj* unequalled
matchmaker *n* (*pl* **-s**) person who schemes to bring about a marriage > **matchmaking** *n* (*pl* **-s**) *adj*
matchmakers *n* ▷ **matchmaker**
matchmaking *n* ▷ **matchmaker**
matchmakings *n* ▷ **matchmaker**
matchstick *n* (*pl* **-s**) wooden part of a match ▶ *adj* (of drawn figures) thin and straight
matchsticks *n* ▷ **matchstick**
matchwood *n* (*pl* **-s**) small splinters
matchwoods *n* ▷ **matchwood**
mate[1] *n* (*pl* **-s**) (*Informal*) friend ▶ *v* (**-tes, -ting, -ted**) pair (animals) or (of animals) be paired for reproduction
mate[2] *n* (*pl* **-s**) checkmate ▶ *v* (**-tes, -ting, -ted**) (CHESS) checkmate
mated *v* ▷ **mate**[1,2]
mates *n, v* ▷ **mate**[1,2]
mating *v* ▷ **mate**[1,2]

material *n* (*pl* **-s**) substance of which a thing is made ▶ *adj* of matter or substance > **materialist** *adj, n* > **materialistic** *adj*
materialism *n* (*pl* **-s**) excessive interest in or desire for money and possessions
materialisms *n* ▷ **materialism**
materialist *adj, n* (*pl* **-s**) ▷ **material**
materialistic *adj* ▷ **material**
materialists *n* ▷ **material**
materialize *v* (**-zes, -zing, -zed**) actually happen > **materialization** *n* (*pl* **-s**)
materialization *n* ▷ **materialize**
materializations *n* ▷ **materialize**
materialized *v* ▷ **materialize**
materializes *v* ▷ **materialize**
materializing *v* ▷ **materialize**
materially *adv* considerably
materials *n* ▷ **material**
maternal *adj* of a mother ▶ *adj* of or for pregnant women
maternities *n* ▷ **maternity**
maternity *n* (*pl* **-ties**) motherhood
matey *adj* (**-tier, -tiest**) (BRIT) (*Informal*) friendly or intimate
mathematics *n* science of number, quantity, shape, and space > **mathematical** *adj* > **mathematically** *adv* > **mathematician** *n* (*pl* **-s**)
mathematical *adj* ▷ **mathematics**
mathematically *adv* ▷ **mathematics**
mathematician *n* ▷ **mathematics**
mathematicians *n* ▷ **mathematics**
maths *n* (*Informal*) mathematics
matier *adj* ▷ **matey**
matiest *adj* ▷ **matey**
matilda *n* (*pl* **-s**) (AUST HIST) swagman's bundle of belongings
matildas *n* ▷ **matilda**
matinée [**mat**-in-nay] *n* (*pl* **-s**) afternoon performance in a theatre or cinema
matinées *n* ▷ **matinée**
matins *pl n* early morning service in various Christian Churches
matriarch [**mate**-ree-ark] *n* (*pl* **-s**) female head of a tribe or family > **matriarchal** *adj*
matriarchal *n* ▷ **matriarch**
matriarchies *n* ▷ **matriarchy**
matriarchs *n* ▷ **matriarch**
matriarchy *n* (*pl* **-chies**) society governed by a female, in which descent is traced through the female line
matrices *n* ▷ **matrix**
matricide *n* (*pl* **-s**) crime of killing one's mother
matricides *n* ▷ **matricide**
matriculate *v* (**-tes, -ting, -ted**) enrol or be enrolled in a college or university > **matriculation** *n* (*pl* **-s**)
matriculated *v* ▷ **matriculate**
matriculates *v* ▷ **matriculate**
matriculating *v* ▷ **matriculate**
matriculation *n* ▷ **matriculate**
matriculations *n* ▷ **matriculate**
matrimonial *adj* ▷ **matrimony**
matrimonies *n* ▷ **matrimony**
matrimony *n* (*pl* **-nies**) marriage > **matrimonial** *adj*
matrix [**may**-trix] *n* (*pl* **-trices**) substance or situation in which something originates, takes form, or is enclosed
matron *n* (*pl* **-s**) staid or dignified married woman > **matronly** *adj*
matrons *n* ▷ **matron**
mats *n, v* ▷ **mat**
matt *adj* dull, not shiny
matted *v* ▷ **mat**
matter *n* (*pl* **-s**) substance of which something is made ▶ *v* (**-s, -ing, -ed**) be of importance
mattered *v* ▷ **matter**
mattering *v* ▷ **matter**
matters *n, v* ▷ **matter**
matting *v* ▷ **mat**
mattock *n* (*pl* **-s**) large pick with one of its blade ends flattened for loosening soil
mattocks *n* ▷ **mattock**
mattress *n* (*pl* **-es**) large stuffed flat case, often with springs, used on or as a bed
mattresses *n* ▷ **mattress**
mature *adj* fully developed or grown-up ▶ *v* (**-res, -ring, -red**) make or become mature > **maturation** *n* (*pl* **-s**)
maturation *n* ▷ **mature**
maturations *n* ▷ **mature**
matured *v* ▷ **mature**
matures *v* ▷ **mature**
maturing *v* ▷ **mature**
maturities *n* ▷ **maturity**
maturity *n* (*pl* **-ties**) state of being mature
maudlin *adj* foolishly or tearfully sentimental
maul *v* (**-s, -ing, -ed**) handle roughly
mauled *v* ▷ **maul**
mauling *v* ▷ **maul**
mauls *v* ▷ **maul**
maunder *v* (**-s, -ing, -ed**) talk or act aimlessly or idly
maundered *v* ▷ **maunder**
maundering *v* ▷ **maunder**
maunders *v* ▷ **maunder**
mausoleum [maw-so-**lee**-um] *n* (*pl* **-s**) stately tomb
mausoleums *n* ▷ **mausoleum**

mauve *adj* (**-r, -est**) pale purple
mauver *adj* ▷ **mauve**
mauvest *adj* ▷ **mauve**
maverick *n* (*pl* **-s**) ▶ *adj* independent and unorthodox (person)
mavericks *n* ▷ **maverick**
maw *n* (*pl* **-s**) animal's mouth, throat, or stomach
maws *n* ▷ **maw**
mawkish *adj* foolishly sentimental

> **max** *n* (**maxes**). Max is a short form of **maximum.** This is a useful word, particularly if you find yourself with an X toward the end of the game, with limited opportunity to play it. Max scores 12 points.

maxim *n* (*pl* **-s**) general truth or principle
maxima *n* ▷ **maximum**
maximal *adj* ▷ **maxim**
maxims *n* ▷ **maxim**
maximum *adj, n* (*pl* **-s, -ma**) greatest possible (amount or number) > **maximal** *adj*
maximize *v* (**-zes, -zing, -zed**) increase to a maximum
maximized *v* ▷ **maximize**
maximizes *v* ▷ **maximize**
maximizing *v* ▷ **maximize**
maximums *n* ▷ **maximum**
may[1] *v* (*past tense* **might**) used as an auxiliary to express possibility, permission, opportunity, etc.
may[2] *n* (*pl* **-s**) ▷ **hawthorn**
mays *n* ▷ **may**[2]
maybe *adv* perhaps, possibly
mayday *n* (*pl* **-s**) international radio distress signal
maydays *n* ▷ **mayday**
mayflies *n* ▷ **mayfly**
mayfly *n* (*pl* **-lies**) short-lived aquatic insect
mayhem *n* (*pl* **-s**) violent destruction or confusion
mayhems *n* ▷ **mayhem**
mayonnaise *n* (*pl* **-s**) creamy sauce of egg yolks, oil, and vinegar
mayonnaises *n* ▷ **mayonnaise**
mayor *n* (*pl* **-s**) head of a municipality
mayoralties *n* ▷ **mayoralty**
mayoralty *n* (*pl* **-ies**) (term of) office of a mayor
mayoress *n* (*pl* **-es**) mayor's wife
mayoresses *n* ▷ **mayoress**
mayors *n* ▷ **mayor**
maypole *n* (*pl* **-s**) pole set up for dancing round on the first day of May to celebrate spring
maypoles *n* ▷ **maypole**
maze *n* (*pl* **-s**) complex network of paths or lines designed to puzzle
mazes *n* ▷ **maze**
mazurka *n* (*pl* **-s**) lively Polish dance
mazurkas *n* ▷ **mazurka**
me *pron* ▷ **I**
mead *n* (*pl* **-s**) alcoholic drink made from honey
meads *n* ▷ **mead**
meadow *n* (*pl* **-s**) piece of grassland
meadows *n* ▷ **meadow**
meadowsweet *n* (*pl* **-s**) plant with dense heads of small fragrant flowers
meadowseets *n* ▷ **meadowsweet**
meagre *adj* scanty or insufficient
meal[1] *n* (*pl* **-s**) occasion when food is served and eaten
meal[2] *n* (*pl* **-s**) grain ground to powder > **mealy -lier, -liest**) ▶ *adj*
mealie *n* (*pl* **-s**) (S AFR) maize
mealier *adj* ▷ **meal**[2]
mealies *n* ▷ **mealie**
mealiest *adj* ▷ **meal**[2]
meals *n* ▷ **meal**[1,2]
mealy *adj* ▷ **meal**[2]
mealymouthed *adj* not outspoken enough
mean[1] *v* (**-s, -ing, meant**) intend to convey or express > **meaningful** *adj* > **meaningless** *adj*
mean[2] *adj* (**-er, -est**) miserly, ungenerous, or petty > **meanly** *adv* > **meanness** *n* (*pl* **-es**)
mean[3] *n* (*pl* **-s**) middle point between two extremes ▶ *pl* method by which something is done ▶ *adj* intermediate in size or quantity
meaner *adj* ▷ **mean**[2]
meanest *adj* ▷ **mean**[2]
meaning *n* (*pl* **-s**) sense, significance
meaningful *adj* ▷ **mean**[1]
meaningless *adj* ▷ **mean**[1]
meanings *n* ▷ **meaning**
meanly *adv* ▷ **mean**[2]
meanness *n* ▷ **mean**[2]
meannesses *n* ▷ **mean**[2]
means *v* ▷ **mean**[1] ▶ *n* ▷ **mean**[3]
meander [mee-**and**-er] *v* (**-s, -ing, -ed**) follow a winding course ▶ *n* (*pl* **-s**) winding course
meandered *v* ▷ **meander**
meandering *v* ▷ **meander**
meanders *v, n* ▷ **meander**
meantime *n* (*pl* **-s**) intervening period ▶ *adv* meanwhile
meantimes *n* ▷ **meantime**
meanwhile *adv* during the intervening period
measles *n* infectious disease producing red spots
measly *adj* (*Informal*) meagre
measure *n* (*pl* **-s**) size or quantity ▶ *v* (**-res, -ring, -red**) determine the size or quantity of

> measurable *adj*
measurable *adj* ▷ **measure**
measured *adj* slow and steady ▶ *v* ▷ **measure**
measurement *n* (*pl* **-s**) measuring
measures *n, v* ▷ **measure**
measuring *v* ▷ **measure**
meat *n* (*pl* **-s**) animal flesh as food
meatier *adj* ▷ **meaty**
meatiest *adj* ▷ **meaty**
meats *n* ▷ **meat**
meaty *adj* (**-tier, -tiest**) (tasting) of or like meat
mechanic *n* (*pl* **-s**) person skilled in repairing or operating machinery
mechanical *adj* of or done by machines **> mechanically** *adv*
mechanically *adv* ▷ **mechanical**
mechanics *n* scientific study of motion and force ▷ **mechanic**
mechanism *n* (*pl* **-s**) way a machine works
mechanisms *n* ▷ **mechanism**
mechanization *n* ▷ **mechanize**
mechanizations *n* ▷ **mechanism**
mechanize *v* (**-zes, -zing, -zed**) equip with machinery **> mechanization** *n* (*pl* **-s**)
mechanized *v* ▷ **mechanize**
mechanizes *v* ▷ **mechanize**
mechanizing *v* ▷ **mechanize**
medal *n* (*pl* **-s**) piece of metal with an inscription etc., given as a reward or memento
medallion *n* (*pl* **-s**) disc-shaped ornament worn on a chain round the neck
medallions *n* ▷ **medallion**
medallist *n* (*pl* **-s**) winner of a medal
medallists *n* ▷ **medallist**
medals *n* ▷ **medal**
meddle *v* (**-les, -ling, -led**) interfere annoyingly **> meddler** *n* (*pl* **-s**) **> meddlesome** *adj*
meddled *v* ▷ **meddle**
meddler *n* ▷ **meddle**
meddlers *n* ▷ **meddle**
meddles *v* ▷ **meddle**
meddlesome *adj* ▷ **meddle**
meddling *v* ▷ **meddle**
media *n* (*pl* **-iae**) ▷ **medium** the mass media collectively
mediae *n* ▷ **media**
mediaeval *adj* ▷ **medieval**
medial *adj* of or in the middle
median *adj, n* (*pl* **-s**) middle (point or line)
medians *n* ▷ **median**
mediate *v* (**-tes, -ting, -ted**) intervene in a dispute to bring about agreement **> mediation** *n* (*pl* **-s**) **> mediator** *n* (*pl* **-s**)
mediated *v* ▷ **mediate**
mediates *v* ▷ **mediate**
mediating *v* ▷ **mediate**
mediation *n* ▷ **mediate**
mediations *n* ▷ **mediate**
mediator *n* ▷ **mediate**
mediators *n* ▷ **mediate**
medic *n* (*pl* **-s**) (*Informal*) doctor or medical student
medics *n* ▷ **medic**
medical *adj* of the science of medicine ▶ *n* (*pl* **-s**) (*Informal*) medical examination **> medically** *adv*
medically *adv* ▷ **medical**
medicals *n* ▷ **medical**
medicate *v* (**-tes, -ting, -ted**) treat with a medicinal substance
medicated *v* ▷ **medicate**
medicates *v* ▷ **medicate**
medicating *v* ▷ **medicate**
medication *n* (*pl* **-s**) (treatment with) a medicinal substance
medications *n* ▷ **medication**
medicine *n* (*pl* **-s**) substance used to treat disease
medicinal [med-**diss**-in-al] *adj* having therapeutic properties
medicines *n* ▷ **medicine**
medieval [med-ee-**eve**-al] *adj* of the Middle Ages
mediocre [mee-dee-**oak**-er] *adj* average in quality **> mediocrity** [mee-dee-**ok**-rit-ee] ▶ *n* (*pl* **-ties**)
mediocrities *n* ▷ **mediocre**
mediocrity *n* ▷ **mediocre**
meditate *v* (**-tes, -ting, -ted**) reflect deeply, esp. on spiritual matters **> meditation** *n* (*pl* **-s**) **> meditative** *adj* **> meditatively** *adv* **> meditator** *n* (*pl* **-s**)
meditated *v* ▷ **meditate**
meditates *v* ▷ **meditate**
meditating *v* ▷ **meditate**
meditation *n* ▷ **meditate**
meditations *n* ▷ **meditate**
meditative *adj* ▷ **meditate**
meditatively *adv* ▷ **meditate**
meditator *n* ▷ **meditate**
meditators *n* ▷ **meditate**
medium *adj* midway between extremes, average ▶ *n* (*pl* **-dia, -diums**) middle state, degree, or condition
mediums *n* ▷ **medium**
medlar *n* (*pl* **-s**) apple-like fruit of a small tree, eaten when it begins to decay
medlars *n* ▷ **medlar**
medley *n* (*pl* **-s**) miscellaneous mixture

medleys *n* ▷ **medley**
medulla [mid-**dull**-la] *n* (*pl* **-las, -lae**) marrow, pith, or inner tissue
medullae *n* ▷ **medulla**
medullas *n* ▷ **medulla**
meek *adj* (**-er, -est**) submissive or humble > **meekly** *adv* > **meekness** *n* (*pl* **-es**)
meeker *adj* ▷ **meek**
meekest *adj* ▷ **meek**
meekly *adv* ▷ **meek**
meekness *n* ▷ **meek**
meeknesses *n* ▷ **meek**
meerkat *n* (*pl* **-s**) S African mongoose
meerkats *n* ▷ **meerkat**
meerschaum [**meer**-shum] *n* (*pl* **-s**) white substance like clay
meerschaums *n* ▷ **meerschaum**
meet[1] *v* (**-s, meeting, met**) come together (with) ▶ *n* (*pl* **-s**) meeting, esp. a sports meeting
meet[2] *adj* (**-er, -est**) (*Obs*) fit or suitable
meeter *adj* ▷ **meet[2]**
meetest *adj* ▷ **meet[2]**
meeting *n* (*pl* **-s**) coming together ▶ *v* ▷ **meet[1]**
meets *v, n* ▷ **meek[1]**
megabyte *n* (*pl* **-s**) (COMPUTERS) 2^{20} or 1 048 576 bytes
megabytes *n* ▷ **megabyte**
megahertz *n* one million hertz
megalith *n* (*pl* **-s**) great stone, esp. as part of a prehistoric monument > **megalithic** *adj*
megalithic *adj* ▷ **megalith**
megaliths *n* ▷ **megalith**
megalomania *n* (*pl* **-s**) craving for or mental delusions of power > **megalomaniac** *adj, n* (*pl* **-s**)
megalomaniac *n* ▷ **megalomania**
megalomaniacs *n* ▷ **megalomania**
megalomanias *n* ▷ **megalomania**
megaphone *n* (*pl* **-s**) cone-shaped instrument used to amplify the voice
megaphones *n* ▷ **megaphone**
megapode *n* (*pl* **-s**) bird of Australia, New Guinea, and adjacent islands
megapodes *n* ▷ **megapode**
megaton *n* (*pl* **-s**) explosive power equal to that of one million tons of TNT
megatons *n* ▷ **megaton**
melaleuca [mel-a-**loo**-ka] *n* (*pl* **-s**) Australian shrub or tree with a white trunk and black branches
melaleucas *n* ▷ **melaleuca**
melancholia [mel-an-**kole**-lee-a] *n* (*pl* **-s**) state of depression
melancholias *n* ▷ **melancholia**
melancholic *adj* ▷ **melancholy**
melancholies *n* ▷ **melancholy**
melancholy [**mel**-an-kol-lee] *n* (*pl* **-lies**) sadness or gloom ▶ *adj* sad or gloomy > **melancholic** *adj, n* (*pl* **-s**)
melange [may-**lahnzh**] *n* (*pl* **-s**) mixture
melanges *n* ▷ **melange**
melanin *n* (*pl* **-s**) dark pigment found in the hair, skin, and eyes of humans and animals
melanins *n* ▷ **melanin**
mêlée [**mel**-lay] *n* (*pl* **-s**) noisy confused fight or crowd
mêlées *n* ▷ **mêlée**
mellifluous [mel-**lif**-flew-uss] *adj* (of sound) smooth and sweet
mellow *adj* soft, not harsh ▶ *v* (**-s, -ing, -ed**) make or become mellow
mellowed *v* ▷ **mellow**
mellowing *v* ▷ **mellow**
mellows *v* ▷ **mellow**
melodic [mel-**lod**-ik] *adj* of melody
melodious [mel-**lode**-ee-uss] *adj* pleasing to the ear
melodrama *n* (*pl* **-s**) play full of extravagant action and emotion > **melodramatic** *adj*
melodramas *n* ▷ **melodrama**
melodramatic *adj* ▷ **melodrama**
melody *n* (*pl* **-dies**) series of musical notes which make a tune
melon *n* (*pl* **-s**) large round juicy fruit with a hard rind
melons *n* ▷ **melon**
melt *v* (**-s, -ing, -ed**) (cause to) become liquid by heat
meltdown *n* (*pl* **-s**) (in a nuclear reactor) melting of the fuel rods, with the possible release of radiation
meltdowns *n* ▷ **meltdown**
melted *v* ▷ **melt**
melting *v* ▷ **melt**
melts *v* ▷ **melt**
member *n* (*pl* **-s**) individual making up a body or society > **membership** *n* (*pl* **-s**)
members *n* ▷ **member**
membership *n* ▷ **member**
memberships *n* ▷ **member**
membrane *n* (*pl* **-s**) thin flexible tissue in a plant or animal body > **membranous** *adj*
membranes *n* ▷ **membrane**
membranous *adj* ▷ **membrane**
memento *n* (*pl* **-tos, -toes**) thing serving to remind, souvenir
mementoes *n* ▷ **memento**
mementos *n* ▷ **memento**
memo *n* (*pl* **-s**) ▷ **memorandum**

memos *n* ▷ **memo**
memoir [**mem**-wahr] *n* (*pl* **-s**) biography or historical account based on personal knowledge ▸ *pl* collection of these
memoirs *n* ▷ **memoir**
memorable *adj* worth remembering, noteworthy > **memorably** *adv*
memorably *adv* ▷ **memorable**
memoranda *n* ▷ **memorandum**
memorandum *n* (*pl* **-dums, -da**) written record or communication within a business
memorandums *n* ▷ **memorandum**
memorial *n* (*pl* **-s**) something serving to commemorate a person or thing ▸ *adj* serving as a memorial
memorials *n* ▷ **memorandum**
memorize *v* (**-zes, -zing, -zed**) commit to memory
memorized *v* ▷ **memorize**
memorizes *v* ▷ **memorize**
memorizing *v* ▷ **memorize**
memory *n* (*pl* **-ries**) ability to remember
men *n* ▷ **man**
menace *n* (*pl* **-s**) threat ▸ *v* (**-ces, -cing, -ced**) threaten, endanger > **menacing** *adj*
menaced *v* ▷ **menace**
menaces *n, v* ▷ **menace**
menacing *v, adj* ▷ **menace**
ménage [may-**nahzh**] *n* (*pl* **-s**) household
ménages *n* ▷ **ménage**
menagerie [min-**naj**-er-ee] *n* (*pl* **-s**) collection of wild animals for exhibition
menageries *n* ▷ **menagerie**
mend *v* (**-s, -ing, -ed**) repair or patch ▸ *n* (*pl* **-s**) mended area
mendacious *adj* ▷ **mendacity**
mendacities *n* ▷ **mendacity**
mendacity *n* (*pl* **-ties**) (tendency to) untruthfulness > **mendacious** *adj*
mended *v* ▷ **mend**
mendicant *adj* begging ▸ *n* (*pl* **-s**) beggar
mendicants *n* ▷ **mendicant**
mending *v* ▷ **mend**
mends *v, n* ▷ **mend**
menhir [**men**-hear] *n* (*pl* **-s**) single upright prehistoric stone
menhirs *n* ▷ **menhir**
menial [**mean**-nee-al] *adj* involving boring work of low status ▸ *n* (*pl* **-s**) person with a menial job
menials *n* ▷ **menial**
meningitis [men-in-**jite**-iss] *n* (*pl* **-es**) inflammation of the membranes of the brain
meningitises *n* ▷ **meningitis**
meniscus *n* (*pl* **-ci**) curved surface of a liquid
menisci *n* ▷ **meniscus**
menopausal *adj* ▷ **menopause**
menopause *n* (*pl* **-s**) time when a woman's menstrual cycle ceases > **menopausal** *adj*
menopauses *n* ▷ **menopause**
menservants *n* ▷ **manservant**
menstruation *n* (*pl* **-s**) approximately monthly discharge of blood and cellular debris from the womb of a nonpregnant woman > **menstruate** *v* (**-tes, -ting, -ted**) > **menstrual** *adj*
menstrual *adj* ▷ **menstruation**
menstruated *v* ▷ **menstruation**
menstruates *v* ▷ **menstruation**
menstruating *v* ▷ **menstruation**
menstruations *n* ▷ **menstruation**
mensuration *n* (*pl* **-s**) measuring, esp. in geometry
mensurations *n* ▷ **mensuration**
mental *adj* of, in, or done by the mind > **mentally** *adv*
mentalities *n* ▷ **mentality**
mentality *n* (*pl* **-ties**) way of thinking
mentally *adv* ▷ **mental**
menthol *n* (*pl* **-s**) organic compound found in peppermint, used medicinally
menthols *n* ▷ **menthol**
mention *v* (**-s, -ing, -ed**) refer to briefly ▸ *n* (*pl* **-s**) brief reference to a person or thing
mentioned *v* ▷ **mention**
mentioning *v* ▷ **mention**
mentions *v, n* ▷ **mention**
mentor *n* (*pl* **-s**) adviser or guide
mentors *n* ▷ **mentor**
menu *n* (*pl* **-s**) list of dishes to be served, or from which to order
menus *n* ▷ **menu**
mercantile *adj* of trade or traders
mercenaries *n* ▷ **mercenary**
mercenary *adj* influenced by greed ▸ *n* (*pl* **-ries**) hired soldier
merchandises *n* ▷ **merchandise**
merchandise *n* (*pl* **-s**) commodities
merchant *n* (*pl* **-s**) person engaged in trade, wholesale trader
merchantman *n* (*pl* **-men**) trading ship
merchantmen *n* ▷ **merchantman**
merchants *n* ▷ **merchant**
merciful *adj* compassionate
merciless *adj* ▷ **mercy**
mercurial *adj* lively, changeable
mercuries *n* ▷ **mercury**
mercury *n* (*pl* **-ries**) (CHEM) silvery liquid metal
mercy *n* (*pl* **-cies**) compassionate treatment of an offender or enemy who is in one's power

>**merciless** *adj*
mere[1] *adj* (**-r, -st**) nothing more than >**merely** *adv*
mere[2] *n* (*pl* **-s**) (BRIT) (*Obs*) lake
merely *adv* ▷ **mere**[1]
merer *adj* ▷ **mere**[1]
meres *n* ▷ **mere**[2]
merest *adj* ▷ **mere**[1]
meretricious *adj* superficially or garishly attractive but of no real value
merganser [mer-**gan**-ser] *n* (*pl* **-s**) large crested diving duck
mergansers *n* ▷ **merganser**
merge *v* (**-ges, -ging, -ged**) combine or blend
merged *v* ▷ **merge**
merger *n* (*pl* **-s**) combination of business firms into one
merges *v* ▷ **merge**
merging *v* ▷ **merge**
mergers *n* ▷ **merger**
meridian *n* (*pl* **-s**) imaginary circle of the earth passing through both poles
meridians *n* ▷ **meridian**
meringue [mer-**rang**] *n* (*pl* **-s**) baked mixture of egg whites and sugar
meringues *n* ▷ **meringue**
merino *n* (*pl* **-s**) breed of sheep with fine soft wool
merinos *n* ▷ **merino**
merit *n* (*pl* **-s**) excellence or worth ▶ *pl* admirable qualities ▶ *v* (**-s, -ing, -ed**) deserve
merited *v* ▷ **merit**
meriting *v* ▷ **merit**
meritocracies *n* ▷ **meritocracy**
meritocracy [mer-it-**tok**-rass-ee] *n* (*pl* **-s**) rule by people of superior talent or intellect
meritorious *adj* deserving praise
merits *n, v* ▷ **merit**
merlin *n* (*pl* **-s**) small falcon
merlins *n* ▷ **merlin**
mermaid *n* (*pl* **-s**) imaginary sea creature with the upper part of a woman and the lower part of a fish
mermaids *n* ▷ **mermaid**
merrier *adj* ▷ **merry**
merriest *adj* ▷ **merry**
merrily *adv* ▷ **merry**
merriment *n* ▷ **merry**
merriments *n* ▷ **merry**
merry *adj* (**-rrier, -rriest**) cheerful or jolly >**merrily** *adv* >**merriment** *n* (*pl* **-s**)
merrymaking *n* (*pl* **-s**) noisy, cheerful celebrations or fun
merrymakings *n* ▷ **merrymaking**
mesdames *n* ▷ **madame**
mesdemoiselles *n* ▷ **mademoiselle**
mesh *n* (*pl* **-es**) network or net ▶ *v* (**-es, -ing, -ed**) (of gear teeth) engage
meshed *v* ▷ **mesh**
meshes *n, v* ▷ **mesh**
meshing *v* ▷ **mesh**
mesmerize *v* (**-zes, -zing, -zed**) hold spellbound
mesmerized *v* ▷ **mesmerize**
mesmerizes *v* ▷ **mesmerize**
mesmerizing *v* ▷ **mesmerize**
meson [**mee**-zon] *n* (*pl* **-s**) elementary atomic particle
mesons *n* ▷ **meson**
mess *n* (*pl* **-es**) untidy or dirty confusion ▶ *v* (**-es, -ing, -ed**) muddle or dirty
message *n* (*pl* **-s**) communication sent
messages *n* ▷ **message**
messaging *n* (*pl* **-s**) sending and receiving of textual communications by mobile phone
messagings *n* ▷ **message**
messed *v* ▷ **mess**
messeigneurs *n* ▷ **monseigneur**
messenger *n* (*pl* **-s**) bearer of a message
messengers *n* ▷ **messenger**
messes *n, v* ▷ **mess**
messiah *n* (*pl* **-s**) promised deliverer >**messianic** *adj*
messiahs *n* ▷ **messiah**
messianic *adj* ▷ **messiah**
messier *adj* ▷ **messy**
messiest *adj* ▷ **messy**
messieurs *n* ▷ **monsieur**
messily *adv* ▷ **messy**
messing *v* ▷ **mess**
messy *adj* (**-ssier, -ssiest**) dirty, confused, or untidy >**messily** *adv*
met *v* ▷ **meet**[1]
metabolic *adj* ▷ **metabolism**
metabolism [met-**tab**-oh-liz-zum] *n* (*pl* **-s**) chemical processes of a living body >**metabolic** *adj*
metabolisms *n* ▷ **metabolism**
metabolize *v* (**-zes, -zing, -zed**) produce or be produced by metabolism
metabolized *v* ▷ **metabolize**
metabolizes *v* ▷ **metabolize**
metabolizing *v* ▷ **metabolize**
metal *n* (*pl* **-s**) chemical element, such as iron or copper, that is malleable and capable of conducting heat and electricity >**metallic** *adj*
metallic *adj* ▷ **metal**
metallurgical *adj* ▷ **metallurgy**
metallurgist *n* ▷ **metallurgy**
metallurgists *n* ▷ **metallurgy**

metallurgy *n* (*pl* **-gies**) scientific study of the structure, properties, extraction, and refining of metals > **metallurgical** *adj* > **metallurgist** *n* (*pl* **-s**)
metals *n* ▷ **metal**
metamorphic *adj* (of rocks) changed in texture or structure by heat and pressure
metamorphose *v* (**-ses, -sing, -sed**) transform
metamorphosed *v* ▷ **metamorphose**
metamorphoses *n, v* ▷ **metamorphosis**
metamorphosing *v* ▷ **metamorphose**
metamorphosis [met-a-**more**-foss-is] *n* (*pl* **-ses**) [-foss-eez] change of form or character
metaphor *n* (*pl* **-s**) figure of speech in which a term is applied to something it does not literally denote in order to imply a resemblance > **metaphorical** *adj* > **metaphorically** *adv*
metaphorically *adv* ▷ **metaphor**
metaphors *n* ▷ **metaphor**
metaphysical *adj* ▷ **metaphysics**
metaphysics *n* branch of philosophy concerned with being and knowing > **metaphysical** *adj*
mete *v* (**-tes, -ting, -ted**) (*usu. with* **out**) deal out as punishment
meted *v* ▷ **mete**
meteor *n* (*pl* **-s**) small fast-moving heavenly body, visible as a streak of incandescence if it enters the earth's atmosphere
meteoric [meet-ee-**or**-rik] *adj* of a meteor
meteorite *n* (*pl* **-s**) meteor that has fallen to earth
meteorites *n* ▷ **meteorite**
meteorological *adj* ▷ **meteorology**
meteorologies *n* ▷ **meteorology**
meteorologist *n* ▷ **meteorology**
meteorologists *n* ▷ **meteorology**
meteorology *n* (*pl* **-gies**) study of the earth's atmosphere, esp. for weather forecasting > **meteorological** *adj* > **meteorologist** *n* (*pl* **-s**)
meteors *n* ▷ **meteor**
meter *n* (*pl* **-s**) instrument for measuring and recording something, such as the consumption of gas or electricity ▶ *v* (**-s, -ing, -ed**) measure by meter
meters *n, v* ▷ **meter**
metes *v* ▷ **mete**
meting *v* ▷ **mete**
methane *n* (*pl* **-s**) colourless inflammable gas
methanes *n* ▷ **methane**
methanol *n* (*pl* **-s**) colourless poisonous liquid used as a solvent and fuel (*also* **methyl alcohol**)
methanols *n* ▷ **methanol**
methinks *v* (*past tense* **methought**) (*Obs*) it seems to me
method *n* (*pl* **-s**) way or manner
methodical *adj* orderly > **methodically** *adv*
methodically *adv* ▷ **methodical**
methodism *n* ▷ **methodist**
methodisms *n* ▷ **methodist**
methodist *n* (*pl* **-s**) member of any of the Protestant churches originated by John Wesley and his followers ▶ *adj* of methodists or their Church > **methodism** *n* (*pl* **-s**)
methodists *n* ▷ **methodist**
methodologies *n* ▷ **methodology**
methodology *n* (*pl* **-gies**) particular method or procedure
methods *n* ▷ **method**
meths *n* (*Informal*) methylated spirits
methyl *n* (*pl* **-s**) (compound containing) a saturated hydrocarbon group of atoms
methyls *n* ▷ **methyl**
meticulous *adj* very careful about details > **meticulously** *adv*
meticulously *adv* ▷ **meticulous**
métier [**met**-ee-ay] *n* (*pl* **-s**) profession or trade
métiers *n* ▷ **métier**
metonymies *n* ▷ **metonymy**
metonymy [mit-**on**-im-ee] *n* (*pl* **-mies**) figure of speech in which one thing is replaced by another associated with it, such as 'the Crown' for 'the queen'
metre *n* (*pl* **-s**) basic unit of length equal to about 1.094 yards (100 centimetres)
metres *n* ▷ **metre**
metric *adj* of the decimal system of weights and measures based on the metre
metrical *adj* of measurement
metrication *n* (*pl* **-s**) conversion to the metric system
metrications *n* ▷ **metrication**
metronome *n* (*pl* **-s**) instrument which marks musical time by means of a ticking pendulum
metronomes *n* ▷ **metronome**
metropolis [mit-**trop**-oh-liss] *n* (*pl* **-es**) chief city of a country or region
metropolises *n* ▷ **metropolis**
metropolitan *adj* of a metropolis
metrosexual *adj, n* (*pl* **-s**) (of) a heterosexual man who is preoccupied with his appearance
metrosexuals *n* ▷ **metrosexual**
mettle *n* (*pl* **-s**) courage or spirit
mettles *n* ▷ **mettle**
mew *n* (*pl* **-s**) cry of a cat ▶ *v* (**-s, -ing, -ed**) utter this cry
mewed *v* ▷ **mew**
mewing *v* ▷ **mew**

mews *n, v* ▷ **mew**

> **mezquit** *n* (**mezquit**). A mezquit is a small spiny tree or shrub. With its combination of Q and Z, mezquit is a very high-scoring word. As it contains seven letters, mezquit can earn you a bonus of 50 points if you manage to use all the letters on your rack to form it. Mezquit scores 28 points.

mezzanine [**mez**-zan-een] *n* (*pl* **-s**) intermediate storey, esp. between the ground and first floor
mezzanines *n* ▷ **mezzanine**
mezzotint [**met**-so-tint] *n* (*pl* **-s**) method of engraving by scraping the roughened surface of a metal plate
mezzotints *n* ▷ **mezzotint**

> **mi** *n* (**mis**). Mi is the third degree of a major scale in music. This isn't a high-scoring word, but can be very helpful when you want to form words in more than one direction. Mi scores 4 points.

miaow [mee-**ow**] *n* (*pl* **-s**) ▶ *v* (**-s, -ing, -wed**) ▷ **mew**
miaowed *v* ▷ **miaow**
miaowing *v* ▷ **miaow**
miaows *v, n* ▷ **miaow**
miasma [mee-**azz**-ma] *n* (*pl* **-mata**) unwholesome or foreboding atmosphere
miasmata *n* ▷ **miasma**
mica [**my**-ka] *n* (*pl* **-s**) glasslike mineral used as an electrical insulator
micas *n* ▷ **mica**
mice *n* ▷ **mouse**
microbe *n* (*pl* **-s**) minute organism, esp. one causing disease > **microbial** *adj*
microbes *n* ▷ **microbe**
microbial *adj* ▷ **microbe**
microchip *n* (*pl* **-s**) small wafer of silicon containing electronic circuits
microchips *n* ▷ **microchip**
microcomputer *n* (*pl* **-s**) computer with a central processing unit contained in one or more silicon chips
microcomputers *n* ▷ **microcomputer**
microcosm *n* (*pl* **-s**) miniature representation of something
microcosms *n* ▷ **microcosm**
microfiche [**my**-kroh-feesh] *n* (*pl* **-s**) microfilm in sheet form
microfiches *n* ▷ **microfiche**
microfilm *n* (*pl* **-s**) miniaturized recording of books or documents on a roll of film
microfilms *n* ▷ **microfilm**
microlight *n* (*pl* **-s**) very small light private aircraft with large wings
microlights *n* ▷ **microlight**
micrometer [my-**krom**-it-er] *n* (*pl* **-s**) instrument for measuring very small distances or angles
micrometers *n* ▷ **micrometer**
micron [**my**-kron] *n* (*pl* **-s**) one millionth of a metre
microns *n* ▷ **micron**
microorganism *n* (*pl* **-ms**) organism of microscopic size
microorganisms *n* ▷ **microorganism**
microphone *n* (*pl* **-s**) instrument for amplifying or transmitting sounds
microphones *n* ▷ **microphone**
microprocessor *n* (*pl* **-s**) integrated circuit acting as the central processing unit in a small computer
microprocessors *n* ▷ **microprocessor**
microscope *n* (*pl* **-s**) instrument with lens(es) which produces a magnified image of a very small object > **microscopic** *adj* too small to be seen except with a microscope > **microscopically** *adv*
microscopes *n* ▷ **microscope**
microscopic *adj* ▷ **microscope**
microscopically *adv* ▷ **microscope**
microscopies *n* ▷ **microscopy**
microscopy *n* (*pl* **-pies**) use of a microscope
microsurgeries *n* ▷ **microsurgery**
microsurgery *n* (*pl* **-ries**) intricate surgery using a special microscope and miniature precision instruments
microwave *n* (*pl* **-s**) electromagnetic wave with a wavelength of a few centimetres, used in radar and cooking ▶ *v* (**-ves, -ving, -ved**) cook in a microwave oven
microwaved *v* ▷ **microwave**
microwaves *n, v* ▷ **microwave**
microwaving *v* ▷ **microwave**
mid *adj* intermediate, middle
midday *n* (*pl* **-s**) noon
middays *n* ▷ **midday**
midden *n* (*pl* **-s**) (BRIT & AUST) dunghill or rubbish heap
middens *n* ▷ **midden**
middle *adj* equidistant from two extremes ▶ *n* (*pl* **-s**) middle point or part
middleman *n* (*pl* **-men**) trader who buys from the producer and sells to the consumer
middlemen *n* ▷ **middleman**
middles *n* ▷ **middle**
middleweight *n* (*pl* **-s**) boxer weighing up to 160lb (professional) or 75kg (amateur)
middleweights *n* ▷ **middleweight**

middling *adj* mediocre
midge *n* (*pl* **-s**) small mosquito-like insect
midges *n* ▷ **midge**
midget *n* (*pl* **-s**) very small person or thing
midgets *n* ▷ **midget**
midland *n* (*pl* **-s**) (BRIT, AUST & US) middle part of a country
midlands *n* ▷ **midland**
midnight *n* (*pl* **-s**) twelve o'clock at night
midnights *n* ▷ **midnight**
midriff *n* (*pl* **-s**) middle part of the body
midriffs *n* ▷ **midriff**
midshipman *n* (*pl* **-men**) naval officer of the lowest commissioned rank
midshipmen *n* ▷ **midshipman**
midsummer *n* (*pl* **-s**) middle of summer
midsummers *n* ▷ **midsummer**
midway *adj*, *adv* halfway
midwife *n* (*pl* **-wives**) trained person who assists at childbirth > **midwifery** *n* (*pl* **-ries**)
midwiferies *n* ▷ **midwife**
midwifery *n* ▷ **midwife**
midwives *n* ▷ **midwife**
midwinter *n* (*pl* **-s**) middle or depth of winter
midwinters *n* ▷ **midwinter**
mien [**mean**] *n* (*pl* **-s**) (*Lit*) person's bearing, demeanour, or appearance
miens *n* ▷ **mien**
miffed *adj* (*Informal*) offended or upset
might[1] ▷ **may**
might[2] *n* (*pl* **-s**) power or strength
mightier *adj* ▷ **mighty**
mightiest *adj* ▷ **mighty**
mightily *adv* ▷ **mighty**
mighty *adj* (**-tier, -tiest**) powerful ▶ *adv* (US & AUST) (*Informal*) very > **mightily** *adv*
migraine [**mee**-grain] *n* (*pl* **-s**) severe headache, often with nausea and visual disturbances
migraines *n* ▷ **migraine**
migrant *n* (*pl* **-s**) person or animal that moves from one place to another ▶ *adj* moving from one place to another
migrants *n* ▷ **migrant**
migrate *v* (**-tes, -ting, -ted**) move from one place to settle in another > **migration** *n* (*pl* **-s**)
migrated *v* ▷ **migrate**
migrates *v* ▷ **migrate**
migrating *v* ▷ **migrate**
migration *n* ▷ **migrate**
migrations *n* ▷ **migrate**
migratory *adj* (of an animal) migrating every year
mike *n* (*pl* **-s**) (*Informal*) microphone
mikes *n* ▷ **mike**
milch *adj* (CHIEFLY BRIT) (of a cow) giving milk
mild *adj* (**-er, -est**) not strongly flavoured > **mildly** *adv* > **mildness** *n* (*pl* **-es**)
milder *adj* ▷ **mild**
mildest *adj* ▷ **mild**
mildew *n* (*pl* **-s**) destructive fungus on plants or things exposed to damp > **mildewed** *adj*
mildewed *adj* ▷ **mildew**
mildews *n* ▷ **mildew**
mildly *adv* ▷ **mild**
mildness *n* ▷ **mild**
mildnesses *n* ▷ **mild**
mile *n* (*pl* **-s**) unit of length equal to 1760 yards or 1.609 kilometres
mileage *n* (*pl* **-s**) distance travelled in miles
mileages *n* ▷ **mileage**
mileometer *n* (*pl* **-s**) (BRIT) device that records the number of miles a vehicle has travelled
mileometers *n* ▷ **mileometer**
miles *n* ▷ **mile**
milestone *n* (*pl* **-s**) significant event
milestones *n* ▷ **milestone**
milieu [meal-**yer**] *n* (*pl* **milieux, milieus**) [meal-**yerz**] environment or surroundings
milieus *n* ▷ **milieu**
milieux *n* ▷ **milieu**
militancies *n* ▷ **militant**
militancy *n* ▷ **militant**
militant *adj* aggressive or vigorous in support of a cause > **militancy** *n* (*pl* **-cies**)
militants *n* ▷ **militant**
militaries *n* ▷ **military**
militarism *n* (*pl* **-s**) belief in the use of military force and methods
militarisms *n* ▷ **militarism**
militarist *n* ▷ **military**
militarists *n* ▷ **military**
militarized *adj* ▷ **military**
military *adj* of or for soldiers, armies, or war ▶ *n* (*pl* **-ries**) armed services > **militarist** *n* (*pl* **-s**) > **militarized** *adj*
militate *v* (**-tes, -ting, -ted**) (*usu. with* **against** *or* **for**) have a strong influence or effect
militated *v* ▷ **militate**
militates *v* ▷ **militate**
militating *v* ▷ **militate**
militia [mill-**ish**-a] *n* (*pl* **-s**) military force of trained citizens for use in emergency only
militias *n* ▷ **militia**
milk *n* (*pl* **-s**) white fluid produced by female mammals to feed their young ▶ *v* (**-s, -ing, -ed**) draw milk from > **milky** *adj* (**-kier, -kiest**)
milked *v* ▷ **milk**
milkier *adj* ▷ **milk**
milkiest *adj* ▷ **milk**
milking *v* ▷ **milk**

milkmaid *n* (*pl* **-s**) (esp. in former times) woman who milks cows
milkmaids *n* ▷ **milkmaid**
milkman *n* (*pl* **-men**) (BRIT, AUST & NZ) man who delivers milk to people's houses
milkmen *n* ▷ **milkman**
milks *n, v* ▷ **milk**
milkshake *n* (*pl* **-s**) frothy flavoured cold milk drink
milkshakes *n* ▷ **milkshake**
milksop *n* (*pl* **-s**) feeble man
milksops *n* ▷ **milk**
milky *adj* ▷ **milk**
mill *n* (*pl* **-s**) factory ▶ *v* (**-s, -ing, -ed**) grind, press, or process in or as if in a mill
milled *v* ▷ **mill**
millennium *n* (*pl* **-nnia, -nniums**) period of a thousand years
millennia *n* ▷ **mill**
millenniums *n* ▷ **mill**
miller *n* (*pl* **-s**) person who works in a mill
millers *n* ▷ **miller**
millet *n* (*pl* **-s**) type of cereal grass
millets *n* ▷ **millet**
millibar *n* (*pl* **-s**) unit of atmospheric pressure
millibars *n* ▷ **millibar**
millimetre *n* (*pl* **-s**) thousandth part of a metre
millimetres *n* ▷ **millimetre**
milliner *n* (*pl* **-s**) maker or seller of women's hats > **millinery** *n* (*pl* **-ries**)
millineries *n* ▷ **milliner**
milliners *n* ▷ **milliner**
millinery *n* ▷ **milliner**
milling *v* ▷ **mill**
million *n* (*pl* **-s**) one thousand thousands > **millionth** *adj, n* (*pl* **-s**)
millionaire *n* (*pl* **-s**) person who owns at least a million pounds, dollars, etc.
millionaires *n* ▷ **millionaire**
millions *n* ▷ **million**
millionths *n* ▷ **million**
millipede *n* (*pl* **-s**) small animal with a jointed body and many pairs of legs
millipedes *n* ▷ **millipede**
mills *n, v* ▷ **mill**
millstone *n* (*pl* **-s**) flat circular stone for grinding corn
millstones *n* ▷ **millstone**
millwheel *n* (*pl* **-s**) waterwheel that drives a mill
millwheels *n* ▷ **millwheel**
milometer *n* (*pl* **-s**) (BRIT) ▷ **mileometer**
milometers *n* ▷ **milometer**
milt *n* (*pl* **-s**) sperm of fish
milts *n* ▷ **milt**
mime *n* (*pl* **-s**) acting without the use of words ▶ *v* (**-mes, -ming, -med**) act in mime
mimed *v* ▷ **mime**
mimes *n, v* ▷ **mime**
miming *v* ▷ **mime**
mimic *v* (**-ics, -icking, -icked**) imitate (a person or manner), esp. for satirical effect ▶ *n* (*pl* **-s**) person or animal that is good at mimicking > **mimicry** *n* (*pl* **-ries**)
mimicked *v* ▷ **mimic**
mimicking *v* ▷ **mimic**
mimicry *n* ▷ **mimic**
mimics *n, v* ▷ **mimic**
mina *n* ▷ **myna**
minas *n* ▷ **myna**
minaret *n* (*pl* **-s**) tall slender tower of a mosque
minarets *n* ▷ **minaret**
mince *v* (**-ces, -cing, -ced**) cut or grind into very small pieces ▶ *n* (*pl* **-s**) minced meat
minced *v* ▷ **mince**
mincemeat *n* (*pl* **-s**) sweet mixture of dried fruit and spices
mincemeats *n* ▷ **mincemeat**
mincer *n* (*pl* **-s**) machine for mincing meat
mincers *n* ▷ **mince**
minces *v, n* ▷ **mince**
mincing *adj* affected in manner ▶ *v* ▷ **mince**
mind *n* (*pl* **-s**) thinking faculties ▶ *v* (**-s, -ing, -ed**) take offence at
minded *adj* having an inclination as specified ▶ *v* ▷ **mind**
minder *n* (*pl* **-s**) (*Informal*) aide or bodyguard
minders *n* ▷ **minder**
mindful *adj* heedful
minding *v* ▷ **mind**
mindless *adj* stupid
minds *n, v* ▷ **mind**
mine¹ *pron* belonging to me
mine² *n* (*pl* **-s**) deep hole for digging out coal, ores, etc. ▶ *v* (**-nes, -ning, -ned**) dig for minerals
mined *v* ▷ **mine**
minefield *n* (*pl* **-s**) area of land or water containing mines
minefields *n* ▷ **minefield**
miner *n* (*pl* **-s**) person who works in a mine
mineral *n* (*pl* **-s**) naturally occurring inorganic substance, such as metal ▶ *adj* of, containing, or like minerals
mineralogies *n* ▷ **mineralogy**
mineralogy [min-er-**al**-a-jee] *n* (*pl* **-gies**) study of minerals
minerals *n* ▷ **mineral**
miners *n* ▷ **miner**
mines *n, v* ▷ **mine**

minestrone [min-ness-**strone**-ee] *n* (*pl* **-s**) soup containing vegetables and pasta

minestrones *n* ▷ **minestrone**

minesweeper *n* (*pl* **-s**) ship for clearing away mines

minesweepers *n* ▷ **minesweeper**

mining *v* ▷ **mine**

minger *n* (*pl* **-s**) (BRIT) (*Informal*) unattractive person

mingers *n* ▷ **minger**

mingier *adj* ▷ **mingy**

mingiest *adj* ▷ **mingy**

minging *adj* (BRIT) (*Informal*) unattractive or unpleasant

mingle *v* (**-les, -ling, -led**) mix or blend

mingled *v* ▷ **mingle**

mingles *v* ▷ **mingle**

mingling *v* ▷ **mingle**

mingy *adj* (**-gier, -giest**) (*Informal*) miserly

mini *n* (*pl* **-s**) ▶ *adj* (**-ier, -iest**) (something) small or miniature

minier *adj* ▷ **mini**

miniest *adj* ▷ **mini**

minis *n* ▷ **mini**

miniature *n* (*pl* **-s**) small portrait, model, or copy ▶ *adj* small-scale > **miniaturist** *n* (*pl* **-s**)

miniatures *n* ▷ **miniature**

miniaturist *n* ▷ **miniature**

miniaturists *n* ▷ **miniature**

miniaturize *v* (**-zes, -zing, -zed**) make to a very small scale

miniaturized *v* ▷ **miniaturize**

miniaturizes *v* ▷ **miniaturize**

miniaturizing *v* ▷ **miniaturize**

minibar *n* (*pl* **-s**) selection of drinks and confectionery provided in a hotel room

minibus *n* (*pl* **-es**) small bus

minibuses *n* ▷ **minibus**

minicab *n* (*pl* **-s**) (BRIT) ordinary car used as a taxi

minicabs *n* ▷ **minicab**

minicomputer *n* (*pl* **-s**) computer smaller than a mainframe but more powerful than a microcomputer

minicomputers *n* ▷ **minicomputer**

minidisc *n* (*pl* **-s**) small recordable compact disc

minidiscs *n* ▷ **minidisc**

minim *n* (*pl* **-s**) (MUSIC) note half the length of a semibreve

minima *n* ▷ **minimum**

minimal *adj* minimum

minimize *v* (**-zes, -zing, -zed**) reduce to a minimum

minimized *v* ▷ **minimize**

minimizes *v* ▷ **minimize**

minimizing *v* ▷ **minimize**

minims *n* ▷ **minim**

minimum *adj, n* (*pl* **-mums, -ma**) least possible (amount or number)

minimums *n* ▷ **minimum**

minion *n* (*pl* **-s**) servile assistant

minions *n* ▷ **minion**

miniseries *n* (*pl* **-ries**) TV programme shown in several parts, often on consecutive days

miniseries *n* ▷ **miniseries**

minister *n* (*pl* **-s**) head of a government department ▶ *v* (**-s, -ing, -ed**) (*foll. by* **to**) attend to the needs of > **ministerial** *adj*

ministered *v* ▷ **minister**

ministerial *adj* ▷ **minister**

ministering *v* ▷ **minister**

ministers *n, v* ▷ **minister**

ministration *n* (*pl* **-s**) giving of help

ministrations *n* ▷ **ministration**

ministries *n* ▷ **ministry**

ministry *n* (*pl* **-tries**) profession or duties of a clergyman

mink *n* stoatlike animal

minnow *n* (*pl* **-s**) small freshwater fish

minnows *n* ▷ **minnow**

minor *adj* lesser ▶ *n* (*pl* **-s**) person regarded legally as a child

minorities *n* ▷ **minority**

minority *n* (*pl* **-ties**) lesser number

minors *n* ▷ **minor**

minster *n* (*pl* **-s**) (BRIT) cathedral or large church

minsters *n* ▷ **minster**

minstrel *n* (*pl* **-s**) medieval singer or musician

minstrels *n* ▷ **minstrel**

mint[1] *n* (*pl* **-s**) plant with aromatic leaves used for seasoning and flavouring

mint[2] *n* place where money is coined ▶ *v* (**-s, -ing, -ed**) make (coins)

minted *v* ▷ **mint**[2]

minting *v* ▷ **mint**[2]

mints *n* ▷ **mint**[1,2] ▶ *v* ▷[2]

minuet [min-new-**wet**] *n* (*pl* **-s**) stately dance

minuets *n* ▷ **minuet**

minus *prep, adj* indicating subtraction ▶ *adj* less than zero ▶ *n* (*pl* **-es**) sign (-) denoting subtraction or a number less than zero

minuses *n* ▷ **minus**

minuscule [**min**-niss-skyool] *adj* very small

minute[1] [**min**-it] *n* (*pl* **-s**) 60th part of an hour or degree ▶ *pl* record of the proceedings of a meeting ▶ *v* (**-tes, -ting, -ted**) record in the minutes

minute[2] [my-**newt**] *adj* (**-r, -st**) very small > **minutely** *adv*

minuted *v* ▷ **minute**[1]
minutely *adv* ▷ **minute**[2]
minuter *adj* ▷ **minute**[2]
minutes *n, v* ▷ **minute**[1]
minutest *adj* ▷ **minute**[2]
minutiae [my-**new**-shee-eye] *pl n* trifling or precise details
minuting *v* ▷ **minute**[1]
minx *n* (*pl* **-es**) bold or flirtatious girl
minxes *n* ▷ **minx**
miracle *n* (*pl* **-s**) wonderful supernatural event > **miraculous** *adj* > **miraculously** *adv*
miracles *n* ▷ **miracle**
miraculous *adj* ▷ **miracle**
miraculously *adv* ▷ **miracle**
mirage [mir-**rahzh**] *n* (*pl* **-s**) optical illusion, esp. one caused by hot air
mirages *n* ▷ **mirage**
mire *n* (*pl* **-s**) swampy ground
mires *n* ▷ **mire**
mirror *n* (*pl* **-s**) coated glass surface for reflecting images ▶ *v* (**-s, -ing, -ed**) reflect in or as if in a mirror
mirrored *v* ▷ **mirror**
mirroring *v* ▷ **mirror**
mirrors *n, v* ▷ **mirror**
mirth *n* (*pl* **-s**) laughter, merriment, or gaiety > **mirthful** *adj* > **mirthless** *adj*
mirthful *adv* ▷ **mirth**
mirthless *adj* ▷ **mirth**
mirths *n* ▷ **mirth**
misadventure *n* (*pl* **-s**) unlucky chance
misadventures *n* ▷ **misadventure**
misanthrope [**miz**-zan-thrope] *n* (*pl* **-s**) person who dislikes people in general > **misanthropic** [miz-zan-**throp**-ik] ▶ *adj* > **misanthropy** [miz-**zan**-throp-ee] ▶ *n* (*pl* **-pies**)
misanthropes *n* ▷ **misanthrope**
misanthropies *n* ▷ **misanthrope**
misanthropic *adj* ▷ **misanthrope**
misanthropy *n* ▷ **misanthrope**
misapprehend *v* (**-s, -ing, -ed**) missunderstand > **misapprehension** *n* (*pl* **-s**)
misapprehended *v* ▷ **misapprehend**
misapprehending *v* ▷ **misapprehend**
misapprehends *v* ▷ **misapprehend**
misapprehension *n* ▷ **misapprehend**
misapprehensions *n* ▷ **misapprehend**
misappropriate *v* (**-tes, -ting, -ted**) take and use (money) dishonestly > **misappropriation** *n* (*pl* **-s**)
misappropriated *v* ▷ **misappropriate**
misappropriates *v* ▷ **misappropriate**
misappropriating *v* ▷ **misappropriate**
misappropriation *n* ▷ **misappropriate**
misappropriations *n* ▷ **misappropriate**
miscarriage *n* (*pl* **-s**) spontaneous premature expulsion of a fetus from the womb
miscarriages *n* ▷ **miscarriage**
miscarried *v* ▷ **miscarry**
miscarries *v* ▷ **miscarry**
miscarry *v* (**-ries, -rying, -ried**) have a miscarriage
miscarrying *v* ▷ **miscarry**
miscast *v* (**-s, -ing, -cast**) cast (a role or actor) in (a play or film) inappropriately
miscasting *v* ▷ **miscast**
miscasts *v* ▷ **miscast**
miscegenation [miss-ij-in-**nay**-shun] *n* (*pl* **-s**) interbreeding of races
miscegenations *n* ▷ **miscegenation**
miscellaneous [miss-sell-**lane**-ee-uss] *adj* mixed or assorted
miscellanies *n* ▷ **miscellany**
miscellany [miss-**sell**-a-nee] *n* (*pl* **-nies**) mixed assortment
mischance *n* (*pl* **-es**) unlucky event
mischances *n* ▷ **mischance**
mischief *n* (*pl* **-s**) annoying but not malicious behaviour
mischiefs *n* ▷ **mischief**
mischievous *adj* full of mischief > **mischievously** *adv*
mischievously *adv* ▷ **mischievous**
miscible [**miss**-sib-bl] *adj* able to be mixed
misconception *n* (*pl* **-s**) wrong idea or belief
misconceptions *n* ▷ **misconception**
misconduct *n* (*pl* **-s**) immoral or unethical behaviour
misconducts *n* ▷ **misconduct**
miscreant [**miss**-kree-ant] *n* (*pl* **-s**) wrongdoer
miscreants *n* ▷ **miscreant**
misdeed *n* (*pl* **-s**) wrongful act
misdeeds *n* ▷ **misdeed**
misdemeanour *n* (*pl* **-s**) minor wrongdoing
misdemeanours *n* ▷ **misdemeanour**
miser *n* (*pl* **-s**) person who hoards money and hates spending it > **miserly** *adj*
miserable *adj* very unhappy, wretched
miseries *adj* ▷ **misery**
miserly *adj* ▷ **miser**
misers *n* ▷ **miser**
misery *n* (*pl* **-ries**) great unhappiness
misfire *v* (**-res, -ring, -red**) (of a firearm or engine) fail to fire correctly
misfired *v* ▷ **misfire**
misfires *v* ▷ **misfire**
misfiring *v* ▷ **misfire**
misfit *n* (*pl* **-s**) person not suited to his or her social environment

misfits *n* ▷ **misfit**
misfortune *n* (*pl* **-s**) (piece of) bad luck
misfortunes *n* ▷ **misfortune**
misgiving *n* (*pl* **-s**) feeling of fear or doubt
misgivings *n* ▷ **misgiving**
misguided *adj* mistaken or unwise
mishandle *v* (**-les, -ling, -led**) handle badly or inefficiently
mishandled *v* ▷ **mishandle**
mishandles *v* ▷ **mishandle**
mishandling *v* ▷ **mishandle**
mishap *n* (*pl* **-s**) minor accident
mishaps *n* ▷ **mishap**
misinform *v* (**-s, -ing, -ed**) give incorrect information to > **misinformation** *n* (*pl* **-s**)
misinformation *n* ▷ **misinform**
misinformations *n* ▷ **misinform**
misinformed *v* ▷ **misinform**
misinforming *v* ▷ **misinform**
misinforms *v* ▷ **misinform**
misjudge *v* (**-ges, -ging, -ged**) judge wrongly or unfairly > **misjudgment, misjudgement** *n* (*pl* **-s**)
misjudged *v* ▷ **misjudge**
misjudgement *n* ▷ **misjudge**
misjudges *v* ▷ **misjudge**
misjudging *v* ▷ **misjudge**
misjudgment *n* ▷ **misjudge**
mislaid *v* ▷ **mislay**
mislay *v* (**-s, -ing, -laid**) lose (something) temporarily
mislaying *v* ▷ **mislay**
mislays *v* ▷ **mislay**
mislead *v* (**-s, -ing, -led**) give false or confusing information to > **misleading** *adj*
misleading *v, adj* ▷ **mislead**
misleads *v* ▷ **mislead**
misled *v* ▷ **mislead**
mismanage *v* (**-ges, -ging, -ged**) organize or run (something) badly > **mismanagement** *n* (*pl* **-s**)
mismanaged *v* ▷ **mismanage**
mismanagement *n* ▷ **mismanage**
mismanagements *n* ▷ **mismanage**
mismanages *v* ▷ **mismanage**
mismanaging *v* ▷ **mismanage**
misnomer [miss-**no**-mer] *n* (*pl* **-s**) incorrect or unsuitable name
misnomers *n* ▷ **misnomer**
misogyny [miss-**oj**-in-ee] *n* (*pl* **-nies**) hatred of women > **misogynist** *n* (*pl* **-s**)
misogynies *n* ▷ **misogyny**
misogynist *n* ▷ **misogyny**
misogynists *n* ▷ **misogyny**
misplace *v* (**-ces, -cing, -ced**) mislay
misplaced *v* ▷ **misplace**
misplaces *v* ▷ **misplace**
misplacing *v* ▷ **misplace**
misprint *n* (*pl* **-s**) printing error
misprints *n* ▷ **misprint**
misrepresent *v* (**-s, -ing, -ed**) represent wrongly or inaccurately
misrepresented *v* ▷ **misrepresent**
misrepresenting *v* ▷ **misrepresent**
misrepresents *v* ▷ **misrepresent**
miss *v* (**-es, -ing, -ed**) fail to notice, hear, hit, reach, find, or catch ▶ *n* (*pl* **-es**) fact or instance of missing
missed *v* ▷ **miss**
misses *v, n* ▷ **miss**
missing *adj* lost or absent ▶ *v* ▷ **miss**
missal *n* (*pl* **-s**) book containing the prayers and rites of the Mass
missals *n* ▷ **missal**
misshapen *adj* badly shaped, deformed
missile *n* (*pl* **-s**) object or weapon thrown, shot, or launched at a target
missiles *n* ▷ **missile**
mission *n* (*pl* **-s**) specific task or duty
missionaries *n* ▷ **mission**
missionary *n* (*pl* **-ries**) person sent abroad to do religious and social work
missions *n* ▷ **mission**
missive *n* (*pl* **-s**) letter
missives *n* ▷ **missive**
misspent *adj* wasted or misused
mist *n* (*pl* **-s**) thin fog
mists *n* ▷ **mist**
mistake *n* (*pl* **-s**) error or blunder ▶ *v* (**-takes, -taking, -took, -taken**) misunderstand
mistaken *v* ▷ **mistake**
mistakes *n, v* ▷ **mistake**
mistaking *v* ▷ **mistake**
mister *n* (*pl* **-s**) an informal form of address for a man
misters *n* ▷ **mister**
mistier *adj* ▷ **misty**
mistiest *adj* ▷ **misty**
mistletoe *n* (*pl* **-s**) evergreen plant with white berries growing as a parasite on trees
mistletoes *n* ▷ **mistletoe**
mistook *v* ▷ **mistake**
mistral *n* (*pl* **-s**) strong dry northerly wind of S France
mistrals *n* ▷ **mistral**
mistress *n* (*pl* **-es**) woman who has a continuing sexual relationship with a married man
mistresses *n* ▷ **mistress**
mistrial *n* (*pl* **-s**) (LAW) trial made void because

of some error
mistrials *n* ▷ **mistrial**
mistrust *v* (**-s, -ing, -ed**) have doubts or suspicions about ▶ *n* (*pl* **-s**) lack of trust > **mistrustful** *adj*
mistrusted *v* ▷ **mistrust**
mistrustful *adj* ▷ **mistrust**
mistrusting *v* ▷ **mistrust**
mistrusts *v, n* ▷ **mistrust**
misty *adj* full of mist
misunderstand *v* (**-stands, -standing, -stood**) fail to understand properly > **misunderstanding** *n* (*pl* **-s**)
misunderstanding *v, n* ▷ **misunderstand**
misunderstandings *n* ▷ **misunderstand**
misunderstands *v* ▷ **misunderstand**
misunderstood *v* ▷ **misunderstand**
misuse *n* (*pl* **-s**) incorrect, improper, or careless use ▶ *v* (**-ses, -sing, -sed**) use wrongly
misused *v* ▷ **misuse**
misuses *n, v* ▷ **misuse**
misusing *v* ▷ **misuse**
mite *n* (*pl* **-s**) very small spider-like animal
mites *n* ▷ **mite**
mitigate *v* (**-tes, -ting, -ted**) make less severe > **mitigation** *n* (*pl* **-s**)
mitigated *v* ▷ **mitigate**
mitigating *v* ▷ **mitigate**
mitigates *v* ▷ **mitigate**
mitigation *n* ▷ **mitigate**
mitigations *n* ▷ **mitigate**
mitre [**my**-ter] *n* (*pl* **-s**) bishop's pointed headdress ▶ *v* (**-res, -ring, -red**) join with a mitre joint
mitred *v* ▷ **mitre**
mitres *n, v* ▷ **mitre**
mitring *v* ▷ **mitre**
mitt *n* (*pl* **-s**) baseball catcher's glove
mitts *n* ▷ **mitt**
mitten *n* (*pl* **-s**) glove with one section for the thumb and one for the four fingers together
mittens *n* ▷ **mitten**
mix *v* (**-es, -ing, -ed**) combine or blend into one mass ▶ *n* (*pl* **-es**) mixture > **mixed** *adj* > **mixup** *n* (*pl* **-s**) > **mixer** *n* (*pl* **-s**)
mixed *v, adj* ▷ **mix**
mixer *n* ▷ **mix**
mixers *n* ▷ **mix**
mixes *v, n* ▷ **mix**
mixing *v* ▷ **mix**
mixture *n* (*pl* **-s**) something mixed
mixtures *n* ▷ **mixture**
mixup *n* ▷ **mix**
mixups *n* ▷ **mix**

miz *n* (**mizzes**). Miz is an informal short form of **misery.** This is a useful word, giving a high score for three letters. Remember that you'll need a blank tile for the second Z if you want to form the plural. Miz scores 14 points.

mizzenmast *n* (*pl* **-s**) (on a vessel with three or more masts) third mast from the bow
mizzenmasts *n* ▷ **mizzenmast**

mm *interj*. Mm is a sound that people make to express satisfaction. This two-letter word with no vowels can be very handy when forming several words at once. Mm scores 6 points.

mnemonic [nim-**on**-ik] *n* (*pl* **-s**) ▶ *adj* (something, such as a rhyme) intended to help the memory
mnemonics *n* ▷ **mnemonic**

mo *n* (**mos**). Mo is an informal short form of **moment.** This word can come in handy when you are trying to play words in more than one direction at once. Mo scores 4 points.

moa *n* (*pl* **-s**) large extinct flightless New Zealand bird
moas *n* ▷ **moa**
moan *n* (*pl* **-s**) low cry of pain ▶ *v* (**-s, -ing, -ed**) make or utter with a moan
moaned *v* ▷ **moan**
moaning *v* ▷ **moan**
moans *n, v* ▷ **moan**
moat *n* (*pl* **-s**) deep wide ditch, esp. round a castle
moats *n* ▷ **moat**
mob *n* (*pl* **-s**) disorderly crowd ▶ *v* (**-s, -bbing, -bbed**) surround in a mob to acclaim or attack
mobbed *v* ▷ **mob**
mobbing *v* ▷ **mob**
mobs *n, v* ▷ **mob**
mobile *adj* able to move ▶ *n* (*pl* **-s**) hanging structure designed to move in air currents > **mobility** *n* (*pl* **-ties**)
mobiles *n* ▷ **mobile**
mobilities *n* ▷ **mobile**
mobility *n* ▷ **mobile**
mobilization *n* ▷ **mobilize**
mobilizations *n* ▷ **mobilize**
mobilize *v* (**-zes, -zing, -zed**) (of the armed services) prepare for active service > **mobilization** *n* (*pl* **-s**)
mobilized *v* ▷ **mobilize**
mobilizes *v* ▷ **mobilize**
mobilizing *v* ▷ **mobilize**
moccasin *n* (*pl* **-s**) soft leather shoe
moccasins *n* ▷ **moccasin**
mocha [**mock**-a] *n* (*pl* **-s**) kind of strong dark

coffee
mochas *n* ▷ **mocha**
mock *v* (**-s, -ing, -ed**) make fun of ▶ *adj* sham or imitation
mocked *v* ▷ **mock**
mockeries *n* ▷ **mockery**
mockery *n* (*pl* **-ries**) derision
mocking *v* ▷ **mock**
mockingbird *n* (*pl* **-s**) N American bird which imitates other birds' songs
mockingbirds *n* ▷ **mockingbird**
mocks *pl n* (*Informal*) (in England and Wales) practice exams taken before public exams ▶ *v* ▷ **mock**
mock-up *n* (*pl* **-s**) full-scale model for test or study
mock-ups *n* ▷ **mock-up**
mode *n* (*pl* **-s**) method or manner
modes *n* ▷ **mode**
model *n* (*pl* **-s**) (miniature) representation ▶ *v* (**-s, -elling, -elled**) make a model of
modelled *n* ▷ **model**
modelling *n* ▷ **model**
models *n* ▷ **model**
modem [**mode**-em] *n* (*pl* **-s**) device for connecting two computers by a telephone line
modems *n* ▷ **modem**
moderate *adj* not extreme ▶ *n* (*pl* **-s**) person of moderate views ▶ *v* (**-tes, -ting, -ted**) make or become less violent or extreme > **moderately** *adv* > **moderation** (*pl* **-s**) *n*
moderated *v* ▷ **moderate**
moderately *adv* ▷ **moderate**
moderates *n, v* ▷ **moderate**
moderating *v* ▷ **moderate**
moderation *n* ▷ **moderate**
moderations *n* ▷ **moderate**
moderator *n* (*pl* **-s**) (Presbyterian Church) minister appointed to preside over a Church court, general assembly, etc.
moderators *n* ▷ **moderate**
modern *adj* (**-er, -est**) of present or recent times > **modernity** *n* (*pl* **-ties**)
moderner *adj* ▷ **modern**
modernest *adj* ▷ **modern**
modernism *n* (*pl* **-s**) (support of) modern tendencies, thoughts, or styles > **modernist** *adj, n* (*pl* **-s**)
modernism *n* ▷ **modern**
modernisms *n* ▷ **modern**
modernist *n* ▷ **modern**
modernists *n* ▷ **modern**
modernities *n* ▷ **modern**
modernity *n* ▷ **modern**
modernization *n* ▷ **modernize**
modernizations *n* ▷ **modernize**
modernize *v* (**-izes, -izing, -ized**) bring up to date > **modernization** *n* (*pl* **-s**)
modest *adj* (**-er, -est**) not vain or boastful > **modestly** *adv* > **modesty** *n* (*pl* **-s**)
modester *adj* ▷ **modest**
modestest *adj* ▷ **modest**
modesties *n* ▷ **modest**
modestly *adv* ▷ **modest**
modesty *n* ▷ **modest**
modicum *n* (*pl* **-s**) small quantity
modicums *n* ▷ **modicum**
modify *v* (**-fies, -fying, -fied**) change slightly > **modification** *n* (*pl* **-s**)
modified *v* ▷ **modify**
modifier *n* (*pl* **-s**) word that qualifies the sense of another
modifiers *n* ▷ **modifier**
modish [**mode**-ish] *adj* in fashion
modulate *v* (**-tes, -ting, -ted**) vary in tone > **modulation** *n* (*pl* **-s**) > **modulator** *n* (*pl* **-s**)
modulated *v* ▷ **modulate**
modulates *v* ▷ **modulate**
modulating *v* ▷ **modulate**
modulation *n* ▷ **modulate**
modulations *n* ▷ **modulate**
module *n* (*pl* **-s**) self-contained unit, section, or component with a specific function
modules *n* ▷ **module**
mogul [**moh**-gl] *n* (*pl* **-s**) important or powerful person
moguls *n* ▷ **mogul**
mohair *n* (*pl* **-s**) fine hair of the Angora goat
mohairs *n* ▷ **mohair**
mohican *n* (*pl* **-s**) punk hairstyle with shaved sides and a stiff central strip of hair, often brightly coloured
mohicans *n* ▷ **mohican**
moieties *n* ▷ **moieties**
moiety [**moy**-it-ee] *n* (*pl* **-ties**) half
moist *adj* (**-er, -est**) slightly wet
moisten *v* (**-s, -ing, -ed**) make or become moist
moistened *v* ▷ **moisten**
moistening *v* ▷ **moisten**
moistens *v* ▷ **moisten**
moister *adj* ▷ **moist**
moistest *adj* ▷ **moist**
moisture *n* (*pl* **-s**) liquid diffused as vapour or condensed in drops
moistures *n* ▷ **moisture**
moisturize *v* (**-zes, -zing, -zed**) add moisture to (the skin etc.)
moisturized *v* ▷ **moisten**
moisturizes *v* ▷ **moisten**

moisturizing *v* ▷ **moisten**
molar *n* (*pl* **-s**) large back tooth used for grinding
molars *n* ▷ **molar**
molasses *n* dark syrup, a by-product of sugar refining
mole[1] *n* (*pl* **-s**) small dark raised spot on the skin
mole[2] *n* (*pl* **-s**) small burrowing mammal
mole[3] *n* (*pl* **-s**) unit of amount of substance
mole[4] *n* (*pl* **-s**) breakwater
molecule [**mol**-lik-kyool] *n* (*pl* **-s**) simplest freely existing chemical unit, composed of two or more atoms > **molecular** [mol-**lek**-yew-lar] ▶ *adj*
molecular *adj* ▷ **molecule**
molecules *n* ▷ **molecule**
moles *n* ▷ **mole**[1,2,3,4]
molest *v* (**-s, -ing, -ed**) interfere with sexually > **molester** *n* (*pl* **-s**) > **molestation** *n* (*pl* **-s**)
molested *v* ▷ **molest**
molester *n* ▷ **molest**
molesters *n* ▷ **molest**
molesting *v* ▷ **molest**
molests *v* ▷ **molest**
moll *n* (*pl* **-s**) (*Slang*) gangster's female accomplice
mollified *v* ▷ **mollify**
mollifies *v* ▷ **mollify**
mollify *v* (**-fies, -fying, -fied**) pacify or soothe
mollifying *v* ▷ **mollify**
molls *n* ▷ **moll**
mollusc *n* (*pl* **-s**) soft-bodied, usu. hard-shelled, animal, such as a snail or oyster
molluscs *n* ▷ **mollusc**
mollycoddle *v* (**-les, -ling, -led**) pamper
mollycoddled *v* ▷ **mollycoddle**
mollycoddles *v* ▷ **mollycoddle**
mollycoddling *v* ▷ **mollycoddle**
molten *adj* liquefied or melted
molybdenum [mol-**lib**-din-um] *n* (*pl* **-s**) (CHEM) hard silvery-white metallic element
molybdenums *n* ▷ **molybdenum**
moment *n* (*pl* **-s**) short space of time
momenta *n* ▷ **momentum**
momentarily *adv* ▷ **momentary**
momentary *adj* lasting only a moment > **momentarily** *adv*
momentous [moh-**men**-tuss] *adj* of great significance
moments *n* ▷ **moment**
momentum *n* (*pl* **-ta**) impetus of a moving body
monarch *n* (*pl* **-s**) sovereign ruler of a state > **monarchical** *adj*
monarchical *adj* ▷ **monarch**
monarchies *n* ▷ **monarchy**
monarchist *n* (*pl* **-s**) supporter of monarchy
monarchists *n* ▷ **monarchist**
monarchs *n* ▷ **monarch**
monarchy *n* (*pl* **-chies**) government by or a state ruled by a sovereign
monasteries *n* ▷ **monastery**
monastery *n* (*pl* **-ries**) residence of a community of monks > **monasticism** *n* (*pl* **-s**)
monastic *adj* of monks, nuns, or monasteries
monasticism *n* ▷ **monastery**
monasticisms *n* ▷ **monastery**
monetarism *n* (*pl* **-s**) theory that inflation is caused by an increase in the money supply > **monetarist** *n* (*pl* **-s**) *adj*
monetarisms *n* ▷ **monetarism**
monetarist *n, adj* ▷ **monetarism**
monetarists *n* ▷ **monetarism**
monetary *adj* of money or currency
money *n* (*pl* **-s**) medium of exchange, coins or banknotes > **moneyed, monied** *adj* rich
moneyed *adj* ▷ **money**
moneys *n* ▷ **money**
mongoose *n* (*pl* **-s**) stoatlike mammal of Asia and Africa that kills snakes
mongooses *n* ▷ **money**
mongrel *n* (*pl* **-s**) animal, esp. a dog, of mixed breed ▶ *adj* of mixed breed or origin
mongrels *n* ▷ **mongrel**
monied *adj* ▷ **money**
monitor *n* (*pl* **-s**) person or device that checks, controls, warns, or keeps a record of something ▶ *v* (**-s, -ing, -ed**) watch and check on
monitored *v* ▷ **monitor**
monitoring *v* ▷ **monitor**
monitors *n, v* ▷ **monitor**
monk *n* (*pl* **-s**) member of an all-male religious community bound by vows > **monkish** *adj*
monkey *n* (*pl* **-s**) long-tailed primate ▶ *v* (**-s, -ing, -ed**) (*usu. foll. by* **about** *or* **around**) meddle or fool
monkeyed *v* ▷ **monkey**
monkeying *v* ▷ **monkey**
monkeys *n, v* ▷ **monkey**
monkish *adj* ▷ **monk**
monks *n* ▷ **monk**
monochrome *adj* (PHOTOG) black-and-white
monocle *n* (*pl* **-s**) eyeglass for one eye only
monocles *n* ▷ **monocle**
monogamies *n* ▷ **monogamy**
monogamy *n* (*pl* **-mies**) custom of being married to one person at a time
monogram *n* (*pl* **-s**) design of combined

letters, esp. a person's initials
monograms *n* ▷ **monogram**
monograph *n* (*pl* **-s**) book or paper on a single subject
monographs *n* ▷ **monograph**
monolith *n* (*pl* **-s**) large upright block of stone > **monolithic** *adj*
monolithic *n* ▷ **monolith**
monoliths *n* ▷ **monolith**
monologue *n* (*pl* **-s**) long speech by one person
monologues *n* ▷ **monologue**
monomania *n* (*pl* **-s**) obsession with one thing > **monomaniac** *n*, *adj*
monomaniac *adj* ▷ **monomania**
monomanias *n* ▷ **monomania**
monoplane *n* (*pl* **-s**) aeroplane with one pair of wings
monoplanes *n* ▷ **monoplane**
monopolies *n* ▷ **monopoly**
monopolize *v* (**-zes, -zing, -zed**) have or take exclusive possession of
monopolized *v* ▷ **monopoly**
monopolizes *v* ▷ **monopoly**
monopolizing *v* ▷ **monopoly**
monopoly *n* (*pl* **-lies**) exclusive possession of or right to do something
monorail *n* (*pl* **-s**) single-rail railway
monorails *n* ▷ **monorail**
monotheism *n* (*pl* **-s**) belief in only one God > **monotheistic** *adj*
monotheisms *n* ▷ **monorail**
monotheistic *adj* ▷ **monotheism**
monotone *n* (*pl* **-s**) unvaried pitch in speech or sound > **monotony** *n* (*pl* **-s**)
monotones *n* ▷ **monotone**
monotonies *n* ▷ **monotone**
monotonous *adj* tedious due to lack of variety > **monotonously** *adv*
monotonously *adv* ▷ **monotous**
monseigneur [mon-sen-**nyur**] *n* (*pl* **messeigneurs**) [may-sen-**nyur**] title of French prelates
monsieur [muss-**syur**] *n* (*pl* **messieurs**) [may-**syur**] French title of address equivalent to *sir* or *Mr*
monsignor *n* (*pl* **-s**) (RC CHURCH) title attached to certain offices
monsignors *n* ▷ **monsignor**
monsoon *n* (*pl* **-s**) seasonal wind of SE Asia
monsoons *n* ▷ **monsoon**
monster *n* (*pl* **-s**) imaginary, usu. frightening, beast ▶ *adj* huge
monsters *n* ▷ **monster**
monstrance *n* (*pl* **-ces**) (RC CHURCH) container in which the consecrated Host is exposed for adoration
monstrances *n* ▷ **monstrance**
monstrocities *n* ▷ **monstrosity**
monstrosity *n* (*pl* **-ties**) large ugly thing
monstrous *adj* unnatural or ugly > **monstrously** *adv*
monstrously *adv* ▷ **monstrous**
montage [**mon**-tahzh] *n* (*pl* **-s**) (making of) a picture composed from pieces of others
montages *n* ▷ **montage**
month *n* (*pl* **-s**) one of the twelve divisions of the calendar year
monthlies *n* ▷ **month**
monthly *adj* happening or payable once a month ▶ *adv* once a month ▶ *n* (*pl* **-lies**) monthly magazine
months *n* ▷ **month**
monument *n* (*pl* **-s**) something, esp. a building or statue, that commemorates something
monumental *adj* large, impressive, or lasting > **monumentally** *adv*
monumentally *adv* ▷ **monumental**
monuments *n* ▷ **monument**
moo *n* (*pl* **-s**) long deep cry of a cow ▶ *v* (**-s, -ing, -ed**) make this noise
mooed *v* ▷ **moo**
mooing *v* ▷ **moo**
moos *n*, *v* ▷ **moo**
mooch *v* (**-es, -ing, -ed**) (*Slang*) loiter about aimlessly
mooched *v* ▷ **mooch**
mooches *v* ▷ **mooch**
mooching *v* ▷ **mooch**
mood[1] *n* (*pl* **-s**) temporary (gloomy) state of mind
mood[2] *n* (GRAMMAR) form of a verb indicating whether it expresses a fact, wish, supposition, or command
moodier *adj* ▷ **moody**
moodiest *adj* ▷ **moody**
moodily *adv* ▷ **moody**
moods *n* ▷ **mood**[1,2]
moody *adj* (**-dier, -iest**) sullen or gloomy > **moodily** *adv*
moon *n* (*pl* **-s**) natural satellite of the earth ▶ *v* (**-s, -ing, -ed**) (*foll. by* **about** *or* **around**) be idle in a listless or dreamy way
mooned *v* ▷ **moon**
mooning *v* ▷ **moon**
moonlight *n* (*pl* **-s**) light from the moon ▶ *v* (**-s, -ing, -ed**) (*Informal*) work at a secondary job, esp. illegally
moonlighted *v* ▷ **moonlight**
moonlighting *v* ▷ **moonlight**
moonlights *n*, *v* ▷ **moonlight**

moons *n, v* ▷ **moon**
moonshine *n* (*pl* **-s**) (US & CANADIAN) illicitly distilled whisky
moonshines *n* ▷ **moonshine**
moonstone *n* (*pl* **-s**) translucent semiprecious stone
moonstones *n* ▷ **moonstone**
moonstruck *adj* slightly mad or odd
moor¹ *n* (*pl* **-s**) (BRIT) tract of open uncultivated ground covered with grass and heather
moor² *v* (**-s, -ing, -ed**) secure (a ship) with ropes etc. > **mooring** *n* (*pl* **-s**)
moored *v* ▷ **moor²**
moorhen *n* (*pl* **-s**) small black water bird
moorhens *n* ▷ **moorhen**
mooring *v, n* ▷ **moor²**
moors *n* ▷ **moor¹** ▶ *v* ▷ **moor²**
moose *n* large N American deer
moot *adj* (**-er, -est**) debatable ▶ *v* (**-s, -ing, -ed**) bring up for discussion
mooted *v* ▷ **moot**
mooter *adj* ▷ **moot**
mootest *adj* ▷ **moot**
mooting *v* ▷ **moot**
moots *v* ▷ **moot**
mop *n* (*pl* **-s**) long stick with twists of cotton or a sponge on the end, used for cleaning ▶ *v* (**-s, -pping, -pped**) clean or soak up with or as if with a mop
mope *v* (**-pes, -ping, -ped**) be gloomy and apathetic
moped *n* (*pl* **-s**) light motorized cycle ▶ *v* ▷ **mope**
mopeds *v* ▷ **mope**
mopes *v* ▷ **mope**
moping *v* ▷ **mope**
mopoke *n* (*pl* **-s**) small spotted owl of Australia and New Zealand
mopokes *n* ▷ **mopoke**
mopped *v* ▷ **mop**
mopping *v* ▷ **mop**
mops *n, v* ▷ **mop**
moraine *n* (*pl* **-s**) accumulated mass of debris deposited by a glacier
moraines *n* ▷ **moraine**
moral *adj* concerned with right and wrong conduct ▶ *n* (*pl* **-s**) lesson to be obtained from a story or event > **morally** *adv*
morale [mor-**rahl**] *n* (*pl* **-s**) degree of confidence or hope of a person or group
morales *n* ▷ **morale**
moralist *n* (*pl* **-s**) person with a strong sense of right and wrong
moralists *n* ▷ **moralist**
moralities *n* ▷ **morality**
morality *n* (*pl* **-ties**) good moral conduct
moralize *v* (**-zes, -zing, -zed**) make moral pronouncements
moralized *v* ▷ **moralize**
moralizes *v* ▷ **moralize**
moralizing *v* ▷ **moralize**
morally *adv* ▷ **moral**
morals *n* ▷ **moral**
morass *n* (*pl* **-es**) marsh
morasses *n* ▷ **morass**
moratoria *n* ▷ **moratorium**
moratorium *n* (*pl* **-ria, -riums**) legally authorized ban or delay
moratoriums *n* ▷ **moratorium**
moray *n* (*pl* **-s**) large voracious eel
morays *n* ▷ **moray**
morbid *adj* unduly interested in death or unpleasant events
mordant *adj* sarcastic or scathing ▶ *n* (*pl* **-s**) substance used to fix dyes
mordants *n* ▷ **mordant**
more *adj* greater in amount or degree ▷ **much, many** ▶ *adv* to a greater extent ▶ *pron* greater or additional amount or number
moreover *adv* in addition to what has already been said
mores [**more**-rayz] *pl n* customs and conventions embodying the fundamental values of a community
morgue *n* (*pl* **-s**) mortuary
morgues *n* ▷ **morgue**
moribund *adj* without force or vitality
morn *n* (*pl* **morns**) (*Poetic*) morning
morns *n* ▷ **morn**
morning *n* (*pl* **-s**) part of the day before noon
mornings *n* ▷ **morning**
morocco *n* (*pl* **-s**) goatskin leather
moroccos *n* ▷ **morocco**
moron *n* (*pl* **-s**) (*Informal*) foolish or stupid person > **moronic** *adj*
moronic *adj* ▷ **moron**
morons *n* ▷ **moron**
morose [mor-**rohss**] *adj* (**-r, -st**) sullen or moody
moroser *adj* ▷ **morose**
morosest *adj* ▷ **morose**
morphia *n* ▷ **morphine**
morphines *n* ▷ **morphine**
morphine, morphia *n* (*pl* **-s**) drug extracted from opium, used as an anaesthetic and sedative
morphological *adj* ▷ **morphology**
morphologies *n* ▷ **morphology**
morphology *n* (*pl* **-gies**) science of forms and structures of organisms or words > **morphological** *adj*

morrow *n* (*pl* **-s**) (*Poetic*) next day
morrows *n* ▷ **morrow**
morse *n* (*pl* **-s**) clasp or fastening
morsel *n* (*pl* **-s**) small piece, esp. of food
morsels *n* ▷ **morsel**
morses *n* ▷ **morse**
mortal *adj* subject to death ▶ *n* (*pl* **-s**) human being > **mortally** *adv*
mortalities *n* ▷ **mortal**
mortality *n* (*pl* **-ties**) state of being mortal
mortally *adj* ▷ **mortal**
mortals *n* ▷ **mortal**
mortar *n* (*pl* **-s**) small cannon with a short range
mortarboard *n* (*pl* **-s**) black square academic cap
mortarboards *n* ▷ **mortarboard**
mortars *n* ▷ **mortar**
mortgage *n* (*pl* **-s**) conditional pledging of property, esp. a house, as security for the repayment of a loan ▶ *v* (**-ges, -ging, -ged**) pledge (property) as security thus
mortgaged *v* ▷ **mortgage**
mortgagee *n* (*pl* **-s**) creditor in a mortgage
mortgagees *n* ▷ **mortgagee**
mortgages *n, v* ▷ **mortgage**
mortgaging *v* ▷ **mortgage**
mortgagor *n* (*pl* **-s**) debtor in a mortgage
mortgagors *n* ▷ **mortgagor**
mortice, mortise [more-tiss] *n* (*pl* **-s**) hole in a piece of wood or stone shaped to receive a matching projection on another piece
mortices *n* ▷ **mortice**
mortification *n* ▷ **mortify**
mortifications *n* ▷ **mortify**
mortified *v* ▷ **mortify**
mortifies *v* ▷ **mortify**
mortify *v* (**-fies, -fying, -fied**) humiliate > **mortification** *n* (*pl* **-s**)
mortifying *v* ▷ **mortify**
mortise *n* ▷ **mortice**
mortises *n* ▷ **mortice**
mortuaries *n* ▷ **mortuary**
mortuary *n* (*pl* **-aries**) building where corpses are kept before burial or cremation
mosaic [mow-**zay**-ik] *n* (*pl* **-s**) design or decoration using small pieces of coloured stone or glass
mosaics *n* ▷ **mosaic**
mosque *n* (*pl* **-s**) Muslim temple
mosques *n* ▷ **mosque**
mosquito *n* (*pl* **-toes, -tos**) blood-sucking flying insect
mosquitoes *n* ▷ **mosquito**
mosquitos *n* ▷ **mosquito**
moss *n* (*pl* **-es**) small flowerless plant growing in masses on moist surfaces > **mossy** *adj* (**-ssier, -ssiest**)
mosses *n* ▷ **moss**
mossier *adj* ▷ **moss**
mossiest *adj* ▷ **moss**
mossy *adj* (**-ssier, -ssiest**) ▷ **moss**
most *n* greatest number or degree ▶ *adj* greatest in number or degree ▷ **much, many** ▶ *adv* in the greatest degree
mostly *adv* for the most part, generally
motel *n* (*pl* **-s**) roadside hotel for motorists
motels *n* ▷ **motel**
motet *n* (*pl* **-s**) short sacred choral song
motets *n* ▷ **motet**
moth *n* (*pl* **-s**) nocturnal insect like a butterfly
mothball *n* (*pl* **-s**) small ball of camphor or naphthalene used to repel moths from stored clothes ▶ *v* (**-ed, -ing, -ed**) store (something operational) for future use
mothballed *v* ▷ **moth**
mothballing *v* ▷ **moth**
mothballs *n, v* ▷ **moth**
moths *n* ▷ **moth**
mother *n* (*pl* **-s**) female parent ▶ *adj* native or inborn ▶ *v* (**-s, -ing, -ed**) look after as a mother > **motherhood** *n* (*pl* **-s**) > **motherly** *adj* > **motherless** *adj*
mothered *v* ▷ **mother**
motherhood *n* ▷ **mother**
motherhoods *n* ▷ **mother**
mothering *v* ▷ **mother**
motherless *adj* ▷ **mother**
motherly *adj* ▷ **mother**
mothers *n, v* ▷ **mother**
mothers-in-law *n* ▷ **mother-in-law**
motif [moh-**teef**] *n* (*pl* **-s**) (recurring) theme or design
motifs *n* ▷ **motif**
motion *n* (*pl* **-s**) process, action, or way of moving ▶ *v* (**-s, -ing, -ed**) direct (someone) by gesture
motioned *v* ▷ **motion**
motioning *v* ▷ **motion**
motionless *adj* not moving
motions *n, v* ▷ **motion**
motivate *v* (**-tes, -ting, -ted**) give incentive to > **motivation** *n* (*pl* **-s**)
motivated *v* ▷ **motivate**
motivates *v* ▷ **motivate**
motivating *v* ▷ **motivate**
motivation *n* ▷ **motivate**
motivations *n* ▷ **motivate**
motive *n* (*pl* **-s**) reason for a course of action ▶ *adj* causing motion

motives *n* ▷ **motive**

motley *adj* miscellaneous

motocross *n* (*pl* **-es**) motorcycle race over a rough course

motocrosses *n* ▷ **motocross**

motor *n* (*pl* **-s**) engine, esp. of a vehicle ▶ *v* (**-s, -ing, -ed**) travel by car > **motorized** *adj* equipped with a motor or motor transport > **motorbike** *n* (*pl* **-s**) > **motorboat** *n* (*pl* **-s**) > **motorcar** *n* (*pl* **-s**) > **motorcycle** *n* (*pl* **-s**) > **motorcyclist** *n* (*pl* **-s**)

motorbike *n* ▷ **motor**

motorbikes *n* ▷ **motor**

motorboat *n* ▷ **motor**

motorboats *n* ▷ **motor**

motorcar *n* ▷ **motor**

motorcars *n* ▷ **motor**

motorcycle *n* ▷ **motor**

motorcycles *n* ▷ **motor**

motorcyclist *n* ▷ **motor**

motorcyclists *n* ▷ **motor**

motored *v* ▷ **motor**

motoring *v* ▷ **motor**

motorist *n* (*pl* **-s**) driver of a car

motorists *n* ▷ **motorist**

motorized *adj* ▷ **motor**

motors *n, v* ▷ **motor**

motorway *n* (*pl* **-s**) main road for fast-moving traffic

motorways *n* ▷ **motorway**

mottled *adj* marked with blotches

motto *n* (*pl* **-ttoes, -ttos**) saying expressing an ideal or rule of conduct

mottoes *n* ▷ **motto**

mottos *n* ▷ **motto**

mould[1] *n* (*pl* **-s**) hollow container in which metal etc. is cast ▶ *v* (**-s, -ing, -ed**) shape

mould[2] *n* (*pl* **-s**) fungal growth caused by dampness

mould[3] *n* (*pl* **-s**) loose soil

moulded *v* ▷ **mould[1]**

moulder *v* (**-s, -ing, -ed**) decay into dust

mouldered *v* ▷ **moulder**

mouldering *v* ▷ **moulder**

moulders *v* ▷ **moulder**

mouldier *adj* ▷ **mouldy**

mouldiest *adj* ▷ **mouldy**

moulding *n* (*pl* **-s**) moulded ornamental edging ▶ *v* ▷ **mould[1]**

moulds *n* ▷ **mould[1,2,3]** ▶ *v* ▷ **mould[1]**

mouldy *adj* (**-dier, -diest**) stale or musty; dull or boring

moult *v* (**-s, -ing, -ed**) shed feathers, hair, or skin to make way for new growth ▶ *n* (*pl* **-s**) process of moulting

moulted *v* ▷ **moult**

moulting *v* ▷ **moult**

moults *v, n* ▷ **moult**

mound *n* (*pl* **-s**) heap, esp. of earth or stones

mounds *n* ▷ **mound**

mount *v* (**-s, -ing, -ed**) climb or ascend ▶ *n* (*pl* **-s**) backing or support on which something is fixed

mountain *n* (*pl* **-s**) hill of great size > **mountainous** *adj* full of mountains *n* (*pl* **-s**) person who climbs mountains > **mountaineering** *n* (*pl* **-s**)

mountaineering *n* ▷ **mountaineer**

mountaineerings *n* ▷ **mountaineer**

mountaineers *n* ▷ **mountaineer**

mountains *n* ▷ **mountain**

mountebank *n* (*pl* **-s**) charlatan or fake

mountebanks *n* ▷ **mountebank**

mounted *v* ▷ **mount**

mounting *v* ▷ **mount**

mounts *v, n* ▷ **mount**

mourn *v* (**-s, -ing, -ed**) feel or express sorrow for (a dead person or lost thing)

mourned *v* ▷ **mourn**

mourner *n* (*pl* **mourners**) person attending a funeral

mourners *n* ▷ **mourner**

mournful *adj* (**-ler, -lest**) sad or dismal > **mournfully** *adv*

mournfuller *adj* ▷ **mournful**

mournfullest *adj* ▷ **mournful**

mournfully *adv* ▷ **mournful**

mourning *n* (*pl* **-s**) grieving ▶ *v* ▷ **mourn**

mournings *n* ▷ **mourning**

mourns *v* ▷ **mourn**

mouse *n* (*pl* **mice**) small long-tailed rodent

mouser *n* (*pl* **-s**) cat used to catch mice

mousers *n* ▷ **mouser**

mousse *n* (*pl* **-s**) dish of flavoured cream whipped and set

mousses *n* ▷ **mousse**

moustache *n* (*pl* **-s**) hair on the upper lip

moustaches *n* ▷ **moustache**

mousy *adj* like a mouse, esp. in hair colour

mouth *n* (*pl* **-s**) opening in the head for eating and issuing sounds ▶ *v* (**-s, -ing, -ed**) form (words) with the lips without speaking

mouthed *v* ▷ **mouth**

mouthful *n* (*pl* **-s**) amount of food or drink put into the mouth at any one time when eating or drinking

mouthfuls *n* ▷ **mouthful**

mouthing *v* ▷ **mouth**

mouthpiece *n* (*pl* **-s**) part of a telephone into which a person speaks

mouthpieces *n* ▷ **mouthpiece**
mouths *n, v* ▷ **mouth**
move *v* (**-ves, -ving, -ved**) change in place or position ▶ *n* (*pl* **-s**) moving > **movable, moveable** *adj*
movement *n* (*pl* **-s**) action or process of moving
movements *n* ▷ **movement**
moved *v* ▷ **move**
moves *v, n* ▷ **move**
movie *n* (*pl* **-s**) (*Informal*) cinema film
movies *n* ▷ **movie**
moving *v* ▷ **move**
mow *v* (**-s, -ing, -ed** *or* **mown**) cut (grass or crops)
mowed *v* ▷ **mow**
mower *n* (*pl* **-s**) machine for cutting grass
mowers *n* ▷ **mower**
mowing *v* ▷ **mow**
mown *v* ▷ **mow**
mows *v* ▷ **mow**

> **moz** *n* (**mozes**). Moz is an old Australian slang word for a jinx or hex. This is an unusual word that is worth remembering as it can be very useful if you have a Z but little chance to play it on a crowded board. Moz scores 14 points.

mozzarella [mot-sa-**rel**-la] *n* (*pl* **-s**) moist white cheese originally made in Italy from buffalo milk
mozzarellas *n* ▷ **mozzarella**

> **mu** *n* (**mus**). Mu is the 12th letter in the Greek alphabet. This is a useful word to remember: it won't score you many points on its own, but it can be very helpful on a crowded board when you need to form words in different directions. Mu scores 4 points.

much *adj* (**more, most**) large amount or degree of ▶ *n* large amount or degree ▶ *adv* (**more, most**) to a great degree
mucilage [**mew**-sill-ij] *n* (*pl* **-s**) gum or glue
mucilages *n* ▷ **mucilage**
muck *n* (*pl* **-s**) dirt, filth > **mucky** *adj*
mucks *n* ▷ **mucks**
mucky *adj* ▷ **mucks**
mucus [**mew**-kuss] *n* (*pl* **-s**) slimy secretion of the mucous membranes
mucuses *n* ▷ **mucus**
mud *n* (*pl* **-s**) wet soft earth > **muddy** *adj*
muddier *adj* ▷ **mud**
muddiest *adj* ▷ **mud**
muddy *adj* (**-ddier, -ddiest**) ▷ **mud**
mudguard *n* (*pl* **-s**) cover over a wheel to prevent mud or water being thrown up by it
mudguards *n* ▷ **mudguard**
muds *n* ▷ **mud**
muddle *v* (**-les, -ling, -led**) (*often foll. by* **up**) confuse ▶ *n* (*pl* **-s**) state of confusion
muddled *v* ▷ **muddle**
muddles *v, n* ▷ **muddle**
muddling *v* ▷ **muddle**
muesli [**mewz**-lee] *n* (*pl* **-s**) mixture of grain, nuts, and dried fruit, eaten with milk
mueslis *n* ▷ **muesli**
muezzin [moo-**ezz**-in] *n* (*pl* **-s**) official who summons Muslims to prayer
muezzins *n* ▷ **muezzin**
muff[1] *n* (*pl* **-s**) tube-shaped covering to keep the hands warm
muff[2] *v* (**-s, -ing, -ed**) bungle (an action)
muffed *v* ▷ **muff**
muffin *n* (*pl* **-s**) light round flat yeast cake
muffing *v* ▷ **muff**
muffins *n* ▷ **muffin**
muffs *n* ▷ **muff**[1] ▶ *v* ▷ **muff**[2]
muffle *v* (**-les, -ling, -led**) wrap up for warmth or to deaden sound
muffled *v* ▷ **muffle**
muffler *n* (*pl* **-s**) (BRIT) scarf
mufflers *n* ▷ **muffle**
muffles *v* ▷ **muffle**
muffling *v* ▷ **muffle**
mufti *n* (*pl* **-s**) civilian clothes worn by a person who usually wears a uniform
muftis *n* ▷ **mufti**
mug[1] *n* (*pl* **-s**) large drinking cup
mug[2] *n* (*pl* **-s**) (*Slang*) face ▶ *v* (**-s, -gging, -gged**) (*Informal*) attack in order to rob > **mugger** *n* (*pl* **-s**)
mug[3] *v* (**-s, -gging, -gged**) (*foll. by* **up**) (*Informal*) study hard
mugged *v* ▷ **mug**[2,3]
mugger *v* ▷ **mug**[2]
muggers *v* ▷ **mug**[2]
muggier *adj* ▷ **muggy**
muggiest *adj* ▷ **muggy**
mugging *v* ▷ **mug**[2,3]
muggins *n* (*Informal*) stupid or gullible person
muggy *adj* (**-ggier, -ggiest**) (of weather) damp and stifling
mugs *n* ▷ **mug**[1,2]
mulatto [mew-**lat**-toe] *n* (*pl* **-tos, -toes**) child of one Black and one White parent
mulattoes *adj* ▷ **mulatto**
mulattos *adj* ▷ **mulatto**
mulberries *n* ▷ **mulberry**
mulberry *n* (*pl* **-rries**) tree whose leaves are used to feed silkworms

mulch *n* (*pl* **-es**) mixture of wet straw, leaves, etc., used to protect the roots of plants ▶ *v* (**-es, -ing, -ed**) cover (land) with mulch
mulched *v* ▷ **mulch**
mulches *n, v* ▷ **mulch**
mulching *v* ▷ **mulch**
mule[1] *n* (*pl* **-s**) offspring of a horse and a donkey > **mulish** *adj* obstinate
mule[2] *n* backless shoe or slipper
mules *n* ▷ **mule[1,2]**
mulga *n* (*pl* **-s**) Australian acacia shrub growing in desert regions
mulgas *n* ▷ **mulga**
mulish *adj* ▷ **mule[1]**
mull *v* (**-s, -ing, -ed**) think (over) or ponder > **mulled** *adj* (of wine or ale) flavoured with sugar and spices and served hot
mullah *n* (*pl* **-s**) Muslim scholar, teacher, or religious leader
mullahs *n* ▷ **mullah**
mulled *v, adj* ▷ **mull**
mullet[1] *n* (*pl* **-s**) edible sea fish
mullet[2] *n* (*pl* **-s**) haircut in which the hair is short at the top and sides and long at the back
mullets *n* ▷ **mullet[1,2]**
mulling *v* ▷ **mull**
mulls *v* ▷ **mull**
mulligatawnies *n* ▷ **mulligatawny**
mulligatawny *n* (*pl* **-nies**) soup made with curry powder
mullion *n* (*pl* **-s**) vertical dividing bar in a window > **mullioned** *adj*
mullioned *adj* ▷ **mullion**
mullions *n* ▷ **mullion**
mulloway *n* (*pl* **-s**) large Australian sea fish, valued for sport and food
mulloways *n* ▷ **mulloway**
multifarious [mull-tee-**fare**-ee-uss] *adj* having many various parts
multiple *adj* having many parts ▶ *n* (*pl* **-s**) quantity which contains another an exact number of times
multiples *n* ▷ **multiple**
multiplex *n* (*pl* **-es**) purpose-built complex containing several cinemas and usu. restaurants and bars ▶ *adj* having many elements, complex
multiplexes *n* ▷ **multiplex**
multiplicities *n* ▷ **multiplicity**
multiplicity *n* (*pl* **-ties**) large number or great variety
multiply *v* (**-lies, -lying, -lied**) (cause to) increase in number, quantity, or degree > **multiplication** *n* (*pl* **-s**)
multiplicand *n* (*pl* **-s**) (MATHS) number to be multiplied
multiplicands *n* ▷ **multiplicand**
multiplication *n* ▷ **multiply**
multiplications *n* ▷ **multiply**
multiplied *v* ▷ **multiply**
multiplies *v* ▷ **multiply**
multiplying *v* ▷ **multiply**
multipurpose *adj* having many uses
multitude *n* (*pl* **-s**) great number
multitudes *n* ▷ **multitude**
multitudinous *adj* very numerous
mum *n* (*pl* **-s**) (*Informal*) mother
mums *n* ▷ **mum**
mumble *v* (**-les, -ling, -led**) speak indistinctly, mutter
mumbled *v* ▷ **mumble**
mumbles *v* ▷ **mumble**
mumbling *v* ▷ **mumble**
mummer *n* (*pl* **-s**) actor in a traditional English folk play or mime
mummers *n* ▷ **mummer**
mummies *n* ▷ **mummer**
mummified *adj* (of a body) preserved as a mummy
mummy[1] *n* (*pl* **-mmies**) body embalmed and wrapped for burial in ancient Egypt
mummy[2] *n* (*pl* **-mmies**) ▷ **mother**
mumps *n* infectious disease with swelling in the glands of the neck
munch *v* (**-es, -ing, -ed**) chew noisily and steadily
munched *v* ▷ **munch**
munches *v* ▷ **munch**
munching *v* ▷ **munch**
mundane *adj* everyday
municipal *adj* relating to a city or town
municipalities *n* ▷ **municipality**
municipality *n* (*pl* **-ties**) city or town with local self-government
munificence *n* ▷ **munificent**
munificences *n* ▷ **munificent**
munificent [mew-**niff**-fiss-sent] *adj* very generous > **munificence** *n* (*pl* **-s**)
muniments *pl n* title deeds or similar documents
munitions *pl n* military stores
munted *adj* (NZ) (*Slang*) destroyed or ruined
mural *n* (*pl* **-s**) painting on a wall
murals *n* ▷ **mural**
murder *n* (*pl* **-s**) unlawful intentional killing of a human being ▶ *v* (**-s, -ing, -ed**) kill in this way > **murderer, murderess** *n* (*pl* **-s**) > **murderous** *adj*
murdered *v* ▷ **murder**

murderer *n* ▷ **murder**
murderers *n* ▷ **murder**
murderess *n* ▷ **murder**
murderesses *n* ▷ **murder**
murdering *v* ▷ **murder**
murderous *adj* ▷ **murder**
murders *v, n* ▷ **murder**
murk *n* (*pl* **-s**) thick darkness
murkier *adj* ▷ **murky**
murkiest *adj* ▷ **murky**
murks *n* ▷ **murk**
murky *adj* (**-kier, -kiest**) dark or gloomy
murmur *v* (**-s, -ing, -ed**) speak or say in a quiet indistinct way ▶ *n* (*pl* **-s**) continuous low indistinct sound
murmured *v* ▷ **murmur**
murmuring *v* ▷ **murmur**
murmurs *v, n* ▷ **murmur**
muscle *n* (*pl* **-s**) tissue in the body which produces movement by contracting
muscles *n* ▷ **muscle**
muscular *adj* with well-developed muscles
muse *v* (**-ses, -sing, -sed**) ponder quietly
mused *v* ▷ **muse**
musing *v* ▷ **muse**
muses *v* ▷ **muse**
museum *n* (*pl* **-s**) building where natural, artistic, historical, or scientific objects are exhibited and preserved
museums *n* ▷ **museum**
mush *n* (*pl* **-es**) soft pulpy mass > **mushy** *adj* (**-shier, -shiest**)
mushes *n* ▷ **mush**
mushier *adj* ▷ **mush**
mushiest *adj* ▷ **mush**
mushroom *n* (*pl* **-s**) edible fungus with a stem and cap ▶ *v* (**-s, -ing, -ed**) grow rapidly
mushroomed *v* ▷ **mushroom**
mushrooming *v* ▷ **mushroom**
mushrooms *n, v* ▷ **mushroom**
mushy (**-shier, -shiest**) *adj* ▷ **mush**
music *n* (*pl* **-s**) art form using a melodious and harmonious combination of notes ▶ *n* (*pl* **-s**) play or film with songs and dancing > **musician** *n* (*pl* **-s**)
musical *adj* of or like music > **musically** *adv*
musically *adv* ▷ **musical**
musician *n* ▷ **music**
musicians *n* ▷ **music**
musicologies *n* ▷ **musicology**
musicologist *n* ▷ **musicology**
musicologists *n* ▷ **musicology**
musicology *n* (*pl* **-gies**) scientific study of music > **musicologist** *n* (*pl* **-s**)
musics *n* ▷ **music**
musk *n* (*pl* **-s**) scent obtained from a gland of the musk deer or produced synthetically > **musky** *adj* (**-kier, -kiest**)
musket *n* (*pl* **-s**) (HIST) long-barrelled gun > **musketeer** *n* (*pl* **-s**)
musketeer *n* ▷ **musket**
musketeers *n* ▷ **musket**
musketries *n* ▷ **musketry**
musketry *n* (*pl* **-ries**) (use of) muskets
muskets *n* ▷ **musket**
muskier *adj* ▷ **musk**
muskiest *adj* ▷ **musk**
muskrat *n* (*pl* **-s**) N American beaver-like rodent
muskrats *n* ▷ **muskrat**
musks *n* ▷ **musk**
musky *adj* (**-kier, -kiest**) ▷ **musk**
muslin *n* (*pl* **-s**) fine cotton fabric
muslins *n* ▷ **muslin**
mussel *n* (*pl* **-s**) edible shellfish with a dark hinged shell
mussels *n* ▷ **mussel**
must[1] *v* used as an auxiliary to express obligation, certainty, or resolution ▶ *n* (*pl* **-s**) essential or necessary thing
must[2] *n* (*pl* **-s**) newly pressed grape juice
musts *n* ▷ **must**[1,2]
mustang *n* (*pl* **-s**) wild horse of SW USA
mustangs *n* ▷ **mustang**
mustard *n* (*pl* **-s**) paste made from the powdered seeds of a plant, used as a condiment
mustards *n* ▷ **mustard**
muster *v* (**-s, -ing, -ed**) assemble ▶ *n* (*pl* **-s**) assembly of military personnel
mustered *v* ▷ **muster**
mustering *v* ▷ **muster**
musters *v, n* ▷ **muster**
mustier *adj* ▷ **musty**
mustiest *adj* ▷ **musty**
mustiness *n* ▷ **musty**
mustinesses *n* ▷ **musty**
musty *adj* (**mustier, mustiest**) smelling mouldy and stale > **mustiness** *n* (*pl* **-es**)
mutabilities *n* ▷ **mutable**
mutability *n* ▷ **mutable**
mutable [**mew**-tab-bl] *adj* liable to change > **mutability** *n* (*pl* **-ties**)
mutant *n* (*pl* **-s**) mutated animal, plant, etc.
mutants *n* ▷ **mutant**
mutate *v* (**-tes, -ting, -ted**) (cause to) undergo mutation
mutated *v* ▷ **mutate**
mutates *v* ▷ **mutate**
mutating *v* ▷ **mutate**

mutation *n* (*pl* **-s**) (genetic) change
mutations *n* ▷ **mutation**
mute *adj* (**-r, -st**) silent ▶ *n* (*pl* **-s**) person who is unable to speak > **mutely** *adv*
muted *adj* (of sound or colour) softened
mutely *adv* ▷ **mute**
muter *adj* ▷ **mute**
mutes *n* ▷ **mute**
mutest *adj* ▷ **mute**
muti [moo-ti] *n* (*pl* **-s**) (S AFR) (*Informal*) medicine, esp. herbal medicine
mutis *n* ▷ **muti**
mutilate [**mew**-till-ate] *v* (**-tes, -ting, -ted**) deprive of a limb or other part > **mutilation** *n* (*pl* **-s**)
mutilated *v* ▷ **mutilate**
mutilates *v* ▷ **mutilate**
mutilating *v* ▷ **mutilate**
mutilation *n* ▷ **mutilate**
mutilations *n* ▷ **mutilate**
mutineer *n* ▷ **mutiny**
mutineers *n* ▷ **mutiny**
mutinied *v* ▷ **mutiny**
mutinies *v* ▷ **mutiny**
mutinous *n* ▷ **mutiny**
mutiny [**mew**-tin-ee] *n* (*pl* **-nies**) rebellion against authority, esp. by soldiers or sailors ▶ *v* (**-nies, -nying, -nied**) commit mutiny > **mutineer** *n* (*pl* **-s**) > **mutinous** *adj*
mutinying *n* ▷ **mutiny**
mutt *n* (*pl* **-s**) (*Slang*) mongrel dog
mutts *n* ▷ **mutt**
mutter *v* (**-s, -ing, -ed**) utter or speak indistinctly ▶ *n* (*pl* **-s**) muttered sound or grumble
muttered *v* ▷ **mutter**
muttering *v* ▷ **mutter**
mutters *v, n* ▷ **mutter**
mutton *n* (*pl* **-s**) flesh of sheep, used as food
muttons *n* ▷ **mutton**
mutual [**mew**-chew-al] *adj* felt or expressed by each of two people about the other > **mutually** *adv*
mutually *adv* ▷ **mutual**

> **mux** *v* (**muxes, muxing, muxed**). Mux is an old American word meaning to make a mess of something. This word is very useful not only because it contains an X, but because its verb forms can enable you to clear your rack of unpromising letters. Mux scores 12 points.
> **muzjik** *n* (**muzjiks**). A muzjik is a Russian peasant. This is a great high-scoring word, combining Z, J and K. If you can play the plural using all of your tiles, you'll get a bonus of 50 points. Muzjik scores 28 points.

muzzle *n* (*pl* **-s**) animal's mouth and nose ▶ *v* (**-les, -ling, -led**) prevent from being heard or noticed
muzzled *v* ▷ **muzzle**
muzzles *n, v* ▷ **muzzle**
muzzling *v* ▷ **muzzle**
muzzy *adj* (**-zzier, -zziest**) confused or muddled
my *adj* belonging to me
myall *n* (*pl* **-s**) Australian acacia with hard scented wood
myalls *n* ▷ **myall**
mycology *n* (*pl* **-gies**) study of fungi
mycologies *n* ▷ **mycology**
myna, mynah, mina *n* (*pl* **-s**) Asian bird which can mimic human speech
mynah *n* ▷ **myna**
mynahs *n* ▷ **myna**
mynas *n* ▷ **myna**
myopia [my-**oh**-pee-a] *n* (*pl* **-s**) short-sightedness > **myopic** [my-**op**-ik] ▶ *adj*
myopias *n* ▷ **myopia**
myopic *adj* ▷ **myopia**
myriad [**mir**-ree-ad] *adj* innumerable ▶ *n* (*pl* **-s**) large indefinite number
myriads *n* ▷ **myriad**
myrrh [**mur**] *n* (*pl* **-s**) aromatic gum used in perfume, incense, and medicine
myrrhs *n* ▷ **myrrh**
myrtle [**mur**-tl] *n* (*pl* **-s**) flowering evergreen shrub
myrtles *n* ▷ **myrtle**
myself *pron* ▷ **I**
mysteries *n* ▷ **mystery**
mysterious *adj* ▷ **mystery**
mysteriously *adv* ▷ **mystery**
mystery *n* (*pl* **-ries**) strange or inexplicable event or phenomenon > **mysterious** *adj* > **mysteriously** *adv*
mystic *n* (*pl* **-s**) person who seeks spiritual knowledge ▶ *adj* mystical > **mysticism** *n* (*pl* **-s**)
mystical *adj* having a spiritual or religious significance beyond human understanding
mysticism *n* ▷ **mystic**
mysticisms *n* ▷ **mystic**
mystics *n* ▷ **mystic**
mystification *v* ▷ **mystify**
mystifications *v* ▷ **mystify**
mystified *v* ▷ **mystify**
mystifies *v* ▷ **mystify**
mystify *v* (**-fies, -fying, -fied**) bewilder or puzzle > **mystification** *n* (*pl* **-s**)
mystifying *v* ▷ **mystify**

mystique [miss-**steek**] *n* (*pl* **-s**) aura of mystery or power
mystiques *n* ▷ **mystique**
myth *n* (*pl* **-s**) tale with supernatural characters, usu. of how the world and mankind began > **mythical, mythic** *adj*
mythic *adj* ▷ **myth**
mythical *adj* ▷ **myth**
mythological *adj* ▷ **mythology**
mythologies *n* ▷ **mythology**
mythology *n* (*pl* **-gies**) myths collectively > **mythological** *adj*
myths *n* ▷ **myth**
myxomatoses *n* ▷ **myxomatosis**
myxomatosis [mix-a-mat-**oh**-siss] *n* (*pl* **-ses**) contagious fatal viral disease of rabbits

N n

Along with R and T, N is one of the most common consonants in Scrabble. As you'll often have it on your rack, it's well worth learning what N can do in different situations. N is useful when you need short words, as it begins two-letter words with every vowel except I, and with Y as well. There are plenty of three-letter words starting with N, but there aren't many high-scoring ones. Remember words like **nab** (5 points), **nag** (4), **nap** (5), **nay** (6), **new** (6), **nib** (5), **nob** (5), **nod** (4) and **now (6).**

na *interj*. Na is a Scots word for **no** or **not.** This word can be very convenient when you need to form words in different directions. Na scores 2 points.

naan *n* (*pl* **-s**) ▷ **nan bread**

naans *n* ▷ **naan**

naartjie [**nahr**-chee] *n* (*pl* **-s**) (S AFR) tangerine

naartjies *n* ▷ **naartjie**

nab *v* (**-s, -bbing, -bbed**) (*Informal*) arrest (someone)

nabbed *v* ▷ **nab**

nabbing *v* ▷ **nab**

nabs *v* ▷ **nab**

nadir *n* (*pl* **-s**) point in the sky opposite the zenith

nadirs *n* ▷ **nadir**

naevi *n* ▷ **naevus**

naevus [**nee**-vuss] *n* (*pl* **-vi**) birthmark or mole

naff *adj* (**-er, -est**) (BRIT) (*Slang*) lacking quality or taste

naffer *adj* ▷ **naff**

naffest *adj* ▷ **naff**

nag[1] *v* (**-s, -gging, -gged**) scold or find fault constantly ▶ *n* (*pl* **-s**) person who nags > **nagging** *adj, n* (*pl* **-s**)

nag[2] *n* (*pl* **-s**) (*Informal*) old horse

nagged *v* ▷ **nag**[1]

nagging *v, adj n* ▷ **nag**[1]

naggings *n* ▷ **nag**[1]

nags *v* ▷ **nag**[1] ▶ *n* ▷ **nag**[1, 2]

naiad [**nye**-ad] *n* (*pl* **-s**) (GREEK MYTH) nymph living in a lake or river

naiads *n* ▷ **naiad**

nail *n* (*pl* **-s**) pointed piece of metal with a head, hit with a hammer to join two objects together ▶ *v* (**-s, -ing, -ed**) attach (something) with nails

nailed *v* ▷ **nail**

nailing *v* ▷ **nail**

nails *n, v* ▷ **nail**

naive [nye-**eev**] *adj* (**-r, -st**) innocent and gullible > **naively** *adv* > **naivety** [nye-**eev**-tee] *n* (*pl* **-ties**), **naïveté** (*pl* **-s**)

naively *adv* ▷ **naive**

naiver *adj* ▷ **naive**

naivest *adj* ▷ **naive**

naïveté *n* ▷ **naive**

naïvetés *n* ▷ **naive**

naiveties *n* ▷ **naive**

naivety *n* ▷ **naive**

naked *adj* (**-er, -est**) without clothes > **nakedness** *n* (*pl* **-es**)

nakeder *adj* ▷ **naked**

nakedest *adj* ▷ **naked**

nakedness *n* ▷ **naked**

nakednesses *n* ▷ **naked**

name *n* (*pl* **-s**) word by which a person or thing is known ▶ *v* (**-mes, -ming, -med**) give a name to

named *v* ▷ **name**

nameless *adj* without a name

namely *adv* that is to say

names *n, v* ▷ **name**

namesake *n* (*pl* **-s**) person with the same name as another

namesakes *n* ▷ **namely**

naming *v* ▷ **name**

nannies *n* ▷ **nanny**

nanny *n* (*pl* **-nnies**) woman whose job is looking after young children

nap[1] *n* (*pl* **-s**) short sleep ▶ *v* (**-s, -pping, -pped**) have a short sleep

nap[2] *n* (*pl* **-s**) raised fibres of velvet or similar cloth

nap3 *n* (*pl* **-s**) card game similar to whist
napalm *n* (*pl* **-s**) highly inflammable jellied petrol, used in bombs
napalms *n* ▷ **napalm**
nape *n* (*pl* **-s**) back of the neck
napes *n* ▷ **nape**
naphtha *n* (*pl* **-s**) liquid mixture distilled from coal tar or petroleum, used as a solvent and in petrol
naphthalene *n* (*pl* **-s**) white crystalline product distilled from coal tar or petroleum, used in disinfectants, mothballs, and explosives
naphthalenes *n* ▷ **naphthalene**
naphthas *n* ▷ **naphtha**
napkin *n* (*pl* **-s**) piece of cloth or paper for wiping the mouth or protecting the clothes while eating
napkins *n* ▷ **napkin**
napped *v* ▷ **nap1**
nappies *n* ▷ **nappy**
napping *v* ▷ **nap1**
nappy *n* (*pl* **-ppies**) piece of absorbent material fastened round a baby's lower torso to absorb urine and faeces
naps *n* ▷ **nap** ▶ *v* ▷ **nap1**
narcissism *n* (*pl* **-s**) exceptional interest in or admiration for oneself > **narcissistic** *adj*
narcissisms *n* ▷ **narcissism**
narcissistic *adj* ▷ **narcissism**
narcissi *n* ▷ **narcissus**
narcissus *n* (*pl* **-cissi**) yellow, orange, or white flower related to the daffodil
narcoses *n* ▷ **narcosis**
narcosis *n* (*pl* **-s**) effect of a narcotic
narcotic *n* (*pl* **-s**) ▶ *adj* (of) a drug, such as morphine or opium, which produces numbness and drowsiness, used medicinally but addictive
narcotics *n* ▷ **narcotic**
nark (*Slang*) *v* (**-s, -ing, -ed**) annoy ▶ *n* (*pl* **-s**) informer or spy
narked *v* ▷ **nark**
narkier *adj* ▷ **narky**
narkiest *adj* ▷ **narky**
narking *v* ▷ **nark**
narks *v*, *n* ▷ **nark**
narky *adj* (*Slang*) (**-kier, -kiest**) irritable or complaining
narrate *v* (**-tes, -ting, -ted**) tell (a story) > **narration** *n* (*pl* **-s**) > **narrator** *n* (*pl* **-s**)
narrated *v* ▷ **narrate**
narrates *v* ▷ **narrate**
narrating *v* ▷ **narrate**
narration *n* ▷ **narrate**
narrations *n* ▷ **narrate**
narrative *n* (*pl* **-s**) account, story
narratives *n* ▷ **narrative**
narrator *n* ▷ **narrate**
narrators *n* ▷ **narrate**
narrow *adj* (**-er, -est**) small in breadth in comparison to length ▶ *v* (**-s, -ing, -ed**) make or become narrow > **narrowly** *adv* > **narrowness** *n* (*pl* **-es**)
narrowed *v* ▷ **narrow**
narrower *adj* ▷ **narrow**
narrowest *adj* ▷ **narrow**
narrowing *v* ▷ **narrow**
narrowly *adv* ▷ **narrow**
narrowness *n* ▷ **narrow**
narrownesses *n* ▷ **narrow**
narrows *v* ▷ **narrow** ▶ *pl n* narrow part of a strait, river, or current
narwhal *n* (*pl* **-s**) arctic whale with a long spiral tusk
narwhals *n* ▷ **narwhal**
nasal *adj* of the nose > **nasally** *adv*
nasally *adv* ▷ **nasal**
nascent *adj* starting to grow or develop
nastier *adj* ▷ **nasty**
nastiest *adj* ▷ **nasty**
nastily *adv* ▷ **nasty**
nastiness *n* ▷ **nasty**
nastinesses *n* ▷ **nasty**
nasturtium *n* (*pl* **-s**) plant with yellow, red, or orange trumpet-shaped flowers
nasturtiums *n* ▷ **nasturtium**
nasty *adj* (**-tier, -tiest**) unpleasant > **nastily** *adv* > **nastiness** *n* (*pl* **-es**)
natal *adj* of or relating to birth
nation *n* (*pl* **nations**) people of one or more cultures or races organized as a single state
nations *n* ▷ **nation**
national *adj* characteristic of a particular nation ▶ *n* (*pl* **-s**) citizen of a nation > **nationally** *adv*
nationalism *n* (*pl* **-s**) policy of national independence > **nationalist** *n* (*pl* **-s**) *adj*
nationalisms *n* ▷ **nationalism**
nationalist *n* ▷ **nationalism**
nationalists *n* ▷ **nationalism**
nationalities *n* ▷ **nationality**
nationality *n* (*pl* **-ties**) fact of being a citizen of a particular nation
nationalization *n* ▷ **nationalize**
nationalizations *n* ▷ **nationalize**
nationalize *v* (**-izes, -izing, -ized**) put (an industry or a company) under state control > **nationalization** *n* (*pl* **-s**)
nationalized *v* ▷ **nationalize**

nationalizes *v* ▷ **nationalize**
nationalizing *v* ▷ **nationalize**
nationally *adv* ▷ **national**
nationals *n* ▷ **national**
native *adj* relating to a place where a person was born ▶ *n* (*pl* **-s**) person born in a specified place
natives *n* ▷ **native**
nativities *n* ▷ **nativity**
nativity *n* (*pl* **-ties**) birth or origin
natter (*Informal*) *v* (**-s, -ing, -ed**) talk idly or chatter ▶ *n* (*pl* **-s**) long idle chat
nattered *v* ▷ **natter**
nattering *v* ▷ **natter**
natters *v, n* ▷ **natter**
nattier *adj* ▷ **natty**
nattiest *adj* ▷ **natty**
natty *adj* (**-ttier, -ttiest**) (*Informal*) smart and spruce
natural *adj* normal or to be expected ▶ *n* (*pl* **-s**) person with an inborn talent or skill
naturalism *n* (*pl* **-s**) movement in art and literature advocating detailed realism > **naturalistic** *adj*
naturalisms *n* ▷ **naturalism**
naturalist *n* (*pl* **-s**) student of natural history
naturalistic *n* ▷ **naturalism**
naturalists *n* ▷ **naturalist**
naturalization *n* ▷ **naturalize**
naturalizations *n* ▷ **naturalize**
naturalize *v* (**-izes, -izing, -ized**) give citizenship to (a person born in another country) > **naturalization** *n* (*pl* **-s**)
naturalized *v* ▷ **naturalize**
naturalizes *v* ▷ **naturalize**
naturalizing *v* ▷ **naturalize**
naturally *adv* of course
naturals *n* ▷ **natural**
nature *n* (*pl* **-s**) whole system of the existence, forces, and events of the physical world that are not controlled by human beings
natures *n* ▷ **nature**
naturism *n* (*pl* **-s**) nudism > **naturist** *n* (*pl* **-s**)
naturisms *n* ▷ **naturism**
naturist *n* ▷ **naturism**
naturists *n* ▷ **naturism**
naught *n* (*pl* **-s**) (*Lit*) nothing
naughtier *adj* ▷ **naughty**
naughtiest *adj* ▷ **naughty**
naughtily *adv* ▷ **naughty**
naughtiness *n* ▷ **naughty**
naughtinesses *n* ▷ **naughty**
naughts *n* ▷ **naught**
naughty *adj* (**-tier, -tiest**) disobedient or mischievous > **naughtily** *adv* > **naughtiness** *n* (*pl* **-es**)
nausea [**naw**-zee-a] *n* (*pl* **-s**) feeling of being about to vomit
nauseas *n* ▷ **nausea**
nauseate *v* (**-tes, -ting, -ted**) make (someone) feel sick
nauseated *v* ▷ **nauseate**
nauseates *v* ▷ **nauseate**
nauseating *v* ▷ **nauseate**
nauseous *adj* as if about to vomit
nautical *adj* of the sea or ships
nautili *n* ▷ **nautilus**
nautilus *n* (*pl* **-luses, -li**) shellfish with many tentacles
nautiluses *n* ▷ **nautilus**
naval *adj* ▷ **navy**
nave *n* (*pl* **-s**) long central part of a church
navel *n* (*pl* **-s**) hollow in the middle of the abdomen where the umbilical cord was attached
navels *n* ▷ **navel**
naves *n* ▷ **nave**
navies *n* ▷ **navy**
navigable *adj* wide, deep, or safe enough to be sailed through
navigate *v* (**-tes, -ting, -ted**) direct or plot the path or position of a ship, aircraft, or car > **navigation** *n* (*pl* **-s**) > **navigator** *n* (*pl* **-s**)
navigated *v* ▷ **navigate**
navigates *v* ▷ **navigate**
navigating *v* ▷ **navigate**
navigation *n* ▷ **navigate**
navigations *n* ▷ **navigate**
navigator *n* ▷ **navigate**
navigators *n* ▷ **navigate**
navvies *n* ▷ **navvy**
navvy *n* (*pl* **-vvies**) (BRIT) labourer employed on a road or a building site
navy *n* (*pl* **-vies**) branch of a country's armed services comprising warships with their crews and organization
nay *interj* (*Obs*) no

> **ne** *adv*. Ne is an old word meaning **not.** This handy little word can be very helpful when you are trying to form several words at once. Ne scores 2 points.

neanderthal [nee-**ann**-der-tahl] *adj* of a type of primitive man that lived in Europe before 12 000 BC
near *prep, adv adj* (**-er, -est**) indicating a place or time not far away ▶ *adj* almost being the thing specified ▶ *v* (**-s, -ing, -ed**) draw close (to) > **nearness** *n* (*pl* **-es**)
nearby *adj* not far away

neared *v* ▷ **near**
nearer *adj* ▷ **near**
nearest *adj* ▷ **near**
nearing *v* ▷ **near**
nearly *adv* almost
nearness *n* ▷ **near**
nearnesses *n* ▷ **near**
nears *v* ▷ **near**
nearside *n* (*pl* **-s**) side of a vehicle that is nearer the kerb
nearsides *n* ▷ **nearside**
neat *adj* (**-er, -est**) tidy and clean > **neatly** *adv* > **neatness** *n* (*pl* **-es**)
neater *adj* ▷ **neat**
neatest *adj* ▷ **neat**
neatly *adv* ▷ **neat**
neatness *n* ▷ **neat**
neatnesses *n* ▷ **neat**
nebula *n* (*pl* **-lae**) (ASTRONOMY) hazy cloud of particles and gases > **nebulous** *adj* vague and unclear
nebulae *n* ▷ **nebula**
nebulous *adj* ▷ **nebula**
necessarily *adv* ▷ **necessary**
necessary *adj* needed to obtain the desired result > **necessarily** *adv*
necessitate *v* (**-tes, -ting, -ted**) compel or require
necessitated *v* ▷ **necessitate**
necessitates *v* ▷ **necessitate**
necessitating *v* ▷ **necessitate**
necessities *n* ▷ **necessity**
necessity *n* (*pl* **-ties**) circumstances that inevitably require a certain result
neck *n* (*pl* **-s**) part of the body joining the head to the shoulders ▶ *v* (**-s, -ing, -ed**) (*Slang*) kiss and cuddle
necked *v* ▷ **neck**
neckerchief *n* (*pl* **-s**) piece of cloth worn tied round the neck
neckerchiefs *n* ▷ **neckerchief**
necking *v* ▷ **neck**
necklace *n* (*pl* **-s**) decorative piece of jewellery worn around the neck
necklaces *n* ▷ **necklace**
necks *n, v* ▷ **neck**
necromancies *n* ▷ **necromancy**
necromancy *n* (*pl* **-cies**) communication with the dead
necropolis [neck-**rop**-pol-liss] *n* (*pl* **-ses**) cemetery
necropolises *n* ▷ **necropolis**
nectar *n* (*pl* **-s**) sweet liquid collected from flowers by bees
nectars *n* ▷ **nectar**
nectarine *n* (*pl* **-s**) smooth-skinned peach
nectarines *n* ▷ **nectarine**
née [nay] *prep* indicating the maiden name of a married woman
need *v* (**-s, -ing, -ed**) require or be in want of ▶ *n* (*pl* **-s**) condition of lacking something
needed *v* ▷ **need**
needful *adj* necessary or required
needier *adj* ▷ **needy**
neediest *adj* ▷ **needy**
needing *v* ▷ **need**
needle *n* (*pl* **-s**) thin pointed piece of metal with an eye through which thread is passed for sewing ▶ *v* (**-les, -ling, -led**) (*Informal*) goad or provoke
needled *v* ▷ **needle**
needles *n, v* ▷ **needle**
needless *adj* unnecessary
needlework *n* (*pl* **-s**) sewing and embroidery
needleworks *n* ▷ **needlework**
needling *v* ▷ **needle**
needs *v, n* ▷ **need** ▶ *adv* (*preceded or foll. by* **must**) necessarily
needy *adj* (**-dier, -diest**) poor, in need of financial support
nefarious [nif-**fair**-ee-uss] *adj* wicked
negate *v* (**-tes, -ting, -ted**) invalidate > **negation** *n* (*pl* **-s**)
negated *v* ▷ **negate**
negates *v* ▷ **negate**
negating *v* ▷ **negate**
negation *n* ▷ **negate**
negations *n* ▷ **negate**
negative *adj* expressing a denial or refusal ▶ *n* (*pl* **-s**) negative word or statement
negatives *n* ▷ **negative**
neglect *v* (**-s, -ing, -ed**) take no care of ▶ *n* (*pl* **-s**) neglecting or being neglected > **neglectful** *adj*
neglected *v* ▷ **neglect**
neglectful *adj* ▷ **neglect**
neglecting *v* ▷ **neglect**
neglects *v, n* ▷ **neglect**
negligee [**neg**-lee-zhay] *n* (*pl* **-s**) woman's lightweight usu. lace-trimmed dressing gown
negligees *n* ▷ **negligee**
negligence *n* (*pl* **-s**) neglect or carelessness > **negligent** *adj* > **negligently** *adv*
negligences *n* ▷ **negligence**
negligent *adj* ▷ **negligence**
negligently *adv* ▷ **negligence**
negligible *adj* so small or unimportant as to be not worth considering
negotiable *adj* ▷ **negotiate**

negotiate *v* (**-tes, -ting, -ted**) discuss in order to reach (an agreement) > **negotiation** *n* (*pl* **-s**) > **negotiator** *n* (*pl* **-s**) > **negotiable** *adj*
negotiated *v* ▷ **negotiate**
negotiates *v* ▷ **negotiate**
negotiating *v* ▷ **negotiate**
negotiation *n* ▷ **negotiate**
negotiations *n* ▷ **negotiate**
negotiator *n* ▷ **negotiate**
negotiators *n* ▷ **negotiate**
neigh *n* (*pl* **-s**) loud high-pitched sound made by a horse ▶ *v* (**-s, -ing, -ed**) make this sound
neighed *v* ▷ **neigh**
neighing *v* ▷ **neigh**
neighs *n, v* ▷ **neigh**
neighbour *n* (*pl* **-s**) person who lives or is situated near another
neighbourhood *n* (*pl* **-s**) district
neighbourhoods *n* ▷ **neighbourhood**
neighbouring *adj* situated nearby
neighbourly *adj* kind, friendly, and helpful
neighbours *n* ▷ **neighbour**
neither *adj, pron* not one nor the other ▶ *conj* not
nemeses *n* ▷ **nemesis**
nemesis [**nem**-miss-iss] *n* (*pl* **-ses**) retribution or vengeance
neo- *combining form* new, recent, or a modern form of
neolith *n* (*pl* **-s**) stone implement from the Neolithic age
neoliths *n* ▷ **neolith**
neologism [nee-**ol**-a-jiz-zum] *n* (*pl* **-s**) newly-coined word or an established word used in a new sense
neologisms *n* ▷ **neologism**
neon *n* (*pl* **-s**) (CHEM) colourless odourless gaseous element used in illuminated signs and lights
neons *n* ▷ **neon**
neophyte *n* (*pl* **-s**) beginner or novice
neophytes *n* ▷ **neophyte**
nephew *n* (*pl* **-s**) son of one's sister or brother
nephews *n* ▷ **nephew**
nephritis [nif-**frite**-tiss] *n* (*pl* **-tises**) inflammation of a kidney
nephritises *n* ▷ **nephritis**
nepotism [**nep**-a-tiz-zum] *n* (*pl* **-s**) favouritism in business shown to relatives and friends
nepotisms *n* ▷ **nepotism**
nerd *n* (*pl* **-s**) (*Slang*) boring person obsessed with a particular subject
nerds *n* ▷ **nerd**
nerve *n* (*pl* **-s**) cordlike bundle of fibres that conducts impulses between the brain and other parts of the body
nerveless *adj* numb, without feeling
nerves *n* ▷ **nerve** ▶ *pl n* anxiety or tension
nervier *adj* ▷ **nervy**
nerviest *adj* ▷ **nervy**
nervous *adj* apprehensive or worried > **nervously** *adv* > **nervousness** *n* (*pl* **-es**)
nervously *adv* ▷ **nervous**
nervousness *n* ▷ **nervous**
nervousnesses *n* ▷ **nervous**
nervy *adj* (**-vier, -viest**) excitable or nervous
nest *n* (*pl* **-s**) place or structure in which birds or certain animals lay eggs or give birth to young ▶ *v* (**-s, -ing, -ed**) make or inhabit a nest
nested *v* ▷ **nest**
nesting *v* ▷ **nest**
nests *v, n* ▷ **nest**
nestle *v* (**-les, -ling, -led**) snuggle
nestled *v* ▷ **nestle**
nestles *v* ▷ **nestle**
nestling *n* (*pl* **-s**) bird too young to leave the nest ▶ *v* ▷ **nestle**
nestlings *n* ▷ **nestling**
net[1] *n* (*pl* **-s**) fabric of meshes of string, thread, or wire with many openings ▶ *v* (**-s, -tting, -tted**) catch (a fish or animal) in a net
net[2], **nett** *adj* left after all deductions ▶ *v* (**-s, -tting, -tted**) yield or earn as a clear profit
netball *n* (*pl* **-s**) team game in which a ball has to be thrown through a net hanging from a ring at the top of a pole
netballs *n* ▷ **netball**
nether *adj* lower
nets *v* ▷ **net**[1, 2]
nets *n* ▷ **net**[1]
nett *adj* ▷ **net**[2]
netted *v* ▷ **net**[1, 2]
netting *v* ▷ **net**[1, 2] ▶ *n* (*pl* **-s**) material made of net
nettings *n* ▷ **netting**
nettle *n* (*pl* **-s**) plant with stinging hairs on the leaves
nettled *adj* irritated or annoyed
nettles *n* ▷ **nettle**
network *n* (*pl* **-s**) system of intersecting lines, roads, etc.
networks *n* ▷ **network**
neural *adj* of a nerve or the nervous system
neuralgia *n* (*pl* **-s**) severe pain along a nerve
neuralgias *n* ▷ **neuralgia**
neuritis [nyoor-**rite**-tiss] *n* (*pl* **-tises**) inflammation of a nerve or nerves
neuritises *n* ▷ **neuritis**
neurologies *n* ▷ **neurology**
neurologist *n* ▷ **neurology**

neurologists *n* ▷ **neurology**
neurology *n* (*pl* **-gies**) scientific study of the nervous system > **neurologist** *n* (*pl* **-s**)
neuroses *n* ▷ **neurosis**
neurosis *n* (*pl* **-ses**) mental disorder producing hysteria, anxiety, depression, or obsessive behaviour
neurotic *adj* emotionally unstable ▶ *n* (*pl* **-s**) neurotic person
neurotics *n* ▷ **neurotic**
neuter *adj* belonging to a particular class of grammatical inflections in some languages ▶ *v* (**-s, -ing, -ed**) castrate (an animal)
neutered *v* ▷ **neuter**
neutering *v* ▷ **neuter**
neuters *v* ▷ **neuter**
neutral *adj* taking neither side in a war or dispute ▶ *n* (*pl* **-s**) neutral person or nation > **neutrality** *n* (*pl* **-ties**)
neutralities *n* ▷ **neutral**
neutrality *n* ▷ **neutral**
neutralize *v* (**-izes, -izing, -ized**) make ineffective or neutral
neutralized *v* ▷ **neutralize**
neutralizes *v* ▷ **neutralize**
neutralizing *v* ▷ **neutralize**
neutrals *n* ▷ **neutral**
neutrino [new-**tree**-no] *n* (*pl* **-nos**) elementary particle with no mass or electrical charge
neutrinos *n* ▷ **neutrino**
neutron *n* (*pl* **-s**) electrically neutral elementary particle of about the same mass as a proton
neutrons *n* ▷ **neutron**
never *adv* at no time
nevertheless *adv* in spite of that
new *adj* (**-er, -est**) not existing before (*foll. by* **to**) ▶ *adv* recently
newbie (*Informal*) *n* (*pl* **-s**) person new to a job, club, etc
newbies *n* ▷ **newbie**
newborn *adj* recently or just born
newcomer *n* (*pl* **-s**) recent arrival or participant
newcomers *n* ▷ **newcomer**
newel *n* (*pl* **-s**) post at the top or bottom of a flight of stairs that supports the handrail
newels *n* ▷ **newel**
newer *adj* ▷ **new**
newest *adj* ▷ **new**
newfangled *adj* objectionably or unnecessarily modern
newlyweds *pl n* recently married couple
newness *n* (*pl* **-es**) novelty
newnesses *n* ▷ **newness**
news *n* important or interesting new happenings
newsagent *n* (*pl* **-s**) (BRIT) shopkeeper who sells newspapers and magazines
newsagents *n* ▷ **newsagent**
newscaster *n* ▷ **newsreader**
newscasters *n* ▷ **newsreader**
newsflash *n* (*pl* **-es**) brief important news item, which interrupts a radio or television programme
newsflashes *n* ▷ **newsflash**
newsier *adj* ▷ **newsy**
newsiest *adj* ▷ **newsy**
newsletter *n* (*pl* **-s**) bulletin issued periodically to members of a group
newsletters *n* ▷ **newsletter**
newspaper *n* (*pl* **-s**) weekly or daily publication containing news
newspapers *n* ▷ **newspaper**
newsprint *n* (*pl* **-s**) inexpensive paper used for newspapers
newsprints *n* ▷ **newsprint**
newsreader, newscaster *n* (*pl* **-s**) person who reads the news on the television or radio
newsreaders *n* ▷ **newsreader**
newsreel *n* (*pl* **-s**) short film giving news
newsreels *n* ▷ **newsreel**
newsroom *n* (*pl* **-s**) room where news is received and prepared for publication or broadcasting
newsrooms *n* ▷ **newsroom**
newsworthy *adj* sufficiently interesting to be reported as news
newsy *adj* (**-sier, -siest**) full of news
newt *n* (*pl* **-s**) small amphibious creature with a long slender body and tail
newton *n* (*pl* **-s**) unit of force
newtons *n* ▷ **newton**
newts *n* ▷ **newt**
next *adj, adv* immediately following
nexus *n* (*pl* **nexus**) connection or link
nib *n* (*pl* **-s**) writing point of a pen
nibble *v* (**-les, -ling, -led**) take little bites (of) ▶ *n* (*pl* **-les**) little bite
nibbled *v* ▷ **nibble**
nibbles *v, n* ▷ **nibble**
nibbling *v* ▷ **nibble**
nibs *n* (*pl* ▷ **nib**
nibses *n* ▷ **nibs**
nice *adj* (**-r, -st**) pleasant > **nicely** *adv* > **niceness** *n* (*pl* **-es**)
nicely *adv* ▷ **nice**
niceness *n* ▷ **nice**
nicenesses *n* ▷ **nice**
nicer *adj* ▷ **nice**

nicest *adj* ▷ **nice**
niceties *n* ▷ **nicety**
nicety *n* (*pl* **-ties**) subtle point
niche [**neesh**] *n* (*pl* **-s**) hollow area in a wall
niches *n* ▷ **niche**
nick *v* (**-s, -ing, -ed**) make a small cut in ▶ *n* (*pl* **-s**) small cut
nicked *v* ▷ **nick**
nickel *n* (*pl* **-s**) (CHEM) silvery-white metal often used in alloys
nickelodeon *n* (*pl* **-s**) (US) early type of jukebox
nickelodeons *n* ▷ **nickelodeon**
nickels *n* ▷ **nickel**
nicking *v* ▷ **nick**
nickname *n* (*pl* **-s**) familiar name given to a person or place ▶ *v* (**-mes, -ming, -med**) call by a nickname
nicknamed *v* ▷ **nickname**
nicknames *n, v* ▷ **nickname**
nicknaming *v* ▷ **nickname**
nicks *v, n* ▷ **nick**
nicotine *n* (*pl* **-s**) poisonous substance found in tobacco
nicotines *n* ▷ **nicotine**
niece *n* (*pl* **-s**) daughter of one's sister or brother
nieces *n* ▷ **niece**
niftier *adj* ▷ **nifty**
niftiest *adj* ▷ **nifty**
nifty *adj* (**-tier, -tiest**) (*Informal*) neat or smart
niggard *n* ▷ **niggardly**
niggardly *adj* stingy > **niggard** *n* (*pl* **-s**) stingy person
niggards *n* ▷ **niggardly**
niggle *v* (**-les, -ling, -led**) worry slightly ▶ *n* (*pl* **-s**) small worry or doubt
niggled *v* ▷ **niggle**
niggles *v, n* ▷ **niggle**
niggling *v* ▷ **niggle**
nigh *adv, prep* (*Lit*) near
night *n* (*pl* **-s**) time of darkness between sunset and sunrise
nightcap *n* (*pl* **-s**) drink taken just before bedtime
nightcaps *n* ▷ **nightcap**
nightclub *n* (*pl* **-s**) establishment for dancing, music, etc., open late at night
nightclubs *n* ▷ **nightclub**
nightdress *n* (*pl* **-es**) woman's loose dress worn in bed
nightdresses *n* ▷ **nightdress**
nightfall *n* (*pl* **-s**) approach of darkness
nightfalls *n* ▷ **nightfall**
nightie *n* (*pl* **-s**) (*Informal*) nightdress
nighties *n* ▷ **nightie**
nightingale *n* (*pl* **-s**) small bird with a musical song usu. heard at night
nightingales *n* ▷ **nightingale**
nightjar *n* (*pl* **-s**) nocturnal bird with a harsh cry
nightjars *n* ▷ **nightjar**
nightlife *n* (*pl* **-s**) entertainment and social activities available at night in a town or city
nightlifes *n* ▷ **nightlife**
nightly *adj, adv* (happening) each night
nightmare *n* (*pl* **-s**) very bad dream
nightmares *n* ▷ **nightmare**
nights *n* ▷ **night**
nightshade *n* (*pl* **-s**) plant with bell-shaped flowers which are often poisonous
nightshades *n* ▷ **nightshade**
nightshirt *n* (*pl* **-s**) long loose shirt worn in bed
nightshirts *n* ▷ **nightshirt**
nihilism [**nye**-ill-liz-zum] *n* (*pl* **-s**) rejection of all established authority and institutions > **nihilist** *n* (*pl* **-s**) > **nihilistic** *adj*
nihilisms *n* ▷ **nihilism**
nihilist *n* ▷ **nihilism**
nihilistic *adj* ▷ **nihilism**
nihilists *n* ▷ **nihilism**
nil *n* (*pl* **-s**) nothing, zero
nils *n* ▷ **nil**
nimbi *n* ▷ **nimbus**
nimble *adj* (**-r, -st**) agile and quick > **nimbly** *adv*
nimbler *adj* ▷ **nimble**
nimblest *adj* ▷ **nimble**
nimbly *adv* ▷ **nimble**
nimbus *n* (*pl* **-bi, -buses**) dark grey rain cloud
nimbuses *n* ▷ **nimbus**
nincompoop *n* (*pl* **-s**) (*Informal*) stupid person
nincompoops *n* ▷ **nincompoop**
nine *adj, n* (*pl* **-s**) one more than eight
ninepins *n* game of skittles
nines *n* ▷ **nine**
nineteen *adj, n* (*pl* **-s**) ten and nine > **nineteenth** *adj, n* (*pl* **-s**)
nineteens *n* ▷ **nineteen**
nineteenth *adj, n* ▷ **nineteen**
nineteenths *n* ▷ **nineteen**
nineties *n* ▷ **ninety**
ninetieth *adj, n* ▷ **ninety**
ninetieths *n* ▷ **ninety**
ninety *adj, n* (*pl* **-ties**) ten times nine > **ninetieth** *adj, n* (*pl* **-s**)
ninth *adj, n* (*pl* **-s**) (of) number nine in a series
ninths *n* ▷ **ninth**
niobium *n* (*pl* **-s**) (CHEM) white superconductive metallic element
niobiums *n* ▷ **niobium**
nip[1] *v* (**-s, -pping, -pped**) (*Informal*) hurry ▶ *n* (*pl*

-s) pinch or light bite
nip² *n* (*pl* **nips**) small alcoholic drink
nipped *v* ▷ **nip¹**
nipper *n* (*pl* **-s**) (BRIT, AUST & NZ) (*Informal*) small child
nippers *n* ▷ **nipper**
nippier *adj* ▷ **nippy**
nippiest *adj* ▷ **nippy**
nipping *v* ▷ **nip¹**
nipple *n* (*pl* **-s**) projection in the centre of a breast
nipples *n* ▷ **nipple**
nippy *adj* (*Informal*) (**-pier, -piest**) frosty or chilly
nips *v* ▷ **nip¹** ▶ *n* ▷ **nip¹, ²**
nirvana [near-**vah**-na] *n* (*pl* **-s**) (BUDDHISM) (HINDUISM) absolute spiritual enlightenment and bliss
nirvanas *n* ▷ **nirvana**
nit *n* (*pl* **-s**) egg or larva of a louse (*Informal*) ▷ **nitwit**
nitrate *n* (*pl* **-s**) compound of nitric acid, used as a fertilizer
nitrates *n* ▷ **nitrate**
nitric, nitrous, nitrogenous *adj* of or containing nitrogen
nitrogen [**nite**-roj-jen] *n* (*pl* **-s**) (CHEM) colourless odourless gas that forms four fifths of the air
nitrogenous *n* ▷ **nitric**
nitrogens *n* ▷ **nitrogen**
nitroglycerin *n* ▷ **nitroglycerine**
nitroglycerine, nitroglycerin *n* (*pl* **-s**) explosive liquid
nitroglycerines *n* ▷ **nitroglycerine**
nitroglycerins *n* ▷ **nitroglycerine**
nitrous *adj* ▷ **nitric**
nits *n* ▷ **nit**
nitwit *n* (*pl* **-s**) (*Informal*) stupid person
nitwits *n* ▷ **nitwit**

> **nix** *n* (**nixes**). A nix is a water sprite in Germanic mythology. This is a handy little word, combining X with two of the most common tiles in the game. If you have an X on your rack, look out for opportunities on the board to play this as there's most likely an N or I available. Nix scores 10 points.

no *interj* expresses denial, disagreement, or refusal ▶ *adj* not any, not a ▶ *adv* not at all ▶ *n* (*pl* **noes, nos**) answer or vote of 'no'
nob *n* (*pl* **-s**) (CHIEFLY BRIT) (*Slang*) person of wealth or social distinction
nobs *n* ▷ **nob**
nobble *v* (**-les, -ling, -led**) (BRIT) (*Slang*) attract the attention of (someone) in order to talk to him or her
nobbled *v* ▷ **nobble**
nobbles *v* ▷ **nobble**
nobbling *v* ▷ **nobble**
nobelium *n* (*pl* **-s**) (CHEM) artificially-produced radioactive element
nobeliums *n* ▷ **nobelium**
nobilities *n* ▷ **nobility**
nobility *n* (*pl* **-ties**) quality of being noble > **nobleman, noblewoman** *n* (*pl* **-men**)
noble *adj* (**-r, -st**) showing or having high moral qualities ▶ *n* (*pl* **-s**) member of the nobility > **nobly** *adv*
nobleman *n* ▷ **nobility**
noblemen *n* ▷ **nobility**
nobler *adj* ▷ **noble**
nobles *n* ▷ **noble**
noblest *adj* ▷ **noble**
noblewoman *n* ▷ **nobility**
noblewomen *n* ▷ **nobility**
nobly *adv* ▷ **noble**
nobodies *n* ▷ **nobody**
nobody *pron* no person ▶ *n* (*pl* **-dies**) person of no importance
nocturnal *adj* of the night
nocturne *n* (*pl* **-s**) short dreamy piece of music
nocturnes *n* ▷ **nocturne**
nod *v* (**-s, -dding, -dded**) lower and raise (one's head) briefly in agreement or greeting ▶ *n* (*pl* **-s**) act of nodding
nodded *v* ▷ **nod**
nodding *v* ▷ **nod**
noddle *n* (*pl* **s**) (CHIEFLY BRIT) (*Informal*) the head
noddles *n* ▷ **noddle**
node *n* (*pl* **-s**) point on a plant stem from which leaves grow
nodes *n* ▷ **node**
nods *v, n* ▷ **nod**
nodule *n* (*pl* **-s**) small knot or lump
nodules *n* ▷ **nodule**
noel *n* (*pl* **-s**) Christmas carol
noels *n* ▷ **noel**
noes *n* ▷ **no**
noggin *n* (*pl* **-s**) (*Informal*) head
noggins *n* ▷ **noggin**
noise *n* (*pl* **-s**) sound, usu. a loud or disturbing one > **noiseless** *adj*
noiseless *adj* ▷ **noise**
noises *n* ▷ **noise**
noisier *adj* ▷ **noisy**
noisiest *adj* ▷ **noisy**
noisily *adv* ▷ **noisy**
noisy *adj* (**-sier, -siest**) making a lot of noise > **noisily** *adv*
noisome *adj* (of smells) offensive
nomad *n* (*pl* **-s**) member of a tribe with no fixed

dwelling place, wanderer > **nomadic** *adj*
nomadic *adj* ▷ **nomad**
nomads *n* ▷ **nomad**
nomenclature *n* (*pl* **-s**) system of names used in a particular subject
nomenclatures *n* ▷ **nomenclature**
nominal *adj* in name only > **nominally** *adv*
nominally *adv* ▷ **nominal**
nominate *v* (**-tes, -ting, -ted**) suggest as a candidate > **nomination** *n* (*pl* **-s**)
nominated *v* ▷ **nominate**
nominates *v* ▷ **nominate**
nominating *v* ▷ **nominate**
nomination *n* ▷ **nominate**
nominations *n* ▷ **nominate**
nominative *n* (*pl* **-s**) form of a noun indicating the subject of a verb
nominatives *n* ▷ **nominative**
nominee *n* (*pl* **-s**) candidate
nominees *n* ▷ **nominee**
non- *prefix* indicating: negation
nonagenarian *n* (*pl* **-s**) person aged between ninety and ninety-nine
nonagenarians *n* ▷ **nonagenarian**
nonaggression *n* (*pl* **-s**) policy of not attacking other countries
nonaggressions *n* ▷ **nonaggression**
nonagon *n* (*pl* **-s**) geometric figure with nine sides
nonagons *n* ▷ **nonagon**
nonalcoholic *adj* containing no alcohol
nonaligned *adj* (of a country) not part of a major alliance or power bloc
nonce *n* (*pl* **-s**) for the present
nonces *n* ▷ **nonce**
nonchalance *n* ▷ **nonchalant**
nonchalances *n* ▷ **nonchalant**
nonchalant *adj* casually unconcerned or indifferent > **nonchalantly** *adv* > **nonchalance** *n* (*pl* **-s**)
nonchalantly *adv* ▷ **nonchalant**
noncombatant *n* (*pl* **-s**) member of the armed forces whose duties do not include fighting
noncombatants *n* ▷ **noncombatant**
noncommittal *adj* not committing oneself to any particular opinion
nonconductor *n* (*pl* **-s**) substance that is a poor conductor of heat, electricity, or sound
nonconductors *n* ▷ **nonconductor**
nonconformist *n* (*pl* **-s**) person who does not conform to generally accepted patterns of behaviour or thought (**N-**) ▸ *adj* (of behaviour or ideas) not conforming to accepted patterns > **nonconformity** *n* (*pl* **-ties**)
nonconformists *n* ▷ **nonconformist**
nonconformities *n* ▷ **nonconformist**
nonconformity *n* ▷ **nonconformist**
noncontributory *adj* (BRIT) denoting a pension scheme for employees, the premiums of which are paid entirely by the employer
nondescript *adj* lacking outstanding features
none *pron* not any
nonentities *n* ▷ **nonentity**
nonentity [non-**enn**-tit-tee] *n* (*pl* **-ties**) insignificant person or thing
nonetheless *adv* despite that, however
nonevent *n* (*pl* **-s**) disappointing or insignificant occurrence
nonevents *n* ▷ **nonevent**
nonflammable *adj* not easily set on fire
nonintervention *n* (*pl* refusal to intervene in the affairs of others
nonpareil [non-par-**rail**] *n* (*pl* **-s**) person or thing that is unsurpassed
nonpareils *n* ▷ **nonpareil**
nonpayment *n* (*pl* **-s**) failure to pay money owed
nonpayments *n* ▷ **nonpayment**
nonplussed *adj* perplexed
nonsense *n* (*pl* **-s**) something that has or makes no sense > **nonsensical** *adj*
nonsenses *n* ▷ **nonsense**
nonsensical *adj* ▷ **nonsense**
nonstandard *adj* denoting language that is not regarded as correct by educated native speakers
nonstarter *n* (*pl* **-s**) person or idea that has little chance of success
nonstarters *n* ▷ **nonstarter**
nonstick *adj* coated with a substance that food will not stick to when cooked
nonstop *adj, adv* without a stop
nontoxic *adj* not poisonous
noodles *pl n* long thin strips of pasta
nook *n* (*pl* **-s**) sheltered place
nooks *n* ▷ **nook**
noon *n* (*pl* **-s**) twelve o'clock midday
noonday *adj* happening at noon
noons *n* ▷ **noon**
noose *n* (*pl* **-s**) loop in the end of a rope, tied with a slipknot
nooses *n* ▷ **noose**
nor *conj* and not
norm *n* (*pl* **-s**) standard that is regarded as normal
normal *adj* usual, regular, or typical > **normally** *adv* > **normality** *n* (*pl* **-ties**) > **normalize** *v* (**-izes, -izing, -ized**)
normalities *n* ▷ **normal**

normality *n* ▷ **normal**
normalized *v* ▷ **normal**
normalizes *v* ▷ **normal**
normalizing *v* ▷ **normal**
normally *adv* ▷ **normal**
norms *n* ▷ **norm**
north *n* (*pl* **-s**) direction towards the North Pole, opposite south ▶ *adj* to or in the north ▶ *adv* in, to, or towards the north > **northerly** *adj* > **northern** *adj* > **northward** *adj, adv* > **northwards** *adv*
northerly *adj* ▷ **north**
northern *adj* ▷ **north**
northerner *n* (*pl* **-s**) person from the north of a country or area
northerners *n* ▷ **northerner**
norths *n* ▷ **north**
northward *adj, adv* ▷ **north**
northwards *adv* ▷ **north**
nos *n* ▷ **no**
nose *n* (*pl* **-s**) organ of smell, used also in breathing ▶ *v* (**-ses, -sing, -sed**) move forward slowly and carefully
nosed *v* ▷ **nose**
nosegay *n* (*pl* **-s**) small bunch of flowers
nosegays *n* ▷ **nosegay**
noses *n, v* ▷ **nose**
nosey, nosy *adj* (*Informal*) (**-sier, -siest**) prying or inquisitive > **nosiness** *n* (*pl* **-es**)
nosier *adj* ▷ **nosey**
nosiest *adj* ▷ **nosey**
nosiness *n* ▷ **nosey**
nosinesses *n* ▷ **nosey**
nosing *v* ▷ **nose**
nosh *n* (*pl* **-es**) (BRIT, AUST & NZ) (*Slang*) food ▶ *v* (**-shes, -shing, -shed**) eat
noshed *v* ▷ **nosh**
noshes *n, v* ▷ **nosh**
noshing *v* ▷ **nosh**
nostalgia *n* (*pl* **-s**) sentimental longing for the past > **nostalgic** *adj*
nostalgias *n* ▷ **nostalgia**
nostalgic *adj* ▷ **nostalgia**
nostril *n* (*pl* **-s**) one of the two openings at the end of the nose
nostrils *n* ▷ **nostril**
nostrum *n* (*pl* **-s**) quack medicine
nostrums *n* ▷ **nostrum**
nosy *adj* (**-sier, -siest**) ▷ **nosey**
not *adv* expressing negation, refusal, or denial
notable *adj* worthy of being noted, remarkable ▶ *n* (*pl* **-s**) person of distinction > **notably** *adv*
notabilities *n* ▷ **notability**
notability *n* (*pl* **-ties**)
notables *n* ▷ **notable**
notably *adv* ▷ **notable**
notaries *n* ▷ **notary**
notary *n* (*pl* **-ries**) person authorized to witness the signing of legal documents
notation *n* (*pl* **-s**) representation of numbers or quantities in a system by a series of symbols
notations *n* ▷ **notation**
notch *n* (*pl* **-es**) V-shaped cut ▶ *v* (**-ches, -ching, -ched**) make a notch in (*foll. by* **up**)
notched *v* ▷ **notch**
notches *n, v* ▷ **notch**
notching *v* ▷ **notch**
note *n* (*pl* **-s**) short letter ▶ *v* (**-tes, -ting, -ted**) notice, pay attention to
notebook *n* (*pl* **-s**) book for writing in
notebooks *n* ▷ **notebook**
noted *v* ▷ **note** ▶ *adj* well-known
notes *n, v* ▷ **note**
noteworthy *adj* worth noting, remarkable
nothing *pron* not anything ▶ *adv* not at all
nothingness *n* (*pl* **-es**) nonexistence
nothingnesses *n* ▷ **nothingness**
notice *n* (*pl* **-s**) observation or attention ▶ *v* (**-ces, -cing, -ced**) observe, become aware of
noticeable *adj* easily seen or detected, appreciable
noticed *v* ▷ **notice**
notices *n, v* ▷ **notice**
noticing *v* ▷ **notice**
notifiable *adj* having to be reported to the authorities
notification *n* ▷ **notify**
notifications *n* ▷ **notify**
notified *v* ▷ **notify**
notifies *v* ▷ **notify**
notify *v* (**-fies, -fying, -fied**) inform > **notification** *n* (*pl* **-s**)
notifying *v* ▷ **notify**
noting *v* ▷ **note**
notion *n* (*pl* **-s**) idea or opinion
notional *adj* speculative, imaginary, or unreal
notions *n* ▷ **notion**
notorieties *n* ▷ **notorious**
notoriety *n* ▷ **notorious**
notorious *adj* well known for something bad > **notoriously** *adv* > **notoriety** *n* (*pl* **-ties**)
notoriously *adv* ▷ **notorious**
notwithstanding *prep* in spite of
nougat *n* (*pl* **-s**) chewy sweet containing nuts and fruit
nougats *n* ▷ **nougat**
nought *n* (*pl* **-s**) figure 0
noughties *pl n* (*Informal*) decade from 2000 to 2009

noughts *n* ▷ **nought**
noun *n* (*pl* **-s**) word that refers to a person, place, or thing
nouns *n* ▷ **noun**
nourish *v* (**-shes, -shing, -shed**) feed > **nourishment** *n* (*pl* **-s**)
nourished *v* ▷ **nourish**
nourishes *v* ▷ **nourish**
nourishing *adj* providing the food necessary for life and growth ▶ *v* ▷ **nourish**
nourishment *n* ▷ **nourish**
nourishments *n* ▷ **nourish**
nova *n* (*pl* **-vae, -vas**) star that suddenly becomes brighter and then gradually decreases to its original brightness
novae *n* ▷ **nova**
novas *n* ▷ **nova**
novel[1] *n* (*pl* **-s**) long fictitious story in book form
novel[2] *adj* fresh, new, or original > **novelist** *n* (*pl* **-s**) writer of novels
novelists *n* ▷ **novelist**
novella *n* (*pl* **-s, -llae**) short novel
novellae *n* ▷ **novella**
novellas *n* ▷ **novella**
novels *n* ▷ **novel**[1]
novelties *n* ▷ **novelty**
novelty *n* (*pl* **-ties**) newness
novena [no-**vee**-na] *n* (*pl* **-s**) (RC CHURCH) set of prayers or services on nine consecutive days
novenas *n* ▷ **novena**
novice *n* (*pl* **-s**) beginner
novices *n* ▷ **novice**
now *adv* at or for the present time ▶ *conj* seeing that, since
nowadays *adv* in these times
nowhere *adv* not anywhere

> **nox** *n* (**noxes**). In chemistry, nox is short for nitrogen oxide. This is an unusual word which can come in useful in the later stages of the game when there isn't much space left, or when you have an X but can't form a longer word with it. Nox scores 10 points.

noxious *adj* poisonous or harmful
nozzle *n* (*pl* **-s**) projecting spout through which fluid is discharged
nozzles *n* ▷ **nozzle**

> **nth** *adv*. In mathematics, nth represents an unspecified ordinal number. Nth is a good word to remember for awkward situations on the board, as it's one of very few three-letter words that doesn't contain a vowel. Nth scores 6 points.

> **nu** *n* nus. Nu is the 13th letter in the Greek alphabet. This word is worth remembering, as it can be really useful when you want to form short words in the process of playing a longer one. Nu scores 2 points.

nuance [**new**-ahnss] *n* (*pl* **-s**) subtle difference in colour, meaning, or tone
nuances *n* ▷ **nuance**
nub *n* (*pl* **-s**) point or gist (of a story etc.)
nubs *n* ▷ **nub**
nubile [**new**-bile] *adj* (of a young woman) sexually attractive
nuclear *adj* of nuclear weapons or energy
nuclei *n* ▷ **nucleus**
nucleus *n* (*pl* **-clei**) centre, esp. of an atom or cell
nude *adj* (**-r, -st**) naked ▶ *n* (*pl* **-s**) naked figure in painting, sculpture, or photography > **nudity** *n* (*pl* **-ties**)
nuder *adj* ▷ **nude**
nudes *n* ▷ **nude**
nudest *adj* ▷ **nude**
nudge *v* (**-dges, -dging, -dged**) push gently, esp. with the elbow ▶ *n* (*pl* **-s**) gentle push or touch
nudged *v* ▷ **nudge**
nudges *v, n* ▷ **nudge**
nudging *v* ▷ **nudge**
nudism *n* (*pl* **-s**) practice of not wearing clothes > **nudist** *n* (*pl* **-s**)
nudisms *n* ▷ **nudism**
nudist *n* ▷ **nudism**
nudists *n* ▷ **nudism**
nudities *n* ▷ **nude**
nudity *n* ▷ **nude**
nugatory [**new**-gat-tree] *adj* of little value
nugget *n* (*pl* **-s**) small lump of gold in its natural state ▶ *v* (**-s, -tting, -tted**) (NZ & S AFR) polish footwear
nuggets *n, v* ▷ **nugget**
nuggetted *v* ▷ **nugget**
nuggetting *v* ▷ **nugget**
nuisance *n* (*pl* **-s**) something or someone that causes annoyance or bother
nuisances *n* ▷ **nuisance**
nuke (*Slang*) *v* (**-kes, -king, -ked**) attack with nuclear weapons ▶ *n* (*pl* **-s**) nuclear weapon
nuked *v* ▷ **nuke**
nukes *v, n* ▷ **nuke**
nuking *v* ▷ **nuke**
null *adj* not legally valid > **nullity** *n* (*pl* **-s**)
nullified *v* ▷ **nullify**
nullifies *v* ▷ **nullify**

nullify *v* (**-fies, -fying, -fied**) make ineffective
nullifying *v* ▷ **nullify**
nullities *n* ▷ **null**
nullity *n* ▷ **null**
numb *adj* (**-er, -est**) without feeling, as through cold, shock, or fear ▶ *v* (**-s, -ing, -ed**) make numb > **numbly** *adv* > **numbness** *n* (*pl* **-es**)
numbat *n* (*pl* **-s**) small Australian marsupial with a long snout and tongue
numbats *n* ▷ **numbat**
numbed *v* ▷ **numb**
number¹ *adj* ▷ **numb**
number² *n* (*pl* **-s**) sum or quantity ▶ *v* (**-s, -ing, -ed**) count
numbered *v* ▷ **number**
numbering *v* ▷ **number**
numberless *adj* too many to be counted
numberplate *n* (*pl* **-s**) plate on a car showing the registration number
numberplates *n* ▷ **numberplate**
numbers *n, v* ▷ **number**
numbest *adj* ▷ **numb**
numbing *v* ▷ **numb**
numbly *adv* ▷ **numb**
numbness *n* ▷ **numb**
numbnesses *n* ▷ **numb**
numbs *v* ▷ **numb**
numbskull *n* (*pl* **-s**) stupid person
numbskulls *n* ▷ **numbskull**
numeracies *n* ▷ **numerate**
numeracy *n* ▷ **numerate**
numeral *n* (*pl* **-s**) word or symbol used to express a sum or quantity
numerals *n* ▷ **numeral**
numerate *adj* able to do basic arithmetic > **numeracy** *n* (*pl* **-cies**)
numeration *n* (*pl* **-s**) act or process of numbering or counting
numerations *n* ▷ **numeration**
numerator *n* (*pl* **-s**) (MATHS) number above the line in a fraction
numerators *n* ▷ **numerator**
numerical *adj* measured or expressed in numbers > **numerically** *adv*
numerically *adv* ▷ **numerical**
numerous *adj* existing or happening in large numbers
numismatist *n* (*pl* **-s**) coin collector
numismatists *n* ▷ **numismatist**
numskull *n* (*pl* **-s**) ▷ **numbskull**
numskulls *n* ▷ **numskull**
nun *n* (*pl* **-s**) female member of a religious order
nuncio *n* (*pl* **-s**) (RC CHURCH) pope's ambassador
nuncios *n* ▷ **nuncio**
nunneries *n* ▷ **nunnery**
nunnery *n* (*pl* **-ries**) convent
nuns *n* ▷ **nun**
nuptial *adj* relating to marriage
nuptials *pl n* wedding
nurse *n* (*pl* **-s**) person employed to look after sick people, usu. in a hospital ▶ *v* (**-ses, -sing, -sed**) look after (a sick person)
nursed *v* ▷ **nurse**
nurseries *n* ▷ **nursery**
nursery *n* (*pl* **-ries**) room where children sleep or play
nurseryman *n* (*pl* **-men**) person who raises plants for sale
nurserymen *n* ▷ **nurseryman**
nurses *n, v* ▷ **nurse**
nursing *v* ▷ **nurse**
nurture *n* (*pl* **-s**) act or process of promoting the development of a child or young plant ▶ *v* (**-res, -ring, -red**) promote or encourage the development of
nurtured *v* ▷ **nurture**
nurtures *n, v* ▷ **nurture**
nurturing *v* ▷ **nurture**
nut *n* (*pl* **-s**) fruit consisting of a hard shell and a kernel
nutcracker *n* (*pl* **-s**) device for cracking the shells of nuts
nutcrackers *n* ▷ **nutcracker**
nuthatch *n* (*pl* **-es**) small songbird
nuthatches *n* ▷ **nuthatch**
nutmeg *n* (*pl* **-s**) spice made from the seed of a tropical tree
nutmeg *n* ▷ **nutmeg**
nutria *n* (*pl* **-s**) fur of the coypu
nutrias *n* ▷ **nutria**
nutrient *n* (*pl* **-s**) substance that provides nourishment
nutrients *n* ▷ **nutrient**
nutriment *n* (*pl* **-s**) food or nourishment required by all living things to grow and stay healthy
nutriments *n* ▷ **nutriment**
nutrition *n* (*pl* **-s**) process of taking in and absorbing nutrients > **nutritional** *adj*
nutritional *adj* ▷ **nutrition**
nutritions *n* ▷ **nutrition**
nutritious, nutritive *adj* nourishing
nutritive *adj* ▷ **nutritious**
nuts *n* ▷ **nut**
nutter *n* (*pl* **-s**) (BRIT) (*Slang*) insane person
nutters *n* ▷ **nutter**
nuttier *adj* ▷ **nutty**
nuttiest *adj* ▷ **nutty**
nutty *adj* (**-ttier, -ttiest**) containing or

resembling nuts

nuzzle *v* (**-les, -ling, -led**) push or rub gently with the nose or snout

nuzzled *v* ▷ **nuzzle**

nuzzles *v* ▷ **nuzzle**

nuzzling *v* ▷ **nuzzle**

ny *adj, adv*. Ny is an old spelling of **nigh.** This word can be useful when you're forming one word adjacent to another, and so need to form two-letter words where the two words meet. Ny is also unusual in that it doesn't contain a vowel. Ny scores 5 points.

nylon *n* (*pl* **-s**) synthetic material used for clothing etc.

nylons *n* ▷ **nylon** ▶ *pl n* stockings made of nylon

nymph *n* (*pl* **-s**) mythical spirit of nature, represented as a beautiful young woman

nymphs *n* ▷ **nymph**

nymphet *n* (*pl* **-s**) sexually precocious young girl

nymphets *n* ▷ **nymphet**

Oo

With eight Os in the bag, you're likely to have at least one on your rack during a game. There are plenty of good two-letter words starting with O. It's worth knowing that O will form a two-letter word in front of every other vowel except A, as well as in front of Y. O also combines well with X, with **ox** (9 points) as the obvious starting point, and several words that refer to **oxygen** (17), including **oxo** (10) and **oxy** (13). Don't forget the short everyday words that begin with O. While **on** and **or** (2 each) won't earn you many points, they can be very helpful when you are trying to score in more than one direction at a time. **Of** and **oh** (5 each) can also prove very useful.

oaf *n* (*pl* **-s**) stupid or clumsy person > **oafish** *adj*
oafish *adj* ▷ **oaf**
oafs *n* ▷ **oaf**
oak *n* (*pl* **-s**) deciduous forest tree > **oaken** *adj*
oaken *adj* ▷ **oak**
oaks *n* ▷ **oak**
oakum *n* (*pl* **-s**) fibre obtained by unravelling old rope
oakums *n* ▷ **oakum**
oar *n* (*pl* **-s**) pole with a broad blade, used for rowing a boat
oars *n* ▷ **oar**
oasis *n* (*pl* **-ses**) fertile area in a desert
oases *n* ▷ **oasis**
oast *n* (*pl* **-s**) (CHIEFLY BRIT) oven for drying hops
oasts *n* ▷ **oast**
oat *n* (*pl* **-s**) hard cereal grown as food ▶ *pl* grain of this cereal
oath *n* (*pl* **-s**) solemn promise, esp. to be truthful in court
oaths *n* ▷ **oath**
oatmeal *adj* pale brownish-cream
oats *n* ▷ **oat**
obbligato [ob-lig-**gah**-toe] *n* (*pl* **-os**) (MUSIC) essential part or accompaniment
obbligatos *n* ▷ **obbligato**
obduracies *n* ▷ **obdurate**
obduracy *n* ▷ **obdurate**
obdurate *adj* hardhearted or stubborn > **obduracy** *n* (*pl* **-cies**)
obedience *n* ▷ **obedient**
obediences *n* ▷ **obedient**
obedient *adj* obeying or willing to obey > **obedience** *n* (*pl* **-s**) > **obediently** *adv*
obediently *adv* ▷ **obedient**
obeisance [oh-**bay**-sanss] *n* (*pl* **-s**) attitude of respect
obeisances *n* ▷ **obeisance**
obelisk [**ob**-bill-isk] *n* (*pl* **-s**) four-sided stone column tapering to a pyramid at the top
obelisks *n* ▷ **obelisk**
obese [oh-**beess**] *adj* (**-r, -st**) very fat > **obesity** *n* (*pl* **-ties**)
obeser *adj* ▷ **obese**
obesest *adj* ▷ **obese**
obesities *n* ▷ **obese**
obesity *n* ▷ **obese**
obey *v* (**-s, -ing, -ed**) carry out instructions or orders
obeyed *v* ▷ **obey**
obeying *v* ▷ **obey**
obeys *v* ▷ **obey**
obfuscate *v* (**-tes, -ting, -ted**) make (something) confusing
obfuscated *v* ▷ **obfuscate**
obfuscates *v* ▷ **obfuscate**
obfuscating *v* ▷ **obfuscate**
obituaries *n* ▷ **obituary**
obituarist *n* ▷ **obituary**
obituarists *n* ▷ **obituary**
obituary *n* (*pl* **-ies**) announcement of someone's death, esp. in a newspaper > **obituarist** *n* (*pl* **-s**)
object[1] *n* (*pl* **-s**) physical thing
object[2] *v* (**-s, -ing, -ed**) express disapproval > **objection** *n* (*pl* **-s**) > **objector** *n* (*pl* **-s**)
objected *v* ▷ **object**[2]
objecting *v* ▷ **object**[2]
objection *n* ▷ **object**[2]
objectionable *adj* unpleasant
objections *n* ▷ **object**[2]
objective *n* (*pl* **-s**) aim or purpose ▶ *adj* not

biased > **objectively** *adv* > **objectivity** *n* (*pl* **-ties**)
objectively *adv* ▷ **objective**
objectives *n* ▷ **objective**
objectivities *n* ▷ **objective**
objectivity *n* ▷ **objective**
objector *n* ▷ **object²**
objectors *n* ▷ **object²**
objects *n, v* ▷ **object¹, ²**
oblation *n* (*pl* **-s**) religious offering
oblations *n* ▷ **oblation**
obligated *adj* obliged to do something
obligation *n* (*pl* **-s**) duty
obligations *n* ▷ **obligation**
obligatory *adj* required by a rule or law
oblige *v* (**-ges, -ging, -ged**) compel (someone) morally or by law to do something
obliged *v* ▷ **oblige**
obliges *v* ▷ **oblige**
obliging *adj* ready to help other people ▶ *v* ▷ **oblige** > **obligingly** *adv*
obligingly *adv* ▷ **oblige**
oblique [oh-**bleak**] *adj* (**-r, -st**) slanting ▶ *n* (*pl* **-s**) the symbol (/) > **obliquely** *adv*
obliquely *adv* ▷ **oblique**
obliquer *adj* ▷ **oblique**
obliques *n* ▷ **oblique**
obliquest *adj* ▷ **oblique**
obliterate *v* (**-tes, -ting, -ted**) wipe out, destroy > **obliteration** *n* (*pl* **-s**)
obliterated *v* ▷ **obliterate**
obliterates *v* ▷ **obliterate**
obliterating *v* ▷ **obliterate**
obliteration *n* ▷ **obliterate**
obliterations *n* ▷ **obliterate**
oblivion *n* (*pl* **-s**) state of being forgotten
oblivions *n* ▷ **oblivion**
oblivious *adj* unaware
oblong *adj* having two long sides, two short sides, and four right angles ▶ *n* (*pl* **-s**) oblong figure
oblongs *n* ▷ **oblong**
obloquies *n* ▷ **obloquy**
obloquy [**ob**-lock-wee] *n* (*pl* **-quies**) verbal abuse
obnoxious *adj* offensive
oboe *n* (*pl* **-s**) double-reeded woodwind instrument > **oboist** *n* (*pl* **-s**)
oboes *n* ▷ **oboe**
oboist *n* ▷ **oboe**
oboists *n* ▷ **oboe**
obscene *adj* (**-r, -st**) portraying sex offensively > **obscenity** *n* (*pl* **-ies**)
obscener *adj* ▷ **obscene**
obscenest *adj* ▷ **obscene**
obscenities *n* ▷ **obscene**
obscenity *n* ▷ **obscene**
obscure *adj* (**-r, -st**) not well known ▶ *v* (**-res, -ring, -red**) make (something) obscure > **obscurity** *n* (*pl* **-ties**)
obscured *v* ▷ **obscure**
obscurer *adj* ▷ **obscure**
obscures *v* ▷ **obscure**
obscurest *adj* ▷ **obscure**
obscuring *v* ▷ **obscure**
obscurities *n* ▷ **obscure**
obscurity *n* ▷ **obscure**
obsequies [**ob**-sick-weez] *pl n* funeral rites
obsequious [ob-**seek**-wee-uss] *adj* overattentive in order to gain favour > **obsequiousness** *n*
obsequiousness *n* ▷ **obsequious**
observe *v* (**-ves, -ving, -ved**) see or notice > **observable** *adj*
observable *adj* ▷ **observe**
observance *n* (*pl* **-s**) observing of a custom
observances *n* ▷ **observance**
observant *adj* quick to notice things
observation *n* (*pl* **-s**) action or habit of observing
observations *n* ▷ **observation**
observatories *n* ▷ **observatory**
observatory *n* (*pl* **-ries**) building equipped for studying the weather and the stars
observed *v* ▷ **observe**
observer *n* (*pl* **-s**) person who observes, esp. one who watches someone or something carefully
observers *n* ▷ **observer**
observes *v* ▷ **observe**
observing *v* ▷ **observe**
obsess *v* (**-es, -ing, -ed**) preoccupy (someone) compulsively > **obsessed** *adj* > **obsessive** *adj* > **obsession** *n* (*pl* **-s**)
obsessed *v, adj* ▷ **obsess**
obsesses *v* ▷ **obsess**
obsessing *v* ▷ **obsess**
obsession *n* ▷ **obsess**
obsessions *n* ▷ **obsess**
obsessive *adj* ▷ **obsess**
obsidian *n* (*pl* **-s**) dark glassy volcanic rock
obsidians *n* ▷ **obsidian**
obsolescence *n* ▷ **obsolescent**
obsolescences *n* ▷ **obsolescent**
obsolescent *adj* becoming obsolete > **obsolescence** *n* (*pl* **-s**)
obsolete *adj* no longer in use
obstacle *n* (*pl* **-s**) something that makes progress difficult
obstacles *n* ▷ **obstacle**
obstetric *adj* ▷ **obstetrics**

obstetrician *n* ▷ **obstetrics**
obstetricians *n* ▷ **obstetrics**
obstetrics *n* branch of medicine concerned with pregnancy and childbirth > **obstetric** *adj* > **obstetrician** *n* (*pl* **-s**)
obstinacy *n* ▷ **obstinate**
obstinacies *n* ▷ **obstinate**
obstinate *adj* stubborn > **obstinately** *adv* > **obstinacy** *n* (*pl* **-cies**)
obstinately *adv* ▷ **obstinate**
obstreperous *adj* unruly, noisy
obstruct *v* (**-s, -ing, -ed**) block with an obstacle > **obstruction** *n* (*pl* **-s**) > **obstructive** *adj*
obstructed *v* ▷ **obstruct**
obstructing *v* ▷ **obstruct**
obstruction *n* ▷ **obstruct**
obstructions *n* ▷ **obstruct**
obstructive *adj* ▷ **obstruct**
obstructs *v* ▷ **obstruct**
obtain *v* (**-s, -ing, -ed**) acquire intentionally > **obtainable** *adj*
obtainable *adj* ▷ **obtain**
obtained *v* ▷ **obtain**
obtaining *v* ▷ **obtain**
obtains *v* ▷ **obtain**
obtrude *v* (**-des, -ding, -ded**) push oneself or one's ideas on others
obtruded *v* ▷ **obtrude**
obtrudes *v* ▷ **obtrude**
obtruding *v* ▷ **obtrude**
obtuse *adj* (**-r, -st**) mentally slow > **obtuseness** *n* (*pl* **-es**)
obtuseness *n* ▷ **obtuse**
obtusenesses *n* ▷ **obtuse**
obtuser *adj* ▷ **obtuse**
obtusest *adj* ▷ **obtuse**
obtrusive *adj* unpleasantly noticeable > **obtrusively** *adv*
obtrusively *adv* ▷ **obstrusive**
obverse *n* (*pl* **-s**) opposite way of looking at an idea
obverses *n* ▷ **obverse**
obviate *v* (**-tes, -ting, -ted**) make unnecessary
obviated *v* ▷ **obviate**
obviates *v* ▷ **obviate**
obviating *v* ▷ **obviate**
obvious *adj* easy to see or understand, evident > **obviously** *adv*
obviously *adv* ▷ **obvious**
ocarina *n* (*pl* **-s**) small oval wind instrument
ocarinas *n* ▷ **ocarina**
occasion *n* (*pl* **-s**) time at which a particular thing happens ▶ *v* (**-s, -ing, -ed**) cause
occasional *adj* happening sometimes > **occasionally** *adv*
occasionally *adv* ▷ **occasional**
occasioned *v* ▷ **occasion**
occasioning *v* ▷ **occasion**
occasions *n, v* ▷ **occasion**
occident *n* (*pl* **occidents**) (*Lit*) west > **occidental** *adj*
occidental *adj* ▷ **occident**
occidents *n* ▷ **occident**
occiput [**ox**-sip-put] *n* (*pl* **-s**) back of the head
occiputs *n* ▷ **occiput**
occlude *v* (**-des, -ding, -ded**) obstruct > **occlusion** *n* (*pl* **-s**)
occluded *v* ▷ **occlude**
occludes *v* ▷ **occlude**
occluding *v* ▷ **occlude**
occlusion *n* ▷ **occlude**
occlusions *n* ▷ **occlude**
occult *adj* relating to the supernatural
occupancies *n* ▷ **occupancy**
occupancy *n* (*pl* **-cies**) (length of) a person's stay in a specified place
occupant *n* (*pl* **-s**) person occupying a specified place
occupants *n* ▷ **occupant**
occupation *n* (*pl* **-s**) profession > **occupational** *adj*
occupational *adj* ▷ **occupation**
occupations *n* ▷ **occupation**
occupied *v* ▷ **occupy**
occupier *n* ▷ **occupy**
occupiers *n* ▷ **occupy**
occupies *v* ▷ **occupy**
occupy *v* (**-pies, -pying, -pied**) live or work in (a building) > **occupier** *n* (*pl* **-s**)
occur *v* (**-s, -rring, -rred**) happen
occurrence *n* (*pl* **-s**) something that occurs
occurrences *n* ▷ **occurrence**
occurred *v* ▷ **occur**
occurring *v* ▷ **occur**
occurs *v* ▷ **occur**
ocean *n* (*pl* **-s**) vast area of sea between continents > **oceanic** *adj*
oceanic *adj* ▷ **ocean**
oceanographies *n* ▷ **oceanography**
oceanography *n* (*pl* **-phies**) scientific study of the oceans
oceans *n* ▷ **ocean**
ocelot [**oss**-ill-lot] *n* (*pl* **-s**) American wild cat with a spotted coat
ocelots *n* ▷ **ocelot**
oche [**ok**-kee] *n* (*pl* **-s**) (DARTS) mark on the floor behind which a player must stand
oches *n* ▷ **oche**
ochre [**oak**-er] *adj, n* (*pl* **-s**) brownish-yellow (earth)

ochres *n* ▷ **ochre**
octagon *n* (*pl* **-s**) geometric figure with eight sides > **octagonal** *adj*
octagonal *adj* ▷ **octagon**
octagons *n* ▷ **octagon**
octahedra *n* ▷ **octahedron**
octahedron [ok-ta-**heed**-ron] *n* (*pl* **-drons, -dra**) three-dimensional geometric figure with eight faces
octahedrons *n* ▷ **octahedra**
octane *n* (*pl* **-s**) hydrocarbon found in petrol
octanes *n* ▷ **octane**
octave *n* (*pl* **-s**) (MUSIC) (interval between the first and) eighth note of a scale
octaves *n* ▷ **octave**
octet *n* (*pl* **-s**) group of eight performers
octets *n* ▷ **octet**
octogenarian *n* (*pl* **-s**) person aged between eighty and eighty-nine
octogenarians *n* ▷ **octogenarian**
octopus *n* (*pl* **-es**) sea creature with a soft body and eight tentacles
octopuses *n* ▷ **octopus**
ocular *adj* relating to the eyes or sight
odd (**-er, -est**) *adj* unusual
odder *adj* ▷ **odd**
oddest *adj* ▷ **odd**
oddities *n* ▷ **oddity**
oddity *n* (*pl* **-ties**) odd person or thing
oddments *pl n* things left over
oddness *n* (*pl* **-es**) quality of being odd
oddnesses *n* ▷ **oddness**
odds *pl n* (ratio showing) the probability of something happening
ode *n* (*pl* **-s**) lyric poem, usu. addressed to a particular subject
odes *n* ▷ **ode**
odious *adj* offensive
odium [**oh**-dee-um] *n* (*pl* **-s**) widespread dislike
odiums *n* ▷ **odium**
odorous *adj* ▷ **odour**
odour *n* (*pl* **-s**) particular smell > **odorous** *adj* > **odourless** *adj*
odourless *adj* ▷ **odour**
odours *n* ▷ **odour**
odyssey [**odd**-iss-ee] *n* (*pl* **-s**) long eventful journey
odysseys *n* ▷ **odyssey**

> **oe** *n* (**oes**). Oe is a Scots word for a grandchild. This is a good word to remember, as it combines two of the most common letters in the game without using any consonants. Oe scores 2 points.

oedema [id-**deem**-a] *n* (*pl* **-mata**) (MED) abnormal swelling
oedemata *n* ▷ **oedema**
oesophagi *n* ▷ **oesophagus**
oesophagus [ee-**soff**-a-guss] *n* (*pl* **-gi**) passage between the mouth and stomach
oestrogen [**ee**-stra-jen] *n* (*pl* **-s**) female hormone that controls the reproductive cycle
oestrogens *n* ▷ **oestrogen**
of *prep* belonging to
off *prep* away from ▶ *adv* away ▶ *adj* not operating ▶ *n* (*pl* **-s**) (CRICKET) side of the field to which the batsman's feet point
offal *n* (*pl* **-s**) edible organs of an animal, such as liver or kidneys
offals *n* ▷ **offal**
offcut *n* (*pl* **-s**) piece remaining after the required parts have been cut out
offcuts *n* ▷ **offcut**
offend *v* (**-s, -ing, -ed**) hurt the feelings of, insult
offence *n* (*pl* **-s**) (cause of) hurt feelings or annoyance
offences *n* ▷ **offence**
offended *v* ▷ **offend**
offender *n* (*pl* **-s**) person who commits a crime
offenders *n* ▷ **offender**
offending *v* ▷ **offend**
offends *v* ▷ **offend**
offensive *adj* disagreeable ▶ *n* (*pl* **-s**) position or action of attack
offensives *n* ▷ **offensive**
offer *v* (**-s, -ing, -ed**) present (something) for acceptance or rejection ▶ *n* (*pl* **-s**) instance of offering something
offering *n* (*pl* **-s**) thing offered
offered *v* ▷ **offer**
offering *v* ▷ **offer**
offerings *n* ▷ **offering**
offers *v, n* ▷ **offer**
offertories *n* ▷ **offertory**
offertory *n* (**-ries**) (CHRISTIANITY) offering of the bread and wine for Communion
offhand *adj* casual, curt ▶ *adv* without preparation
office *n* (*pl* **-s**) room or building where people work at desks
officer *n* (*pl* **-s**) person in authority in the armed services
officers *n* ▷ **officer**
offices *n* ▷ **office**
official *adj* of a position of authority ▶ *n* (*pl* **-s**) person who holds a position of authority > **officially** *adv*
officialdom *n* (*pl* **-s**) officials collectively
officialdoms *n* ▷ **officialdom**

officially *adv* ▷ **official**
officials *n* ▷ **official**
officiate *v* (**-tes, -ting, -ted**) act in an official role
officiated *v* ▷ **officiate**
officiates *v* ▷ **officiate**
officiating *v* ▷ **officiate**
officious *adj* interfering unnecessarily
offing *n* (*pl* **-s**) area of the sea visible from the shore
offings *n* ▷ **offing**
offs *n* ▷ **off**
offset *v* (**-sets, -setting, -set**) cancel out, compensate for
offsets *v* ▷ **offset**
offsetting *v* ▷ **offset**
offshoot *n* (*pl* **-s**) something developed from something else
offshoots *n* ▷ **offshoot**
offside *adj, adv* (SPORT) (positioned) illegally ahead of the ball
offspring *n* (*pl* **-s**) child
offsprings *n* ▷ **offspring**
oft *adv* (*Poetic*) often
often *adv* frequently, much of the time
ogle *v* (**-les, -ling, -led**) stare at (someone) lustfully
ogled *v* ▷ **ogle**
ogles *v* ▷ **ogle**
ogling *v* ▷ **ogle**
ogre *n* (*pl* **-s**) giant that eats human flesh
ogres *n* ▷ **ogre**
oh *interj* exclamation of surprise, pain, etc.
ohm *n* (*pl* **-s**) unit of electrical resistance
ohms *n* ▷ **ohm**

> **oi** *interj*. Oi is something people shout to attract attention. This is a good word to remember, as it combines two of the most common letters in the game without using any consonants. Oi scores 2 points.

oil *n* (*pl* **-s**) viscous liquid, insoluble in water and usu. flammable ▷ **petroleum** ▶ *pl* oil-based paints used in art ▶ *v* (**-s, -ing, -ed**) lubricate (a machine) with oil > **oily** *adj* (**-lier, -liest**)
oiled *v* ▷ **oil**
oilfield *n* (**-s**) area containing oil reserves
oilfields *n* ▷ **oilfield**
oilier *adj* ▷ **oil**
oiliest *adj* ▷ **oil**
oiling *v* ▷ **oil**
oils *n, v* ▷ **oil**
oilskin *n* (*pl* **-s**) (garment made from) waterproof material
oilskins *n* ▷ **oilskin**
oily *adj* ▷ **oil**
ointment *n* (*pl* **-s**) greasy substance used for healing skin or as a cosmetic
ointments *n* ▷ **ointment**
okapi [ok-**kah**-pee] *n* (*pl* **-s**) African animal related to the giraffe but with a shorter neck
okapis *n* ▷ **okapi**
okra *n* (*pl* **-s**) tropical plant with edible green pods
okras *n* ▷ **okra**
okay (*Informal*) *interj* expression of approval ▶ *v* (**-s, -ing, -ed**) approve (something) ▶ *n* (*pl* **-s**) approval
okayed *v* ▷ **okay**
okaying *v* ▷ **okay**
okays *v, n* ▷ **okay**
old *adj* (**-er, -est**) having lived or existed for a long time
olden *adj* old
older *adj* ▷ **old**
oldest *adj* ▷ **old**
oldie *n* (*pl* **-s**) (*Informal*) old but popular song or film
oldies *n* ▷ **oldie**
oleaginous [ol-lee-**aj**-in-uss] *adj* oily, producing oil
oleander [ol-lee-**ann**-der] *n* (*pl* **-s**) Mediterranean flowering evergreen shrub
oleanders *n* ▷ **oleander**
olfactory *adj* relating to the sense of smell
oligarchic *adj* ▷ **oiligarchy**
oligarchical *adj* ▷ **oligarchy**
oligarchies *n* ▷ **oligarchy**
oligarchy [**ol**-lee-gark-ee] *n* (*pl* **-ies**) government by a small group of people > **oligarchic, oligarchical** *adj*
olive *n* (*pl* **-s**) small green or black fruit used as food or pressed for its oil ▶ *adj* greyish-green
olives *n* ▷ **olive**
ombudsman *n* (*pl* **-men**) official who investigates complaints against government organizations
ombudsmen *n* ▷ **ombudsman**
omelette *n* (*pl* **-s**) dish of eggs beaten and fried
omelettes *n* ▷ **omelette**
omen *n* (*pl* (*pl* **-s**) happening or object thought to foretell success or misfortune
omens *n* ▷ **omen**
ominous *adj* worrying, seeming to foretell misfortune
omit *v* (**-s, -tting, -tted**) leave out > **omission** *n* (*pl* **-s**)
omission *n* ▷ **omit**
omissions *n* ▷ **omit**

omits *v* ▷ **omit**
omitted *v* ▷ **omit**
omitting *v* ▷ **omit**
omnibus *n* (*pl* **-es**) several books or TV or radio programmes made into one
omnibuses *n* ▷ **omnibus**
omnipotence *n* ▷ **omnipotent**
omnipotences *n* ▷ **omnipotent**
omnipotent *adj* having unlimited power > **omnipotence** *n* (*pl* **-s**)
omnipresence *n* ▷ **omnipresent**
omnipresences *n* ▷ **omnipresent**
omnipresent *adj* present everywhere > **omnipresence** *n* (*pl* **-s**)
omniscience *n* ▷ **omniscient**
omnisciences *n* ▷ **omniscient**
omniscient [om-**niss**-ee-ent] *adj* knowing everything > **omniscience** *n* (*pl* **-s**)
omnivore *n* (*pl* **-s**) omnivorous animal
omnivores *n* ▷ **omnivore**
omnivorous [om-**niv**-vor-uss] *adj* eating food obtained from both animals and plants
on *prep* indicating position above, attachment, closeness, etc. ▶ *adv* in operation ▶ *adj* operating ▶ *n* (*pl* **-s**) (CRICKET) side of the field on which the batsman stands
once *adv* on one occasion ▶ *conj* as soon as
oncogene [**on**-koh-jean] *n* (*pl* **-s**) gene that can cause cancer when abnormally activated
oncogenes *n* ▷ **oncogene**
oncoming *adj* approaching from the front
one *adj* single, lone ▶ *n* (*pl* **-s**) number or figure 1 ▶ *pron* any person
oneness *n* (*pl* **-es**) unity
onenesses *n* ▷ **oneness**
onerous [**own**-er-uss] *adj* (of a task) difficult to carry out
ones *n* ▷ **one**
oneself *pron* ▷ **one**
ongoing *adj* in progress, continuing
onion *n* (*pl* **-s**) strongly flavoured edible bulb
onions *n* ▷ **onion**
online *adj* (of a computer) directly controlled by a central processor
onlooker *n* (*pl* **-s**) person who watches without taking part
onlookers *n* ▷ **onlooker**
only *adj* alone of its kind ▶ *adv* exclusively ▶ *conj* but
onomatopoeia [on-a-mat-a-**pee**-a] *n* (*pl* **-s**) use of a word which imitates the sound it represents, such as *hiss* > **onomatopoeic** *adj*
onomatopoeias *n* ▷ **onomatopoeia**
onomatopoeic *adj* ▷ **onomatopoeia**
onset *n* (*pl* **-s**) beginning
onsets *n* ▷ **onset**
onslaught *n* (*pl* **-s**) violent attack
onslaughts *n* ▷ **onslaught**
onto *prep* to a position on
ontological *adj* ▷ **ontology**
ontologies *n* ▷ **ontology**
ontology *n* (*pl* **-gies**) branch of philosophy concerned with existence > **ontological** *adj*
onus [**own**-uss] *n* (*pl* **-es**) responsibility or burden
onuses *n* ▷ **onus**
onward *adj* directed or moving forward ▶ *adv* (*also* **onwards**) ahead, forward
onwards *see* ▷ **onward**
onyx *n* (*pl* **-es**) type of quartz with coloured layers
onyxes *n* ▷ **onyx**

> **oo** *n* (**oos**). Oo is a Scots word for **wool.** This is a good word to remember, as it combines two of the most common letters in the game without using any consonants. Oo scores two points.

oodles *pl n* (*Informal*) great quantities
ooze[1] *v* (**-zes, -zing, -zed**) flow slowly ▶ *n* (*pl* **-s**) sluggish flow > **oozy** *adj* (**-zier, -ziest**)
ooze[2] *n* (**-s**) soft mud at the bottom of a lake or river
oozed *v* ▷ **ooze**
oozes *v, n* ▷ **ooze**[1, 2]
oozier *adj* ▷ **ooze**[1]
ooziest *adj* ▷ **ooze**[1]
oozing *v* ▷ **ooze**
oozy *adj* ▷ **ooze**[1]
opacities *n* ▷ **opaque**
opacity *n* ▷ **opaque**
opal *n* (*pl* **-s**) iridescent precious stone
opalescent *adj* iridescent like an opal
opals *n* ▷ **opal**
opaque *adj* (**-r, -st**) not able to be seen through, not transparent > **opacity** *n* (**-ties**)
opaquer *adj* ▷ **opaque**
opaquest *adj* ▷ **opaque**
open *adj* (**-er, -est**) not closed ▶ *v* (**-s, -ing, -ed**) (cause to) become open ▶ *n* (*pl* **-s**) (SPORT) competition which all may enter
opened *v* ▷ **open**
opener *n* instrument for opening containers
openest *adj* ▷ **open**
opening *n* (*pl* **-s**) opportunity ▶ *adj* first ▶ *v* ▷ **open**
openings *n* ▷ **opening**
openly *adv* without concealment
opens *v, n* ▷ **open**
opera[1] *n* (*pl* **-s**) drama in which the text is sung to an orchestral accompaniment > **operatic**

adj
opera² *n* ▷ **opus**
operas *n* ▷ **opera**
operate *v* (**-tes, -ting, -ted**) (cause to) work > **operator** *n* (*pl* **-s**)
operated *v* ▷ **operate**
operates *v* ▷ **operate**
operatic *adj* ▷ **opera¹**
operating *v* ▷ **operate**
operation *n* (*pl* **-s**) method or procedure of working
operational *adj* in working order
operations *n* ▷ **operation**
operative *adj* working ▶ *n* (*pl* **-s**) worker with a special skill
operatives *n* ▷ **operative**
operator *n* ▷ **operate**
operators *n* ▷ **operate**
operetta *n* (*pl* **-s**) light-hearted comic opera
operettas *n* ▷ **operetta**
ophthalmic *adj* relating to the eye
ophthalmologies *n* ▷ **ophthalmology**
ophthalmologist *n* ▷ **ophthalmology**
ophthalmologists *n* ▷ **ophthalmology**
ophthalmology *n* (*pl* **-gies**) study of the eye and its diseases > **ophthalmologist** *n* (*pl* **-s**)
opiate *n* (*pl* **-s**) narcotic drug containing opium
opiates *n* ▷ **opiate**
opine *v* (**-nes, -ning, -ned**) (*Old-fashioned*) express an opinion
opined *v* ▷ **opine**
opines *v* ▷ **opine**
opining *v* ▷ **opine**
opinion *n* (*pl* **-s**) personal belief or judgment
opinionated *adj* having strong opinions
opinions *n* ▷ **opinion**
opium *n* (*pl* **-s**) addictive narcotic drug made from poppy seeds
opiums *n* ▷ **opium**
opossum *n* (*pl* **-s**) small marsupial of America or Australasia
opossums *n* ▷ **opossum**
opponent *n* (*pl* **-s**) person one is working against in a contest, battle, or argument
opponents *n* ▷ **opponent**
opportune *adj* happening at a suitable time
opportunism *n* ▷ **opportunist**
opportunisms, ▷ **opportunist**
opportunist *n* (*pl* **-s**) ▶ *adj* (person) doing whatever is advantageous without regard for principles > **opportunism** *n* (*pl* **-s**)
opportunists *n* ▷ **opportunist**
opportunities *n* ▷ **opportunity**
opportunity *n* (*pl* **-ties**) favourable time or condition
oppose *v* (**-ses, -sing, -sed**) work against
opposed *v* ▷ **oppose**
opposes *v* ▷ **oppose**
opposing *v* ▷ **oppose**
opposition *n* (*pl* **-s**) obstruction or hostility
oppositions *n* ▷ **opposition**
opposite *adj* situated on the other side ▶ *n* (*pl* **-s**) person or thing that is opposite ▶ *prep* facing ▶ *adv* on the other side
opposites *n* ▷ **opposite**
oppress *v* (**-es, -ing, -ed**) control by cruelty or force > **oppression** *n* (*pl* **-s**) > **oppressor** *n* (*pl* **-s**)
oppressed *v* ▷ **oppress**
oppresses *v* ▷ **oppress**
oppressing *v* ▷ **oppress**
oppression *n* ▷ **oppress**
oppressions *n* ▷ **oppress**
oppressive *adj* tyrannical > **oppressively** *adv*
oppressively *adv* ▷ **oppressive**
oppressor *n* ▷ **oppress**
oppressors *n* ▷ **oppress**
opprobrium [op-**probe**-ree-um] *n* (*pl* **-s**) state of being criticized severely for wrong one has done
opprobriums *n* ▷ **opprobrium**
opt *v* (**-s, -ing, -ed**) show a preference, choose
opted *v* ▷ **opt**
opting *v* ▷ **opt**
opts *v* ▷ **opt**
optic *adj* relating to the eyes or sight > **optical** *adj*
optical *adj* ▷ **optic**
optics *n* science of sight and light
optician *n* (*pl* **-s**) (*also* **ophthalmic optician**) person qualified to prescribe glasses (*also* **dispensing optician**)
opticians *n* ▷ **optician**
optimism *n* (*pl* **-s**) tendency to take the most hopeful view > **optimist** *n* (*pl* **-s**) > **optimistic** *adj* > **optimistically** *adv*
optimisms *n* ▷ **optimism**
optimist *n* ▷ **optimism**
optimistic *adj* ▷ **optimism**
optimistically *adv* ▷ **optimism**
optimists *n* ▷ **optimism**
optima *n* ▷ **optimum**
optimal *adj* ▷ **optimum**
optimize *v* (**-zes, -zing, -zed**) make the most of
optimized *v* ▷ **optimize**
optimizes *v* ▷ **optimize**
optimizing *v* ▷ **optimize**
optimum *n* (*pl* **-ma, -mums**) best possible conditions ▶ *adj* most favourable > **optimal** *adj*

optimums *n* ▷ **optimum**
option *n* (*pl* **-s**) choice
optional *adj* possible but not compulsory
options *n* ▷ **option**
optometries *n* ▷ **optometry**
optometrist *n* (*pl* **-s**) person qualified to prescribe glasses > **optometry** *n* (**-ries**)
optometrists *n* ▷ **optometrist**
optometry *n* ▷ **optometrist**
opulence *n* ▷ **opulent**
opulences *n* ▷ **opulent**
opulent [**op**-pew-lent] *adj* having or indicating wealth > **opulence** *n* (**-s**)
opus *n* (*pl* **opuses, opera**) artistic creation, esp. a musical work
opuses *n* ▷ **opus**
or *conj* used to join alternatives
oracle *n* (*pl* **-s**) shrine of an ancient god > **oracular** *adj*
oracles *n* ▷ **oracle**
oracular *adj* ▷ **oracle**
oral *adj* spoken ▶ *n* (*pl* **-s**) spoken examination > **orally** *adv*
orally *adv* ▷ **oral**
orals *n* ▷ **oral**
orange *n* (*pl* **-s**) reddish-yellow citrus fruit ▶ *adj* reddish-yellow
orangeade *n* (BRIT) orange-flavoured, usu. fizzy drink
orangeades *n* ▷ **orangeade**
orangeries *n* ▷ **orangery**
orangery *n* (*pl* **-ries**) greenhouse for growing orange trees
oranges *n* ▷ **orange**
oration *n* (*pl* **-s**) formal speech
orations *n* ▷ **oration**
orator [**or**-rat-tor] *n* (*pl* **-s**) skilful public speaker
oratorical *adj* ▷ **oratory**
oratories *n* ▷ **oratory**[1, 2]
oratorio [or-rat-**tor**-ee-oh] *n* (*pl* **-s**) musical composition for choir and orchestra, usu. with a religious theme
oratorios *n* ▷ **oratorio**
orators *n* ▷ **orator**
oratory[1] [**or**-rat-tree] *n* (*pl* **-ries**) art of making speeches > **oratorical** *adj*
oratory[2] *n* (*pl* **-ries**) small private chapel
orb *n* (*pl* **-s**) ceremonial decorated sphere with a cross on top, carried by a monarch
orbs *n* ▷ **orb**
orbit *n* (*pl* **-s**) curved path of a planet, satellite, or spacecraft around another body ▶ *v* (**-s, -ing, -ed**) move in an orbit around > **orbital** *adj*
orbital *adj* ▷ **orbit**
orbited *v* ▷ **orbit**
orbiting *v* ▷ **orbit**
orbits *n, v* ▷ **orbit**
orchard *n* (*pl* **-s**) area where fruit trees are grown
orchards *n* ▷ **orchard**
orchestra *n* (*pl* **-s**) large group of musicians, esp. playing a variety of instruments (*also* **orchestra pit**) > **orchestral** *adj*
orchestral *adj* ▷ **orchestra**
orchestras *n* ▷ **orchestra**
orchestrate *v* (**-tes, -ting, -ted**) arrange (music) for orchestra > **orchestration** *n* (*pl* **-s**)
orchestrated *v* ▷ **orchestrate**
orchestrates *v* ▷ **orchestrate**
orchestrating *v* ▷ **orchestrate**
orchestration *n* ▷ **orchestrate**
orchestrations *n* ▷ **orchestrate**
orchid *n* (*pl* **-s**) plant with flowers that have unusual lip-shaped petals
orchids *n* ▷ **orchid**
ordain *v* (**-s, -ing, -ed**) make (someone) a member of the clergy
ordained *v* ▷ **ordain**
ordaining *v* ▷ **ordain**
ordains *v* ▷ **ordain**
ordeal *n* (*pl* **-s**) painful or difficult experience
ordeals *n* ▷ **ordeal**
order *n* (*pl* **-s**) instruction to be carried out ▶ *v* (**-s, -ing, -ed**) give an instruction to
orderlies *n* ▷ **orderly**
orderliness *n* ▷ **orderly**
orderlinesses *n* ▷ **orderly**
orderly *adj* well-organized ▶ *n* (*pl* **-lies**) male hospital attendant > **orderliness** *n* (*pl* **-es**)
ordered *v* ▷ **order**
ordering *v* ▷ **order**
orders *n, v* ▷ **order**
ordinance *n* (*pl* **-s**) official rule or order
ordinances *n* ▷ **ordinance**
ordinarily *adv* ▷ **ordinary**
ordinary *adj* usual or normal > **ordinarily** *adv*
ordination *n* (*pl* **-s**) act of making someone a member of the clergy
ordinations *n* ▷ **ordination**
ordnance *n* (*pl* **-s**) weapons and military supplies
ordnances *n* ▷ **ordnance**
ordure *n* (*pl* **-s**) excrement
ordures *n* ▷ **ordure**
ore *n* (*pl* **-s**) (rock containing) a mineral which yields metal
ores *n* ▷ **ore**
oregano [or-rig-**gah**-no] *n* (*pl* **-nos**) sweet-smelling herb used in cooking
oreganos *n* ▷ **oregano**

organ *n* (*pl* **-s**) part of an animal or plant that has a particular function, such as the heart or lungs
organdie *n* (*pl* **-s**) fine cotton fabric
organdies *n* ▷ **organdie**
organic *adj* of or produced from animals or plants (CHEM) > **organically** *adv*
organically *adv* ▷ **organic**
organism *n* (**-s**) any living animal or plant
organisms *n* ▷ **organism**
organist *n* (*pl* **-s**) organ player
organists *n* ▷ **organist**
organization *n* (*pl* **-s**) group of people working together > **organizational** *adj*
organizational *adj* ▷ **organization**
organizations *n* ▷ **organization**
organize *v* (**-zes, -zing, -zed**) make arrangements for > **organizer** *n* (*pl* **-s**)
organized *v* ▷ **organize**
organizer *n* ▷ **organize**
organizers *n* ▷ **organize**
organizes *v* ▷ **organize**
organizing *v* ▷ **organize**
organs *n* ▷ **organ**
orgasm *n* (*pl* **-s**) most intense point of sexual pleasure > **orgasmic** *adj*
orgasmic *adj* ▷ **orgasm**
orgasms *n* ▷ **orgasm**
orgiastic *adj* ▷ **orgy**
orgies *n* ▷ **orgy**
orgy *n* (*pl* **-gies**) party involving promiscuous sexual activity > **orgiastic** *adj*
orient[1], **orientate** *v* (**-s, -ing, -ed**) position (oneself) according to one's surroundings > **orientation** *n* (*pl* **-s**)
orient[2] *n* (*pl* **-s**) (*Lit*) east > **oriental** *adj*
oriental *adj* ▷ **orient**[2]
orientate *v* ▷ **orient**
orientated *v* ▷ **orient**
orientates *v* ▷ **orient**
orientating *v* ▷ **orient**
orientation *n* ▷ **orient**
orientations *n* ▷ **orient**
oriented *v* ▷ **orient**
orienteering *n* (*pl* **-s**) sport in which competitors hike over a course using a compass and map
orienteerings *n* ▷ **orienteering**
orienting *v* ▷ **orient**
orients *v* ▷ **orient**
Orients *n* ▷ **Orient**
Orientalist *n* (*pl* **-s**) specialist in the languages and history of the Far East
Orientalists *n* ▷ **Orientalist**
orifice [or-rif-fiss] *n* (*pl* **-s**) opening or hole
orifices *n* ▷ **orifice**
origami [or-rig-**gah**-mee] *n* (*pl* **-mis**) Japanese decorative art of paper folding
origamis *n* ▷ **origami**
origin *n* (*pl* **-s**) point from which something develops
original *adj* first or earliest ▶ *n* (*pl* **-s**) first version, from which others are copied > **originality** *n* (*pl* **-ies**) > **originally** *adv*
originalities *n* ▷ **original**
originality *n* ▷ **original**
originally *adv* ▷ **original**
originals *n* ▷ **original**
originate *v* (**-tes, -ting, -ted**) come or bring into existence > **origination** *n* (*pl* **-s**) > **originator** *n* (*pl* **-s**)
originated *v* ▷ **originate**
originates *v* ▷ **originate**
originating *v* ▷ **originate**
origination *n* ▷ **origination**
originations *n* ▷ **originate**
originator *n* ▷ **originate**
originator *n* ▷ **originate**
origins *n* ▷ **origin**
oriole *n* (*pl* **-s**) tropical or American songbird
orioles *n* ▷ **oriole**
ormolu *n* (*pl* **-lus**) gold-coloured alloy used for decoration
ormulus *n* ▷ **ormulu**
ornament *n* (*pl* **-s**) decorative object ▶ *v* (**-s, -ing, -ed**) decorate > **ornamental** *adj* > **ornamentation** *n* (*pl* **-s**)
ornamental *adj* ▷ **ornament**
ornamentation *n* ▷ **ornament**
ornamentations *n* ▷ **ornament**
ornamented *v* ▷ **ornament**
ornamenting *v* ▷ **ornament**
ornaments *n, v* ▷ **ornament**
ornate *adj* highly decorated, elaborate
ornithological *adj* ▷ **ornithology**
ornithologies *n* ▷ **ornithology**
ornithologist *n* ▷ **ornithology**
ornithologists *n* ▷ **ornithology**
ornithology *n* (*pl* **-gies**) study of birds > **ornithological** *adj* > **ornithologist** *n* (*pl* **-s**)
orphan *n* (*pl* **-s**) child whose parents are dead
orphanage *n* (*pl* **-s**) children's home for orphans
orphanages *n* ▷ **orphanage**
orphaned *adj* having no living parents
orphans *n* ▷ **orphan**
orreries *n* ▷ **orrery**
orrery *n* (*pl* **-ries**) mechanical model of the solar system
orris *n* (*pl* **-es**) kind of iris (*also* **orris root**)

orrises *n* ▷ **orris**
orthodontics *n* (*pl* branch of dentistry concerned with correcting irregular teeth > **orthodontist** *n* (*pl* **-s**)
orthodontist *n* ▷ **orthodontics**
orthodontists *n* ▷ **orhtodontics**
orthodox *adj* conforming to established views > **orthodoxy** *n* (*pl* **-ies**)
orthodoxies *n* ▷ **orthodox**
orthodoxy *n* ▷ **orthodox**
orthography *n* (*pl* **-phies**) correct spelling
orthographies *n* ▷ **orthography**
orthopaedic *adj* ▷ **orthopaedics**
orthopaedics *n* (*pl* branch of medicine concerned with disorders of the bones or joints > **orthopaedic** *adj*
oryx *n* (*pl* **-es**) large African antelope
oryxes *n* ▷ **oryx**

os *n* (**ossa**). Os is a technical word for **bone.** This word won't score many points on its own, but will allow you to connect a word beginning with O to one ending in S (e.g. most plurals). Os scores 2 points.

oscillate [**oss**-ill-late] *v* (**-tes, -ting, -ted**) swing back and forth > **oscillation** *n* (*pl* **-s**) > **oscillator** *n* (*pl* **-s**)
oscillated *v* ▷ **oscillate**
oscillates *v* ▷ **oscillate**
oscillating *v* ▷ **oscillate**
oscillation *n* ▷ **oscillate**
oscillation *n* ▷ **oscillate**
oscillations *n* ▷ **oscillate**
oscillator *n* ▷ **oscillate**
oscillators *n* ▷ **oscillate**
oscilloscope [oss-**sill**-oh-scope] *n* (*pl* **-s**) instrument that shows the shape of a wave on a cathode-ray tube
oscilloscopes *n* ▷ **oscilloscope**
osier [**oh**-zee-er] *n* (*pl* **-s**) willow tree
osiers *n* ▷ **osier**
osmium *n* (*pl* **-s**) (CHEM) heaviest known metallic element
osmiums *n* ▷ **osmium**
osmosis *n* (*pl* **-ses**) movement of a liquid through a membrane from a lower to a higher concentration > **osmotic** *adj*
osmoses *n* ▷ **osmosis**
osmotic *adj* ▷ **osmosis**
osprey *n* (*pl* **-s**) large fish-eating bird of prey
ospreys *n* ▷ **osprey**
ossification *n* ▷ **ossify**
ossifications *n* ▷ **ossify**
ossified *v* ▷ **ossify**
ossifies *v* ▷ **ossify**
ossify *v* (**-fies, -fying, -fied**) (cause to) become bone, harden > **ossification** *n* (*pl* **-s**)
ossifying *v* ▷ **ossify**
ostensible *adj* apparent, seeming > **ostensibly** *adv*
ostensibly *adv* ▷ **ostensible**
ostentation *n* (*pl* **-s**) pretentious display > **ostentatious** *adj* > **ostentatiously** *adv*
ostentations *n* ▷ **ostentation**
ostentatious *adj* ▷ **ostentation**
ostentatiously *adv* ▷ **ostentation**
osteopath *n* ▷ **osteopathy**
osteopathies *n* ▷ **osteopathy**
osteopaths *n* ▷ **osteopathy**
osteopathy *n* (*pl* **-thies**) medical treatment involving manipulation of the joints > **osteopath** *n* (*pl* **-s**)
osteoporosis *n* (*pl* **-ses**) brittleness of the bones, caused by lack of calcium
osteoporoses *n* ▷ **osteoporosis**
ostracism *n* ▷ **ostracize**
ostracisms *n* ▷ **ostracize**
ostracize *v* (**-zes, -zing, -zed**) exclude (a person) from a group > **ostracism** *n* (*pl* **-s**)
ostracized *v* ▷ **ostracize**
ostracizes *v* ▷ **ostracize**
ostracizing *v* ▷ **ostracize**
ostrich *n* (*pl* **-es**) large African bird that runs fast but cannot fly
ostriches *n* ▷ **ostrich**
other *adj* remaining in a group of which one or some have been specified ▶ *n* (*pl* **-s**) other person or thing
others *n* ▷ **other**
otherwise *conj* or else, if not ▶ *adv* differently, in another way
otherworldly *adj* concerned with spiritual rather than practical matters
otiose [**oh**-tee-oze] *adj* not useful
otter *n* (*pl* **-s**) small brown freshwater mammal that eats fish
otters *n* ▷ **otter**
ottoman *n* (*pl* **-mans**) storage chest with a padded lid for use as a seat
ottomans *n* ▷ **ottoman**

ou *n* (**ous**). Ou is a South African slang word for a man. This word doesn't score many points, but is very useful when you are trying to form words in more than one direction. Ou scores 2 points.

oubliette [oo-blee-**ett**] *n* (*pl* **-s**) dungeon entered only by a trapdoor
oubliettes *n* ▷ **oubliette**
ouch *interj* exclamation of sudden pain

ought *v* used to express: obligation
ounce *n* (*pl* **-s**) unit of weight equal to one sixteenth of a pound (28.4 grams)
ounces *n* ▷ **ounce**
our *adj* belonging to us
ours *pron* thing(s) belonging to us
ourselves *pron* ▷ **we, us**
ousel *n* (*pl* **-s**) ▷ **dipper**
ousels *n* ▷ **ousel**
oust *v* (**-s, -ing, -ed**) force (someone) out, expel
ousted *v* ▷ **oust**
ousting *v* ▷ **oust**
ousts *v* ▷ **oust**
out *adv, adj* denoting movement or distance away from, a state of being used up or extinguished, public availability, etc. ▶ *v* (**-s, -ing, -ed**) (*Informal*) name (a public figure) as being homosexual
outback *n* (*pl* **-s**) remote bush country of Australia
outbacks *n* ▷ **outback**
outbid *v* (**-bids, -bidding, -bid, -bidden**) offer a higher price than
outbid *v* ▷ **outbid**
outbidden *v* ▷ **outbid**
outbidding *v* ▷ **outbid**
outbids *v* ▷ **outbid**
outbreak *n* (*pl* **-s**) sudden occurrence (of something unpleasant)
outbreaks *n* ▷ **outbreak**
outburst *n* (*pl* **-s**) sudden expression of emotion
outbursts *n* ▷ **outburst**
outcast *n* (*pl* **-s**) person rejected by a particular group
outcasts *n* ▷ **outcast**
outclass *v* (**-es, -ing, -ed**) surpass in quality
outclassed *v* ▷ **outclass**
outclasses *v* ▷ **outclass**
outclassing *v* ▷ **outclass**
outcome *n* (*pl* **-s**) result
outcomes *n* ▷ **outcome**
outcries *n* ▷ **outcry**
outcrop *n* (*pl* **-s**) part of a rock formation that sticks out of the earth
outcrops *n* ▷ **outcrop**
outcry *n* (*pl* **-ries**) vehement or widespread protest
outdo *v* (**-does, -doing, -did, -done**) surpass in performance
outdid *v* ▷ **outdo**
outdoes *v* ▷ **outdo**
outdoing *v* ▷ **outdo**
outdone *v* ▷ **outdo**
outdoor *adj* ▷ **outdoors**
outdoors *adv* in(to) the open air ▶ *n* (*pl* the open air > **outdoor** *adj*
outed *v* ▷ **out**
outer *adj* on the outside
outermost *adj* furthest out
outface *v* (**-ces, -cing, -ced**) subdue or disconcert (someone) by staring
outfaced *v* ▷ **outface**
outfaces *v* ▷ **outface**
outfacing *v* ▷ **outface**
outfield *n* (*pl* **-s**) (CRICKET) area far from the pitch
outfields *n* ▷ **outfield**
outfit *n* (*pl* **-s**) matching set of clothes
outfits *n* ▷ **outfit**
outfitter *n* (*pl* **-s**) supplier of men's clothes
outfitters *n* ▷ **outfitter**
outflank *v* (**-s, -ing, -ed**) get round the side of (an enemy army)
outflanked *v* ▷ **outflank**
outflanking *v* ▷ **outflank**
outflanks *v* ▷ **outflank**
outgoing *adj* leaving
outgoings *pl n* expenses
outgrow *v* (**-grows, -growing, -grew, -grown**) become too large or too old for
outgrew *v* ▷ **outgrow**
outgrowing *v* ▷ **outgrow**
outgrown *v* ▷ **outgrow**
outgrows *v* ▷ **outgrow**
outgrowth *n* natural development
outgrowths *n* ▷ **outgrowth**
outhouse *n* (*pl* **-s**) building near a main building
outhouses *n* ▷ **outhouse**
outing *n* (*pl* **-s**) leisure trip ▶ *v* ▷ **out**
outings *n* ▷ **outing**

> **outjinx** *v* (**outjinxes, outjinxing, outjinxed**). Outjinx means to outmanoeuvre. If someone else plays **jinx,** you can outjinx them by adding O, U and T! If you can form the whole word using all of your letters, you'll get a 50-point bonus. Outjinx scores 21 points.

outlandish *adj* extremely unconventional
outlaw *n* (*pl* **-s**) (HIST) criminal deprived of legal protection, bandit ▶ *v* (**-s, -ing, -ed**) make illegal (HIST)
outlawed *v* ▷ **outlaw**
outlawing *v* ▷ **outlaw**
outlaws *n, v* ▷ **outlaw**
outlay *n* (*pl* **-s**) expenditure
outlays *n* ▷ **outlay**
outlet *n* (*pl* **-s**) means of expressing emotion
outlets *n* ▷ **outlet**

outline *n* (*pl* **-s**) short general explanation ▶ *v* (**-nes, -ning, -ned**) summarize
outlined *v* ▷ **outline**
outlines *n, v* ▷ **outline**
outlining *v* ▷ **outline**
outlook *n* (*pl* **-s**) attitude
outlooks *n* ▷ **outlook**
outlying *adj* distant from the main area
outmanoeuvre *v* (**-res, -ring, -red**) get an advantage over
outmanoeuvred *v* ▷ **outmanoeuvre**
outmanoeuvres *v* ▷ **outmanoeuvre**
outmanoeuvring *v* ▷ **outmanoeuvre**
outmoded *adj* no longer fashionable or accepted
outnumber *v* (**-s, -ing, -ed**) exceed in number
outnumbered *v* ▷ **outnumber**
outnumbering *v* ▷ **outnumber**
outnumbers *v* ▷ **outnumber**
outpatient *n* (*pl* **-s**) patient who does not stay in hospital overnight
outpatients *n* ▷ **outpatient**
outpost *n* (*pl* **-s**) outlying settlement
outposts *n* ▷ **outpost**
outpouring *n* (*pl* **-s**) passionate outburst
outpourings *n* ▷ **outpouring**
output *n* (*pl* **-s**) amount produced ▶ *v* (**-puts, -putting, -putted**) (COMPUTERS) produce (data) at the end of a process
outputted *v* ▷ **output**
outputting *v* ▷ **output**
outputs *n, v* ▷ **output**
outrage *n* (*pl* **-s**) great moral indignation ▶ *v* (**-s, -ing, -ed**) offend morally
outraged *v* ▷ **outrage**
outrageous *adj* shocking > **outrageously** *adv*
outrageously *adv* ▷ **outrageous**
outrages *n, v* ▷ **outrage**
outraging *v* ▷ **outrage**
outré [oo-tray] *adj* shockingly eccentric
outrider *n* (*pl* **-s**) motorcyclist acting as an escort
outriders *n* ▷ **outrider**
outrigger *n* (*pl* **-s**) stabilizing frame projecting from a boat
outriggers *n* ▷ **outrigger**
outright *adj, adv* absolute(ly)
outrun *v* (**-runs, -running, -ran, -run**) run faster than
outran *v* ▷ **outrun**
outrun *v* ▷ **outrun**
outrunning *v* ▷ **outrun**
outruns *v* ▷ **outrun**
outs *v* ▷ **out**
outset *n* (*pl* **-s**) beginning
outsets *n* ▷ **outset**
outshine *v* (**-shines, -shining, -shone**) surpass (someone) in excellence
outshines *v* ▷ **outshine**
outshining *v* ▷ **outshine**
outshone *v* ▷ **outshine**
outside *prep, adj adv* indicating movement to or position on the exterior ▶ *adj* unlikely ▶ *n* (*pl* **-s**) external area or surface
outsider *n* (*pl* **-s**) person outside a specific group
outsiders *n* ▷ **outsider**
outsides *n* ▷ **outside**
outsize, outsized *adj* larger than normal
outsized *adj* ▷ **outsize**
outskirts *pl n* outer areas, esp. of a town
outsmart *v* (**-s, -ing, -ed**) (*Informal*) outwit
outsmarted *v* ▷ **outsmart**
outsmarting *v* ▷ **outsmart**
outsmarts *v* ▷ **outsmart**
outspan *v* (**-s, -nning, -nned**) (S AFR) relax
outspanned *v* ▷ **outspan**
outspanning *v* ▷ **outspan**
outspans *v* ▷ **outspan**
outspoken *adj* tending to say what one thinks
outstanding *adj* excellent
outstrip *v* (**-s, -pping, -pped**) surpass
outstripped *v* ▷ **outstrip**
outstripping *v* ▷ **outstrip**
outstrips *v* ▷ **outstrip**
outtake *n* (*pl* **-s**) unreleased take from a recording session, film, or TV programme
outtakes *n* ▷ **outtake**
outward *adj* apparent ▶ *adv* (*also* **outwards**) away from somewhere > **outwardly** *adv*
outwardly *adv* ▷ **outward**
outweigh *v* (**-s, -ing, -ed**) be more important, significant, or influential than
outweighed *v* ▷ **outweigh**
outweighing *v* ▷ **outweigh**
outweighs *v* ▷ **outweigh**
outwit *v* (**-s, -tting, -tted**) get the better of (someone) by cunning
outwits *v* ▷ **outwit**
outwitted *v* ▷ **outwit**
outwitting *v* ▷ **outwit**
ouzel [ooze-el] *n* (*pl* **-s**) ▷ **dipper**
ouzels *n* ▷ **ouzel**
ova *n* ▷ **ovum**
oval *adj* egg-shaped ▶ *n* (*pl* **-s**) anything that is oval in shape
ovals *n* ▷ **oval**
ovarian *adj* ▷ **ovary**
ovaries *n* ▷ **ovary**
ovary *n* (*pl* **-ries**) female egg-producing organ

> **ovarian** *adj*
ovation *n* (*pl* **-s**) enthusiastic round of applause
ovations *n* ▷ **ovation**
oven *n* (*pl* **-s**) heated compartment or container for cooking or for drying or firing ceramics
ovens *n* ▷ **oven**
over *prep, adv* indicating position on the top of, movement to the other side of, amount greater than, etc. ▶ *adj* finished ▶ *n* (*pl* **-s**) (CRICKET) series of six balls bowled from one end
overall *adj, adv* in total ▶ *n* (*pl* **-s**) coat-shaped protective garment ▶ *pl* protective garment consisting of trousers with a jacket or bib and braces attached
overalls *n* ▷ **overall**
overarm *adj, adv* (thrown) with the arm above the shoulder
overawe *v* (**-wes, -wing, -wed**) affect (someone) with an overpowering sense of awe
overawed *v* ▷ **overawe**
overawes *v* ▷ **overawe**
overawing *v* ▷ **overawe**
overbalance *v* (**-ces, -cing, -ced**) lose balance
overbalanced *v* ▷ **overbalance**
overbalances *v* ▷ **overbalance**
overbalancing *v* ▷ **overbalance**
overbearing *adj* unpleasantly forceful
overblown *adj* excessive
overboard *adv* from a boat into the water
overcame *v* ▷ **overcome**
overcast *adj* (of the sky) covered by clouds
overcoat *n* (*pl* **-s**) heavy coat
overcoats *n* ▷ **overcoat**
overcome *v* (**-comes, -coming, -came, -come**) gain control over after an effort
overcomes *v* ▷ **overcome**
overcoming *v* ▷ **overcome**
overcrowded *adj* containing more people or things than is desirable
overdid *v* ▷ **overdo**
overdo *v* (**-does, -doing, -did, -done**) do to excess
overdoes *v* ▷ **overdo**
overdoing *v* ▷ **overdo**
overdone *v* ▷ **overdo**
overdose *n* (*pl* **-s**) excessive dose of a drug ▶ *v* (**-ses, -sing, -sed**) take an overdose
overdosed *n* ▷ **overdose**
overdoses *n, v* ▷ **overdose**
overdosing *v* ▷ **overdose**
overdraft *n* (*pl* **-s**) overdrawing
overdrafts *n* ▷ **overdraft**
overdraw *v* (**-draws, -drawing, -drew, -drawn**) withdraw more money than is in (one's bank account)
overdrawing *v* ▷ **overdraw**
overdrawn *v* ▷ **overdraw**
overdraws *v* ▷ **overdraw**
overdrew *v* ▷ **overdraw**
overdrawn *adj* having overdrawn one's account
overdrive *n* (*pl* **-s**) very high gear in a motor vehicle
overdrives *n* ▷ **overdrive**
overdue *adj* still due after the time allowed
overgrown *adj* thickly covered with plants and weeds
overhaul *v* (**-s, -ing, -ed**) examine and repair ▶ *n* (*pl* **-s**) examination and repair
overhauled *v* ▷ **overhaul**
overhauling *v* ▷ **overhaul**
overhauls *v, n* ▷ **overhaul**
overhead *adv, adj* above one's head
overheads *pl n* general cost of maintaining a business
overhear *v* (**-hears, -hearing, -heard**) hear (a speaker or remark) unintentionally or without the speaker's knowledge
overheard *v* ▷ **overhear**
overhearing *v* ▷ **overhear**
overhears *v* ▷ **overhear**
overjoyed *adj* extremely pleased
overkill *n* (*pl* **-s**) treatment that is greater than required
overkills *n* ▷ **overkill**
overland *adj, adv* by land
overlap *v* (**-s, -pping, -pped**) share part of the same space or period of time (as) ▶ *n* (*pl* **-s**) area overlapping
overlapped *v* ▷ **overlap**
overlapping *v* ▷ **overlap**
overlaps *v, n* ▷ **overlap**
overleaf *adv* on the back of the current page
overlook *v* (**-s, -ing, -ed**) fail to notice
overlooked *v* ▷ **overlook**
overlooking *v* ▷ **overlook**
overlooks *v* ▷ **overlook**
overly *adv* excessively
overnight *adj, adv* (taking place) during one night
overpower *v* (**-s, -ing, -ed**) subdue or overcome (someone)
overpowered *v* ▷ **overpower**
overpowering *v* ▷ **overpower**
overpowers *v* ▷ **overpower**
overran *v* ▷ **overrun**

overreach *v* (**-es, -ing, -ed**) fail by trying to be too clever
overreached *v* ▷ **overreach**
overreaches *v* ▷ **overreach**
overreaching *v* ▷ **overreach**
override *v* (**-rides, -riding, -rode, -ridden**) overrule
overridden *v* ▷ **override**
overrides *v* ▷ **override**
overriding *v* ▷ **override**
overrode *v* ▷ **override**
overrule *v* (**-les, -ling, -led**) reverse the decision of (a person with less power)
overruled *v* ▷ **overrule**
overrules *v* ▷ **overrule**
overruling *v* ▷ **overrule**
overrun *v* (**-runs, -running, -ran, -run**) spread over (a place) rapidly
overrunning *v* ▷ **overrun**
overruns *v* ▷ **overrun**
overs *n* ▷ **over**
oversaw *v* ▷ **oversee**
overseas *adv, adj* to, of, or from a distant country
oversee *v* (**-sees, -seeing, -saw, -seen**) watch over from a position of authority > **overseer** *n* (**-s**)
overseeing *v* ▷ **oversee**
overseen *v* ▷ **oversee**
overseer *n* ▷ **oversee**
overseers *n* ▷ **oversee**
oversees *v* ▷ **oversee**
overshadow *v* (**-s, -ing, -ed**) reduce the significance of (a person or thing) by comparison
overshadowed *v* ▷ **overshadow**
overshadowing *v* ▷ **overshadow**
overshadows *v* ▷ **overshadow**
oversight *n* (*pl* **-s**) mistake caused by not noticing something
oversights *n* ▷ **oversight**
overspill *n* (*pl* **-s**) (BRIT) rehousing of people from crowded cities in smaller towns
overspills *n* ▷ **overspill**
overstay *v* (**-s, -ing, -ed**) stay longer than one's host or hostess would like
overstayed *v* ▷ **overstay**
overstayer *n* (**-s**) (NZ) person who remains in New Zealand after their permit has expired
overstayers *n* ▷ **overstyer**
overstaying *v* ▷ **overstay**
overstays *v* ▷ **overstay**
overt *adj* open, not hidden > **overtly** *adv*
overtly *adv* ▷ **overt**
overtake *v* (**-takes, -taking, -took, -taken**) move past (a vehicle or person) travelling in the same direction
overtaken *v* ▷ **overtake**
overtakes *v* ▷ **overtake**
overtaking *v* ▷ **overtake**
overtook *v* ▷ **overtake**
overthrew *v* ▷ **overthrow**
overthrow *v* (**-throws, -throwing, -threw, -thrown**) defeat and replace ▶ *n* (*pl* **-s**) downfall, destruction
overthrowing *v* ▷ **overthrow**
overthrown *v* ▷ **overthrow**
overthrows *v, n* ▷ **overthrow**
overtime *n, adv* (*pl* **-s**) (paid work done) in addition to one's normal working hours
overtimes *n* ▷ **overtime**
overtone *n* (*pl* **-s**) additional meaning
overtones *n* ▷ **overtone**
overture *n* (*pl* **-s**) (MUSIC) orchestral introduction ▶ *pl* opening moves in a new relationship
overtures *n* ▷ **overture**
overturn *v* (**-s, -ing, -ed**) turn upside down
overturned *v* ▷ **overturn**
overturning *v* ▷ **overturn**
overturns *v* ▷ **overturn**
overweight *adj* weighing more than is healthy
overwhelm *v* (**-s, -ing, -ed**) overpower, esp. emotionally > **overwhelming** *adj* > **overwhelmingly** *adv*
overwhelmed *v* ▷ **overwhelm**
overwhelming *v, adj* ▷ **overwhelm**
overwhelmingly *adv* ▷ **overwhelm**
overwhelms *v* ▷ **overwhelm**
overwrought *adj* nervous and agitated
ovoid [**oh**-void] *adj* egg-shaped
ovulate [**ov**-yew-late] *v* (**-tes, -ting, -ted**) produce or release an egg cell from an ovary > **ovulation** *n* (**-s**)
ovulated *v* ▷ **ovulate**
ovulates *v* ▷ **ovulate**
ovulating *v* ▷ **ovulate**
ovulation *n* ▷ **ovulate**
ovulations *n* ▷ **ovulate**
ovum [**oh**-vum] *n* (*pl* **ova**) unfertilized egg cell
owe *v* (**owes, owing, owed**) be obliged to pay (a sum of money) to (a person)
owed *v* ▷ **owe**
owes *v* ▷ **owe**
owing *v* ▷ **owe**
owl *n* (*pl* **-s**) night bird of prey > **owlish** *adj*
owlish *adj* ▷ **owl**
owls *n* ▷ **owl**
own *adj* used to emphasize possession

▸ *v* (**-s, -ing, -ed**) possess > **owner** *n* (*pl* **-s**) > **ownership** *n* (*pl* **-s**)
owned *v* ▷ **own**
owner *n* ▷ **own**
owners *n* ▷ **own**
ownership *n* ▷ **own**
ownerships *n* ▷ **own**
owning *v* ▷ **own**
owns *v* ▷ **own**
ox *n* (*pl* **oxen**) castrated bull
oxen *n* ▷ **ox**
oxide *n* (*pl* **-s**) compound of oxygen and one other element
oxides *n* ▷ **oxide**
oxidize *v* (**-zes, -zing, -zed**) combine chemically with oxygen, as in burning or rusting
oxidized *v* ▷ **oxidize**
oxidizes *v* ▷ **oxidize**
oxidizing *v* ▷ **oxidize**
oxygen *n* (*pl* **-s**) (CHEM) gaseous element essential to life and combustion
oxygenate *v* (**-tes, -ting, -ted**) add oxygen to
oxygenated *v* ▷ **oxygenate**
oxygenates *v* ▷ **oxygenate**
oxygenating *v* ▷ **oxygenate**
oxygens *n* ▷ **oxygen**
oxymora *n* ▷ **oxymoron**
oxymoron [ox-see-**more**-on] *n* (*pl* **-mora, -morons**) figure of speech that combines two apparently contradictory ideas
oxymorons *n* ▷ **oxymoron**
oyez *interj* (HIST) shouted three times by a public crier, listen
oyster *n* (*pl* **-s**) edible shellfish
oystercatcher *n* (*pl* **-s**) wading bird with black-and-white feathers
oystercatchers *n* ▷ **oystercatcher**
oysters *n* ▷ **oyster**
ozone *n* (*pl* **-s**) strong-smelling form of oxygen
ozones *n* ▷ **ozone**

Pp

P forms a two-letter word in front of every vowel except U, which makes it very useful for joining a new word to one already on the board. It also forms several three-letter words with X: **pax, pix, pox** (12 points each) and **pyx** (15). You should also remember one of the strangest words in Scrabble – **pH** (7), which is valid because it doesn't start with a capital letter. When you have the letter P on your rack, look for an H on the board, as they may allow you to play a word beginning or ending in PH, adding to your options.

pa *n* (*pl* **-s**) (NZ) (formerly) a fortified Maori settlement
pace *n* (*pl* **-s**) single step in walking ▶ *v* (**-ces, -cing, -ced**) walk up and down, esp. in anxiety
paced *v* ▷ **pace**
pacemaker *n* (*pl* **-s**) electronic device surgically implanted in a person with heart disease to regulate the heartbeat
pacemakers *n* ▷ **pacemaker**
paces *n*, *v* ▷ **pace**
pachyderm [**pak**-ee-durm] *n* (*pl* **-s**) thick-skinned animal such as an elephant
pachyderms *n* ▷ **pachyderm**
pacification *n* ▷ **pacify**
pacifications *n* ▷ **pacify**
pacified *v* ▷ **pacify**
pacifies *v* ▷ **pacify**
pacifism *n* ▷ **pacifist**
pacifisms *n* ▷ **pacifist**
pacifist *n* (*pl* **-s**) person who refuses on principle to take part in war > **pacifism** *n* (*pl* **-s**)
pacifists *n* ▷ **pacifist**
pacify *v* (**-fies, -fying, -fied**) soothe, calm > **pacification** *n* (*pl* **-s**)
pacifying *v* ▷ **pacify**
pacing *v* ▷ **pace**
pack *v* (**-s, -ing, -ed**) put (clothes etc.) together in a suitcase or bag ▶ *n* (*pl* **-s**) bag carried on a person's or animal's back
packed *v* ▷ **pack**
packing *v* ▷ **pack**
packs *v*, *n* ▷ **pack**
package *n* (*pl* **-s**) small parcel ▶ *v* (**-ges, -ging, -ged**) put into a package > **packaging** *n* (*pl* **-s**)
packaged *v* ▷ **package**
packages *n*, *v* ▷ **package**
packaging *v*, *n* ▷ **package**
packagings *n* ▷ **package**
packet *n* (*pl* **-s**) small container (and contents)
packets *n* ▷ **packet**
packhorse *n* (*pl* **-s**) horse used for carrying goods
packhorses *n* ▷ **packhorse**
pact *n* (*pl* **-s**) formal agreement
pacts *n* ▷ **pact**
pad *n* (*pl* **-s**) piece of soft material used for protection, support, absorption of liquid, etc. ▶ *v* (**padding, padded**) protect or fill with soft material
padded *v* ▷ **pad**
paddies *n* ▷ **paddy**
padding *n* (*pl* **-s**) soft material used to pad something ▶ *v* ▷ **pad**
paddings *n* ▷ **padding**
paddle[1] *n* (*pl* **-s**) short oar with a broad blade at one or each end ▶ *v* (**-les, -ling, -led**) move (a canoe etc.) with a paddle
paddle[2] *v* (**-les, -ling, -led**) walk barefoot in shallow water
paddled *v* ▷ **paddle[1, 2]**
paddles *n*, *v* ▷ **paddle[1, 2]**
paddling *v* ▷ **paddle[1, 2]**
paddock *n* (*pl* **-s**) small field or enclosure for horses
paddocks *n* ▷ **paddock**
paddy *n* (*pl* **-ies**) (BRIT) (*Informal*) fit of temper
paddymelons *n* ▷ **pademelon**
pademelon, paddymelon [**pad**-ee-mel-an] *n* (*pl* **-s**) small Australian wallaby
pademelons *n* ▷ **pademelon**
padlock *n* (*pl* **-s**) detachable lock with a hinged

hoop fastened over a ring on the object to be secured
padlocks *n* ▷ **padlock**
padre [**pah**-dray] *n* (*pl* **-s**) chaplain to the armed forces
padres *n* ▷ **padre**
pads *v*, *n* ▷ **pad**
paean [**pee**-an] *n* (*pl* **-s**) song of triumph or thanksgiving
paeans *n* ▷ **paean**
paediatrics *n* branch of medicine concerned with diseases of children > **paediatrician** *n*
paella [pie-**ell**-a] *n* (*pl* **-s**) Spanish dish of rice, chicken, shellfish, and vegetables
paellas *n* ▷ **paella**
pagan *n* (*pl* **-s**) ▶ *adj* (person) not belonging to one of the world's main religions
pagans *n* ▷ **pagan**
page[1] *n* (*pl* **-s**) (one side of) a sheet of paper forming a book etc.
page[2] *n* (*also* **pageboy**) small boy who attends a bride at her wedding ▶ *v* (**-ges, -ging, -ged**) summon (someone) by bleeper or loudspeaker, in order to pass on a message
pageant *n* (*pl* **-s**) parade or display of people in costume, usu. illustrating a scene from history > **pageantry** *n* (*pl* **-ries**)
pageantries *n* ▷ **pageant**
pageantry *n* ▷ **pageant**
pageants *n* ▷ **pageant**
paged *v* ▷ **page**[2]
pages *n*, *v* ▷ **page**[1, 2]
pagination *n* (*pl* **-s**) numbering of the pages of a book etc.
paginations *n* ▷ **pagination**
paging *v* ▷ **page**[2]
pagoda *n* (*pl* **-s**) pyramid-shaped Asian temple or tower
pagodas *n* ▷ **pagoda**
paid *v* ▷ **pay**
pail *n* (*pl* **-s**) (contents of) a bucket
pails *n* ▷ **pail**
pain *n* (*pl* **-s**) physical or mental suffering ▶ *pl* trouble, effort > **painful** *adj* > **painfully** *adv* > **painless** *adj* > **painlessly** *adv*
painful *adj* ▷ **pain**
painfully *adv* ▷ **pain**
painkiller *n* (*pl* **-s**) drug that relieves pain
painkillers *n* ▷ **painkiller**
painless *adj* ▷ **pain**
painlessly *adv* ▷ **pain**
pains *n* ▷ **pain**
painstaking *adj* extremely thorough and careful
paint *n* (*pl* **-s**) coloured substance, spread on a surface with a brush or roller ▶ *v* (**-s, -ing, -ed**) colour or coat with paint > **painter** *n* (*pl* **-s**) > **painting** *n* (*pl* **-s**)
painted *v* ▷ **paint**
painter[1] *n* ▷ **paint**
painter[2] *n* (*pl* **-s**) rope at the front of a boat, for tying it up
painters *n* ▷ **paint painter**[2]
painting *v*, *n* ▷ **paint**
paintings *n* ▷ **paint**
paints *n*, *v* ▷ **paint**
pair *n* (*pl* **-s**) set of two things matched for use together ▶ *v* (**-s, -ing, -ed**) group or be grouped in twos
paired *v* ▷ **pair**
pairing *v* ▷ **pair**
pairs *n*, *v* ▷ **pair**
pakeha [**pah**-kee-ha] *n* (*pl* **-s**) (NZ) New Zealander who is not of Maori descent
pakehas *n* ▷ **pakeha**
pal *n* (*pl* **-s**) (*Informal*) (*Old-fashioned in NZ*) friend
pals *n* ▷ **pal**
palace *n* (*pl* **-s**) residence of a king, bishop, etc.
palaces *n* ▷ **palace**
palaeographies *n* ▷ **palaeography**
palaeography [pal-ee-**og**-ra-fee] *n* (*pl* **-ies**) study of ancient manuscripts
palaeolithic [pal-ee-oh-**lith**-ik] *adj* of the Old Stone Age
palaeontologies *n* ▷ **palaeontology**
palaeontology [pal-ee-on-**tol**-a-jee] *n* (*pl* **-ies**) study of past geological periods and fossils
palagi [pa-**lang**-gee] *n* (*pl* **-s**) (NZ) Samoan name for a pakeha
palagis *n* ▷ **palagi**
palatable *adj* pleasant to taste
palate *n* (*pl* **-s**) roof of the mouth
palates *n* ▷ **palate**
palatial *adj* like a palace, magnificent
palaver [pal-**lah**-ver] *n* (*pl* **-s**) time-wasting fuss
palavers *n* ▷ **palaver**
pale[1] *adj* (**-er, -est**) light, whitish ▶ *v* (**-les, -ling, -led**) become pale
pale[2] *n* (*pl* **-s**) wooden or metal post used in fences
paled *v* ▷ **pale**
paler *adj* ▷ **pale**[1]
pales *v* ▷ **pale**[1, 2]
palest *adj* ▷ **pale**[1]
paling *v* ▷ **pale**
palette *n* (*pl* **-s**) artist's flat board for mixing colours on
palettes *n* ▷ **palette**
palindrome *n* (*pl* **-s**) word or phrase that reads the same backwards as forwards

palindromes *n* ▷ **palindrome**
paling *n* (*pl* **-s**) wooden or metal post used in fences
palings *n* ▷ **paling**
palisade *n* (*pl* **-s**) fence made of wooden posts driven into the ground
palisades *n* ▷ **palisade**
pall[1] *n* (*pl* **-s**) cloth spread over a coffin
pall[2] *v* (**-s, -ing, -ed**) become boring
pallbearer *n* (*pl* **-s**) person who helps to carry the coffin at a funeral
pallbearers *n* ▷ **pallbearer**
palled *v* ▷ **pall**[2]
palling *v* ▷ **pall**[2]
palls *n* ▷ **pall**[1] ▶ *v* ▷ **pall**[2]
palladium *n* (*pl* **-s**) (CHEM) silvery-white element of the platinum metal group
palladiums *n* ▷ **palladium**
pallet[1] *n* (*pl* **-s**) portable platform for storing and moving goods
pallet[2] *n* straw-filled mattress or bed
pallets *n* ▷ **pallet**[1, 2]
palliate *v* (**-tes, -ting, -ted**) lessen the severity of (something) without curing it
palliated *v* ▷ **palliate**
palliates *v* ▷ **palliate**
palliating *v* ▷ **palliate**
palliative *adj* giving temporary or partial relief ▶ *n* (*pl* **-s**) something, for example a drug, that palliates
palliatives *n* ▷ **palliative**
pallid *adj* (**-er, -est**) pale, esp. because ill or weak > **pallor** *n* (*pl* **-s**)
pallider *adj* ▷ **pallid**
pallidest *adj* ▷ **pallid**
pallier *adj* ▷ **pally**
palliest *adj* ▷ **pally**
pallor *n* ▷ **pallid**
pallors *n* ▷ **pallid**
pally *adj* (**-llier, -lliest**) (*Informal*) on friendly terms
palm[1] *n* (*pl* **-s**) inner surface of the hand
palm[2] *n* (*pl* **-s**) tropical tree with long pointed leaves growing out of the top of a straight trunk
palmist *n* ▷ **palmistry**
palmistries *n* ▷ **palmistry**
palmistry *n* (*pl* **-ries**) fortune-telling from lines on the palm of the hand > **palmist** *n* (*pl* **-s**)
palmists *n* ▷ **palmistry**
palms *n* ▷ **palm**[1, 2]
palmtop *adj* (of a computer) small enough to be held in the hand ▶ *n* (*pl* **-s**) computer small enough to be held in the hand
palmtops *n* ▷ **palmtop**
palomino *n* (*pl* **-s**) gold-coloured horse with a white mane and tail
palominos *n* ▷ **palomino**
palpable *adj* obvious > **palpably** *adv*
palpably *adv* ▷ **palpable**
palpate *v* (**-tes, -ting, -ted**) (MED) examine (an area of the body) by touching
palpated *v* ▷ **palpate**
palpates *v* ▷ **palpate**
palpating *v* ▷ **palpate**
palpitate *v* (**-tes, -ting, -ted**) (of the heart) beat rapidly > **palpitation** *n* (*pl* **-s**)
palpitated *v* ▷ **palpitate**
palpitates *v* ▷ **palpitate**
palpitating *v* ▷ **palpitate**
palpitation *n* ▷ **palpitate**
palpitations *v* ▷ **palpitate**
palsied *adj* affected with palsy
palsies *n* ▷ **palsy**
palsy [**pawl**-zee] *n* (*pl* **-sies**) paralysis
paltrier *adj* ▷ **paltry**
paltriest *adj* ▷ **paltry**
paltry *adj* (**-rier, -riest**) insignificant
pampas *pl n* vast grassy plains in S America
pamper *v* (**-s, -ing, -ed**) treat (someone) with great indulgence, spoil
pampered *v* ▷ **pamper**
pampering *v* ▷ **pamper**
pampers *v* ▷ **pamper**
pamphlet *n* (*pl* **-s**) thin paper-covered booklet
pamphleteer *n* (*pl* **-s**) writer of pamphlets
pamphleteers *n* ▷ **pamphleteer**
pamphlets *n* ▷ **pamphlet**
pan[1] *n* (*pl* **-s**) wide long-handled metal container used in cooking ▶ *v* (**-s, -nning, -nned**) sift gravel from (a river) in a pan to search for gold (*Informal*)
pan[2] *v* (**-s, -nning, -nned**) (of a film camera) be moved slowly so as to cover a whole scene or follow a moving object
panacea [pan-a-**see**-a] *n* (*pl* **-s**) remedy for all diseases or problems
panaceas *n* ▷ **panacea**
panache [pan-**ash**] *n* (*pl* **-s**) confident elegant style
panaches *n* ▷ **panache**
panatella *n* (*pl* **-s**) long slender cigar
panatellas *n* ▷ **panatella**
pancake *n* (*pl* **-s**) thin flat circle of fried batter
pancakes *n* ▷ **pancake**
panchromatic *adj* (PHOTOG) sensitive to light of all colours
pancreas [**pang**-kree-ass] *n* (*pl* **-es**) large gland behind the stomach that produces insulin and helps digestion > **pancreatic** *adj*

pancreases *n* ▷ **pancreas**
pancreatic *adj* ▷ **pancreas**
panda *n* (*pl* **-s**) large black-and-white bearlike mammal from China
pandas *n* ▷ **panda**
pandemic *adj* (of a disease) occurring over a wide area
pandemonium *n* (*pl* **-s**) wild confusion, uproar
pandemoniums *n* ▷ **pandemonium**
pander[1] *v* (**-s, -ing, -ed**) (*foll. by* **to**) indulge (a person his or her desires)
pander[2] *n* (*pl* **-s**) (*Old-fashioned*) person who procures a sexual partner for someone
pandered *v* ▷ **pander**
pandering *v* ▷ **pander**
panders *v, n* ▷ **pander**[1, 2]
pane *n* (*pl* **-s**) sheet of glass in a window or door
panes *n* ▷ **pane**
panegyric [pan-ee-**jire**-ik] *n* (*pl* **-s**) formal speech or piece of writing in praise of someone or something
panegyrics *n* ▷ **panegyric**
panel *n* (*pl* **-s**) flat distinct section of a larger surface, for example in a door ▶ *v* (**-s, -lling, -lled**) cover or decorate with panels
panelled *v* ▷ **panel**
panelling *n* (*pl* **-s**) panels collectively, esp. on a wall ▶ *v* ▷ **panel**
panellings *n* ▷ **panelling**
panellist *n* (*pl* **-s**) member of a panel
panellists *n* ▷ **panellist**
panels *n* ▷ **panel**
pang *n* (*pl* **-s**) sudden sharp feeling of pain or sadness
pangs *n* ▷ **pang**
pangolin *n* (*pl* **-s**) animal of tropical countries with a scaly body and a long snout for eating ants and termites (*also* **scaly anteater**)
pangolins *n* ▷ **pangolin**
panic *n* (*pl* **-s**) sudden overwhelming fear, often affecting a whole group of people ▶ *v* (**-s, -cking, -cked**) feel or cause to feel panic > **panicky** *adj* (**-ier, -iest**)
panicked *v* ▷ **panic**
panickier *adj* ▷ **panic**
panickiest *adj* ▷ **panic**
panicking *v* ▷ **panic**
panicky *adj* ▷ **panic**
panics *n, v* ▷ **panic**
panic-stricken *adj* ▷ **panic**
pannier *n* (*pl* **-s**) bag fixed on the back of a cycle
panniers *n* ▷ **pannier**
panoplies *n* ▷ **panoply**
panoply *n* (*pl* **-ies**) magnificent array
panorama *n* (*pl* **-s**) wide unbroken view of a scene > **panoramic** *adj*
panoramas *n* ▷ **panorama**
panoramic *adj* ▷ **panorama**
pansies *n* ▷ **pansy**
pansy *n* (*pl* **-sies**) small garden flower with velvety purple, yellow, or white petals
pant *v* (**-s, -ing, -ed**) breathe quickly and noisily during or after exertion
pantaloons *pl n* baggy trousers gathered at the ankles
pantechnicon *n* (*pl* **-s**) large van for furniture removals
pantechnicons *n* ▷ **pantechnicon**
panted *v* ▷ **pant**
pantheism *n* (*pl* **-s**) belief that God is present in everything > **pantheist** *n* (*pl* **-s**) > **pantheistic** *adj*
pantheisms *n* ▷ **pantheism**
pantheist *n* ▷ **pantheism**
pantheistic *adj* ▷ **pantheism**
pantheists *n* ▷ **pantheism**
pantheon *n* (*pl* **-s**) (in ancient Greece and Rome) temple built to honour all the gods
pantheons *n* ▷ **pantheon**
panther *n* (*pl* **-s**) leopard, esp. a black one
panthers *n* ▷ **panther**
panties *pl n* women's underpants
pantile *n* (*pl* **-s**) roofing tile with an S-shaped cross section
pantiles *n* ▷ **pantile**
panting *v* ▷ **pant**
pantomime *n* (*pl* **-s**) play based on a fairy tale, performed at Christmas time
pantomimes *n* ▷ **pantomime**
pantries *n* ▷ **pantry**
pantry *n* (*pl* **-ries**) small room or cupboard for storing food
pants *v* ▷ **pant**
pants *pl n* undergarment for the lower part of the body
pap *n* (*pl* **-s**) soft food for babies or invalids
papacies *n* ▷ **papacy**
paps *n* ▷ **pap**
papacy [**pay**-pa-see] *n* (*pl* **-cies**) position or term of office of a pope
papal *adj* of the pope
paparazzi *n* ▷ **paparazzo**
paparazzo [pap-a-**rat**-so] *n* (*pl* **-razzi**) photographer specializing in candid photographs of famous people
papaya [pa-**pie**-ya] *n* (*pl* **-s**) large sweet West Indian fruit
papayas *n* ▷ **papaya**
paper *n* (*pl* **-s**) material made in sheets from wood pulp or other fibres ▶ *pl* personal

documents ▶ *v* (**-s, -ing, -ed**) cover (walls) with wallpaper
paperback *n* (*pl* **-s**) book with covers made of flexible card
paperbacks *n* ▷ **paperback**
papering *v* ▷ **paper**
papered *v* ▷ **paper**
papers *n, v* ▷ **paper**
paperweight *n* (*pl* **-s**) heavy decorative object placed on top of loose papers
paperweights *n* ▷ **paperweight**
paperwork *n* (*pl* **-s**) clerical work, such as writing reports and letters
paperworks *n* ▷ **paperwork**
papoose *n* (*pl* **-s**) Native American child
papooses *n* ▷ **papoose**
paprika *n* (*pl* **-s**) mild powdered seasoning made from red peppers
paprikas *n* ▷ **paprika**
papyri *n* ▷ **papyrus**
papyrus [pap-**ire**-uss] *n* (*pl* **-ri, -ruses**) tall water plant
papyruses *n* ▷ **papyrus**
par *n* (*pl* **-s**) usual or average condition
parable *n* (*pl* **-s**) story that illustrates a religious teaching
parables *n* ▷ **parable**
parabola [par-**ab**-bol-a] *n* (*pl* **-s**) regular curve resembling the course of an object thrown forward and up > **parabolic** *adj*
parabolas *n* ▷ **parabola**
parabolic *adj* ▷ **parabola**
paracetamol *n* (*pl* **-s**) mild pain-relieving drug
paracetamols *n* ▷ **paracetamol**
parachute *n* (*pl* **-s**) large fabric canopy that slows the descent of a person or object from an aircraft ▶ *v* (**-tes, -ting, -ted**) land or drop by parachute > **parachutist** *n* (*pl* **-s**)
parachuted *n, v* ▷ **parachute**
parachutes *v* ▷ **parachute**
parachuting *v* ▷ **parachute**
parachutist *n* ▷ **parachute**
parachutists *n* ▷ **parachute**
parade *n* (*pl* **-s**) procession or march ▶ *v* (**-des, -ding, -ded**) display or flaunt
paraded *v* ▷ **parade**
parades *n, v* ▷ **parade**
parading *v* ▷ **parade**
paradigm [**par**-a-dime] *n* (*pl* **-s**) example or model
paradigms *n* ▷ **paradigm**
paradise *n* (*pl* **-s**) heaven
paradises *n* ▷ **paradise**
paradox *n* (*pl* **-xes**) statement that seems self-contradictory but may be true > **paradoxical** *adj* > **paradoxically** *adv*
paradoxes *n* ▷ **paradox**
paradoxical *adj* ▷ **paradox**
paradoxically *adv* ▷ **paradox**
paraffin *n* (*pl* **-s**) (BRIT & S AFR) liquid mixture distilled from petroleum and used as a fuel or solvent
paraffins *n* ▷ **paraffin**
paragliding *n* (*pl* **-s**) cross-country gliding wearing a parachute shaped like wings
paraglidings *n* ▷ **paragliding**
paragon *n* (*pl* **-s**) model of perfection
paragons *n* ▷ **paragon**
paragraph *n* (*pl* **-s**) section of a piece of writing starting on a new line
paragraphs *n* ▷ **paragraph**
parakeet *n* (*pl* **-s**) small long-tailed parrot
parakeets *n* ▷ **parakeet**
parallax *n* (*pl* **-es**) apparent change in an object's position due to a change in the observer's position
parallaxes *n* ▷ **parallax**
parallel *adj* separated by an equal distance at every point ▶ *n* (*pl* **-s**) line separated from another by an equal distance at every point ▶ *v* (**-s, -ing, -ed**) correspond to
paralleled *n* ▷ **parallel**
paralleling *v* ▷ **parallel**
parallels *n, v* ▷ **parallel**
parallelogram *n* (*pl* **-s**) four-sided geometric figure with opposite sides parallel
parallelograms *n* ▷ **parallelogram**
paralyse *v* (**-ses, -sing, -sed**) affect with paralysis
paralysed *v* ▷ **paralyse**
paralyses *v* ▷ **paralyse** ▶ *n* ▷ **paralysis**
paralysing ▷ **paralyse**
paralysis *n* (*pl* **-ses**) inability to move or feel, because of damage to the nervous system
paralytic *n* (*pl* **-s**) ▶ *adj* (person) affected with paralysis
paralytics *n* ▷ **paralytic**
paramedic *n* (*pl* **-s**) person working in support of the medical profession > **paramedical** *adj*
paramedical *n* ▷ **paramedic**
paramedics *n* ▷ **paramedic**
parameter [par-**am**-it-er] *n* (*pl* **-s**) limiting factor, boundary
parameters *n* ▷ **parameter**
paramilitary *adj* organized on military lines
paramount *adj* of the greatest importance
paramour *n* (*pl* **-s**) (*Old-fashioned*) lover, esp. of a person married to someone else
paramours *n* ▷ **paramour**
paranoia *n* (*pl* **-s**) mental illness causing

delusions of grandeur or persecution (*Informal*) > **paranoid, paranoiac** *adj, n* (*pl* **-s**)
paranoiac *adj, n* ▷ **paranoia**
paranoiacs *n* ▷ **paranoia**
paranoias *n* ▷ **paranoia**
paranoid *adj, n* ▷ **paranoia**
paranoids *n* ▷ **paranoia**
paranormal *adj* beyond scientific explanation
parapet *n* (*pl* **-s**) low wall or railing along the edge of a balcony or roof
parapets *n* ▷ **parapet**
paraphernalia *n* (*pl* **-s**) personal belongings or bits of equipment
paraphernalias *n* ▷ **paraphernalia**
paraphrase *v* (**-ses, -sing, -sed**) put (a statement or text) into other words
paraphrased *v* ▷ **paraphrase**
paraphrases *v* ▷ **paraphrase**
paraphrasing *v* ▷ **paraphrase**
paraplegia [par-a-**pleej**-ya] *n* (*pl* **-s**) paralysis of the lower half of the body > **paraplegic** *adj, n* (*pl* **-s**)
paraplegias *n* ▷ **paraplegia**
paraplegic *adj, n* ▷ **paraplegia**
paraplegics *n* ▷ **paraplegia**
parapsychologies *n* ▷ **parapsychology**
parapsychology *n* (*pl* **-gies**) study of mental phenomena such as telepathy
parasite *n* (*pl* **-s**) animal or plant living in or on another > **parasitic** *adj*
parasites *n* ▷ **parasite**
parasitic *adj* ▷ **parasite**
parasol *n* (*pl* **-s**) umbrella-like sunshade
parasols *n* ▷ **parasol**
paratrooper *n* (*pl* **-s**) soldier trained to be dropped by parachute into a battle area > **paratroops** *pl n*
paratroopers *n* ▷ **paratrooper**
paratroops *n* ▷ **paratrooper**
parboil *v* (**-s, -ing, -ed**) boil until partly cooked
parboiled *v* ▷ **parboil**
parboiling *v* ▷ **parboil**
parboils *v* ▷ **parboil**
parcel *n* (*pl* **-s**) something wrapped up, package ▶ *v* (**-s, -lling, -lled**) (*often foll. by* **up**) wrap up
parcelled *v* ▷ **parcel**
parcelling *v* ▷ **parcel**
parcels *n, v* ▷ **parcel**
parch *v* (**-es, -ing, -ed**) make very hot and dry
parched *v* ▷ **parch**
parches *v* ▷ **parch**
parching *v* ▷ **parch**
parchment *n* (*pl* **-s**) thick smooth writing material made from animal skin
parchments *n* ▷ **parchment**
pardon *v* (**-s, -ing, -ed**) forgive, excuse ▶ *n* (*pl* **-s**) forgiveness > **pardonable** *adj*
pardonable *adj* ▷ **pardon**
pardoned *v* ▷ **pardon**
pardoning *v* ▷ **pardon**
pardons *v, n* ▷ **pardon**
pare *v* (**-res, -ring, -red**) cut off the skin or top layer of (*often foll. by* **down**)
pared *v* ▷ **pare**
pares *v* ▷ **pare**
paring *v* ▷ **pare** ▶ *n* (*pl* **-s**) piece pared off
parings *n* ▷ **pareing**
parent *n* (*pl* **-s**) father or mother > **parental** *adj* > **parenthood** *n* (*pl* **-s**)
parentage *n* (*pl* **-s**) ancestry or family
parentages *n* ▷ **parentage**
parental *adj* ▷ **parent**
parenthood *n* ▷ **parent**
parenthoods *n* ▷ **parent**
parenting *n* (*pl* **-s**) activity of bringing up children
parentings *n* ▷ **parenting**
parents *n* ▷ **parent**
parenthesis [par-**en**-thiss-iss] *n* (*pl* **-ses**) word or sentence inserted into a passage, marked off by brackets or dashes ▶ *pl* round brackets, ( ) > **parenthetical** *adj*
parentheses *n* ▷ **parenthesis**
parenthetical *adj* ▷ **parenthesis**
pariah [par-**rye**-a] *n* (*pl* **-s**) social outcast
pariahs *n* ▷ **pariah**
parietal [par-**rye**-it-al] *adj* of the walls of a body cavity such as the skull
parish *n* (*pl* **-es**) area that has its own church and a priest or pastor
parishes *n* ▷ **parish**
parishioner *n* (*pl* **-s**) inhabitant of a parish
parishioners *n* ▷ **parishioner**
parities *n* ▷ **parity**
parity *n* (*pl* **-ties**) equality or equivalence
park *n* (*pl* **-s**) area of open land for recreational use by the public ▶ *v* (**-s, -ing, -ed**) stop and leave (a vehicle) temporarily
parked *v* ▷ **park**
parking *v* ▷ **park**
parks *n, v* ▷ **park**
parka *n* (*pl* **-s**) large waterproof jacket with a hood
parkas *n* ▷ **parka**
parkier *adj* ▷ **parky**
parkiest *adj* ▷ **parky**
parky *adj* (**-kier, -kiest**) (BRIT) (*Informal*) (of the weather) chilly
parlance *n* (*pl* **-s**) particular way of speaking,

idiom
parlances *n* ▷ **parlance**
parley *n* (*pl* **-s**) meeting between leaders or representatives of opposing forces to discuss terms ▶ *v* (**-s, -ing, -ed**) have a parley
parleyed *v* ▷ **parley**
parleying *v* ▷ **parley**
parleys *n, v* ▷ **parley**
parliament *n* (*pl* **-s**) law-making assembly of a country > **parliamentary** *adj*
parliamentary *adj* ▷ **parliament**
parliaments *n* ▷ **parliament**
parlour *n* (*pl* **-s**) (*Old-fashioned*) living room for receiving visitors
parlours *n* ▷ **parlour**
parlous *adj* (*Old-fashioned*) dire
parochial *adj* narrow in outlook > **parochialism** *n* (*pl* **-s**)
parochialism *n* ▷ **parochial**
parochialisms *n* ▷ **parochial**
parodied *v* ▷ **parody**
parodies *n, v* ▷ **parody**
parody *n* (*pl* **-dies**) exaggerated and amusing imitation of someone else's style ▶ *v* (**-ies, -ying, -ied**) make a parody of
parodying *v* ▷ **parody**
parole *n* (*pl* **-s**) early freeing of a prisoner on condition that he or she behaves well ▶ *v* (**-les, -ling, -led**) put on parole
paroled *v* ▷ **parole**
paroles *n, v* ▷ **parole**
paroling *v* ▷ **parole**
paroxysm *n* (*pl* **-s**) uncontrollable outburst of rage, delight, etc.
paroxysms *n* ▷ **paroxysm**
parquet [**par**-kay] *n* (*pl* **-s**) floor covering made of wooden blocks arranged in a geometric pattern > **parquetry** *n* (*pl* **-ies**)
parquetries *n* ▷ **parquet**
parquetry *n* ▷ **parquet**
parquets *n* ▷ **parquet**
parricide *n* (*pl* **-s**) crime of killing either of one's parents
parricides *n* ▷ **parricide**
parried *v* ▷ **parry**
parries *v* ▷ **parry**
parrot *n* (*pl* **-s**) tropical bird with a short hooked beak and an ability to imitate human speech ▶ *v* (**-s, -ing, -ed**) repeat (someone else's words) without thinking
parroted *v* ▷ **parrot**
parroting *v* ▷ **parrot**
parrots *n, v* ▷ **parrot**
parry *v* (**-rries, -rrying, -rried**) ward off (an attack)
parrying *v* ▷ **parry**
pars *n* ▷ **par**
parse [**parz**] *v* (**-ses, -sing, -sed**) analyse (a sentence) in terms of grammar
parsed *v* ▷ **parse**
parses *v* ▷ **parse**
parsing *v* ▷ **parse**
parsimonies *n* ▷ **parsimony**
parsimonious *adj* ▷ **parsimony**
parsimony *n* (*pl* **-nies**) extreme caution in spending money > **parsimonious** *adj*
parsley *n* (*pl* **-s**) herb used for seasoning and decorating food
parsleys *n* ▷ **parsley**
parsnip *n* (*pl* **-s**) long tapering cream-coloured root vegetable
parsnips *n* ▷ **parsnip**
parson *n* (*pl* **-s**) Anglican parish priest
parsons *n* ▷ **parson**
parsonage *n* (*pl* **-s**) parson's house
parsonages *n* ▷ **parsonage**
part *n* (*pl* **-s**) one of the pieces that make up a whole ▶ *v* (**-s, -ing, -ed**) divide or separate
partake *v* (**-takes, -taking, -took, -taken**) (*foll. by* **of**) take (food or drink)
partaken *v* ▷ **partake**
partakes *v* ▷ **partake**
partaking *v* ▷ **partake**
partial *adj* not complete > **partiality** *n* (*pl* **-ties**) > **partially** *adv*
partialities *n* ▷ **partial**
partiality *n* ▷ **partial**
partially *adv* ▷ **partial**
parted *v* ▷ **part**
participate *v* (**-tes, -ting, -ted**) become actively involved > **participant** *n* (*pl* **-s**) > **participation** *n* (*pl* **-s**)
participant *n* ▷ **participate**
participants *n* ▷ **participate**
participated *v* ▷ **participate**
participates *v* ▷ **participate**
participating *v* ▷ **participate**
participation *n* ▷ **participation**
participations *n* ▷ **participations**
participle *n* (*pl* **-s**) form of a verb used in compound tenses or as an adjective
participles *n* ▷ **participle**
particle *n* (*pl* **-s**) extremely small piece or amount
particles *n* ▷ **particle**
particular *adj* relating to one person or thing, not general ▶ *n* (*pl* **-s**) item of information, detail > **particularly** *adv*
particularize *v* (**-zes, -zing, -zed**) give details about

particularized *v* ▷ **particularize**
particularizes *v* ▷ **particularize**
particularizing *v* ▷ **particularize**
particularly *adv* ▷ **particular**
particulars *n* ▷ **particular**
parties *n* ▷ **party**
parting *n* (*pl* **-s**) occasion when one person leaves another ▶ *v* ▷ **part**
partings *n* ▷ **parting**
partisan *n* (*pl* **-s**) strong supporter of a party or group ▶ *adj* prejudiced or one-sided
partisans *n* ▷ **partisan**
partition *n* (*pl* **-s**) screen or thin wall that divides a room ▶ *v* (**-s, -ing, -ed**) divide with a partition
partitioned *v* ▷ **partition**
partitioning *v* ▷ **partition**
partitions *n, v* ▷ **partition**
partly *adv* not completely
partner *n* (*pl* **-s**) either member of a couple in a relationship or activity ▶ *v* (**-s, -ing, -ed**) be the partner of
partnered *v* ▷ **partner**
partnering *v* ▷ **partner**
partners *n, v* ▷ **partner**
partnership *n* (*pl* **-s**) joint business venture between two or more people
partnerships *n* ▷ **partnership**
partook *v* ▷ **partake**
partridge *n* (*pl* **-s**) game bird of the grouse family
partridges *n* ▷ **partridge**
parts *n, v* ▷ **part**
parturition *n* (*pl* **-s**) act of giving birth
party *n* (*pl* **-ties**) social gathering for pleasure
parvenu [**par**-ven-new] *n* (*pl* **-s**) person newly risen to a position of power or wealth
parvenus *n* ▷ **parvenu**
pas *n* ▷ **pa**
pascal *n* (*pl* **-s**) unit of pressure
pascals *n* ▷ **pascal**
paspalum [pass-**pale**-um] *n* (*pl* **-s**) (AUST & NZ) type of grass with wide leaves
paspalums *n* ▷ **paspalum**
pass *v* (**-es, -ing, -ed**) go by, past, or through (SPORT) ▶ *n* (*pl* **-es**) successful result in a test or examination
passable *adj* (just) acceptable
passage *n* (*pl* **-s**) channel or opening providing a way through
passages *n* ▷ **passage**
passageway *n* (*pl* **-s**) passage or corridor
passageways *n* ▷ **passageway**
passbook *n* (*pl* **-s**) book issued by a bank or building society for keeping a record of deposits and withdrawals
passbooks *n* ▷ **passbook**
passé [**pas**-say] *adj* out-of-date
passed *v* ▷ **pass**
passenger *n* (*pl* **-s**) person travelling in a vehicle driven by someone else
passengers *n* ▷ **passenger**
passes *v, n* ▷ **pass**
passim *adv* (LATIN) everywhere, throughout
passing *adj* brief or transitory ▶ *v* ▷ **pass**
passion *n* (*pl* **-s**) intense sexual love > **passionate** *adj*
passionate *adj* ▷ **passion**
passionflower *n* (*pl* **-s**) tropical American plant
passionflowers *n* ▷ **passionflower**
passions *n* ▷ **passion**
passive *adj* not playing an active part > **passivity** *n* (*pl* **-ties**)
passivities *n* ▷ **passive**
passivity *n* ▷ **passive**
passport *n* (*pl* **-s**) official document of nationality granting permission to travel abroad
passports *n* ▷ **passport**
password *n* (*pl* **-s**) secret word or phrase that ensures admission
passwords *n* ▷ **password**
past *adj* of the time before the present ▶ *n* (*pl* **-s**) period of time before the present ▶ *adv* by, along ▶ *prep* beyond
pasta *n* (*pl* **-s**) type of food, such as spaghetti, that is made in different shapes from flour and water
pastas *n* ▷ **pasta**
paste *n* (*pl* **-s**) moist soft mixture, such as toothpaste ▶ *v* (**-tes, -ting, -ted**) fasten with paste
pasteboard *n* (*pl* **-s**) stiff thick paper
pasteboards *n* ▷ **pasteboard**
pasted *v* ▷ **paste**
pastel *n* (*pl* **-s**) coloured chalk crayon for drawing ▶ *adj* pale and delicate in colour
pastels *n* ▷ **pastel**
pastes *n, v* ▷ **paste**
pasteurize *v* (**-zes, -zing, -zed**) sterilize by heating > **pasteurization** *n* (*pl* **-s**)
pasteurization *n* ▷ **pasteurize**
pasteurizations *n* ▷ **pasteurize**
pasteurized *v* ▷ **pasteurize**
pasteurizes *v* ▷ **pasteurize**
pasteurizing *v* ▷ **pasteurize**
pastiche [pass-**teesh**] *n* (*pl* **-s**) work of art that mixes styles or copies the style of another artist
pastiches *n* ▷ **pastiche**

pastier *adj* ▷ **pasty**[1]
pasties *n* ▷ **pasty**[2]
pastiest *adj* ▷ **pasty**[1]
pastille *n* (*pl* **-s**) small fruit-flavoured and sometimes medicated sweet
pastilles *n* ▷ **pastille**
pastime *n* (*pl* **-s**) activity that makes time pass pleasantly
pastimes *n* ▷ **pastime**
pasting *n* (*pl* **-s**) (*Informal*) heavy defeat ▶ *v* ▷ **paste**
pastings *n* ▷ **pasting**
pastor *n* (*pl* **-s**) member of the clergy in charge of a congregation
pastoral *adj* of or depicting country life
pastors *n* ▷ **pastor**
pastrami *n* (*pl* **-s**) highly seasoned smoked beef
pastramis *n* ▷ **pastrami**
pastries *n* ▷ **pastry**
pastry *n* (*pl* **-ries**) baking dough made of flour, fat, and water
pasts *n* ▷ **past**
pasture *n* (*pl* **-s**) grassy land for farm animals to graze on
pastures *n* ▷ **pasture**
pasty[1] [**pay**-stee] *adj* (**-tier, -tiest**) (of a complexion) pale and unhealthy
pasty[2] [**pass**-tee] *n* (*pl* **-ties**) round of pastry folded over a savoury filling
pat[1] *v* (**-s, -tting, -tted**) tap lightly ▶ *n* (*pl* **-s**) gentle tap or stroke
pat[2] *adj* quick, ready, or glib
patch *n* (*pl* **-es**) piece of material sewn on a garment ▶ *v* (**-es, -ing, -ed**) mend with a patch
patched *v* ▷ **patch**
patches *n, v* ▷ **patch**
patchier *adj* ▷ **patchy**
patchiest *adj* ▷ **patchy**
patching *v* ▷ **patch**
patchwork *n* (*pl* **-s**) needlework made of pieces of different materials sewn together
patchworks *n* ▷ **patchwork**
patchy *adj* (**-hier, -hiest**) of uneven quality or intensity
pate *n* (*pl* **-s**) (*Old-fashioned*) head
pates *n* ▷ **pate**
pâté [**pat**-ay] *n* (*pl* **-s**) spread of finely minced liver etc.
pâtés *n* ▷ **pâté**
patella *n* (*pl* **-ae**) kneecap
patellae *n* ▷ **patella**
patent *n* (*pl* **-s**) document giving the exclusive right to make or sell an invention ▶ *adj* open to public inspection ▶ *v* (**-s, -ing, -ed**) obtain a patent for
patented *v* ▷ **patent**
patenting *v* ▷ **patent**
patently *adv* obviously
patents *n, v* ▷ **patent**
paternal *adj* fatherly
paternities *n* ▷ **paternity**
paternity *n* (*pl* **-ties**) fact or state of being a father
paternalism *n* (*pl* **-s**) authority exercised in a way that limits individual responsibility > **paternalistic** *adj*
paternalisms *n* ▷ **paternalism**
paternalistic *adj* ▷ **paternalism**
path *n* (*pl* **-s**) surfaced walk or track
pathname *n* (*pl* **-s**) (COMPUTERS) file name listing the sequence of directories leading to a particular file or directory
pathnames *n* ▷ **pathname**
paths *n* ▷ **path**
pathetic *adj* causing feelings of pity or sadness > **pathetically** *adv*
pathetically *adv* ▷ **pathetic**
pathogen *n* (*pl* **-s**) thing that causes disease > **pathogenic** *adj*
pathogenic *adj* ▷ **pathogen**
pathogens *n* ▷ **pathogen**
pathologies *n* ▷ **pathology**
pathology *n* (*pl* **-gies**) scientific study of diseases > **pathologist** *n* (*pl* **-s**)
pathological *adj* of pathology
pathologist *n* ▷ **pathology**
pathologists *n* ▷ **pathology**
pathos *n* (*pl* **-es**) power of arousing pity or sadness
pathoses *n* ▷ **pathos**
patience *n* (*pl* **-s**) quality of being patient
patiences *n* ▷ **patience**
patient *adj* enduring difficulties or delays calmly ▶ *n* (*pl* **-s**) person receiving medical treatment
patients *n* ▷ **patient**
patina *n* (*pl* **-s**) fine layer on a surface
patinas *n* ▷ **patina**
patio *n* (*pl* **-os**) paved area adjoining a house
patios *n* ▷ **patio**
patois [**pat**-wah] *n* (*pl* **patois**) [**pat**-wahz] regional dialect, esp. of French
patriarch *n* (*pl* **-s**) male head of a family or tribe > **patriarchal** *adj*
patriarchal *adj* ▷ **patriarch**
patriarchies *n* ▷ **patriarchy**
patriarchs *n* ▷ **patriarch**
patriarchy *n* (*pl* **-hies**) society in which men have most of the power

patrician *n* (*pl* **-s**) member of the nobility ▶ *adj* of noble birth
patricians *n* ▷ **patrician**
patricide *n* (*pl* **-s**) crime of killing one's father
patricides *n* ▷ **patricide**
patrimonies *n* ▷ **patrimony**
patrimony *n* (*pl* **-nies**) property inherited from ancestors
patriot *n* (*pl* **-s**) person who loves his or her country and supports its interests > **patriotic** *adj* > **patriotism** *n* (*pl* **-s**)
patriotic *adj* ▷ **patriot**
patriotism *n* ▷ **patriot**
patriotisms *n* ▷ **patriot**
patriots *n* ▷ **patriot**
patrol *n* (*pl* **-s**) regular circuit by a guard ▶ *v* (**-s, -lling, -lled**) go round on guard, or reconnoitring
patrolled *v* ▷ **patrol**
patrolling *v* ▷ **patrol**
patrols *n, v* ▷ **patrol**
patron *n* (*pl* **-s**) person who gives financial support to charities, artists, etc.
patronage *n* (*pl* **-s**) support given by a patron
patronages *n* ▷ **patronage**
patronize *v* (**-zes, -zing, -zed**) treat in a condescending way
patronized *v* ▷ **patronize**
patronizes *v* ▷ **patronize**
patronizing *v* ▷ **patronize**
patrons *n* ▷ **patron**
patronymic *n* (*pl* **-s**) name derived from one's father or a male ancestor
patronymics *n* ▷ **patronymic**
pats *v, n* ▷ **pat**[1]
patted *v* ▷ **pat**[1]
patter[1] *v* (**-s, -ing, -ed**) make repeated soft tapping sounds ▶ *n* (*pl* **-s**) quick succession of taps
patter[2] *n* (*pl* **-s**) glib rapid speech
pattered *v* ▷ **patter**[1]
pattering *v* ▷ **patter**[1]
patters *v, n* ▷ **patter**[1, 2]
pattern *n* (*pl* **-s**) arrangement of repeated parts or decorative designs
patterned *adj* decorated with a pattern
patterns *n* ▷ **pattern**
patties *n* ▷ **patty**
patting *v* ▷ **pat**[1]
patty *n* (*pl* **-tties**) small flattened cake of minced food
paucities *n* ▷ **paucity**
paucity *n* (*pl* **-ties**) scarcity
paunch *n* (*pl* **-es**) protruding belly
paunches *n* ▷ **paunch**
pauper *n* (*pl* **-s**) very poor person
paupers *n* ▷ **pauper**
pause *v* (**-ses, -sing, -sed**) stop for a time ▶ *n* (*pl* **-s**) stop or rest in speech or action
paused *v* ▷ **pause**
pauses *v, n* ▷ **pause**
pausing *v* ▷ **pause**
pave *v* (**-ves, -ving, -ved**) form (a surface) with stone or brick
paved *v* ▷ **pave**
pavement *n* (*pl* **-s**) paved path for pedestrians
pavements *n* ▷ **pavement**
paves *v* ▷ **pave**
paving *v* ▷ **pave**
pavilion *n* (*pl* **-s**) building on a playing field etc.
pavilions *n* ▷ **pavilion**
paw *n* (*pl* **-s**) animal's foot with claws and pads ▶ *v* (**-s, -ing, -ed**) scrape with the paw or hoof
pawed *v* ▷ **paw**
pawing *v* ▷ **paw**
paws *n, v* ▷ **paw**
pawn[1] *v* (**-s, -ing, -ed**) deposit (an article) as security for money borrowed
pawn[2] *n* (*pl* **-s**) chessman of the lowest value
pawnbroker *n* (*pl* **-s**) lender of money on goods deposited
pawnbrokers *n* ▷ **pawnbroker**
pawned *v* ▷ **pawn**[1]
pawning *v* ▷ **pawn**[1]
pawns *v, n* ▷ **pawn**[1, 2]
pay *v* (**-s, -ing, paid**) give money etc. in return for goods or services ▶ *n* (*pl* **-s**) wages or salary
payable *adj* due to be paid
payee *n* (*pl* **-s**) person to whom money is paid or due
payees *n* ▷ **payee**
paying *v* ▷ **pay**
payload *n* (*pl* **-s**) passengers or cargo of an aircraft
payloads *n* ▷ **payload**
payment *n* (*pl* **-s**) act of paying
payments *n* ▷ **payment**
payola *n* (*pl* **-s**) (CHIEFLY US) (*Informal*) bribe to get special treatment, esp. to promote a commercial product
pays *v, n* ▷ **pay**
payolas *n* ▷ **payola**

pax *n* (**paxes**). A pax is a period of peace, especially when there is one dominant nation. If you have a P and an X on your rack, there is likely to be an A available on the board. Pax gives a decent score for a three-letter word, so watch out for chances to play it on a bonus square. Pax scores 12 points.

pe *n* (**pes**). Pe is the 17th letter in the Hebrew alphabet. This is a very handy word because it allows you to connect words beginning with P to those ending in E, or vice versa and E is the most common tile in the game. Pe scores 4 points.

pea *n* (*pl* **-s**) climbing plant with seeds growing in pods
peas *n* ▷ **pea**
peace *n* (*pl* **-s**) calm, quietness > **peaceful** *adj* > **peacefully** *adv*
peaceable *adj* inclined towards peace > **peaceably** *adv*
peaceably *adv* ▷ **peaceable**
peaceful *adj* ▷ **peace**
peacefully *adv* ▷ **peace**
peaces *n* ▷ **peace**
peach *n* (*pl* **-es**) soft juicy fruit with a stone and a downy skin ▶ *adj* pinkish-orange
peaches *n* ▷ **peach**
peacock *n* (*pl* **-s**) large male bird with a brilliantly coloured fanlike tail > **peahen** *n fem* (*pl* **-s**)
peacocks *n* ▷ **peacock**
peahen *n* ▷ **peacock**
peahens *n* ▷ **peacock**
peak *n* (*pl* **-s**) pointed top, esp. of a mountain ▶ *v* (**-s, -ing, -ed**) form or reach a peak ▶ *adj* of or at the point of greatest demand > **peaked** *adj*
peaked *adj, v* ▷ **peak**
peakier *adj* ▷ **peaky**
peakiest *adj* ▷ **peaky**
peaking *v* ▷ **peak**
peaks *n, v* ▷ **peak**
peaky *adj* (**-kier, -kiest**) pale and sickly
peal *n* (*pl* **-s**) long loud echoing sound, esp. of bells or thunder ▶ *v* (**-s, -ing, -ed**) sound with a peal or peals
pealed *v* ▷ **peal**
pealing *v* ▷ **peal**
peals *n, v* ▷ **peal**
peanut *n* (*pl* **-s**) pea-shaped nut that ripens underground ▶ *pl* (*Informal*) trifling amount of money
peanuts *n* ▷ **peanut**
pear *n* (*pl* **-s**) sweet juicy fruit with a narrow top and rounded base
pears *n* ▷ **pear**
pearl *n* (*pl* **-s**) hard round shiny object found inside some oyster shells and used as a jewel > **pearly** *adj* (**-lier, -liest**)
pearlier *adj* ▷ **pearl**
pearliest *adj* ▷ **peral**
pearls *n* ▷ **pearl**
pearly *adj* ▷ **pearl**
peasant *n* (*pl* **-s**) person working on the land, esp. in poorer countries or in the past
peasantries *n* ▷ **peasantry**
peasantry *n* (*pl* **-ries**) peasants collectively
peasants *n* ▷ **peasant**
peat *n* (*pl* **-s**) decayed vegetable material found in bogs, used as fertilizer or fuel
peats *n* ▷ **peat**
pebble *n* (*pl* **-s**) small roundish stone > **pebbly** *adj* (**-lier, -liest**)
pebbles *n* ▷ **pebble**
pebblier *adj* ▷ **pebble**
pebbliest *adj* ▷ **pebble**
pebbly *adj* ▷ **pebble**
pecan [**pee**-kan] *n* (*pl* **-s**) edible nut of a N American tree
pecans *n* ▷ **pecan**
peccadillo *n* (*pl* **-lloes, -llos**) trivial misdeed
peccadilloes *n* ▷ **peccadillo**
peccadillos *n* ▷ **peccadillo**
peck *v* (**-s, -ing, -ed**) strike or pick up with the beak ▶ *n* (*pl* **-s**) pecking movement
pecked *v* ▷ **peck**
pecking *v* ▷ **peck**
peckish *adj* (*Informal*) slightly hungry
pecks *v, n* ▷ **peck**
pecs *pl n* (*Informal*) pectoral muscles
pectin *n* (*pl* **-s**) substance in fruit that makes jam set
pectins *n* ▷ **pectin**
pectoral *adj* of the chest or thorax ▶ *n* (*pl* **-s**) pectoral muscle or fin
pectorals *n* ▷ **pectoral**
peculiar *adj* strange
peculiarities *n* ▷ **peculiarity**
peculiarity *n* (*pl* **-ties**) oddity, eccentricity
pecuniary *adj* relating to, or consisting of, money
pedagogue *n* (*pl* **-s**) schoolteacher, esp. a pedantic one
pedagogues *n* ▷ **pedagogue**
pedal *n* (*pl* **-s**) foot-operated lever used to control a vehicle or machine, or to modify the tone of a musical instrument ▶ *v* (**-s, -lling, -lled**) propel (a bicycle) by using its pedals
pedalled *v* ▷ **pedal**
pedalling *v* ▷ **pedal**
pedals *n* ▷ **pedal**
pedant *n* (*pl* **-s**) person who is excessively concerned with details and rules, esp. in academic work > **pedantic** *adj* > **pedantry** *n* (*pl* **-ries**)
pedantic *adj* ▷ **pedant**

pedantries *n* ▷ **pedant**
pedantry *n* ▷ **pedant**
pedants *n* ▷ **pedant**
peddle *v* (**-les, -ling, -led**) sell (goods) from door to door
peddled *v* ▷ **peddle**
peddles *v* ▷ **peddle**
peddling *v* ▷ **peddle**
peddler *n* (*pl* **-s**) person who sells illegal drugs
peddlers *n* ▷ **peddler**
pedestal *n* (*pl* **-s**) base supporting a column, statue, etc.
pedestals *n* ▷ **pedestal**
pedestrian *n* (*pl* **-s**) person who walks ▶ *adj* dull, uninspiring
pedestrians *n* ▷ **pedestrian**
pedicure *n* (*pl* **-s**) medical or cosmetic treatment of the feet
pedicures *n* ▷ **pedicure**
pedigree *n* (*pl* **-s**) register of ancestors, esp. of a purebred animal
pedigrees *n* ▷ **pedigree**
pediment *n* (*pl* **-s**) triangular part over a door etc.
pediments *n* ▷ **pediment**
pedlar *n* (*pl* **-s**) person who sells goods from door to door
pedlars *n* ▷ **pedlar**
pee (*Informal*) *v* (**-s, -ing, peed**) urinate ▶ *n* (**-s**) act of urinating
peed *v* ▷ **pee**
peeing *v* ▷ **pee**
pees *v, n* ▷ **pee**
peek *v, n* (*pl* **-s**) peep or glance
peeks *n* ▷ **peek**
peel *v* (**-s, -ing, -ed**) remove the skin or rind of (a vegetable or fruit) ▶ *n* (*pl* **-s**) rind or skin > **peelings** *pl n*
peeled *v* ▷ **peel**
peeling *v* ▷ **peel**
peelings *n* ▷ **peel**
peels *v, n* ▷ **peel**
peep[1] *v* (**-s, -ing, -ed**) look slyly or quickly ▶ *n* (*pl* **-s**) peeping look
peep[2] *v* (**-s, -ing, -ed**) make a small shrill noise ▶ *n* (**-s**) small shrill noise
peeped *v* ▷ **peep**[1, 2]
peeping *v* ▷ **peep**[1, 2]
peeps *v, n* ▷ **peep**[1, 2]
peer[1] *n* (*pl* **-s**), *fem* **peeress** (*pl* **-es**) (in Britain) member of the nobility
peer[2] *v* (**-s, -ing, -ed**) look closely and intently
peerage *n* (BRIT) whole body of peers
peerages *n* ▷ **peerage**
peered *v* ▷ **peer**[2]
peeress *n* ▷ **peer**
peeresses *n* ▷ **peer**
peering *v* ▷ **peer**[2]
peerless *adj* unequalled, unsurpassed
peers *n, v* ▷ **peer**[1, 2]
peers *v* ▷ **peer**
peering *v* ▷ **peer**
peered *v* ▷ **peer**
peeved *adj* (*Informal*) annoyed
peevish *adj* fretful or irritable > **peevishly** *adv*
peevishly *adv* ▷ **peevish**
peewee *n* (*pl* **-s**) black-and-white Australian bird
peewees *n* ▷ **peewee**
peewit *n* (*pl* **-s**) ▷ **lapwing**
peewits *n* ▷ **peewit**
peg *n* (*pl* **-s**) pin or clip for joining, fastening, marking, etc. ▶ *v* (**-s, -gging, -gged**) fasten with pegs
pegged *v* ▷ **peg**
pegging *v* ▷ **peg**
pegs *n, v* ▷ **peg**
peignoir [**pay**-nwahr] *n* (*pl* **-s**) woman's light dressing gown
peignoirs *n* ▷ **peignoir**
pejorative [pij-**jor**-a-tiv] *adj* (of words etc.) with an insulting or critical meaning
pelargonium *n* (*pl* **-s**) plant with red, white, purple, or pink flowers
pelargoniums *n* ▷ **pelargonium**
pelican *n* (*pl* **-s**) large water bird with a pouch beneath its bill for storing fish
pelicans *n* ▷ **pelican**
pellagra *n* (*pl* **-s**) disease caused by lack of vitamin B
pellagras *n* ▷ **pellagra**
pellet *n* (*pl* **-s**) small ball of something
pellets *n* ▷ **pellet**
pellucid *adj* very clear
pelmet *n* (*pl* **-s**) ornamental drapery or board, concealing a curtain rail
pelmets *n* ▷ **pelmet**
pelt[1] *v* (**-s, -ing, -ed**) throw missiles at
pelt[2] *n* (*pl* **-s**) skin of a fur-bearing animal
pelted *v* ▷ **pelt**[1]
pelting *v* ▷ **pelt**[1]
pelts *v, n* ▷ **pelt**[1, 2]
pelvic *adj* ▷ **pelvis**
pelvis *n* (*pl* **-es**) framework of bones at the base of the spine, to which the hips are attached > **pelvic** *adj*
pelvises *n* ▷ **pelvis**
pen[1] *n* (*pl* **-s**) instrument for writing in ink ▶ *v* (**-s, -nning, -nned**) write or compose
pen[2] *n* small enclosure for domestic animals

▸ *v* (**-s, -nning, -nned**) put or keep in a pen
pen³ *n* (*pl* **-s**) female swan
penal [**pee**-nal] *adj* of or used in punishment
penalize (**-zes, -zing, -zed**) *v* impose a penalty on
penalized *v* ▹ **penalize**
penalizes *v* ▹ **penalize**
penalizing *v* ▹ **penalize**
penalties *n* ▹ **penalty**
penalty *n* (*pl* **-ties**) punishment for a crime or offence
penance *n* (*pl* (*pl* **-s**) voluntary self-punishment to make amends for wrongdoing
penances *n* ▹ **penance**
pence *n* (BRIT) ▹ **penny**
penchant [**pon**-shon] *n* (*pl* **-s**) inclination or liking
penchants *n* ▹ **penchant**
pencil *n* (*pl* **-s**) thin cylindrical instrument containing graphite, for writing or drawing ▸ *v* (**-s, -lling, -lled**) draw, write, or mark with a pencil
pencilled *v* ▹ **pencil**
pencilling *v* ▹ **pencil**
pencils *n, v* ▹ **pencil**
pendant *n* (*pl* **-s**) ornament worn on a chain round the neck
pendants *n* ▹ **pendant**
pendent *adj* hanging
pending *prep* while waiting for ▸ *adj* not yet decided or settled
pendulous *adj* hanging, swinging
pendulum *n* (*pl* **-s**) suspended weight swinging to and fro, esp. as a regulator for a clock
pendulums *n* ▹ **pendulum**
penetrate *v* (**-tes, -ting, -ted**) find or force a way into or through > **penetration** *n* (*pl* **-s**)
penetrable *adj* capable of being penetrated
penetrated *v* ▹ **penetrate**
penetrates *v* ▹ **penetrate**
penetrating *adj* (of a sound) loud and unpleasant ▸ *v* ▹ **penetrate**
penetration *n* ▹ **penetrate**
penetrations *n* ▹ **penetrate**
penguin *n* (*pl* **-s**) flightless black-and-white sea bird of the southern hemisphere
penguins *n* ▹ **penguin**
penicillin *n* (*pl* **-s**) antibiotic drug effective against a wide range of diseases and infections
penicillins *n* ▹ **penicillin**
peninsula *n* (*pl* **-s**) strip of land nearly surrounded by water > **peninsular** *adj*
penisular *adj* ▹ **penisula**
peninsulas *n* ▹ **peninsula**
penis *n* (*pl* **-es**) organ of copulation and urination in male mammals
penises *n* ▹ **penis**
penitence *n* ▹ **penitent**
penitences *n* ▹ **penitent**
penitent *adj* feeling sorry for having done wrong ▸ *n* (*pl* **-s**) someone who is penitent > **penitence** *n* (*pl* **-s**)
penitentiaries *n* ▹ **penitentiary**
penitentiary *n* (*pl* **-ries**) (US) prison ▸ *adj* (*also* **penitential**) relating to penance
penitents *n* ▹ **penitent**
penknife *n* (*pl* **-knives**) small knife with blade(s) that fold into the handle
penknives *n* ▹ **penknife**
pennant *n* (*pl* **-s**) long narrow flag
pennants *n* ▹ **pennant**
penned *v* ▹ **pen¹, ²**
pennies *n* ▹ **penny**
penniless *adj* very poor
penning *v* ▹ **pen¹, ²**
penny *n* (*pl* **pence, pennies**) British bronze coin worth one hundredth of a pound
pens *n* ▹ **pen¹, ², ³**
pension¹ *n* (*pl* **-s**) regular payment to people above a certain age, retired employees, widows, etc. > **pensionable** *adj*
pension² [**pon**-syon] *n* (*pl* **-s**) boarding house in Europe
pensionable *adj* ▹ **pension**
pensioner *n* (*pl* **-s**) person receiving a pension
pensioners *n* ▹ **pension**
pensions *n* ▹ **pension¹, ²**
pensive *adj* deeply thoughtful, often with a tinge of sadness
pentagon *n* (*pl* **-s**) geometric figure with five sides > **pentagonal** *adj*
pentagonal *adj* ▹ **pentagon**
pentagons *n* ▹ **pentagon**
pentameter [pen-**tam**-it-er] *n* (*pl* **-s**) line of poetry with five metrical feet
pentameters *n* ▹ **pentameter**
penthouse *n* (*pl* **-s**) flat built on the roof or top floor of a building
penthouses *n* ▹ **penthouse**
penultimate *adj* second last
penumbra *n* (*pl* **-brae, -bras**) (in an eclipse) the partially shadowed region which surrounds the full shadow
penumbrae *n* ▹ **penumbra**
penumbras *n* ▹ **penumbra**
penuries *n* ▹ **penury**
penurious *adj* ▹ **penury**
penury *n* (*pl* **-ries**) extreme poverty

> **penurious** *adj*
peonies *n* ▷ **peony**
peony *n* (*pl* **-nies**) garden plant with showy red, pink, or white flowers
people *pl n* persons generally ▶ *n* (*pl* **-s**) race or nation ▶ *v* (**-les, -ling, -led**) provide with inhabitants
peopled *v* ▷ **people**
peoples *n, v* ▷ **people**
peopling *v* ▷ **people**
pep *n* (*pl* **-s**) (*Informal*) high spirits, energy, or enthusiasm
pepper *n* (*pl* **-s**) sharp hot condiment made from the fruit of an East Indian climbing plant ▶ *v* (**-s, -ing, -ed**) season with pepper
peppercorn *n* dried berry of the pepper plant
peppercorns *n* ▷ **peppercorn**
peppered *v* ▷ **pepper**
pepperier *adj* ▷ **peppery**
pepperiest *adj* ▷ **peppery**
peppering *v* ▷ **pepper**
peppermint *n* (*pl* **-s**) plant that yields an oil with a strong sharp flavour
peppermints *n* ▷ **peppermint**
peppers *n, v* ▷ **pepper**
peppery *adj* (**-rier, -riest**) tasting of pepper
peps *n* ▷ **pep**
peptic *adj* relating to digestion or the digestive juices
per *prep* for each
perambulate *v* (**-tes, -ting, -ted**) (*Old-fashioned*) walk through or about (a place) > **perambulation** *n* (*pl* **-s**)
perambulated *v* ▷ **perambulate**
perambulates *v* ▷ **perambulate**
perambulating *v* ▷ **perambulate**
perambulation *n* ▷ **perambulate**
perambulations *n* ▷ **perambulate**
perambulator *n* (*pl* **-s**) pram
perambulators *n* ▷ **perambulator**
perceive *v* (**-ves, -ving, -ved**) become aware of (something) through the senses
perceived *v* ▷ **perceive**
perceives *v* ▷ **perceive**
perceiving *v* ▷ **perceive**
perceptible *adj* discernible, recognizable
perception *n* (*pl* **-s**) act of perceiving > **perceptive** *adj*
perceptions *n* ▷ **perception**
perceptive *adj* ▷ **perception**
perch¹ *n* (*pl* **-es**) resting place for a bird ▶ *v* (**-es, -ing, -ed**) alight, rest, or place on or as if on a perch
perch² *n* (*pl* **-es**) any of various edible fishes
perchance *adv* (*Old-fashioned*) perhaps
perches *n, v* ▷ **perch¹, ²**
perching *v* ▷ **perch¹, ²**
perched *v* ▷ **perch¹, ²**
percipient *adj* quick to notice things, observant
percolate *v* (**-tes, -ting, -ted**) pass or filter through small holes > **percolation** *n*
percolated *v* ▷ **percolate**
percolates *v* ▷ **percolate**
percolating *v* ▷ **percolate**
percolation *n* ▷ **percolate**
percolations *n* ▷ **percolate**
percolator *n* (*pl* **-s**) coffeepot in which boiling water is forced through a tube and filters down through coffee
percolators *n* ▷ **percolator**
percussion *n* (*pl* **-s**) striking of one thing against another
percussions *n* ▷ **percussion**
perdition *n* (*pl* **-s**) (CHRISTIANITY) spiritual ruin
perditions *n* ▷ **perdition**
peregrination *n* (*pl* **-s**) (*Obs*) travels, roaming
peregrinations *n* ▷ **peregrination**
peremptory *adj* authoritative, imperious
perennial *adj* lasting through many years ▶ *n* (*pl* **-s**) plant lasting more than two years > **perennially** *adv*
perennially *adv* ▷ **perennial**
perennials *n* ▷ **perennial**
perfect *adj* (**-er, -est**) having all the essential elements ▶ *n* (*pl* **-s**) (GRAMMAR) perfect tense ▶ *v* (**-s, -ing, -ed**) improve > **perfectly** *adv*
perfected *n* ▷ **perfect**
perfecter *adj* ▷ **perfect**
perfectest *adj* ▷ **perfect**
perfecting *v* ▷ **perfect**
perfection *n* (*pl* **-s**) state of being perfect
perfectionist *n* (*pl* **-s**) person who demands the highest standards of excellence > **perfectionism** *n* (*pl* **-s**)
perfectionism *n* ▷ **perfectionist**
perfectionisms *n* ▷ **perfectionist**
perfectionists *n* ▷ **perfectionist**
perfections *n* ▷ **perfection**
perfectly *adv* ▷ **perfect**
perfects *n, v* ▷ **perfect**
perfidious *adj* (*Lit*) treacherous, disloyal > **perfidy** *n* (*pl* **-ies**)
perfidies *n* ▷ **perfidious**
perfidy *n* ▷ **perfidious**
perforate *v* (**-es, -ing, -ed**) make holes in > **perforation** *n* (*pl* **-s**)
perforated *v* ▷ **perforate**
perforates *v* ▷ **perforate**
perforating *v* ▷ **perforate**

perforation *n* ▷ **perforate**
perforations *n* ▷ **perforate**
perforce *adv* of necessity
perform *v* (**-s, -ing, -ed**) carry out (an action) > **performance** *n* (*pl* **-s**) > **performer** *n* (*pl* **-s**)
performance *n* ▷ **perform**
performances *n* ▷ **perform**
performed *v* ▷ **perform**
performer *n* ▷ **perform**
performers *n* ▷ **perform**
performing *v* ▷ **perform**
performs *v* ▷ **perform**
perfume *n* (*pl* **-s**) liquid cosmetic worn for its pleasant smell ▶ *v* (**-es, -ing, -ed**) give a pleasant smell to
perfumed *v* ▷ **perfume**
perfumeries *n* ▷ **perfumery**
perfumery *n* (*pl* **-ries**) perfumes in general
perfumes *n, v* ▷ **perfume**
perfuming *v* ▷ **perfume**
perfunctorily *adv* ▷ **perfunctory**
perfunctory *adj* done only as a matter of routine, superficial > **perfunctorily** *adv*
pergola *n* (*pl* **-s**) arch or framework of trellis supporting climbing plants
pergolas *n* ▷ **pergola**
perhaps *adv* possibly, maybe
pericardia *n* ▷ **pericardum**
pericardium *n* (*pl* **-dia**) membrane enclosing the heart
perihelia *n* ▷ **perihelion**
perihelion *n* (*pl* **-lia**) point in the orbit of a planet or comet that is nearest to the sun
peril *n* (*pl* **-s**) great danger > **perilous** *adj* > **perilously** *adv*
perilous *adj* ▷ **peril**
perilously *adv* ▷ **peril**
perils *n* ▷ **peril**
perimeter [per-**rim**-it-er] *n* (*pl* **-s**) (length of) the outer edge of an area
perimeters *n* ▷ **perimeter**
perinatal *adj* of or in the weeks shortly before or after birth
period *n* (*pl* **-s**) particular portion of time (US) ▶ *adj* (of furniture, dress, a play, etc.) dating from or in the style of an earlier time
periodic *adj* recurring at intervals
periodical *n* (*pl* **-s**) magazine issued at regular intervals ▶ *adj* periodic
periodicals *n* ▷ **periodical**
periods *n* ▷ **period**
peripatetic [per-rip-a-**tet**-ik] *adj* travelling about from place to place
peripheral [per-**if**-er-al] *adj* unimportant, not central
peripheries *n* ▷ **periphery**
periphery [per-**if**-er-ee] *n* (*pl* **-ries**) boundary or edge
periscope *n* (*pl* **-s**) instrument used, esp. in submarines, to give a view of objects on a different level
periscopes *n* ▷ **periscope**
perish *v* (**-es, -ing, -ed**) be destroyed or die
perishable *adj* liable to rot quickly
perished *v* ▷ **perish**
perishes *v* ▷ **perish**
perishing *adj* (*Informal*) very cold ▶ *v* ▷ **perish**
peritonea *n* ▷ **peritoneum**
peritoneum [per-rit-toe-**nee**-um] *n* (*pl* **-nea, -neums**) membrane lining the internal surface of the abdomen
peritoneums *n* ▷ **peritoneum**
peritonitis [per-rit-tone-**ite**-iss] *n* (*pl* **-tises**) inflammation of the peritoneum
peritonitises *n* ▷ **peritonitis**
periwinkle[1] *n* (*pl* **-s**) small edible shellfish, the winkle
periwinkle[2] *n* (*pl* **-s**) plant with trailing stems and blue flowers
periwinkles *n* ▷ **periwinkle**[1, 2]
perjuries *n* ▷ **perjury**
perjury *n* (*pl* **-ies**) act or crime of lying while under oath in a court
perk *n* (*pl* **-s**) (*Informal*) incidental benefit gained from a job, such as a company car
perkier *adj* ▷ **perk**
perkiest *adj* ▷ **perk**
perks *n* ▷ **perk**
perky *adj* (**-kier, -kiest**) lively or cheerful
perlemoen *n* (*pl* **-s**) (S AFR) edible sea creature with a shell lined with mother of pearl
perlemoens *n* ▷ **perlemoen**
perm *n* (*pl* **-s**) long-lasting curly hairstyle produced by treating the hair with chemicals ▶ *v* (**-s, -ing, -ed**) give (hair) a perm
permafrost *n* (*pl* **-s**) permanently frozen ground
permafrosts *n* ▷ **permafrost**
permanence *n* ▷ **permanent**
permanences *n* ▷ **permanent**
permanent *adj* lasting forever > **permanence** *n* (*pl* **-s**) > **permanently** *adv*
permanently *adv* ▷ **permanent**
permeate *v* (**-tes, -ting, -ted**) pervade or pass through the whole of (something)
permeable *adj* able to be permeated, esp. by liquid
permeated *v* ▷ **permeate**
permeates *v* ▷ **permeate**
permeating *v* ▷ **permeate**

permed *v* ▷ **perm**
perming *v* ▷ **perm**
permissible *adj* ▷ **permit**
permission *n* (*pl* **-s**) authorization to do something
permissions *n* ▷ **permission**
permissive *adj* (excessively) tolerant, esp. in sexual matters
permit *v* (**-s, -tting, -tted**) give permission, allow ▶ *n* (*pl* **-s**) document giving permission to do something > **permissible** *adj*
permits *v, n* ▷ **permit**
permitted *v* ▷ **permit**
permitting *v* ▷ **permit**
perms *n, v* ▷ **perm**
permutation *n* (*pl* **-s**) any of the ways a number of things can be arranged or combined
permutations *n* ▷ **permutation**
pernicious *adj* wicked
pernickety *adj* (*Informal*) (excessively) fussy about details
peroration *n* (*pl* **-s**) concluding part of a speech, usu. summing up the main points
perorations *n* ▷ **peroration**
peroxide *n* (*pl* **-s**) hydrogen peroxide used as a hair bleach
peroxides *n* ▷ **peroxide**
perpendicular *adj* at right angles to a line or surface ▶ *n* (*pl* **-s**) line or plane at right angles to another
perpendiculars *n* ▷ **perpendicular**
perpetrate *v* (**-tes, -ting, -ted**) commit or be responsible for (a wrongdoing) > **perpetration** *n* (*pl* **-s**) > **perpetrator** *n* (*pl* **-s**)
perpetrated *v* ▷ **perpetrate**
perpetrates *v* ▷ **perpetrate**
perpetrating *v* ▷ **perpetrate**
perpetration *n* ▷ **perpetrate**
perpetrations *n* ▷ **perpetrate**
perpetrator *n* ▷ **perpetrate**
perpetrators *n* ▷ **perpetrate**
perpetual *adj* lasting forever > **perpetually** *adv*
perpetually *adv* ▷ **perpetual**
perpetuate *v* (**-tes, -ting, -ted**) cause to continue or be remembered > **perpetuation** *n* (*pl* **-s**)
perpetuated *v* ▷ **perpetuate**
perpetuates *v* ▷ **perpetuate**
perpetuating *v* ▷ **perpetuate**
perpetuation *n* ▷
perpetuations *n* ▷
perplex *v* (**-es, -ing, -ed**) puzzle, bewilder > **perplexity** *n* (*pl* **-ties**)
perplexed *v* ▷ **perplex**
perplexes *v* ▷ **perplex**
perplexing *v* ▷ **perplex**
perplexities *n* ▷ **perplex**
perplexity *n* ▷ **perplex**
perquisite *n* (*pl* **-s**) (*Formal*) ▷ **perk**
perquisites *n* ▷ **perquisite**
perries *n* ▷ **perry**
perry *n* (*pl* **-rries**) alcoholic drink made from fermented pears
persecute *v* (**-tes, -ting, -ted**) treat cruelly because of race, religion, etc. > **persecution** *n* (*pl* **-s**) > **persecutor** *n* (*pl* **-s**)
persecuted *v* ▷ **persecute**
persecutes *v* ▷ **persecute**
persecuting *v* ▷ **persecute**
persecution *n* ▷ **persecute**
persecutions *n* ▷ **persecute**
persecutor *n* ▷ **persecute**
persecutors *n* ▷ **persecute**
persevere *v* (**-res, -ring, -red**) keep making an effort despite difficulties > **perseverance** *n* (*pl* **-s**)
perseverance *n* ▷ **persevere**
perseverances *n* ▷ **persevere**
persevered *v* ▷ **persevere**
perseveres *v* ▷ **persevere**
persevering *v* ▷ **persevere**
persimmon *n* (*pl* **-s**) sweet red tropical fruit
persimmons *n* ▷ **persimmon**
persist *v* (**-s, -ing, -ed**) continue to be or happen, last > **persistent** *adj* > **persistently** *adv* > **persistence** *n* (*pl* **-s**)
persisted *v* ▷ **persist**
persistence *adj* ▷ **persist**
persistences *adj* ▷ **persist**
persistent *adj* ▷ **persist**
persistently *v* ▷ **persist**
persisting *v* ▷ **persist**
persists *v* ▷ **persist**
person *n* (*pl* **-s**) human being
persons *n* ▷ **person**
persona [per-**soh**-na] *n* (*pl* **-nae**) [-nee] someone's personality as presented to others
personable *adj* pleasant in appearance and personality
personae *n* ▷ **persona**
personage *n* (*pl* **-s**) important person
personages *n* ▷ **personage**
personal *adj* individual or private
personalities *n* ▷ **personality**
personality *n* (*pl* **-ties**) person's distinctive characteristics
personally *adv* directly, not by delegation to others
personification *n* ▷ **personify**

personifications *n* ▷ **personify**
personified *v* ▷ **personify**
personifies *v* ▷ **personify**
personify *v* (**-fies, -fying, -fied**) give human characteristics to > **personification** *n* (*pl* **-s**)
personifying *v* ▷ **personify**
personnel *n* (*pl* **-s**) people employed in an organization
personnels *n* ▷ **personnel**
perspective *n* (*pl* **-s**) view of the relative importance of situations or facts
perspectives *n* ▷ **perspective**
perspicacious *adj* having quick mental insight > **perspicacity** *n* (*pl* **-ties**)
perspicacities *n* ▷ **perspicacious**
perspicacity *n* ▷ **perspicacious**
perspiration *n* ▷ **perspire**
perspirations *n* ▷ **perspire**
perspire *v* (**-res, -ring, -red**) sweat > **perspiration** *n* (*pl* **-s**)
perspired *v* ▷ **perspire**
perspires *v* ▷ **perspire**
perspiring *v* ▷ **perspire**
persuade *v* (**-des, -ding, -ded**) make (someone) do something by argument, charm, etc. > **persuasive** *adj*
persuasion *n* (*pl* **-s**) act of persuading
persuasions *n* ▷ **persuasion**
persuasive *adj* ▷ **persuade**
persuaded *v* ▷ **persuade**
persuades *v* ▷ **persuade**
persuading *v* ▷ **persuade**
pert *adj* (**-er, -est**) saucy and cheeky
pertain *v* (**-s, -ing, -ed**) belong or be relevant (to)
pertained *v* ▷ **pertain**
pertaining *v* ▷ **pertain**
pertains *v* ▷ **pertain**
perter *adj* ▷ **pert**
pertest *adj* ▷ **pert**
pertinacious *adj* (*Formal*) very persistent and determined > **pertinacity** *n* (*pl* **-ties**)
pertinacities *n* ▷ **pertinacious**
pertinacity *n* ▷ **pertinacious**
pertinence *n* ▷ **pertinent**
pertinences *n* ▷ **pertinent**
pertinent *adj* relevant > **pertinence** *n* (*pl* **-s**)
perturb *v* (**-s, -ing, -ed**) disturb greatly > **perturbation** *n* (*pl* **-s**)
perturbation *n* ▷ **perturb**
perturbation *n* ▷ **perturb**
perturbed *v* ▷ **perturb**
perturbing *v* ▷ **perturb**
perturbs *v* ▷ **perturb**
perusal *n* ▷ **peruse**
perusals *n* ▷ **peruse**
peruse *v* (**-ses, -sing, -sed**) read in a careful or leisurely manner > **perusal** *n* (*pl* **-s**)
perused *v* ▷ **peruse**
peruses *v* ▷ **peruse**
perusing *v* ▷ **peruse**
pervade *v* (**-des, -ding, -ded**) spread right through (something) > **pervasive** *adj*
pervaded *v* ▷ **pervade**
pervades *v* ▷ **pervade**
pervading *v* ▷ **pervade**
pervasive *adj* ▷ **pervade**
perverse *adj* (**-r, -st**) deliberately doing something different from what is thought normal or proper > **perversely** *adv* > **perversity** *n* (*pl* **-ties**)
perversely *n* ▷ **perverse**
perverser *adj* ▷ **perverse**
perversest *adj* ▷ **perverse**
perversion *n* (*pl* **-s**) sexual act or desire considered abnormal
perversions *n* ▷ **perversion**
perversities *n* ▷ **perverse**
perversity *n* ▷ **perverse**
pervert *v* (**-s, -ing, -ed**) use or alter for a wrong purpose ▶ *n* (*pl* **-s**) person who practises sexual perversion
perverted *v* ▷ **pervert**
perverting *v* ▷ **pervert**
perverts *v, n* ▷ **pervert**
pervious *adj* able to be penetrated, permeable
peseta [pa-**say**-ta] *n* (*pl* **-s**) former monetary unit of Spain
pesetas *n* ▷ **peseta**
pessaries *n* ▷ **pessary**
pessary *n* (*pl* **-ries**) appliance worn in the vagina, either to prevent conception or to support the womb
pessimism *n* (*pl* **-s**) tendency to expect the worst in all things > **pessimist** *n* (*pl* **-s**) > **pessimistic** *adj* > **pessimistically** *adv*
pessimisms *n* ▷ **pessimism**
pessimist *n* ▷ **pessimism**
pessimistic *adj* ▷ **pessimism**
pessimistically *adv* ▷ **pessimism**
pessimists *n* ▷ **pessimism**
pest *n* (*pl* **-s**) annoying person
pesticide *n* (*pl* **-s**) chemical for killing insect pests
pesticides *n* ▷ **pesticide**
pester *v* (**-s, -ing, -ed**) annoy or nag continually
pestered *v* ▷ **pester**
pestering *v* ▷ **pester**
pesters *v* ▷ **pester**
pestilence *n* (*pl* **-s**) deadly epidemic disease

pestilences *n* ▷ **pestilence**
pestilent *adj* annoying, troublesome > **pestilential** *adj*
pestilential *adj* ▷ **pestilent**
pestle *n* (*pl* **-s**) club-shaped implement for grinding things to powder in a mortar
pestles *n* ▷ **pestle**
pests *n* ▷ **pest**
pet *n* (*pl* **-s**) animal kept for pleasure and companionship ▶ *adj* particularly cherished ▶ *v* (**-s, -tting, -tted**) treat as a pet
petal *n* (*pl* **-s**) one of the brightly coloured outer parts of a flower > **petalled** *adj*
petalled *adj* ▷ **petal**
petals *n* ▷ **petal**
petard *n* (*pl* **-s**) being the victim of one's own schemes
petards *n* ▷ **petard**
petite *adj* (of a woman) small and dainty
petition *n* (*pl* **-s**) formal request, esp. one signed by many people and presented to parliament ▶ *v* (**-s, -ing, -ed**) present a petition to > **petitioner** *n* (*pl* **-s**)
petitioned *v* ▷ **petition**
petitioner *n* ▷ **petition**
petitioners *n* ▷ **petition**
petitioning *v* ▷ **petition**
petitions *n, v* ▷ **petition**
petrel *n* (*pl* **-s**) sea bird with a hooked bill and tubular nostrils
petrels *n* ▷ **petrel**
petrification *n* ▷ **petrify**
petrifications *n* ▷ **petrify**
petrified *v* ▷ **petrify**
petrifies *v* ▷ **petrify**
petrify *v* (**-fies, -fying, -fied**) frighten severely > **petrification** *n* (*pl* **-s**)
petrochemical *n* (*pl* **-s**) substance, such as acetone, obtained from petroleum
petrochemicals *n* ▷ **petrochemical**
petrol *n* (*pl* **-s**) flammable liquid obtained from petroleum, used as fuel in internal-combustion engines
petroleum *n* (*pl* **-s**) thick dark oil found underground
petroleums *n* ▷ **petroleums**
petrols *n* ▷ **petrol**
pets *n, v* ▷ **pet**
petted *v* ▷ **pet**
petticoat *n* (*pl* **-s**) woman's skirt-shaped undergarment
petticoats *n* ▷ **petticoat**
pettier *adj* ▷ **petty**
pettiest *adj* ▷ **petty**
pettifogging *adj* excessively concerned with unimportant detail
pettiness *n* ▷ **petty**
pettinesses *n* ▷ **petty**
petting *v* ▷ **pet**
petty *adj* (**-ttier, -ttiest**) unimportant, trivial > **pettiness** *n* (*pl* **-es**)
petulance *n* ▷ **petulant**
petulances *n* ▷ **petulant**
petulant *adj* childishly irritable or peevish > **petulance** *n* (*pl* **-s**) > **petulantly** *adv*
petulantly *adv* ▷ **petulant**
petunia *n* (*pl* **-s**) garden plant with funnel-shaped flowers
petunias *n* ▷ **petunia**
pew *n* (*pl* **-s**) fixed benchlike seat in a church
pews *n* ▷ **pew**
pewter *n* (*pl* **-s**) greyish metal made of tin and lead
pewters *n* ▷ **pewter**
phalanger *n* (*pl* **-s**) long-tailed Australian tree-dwelling marsupial
phalangers *n* ▷ **phalanger**
phalanx *n* (*pl* **-es**) closely grouped mass of people
phalanxes *n* ▷ **phalanx**
phalli *n* ▷ **phallus**
phallic *adj* ▷ **phallic**
phallus *n* (*pl* **-lluses, -lli**) penis, esp. as a symbol of reproductive power in primitive rites > **phallic** *adj*
phalluses *n* ▷ **phallus**
phantasm *n* (*pl* **-s**) unreal vision, illusion > **phantasmal** *adj*
phantasmal *adj* ▷ **phantasm**
phantasms *n* ▷ **phantasm**
phantasmagoria *n* (*pl* **-s**) shifting medley of dreamlike figures
phantasmagorias *n* ▷ **phantasmagoria**
phantom *n* (*pl* **-s**) ghost
phantoms *n* ▷ **phantom**
pharmaceutical *adj* of pharmacy
pharmacies *n* ▷ **pharmacy**
pharmacist *n* (*pl* **-s**) person qualified to prepare and sell drugs and medicines
pharmacists *n* ▷ **pharmacist**
pharmacological *adj* ▷ **pharmacology**
pharmacologies *n* ▷ **pharmacology**
pharmacologist *n* ▷ **pharmacology**
pharmacologists *n* ▷ **pharmacology**
pharmacology *n* (*pl* **-gies**) study of drugs > **pharmacological** *adj* > **pharmacologist** *n* (*pl* **-s**)
pharmacopoeia [far-ma-koh-**pee**-a] *n* (*pl* **-s**) book with a list of and directions for the use of drugs

pharmacopoeias *n* ▷ **pharmacopoeia**
pharmacy *n* (*pl* **-cies**) preparation and dispensing of drugs and medicines
pharynges *n* ▷ **pharynx**
pharyngitis [far-rin-**jite**-iss] *n* (*pl* **-tes**) inflammation of the pharynx
pharyngitises *n* ▷ **pharynx**
pharynx [**far**-rinks] *n* (*pl* **-nges, -nxes**) cavity forming the back part of the mouth
pharynxes ▷ **pharynx**
phase *n* (*pl* **-s**) any distinct or characteristic stage in a development or chain of events ▶ *v* (**-ses, -sing, -sed**) arrange or carry out in stages or to coincide with something else
phased *v* ▷ **phase**
phases *n*, *v* ▷ **phase**
phasing *v* ▷ **phase**
pheasant *n* (*pl* **-s**) game bird with bright plumage
pheasants *n* ▷ **pheasant**
phenobarbitone *n* (*pl* **-s**) drug inducing sleep or relaxation
phenobarbitones *n* ▷ **phenobarbitone**
phenol *n* (*pl* **-s**) chemical used in disinfectants and antiseptics
phenols *n* ▷ **phenol**
phenomena *n* ▷ **phenomenon**
phenomenal *adj* extraordinary, outstanding > **phenomenally** *adv*
phenomenally *adv* ▷ **phenomenal**
phenomenon *n* (*pl* **-mena**) anything appearing or observed
phial *n* (*pl* **-s**) small bottle for medicine etc.
phials *n* ▷ **phial**
philadelphus *n* (*pl* **-es**) shrub with sweet-scented flowers
philadelphuses *n* ▷ **philadelphus**
philanderer *n* (*pl* **-s**) man who flirts or has many casual love affairs > **philandering** *adj*, *n* (*pl* **-s**)
philanderers *n* ▷ **philanderer**
philandering *n* ▷ **philanderer**
philanderings *n* ▷ **philanderer**
philanthropic *adj* ▷ **philanthropy**
philanthropies *n* ▷ **philanthropy**
philanthropist *n* ▷ **philanthropy**
philanthropists *n* ▷ **philanthropy**
philanthropy *n* (*pl* **-pies**) practice of helping people less well-off than oneself > **philanthropic** *adj* > **philanthropist** *n* (*pl* **-s**)
philatelies *n* ▷ **philately**
philatelist *n* ▷ **philately**
philatelists *n* ▷ **philately**
philately [fill-**lat**-a-lee] *n* (*pl* **-lies**) stamp collecting > **philatelist** *n* (*pl* **-s**)
philharmonic *adj* (in names of orchestras etc.) music-loving
philistine *adj*, *n* (*pl* **-s**) boorishly uncultivated (person) > **philistinism** *n* (*pl* **-s**)
philistines *n* ▷ **philistine**
philistinism *n* ▷ **philistine**
philistinisms *n* ▷ **philistine**
philological *adj* ▷ **philology**
philologies *n* ▷ **philology**
philologist *n* ▷ **philology**
philologists *n* ▷ **philology**
philology *n* (*pl* **-gies**) science of the structure and development of languages > **philological** *adj* > **philologist** *n* (*pl* **-s**)
philosopher *n* (*pl* **-s**) person who studies philosophy
philosophers *n* ▷ **philosopher**
philosophize *v* (**-zes, -zing, -zed**) discuss in a philosophical manner
philosophized *v* ▷ **philosophize**
philosophizes *v* ▷ **philosophize**
philosophizing *v* ▷ **philosophize**
philosophic *adj* ▷ **philosophy**
philosophical *adj* ▷ **philosophy**
philosophically *adv* ▷ **philosophy**
philosophies *n* ▷ **philosophy**
philosophy *n* (*pl* **-phies**) study of the meaning of life, knowledge, thought, etc. > **philosophical, philosophic** *adj* of philosophy > **philosophically** *adv*
philtre *n* (*pl* **-s**) magic drink supposed to arouse love in the person who drinks it
philtres *n* ▷ **philtre**
phlebitis [fleb-**bite**-iss] *n* (*pl* **-es**) inflammation of a vein
phlebitises *n* ▷ **phlebitis**
phlegm [**flem**] *n* (*pl* **-s**) thick yellowish substance formed in the nose and throat during a cold
phlegmatic [fleg-**mat**-ik] *adj* not easily excited, unemotional > **phlegmatically** *adv*
phlematically *adv* ▷ **phlegmatic**
phlegms *n* ▷ **phlegm**
phlox *n* (*pl* **phlox, -xes**) flowering garden plant
phloxes *n* ▷ **phlox**
phobia *n* (*pl* **-s**) intense and unreasoning fear or dislike
phobias *n* ▷ **phobia**
phoenix *n* (*pl* **-es**) legendary bird said to set fire to itself and rise anew from its ashes
phoenixes *n* ▷ **phoenix**
phone *n*, *v* (**-nes, -ning, -ned**) (*Informal*) telephone
phonecard *n* (*pl* **-s**) card used to operate certain public telephones

phonecards *n* ▷ **phonecard**
phoned *v* ▷ **phone**
phones *v* ▷ **phone**
phonetic *adj* of speech sounds > **phonetically** *adv*
phonetically *adv* ▷ **phonetic**
phonetics *n* science of speech sounds
phoney, phony (*Informal*) *adj* (**-nier, -niest**) not genuine ▶ *n* (*pl* **-neys, -nies**) phoney person or thing
phoneys *n* ▷ **phoney**
phonier *adj* ▷ **phoney**
phonies *n* ▷ **phoney**
phoniest *adj* ▷ **phoney**
phoning *v* ▷ **phone**
phonograph *n* (*pl* **-s**) (US) (*old-fashioned*) record player
phonographs *n* ▷ **phonograph**
phony *adj* ▷ **phony**
phosphorescence *n* (*pl* **-s**) faint glow in the dark > **phosphorescent** *adj*
phosphorescences *n* ▷ **phosphorescence**
phosphorescent *adj* ▷ **phosphorescence**
phosphate *n* (*pl* **-s**) compound of phosphorus
phosphates *n* ▷ **phosphate**
phosphorus *n* (*pl* **-es**) (CHEM) toxic flammable nonmetallic element which appears luminous in the dark
phosphoruses *n* ▷ **phosphorus**
photo *n* (*pl* **-s**) ▷ **photograph**
photocopied *v* ▷ **photocopy**
photocopier *n* ▷ **photocopy**
photocopiers *n* ▷ **photocopy**
photocopies *n, v* ▷ **photocopy**
photocopy *n* (*pl* **-pies**) photographic reproduction ▶ *v* (**-pies, -pying, -pied**) make a photocopy of > **photocopier** *n* (*pl* **-s**)
photocopying *v* ▷ **photocopy**
photoelectric *adj* using or worked by electricity produced by the action of light
photogenic *adj* always looking attractive in photographs
photograph *n* (*pl* **-s**) picture made by the chemical action of light on sensitive film ▶ *v* (**-s, -ing, -ed**) take a photograph of > **photographic** *adj*
photographed *v* ▷ **photograph**
photographer *n* (*pl* **-s**) person who takes photographs, esp. professionally
photographers *n* ▷ **photographer**
photographic *adj* ▷ **photograph**
photographing *v* ▷ **photograph**
photographs *n, v* ▷ **photograph**
photographies *n* ▷ **photography**
photography *n* (*pl* **-s**) art of taking photographs
photos *n* ▷ **photo**
photostat *n* (*pl* **-s**) copy made by photocopying machine
photostats *n* ▷ **photostat**
photosyntheses *n* ▷ **photosynthesis**
photosynthesis *n* (*pl* **-ses**) process by which a green plant uses sunlight to build up carbohydrate reserves
phrase *n* (*pl* **-s**) group of words forming a unit of meaning, esp. within a sentence ▶ *v* (**-ses, -sing, -sed**) express in words
phrased *v* ▷ **phrase**
phrases *n, v* ▷ **phrase**
phrasing *v* ▷ **phrase**
phraseologies *n* ▷ **phraseology**
phraseology *n* (*pl* **-gies**) way in which words are used
physical *adj* of the body, as contrasted with the mind or spirit > **physically** *adv*
physically *adv* ▷ **physical**
physician *n* (*pl* **-s**) doctor of medicine
physicians *n* ▷ **physician**
physics *n* science of the properties of matter and energy
physicist *n* (*pl* **-s**) person skilled in or studying physics
physicists *n* ▷ **physicist**
physiognomies *n* ▷ **physiognomy**
physiognomy [fiz-ee-**on**-om-ee] *n* (*pl* **-mies**) face
physiological *adj* ▷ **physiology**
physiologies *n* ▷ **physiology**
physiologist *n* ▷ **physiology**
physiologists *n* ▷ **physiology**
physiology *n* (*pl* **-gies**) science of the normal function of living things > **physiological** *adj* > **physiologist** *n* (*pl* **-s**)
physiotherapies *n* ▷ **physiotherapy**
physiotherapist *n* ▷ **physiotherapy**
physiotherapists *n* ▷ **physiotherapy**
physiotherapy *n* (*pl* **-pies**) treatment of disease or injury by physical means such as massage, rather than by drugs > **physiotherapist** *n* (*pl* **-s**)
physique *n* (*pl* **-s**) person's bodily build and muscular development
physiques *n* ▷ **physique**
pi *n* (*pl* **-s**) (MATHS) ratio of the circumference of a circle to its diameter
pis *n* ▷ **pi**
pianissimo *adv* (MUSIC) very quietly
piano[1] *n* (*pl* **-os**) musical instrument with strings which are struck by hammers worked by a keyboard (*also* **pianoforte**) (*pl* **-s**) > **pianist**

n (*pl* **-s**)
pianist *n* ▷ **piano[1]**
pianists *n* ▷ **piano[1]**
piano[2] *adv* (MUSIC) quietly
pianoforte *n* ▷ **piano[1]**
pianofortes *n* ▷ **piano[1]**
pianos *n* ▷ **piano[1]**
piazza *n* (*pl* **-s**) square or marketplace, esp. in Italy
piazzas *n* ▷ **piazza**
pic *n* (*pl* **-s, pix**) (*Informal*) photograph or illustration
picador *n* (*pl* **-s**) mounted bullfighter with a lance
picadors *n* ▷ **picador**
picaresque *adj* denoting a type of fiction in which the hero, a rogue, has a series of adventures
piccalilli *n* (*pl* **-s**) pickle of vegetables in mustard sauce
piccalillis *n* ▷ **piccalilli**
piccolo *n* (*pl* **-os**) small flute
piccolos *n* ▷ **piccolo**
pick[1] *v* (**-s, -ing, -ed**) choose ▶ *n* (*pl* **-s**) choice
pick[2] *n* (*pl* **-s**) tool with a curved iron crossbar and wooden shaft, for breaking up hard ground or rocks
pickaxe *n* (*pl* **-s**) large pick
pickaxes *n* ▷ **pickaxe**
picked *v* ▷ **pick[1]**
picket *n* (*pl* **-s**) person or group standing outside a workplace to deter would-be workers during a strike ▶ *v* (**-s, -ing, -ed**) form a picket outside (a workplace)
picketed *v* ▷ **picket**
picketing *v* ▷ **picket**
pickets *n, v* ▷ **picket**
picking *v* ▷ **pick[1]**
pickings *pl n* money easily acquired
pickle *n* (*pl* **-s**) food preserved in vinegar or salt water ▶ *v* (**-les, -ling, -led**) preserve in vinegar or salt water
pickled *adj* (of food) preserved ▶ *n* ▷ **pickle**
pickles *n, v* ▷ **pickle**
pickling *v* ▷ **pickle**
pickpocket *n* (*pl* **-s**) thief who steals from someone's pocket
pickpockets *n* ▷ **pickpocket**
picks *n, v* ▷ **pick[1, 2]**
picnic *n* (*pl* **-s**) informal meal out of doors ▶ *v* (**-s, -cking, -cked**) have a picnic
picknicked *v* ▷ **picnic**
picknicking *v* ▷ **picnic**
picnics *n, v* ▷ **picnic**
pics *n* ▷ **pic**
pictorial *adj* of or in painting or pictures
picture *n* (*pl* **-s**) drawing or painting ▶ *pl* cinema ▶ *v* (**-res, -ring, -red**) visualize, imagine
pictured *v* ▷ **picture**
pictures *n, v* ▷ **picture**
picturesque *adj* (of a place or view) pleasant to look at
picturing *v* ▷ **picture**
piddle *v* (**-les, -ling, -led**) (*Informal*) urinate
piddled *v* ▷ **piddle**
piddles *v* ▷ **piddle**
piddling *v* ▷ **piddle**
pidgin *n* (*pl* **-s**) language, not a mother tongue, made up of elements of two or more other languages
pidgins *n* ▷ **pidgin**
pie *n* (*pl* **-s**) dish of meat, fruit, etc. baked in pastry
pies *n* ▷ **pie**
piebald *adj, n* (*pl* **-s**) (horse) with irregular black-and-white markings
piebalds *n* ▷ **piebald**
piece *n* (*pl* **-s**) separate bit or part
pieces *n* ▷ **piece**
piecemeal *adv* bit by bit
piecework *n* (*pl* **-s**) work paid for according to the quantity produced
pieceworks *n* ▷ **piecework**
pied *adj* having markings of two or more colours
pier *n* (*pl* **-s**) platform on stilts sticking out into the sea
piers *n* ▷ **pier**
pierce *v* (**-ces, -cing, -ced**) make a hole in or through with a sharp instrument
pierced *v* ▷ **pierce**
pierces *v* ▷ **pierce**
piercing *adj* (of a sound) shrill and high-pitched ▶ *v* ▷ **pierce**
pierrot [**pier**-roe] *n* (*pl* **-s**) pantomime clown with a whitened face
pierrots *n* ▷ **pierrot**
pieties *n* ▷ **piety**
piety *n* (*pl* **-ties**) deep devotion to God and religion
piffle *n* (*pl* **-s**) (*Informal*) nonsense
piffles *n* ▷ **piffle**
pig *n* (*pl* **-s**) animal kept and killed for pork, ham, and bacon
pigeon[1] *n* (*pl* **-s**) bird with a heavy body and short legs, sometimes trained to carry messages
pigeon[2] *n* (*Informal*) concern or responsibility

pigeonhole *n* **(-s)** compartment for papers in a desk etc. ▶ *v* **(-les, -ling, -led)** classify
pigeonholed *v* ▷ **pigeonhole**
pigeonholing *v* ▷ **pigeonhole**
pigeonholes *n, v* ▷ **pigeonhole**
pigeons *n* ▷ **pigeon[1, 2]**
piggeries *n* ▷ **piggery**
piggery *n* (*pl* **-ries**) place for keeping and breeding pigs
piggier *adj* ▷ **piggy**
piggiest *adj* ▷ **piggy**
piggish, piggy (-ggier, -ggiest) *adj* (*Informal*) dirty
piggy *adj* ▷ **piggish**
piggyback *n* (*pl* **-s**) ride on someone's shoulders ▶ *adv* carried on someone's shoulders
piggybacks *n* ▷ **piggyback**
pigment *n* (*pl* **-s**) colouring matter, paint or dye > **pigmentation** *n* (*pl* **-s**)
pigmentation *n* ▷ **pigment**
pigmentations *n* ▷ **pigment**
pigments *n* ▷ **pigment**
pigmies *n* ▷ **pigmy**
pigmy *n* (*pl* **-mies**) ▷ **pygmy**
pigs *n* ▷ **pig**
pigtail *n* (*pl* **-s**) plait of hair hanging from the back or either side of the head
pigtails *n* ▷ **pigtail**
pike[1] *n* (*pl* **-s**) large predatory freshwater fish
pike[2] *n* (*pl* **-s**) (HIST) long-handled spear
pikes *n* ▷ **pike[1, 2]**
pikelet *n* (*pl* **-s**) (AUST & NZ) small thick pancake
pikelets *n* ▷ **pikelet**
piker *n* (*pl* **-s**) (AUST & NZ) (*Slang*) shirker
pikers *n* ▷ **piker**
pilaster *n* (*pl* **-s**) square column, usu. set in a wall
pilasters *n* ▷ **pilaster**
pilau, pilaf, pilaff *n* (*pl* **-s**) Middle Eastern dish of meat, fish, or poultry boiled with rice, spices, etc.
pilaffs *n* ▷ **pilaff**
pilafs *n* ▷ **pilaf**
pilchard *n* (*pl* **-s**) small edible sea fish of the herring family
pilchards *n* ▷ **pilchard**
pile[1] *n* (*pl* **-s**) number of things lying on top of each other ▶ *v* **(-les, -ling, -led)** collect into a pile
pile[2] *n* (*pl* **-s**) beam driven into the ground, esp. as a foundation for building
pile[3] *n* (*pl* **-s**) fibres of a carpet or a fabric, esp. velvet, that stand up from the weave
piled *v* ▷ **pile[1]**
piling *v* ▷ **pile[1]**
piles *pl n* swollen veins in the rectum, haemorrhoids ▶ *v, n* ▷ **pile[1, 2, 3]**
pilfer *v* **(-s, -ing, -ed)** steal in small quantities
pilfered *v* ▷ **pilfer**
pilfering *v* ▷ **pilfer**
pilfers *v* ▷ **pilfer**
pilgrim *n* (*pl* **-s**) person who journeys to a holy place > **pilgrimage** *n* (*pl* **-s**)
pilgrimage *n* ▷ **pilgrim**
pilgrimages *n* ▷ **pilgrim**
pilgrims *n* ▷ **pilgrim**
pill *n* (*pl* **-s**) small ball of medicine swallowed whole
pills *n* ▷ **pill**
pillage *v* **(-ges, -ging, -ged)** steal property by violence in war ▶ *n* (*pl* **-s**) violent seizure of goods, esp. in war
pillaged *v* ▷ **pillage**
pillages *v, n* ▷ **pillage**
pillaging *v* ▷ **pillage**
pillar *n* (*pl* **-s**) upright post, usu. supporting a roof
pillars *n* ▷ **pillar**
pillion *n* (*pl* **-s**) seat for a passenger behind the rider of a motorcycle
pillions *n* ▷ **pillion**
pilloried *v* ▷ **pillory**
pillories *n, v* ▷ **pillory**
pillory *n* (*pl* **-ries**) (HIST) frame with holes for the head and hands in which an offender was locked and exposed to public abuse ▶ *v* **(-ies, -ying, -ied)** ridicule publicly
pillow *n* (*pl* **-s**) stuffed cloth bag for supporting the head in bed ▶ *v* **(-s, -ing, -ed)** rest as if on a pillow
pillowcase, pillowslip *n* (*pl* **-s**) removable cover for a pillow
pillowcases *n* ▷ **pillowcase**
pillowed *v* ▷ **pillow**
pillowing *v* ▷ **pillow**
pillows *n, v* ▷ **pillow**
pillowslip *n* ▷ **pillowcase**
pillowslips *n* ▷ **pillowcase**
pilot *n* (*pl* **-s**) person qualified to fly an aircraft or spacecraft ▶ *adj* experimental and preliminary ▶ *v* **(-s, -ing, -ed)** act as the pilot of
piloted *v* ▷ **pilot**
piloting *v* ▷ **pilot**
pilots *n, v* ▷ **pilot**
pimento *n* (*pl* **-tos**) mild-tasting red pepper
pimentos *n* ▷ **pimento**
pimp *n* (*pl* **-s**) man who gets customers for a prostitute in return for a share of his or her earnings ▶ *v* **(-s, -ing, -ed)** act as a pimp

pimped *v* ▷ **pimp**
pimpernel *n* (*pl* **-s**) wild plant with small star-shaped flowers
pimpernels *n* ▷ **pimpernel**
pimping *v* ▷ **pimp**
pimple *n* (*pl* **-s**) small pus-filled spot on the skin **> pimply** *adj* (**-lier, -liest**)
pimples *n* ▷ **pimple**
pimplier *v* ▷ **pimple**
pimpliest *v* ▷ **pimple**
pimply *v* ▷ **pimple**
pimps *n, v* ▷ **pimp**
pin *n* (*pl* **-s**) short thin piece of stiff wire with a point and head, for fastening things ▶ *v* (**-s, pinning, pinned**) fasten with a pin
pinafore *n* (*pl* **-s**) apron
pinafores *n* ▷ **pinafore**
pinball *n* (*pl* **-s**) electrically operated table game in which a small ball is shot through various hazards
pinballs *n* ▷ **pinball**
pincers *pl n* tool consisting of two hinged arms, for gripping
pinch *v* (**-es, -ing, -ed**) squeeze between finger and thumb ▶ *n* (*pl* **-es**) act of pinching
pinchbeck *n* (*pl* **-s**) alloy of zinc and copper, used as imitation gold
pinchbecks *n* ▷ **pinchbeck**
pinched *v* ▷ **pinch**
pinches *v, n* ▷ **pinch**
pinching *v* ▷ **pinch**
pinned *v* ▷ **pin**
pinning *v* ▷ **pin**
pins *n, v* ▷ **pin**
pine¹ *n* (*pl* **-s**) evergreen coniferous tree
pine² *v* (**-nes, -ning, -ned**) (*foll. by* **for**) feel great longing (for)
pineapple *n* (*pl* **-s**) large tropical fruit with juicy yellow flesh and a hard skin
pineapples *n* ▷ **pineapple**
pined *v* ▷ **pine²**
pines *n, v* ▷ **pine¹, ²**
ping *v* (**-s, -ing, -ed**) ▶ *n* (*pl* **-s**) (make) a short high-pitched sound
pinged *v* ▷ **ping**
pinging *v* ▷ **ping**
pings *v, n* ▷ **ping**
pining *v* ▷ **pine²**
pinion¹ *n* (*pl* **-s**) bird's wing ▶ *v* (**-s, -ing, -ed**) immobilize (someone) by tying or holding his or her arms
pinion² *n* (*pl* **-s**) small cogwheel
pinioned *v* ▷ **pinion**
pinioning *v* ▷ **pinion**
pinions *n, v* ▷ **pinion¹, ²**
pink *n* (*pl* **-s**) pale reddish colour ▶ *adj* (**-er, -est**) of the colour pink ▶ *v* (**-s, -ing, -ed**) (of an engine) make a metallic noise because not working properly, knock
pinked *v* ▷ **pink**
pinker *adj* ▷ **pink**
pinkest *adj* ▷ **pink**
pinking *v* ▷ **pink**
pinks *n, v* ▷ **pink**
pinnacle *n* (*pl* **-s**) highest point of fame or success
pinnacles *n* ▷ **pinnacle**
pinotage [**pin**-no-tajj] *n* (*pl* **-s**) blended red wine of S Africa
pinotages *n* ▷ **pinotage**
pinpoint *v* (**-s, -ing, -ed**) locate or identify exactly
pinpointed *v* ▷ **pinpoint**
pinpointing *v* ▷ **pinpoint**
pinpoints *v* ▷ **pinpoint**
pinstripe *n* (*pl* **-s**) very narrow stripe in fabric
pinstripes *n* ▷ **pinstripe**
pint *n* (*pl* **-s**) liquid measure, 1/8 gallon (.568 litre)
pints *n* ▷ **pint**
pioneer *n* (*pl* **-s**) explorer or early settler of a new country ▶ *v* (**-s, -ing, -ed**) be the pioneer or leader of
pioneered *v* ▷ **pioneer**
pioneering *v* ▷ **pioneer**
pioneers *n, v* ▷ **pioneer**
pious *adj* deeply religious, devout
pip¹ *n* (*pl* **-s**) small seed in a fruit
pip² *n* high-pitched sound used as a time signal on radio (*Informal*)
pips *n* ▷ **pip¹, ²**
pipe *n* (*pl* **-s**) tube for conveying liquid or gas ▶ *pl* bagpipes ▶ *v* (**-pes, -ping, -ped**) play on a pipe
piped *v* ▷ **pipe**
piper *n* (*pl* **-s**) player on a pipe or bagpipes
pipers *n* ▷ **piper**
piping *n* (*pl* **-s**) system of pipes ▶ *v* ▷ **pipe**
pipings *n* ▷ **piping**
pipeline *n* (*pl* **-s**) long pipe for transporting oil, water, etc.
pipelines *n* ▷ **pipeline**
pipes *n, v* ▷ **pipe**
pipette *n* (*pl* **-s**) slender glass tube used to transfer or measure fluids
pipettes *n* ▷ **pipette**
pipi *n* (*pl* **-s**) (AUST) mollusc often used as bait
pipit *n* (*pl* **-s**) small brownish songbird
pipits *n* ▷ **pipit**
pippin *n* (*pl* **-s**) type of eating apple

pippins *n* ▷ **pippin**
pips *n* ▷ **pip^{1,2}**
piquancies *n* ▷ **piquant**
piquancy *n* ▷ **piquant**
piquant [**pee**-kant] *adj* having a pleasant spicy taste > **piquancy** *n* (*pl* **-cies**)
pique [**peek**] *n* (*pl* **-s**) feeling of hurt pride, baffled curiosity, or resentment ▶ *v* (**-ques, -quing, -qued**) hurt the pride of
piqué [**pee**-kay] *n* (*pl* **-s**) stiff ribbed cotton fabric
piqued *v* ▷ **pique**
piques *n, v* ▷ **pique**
piqués *n* ▷ **piqué**
piquing *v* ▷ **pique**
piquet [pik-**ket**] *n* (*pl* **-s**) card game for two
piquets *n* ▷ **piquet**
piracies *n* ▷ **pirate**
piracy *n* ▷ **pirate**
piranha *n* (*pl* **-s**) small fierce freshwater fish of tropical America
piranhas *n* ▷ **piranha**
pirate *n* (*pl* **-s**) sea robber ▶ *v* (**-tes, -ting, -ted**) sell or reproduce (artistic work etc.) illegally > **piracy** *n* (*pl* **-cies**) > **piratical** *adj*
pirated *v* ▷ **pirate**
pirates *n, v* ▷ **pirate**
piratical *adj* ▷ **pirate**
pirating *v* ▷ **pirate**
pirouette *v, n* (*pl* **-s**) (make) a spinning turn balanced on the toes of one foot
pirouettes *n* ▷ **pirouette**
pistachio *n* (*pl* **-s**) edible nut of a Mediterranean tree
pistachios *n* ▷ **pistachio**
piste [**peest**] *n* (*pl* **-s**) ski slope
pistes *n* ▷ **piste**
pistil *n* (*pl* **-s**) seed-bearing part of a flower
pistils *n* ▷ **pistil**
pistol *n* (*pl* **-s**) short-barrelled handgun
pistols *n* ▷ **pistol**
piston *n* (*pl* **-s**) cylindrical part in an engine that slides to and fro in a cylinder
pistons *n* ▷ **piston**
pit *n* (*pl* **-s**) deep hole in the ground ▷ **orchestra pit** ▶ *v* (**-s, -tting, -tteds**) mark with small dents or scars
pitch^1 *v* (**-es, -ing, -ed**) throw, hurl ▶ *n* (*pl* **-es**) area marked out for playing sport
pitch^2 *n* dark sticky substance obtained from tar
pitched *v* ▷ **pitch^1**
pitches *v, n* ▷ **pitch^1**
pitching *v* ▷ **pitch^1**
pitchblende *n* (*pl* **-s**) mineral composed largely of uranium oxide, yielding radium
pitchblendes *n* ▷ **pitchblende**
pitcher *n* (*pl* **-s**) large jug with a narrow neck
pitchers *n* ▷ **pitcher**
pitchfork *n* (*pl* **-s**) large long-handled fork for lifting hay ▶ *v* (**-s, -ing, -ed**) thrust abruptly or violently
pitchforked *v* ▷ **pitchfork**
pitchforking *v* ▷ **pitchfork**
pitchforks *n, v* ▷ **pitchfork**
piteous, pitiable *adj* arousing pity
pitfall *n* (*pl* **-s**) hidden difficulty or danger
pitfalls *n* ▷ **pitfall**
pith *n* (*pl* **-s**) soft white lining of the rind of oranges etc.
pithier *adj* ▷ **pithy**
pithiest *adj* ▷ **pithy**
piths *n* ▷ **pith**
pithy *adj* (**-thier, -thiest**) short and full of meaning
pitiable *adj* ▷ **piteous**
pitied *v* ▷ **pity**
pities *n, v* ▷ **pity**
pitiful *adj* arousing pity > **pitifully** *adv*
pitifully *adv* ▷ **pitiful**
pitiless *adj* feeling no pity or mercy > **pitilessly** *adv*
pitilessly *adv* ▷ **pitiless**
piton [**peet**-on] *n* (*pl* **-s**) metal spike used in climbing to secure a rope
pitons *n* ▷ **piton**
pits *n, v* ▷ **pit**
pittance *n* (*pl* **-s**) very small amount of money
pittances *n* ▷ **pittance**
pitted *v* ▷ **pit**
pitting *v* ▷ **pit**
pituitaries *n* ▷ **pituitary**
pituitary *n* (*pl* **-ies**) gland at the base of the brain, that helps to control growth
pity *n* (*pl* **-ties**) sympathy or sorrow for others' suffering ▶ *v* (**-ies, -ying, -ied**) feel pity for
pitying *v* ▷ **pity**
pivot *n* (*pl* **-s**) central shaft on which something turns ▶ *v* (**-s, -ing, -ed**) provide with or turn on a pivot
pivotal *adj* of crucial importance
pivoted *v* ▷ **pivot**
pivoting *v* ▷ **pivot**
pivots *n, v* ▷ **pivot**
pix *n* (*Informal*) ▷ **pic**
pixie *n* (*pl* **-s**) (in folklore) fairy
pixies *n* ▷ **pixie**
pizza *n* (*pl* **-s**) flat disc of dough covered with a wide variety of savoury toppings and baked
pizzas *n* ▷ **pizza**

pizzazz *n* (*pl* **-es**) (*Informal*) attractive combination of energy and style
pizzazzes *n* ▷ **pizzazz**
pizzicato [pit-see-**kah**-toe] *adj* (MUSIC) played by plucking the string of a violin etc. with the finger
placard *n* (*pl* **-s**) notice that is carried or displayed in public
placards *n* ▷ **placard**
placate *v* (**-tes, -ting, -ted**) make (someone) stop feeling angry or upset > **placatory** *adj*
placated *v* ▷ **placate**
placates *v* ▷ **placate**
placating *v* ▷ **placate**
placatory *adj* ▷ **placate**
place *n* (*pl* **-s**) particular part of an area or space ▶ *v* (**-ces, -cing, -ced**) put in a particular place
placed *v* ▷ **place**
places *n, v* ▷ **place**
placebo [plas-**see**-bo] *n* (*pl* **-bos, -boes**) sugar pill etc. given to an unsuspecting patient instead of an active drug
placeboes *n* ▷ **placebo**
placebos *n* ▷ **placebo**
placenta [plass-**ent**-a] *n* (*pl* **-tas, -tae**) organ formed in the womb during pregnancy, providing nutrients for the fetus > **placental** *adj*
placentae *n* ▷ **placenta**
placental *adj* ▷ **placenta**
placentas *n* ▷ **placenta**
placid *adj* (**-er, -est**) not easily excited or upset, calm > **placidity** *n* (*pl* **-ties**)
placider *adj* ▷ **placid**
placidest *adj* ▷ **placid**
placidities *n* ▷ **placid**
placidity *n* ▷ **placid**
placing *v* ▷ **place**
plagiarize [**play**-jer-ize] *v* (**-zes, -zing, -zed**) steal ideas, passages, etc. from (someone else's work) and present them as one's own > **plagiarism** *n* (*pl* **-s**)
plagiarism *n* ▷ **plagiarize**
plagiarisms *n* ▷ **plagiarize**
plagiarized *v* ▷ **plagiarize**
plagiarizes *v* ▷ **plagiarize**
plagiarizing *v* ▷ **plagiarize**
plague *n* (*pl* **-s**) fast-spreading fatal disease ▶ *v* (**-gues, -guing, -gued**) trouble or annoy continually
plagued *v* ▷ **plague**
plagues *n, v* ▷ **plague**
plaguing *v* ▷ **plague**
plaice *n* (*pl* **plaice**) edible European flatfish
plaid *n* (*pl* **-s**) long piece of tartan cloth worn as part of Highland dress
plaids *n* ▷ **plaid**
plain (**-er, -est**) *adj* easy to see or understand ▶ *n* (*pl* **-s**) large stretch of level country > **plainly** *adv* > **plainness** *n* (*pl* **-es**)
plainer *adj* ▷ **plain**
plainest *adj* ▷ **plain**
plainly *adj* ▷ **plain**
plainness *n* ▷ **plain**
plainnesses *n* ▷ **plain**
plains *n* ▷ **plain**
plainsong *n* (*pl* **-s**) unaccompanied singing, esp. in a medieval church
plainsongs *n* ▷ **plainsong**
plaintiff *n* (*pl* **-s**) person who sues in a court of law
plaintiffs *n* ▷ **plaintiff**
plaintive *adj* sad, mournful > **plaintively** *adv*
plaintively *adv* ▷ **plaintive**
plait [**platt**] *n* (*pl* **-s**) intertwined length of hair ▶ *v* (**-s, -ing, -ed**) intertwine separate strands in a pattern
plaited *v* ▷ **plait**
plaiting *v* ▷ **plait**
plaits *n, v* ▷ **plait**
plan *n* (*pl* **-s**) way thought out to do or achieve something ▶ *v* (**-s, -nning, -nned**) arrange beforehand > **planner** *n* (*pl* **-s**)
plane[1] *n* (*pl* **-s**) aeroplane ▶ *adj* perfectly flat or level ▶ *v* (**-nes, -ning, -ned**) glide or skim
plane[2] *n* (*pl* **-s**) tool for smoothing wood ▶ *v* (**-nes, -ning, -ned**) smooth (wood) with a plane
plane[3] *n* (*pl* **-s**) tree with broad leaves
planed *v* ▷ **plane**[1, 2]
planes *n, v* ▷ **plane**[1, 2, 3]
planet *n* (*pl* **-s**) large body in space that revolves round the sun or another star > **planetary** *adj*
planetaria *n* ▷ **planetarium**
planetarium *n* (*pl* **-iums, -ia**) building where the movements of the stars, planets, etc. are shown by projecting lights on the inside of a dome
planetariums *n* ▷ **planetarium**
planetary *adj* ▷ **planet**
planets *n* ▷ **planet**
plangent *adj* (of sounds) mournful and resounding
planing *v* ▷ **plane**[1, 2]
plank *n* (*pl* **-s**) long flat piece of sawn timber
planks *n* ▷ **plank**
plankton *n* (*pl* **-s**) minute animals and plants floating in the surface water of a sea or lake

plops *n, v* ▷ **plop**
plot¹ *n* (*pl* **-s**) secret plan to do something illegal or wrong ▶ *v* (**-s, -tting, -tted**) plan secretly, conspire
plot² *n* (**-s**) small piece of land
plotted *v* ▷ **plot¹**
plotting *v* ▷ **plot¹**
plots *n, v* ▷ **plot¹, ²**
plough *n* (*pl* **-s**) agricultural tool for turning over soil ▶ *v* (**-s, -ing, -ed**) turn over (earth) with a plough > **ploughman** *n* (*pl* **-men**)
ploughed *v* ▷ **plough**
ploughing *v* ▷ **plough**
ploughman *n* ▷ **plough**
ploughmen *n* ▷ **plough**
ploughs *n, v* ▷ **plough**
ploughshare *n* (*pl* **-s**) blade of a plough
ploughshares *n* ▷ **ploughshare**
plover *n* (*pl* **-s**) shore bird with a straight bill and long pointed wings
plovers *n* ▷ **plover**
ploy *n* (*pl* **-s**) manoeuvre designed to gain an advantage
ploys *n* ▷ **ploy**
pluck *v* (**-s, -ing, -ed**) pull or pick off ▶ *n* (*pl* **-s**) courage
plucked *v* ▷ **pluck**
pluckier *adj* ▷ **plucky**
pluckiest *adj* ▷ **plucky**
pluckily *adj* ▷ **plucky**
plucking *v* ▷ **pluck**
plucks *v, n* ▷ **pluck**
plucky *adj* (**-kier, -kiest**) brave > **pluckily** *adv*
plug *n* (*pl* **-s**) thing fitting into and filling a hole ▶ *v* (**-s, -gging, -gged**) block or seal (a hole or gap) with a plug
plugged *v* ▷ **plug**
plugging *v* ▷ **plug**
plugs *n, v* ▷ **plug**
plum *n* (*pl* **-s**) oval usu. dark red fruit with a stone in the middle ▶ *adj* dark purplish-red
plumage *n* (*pl* **-s**) bird's feathers
plumages *n* ▷ **plumage**
plumb *v* (**-s, -ing, -ed**) understand (something obscure) ▶ *adv* exactly
plumbed *v* ▷ **plumb**
plumber *n* (*pl* **-s**) person who fits and repairs pipes and fixtures for water and drainage systems
plumbers *n* ▷ **plumber**
plumbing *n* pipes and fixtures used in water and drainage systems ▶ *v* ▷ **plumb**
plumbs *v* ▷ **plumb**
plume *n* (*pl* **-s**) feather, esp. one worn as an ornament
plumes *n* ▷ **plume**
plummet *v* (**-s, -ing, -ed**) plunge downward
plummeted *v* ▷ **plummet**
plummeting *v* ▷ **plummet**
plummets *v* ▷ **plummet**
plump¹ *adj* (**-er, -est**) moderately or attractively fat > **plumpness** *n* (*pl* **-es**)
plump² *v* (**-s, -ing, -ed**) sit or fall heavily and suddenly
plumper *adj* ▷ **plump¹**
plumpest *adj* ▷ **plump¹**
plumped *v* ▷ **plump²**
plumping *v* ▷ **plump²**
plumpness *n* ▷ **plump**
plumpnesses *n* ▷ **plump**
plumps *v* ▷ **plump²**
plums *n* ▷ **plum**
plunder *v* (**-s, -ing, -ed**) take by force, esp. in time of war ▶ *n* (*pl* **-s**) things plundered, spoils
plundered *v* ▷ **plunder**
plundering *v* ▷ **plunder**
plunders *v, n* ▷ **plunder**
plunge *v* (**-ges, -ging, -ged**) put or throw forcibly or suddenly (into) ▶ *n* (*pl* **-s**) plunging, dive
plunged *v* ▷ **plunge**
plunger *n* (*pl* **-s**) rubber suction cup used to clear blocked pipes
plungers *n* ▷ **plunger**
plunges *v, n* ▷ **plunge**
plunging *v* ▷ **plunge**
pluperfect *adj, n* (*pl* **-s**) (GRAMMAR) (tense) expressing an action completed before a past time, e.g. *had gone* in *his wife had gone already*
pluperfects *n* ▷ **pluperfect**
plural *adj* of or consisting of more than one ▶ *n* (*pl* **-s**) word indicating more than one
plurals *n* ▷ **plural**
pluralism *n* (*pl* **-s**) existence and toleration of a variety of peoples, opinions, etc. in a society > **pluralist** *n* (*pl* **-s**) > **pluralistic** *adj*
pluralisms *n* ▷ **pluralism**
pluralist *n* ▷ **pluralism**
pluralists *n* ▷ **pluralism**
pluralistic *adj* ▷ **pluralism**
plus *prep, adj* indicating addition ▶ *adj* more than zero ▶ *n* (*pl* **-es**) sign (+) denoting addition
pluses *n* ▷ **plus**
plush *n* (*pl* **-es**) fabric with long velvety pile ▶ *adj* (**-er, -est**) (*also* **plushy**) (**-ier, -iest**) luxurious
plusher *adj* ▷ **plush**
plushest *adj* ▷ **plush**
plushes *n* ▷ **plush**

plushier *adj* ▷ **plush**
plushiest *adj* ▷ **plush**
plutocrat *n* (*pl* **-s**) person who is powerful because of being very rich > **plutocratic** *adj*
plutocratic *adj* ▷ **plutocrat**
plutocrats *n* ▷ **plutocrat**
plutonium *n* (*pl* **-s**) (CHEM) radioactive metallic element used esp. in nuclear reactors and weapons
plutoniums *n* ▷ **plutonium**
ply[1] *v* (**-ies, -ying, -ied**) work at (a job or trade)
ply[2] *n* (*pl* **-ies**) thickness of wool, fabric, etc.
plying *v* ▷ **ply**[1]
plywood *n* (*pl* **-s**) board made of thin layers of wood glued together
plywoods *n* ▷ **plywood**
pneumatic *adj* worked by or inflated with wind or air
pneumonia *n* (*pl* **-s**) inflammation of the lungs
pneumonias *n* ▷ **pneumonia**

> **po** *n* (**pos**). A po is an informal word for a chamber pot. This is a good word to have ready in case you see an opportunity to play a good word beginning with P next to a word ending in O, or vice versa. Po scores 4 points.

poach[1] *v* (**-es, -ing, -ed**) catch (animals) illegally on someone else's land
poach[2] *v* (**-es, -ing, -ed**) simmer (food) gently in liquid
poached *v* ▷ **poach**
poacher *n* (*pl* **-s**) person who catches animals illegally on someone else's land
poachers *n* ▷ **poacher**
poaches *v* ▷ **poach**
poaching *v* ▷ **poach**
pocket *n* (*pl* **-s**) small bag sewn into clothing for carrying things ▸ *v* (**-s, -ing, -ed**) put into one's pocket ▸ *adj* small
pocketed *v* ▷ **pocket**
pocketing *v* ▷ **pocket**
pockets *n, v* ▷ **pocket**
pockmarked *adj* (of the skin) marked with hollow scars where diseased spots have been
pod *n* (*pl* **-s**) long narrow seed case of peas, beans, etc.
podgier *adj* ▷ **podgy**
podgiest *adj* ▷ **podgy**
pods *n* ▷ **pod**
podgy *adj* (**-gier, -giest**) short and fat
podia *n* ▷ **podium**
podium *n* (*pl* **-diums, -dia**) small raised platform for a conductor or speaker
podiums *n* ▷ **podium**
poem *n* (*pl* **-s**) imaginative piece of writing in rhythmic lines
poems *n* ▷ **poem**
poep *n* (*pl* **-s**) (S AFR) (*Slang*) emission of gas from the anus
poeps *n* ▷ **poep**
poesies *n* ▷ **poesy**
poesy *n* (*pl* **-sies**) (*Obs*) poetry
poet *n* (*pl* **-s**) writer of poems
poetic, poetical *adj* of or like poetry > **poetically** *adv*
poetical *adj* ▷ **poetic**
poetically *adv* ▷ **poetic**
poetries *n* ▷ **poetry**
poetry *n* (*pl* **-ries**) poems
poets *n* ▷ **poet**
pogrom *n* (*pl* **-s**) organized persecution and massacre
pogroms *n* ▷ **pogrom**
poignancies *n* ▷ **poignant**
poignancy *n* ▷ **poignant**
poignant *adj* sharply painful to the feelings > **poignancy** *n* (*pl* **-cies**)
poinsettia *n* (*pl* **-s**) Central American shrub widely grown for its clusters of scarlet leaves, which resemble petals
poinsettias *n* ▷ **poinsettia**
point *n* (*pl* **-s**) main idea in a discussion, argument, etc. ▸ *v* (**-s, -ing, -ed**) show the direction or position of something or draw attention to it by extending a finger or other pointed object towards it
pointed *adj* having a sharp end ▸ *v* ▷ **point** > **pointedly** *adv*
pointedly *adv* ▷ **pointed**
pointer *n* (*pl* **-s**) helpful hint
pointers *n* ▷ **pointer**
pointing *v* ▷ **point**
pointless *adj* meaningless, irrelevant
points *n, v* ▷ **point**
poise *n* (*pl* **-s**) calm dignified manner
poised *adj* absolutely ready
poises *n* ▷ **poise**
poison *n* (*pl* **-s**) substance that kills or injures when swallowed or absorbed ▸ *v* (**-s, -ing, -ed**) give poison to > **poisoner** *n* (*pl* **-s**) > **poisonous** *adj*
poisoned *v* ▷ **poison**
poisoner *n* ▷ **poison**
poisoners *n* ▷ **poison**
poisoning *v* ▷ **poison**
poisonous *adj* ▷ **poison**
poisons *n, v* ▷ **poison**
poke *v* (**-kes, -king, -ked**) jab or prod with one's finger, a stick, etc. ▸ *n* (*pl* **-s**) poking

poked *v* ▷ **poke**
poker¹ *n* (*pl* **-s**) metal rod for stirring a fire
poker² *n* (*pl* **-s**) card game in which players bet on the hands dealt
pokers *n* ▷ **poker¹, ²**
pokier *adj* ▷ **poky**
pokiest *adj* ▷ **poky**
poking *v* ▷ **poke**
pokes *v, n* ▷ **poke**
poky *adj* (**-kier, -kiest**) small and cramped
polar *adj* of or near either of the earth's poles
polarize *v* (**-zes, -zing, -zed**) form or cause to form into groups with directly opposite views > **polarization** *n* (*pl* **-s**)
polarization *n* ▷ **polarize**
polarizations *n* ▷ **polarize**
polarized *v* ▷ **polarize**
polarizes *v* ▷ **polarize**
polarizing *v* ▷ **polarize**
polder *n* (*pl* **-s**) land reclaimed from the sea, esp. in the Netherlands
polders *n* ▷ **polder**
pole¹ *n* (*pl* **-s**) long rounded piece of wood etc.
pole² *n* (*pl* **-s**) point furthest north or south on the earth's axis of rotation
poleaxe *v* (**-xes, -xing, -xed**) hit or stun with a heavy blow
poleaxed *v* ▷ **poleaxe**
poleaxes *v* ▷ **poleaxe**
poleaxing *v* ▷ **poleaxe**
polecat *n* (*pl* **-s**) small animal of the weasel family
polecats *n* ▷ **polecat**
polemic [pol-**em**-ik] *n* (*pl* **-s**) fierce attack on or defence of a particular opinion, belief, etc. > **polemical** *adj*
polemical *adj* ▷ **polemic**
polemics *n* ▷ **polemic**
poles *n* ▷ **pole¹, ²**
police *n* organized force in a state which keeps law and order ▶ *v* (**-ces, -cing, -ced**) control or watch over with police or a similar body
policed *v* ▷ **police**
policeman, policewoman *n* (*pl* **-men, -women**) member of a police force
policemen *n* ▷ **policeman**
polices *v* ▷ **police**
policewomen *n* ▷ **policeman**
policies *n* ▷ **policy¹, ²**
policing *v* ▷ **police**
policy¹ *n* (*pl* **-cies**) plan of action adopted by a person, group, or state
policy² *n* (*pl* **-cies**) document containing an insurance contract
polio *n* (*pl* **-s**) disease affecting the spinal cord, which often causes paralysis (*also* **poliomyelitis**)
polios *n* ▷ **polio**
polish *v* (**-es, -ing, -ed**) make smooth and shiny by rubbing ▶ *n* (*pl* **-es**) substance used for polishing
polished *adj* accomplished ▶ *v* ▷ **polish**
polishing *v* ▷ **polish**
polishes *v, n* ▷ **polish**
polite *adj* showing consideration for others in one's manners, speech, etc. > **politely** *adv* > **politeness** *n* (*pl* **-es**)
politely *adv* ▷ **polite**
politeness *n* ▷ **polite**
politenesses *n* ▷ **politeness**
politic *adj* wise and likely to prove advantageous
political *adj* of the state, government, or public administration > **politically** *adv*
politically *adv* ▷ **political**
politician *n* (*pl* **-s**) person actively engaged in politics, esp. a member of parliament
politicians *n* ▷ **politician**
politics *n* winning and using of power to govern society
polka *n* (*pl* **-s**) lively 19th-century dance
polkas *n* ▷ **polka**
poll *n* (*pl* **-s**) (*also* **opinion poll**) questioning of a random sample of people to find out general opinion ▶ *v* (**-s, -ing, -ed**) receive (votes)
pollarded *adj* (of a tree) growing very bushy because its top branches have been cut short
polled *v* ▷ **poll**
pollen *n* (*pl* **-s**) fine dust produced by flowers to fertilize other flowers
pollens ▷
pollinate *v* (**-tes, -ting, -ted**) fertilize with pollen
pollinated *v* ▷ **pollinate**
pollinates *v* ▷ **pollinate**
pollinating *v* ▷ **pollinate**
polling *v* ▷ **poll**
polls *n, v* ▷ **poll**
pollster *n* (*pl* **-s**) person who conducts opinion polls
pollsters *n* ▷ **pollster**
pollute *v* (**-tes, -ting, -ted**) contaminate with something poisonous or harmful > **pollution** *n* (*pl* **-s**)
pollutant *n* (*pl* **-s**) something that pollutes
pollutants *n* ▷ **pollutant**
polluted *v* ▷ **pollute**
pollutes *v* ▷ **pollute**
polluting *v* ▷ **pollute**
pollution *n* ▷ **pollute**

pollutions *n* ▷ **pollute**
polo *n* (*pl* **-s**) game like hockey played by teams of players on horseback
polonaise *n* (*pl* **-s**) old stately dance
polonaises *n* ▷ **polonaise**
polonium *n* (*pl* **-s**) (CHEM) radioactive element that occurs in trace amounts in uranium ores
poloniums *n* ▷ **polonium**
polos *n* ▷ **polo**
poltergeist *n* (*pl* **-s**) spirit believed to move furniture and throw objects around
poltergeists *n* ▷ **poltergeist**
poltroon *n* (*pl* **-s**) (*Obs*) utter coward
poltroons *n* ▷ **poltroon**
polyandries *n* ▷ **polyandry**
polyandry *n* (*pl* **-ries**) practice of having more than one husband at the same time
polyanthus *n* (*pl* **-es**) garden primrose
polyanthuses *n* ▷ **polyanthus**
polychromatic *adj* many-coloured
polyester *n* (*pl* **-s**) synthetic material used to make plastics and textile fibres
polyesters *n* ▷ **polyester**
polygamies *n* ▷ **polygamy**
polygamist *n* ▷ **polygamy**
polygamists *n* ▷ **polygamy**
polygamous *adj* ▷ **polygamy**
polygamy [pol-**ig**-a-mee] *n* (*pl* **-mies**) practice of having more than one husband or wife at the same time > **polygamous** *adj* > **polygamist** *n* (*pl* **-s**)
polyglot *adj*, *n* (*pl* **-s**) (person) able to speak or write several languages
polyglots *n* ▷ **polyglot**
polygon *n* (*pl* **-s**) geometrical figure with three or more angles and sides > **polygonal** *adj*
polygonal *adj* ▷ **polygon**
polygons *n* ▷ **polygon**
polyhedra *n* ▷ **polyhedron**
polyhedron *n* (*pl* **-rons, -ra**) solid figure with four or more sides
polyhedrons *n* ▷ **polyhedron**
polymer *n* (*pl* **-s**) chemical compound with large molecules made of simple molecules of the same kind
polymerize *v* **(-zes, -zing, -zed)** form into polymers > **polymerization** *n* (*pl* **-s**)
polymerization *n* ▷ **polymerize**
polymerizations *n* ▷ **polymerize**
polymerized *v* ▷ **polymerize**
polymerizes *v* ▷ **polymerize**
polymerizing *v* ▷ **polymerize**
polymers *n* ▷ **polymer**
polyp *n* (*pl* **-s**) small simple sea creature with a hollow cylindrical body
polyps *n* ▷ **polyp**
polyphonic *adj* (MUSIC) consisting of several melodies played simultaneously
polystyrene *n* (*pl* **-s**) synthetic material used esp. as white rigid foam for packing and insulation
polystyrenes *n* ▷ **polystyrene**
polytechnic *n* (*pl* **-s**) (in New Zealand and formerly in Britain) college offering courses in many subjects at and below degree level
polytechnics *n* ▷ **polytechnic**
polytheism *n* (*pl* **-s**) belief in many gods > **polytheistic** *adj*
polytheisms *n* ▷ **polytheism**
polytheistic *n* ▷ **polytheism**
polythene *n* (*pl* **-s**) light plastic used for bags etc.
polythenes *n* ▷ **polythene**
polyunsaturated *adj* of a group of fats that do not form cholesterol in the blood
polyurethane *n* (*pl* **-s**) synthetic material used esp. in paints
polyurethanes *n* ▷ **polyurethane**
pom *n* (*pl* **-s**) (AUST & NZ) (*Slang*) person from England (*also* **pommy**) (*pl* **-mmies**)
pomander *n* (*pl* **-s**) (container for) a mixture of sweet-smelling petals, herbs, etc.
pomanders *n* ▷ **pomander**
pomegranate *n* (*pl* **-s**) round tropical fruit with a thick rind containing many seeds in a red pulp
pomegranates *n* ▷ **pomegranate**
pommel *n* (*pl* **-s**) raised part on the front of a saddle
pommels *n* ▷ **pommel**
pommies *n* ▷ **pom**
pommy *n* ▷ **pom**
poms *n* ▷ **pom**
pomp *n* (*pl* **-s**) stately display or ceremony
pomps *n* ▷ **pomp**
pompom *n* (*pl* **-s**) decorative ball of tufted wool, silk, etc.
pompoms *n* ▷ **pompom**
pomposities *n* ▷ **pompous**
pomposity *n* ▷ **pompous**
pompous *adj* foolishly serious and grand, self-important > **pompously** *adv* > **pomposity** *n* (*pl* **-ties**)
pompously *adv* ▷ **pompous**
poncho *n* (*pl* **-os**) loose circular cloak with a hole for the head
ponchos *n* ▷ **poncho**
pond *n* (*pl* **-s**) small area of still water
ponds *n* ▷ **pond**
ponder *v* **(-s, -ing, -ed)** think thoroughly or

deeply (about)
pondered *v* ▷ **ponder**
pondering *v* ▷ **ponder**
ponderous *adj* serious and dull > **ponderously** *adv*
ponderously *adv* ▷ **ponderous**
ponders *v* ▷ **ponder**
pong *v, n* (*pl* **-s**) (*Informal*) (give off) a strong unpleasant smell
pongs *n* ▷ **pong**
ponies *n* ▷ **pony**
pontiff *n* (*pl* **-s**) the Pope
pontiffs *n* ▷ **pontiff**
pontificate *v* (**-tes, -ting, -ted**) state one's opinions as if they were the only possible correct ones ▶ *n* (*pl* **-s**) period of office of a Pope
pontificated *v* ▷ **pontificate**
pontificates *v, n* ▷ **pontificate**
pontificating *v* ▷ **pontificate**
pontoon[1] *n* (*pl* **-s**) floating platform supporting a temporary bridge
pontoon[2] *n* (*pl* **-s**) gambling card game
pontoons *n* ▷ **pontoon**[1, 2]
pony *n* (*pl* **-nies**) small horse
ponytail *n* (*pl* **-s**) long hair tied in one bunch at the back of the head
ponytails *n* ▷ **ponytail**
poodle *n* (*pl* **-s**) dog with curly hair often clipped fancifully
poodles *n* ▷ **poodle**
pool[1] *n* (*pl* **-s**) small body of still water
pool[2] *n* (*pl* **-s**) shared fund or group of workers or resources ▶ *pl* (BRIT) ▷ **football pools** ▶ *v* (**-s, -ing, -ed**) put in a common fund
pooled *v* ▷ **pool**[2]
pooling *v* ▷ **pool**[2]
pools *n, v* ▷ **pool**[1, 2]
poop *n* (*pl* **-s**) raised part at the back of a sailing ship
poops *n* ▷ **poop**
poor *adj* having little money and few possessions
poorlier *adj* ▷ **poorly**
poorliest *adj* ▷ **poorly**
poorly *adv* in a poor manner ▶ *adj* (**-lier, -liest**) not in good health
pop[1] *v* (**-s, -pping, -pped**) make or cause to make a small explosive sound (*Informal*) ▶ *n* small explosive sound (BRIT)
pop[2] *n* (*pl* **-s**) music of general appeal, esp. to young people
pop[3] *n* (*pl* **-s**) (*Informal*) father
popcorn *n* (*pl* **-s**) grains of maize heated until they puff up and burst
popcorns *n* ▷ **popcorn**
pope *n* (*pl* **-s**) head of the Roman Catholic Church
popes *n* ▷ **pope**
poplar *n* (*pl* **-s**) tall slender tree
poplars *n* ▷ **poplar**
poplin *n* (*pl* **-s**) ribbed cotton material
poplins *n* ▷ **poplin**
poppadom *n* (*pl* **-s**) thin round crisp Indian bread
poppadoms *n* ▷ **poppadom**
popped *v* ▷ **pop**[1]
poppies *n* ▷ **poppy**
popping *v* ▷ **pop**[1]
poppy *n* (*pl* **-ppies**) plant with a large red flower
pops *n* ▷ **pop**
populace *n* (*pl* **-s**) the ordinary people
populaces *n* ▷ **populace**
popular *adj* widely liked and admired > **popularly** *adv* > **popularity** *n* (*pl* **-ties**)
popularize *v* (**-zes, -zing, -zed**) make popular
popularized *v* ▷ **popularize**
popularizes *v* ▷ **popularize**
popularizing *v* ▷ **popularize**
popularities *n* ▷ **popular**
popularity *n* ▷ **popular**
popularly *adv* ▷ **popular**
populate *v* (**-tes, -ting, -ted**) live in, inhabit
populated *v* ▷ **populate**
populates *v* ▷ **populate**
populating *v* ▷ **populate**
population *n* (*pl* **-s**) all the people who live in a particular place
populations *n* ▷ **population**
populous *adj* densely populated
porbeagle *n* (*pl* **-s**) kind of shark
porbeagles *n* ▷ **porbeagle**
porcelain *n* (*pl* **-s**) fine china
porcelains *n* ▷ **porcelain**
porch *n* (*pl* **-es**) covered approach to the entrance of a building
porches *n* ▷ **porch**
porcine *adj* of or like a pig
porcupine *n* (*pl* **-s**) animal covered with long pointed quills
porcupines *n* ▷ **porcupine**
pore *n* (*pl* **-s**) tiny opening in the skin or in the surface of a plant
pores *n* ▷ **pore**
pork *n* (*pl* **-s**) pig meat
porker *n* (*pl* **-s**) pig raised for food
porkers *n* ▷ **porker**
porks *n* ▷ **pork**
porn, porno *adj, n* (*pl* **-s**) (*Informal*) ▷ **pornography, pornographic**

pornographies *n* ▷ **pornography**
pornography *n* (*pl* **-hies**) writing, films, or pictures designed to be sexually exciting > **pornographic** *adj*
pornographer *n* (*pl* **-s**) producer of pornography
pornographers *n* ▷ **pornographer**
pornographic *n* ▷ **pornography**
pornos *n* ▷ **porn**
porns *n* ▷ **porn**
porosities *n* ▷ **porous**
porosity *n* ▷ **porous**
porous *adj* allowing liquid to pass through gradually > **porosity** *n* (*pl* **-ties**)
porphyries *n* ▷ **porphyry**
porphyry [**por**-fir-ee] *n* (*pl* **-ries**) reddish rock with large crystals in it
porpoise *n* (*pl* **-s**) fishlike sea mammal
porpoises *n* ▷ **porpoise**
porridge *n* (*pl* **-s**) breakfast food made of oatmeal cooked in water or milk
porridges *n* ▷ **porridge**
port¹ *n* (*pl* **-s**) (town with) a harbour
port² *n* (*pl* **-s**) left side of a ship or aircraft when facing the front of it
port³ *n* (*pl* **-s**) strong sweet wine, usu. red
port⁴ *n* (*pl* **-s**) opening in the side of a ship
portabilities *n* ▷ **portable**
portability *n* ▷ **portable**
portable *adj* easily carried > **portability** *n* (*pl* **-ties**)
portal *n* (*pl* **-s**) large imposing doorway or gate
portals *n* ▷ **portal**
portcullis *n* (*pl* **-es**) grating suspended above a castle gateway, that can be lowered to block the entrance
portcullises *n* ▷ **portcullis**
portend *v* (**-s, -ing, -ed**) be a sign of
portended *v* ▷ **portend**
portending *v* ▷ **portend**
portends *v* ▷ **portend**
portent *n* (*pl* **-s**) sign of a future event
portentous *adj* of great or ominous significance
portents *n* ▷ **portent**
porter¹ *n* (*pl* **-s**) man who carries luggage
porter² *n* (*pl* **-s**) doorman or gatekeeper of a building
porters *n* ▷ **porter¹, ²**
portfolio *n* (*pl* **-s**) (flat case for carrying) examples of an artist's work
portfolios *n* ▷ **portfolio**
porthole *n* (*pl* **-s**) small round window in a ship or aircraft
portholes *n* ▷ **porthole**
portico *n* (*pl* **-coes, -cos**) porch or covered walkway with columns supporting the roof
porticoes *n* ▷ **portico**
porticos *n* ▷ **portico**
portion *n* (*pl* **-s**) part or share
portions *n* ▷ **portion**
portlier *adj* ▷ **portly**
portliest *adj* ▷ **portly**
portly *adj* (**-lier, -liest**) rather fat
portmanteau *n* (*pl* **-eaus, -eaux**) (*Old-fashioned*) large suitcase that opens into two compartments ▶ *adj* combining aspects of different things
portmanteaus *n* ▷ **portmanteau**
portmanteaux *n* ▷ **portmanteau**
portrait *n* (*pl* **-s**) picture of a person
portraits *n* ▷ **portrait**
portray *v* (**-s, -ing, -ed**) describe or represent by artistic means, as in writing or film > **portrayal** *n* (*pl* **-s**)
portrayal *n* ▷ **portray**
portrayals *n* ▷ **portray**
portrayed *v* ▷ **portray**
portraying *v* ▷ **portray**
portrays *v* ▷ **portray**
ports *n* ▷ **port¹, ², ³, ⁴**
pose *v* (**-ses, -sing, -sed**) place in or take up a particular position to be photographed or drawn ▶ *n* (*pl* **-s**) position while posing
posed *v* ▷ **pose**
poser *n* (*pl* **-s**) puzzling question
posers *n* ▷ **poser**
poses *v, n* ▷ **pose**
poseur *n* (*pl* **-s**) person who behaves in an affected way to impress others
poseurs *n* ▷ **poseur**
posies *n* ▷ **posy**
posing *v* ▷ **pose**
posh *adj* (*Informal*) smart, luxurious
posit [**pozz**-it] *v* (**-s, -ing, -ed**) lay down as a basis for argument
posited *v* ▷ **posit**
positing *v* ▷ **posit**
position *n* (*pl* **-s**) place ▶ *v* (**-s, -ing, -ed**) place
positioned *v* ▷ **position**
positioning *v* ▷ **position**
positions *n, v* ▷ **position**
posits *v* ▷ **posit**
positive *adj* feeling no doubts, certain (MATHS) > **positively** *adv*
positively *adv* ▷ **positive**
positron *n* (*pl* **-s**) (PHYSICS) particle with same mass as electron but positive charge
positrons *n* ▷ **positron**
posse [**poss**-ee] *n* (*pl* **-s**) (US) group of men

organized to maintain law and order
posses *n* ▷ **posse**
possess *v* (**-es, -ing, -ed**) have as one's property > **possessor** *n* (*pl* **-s**)
possessed *v* ▷ **possess**
possesses *v* ▷ **possess**
possessing *v* ▷ **possess**
possession *n* (*pl* **-s**) state of possessing, ownership ▶ *pl* things a person possesses
possessions *n* ▷ **possession**
possessive *adj* wanting all the attention or love of another person > **possessiveness** *n*
possessiveness *n* ▷ **possessive**
possessor *n* ▷ **possess**
possessors *n* ▷ **possess**
possibilities *n* ▷ **possibility**
possibility *n* ▷ **possible**
possible *adj* able to exist, happen, or be done ▶ *n* (*pl* **-s**) person or thing that might be suitable or chosen > **possibility** *n* (*pl* **-ties**)
possibles *n* ▷ **possible**
possibly *adv* perhaps, not necessarily
possum *n* (*pl* **-s**) ▷ **opossum** (AUST & NZ) ▷ **phalanger**
possums *n* ▷ **possum**
post¹ *n* (*pl* **-s**) official system of delivering letters and parcels ▶ *v* (**-s, -ing, -ed**) send by post > **postal** *adj*
post² *n* (*pl* **-s**) length of wood, concrete, etc. fixed upright to support or mark something ▶ *v* (**-s, -ing, -ed**) put up (a notice) in a public place
post³ *n* (*pl* **-s**) job ▶ *v* (**-s, -ing, -ed**) send (a person) to a new place to work
postage *n* charge for sending a letter or parcel by post
postages *n* ▷ **postage**
postal *adj* ▷ **post¹**
postbag *n* (*pl* **-s**) postman's bag
postbags *n* ▷ **postbag**
postcard *n* (*pl* **-s**) card for sending a message by post without an envelope
postcards *n* ▷ **postcard**
postcode *n* system of letters and numbers used to aid the sorting of mail
postcodes *n* ▷ **postcode**
postdate *v* (**-tes, -ting, -ted**) write a date on (a cheque) that is later than the actual date
postdated *v* ▷ **postdate**
postdates *v* ▷ **postdate**
postdating *v* ▷ **postdate**
posted *v* ▷ **post¹, ², ³**
poster *n* (*pl* **-s**) large picture or notice stuck on a wall
posterior *n* (*pl* **-s**) buttocks ▶ *adj* behind, at the back of
posteriors *n* ▷ **posterior**
posterities *n* ▷ **posterity**
posterity *n* (*pl* **-ties**) future generations, descendants
postern *n* (*pl* **-s**) small back door or gate
posterns *n* ▷ **postern**
posters *n* ▷ **poster**
postgraduate *n* (*pl* **-s**) person with a degree who is studying for a more advanced qualification
postgraduates *n* ▷ **postgraduate**
posthaste *adv* with great speed
posthumous [poss-tume-uss] *adj* occurring after one's death > **posthumously** *adv*
posthumously *adv* ▷ **posthumous**
postie *n* (*pl* **-s**) (SCOT, AUST & NZ) (*Informal*) postman
posties *n* ▷ **postie**
postilion, postillion *n* (*pl* **-s**) (HIST) person riding one of a pair of horses drawing a carriage
postilions *n* ▷ **postilion**
postillion *n* ▷ **postilion**
postillions *n* ▷ **postilion**
posting *v* ▷ **post¹, ², ³**
postman, postwoman *n* (*pl* **-men, -women**) person who collects and delivers post
postmark *n* (*pl* **-s**) official mark stamped on letters showing place and date of posting
postmarks *n* ▷ **postmark**
postmen *n* ▷ **postman**
postmaster, postmistress *n* (*pl* **-s, -es**) (in some countries) official in charge of a post office
postmasters *n* ▷ **postmaster**
postmistress *n* ▷ **postmaster**
postmistresses *n* ▷ **postmaster**
postmortem ▶ *n* (*pl* **-s**) medical examination of a body to establish the cause of death
postmortems *n* ▷ **postmortem**
postnatal *adj* occurring after childbirth
postpone *v* (**-nes, -ning, -ned**) put off to a later time > **postponement** *n* (*pl* **-s**)
postponed *v* ▷ **postpone**
postponement *n* ▷ **postpone**
postponements *n* ▷ **postpone**
postpones *v* ▷ **postpone**
postponing *v* ▷ **postpone**
posts *n, v* ▷ **post¹, ², ³**
postscript *n* (*pl* **-s**) passage added at the end of a letter
postscripts *n* ▷ **postscript**
postulant *n* (*pl* **-s**) candidate for admission to a religious order

postulants *n* ▷ **postulant**
postulate *v* (**-tes, -ting, -ted**) assume to be true as the basis of an argument or theory
postulated *v* ▷ **postulate**
postulates *v* ▷ **postulate**
postulating *v* ▷ **postulate**
posture *n* (*pl* **-s**) position or way in which someone stands, walks, etc. ▶ *v* (**-res, -ring, -red**) behave in an exaggerated way to get attention
postured *v* ▷ **posture**
postures *n, v* ▷ **posture**
posturing *v* ▷ **posture**
postwomen *n* ▷ **postman**
posy *n* (*pl* **-sies**) small bunch of flowers
pot[1] *n* (*pl* **-s**) round deep container ▶ *pl* (*Informal*) large amount ▶ *v* (**-s, -tting, -tted**) plant in a pot
pot[2] *n* (*Slang*) cannabis
potted *adj* grown in a pot ▶ *v* ▷ **pot**[1]
potting *v* ▷ **pot**[1]
pots *n* ▷ **pot**[1]
potable [**pote**-a-bl] *adj* drinkable
potash *n* (*pl* **-es**) white powdery substance obtained from ashes and used as fertilizer
potashes *n* ▷ **potash**
potassium *n* (*pl* **-s**) (CHEM) silvery metallic element
potassiums *n* ▷ **potassium**
potato ▶ *n* (*pl* **-oes**) roundish starchy vegetable that grows underground
potatoes *n* ▷ **potato**
poteen *n* (*pl* **-s**) (in Ireland) illegally made alcoholic drink
poteens *n* ▷ **poteen**
potencies *n* ▷ **potent**
potency *n* ▷ **potent**
potent *adj* having great power or influence > **potency** *n* (*pl* **-cies**)
potentate *n* (*pl* **-s**) ruler or monarch
potentates *n* ▷ **potentate**
potential *adj* possible but not yet actual ▶ *n* (*pl* **-s**) ability or talent not yet fully used > **potentially** *adv* > **potentiality** *n* (*pl* **-ties**)
potentialities *n* ▷ **potential**
potentiality *n* ▷ **potential**
potentially *adv* ▷ **potential**
potentials *n* ▷ **potential**
pothole *n* (*pl* **-s**) hole in the surface of a road
potholer *n* ▷ **potholing**
potholers *n* ▷ **potholing**
potholes *n* ▷ **pothole**
potholing *n* (*pl* **-s**) sport of exploring underground caves > **potholer** *n* (*pl* **-s**)
potholings *n* ▷ **potholing**
potion *n* (*pl* **-s**) dose of medicine or poison
potions *n* ▷ **potion**
potoroo *n* (*pl* **-s**) Australian leaping rodent
potoroos *n* ▷ **potoroo**
potpourri [po-**poor**-ee] *n* (*pl* **-s**) fragrant mixture of dried flower petals
potpourris *n* ▷ **potpourri**
pottage *n* (*pl* **-s**) (*Old-fashioned*) thick soup or stew
pottages *n* ▷ **pottage**
potter[1] *n* (*pl* **-s**) person who makes pottery
potter[2] *v* (**-s, -ing, -ed**) be busy in a pleasant but aimless way
pottered *v* ▷ **potter**[2]
potteries *n* ▷ **pottery**
pottering *v* ▷ **potter**[2]
potters *n, v* ▷ **potter**[1, 2]
pottery *n* (*pl* **-ries**) articles made from baked clay
pottier *adj* ▷ **potty**
potties *n* ▷ **potty**[2]
pottiest *adj* ▷ **potty**
potty[1] *adj* (**-ttier, -ttiest**) (*Informal*) crazy or silly
potty[2] *n* (*pl* **-tries**) bowl used by a small child as a toilet
pouch *n* (*pl* **-es**) small bag
pouches *n* ▷ **pouch**
pouf, pouffe [**poof**] *n* (*pl* **-s**) large solid cushion used as a seat
pouffe *n* ▷ **pouf**
pouffes *n* ▷ **pouf**
poufs *n* ▷ **pouf**
poulterer *n* (*pl* **-s**) (BRIT) person who sells poultry
poulterers *n* ▷ **poulterer**
poultice [**pole**-tiss] *n* (*pl* **-s**) moist dressing, often heated, applied to inflamed skin
poultices *n* ▷ **poultice**
poultries *n* ▷ **poultry**
poultry *n* (*pl* **-ries**) domestic fowls
pounce *v* (**-ces, -cing, -ced**) spring upon suddenly to attack or capture ▶ *n* (*pl* **-s**) pouncing
pounced *v* ▷ **pounce**
pouncing *v* ▷ **pounce**
pounces *v, n* ▷ **pounce**
pound[1] *n* (*pl* **-s**) monetary unit of Britain and some other countries
pound[2] *v* (**-s, -ing, -ed**) hit heavily and repeatedly
pound[3] *n* (*pl* **-s**) enclosure for stray animals or officially removed vehicles
pounded *v* ▷ **pound**[2]
pounding *v* ▷ **pound**[2]
pounds *n, v* ▷ **pound**[1, 3]

pour *v* (**-s, -ing, -ed**) flow or cause to flow out in a stream
poured *v* ▷ **pour**
pouring *v* ▷ **pour**
pours *v* ▷ **pour**
pout *v* (**-s, -ing, -ed**) thrust out one's lips, look sulky ▶ *n* (*pl* **-s**) pouting look
pouted *v* ▷ **pout**
pouting *v* ▷ **pout**
pouts *v, n* ▷ **pout**
poverties *n* ▷ **poverty**
poverty *n* (*pl* **-ties**) state of being without enough food or money
powder *n* (*pl* **-s**) substance in the form of tiny loose particles ▶ *v* (**-s, -ing, -ed**) apply powder to > **powdery** *adj* (**-rier, -riest**)
powdered *adj, v* ▷ **powder**
powderier *adj* ▷ **powder**
powderiest *adj* ▷ **powder**
powdering *v* ▷ **powder**
powders *n, v* ▷ **powder**
power *n* (*pl* **-s**) ability to do or act > **powerful** *adj* > **powerless** *adj*
powered *adj* having or operated by mechanical or electrical power
powerful *adj* ▷ **power**
powerless *adj* ▷ **power**
powers *n* ▷ **power**
powwow *n* (*pl* **-s**) (*Informal*) talk or conference
powwows *n* ▷ **powwow**
pox *n* (*pl* **-es**) disease in which skin pustules form
poxes *n* ▷ **pox**

poz *adj*. Poz is an old-fashioned short form of **positive.** This is a good word for a crowded board towards the end of the game, especially if you can form another word in the process, or form it on a bonus square. Poz scores 24 points.

practicabilities *n* ▷ **practicable**
practicability *n* ▷ **practicable**
practicable *adj* capable of being done successfully > **practicability** *n* (*pl* **-ties**)
practical *adj* involving experience or actual use rather than theory ▶ *n* (*pl* **-s**) examination in which something has to be done or made > **practically** *adv*
practically *adv* ▷ **practical**
practicals *n* ▷ **practical**
practice *n* (*pl* **-s**) something done regularly or habitually
practices *n* ▷ **practice**
practise *v* (**-ses, -sing, -sed**) do repeatedly so as to gain skill
practised *v* ▷ **practise**
practises *v* ▷ **practise**
practising *v* ▷ **practise**
practitioner *n* (*pl* **-s**) person who practises a profession
practitioners *n* ▷ **practitioner**
pragmatic *adj* concerned with practical consequences rather than theory > **pragmatism** *n* (*pl* **-s**) > **pragmatist** *n* (*pl* **-s**)
pragmatism *n* ▷ **pragmatic**
pragmatisms *n* ▷ **pragmatic**
pragmatist *n* ▷ **pragmatic**
pragmatists *n* ▷ **pragmatic**
prairie *n* (*pl* **-s**) large treeless area of grassland, esp. in N America and Canada
prairies *n* ▷ **prairie**
praise *v* (**-ses, -sing, -sed**) express approval or admiration of (someone or something) ▶ *n* (*pl* **-s**) something said or written to show approval or admiration > **praiseworthy** *adj*
praised *v* ▷ **praise**
praises *v, n* ▷ **praise**
praiseworthy *adj* ▷ **praise**
praising *v* ▷ **praise**
praline [**prah**-leen] *n* (*pl* **-s**) sweet made of nuts and caramelized sugar
pralines *n* ▷ **praline**
pram *n* (*pl* **-s**) four-wheeled carriage for a baby, pushed by hand
prams *n* ▷ **pram**
prance *v* (**-ces, -cing, -ced**) walk with exaggerated bouncing steps
pranced *v* ▷ **prance**
prances *v* ▷ **prance**
prancing *v* ▷ **prance**
prang *v, n* (*pl* **-s**) (*Slang*) (have) a crash in a car or aircraft
prangs *n* ▷ **prang**
prank *n* (*pl* **-s**) mischievous trick
pranks *n* ▷ **prank**
prat *n* (*pl* **-s**) (BRIT, AUST & NZ) (*Informal*) stupid person
prats *n* ▷ **prat**
prattle *v* (**-les, -ling, -led**) chatter in a childish or foolish way ▶ *n* (*pl* **-s**) childish or foolish talk
prattled *v* ▷ **prattle**
prattles *v, n* ▷ **prattle**
prattling *v* ▷ **prattle**
prawn *n* (*pl* **-s**) edible shellfish like a large shrimp
prawns *n* ▷ **prawn**
praxis *n* (*pl* **praxises**) practice as opposed to theory
praxises *n* ▷ **praxis**
pray *v* (**-s, -ing, -ed**) say prayers

prayed *v* ▷ **pray**
prayer *n* (*pl* **-s**) thanks or appeal addressed to one's God
prayers *n* ▷ **prayer**
praying *v* ▷ **pray**
prays *v* ▷ **pray**
preach *v* (**-es, -ing, -ed**) give a talk on a religious theme as part of a church service
preached *v* ▷ **preach**
preaches *v* ▷ **preach**
preaching *v* ▷ **preach**
preacher *n* (*pl* **-s**) person who preaches, esp. in church
preachers *n* ▷ **preacher**
preamble *n* (*pl* **-s**) introductory part to something said or written
preambles *n* ▷ **preamble**
prearranged *adj* arranged beforehand
prebendaries *n* ▷ **prebendary**
prebendary *n* (*pl* **-ries**) clergyman who is a member of the chapter of a cathedral
precarious *adj* insecure, unsafe, likely to fall or collapse > **precariously** *adv*
precariously *adv* ▷ **precarious**
precaution *n* (*pl* **-s**) action taken in advance to prevent something bad happening > **precautionary** *adj*
precautionary *adj* ▷ **precaution**
precautions *n* ▷ **precaution**
precede *v* (**-des, -ding, -ded**) go or be before
preceded *v* ▷ **precede**
precedence [**press**-ee-denss] *n* (*pl* **-s**) formal order of rank or position
precedences *n* ▷ **precedence**
precedent *n* (*pl* **-s**) previous case or occurrence regarded as an example to be followed
precedents *n* ▷ **precedent**
precedes *v* ▷ **precede**
preceding *v* ▷ **precede**
precentor *n* (*pl* **-s**) person who leads the singing in a church
precentors *n* ▷ **precentor**
precept *n* (*pl* **-s**) rule of behaviour > **preceptive** *adj*
preceptive *adj* ▷ **precept**
precepts *n* ▷ **precept**
precinct *n* (*pl* **-s**) (BRIT, AUST & S AFR) area in a town closed to traffic ▶ *pl* surrounding region
precincts *n* ▷ **precinct**
precious *adj* of great value and importance
precipice *n* (*pl* **-s**) very steep face of cliff or rockface
precipices *n* ▷ **precipice**
precipitate *v* (**-tes, -ting, -ted**) cause to happen suddenly ▶ *adj* done rashly or hastily ▶ *n* (*pl* **-s**) (CHEM) substance precipitated from a solution > **precipitately** *adv* > **precipitation** *n* (*pl* **-s**) precipitating
precipitated *v, n* ▷ **precipitate**
precipitately *adv* ▷ **precipitate**
precipitates *v, n* ▷ **precipitate**
precipitating *v* ▷ **precipitate**
precipitation *n* ▷ **precipitate**
precipitations *n* ▷ **precipitate**
precipitous *adj* sheer
précis [**pray**-see] *n* (*pl* **précis**) short written summary of a longer piece ▶ *v* (**-ses, -sing, -sed**) make a précis of
precise *adj* (**-r, -st**) exact, accurate in every detail > **precisely** *adv* > **precision** *n* (*pl* **-s**)
précised *v* ▷ **précis**
précises *v* ▷ **précis**
precisely *adv* ▷ **precise**
preciser *adj* ▷ **precise**
precisest *adj* ▷ **precise**
précising *v* ▷ **précis**
precision *n* ▷ **precise**
precisions *n* ▷ **precise**
preclude *v* (**-des, -ding, -ded**) make impossible to happen
precluded *v* ▷ **preclude**
precludes *v* ▷ **preclude**
precluding *v* ▷ **preclude**
precocious *adj* having developed or matured early or too soon > **precocity** *n* (*pl* **-ties**)
precocities *n* ▷ **precocious**
precocity *n* ▷ **precocious**
precognition *n* (*pl* **-s**) alleged ability to foretell the future
precognitions *n* ▷ **precognition**
preconceived *adj* (of an idea) formed without real experience or reliable information > **preconception** *n* (*pl* **-s**)
preconception *n* ▷ **preconceived**
preconceptions *n* ▷ **preconcieve**
precondition *n* (*pl* **-s**) something that must happen or exist before something else can
preconditions *n* ▷ **precondition**
precursor *n* (*pl* **-s**) something that precedes and is a signal of something else, forerunner
precursors *n* ▷ **precursor**
predate *v* (**-tes, -ting, -ted**) occur at an earlier date than
predated *v* ▷ **predate**
predates *v* ▷ **predate**
predating *v* ▷ **predate**
predator *n* (*pl* **-s**) predatory animal
predators *n* ▷ **predators**
predatory [**pred**-a-tree] *adj* habitually hunting and killing other animals for food

predecease *v* (**-ses, -sing, -sed**) die before (someone else)
predeceased *v* ▷ **predecease**
predeceases *v* ▷ **predecease**
predeceasing *v* ▷ **predecease**
predecessor *n* (*pl* **-s**) person who precedes another in an office or position
predecessors *n* ▷ **predecessor**
predestination *n* (*pl* **-s**) (THEOLOGY) belief that future events have already been decided by God or fate > **predestined** *adj*
predestinations *n* ▷ **predestine**
predestined *adj* ▷ **predestination**
predetermined *adj* decided in advance
predicament *n* (*pl* **-s**) embarrassing or difficult situation
predicaments *n* ▷ **predicament**
predicate *n* (*pl* **-tes**) (GRAMMAR) part of a sentence in which something is said about the subject, e.g. *went home* in *I went home* ▶ *v* (**-tes, -ting, -ted**) declare or assert
predicated *v* ▷ **predicate**
predicates *n, v* ▷ **predicate**
predicating *v* ▷ **predicate**
predict *v* (**-s, -ing, -ed**) tell about in advance, prophesy > **predictable** *adj* > **prediction** *n* (*pl* **-s**)
predictable *adj* ▷ **predict**
predicted *v* ▷ **predict**
predicting *v* ▷ **predict**
prediction *n* ▷ **predict**
predictions *n* ▷ **predict**
predictive *adj* relating to or able to make predictions
predicts *v* ▷ **predict**
predilection *n* (*pl* **-s**) (*Formal*) preference or liking
predilections *n* ▷ **predilection**
predispose *v* (**-ses, -sing, -sed**) influence (someone) in favour of something > **predisposition** *n* (*pl* **-s**)
predisposed *v* ▷ **predispose**
predisposes *v* ▷ **predispose**
predisposing *v* ▷ **predispose**
predisposition *n* ▷ **predispose**
predispositions *n* ▷ **predispose**
predominate *v* (**-tes, -ting, -ted**) be the main or controlling element > **predominance** *n* (*pl* **-s**) > **predominant** *adj* > **predominantly** *adv*
predominance *n* ▷ **predominances**
predominances *n* ▷ **predominance**
predominant *n* ▷ **predominate**
predominantly *adv* ▷ **predominate**
predominated *v* ▷ **predominate**
predominates *v* ▷ **predominate**
predominating *v* ▷ **predominate**
preen *v* (**-s, -ing, -ed**) (of a bird) clean or trim (feathers) with the beak
preened *v* ▷ **preen**
preening *v* ▷ **preen**
preens *v* ▷ **preen**
prefab *n* (*pl* **-s**) prefabricated house
prefabricated *adj* (of a building) manufactured in shaped sections for rapid assembly on site
prefabs *n* ▷ **prefab**
preface [**pref**-iss] *n* (*pl* **-s**) introduction to a book ▶ *v* (**-ces, -cing, -ced**) serve as an introduction to (a book, speech, etc.) > **prefatory** *adj*
prefaced *v* ▷ **preface**
prefaces *n, v* ▷ **preface**
prefacing *v* ▷ **preface**
prefatory *adj* ▷ **preface**
prefect *n* (*pl* **-s**) senior pupil in a school, with limited power over others
prefects *n* ▷ **prefect**
prefecture *n* (*pl* **-s**) office or area of authority of a prefect
prefectures *n* ▷ **prefecture**
prefer *v* (**-s, -rring, -rred**) like better > **preference** *n* (*pl* **-s**)
preferable *adj* more desirable > **preferably** *adv*
preferably *adv* ▷ **preferable**
preference *n* ▷ **prefer**
preferences *n* ▷ **prefer**
preferential *adj* showing preference
preferment *n* (*pl* **-s**) promotion or advancement
preferments *n* ▷ **preferment**
preferred *v* ▷ **prefer**
preferring *v* ▷ **prefer**
prefers *v* ▷ **prefer**
prefigure *v* (**-res, -ring, -red**) represent or suggest in advance
prefigured *v* ▷ **prefigure**
prefigures *v* ▷ **prefigure**
prefiguring *v* ▷ **prefigure**
prefix *n* (*pl* **-es**) letter or group of letters put at the beginning of a word to make a new word, such as *un-* in *unhappy* ▶ *v* (**-es, -ing, -ed**) put as an introduction or prefix (to)
prefixed *v* ▷ **prefix**
prefixes *n, v* ▷ **prefix**
prefixing *v* ▷ **prefix**
pregnacies *n* ▷ **pregnant**
pregnancy *n* ▷ **pregnant**
pregnant *adj* carrying a fetus in the womb > **pregnancy** *n* (*pl* **-cies**)
prehensile *adj* capable of grasping

prehistoric *adj* of the period before written history begins > **prehistory** *n* (*pl* **-ries**)
prehistories *n* ▷ **prehistoric**
prehistory *n* ▷ **prehistoric**
prejudice *n* (*pl* **-s**) unreasonable or unfair dislike or preference ▶ *v* (**-ces, -cing, -ced**) cause (someone) to have a prejudice > **prejudicial** *adj* disadvantageous, harmful
prejudiced *v* ▷ **prejudice**
prejudicial *adj* ▷ **prejudice**
prejudicing *v* ▷ **prejudice**
prejudices *n, v* ▷ **prejudice**
prelate [**prel**-it] *n* (*pl* **-s**) bishop or other churchman of high rank
prelates *n* ▷ **prelate**
preliminaries *n* ▷ **preliminary**
preliminary *adj* happening before and in preparation, introductory ▶ *n* (*pl* **-ries**) preliminary remark, contest, etc.
prelude *n* (*pl* **-s**) introductory movement in music
preludes *n* ▷ **prelude**
premarital *adj* occurring before marriage
premature *adj* happening or done before the normal or expected time > **prematurely** *adv*
prematurely *adv* ▷ **premature**
premeditated *adj* planned in advance > **premeditation** *n* (*pl* **-s**)
premeditation *n* ▷ **premeditated**
premeditations *n* ▷ **premeditated**
premenstrual *adj* occurring or experienced before a menstrual period
premier *n* (*pl* **-s**) prime minister ▶ *adj* chief, leading > **premiership** *n* (*pl* **-s**)
première *n* (*pl* **-s**) first performance of a play, film, etc.
premières *n* ▷ **première**
premiers *n* ▷ **premier**
premiership *n* ▷ **premier**
premierships *n* ▷ **premier**
premise, premiss *n* (*pl* **-s, -es**) statement assumed to be true and used as the basis of reasoning
premises *n* ▷ **premise**
premises *pl n* house or other building and its land
premisses *n* ▷ **premise**
premium *n* (*pl* **-s**) additional sum of money, as on a wage or charge
premiums *n* ▷ **premium**
premonition *n* (*pl* **-s**) feeling that something unpleasant is going to happen; foreboding > **premonitory** *adj*
premonitions *n* ▷ **premonition**
premonitory *adj* ▷ **premonition**
prenatal *adj* before birth, during pregnancy
preoccupied *v* ▷ **preoccupy**
preoccupies *v* ▷ **preoccupy**
preoccupy *v* (**-pied, -pying, -pied**) fill the thoughts or attention of (someone) to the exclusion of other things > **preoccupation** *n* (*pl* **-s**)
preoccupation *n* ▷ **preoccupy**
preoccupations *n* ▷ **preoccupy**
preoccupying *v* ▷ **preoccupy**
preordained *adj* decreed or determined in advance
prep. preparatory
prepacked *adj* sold already wrapped
prepaid *adj* paid for in advance
prepare *v* (**-res, -ring, -red**) make or get ready
preparation *n* (*pl* **-s**) preparing
preparations *n* ▷ **preparation**
preparatory [prip-**par**-a-tree] *adj* preparing for
prepared *adj* willing ▶ *v* ▷ **prepare**
prepares *v* ▷ **prepare**
preparing *v* ▷ **prepare**
preponderance *n* (*pl* **-s**) greater force, amount, or influence > **preponderant** *adj*
preponderances *adj* ▷ **preponderance**
preponderant *adj* ▷ **preponderance**
preposition *n* (*pl* **-s**) word used before a noun or pronoun to show its relationship with other words, such as *by* in *go by bus* > **prepositional** *adj*
prepositional *n* ▷ **preposition**
prepositions *n* ▷ **preposition**
prepossessing *adj* making a favourable impression, attractive
preposterous *adj* utterly absurd
prepuce [**pree**-pyewss] *n* (*pl* **-s**) retractable fold of skin covering the tip of the penis, foreskin
prepuces *n* ▷ **prepuce**
prerecorded *adj* recorded in advance to be played or broadcast later
prerequisite *adj, n* (*pl* **-s**) (something) required before something else is possible
prerequisites *n* ▷ **prerequisite**
prerogative *n* (*pl* **-s**) special power or privilege
prerogatives *n* ▷ **prerogative**
presage [**press**-ij] *v* (**-ges, -ging, -ged**) be a sign or warning of
presaged *v* ▷ **presage**
presages *v* ▷ **presage**
presaging *v* ▷ **presage**
presbyteries *n* ▷ **presbytery**
presbytery *n* (*pl* **-ies**) (PRESBYTERIAN CHURCH) local church court
prescience [**press**-ee-enss] *n* (*pl* **-s**) knowledge of events before they happen > **prescient** *adj*

presciences *n* ▷ **prescience**
prescient *adj* ▷ **prescience**
prescribe *v* (**-bes, -bing, -bed**) recommend the use of (a medicine)
prescribed *v* ▷ **prescribe**
prescribes *v* ▷ **prescribe**
prescribing *v* ▷ **prescribe**
prescription *n* written instructions from a doctor for the making up and use of a medicine
prescriptions *n* ▷ **prescription**
prescriptive *adj* laying down rules
presence *n* (*pl* **-s**) fact of being in a specified place
presences *n* ▷ **presence**
present[1] *adj* being in a specified place ▶ *n* (*pl* **-s**) present time or tense
present[2] *n* something given to bring pleasure to another person ▶ *v* (**-s, -ing, -ed**) introduce formally or publicly > **presentation** *n* (*pl* **-s**)
presentable *adj* attractive, neat, fit for people to see
presented *n* ▷ **present**[2]
presenter *n* (*pl* **-s**) person introducing a TV or radio show
presenters *n* ▷ **presenter**
presentiment [priz-**zen**-tim-ent] *n* (*pl* **-s**) sense of something unpleasant about to happen
presentiments *n* ▷ **presentiment**
presenting *v* ▷ **present**[2]
presently *adv* soon (US & SCOT)
presents *n, v* ▷ **present**[1, 2]
preserve *v* (**-ves, -ving, -ved**) keep from being damaged, changed, or ended ▶ *n* (*pl* **-s**) area of interest restricted to a particular person or group > **preservation** *n* (*pl* **-s**)
preservation *n* ▷ **preserve**
preservations *n* ▷ **preserve**
preservative *n* (*pl* **-s**) chemical that prevents decay
preservatives *n* ▷ **preservative**
preserved *v* ▷ **preserve**
preserves *v, n* ▷ **preserve**
preserving *v* ▷ **preserve**
preshrunk *adj* (of fabric or a garment) having been shrunk during manufacture so that further shrinkage will not occur when washed
preside *v* (**-des, -ding, -ded**) be in charge, esp. of a meeting
presided *v* ▷ **preside**
presidencies *n* ▷ **president**
presidency *n* ▷ **president**
president *n* (*pl* **-s**) head of state in many countries > **presidential** *adj* > **presidency** *n* (*pl* **-cies**)
presidential *n* ▷ **president**
presidents *n* ▷ **president**
presides *v* ▷ **preside**
presiding *v* ▷ **preside**
press *v* (**-es, -ing, -ed**) apply force or weight to ▶ *n* (*pl* **-es**) printing machine
pressed *v* ▷ **press**
presses *v, n* ▷ **press**
pressing *adj* urgent ▶ *v* ▷ **press**
presses *n* ▷ **press**
pressure *n* (*pl* **-s**) force produced by pressing
pressures *n* ▷ **pressure**
prestidigitation *n* (*pl* **-s**) skilful quickness with the hands, conjuring
prestidigitations *n* ▷ **prestidigitation**
prestige *n* (*pl* **-s**) high status or respect resulting from success or achievements > **prestigious** *adj*
prestiges *n* ▷ **prestige**
prestigious *adj* ▷ **prestige**
presumed *v* ▷ **presume**
presto *adv* (MUSIC) very quickly
prestressed *adj* (of concrete) containing stretched steel wires to strengthen it
presume *v* (**-mes, -ing, -med**) suppose to be the case
presumably *adv* one supposes (that)
presumed *v* ▷ **presume**
presumes *v* ▷ **presume**
presuming *v* ▷ **presume**
presumption (*pl* **-s**) *n* bold insolent behaviour
presumption *n* ▷ **presumption**
presumptive *adj* assumed to be true or valid until the contrary is proved
presumptuous *adj* doing things one has no right to do
presuppose *v* (**-ses, -sing, -sed**) need as a previous condition in order to be true > **presupposition** *n* (*pl* **-s**)
presupposed *v* ▷ **presuppose**
presupposes *v* ▷ **presuppose**
presupposing *v* ▷ **presuppose**
presupposition *v* ▷ **presuppose**
presuppositions *v* ▷ **presuppose**
pretence *n* (*pl* **-s**) behaviour intended to deceive, pretending
pretences *n* ▷ **pretence**
pretend *v* (**-s, -ing, -ed**) claim or give the appearance of (something untrue) to deceive or in play
pretended *v* ▷ **pretend**
pretender *n* (*pl* **-s**) person who makes a false or disputed claim to a position of power
pretenders *n* ▷ **pretender**

pretending *v* ▷ **pretend**
pretends *v* ▷ **pretend**
pretension *n* ▷ **pretentious**
pretensions *n* ▷ **pretentious**
pretentious *adj* making (unjustified) claims to special merit or importance > **pretension** *n* (*pl* **-s**)
preternatural *adj* beyond what is natural, supernatural
pretext *n* (*pl* **-s**) false reason given to hide the real one
pretexts *n* ▷ **pretext**
prettier *adj* ▷ **pretty**
prettiest *adj* ▷ **pretty**
prettily *adv* ▷ **pretty**
prettiness *n* ▷ **pretty**
prettinesses *n* ▷ **pretty**
pretty *adj* (**-ttier, -ttiest**) pleasing to look at ▶ *adv* fairly, moderately > **prettily** *adv* > **prettiness** *n* (*pl* **-es**)
pretzel *n* (*pl* **-s**) brittle salted biscuit
pretzels *n* ▷ **pretzel**
prevail *v* (**-s, -ing, -ed**) gain mastery
prevailed *v* ▷ **prevail**
prevailing *adj* widespread ▶ *v* ▷ **prevail**
prevails *v* ▷ **prevail**
prevalence *n* ▷ **prevalent**
prevalences *n* ▷ **prevalent**
prevalent *adj* widespread, common > **prevalence** *n* (*pl* **-s**)
prevaricate *v* (**-tes, -ting, -ted**) avoid giving a direct or truthful answer > **prevarication** *n* (*pl* **-s**)
prevaricated *v* ▷ **prevaricate**
prevaricates *v* ▷ **prevaricate**
prevaricating *v* ▷ **prevaricate**
prevarication *n* ▷ **prevaricate**
prevarications *n* ▷ **prevaricate**
prevent *v* (**-s, -ing, -ed**) keep from happening or doing > **preventable** *adj* > **prevention** *n* (*pl* **-s**) > **preventive** *adj*, *n* (*pl* **-s**)
preventable *adj* ▷ **prevent**
prevented *v* ▷ **prevent**
preventing *v* ▷ **prevent**
prevention *n* ▷ **prevent**
preventions *n* ▷ **prevent**
preventive *adj*, *n* ▷ **prevent**
preventives *n* ▷ **prevent**
prevents *v* ▷ **prevent**
preview *n* (*pl* **-s**) advance showing of a film or exhibition before it is shown to the public
previews *n* ▷ **preview**
previous *adj* coming or happening before > **previously** *adv*
previously *adv* ▷ **previous**
prey *n* (*pl* **-s**) animal hunted and killed for food by another animal
preys *n* ▷ **prey**
price *n* (*pl* **-s**) amount of money for which a thing is bought or sold ▶ *v* (**-ces, -cing, -ced**) fix or ask the price of
priced *v* ▷ **price**
priceless *adj* very valuable
prices *n*, *v* ▷ **price**
pricier *adj* ▷ **pricey**
priciest *adj* ▷ **pricey**
pricing *v* ▷ **price**
pricey *adj* (**-cier, -ciest**) (*Informal*) expensive
prick *v* (**-s, -ing, -ed**) pierce lightly with a sharp point ▶ *n* (*pl* **-s**) sudden sharp pain caused by pricking
pricked *v* ▷ **prick**
pricking *v* ▷ **prick**
prickle *n* (*pl* **-s**) thorn or spike on a plant ▶ *v* (**-les, -ling, -led**) have a tingling or pricking sensation > **prickly** *adj* (**-lier, -liest**)
prickled *v* ▷ **prickle**
prickles *n*, *v* ▷ **prickle**
pricklier *adj* ▷ **prickle**
prickliest *adj* ▷ **prickle**
prickling *v* ▷ **prickle**
prickly *adj* ▷ **prickle**
pricks *v*, *n* ▷ **prick**
pride *n* (*pl* **-s**) feeling of pleasure and satisfaction when one has done well
prides *n* ▷ **pride**
pried *v* ▷ **pry**
pries *v* ▷ **pry**
priest *n* (*pl* **-s**) (in the Christian church) a person who can administer the sacraments and preach > **priestess** *n fem* (*pl* **-es**) > **priesthood** *n* (*pl* **-s**) > **priestly** *adj* (**-lier, -liest**)
priestess *n* ▷ **priest**
priestesses *n* ▷ **priest**
priesthood *n* ▷ **priest**
priesthoods *n* ▷ **priest**
priestlier *adj* ▷ **priest**
priestliest *adj* ▷ **priest**
priestly *adj* ▷ **priest**
priests *n* ▷ **priest**
prig *n* (*pl* **-s**) self-righteous person who acts as if superior to others > **priggish** *adj* > **priggishness** *n* (*pl* **-s**)
priggish *adj* ▷ **prig**
priggishness *n* ▷ **prig**
prigishnesses *n* ▷ **prig**
prigs *n* ▷ **prig**
prim *adj* (**-mmer, -mmest**) formal, proper, and rather prudish > **primly** *adv*
primacies *n* ▷ **primacy**

primacy *n* (*pl* **-ies**) state of being first in rank, grade, etc.
primaeval *adj* ▷ **primeval**
primal *adj* of basic causes or origins
primarily *adv* ▷ **primary**
primary *adj* chief, most important > **primarily** *adv*
primate[1] *n* (*pl* **-s**) member of an order of mammals including monkeys and humans
primate[2] *n* (*pl* **-s**) archbishop
primates *n* ▷ **primate**[1, 2]
prime *adj* main, most important ▶ *n* (*pl* **-s**) time when someone is at his or her best or most vigorous ▶ *v* (**-mes, -ming, -med**) give (someone) information in advance to prepare them for something
primed *v* ▷ **prime**
primer *n* (*pl* **-s**) special paint applied to bare wood etc. before the main paint
primers *n* ▷ **primer**
primes *n, v* ▷ **prime**
priming *v* ▷ **prime**
primeval [prime-**ee**-val] *adj* of the earliest age of the world
primitive *adj* of an early simple stage of development
primly *adv* ▷ **prim**
primmer *adj* ▷ **prim**
primmest *adj* ▷ **prim**
primogeniture *n* (*pl* **-s**) system under which the eldest son inherits all his parents' property
primogenitures *n* ▷ **primogeniture**
primordial *adj* existing at or from the beginning
primrose *n* (*pl* **-s**) pale yellow spring flower
primroses *n* ▷ **primrose**
primula *n* (*pl* **-s**) type of primrose with brightly coloured flowers
primulas *n* ▷ **primula**
prince *n* (*pl* **-s**) male member of a royal family, esp. the son of the king or queen
princelier *adj* ▷ **princely**
princeliest *adj* ▷ **princely**
princely *adj* (**-lier, -liest**) of or like a prince
princess *n* (*pl* **-es**) female member of a royal family, esp. the daughter of the king or queen
princes *n* ▷ **prince**
princesses *n* ▷ **princess**
principal *adj* main, most important ▶ *n* (*pl* **-s**) head of a school or college > **principally** *adv*
principalities *n* ▷ **principality**
principality *n* (*pl* **-ties**) territory ruled by a prince
principally *adv* ▷ **principal**
principals *n* ▷ **principal**
principle *n* (*pl* **-s**) moral rule guiding behaviour
principles *n* ▷ **principle**
print *v* (**-s, -ing, -ed**) reproduce (a newspaper, book, etc.) in large quantities by mechanical or electronic means ▶ *n* (*pl* **-s**) printed words etc. > **printing** *n* (*pl* **-s**)
printed *v* ▷ **print**
printer *n* (*pl* **-s**) person or company engaged in printing
printers *n* ▷ **printer**
printing *n, v* ▷ **print**
printings *n* ▷ **print**
prints *v* ▷ **print**
printing *v* ▷ **print**
printed *v* ▷ **print**
prints *n* ▷ **print**
prior[1] *adj* earlier
prior[2] *n* (*pl* **-s**) head monk in a priory
prioress *n* (*pl* **-es**) deputy head nun in a convent
prioresses *n* ▷ **prioress**
priories *n* ▷ **priory**
priors *n* ▷ **prior**[2]
priory *n* (*pl* **-ries**) place where certain orders of monks or nuns live
priors *n* ▷ **prior**
priorities *n* ▷ **priority**
priority *n* (*pl* **-ties**) most important thing that must be dealt with first
prise *v* (**-ses, -sing, -sed**) force open by levering
prised *v* ▷ **prise**
prises *v* ▷ **prise**
prising *v* ▷ **prise**
prism *n* (*pl* **-s**) transparent block usu. with triangular ends and rectangular sides, used to disperse light into a spectrum or refract it in optical instruments
prismatic *adj* of or shaped like a prism
prisms *n* ▷ **prism**
prison *n* (*pl* **-s**) building where criminals and accused people are held
prisons *n* ▷ **prison**
prisoner *n* (*pl* **-s**) person held captive
prisoners *n* ▷ **prisoner**
prissier *adj* ▷ **prissy**
prissiest *adj* ▷ **prissy**
prissily *adv* ▷ **prissy**
prissy *adj* (**-ssier, -ssiest**) prim, correct, and easily shocked > **prissily** *adv*
pristine *adj* clean, new, and unused
privacies *n* ▷ **private**
privacy *n* ▷ **private**
private *adj* for the use of one person or group only ▶ *n* (*pl* **-s**) soldier of the lowest rank

>**privately** *adv* > **privacy** *n* (*pl* **-cies**)
privately *adv* ▷ **private**
privates *n* ▷ **private**
privateer *n* (*pl* **-s**) (HIST) privately owned armed vessel authorized by the government to take part in a war
privateers *n* ▷ **privateer**
privation *n* (*pl* **-s**) loss or lack of the necessities of life
privations *n* ▷ **privation**
privatization *n* ▷ **privatize**
privatizations *n* ▷ **privatize**
privatize *v* (**-zes, -zing, -zed**) sell (a publicly owned company) to individuals or a private company > **privatization** *n* (*pl* **-s**)
privatized *v* ▷ **privatize**
privatizes *v* ▷ **privatize**
privatizing *v* ▷ **privatize**
privet *n* (*pl* **-s**) bushy evergreen shrub used for hedges
privets *n* ▷ **privet**
privier *adj* ▷ **privy**
privies *n* ▷ **privy**
priviest *adj* ▷ **privy**
privilege *n* (*pl* **-s**) advantage or favour that only some people have
privileged *adj* enjoying a special right or immunity
privileges *n* ▷ **privilege**
privy *adj* (**-vier, -viest**) sharing knowledge of something secret ▶ *n* (*pl* **-ies**) (*Obs*) toilet, esp. an outside one
prize[1] *n* (*pl* **-s**) reward given for success in a competition etc. ▶ *adj* winning or likely to win a prize
prize[2] *v* (**-zes, -zing, -zed**) value highly
prize[3] *v* ▷ **prise**
prized *v* ▷ **prize**
prizefighter *n* (*pl* **-s**) boxer who fights for money
prizefighters *n* ▷ **prizefighter**
prizes *n, v* ▷ **prize**[1, 2]
prizing *v* ▷ **prize**[2]
pro[1] *adv, prep* in favour of
pro[2] *n* (*pl* **-s**) (*Informal*) professional
probabilities *n* ▷ **probable**
probabilitity *n* ▷ **probable**
probable *adj* likely to happen or be true > **probability** *n* (*pl* **-ties**)
probably *adv* in all likelihood
probate *n* (*pl* **-s**) process of proving the validity of a will
probates *n* ▷ **probate**
probation *n* (*pl* **-s**) system of dealing with law-breakers, esp. juvenile ones, by placing them under supervision
probationer *n* (*pl* **-s**) person on probation
probationers *n* ▷ **probationer**
probations *n* ▷ **probation**
probe *v* (**-bes, -bing, -bed**) search into or examine closely ▶ *n* (*pl* **-s**) surgical instrument used to examine a wound, cavity, etc.
probed *v* ▷ **probe**
probes *v, n* ▷ **probe**
probing *v* ▷ **probe**
probiotic *adj, n* (*pl* **-s**) (of) a bacterium that protects the body from harmful bacteria
probiotics *n* ▷ **probiotic**
probities *n* ▷ **probity**
probity *n* (*pl* **-ties**) honesty, integrity
problem *n* (*pl* **-s**) something difficult to deal with or solve > **problematic, problematical** *adj*
problematic *adj* ▷ **problem**
problematical *adj* ▷ **problem**
problems *n* ▷ **problem**
proboscis [pro-**boss**-iss] *n* (*pl* **-scises**) long trunk or snout
proboscises *n* ▷ **proboscis**
procedural *adj* ▷ **procedure**
procedure *n* (*pl* **-s**) way of doing something, esp. the correct or usual one > **procedural** *adj*
procedures *n* ▷ **procedure**
proceed *v* (**-s, -ing, -ed**) start or continue doing
proceeded *v* ▷ **proceed**
proceeds *pl n* money obtained from an event or activity ▶ *v* ▷ **proceed**
proceeding *v* ▷ **proceed**
proceedings *pl n* organized or related series of events
process *n* (*pl* **-es**) series of actions or changes ▶ *v* (**-es, -ing, -ed**) handle or prepare by a special method of manufacture > **processor** *n* (*pl* **-s**)
processed *adj* (of food) treated to prevent it decaying ▶ *v* ▷ **process**
processes *n, v* ▷ **process**
processing *v* ▷ **process**
procession *n* (*pl* **-s**) line of people or vehicles moving forward together in order
processions *n* ▷ **procession**
processor *n* ▷ **process**
processors *n* ▷ **process**
proclaim *v* (**-s, -ing, -ed**) declare publicly > **proclamation** *n* (*pl* **-s**)
proclaimed *v* ▷ **proclaim**
proclaiming *v* ▷ **proclaim**
proclaims *v* ▷ **proclaim**
proclamation *n* ▷ **proclaim**
proclamations *n* ▷ **proclaim**

proclivities *n* ▷ **proclivity**
proclivity *n* (*pl* **-ties**) inclination, tendency
procrastinate *v* (**-tes, -ting, -ted**) put off taking action, delay > **procrastination** *n* (*pl* **-s**)
procrastinated *v* ▷ **procrastinate**
procrastinates *v* ▷ **procrastinate**
procrastinating *v* ▷ **procrastinate**
procrastination *n* ▷ **procrastinate**
procrastinations *n* ▷ **procrastinate**
procreate *v* (**-tes, -ting, -ted**) (*Formal*) produce offspring > **procreation** *n* (*pl* **-s**)
procreated *v* ▷ **procreate**
procreates *v* ▷ **procreate**
procreating *v* ▷ **procreate**
procreation *n* ▷ **procreate**
procreations *n* ▷ **procreate**
procure *v* (**-res, -ring, -red**) get, provide > **procurement** *n* (*pl* **-s**)
procured *v* ▷ **procure**
procurement *n* ▷ **procure**
procurements *n* ▷ **procure**
procurer, procuress *n* (*pl* **-s, -es**) person who obtains people to act as prostitutes
procurers *n* ▷ **procurer**
procures *v* ▷ **procure**
procuress *n* ▷ **procurer**
procuresses *n* ▷ **procurer**
procuring *v* ▷ **procure**
prod *v* (**-s, -dding, -dded**) poke with something pointed ▶ *n* (*pl* **-s**) prodding
prodded *v* ▷ **prod**
prodding *v* ▷ **prod**
prodigal *adj* recklessly extravagant, wasteful > **prodigality** *n* (*pl* **-s**)
prodigalities *n* ▷ **prodigal**
prodigality *n* ▷ **prodigal**
prodigies *n* ▷ **prodigy**
prodigious *adj* very large, immense > **prodigiously** *adv*
prodigiously *adv* ▷ **prodigious**
prodigy *n* (*pl* **-gies**) person with some marvellous talent
prods *v, n* ▷ **prod**
produce *v* (**-ces, -cing, -ced**) bring into existence ▶ *n* (*pl* **-s**) food grown for sale
produced *v* ▷ **produce**
producer *n* (*pl* **-s**) person with control over the making of a film, record, etc.
producers *n* ▷ **producer**
produces *v, n* ▷ **produce**
producing *v* ▷ **produce**
product *n* (*pl* **-s**) something produced
production *n* (*pl* **-s**) producing
productions *n* ▷ **production**
productive *adj* producing large quantities > **productivity** *n* (*pl* **-ies**)
productivities *n* ▷ **productive**
productivity *n* ▷ **productive**
products *n* ▷ **product**
profane *adj* showing disrespect for religion or holy things ▶ *v* (**-nes, -ning, -ned**) treat (something sacred) irreverently, desecrate
profanation *n* (*pl* **-s**) act of profaning
profanations *n* ▷ **profanation**
profaned *v* ▷ **profane**
profanes *v* ▷ **profane**
profaning *v* ▷ **profane**
profanities *n* ▷ **profanity**
profanity *n* (*pl* **-ties**) profane talk or behaviour, blasphemy
profess *v* (**-es, -ing, -ed**) state or claim (something as true), sometimes falsely > **professed** *adj* supposed
professed *v, adj* ▷ **profess**
professes *v* ▷ **profess**
professing *v* ▷ **profess**
profession *n* (*pl* **-s**) type of work, such as being a doctor, that needs special training
professional *adj* working in a profession ▶ *n* person who works in a profession > **professionally** *adv* > **professionalism** *n* (*pl* **-s**)
professionally *adv* ▷ **professional**
professionalism *n* ▷ **professional**
professionalisms *n* ▷ **professional**
professions *n* ▷ **profession**
professor *n* (*pl* **-s**) teacher of the highest rank in a university > **professorial** *adj* > **professorship** *n* (*pl* **-s**)
professorial *adj* ▷ **professor**
professors *n* ▷ **professor**
professorship *n* ▷ **professor**
professorships *n* ▷ **professor**
proffer *v* (**-s, -ing, -ed**) offer
proffered *v* ▷ **proffer**
proffering *v* ▷ **proffer**
proffers *v* ▷ **proffer**
proficiencies *n* ▷ **proficient**
proficiency *n* ▷ **proficient**
proficient *adj* skilled, expert > **proficiency** *n* (*pl* **-cies**)
profile *n* (*pl* **-s**) outline, esp. of the face, as seen from the side
profiles *n* ▷ **profile**
profit *n* (*pl* **-s**) money gained ▶ *v* (**-s, -ing, -ed**) gain or benefit
profitable *adj* making profit > **profitably** *adv* > **profitability** *n* (*pl* **-ties**)
profitabilities *n* ▷ **profitable**
profitability *n* ▷ **profitable**

profitably *adv* ▷ **profitable**
profited *v* ▷ **profit**
profiteer *n* (*pl* **-s**) person who makes excessive profits at the expense of the public > **profiteering** *n* (*pl* **-s**)
profiteering *n* ▷ **profiteer**
profiteerings *n* ▷ **profiteer**
profiteers *n* ▷ **profiteer**
profiting *v* ▷ **profit**
profits *n, v* ▷ **profit**
profligacies *n* ▷ **profligate**
profligacy *n* ▷ **profligate**
profligate *adj* recklessly extravagant ▶ *n* (*pl* **-s**) profligate person > **profligacy** *n* (*pl* **-cies**)
profligates *n* ▷ **profligate**
profound *adj* (**-er, -est**) showing or needing great knowledge > **profundity** *n* (*pl* **-ties**)
profounder *adj* ▷ **profound**
profoundest *adj* ▷ **profound**
profundities *n* ▷ **profound**
profundity *n* ▷ **profound**
profuse *adj* plentiful > **profusion** *n* (*pl* **-s**)
profusion *n* ▷ **profuse**
profusions *n* ▷ **profuse**
progenies *n* ▷ **progeny**
progeny [**proj**-in-ee] *n* (*pl* **-nies**) children
progenitor [pro-**jen**-it-er] *n* (*pl* **-s**) ancestor
progenitors *n* ▷ **progenitor**
progesterone *n* (*pl* **-s**) hormone which prepares the womb for pregnancy and prevents further ovulation
progesterones *n* ▷ **progesterone**
prognoses *n* ▷ **prognosis**
prognosis *n* (*pl* **-noses**) doctor's forecast about the progress of an illness
prognostication *n* (*pl* **-s**) forecast or prediction
prognostications *n* ▷ **prognostication**
program *n* (*pl* **-s**) sequence of coded instructions for a computer ▶ *v* (**-s, -mming, --mmed**) arrange (data) so that it can be processed by a computer > **programmer** *n* (*pl* **-s**) > **programmable** *adj*
programmable *adj* ▷ **program**
programmed *v* ▷ **program**
programmer *n* ▷ **program**
programmers *n* ▷ **program**
programming *v* ▷ **program**
programs *n, v* ▷ **program**
programme *n* (*pl* **-s**) planned series of events
programmes *n* ▷ **programme**
progress *n* (*pl* **-es**) improvement, development ▶ *v* (**-es, -ing, -ed**) become more advanced or skilful > **progression** *n* (*pl* **-s**)
progressed *v* ▷ **progress**
progresses *v* ▷ **progress**
progressing *v* ▷ **progress**
progression *n* ▷ **progress**
progressions *n* ▷ **progress**
progressive *adj* favouring political or social reform > **progressively** *adv*
progressively *adv* ▷ **progressive**
prohibit *v* (**-s, -ing, -ed**) forbid or prevent from happening
prohibited *v* ▷ **prohibit**
prohibiting *v* ▷ **prohibit**
prohibition *n* (*pl* **-s**) act of forbidding
prohibitions *n* ▷ **prohibition**
prohibitive *adj* (of prices) too high to be affordable > **prohibitively** *adv*
prohibitively *adv* ▷ **prohibitive**
prohibits *v* ▷ **prohibit**
project *n* (*pl* **projects**) planned scheme to do or examine something over a period ▶ *v* (**-s, -ing, -ed**) make a forecast based on known data > **projection** *n* (*pl* **-s**)
projected *v* ▷ **project**
projectile *n* (*pl* **-s**) object thrown as a weapon or fired from a gun
projectiles *n* ▷ **projectile**
projecting *v* ▷ **project**
projection *n* ▷ **project**
projectionist *n* (*pl* **-s**) person who operates a projector
projectionists *n* ▷ **projectionist**
projections *n* ▷ **project**
projector *n* (*pl* **-s**) apparatus for projecting photographic images, films, or slides on a screen
projectors *n* ▷ **projector**
projects *n, v* ▷ **project**
prolapse *n* (*pl* **-s**) slipping down of an internal organ of the body from its normal position
prolapses *n* ▷ **prolapse**
prole *adj, n* (*pl* **-s**) (CHIEFLY BRIT) (*Slang*) proletarian
proles *n* ▷ **prole**
proletariat [pro-lit-**air**-ee-at] *n* (*pl* **-s**) working class > **proletarian** *adj, n* (*pl* **-s**)
proletarian *n* ▷ **proletariat**
proletarians *n* ▷ **proletariat**
proletariats *n* ▷ **proletariat**
proliferate *v* (**-tes, -ting, -ted**) grow or reproduce rapidly > **proliferation** *n* (*pl* **-s**)
proliferated *v* ▷ **proliferate**
proliferates *v* ▷ **proliferate**
proliferating *v* ▷ **proliferate**
proliferation *n* ▷ **proliferate**
proliferations *n* ▷ **proliferate**
prolific *adj* very productive > **prolifically** *adv*

prolifically *adv* ▷ **prolific**
prolix *adj* (of speech or a piece of writing) overlong and boring
prologue *n* (*pl* **-s**) introduction to a play or book
prologues *n* ▷ **prologue**
prolong *v* (**-s, -ing, -ed**) make (something) last longer > **prolongation** *n* (*pl* **-s**)
prolongation *n* ▷ **prolong**
prolongations *n* ▷ **prolong**
prolonged *v* ▷ **prolong**
prolonging *v* ▷ **prolong**
prolongs *v* ▷ **prolong**
prom *n* (*pl* **-s**) ▷ **promenade**
promenade *n* (*pl* **-s**) (CHIEFLY BRIT) paved walkway along the seafront at a holiday resort ▶ *v* (**-des, -ding, -ded**) ▶ *n* (*Old-fashioned*) (take) a leisurely walk
promenaded *v* ▷ **promenade**
promenades *n, v* ▷ **promenade**
promenading *v* ▷ **promenade**
prominence *n* ▷ **prominent**
prominences *n* ▷ **prominent**
prominent *adj* very noticeable > **prominently** *adv* > **prominence** *n* (*pl* **-s**)
prominently *adv* ▷ **prominent**
promiscuities *n* ▷ **promiscuous**
promiscuity *n* ▷ **promiscuous**
promiscuous *adj* having many casual sexual relationships > **promiscuity** *n* (*pl* **-ties**)
promise *v* (**-ses, -sing, -sed**) say that one will definitely do or not do something ▶ *n* (*pl* **-s**) undertaking to do or not to do something
promised *v* ▷ **promise**
promises *v* ▷ **promise**
promising *adj* likely to succeed or turn out well ▶ *v* ▷ **promise**
promo *n* (*pl* **-os**) (*Informal*) short film to promote a product
promontories *n* ▷ **promontory**
promontory *n* (*pl* **-ries**) point of high land jutting out into the sea
promos *n* ▷ **promo**
promote *v* (**-tes, -ting, -ted**) help to make (something) happen or increase > **promotion** *n* (*pl* **-s**) > **promotional** *adj*
promoted *v* ▷ **promote**
promoter *n* (*pl* **-s**) person who organizes or finances an event etc.
promoters *n* ▷ **promoter**
promotes *v* ▷ **promote**
promoting *v* ▷ **promote**
promotion *n* ▷ **promote**
promotional *adj* ▷ **promote**
promotions *n* ▷ **promote**
prompt *v* (**-s, -ing, -ed**) cause (an action) ▶ *adj* done without delay ▶ *adv* exactly > **promptness** *n* (*pl* **-es**)
prompted *v* ▷ **prompt**
prompter, prompt *n* (*pl* **-s**) person offstage who prompts actors
prompter *n* ▷ **prompter**
prompting *v* ▷ **prompt**
promptly *adv* immediately, without delay
promptness *n* ▷ **prompt**
promptnesses *n* ▷ **prompt**
prompts *v, n* ▷ **prompt**
proms *n* ▷ **prom**
promulgate *v* (**-tes, -ting, -ted**) put (a law etc.) into effect by announcing it officially > **promulgation** *n* (*pl* **-s**)
promulgated *v* ▷ **promulgate**
promulgates *v* ▷ **promulgate**
promulgating *v* ▷ **promulgate**
promulgation *n* ▷ **promulgate**
promulgations *n* ▷ **promulgate**
prone *adj* (**-r, -st**) (*foll. by* **to**) likely to do or be affected by (something)
proner *adj* ▷ **prone**
pronest *adj* ▷ **prone**
prong *n* (*pl* **-s**) one spike of a fork or similar instrument > **pronged** *adj*
pronged *adj* ▷ **prong**
prongs *n* ▷ **prong**
pronoun *n* (*pl* **-s**) word, such as *she* or *it*, used to replace a noun
pronouns *n* ▷ **pronoun**
pronounce *v* (**-ces, -cing, -ced**) form the sounds of (words or letters), esp. clearly or in a particular way > **pronounceable** *adj*
pronouncable *adj* ▷ **pronounce**
pronounced *adj* very noticeable ▶ *v* ▷ **pronounce**
pronounces *v* ▷ **pronounce**
pronouncement *n* (*pl* **-s**) formal announcement
pronouncements *n* ▷ **pronouncement**
pronouncing *v* ▷ **pronounce**
pronunciation *n* (*pl* **-s**) way in which a word or language is pronounced
pronunciations *n* ▷ **pronunciation**
pronto *adv* (*Informal*) at once
proof *n* (*pl* **-s**) evidence that shows that something is true or has happened ▶ *adj* able to withstand
proofread *v* (**-s, -ing, -read**) read and correct (printer's proofs) > **proofreader** *n* (*pl* **-s**)
proofreader *n* ▷ **proofread**
proofreaders *n* ▷ **proofread**
proofreading *v* ▷ **proofread**

proofreads *v* ▷ **proofread**
proofs *n* ▷ **proof**
prop[1] *v* (**-s, -pping, -pped**) support (something) so that it stays upright or in place ▶ *n* (*pl* **-s**) pole, beam, etc. used as a support
prop[2] *n* (*pl* **-s**) movable object used on the set of a film or play
prop[3] *n* (*pl* **-s**) (*Informal*) propeller
propaganda *n* (*pl* **-s**) (organized promotion of) information to assist or damage the cause of a government or movement > **propagandist** *n* (*pl* **-s**)
propagandas *n* ▷ **propaganda**
propagandist *n* ▷ **propaganda**
propagandists *n* ▷ **propaganda**
propagate *v* (**-tes, -ting, -ted**) spread (information and ideas) > **propagation** *n* (*pl* **-s**)
propagated *v* ▷ **propagate**
propagates *v* ▷ **propagate**
propagating *v* ▷ **propagate**
propagation *n* ▷ **propagate**
propagations *n* ▷ **propagate**
propane *n* (*pl* **-s**) flammable gas found in petroleum and used as a fuel
propanes *n* ▷ **propane**
propel *v* (**-s, -lling, -lled**) cause to move forward
propellant *n* (*pl* **-s**) something that provides or causes propulsion
propellants *n* ▷ **propellant**
propelled *v* ▷ **propel**
propeller *n* (*pl* **-s**) revolving shaft with blades for driving a ship or aircraft
propellers *n* ▷ **propeller**
propelling *v* ▷ **propel**
propels *v* ▷ **propel**
propped *v* ▷ **prop**[1]
propping *v* ▷ **prop**[1]
props *v, n* ▷ **prop**[1, 2, 3]
propulsion *n* (*pl* **-s**) method by which something is propelled
propulsions *n* ▷ **propulsion**
propensities *n* ▷ **propensity**
propensity *n* (*pl* **-ies**) natural tendency
proper *adj* (**-er, -est**) real or genuine > **properly** *adv*
properer *adj* ▷ **proper**
properest *adj* ▷ **proper**
properly *adv* ▷ **proper**
properties *n* ▷ **property**
property *n* (*pl* **-ties**) something owned
prophecies *n* ▷ **prophecy**
prophecy *n* (*pl* **-cies**) prediction
prophesied *v* ▷ **prophesy**
prophesies *v* ▷ **prophesy**
prophesy *v* (**-sies, -sying, -sied**) foretell
prophesying *v* ▷ **prophesy**
prophet *n* (*pl* **-s**) person supposedly chosen by God to spread His word > **prophetic** *adj* > **prophetically** *adv*
prophetic *adj* ▷ **prophet**
prophetically *adv* ▷ **prophet**
prophets *n* ▷ **prophet**
prophylactic *n* (*pl* **-s**) ▶ *adj* (drug) used to prevent disease
prophylactics *n* ▷ **prophylactic**
propitiate *v* (**-tes, -ting, -ted**) appease, win the favour of > **propitiation** *n*
propitiated *v* ▷ **propitiate**
propitiates *v* ▷ **propitiate**
propitiating *v* ▷ **propitiate**
propitiation *n* ▷ **propitiate**
propitiations *n* ▷ **propitiate**
propitious *adj* favourable or auspicious
proponent *n* (*pl* **-s**) person who argues in favour of something
proponents *n* ▷ **proponent**
proportion *n* (*pl* **-s**) relative size or extent ▶ *pl* dimensions or size ▶ *v* (**-s, -ing, -ed**) adjust in relative amount or size
proportional, proportionate *adj* being in proportion > **proportionally, proportionately** *adv*
proportionally *adv* ▷ **proportional**
proportionate *adj* ▷ **proportional**
proportionately *adv* ▷ **proportional**
proportioned *v* ▷ **proportion**
proportioning *v* ▷ **proportion**
proportions *n, v* ▷ **proportion**
propose *v* (**-ses, -sing, -sed**) put forward for consideration > **proposal** *n* (*pl* **-s**)
proposal *n* ▷ **propose**
proposals *n* ▷ **propose**
proposed *v* ▷ **propose**
proposes *v* ▷ **propose**
proposing *v* ▷ **propose**
proposition *n* (*pl* **-s**) offer ▶ *v* (**-s, -ing, -ed**) (*Informal*) ask (someone) to have sexual intercourse
propositioned *v* ▷ **proposition**
propositioning *v* ▷ **proposition**
propositions *n, v* ▷ **proposition**
propound *v* (**-s, -ing, -ed**) put forward for consideration
propounded *v* ▷ **propound**
propounding *v* ▷ **propound**
propounds *v* ▷ **propound**
proprietor *n* (*pl* **-s**) owner of a business establishment > **proprietress** *n fem* (*pl* **-es**)
proprietary *adj* made and distributed under

a trade name
proprieties *n* ▷ **propriety**
proprietors *n* ▷ **proprietor**
proprietress *n* ▷ **proprietor**
proprietresses *n* ▷ **proprietor**
propriety *n* (*pl* **-ties**) correct conduct
propulsion *n* ▷ **propel**
prorogue *v* (**-gues, -guing, -gued**) suspend (parliament) without dissolving it
> **prorogation** *n* (*pl* **-s**)
prorogation *n* ▷ **prorogue**
prorogations *n* ▷ **prorogue**
prorogued *v* ▷ **prorogue**
prorogues *v* ▷ **prorogue**
proroguing *v* ▷ **prorogue**
pros *n* ▷ **pro**
prosaic [pro-**zay**-ik] *adj* lacking imagination, dull > **prosaically** *adv*
prosaically *adv* ▷ **prosaic**
proscenia *n* ▷ **proscenium**
proscenium *n* (*pl* **-nia, -niums**) arch in a theatre separating the stage from the auditorium
prosceniums *n* ▷ **proscenium**
proscribe *v* (**-bes, -bing, -bed**) prohibit, outlaw > **proscription** *n* (*pl* **-s**) > **proscriptive** *adj*
proscribed *v* ▷ **proscribe**
proscribes *v* ▷ **proscribe**
proscribing *v* ▷ **proscribe**
proscription *n* ▷ **proscribe**
proscriptions *n* ▷ **proscribe**
proscriptive *adj* ▷ **proscribe**
prose *n* (*pl* **-s**) ordinary speech or writing in contrast to poetry
proses *n* ▷ **prose**
prosecute *v* (**-tes, -ting, -ted**) bring a criminal charge against > **prosecution** *n* (*pl* **-s**) > **prosecutor** *n* (*pl* **-s**)
prosecuted *v* ▷ **prosecute**
prosecutes *v* ▷ **prosecute**
prosecuting *v* ▷ **prosecute**
prosecution *n* ▷ **prosecute**
prosecutions *n* ▷ **prosecute**
prosecutor *n* ▷ **prosecute**
prosecutors *n* ▷ **prosecute**
proselyte [**pross**-ill-ite] *n* (*pl* **-s**) recent convert
proselytes *n* ▷ **proselyte**
proselytize [**pross**-ill-it-ize] *v* (**-zes, -zing, -zed**) attempt to convert
proselytized *v* ▷ **proselytize**
proselytized *v* ▷ **proselytize**
proselytizing *v* ▷ **proselytize**
prospect *n* (*pl* **-s**) something anticipated (*Old-fashioned*) ▶ *pl* probability of future success ▶ *v* (**-s, -ing, -ed**) explore, esp. for gold > **prospector** *n* (*pl* **-s**)
prospected *v* ▷ **prospect**
prospecting *v* ▷ **prospect**
prospective *adj* future
prospector *n* ▷ **prospect**
prospectors *n* ▷ **prospect**
prospects *n, v* ▷ **prospect**
prospectus *n* (*pl* **-es**) booklet giving details of a university, company, etc.
prospectuses *n* ▷ **prospectus**
prosper *v* (**-s, -ing, -ed**) be successful
> **prosperous** *adj*
prospered *v* ▷ **prosper**
prospering *v* ▷ **prosper**
prosperities *n* ▷ **prosperity**
prosperity *n* success and wealth
prosperous *adj* ▷ **prosper**
prospers *v* ▷ **prosper**
prostate *n* (*pl* **-s**) gland in male mammals that surrounds the neck of the bladder
prostates *n* ▷ **prostate**
prostheses *n* ▷ **prosthesis**
prosthesis [pross-**theess**-iss] *n* (*pl* **-ses**) [-seez] artificial body part, such as a limb or breast
> **prosthetic** *adj*
prosthetic *adj* ▷ **prosthesis**
prostitute *n* (*pl* **-s**) person who offers sexual intercourse in return for payment
▶ *v* (**-tes, -ting, -ted**) make a prostitute of
> **prostitution** *n* (*pl* **-s**)
prostituted *v* ▷ **prostitute**
prostitutes *n, v* ▷ **prostitute**
prostituting *v* ▷ **prostitute**
prostitution *n* ▷ **prostitute**
prostitutions *n* ▷ **prostitute**
prostrate *adj* lying face downwards ▶ *v* (**-tes, -ting, -ted**) lie face downwards > **prostration** *n* (*pl* **-s**)
prostrated *v* ▷ **prostrate**
prostrates *v* ▷ **prostrate**
prostrating *v* ▷ **prostrate**
prostration *n* ▷ **prostrate**
prostrations *n* ▷ **prostrate**
protagonist *n* (*pl* **-s**) supporter of a cause
protagonists *n* ▷ **protagonist**
protea [**pro**-tee-a] *n* (*pl* **-s**) African shrub with showy flowers
protean [pro-**tee**-an] *adj* constantly changing
proteas *n* ▷ **protea**
protect *v* (**-s, -ing, -ed**) defend from trouble, harm, or loss > **protection** *n* (*pl* **-s**)
protected *v* ▷ **protect**
protecting *v* ▷ **protect**
protection *n* ▷ **protect**
protectionism *n* policy of protecting

industries by taxing competing imports **> protectionist** *n* (*pl* **-s**) *adj*
protectionisms *n* ▷ **protectionism**
protectionist *n* ▷ **protectionism**
protectionists *n* ▷ **protectionism**
protections *n* ▷ **protect**
protective *adj* giving protection
protector *n* (*pl* **-s**) person or thing that protects
protectorate *n* (*pl* **-s**) territory largely controlled by a stronger state
protectorates *n* ▷ **protectorate**
protectors *n* ▷ **protector**
protects *v* ▷ **protect**
protégé, *fem* **protégée** [**pro**-ti-zhay] *n* (*pl* **-s**) person who is protected and helped by another
protégés *n* ▷ **protégé**
protein *n* (*pl* **-s**) any of a group of complex organic compounds that are essential for life
proteins *n* ▷ **protein**
protest *n* (*pl* **-s**) declaration or demonstration of objection ▶ *v* (**-s, -ing, -ed**) object, disagree
protestant *n* (*pl* **-s**) one who protests
protestants *n* ▷ **protestant**
protestation *n* (*pl* **-s**) strong declaration
protestations *n* ▷ **protestation**
protested *v* ▷ **protest**
protesting *v* ▷ **protest**
protests *n, v* ▷ **protest**
protocol *n* (*pl* **-s**) rules of behaviour for formal occasions
protocols *n* ▷ **protocol**
proton *n* (*pl* **-s**) positively charged particle in the nucleus of an atom
protons *n* ▷ **proton**
protoplasm *n* (*pl* **-s**) substance forming the living contents of a cell
protoplasms *n* ▷ **protoplasm**
prototype *n* (*pl* **-s**) original or model to be copied or developed
prototypes *n* ▷ **prototype**
protozoa *n* ▷ **protozoan**
protozoan [pro-toe-**zoe**-an] *n* (*pl* **-zoa**) microscopic one-celled creature
protracted *adj* lengthened or extended
protractor *n* (*pl* **-s**) instrument for measuring angles
protractors *n* ▷ **protractor**
protrude *v* (**-des, -ding, -ded**) stick out, project **> protrusion** *n* (*pl* **-s**)
protruded *v* ▷ **protrude**
protrudes *v* ▷ **protrude**
protruding *v* ▷ **protrude**
protrusion *n* ▷ **protrude**
protrusions *n* ▷ **protrude**
protuberance *n* ▷ **protuberant**
protuberances *n* ▷ **protuberant**
protuberant *adj* swelling out, bulging **> protuberance** *n* (*pl* **-s**)
proud *adj* (**-er, -est**) feeling pleasure and satisfaction **> proudly** *adv*
prouder *adj* ▷ **proud**
proudest *adj* ▷ **proud**
proudly *adv* ▷ **proud**
prove *v* (**-ves, -ving, -ved** *or* **-ven**) establish the validity of
proved *v* ▷ **prove**
proven *adj* known from experience to work ▶ *v* ▷ **prove**
provenance [**prov**-in-anss] *n* (*pl* **-s**) place of origin
provenances *n* ▷ **provenance**
provender *n* (*pl* **-s**) (*Old-fashioned*) fodder
provenders *n* ▷ **provender**
proverb *n* (*pl* **-s**) short saying that expresses a truth or gives a warning **> proverbial** *adj*
proverbial *adj* ▷ **proverb**
proverbs *n* ▷ **proverb**
proves *v* ▷ **prove**
provide *v* (**-des, -ding, -ded**) make available **> provider** *n* (*pl* **-s**)
provided *v* ▷ **provide**
providence *n* (*pl* **-s**) God or nature seen as a protective force that arranges people's lives
providences *n* ▷ **providence**
provident *adj* thrifty
providential *adj* lucky
provider *n* ▷ **provide**
providers *n* ▷ **provide**
provides *v* ▷ **provide**
providing *v* ▷ **provide**
province *n* (*pl* **-s**) area governed as a unit of a country or empire ▶ *pl* parts of a country outside the capital
provincial *adj* of a province or the provinces ▶ *n* (*pl* **-s**) unsophisticated person
provincialism *n* (*pl* **-s**) narrow-mindedness and lack of sophistication
provincialisms *n* ▷ **provincialism**
provincials *n* ▷ **provincial**
provinces *n* ▷ **province**
proving *v* ▷ **prove**
provision *n* (*pl* **-s**) act of supplying something ▶ *pl* food ▶ *v* (**-s, -ing, -ed**) supply with food
provisional *adj* temporary or conditional **> provisionally** *adv*
provisionally *adv* ▷ **provisional**
provisioned *v* ▷ **provision**
provisioning *v* ▷ **provision**

provisions *n, v* ▷ **provision**
proviso [pro-**vize**-oh] *n* (*pl* **-sos, -soes**) condition, stipulation
provisoes *n* ▷ **proviso**
provisos *n* ▷ **proviso**
provocation *n* ▷ **provoke**
provocations *n* ▷ **provoke**
provocative *adj* ▷ **provoke**
provoke *v* (**-kes, -king, -ked**) deliberately anger > **provocation** *n* (*pl* **-s**) > **provocative** *adj*
provoked *v* ▷ **provoke**
provokes *v* ▷ **provoke**
provoking *v* ▷ **provoke**
provost *n* (*pl* **-s**) head of certain university colleges in Britain
provosts *n* ▷ **provost**
prow *n* (*pl* **-s**) bow of a vessel
prows *n* ▷ **prow**
prowess *n* (*pl* **-es**) superior skill or ability
prowesses *n* ▷ **prowess**
prowl *v* (**-s, -ing, -ed**) move stealthily around a place as if in search of prey or plunder ▶ *n* (*pl* **-s**) prowling
prowled *v* ▷ **prowl**
prowler *n* (*pl* **-s**) person who moves stealthily around a place as if in search of prey or plunder
prowlers *n* ▷ **prowler**
prowling *v* ▷ **prowl**
prowls *v, n* ▷ **prowl**
proxies *n* ▷ **proxy**
proximate *n* ▷ **proximity**
proximities *n* ▷ **proximity**
proximity *n* (*pl* **-ties**) nearness in space or time > **proximate** *adj*
proxy *n* (*pl* **-xies**) person authorized to act on behalf of someone else
prude *n* (*pl* **-s**) person who is excessively modest, prim, or proper > **prudish** *adj* > **prudery** *n* (*pl* **-ries**)
prudence *n* ▷ **prudent**
prudences *n* ▷ **prudent**
prudent *adj* cautious, discreet, and sensible > **prudence** *n* (*pl* **-s**)
prudential *adj* (*Old-fashioned*) prudent
prudes *n* ▷ **prude**
pruderies *n* ▷ **prude**
prudery *n* ▷ **prude**
prudish *adj* ▷ **prude**
prune[1] *n* (*pl* **-s**) dried plum
prune[2] *v* (**-nes, -ning, -ned**) cut off dead parts or excessive branches from (a tree or plant)
pruned *v* ▷ **prune**
prunes *n, v* ▷ **prune**[1, 2]
pruning *v* ▷ **prune**
prurience *n* ▷ **prurient**
pruriences *n* ▷ **prurient**
prurient *adj* excessively interested in sexual matters > **prurience** *n* (*pl* **-s**)
pry *v* (**prys, prying, pried**) make an impertinent or uninvited inquiry into a private matter
prying *v* ▷ **pry**
psalm *n* (*pl* **-s**) sacred song
psalmist *n* (*pl* **-s**) writer of psalms
psalmists *n* ▷ **psalmist**
psalms *n* ▷ **psalm**
psalter *n* (*pl* **-s**) book containing (a version of) psalms from the Bible
psalteries *n* ▷ **psalter**
psaltery *n* (*pl* **-ries**) ancient instrument played by plucking strings
psalters *n* ▷ **psalter**
psephologies *n* ▷ **psephology**
psephology [sef-**fol**-a-jee] *n* (*pl* **-gies**) statistical study of elections
pseud *n* (*pl* **-s**) (*Informal*) pretentious person
pseuds *n* ▷ **pseud**
pseudonym *n* (*pl* **-s**) fictitious name adopted esp. by an author > **pseudonymous** *adj*
pseudonymous *adj* ▷ **pseudonym**
pseudonyms *n* ▷ **pseudonym**

> **psi** *n* (**psis**). Psi is the 23rd letter of the Greek alphabet. This word can be useful if you have a difficult rack, especially if you can form another word at the same time. Psi scores 5 points.

psittacosis *n* (*pl* **-ses**) disease of parrots that can be transmitted to humans
psittacoses *n* ▷ **psittacosis**

> **pst** *interj*. Pst is a sound people make when they want to draw someone's attention to something without making too much noise. This is a useful word to remember because it doesn't use any vowels, and so can be useful if you have no vowels on your rack. Pst scores 5 points.

psyche [**sye**-kee] *n* (*pl* **-s**) human mind or soul
psychedelic *adj* denoting a drug that causes hallucinations
psyche *n* ▷ **psyche**
psychiatric *adj* ▷ **psychiatry**
psychiatries *n* ▷ **psychiatry**
psychiatrist *n* ▷ **psychiatry**
psychiatrists *n* ▷ **psychiatry**
psychiatry *n* (*pl* **-ries**) branch of medicine concerned with mental disorders > **psychiatric** *adj* > **psychiatrist** *n*

psychic *adj* (*also* **psychical**) having mental powers which cannot be explained by natural laws ▶ *n* (*pl* **-s**) person with psychic powers
psychics *n* ▷ **psychic**
psycho *n* (*pl* **-s**) (*Informal*) psychopath
psychoanalyse *v* ▷ **psychoanalysis**
psychoanalysed *v* ▷ **psychoanalysis**
psychoanalyses *n, v* ▷ **psychoanalysis**
psychoanalysing *v* ▷ **psychoanalysis**
psychoanalysis *n* (*pl* **-ses**) method of treating mental and emotional disorders by discussion and analysis of one's thoughts and feelings > **psychoanalyse** *v* (**-ses, -sing, -sed**) > **psychoanalyst** *n* (*pl* **-s**)
psychoanalyst *n* ▷ **psychoanalysis**
psychoanalysts *n* ▷ **psychoanalysis**
psychological *adj* of or affecting the mind > **psychologically** *adv*
psychologically *adv* ▷ **psychological**
psychologies *n* ▷ **psychology**
psychologist *n* ▷ **psychology**
psychologists *n* ▷ **psychology**
psychology *n* (*pl* **-gies**) study of human and animal behaviour > **psychologist** *n* (*pl* **-s**)
psychopath *n* (*pl* **-s**) person afflicted with a personality disorder causing him or her to commit antisocial or violent acts > **psychopathic** *adj*
psychopathic *adj* ▷ **psychopath**
psychopaths *n* ▷ **psychopath**
psychos *n* ▷ **psycho**
psychoses *n* ▷ **psychosis**
psychosis *n* (*pl* **-ses**) severe mental disorder in which the sufferer's contact with reality becomes distorted > **psychotic** *adj*
psychosomatic *adj* (of a physical disorder) thought to have psychological causes
psychotherapeutic *adj* ▷ **psychotherapy**
psychotherapies *n* ▷ **psychotherapy**
psychotherapist *n* ▷ **psychotherapy**
psychotherapists *n* ▷ **psychotherapy**
psychotherapy *n* (*pl* **-pies**) treatment of nervous disorders by psychological methods > **psychotherapeutic** *adj* > **psychotherapist** *n*
psychotic *adj* ▷ **psychosis**
ptarmigan [**tar**-mig-an] *n* (*pl* **-s**) bird of the grouse family which turns white in winter
ptarmigans *n* ▷ **ptarmigan**
pterodactyl [terr-roe-**dak**-til] *n* (*pl* **-s**) extinct flying reptile with batlike wings
pterodactyls *n* ▷ **pterodactyl**
ptomaine [**toe**-main] *n* (*pl* **-s**) any of a group of poisonous alkaloids found in decaying matter
ptomaines *n* ▷ **ptomaine**
pub *n* (*pl* **-s**) building with a bar licensed to sell alcoholic drinks
pubertal *adj* ▷ **puberty**
puberties *n* ▷ **puberty**
puberty *n* (*pl* **-ties**) beginning of sexual maturity > **pubertal** *adj*
pubic *adj* of the lower abdomen
public *adj* of or concerning the people as a whole ▶ *n* (*pl* **-s**) the community, people in general > **publicly** *adv*
publican *n* (*pl* **-s**) (BRIT, AUST & NZ) person who owns or runs a pub
publicans *n* ▷ **publican**
publication *n* ▷ **publish**
publications *n* ▷ **publish**
publicist *n* (*pl* **-s**) person, esp. a press agent or journalist, who publicizes something
publicists *n* ▷ **publicist**
publicities *n* ▷ **publicity**
publicity *n* (*pl* **-ties**) process or information used to arouse public attention
publicize *v* (**-zes, -zing, -zed**) bring to public attention
publicized *v* ▷ **publicize**
publicizes *v* ▷ **publicize**
publicizing *v* ▷ **publicize**
publicly *adv* ▷ **public**
publics *n* ▷ **public**
publish *v* (**-es, -ing, -ed**) produce and issue (printed matter) for sale > **publication** *n* (*pl* **-s**) > **publisher** *n* (*pl* **-s**)
published *v* ▷ **publish**
publisher *n* ▷ **publish**
publishers *n* ▷ **publish**
publishes *v* ▷ **publish**
publishing *v* ▷ **publish**
pubs *n* ▷ **pub**
puce *adj* (**pucer, pucest**) purplish-brown
pucer *adj* ▷ **puce**
pucest *adj* ▷ **puce**
puck[1] *n* (*pl* **-s**) small rubber disc used in ice hockey
puck[2] *n* (*pl* **-s**) mischievous or evil spirit > **puckish** *adj*
pucker *v* (**-s, -ing, -ed**) gather into wrinkles ▶ *n* (*pl* **-s**) wrinkle or crease
puckered *v* ▷ **pucker**
puckering *v* ▷ **pucker**
puckers *v, n* ▷ **pucker**
puckish *adj* ▷ **puck**[2]
pucks *n* ▷ **puck**[1, 2]
pudding *n* (*pl* **-s**) dessert, esp. a cooked one served hot
puddings *n* ▷ **pudding**
puddle *n* (*pl* **-s**) small pool of water, esp. of rain

puddles *n* ▷ **puddle**
puerile *adj* silly and childish
puerperal [pew-**er**-per-al] *adj* concerning the period following childbirth
puff *n* (*pl* **-s**) (sound of) a short blast of breath, wind, etc. ▶ *v* (**-s, -ing, -ed**) blow or breathe in short quick draughts > **puffy** *adj* (**-ffier, -ffiest**)
puffball *n* (*pl* **-s**) ball-shaped fungus
puffballs *n* ▷ **puffball**
puffed *v* ▷ **puff**
puffier *adj* ▷ **puff**
puffiest *adj* ▷ **puff**
puffin *n* (*pl* **-s**) black-and-white sea bird with a brightly-coloured beak
puffins *n* ▷ **puffin**
puffing *v* ▷ **puff**
puffs *n, v* ▷ **puff**
puffy *adj* ▷ **puff**
pug *n* (*pl* **-s**) small snub-nosed dog
pugs *n* ▷ **pug**
pugilist [**pew**-jil-ist] *n* (*pl* **-s**) boxer > **pugilism** *n* (*pl* **-s**) > **pugilistic** *adj*
pugilism *n* ▷ **pugilist**
pugilisms *n* ▷ **pugilist**
pugilistic *adj* ▷ **pugilist**
pugilists *n* ▷ **pugilist**
pugnacious *adj* ready and eager to fight > **pugnacity** *n* (*pl* **-ties**)
pugnacities *n* ▷ **pugnacious**
pugnacity *n* ▷ **pugnacious**
puissance [**pwee**-sonce] *n* (*pl* **-s**) showjumping competition that tests a horse's ability to jump large obstacles
puissances *n* ▷ **puissance**
puke (*Slang*) *v* (**-kes, -king, -ked**) vomit ▶ *n* (*pl* **-s**) act of vomiting
puked *v* ▷ **puke**
pukes *v, n* ▷ **puke**
puking *v* ▷ **puke**
pulchritude *n* (*pl* **-s**) (*Lit*) beauty
pulchritudes *n* ▷ **pulchritude**
pull *v* (**-s, -ing, -ed**) exert force on (an object) to move it towards the source of the force ▶ *n* (*pl* **-s**) act of pulling
pulled *v* ▷ **pull**
pullet *n* (*pl* **-s**) young hen
pullets *n* ▷ **pullet**
pulley *n* (*pl* **-s**) wheel with a grooved rim in which a belt, chain, or piece of rope runs in order to lift weights by a downward pull
pulleys *n* ▷ **pulley**
pulling *v* ▷ **pull**
pullover *n* (*pl* **-s**) sweater that is pulled on over the head
pullovers *n* ▷ **pullover**
pulls *v, n* ▷ **pull**
pulmonary *adj* of the lungs
pulp *n* (*pl* **-s**) soft wet substance made from crushed or beaten matter ▶ *v* (**-s, -ing, -ed**) reduce to pulp
pulped *v* ▷ **pulp**
pulping *v* ▷ **pulp**
pulpit *n* (*pl* **-s**) raised platform for a preacher
pulpits *n* ▷ **pulpit**
pulps *n, v* ▷ **pulp**
pulsar *n* (*pl* **-s**) small dense star which emits regular bursts of radio waves
pulsars *n* ▷ **pulsar**
pulsate *v* ▷ **pulse**[1]
pulsated *v* ▷ **pulse**[1]
pulsates *v* ▷ **pulse**[1]
pulsating *v* ▷ **pulse**[1]
pulsation *n* ▷ **pulse**[1]
pulsations *n* ▷ **pulse**[1]
pulse[1] *n* (*pl* **-s**) regular beating of blood through the arteries at each heartbeat > **pulsate** *v* (**-s, -ing, -ed**) throb, quiver > **pulsation** *n* (*pl* **-s**)
pulse[2] *n* (**-s**) edible seed of a pod-bearing plant such as a bean or pea
pulses *n* ▷ **pulse**[1, 2]
pulverize *v* (**-zes, -zing, -zed**) reduce to fine pieces
pulverized *v* ▷ **pulverize**
pulverizes *v* ▷ **pulverize**
pulverizing *v* ▷ **pulverize**
puma *n* (*pl* **-s**) large American wild cat with a greyish-brown coat
pumas *n* ▷ **puma**
pumice [**pumm**-iss] *n* (*pl* **-s**) light porous stone used for scouring
pumices *n* ▷ **pumice**
pummel *v* (**-s, -lling, -lled**) strike repeatedly with or as if with the fists
pummelled *v* ▷ **pummel**
pummelling *v* ▷ **pummel**
pummels *v* ▷ **pummel**
pump[1] *n* (*pl* **-s**) machine used to force a liquid or gas to move in a particular direction ▶ *v* (**-s, -ing, -ed**) raise or drive with a pump
pump[2] *n* (*pl* **-s**) light flat-soled shoe
pumped *v* ▷ **pump**
pumping *v* ▷ **pump**
pumpkin *n* (*pl* **-s**) large round fruit with an orange rind, soft flesh, and many seeds
pumpkins *n* ▷ **pumpkin**
pumps *n, v* ▷ **pump**[1, 2]
pun *n* (*pl* **-s**) use of words to exploit double meanings for humorous effect ▶ *v* (**-s, -nning, -nned**) make puns

punch[1] *v* (**-es, -ing, -ed**) strike at with a clenched fist ▶ *n* (*pl* **-es**) blow with a clenched fist (*Informal*)
punch[2] *n* (*pl* **-es**) tool or machine for shaping, piercing, or engraving ▶ *v* (**-es, -ing, -ed**) pierce, cut, stamp, shape, or drive with a punch
punch[3] *n* (*pl* **-es**) drink made from a mixture of wine, spirits, fruit, sugar, and spices
punched *v* ▷ **punch**[1, 2]
punches *v, n* ▷ **punch**
punchier *adj* ▷ **punchy**
punchiest *adj* ▷ **punchy**
punching *v* ▷ **punch**[1, 2]
punchy *adj* (**-chier, -chiest**) forceful
punctilious *adj* paying great attention to correctness in etiquette
punctual *adj* arriving or taking place at the correct time > **punctuality** *n* (*pl* **-ties**) > **punctually** *adv*
punctualities *n* ▷ **punctual**
punctuality *n* ▷ **punctual**
punctually *adv* ▷ **punctual**
punctuate *v* (**-tes, -ting, -ted**) put punctuation marks in
punctuated *v* ▷ **punctuate**
punctuates *v* ▷ **punctuate**
punctuating *v* ▷ **punctuate**
punctuation *n* (*pl* **-s**) (use of) marks such as commas, colons, etc. in writing, to assist in making the sense clear
punctuations *n* ▷ **punctuation**
puncture *n* (*pl* **-s**) small hole made by a sharp object, esp. in a tyre ▶ *v* (**-res, -ring, -red**) pierce a hole in
punctured *v* ▷ **puncture**
punctures *n, v* ▷ **puncture**
puncturing *v* ▷ **puncture**
pundit *n* (*pl* **-s**) expert who speaks publicly on a subject
pundits *n* ▷ **pundit**
pungencies *n* ▷ **pungent**
pungency *n* ▷ **pungent**
pungent *adj* having a strong sharp bitter flavour > **pungency** *n* (*pl* **-cies**)
punier *adj* ▷ **puny**
puniest *adj* ▷ **puny**
punish *v* (**-es, -ing, -ed**) cause (someone) to suffer or undergo a penalty for some wrongdoing > **punishment** *n* (*pl* **-s**)
punished *v* ▷ **punish**
punishes *v* ▷ **punish**
punishing *adj* harsh or difficult ▶ *v* ▷ **punish**
punishment *n* ▷ **punish**
punishments *n* ▷ **punish**
punitive [**pew**-nit-tiv] *adj* relating to punishment
punk *n* (*pl* **-s**) anti-Establishment youth movement and style of rock music of the late 1970s
punks *n* ▷ **punk**
punned *v* ▷ **pun**
punnet *n* (*pl* **-s**) small basket for fruit
punnets *n* ▷ **punnet**
punning *v* ▷ **pun**
puns *n, v* ▷ **pun**
punt[1] *n* (*pl* **-s**) open flat-bottomed boat propelled by a pole ▶ *v* (**-s, -ing, -ed**) travel in a punt
punt[2] (SPORT) *n* (*pl* **-s**) kick of a ball before it touches the ground when dropped from the hands ▶ *v* (**-s, -ing, -ed**) kick (a ball) in this way
punt[3] *n* (*pl* **-s**) former monetary unit of the Irish Republic
punted *v* ▷ **punt**
punter *n* (*pl* **-s**) person who bets
punters *n* ▷ **punter**
punting *v* ▷ **punt**
punts *n, v* ▷ **punt**[1, 2, 3]
puny *adj* (**-nier, -niest**) small and feeble
pup *n* (*pl* **-s**) young of certain animals, such as dogs and seals
pupa *n* (*pl* **-pae, -pas**) insect at the stage of development between a larva and an adult
pupae *n* ▷ **pupa**
pupas *n* ▷ **pupa**
pupil[1] *n* (*pl* **-s**) person who is taught by a teacher
pupil[2] *n* (*pl* **-s**) round dark opening in the centre of the eye
pupils *n* ▷ **pupil**[1, 2]
puppet *n* (*pl* **-s**) small doll or figure moved by strings or by the operator's hand > **puppeteer** *n* (*pl* **-s**)
puppeteer *n* ▷ **puppet**
puppeteers *n* ▷ **puppet**
puppets *n* ▷ **puppet**
puppies *n* ▷ **puppy**
puppy *n* (*pl* **-ppies**) young dog
pups *n* ▷ **pup**
purchase *v* (**-ses, -sing, -sed**) obtain by payment ▶ *n* (*pl* **-s**) thing that is bought > **purchaser** *n* (*pl* **-s**)
purchased *v* ▷ **purchase**
purchaser *n* ▷ **purchase**
purchasers *n* ▷ **purchase**
purchases *v, n* ▷ **purchase**
purchasing *v* ▷ **purchase**
purdah *n* (*pl* **-s**) Muslim and Hindu custom of keeping women in seclusion, with clothing

that conceals them completely when they go out

purdahs *n* ▷ **purdah**

pure *adj* (**-r, -st**) unmixed, untainted > **purely** *adv* > **purity** *n* (*pl* **-ies**)

purely *adv* ▷ **pure**

purée [**pure**-ray] *n* (*pl* **-s**) pulp of cooked food ▶ *v* (**-s, -réeing, -réed**) make into a purée

puréed *v* ▷ **purée**

puréeing *v* ▷ **purée**

purées *n, v* ▷ **purée**

purer *adj* ▷ **pure**

purest *adj* ▷ **pure**

purgatorial *adj* ▷ **purgatory**

purgatories *n* ▷ **purgatory**

purgatory *n* (*pl* **-ries**) place or state of temporary suffering > **purgatorial** *adj*

purge *v* (**-ges, -ging, -ged**) rid (a thing or place) of (unwanted things or people) ▶ *n* (*pl* **-s**) purging

purgative *n, adj* (medicine) designed to cause defecation

purgatives *n* ▷ **purgative**

purged *v* ▷ **purge**

purges *v, n* ▷ **purge**

purging *v* ▷ **purge**

purification *n* ▷ **purify**

purifications *n* ▷ **purify**

purified *v* ▷ **purify**

purifies *v* ▷ **purify**

purify *v* (**-fies, -fying, -fied**) make or become pure > **purification** *n* (*pl* **-s**)

purifying *v* ▷ **purify**

purist *n* (*pl* **-s**) person concerned with strict obedience to the traditions of a subject

purists *n* ▷ **purist**

puritan *n* (*pl* **-s**) person with strict moral and religious principles > **puritanical** *adj* > **puritanism** *n* (*pl* **-s**)

puritanical *adj* ▷ **puritan**

puritanism *n* ▷ **puritan**

puritanisms *n* ▷ **puritan**

puritans *n* ▷ **puritan**

purities *n* ▷ **pure**

purity *n* ▷ **pure**

purl *n* (*pl* **-s**) stitch made by knitting a plain stitch backwards ▶ *v* (**-s, -ing, -ed**) knit in purl

purled *v* ▷ **purl**

purlieus [**per**-lyooz] *pl n* (*Lit*) outskirts

purling *v* ▷ **purl**

purloin *v* (**-s, -ing, -ed**) steal

purloined *v* ▷ **purloin**

purloining *v* ▷ **purloin**

purloins *v* ▷ **purloin**

purls *n, v* ▷ **purl**

purple *adj, n* (*pl* **-s**) (of) a colour between red and blue

purples *n* ▷ **purple**

purport *v* (**-s, -ing, -ed**) claim (to be or do something) ▶ *n* (*pl* **-s**) apparent meaning, significance

purported *v* ▷ **purport**

purporting *v* ▷ **purport**

purports *v, n* ▷ **purport**

purpose *n* (*pl* **-s**) reason for which something is done or exists

purposely *adv* intentionally

purposes *n* ▷ **purpose**

purr *v* (**-s, -ing, -ed**) (of cats) make low vibrant sound, usu. when pleased ▶ *n* (*pl* **-s**) this sound

purred *v* ▷ **purr**

purring *v* ▷ **purr**

purrs *v, n* ▷ **purr**

purse *n* (*pl* **-s**) small bag for money (US & NZ) ▶ *v* (**-ses, -sing, -sed**) draw (one's lips) together into a small round shape

pursed *v* ▷ **purse**

purser *n* (*pl* **-s**) ship's officer who keeps the accounts

pursers *n* ▷ **purser**

purses *n, v* ▷ **purse**

pursing *v* ▷ **purse**

pursue *v* (**-sues, -suing, -sued**) chase > **pursuer** *n* (*pl* **-s**)

pursued *v* ▷ **pursue**

pursuer *n* ▷ **pursue**

pursuers *n* ▷ **pursue**

pursues *v* ▷ **pursue**

pursuing *v* ▷ **pursue**

pursuit *n* (*pl* **-s**) pursuing

pursuits *n* ▷ **pursuit**

purulent [**pure**-yoo-lent] *adj* of or containing pus

purvey *v* (**-s, -ing, -ed**) supply (provisions) > **purveyor** *n* (*pl* **-s**)

purveyed *v* ▷ **purvey**

purveying *v* ▷ **purvey**

purveyor *n* ▷ **purvey**

purveyors *n* ▷ **purvey**

purveys *v* ▷ **purvey**

purview *n* (*pl* **-s**) scope or range of activity or outlook

purviews *n* ▷ **purview**

pus *n* (*pl* **-es**) yellowish matter produced by infected tissue

puses *n* ▷ **pus**

push *v* (**-es, -ing, -ed**) move or try to move by steady force (*Informal*) ▶ *n* (*pl* **-es**) act of pushing

pushed *v* ▷ **push**
pusher *n* (*pl* **-s**) person who sells illegal drugs
pushers *n* ▷ **pusher**
pushes *v, n* ▷ **push**
pushier *adj* ▷ **pushy**
pushiest *adj* ▷ **pushy**
pushing *v* ▷ **push**
pushy *adj* (**-shier, -shiest**) too assertive or ambitious
pushchair *n* (*pl* **-s**) (BRIT) folding chair on wheels for a baby
pushchairs *n* ▷ **pushchair**
pusillanimous *adj* timid and cowardly > **pusillanimity** *n* (*pl* **-ies**)
pusillanimities *n* ▷ **pusillanimous**
pusillanimity *n* ▷ **pusillanimous**
puss, pussy *n* (*pl* **-es, -ies**) (*Informal*) cat
pusses *n* ▷ **puss**
pussies *n* ▷ **puss**
pussyfoot *v* (**-s, -ing, -ed**) (*Informal*) behave too cautiously
pussyfooted *v* ▷ **pussyfoot**
pussyfooting *v* ▷ **pussyfoot**
pussyfoots *v* ▷ **pussyfoot**
pustule *n* (*pl* **-s**) pimple containing pus
pustules *n* ▷ **pustule**
put *v* (**puts, putting, put**) cause to be (in a position, state, or place) ▶ *n* (*pl* **-s**) throw in putting the shot
putative *adj* reputed, supposed
putrefied *v* ▷ **putrify**
putrefies *v* ▷ **putrify**
putrefy *v* (**-fies, -fying, -fied**) rot and produce an offensive smell > **putrefaction** *n* (*pl* **-s**)
putrefaction *n* ▷ **putrefy**
putrefactions *n* ▷ **putrefy**
putrefying *v* ▷ **putrefy**
putrescent *adj* rotting
putrid *adj* rotten and foul-smelling
puts *v, n* ▷ **put**
putsch *n* (*pl* **-es**) sudden violent attempt to remove a government from power
putsches *n* ▷ **putsch**
putt (GOLF) *n* (*pl* **-s**) stroke on the putting green to roll the ball into or near the hole ▶ *v* (**-s, -ing, -ed**) strike (the ball) in this way
putted *n, v* ▷ **putt**
putter *n* (*pl* **-s**) golf club for putting
putters *n* ▷ **putter**
putties *n* ▷ **putty**
putting *v* ▷ **put putt**
putts *v, n* ▷ **putt**
putty *n* (*pl* **-ies**) adhesive used to fix glass into frames and fill cracks in woodwork
puzzle *v* (**-les, -ling, -led**) perplex and confuse or be perplexed or confused ▶ *n* (*pl* **-s**) problem that cannot be easily solved > **puzzlement** *n* (*pl* **-s**) > **puzzling** *adj*
puzzled *v* ▷ **puzzle**
puzzlement *n* ▷ **puzzle**
puzzlements *n* ▷ **puzzle**
puzzles *v, n* ▷ **puzzle**
puzzling *v, adj* ▷ **puzzle**
pygmies *n* ▷ **pygmy**
pygmy *n* (*pl* **-ies**) something that is a very small example of its type ▶ *adj* (**p-**) very small
pyjamas *pl n* loose-fitting trousers and top worn in bed
pylon *n* (*pl* **-s**) steel tower-like structure supporting electrical cables
pylons *n* ▷ **pylon**
pyramid *n* (*pl* **-s**) solid figure with a flat base and triangular sides sloping upwards to a point > **pyramidal** *adj*
pyramidal *adj* ▷ **pyramid**
pyramids *n* ▷ **pyramid**
pyre *n* (*pl* **-s**) pile of wood for burning a corpse on
pyres *n* ▷ **pyre**
pyromania *n* (*pl* **-s**) uncontrollable urge to set things on fire > **pyromaniac** *n* (*pl* **-s**)
pyromanias *n* ▷ **pyromania**
pyromaniac *n* ▷ **pyromania**
pyromaniacs *n* ▷ **pyromania**
pyrotechnics *n* art of making fireworks > **pyrotechnic** *adj*
pyrotechnic *adj* ▷ **pyrotechnics**
python *n* (*pl* **-s**) large nonpoisonous snake that crushes its prey
pythons *n* ▷ **python**

> **pyx** *n* (**pyxes**). A **pyx** is a container used for testing the weight of coins. This word can also be spelt **pix.** It's a great word to know as it earns a good score and doesn't use any vowels very helpful if you have a difficult rack. Pyx scores 15 points.

Qq

With a value of 10 points, Q is one of the best tiles to have on your rack. It can, however, be a difficult letter to use, especially if you don't have a U to play it with. It's therefore a good idea to remember the short words beginning with Q that don't need a U. This is easy, as there's only one two-letter word starting with Q: **qi** (11 points). There are three three-letter words, only one of which needs a U: **qua** (12). The other two are **qat** and **qis** (12 each). If you do have a U, remember **quiz** (22), which is a very useful word. If you have a blank tile for the second Z, you may be able to form its plural or verb inflections: **quizzes** (24), **quizzed** (25) and **quizzing** (26). This is especially worth remembering in case someone else plays quiz. Don't forget **quartz** (24) either.

qat *n* (**qats**). Qat is a shrub that grows in Africa and Arabia. This is a great word as it combines Q with two of the most common letters in the game, and thus is very handy if there isn't a U on your rack or the board. Qat scores 12 points.

qi *n* (**qis**). In Chinese medicine, qi is vital energy believed to circulate in the body. This is an exceptionally useful word, as it's the only two-letter word containing Q, and doesn't contain a U. The plural is one of only three three-letter words that begin with Q. As I is one of the more common tiles on the board, it's highly likely that you will be able to play qi if you have a Q. Qi scores 11 points.

qua *prep*. Qua means in the capacity of. This is the only three-letter word beginning with Q that needs a U, and is useful when you have a U, or there is a U on the board, but don't have any promising tiles to go with it. Qua scores 12 points.

quack[1] *v* (**-s, -ing, -ed**) (of a duck) utter a harsh guttural sound ▶ *n* (*pl* **-s**) sound made by a duck

quack[2] *n* (*pl* **-s**) unqualified person who claims medical knowledge

quacked *v* ▷ **quack**[1]

quacking *v* ▷ **quack**[1]

quacks *v* ▷ **quack**[1] ▶ *n* ▷ **quack**[1, 2]

quad *n* (*pl* **-s**) ▷ **quadrangle** ▶ *adj* ▷ **quadraphonic**

quadrangle *n* (*pl* **-s**) (*also* **quad**) rectangular courtyard with buildings on all four sides > **quadrangular** *adj*

quadrangles *n* ▷ **quadrangle**

quadrangular *adj* ▷ **quadrangle**

quadrant *n* (*pl* **-s**) quarter of a circle

quadrants *n* ▷ **quadrant**

quadraphonic *adj* (*also* **quad**) using four independent channels to reproduce or record sound

quadratic (MATHS) *n* (*pl* **-s**) equation in which the variable is raised to the power of two, but nowhere raised to a higher power ▶ *adj* of the second power

quadratics *n* ▷ **quadratic**

quadrennial *adj* occurring every four years

quadrilateral *adj* having four sides ▶ *n* (*pl* **-s**) polygon with four sides

quadrilaterals *n* ▷ **quadrilateral**

quadrille *n* (*pl* **-s**) square dance for four couples

quadrilles *n* ▷ **quadrille**

quadriplegia *n* (*pl* **-s**) paralysis of all four limbs

quadriplegias *n* ▷ **quadriplegia**

quadruped [**kwod**-roo-ped] *n* (*pl* **-s**) any animal with four legs

quadrupeds *n* ▷ **quadruped**

quadruple *v* (**-les, -ling, -led**) multiply by four ▶ *adj* four times as much or as many

quadrupled *v* ▷ **quadruple**

quadruples *v* ▷ **quadruple**

quadruplet *n* (*pl* **-s**) one of four offspring born

at one birth
quadruplets *n* ▷ **quadruplet**
quadrupling *v* ▷ **quadruple**
quads *n* ▷ **quad**
quaff [**kwoff**] *v* (**-s, -ing, -ed**) drink heartily or in one draught
quaffed *v* ▷ **quaff**
quaffing *v* ▷ **quaff**
quaffs *v* ▷ **quaff**
quagmire [**kwog**-mire] *n* (*pl* **-s**) soft wet area of land
quagmires *n* ▷ **quagmire**
quail[1] *n* (*pl* **-s**) small game bird of the partridge family
quail[2] *v* (**-s, -ing, -ed**) shrink back with fear
quailed *v* ▷ **quail**
quailing *v* ▷ **quail**
quails *n* ▷ **quail**[1] ▶ *v* ▷ **quail**[2]
quaint *adj* (**-er, -est**) attractively unusual, esp. in an old-fashioned style > **quaintly** *adv*
quainter *adj* ▷ **quaint**
quaintest *adj* ▷ **quaint**
quaintly *adv* ▷ **quaint**
quake *v* (**-kes, -king, -ked**) shake or tremble with or as if with fear ▶ *n* (*pl* **-s**) (*Informal*) earthquake
quaked *v, n* ▷ **quake**
quakes *v* ▷ **quake**
quaking *v* ▷ **quake**
qualification *n* (*pl* **-s**) official record of achievement in a course or examination
qualifications *n* ▷ **qualification**
qualified *v, adj* ▷ **qualify**
qualifies *v* ▷ **qualify**
qualify *v* (**-fies, -fying, -fied**) provide or be provided with the abilities necessary for a task, office, or duty > **qualified** *adj*
qualifying *v* ▷ **qualify**
qualitative *adj* of or relating to quality
qualities *n* ▷ **quality**
quality *n* (*pl* **-ties**) degree or standard of excellence ▶ *adj* excellent or superior
qualm [**kwahm**] *n* (*pl* **-s**) pang of conscience
qualms *n* ▷ **qualm**
quandaries *n* ▷ **quandary**
quandary *n* (*pl* **-ries**) difficult situation or dilemma
quandong [**kwon**-dong] *n* (*pl* **-s**) small Australian tree with edible fruit and nuts used in preserves
quandongs *n* ▷ **quandong**
quango *n* (*pl* **-s**) (CHIEFLY BRIT) quasi-autonomous nongovernmental organization: any partly independent official body set up by a government
quangos *n* ▷ **quango**
quanta *n* ▷ **quantum**
quantifiable *adj* ▷ **quantify**
quantification *n* ▷ **quantify**
quantifications *n* ▷ **quantify**
quantified *v* ▷ **quantify**
quantifies *v* ▷ **quantify**
quantify *v* (**-fies, -fying, -fied**) discover or express the quantity of > **quantifiable** *adj* > **quantification** *n* (*pl* **-s**)
quantifying *v* ▷ **quantify**
quantitative *adj* of or relating to quantity
quantities *n* ▷ **quantity**
quantity *n* (*pl* **-ties**) specified or definite amount or number
quantum *n* (*pl* **-ta**) desired or required amount, esp. a very small one
quarantine *n* (*pl* **-s**) period of isolation of people or animals to prevent the spread of disease ▶ *v* (**-nes, -ning, -ned**) isolate in or as if in quarantine
quarantined *v* ▷ **quarantine**
quarantines *n, v* ▷ **quarantine**
quarantining *v* ▷ **quarantine**
quark *n* (*pl* **-s**) (PHYSICS) subatomic particle thought to be the fundamental unit of matter
quarks *n* ▷ **quark**
quarrel *n* (*pl* **-s**) angry disagreement ▶ *v* (**-s, -lling, -lled**) have a disagreement or dispute > **quarrelsome** *adj*
quarrelled *v* ▷ **quarrel**
quarrelling *v* ▷ **quarrel**
quarrels *n, v* ▷ **quarrel**
quarrelsome *adj* ▷ **quarrel**
quarried *v* ▷ **quarry**[1]
quarries *n* ▷ **quarry**[1, 2] ▶ *v* ▷ **quarry**[1]
quarry[1] *n* (*pl* **-rries**) place where stone is dug from the surface of the earth ▶ *v* (**-rries, -rrying, -rried**) extract (stone) from a quarry
quarry[2] *n* (*pl* **-rries**) person or animal that is being hunted
quart *n* (*pl* **-s**) unit of liquid measure equal to two pints (1.136 litres)
quarter *n* (*pl* **-s**) one of four equal parts of something ▶ *v* (**-s, -ing, -ed**) divide into four equal parts
quarterdeck *n* (*pl* **-s**) (NAUT) rear part of the upper deck of a ship
quarterdecks *n* ▷ **quarterdeck**
quartered *v* ▷ **quarter**
quarterfinal *n* (*pl* **-s**) round before the semifinal in a competition
quarterfinals *n* ▷ **quarterfinal**
quartering *v* ▷ **quarter**

quarterlies *n* ▷ **quarterly**
quarterly *adj* occurring, due, or issued at intervals of three months ▶ *n* (*pl* **-lies**) magazine issued every three months ▶ *adv* once every three months
quartermaster *n* (*pl* **-s**) military officer responsible for accommodation, food, and equipment
quartermasters *n* ▷ **quartermaster**
quarters *n, v* ▷ **quarter**
quartet *n* (*pl* **-s**) group of four performers
quartets *n* ▷ **quartet**
quarto *n* (*pl* **-s**) book size in which the sheets are folded into four leaves
quarto *n* ▷ **quarto**
quarts *n* ▷ **quart**
quartz *n* (*pl* **-es**) hard glossy mineral
quartzes *n* ▷ **quartz**
quasar [**kway**-zar] *n* (*pl* **-s**) extremely distant starlike object that emits powerful radio waves
quasars *n* ▷ **quasar**
quash *v* (**-shes, -shing, -shed**) annul or make void
quashed *v* ▷ **quash**
quashes *v* ▷ **quash**
quashing *v* ▷ **quash**
quatrain *n* (*pl* **-s**) stanza or poem of four lines
quatrains *n* ▷ **quatrain**
quaver *v* (**-s, -ing, -ed**) (of a voice) quiver or tremble ▶ *n* (*pl* **-s**) (MUSIC) note half the length of a crotchet
quavered *v* ▷ **quaver**
quavering *v* ▷ **quaver**
quavers *v, n* ▷ **quaver**
quay [**kee**] *n* (*pl* **-s**) wharf built parallel to the shore
quays *n* ▷ **quay**
queasier *adj* ▷ **queasy**
queasiest *adj* ▷ **queasy**
queasiness *n* ▷ **queasy**
queasinesses *n* ▷ **queasy**
queasy *adj* (**-sier, -siest**) having the feeling that one is about to vomit > **queasiness** *n* (*pl* **-es**)
queen *n* (*pl* **-s**) female sovereign who is the official ruler or head of state > **queenly** *adj*
queenly *adj* ▷ **queen**
queens *n* ▷ **queen**
queer *adj* (**-er, -est**) not normal or usual
queerer *adj* ▷ **queer**
queerest *adj* ▷ **queer**
quell *v* (**-s, -ing, -ed**) suppress
quelled *v* ▷ **quell**
quelling *v* ▷ **quell**
quells *v* ▷ **quell**
quench *v* (**-es, -ing, -ed**) satisfy (one's thirst)
quenched *v* ▷ **quench**
quenches *v* ▷ **quench**
quenching *v* ▷ **quench**
queried *v* ▷ **query**
queries *n, v* ▷ **query**
quern *n* (*pl* **-s**) stone hand mill for grinding corn
querns *n* ▷ **quern**
querulous [**kwer**-yoo-luss] *adj* complaining or whining > **querulously** *adv*
querulously *adv* ▷ **querulous**
query *n* (*pl* **-ries**) question, esp. one raising doubt ▶ *v* (**-ries, -rying, -ried**) express uncertainty, doubt, or an objection concerning (something)
querying *v* ▷ **query**
quest *n* (*pl* **-s**) long and difficult search ▶ *v* (**-s, -ing, -ed**) (*foll. by* **for** *or* **after**) go in search of
quested *v* ▷ **quest**
questing *v* ▷ **quest**
question *n* (*pl* **-s**) form of words addressed to a person in order to obtain an answer ▶ *v* (**-s, -ing, -ed**) put a question or questions to (a person)
questionable *adj* of disputable value or authority > **questionably** *adv*
questionably *adv* ▷ **questionable**
questioned *v* ▷ **question**
questioning *v* ▷ **question**
questionnaire *n* (*pl* **-s**) set of questions on a form, used to collect information from people
questionnaires *n* ▷ **questionnaire**
questions *n, v* ▷ **question**
quests *n, v* ▷ **quest**

> **quetzal** or **quezal** *n* (**quetzals, quezales, quezals**). The quetzal is a crested bird of Central and South America. This is a great word if you can get the tiles for it, so it's well worth remembering both spellings and the three plural forms. If you can use all your letters to play quetzal or quezals, you'll earn a bonus of 50 points. Quetzal scores 25 points.

queue *n* (*pl* **-s**) line of people or vehicles waiting for something ▶ *v* (**queues, queuing** *or* **queueing, queued**) (*often foll. by* **up**) form or remain in a line while waiting
queued *v* ▷ **queue**
queueing *v* ▷ **queue**
queues *n, v* ▷ **queue**
queuing *v* ▷ **queue**
quibble *v* (**-les, -ling, -led**) make trivial

objections ▶ *n* (*pl* **-s**) trivial objection
quibbled *v* ▷ **quibble**
quibbles *v, n* ▷ **quibble**
quibbling *v* ▷ **quibble**
quiche [**keesh**] *n* (*pl* **-s**) savoury flan with an egg custard filling to which vegetables etc. are added
quiches *n* ▷ **quiche**
quick *adj* (**-er, -est**) speedy, fast ▶ *n* (*pl* **-s**) area of sensitive flesh under a nail ▶ *adv* (*Informal*) in a rapid manner > **quickly** *adv*
quicken *v* (**-s, -ing, -ed**) make or become faster
quickened *v* ▷ **quicken**
quickening *v* ▷ **quicken**
quickens *v* ▷ **quicken**
quicker *adj* ▷ **quick**
quickest *adj* ▷ **quick**
quicklime *n* (*pl* **-s**) white solid used in the manufacture of glass and steel
quicklimes *n* ▷ **quicklime**
quickly *adv* ▷ **quick**
quicks *n* ▷ **quick**
quicksand *n* (*pl* **-s**) deep mass of loose wet sand that sucks anything on top of it into it
quicksands *n* ▷ **quicksand**
quicksilver *n* (*pl* **-s**) mercury
quicksilvers *n* ▷ **quicksilver**
quickstep *n* (*pl* **-s**) fast modern ballroom dance
quicksteps *n* ▷ **quickstep**
quid *n* (*pl* **quid, -s**) (BRIT) (*Slang*) pound (sterling)
quids *n* ▷ **quid**
quiescence *n* ▷ **quiescent**
quiescences *n* ▷ **quiescent**
quiescent [kwee-**ess**-ent] *adj* quiet, inactive, or dormant > **quiescence** *n* (*pl* **-s**)
quiet *adj* (**-er, -est**) with little noise ▶ *n* (*pl* **-s**) quietness ▶ *v* (**-s, -ing, -ed**) make or become quiet > **quietly** *adv* > **quietness** *n* (*pl* **-es**)
quieted *v* ▷ **quiet**
quieten *v* (**-s, -ing, -ed**) (*often foll. by* **down**) make or become quiet
quieter *adj* ▷ **quiet**
quietest *adj* ▷ **quiet**
quieting *v* ▷ **quiet**
quietism *n* (*pl* **-s**) passivity and calmness of mind towards external events
quietisms *n* ▷ **quietism**
quietly *adv* ▷ **quiet**
quietness *n* ▷ **quiet**
quietnesses *n* ▷ **quiet**
quiets *v, n* ▷ **quiet**
quietude *n* (**-s**) quietness, peace, or tranquillity
quietudes *n* ▷ **quietude**
quiff *n* (*pl* **-s**) tuft of hair brushed up above the forehead
quiffs *n* ▷ **quiff**
quill *n* (*pl* **-s**) pen made from the feather of a bird's wing or tail
quills *n* ▷ **quill**
quilt *n* (*pl* **-s**) padded covering for a bed
quilted *adj* consisting of two layers of fabric with a layer of soft material between them
quilts *n* ▷ **quilt**
quince *n* (*pl* **-s**) acid-tasting pear-shaped fruit
quinces *n* ▷ **quince**
quinine *n* (*pl* **-s**) bitter drug used as a tonic and formerly to treat malaria
quinines *n* ▷ **quinine**
quinquennial *adj* occurring every five years
quins *n* ▷ **quin**
quinsies *n* ▷ **quinsy**
quinsy *n* (*pl* **-sies**) inflammation of the throat or tonsils
quintessence *n* (*pl* **-s**) most perfect representation of a quality or state > **quintessential** *adj*
quintessences *n* ▷ **quintessence**
quintessential *adj* ▷ **quintessence**
quintet *n* (*pl* **-s**) group of five performers
quintets *n* ▷ **quintet**
quintuplet *n* (*pl* **-s**) one of five offspring born at one birth
quintuplets *n* ▷ **quintuplet**

quinze *n* (**quinzes**). Quinze is a card game. This is a high-scoring word, and if you can use all of your tiles to form the plural, you'll get a 50-points bonus. Quinze scores 24 points.

quip *n* (*pl* **-s**) witty saying ▶ *v* (**-s, -pping, -pped**) make a quip
quipped *v* ▷ **quip**
quipping *v* ▷ **quip**
quips *n, v* ▷ **quip**
quire *n* (*pl* **-s**) set of 24 or 25 sheets of paper
quires *n* ▷ **quire**
quirk *n* (*pl* **-s**) peculiarity of character > **quirky** *adj* (**-kier, -kiest**)
quirks *n* ▷ **quirk**
quirky *adj* ▷ **quirk**
quisling *n* (*pl* **-s**) traitor who aids an occupying enemy force
quislings *n* ▷ **quisling**
quit *v* (**quits, quitting, quit**) stop (doing something)
quite *adv* somewhat ▶ *interj* expression of agreement
quits *adj* (*Informal*) on an equal footing ▶ *v* ▷ **quit**
quitter *n* (*pl* **-s**) person who lacks perseverance

quitters *n* ▷ **quitter**
quitting *v* ▷ **quit**
quiver[1] *v* (**-s, -ing, -ed**) shake with a tremulous movement ▶ *n* (*pl* **-s**) shaking or trembling
quiver[2] *n* (*pl* **-s**) case for arrows
quivered *v* ▷ **quiver**[1]
quivering *v* ▷ **quiver**[1]
quivers *v* ▷ **quiver**[1] ▶ *n* ▷ **quiver**[1, 2]

quixote *n* (**quixotes**). A quixote is an impractically idealistic person. This is a high-scoring word; if you have all the letters to play it, and can place them on the board, you'll score a 50-point bonus for using all of your tiles. Quixote scores 23 points.

quixotic [kwik-**sot**-ik] *adj* romantic and unrealistic > **quixotically** *adv*
quixotically *adv* ▷ **quixotic**
quiz *n* (*pl* **-zzes**) entertainment in which the knowledge of the players is tested by a series of questions ▶ *v* (**-zzes, -zzing, -zzed**) investigate by close questioning
quizzed *v* ▷ **quiz**
quizzes *n, v* ▷ **quiz**
quizzical *adj* questioning and mocking > **quizzically** *adv*
quizzically *adv* ▷ **quizzical**
quizzing *v* ▷ **quiz**
quod *n* (*pl* **-s**) (BRIT) (*Slang*) jail
quods *n* ▷ **quod**
quoit *n* (*pl* **-s**) large ring used in the game of quoits ▶ *pl* game in which quoits are tossed at a stake in the ground in attempts to encircle it
quoits *n* ▷ **quoit**
quokka *n* (*pl* **-s**) small Australian wallaby
quokkas *n* ▷ **quokka**
quorum *n* (*pl* **-s**) minimum number of people required to be present at a meeting before any transactions can take place
quorums *n* ▷ **quorum**
quota *n* (*pl* **-s**) share that is due from, due to, or allocated to a group or person
quotable *adj* ▷ **quote**
quotas *n* ▷ **quota**
quotation *n* (*pl* **-s**) written or spoken passage repeated exactly in a later work, speech, or conversation
quotations *n* ▷ **quotation**
quote *v* (**-tes, -ting, -ted**) repeat (words) exactly from (an earlier work, speech, or conversation) ▶ *n* (*pl* **-s**) (*Informal*) quotation > **quotable** *adj*
quoted *v* ▷ **quote**
quotes *v, n* ▷ **quote**
quoth *v* (*Obs*) said
quotidian *adj* daily
quotient *n* (*pl* **-s**) result of the division of one number or quantity by another
quotients *n* ▷ **quotient**
quoting *v* ▷ **quote**

Rr

R is one of the most common consonants in Scrabble, along with N and T. Despite this, however, there is only one two-letter word beginning with R: **re** (2 points). This is worth remembering, as you won't need to waste time trying to think of others. There are some good three-letter words with R, however, some of which are quite unusual: **raj, rax, rex** (10 each), **rez** and **riz** (12 each). Also, don't forget common words like **raw, ray** and **row** (6 each).

rabbi [**rab**-bye] *n* (*pl* **-s**) Jewish spiritual leader > **rabbinical** *adj*
rabbinical *adj* ▷ **rabbi**
rabbis *n* ▷ **rabbi**
rabbit *n* (*pl* **-s**) small burrowing mammal with long ears
rabbits *n* ▷ **rabbit**
rabble *n* (*pl* **-s**) disorderly crowd of noisy people
rabbles *n* ▷ **rabble**
rabid *adj* (**-er, -est**) fanatical > **rabidly** *adv*
rabider *adj* ▷ **rabid**
rabidest *adj* ▷ **rabid**
rabidly *adv* ▷ **rabid**
rabies [**ray**-beez] *n* usu. fatal viral disease transmitted by dogs and certain other animals
raccoon *n* (*pl* **-s**) small N American mammal with a long striped tail
raccoons *n* ▷ **raccoon**
race[1] *n* (*pl* **-s**) contest of speed ▶ *pl* meeting for horse racing ▶ *v* (**-ces, -cing, -ced**) compete with in a race > **racer** *n* (*pl* **-s**) > **racecourse** *n* (*pl* **-s**) > **racehorse** *n* (*pl* **-s**) > **racetrack** *n* (*pl* **-s**)
race[2] *n* (*pl* **-s**) group of people of common ancestry with distinguishing physical features, such as skin colour > **racial** *adj*
raced *n, v* ▷ **race**[1]
racecourse *n* ▷ **race**[1]
racecourses *n* ▷ **race**[1]
raced *n, v* ▷ **race**[1]
racehorse *n* ▷ **race**[1]
racehorses *n* ▷ **race**[1]
raceme [rass-**eem**] *n* (*pl* **-s**) cluster of flowers along a central stem, as in the foxglove
racemes *n* ▷ **raceme**
racer *n* ▷ **race**[1]
racers *n* ▷ **race**[1]
races *n* ▷ **race**[1, 2] ▶ *v* ▷ **race**[1]
racetrack *n* ▷ **race**[1]
racetracks *n* ▷ **race**[1]
racial *adj* ▷ **race**[2]
racialism *n* ▷ **racism**
racialisms *adj, n* ▷ **racism**
racialist *n* ▷ **racism**
racialists *n* ▷ **racism**
racier *adj* ▷ **racy**
raciest *adj* ▷ **racy**
racing *v* ▷ **race**
racism, racialism *n* (*pl* **-s**) hostile attitude or behaviour to members of other races, based on a belief in the innate superiority of one's own race > **racist, racialist** *adj, n* (*pl* **-s**)
racisms *n* ▷ **racism**
racist *n* ▷ **racism**
racists *n* ▷ **racism**
rack *n* (*pl* **-s**) framework for holding particular articles, such as coats or luggage (HIST) ▶ *v* (**-s, -ing, -ed**) cause great suffering to
racked *v* ▷ **rack**
racket[1] *n* (*pl* **-s**) noisy disturbance
racket[2]**, racquet** *n* (**-s**) bat with strings stretched in an oval frame, used in tennis etc.
racketeer *n* (*pl* **-s**) person making illegal profits
racketeers *n* ▷ **racketeer**
rackets *n* ball game played in a paved walled court ▶ *n* ▷ **racket**[1, 2]
racking *v* ▷ **rack**
racks *n, v* ▷ **rack**
raconteur [rak-on-**tur**] *n* (*pl* **-s**) skilled storyteller
raconteurs *n* ▷ **raconteur**
racquet *n* ▷ **racket**[2]
racquets *n* ▷ **racket**[2]
racy *adj* (**-cier, -ciest**) slightly shocking
radar *n* (*pl* **-s**) device for tracking distant objects by bouncing high-frequency radio

pulses off them
radars *n* ▷ **radar**
radial *adj* spreading out from a common central point
radiance *n* ▷ **radiant**
radiances *n* ▷ **radiant**
radiant *adj* looking happy > **radiance** *n* (**-s**)
radiate *v* (**-tes, -ting, -ted**) spread out from a centre
radiated *v* ▷ **radiate**
radiates *v* ▷ **radiate**
radiating *v* ▷ **radiate**
radiation *n* (*pl* **-s**) transmission of energy from one body to another
radiations *n* ▷ **radiation**
radiator *n* (**-s**) (BRIT) arrangement of pipes containing hot water or steam to heat a room
radiators *n* ▷ **radiator**
radical *adj* fundamental ▶ *n* (*pl* **-s**) person advocating fundamental (political) change > **radically** *adv* > **radicalism** *n* (**-s**)
radicalism *n* ▷ **radical**
radicalisms *n* ▷ **radical**
radically *adv* ▷ **radical**
radicals *n* ▷ **radical**
radicle *n* (*pl* **-s**) small or developing root
radicles *n* ▷ **radicle**
radii *n* ▷ **radius**
radio *n* (*pl* **-s**) use of electromagnetic waves for broadcasting, communication, etc. ▶ *v* (**-s, -ing, -ed**) transmit (a message) by radio
radioactive *adj* emitting radiation as a result of nuclear decay > **radioactivity** *n* (*pl* **-ies**)
radioactivities *n* ▷ **radioactive**
radioactivity *n* ▷ **radioactive**
radioed *v* ▷ **radio**
radiographer *n* ▷ **radiography**
radiographers *n* ▷ **radiography**
radiographies *n* ▷ **radiography**
radiography [ray-dee-**og**-ra-fee] *n* (*pl* **-phies**) production of an image on a film or plate by radiation > **radiographer** *n* (*pl* **-s**)
radioing *v* ▷ **radio**
radiologies *n* ▷ **radiology**
radiologist *n* ▷ **radiology**
radiologists *n* ▷ **radiology**
radiology [ray-dee-**ol**-a-jee] *n* (*pl* **-gies**) science of using x-rays in medicine > **radiologist** *n* (*pl* **-s**)
radios *n, v* ▷ **radio**
radiotherapies *n* ▷ **radiotherapy**
radiotherapist *n* ▷ **radiotherapy**
radiotherapists *n* ▷ **radiotherapy**
radiotherapy *n* (*pl* **-pies**) treatment of disease, esp. cancer, by radiation > **radiotherapist** *n* (*pl* **-s**)
radish *n* (*pl* **-es**) small hot-flavoured root vegetable eaten raw in salads
radishes *n* ▷ **radish**
radium *n* (*pl* **-s**) (CHEM) radioactive metallic element
radiums *n* ▷ **radiums**
radius *n* (*pl* **radii, radiuses**) (length of) a straight line from the centre to the circumference of a circle
radiuses *n* ▷ **radius**
radon [**ray**-don] *n* (*pl* **-s**) (CHEM) radioactive gaseous element
radons *n* ▷ **radon**
raffia *n* (*pl* **-s**) prepared palm fibre for weaving mats etc.
raffias *n* ▷ **raffia**
raffish *adj* slightly disreputable
raffle *n* (*pl* **-s**) lottery with goods as prizes ▶ *v* (**-les, -ling, -led**) offer as a prize in a raffle
raffled *v* ▷ **raffle**
raffles *n, v* ▷ **raffle**
raffling *v* ▷ **raffle**
raft *n* (*pl* **-s**) floating platform of logs, planks, etc.
rafter *n* (*pl* **-s**) one of the main beams of a roof
rafters *n* ▷ **rafter**
rafts *n* ▷ **raft**
rag[1] *n* (*pl* **-s**) fragment of cloth ▶ *pl* tattered clothing
rag[2] (BRIT) *v* (**-s, -gging, -gged**) tease ▶ *adj, n* (*pl* **-s**) (of) events organized by students to raise money for charities
rage *n* (*pl* **-s**) violent anger or passion ▶ *v* (**-ges, -ging, -ged**) speak or act with fury
raged *v* ▷ **rage**
rages *n, v* ▷ **rage**
ragamuffin *n* (*pl* **-s**) ragged dirty child
ragamuffins *n* ▷ **ragamuffin**
ragged [**rag**-gid] *adj* dressed in shabby or torn clothes ▶ *v* ▷ **rag**[2]
ragging *v* ▷ **rag**[2]
raging *v* ▷ **rage**
raglan *adj* (of a sleeve) joined to a garment by diagonal seams from the neck to the underarm
ragout [rag-**goo**] *n* (*pl* **-s**) richly seasoned stew of meat and vegetables
ragouts *n* ▷ **ragout**
rags *n, v* ▷ **rag**[1, 2]
ragtime *n* (*pl* **-s**) style of jazz piano music
ragtimes *n* ▷ **ragtime**
raid *n* (*pl* **-s**) sudden surprise attack or search ▶ *v* (**-s, -ing, -ed**) make a raid on > **raider** *n*

(*pl* **-s**)
raided *v* ▷ **raid**
raider *n* ▷ **raid**
raiders *n* ▷ **raid**
raiding *v* ▷ **raid**
raids *n*, *v* ▷ **raid**
rail[1] *n* (*pl* **-s**) horizontal bar, esp. as part of a fence or track
rail[2] *v* (**-s, -ing, -ed**) (*foll. by* **at** *or* **against**) complain bitterly or loudly
rail[3] *n* (*pl* **-s**) small marsh bird
railed *v* ▷ **rail**[2]
railing *n* (*pl* **-s**) fence made of rails supported by posts ▶ *v* ▷ **rail**[2]
railings *n* ▷ **railing**
railleries *n* ▷ **raillery**
raillery *n* (*pl* **-ies**) teasing or joking
rails *n* ▷ **rail**[1, 2, 3] ▶ *v* ▷ **rail**[2]
railway *n* (*pl* **-s**) track of iron rails on which trains run
railways *n* ▷ **railway**
raiment *n* (*pl* **-s**) (*Obs*) clothing
raiments *n* ▷ **raiment**
rain *n* (*pl* **-s**) water falling in drops from the clouds ▶ *v* (**-s, -ing, -ed**) fall or pour down as rain > **rainy** *adj* (**-nier, -niest**)
rainbow *n* (*pl* **-s**) arch of colours in the sky
rainbows *n* ▷ **rainbow**
raincoat *n* (*pl* **-s**) water-resistant overcoat
raincoats *n* ▷ **raincoat**
rained *v* ▷ **rain**
rainier *adj* ▷ **rainy**
rainiest *adj* ▷ **rainy**
rainfall *n* (*pl* **-s**) amount of rain
rainfalls *n* ▷ **rainfall**
rainforest *n* (*pl* **-s**) dense forest in tropical and temperate areas
rainforests *n* ▷ **rainforest**
raining *v* ▷ **rain**
rains *n*, *v* ▷ **rain**
rainy *adj* ▷ **rain**
raise *v* (**-ses, -sing, -sed**) lift up
raised *v* ▷ **raise**
raises *v* ▷ **raise**
raisin *n* (*pl* **-s**) dried grape
raising *v* ▷ **raise**
raisins *n* ▷ **raisin**

> **raj** *n* (**rajes**). Raj is an Indian word for government. This word can be very useful when there isn't much space on the board. If you can't play raj, remember that it's just **jar** backwards you might be able to fit that in somewhere. Raj scores 10 points.

raja, rajah *n* (*pl* **-s**) (HIST) Indian prince or ruler
rajah *n* ▷ **raja**
rajahs *n* ▷ **raja**
rajas *n* ▷ **raja**
rake[1] *n* (*pl* **-s**) tool with a long handle and a crosspiece with teeth, used for smoothing earth or gathering leaves, hay, etc. ▶ *v* (**-kes, -king, -ked**) gather or smooth with a rake
rake[2] *n* (*pl* **-s**) dissolute or immoral man
raked *v* ▷ **rake**[1]
rakes *n*, *v* ▷ **rake**[1, 2] ▶ *v* ▷ **rake**[1]
raking *v* ▷ **rake**[1]
rakish *adj* dashing or jaunty
rallied *v* ▷ **rally**
rallies *n*, *v* ▷ **rally**
rally *n* (*pl* **-ies**) large gathering of people for a meeting ▶ *v* (**-ies, -ying, -ied**) bring or come together after dispersal or for a common cause
rallying *v* ▷ **rally**
ram *n* (*pl* **-s**) male sheep ▶ *v* (**-s, -mming, -mmed**) strike against with force
ramble *v* (**-les, -ling, -led**) walk without a definite route ▶ *n* (*pl* **-s**) walk, esp. in the country
rambled *v* ▷ **ramble**
rambler *n* (*pl* **-s**) person who rambles
ramblers *n* ▷ **rambler**
rambles *v*, *n* ▷ **ramble**
rambling *v* ▷ **ramble**
ramekin [ram-ik-in] *n* (*pl* **-s**) small ovenproof dish for a single serving of food
ramekins *n* ▷ **ramekin**
ramifications *pl n* consequences resulting from an action
rammed *v* ▷ **ram**
ramming *v* ▷ **ram**
ramp *n* (*pl* **-s**) slope joining two level surfaces
rampage *v* (**-ges, -ging, -ged**) dash about violently
rampaged *v* ▷ **rampage**
rampages *v* ▷ **rampage**
rampaging *v* ▷ **rampage**
rampant *adj* growing or spreading uncontrollably
rampart *n* (*pl* **-s**) mound or wall for defence
ramparts *n* ▷ **rampart**
ramps *n* ▷ **ramp**
rams *n*, *v* ▷ **ram**
ramshackle *adj* tumbledown, rickety, or makeshift
ran *v* ▷ **run**
ranch *n* (*pl* **-es**) large cattle farm in the American West > **rancher** *n* (*pl* **-s**)
rancher *n* ▷ **ranch**
ranchers *n* ▷ **ranch**

ranches *n* ▷ **ranch**
rancid *adj* (of butter, bacon, etc.) stale and having an offensive smell > **rancidity** *n* (*pl* **-ies**)
rancidities *n* ▷ **rancidity**
rancidity *n* ▷ **rancid**
rancorous *adj* ▷ **rancour**
rancour *n* (*pl* **-s**) deep bitter hate > **rancorous** *adj*
rancours *n* ▷ **rancour**
rand *n* (*pl* **-s**) monetary unit of S Africa
randier *adj* ▷ **randy**
randiest *adj* ▷ **randy**
random *adj* made or done by chance or without plan
rands *n* ▷ **rand**
randy *adj* (**-ier, -iest**) (*Informal*) sexually aroused
rang *v* ▷ **ring**[1]
range *n* (*pl* **-s**) limits of effectiveness or variation ▶ *v* (**-ges, -ging, -ged**) vary between one point and another
ranged *v* ▷ **range**
ranger *n* (*pl* **-s**) official in charge of a nature reserve etc.
rangers *n* ▷ **ranger**
rangefinder *n* (*pl* **-s**) instrument for finding how far away an object is
rangefinders *n* ▷ **rangefinder**
ranges *n, v* ▷ **range**
rangier *adj* ▷ **rangy**
rangiest *adj* ▷ **rangy**
ranging *v* ▷ **range**
rangy [**rain**-jee] *adj* (**-ier, -iest**) having long slender limbs
rank[1] *n* (*pl* **-s**) relative place or position ▶ *v* (**-s, -ing, -ed**) have a specific rank or position
rank[2] *adj* complete or absolute
ranked *v* ▷ **rank**
ranking *v* ▷ **rank**
rankle *v* (**-les, -ling, -led**) continue to cause resentment or bitterness
rankled *v* ▷ **rankle**
rankles *v* ▷ **rankle**
rankling *v* ▷ **rankle**
ranks *n, v* ▷ **rank**[1]
ransack *v* (**-s, -ing, -ed**) search thoroughly
ransacked *v* ▷ **ransack**
ransacking *v* ▷ **ransack**
ransacks *v* ▷ **ransack**
ransom *n* (*pl* **-s**) money demanded in return for the release of someone who has been kidnapped
ransoms *n* ▷ **ransom**
rant *v* (**-s, -ing, -ed**) talk in a loud and excited way > **ranter** *n* (*pl* **-s**)
ranted *v* ▷ **rant**
ranter *n* ▷ **rant**
ranters *n* ▷ **rant**
ranting *v* ▷ **rant**
rants *v* ▷ **rant**
rap *v* (**-s, -pping, -pped**) hit with a sharp quick blow ▶ *n* (*pl* **-s**) quick sharp blow > **rapper** *n* (*pl* **-s**)
rapacious *adj* greedy or grasping > **rapacity** *n* (*pl* **-ies**)
rapacities *n* ▷ **rapacious**
rapacity *n* ▷ **rapacious**
rape[1] *v* (**-pes, -ping, -ped**) force to submit to sexual intercourse ▶ *n* (*pl* **-s**) act of raping > **rapist** *n* (*pl* **-s**)
rape[2] *n* (*pl* **-s**) plant with oil-yielding seeds, also used as fodder
raped *v* ▷ **rape**[1]
rapes *v* ▷ **rape**[1] ▶ *n* ▷ **rape**[1,2]
rapid *adj* (**-er, -est**) quick, swift > **rapidly** *adv* > **rapidity** *n* (*pl* **-ies**)
rapider *adj* ▷ **rapid**
rapidest *adj* ▷ **rapid**
rapidities *n* ▷ **rapid**
rapidity *n* ▷ **rapid**
rapidly *adv* ▷ **rapid**
rapids *pl n* part of a river with a fast turbulent current
rapier [**ray**-pyer] *n* (*pl* **-s**) fine-bladed sword
rapiers *n* ▷ **rapier**
raping *v* ▷ **rape**[1]
rapist *n* ▷ **rape**[1]
rapists *n* ▷ **rape**[1]
rapped *v* ▷ **rap**
rapper *n* ▷ **rap**
rappers *n* ▷ **rap**
rapping *v* ▷ **rap**
rapport [rap-**pore**] *n* (*pl* **-s**) harmony or agreement
rapports *n* ▷ **rapport**
rapprochement [rap-**prosh**-mong] *n* (*pl* **-s**) re-establishment of friendly relations, esp. between nations
rapprochements *n* ▷ **rapprochement**
raps *v, n* ▷ **rap**
rapt *adj* engrossed or spellbound
rapture *n* (*pl* **-s**) ecstasy > **rapturous** *adj*
raptures *n* ▷ **rapture**
rapturous *adj* ▷ **rapture**
rare[1] *adj* (**-r, -st**) uncommon > **rarity** *n* (*pl* **-ies**)
rare[2] *adj* (**-r, -st**) (of meat) lightly cooked
rarebit *n* (*pl* **-s**) dish of melted cheese on toast
rarebits *n* ▷ **rarebit**
rarefied [**rare**-if-ide] *adj* highly specialized, exalted

rarely *adv* seldom
rarer *adj* ▷ **rare**[1,2]
rarest *adj* ▷ **rare**[1,2]
raring *adj* enthusiastic, willing, or ready to
rarities *n* ▷ **rare**[1]
rarity *n* ▷ **rare**[1]
rascal *n* (*pl* **-s**) rogue > **rascally** *adj* (**-ier, -iest**)
rascalliest *adj* ▷ **rascal**
rascally *adj* ▷ **rascal**
rascals *n* ▷ **rascal**
rash[1] *adj* (**-er, -est**) hasty, reckless, or incautious > **rashly** *adv*
rash[2] *n* (*pl* **-es**) eruption of spots or patches on the skin
rasher *n* (*pl* **-s**) thin slice of bacon ▶ *adj* ▷ **rash**[1]
rashers *n* ▷ **rasher**
rashes *n* ▷ **rash**[2]
rashest *adj* ▷ **rash**[1]
rashly *adv* ▷ **rash**[1]
rasp *n* (*pl* **-s**) harsh grating noise ▶ *v* (**-s, -ing, -ed**) speak in a grating voice
raspberries *n* ▷ **raspberry**
raspberry *n* (*pl* **-ies**) red juicy edible berry (*Informal*)
rasped *v* ▷ **rasp**
rasping *v* ▷ **rasp**
rasps *n, v* ▷ **rasp**
rat *n* (*pl* **-s**) small rodent (*Informal*) ▶ *v* (**-s, -tting, -tted**) (*Informal*) inform (on)
ratafia [rat-a-**fee**-a] *n* (*pl* **-s**) liqueur made from fruit
ratafias *n* ▷ **ratafia**
ratatouille [rat-a-**twee**] *n* (*pl* **-s**) vegetable casserole of tomatoes, aubergines, etc.
ratatouilles *n* ▷ **ratatouille**
ratchet *n* (*pl* **-s**) set of teeth on a bar or wheel allowing motion in one direction only
ratchets *n* ▷ **ratchet**
rate *n* (*pl* **-s**) degree of speed or progress ▶ *pl* local tax on business ▶ *v* (**-tes, -ting, -ted**) consider or value > **ratepayer** *n* (*pl* **-s**)
rateable *adj* able to be rated
rated *v* ▷ **rate**
ratepayer *n* ▷ **rate**
ratepayers *n* ▷ **rate**
rates *n, v* ▷ **rate**
rather *adv* to some extent
ratification *n* ▷ **ratify**
ratifications *n* ▷ **ratify**
ratified *v* ▷ **ratify**
ratifies *v* ▷ **ratify**
ratify *v* (**-ies, -ying, -ied**) give formal approval to > **ratification** *n* (*pl* **-s**)
ratifiying *v* ▷ **ratify**
rating *n* (*pl* **-s**) valuation or assessment ▶ *pl* size of the audience for a TV programme ▶ *v* ▷ **rate**
ratings *n* ▷ **rating**
ratio *n* (*pl* **-s**) relationship between two numbers or amounts expressed as a proportion
ration *n* (*pl* **-s**) fixed allowance of food etc. ▶ *v* (**-s, -ing, -ed**) limit to a certain amount per person
rational *adj* reasonable, sensible > **rationally** *adv* > **rationality** *n* (*pl* **-ies**)
rationale [rash-a-**nahl**] *n* (*pl* **-s**) reason for an action or decision
rationales *n* ▷ **rationale**
rationalism *n* (*pl* **-s**) philosophy that regards reason as the only basis for beliefs or actions > **rationalist** *n* (*pl* **-s**)
rationalisms *n* ▷ **rationalism**
rationalist *n* ▷ **rationalism**
rationalists *n* ▷ **rationalism**
rationalities *n* ▷ **rational**
rationality *n* ▷ **rational**
rationalize *v* (**-zes, -zing, -zed**) justify by plausible reasoning > **rationalization** *n* (*pl* **-s**)
rationalization *n* ▷ **rationalize**
rationalizations *n* ▷ **rationalize**
rationalized *v* ▷ **rationalize**
rationalizes *v* ▷ **rationalize**
rationalizing *v* ▷ **rationalize**
rationally *adv* ▷ **rational**
rationed *v* ▷ **ration**
rationing *v* ▷ **ration**
rations *n, v* ▷ **ration**
ratios *n* ▷ **ratio**
rats *n* ▷ **rat**
rattan *n* (*pl* **-s**) climbing palm with jointed stems used for canes
rattans *n* ▷ **rattan**
ratted *v* ▷ **rat**
rattier *adj* ▷ **ratty**
rattiest *adj* ▷ **ratty**
ratting *v* ▷ **rat**
rattle *v* (**-les, -ling, -led**) give out a succession of short sharp sounds ▶ *n* (*pl* **-s**) short sharp sound
rattled *v* ▷ **rattle**
rattlesnake *n* (*pl* **-s**) poisonous snake with loose horny segments on the tail that make a rattling sound
rattlesnakes *n* ▷ **rattlesnake**
rattles *v, n* ▷ **rattle**
rattling *v* ▷ **rattle**
ratty *adj* (**-ier, -iest**) (BRIT & NZ) (*Informal*) bad-tempered, irritable
raucous *adj* hoarse or harsh

raunchier *adj* ▷ **raunchy**
raunchiest *adj* ▷ **raunchy**
raunchy *adj* (**-chier, -chiest**) (*Slang*) earthy, sexy
ravage *v* (**-ges, -ging, -ged**) cause extensive damage to
ravaged *v* ▷ **ravage**
ravages *pl n* damaging effects ▶ *v* ▷ **ravage**
ravaging *v* ▷ **ravage**
rave *v* (**-ves, -ving, -ved**) talk wildly or with enthusiasm ▶ *n* (*pl* **-s**) (*Slang*) large-scale party with electronic dance music
raved *v* ▷ **rave**
ravel *v* (**-s, -lling, -lled**) tangle or become entangled
ravelled *v* ▷ **ravel**
ravelling *v* ▷ **ravel**
ravels *v* ▷ **ravel**
raven *n* (*pl* **-s**) black bird like a large crow ▶ *adj* (of hair) shiny black
ravens *n* ▷ **raven**
ravenous *adj* very hungry
raves *v, n* ▷ **rave**
ravine [rav-**veen**] *n* (*pl* **-s**) narrow steep-sided valley worn by a stream
ravines *n* ▷ **ravine**
raving *adj* delirious ▶ *v* ▷ **rave**
ravioli *pl n* small squares of pasta with a savoury filling
ravish *v* (**-es, -ing, -ed**) enrapture
ravished *v* ▷ **ravish**
ravishes *v* ▷ **ravish**
ravishing *adj, v* ▷ **ravish**
raw *adj* (**-er, -est**) uncooked
rawer *adj* ▷ **raw**
rawest *adj* ▷ **raw**
rawhide *n* (*pl* **-s**) untanned hide
rawhides *n* ▷ **rawhide**

> **rax** *v* (**raxes, raxing, raxed**). Rax is a Scots word that means to stretch or extend. This is a good word to have ready when you have an X on your rack, as there is probably an A or R on the board already. The verb forms can also help you to get a better score. Rax scores 10 points.

ray[1] *n* (*pl* **-s**) single line or narrow beam of light
ray[2] *n* (*pl* **-s**) large sea fish with a flat body and a whiplike tail
rays *n* ▷ **ray**[1, 2]
rayon *n* (*pl* **-s**) (fabric made of) a synthetic fibre
rayons *n* ▷ **rayon**
raze *v* (**-zes, -zing, -zed**) destroy (buildings or a town) completely
razed *v* ▷ **raze**
razes *v* ▷ **raze**
razing *v* ▷ **raze**
razor *n* (*pl* **-s**) sharp instrument for shaving
razorbill *n* (*pl* **-s**) sea bird of the North Atlantic with a stout sideways flattened bill
razorbills *n* ▷ **razorbill**
razors *n* ▷ **razor**

> **re** *n* (**res**). Re is a musical note. This is the only two-letter word beginning with R, and so is a good one to remember. Re is very useful as it allows you to connect a word beginning with R to one ending in E, or vice versa and R and E are two of the most common tiles in the game. Re scores 2 points.

reach *v* (**-es, -ing, -ed**) arrive at ▶ *n* (*pl* **-es**) distance that one can reach; stretch of a river > **reachable** *adj*
reachable *adj* ▷ **reach**
reached *v* ▷ **reach**
reaches *v, n* ▷ **reach**
reaching *v* ▷ **reach**
react *v* (**-s, -ing, -ed**) act in response (to) (*foll. by* **against**)
reactance *n* (*pl* **-s**) (ELECTRICITY) resistance to the flow of an alternating current caused by the inductance or capacitance of the circuit
reactances *n* ▷ **reactance**
reacted *v* ▷ **react**
reacting *v* ▷ **react**
reaction *n* (*pl* **-s**) physical or emotional response to a stimulus
reactionaries *n* ▷ **reactionary**
reactionary *n, adj* (*pl* **-ies**) (person) opposed to change, esp. in politics
reactionary *n* ▷ **reaction**
reactions *n* ▷ **reaction**
reactive *adj* chemically active
reactor *n* (*pl* **-s**) apparatus in which a nuclear reaction is maintained and controlled to produce nuclear energy
reactors *n* ▷ **reactor**
reacts *v* ▷ **react**
read *v* (**-s, -ing, read**) look at and understand or take in (written or printed matter) ▶ *n* matter suitable for reading > **reading** *n* (*pl* **-s**)
readable *adj* enjoyable to read
reader *n* (*pl* **-s**) person who reads
readers *n* ▷ **reader**
readership *n* (*pl* **-s**) readers of a publication collectively
readerships *n* ▷ **readership**
readier *adj* ▷ **ready**
readiest *adj* ▷ **ready**
readily *adv* ▷ **ready**
readiness *n* ▷ **ready**

readinesses *n* ▷ **ready**
reading *n, v* ▷ **read**
readings *n* ▷ **read**
readjust *v* (**-s, -ing, -ed**) adapt to a new situation > **readjustment** *n* (*pl* **-s**)
readjusted *v* ▷ **readjust**
readjusting *v* ▷ **readjust**
readjustment *n* ▷ **readjust**
readjustments *n* ▷ **readjust**
readjusts *v* ▷ **readjust**
reads *v* ▷ **read**
ready *adj* (**-dier, -diest**) prepared for use or action > **readily** *adv* > **readiness** *n* (*pl* **-es**)
reagent [ree-**age**-ent] *n* (*pl* **-s**) chemical substance that reacts with another, used to detect the presence of the other
reagents *n* ▷ **reagent**
real *adj* (**-er, -est**) existing in fact
realism *n* ▷ **realistic**
realisms *n* ▷ **realistic**
realist *n* > **realistic**
realistically *adv* ▷ **realistic**
realists *n* ▷ **realistic**
realistic *adj* seeing and accepting things as they really are, practical > **realistically** *adv* > **realism** *n* (*pl* **-s**) > **realist** *n* (*pl* **-s**)
realities *n* ▷ **reality**
reality *n* (*pl* **-ies**) state of things as they are
realize *v* (**-zes, -zing, -zed**) become aware or grasp the significance of > **realization** *n* (*pl* **-s**)
realization *n* ▷ **realize**
realizations *n* ▷ **realize**
realized *v* ▷ **realize**
realizes *v* ▷ **realize**
realizing *v* ▷ **realize**
really *adv* very ▶ *interj* exclamation of dismay, doubt, or surprise
realm *n* (*pl* **-s**) kingdom
realms *n* ▷ **realm**
ream *n* (*pl* **-s**) twenty quires of paper, generally 500 sheets ▶ *pl* (*Informal*) large quantity (of written matter)
reams *n* ▷ **ream**
reap *v* (**-s, -ing, -ed**) cut and gather (a harvest) > **reaper** *n* (*pl* **-s**)
reaped *v* ▷ **reap**
reaper *n* ▷ **reap**
reapers *n* ▷ **reap**
reaping *v* ▷ **reap**
reappear *v* (**-s, -ing, -ed**) appear again > **reappearance** *n* (*pl* **-s**)
reappearance *n* ▷ **reappear**
reappearances *n* ▷ **reappear**
reappeared *v* ▷ **reappear**
reappearing *v* ▷ **reappear**
reappears *v* ▷ **reappear**
reaps *v* ▷ **reap**
rear[1] *n* (*pl* **-s**) back part > **rearmost** *adj*
rear[2] *v* (**-s, -ing, -ed**) care for and educate (children)
reared *v* ▷ **rear**
rearguard *n* (*pl* **-s**) troops protecting the rear of an army
rearguards *n* ▷ **rearguard**
rearing *v* ▷ **rear**
rearmost *adj* ▷ **rear**[1]
rearrange *v* (**-ges, -ging, -ged**) organize differently, alter > **rearrangement** *n* (*pl* **-s**)
rearranged *v* ▷ **rearrange**
rearrangement *n* ▷ **rearrange**
rearrangements *n* ▷ **rearrange**
rearranges *v* ▷ **rearrange**
rearranging *v* ▷ **rearrange**
rears *n* ▷ **rear**[1] ▶ *v* ▷ **rear**[2]
reason *n* (*pl* **-s**) cause or motive ▶ *v* (**-s, -ing, -ed**) think logically in forming conclusions
reasonable *adj* sensible > **reasonably** *adv*
reasoned *v* ▷ **reason**
reasoning *v* ▷ **reason**
reasons *n, v* ▷ **reason**
reassess *v* (**-es, -ing, -ed**) reconsider the value or importance of
reassessed *v* ▷ **reassess**
reassesses *v* ▷ **reassess**
reassessing *v* ▷ **reassess**
reassure *v* (**-res, -ring, -red**) restore confidence to > **reassurance** *n* (*pl* **-s**)
reassurance *n* ▷ **reassure**
reassurances *n* ▷ **reassure**
reassured *v* ▷ **reassure**
reassures *v* ▷ **reassure**
reassuring *v* ▷ **reassure**
rebate *n* (*pl* **-s**) discount or refund
rebates *n* ▷ **rebate**
rebel *v* (**-s, -lling, -lled**) revolt against the ruling power ▶ *n* (*pl* **-s**) person who rebels > **rebellious** *adj*
rebelled *v* ▷ **rebel**
rebelling *v* ▷ **rebel**
rebellion *n* (*pl* **-s**) organized open resistance to authority
rebellions *n* ▷ **rebellion**
rebellious *adj* ▷ **rebel**
rebels *v, n* ▷ **rebel**
rebore, reboring *n* (*pl* **-s**) boring of a cylinder to restore its true shape
rebores *n* ▷ **rebore**
reboring *n* ▷ **rebore**
reborings *n* ▷ **rebore**
rebound *v* (**-s, -ing, -ed**) spring back

rebounded *v* ▷ **rebound**
rebounding *v* ▷ **rebound**
rebounds *v* ▷ **rebound**
rebuff *v* (**-s, -ing, -ed**) reject or snub ▶ *n* (*pl* **-s**) blunt refusal, snub
rebuffed *v* ▷ **rebuff**
rebuffing *v* ▷ **rebuff**
rebuffs *v, n* ▷ **rebuff**
rebuke *v* (**-kes, -king, -ked**) scold sternly ▶ *n* (*pl* **-s**) stern scolding
rebuked *v* ▷ **rebuke**
rebukes *v, n* ▷ **rebuke**
rebuking *v* ▷ **rebuke**
rebus *n* (*pl* **-es**) puzzle consisting of pictures and symbols representing words or syllables
rebuses *n* ▷ **rebus**
rebut *v* (**-s, -tting, -tted**) prove that (a claim) is untrue > **rebuttal** *n* (*pl* **-s**)
rebuts *v* ▷ **rebut**
rebuttal *n* ▷ **rebut**
rebuttals *n* ▷ **rebut**
rebutted *v* ▷ **rebut**
rebutting *v* ▷ **rebut**
recalcitrant *adj* wilfully disobedient > **recalcitrance** *n* (*pl* **-s**)
recalcitrance *n* ▷ **recalcitrant**
recalcitrances *n* ▷ **recalcitrant**
recall *v* (**-s, -ing, -ed**) recollect or remember ▶ *n* (*pl* (*pl* **-s**) ability to remember
recalled *v* ▷ **recall**
recalling *v* ▷ **recall**
recalls *v, n* ▷ **recall**
recant *v* (**-s, -ing, -ed**) withdraw (a statement or belief) publicly > **recantation** *n* (*pl* **-s**)
recantation *n* ▷ **recant**
recantations *n* ▷ **recant**
recanted *v* ▷ **recant**
recanting *v* ▷ **recant**
recants *v* ▷ **recant**
recap (*Informal*) *v* (**-s, -pping, -pped**) recapitulate ▶ *n* (*pl* **-s**) recapitulation
recapitulate *v* (**-tes, -ting, -ted**) state again briefly, repeat > **recapitulation** *n* (*pl* **-s**)
recapitulated *v* ▷ **recapitulate**
recapitulates *v* ▷ **recapitulate**
recapitulating *v* ▷ **recapitulate**
recapitulation *n* ▷ **recapitulate**
recapitulations *n* ▷ **recapitulate**
recapped *v* ▷ **recap**
recapping *v* ▷ **recap**
recaps *v, n* ▷ **recap**
recapture *v* (**-res, -ring, -red**) experience again
recaptured *v* ▷ **recapture**
recaptures *v* ▷ **recapture**
recapturing *v* ▷ **recapture**
recce (CHIEFLY BRIT) (*Slang*) *v* (**-s, -ceing, -ced** *or* **-ceed**) reconnoitre ▶ *n* (*pl* **-s**) reconnaissance
recced *v* ▷ **recce**
recceed *v* ▷ **recce**
recceing *v* ▷ **recce**
recces *v, n* ▷ **recce**
recede *v* (**-des, -ding, -ded**) move to a more distant place
receded *v* ▷ **recede**
recedes *v* ▷ **recede**
receding *v* ▷ **recede**
receipt *n* (*pl* **-s**) written acknowledgment of money or goods received
receipts *n* ▷ **receipt**
receive *v* (**-ves, -ving, -ved**) take, accept, or get
received *adj* generally accepted ▶ *v* ▷ **receive**
receiver *n* (*pl* **-s**) part of telephone that is held to the ear
receivers *n* ▷ **receiver**
receivership *n* (*pl* **-s**) state of being administered by a receiver
receiverships *n* ▷ **receivership**
receives *v* ▷ **receive**
receiving *v* ▷ **receive**
recent *adj* (**-er, -est**) having happened lately > **recently** *adv*
recenter *adj* ▷ **recent**
recentest *adj* ▷ **recent**
recently *adv* ▷ **recent**
receptacle *n* (*pl* **-s**) object used to contain something
receptacles *n* ▷ **receptacle**
reception *n* (*pl* **-s**) area for receiving guests, clients, etc.
receptionist *n* (*pl* **-s**) person who receives guests, clients, etc.
receptionists *n* ▷ **receptionist**
receptions *n* ▷ **reception**
receptive *adj* willing to accept new ideas, suggestions, etc. > **receptivity** *n* (*pl* **-ies**)
receptivities *n* ▷ **receptive**
receptivity *n* ▷ **receptive**
recess *n* (*pl* **-es**) niche or alcove
recessed *adj* hidden or placed in a recess
recesses *n* ▷ **recess**
recession *n* (*pl* **-s**) period of economic difficulty when little is being bought or sold
recessions *n* ▷ **recession**
recessive *adj* receding
recherché [rish-**air**-shay] *adj* refined or elegant
recidivism *n* (*pl* **-s**) habitual relapse into crime > **recidivist** *n* (*pl* **-s**)
recidivisms *n* ▷ **recidivism**
recidivist *n* ▷ **recidivism**
recidivists *n* ▷ **recidivism**

recipe *n* (*pl* **-s**) directions for cooking a dish
recipes *n* ▷ **recipe**
recipient *n* (*pl* **-s**) person who receives something
recipients *n* ▷ **recipient**
reciprocal [ris-**sip**-pro-kl] *adj* mutual > **reciprocally** *adv*
reciprocally *adv* ▷ **reciprocal**
reciprocate *v* (**-tes, -ting, -ted**) give or feel in return > **reciprocation** *n* (*pl* **-s**) > **reciprocity** *n* (*pl* **-s**)
reciprocated *v* ▷ **reciprocate**
reciprocates *v* ▷ **reciprocate**
reciprocating *v* ▷ **reciprocate**
reciprocation *n* ▷ **reciprocate**
reciprocations *n* ▷ **reciprocate**
reciprocities *n* ▷ **reciprocate**
reciprocity *n* ▷ **reciprocate**
recital *n* (*pl* **-s**) musical performance by a soloist or soloists
recitals *n* ▷ **recital**
recitation *n* (*pl* **-s**) recital, usu. from memory, of poetry or prose
recitations *n* ▷ **recitation**
recitative [ress-it-a-**teev**] *n* (*pl* **-s**) speechlike style of singing, used esp. for narrative passages in opera
recitatives *n* ▷ **recitative**
recite *v* (**-tes, -ting, -ted**) repeat (a poem etc.) aloud to an audience
recited *v* ▷ **recite**
recites *v* ▷ **recite**
reciting *v* ▷ **recite**
reckless *adj* heedless of danger > **recklessly** *adv* > **recklessness** *n* (*pl* **-s**)
recklessly *adv* ▷ **reckless**
recklessness *n* ▷ **reckless**
recklessnesses *n* ▷ **reckless**
reckon *v* (**-s, -ing, -ed**) consider or think > **reckoning** *n* (*pl* **-s**)
reckoned *v* ▷ **reckon**
reckoning *v, n* ▷ **reckon**
reckonings *n* ▷ **reckon**
reckons *v* ▷ **reckon**
reclaim *v* (**-s, -ing, -ed**) regain possession of > **reclamation** *n* (*pl* **-s**)
reclaimed *v* ▷ **reclaim**
reclaiming *v* ▷ **reclaim**
reclaims *v* ▷ **reclaim**
reclamation *n* ▷ **reclaim**
reclamations *n* ▷ **reclaim**
recline *v* (**-nes, -ning, -ned**) rest in a leaning position > **reclining** *adj*
reclined *v* ▷ **recline**
reclines *v* ▷ **recline**
reclining *v, adj* ▷ **recline**
recluse *n* (*pl* **-s**) person who avoids other people > **reclusive** *adj*
recluses *n* ▷ **recluse**
reclusive *adj* ▷ **recluse**
recognition *n* ▷ **recognize**
recognitions *n* ▷ **recognize**
recognizable *adj* ▷ **recognize**
recognizance [rik-**og**-nizz-anss] *n* (*pl* **-s**) undertaking before a court to observe some condition
recognizances *n* ▷ **recognizance**
recognize *v* (**-zes, -zing, -zed**) identify as (a person or thing) already known > **recognition** *n* (*pl* **-s**) > **recognizable** *adj*
recognized *v* ▷ **recognize**
recognizes *v* ▷ **recognize**
recognizing *v* ▷ **recognize**
recoil *v* (**-s, -ing, -ed**) jerk or spring back ▶ *n* (*pl* **-s**) backward jerk
recoiled *v* ▷ **recoil**
recoiling *v* ▷ **recoil**
recoils *v, n* ▷ **recoil**
recollect *v* (**-s, -ing, -ed**) call back to mind, remember > **recollection** *n* (*pl* **-s**)
recollected *v* ▷ **recollect**
recollecting *v* ▷ **recollect**
recollection *n* ▷ **recollect**
recollections *n* ▷ **recollect**
recollects *v* ▷ **recollect**
recommend *v* (**-s, -ing, -ed**) advise or counsel > **recommendation** *n* (*pl* **-s**)
recommendation *n* ▷ **recommend**
recommendations *n* ▷ **recommend**
recommended *v* ▷ **recommend**
recommending *v* ▷ **recommend**
recommends *v* ▷ **recommend**
recompense *v* (**-ses, -sing, -sed**) pay or reward ▶ *n* (*pl* **-s**) compensation
recompensed *v* ▷ **recompense**
recompenses *v, n* ▷ **recompense**
recompensing *v* ▷ **recompense**
reconcile *v* (**-les, -ling, -led**) harmonize (conflicting beliefs etc.) > **reconciliation** *n* (*pl* **-s**)
reconciled *v* ▷ **reconcile**
reconciles *v* ▷ **reconcile**
reconciliation *n* ▷ **reconcile**
reconciliations *n* ▷ **reconcile**
reconciling *v* ▷ **reconcile**
recondite *adj* difficult to understand
recondition *v* (**-s, -ing, -ed**) restore to good condition or working order
reconditioned *v* ▷ **recondition**
reconditioning *v* ▷ **recondition**

reconditions *v* ▷ **recondition**
reconnaissance [rik-**kon**-iss-anss] *n* (*pl* **-s**) survey for military or engineering purposes
reconnaissances *n* ▷ **reconnaissance**
reconnoitre [rek-a-**noy**-ter] *v* (**-res, -ring, -red**) make a reconnaissance of
reconnoitred *v* ▷ **reconnoitre**
reconnoitres *v* ▷ **reconnoitre**
reconnoitring *v* ▷ **reconnoitre**
reconsider *v* (**-s, -ing, -ed**) think about again, consider changing
reconsidered *v* ▷ **reconsider**
reconsidering *v* ▷ **reconsider**
reconsiders *v* ▷ **reconsider**
reconstitute *v* (**-tes, -ting, -ted**) reorganize > **reconstitution** *n* (*pl* **-s**)
reconstituted *v* ▷ **reconstitute**
reconstitutes *v* ▷ **reconstitute**
reconstituting *v* ▷ **reconstitute**
reconstitution *n* ▷ **reconstitute**
reconstitutions *n* ▷ **reconstitute**
reconstruct *v* (**-s, -ing, -ed**) rebuild > **reconstruction** *n* (*pl* **-s**)
reconstructed *v* ▷ **reconstruct**
reconstructing *v* ▷ **reconstruct**
reconstruction *n* ▷ **reconstruct**
reconstructions *n* ▷ **reconstruct**
reconstructs *v* ▷ **reconstruct**
record *n* (*pl* **-s**) [**rek**-ord] document or other thing that preserves information ▶ *v* (**-s, -ing, -ed**) [rik-**kord**] put in writing > **recording** *n* (*pl* **-s**)
recorded *v* ▷ **record**
recorder *n* (*pl* **-s**) person or machine that records, esp. a video, cassette, or tape recorder
recorders *n* ▷ **recorder**
recording *v* ▷ **record**
records *n, v* ▷ **record**
recount *v* (**-s, -ing, -ed**) tell in detail
recounted *v* ▷ **recount**
recounting *v* ▷ **recount**
recounts *v* ▷ **recount**
recoup [rik-**koop**] *v* (**-s, -ing, -ed**) regain or make good (a loss)
recouped *v* ▷ **recoup**
recouping *v* ▷ **recoup**
recoups *v* ▷ **recoup**
recourse *n* (*pl* **-s**) source of help
recourses *n* ▷ **recourse**
recover *v* (**-s, -ing, -ed**) become healthy again > **recovery** *n* (*pl* **-ies**) > **recoverable** *adj*
recoverable *adj* ▷ **recover**
recovered *v* ▷ **recover**
recoveries *n* ▷ **recover**
recovering *v* ▷ **recover**
recovers *v* ▷ **recover**
recovery *v* ▷ **recover**
recreation *n* (*pl* **-s**) agreeable or refreshing occupation, relaxation, or amusement > **recreational** *adj*
recreational *adj* ▷ **recreation**
recreations *n* ▷ **recreation**
recrimination *n* (*pl* **-s**) mutual blame > **recriminatory** *adj*
recriminations *n* ▷ **recrimination**
recriminatory *adj* ▷ **recrimination**
recruit *v* (**-s, -ing, -ed**) enlist (new soldiers, members, etc.) ▶ *n* (*pl* **-s**) newly enlisted soldier > **recruitment** *n* (*pl* **-s**)
recruited *v* ▷ **recruit**
recruiting *v* ▷ **recruit**
recruitment *n* ▷ **recruit**
recruitments *n* ▷ **recruit**
recruits *v, n* ▷ **recruit**
recta *n* ▷ **rectum**
rectangle *n* (*pl* **-s**) oblong four-sided figure with four right angles > **rectangular** *adj*
rectangles *n* ▷ **rectangle**
rectangular *adj* ▷ **rectangle**
rectification *n* ▷ **rectify**
rectifications *n* ▷ **rectify**
rectified *v* ▷ **rectify**
rectifier *n* ▷ **rectify**
rectifiers *n* ▷ **rectify**
rectifies *v* ▷ **rectify**
rectify *v* (**-ies, -ying, -ied**) put right, correct (CHEM) (ELECTRICITY) > **rectification** *n* (*pl* **-s**)
rectifying *v* ▷ **rectify**
rectilinear *adj* in a straight line
rectitude *n* (*pl* **-s**) moral correctness
rectitudes *n* ▷ **rectitude**
recto *n* (*pl* **-os**) right-hand page of a book
rector *n* (*pl* **-s**) clergyman in charge of a parish
rectories *n* ▷ **rectory**
rectors *n* ▷ **rector**
rectory *n* (*pl* **-s**) rector's house
rectos *n* ▷ **recto**
rectum *n* (*pl* **-tums, -ta**) final section of the large intestine
rectums *n* ▷ **rectum**
recumbent *adj* lying down
recuperate *v* (**-tes, -ting, -ted**) recover from illness > **recuperation** *n* (*pl* **-s**) > **recuperative** *adj*
recuperated *v* ▷ **recuperate**
recuperates *v* ▷ **recuperate**
recuperating *v* ▷ **recuperate**
recuperation *n* ▷ **recuperate**
recuperations *n* ▷ **recuperate**

recuperative *adj* ▷ **recuperate**
recur *v* (**-s, -rring, -rred**) happen again > **recurrence** *n* (*pl* **-s**) repetition > **recurrent** *adj*
recurred *v* ▷ **recur**
recurrence *n* ▷ **recur**
recurrences *n* ▷ **recur**
recurrent *adj* ▷ **recur**
recurring *v* ▷ **recur**
recurs *v* ▷ **recur**
recycle *v* (**-les, -ling, -led**) reprocess (used materials) for further use > **recyclable** *adj*
recyclable *adj* ▷ **recycle**
recycled *v* ▷ **recycle**
recycles *v* ▷ **recycle**
recycling *v* ▷ **recycle**
red *adj* (**-dder, -ddest**) of a colour varying from crimson to orange and seen in blood, fire, etc. ▶ *n* (*pl* **-s**) red colour > **reddish** *adj* > **redness** *n* (*pl* **-es**)
redbrick *adj* (of a university in Britain) founded in the late 19th or early 20th century
redcoat *n* (*pl* **-s**) (HIST) British soldier
redcoats *n* ▷ **redcoat**
redcurrant *n* (*pl* **-s**) small round edible red berry
redcurrants *n* ▷ **redcurrant**
redden *v* (**-s, -ing, -ed**) make or become red
reddened *v* ▷ **redden**
reddening *v* ▷ **redden**
reddens *v* ▷ **redden**
redder *adj* ▷ **red**
reddest *adj* ▷ **red**
reddish *adj* ▷ **red**
redeem *v* (**-s, -ing, -ed**) make up for > **redeemable** *adj* > **redemption** *n* (*pl* **-s**) > **redemptive** *adj*
redeemable *adj* ▷ **reddem**
redeemed *v* ▷ **redeem**
redeeming *v* ▷ **redeem**
redeems *v* ▷ **redeem**
redemption *adj* ▷ **reddem**
redemptions *adj* ▷ **reddem**
redemptive *adj* ▷ **reddem**
redeploy *v* (**-s, -ing, -ed**) assign to a new position or task > **redeployment** *n* (*pl* **-s**)
redeployed *v* ▷ **redeploy**
redeploying *v* ▷ **redeploy**
redeployment *n* ▷ **redeploy**
redeployment *n* ▷ **redeploy**
redeploys *v* ▷ **redeploy**
redevelop *v* (**-s, -ing, -ed**) rebuild or renovate (an area or building) > **redevelopment** *n* (*pl* **-s**)
redeveloped *v* ▷ **redevelop**
redeveloping *v* ▷ **redevelop**
redevelopment *n* ▷ **redevelop**
redevelopments *n* ▷ **redevelop**
redevelops *v* ▷ **redevelop**
redness *n* ▷ **red**
redolent *adj* reminiscent (of)
redouble *v* (**-les, -ling, -led**) increase, multiply, or intensify
redoubled *v* ▷ **redouble**
redoubles *v* ▷ **redouble**
redoubling *v* ▷ **redouble**
redoubt *n* (*pl* **-s**) small fort defending a hilltop or pass
redoubtable *adj* formidable
redoubts *n* ▷ **redoubt**
redound *v* (**-s, -ing, -ed**) cause advantage or disadvantage (to)
redounded *v* ▷ **redound**
redounding *v* ▷ **redound**
redounds *v* ▷ **redound**
redox *n* (*pl* **-es**) chemical reaction in which one substance is reduced and the other is oxidized
redoxes *n* ▷ **redox**
redress *v* (**-es, -ing, -ed**) make amends for ▶ *n* (*pl* **-es**) compensation or amends
redressed *v* ▷ **redress**
redresses *v, n* ▷ **redress**
redressing *v* ▷ **redress**
reds *n* ▷ **red**
reduce *v* (**-ces, -cing, -ced**) bring down, lower > **reducible** *adj* > **reduction** *n* (*pl* **-s**)
reduced *v* ▷ **reduce**
reduces *v* ▷ **reduce**
reducible *adj* ▷ **reduce**
reducing *v* ▷ **reduce**
reduction *n* ▷ **reduce**
reductions *n* ▷ **reduce**
redundancies *n* ▷ **redundant**
redundancy *n* ▷ **redundant**
redundant *adj* (of a worker) no longer needed > **redundancy** *n* (*pl* **-s**)
reed *n* (*pl* **-s**) tall grass that grows in swamps and shallow water
reedier *adj* ▷ **reedy**
reediest *n* ▷ **reedy**
reeds *n* ▷ **reed**
reedy (**-dier, -diest**) *adj* harsh and thin in tone
reef¹ *n* (*pl* **-s**) ridge of rock or coral near the surface of the sea
reef² *n* (*pl* **-s**) part of a sail which can be rolled up to reduce its area ▶ *v* (**-s, -ing, -ed**) take in a reef of
reefed *v* ▷ **reef²**
reefer *n* (*pl* **-s**) short thick jacket worn esp. by sailors

reefers *n* ▷ **reefer**
reefing *v* ▷ **reef**[2]
reefs *n* ▷ **reef**[1,2] ▶ *v* ▷ **reef**[2]
reek *v* (**-s, -ing, -ed**) smell strongly ▶ *n* (*pl* **-s**) strong unpleasant smell
reeked *v* ▷ **reek**
reeking *v* ▷ **reek**
reeks *v, n* ▷ **reek**
reel[1] *n* (*pl* **-s**) cylindrical object on which film, tape, thread, or wire is wound
reel[2] *v* (**-s, -ing, -ed**) stagger, sway, or whirl
reel[3] *n* (*pl* **-s**) lively Scottish dance
reeled *v* ▷ **reel**[2]
reeling *v* ▷ **reel**[2]
reels *n* ▷ **reel**[1,3] ▶ *v* ▷ **reel**[2]
ref *n* (*pl* **-s**) (*Informal*) referee in sport
refectories *n* ▷ **refectory**
refectory *n* (*pl* **-ies**) room for meals in a college etc.
refer *v* (**-s, -rring, -rred**) (*foll. by* **to**) allude (to) > **referral** *n* (*pl* **-s**)
referee *n* (*pl* **-s**) umpire in sports, esp. soccer or boxing ▶ *v* (**-s, -ing, -eed**) act as referee of
refereed *v* ▷ **referee**
refereeing *v* ▷ **referee**
referees *n, v* ▷ **referee**
reference *n* (*pl* **-s**) act of referring
references *n* ▷ **reference**
referenda *n* ▷ **referendum**
referendum *n* (*pl* **-dums, -da**) direct vote of the electorate on an important question
referendums *n* ▷ **referendum**
referral *n* ▷ **refer**
referrals *n* ▷ **refer**
referred *v* ▷ **refer**
referring *v* ▷ **refer**
refers *v* ▷ **refer**
refill *v* (**-s, -ing, -ed**) fill again ▶ *n* (*pl* **-s**) second or subsequent filling
refilled *v* ▷ **refill**
refilling *v* ▷ **refill**
refills *v, n* ▷ **refill**
refine *v* (**-nes, -ning, -ned**) purify
refined *adj* cultured or polite ▶ *v* ▷ **refine**
refinement *n* (*pl* **-s**) improvement or elaboration
refinements *n* ▷ **refinement**
refineries *n* ▷ **refinery**
refinery *n* (*pl* **-ies**) place where sugar, oil, etc. is refined
refines *v* ▷ **refine**
refining *v* ▷ **refine**
reflate *v* ▷ **reflation**
reflated *v* ▷ **reflation**
reflates *v* ▷ **reflation**
reflating *v* ▷ **reflation**
reflation *n* (*pl* **-s**) increase in the supply of money and credit designed to encourage economic activity > **reflate** *v* (**-tes, -ting, -ted**) > **reflationary** *adj*
reflationary *adj* ▷ **reflation**
reflations *n* ▷ **reflation**
reflect *v* (**-s, -ing, -ed**) throw back, esp. rays of light, heat, etc.
reflected *v* ▷ **reflect**
reflecting *v* ▷ **reflect**
reflection *n* (*pl* **-s**) act of reflecting
reflections *n* ▷ **reflect**
reflective *adj* quiet, contemplative
reflector *n* (*pl* **-s**) polished surface for reflecting light etc.
reflectors *n* ▷ **reflector**
reflects *v* ▷ **reflect**
reflex *n* (*pl* **-es**) involuntary response to a stimulus or situation ▶ *adj* (of a muscular action) involuntary
reflexes *n* ▷ **reflex**
reflexive *adj* (GRAMMAR) denoting a verb whose subject is the same as its object
reflexologies *n* ▷ **reflexology**
reflexology *n* (*pl* **-ies**) foot massage as a therapy in alternative medicine
reform *n* (*pl* **-s**) improvement ▶ *v* (**-s, -ing, -ed**) improve > **reformer** *n* (*pl* **-s**)
reformation *n* (*pl* **-s**) act or instance of something being reformed
reformations *n* ▷ **reformation**
reformatories *n* ▷ **reformatory**
reformatory *n* (*pl* **-s**) (formerly) institution for reforming young offenders
reformed *v* ▷ **reform**
reformer *n* ▷ **reform**
reformers *n* ▷ **reform**
reforming *v* ▷ **reform**
reforms *n, v* ▷ **reform**
refract *v* (**-s, -ing, -ed**) change the course of (light etc.) passing from one medium to another > **refraction** *n* (*pl* **-s**) > **refractive** *adj* > **refractor** *n* (*pl* **-s**)
refracted *v* ▷ **refract**
refracting *v* ▷ **refract**
refraction *n* ▷ **refract**
refractions *n* ▷ **refract**
refractive *adj* ▷ **refract**
refractor *n* ▷ **refract**
refractors *n* ▷ **refract**
refractory *adj* unmanageable or rebellious
refracts *v* ▷ **refract**
refrain[1] *v* (**-s, -ing, -ed**) keep oneself from doing
refrain[2] *n* (*pl* **-s**) frequently repeated part of

a song
refrained *v* ▷ **refrain**[1]
refraining *v* ▷ **refrain**[1]
refrains *n* ▷ **refrain**[1, 2] ▶ *v* ▷ **refrain**[2]
refresh *v* (**-es, -ing, -ed**) revive or reinvigorate, as through food, drink, or rest > **refresher** *n* (*pl* **-s**)
refreshed *v* ▷ **refresh**
refresher *n* ▷ **refresh**
refreshers *n* ▷ **refresh**
refreshes *v* ▷ **refresh**
refreshing *adj* having a reviving effect ▶ *v* ▷ **refresh**
refreshment *n* (*pl* **-s**) something that refreshes, esp. food or drink
refreshments *n* ▷ **refreshment**
refrigerate *v* (**-tes, -ting, -ted**) cool or freeze in order to preserve > **refrigeration** *n* (*pl* **-s**)
refrigerated *v* ▷ **refrigerate**
refrigerates *v* ▷ **refrigerate**
refrigerating *v* ▷ **refrigerate**
refrigeration *n* ▷ **refrigerate**
refrigerations *n* ▷ **refrigerate**
refrigerator *n* (*pl* **-s**) ▷ **fridge**
refrigerators *n* ▷ **refrigerator**
refs *n* ▷ **ref**
refuge *n* (*pl* **-s**) (source of) shelter or protection
refugee *n* (*pl* **-s**) person who seeks refuge, esp. in a foreign country
refugees *n* ▷ **refugee**
refuges *n* ▷ **refuge**
refulgent *adj* shining, radiant
refund *v* (**-s, -ing, -ed**) pay back ▶ *n* (*pl* **-s**) return of money
refunded *v* ▷ **refund**
refunding *v* ▷ **refund**
refunds *v, n* ▷ **refund**
refurbish *v* (**-es, -ing, -ed**) renovate and brighten up
refurbished *v* ▷ **refurbish**
refurbishes *v* ▷ **refurbish**
refurbishing *v* ▷ **refurbish**
refusal *n* (*pl* **-s**) denial of anything demanded or offered
refusals *n* ▷ **refusal**
refuse[1] *v* (**-ses, -sing, -sed**) decline, deny, or reject
refuse[2] *n* (*pl* **-s**) rubbish or useless matter
refused *v* ▷ **refuse**[1]
refuses *v* > **refuse**[1] ▶ *n* ▷ **refuse**[2]
refusing *v* ▷ **refuse**[1]
refute *v* (**-tes, -ting, -ted**) disprove > **refutation** *n* (*pl* **-s**)
refutation *n* ▷ **refute**
refutations *n* ▷ **refute**
refuted *v* ▷ **refute**
refutes *v* ▷ **refute**
refuting *v* ▷ **refute**
regain *v* (**-s, -ing, -ed**) get back or recover
regained *v* ▷ **regain**
regaining *v* ▷ **regain**
regains *v* ▷ **regain**
regal *adj* of or like a king or queen > **regally** *adv*
regalia *pl n* ceremonial emblems of royalty or high office
regale *v* (**-les, -ling, -led**) entertain (someone) with stories etc.
regaled *v* ▷ **regale**
regales *v* ▷ **regale**
regaling *v* ▷ **regale**
regally *adv* ▷ **regal**
regard *v* (**-s, -ing, -ed**) consider ▶ *n* (*pl* **-s**) respect or esteem ▶ *pl* expression of goodwill
regarded *v* ▷ **regard**
regarding in respect of, concerning *v* ▷ **regard**
regardless *adj* heedless ▶ *adv* in spite of everything
regards *v, n* ▷ **regard**
regatta *n* (*pl* **-s**) meeting for yacht or boat races
regattas *n* ▷ **regatta**
regenerate *v* (**-tes, -ting, -ted**) (cause to) undergo spiritual, moral, or physical renewal > **regeneration** *n* (*pl* **-s**) > **regenerative** *adj*
regenerated *v* ▷ **regenerate**
regenerates *v* ▷ **regenerate**
regenerating *v* ▷ **regenerate**
regeneration *n* ▷ **regenerate**
regenerations *n* ▷ **regenerate**
regenerative *adj* ▷ **regenerate**
regencies *n* ▷ **regency**
regency *n* (*pl* **-ies**) status or period of office of a regent
regent *n* (*pl* **-s**) ruler of a kingdom during the absence, childhood, or illness of its monarch ▶ *adj* ruling as a regent
regents *n* ▷ **regent**
reggae *n* (*pl* **-s**) style of Jamaican popular music with a strong beat
reggaes *n* ▷ **reggae**
regicide *n* (*pl* **-s**) killing of a king
regicides *n* ▷ **regicide**
regime [ray-**zheem**] *n* (*pl* **-s**) system of government
regimen *n* (*pl* **-s**) prescribed system of diet etc.
regimens *n* ▷ **regimen**
regiment *n* (*pl* **-s**) organized body of troops as a unit of the army > **regimental** *adj* > **regimentation** *n* (*pl* **-s**)
regimental *adj* ▷ **regiment**
regimentation *n* ▷ **regiment**

regimentations *n* ▷ **regiment**
regimented *adj* very strictly controlled
regiments *n* ▷ **regiment**
regimes *n* ▷ **regime**
region *n* (*pl* **-s**) administrative division of a country > **regional** *adj*
regional *adj* ▷ **region**
regions *n* ▷ **region**
register *n* (*pl* **-s**) (book containing) an official list or record of things ▶ *v* (**-s, -ing, -ed**) enter in a register or set down in writing > **registration** *n* (*pl* **-s**)
registered *v* ▷ **register**
registering *v* ▷ **register**
registers *n, v* ▷ **register**
registrar *n* (*pl* **-s**) keeper of official records
registrars *n* ▷ **registrar**
registration *n* ▷ **register**
registrations *n* ▷ **registers**
regress *v* (**-es, -ing, -ed**) revert to a former worse condition
regressed *v* ▷ **regress**
regresses *v* ▷ **regress**
regressing *v* ▷ **regress**
regression *n* (*pl* **-s**) act of regressing (PSYCHOL) > **regressive** *adj*
regressions *n* ▷ **regression**
regressive *adj* ▷ **regression**
regret *v* (**-s, -tting, -tted**) feel sorry about ▶ *n* (*pl* **-s**) feeling of repentance, guilt, or sorrow > **regretful** *adj* > **regrettable** *adj*
regretful *adj* ▷ **regret**
regrets *v* ▷ **regret**
regrettable *adj* ▷ **regret**
regretted *v* ▷ **regret**
regretting *v* ▷ **regret**
regular *adj* normal, customary, or usual ▶ *n* (*pl* **-s**) regular soldier > **regularity** *n* (*pl* **-s**) > **regularize** *v* (**-zes, -zing, -zed**) > **regularly** *adv*
regularities *n* ▷ **regular**
regularity *n* ▷ **regular**
regularize *v* ▷ **regular**
regularized *v* ▷ **regular**
regularizes *v* ▷ **regular**
regularizing *v* ▷ **regular**
regularly *adv* ▷ **regular**
regulars *n* ▷ **regular**
regulate *v* (**-tes, -ting, -ted**) control, esp. by rules
regulated *v* ▷ **regulate**
regulates *v* ▷ **regulate**
regulating *v* ▷ **regulate**
regulation *n* (*pl* **-s**) rule
regulations *n* ▷ **regulation**
regulator *n* (*pl* **-s**) device that automatically controls pressure, temperature, etc.
regulators *n* ▷ **regulator**
regurgitate *v* (**-tes, -ting, -ted**) vomit > **regurgitation** *n* (*pl* **-s**)
regurgitated *v* ▷ **regurgitate**
regurgitates *v* ▷ **regurgitate**
regurgitating *v* ▷ **regurgitate**
regurgitation *n* ▷ **regurgitate**
regurgitations *n* ▷ **regurgitate**
rehabilitate *v* (**-tes, -ting, -ted**) help (a person) to readjust to society after illness, imprisonment, etc. > **rehabilitation** *n* (*pl* **-s**)
rehabilitated *v* ▷ **rehabilitate**
rehabilitates *v* ▷ **rehabilitate**
rehabilitating *v* ▷ **rehabilitate**
rehabilitation *n* ▷ **rehabilitate**
rehabilitations *n* ▷ **rehabilitate**
rehash *v* (**-es, -ing, -ed**) rework or reuse ▶ *n* (*pl* **-es**) old ideas presented in a new form
rehashed *v* ▷ **rehash**
rehashes *v, n* ▷ **rehash**
rehashing *v* ▷ **rehash**
rehearse *v* (**-ses, -sing, -sed**) practise (a play, concert, etc.) > **rehearsal** *n* (*pl* **-s**)
rehearsal *n* ▷ **rehearse**
rehearsals *n* ▷ **rehearse**
rehearsed *v* ▷ **rehearse**
rehearses *v* ▷ **rehearse**
rehearsing *v* ▷ **rehearse**
rehouse *v* (**-ses, -sing, -sed**) provide with a new (and better) home
rehoused *v* ▷ **rehouse**
rehouses *v* ▷ **rehouse**
rehousing *v* ▷ **rehouse**
reign *n* (*pl* **-s**) period of a sovereign's rule ▶ *v* (**-s, -ing, -ed**) rule (a country)
reigned *v* ▷ **reign**
reigning *v* ▷ **reign**
reigns *n, v* ▷ **reign**
reimburse *v* (**-ses, -sing, -sed**) refund, pay back > **reimbursement** *n* (*pl* **-s**)
reimbursed *v* ▷ **reimburse**
reimbursement *n* ▷ **reimburse**
reimbursements *n* ▷ **reimburse**
reimburses *v* ▷ **reimburse**
reimbursing *v* ▷ **reimburse**
rein *v* (**-s, -ing, -ed**) check or manage with reins
reincarnation *n* (*pl* **-s**) rebirth of a soul in successive bodies > **reincarnate** *v* (**-tes, -ting, -ted**)
reincarnate *v* ▷ **reincarnation**
reincarnated *v* ▷ **reincarnation**
reincarnates *v* ▷ **reincarnation**
reincarnating *v* ▷ **reincarnation**

reincarnations *n* ▷ **reincarnation**
reindeer *n* (*pl* **-deer, -deers**) deer of arctic regions with large branched antlers
reindeers *n* ▷ **reindeer**
reined *v* ▷ **rein**
reining *v* ▷ **rein**
reinforce *v* (**-ces, -cing, -ced**) strengthen with new support, material, or force > **reinforcement** *n* (*pl* **-s**)
reinforced *v* ▷ **reinforce**
reinforcement *n* ▷ **reinforce**
reinforcements *n* ▷ **reinforce**
reinforces *v* ▷ **reinforce**
reinforcing *v* ▷ **reinforce**
reins *pl n* narrow straps attached to a bit to guide a horse ▶ *v* ▷ **rein**
reinstate *v* (**-tes, -ting, -ted**) restore to a former position > **reinstatement** *n* (*pl* **-s**)
reinstated *v* ▷ **reinstate**
reinstatement *n* ▷ **reinstate**
reinstatements *n* ▷ **reinstate**
reinstates *v* ▷ **reinstate**
reinstating *v* ▷ **reinstate**
reiterate *v* (**-tes, -ting, -ted**) repeat again and again > **reiteration** *n* (*pl* **-s**)
reiterated *v* ▷ **reiterate**
reiterates *v* ▷ **reiterate**
reiterating *v* ▷ **reiterate**
reiteration *n* ▷ **reiterate**
reiterations *n* ▷ **reiterate**
reject *v* (**-s, -ing, -ed**) refuse to accept or believe ▶ *n* (*pl* **-s**) person or thing rejected as not up to standard > **rejection** *n* (*pl* **-s**)
rejected *v* ▷ **reject**
rejecting *v* ▷ **reject**
rejection *n* ▷ **reject**
rejections *n* ▷ **reject**
rejects *v, n* ▷ **reject**
rejig *v* (**-s, -gging, -gged**) re-equip (a factory or plant)
rejigged *v* ▷ **rejig**
rejigging *v* ▷ **rejig**
rejigs *v* ▷ **rejig**
rejoice *v* (**-ces, -cing, -ced**) feel or express great happiness
rejoiced *v* ▷ **rejoice**
rejoices *v* ▷ **rejoice**
rejoicing *v* ▷ **rejoice**
rejoin[1] *v* (**-s, -ing, -ed**) join again
rejoin[2] *v* (**-s, -ing, -ed**) reply
rejoinder (*pl* **-s**) *n* answer, retort
rejoinders *n* ▷ **rejoinder**
rejoined *v* ▷ **rejoin**[1, 2]
rejoining *v* ▷ **rejoin**[1, 2]
rejoins *v* ▷ **rejoin**[1, 2]
rejuvenate *v* (**-tes, -ting, -ted**) restore youth or vitality to > **rejuvenation** *n* (*pl* **-s**)
rejuvenated *v* ▷ **rejuvenate**
rejuvenates *v* ▷ **rejuvenate**
rejuvenating *v* ▷ **rejuvenate**
rejuvenation *n* ▷ **rejuvenate**
rejuvenations *v* ▷ **rejuvenate**
relapse *v* (**-ses, -sing, -sed**) fall back into bad habits, illness, etc. ▶ *n* (*pl* **-s**) return of bad habits, illness, etc.
relapsed *v* ▷ **relapse**
relapses *v, n* ▷ **relapse**
relapsing *v* ▷ **relapse**
relate *v* (**-tes, -ting, -ted**) establish a relation between > **related** *adj*
related *adj, v* ▷ **relate**
relates *v* ▷ **relate**
relating *v* ▷ **relate**
relation *n* (*pl* **-s**) connection between things ▶ *pl* social or political dealings
relations *n* ▷ **relation**
relationship *n* (*pl* **-s**) dealings and feelings between people or countries
relationships *n* ▷ **relationship**
relative *adj* dependent on relation to something else, not absolute ▶ *n* (*pl* **-s**) person connected by blood or marriage > **relatively** *adv*
relatively *adv* ▷ **relative**
relatives *n* ▷ **relative**
relativities *n* ▷ **relativity**
relativity *n* (*pl* **-ies**) subject of two theories of Albert Einstein, dealing with relationships of space, time, and motion, and acceleration and gravity
relax *v* (**-es, -ing, -ed**) make or become looser, less tense, or less rigid > **relaxing** *adj* > **relaxation** *n* (*pl* **-s**)
relaxation *n* ▷ **relax**
relaxations *n* ▷ **relax**
relaxed *v* ▷ **relax**
relaxes *v* ▷ **relax**
relaxing *v, adj* ▷ **relax**
relay *n* (*pl* **-s**) fresh set of people or animals relieving others ▶ *v* (**-s, -ing, -ed**) pass on (a message)
relayed *v* ▷ **relay**
relaying *v* ▷ **relay**
relays *n, v* ▷ **relay**
release *v* (**-ses, -sing, -sed**) set free ▶ *n* (*pl* **-s**) setting free
released *v* ▷ **release**
releases *v, n* ▷ **release**
releasing *v* ▷ **release**
relegate *v* (**-tes, -ting, -ted**) put in a less

important position > **relegation** *n* (*pl* **-s**)
relegated *v* ▷ **relegate**
relegates *v* ▷ **relegate**
relegating *v* ▷ **relegate**
relegation *n* ▷ **relegate**
relegations *n* ▷ **relegate**
relent *v* (**-s, -ing, -ed**) give up a harsh intention, become less severe
relented *v* ▷ **relent**
relenting *v* ▷ **relent**
relentless *adj* unremitting
relents *v* ▷ **relent**
relevance *n* ▷ **relevant**
relevances *n* ▷ **relevant**
relevant *adj* to do with the matter in hand > **relevance** *n* (*pl* **-s**)
reliabilities *n* ▷ **reliable**
reliability *n* ▷ **reliable**
reliable *adj* able to be trusted, dependable > **reliably** *adv* > **reliability** *n* (*pl* **-ies**)
reliably *adv* ▷ **reliable**
reliance *n* (*pl* **-s**) dependence, confidence, or trust > **reliant** *adj*
reliances *n* ▷ **reliance**
reliant *adj* ▷ **reliance**
relic *n* (*pl* **-s**) something that has survived from the past ▶ *pl* remains or traces
relics *n* ▷ **relic**
relict *n* (*pl* **-s**) (*Obs*) widow
relicts *n* ▷ **relict**
relied *v* ▷ **rely**
relief *n* (*pl* **-s**) gladness at the end or removal of pain, distress, etc.
reliefs *n* ▷ **relief**
relies *v* ▷ **rely**
relieve *v* (**-ves, -ving, -ved**) bring relief to
relieved *v* ▷ **relieve**
relieves *v* ▷ **relieve**
relieving *v* ▷ **relieve**
religion *n* (*pl* **-s**) system of belief in and worship of a supernatural power or god
religious *adj* of religion > **religiously** *adv*
religiously *adv* ▷ **religious**
religions *n* ▷ **religion**
relinquish *v* (**-es, -ing, -ed**) give up or abandon
relinquished *v* ▷ **relinquish**
relinquishes *v* ▷ **relinquish**
relinquishing *v* ▷ **relinquish**
reliquaries *n* ▷ **reliquary**
reliquary *n* (*pl* **-ies**) case or shrine for holy relics
relish *v* (**-es, -ing, -ed**) enjoy, like very much ▶ *n* (*pl* **-es**) liking or enjoyment
relished *v* ▷ **relish**
relishes *v, n* ▷ **relish**
relishing *v* ▷ **relish**
relocate *v* (**-tes, -ting, -ted**) move to a new place to live or work > **relocation** *n* (*pl* **-s**)
relocated *v* ▷ **relocate**
relocates *v* ▷ **relocate**
relocating *v* ▷ **relocate**
relocation *n* ▷ **relocate**
relocations *n* ▷ **relocate**
reluctance *n* ▷ **reluctant**
reluctances *n* ▷ **reluctant**
reluctant *adj* unwilling or disinclined > **reluctantly** *adv* > **reluctance** *n* (*pl* **-s**)
reluctantly *adv* ▷ **reluctant**
rely *v* (**-ies, -ying, -ied**) depend (on)
relying *v* ▷ **rely**
remain *v* (**-s, -ing, -ed**) continue
remainder *n* (*pl* **-s**) part which is left ▶ *v* (**-s, -ing, -ed**) offer (copies of a poorly selling book) at reduced prices
remaindered *v* ▷ **remainders**
remaindering *v* ▷ **remainders**
remainders *n, v* ▷ **remainders**
remained *v* ▷ **remain**
remaining *v* ▷ **remain**
remains *pl n* relics, esp. of ancient buildings ▶ *v* ▷ **remain**
remand *v* (**-s, -ing, -ed**) send back into custody or put on bail before trial
remanded *v* ▷ **remand**
remanding *v* ▷ **remand**
remands *v* ▷ **remand**
remark *v* (**-s, -ing, -ed**) make a casual comment (on) ▶ *n* (*pl* **-s**) observation or comment
remarkable *adj* worthy of note or attention > **remarkably** *adv*
remarkably *adv* ▷ **remarkable**
remarked *v* ▷ **remark**
remarking *v* ▷ **remark**
remarks *v, n* ▷ **remark**
remedial *adj* intended to correct a specific disability, handicap, etc.
remedied *v* ▷ **remedy**
remedies *n, v* ▷ **remedy**
remedy *n* (*pl* **-ies**) means of curing pain or disease ▶ *v* (**-ies, -ying, -ied**) put right
remedying *v* ▷ **remedy**
remember *v* (**-s, -ing, -ed**) retain in or recall to one's memory
remembered *v* ▷ **remember**
remembering *v* ▷ **remember**
remembers *v* ▷ **remember**
remembrance *n* (*pl* **-s**) memory
remembrances *n* ▷ **remembrance**
remind *v* (**-s, -ing, -ed**) cause to remember
reminded *v* ▷ **remind**
reminder *n* (*pl* **-s**) something that recalls the

past
reminders *n* ▷ **reminder**
reminding *v* ▷ **remind**
reminds *v* ▷ **remind**
reminisce *v* (**-ces, -cing, -ced**) talk or write of past times, experiences, etc.
reminisced *v* ▷ **reminisce**
reminiscence *n* (*pl* **-s**) remembering ▸ *pl* memoirs
reminiscences *n* ▷ **reminiscence**
reminiscent *adj* reminding or suggestive (of)
reminisces *v* ▷ **reminisce**
reminiscing *v* ▷ **reminisce**
remiss *adj* negligent or careless
remission *n* (*pl* **-s**) reduction in the length of a prison term
remissions *n* ▷ **remission**
remit *v* (**-s, -tting, -tted**) send (money) for goods, services, etc., esp. by post ▸ *n* (*pl* **-s**) [**ree**-mitt] area of competence or authority
remits *v, n* ▷ **remit**
remittance *n* (*pl* **-s**) money sent as payment
remittances *n* ▷ **remittance**
remitted *v* ▷ **remit**
remitting *v* ▷ **remit**
remnant *n* (*pl* **-s**) small piece, esp. of fabric, left over
remnants *n* ▷ **remnant**
remonstrance *n* ▷ **remonstrate**
remonstrances *n* ▷ **remonstrate**
remonstrate *v* (**-tes, -ting, -ted**) argue in protest > **remonstrance** *n* (*pl* **-s**)
remonstrated *v* ▷ **remonstrate**
remonstrates *v* ▷ **remonstrate**
remonstrating *v* ▷ **remonstrate**
remorse *n* (*pl* **-s**) feeling of sorrow and regret for something one did > **remorseful** *adj*
remorseful *adj* ▷ **remorse**
remorseless *adj* pitiless > **remorselessly** *adv*
remorselessly *adv* ▷ **remorseless**
remorses *n* ▷ **remorse**
remote *adj* (**-er, -est**) far away, distant > **remotely** *adv*
remoter *adj* ▷ **remote**
remotest *adj* ▷ **remote**
remotely *adv* ▷ **remote**
remould *v* (**-s, -ing, -ed**) (BRIT) renovate (a worn tyre) ▸ *n* (*pl* **-s**) (BRIT) renovated tyre
remoulded *v* ▷ **remould**
remoulding *v* ▷ **remould**
remoulds *v, n* ▷ **remould**
remove *v* (**-ves, -ving, -ved**) take away or off ▸ *n* (*pl* **-s**) degree of difference > **removable** *adj*
removable *adj* ▷ **remove**
removal *n* (*pl* **-s**) removing, esp. changing residence
removals *n* ▷ **removal**
removed *v* ▷ **remove**
removes *v, n* ▷ **remove**
removing *v* ▷ **remove**
remunerate *v* (**-tes, -ting, -ted**) reward or pay > **remunerative** *adj*
remunerated *v* ▷ **remunerate**
remunerates *v* ▷ **remunerate**
remunerating *v* ▷ **remunerate**
remuneration *n* (*pl* **-s**) reward or payment
remunerations *n* ▷ **remuneration**
remunerative *adj* ▷ **remuneration**
renaissance *n* (*pl* **-s**) revival or rebirth
renaissances *n* ▷ **renaissance**
renal [**ree**-nal] *adj* of the kidneys
renascent *adj* becoming active or vigorous again
rend *v* (**-s, -ing, rent**) tear or wrench apart
render *v* (**-s, -ing, -ed**) cause to become
rendered *v* ▷ **render**
rendering *v* ▷ **render**
renders *v* ▷ **render**
rendezvous [**ron**-day-voo] *n* (*pl* **-vous**) appointment ▸ *v* (**-vous, -vousing, -voused**) meet as arranged
rendezvoused *v* ▷ **rendezvous**
rendezvousing *v* ▷ **rendezvous**
rending *v* ▷ **rend**
rendition *n* (*pl* **-s**) performance
renditions *n* ▷ **rendition**
rends *v* ▷ **rend**
renegade *n* (*pl* **-s**) person who deserts a cause
renegades *n* ▷ **renegade**
renege [rin-**nayg**] *v* (**-ges, -ging, -ged**) go back (on a promise etc.)
reneged *v* ▷ **renege**
reneges *v* ▷ **renege**
reneging *v* ▷ **renege**
renew *v* (**-s, -ing, -ed**) begin again > **renewable** *adj* > **renewal** *n* (*pl* **-s**)
renewable *adj* ▷ **renew**
renewal *n* ▷ **renew**
renewals *n* ▷ **renew**
renewed *v* ▷ **renew**
renewing *v* ▷ **renew**
renews *v* ▷ **renew**
rennet *n* (*pl* **-s**) substance for curdling milk to make cheese
rennets *n* ▷ **rennet**
renounce *v* (**-ces, -cing, -ced**) give up (a belief, habit, etc.) voluntarily > **renunciation** *n* (*pl* **-s**)
renounced *v* ▷ **renounce**
renounces *v* ▷ **renounce**
renouncing *v* ▷ **renounce**

renovate *v* (**-tes, -ting, -ted**) restore to good condition > **renovation** *n* (*pl* **-s**)
renovated *v* ▷ **renovate**
renovates *v* ▷ **renovate**
renovating *v* ▷ **renovate**
renovation *n* ▷ **renovate**
renovations *n* ▷ **renovate**
renown *n* (*pl* **-s**) widespread good reputation
renowned *adj* famous
renowns *n* ▷ **renown**
rent¹ *v* (**-s, -ing, -ed**) give or have use of in return for regular payments ▶ *n* (*pl* **-s**) regular payment for use of land, a building, machine, etc.
rent² *n* (*pl* **-s**) tear or fissure ▶ *v* ▷ **rend**
rental *n* (*pl* **-s**) sum payable as rent
rentals *n* ▷ **rental**
rented *v* ▷ **rent¹**
renting *v* ▷ **rent¹**
rents *v* ▷ **rent¹** ▶ *n* ▷ **rent²**
renunciation *n* ▷ **renounce**
renunciations *n* ▷ **renounce**
reorganize *v* (**-zes, -zing, -zed**) organize in a new and more efficient way > **reorganization** *n* (*pl* **-s**)
reorganization *n* ▷ **reorganize**
reorganizations *n* ▷ **reorganize**
reorganized *v* ▷ **reorganize**
reorganizes *v* ▷ **reorganize**
reorganizing *v* ▷ **reorganize**
rep¹ *n* (*pl* **-s**) repertory company
rep² *n* (*pl* **-s**) ▷ **representative**
repair¹ *v* (**-s, -ing, -ed**) restore to good condition, mend ▶ *n* (*pl* **-s**) act of repairing
repair² *v* (**-s, -ing, -ed**) go (to)
repaired *v* ▷ **repair¹, ²**
repairing *v* ▷ **repair¹, ²**
repairs *v* ▷ **repair¹, ²** ▶ *n* ▷ **repair¹**
reparation *n* (*pl* **-s**) something done or given as compensation
reparations *n* ▷ **reparation**
repartee *n* (*pl* **-s**) interchange of witty retorts
repartees *n* ▷ **repartee**
repast *n* (*pl* **-s**) meal
repasts *n* ▷ **repast**
repatriate *v* (**-tes, -ting, -ted**) send (someone) back to his or her own country > **repatriation** *n* (*pl* **-s**)
repatriated *v* ▷ **repatriate**
repatriates *v* ▷ **repatriate**
repatriating *v* ▷ **repatriate**
repatriation *n* ▷ **repatriate**
repatriations *n* ▷ **repatriate**
repay *v* (**-s, -ing, -paid**) pay back, refund > **repayable** *adj* > **repayment** *n* (*pl* **-s**)
repayable *adj* ▷ **repay**
repaying *v* ▷ **repay**
repayment *n* ▷ **repay**
repayments *n* ▷ **repay**
repays *v* ▷ **repay**
repeal *v* (**-s, -ing, -ed**) cancel (a law) officially ▶ *n* (*pl* **-s**) act of repealing
repealed *v* ▷ **repeal**
repealing *v* ▷ **repeal**
repeals *v, n* ▷ **repeal**
repeat *v* (**-s, -ing, -ed**) say or do again ▶ *n* (*pl* **-s**) act or instance of repeating > **repeatedly** *adv*
repeated *v* ▷ **repeat**
repeatedly *adv* ▷ **repeat**
repeater *n* (*pl* **-s**) firearm that may be discharged many times without reloading
repeaters *n* ▷ **repeater**
repeating *v* ▷ **repeat**
repeats *v, n* ▷ **repeat**
repel *v* (**-s, -lling, -lled**) be disgusting to
repelled *v* ▷ **repel**
repellent *adj* distasteful ▶ *n* (*pl* **-s**) something that repels, esp. a chemical to repel insects
repellents *n* ▷ **repellent**
repelling *v* ▷ **repel**
repels *v* ▷ **repel**
repent *v* (**-s, -ing, -ed**) feel regret for (a deed or omission) > **repentance** *n* (*pl* **-s**) > **repentant** *adj*
repentance *n* ▷ **repent**
repentances *n* ▷ **repent**
repentant *adj* ▷ **repent**
repented *v* ▷ **repent**
repenting *v* ▷ **repent**
repents *v* ▷ **repent**
repercussions *pl n* indirect effects, often unpleasant
repertoire *n* (*pl* **-s**) stock of plays, songs, etc. that a player or company can give
repertoires *n* ▷ **repertoire**
repertories *n* ▷ **repertory**
repertory *n* (*pl* **-ies**) repertoire
repetition *n* (*pl* **-s**) act of repeating
repetitions *n* ▷ **repetition**
repetitious *adj* ▷ **repetitive**
repetitive, repetitious *adj* full of repetition
rephrase *v* (**-ses, -sing, -sed**) express in different words
rephrased *v* ▷ **rephrase**
rephrases *v* ▷ **rephrase**
rephrasing *v* ▷ **rephrase**
repine *v* (**-nes, -ning, -ned**) fret or complain
repined *v* ▷ **repine**
repines *v* ▷ **repine**
repining *v* ▷ **repine**

replace *v* (**-ces, -cing, -ced**) substitute for > **replacement** *n* (*pl* **-s**)
replaced *v* ▷ **replace**
replacement *n* ▷ **replace**
replacements *n* ▷ **replace**
replaces *v* ▷ **replace**
replacing *v* ▷ **replace**
replay *n* (*pl* **-s**) immediate reshowing on TV of an incident in sport, esp. in slow motion ▶ *v* (**-s, -ing, -ed**) play (a match, recording, etc.) again
replayed *v* ▷ **replay**
replaying *v* ▷ **replay**
replays *n, v* ▷ **replay**
replenish *v* (**-es, -ing, -ed**) fill up again, resupply > **replenishment** *n* (*pl* **-s**)
replenished *v* ▷ **replenish**
replenishes *v* ▷ **replenish**
replenishing *v* ▷ **replenish**
replenishment *n* ▷ **replenish**
replenishments *n* ▷ **replenish**
replete *adj* filled or gorged
replica *n* (*pl* **-s**) exact copy
replicas *n* ▷ **replica**
replicate *v* (**-s, -ing, -ed**) make or be a copy of
replicated *v* ▷ **replicate**
replicates *v* ▷ **replicate**
replicating *v* ▷ **replicate**
replied *v* ▷ **reply**
replies *v, n* ▷ **reply**
reply *v* (**-ies, -ying, -ied**) answer or respond ▶ *n* (*pl* **-ies**) answer or response
replying *v* ▷ **reply**
report *v* (**-s, -ing, -ed**) give an account of ▶ *n* (*pl* **-s**) account or statement
reported *v* ▷ **report**
reportedly *adv* according to rumour
reporter *n* (*pl* **-s**) person who gathers news for a newspaper, TV, etc.
reporters *n* ▷ **reporter**
reporting *v* ▷ **report**
reports *v, n* ▷ **report**
repose *n* (*pl* **-s**) peace ▶ *v* (**-ses, -sing, -sed**) lie or lay at rest
reposed *v* ▷ **repose**
reposes *n, v* ▷ **repose**
reposing *v* ▷ **repose**
repositories *n* ▷ **repository**
repository *n* (*pl* **-ies**) place where valuables are deposited for safekeeping, store
repossess *v* (**-es, -ing, -ed**) (of a lender) take back property from a customer who is behind with payments > **repossession** *n* (*pl* **-s**)
repossessed *v* ▷ **repossess**
repossesses *v* ▷ **repossess**
repossessing *v* ▷ **repossess**
repossession *n* ▷ **repossess**
repossessions *n* ▷ **repossess**
reprehensible *adj* open to criticism, unworthy
represent *v* (**-s, -ing, -ed**) act as a delegate or substitute for > **representation** *n* (*pl* **-s**)
representation *n* ▷ **represent**
representations *n* ▷ **represent**
representative *n* (*pl* **-s**) person chosen to stand for a group ▶ *adj* typical
representatives *n* ▷ **representative**
represented *v* ▷ **represent**
representing *v* ▷ **represent**
represents *v* ▷ **represent**
repress *v* (**-es, -ing, -ed**) keep (feelings) in check > **repression** *n* (*pl* **-s**) > **repressive** *adj*
repressed *v* ▷ **repress**
represses *v* ▷ **repress**
repressing *v* ▷ **repress**
repression *n* ▷ **repress**
repressions *n* ▷ **repress**
repressive *adj* ▷ **repress**
reprieve *v* (**-ves, -ving, -ved**) postpone the execution of (a condemned person) ▶ *n* (*pl* **-s**) (document granting) postponement or cancellation of a punishment
reprieved *v* ▷ **reprieve**
reprieves *v, n* ▷ **reprieve**
reprieving *v* ▷ **reprieve**
reprimand *v* (**-s, -ing, -ed**) blame (someone) officially for a fault ▶ *n* (*pl* **-s**) official blame
reprimanded *v* ▷ **reprimand**
reprimanding *v* ▷ **reprimand**
reprimands *v, n* ▷ **reprimand**
reprint *v* (**-s, -ing, -ed**) print further copies of (a book) ▶ *n* (*pl* **-s**) reprinted copy
reprinted *v* ▷ **reprint**
reprinting *v* ▷ **reprint**
reprints *v, n* ▷ **reprint**
reprisal *n* (*pl* **-s**) retaliation
reprisals *n* ▷ **reprisal**
reproach *n, v* (**-es, -ing, -ed**) blame, rebuke > **reproachful** *adj* > **reproachfully** *adv*
reproached *v* ▷ **reproach**
reproaches *v* ▷ **reproach**
reproachful *adj* ▷ **reproach**
reproachfully *adv* ▷ **reproach**
reproaching *v* ▷ **reproach**
reprobate *adj, n* (*pl* **-s**) depraved or disreputable (person)
reprobates *n* ▷ **reprobate**
reproduce *v* (**-ces, -cing, -ced**) produce a copy of > **reproducible** *adj*
reproduced *v* ▷ **reproduce**

reproduces *v* ▷ **reproduce**
reproducible *adj* ▷ **reproduce**
reproducing *v* ▷ **reproduce**
reproduction *n* (*pl* **-s**) process of reproducing > **reproductive** *adj*
reproductions *n* ▷ **reproduction**
reproductive *adj* ▷ **reproduction**
reproof *n* (*pl* **-s**) severe blaming of someone for a fault
reproofs *n* ▷ **reproof**
reprove *v* (**-ves, -ving, -ved**) speak severely to (someone) about a fault
reproved *v* ▷ **reprove**
reproves *v* ▷ **reprove**
reproving *v* ▷ **reprove**
reps *n* ▷ **rep**[1, 2]
reptile *n* (*pl* **-s**) cold-blooded egg-laying vertebrate with horny scales or plates, such as a snake or tortoise > **reptilian** *adj*
reptiles *n* ▷ **reptile**
reptilian *adj* ▷ **reptile**
republic *n* (*pl* **-s**) form of government in which the people or their elected representatives possess the supreme power
republican *n* (*pl* **-s**) supporter or advocate of a republic > **republicanism** *n* (*pl* **-s**)
republicans *n* ▷ **republican**
republicanism *n* ▷ **republican**
republicanisms *n* ▷ **republican**
republics *n* ▷ **republic**
repudiate [rip-**pew**-dee-ate] *v* (**-tes, -ting, -ted**) reject the authority or validity of > **repudiation** *n* (*pl* **-s**)
repudiated *v* ▷ **repudiate**
repudiates *v* ▷ **repudiate**
repudiating *v* ▷ **repudiate**
repudiation *n* ▷ **repudiate**
repudiations *n* ▷ **repudiate**
repugnance *n* ▷ **repugnant**
repugnances *n* ▷ **repugnant**
repugnant *adj* offensive or distasteful > **repugnance** *n* (*pl* **-s**)
repulse *v* (**-ses, -sing, -sed**) be disgusting to ▶ *n* (*pl* **-s**) driving back
repulsed *v* ▷ **repulse**
repulsing *v* ▷ **repulse**
repulses *v, n* ▷ **repulse**
repulsion *n* (*pl* **-s**) distaste or aversion
repulsions *n* ▷ **repulsion**
repulsive *adj* loathsome, disgusting
reputable *adj* of good reputation, respectable
reputation *n* (*pl* **-s**) estimation in which a person is held
reputations *n* ▷ **reputation**
repute *n* (*pl* **-s**) reputation
reputed *adj* supposed > **reputedly** *adv*
reputedly *adv* ▷ **reputed**
reputes *n* ▷ **repute**
request *v* (**-s, -ing, -ed**) ask ▶ *n* (*pl* **-s**) asking
requested *v* ▷ **request**
requesting *v* ▷ **request**
requests *v, n* ▷ **request**
requiem [**rek**-wee-em] *n* (*pl* **-s**) Mass for the dead
requiems *n* ▷ **requiem**
require *v* (**-res, -ring, -red**) want or need
required *v* ▷ **require**
requirement *n* (*pl* **-s**) essential condition
requirements *n* ▷ **requirement**
requires *v* ▷ **require**
requiring *v* ▷ **require**
requisite [**rek**-wizz-it] *adj* necessary, essential ▶ *n* (*pl* **-s**) essential thing
requisites *n* ▷ **requisite**
requisition *v* (**-s, -ing, -ed**) demand (supplies) ▶ *n* (*pl* **-s**) formal demand, such as for materials or supplies
requisitioned *v* ▷ **requisition**
requisitioning *v* ▷ **requisition**
requisitions *v, n* ▷ **requisition**
requite *v* (**-tes, -ting, -ted**) return to someone (the same treatment or feeling as received)
requited *v* ▷ **requite**
requites *v* ▷ **requite**
requiting *v* ▷ **requite**
reredos [**rear**-doss] *n* (*pl* **-es**) ornamental screen behind an altar
reredoses *n* ▷ **reredos**
resat *v* ▷ **resit**
rescind *v* (**-s, -ing, -ed**) annul or repeal
rescinded *v* ▷ **rescind**
rescinding *v* ▷ **rescind**
rescinds *v* ▷ **rescind**
rescue *v* (**-cues, -cuing, -cued**) deliver from danger or trouble, save ▶ *n* (*pl* **-s**) rescuing > **rescuer** *n* (*pl* **-s**)
rescued *v* ▷ **rescue**
rescuer *n* ▷ **rescue**
rescuers *n* ▷ **rescue**
rescues *v, n* ▷ **rescue**
rescuing *v* ▷ **rescue**
research *n* (*pl* **-es**) systematic investigation to discover facts or collect information ▶ *v* (**-es, -ing, -ed**) carry out investigations > **researcher** *n* (*pl* **-s**)
researched *v* ▷ **research**
researcher *n* ▷ **research**
researchers *n* ▷ **research**
researches *n, v* ▷ **research**
researching *v* ▷ **research**

resemblance *n* ▷ **resemble**
resemblances *n* ▷ **resemble**
resemble *v* (**-les, -ling, -led**) be or look like > **resemblance** *n* (*pl* **-s**)
resembled *v* ▷ **resemble**
resembles *v* ▷ **resemble**
resembling *v* ▷ **resemble**
resent *v* (**-s, -ing, -ed**) feel bitter about > **resentful** *adj* > **resentment** *n* (*pl* **-s**)
resented *v* ▷ **resent**
resentful *adj* ▷ **resent**
resenting *v* ▷ **resent**
resentment *n* ▷ **resent**
resentments *n* ▷ **resent**
resents *v* ▷ **resent**
reservation *n* (*pl* **-s**) doubt
reservations *n* ▷ **reservation**
reserve *v* (**-ves, -ving, -ved**) set aside, keep for future use ▶ *n* (*pl* **-s**) something, esp. money or troops, kept for emergencies (SPORT)
reserved *adj* not showing one's feelings, lacking friendliness ▶ *v* ▷ **reserve**
reserves *v, n* ▷ **reserve**
reserving *v* ▷ **reserve**
reservist *n* (*pl* **-s**) member of a military reserve
reservists *n* ▷ **reservist**
reservoir *n* (*pl* **-s**) natural or artificial lake storing water for community supplies
reservoirs *n* ▷ **reservoir**
reshuffle *n* (*pl* **-s**) reorganization ▶ *v* (**-s, -ing, -ed**) reorganize
reshuffled *n* ▷ **reshuffle**
reshuffles *n, v* ▷ **reshuffle**
reshuffling *v* ▷ **reshuffle**
reside *v* (**-des, -ding, -ded**) dwell permanently
resided *v* ▷ **reside**
residence *n* (*pl* **-s**) home or house
residences *n* ▷ **residence**
resident *n* (*pl* **-s**) person who lives in a place ▶ *adj* living in a place
residential *adj* (of part of a town) consisting mainly of houses
residents *n* ▷ **resident**
resides *v* ▷ **reside**
residing *v* ▷ **reside**
residue *n* (*pl* **-s**) what is left, remainder > **residual** *adj*
residual *adj* ▷ **residue**
residues *n* ▷ **residue**
resign *v* (**-s, -ing, -ed**) give up office, a job, etc.
resignation *n* (*pl* **-s**) resigning
resignations *n* ▷ **resignation**
resigned *adj* content to endure ▶ *v* ▷ **resign**
resigning *v* ▷ **resign**
resigns *v* ▷ **resign**
resilience *n* ▷ **resilient**
resiliences *n* ▷ **resilient**
resilient *adj* (of a person) recovering quickly from a shock etc. > **resilience** *n* (*pl* **-s**)
resin [**rezz**-in] *n* (*pl* **-s**) sticky substance from plants, esp. pines > **resinous** *adj*
resinous *adj* ▷ **resin**
resins *n* ▷ **resin**
resist *v* (**-s, -ing, -ed**) withstand or oppose > **resistant** *adj* > **resistible** *adj*
resistance *n* (*pl* **-s**) act of resisting
resistances *n* ▷ **resistance**
resistant *adj* ▷ **resist**
resisted *v* ▷ **resist**
resistible *adj* ▷ **resist**
resisting *v* ▷ **resist**
resistor *n* (*pl* **-s**) component of an electrical circuit producing resistance
resistors *n* ▷ **resistor**
resists *v* ▷ **resist**
resit *v* (**-s, -tting, -sat**) take (an exam) again ▶ *n* (*pl* **-s**) exam that has to be taken again
resitting *v* ▷ **resit**
resits *v, n* ▷ **resit**
resolute *adj* firm in purpose > **resolutely** *adv*
resolutely *adv* ▷ **resolute**
resolution *n* (*pl* **-s**) firmness of conduct or character
resolutions *n* ▷ **resolution**
resolve *v* (**-ves, -ving, -ved**) decide with an effort of will
resolved *adj* determined ▶ *v* ▷ **resolve**
resolves *v* ▷ **resolve**
resolving *v* ▷ **resolve**
resonance *n* (*pl* **-s**) echoing, esp. with a deep sound > **resonant** *adj* > **resonate** *v* (**-tes, -ting, -ted**)
resonances *n* ▷ **resonance**
resonant *adj* ▷ **resonance**
resonate *v* ▷ **resonance**
resonated *v* ▷ **resonance**
resonates *v* ▷ **resonance**
resonating *v* ▷ **resonance**
resort *v* (**-s, -ing, -ed**) have recourse (to) for help etc. ▶ *n* (*pl* **-s**) place for holidays
resorted *v* ▷ **resort**
resorting *v* ▷ **resort**
resorts *v, n* ▷ **resort**
resound [riz-**zownd**] *v* (**-s, -ing, -ed**) echo or ring with sound
resounded *v* ▷ **resound**
resounding *adj* echoing ▶ *v* ▷ **resound**
resounds *v* ▷ **resound**
resource *n* (*pl* **-s**) thing resorted to for support ▶ *pl* sources of economic wealth

> **resourceful** *adj* > **resourcefulness** *n*
resourceful *adj* ▷ **resource**
resourcefulness *n* ▷ **resource**
resources *n* ▷ **resource**
respect *n* (*pl* **-s**) consideration ▶ *v* (**-s, -ing, -ed**) treat with esteem > **respecter** *n* (*pl* **-s**) > **respectful** *adj*
respectable *adj* worthy of respect > **respectably** *adv* > **respectability** *n* (*pl* **-ies**)
respectabilities *n* ▷ **respectable**
respectability *n* ▷ **respectable**
respectably *adv* ▷ **respectable**
respected *v* ▷ **respect**
respecter *n* ▷ **respect**
respecters *n* ▷ **respect**
respectful *adj* ▷ **respect**
respecting *prep* concerning ▶ *v* ▷ **respect**
respective *adj* relating separately to each of those in question > **respectively** *adv*
respectively *adv* ▷ **respective**
respects *n, v* ▷ **respect**
respiration [ress-per-**ray**-shun] *n* (*pl* **-s**) breathing > **respiratory** *adj*
respirations *n* ▷ **respiration**
respirator *n* apparatus worn over the mouth and breathed through as protection against dust, poison gas, etc., or to provide artificial respiration
respirators *n* ▷ **respirator**
respiratory *adj* ▷ **respiration**
respire *v* (**-res, -ring, -red**) breathe
respired *v* ▷ **respire**
respires *v* ▷ **respire**
respiring *v* ▷ **respire**
respite *n* (*pl* **-s**) pause, interval of rest
respites *n* ▷ **respite**
resplendence *n* ▷ **resplendent**
resplendences *n* ▷ **resplendent**
resplendent *adj* brilliant or splendid > **resplendence** *n* (*pl* **-s**)
respond *v* (**-s, -ing, -ed**) answer
responded *v* ▷ **respond**
respondent *n* (*pl* **-s**) (LAW) defendant
respondents *n* ▷ **respondent**
responding *v* ▷ **respond**
responds *v* ▷ **respond**
response *n* (*pl* **-s**) answer
responses *n* ▷ **response**
responsibilities *n* ▷ **responsibility**
responsibility *n* (*pl* **-ies**) state of being responsible
responsible *adj* having control and authority > **responsibly** *adv*
responsibly *adv* ▷ **responsible**
responsive *adj* readily reacting to some influence > **responsiveness** *n*
responsiveness *n* ▷ **responsive**
rest[1] *n* (*pl* **-s**) freedom from exertion etc. ▶ *v* (**-s, -ing, -ed**) take a rest > **restful** *adj* > **restless** *adj*
rest[2] *n* what is left ▶ *v* (**-s, -ing, -ed**) remain, continue to be
restaurant *n* (*pl* **-s**) commercial establishment serving meals
restaurants *n* ▷ **restaurant**
restaurateur [rest-er-a-**tur**] *n* (*pl* **-s**) person who owns or runs a restaurant
restaurateurs *n* ▷ **restaurateur**
rested *v* ▷ **rest**[1, 2]
restful (**-ler, -lest**) *adj* ▷ **rest**[1]
restfuller *adj* ▷ **restful**
restfullest *adj* ▷ **restful**
resting *v* ▷ **rest**[1, 2]
restitution *n* (*pl* **-s**) giving back
restitutions *n* ▷ **restitution**
restive *adj* restless or impatient
restless *adj* ▷ **rest**[1]
restore *v* (**-res, -ring, -red**) return (a building, painting, etc.) to its original condition > **restoration** *n* (*pl* **-s**) > **restorer** *n* (*pl* **-s**)
restoration *n* ▷ **restore**
restorations *n* ▷ **restore**
restorative *adj* restoring ▶ *n* (*pl* **-s**) food or medicine to strengthen etc.
restoratives *n* ▷ **restorative**
restored *v* ▷ **restore**
restorer *n* ▷ **restore**
restorers *n* ▷ **restore**
restores *v* ▷ **restore**
restoring *v* ▷ **restore**
restrain *v* (**-s, -ing, -ed**) hold (someone) back from action
restrained *adj* not displaying emotion ▶ *v* ▷ **restrain**
restraining *v* ▷ **restrain**
restrains *v* ▷ **restrain**
restraint *n* (*pl* **-s**) control, esp. self-control
restraints *n* ▷ **restraint**
restrict *v* (**-s, -ing, -ed**) confine to certain limits > **restriction** *n* (*pl* **-s**) > **restrictive** *adj*
restricted *v* ▷ **restrict**
restricting *v* ▷ **restrict**
restriction *n* ▷ **restrict**
restrictions *n* ▷ **restrict**
restrictive *adj* ▷ **restrict**
restricts *v* ▷ **restrict**
restructure *v* (**-res, -ring, -red**) organize in a different way
restructured *v* ▷ **restructure**
restructures *v* ▷ **restructure**
restructuring *v* ▷ **restructure**

rests *n, v* ▷ **rest**[1, 2]
result *n* (*pl* **-s**) outcome or consequence ▶ *v* (**-s, -ing, -ed**) (*foll. by* **from**) be the outcome or consequence (of) > **resultant** *adj*
resultant *adj* ▷ **result**
resulted *v* ▷ **result**
resulting *v* ▷ **result**
results *n, v* ▷ **result**
resume *v* (**-mes, -ming, -med**) begin again > **resumption** *n* (*pl* **-s**)
résumé [rezz-yew-may] *n* (*pl* **-s**) summary
resumed *v* ▷ **resume**
resumes *v* ▷ **resume**
résumés *n* ▷ **résumé**
resuming *v* ▷ **resume**
resumption *n* ▷ **resume**
resumptions *n* ▷ **resume**
resurgence *n* (*pl* **-s**) rising again to vigour > **resurgent** *adj*
resurgences *n* ▷ **resurgence**
resurgent *adj* ▷ **resurgence**
resurrect *v* (**-s, -ing, -ed**) restore to life
resurrected *v* ▷ **resurrect**
resurrecting *v* ▷ **resurrect**
resurrection *n* (*pl* **-s**) rising again (esp. from the dead)
resurrections *n* ▷ **resurrection**
resurrects *v* ▷ **resurrect**
resuscitate [ris-**suss**-it-tate] *v* (**-tes, -ting, -ted**) restore to consciousness > **resuscitation** *n* (*pl* **-s**)
resuscitated *v* ▷ **resuscitate**
resuscitates *v* ▷ **resuscitate**
resuscitating *v* ▷ **resuscitate**
resuscitation *n* ▷ **resuscitate**
resuscitations *n* ▷ **resuscitate**
retail *n* (*pl* **-s**) selling of goods individually or in small amounts to the public ▶ *adv* by retail ▶ *v* (**-s, -ing, -ed**) sell or be sold retail
retailed *v* ▷ **retail**
retailer *n* (*pl* **-s**) person or company that sells goods to the public
retailers *n* ▷ **retailer**
retailing *v* ▷ **retail**
retails *n, v* ▷ **retail**
retain *v* (**-s, -ing, -ed**) keep in one's possession
retained *v* ▷ **retain**
retainer *n* (*pl* **-s**) fee to retain someone's services
retainers *n* ▷ **retainer**
retaining *v* ▷ **retain**
retains *v* ▷ **retain**
retaliate *v* (**-tes, -ting, -ted**) repay an injury or wrong in kind > **retaliation** *n* (*pl* **-s**) > **retaliatory** *adj*
retaliated *v* ▷ **retaliate**
retaliates *v* ▷ **retaliate**
retaliating *v* ▷ **retaliate**
retaliation *n* ▷ **retaliate**
retaliations *n* ▷ **retaliate**
retaliatory *adj* ▷ **retaliate**
retard *v* (**-s, -ing, -ed**) delay or slow (progress or development) > **retardation** *n* (*pl* **-s**)
retardation *n* ▷ **retard**
retardations *n* ▷ **retard**
retarded *adj* underdeveloped, esp. mentally ▶ *v* ▷ **retard**
retarding *v* ▷ **retard**
retards *v* ▷ **retard**
retch *v* (**-es, -ing, -ed**) try to vomit
retched *v* ▷ **retch**
retches *v* ▷ **retch**
retching *v* ▷ **retch**
rethink *v* (**-s, -ing, -thought**) consider again, esp. with a view to changing one's tactics
rethinks *v* ▷ **rethink**
rethinking *v* ▷ **rethink**
rethought *v* ▷ **rethink**
reticence *n* ▷ **reticent**
reticences *n* ▷ **reticent**
reticent *adj* uncommunicative, reserved > **reticence** *n* (*pl* **-s**)
retina *n* (*pl* **-nas, -nae**) light-sensitive membrane at the back of the eye
retinae *n* ▷ **retina**
retinas *n* ▷ **retina**
retinue *n* (*pl* **-s**) band of attendants
retinues *n* ▷ **retinue**
retire *v* (**-res, -ring, -red**) (cause to) give up office or work, esp. through age > **retirement** *n* (*pl* **-s**)
retired *adj* having retired from work etc. ▶ *v* ▷ **retire**
retirement *n* ▷ **retire**
retirements *n* ▷ **retire**
retires *v* ▷ **retire**
retiring *adj* shy ▶ *v* ▷ **retire**
retort[1] *v* (**-s, -ing, -ed**) reply quickly, wittily, or angrily ▶ *n* (*pl* **-s**) quick, witty, or angry reply
retort[2] *n* (*pl* **-s**) glass container with a bent neck used for distilling
retorted *v* ▷ **retort**[1]
retorting *v* ▷ **retort**[1]
retorts *v* ▷ **retort**[1] ▶ *n* ▷ **retort**[1, 2]
retouch *v* (**-es, -ing, -ed**) restore or improve by new touches, esp. of paint
retouched *v* ▷ **retouch**
retouches *v* ▷ **retouch**
retouching *v* ▷ **retouch**
retrace *v* (**-ces, -cing, -ced**) go back over (a

route etc.) again
retraced *v* ▷ **retrace**
retraces *v* ▷ **retrace**
retracing *v* ▷ **retrace**
retract *v* (**-s, -ing, -ed**) withdraw (a statement etc.) > **retraction** *n* (*pl* **-s**)
retractable, retractile *adj* able to be retracted
retracted *v* ▷ **retract**
retractile *adj* ▷ **retractable**
retracting *v* ▷ **retract**
retracts *v* ▷ **retract**
retraction *n* ▷ **retract**
retractions *n* ▷ **retract**
retread *v* (**-s, -ing, -ed**) ▶ *n* (*pl* **-s**) ▷ **remould**
retreaded *v* ▷ **retread**
retreading *v* ▷ **retread**
retreads *v, n* ▷ **retread**
retreat *v* (**-s, -ing, -ed**) move back from a position, withdraw ▶ *n* (*pl* **-s**) act of or military signal for retiring or withdrawal
retreated *v* ▷ **retreat**
retreating *v* ▷ **retreat**
retreats *v, n* ▷ **retreat**
retrench *v* (**-es, -ing, -ed**) reduce expenditure, cut back > **retrenchment** *n* (*pl* **-s**)
retrenched *v* ▷ **retrench**
retrenches *v* ▷ **retrench**
retrenching *v* ▷ **retrench**
retrenchment *n* ▷ **retrench**
retrenchments *n* ▷ **retrench**
retrial *n* (*pl* **-s**) second trial of a case or defendant in a court of law
retrials *n* ▷ **retrial**
retribution *n* (*pl* **-s**) punishment or vengeance for evil deeds > **retributive** *adj*
retributions *n* ▷ **retribution**
retributive *adj* ▷ **retributions**
retrieve *v* (**-ves, -ving, -ved**) fetch back again > **retrievable** *adj* > **retrieval** *n* (*pl* **-s**)
retrievable *adj* ▷ **retrieve**
retrieval *n* ▷ **retrieve**
retrievals *n* ▷ **retrieve**
retrieved *v* ▷ **retrieve**
retriever *n* (*pl* **-s**) dog trained to retrieve shot game
retrievers *n* ▷ **retrieve**
retrieves *v* ▷ **retrieve**
retrieving *v* ▷ **retrieve**
retroactive *adj* effective from a date in the past
retrograde *adj* tending towards an earlier worse condition
retrogressive *adj* going back to an earlier worse condition > **retrogression** *n* (*pl* **-s**)
retrogression *n* ▷ **retrogressive**
retrogressions *n* ▷ **retrogressive**
retrorocket *n* (*pl* **-s**) small rocket engine used to slow a spacecraft
retrorockets *n* ▷ **retrorocket**
retrospective *adj* looking back in time ▶ *n* (*pl* **-s**) exhibition of an artist's life's work
retrospectives *n* ▷ **retrospective**
retroussé [rit-**troo**-say] *adj* (of a nose) turned upwards
retsina *n* (*pl* **-s**) Greek wine flavoured with resin
retsinas *n* ▷ **retsina**
return *v* (**-s, -ing, -ed**) go or come back ▶ *n* (*pl* **-s**) returning > **returnable** *adj*
returnable *adj* ▷ **return**
returned *v* ▷ **return**
returning *v* ▷ **return**
returns *v, n* ▷ **return**
reunion *n* (*pl* **-s**) meeting of people who have been apart
reunions *n* ▷ **reunion**
reunite *v* (**-tes, -ting, -ted**) bring or come together again after a separation
reunited *v* ▷ **reunite**
reunites *v* ▷ **reunite**
reuniting *v* ▷ **reunite**
reuse *v* (**-ses, -sing, -sed**) use again > **reusable** *adj*
reusable *adj* ▷ **reuse**
reused *v* ▷ **reuse**
reuses *v* ▷ **reuse**
reusing *v* ▷ **reuse**
rev (*Informal*) *n* (*pl* **-s**) revolution (of an engine) ▶ *v* (**-s, -vving, -vved**) (*foll. by* **up**) increase the speed of revolution of (an engine)
revalue *v* (**-ues, -uing, -ued**) adjust the exchange value of (a currency) upwards > **revaluation** *n* (*pl* **-s**)
revaluation *n* ▷ **revalue**
revaluations *n* ▷ **revalue**
revalued *v* ▷ **revalue**
revalues *v* ▷ **revalue**
revaluing *v* ▷ **revalue**
revamp *v* (**-s, -ing, -ed**) renovate or restore
revamped *v* ▷ **revamp**
revamping *v* ▷ **revamp**
revamps *v* ▷ **revamp**
reveal *v* (**-s, -ing, -ed**) make known > **revelation** *n* (*pl* **-s**)
revealed *v* ▷ **reveal**
revealing *v* ▷ **reveal**
reveals *v* ▷ **reveal**
reveille [riv-**val**-ee] *n* (*pl* **-s**) morning bugle call to waken soldiers
reveilles *n* ▷ **reveille**

revel *v* (**-s, -lling, -lled**) take pleasure (in) > **reveller** *n* (*pl* **-s**)
revelation *n* ▷ **revel**
revelations *n* ▷ **revel**
revelled *v* ▷ **revel**
reveller *n* ▷ **revel**
revellers *n* ▷ **revel**
revelling *v* ▷ **revel**
revelries *n* ▷ **revelry**
revelry *n* (*pl* **-s**) festivity
revels *pl n* merrymaking ▶ *v* ▷ **revel**
revenge *n* (*pl* **-s**) retaliation for wrong done ▶ *v* (**-ges, -ging, -ged**) make retaliation for > **revengeful** *adj*
revenged *v* ▷ **revenge**
revengeful *adj* ▷ **revenge**
revenges *n, v* ▷ **revenge**
revenging *v* ▷ **revenge**
revenue *n* (*pl* **-s**) income, esp. of a state
revenues *n* ▷ **revenue**
reverberate *v* (**-tes, -ting, -ted**) echo or resound > **reverberation** *n* (*pl* **-s**)
reverberated *v* ▷ **reverberate**
reverberates *v* ▷ **reverberate**
reverberating *v* ▷ **reverberate**
reverberation *n* ▷ **reverberate**
reverberations *n* ▷ **reverberate**
revere *v* (**-s, -ing, -ed**) be in awe of and respect greatly
revered *v* ▷ **revere**
reverence *n* (*pl* **-s**) awe mingled with respect and esteem
reverences *n* ▷ **reverence**
reverent *adj* showing reverence > **reverently** *adv*
reverential *adj* marked by reverence
reverently *adv* ▷ **reverent**
reveres *v* ▷ **revere**
revering *v* ▷ **revere**
reverie *n* (*pl* **-s**) absent-minded daydream
reveries *n* ▷ **reverie**
revers [riv-**veer**] *n* (*pl* **-s**) turned back part of a garment, such as the lapel
reverse *v* (**-ses, -sing, -sed**) turn upside down or the other way round ▶ *n* (*pl* **-s**) opposite ▶ *adj* opposite or contrary > **reversal** *n* (*pl* **-s**) > **reversible** *adj*
reversal *n* ▷ **reverse**
reversals *n* ▷ **reverse**
reversed *v* ▷ **reverse**
reverses *v, n* ▷ **reverse**
reversible *adj* ▷ **reverse**
reversing *v* ▷ **reverse**
reversion *n* ▷ **revert**
reversions *n* ▷ **revert**
revert *v* (**-s, -ing, -ed**) return to a former state > **reversion** *n* (*pl* **-s**)
reverted *v* ▷ **revert**
reverting *v* ▷ **revert**
reverts *v* ▷ **revert**
review *n* (*pl* **-s**) critical assessment of a book, concert, etc. ▶ *v* (**-s, -ing, -ed**) hold or write a review of
reviewed *v* ▷ **review**
reviewer *n* (*pl* **-s**) writer of reviews
reviewers *n* ▷ **reviewer**
reviewing *v* ▷ **review**
reviews *n, v* ▷ **review**
revile *v* (**-les, -ling, -led**) be abusively scornful of
reviled *v* ▷ **revile**
reviles *v* ▷ **revile**
reviling *v* ▷ **revile**
revise *v* (**-ses, -sing, -sed**) change or alter > **revision** *n* (*pl* **-s**)
revised *v* ▷ **revise**
revises *v* ▷ **revise**
revising *v* ▷ **revise**
revision *n* ▷ **revive**
revisions *n* ▷ **revive**
revival *n* (*pl* **-s**) reviving or renewal > **revivalism** *n* (*pl* **-s**) > **revivalist** *n* (*pl* **-s**)
revivalism *n* ▷ **revival**
revivalisms *n* ▷ **revival**
revivalists *n* ▷ **revival**
revivalist *n* ▷ **revival**
revivals *n* ▷ **revival**
revive *v* (**-ves, -ving, -ved**) bring or come back to life, vigour, use, etc.
revived *v* ▷ **revive**
revives *v* ▷ **revive**
reviving *v* ▷ **revive**
revocation *n* ▷ **revoke**
revocations *n* ▷ **revoke**
revoke *v* (**-kes, -king, -ked**) cancel (a will, agreement, etc.) > **revocation** *n* (*pl* **-s**)
revoked *v* ▷ **revoke**
revokes *v* ▷ **revoke**
revoking *v* ▷ **revoke**
revolt *n* (*pl* **-s**) uprising against authority ▶ *v* (**-s, -ing, -ed**) rise in rebellion
revolted *v* ▷ **revolt**
revolting *adj* disgusting, horrible ▶ *v* ▷ **revolt**
revolts *n, v* ▷ **revolt**
revolution *n* (*pl* **-s**) overthrow of a government by the governed
revolutionaries *n* ▷ **revolutionary**
revolutionary *adj* advocating or engaged in revolution ▶ *n* (*pl* **-ies**) person advocating or engaged in revolution

revolutionize *v* (**-zes, -zing, -zed**) change considerably
revolutionized *v* ▷ **revolutionize**
revolutionizes *v* ▷ **revolutionize**
revolutionizing *v* ▷ **revolutionize**
revolutions *n* ▷ **revolution**
revolve *v* (**-ves, -ving, -ved**) turn round, rotate
revolved *v* ▷ **revolve**
revolver *n* (*pl* **-s**) repeating pistol
revolvers *n* ▷ **revolver**
revolves *v* ▷ **revolve**
revolving *v* ▷ **revolve**
revs *n, v* ▷ **rev**
revue *n* (*pl* **-s**) theatrical entertainment with topical sketches and songs
revues *n* ▷ **revue**
revulsion *n* (*pl* **-s**) strong disgust
revulsions *n* ▷ **revulsion**
revved *v* ▷ **rev**
revving *v* ▷ **rev**
reward *n* (*pl* **-s**) something given in return for a service ▸ *v* (**-s, -ing, -ed**) pay or give something to (someone) for a service, information, etc.
rewarded *v* ▷ **reward**
rewarding *v* ▷ **reward**
rewards *n, v* ▷ **reward**
rewind *v* (**-s, -ing, -wound**) run (a tape or film) back to an earlier point in order to replay
rewinding *v* ▷ **rewind**
rewinds *v* ▷ **rewind**
rewire *v* (**-res, -ring, -red**) provide (a house, engine, etc.) with new wiring
rewired *v* ▷ **rewire**
rewires *v* ▷ **rewire**
rewiring *v* ▷ **rewire**
rewound *v* ▷ **rewind**
rewrite *v* (**-tes, -ting, -wrote, -written**) write again in a different way ▸ *n* (*pl* **-s**) something rewritten
rewrites *v, n* ▷ **rewrite**
rewriting *v* ▷ **rewrite**
rewritten *v* ▷ **rewrite**
rewrote *v* ▷ **rewrite**

> **rex** *n* (**rexes**). Rex is a Latin word for king. This is a very useful word, as it combines X with two of the most common letters on the board, making it one to look for when you get an X. Rex scores 10 points.
> **rez** *n* (**rezes**). Rez is a short informal word for reservation. Combining Z with two of the most common tiles on the board, this is one of the first words to think about when you draw a Z and don't have the letters for a longer word. Rez scores 12 points.

rhapsodic *adj* ▷ **rhapsody**
rhapsodies *n* ▷ **rhapsody**
rhapsodize *v* (**-zes, -zing, -zed**) speak or write with extravagant enthusiasm
rhapsodized *v* ▷ **rhapsodize**
rhapsodizes *v* ▷ **rhapsodize**
rhapsodizing *v* ▷ **rhapsodize**
rhapsody *n* (*pl* **-ies**) freely structured emotional piece of music > **rhapsodic** *adj*
rhea [**ree**-a] *n* (*pl* **-s**) S American three-toed ostrich
rheas *n* ▷ **rhea**
rhenium *n* (*pl* **-s**) (CHEM) silvery-white metallic element with a high melting point
rheniums *n* ▷ **rhenium**
rheostat *n* (*pl* **-s**) instrument for varying the resistance of an electrical circuit
rheostats *n* ▷ **rheostat**
rhesus [**ree**-suss] *n* (*pl* **-es**) small long-tailed monkey of S Asia
rhesuses *n* ▷ **rhesus**
rhetoric *n* (*pl* **-s**) art of effective speaking or writing
rhetorical *adj* (of a question) not requiring an answer > **rhetorically** *adv*
rhetorically *adv* ▷ **rhetorical**
rhetorics *n* ▷ **rhetoric**
rheumatic *n, adj* (*pl* **-s**) (person) affected by rheumatism
rheumatics *n* ▷ **rheumatic**
rheumatism *n* (*pl* **-s**) painful inflammation of joints or muscles
rheumatisms *n* ▷ **rheumatism**
rheumatoid *adj* of or like rheumatism
rhinestone *n* (*pl* **-s**) imitation diamond
rhinestones *n* ▷ **rhinestone**
rhino *n* (*pl* **-s**) rhinoceros
rhinoceros *n* (*pl* **-oses, -os**) large thick-skinned animal with one or two horns on its nose
rhinoceroses *n* ▷ **rhinoceros**
rhinos *n* ▷ **rhino**
rhizome *n* (*pl* **-s**) thick underground stem producing new plants
rhizomes *n* ▷ **rhizome**

> **rho** *n* (**rhos**). Rho is the 17th letter of the Greek alphabet. It's useful to remember words that start with RH, as there are quite a few that can come in useful. If you or someone else plays rho, remember that it could be expanded to **rhodium, rhombus** or **rhomboid.** Rho scores 6 points.

rhodium *n* (*pl* **-s**) (CHEM) hard metallic element

rhodiums *n* ▷ **rhodium**
rhododendron *n* (*pl* **-s**) evergreen flowering shrub
rhododendrons *n* ▷ **rhododendron**
rhombi *n* ▷ **rhombus**
rhomboid *n* (*pl* **-s**) parallelogram with adjacent sides of unequal length
rhomboids *n* ▷ **rhomboid**
rhombus *n* (*pl* **-buses, -bi**) parallelogram with sides of equal length but no right angles, diamond-shaped figure
rhombuses *n* ▷ **rhombus**
rhubarb *n* (*pl* **-s**) garden plant of which the fleshy stalks are cooked as fruit
rhubarbs *n* ▷ **rhubarb**

rhy *n* (**rhys**). Rhy is an alternative spelling of rye. This is a useful word as it doesn't contain a vowel, and so can be helpful when you have a poor combination of tiles on your rack. Rhy scores 9 points.

rhyme *n* (*pl* **-s**) sameness of the final sounds at the ends of lines of verse, or in words ▶ *v* (**-mes, -ming, -med**) make a rhyme
rhymed *v* ▷ **rhyme**
rhymes *n, v* ▷ **rhyme**
rhyming *v* ▷ **rhyme**
rhythm *n* (*pl* **-s**) any regular movement or beat > **rhythmic, rhythmical** *adj* > **rhythmically** *adv*
rhythmic *adj* ▷ **rhythm**
rhythmical *adj* ▷ **rhythm**
rhythmically *adv* ▷ **rhythm**
rhythms *n* ▷ **rhythm**
rib¹ *n* (*pl* **-s**) one of the curved bones forming the framework of the upper part of the body ▶ *v* (**-s, -bbing, -bbed**) provide or mark with ribs > **ribbed** *adj* > **ribbing** *n* (*pl* **-s**)
rib² *v* (**-s, -bbing, -bbed**) (*Informal*) tease or ridicule > **ribbing** *n* (*pl* **-s**)
ribald *adj* humorously or mockingly rude or obscene > **ribaldry** *n* (*pl* **-s**)
ribaldries *n* ▷ **ribald**
ribaldry *n* ▷ **ribald**
ribbed *v, adj* ▷ **rib**¹, ²
ribbing *v, n* ▷ **rib**¹, ²
ribbings *n* ▷ **rib**¹, ²
ribbon *n* (*pl* **-s**) narrow band of fabric used for trimming, tying, etc.
ribbons *n* ▷ **ribbon**
ribcage *n* (*pl* **-s**) bony structure of ribs enclosing the lungs
ribcages *n* ▷ **ribcage**
riboflavin [rye-boe-**flay**-vin] *n* (*pl* **-s**) form of vitamin B
riboflavins *n* ▷ **riboflavin**
ribs *n, v* ▷ **rib**¹, ²
rice *n* (*pl* **-s**) cereal plant grown on wet ground in warm countries
rices *n* ▷ **rice**
rich *adj* (**-er, -est**) owning a lot of money or property, wealthy > **richness** *n* (*pl* **-es**)
richer *adj* ▷ **rich**
riches *pl n* wealth
richest *adj* ▷ **rich**
richly *adv* elaborately
richness *n* ▷ **rich**
richnesses *n* ▷ **rich**
rick¹ *n* (*pl* **-s**) stack of hay etc.
rick² *v, n* (**-s, -ing, -ed**) sprain or wrench
ricked *v* ▷ **rick**²
ricketier *adj* ▷ **rickety**
ricketiest *adj* ▷ **rickety**
rickets *n* disease of children marked by softening of the bones, bow legs, etc., caused by vitamin D deficiency
rickety *adj* (**-tier, -tiest**) shaky or unstable
ricking *v* ▷ **rick**¹
ricks *n* ▷ **rick**¹ ▶ *v* ▷ **rick**²
rickshaw *n* (*pl* **-s**) light two-wheeled man-drawn Asian vehicle
rickshaws *n* ▷ **rickshaw**
ricochet [**rik**-osh-ay] *v* (**-s, -ing, -ed**) (of a bullet) rebound from a solid surface ▶ *n* (*pl* **-s**) such a rebound
ricocheted *v* ▷ **ricochet**
ricocheting *v* ▷ **ricochet**
ricochets *v, n* ▷ **ricochet**
rid *v* (**-s, -dding, rid**) clear or relieve (of)
ridden *v* ▷ **ride** ▶ *adj* afflicted or affected by the thing specified
ridding *v* ▷ **rid**
riddle¹ *n* (*pl* **-s**) question made puzzling to test one's ingenuity
riddle² *v* (**-les, -ling, -led**) pierce with many holes ▶ *n* (*pl* **-s**) coarse sieve for gravel etc.
riddled *v* ▷ **riddle**²
riddles *n* ▷ **riddle**¹, ² ▶ *v* ▷ **riddle**²
riddling *v* ▷ **riddle**²
ride *v* (**-des, -ding, rode, ridden**) sit on and control or propel (a horse, bicycle, etc.) ▶ *n* (*pl* **-s**) journey on a horse etc., or in a vehicle
rider *n* (*pl* **-s**) person who rides
riders *n* ▷ **rider**
rides *v, n* ▷ **ride**
ridge *n* (*pl* **-s**) long narrow hill > **ridged** *adj*
ridged *adj* ▷ **ridge**
ridges *n* ▷ **ridge**
ridicule *n* (*pl* **-s**) treatment of a person or thing as ridiculous ▶ *v* (**-les, -ling, -led**) laugh at,

make fun of
ridiculed *v* ▷ **ridicule**
ridicules *n, v* ▷ **ridicule**
ridiculing *v* ▷ **ridicule**
ridiculous *adj* deserving to be laughed at, absurd
riding¹ *v* ▷ **ride**
riding² *n* (*pl* **-s**) (in Canada) parliamentary constituency
ridings *n* ▷ **riding**
rids *v* ▷ **rid**
riesling *n* (*pl* **-s**) type of white wine
rieslings *n* ▷ **riesling**
rife *adj* (**-r, -st**) widespread or common
rifer *adj* ▷ **rife**
rifest *adj* ▷ **rife**
riff *n* (*pl* **-s**) (JAZZ, ROCK) short repeated melodic figure
riffle *v* (**-les, -ling, -led**) flick through (pages etc.) quickly
riffled *v* ▷ **riffle**
riffles *v* ▷ **riffle**
riffling *v* ▷ **riffle**
riffraff *n* (*pl* **-s**) rabble, disreputable people
riffraffs *n* ▷ **riffraff**
riffs *n* ▷ **riff**
rifle¹ *n* (*pl* **-s**) firearm with a long barrel
rifle² *v* (**-les, -ling, -led**) search and rob
rifled *v* ▷ **rifle²**
rifles *n* ▷ **rifle¹** ▶ *v* ▷ **rifle²**
rifling *v* ▷ **rifle²**
rift *n* (*pl* **-s**) break in friendly relations
rifts *n* ▷ **rift**
rig *v* (**-s, -gging, -gged**) arrange in a dishonest way ▶ *n* (*pl* **-s**) apparatus for drilling for oil and gas
rigged *v* ▷ **rig**
rigging *n* ship's spars and ropes ▶ *v* ▷ **rig**
right *adj* (**-er, -est**) just ▶ *adv* properly ▶ *n* (*pl* **-s**) claim, title, etc. allowed or due ▶ *v* (**-s, -ing, -ed**) bring or come back to a normal or correct state > **rightly** *adv* > **rightful** *adj* > **rightfully** *adv*
righted *v* ▷ **right**
righteous [**rye**-chuss] *adj* upright, godly, or virtuous > **righteousness** *n* (*pl* **-s**)
righteousness *n* ▷ **righteous**
righteousnesses *n* ▷ **righteous**
righter *adj* ▷ **right**
rightest *adj* ▷ **right**
rightful *adj* ▷ **right**
rightfully *adv* ▷ **right**
righting *v* ▷ **right**
rightist *n* (*pl* **-s**) ▶ *adj* (person) on the political right
rightists *n* ▷ **rightist**
rightly *adv* ▷ **right**
rights *n, v* ▷ **right**
rigid *adj* (**-er, -est**) inflexible or strict > **rigidly** *adv* > **rigidity** *n* (*pl* **-s**)
rigider *adj* ▷ **rigid**
rigidest *adj* ▷ **rigid**
rigidities *n* ▷ **rigid**
rigidity *n* ▷ **rigid**
rigidly *n* ▷ **rigid**
rigmarole *n* (*pl* **-s**) long complicated procedure
rigmaroles *n* ▷ **rigmarole**
rigorous *adj* harsh, severe, or stern
rigour *n* (*pl* **-s**) harshness, severity, or strictness
rigours *n* ▷ **rigour**
rigs *v, n* ▷ **rig**
rile *v* (**-les, -ling, -led**) anger or annoy
riled *v* ▷ **rile**
riles *v* ▷ **rile**
riling *v* ▷ **rile**
rill *n* (*pl* **-s**) small stream
rills *n* ▷ **rill**
rim *n* (*pl* **-s**) edge or border > **rimmed** *adj*
rime *n* (*pl* **-s**) (*Lit*) hoarfrost
rimes *n* ▷ **rime**
rimmed *adj* ▷ **rim**
rims *n* ▷ **rim**
rimu *n* (*pl* **-s**) (NZ) New Zealand tree whose wood is used for building and furniture
rimus *n* ▷ **rimu**
rind *n* (*pl* **-s**) tough outer coating of fruits, cheese, or bacon
rinds *n* ▷ **rind**
ring¹ *v* (**-s, -ing, rang, rung**) give out a clear resonant sound, as a bell ▶ *n* (*pl* **-s**) ringing
ring² *n* (*pl* **-s**) circle of gold etc., esp. for a finger ▶ *v* (**-s, -ing, -ed**) put a ring round
ringed *v* ▷ **ring²**
ringer *n* (*pl* **-s**) (BRIT, AUST & NZ) (*Slang*) person or thing apparently identical to another
ringers *n* ▷ **ringer**
ringing *v* ▷ **ring¹, ²**
ringleader *n* (*pl* **-s**) instigator of a mutiny, riot, etc.
ringleaders *n* ▷ **ringleader**
ringlet *n* (*pl* **-s**) curly lock of hair
ringlets *n* ▷ **ringlet**
rings *n, v* ▷ **ring¹, ²**
ringside *n* (*pl* **-s**) row of seats nearest a boxing or circus ring
ringsides *n* ▷ **ringside**
ringtail *n* (*pl* **-s**) (AUST) possum with a curling tail used to grip branches while climbing
ringtails *n* ▷ **ringtail**

ringtone *n* (*pl* **-s**) tune played by a mobile phone when it receives a call
ringtones *n* ▷ **ringtone**
ringworm *n* (*pl* **-s**) fungal skin disease in circular patches
ringworms *n* ▷ **ringworm**
rink *n* (*pl* **-s**) sheet of ice for skating or curling
rinks *n* ▷ **rink**
rinse *v* (**-ses, -sing, -sed**) remove soap from (washed clothes, hair, etc.) by applying clean water ▶ *n* (*pl* **-s**) rinsing
rinsed *v* ▷ **rinse**
rinses *v, n* ▷ **rinse**
rinsing *v* ▷ **rinse**
riot *n* (*pl* **-s**) disorderly unruly disturbance ▶ *v* (**-s, -ing, -ed**) take part in a riot
rioted *v* ▷ **riot**
rioting *v* ▷ **riot**
riotous *adj* unrestrained
riots *n, v* ▷ **riot**
rip *v* (**-s, -pping, -pped**) tear violently (*Informal*) ▶ *n* (*pl* **-s**) split or tear
riparian [rip-**pair**-ee-an] *adj* of or on the banks of a river
ripcord *n* (*pl* **-s**) cord pulled to open a parachute
ripcords *n* ▷ **ripcord**
ripe *adj* (**-er, -est**) ready to be reaped, eaten, etc.
ripen *v* (**-s, -ing, -ed**) grow ripe
ripened *v* ▷ **ripen**
ripening *v* ▷ **ripen**
ripens *v* ▷ **ripen**
riper *adj* ▷ **ripe**
ripest *adj* ▷ **ripe**
riposte [rip-**posst**] *n* (*pl* **-s**) verbal retort ▶ *v* (**-tes, -ting, -ted**) make a riposte
riposted *v* ▷ **riposte**
ripostes *n, v* ▷ **riposte**
riposting *v* ▷ **riposte**
ripped *v* ▷ **rip**
ripping *v* ▷ **rip**
ripple *n* (*pl* **-s**) slight wave or ruffling of a surface ▶ *v* (**-les, -ling, -led**) flow or form into little waves (on)
rippled *v* ▷ **ripple**
ripples *n, v* ▷ **ripple**
rippling *v* ▷ **ripple**
rips *v, n* ▷ **rip**
rise *v* (**-ses, -sing, rose, risen**) get up from a lying, sitting, or kneeling position ▶ *n* (*pl* **-s**) rising
risen *v* ▷ **rise**
riser *n* (*pl* **-s**) person who rises, esp. from bed
risers *n* ▷ **riser**
rises *v, n* ▷ **rise**
rising *n* (*pl* **-s**) revolt ▶ *adj* increasing in rank or maturity ▶ *v* ▷ **rise**
risings *n* ▷ **rising**
risible [**riz**-zib-bl] *adj* causing laughter, ridiculous
risk *n* (*pl* **-s**) chance of disaster or loss ▶ *v* (**-s, -ing, -ed**) act in spite of the possibility of (injury or loss)
risked *v* ▷ **risk**
riskier *adj* ▷ **risky**
riskiest *adj* ▷ **risky**
risking *v* ▷ **risk**
risks *n, v* ▷ **risk**
risky *adj* (**-kier, -kiest**) full of risk, dangerous
risotto *n* (*pl* **-s**) dish of rice cooked in stock with vegetables, meat, etc.
risottos *n* ▷ **risotto**
risqué [**risk**-ay] *adj* bordering on indecency
rissole *n* (*pl* **-s**) cake of minced meat, coated with breadcrumbs and fried
rissoles *n* ▷ **rissole**
rite *n* (*pl* **-s**) formal practice or custom, esp. religious
rites *n* ▷ **rite**
ritual *n* (*pl* **-s**) prescribed order of rites ▶ *adj* concerning rites > **ritually** *adv*
ritualistic *adj* like a ritual
ritually *adv* ▷ **ritual**
rituals *n* ▷ **ritual**
ritzier *adj* ▷ **ritzy**
ritziest *adj* ▷ **ritzy**
ritzy *adj* (**-zier, -ziest**) (*Slang*) luxurious or elegant
rival *n* (*pl* **-s**) person or thing that competes with or equals another for favour, success, etc. ▶ *adj* in the position of a rival ▶ *v* (**-s, -lling, -lled**) (try to) equal
rivalled *v* ▷ **rival**
rivalling *v* ▷ **rival**
rivalries *n* ▷ **rivalry**
rivalry *n* (*pl* **-s**) keen competition
rivals *v, n* ▷ **rival**
riven *adj* split apart
river *n* (*pl* **-s**) large natural stream of water
rivers *n* ▷ **river**
rivet [**riv**-vit] *n* (*pl* **-s**) bolt for fastening metal plates, the end being put through holes and then beaten flat ▶ *v* (**-s, -ing, -ed**) fasten with rivets
riveted *v* ▷ **rivet**
riveting *adj* very interesting and exciting ▶ *v* ▷ **rivet**
rivets *n, v* ▷ **rivet**
rivulet *n* (*pl* **-s**) small stream
rivulets *n* ▷ **rivulet**

riz *v*. Riz is the past tense of rise in some US dialects. This unusual word can be very useful if you get a Z in the later stages of the game, as you will probably be able to find either I or R on the board already. Riz scores 12 points.

roach *n* (*pl* **-es**) Eurasian freshwater fish
roaches *n* ▷ **roach**
road *n* (*pl* **-s**) way prepared for passengers, vehicles, etc.
roadblock *n* (*pl* **-s**) barricade across a road to stop traffic for inspection etc.
roadblocks *n* ▷ **roadblock**
roadhouse *n* (*pl* **-s**) (BRIT, AUST & S AFR) pub or restaurant on a country road
roadhouses *n* ▷ **roadhouse**
roadie *n* (*pl* **-s**) (BRIT, AUST & NZ) (*Informal*) person who transports and sets up equipment for a band
roadies *n* ▷ **roadie**
roads *n* ▷ **road**
roadside *n* (*pl* **-s**) ▶ *adj* by the road
roadsides *n* ▷ **roadside**
roadway *n* (*pl* **-s**) the part of a road used by vehicles
roadways *n* ▷ **roadway**
roadworks *pl n* repairs to a road, esp. blocking part of the road
roadworthy *adj* (of a vehicle) mechanically sound
roam *v* (**-s, -ing, -ed**) wander about
roamed *v* ▷ **roam**
roaming *v* ▷ **roam**
roams *v* ▷ **roam**
roan *adj* (of a horse) having a brown or black coat sprinkled with white hairs ▶ *n* (*pl* **-s**) roan horse
roans *n* ▷ **roan**
roar *v* (**-s, -ing, -ed**) make or utter a loud deep hoarse sound like that of a lion ▶ *n* (*pl* **-s**) such a sound
roared *v* ▷ **roar**
roaring *v* ▷ **roar**
roars *v, n* ▷ **roar**
roast *v* (**-s, -ing, -ed**) cook by dry heat, as in an oven ▶ *n* (*pl* **-s**) roasted joint of meat ▶ *adj* roasted
roasted *v* ▷ **roast**
roasting (*Informal*) *adj* extremely hot ▶ *n* (*pl* **-s**) severe criticism or scolding ▶ *v* ▷ **roast**
roastings *n* ▷ **roasting**
roasts *v, n* ▷ **roast**
rob *v* (**-s, -bbing, -bbed**) steal from > **robber** *n* (*pl* **-s**) > **robbery** *n* (*pl* **-ies**)
robbed *v* ▷ **rob**
robber *n* ▷ **rob**
robberies *n* ▷ **rob**
robbers *n* ▷ **rob**
robbery *n* ▷ **rob**
robbing *v* ▷ **rob**
robe *n* (*pl* **-s**) long loose outer garment ▶ *v* (**-bes, -bing, -bed**) put a robe on
robed *v* ▷ **robe**
robes *v, n* ▷ **robe**
robin *n* (*pl* **-s**) small brown bird with a red breast
robing *v* ▷ **robe**
robins *n* ▷ **robin**
robot *n* (*pl* **-s**) automated machine, esp. one performing functions in a human manner > **robotic** *adj*
robotic *adj* ▷ **robot**
robotics *n* science of designing and using robots
robots *n* ▷ **robot**
robs *v* ▷ **rob**
robust *adj* (**-er, -est**) very strong and healthy > **robustly** *adv* > **robustness** *n* (*pl* **-s**)
robuster *adj* ▷ **robust**
robustest *adj* ▷ **robust**
robustly *adv* ▷ **robust**
robustness *n* ▷ **robust**
robustnesses *n* ▷ **robust**
roc *n* (*pl* **-s**) monstrous bird of Arabian mythology
rock[1] *n* (*pl* **-s**) hard mineral substance that makes up part of the earth's crust, stone
rock[2] *v* (**-s, -ing, -ed**) (cause to) sway to and fro ▶ *n* style of pop music with a heavy beat
rocked *v* ▷ **rock**[2]
rocker *n* (*pl* **-s**) rocking chair
rockeries *n* ▷ **rockery**
rockers *n* ▷ **rocker**
rockery *n* (*pl* **-ies**) mound of stones in a garden for rock plants
rocket *n* (*pl* **-s**) self-propelling device powered by the burning of explosive contents (used as a firework, weapon, etc.) ▶ *v* (**-s, -ing, -ed**) move fast, esp. upwards, like a rocket
rocketed *v* ▷ **rocket**
rocketing *v* ▷ **rocket**
rockets *n, v* ▷ **rocket**
rockier *adj* ▷ **rocky**[1], **rocky**[2]
rockiest *adj* ▷ **rocky**[1], **rocky**[2]
rocking *v* ▷ **rock**[2]
rocks *n* ▷ **rock**[1] ▶ *v* ▷ **rock**[2]
rocky[1] *adj* (**-ier, -iest**) having many rocks
rocky[2] *adj* (**-ier, -iest**) shaky or unstable
rococo [rok-**koe**-koe] *adj* (of furniture, architecture, etc.) having much elaborate

decoration in an early 18th-century style
rocs *n* ▷ **roc**
rod *n* (*pl* **-s**) slender straight bar, stick
rode *v* ▷ **ride**
rodent *n* (*pl* **-s**) animal with teeth specialized for gnawing, such as a rat, mouse, or squirrel
rodents *n* ▷ **rodent**
rodeo *n* (*pl* **-s**) display of skill by cowboys, such as bareback riding
rodeos *n* ▷ **rodeo**
rods *n* ▷ **rod**
roe¹ *n* (*pl* **-s**) mass of eggs in a fish, sometimes eaten as food
roe² *n* (*pl* **-s**) small species of deer
roentgen [**ront**-gan] *n* (*pl* **-s**) unit measuring a radiation dose
roentgens *n* ▷ **roentgen**
roes *n* ▷ **roe¹, ²**
rogue *n* (*pl* **-s**) dishonest or unprincipled person ▶ *adj* (of a wild beast) having a savage temper and living apart from the herd > **roguish** *adj*
rogues *n* ▷ **rogue**
roguish *adj* ▷ **rogee**
roister *v* (**-s, -ing, -ed**) make merry noisily or boisterously
roistered *v* ▷ **roister**
roistering *v* ▷ **roister**
roisters *v* ▷ **roister**

> **rok** *n* (**roks**). Rok is an alternative spelling of **roc.** This uncommon word can be helpful if you have a K without the tiles needed for a longer word. Rok scores 7 points.

role *n* (*pl* **-s**) task or function
roles *n* ▷ **role**
roll *v* (**-s, -ing, -ed**) move by turning over and over ▶ *n* (*pl* **-s**) act of rolling over or from side to side
rolled *v* ▷ **roll**
roller *n* (*pl* **-s**) rotating cylinder used for smoothing or supporting a thing to be moved, spreading paint, etc.
rollers *n* ▷ **roller**
rollicking *adj* boisterously carefree
rolling *v* ▷ **roll**
rolls *v, n* ▷ **roll**
roman *n* roman type or print
romance *n* (*pl* **-s**) love affair
romances *n* ▷ **romance**
romantic *adj* of or dealing with love ▶ *n* (*pl* **-s**) romantic person or artist > **romantically** *adv* > **romanticism** *n* (*pl* **-s**)
romantically *adv* ▷ **romantic**
romanticism *n* ▷ **romantic**
romanticisms *n* ▷ **romantic**
romanticize *v* (**-zes, -zing, -zed**) describe or regard in an idealized and unrealistic way
romanticized *v* ▷ **romanticize**
romanticizes *v* ▷ **romanticize**
romanticizing *v* ▷ **romanticize**
romantics *n* ▷ **romantic**
romp *v* (**-s, -ing, -ed**) play wildly and joyfully ▶ *n* (*pl* **-s**) boisterous activity
romped *v* ▷ **romp**
rompers *pl n* child's overalls
romping *v* ▷ **romp**
romps *v, n* ▷ **romp**
rondo *n* (*pl* **-s**) piece of music with a leading theme continually returned to
rondos *n* ▷ **rondo**
roo *n* (*pl* **-s**) (AUST) (*Informal*) kangaroo
rood *n* (*pl* **-s**) (CHRISTIANITY) the Cross
roods *n* ▷ **rood**
roof *n* (*pl* **-s**) outside upper covering of a building, car, etc. ▶ *v* put a roof on
roofs *n* ▷ **roofs**
rooibos [**roy**-boss] *n* (*pl* **-es**) (S AFR) tea prepared from the dried leaves of an African plant
rooiboses *n* ▷ **rooibos**
rook¹ *n* (*pl* **-s**) Eurasian bird of the crow family
rook² *n* (*pl* **-s**) chess piece shaped like a castle
rookeries *n* ▷ **rookery**
rookery *n* (*pl* **-ies**) colony of rooks, penguins, or seals
rookie *n* (*pl* **-s**) (*Informal*) new recruit
rookies *n* ▷ **rookie**
rooks *n* ▷ **rook**
room *n* (*pl* **-s**) enclosed area in a building ▶ *pl* lodgings
roomier *adj* ▷ **roomy**
roomiest *adj* ▷ **roomy**
rooms *n* ▷ **room**
roomy *adj* (**-ier, -iest**) spacious
roos *n* ▷ **roo**
roost *n* (*pl* **-s**) perch for fowls ▶ *v* (**-s, -ing, -ed**) perch
roosted *v* ▷ **roost**
rooster *n* (*pl* **-s**) domestic cock
roosters *n* ▷ **rooster**
roosting *v* ▷ **roost**
roosts *v, n* ▷ **roost**
root¹ *n* (*pl* **-s**) part of a plant that grows down into the earth obtaining nourishment ▶ *pl* person's sense of belonging ▶ *v* (**-s, -ing, -ed**) establish a root and start to grow
root² *v* (**-s, -ing, -ed**) dig or burrow
rooted *v* ▷ **root¹, ²**
rooting *v* ▷ **root¹, ²**
rootless *adj* having no sense of belonging

roots *n* ▷ **root**[1] ▶ *v* ▷ **root**[1, 2]
rope *n* (*pl* **-s**) thick cord
ropes *n* ▷ **rope**
ropey, ropy *adj* (**-pier, -piest**) (BRIT) (*Informal*) inferior or inadequate
ropier *adj* ▷ **ropy**
ropiest *adj* ▷ **ropy**
ropy *adj* ▷ **ropey**
rorqual *n* (*pl* **-s**) toothless whale with a dorsal fin
rorquals *n* ▷ **rorqual**
rort (AUST) (*Informal*) *n* (*pl* **-s**) dishonest scheme ▶ *v* (**-s, -ing, -ed**) take unfair advantage of something
rorted *v* ▷ **rort**
rorting *v* ▷ **rort**
rorts *n*, *v* ▷ **rort**
rosaries *n* ▷ **rosary**
rosary *n* (*pl* **-ies**) series of prayers
rose[1] *n* (*pl* **-s**) shrub or climbing plant with prickly stems and fragrant flowers ▶ *adj* pink
rose[2] *v* ▷ **rise**
roseate [**roe**-zee-ate] *adj* rose-coloured
rosehip *n* (*pl* **-s**) berry-like fruit of a rose plant
rosehips *n* ▷ **rosehip**
rosella *n* (*pl* **-s**) type of Australian parrot
rosellas *n* ▷ **rosella**
rosemaries *n* ▷ **rosemary**
rosemary *n* (*pl* **-ies**) fragrant flowering shrub
roses *n* ▷ **rose**[1]
rosette *n* (*pl* **-s**) rose-shaped ornament, esp. a circular bunch of ribbons
rosettes *n* ▷ **rosette**
rosewood *n* (*pl* **-s**) fragrant wood used to make furniture
rosewoods *n* ▷ **rosewood**
rosier *adj* ▷ **rosy**
rosiest *adj* ▷ **rosy**
rosin [**rozz**-in] *n* (*pl* **-s**) resin used for treating the bows of violins etc.
rosins *n* ▷ **rosin**
roster *n* (*pl* **-s**) list of people and their turns of duty
rosters *n* ▷ **roster**
rostra *n* ▷ **rostrum**
rostrum *n* (*pl* **-trums, -tra**) platform or stage
rostrums *n* ▷ **rostrum**
rosy *adj* (**-sier, -siest**) pink-coloured
rot *v* (**-s, -tting, -tted**) decompose or decay ▶ *n* (*pl* **-s**) decay (*Informal*)
rota *n* (*pl* **-s**) list of people who take it in turn to do a particular task
rotas *n* ▷ **rota**
rotary *adj* revolving
rotate *v* (**-tes, -ting, -ted**) (cause to) move round a centre or on a pivot > **rotation** *n* (*pl* **-s**)
rotated *v* ▷ **rotate**
rotates *v* ▷ **rotate**
rotating *v* ▷ **rotate**
rotation *n* ▷ **rotate**
rotations *n* ▷ **rotate**
rote *n* (*pl* **-s**) mechanical repetition
rotes *n* ▷ **rote**
rotisserie *n* (*pl* **-s**) rotating spit for cooking meat
rotisseries *n* ▷ **rotisserie**
rotor *n* (*pl* **-s**) revolving portion of a dynamo, motor, or turbine
rotors *n* ▷ **rotor**
rots *v*, *n* ▷ **rot**
rotted *v* ▷ **rot**
rotten *adj* (**-er, -est**) decaying (*Informal*)
rottener *adj* ▷ **rotten**
rottenest *adj* ▷ **rotten**
rotter *n* (*pl* **-s**) (CHIEFLY BRIT) (*Slang*) despicable person
rotters *n* ▷ **rotter**
rotting *v* ▷ **rot**
rotund [roe-**tund**] *adj* round and plump > **rotundity** *n* (*pl* **-ies**)
rotunda *n* (*pl* **-s**) circular building or room, esp. with a dome
rotundas *n* ▷ **rotunda**
rotundities *n* ▷ **rotund**
rotundity *n* ▷ **rotund**
rouble [**roo**-bl] *n* (*pl* **-s**) monetary unit of Russia, Belarus, and Tajikistan
roubles *n* ▷ **rouble**
roué [**roo**-ay] *n* (*pl* **-s**) man given to immoral living
roués *n* ▷ **roué**
rouge *n* (*pl* **-s**) red cosmetic used to colour the cheeks
rouges *n* ▷ **rouge**
rough *adj* (**-er, -est**) uneven or irregular ▶ *v* (**-s, -ing, -ed**) make rough ▶ *n* (*pl* **-s**) rough state or area > **roughen** *v* (**-s, -ing, -ed**) > **roughly** *adv* > **roughness** *n* (*pl* **-s**)
roughage *n* (*pl* **-s**) indigestible constituents of food which aid digestion
roughages *n* ▷ **roughage**
roughcast *n* (*pl* **-s**) mixture of plaster and small stones for outside walls ▶ *v* (**-s, -ing, -cast**) coat with this
roughcasting *v* ▷ **roughcast**
roughcasts *n*, *v* ▷ **roughcast**
roughed *v* ▷ **rough**
roughen *v* ▷ **rough**
roughened *v* ▷ **rough**
roughening *v* ▷ **rough**

roughens *v* ▷ **rough**
rougher *adj* ▷ **rough**
roughest *adj* ▷ **rough**
roughhouse *n* (*pl* **-s**) (CHIEFLY US) (*Slang*) fight
roughhouses *n* ▷ **roughhouse**
roughing *v* ▷ **rough**
roughly *adv* ▷ **rough**
roughness *n* ▷ **rough**
roughnesses *n* ▷ **rough**
roughs *v, n* ▷ **rough**
roughshod *adv* with total disregard
roulette *n* (*pl* **-s**) gambling game played with a revolving wheel and a ball
roulettes *n* ▷ **roulette**
round *adj* (**-er, -est**) spherical, cylindrical, circular, or curved ▶ *adv, prep* indicating an encircling movement, presence on all sides, etc. ▶ *v* (**-s, -ing, -ed**) move round ▶ *n* (*pl* **-s**) customary course, as of a milkman
roundabout *n* (*pl* **-s**) road junction at which traffic passes round a central island ▶ *adj* not straightforward
roundabouts *n* ▷ **roundabout**
rounded *v* ▷ **round**
roundel *n* (*pl* **-s**) small disc
roundelay *n* (*pl* **-s**) simple song with a refrain
roundelays *n* ▷ **roundelay**
roundels *n* ▷ **roundel**
rounder *adj* ▷ **round**
roundest *adj* ▷ **round**
rounders *n* bat-and-ball team game
rounding *v* ▷ **round**
roundly *adv* thoroughly
rounds *v, n* ▷ **round**
rouse¹ [rhymes with **cows**] *v* (**-ses, -sing, -sed**) wake up
rouse² [rhymes with **mouse**] *v* (**-ses, -sing, -sed**) (*foll. by* **on**) (AUST) scold or rebuke
rouseabout *n* (*pl* **-s**) (AUST & NZ) labourer in a shearing shed
rouseabouts *n* ▷ **rouseabout**
roused *v* ▷ **rouse¹, ²**
rouses *v* ▷ **rouse¹, ²**
rousing *v* ▷ **rouse¹, ²**
roustabout *n* (*pl* **-s**) labourer on an oil rig
roustabouts *n* ▷ **roustabout**
rout *n* (*pl* **-s**) overwhelming defeat ▶ *v* (**-s, -ing, -ed**) defeat and put to flight
route *n* (*pl* **-s**) roads taken to reach a destination
routed *v* ▷ **rout**
routes *n* ▷ **route**
routine *n* (*pl* **-s**) usual or regular method of procedure ▶ *adj* ordinary or regular
routines *n* ▷ **routine**
routing *v* ▷ **rout**
routs *n, v* ▷ **rout**
roux [roo] *n* (*pl* **roux**) fat and flour cooked together as a basis for sauces
rove *v* (**-ves, -ving, -ved**) wander
roved *v* ▷ **rove**
rover *n* (*pl* **-s**) wanderer, traveller
rovers *n* ▷ **rover**
roves *v* ▷ **rove**
roving *v* ▷ **rove**
row¹ [rhymes with **go**] *n* (*pl* **-s**) straight line of people or things
row² [rhymes with **go**] *v* (**-s, -ing, -ed**) propel (a boat) by oars ▶ *n* (**-s**) spell of rowing
row³ [rhymes with **now**] (*Informal*) *n* (**-s**) dispute ▶ *v* (**-s, -ing, -ed**) quarrel noisily
rowan *n* (*pl* **-s**) tree producing bright red berries, mountain ash
rowans *n* ▷ **rowan**
rowdier *adj* ▷ **rowdy**
rowdiest *adj* ▷ **rowdy**
rowdies *n* ▷ **rowdy**
rowdy *adj* (**-dier, -diest**) disorderly, noisy, and rough ▶ *n* (*pl* **-ies**) person like this
rowed *v* ▷ **row², ³**
rowel [rhymes with **towel**] *n* (*pl* **-s**) small spiked wheel on a spur
rowels *n* ▷ **rowel**
rowing *v* ▷ **row², ³**
rowlock [**rol**-luk] *n* (*pl* **-s**) device on a boat that holds an oar in place
rowlocks *n* ▷ **rowlock**
rows *n* ▷ **row¹, ², ³** ▶ *v* ▷ **row², ³**
royal *adj* (**-ler, -lest**) of, befitting, or supported by a king or queen ▶ *n* (*pl* **-s**) (*Informal*) member of a royal family > **royally** *adv*
royalist *n* (*pl* **-s**) supporter of monarchy
royalists *n* ▷ **royalist**
royaller *adj* ▷ **royal**
royallest *adj* ▷ **royal**
royally *adv* ▷ **royal**
royals *n* ▷ **royal**
royalties *n* ▷ **royalty**
royalty *n* (*pl* **-ies**) royal people
rub *v* (**-s, -bbing, -bbed**) apply pressure and friction to (something) with a circular or backwards-and-forwards movement ▶ *n* (**-s**) act of rubbing
rubato *adv, n* (*pl* **-s**) (MUSIC) (with) expressive flexibility of tempo
rubatos *n* ▷ **rubato**
rubbed *v* ▷ **rub**
rubber¹ *n* (*pl* **-s**) strong waterproof elastic material, orig. made from the dried sap of a tropical tree, now usu. synthetic ▶ *adj* made

of or producing rubber > **rubbery** *adj* (**-rier, -riest**)
rubber² *n* (*pl* **-s**) match consisting of three games of bridge, whist, etc.
rubberier *adj* ▷ **rubber¹**
rubberiest *adj* ▷ **rubber¹**
rubberneck *v* (**-s, -ing, -ed**) stare with unthinking curiosity
rubbernecked *v* ▷ **rubberneck**
rubbernecking *v* ▷ **rubberneck**
rubbernecks *v* ▷ **rubberneck**
rubbers *n* ▷ **rubber¹, ²**
rubbery *adj* ▷ **rubber¹**
rubbing *v* ▷ **rub**
rubbish *n* (*pl* **-es**) waste matter > **rubbishy** *adj*
rubbishes *n* ▷ **rubbish**
rubbishy *adj* ▷ **rubbish**
rubble *n* (*pl* **-s**) fragments of broken stone, brick, etc.
rubbles *n* ▷ **rubble**
rubella *n* (*pl* **-s**) ▷ **German measles**
rubellas *n* ▷ **rubella**
rubicund *adj* ruddy
rubidium *n* (*pl* **-s**) (CHEM) soft highly reactive radioactive element
rubidiums *n* ▷ **rubidium**
rubies *n* ▷ **ruby**
rubric *n* (*pl* **-s**) heading or explanation inserted in a text
rubrics *n* ▷ **rubric**
rubs *v, n* ▷ **rub**
ruby *n* (*pl* **-ies**) red precious gemstone ▶ *adj* deep red
ruck¹ *n* (*pl* **-s**) rough crowd of common people
ruck² *n, v* (**-s, -ing, -ed**) wrinkle or crease
rucked *v* ▷ **ruck²**
rucking *v* ▷ **ruck²**
rucks *n* ▷ **ruck¹, ²** ▶ *v* ▷ **ruck²**
rucksack *n* (*pl* **-s**) (BRIT, AUST & S AFR) large pack carried on the back
rucksacks *n* ▷ **rucksack**
ructions *pl n* (*Informal*) noisy uproar
rudder *n* (*pl* **-s**) vertical hinged piece at the stern of a boat or at the rear of an aircraft, for steering
rudders *n* ▷ **rudder**
ruddier *adj* ▷ **ruddy**
ruddiest *adj* ▷ **ruddy**
ruddy *adj* (**-dier, -diest**) of a fresh healthy red colour
rude *adj* (**-r, -st**) impolite or insulting > **rudely** *adv* > **rudeness** *n* (*pl* **-s**)
rudely *adv* ▷ **rude**
rudeness *n* ▷ **rude**
rudenesses *n* ▷ **rude**
ruder *adj* ▷ **rude**
rudest *adj* ▷ **rude**
rudimentary *adj* basic, elementary
rudiments *pl n* simplest and most basic stages of a subject
rue¹ *v* (**rues, ruing, rued**) feel regret for
rue² *n* (*pl* **-s**) plant with evergreen bitter leaves
rueful *adj* regretful or sorry > **ruefully** *adv*
ruefully *adv* ▷ **rueful**
rued *v* ▷ **rue¹**
rues *v* ▷ **rue¹** ▶ *n* ▷ **rue²**
ruff *n* (*pl* **-s**) starched and frilled collar
ruffian *n* (*pl* **-s**) violent lawless person
ruffians *n* ▷ **ruffian**
ruffle *v* (**-les, -ling, -led**) disturb the calm of ▶ *n* (*pl* **-s**) frill or pleat
ruffled *v* ▷ **ruffle**
ruffles *v, n* ▷ **ruffle**
ruffling *v* ▷ **ruffle**
ruffs *n* ▷ **ruff**
rug *n* (*pl* **-s**) small carpet
rugbies *n* ▷ **rugby**
rugby *n* (*pl* **-ies**) form of football played with an oval ball which may be handled by the players
rugged [**rug**-gid] *adj* rocky or steep
rugger *n* (*pl* **-s**) (CHIEFLY BRIT) (*Informal*) rugby
ruggers *n* ▷ **rugger**
rugs *n* ▷ **rug**
ruin *v* (**-s, -ing, -ed**) destroy or spoil completely ▶ *n* (*pl* **-s**) destruction or decay
ruination *n* (*pl* **-s**) act of ruining
ruinations *n* ▷ **ruination**
ruined *v* ▷ **ruin**
ruing *v* ▷ **rue¹**
ruining *v* ▷ **ruin**
ruinous *adj* causing ruin > **ruinously** *adv*
ruinously *adv* ▷ **ruinous**
ruins *v, n* ▷ **ruin**
rule *n* (*pl* **-s**) statement of what is allowed, for example in a game or procedure ▶ *v* (**-les, -ling, -led**) govern
ruled *v* ▷ **rule**
ruler *n* (*pl* **-s**) person who governs
rulers *n* ▷ **ruler**
rules *n, v* ▷ **rule**
ruling *n* (*pl* **-s**) formal decision ▶ *v* ▷ **rule**
rulings *n* ▷ **ruling**
rum *n* (*pl* **-s**) alcoholic drink distilled from sugar cane
rumba *n* (*pl* **-s**) lively ballroom dance of Cuban origin
rumbas *n* ▷ **rumba**
rumble *v* (**-les, -ling, -led**) make a low continuous noise (BRIT) (*Informal*) ▶ *n* (*pl* **-s**) deep resonant sound

rumbled *v* ▷ **rumble**
rumbles *v, n* ▷ **rumble**
rumbling *v* ▷ **rumble**
rumbustious *adj* boisterous or unruly
ruminate *v* (**-tes, -ting, -ted**) chew the cud
ruminant *adj, n* (*pl* **-s**) cud-chewing (animal, such as a cow, sheep, or deer)
ruminants *n* ▷ **ruminant**
ruminated *v* ▷ **ruminate**
ruminates *v* ▷ **ruminate**
ruminating *v* ▷ **ruminate**
rumination *n* (*pl* **-s**) quiet meditation and reflection > **ruminative** *adj*
ruminations *n* ▷ **rumination**
ruminative *adj* ▷ **rumination**
rummage *v* (**-ges, -ging, -ged**) search untidily and at length ▶ *n* (*pl* **-s**) untidy search through a collection of things
rummaged *v* ▷ **rummage**
rummages *v, n* ▷ **rummage**
rummaging *v* ▷ **rummage**
rummies *n* ▷ **rummy**
rummy *n* (*pl* **-ies**) card game in which players try to collect sets or sequences
rumour *n* (*pl* **-s**) unproved statement
rumoured *adj* suggested by rumour
rumours *n* ▷ **rumour**
rump *n* (*pl* **-s**) buttocks
rumple *v* (**-les, -ling, -led**) make untidy, crumpled, or dishevelled
rumpled *v* ▷ **rumple**
rumples *v* ▷ **rumple**
rumpling *v* ▷ **rumple**
rumps *n* ▷ **rump**
rumpus *n* (*pl* **-es**) noisy commotion
rumpuses *n* ▷ **rumpus**
rums *n* ▷ **rum**
run *v* (**runs, running, ran, run**) move with a more rapid gait than walking ▶ *n* (*pl* **-s**) act or spell of running
rune *n* (*pl* **-s**) any character of the earliest Germanic alphabet > **runic** *adj*
runes *n* ▷ **rune**
rung[1] *n* (*pl* **-s**) crossbar on a ladder
rung[2] *v* ▷ **ring**[1]
rungs *n* ▷ **rung**[1]
runic *adj* ▷ **rune**
runnel *n* (*pl* **-s**) small brook
runnels *n* ▷ **runnel**
runner *n* (*pl* **-s**) competitor in a race
runners *n* ▷ **runner**
runnier *adj* ▷ **runny**
runniest *adj* ▷ **runny**
running *adj* continuous ▶ *n* (*pl* **-s**) act of moving or flowing quickly ▶ *v* ▷ **run**
runnings *n* ▷ **running**
runny *adj* (**-nier, -niest**) tending to flow
runs *v, n* ▷ **run**
runt *n* (*pl* **-s**) smallest animal in a litter
runts *n* ▷ **runt**
runway *n* (*pl* **-s**) hard level roadway where aircraft take off and land
runways *n* ▷ **runway**
rupee *n* (*pl* **-s**) monetary unit of India and Pakistan
rupees *n* ▷ **rupee**
rupture *n* (*pl* **-s**) breaking, breach ▶ *v* (**-res, -ring, -red**) break, burst, or sever
ruptured *v* ▷ **rupture**
ruptures *n, v* ▷ **rupture**
rupturing *v* ▷ **rupture**
rural *adj* in or of the countryside
ruse [**rooz**] *n* (*pl* **-s**) stratagem or trick
ruses *n* ▷ **ruse**
rush[1] *v* (**-es, -ing, -ed**) move or do very quickly ▶ *n* (*pl* **-es**) sudden quick or violent movement ▶ *pl* first unedited prints of a scene for a film ▶ *adj* done with speed, hasty
rush[2] *n* (*pl* **-es**) marsh plant with a slender pithy stem
rushed *v* ▷ **rush**[1]
rushes *v, n* ▷ **rush**[1, 2]
rushier *adj* ▷ **rushy**
rushiest *adj* ▷ **rushy**
rushing *v* ▷ **rush**[1]
rushy *adj* (**-shier, -shiest**) full of rushes
rusk *n* (*pl* **-s**) hard brown crisp biscuit, used esp. for feeding babies
rusks *n* ▷ **rusk**
russet *adj* reddish-brown ▶ *n* (*pl* **-s**) apple with rough reddish-brown skin
russets *n* ▷ **russet**
rust *n* (*pl* **-s**) reddish-brown coating formed on iron etc. that has been exposed to moisture ▶ *adj* reddish-brown ▶ *v* (**-s, -ing, -ed**) become coated with rust
rusted *v* ▷ **rust**
rustic *adj* of or resembling country people ▶ *n* (*pl* **-s**) person from the country
rustics *n* ▷ **rustic**
rustier *adj* ▷ **rusty**
rustiest *adj* ▷ **rusty**
rusting *v* ▷ **rust**
rustle[1] *v, n* (*pl* **-s**) (make) a low whispering sound
rustle[2] *v* (**-les, -ling, -led**) (US) steal (cattle)
rustled *v* ▷ **rustle**
rustler *n* (*pl* **-s**) (US) cattle thief
rustlers *n* ▷ **rustler**
rustles *n, v* ▷ **rustle**

rustling *v* ▷ **rustle**
rusts *n, v* ▷ **rust**
rusty *adj* (**-tier, -tiest**) coated with rust
rut[1] *n* (*pl* **-s**) furrow made by wheels
rut[2] *n* recurrent period of sexual excitability in male deer ▶ *v* (**-s, -tting, -tted**) be in a period of sexual excitability
ruthenium *n* (*pl* **-s**) (CHEM) rare hard brittle white element
rutheniums *n* ▷ **ruthenium**
ruthless *adj* pitiless, merciless > **ruthlessly** *adv* > **ruthlessness** *n* (*pl* **-es**)
ruthlessly *adv* ▷ **ruthless**
ruthlessness *n* ▷ **ruthless**
ruthlessnesses *n* ▷ **ruthless**
ruts *n* ▷ **rut**[1, 2] ▶ *v* ▷ **rut**[2]
rutted *v* ▷ **rut**[2]
rutting *v* ▷ **rut**[2]
rye *n* (*pl* **-s**) kind of grain used for fodder and bread
ryes *n* ▷ **rye**

Ss

S begins only four two-letter words, **sh** (5 points), **si, so** and **st** (2 each). These are easy to remember, and it's worth noting that two of them, **sh** and **st,** don't use any vowels. Interestingly, there are quite a few three-letter words beginning with S that don't contain vowels, some of which give good scores. These are **shh** (9), **shy** (9), **sky** (10), **sly** (6), **sny** (6), **spy** (8), **sty** (6), **swy** (9) and **syn** (6). S also forms a number of three-letter words with X. These are easy to remember as they use every vowel except U: **sax, sex, six** and **sox** (10 each). Apart from the two- and three-letter words, don't forget **squeeze** (25), which uses the two highest-scoring tiles in the game.

sabbath *n* (*pl* **-s**) day of worship and rest: Saturday for Jews, Sunday for Christians
sabbaths *n* ▷ **sabbath**
sabbatical *adj*, *n* (*pl* **-s**) (denoting) leave for study
sabbaticals *n* ▷ **sabbatical**
sable *n* (*pl* **-s**) dark fur from a small weasel-like Arctic animal ▶ *adj* black
sables *n* ▷ **sable**
sabot [**sab**-oh] *n* (*pl* **-s**) wooden shoe traditionally worn by peasants in France
sabotage *n* (*pl* **-s**) intentional damage done to machinery, systems, etc. ▶ *v* (**-ges, -ging, -ged**) damage intentionally
sabotaged *v* ▷ **sabotage**
sabotages *n*, *v* ▷ **sabotage**
sabotaging *v* ▷ **sabotage**
saboteur *n* (*pl* **-s**) person who commits sabotage
saboteurs *n* ▷ **saboteur**
sabots *n* ▷ **sabot**
sabre *n* (*pl* **-s**) curved cavalry sword
sabres *n* ▷ **sabre**
sac *n* (*pl* **-s**) pouchlike structure in an animal or plant
saccharin *n* (*pl* **-s**) artificial sweetener > **saccharine** *adj* excessively sweet
saccharine *adj* ▷ **saccharin**
saccharins *n* ▷ **saccharin**
sacerdotal *adj* of priests
sachet *n* (*pl* **-s**) small envelope or bag containing a single portion
sachets *n* ▷ **sachet**
sack[1] *n* (*pl* **-s**) large bag made of coarse material ▶ *v* (**-s, -ing, -ed**) (*Informal*) dismiss
sack[2] *n* (*pl* **-s**) plundering of a captured town ▶ *v* (**-s, -ing, -ed**) plunder (a captured town)
sackcloth *n* (*pl* **-s**) coarse fabric used for sacks, formerly worn as a penance
sackcloths *n* ▷ **sackcloth**
sacked *v* ▷ **sack**[1, 2]
sacking *v* ▷ **sack**[1, 2]
sacks *v*, *n* ▷ **sack**[1, 2]
sacra *n* ▷ **sacrum**
sacrament *n* (*pl* **-s**) ceremony of the Christian Church, esp. Communion > **sacramental** *adj*
sacramental *adj* ▷ **sacrament**
sacraments *n* ▷ **sacrament**
sacred *adj* holy
sacrifice *n* (*pl* **-s**) giving something up ▶ *v* (**-es, -ing, -ced**) offer as a sacrifice > **sacrificial** *adj*
sacrificed *v* ▷ **sacrifice**
sacrifices *n*, *v* ▷ **sacrifice**
sacrificial *adj* ▷ **sacrifice**
sacrificing *v* ▷ **sacrifice**
sacrilege *n* (*pl* **-s**) misuse or desecration of something sacred > **sacrilegious** *adj*
sacrileges *n* ▷ **sacrilege**
sacrilegious *adj* ▷ **sacrilege**
sacristan *n* (*pl* **-s**) person in charge of the contents of a church
sacristans *n* ▷ **sacristan**
sacristies *n* ▷ **sacristy**
sacristy *n* (*pl* **-ties**) room in a church where sacred objects are kept
sacrosanct *adj* regarded as sacred, inviolable
sacrum [**say**-krum] *n* (*pl* **-cra**) wedge-shaped bone at the base of the spine
sacs *n* ▷ **sac**
sad *adj* (**-dder, -ddest**) sorrowful, unhappy

> **sadly** *adv* > **sadness** *n* (*pl* **-es**)
sadden *v* (**-s, -ing, -ed**) make sad
saddened *v* ▷ **sadden**
saddening *v* ▷ **sadden**
saddens *v* ▷ **sadden**
sadder *adj* ▷ **sad**
saddest *adj* ▷ **sad**
saddle *n* (*pl* **-les**) rider's seat on a horse or bicycle ▶ *v* (**-les, -ling, -led**) put a saddle on (a horse)
saddled *v* ▷ **saddle**
saddler *n* (*pl* **-s**) maker or seller of saddles
saddlers *n* ▷ **saddler**
saddles *n, v* ▷ **saddle**
saddling *v* ▷ **saddle**
saddo *n* (*pl* **-s, -es**) (BRIT) (*Informal*) socially inadequate or pathetic person
saddoes *n* ▷ **saddo**
saddos *n* ▷ **saddo**
sadism [**say**-dizz-um] *n* (*pl* **-s**) gaining of (sexual) pleasure from inflicting pain > **sadist** *n* (*pl* **-s**) > **sadistic** *adj* > **sadistically** *adv*
sadisms *n* ▷ **sadism**
sadist *n* ▷ **sadism**
sadistic *adj* ▷ **sadism**
sadistically *adv* ▷ **sadism**
sadists *n* ▷ **sadism**
sadly *adv* ▷ **sad**
sadness *n* ▷ **sad**
sadnesses *n* ▷ **sad**
sadomasochism *n* (*pl* **-s**) combination of sadism and masochism > **sadomasochist** *n* (*pl* **-s**)
sadomasochisms *n* ▷ **sadomasochism**
sadomasochist *n* ▷ **sadomasochism**
sadomasochists *n* ▷ **sadomasochism**
safari *n* (*pl* **-s**) expedition to hunt or observe wild animals, esp. in Africa
safaris *n* ▷ **safari**
safe *adj* (**-r, -st**) secure, protected ▶ *n* (*pl* **-s**) strong lockable container > **safely** *adv*
safeguard *v* (**-s, -ing, -ed**) protect ▶ *n* (*pl* **-s**) protection
safeguarded *v* ▷ **safeguard**
safeguarding *v* ▷ **safeguard**
safeguards *v, n* ▷ **safeguard**
safekeeping *n* (*pl* **-s**) protection
safekeepings *n* ▷ **safekeeping**
safely *adv* ▷ **safe**
safer *adj* ▷ **safe**
safes *n* ▷ **safe**
safest *adj* ▷ **safe**
safeties *n* ▷ **safety**
safety *n* (*pl* **-ties**) state of being safe
saffron *n* (*pl* **-s**) orange-coloured flavouring obtained from a crocus ▶ *adj* orange
saffrons *n* ▷ **saffron**
sag *v* (**sags, sagging, sagged**) sink in the middle ▶ *n* (*pl* **-s**) droop
saga [**sah**-ga] *n* (*pl* **-s**) legend of Norse heroes
sagacious *adj* wise > **sagacity** *n* (*pl* **-ties**)
sagacities *n* ▷ **sagacious**
sagacity *n* ▷ **sagacious**
sagas *n* ▷ **saga**
sage[1] *n* (*pl* **-s**) very wise man ▶ *adj* (**-r, -st**) (*Lit*) wise > **sagely** *adv*
sage[2] *n* (*pl* **-s**) aromatic herb with grey-green leaves
sagely *adv* ▷ **sage**[1]
sager *adj* ▷ **sage**[1]
sages *n* ▷ **sage**[1, 2]
sagest *adj* ▷ **sage**[1]
sagged *v* ▷ **sag**
sagging *v* ▷ **sag**
sago *n* (*pl* **-s**) starchy cereal from the powdered pith of the sago palm tree
sagos *n* ▷ **sago**
sags *v, n* ▷ **sag**
said *v* ▷ **say**
sail *n* (*pl* **-s**) sheet of fabric stretched to catch the wind for propelling a sailing boat ▶ *v* (**-s, -ing, -ed**) travel by water
sailboard *n* (*pl* **-s**) board with a mast and single sail, used for windsurfing
sailboards *n* ▷ **sailboard**
sailed *v* ▷ **sail**
sailing *v* ▷ **sail**
sailor *n* (*pl* **-s**) member of a ship's crew
sailors *n* ▷ **sailor**
sails *n, v* ▷ **sail**
saint *n* (*pl* **-s**) (CHRISTIANITY) person venerated after death as specially holy > **saintly** *adj* > **saintliness** *n* (*pl* **-es**)
saintliness *n* ▷ **saint**
saintlinesses *n* ▷ **saint**
saintly *adj* ▷ **saint**
saints *n* ▷ **saint**
sake[1] *n* (*pl* **-s**) benefit
sake[2], **saki** [**sah**-kee] *n* (*pl* **-s**) Japanese alcoholic drink made from fermented rice
sakes *n* ▷ **sake**[1, 2]
saki *n* ▷ **sake**[2]
sakis *n* ▷ **sake**[2]
salaam [sal-**ahm**] *n* (*pl* **-s**) low bow of greeting among Muslims
salaams *n* ▷ **salaam**
salacious *adj* excessively concerned with sex
salad *n* (*pl* **-s**) dish of raw vegetables, eaten as a meal or part of a meal
salads *n* ▷ **salad**

salamander *n* (*pl* **-s**) amphibian which looks like a lizard
salamanders *n* ▷ **salamander**
salami *n* (*pl* **-s**) highly spiced sausage
salamis *n* ▷ **salami**
salaried *adj* ▷ **salary**
salaries *n* ▷ **salary**
salary *n* (*pl* **-ries**) fixed regular payment, usu. monthly, to an employee > **salaried** *adj*
sale *n* (*pl* **-s**) exchange of goods for money > **saleable** *adj* fit or likely to be sold
saleable *adj* ▷ **sale**
sales *n* ▷ **sale**
salesman, saleswoman (*pl* **-men, -women**) > **salesperson** (*pl* **-people**) *n* person who sells goods
salesmanship *n* (*pl* **-s**) skill in selling
salesmanships *n* ▷ **salesmanship**
salesmen *n* ▷ **salesman**
salespeople *n* ▷ **salesman**
salesperson *n* ▷ **salesman**
saleswoman *n* ▷ **salesman**
saleswomen *n* ▷ **salesman**
salient [say-lee-ent] *adj* prominent, noticeable ▶ *n* (*pl* **-s**) (MIL) projecting part of a front line
salients *n* ▷ **salient**
saline [say-line] *adj* containing salt > **salinity** *n* (*pl* **-ties**)
salinities *n* ▷ **saline**
salinity *n* ▷ **saline**
saliva *n* (*pl* **-s**) liquid that forms in the mouth, spittle > **salivary** *adj*
salivary *adj* ▷ **saliva**
salivas *n* ▷ **saliva**
salivate *v* (**-tes, -ting, -ted**) produce saliva
salivated *v* ▷ **salivate**
salivates *v* ▷ **salivate**
salivating *v* ▷ **salivate**
sallee *n* (*pl* **-s**) (AUST) SE Australian eucalyptus with a pale grey bark
sallees *n* ▷ **sallee**
sallied *v* ▷ **sally**
sallies *n, v* ▷ **sally**
sallow *adj* (**-er, -est**) of an unhealthy pale or yellowish colour
sallower *adj* ▷ **sallow**
sallowest *adj* ▷ **sallow**
sally *n* (*pl* **-lies**) witty remark ▶ *v* (**-lies, -lying, -lied**) (*foll. by* **forth**) rush out
sallying *v* ▷ **sally**
salmon *n* (*pl* **-s**) large fish with orange-pink flesh valued as food ▶ *adj* orange-pink
salmonella *n* (*pl* **-lae**) bacterium causing food poisoning
salmonellae *n* ▷ **salmonella**
salmons *n* ▷ **salmon**
salon *n* (*pl* **-s**) commercial premises of a hairdresser, beautician, etc.
salons *n* ▷ **salon**
saloon *n* (*pl* **-s**) two-door or four-door car with body closed off from rear luggage area
saloons *n* ▷ **saloon**
salt *n* (*pl* **-s**) white crystalline substance used to season food ▶ *v* (**-s, -ing, -ed**) season or preserve with salt > **salty** *adj* (**-tier, -tiest**)
saltbush *n* (*pl* **-es**) shrub that grows in alkaline desert regions
saltbushes *n* ▷ **saltbush**
salted *v* ▷ **salt**
saltier *adj* ▷ **salt**
saltiest *adj* ▷ **salt**
salting *v* ▷ **salt**
saltire *n* (*pl* **-s**) (HERALDRY) diagonal cross on a shield
saltires *n* ▷ **saltire**
saltpetre *n* (*pl* **-s**) compound used in gunpowder and as a preservative
saltpetres *n* ▷ **saltpetre**
salts *n, v* ▷ **salt**
salty *adj* ▷ **salt**
salubrious *adj* favourable to health
saluki *n* (*pl* **-s**) tall hound with a silky coat
salukis *n* ▷ **saluki**
salutary *adj* producing a beneficial result
salutation *n* (*pl* **-s**) greeting by words or actions
salutations *n* ▷ **salutation**
salute *n* (*pl* **-s**) motion of the arm as a formal military sign of respect ▶ *v* (**-tes, -ting, -ted**) greet with a salute
saluted *v* ▷ **salute**
salutes *n, v* ▷ **salute**
saluting *v* ▷ **salute**
salvage *n* (*pl* **-s**) saving of a ship or other property from destruction ▶ *v* (**-ges, -ging, -ged**) save from destruction or waste
salvaged *v* ▷ **salvage**
salvages *n, v* ▷ **salvage**
salvaging *v* ▷ **salvage**
salvation *n* (*pl* **-s**) fact or state of being saved from harm or the consequences of sin
salvations *n* ▷ **salvation**
salve *n* (*pl* **-s**) healing or soothing ointment ▶ *v* (**-ves, -ving, -ved**) soothe or appease
salved *v* ▷ **salve**
salver *n* (*pl* **-s**) (silver) tray on which something is presented
salvers *n* ▷ **salver**
salves *n, v* ▷ **salve**
salvia *n* (*pl* **-s**) plant with blue or red flowers

salvias *n* ▷ **salvia**
salving *v* ▷ **salve**
salvo *n* (*pl* **-s, -es**) simultaneous discharge of guns etc.
salvoes *n* ▷ **salvo**
salvos *n* ▷ **salvo**
samaritan *n* (*pl* **-s**) person who helps people in distress
samaritans *n* ▷ **samaritan**
samba *n* (*pl* **-s**) lively Brazilian dance
sambas *n* ▷ **samba**
same *adj* identical, not different, unchanged **> sameness** *n* (*pl* **-es**)
sameness *n* ▷ **same**
samenesses *n* ▷ **same**
samovar *n* (*pl* **-s**) Russian tea urn
samovars *n* ▷ **samovar**
sampan *n* (*pl* **-s**) small boat with oars used in China
sampans *n* ▷ **sampan**
samphire *n* (*pl* **-s**) plant found on rocks by the seashore
samphires *n* ▷ **samphire**
sample *n* (*pl* **-s**) part taken as representative of a whole ▶ *v* (**-les, -ling, -led**) take and test a sample of **> sampling** *n* (*pl* **-s**)
sampled *v* ▷ **sample**
sampler *n* (*pl* **-s**) piece of embroidery showing the embroiderer's skill
samplers *n* ▷ **sampler**
samples *v, n* ▷ **sample**
sampling *v, n* ▷ **sample**
samplings *n* ▷ **sample**
samurai *n* (*pl* **-rai**) member of an ancient Japanese warrior caste
sanatoria *n* ▷ **sanatorium**
sanatorium *n* (*pl* **-riums, -ria**) institution for invalids or convalescents
sanatoriums *n* ▷ **sanatorium**
sancta *n* ▷ **sanctum**
sanctified *v* ▷ **sanctify**
sanctifies *v* ▷ **sanctify**
sanctify *v* (**-fies, -fying, -fied**) make holy
sanctifying *v* ▷ **sanctify**
sanctimonious *adj* pretending to be religious and virtuous
sanction *n* (*pl* **-s**) permission, authorization ▶ *v* (**-s, -ing, -ed**) allow, authorize
sanctioned *v* ▷ **sanction**
sanctioning *v* ▷ **sanction**
sanctions *n, v* ▷ **sanction**
sanctities *n* ▷ **sanctity**
sanctity *n* (*pl* **-ties**) sacredness, inviolability
sanctuaries *n* ▷ **sanctuary**
sanctuary *n* (*pl* **-ries**) holy place
sanctum *n* (*pl* **-tums, -ta**) sacred place
sanctums *n* ▷ **sanctum**
sand *n* (*pl* **-s**) substance consisting of small grains of rock, esp. on a beach or in a desert ▶ *v* (**-s, -ing, -ed**) smooth with sandpaper
sandal *n* (*pl* **-s**) light shoe consisting of a sole attached by straps
sandals *n* ▷ **sandal**
sandalwood *n* (*pl* **-s**) sweet-scented wood
sandalwoods *n* ▷ **sandalwood**
sandbag *n* (*pl* **-s**) bag filled with sand, used as protection against gunfire or flood water
sandbags *n* ▷ **sandbag**
sandblast *v* (**-s, -ing, -ed**) ▶ *n* (*pl* **-s**) (clean with) a jet of sand blown from a nozzle under pressure
sandblasted *v* ▷ **sandblast**
sandblasting *v* ▷ **sandblast**
sandblasts *v, n* ▷ **sandblast**
sanded *v* ▷ **sand**
sander *n* (*pl* **-s**) power tool for smoothing surfaces
sanders *n* ▷ **sander**
sandier *adj* ▷ **sandy**
sandiest *adj* ▷ **sandy**
sanding *v* ▷ **sand**
sandpaper *n* (*pl* **-s**) paper coated with sand for smoothing a surface
sandpapers *n* ▷ **sandpaper**
sandpiper *n* (*pl* **-s**) shore bird with a long bill and slender legs
sandpipers *n* ▷ **sandpiper**
sands *n, v* ▷ **sand** ▶ *pl n* stretches of sand forming a beach or desert
sandstone *n* (*pl* **-s**) rock composed of sand
sandstones *n* ▷ **sandstone**
sandstorm *n* (*pl* **-s**) desert wind that whips up clouds of sand
sandstorms *n* ▷ **sandstorm**
sandwich *n* (*pl* **-es**) two slices of bread with a layer of food between ▶ *v* (**-es, -ing, -ed**) insert between two other things
sandwiched *v* ▷ **sandwich**
sandwiches *n, v* ▷ **sandwich**
sandwiching *v* ▷ **sandwich**
sandy *adj* (**-dier, -diest**) covered with sand
sane *adj* (**-r, -st**) of sound mind **> sanity** *n* (*pl* **-ties**)
saner *adj* ▷ **sane**
sanest *adj* ▷ **sane**
sang *v* ▷ **sing**
sangoma *n* (*pl* **-s**) (S AFR) witch doctor or herbalist
sangomas *n* ▷ **sangoma**
sanguinary *adj* accompanied by bloodshed

sanguine *adj* cheerful, optimistic
sanitary *adj* promoting health by getting rid of dirt and germs
sanitation *n* (*pl* **-s**) sanitary measures, esp. drainage or sewerage
sanitations *n* ▷ **sanitation**
sanities *n* ▷ **sane**
sanity *n* ▷ **sane**
sank *v* ▷ **sink**
sap[1] *n* (*pl* **-s**) moisture that circulates in plants
sap[2] *v* (**saps, sapping, sapped**) undermine
sapient [**say**-pee-ent] *adj* (*Lit*) wise, shrewd
sapling *n* (*pl* **-s**) young tree
saplings *n* ▷ **sapling**
sapped *v* ▷ **sap**[2]
sapper *n* (*pl* **-s**) soldier in an engineering unit
sappers *n* ▷ **sapper**
sapphire *n* (*pl* **-s**) blue precious stone ▶ *adj* deep blue
sapphires *n* ▷ **sapphire**
sapping *v* ▷ **sap**[2]
saps *n* ▷ **sap**[1] ▶ *v* ▷ **sap**[2]
saraband *n* ▷ **sarabande**
sarabande, saraband *n* (*pl* **-s**) slow stately Spanish dance
sarabandes *n* ▷ **sarabande**
sarabands *n* ▷ **sarabande**
sarcasm *n* (*pl* **-s**) (use of) bitter or wounding ironic language > **sarcastic** *adj* > **sarcastically** *adv*
sarcasms *n* ▷ **sarcasm**
sarcastic *adj* ▷ **sarcasm**
sarcastically *adv* ▷ **sarcasm**
sarcophagi *n* ▷ **sarcophagus**
sarcophagus *n* (*pl* **-gi, -guses**) stone coffin
sarcophaguses *n* ▷ **sarcophagus**
sardine *n* (*pl* **-s**) small fish of the herring family, usu. preserved tightly packed in tins
sardines *n* ▷ **sardine**
sardonic *adj* mocking or scornful > **sardonically** *adv*
sardonically *adv* ▷ **sardonic**
saree *n* ▷ **sari**
sarees *n* ▷ **sari**
sargasso *n* ▷ **sargassum**
sargassos *n* ▷ **sargassum**
sargassum, sargasso *n* (*pl* **-s**) type of floating seaweed
sargassums *n* ▷ **sargassum**
sari, saree *n* (*pl* **-s**) long piece of cloth draped around the body and over one shoulder, worn by Hindu women
saris *n* ▷ **sari**
sarmie *n* (*pl* **-s**) (S AFR) (*Slang*) sandwich
sarmies *n* ▷ **sarmie**
sarong *n* (*pl* **-s**) long piece of cloth tucked around the waist or under the armpits, worn esp. in Malaysia
sarongs *n* ▷ **sarong**
sarsaparilla *n* (*pl* **-s**) soft drink, orig. made from the root of a tropical American plant
sarsaparillas *n* ▷ **sarsaparilla**
sartorial *adj* of men's clothes or tailoring
sash[1] *n* (*pl* **-es**) decorative strip of cloth worn round the waist or over one shoulder
sash[2] *n* (*pl* **-es**) wooden frame containing the panes of a window
sashes *n* ▷ **sash**[1, 2]
sassafras *n* (*pl* **-rases**) American tree with aromatic bark used medicinally
sassafrases *n* ▷ **sassafras**
sat *v* ▷ **sit**
satanic *adj* of Satan
satanism *n* (*pl* **-s**) worship of Satan
satanisms *n* ▷ **satanism**
satay, saté [**sat**-ay] *n* (*pl* **-s**) Indonesian and Malaysian dish consisting of pieces of chicken, pork, etc., grilled on skewers and served with peanut sauce
satays *n* ▷ **satay**
satchel *n* (*pl* **-s**) bag, usu. with a shoulder strap, for carrying books
satchels *n* ▷ **satchel**
sate *v* (**-tes, -ting, -ted**) satisfy (a desire or appetite) fully
sated *v* ▷ **sate**
satellite *n* (*pl* **-s**) man-made device orbiting in space ▶ *adj* of or used in the transmission of television signals from a satellite to the home
satellites *n* ▷ **satellite**
sates *v* ▷ **sate**
satiate [**say**-she-ate] *v* (**-tes, -ting, -ted**) provide with more than enough, so as to disgust
satiated *v* ▷ **satiate**
satiates *v* ▷ **satiate**
satiating *v* ▷ **satiate**
satieties *n* ▷ **satiety**
satiety [sat-**tie**-a-tee] *n* (*pl* **-ties**) feeling of having had too much
satin *n* (*pl* **-s**) silky fabric with a glossy surface on one side
sating *v* ▷ **sate**
satins *n* ▷ **satin**
satinwood *n* (*pl* **-s**) tropical tree yielding hard wood
satinwoods *n* ▷ **satinwood**
satiny *adj* of or like satin
satire *n* (*pl* **-s**) use of ridicule to expose vice or folly > **satirical** *adj* > **satirist** *n* (*pl* **-s**)

satires *n* ▷ **satire**
satirical *adj* ▷ **satire**
satirist *n* ▷ **satire**
satirists *n* ▷ **satire**
satirize *v* (**-zes, -zing, -zed**) ridicule by means of satire
satirized *v* ▷ **satirize**
satirizes *v* ▷ **satirize**
satirizing *v* ▷ **satirize**
satisfaction *n* ▷ **satisfy**
satisfactions *n* ▷ **satisfy**
satisfactory *adj* ▷ **satisfy**
satisfied *v* ▷ **satisfy**
satisfies *v* ▷ **satisfy**
satisfy *v* (**-fies, -fying, -fied**) please, content > **satisfaction** *n* (*pl* **-s**) > **satisfactory** *adj*
satisfying *v* ▷ **satisfy**
satnav *n* (*pl* **-s**) (MOTORING) (*Informal*) satellite navigation
satnavs *n* ▷ **satnav**
satsuma *n* (*pl* **-s**) kind of small orange
satsumas *n* ▷ **satsuma**
saturate *v* (**-tes, -ting, -ted**) soak thoroughly > **saturation** *n* (*pl* **-s**)
saturated *v* ▷ **saturate**
saturates *v* ▷ **saturate**
saturating *v* ▷ **saturate**
saturation *n* ▷ **saturate**
saturations *n* ▷ **saturate**
saturnalia *n* (*pl* **-s**) wild party or orgy
saturnalias *n* ▷ **saturnalia**
saturnine *adj* gloomy in temperament or appearance
satyr *n* (*pl* **-s**) woodland god, part man, part goat
satyrs *n* ▷ **satyr**
sauce *n* (*pl* **-s**) liquid added to food to enhance flavour
saucepan *n* (*pl* **-s**) cooking pot with a long handle
saucepans *n* ▷ **saucepan**
saucer *n* (*pl* **-s**) small round dish put under a cup
saucers *n* ▷ **saucer**
sauces *n* ▷ **sauce**
saucier *adj* ▷ **saucy**
sauciest *adj* ▷ **saucy**
saucily *adv* ▷ **saucy**
saucy *adj* (**-cier, -ciest**) impudent > **saucily** *adv*
sauerkraut *n* (*pl* **-s**) shredded cabbage fermented in brine
sauerkrauts *n* ▷ **sauerkraut**
sauna *n* (*pl* **-s**) Finnish-style steam bath
saunas *n* ▷ **sauna**
saunter *v* (**-s, -ing, -ed**) walk in a leisurely manner, stroll ▶ *n* (*pl* **-s**) leisurely walk
sauntered *v* ▷ **saunter**
sauntering *v* ▷ **saunter**
saunters *v, n* ▷ **saunter**
sausage *n* (*pl* **-s**) minced meat in an edible tube-shaped skin
sausages *n* ▷ **sausage**
sauté [so-tay] *v* (**-tés, -téing** *or* **-téeing, -téed**) fry quickly in a little fat
sautéed *v* ▷ **sauté**
sautéeing *v* ▷ **sauté**
sautéing *v* ▷ **sauté**
sautés *v* ▷ **sauté**
savage *adj* (**-r, -st**) wild, untamed ▶ *n* (*pl* **-s**) uncivilized person ▶ *v* (**-ges, -ging, -ged**) attack ferociously > **savagely** *adv* > **savagery** *n* (*pl* **-ries**)
savaged *v* ▷ **savage**
savagely *adv* ▷ **savage**
savager *adj* ▷ **savage**
savageries *n* ▷ **savage**
savagery *n* ▷ **savage**
savages *n, v* ▷ **savage**
savagest *adj* ▷ **savage**
savaging *v* ▷ **savage**
savanna *n* ▷ **savannah**
savannah, savanna *n* (*pl* **-s**) extensive open grassy plain in Africa
savannahs *n* ▷ **savannah**
savannas *n* ▷ **savanna**
savant *n* (*pl* **-s**) learned person
savants *n* ▷ **savant**
save *v* (**-ves, -ving, -ved**) rescue or preserve from harm, protect ▶ *n* (*pl* **-s**) (SPORT) act of preventing a goal > **saver** *n* (*pl* **-s**)
saved *v* ▷ **save**
saveloy *n* (*pl* **-s**) (BRIT, AUST & NZ) spicy smoked sausage
saveloys *n* ▷ **saveloy**
saver *n* ▷ **save**
savers *n* ▷ **save**
saves *v, n* ▷ **save**
saving *v* ▷ **save** ▶ *n* (*pl* **-s**) economy
savings *n pl* money put by for future use
saviour *n* (*pl* **-s**) person who rescues another
saviours *n* ▷ **saviour**
savories *n* ▷ **savory**
savory *n* (*pl* **-ries**) aromatic herb used in cooking
savour *v* (**-s, -ing, -ed**) enjoy, relish (*foll. by* **of**) ▶ *n* (*pl* **-s**) characteristic taste or odour
savoured *v* ▷ **savour**
savourier *adj* ▷ **savoury**
savouries *n* ▷ **savoury**
savouriest *adj* ▷ **savoury**

savouring *v* ▷ **savour**
savours *v, n* ▷ **savour**
savoury *adj* (**-rier, -riest**) salty or spicy ▶ *n* (*pl* **-ries**) savoury dish served before or after a meal
savoy *n* (*pl* **-s**) variety of cabbage
savoys *n* ▷ **savoy**
savvied *v* ▷ **savvy**
savvies *v, n* ▷ **savvy**
savvy (*Slang*) *v* (**-vies, -vying, -vied**) understand ▶ *n* (*pl* **-vies**) understanding, intelligence
savvying *v* ▷ **savvy**
saw¹ *n* (*pl* **-s**) cutting tool with a toothed metal blade ▶ *v* (**-s, -ing, -ed, -ed** *or* **sawn**) cut with a saw
saw² ▷ **see¹**
saw³ *n* (*pl* **-s**) wise saying, proverb
sawdust *n* (*pl* **-s**) fine wood fragments made in sawing
sawdusts *n* ▷ **sawdust**
sawed *v* ▷ **saw¹**
sawfish *n* (*pl* **-es**) fish with a long toothed snout
sawfishes *n* ▷ **sawfish**
sawing *v* ▷ **saw¹**
sawmill *n* (*pl* **-s**) mill where timber is sawn into planks
sawmills *n* ▷ **sawmill**
sawn *v* ▷ **saw¹**
saws *n* ▷ **saw¹,³** ▶ *v* ▷ **saw¹**
sawyer *n* (*pl* **-s**) person who saws timber for a living
sawyers *n* ▷ **sawyer**
sax *n* (*pl* **-es**) (*Informal*) ▷ **saxophone**
saxes *n* ▷ **sax**
saxifrage *n* (*pl* **-s**) alpine rock plant with small flowers
saxifrages *n* ▷ **saxifrage**
saxophone *n* (*pl* **-s**) brass wind instrument with keys and a curved body > **saxophonist** *n* (*pl* **-s**)
saxophones *n* ▷ **saxophone**
saxophonist *n* ▷ **saxophone**
saxophonists *n* ▷ **saxophone**
say *v* (**-s, -ing, said**) speak or utter ▶ *n* (*pl* **-s**) right or chance to speak
saying *n* (*pl* **-s**) maxim, proverb ▶ *v* ▷ **say**
sayings *n* ▷ **saying**
says *v, n* ▷ **say**

> **saz** *n* (**sazes**). A saz is a Turkish musical instrument. This is a very useful word, and one to remember for when you get a Z in the later stages of the game, with little space left on the board. Saz scores 12 points.

scab *n* (*pl* **-s**) crust formed over a wound
scabbard *n* (*pl* **-s**) sheath for a sword or dagger
scabbards *n* ▷ **scabbard**
scabbier *adj* ▷ **scabby**
scabbiest *adj* ▷ **scabby**
scabby *adj* (**-bbier, -bbiest**) covered with scabs
scabies [**skay**-beez] *n* itchy skin disease
scabrous [**skay**-bruss] *adj* rough and scaly
scabs *n* ▷ **scab**
scaffold *n* (*pl* **-s**) temporary platform for workmen
scaffolding *n* (*pl* **-s**) (materials for building) scaffolds
scaffoldings *n* ▷ **scaffolding**
scaffolds *n* ▷ **scaffold**
scalar *n* (*pl* **-s**) ▶ *adj* (variable quantity) having magnitude but no direction
scalars *n* ▷ **scalar**
scald *v* (**-s, -ing, -ed**) burn with hot liquid or steam ▶ *n* (*pl* **-s**) injury by scalding
scalded *v* ▷ **scald**
scalding *v* ▷ **scald**
scalds *v, n* ▷ **scald**
scale¹ *n* (*pl* **-s**) one of the thin overlapping plates covering fishes and reptiles ▶ *v* (**-les, -ling, -led**) remove scales from > **scaly** *adj* (**-lier, -liest**)
scale² *n* (*pl* **-s**) (*often pl* weighing instrument
scale³ *n* (*pl* **-s**) graduated table or sequence of marks at regular intervals, used as a reference in making measurements ▶ *v* (**-les, -ling, -led**) climb
scaled *v* ▷ **scale¹,³**
scalene *adj* (of a triangle) with three unequal sides
scales *n* ▷ **scale¹,²,³** ▶ *v* ▷ **scale¹,³**
scalier *adj* ▷ **scale¹**
scaliest *adj* ▷ **scale¹**
scaling *v* ▷ **scale¹,³**
scallop *n* (*pl* **-s**) edible shellfish with two fan-shaped shells
scalloped *adj* decorated with small curves along the edge
scallops *n* ▷ **scallop**
scallywag *n* (*pl* **-s**) (*Informal*) scamp, rascal
scallywags *n* ▷ **scallywag**
scalp *n* (*pl* **-s**) skin and hair on top of the head ▶ *v* (**-s, -ing, -ed**) cut off the scalp of
scalped *v* ▷ **scalp**
scalpel *n* (*pl* **-s**) small surgical knife
scalpels *n* ▷ **scalpel**
scalping *v* ▷ **scalp**
scalps *n, v* ▷ **scalp**
scaly *adj* ▷ **scale¹**
scam *n* (*pl* **-s**) (*Informal*) dishonest scheme

scamp *n* (*pl* **-s**) mischievous child
scamper *v* (**-s, -ing, -ed**) run about hurriedly or in play ▶ *n* (*pl* **-s**) scampering
scampered *v* ▷ **scamper**
scampering *v* ▷ **scamper**
scampers *v, n* ▷ **scamper**
scampi *pl n* large prawns
scamps *n* ▷ **scamp**
scams *n* ▷ **scam**
scan *v* (**-s, -nning, -nned**) scrutinize carefully ▶ *n* (*pl* **-s**) scanning
scandal *n* (*pl* **-s**) disgraceful action or event > **scandalous** *adj*
scandalize *v* (**-zes, -zing, -zed**) shock by scandal
scandalized *v* ▷ **scandalize**
scandalizes *v* ▷ **scandalize**
scandalizing *v* ▷ **scandalize**
scandalous *adj* ▷ **scandal**
scandals *n* ▷ **scandal**
scandium *n* (*pl* **-s**) (CHEM) rare silvery-white metallic element
scandiums *n* ▷ **scandium**
scanned *v* ▷ **scan**
scanner *n* (*pl* **-s**) electronic device used for scanning
scanners *n* ▷ **scanner**
scanning *v* ▷ **scan**
scans *v, n* ▷ **scan**
scansion *n* (*pl* **-s**) metrical scanning of verse
scansions *n* ▷ **scansion**
scant *adj* (**-er, -est**) barely sufficient, meagre
scanter *adj* ▷ **scant**
scantest *adj* ▷ **scant**
scantier *adj* ▷ **scanty**
scantiest *adj* ▷ **scanty**
scantily *n* ▷ **scanty**
scanty *adj* (**-tier, -tiest**) barely sufficient or not sufficient > **scantily** *adv*
scapegoat *n* (*pl* **-s**) person made to bear the blame for others
scapegoats *n* ▷ **scapegoat**
scapula *n* (*pl* **-lae, -las**) shoulder blade > **scapular** *adj*
scapulae *n* ▷ **scapula**
scapular *adj* ▷ **scapula**
scapulas *n* ▷ **scapula**
scar *n* (*pl* **-s**) mark left by a healed wound ▶ *v* (**-s, -rring, -rred**) mark or become marked with a scar
scarab *n* (*pl* **-s**) sacred beetle of ancient Egypt
scarabs *n* ▷ **scarab**
scarce *adj* (**-r, -st**) insufficient to meet demand > **scarcity** *n* (*pl* **-ties**)
scarcely *adv* hardly at all
scarcer *adj* ▷ **scarce**
scarcest *adj* ▷ **scarce**
scarcities *n* ▷ **scarce**
scarcity *n* ▷ **scarce**
scare *v* (**-res, -ring, -red**) frighten or be frightened ▶ *n* (*pl* **-s**) fright, sudden panic
scarecrow *n* (*pl* **-s**) figure dressed in old clothes, set up to scare birds away from crops
scarecrows *n* ▷ **scarecrow**
scared *v* ▷ **scare**
scaremonger *n* (*pl* **-s**) person who spreads alarming rumours
scaremongers *n* ▷ **scaremonger**
scares *v, n* ▷ **scare**
scarf[1] *n* (*pl* **scarves, -s**) piece of material worn round the neck, head, or shoulders
scarf[2] *n* (*pl* **-s**) joint between two pieces of timber made by notching the ends and fastening them together ▶ *v* (**-s, -ing, -ed**) join in this way
scarfed *v* ▷ **scarf**[2]
scarfing *v* ▷ **scarf**[2]
scarfs *n* ▷ **scarf**[1, 2] ▶ *v* ▷ **scarf**[2]
scarier *adj* ▷ **scary**
scariest *adj* ▷ **scary**
scarification *n* ▷ **scarify**
scarifications *n* ▷ **scarify**
scarified *v* ▷ **scarify**
scarifies *v* ▷ **scarify**
scarify *v* (**-fies, -fying, -fied**) scratch or cut slightly all over > **scarification** *n* (*pl* **-s**)
scarifying *v* ▷ **scarify**
scaring *v* ▷ **scare**
scarlatina *n* (*pl* **-s**) scarlet fever
scarlatinas *n* ▷ **scarlatina**
scarlet *adj, n* (*pl* **-s**) brilliant red
scarlets *n* ▷ **scarlet**
scarp *n* (*pl* **-s**) steep slope
scarper *v* (**-s, -ing, -ed**) (BRIT) (*Slang*) run away
scarpered *v* ▷ **scarper**
scarpering *v* ▷ **scarper**
scarpers *v* ▷ **scarper**
scarps *n* ▷ **scarp**
scarred *v* ▷ **scar**
scarring *v* ▷ **scar**
scars *n, v* ▷ **scar**
scarves *n* ▷ **scarf**[1]
scary *adj* (**-rier, -riest**) (*Informal*) frightening
scat[1] *v* (**-s, -tting, -tted**) (*Informal*) go away
scat[2] *n* (*pl* **-s**) jazz singing using improvised vocal sounds instead of words
scathing *adj* harshly critical
scatological *adj* preoccupied with obscenity, esp. with references to excrement > **scatology** *n* (*pl* **-gies**)

scatologies *n* ▷ **scatology**
scatology *n* ▷ **scatological**
scats *n* ▷ **scat²** ▶ *v* ▷ **scat¹**
scatted *v* ▷ **scat¹**
scatter *v* (**-s, -ing, -ed**) throw about in various directions
scatterbrain *n* (*pl* **-s**) empty-headed person
scatterbrains *n* ▷ **scatterbrain**
scattered *v* ▷ **scatter**
scattering *v* ▷ **scatter**
scatters *v* ▷ **scatter**
scattier *adj* ▷ **scatty**
scattiest *adj* ▷ **scatty**
scatting *v* ▷ **scat¹**
scatty *adj* (**-tier, -tiest**) (*Informal*) empty-headed
scavenge *v* (**-ges, -ging, -ged**) search for (anything usable) among discarded material
scavenged *v* ▷ **scavenge**
scavenger *n* (*pl* **-s**) person who scavenges
scavengers *n* ▷ **scavenger**
scavenges *v* ▷ **scavenge**
scavenging *v* ▷ **scavenge**
scenario *n* (*pl* **-rios**) summary of the plot of a play or film
scenarios *n* ▷ **scenario**
scene *n* (*pl* **-s**) place of action of a real or imaginary event
sceneries *n* ▷ **scenery**
scenery *n* (*pl* **-ries**) natural features of a landscape
scenes *n* ▷ **scene**
scenic *adj* picturesque
scent *n* (*pl* **-s**) pleasant smell ▶ *v* (**-s, -ing, -ed**) detect by smell
scented *v* ▷ **scent**
scenting *v* ▷ **scent**
scents *n, v* ▷ **scent**
sceptic [**skep**-tik] *n* (*pl* **-s**) person who habitually doubts generally accepted beliefs > **sceptical** *adj* > **sceptically** *adv* > **scepticism** *n* (*pl* **-s**)
sceptical *adj* ▷ **sceptic**
sceptically *adv* ▷ **sceptic**
scepticism *n* ▷ **sceptic**
scepticisms *n* ▷ **sceptic**
sceptics *n* ▷ **sceptic**
sceptre *n* (*pl* **-s**) ornamental rod symbolizing royal power
sceptres *n* ▷ **sceptre**
schedule *n* (*pl* **-s**) plan of procedure for a project ▶ *v* (**-les, -ling, -led**) plan to occur at a certain time
scheduled *v* ▷ **schedule**
schedules *n, v* ▷ **schedule**
scheduling *v* ▷ **schedule**
schema *n* (*pl* **-mata**) overall plan or diagram
schematic *adj* presented as a plan or diagram
scheme *n* (*pl* **-s**) systematic plan ▶ *v* (**-mes, -ming, -med**) plan in an underhand manner > **scheming** *adj, n* (*pl* **-s**)
schemed *v* ▷ **scheme**
schemes *n, v* ▷ **scheme**
scheming *v, adj n* ▷ **scheme**
schemings *n* ▷ **scheme**
scherzi *n* ▷ **scherzo**
scherzo [**skairt**-so] *n* (*pl* **-zos, -zi**) brisk lively piece of music
scherzos *n* ▷ **scherzo**
schism [**skizz**-um] *n* (*pl* **-s**) (group resulting from) division in an organization > **schismatic** *adj, n* (*pl* **-s**)
schismatic *adj, n* ▷ **schism**
schismatics *n* ▷ **schism**
schisms *n* ▷ **schism**
schist [**shist**] *n* (*pl* **-s**) crystalline rock which splits into layers
schists *n* ▷ **schist**
schizoid *adj* abnormally introverted ▶ *n* (*pl* **-s**) schizoid person
schizoids *n* ▷ **schizoid**
schizophrenia *n* (*pl* **-s**) mental disorder involving deterioration of or confusion about the personality > **schizophrenic** *adj, n* (*pl* **-s**)
schizophrenias *n* ▷ **schizophrenia**
schizophrenic *adj, n* ▷ **schizophrenia**
schizophrenics *n* ▷ **schizophrenia**
schmaltz *n* (*pl* **-es**) excessive sentimentality > **schmaltzy** *adj* (**-zier, -ziest**)
schmaltzes *n* ▷ **schmaltz**
schmaltzier *adj* ▷ **schmaltz**
schmaltziest *adj* ▷ **schmaltz**
schmaltzy *adj* ▷ **schmaltz**
schnapps *n* (*pl* **-es**) strong alcoholic spirit
schnappses *n* ▷ **schnapps**
schnitzel *n* (*pl* **-s**) thin slice of meat, esp. veal
schnitzels *n* ▷ **schnitzel**
scholar *n* (*pl* **-s**) learned person
scholarly *adj* learned
scholars *n* ▷ **scholar**
scholarship *n* (*pl* **-s**) learning
scholarships *n* ▷ **scholarship**
scholastic *adj* of schools or scholars
school¹ *n* (*pl* **-s**) place where children are taught or instruction is given in a subject ▶ *v* (**-s, -ing, -ed**) educate or train
school² *n* (*pl* **-s**) shoal of fish, whales, etc.
schooled *v* ▷ **school¹**
schoolie *n* (*pl* **-s**) (AUST) schoolteacher or high-school student

schoolies *n* ▷ **schoolie**
schooling *v* ▷ **school**[1]
schools *n* ▷ **school**[1, 2] ▶ *v* ▷ **school**[1]
schooner *n* (*pl* **-s**) sailing ship rigged fore-and-aft
schooners *n* ▷ **schooner**
sciatic *adj* of the hip
sciatica *n* (*pl* **-s**) severe pain in the large nerve in the back of the leg
sciaticas *n* ▷ **sciatica**
science *n* (*pl* **-s**) systematic study and knowledge of natural or physical phenomena
sciences *n* ▷ **science**
scientific *adj* of science > **scientifically** *adv*
scientifically *adv* ▷ **scientific**
scientist *n* (*pl* **-s**) person who studies or practises a science
scientists *n* ▷ **scientist**
scimitar *n* (*pl* **-s**) curved oriental sword
scimitars *n* ▷ **scimitar**
scintillate *v* (**-tes, -ting, -ted**) give off sparks
scintillated *v* ▷ **scintillate**
scintillates *v* ▷ **scintillate**
scintillating *adj* very lively and amusing ▶ *v* ▷ **scintillate**
scion [**sy**-on] *n* (*pl* **-s**) descendant or heir
scions *n* ▷ **scion**
scissors *pl n* cutting instrument with two crossed pivoted blades
scleroses *n* ▷ **sclerosis**
sclerosis *n* (*pl* **-ses**) abnormal hardening of body tissues
scoff[1] *v* (**-s, -ing, -ed**) express derision
scoff[2] *v* (**-s, -ing, -ed**) (*Informal*) eat rapidly
scoffed *v* ▷ **scoff**[1, 2]
scoffing *v* ▷ **scoff**[1, 2]
scoffs *v* ▷ **scoff**[1, 2]
scold *v* (**-s, -ing, -ed**) find fault with, reprimand ▶ *n* (*pl* **-s**) person who scolds > **scolding** *n* (*pl* **-s**)
scolded *v* ▷ **scold**
scolding *v, n* ▷ **scold**
scoldings *n* ▷ **scold**
scolds *v, n* ▷ **scold**
sconce *n* (*pl* **-s**) bracket on a wall for holding candles or lights
sconces *n* ▷ **sconce**
scone *n* (*pl* **-s**) small plain cake baked in an oven or on a griddle
scones *n* ▷ **scone**
scoop *n* (*pl* **-s**) shovel-like tool for ladling or hollowing out ▶ *v* (**-s, -ing, -ed**) take up or hollow out with or as if with a scoop
scooped *v* ▷ **scoop**
scooping *v* ▷ **scoop**
scoops *n, v* ▷ **scoop**
scoot *v* (**-s, -ing, -ed**) (*Slang*) leave or move quickly
scooted *v* ▷ **scoot**
scooter *n* (*pl* **-s**) child's vehicle propelled by pushing on the ground with one foot
scooters *n* ▷ **scooter**
scooting *v* ▷ **scoot**
scoots *v* ▷ **scoot**
scope *n* (*pl* **-s**) opportunity for using abilities
scopes *n* ▷ **scope**
scorch *v* (**-es, -ing, -ed**) burn on the surface ▶ *n* (*pl* **-es**) slight burn
scorched *v* ▷ **scorch**
scorcher *n* (*pl* **-s**) (*Informal*) very hot day
scorchers *n* ▷ **scorcher**
scorches *v, n* ▷ **scorch**
scorching *v* ▷ **scorch**
score *n* (*pl* **-s**) points gained in a game or competition ▶ *v* (**-res, -ring, -red**) gain (points) in a game
scored *v* ▷ **score**
scores *n, v* ▷ **score** ▶ *pl n* lots
scoring *v* ▷ **score**
scorn *n* (*pl* **-s**) open contempt ▶ *v* (**-s, -ing, -ed**) despise > **scornful** *adj* > **scornfully** *adv*
scorned *v* ▷ **scorn**
scornful *adj* ▷ **scorn**
scornfully *adv* ▷ **scorn**
scorning *v* ▷ **scorn**
scorns *n, v* ▷ **scorn**
scorpion *n* (*pl* **-s**) small lobster-shaped animal with a sting at the end of a jointed tail
scorpions *n* ▷ **scorpion**
scotch *v* (**-es, -ing, -ed**) put an end to
scotched *v* ▷ **scotch**
scotches *v* ▷ **scotch**
scotching *v* ▷ **scotch**
scoundrel *n* (*pl* **-s**) (*Old-fashioned*) cheat or deceiver
scoundrels *n* ▷ **scoundrel**
scour[1] *v* (**-s, -ing, -ed**) clean or polish by rubbing with something rough
scour[2] *v* (**-s, -ing, -ed**) search thoroughly and energetically
scoured *v* ▷ **scour**[1, 2]
scourer *n* (*pl* **-s**) small rough nylon pad used for cleaning pots and pans
scourers *n* ▷ **scourer**
scourge *n* (*pl* **-s**) person or thing causing severe suffering ▶ *v* (**-ges, -ging, -ged**) cause severe suffering to
scourged *v* ▷ **scourge**
scourges *n, v* ▷ **scourge**
scourging *v* ▷ **scourge**
scouring *v* ▷ **scour**[1, 2]

scours *v* ▷ **scour**[1, 2]
scout *n* (*pl* **-s**) person sent out to reconnoitre ▶ *v* (**-s, -ing, -ed**) act as a scout
scouted *v* ▷ **scout**
scouting *v* ▷ **scout**
scouts *n, v* ▷ **scout**
scowl *v* (**-s, -ing, -ed**) ▶ *n* (*pl* **-s**) (have) an angry or sullen expression
scowled *v* ▷ **scowl**
scowling *v* ▷ **scowl**
scowls *v, n* ▷ **scowl**
scrabble *v* (**-les, -ling, -led**) scrape at with the hands, feet, or claws
scrabbled *v* ▷ **scrabble**
scrabbles *v* ▷ **scrabble**
scrabbling *v* ▷ **scrabble**
scrag *n* (*pl* **-s**) thin end of a neck of mutton
scraggier *adj* ▷ **scraggy**
scraggiest *adj* ▷ **scraggy**
scraggy *adj* (**-ggier, -ggiest**) thin, bony
scrags *n* ▷ **scrag**
scram *v* (**-s, -mming, -mmed**) (*Informal*) go away quickly
scramble *v* (**-les, -ling, -led**) climb or crawl hastily or awkwardly ▶ *n* (*pl* **-les**) scrambling
scrambled *v* ▷ **scramble**
scrambler *n* (*pl* **-s**) electronic device that makes transmitted speech unintelligible
scramblers *n* ▷ **scrambler**
scrambles *v, n* ▷ **scramble**
scrambling *v* ▷ **scramble**
scrammed *v* ▷ **scram**
scramming *v* ▷ **scram**
scrams *v* ▷ **scram**
scrap[1] *n* (*pl* **-s**) small piece ▶ *v* (**-s, -pping, -pped**) discard as useless
scrap[2] *n* (*pl* **-s**) ▶ *v* (**-s, -pping, -pped**) (*Informal*) fight or quarrel
scrapbook *n* (*pl* **-s**) book with blank pages in which newspaper cuttings or pictures are stuck
scrapbooks *n* ▷ **scrapbook**
scrape *v* (**-pes, -ping, -ped**) rub with something rough or sharp ▶ *n* (*pl* **-s**) act or sound of scraping > **scraper** *n* (*pl* **-s**)
scraped *v* ▷ **scrape**
scraper *n* ▷ **scrape**
scrapers *n* ▷ **scrape**
scrapes *v, n* ▷ **scrape**
scraping *v* ▷ **scrape**
scrapped *v* ▷ **scrap**[1, 2]
scrappier *adj* ▷ **scrappy**
scrappiest *adj* ▷ **scrappy**
scrapping *v* ▷ **scrap**[1, 2]
scrappy *adj* (**-ppier, -ppiest**) fragmentary, disjointed
scraps *v* ▷ **scrap**[1, 2] ▶ *n* ▷ **scrap**[1, 2] ▶ *pl n* leftover food
scratch *v* (**-es, -ing, -ed**) mark or cut with claws, nails, or anything rough or sharp ▶ *n* (*pl* **-es**) wound, mark, or sound made by scratching ▶ *adj* put together at short notice > **scratchy** *adj* (**-chier, -chiest**)
scratchcard *n* (*pl* **-s**) ticket that reveals whether or not the holder has won a prize when the surface is removed by scratching
scratchcards *n* ▷ **scratchcard**
scratched *v* ▷ **scratch**
scratches *v, n* ▷ **scratch**
scratchier *adj* ▷ **scratch**
scratchiest *adj* ▷ **scratch**
scratching *v* ▷ **scratch**
scratchy *adj* ▷ **scratch**
scrawl *v* (**-s, -ing, -ed**) write carelessly or hastily ▶ *n* (*pl* **-s**) scribbled writing
scrawled *v* ▷ **scrawl**
scrawling *v* ▷ **scrawl**
scrawls *v, n* ▷ **scrawl**
scrawnier *adj* ▷ **scrawny**
scrawniest *adj* ▷ **scrawny**
scrawny *adj* (**-nier, -niest**) thin and bony
scream *v* (**-s, -ing, -ed**) utter a piercing cry, esp. of fear or pain ▶ *n* (*pl* **-s**) shrill piercing cry
screamed *v* ▷ **scream**
screaming *v* ▷ **scream**
screams *v, n* ▷ **scream**
scree *n* (*pl* **-s**) slope of loose shifting stones
screech *v* (**-es, -ing, -ed**) ▶ *n* (*pl* **-es**) (utter) a shrill cry
screeched *v* ▷ **screech**
screeches *v, n* ▷ **screech**
screeching *v* ▷ **screech**
screed *n* (*pl* **-s**) long tedious piece of writing
screeds *n* ▷ **screed**
screen *n* (*pl* **-s**) surface of a television set, VDU, etc., on which an image is formed ▶ *v* (**-s, -ing, -ed**) shelter or conceal with or as if with a screen
screened *v* ▷ **screen**
screening *v* ▷ **screen**
screens *n, v* ▷ **screen**
screes *n* ▷ **scree**
screw *n* (*pl* **-s**) metal pin with a spiral ridge along its length, twisted into materials to fasten them together ▶ *v* (**-s, -ing, -ed**) turn (a screw)
screwdriver *n* (*pl* **-s**) tool for turning screws
screwdrivers *n* ▷ **screwdriver**
screwed *v* ▷ **screw**
screwier *adj* ▷ **screwy**

screwiest *adj* ▷ **screwy**
screwing *v* ▷ **screw**
screws *n, v* ▷ **screw**
screwy *adj* (**-wier, -wiest**) (*Informal*) crazy or eccentric
scribble *v* (**-les, -ling, -led**) write hastily or illegibly ▶ *n* (*pl* **-s**) something scribbled
scribbled *v* ▷ **scribble**
scribbles *v, n* ▷ **scribble**
scribbling *v* ▷ **scribble**
scribe *n* (*pl* **-s**) person who copied manuscripts before the invention of printing
scribes *n* ▷ **scribe**
scrimmage *n* (*pl* **-s**) rough or disorderly struggle
scrimmages *n* ▷ **scrimmage**
scrimp *v* (**-s, -ing, -ed**) be very economical
scrimped *v* ▷ **scrimp**
scrimping *v* ▷ **scrimp**
scrimps *v* ▷ **scrimp**
scrip *n* (*pl* **-s**) certificate representing a claim to stocks or shares
scrips *n* ▷ **scrip**
script *n* (*pl* **-s**) text of a film, play, or TV programme
scripts *n* ▷ **script**
scriptural *adj* ▷ **scripture**
scripture *n* (*pl* **-s**) sacred writings of a religion > **scriptural** *adj*
scriptures *n* ▷ **scripture**
scrofula *n* (*pl* **-s**) tuberculosis of the lymphatic glands > **scrofulous** *adj*
scrofulas *n* ▷ **scrofula**
scrofulous *adj* ▷ **scrofula**
scroggin *n* (*pl* **-s**) (NZ) mixture of nuts and dried fruits
scroggins *n* ▷ **scroggin**
scroll *n* (*pl* **-s**) roll of parchment or paper ▶ *v* (**-s, -ing, -ed**) move (text) up or down on a VDU screen
scrolled *v* ▷ **scroll**
scrolling *v* ▷ **scroll**
scrolls *n, v* ▷ **scroll**
scrota *n* ▷ **scrotum**
scrotum *n* (*pl* **-ta, -tums**) pouch of skin containing the testicles
scrotums *n* ▷ **scrotum**
scrounge *v* (**-ges, -ging, -ged**) (*Informal*) get by cadging or begging > **scrounger** *n* (*pl* **-s**)
scrounged *v* ▷ **scrounge**
scrounger *n* ▷ **scrounge**
scroungers *n* ▷ **scrounge**
scrounges *v* ▷ **scrounge**
scrounging *v* ▷ **scrounge**
scrub[1] *v* (**-s, -bbing, -bbed**) clean by rubbing, often with a hard brush and water ▶ *n* (*pl* **-s**) scrubbing
scrub[2] *n* (*pl* **-s**) stunted trees
scrubbed *v* ▷ **scrub[1]**
scrubbier *adj* ▷ **scrubby**
scrubbiest *adj* ▷ **scrubby**
scrubbing *v* ▷ **scrub[1]**
scrubby *adj* (**-bbier, -bbiest**) covered with scrub
scrubs *v* ▷ **scrub[1]** ▶ *n* ▷ **scrub[1, 2]**
scruff[1] *n* (*pl* **-s**) nape (of the neck)
scruff[2] *n* (*pl* **-s**) (*Informal*) untidy person
scruffier *adj* ▷ **scruffy**
scruffiest *adj* ▷ **scruffy**
scruffs *n* ▷ **scruff[1, 2]**
scruffy *adj* (**-ffier, -ffiest**) unkempt or shabby
scrum, scrummage *n* (*pl* **-s**) (RUGBY) restarting of play in which opposing packs of forwards push against each other to gain possession of the ball
scrummage *n* ▷ **scrum**
scrummages *n* ▷ **scrum**
scrumptious *adj* (*Informal*) delicious
scrums *n* ▷ **scrum**
scrunch *v* (**-es, -ing, -ed**) crumple or crunch or be crumpled or crunched ▶ *n* (*pl* **-es**) act or sound of scrunching
scrunched *v* ▷ **scrunch**
scrunches *v, n* ▷ **scrunch**
scrunching *v* ▷ **scrunch**
scruple *n* (*pl* **-s**) doubt produced by one's conscience or morals ▶ *v* (**-les, -ling, -led**) have doubts on moral grounds
scrupled *v* ▷ **scruple**
scruples *n, v* ▷ **scruple**
scrupling *v* ▷ **scruple**
scrupulous *adj* very conscientious > **scrupulously** *adv*
scrupulously *adv* ▷ **scrupulous**
scrutinies *n* ▷ **scrutiny**
scrutinize *v* (**-zes, -zing, -zed**) examine closely
scrutinized *v* ▷ **scrutinize**
scrutinizes *v* ▷ **scrutinize**
scrutinizing *v* ▷ **scrutinize**
scrutiny *n* (*pl* **-nies**) close examination
scud *v* (**-s, -dding, -dded**) move along swiftly
scudded *v* ▷ **scud**
scudding *v* ▷ **scud**
scuds *v* ▷ **scud**
scuff *v* (**-s, -ing, -ed**) drag (the feet) while walking ▶ *n* (*pl* **-s**) mark caused by scuffing
scuffed *v* ▷ **scuff**
scuffing *v* ▷ **scuff**
scuffle *v* (**-les, -ling, -led**) fight in a disorderly manner ▶ *n* (*pl* **-s**) disorderly struggle

scuffled *v* ▷ **scuffle**
scuffles *v, n* ▷ **scuffle**
scuffling *v* ▷ **scuffle**
scuffs *v, n* ▷ **scuff**
scull *n* (*pl* **-s**) small oar ▶ *v* (**-s, -ing, -ed**) row (a boat) using sculls
sculled *v* ▷ **scull**
sculleries *n* ▷ **scullery**
scullery *n* (*pl* **-ries**) small room where washing-up and other kitchen work is done
sculling *v* ▷ **scull**
sculls *n, v* ▷ **scull**
sculptor *n* ▷ **sculpture**
sculptors *n* ▷ **sculpture**
sculptress *n* ▷ **sculpture**
sculptresses *n* ▷ **sculpture**
sculptural *adj* ▷ **sculpture**
sculpture *n* (*pl* **-s**) art of making figures or designs in wood, stone, etc. ▶ *v* (**-res, -ring, -red**) (*also* **sculpt**) represent in sculpture > **sculptor, sculptress** *n* (*pl* **-s, -es**) > **sculptural** *adj*
sculptured *v* ▷ **sculpture**
sculptures *n, v* ▷ **sculpture**
sculpturing *v* ▷ **sculpture**
scum *n* (*pl* **-s**) impure or waste matter on the surface of a liquid > **scummy** *adj* (**-mmier, -mmiest**)
scummier *adj* ▷ **scum**
scummiest *adj* ▷ **scum**
scummy *adj* ▷ **scum**
scums *n* ▷ **scum**
scungier *adj* ▷ **scungy**
scungiest *adj* ▷ **scungy**
scungy *adj* (**-ier, -iest**) (AUST & NZ) (*Informal*) sordid or dirty
scupper *v* (**-s, -ing, -ed**) (*Informal*) defeat or ruin
scuppered *v* ▷ **scupper**
scuppering *v* ▷ **scupper**
scuppers *v* ▷ **scupper**
scurf *n* (*pl* **-s**) flaky skin on the scalp
scurfs *n* ▷ **scurf**
scurried *v* ▷ **scurry**
scurries *v, n* ▷ **scurry**
scurrilous *adj* untrue and defamatory
scurry *v* (**-ries, -rying, -ried**) move hastily ▶ *n* (*pl* **-ries**) act or sound of scurrying
scurrying *v* ▷ **scurry**
scurvies *n* ▷ **scurvy**
scurvy *n* (*pl* **-vies**) disease caused by lack of vitamin C
scut *n* (*pl* **-s**) short tail of the hare, rabbit, or deer
scuts *n* ▷ **scut**
scuttle¹ *n* (*pl* **-s**) fireside container for coal
scuttle² *v* (**-les, -ling, -led**) run with short quick steps ▶ *n* (*pl* **-s**) hurried run
scuttle³ *v* (**-les, -ling, -ed**) make a hole in (a ship) to sink it
scuttled *v* ▷ **scuttle²,³**
scuttles *n* ▷ **scuttle¹,²** ▶ *v* ▷ **scuttle²,³**
scuttling *v* ▷ **scuttle²,³**
scythe *n* (*pl* **-s**) long-handled tool with a curved blade for cutting grass ▶ *v* (**-thes, -thing, -thed**) cut with a scythe
scythed *v* ▷ **scythe**
scythes *n, v* ▷ **scythe**
scything *v* ▷ **scythe**
sea *n* (*pl* **-s**) mass of salt water covering three quarters of the earth's surface
seaboard *n* (*pl* **-s**) coast
seaboards *n* ▷ **seaboard**
seafaring *adj* working or travelling by sea
seafood *n* (*pl* **-s**) edible saltwater fish or shellfish
seafoods *n* ▷ **seafood**
seagull *n* (*pl* **-s**) gull
seagulls *n* ▷ **seagull**
seal¹ *n* (*pl* **-s**) piece of wax, lead, etc. with a special design impressed upon it, attached to a letter or document as a mark of authentication ▶ *v* (**-s, -ing, -ed**) close with or as if with a seal
seal² *n* (*pl* **-s**) amphibious mammal with flippers as limbs > **sealskin** *n* (*pl* **-s**)
sealant *n* (*pl* **-s**) any substance used for sealing
sealants *n* ▷ **sealant**
sealed *v* ▷ **seal¹**
sealing *v* ▷ **seal¹**
seals *n* ▷ **seal¹,²** ▶ *v* ▷ **seal¹**
sealskin *n* ▷ **seal²**
sealskins *n* ▷ **seal²**
seam *n* (*pl* **-s**) line where two edges are joined, as by stitching ▶ *v* (**-s, -ing, -ed**) mark with furrows or wrinkles > **seamless** *adj*
seaman *n* (*pl* **-men**) sailor
seamed *v* ▷ **seam**
seamen *n* ▷ **seaman**
seamier *adj* ▷ **seamy**
seamiest *adj* ▷ **seamy**
seaming *v* ▷ **seam**
seamless *adj* ▷ **seam**
seams *n, v* ▷ **seam**
seamstress *n* (*pl* **-es**) woman who sews, esp. professionally
seamstresses *n* ▷ **seamstress**
seamy *adj* (**-mier, -miest**) sordid
seance [say-anss] *n* (*pl* **-s**) meeting at which spiritualists attempt to communicate with the dead

seances *n* ▷ **seance**
seaplane *n* (*pl* **-s**) aircraft designed to take off from and land on water
seaplanes *n* ▷ **seaplane**
sear *v* (**-s, -ing, -ed**) scorch, burn the surface of
search *v* (**-es, -ing, -ed**) examine closely in order to find something ▶ *n* (*pl* **-es**) searching
searched *v* ▷ **search**
searches *v, n* ▷ **search**
searching *adj* keen or thorough ▶ *v* ▷ **search**
searchlight *n* (*pl* **-s**) powerful light with a beam that can be shone in any direction
searchlights *n* ▷ **searchlight**
seared *v* ▷ **sear**
searing *adj* (of pain) very sharp ▶ *v* ▷ **sear**
sears *v* ▷ **sear**
seas *n* ▷ **sea**
seasick *adj* suffering from nausea caused by the motion of a ship > **seasickness** *n* (*pl* **-es**)
seasickness *n* ▷ **seasick**
seasicknesses *n* ▷ **seasick**
seaside *n* (*pl* **-s**) area, esp. a holiday resort, on the coast
seasides *n* ▷ **seaside**
season *n* (*pl* **-s**) one of four divisions of the year, each of which has characteristic weather conditions ▶ *v* (**-s, -ing, -ed**) flavour with salt, herbs, etc.
seasonable *adj* appropriate for the season
seasonal *adj* depending on or varying with the seasons
seasoned *adj* experienced ▶ *v* ▷ **season**
seasoning *v* ▷ **season** ▶ *n* (*pl* **-s**) salt, herbs, etc. added to food to enhance flavour
seasonings *n* ▷ **seasoning**
seasons *n, v* ▷ **season**
seat *n* (*pl* **-s**) thing designed or used for sitting on ▶ *v* (**-s, -ing, -ed**) cause to sit
seated *v* ▷ **seat**
seating *v* ▷ **seat**
seats *n, v* ▷ **seat**
seaweed *n* (*pl* **-s**) plant growing in the sea
seaweeds *n* ▷ **seaweed**
seaworthy *adj* (of a ship) in fit condition for a sea voyage
sebaceous *adj* of, like, or secreting fat or oil
secateurs *pl n* small pruning shears
secede *v* (**-des, -ding, -ded**) withdraw formally from a political alliance or federation > **secession** *n* (*pl* **-s**)
seceded *v* ▷ **secede**
secedes *v* ▷ **secede**
seceding *v* ▷ **secede**
secession *n* ▷ **secede**
secessions *n* ▷ **secede**
seclude *v* (**-des, -ding, -ded**) keep (a person) from contact with others
secluded *adj* private, sheltered ▶ *v* ▷ **seclude** > **seclusion** *n* (*pl* **-s**)
secludes *v* ▷ **seclude**
secluding *v* ▷ **seclude**
seclusion *n* ▷ **secluded**
seclusions *n* ▷ **secluded**
second[1] *adj* coming directly after the first ▶ *n* (*pl* **-s**) person or thing coming second ▶ *v* (**-s, -ing, -ed**) express formal support for (a motion proposed in a meeting) > **secondly** *adv*
second[2] *n* (*pl* **-s**) sixtieth part of a minute of an angle or time
second[3] [si-**kond**] *v* (**-s, -ing, -ed**) transfer (a person) temporarily to another job > **secondment** *n* (*pl* **-s**)
secondary *adj* of less importance
seconded *v* ▷ **second**[1,3]
secondhand *adj* bought after use by another
seconding *v* ▷ **second**[1,3]
secondly *adv* ▷ **second**[1]
secondment *n* ▷ **second**[3]
secondments *n* ▷ **second**[3]
seconds *v* ▷ **second**[1,3] ▶ *n* ▷ **second**[1,2] ▶ *pl n* inferior goods
secrecies *n* ▷ **secret**
secrecy *n* ▷ **secret**
secret *adj* kept from the knowledge of others ▶ *n* (*pl* **-s**) something kept secret > **secretly** *adv* > **secrecy** *n* (*pl* **-cies**)
secretarial *adj* ▷ **secretary**
secretariat *n* (*pl* **-s**) administrative office or staff of a legislative body
secretariats *n* ▷ **secretariat**
secretaries *n* ▷ **secretary**
secretary *n* (*pl* **-ries**) person who deals with correspondence and general clerical work > **secretarial** *adj*
secrete[1] *v* (**-tes, -ting, -ted**) (of an organ, gland, etc.) produce and release (a substance) > **secretion** *n* (*pl* **-s**) > **secretory** [sek-**reet**-or-ee] *adj*
secrete[2] *v* (**-tes, -ting, -ted**) hide or conceal
secreted *v* ▷ **secrete**[1,2]
secretes *v* ▷ **secrete**[1,2]
secreting *v* ▷ **secrete**[1,2]
secretion *n* ▷ **secrete**[1]
secretions *n* ▷ **secrete**[1]
secretive *adj* inclined to keep things secret > **secretiveness** *n* (*pl* **-es**)
secretiveness *n* ▷ **secretive**
secretivenesses *n* ▷ **secretive**
secretly *adv* ▷ **secret**

secretory *adj* ▷ **secrete**[1]
secrets *n* ▷ **secret**
sect *n* (*pl* **-s**) subdivision of a religious or political group, esp. one with extreme beliefs
sectarian *adj* of a sect
section *n* (*pl* **-s**) part cut off ▶ *v* (**-s, -ing, -ed**) cut or divide into sections > **sectional** *adj*
sectional *adj* ▷ **section**
sectioned *v* ▷ **section**
sectioning *v* ▷ **section**
sections *n, v* ▷ **section**
sector *n* (*pl* **-s**) part or subdivision
sectors *n* ▷ **sector**
sects *n* ▷ **sect**
secular *adj* worldly, as opposed to sacred
secure *adj* (**-r, -st**) free from danger ▶ *v* (**-res, -ring, -red**) obtain > **securely** *adv*
secured *v* ▷ **secure**
securely *adv* ▷ **secure**
securer *adj* ▷ **secure**
secures *v* ▷ **secure**
securest *adj* ▷ **secure**
securing *v* ▷ **secure**
securities *n* ▷ **security**
security *n* (*pl* **-ties**) precautions against theft, espionage, or other danger
sedan *n* (*pl* **-s**) (US, AUST & NZ) two-door or four-door car with the body closed off from the rear luggage area
sedans *n* ▷ **sedan**
sedate[1] *adj* (**-r, -st**) calm and dignified > **sedately** *adv*
sedate[2] *v* (**-tes, -ting, -ted**) give a sedative drug to > **sedation** *n* (*pl* **-s**)
sedated *v* ▷ **sedate**[2]
sedately *adv* ▷ **sedate**[1]
sedater *adj* ▷ **sedate**[1]
sedates *v* ▷ **sedate**[2]
sedatest *adj* ▷ **sedate**[1]
sedating *v* ▷ **sedate**[2]
sedation *n* ▷ **sedate**[2]
sedations *n* ▷ **sedate**[2]
sedative *adj* having a soothing or calming effect ▶ *n* (*pl* **-s**) sedative drug
sedatives *n* ▷ **sedative**
sedentary *adj* done sitting down, involving little exercise
sedge *n* (*pl* **-s**) coarse grasslike plant growing on wet ground
sedges *n* ▷ **sedge**
sediment *n* (*pl* **-s**) matter which settles to the bottom of a liquid > **sedimentary** *adj*
sedimentary *adj* ▷ **sediment**
sediments *n* ▷ **sediment**
sedition *n* (*pl* **-s**) speech or action encouraging rebellion against the government > **seditious** *adj*
seditions *n* ▷ **sedition**
seditious *adj* ▷ **sedition**
seduce *v* (**-ces, -cing, -ced**) persuade into sexual intercourse > **seducer, seductress** *n* (*pl* **-s, -es**) > **seduction** *n* (*pl* **-s**) > **seductive** *adj*
seduced *v* ▷ **seduce**
seducer *n* ▷ **seduce**
seducers *n* ▷ **seduce**
seduces *v* ▷ **seduce**
seducing *v* ▷ **seduce**
seduction *n* ▷ **seduce**
seductions *n* ▷ **seduce**
seductive *adj* ▷ **seduce**
seductress *n* ▷ **seduce**
seductresses *n* ▷ **seduce**
sedulous *adj* diligent or persevering > **sedulously** *adv*
sedulously *adv* ▷ **sedulous**
see[1] *v* (**-s, -ing, saw, seen**) perceive with the eyes or mind
see[2] *n* (*pl* **-s**) diocese of a bishop
seed *n* (*pl* **-s**) mature fertilized grain of a plant ▶ *v* (**-s, -ing, -ed**) sow with seed
seeded *v* ▷ **seed**
seedier *adj* ▷ **seedy**
seediest *adj* ▷ **seedy**
seeding *v* ▷ **seed**
seedling *n* (*pl* **-s**) young plant raised from a seed
seedlings *n* ▷ **seedling**
seeds *n, v* ▷ **seed**
seedy *adj* (**-dier, -diest**) shabby
seeing *conj* in view of the fact that ▶ *v* ▷ **see**[1]
seek *v* (**-s, -ing, sought**) try to find or obtain
seeking *v* ▷ **seek**
seeks *v* ▷ **seek**
seem *v* (**-s, -ing, -ed**) appear to be
seemed *v* ▷ **seem**
seeming *adj* apparent but not real > **seemingly** *adv, v* ▷ **seem**
seemingly *adv* ▷ **seeming**
seemlier *adj* ▷ **seemly**
seemliest *adj* ▷ **seemly**
seemly *adj* (**-lier, -liest**) proper or fitting
seems *v* ▷ **seem**
seen *v* ▷ **see**[1]
seep *v* (**-s, -ing, -ed**) trickle through slowly, ooze > **seepage** *n* (*pl* **-s**)
seepage *n* ▷ **seep**
seepages *n* ▷ **seep**
seeped *v* ▷ **seep**
seeping *v* ▷ **seep**
seeps *v* ▷ **seep**

seer *n* (*pl* **-s**) prophet
seers *n* ▷ **seer**
seersucker *n* (*pl* **-s**) light cotton fabric with a slightly crinkled surface
seersuckers *n* ▷ **seersucker**
sees *n* ▷ **see²** ▶ *v* ▷ **see¹**
seesaw *n* (*pl* **-s**) plank balanced in the middle so that two people seated on either end ride up and down alternately ▶ *v* (**-s, -ing, -ed**) move up and down
seesawed *v* ▷ **seesaw**
seesawing *v* ▷ **seesaw**
seesaws *n, v* ▷ **seesaw**
seethe *v* (**-thes, -thing, -thed**) be very agitated
seethed *v* ▷ **seethe**
seethes *v* ▷ **seethe**
seething *v* ▷ **seethe**
segment *n* (*pl* **-s**) one of several sections into which something may be divided ▶ *v* (**-s, -ing, -ed**) divide into segments > **segmentation** *n* (*pl* **-s**)
segmentation *n* ▷ **segment**
segmentations *n* ▷ **segment**
segmented *v* ▷ **segment**
segmenting *v* ▷ **segment**
segments *n, v* ▷ **segment**
segregate *v* (**-tes, -ting, -ted**) set apart > **segregation** *n* (*pl* **-s**)
segregated *v* ▷ **segregate**
segregates *v* ▷ **segregate**
segregating *v* ▷ **segregate**
segregation *n* ▷ **segregate**
segregations *n* ▷ **segregate**
seine [**sane**] *n* (*pl* **-s**) large fishing net that hangs vertically from floats
seines *n* ▷ **seine**
seismic *adj* relating to earthquakes
seismograph, seismometer *n* (*pl* **-s**) instrument that records the strength of earthquakes
seismographs *n* ▷ **seismograph**
seismological *adj* ▷ **seismology**
seismologies *n* ▷ **seismology**
seismologist *n* ▷ **seismology**
seismologists *n* ▷ **seismology**
seismology *n* (*pl* **-gies**) study of earthquakes > **seismological** *adj* > **seismologist** *n* (*pl* **-s**)
seismometer *n* ▷ **seismograph**
seismometers *n* ▷ **seismograph**
seize *v* (**-zes, -zing, -zed**) take hold of forcibly or quickly (*usu. foll. by* **up**)
seized *v* ▷ **seize**
seizes *v* ▷ **seize**
seizing *v* ▷ **seize**
seizure *n* (*pl* **-s**) sudden violent attack of an illness
seizures *n* ▷ **seizure**
seldom *adv* not often, rarely
select *v* (**-s, -ing, -ed**) pick out or choose ▶ *adj* chosen in preference to others > **selector** *n* (*pl* **-s**)
selected *v* ▷ **select**
selecting *v* ▷ **select**
selection *n* (*pl* **-s**) selecting
selections *n* ▷ **selection**
selective *adj* chosen or choosing carefully > **selectively** *adv* > **selectivity** *n* (*pl* **-ties**)
selectively *adv* ▷ **selective**
selectivities *n* ▷ **selective**
selectivity *n* ▷ **selective**
selector *n* ▷ **select**
selectors *n* ▷ **select**
selects *v* ▷ **select**
selenium *n* (*pl* **-s**) (CHEM) nonmetallic element with photoelectric properties
seleniums *n* ▷ **selenium**
self *n* (*pl* **selves**) distinct individuality or identity of a person or thing
selfish *adj* caring too much about oneself and not enough about others > **selfishly** *adv* > **selfishness** *n* (*pl* **-es**)
selfishly *adv* ▷ **selfish**
selfishness *n* ▷ **selfish**
selfishnesses *n* ▷ **selfish**
selfless *adj* unselfish
selfsame *adj* the very same
sell *v* (**-s, -ing, sold**) exchange (something) for money (*foll. by* **for**) ▶ *n* (*pl* **-s**) manner of selling > **seller** *n* (*pl* **-s**)
seller *n* ▷ **sell**
sellers *n* ▷ **sell**
selling *v* ▷ **sell**
sellotape *n* (*pl* **-s**)® type of adhesive tape ▶ *v* (**-pes, -ping, -ped**) stick with sellotape
sellotaped *v* ▷ **sellotape**
sellotapes *n, v* ▷ **sellotape**
sellotaping *v* ▷ **sellotape**
sellout *n* (*pl* **-s**) performance of a show etc. for which all the tickets are sold
sellouts *n* ▷ **sellout**
sells *v, n* ▷ **sell**
selvage, selvedge *n* (*pl* **-s**) edge of cloth, woven so as to prevent unravelling
selvages *n* ▷ **selvage**
selvedge *n* ▷ **selvage**
selvedges *n* ▷ **selvage**
selves *n* ▷ **self**
semantic *adj* relating to the meaning of words
semantics *n* study of linguistic meaning
semaphore *n* (*pl* **-s**) system of signalling by

holding two flags in different positions to represent letters of the alphabet
semaphores *n* ▷ **semaphore**
semblance *n* (*pl* **-s**) outward or superficial appearance
semblances *n* ▷ **semblance**
semen *n* (*pl* **-s**) sperm-carrying fluid produced by male animals
semens *n* ▷ **semen**
semester *n* (*pl* **-s**) either of two divisions of the academic year
semesters *n* ▷ **semester**
semi *n* (*pl* **-s**) (BRIT & S AFR) (*Informal*) semidetached house
semibreve *n* (*pl* **-s**) musical note four beats long
semibreves *n* ▷ **semibreve**
semicolon *n* (*pl* **-s**) the punctuation mark (;)
semicolons *n* ▷ **semicolon**
semiconductor *n* (*pl* **-s**) substance with an electrical conductivity that increases with temperature
semiconductors *n* ▷ **semiconductor**
semidetached *adj* (of a house) joined to another on one side
semifinal *n* (*pl* **-s**) match or round before the final > **semifinalist** *n* (*pl* **-s**)
semifinalist *n* ▷ **semifinal**
semifinalists *n* ▷ **semifinal**
semifinals *n* ▷ **semifinal**
seminal *adj* original and influential
seminar *n* (*pl* **-s**) meeting of a group of students for discussion
seminaries *n* ▷ **seminary**
seminars *n* ▷ **seminar**
seminary *n* (*pl* **-ries**) college for priests
semiprecious *adj* (of gemstones) having less value than precious stones
semiquaver *n* (*pl* **-s**) musical note half the length of a quaver
semiquavers *n* ▷ **semiquaver**
semis *n* ▷ **semi**
semitone *n* (*pl* **-s**) smallest interval between two notes in Western music
semitones *n* ▷ **semitone**
semitrailer *n* (*pl* **-s**) (AUST) large truck in two separate sections joined by a pivoted bar
semitrailers *n* ▷ **semitrailer**
semolina *n* (*pl* **-s**) hard grains of wheat left after the milling of flour, used to make puddings and pasta
semolinas *n* ▷ **semolina**
senate *n* (*pl* **-s**) upper house of some parliaments; governing body of some universities
senates *n* ▷ **senate**
senator *n* (*pl* **-s**) member of a senate > **senatorial** *adj*
senatorial *adj* ▷ **senator**
senators *n* ▷ **senator**
send *v* (**-s, -ing, sent**) cause (a person or thing) to go to or be taken or transmitted to a place
sending *v* ▷ **send**
sendoff *n* (*pl* **-s**) demonstration of good wishes at a person's departure
sendoffs *n* ▷ **sendoff**
sends *v* ▷ **send**
sendup *n* (*pl* **-s**) (*Informal*) imitation
sendups *n* ▷ **sendup**
senile *adj* mentally or physically weak because of old age > **senility** *n* (*pl* **-ties**)
senilities *n* ▷ **senile**
senility *n* ▷ **senile**
senior *adj* superior in rank or standing ▶ *n* (*pl* **-s**) senior person > **seniority** *n* (*pl* **-ties**)
seniorities *n* ▷ **senior**
seniority *n* ▷ **senior**
seniors *n* ▷ **senior**
senna *n* (*pl* **-s**) tropical plant
sennas *n* ▷ **senna**
señor [sen-**nyor**] *n* (*pl* **-ores**) Spanish term of address equivalent to *sir* or *Mr*
señora [sen-**nyor**-a] *n* (*pl* **-s**) Spanish term of address equivalent to *madam* or *Mrs*
señoras *n* ▷ **señora**
señorita [sen-nyor-**ee**-ta] *n* (*pl* **-s**) Spanish term of address equivalent to *madam* or *Miss*
señoritas *n* ▷ **señorita**
señors *n* ▷ **señor**
sensation *n* (*pl* **-s**) ability to feel things physically
sensational *adj* causing intense shock, anger, or excitement
sensationalism *n* (*pl* **-s**) deliberate use of sensational language or subject matter > **sensationalist** *adj*, *n* (*pl* **-s**)
sensationalisms *n* ▷ **sensationalism**
sensationalist *adj*, *n* ▷ **sensationalism**
sensationalists *n* ▷ **sensationalism**
sensations *n* ▷ **sensation**
sense *n* (*pl* **-s**) any of the faculties of perception or feeling (sight, hearing, touch, taste, or smell ▶ *v* (**-ses, -sing, -sed**) perceive > **senseless** *adj*
sensed *v* ▷ **sense**
senseless *adj* ▷ **sense**
senses *n*, *v* ▷ **sense**
sensibilities *n* ▷ **sensibility**
sensibility *n* (*pl* **-ties**) ability to experience deep feelings

sensible *adj* (**-r, -st**) having or showing good sense > **sensibly** *adv*
sensibler *adj* ▷ **sensible**
sensiblest *adj* ▷ **sensible**
sensibly *adv* ▷ **sensible**
sensing *v* ▷ **sense**
sensitive *adj* easily hurt or offended > **sensitively** *adv* > **sensitivity** *n* (*pl* **-s**)
sensitively *adv* ▷ **sensitive**
sensitivities *n* ▷ **sensitive**
sensitivity *n* ▷ **sensitive**
sensitize *v* (**-zes, -zing, -zed**) make sensitive
sensitized *v* ▷ **sensitize**
sensitizes *v* ▷ **sensitize**
sensitizing *v* ▷ **sensitize**
sensor *n* (*pl* **-s**) device that detects or measures the presence of something, such as radiation
sensors *n* ▷ **sensor**
sensory *adj* of the senses or sensation
sensual *adj* giving pleasure to the body and senses rather than the mind > **sensually** *adv* > **sensuality** *n* (*pl* **-ties**) > **sensualist** *n* (*pl* **-s**)
sensualist *n* ▷ **sensual**
sensualists *n* ▷ **sensual**
sensualities *n* ▷ **sensual**
sensuality *n* ▷ **sensual**
sensually *adj* ▷ **sensual**
sensuous *adj* pleasing to the senses > **sensuously** *adv*
sensuously *adv* ▷ **sensuous**
sent *v* ▷ **send**
sentence *n* (*pl* **-s**) sequence of words capable of standing alone as a statement, question, or command ▶ *v* (**-ces, -cing, -ced**) pass sentence on (a convicted person)
sentenced *v* ▷ **sentence**
sentences *n, v* ▷ **sentence**
sentencing *n, v* ▷ **sentence**
sententious *adj* trying to sound wise
sentience *n* ▷ **sentient**
sentiences *n* ▷ **sentient**
sentient [**sen**-tee-ent] *adj* capable of feeling > **sentience** *n* (*pl* **-s**)
sentiment *n* (*pl* **-s**) thought, opinion, or attitude
sentimental *adj* excessively romantic or nostalgic > **sentimentalism** *n* (*pl* **-s**) > **sentimentality** *n* (*pl* **-ties**)
sentimentalism *n* ▷ **sentimental**
sentimentalisms *n* ▷ **sentimental**
sentimentalities *n* ▷ **sentimentality**
sentimentality *n* ▷ **sentimental**
sentimentalize *v* (**-zes, -zing, -zed**) make sentimental
sentimentalized *v* ▷ **sentimentalize**
sentimentalizes *v* ▷ **sentimentalize**
sentiments *n* ▷ **sentiment**
sentinel *n* (*pl* **-s**) sentry
sentinels *n* ▷ **sentinel**
sentries *n* ▷ **sentry**
sentry *n* (*pl* **-tries**) soldier on watch
sepal *n* (*pl* **-s**) leaflike division of the calyx of a flower
sepals *n* ▷ **sepal**
separable *adj* ▷ **separate**
separate *v* (**-tes, -ting, -ted**) act as a barrier between ▶ *adj* not the same, different > **separable** *adj* > **separately** *adv*
separated *v* ▷ **separate**
separately *adv* ▷ **separate**
separates *v* ▷ **separate**
separating *v* ▷ **separate**
separation *n* (*pl* **-s**) separating or being separated
separations *n* ▷ **separation**
separatism *n* ▷ **separatist**
separatisms *n* ▷ **separatist**
separatist *n* (*pl* **-s**) person who advocates the separation of a group from an organization or country > **separatism** *n* (*pl* **-s**)
separatists *n* ▷ **separatist**
sepia *adj, n* (*pl* **-s**) reddish-brown (pigment)
sepias *n* ▷ **sepia**
sepses *n* ▷ **sepsis**
sepsis *n* (*pl* **-ses**) poisoning caused by pus-forming bacteria
septet *n* (*pl* **-s**) group of seven performers
septets *n* ▷ **septet**
septic *adj* (of a wound) infected
septicaemia [sep-tis-**see**-mee-a] *n* (*pl* **-s**) infection of the blood
septicaemias *n* ▷ **septicaemia**
septuagenarian *n* (*pl* **-s**) person aged between seventy and seventy-nine
septuagenarians *n* ▷ **septuagenarian**
sepulchral [sip-**pulk**-ral] *adj* gloomy
sepulchre [**sep**-pull-ker] *n* (*pl* **-s**) tomb or burial vault
sepulchres *n* ▷ **sepulchre**
sequel *n* (*pl* **-s**) novel, play, or film that continues the story of an earlier one
sequels *n* ▷ **sequel**
sequence *n* (*pl* **-s**) arrangement of two or more things in successive order > **sequential** *adj*
sequences *n* ▷ **sequence**
sequential *adj* ▷ **sequence**
sequester *v* (**-s, -ing, -ed**) seclude
sequestered *v* ▷ **sequester**
sequestering *v* ▷ **sequester**
sequesters *v* ▷ **sequester**

sequestrate *v* (**-tes, -ting, -ted**) confiscate (property) until its owner's debts are paid or a court order is complied with > **sequestration** *n* (*pl* **-s**)
sequestrated *v* ▷ **sequestrate**
sequestrates *v* ▷ **sequestrate**
sequestrating *v* ▷ **sequestrate**
sequestration *n* ▷ **sequestrate**
sequestrations *n* ▷ **sequestrate**
sequin *n* (*pl* **-s**) small ornamental metal disc on a garment > **sequined** *adj*
sequined *adj* ▷ **sequin**
sequins *n* ▷ **sequin**
sequoia *n* (*pl* **-s**) giant Californian coniferous tree
sequoias *n* ▷ **sequoia**
seraglio [sir-**ah**-lee-oh] *n* (*pl* **-s**) harem of a Muslim palace
seraglios *n* ▷ **seraglio**
seraph *n* (*pl* **-s, -aphim**) member of the highest order of angels > **seraphic** *adj*
seraphic *adj* ▷ **seraph**
seraphim *n* ▷ **seraph**
seraphs *n* ▷ **seraph**
serenade *n* (*pl* **-s**) music played or sung to a woman by a lover ▶ *v* (**-des, -ding, -ded**) sing or play a serenade to (someone)
serenaded *v* ▷ **serenade**
serenades *n, v* ▷ **serenade**
serenading *v* ▷ **serenade**
serendipities *n* ▷ **serendipity**
serendipity *n* (*pl* **-ties**) gift of making fortunate discoveries by accident
serene *adj* (**-r, -st**) calm, peaceful > **serenely** *adv* > **serenity** *n* (*pl* **-ties**)
serenely *adv* ▷ **serene**
serener *adj* ▷ **serene**
serenest *adj* ▷ **serene**
serenities *n* ▷ **serene**
serenity *n* ▷ **serene**
serf *n* (*pl* **-s**) medieval farm labourer who could not leave the land he worked on > **serfdom** *n* (*pl* **-s**)
serfdom *n* ▷ **serf**
serfdoms *n* ▷ **serf**
serfs *n* ▷ **serf**
serge *n* (*pl* **-s**) strong woollen fabric
sergeant *n* (*pl* **-s**) noncommissioned officer in the army
sergeants *n* ▷ **sergeant**
serges *n* ▷ **serge**
serial *n* (*pl* **-s**) story or play produced in successive instalments ▶ *adj* of or forming a series
serialize *v* (**-zes, -zing, -zed**) publish or present as a serial
serialized *v* ▷ **serialize**
serializes *v* ▷ **serialize**
serializing *v* ▷ **serialize**
serials *n* ▷ **serial**
series *n* (*pl* **series**) group or succession of related things, usu. arranged in order
serious *adj* giving cause for concern > **seriously** *adv* > **seriousness** *n* (*pl* **-es**)
seriously *adv* ▷ **serious**
seriousness *n* ▷ **serious**
seriousnesses *n* ▷ **serious**
sermon *n* (*pl* **-s**) speech on a religious or moral subject by a clergyman in a church service
sermonize *v* (**-zes, -zing, -zed**) make a long moralizing speech
sermonized *v* ▷ **sermonize**
sermonizes *v* ▷ **sermonize**
sermonizing *v* ▷ **sermonize**
sermons *n* ▷ **sermon**
serpent *n* (*pl* **-s**) (*Lit*) snake
serpentine *adj* twisting like a snake
serpents *n* ▷ **serpent**
serrated *adj* having a notched or sawlike edge
serried *adj* in close formation
serum [**seer**-um] *n* (*pl* **-s**) watery fluid left after blood has clotted
serums *n* ▷ **serum**
servant *n* (*pl* **-s**) person employed to do household work for another
servants *n* ▷ **servant**
serve *v* (**-s, -ing, -ed**) work for (a person, community, or cause) ▶ *n* (*pl* **-s**) (TENNIS ETC.) act of serving the ball
served *v* ▷ **serve**
server *n* (*pl* **-s**) player who serves in racket games
servers *n* ▷ **server**
serves *n, v* ▷ **serve**
service *n* (*pl* **-s**) system that provides something needed by the public ▶ *v* (**-ces, -cing, -ced**) overhaul (a machine or vehicle)
serviceable *adj* useful or helpful
serviced *v* ▷ **service**
serviceman, servicewoman *n* (*pl* **-men, -women**) member of the armed forces
servicemen *n* ▷ **serviceman**
services *n, v* ▷ **service** ▶ *pl n* armed forces
servicewoman *n* ▷ **serviceman**
servicewomen *n* ▷ **serviceman**
servicing *v* ▷ **service**
serviette *n* (*pl* **-s**) table napkin
serviettes *n* ▷ **serviette**
servile *adj* too eager to obey people, fawning > **servility** *n* (*pl* **-s**)

servilities *n* ▷ **servile**
servility *n* ▷ **servile**
serving *v* ▷ **serve**
servitude *n* (*pl* **-s**) bondage or slavery
servitudes *n* ▷ **servitude**
sesame [**sess**-am-ee] *n* (*pl* **-s**) plant cultivated for its seeds and oil, which are used in cooking
sesames *n* ▷ **sesame**
session *n* (*pl* **-s**) period spent in an activity
sessions *n* ▷ **session**
set[1] *v* (**-s, -tting, set**) put in a specified position or state ▶ *n* (*pl* **-s**) scenery used in a play or film ▶ *adj* fixed or established beforehand
set[2] *n* (*pl* **-s**) number of things or people grouped or belonging together
setback *n* (*pl* **-s**) anything that delays progress
setbacks *n* ▷ **setback**
sets *v* ▷ **set**[1] ▶ *n* ▷ **set**[2]
sett, set *n* (*p* **-s**) badger's burrow
settee *n* (*pl* **-s**) couch
settees *n* ▷ **settee**
setter *n* (*pl* **-s**) long-haired gun dog
setters *n* ▷ **setter**
setting *n* (*pl* **-s**) background or surroundings ▶ *v* ▷ **set**
settings *n* ▷ **setting**
settle[1] *v* (**-les, -ling, -led**) arrange or put in order
settle[2] *n* (*pl* **-s**) long wooden bench with high back and arms
settled *v* ▷ **settle**[1]
settlement *n* (*pl* **-s**) act of settling
settlements *n* ▷ **settlement**
settler *n* (*pl* **-s**) colonist
settlers *n* ▷ **settler**
settles *v* ▷ **settle**[1] ▶ *n* ▷ **settle**[2]
settling *v* ▷ **settle**[1]
setts *n* ▷ **sett**
setup *n* (*pl* **-s**) way in which anything is organized or arranged
setups *n* ▷ **setup**
seven *adj, n* (*pl* **-s**) one more than six
sevens *n* ▷ **seven**
seventeen *adj, n* (*pl* **-s**) ten and seven > **seventeenth** *adj, n* (*pl* **-s**)
seventeens *n* ▷ **seventeen**
seventeenth *n* ▷ **seventeen**
seventeenths *n* ▷ **seventeen**
seventh *adj, n* (*pl* **-s**) (of) number seven in a series
sevenths *n* ▷ **seventh**
seventies *n* ▷ **seventy**
seventieth *n* ▷ **seventy**
seventieths *n* ▷ **seventy**
seventy *adj, n* (*pl* **-ties**) ten times seven > **seventieth** *adj, n* (*pl* **-s**)
sever *v* (**-s, -ing, -ed**) cut through or off > **severance** *n* (*pl* **-s**)
several *adj* some, a few
severally *adv* separately
severance *n* ▷ **sever**
severances *n* ▷ **sever**
severe *adj* (**-r, -st**) strict or harsh > **severely** *adv* > **severity** *n* (*pl* **-ties**)
severed *v* ▷ **sever**
severely *adv* ▷ **severe**
severer *adj* ▷ **severe**
severest *adj* ▷ **severe**
severing *v* ▷ **sever**
severities *n* ▷ **severe**
severity *n* ▷ **severe**
severs *v* ▷ **sever**
sew *v* (**-s, -ing, -ed, sewn** *or* **-ed**) join with thread repeatedly passed through with a needle
sewage *n* (*pl* **-s**) waste matter or excrement carried away in sewers
sewages *n* ▷ **sewage**
sewed *v* ▷ **sew**
sewer *n* (*pl* **-s**) drain to remove waste water and sewage > **sewerage** *n* (*pl* **-s**) system of sewers
sewerage *n* ▷ **sewer**
sewerages *n* ▷ **sewer**
sewers *n* ▷ **sewer**
sewing *v* ▷ **sew**
sewn *v* ▷ **sew**
sews *v* ▷ **sew**
sex *n* (*pl* **-es**) state of being male or female ▶ *v* (**-es, -ing, -ed**) find out the sex of > **sexual** *adj* > **sexually** *adv* > **sexuality** *n* (*pl* **-ties**)
sexagenarian *n* (*pl* **-s**) person aged between sixty and sixty-nine
sexagenarians *n* ▷ **sexagenarian**
sexed *v* ▷ **sex**
sexes *n, v* ▷ **sex**
sexier *adj* ▷ **sexy**
sexiest *adj* ▷ **sexy**
sexing *v* ▷ **sex**
sexism *n* (*pl* **-s**) discrimination on the basis of a person's sex > **sexist** *adj, n* (*pl* **-s**)
sexisms *n* ▷ **sexism**
sexist *n* ▷ **sexism**
sexists *n* ▷ **sexism**
sextant *n* (*pl* **-s**) navigator's instrument for measuring angles, as between the sun and horizon, to calculate one's position
sextants *n* ▷ **sextant**
sextet *n* (*pl* **-s**) group of six performers

sextets *n* ▷ **sextet**
sexton *n* (*pl* **-s**) official in charge of a church and churchyard
sextons *n* ▷ **sexton**
sexual *adj* ▷ **sex**
sexualities *n* ▷ **sex**
sexuality *n* ▷ **sex**
sexually *adv* ▷ **sex**
sexy *adj* (**-xier, -xiest**) sexually exciting or attractive

> **sez** *v*. Sez is an short informal form of **says.** This word can be very useful when there isn't much space on the board, as it gives a good score. Sez scores 12 points.
> **sh** *interj*. Sh is a sound people make to request silence or quiet. This is one of two two-letter words beginning with S that do not contain a vowel. It's useful when you want to connect a word beginning with H to one ending in S or vice versa. Sh scores 5 points.

shabbier *adj* ▷ **shabby**
shabbiest *adj* ▷ **shabby**
shabbily *adv* ▷ **shabby**
shabbiness *n* ▷ **shabby**
shabbinesses *n* ▷ **shabby**
shabby *adj* (**-bier, -biest**) worn or dilapidated in appearance > **shabbily** *adv* > **shabbiness** *n* (*pl* **-es**)
shack *n* (*pl* **-s**) rough hut
shackle *n* (*pl* **-s**) one of a pair of metal rings joined by a chain, for securing a person's wrists or ankles ▶ *v* (**-les, -ling, -led**) fasten with shackles
shackled *v* ▷ **shackle**
shackles *n, v* ▷ **shackle**
shackling *v* ▷ **shackle**
shacks *n* ▷ **shack**
shad *n* (*pl* **-s**) herring-like fish
shade *n* (*pl* **-s**) relative darkness ▶ *v* (**-des, -ding, -ded**) screen from light > **shady** *adj* (**-dier, -diest**) situated in or giving shade
shaded *v* ▷ **shade**
shades *n, v* ▷ **shade** ▶ *pl n* (*Slang*) sunglasses
shadier *adj* ▷ **shade**
shadiest *adj* ▷ **shade**
shading *v* ▷ **shade**
shadow *n* (*pl* **-s**) dark shape cast on a surface when something stands between a light and the surface ▶ *v* (**-s, -ing, -ed**) cast a shadow over > **shadowy** *adj* (**-wier, -wiest**)
shadowboxing *n* (*pl* **-s**) boxing against an imaginary opponent for practice
shadowboxings *n* ▷ **shadowboxing**
shadowed *v* ▷ **shadow**
shadowier *adj* ▷ **shadow**
shadowiest *adj* ▷ **shadow**
shadowing *v* ▷ **shadow**
shadows *n, v* ▷ **shadow**
shadowy *adj* ▷ **shadow**
shads *n* ▷ **shad**
shady *adj* ▷ **shade**
shaft *n* (*pl* **-s**) long narrow straight handle of a tool or weapon
shafts *n* ▷ **shaft**
shag[1] *n* (*pl* **-s**) coarse shredded tobacco ▶ *adj* (of a carpet) having a long pile
shag[2] *n* (*pl* **-s**) kind of cormorant
shaggier *adj* ▷ **shaggy**
shaggiest *adj* ▷ **shaggy**
shaggy *adj* (**-ggier, -ggiest**) covered with rough hair or wool
shagreen *n* (*pl* **-s**) sharkskin
shagreens *n* ▷ **shagreen**
shags *n* ▷ **shag**[1, 2]
shah *n* (*pl* **-s**) formerly, ruler of Iran
shahs *n* ▷ **shah**
shake *v* (**-kes, -king, shook,-en**) move quickly up and down or back and forth ▶ *n* (*pl* **-s**) shaking (*Informal*)
shaken *v* ▷ **shake**
shakes *v, n* ▷ **shake**
shakier *adj* ▷ **shaky**
shakiest *adj* ▷ **shaky**
shakily *adv* ▷ **shaky**
shaking *v* ▷ **shake**
shaky *adj* (**-kier, -kiest**) unsteady > **shakily** *adv*
shale *n* (*pl* **-s**) flaky sedimentary rock
shales *n* ▷ **shale**
shall *v* (*past tense* **should**) used as an auxiliary to make the future tense or to indicate intention, obligation, or inevitability
shallot *n* (*pl* **-s**) kind of small onion
shallots *n* ▷ **shallot**
shallow *adj* (**-er, -est**) not deep > **shallowness** *n* (*pl* **-es**)
shallower *adj* ▷ **shallow**
shallowest *adj* ▷ **shallow**
shallowness *n* ▷ **shallow**
shallownesses *n* ▷ **shallow**
shallows *pl n* area of shallow water
sham *n* (*pl* **-s**) thing or person that is not genuine ▶ *adj* not genuine ▶ *v* (**-s, -mming, -mmed**) fake, feign
shamble *v* (**-les, -ling, -led**) walk in a shuffling awkward way
shambled *v* ▷ **shamble**
shambles *n* (*pl* disorderly event or place ▶ *v* ▷ **shamble**

shambling *v* ▷ **shamble**
shame *n* (*pl* **-s**) painful emotion caused by awareness of having done something dishonourable or foolish ▶ *v* (**-mes, -ming, -med**) cause to feel shame ▶ *interj* (S AFR) (*Informal*) exclamation of sympathy or endearment
shamed *v* ▷ **shame**
shamefaced *adj* looking ashamed
shameful *adj* causing or deserving shame > **shamefully** *adv*
shamefully *adv* ▷ **shameful**
shameless *adj* with no sense of shame
shames *n, v* ▷ **shame**
shaming *v* ▷ **shame**
shammed *v* ▷ **sham**
shammies *n* ▷ **shammy**
shamming *v* ▷ **sham**
shammy *n* (*pl* **-mies**) (*Informal*) piece of chamois leather
shampoo *n* (*pl* **-s**) liquid soap for washing hair, carpets, or upholstery ▶ *v* (**-s, -ing, -ed**) wash with shampoo
shampooed *v* ▷ **shampoo**
shampooing *v* ▷ **shampoo**
shampoos *n, v* ▷ **shampoo**
shamrock *n* (*pl* **-s**) clover leaf, esp. as the Irish emblem
shamrocks *n* ▷ **shamrock**
shams *n, v* ▷ **sham**
shandies *n* ▷ **shandy**
shandy *n* (*pl* **-dies**) drink made of beer and lemonade
shanghai *v* (**-hais, -haiing, -haied**) force or trick (someone) into doing something ▶ *n* (*pl* **-s**) (AUST & NZ) catapult
shanghaied *v* ▷ **shanghai**
shanghaiing *v* ▷ **shanghai**
shanghais *v, n* ▷ **shanghai**
shank *n* (*pl* **-s**) lower leg
shanks *n* ▷ **shank**
shanties *n* ▷ **shanty**[1, 2]
shantung *n* (*pl* **-s**) soft Chinese silk with a knobbly surface
shantungs *n* ▷ **shantung**
shanty[1] *n* (*pl* **-ties**) shack or crude dwelling
shanty[2] *n* (*pl* **-ties**) sailor's traditional song
shantytown *n* (*pl* **-s**) slum consisting of shanties
shantytowns *n* ▷ **shantytown**
shape *n* (*pl* **-s**) outward form of an object ▶ *v* (**-pes, -ping, -ped**) form or mould > **shapeless** *adj*
shaped *v* ▷ **shape**
shapeless *adj* ▷ **shape**
shapelier *adj* ▷ **shapely**
shapeliest *adj* ▷ **shapely**
shapely *adj* (**-lier, -liest**) having an attractive shape
shapes *n, v* ▷ **shape**
shaping *v* ▷ **shape**
shard *n* (*pl* **-s**) broken piece of pottery or glass
shards *n* ▷ **shard**
share[1] *n* (*pl* **-s**) part of something that belongs to or is contributed by a person ▶ *v* (**-res, -ring, -red**) give or take a share of (something) > **shareholder** *n* (*pl* **-s**)
share[2] *n* (*pl* **-s**) blade of a plough
shared *v* ▷ **share**[1]
shareholder *n* ▷ **share**[1]
shareholders *n* ▷ **share**[1]
sharemilker *n* (*pl* **-s**) (NZ) person who works on a dairy farm belonging to someone else
sharemilkers *n* ▷ **sharemilker**
shares *v* ▷ **share**[1] ▶ *n* ▷ **share**[1, 2]
sharing *v* ▷ **share**[1]
shark *n* (*pl* **-s**) large usu. predatory sea fish
sharks *n* ▷ **shark**
sharkskin *n* (*pl* **-s**) stiff glossy fabric
sharkskins *n* ▷ **sharkskin**
sharp *adj* having a keen cutting edge or fine point ▶ *adv* promptly ▶ *n* (*pl* **-s**) (MUSIC) symbol raising a note one semitone above natural pitch > **sharply** *adv* > **sharpness** *n* (*pl* **-es**)
sharpen *v* (**-s, -ing, -ed**) make or become sharp or sharper > **sharpener** *n* (*pl* **-s**)
sharpened *v* ▷ **sharpen**
sharpener *n* ▷ **sharpen**
sharpeners *n* ▷ **sharpen**
sharpening *v* ▷ **sharpen**
sharpens *v* ▷ **sharpen**
sharply *adv* ▷ **sharp**
sharpness *n* ▷ **sharp**
sharpnesses *n* ▷ **sharp**
sharps *n* ▷ **sharp**
sharpshooter *n* (*pl* **-s**) marksman
sharpshooters *n* ▷ **sharpshooter**
shatter *v* (**-s, -ing, -ed**) break into pieces
shattered *adj* (*Informal*) completely exhausted ▶ *v* ▷ **shatter**
shattering *v* ▷ **shatter**
shatters *v* ▷ **shatter**
shave *v* (**-ves, -ving, -ved, -ved** *or* **shaven**) remove (hair) from (the face, head, or body) with a razor or shaver ▶ *n* (*pl* **-s**) shaving
shaved *v* ▷ **shave**
shaven *v* ▷ **shave**
shaver *n* (*pl* **-s**) electric razor
shavers *n* ▷ **shaver**
shaves *v, n* ▷ **shave**

shaving *v* ▷ **shave**
shavings *pl n* parings
shawl *n* (*pl* **-s**) piece of cloth worn over a woman's head or shoulders or wrapped around a baby
shawls *n* ▷ **shawl**
she *pron* refers to: female person or animal previously mentioned
sheaf *n* (*pl* **sheaves**) bundle of papers
shear *v* (**-s, -ing, -ed, -ed** *or* **shorn**) clip hair or wool from > **shearer** *n* (*pl* **-s**)
sheared *v* ▷ **shear**
shearer *n* ▷ **shear**
shearers *n* ▷ **shear**
shearing *v* ▷ **shear**
shears *pl n* large scissors or a cutting tool shaped like these ▶ *v* ▷ **shear**
shearwater *n* (*pl* **-s**) medium-sized sea bird
shearwaters *n* ▷ **shearwater**
sheath *n* (*pl* **-s**) close-fitting cover, esp. for a knife or sword
sheathe *v* (**-thes, -thing, -thed**) put into a sheath
sheathed *v* ▷ **sheathe**
sheathes *v* ▷ **sheathe**
sheathing *v* ▷ **sheathe**
sheaths *n* ▷ **sheath**
sheaves *n* ▷ **sheaf**
shebeen *n* (*pl* **-s**) (SCOT, IRISH & S AFR) place where alcohol is sold illegally
shebeens *n* ▷ **shebeen**
shed[1] *n* (*pl* **-s**) building used for storage or shelter or as a workshop
shed[2] *v* (**-s, -dding, shed**) pour forth (tears)
shedding *v* ▷ **shed**[2]
sheds *n* ▷ **shed**[1] ▶ *v* ▷ **shed**[2]
sheen *n* (*pl* **-s**) glistening brightness on the surface of something
sheens *n* ▷ **sheen**
sheep *n* (*pl* **sheep**) ruminant animal bred for wool and meat
sheepdog *n* (*pl* **-s**) dog used for herding sheep
sheepdogs *n* ▷ **sheepdog**
sheepish *adj* embarrassed because of feeling foolish > **sheepishly** *adv*
sheepishly *adv* ▷ **sheepish**
sheepskin *n* (*pl* **-s**) skin of a sheep with the fleece still on, used for clothing or rugs
sheepskins *n* ▷ **sheepskin**
sheer[1] *adj* (**-er, -est**) absolute, complete
sheer[2] *v* (**-s, -ing, -ed**) change course suddenly
sheered *v* ▷ **sheer**[2]
sheerer *adj* ▷ **sheer**[1]
sheerest *adj* ▷ **sheer**[1]
sheering *v* ▷ **sheer**[2]
sheers *v* ▷ **sheer**[2]
sheet[1] *n* (*pl* **-s**) large piece of cloth used as an inner bed cover
sheet[2] *n* (*pl* **-s**) rope for controlling the position of a sail
sheets *n* ▷ **sheet**[1, 2]
sheikdom *n* ▷ **sheikh**
sheikdoms *n* ▷ **sheikh**
sheikh, sheik [shake] *n* (*pl* **-s**) Arab chief > **sheikhdom, sheikdom** *n* (*pl* **-s**)
sheikhdoms *n* ▷ **sheikhdom**
sheikhs *n* ▷ **sheikh**
sheiks *n* ▷ **sheikh**
sheila *n* (*pl* **-s**) (AUST & NZ) (*Slang*) girl or woman
sheilas *n* ▷ **sheila**
shekel *n* (*pl* **-s**) monetary unit of Israel
shekels *n* ▷ **shekel** ▶ *pl n* (*Informal*) money
shelf *n* (*pl* **-ves**) board fixed horizontally for holding things
shell *n* (*pl* **-s**) hard outer covering of an egg, nut, or certain animals ▶ *v* (**-s, -lling, -lled**) take the shell from
shellac *n* (*pl* **-s**) resin used in varnishes ▶ *v* (**-cs, -cking, -cked**) coat with shellac
shellacked *v* ▷ **shellac**
shellacking *v* ▷ **shellac**
shellacs *n, v* ▷ **shellac**
shelled *v* ▷ **shell**
shellfish *n* (*pl* **-s**) sea-living animal, esp. one that can be eaten, with a shell
shellfishes *n* ▷ **shellfish**
shelling *v* ▷ **shell**
shells *n, v* ▷ **shell**
shelter *n* (*pl* **-s**) structure providing protection from danger or the weather ▶ *v* (**-s, -ing, -ed**) give shelter to
sheltered *v* ▷ **shelter**
sheltering *v* ▷ **shelter**
shelters *n, v* ▷ **shelter**
shelve[1] *v* (**-ves, -ving, -ved**) put aside or postpone
shelve[2] *v* (**-ves, -ving, -ved**) slope
shelved *v* ▷ **shelve**[1, 2]
shelves *v* ▷ **shelve**[1, 2] ▶ *n* ▷ **shelf**
shelving *n* (*pl* **-s**) (material for) shelves ▶ *v* ▷ **shelve**[1, 2]
shenanigans *pl n* (*Informal*) mischief or nonsense
shepherd *n* (*pl* **-s**) person who tends sheep ▶ *v* (**-s, -ing, -ed**) guide or watch over (people) > **shepherdess** *n fem* (*pl* **-s**)
shepherded *v* ▷ **shepherd**
shepherdess *n* ▷ **shepherd**
shepherdesses *n* ▷ **shepherd**
shepherding *v* ▷ **shepherd**

shepherds *n, v* ▷ **shepherd**
sherbet *n* (*pl* **-s**) (BRIT, AUST & NZ) fruit-flavoured fizzy powder
sherbets *n* ▷ **sherbet**
sheriff *n* (*pl* **-s**) (in the US) chief law enforcement officer of a county
sheriffs *n* ▷ **sheriff**
sherries *n* ▷ **sherry**
sherry *n* (*pl* **-ries**) pale or dark brown fortified wine

> **shh** *interj*. Shh is a sound people make to request silence or quiet. As it doesn't contain a vowel, shh can help you to clear an unpromising rack. Shh scores 9 points.

shibboleth *n* (*pl* **-s**) slogan or principle, usu. considered outworn, characteristic of a particular group
shibboleths *n* ▷ **shibboleth**
shied *v* ▷ **shy**[1, 2]
shield *n* (*pl* **-s**) piece of armour carried on the arm to protect the body from blows or missiles ▶ *v* (**-s, -ing, -ed**) protect
shielded *v* ▷ **shield**
shielding *v* ▷ **shield**
shields *n, v* ▷ **shield**
shies *v* ▷ **shy**[1, 2] ▶ *n* ▷ **shy**[2]
shift *v* (**-s, -ing, -ed**) move ▶ *n* (*pl* **-s**) shifting
shifted *v* ▷ **shift**
shiftier *adj* ▷ **shifty**
shiftiest *adj* ▷ **shifty**
shiftiness *n* ▷ **shifty**
shiftinesses *n* ▷ **shifty**
shifting *v* ▷ **shift**
shiftless *adj* lacking in ambition or initiative
shifts *v, n* ▷ **shift**
shifty *adj* (**-tier, -tiest**) evasive or untrustworthy > **shiftiness** *n* (*pl* **-es**)
shillelagh [shil-**lay**-lee] *n* (*pl* **-s**) (in Ireland) a cudgel
shillelaghs *n* ▷ **shillelagh**
shilling *n* (*pl* **-s**) former British coin, replaced by the 5p piece
shillings *n* ▷ **shilling**
shillyshallied *v* ▷ **shillyshally**
shillyshallies *v* ▷ **shillyshally**
shillyshally *v* (**-lies, -lying, -lied**) (*Informal*) be indecisive
shillyshallying *v* ▷ **shillyshally**
shimmer *v* (**-s, -ing, -ed**) ▶ *n* (*pl* **-s**) (shine with) a faint unsteady light
shimmered *v* ▷ **shimmer**
shimmering *v* ▷ **shimmer**
shimmers *v, n* ▷ **shimmer**
shin *n* (*pl* **-s**) front of the lower leg ▶ *v* (**-s, -nning, -nned**) climb by using the hands or arms and legs
shinbone *n* (*pl* **-s**) tibia
shinbones *n* ▷ **shinbone**
shindig *n* (*pl* **-s**) (*Informal*) noisy party
shindigs *n* ▷ **shindig**
shine *v* (**-s, -ing, shone**) give out or reflect light ▶ *n* (*pl* **-s**) brightness or lustre > **shiny** *adj* (**-nier, -niest**)
shiner *n* (*pl* **-s**) (*Informal*) black eye
shiners *n* ▷ **shiner**
shines *v, n* ▷ **shine**
shingle[1] *n* (*pl* **-s**) wooden roof tile ▶ *v* (**-les, -ling, -led**) cover (a roof) with shingles
shingle[2] *n* (*pl* **-s**) coarse gravel found on beaches
shingled *v* ▷ **shingle**[1]
shingles *n* disease causing a rash of small blisters along a nerve ▷ **shingle**[1, 2] ▶ *v* ▷ **shingle**[1]
shingling *v* ▷ **shingle**[1]
shinier *adj* ▷ **shine**
shiniest *adj* ▷ **shine**
shining *v* ▷ **shine**
shinned *v* ▷ **shin**
shinning *v* ▷ **shin**
shins *n, v* ▷ **shin**
shinties *n* ▷ **shinty**
shinty *n* (*pl* **-ties**) game like hockey
shiny *adj* ▷ **shine**
ship *n* (*pl* **-s**) large seagoing vessel ▶ *v* (**-s, -pping, -pped**) send or transport by carrier, esp. a ship
shipment *n* (*pl* **-s**) act of shipping cargo
shipments *n* ▷ **shipment**
shipped *v* ▷ **ship**
shipping *n* (*pl* **-s**) freight transport business ▶ *v* ▷ **ship**
shippings *n* ▷ **shipping**
ships *n, v* ▷ **ship**
shipshape *adj* orderly or neat
shipwreck *n* (*pl* **-s**) destruction of a ship through storm or collision ▶ *v* (**-s, -ing, -ed**) cause to undergo shipwreck
shipwrecked *v* ▷ **shipwreck**
shipwrecking *v* ▷ **shipwreck**
shipwrecks *n, v* ▷ **shipwreck**
shipyard *n* (*pl* **-s**) place where ships are built
shipyards *n* ▷ **shipyard**
shire *n* (*pl* **-s**) (BRIT) county
shires *n* ▷ **shire**
shirk *v* (**-s, -ing, -ed**) avoid (duty or work) > **shirker** *n* (*pl* **-s**)
shirked *v* ▷ **shirk**
shirker *n* ▷ **shirk**

shirkers *n* ▷ **shirk**
shirking *v* ▷ **shirk**
shirks *v* ▷ **shirk**
shirt *n* (*pl* **-s**) garment for the upper part of the body
shirtier *adj* ▷ **shirty**
shirtiest *adj* ▷ **shirty**
shirts *n* ▷ **shirt**
shirty *adj* (**-tier, -tiest**) (CHIEFLY BRIT) (*Slang*) bad-tempered or annoyed
shiver[1] *v* (**-s, -ing, -ed**) tremble, as from cold or fear ▶ *n* (*pl* **-s**) shivering
shiver[2] *v* (**-s, -ing, -ed**) splinter into pieces
shivered *v* ▷ **shiver**[1, 2]
shivering *v* ▷ **shiver**[1, 2]
shivers *v* ▷ **shiver**[1, 2] ▶ *n* ▷ **shiver**[1]
shoal[1] *n* (*pl* **-s**) large number of fish swimming together
shoal[2] *n* (*pl* **-s**) stretch of shallow water
shoals *n* ▷ **shoal**[1, 2]
shock[1] *v* (**-s, -ing, -ed**) horrify, disgust, or astonish ▶ *n* (*pl* **-s**) sudden violent emotional disturbance > **shocker** *n* (*pl* **-s**)
shock[2] *n* (*pl* **-s**) bushy mass (of hair)
shocked *v* ▷ **shock**[1]
shocker *n* ▷ **shock**[1]
shockers *n* ▷ **shock**[1]
shocking *adj* causing horror, disgust, or astonishment ▶ *v* ▷ **shock**[1]
shocks *v* ▷ **shock**[1] ▶ *n* ▷ **shock**[1, 2]
shod *v* ▷ **shoe**
shoddier *adj* ▷ **shoddy**
shoddiest *adj* ▷ **shoddy**
shoddy *adj* (**-dier, -diest**) made or done badly
shoe *n* (*pl* **-s**) outer covering for the foot, ending below the ankle ▶ *v* (**shoes, shoeing, shod**) fit with a shoe or shoes
shoehorn *n* (*pl* **-s**) smooth curved implement inserted at the heel of a shoe to ease the foot into it
shoehorns *n* ▷ **shoehorn**
shoeing *v* ▷ **shoe**
shoes *n, v* ▷ **shoe**
shoestring *n* (*pl* **-s**) (*foll. by* **on a**) using a very small amount of money
shoestrings *n* ▷ **shoestring**
shone *v* ▷ **shine**
shonkier *adj* ▷ **shonky**
shonkiest *adj* ▷ **shonky**
shonky *adj* (**-kier, -kiest**) (AUST & NZ) (*Informal*) unreliable or unsound
shoo *interj* go away! ▶ *v* (**-s, -ing, -ed**) drive away as by saying 'shoo'
shooed *v* ▷ **shoo**
shooing *v* ▷ **shoo**
shook *v* ▷ **shake**
shoos *v* ▷ **shoo**
shoot *v* (**-s, -ing, shot**) hit, wound, or kill with a missile fired from a weapon ▶ *n* (*pl* **-s**) new branch or sprout of a plant
shooting *v* ▷ **shoot**
shoots *v, n* ▷ **shoot**
shop *n* (*pl* **-s**) place for sale of goods and services ▶ *v* (**-s, -pping, -pped**) visit a shop or shops to buy goods
shoplifter *n* (*pl* **-s**) person who steals from a shop
shoplifters *n* ▷ **shoplifter**
shopped *v* ▷ **shop**
shopping *v* ▷ **shop**
shops *n, v* ▷ **shop**
shopsoiled *adj* soiled or faded from being displayed in a shop
shore[1] *n* (*pl* **-s**) edge of a sea or lake
shore[2] *v* (**-res, -ring, -red**) (*foll. by* **up**) prop or support
shored *v* ▷ **shore**[2]
shores *n* ▷ **shore**[1] ▶ *v* ▷ **shore**[2]
shoring *v* ▷ **shore**[2]
shorn *v* ▷ **shear**
short *adj* (**-er, -est**) not long ▶ *adv* abruptly ▶ *n* (*pl* **-s**) drink of spirits
shortage *n* (*pl* **-s**) deficiency
shortages *n* ▷ **shortage**
shortbread, shortcake *n* (*pl* **-s**) crumbly biscuit made with butter
shortbreads *n* ▷ **shortbread**
shortcake *n* ▷ **shortbread**
shortcakes *n* ▷ **shortbread**
shortchange *v* (**-ges, -ging, -ed**) give (someone) less than the correct amount of change
shortchanged *v* ▷ **shortchange**
shortchanges *v* ▷ **shortchange**
shortchanging *v* ▷ **shortchange**
shortcoming *n* (*pl* **-s**) failing or defect
shortcomings *n* ▷ **shortcoming**
shorten *v* (**-s, -ing, -ed**) make or become shorter
shortened *v* ▷ **shorten**
shortening *v* ▷ **shorten**
shortens *v* ▷ **shorten**
shorter *adj* ▷ **short**
shortest *adj* ▷ **short**
shortfall *n* (*pl* **-s**) deficit
shortfalls *n* ▷ **shortfall**
shorthand *n* (*pl* **-s**) system of rapid writing using symbols to represent words
shorthanded *adj* not having enough workers
shorthands *n* ▷ **shorthand**

shortlist *v* (**-s, -ing, -ed**) put on a short list
shortlisted *v* ▷ **shortlist**
shortlisting *v* ▷ **shortlist**
shortlists *v* ▷ **shortlist**
shortly *adv* soon
shorts *n* ▷ **short** ▶ *pl n* short trousers
shortsighted *adj* unable to see distant things clearly
shot *n* (*pl* **-s**) shooting ▶ *v* ▷ **shoot**
shotgun *n* (*pl* **-s**) gun for firing a charge of shot at short range
shotguns *n* ▷ **shotgun**
shots *n* ▷ **shot**
should *v* ▷ **shall**
shoulder *n* (*pl* **-s**) part of the body to which an arm, foreleg, or wing is attached ▶ *v* (**-s, -ing, -ed**) bear (a burden or responsibility)
shouldered *v* ▷ **shoulder**
shouldering *v* ▷ **shoulder**
shoulders *n, v* ▷ **shoulder**
shout *n* (*pl* **-s**) loud cry (*Informal*) ▶ *v* (**-s, -ing, -ed**) cry out loudly
shouted *v* ▷ **shout**
shouting *v* ▷ **shout**
shouts *n, v* ▷ **shout**
shove *v* (**-ves, -ving, -ved**) push roughly ▶ *n* (*pl* **-s**) rough push
shoved *v* ▷ **shove**
shovel *n* (*pl* **-s**) tool for lifting or moving loose material ▶ *v* (**-s, -lling, -lled**) lift or move as with a shovel
shovelled *v* ▷ **shovel**
shovelling *v* ▷ **shovel**
shovels *n, v* ▷ **shovel**
shoves *n* ▷ **shove**
shoving *v* ▷ **shove**
show *v* (**-s, -ing, -ed, shown** *or* **showed**) make, be, or become noticeable or visible ▶ *n* (*pl* **-s**) public exhibition
showcase *n* (*pl* **-s**) situation in which something is displayed to best advantage
showcases *n* ▷ **showcase**
showdown *n* (*pl* **-s**) confrontation that settles a dispute
showdowns *n* ▷ **showdown**
showed *v* ▷ **show**
shower *n* (*pl* **-s**) kind of bath in which a person stands while being sprayed with water ▶ *v* (**-s, -ing, -ed**) wash in a shower > **showery** *adj* (**-rier, -riest**)
showered *v* ▷ **shower**
showerier *adj* ▷ **shower**
showeriest *adj* ▷ **shower**
showering *v* ▷ **shower**
showers *n, v* ▷ **shower**
showery *adj* ▷ **shower**
showier *adj* ▷ **showy**
showiest *adj* ▷ **showy**
showily *adv* ▷ **showy**
showing *v* ▷ **show**
showjumping *n* (*pl* **-s**) competitive sport of riding horses to demonstrate skill in jumping
showjumpings *n* ▷ **showjumping**
showman *n* (*pl* **-men**) man skilled at presenting anything spectacularly > **showmanship** *n* (*pl* **-s**)
showmanship *n* ▷ **showman**
showmanships *n* ▷ **showman**
showmen *n* ▷ **showman**
shown *v* ▷ **show**
showoff *n* (*pl* **-s**) (*Informal*) person who shows off
showoffs *n* ▷ **showoff**
showpiece *n* (*pl* **-s**) excellent specimen shown for display or as an example
showpieces *n* ▷ **showpiece**
showroom *n* (*pl* **-s**) room in which goods for sale are on display
showrooms *n* ▷ **showroom**
shows *v, n* ▷ **show**
showy *adj* (**-wier, -wiest**) gaudy > **showily** *adv*
shrank *v* ▷ **shrink**
shrapnel *n* (*pl* **-s**) artillery shell filled with pellets which scatter on explosion
shrapnels *n* ▷ **shrapnel**
shred *n* (*pl* **-s**) long narrow strip torn from something ▶ *v* (**-s, -dding, -dded** *or* **shred**) tear to shreds
shredded *v* ▷ **shred**
shredding *v* ▷ **shred**
shreds *n, v* ▷ **shred**
shrew *n* (*pl* **-s**) small mouselike animal > **shrewish** *adj*
shrewd *adj* (**-er, -est**) clever and perceptive > **shrewdly** *adv* > **shrewdness** *n* (*pl* **-es**)
shrewder *adj* ▷ **shrewd**
shrewdest *adj* ▷ **shrewd**
shrewdly *adv* ▷ **shrewd**
shrewdness *n* ▷ **shrewd**
shrewdnesses *n* ▷ **shrewd**
shrewish *adj* ▷ **shrew**
shrews *n* ▷ **shrew**
shriek *n* (*pl* **-s**) shrill cry ▶ *v* (**-s, -ing, -ed**) utter (with) a shriek
shrieked *v* ▷ **shriek**
shrieking *v* ▷ **shriek**
shrieks *n, v* ▷ **shriek**
shrike *n* (*pl* **-s**) songbird with a heavy hooked bill
shrikes *n* ▷ **shrike**

shrill *adj* (**-er, -est**) (of a sound) sharp and high-pitched > **shrillness** *n* (*pl* **-es**) > **shrilly** *adv*

shriller *adj* ▷ **shrill**

shrillest *adj* ▷ **shrill**

shrillness *n* ▷ **shrill**

shrillnesses *n* ▷ **shrill**

shrilly *adv* ▷ **shrill**

shrimp *n* (*pl* **-s**) small edible shellfish (*Informal*)

shrimping *n* (*pl* **-s**) fishing for shrimps

shrimpings *n* ▷ **shrimping**

shrimps *n* ▷ **shrimp**

shrine *n* (*pl* **-s**) place of worship associated with a sacred person or object

shrines *n* ▷ **shrine**

shrink *v* (**-s, -ing, shrank** *or* **shrunk, shrunk** *or* **shrunken**) become or make smaller ▸ *n* (*pl* **-s**) (*Slang*) psychiatrist

shrinkage *n* (*pl* **-s**) decrease in size, value, or weight

shrinkages *n* ▷ **shrinkage**

shrinking *v* ▷ **shrink**

shrinks *v, n* ▷ **shrink**

shrivel *v* (**-s, -lling, -lled**) shrink and wither

shrivelled *v* ▷ **shrivel**

shrivelling *v* ▷ **shrivel**

shrivels *v* ▷ **shrivel**

shroud *n* (*pl* **-s**) piece of cloth used to wrap a dead body ▸ *v* (**-s, -ing, -ed**) conceal

shrouded *v* ▷ **shroud**

shrouding *v* ▷ **shroud**

shrouds *n, v* ▷ **shroud**

shrub *n* (*pl* **-s**) woody plant smaller than a tree

shrubberies *n* ▷ **shrubbery**

shrubbery *n* (*pl* **-ries**) area planted with shrubs

shrubs *n* ▷ **shrub**

shrug *v* (**-s, -gging, -gged**) raise and then drop (the shoulders) as a sign of indifference, ignorance, or doubt ▸ *n* (*pl* **-s**) shrugging

shrugged *v* ▷ **shrug**

shrugging *v* ▷ **shrug**

shrugs *v, n* ▷ **shrug**

shrunk *v* ▷ **shrink**

shrunken *v* ▷ **shrink**

shudder *v* (**-s, -ing, -ed**) shake or tremble violently, esp. with horror ▸ *n* (*pl* **-s**) shaking or trembling

shuddered *v* ▷ **shudder**

shuddering *v* ▷ **shudder**

shudders *v, n* ▷ **shudder**

shuffle *v* (**-les, -ling, -led**) walk without lifting the feet ▸ *n* (*pl* **-s**) shuffling

shuffled *v* ▷ **shuffle**

shuffles *v, n* ▷ **shuffle**

shuffling *v* ▷ **shuffle**

shun *v* (**-s, -nning, -nned**) avoid

shunned *v* ▷ **shun**

shunning *v* ▷ **shun**

shuns *v* ▷ **shun**

shunt *v* (**-s, -ing, -ed**) move (objects or people) to a different position

shunted *v* ▷ **shunt**

shunting *v* ▷ **shunt**

shunts *v* ▷ **shunt**

shush *interj* be quiet!

shut *v* (**-s, -tting, shut**) bring together or fold, close

shutdown *n* (*pl* **-s**) closing

shutdowns *n* ▷ **shutdown**

shuts *v* ▷ **shut**

shutter *n* (*pl* **-s**) hinged doorlike cover for closing off a window

shutters *n* ▷ **shutter**

shutting *v* ▷ **shut**

shuttle *n* (*pl* **-s**) vehicle going to and fro over a short distance ▸ *v* (**-les, -ling, -led**) travel by or as if by shuttle

shuttlecock *n* (*pl* **-s**) small light cone with feathers stuck in one end, struck to and fro in badminton

shuttlecocks *n* ▷ **shuttlecock**

shuttled *v* ▷ **shuttle**

shuttles *n, v* ▷ **shuttle**

shuttling *v* ▷ **shuttle**

shy[1] *adj* (**-er, -est**) not at ease in company (*foll. by* **of**) ▸ *v* (**shies, shying, shied**) start back in fear (*foll. by* **away from**) > **shyly** *adv* > **shyness** *n* (*pl* **-es**)

shy[2] *v* (**shies, shying, shied**) throw ▸ *n* (*pl* **shies**) throw

shyer *adj* ▷ **shy**[1]

shyest *adj* ▷ **shy**[1]

shying *v* ▷ **shy**[1, 2]

shyly *adv* ▷ **shy**[1]

shyness *n* ▷ **shy**[1]

shynesses *n* ▷ **shy**[1]

si *n* (**sis**). Si means the same as **te**, a musical note This is an unusual word which can be helpful when you want to form words in more than one direction Si scores 2 points

sibilant *adj* hissing ▸ *n* (*pl* **-s**) consonant pronounced with a hissing sound

sibilants *n* ▷ **sibilant**

sibling *n* (*pl* **-s**) brother or sister

siblings *n* ▷ **sibling**

sibyl *n* (*pl* **-s**) (in ancient Greece and Rome) prophetess

sibyls *n* ▷ **sibyl**

sic (LATIN) thus: used to indicate that an odd spelling or reading is in fact accurate

sick *adj* (**-er, -est**) vomiting or likely to vomit
> **sickness** *n* (*pl* **-es**)
sicken *v* (**-s, -zing, -ed**) make nauseated or disgusted
sickened *v* ▷ **sicken**
sickening *v* ▷ **sicken**
sickens *v* ▷ **sicken**
sicker *adj* ▷ **sick**
sickest *adj* ▷ **sick**
sickle *n* (*pl* **-s**) tool with a curved blade for cutting grass or grain
sickles *n* ▷ **sickle**
sicklier *adj* ▷ **sickly**
sickliest *adj* ▷ **sickly**
sickly *adj* (**-lier, -liest**) unhealthy, weak
sickness *n* ▷ **sick**
sicknesses *n* ▷ **sick**
side *n* (*pl* **-s**) line or surface that borders anything ▶ *adj* at or on the side
sideboard *n* (*pl* **-s**) piece of furniture for holding plates, cutlery, etc. in a dining room
sideboards *n* ▷ **sideboard** ▶ *pl n* ▷ **sideburns**
sideburns, sideboards *pl n* man's side whiskers
sidekick *n* (*pl* **-s**) (*Informal*) close friend or associate
sidekicks *n* ▷ **sidekick**
sidelight *n* (*pl* **-s**) either of two small lights on the front of a vehicle
sidelights *n* ▷ **sidelight**
sideline *n* (*pl* **-s**) subsidiary interest or source of income
sidelines *n* ▷ **sideline**
sidelong *adj* sideways ▶ *adv* obliquely
sidereal [side-**eer**-ee-al] *adj* of or determined with reference to the stars
sides *n* ▷ **side**
sidesaddle *n* (*pl* **-s**) saddle designed to allow a woman rider to sit with both legs on the same side of the horse
sidesaddles *n* ▷ **sidesaddle**
sidestep *v* (**-s, -pping, -pped**) dodge (an issue)
sidestepped *v* ▷ **sidestep**
sidestepping *v* ▷ **sidestep**
sidesteps *v* ▷ **sidestep**
sidetrack *v* (**-s, -ing, -ed**) divert from the main topic
sidetracked *v* ▷ **sidetrack**
sidetracking *v* ▷ **sidetrack**
sidetracks *v* ▷ **sidetrack**
sidewalk *n* (*pl* **-s**) (US) paved path for pedestrians, at the side of a road
sidewalks *n* ▷ **sidewalk**
sideways *adv* to or from the side
siding *n* (*pl* **-s**) short stretch of railway track on which trains or wagons are shunted from the main line
sidings *n* ▷ **siding**
sidle *v* (**-les, -ling, -led**) walk in a furtive manner
sidled *v* ▷ **sidle**
sidles *v* ▷ **sidle**
sidling *v* ▷ **sidle**
siege *n* (*pl* **-s**) surrounding and blockading of a place
sieges *n* ▷ **siege**
sienna *n* (*pl* **-s**) reddish- or yellowish-brown pigment made from natural earth
siennas *n* ▷ **sienna**
sierra *n* (*pl* **-s**) range of mountains in Spain or America with jagged peaks
sierras *n* ▷ **sierra**
siesta *n* (*pl* **-s**) afternoon nap, taken in hot countries
siestas *n* ▷ **siesta**
sieve [**siv**] *n* (*pl* **-s**) utensil with mesh through which a substance is sifted or strained ▶ *v* (**-ves, -ving, -ved**) sift or strain through a sieve
sieved *v* ▷ **sieve**
sieves *n, v* ▷ **sieve**
sieving *v* ▷ **sieve**
sift *v* (**-s, -ing, -ed**) remove the coarser particles from a substance with a sieve
sifted *v* ▷ **sift**
sifting *v* ▷ **sift**
sifts *v* ▷ **sift**
sigh *n* (*pl* **-s**) long audible breath expressing sadness, tiredness, relief, or longing ▶ *v* (**-s, -ing, -ed**) utter a sigh
sighed *v* ▷ **sigh**
sighing *v* ▷ **sigh**
sighs *n, v* ▷ **sigh**
sight *n* (*pl* **-s**) ability to see ▶ *v* (**-s, -ing, -ed**) catch sight of
sighted *v* ▷ **sight**
sighting *v* ▷ **sight**
sightless *adj* blind
sights *n, v* ▷ **sight**
sightseeing *n* (*pl* **-s**) visiting places of interest
> **sightseer** *n* (*pl* **-s**)
sightseeings *n* ▷ **sightseeing**
sightseer *n* ▷ **sightseeing**
sightseers *n* ▷ **sightseeing**
sign *n* (*pl* **-s**) indication of something not immediately or outwardly observable ▶ *v* (**-s, -ing, -ed**) write (one's name) on (a document or letter) to show its authenticity or one's agreement
signal *n* (*pl* **-s**) sign or gesture to convey information ▶ *adj* (*Formal*) very important

▶ *v* (**-s, -lling, -lled**) convey (information) by signal > **signally** *adv*
signalled *v* ▷ **signal**
signalling *v* ▷ **signal**
signally *adv* ▷ **signal**
signalman *n* (*pl* **-men**) railwayman in charge of signals and points
signalmen *n* ▷ **signalman**
signals *n, v* ▷ **signal**
signatories *n* ▷ **signatory**
signatory *n* (*pl* **-ries**) one of the parties who sign a document
signature *n* (*pl* **-s**) person's name written by himself or herself in signing something
signatures *n* ▷ **signature**
signed *v* ▷ **sign**
signet *n* (*pl* **-s**) small seal used to authenticate documents
signets *n* ▷ **signet**
significance *n* ▷ **significant**
significances *n* ▷ **significant**
significant *adj* important > **significantly** *adv* > **significance** *n* (*pl* **-s**)
significantly *adv* ▷ **significant**
signification *n* ▷ **signify**
significations *n* ▷ **signify**
signified *v* ▷ **signify**
signifies *v* ▷ **signify**
signify *v* (**-fies, -fying, -fied**) indicate or suggest > **signification** *n* (*pl* **-s**)
signifying *v* ▷ **signify**
signing *n* (*pl* **-s**) system of communication by gestures, as used by deaf people ▶ *v* ▷ **sign**
signings *n* ▷ **signing**
signor [see-**nyor**] *n* (*pl* **-s**) Italian term of address equivalent to *sir* or *Mr*
signora [see-**nyor**-a] *n* (*pl* **-s**) Italian term of address equivalent to *madam* or *Mrs*
signoras *n* ▷ **signora**
signorina [see-nyor-**ee**-na] *n* (*pl* **-s**) Italian term of address equivalent to *madam* or *Miss*
signorinas *n* ▷ **signorina**
signors *n* ▷ **signor**
signpost *n* (*pl* **-s**) post bearing a sign that shows the way
signposts *n* ▷ **signpost**
signs *n, v* ▷ **sign**
silage [**sile**-ij] *n* (*pl* **-s**) fodder crop harvested while green and partially fermented in a silo or plastic bags
silages *n* ▷ **silage**
silence *n* (*pl* **-s**) absence of noise or speech ▶ *v* (**-ces, -cing, -ced**) make silent > **silent** *adj* > **silently** *adv*
silenced *v* ▷ **silence**
silencer *n* (*pl* **-s**) device to reduce the noise of an engine exhaust or gun
silencers *n* ▷ **silencer**
silences *n, v* ▷ **silence**
silencing *v* ▷ **silence**
silent *adj* ▷ **silencet**
silently *adv* ▷ **silence**
silhouette *n* (*pl* **-s**) outline of a dark shape seen against a light background ▶ *v* (**-s, -ing, -ed**) show in silhouette
silhouetted *v* ▷ **silhouette**
silhouettes *n, v* ▷ **silhouette**
silhouetting *v* ▷ **silhouette**
silica *n* (*pl* **-s**) hard glossy mineral found as quartz and in sandstone
silicas *n* ▷ **silica**
silicon *n* (*pl* **-s**) (CHEM) brittle nonmetallic element widely used in chemistry and industry
silicone *n* (*pl* **-s**) tough synthetic substance made from silicon and used in lubricants, paints, and resins
silicones *n* ▷ **silicone**
silicons *n* ▷ **silicon**
silicoses *n* ▷ **silicosis**
silicosis *n* (*pl* **-ses**) lung disease caused by inhaling silica dust
silk *n* (*pl* **-s**) fibre made by the larva of a certain moth
silken *adj* ▷ **silky**
silkier *adj* ▷ **silky**
silkiest *adj* ▷ **silky**
silks *n* ▷ **silk**
silky (**-ier, -iest**), **silken** *adj* of or like silk
sill *n* (*pl* **-s**) ledge at the bottom of a window or door
sillier *adj* ▷ **silly**
silliest *adj* ▷ **silly**
silliness *n* ▷ **silly**
sillinesses *n* ▷ **silly**
sills *n* ▷ **sill**
silly *adj* (**-lier, -liest**) foolish > **silliness** *n* (*pl* **-es**)
silo *n* (*pl* **-los**) pit or airtight tower for storing silage or grains
silos *n* ▷ **silo**
silt *n* (*pl* **-s**) mud deposited by moving water ▶ *v* (**-s, -ing, -ed**) (*foll. by* **up**) fill or be choked with silt
silted *v* ▷ **silt**
silting *v* ▷ **silt**
silts *n, v* ▷ **silt**
silvan *adj* ▷ **sylvan**
silver *n* (*pl* **-s**) white precious metal ▶ *adj* made of or of the colour of silver
silverbeet *n* (*pl* **-s**) (AUST & NZ) leafy green

vegetable with white stalks
silverbeets *n* ▷ **silverbeet**
silverfish *n* (*pl* **-es**) small wingless silver-coloured insect
silverfishes *n* ▷ **silverfish**
silvers *n* ▷ **silver**
silverside *n* (*pl* **-s**) cut of beef from below the rump and above the leg
silversides *n* ▷ **silverside**
sim *n* (*pl* **-s**) computer game that simulates an activity such as flying or playing a sport
simian *adj, n* (*pl* **-s**) (of or like) a monkey or ape
simians *n* ▷ **simian**
similar *adj* alike but not identical > **similarity** *n* (*pl* **-s**) > **similarly** *adv*
similarities *n* ▷ **similar**
similarity *n* ▷ **similar**
similarly *adv* ▷ **similar**
simile [**sim**-ill-ee] *n* (*pl* **-s**) figure of speech comparing one thing to another, using 'as' or 'like'
similes *n* ▷ **simile**
similitude *n* (*pl* **-s**) similarity, likeness
similitudes *n* ▷ **similitude**
simmer *v* (**-s, -ing, -ed**) cook gently at just below boiling point
simmered *v* ▷ **simmer**
simmering *v* ▷ **simmer**
simmers *v* ▷ **simmer**
simper *v* (**-s, -ing, -ed**) smile in a silly or affected way ▶ *n* (*pl* **-s**) simpering smile
simpered *v* ▷ **simper**
simpering *v* ▷ **simper**
simpers *v, n* ▷ **simper**
simple *adj* (**-r, -st**) easy to understand or do > **simply** *adv* > **simplicity** *n* (*pl* **-ties**)
simpler *adj* ▷ **simple**
simplest *adj* ▷ **simple**
simpleton *n* (*pl* **-s**) foolish or half-witted person
simpletons *n* ▷ **simpleton**
simplicities *n* ▷ **simple**
simplicity *n* ▷ **simple**
simplification *n* ▷ **simplify**
simplifications *n* ▷ **simplify**
simplified *v* ▷ **simplify**
simplifies *v* ▷ **simplify**
simplify *v* (**-fies, -fying, -fied**) make less complicated > **simplification** *n* (*pl* **-s**)
simplifying *v* ▷ **simplify**
simplistic *adj* too simple or naive
simply *adv* ▷ **simpl**
sims *n* ▷ **sim**
simulate *v* (**-tes, -ting, -ted**) make a pretence of > **simulation** *n* (*pl* **-s**) > **simulator** *n* (*pl* **-s**)
simulated *v* ▷ **simulate**
simulates *v* ▷ **simulate**
simulating *v* ▷ **simulate**
simulation *n* ▷ **simulate**
simulations *n* ▷ **simulate**
simulator *n* ▷ **simulate**
simulators *n* ▷ **simulate**
simultaneous *adj* occurring at the same time > **simultaneously** *adv*
simultaneously *adv* ▷ **simultaneous**
sin[1] *n* (*pl* **-s**) breaking of a religious or moral law ▶ *v* (**-s, -nning, -nned**) commit a sin > **sinner** *n* (*pl* **-s**)
sin[2] (MATHS) sine
since *prep* during the period of time after ▶ *conj* from the time when ▶ *adv* from that time
sincere *adj* (**-r, -st**) without pretence or deceit > **sincerely** *adv* > **sincerity** *n* (*pl* **-ties**)
sincerely *adv* ▷ **sincere**
sincerer *adj* ▷ **sincere**
sincerest *adj* ▷ **sincere**
sincerities *n* ▷ **sincere**
sincerity *n* ▷ **sincere**
sine *n* (*pl* **-s**) (in trigonometry) ratio of the length of the opposite side to that of the hypotenuse in a right-angled triangle
sinecure [**sin**-ee-cure] *n* (*pl* **-s**) paid job with minimal duties
sinecures *n* ▷ **sinecure**
sines *n* ▷ **sine**
sinew *n* (*pl* **-s**) tough fibrous tissue joining muscle to bone > **sinewy** *adj* (**-wier, -wiest**)
sinewier *adj* ▷ **sinew**
sinewiest *adj* ▷ **sinew**
sinews *n* ▷ **sinew**
sinewy *adj* ▷ **sinew**
sinful *adj* guilty of sin > **sinfully** *adv*
sinfully *adv* ▷ **sinful**
sing *v* (**-s, -ing, sang, sung**) make musical sounds with the voice
singe *v* (**-ges, -geing, -ged**) burn the surface of ▶ *n* (*pl* **-s**) superficial burn
singed *v* ▷ **singe**
singeing *v* ▷ **singe**
singer *n* (*pl* **-s**) person who sings, esp. professionally
singers *n* ▷ **singer**
singes *v, n* ▷ **singe**
singing *v* ▷ **sing**
single *adj* one only ▶ *n* (*pl* **-s**) single thing ▶ *v* (**-les, -ling, -led**) (*foll. by* **out**) pick out from others > **singly** *adv*
singled *v* ▷ **single**
singles *n, v* ▷ **single** ▶ *pl n* game between two players

singlet *n* (*pl* **-s**) sleeveless vest
singlets *n* ▷ **singlet**
singling *v* ▷ **single**
singly *adv* ▷ **single**
sings *v* ▷ **sing**
singsong *n* (*pl* **-s**) informal singing session ▶ *adj* (of the voice) repeatedly rising and falling in pitch
singsongs *n* ▷ **singsong**
singular *adj* (of a word or form) denoting one person or thing ▶ *n* (*pl* **-s**) singular form of a word > **singularity** *n* (*pl* **-ties**) > **singularly** *adv*
singularities *n* ▷ **singular**
singularity *n* ▷ **singular**
singularly *adv* ▷ **singular**
singulars *n* ▷ **singular**
sinister *adj* threatening or suggesting evil or harm
sink *v* (**-s, -ing, sank, sunk** *or* **sunken**) submerge (in liquid) ▶ *n* (*pl* **-s**) fixed basin with a water supply and drainage pipe
sinker *n* (*pl* **-s**) weight for a fishing line
sinkers *n* ▷ **sinker**
sinking *v* ▷ **sink**
sinks *v, n* ▷ **sink**
sinned *v* ▷ **sin**[1]
sinner *n* ▷ **sin**[1]
sinners *n* ▷ **sin**[1]
sinning *v* ▷ **sin**[1]
sins *n, v* ▷ **sin**[1]
sinuous *adj* curving > **sinuously** *adv*
sinuously *adv* ▷ **sinuous**
sinus [**sine**-uss] *n* (*pl* **-nuses**) hollow space in a bone, esp. an air passage opening into the nose
sinuses *n* ▷ **sinus**
sip *v* (**-s, -pping, -pped**) drink in small mouthfuls ▶ *n* (*pl* **-s**) amount sipped
siphon *n* (*pl* **-s**) bent tube which uses air pressure to draw liquid from a container ▶ *v* (**-s, -ing, -ed**) draw off thus
siphoned *v* ▷ **siphon**
siphoning *v* ▷ **siphon**
siphons *n, v* ▷ **siphon**
sipped *v* ▷ **sip**
sipping *v* ▷ **sip**
sips *v, n* ▷ **sip**
sir *n* (*pl* **-s**) polite term of address for a man
sire *n* (*pl* **-s**) male parent of a horse or other domestic animal ▶ *v* (**-res, -ring, -red**) father
sired *v* ▷ **sire**
siren *n* (*pl* **-s**) device making a loud wailing noise as a warning
sirens *n* ▷ **siren**
sires *n, v* ▷ **sire**
siring *v* ▷ **sire**
sirloin *n* (*pl* **-s**) prime cut of loin of beef
sirloins *n* ▷ **sirloin**
sirocco *n* (*pl* **-s**) hot wind blowing from N Africa into S Europe
siroccos *n* ▷ **sirocco**
sirs *n* ▷ **sir**
sis *interj* (S AFR) (*Informal*) exclamation of disgust
sisal [**size**-al] *n* (*pl* **-s**) (fibre of) plant used in making ropes
sisals *n* ▷ **sisal**
siskin *n* (*pl* **-s**) yellow-and-black finch
siskins *n* ▷ **siskin**
sissier *adj* ▷ **sissy**
sissies *n* ▷ **sissy**
sissiest *adj* ▷ **sissy**
sissy *adj* (**-ssier, -ssiest**) ▶ *n* (*pl* **-ssies**) weak or cowardly (person)
sister *n* (*pl* **-s**) girl or woman with the same parents as another person ▶ *adj* closely related, similar > **sisterly** *adj*
sisterhood *n* (*pl* **-s**) state of being a sister
sisterhoods *n* ▷ **sisterhood**
sisterly *adj* ▷ **sister**
sisters *n* ▷ **sister**
sit *v* (**-s, -tting, sat**) rest one's body upright on the buttocks
sitar *n* (*pl* **-s**) Indian stringed musical instrument
sitars *n* ▷ **sitar**
sitcom *n* (*pl* **-s**) (*Informal*) situation comedy
sitcoms *n* ▷ **sitcom**
site *n* (*pl* **-s**) place where something is, was, or is intended to be located ▷ **website** ▶ *v* (**-tes, -ting, -ted**) provide with a site
sited *v* ▷ **site**
sites *n, v* ▷ **site**
siting *v* ▷ **site**
sits *v* ▷ **sit**
sitting *v* ▷ **sit**
situate *v* (**-tes, -ting, -ted**) place
situated *v* ▷ **situate**
situates *v* ▷ **situate**
situating *v* ▷ **situate**
situation *n* (*pl* **-s**) state of affairs
situations *n* ▷ **situation**
six *adj, n* (*pl* **-es**) one more than five
sixes *n* ▷ **six**
sixteen *adj, n* (*pl* **-s**) six and ten > **sixteenth** *adj, n* (*pl* **-s**)
sixteens *n* ▷ **sixteen**
sixteenth *n* ▷ **sixteen**
sixteenths *n* ▷ **sixteen**
sixth *adj, n* (*pl* **-s**) (of) number six in a series
sixths *n* ▷ **sixth**

sixties *n* ▷ **sixty**
sixtieth *n* ▷ **sixty**
sixtieths *n* ▷ **sixty**
sixty *adj, n* (*pl* **-s**) six times ten > **sixtieth** *adj, n* (*pl* **-s**)
sizable *adj* ▷ **sizeable**
size[1] *n* (*pl* **-s**) dimensions, bigness ▶ *v* (**-zes, -zing, -zed**) arrange according to size
size[2] *n* (*pl* **-s**) gluey substance used as a protective coating
sizeable, sizable *adj* quite large
sized *v* ▷ **size**[1]
sizes *n* ▷ **size**[1, 2] ▶ *v* ▷ **size**[1]
sizing *v* ▷ **size**[1]
sizzle *v* (**-les, -ling, -led**) make a hissing sound like frying fat
sizzled *v* ▷ **sizzle**
sizzles *v* ▷ **sizzle**
sizzling *v* ▷ **sizzle**
skankier *adj* ▷ **skanky**
skankiest *adj* ▷ **skanky**
skanky *adj* (**-kier, -kiest**) (*Slang*) dirty or unnattractive
skate[1] *n* (*pl* **-s**) boot with a steel blade or sets of wheels attached to the sole for gliding over ice or a hard surface ▶ *v* (**-tes, -ting, -ted**) glide on or as if on skates
skate[2] *n* (*pl* **-s**) large marine flatfish
skateboard *n* (*pl* **-s**) board mounted on small wheels for riding on while standing up > **skateboarding** *n* (*pl* **-s**)
skateboarding *n* ▷ **skateboard**
skateboardings *n* ▷ **skateboard**
skateboards *n* ▷ **skateboard**
skated *v* ▷ **skate**[1]
skates *n* ▷ **skate**[1, 2] ▶ *v* ▷ **skate**[1]
skating *v* ▷ **skate**[1]
skedaddle *v* (**-les, -ling, -led**) (*Informal*) run off
skedaddled *v* ▷ **skedaddle**
skedaddles *v* ▷ **skedaddle**
skedaddling *v* ▷ **skedaddle**
skein *n* (*pl* **-s**) yarn wound in a loose coil
skeins *n* ▷ **skein**
skeletal *adj* ▷ **skeleton**
skeleton *n* (*pl* **-s**) framework of bones inside a person's or animal's body ▶ *adj* reduced to a minimum > **skeletal** *adj*
skeletons *n* ▷ **skeleton**
sketch *n* (*pl* **-es**) rough drawing ▶ *v* (**-es, -ing, -ed**) make a sketch (of)
sketched *v* ▷ **sketch**
sketches *n, v* ▷ **sketch**
sketchier *adj* ▷ **sketchy**
sketchiest *adj* ▷ **sketchy**
sketching *v* ▷ **sketch**
sketchy *adj* (**-chier, -chiest**) incomplete or inadequate
skew *v* (**-s, -ing, -ed**) make slanting or crooked ▶ *adj* slanting or crooked
skewed *v* ▷ **skew**
skewer *n* (*pl* **-s**) pin to hold meat together during cooking ▶ *v* (**-s, -ing, -ed**) fasten with a skewer
skewered *v* ▷ **skewer**
skewering *v* ▷ **skewer**
skewers *n, v* ▷ **skewer**
skewing *v* ▷ **skew**
skews *v* ▷ **skew**
skewwhiff *adj* (BRIT) (*Informal*) slanting or crooked
ski *n* (*pl* **-s**) one of a pair of long runners fastened to boots for gliding over snow or water ▶ *v* (**skis, skiing, skied**) travel on skis > **skier** *n* (*pl* **-s**)
skid *v* (**-s, -dding, -dded**) (of a moving vehicle) slide sideways uncontrollably ▶ *n* (*pl* **-s**) skidding
skidded *v* ▷ **skid**
skidding *v* ▷ **skid**
skids *v, n* ▷ **skid**
skied *v* ▷ **ski**
skier *n* ▷ **ski**
skiers *n* ▷ **ski**
skies *n* ▷ **sky**
skiff *n* (*pl* **-s**) small boat
skiffs *n* ▷ **skiff**
skiing *v* ▷ **ski**
skilful *adj* having or showing skill > **skilfully** *adv*
skilfully *adv* ▷ **skilful**
skill *n* (*pl* **-s**) special ability or expertise > **skilled** *adj*
skilled *adj* ▷ **skill**
skillet *n* (*pl* **-s**) small frying pan or shallow cooking pot
skillets *n* ▷ **skillet**
skills *n* ▷ **skill**
skim *v* (**-s, -mming, -mmed**) remove floating matter from the surface of (a liquid)
skimmed *v* ▷ **skim**
skimming *v* ▷ **skim**
skimp *v* (**-s, -ing, -ed**) not invest enough time, money, material, etc.
skimped *v* ▷ **skimp**
skimpier *adj* ▷ **skimpy**
skimpiest *adj* ▷ **skimpy**
skimping *v* ▷ **skimp**
skimps *v* ▷ **skimp**
skimpy *adj* (**-pier, -piest**) scanty or insufficient
skims *v* ▷ **skim**

skin *n* (*pl* **-s**) outer covering of the body ▶ *v* (**-s, -nning, -nned**) remove the skin of > **skinless** *adj*
skinflint *n* (*pl* **-s**) miser
skinflints *n* ▷ **skinflint**
skinhead *n* (*pl* **-s**) youth with very short hair
skinheads *n* ▷ **skinhead**
skinless *adj* ▷ **skin**
skinned *v* ▷ **skin**
skinnier *adj* ▷ **skinny**
skinniest *adj* ▷ **skinny**
skinning *v* ▷ **skin**
skinny *adj* (**-nnier, -nniest**) thin
skins *n, v* ▷ **skin**
skint *adj* (BRIT) (*Slang*) having no money
skip[1] *v* (**-s, -pping, -pped**) leap lightly from one foot to the other ▶ *n* (*pl* **-s**) skipping
skip[2] *n* (*pl* **-s**) large open container for builders' rubbish
skipped *v* ▷ **skip**[1]
skipper *n* (*pl* **-s**) ▶ *v* (**-s, -ing, -ed**) captain
skippered *v* ▷ **skipper**
skippering *v* ▷ **skipper**
skippers *n, v* ▷ **skipper**
skipping *v* ▷ **skip**[1]
skips *v* ▷ **skip**[1] ▶ *n* ▷ **skip**[1,2]
skirl *n* (*pl* **-s**) sound of bagpipes
skirls *n* ▷ **skirl**
skirmish *n* (*pl* **-es**) brief or minor fight or argument ▶ *v* (**-es, -ing, -ed**) take part in a skirmish
skirmished *v* ▷ **skirmish**
skirmishes *n, v* ▷ **skirmish**
skirmishing *v* ▷ **skirmish**
skirt *n* (*pl* **-s**) woman's garment hanging from the waist ▶ *v* (**-s, -ing, -ed**) border
skirted *v* ▷ **skirt**
skirting *v* ▷ **skirt**
skirts *n, v* ▷ **skirt**
skis *n, v* ▷ **ski**
skit *n* (*pl* **-s**) brief satirical sketch
skite *v* (**-tes, -ting, -ted**) ▶ *n* (*pl* **-s**) (AUST & NZ) boast
skited *v* ▷ **skite**
skites *v, n* ▷ **skite**
skiting *v* ▷ **skite**
skits *n* ▷ **skit**
skittish *adj* playful or lively
skittle *n* (*pl* **-s**) bottle-shaped object used as a target in some games
skittles *n* ▷ **skittle** ▶ *pl n* game in which players try to knock over skittles by rolling a ball at them
skive *v* (**-ves, -ving, -ved**) (BRIT) (*Informal*) evade work or responsibility
skived *v* ▷ **skive**
skives *v* ▷ **skive**
skiving *v* ▷ **skive**
skivvies *n* ▷ **skivvy**
skivvy *n* (*pl* **-vies**) (BRIT) female servant who does menial work
skua *n* (*pl* **-s**) large predatory gull
skuas *n* ▷ **skua**
skulduggeries *n* ▷ **skulduggery**
skulduggery *n* (*pl* **-ries**) (*Informal*) trickery
skulk *v* (**-s, -ing, -ed**) move stealthily
skulked *v* ▷ **skulk**
skulking *v* ▷ **skulk**
skulks *v* ▷ **skulk**
skull *n* (*pl* **-s**) bony framework of the head
skullcap *n* (*pl* **-s**) close-fitting brimless cap
skullcaps *n* ▷ **skullcap**
skulls *n* ▷ **skull**
skunk *n* (*pl* **-s**) small black-and-white N American mammal which emits a foul-smelling fluid when attacked
skunks *n* ▷ **skunk**
sky *n* (*pl* **skies**) upper atmosphere as seen from the earth
skydiving *n* (*pl* **-s**) sport of jumping from an aircraft and performing manoeuvres before opening one's parachute
skydivings *n* ▷ **skydiving**
skylark *n* (*pl* **-s**) lark that sings while soaring at a great height
skylarks *n* ▷ **skylark**
skylight *n* (*pl* **-s**) window in a roof or ceiling
skylights *n* ▷ **skylight**
skyscraper *n* (*pl* **-s**) very tall building
skyscrapers *n* ▷ **skyscraper**
slab *n* (*pl* **-s**) broad flat piece
slabs *n* ▷ **slab**
slack *adj* (**-er, -est**) not tight ▶ *n* (*pl* **-s**) slack part ▶ *v* (**-s, -ing, -ed**) neglect one's work or duty > **slacker** *n* (*pl* **-s**) > **slackness** *n* (*pl* **-es**)
slacked *v* ▷ **slack**
slacken *v* (**-s, -ing, -ed**) make or become slack
slackened *v* ▷ **slacken**
slackening *v* ▷ **slacken**
slackens *v* ▷ **slacken**
slacker *n, adj* ▷ **slack**
slackers *n* ▷ **slack**
slackest *adj* ▷ **slack**
slacking *v* ▷ **slack**
slackness *n* ▷ **slack**
slacknesses *n* ▷ **slack**
slacks *n, v* ▷ **slack** ▶ *pl n* informal trousers
slag *n* (*pl* **-s**) waste left after metal is smelted ▶ *v* (**-s, -gging, -gged**) (*foll. by* **off**) (BRIT, AUST & NZ) (*Slang*) criticize

slagged *v* ▷ **slag**
slagging *v* ▷ **slag**
slags *n, v* ▷ **slag**
slain *v* ▷ **slay**
slake *v* (**-kes, -king, -ked**) satisfy (thirst or desire)
slaked *v* ▷ **slake**
slakes *v* ▷ **slake**
slaking *v* ▷ **slake**
slalom *n* (*pl* **-s**) skiing or canoeing race over a winding course
slaloms *n* ▷ **slalom**
slam *v* (**-s, -mming, -mmed**) shut, put down, or hit violently and noisily ▶ *n* (*pl* **-s**) act or sound of slamming
slammed *v* ▷ **slam**
slamming *v* ▷ **slam**
slams *v, n* ▷ **slam**
slander *n* (*pl* **-s**) false and malicious statement about a person ▶ *v* (**-s, -ing, -ed**) utter slander about > **slanderous** *adj*
slandered *v* ▷ **slander**
slandering *v* ▷ **slander**
slanderous *adj* ▷ **slander**
slanders *n, v* ▷ **slander**
slang *n* (*pl* **-s**) very informal language > **slangy** *adj* (**-gier, -giest**)
slangier *adj* ▷ **slang**
slangiest *adj* ▷ **slang**
slangs *n* ▷ **slang**
slangy *adj* ▷ **slang**
slant *v* (**-s, -ing, -ed**) lean at an angle, slope ▶ *n* (*pl* **-s**) slope > **slanting** *adj*
slanted *v* ▷ **slant**
slanting *v, adj* ▷ **slant**
slants *v, n* ▷ **slant**
slap *n* (*pl* **-s**) blow with the open hand or a flat object ▶ *v* (**-s, -pping, -pped**) strike with the open hand or a flat object
slapdash *adj* careless and hasty
slaphappy *adj* (*Informal*) cheerfully careless
slapped *v* ▷ **slap**
slapping *v* ▷ **slap**
slaps *n, v* ▷ **slap**
slapstick *n* (*pl* **-s**) boisterous knockabout comedy
slapsticks *n* ▷ **slapstick**
slash *v* (**-es, -ing, -ed**) cut with a sweeping stroke ▶ *n* (*pl* **-es**) sweeping stroke
slashed *v* ▷ **slash**
slashes *v, n* ▷ **slash**
slashing *v* ▷ **slash**
slat *n* (*pl* **-s**) narrow strip of wood or metal
slate[1] *n* (*pl* **-s**) rock which splits easily into thin layers
slate[2] *v* (**-tes, -ting, -ted**) (*Informal*) criticize harshly
slated *v* ▷ **slate**[2]
slates *n* ▷ **slate**[1] ▶ *v* ▷ **slate**[2]
slating *v* ▷ **slate**[2]
slats *n* ▷ **slat**
slattern *n* (*pl* **-s**) (*Old-fashioned*) slovenly woman > **slatternly** *adj*
slatternly *adv* ▷ **slattern**
slatterns *n* ▷ **slattern**
slaughter *v* (**-s, -ing, -ed**) kill (animals) for food ▶ *n* (*pl* **-s**) slaughtering
slaughtered *v* ▷ **slaughter**
slaughterhouse *n* (*pl* **-s**) place where animals are killed for food
slaughterhouses *n* ▷ **slaughterhouse**
slaughtering *v* ▷ **slaughter**
slaughters *v, n* ▷ **slaughter**
slave *n* (*pl* **-s**) person owned by another for whom he or she has to work ▶ *v* (**-ves, -ing, -ved**) work like a slave
slaved *v* ▷ **slave**
slaver *n* (*pl* **-s**) person or ship engaged in the slave trade ▶ *v* [**slav**-ver] (**-s, -ing, -ed**) dribble saliva from the mouth
slavered *v* ▷ **slaver**
slaveries *n* ▷ **slavery**
slavering *v* ▷ **slaver**
slavers *n, v* ▷ **slaver**
slavery *n* (*pl* **-ries**) state or condition of being a slave
slaves *v, n* ▷ **slave**
slaving *v* ▷ **slave**
slavish *adj* of or like a slave
slay *v* (**-s, -ing, slew, slain**) kill
slaying *v* ▷ **slay**
slays *v* ▷ **slay**
sleazes *n* ▷ **sleaze**
sleazier *adj* ▷ **sleazy**
sleaziest *adj* ▷ **sleazy**
sleazy *adj* (**-zier, -ziest**) run-down or sordid > **sleaze** *n* (*pl* **-s**)
sled *n* (*pl* **-s**) ▶ *v* (**-s, -dding, -dded**) ▷
sledded *v* ▷ **sled**
sledding *v* ▷ **sled**
sledge[1] *n* (*pl* **-s**) carriage on runners for sliding on snow ▶ *v* (**-dges, -dging, -dged**) travel by sledge
sledge[2], **sledgehammer** *n* (*pl* **-s**) heavy hammer with a long handle
sledged *v* ▷ **sledge**[1]
sledgehammer *n* ▷ **sledge**
sledgehammers *n* ▷ **sledge**
sledges *n* ▷ **sledge**[1, 2] ▶ *v* ▷ **sledge**[1]
sledging *v* ▷ **sledge**[1]

sleds *n, v* ▷ **sled**
sleek *adj* (**-er, -est**) glossy, smooth, and shiny
sleeker *adj* ▷ **sleek**
sleekest *adj* ▷ **sleek**
sleep *n* (*pl* **-s**) state of rest characterized by unconsciousness ▶ *v* (**-s, -ing, slept**) be in or as if in a state of sleep > **sleepy** *adj* (**-pier, -piest**) > **sleepily** *adv* > **sleepiness** *n* (*pl* **-es**) > **sleepless** *adj*
sleeper *n* (*pl* **-s**) railway car fitted for sleeping in
sleepers *n* ▷ **sleeper**
sleepier *adj* ▷ **sleep**
sleepiest *adj* ▷ **sleep**
sleepily *adv* ▷ **sleep**
sleepiness *n* ▷ **sleep**
sleepinesses *n* ▷ **sleep**
sleeping *v* ▷ **sleep**
sleepless *adj* ▷ **sleep**
sleepout *n* (*pl* **-s**) (NZ) small building for sleeping in
sleepouts *n* ▷ **sleepout**
sleepover *n* (*pl* **-s**) occasion when a person stays overnight at a friend's house
sleepovers *n* ▷ **sleepover**
sleeps *n, v* ▷ **sleep**
sleepy *adj* ▷ **sleep**
sleet *n* (*pl* **-s**) rain and snow or hail falling together
sleets *n* ▷ **sleet**
sleeve *n* (*pl* **-s**) part of a garment which covers the arm > **sleeveless** *adj*
sleeveless *adj* ▷ **sleeve**
sleeves *n* ▷ **sleeve**
sleigh *n* (*pl* **-s**) ▶ *v* (**-s, -ing, -ed**) sledge
sleighed *v* ▷ **sleigh**
sleighing *v* ▷ **sleigh**
sleighs *n, v* ▷ **sleigh**
slender *adj* (**-er, -est**) slim
slenderer *adj* ▷ **slender**
slenderest *adj* ▷ **slender**
slept *v* ▷ **sleep**
sleuth [slooth] *n* (*pl* **-s**) detective
sleuths *n* ▷ **sleuth**
slew[1] *v* ▷ **slay**
slew[2] *v* (**-s, -ing, -ed**) twist or swing round
slewed *v* ▷ **slew[2]**
slewing *v* ▷ **slew[2]**
slews *v* ▷ **slew[2]**
slice *n* (*pl* **-s**) thin flat piece cut from something ▶ *v* (**-ces, -cing, -ced**) cut into slices
sliced *v* ▷ **slice**
slices *n, v* ▷ **slice**
slicing *v* ▷ **slice**
slick *adj* (**-er, -est**) persuasive and glib ▶ *n* (*pl* **-s**) patch of oil on water ▶ *v* (**-s, -ing, -ed**) make smooth or sleek
slicked *v* ▷ **slick**
slicker *adj* ▷ **slick**
slickest *adj* ▷ **slick**
slicking *v* ▷ **slick**
slicks *n, v* ▷ **slick**
slid *v* ▷ **slide**
slide *v* (**-des, -ding, slid**) slip smoothly along (a surface) ▶ *n* (*pl* **-s**) sliding
slides *v, n* ▷ **slide**
sliding *v* ▷ **slide**
slier *adj* ▷ **sly**
sliest *adj* ▷ **sly**
slight *adj* (**-er, -est**) small in quantity or extent ▶ *v* (**-s, -ing, -ed**) ▶ *n* (*pl* **-s**) snub > **slightly** *adv*
slighted *v* ▷ **slight**
slighter *adj* ▷ **slight**
slightest *adj* ▷ **slight**
slighting *v* ▷ **slight**
slightly *adv* ▷ **slight**
slights *v, n* ▷ **slight**
slim *adj* (**-mmer, -mmest**) not heavy or stout, thin ▶ *v* (**-s, -mming, -mmed**) make or become slim by diet and exercise > **slimmer** *n* (*pl* **-s**)
slime *n* (*pl* **-s**) unpleasant thick slippery substance
slimes *n* ▷ **slime**
slimier *adj* ▷ **slimy**
slimiest *adj* ▷ **slimy**
slimmed *v* ▷ **slim**
slimmer *adj, n* ▷ **slim**
slimmers *n* ▷ **slim**
slimmest *adj* ▷ **slim**
slimming *v* ▷ **slim**
slims *v* ▷ **slim**
slimy *adj* (**-mier, -miest**) of, like, or covered with slime
sling[1] *n* (*pl* **-s**) bandage hung from the neck to support an injured hand or arm ▶ *v* (**-s, -ing, slung**) throw
sling[2] *n* (*pl* **-s**) sweetened drink with a spirit base
slinging *v* ▷ **sling[1]**
slings *n* ▷ **sling[1,2]** ▶ *v* ▷ **sling[1]**
slink *v* (**-s, -ing, slunk**) move furtively or guiltily
slinkier *adj* ▷ **slinky**
slinkiest *adj* ▷ **slinky**
slinking *v* ▷ **slink**
slinks *v* ▷ **slink**
slinky *adj* (**-kier, -kiest**) (of clothes) figure-hugging
slip[1] *v* (**-s, -pping, -pped**) lose balance by sliding ▶ *n* (*pl* **-s**) slipping
slip[2] *n* (*pl* **-s**) small piece (of paper)

slip[3] *n* (*pl* **-s**) clay mixed with water used for decorating pottery
slipknot *n* (*pl* **-s**) knot tied so that it will slip along the rope round which it is made
slipknots *n* ▷ **slipknot**
slipped *v* ▷ **slip**[1]
slipper *n* (*pl* **-s**) light shoe for indoor wear
slipperier *adj* ▷ **slippery**
slipperiest *adj* ▷ **slippery**
slippers *n* ▷ **slipper**
slippery *adj* (**-rier, -riest**) so smooth or wet as to cause slipping or be difficult to hold
slippier *adj* ▷ **slippy**
slippiest *adj* ▷ **slippy**
slipping *v* ▷ **slip**[1]
slippy *adj* (**-ppier, -ppiest**) (*Informal*) slippery
slips *n* ▷ **slip**[1, 2, 3] ▶ *v* ▷ **slip**[1]
slipshod *adj* (of an action) careless
slipstream *n* (*pl* **-s**) stream of air forced backwards by a fast-moving object
slipstreams *n* ▷ **slipstream**
slipway *n* (*pl* **-s**) launching slope on which ships are built or repaired
slipways *n* ▷ **slipway**
slit *n* (*pl* **-s**) long narrow cut or opening ▶ *v* (**-s, -tting, slit**) make a long straight cut in
slither *v* (**-s, -ing, -ed**) slide unsteadily
slithered *v* ▷ **slither**
slithering *v* ▷ **slither**
slithers *v* ▷ **slither**
slits *n, v* ▷ **slit**
slitting *v* ▷ **slit**
sliver [**sliv**-ver] *n* (*pl* **-s**) small thin piece
slivers *n* ▷ **sliver**
slob *n* (*pl* **-s**) (*Informal*) lazy and untidy person > **slobbish** *adj*
slobber *v* (**-s, -ing, -ed**) dribble or drool > **slobbery** *adj*
slobbered *v* ▷ **slobber**
slobbering *v* ▷ **slobber**
slobbers *v* ▷ **slobber**
slobbery *adj* ▷ **slobber**
slobbish *adj* ▷ **slob**
slobs *n* ▷ **slob**
sloe *n* (*pl* **-s**) sour blue-black fruit
sloes *n* ▷ **sloe**
slog *v* (**-s, -gging, -gged**) work hard and steadily ▶ *n* (*pl* **-s**) long and exhausting work or walk
slogan *n* (*pl* **-s**) catchword or phrase used in politics or advertising
slogans *n* ▷ **slogan**
slogged *v* ▷ **slog**
slogging *v* ▷ **slog**
slogs *v, n* ▷ **slog**
sloop *n* (*pl* **-s**) small single-masted ship
sloops *n* ▷ **sloop**
slop *v* (**-s, -pping, -pped**) splash or spill ▶ *n* (*pl* **-s**) spilt liquid
slope *v* (**-pes, -ping, -ped**) slant ▶ *n* (*pl* **-s**) sloping surface
sloped *v* ▷ **slope**
slopes *v, n* ▷ **slope** ▶ *pl n* hills
sloping *v* ▷ **slope**
slopped *v* ▷ **slop**
sloppier *adj* ▷ **sloppy**
sloppiest *adj* ▷ **sloppy**
slopping *v* ▷ **slop**
sloppy *adj* (**-ppier, -ppiest**) careless or untidy
slops *v, n* ▷ **slop** ▶ *pl n* liquid refuse and waste food used to feed animals
slosh *v* (**-es, -ing, -ed**) splash carelessly ▶ *n* (*pl* **-es**) splashing sound
sloshed *adj* (*Slang*) drunk ▶ *v* ▷ **slosh**
sloshes *v, n* ▷ **slosh**
sloshing *v* ▷ **slosh**
slot *n* (*pl* **-s**) narrow opening for inserting something ▶ *v* (**-s, -tting, -tted**) make a slot or slots in
sloth [rhymes with **both**] *n* (*pl* **-s**) slow-moving animal of tropical America
slothful *adj* lazy or idle
sloths *n* ▷ **sloth**
slots *n, v* ▷ **slot**
slotted *v* ▷ **slot**
slotting *v* ▷ **slot**
slouch *v* (**-es, -ing, -ed**) sit, stand, or move with a drooping posture ▶ *n* (*pl* **-es**) drooping posture
slouched *v* ▷ **slouch**
slouches *v, n* ▷ **slouch**
slouching *v* ▷ **slouch**
slough[1] [rhymes with **now**] *n* (*pl* **-s**) bog
slough[2] [**sluff**] *v* (**-s, -ing, -ed**) (of a snake) shed (its skin) or (of a skin) be shed
sloughed *v* ▷ **slough**[2]
sloughing *v* ▷ **slough**[2]
sloughs *n* ▷ **slough**[1] ▶ *v* ▷ **slough**[2]
sloven *n* (*pl* **-s**) habitually dirty or untidy person
slovenlier *adj* ▷ **slovenly**
slovenliest *adj* ▷ **slovenly**
slovenly *adj* (**-lier, -liest**) dirty or untidy
slovens *n* ▷ **sloven**
slow *adj* (**-er, -est**) taking a longer time than is usual or expected ▶ *v* (**-s, -ing, -ed**) reduce the speed (of) > **slowly** *adv* > **slowness** *n* (*pl* **-es**)
slowcoach *n* (*pl* **-es**) (*Informal*) person who moves or works slowly
slowcoaches *n* ▷ **slowcoach**

slowed *v* ▷ **slow**
slower *adj* ▷ **slow**
slowest *adj* ▷ **slow**
slowing *v* ▷ **slow**
slowly *adv* ▷ **slow**
slowness *n* ▷ **slow**
slownesses *n* ▷ **slow**
slows *v* ▷ **slow**
slowworm *n* (*pl* **-s**) small legless lizard
slowworms *n* ▷ **slowworm**
sludge *n* (*pl* **-s**) thick mud
sludges *n* ▷ **sludge**
slug[1] *n* (*pl* **-s**) land snail with no shell
slug[2] *n* (*pl* **-s**) bullet (*Informal*)
slug[3] *v* (**-s, -gging, -gged**) hit hard ▶ *n* (*pl* **-s**) heavy blow
sluggard *n* (*pl* **-s**) lazy person
sluggards *n* ▷ **sluggard**
slugged *v* ▷ **slug**[3]
slugging *v* ▷ **slug**[3]
sluggish *adj* slow-moving, lacking energy > **sluggishly** *adv* > **sluggishness** *n* (*pl* **-es**)
sluggishly *adv* ▷ **sluggish**
sluggishness *n* ▷ **sluggish**
sluggishnesses *n* ▷ **sluggish**
slugs *n* ▷ **slug**[1, 2, 3] ▶ *v* ▷ **slug**[3]
sluice *n* (*pl* **-s**) channel carrying off water ▶ *v* (**-ces, -cing, -ced**) pour a stream of water over or through
sluiced *v* ▷ **sluice**
sluices *n, v* ▷ **sluice**
sluicing *v* ▷ **sluice**
slum *n* (*pl* **-s**) squalid overcrowded house or area ▶ *v* (**-s, -mming, -mmed**) temporarily and deliberately experience poorer places or conditions than usual
slumber *v* (**-s, -ing, -ed**) ▶ *n* (*pl* **-s**) (*Lit*) sleep
slumbered *v* ▷ **slumber**
slumbering *v* ▷ **slumber**
slumbers *v, n* ▷ **slumber**
slummed *v* ▷ **slum**
slumming *v* ▷ **slum**
slump *v* (**-s, -ing, -ed**) (of prices or demand) decline suddenly ▶ *n* (*pl* **-s**) sudden decline in prices or demand
slumped *v* ▷ **slump**
slumping *v* ▷ **slump**
slumps *v, n* ▷ **slump**
slums *n, v* ▷ **slum**
slung *v* ▷ **sling**[1]
slunk *v* ▷ **slink**
slur *v* (**-s, -rring, -rred**) pronounce or utter (words) indistinctly ▶ *n* (*pl* **-s**) slurring of words
slurp (*Informal*) *v* (**-s, -ing, -ed**) eat or drink noisily ▶ *n* (*pl* **-s**) slurping sound
slurped *v* ▷ **slurp**
slurping *v* ▷ **slurp**
slurps *v, n* ▷ **slurp**
slurred *v* ▷ **slur**
slurries *n* ▷ **slurry**
slurring *v* ▷ **slur**
slurry *n* (*pl* **-ries**) muddy liquid mixture
slurs *v, n* ▷ **slur**
slush *n* (*pl* **-es**) watery muddy substance > **slushy** *adj* (**-shier, -shiest**)
slushes *n* ▷ **slush**
slushier *adj* ▷ **slush**
slushiest *adj* ▷ **slush**
slushy *adj* ▷ **slush**
sly *adj* (**slyer, slyest** *or* **slier, sliest**) crafty > **slyly** *adv* > **slyness** *n* (*pl* **-es**)
slyer *adj* ▷ **sly**
slyest *adj* ▷ **sly**
slyly *adv* ▷ **sly**
slyness *n* ▷ **sly**
slynesses *n* ▷ **sly**
smack[1] *v* (**-s, -ing, -ed**) slap sharply ▶ *n* (*pl* **-s**) sharp slap ▶ *adv* (*Informal*) squarely or directly
smack[2] *n* (*pl* **-s**) slight flavour or trace ▶ *v* (**-s, -ing, -ed**) have a slight flavour or trace (of)
smack[3] *n* (*pl* **-s**) small single-masted fishing boat
smacked *v* ▷ **smack**[1, 2]
smacker *n* (*pl* **-s**) (*Slang*) loud kiss
smackers *n* ▷ **smacker**
smacking *v* ▷ **smack**[1, 2]
smacks *n* ▷ **smack**[1, 2, 3] ▶ *v* ▷ **smack**[1, 2]
small *adj* (**-er, -est**) not large in size, number, or amount ▶ *n* (*pl* **-s**) narrow part of the lower back > **smallness** *n* (*pl* **-es**)
smaller *adj* ▷ **small**
smallest *adj* ▷ **small**
smallholding *n* (*pl* **-s**) small area of farming land
smallholdings *n* ▷ **smallholding**
smallness *n* ▷ **small**
smallnesses *n* ▷ **small**
smallpox *n* (*pl* **-es**) contagious disease with blisters that leave scars
smallpoxes *n* ▷ **smallpox**
smalls *n* ▷ **small** ▶ *pl n* (*Informal*) underwear
smarmier *adj* ▷ **smarmy**
smarmiest *adj* ▷ **smarmy**
smarmy *adj* (**-mier, -miest**) (*Informal*) unpleasantly suave or flattering
smart *adj* (**-er, -est**) well-kept and neat ▶ *v* (**-s, -ing, -ed**) feel or cause stinging pain ▶ *n* (*pl* **-s**) stinging pain > **smartly** *adv* > **smartness** *n* (*pl* **-es**)

smarted *v* ▷ **smart**
smarten *v* **(-s, -ing, -ed)** make or become smart
smartened *v* ▷ **smarten**
smartening *v* ▷ **smarten**
smartens *v* ▷ **smarten**
smarter *adj* ▷ **smart**
smartest *adj* ▷ **smart**
smarting *v* ▷ **smart**
smartly *adv* ▷ **smart**
smartness *n* ▷ **smart**
smartnesses *n* ▷ **smart**
smarts *v, n* ▷ **smart**
smash *v* **(-es, -ing, -ed)** break violently and noisily ▶ *n* (*pl* **-es**) act or sound of smashing
smashed *v* ▷ **smash**
smasher *n* (*pl* **-s**) (*Informal*) attractive person or thing
smashers *n* ▷ **smasher**
smashes *v, n* ▷ **smash**
smashing *adj* (*Informal*) excellent ▶ *v* ▷ **smash**
smattering *n* (*pl* **-s**) slight knowledge
smatterings *n* ▷ **smattering**
smear *v* **(-s, -ing, -ed)** spread with a greasy or sticky substance ▶ *n* (*pl* **-s**) dirty mark or smudge
smeared *v* ▷ **smear**
smearing *v* ▷ **smear**
smears *v, n* ▷ **smear**
smell *v* **(-s, -ing, smelt** *or* **-ed)** perceive (a scent or odour) by means of the nose ▶ *n* (*pl* **-s**) ability to perceive odours by the nose
smelled *v* ▷ **smell**
smellier *adj* ▷ **smelly**
smelliest *adj* ▷ **smelly**
smelling *v* ▷ **smell**
smells *v, n* ▷ **smell**
smelly *adj* **(-llier, -lliest)** having a nasty smell
smelt¹ *v* **(-s, -ing, -ed)** extract (a metal) from (an ore) by heating
smelt² *n* (*pl* **smelt**) small fish of the salmon family
smelt³ *v* ▷ **smell**
smelted *v* ▷ **smelt¹**
smelter *n* (*pl* **-s**) industrial plant where smelting is carried out
smelters *n* ▷ **smelter**
smelting *v* ▷ **smelt¹**
smelts *v* ▷ **smelt¹**
smile *n* (*pl* **-s**) turning up of the corners of the mouth to show pleasure, amusement, or friendliness ▶ *v* **(-les, -ing, -led)** give a smile
smiled *v* ▷ **smile**
smiles *n, v* ▷ **smile**
smiley *n* (*pl* **-s**) symbol depicting a smile or other facial expression, used in e-mail
smileys *n* ▷ **smiley**
smiling *v* ▷ **smile**
smirch *v* **(-es, -ing, -ed)** ▶ *n* (*pl* **-es**) stain
smirched *v* ▷ **smirch**
smirches *v, n* ▷ **smirch**
smirching *v* ▷ **smirch**
smirk *n* (*pl* **-s**) smug smile ▶ *v* **(-s, -ing, -ed)** give a smirk
smirked *v* ▷ **smirk**
smirking *v* ▷ **smirk**
smirks *n, v* ▷ **smirk**
smite *v* **(-tes, -ting, smote, smitten)** (*Old-fashioned*) strike hard
smites *v* ▷ **smite**
smith *n* (*pl* **-s**) worker in metal
smithereens *pl n* shattered fragments
smithies *n* ▷ **smithy**
smiths *n* ▷ **smith**
smithy *n* (*pl* **-thies**) blacksmith's workshop
smiting *v* ▷ **smite**
smitten *v* ▷ **smite**
smock *n* (*pl* **-s**) loose overall ▶ *v* **(-s, -ing, -ed)** gather (material) by sewing in a honeycomb pattern > **smocking** *n* (*pl* **-s**)
smocked *v* ▷ **smock**
smocking *v, n* ▷ **smock**
smockings *n* ▷ **smock**
smocks *n, v* ▷ **smock**
smog *n* (*pl* **-s**) mixture of smoke and fog
smogs *n* ▷ **smog**
smoke *n* (*pl* **-s**) cloudy mass that rises from something burning ▶ *v* **(-kes, -king, -ked)** give off smoke > **smokeless** *adj* > **smoker** *n* (*pl* **-s**) > **smoky** *adj* **(-kier, -kiest)**
smoked *v* ▷ **smoke**
smokeless *adj* ▷ **smoke**
smoker *n* ▷ **smok**
smokers *n* ▷ **smok**
smokes *n, v* ▷ **smoke**
smokier *adj* ▷ **smoke**
smokiest *adj* ▷ **smoke**
smoking *v* ▷ **smoke**
smoky *adj* ▷ **smoke**
smooch (*Informal*) *v* **(-es, -ing, -ed)** kiss and cuddle ▶ *n* (*pl* **-es**) smooching
smooched *v* ▷ **smooch**
smooches *v, n* ▷ **smooch**
smooching *v* ▷ **smooch**
smooth *adj* **(-er, -est)** even in surface, texture, or consistency ▶ *v* **(-s, -ing, -ed)** make smooth > **smoothly** *adv*
smoothed *v* ▷ **smooth**
smoother *adj* ▷ **smooth**
smoothest *adj* ▷ **smooth**

smoothie *n* (*pl* **-thies**) (*Informal*) charming but possibly insincere man
smoothies *n* ▷ **smoothie**
smoothing *v* ▷ **smooth**
smoothly *adv* ▷ **smooth**
smooths *v* ▷ **smooth**
smorgasbord *n* (*pl* **-s**) buffet meal of assorted dishes
smorgasbords *n* ▷ **smorgasbord**
smote *v* ▷ **smite**
smother *v* (**-s, -ing, -ed**) suffocate or stifle
smothered *v* ▷ **smother**
smothering *v* ▷ **smother**
smothers *v* ▷ **smother**
smoulder *v* (**-s, -ing, -ed**) burn slowly with smoke but no flame
smouldered *v* ▷ **smoulder**
smouldering *v* ▷ **smoulder**
smoulders *v* ▷ **smoulder**
smudge *v* (**-ges, -ging, -ged**) make or become smeared or soiled ▶ *n* (*pl* **-s**) dirty mark > **smudgy** *adj* (**-gier, -giest**)
smudged *v* ▷ **smudge**
smudges *v, n* ▷ **smudge**
smudgier *adj* ▷ **smudge**
smudgiest *adj* ▷ **smudge**
smudging *v* ▷ **smudge**
smudgy *adj* ▷ **smudge**
smug *adj* (**-gger, -ggest**) self-satisfied > **smugly** *adv* > **smugness** *n* (*pl* **-es**)
smugger *adj* ▷ **smug**
smuggest *adj* ▷ **smug**
smuggle *v* (**-les, -ling, -led**) import or export (goods) secretly and illegally > **smuggler** *n* (*pl* **-s**)
smuggled *v* ▷ **smuggle**
smuggler *n* ▷ **smuggle**
smugglers *n* ▷ **smuggle**
smuggles *v* ▷ **smuggle**
smuggling *v* ▷ **smuggle**
smugly *adv* ▷ **smug**
smugness *n* ▷ **smug**
smugnesses *n* ▷ **smug**
smut *n* (*pl* **-s**) obscene jokes, pictures, etc. > **smutty** *adj* (**-ttier, -ttiest**)
smuts *n* ▷ **smut**
smuttier *adj* ▷ **smut**
smuttiest *adj* ▷ **smut**
smutty *adj* ▷ **smut**
snack *n* (*pl* **-s**) light quick meal
snacks *n* ▷ **snack**
snaffle *n* (*pl* **-s**) jointed bit for a horse ▶ *v* (**-les, -ling, -led**) (BRIT, AUST & NZ) (*Slang*) steal
snaffled *v* ▷ **snaffle**
snaffles *n, v* ▷ **snaffle**
snaffling *v* ▷ **snaffle**
snag *n* (*pl* **-s**) difficulty or disadvantage ▶ *v* (**-s, -gging, -gged**) catch or tear on a point
snagged *v* ▷ **snag**
snagging *v* ▷ **snag**
snags *n, v* ▷ **snag**
snail *n* (*pl* **-s**) slow-moving mollusc with a spiral shell
snails *n* ▷ **snail**
snake *n* (*pl* **-s**) long thin scaly limbless reptile ▶ *v* (**-kes, -king, -ked**) move in a winding course like a snake
snaked *v* ▷ **snake**
snakes *n, v* ▷ **snake**
snakier *adj* ▷ **snaky**
snakiest *adj* ▷ **snaky**
snaking *v* ▷ **snake**
snaky *adj* (**-kier, -kiest**) twisted or winding
snap *v* (**-s, -pping, -pped**) break suddenly ▶ *n* (*pl* **-s**) act or sound of snapping ▶ *adj* made on the spur of the moment
snapdragon *n* (*pl* **-s**) plant with flowers that can open and shut like a mouth
snapdragons *n* ▷ **snapdragon**
snapped *v* ▷ **snap**
snapper *n* (*pl* **-s**) food fish of Australia and New Zealand with a pinkish body covered with blue spots
snappers *n* ▷ **snapper**
snappier *adj* ▷ **snappy**
snappiest *adj* ▷ **snappy**
snapping *v* ▷ **snap**
snappish *adj* ▷ **snappy**
snappy *adj* (**-ppier, -ppiest**) (*also* **snappish**) irritable
snaps *v, n* ▷ **snap**
snapshot *n* (*pl* **-s**) informal photograph
snapshots *n* ▷ **snapshot**
snare *n* (*pl* **-s**) trap with a noose ▶ *v* (**-res, -ring, -red**) catch in or as if in a snare
snared *v* ▷ **snare**
snares *n, v* ▷ **snare**
snaring *v* ▷ **snare**
snarl[1] *v* (**-s, -ing, -ed**) (of an animal) growl with bared teeth ▶ *n* (*pl* **-s**) act or sound of snarling
snarl[2] *n* (*pl* **-s**) tangled mess ▶ *v* (**-s, -ing, -ed**) make tangled
snarled *v* ▷ **snarl[1, 2]**
snarling *v* ▷ **snarl[1, 2]**
snarls *n, v* ▷ **snarl[1, 2]**
snatch *v* (**-es, -ing, -ed**) seize or try to seize suddenly ▶ *n* (*pl* **-es**) snatching
snatched *v* ▷ **snatch**
snatches *v, n* ▷ **snatch**
snatching *v* ▷ **snatch**

snazzier *adj* ▷ **snazzy**
snazziest *adj* ▷ **snazzy**
snazzy *adj* (**-zzier, -zziest**) (*Informal*) stylish and flashy
sneak *v* (**-s, -ing, -ed**) move furtively ▶ *n* (*pl* **-s**) cowardly or underhand person > **sneaky** *adj* (**-kier, -kiest**)
sneaked *v* ▷ **sneak**
sneakers *pl n* canvas shoes with rubber soles
sneakier *adj* ▷ **sneak**
sneakiest *adj* ▷ **sneak**
sneaking *adj* slight but persistent ▶ *v* ▷ **sneak**
sneaks *v, n* ▷ **sneak**
sneaky *adj* ▷ **sneak**
sneer *n* (*pl* **-s**) contemptuous expression or remark ▶ *v* (**-s, -ing, -ed**) show contempt by a sneer
sneered *v* ▷ **sneer**
sneering *v* ▷ **sneer**
sneers *n, v* ▷ **sneer**
sneeze *v* (**-zes, -zing, -zed**) expel air from the nose suddenly, involuntarily, and noisily ▶ *n* (*pl* **-s**) act or sound of sneezing
sneezed *v* ▷ **sneeze**
sneezes *v, n* ▷ **sneeze**
sneezing *v* ▷ **sneeze**
snicker *n* (*pl* **-s**) ▶ *v* (**-s, -ing, -ed**) ▷ **snigger**
snickered *v* ▷ **snicker**
snickering *v* ▷ **snicker**
snickers *n, v* ▷ **snicker**
snide *adj* (**-r, -st**) critical in an unfair and nasty way
snider *adj* ▷ **snide**
snidest *adj* ▷ **snide**
sniff *v* (**-s, -ing, -ed**) inhale through the nose in short audible breaths ▶ *n* (*pl* **-s**) act or sound of sniffing
sniffed *v* ▷ **sniff**
sniffing *v* ▷ **sniff**
sniffle *v* (**-les, -ling, -led**) sniff repeatedly, as when suffering from a cold ▶ *n* (*pl* **-s**) slight cold
sniffled *v* ▷ **sniffle**
sniffles *v, n* ▷ **sniffle**
sniffling *v* ▷ **sniffle**
sniffs *v, n* ▷ **sniff**
snifter *n* (*pl* **-s**) (*Informal*) small quantity of alcoholic drink
snifters *n* ▷ **snifter**
snigger *n* (*pl* **-s**) sly disrespectful laugh, esp. one partly stifled ▶ *v* (**-s, -ing, -ed**) utter a snigger
sniggered *v* ▷ **snigger**
sniggering *v* ▷ **snigger**
sniggers *n, v* ▷ **snigger**
snip *v* (**-s, -pping, -pped**) cut in small quick strokes with scissors or shears ▶ *n* (*pl* **-s**) (*Informal*) bargain
snipe *n* (*pl* **-s**) wading bird with a long straight bill ▶ *v* (**-pes, -ping, -ped**) (*foll. by* **at**) shoot at (a person) from cover
sniped *v* ▷ **snipe**
sniper *n* (*pl* **-s**) person who shoots at someone from cover
snipers *n* ▷ **sniper**
snipes *n, v* ▷ **snipe**
sniping *v* ▷ **snipe**
snipped *v* ▷ **snip**
snippet *n* (*pl* **-s**) small piece
snippets *n* ▷ **snippet**
snipping *v* ▷ **snip**
snips *v, n* ▷ **snip**
snitch (*Informal*) *v* (**-es, -ing, -ed**) act as an informer ▶ *n* (*pl* **-es**) informer
snitched *v* ▷ **snitch**
snitches *v, n* ▷ **snitch**
snitching *v* ▷ **snitch**
snivel *v* (**-s, -lling, -lled**) cry in a whining way
snivelled *v* ▷ **snivel**
snivelling *v* ▷ **snivel**
snivels *v* ▷ **snivel**
snob *n* (*pl* **-s**) person who judges others by social rank > **snobbery** *n* (*pl* **-ries**) > **snobbish** *adj*
snobberies *n* ▷ **snob**
snobbery *n* ▷ **snob**
snobbish *adj* ▷ **snob**
snobs *n* ▷ **snob**
snoek *n* (*pl* **-s**) (S AFR) edible marine fish
snoeks *n* ▷ **snoek**
snood *n* (*pl* **-s**) pouch, often of net, loosely holding a woman's hair at the back
snoods *n* ▷ **snood**
snook *n* (*pl* **-s**) gesture of contempt
snooker *n* (*pl* **-s**) game played on a billiard table ▶ *v* (**-s, -ing, -ed**) leave (a snooker opponent) in a position such that another ball blocks the target ball
snookered *v* ▷ **snooker**
snookering *v* ▷ **snooker**
snookers *n, v* ▷ **snooker**
snooks *n* ▷ **snook**
snoop (*Informal*) *v* (**-s, -ing, -ed**) pry ▶ *n* (*pl* **-s**) snooping > **snooper** *n* (*pl* **-s**)
snooped *v* ▷ **snoop**
snooper *n* ▷ **snoop**
snoopers *n* ▷ **snoop**
snooping *v* ▷ **snoop**
snoops *v, n* ▷ **snoop**
snootier *adj* ▷ **snooty**

snootiest *adj* ▷ **snooty**
snooty *adj* (**-tier, -tiest**) (*Informal*) haughty
snooze (*Informal*) *v* (**-zes, -zing, -zed**) take a brief light sleep ▶ *n* (*pl* **-s**) brief light sleep
snoozed *v* ▷ **snooze**
snoozes *v, n* ▷ **snooze**
snoozing *v* ▷ **snooze**
snore *v* (**-res, -ring, -red**) make snorting sounds while sleeping ▶ *n* (*pl* **-s**) sound of snoring
snored *v* ▷ **snore**
snores *v, n* ▷ **snore**
snoring *v* ▷ **snore**
snorkel *n* (*pl* **-s**) tube allowing a swimmer to breathe while face down on the surface of the water ▶ *v* (**-s, -lling, -lled**) swim using a snorkel
snorkelled *v* ▷ **snorkel**
snorkelling *v* ▷ **snorkel**
snorkels *n, v* ▷ **snorkel**
snort *v* (**-s, -ing, -ed**) exhale noisily through the nostrils ▶ *n* (*pl* **-s**) act or sound of snorting
snorted *v* ▷ **snort**
snorting *v* ▷ **snort**
snorts *v, n* ▷ **snort**
snot *n* (*pl* **-s**) (*Slang*) mucus from the nose
snots *n* ▷ **snot**
snout *n* (*pl* **-s**) animal's projecting nose and jaws
snouts *n* ▷ **snout**
snow *n* (*pl* **-s**) frozen vapour falling from the sky in flakes ▶ *v* (**-s, -ing, -ed**) fall as or like snow > **snowy** *adj* (**-wier, -wiest**)
snowball *n* (*pl* **-s**) snow pressed into a ball for throwing ▶ *v* (**-s, -ing, -ed**) increase rapidly
snowballed *v* ▷ **snowball**
snowballing *v* ▷ **snowball**
snowballs *n, v* ▷ **snowball**
snowboard *n* (*pl* **-s**) board on which a person stands to slide across the snow > **snowboarding** *n* (*pl* **-s**)
snowboarding *n* ▷ **snowboard**
snowboardings *n* ▷ **snowboard**
snowboards *n* ▷ **snowboard**
snowdrift *n* (*pl* **-s**) bank of deep snow
snowdrifts *n* ▷ **snowdrift**
snowdrop *n* (*pl* **-s**) small white bell-shaped spring flower
snowdrops *n* ▷ **snowdrop**
snowed *v* ▷ **snow**
snowflake *n* (*pl* **-s**) single crystal of snow
snowflakes *n* ▷ **snowflake**
snowier *adj* ▷ **snow**
snowiest *adj* ▷ **snow**
snowing *v* ▷ **snow**
snowman *n* (*pl* **-men**) figure shaped out of snow
snowmen *n* ▷ **snowman**
snowplough *n* (*pl* **-s**) vehicle for clearing away snow
snowploughs *n* ▷ **snowplough**
snows *n, v* ▷ **snow**
snowshoes *pl n* racket-shaped shoes for travelling on snow
snowy *adj* ▷ **snow**
snub *v* (**-s, -bbing, -bbed**) insult deliberately ▶ *n* (*pl* **-s**) deliberate insult ▶ *adj* (of a nose) short and blunt
snubbed *v* ▷ **snub**
snubbing *v* ▷ **snub**
snubs *v, n* ▷ **snub**
snuff[1] *n* (*pl* **-s**) powdered tobacco for sniffing up the nostrils
snuff[2] *v* (**-s, -ing, -ed**) extinguish (a candle)
snuffed *v* ▷ **snuff**[2]
snuffing *v* ▷ **snuff**[2]
snuffle *v* (**-les, -ling, -led**) breathe noisily or with difficulty
snuffled *v* ▷ **snuffle**
snuffles *v* ▷ **snuffle**
snuffling *v* ▷ **snuffle**
snuffs *n* ▷ **snuff**[1] ▶ *v* ▷ **snuff**[2]
snug *adj* (**-gger, -ggest**) warm and comfortable ▶ *n* (*pl* **-s**) (in Britain and Ireland) small room in a pub > **snugly** *adv*
snugger *adj* ▷ **snug**
snuggest *adj* ▷ **snug**
snuggle *v* (**-les, -ling, -led**) nestle into a person or thing for warmth or from affection
snuggled *v* ▷ **snuggle**
snuggles *v* ▷ **snuggle**
snuggling *v* ▷ **snuggle**
snugly *adv* ▷ **snug**
snugs *n* ▷ **snug**

> **sny** *n* (**snys**). Sny is a Canadian word for a side channel of a river. This word doesn't contain a vowel, so it can help you to clear an awkward rack. Sny scores 6 points.

so *adv* to such an extent ▶ *conj* in order that ▶ *interj* exclamation of surprise, triumph, or realization
soak *v* (**-s, -ing, -ed**) make wet ▶ *n* (*pl* **-s**) soaking > **soaking** *n* (*pl* **-s**) *adj*
soaked *v* ▷ **soak**
soaking *v, n, adj* ▷ **soak**
soakings *n* ▷ **soak**
soaks *v, n* ▷ **soak**
soap *n* (*pl* **-s**) compound of alkali and fat, used with water as a cleaning agent ▶ *v* (**-s, -ing,**

-ed) apply soap to > **soapy** *adj* (**-pier, -piest**)

soaped *v* ▷ **soap**

soapier *adj* ▷ **soap**

soapiest *adj* ▷ **soap**

soaping *v* ▷ **soap**

soaps *n, v* ▷ **soap**

soapy *adj* ▷ **soap**

soar *v* (**-s, -ing, -ed**) rise or fly upwards

soared *v* ▷ **soar**

soaring *v* ▷ **soar**

soars *v* ▷ **soar**

sob *v* (**-s, -bbing, -bbed**) weep with convulsive gasps ▶ *n* (*pl* **-s**) act or sound of sobbing

sobbed *v* ▷ **sob**

sobbing *v* ▷ **sob**

sober *adj* (**-er, -est**) not drunk ▶ *v* (**-s, -ing, -ed**) make or become sober > **soberly** *adv*

sobered *v* ▷ **sober**

soberer *adj* ▷ **sober**

soberest *adj* ▷ **sober**

sobering *v* ▷ **sober**

soberly *adv* ▷ **sober**

sobers *v* ▷ **sober**

sobrieties *n* ▷ **sobriety**

sobriety *n* (*pl* **-ties**) state of being sober

sobriquet [**so**-brik-ay] *n* (*pl* **-s**) nickname

sobriquets *n* ▷ **sobriquet**

sobs *v, n* ▷ **sob**

soccer *n* (*pl* **-s**) football played by two teams of eleven kicking a spherical ball

soccers *n* ▷ **soccer**

sociabilities *n* ▷ **sociable**

sociability *n* ▷ **sociable**

sociable *adj* friendly or companionable > **sociability** *n* (*pl* **-ties**) > **sociably** *adv*

sociably *adv* ▷ **sociable**

social *adj* living in a community ▶ *n* (*pl* **-s**) informal gathering > **socially** *adv*

socialism *n* (*pl* **-s**) political system which advocates public ownership of industries, resources, and transport

socialisms *n* ▷ **socialism**

socialist *n* (*pl* **-s**) ▶ *adj*

socialists *n* ▷ **socialist**

socialite *n* (*pl* **-s**) member of fashionable society

socialites *n* ▷ **socialite**

socialize *v* (**-zes, -zing, -zed**) meet others socially

socialized *v* ▷ **socialize**

socializes *v* ▷ **socialize**

socializing *v* ▷ **socialize**

socially *adv* ▷ **social**

socials *n* ▷ **social**

societies *n* ▷ **society**

society *n* (*pl* **-ties**) human beings considered as a group

sociological *adj* ▷ **sociology**

sociologies *n* ▷ **sociology**

sociologist *n* ▷ **sociology**

sociologists *n* ▷ **sociology**

sociology *n* (*pl* **-gies**) study of human societies > **sociological** *adj* > **sociologist** *n* (*pl* **-s**)

sock[1] *n* (*pl* **-s**) knitted covering for the foot

sock[2] (*Slang*) *v* (**-s, -ing, -ed**) hit hard ▶ *n* (*pl* **-s**) hard blow

socked *v* ▷ **sock**[2]

socket *n* (*pl* **-s**) hole or recess into which something fits

sockets *n* ▷ **socket**

socking *v* ▷ **sock**[2]

socks *v* ▷ **sock**[2] ▶ *n* ▷ **sock**[1, 2]

sod *n* (*pl* **-s**) (piece of) turf

soda *n* (*pl* **-s**) compound of sodium

sodas *n* ▷ **soda**

sodden *adj* soaked

sodium *n* (*pl* **-s**) (CHEM) silvery-white metallic element

sodiums *n* ▷ **sodium**

sods *n* ▷ **sod**

sofa *n* (*pl* **-s**) couch

sofas *n* ▷ **sofa**

soft *adj* (**-er, -s**) easy to shape or cut > **softly** *adv*

soften *v* (**-s, -ing, -ed**) make or become soft or softer

softened *v* ▷ **soften**

softening *v* ▷ **soften**

softens *v* ▷ **soften**

softer *adj* ▷ **soft**

softest *adj* ▷ **soft**

softly *adv* ▷ **soft**

software *n* (*pl* **-s**) computer programs

softwares *n* ▷ **software**

softwood *n* (*pl* **-s**) wood of a coniferous tree

softwoods *n* ▷ **softwood**

soggier *adj* ▷ **soggy**

soggiest *adj* ▷ **soggy**

sogginess *n* ▷ **soggy**

sogginesses *n* ▷ **soggy**

soggy *adj* (**-ggier, -ggiest**) soaked > **sogginess** *n* (*pl* **-es**)

soigné, *fem* **soignée** [**swah**-nyay] *adj* well-groomed, elegant

soil[1] *n* (*pl* **-s**) top layer of earth

soil[2] *v* (**-s, -ing, -ed**) make or become dirty

soiled *v* ▷ **soil**

soiling *v* ▷ **soil**

soils *n* ▷ **soil**[1] ▶ *v* ▷ **soil**[2]

soiree [**swah**-ray] *n* (*pl* **-s**) evening party or gathering

soirees *n* ▷ **soiree**
sojourn [**soj**-urn] *n* (*pl* **-s**) temporary stay ▶ *v* (**-s, -ing, -ed**) stay temporarily
sojourned *v* ▷ **sojourn**
sojourning *v* ▷ **sojourn**
sojourns *n, v* ▷ **sojourn**
solace [**sol**-iss] *n, v* (**-ces, -cing, -ced**) comfort in distress
solaced *v* ▷ **solace**
solaces *v* ▷ **solace**
solacing *v* ▷ **solace**
solar *adj* of the sun
solaria *n* ▷ **solarium**
solarium *n* (*pl* **-riums, -ria**) place with beds and ultraviolet lights used for acquiring an artificial suntan
solariums *n* ▷ **solarium**
sold *v* ▷ **sell**
solder *n* (*pl* **-s**) soft alloy used to join two metal surfaces ▶ *v* (**-s, -ing, -ed**) join with solder
soldered *v* ▷ **solder**
soldering *v* ▷ **solder**
solders *n, v* ▷ **solder**
soldier *n* (*pl* **-s**) member of an army ▶ *v* (**-s, -ing, -ed**) serve in an army > **soldierly** *adj*
soldiered *v* ▷ **soldier**
soldiering *v* ▷ **soldier**
soldierly *adj* ▷ **soldier**
soldiers *n, v* ▷ **soldier**
sole¹ *adj* one and only
sole² *n* (*pl* **-s**) underside of the foot ▶ *v* (**-les, -ling, -led**) provide (a shoe) with a sole
sole³ *n* (*pl* **-s**) small edible flatfish
solecism [**sol**-iss-izz-um] *n* (*pl* **-s**) minor grammatical mistake
solecisms *n* ▷ **solecism**
soled *v* ▷ **sole²**
solely *adv* only, completely
solemn *adj* (**-er, -est**) serious, deeply sincere > **solemnly** *adv* > **solemnity** *n* (*pl* **-ties**)
solemner *adj* ▷ **solemn**
solemnest *adj* ▷ **solemn**
solemnities *n* ▷ **solemn**
solemnity *n* ▷ **solemn**
solemnly *adv* ▷ **solemn**
solenoid [**sole**-in-oid] *n* (*pl* **-s**) coil of wire magnetized by passing a current through it
solenoids *n* ▷ **solenoid**
soles *n* ▷ **sole²,³** ▶ *v* ▷ **sole²**
solicit *v* (**-s, -ing, -ed**) request > **solicitation** *n* (*pl* **-s**)
solicitation *n* ▷ **solicit**
solicitations *n* ▷ **solicit**
solicited *v* ▷ **solicit**
soliciting *v* ▷ **solicit**
solicitor *n* (*pl* **-s**) (BRIT, AUST & NZ) lawyer who advises clients and prepares documents and cases
solicitors *n* ▷ **solicitor**
solicitous *adj* anxious about someone's welfare > **solicitude** *n* (*pl* **-s**)
solicits *v* ▷ **solicit**
solicitude *n* ▷ **solicitous**
solicitudes *n* ▷ **solicitous**
solid *adj* (**-er, -est**) (of a substance) keeping its shape ▶ *n* (*pl* **-s**) three-dimensional shape > **solidity** *n* (*pl* **-ties**) > **solidly** *adv*
solidarities *n* ▷ **solidarity**
solidarity *n* (*pl* **-ties**) agreement in aims or interests, total unity
solider *adj* ▷ **solid**
solidest *adj* ▷ **solid**
solidified *v* ▷ **solidify**
solidifies *v* ▷ **solidify**
solidify *v* (**-fies, -fying, -fied**) make or become solid or firm
solidifying *v* ▷ **solidify**
solidities *n* ▷ **solid**
solidity *n* ▷ **solid**
solidly *adv* ▷ **solid**
solids *n* ▷ **solid**
soliloquies *n* ▷ **soliloquy**
soliloquy *n* (*pl* **-quies**) speech made by a person while alone, esp. in a play
soling *v* ▷ **sole²**
solipsism *n* (*pl* **-s**) doctrine that the self is the only thing known to exist > **solipsist** *n* (*pl* **-s**)
solipsisms *n* ▷ **solipsism**
solipsist *n* ▷ **solipsism**
solipsists *n* ▷ **solipsism**
solitaire *n* (*pl* **-s**) game for one person played with pegs set in a board
solitaires *n* ▷ **solitaire**
solitary *adj* alone, single
solitude *n* (*pl* **-s**) state of being alone
solitudes *n* ▷ **solitude**
solo *n* (*pl* **-s**) music for one performer ▶ *adj* done alone ▶ *adv* by oneself, alone > **soloist** *n* (*pl* **-s**)
soloist *n* ▷ **solo**
soloists *n* ▷ **solo**
solos *n* ▷ **solo**
solstice *n* (*pl* **-s**) either the shortest (in winter) or longest (in summer) day of the year
solstices *n* ▷ **solstice**
solubilities *n* ▷ **soluble**
solubility *n* ▷ **soluble**
soluble *adj* able to be dissolved > **solubility** *n* (*pl* **-ties**)
solution *n* (*pl* **-s**) answer to a problem
solutions *n* ▷ **solution**

solvable *adj* ▷ **solve**
solve *v* (**-ves, -ving, -ved**) find the answer to (a problem) > **solvable** *adj*
solved *v* ▷ **solve**
solvencies *n* ▷ **solvent**
solvency *n* ▷ **solvent**
solvent *adj* having enough money to pay one's debts ▶ *n* (*pl* **-s**) liquid capable of dissolving other substances > **solvency** *n* (*pl* **-cies**)
solvents *n* ▷ **solvent**
solves *v* ▷ **solve**
solving *v* ▷ **solve**
sombre *adj* (**-r, -st**) dark, gloomy
sombrer *adj* ▷ **sombre**
sombrero *n* (*pl* **-s**) wide-brimmed Mexican hat
sombreros *n* ▷ **sombrero**
sombrest *adj* ▷ **sombre**
some *adj* unknown or unspecified (*Informal*) ▶ *pron* certain unknown or unspecified people or things
somebodies *n* ▷ **somebody**
somebody *pron* some person ▶ *n* (*pl* **-dies**) important person
somehow *adv* in some unspecified way
someone *pron* somebody
somersault *n* (*pl* **-s**) leap or roll in which the trunk and legs are turned over the head ▶ *v* (**-s, -ing, -ed**) perform a somersault
somersaulted *v* ▷ **somersault**
somersaulting *v* ▷ **somersault**
somersaults *n, v* ▷ **somersault**
something *pron* unknown or unspecified thing or amount
sometime *adv* at some unspecified time ▶ *adj* former
sometimes *adv* from time to time, now and then
somewhat *adv* to some extent, rather
somewhere *adv* in, to, or at some unspecified or unknown place
somnambulism *n* ▷ **somnambulist**
somnambulisms *n* ▷ **somnambulist**
somnambulist *n* (*pl* **-s**) person who walks in his or her sleep > **somnambulism** *n* (*pl* **-s**)
somnambulists *n* ▷ **somnambulist**
somnolent *adj* drowsy
son *n* (*pl* **-s**) male offspring
sonar *n* (*pl* **-s**) device for detecting underwater objects by the reflection of sound waves
sonars *n* ▷ **sonar**
sonata *n* (*pl* **-s**) piece of music in several movements for one instrument with or without piano
sonatas *n* ▷ **sonata**
song *n* (*pl* **-s**) music for the voice
songbird *n* (*pl* **-s**) any bird with a musical call
songbirds *n* ▷ **songbird**
songs *n* ▷ **song**
songster, songstress *n* (*pl* **-s, -es**) singer
songsters *n* ▷ **songster**
songstress *n* ▷ **songster**
songstresses *n* ▷ **songster**
sonic *adj* of or producing sound
sonnet *n* (*pl* **-s**) fourteen-line poem with a fixed rhyme scheme
sonnets *n* ▷ **sonnet**
sonorities *n* ▷ **sonorous**
sonority *n* ▷ **sonorous**
sonorous *adj* (of sound) deep or resonant > **sonorously** *adv* > **sonority** *n* (*pl* **-ties**)
sonorously *adv* ▷ **sonorous**
sons *n* ▷ **son**
soon *adv* in a short time
sooner *adv* rather
soot *n* (*pl* **-s**) black powder formed by the incomplete burning of an organic substance > **sooty** *adj* (**-tier, -tiest**)
soothe *v* (**-thes, -thing, -thed**) make calm
soothed *v* ▷ **soothe**
soothes *v* ▷ **soothe**
soothing *v* ▷ **soothe**
soothsayer *n* (*pl* **-s**) seer or prophet
soothsayers *n* ▷ **soothsayer**
sootier *adj* ▷ **soot**
sootiest *adj* ▷ **soot**
soots *n* ▷ **soot**
sooty *adj* ▷ **soot**
sop *n* (*pl* **-s**) concession to pacify someone ▶ *v* (**-s, -pping, -pped**) mop up or absorb (liquid)
sophism *n* ▷ **sophistry**
sophisms *n* ▷ **sophistry**
sophist *n* (*pl* **-s**) person who uses clever but invalid arguments
sophisticate *v* (**-tes, -ting, -ted**) make less natural or innocent ▶ *n* (*pl* **-s**) sophisticated person
sophisticated *adj* having or appealing to refined or cultured tastes and habits ▶ *v* ▷ **sophisticate** > **sophistication** *n* (*pl* **-s**)
sophisticates *v, n* ▷ **sophisticate**
sophisticating *v* ▷ **sophisticate**
sophistication *n* ▷ **sophisticated**
sophistications *n* ▷ **sophisticated**
sophistries *n* ▷ **sophistry**
sophistry, sophism *n* (*pl* **-ries, -s**) clever but invalid argument
sophists *n* ▷ **sophist**
sophomore *n* (*pl* **-s**) (US) student in second year at college
sophomores *n* ▷ **sophomore**

soporific *adj* causing sleep ▶ *n* (*pl* **-s**) drug that causes sleep
soporifics *n* ▷ **soporific**
sopped *v* ▷ **sop**
soppier *adj* ▷ **soppy**
soppiest *adj* ▷ **soppy**
sopping *adj* completely soaked ▶ *v* ▷ **sop**
soppy *adj* (**soppier, soppiest**) (*Informal*) oversentimental
soprano *n* (*pl* **-s**) (singer with) the highest female or boy's voice
sopranos *n* ▷ **soprano**
sops *n, v* ▷ **sop**
sorbet *n* (*pl* **-s**) flavoured water ice
sorbets *n* ▷ **sorbet**
sorcerer *n* (*pl* **-s**) magician > **sorceress** *n fem* (*pl* **-s**)
sorcerers *n* ▷ **sorcerer**
sorceress *n* ▷ **sorcerer**
sorceresses *n* ▷ **sorcerer**
sorceries *n* ▷ **sorcery**
sorcery *n* (*pl* **-ries**) witchcraft or magic
sordid *adj* (**-er, -est**) dirty, squalid > **sordidly** *adv* > **sordidness** *n* (*pl* **-es**)
sordider *adj* ▷ **sordid**
sordidest *adj* ▷ **sordid**
sordidly *adv* ▷ **sordid**
sordidness *n* ▷ **sordid**
sordidnesses *n* ▷ **sordid**
sore *adj* (**-r, -st**) painful ▶ *n* (*pl* **-s**) painful area on the body ▶ *adv* (*Obs*) greatly > **soreness** *n* (*pl* **-es**)
sorely *adv* greatly
soreness *n* ▷ **sore**
sorenesses *n* ▷ **sore**
sorer *adj* ▷ **sore**
sores *n* ▷ **sore**
sorest *adj* ▷ **sore**
sorghum *n* (*pl* **-s**) kind of grass cultivated for grain
sorghums *n* ▷ **sorghum**
sorrel *n* (*pl* **-s**) bitter-tasting plant
sorrels *n* ▷ **sorrel**
sorrier *adj* ▷ **sorry**
sorriest *adj* ▷ **sorry**
sorrow *n* (*pl* **-s**) grief or sadness ▶ *v* (**-s, -ing, -ed**) grieve > **sorrowful** *adj* > **sorrowfully** *adv*
sorrowed *v* ▷ **sorrow**
sorrowful *adj* ▷ **sorrow**
sorrowfully *adv* ▷ **sorrow**
sorrowing *v* ▷ **sorrow**
sorrows *n, v* ▷ **sorrow**
sorry *adj* (**-rier, -riest**) feeling pity or regret
sort *n* (*pl* **-s**) group all sharing certain qualities or characteristics ▶ *v* (**-s, -ing, -ed**) arrange according to kind
sorted *v* ▷ **sort**
sortie *n* (*pl* **-s**) relatively short return trip
sorties *n* ▷ **sortie**
sorting *v* ▷ **sort**
sorts *n, v* ▷ **sort**
sot *n* (*pl* **-s**) habitual drunkard
sots *n* ▷ **sot**
soubriquet [**so**-brik-ay] *n* (*pl* **-s**) ▷ **sobriquet**
soubriquets *n* ▷ **soubriquet**
soufflé [**soo**-flay] *n* (*pl* **-s**) light fluffy dish made with beaten egg whites and other ingredients
soufflés *n* ▷ **soufflé**
sough [rhymes with **now**] *v* (**-s, -ing, -ed**) (of the wind) make a sighing sound
soughed *v* ▷ **sough**
soughing *v* ▷ **sough**
soughs *v* ▷ **sough**
sought [**sawt**] *v* ▷ **seek**
souk [**sook**] *n* (*pl* **-s**) marketplace in Muslim countries, often open-air
souks *n* ▷ **souk**
soul *n* (*pl* **-s**) spiritual and immortal part of a human being
soulful *adj* full of emotion
soulless *adj* lacking human qualities, mechanical
souls *n* ▷ **soul**
sound[1] *n* (*pl* **-s**) something heard, noise ▶ *v* (**-s, -ing, -ed**) make or cause to make a sound
sound[2] *adj* (**-er, -est**) in good condition > **soundly** *adv*
sound[3] *v* (**-s, -ing, -ed**) find the depth of (water etc.)
sound[4] *n* (*pl* **-s**) channel or strait
sounded *v* ▷ **sound**[1, 3]
sounder *adj* ▷ **sound**[2]
soundest *adj* ▷ **sound**[2]
sounding *v* ▷ **sound**[1, 3]
soundings *pl n* measurements of depth taken by sounding
soundly *adv* ▷ **sound**[2]
soundproof *adj* not penetrable by sound ▶ *v* (**-s, -ing, -ed**) make soundproof
soundproofed *v* ▷ **soundproof**
soundproofing *v* ▷ **soundproof**
soundproofs *v* ▷ **soundproof**
sounds *n* ▷ **sound**[1, 4] ▶ *v* ▷ **sound**[1, 3]
soundtrack *n* (*pl* **-s**) recorded sound accompaniment to a film
soundtracks *n* ▷ **soundtrack**
soup *n* (*pl* **-s**) liquid food made from meat, vegetables, etc. > **soupy** *adj* (**-pier, -piest**)
soupçon [**soop**-sonn] *n* (*pl* **-s**) small amount

soupçons *n* ▷ **soupçon**
soupier *adj* ▷ **soup**
soupiest *adj* ▷ **soup**
soups *n* ▷ **soup**
soupy *adj* ▷ **soup**
sour *adj* (**-er, -est**) sharp-tasting ▶ *v* (**-s, -ing, -ed**) make or become sour > **sourly** *adv* > **sourness** *n* (*pl* **-s**)
source *n* (*pl* **-s**) origin or starting point
sources *n* ▷ **source**
soured *v* ▷ **sour**
sourer *adj* ▷ **sour**
sourest *adj* ▷ **sour**
souring *v* ▷ **sour**
sourly *adv* ▷ **sour**
sourness *n* ▷ **sour**
sournesses *n* ▷ **sour**
sours *v* ▷ **sour**
souse *v* (**-ses, -sing, -sed**) plunge (something) into liquid
soused *v* ▷ **souse**
souses *v* ▷ **souse**
sousing *v* ▷ **souse**
soutane [soo-**tan**] *n* (*pl* **-s**) Roman Catholic priest's cassock
soutanes *n* ▷ **soutane**
south *n* (*pl* **-s**) direction towards the South Pole, opposite north ▶ *adj* to or in the south ▶ *adv* in, to, or towards the south > **southerly** *adj* > **southern** *adj* > **southward** *adj, adv* > **southwards** *adv*
southerly *adj* ▷ **south**
southern *adj* ▷ **south**
southerner *n* (*pl* **-s**) person from the south of a country or area
southerners *n* ▷ **southerner**
southpaw *n* (*pl* **-s**) (*Informal*) left-handed person, esp. a boxer
southpaws *n* ▷ **southpaw**
souths *n* ▷ **south**
southward *adj, adv* ▷ **south**
southwards *adv* ▷ **south**
souvenir *n* (*pl* **-s**) keepsake, memento
souvenirs *n* ▷ **souvenir**
sou'wester *n* (*pl* **-s**) seaman's waterproof hat covering the head and back of the neck
sou'westers *n* ▷ **sou'wester**
sovereign *n* (*pl* **-s**) king or queen ▶ *adj* (of a state) independent > **sovereignty** *n* (*pl* **-ties**)
sovereigns *n* ▷ **sovereign**
sovereignties *n* ▷ **sovereign**
sovereignty *n* ▷ **sovereign**
soviet *n* (*pl* **-s**) formerly, elected council at various levels of government in the USSR ▶ *adj*
soviets *n* ▷ **soviet**
sow[1] [rhymes with **know**] *v* (**-s, -ing, -ed, sown** *or* **-ed**) scatter or plant (seed) in or on (the ground)
sow[2] [rhymes with **cow**] *n* (*pl* **-s**) female adult pig
sowed *v* ▷ **sow**[1]
sowing *v* ▷ **sow**[1]
sown *v* ▷ **sow**[1]
sows *n* ▷ **sow**[2] ▶ *v* ▷ **sow**[1]

sox *pl n*. Sox is an informal word for **socks.** This is a good word to remember for when you find an X on your rack without the space or tiles to play a longer word. Sox scores 10 points.

soya *n* (*pl* **-s**) plant whose edible bean is used for food and as a source of oil
soyas *n* ▷ **soya**
sozzled *adj* (BRIT, AUST & NZ) (*Slang*) drunk
spa *n* (*pl* **-s**) resort with a mineral-water spring
space *n* (*pl* **-s**) unlimited expanse in which all objects exist and move ▶ *v* (**-ces, -cing, -ced**) place at intervals
spacecraft, spaceship *n* (*pl* **-s**) vehicle for travel beyond the earth's atmosphere
spacecrafts *n* ▷ **spacecraft**
spaced *v* ▷ **space**
spaces *n, v* ▷ **space**
spaceship *n* ▷ **spacecraft**
spaceships *n* ▷ **spacecraft**
spacesuit *n* (*pl* **-s**) sealed pressurized suit worn by an astronaut
spacesuits *n* ▷ **spacesuit**
spacing *v* ▷ **space**
spacious *adj* having a large capacity or area
spade[1] *n* (*pl* **-s**) tool for digging
spade[2] *n* (*pl* **-s**) playing card of the suit marked with black leaf-shaped symbols
spades *n* ▷ **spade**[1, 2]
spadework *n* (*pl* **-s**) hard preparatory work
spadeworks *n* ▷ **spadework**
spaghetti *n* (*pl* **-s**) pasta in the form of long strings
spaghettis *n* ▷ **spaghetti**
span *n* (*pl* **-s**) space between two points ▶ *v* (**-s, -nning, -nned**) stretch or extend across
spangle *n* (*pl* **-les**) small shiny metallic ornament ▶ *v* (**-les, -ling, -led**) decorate with spangles
spangled *v* ▷ **spangle**
spangles *n, v* ▷ **spangle**
spangling *v* ▷ **spangle**
spaniel *n* (*pl* **-s**) dog with long ears and silky hair
spaniels *n* ▷ **spaniel**

spank *v* (**-s, -ing, -ed**) slap with the open hand, on the buttocks or legs ▶ *n* (*pl* **-s**) such a slap > **spanking** *n* (*pl* **-s**)
spanked *v* ▷ **spank**
spanking *adj* (*Informal*) outstandingly fine or smart ▶ *v* ▷ **spank** ▶ *n* ▷ **spank**
spankings *n* ▷ **spank**
spanks *v*, *n* ▷ **spank**
spanned *v* ▷ **span**
spanner *n* (*pl* **-s**) tool for gripping and turning a nut or bolt
spanners *n* ▷ **spanner**
spanning *v* ▷ **span**
spans *n*, *v* ▷ **span**
spar¹ *n* (*pl* **-s**) pole used as a ship's mast, boom, or yard
spar² *v* (**-s, -rring, -rred**) box or fight using light blows for practice
spare *adj* extra ▶ *n* (*pl* **-s**) duplicate kept in case of damage or loss ▶ *v* (**-res, -ring, -red**) refrain from punishing or harming
spared *v* ▷ **spare**
spares *n*, *v* ▷ **spare**
sparing *adj* economical ▶ *v* ▷ **spare**
spark *n* (*pl* **-s**) fiery particle thrown out from a fire or caused by friction ▶ *v* (**-s, -ing, -ed**) give off sparks
sparked *v* ▷ **spark**
sparkie *n* (*pl* **-s**) (NZ) (*Informal*) electrician
sparkies *n* ▷ **sparkie**
sparking *v* ▷ **spark**
sparkle *v* (**-les, -ling, -led**) glitter with many points of light ▶ *n* (*pl* **-s**) sparkling points of light
sparkled *v* ▷ **sparkle**
sparkler *n* (*pl* **-s**) hand-held firework that emits sparks
sparklers *n* ▷ **sparkler**
sparkles *v*, *n* ▷ **sparkle**
sparkling *adj* (of wine or mineral water) slightly fizzy ▶ *v* ▷ **sparkle**
sparks *v*, *n* ▷ **spark**
sparred *v* ▷ **spar²**
sparring *v* ▷ **spar²**
sparrow *n* (*pl* **-s**) small brownish bird
sparrowhawk *n* (*pl* **-s**) small hawk
sparrowhawks *n* ▷ **sparrowhawk**
sparrows *n* ▷ **sparrow**
spars *n* ▷ **spar¹** ▶ *v* ▷ **spar²**
sparse *adj* (**-r, -st**) thinly scattered > **sparsely** *adv* > **sparseness** *n* (*pl* **-es**)
sparsely *adv* ▷ **sparse**
sparseness *n* ▷ **sparse**
sparsenesses *n* ▷ **sparse**
sparser *adj* ▷ **sparse**
sparsest *adj* ▷ **sparse**
spartan *adj* strict and austere
spas *n* ▷ **spa**
spasm *n* (*pl* **-s**) involuntary muscular contraction
spasmodic *adj* occurring in spasms > **spasmodically** *adv*
spasmodically *adv* ▷ **spasmodic**
spasms *n* ▷ **spasm**
spastic *n* (*pl* **-s**) person with cerebral palsy ▶ *adj* suffering from cerebral palsy
spastics *n* ▷ **spastic**
spat¹ *n* (*pl* **-s**) slight quarrel
spat² *v* ▷ **spit¹**
spate *n* (*pl* **-s**) large number of things happening within a period of time
spates *n* ▷ **spate**
spatial *adj* of or in space
spats *pl n* coverings formerly worn over the ankle and instep ▶ *n* ▷ **spat¹**
spatter *v* (**-s, -ing, -ed**) scatter or be scattered in drops over (something) ▶ *n* (*pl* **-s**) spattering sound
spattered *v* ▷ **spatter**
spattering *v* ▷ **spatter**
spatters *n*, *v* ▷ **spatter**
spatula *n* (*pl* **-s**) utensil with a broad flat blade for spreading or stirring
spatulas *n* ▷ **spatula**
spawn *n* (*pl* **-s**) jelly-like mass of eggs of fish, frogs, or molluscs ▶ *v* (**-s, -ing, -ed**) (of fish, frogs, or molluscs) lay eggs
spawned *v* ▷ **spawn**
spawning *v* ▷ **spawn**
spawns *n*, *v* ▷ **spawn**
spay *v* (**-s, -ing, -ed**) remove the ovaries from (a female animal)
spayed *v* ▷ **spay**
spaying *v* ▷ **spay**
spays *v* ▷ **spay**
speak *v* (**-s, -ing, spoke, spoken**) say words, talk
speaker *n* (*pl* **-s**) person who speaks, esp. at a formal occasion
speakers *n* ▷ **speaker**
speaking *v* ▷ **speak**
speaks *v* ▷ **speak**
spear¹ *n* (*pl* **-s**) weapon consisting of a long shaft with a sharp point ▶ *v* (**-s, -ing, -ed**) pierce with or as if with a spear
spear² *n* (*pl* **-s**) slender shoot
speared *v* ▷ **spear¹**
spearhead *v* (**-es, -ing, -ed**) lead (an attack or campaign) ▶ *n* (*pl* **-s**) leading force in an attack or campaign
spearheaded *v* ▷ **spearhead**

spearheading *v* ▷ **spearhead**
spearheads *v, n* ▷ **spearhead**
spearing *v* ▷ **spear**[1]
spearmint *n* (*pl* **-s**) type of mint
spearmints *n* ▷ **spearmint**
spears *n* ▷ **spear**[1, 2] ▶ *v* ▷ **spear**[1]
spec *n* (*pl* **-s**) (*Informal*) speculation
special *adj* distinguished from others of its kind > **specially** *adv*
specialist *n* (*pl* **-s**) expert in a particular activity or subject
specialists *n* ▷ **specialist**
specialities *n* ▷ **speciality**
speciality *n* (*pl* **-ties**) special interest or skill
specialization *n* ▷ **specialize**
specializations *n* ▷ **specialize**
specialize *v* (**-zes, -zing, -zed**) be a specialist > **specialization** *n* (*pl* **-s**)
specialized *v* ▷ **specialize**
specializes *v* ▷ **specialize**
specializing *v* ▷ **specialize**
specially *adv* ▷ **special**
specie *n* coins as distinct from paper money
species *n* (*pl* **species**) group of plants or animals that are related closely enough to interbreed naturally
specific *adj* particular, definite ▶ *n* (*pl* **-s**) drug used to treat a particular disease > **specifically** *adv*
specifically *adv* ▷ **specific**
specification *n* (*pl* **-s**) detailed description of something to be made or done
specifications *n* ▷ **specification**
specifics *n* ▷ **specific** ▶ *pl n* particular details
specified *v* ▷ **specify**
specifies *v* ▷ **specify**
specify *v* (**-fies, -fying, -fied**) refer to or state specifically
specifying *v* ▷ **specify**
specimen *n* (*pl* **-s**) individual or part typifying a whole
specimens *n* ▷ **specimen**
specious [**spee**-shuss] *adj* apparently true, but actually false
speck *n* (*pl* **-s**) small spot or particle
speckle *n* (*pl* **-s**) small spot ▶ *v* (**-les, -ling, -led**) mark with speckles
speckled *v* ▷ **speckle**
speckles *n, v* ▷ **speckle**
speckling *v* ▷ **speckle**
specks *n* ▷ **speck**
specs *pl n* (*Informal*) ▷ **spectacles** ▶ *n* ▷ **spec**
spectacle *n* (*pl* **-s**) strange, interesting, or ridiculous sight
spectacles *n* ▷ **spectacle** ▶ *pl n* pair of glasses for correcting faulty vision
spectacles *n* ▷ **spectacle**
spectacular *adj* impressive ▶ *n* (*pl* **-s**) spectacular public show > **spectacularly** *adv*
spectacularly *adv* ▷ **spectacular**
spectaculars *n* ▷ **spectacular**
spectate *v* (**-tes, -ting, -ted**) watch
spectated *v* ▷ **spectate**
spectates *v* ▷ **spectate**
spectating *v* ▷ **spectate**
spectator *n* (*pl* **-s**) person viewing anything, onlooker
spectators *n* ▷ **spectator**
spectra *n* ▷ **spectrum**
spectral *adj* ▷ **spectre**
spectre *n* (*pl* **-s**) ghost > **spectral** *adj*
spectres *n* ▷ **spectre**
spectroscope *n* (*pl* **-s**) instrument for producing or examining spectra
spectroscopes *n* ▷ **spectroscope**
spectrum *n* (*pl* **-tra**) range of different colours, radio waves, etc. in order of their wavelengths
speculate *v* (**-tes, -ting, -ted**) guess, conjecture > **speculation** *n* (*pl* **-s**) > **speculative** *adj* > **speculator** *n* (*pl* **-s**)
speculated *v* ▷ **speculate**
speculates *v* ▷ **speculate**
speculating *v* ▷ **speculate**
speculation *n* ▷ **speculate**
speculations *n* ▷ **speculate**
speculative *adj* ▷ **speculate**
speculator *n* ▷ **speculate**
speculators *n* ▷ **speculate**
sped *v* ▷ **speed**
speech *n* (*pl* **-es**) act, power, or manner of speaking
speeches *n* ▷ **speech**
speechless *adj* unable to speak because of great emotion
speed *n* (*pl* **-s**) swiftness ▶ *v* (**-s, -ing, sped** *or* **-ed**) go quickly
speedboat *n* (*pl* **-s**) light fast motorboat
speedboats *n* ▷ **speedboat**
speeded *v* ▷ **speed**
speedier *adj* ▷ **speedy**
speediest *adj* ▷ **speedy**
speedily *adv* ▷ **speedy**
speeding *v* ▷ **speed**
speedometer *n* (*pl* **-s**) instrument to show the speed of a vehicle
speedometers *n* ▷ **speedometer**
speeds *n, v* ▷ **speed**
speedway *n* (*pl* **-s**) track for motorcycle racing
speedways *n* ▷ **speedway**

speedwell *n* (*pl* **-s**) plant with small blue flowers
speedwells *n* ▷ **speedwell**
speedy *adj* (**-dier, -diest**) prompt > **speedily** *adv*
speleologies *n* ▷ **speleology**
speleology *n* (*pl* **-gies**) study and exploration of caves
spell[1] *v* (**-s, -ing, spelt** *or* **-ed**) give in correct order the letters that form (a word)
spell[2] *n* (*pl* **-s**) formula of words supposed to have magic power
spell[3] *n* (*pl* **-s**) period of time of weather or activity
spellbound *adj* entranced
spellchecker *n* (*pl* **-s**) (COMPUTING) program that highlights wrongly spelled words in a word-processed document
spellcheckers *n* ▷ **spellchecker**
spelled *v* ▷ **spell**[1]
spelling *n* (*pl* **-s**) way a word is spelt ▶ *v* ▷ **spell**[1]
spellings *n* ▷ **spelling**
spells *v* ▷ **spell**[1] ▶ *n* ▷ **spell**[2, 3]
spelt *v* ▷ **spell**[1]
spend *v* (**-s, -ing, spent**) pay out (money)
spending *v* ▷ **spend**
spends *v* ▷ **spend**
spendthrift *n* (*pl* **-s**) person who spends money wastefully
spendthrifts *n* ▷ **spendthrift**
spent *v* ▷ **spend**
sperm *n* (*pl* **-s** *or* **sperm**) male reproductive cell
spermaceti [sper-ma-**set**-ee] *n* (*pl* **-s**) waxy solid obtained from the sperm whale
spermacetis *n* ▷ **spermaceti**
spermatozoa *n* ▷ **spermatozoon**
spermatozoon [sper-ma-toe-**zoe**-on] *n* (*pl* **-zoa**) sperm
spermicide *n* (*pl* **-s**) substance that kills sperm
spermicides *n* ▷ **spermicide**
sperms *n* ▷ **sperm**
spew *v* (**-s, -ing, -ed**) vomit
spewed *v* ▷ **spew**
spewing *v* ▷ **spew**
spews *v* ▷ **spew**
sphagnum *n* (*pl* **-s**) moss found in bogs
sphagnums *n* ▷ **sphagnum**
sphere *n* (*pl* **-s**) perfectly round solid object > **spherical** *adj*
spheres *n* ▷ **sphere**
spherical *adj* ▷ **sphere**
sphincter *n* (*pl* **-s**) ring of muscle which controls the opening and closing of a hollow organ
sphincters *n* ▷ **sphincter**
sphinx *n* (*pl* **-es**) enigmatic person
sphinxes *n* ▷ **sphinx**
spice *n* (*pl* **-s**) aromatic substance used as flavouring ▶ *v* (**-ces, -cing, -ced**) flavour with spices
spiced *v* ▷ **spice**
spices *n, v* ▷ **spice**
spicier *adj* ▷ **spicy**
spiciest *adj* ▷ **spicy**
spicing *v* ▷ **spice**
spicy *adj* (**-cier, -ciest**) flavoured with spices
spider *n* (*pl* **-s**) small eight-legged creature which spins a web to catch insects for food > **spidery** *adj*
spiders *n* ▷ **spider**
spidery *adj* ▷ **spider**
spied *v* ▷ **spy**
spiel *n* (*pl* **-s**) speech made to persuade someone to do something
spiels *n* ▷ **spiel**
spies *v, n* ▷ **spy**
spigot *n* (*pl* **-s**) stopper for, or tap fitted to, a cask
spigots *n* ▷ **spigot**
spike *n* (*pl* **-s**) sharp point ▶ *v* (**-kes, -king, -ked**) put spikes on > **spiky** *adj* (**-kier, -kiest**)
spiked *v* ▷ **spike**
spikes *n, v* ▷ **spike** ▶ *pl n* sports shoes with spikes for greater grip
spikier *adj* ▷ **spike**
spikiest *adj* ▷ **spike**
spiking *v* ▷ **spike**
spiky *adj* ▷ **spike**
spill[1] *v* (**-s, -ing, spilt** *or* **spilled**) pour from or as if from a container ▶ *n* (*pl* **-s**) fall > **spillage** *n* (*pl* **-s**)
spill[2] *n* (*pl* **-s**) thin strip of wood or paper for lighting pipes or fires
spillage *n* ▷ **spill**[1]
spillages *n* ▷ **spill**[1]
spilled *v* ▷ **spill**[1]
spilling *v* ▷ **spill**[1]
spills *n* ▷ **spill**[1, 2] ▶ *v* ▷ **spill**[1]
spilt *v* ▷ **spill**[1]
spin *v* (**-s, -nning, spun**) revolve or cause to revolve rapidly ▶ *n* (*pl* **-s**) revolving motion > **spinner** *n* (*pl* **-s**)
spinach *n* (*pl* **-es**) dark green leafy vegetable
spinaches *n* ▷ **spinach**
spinal *adj* of the spine
spindle *n* (*pl* **-s**) rotating rod that acts as an axle
spindles *n* ▷ **spindle**
spindlier *adj* ▷ **spindly**
spindliest *adj* ▷ **spindly**
spindly *adj* (**-lier, -liest**) long, slender, and frail

spine *n* (*pl* **-s**) backbone
spineless *adj* lacking courage
spines *n* ▷ **spine**
spinet *n* (*pl* **-s**) small harpsichord
spinets *n* ▷ **spinet**
spinier *adj* ▷ **spiny**
spiniest *adj* ▷ **spiny**
spinifex *n* (*pl* **-es**) coarse spiny Australian grass
spinifexes *n* ▷ **spinifex**
spinnaker *n* (*pl* **-s**) large sail on a racing yacht
spinnakers *n* ▷ **spinnaker**
spinner *n* ▷ **spin**
spinners *n* ▷ **spin**
spinney *n* (*pl* **-s**) (CHIEFLY BRIT) small wood
spinneys *n* ▷ **spinney**
spinning *v* ▷ **spin**
spins *v, n* ▷ **spin**
spinster *n* (*pl* **-s**) unmarried woman
spinsters *n* ▷ **spinster**
spiny *adj* (**-nier, -niest**) covered with spines
spiral *n* (*pl* **-s**) continuous curve formed by a point winding about a central axis at an ever-increasing distance from it ▶ *v* (**-s, -lling, -lled**) move in a spiral ▶ *adj* having the form of a spiral
spiralled *v* ▷ **spiral**
spiralling *v* ▷ **spiral**
spirals *n, v* ▷ **spiral**
spire *n* (*pl* **-s**) pointed part of a steeple
spires *n* ▷ **spire**
spirit¹ *n* (*pl* **-s**) nonphysical aspect of a person concerned with profound thoughts ▶ *v* (**-s, -ing, -ed**) carry away mysteriously
spirit² *n* (*pl* **-s**) liquid obtained by distillation
spirited *adj* lively ▶ *v* ▷ **spirit¹**
spiriting *v* ▷ **spirit¹**
spirits *n* ▷ **spirit¹, ²** ▶ *pl n* emotional state ▶ *v* ▷ **spirit¹**
spiritual *adj* relating to the spirit ▶ *n* (*pl* **-s**) type of religious folk song originating among Black slaves in America > **spiritually** *adv* > **spirituality** *n* (*pl* **-ties**)
spiritualism *n* (*pl* **-s**) belief that the spirits of the dead can communicate with the living > **spiritualist** *n* (*pl* **-s**)
spiritualisms *n* ▷ **spiritualism**
spiritualist *n* ▷ **spiritualism**
spiritualists *n* ▷ **spiritualism**
spiritualities *n* ▷ **spiritual**
spirituality *n* ▷ **spiritual**
spiritually *adv* ▷ **spiritual**
spirituals *n* ▷ **spiritual**
spit¹ *v* (**-s, -tting, spat**) eject (saliva or food) from the mouth ▶ *n* (*pl* **-s**) saliva
spit² *n* (*pl* **-s**) sharp rod on which meat is skewered for roasting
spite *n* (*pl* **-s**) deliberate nastiness ▶ *v* (**-tes, -ting, -ted**) annoy or hurt from spite > **spiteful** *adj* > **spitefully** *adv*
spited *v* ▷ **spite**
spiteful *adj* ▷ **spite**
spitefully *adv* ▷ **spite**
spites *n, v* ▷ **spite**
spitfire *n* (*pl* **-s**) person with a fiery temper
spitfires *n* ▷ **spitfire**
spiting *v* ▷ **spite**
spits *n* ▷ **spit¹, ²** ▶ *v* ▷ **spit¹**
spitting *v* ▷ **spit¹**
spittle *n* (*pl* **-s**) fluid produced in the mouth, saliva
spittles *n* ▷ **spittle**
spittoon *n* (*pl* **-s**) bowl to spit into
spittoons *n* ▷ **spittoon**
spiv *n* (*pl* **-s**) (BRIT, AUST & NZ) (*Slang*) smartly dressed man who makes a living by shady dealings
spivs *n* ▷ **spiv**
splash *v* (**-es, -ing, -ed**) scatter liquid on (something) ▶ *n* (*pl* **-es**) splashing sound
splashed *v* ▷ **splash**
splashes *v, n* ▷ **splash**
splashing *v, n* ▷ **splash**
splatter *v* (**-s, -ing, -ed**) ▶ *n* (*pl* **-s**) splash
splattered *v* ▷ **splatter**
splattering *v* ▷ **splatter**
splatters *v, n* ▷ **splatter**
splay *v* (**-s, -ing, -ed**) spread out, with ends spreading in different directions
splayed *v* ▷ **splay**
splaying *v* ▷ **splay**
splays *v* ▷ **splay**
spleen *n* (*pl* **-s**) abdominal organ which filters bacteria from the blood
spleens *n* ▷ **spleen**
splendid *adj* (**-er, -est**) excellent > **splendidly** *adv* > **splendour** *n* (*pl* **-s**)
splendider *adj* ▷ **splendid**
splendidest *adj* ▷ **splendid**
splendidly *adv* ▷ **splendid**
splendour *n* ▷ **splendid**
splendours *n* ▷ **splendid**
splenetic *adj* spiteful or irritable
splice *v* (**-ces, -cing, -ced**) join by interweaving or overlapping ends
spliced *v* ▷ **splice**
splices *v* ▷ **splice**
splicing *v* ▷ **splice**
splint *n* (*pl* **-s**) rigid support for a broken bone
splinter *n* (*pl* **-s**) thin sharp piece broken off, esp. from wood ▶ *v* (**-s, -ing, -ed**) break into

fragments
splintered *v* ▷ **splinter**
splintering *v* ▷ **splinter**
splinters *n, v* ▷ **splinter**
splints *n* ▷ **splint**
split *v* (**-s, -tting, split**) break into separate pieces ▶ *n* (*pl* **-s**) crack or division caused by splitting
splits *v* ▷ **split** ▶ *n* ▷ **split** ▶ *pl n* act of sitting with the legs outstretched in opposite directions
splitting *v* ▷ **split**
splodge *n* (*pl* **-s**) ▶ *v* (**-ges, -ging, -ged**) ▷ **splotch**
splodged *v* ▷ **splodge**
splodges *n, v* ▷ **splodge**
splodging *v* ▷ **splodge**
splotch *n* (*pl* **-s**) ▶ *v* (**-ches, -ching, -ched**) splash, daub
splotched *v* ▷ **splotch**
splotches *n, v* ▷ **splotch**
splotching *v* ▷ **splotch**
splurge *v* (**-ges, -ging, -ged**) spend money extravagantly ▶ *n* (*pl* **-s**) bout of extravagance
splurged *v* ▷ **splurge**
splurges *v, n* ▷ **splurge**
splurging *v* ▷ **splurge**
splutter *v* (**-s, -ing, -ed**) utter with spitting or choking sounds ▶ *n* (*pl* **-s**) spluttering
spluttered *v* ▷ **splutter**
spluttering *v* ▷ **splutter**
splutters *v, n* ▷ **splutter**
spoil *v* (**-s, -ing, -spoilt** *or* **-ed**) damage
spoiled *v* ▷ **spoil**
spoiling *v* ▷ **spoil**
spoils *pl n* booty ▶ *v* ▷ **spoil**
spoilsport *n* (*pl* **-s**) person who spoils the enjoyment of others
spoilsports *n* ▷ **spoilsport**
spoilt *v* ▷ **spoil**
spoke¹ *v* ▷ **speak**
spoke² *n* (*pl* **-s**) bar joining the hub of a wheel to the rim
spoken *v* ▷ **speak**
spokes *n* ▷ **spoke²**
spokesman, spokeswoman, spokesperson *n* (*pl* **-men, -women, -persons, -people**) person chosen to speak on behalf of a group
spokesmen *n* ▷ **spokesman**
spokespeople *n* ▷ **spokesman**
spokesperson *n* ▷ **spokesman**
spokespersons *n* ▷ **spokesman**
spokeswoman *n* ▷ **spokesman**
spokeswomen *n* ▷ **spokesman**
spoliation *n* (*pl* **-s**) plundering
spoliations *n* ▷ **spoliation**
sponge *n* (*pl* **-s**) sea animal with a porous absorbent skeleton ▶ *v* (**-ges, -ging, -ged**) wipe with a sponge > **spongy** *adj* (**-gier, -giest**)
sponged *v* ▷ **sponge**
sponger *n* (*pl* **-s**) (*Slang*) person who sponges on others
spongers *n* ▷ **sponger**
sponges *n, v* ▷ **sponge**
spongier *adj* ▷ **sponge**
spongiest *adj* ▷ **sponge**
sponging *v* ▷ **sponge**
spongy *adj* ▷ **sponge**
sponsor *n* (*pl* **-s**) person who promotes something ▶ *v* (**-s, -ing, -ed**) act as a sponsor for > **sponsorship** *n* (*pl* **-s**)
sponsored *v* ▷ **sponsor**
sponsoring *v* ▷ **sponsor**
sponsors *n, v* ▷ **sponsor**
sponsorship *n* ▷ **sponsor**
sponsorships *n* ▷ **sponsor**
spontaneities *n* ▷ **spontaneous**
spontaneity *n* ▷ **spontaneous**
spontaneous *adj* not planned or arranged > **spontaneously** *adv* > **spontaneity** *n* (*pl* **-ties**)
spontaneously *adv* ▷ **spontaneous**
spoof *n* (*pl* **-s**) mildly satirical parody
spoofs *n* ▷ **spoof**
spook *n* (*pl* **-s**) (*Informal*) ghost > **spooky** *adj* (**-kier, -kiest**)
spookier *adj* ▷ **spook**
spookiest *adj* ▷ **spook**
spooks *n* ▷ **spook**
spooky *adj* ▷ **spook**
spool *n* (*pl* **-s**) cylinder round which something can be wound
spools *n* ▷ **spool**
spoon *n* (*pl* **-s**) shallow bowl attached to a handle for eating, stirring, or serving food ▶ *v* (**-s, -ing, -ed**) lift with a spoon > **spoonful** *n* (*pl* **-s**)
spoonbill *n* (*pl* **-s**) wading bird of warm regions with a long flat bill
spoonbills *n* ▷ **spoonbill**
spooned *v* ▷ **spoon**
spoonerism *n* (*pl* **-s**) accidental changing over of the initial sounds of a pair of words, such as *half-warmed fish* for *half-formed wish*
spoonerisms *n* ▷ **spoonerism**
spoonful *n* ▷ **spoon**
spoonfuls *n* ▷ **spoon**
spooning *v* ▷ **spoon**
spoons *n, v* ▷ **spoon**
spoor *n* (*pl* **-s**) trail of an animal
spoors *n* ▷ **spoor**

sporadic *adj* intermittent, scattered >**sporadically** *adv*
sporadically *adv* ▷ **sporadic**
spore *n* (*pl* **-s**) minute reproductive body of some plants
spores *n* ▷ **spore**
sporran *n* (*pl* **-s**) pouch worn in front of a kilt
sporrans *n* ▷ **sporran**
sport *n* (*pl* **-s**) activity for pleasure, competition, or exercise *v* (**-s, -ing, -ed**) wear proudly > **sporty** *adj* (**-tier, -tiest**)
sported *v* ▷ **sport**
sportier *adj* ▷ **sport**
sportiest *adj* ▷ **sport**
sporting *adj* of sport ▶ *v* ▷ **sport**
sportive *adj* playful
sports *n*, *v* ▷ **sport**
sportsman, sportswoman *n* (*pl* **-men, -women**) person who plays sports >**sportsmanlike** *adj* > **sportsmanship** *n* (*pl* **-s**)
sportsmanlike *adj* ▷ **sportsman**
sportsmanship *n* ▷ **sportsman**
sportsmanships *n* ▷ **sportsman**
sportsmen *n* ▷ **sportsman**
sportswoman *n* ▷ **sportsman**
sportswomen *n* ▷ **sportsman**
sporty *adj* ▷ **sport**
spot *n* (*pl* **-s**) small mark on a surface (*Informal*) ▶ *v* (**-s, -tting, -tted**) notice
spotless *adj* absolutely clean > **spotlessly** *adv*
spotlessly *adv* ▷ **spotless**
spotlight *n* (*pl* **-s**) powerful light illuminating a small area
spotlights *n* ▷ **spotlight**
spots *n*, *v* ▷ **spot**
spotted *v* ▷ **spot**
spottier *adj* ▷ **spotty**
spottiest *adj* ▷ **spotty**
spotting *v* ▷ **spot**
spotty *adj* (**-ttier, -ttiest**) with spots
spouse *n* (*pl* **-s**) husband or wife
spouses *n* ▷ **spouse**
spout *v* (**-s, -ing, -ed**) pour out in a stream or jet (*Slang*) ▶ *n* (*pl* **-s**) projecting tube or lip for pouring liquids
spouted *v* ▷ **spout**
spouting *v* ▷ **spout**
spouts *v*, *n* ▷ **spout**
sprain *v* (**-s, -ing, -ed**) injure (a joint) by a sudden twist ▶ *n* (*pl* **-s**) such an injury
sprained *v* ▷ **sprain**
spraining *v* ▷ **sprain**
sprains *v*, *n* ▷ **sprain**
sprang *v* ▷ **spring**
sprat *n* (*pl* **-s**) small sea fish
sprats *n* ▷ **sprat**
sprawl *v* (**-s, -ing, -ed**) lie or sit with the limbs spread out ▶ *n* (*pl* **-s**) part of a city that has spread untidily over a large area
sprawled *v* ▷ **sprawl**
sprawling *v* ▷ **sprawl**
sprawls *v*, *n* ▷ **sprawl**
spray[1] *n* (*pl* **-s**) (device for producing) fine drops of liquid ▶ *v* (**-s, -ing, -ed**) scatter in fine drops
spray[2] *n* (*pl* **-s**) branch with buds, leaves, flowers, or berries
sprayed *v* ▷ **spray[1]**
spraying *v* ▷ **spray[1]**
sprays *v* ▷ **spray[1]** ▶ *n* ▷ **spray[1, 2]**
spread *v* (**-s, -ing, spread**) open out or be displayed to the fullest extent ▶ *n* (*pl* **-s**) spreading (*Informal*)
spreading *v* ▷ **spread**
spreads *v*, *n* ▷ **spread**
spreadsheet *n* (*pl* **-s**) computer program for manipulating figures
spreadsheets *n* ▷ **spreadsheet**
spree *n* (*pl* **-s**) session of overindulgence, usu. in drinking or spending money
sprees *n* ▷ **spree**
sprier *adj* ▷ **spry**
spriest *adj* ▷ **spry**
sprig *n* (*pl* **-s**) twig or shoot
sprightlier *adj* ▷ **sprightly**
sprightliest *adj* ▷ **sprightly**
sprightliness *n* ▷ **sprightly**
sprightlinesses *n* ▷ **sprightly**
sprightly *adj* (**-lier, -liest**) lively and brisk > **sprightliness** *n* (*pl* **-es**)
sprigs *n* ▷ **sprig**
spring *v* (**-s, -ing, sprang** *or* **sprung**) move suddenly upwards or forwards in a single motion, jump ▶ *n* (*pl* **-s**) season between winter and summer
springboard *n* (*pl* **-s**) flexible board used to gain height or momentum in diving or gymnastics
springboards *n* ▷ **springboard**
springbok *n* (*pl* **-s**) S African antelope
springboks *n* ▷ **springbok**
springer *n* (*pl* **-s**) small spaniel
springers *n* ▷ **springer**
springier *adj* ▷ **springy**
springiest *adj* ▷ **springy**
springing *v* ▷ **spring**
springs *v*, *n* ▷ **springs**
springy *adj* (**-gier, -giest**) elastic
sprinkle *v* (**-les, -ling, -led**) scatter (liquid or powder) in tiny drops or particles over (something) > **sprinkler** *n* (*pl* **-s**)

sprinkled *v* ▷ **sprinkle**
sprinkler *n* ▷ **sprinkle**
sprinklers *n* ▷ **sprinkle**
sprinkles *v* ▷ **sprinkle**
sprinkling *v* ▷ **sprinkle** ▶ *n* (*pl* **-s**) small quantity or number
sprinklings *n* ▷ **sprinkling**
sprint *n* (*pl* **-s**) short race run at top speed ▶ *v* (**-s, -ing, -ed**) run a short distance at top speed > **sprinter** *n* (*pl* **-s**)
sprinted *v* ▷ **sprint**
sprinter *n* ▷ **sprint**
sprinters *n* ▷ **sprint**
sprinting *v* ▷ **sprint**
sprints *n, v* ▷ **sprint**
sprite *n* (*pl* **-s**) elf
sprites *n* ▷ **sprite**
sprocket *n* (*pl* **-s**) wheel with teeth on the rim, that drives or is driven by a chain
sprockets *n* ▷ **sprocket**
sprout *v* (**-s, -ing, -ed**) put forth shoots ▶ *n* (*pl* **-s**) shoot
sprouted *v* ▷ **sprout**
sprouting *v* ▷ **sprout**
sprouts *v, n* ▷ **sprout**
spruce[1] *n* (*pl* **-s**) kind of fir
spruce[2] *adj* (**-r, -st**) neat and smart
sprucer *adj* ▷ **spruce**[2]
spruces *n* ▷ **spruce**[1]
sprucest *adj* ▷ **spruce**[2]
sprung *v* ▷ **spring**
spry *adj* (**-yer, -yest** *or* **sprier**) (**spriest**) active or nimble
spryer *adj* ▷ **spry**
spryest *adj* ▷ **spry**
spud *n* (*pl* **-s**) (*Informal*) potato
spuds *n* ▷ **spud**
spume *n* (*pl* **-s**) ▶ *v* (**-mes, -ming, -med**) froth
spumed *v* ▷ **spume**
spumes *v, n* ▷ **spume**
spuming *v* ▷ **spume**
spun *v* ▷ **spin**
spunk *n* (*pl* **-s**) (*Informal*) courage, spirit > **spunky** *adj* (**-kier, -kiest**)
spunkier *adj* ▷ **spunk**
spunkiest *adj* ▷ **spunk**
spunks *n* ▷ **spunk**
spunky *adj* ▷ **spunk**
spur *n* (*pl* **-s**) stimulus or incentive ▶ *v* (**-s, -rring, -rred**) urge on, incite (someone)
spurge *n* (*pl* **-s**) plant with milky sap
spurges *n* ▷ **spurge**
spurious *adj* not genuine
spurn *v* (**-s, -ing, -ed**) reject with scorn
spurned *v* ▷ **spurn**
spurning *v* ▷ **spurn**
spurns *v* ▷ **spurn**
spurred *v* ▷ **spur**
spurring *v* ▷ **spur**
spurs *n, v* ▷ **spur**
spurt *v* (**-s, -ing, -ed**) gush or cause to gush out in a jet ▶ *n* (*pl* **-s**) short sudden burst of activity or speed
spurted *v* ▷ **spurt**
spurting *v* ▷ **spurt**
spurts *v, n* ▷ **spurt**
sputa *n* ▷ **sputum**
sputnik *n* (*pl* **-s**) early Soviet artificial satellite
sputniks *n* ▷ **sputnik**
sputter *v* (**-es, -ing, -ed**) ▶ *n* (*pl* **-s**) splutter
sputtered *v* ▷ **sputter**
sputtering *v* ▷ **sputter**
sputters *v, n* ▷ **sputter**
sputum *n* (*pl* **-ta**) spittle, usu. mixed with mucus
spy *n* (*pl* **spies**) person employed to obtain secret information ▶ *v* (**spies, spying, spied**) act as a spy
spying *v* ▷ **spy**
squabble *v* (**-les, -ling, -led**) ▶ *n* (*pl* **-s**) (engage in) a petty or noisy quarrel
squabbled *v* ▷ **squabble**
squabbles *v, n* ▷ **squabble**
squabbling *v* ▷ **squabble**
squad *n* (*pl* **-s**) small group of people working or training together
squadron *n* (*pl* **-s**) division of an air force, fleet, or cavalry regiment
squadrons *n* ▷ **squadron**
squads *n* ▷ **squad**
squalid *adj* (**-er, -est**) dirty and unpleasant
squalider *adj* ▷ **squalid**
squalidest *adj* ▷ **squalid**
squall[1] *n* (*pl* **-s**) sudden strong wind
squall[2] *v* (**-s, -ing, -ed**) cry noisily, yell ▶ *n* (*pl* **-s**) harsh cry
squalled *v* ▷ **squall**[2]
squalling *v* ▷ **squall**[2]
squalls *v* ▷ **squall**[2] ▶ *n* ▷ **squall**[1, 2]
squalor *n* (*pl* **-s**) disgusting dirt and filth
squalors *n* ▷ **squalor**
squander *v* (**-s, -ing, -ed**) waste (money or resources)
squandered *v* ▷ **squander**
squandering *v* ▷ **squander**
squanders *v* ▷ **squander**
square *n* (*pl* **-s**) geometric figure with four equal sides and four right angles ▶ *adj* square in shape ▶ *v* (**-res, -ring, -red**) multiply (a number) by itself ▶ *adv* squarely, directly

squared *v* ▷ **square**
squarely *adv* in a direct way
squares *n, v* ▷ **square**
squaring *v* ▷ **square**
squash[1] *v* (**-es, -ing, -ed**) crush flat ▶ *n* (*pl* **-es**) sweet fruit drink diluted with water > **squashy** *adj* (**-shier, -shiest**)
squash[2] *n* (*pl* **-es**) marrow-like vegetable
squashed *v* ▷ **squash[1]**
squashes *n* ▷ **squash[1, 2]** ▶ *v* ▷ **squash[1]**
squashier *adj* ▷ **squash[1]**
squashiest *adj* ▷ **squash[1]**
squashing *v* ▷ **squash[1]**
squashy *adj* ▷ **squash[1]**
squat *v* (**-s, -tting, -tted**) crouch with the knees bent and the weight on the feet ▶ *n* (*pl* **-s**) place where squatters live ▶ *adj* (**-tter, -ttest**) short and broad
squats *v, n* ▷ **squat**
squatted *v* ▷ **squat**
squatter *n* (*pl* **-s**) illegal occupier of unused premises ▶ *adj* ▷ **squat**
squatters *n* ▷ **squatter**
squattest *n* ▷ **squat**
squatting *v* ▷ **squat**
squaw *n* (*pl* **-s**) (*Offens*) Native American woman
squawk *n* (*pl* **-s**) loud harsh cry ▶ *v* (**-s, -ing, -ed**) utter a squawk
squawked *v* ▷ **squawk**
squawking *v* ▷ **squawk**
squawks *v* ▷ **squawk**
squaws *n* ▷ **squaw**
squeak *n* (*pl* **-s**) short shrill cry or sound ▶ *v* (**-s, -ing, -ed**) make or utter a squeak > **squeaky** *adj* (**-kier, -kiest**)
squeaked *v* ▷ **squeak**
squeakier *adj* ▷ **squeak**
squeakiest *adj* ▷ **squeak**
squeaking *v* ▷ **squeak**
squeaks *n, v* ▷ **squeak**
squeaky *adj* ▷ **squeak**
squeal *n* (*pl* **-s**) long shrill cry or sound ▶ *v* (**-s, -ing, -ed**) make or utter a squeal (*Slang*)
squealed *v* ▷ **squeal**
squealing *v* ▷ **squeal**
squeals *n, v* ▷ **squeal**
squeamish *adj* easily sickened or shocked
squeegee *n* (*pl* **-s**) tool with a rubber blade for clearing water from a surface
squeegees *n* ▷ **squeegee**
squeeze *v* (**-zes, -zing, -zed**) grip or press firmly ▶ *n* (*pl* **-s**) squeezing
squeezed *v* ▷ **squeeze**
squeezes *v, n* ▷ **squeeze**
squeezing *v* ▷ **squeeze**
squelch *v* (**-es, -ing, -ed**) make a wet sucking sound, as by walking through mud ▶ *n* (*pl* **-es**) squelching sound
squelched *v* ▷ **squelch**
squelches *n* ▷ **squelch**
squelching *v* ▷ **squelch**
squib *n* (*pl* **-s**) small firework that hisses before exploding
squibs *n* ▷ **squib**
squid *n* (*pl* **-s**) sea creature with a long soft body and ten tentacles
squids *n* ▷ **squid**
squiggle *n* (*pl* **-s**) wavy line > **squiggly** *adj* (**-lier, -liest**)
squiggles *n* ▷ **squiggle**
squigglier *adj* ▷ **squiggle**
squiggliest *adj* ▷ **squiggle**
squiggly *adj* ▷ **squiggle**
squint *v* (**-s, -ing, -ed**) have eyes which face in different directions ▶ *n* (*pl* **-s**) squinting condition of the eye ▶ *adj* crooked (**-er, -est**)
squinted *v* ▷ **squint**
squinter *adj* ▷ **squint**
squintest *adj* ▷ **squint**
squinting *v* ▷ **squint**
squints *v, n* ▷ **squint**
squire *n* (*pl* **-s**) country gentleman, usu. the main landowner in a community
squires *n* ▷ **squire**
squirm *v* (**-s, -ing, -ed**) wriggle, writhe ▶ *n* (*pl* **-s**) wriggling movement
squirmed *v* ▷ **squirm**
squirming *v* ▷ **squirm**
squirms *v, n* ▷ **squirm**
squirrel *n* (*pl* **-s**) small bushy-tailed tree-living animal
squirrels *n* ▷ **squirrel**
squirt *v* (**-s, -ing, -ed**) force (a liquid) or (of a liquid) be forced out of a narrow opening ▶ *n* (*pl* **-s**) jet of liquid
squirted *v* ▷ **squirt**
squirting *v* ▷ **squirt**
squirts *n, v* ▷ **squirt**
squish *v* (**-es, -ing, -ed**) ▶ *n* (*pl* **-es**) (make) a soft squelching sound > **squishy** *adj* (**-shier, -shiest**)
squished *v* ▷ **squish**
squishes *n, v* ▷ **squish**
squishier *adj* ▷ **squish**
squishiest *adj* ▷ **squish**
squishing *v* ▷ **squish**
squishy *adj* ▷ **squish**

squiz *n* (**squizzes**). Squiz is an informal word for a look or glance. This is a useful word to remember, both for when you have the most of the tiles to form it and when someone else plays **quiz** which you can then add an S to for a good score. Squiz scores 23 points.

st *interj*. St is a sound people make to request silence or quiet. This is one of two two-letter words beginning with S that do not contain a vowel. It's useful when you want to connect a word beginning with H to one ending in T or vice versa. St scores 2 points.

stab *v* (**-s, -bbing, -bbed**) pierce with something pointed ▶ *n* (*pl* **-s**) stabbing
stabbed *v* ▷ **stab**
stabbing *v* ▷ **stab**
stabilities *n* ▷ **stable[2]**
stability *n* ▷ **stable[2]**
stabilization *n* ▷ **stabilize**
stabilizations *n* ▷ **stabilize**
stabilize *v* (**-zes, -zing, -zed**) make or become stable > **stabilization** *n* (*pl* **-s**)
stabilized *v* ▷ **stabilize**
stabilizer *n* (*pl* **-s**) device for stabilizing a child's bicycle, an aircraft, or a ship
stabilizers *n* ▷ **stabilizer**
stabilizes *v* ▷ **stabilize**
stabilizing *v* ▷ **stabilize**
stable[1] *n* (*pl* **-s**) building in which horses are kept ▶ *v* (**-les, -ling, -led**) put or keep (a horse) in a stable
stable[2] *adj* (**-r, -st**) firmly fixed or established > **stability** *n* (*pl* **-ties**)
stabled *v* ▷ **stable[1]**
stabler *adj* ▷ **stable[2]**
stables *n, v* ▷ **stable[1]**
stablest *adj* ▷ **stable[2]**
stabling *v* ▷ **stable[1]**
stabs *v, n* ▷ **stab**
staccato [stak-ah-toe] *adv* (MUSIC) with the notes sharply separated ▶ *adj* consisting of short abrupt sounds
stack *n* (*pl* **-s**) ordered pile ▶ *v* (**-s, -ing, -ed**) pile in a stack
stacked *v* ▷ **stack**
stacking *v* ▷ **stack**
stacks *n, v* ▷ **stack**
stadia *n* ▷ **stadium**
stadium *n* (*pl* **-diums, -dia**) sports arena with tiered seats for spectators
stadiums *n* ▷ **stadium**
staff[1] *n* (*pl* **-s**) people employed in an organization ▶ *v* (**-s, -ing, -ed**) supply with personnel
staff[2] *n* (*pl* **staves**) set of five horizontal lines on which music is written
staffed *v* ▷ **staff[1]**
staffing *v* ▷ **staff[1]**
staffs *n, v* ▷ **staff[1]**
stag *n* (*pl* **-s**) adult male deer
stage *n* (*pl* **-s**) step or period of development ▶ *v* (**-ges, -ging, -ged**) put (a play) on stage
stagecoach *n* (*pl* **-es**) large horse-drawn vehicle formerly used to carry passengers and mail
stagecoaches *n* ▷ **stagecoach**
staged *v* ▷ **stage**
stages *n, v* ▷ **stage**
stagey *adj* (**-gier, -giest**) overtheatrical
stagger *v* (**-s, -ing, -ed**) walk unsteadily ▶ *n* (*pl* **-s**) staggering
staggered *v* ▷ **stagger**
staggering *v* ▷ **stagger**
staggers *v, n* ▷ **stagger**
stagier *adj* ▷ **stagey**
stagiest *adj* ▷ **stagey**
staging *v* ▷ **stage**
stagnant *adj* (of water or air) stale from not moving
stagnate *v* (**-tes, -ting, -ted**) be stagnant > **stagnation** *n* (*pl* **-s**)
stagnated *v* ▷ **stagnate**
stagnates *v* ▷ **stagnate**
stagnating *v* ▷ **stagnate**
stagnation *n* ▷ **stagnate**
stagnations *n* ▷ **stagnate**
stags *n* ▷ **stag**
staid *adj* (**-er, -est**) sedate, serious, and rather dull
staider *adj* ▷ **staid**
staidest *adj* ▷ **staid**
stain *v* (**-s, -ing, -ed**) discolour, mark ▶ *n* (*pl* **-s**) discoloration or mark > **stainless** *adj*
stained *v* ▷ **stain**
staining *v* ▷ **stain**
stainless *adj* ▷ **stain**
stains *v, n* ▷ **stain**
staircase, stairway *n* (*pl* **-s**) flight of stairs with a handrail or banisters
staircases *n* ▷ **staircase**
stairs *pl n* flight of steps between floors, usu. indoors
stairway *n* ▷ **staircase**
stairways *n* ▷ **staircase**
stake[1] *n* (*pl* **-s**) pointed stick or post driven into the ground as a support or marker ▶ *v* (**-kes, -king, -ked**) support or mark out with stakes
stake[2] *n* (*pl* **-s**) money wagered ▶ *v* (**-kes, -king, -ked**) wager, risk
staked *v* ▷ **stake[1, 2]**

stakeholder *n* (*pl* **-s**) person who has a concern or interest in something, esp. a business
stakeholders *n* ▷ **stakeholder**
stakes *v* ▷ **stake**[1, 2] ▶ *n* ▷ **stake**[1, 2]
staking *v* ▷ **stake**[1, 2]
stalactite *n* (*pl* **-s**) lime deposit hanging from the roof of a cave
stalactites *n* ▷ **stalactite**
stalagmite *n* (*pl* **-s**) lime deposit sticking up from the floor of a cave
stalagmites *n* ▷ **stalagmite**
stale *adj* (**-r, -st**) not fresh > **staleness** *n* (*pl* **-es**)
stalemate *n* (*pl* **-s**) (CHESS) position in which any of a player's moves would put his king in check, resulting in a draw
stalemates *n* ▷ **stalemate**
staleness *n* ▷ **stale**
stalenesses *n* ▷ **stale**
staler *adj* ▷ **stale**
stalest *adj* ▷ **stale**
stalk[1] *n* (*pl* **-s**) plant's stem
stalk[2] *v* (**-s, -ing, -ed**) follow or approach stealthily
stalked *v* ▷ **stalk**[2]
stalker *n* (*pl* **-s**) person who follows or stealthily approaches a person or an animal
stalkers *n* ▷ **stalker**
stalking *v* ▷ **stalk**[2]
stalking-horse *n* (*pl* **-s**) pretext
stalking-horses *n* ▷ **stalking-horse**
stalks *n* ▷ **stalk**[1] ▶ *v* ▷ **stalk**[2]
stall[1] *n* (*pl* **-s**) small stand for the display and sale of goods ▶ *v* (**-s, -ing, -ed**) stop (a motor vehicle or engine) or (of a motor vehicle or engine) stop accidentally
stall[2] *v* (**-s, -ing, -ed**) employ delaying tactics
stalled *v* ▷ **stall**[1, 2]
stalling *v* ▷ **stall**[1, 2]
stallion *n* (*pl* **-s**) uncastrated male horse
stallions *n* ▷ **stallion**
stalls *n* ▷ **stall**[1] ▶ *v* ▷ **stall**[1, 2] ▶ *pl n* ground-floor seats in a theatre or cinema
stalwart [**stawl**-wart] *adj* strong and sturdy ▶ *n* (*pl* **-s**) stalwart person
stalwarts *n* ▷ **stalwart**
stamen *n* (*pl* **-s**) pollen-producing part of a flower
stamens *n* ▷ **stamen**
stamina *n* (*pl* **-s**) enduring energy and strength
staminas *n* ▷ **stamina**
stammer *v* (**-s, -ing, ed**) speak or say with involuntary pauses or repetition of syllables ▶ *n* (*pl* **-s**) tendency to stammer
stammered *v* ▷ **stammer**
stammering *v* ▷ **stammer**
stammers *v, n* ▷ **stammer**
stamp *n* (*pl* **-s**) piece of gummed paper stuck to an envelope or parcel to show that the postage has been paid ▶ *v* (**-s, -ing, -ed**) bring (one's foot) down forcefully
stamped *v* ▷ **stamp**
stampede *n* (*pl* **-s**) sudden rush of frightened animals or of a crowd ▶ *v* (**-des, -ding, -ded**) (cause to) take part in a stampede
stampeded *v* ▷ **stampede**
stampedes *n, v* ▷ **stampede**
stampeding *v* ▷ **stampede**
stamping *v* ▷ **stamp**
stamps *n, v* ▷ **stamp**
stance *n* (*pl* **-s**) attitude
stances *n* ▷ **stance**
stanch [stahnch] *v* (**-es, -ing, -ed**) ▷ **staunch**[2]
stanched *v* ▷ **stanch**
stanches *v* ▷ **stanch**
stanching *v* ▷ **stanch**
stanchion *n* (*pl* **-s**) upright bar used as a support
stanchions *n* ▷ **stanchion**
stand *v* (**-s, -ing, stood**) be in, rise to, or place in an upright position ▶ *n* (*pl* **-s**) stall for the sale of goods
standard *n* (*pl* **-s**) level of quality ▶ *adj* usual, regular, or average
standardization *n* ▷ **standardize**
standardize *v* (**-zes, -zing, -zed**) cause to conform to a standard > **standardization** *n* (*pl* **-s**)
standardized *v* ▷ **standardize**
standardizes *v* ▷ **standardize**
standardizing *v* ▷ **standardize**
standards *n* ▷ **standard**
standing *adj* permanent, lasting ▶ *n* (*pl* **-s**) reputation or status ▶ *v* ▷ **stand**
standings *n* ▷ **standing**
standoffish *adj* reserved or haughty
standpipe *n* (*pl* **-s**) tap attached to a water main to provide a public water supply
standpipes *n* ▷ **standpipe**
standpoint *n* (*pl* **-s**) point of view
standpoints *n* ▷ **standpoint**
stands *v, n* ▷ **stand**
standstill *n* (*pl* **-s**) complete halt
standstills *n* ▷ **standstill**
stank *v* ▷ **stink**
stanza *n* (*pl* **-s**) verse of a poem
stanzas *n* ▷ **stanza**
staple[1] *n* (*pl* **-s**) U-shaped piece of metal used to fasten papers or secure things ▶ *v* (**-les, -ling, -led**) fasten with staples
staple[2] *adj* of prime importance, principal ▶ *n*

(*pl* **-s**) main constituent of anything
stapled *v* ▷ **staple**[1]
stapler *n* (*pl* **-s**) small device for fastening papers together
staplers *n* ▷ **stapler**
staples *n* ▷ **staple**[1, 2] ▶ *v* ▷ **staple**[1]
stapling *v* ▷ **staple**[1]
star *n* (*pl* **-s**) hot gaseous mass in space, visible in the night sky as a point of light ▶ *v* (**-s, -rring, -rred**) feature or be featured in a main role ▶ *adj* leading, famous
starboard *n* (*pl* **-s**) right-hand side of a ship, when facing forward ▶ *adj* of or on this side
starboards *n* ▷ **starboard**
starch *n* (*pl* **-es**) carbohydrate forming the main food element in bread, potatoes, etc., and used mixed with water for stiffening fabric ▶ *v* (**-es, -ing, -ed**) stiffen (fabric) with starch
starched *v* ▷ **starch**
starches *n, v* ▷ **starch**
starchier *adj* ▷ **starchy**
starchiest *adj* ▷ **starchy**
starching *v* ▷ **starch**
starchy *adj* (**-chier, -chiest**) containing starch
stardom *n* (*pl* **-s**) status of a star in the entertainment or sports world
stardoms *n* ▷ **stardom**
stare *v* (**-res, -ring, -red**) look or gaze fixedly (at) ▶ *n* (*pl* **-s**) fixed gaze
stared *v* ▷ **stare**
stares *v, n* ▷ **stare**
starfish *n* (*pl* **-es**) star-shaped sea creature
starfishes *n* ▷ **starfish**
staring *v* ▷ **stare**
stark *adj* (**-er, -est**) harsh, unpleasant, and plain ▶ *adv* completely
starker *adj* ▷ **stark**
starkest *adj* ▷ **stark**
starling *n* (*pl* **-s**) songbird with glossy black speckled feathers
starlings *n* ▷ **starling**
starred *v* ▷ **star**
starrier *adj* ▷ **starry**
starriest *adj* ▷ **starry**
starring *v* ▷ **star**
starry *adj* (**-rrier, -rriest**) full of or like stars
stars *n, v* ▷ **star** ▶ *pl n* astrological forecast, horoscope
start *v* (**-s, -ing, -ed**) take the first step, begin ▶ *n* (*pl* **-s**) first part of something
started *v* ▷ **start**
starter *n* (*pl* **-s**) first course of a meal
starters *n* ▷ **starter**
starting *v* ▷ **start**
startle *v* (**-les, -ling, -led**) slightly surprise or frighten
startled *v* ▷ **startle**
startles *v* ▷ **startle**
startling *v* ▷ **startle**
starts *v, n* ▷ **start**
starvation *n* ▷ **starve**
starvations *n* ▷ **starve**
starve *v* (**-ves, -ving, -ved**) die or suffer or cause to die or suffer from hunger > **starvation** *n* (*pl* **-s**)
starved *v* ▷ **starve**
starves *v* ▷ **starve**
starving *v* ▷ **starve**
stash (*Informal*) *v* (**-es, -ing, -ed**) store in a secret place ▶ *n* (*pl* **-es**) secret store
stashed *v* ▷ **stash**
stashes *v, n* ▷ **stash**
stashing *v* ▷ **stash**
state *n* (*pl* **-s**) condition of a person or thing ▶ *adj* of or concerning the State ▶ *v* (**-tes, -ting, -ted**) express in words
stated *v* ▷ **state**
statehouse *n* (*pl* **-s**) (NZ) publicly-owned house rented to a low-income tenant
statehouses *n* ▷ **statehouse**
statelier *adj* ▷ **stately**
stateliest *adj* ▷ **stately**
stately *adj* (**-lier, -liest**) dignified or grand
statement *n* (*pl* **-s**) something stated
statements *n* ▷ **statement**
stateroom *n* (*pl* **-s**) private cabin on a ship
staterooms *n* ▷ **stateroom**
states *n, v* ▷ **state**
statesman, stateswoman *n* (*pl* **-men, -women**) experienced and respected political leader > **statesmanship** *n* (*pl* **-s**)
statesmanship *n* ▷ **statesman**
statesmanships *n* ▷ **statesman**
statesmen *n* ▷ **statesman**
stateswoman *n* ▷ **statesman**
stateswomen *n* ▷ **statesman**
static *adj* stationary or inactive ▶ *n* (*pl* **-s**) crackling sound or speckled picture caused by interference in radio or television reception
statics *n* ▷ **static**
stating *v* ▷ **state**
station *n* (*pl* **-s**) place where trains stop for passengers ▶ *v* (**-s, -ing, -ed**) assign (someone) to a particular place
stationary *adj* not moving
stationed *v* ▷ **station**
stationer *n* (*pl* **-s**) dealer in stationery
stationeries *n* ▷ **stationery**

stationers *n* ▷ **stationer**

stationery *n* (*pl* **-ries**) writing materials such as paper and pens

stationing *v* ▷ **station**

stations *n*, *v* ▷ **station**

statistic *n* (*pl* **-s**) numerical fact collected and classified systematically > **statistical** *adj* > **statistically** *adv*

statistical *adj* ▷ **statistic**

statistically *adv* ▷ **statistic**

statistician *n* (*pl* **-s**) person who compiles and studies statistics

statisticians *n* ▷ **statistician**

statistics *n* ▷ **statistic**

statuaries *n* ▷ **statuary**

statuary *n* (*pl* **-ries**) statues collectively

statue *n* (*pl* **-s**) large sculpture of a human or animal figure

statues *n* ▷ **statue**

statuesque *adj* (of a woman) tall and well-proportioned

statuette *n* (*pl* **-s**) small statue

statuettes *n* ▷ **statuette**

stature *n* (*pl* **-s**) person's height

statures *n* ▷ **stature**

status *n* (*pl* **-ses**) social position

statuses *n* ▷ **status**

statute *n* (*pl* **-s**) written law > **statutory** *adj* required or authorized by law

statutes *n* ▷ **statute**

statutory *adj* ▷ **statute**

staunch[1] *adj* (**-er, -est**) loyal, firm

staunch[2], **stanch** *v* (**-ches, -ching, -ched**) stop (a flow of blood)

staunched *v* ▷ **staunch**[2]

stauncher *adj* ▷ **staunch**[1]

staunches *v* ▷ **staunch**[2]

staunchest *adj* ▷ **staunch**[1]

staunching *v* ▷ **staunch**[2]

stave *n* (*pl* **-s**) one of the strips of wood forming a barrel

staves *n* ▷ **staff**[2]

stay[1] *v* (**-s, -ing, -ed**) remain in a place or condition ▶ *n* (*pl* **-s**) period of staying in a place

stay[2] *n* (*pl* **-s**) prop or buttress

stay[3] *n* (*pl* **-s**) rope or wire supporting a ship's mast

stayed *v* ▷ **stay**[1]

staying *v* ▷ **stay**[1]

stays *n* ▷ **stay**[1, 2, 3] ▶ *v* ▷ **stay**[1] ▶ *pl n* corset

stead *n* (*pl* **-s**) in someone's place

steadfast *adj* firm, determined > **steadfastly** *adv*

steadfastly *adv* ▷ **steadfast**

steadied *v* ▷ **steady**

steadier *adj* ▷ **steady**

steadiest *adj* ▷ **steady**

steadily *adv* ▷ **steady**

steadiness *n* ▷ **steady**

steadinesses *n* ▷ **steady**

steads *n* ▷ **stead**

steady *adj* (**-dier, -diest**) not shaky or wavering ▶ *v* (**-dies, -dying, -died**) make steady ▶ *adv* in a steady manner > **steadily** *adv* > **steadiness** *n* (*pl* **-es**)

steadying *v* ▷ **steady**

steak *n* (*pl* **-s**) thick slice of meat, esp. beef

steaks *n* ▷ **steak**

steal *v* (**-s, -ing, stole, stolen**) take unlawfully or without permission

stealing *v* ▷ **steal**

steals *v* ▷ **steal**

stealth *n* (*pl* **-s**) secret or underhand behaviour ▶ *adj* (of technology) able to render an aircraft almost invisible to radar > **stealthy** *adj* (**-thier, -thiest**) > **stealthily** *adv*

stealthier *adj* ▷ **stealth**

stealthiest *adj* ▷ **stealth**

stealthily *adv* ▷ **stealth**

stealths *n* ▷ **stealth**

stealthy *adj* ▷ **stealth**

steam *n* (*pl* **-s**) vapour into which water changes when boiled ▶ *v* (**-s, -ing, -ed**) give off steam

steamed *v* ▷ **steam**

steamer *n* (*pl* **-s**) steam-propelled ship

steamers *n* ▷ **steamer**

steaming *v* ▷ **steam**

steamroller *n* (*pl* **-s**) steam-powered vehicle with heavy rollers, used to level road surfaces ▶ *v* (**-s, -ing, -ed**) use overpowering force to make (someone) do what one wants

steamrollered *v* ▷ **steamroller**

steamrollering *v* ▷ **steamroller**

steamrollers *n*, *v* ▷ **steamroller**

steams *n*, *v* ▷ **steam**

steed *n* (*pl* **-s**) (*Lit*) horse

steeds *n* ▷ **steed**

steel *n* (*pl* **-s**) hard malleable alloy of iron and carbon ▶ *v* (**-s, -ing, -ed**) prepare (oneself) for something unpleasant > **steely** *adj* (**-lier, -liest**)

steeled *v* ▷ **steel**

steelier *adj* ▷ **steel**

steeliest *adj* ▷ **steel**

steeling *v* ▷ **steel**

steels *n*, *v* ▷ **steel**

steely *adj* ▷ **steel**

steep[1] *adj* (**-er, -est**) sloping sharply > **steeply**

adv > **steepness** *n* (*pl* **-es**)
steep² *v* (**-s, -ing, -ed**) soak or be soaked in liquid
steeped *v* ▷ **steep²**
steeper *adj* ▷ **steep¹**
steepest *adj* ▷ **steep¹**
steeping *v* ▷ **steep²**
steeple *n* (*pl* **-s**) church tower with a spire
steeplechase *n* (*pl* **-s**) horse race with obstacles to jump
steeplechases *n* ▷ **steeplechase**
steeplejack *n* (*pl* **-s**) person who repairs steeples and chimneys
steeplejacks *n* ▷ **steeplejack**
steeples *n* ▷ **steeple**
steeply *n* ▷ **steep¹**
steepness *n* ▷ **steep¹**
steepnesses *n* ▷ **steep¹**
steeps *v* ▷ **steep²**
steer¹ *v* (**-s, -ing, -ed**) direct the course of (a vehicle or ship)
steer² *n* (*pl* **-s**) castrated male ox
steerage *n* (*pl* **-s**) cheapest accommodation on a passenger ship
steerages *n* ▷ **steerage**
steered *v* ▷ **steer¹**
steering *v* ▷ **steer¹**
steers *v* ▷ **steer¹** ▶ *n* ▷ **steer²**
stein [**stine**] *n* (*pl* **-s**) earthenware beer mug
steins *n* ▷ **stein**
stellar *adj* of stars
stem¹ *n* (*pl* **-s**) long thin central part of a plant ▶ *v* (**-s, -mming, -mmed**) originate from
stem² *v* (**-s, -mming, -mmed**) stop (the flow of something)
stemmed *v* ▷ **stem¹, ²**
stemming *v* ▷ **stem¹, ²**
stems *v* ▷ **stem¹, ²** ▶ *n* ▷ **stem¹**
stench *n* (*pl* **-es**) foul smell
stenches *n* ▷ **stench**
stencil *n* (*pl* **-s**) thin sheet with cut-out pattern through which ink or paint passes to form the pattern on the surface below ▶ *v* (**-s, -lling, -lled**) make (a pattern) with a stencil
stencilled *v* ▷ **stencil**
stencilling *v* ▷ **stencil**
stencils *n, v* ▷ **stencil**
stenographer *n* (*pl* **-s**) shorthand typist
stenographers *n* ▷ **stenographer**
stent *n* (*pl* **-s**) surgical implant used to keep an artery open
stentorian *adj* (of a voice) very loud
stents *n* ▷ **stent**
step *v* (**-s, -pping, -pped**) move and set down the foot, as when walking ▶ *n* (*pl* **-s**) stepping
stepladder *n* (*pl* **-s**) folding portable ladder with supporting frame
stepladders *n* ▷ **stepladder**
stepped *v* ▷ **step**
steppes *pl n* wide grassy treeless plains in Russia and Ukraine
stepping *v* ▷ **step**
steps *pl n* stepladder ▶ *n, v* ▷ **step**
stereo *adj* ▷ **stereophonic** ▶ *n* (*pl* **-s**) stereophonic record player
stereophonic *adj* using two separate loudspeakers to give the effect of naturally distributed sound
stereos *n* ▷ **stereo**
stereotype *n* (*pl* **-s**) standardized idea of a type of person or thing ▶ *v* (**-pes, -ping, -ped**) form a stereotype of
stereotyped *v* ▷ **stereotype**
stereotypes *n, v* ▷ **stereotype**
stereotyping *v* ▷ **stereotype**
sterile *adj* free from germs > **sterility** *n* (*pl* **-ties**)
sterilities *n* ▷ **sterile**
sterility *n* ▷ **sterile**
sterilization *n* ▷ **sterilize**
sterilizations *n* ▷ **sterilize**
sterilize *v* (**-zes, -zing, -zed**) make sterile > **sterilization** *n* (*pl* **-s**)
sterilized *v* ▷ **sterilize**
sterilizes *v* ▷ **sterilize**
sterilizing *v* ▷ **sterilize**
sterling *n* (*pl* **-s**) British money system ▶ *adj* genuine and reliable
sterlings *n* ▷ **sterling**
stern¹ *adj* (**-er, -est**) severe, strict > **sternly** *adv* > **sternness** *n* (*pl* **-es**)
stern² *n* (*pl* **-s**) rear part of a ship
sterna *n* ▷ **sternum**
sterner *adj* ▷ **stern¹**
sternest *adj* ▷ **stern¹**
sternly *adv* ▷ **stern¹**
sternness *n* ▷ **stern¹**
sternnesses *n* ▷ **stern¹**
sterns *n* ▷ **stern²**
sternum *n* (*pl* **-na, -nums**) ▷ **breastbone**
sternums *n* ▷ **sternum**
steroid *n* (*pl* **-s**) organic compound containing a carbon ring system, such as many hormones
steroids *n* ▷ **steroid**
stethoscope *n* (*pl* **-s**) medical instrument for listening to sounds made inside the body
stethoscopes *n* ▷ **stethoscope**
stevedore *n* (*pl* **-s**) person who loads and unloads ships
stevedores *n* ▷ **stevedore**

stew *n* (*pl* **-s**) food cooked slowly in a closed pot ▶ *v* (**-s, -ing, -ed**) cook slowly in a closed pot
steward *n* (*pl* **-s**) person who looks after passengers on a ship or aircraft > **stewardess** *n fem* (*pl* **-es**)
stewardess *n* ▷ **steward**
stewardesses *n* ▷ **steward**
stewards *n* ▷ **steward**
stewed *v* ▷ **stew**
stewing *v* ▷ **stew**
stews *n, v* ▷ **stew**
stick[1] *n* (*pl* **-s**) long thin piece of wood
stick[2] *v* (**-s, -ing, stuck**) push (a pointed object) into (something)
sticker *n* (*pl* **-s**) adhesive label or sign
stickers *n* ▷ **sticker**
stickier *adj* ▷ **sticky**
stickiest *adj* ▷ **sticky**
sticking *v* ▷ **stick[2]**
stickleback *n* (*pl* **-s**) small fish with sharp spines on its back
sticklebacks *n* ▷ **stickleback**
stickler *n* (*pl* **-s**) person who insists on something
sticklers *n* ▷ **stickler**
sticks *n* ▷ **stick[1]** ▶ *v* ▷ **stick[2]**
stickup *n* (*pl* **-s**) (*Slang*) robbery at gunpoint
stickups *n* ▷ **stickup**
sticky *adj* (**-ckier, -ckiest**) covered with an adhesive substance
sties *n* ▷ **sty**
stiff *adj* (**-er, -est**) not easily bent or moved ▶ *n* (*pl* **-s**) (*Slang*) corpse > **stiffly** *adv* > **stiffness** *n* (*pl* **-es**)
stiffen *v* (**-s, -ing, -ed**) make or become stiff
stiffened *v* ▷ **stiffen**
stiffening *v* ▷ **stiffen**
stiffens *v* ▷ **stiffen**
stiffer *adj* ▷ **stiff**
stiffest *adj* ▷ **stiff**
stiffly *adv* ▷ **stiff**
stiffness *n* ▷ **stiff**
stiffnesses *n* ▷ **stiff**
stiffs *n* ▷ **stiff**
stifle *v* (**-les, -ling, -led**) suppress
stifled *v* ▷ **stifle**
stifles *v* ▷ **stifle**
stifling *v* ▷ **stifle**
stigma *n* (*pl* **-mas, -mata**) mark of social disgrace
stigmas *n* ▷ **stigma**
stigmata *pl n* marks resembling the wounds of the crucified Christ ▶ *n* ▷ **stigma**
stigmatize *v* (**-zes, -zing, -zed**) mark as being shameful
stigmatized *v* ▷ **stigmatize**
stigmatizes *v* ▷ **stigmatize**
stigmatizing *v* ▷ **stigmatize**
stile *n* (*pl* **-s**) set of steps allowing people to climb a fence
stiles *n* ▷ **stile**
stiletto *n* (*pl* **-s**) high narrow heel on a woman's shoe
stilettos *n* ▷ **stiletto**
still[1] *adv* now or in the future as before ▶ *adj* (**-er, -est**) motionless ▶ *n* (*pl* **-s**) photograph from a film scene ▶ *v* (**-s, -ing, -ed**) make still > **stillness** *n* (*pl* **-es**)
still[2] *n* (*pl* **-s**) apparatus for distilling alcoholic drinks
stillborn *adj* born dead
stilled *v* ▷ **still[1]**
stiller *adj* ▷ **still[1]**
stillest *adj* ▷ **still[1]**
stilling *v* ▷ **still[1]**
stillness *n* ▷ **still[1]**
stillnesses *n* ▷ **still[1]**
stills *n* ▷ **still[1, 2]** ▶ *v* ▷ **still[1]**
stilted *adj* stiff and formal in manner
stilts *pl n* pair of poles with footrests for walking raised from the ground
stimulant *n* (*pl* **-s**) something, such as a drug, that acts as a stimulus
stimulants *n* ▷ **stimulant**
stimulate *v* (**-tes, -ting, -ted**) act as a stimulus (on) > **stimulation** *n* (*pl* **-s**)
stimulated *v* ▷ **stimulate**
stimulates *v* ▷ **stimulate**
stimulating *v* ▷ **stimulate**
stimulation *n* ▷ **stimulate**
stimulations *n* ▷ **stimulate**
stimuli *n* ▷ **stimulus**
stimulus *n* (*pl* **-li**) something that rouses a person or thing to activity
sting *v* (**-s, -ing, stung**) (of certain animals or plants) wound by injecting with poison ▶ *n* (*pl* **-s**) wound or pain caused by or as if by stinging
stingier *adj* ▷ **stingy**
stingiest *adj* ▷ **stingy**
stinginess *n* ▷ **stingy**
stinginesses *n* ▷ **stingy**
stinging *v* ▷ **sting**
stings *v, n* ▷ **sting**
stingy *adj* (**-gier, -giest**) mean or miserly > **stinginess** *n* (*pl* **-es**)
stink *n* (*pl* **-s**) strong unpleasant smell ▶ *v* (**-s, -ing, stank** *or* **stunk**) (**stunk**) give off a strong unpleasant smell
stinking *v* ▷ **stink**

stinks *n, v* ▷ **stink**
stint *v* (**-s, -ing, -ed**) (*foll. by* **on**) be miserly with (something) ▸ *n* (*pl* **-s**) allotted amount of work
stinted *v* ▷ **stint**
stinting *v* ▷ **stint**
stints *v, n* ▷ **stint**
stipend [**sty**-pend] *n* (*pl* **-s**) regular allowance or salary, esp. that paid to a clergyman > **stipendiary** *adj* receiving a stipend
stipendiary *adj* ▷ **stipend**
stipends *n* ▷ **stipend**
stipple *v* (**-les, -ling, -led**) paint, draw, or engrave using dots
stippled *v* ▷ **stipple**
stipples *v* ▷ **stipple**
stippling *v* ▷ **stipple**
stipulate *v* (**-tes, -ting, -ted**) specify as a condition of an agreement > **stipulation** *n* (*pl* **-s**)
stipulated *v* ▷ **stipulate**
stipulates *v* ▷ **stipulate**
stipulating *v* ▷ **stipulate**
stipulation *n* ▷ **stipulate**
stipulations *n* ▷ **stipulate**
stir *v* (**-s, -rring, -rred**) mix up (a liquid) by moving a spoon etc. around in it ▸ *n* (*pl* **-s**) a stirring
stirred *v* ▷ **stir**
stirring *v* ▷ **stir**
stirrup *n* (*pl* **-s**) metal loop attached to a saddle for supporting a rider's foot
stirrups *n* ▷ **stirrup**
stirs *v, n* ▷ **stir**
stitch *n* (*pl* **-es**) link made by drawing thread through material with a needle ▸ *v* (**-es, -ing, -ed**) sew
stitched *v* ▷ **stitch**
stitches *n, v* ▷ **stitch**
stitching *v* ▷ **stitch**
stoat *n* (*pl* **-s**) small mammal of the weasel family, with brown fur that turns white in winter
stoats *n* ▷ **stoat**
stock *n* (*pl* **-s**) total amount of goods available for sale in a shop ▸ *adj* kept in stock, standard ▸ *v* (**-s, -ing, -ed**) keep for sale or future use
stockade *n* (*pl* **-s**) enclosure or barrier made of stakes
stockades *n* ▷ **stockade**
stockbroker *n* (*pl* **-s**) person who buys and sells stocks and shares for customers
stockbrokers *n* ▷ **stockbroker**
stocked *v* ▷ **stock**
stockier *adj* ▷ **stocky**
stockiest *adj* ▷ **stocky**
stocking *n* (*pl* **-s**) close-fitting covering for the foot and leg ▸ *v* ▷ **stock**
stockings *n* ▷ **stocking**
stockist *n* (*pl* **-s**) dealer who stocks a particular product
stockists *n* ▷ **stockist**
stockpile *v* (**-les, -ling, -led**) store a large quantity of (something) for future use ▸ *n* (*pl* **-s**) accumulated store
stockpiled *v* ▷ **stockpile**
stockpiles *v, n* ▷ **stockpile**
stockpiling *v* ▷ **stockpile**
stocks *n pl* (HIST) instrument of punishment consisting of a wooden frame with holes into which the hands and feet of the victim were locked ▸ *n, v* ▷ **stock**
stocktaking *n* (*pl* **-s**) counting and valuing of the goods in a shop
stocktakings *n* ▷ **stocktaking**
stocky *adj* (**-ckier, -ckiest**) (of a person) broad and sturdy
stodge *n* (*pl* **-s**) (BRIT, AUST & NZ) heavy starchy food
stodges *n* ▷ **stodge**
stodgier *adj* ▷ **stodgy**
stodgiest *adj* ▷ **stodgy**
stodgy *adj* (**-gier, -giest**) (of food) heavy and starchy
stoep [**stoop**] *n* (*pl* **-s**) (S AFR) verandah
stoeps *n* ▷ **stoep**
stoic [**stow**-ik] *n* (*pl* **-s**) person who suffers hardship without showing his or her feelings ▸ *adj* (*also* **stoical**) suffering hardship without showing one's feelings > **stoically** *adv* > **stoicism** [**stow**-iss-izz-um] *n* (*pl* **-s**)
stoical *adj* ▷ **stoic**
stoically *adv* ▷ **stoic**
stoicism *n* ▷ **stoic**
stoicisms *n* ▷ **stoic**
stoics *n* ▷ **stoic**
stoke *v* (**-kes, -king, -ked**) feed and tend (a fire or furnace) > **stoker** *n* (*pl* **-s**)
stoked *v* ▷ **stoke**
stoker *n* ▷ **stoke**
stokers *n* ▷ **stoke**
stokes *v* ▷ **stoke**
stoking *v* ▷ **stoke**
stole¹ *v* ▷ **steal**
stole² *n* (*pl* **-s**) long scarf or shawl
stolen *v* ▷ **steal**
stoles *n* ▷ **stole²**
stolid *adj* (**-er, -est**) showing little emotion or interest > **stolidly** *adv*
stolider *adj* ▷ **stolid**

stolidest *adj* ▷ **stolid**
stolidly *adv* ▷ **stolid**
stomach *n* (*pl* **-s**) organ in the body which digests food ▶ *v* (**-s, -ing, -ed**) put up with
stomached *v* ▷ **stomach**
stomaching *v* ▷ **stomach**
stomachs *n, v* ▷ **stomach**
stomp *v* (**-s, -ing, -ed**) (*Informal*) tread heavily
stomped *v* ▷ **stomp**
stomping *v* ▷ **stomp**
stomps *v* ▷ **stomp**
stone *n* (*pl* **-s**) material of which rocks are made ▶ *v* (**-nes, -ning, -ned**) throw stones at
stoned *adj* (*Slang*) under the influence of alcohol or drugs ▶ *v* ▷ **stone**
stones *n, v* ▷ **stone**
stonewall *v* (**-s, -ing, -ed**) obstruct or hinder discussion
stonewalled *v* ▷ **stonewall**
stonewalling *v* ▷ **stonewall**
stonewalls *v* ▷ **stonewall**
stoneware *n* (*pl* **-s**) hard kind of pottery fired at a very high temperature
stonewares *n* ▷ **stoneware**
stonier *adj* ▷ **stony**
stoniest *adj* ▷ **stony**
stonily *adv* ▷ **stony**
stoning *v* ▷ **stone**
stony *adj* (**-nier, -niest**) of or like stone > **stonily** *adv*
stood *v* ▷ **stand**
stooge *n* (*pl* **-es**) actor who feeds lines to a comedian or acts as the butt of his jokes
stooges *n* ▷ **stooge**
stool *n* (*pl* **-s**) chair without arms or back
stools *n* ▷ **stool**
stoop *v* (**-s, -ing, -ed**) bend (the body) forward and downward ▶ *n* (*pl* **-s**) stooping posture
stooped *v* ▷ **stoop**
stooping *v* ▷ **stoop**
stoops *v, n* ▷ **stoop**
stop *v* (**-s, -pping, -pped**) cease or cause to cease from doing (something) ▶ *n* (*pl* **-s**) stopping or being stopped > **stoppage** *n* (*pl* **-s**)
stopcock *n* (*pl* **-s**) valve to control or stop the flow of fluid in a pipe
stopcocks *n* ▷ **stopcock**
stopgap *n* (*pl* **-s**) temporary substitute
stopgaps *n* ▷ **stopgap**
stopover *n* (*pl* **-s**) short break in a journey
stopovers *n* ▷ **stopover**
stoppage *n* ▷ **stop**
stoppages *n* ▷ **stop**
stopped *v* ▷ **stop**
stopper *n* (*pl* **-s**) plug for closing a bottle etc.
stoppers *n* ▷ **stopper**
stopping *v* ▷ **stop**
stops *v, n* ▷ **stop**
stopwatch *n* (*pl* **-es**) watch which can be stopped instantly for exact timing of a sporting event
stopwatches *n* ▷ **stopwatch**
storage *n* (*pl* **-s**) storing
storages *n* ▷ **storage**
store *v* (**-res, -ring, -red**) collect and keep (things) for future use ▶ *n* (*pl* **-s**) shop
stored *v* ▷ **store**
stores *v, n* ▷ **store** ▶ *n pl* stock of provisions
storey *n* (*pl* **-s**) floor or level of a building
storeys *n* ▷ **storey**
stories *n* ▷ **story**
storing *v* ▷ **store**
stork *n* (*pl* **-s**) large wading bird
storks *n* ▷ **stork**
storm *n* (*pl* **-s**) violent weather with wind, rain, or snow ▶ *v* (**-s, -ing, -ed**) attack or capture (a place) suddenly
stormed *v* ▷ **storm**
stormier *adj* ▷ **stormy**
stormiest *adj* ▷ **stormy**
storming *v* ▷ **storm**
storms *n, v* ▷ **storm**
stormy *adj* (**-mier, -miest**) characterized by storms
story *n* (*pl* **-ries**) description of a series of events told or written for entertainment
stoup [**stoop**] *n* (*pl* **-s**) small basin for holy water
stoups *n* ▷ **stoup**
stout *adj* (**-er, -est**) fat ▶ *n* (*pl* **-s**) strong dark beer > **stoutly** *adv*
stouter *adj* ▷ **stout**
stoutest *adj* ▷ **stout**
stoutly *adv* ▷ **stout**
stouts *n* ▷ **stout**
stove *n* (*pl* **-s**) apparatus for cooking or heating
stoves *n* ▷ **stove**
stow *v* (**-s, -ing, -ed**) pack or store
stowaway *n* (*pl* **-s**) person who hides on a ship or aircraft in order to travel free
stowaways *n* ▷ **stowaway**
stowed *v* ▷ **stow**
stowing *v* ▷ **stow**
stows *v* ▷ **stow**
straddle *v* (**-les, -ling, -led**) have one leg or part on each side of (something)
straddled *v* ▷ **straddle**
straddles *v* ▷ **straddle**
straddling *v* ▷ **straddle**
strafe *v* (**-fes, -fing, -fed**) attack (an enemy) with machine guns from the air

strafed *v* ▷ **strafe**
strafes *v* ▷ **strafe**
strafing *v* ▷ **strafe**
straggle *v* (**-les, -ling, -led**) go or spread in a rambling or irregular way > **straggler** *n* (*pl* **-s**) > **straggly** *adj* (**-lier, -liest**)
straggled *v* ▷ **straggle**
straggler *n* ▷ **straggle**
stragglers *n* ▷ **straggle**
straggles *v* ▷ **straggle**
stragglier *adj* ▷ **straggle**
straggliest *adj* ▷ **straggle**
straggling *v* ▷ **straggle**
straggly *adj* ▷ **straggle**
straight *adj* (**-er, -est**) not curved or crooked ▶ *adv* in a straight line ▶ *n* (*pl* **-s**) straight part, esp. of a racetrack > **straighten** *v* (**-s, -ing, -ed**)
straightaway *adv* immediately
straighten *v* ▷ **straight**
straightened *v* ▷ **straight**
straightening *v* ▷ **straight**
straightens *v* ▷ **straighn**
straighter *adj* ▷ **straight**
straightest *adj* ▷ **straight**
straightforward *adj* honest, frank
straightlaced *adj* ▷ **straitlaced**
straights *n* ▷ **straight**
strain[1] *v* (**-s, -ing, -ed**) cause (something) to be used or tested beyond its limits ▶ *n* (*pl* **-s**) tension or tiredness
strain[2] *n* (*pl* **-s**) breed or race
strained *adj* not natural, forced ▶ *v* ▷ **strain**[1]
strainer *n* (*pl* **-s**) sieve
strainers *n* ▷ **strainer**
straining *v* ▷ **strain**[1]
strains *n* ▷ **strain**[1, 2] ▶ *v* ▷ **strain**[1]
strait *n* (*pl* **-s**) position of acute difficulty
straitened *adj* not having much money
straitjacket *n* (*pl* **-s**) strong jacket with long sleeves used to bind the arms of a violent person
straitjackets *n* ▷ **straitjacket**
straitlaced, straightlaced *adj* prudish or puritanical
straits *n* ▷ **strait** ▶ *n pl* narrow channel connecting two areas of sea
strand[1] *v* (**-s, -ing, -ed**) run aground ▶ *n* (*pl* **-s**) (*Poetic*) shore
strand[2] *n* (*pl* **-s**) single thread of string, wire, etc.
stranded *v* ▷ **strand**[1]
stranding *v* ▷ **strand**[1]
strands *n* ▷ **strand**[1, 2] ▶ *v* ▷ **strand**[1]
strange *adj* (**-r, -st**) odd or unusual > **strangely** *adv* > **strangeness** *n* (*pl* **-es**)
strangely *adv* ▷ **strange**
strangeness *n* ▷ **strange**
strangenesses *n* ▷ **strange**
stranger *n* (*pl* **-s**) person who is not known or is new to a place or experience ▶ *adj* ▷ **strange**
strangers *n* ▷ **stranger**
strangest *adj* ▷ **strange**
strangle *v* (**-les, -ling, -led**) kill by squeezing the throat > **strangler** *n* (*pl* **-s**)
strangled *v* ▷ **strangle**
stranglehold *n* (*pl* **-s**) strangling grip in wrestling
strangleholds *n* ▷ **stranglehold**
strangler *n* ▷ **strangle**
stranglers *n* ▷ **strangle**
strangles *v* ▷ **strangle**
strangling *v* ▷ **strangle**
strangulation *n* (*pl* **-s**) strangling
strangulations *n* ▷ **strangulation**
strap *n* (*pl* **-s**) strip of flexible material for lifting, fastening, or holding in place ▶ *v* (**-s, -pping, -pped**) fasten with a strap or straps
strapped *n* ▷ **strap**
strapping *adj* tall and sturdy ▶ *v* ▷ **strap**
straps *n, v* ▷ **strap**
strata *n* ▷ **stratum**
stratagem *n* (*pl* **-s**) clever plan, trick
stratagems *n* ▷ **stratagem**
strategic [strat-**ee**-jik] *adj* advantageous > **strategically** *adv*
strategically *adv* ▷ **strategic**
strategies *n* ▷ **strategy**
strategist *n* ▷ **strategy**
strategists *n* ▷ **strategy**
strategy *n* (*pl* **-gies**) overall plan > **strategist** *n* (*pl* **-s**)
strathspey *n* (*pl* **-s**) Scottish dance with gliding steps
strathspeys *n* ▷ **strathspey**
stratification *n* ▷ **stratified**
stratifications *n* ▷ **stratified**
stratified *adj* divided into strata > **stratification** *n* (*pl* **-s**)
stratosphere *n* (*pl* **-s**) atmospheric layer between about 15 and 50 kilometres above the earth
stratospheres *n* ▷ **stratosphere**
stratum [**strah**-tum] *n* (*pl* **-ta**) layer, esp. of rock
straw *n* (*pl* **-s**) dried stalks of grain
strawberries *n* ▷ **strawberry**
strawberry *n* (*pl* **-ries**) sweet fleshy red fruit with small seeds on the outside
straws *n* ▷ **straw**
stray *v* (**-s, -ing, -ed**) wander ▶ *adj* having strayed ▶ *n* (*pl* **-s**) stray animal

strayed *v* ▷ **stray**
straying *v* ▷ **stray**
strays *v, n* ▷ **stray**
streak *n* (*pl* **-s**) long band of contrasting colour or substance ▶ *v* (**-s, -ing, -ed**) mark with streaks > **streaker** *n* (*pl* **-s**) > **streaky** *adj* (**-kier, -kiest**)
streaked *v* ▷ **streak**
streaker *n* ▷ **streak**
streakers *n* ▷ **streak**
streakier *adj* ▷ **streak**
streakiest *adj* ▷ **streak**
streaking *v* ▷ **streak**
streaks *n, v* ▷ **streak**
streaky *adj* ▷ **streak**
stream *n* (*pl* **-s**) small river ▶ *v* (**-s, -ing, -ed**) flow steadily
streamed *v* ▷ **stream**
streamer *n* (*pl* **-s**) strip of coloured paper that unrolls when tossed
streamers *n* ▷ **streamer**
streaming *v* ▷ **stream**
streamline *v* (**-nes, -ning, -ned**) make more efficient by simplifying
streamlined *v* ▷ **streamline**
streamlines *v* ▷ **streamline**
streamlining *v* ▷ **streamline**
streams *n, v* ▷ **stream**
street *n* (*pl* **-s**) public road, usu. lined with buildings
streetcar *n* (US) tram
streetcars *n* ▷ **streetcar**
streets *n* ▷ **street**
streetwise *adj* knowing how to survive in big cities
strength *n* (*pl* **-s**) quality of being strong > **strengthen** *v* (**-s, -ing, -ed**)
strengthen *v* ▷ **strength**
strengthened *v* ▷ **strength**
strengthening *v* ▷ **strength**
strengthens *v* ▷ **strength**
strengths *n* ▷ **strength**
strenuous *adj* requiring great energy or effort > **strenuously** *adv*
strenuously *adv* ▷ **strenuous**
streptococci *n* ▷ **streptococcus**
streptococcus [strep-toe-**kok**-uss] *n* (*pl* **-cocci**) bacterium occurring in chains, many species of which cause disease
stress *n* (*pl* **-es**) tension or strain ▶ *v* (**-es, -ing, -ed**) emphasize
stressed *v* ▷ **stress**
stresses *n, v* ▷ **stress**
stressing *v* ▷ **stress**
stretch *v* (**-es, -ing, -ed**) extend or be extended ▶ *n* (*pl* **-es**) stretching > **stretchy** *adj* (**-chier, -chiest**)
stretched *v* ▷ **stretch**
stretcher *n* (*pl* **-s**) frame covered with canvas, on which an injured person is carried
stretchers *n* ▷ **stretcher**
stretches *v, n* ▷ **stretch**
stretchier *adj* ▷ **stretch**
stretchiest *adj* ▷ **stretch**
stretching *v* ▷ **stretch**
stretchy *adj* ▷ **stretch**
strew *v* (**-s, -ing, -ed** *or* **strewn**) scatter (things) over a surface
strewed *v* ▷ **strew**
strewing *v* ▷ **strew**
strewn *v* ▷ **strew**
strews *v* ▷ **strew**
striated *adj* having a pattern of scratches or grooves
stricken *adj* seriously affected by disease, grief, pain, etc.
strict *adj* (**-er, -est**) stern or severe > **strictly** *adv* > **strictness** *n* (*pl* **-es**)
stricter *adj* ▷ **strict**
strictest *adj* ▷ **strict**
strictly *adv* ▷ **strict**
strictness *n* ▷ **strict**
strictnesses *n* ▷ **strict**
stricture *n* (*pl* **-s**) severe criticism
strictures *n* ▷ **stricture**
stridden *v* ▷ **stride**
stride *v* (**-des, -ding, strode, stridden**) walk with long steps ▶ *n* (*pl* **-s**) long step
stridencies *n* ▷ **strident**
stridency *n* ▷ **strident**
strident *adj* loud and harsh > **stridently** *adv* > **stridency** *n* (*pl* **-cies**)
stridently *adv* ▷ **strident**
strides *v, n* ▷ **stride** ▶ *n pl* progress
striding *v* ▷ **stride**
strife *n* (*pl* **-s**) conflict, quarrelling
strifes *n* ▷ **strife**
strike *v* (**-kes, -king, struck**) cease work as a protest ▶ *n* (*pl* **-s**) stoppage of work as a protest
striker *n* (*pl* **-s**) striking worker
strikers *n* ▷ **striker**
strikes *v, n* ▷ **strike**
striking *adj* impressive ▶ *v* ▷ **strike**
string *n* (*pl* **-s**) thin cord used for tying ▶ *v* (**-s, -ing, strung**) provide with a string or strings
stringed *adj* (of a musical instrument) having strings that are plucked or played with a bow
stringencies *n* ▷ **stringent**
stringency *n* ▷ **stringent**

stringent [**strin**-jent] *adj* strictly controlled or enforced > **stringently** *adv* > **stringency** *n* (*pl* **-cies**)
stringently *adv* ▷ **stringent**
stringier *adj* ▷ **stringy**
stringiest *adj* ▷ **stringy**
stringing *v* ▷ **string**
strings *n, v* ▷ **string** ▶ *n pl* restrictions or conditions
stringy *adj* (**-gier, -giest**) like string
stringybark *n* (*pl* **-s**) Australian eucalyptus with a fibrous bark
stringybarks *n* ▷ **stringybark**
strip[1] *v* (**-s, -pping, -pped**) take (the covering or clothes) off
strip[2] *n* (*pl* **-s**) long narrow piece
stripe *n* (*pl* **-s**) long narrow band of contrasting colour or substance > **striped, stripy, stripey** *adj* (**-pier, -piest**)
striped *adj* ▷ **stripe**
stripes *n* ▷ **stripe**
stripey *adj* ▷ **stripe**
stripier *adj* ▷ **stripe**
stripiest *adj* ▷ **stripe**
stripling *n* (*pl* **-s**) youth
striplings *n* ▷ **stripling**
stripped *v* ▷ **strip**[1]
stripper *n* (*pl* **-s**) person who performs a striptease
strippers *n* ▷ **stripper**
stripping *v* ▷ **strip**[1]
strips *v* ▷ **strip**[1] ▶ *n* ▷ **strip**[2]
striptease *n* (*pl* **-s**) entertainment in which a performer undresses to music
stripteases *n* ▷ **striptease**
stripy *adj* ▷ **stripe**
strive *v* (**-ves, -ving, strove, striven**) make a great effort
striven *v* ▷ **strive**
strives *v* ▷ **strive**
striving *v* ▷ **strive**
strobe *n* (*pl* **-s**) ▷ **stroboscope**
strobes *n* ▷ **strobe**
stroboscope *n* (*pl* **-s**) instrument producing a very bright flashing light
stroboscopes *n* ▷ **stroboscope**
strode *v* ▷ **stride**
stroke *v* (**-kes, -king, -ked**) touch or caress lightly with the hand ▶ *n* (*pl* **-s**) light touch or caress with the hand
stroked *v* ▷ **stroke**
strokes *v, n* ▷ **stroke**
stroking *v* ▷ **stroke**
stroll *v* (**-s, -ing, -ed**) walk in a leisurely manner ▶ *n* (*pl* **-s**) leisurely walk
strolled *v* ▷ **stroll**
strolling *v* ▷ **stroll**
strolls *v, n* ▷ **stroll**
strong *adj* (**-er, -est**) having physical power > **strongly** *adv*
stronger *adj* ▷ **strong**
strongest *adj* ▷ **strong**
stronghold *n* (*pl* **-s**) area of predominance of a particular belief
strongholds *n* ▷ **stronghold**
strongly *adv* ▷ **strong**
strongroom *n* (*pl* **-s**) room designed for the safekeeping of valuables
strongrooms *n* ▷ **strongroom**
strontium *n* (*pl* **-s**) (CHEM) silvery-white metallic element
strontiums *n* ▷ **strontium**
strop *n* (*pl* **-s**) leather strap for sharpening razors
stroppier *adj* ▷ **stroppy**
stroppiest *adj* ▷ **stroppy**
stroppy *adj* (**-pier, -piest**) (*Slang*) angry or awkward
strops *n* ▷ **strop**
strove *v* ▷ **strive**
struck *v* ▷ **strike**
structural *adj* ▷ **structure**
structuralism *n* (*pl* **-s**) approach to literature, social sciences, etc., which sees changes in the subject as caused and organized by a hidden set of universal rules > **structuralist** *n* (*pl* **-s**) *adj*
structuralisms *n* ▷ **structuralism**
structuralist *n, adj* ▷ **structuralism**
structuralists *n* ▷ **structuralism**
structure *n* (*pl* **-s**) complex construction ▶ *v* (**-res, -ring, -red**) give a structure to > **structural** *adj*
structured *v* ▷ **structure**
structures *n, v* ▷ **structure**
structuring *v* ▷ **structure**
strudel *n* (*pl* **-s**) thin sheet of filled dough rolled up and baked, usu. with an apple filling
strudels *n* ▷ **strudel**
struggle *v* (**-les, -ling, -led**) work, strive, or make one's way with difficulty ▶ *n* (*pl* **-s**) striving
struggled *v* ▷ **struggle**
struggles *v, n* ▷ **struggle**
struggling *v* ▷ **struggle**
strum *v* (**-s, -mming, -mmed**) play (a guitar or banjo) by sweeping the thumb or a plectrum across the strings
strummed *v* ▷ **strum**
strumming *v* ▷ **strum**

strumpet *n* (*pl* **-s**) (*Old-fashioned*) prostitute
strumpets *n* ▷ **strumpet**
strums *v* ▷ **strum**
strung *v* ▷ **string**
strut *v* (**-s, -tting, -tted**) walk pompously, swagger ▶ *n* (*pl* **-s**) bar supporting a structure
struts *v, n* ▷ **strut**
strutted *v* ▷ **strut**
strutting *v* ▷ **strut**
strychnine [**strik**-neen] *n* (*pl* **-s**) very poisonous drug used in small quantities as a stimulant
strychnines *n* ▷ **strychnine**
stub *n* (*pl* **-s**) short piece left after use ▶ *v* (**-s, -bbing, -bbed**) strike (the toe) painfully against an object
stubbed *v* ▷ **stub**
stubbier *adj* ▷ **stubby**
stubbiest *adj* ▷ **stubby**
stubbing *v* ▷ **stub**
stubble *n* (*pl* **-s**) short stalks of grain left in a field after reaping > **stubbly** *adj* (**-lier, -liest**)
stubbles *n* ▷ **stubble**
stubblier *adj* ▷ **stubble**
stubbliest *adj* ▷ **stubble**
stubbly *adj* ▷ **stubble**
stubborn *adj* (**-er, -est**) refusing to agree or give in > **stubbornly** *adv* > **stubbornness** *n* (*pl* **-es**)
stubborner *adj* ▷ **stubborn**
stubbornest *adj* ▷ **stubborn**
stubbornly *adv* ▷ **stubborn**
stubbornness *n* ▷ **stubborn**
stubbornnesses *n* ▷ **stubborn**
stubby *adj* (**-bbier, -bbiest**) short and broad
stubs *n, v* ▷ **stub**
stucco *n* (*pl* **-oes**) plaster used for coating or decorating walls
stuccoes *n* ▷ **stucco**
stuck *v* ▷ **stick²**
stud¹ *n* (*pl* **-s**) small piece of metal attached to a surface for decoration ▶ *v* (**-s, -dding, -dded**) set with studs
stud² *n* (*pl* **-s**) male animal, esp. a stallion, kept for breeding
studded *v* ▷ **stud¹**
studding *v* ▷ **stud¹**
student *n* (*pl* **-s**) person who studies a subject, esp. at university
students *n* ▷ **student**
studied *adj* carefully practised or planned ▶ *v* ▷ **study**
studies *v, n* ▷ **study**
studio *n* (*pl* **-s**) workroom of an artist or photographer
studios *n* ▷ **studio**
studious *adj* fond of study > **studiously** *adv*
studiously *adv* ▷ **studious**
studs *n* ▷ **stud¹, ²** ▶ *v* ▷ **stud¹**
study *v* (**-dies, -dying, -died**) be engaged in learning (a subject) ▶ *n* (*pl* **-dies**) act or process of studying
studying *v* ▷ **study**
stuff *n* (*pl* **-s**) substance or material ▶ *v* (**-s, -ing, -ed**) pack, cram, or fill completely
stuffed *v* ▷ **stuff**
stuffier *adj* ▷ **stuffy**
stuffiest *adj* ▷ **stuffy**
stuffing *n* (*pl* **-s**) seasoned mixture with which food is stuffed ▶ *v* ▷ **stuff**
stuffings *n* ▷ **stuffing**
stuffs *n, v* ▷ **stuff**
stuffy *adj* (**-ffier, -ffiest**) lacking fresh air
stultifying *adj* very boring and repetitive
stumble *v* (**-les, -ling, -led**) trip and nearly fall ▶ *n* (*pl* **-s**) stumbling
stumbled *v* ▷ **stumble**
stumbles *n* ▷ **stumble**
stumbling *v* ▷ **stumble**
stump *n* (*pl* **-s**) base of a tree left when the main trunk has been cut away ▶ *v* (**-s, -ing, -ed**) baffle
stumped *v* ▷ **stump**
stumpier *adj* ▷ **stumpy**
stumpiest *adj* ▷ **stumpy**
stumping *v* ▷ **stump**
stumps *n, v* ▷ **stump**
stumpy *adj* (**-pier, -piest**) short and thick
stun *v* (**-s, -nning, -nned**) shock or overwhelm
stung *v* ▷ **sting**
stunk *v* ▷ **stink**
stunned *v* ▷ **stun**
stunning *adj* very attractive or impressive ▶ *v* ▷ **stun**
stuns *v* ▷ **stun**
stunt¹ *v* (**-ts, -ing, -ed**) prevent or impede the growth of > **stunted** *adj*
stunt² *n* (*pl* **-s**) acrobatic or dangerous action
stunted *v, adj* ▷ **stunt¹**
stunting *v* ▷ **stunt¹**
stunts *v* ▷ **stunt¹** ▶ *n* ▷ **stunt²**
stupefaction *n* ▷ **stupefy**
stupefactions *n* ▷ **stupefy**
stupefied *v* ▷ **stupefy**
stupefies *v* ▷ **stupefy**
stupefy *v* (**-fies, -fying, -fied**) make insensitive or lethargic > **stupefaction** *n* (*pl* **-s**)
stupefying *v* ▷ **stupefy**
stupendous *adj* very large or impressive > **stupendously** *adv*
stupendously *adv* ▷ **stupendous**

stupid *adj* (**-er, -est**) lacking intelligence > **stupidity** *n* (*pl* **-ties**) > **stupidly** *adv*
stupider *adj* ▷ **stupid**
stupidest *adj* ▷ **stupid**
stupidities *n* ▷ **stupid**
stupidity *n* ▷ **stupid**
stupidly *adv* ▷ **stupid**
stupor *n* (*pl* **-s**) dazed or unconscious state
stupors *n* ▷ **stupor**
sturdier *adj* ▷ **sturdy**
sturdiest *adj* ▷ **sturdy**
sturdily *adv* ▷ **sturdy**
sturdy *adj* (**-dier, -diest**) healthy and robust > **sturdily** *adv*
sturgeon *n* (*pl* **-s**) fish from which caviar is obtained
sturgeons *n* ▷ **sturgeon**
stutter *v* (**-s, -ing, -ed**) speak with repetition of initial consonants ▶ *n* (*pl* **-s**) tendency to stutter
stuttered *v* ▷ **stutter**
stuttering *v* ▷ **stutter**
stutters *v, n* ▷ **stutter**
sty *n* (*pl* **sties**) pen for pigs
stye *n* (*pl* **styes**) inflammation at the base of an eyelash
styes *n* ▷ **stye**
style *n* (*pl* **-s**) shape or design ▶ *v* (**-les, -ling, -led**) shape or design
styled *v* ▷ **style**
styles *n, v* ▷ **style**
styli *n* ▷ **stylus**
styling *v* ▷ **style**
stylish *adj* smart, elegant, and fashionable > **stylishly** *adv*
stylishly *adv* ▷ **stylish**
stylist *n* (*pl* **-s**) hairdresser
stylistic *adj* of literary or artistic style
stylists *n* ▷ **stylist**
stylize *v* (**-zes, -zing, -zed**) cause to conform to an established stylistic form
stylized *v* ▷ **stylize**
stylizes *v* ▷ **stylize**
stylizing *v* ▷ **stylize**
stylus *n* (*pl* **-li, -luses**) needle-like device on a record player that rests in the groove of the record and picks up the sound signals
styluses *n* ▷ **stylus**
stymie *v* (**-mies, -mieing, -mied**) hinder or thwart
stymied *v* ▷ **stymie**
stymieing *v* ▷ **stymie**
stymies *v* ▷ **stymie**
styptic *n* (*pl* **-s**) ▶ *adj* (drug) used to stop bleeding
styptics *n* ▷ **styptic**
suave [swahv] *adj* smooth and sophisticated in manner > **suavely** *adv*
suavely *adv* ▷ **suave**
sub *n* (*pl* **-s**) subeditor ▶ *v* (**-s, -bbing, -bbed**) act as a substitute
subaltern *n* (*pl* **-s**) British army officer below the rank of captain
subalterns *n* ▷ **subaltern**
subatomic *adj* of or being one of the particles which make up an atom
subbed *v* ▷ **sub**
subbing *v* ▷ **sub**
subcommittee *n* (*pl* **-s**) small committee formed from some members of a larger committee
subcommittees *n* ▷ **subcommittee**
subconscious *adj* happening or existing without one's awareness ▶ *n* (*pl* **-es**) (PSYCHOANALYSIS) that part of the mind of which one is not aware but which can influence one's behaviour > **subconsciously** *adv*
subconsciouses *n* ▷ **subconscious**
subconsciously *adv* ▷ **subconscious**
subcontinent *n* (*pl* **-s**) large land mass that is a distinct part of a continent
subcontinents *n* ▷ **subcontinent**
subcontract *n* (*pl* **-s**) secondary contract by which the main contractor for a job puts work out to others ▶ *v* (**-s, -ing, -ed**) put out (work) on a subcontract > **subcontractor** *n* (*pl* **-s**)
subcontracted *v* ▷ **subcontract**
subcontracting *v* ▷ **subcontract**
subcontractor *n* ▷ **subcontract**
subcontractors *n* ▷ **subcontract**
subcontracts *n, v* ▷ **subcontract**
subcutaneous [sub-cute-**ayn**-ee-uss] *adj* under the skin
subdivide *v* (**-des, -ding, -ded**) divide (a part of something) into smaller parts > **subdivision** *n* (*pl* **-s**)
subdivided *v* ▷ **subdivide**
subdivides *v* ▷ **subdivide**
subdividing *v* ▷ **subdivide**
subdivision *n* ▷ **subdivide**
subdivisions *n* ▷ **subdivide**
subdue *v* (**-dues, -duing, -dued**) overcome
subdued *v* ▷ **subdue**
subdues *v* ▷ **subdue**
subduing *v* ▷ **subdue**
subeditor *n* (*pl* **-s**) person who checks and edits text for a newspaper or magazine
subeditors *n* ▷ **subeditor**
subject *n* (*pl* **-s**) person or thing being dealt

with or studied ▶ *adj* being under the rule of a monarch or government ▶ *v* (**-s, -ing, -ed**) (*foll. by* **to**) cause to undergo > **subjection** *n* (*pl* **-s**)
subjected *v* ▷ **subject**
subjecting *v* ▷ **subject**
subjection *n* ▷ **subject**
subjections *n* ▷ **subject**
subjective *adj* based on personal feelings or prejudices > **subjectively** *adv*
subjectively *adv* ▷ **subjective**
subjects *n, v* ▷ **subject**
subjugate *v* (**-tes, -ting, -ted**) bring (a group of people) under one's control > **subjugation** *n* (*pl* **-s**)
subjugated *v* ▷ **subjugate**
subjugates *v* ▷ **subjugate**
subjugating *v* ▷ **subjugate**
subjugation *n* ▷ **subjugate**
subjugations *n* ▷ **subjugate**
subjunctive (GRAMMAR) *n* (*pl* **-s**) mood of verbs used when the content of the clause is doubted, supposed, or wished ▶ *adj* in or of that mood
subjunctives *n* ▷ **subjunctive**
sublet *v* (**-s, -letting, -let**) rent out (property rented from someone else)
sublets *v* ▷ **sublet**
subletting *v* ▷ **sublet**
sublimate *v* (**-tes, -ting, -ted**) (PSYCHOL) direct the energy of (a strong desire, esp. a sexual one) into socially acceptable activities > **sublimation** *n* (*pl* **-s**)
sublimated *v* ▷ **sublimate**
sublimates *v* ▷ **sublimate**
sublimating *v* ▷ **sublimate**
sublimation *n* ▷ **sublimate**
sublimations *n* ▷ **sublimate**
sublime *adj* (**-r, -st**) of high moral, intellectual, or spiritual value ▶ *v* (**-mes, -ming, -med**) (CHEM) change from a solid to a vapour without first melting > **sublimely** *adv*
sublimed *v* ▷ **sublime**
sublimely *adv* ▷ **sublime**
sublimer *adj* ▷ **sublime**
sublimes *v* ▷ **sublime**
sublimest *adj* ▷ **sublime**
subliminal *adj* relating to mental processes of which the individual is not aware
subliming *v* ▷ **sublime**
submarine *n* (*pl* **-s**) vessel which can operate below the surface of the sea ▶ *adj* below the surface of the sea
submarines *n* ▷ **submarine**
submerge *v* (**-ges, -ging, -ged**) put or go below the surface of water or other liquid > **submersion** *n* (*pl* **-s**)
submerged *v* ▷ **submerge**
submerges *v* ▷ **submerge**
submerging *v* ▷ **submerge**
submersion *n* ▷ **submerge**
submersions *n* ▷ **submerge**
submission *n* (*pl* **-s**) submitting
submissions *n* ▷ **submission**
submissive *adj* meek and obedient
submit *v* (**-s, -tting, -tted**) surrender
submits *v* ▷ **submit**
submitted *v* ▷ **submit**
submitting *v* ▷ **submit**
subordinate *adj* of lesser rank or importance ▶ *n* (*pl* **-s**) subordinate person or thing ▶ *v* (**-tes, -ting, -ted**) make or treat as subordinate > **subordination** *n* (*pl* **-s**)
subordinated *v* ▷ **subordinate**
subordinates *n, v* ▷ **subordinate**
subordinating *v* ▷ **subordinate**
subordination *n* ▷ **subordinate**
subordinations *n* ▷ **subordinate**
suborn *v* (**-s, -ing, -ed**) (*Formal*) bribe or incite (a person) to commit a wrongful act
suborned *v* ▷ **suborn**
suborning *v* ▷ **suborn**
suborns *v* ▷ **suborn**
subpoena [sub-**pee**-na] *n* (*pl* **-s**) writ requiring a person to appear before a lawcourt ▶ *v* (**-nas, -naing, -naed**) summon (someone) with a subpoena
subpoenaed *v* ▷ **subpoena**
subpoenaing *v* ▷ **subpoena**
subpoenas *n, v* ▷ **subpoena**
subs *n, v* ▷ **sub**
subscribe *v* (**-bes, -bing, -bed**) pay (a subscription) > **subscriber** *n* (*pl* **-s**)
subscribed *v* ▷ **subscribe**
subscriber *n* ▷ **subscribe**
subscribers *n* ▷ **subscribe**
subscribes *v* ▷ **subscribe**
subscribing *v* ▷ **subscribe**
subscription *n* (*pl* **-s**) payment for issues of a publication over a period
subscriptions *n* ▷ **subscription**
subsection *n* (*pl* **-s**) division of a section
subsections *n* ▷ **subsection**
subsequent *adj* occurring after, succeeding > **subsequently** *adv*
subsequently *adv* ▷ **subsequent**
subservience *n* ▷ **subservient**
subserviences *n* ▷ **subservient**
subservient *adj* submissive, servile > **subservience** *n* (*pl* **-s**)
subside *v* (**-des, -ding, -ded**) become less

intense
subsided *v* ▷ **subside**
subsidence *n* (*pl* **-s**) act or process of subsiding
subsidences *n* ▷ **subsidence**
subsides *v* ▷ **subside**
subsidiaries *n* ▷ **subsidiary**
subsidiary *adj* of lesser importance ▶ *n* (*pl* **-ries**) subsidiary person or thing
subsidies *n* ▷ **subsidy**
subsiding *v* ▷ **subside**
subsidize *v* (**-izes, -izing, -ized**) help financially
subsidized *v* ▷ **subsidize**
subsidizes *v* ▷ **subsidize**
subsidizing *v* ▷ **subsidize**
subsidy *n* (*pl* **-dies**) financial aid
subsist *v* (**-s, -ing, -ed**) manage to live > **subsistence** *n* (*pl* **-s**)
subsisted *v* ▷ **subsist**
subsistence *n* ▷ **subsist**
subsistences *n* ▷ **subsist**
subsisting *v* ▷ **subsist**
subsists *v* ▷ **subsist**
subsonic *adj* moving at a speed less than that of sound
substance *n* (*pl* **-s**) physical composition of something
substances *n* ▷ **substance**
substantial *adj* of considerable size or value > **substantially** *adv*
substantially *adv* ▷ **substantial**
substantiate *v* (**-tes, -ting, -ted**) support (a story) with evidence > **substantiation** *n* (*pl* **-s**)
substantiated *v* ▷ **substantiate**
substantiates *v* ▷ **substantiate**
substantiating *v* ▷ **substantiate**
substantiation *n* ▷ **substantiate**
substantiations *n* ▷ **substantiate**
substantive *n* (*pl* **-s**) noun ▶ *adj* of or being the essential element of a thing
substantives *n* ▷ **substantive**
substitute *v* (**-tes, -ting, -ted**) take the place of or put in place of another ▶ *n* (*pl* **-s**) person or thing taking the place of (another) > **substitution** *n* (*pl* **-s**)
substituted *v* ▷ **substitute**
substitutes *v, n* ▷ **substitute**
substituting *v* ▷ **substitute**
substitution *n* ▷ **substitute**
substitutions *n* ▷ **substitute**
subsume *v* (**-mes, -ming, -med**) include (an idea, case, etc.) under a larger classification or group
subsumed *v* ▷ **subsume**
subsumes *v* ▷ **subsume**
subsuming *v* ▷ **subsume**
subterfuge *n* (*pl* **-s**) trick used to achieve an objective
subterfuges *n* ▷ **subterfuge**
subterranean *adj* underground
subtitle *n* (*pl* **-s**) secondary title of a book ▶ *v* (**-les, -ling, -led**) provide with a subtitle or subtitles
subtitled *v* ▷ **subtitle**
subtitles *v, n* ▷ **subtitle** ▶ *pl n* printed translation at the bottom of the picture in a film with foreign dialogue
subtitling *v* ▷ **subtitle**
subtle *adj* (**-r, -st**) not immediately obvious > **subtly** *adv* > **subtlety** *n* (*pl* **-ties**)
subtler *adj* ▷ **subtle**
subtlest *adj* ▷ **subtle**
subtleties *n* ▷ **subtle**
subtlety *n* ▷ **subtle**
subtly *adv* ▷ **subtle**
subtract *v* (**-s, -ing, -ed**) take (one number or quantity) from another > **subtraction** *n* (*pl* **-s**)
subtracted *v* ▷ **subtract**
subtracting *v* ▷ **subtract**
subtraction *n* ▷ **subtract**
subtractions *n* ▷ **subtract**
subtracts *v* ▷ **subtract**
subtropical *adj* of the regions bordering on the tropics
suburb *n* (*pl* **-s**) residential area on the outskirts of a city
suburban *adj* of or inhabiting a suburb
suburbia *n* (*pl* **-s**) suburbs and their inhabitants
suburbias *n* ▷ **suburbia**
suburbs *n* ▷ **suburb**
subvention *n* (*pl* **-s**) (*Formal*) subsidy
subventions *n* ▷ **subvention**
subversion *n* ▷ **subvert**
subversions *n* ▷ **subvert**
subversive *adj, n* ▷ **subvert**
subversives *n* ▷ **subvert**
subvert *v* (**-s, -ing, -ed**) overthrow the authority of > **subversion** *n* (*pl* **-s**) > **subversive** *adj, n* (*pl* **-s**)
subverted *v* ▷ **subvert**
subverting *v* ▷ **subvert**
subverts *v* ▷ **subvert**
subway *n* (*pl* **-s**) passage under a road or railway
subways *n* ▷ **subway**
succeed *v* (**-s, -ing, -ed**) accomplish an aim
succeeded *v* ▷ **succeed**
succeeding *v* ▷ **succeed**
succeeds *v* ▷ **succeed**
success *n* (*pl* **-es**) achievement of something

attempted
successes *n* ▷ **success**
successful *adj* having success > **successfully** *adv*
successfully *adv* ▷ **successful**
succession *n* (*pl* **-s**) series of people or things following one another in order
successions *n* ▷ **succession**
successive *adj* consecutive > **successively** *adv*
successively *adv* ▷ **successive**
successor *n* (*pl* **-s**) person who succeeds someone in a position
successors *n* ▷ **successor**
succinct *adj* (**-er, -est**) brief and clear > **succinctly** *adv*
succincter *adj* ▷ **succinct**
succinctest *adj* ▷ **succinct**
succinctly *adv* ▷ **succinct**
succour *v* (**-s, -ing, -ed**) ▶ *n* (*pl* **-s**) help in distress
succoured *v* ▷ **succour**
succouring *v* ▷ **succour**
succours *v, n* ▷ **succour**
succulence *n* ▷ **succulent**
succulences *n* ▷ **succulent**
succulent *adj* juicy and delicious ▶ *n* (*pl* **-s**) succulent plant > **succulence** *n* (*pl* **-s**)
succulent *n* ▷ **succulent**
succulents *n* ▷ **succulent**
succumb *v* (**-s, -ing, -ed**) (*foll. by* **to**) give way (to something overpowering)
succumbed *v* ▷ **succumb**
succumbing *v* ▷ **succumb**
succumbs *v* ▷ **succumb**
such *adj* of the kind specified ▶ *pron* such things
suchlike *pron* such or similar things
suck *v* (**-s, -ing, -ed**) draw (liquid or air) into the mouth ▶ *n* (*pl* **-s**) sucking
sucked *v* ▷ **suck**
sucker *n* (*pl* **-s**) (*Slang*) person who is easily deceived or swindled
suckers *n* ▷ **sucker**
sucking *v* ▷ **suck**
suckle *v* (**-les, -ling, -led**) feed at the breast
suckled *v* ▷ **suckle**
suckles *v* ▷ **suckle**
suckling *n* (*pl* **-s**) unweaned baby or young animal ▶ *v* ▷ **suckle**
sucklings *n* ▷ **suckling**
sucks *v, n* ▷ **suck**
sucrose [**soo**-kroze] *n* (*pl* **-s**) chemical name for sugar
sucroses *n* ▷ **sucrose**
suction *n* (*pl* **-s**) sucking
suctions *n* ▷ **suction**
sudden *adj* done or occurring quickly and unexpectedly > **suddenly** *adv* > **suddenness** *n* (*pl* **-es**)
suddenly *adv* ▷ **sudden**
suddenness *n* ▷ **suddenness**
suddennesses *n* ▷ **suddenness**
sudorific [syoo-dor-**if**-ik] *n* (*pl* **-s**) ▶ *adj* (drug) causing sweating
sudorifics *n* ▷ **sudorific**
suds *pl n* froth of soap and water, lather
sue *v* (**-ues, -uing, -ued**) start legal proceedings against
sued *v* ▷ **sue**
suede *n* (*pl* **-s**) leather with a velvety finish on one side
suedes *n* ▷ **suede**
sues *v* ▷ **sue**
suet *n* (*pl* **-s**) hard fat obtained from sheep and cattle, used in cooking
suets *n* ▷ **suet**
suffer *v* (**-s, -ing, -ed**) undergo or be subjected to > **sufferer** *n* (*pl* **-s**) > **suffering** *n* (*pl* **-s**) > **sufferance** *n* (*pl* **-s**)
sufferance *n* ▷ **suffer**
sufferances *n* ▷ **suffer**
suffered *v* ▷ **suffer**
sufferer *n* ▷ **suffer**
sufferers *n* ▷ **suffer**
suffering *n, v* ▷ **suffer**
sufferings *n* ▷ **suffer**
suffers *v* ▷ **suffer**
suffice [suf-**fice**] *v* (**-ces, -cing, -ced**) be enough for a purpose
sufficed *v* ▷ **suffice**
suffices *v* ▷ **suffice**
sufficiencies *n* ▷ **sufficiency**
sufficiency *n* (*pl* **-cies**) adequate amount
sufficient *adj* enough, adequate > **sufficiently** *adv*
sufficiently *adv* ▷ **sufficient**
sufficing *v* ▷ **suffice**
suffix *n* (*pl* **-es**) letter or letters added to the end of a word to form another word, such as *-s* and *-ness* in *dogs* and *softness*
suffixes *n* ▷ **suffix**
suffocate *v* (**-tes, -ting, -ted**) kill or be killed by deprivation of oxygen > **suffocation** *n* (*pl* **-s**)
suffocated *v* ▷ **suffocate**
suffocates *v* ▷ **suffocate**
suffocating *v* ▷ **suffocate**
suffocation *n* ▷ **suffocate**
suffocations *n* ▷ **suffocate**
suffragan *n* (*pl* **-s**) bishop appointed to assist an archbishop

suffragans *n* ▷ **suffragan**
suffrage *n* (*pl* **-s**) right to vote in public elections
suffrages *n* ▷ **suffrage**
suffragette *n* (*pl* **-s**) (in Britain in the early 20th century) a woman who campaigned militantly for the right to vote
suffragettes *n* ▷ **suffragette**
suffuse *v* (**-ses, -sing, -sed**) spread through or over (something) > **suffusion** *n* (*pl* **-s**)
suffused *v* ▷ **suffuse**
suffuses *v* ▷ **suffuse**
suffusing *v* ▷ **suffuse**
suffusion *n* ▷ **suffuse**
suffusions *n* ▷ **suffuse**
sugar *n* (*pl* **-s**) sweet crystalline carbohydrate found in many plants and used to sweeten food and drinks ▶ *v* (**-s, -ing, -ed**) sweeten or cover with sugar > **sugary** *adj* (**-rier, -riest**)
sugared *v* ▷ **sugar**
sugarier *adj* ▷ **sugar**
sugariest *adj* ▷ **sugar**
sugaring *v* ▷ **sugar**
sugars *n, v* ▷ **sugar**
sugary *adj* ▷ **sugar**
suggest *v* (**-s, -ing, -ed**) put forward (an idea) for consideration
suggested *v* ▷ **suggest**
suggestible *adj* easily influenced
suggesting *v* ▷ **suggest**
suggestion *n* (*pl* **-s**) thing suggested
suggestions *n* ▷ **suggestion**
suggestive *adj* suggesting something indecent > **suggestively** *adv*
suggestively *adv* ▷ **suggestive**
suggests *v* ▷ **suggest**
suicidal *adj* liable to commit suicide > **suicidally** *adv*
suicidally *adv* ▷ **suicide**
suicide *n* (*pl* **-s**) killing oneself intentionally
suicides *n* ▷ **suicide**
suing *v* ▷ **sue**
suit *n* (*pl* **-s**) set of clothes designed to be worn together ▶ *v* (**-s, -ing, -ed**) be appropriate for
suitabilities *n* ▷ **suitable**
suitability *n* ▷ **suitable**
suitable *adj* appropriate or proper > **suitably** *adv* > **suitability** *n* (*pl* **-ties**)
suitably *adv* ▷ **suitable**
suitcase *n* (*pl* **-s**) portable travelling case for clothing
suitcases *n* ▷ **suitcase**
suite *n* (*pl* **-s**) set of connected rooms in a hotel
suited *v* ▷ **suit**
suites *n* ▷ **suite**
suiting *v* ▷ **suit**
suitor *n* (*pl* **-s**) (*Old-fashioned*) man who is courting a woman
suitors *n* ▷ **suitor**
suits *n, v* ▷ **suit**
sulk *v* (**-s, -ing, -ed**) be silent and sullen because of resentment or bad temper ▶ *n* (*pl* **-s**) resentful or sullen mood > **sulky** *adj* (**-kier, -kiest**) > **sulkily** *adv*
sulked *v* ▷ **sulk**
sulkier *adj* ▷ **sulk**
sulkiest *adj* ▷ **sulk**
sulkily *adv* ▷ **sulk**
sulking *v* ▷ **sulk**
sulks *v, n* ▷ **sulk**
sulky *adj* ▷ **sulk**
sullen *adj* (**-er, -est**) unwilling to talk or be sociable > **sullenly** *adv* > **sullenness** *n* (*pl* **-es**)
sullener *adj* ▷ **sullen**
sullenest *adj* ▷ **sullen**
sullenly *adv* ▷ **sullen**
sullenness *n* ▷ **sullen**
sullennesses *n* ▷ **sullen**
sullied *v* ▷ **sully**
sullies *v* ▷ **sully**
sully *v* (**-lies, -lying, -lied**) ruin (someone's reputation)
sullying *v* ▷ **sully**
sulphate *n* (*pl* **-s**) salt or ester of sulphuric acid
sulphates *n* ▷ **sulphate**
sulphide *n* (*pl* **-s**) compound of sulphur with another element
sulphides *n* ▷ **sulphide**
sulphite *n* (*pl* **-s**) salt or ester of sulphurous acid
sulphites *n* ▷ **sulphite**
sulphonamide [sulf-**on**-a-mide] *n* (*pl* **-s**) any of a class of drugs that prevent the growth of bacteria
sulphonamides *n* ▷ **sulphonamide**
sulphur *n* (*pl* **-s**) (CHEM) pale yellow nonmetallic element
sulphuric, sulphurous *adj* of or containing sulphur
sulphurous *adj* ▷ **sulphuric**
sulphurs *n* ▷ **sulphur**
sultan *n* (*pl* **-s**) sovereign of a Muslim country
sultana *n* (*pl* **-s**) kind of raisin
sultanas *n* ▷ **sultana**
sultanate *n* (*pl* **-s**) territory of a sultan
sultanates *n* ▷ **sultanate**
sultans *n* ▷ **sultan**
sultrier *n* ▷ **sultry**
sultriest *n* ▷ **sultry**
sultry *adj* (**-trier, -triest**) (of weather or

climate) hot and humid
sum *n* (*pl* **-s**) result of addition, total
summaries *n* ▷ **summary**
summarily *adv* ▷ **summary**
summarize *v* (**-izes, -izing, -ized**) make or be a summary of (something)
summarized *v* ▷ **summarize**
summarizes *v* ▷ **summarize**
summarizing *v* ▷ **summarize**
summary *n* (*pl* **-ries**) brief account giving the main points of something ▶ *adj* done quickly, without formalities > **summarily** *adv*
summation *n* (*pl* **-s**) summary
summations *n* ▷ **summation**
summer *n* (*pl* **-s**) warmest season of the year, between spring and autumn > **summery** *adj* (**-rier, -riest**)
summerhouse *n* (*pl* **-s**) small building in a garden
summerhouses *n* ▷ **summerhouse**
summerier *adj* ▷ **summer**
summeriest *adj* ▷ **summer**
summers *n* ▷ **summer**
summertime *n* (*pl* **-s**) period or season of summer
summertimes *n* ▷ **summertime**
summery *adj* ▷ **summer**
summit *n* (*pl* **-s**) top of a mountain or hill
summits *n* ▷ **summit**
summon *v* (**-s, -ing, -ed**) order (someone) to come
summoned *v* ▷ **summon**
summoning *v* ▷ **summon**
summons *n* (*pl* **-es**) command summoning someone ▶ *v* (**-es, -ing, -ed**) order (someone) to appear in court ▶ *v* ▷ **summon**
summonsed *n* ▷ **summons**
summonses *v, n* ▷ **summons**
summonsing *v* ▷ **summons**
sumo *n* (*pl* **-s**) Japanese style of wrestling
sumos *n* ▷ **sumo**
sump *n* (*pl* **-s**) container in an internal-combustion engine into which oil can drain
sumps *n* ▷ **sump**
sumptuous *adj* lavish, magnificent > **sumptuously** *adv*
sumptuously *adv* ▷ **sumptuous**
sums *n* ▷ **sum**
sun *n* (*pl* **-s**) star around which the earth and other planets revolve ▶ *v* (**-s, sunning, sunned**) expose (oneself) to the sun's rays > **sunless** *adj*
sunbathe *v* (**-thes, -thing, -thed**) lie in the sunshine in order to get a suntan
sunbathed *v* ▷ **sunbathe**
sunbathes *v* ▷ **sunbathe**
sunbathing *v* ▷ **sunbathe**
sunbeam *n* (*pl* **-s**) ray of sun
sunbeams *n* ▷ **sunbeam**
sunburn *n* (*pl* **-s**) painful reddening of the skin caused by overexposure to the sun > **sunburnt, sunburned** *adj*
sunburned *adj* ▷ **sunburn**
sunburns *n* ▷ **sunburn**
sunburnt *adj* ▷ **sunburn**
sundae *n* (*pl* **-s**) ice cream topped with fruit etc.
sundaes *n* ▷ **sundae**
sundial *n* (*pl* **-s**) device showing the time by means of a pointer that casts a shadow on a marked dial
sundials *n* ▷ **sundial**
sundown *n* (*pl* **-s**) sunset
sundowns *n* ▷ **sundown**
sundries *pl n* several things of various sorts
sundry *adj* several, various
sunflower *n* (*pl* **-s**) tall plant with large golden flowers
sunflowers *n* ▷ **sunflower**
sung *v* ▷ **sing**
sunk *v* ▷ **sink**
sunken *v* ▷ **sink**
sunless *adj* ▷ **sun**
sunned *v* ▷ **sun**
sunnier *adj* ▷ **sunny**
sunniest *adj* ▷ **sunny**
sunning *v* ▷ **sun**
sunny *adj* (**-nnier, -nniest**) full of or exposed to sunlight
sunrise *n* (*pl* **-s**) daily appearance of the sun above the horizon
sunrises *n* ▷ **sunrise**
suns *n, v* ▷ **sun**
sunset *n* (*pl* **-s**) daily disappearance of the sun below the horizon
sunsets *n* ▷ **sunset**
sunshine *n* (*pl* **-s**) light and warmth from the sun
sunshines *n* ▷ **sunshine**
sunspot *n* (*pl* **-s**) dark patch appearing temporarily on the sun's surface
sunspots *n* ▷ **sunspot**
sunstroke *n* (*pl* **-s**) illness caused by prolonged exposure to intensely hot sunlight
sunstrokes *n* ▷ **sunstroke**
suntan *n* (*pl* **-s**) browning of the skin caused by exposure to the sun
suntans *n* ▷ **suntan**
sup *v* (**-s, -pping, -pped**) take (liquid) by sips ▶ *n* (*pl* **-s**) sip

super *adj* (*Informal*) excellent
superannuated *adj* discharged with a pension, owing to old age or illness
superannuation *n* (*pl* **-s**) regular payment by an employee into a pension fund
superannuations *n* ▷ **superannuation**
superb *adj* excellent, impressive, or splendid > **superbly** *adv*
superbly *adv* ▷ **superb**
superbug *n* (*pl* **-s**) (*Informal*) bacterium resistant to antibiotics
superbugs *n* ▷ **superbug**
supercharged *adj* (of an engine) having a supercharger
supercharger *n* (*pl* **-s**) device that increases the power of an internal-combustion engine by forcing extra air into it
superchargers *n* ▷ **supercharger**
supercilious *adj* showing arrogant pride or scorn
superconductor *n* (*pl* **-s**) substance which has almost no electrical resistance at very low temperatures
superconductors *n* ▷ **superconductor**
superficial *adj* not careful or thorough > **superficially** *adv* > **superficiality** *n* (*pl* **-ties**)
superficialities *n* ▷ **superficial**
superficiality *n* ▷ **superficial**
superficially *adv* ▷ **superficial**
superfluities *n* ▷ **superfluous**
superfluity *n* ▷ **superfluous**
superfluous [soo-**per**-flew-uss] *adj* more than is needed > **superfluity** *n* (*pl* **-ties**)
superhuman *adj* beyond normal human ability or experience
superimpose *v* (**-ses, -sing, -sed**) place (something) on or over something else
superimposed *v* ▷ **superimpose**
superimposes *v* ▷ **superimpose**
superimposing *v* ▷ **superimpose**
superintend *v* (**-s, -ing, -ed**) supervise (a person or activity)
superintended *v* ▷ **superintend**
superintendent *n* (*pl* **-s**) senior police officer
superintendents *n* ▷ **superintendent**
superintending *v* ▷ **superintend**
superintends *v* ▷ **superintend**
superior *adj* greater in quality, quantity, or merit ▶ *n* (*pl* **-s**) person of greater rank or status > **superiority** *n* (*pl* **-ties**)
superiorities *n* ▷ **superior**
superiority *n* ▷ **superior**
superiors *n* ▷ **superior**
superlative [soo-**per**-lat-iv] *adj* of outstanding quality ▶ *n* (*pl* **-s**) (GRAMMAR) word expressing this
superlatives *n* ▷ **superlative**
superman *n* (*pl* **-men**) man with great physical or mental powers
supermarket *n* (*pl* **-s**) large self-service store selling food and household goods
supermarkets *n* ▷ **supermarket**
supermen *n* ▷ **superman**
supermodel *n* (*pl* **-s**) famous and highly-paid fashion model
supermodels *n* ▷ **supermodel**
supernatural *adj* of or relating to things beyond the laws of nature
supernova *n* (*pl* **-vae, -vas**) star that explodes and briefly becomes exceptionally bright
supernovae *n* ▷ **supernova**
supernovas *n* ▷ **supernova**
supernumeraries *n* ▷ **supernumerary**
supernumerary *adj* exceeding the required or regular number ▶ *n* (*pl* **-ries**) supernumerary person or thing
superpower *n* (*pl* **-s**) extremely powerful nation
superpowers *n* ▷ **superpower**
superscript *n* (*pl* **-s**) ▶ *adj* (character) printed above the line
superscripts *n* ▷ **superscript**
supersede *v* (**-des, -ding, -ded**) replace, supplant
superseded *v* ▷ **supersede**
supersedes *v* ▷ **supersede**
superseding *v* ▷ **supersede**
supersonic *adj* of or travelling at a speed greater than the speed of sound
superstition *n* (*pl* **-s**) belief in omens, ghosts, etc. > **superstitious** *adj*
superstitions *n* ▷ **superstition**
superstitious *adj* ▷ **superstition**
superstore *n* (*pl* **-s**) large supermarket
superstores *n* ▷ **superstore**
superstructure *n* (*pl* **-s**) structure erected on something else
superstructures *n* ▷ **superstructure**
supervene *v* (**-nes, -ning, -ned**) occur as an unexpected development
supervened *v* ▷ **supervene**
supervenes *v* ▷ **supervene**
supervening *v* ▷ **supervene**
supervise *v* (**-ses, -sing, -sed**) watch over to direct or check > **supervision** *n* (*pl* **-s**) > **supervisor** *n* (*pl* **-s**) > **supervisory** *adj*
supervised *v* ▷ **supervise**
supervises *v* ▷ **supervise**
supervising *v* ▷ **supervise**
supervision *n* ▷ **supervise**

supervisions *n* ▷ **supervise**
supervisor *n* ▷ **supervise**
supervisors *n* ▷ **supervise**
supervisory *adj* ▷ **supervise**
supine *adj* lying flat on one's back
supped *v* ▷ **sup**
supper *n* (*pl* **-s**) light evening meal
suppers *n* ▷ **supper**
supping *v* ▷ **sup**
supplant *v* (**-s, -ing, -ed**) take the place of, oust
supplanted *v* ▷ **supplant**
supplanting *v* ▷ **supplant**
supplants *v* ▷ **supplant**
supple *adj* (**-r, -st**) (of a person) moving and bending easily and gracefully > **suppleness** *n* (*pl* **-es**)
supplement *n* (*pl* **-s**) thing added to complete something or make up for a lack ▶ *v* (**-s, -ing, -ed**) provide or be a supplement to (something) > **supplementary** *adj*
supplementary *adj* ▷ **supplement**
supplemented *v* ▷ **supplement**
supplementing *v* ▷ **supplement**
supplements *n, v* ▷ **supplement**
suppleness *n* ▷ **supple**
supplenesses *n* ▷ **supple**
suppler *adj* ▷ **supple**
supplest *adj* ▷ **supple**
supplicant *n* (*pl* **-s**) person who makes a humble request
supplicants *n* ▷ **supplicant**
supplication *n* (*pl* **-s**) humble request
supplications *n* ▷ **supplication**
supplied *v* ▷ **supply**
supplier *n* ▷ **supply**
suppliers *n* ▷ **supply**
supplies *pl n* food or equipment ▶ *v* ▷ **supply**
supply *v* (**-lies, -lying, -lied**) provide with something required ▶ *n* (*pl* **-lies**) supplying > **supplier** *n* (*pl* **-s**)
supplying *v* ▷ **supply**
support *v* (**-s, -ing, -ed**) bear the weight of ▶ *n* (*pl* **-s**) supporting > **supportive** *adj*
supported *v* ▷ **support**
supporter *n* (*pl* **-s**) person who supports a team, principle, etc.
supporters *n* ▷ **supporter**
supporting *v* ▷ **support**
supportive *adj* ▷ **support**
supports *v, n* ▷ **support**
suppose *v* (**-ses, -sing, -sed**) presume to be true
supposed *adj* presumed to be true without proof, doubtful ▶ *v* ▷ **suppose** > **supposedly** *adv*
supposedly *adv* ▷ **supposed**
supposes *v* ▷ **suppose**
supposing *v* ▷ **suppose**
supposition *n* (*pl* **-s**) supposing
suppositions *n* ▷ **supposition**
suppositories *n* ▷ **suppository**
suppository *n* (*pl* **-ries**) solid medication inserted into the rectum or vagina and left to melt
suppress *v* (**-es, -ing, -ed**) put an end to > **suppression** *n* (*pl* **-s**)
suppressed *v* ▷ **suppress**
suppresses *v* ▷ **suppress**
suppressing *v* ▷ **suppress**
suppression *n* ▷ **suppress**
suppressions *n* ▷ **suppress**
suppurate *v* (**-tes, -ting, -ted**) (of a wound etc.) produce pus
suppurated *v* ▷ **suppurate**
suppurates *v* ▷ **suppurate**
suppurating *v* ▷ **suppurate**
supremacies *n* ▷ **supremacy**
supremacy *n* (*pl* **-cies**) supreme power
supreme *adj* highest in authority, rank, or degree
supremely *adv* extremely
supremo *n* (*pl* **-s**) (*Informal*) person in overall authority
supremos *n* ▷ **supremo**
sups *n, v* ▷ **sup**

> **suq** *n* (**suqs**). A suq is an open-air marketplace in Arabic-speaking countries. This unusual word can be very useful. Usually, when you have a Q and a U, you will be looking to play words with QU in them. But look out for opportunities to play suq instead. Suq scores 12 points.

surcharge *n* (*pl* **-s**) additional charge
surcharges *n* ▷ **surcharge**
surd *n* (*pl* **-s**) (MATHS) number that cannot be expressed in whole numbers
surds *n* ▷ **surd**
sure *adj* (**-r, -st**) free from uncertainty or doubt ▶ *adv, interj* (*Informal*) certainly
surefooted *adj* unlikely to slip or stumble
surely *adv* it must be true that
surer *adj* ▷ **sure**
surest *adj* ▷ **sure**
sureties *n* ▷ **surety**
surety *n* (*pl* **-ties**) person who takes responsibility, or thing given as a guarantee, for the fulfilment of another's obligation
surf *n* (*pl* **-s**) foam caused by waves breaking on the shore ▶ *v* (**-s, -ing, -ed**) take part in surfing > **surfer** *n* (*pl* **-s**)

surface *n* (*pl* **-s**) outside or top of an object ▶ *v* (**-ces, -cing, -ced**) rise to the surface
surfaced *v* ▷ **surface**
surfaces *n, v* ▷ **surface**
surfacing *v* ▷ **surface**
surfboard *n* (*pl* **-s**) long smooth board used in surfing
surfboards *n* ▷ **surfboard**
surfed *v* ▷ **surf**
surfeit *n* (*pl* **-s**) excessive amount
surfeits *n* ▷ **surfeit**
surfer *n* ▷ **surf**
surfers *n* ▷ **surf**
surfing *n* (*pl* **-s**) sport of riding towards the shore on a surfboard on the crest of a wave ▶ *v* ▷ **surf**
surfings *n* ▷ **surfing**
surfs *n, v* ▷ **surf**
surge *n* (*pl* **-s**) sudden powerful increase ▶ *v* (**-ges, -ging, -ged**) increase suddenly
surged *v* ▷ **surge**
surgeon *n* (*pl* **-s**) doctor who specializes in surgery
surgeons *n* ▷ **surgeon**
surgeries *n* ▷ **surgery**
surgery *n* (*pl* **-ries**) treatment in which the patient's body is cut open in order to treat the affected part > **surgical** *adj* > **surgically** *adv*
surges *n, v* ▷ **surge**
surgical *adj* ▷ **surgery**
surgically *adv* ▷ **surgery**
surging *v* ▷ **surge**
surlier *adj* ▷ **surly**
surliest *adj* ▷ **surly**
surliness *n* ▷ **surly**
surlinesses *n* ▷ **surly**
surly *adj* (**-lier, -liest**) ill-tempered and rude > **surliness** *n* (*pl* **-es**)
surmise *v* (**-ises, -ising, -ised**) ▶ *n* (*pl* **-s**) guess, conjecture
surmised *v* ▷ **surmise**
surmises *n, v* ▷ **surmise**
surmising *v* ▷ **surmise**
surmount *v* (**-s, -ing, -ed**) overcome (a problem) > **surmountable** *adj*
surmountable *adj* ▷ **surmount**
surmounted *v* ▷ **surmount**
surmounting *v* ▷ **surmount**
surmounts *v* ▷ **surmount**
surname *n* (*pl* **-s**) family name
surnames *n* ▷ **surname**
surpass *v* (**-es, -ing, -ed**) be greater than or superior to
surpassed *v* ▷ **surpass**
surpasses *v* ▷ **surpass**
surpassing *v* ▷ **surpass**
surplice *n* (*pl* **-s**) loose white robe worn by clergymen and choristers
surplices *n* ▷ **surplice**
surplus *n* (*pl* **-es**) amount left over in excess of what is required
surpluses *n* ▷ **surplus**
surprise *n* (*pl* **-ses**) unexpected event ▶ *v* (**-ses, -sing, -sed**) cause to feel amazement or wonder
surprised *v* ▷ **surprise**
surprises *n, v* ▷ **surprise**
surprising *v* ▷ **surprise**
surreal *adj* bizarre > **surrealist** *n* (*pl* **-s**) *adj* > **surrealistic** *adj*
surrealism *n* (*pl* **-s**) movement in art and literature involving the combination of incongruous images, as in a dream
surrealisms *n* ▷ **surrealism**
surrealist *n, adj* ▷ **surreal**
surrealistic *adj* ▷ **surreal**
surrealists *n* ▷ **surreal**
surrender *v* (**-s, -ing, -ed**) give oneself up ▶ *n* (*pl* **-s**) surrendering
surrendered *v* ▷ **surrender**
surrendering *v* ▷ **surrender**
surrenders *v, n* ▷ **surrender**
surreptitious *adj* done secretly or stealthily > **surreptitiously** *adv*
surreptitiously *adv* ▷ **surreptitious**
surrogate *n* (*pl* **-s**) substitute
surrogates *n* ▷ **surrogate**
surround *v* (**-s, -ing, -ed**) be, come, or place all around (a person or thing) ▶ *n* (*pl* **-s**) border or edging
surrounded *v* ▷ **surround**
surrounding *v* ▷ **surround**
surroundings *pl n* area or environment around a person, place, or thing
surrounds *v, n* ▷ **surround**
surveillance *n* (*pl* **-s**) close observation
surveillances *n* ▷ **surveillance**
survey *v* (**-s, -ing, -ed**) view or consider in a general way ▶ *n* (*pl* **-s**) surveying > **surveyor** *n* (*pl* **-s**)
surveyed *v* ▷ **survey**
surveying *v* ▷ **survey**
surveyor *n* ▷ **survey**
surveyors *n* ▷ **survey**
surveys *v, n* ▷ **survey**
survival *n* (*pl* **-s**) condition of having survived
survivals *n* ▷ **survival**
survive *v* (**-ves, -ing, -ved**) continue to live or exist after (a difficult experience) > **survivor** *n* (*pl* **-s**)

survived *v* ▷ **survive**
survives *v* ▷ **survive**
surviving *v* ▷ **survive**
survivor *n* ▷ **survive**
survivors *n* ▷ **survive**
susceptibilities *n* ▷ **susceptible**
susceptibility *n* ▷ **susceptible**
susceptible *adj* liable to be influenced or affected by > **susceptibility** *n* (*pl* **-ties**)
sushi [**soo**-shee] *n* (*pl* **-s**) Japanese dish of small cakes of cold rice with a topping of raw fish
sushis *n* ▷ **sushi**
suspect *v* (**-s, -ing, -ed**) believe (someone) to be guilty without having any proof ▶ *adj* not to be trusted ▶ *n* (*pl* **-s**) person who is suspected
suspected *v* ▷ **suspect**
suspecting *v* ▷ **suspect**
suspects *v, n* ▷ **suspect**
suspend *v* (**-s, -ing, -ed**) hang from a high place
suspended *v* ▷ **suspend**
suspenders *pl n* straps for holding up stockings
suspending *v* ▷ **suspend**
suspends *v* ▷ **suspend**
suspense *n* (*pl* **-s**) state of uncertainty while awaiting news, an event, etc.
suspenses *n* ▷ **suspense**
suspension *n* (*pl* **-s**) suspending or being suspended
suspensions *n* ▷ **suspension**
suspicion *n* (*pl* **-s**) feeling of not trusting a person or thing
suspicions *n* ▷ **suspicion**
suspicious *adj* feeling or causing suspicion > **suspiciously** *adv*
suspiciously *adv* ▷ **suspicious**
sustain *v* (**-s, -ing, -ed**) maintain or prolong
sustained *v* ▷ **sustain**
sustaining *v* ▷ **sustain**
sustains *v* ▷ **sustain**
sustenance *n* (*pl* **-s**) food
sustenances *n* ▷ **sustenance**
suture [**soo**-cher] *n* (*pl* **-s**) stitch joining the edges of a wound
sutures *n* ▷ **suture**
suzerain *n* (*pl* **-s**) state or sovereign with limited authority over another self-governing state > **suzerainty** *n* (*pl* **-ties**)
suzerains *n* ▷ **suzerain**
suzerainties *n* ▷ **suzerain**
suzerainty *n* ▷ **suzerain**
svelte *adj* (**-r, -st**) attractively or gracefully slim
svelter *adj* ▷ **svelte**
sveltest *adj* ▷ **svelte**
swab *n* (*pl* **-s**) small piece of cotton wool used to apply medication, clean a wound, etc. ▶ *v* (**-s, -bbing, -bbed**) clean (a wound) with a swab
swabbed *v* ▷ **swab**
swabbing *v* ▷ **swab**
swabs *n, v* ▷ **swab**
swaddle *v* (**-les, -ling, -led**) wrap (a baby) in swaddling clothes
swaddled *v* ▷ **swaddle**
swaddles *v* ▷ **swaddle**
swaddling *v* ▷ **swaddle**
swag *n* (*pl* **-s**) (*Slang*) stolen property
swagger *v* (**-s, -ing, -ed**) walk or behave arrogantly ▶ *n* (*pl* **-s**) arrogant walk or manner
swaggered *v* ▷ **swagger**
swaggering *v* ▷ **swagger**
swaggers *v, n* ▷ **swagger**
swagman *n* (*pl* **-men**) (AUST HIST) tramp who carries his belongings in a bundle on his back
swagmen *n* ▷ **swagman**
swags *n* ▷ **swag**
swain *n* (*pl* **-s**) (*Poetic*) suitor
swains *n* ▷ **swain**
swallow^{1} *v* (**-s, -ing, -ed**) cause to pass down one's throat ▶ *n* (*pl* **-s**) swallowing
swallow^{2} *n* (*pl* **-s**) small migratory bird with long pointed wings and a forked tail
swallowed *v* ▷ **swallow**^{1}
swallowing *v* ▷ **swallow**^{1}
swallows *v* ▷ **swallow**^{1} ▶ *n* ▷ **swallow**^{1,2}
swam *v* ▷ **swim**
swamp *n* (*pl* **-s**) watery area of land, bog ▶ *v* (**-s, -ing, -ed**) cause (a boat) to fill with water and sink > **swampy** *adj* (**-pier, -piest**)
swamped *v* ▷ **swamp**
swampier *adj* ▷ **swamp**
swampiest *adj* ▷ **swamp**
swamping *v* ▷ **swamp**
swamps *n, v* ▷ **swamp**
swampy *adj* ▷ **swamp**
swan *n* (*pl* **-s**) large usu. white water bird with a long graceful neck ▶ *v* (**-s, -nning, -nned**) (*Informal*) wander about idly
swank (*Slang*) *v* (**-s, -ing, -ed**) show off or boast ▶ *n* (*pl* **-s**) showing off or boasting
swanked *v* ▷ **swank**
swankier *adj* ▷ **swanky**
swankiest *adj* ▷ **swanky**
swanking *v* ▷ **swank**
swanks *v, n* ▷ **swank**
swanky *adj* (**-kier, -kiest**) (*Slang*) expensive and showy, stylish
swanned *n* ▷ **swan**
swanning *n* ▷ **swan**
swans *n, v* ▷ **swan**

swap *v* (**-s, -pping, -pped**) exchange (something) for something else ▶ *n* (*pl* **-s**) exchange
swapped *v* ▷ **swap**
swapping *v* ▷ **swap**
swaps *v, n* ▷ **swap**
sward *n* (*pl* **-s**) stretch of short grass
swards *n* ▷ **sward**
swarm¹ *n* (*pl* **-s**) large group of bees or other insects ▶ *v* (**-s, -ing, -ed**) move in a swarm
swarm² *v* (**-s, -ing, -ed**) (*foll. by* **up**) climb (a ladder or rope) by gripping with the hands and feet
swarmed *v* ▷ **swarm¹, ²**
swarming *v* ▷ **swarm¹, ²**
swarms *v* ▷ **swarm¹, ²** ▶ *n* ▷ **swarm¹**
swarthier *adj* ▷ **swarthy**
swarthiest *adj* ▷ **swarthy**
swarthy *adj* (**-thier, -thiest**) dark-complexioned
swashbuckler *n* ▷ **swashbuckling**
swashbucklers *n* ▷ **swashbuckling**
swashbuckling *adj* having the exciting behaviour of pirates, esp. those depicted in films > **swashbuckler** *n* (*pl* **-s**)
swastika *n* (*pl* **-s**) symbol in the shape of a cross with the arms bent at right angles, used as the emblem of Nazi Germany
swastikas *n* ▷ **swastika**
swat *v* (**-s, -tting, -tted**) hit sharply ▶ *n* (*pl* **-s**) sharp blow
swatch *n* (*pl* **-es**) sample of cloth
swatches *n* ▷ **swatch**
swath [swawth] *n* (*pl* **-s**) ▷ **swathe**
swathe *v* (**-thes, -thing, -thed**) wrap in bandages or layers of cloth ▶ *n* (*pl* **-s**) long strip of cloth wrapped around something (*also* **swath**)
swathed *v* ▷ **swathe**
swathes *v, n* ▷ **swathe**
swathing *v* ▷ **swathe**
swaths *n* ▷ **swath**
swats *v, n* ▷ **swat**
swatted *v* ▷ **swat**
swatting *v* ▷ **swat**
sway *v* (**-s, -ing, -ed**) swing to and fro or from side to side ▶ *n* (*pl* **-s**) power or influence
swayed *v* ▷ **sway**
swaying *v* ▷ **sway**
sways *v, n* ▷ **sway**
swear *v* (**-s, -ing, swore, sworn**) use obscene or blasphemous language
swearing *v* ▷ **swear**
swears *v* ▷ **swear**
swearword *n* (*pl* **-s**) word considered obscene or blasphemous
swearwords *n* ▷ **swearword**
sweat *n* (*pl* **-s**) salty liquid given off through the pores of the skin ▶ *v* (**-s, -ing, -ed**) have sweat coming through the pores > **sweaty** *adj* (**-tier, -tiest**)
sweatband *n* (*pl* **-s**) strip of cloth tied around the forehead or wrist to absorb sweat
sweatbands *n* ▷ **sweatband**
sweated *v* ▷ **sweat**
sweater *n* (*pl* **-s**) (woollen) garment for the upper part of the body
sweaters *n* ▷ **sweater**
sweatier *adj* ▷ **sweat**
sweatiest *adj* ▷ **sweat**
sweating *v* ▷ **sweat**
sweats *n, v* ▷ **sweat**
sweatshirt *n* (*pl* **-s**) long-sleeved cotton jersey
sweatshirts *n* ▷ **sweatshirt**
sweatshop *n* (*pl* **-s**) place where employees work long hours in poor conditions for low pay
sweatshops *n* ▷ **sweatshop**
sweaty *adj* ▷ **sweat**
swede *n* (*pl* **-des**) kind of turnip
swedes *n* ▷ **swede**
sweep *v* (**-s, -ing, swept**) remove dirt from (a floor) with a broom ▶ *n* (*pl* **-s**) sweeping
sweeping *adj* wide-ranging ▶ *v* ▷ **sweep**
sweeps *v, n* ▷ **sweep**
sweepstake *n* (*pl* **-s**) lottery in which the stakes of the participants make up the prize
sweepstakes *n* ▷ **sweepstake**
sweet *adj* (**-er, -est**) tasting of or like sugar ▶ *n* (*pl* **-s**) shaped piece of food consisting mainly of sugar > **sweetly** *adv* > **sweetness** *n* (*pl* **-es**) > **sweeten** *v* (**-s, -ing, -ed**)
sweetbread *n* (*pl* **-s**) animal's pancreas used as food
sweetbreads *n* ▷ **sweetbread**
sweetened *v* ▷ **sweet**
sweetener *n* (*pl* **-s**) sweetening agent that does not contain sugar
sweeteners *n* ▷ **sweetener**
sweetening *v* ▷ **sweet**
sweetens *v* ▷ **sweet**
sweetheart *n* (*pl* **-s**) lover
sweethearts *n* ▷ **sweetheart**
sweetly *adv* ▷ **sweet**
sweetmeat *n* (*pl* **-s**) (*Old-fashioned*) sweet delicacy such as a small cake
sweetmeats *n* ▷ **sweetmeat**
sweetness *n* ▷ **sweet**
sweetnesses *n* ▷ **sweet**
sweets *n* ▷ **sweet**

swell *v* (**-lls, -lling, -lled, swollen** *or* **swelled**) expand or increase ▶ *n* (*pl* **-s**) swelling or being swollen ▶ *adj* (**-er, -est**) (US) (*Slang*) excellent or fine
swelled *v* ▷ **swell**
sweller *adj* ▷ **swell**
swellest *adj* ▷ **swell**
swelling *n* (*pl* **-s**) enlargement of part of the body, caused by injury or infection ▶ *v* ▷ **swell**
swells *v, n* ▷ **swell**
swelter *v* (**-s, -ing, -ed**) feel uncomfortably hot
sweltered *v* ▷ **swelter**
sweltering *adj* uncomfortably hot ▶ *v* ▷ **swelter**
swelters *v* ▷ **swelter**
swept *v* ▷ **sweep**
swerve *v* (**-ves, -ving, -ved**) turn aside from a course sharply or suddenly ▶ *n* (*pl* **-s**) swerving
swerved *v* ▷ **swerve**
swerves *v, n* ▷ **swerve**
swerving *v* ▷ **swerve**
swift *adj* (**-er, -est**) moving or able to move quickly ▶ *n* (*pl* **-s**) fast-flying bird with pointed wings > **swiftly** *adv* > **swiftness** *n* (*pl* **-es**)
swifter *adj* ▷ **swift**
swiftest *adj* ▷ **swift**
swiftly *adv* ▷ **swift**
swiftness *n* ▷ **swift**
swiftnesses *n* ▷ **swift**
swifts *n* ▷ **swift**
swig *n* (*pl* **-s**) large mouthful of drink ▶ *v* (**-s, -gging, -gged**) drink in large mouthfuls
swigged *v* ▷ **swig**
swigging *v* ▷ **swig**
swigs *n, v* ▷ **swig**
swill *v* (**-s, -ing, -ed**) drink greedily ▶ *n* (*pl* **-s**) sloppy mixture containing waste food, fed to pigs
swilled *v* ▷ **swill**
swilling *v* ▷ **swill**
swills *v, n* ▷ **swill**
swim *v* (**-s, -mming, swam, swum**) move along in water by movements of the limbs ▶ *n* (*pl* **-s**) act or period of swimming > **swimmer** *n* (*pl* **-s**)
swimmer *n* ▷ **swim**
swimmers *n* ▷ **swim**
swimming *v* ▷ **swim**
swimmingly *adv* successfully and effortlessly
swims *v, n* ▷ **swim**
swindle *v* (**-les, -ling, -led**) cheat (someone) out of money ▶ *n* (*pl* **-s**) instance of swindling > **swindler** *n* (*pl* **-s**)
swindled *v* ▷ **swindle**
swindler *n* ▷ **swindle**
swindlers *n* ▷ **swindle**
swindles *v, n* ▷ **swindle**
swindling *v* ▷ **swindle**
swine *n* (*pl* **-s**) contemptible person
swines *n* ▷ **swine**
swing *v* (**-s, -ing, swung**) move to and fro, sway ▶ *n* (*pl* **-s**) swinging
swingeing [**swin**-jing] *adj* punishing, severe
swinging *v* ▷ **swing**
swings *v, n* ▷ **swing**
swipe *v* (**-ipes, -iping, -iped**) strike (at) with a sweeping blow ▶ *n* (*pl* **-s**) hard blow
swiped *v* ▷ **swipe**
swipes *v, n* ▷ **swipe**
swiping *v* ▷ **swipe**
swirl *v* (**-s, -ing, -ed**) turn with a whirling motion ▶ *n* (*pl* **-s**) whirling motion
swirled *v* ▷ **swirl**
swirling *v* ▷ **swirl**
swirls *v, n* ▷ **swirl**
swish *v* (**-es, -ing, -ed**) move with a whistling or hissing sound ▶ *n* (*pl* **-es**) whistling or hissing sound ▶ *adj* (**-er, -est**) (*Informal*) fashionable, smart
swished *v* ▷ **swish**
swisher *adj* ▷ **swish**
swishes *v, n* ▷ **swish**
swishest *adj* ▷ **swish**
swishing *v* ▷ **swish**
switch *n* (*pl* **-es**) device for opening and closing an electric circuit ▶ *v* (**-ches, -ching, -ched**) change abruptly
switchback *n* (*pl* **-s**) road or railway with many sharp hills or bends
switchbacks *n* ▷ **switchback**
switchboard *n* (*pl* **-s**) installation in a telephone exchange or office where telephone calls are connected
switchboards *n* ▷ **switchboard**
switched *v* ▷ **switch**
switches *n, v* ▷ **switch**
switching *v* ▷ **switch**
swivel *v* (**-s, -elling, -elled**) turn on a central point ▶ *n* (*pl* **-s**) coupling device that allows an attached object to turn freely
swivelled *v* ▷ **swivel**
swivelling *v* ▷ **swivel**
swivels *v, n* ▷ **swivel**
swollen *v* ▷ **swell**
swoon *v* (**-s, -ing, -ed**) ▶ *n* (*pl* **-s**) faint
swooned *v* ▷ **swoon**
swooning *v* ▷ **swoon**
swoons *v, n* ▷ **swoon**
swoop *v* (**-s, -ing, -ed**) sweep down or pounce on suddenly ▶ *n* (*pl* **-s**) swooping
swooped *v* ▷ **swoop**

swooping *v* ▷ **swoop**
swoops *v, n* ▷ **swoop**
swop *v* (**-s, -pping, -pped**) ▶ *n* (*pl* **-s**) ▷ **swap**
swopped *v* ▷ **swop**
swopping *v* ▷ **swop**
swops *v, n* ▷ **swop**
sword *n* (*pl* **-s**) weapon with a long sharp blade
swordfish *n* (*pl* **-es**) large fish with a very long upper jaw
swordfishes *n* ▷ **swordfish**
swords *n* ▷ **sword**
swordsman *n* (*pl* **-men**) person skilled in the use of a sword
swordsmen *n* ▷ **swordsman**
swore *v* ▷ **swear**
sworn *v* ▷ **swear** ▶ *adj* bound by or as if by an oath
swot (*Informal*) *v* (**-s, -tting, -tted**) study hard ▶ *n* (*pl* **-s**) person who studies hard
swots *v, n* ▷ **swot**
swotted *v* ▷ **swot**
swotting *v* ▷ **swot**
swum *v* ▷ **swim**
swung *v* ▷ **swing**

swy *n* (**swys**). Swy is an Australian gambling game. This is a very unusual word which doesn't contain a vowel, so it can be useful in helping you to clear a difficult rack. Swy scores 9 points.

sybarite [**sib**-bar-ite] *n* (*pl* **-s**) lover of luxury > **sybaritic** *adj*
sybarites *n* ▷ **sybarite**
sybaritic *adj* ▷ **sybarite**
sycamore *n* (*pl* **-s**) tree with five-pointed leaves and two-winged fruits
sycamores *n* ▷ **sycamore**
sycophancies *n* ▷ **sycophant**
sycophancy *n* ▷ **sycophant**
sycophant *n* (*pl* **-s**) person who uses flattery to win favour from people with power or influence > **sycophantic** *adj* > **sycophancy** *n* (*pl* **-cies**)
sycophantic *adj* ▷ **sycophant**
sycophants *n* ▷ **sycophant**
syllabi *n* ▷ **syllabus**
syllabic *adj* ▷ **syllable**
syllable *n* (*pl* **-s**) part of a word pronounced as a unit > **syllabic** *adj*
syllables *n* ▷ **syllable**
syllabub *n* (*pl* **-s**) dessert of beaten cream, sugar, and wine
syllabubs *n* ▷ **syllabub**
syllabus *n* (*pl* **-buses, -bi**) list of subjects for a course of study
syllabuses *n* ▷ **syllabus**
syllogism *n* (*pl* **-s**) form of logical reasoning consisting of two premises and a conclusion
syllogisms *n* ▷ **syllogism**
sylph *n* (*pl* **-s**) slender graceful girl or woman > **sylphlike** *adj*
sylphlike *adj* ▷ **sylph**
sylphs *n* ▷ **sylph**
sylvan *adj* (*Lit*) relating to woods and trees
symbioses *n* ▷ **symbiosis**
symbiosis *n* (*pl* **-oses**) close association of two species living together to their mutual benefit > **symbiotic** *adj*
symbiotic *adj* ▷ **symbiosis**
symbol *n* (*pl* **-s**) sign or thing that stands for something else > **symbolic** *adj* > **symbolically** *adv*
symbolic *adj* ▷ **symbol**
symbolically *adv* ▷ **symbol**
symbolism *n* (*pl* **-s**) representation of something by symbols > **symbolist** *n* (*pl* **-s**) *adj*
symbolisms *n* ▷ **symbolism**
symbolist *n* ▷ **symbolism**
symbolists *n* ▷ **symbolism**
symbolize *v* (**-izes, -izing, -ized**) be a symbol of
symbolized *v* ▷ **symbolize**
symbolizes *v* ▷ **symbolize**
symbolizing *v* ▷ **symbolize**
symbols *n* ▷ **symbol**
symmetrical *adj* ▷ **symmetry**
symmetrically *adv* ▷ **symmetry**
symmetries *n* ▷ **symmetry**
symmetry *n* (*pl* **-tries**) state of having two halves that are mirror images of each other > **symmetrical** *adj* > **symmetrically** *adv*
sympathetic *adj* feeling or showing sympathy > **sympathetically** *adv*
sympathetically *adv* ▷ **sympathetic**
sympathies *n* ▷ **sympathy**
sympathize *v* (**-zes, -izing, -ized**) feel or express sympathy > **sympathizer** *n* (*pl* **-s**)
sympathized *v* ▷ **sympathize**
sympathizer *n* ▷ **sympathize**
sympathizers *n* ▷ **sympathize**
sympathizes *v* ▷ **sympathize**
sympathizing *v* ▷ **sympathize**
sympathy *n* (*pl* **-thies**) compassion for someone's pain or distress
symphonic *adj* ▷ **symphony**
symphonies *n* ▷ **symphony**
symphony *n* (*pl* **-nies**) composition for orchestra, with several movements > **symphonic** *adj*
symposia *n* ▷ **symposium**
symposium *n* (*pl* **-iums, -sia**) conference for

discussion of a particular topic
symposiums *n* ▷ **symposium**
symptom *n* (*pl* **-s**) sign indicating the presence of an illness > **symptomatic** *adj*
symptomatic *adj* ▷ **symptom**
symptoms *n* ▷ **symptom**

syn *adv*. (**Syn**) is a Scots word for **since.** This is a good word to remember for when you have a shortage of vowels. Syn scores 6 points.

synagogue *n* (*pl* **-s**) Jewish place of worship and religious instruction
synagogues *n* ▷ **synagogue**
sync, synch (*Informal*) *n* (*pl* **-s**) synchronization ▶ *v* (**-s, -ing, -ed**) synchronize
synced *v* ▷ **sync**
synched *v* ▷ **sync**
synching *v* ▷ **sync**
synchromesh *adj* (of a gearbox) having a device that synchronizes the speeds of gears before they engage
synchronization *n* ▷ **synchronize**
synchronizations *n* ▷ **synchronize**
synchronize *v* (**-izes, -izing, -ized**) (of two or more people) perform (an action) at the same time > **synchronization** *n* (*pl* **-s**)
synchronized *v* ▷ **synchronize**
synchronizes *v* ▷ **synchronize**
synchronizing *v* ▷ **synchronize**
synchronous *adj* happening or existing at the same time
synchs *n, v* ▷ **sync**
syncing *v* ▷ **sync**
syncopate *v* (**-tes, -ting, -ted**) (MUSIC) stress the weak beats in (a rhythm) instead of the strong ones > **syncopation** *n* (*pl* **-s**)
syncopated *v* ▷ **syncopate**
syncopates *v* ▷ **syncopate**
syncopating *v* ▷ **syncopate**
syncopation *n* ▷ **syncopate**
syncopations *n* ▷ **syncopate**
syncope [sing-kop-ee] *n* (*pl* **-s**) (MED) a faint
syncopes *n* ▷ **syncope**
syncs *n, v* ▷ **sync**
syndicate *n* (*pl* **-s**) group of people or firms undertaking a joint business project ▶ *v* (**-tes, -ting, -ted**) publish (material) in several newspapers > **syndication** *n* (*pl* **-s**)
syndicated *v* ▷ **syndicate**
syndicates *n, v* ▷ **syndicate**
syndicating *v* ▷ **syndicate**
syndication *n* ▷ **syndicate**
syndications *n* ▷ **syndicate**
syndrome *n* (*pl* **-s**) combination of symptoms indicating a particular disease
syndromes *n* ▷ **syndrome**
synergies *n* ▷ **synergy**
synergy *n* (*pl* **-gies**) potential ability for people or groups to be more successful working together than on their own
synod *n* (*pl* **-s**) church council
synods *n* ▷ **synod**
synonym *n* (*pl* **-s**) word with the same meaning as another > **synonymous** *adj*
synonymous *adj* ▷ **synonym**
synonyms *n* ▷ **synonym**
synopses *n* ▷ **synopsis**
synopsis *n* (*pl* **-ses**) summary or outline
syntactic *adj* ▷ **syntax**
syntax *n* (*pl* **-es**) (GRAMMAR) way in which words are arranged to form phrases and sentences > **syntactic** *adj*
syntaxes *n* ▷ **syntax**
syntheses *n* ▷ **synthesis**
synthesis *n* (*pl* **-ses**) combination of objects or ideas into a whole
synthesize *v* (**-izes, -izing, -ized**) produce by synthesis
synthesized *v* ▷ **synthesize**
synthesizer *n* (*pl* **-s**) electronic musical instrument producing a range of sounds
synthesizers *n* ▷ **synthesizer**
synthesizes *v* ▷ **synthesize**
synthesizing *v* ▷ **synthesize**
synthetic *adj* (of a substance) made artificially > **synthetically** *adv*
synthetically *adv* ▷ **synthetic**
syphilis *n* (*pl* **-es**) serious sexually transmitted disease > **syphilitic** *adj*
syphilises *n* ▷ **syphilis**
syphilitic *adj* ▷ **syphilis**
syphon *n* (*pl* **-s**) ▶ *v* (**-s, -ing, -ed**) ▷ **siphon**
syphoned *v* ▷ **syphon**
syphoning *v* ▷ **syphon**
syphons *n, v* ▷ **syphon**
syringe *n* (*pl* **-s**) device for withdrawing or injecting fluids, consisting of a hollow cylinder, a piston, and a hollow needle ▶ *v* (**-ges, -ging, -ged**) wash out or inject with a syringe
syringed *v* ▷ **syringe**
syringes *n, v* ▷ **syringe**
syringing *v* ▷ **syringe**
syrup *n* (*pl* **-s**) solution of sugar in water > **syrupy** *adj* (**-pier, -piest**)
syrupier *adj* ▷ **syrup**
syrupiest *adj* ▷ **syrup**
syrups *n* ▷ **syrup**
syrupy *adj* ▷ **syrup**
system *n* (*pl* **-s**) method or set of methods

> **systematic** *adj* > **systematically** *adv*
systematic *adj* ▷ **system**
systematically *adv* ▷ **system**
systematization *n* ▷ **systematize**
systematizations *n* ▷ **systematize**
systematize *v* (**-izes, -izing, -ized**) organize using a system
systematization *n* (*pl* **-s**) systemizing
systematized *v* ▷ **systematize**
systematizes *v* ▷ **systematize**
systematizing *v* ▷ **systematize**
systemic *adj* affecting the entire animal or body
systems *n* ▷ **system**
systole [**siss**-tol-ee] *n* (*pl* **-s**) regular contraction of the heart as it pumps blood > **systolic** *adj*
systoles *n* ▷ **systole**
systolic *adj* ▷ **systole**

Tt

T is one of the most common consonants in Scrabble. There are only four two-letter words that begin with T, but they are easy to remember as there is one for every vowel except U. Like S, T begins a number of three-letter words that don't use vowels, which are well worth remembering. These are: **thy** (6 points), **try** (6), **tsk** (7), **twp** (8) and **tyg** (7). There are also some useful three-letter words using X: **tax, tix** and **tux** (10 each). If you have an X during a game, remember words like **text** (11), **texts** (12), **textile** (14), **textual** (14) and **texture** (14). The last three of these have seven letters, and so will earn you 50-point bonuses if you use all your tiles to form them.

ta *interj* (*Informal*) thank you
tab *n* (*pl* **-s**) small flap or projecting label
tabard *n* (*pl* **-s**) short sleeveless tunic decorated with a coat of arms, worn in medieval times
tabards *n* ▷ **tabard**
tabbies *n* ▷ **tabby**
tabby *n* (*pl* **-bbies**) ▶ *adj* (cat) with dark stripes on a lighter background
tabernacle *n* (*pl* **-s**) portable shrine of the Israelites
tabernacles *n* ▷ **tabernacle**
tabla *n* (*pl* **-bla, -blas**) one of a pair of Indian drums played with the hands
tablas *n* ▷ **tabla**
table *n* (*pl* **-s**) piece of furniture with a flat top supported by legs ▶ *v* (**-les, -ling, -led**) submit (a motion) for discussion by a meeting
tabled *v* ▷ **table**
tableland *n* (*pl* **-s**) high plateau
tablelands *n* ▷ **tableland**
tablespoon *n* (*pl* **-s**) large spoon for serving food
tablespoons *n* ▷ **tablespoon**
tableau [**tab**-loh] *n* (*pl* **-leaux**) silent motionless group arranged to represent some scene
tableaux *n* ▷ **tableau**
tabled *v* ▷ **table**
tables *n, v* ▷ **table**
tablet *n* (*pl* **-s**) pill of compressed medicinal substance
tablets *n* ▷ **tablet**
tabling *v* ▷ **table**
tabloid *n* (*pl* **-s**) small-sized newspaper with many photographs and a concise, usu. sensational style
tabloids *n* ▷ **tabloid**
taboo *n* (*pl* **-s**) prohibition resulting from religious or social conventions ▶ *adj* forbidden by a taboo
taboos *n* ▷ **taboo**
tabs *n* ▷ **tab**
tabular *adj* arranged in a table
tabulate *v* (**-tes, -ting, -ted**) arrange (information) in a table > **tabulation** *n* (*pl* **-s**)
tabulated *v* ▷ **tabulate**
tabulates *v* ▷ **tabulate**
tabulating *v* ▷ **tabulate**
tabulation *n* ▷ **tabulate**
tabulations *n* ▷ **tabulate**
tachograph *n* (*pl* **-s**) device for recording the speed and distance travelled by a motor vehicle
tachographs *n* ▷ **tachograph**
tachometer *n* (*pl* **-s**) device for measuring speed, esp. that of a revolving shaft
tachometers *n* ▷ **tachometer**
tacit [**tass**-it] *adj* implied but not spoken > **tacitly** *adv*
tacitly *adv* ▷ **tacit**
taciturn [**tass**-it-turn] *adj* habitually uncommunicative > **taciturnity** *n* (*pl* **-ties**)
taciturnities *n* ▷ **taciturn**
taciturnity *n* ▷ **taciturn**
tack[1] *n* (*pl* **-s**) short nail with a large head ▶ *v* (**-s, -ing, -ed**) fasten with tacks
tack[2] *n* (*pl* **-s**) course of a ship sailing obliquely into the wind ▶ *v* (**-s, -ing, -ed**) sail into the wind on a zigzag course
tack[3] *n* (*pl* **-s**) riding harness for horses
tacked *v* ▷ **tack**[1, 2]
tackier *adj* ▷ **tacky**[1, 2]

tackies, takkies *pl n* (*sing* **tacky**) (S AFR) (*Informal*) tennis shoes or plimsolls
tackiest *adj* ▷ **tacky**[1, 2]
tacking *v* ▷ **tack**[1, 2]
tackle *v* (**-les, -ling, -led**) deal with (a task) (SPORT) ▶ *n* (*pl* **-les**) (SPORT) act of tackling an opposing player
tackled *v* ▷ **tackle**
tackles *v, n* ▷ **tackle**
tackling *v* ▷ **tackle**
tacks *n* ▷ **tack**[1, 2, 3] ▶ *v* ▷ **tack**[1, 2]
tacky[1] *adj* (**-ckier, -ckiest**) slightly sticky
tacky[2] *adj* (**-ckier, -ckiest**) (*Informal*) vulgar and tasteless
tacky[3] *n* ▷ **tackies**
taco [**tah**-koh] *n* (*pl* **-s**) (MEXICAN COOKERY) tortilla fried until crisp, served with a filling
tacos *n* ▷ **taco**
tact *n* (*pl* **-s**) skill in avoiding giving offence > **tactful** *adj* > **tactfully** *adv* > **tactless** *adj* > **tactlessly** *adv*
tactful *adj* ▷ **tact**
tactfully *adv* ▷ **tact**
tactic *n* (*pl* **-s**) method or plan to achieve an end > **tactical** *adj* > **tactician** *n* (*pl* **-s**)
tactical *adj* ▷ **tactic**
tactician *n* ▷ **tactic**
tacticians *n* ▷ **tactic**
tactics *pl n* art of directing military forces in battle ▶ *n* ▷ **tactic**
tactile *adj* of or having the sense of touch
tactless *adj* ▷ **tact**
tactlessly *adv* ▷ **tact**
tacts *n* ▷ **tact**
tadpole *n* (*pl* **-s**) limbless tailed larva of a frog or toad
tadpoles *n* ▷ **tadpole**
taffeta *n* (*pl* **-s**) shiny silk or rayon fabric
taffetas *n* ▷ **taffeta**
tag[1] *n* (*pl* **-s**) label bearing information ▶ *v* (**-s, -gging, -gged**) attach a tag to
tag[2] *n* (*pl* **-s**) children's game where the person being chased becomes the chaser upon being touched ▶ *v* (**-s, -gging, -gged**) touch and catch in this game
tagged *v* ▷ **tag**[1, 2]
tagging *v* ▷ **tag**[1, 2]
tagliatelle *n* pasta in long narrow strips
tags *n, v* ▷ **tag**[1, 2]
tail *n* (*pl* **-s**) rear part of an animal's body, usu. forming a flexible appendage ▶ *adj* at the rear ▶ *v* (**-s, -ing, -ed**) (*Informal*) follow (someone) secretly > **tailless** *adj*
tailback *n* (*pl* **-s**) (BRIT) queue of traffic stretching back from an obstruction
tailbacks *n* ▷ **tailback**
tailboard *n* (*pl* **-s**) removable or hinged rear board on a truck etc.
tailboards *n* ▷ **tailboard**
tailed *v* ▷ **tail**
tailing *v* ▷ **tail**
tailless *adj* ▷ **tail**
tailor *n* (*pl* **-s**) person who makes men's clothes ▶ *v* (**-s, -ing, -ed**) adapt to suit a purpose
tailored *v* ▷ **tailor**
tailoring *v* ▷ **tailor**
tailors *n, v* ▷ **tailor**
tailplane *n* (*pl* **-s**) small stabilizing wing at the rear of an aircraft
tailplanes *n* ▷ **tailplane**
tails *adv* with the side of a coin uppermost that does not have a portrait of a head on it ▶ *pl n* (*Informal*) tail coat ▶ *n, v* ▷ **tail**
tailspin *n* (*pl* **-s**) uncontrolled spinning dive of an aircraft
tailspins *n* ▷ **tailspin**
tailwind *n* (*pl* **-s**) wind coming from the rear
tailwinds *n* ▷ **tailwind**
taint *v* (**-s, -ing, -ed**) spoil with a small amount of decay, contamination, or other bad quality ▶ *n* (*pl* **-s**) something that taints
tainted *v* ▷ **taint**
tainting *v* ▷ **taint**
taints *v, n* ▷ **taint**
taipan *n* (*pl* **-s**) large poisonous Australian snake
taipans *n* ▷ **taipan**

> **taj** *n* (**tajes**). A taj is a tall conical cap worn by some Muslims. This unusual word can be helpful if you are struggling to use J because there aren't any good opportunities for longer words on the board. Taj scores 10 points.

take *v* (**takes, taking, took, taken**) remove from a place ▶ *n* (*pl* **-s**) one of a series of recordings from which the best will be used
takeaway *n* (*pl* **-s**) shop or restaurant selling meals for eating elsewhere
takeaways *n* ▷ **takeaway**
taken *v* ▷ **take**
takeoff *n* (*pl* **-s**) (of an aircraft) act of leaving the ground
takeoffs *n* ▷ **takeoff**
takeover *n* (*pl* **-s**) act of taking control of a company by buying a large number of its shares
takeovers *n* ▷ **takeover**
takes *v, n* ▷ **take**
taking *adj* charming ▶ *v* ▷ **take**

takings *pl n* money received by a shop
takkies *pl n* ▷ **tackies**
talc *n* (*pl* **-s**) talcum powder
talcs *n* ▷ **talc**
tale *n* (*pl* **-s**) story
talent *n* (*pl* **-s**) natural ability > **talented** *adj*
talented *adj* ▷ **talent**
talents *n* ▷ **talent**
tales *n* ▷ **tale**
talisman *n* (*pl* **-s**) object believed to have magic power > **talismanic** *adj*
talismanic *adj* ▷ **talisman**
talismans *n* ▷ **talisman**
talk *v* (**-s, -ing, -ed**) express ideas or feelings by means of speech ▶ *n* (*pl* **-s**) speech or lecture
talkative *adj* fond of talking
talkback *n* (*pl* **-s**) (NZ) broadcast in which telephone comments or questions from the public are transmitted live
talkbacks *n* ▷ **talkback**
talked *v* ▷ **talk**
talker *n* (*pl* **-s**) person who talks
talkers *n* ▷ **talker**
talking *v* ▷ **talk**
talks *v, n* ▷ **talk**
tall (**-er, -est**) *adj* higher than average
tallboy *n* (*pl* **-s**) high chest of drawers
tallboys *n* ▷ **tallboy**
taller *adj* ▷ **tall**
tallest *adj* ▷ **tall**
tallied *v* ▷ **tally**
tallies *v, n* ▷ **tally**
tallow *n* (*pl* **-s**) hard animal fat used to make candles
tallows *n* ▷ **tallow**
tally *v* (**-llies, -llying, -llied**) (of two things) correspond ▶ *n* (*pl* **-lies**) record of a debt or score
tallying *v* ▷ **tally**
talon *n* (*pl* **-s**) bird's hooked claw
talons *n* ▷ **talon**
tamarind *n* (*pl* **-s**) tropical tree
tamarinds *n* ▷ **tamarind**
tamarisk *n* (*pl* **-s**) evergreen shrub with slender branches and feathery flower clusters
tamarisks *n* ▷ **tamarisk**
tambourine *n* (*pl* **-s**) percussion instrument like a small drum with jingling metal discs attached
tambourines *n* ▷ **tambourine**
tame *adj* (**-r, -est**) (of animals) brought under human control ▶ *v* (**-mes, -ming, -med**) make tame > **tamely** *adv*
tamed *v* ▷ **tame**
tamely *adv* ▷ **tame**
tamer *n* (*pl* **-s**) person who tames wild animals ▶ *adj* ▷ **tame**
tamers *n* ▷ **tamer**
tames *v* ▷ **tame**
tamest *adj* ▷ **tame**
taming *v* ▷ **tame**
tamp *v* (**-s, -ing, -ed**) pack down by repeated taps
tamped *v* ▷ **tamp**
tamper *v* (**-s, -ing, -ed**) (*foll. by* **with**) interfere
tampered *v* ▷ **tamper**
tampering *v* ▷ **tamper**
tampers *v* ▷ **tamper**
tamping *v* ▷ **tamp**
tampon *n* (*pl* **-s**) absorbent plug of cotton wool inserted into the vagina during menstruation
tampons *n* ▷ **tampon**
tamps *v* ▷ **tamp**
tan *n* (*pl* **-s**) brown coloration of the skin from exposure to sunlight ▶ *v* (**-s, -nning, -nned**) (of skin) go brown from exposure to sunlight ▶ *adj* (**-ner, -nest**) yellowish-brown
tandem *n* (*pl* **-s**) bicycle for two riders, one behind the other
tandems *n* ▷ **tandem**
tandoori *adj* (of food) cooked in an Indian clay oven
tang *n* (*pl* **-s**) strong taste or smell > **tangy** *adj* (**-gier, -giest**)
tangent *n* (*pl* **-s**) line that touches a curve without intersecting it
tangential *adj* of superficial relevance only > **tangentially** *adv*
tangentially *adv* ▷ **tangential**
tangents *n* ▷ **tangent**
tangerine *n* (*pl* **-s**) small orange-like fruit of an Asian citrus tree
tangerines *n* ▷ **tangerine**
tangible *adj* able to be touched > **tangibly** *adv*
tangibly *adv* ▷ **tangible**
tangier *adj* ▷ **tang**
tangiest *adj* ▷ **tang**
tangle *n* (*pl* **-les**) confused mass or situation ▶ *v* (**-les, -ling, -led**) twist together in a tangle
tangled *v* ▷ **tangle**
tangles *n, v* ▷ **tangle**
tangling *v* ▷ **tangle**
tango *n* (*pl* **-gos**) S American dance ▶ *v* (**-goes, -going, -goed**) dance a tango
tangoed *v* ▷ **tango**
tangoes *v* ▷ **tango**
tangoing *v* ▷ **tango**
tangos *v* ▷ **tango**
tangs *n* ▷ **tang**

tangy *adj* ▷ **tang**
taniwha [**tun**-ee-fah] *n* (*pl* **-s**) (NZ) mythical Maori monster that lives in water
taniwhas *n* ▷ **taniwha**
tank *n* (*pl* **-s**) container for liquids or gases
tankard *n* (*pl* **-s**) large beer-mug, often with a hinged lid
tankards *n* ▷ **tankard**
tanker *n* (*pl* **-s**) ship or truck for carrying liquid in bulk
tankers *n* ▷ **tanker**
tanks *n* ▷ **tank**
tanned *v* ▷ **tan**
tanner *adj* ▷ **tan**
tanneries *n* ▷ **tannery**
tannery *n* (*pl* **-ries**) place where hides are tanned
tannest *adj* ▷ **tan**
tannin *n* (*pl* **-s**) vegetable substance used in tanning
tanning *v* ▷ **tan**
tannins *n* ▷ **tannin**
tans *n, v* ▷ **tan**
tansies *n* ▷ **tansy**
tansy *n* (*pl* **-sies**) yellow-flowered plant
tantalize *v* (**-zes, -zing, -zed**) torment by showing but withholding something desired > **tantalizing** *adj* > **tantalizingly** *adv*
tantalized *v* ▷ **tantalize**
tantalizes *v* ▷ **tantalize**
tantalizing *v, adj* ▷ **tantalize**
tantalizingly *adv* ▷ **tantalize**
tantalum *n* (*pl* **-s**) (CHEM) hard greyish-white metallic element
tantalums *n* ▷ **tantalum**
tantamount *adj* equivalent in effect to
tantrum *n* (*pl* **-s**) childish outburst of temper
tantrums *n* ▷ **tantrum**
tap[1] *v* (**taps, tapping, -pped**) knock lightly and usu. repeatedly ▶ *n* (*pl* **-s**) light knock
tap[2] *n* (*pl* **-s**) valve to control the flow of liquid from a pipe or cask ▶ *v* (**taps, tapping, tapped**) listen in on (a telephone call) secretly by making an illegal connection
tape *n* (*pl* **-s**) narrow long strip of material ▶ *v* (**tapes, taping, taped**) record on magnetic tape
taped *v* ▷ **tape**
taper *v* (**-s, -ing, -ed**) become narrower towards one end ▶ *n* (*pl* **-s**) long thin candle
tapered *v* ▷ **taper**
tapering *v* ▷ **taper**
tapers *v, n* ▷ **taper**
tapes *n, v* ▷ **tape**
tapestries *n* ▷ **tapestry**
tapestry *n* (*pl* **-tries**) fabric decorated with coloured woven designs
tapeworm *n* (*pl* **-s**) long flat parasitic worm living in the intestines of vertebrates
tapeworms *n* ▷ **tapeworm**
tapioca *n* (*pl* **-s**) beadlike starch made from cassava root, used in puddings
tapiocas *n* ▷ **tapioca**
taping *v* ▷ **tape**
tapir [**tape**-er] *n* (*pl* **-s**) piglike mammal of tropical America and SE Asia, with a long snout
tapirs *n* ▷ **tapir**
tapped *v* ▷ **tap**[1, 2]
tappet *n* (*pl* **-s**) short steel rod in an engine, transferring motion from one part to another
tappets *n* ▷ **tappet**
tapping *v* ▷ **tap**[1, 2]
taproot *n* (*pl* **-s**) main root of a plant, growing straight down
taproots *n* ▷ **taproot**
taps *n, v* ▷ **tap**[1, 2]
tar *n* (*pl* **-rs**) thick black liquid distilled from coal etc. ▶ *v* (**-s, -rring, -rred**) coat with tar
taramasalata *n* (*pl* **-s**) creamy pink pâté made from fish roe
taramasalatas *n* ▷ **taramasalata**
tarantella *n* (*pl* **-s**) lively Italian dance
tarantellas *n* ▷ **tarantella**
tarantula *n* (*pl* **-s**) large hairy spider with a poisonous bite
tarantulas *n* ▷ **tarantula**
tardier *adj* ▷ **tardy**
tardiest *adj* ▷ **tardy**
tardily *adv* ▷ **tardy**
tardiness *n* ▷ **tardy**
tardinesses *n* ▷ **tardy**
tardy *adj* (**-dier, -diest**) slow or late > **tardily** *adv* > **tardiness** *n* (*pl* **-es**)
tare *n* (*pl* **-s**) type of vetch plant
tares *n* ▷ **tare**
target *n* (*pl* **-s**) object or person a missile is aimed at ▶ *v* (**-gets, -geting, -geted**) aim or direct
targeted *v* ▷ **target**
targeting *v* ▷ **target**
targets *n, v* ▷ **target**
tariff *n* (*pl* **-s**) tax levied on imports
tariffs *n* ▷ **tariff**
tarn *n* (*pl* **-s**) small mountain lake
tarnish *v* (**-shes, -shing, -shed**) make or become stained or less bright ▶ *n* (*pl* **-es**) discoloration or blemish
tarnished *v* ▷ **tarnish**
tarnishes *v, n* ▷ **tarnish**

tarnishing *v* ▷ **tarnish**
tarns *n* ▷ **tarn**
tarot [tarr-oh] *n* (*pl* **-s**) special pack of cards used mainly in fortune-telling
tarots *n* ▷ **tarot**
tarpaulin *n* (*pl* **-s**) (sheet of) heavy waterproof fabric
tarpaulins *n* ▷ **tarpaulin**
tarragon *n* (*pl* **-s**) aromatic herb
tarragons *n* ▷ **tarragon**
tarred *v* ▷ **tar**
tarried *v* ▷ **tarry**
tarries *v* ▷ **tarry**
tarring *v* ▷ **tar**
tarry *v* (**tarries, tarrying, tarried**) (*Old-fashioned*) linger or delay
tarrying *v* ▷ **tarry**
tars *n, v* ▷ **tar**
tarsi *n* ▷ **tarsus**
tarsus *n* (*pl* **-si**) bones of the heel and ankle collectively
tart[1] *n* (*pl* **-s**) pie or flan with a sweet filling
tart[2] *adj* (**-er, -est**) sharp or bitter > **tartly** *adv* > **tartness** *n* (*pl* **-es**)
tart[3] *n* (*pl* **-s**) (*Informal*) sexually provocative or promiscuous woman
tartan *n* (*pl* **-s**) design of straight lines crossing at right angles, esp. one associated with a Scottish clan
tartans *n* ▷ **tartan**
tartar[1] *n* (*pl* **-s**) hard deposit on the teeth
tartar[2] *n* (*pl* **-s**) fearsome or formidable person
tartars *n* ▷ **tartar**[1, 2]
tarter *adj* ▷ **tart**[2]
tartest *adj* ▷ **tart**[2]
tartly *adv* ▷ **tart**[2]
tartness *n* ▷ **tart**[2]
tartnesses *n* ▷ **tart**[2]
tartrazine [tar-traz-zeen] *n* (*pl* **-s**) artificial yellow dye used in food etc.
tartrazines *n* ▷ **tartrazine**
tarts *n* ▷ **tart**[1, 3]
task *n* (*pl* **-s**) (difficult or unpleasant) piece of work to be done
taskmaster *n* (*pl* **-s**) person who enforces hard work
taskmasters *n* ▷ **taskmaster**
tasks *n* ▷ **task**
tassel *n* (*pl* **-s**) decorative fringed knot of threads
tassels *n* ▷ **tassel**
taste *n* (*pl* **-s**) sense by which the flavour of a substance is distinguished in the mouth ▶ *v* (**-tes, -ting, -ted**) distinguish the taste of (a substance)
tasted *v* ▷ **taste**
tasteful *adj* having or showing good taste > **tastefully** *adv*
tastefully *adv* ▷ **tasteful**
tasteless *adj* bland or insipid > **tastelessly** *adv*
tastelessly *adv* ▷ **tasteless**
tastes *n, v* ▷ **taste**
tastier *adj* ▷ **tasty**
tastiest *adj* ▷ **tasty**
tasting *v* ▷ **taste**
tasty *adj* (**-tier, -tiest**) pleasantly flavoured
tat *n* (*pl* **-s**) (BRIT) tatty or tasteless article(s)
tats *n* ▷ **tat**
tattered *adj* ragged or torn
tattier *n* ▷ **tatty**
tattiest *n* ▷ **tatty**
tattle *v* (**-les, -ling, -led**), *n* (*pl* **-les**) (BRIT, AUST & NZ) gossip or chatter
tattled *v* ▷ **tattle**
tattles *n* ▷ **tattle**
tattling *v* ▷ **tattle**
tattoo[1] *n* (*pl* **-s**) pattern made on the body by pricking the skin and staining it with indelible inks ▶ *v* (**-toos, -tooing, -tooed**) make such a pattern on the skin > **tattooist** *n* (*pl* **-s**)
tattoo[2] *n* (*pl* **-s**) military display or pageant
tattooed *n* ▷ **tattoo**[1]
tattooing *n* ▷ **tattoo**[1]
tattooist *n* ▷ **tattoo**[1]
tattooists *n* ▷ **tattoo**[1]
tattoos *n* ▷ **tattoo**[1, 2] ▶ *v* ▷ **tattoo**[1]
tatty *adj* (**-tier, -tiest**) shabby or worn out
taught *v* ▷ **teach**
taunt *v* (**-s, -ing, -ed**) tease with jeers ▶ *n* (*pl* **-s**) jeering remark
taunted *v* ▷ **taunt**
taunting *v* ▷ **taunt**
taunts *v, n* ▷ **taunt**
taupe *adj* brownish-grey
taut *adj* (**-er, -est**) drawn tight
tauten *v* (**-s, -ing, -ed**) make or become taut
tautened *v* ▷ **tauten**
tautening *v* ▷ **tauten**
tautens *v* ▷ **tauten**
tauter *adj* ▷ **taut**
tautest *adj* ▷ **taut**
tautological *adj* ▷ **tautology**
tautologies *n* ▷ **tautology**
tautology *n* (*pl* **-gies**) use of words which merely repeat something already stated > **tautological** *adj*
tavern *n* (*pl* **-s**) (*Old-fashioned*) pub
taverns *n* ▷ **tavern**
tawdrier *adj* ▷ **tawdry**

tawdriest *adj* ▷ **tawdry**

tawdry *adj* (**-drier, -driest**) cheap, showy, and of poor quality

tawnier *adj* ▷ **tawny**

tawniest *adj* ▷ **tawny**

tawny *adj* (**-nier, -niest**) yellowish-brown

tax *n* (*pl* **-es**) compulsory payment levied by a government on income, property, etc. to raise revenue ▶ *v* (**-es, -ing, -ed**) levy a tax on > **taxable** *adj* > **taxpayer** *n* (*pl* **-s**)

taxable *adj* ▷ **tax**

taxation *n* (*pl* **-s**) levying of taxes

taxations *n* ▷ **taxation**

taxed *v* ▷ **tax**

taxes *n, v* ▷ **tax**

taxi *n* (*pl* **-s**) car with a driver that may be hired to take people to any specified destination ▶ *v* (**taxis, taxiing, taxied**) (of an aircraft) run along the ground before taking off or after landing

taxidermies *n* ▷ **taxidermy**

taxidermist *n* ▷ **taxidermy**

taxidermists *n* ▷ **taxidermy**

taxidermy *n* (*pl* **-mies**) art of stuffing and mounting animal skins to give them a lifelike appearance > **taxidermist** *n* (*pl* **-s**)

taxied *v* ▷ **taxi**

taxiing *v* ▷ **taxi**

taxing *v* ▷ **tax**

taxis *n, v* ▷ **taxi**

taxonomic *adj* ▷ **taxonomy**

taxonomies *n* ▷ **taxonomy**

taxonomist *n* ▷ **taxonomy**

taxonomists *n* ▷ **taxonomy**

taxonomy *n* (*pl* **-mies**) classification of plants and animals into groups > **taxonomic** *adj* > **taxonomist** *n* (*pl* **-s**)

taxpayer *n* ▷ **tax**

taxpayers *n* ▷ **tax**

> **te** *n* (**tes**). Te is the seventh note of a musical scale. Although it won't earn you many points on its own, te is extremely useful as it allows you to connect a word beginning with T to one ending in E, or vice versa, which is very helpful as T and E are two of the most common tiles in the game. Te scores 2 points.

tea *n* (*pl* **-s**) drink made from infusing the dried leaves of an Asian bush in boiling water

teapot *n* (*pl* **-s**) container with a lid, spout, and handle for making and serving tea

teapots *n* ▷ **teapot**

teaspoon *n* (*pl* **-s**) small spoon for stirring tea

teaspoons *n* ▷ **teaspoon**

teach *v* (**-es, -ing, taught**) tell or show (someone) how to do something > **teaching** *n* (*pl* **-s**)

teacher *n* (*pl* **-s**) person who teaches, esp. in a school

teachers *n* ▷ **teacher**

teaches *v* ▷ **teach**

teaching *v, n* ▷ **teach**

teachings *n* ▷ **teach**

teak *n* (*pl* **-s**) very hard wood of an E Indian tree

teaks *n* ▷ **teak**

teal *n* (*pl* **-s**) kind of small duck

teals *n* ▷ **teal**

team *n* (*pl* **-s**) group of people forming one side in a game

teams *n* ▷ **team**

teamster *n* (*pl* **-s**) (US) commercial vehicle driver

teamsters *n* ▷ **teamster**

teamwork *n* (*pl* **-s**) cooperative work by a team

teamworks *n* ▷ **teamwork**

tear[1], **teardrop** *n* (*pl* **-s**) drop of fluid appearing in and falling from the eye

tear[2] *v* (**-s, -ing, tore, torn**) rip a hole in ▶ *n* (*pl* **-s**) hole or split

tearaway *n* (*pl* **-s**) wild or unruly person

tearaways *n* ▷ **tearaway**

teardrop *n* ▷ **tear**[1]

teardrops *n* ▷ **tear**[1]

tearful *adj* weeping or about to weep

tearing *v* ▷ **tear**[2]

tears *n* ▷ **tear**[1, 2] ▶ *v* ▷ **tear**[2]

teas *n* ▷ **tea**

tease *v* (**-ses, -sing, -sed**) make fun of (someone) in a provoking or playful way ▶ *n* (*pl* **-s**) person who teases > **teasing** *adj, n* (*pl* **-s**)

teased *v* ▷ **tease**

teasel, teazel, teazle *n* (*pl* **-s**) plant with prickly leaves and flowers

teasels *n* ▷ **teasel**

teases *v, n* ▷ **tease**

teasing *v, adj n* ▷ **tease**

teasings *n* ▷ **tease**

teat *n* (*pl* **-s**) nipple of a breast or udder

teats *n* ▷ **teat**

teazel *n* ▷ **teasel**

teazels *n* ▷ **teasel**

teazle *n* ▷ **teasel**

teazles *n* ▷ **teasel**

tech *n* (*pl* **-s**) (*Informal*) technical college

techie (*Informal*) *n* (*pl* **-s**) person who is skilled in the use of technology ▶ *adj* relating to or skilled in the use of technology

techies *n* ▷ **techie**

technetium [tek-**neesh**-ee-um] *n* (*pl* **-s**) (CHEM)

artificially produced silvery-grey metallic element
technetiums *n* ▷ **technetium**
technical *adj* of or specializing in industrial, practical, or mechanical arts and applied sciences > **technically** *adv*
technicalities *n* ▷ **technicality**
technicality *n* (*pl* **-s**) petty point based on a strict application of rules
technically *adv* ▷ **technical**
technician *n* (*pl* **-s**) person skilled in a particular technical field
technicians *n* ▷ **technician**
technicolor *adj* garishly coloured
technique *n* (*pl* **-s**) method or skill used for a particular task
techniques *n* ▷ **technique**
techno *n* (*pl* **-s**) type of electronic dance music with a very fast beat
technocracies *n* ▷ **technocracy**
technocracy *n* (*pl* **-cies**) government by technical experts > **technocrat** *n* (*pl* **-s**)
technocrat *n* ▷ **technocracy**
technocrats *n* ▷ **technocracy**
technological *adj* ▷ **technology**
technologies *n* ▷ **technology**
technologist *n* ▷ **technology**
technologists *n* ▷ **technology**
technology *n* (*pl* **-gies**) application of practical or mechanical sciences to industry or commerce > **technological** *adj* > **technologist** *n* (*pl* **-s**)
technos *n* ▷ **techno**
techs *n* ▷ **tech**
tectonics *n* study of the earth's crust and the forces affecting it
teddies *n* ▷ **teddy**
teddy *n* (*pl* **-dies**) teddy bear
tedious *adj* causing fatigue or boredom > **tediously** *adv*
tediously *adv* ▷ **tedious**
tedium *n* (*pl* **-s**) monotony
tediums *n* ▷ **tedium**
tee *n* (*pl* **-s**) small peg from which a golf ball can be played at the start of each hole
teem[1] *v* (**-s, -ing, -ed**) be full of
teem[2] *v* (**-s, -ing, -ed**) rain heavily
teemed *v* ▷ **teem[1, 2]**
teeming *v* ▷ **teem[1, 2]**
teems *v* ▷ **teem[1, 2]**
teenage *adj* ▷ **teenager**
teenager *n* (*pl* **-s**) person aged between 13 and 19 > **teenage** *adj*
teenagers *n* ▷ **teenager**
teens *pl n* period of being a teenager
teepee *n* (*pl* **-s**) ▷ **tepee**
teepees *n* ▷ **teepee**
tees *n* ▷ **tee**
teeter *v* (**-s, -ing, -ed**) wobble or move unsteadily
teetered *v* ▷ **teeter**
teetering *v* ▷ **teeter**
teeters *v* ▷ **teeter**
teeth *n* ▷ **tooth**
teethe *v* (**-thes, -thing, -thed**) (of a baby) grow his or her first teeth
teethed *v* ▷ **teethe**
teethes *v* ▷ **teethe**
teething *v* ▷ **teethe**
teetotal *adj* drinking no alcohol > **teetotaller** *n* (*pl* **-s**)
teetotaller *n* ▷ **teetotal**
teetotallers *n* ▷ **teetotal**
telecommunications *n* communications using telephone, radio, television, etc.
telegram *n* (*pl* **-s**) formerly, a message sent by telegraph
telegrams *n* ▷ **telegram**
telegraph *n* (*pl* **-s**) formerly, a system for sending messages over a distance along a cable ▶ *v* (**-s, -ing, -ed**) communicate by telegraph > **telegraphic** *adj* > **telegraphist** *n* (*pl* **-s**)
telegraphed *v* ▷ **telegraph**
telegraphic *adj* ▷ **telegraph**
telegraphies *n* ▷ **telegraphy**
telegraphing *v* ▷ **telegraph**
telegraphist *n* ▷ **telegraph**
telegraphists *n* ▷ **telegraph**
telegraphs *n, v* ▷ **telegraph**
telegraphy *n* (*pl* **-phies**) science or use of a telegraph
telekinesis *n* (*pl* **-eses**) movement of objects by thought or willpower
telekineses *n* ▷ **telekinesis**
telemetries *n* ▷ **telemetry**
telemetry *n* (*pl* **-tries**) use of electronic devices to record or measure a distant event and transmit the data to a receiver
teleological *adj* ▷ **teleology**
teleologies *n* ▷ **teleology**
teleology *n* (*pl* **-gies**) belief that all things have a predetermined purpose > **teleological** *adj*
telepathic *adj* ▷ **telepathy**
telepathically *adv* ▷ **telepathy**
telepathies *n* ▷ **telepathy**
telepathy *n* (*pl* **-thies**) direct communication between minds > **telepathic** *adj* > **telepathically** *adv*
telephone *n* (*pl* **-s**) device for transmitting

sound over a distance ▶ *v* (**-nes, -ning, -ned**) call or talk to (a person) by telephone > **telephony** *n* (*pl* **-nies**) > **telephonic** *adj*
telephoned *v* ▷ **telephone**
telephones *n, v* ▷ **telephone**
telephonic *adj* ▷ **telephone**
telephonies *n* ▷ **telephone**
telephoning *v* ▷ **telephone**
telephonist *n* (*pl* **-s**) person operating a telephone switchboard
telephonists *n* ▷ **telephonist**
telephony *n* ▷ **telephone**
teleprinter *n* (*pl* **-s**) (BRIT) apparatus like a typewriter for sending and receiving typed messages by wire
teleprinters *n* ▷ **teleprinter**
telesales *n* selling of a product or service by telephone
telescope *n* (*pl* **-s**) optical instrument for magnifying distant objects ▶ *v* (**-pes, -ping, -ped**) shorten > **telescopic** *adj*
telescoped *v* ▷ **telescope**
telescopes *n, v* ▷ **telescope**
telescopic *adj* ▷ **telescope**
telescoping *v* ▷ **telescope**
televise *v* (**-ses, -sing, -sed**) broadcast on television
televised *v* ▷ **televise**
televises *v* ▷ **televise**
televising *v* ▷ **televise**
television *n* (*pl* **-s**) system of producing a moving image and accompanying sound on a distant screen > **televisual** *adj*
televisions *n* ▷ **television**
televisual *adj* ▷ **television**
telex *n* (*pl* **-es**) international communication service using teleprinters ▶ *v* (**-es, -ing, -ed**) transmit by telex
telexed *v* ▷ **telex**
telexes *n, v* ▷ **telex**
telexing *v* ▷ **telex**
tell *v* (**-s, -lling, told**) make known in words
teller *n* (*pl* **-s**) narrator
tellers *n* ▷ **teller**
tellies *n* ▷ **telly**
telling *adj* having a marked effect ▶ *v* ▷ **tell**
tells *v* ▷ **tell**
telltale *n* (*pl* **-s**) person who reveals secrets ▶ *adj* revealing
telltales *n* ▷ **telltale**
tellurium *n* (*pl* **-s**) (CHEM) brittle silvery-white nonmetallic element
telluriums *n* ▷ **tellurium**
telly *n* (*pl* **-lies**) (*Informal*) television
temerities *n* ▷ **temerity**
temerity [tim-**merr**-it-tee] *n* (*pl* **-ties**) boldness or audacity
temp (BRIT) (*Informal*) *n* (*pl* **-s**) temporary employee, esp. a secretary ▶ *v* (**-s, -ing, -ed**) work as a temp
temped *v* ▷ **temp**
temper *n* (*pl* **-s**) outburst of anger ▶ *v* (**-s, -ing, -ed**) make less extreme
tempera *n* (*pl* **-s**) painting medium for powdered pigments
temperas *n* ▷ **tempera**
temperament *n* (*pl* **-s**) person's character or disposition
temperamental *adj* having changeable moods > **temperamentally** *adv*
temperamentally *adv* ▷ **temperamental**
temperaments *n* ▷ **temperament**
temperance *n* (*pl* **-s**) moderation
temperances *n* ▷ **temperance**
temperate *adj* (of climate) not extreme
temperature *n* (*pl* **-s**) degree of heat or cold
temperatures *n* ▷ **temperature**
tempered *v* ▷ **temper**
tempering *v* ▷ **temper**
tempers *n, v* ▷ **temper**
tempest *n* (*pl* **-s**) violent storm
tempests *n* ▷ **tempest**
tempestuous *adj* violent or stormy
tempi *n* ▷ **tempo**
temping *v* ▷ **temp**
template *n* (*pl* **-s**) pattern used to cut out shapes accurately
templates *n* ▷ **template**
temple[1] *n* (*pl* **-s**) building for worship
temple[2] *n* (*pl* **-s**) region on either side of the forehead
temples *n* ▷ **temple[1, 2]**
tempo *n* (*pl* **-pi, -pos**) rate or pace
temporal *adj* of time
temporarily *adv* ▷ **temporary**
temporary *adj* lasting only for a short time > **temporarily** *adv*
temporize *v* (**-zes, -zing, -zed**) gain time by negotiation or evasiveness
temporized *v* ▷ **temporize**
temporizes *v* ▷ **temporize**
temporizing *v* ▷ **temporize**
tempos *n* ▷ **tempo**
temps *n, v* ▷ **temp**
tempt *v* (**-s, -ing, -ed**) entice (a person) to do something wrong > **tempter, temptress** *n* (*pl* **-s, -es**)
temptation *n* (*pl* **-s**) tempting
temptations *n* ▷ **temptation**
tempted *v* ▷ **tempt**

tempter *n* ▷ **tempt**
tempters *n* ▷ **tempt**
tempting *adj* attractive or inviting ▶ *v* ▷ **tempt**
temptress *n* ▷ **tempt**
temptresses *n* ▷ **tempt**
tempts *v* ▷ **tempt**
ten *adj, n* (*pl* **-s**) one more than nine
tenable *adj* able to be upheld or maintained
tenacious *adj* holding fast > **tenaciously** *adv* > **tenacity** *n* (*pl* **-ties**)
tenaciously *adv* ▷ **tenacious**
tenacities *n* ▷ **tenacious**
tenacity *n* ▷ **tenacious**
tenancies *n* ▷ **tenant**
tenancy *n* ▷ **tenant**
tenant *n* (*pl* **-s**) person who rents land or a building > **tenancy** *n* (*pl* **-cies**)
tenants *n* ▷ **tenant**
tench *n* (*pl* **-es**) freshwater game fish of the carp family
tenches *n* ▷ **tench**
tend[1] *v* (**-s, -ing, -ed**) be inclined
tend[2] *v* (**-s, -ing, -ed**) take care of
tended *v* ▷ **tend**[1, 2]
tendencies *n* ▷ **tendency**
tendency *n* (*pl* **-cies**) inclination to act in a certain way > **tendentious** *adj* biased, not impartial
tendentious *adj* ▷ **tendency**
tender[1] *adj* (**-er, -est**) not tough > **tenderly** *adv* > **tenderness** *n* (*pl* **-es**)
tender[2] *v* (**-s, -ing, -ed**) offer ▶ *n* (*pl* **-s**) such an offer
tender[3] *n* (*pl* **-s**) small boat that brings supplies to a larger ship in a port
tendered *v* ▷ **tender**[2]
tenderer *adj* ▷ **tender**[1]
tenderest *adj* ▷ **tender**[1]
tendering *v* ▷ **tender**[2]
tenderize *v* (**-zes, -zing, -zed**) soften (meat) by pounding or treatment with a special substance
tenderized *v* ▷ **tenderize**
tenderizes *v* ▷ **tenderize**
tenderizing *v* ▷ **tenderize**
tenderly *adv* ▷ **tender**[1]
tenderness *n* ▷ **tender**[1]
tendernesses *n* ▷ **tender**[1]
tenders *n* ▷ **tender**[2, 3] ▶ *v* ▷ **tender**[2]
tending *v* ▷ **tend**[1, 2]
tendon *n* (*pl* **-s**) strong tissue attaching a muscle to a bone
tendons *n* ▷ **tendon**
tendril *n* (*pl* **-s**) slender stem by which a climbing plant clings
tendrils *n* ▷ **tendril**
tends *v* ▷ **tend**[1, 2]
tenement *n* (*pl* **-s**) (esp. in Scotland or the US) building divided into several flats
tenements *n* ▷ **tenement**
tenet [**ten**-nit] *n* (*pl* **-s**) doctrine or belief
tenets *n* ▷ **tenet**
tenner *n* (*pl* **-s**) (BRIT) (*Informal*) ten-pound note
tenners *n* ▷ **tenner**
tennis *n* (*pl* **-es**) game in which players use rackets to hit a ball back and forth over a net
tennises *n* ▷ **tennis**
tenon *n* (*pl* **-s**) projecting end on a piece of wood fitting into a slot in another
tenons *n* ▷ **tenon**
tenor *n* (*pl* **-s**) (singer with) the second highest male voice ▶ *adj* (of a voice or instrument) between alto and baritone
tenors *n* ▷ **tenor**
tens *n* ▷ **ten**
tense[1] *adj* (**-r, -st**) emotionally strained ▶ *v* (**-ses, -sing, -sed**) make or become tense
tense[2] *n* (*pl* **-s**) (GRAMMAR) form of a verb showing the time of action
tensed *v* ▷ **tense**[1]
tenser *adj* ▷ **tense**[1]
tenses *n* ▷ **tense**[2] ▶ *v* ▷ **tense**[1]
tensest *adj* ▷ **tense**[1]
tensile *adj* of tension
tensing *v* ▷ **tense**[1]
tension *n* (*pl* **-s**) hostility or suspense
tensions *n* ▷ **tension**
tent *n* (*pl* **-s**) portable canvas shelter
tentacle *n* (*pl* **-s**) flexible organ of many invertebrates, used for grasping, feeding, etc.
tentacles *n* ▷ **tentacle**
tentative *adj* provisional or experimental > **tentatively** *adv*
tentatively *adv* ▷ **tentative**
tenterhooks *pl n* tension
tenth *adj, n* (*pl* **-s**) (of) number ten in a series
tenths *n* ▷ **tenth**
tents *n* ▷ **tent**
tenuous *adj* slight or flimsy > **tenuously** *adv*
tenuously *adv* ▷ **tenuous**
tenure *n* (*pl* **-s**) (period of) the holding of an office or position
tenures *n* ▷ **tenure**
tepee, teepee [**tee**-pee] *n* (*pl* **-s**) cone-shaped tent, formerly used by Native Americans
tepees *n* ▷ **tepee**
tepid *adj* (**-er, -est**) slightly warm
tepider *adj* ▷ **tepid**
tepidest *adj* ▷ **tepid**
tequila *n* (*pl* **-s**) Mexican alcoholic drink

tequilas *n* ▷ **tequila**
tercentenaries *n* ▷ **tercentenary**
tercentenary *adj, n* (*pl* **-ries**) (of) a three hundredth anniversary
term *n* (*pl* **-s**) word or expression ▶ *v* (**-s, -ing, -ed**) name or designate
termed *v* ▷ **term**
terminal *adj* (of an illness) ending in death ▶ *n* (*pl* **-s**) place where people or vehicles begin or end a journey > **terminally** *adv*
terminally *adv* ▷ **terminal**
terminals *n* ▷ **terminal**
terminate *v* (**-tes, -ting, -ted**) bring or come to an end > **termination** *n* (*pl* **-s**)
terminated *v* ▷ **terminate**
terminates *v* ▷ **terminate**
terminating *v* ▷ **terminate**
termination *n* ▷ **terminate**
terminations *n* ▷ **terminate**
terming *v* ▷ **term**
termini *n* ▷ **terminus**
terminologies *n* ▷ **terminology**
terminology *n* (*pl* **-gies**) technical terms relating to a subject
terminus *n* (*pl* **-ni, -nuses**) railway or bus station at the end of a line
terminuses *n* ▷ **terminus**
termite *n* (*pl* **-s**) white antlike insect that destroys timber
termites *n* ▷ **termite**
terms *n, v* ▷ **term** ▶ *pl n* conditions
tern *n* (*pl* **-s**) gull-like sea bird with a forked tail and pointed wings
ternary *adj* consisting of three parts
terns *n* ▷ **tern**
terrace *n* (*pl* **-s**) row of houses built as one block ▶ *v* (**-ces, -cing, -ced**) form into or provide with a terrace
terraced *v* ▷ **terrace**
terraces *n, v* ▷ **terrace** ▶ *pl n* (*also* **terracing**) tiered area in a stadium where spectators stand
terracing *v* ▷ **terrace**
terracotta *adj, n* (*pl* **-s**) (made of) brownish-red unglazed pottery ▶ *adj* brownish-red
terracottas *n* ▷ **terracotta**
terrain *n* (*pl* **-s**) area of ground, esp. with reference to its physical character
terrains *n* ▷ **terrain**
terrapin *n* (*pl* **-s**) small turtle-like reptile
terrapins *n* ▷ **terrapin**
terraria *n* ▷ **terrarium**
terrarium *n* (*pl* **-raria, -rariums**) enclosed container for small plants or animals
terrariums *n* ▷ **terrarium**
terrazzo *n* (*pl* **-s**) floor of marble chips set in mortar and polished
terrazzos *n* ▷ **terrazzo**
terrestrial *adj* of the earth
terrible *adj* very serious > **terribly** *adv*
terribly *adv* ▷ **terrible**
terrier *n* (*pl* **-s**) any of various breeds of small active dog
terriers *n* ▷ **terrier**
terries *n* ▷ **terry**
terrific *adj* great or intense
terrified *v, adj* ▷ **terrify**
terrifies *v* ▷ **terrify**
terrify *v* (**-fies, -fying, -fied**) fill with fear > **terrified** *adj* > **terrifying** *adj*
terrifying *v, adj* ▷ **terrify**
terrine [terr-**reen**] *n* (*pl* **-s**) earthenware dish with a lid
terrines *n* ▷ **terrine**
territorial *adj* ▷ **territory**
territories *n* ▷ **territory**
territory *n* (*pl* **-ries**) district > **territorial** *adj*
terror *n* (*pl* **-s**) great fear
terrorism *n* (*pl* **-s**) use of violence and intimidation to achieve political ends > **terrorist** *n* (*pl* **-s**) *adj*
terrorisms *n* ▷ **terrorism**
terrorist *n, adj* ▷ **terrorism**
terrorists *n* ▷ **terrorism**
terrorize *v* (**-zes, -zing, -zed**) force or oppress by fear or violence
terrorized *v* ▷ **terrorize**
terrorizes *v* ▷ **terrorize**
terrorizing *v* ▷ **terrorize**
terrors *n* ▷ **terror**
terry *n* (*pl* **-ries**) fabric with small loops covering both sides, used esp. for making towels
terse *adj* (**-r, -st**) neat and concise > **tersely** *adv*
tersely *adv* ▷ **terse**
terser *adj* ▷ **terse**
tersest *adj* ▷ **terse**
tertiary [**tur**-shar-ee] *adj* third in degree, order, etc.
tessellated *adj* paved or inlaid with a mosaic of small tiles
test *v* (**-s, -ing, -ed**) try out to ascertain the worth, capability, or endurance of ▶ *n* (*pl* **-s**) critical examination > **testing** *adj*
testament *n* (*pl* **-s**) proof or tribute
testaments *n* ▷ **testament**
testator [test-**tay**-tor], *fem* **testatrix** [test-**tay**-triks] *n* (*pl* **-s, -xes**) maker of a will
testators *n* ▷ **testator**
testatrix *n* ▷ **testator**

testatrixes *n* ▷ **testator**
tested *v* ▷ **test**
testes *n* ▷ **testis**
testicle *n* (*pl* **-s**) either of the two male reproductive glands
testicles *n* ▷ **testicle**
testier *adj* ▷ **testy**
testiest *adj* ▷ **testy**
testified *v* ▷ **testify**
testifies *v* ▷ **testify**
testify *v* (**-fies, -fying, -fied**) give evidence under oath
testifying *v* ▷ **testify**
testily *adv* ▷ **testy**
testimonial *n* (*pl* **-s**) recommendation of the worth of a person or thing
testimonials *n* ▷ **testimonial**
testimonies *n* ▷ **testimony**
testimony *n* (*pl* **-nies**) declaration of truth or fact
testiness *n* ▷ **testy**
testinesses *n* ▷ **testy**
testing *v, adj* ▷ **test**
testis *n* (*pl* **-tes**) testicle
testosterone *n* (*pl* **-s**) male sex hormone secreted by the testes
testosterones *n* ▷ **testosterone**
tests *v, n* ▷ **test**
testy *adj* (**-tier, -tiest**) irritable or touchy > **testily** *adv* > **testiness** *n* (*pl* **-es**)
tetanus *n* (*pl* **-es**) acute infectious disease producing muscular spasms and convulsions
tetanuses *n* ▷ **tetanus**
tether *n* (*pl* **-s**) rope or chain for tying an animal to a spot ▶ *v* (**-s, -ing, -ed**) tie up with rope
tethered *v* ▷ **tether**
tethering *v* ▷ **tether**
tethers *n, v* ▷ **tether**
tetrahedra *n* ▷ **tetrahedron**
tetrahedron [tet-ra-**heed**-ron] *n* (*pl* **-drons, -dra**) solid figure with four faces
tetrahedrons *n* ▷ **tetrahedron**
tetralogies *n* ▷ **tetralogy**
tetralogy *n* (*pl* **-gies**) series of four related works
text *n* (*pl* **-s**) main body of a book as distinct from illustrations etc. ▶ *v* (**-s, -ing, -ed**) send a text message to (someone) > **textual** *adj*
textbook *n* (*pl* **-s**) standard book on a particular subject ▶ *adj* perfect
textbooks *n* ▷ **textbook**
texted *v* ▷ **text**
textile *n* (*pl* **-s**) fabric or cloth, esp. woven
textiles *n* ▷ **textile**
texting *v* ▷ **text**
texts *n, v* ▷ **text**
textual *adj* ▷ **text**
textural *adj* ▷ **texture**
texture *n* (*pl* **-s**) structure, feel, or consistency > **textured** *adj* > **textural** *adj*
textured *adj* ▷ **texture**
textures *n* ▷ **texture**
thalidomide [thal-**lid**-oh-mide] *n* (*pl* **-s**) drug formerly used as a sedative, but found to cause abnormalities in developing fetuses
thalidomides *n* ▷ **thalidomide**
thallium *n* (*pl* **-s**) (CHEM) highly toxic metallic element
thalliums *n* ▷ **thallium**
than *conj, prep* used to introduce the second element of a comparison
thane *n* (*pl* **-s**) (HIST) Anglo-Saxon or medieval Scottish nobleman
thanes *n* ▷ **thane**
thank *v* (**-s, -ing, -ed**) express gratitude to
thanked *v* ▷ **thank**
thankful *adj* grateful
thanking *v* ▷ **thank**
thankless *adj* unrewarding or unappreciated
thanks *pl n* words of gratitude ▶ *interj* polite expression of gratitude ▶ *v* ▷ **thank**
that *adj, pron* used to refer to something already mentioned or familiar, or further away ▶ *conj* used to introduce a clause ▶ *pron* used to introduce a relative clause
thatch *n* (*pl* **-es**) roofing material of reeds or straw ▶ *v* (**-ches, -ching, -ched**) roof (a house) with reeds or straw
thatched *v* ▷ **thatch**
thatches *n, v* ▷ **thatch**
thatching *v* ▷ **thatch**
thaw *v* (**-s, -ing, -ed**) make or become unfrozen ▶ *n* (*pl* **-s**) thawing
thawed *v* ▷ **thaw**
thawing *v* ▷ **thaw**
thaws *n, v* ▷ **thaw**
the *adj* the definite article, used before a noun
theatre *n* (*pl* **-s**) place where plays etc. are performed
theatres *n* ▷ **theatre**
theatrical *adj* of the theatre > **theatrically** *adv* > **theatricality** *n* (*pl* **-ties**)
theatricalities *n* ▷ **theatrical**
theatricality *n* ▷ **theatrical**
theatrically *adv* ▷ **theatrical**
theatricals *pl n* (amateur) dramatic performances
thee *pron* (*Obs*) you
theft *n* (*pl* **-s**) act or an instance of stealing

thefts *n* ▷ **theft**
their *adj* of or associated with them
theirs *pron* (thing or person) belonging to them
theism [**thee**-iz-zum] *n* (*pl* **-s**) belief in a God or gods > **theist** *n* (*pl* **-s**) *adj* > **theistic** *adj*
theisms *n* ▷ **theism**
theist *n, adj* ▷ **theism**
theistic *adj* ▷ **theism**
theists *n* ▷ **theism**
them *pron* refers to people or things other than the speaker or those addressed
thematic *adj* ▷ **theme**
theme *n* (*pl* **-s**) main idea or subject being discussed > **thematic** *adj*
themes *n* ▷ **theme**
themselves *pron* ▷ **they, them**
then *adv* at that time
thence *adv* from that place or time
theocracies *n* ▷ **theocracy**
theocracy *n* (*pl* **-cies**) government by a god or priests > **theocratic** *adj*
theocratic *adj* ▷ **theocracy**
theodolite [thee-**odd**-oh-lite] *n* (*pl* **-s**) surveying instrument for measuring angles
theodolites *n* ▷ **theodolite**
theologian *n* ▷ **theology**
theologians *n* ▷ **theology**
theological *adj* ▷ **theology**
theologically *adv* ▷ **theology**
theologies *n* ▷ **theology**
theology *n* (*pl* **-gies**) study of religions and religious beliefs > **theologian** *n* (*pl* **-s**) > **theological** *adj* > **theologically** *adv*
theorem *n* (*pl* **-s**) proposition that can be proved by reasoning
theorems *n* ▷ **theorem**
theoretical *adj* based on theory rather than practice or fact > **theoretically** *adv*
theoretically *adv* ▷ **theoretical**
theories *n* ▷ **theory**
theorist *n* ▷ **theory**
theorists *n* ▷ **theory**
theorize *v* (**-zes, -zing, -zed**) form theories, speculate
theorized *v* ▷ **theorize**
theorizes *v* ▷ **theorize**
theorizing *v* ▷ **theorize**
theory *n* (*pl* **-ries**) set of ideas to explain something > **theorist** *n* (*pl* **-s**)
theosophical *adj* ▷ **theosophy**
theosophies *n* ▷ **theosophy**
theosophy *n* (*pl* **-phies**) religious or philosophical system claiming to be based on intuitive insight into the divine nature > **theosophical** *adj*
therapeutic [ther-rap-**pew**-tik] *adj* curing
therapeutics *n* art of curing
therapies *n* ▷ **therapy**
therapist *n* ▷ **therapy**
therapists *n* ▷ **therapy**
therapy *n* (*pl* **-pies**) curing treatment > **therapist** *n* (*pl* **-s**)
there *adv* in or to that place
thereby *adv* by that means
therefore *adv* consequently, that being so
thereupon *adv* immediately after that
therm *n* (*pl* **-s**) unit of measurement of heat
thermal *adj* of heat ▸ *n* (*pl* **-s**) rising current of warm air
thermals *n* ▷ **thermal**
thermodynamics *n* scientific study of the relationship between heat and other forms of energy
thermometer *n* (*pl* **-s**) instrument for measuring temperature
thermometers *n* ▷ **thermometer**
thermonuclear *adj* involving nuclear fusion
thermoplastic *adj* (of a plastic) softening when heated and resetting on cooling
thermosetting *adj* (of a plastic) remaining hard when heated
thermostat *n* (*pl* **-s**) device for automatically regulating temperature > **thermostatic** *adj*
thermostatic *adj* ▷ **thermostat**
thermostats *n* ▷ **thermostat**
therms *n* ▷ **therm**
thesaurus [thiss-**sore**-uss] *n* (*pl* **-ruses**) book containing lists of synonyms and related words
thesauruses *n* ▷ **thesaurus**
these *adj, pron* ▷ **this**
theses *n* ▷ **thesis**
thesis *n* (*pl* **theses**) written work submitted for a degree
thespian *n* (*pl* **-s**) actor or actress ▸ *adj* of the theatre
thespians *n* ▷ **thespian**
they *pron* refers to: people or things other than the speaker or people addressed
thiamine *n* (*pl* **-s**) vitamin found in the outer coat of rice and other grains
thiamines *n* ▷ **thiamine**
thick *adj* (**-er, -est**) of great or specified extent from one side to the other > **thickly** *adv*
thicken *v* (**-s, -ing, -ed**) make or become thick or thicker
thickened *v* ▷ **thicken**
thickening *v* ▷ **thicken**
thickens *v* ▷ **thicken**

thicker *adj* ▷ **thick**
thickest *adj* ▷ **thick**
thicket *n* (*pl* **-s**) dense growth of small trees
thickets *n* ▷ **thicket**
thickly *adv* ▷ **thick**
thickness *n* (*pl* **-es**) state of being thick
thicknesses *n* ▷ **thickness**
thickset *adj* stocky in build
thief *n* (*pl* **thieves**) person who steals
thieve *v* (**-ves, -ving, -ved**) steal > **thieving** *adj*
thieved *v* ▷ **thieve**
thieves *v* ▷ **thieve** ▶ *n* ▷ **thief**
thieving *v, adj* ▷ **thieve**
thigh *n* (*pl* **-s**) upper part of the human leg
thighs *n* ▷ **thigh**
thimble *n* (*pl* **-s**) cap protecting the end of the finger when sewing
thimbles *n* ▷ **thimble**
thin *adj* (**-nner, -nnest**) not thick ▶ *v* (**-s, -nning, -nned**) make or become thin > **thinly** *adv* > **thinness** *n* (*pl* **-es**)
thine *pron, adj* (*Obs*) (something) of or associated with you (thou)
thing *n* (*pl* **-s**) material object
things *n* ▷ **thing** ▶ *pl n* possessions, clothes, etc.
think *v* (**-s, -ing, thought**) consider, judge, or believe > **thinker** *n* (*pl* **-s**) > **thinking** *adj, n* (*pl* **-s**)
thinker *n* ▷ **think**
thinkers *n* ▷ **think**
thinking *v, adj, n* ▷ **think**
thinkings *n* ▷ **think**
thinks *v* ▷ **think**
thinly *adv* ▷ **thin**
thinned *v* ▷ **thin**
thinner *adj* ▷ **thin**
thinness *n* ▷ **thin**
thinnesses *n* ▷ **thin**
thinnest *adj* ▷ **thin**
thinning *v* ▷ **thin**
thins *v* ▷ **thin**
third *adj* of number three in a series ▶ *n* (*pl* **-s**) one of three equal parts
thirds *n* ▷ **third**
thirst *n* (*pl* **-s**) desire to drink ▶ *v* (**-s, -ing, -ed**) feel thirst > **thirsty** *adj* (**-tier, -tiest**) > **thirstily** *adv*
thirsted *v* ▷ **thirst**
thirstier *adj* ▷ **thirst**
thirstiest *adj* ▷ **thirst**
thirstily *adv* ▷ **thirst**
thirsting *v* ▷ **thirst**
thirsts *n, v* ▷ **thirst**
thirsty *adj* (**-tier, -tiest**) ▷ **thirst**
thirteen *adj, n* (*pl* **-s**) three plus ten > **thirteenth** *adj, n* (*pl* **-s**)
thirteens *n* ▷ **thirteen**
thirteenth *n* ▷ **thirteen**
thirteenths *n* ▷ **thirteen**
thirties *n* ▷ **thirty**
thirtieth *n* ▷ **thirty**
thirtieths *n* ▷ **thirty**
thirty *adj, n* (*pl* **-ties**) three times ten > **thirtieth** *adj, n* (*pl* **-s**)
this *adj, pron* used to refer to a thing or person nearby, just mentioned, or about to be mentioned ▶ *adj* used to refer to the present time
thistle *n* (*pl* **-s**) prickly plant with dense flower heads
thistles *n* ▷ **thistle**
thither *adv* (*Obs*) to or towards that place
thong *n* (*pl* **-s**) thin strip of leather etc.
thongs *n* ▷ **thong**
thoraces *n* ▷ **thorax**
thoracic *adj* ▷ **thorax**
thorax *n* (*pl* **-xes, -races**) part of the body between the neck and the abdomen > **thoracic** *adj*
thoraxes *n* ▷ **thorax**
thorn *n* (*pl* **-s**) prickle on a plant > **thorny** *adj* (**-ier, -iest**)
thornier *adj* ▷ **thorn**
thorniest *adj* ▷ **thorn**
thorns *n* ▷ **thorn**
thorny *adj* ▷ **thorn**
thorough *adj* complete > **thoroughly** *adv* > **thoroughness** *n* (*pl* **-es**)
thoroughbred *n* (*pl* **-s**) ▶ *adj* (animal) of pure breed
thoroughbreds *n* ▷ **thoroughbred**
thoroughfare *n* (*pl* **-s**) way through from one place to another
thoroughfares *n* ▷ **thoroughfare**
thoroughly *adv* ▷ **thorough**
thoroughness *n* ▷ **thorough**
thoroughnesses *n* ▷ **thorough**
those *adj, pron* ▷ **that**
thou *pron* (*Obs*) you
though *conj* despite the fact that ▶ *adv* nevertheless
thought *v* ▷ **think** ▶ *n* (*pl* **-s**) thinking > **thoughtful** *adj* considerate
thoughtful *adj* ▷ **thought**
thoughtless *adj* inconsiderate
thoughts *n* ▷ **thought**
thousand *adj, n* (*pl* **-s**) ten hundred
thousands *n* ▷ **thousand**
thousandth *adj, n* (*pl* **-s**) (of) number one

thousand in a series
thousandths *n* ▷ **thousandth**
thrall *n* (*pl* **-s**) state of being in the power of another person
thralls *n* ▷ **thrall**
thrash *v* (**-es, -ing, -ed**) beat, esp. with a stick or whip
thrashed *v* ▷ **thrash**
thrashes *v* ▷ **thrash**
thrashing *n* (*pl* **-s**) severe beating ▶ *v* ▷ **thrash**
thread *n* (*pl* **-s**) fine strand or yarn ▶ *v* (**-s, -ing, -ed**) pass thread through
threadbare *adj* (of fabric) with the nap worn off
threaded *v* ▷ **thread**
threading *v* ▷ **thread**
threads *n, v* ▷ **thread**
threat *n* (*pl* **-s**) declaration of intent to harm
threaten *v* (**-s, -ing, -ed**) make or be a threat to
threatened *v* ▷ **threaten**
threatening *v* ▷ **threaten**
threatens *v* ▷ **threaten**
threats *n* ▷ **threat**
three *adj, n* (*pl* **-s**) one more than two
threes *n* ▷ **three**
threesome *n* (*pl* **-s**) group of three
threesomes *n* ▷ **threesome**
threnodies *n* ▷ **threnody**
threnody *n* (*pl* **-dies**) lament for the dead
thresh *v* (**-es, -ing, -ed**) beat (wheat etc.) to separate the grain from the husks and straw
threshed *v* ▷ **thresh**
threshes *v* ▷ **thresh**
threshing *v* ▷ **thresh**
threshold *n* (*pl* **-s**) bar forming the bottom of a doorway
thresholds *n* ▷ **threshold**
threw *v* ▷ **throw**
thrice *adv* (*Lit*) three times
thrift *n* (*pl* **-s**) wisdom and caution with money > **thrifty** *adj*
thrifts *n* ▷ **thrift**
thrifty *adj* ▷ **thrif**
thrill *n* (*pl* **-s**) sudden feeling of excitement ▶ *v* (**-s, -ing, -ed**) (cause to) feel a thrill > **thrilling** *adj*
thrilled *v* ▷ **thrill**
thriller *n* (*pl* **-s**) book, film, etc. with an atmosphere of mystery or suspense
thrillers *n* ▷ **thriller**
thrilling *v, adj* ▷ **thrill**
thrills *n, v* ▷ **thrill**
thrive *v* (**-ves, -ving, -ved** *or* **throve**, **thrived** *or* **thriven**) flourish or prosper
thrived *v* ▷ **thrive**
thriven *v* ▷ **thrive**
thrives *v* ▷ **thrive**
thriving *v* ▷ **thrive**
throat *n* (*pl* **-s**) passage from the mouth and nose to the stomach and lungs
throatier *adj* ▷ **throaty**
throatiest *adj* ▷ **throaty**
throats *n* ▷ **throat**
throaty *adj* (**-tier, -tiest**) (of the voice) hoarse
throb *v* (**-s, -bbing, -bbed**) pulsate repeatedly ▶ *n* (*pl* **-s**) throbbing
throbbed *v* ▷ **throb**
throbbing *v* ▷ **throb**
throbs *v, n* ▷ **throb**
throes *pl n* violent pangs or pains
thrombosis *n* (*pl* **-oses**) forming of a clot in a blood vessel or the heart
thromboses *n* ▷ **thrombosis**
throne *n* (*pl* **-s**) ceremonial seat of a monarch or bishop
thrones *n* ▷ **throne**
throng *n* (*pl* **-s**) ▶ *v* (**-s, -ing, -ed**) crowd
thronged *v* ▷ **throng**
thronging *v* ▷ **throng**
throngs *n, v* ▷ **throng**
throstle *n* (*pl* **-s**) song thrush
throstles *n* ▷ **throstle**
throttle *n* (*pl* **-s**) device controlling the amount of fuel entering an engine ▶ *v* (**-les, -ling, -led**) strangle
throttled *v* ▷ **throttle**
throttles *n, v* ▷ **throttle**
throttling *v* ▷ **throttle**
through *prep* from end to end or side to side of ▶ *adj* finished
throughout *prep, adv* in every part (of)
throughput *n* (*pl* **-s**) amount of material processed
throughputs *n* ▷ **throughput**
throve *v* ▷ **thrive**
throw *v* (**-s, -ing, threw, thrown**) hurl through the air ▶ *n* (*pl* **-s**) throwing
throwaway *adj* done or said casually
throwback *n* (*pl* **-s**) person or thing that reverts to an earlier type
throwbacks *n* ▷ **throwback**
throwing *v* ▷ **throw**
thrown *v* ▷ **throw**
throws *v, n* ▷ **throw**
thrush[1] *n* (*pl* **-es**) brown songbird
thrush[2] *n* (*pl* **-es**) fungal disease of the mouth or vagina
thrushes *n* ▷ **thrush[1, 2]**
thrust *v* (**-s, -ing, thrust**) push forcefully ▶ *n* (*pl* **-s**) forceful stab

thrusting *v* ▷ **thrust**
thrusts *v*, *n* ▷ **thrust**
thud *n* (*pl* **-s**) dull heavy sound ▶ *v* (**-s, -dding, -dded**) make such a sound
thudded *v* ▷ **thud**
thudding *v* ▷ **thud**
thuds *n*, *v* ▷ **thud**
thug *n* (*pl* **-s**) violent man, esp. a criminal > **thuggery** *n* (*pl* **-ries**) > **thuggish** *adj*
thuggeries *n* ▷ **thug**
thuggery *n* ▷ **thug**
thuggish *adj* ▷ **thug**
thugs *n* ▷ **thug**
thumb *n* (*pl* **-s**) short thick finger set apart from the others ▶ *v* (**-s, -ing, -ed**) touch or handle with the thumb
thumbed *v* ▷ **thumb**
thumbing *v* ▷ **thumb**
thumbs *n*, *v* ▷ **thumb**
thump *n* (*pl* **-s**) (sound of) a dull heavy blow ▶ *v* (**-s, -ing, -ed**) strike heavily
thumped *v* ▷ **thump**
thumping *v* ▷ **thump**
thumps *n*, *v* ▷ **thump**
thunder *n* (*pl* **-s**) loud noise accompanying lightning ▶ *v* (**-s, -ing, -ed**) rumble with thunder > **thunderous** *adj* > **thundery** (**-rier, -riest**) *adj*
thunderbolt *n* (*pl* **-s**) lightning flash
thunderbolts *n* ▷ **thunderbolt**
thunderclap *n* (*pl* **-s**) peal of thunder
thunderclaps *n* ▷ **thunderclap**
thundered *v* ▷ **thunder**
thunderier *adj* ▷ **thunder**
thunderiest *adj* ▷ **thunder**
thundering *v* ▷ **thunder**
thunderous *adj* ▷ **thunder**
thunders *v*, *n* ▷ **thunder**
thunderstruck *adj* amazed
thundery *adj* ▷ **thunder**
thus *adv* therefore
thwack *v* (**-s, -ing, -ed**) ▶ *n* (*pl* **-s**) whack
thwacked *v* ▷ **thwack**
thwacking *v* ▷ **thwack**
thwacks *v*, *n* ▷ **thwack**
thwart *v* (**-s, -ing, -ed**) foil or frustrate ▶ *n* (*pl* **-s**) seat across a boat
thwarted *v* ▷ **thwart**
thwarting *v* ▷ **thwart**
thwarts *v*, *n* ▷ **thwart**
thy *adj* (*Obs*) of or associated with you (thou)
thylacine *n* (*pl* **-s**) extinct doglike Tasmanian marsupial
thylacines *n* ▷ **thylacine**
thyme [**time**] *n* (*pl* **-s**) aromatic herb
thymes *n* ▷ **thyme**
thymi *n* ▷ **thymus**
thymus *n* (*pl* **-muses, -mi**) small gland at the base of the neck
thymuses *n* ▷ **thymus**
thyroid *adj*, *n* (*pl* **-s**) (of) a gland in the neck controlling body growth
thyroids *n* ▷ **thyroid**
thyself *pron* (*Obs*) ▷ **thou**

ti *n* (**tis**). Ti means the same as **te.** This is a useful word when you want to form words in more than one direction. Ti scores 2 points.

tiara *n* (*pl* **-s**) semicircular jewelled headdress
tiaras *n* ▷ **tiara**
tibia *n* (*pl* **-biae, -bias**) inner bone of the lower leg > **tibial** *adj*
tibiae *n* ▷ **tibia**
tibial *adj* ▷ **tibia**
tibias *n* ▷ **tibia**
tic *n* (*pl* **-s**) spasmodic muscular twitch
tick[1] *n* (*pl* **-s**) mark (✓) used to check off or indicate the correctness of something ▶ *v* (**-s, -ing, -ed**) mark with a tick
tick[2] *n* (*pl* **-s**) tiny bloodsucking parasitic animal
tick[3] *n* (*pl* **-s**) (*Informal*) credit or account
ticked *v* ▷ **tick[1]**
ticket *n* (*pl* **-s**) card or paper entitling the holder to admission, travel, etc. (CHIEFLY US & NZ) ▶ *v* (**-s, -ing, -ed**) attach or issue a ticket to
ticketed *v* ▷ **ticket**
ticketing *v* ▷ **ticket**
tickets *n*, *v* ▷ **ticket**
ticking *n* (*pl* **-s**) strong material for mattress covers ▶ *v* ▷ **tick[1]**
tickings *n* ▷ **ticking**
tickle *v* (**-les, -ling, -led**) touch or stroke (a person) to produce laughter ▶ *n* (*pl* **-s**) tickling
tickled *v* ▷ **tickle**
tickles *v*, *n* ▷ **tickle**
tickling *v* ▷ **tickle**
ticklish *adj* sensitive to tickling
ticks *v* ▷ **tick[1]** ▶ *n* ▷ **tick[1, 2, 3]**
ticktack *n* (*pl* **-s**) (BRIT) bookmakers' sign language
ticktacks *n* ▷ **ticktack**
tics *n* ▷ **tic**
tidal *adj* ▷ **tide**
tiddler *n* (*pl* **-s**) (*Informal*) very small fish
tiddlers *n* ▷ **tiddler**
tiddlier *adj* ▷ **tiddly[1, 2]**
tiddliest *adj* ▷ **tiddly[1, 2]**
tiddly[1] *adj* (**-dlier, -dliest**) tiny
tiddly[2] *adj* (**-dlier, -dliest**) (*Informal*) slightly

drunk
tiddlywink *n* small plastic disc
tiddlywinks *n* game in which players try to flip small plastic discs into a cup
tide *n* (*pl* **-s**) rise and fall of the sea caused by the gravitational pull of the sun and moon **> tidal** *adj*
tides *n* ▷ **tide**
tidied *v* ▷ **tidy**
tidier *adj* ▷ **tidy**
tidies *v* ▷ **tidy**
tidiest *adj* ▷ **tidy**
tidily *adv* ▷ **tidy**
tidiness *n* ▷ **tidy**
tidinesses *n* ▷ **tidy**
tidings *pl n* news
tidy *adj* (**-dier, -diest**) neat and orderly ▶ *v* (**-dies, -dying, -died**) put in order **> tidily** *adv* **> tidiness** *n* (*pl* **-es**)
tidying *v* ▷ **tidy**
tie *v* (**ties, tying, tied**) fasten or be fastened with string, rope, etc. ▶ *n* (*pl* **-s**) long narrow piece of material worn knotted round the neck
tied *v* ▷ **tie** ▶ *adj* (BRIT) (of a cottage etc.) rented to the tenant only as long as he or she is employed by the owner
tier *n* (*pl* **-s**) one of a set of rows placed one above and behind the other
tiers *n* ▷ **tier**
ties *v, n* ▷ **tie**
tiff *n* (*pl* **-s**) petty quarrel
tiffs *n* ▷ **tiff**
tiger *n* (*pl* **-s**) large yellow-and-black striped Asian cat
tigers *n* ▷ **tiger**
tight *adj* (**-er, -est**) stretched or drawn taut **> tightly** *adv*
tighten *v* (**-s, -ing, -ed**) make or become tight or tighter
tightened *v* ▷ **tighten**
tightening *v* ▷ **tighten**
tightens *v* ▷ **tighten**
tighter *adj* ▷ **tight**
tightest *adj* ▷ **tight**
tightly *adv* ▷ **tight**
tightrope *n* (*pl* **-s**) rope stretched taut on which acrobats perform
tightropes *n* ▷ **tightrope**
tights *pl n* one-piece clinging garment covering the body from the waist to the feet
tigress *n* (*pl* **-s**) female tiger
tigresses *n* ▷ **tigress**
tiki *n* (*pl* **-s**) (NZ) small carving of a grotesque person worn as a pendant
tikis *n* ▷ **tiki**
tikka *adj* (INDIAN COOKERY) marinated in spices and dry-roasted
tilde *n* (*pl* **-s**) mark (~) used in Spanish to indicate that the letter 'n' is to be pronounced in a particular way
tildes *n* ▷ **tilde**
tile *n* (*pl* **-s**) flat piece of ceramic, plastic, etc. used to cover a roof, floor, or wall ▶ *v* (**-les, -ling, -led**) cover with tiles **> tiled** *adj*
tiled *v, adj* ▷ **tile**
tiles *n, v* ▷ **tile**
tiling *n* (*pl* **-s**) tiles collectively ▶ *v* ▷ **tile**
tilings *n* ▷ **tiling**
till[1] *conj, prep* until
till[2] *v* (**-s, -ing, -ed**) cultivate (land) **> tillage** *n* (*pl* **-s**)
till[3] *n* (*pl* **-s**) drawer for money, usu. in a cash register
tillage *n* ▷ **till**[2]
tillages *n* ▷ **till**[2]
tilled *v* ▷ **till**[2]
tiller *n* (*pl* **-s**) lever to move a rudder of a boat
tillers *n* ▷ **tiller**
tilling *v* ▷ **till**[2]
tills *v* ▷ **till**[2] ▶ *n* ▷ **till**[3]
tilt *v* (**-s, -ing, -ed**) slant at an angle ▶ *n* (*pl* **-s**) slope
tilted *v* ▷ **tilt**
tilting *v* ▷ **tilt**
tilts *v, n* ▷ **tilt**
timber *n* (*pl* **-s**) wood as a building material **> timbered** *adj*
timbered *adj* ▷ **timber**
timbers *n* ▷ **timber**
timbre [**tam**-bra] *n* (*pl* **-s**) distinctive quality of sound of a voice or instrument
timbres *n* ▷ **timbre**
time *n* (*pl* **-s**) past, present, and future as a continuous whole ▶ *v* (**-mes, -ming, -med**) note the time taken by
timed *v* ▷ **time**
timeless *adj* unaffected by time
timelier *adj* ▷ **timely**
timeliest *adj* ▷ **timely**
timely *adj* (**-lier, -liest**) at the appropriate time
timepiece *n* (*pl* **-s**) watch or clock
timepieces *n* ▷ **timepiece**
times *n, v* ▷ **time**
timeserver *n* (*pl* **-s**) person who changes his or her views to gain support or favour
timeservers *n* ▷ **timeserver**
timetable *n* (*pl* **-s**) plan showing the times when something takes place, the departure and arrival times of trains or buses, etc.

timetables *n* ▷ **timetable**
timid *adj* (**-er, -est**) easily frightened > **timidly** *adv* > **timidity** *n* (*pl* **-dies**)
timider *adj* ▷ **timid**
timidest *adj* ▷ **timid**
timidities *n* ▷ **timid**
timidity *n* ▷ **timid**
timidly *adv* ▷ **timid**
timing *v* ▷ **time**
timorous *adj* timid
timpani [**tim**-pan-ee] *pl n* set of kettledrums > **timpanist** *n* (*pl* **-s**)
timpanist *n* ▷ **timpani**
timpanists *n* ▷ **timpani**
tin *n* (*pl* **-s**) soft metallic element
tincture *n* (*pl* **-s**) medicinal extract in a solution of alcohol
tinctures *n* ▷ **tincture**
tinder *n* (*pl* **-s**) dry easily-burning material used to start a fire > **tinderbox** *n* (*pl* **-es**)
tinderbox *n* ▷ **tinder**
tinderboxes *n* ▷ **tinder**
tinders *n* ▷ **tinder**
tine *n* (*pl* **-s**) prong of a fork or antler
tines *n* ▷ **tine**
ting *n* (*pl* **-s**) high metallic sound, as of a small bell
tinge *n* (*pl* **-s**) slight tint ▶ *v* (**-ges, -geing, -ged**) give a slight tint or trace to
tinged *v* ▷ **tinge**
tinges *n, v* ▷ **tinge**
tinging *v* ▷ **tinge**
tingle *v* (**-les, -ling, -led**) ▶ *n* (*pl* **-s**) (feel) a prickling or stinging sensation
tingled *v* ▷ **tingle**
tingles *v, n* ▷ **tingle**
tingling *v* ▷ **tingle**
tings *n* ▷ **ting**
tinier *adj* ▷ **tiny**
tiniest *adj* ▷ **tiny**
tinker *n* (*pl* **-s**) travelling mender of pots and pans ▶ *v* (**-s, -ing, -ed**) fiddle with (an engine etc.) in an attempt to repair it
tinkered *v* ▷ **tinker**
tinkering *v* ▷ **tinker**
tinkers *n, v* ▷ **tinker**
tinkle *v* (**-les, -ling, -led**) ring with a high tinny sound like a small bell ▶ *n* (*pl* **-s**) this sound or action
tinkled *v* ▷ **tinkle**
tinkles *v, n* ▷ **tinkle**
tinkling *v* ▷ **tinkle**
tinned *adj* (of food) preserved by being sealed in a tin
tinnier *adj* ▷ **tinny**
tinniest *adj* ▷ **tinny**
tinny *adj* (**-nnier, -nniest**) (of sound) thin and metallic
tinpot *adj* (*Informal*) worthless or unimportant
tins *n* ▷ **tin**
tinsel *n* (*pl* **-s**) decorative metallic strips or threads
tinsels *n* ▷ **tinsel**
tint *n* (*pl* **-s**) (pale) shade of a colour ▶ *v* (**-s, -ing, -ed**) give a tint to
tinted *v* ▷ **tint**
tinting *v* ▷ **tint**
tints *n, v* ▷ **tint**
tiny *adj* (**-ier, -iest**) very small
tip[1] *n* (*pl* **-s**) narrow or pointed end of anything ▶ *v* (**-s, -pping, -pped**) put a tip on
tip[2] *n* (*pl* **-s**) money given in return for service ▶ *v* (**-s, -pping, -pped**) give a tip to
tip[3] *v* (**-s, -pping, -pped**) tilt or overturn ▶ *n* (*pl* **-s**) rubbish dump
tipped *v* ▷ **tip**[1,2,3]
tipping *v* ▷ **tip**[1,2,3]
tipple *v* (**-les, -ling, -led**) drink alcohol habitually, esp. in small quantities ▶ *n* (*pl* **-s**) alcoholic drink > **tippler** *n* (*pl* **-s**)
tippled *v* ▷ **tipple**
tippler *n* ▷ **tipple**
tipplers *n* ▷ **tipple**
tipples *v, n* ▷ **tipple**
tippling *v* ▷ **tipple**
tips *n, v* ▷ **tip**[1,2,3]
tipsier *adj* ▷ **tipsy**
tipsiest *adj* ▷ **tipsy**
tipster *n* (*pl* **-s**) person who sells tips about races
tipsters *n* ▷ **tipster**
tipsy *adj* (**-sier, -siest**) slightly drunk
tiptoe *v* (**-toes, -toeing, -toed**) walk quietly with the heels off the ground
tiptoed *v* ▷ **tiptoe**
tiptoeing *v* ▷ **tiptoe**
tiptoes *v* ▷ **tiptoe**
tiptop *adj* of the highest quality or condition
tirade *n* (*pl* **-s**) long angry speech
tirades *n* ▷ **tirade**
tire *v* (**-res, -ring, -red**) reduce the energy of, as by exertion > **tiring** *adj*
tired *adj* (**-er, -est**) exhausted ▶ *v* ▷ **tire**
tireder *adj* ▷ **tired**
tiredest *adj* ▷ **tired**
tireless *adj* energetic and determined
tires *v* ▷ **tire**
tiresome *adj* boring and irritating
tiring *v, adj* ▷ **tire**
tissue *n* (*pl* **-s**) substance of an animal body

or plant
tissues *n* ▷ **tissue**
tit[1] *n* (*pl* **-s**) any of various small songbirds
tit[2] *n* (*pl* **-s**) (*Slang*) female breast
titanic *adj* huge or very important
titanium *n* (*pl* **-s**) (CHEM) strong light metallic element used to make alloys
titaniums *n* ▷ **titanium**
titbit *n* (*pl* **-s**) tasty piece of food
titbits *n* ▷ **titbit**
tithe *n* (*pl* **-s**) esp. formerly, one tenth of one's income or produce paid to the church as a tax
tithes *n* ▷ **tithe**
titian [**tish**-an] *adj* (of hair) reddish-gold
titillate *v* (**-tes, -ting, -ted**) excite or stimulate pleasurably > **titillating** *adj* > **titillation** *n* (*pl* **-s**)
titillated *v* ▷ **titillate**
titillates *v* ▷ **titillate**
titillating *v, adj* ▷ **titillate**
titillation *n* ▷ **titillate**
titillations *n* ▷ **titillate**
titivate *v* (**-tes, -ting, -ted**) smarten up
titivated *v* ▷ **titivate**
titivates *v* ▷ **titivate**
titivating *v* ▷ **titivate**
title *n* (*pl* **-s**) name of a book, film, etc.
titled *adj* aristocratic
titles *n* ▷ **title**
tits *n* ▷ **tit**[1, 2]
titter *v* (**-s, -ing, -ed**) laugh in a suppressed way ▶ *n* (*pl* **-s**) suppressed laugh
tittered *v* ▷ **titter**
tittering *v* ▷ **titter**
titters *v, n* ▷ **titter**
titular *adj* in name only
tizzies *n* ▷ **tizzy**
tizzy *n* (*pl* **-zies**) (*Informal*) confused or agitated state

tix *pl n*. Tix is an informal word for **tickets.** This is a good word if you are struggling to use an X towards the end of a game.

to *prep* indicating movement towards, equality or comparison, etc. ▶ *adv* to a closed position
toad *n* (*pl* **-s**) animal like a large frog
toadied *v* ▷ **toady**
toadies *n, v* ▷ **toady**
toads *n* ▷ **toad**
toadstool *n* (*pl* **-s**) poisonous fungus like a mushroom
toadstools *n* ▷ **toadstool**
toady *n* (*pl* **-dies**) ingratiating person ▶ *v* (**-dies, -dying, -died**) be ingratiating
toadying *v* ▷ **toady**
toast[1] *n* (*pl* **-s**) sliced bread browned by heat ▶ *v* (**-s, -ing, -ed**) brown (bread) by heat
toast[2] *n* (*pl* **-s**) tribute or proposal of health or success marked by people raising glasses and drinking together ▶ *v* (**-s, -ing, -ed**) drink a toast to
toasted *v, n* ▷ **toast**[1, 2]
toaster *n* (*pl* **-s**) electrical device for toasting bread
toasters *n* ▷ **toaster**
toasting *n, v* ▷ **toast**[1, 2]
toasts *n, v* ▷ **toast**[1, 2]
tobacco *n* (*pl* **-os, -oes**) plant with large leaves dried for smoking
tobaccoes *n* ▷ **tobacco**
tobacconist *n* (*pl* **-s**) person or shop selling tobacco, cigarettes, etc.
tobacconists *n* ▷ **tobacconist**
tobaccos *n* ▷ **tobacco**
toboggan *n* (*pl* **-s**) narrow sledge for sliding over snow ▶ *v* (**-s, -ing, -ed**) ride a toboggan
tobogganed *v* ▷ **toboggan**
tobogganing *v* ▷ **toboggan**
toboggans *n, v* ▷ **toboggan**
toccata [tok-**kah**-ta] *n* (*pl* **-s**) rapid piece of music for a keyboard instrument
toccatas *n* ▷ **toccata**
today *n* (*pl* **-s**) this day ▶ *adv* on this day
todays *n* ▷ **today**
toddies *n* ▷ **toddy**
toddle *v* (**-les, -ling, -led**) walk with short unsteady steps
toddled *v* ▷ **toddle**
toddler *n* (*pl* **-s**) child beginning to walk
toddlers *n* ▷ **toddler**
toddles *v* ▷ **toddle**
toddling *v* ▷ **toddle**
toddy *n* (*pl* **-dies**) sweetened drink of spirits and hot water
toe *n* (*pl* **-s**) digit of the foot ▶ *v* (**toes, toeing, toed**) touch or kick with the toe
toed *v* ▷ **toe**
toeing *v* ▷ **toe**
toes *n, v* ▷ **toe**
toff *n* (*pl* **-s**) (BRIT) (*Slang*) well-dressed or upper-class person
toffee *n* (*pl* **-s**) chewy sweet made of boiled sugar
toffees *n* ▷ **toffee**
toffs *n* ▷ **toff**
tofu *n* (*pl* **-s**) soft food made from soya-bean curd
tofus *n* ▷ **tofu**
tog *n* (*pl* **-s**) unit for measuring the insulating

power of duvets
toga [**toe**-ga] *n* (*pl* **-s**) garment worn by citizens of ancient Rome
togas *n* ▷ **toga**
together *adv* in company ▶ *adj* (*Informal*) organized
toggle *n* (*pl* **-s**) small bar-shaped button inserted through a loop for fastening
toggles *n* ▷ **toggle**
togs *n* ▷ **tog**
toil *n* (*pl* **-s**) hard work ▶ *v* (**-s, -ing, -ed**) work hard
toiled *v* ▷ **toil**
toilet *n* (*pl* **-s**) (room with) a bowl connected to a drain for receiving and disposing of urine and faeces
toiletries *n* ▷ **toiletry**
toiletry *n* (*pl* **-ries**) object or cosmetic used to clean or groom oneself
toilets *n* ▷ **toilet**
toiling *v* ▷ **toil**
toils *n, v* ▷ **toil**
token *n* (*pl* **-s**) sign or symbol ▶ *adj* nominal or slight
tokenism *n* (*pl* **-s**) policy of making only a token effort, esp. to comply with a law
tokenisms *n* ▷ **tokenism**
tokens *n* ▷ **token**
told *v* ▷ **tell**
tolerable *adj* bearable > **tolerably** *adv*
tolerably *adv* ▷ **tolerable**
tolerance *n* (*pl* **-s**) acceptance of other people's rights to their own opinions or actions > **tolerant** *adj* > **tolerantly** *adv* > **toleration** *n* (*pl* **-s**)
tolerances *n* ▷ **tolerance**
tolerant *adj* ▷ **tolerance**
tolerantly *adv* ▷ **tolerance**
tolerate *v* (**-tes, -ting, -ted**) allow to exist or happen
tolerated *v* ▷ **tolerate**
tolerates *v* ▷ **tolerate**
tolerating *v* ▷ **tolerate**
toleration *n* ▷ **tolerance**
tolerations *n* ▷ **tolerance**
toll¹ *v* (**-s, -ing, -ed**) ring (a bell) slowly and regularly, esp. to announce a death ▶ *n* (*pl* **-s**) tolling
toll² *n* (*pl* **-s**) charge for the use of a bridge or road
tolled *v* ▷ **toll¹**
tolling *v* ▷ **toll¹**
tolls *n* ▷ **toll¹, ²** ▶ *v* ▷ **toll¹**
tom *n* (*pl* **-s**) male cat
tomahawk *n* (*pl* **-s**) fighting axe of the Native Americans
tomahawks *n* ▷ **tomahawk**
tomato *n* (*pl* **-es**) red fruit used in salads and as a vegetable
tomatoes *n* ▷ **tomato**
tomb *n* (*pl* **-s**) grave
tombola *n* (*pl* **-s**) lottery with tickets drawn from a revolving drum
tombolas *n* ▷ **tombola**
tomboy *n* (*pl* **-s**) girl who acts or dresses like a boy
tomboys *n* ▷ **tomboy**
tombs *n* ▷ **tomb**
tombstone *n* (*pl* **-s**) gravestone
tombstones *n* ▷ **tombstone**
tome *n* (*pl* **-s**) large heavy book
tomes *n* ▷ **tome**
tomfooleries *n* ▷ **tomfoolery**
tomfoolery *n* (*pl* **-ries**) foolish behaviour
tomorrow *adv, n* (*pl* **-s**) (on) the day after today
tomorrows *n* ▷ **tomorrow**
toms *n* ▷ **tom**
ton *n* (*pl* **-s**) unit of weight equal to 2240 pounds or 1016 kilograms or, in the US, 2000 pounds or 907 kilograms
tonal *adj* (MUSIC) written in a key > **tonality** *n* (*pl* **-ties**)
tonalities *n* ▷ **tonal**
tonality *n* ▷ **tonal**
tone *n* (*pl* **-s**) sound with reference to its pitch, volume, etc. ▶ *v* (**-nes, -ning, -ned**) harmonize (with) > **toneless** *adj*
toned *v* ▷ **tone**
toneless *adj* ▷ **tone**
tones *n, v* ▷ **tone**
tongs *pl n* large pincers for grasping and lifting
tongue *n* (*pl* **-s**) muscular organ in the mouth, used in speaking and tasting
tongues *n* ▷ **tongue**
tonic *n* (*pl* **-s**) medicine to improve body tone ▶ *adj* invigorating
tonics *n* ▷ **tonic**
tonight *adv, n* (*pl* **-s**) (in or during) the night or evening of this day
tonights *n* ▷ **tonight**
toning *v* ▷ **tone**
tonnage *n* (*pl* **-s**) weight capacity of a ship
tonnages *n* ▷ **tonnage**
tonne [**tunn**] *n* (*pl* **-s**) unit of weight equal to 1000 kilograms
tonnes *n* ▷ **tonne**
tons *n* ▷ **ton**
tonsil *n* (*pl* **-s**) small gland in the throat
tonsillectomies *n* ▷ **tonsillectomy**
tonsillectomy *n* (*pl* **-mies**) surgical removal

of the tonsils
tonsillitis *n* (*pl* **-tises**) inflammation of the tonsils
tonsillitises *n* ▷ **tonsillitis**
tonsils *n* ▷ **tonsil**
tonsure *n* (*pl* **-s**) shaving of all or the top of the head as a religious or monastic practice > **tonsured** *adj*
tonsured *adj* ▷ **tonsure**
tonsures *n* ▷ **tonsure**
too *adv* also, as well
took *v* ▷ **take**
tool *n* (*pl* **-s**) implement used by hand
tools *n* ▷ **tool**
toot *n* (*pl* **-s**) short hooting sound ▶ *v* (**-s, -ing, -ed**) (cause to) make such a sound
tooted *v* ▷ **toot**
tooth *n* (*pl* **teeth**) bonelike projection in the jaws of most vertebrates for biting and chewing > **toothless** *adj*
toothless *adj* ▷ **tooth**
toothpaste *n* (*pl* **-s**) paste used to clean the teeth
toothpastes *n* ▷ **toothpaste**
toothpick *n* (*pl* **-s**) small stick for removing scraps of food from between the teeth
toothpicks *n* ▷ **toothpick**
tooting *v* ▷ **toot**
toots *n, v* ▷ **toot**
top¹ *n* (*pl* **-s**) highest point or part ▶ *adj* at or of the top ▶ *v* (**-s, -pping, -pped**) form a top on
top² *n* (*pl* **-s**) toy which spins on a pointed base
topaz [**toe**-pazz] *n* (*pl* **-es**) semiprecious stone in various colours
topazes *n* ▷ **topaz**
topee, topi [**toe**-pee] *n* (*pl* **-s**) lightweight hat worn in tropical countries
topees *n* ▷ **topee**
topi *n* ▷ **topee**
topiaries *n* ▷ **topiary**
topiary [**tope**-yar-ee] *n* (*pl* **-ries**) art of trimming trees and bushes into decorative shapes
topic *n* (*pl* **-s**) subject of a conversation, book, etc.
topical *adj* relating to current events > **topicality** *n* (*pl* **-ties**)
topicalities *n* ▷ **topical**
topicality *n* ▷ **topical**
topics *n* ▷ **topic**
topis *n* ▷ **topee**
topless *adj* (of a costume or woman) with no covering for the breasts
topmost *adj* highest or best
topographer *n* ▷ **topography**
topographers *n* ▷ **topography**
topographical *adj* ▷ **topography**
topographies *n* ▷ **topography**
topography *n* (*pl* **-phies**) (science of describing) the surface features of a place > **topographer** *n* (*pl* **-s**) > **topographical** *adj*
topological *adj* ▷ **topology**
topologies *n* ▷ **topology**
topology *n* (*pl* **-gies**) geometry of the properties of a shape which are unaffected by continuous distortion > **topological** *adj*
topped *n* ▷ **top¹**
topping *n* (*pl* **-s**) sauce or garnish for food ▶ *v* ▷ **top¹**
toppings *n* ▷ **topping**
topple *v* (**-les, -ling, -led**) (cause to) fall over
toppled *v* ▷ **topple**
topples *v* ▷ **topple**
toppling *v* ▷ **topple**
top-notch *adj* excellent, first-class
tops *n* ▷ **top¹, ²** ▶ *v* ▷ **top¹**
topsoil *n* (*pl* **-s**) surface layer of soil
topsoils *n* ▷ **topsoil**
toque [**toke**] *n* (*pl* **-s**) small round hat
toques *n* ▷ **toque**
tor *n* (*pl* **-s**) high rocky hill
torch *n* (*pl* **-es**) small portable battery-powered lamp ▶ *v* (**-es, -ing, -ed**) (*Informal*) deliberately set (a building) on fire
torched *v* ▷ **torch**
torches *n, v* ▷ **torch**
torching *v* ▷ **torch**
tore *v* ▷ **tear²**
toreador [**torr**-ee-a-dor] *n* (*pl* **-s**) bullfighter
toreadors *n* ▷ **toreador**
torment *v* (**-s, -ing, -ed**) cause (someone) great suffering ▶ *n* (*pl* **-s**) great suffering > **tormentor** *n* (*pl* **-s**)
tormented *v* ▷ **torment**
tormenting *v* ▷ **torment**
tormentor *n* ▷ **torment**
tormentors *n* ▷ **torment**
torments *v, n* ▷ **torment**
torn *v* ▷ **tear²**
tornado *n* (*pl* **-s, -es**) violent whirlwind
tornadoes *n* ▷ **tornado**
tornados *n* ▷ **tornado**
torpedo *n* (*pl* **-es**) self-propelled underwater missile ▶ *v* (**-es, -ing, -ed**) attack or destroy with or as if with torpedoes
torpedoed *v* ▷ **torpedo**
torpedoes *n, v* ▷ **torpedo**
torpedoing *v* ▷ **torpedo**
torpid *adj* sluggish and inactive
torpor *n* (*pl* **-s**) torpid state
torpors *n* ▷ **torpor**

torque [tork] *n* (*pl* **-s**) force causing rotation

torques *n* ▷ **torque**

torrent *n* (*pl* **-s**) rushing stream

torrential *adj* (of rain) very heavy

torrents *n* ▷ **torrent**

torrid *adj* (**-er, -est**) very hot and dry

torrider *adj* ▷ **torrid**

torridest *adj* ▷ **torrid**

tors *n* ▷ **tor**

torsion *n* (*pl* **-s**) twisting of a part by equal forces being applied at both ends but in opposite directions

torsions *n* ▷ **torsion**

torso *n* (*pl* **-s**) trunk of the human body

torsos *n* ▷ **torso**

tort *n* (*pl* **-s**) (LAW) civil wrong or injury for which damages may be claimed

tortilla *n* (*pl* **-s**) thin Mexican pancake

tortillas *n* ▷ **tortilla**

tortoise *n* (*pl* **-s**) slow-moving land reptile with a dome-shaped shell

tortoises *n* ▷ **tortoise**

tortoiseshell *n* (*pl* **-s**) mottled brown shell of a turtle, used for making ornaments ▶ *adj* having brown, orange, and black markings

tortoiseshells *n* ▷ **tortoiseshell**

torts *n* ▷ **tort**

tortuous *adj* winding or twisting

torture *v* (**-res, -ring, -red**) cause (someone) severe pain or mental anguish ▶ *n* (*pl* **-s**) severe physical or mental pain > **torturer** *n* (*pl* **-s**)

tortured *v* ▷ **torture**

torturer *n* ▷ **torture**

torturers *n* ▷ **torture**

tortures *v, n* ▷ **torture**

torturing *v* ▷ **torture**

toss *v* (**-es, -ing, -ed**) throw lightly ▶ *n* (*pl* **-es**) tossing

tossed *v* ▷ **toss**

tosses *v, n* ▷ **toss**

tossing *v* ▷ **toss**

tot[1] *n* (*pl* **-s**) small child

tot[2] *v* (**-s, -tting, -tted**) add (numbers) together

total *n* (*pl* **-s**) whole, esp. a sum of parts ▶ *adj* complete ▶ *v* (**-s, -lling, -lled**) amount to > **totally** *adv* > **totality** *n* (*pl* **-ties**)

totalitarian *adj* of a dictatorial one-party government > **totalitarianism** *n* (*pl* **-s**)

totalitarianism *n* ▷ **totalitarian**

totalitarianisms *n* ▷ **totalitarian**

totalities *n* ▷ **total**

totality *n* ▷ **total**

totalled *v* ▷ **total**

totalling *v* ▷ **total**

totally *adv* ▷ **total**

totals *n, v* ▷ **total**

tote[1] *v* (**-tes, -ting, -ted**) carry (a gun etc.)

tote[2] *n* (*pl* **-s**) ▷ **totalizator**

toted *v* ▷ **tote**[1]

totem *n* (*pl* **-s**) tribal badge or emblem

totems *n* ▷ **totem**

totes *v* ▷ **tote**[1] ▶ *n* ▷ **tote**[2]

toting *v* ▷ **tote**[1]

tots *n* ▷ **tot**[1] ▶ *v* ▷ **tot**[2]

totted *v* ▷ **tot**[2]

totter *v* (**-s, -ing, -ed**) move unsteadily

tottered *v* ▷ **totter**

tottering *v* ▷ **totter**

totters *v* ▷ **totter**

totting *v* ▷ **tot**[2]

toucan *n* (*pl* **-s**) tropical American bird with a large bill

toucans *n* ▷ **toucan**

touch *v* (**-es, -ing, -ed**) come into contact with ▶ *n* (*pl* **-es**) sense by which an object's qualities are perceived when they come into contact with part of the body ▶ *adj* of a non-contact version of particular sport

touché [too-shay] *interj* acknowledgment of the striking home of a remark or witty reply

touched *adj* emotionally moved ▶ *v* ▷ **touch**

touches *v, n* ▷ **touch**

touchier *adj* ▷ **touchy**

touchiest *adj* ▷ **touchy**

touching *adj* emotionally moving ▶ *v* ▷ **touch**

touchline *n* (*pl* **-s**) side line of the pitch in some games

touchlines *n* ▷ **touchline**

touchstone *n* (*pl* **-s**) standard by which a judgment is made

touchstones *n* ▷ **touchstone**

touchy *adj* (**-chier, -chiest**) easily offended

tough *adj* (**-er, -est**) strong or resilient ▶ *n* (*pl* **-s**) (*Informal*) rough violent person > **toughness** *n* (*pl* **-es**)

toughen *v* (**-s, -ing, -ed**) make or become tough or tougher

toughened *v* ▷ **toughen**

toughening *v* ▷ **toughen**

toughens *v* ▷ **toughen**

tougher *adj* ▷ **tough**

toughest *adj* ▷ **tough**

toughness *n* ▷ **tough**

toughnesses *n* ▷ **tough**

toughs *n* ▷ **tough**

toupee [too-pay] *n* (*pl* **-s**) small wig

toupees *n* ▷ **toupee**

tour *n* (*pl* **-s**) journey visiting places of interest along the way ▶ *v* (**-s, -ing, -ed**) make a tour

(of)
toured *v* ▷ **tour**
touring *v* ▷ **tour**
tourism *n* (*pl* **-s**) tourist travel as an industry
tourisms *n* ▷ **tourism**
tourist *n* (*pl* **-s**) person travelling for pleasure
tourists *n* ▷ **tourist**
touristy *adj* (*Informal*) (*often derogatory*) full of tourists or tourist attractions
tournament *n* (*pl* **-s**) sporting competition with several stages to decide the overall winner
tournaments *n* ▷ **tournament**
tourniquet [**tour**-nick-kay] *n* (*pl* **-s**) something twisted round a limb to stop bleeding
tourniquets *n* ▷ **tourniquet**
tours *n, v* ▷ **tour**
tousled *adj* ruffled and untidy
tout [rhymes with **shout**] *v* (**-s, -ing, -ed**) seek business in a persistent manner ▶ *n* (*pl* **-s**) person who sells tickets for a popular event at inflated prices
touted *v* ▷ **tout**
touting *v* ▷ **tout**
touts *v, n* ▷ **tout**
tow¹ *v* (**-s, -ing, -ed**) drag, esp. by means of a rope ▶ *n* (*pl* **-s**) towing
tow² *n* (*pl* **-s**) fibre of hemp or flax
toward *n* ▷ **towards**
towards, toward *prep* in the direction of
towbar *n* (*pl* **-s**) metal bar on a car for towing vehicles
towbars *n* ▷ **towbar**
towed *v* ▷ **tow¹**
towel *n* (*pl* **-s**) cloth for drying things
towelling *n* (*pl* **-s**) material used for making towels
towellings *n* ▷ **towelling**
towels *n* ▷ **towel**
tower *n* (*pl* **-s**) tall structure, often forming part of a larger building
towers *n* ▷ **tower**
towing *v* ▷ **tow¹**
town *n* (*pl* **-s**) group of buildings larger than a village
towns *n* ▷ **town**
township *n* (*pl* **-s**) small town
townships *n* ▷ **township**
towpath *n* (*pl* **-s**) path beside a canal or river, originally for horses towing boats
towpaths *n* ▷ **towpath**
tows *n* ▷ **tow¹, ²** ▶ *v* ▷ **tow¹**
toxaemia [tox-**seem**-ya] *n* (*pl* **-s**) blood poisoning
toxaemias *n* ▷ **toxaemia**
toxic *adj* poisonous > **toxicity** *n* (*pl* **-ties**)
toxicities *n* ▷ **toxic**
toxicity *n* ▷ **toxic**
toxicologies *n* ▷ **toxicology**
toxicology *n* (*pl* **-gies**) study of poisons
toxin *n* (*pl* **-s**) poison of bacterial origin
toxins *n* ▷ **toxin**
toy *n* (*pl* **-s**) something designed to be played with ▶ *adj* (of a dog) of a variety much smaller than is normal for that breed ▶ *v* (**-s, -ing, -ed**) play
toyed *v* ▷ **toy**
toying *v* ▷ **toy**
toys *n, v* ▷ **toy**
trace *v* (**-ces, -cing, -ced**) track down and find ▶ *n* (*pl* **-s**) track left by something > **traceable** *adj*
traceable *adj* ▷ **trace**
traced *v* ▷ **trace**
tracer *n* (*pl* **-s**) projectile which leaves a visible trail
traceries *n* ▷ **tracery**
tracers *n* ▷ **tracer**
tracery *n* (*pl* **-ries**) pattern of interlacing lines
traces *v, n* ▷ **trace** ▶ *pl n* strap by which a horse pulls a vehicle
trachea [track-**kee**-a] *n* (*pl* **-cheae**) windpipe
tracheae *n* ▷ **trachea**
tracheotomies *n* ▷ **tracheotomy**
tracheotomy [track-ee-**ot**-a-mee] *n* (*pl* **-mies**) surgical incision into the trachea
tracing *n* (*pl* **-s**) traced copy ▶ *v* ▷ **trace**
track *n* (*pl* **-s**) rough road or path ▶ *v* (**-s, -ing, -ed**) follow the trail or path of
tracked *v* ▷ **track**
tracking *v* ▷ **track**
tracks *n, v* ▷ **track**
tracksuit *n* (*pl* **-s**) warm loose-fitting suit worn by athletes etc., esp. during training
tracksuits *n* ▷ **tracksuit**
tract¹ *n* (*pl* **-s**) wide area
tract² *n* (*pl* **-s**) pamphlet, esp. a religious one
tractable *adj* easy to manage or control
traction *n* (*pl* **-s**) pulling, esp. by engine power
tractions *n* ▷ **traction**
tractor *n* (*pl* **-s**) motor vehicle with large rear wheels for pulling farm machinery
tractors *n* ▷ **tractor**
tracts *n* ▷ **tract¹, ²**
trade *n* (*pl* **-s**) buying, selling, or exchange of goods ▶ *v* (**-des, -ding, -ded**) buy and sell > **trader** *n* (*pl* **-s**) > **trading** *n* (*pl* **-s**)
traded *v* ▷ **trade**
trademark *n* (*pl* **-s**) (legally registered) name or symbol used by a firm to distinguish its

goods
trademarks *n* ▷ **trademark**
trader *n* ▷ **trade**
traders *n* ▷ **trade**
trades *n, v* ▷ **trade**
tradesman *n* (*pl* **-men**) skilled worker
tradesmen *n* ▷ **tradesman**
trading *v, n* ▷ **trade**
tradings *n* ▷ **trad**
tradition *n* (*pl* **-s**) body of beliefs, customs, etc. handed down from generation to generation > **traditional** *adj* > **traditionally** *adv*
traditional *adj* ▷ **tradition**
traditionally *adv* ▷ **tradition**
traditions *n* ▷ **tradition**
traduce *v* (**-ces, -cing, -ced**) slander
traduced *v* ▷ **traduce**
traduces *v* ▷ **traduce**
traducing *v* ▷ **traduce**
traffic *n* (*pl* **-s**) vehicles coming and going on a road ▶ *v* (**-s, -cking, -cked**) trade, usu. illicitly > **trafficker** *n* (*pl* **-s**)
trafficked *v* ▷ **traffic**
trafficker *n* ▷ **traffic**
traffickers *n* ▷ **traffic**
trafficking *v* ▷ **traffic**
traffics *n, v* ▷ **traffic**
tragedian [traj-**jee**-dee-an], **tragedienne** [traj-jee-dee-**enn**] *n* (*pl* **-s**) person who acts in or writes tragedies
tragedians *n* ▷ **tragedian**
tragedies *n* ▷ **tragedy**
tragedy *n* (*pl* **-dies**) shocking or sad event
tragic *adj* of or like a tragedy > **tragically** *adv*
tragically *adv* ▷ **tragic**
tragicomedies *n* ▷ **tragicomedy**
tragicomedy *n* (*pl* **-s**) play with both tragic and comic elements
trail *n* (*pl* **-s**) path, track, or road ▶ *v* (**-s, -ing, -ed**) drag along the ground
trailed *v* ▷ **trail**
trailer *n* (*pl* **-s**) vehicle designed to be towed by another vehicle
trailers *n* ▷ **trailer**
trailing *v* ▷ **trail**
trails *n, v* ▷ **trail**
train *v* (**-s, -ing, -ed**) instruct in a skill ▶ *n* (*pl* **-s**) line of railway coaches or wagons drawn by an engine
trained *v* ▷ **train**
trainee *n* (*pl* **-s**) person being trained
trainees *n* ▷ **trainee**
trainer *n* (*pl* **-s**) person who trains an athlete or sportsman
trainers *n* ▷ **trainer**
training *v* ▷ **train**
trains *v, n* ▷ **train**
traipse *v* (**-pses, -psing, -psed**) (*Informal*) walk wearily
traipsed *v* ▷ **traipse**
traipses *v* ▷ **traipse**
traipsing *v* ▷ **traipse**
trait *n* (*pl* **-s**) characteristic feature
traitor *n* (*pl* **-s**) person guilty of treason or treachery > **traitorous** *adj*
traitorous *adj* ▷ **traitor**
traitors *n* ▷ **traitor**
traits *n* ▷ **trait**
trajectories *n* ▷ **trajectory**
trajectory *n* (*pl* **-ries**) line of flight, esp. of a projectile
tram *n* (*pl* **-s**) public transport vehicle powered by an overhead wire and running on rails laid in the road
tramlines *pl n* track for trams
tramp *v* (**-s, -ing, -ed**) travel on foot, hike ▶ *n* (*pl* **-s**) homeless person who travels on foot
tramped *v* ▷ **tramp**
tramping *v* ▷ **tramp**
trample *v* (**-les, -ling, -led**) tread on and crush
trampled *v* ▷ **trample**
tramples *v* ▷ **trample**
trampling *v* ▷ **trample**
trampoline *n* (*pl* **-s**) tough canvas sheet attached to a frame by springs, used by acrobats etc. ▶ *v* (**-nes, -ning, -ned**) bounce on a trampoline
trampolined *v* ▷ **trampoline**
trampolines *n, v* ▷ **trampoline**
trampolining *v* ▷ **trampoline**
tramps *n* ▷ **tramp**
trams *n* ▷ **tram**
trance *n* (*pl* **-s**) unconscious or dazed state
trances *n* ▷ **trance**
tranche *n* (*pl* **-s**) portion of something large, esp. a sum of money
tranches *n* ▷ **tranche**
tranquil *adj* (**-ler, -lest**) calm and quiet > **tranquilly** *adv* > **tranquillity** *n* (*pl* **-ties**)
tranquiller *adj* ▷ **tough**
tranquillest *adj* ▷ **tough**
tranquillities *n* ▷ **tranquil**
tranquillity *n* ▷ **tranquil**
tranquillize *v* (**-zes, -zing, -zed**) make calm
tranquillized *v* ▷ **tranquillize**
tranquillizer *n* (*pl* **-s**) drug which reduces anxiety or tension
tranquillizers *n* ▷ **tranquillizer**
tranquillizes *v* ▷ **tranquillize**
tranquillizing *v* ▷ **tranquillize**

tranquilly *adv* ▷ **tranquil**

transact *v* (**-s, -ing, -ed**) conduct or negotiate (a business deal)

transacted *v* ▷ **transact**

transacting *v* ▷ **transact**

transaction *n* (*pl* **-s**) business deal transacted

transactions *n* ▷ **transaction**

transacts *v* ▷ **transact**

transatlantic *adj* on, from, or to the other side of the Atlantic

transceiver *n* (*pl* **-s**) transmitter and receiver of radio or electronic signals

transceivers *n* ▷ **transceiver**

transcend *v* (**-s, -ing, -ed**) rise above > **transcendence** *n* (*pl* **-s**) > **transcendent** *adj*

transcended *v* ▷ **transcend**

transcendence *n* ▷ **transcend**

transcendences *n* ▷ **transcend**

transcendent *adj* ▷ **transcend**

transcendental *adj* based on intuition rather than experience

transcending *v* ▷ **transcend**

transcends *v* ▷ **transcend**

transcribe *v* (**-bes, -bing, -bed**) write down (something said)

transcribed *v* ▷ **transcribe**

transcribes *v* ▷ **transcribe**

transcribing *v* ▷ **transcribe**

transcript *n* (*pl* **-s**) copy

transcripts *n* ▷ **transcript**

transducer *n* (*pl* **-s**) device that converts one form of energy to another

transducers *n* ▷ **transducer**

transept *n* (*pl* **-s**) either of the two shorter wings of a cross-shaped church

transepts *n* ▷ **transept**

transexual *n* ▷ **transsexual**

transexuals *n* ▷ **transsexual**

transfer *v* (**-fers, -ferring, -ferred**) move or send from one person or place to another ▶ *n* (*pl* **-s**) transferring > **transferable** *adj*

transferable *adj* ▷ **transfer**

transference *n* (*pl* **-s**) transferring

transferences *n* ▷ **transference**

transferred *v* ▷ **transfer**

transferring *v* ▷ **transfer**

transfers *v*, *n* ▷ **transfer**

transfiguration *n* ▷ **transfigure**

transfigurations *n* ▷ **transfigure**

transfigure *v* (**-res, -ring, -red**) change in appearance > **transfiguration** *n* (*pl* **-s**)

transfigured *v* ▷ **transfigure**

transfigures *v* ▷ **transfigure**

transfiguring *v* ▷ **transfigure**

transfix *v* (**-es, -ing, -ed**) astound or stun

transfixed *v* ▷ **transfix**

transfixes *v* ▷ **transfix**

transfixing *v* ▷ **transfix**

transform *v* (**-s, -ing, -ed**) change the shape or character of > **transformation** *n* (*pl* **-s**)

transformation *n* ▷ **transform**

transformations *n* ▷ **transform**

transformed *v* ▷ **transform**

transformer *n* (*pl* **-s**) device for changing the voltage of an alternating current

transformers *n* ▷ **transformer**

transforming *v* ▷ **transform**

transforms *v* ▷ **transform**

transfuse *v* (**-ses, -sing, -sed**) give a transfusion to

transfused *v* ▷ **transfuse**

transfuses *v* ▷ **transfuse**

transfusing *v* ▷ **transfuse**

transfusion *n* (*pl* **-s**) injection of blood into the blood vessels of a patient

transfusions *n* ▷ **transfusion**

transgress *v* (**-es, -ing, -ed**) break (a moral law) > **transgression** *n* (*pl* **-s**) > **transgressor** *n* (*pl* **-s**)

transgressed *v* ▷ **transgress**

transgresses *v* ▷ **transgress**

transgressing *v* ▷ **transgress**

transgression *n* ▷ **transgress**

transgressions *n* ▷ **transgress**

transgressor *n* ▷ **transgress**

transgressors *n* ▷ **transgress**

transience *n* ▷ **transient**

transiences *n* ▷ **transient**

transient *adj* lasting only for a short time > **transience** *n* (*pl* **-s**)

transistor *n* (*pl* **-s**) semiconducting device used to amplify electric currents

transistors *n* ▷ **transistor**

transit *n* (*pl* **-s**) movement from one place to another

transition *n* (*pl* **-s**) change from one state to another > **transitional** *adj*

transitional *adj* ▷ **transition**

transitions *n* ▷ **transition**

transitive *adj* (GRAMMAR) (of a verb) requiring a direct object

transitory *adj* not lasting long

transits *n* ▷ **transit**

translate *v* (**-tes, -ting, -ted**) turn from one language into another > **translation** *n* (*pl* **-s**) > **translator** *n* (*pl* **-s**)

translated *v* ▷ **translate**

translates *v* ▷ **translate**

translating *v* ▷ **translate**

translation *n* ▷ **translat**

translations *n* ▷ **translat**
translator *n* ▷ **translate**
translators *n* ▷ **translate**
transliterate *v* (**-tes, -ting, -ted**) convert to the letters of a different alphabet > **transliteration** *n* (*pl* **-s**)
transliterated *v* ▷ **transliterate**
transliterates *v* ▷ **transliterate**
transliterating *v* ▷ **transliterate**
transliteration *n* ▷ **transliterate**
translucence *n* ▷ **translucence**
translucences *n* ▷ **translucent**
translucencies *n* ▷ **translucent**
translucency *n* ▷ **translucent**
translucent *adj* letting light pass through, but not transparent > **translucency, translucence** *n* (*pl* **-cies, -ces**)
transmigrate *v* (**-tes, -ting, -ted**) (of a soul) pass into another body > **transmigration** *n* (*pl* **-s**)
transmigrated *v* ▷ **transmigrate**
transmigrates *v* ▷ **transmigrate**
transmigrating *v* ▷ **transmigrate**
transmigration *n* ▷ **transmigrate**
transmigrations *n* ▷ **transmigrate**
transmission *n* (*pl* **-s**) transmitting
transmissions *n* ▷ **transmission**
transmit *v* (**-mits, -mitting, -mitted**) pass (something) from one person or place to another > **transmittable** *adj* > **transmitter** *n* (*pl* **-s**)
transmits *v* ▷ **transmit**
transmittable *adj* ▷ **transmit**
transmitted *v* ▷ **transmit**
transmitter *n* ▷ **transmit**
transmitters *n* ▷ **transmit**
transmitting *v* ▷ **transmit**
transmogrified *v* ▷ **transmogrify**
transmogrifies *v* ▷ **transmogrify**
transmogrify *v* (**-fies, -fying, -fied**) (*Informal*) change completely
transmogrifying *v* ▷ **transmogrify**
transmutation *n* ▷ **transmute**
transmutations *n* ▷ **transmute**
transmute *v* (**-tes, -ting, -ted**) change the form or nature of > **transmutation** *n* (*pl* **-s**)
transmuted *v* ▷ **transmute**
transmutes *v* ▷ **transmute**
transmuting *v* ▷ **transmute**
transom *n* (*pl* **-s**) horizontal bar across a window
transoms *n* ▷ **transom**
transparencies *n* ▷ **transparency**
transparency *n* (*pl* **-cies**) transparent quality
transparent *adj* able to be seen through, clear > **transparently** *adv*
transparently *adv* ▷ **transparent**
transpiration *n* ▷ **transpire**
transpirations *n* ▷ **transpire**
transpire *v* (**-res, -ring, -red**) become known > **transpiration** *n* (*pl* **-s**)
transpired *v* ▷ **transpire**
transpires *v* ▷ **transpire**
transpiring *v* ▷ **transpire**
transplant *v* (**-s, -ing, -ed**) transfer (an organ or tissue) surgically from one part or body to another ▶ *n* (*pl* **-s**) surgical transplanting > **transplantation** *n* (*pl* **-s**)
transplantation *n* ▷ **transplant**
transplantations *n* ▷ **transplant**
transplanted *v* ▷ **transplant**
transplanting *v* ▷ **transplant**
transplants *v, n* ▷ **transplant**
transport *v* (**-s, -ing, -ed**) convey from one place to another ▶ *n* (*pl* **-s**) business or system of transporting > **transportation** *n* (*pl* **-s**)
transportation *n* ▷ **transport**
transportations *n* ▷ **transport**
transported *v* ▷ **transport**
transporter *n* (*pl* **-s**) large goods vehicle
transporters *n* ▷ **transporter**
transporting *v* ▷ **transport**
transports *v, n* ▷ **transport**
transpose *v* (**-ses, -sing, -sed**) interchange two things > **transposition** *n* (*pl* **-s**)
transposed *v* ▷ **transpose**
transposes *v* ▷ **transpose**
transposing *v* ▷ **transpose**
transposition *n* ▷ **transpose**
transpositions *n* ▷ **transpose**
transsexual, transexual *n* (*pl* **-s**) person of one sex who believes his or her true identity is of the opposite sex
transsexuals *n* ▷ **transsexual**
transuranic [tranz-yoor-**ran**-ik] *adj* (of an element) having an atomic number greater than that of uranium
transverse *adj* crossing from side to side
transvestite *n* (*pl* **-s**) person who seeks sexual pleasure by wearing the clothes of the opposite sex > **transvestism** *n* (*pl* **-s**)
transvestism *n* ▷ **transvestite**
transvestisms *n* ▷ **transvestite**
transvestites *n* ▷ **transvestite**
trap *n* (*pl* **-s**) device for catching animals ▶ *v* (**-s, -pping, -pped**) catch
trapdoor *n* (*pl* **-s**) door in floor or roof
trapdoors *n* ▷ **trapdoor**
trapeze *n* (*pl* **-s**) horizontal bar suspended from two ropes, used by circus acrobats

trapezes *n* ▷ **trapeze**
trapezia *n* ▷ **trapezium**
trapezium *n* (*pl* **-ziums, -zia**) quadrilateral with two parallel sides of unequal length
trapeziums *n* ▷ **trapezium**
trapezoid [**trap**-piz-zoid] *n* (*pl* **-s**) quadrilateral with no sides parallel
trapezoids *n* ▷ **trapezoid**
trapped *n* ▷ **trap**
trapper *n* (*pl* **-s**) person who traps animals for their fur
trappers *n* ▷ **trapper**
trapping *n* ▷ **trap**
trappings *pl n* accessories that symbolize an office or position
traps *n, v* ▷ **trap**
trash *n* (*pl* **-es**) anything worthless > **trashy** *adj* (**-shier, -shiest**)
trashes *n* ▷ **trash**
trashier *adj* ▷ **trash**
trashiest *adj* ▷ **trash**
trashy *adj* ▷ **trash**
trauma [**traw**-ma] *n* (*pl* **-mata, -s**) emotional shock > **traumatic** *adj* > **traumatize** *v* (**-zes, -zing, -zed**)
traumas *n* ▷ **trauma**
traumata *n* ▷ **trauma**
traumatic *adj* ▷ **trauma**
traumatized *v* ▷ **trauma**
traumatizes *v* ▷ **trauma**
traumatizing *v* ▷ **trauma**
travail *n* (*pl* **-s**) (*Lit*) labour or toil
travails *n* ▷ **travail**
travel *v* (**-s, -lling, -lled**) go from one place to another, through an area, or for a specified distance ▶ *n* (*pl* **-s**) travelling, esp. as a tourist > **traveller** *n* (*pl* **-s**)
travelled *v* ▷ **travel**
traveller *n* ▷ **travel**
travellers *n* ▷ **travel**
travelling *v* ▷ **travel**
travelogue *n* (*pl* **-s**) film or talk about someone's travels
travelogues *n* ▷ **travelogue**
travels *v, n* ▷ **travel** ▶ *pl n* (account of) travelling
traverse *v* (**-ses, -sing, -sed**) move over or back and forth over
traversed *v* ▷ **traverse**
traverses *v* ▷ **traverse**
traversing *v* ▷ **traverse**
travesties *n* ▷ **travesty**
travesty *n* (*pl* **-ties**) grotesque imitation or mockery
trawl *n* (*pl* **-s**) net dragged at deep levels behind a fishing boat ▶ *v* (**-s, -ing, -ed**) fish with such a net
trawled *v* ▷ **trawl**
trawler *n* (*pl* **-s**) trawling boat
trawlers *n* ▷ **trawler**
trawling *v* ▷ **trawl**
trawls *n, v* ▷ **trawl**
tray *n* (*pl* **-s**) flat board, usu. with a rim, for carrying things
trays *n* ▷ **tray**
treacheries *n* ▷ **treachery**
treacherous *adj* disloyal > **treacherously** *adv*
treacherously *adv* ▷ **treacherous**
treachery *n* (*pl* **-ries**) wilful betrayal
treacle *n* (*pl* **-s**) thick dark syrup produced when sugar is refined > **treacly** *adj* (**-lier, -liest**)
treacles *n* ▷ **treacle**
treaclier *adj* ▷ **treacle**
treacliest *adj* ▷ **treacle**
treacly *adj* ▷ **treacle**
tread *v* (**-s, -ing, trod, trodden** *or* **trod**) set one's foot on ▶ *n* (*pl* **-s**) way of walking or dancing
treading *v* ▷ **tread**
treadle [**tred**-dl] *n* (*pl* **-s**) lever worked by the foot to turn a wheel
treadles *n* ▷ **treadle**
treadmill *n* (*pl* **-s**) (HIST) cylinder turned by treading on steps projecting from it
treadmills *n* ▷ **treadmill**
treads *v, n* ▷ **tread**
treason *n* (*pl* **-s**) betrayal of one's sovereign or country > **treasonable** *adj*
treasonable *adj* ▷ **treason**
treasons *n* ▷ **treason**
treasure *n* (*pl* **-s**) collection of wealth, esp. gold or jewels ▶ *v* (**-res, -ring, -red**) prize or cherish
treasured *v* ▷ **treasure**
treasurer *n* (*pl* **-s**) official in charge of funds
treasurers *n* ▷ **treasurer**
treasures *n, v* ▷ **treasure**
treasuries *n* ▷ **treasury**
treasuring *v* ▷ **treasure**
treasury *n* (*pl* **-ries**) storage place for treasure
treat *v* (**-s, -ing, -ed**) deal with or regard in a certain manner ▶ *n* (*pl* **-s**) pleasure, entertainment, etc. given or paid for by someone else
treated *v* ▷ **treat**
treaties *n* ▷ **treaty**
treating *v* ▷ **treat**
treatise [**treat**-izz] *n* (*pl* **-s**) formal piece of writing on a particular subject
treatises *n* ▷ **treatise**
treatment *n* (*pl* **-s**) medical care

treatments *n* ▷ **treatment**
treats *v, n* ▷ **treat**
treaty *n* (*pl* **-ties**) signed contract between states
treble *adj* triple (MUSIC) ▸ *n* (*pl* **-s**) (singer with or part for) a soprano voice ▸ *v* (**-les, -ling, -led**) increase three times > **trebly** *adv*
trebled *v* ▷ **treble**
trebles *n, v* ▷ **treble**
trebling *v* ▷ **treble**
trebly *adv* ▷ **treble**
tree *n* (*pl* **-s**) large perennial plant with a woody trunk > **treeless** *adj*
treeless *adj* ▷ **tree**
trees *n* ▷ **tree**
trefoil [**tref**-foil] *n* (*pl* **-s**) plant, such as clover, with a three-lobed leaf
trefoils *n* ▷ **trefoil**
trek *n* (*pl* **-s**) long difficult journey, esp. on foot ▸ *v* (**-s, -kking, -kked**) make such a journey
trekked *v* ▷ **trek**
trekking *v* ▷ **trek**
treks *n, v* ▷ **trek**
trellis *n* (*pl* **-ises**) framework of horizontal and vertical strips of wood
trellises *n* ▷ **trellis**
tremble *v* (**-les, -ling, -led**) shake or quiver ▸ *n* (*pl* **-les**) trembling > **trembling** *adj*
trembled *v* ▷ **tremble**
trembles *v, n* ▷ **tremble**
trembling *v, adj* ▷ **tremble**
tremendous *adj* huge > **tremendously** *adv*
tremendously *adv* ▷ **tremendous**
tremolo *n* (*pl* **-s**) (MUSIC) quivering effect in singing or playing
tremolos *n* ▷ **tremolo**
tremor *n* (*pl* **-s**) involuntary shaking
tremors *n* ▷ **tremor**
tremulous *adj* trembling, as from fear or excitement
trench *n* (*pl* **-es**) long narrow ditch, esp. one used as a shelter in war
trenchant *adj* incisive
trencher *n* (*pl* **-s**) (HIST) wooden plate for serving food
trencherman *n* (*pl* **-men**) hearty eater
trenchermen *n* ▷ **trencherman**
trenchers *n* ▷ **trencher**
trenches *n* ▷ **trench**
trend *n* (*pl* **-s**) general tendency or direction
trendier *adj* ▷ **trendy**
trendies *n* ▷ **trendy**
trendiest *adj* ▷ **trendy**
trendiness *n* ▷ **trendy**
trendinesses *n* ▷ **trendy**
trends *n* ▷ **trend**
trendy *adj* (**-dier, -diest**) ▸ *n* (*pl* **-dies**) (*Informal*) consciously fashionable (person) > **trendiness** *n* (*pl* **-es**)
trepidation *n* (*pl* **-s**) fear or anxiety
trepidations *n* ▷ **trepidation**
trespass *v* (**-es, -ing, -ed**) go onto another's property without permission ▸ *n* (*pl* **-es**) trespassing > **trespasser** *n* (*pl* **-s**)
trespassed *v* ▷ **trespass**
trespasser *n* ▷ **trespass**
trespassers *n* ▷ **trespass**
trespasses *v, n* ▷ **trespass**
trespassing *v* ▷ **trespass**
tresses *pl n* long flowing hair
trestle *n* (*pl* **-s**) board fixed on pairs of spreading legs, used as a support
trestles *n* ▷ **trestle**
trevallies *n* ▷ **trevally**
trevally *n* (*pl* **-lies**) (AUST & NZ) any of various food and game fishes
trews *pl n* close-fitting tartan trousers
triad *n* (*pl* **-s**) group of three
triads *n* ▷ **triad**
trial *n* (*pl* **-s**) investigation of a case before a judge
trials *n* ▷ **trial** ▸ *pl n* sporting competition for individuals
triangle *n* (*pl* **-s**) geometric figure with three sides > **triangular** *adj*
triangles *n* ▷ **triangle**
triangular *adj* ▷ **triangle**
tribal *adj* ▷ **tribe**
tribalism *n* (*pl* **-s**) loyalty to a tribe
tribalisms *n* ▷ **tribalism**
tribe *n* (*pl* **-s**) group of clans or families believed to have a common ancestor > **tribal** *adj*
tribes *n* ▷ **tribe**
tribulation *n* (*pl* **-s**) great distress
tribulations *n* ▷ **tribulation**
tribunal *n* (*pl* **-s**) board appointed to inquire into a specific matter
tribunals *n* ▷ **tribunal**
tribune *n* (*pl* **-s**) people's representative, esp. in ancient Rome
tribunes *n* ▷ **tribune**
tributaries *n* ▷ **tributary**
tributary *n* (*pl* **-ries**) stream or river flowing into a larger one ▸ *adj* (of a stream or river) flowing into a larger one
tribute *n* (*pl* **-s**) sign of respect or admiration
tributes *n* ▷ **tribute**
trice *n* (*pl* **-s**) moment
triceps *n* (*pl* **-pses**) muscle at the back of the upper arm

tricepses *n* ▷ **triceps**
trices *n* ▷ **trice**
trichologies *n* ▷ **trichology**
trichologist *n* ▷ **trichology**
trichologists *n* ▷ **trichology**
trichology [trick-**ol**-a-jee] *n* (*pl* **-gies**) study and treatment of hair and its diseases **> trichologist** *n* (*pl* **-s**)
trick *n* (*pl* **-s**) deceitful or cunning action or plan ▶ *v* (**-s, -ing, -ed**) cheat or deceive **> trickery** *n* (*pl* **-ries**) **> trickster** *n* (*pl* **-s**)
tricked *v* ▷ **trick**
trickeries *n* ▷ **trick**
trickery *n* ▷ **trick**
trickier *adj* ▷ **tricky**
trickiest *adj* ▷ **tricky**
tricking *v* ▷ **trick**
trickle *v* (**-les, -ling, -led**) (cause to) flow in a thin stream or drops ▶ *n* (*pl* **-s**) gradual flow
trickled *v* ▷ **trickle**
trickles *v, n* ▷ **trickle**
trickling *v* ▷ **trickle**
tricks *n, v* ▷ **trick**
trickster *n* ▷ **trick**
tricksters *n* ▷ **trick**
tricky *adj* (**-kier, -kiest**) difficult, needing careful handling
tricolour [**trick**-kol-lor] *n* (*pl* **-s**) three-coloured striped flag
tricolours *n* ▷ **tricolour**
tricycle *n* (*pl* **-s**) three-wheeled cycle
tricycles *n* ▷ **tricycle**
trident *n* (*pl* **-s**) three-pronged spear
tridents *n* ▷ **trident**
tried *v* ▷ **try**
triennial *adj* happening every three years
tries *v, n* ▷ **try**
trifle *n* (*pl* **-s**) insignificant thing or amount
trifles *n* ▷ **trifle**
trifling *adj* insignificant
trigger *n* (*pl* **-s**) small lever releasing a catch on a gun or machine ▶ *v* (**-s, -ing, -ed**) (*usu. foll. by* **off**) set (an action or process) in motion
triggered *v* ▷ **trigger**
triggering *v* ▷ **trigger**
triggers *n, v* ▷ **trigger**
trigonometries *n* ▷ **trigonometry**
trigonometry *n* (*pl* **-ries**) branch of mathematics dealing with relations of the sides and angles of triangles
trike *n* (*pl* **-s**) (*Informal*) tricycle
trikes *n* ▷ **trike**
trilateral *adj* having three sides
trilbies *n* ▷ **trilby**
trilby *n* (*pl* **-bies**) man's soft felt hat
trill *n* (*pl* **-s**) (MUSIC) rapid alternation between two notes ▶ *v* (**-s, -ing, -ed**) play or sing a trill
trilled *v* ▷ **trill**
trilling *v* ▷ **trill**
trillion *n* (*pl* **-s**) one million million, 10^{12}
trillions *n* ▷ **trillion**
trills *n, v* ▷ **trill**
trilobite [**trile**-oh-bite] *n* (*pl* **-s**) small prehistoric sea animal
trilobites *n* ▷ **trilobite**
trilogies *n* ▷ **trilogy**
trilogy *n* (*pl* **-gies**) series of three related books, plays, etc.
trim *adj* (**-mmer, -mmest**) neat and smart ▶ *v* (**-s, -mming, -mmed**) cut or prune into good shape ▶ *n* (*pl* **-s**) decoration
trimaran [**trime**-a-ran] *n* (*pl* **-s**) three-hulled boat
trimarans *n* ▷ **trimaran**
trimmed *v* ▷ **trim**
trimmer *adj* ▷ **trim**
trimmest *adj* ▷ **trim**
trimming *n* (*pl* **-s**) decoration ▶ *v* ▷ **trim**
trimmings *n* ▷ **trimming** ▶ *pl n* usual accompaniments
trims *v, n* ▷ **trim**
trinities *n* ▷ **trinity**
trinitrotoluene *n* (*pl* **-s**) TNT
trinitrotoluenes *n* ▷ **trinitrotoluene**
trinity *n* (*pl* **-ties**) group of three
trinket *n* (*pl* **-s**) small or worthless ornament or piece of jewellery
trinkets *n* ▷ **trinket**
trio *n* (*pl* **-s**) group of three
trios *n* ▷ **trio**
trip *n* (*pl* **-s**) journey to a place and back, esp. for pleasure ▶ *v* (**-s, -pping, -pped**) (cause to) stumble
tripe *n* (*pl* **-s**) stomach of a cow used as food
tripes *n* ▷ **tripe**
triple *adj* having three parts ▶ *v* (**-les, -ling, -led**) increase three times
tripled *v* ▷ **triple**
triples *v* ▷ **triple**
triplet *n* (*pl* **-s**) one of three babies born at one birth
triplets *n* ▷ **triplet**
triplicate *adj* triple
tripling *v* ▷ **triple**
tripod [**tripe**-pod] *n* (*pl* **-s**) three-legged stand, stool, etc.
tripods *n* ▷ **tripod**
tripos [**tripe**-poss] *n* (*pl* **-poses**) final examinations for an honours degree at Cambridge University
triposes *n* ▷ **tripos**

tripped *v* ▷ **trip**
tripper *n* (*pl* **-s**) tourist
trippers *n* ▷ **tripper**
tripping *v* ▷ **trip**
trips *n*, *v* ▷ **trip**
triptych [**trip**-tick] *n* (*pl* **-s**) painting or carving on three hinged panels, often forming an altarpiece
triptychs *n* ▷ **triptych**
trite *adj* (of a remark or idea) commonplace and unoriginal
tritium *n* (*pl* **-s**) radioactive isotope of hydrogen
tritiums *n* ▷ **tritium**
triumph *n* (*pl* **-s**) (happiness caused by) victory or success ▶ *v* (**-s, -ing, -ed**) be victorious or successful
triumphal *adj* celebrating a triumph
triumphant *adj* feeling or showing triumph
triumphed *v* ▷ **triumph**
triumphing *v* ▷ **triumph**
triumphs *n*, *v* ▷ **triumph**
triumvirate [try-**umm**-vir-rit] *n* (*pl* **-s**) group of three people in joint control
triumvirates *n* ▷ **triumvirate**
trivet [**triv**-vit] *n* (*pl* **-s**) metal stand for a pot or kettle
trivets *n* ▷ **trivet**
trivia *pl n* trivial things or details
trivial *adj* of little importance > **trivially** *adv* > **triviality** *n* (*pl* **-ties**)
trivialities *n* ▷ **trivial**
triviality *n* ▷ **trivial**
trivialize *v* (**-zes, -zing, -zed**) make (something) seem less important or complex than it is
trivialized *v* ▷ **trivialize**
trivializes *v* ▷ **trivialize**
trivializing *v* ▷ **trivialize**
trivially *adv* ▷ **trivial**
trod *v* ▷ **tread**
trodden *v* ▷ **tread**
troglodyte *n* (*pl* **-s**) cave dweller
troglodytes *n* ▷ **troglodyte**
troika *n* (*pl* **-s**) Russian vehicle drawn by three horses abreast
troikas *n* ▷ **troika**
troll *n* (*pl* **-s**) giant or dwarf in Scandinavian folklore
trolley *n* (*pl* **-s**) small wheeled table for food and drink
trolleys *n* ▷ **trolley**
trollop *n* (*pl* **-s**) (*Old-fashioned*) promiscuous or slovenly woman
trollops *n* ▷ **trollop**
trolls *n* ▷ **troll**
trombone *n* (*pl* **-s**) brass musical instrument with a sliding tube > **trombonist** *n* (*pl* **-s**)
trombones *n* ▷ **trombone**
trombonist *n* ▷ **trombone**
trombonists *n* ▷ **trombone**
troop *n* (*pl* **-s**) large group ▶ *v* (**-s, -ing, -ed**) move in a crowd
trooped *v* ▷ **troop**
trooper *n* (*pl* **-s**) cavalry soldier
troopers *n* ▷ **trooper**
trooping *v* ▷ **troop**
troops *n*, *v* ▷ **troop** ▶ *pl n* soldiers
trope *n* (*pl* **-s**) figure of speech
tropes *n* ▷ **trope**
trophies *n* ▷ **trophy**
trophy *n* (*pl* **-phies**) cup, shield, etc. given as a prize
tropic *n* (*pl* **-s**) either of two lines of latitude at $23\frac{1}{2}$°N (**tropic of Cancer**) or $23\frac{1}{2}$°S (**tropic of Capricorn**) ▶ *pl n* part of the earth's surface between these lines
tropical *adj* of or in the tropics
tropics *n* ▷ **tropic**
trot *v* (**-s, -tting, -tted**) (of a horse) move at a medium pace, lifting the feet in diagonal pairs ▶ *n* (*pl* **-s**) trotting
troth [rhymes with **growth**] *n* (*pl* **-s**) (*Obs*) pledge of devotion, esp. a betrothal
troths *n* ▷ **troth**
trots *v*, *n* ▷ **trot**
trotted *v* ▷ **trot**
trotter *n* (*pl* **-s**) pig's foot
trotters *n* ▷ **trotter**
trotting *v* ▷ **trot**
troubadour [**troo**-bad-oor] *n* (*pl* **-s**) medieval travelling poet and singer
troubadours *n* ▷ **troubadour**
trouble *n* (*pl* **-s**) (cause of) distress or anxiety ▶ *v* (**-les, -ling, -led**) (cause to) worry > **troubled** *adj* > **troublesome** *adj*
troubled *v*, *adj* ▷ **trouble**
troubles *n*, *v* ▷ **trouble**
troubleshooter *n* (*pl* **-s**) person employed to locate and deal with faults or problems
troubleshooters *n* ▷ **troubleshooter**
troublesome *adj* ▷ **trouble**
troubling *v* ▷ **trouble**
trough [**troff**] *n* (*pl* **-s**) long open container, esp. for animals' food or water
troughs *n* ▷ **trough**
trounce *v* (**-ces, -cing, -ced**) defeat utterly
trounced *v* ▷ **trounce**
trounces *v* ▷ **trounce**
trouncing *v* ▷ **trounce**

troupe [troop] *n* (*pl* **-s**) company of performers **>trouper** *n* (*pl* **-s**)
trouper *n* ▷ **troupe**
troupers *n* ▷ **troupe**
troupes *n* ▷ **troupe**
trouser *adj* of trousers
trousers *pl n* two-legged outer garment with legs reaching usu. to the ankles
trousseau [troo-so] *n* (*pl* **-seaux, -seaus**) bride's collection of clothing etc. for her marriage
trousseaus *n* ▷ **trousseau**
trousseaux *n* ▷ **trousseau**
trout *n* (*pl* **trout, trouts**) game fish related to the salmon
trouts *n* ▷ **trout**
trowel *n* (*pl* **-s**) hand tool with a wide blade for spreading mortar, lifting plants, etc.
trowels *n* ▷ **trowel**
truancies *n* ▷ **truant**
truancy *n* ▷ **truant**
truant *n* (*pl* **-s**) pupil who stays away from school without permission **>truancy** *n* (*pl* **-cies**)
truants *n* ▷ **truant**
truce *n* (*pl* **-s**) temporary agreement to stop fighting
truces *n* ▷ **truce**
truck¹ *n* (*pl* **-s**) railway goods wagon
truck² *n* (*pl* **-s**) commercial goods
trucker *n* (*pl* **-s**) truck driver
truckers *n* ▷ **trucker**
trucks *n* ▷ **truck¹, ²**
truculence *n* ▷ **truculent**
truculences *n* ▷ **truculent**
truculent [truck-yew-lent] *adj* aggressively defiant **>truculence** *n* (*pl* **-s**)
trudge *v* (**-dges, -dging, -dged**) walk heavily or wearily ▶ *n* (*pl* **-s**) long tiring walk
trudged *v* ▷ **trudge**
trudges *v, n* ▷ **trudge**
trudging *v* ▷ **trudge**
true *adj* (**truer, truest**) in accordance with facts **>truly** *adv*
truer *adj* ▷ **true**
truest *adj* ▷ **true**
truffle *n* (*pl* **-s**) edible underground fungus
truffles *n* ▷ **truffle**
trug *n* (*pl* **-s**) (BRIT) long shallow basket used by gardeners
trugs *n* ▷ **trug**
truism *n* (*pl* **-s**) self-evident truth
truisms *n* ▷ **truism**
truly *adv* ▷ **true**
trump¹ *n* (*pl* **-s**) ▶ *adj* (card) of the suit outranking the others ▶ *v* (**-s, -ing, -ed**) play a trump card on (another card)
trump² *n* (*pl* **-s**) (*Lit*) (sound of) a trumpet
trumped *v* ▷ **trump¹**
trumpet *n* (*pl* **-s**) valved brass instrument with a flared tube ▶ *v* (**-s, -ing, -ed**) proclaim loudly **>trumpeter** *n* (*pl* **-s**)
trumpeted *v* ▷ **trumpet**
trumpeter *n* ▷ **trumpet**
trumpeters *n* ▷ **trumpet**
trumpeting *v* ▷ **trumpet**
trumpets *n, v* ▷ **trumpet**
trumping *v* ▷ **trump¹**
trumps *n* ▷ **trump¹, ²** ▶ *pl n* suit outranking the others ▶ *v* ▷ **trump¹**
truncate *v* (**-tes, -ting, -ted**) cut short
truncated *v* ▷ **truncate**
truncates *v* ▷ **truncate**
truncating *v* ▷ **truncate**
truncheon *n* (*pl* **-s**) club carried by a policeman
truncheons *n* ▷ **truncheon**
trundle *v* (**-les, -ling, -led**) move heavily on wheels
trundled *v* ▷ **trundle**
trundles *v* ▷ **trundle**
trundling *v* ▷ **trundle**
trunk *n* (*pl* **-s**) main stem of a tree
trunks *n* ▷ **trunk** ▶ *pl n* man's swimming shorts
truss *v* (**-es, -ing, -ed**) tie or bind up ▶ *n* (*pl* **-es**) device for holding a hernia in place
trussed *v* ▷ **truss**
trusses *v, n* ▷ **truss**
trussing *v* ▷ **truss**
trust *v* (**-s, -ing, -ed**) believe in and rely on ▶ *n* (*pl* **-s**) confidence in the truth, reliability, etc. of a person or thing
trusted *v* ▷ **trust**
trustee *n* (*pl* **-s**) person holding property on another's behalf
trustees *n* ▷ **trustee**
trustful, trusting *adj* inclined to trust others
trustier *adj* ▷ **trusty**
trustiest *adj* ▷ **trusty**
trusting *v* ▷ **trust** ▶ *adj* ▷ **trustful**
trusts *n, v* ▷ **trust**
trustworthy *adj* reliable or honest
trusty *adj* (**-tier, -tiest**) faithful or reliable
truth *n* (*pl* **-s**) state of being true
truthful *adj* honest **>truthfully** *adv*
truthfully *adv* ▷ **truthful**
truths *n* ▷ **truth**
try *v* (**tries, trying, tried**) make an effort or attempt ▶ *n* (*pl* **tries**) attempt or effort
trying *adj* (*Informal*) difficult or annoying ▶ *v* ▷ **try**
tryst *n* (*pl* **-s**) arrangement to meet
trysts *n* ▷ **tryst**

tsar, czar [**zahr**] *n* (*pl* **-s**) (HIST) Russian emperor
tsars *n* ▷ **tsar**

tsk *interj*. Tsk is a sound people make to show disapproval. This is a useful word because it enables you to play K without using vowels, which is handy if your rack is low on vowel tiles. Tsk scores 7 points.

tsunami *n* (*pl* **-mis, -mi**) tidal wave, usu. caused by an earthquake under the sea
tsunamis *n* ▷ **tsunami**
tuatara *n* (*pl* **-s**) large lizard-like New Zealand reptile
tuataras *n* ▷ **tuatara**
tub *n* (*pl* **-s**) open, usu. round container
tuba [**tube**-a] *n* (*pl* **-s**) valved low-pitched brass instrument
tubas *n* ▷ **tuba**
tubbier *adj* ▷ **tubby**
tubbiest *adj* ▷ **tubby**
tubby *adj* (**tubbier, tubbiest**) (of a person) short and fat
tube *n* (*pl* **-s**) hollow cylinder
tuber [**tube**-er] *n* (*pl* **-s**) fleshy underground root of a plant such as a potato > **tuberous** *adj*
tubercle [**tube**-er-kl] *n* (*pl* **-s**) small rounded swelling
tubercles *n* ▷ **tubercle**
tubercular *adj* ▷ **tuberculosis**
tuberculin *n* (*pl* **-s**) extract from a bacillus used to test for tuberculosis
tuberculins *n* ▷ **tuberculin**
tuberculosis [tube-berk-yew-**lohss**-iss] *n* (*pl* **-ses**) infectious disease causing tubercles, esp. in the lungs > **tubercular** *adj*
tuberculoses *n* ▷ **tuberculosis**
tuberous *adj* ▷ **tuber**
tubers *n* ▷ **tuber**
tubes *n* ▷ **tube**
tubing *n* (*pl* **-s**) length of tube
tubings *n* ▷ **tubing**
tubs *n* ▷ **tub**
tubular [**tube**-yew-lar] *adj* of or shaped like a tube
tuck *v* (**-s, -ing, -ed**) push or fold into a small space ▶ *n* (*pl* **-s**) stitched fold
tucked *v* ▷ **tuck**
tucker *n* (*pl* **-s**) (AUST & NZ) (*Informal*) food
tuckers *n* ▷ **tucker**
tucking *v* ▷ **tuck**
tucks *v, n* ▷ **tuck**
tufa [**tew**-fa] *n* (*pl* **-s**) porous rock formed as a deposit from springs
tufas *n* ▷ **tufa**
tuffet *n* (*pl* **-s**) small mound or seat
tuffets *n* ▷ **tuffet**
tuft *n* (*pl* **-s**) bunch of feathers, grass, hair, etc. held or growing together at the base
tufts *n* ▷ **tuft**
tug *v* (**-s, -gging, -gged**) pull hard ▶ *n* (*pl* **-s**) hard pull
tugged *v* ▷ **tug**
tugging *v* ▷ **tug**
tugs *v, n* ▷ **tug**
tuition *n* (*pl* **-s**) instruction, esp. received individually or in a small group
tuitions *n* ▷ **tuition**
tulip *n* (*pl* **-s**) plant with bright cup-shaped flowers
tulips *n* ▷ **tulip**
tulle [**tewl**] *n* (*pl* **-s**) fine net fabric of silk etc.
tulles *n* ▷ **tulle**
tumble *v* (**-les, -ling, -led**) (cause to) fall, esp. awkwardly or violently ▶ *n* (*pl* **-s**) fall
tumbled *v* ▷ **tumble**
tumbledown *adj* dilapidated
tumbler *n* (*pl* **-s**) stemless drinking glass
tumblers *n* ▷ **tumbler**
tumbles *v, n* ▷ **tumble**
tumbling *v* ▷ **tumble**
tumbrel *n* ▷ **tumbril**
tumbrels *n* ▷ **tumbril**
tumbril, tumbrel *n* (*pl* **-s**) farm cart used during the French Revolution to take prisoners to the guillotine
tumbrils *n* ▷ **tumbril**
tumescent [tew-**mess**-ent] *adj* swollen or becoming swollen
tummies *n* ▷ **tummy**
tummy *n* (*pl* **-mies**) (*Informal*) stomach
tumour [**tew**-mer] *n* (*pl* **-s**) abnormal growth in or on the body
tumours *n* ▷ **tumour**
tumuli *n* ▷ **tumulus**
tumult *n* (*pl* **-s**) uproar or commotion > **tumultuous** [tew-**mull**-tew-uss] ▶ *adj*
tumults *n* ▷ **tumult**
tumultuous *adj* ▷ **tumult**
tumulus *n* (*pl* **-li**) burial mound
tun *n* (*pl* **-s**) large beer cask
tuna *n* (*pl* **-s**) large marine food fish
tunas *n* ▷ **tuna**
tundra *n* (*pl* **-s**) vast treeless Arctic region with permanently frozen subsoil
tundras *n* ▷ **tundra**
tune *n* (*pl* **-s**) (pleasing) sequence of musical notes ▶ *v* (**-nes, -ning, -ned**) adjust (a musical instrument) so that it is in tune > **tuneful** *adj* > **tunefully** *adv* > **tuneless** *adj* > **tuner** *n* (*pl* **-s**)
tuned *v* ▷ **tune**

tuneful *adj* ▷ **tune**
tunefully *adv* ▷ **tune**
tuneless *adj* ▷ **tune**
tuner *n* ▷ **tune**
tuners *n* ▷ **tune**
tunes *n, v* ▷ **tune**
tungsten *n* (*pl* **-s**) (CHEM) greyish-white metal
tungstens *n* ▷ **tungsten**
tunic *n* (*pl* **-s**) close-fitting jacket forming part of some uniforms
tunics *n* ▷ **tunic**
tuning *v* ▷ **tune**
tunnel *n* (*pl* **-s**) underground passage ▶ *v* (**-s, -lling, -lled**) make a tunnel (through)
tunnelled *v* ▷ **tunnel**
tunnelling *v* ▷ **tunnel**
tunnels *n, v* ▷ **tunnel**
tunnies *n* ▷ **tunny**
tunny *n* (*pl* **-nies, -ny**) tuna
tuns *n* ▷ **tun**
tup *n* (*pl* **-s**) male sheep
tups *n* ▷ **tup**
turban *n* (*pl* **-s**) Muslim, Hindu, or Sikh man's head covering, made by winding cloth round the head
turbans *n* ▷ **turban**
turbid *adj* muddy, not clear
turbine *n* (*pl* **-s**) machine or generator driven by gas, water, etc. turning blades
turbines *n* ▷ **turbine**
turbot *n* (*pl* **-s**) large European edible flatfish
turbots *n* ▷ **turbot**
turbulence *n* (*pl* **-s**) confusion, movement, or agitation > **turbulent** *adj*
turbulences *n* ▷ **turbulence**
turbulent *adj* ▷ **turbulence**
tureen *n* (*pl* **-s**) serving dish for soup
tureens *n* ▷ **tureen**
turf *n* (*pl* **-s, turves**) short thick even grass ▶ *v* (**-s, -ing, -ed**) cover with turf
turfed *v* ▷ **turf**
turfing *v* ▷ **turf**
turfs *n, v* ▷ **turf**
turgid [tur-jid] *adj* (**-er, -est**) (of language) pompous
turgider *adj* ▷ **turgid**
turgidest *adj* ▷ **turgid**
turkey *n* (*pl* **-s**) large bird bred for food
turkeys *n* ▷ **turkey**
turmeric *n* (*pl* **-s**) yellow spice obtained from the root of an Asian plant
turmerics *n* ▷ **turmeric**
turmoil *n* (*pl* **-s**) agitation or confusion
turmoils *n* ▷ **turmoil**
turn *v* (**-s, -ing, -ed**) change the position or direction (of) ▶ *n* (*pl* **-s**) turning > **turner** *n* (*pl* **-s**)
turncoat *n* (*pl* **-s**) person who deserts one party or cause to join another
turncoats *n* ▷ **turncoat**
turned *v* ▷ **turn**
turner *n* ▷ **turn**
turners *n* ▷ **turn**
turning *n* (*pl* **-s**) road or path leading off a main route ▶ *v* ▷ **turn**
turnings *n* ▷ **turning**
turnip *n* (*pl* **-s**) root vegetable with orange or white flesh
turnips *n* ▷ **turnip**
turnout *n* (*pl* **-s**) number of people appearing at a gathering
turnouts *n* ▷ **turnout**
turnover *n* (*pl* **-s**) total sales made by a business over a certain period
turnovers *n* ▷ **turnover**
turnpike *n* (*pl* **-s**) (BRIT) road where a toll is collected at barriers
turnpikes *n* ▷ **turnpike**
turns *v, n* ▷ **turn**
turnstile *n* (*pl* **-s**) revolving gate for admitting one person at a time
turnstiles *n* ▷ **turnstile**
turntable *n* (*pl* **-s**) revolving platform
turntables *n* ▷ **turntable**
turnup *n* (*pl* **-s**) turned-up fold at the bottom of a trouser leg
turnups *n* ▷ **turnup**
turpentine *n* (*pl* **-s**) (oil made from) the resin of certain trees
turpentines *n* ▷ **turpentine**
turpitude *n* (*pl* **-s**) wickedness
turpitudes *n* ▷ **turpitude**
turps *n* turpentine oil
turquoise *adj* blue-green ▶ *n* (*pl* **-s**) blue-green precious stone
turquoises *n* ▷ **turquoise**
turret *n* (*pl* **-s**) small tower
turrets *n* ▷ **turret**
turtle *n* (*pl* **-s**) sea tortoise
turtledove *n* (*pl* **-s**) small wild dove
turtledoves *n* ▷ **turtledove**
turtleneck *n* (*pl* **-s**) (sweater with) a round high close-fitting neck
turtlenecks *n* ▷ **turtleneck**
turtles *n* ▷ **turtle**
turves *n* ▷ **turf**
tusk *n* (*pl* **-s**) long pointed tooth of an elephant, walrus, etc.
tusks *n* ▷ **tusk**
tussle *n* (*pl* **-s**) ▶ *v* (**-les, -ling, -led**) fight or

scuffle
tussled *v* ▷ **tussle**
tussles *n, v* ▷ **tussle**
tussling *v* ▷ **tussle**
tussock *n* (*pl* **-s**) tuft of grass
tussocks *n* ▷ **tussock**
tutelage [**tew**-till-lij] *n* (*pl* **-s**) instruction or guidance, esp. by a tutor > **tutelary** [**tew**-till-lar-ee] ▶ *adj*
tutelages *n* ▷ **tutelage**
tutelary *adj* ▷ **tutelage**
tutor *n* (*pl* **-s**) person teaching individuals or small groups ▶ *v* (**-s, -ing, -ed**) act as a tutor to
tutored *v* ▷ **tutor**
tutorial *n* (*pl* **-s**) period of instruction with a tutor
tutorials *n* ▷ **tutorial**
tutoring *v* ▷ **tutor**
tutors *n, v* ▷ **tutor**
tutu *n* (*pl* **-s**) short stiff skirt worn by ballerinas
tutus *n* ▷ **tutu**

> **tux** *n* (**tuxes**). Tux is a short form of **tuxedo.** This is a very useful word, as U and T are common tiles, so look for opportunities to play it when you get an X. Tux scores 10 points.

tuxedo *n* (*pl* **-s**) (US & AUST) dinner jacket
tuxedos *n* ▷ **tuxedo**
twaddle *n* (*pl* **-s**) silly or pretentious talk or writing
twaddles *n* ▷ **twaddle**
twain *n* (*pl* **-s**) (*Obs*) two
twains *n* ▷ **twain**
twang *n* (*pl* **-s**) sharp ringing sound ▶ *v* (**-s, -ing, -ed**) (cause to) make a twang
twanged *v* ▷ **twang**
twanging *v* ▷ **twang**
twangs *n, v* ▷ **twang**
tweak *v* (**-s, -ing, -ed**) pinch or twist sharply ▶ *n* (*pl* **-s**) tweaking
tweaked *v* ▷ **tweak**
tweaking *v* ▷ **tweak**
tweaks *v, n* ▷ **tweak**
twee *adj* (*Informal*) (**-r, -st**) too sentimental, sweet, or pretty
tweed *n* (*pl* **-s**) thick woollen cloth > **tweedy** *adj* (**-dier, -diest**)
tweedier *adj* ▷ **tweed**
tweediest *adj* ▷ **tweed**
tweeds *n* ▷ **tweed** ▶ *pl n* suit of tweed
tweedy *adj* ▷ **tweed**
tweer *adj* ▷ **twee**
tweest *adj* ▷ **twee**
tweet *n* (*pl* **-s**) ▶ *v* (**-s, -ing, -ed**) chirp
tweeted *v* ▷ **tweet**
tweeter *n* (*pl* **-s**) loudspeaker reproducing high-frequency sounds
tweeters *n* ▷ **tweeter**
tweeting *v* ▷ **tweet**
tweets *n, v* ▷ **tweet**
tweezers *pl n* small pincer-like tool
twelfth *adj, n* (*pl* **-s**) (of) number twelve in a series
twelfths *n* ▷ **twelfth**
twelve *adj, n* (*pl* **-s**) two more than ten
twelves *n* ▷ **twelve**
twenties *n* ▷ **twenty**
twentieth *adj, n* ▷ **twenty**
twentieths *n* ▷ **twenty**
twenty *adj, n* (*pl* **-ties**) two times ten > **twentieth** *adj, n* (*pl* **-s**)
twerp *n* (*pl* **-s**) (*Informal*) silly person
twerps *n* ▷ **twerp**
twice *adv* two times
twiddle *v* (**-les, -ling, -led**) fiddle or twirl in an idle way
twiddled *v* ▷ **twiddle**
twiddles *v* ▷ **twiddle**
twiddling *v* ▷ **twiddle**
twig[1] *n* (*pl* **-s**) small branch or shoot
twig[2] *v* (**-s, -gging, -gged**) (*Informal*) realize or understand
twigged *v* ▷ **twig**[1]
twigging *v* ▷ **twig**[1]
twigs *n* ▷ **twig**[1] ▶ *v* ▷ **twig**[2]
twilight *n* (*pl* **-s**) soft dim light just after sunset
twilights *n* ▷ **twilight**
twill *n* (*pl* **-s**) fabric woven to produce parallel ridges
twills *n* ▷ **twill**
twin *n* (*pl* **-s**) one of a pair, esp. of two children born at one birth ▶ *v* (**-s, -nning, -nned**) pair or be paired
twine *n* (*pl* **-es**) string or cord ▶ *v* (**-nes, -ning, -ned**) twist or coil round
twined *v* ▷ **twine**
twines *n, v* ▷ **twine**
twining *v* ▷ **twine**
twinge *n* (*pl* **-s**) sudden sharp pain or emotional pang
twinges *n* ▷ **twinge**
twinkle *v* (**-les, -ling, -led**) shine brightly but intermittently ▶ *n* (*pl* **-les**) flickering brightness
twinkled *v* ▷ **twinkle**
twinkles *v, n* ▷ **twinkle**
twinkling *v* ▷ **twinkle**
twinned *v* ▷ **twin**
twinning *v* ▷ **twin**
twins *n, v* ▷ **twin**

twirl *v* (**-s, -ing, -ed**) turn or spin around quickly
twirled *v* ▷ **twirl**
twirling *v* ▷ **twirl**
twirls *v* ▷ **twirl**
twist *v* (**-s, -ing, -ed**) turn out of the natural position ▶ *n* (*pl* **-s**) twisting
twisted *adj* (of a person) cruel or perverted ▶ *v* ▷ **twist**
twister *n* (*pl* **-s**) (BRIT) (*Informal*) swindler
twisters *n* ▷ **twister**
twisting *v* ▷ **twist**
twists *v, n* ▷ **twist**
twit[1] *v* (**-s, -tting, -tted**) poke fun at (someone)
twit[2] *n* (*pl* **-s**) (*Informal*) foolish person
twitch *v* (**-es, -ing, -ed**) move spasmodically ▶ *n* (*pl* **-es**) nervous muscular spasm
twitched *v* ▷ **twitch**
twitches *v, n* ▷ **twitch**
twitching *v* ▷ **twitch**
twits *n* ▷ **twit**[2] ▶ *v* ▷ **twit**[1]
twitted *v* ▷ **twit**[1]
twitter *v* (**-s, -ing, -ed**) (of birds) utter chirping sounds ▶ *n* (*pl* **-s**) act or sound of twittering
twittered *v* ▷ **twitter**
twittering *v* ▷ **twitter**
twitters *v, n* ▷ **twitter**
twitting *v* ▷ **twit**[1]
two *adj, n* (*pl* **-s**) one more than one
twos *n* ▷ **two**

> **twp** *adj*. This is a Welsh word that means stupid or daft. This is a useful word because it contains no vowels, and can thus help when you have an awkward rack. Twp scores 8 points.

tycoon *n* (*pl* **-s**) powerful wealthy businessman
tycoons *n* ▷ **tycoon**

> **tyg** *n* (**tygs**). A tyg is a cup with more than one handle. This word is useful because it uses no vowels, and can thus help when you are short of them. Tyg scores 7 points.

tying *v* ▷ **tie**
tyke *n* (*pl* **-s**) (BRIT, AUST & NZ) (*Informal*) small cheeky child
tykes *n* ▷ **tyke**
type *n* (*pl* **-s**) class or category ▶ *v* (**-pes, -ping, -ped**) print with a typewriter or word processor
typecast *v* (**-s, -ing, -ed**) continually cast (an actor or actress) in similar roles
typecasted *v* ▷ **typecast**
typecasting *v* ▷ **typecast**
typecasts *v* ▷ **typecast**
typed *v* ▷ **type**
types *n, v* ▷ **type**
typewriter *n* (*pl* **-s**) machine which prints a character when the appropriate key is pressed
typewriters *n* ▷ **typewriter**
typing *v* ▷ **type**
typist *n* (*pl* **-s**) person who types with a typewriter or word processor
typists *n* ▷ **typist**
typhoon *n* (*pl* **-s**) violent tropical storm
typhoons *n* ▷ **typhoon**
typhus *n* (*pl* **-uses**) infectious feverish disease
typhuses *n* ▷ **typhus**
typical *adj* true to type, characteristic > **typically** *adv*
typically *adv* ▷ **typical**
typified *v* ▷ **typify**
typifies *v* ▷ **typify**
typify *v* (**-fies, -fying, -fied**) be typical of
typifying *v* ▷ **typify**
typographer *n* ▷ **typography**
typographers *n* ▷ **typography**
typographical *adj* ▷ **typography**
typographies *n* ▷ **typography**
typography *n* (*pl* **-phies**) art or style of printing > **typographical** *adj* > **typographer** *n* (*pl* **-s**)
tyrannical *adj* like a tyrant, oppressive
tyrannies *n* ▷ **tyranny**
tyrannize *v* (**-zes, -zing, -zed**) exert power (over) oppressively or cruelly > **tyrannous** *adj*
tyrannized *v* ▷ **tyrannize**
tyrannizes *v* ▷ **tyrannize**
tyrannizing *v* ▷ **tyrannize**
tyrannosaurus [tirr-ran-oh-**sore**-uss] *n* (*pl* **-es**) large two-footed flesh-eating dinosaur
tyrannosauruses *n* ▷ **tyrannosaurus**
tyrannous *n* ▷ **tyrannize**
tyranny *n* (*pl* **-nies**) tyrannical rule
tyrant *n* (*pl* **-s**) oppressive or cruel ruler
tyrants *n* ▷ **tyrant**
tyre *n* (*pl* **-s**) rubber ring, usu. inflated, over the rim of a vehicle's wheel to grip the road
tyres *n* ▷ **tyre**
tyro *n* (*pl* **-ros**) novice or beginner
tyros *n* ▷ **tyro**

> **tzaddiq** *n* (**tzaddiqim, tzaddiqs**). A tzaddiq is a Hasidic Jewish leader. This is a fantastic word if you can get the necessary tiles. If someone has played add, you might be able to form it around that; if you can form the whole word using all your tiles you'll earn a 50-point bonus. Tzaddiq scores 27 points.

Uu

U can be a difficult tile to use effectively. Although there are quite a few two-letter words beginning with U, most of them are quite unusual, and so difficult to remember. Only **up** (4 points) and **us** (2) are immediately obvious, so it's well worth learning words like **ug** (3), **uh** (5), **um** (4), and **un**, **ur** and **ut** (2 each). Three-letter words beginning with U can also be difficult to remember. If you are trying to use a Q, X or Z, bear in mind that there aren't any valid three-letter words with these letters that start with U. Knowing this can save you valuable time. It's also helpful to remember that there aren't any particularly high-scoring two- or three-letter words starting with U.

ubiquities *n* ▷ **ubiquitous**

ubiquitous [yew-**bik**-wit-uss] *adj* being or seeming to be everywhere at once > **ubiquity** *n* (*pl* **-ties**)

ubiquity *n* ▷ **ubiquitous**

udder *n* (*pl* **-s**) large baglike milk-producing gland of cows, sheep, or goats

udders *n* ▷ **udder**

ug *v* (**ugs, ugging, ugged**). Ug is an old word meaning to loathe. The different verb forms of this word can be useful, and remember that if someone plays ug or its inflections, you can put B, L, M or T in front of it to form another valid word. Ug scores 3 points.

ugh *interj*. Ugh is a sound that people make when they dislike something or are disgusted by it. Together with uke, this is the highest-scoring three-letter word starting with U. Ugh scores 7 points.

uglier *adj* ▷ **ugly**

ugliest *adj* ▷ **ugly**

ugliness *n* ▷ **ugly**

uglinesses *n* ▷ **ugly**

ugly *adj* (**-lier, -liest**) of unpleasant appearance > **ugliness** *n* (*pl* **-es**)

uh *interj*. Uh is a sound that people make when they are unsure about something. This useful little word can help when you are trying to form words in more than one direction. Uh scores 5 points.

uke *n* (**ukes**). Uke is a short form of ukulele. Together with ugh, this is the highest-scoring three-letter word starting with U. Uke scores 7 points.

ukelele *n* ▷ **ukulele**

ukeleles *n* ▷ **ukulele**

ukulele, ukelele [yew-kal-**lay**-lee] *n* (*pl* **-s**) small guitar with four strings

ukuleles *n* ▷ **ukulele**

ulcer *n* (*pl* **-s**) open sore on the surface of the skin or mucous membrane. > **ulceration** *n* (*pl* **-s**)

ulcerated *adj* made or becoming ulcerous

ulceration *n* ▷ **ulcer**

ulcerations *n* ▷ **ulcer**

ulcerous *adj* of, like, or characterized by ulcers

ulcers *n* ▷ **ulcer**

ulna *n* (*pl* **-nae, -nas**) inner and longer of the two bones of the human forearm

ulnae *n* ▷ **ulna**

ulnas *n* ▷ **ulna**

ulterior *adj* (of an aim, reason, etc.) concealed or hidden

ultimate *adj* final in a series or process > **ultimately** *adv*

ultimately *adv* ▷ **ultimate**

ultimatum [ult-im-**may**-tum] *n* (*pl* **-s**) final warning stating that action will be taken unless certain conditions are met

ultimatums *n* ▷ **ultimatum**

ultramarine *adj* vivid blue

ultrasonic *adj* of or producing sound waves with a higher frequency than the human ear can hear

ultraviolet *adj*, *n* (*pl* **-s**) (of) light beyond the limit of visibility at the violet end of the spectrum

ultraviolets *n* ▷ **ultraviolet**

ululate [**yewl**-yew-late] *v* (**-tes, -ting, -ted**) howl

or wail > **ululation** *n* (*pl* **-s**)
ululated *v* ▷ **ululate**
ululates *v* ▷ **ululate**
ululating *v* ▷ **ululate**
ululation *n* ▷ **ululate**
ululations *n* ▷ **ululate**

um *interj*. Um is a sound people make when hesitating in speech. If someone plays this word, remember that lots of words end in UM (dictum, podium and rostrum, for example) and look out for chances to play them. Um scores 4 points.

umber *adj* dark brown to reddish-brown
umbilical *adj* of the navel
umbrella *n* (*pl* **-s**) portable device used for protection against rain, consisting of a folding frame covered in material attached to a central rod
umbrellas *n* ▷ **umbrella**
umpire *n* (*pl* **-s**) official who rules on the playing of a game ▸ *v* (**-res, -ring, -red**) act as umpire in (a game)
umpired *v* ▷ **umpire**
umpires *n*, *v* ▷ **umpire**
umpiring *v* ▷ **umpire**
umpteen *adj* (*Informal*) very many > **umpteenth** *n* (*pl* **-s**) *adj*
umpteenth *n*, *adj* ▷ **umpteen**
umpteenths *n* ▷ **umpteen**

un *pron*. Un is a dialect word for one. If someone plays this, remember that you can form lots of words by placing letters after UN. Un scores 2 points.

unable *adj* lacking the necessary power, ability, or authority to (do something)
unaccountable *adj* unable to be explained > **unaccountably** *adv*
unaccountably *adv* ▷ **unaccountable**
unadulterated *adj* with nothing added, pure
unanimities *n* ▷ **unanimous**
unanimity *n* ▷ **unanimous**
unanimous [yew-**nan**-im-uss] *adj* in complete agreement > **unanimity** *n* (*pl* **-ties**)
unarmed *adj* without weapons
unassuming *adj* modest or unpretentious
unaware *adj* not aware or conscious
unawares *adv* by surprise
unbalanced *adj* biased or one-sided
unbearable *adj* not able to be endured > **unbearably** *adv*
unbearably *adv* ▷ **unbearable**
unbeknown *adv* without the knowledge of (a person)
unbend *v* (**-s, -ing, unbent**) (*Informal*) become less strict or more informal in one's attitudes or behaviour > **unbending** *adj*
unbending *v*, *adj* ▷ **unbend**
unbends *v* ▷ **unbend**
unbent *v* ▷ **unbend**
unbidden *adj* not ordered or asked
unborn *adj* not yet born
unbosom *v* (**-s, -ing, -ed**) relieve (oneself) of (secrets or feelings) by telling someone
unbosomed *v* ▷ **unbosom**
unbosoming *v* ▷ **unbosom**
unbosoms *v* ▷ **unbosom**
unbridled *adj* (of feelings or behaviour) not controlled in any way
unburden *v* (**-s, -ing, -ed**) relieve (one's mind or oneself) of a worry by confiding in someone
unburdened *v* ▷ **unburden**
unburdening *v* ▷ **unburden**
unburdens *v* ▷ **unburden**
uncannier *adj* ▷ **uncanny**
uncanniest *adj* ▷ **uncanny**
uncannily *adv* ▷ **uncanny**
uncanny *adj* (**-nnier, -nniest**) weird or mysterious > **uncannily** *adv*
unceremonious *adj* relaxed and informal > **unceremoniously** *adv*
unceremoniously *adv* ▷ **unceremonious**
uncertain *adj* not able to be accurately known or predicted > **uncertainty** *n* (*pl* **-ties**)
uncertainties *n* ▷ **uncertain**
uncertainty *n* ▷ **uncertain**
uncle *n* (*pl* **-s**) brother of one's father or mother
unclean *adj* lacking moral, spiritual, or physical cleanliness
uncles *n* ▷ **uncle**
uncomfortable *adj* not physically relaxed
uncommon *adj* (**-er, -est**) not happening or encountered often > **uncommonly** *adv*
uncommoner *adj* ▷ **uncommon**
uncommonest *adj* ▷ **uncommon**
uncommonly *adv* ▷ **uncommon**
uncompromising *adj* not prepared to compromise
unconcerned *adj* lacking in concern or involvement > **unconcernedly** *adv*
unconcernedly *adv* ▷ **unconcerned**
unconditional *adj* without conditions or limitations
unconscionable *adj* having no principles, unscrupulous
unconscious *adj* lacking normal awareness through the senses ▸ *n* (*pl* **-es**) part of the mind containing instincts and ideas that exist without one's awareness > **unconsciously** *adv* > **unconsciousness** *n*

(*pl* **-es**)
unconsciouses *n* ▷ **unconscious**
unconsciously *adv* ▷ **unconscious**
unconsciousness *n* ▷ **unconscious**
unconsciousnesses *n* ▷ **unconscious**
uncooperative *adj* not willing to help other people with what they are doing
uncouth *adj* (**-er, -est**) lacking in good manners, refinement, or grace
uncouther *adj* ▷ **uncouth**
uncouthest *adj* ▷ **uncouth**
uncover *v* (**-s, -ing, -ed**) reveal or disclose
uncovered *v* ▷ **uncover**
uncovering *v* ▷ **uncover**
uncovers *v* ▷ **uncover**
unction *n* (*pl* **-s**) act of anointing with oil in sacramental ceremonies
unctions *n* ▷ **unction**
unctuous *adj* pretending to be kind and concerned
undecided *adj* not having made up one's mind
undeniable *adj* unquestionably true > **undeniably** *adv*
undeniably *adv* ▷ **undeniable**
under *prep, adv* indicating movement to or position beneath the underside or base ▶ *prep* less than
underage *adj* below the required or standard age
underarm *adj* (SPORT) denoting a style of throwing, bowling, or serving in which the hand is swung below shoulder level ▶ *adv* (SPORT) in an underarm style
undercarriage *n* (*pl* **-s**) landing gear of an aircraft
undercarriages *n* ▷ **undercarriage**
underclass *n* (*pl* **-es**) class consisting of the most disadvantaged people, such as the long-term unemployed
underclasses *n* ▷ **underclass**
undercoat *n* (*pl* **-s**) coat of paint applied before the final coat
undercoats *n* ▷ **undercoat**
undercover *adj* done or acting in secret
undercurrent *n* (*pl* **-s**) current that is not apparent at the surface
undercurrents *n* ▷ **undercurrent**
undercut *v* (**-cuts, -cutting, -cut**) charge less than (a competitor) to obtain trade
undercuts *v* ▷ **undercut**
undercutting *v* ▷ **undercut**
underdog *n* (*pl* **-s**) person or team in a weak or underprivileged position
underdogs *n* ▷ **underdog**
underdone *adj* not cooked enough
underestimate *v* (**-tes, -ting, -ted**) make too low an estimate of
underestimated *v* ▷ **underestimate**
underestimates *v* ▷ **underestimate**
underestimating *v* ▷ **underestimate**
underfoot *adv* under the feet
undergarment *n* (*pl* **-s**) any piece of underwear
undergarments *n* ▷ **undergarment**
undergo *v* (**-goes, -going, -went, -gone**) experience, endure, or sustain
undergoes *v* ▷ **undergo**
undergoing *v* ▷ **undergo**
undergone *v* ▷ **undergo**
undergraduate *n* (*pl* **-s**) person studying in a university for a first degree
undergraduates *n* ▷ **undergraduate**
underground *adj* occurring, situated, used, or going below ground level ▶ *n* (*pl* **-s**) electric passenger railway operated in underground tunnels
undergrounds *n* ▷ **underground**
undergrowth *n* (*pl* **-s**) small trees and bushes growing beneath taller trees in a wood or forest
undergrowths *n* ▷ **undergrowth**
underhand *adj* sly, deceitful, and secretive
underlain *v* ▷ **underlie**
underlay *v* ▷ **underlie**
underlie *v* (**-lies, -lying, -lay, underlain**) lie or be placed under > **underlying** *adj* fundamental or basic
underlies *v* ▷ **underlie**
underline *v* (**-s, -ning, -d**) draw a line under
underlined *v* ▷ **underline**
underlines *v* ▷ **underline**
underling *n* (*pl* **-s**) subordinate
underlings *n* ▷ **underling**
underlining *v* ▷ **underline**
underlying *v, adj* ▷ **underlie**
undermine *v* (**-nes, -ning, -ned**) weaken gradually
undermined *v* ▷ **undermine**
undermines *v* ▷ **undermine**
undermining *v* ▷ **undermine**
underneath *prep, adv* under or beneath ▶ *adj, n* (*pl* **-s**) lower (part or surface)
underneaths *n* ▷ **underneath**
underpants *pl n* man's undergarment for the lower part of the body
underpass *n* (*pl* **-es**) section of a road that passes under another road or a railway line
underpasses *n* ▷ **underpass**
underpin *v* (**-pins, -pinning, -pinned**) give strength or support to

underpinned *v* ▷ **underpin**
underpinning *v* ▷ **underpin**
underpins *v* ▷ **underpin**
underprivileged *adj* lacking the rights and advantages of other members of society
underrate *v* (**-tes, -ting, -ted**) not realize the full potential of > **underrated** *adj*
underrated *v, adj* ▷ **underrate**
underrates *v* ▷ **underrate**
underrating *v* ▷ **underrate**
underseal *n* (*pl* **-s**) (CHIEFLY BRIT) coating of tar etc. applied to the underside of a motor vehicle to prevent corrosion
underseals *n* ▷ **underseal**
underside *n* (*pl* **-s**) bottom or lower surface
undersides *n* ▷ **underside**
understand *v* (**-s, -ing, -stood**) know and comprehend the nature or meaning of > **understandable** *adj* > **understandably** *adv*
understandable *adj* ▷ **understand**
understandably *adj* ▷ **understand**
understanding *n* (*pl* **-s**) ability to learn, judge, or make decisions ▶ *adj* kind and sympathetic ▶ *v* ▷ **understand**
understandings *n* ▷ **understanding**
understands *v* ▷ **understand**
understate *v* (**-tes, -ting, -ted**) describe or represent (something) in restrained terms > **understatement** *n* (*pl* **-s**)
understated *v* ▷ **understate**
understatement *n* ▷ **understate**
understatements *n* ▷ **understate**
understates *v* ▷ **understate**
understating *v* ▷ **understate**
understood *v* ▷ **understand**
understudied *v* ▷ **understudy**
understudies *n, v* ▷ **understudy**
understudy *n* (*pl* **-dies**) actor who studies a part in order to be able to replace the usual actor if necessary ▶ *v* (**-dies, -dying, -died**) act as an understudy for
understudying *v* ▷ **understudy**
undertake *v* (**-takes, -taking, -took, -taken**) agree or commit oneself to (something) or to do (something)
undertaken *v* ▷ **undertake**
undertaker *n* (*pl* **-s**) person whose job is to prepare corpses for burial or cremation and organize funerals
undertakers *n* ▷ **undertaker**
undertakes *v* ▷ **undertake**
undertaking *n* (*pl* **-s**) task or enterprise ▶ *v* ▷ **undertake**
undertakings *n* ▷ **undertaking**
undertone *n* (*pl* **-s**) quiet tone of voice
undertones *n* ▷ **undertone**
undertook *v* ▷ **undertake**
undertow *n* (*pl* **-s**) strong undercurrent flowing in a different direction from the surface current
undertows *n* ▷ **undertow**
underwear *n* (*pl* **-s**) clothing worn under the outer garments and next to the skin
underwears *n* ▷ **underwear**
underwent *v* ▷ **undergo**
underworld *n* (*pl* **-s**) criminals and their associates
underworlds *n* ▷ **underworld**
underwrite *v* (**-writes, -writing, -wrote, -written**) accept financial responsibility for (a commercial project)
underwriter *n* (*pl* **-s**) person who underwrites (esp. an insurance policy)
underwriters *n* ▷ **underwriter**
underwrites *v* ▷ **underwrite**
underwriting *v* ▷ **underwrite**
underwritten *v* ▷ **underwrite**
underwrote *v* ▷ **underwrite**
undesirable *adj* not desirable or pleasant, objectionable ▶ *n* (*pl* **-s**) objectionable person
undesirables *n* ▷ **undesirable**
undid *v* ▷ **undo**
undo *v* (**-does, -doing, -did, -done**) open, unwrap > **undone** *adj*
undoes *v* ▷ **undo**
undoing *n* (*pl* **-s**) cause of someone's downfall ▶ *v* ▷ **undo**
undoings *n* ▷ **undoing**
undone *v, adj* ▷ **undo**
undoubted *adj* certain or indisputable > **undoubtedly** *adv*
undoubtedly *adv* ▷ **undoubted**
undue *adj* greater than is reasonable, excessive > **unduly** *adv*
undulate *v* (**-tes, -ting, -ted**) move in waves > **undulation** *n* (*pl* **-s**)
undulated *v* ▷ **undulate**
undulates *v* ▷ **undulate**
undulating *v* ▷ **undulate**
undulation *n* ▷ **undulate**
undulations *n* ▷ **undulate**
unduly *adv* ▷ **undue**
undying *adj* never ending, eternal
unearth *v* (**-s, -ing, -ed**) reveal or discover by searching
unearthed *v* ▷ **unearth**
unearthing *v* ▷ **unearth**
unearthly *adj* ghostly or eerie
unearths *v* ▷ **unearth**
unease *n* (*pl* **-s**) feeling of anxiety

uneases *n* ▷ **unease**
uneasier *adj* ▷ **uneasy**
uneasiest *adj* ▷ **uneasy**
uneasily *adv* ▷ **uneasy**
uneasiness *n* ▷ **uneasy**
uneasinesses *n* ▷ **uneasy**
uneasy *adj* **(-sier, -siest)** (of a person) anxious or apprehensive > **uneasily** *adv* > **uneasiness** *n* (*pl* **-es**)
unemployed *adj* out of work > **unemployment** *n* (*pl* **-s**)
unemployment *n* ▷ **unemployed**
unemployments *n* ▷ **unemployed**
unequivocal *adj* completely clear in meaning > **unequivocally** *adv*
unequivocally *adv* ▷ **unequivocal**
unerring *adj* never mistaken, consistently accurate
unexceptionable *adj* beyond criticism or objection
unfailing *adj* continuous or reliable > **unfailingly** *adv*
unfailingly *adv* ▷ **unfailing**
unfair *adj* **(-er, -est)** not right, fair, or just > **unfairly** *adv* > **unfairness** *n* (*pl* **-es**)
unfairer *adj* ▷ **unfair**
unfairest *adj* ▷ **unfair**
unfairly *adv* ▷ **unfair**
unfairness *n* ▷ **unfair**
unfairnesses *n* ▷ **unfair**
unfaithful *adj* having sex with someone other than one's regular partner > **unfaithfulness** *n* (*pl* **-es**)
unfaithfulness *n* ▷ **unfaithful**
unfaithfulnesses *n* ▷ **unfaithful**
unfeeling *adj* without sympathy
unfit *adj* unqualified or unsuitable
unflappabilities *n* ▷ **unflappable**
unflappability *n* ▷ **unflappable**
unflappable *adj* (*Informal*) not easily upset > **unflappability** *n* (*pl* **-ties**)
unfold *v* **(-s, -ing, -ed)** open or spread out from a folded state
unfolded *v* ▷ **unfold**
unfolding *v* ▷ **unfold**
unfolds *v* ▷ **unfold**
unforgettable *adj* impossible to forget, memorable
unfortunate *adj* unlucky, unsuccessful, or unhappy > **unfortunately** *adv*
unfortunately *adv* ▷ **unfortunate**
unfrock *v* **(-s, -ing, -ed)** deprive (a priest in holy orders) of his or her priesthood
unfrocked *v* ▷ **unfrock**
unfrocking *v* ▷ **unfrock**
unfrocks *v* ▷ **unfrock**
ungainlier *adj* ▷ **ungainly**
ungainliest *adj* ▷ **ungainly**
ungainly *adj* **(-lier, -liest)** lacking grace when moving
ungodlier *adj* ▷ **ungodly**
ungodliest *adj* ▷ **ungodly**
ungodly *adj* **(-lier, -liest)** (*Informal*) unreasonable or outrageous
ungrateful *adj* not grateful or thankful
unguarded *adj* not protected
unguent [ung-gwent] *n* (*pl* **-s**) (*Lit*) ointment
unguents *n* ▷ **unguent**
unhand *v* **(-s, -ing, -ed)** (*Old-fashioned or lit*) release from one's grasp
unhanded *v* ▷ **unhand**
unhanding *v* ▷ **unhand**
unhands *v* ▷ **unhand**
unhappier *adj* ▷ **unhappy**
unhappiest *adj* ▷ **unhappy**
unhappily *adv* ▷ **unhappy**
unhappiness *n* ▷ **unhappy**
unhappinesses *n* ▷ **unhappy**
unhappy *adj* **(-ppier, -ppiest)** sad or depressed > **unhappily** *adv* > **unhappiness** *n* (*pl* **-es**)
unhealthier *adj* ▷ **unhealthy**
unhealthiest *adj* ▷ **unhealthy**
unhealthy *adj* **(-thier, -thiest)** likely to cause poor health
unhinge *v* **(-ges, -ging, -ged)** derange or unbalance (a person or his or her mind)
unhinged *v* ▷ **unhinge**
unhinges *v* ▷ **unhinge**
unhinging *v* ▷ **unhinge**
unicorn *n* (*pl* **-s**) imaginary horselike creature with one horn growing from its forehead
unicorns *n* ▷ **unicorn**
unification *n* ▷ **unify**
unifications *n* ▷ **unify**
unified *v* ▷ **unify**
unifies *v* ▷ **unify**
uniform *n* (*pl* **-s**) special identifying set of clothes for the members of an organization, such as soldiers ▶ *adj* regular and even throughout, unvarying > **uniformly** *adv* > **uniformity** *n* (*pl* **-ties**)
uniformities *n* ▷ **uniform**
uniformity *n* ▷ **uniform**
uniformly *adv* ▷ **uniform**
uniforms *n* ▷ **uniform**
unify *v* **(-fies, -fying, -fied)** make or become one > **unification** *n* (*pl* **-s**)
unifying *v* ▷ **unify**
unilateral *adj* made or done by only one person or group > **unilaterally** *adv*

unilaterally *adv* ▷ **unilateral**
unimpeachable *adj* completely honest and reliable
uninterested *adj* having or showing no interest in someone or something
union *n* (*pl* **-s**) uniting or being united
unionist *n* (*pl* **-s**) member or supporter of a trade union
unionists *n* ▷ **unionist**
unionization *n* ▷ **unionize**
unionizations *n* ▷ **unionize**
unionize *v* (**-zes, -zing, -zed**) organize (workers) into a trade union > **unionization** *n* (*pl* **-s**)
unionized *v* ▷ **unionize**
unionizes *v* ▷ **unionize**
unionizing *v* ▷ **unionize**
unions *n* ▷ **union**
unique [yoo-**neek**] *adj* being the only one of a particular type > **uniquely** *adv*
uniquely *adv* ▷ **unique**
unisex *adj* designed for use by both sexes
unison *n* (*pl* **-s**) complete agreement
unisons *n* ▷ **unison**
unit *n* (*pl* **-s**) single undivided entity or whole
unitary *adj* consisting of a single undivided whole
unite *v* (**-tes, -ting, -ted**) make or become an integrated whole
united *v* ▷ **unite**
unites *v* ▷ **unite**
unities *n* ▷ **unity**
uniting *v* ▷ **unite**
units *n* ▷ **unit**
unity *n* (*pl* **-ties**) state of being one
universal *adj* of or typical of the whole of mankind or of nature > **universally** *adv* > **universality** *n* (*pl* **-ties**)
universalities *n* ▷ **universal**
universality *n* ▷ **universal**
universally *adv* ▷ **universal**
universe *n* (*pl* **-s**) whole of all existing matter, energy, and space
universes *n* ▷ **universe**
universities *n* ▷ **university**
university *n* (*pl* **-ties**) institution of higher education with the authority to award degrees
unkempt *adj* (of the hair) not combed
unknown *adj* not known ▶ *n* (*pl* **-s**) unknown person, quantity, or thing
unknowns *n* ▷ **unknown**
unleaded *adj* (of petrol) containing less tetraethyl lead, in order to reduce environmental pollution
unless *conj* except under the circumstances that
unlike *adj* dissimilar or different ▶ *prep* not like or typical of
unlikely *adj* improbable
unload *v* (**-s, -ing, -ed**) remove (cargo) from (a ship, truck, or plane)
unloaded *v* ▷ **unload**
unloading *v* ▷ **unload**
unloads *v* ▷ **unload**
unmask *v* (**-s, -ing, -ed**) remove the mask or disguise from
unmasked *v* ▷ **unmask**
unmasking *v* ▷ **unmask**
unmasks *v* ▷ **unmask**
unmentionable *adj* unsuitable as a topic of conversation
unmistakable, unmistakeable *adj* not ambiguous, clear > **unmistakably, unmistakeably** *adv*
unmistakably *adv* ▷ **unmistakable**
unmistakeable *adj* ▷ **unmistakable**
unmistakeably *adv* ▷ **unmistakable**
unmitigated *adj* not reduced or lessened in severity etc.
unmoved *adj* not affected by emotion, indifferent
unnatural *adj* strange and frightening because not usual
unnerve *v* (**-ves, -ving, -ved**) cause to lose courage, confidence, or self-control
unnerved *v* ▷ **unnerve**
unnerves *v* ▷ **unnerve**
unnerving *v* ▷ **unnerve**
unnumbered *adj* countless
unorthodox *adj* (of ideas, methods, etc.) unconventional and not generally accepted
unpack *v* (**-s, -ing, -ed**) remove the contents of (a suitcase, trunk, etc.)
unpacked *v* ▷ **unpack**
unpacking *v* ▷ **unpack**
unpacks *v* ▷ **unpack**
unparalleled *adj* not equalled, supreme
unpick *v* (**-s, -ing, -ed**) undo (the stitches) of (a piece of sewing)
unpicked *v* ▷ **unpick**
unpicking *v* ▷ **unpick**
unpicks *v* ▷ **unpick**
unpleasant *adj* not pleasant or agreeable > **unpleasantly** *adv* > **unpleasantness** *n* (*pl* **-s**)
unpleasantly *adv* ▷ **unpleasant**
unpleasantness *n* ▷ **unpleasant**
unpleasantnesses *n* ▷ **unpleasant**
unprintable *adj* unsuitable for printing for reasons of obscenity or libel

unprofessional *adj* contrary to the accepted code of a profession > **unprofessionally** *adv*
unprofessionally *adv* ▷ **unprofessional**
unqualified *adj* lacking the necessary qualifications
unravel *v* (**-vels, -velling, -velled**) reduce (something knitted or woven) to separate strands
unravelled *v* ▷ **unravel**
unravelling *v* ▷ **unravel**
unravels *v* ▷ **unravel**
unremitting *adj* never slackening or stopping
unrequited *adj* not returned
unrest *n* (*pl* **-s**) rebellious state of discontent
unrests *n* ▷ **unrest**
unrivalled *adj* having no equal
unroll *v* (**-s, -ing, -ed**) open out or unwind (something rolled or coiled) or (of something rolled or coiled) become opened out or unwound
unrolled *v* ▷ **unroll**
unrolling *v* ▷ **unroll**
unrolls *v* ▷ **unroll**
unrulier *adj* ▷ **unruly**
unruliest *adj* ▷ **unruly**
unruly *adj* (**-lier, -liest**) difficult to control or organize
unsavoury *adj* distasteful or objectionable
unscathed *adj* not harmed or injured
unscrupulous *adj* prepared to act dishonestly, unprincipled
unseat *v* (**-s, -ing, -ed**) throw or displace from a seat or saddle
unseated *v* ▷ **unseat**
unseating *v* ▷ **unseat**
unseats *v* ▷ **unseat**
unsettled *adj* lacking order or stability
unsightlier *adj* ▷ **unsightly**
unsightliest *adj* ▷ **unsightly**
unsightly *adj* (**-lier, -liest**) unpleasant to look at
unsociable *adj* ▷ **unsocial**
unsocial *adj* (*also* **unsociable**) avoiding the company of other people
unsound *adj* unhealthy or unstable
unstable *adj* (**-r, -st**) lacking stability or firmness
unstabler *adj* ▷ **unstable**
unstablest *adj* ▷ **unstable**
unsuitable *adj* not right or appropriate for a particular purpose > **unsuitably** *adv*
unsuitably *adv* ▷ **unsuitable**
unsuited *adj* not appropriate for a particular task or situation
unswerving *adj* firm, constant, not changing
unthinkable *adj* out of the question, inconceivable
untidier *adj* ▷ **untidy**
untidiest *adj* ▷ **untidy**
untidily *adv* ▷ **untidy**
untidiness *n* ▷ **untidy**
untidinesses *n* ▷ **untidy**
untidy *adj* (**-dier, -diest**) messy and disordered > **untidily** *adv* > **untidiness** *n* (*pl* **-es**)
untie *v* (**-ties, -tying, -tied**) open or free (something that is tied)
untied *v* ▷ **untie**
unties *v* ▷ **untie**
until *conj* up to the time that ▶ *prep* in or throughout the period before
untimelier *adj* ▷ **untimely**
untimeliest *adj* ▷ **untimely**
untimely *adj* (**-lier, -liest**) occurring before the expected or normal time
unto *prep* (*Old-fashioned*) to
untold *adj* incapable of description
untouchable *adj* above reproach or suspicion ▶ *n* (*pl* **-s**) member of the lowest Hindu caste in India
untouchables *n* ▷ **untouchable**
untoward *adj* causing misfortune or annoyance
untrue *adj* (**-r, -st**) incorrect or false
untruer *adj* ▷ **untrue**
untruest *adj* ▷ **untrue**
untruth *n* (*pl* **-s**) statement that is not true, lie
untruths *n* ▷ **untruth**
untying *v* ▷ **untie**
unusual *adj* uncommon or extraordinary > **unusually** *adv*
unusually *adv* ▷ **unusual**
unutterable *adj* incapable of being expressed in words > **unutterably** *adv*
unutterably *adv* ▷ **unutterable**
unvarnished *adj* not elaborated upon
unwieldier *adj* ▷ **unwieldy**
unwieldiest *adj* ▷ **unwieldy**
unwieldy *adj* (**-dier, -diest**) too heavy, large, or awkward to be easily handled
unwind *v* (**-s, -ing, unwound**) relax after a busy or tense time
unwinding *v* ▷ **unwind**
unwinds *v* ▷ **unwind**
unwitting *adj* not intentional > **unwittingly** *adv*
unwittingly *adv* ▷ **unwitting**
unwonted *adj* out of the ordinary
unworthier *adj* ▷ **unworthy**
unworthiest *adj* ▷ **unworthy**
unworthy *adj* (**-thier, -thiest**) not deserving

or worthy
unwound *v* ▷ **unwind**
unwrap *v* (**-s, -pping, -pped**) remove the wrapping from (something)
unwrapped *v* ▷ **unwrap**
unwrapping *v* ▷ **unwrap**
unwraps *v* ▷ **unwrap**
unwritten *adj* not printed or in writing
up *prep, adv* indicating movement to or position at a higher place ▸ *adv* indicating readiness, intensity or completeness, etc. ▸ *adj* of a high or higher position ▸ *v* (**-s, -pping, -pped**) increase or raise ▸ *adv* (*also* **upwards**) from a lower to a higher place, level, or condition
upbeat *adj* (*Informal*) cheerful and optimistic ▸ *n* (*pl* **-s**) (MUSIC) unaccented beat
upbeats *n* ▷ **upbeat**
upbraid *v* (**-s, -ing, -ded**) scold or reproach
upbraided *v* ▷ **upbraid**
upbraiding *v* ▷ **upbraid**
upbraids *v* ▷ **upbraid**
upbringing *n* (*pl* **-s**) education of a person during the formative years
upbringings *n* ▷ **upbringing**
update *v* (**-tes, -ting, -ted**) bring up to date
updated *v* ▷ **update**
updates *v* ▷ **update**
updating *v* ▷ **update**
upend *v* (**-s, -ing, -ed**) turn or set (something) on its end
upended *v* ▷ **upend**
upending *v* ▷ **upend**
upends *v* ▷ **upend**
upfront *adj* open and frank ▸ *adv, adj* (of money) paid out at the beginning of a business arrangement
upgrade *v* (**-des, -ding, -ded**) promote (a person or job) to a higher rank
upgraded *v* ▷ **upgrade**
upgrades *v* ▷ **upgrade**
upgrading *v* ▷ **upgrade**
upheaval *n* (*pl* **-s**) strong, sudden, or violent disturbance
upheavals *n* ▷ **upheaval**
upheld *v* ▷ **uphold**
uphill *adj* sloping or leading upwards ▸ *adv* up a slope ▸ *n* (*pl* **-s**) (S AFR) difficulty
uphills *n* ▷ **uphill**
uphold *v* (**-s, -ing, upheld**) maintain or defend against opposition > **upholder** *n* (*pl* **-s**)
upholder *n* ▷ **uphold**
upholders *n* ▷ **uphold**
upholding *v* ▷ **uphold**
upholds *v* ▷ **uphold**
upholster *v* (**-s, -ing, -ed**) fit (a chair or sofa) with padding, springs, and covering > **upholsterer** *n* (*pl* **-s**)
upholstered *v* ▷ **upholster**
upholsterer *n* ▷ **upholster**
upholsterers *n* ▷ **upholster**
upholsteries *n* ▷ **upholstery**
upholstering *v* ▷ **upholster**
upholsters *v* ▷ **upholster**
upholstery *n* (*pl* **-ries**) soft covering on a chair or sofa
upkeep *n* (*pl* **-s**) act, process, or cost of keeping something in good repair
upkeeps *n* ▷ **upkeep**
upland *adj* of or in an area of high or relatively high ground > **uplands** *pl n* area of high or relatively high ground
uplands *pl n* ▷ **upland**
uplift *v* (**-s, -ing, -ed**) raise or lift up ▸ *n* (*pl* **-s**) act or process of improving moral, social, or cultural conditions > **uplifting** *adj*
uplifted *v* ▷ **uplift**
uplifting *v, adj* ▷ **uplift**
uplifts *v, n* ▷ **uplift**
upload *v* (**-s, -ing, -ed**) transfer (data or a program) from one's own computer into the memory of another computer
uploaded *v* ▷ **upload**
uploading *v* ▷ **upload**
uploads *v* ▷ **upload**
upon *prep* on
upped *v* ▷ **up**
upper *adj* higher or highest in physical position, wealth, rank, or status ▸ *n* (*pl* **-s**) part of a shoe above the sole
uppermost *adj* highest in position, power, or importance ▸ *adv* in or into the highest place or position
uppers *n* ▷ **upper**
upping *v* ▷ **up**
uppish, uppity *adj* (BRIT) (*Informal*) snobbish, arrogant, or presumptuous
uppity *adj* ▷ **uppish**
upright *adj* vertical or erect ▸ *adv* vertically or in an erect position ▸ *n* (*pl* **-s**) vertical support, such as a post > **uprightness** *n* (*pl* **-s**)
uprightness *n* ▷ **upright**
uprightnesses *n* ▷ **upright**
uprights *n* ▷ **upright**
uprising *n* (*pl* **-s**) rebellion or revolt
uprisings *n* ▷ **uprising**
uproar *n* (*pl* **-s**) disturbance characterized by loud noise and confusion
uproarious *adj* very funny > **uproariously** *adv*
uproariously *adv* ▷ **uproarious**

uproars *n* ▷ **uproar**
uproot *v* (**-s, -ing, -ed**) pull up by or as if by the roots
uprooted *v* ▷ **uproot**
uprooting *v* ▷ **uproot**
uproots *v* ▷ **uproot**
ups *v* ▷ **up**
upset *adj* emotionally or physically disturbed or distressed ▶ *v* (**-s, -tting, upset**) tip over ▶ *n* (*pl* **-s**) unexpected defeat or reversal > **upsetting** *adj*
upsets *v, n* ▷ **upset**
upsetting *v, adj* ▷ **upset**
upshot *n* (*pl* **-s**) final result or conclusion
upshots *n* ▷ **upshot**
upstage *adj* at the back half of the stage ▶ *v* (**-ges, -ging, -ged**) (*Informal*) draw attention to oneself from (someone else)
upstaged *v* ▷ **upstage**
upstages *v* ▷ **upstage**
upstaging *v* ▷ **upstage**
upstairs *adv* to or on an upper floor of a building ▶ *n* upper floor
upstanding *adj* of good character
upstart *n* (*pl* **-s**) person who has risen suddenly to a position of power and behaves arrogantly
upstarts *n* ▷ **upstart**
upstream *adv, adj* in or towards the higher part of a stream
upsurge *n* (*pl* **-s**) rapid rise or swell
upsurges *n* ▷ **upsurge**
uptake *n* (*pl* **-s**) (*Informal*) quick *or* slow to understand or learn
uptakes *n* ▷ **uptake**
uptight *adj* (*Informal*) nervously tense, irritable, or angry
upturn *n* (*pl* **-s**) upward trend or improvement > **upturned** *adj* facing upwards
upturned *adj* ▷ **upturn**
upturns *n* ▷ **upturn**
upward *adj* directed or moving towards a higher place or level
upwards *adv* ▷ **up**

> **ur** *interj*. Ur is a sound people make when hesitating in speech. If someone plays this, you may be able to use it to form words that begin with UR. Ur is also handy for connecting words beginning with U to those ending in R. Ur scores 2 points.

uranium *n* (*pl* **-s**) (CHEM) radioactive silvery-white metallic element, used chiefly as a source of nuclear energy
uraniums *n* ▷ **uranium**
urban *adj* of or living in a city or town
urbane *adj* (**-r, -st**) characterized by courtesy, elegance, and sophistication > **urbanity** *n* (*pl* **-ties**)
urbaner *adj* ▷ **urbane**
urbanest *adj* ▷ **urbane**
urbanities *n* ▷ **urbane**
urbanity *n* ▷ **urbane**
urbanization *n* ▷ **urbanize**
urbanizations *n* ▷ **urbanize**
urbanize *v* (**-zes, -zing, -zed**) make (a rural area) more industrialized and urban > **urbanization** *n* (*pl* **-s**)
urbanized *v* ▷ **urbanize**
urbanizes *v* ▷ **urbanize**
urbanizing *v* ▷ **urbanize**
urchin *n* (*pl* **-s**) mischievous child
urchins *n* ▷ **urchin**
urethra [yew-**reeth**-ra] *n* (*pl* **-rae**) canal that carries urine from the bladder out of the body
urethrae *n* ▷ **urethra**
urge *n* (*pl* **-s**) strong impulse, inner drive, or yearning ▶ *v* (**-urges, -urging, -urged**) plead with or press (a person to do something)
urged *v* ▷ **urge**
urgencies *n* ▷ **urgent**
urgency *n* ▷ **urgent**
urgent *adj* requiring speedy action or attention > **urgency** *n* (*pl* **-cies**) > **urgently** *adv*
urgently *adv* ▷ **urgent**
urges *n, v* ▷ **urge**
urging *v* ▷ **urge**
urinal *n* (*pl* **-s**) sanitary fitting used by men for urination
urinals *n* ▷ **urine**
urinary *adj* ▷ **urine**
urinate *v* (**-tes, -ting, -ted**) discharge urine > **urination** *n* (*pl* **-s**)
urinated *v* ▷ **urinate**
urinates *v* ▷ **urinate**
urinating *v* ▷ **urinate**
urination *n* ▷ **urinate**
urinations *n* ▷ **urinate**
urine *n* (*pl* **-s**) pale yellow fluid excreted by the kidneys to the bladder and passed as waste from the body > **urinary** *adj*
urines *n* ▷ **urine**
urn *n* (*pl* **-s**) vase used as a container for the ashes of the dead
urns *n* ▷ **urn**
ursine *adj* of or like a bear
us *pron* ▷ **we**
usable *adj* able to be used
usage *n* (*pl* **-s**) regular or constant use
usages *n* ▷ **usage**

use *v* (**-ses, -sing, -sed**) put into service or action ▶ *n* (*pl* **-s**) using or being used > **user** *n* (*pl* **-s**) > **useful** *adj* > **usefully** *adv* > **usefulness** *n* (*pl* **-es**) > **useless** *adj* > **uselessly** *adv* > **uselessness** *n* (*pl* **-es**)
used *adj* second-hand ▶ *v* ▷ **use**
useful *adj* ▷ **use**
usefully *adv* ▷ **use**
usefulness *n* ▷ **use**
usefulnesses *n* ▷ **use**
useless *adj* ▷ **use**
uselessly *adv* ▷ **use**
uselessness *n* ▷ **use**
uselessnesses *n* ▷ **use**
user *n* ▷ **use**
username *n* (*pl* **-s**) (COMPUTERS) name entered into a computer for identification purposes
usernames *n* ▷ **username**
users *n* ▷ **use**
uses *v, n* ▷ **use**
usher *n* (*pl* **-s**) official who shows people to their seats, as in a church ▶ *v* (**-s, -ing, -ed**) conduct or escort
ushered *v* ▷ **usher**
usherette *n* (*pl* **-s**) female assistant in a cinema who shows people to their seats
usherettes *n* ▷ **usherette**
ushering *v* ▷ **usher**
ushers *n, v* ▷ **usher**
using *v* ▷ **use**
usual *adj* of the most normal, frequent, or regular type
usually *adv* most often, in most cases
usurer *n* ▷ **usury**
usurers *n* ▷ **usury**
usuries *n* ▷ **usury**
usurp [yewz-**zurp**] *v* (**-s, -ing, -ed**) seize (a position or power) without authority > **usurpation** *n* (*pl* **-s**) > **usurper** *n* (*pl* **-s**)
usurpation *n* ▷ **usurp**
usurpations *n* ▷ **usurp**
usurped *v* ▷ **usurp**
usurper *n* ▷ **usurp**
usurpers *n* ▷ **usurp**
usurping *v* ▷ **usurp**
usurps *v* ▷ **usurp**
usury *n* (*pl* **-ries**) practice of lending money at an extremely high rate of interest > **usurer** [**yewz**-yoor-er] ▶ *n* (*pl* **-s**)

> **ut** *n* (**uts**). Ut is a musical note. This unusual word is useful for connecting words beginning with U to those ending with T. Ut scores 2 points.

ute [yoot] *n* (*pl* **-s**) (AUST & NZ) (*Informal*) utility truck
utensil *n* (*pl* **-s**) tool or container for practical use
utensils *n* ▷ **utensil**
uteri *n* ▷ **uterus**
uterine *adj* ▷ **uterus**
uterus [**yew**-ter-russ] *n* (*pl* **uteri**) womb > **uterine** *adj*
utes *n* ▷ **ute**
utilitarian *adj* useful rather than beautiful
utilitarianism *n* (*pl* **-s**) (ETHICS) doctrine that the right action is the one that brings about the greatest good for the greatest number of people
utilitarianisms *n* ▷ **utilitarianism**
utilities *n* ▷ **utility**
utility *n* (*pl* **-ties**) usefulness ▶ *adj* designed for use rather than beauty
utilization *n* ▷ **utilize**
utilizations *n* ▷ **utilize**
utilize *v* (**-zes, -zing, -zed**) make practical use of > **utilization** *n* (*pl* **-s**)
utilized *v* ▷ **utilize**
utilizes *v* ▷ **utilize**
utilizing *v* ▷ **utilize**
utmost, uttermost *adj, n* (*pl* **-s**) (of) the greatest possible degree or amount
utmosts *n* ▷ **utmost**
utopia [yew-**tope**-ee-a] *n* (*pl* **-s**) any real or imaginary society, place, or state considered to be perfect or ideal > **utopian** *adj*
utopian *adj* ▷ **utopia**
utopias *n* ▷ **utopia**
utter[1] *v* (**-s, -ing, -ed**) express (something) in sounds or words
utter[2] *adj* total or absolute > **utterly** *adv*
utterance *n* (*pl* **-s**) something uttered
utterances *n* ▷ **utterance**
uttered *v* ▷ **utter**[1]
uttering *v* ▷ **utter**[1]
utterly *adv* ▷ **utter**[2]
uttermost *adj, n* (*pl* **-s**) ▷ **utmost**
uttermosts *n* ▷ **uttermost**
utters *v* ▷ **utter**[1]
uvula [**yew**-view-la] *n* (*pl* **-s**) small fleshy part of the soft palate that hangs in the back of the throat > **uvular** *adj*
uvular *adj* ▷ **uvula**
uvulas *n* ▷ **uvula**
uxorious [ux-**or**-ee-uss] *adj* excessively fond of or dependent on one's wife

Vv

If you have a V on your rack, the first thing to remember is that there are no valid two-letter words beginning with V. In fact, there are no two-letter words that end in V either, so you can't form any two-letter words using V. Remembering this will stop you wasting time trying to think of some. While V is useless for two-letter words, it does start some good three-letter words. **Vex** and **vox** (13 points each) are the best of these, while **vaw, vow** and **vly** (9 each) are also useful.

vac *n* (**vacs**). Vac is a short form of vacuum cleaner. This word can prove useful when you have a V but not much space to play it in. Remember that if you have the letters for vac, you might be able to form **cave** using an E that is already on the board. Vac scores 8 points.

vacancies *n* ▷ **vacancy**

vacancy *n* (*pl* **-cies**) unfilled job

vacant *adj* (of a toilet, room, etc.) unoccupied > **vacantly** *adv*

vacantly *adv* ▷ **vacant**

vacate *v* (**-tes, -ting, -ted**) cause (something) to be empty by leaving

vacated *v* ▷ **vacate**

vacates *v* ▷ **vacate**

vacating *v* ▷ **vacate**

vacation *n* time when universities and law courts are closed

vacations *n* ▷ **vacation**

vaccinate *v* (**-tes, -ting, -ted**) inject with a vaccine > **vaccination** *n* (*pl* **-s**)

vaccinated *v* ▷ **vaccinate**

vaccinates *v* ▷ **vaccinate**

vaccinating *v* ▷ **vaccinate**

vaccination *n* ▷ **vaccinate**

vaccinations *n* ▷ **vaccinate**

vaccine *n* (*pl* **-s**) substance designed to cause a mild form of a disease to make a person immune to the disease itself

vaccines *n* ▷ **vaccine**

vacillate [vass-ill-late] *v* (**-tes, -ting, -ted**) keep changing one's mind or opinions > **vacillation** *n* (*pl* **-s**)

vacillated *v* ▷ **vacillate**

vacillates *v* ▷ **vacillate**

vacillating *v* ▷ **vacillate**

vacillation *n* ▷ **vacillate**

vacillations *n* ▷ **vacillate**

vacua *n* ▷ **vacuum**

vacuous *adj* not expressing intelligent thought > **vacuity** *n* (*pl* **-ties**)

vacuum *n* (*pl* **-cuums, -cua**) empty space from which all or most air or gas has been removed ▶ *v* (**-s, -ing, -ed**) clean with a vacuum cleaner

vacuumed *v* ▷ **vacuum**

vacuuming *v* ▷ **vacuum**

vacuums *n* ▷ **vacuum**

vagabond *n* (*pl* **-s**) person with no fixed home, esp. a beggar

vagabonds *n* ▷ **vagabond**

vagaries *n* ▷ **vagary**

vagary [vaig-a-ree] *n* (*pl* **-ries**) unpredictable change

vagina [vaj-jine-a] *n* (*pl* **-s**) (in female mammals) passage from the womb to the external genitals > **vaginal** *adj*

vaginal *adj* ▷ **vagina**

vaginas *n* ▷ **vagina**

vagrancies *n* ▷ **vagrancy**

vagrancy *n* ▷ **vagrant**

vagrant [vaig-rant] *n* (*pl* **-s**) person with no settled home ▶ *adj* wandering > **vagrancy** *n* (*pl* **-cies**)

vagrants *n* ▷ **vagrant**

vague *adj* (**-guer, -guest**) not clearly explained > **vaguely** *adv*

vaguely *adv* ▷ **vague**

vaguer *adj* ▷ **vague**

vaguest *adj* ▷ **vague**

vain *adj* (**-er, -est**) excessively proud, esp. of one's appearance

vainer *adj* ▷ **vain**

vainest *adj* ▷ **vain**

vainglorious *adj* (*Lit*) boastful

valance [**val**-lenss] *n* (*pl* **-s**) piece of drapery round the edge of a bed
valances *n* ▷ **valance**
vale *n* (*pl* **-s**) (*Lit*) valley
valediction *n* (*pl* **-s**) farewell speech
valedictions *n* ▷ **valediction**
valedictory [val-lid-**dik**-tree] *adj* (of a speech, performance, etc.) intended as a farewell
valence [**vale**-ence] *n* (*pl* **-s**) molecular bonding between atoms
valences *n* ▷ **valence**
valencies *n* ▷ **valency**
valency *n* (*pl* **-cies**) power of an atom to make molecular bonds
valentine *n* (*pl* **-s**) (person to whom one sends) a romantic card on Saint Valentine's Day, 14th February
valentines *n* ▷ **valentine**
valerian *n* (*pl* **-s**) herb used as a sedative
valerians *n* ▷ **valerian**
vales *n* ▷ **vale**
valet *n* (*pl* **-s**) man's personal male servant
valets *n* ▷ **valet**
valetudinarian [val-lit-yew-din-**air**-ee-an] *n* (*pl* **-s**) person with a long-term illness
valetudinarians *n* ▷ **valetudinarian**
valiant *adj* brave or courageous
valid *adj* (**-er, -est**) soundly reasoned > **validity** *n* (*pl* **-ies**)
validate *v* (**-tes, -ting, -ted**) make valid > **validation** *n* (*pl* **-s**)
validated *v* ▷ **validate**
validates *v* ▷ **validate**
validating *v* ▷ **validate**
validation *n* ▷ **validate**
validations *n* ▷ **validate**
valider *adj* ▷ **valid**
validest *adj* ▷ **valid**
validities *n* ▷ **valid**
validity *n* ▷ **valid**
valise [val-**leez**] *n* (*pl* **-s**) (*Old-fashioned*) small suitcase
valises *n* ▷ **valise**
valley *n* (*pl* **-s**) low area between hills, often with a river running through it
valleys *n* ▷ **valley**
valour *n* (*pl* **-s**) (*Lit*) bravery
valours *n* ▷ **valour**
valuable *adj* having great worth
valuables *pl n* valuable personal property
valuation *n* (*pl* **-s**) assessment of worth
valuations *n* ▷ **valuation**
value *n* (*pl* **-s**) importance, usefulness ▶ *pl* moral principles ▶ *v* (**-ues, -uing, -ued**) assess the worth or desirability of > **valueless** *adj* > **valuer** *n* (*pl* **-s**)
valued *v* ▷ **value**
valueless *adj* ▷ **value**
valuer *n* ▷ **value**
valuers *n* ▷ **value**
values *n, v* ▷ **value**
valuing *v* ▷ **value**
valve *n* (*pl* **-s**) device to control the movement of fluid through a pipe > **valvular** *adj*
valves *n* ▷ **valve**
valvular *adj* ▷ **valve**
vamp¹ *n* (*pl* **-s**) (*Informal*) sexually attractive woman who seduces men
vamp² *v* (**-s, -ing, -ed**) make (a story, piece of music, etc.) seem new by inventing additional parts
vamped *v* ▷ **vamp²**
vamping *v* ▷ **vamp²**
vampire *n* (*pl* **-s**) (in folklore) corpse that rises at night to drink the blood of the living
vampires *n* ▷ **vampire**
vamps *n, v* ▷ **vamp¹, ²**
van¹ *n* (*pl* **-s**) motor vehicle for transporting goods
van² *n* (*pl* **-s**) ▷ **vanguard**
vanadium *n* (*pl* **-s**) (CHEM) metallic element, used in steel
vanadiums *n* ▷ **vanadium**
vandal *n* (*pl* **-s**) person who deliberately damages property > **vandalism** *n* (*pl* **-s**) > **vandalize** *v* (**-zes, -zing, -zed**)
vandalism *n* ▷ **vandal**
vandalisms *n* ▷ **vandal**
vandalize *n* ▷ **vandal**
vandalized *n* ▷ **vandal**
vandalizes *n* ▷ **vandal**
vandalizing *v* ▷ **vandal**
vandals *n* ▷ **vandal**
vane *n* (*pl* **-s**) flat blade on a rotary device such as a weathercock or propeller
vanes *n* ▷ **vane**
vanguard *n* (*pl* **-s**) unit of soldiers leading an army
vanguards *n* ▷ **vanguard**
vanilla *n* (*pl* **-s**) seed pod of a tropical climbing orchid, used for flavouring
vanillas *n* ▷ **vanilla**
vanish *v* (**-es, -ing, -ed**) disappear suddenly or mysteriously
vanished *v* ▷ **vanish**
vanishes *v* ▷ **vanish**
vanishing *v* ▷ **vanish**
vanities *n* ▷ **vanity**
vanity *n* (*pl* **-ies**) (display of) excessive pride
vanquish *v* (**-es, -ing, -ed**) (*Lit*) defeat

(someone) utterly
vanquished *v* ▷ **vanquish**
vanquishes *v* ▷ **vanquish**
vanquishing *v* ▷ **vanquish**
vans *n* ▷ **van**[1, 2]
vantage *n* (*pl* **-s**) position that gives one an overall view
vantages *n* ▷ **vantage**
vapid *adj* (**-er, -est**) lacking character, dull
vapider *adj* ▷ **vapid**
vapidest *adj* ▷ **vapid**
vaporize *v* ▷ **vapour**
vaporized *v* ▷ **vapour**
vaporizer *n* ▷ **vapour**
vaporizers *n* ▷ **vapour**
vaporizes *v* ▷ **vapour**
vaporizing *v* ▷ **vapour**
vaporous *adj* ▷ **vapour**
vapour *n* (*pl* **-s**) moisture suspended in air as steam or mist > **vaporize** *v* (**-zes, -zing, -zed**) > **vaporizer** *n* (*pl* **-s**) > **vaporous** *adj*
vapours *n* ▷ **vapour**
variabilities *n* ▷ **variable**
variability *n* ▷ **variable**
variable *adj* not always the same, changeable ▶ *n* (*pl* **-s**) (MATHS) expression with a range of values > **variability** *n* (*pl* **-ties**)
variables *n* ▷ **variable**
variant *adj* differing from a standard or type ▶ *n* (*pl* **-s**) something that differs from a standard or type
variants *n* ▷ **variant**
variation *n* (*pl* **-s**) something presented in a slightly different form
variations *n* ▷ **variation**
varied *v, adj* ▷ **vary**
variegated *adj* having patches or streaks of different colours > **variegation** *n* (*pl* **-s**)
variegation *n* ▷ **variegate**
variegations *n* ▷ **variegate**
varies *adj* ▷ **vary**
varieties *n* ▷ **variety**
variety *n* (*pl* **-ies**) state of being diverse or various
various *adj* of several kinds > **variously** *adv*
variously *adv* ▷ **various**
varnish *n* (*pl* **-es**) solution of oil and resin, put on a surface to make it hard and glossy ▶ *v* (**-es, -ing, -ed**) apply varnish to
varnished *v* ▷ **varnish**
varnishes *n, v* ▷ **varnish**
varnishing *v* ▷ **varnish**
vary *v* (**-ries, -rying, -ried**) change > **varied** *adj*
varying *v* ▷ **vary**
vascular *adj* (BIOL) relating to vessels
vase *n* (*pl* **-s**) ornamental jar, esp. for flowers
vasectomies *n* ▷ **vasectomy**
vasectomy *n* (*pl* **-mies**) surgical removal of part of the vas deferens, as a contraceptive method
vases *n* ▷ **vase**
vassal *n* (*pl* **-s**) (HIST) man given land by a lord in return for military service > **vassalage** *n* (*pl* **-s**)
vassalage *n* ▷ **vassal**
vassalages *n* ▷ **vassal**
vassals *n* ▷ **vassal**
vast *adj* (**-er, -est**) extremely large > **vastly** *adv* > **vastness** *n* (*pl* **-es**)
vaster *adj* ▷ **vast**
vastest *adj* ▷ **vast**
vastly *adv* ▷ **vast**
vastness *n* ▷ **vast**
vastnesses *n* ▷ **vast**
vat *n* (*pl* **-s**) large container for liquids
vats *n* ▷ **vat**
vaudeville *n* (*pl* **-s**) variety entertainment of songs and comic turns
vaudevilles *n* ▷ **vaudeville**
vault[1] *n* (*pl* **-s**) secure room for storing valuables
vault[2] *v* (**-s, -ing, -ed**) jump over (something) by resting one's hand(s) on it. ▶ *n* such a jump
vaulted *adj* having an arched roof ▶ *v* ▷ **vault**[2]
vaulting *v* ▷ **vault**[2]
vaults *n, v* ▷ **vault**[1, 2]
vaunt *v* (**-s, -ing, -ed**) describe or display (success or possessions) boastfully > **vaunted** *adj*
vaunted *adj, v* ▷ **vaunt**
vaunting *v* ▷ **vaunt**
vaunts *v* ▷ **vaunt**

> **vaw** *n* (**vaws**). Vaw is a letter of the Hebrew alphabet. This is a very unusual word that can be useful when you are short of options. If you have the tiles for vaw, look out for opportunities to play **wave** or **wavy** using an E or Y that is already on the board. Vaw scores 9 points.

veal *n* (*pl* **-s**) calf meat
veals *n* ▷ **veal**
vector *n* (*pl* **-s**) (MATHS) quantity that has size and direction, such as force
vectors *n* ▷ **vector**
veer *v* (**-s, -ing, -ed**) change direction suddenly
veered *v* ▷ **veer**
veering *v* ▷ **veer**
veers *v* ▷ **veer**

> **veg** *n* (**veges**). Veg is a short form of **vegetable.** If someone plays this, look

out for opportunities to form **vegan** or **vegetate** from it. Veg scores 7 points.

vegan [**vee**-gan] *n* (*pl* **-s**) person who eats no meat, fish, eggs, or dairy products ▶ *adj* suitable for a vegan > **veganism** *n* (*pl* **-s**)
veganism *n* ▷ **vegan**
veganisms *n* ▷ **vegan**
vegans *n* ▷ **vegan**
vegetable *n* (*pl* **-s**) edible plant ▶ *adj* of or like plants or vegetables
vegetables *n* ▷ **vegetable**
vegetarian *n* (*pl* **-s**) person who eats no meat or fish ▶ *adj* suitable for a vegetarian > **vegetarianism** *n* (*pl* **-s**)
vegetarianism *n* ▷ **vegetarian**
vegetarianisms *n* ▷ **vegetarian**
vegetarians *n* ▷ **vegetarian**
vegetate *v* (**-tes, -ting, -ted**) live a dull boring life with no mental stimulation
vegetated *v* ▷ **vegetate**
vegetates *v* ▷ **vegetate**
vegetating *v* ▷ **vegetate**
vegetation *n* (*pl* **-s**) plant life of a given place
vegetations *n* ▷ **vegetation**
vehemence *n* ▷ **vehement**
vehemences *n* ▷ **vehement**
vehement *adj* expressing strong feelings > **vehemence** *n* (*pl* **-s**) > **vehemently** *adv*
vehemently *adv* ▷ **vehement**
vehicle *n* (*pl* **-s**) machine, esp. with an engine and wheels, for carrying people or objects > **vehicular** *adj*
vehicles *n* ▷ **vehicle**
vehicular *adj* ▷ **vehicle**
veil *n* (*pl* **-s**) piece of thin cloth covering the head or face ▶ *v* (**-s, -ing, -ed**) cover with or as if with a veil
veiled *adj* disguised ▶ *v* ▷ **veil**
veiling *v* ▷ **veil**
veils *n*, *v* ▷ **veil**
vein *n* (*pl* **-s**) tube that takes blood to the heart > **veined** *adj*
veined *adj* ▷ **vein**
veins *n* ▷ **vein**
veld, veldt *n* (*pl* **-s**) high grassland in southern Africa
velds *n* ▷ **veld**
veldskoen, velskoen *n* (*pl* **-s**) (S AFR) leather ankle boot
veldskoens *n* ▷ **veldskoen**
veldts *n* ▷ **veld**
vellum *n* (*pl* **-s**) fine calfskin parchment
vellums *n* ▷ **vellum**
velocities *n* ▷ **velocity**
velocity *n* (*pl* **-ties**) speed of movement in a given direction
velour, velours [vel-**loor**] *n* (*pl* **-s**) fabric similar to velvet
velours *n* ▷ **velour**
velskoen *n* ▷ **veldskoen**
velskoens *n* ▷ **veldskoen**
velvet *n* (*pl* **-s**) fabric with a thick soft pile
velveteen *n* (*pl* **-s**) cotton velvet
velveteens *n* ▷ **velveteen**
velvetier *adj* ▷ **velvety**
velvetiest *adj* ▷ **velvety**
velvets *n* ▷ **velvet**
velvety *adj* (**-tier, -tiest**) soft and smooth
venal *adj* easily bribed
vend *v* (**-s, -ing, -ed**) sell > **vendor** *n* (*pl* **-s**)
vended *v* ▷ **vend**
vendetta *n* (*pl* **-s**) prolonged quarrel between families, esp. one involving revenge killings
vendettas *n* ▷ **vendetta**
vending *v* ▷ **vend**
vendor *n* ▷ **vend**
vendors *n* ▷ **vend**
vends *v* ▷ **vend**
veneer *n* (*pl* **-s**) thin layer of wood etc. covering a cheaper material
veneers *n* ▷ **veneer**
venerable *adj* worthy of deep respect
venerate *v* (**-tes, -ting, -ted**) hold (a person) in deep respect > **veneration** *n* (*pl* **-s**)
venerated *v* ▷ **venerate**
venerates *v* ▷ **venerate**
venerating *v* ▷ **venerate**
veneration *n* ▷ **venerate**
venerations *n* ▷ **venerate**
vengeance *n* (*pl* **-s**) revenge
vengeances *n* ▷ **vengeance**
vengeful *adj* wanting revenge
venial [**veen**-ee-al] *adj* (of a sin or fault) easily forgiven
venison *n* (*pl* **-s**) deer meat
venisons *n* ▷ **venison**
venom *n* (*pl* **-s**) malice or spite > **venomous** *adj*
venomous *adj* ▷ **venom**
venoms *n* ▷ **venom**
venous *adj* (ANAT) of veins
vent¹ *n* (*pl* **-s**) outlet releasing fumes or fluid ▶ *v* (**-s, -ing, -ed**) express (an emotion) freely
vent² *n* (*pl* **-s**) vertical slit in a jacket
vented *v* ▷ **vent¹**
ventilate *v* (**-tes, -ting, -ted**) let fresh air into > **ventilation** *n* (*pl* **-s**) > **ventilator** *n* (*pl* **-s**)
ventilated *v* ▷ **ventilate**
ventilates *v* ▷ **ventilate**
ventilating *v* ▷ **ventilate**
ventilation *n* ▷ **ventilate**

ventilations *n* ▷ **ventilate**
ventilator *n* ▷ **ventilate**
ventilators *n* ▷ **ventilate**
venting *v* ▷ **vent**[1]
ventral *adj* relating to the front of the body
ventricle *n* (*pl* **-s**) (ANAT) one of the four cavities of the heart or brain
ventricles *n* ▷ **ventricle**
ventriloquism *n* ▷ **ventriloquist**
ventriloquisms *n* ▷ **ventriloquist**
ventriloquist *n* (*pl* **-s**) entertainer who can speak without moving his or her lips, so that a voice seems to come from elsewhere **> ventriloquism** *n* (*pl* **-s**)
ventriloquists *n* ▷ **ventriloquist**
vents *n, v* ▷ **vent**[1, 2]
venture *n* (*pl* **-s**) risky undertaking, esp. in business ▸ *v* (**-res, -ring, -red**) do something risky
ventured *v* ▷ **venture**
ventures *n, v* ▷ **venture**
venturesome *adj* daring
venturing *v* ▷ **venture**
venue *n* (*pl* **-s**) place where an organized gathering is held
venues *n* ▷ **venue**
veracious *adj* ▷ **veracity**
veracities *n* ▷ **veracity**
veracity *n* (*pl* **-ties**) habitual truthfulness **> veracious** *adj*
veranda *n* ▷ **verandah**
verandah, veranda *n* (*pl* **-s**) open porch attached to a house
verandahs *n* ▷ **verandah**
verandas *n* ▷ **verandah**
verb *n* (*pl* **-s**) word that expresses the idea of action, happening, or being
verbal *adj* spoken **> verbally** *adv*
verbalize *v* (**-s, -ing, -ed**) express (something) in words
verbalized *v* ▷ **verbalize**
verbalizes *n* ▷ **verbalize**
verbalizing *v* ▷ **verbalize**
verbally *adv* ▷ **verbal**
verbatim [verb-**bait**-im] *adv, adj* word for word
verbena *n* (*pl* **-s**) plant with sweet-smelling flowers
verbenas *n* ▷ **verbena**
verbiage *n* (*pl* **-s**) excessive use of words
verbiages *n* ▷ **verbiage**
verbose [verb-**bohss**] *adj* (**-r, -st**) speaking at tedious length **> verbosity** *n* (*pl* **-ties**)
verboser *adj* ▷ **verbose**
verbosest *adj* ▷ **verbose**
verbosities *n* ▷ **verbose**
verbosity *n* ▷ **verbose**
verbs *n* ▷ **verb**
verdant *adj* (*Lit*) covered in green vegetation
verdict *n* (*pl* **-s**) decision of a jury
verdicts *n* ▷ **verdict**
verdigris [**ver**-dig-riss] *n* (*pl* **-es**) green film on copper, brass, or bronze
verdigrises *n* ▷ **verdigris**
verdure *n* (*pl* **-s**) (*Lit*) flourishing green vegetation
verdures *n* ▷ **verdure**
verge *n* (*pl* **-s**) grass border along a road
verger *n* (*pl* **-s**) (C OF E) church caretaker
vergers *n* ▷ **verger**
verges *n* ▷ **verge**
verifiable *adj* ▷ **verify**
verification *n* ▷ **verify**
verifications *n* ▷ **verify**
verified *v* ▷ **verify**
verifies *v* ▷ **verify**
verify *v* (**-fies, -fying, -fied**) check the truth or accuracy of **> verifiable** *adj* **> verification** *n* (*pl* **-s**)
verifying *v* ▷ **verify**
verily *adv* (*Obs*) in truth
verisimilitude *n* (*pl* **-s**) appearance of being real or true
verisimilitudes *n* ▷ **verisimilitude**
veritable *adj* rightly called, without exaggeration **> veritably** *adv*
veritably *adv* ▷ **veritable**
verities *n* ▷ **verity**
verity *n* (*pl* **-ies**) true statement or principle
vermicelli [ver-me-**chell**-ee] *n* (*pl* **-s**) fine strands of pasta
vermicellis *n* ▷ **vermicelli**
vermiform *adj* shaped like a worm
vermilion *adj* orange-red
vermin *pl n* (*pl* **-s**) animals, esp. insects and rodents, that spread disease or cause damage **> verminous** *adj*
verminous *adj* ▷ **vermin**
vermins *n* ▷ **vermin**
vermouth [**ver**-muth] *n* (*pl* **-s**) wine flavoured with herbs
vermouths *n* ▷ **vermouth**
vernacular [ver-**nak**-yew-lar] *n* (*pl* **-s**) most widely spoken language of a particular people or place
vernaculars *n* ▷ **vernacular**
vernal *adj* occurring in spring
vernier [**ver**-nee-er] *n* (*pl* **-s**) movable scale on a graduated measuring instrument for taking readings in fractions
verniers *n* ▷ **vernier**

veronica *n* (*pl* **-s**) plant with small blue, pink, or white flowers
veronicas *n* ▷ **veronica**
verruca [ver-**roo**-ka] *n* (*pl* **-s**) wart, usu. on the foot
verrucas *n* ▷ **verruca**
versatile *adj* having many skills or uses
> **versatility** *n* (*pl* **-ties**)
versatilities *n* ▷ **versatile**
versatility *n* ▷ **versatile**
verse *n* (*pl* **-s**) group of lines forming part of a song or poem
verses *n* ▷ **verse**
versification *n* (*pl* **-s**) writing in verse
versifications *n* ▷ **versification**
version *n* (*pl* **-s**) form of something, such as a piece of writing, with some differences from other forms
versions *n* ▷ **version**
verso *n* (*pl* **-s**) left-hand page of a book
versos *n* ▷ **verso**
versus *prep* in opposition to or in contrast with
vertebra *n* (*pl* **-rae**) one of the bones that form the spine > **vertebral** *adj*
vertebrae *n* ▷ **vertabra**
vertebral *adj* ▷ **vertebra**
vertebrate *n*, *adj* (*pl* **-s**) (animal) having a spine
vertebrates *n* ▷ **vertebrate**
vertex *n* (*pl* **-texes, -tices**) (MATHS) point on a geometric figure where the sides form an angle
vertexes *n* ▷ **vertex**
vertical *adj* straight up and down ▶ *n* (*pl* **-s**) vertical direction
verticals *n* ▷ **vertical**
vertices *n* ▷ **vertex**
vertiginous *adj* ▷ **vertigo**
vertigo *n* (*pl* **-s**) dizziness, usu. when looking down from a high place > **vertiginous** *adj*
vertigoes *n* ▷ **vertigo**
vervain *n* (*pl* **-s**) plant with spikes of blue, purple, or white flowers
vervains *n* ▷ **vervain**
verve *n* (*pl* **-s**) enthusiasm or liveliness
verves *n* ▷ **verve**
very *adv* more than usually, extremely ▶ *adj* absolute, exact
vesicle *n* (*pl* **-s**) (BIOL) sac or small cavity, esp. one containing fluid
vesicles *n* ▷ **vesicle**
vespers *pl n* (RC CHURCH) (service of) evening prayer
vessel *n* (*pl* **-s**) ship
vessels *n* ▷ **vessel**
vest *n* (*pl* **-s**) undergarment worn on the top half of the body ▶ *v* (**-s, -ing, -ed**) (*foll. by* **in** *or* **with**) give (authority) to (someone)
vested *v* ▷ **vest**
vestibule *n* (*pl* **-s**) small entrance hall
vestibules *n* ▷ **vestibule**
vestige [**vest**-ij] *n* (*pl* **-s**) small amount or trace
> **vestigial** *adj*
vestiges *n* ▷ **vestige**
vestigial *adj* ▷ **vestige**
vesting *v* ▷ **vest**
vestments *pl n* priest's robes
vestries *n* ▷ **vestry**
vestry *n* (*pl* **-ies**) room in a church used as an office by the priest or minister
vests *n*, *v* ▷ **vest**
vet[1] *n* (*pl* **-s**) ▷ **veterinary surgeon** ▶ *v* (**-s, -tting, -tted**) check the suitability of
vet[2] *n* (*pl* **-s**) (US, AUST & NZ) military veteran
vetch *n* (*pl* **-es**) climbing plant with a beanlike fruit used as fodder
vetches *n* ▷ **vetch**
veteran *n* (*pl* **-s**) person with long experience in a particular activity, esp. military service ▶ *adj* long-serving
veterans *n* ▷ **veteran**
veterinary *adj* concerning animal health
veto *n* (*pl* **-es**) official power to cancel a proposal ▶ *v* (**-es, -ing, -ed**) enforce a veto against
vetoed *v* ▷ **veto**
vetoes *n*, *v* ▷ **veto**
vetoing *v* ▷ **veto**
vets *n*, *v* ▷ **vet**[1, 2]
vetted *v* ▷ **vet**[1]
vetting *v* ▷ **vet**[1]
vex *v* (**-es, -ing, -ed**) frustrate, annoy
vexation *n* (*pl* **-s**) something annoying
> **vexatious** *adj*
vexations *n* ▷ **vexation**
vexatious *adj* ▷ **vexation**
vexed *v* ▷ **vex**
vexes *v* ▷ **vex**
vexing *v* ▷ **vex**
via *prep* by way of
viabilities *n* ▷ **viable**
viability *n* ▷ **viable**
viable *adj* able to be put into practice
> **viability** *n* (*pl* **-ties**)
viaduct *n* (*pl* **-s**) bridge over a valley
viaducts *n* ▷ **viaduct**
vial *n* (*pl* **-s**) ▷ **phial**
vials *n* ▷ **vial**
viands *pl n* (*Obs*) food
vibes *pl n* (*Informal*) emotional reactions

between people
vibrant [**vibe**-rant] *adj* vigorous in appearance, energetic
vibraphone *n* (*pl* **-s**) musical instrument with metal bars that resonate electronically when hit
vibraphones *n* ▷ **vibraphone**
vibrate *v* (**-tes, -ting, -ted**) move back and forth rapidly > **vibration** *n* (*pl* **-s**)
vibrated *v* ▷ **vibrate**
vibrates *v* ▷ **vibrate**
vibrating *v* ▷ **vibrate**
vibration *n* ▷ **vibrate**
vibrations *n* ▷ **vibrate**
vibrato *n* (*pl* **-s**) (MUSIC) rapid fluctuation in the pitch of a note
vibrator *n* (*pl* **-s**) device that produces vibratory motion, used for massage or as a sex aid > **vibratory** *adj*
vibrators *n* ▷ **vibrate**
vibratos *n* ▷ **vibrato**
vicar *n* (*pl* **-s**) (C OF E) member of the clergy in charge of a parish
vicarage *n* (*pl* **-s**) vicar's house
vicarages *n* ▷ **vicarage**
vicarious [vick-**air**-ee-uss] *adj* felt indirectly by imagining what another person experiences > **vicariously** *adv*
vicariously *adv* ▷ **vicarious**
vicars *n* ▷ **vicar**
vice[1] *n* (*pl* **-s**) immoral or evil habit or action
vice[2] *n* (*pl* **-s**) tool with a pair of jaws for holding an object while working on it
vice[3] *adj* serving in place of
viceregal *adj* ▷ **viceroy**
viceroy *n* (*pl* **-s**) governor of a colony who represents the monarch > **viceregal** *adj*
viceroys *n* ▷ **viceroy**
vices *n* ▷ **vice**[1, 2]
vicinities *n* ▷ **vicinity**
vicinity [viss-**in**-it-ee] *n* (*pl* **-ties**) surrounding area
vicious *adj* cruel and violent > **viciously** *adv*
viciously *adv* ▷ **vicious**
vicissitudes [viss-**iss**-it-yewds] *pl n* changes in fortune
victim *n* (*pl* **-s**) person or thing harmed or killed
victimization *n* ▷ **victimize**
victimizations *n* ▷ **victimize**
victimize *v* (**-zes, -zing, -zed**) punish unfairly > **victimization** *n* (*pl* **-s**)
victimized *v* ▷ **victimize**
victimizes *v* ▷ **victimize**
victimizing *v* ▷ **victimize**
victims *n* ▷ **victim**
victor *n* (*pl* **-s**) person who has defeated an opponent, esp. in war or in sport
victories *n* ▷ **victory**
victorious *adj* ▷ **victory**
victors *n* ▷ **victor**
victory *n* (*pl* **-ries**) winning of a battle or contest > **victorious** *adj*
victuals [**vit**-tals] *pl n* (*Old-fashioned*) food and drink
vicuña [vik-**koo**-nya] *n* (*pl* **-s**) S American animal like the llama
vicuñas *n* ▷ **vicuña**
video *n* (*pl* **-s**) ▷ **video cassette (recorder)** ▶ *v* (**-s, -ing, -ed**) record (a TV programme or event) on video ▶ *adj* relating to or used in producing television images
videoed *v* ▷ **video**
videoing *v* ▷ **video**
videos *n, v* ▷ **video**
videotext *n* (*pl* **-s**) means of representing on a TV screen information that is held in a computer
videotexts *n* ▷ **videotext**
vie *v* (**vies, vying, vied**) compete (with someone)
vied *v* ▷ **vie**
vies *v* ▷ **vie**
view *n* (*pl* **-s**) opinion or belief ▶ *v* (**-s, -ing, -ed**) think of (something) in a particular way
viewdata *n* (*pl* **-as**)® videotext service linking users to a computer by telephone
viewdatas *n* ▷ **viewdatas**
viewed *v* ▷ **view**
viewer *n* person who watches television
viewers *n* ▷ **viewer**
viewfinder *n* (*pl* **-s**) window on a camera showing what will appear in a photograph
viewfinders *n* ▷ **viewfinder**
viewing *v* ▷ **view**
views *n, v* ▷ **view**
vigil [**vij**-ill] *n* (*pl* **-s**) night-time period of staying awake to look after a sick person, pray, etc.
vigilance *n* ▷ **vigilant**
vigilances *n* ▷ **vigilant**
vigilant *adj* watchful in case of danger > **vigilance** *n* (*pl* **-s**)
vigilante [vij-ill-**ant**-ee] *n* (*pl* **-s**) person, esp. as one of a group, who takes it upon himself or herself to enforce the law
vigilantes *n* ▷ **vigilante**
vigils *n* ▷ **vigil**
vignette [vin-**yet**] *n* (*pl* **-s**) concise description of the typical features of something
vignettes *n* ▷ **vignette**

vigorous *adj* ▷ **vigour**
vigorously *adv* ▷ **vigour**
vigour *n* (*pl* **-s**) physical or mental energy > **vigorous** *adj* > **vigorously** *adv*
vigours *n* ▷ **vigour**
viking *n* (*pl* **-s**) (HIST) seafaring raider and settler from Scandinavia
vikings *n* ▷ **viking**
vile (**-r, -st**) *adj* very wicked > **vilely** *adv* > **vileness** *n* (*pl* **-s**)
vilely *adv* ▷ **vile**
vileness *n* ▷ **vile**
vilenesses *n* ▷ **vile**
viler *adj* ▷ **vile**
vilest *adj* ▷ **vile**
vilification *n* ▷ **vilify**
vilifications *n* ▷ **vilify**
vilified *v* ▷ **vilify**
vilifies *v* ▷ **vilify**
vilify *v* (**-fies, -fying, -fied**) attack the character of > **vilification** *n* (*pl* **-s**)
vilifying *v* ▷ **vilify**
villa *n* (*pl* **-s**) large house with gardens
village *n* (*pl* **-s**) small group of houses in a country area > **villager** *n* (*pl* **-s**)
villager *n* ▷ **village**
villagers *n* ▷ **village**
villages *n* ▷ **village**
villain *n* (*pl* **-s**) wicked person > **villainous** *adj* > **villainy** *n* (*pl* **-nies**)
villianies *n* ▷ **villian**
villainous *adj* ▷ **villain**
villains *n* ▷ **villain**
villas *n* ▷ **villa**
villein [**vill**-an] *n* (*pl* **-s**) (HIST) peasant bound in service to his lord
villeins *n* ▷ **villein**
villiany *n* ▷ **villian**

> **vim** *n* (**vims**). Vim means vigour or energy. This word can be helpful when you're stuck with unpromising letters, and gives a reasonable score for a three-letter word. Vim scores 8 points.

vinaigrette *n* (*pl* **-s**) salad dressing of oil and vinegar
vinaigrettes *n* ▷ **vinaigrette**
vindicate *v* (**-tes, -ting, -ted**) clear (someone) of guilt > **vindication** *n* (*pl* **-s**)
vindicated *v* ▷ **vindicate**
vindicates *v* ▷ **vindicate**
vindicating *v* ▷ **vindicate**
vindication *n* ▷ **vindicate**
vindications *n* ▷ **vindicate**
vindictive *adj* maliciously seeking revenge > **vindictiveness** *n* (*pl* **-es**) > **vindictively** *adv*
vindictively *adv* ▷ **vindictive**
vindictiveness *n* ▷ **vindictive**
vindictivenesses *n* ▷ **vindictive**
vine *n* (*pl* **-s**) climbing plant, esp. one producing grapes
vinegar *n* (*pl* **-s**) acid liquid made from wine, beer, or cider > **vinegary** *adj*
vinegars *n* ▷ **vinegar**
vinegary *adj* ▷ **vinegar**
vines *n* ▷ **vine**
vineyard [**vinn**-yard] *n* (*pl* **-s**) plantation of grape vines, esp. for making wine
vineyards *n* ▷ **vineyard**
vino [**vee**-noh] *n* (*pl* **-s**) (*Informal*) wine
vinos *n* ▷ **vino**
vintage *n* (*pl* **-s**) wine from a particular harvest of grapes ▶ *adj* best and most typical
vintages *n* ▷ **vintage**
vintner *n* (*pl* **-s**) dealer in wine
vintners *n* ▷ **vintner**
vinyl [**vine**-ill] *n* (*pl* **-s**) type of plastic, used in mock leather and records
vinyls *n* ▷ **vinyl**
viol [**vie**-oll] *n* (*pl* **-s**) early stringed instrument preceding the violin
viola[1] [vee-**oh**-la] *n* (*pl* **-s**) stringed instrument lower in pitch than a violin
viola[2] [**vie**-ol-la] *n* (*pl* **-s**) variety of pansy
violas *n* ▷ **viola**[1, 2]
violate *v* (**-tes, -ting, -ted**) break (a law or agreement) > **violation** *n* > **violator** *n*
violated *v* ▷ **violate**
violates *v* ▷ **violate**
violating *v* ▷ **violate**
violation *n* ▷ **violate**
violations *n* ▷ **violate**
violator *n* ▷ **violate**
violators *n* ▷ **violate**
violence *n* (*pl* **-s**) use of physical force, usu. intended to cause injury or destruction > **violent** *adj* > **violently** *adv*
violences *n* ▷ **violence**
violent *adj* ▷ **violence**
violently *adv* ▷ **violent**
violet *n* (*pl* **-s**) plant with bluish-purple flowers ▶ *adj* bluish-purple
violets *n* ▷ **violet**
violin *n* (*pl* **-s**) small four-stringed musical instrument played with a bow. > **violinist** *n* (*pl* **-s**)
violinist *n* ▷ **violin**
violinists *n* ▷ **violin**
violins *n* ▷ **violin**
viols *n* ▷ **viol**
viper *n* (*pl* **-s**) poisonous snake

vipers *n* ▷ **viper**
virago [vir-**rah**-go] *n* (*pl* **-goes, -gos**) aggressive woman
viragoes *n* ▷ **virago**
viragos *n* ▷ **virago**
viral *adj* of or caused by a virus
virgin *n* (*pl* **-s**) person, esp. a woman, who has not had sexual intercourse ▶ *adj* not having had sexual intercourse > **virginity** *n* (*pl* **-ties**)
virginal *adj* like a virgin ▶ *n* early keyboard instrument like a small harpsichord
virginities *n* ▷ **virgin**
virginity *n* ▷ **virgin**
virgins *n* ▷ **virgin**
virile *adj* having the traditional male characteristics of physical strength and a high sex drive > **virility** *n* (*pl* **-ties**)
virilities *n* ▷ **virile**
virility *n* ▷ **virile**
virologies *n* ▷ **virology**
virologies *n* ▷ **virology**
virology *n* (*pl* **-gies**) study of viruses
virtual *adj* having the effect but not the form of > **virtually** *adv* practically, almost
virtually *adv* ▷ **virtual**
virtue *n* (*pl* **-s**) moral goodness
virtues *n* ▷ **virtue**
virtuosi *n* ▷ **virtuoso**
virtuosities *n* ▷ **virtuoso**
virtuosity *n* ▷ **virtuoso**
virtuoso *n* (*pl* **-sos, -si**) person with impressive esp. musical skill > **virtuosity** *n* (*pl* **-ies**)
virtuosos *n* ▷ **virtuoso**
virtuous *adj* morally good > **virtuously** *adv*
virtuously *adv* ▷ **virtuous**
virulent [**vir**-yew-lent] *adj* very infectious
virus *n* (*pl* **-es**) microorganism that causes disease in humans, animals, and plants
viruses *n* ▷ **virus**
visa *n* (*pl* **-s**) permission to enter a country, granted by its government and shown by a stamp on one's passport
visage [**viz**-zij] *n* (*pl* **-s**) (*Lit*) face
visages *n* ▷ **visage**
visas *n* ▷ **visa**
viscera [**viss**-er-a] *pl n* large abdominal organs
visceral [**viss**-er-al] *adj* instinctive
viscid [**viss**-id] *adj* sticky
viscose *n* (*pl* **-s**) synthetic fabric made from cellulose
viscoses *n* ▷ **viscose**
viscosities *n* ▷ **viscous**
viscosity *n* ▷ **viscous**
viscount [**vie**-count] *n* (*pl* **-s**) British nobleman ranking between an earl and a baron
viscountess [**vie**-count-iss] *n* (*pl* **-es**) woman holding the rank of viscount in her own right
viscountesses *n* ▷ **viscountess**
viscounts *n* ▷ **viscount**
viscous *adj* thick and sticky > **viscosity** *n* (*pl* **-ties**)
visibilities *n* ▷ **visibility**
visibility *n* (*pl* **-ties**) range or clarity of vision
visible *adj* able to be seen > **visibly** *adv*
visibly *adv* ▷ **visible**
vision *n* (*pl* **-s**) ability to see
visionaries *n* ▷ **visionary**
visionary *adj* showing foresight ▶ *n* (*pl* **-ries**) visionary person
visions *n* ▷ **vision**
visit *v* (**-s, -ing, -ed**) go or come to see ▶ *n* instance of visiting > **visitor** *n* (*pl* **-s**)
visitation *n* (*pl* **-s**) formal visit or inspection
visitations *n* ▷ **visitation**
visited *v* ▷ **visit**
visiting *v* ▷ **visit**
visitor *n* ▷ **visit**
visitors *n* ▷ **visit**
visits *v* ▷ **visit**
visor [**vize**-or] *n* (*pl* **-s**) transparent part of a helmet that pulls down over the face
visors *n* ▷ **visor**
vista *n* (*pl* **-s**) (beautiful) extensive view
vistas *n* ▷ **vista**
visual *adj* done by or used in seeing
visualization *n* ▷ **visualize**
visualizations *n* ▷ **visualize**
visualize *v* (**-zes, -zing, -zed**) form a mental image of > **visualization** *n* (*pl* **-s**)
visualized *v* ▷ **visualize**
visualizes *v* ▷ **visualize**
visualizing *v* ▷ **visualize**
vital *adj* essential or highly important > **vitally** *adv*
vitalities *n* ▷ **vitality**
vitality *n* (*pl* **-ties**) physical or mental energy
vitally *adv* ▷ **vital**
vitals *pl n* bodily organs necessary to maintain life
vitamin *n* (*pl* **-s**) one of a group of substances that are essential in the diet for specific body processes
vitamins *n* ▷ **vitamin**
vitiate [**vish**-ee-ate] *v* (**-tes, -ting, -ted**) spoil the effectiveness of
vitiated *v* ▷ **vitiate**
vitiates *v* ▷ **vitiate**
vitiating *v* ▷ **vitiate**
viticulture *n* (*pl* **-s**) cultivation of grapevines
viticultures *n* ▷ **viticulture**

vitreous *adj* like or made from glass
vitriol *n* (*pl* **-s**) language expressing bitterness and hatred > **vitriolic** *adj*
vitriolic *adj* ▷ **vitriol**
vitriols *n* ▷ **vitriol**
vituperation *n* ▷ **vituperative**
vituperations *n* ▷ **vituperative**
vituperative [vite-**tyew**-pra-tiv] *adj* bitterly abusive > **vituperation** *n* (*pl* **-s**)
viva¹ *interj* long live (a person or thing)
viva² *n* (*pl* **-s**) (BRIT) examination in the form of an interview
vivace [viv-**vah**-chee] *adv* (MUSIC) in a lively manner
vivacious *adj* full of energy and enthusiasm > **vivacity** *n* (*pl* **-ties**)
vivacities *n* ▷ **vivacious**
vivacity *n* ▷ **vivacious**
vivas *n* ▷ **viva**²
vivid *adj* (**-er, -est**) very bright > **vividly** *adv* > **vividness** *n* (*pl* **-es**)
vivider *adj* ▷ **vivd**
vividest *adj* ▷ **vivd**
vividly *adv* ▷ **vivd**
vividness *n* ▷ **vivid**
vividnesses *n* ▷ **vivid**
vivisection *n* (*pl* **-s**) performing surgical experiments on living animals > **vivisectionist** *n* (*pl* **-s**)
vivisectionist *n* ▷ **vivisection**
vivisectionists *n* ▷ **vivisection**
vivisections *n* ▷ **vivisection**
vixen *n* (*pl* **-s**) female fox
vixens *n* ▷ **vixen**
vizier [viz-**zeer**] *n* (*pl* **-s**) high official in certain Muslim countries
viziers *n* ▷ **vizier**
vizor *n* (*pl* **-s**) ▷ **visor**
vizors *n* ▷ **vizor**

vly *n* (**vlys**). Vly is a South African word meaning an area of low marshy ground. This is a good word to remember because it doesn't contain any vowels, making it useful when you are short of vowel tiles. Vly scores 9 points.

vocabularies *n* ▷ **vocabulary**
vocabulary *n* (*pl* **-ries**) all the words that a person knows
vocal *adj* relating to the voice
vocalist *n* (*pl* **-s**) singer
vocalists *n* ▷ **vocalist**
vocalization *n* ▷ **vocalize**
vocalizations *n* ▷ **vocalize**
vocalize *v* (**-zes, -zing, -zed**) express with or use the voice > **vocalization** *n* (*pl* **-s**)
vocalizes *v* ▷ **vocalize**
vocalizes *v* ▷ **vocalize**
vocalizing *v* ▷ **vocalize**
vocally *adv* ▷ **vocal**
vocals *pl n* singing part of a piece of pop music > **vocally** *adv*
vocation *n* (*pl* **-s**) profession or trade
vocational *adj* directed towards a particular profession or trade
vocations *n* ▷ **vocation**
vociferous *adj* shouting, noisy
vodka *n* (*pl* **-s**) (Russian) spirit distilled from potatoes or grain
vodkas *n* ▷ **vodka**
vogue *n* (*pl* **-s**) popular style
vogues *n* ▷ **vogue**
voice *n* (*pl* **-s**) (quality of) sound made when speaking or singing ▶ *v* (**-ces, -cing, -ced**) express verbally > **voiceless** *adj*
voiced *v* ▷ **voice**
voiceless *adj* ▷ **voice**
voices *n, v* ▷ **voice**
voicing *v* ▷ **voice**
void *adj* not legally binding ▶ *n* (*pl* **-s**) empty space ▶ *v* (**-s, -ing, -ed**) make invalid
voided *v* ▷ **void**
voiding *v* ▷ **void**
voids *n, v* ▷ **void**
voile [**voyl**] *n* (*pl* **-s**) light semitransparent fabric
voiles *n* ▷ **voile**
volatile *adj* liable to sudden change, esp. in behaviour > **volatility** *n* (*pl* **-ties**)
volatilities *n* ▷ **volatile**
volatility *n* ▷ **volatile**
volcanic *adj* ▷ **volcano**
volcano *n* (*pl* **-noes, -nos**) mountain with a vent through which lava is ejected > **volcanic** *adj*
volcanoes *n* ▷ **volcano**
volcanos *n* ▷ **volcano**
vole *n* (*pl* **-s**) small rodent
voles *n* ▷ **vole**
volition *n* (*pl* **-s**) ability to decide things for oneself
volitions *n* ▷ **volition**
volley *n* (*pl* **-s**) simultaneous discharge of ammunition ▶ *v* (**-s, -ing, -ed**) discharge (ammunition) in a volley
volleyball *n* (*pl* **-s**) team game where a ball is hit with the hands over a high net
volleyballs *n* ▷ **volleyball**
volleyed *v* ▷ **volley**
volleying *v* ▷ **volley**

volleys *n, v* ▷ **volley**
volt *n* (*pl* **-s**) unit of electric potential
voltage *n* (*pl* **-s**) electric potential difference expressed in volts
voltages *n* ▷ **voltage**
voltmeter *n* instrument for measuring voltage
voltmeters *n* ▷ **voltmeter**
volts *n* ▷ **volt**
volubilities *n* ▷ **voluble**
volubility *n* ▷ **voluble**
voluble *adj* talking easily and at length > **volubility** *n* (*pl* **-ties**) > **volubly** *adv*
volubly *adv* ▷ **voluble**
volume *n* (*pl* **-s**) size of the space occupied by something
volumes *n* ▷ **volume**
volumetric *adj* relating to measurement by volume
voluminous *adj* (of clothes) large and roomy
voluntaries *n* ▷ **voluntary**
voluntarily *adv* ▷ **voluntary**
voluntary *adj* done by choice ▶ *n* (*pl* **-ries**) organ solo in a church service > **voluntarily** *adv*
volunteer *n* (*pl* **-s**) person who offers voluntarily to do something ▶ *v* (**-s, -ing, -ed**) offer one's services
volunteered *v* ▷ **volunteer**
volunteering *v* ▷ **volunteer**
volunteers *n, v* ▷ **volunteer**
voluptuaries *n* ▷ **voluptuary**
voluptuary *n* (*pl* **-ries**) person devoted to sensual pleasures
voluptuous *adj* (of a woman) sexually alluring through fullness of figure
volute *n* (*pl* **-s**) spiral or twisting turn, form, or object
volutes *n* ▷ **volute**
vomit *v* (**-s, -ing, -ed**) eject (the contents of the stomach) through the mouth ▶ *n* (*pl* **-s**) matter vomited
vomited *v* ▷ **vomit**
vomiting *v* ▷ **vomit**
vomits *v, n* ▷ **vomit**
voodoo *n* (*pl* **-s**) religion involving ancestor worship and witchcraft, practised by Black people in the West Indies, esp. in Haiti.
voodoos *n* ▷ **voodoo**
voracious *adj* craving great quantities of food > **voraciously** *adv* > **voracity** *n* (*pl* **-ties**)
voraciously *adv* ▷ **voracious**
voracities *n* ▷ **voracious**
voracity *n* ▷ **voracious**
vortex *n* (*pl* **-texes, -tices**) whirlpool
vortexes *n* ▷ **vortex**
vortices *n* ▷ **vortex**
vote *n* (*pl* **-s**) choice made by a participant in a shared decision, esp. in electing a candidate ▶ *v* (**-tes, -ting, -ted**) make a choice by a vote > **voter** *n* (*pl* **-s**)
voted *v* ▷ **vote**
voter *n* ▷ **vote**
voters *n* ▷ **vote**
votes *n, v* ▷ **vote**
voting *v* ▷ **vote**
votive *adj* done or given to fulfil a vow
vouch *v* (**-es, -ing, -ed**) give one's personal assurance about
vouched *v* ▷ **vouch**
voucher *n* (*pl* **-s**) ticket used instead of money to buy specified goods
vouchers *n* ▷ **voucher**
vouches *v* ▷ **vouch**
vouching *v* ▷ **vouch**
vouchsafe *v* (**-fes, -fing, -fed**) (*Old-fashioned*) give, entrust
vouchsafed *v* ▷ **vouchsafe**
vouchsafes *v* ▷ **vouchsafe**
vouchsafing *v* ▷ **vouchsafe**
vow *n* (*pl* **-s**) solemn and binding promise ▶ *pl* formal promises made when marrying or entering a religious order ▶ *v* (**-s, -ing, -ed**) promise solemnly
vowed *v* ▷ **vow**
vowel *n* (*pl* **-s**) speech sound made without obstructing the flow of breath
vowels *n* ▷ **vowel**
vowing *v* ▷ **vow**
vows *n, v* ▷ **vow**

vox *n* (**voces**). Vox means a voice or sound. Along with **vex,** this is the highest-scoring three-letter word beginning with V. Vox scores 13 points.

voyage *n* (*pl* **-s**) long journey by sea or in space ▶ *v* (**-ges, -ging, -ged**) make a voyage > **voyager** *n* (*pl* **-s**)
voyaged *v* ▷ **voyage**
voyager *n* ▷ **voyager**
voyagers *n* ▷ **voyager**
voyages *n, v* ▷ **voyage**
voyaging *v* ▷ **voyage**
voyeur *n* (*pl* **-s**) person who obtains pleasure from watching people undressing or having sex > **voyeurism** *n* (*pl* **-s**)
voyeurism *n* ▷ **voyeur**
voyeurisms *n* ▷ **voyeur**
voyeurs *n* ▷ **voyeur**

vug *n* (**vugs**). A vug is a small cavity in a rock. This is a very unusual word that can be useful when you have an uninspiring combination of letters. Vug scores 7 points.

vulcanize *v* (**-zes, -zing, -zed**) strengthen (rubber) by treating it with sulphur
vulcanized *v* ▷ **vulcanize**
vulcanizes *v* ▷ **vulcanize**
vulcanizing *v* ▷ **vulcanize**
vulgar *adj* (**-er, -est**) showing lack of good taste, decency, or refinement > **vulgarly** *adv* > **vulgarity** *n* (*pl* **-ies**)
vulgarer *adj* ▷ **vulgar**
vulgarest *adj* ▷ **vulgar**
vulgarian *n* (*pl* **-s**) vulgar (rich) person
vulgarians *n* ▷ **vulgarian**
vulgarities *n* ▷ **vulgar**
vulgarities *n* ▷ **vulgar**
vulgarly *adv* ▷ **vulgar**
vulnerabilities *n* ▷ **vulnerable**
vulnerability *n* ▷ **vulnerable**
vulnerable *adj* liable to be physically or emotionally hurt > **vulnerability** *n* (*pl* **-s**)
vulpine *adj* of or like a fox
vulture *n* (*pl* **-s**) large bird that feeds on the flesh of dead animals
vultures *n* ▷ **vulture**
vulva *n* (*pl* **-vae**) woman's external genitals
vulvae *n* ▷ **vulva**
vying *v* ▷ **vie**

Ww

W is a useful tile to have on your rack as it earns 4 points on its own and produces a number of high-scoring short words. There are, however, only two two-letter words begin with W: **we** and **wo** (5 points each). If you know this, though, you won't waste time looking for others. There are lots of everyday three-letter words that earn good scores: **wax** (13) with its two old-fashioned variants **wex** and **wox** (also 13 each) and **way, who, why, wow** and **wry** (9 each). Don't forget **wok** (10) either, which can be as useful on the Scrabble board as in the kitchen!

wackier *adj* ▷ **wacky**
wackiest *adj* ▷ **wacky**
wackiness *n* ▷ **wacky**
wackinesses *n* ▷ **wacky**
wacky *adj* (**-ckier, -ckiest**) (*Informal*) eccentric or funny > **wackiness** *n* (*pl* **-es**)
wad *n* (*pl* **-s**) small mass of soft material
waddies *n* ▷ **waddy**
wadding *n* (*pl* **-s**) soft material used for padding or stuffing
waddings *n* ▷ **wadding**
waddle *v* (**-les, -ling, -led**) walk with short swaying steps ▸ *n* (*pl* **-s**) swaying walk
waddled *v, n* ▷ **waddle**
waddles *v* ▷ **waddle**
waddling *v* ▷ **waddle**
waddy *n* (*pl* **-ies**) heavy wooden club used by Australian Aborigines
wade *v* (**-des, -ding, -ded**) walk with difficulty through water or mud
waded *v* ▷ **wade**
wader *n* (*pl* **-s**) long-legged water bird ▸ *pl* angler's long waterproof boots
waders *n* ▷ **wader**
wades *v* ▷ **wade**
wadi [**wod**-dee] *n* (*pl* **-s**) (in N Africa and Arabia) river which is dry except in the wet season
wading *v* ▷ **wade**
wadis *n* ▷ **wadi**
wads *n* ▷ **wad**
wafer *n* (*pl* **-s**) thin crisp biscuit
wafers *n* ▷ **wafer**
waffle[1] (*Informal*) *v* (**-les, -ling, -led**) speak or write in a vague wordy way ▸ *n* (*pl* **-s**) vague wordy talk or writing
waffle[2] *n* (*pl* **-s**) square crisp pancake with a gridlike pattern
waffled *v* ▷ **waffle**[1]
waffles *v, n* ▷ **waffle**[1, 2]
waffling *v* ▷ **waffle**[1]
waft *v* (**-s, -ing, -ed**) drift or carry gently through the air ▸ *n* (*pl* **-s**) something wafted
wafted *v* ▷ **waft**
wafting *v* ▷ **waft**
wafts *v, n* ▷ **waft**
wag *v* (**-s, -gging, -gged**) move rapidly from side to side ▸ *n* (*pl* **-s**) wagging movement
wage *n* (*pl* **-s**) (*often pl* payment for work done, esp. when paid weekly ▸ *v* (**-ges, -ging, -ged**) engage in (an activity)
waged *v* ▷ **wage**
wager *n, v* (**-s, -ing, -ed**) bet on the outcome of something
wagered *v* ▷ **wager**
wagering *v* ▷ **wager**
wagers *n, v* ▷ **wager**
wages *n, v* ▷ **wage**
wagged *v* ▷ **wag**
wagging *v* ▷ **wag**
waggle *v* (**-les, -ling, -led**) move with a rapid shaking or wobbling motion
waggled *v* ▷ **waggle**
waggles *v* ▷ **waggle**
waggling *v* ▷ **waggle**
waggon *n* ▷ **wagon**
waggons *n* ▷ **wagon**
waging *v* ▷ **wage**
wagon, waggon *n* (*pl* **-s**) four-wheeled vehicle for heavy loads
wagons *n* ▷ **wagon**
wags *v* ▷ **wag**
wagtail *n* (*pl* **-s**) small long-tailed bird
wagtail *n* ▷ **wagtails**
wahoo *n* (*pl* **-s**) food and game fish of tropical

seas

wahoos *n* ▷ **wahoo**

waif *n* (*pl* **-s**) young person who is, or seems, homeless or neglected

waifs *n* ▷ **waif**

wail *v* (**-s, -ing, -ed**) cry out in pain or misery ▶ *n* (*pl* **-s**) mournful cry

wailed *v* ▷ **wail**

wailing *v* ▷ **wail**

wails *v, n* ▷ **wail**

wain *n* (*pl* **-s**) (*Poetic*) farm wagon

wains *n* ▷ **wain**

wainscot, wainscoting *n* (*pl* **-s**) wooden lining of the lower part of the walls of a room

wainscoting *n* ▷ **wainscot**

wainscotings *n* ▷ **wainscot**

wainscots *n* ▷ **wainscot**

waist *n* (*pl* **-s**) part of the body between the ribs and hips

waistband *n* (*pl* **-s**) band of material sewn on to the waist of a garment to strengthen it

waistbands *n* ▷ **waistband**

waistcoat *n* (*pl* **-s**) sleeveless garment which buttons up the front, usu. worn over a shirt and under a jacket

waistcoats *n* ▷ **waistcoat**

waistline *n* (*pl* **-s**) (size of) the waist of a person or garment

waistlines *n* ▷ **waistline**

waists *n* ▷ **waist**

wait *v* (**-s, -ing, -ed**) remain inactive in expectation (of something) ▶ *n* (*pl* **-s**) act or period of waiting

waited *v* ▷ **wait**

waiter *n* (*pl* **-s**) man who serves in a restaurant etc. > **waitress** *n fem* (*pl* **-es**)

waiters *n* ▷ **waiter**

waiting *v* ▷ **wait**

waitress *n* ▷ **waiter**

waitresses *n* ▷ **waiter**

waits *v, n* ▷ **wait**

waive *v* (**-ves, -ving, -ved**) refrain from enforcing (a law, right, etc.)

waived *v* ▷ **waive**

waiver *n* (*pl* **-s**) act or instance of voluntarily giving up a claim, right, etc.

waivers *n* ▷ **waiver**

waives *v* ▷ **waive**

waiving *v* ▷ **waive**

waka *n* (*pl* **-s**) (NZ) Maori canoe

wakas *n* ▷ **waka**

wake[1] *v* (**-kes, -king, woke, woken**) rouse from sleep or inactivity ▶ *n* (*pl* **-s**) vigil beside a corpse the night before the funeral > **wakeful** *adj*

wake[2] *n* (*pl* **-s**) track left by a moving ship

wakeful *adj* ▷ **wake**[1]

waken *v* (**-s, -ing, -ed**) wake

wakened *v* ▷ **waken**

wakening *v* ▷ **waken**

wakens *v* ▷ **waken**

wakes *n* ▷ **wake**[1, 2]

waking *v* ▷ **wake**[1]

walk *v* (**-s, -ing, -ed**) move on foot with at least one foot always on the ground ▶ *n* (*pl* **-s**) act or instance of walking > **walker** *n* (*pl* **-s**)

walkabout *n* (*pl* **-s**) informal walk among the public by royalty etc.

walkabouts *n* ▷ **walkabout**

walked *v* ▷ **walk**

walker *n* ▷ **walk**

walkers *n* ▷ **walk**

walking *v* ▷ **walk**

walkout *n* (*pl* **-s**) strike

walkouts *n* ▷ **walkout**

walkover *n* (*pl* **-s**) easy victory

walkovers *n* ▷ **walkover**

walks *v, n* ▷ **walk**

wall *n* (*pl* **-s**) structure of brick, stone, etc. used to enclose, divide, or support ▶ *v* (**-s, -ing, -ed**) enclose or seal with a wall or walls

wallabies *n* ▷ **wallaby**

wallaby *n* (*pl* **-bies**) marsupial like a small kangaroo

wallaroo *n* (*pl* **-s**) large stocky Australian kangaroo of rocky regions

wallaroos *n* ▷ **wallaroo**

walled *v* ▷ **wall**

wallet *n* (*pl* **-s**) small folding case for paper money, documents, etc.

wallets *n* ▷ **wallet**

walleye *n* (*pl* **-s**) fish with large staring eyes (*also* **dory**)

walleyes *n* ▷ **walleye**

wallflower *n* (*pl* **-s**) fragrant garden plant

wallflowers *n* ▷ **wallflower**

wallies *n* ▷ **wally**

walling *v* ▷ **wall**

wallop (*Informal*) *v* (**-s, -ing, -ed**) hit hard ▶ *n* (*pl* **-s**) hard blow

walloped *v* ▷ **wallop**

walloping (*Informal*) *n* thrashing ▶ *adj* large or great ▶ *v* ▷ **wallop**

wallops *v, n* ▷ **wallop**

wallow *v* (**-s, -ing, -ed**) revel in an emotion ▶ *n* (*pl* **-s**) act or instance of wallowing

wallowed *v* ▷ **wallow**

wallowing *v* ▷ **wallow**

wallows *v, n* ▷ **wallow**

wallpaper *n* (*pl* **-s**) decorative paper to cover

interior walls
wallpapers *n* ▷ **wallpaper**
walls *n*, *v* ▷ **wall**
wally *n* (*pl* **-ies**) (BRIT) (*Slang*) stupid person
walnut *n* (*pl* **-s**) edible nut with a wrinkled shell
walnuts *n* ▷ **walnut**
walrus *n* (*pl* **-ruses, -rus**) large sea mammal with long tusks
walruses *n* ▷ **walrus**
waltz *n* (*pl* **-es**) ballroom dance ▶ *v* (**-zes, -zing, -zed**) dance a waltz
waltzed *v* ▷ **waltz**
waltzes *n*, *v* ▷ **waltz**
waltzing *v* ▷ **waltz**
wampum [**wom**-pum] *n* (*pl* **-s**) shells woven together, formerly used by Native Americans for money and ornament
wampums *n* ▷ **wampum**
wan [rhymes with **swan**] *adj* (**-nner, -nnest**) pale and sickly looking
wand *n* (*pl* **-s**) thin rod, esp. one used in performing magic tricks
wander *v* (**-s, -ing, -ed**) move about without a definite destination or aim ▶ *n* (*pl* **-s**) act or instance of wandering > **wanderer** *n* (*pl* **-s**)
wandered *v* ▷ **wander**
wanderer *n* ▷ **wander**
wanderers *n* ▷ **wander**
wandering *v* ▷ **wander**
wanderlust *n* (*pl* **-s**) great desire to travel
wanderlusts *n* ▷ **wanderlust**
wanders *v*, *n* ▷ **wander**
wands *n* ▷ **wand**
wane *v* (**-nes, -ning, -ned**) decrease gradually in size or strength
waned *v* ▷ **wane**
wanes *v* ▷ **wane**
wangle *v* (**-les, -ling, -led**) (*Informal*) get by devious methods
wangled *v* ▷ **wangle**
wangles *v* ▷ **wangle**
wangling *v* ▷ **wangle**
waning *v* ▷ **wane**
wanner *adj* ▷ **wan**
wannest *adj* ▷ **wan**
want *v* (**-s, -ing, -ed**) need or long for ▶ *n* (*pl* **-s**) act or instance of wanting
wanted *adj* sought by the police ▶ *v* ▷ **want**
wanting *adj* lacking ▶ *v* ▷ **want**
wanton *adj* (**-er, -est**) without motive, provocation, or justification
wantoner *adj* ▷ **wanton**
wantonest *adj* ▷ **wanton**
wants *v*, *n* ▷ **want**
war *n* (*pl* **-s**) fighting between nations ▶ *adj* of, like, or caused by war ▶ *v* (**-s, -rring, -rred**) conduct a war > **warring** *adj*
waratah *n* (*pl* **-s**) Australian shrub with crimson flowers
waratahs *n* ▷ **waratah**
warble *v* (**-les, -ling, -led**) sing in a trilling voice
warbled *v* ▷ **warble**
warbler *n* (*pl* **-s**) any of various small songbirds
warblers *n* ▷ **warbler**
warbles *v* ▷ **warble**
warbling *v* ▷ **warble**
ward *n* (*pl* **-s**) room in a hospital for patients needing a similar kind of care
warden *n* (*pl* **-s**) person in charge of a building and its occupants
wardens *n* ▷ **warden**
warder *n* (*pl* **-s**) prison officer > **wardress** *n fem* (*pl* **-es**)
warders *n* ▷ **warder**
wardress *n* ▷ **warder**
wardresses *n* ▷ **warder**
wardrobe *n* (*pl* **-s**) cupboard for hanging clothes in
wardrobes *n* ▷ **wardrobe**
wardroom *n* (*pl* **-s**) officers' quarters on a warship
wardrooms *n* ▷ **wardroom**
wards *n* ▷ **ward**
ware *n* (*pl* **-s**) articles of a specified type or material ▶ *pl* goods for sale
warehouse *n* (*pl* **-s**) building for storing goods prior to sale or distribution
warehouses *n* ▷ **warehouse**
wares *n* ▷ **ware**
warfare *n* (*pl* **-s**) fighting or hostilities
warfares *n* ▷ **warfare**
warhead *n* (*pl* **-s**) explosive front part of a missile
warheads *n* ▷ **warhead**
warier *adj* ▷ **wary**
wariest *n* ▷ **wary**
warily *adv* ▷ **wary**
wariness *n* ▷ **wary**
warinesses *n* ▷ **wary**
warlike *adj* of or relating to war
warlock *n* (*pl* **-s**) man who practises black magic
warlocks *n* ▷ **warlock**
warm *adj* (**-er, -est**) moderately hot ▶ *v* (**-s, -ing, -ed**) make or become warm > **warmly** *adv*
warmed *v* ▷ **warm**
warmer *adj* ▷ **warm**
warmest *adj* ▷ **warm**
warming *v* ▷ **warm**
warmly *adv* ▷ **warm**

warmonger *n* (*pl* **-s**) person who encourages war
warmongers *n* ▷ **warmonger**
warms *v* ▷ **warm**
warmth *n* (*pl* **-s**) mild heat
warmths *n* ▷ **warmth**
warn *v* (**-s, -ing, -ed**) make aware of possible danger or harm
warned *v* ▷ **warn**
warning *n* (*pl* **-s**) something that warns ▶ *v* ▷ **warn**
warnings *n* ▷ **warning**
warns *v* ▷ **warn**
warp *v* (**-s, -ing, -ed**) twist out of shape ▶ *n* (*pl* **-s**) state of being warped
warped *v* ▷ **warp**
warping *v* ▷ **warp**
warps *v, n* ▷ **warp**
warrant *n* (*pl* **-s**) (document giving) official authorization ▶ *v* (**-s, -ing, -ed**) make necessary
warranted *v* ▷ **warrant**
warranties *n* ▷ **warranty**
warranting *v* ▷ **warrant**
warrants *n, v* ▷ **warrant**
warranty *n* (*pl* **-ties**) (document giving) a guarantee
warred *v* ▷ **war**
warren *n* (*pl* **-s**) series of burrows in which rabbits live
warrens *n* ▷ **warren**
warrigal (AUST) *n* (*pl* **-s**) dingo ▶ *adj* wild
warrigals *n* ▷ **warrigal**
warring *v* ▷ **war**
warrior *n* (*pl* **-s**) person who fights in a war
warriors *n* ▷ **warrior**
wars *n, v* ▷ **war**
warship *n* (*pl* **-s**) ship designed and equipped for naval combat
warships *n* ▷ **warship**
wart *n* (*pl* **-s**) small hard growth on the skin
warts *n* ▷ **wart**
wary [ware-ree] *adj* (**-rier, -riest**) watchful or cautious > **warily** *adv* > **wariness** *n* (*pl* **-es**)
was *v* ▷ **be**
wash *v* (**-es, -ing, -ed**) clean (oneself, clothes, etc.) with water and usu. soap (*Informal*) ▶ *n* (*pl* **-es**) act or process of washing > **washable** *adj*
washable *adj* ▷ **wash**
washed *v* ▷ **wash**
washer *n* (*pl* **-s**) ring put under a nut or bolt or in a tap as a seal
washers *n* ▷ **washer**
washes *v, n* ▷ **wash**
washing *n* (*pl* **-s**) clothes to be washed ▶ *v* ▷ **wash**
washings *n* ▷ **washing**
washout *n* (*pl* **-s**) (*Informal*) complete failure
washouts *n* ▷ **washouts**
wasp *n* (*pl* **-s**) stinging insect with a slender black-and-yellow striped body
waspish *adj* bad-tempered
wasps *n* ▷ **wasp**
wastage *n* (*pl* **-s**) loss by wear or waste
wastages *n* ▷ **wastage**
waste *v* (**-tes, -ting, -ted**) use pointlessly or thoughtlessly ▶ *n* (*pl* **-s**) act of wasting or state of being wasted ▶ *pl* desert ▶ *adj* rejected as worthless or surplus to requirements
wasted *v* ▷ **waste**
wasteful *adj* extravagant > **wastefully** *adv*
wastefully *adv* ▷ **waste**
waster, wastrel *n* (*pl* **-s**) layabout
wasters *n* ▷ **waster**
wastes *v, n* ▷ **waste**
wasting *v* ▷ **waste**
wastrel *n* ▷ **waster**
wastrels *n* ▷ **waster**
watch *v* (**-es, -ing, -ed**) look at closely ▶ *n* (*pl* **-es**) portable timepiece for the wrist or pocket > **watchable** *adj* > **watcher** *n* (*pl* **-s**)
watchable *adj* ▷ **watch**
watchdog *n* (*pl* **-s**) dog kept to guard property
watchdogs *n* ▷ **watchdog**
watched *v* ▷ **watch**
watcher *n* ▷ **watch**
watchers *n* ▷ **watch**
watches *v, n* ▷ **watch**
watchful *adj* vigilant or alert > **watchfully** *adv*
watchfully *adv* ▷ **watchful**
watching *v* ▷ **watch**
watchman *n* (*pl* **-men**) man employed to guard a building or property
watchmen *n* ▷ **watchman**
watchword *n* (*pl* **-s**) word or phrase that sums up the attitude of a particular group
watchwords *n* ▷ **watchword**
water *n* (*pl* **-s**) clear colourless tasteless liquid that falls as rain and forms rivers etc. ▶ *v* (**-s, -ing, -ed**) put water on or into > **watery** *adj* (**-rier, -riest**)
watercolour *n* (*pl* **-s**) paint thinned with water
watercolours *n* ▷ **watercolour**
watercourse *n* (*pl* **-s**) bed of a stream or river
watercourses *n* ▷ **watercourse**
watercress *n* (*pl* **-es**) edible plant growing in clear ponds and streams
watercresses *n* ▷ **watercress**
watered *v* ▷ **water**
waterfall *n* (*pl* **-s**) place where the waters of a

river drop vertically
waterfalls *n* ▷ **waterfall**
waterfront *n* (*pl* **-s**) part of a town alongside a body of water
waterfronts *n* ▷ **waterfront**
waterier *adj* ▷ **watery**
wateriest *adj* ▷ **watery**
watering *v* ▷ **water**
watermark *n* (*pl* **-s**) faint translucent design in a sheet of paper
watermarks *n* ▷ **watermark**
watermelon *n* (*pl* **-s**) melon with green skin and red flesh
watermelons *n* ▷ **watermelon**
waterproof *adj* not letting water through ▶ *n* (*pl* **-s**) waterproof garment ▶ *v* (**-s, -ing, -ed**) make waterproof
waterproofed *v* ▷ **waterproof**
waterproofing *v* ▷ **waterproof**
waterproofs *n, v* ▷ **waterproof**
waters *n, v* ▷ **water**
watershed *n* (*pl* **-s**) important period or factor serving as a dividing line
watersheds *n* ▷ **watershed**
watersider *n* (*pl* **-s**) (NZ) person employed to load and unload ships
watersiders *n* ▷ **watersider**
waterskiing *n* (*pl* **-s**) sport of riding over water on skis towed by a speedboat
waterskiings *n* ▷ **waterskiing**
watertight *adj* not letting water through
watery *adj* ▷ **water**
watt [wott] *n* (*pl* **-s**) unit of power
wattage *n* (*pl* **-s**) electrical power expressed in watts
wattages *n* ▷ **wattage**
wattle [wott-tl] *n* (*pl* **-s**) branches woven over sticks to make a fence making fences
wattles *n* ▷ **wattle**
watts *n* ▷ **watt**
wave *v* (**-ves, -ving, -ved**) move the hand to and fro as a greeting or signal ▶ *n* (*pl* **-s**) moving ridge on water > **wavy** *adj* (**-vier, -viest**)
waved *v* ▷ **wave**
wavelength *n* (*pl* **-s**) distance between the same points of two successive waves
wavelengths *n* ▷ **wavelength**
waver *v* (**-s, -ing, -ed**) hesitate or be irresolute > **waverer** *n* (*pl* **-s**)
wavered *v* ▷ **waver**
waverer *n* ▷ **waver**
waverers *n* ▷ **waver**
wavering *v* ▷ **waver**
wavers *v* ▷ **waver**
waves *v, n* ▷ **wave**
wavier *adj* ▷ **wave**
waviest *adj* ▷ **wave**
waving *v* ▷ **wave**
wavy *adj* ▷ **wave**
wax[1] *n* (*pl* **-es**) solid shiny fatty or oily substance used for sealing, making candles, etc. ▶ *v* (**-es, -ing, -ed**) coat or polish with wax > **waxy** *adj* (**-xier, -xiest**)
wax[2] *v* (**-es, -ing, -ed**) increase in size or strength
waxed *v* ▷ **wax**[1, 2]
waxen *adj* made of or like wax
waxes *n, v* ▷ **wax**[1, 2]
waxier *adj* ▷ **wax**
waxiest *adj* ▷ **wax**
waxing *v* ▷ **wax**[1, 2]
waxwork *n* (*pl* **-s**) lifelike wax model of a (famous) person ▶ *pl* place exhibiting these
waxworks *n* ▷ **waxwork**
waxy *adj* ▷ **wax**[1]
way *n* (*pl* **-s**) manner or method
wayfarer *n* (*Lit*) traveller
wayfarers *n* ▷ **wayfarer**
waylaid *v* ▷ **waylay**
waylay *v* (**-lays, -laying, -laid**) lie in wait for and accost or attack
waylaying *v* ▷ **waylay**
waylays *v* ▷ **waylay**
ways *n* ▷ **way**
wayside *adj, n* (*pl* **-s**) (situated by) the side of a road
waysides *n* ▷ **wayside**
wayward *adj* erratic, selfish, or stubborn > **waywardness** *n* (*pl* **-es**)
waywardness *n* ▷ **waywardness**
waywardnesses *n* ▷ **wayward**
we *pron* (*used as the subject of a verb*) the speaker or writer and one or more others
weak *adj* (**-er, -est**) lacking strength
weaken *v* (**-s, -ing, -ed**) make or become weak
weakened *v* ▷ **weaken**
weakening *v* ▷ **weaken**
weakens *v* ▷ **weaken**
weaker *adj* ▷ **weak**
weakest *adj* ▷ **weak**
weakling *n* feeble person or animal
weaklings *n* ▷ **weakling**
weakly *adv* feebly
weakness *n* (**-es**) being weak
weaknesses *n* ▷ **weakness**
weal *n* (*pl* **-s**) raised mark left on the skin by a blow
weals *n* ▷ **weal**
wealth *n* (*pl* **-s**) state of being rich > **wealthy** *adj* (**-thier, -thiest**)

wealthier *adj* ▷ **wealth**
wealthiest *adj* ▷ **wealth**
wealthy *adj* ▷ **wealth**
wean *v* (**-s, -ing, -ed**) accustom (a baby or young mammal) to food other than mother's milk
weaned *v* ▷ **wean**
weaning *v* ▷ **wean**
weans *v* ▷ **wean**
weapon *n* (*pl* **-s**) object used in fighting
weaponries *n* ▷ **weapon**
weaponry *n* (*pl* **-ries**) weapons collectively
weapons *n* ▷ **weapon**
wear *v* (**-s, -ing, wore, worn**) have on the body as clothing or ornament ▶ *n* (*pl* **-s**) clothes suitable for a particular time or purpose > **wearer** *n* (*pl* **-s**)
wearer *n* ▷ **wear**
wearers *n* ▷ **wear**
wearied *v* ▷ **weary**
wearier *adj* ▷ **weary**
wearies *v* ▷ **weary**
weariest *adj* ▷ **weary**
wearily *adv* ▷ **weary**
weariness *n* ▷ **weary**
wearinesses *n* ▷ **weary**
wearing *v* ▷ **wear**
wearisome *adj* tedious
wears *n, v* ▷ **wear**
weary *adj* (**-rier, -riest**) tired or exhausted ▶ *v* (**-ries, -rying, -ried**) make or become weary > **wearily** *adv* > **weariness** *n* (*pl* **-es**)
wearying *v* ▷ **weary**
weasel *n* (*pl* **-s**) small carnivorous mammal with a long body and short legs
weasels *n* ▷ **weasel**
weather *n* (*pl* **-s**) day-to-day atmospheric conditions of a place ▶ *v* (**-s, -ing, -ed**) (cause to) be affected by the weather
weathercock, weathervane *n* device that revolves to show the direction of the wind
weathercocks *n* ▷ **weathercock**
weathered *v* ▷ **weather**
weathering *v* ▷ **weather**
weathers *v, n* ▷ **weather**
weathervanes *n* ▷ **weathervane**
weave *v* (**-s, -ving, wove** *or* **weaved, woven** *or* **weaved**) make (fabric) by interlacing (yarn) on a loom > **weaver** *n* (*pl* **-s**)
weaved *v* ▷ **weave**
weaver *n* ▷ **weave**
weavers *n* ▷ **weave**
weaves *v* ▷ **weave**
web *n* (*pl* **-s**) net spun by a spider > **webbed** *adj*
webbed *adj* ▷ **web**
webbing *n* (*pl* **-s**) strong fabric woven in strips
webbings *n* ▷ **web**
webcam *n* (*pl* **-s**) camera that transmits images over the Internet
webcams *n* ▷ **webcam**
webcast *n* (*pl* **-s**) broadcast of an event over the Internet
webcasts *n* ▷ **webcast**
weblog *n* (*pl* **-s**) person's online journal (*also* **blog**)
weblogs *n* ▷ **weblog**
webs *n* ▷ **web**
website *n* (*pl* **-s**) group of connected pages on the World Wide Web
websites *n* ▷ **website**
wed *v* (**-s, -dding, -dded** *or* **wed**) marry
wedded *v* ▷ **wed**
wedding *n* (*pl* **-s**) act or ceremony of marriage ▶ *v* ▷ **wed**
weddings *n* ▷ **wedding**
wedge *n* (*pl* **wedges**) piece of material thick at one end and thin at the other ▶ *v* (**-ges, -ging, -ged**) fasten or split with a wedge
wedged *v* ▷ **wedge**
wedges *n, v* ▷ **wedge**
wedging *v* ▷ **wedge**
wedlock *n* (*pl* **-s**) marriage
wedlocks *n* ▷ **wedlock**
wee *adj* (**-r, -st**) (BRIT, AUST & NZ) (*Informal*) small or short
weed *n* (*pl* **-s**) plant growing where undesired (*Informal*) ▶ *v* (**-s, -ing, -ed**) clear of weeds
weeded *v* ▷ **weed**
weedier *adj* ▷ **weedy**
weediest *adj* ▷ **weddy**
weeding *v* ▷ **weed**
weeds *n, v* ▷ **weed** ▶ *pl n* (*Obs*) widow's mourning clothes
weedy *adj* (**-dier, -diest**) (*Informal*) (of a person) thin and weak
week *n* (*pl* **-s**) period of seven days, esp. one beginning on a Sunday
weekday *n* (*pl* **-s**) any day of the week except Saturday or Sunday
weekdays *n* ▷ **weekday**
weekend *n* (*pl* **-s**) Saturday and Sunday
weekends *n* ▷ **weekend**
weeklies *n* ▷ **weekly**
weekly *adj, adv* happening, done, etc. once a week ▶ *n* (*pl* **-lies**) newspaper or magazine published once a week
weeks *n* ▷ **week**
weep *v* (**-s, -ing, wept**) shed tears
weepier *adj* ▷ **weepy**
weepiest *adj* ▷ **weepy**

weeping *v* ▷ **weep**
weeps *v* ▷ **weep**
weepy *adj* (**-pier, -piest**) liable to cry
weer *adj* ▷ **wee**
weest *adj* ▷ **wee**
weevil *n* (*pl* **-s**) small beetle which eats grain etc.
weevils *n* ▷ **weevil**
weft *n* (*pl* **-s**) cross threads in weaving
wefts *n* ▷ **weft**
weigh *v* (**-s, -ing, -ed**) have a specified weight
weighbridge *n* (*pl* **-s**) machine for weighing vehicles by means of a metal plate set into the road
weighbridges *n* ▷ **weighbridge**
weighed *v* ▷ **weigh**
weighing *v* ▷ **weigh**
weighs *v* ▷ **weigh**
weight *n* (*pl* **-s**) heaviness of an object ▶ *v* (**-s, -ing, -ed**) add weight to > **weightless** *adj* > **weightlessness** *n*
weighted *v* ▷ **weight**
weightier *adj* ▷ **weighty**
weightiest *adj* ▷ **weighty**
weightily *adv* ▷ **weighty**
weighting *v* ▷ **weight** ▶ *n* (*pl* **-s**) (BRIT) extra allowance paid in special circumstances
weightings *n* ▷ **weighting**
weightless *adj* ▷ **weight**
weightlessness *n* ▷ **weight**
weights *n, v* ▷ **weight**
weighty *adj* (**-tier, -tiest**) important or serious > **weightily** *adv*
weir *n* (*pl* **-s**) river dam
weird (**-er, -est**) *adj* strange or bizarre
weirder *adj* ▷ **weird**
weirdest *adj* ▷ **weird**
weirdo *n* (*pl* **-s**) (*Informal*) peculiar person
weirdos *n* ▷ **weirdo**
weirs *n* ▷ **weir**
welch *v* (**-es, -ing, -ed**) ▷ **welsh**
welched *v* ▷ **welch**
welches *v* ▷ **welch**
welching *v* ▷ **welch**
welcome *v* (**-mes, -ming, -med**) greet with pleasure ▶ *n* (*pl* **-s**) kindly greeting ▶ *adj* received gladly
welcomed *v* ▷ **welcome**
welcomes *v, n* ▷ **welcome**
welcoming *v* ▷ **welcome**
weld *v* (**-s, -ing, -ed**) join (pieces of metal or plastic) by softening with heat ▶ *n* (*pl* **-s**) welded joint > **welder** *n* (*pl* **-s**)
welded *v* ▷ **weld**
welder *n* ▷ **weld**
welders *n* ▷ **weld**
welding *v* ▷ **weld**
welds *v, n* ▷ **weld**
welfare *n* (*pl* **-s**) wellbeing
welfares *n* ▷ **welfare**
well[1] *adv* (**better, best**) satisfactorily ▶ *adj* in good health ▶ *interj* exclamation of surprise, interrogation, etc.
well[2] *n* (*pl* **-s**) hole sunk into the earth to reach water, oil, or gas ▶ *v* (**-s, -ing, -ed**) flow upwards or outwards
wellbeing *n* (*pl* **-s**) state of being well, happy, or prosperous
wellbeings *n* ▷ **wellbeing**
welled *v* ▷ **well**[2]
wellies *pl n* (BRIT & AUST) (*Informal*) wellingtons
welling *v* ▷ **well**[2]
wellingtons *pl n* (BRIT & AUST) high waterproof rubber boots
wells *n, v* ▷ **well**[2]
welsh *v* (**-es, -ing, -ed**) fail to pay a debt or fulfil an obligation
welshed *v* ▷ **welsh**
welshes *v* ▷ **welsh**
welshing *v* ▷ **welsh**
welt *n* (*pl* **-s**) raised mark on the skin produced by a blow
welter *n* (*pl* **-s**) jumbled mass
welters *n* ▷ **welter**
welterweight *n* (*pl* **-s**) boxer weighing up to 147lb (professional) or 67kg (amateur)
welterweights *n* ▷ **welterweight**
welts *n* ▷ **welt**
wen *n* (*pl* **-s**) cyst on the scalp
wench *n* (*pl* **-es**) (*facetious*) young woman
wenches *n* ▷ **wench**
wend *v* (**-s, -ing, -ed**) go or travel
wended *v* ▷ **wend**
wending *v* ▷ **wend**
wends *v* ▷ **wend**
wens *n* ▷ **wen**
went *v* ▷ **go**
wept *v* ▷ **weep**
were *v* form of the past tense of **be** used after *we, you, they,* or a plural noun ▷ **be**
werewolf *n* (*pl* **-wolves**) (in folklore) person who can turn into a wolf
werewolves *n* ▷ **werewolf**
west *n* (*pl* **-s**) (direction towards) the part of the horizon where the sun sets ▶ *adj* to or in the west ▶ *adv* in, to, or towards the west > **westerly** *adj* > **westward** *adj, adv* > **westwards** *adv*
westerly *adj* ▷ **west**
western *adj* of or in the west ▶ *n* (*pl* **-s**) film or

story about cowboys in the western US
westernize *v* (**-zes, -zing, -zed**) adapt to the customs and culture of the West
westernized *v* ▷ **westernize**
westernizes *v* ▷ **westernize**
westernizing *v* ▷ **westernize**
westerns *n* ▷ **western**
wests *n* ▷ **west**
westward *adj* ▷ **west**
westwards *adv* ▷ **west**
wet *adj* (**-tter, -ttest**) covered or soaked with water or another liquid (BRIT) (*Informal*) ▶ *n* moisture or rain (BRIT) (*Informal*) ▶ *v* (**-s, -tting, wet** *or* **wetted**) make wet
wetland *n* (*pl* **-s**) area of marshy land
wetlands *n* ▷ **wetland**
wetted *v* ▷ **wet**
wetter *adj* ▷ **wet**
wettest *adj* ▷ **wet**
wetting *v* ▷ **wet**

wex *n* (**wexes**). Wex is an old word for **wax.** This gives a very good score for a three-letter word, and is a good one to look for when you have an X. Wex scores 13 points.

whack *v* (**-s, -ing, -ed**) strike with a resounding blow ▶ *n* (*pl* **-s**) such a blow
whacked *adj* exhausted ▶ *v* ▷ **whack**
whacking *adj* (*Informal*) huge ▶ *v* ▷ **whack**
whacks *v, n* ▷ **whack**
whale *n* (*pl* **-s**) large fish-shaped sea mammal
whaler *n* ship or person involved in whaling
whalers *n* ▷ **whaler**
whales *n* ▷ **whale**
whaling *n* (*pl* **-s**) hunting of whales for food and oil
whalings *n* ▷ **whaling**
wharf *n* (*pl* **wharves, wharfs**) platform at a harbour for loading and unloading ships
wharfie *n* (*pl* **-s**) (AUST) person employed to load and unload ships
wharfies *n* ▷ **wharfie**
wharfs *n* ▷ **wharf**
wharves *n* ▷ **wharf**
what *pron* which thing ▶ *interj* exclamation of anger, surprise, etc. ▶ *adv* in which way, how much
whatnot *n* (*pl* **-s**) (*Informal*) similar unspecified things
whatnots *n* ▷ **whatnot**
whatsoever *adj* at all
wheat *n* (*pl* **-s**) grain used in making flour, bread, and pasta > **wheaten** *adj*
wheatear *n* (*pl* **-s**) small songbird
wheatears *n* ▷ **wheatear**
wheaten *adj* ▷ **wheat**
wheats *n* ▷ **wheat**
wheedle *v* (**-les, -ling, -led**) coax or cajole
wheedled *v* ▷ **wheedle**
wheedles *v* ▷ **wheedle**
wheedling *v* ▷ **wheedle**
wheel *n* (*pl* **-s**) disc that revolves on an axle ▶ *v* (**-s, -ing, -ed**) push or pull (something with wheels)
wheelbarrow *n* (*pl* **-s**) shallow box for carrying loads, with a wheel at the front and two handles
wheelbarrows *n* ▷ **wheelbarrow**
wheelbase *n* (*pl* **-s**) distance between a vehicle's front and back axles
wheelbases *n* ▷ **wheelbase**
wheelchair *n* (*pl* **-s**) chair mounted on wheels for use by people who cannot walk
wheelchairs *n* ▷ **wheelchair**
wheeled *v* ▷ **wheel**
wheeling *v* ▷ **wheel**
wheels *n, v* ▷ **wheel**
wheeze *v* (**-zes, -zing, -zed**) breathe with a hoarse whistling noise ▶ *n* (*pl* **-s**) wheezing sound (*Informal*) > **wheezy** *adj* (**-zier, -ziest**)
wheezed *v* ▷ **wheeze**
wheezes *v, n* ▷ **wheeze**
wheezier *adj* ▷ **wheeze**
wheeziest *adj* ▷ **wheeze**
wheezing *v* ▷ **wheeze**
wheezy *adj* ▷ **wheeze**
whelk *n* (*pl* **-s**) edible snail-like shellfish
whelks *n* ▷ **whelk**
whelp *n* (*pl* **-s**) pup or cub ▶ *v* (**-s, -ing, -ed**) (of an animal) give birth
whelped *v* ▷ **whelp**
whelping *v* ▷ **whelp**
whelps *n, v* ▷ **whelp**
when *adv* at what time? ▶ *conj* at the time that ▶ *pron* at which time
whence *adv, conj* (*Obs*) from what place or source
whenever *adv, conj* at whatever time
where *adv* in, at, or to what place? ▶ *pron* in, at, or to which place ▶ *conj* in the place at which
whereabouts *n* present position ▶ *adv* at what place
whereas *conj* but on the other hand
whereby *pron* by which
wherefore (*Obs*) *adv* why ▶ *conj* consequently
whereupon *conj* at which point
wherever *conj, adv* at whatever place
wherewithal *n* (*pl* **-s**) necessary funds, resources, etc.
wherewithals *n* ▷ **wherewithals**

whet *v* (**-s, -tting, -tted**) sharpen (a tool)
whether *conj* used to introduce an indirect question or a clause expressing doubt or choice
whets *v* ▷ **whet**
whetstone *n* (*pl* **-s**) stone for sharpening tools
whetstones *n* ▷ **whetstone**
whetted *v* ▷ **whet**
whetting *v* ▷ **whet**
whey [**way**] *n* (*pl* **-s**) watery liquid that separates from the curd when milk is clotted
wheys *n* ▷ **whey**
which *adj, pron* used to request or refer to a choice from different possibilities ▶ *pron* used to refer to a thing already mentioned
whichever *adj, pron* any out of several
whiff *n* (*pl* **-s**) puff of air or odour
whiffs *n* ▷ **whiff**
whig *n* (*pl* **-s**) member of a British political party of the 18th–19th centuries that sought limited reform
whigs *n* ▷ **whig**
while *conj* at the same time that ▶ *n* (*pl* **-s**) period of time
whiles *n* ▷ **while**
whilst *conj* while
whim *n* (*pl* **-s**) sudden fancy
whimper *v* (**-s, -ing, -ed**) cry in a soft whining way ▶ *n* (*pl* **-s**) soft plaintive whine
whimpered *v* ▷ **whimper**
whimpering *v* ▷ **whimper**
whimpers *v, n* ▷ **whimper**
whims *n* ▷ **whim**
whimsical *adj* unusual, playful, and fanciful
whimsies *n* ▷ **whimsy**
whimsy *n* (*pl* **-ies**) capricious idea
whin *n* (*pl* **-s**) (BRIT) gorse
whine *n* (*pl* **-s**) high-pitched plaintive cry ▶ *v* (**-nes, -ning, -ned**) make such a sound > **whining** *n, adj* (*pl* **-s**)
whined *v* ▷ **whine**
whines *n, v* ▷ **whine**
whinge (BRIT, AUST & NZ) (*Informal*) *v* (**-ges, -geing, -ged**) complain ▶ *n* (*pl* **-s**) complaint
whinged *v* ▷ **whinge**
whingeing *v* ▷ **whinge**
whinges *v, n* ▷ **whinge**
whining *v, n adj* ▷ **whine**
whinings *n* ▷ **whine**
whinnied *v* ▷ **whinny**
whinnies *v, n* ▷ **whinny**
whinny *v* (**-nnies, -nnying, -nnied**) neigh softly ▶ *n* (*pl* **-nnies**) soft neigh
whinnying *v* ▷ **whinny**
whins *n* ▷ **whin**
whip *n* (*pl* **-s**) cord attached to a handle, used for beating animals or people ▶ *v* (**-s, -pping, -pped**) strike with a whip, strap, or cane
whipped *v* ▷ **whip**
whippet *n* (*pl* **-s**) racing dog like a small greyhound
whippets *n* ▷ **whippet**
whipping *v* ▷ **whip**
whips *v, n* ▷ **whip**
whir *v* ▷ **whirr**
whirl *v* (**-s, -ing, -ed**) spin or revolve ▶ *n* (*pl* **-s**) whirling movement
whirled *v* ▷ **whirl**
whirling *v* ▷ **whirl**
whirlpool *n* (*pl* **-s**) strong circular current of water
whirlpools *n* ▷ **whirlpool**
whirls *v, n* ▷ **whirl**
whirlwind *n* (*pl* **-s**) column of air whirling violently upwards in a spiral ▶ *adj* much quicker than normal
whirlwinds *n* ▷ **whirlwind**
whirr, whir *n* (*pl* **-s**) prolonged soft buzz ▶ *v* (**-s, -rring, -rred**) (cause to) make a whirr
whirred *v* ▷ **whirr**
whirring *v* ▷ **whirr**
whirrs *n, v* ▷ **whirr**
whirs *n* ▷ **whirr**
whisk *v* (**-s, -ing, -ed**) move or remove quickly ▶ *n* (*pl* **-s**) egg-beating utensil
whisked *v* ▷ **whisk**
whisker *n* (*pl* **-s**) any of the long stiff hairs on the face of a cat or other mammal ▶ *pl* hair growing on a man's face
whiskers *n* ▷ **whisker**
whiskey *n* (*pl* **-s**) Irish or American whisky
whiskeys *n* ▷ **whiskey**
whiskies *n* ▷ **whisky**
whisking *v, v* ▷ **whisk**
whisks *n* ▷ **whisk**
whisky *n* (*pl* **-ies**) spirit distilled from fermented cereals
whisper *v* (**-s, -ing, -ed**) speak softly, without vibration of the vocal cords ▶ *n* (*pl* **-s**) soft voice (*Informal*)
whispered *v* ▷ **whisper**
whispering *v* ▷ **whisper**
whispers *v, n* ▷ **whisper**
whist *n* (*pl* **-s**) card game in which one pair of players tries to win more tricks than another pair
whistle *v* (**-les, -ling, -led**) produce a shrill sound, esp. by forcing the breath through pursed lips ▶ *n* (*pl* **-s**) whistling sound > **whistling** *n, adj* (*pl* **-s**)

whistled *v* ▷ **whistle**
whistles *v, n* ▷ **whistle**
whistling *v, n* ▷ **whistle**
whistlings *n* ▷ **whistle**
whists *n* ▷ **whist**
whit *n* (*pl* **-s**) not the slightest amount
white *adj* (**-r, -st**) of the colour of snow ▶ *n* (*pl* **-s**) colour of snow > **whiteness** *n* (*pl* **-es**) > **whitish** *adj*
whitebait *n* (*pl* **-s**) small edible fish
whitebaits *n* ▷ **whitebait**
whiten *v* (**-s, -ing, -ed**) make or become white or whiter
whitened *v* ▷ **whiten**
whiteness *n* ▷ **white**
whitenesses *n* ▷ **white**
whitening *v* ▷ **whiten**
whitens *v* ▷ **whiten**
whiter *adj* ▷ **white**
whites *n* ▷ **white**
whitest *adj* ▷ **white**
whitewash *n* (*pl* **-es**) substance for whitening walls ▶ *v* (**-es, -ing, -ed**) cover with whitewash
whitewashed *v* ▷ **whitewash**
whitewashes *n, v* ▷ **whitewash**
whitewashing *v* ▷ **whitewash**
whither *adv* (*Obs*) to what place
whiting *n* (*pl* **-s**) edible sea fish
whitings *n* ▷ **whiting**
whitish *adj* ▷ **white**
whittle *v* (**-les, -ling, -led**) cut or carve (wood) with a knife
whittled *v* ▷ **whittle**
whittles *v* ▷ **whittle**
whittling *v* ▷ **whittle**
whiz *v* ▷ **whizz**
whizz, whiz *v* (**-es, -ing, -ed**) make a loud buzzing sound (*Informal*) ▶ *n* (*pl* **-es**) loud buzzing sound (*Informal*)
whizzed *v* ▷ **whizz**
whizzes *v, n* ▷ **whizz**
whizzing *v* ▷ **whizz**
who *pron* which person
whodunnit, whodunit [hoo-**dun**-nit] *n* (*pl* **-s**) (*Informal*) detective story, play, or film
whodunnits *n* ▷ **whodunnit**
whoever *pron* any person who
whole *adj* containing all the elements or parts ▶ *n* (*pl* **-s**) complete thing or system > **wholly** *adv*
wholefood *n* (*pl* **-s**) food that has been processed as little as possible
wholefoods *n* ▷ **wholefood**
wholehearted *adj* sincere or enthusiastic
wholemeal *adj* (of flour) made from the whole wheat grain
wholes *n* ▷ **whole**
wholesale *adj, adv* dealing by selling goods in large quantities to retailers > **wholesaler** *n* (*pl* **-s**)
wholesaler *n* ▷ **wholesale**
wholesalers *n* ▷ **wholesale**
wholesome *adj* physically or morally beneficial
wholly *adv* ▷ **whole**
whom *pron* ▷ **who**
whoop *v, n* (*pl* **-s**) shout or cry to express excitement
whoopee *interj* (*Informal*) cry of joy
whoops *n* ▷ **whoop**
whopper *n* (*pl* **-s**) (*Informal*) anything unusually large > **whopping** *adj*
whoppers *n* ▷ **whopper**
whopping *adj* ▷ **whopper**
whore [**hore**] *n* (*pl* **-s**) prostitute
whores *n* ▷ **whore**
whorl *n* (*pl* **-s**) ring of leaves or petals
whorls *n* ▷ **whorl**
whose *pron* of whom or of which
why *adv* for what reason ▶ *pron* because of which
wick *n* (*pl* **-s**) cord through a lamp or candle which carries fuel to the flame
wicked (**-er, -est**) *adj* morally bad > **wickedly** *adv* > **wickedness** *n* (*pl* **-s**)
wickedly *adv* ▷ **wicked**
wickedness *n* ▷ **wicked**
wickednesses *n* ▷ **wicked**
wicker *adj* made of woven cane > **wickerwork** *n* (*pl* **-s**)
wickerwork *n* ▷ **wicker**
wickerworks *n* ▷ **wicker**
wicket *n* (*pl* **-s**) set of three cricket stumps and two bails
wickets *n* ▷ **wicket**
wicks *n* ▷ **wick**
wide *adj* (**-r, -st**) large from side to side ▶ *adv* to the full extent > **widely** *adv*
widely *adv* ▷ **wide**
widen *v* (**-s, -ing, -ed**) make or become wider
widened *v* ▷ **widen**
widening *v* ▷ **widen**
widens *v* ▷ **widen**
wider *adj* ▷ **wide**
widespread *adj* affecting a wide area or a large number of people
widest *adj* ▷ **wide**
widgeon *n* (*pl* **-s**) ▷ **wigeon**
widgeons *n* ▷ **widgeon**
widow *n* (*pl* **-s**) woman whose husband is dead

and who has not remarried > **widowed** *adj* > **widowhood** *n* (*pl* **-s**)

widowed *adj* ▷ **widow**

widower *n* (*pl* **-s**) man whose wife is dead and who has not remarried

widowers *n* ▷ **widower**

widowhood *n* ▷ **widow**

widowhoods *n* ▷ **widow**

widows *n* ▷ **widow**

width *n* (*pl* **-s**) distance from side to side

widths *n* ▷ **width**

wield *v* (**-s, -ing, -ed**) hold and use (a weapon)

wielded *v* ▷ **wield**

wielding *v* ▷ **wield**

wields *v* ▷ **wield**

wife *n* (*pl* **wives**) woman to whom a man is married

wig *n* (*pl* **-s**) artificial head of hair

wigeon *n* (*pl* **-s**) duck found in marshland

wigeons *n* ▷ **wigeon**

wiggle *v* (**-les, -ling, -led**) move jerkily from side to side ▶ *n* (*pl* **-les**) wiggling movement

wiggled *v* ▷ **wiggle**

wiggles *v, n* ▷ **wiggle**

wiggling *v* ▷ **wiggle**

wigs *n* ▷ **wig**

wigwam *n* (*pl* **-s**) Native American's tent

wigwams *n* ▷ **wigwam**

wild *adj* (**-er, -est**) (of animals) not tamed or domesticated > **wildly** *adv* > **wildness** *n* (*pl* **-es**)

wildcat *n* (*pl* **-s**) European wild animal like a large domestic cat

wildcats *n* ▷ **wildcat**

wildebeest *n* (*pl* **-s**) gnu

wildebeests *n* ▷ **wildebeest**

wilder *adj* ▷ **wild**

wilderness *n* (*pl* **-es**) uninhabited uncultivated region

wildernesses *n* ▷ **wilderness**

wildest *adj* ▷ **wild**

wildlife *n* (*pl* **-s**) wild animals and plants collectively

wildlifes *n* ▷ **wildlife**

wildly *adv* ▷ **wild**

wildness *n* ▷ **wild**

wildnesses *n* ▷ **wild**

wilds *pl n* desolate or uninhabited place

wiles *pl n* tricks or ploys

wilful *adj* headstrong or obstinate > **wilfully** *adv*

wilfully *adv* ▷ **wilful**

wilier *adj* ▷ **wily**

wiliest *adj* ▷ **wily**

will[1] *v* (*past* **would**) used as an auxiliary to form the future tense or to indicate intention, ability, or expectation

will[2] *n* (*pl* **-s**) strong determination ▶ *v* (**-s, -ing, -ed**) use one's will in an attempt to do (something)

willed *v* ▷ **will**[2]

willing *adj* ready or inclined (to do something) ▶ *v* ▷ **will**[2] > **willingly** *adv* > **willingness** *n* (*pl* **-es**)

willingly *adv* ▷ **willing**

willingness *n* ▷ **willing**

willingnesses *n* ▷ **willing**

willow *n* (*pl* **-s**) tree with thin flexible branches

willowier *adj* ▷ **willowy**

willowiest *adj* ▷ **willowy**

willows *n* ▷ **willow**

willowy *adj* (**-wier, -wiest**) slender and graceful

willpower *n* (*pl* **-s**) ability to control oneself and one's actions

willpowers *n* ▷ **willpower**

wills *n, v* ▷ **will**[2]

wilt *v* (**-s, -ing, -ed**) (cause to) become limp or lose strength

wilted *v* ▷ **wilt**

wilting *v* ▷ **wilt**

wilts *v* ▷ **wilt**

wily *adj* (**-lier, -liest**) crafty or sly

wimp *n* (*pl* **-s**) (*Informal*) feeble ineffectual person

wimple *n* (*pl* **-s**) garment framing the face, worn by medieval women and now by nuns

wimples *n* ▷ **wimple**

wimps *n* ▷ **wimp**

win *v* (**-s, -nning, won**) come first in (a competition, fight, etc.) ▶ *n* (*pl* **-s**) victory, esp. in a game > **winner** *n* (*pl* **-s**)

wince *v* (**-ces, -cing, -ced**) draw back, as if in pain ▶ *n* (*pl* **-s**) wincing

winced *v* ▷ **wince**

winces *v, n* ▷ **wince**

winch *n* (*pl* **-es**) machine for lifting or hauling using a cable or chain wound round a drum ▶ *v* (**-es, -ing, -ed**) lift or haul using a winch

winched *v* ▷ **winch**

winches *n, v* ▷ **winch**

winching *v* ▷ **winch**

wincing *v* ▷ **wince**

wind[1] *n* (*pl* **-s**) current of air ▶ *v* (**-s, -ing, -ed**) render short of breath > **windy** *adj* (**-dier, -diest**)

wind[2] *v* (**-s, -ing, wound**) coil or wrap around

winded *v* ▷ **wind**[1]

windfall *n* (*pl* **-s**) unexpected good luck

windfalls *n* ▷ **windfall**

windier *adj* ▷ **wind**[1]

windiest *adj* ▷ **wind**[1]
winding *v* ▷ **wind**[1, 2]
windlass *n* (*pl* **-es**) winch worked by a crank
windlasses *n* ▷ **windlass**
windmill *n* (*pl* **-s**) machine for grinding or pumping driven by sails turned by the wind
windmills *n* ▷ **windmill**
window *n* (*pl* **-s**) opening in a wall to let in light or air
windows *n* ▷ **window**
windpipe *n* (*pl* **-s**) tube linking the throat and the lungs
windpipes *n* ▷ **windpipe**
winds *n, v* ▷ **wind**[1, 2]
windscreen *n* (*pl* **-s**) front window of a motor vehicle
windscreens *n* ▷ **windscreen**
windsock *n* (*pl* **-s**) cloth cone on a mast at an airfield to indicate wind direction
windsocks *n* ▷ **windsock**
windsurfing *n* (*pl* **-s**) sport of riding on water using a surfboard propelled and steered by a sail
windsurfings *n* ▷ **windsurfing**
windward *adj, n* (*pl* **-s**) (of or in) the direction from which the wind is blowing
windwards *n* ▷ **windward**
windy *adj* ▷ **wind**[1]
wine *n* (*pl* **-s**) alcoholic drink made from fermented grapes
wines *n* ▷ **wine**
wing *n* (*pl* **-s**) one of the limbs or organs of a bird, insect, or bat that are used for flying ▶ *pl* sides of a stage ▶ *v* (**-s, -ing, -ed**) fly > **winged** *adj*
winged *v, adj* ▷ **wing**
winger *n* (*pl* **-s**) (SPORT) player positioned on the side of the pitch
wingers *n* ▷ **winger**
winging *v* ▷ **wing**
wings *n, v* ▷ **wing**
wink *v* (**-s, -ing, -ed**) close and open (an eye) quickly as a signal ▶ *n* (*pl* **-s**) winking
winked *v* ▷ **wink**
winking *v* ▷ **wink**
winkle *n* (*pl* **-s**) shellfish with a spiral shell
winkles *n* ▷ **winkle**
winks *v, n* ▷ **wink**
winner *n* ▷ **win**
winners *n* ▷ **win**
winning *adj* gaining victory ▶ *v* ▷ **win**
winnings *pl n* sum won, esp. in gambling
winnow *v* (**-s, -ing, -ed**) (*pl* **-s**) separate (chaff) from (grain)
winnowed *v* ▷ **winnow**
winnowing *v* ▷ **winnow**
winnows *v, n* ▷ **winnow**
winsome *adj* (**-r, -st**) charming or winning
winsomer *adj* ▷ **winsome**
winsomest *adj* ▷ **winsome**
winter *n* (*pl* **-s**) coldest season ▶ *v* (**-s, -ing, -ed**) spend the winter
wintered *v* ▷ **winter**
wintering *v* ▷ **winter**
winters *n, v* ▷ **winter**
wintrier *adj* ▷ **wintry**
wintriest *adj* ▷ **wintry**
wintry *adj* (**-rier, -riest**) of or like winter
wipe *v* (**-pes, -ping, -ped**) clean or dry by rubbing ▶ *n* (*pl* **-s**) wiping
wiped *v* ▷ **wipe**
wipes *v, n* ▷ **wipe**
wiping *v* ▷ **wipe**
wire *n* (*pl* **-s**) thin flexible strand of metal (*Obs*) ▶ *v* (**-res, -ring, -red**) equip with wires
wired *v* ▷ **wire**
wirehaired *adj* (of a dog) having a stiff wiry coat
wireless *n* (*pl* **-es**) (*Old-fashioned*) ▷ **radio** ▶ *adj* (of a computer network) connected by radio rather than by cables or fibre optics
wirelesses *n* ▷ **wireless**
wires *n, v* ▷ **wire**
wirier *adj* ▷ **wiry**
wiriest *adj* ▷ **wiry**
wiring *n* (*pl* **-s**) system of wires ▶ *v* ▷ **wire**
wirings *n* ▷ **wiring**
wiry *adj* (**-rier, -riest**) lean and tough
wisdom *n* (*pl* **-s**) good sense and judgment
wisdoms *n* ▷ **wisdom**
wise[1] *adj* (**-r, -st**) having wisdom > **wisely** *adv*
wise[2] *n* (*pl* **-s**) (*Obs*) manner
wiseacre *n* (*pl* **-s**) person who wishes to seem wise
wiseacres *n* ▷ **wiseacres**
wisecrack (*Informal*) *n* (*pl* **-s**) clever, sometimes unkind, remark ▶ *v* (**-s, -ing, -ed**) make a wisecrack
wisecracked *v* ▷ **wisecrack**
wisecracking *v* ▷ **wisecrack**
wisecracks *n, v* ▷ **wisecrack**
wisely *adv* ▷ **wise**[1]
wiser *adj* ▷ **wise**[1]
wises *n* ▷ **wise**[2]
wisest *adj* ▷ **wise**[1]
wish *v* (**-es, -ing, -ed**) want or desire ▶ *n* (*pl* **-es**) expression of a desire
wishbone *n* (*pl* **-s**) V-shaped bone above the breastbone of a fowl
wishbones *n* ▷ **wishbone**

wished *v* ▷ **wish**
wishes *v, n* ▷ **wish**
wishful *adj* too optimistic
wishing *v* ▷ **wish**
wisp *n* (*pl* **-s**) light delicate streak > **wispy** *adj* (**-pier, -piest**)
wispier *adj* ▷ **wisp**
wispiest *adj* ▷ **wisp**
wisps *n* ▷ **wisp**
wispy *adj* ▷ **wisp**
wisteria *n* (*pl* **-s**) climbing shrub with blue or purple flowers
wisterias *n* ▷ **wisteria**
wistful *adj* sadly longing > **wistfully** *adv*
wistfully *adv* ▷ **wistful**
wit *n* (*pl* **-s**) ability to use words or ideas in a clever and amusing way
witch *n* (*pl* **-es**) person, usu. female, who practises (black) magic
witchcraft *n* (*pl* **-s**) use of magic
witchcrafts *n* ▷ **witchcraft**
witches *n* ▷ **witch**
with *prep* indicating presence alongside, possession, means of performance, characteristic manner, etc.
withdraw *v* (**-drawing, -drew, -drawn**) take or move out or away > **withdrawal** *n* (*pl* **-s**)
withdrawal *n* ▷ **withdraw**
withdrawals *n* ▷ **withdraw**
withdrawn *adj* unsociable ▶ *v* ▷ **withdraw**
withdraws *v* ▷ **withdraw**
withdrew *v* ▷ **withdraw**
wither *v* (**-s, -ing, -ed**) wilt or dry up
withered *v* ▷ **wither**
withering *adj* (of a look or remark) scornful ▶ *v* ▷ **wither**
withers *v* ▷ **wither** ▶ *pl n* ridge between a horse's shoulder blades
withheld *v* ▷ **withhold**
withhold *v* (**-s, -ing, -held**) refrain from giving
withholding *v* ▷ **withhold**
withholds *v* ▷ **withhold**
within *prep, adv* in or inside
without *prep* not accompanied by, using, or having
withstand *v* (**-s, -ing, -stood**) oppose or resist successfully
withstanding *v* ▷ **withstand**
withstands *v* ▷ **wwithstand**
withstood *v* ▷ **wwithstand**
witless *adj* foolish
witness *n* (*pl* **-es**) person who has seen something happen ▶ *v* (**-es, -ing, -ed**) see at first hand
witnessed *v* ▷ **witness**
witnesses *n, v* ▷ **witness**
witnessing *v* ▷ **witness**
wits *n* ▷ **wit**
witter *v* (**-s, -ing, -ed**) (CHIEFLY BRIT) chatter pointlessly or at unnecessary length
wittered *v* ▷ **witter**
wittering *v* ▷ **witter**
witters *v* ▷ **witter**
witticism *n* (*pl* **-s**) witty remark
witticisms *n* ▷ **witticism**
wittier *adj* ▷ **witty**
wittiest *adj* ▷ **witty**
wittily *adv* ▷ **witty**
wittingly *adv* intentionally
witty *adj* (**-ttier, -ttiest**) clever and amusing > **wittily** *adv*
wives *n* ▷ **wife**

> **wiz** *n* (**wizzes**). Wiz is a short form of **wizard.** This is the highest-scoring three-letter word beginning with W, and can be especially useful when there isn't much room to manoeuvre. Wiz scores 15 points.

wizard *n* (*pl* **-s**) magician > **wizardry** *n* (*pl* **-ies**)
wizardries *n* ▷ **wizard**
wizardry *n* ▷ **wizard**
wizards *n* ▷ **wizard**
wizened [**wiz**-zend] *adj* shrivelled or wrinkled

> **wo** *n* (**wos**). Wo is an old-fashioned spelling of **woe.** This unusual word is handy for joining words ending in W to those beginning in O. Wo scores 5 points.

woad *n* (*pl* **-s**) blue dye obtained from a plant, used by the ancient Britons as a body dye
woads *n* ▷ **woad**
wobbegong *n* (*pl* **-s**) Australian shark with brown-and-white skin
wobbegongs *n* ▷ **wobbegong**
wobble *v* (**-les, -ling, -led**) move unsteadily ▶ *n* (*pl* **-s**) wobbling movement or sound > **wobbly** *adj* (**-lier, -liest**)
wobbled *v* ▷ **wobble**
wobbles *v, n* ▷ **wobble**
wobblier *adj* ▷ **wobble**
wobbliest *adj* ▷ **wobble**
wobbling *v* ▷ **wobble**
wobbly *adj* ▷ **wobble**
wodge *n* (*pl* **-s**) (*Informal*) thick lump or chunk
wodges *n* ▷ **wodge**
woe *n* (*pl* **-s**) grief
woebegone *adj* looking miserable
woeful *adj* extremely sad > **woefully** *adv*
woefully *adv* ▷ **woeful**
woes *n* ▷ **woe**

wok *n* (*pl* **-s**) bowl-shaped Chinese cooking pan, used for stir-frying
woke *v* ▷ **wake**[1]
woken *v* ▷ **wake**[1]
woks *n* ▷ **wok**
wold *n* (*pl* **-s**) high open country
wolds *n* ▷ **wold**
wolf *n* (*pl* **wolves**) wild predatory canine mammal ▶ *v* eat ravenously
wolverine *n* (*pl* **-s**) carnivorous mammal of Arctic regions
wolverines *n* ▷ **wolverine**
wolves *n* ▷ **wolf**
woman *n* (*pl* **women**) adult human female > **womanhood** *n* (*pl* **-s**)
womanhood *n* ▷ **woman**
womanhoods *n* ▷ **woman**
womanish *adj* effeminate
womanizer *n* ▷ **womanizing**
womanizers *n* ▷ **womanizing**
womanizing *n* (*pl* **-s**) practice of indulging in casual affairs with women > **womanizer** *n* (*pl* **-s**)
womanizings *n* ▷ **womanizing**
womanly *adj* having qualities traditionally associated with a woman
womb *n* (*pl* **-s**) hollow organ in female mammals where babies are conceived and develop
wombat *n* (*pl* **-s**) small heavily-built burrowing Australian marsupial
wombats *n* ▷ **wombat**
wombs *n* ▷ **womb**
women *n* ▷ **woman**
won *v* ▷ **win**
wonder *v* (**-s, -ing, -ed**) be curious about ▶ *n* (*pl* **-s**) wonderful thing ▶ *adj* spectacularly successful > **wonderment** *n* (*pl* **-s**)
wondered *v* ▷ **wonder**
wonderful *adj* very fine > **wonderfully** *adv*
wonderfully *adv* ▷ **wonderful**
wondering *v* ▷ **wonder**
wonderment *n* ▷ **wonder**
wonderments *n* ▷ **wonder**
wonders *v, n* ▷ **wonder**
wondrous *adj* (*Old-fashioned*) wonderful
wonkier *adj* ▷ **wonky**
wonkiest *adj* ▷ **wonky**
wonky *adj* (**-kier, -kiest**) (BRIT, AUST & NZ) (*Informal*) shaky or unsteady
wont [rhymes with **don't**] *adj* accustomed ▶ *n* (*pl* **-s**) custom
wonts *n* ▷ **wont**
woo *v* (**-s, -ing, -ed**) try to persuade (*Old-fashioned*)
wood *n* (*pl* **-s**) substance trees are made of, used in carpentry and as fuel > **woody** *adj* (**-dier, -diest**)
woodbine *n* (*pl* **-s**) honeysuckle
woodbines *n* ▷ **woodbine**
woodcock *n* (*pl* **-s**) game bird
woodcocks *n* ▷ **woodcook**
woodcut *n* (*pl* **-s**) (print made from) an engraved block of wood
woodcuts *n* ▷ **woodcut**
wooded *adj* covered with trees
wooden *adj* made of wood
woodier *adj* ▷ **wood**
woodiest *adj* ▷ **wood**
woodland *n* (*pl* **-s**) forest
woodlands *n* ▷ **woodland**
woodlice *n* ▷ **woodlouse**
woodlouse *n* (*pl* **-lice**) small insect-like creature with many legs
woodpecker *n* (*pl* **-s**) bird which searches tree trunks for insects
woodpeckers *n* ▷ **woodpecker**
woods *n* ▷ **wood**
woodwind *adj, n* (*pl* **-s**) (of) a type of wind instrument made of wood
woodwinds *n* ▷ **woodwind**
woodworm *n* insect larva that bores into wood
woodworms *n* ▷ **woodworm**
woody *adj* ▷ **wood**
wooed *v* ▷ **woo**
woof[1] *n* (*pl* **-s**) cross threads in weaving
woof[2] *n* (*pl* **-s**) barking noise made by a dog
woofer *n* (*pl* **-s**) loudspeaker reproducing low-frequency sounds
woofers *n* ▷ **woofer**
woofs *n* ▷ **woof**[1,2]
wooing *v* ▷ **woo**
wool *n* (*pl* **-s**) soft hair of sheep, goats, etc. > **woollen** *adj*
woollen *adj* ▷ **wool**
woollier *adj* ▷ **woolly**
woolliest *adj* ▷ **woolly**
woolly *adj* (**-llier, -lliest**) of or like wool ▶ *n* knitted woollen garment
wools *n* ▷ **wool**
woomera *n* (*pl* **-s**) notched stick used by Australian Aborigines to aid the propulsion of a spear
woomeras *n* ▷ **woomera**
woos *v* ▷ **woo**
woozier *adj* ▷ **woozy**
wooziest *adj* ▷ **woozy**
woozy *adj* (**-zier, -ziest**) (*Informal*) weak, dizzy, and confused

word *n* (*pl* **-s**) smallest single meaningful unit of speech or writing ▸ *v* (**-s, -ing, -ed**) express in words
worded *v* ▷ **word**
wordier *adj* ▷ **wordy**
wordiest *adj* ▷ **wordy**
wording *n* (*pl* **-s**) choice and arrangement of words ▸ *v* ▷ **word**
wordings *n* ▷ **wording**
words *n, v* ▷ **word**
wordy *adj* (**-dier, -diest**) using too many words
wore *v* ▷ **wear**
work *n* (*pl* **-s**) physical or mental effort directed to making or doing something ▸ *pl* factory (*Informal*) ▸ *adj* of or for work ▸ *v* (**-s, -ing, -ed**) (cause to) do work > **workable** *adj* > **worker** *n* (*pl* **-s**)
workable *adj* ▷ **work**
workaholic *n* (*pl* **-s**) person obsessed with work
workaholics *n* ▷ **workaholic**
worked *v* ▷ **work**
worker *n* ▷ **work**
workers *n* ▷ **work**
workhorse *n* (*pl* **-s**) person or thing that does a lot of dull or routine work
workhorses *n* ▷ **workhorse**
workhouse *n* (*pl* **-s**) (in England, formerly) institution where the poor were given food and lodgings in return for work
workhouses *n* ▷ **workhouse**
working *v* ▷ **work**
workman *n* (*pl* **-men**) manual worker
workmanship *n* (*pl* **-s**) skill with which an object is made
workmanships *n* ▷ **workmanship**
workmen *n* ▷ **workman**
works *n, v* ▷ **work**
workshop *n* (*pl* **-s**) room or building for a manufacturing process
workshops *n* ▷ **w**
worktop *n* (*pl* **-s**) surface in a kitchen, used for food preparation
worktops *n* ▷ **worktop**
world *n* (*pl* **-s**) the planet earth ▸ *adj* of the whole world
worldlier *adj* ▷ **worldly**
worldliest *adj* ▷ **worldly**
worldly *adj* (**-ier, -iest**) not spiritual
worlds *n* ▷ **world**
worm *n* (*pl* **-s**) small limbless invertebrate animal ▸ *pl* illness caused by parasitic worms in the intestines ▸ *v* (**-s, -ing, -ed**) rid of worms > **wormy** *adj* (**-mier, -miest**)
wormed *v* ▷ **worm**
wormier *adj* ▷ **worm**
wormiest *adj* ▷ **worm**
worming *v* ▷ **worm**
worms *n, v* ▷ **worm**
wormwood *n* (*pl* **-s**) bitter plant
wormwoods *n* ▷ **wormwood**
wormy *adj* ▷ **worm**
worn *v* ▷ **wear**
worried *v, adj* ▷ **worry**
worries *v, n* ▷ **worry**
worry *v* (**-ies, -ying, -ied**) (cause to) be anxious or uneasy ▸ *n* (*pl* **-ies**) (cause of) anxiety or concern > **worried** *adj* > **worrying** *adj, n*
worrying *v, adj* ▷ **worry**
worse *adj, adv* ▷ **bad, badly**
worsen *v* (**-s, -ing, -ed**) make or grow worse
worsened *v* ▷ **worsen**
worsening *v* ▷ **worsen**
worsens *v* ▷ **worsen**
worship *v* (**-s, -pping, -pped**) show religious devotion to ▸ *n* (*pl* **-s**) act or instance of worshipping > **worshipper** *n* (*pl* **-s**)
worshipful *adj* worshipping
worshipped *v* ▷ **worship**
worshipper *n* ▷ **worship**
worshippers *n* ▷ **worship**
worshipping *v* ▷ **worship**
worships *v, n* ▷ **worship**
worst *adj, adv* ▷ **bad, badly** ▸ *n* worst thing
worsted [**wooss**-tid] *n* (*pl* **-s**) type of woollen yarn or fabric
worsteds *n* ▷ **worsted**
worth *prep* having a value of ▸ *n* (*pl* **-s**) value or price > **worthless** *adj*
worthier *adj* ▷ **worthy**
worthiest *adj* ▷ **worthy**
worthily *adv* ▷ **worthy**
worthiness *n* ▷ **worthy**
worthinesses *n* ▷ **worthy**
worthless *adj* ▷ **worth**
worths *n* ▷ **worth**
worthwhile *adj* worth the time or effort involved
worthy *adj* (**-thier, -thiest**) deserving admiration or respect ▸ *n* (*Informal*) notable person > **worthily** *adv* > **worthiness** *n* (*pl* **-es**)
would *v* ▷ **will**[1]
wound[1] *n* (*pl* **-s**) injury caused by violence ▸ *v* (**-s, -ing, -ed**) inflict a wound on
wound[2] *v* ▷ **wind**[2]
wounded *v* ▷ **wound**[1]
wounding *v* ▷ **wound**[1]
wounds *n, v* ▷ **wound**[1]
wove *v* ▷ **weave**
woven *v* ▷ **weave**

wow *interj* exclamation of astonishment ▶ *n* (*pl* **-s**) (*Informal*) astonishing person or thing
wows *n* ▷ **wow**
wowser *n* (*pl* **-s**) (AUST & NZ) (*Slang*) puritanical person
wowsers *n* ▷ **wowser**

wox *n* (**woxes**). Wox is an old past tense of the verb **wax.** This gives a very good score for a three-letter word, and is a good one to look for when you have an X. Wox scores 13 points.

wrack *n* (*pl* **-s**) seaweed
wracks *n* ▷ **wrack**
wraith *n* (*pl* **-s**) ghost
wraiths *n* ▷ **wraith**
wrangle *v* (**-les, -ling, -led**) argue noisily ▶ *n* (*pl* **-s**) noisy argument
wrangled *v* ▷ **wrangle**
wrangles *v, n* ▷ **wrangle**
wrangling *v* ▷ **wrangle**
wrap *v* (**-s, -pping, -pped**) fold (something) round (a person or thing) so as to cover ▶ *n* (*pl* **-s**) garment wrapped round the shoulders
wrapped *v* ▷ **wrap**
wrapper *n* (*pl* **-s**) cover for a product
wrappers *n* ▷ **wrapper**
wrapping *n* (*pl* **-s**) material used to wrap ▶ *v* ▷ **wrap**
wrappings *n* ▷ **wrapping**
wraps *v, n* ▷ **wrap**
wrasse *n* (*pl* **-s**) colourful sea fish
wrasses *n* ▷ **wrasse**
wrath [**roth**] *n* (*pl* **-s**) intense anger > **wrathful** *adj*
wrathful *adj* ▷ **wrath**
wraths *n* ▷ **wrath**
wreak *v* (**-s, -ing, -ed**) cause (chaos)
wreaked *v* ▷ **wreak**
wreaking *v* ▷ **wreak**
wreaks *v* ▷ **wreak**
wreath *n* (*pl* **-s**) twisted ring or band of flowers or leaves used as a memorial or tribute
wreathed *adj* surrounded or encircled
wreaths *n* ▷ **wreath**
wreck *v* (**-s, -ing, -ed**) destroy ▶ *n* (*pl* **-s**) remains of something that has been destroyed or badly damaged, esp. a ship > **wrecker** *n* (*pl* **-s**)
wreckage *n* (*pl* **-s**) wrecked remains
wreckages *n* ▷ **wreckage**
wrecked *v* ▷ **wreck**
wrecker *n* ▷ **wreck**
wreckers *n* ▷ **wreck**
wrecking *v* ▷ **wreck**
wrecks *v, n* ▷ **wreck**
wren *n* (*pl* **-s**) small brown songbird
wrench *v* (**-es, -ing, -ed**) twist or pull violently ▶ *n* (*pl* **-es**) violent twist or pull
wrenched *v* ▷ **wrench**
wrenches *v, n* ▷ **wrench**
wrenching *v* ▷ **wrench**
wrens *n* ▷ **wren**
wrest *v* (**-s, -ing, -ed**) twist violently
wrested *v* ▷ **wrest**
wresting *v* ▷ **wrest**
wrestle *v* (**-les, -ling, -led**) fight, esp. as a sport, by grappling with and trying to throw down an opponent > **wrestler** *n* (*pl* **-s**) > **wrestling** *n* (*pl* **-s**)
wrestled *v* ▷ **wrestle**
wrestler *n* ▷ **wrestle**
wrestlers *n* ▷ **wrestle**
wrestles *v* ▷ **wrestle**
wrestling *v, n* ▷ **wrestle**
wrestlings *n* ▷ **wrestle**
wrests *v* ▷ **wrest**
wretch *n* (*pl* **-es**) despicable person
wretched [**retch**-id] *adj* (**-er, -est**) miserable or unhappy > **wretchedly** *adv* > **wretchedness** *n* (*pl* **-es**)
wretcheder *adj* ▷ **wretched**
wretchedest *adj* ▷ **wretched**
wretchedly *adv* ▷ **wretched**
wretchedness *n* ▷ **wretched**
wretchednesses *n* ▷ **wretched**
wretches *n* ▷ **wretch**
wrier *adj* ▷ **wry**
wriest *adj* ▷ **wry**
wriggle *v* (**-les, -ling, -led**) move with a twisting action ▶ *n* (*pl* **-s**) wriggling movement
wriggled *v* ▷ **wriggle**
wriggles *v, n* ▷ **wriggle**
wriggling *v* ▷ **wriggle**
wright *n* (*pl* **-s**) maker
wrights *n* ▷ **wright**
wring *v* (**-s, -ing, wrung**) twist, esp. to squeeze liquid out of
wringing *v* ▷ **wring**
wrings *v* ▷ **wring**
wrinkle *n* (*pl* **-s**) slight crease, esp. one in the skin due to age ▶ *v* (**-les, -ling, -led**) make or become slightly creased > **wrinkly** *adj* (**-lier, -liest**)
wrinkled *v* ▷ **wrinkle**
wrinkles *n, v* ▷ **wrinkle**
wrinklier *adj* ▷ **wrinkle**
wrinkliest *adj* ▷ **wrinkle**
wrinkling *v* ▷ **wrinkle**
wrinkly *adj* ▷ **wrinkle**
wrist *n* (*pl* **-s**) joint between the hand and

the arm
wrists *n* ▷ **wrist**
wristwatch *n* (*pl* **-es**) watch worn on the wrist
wristwatches *n* ▷ **wristwatch**
writ *n* (*pl* **-s**) written legal command
write *v* (**-tes, -ting, wrote, written**) mark paper etc. with symbols or words > **writing** *n* (*pl* **-s**)
writer *n* (*pl* **-s**) author
writers *n* ▷ **writer**
writhe *v* (**-thes, -thing, -thed**) twist or squirm in or as if in pain
writhed *v* ▷ **writhe**
writhes *v* ▷ **writhe**
writhing *v* ▷ **writhe**
writing *v, n* ▷ **write**
writings *n* ▷ **write**
writs *n* ▷ **writ**
written *v* ▷ **write**
wrong *adj* incorrect or mistaken ▶ *adv* in a wrong manner ▶ *n* (*pl* **-s**) something immoral or unjust ▶ *v* (**-s, -ing, -ed**) treat unjustly > **wrongly** *adv* > **wrongful** *adj* > **wrongfully** *adv*
wrongdoer *n* ▷ **wrongdoing**
wrongdoers *n* ▷ **wrongdoing**
wrongdoing *n* (*pl* **-s**) immoral or illegal behaviour > **wrongdoer** *n* (*pl* **-s**)
wrongdoings *n* ▷ **wrongdoing**
wronged *v* ▷ **wrong**
wrongful *adj* ▷ **wrong**
wrongfully *adv* ▷ **wrong**
wronging *v* ▷ **wrong**
wrongly *adv* ▷ **wrong**
wrongs *n, v* ▷ **wrong**
wrote *v* ▷ **write**
wrought [**rawt**] *v* (*Lit*) ▷ **work** ▶ *adj* (of metals) shaped by hammering or beating
wrung *v* ▷ **wring**
wry *adj* (**wrier, wriest** *or* **wryer**) (**wryest**) drily humorous > **wryly** *adv*
wryer *adj* ▷ **wry**
wryest *adj* ▷ **wry**
wryly *adv* ▷ **wry**

wye *n* (**wyes**). Wye is the letter Y. If you have W and Y on your rack, look for an E on the board that will allow you to play this especially if you can land on a bonus square as a result. Wye scores 9 points.

Xx

Worth 8 points on its own, X is one of the best tiles in the game. It doesn't, however, start many two- and three-letter words. There are only two valid two-letter words, **xi** and **xu** (9 points each), beginning with X, and only one three-letter word, **xis.** Therefore, if you have an X on your rack and need to play short words, you're probably better off thinking of words that end in X or have X in them rather than those that start with X.

xebec *n* (**xebecs**). A xebec is an Algerian ship. This is a good high-scoring word. If you have an X, you'll probably only need one E as well as B and C to play it, as there is likely to be an available E on the board already. Xebec scores 16 points.

xenon *n* (*pl* **-s**) (CHEM) colourless odourless gas found in very small quantities in the air

xenons *n* ▷ **xenon**

xenophobia [zen-oh-**fobe**-ee-a] *n* (*pl* **-s**) fear or hatred of people from other countries

xenophobias *n* ▷ **xenophobia**

xi *n* (**xis**). Xi is the 14th letter of the Greek alphabet. The plural of this word is the only three-letter word that starts with X. Xi scores 9 points.

xoanon *n* (**xoanons**) A xoanon is a primitive carving of a god. If you have all the tiles for the plural, and are able to place them all on the board, you'll earn a 50-point bonus. Xoanon scores 13 points.

xu *n* (**xu**). The xu is a unit of currency in Vietnam. The plural form of this word is the same as its singular, so be sure to challenge anyone who adds an S to it! Xu scores 9 points.

xylem [**zy**-lem] *n* (*pl* **-s**) plant tissue that conducts water and minerals from the roots to all other parts

xylems *n* ▷ **xylem**

xylophone [**zile**-oh-fone] *n* (*pl* **-s**) musical instrument made of a row of wooden bars played with hammers

xylophones *n* ▷ **xylophone**

Yy

Y is a useful tile to have on your rack. It's worth 4 points on its own, and so often gives you good scores. There are only four two-letter words beginning with Y, but these are easy to remember as there's one for every vowel except I: **ya, ye, yo** and **yu** (5 points each). There are quite a few useful three-letter words: **yew** (9) and **yob** (8) and remember that yob was originally **boy** backwards: if you can't fit in yob, you may be able to use boy instead. And while his half-brother the **zo** (or **dzo** or **dso** or **zho**) gets all the attention, don't forget that the **yak** (10) earns quite a decent score!

ya *interj* (S AFR) yes
yabbies *n* ▷ **yabby**
yabby *n* (*pl* **-bbies**) (AUST) small freshwater crayfish
yacht [**yott**] *n* (*pl* **-s**) large boat with sails or an engine, used for racing or pleasure cruising > **yachting** *n* (*pl* **-s**) > **yachtsman** *n* (*pl* **-men**) > **yachtswoman** *n* (*pl* **-women**)
yachting *n* ▷ **yacht**
yachtings *n* ▷ **yacht**
yachts *n* ▷ **yacht**
yachtsman *n* ▷ **yacht**
yachtsmen *n* ▷ **yacht**
yachtswoman *n* ▷ **yacht**
yachtswomen *n* ▷ **yacht**
yak¹ *n* (*pl* **-s**) Tibetan ox with long shaggy hair
yak² *v* (**yaks, yakking, yakked**) (*Slang*) talk continuously about unimportant matters
yakka *n* (*pl* **-s**) (AUST & NZ) (*Informal*) work
yakkas *n* ▷ **yakka**
yakked *v* ▷ **yak²**
yakking *v* ▷ **yak²**
yaks *n* ▷ **yak¹** ▶ *v* ▷ **yak²**
yam *n* (*pl* **-s**) tropical root vegetable
yams *n* ▷ **yam**
yank *v* (**-s, -ing, -ed**) pull or jerk suddenly ▶ *n* (*pl* **-s**) sudden pull or jerk
yanked *v* ▷ **yank**
yanking *v* ▷ **yank**
yanks *v, n* ▷ **yank**
yap *v* (**-s, -pping, -pped**) bark with a high-pitched sound (*Informal*) ▶ *n* (*pl* **-s**) high-pitched bark
yapped *v* ▷ **yap**
yapping *v* ▷ **yap**
yaps *v* ▷ **yap**
yard¹ *n* (*pl* **-s**) unit of length equal to 36 inches or about 91.4 centimetres > **yardstick** *n* (*pl* **-s**) standard against which to judge other people or things
yard² *n* (*pl* **-s**) enclosed area, usu. next to a building and often used for a particular purpose
yards *n* ▷ **yard¹, ²**
yardstick *n* ▷ **yard¹**
yardsticks *n* ▷ **yard¹**
yarmulke [**yar**-mull-ka] *n* (*pl* **-s**) skullcap worn by Jewish men
yarmulkes *n* ▷ **yarmulke**
yarn *n* (*pl* **-s**) thread used for knitting or making cloth
yarns *n* ▷ **yarn**
yashmak *n* (*pl* **-s**) veil worn by a Muslim woman to cover her face in public
yashmaks *n* ▷ **yashmak**
yaw *v* (**-s, -ing, -ed**) (of an aircraft or ship) turn to one side or from side to side while moving
yawed *v* ▷ **yaw**
yawing *v* ▷ **yaw**
yawl *n* (*pl* **-s**) two-masted sailing boat
yawls *n* ▷ **yawl**
yawn *v* (**-s, -ing, -ed**) open the mouth wide and take in air deeply, often when sleepy or bored ▶ *n* (*pl* **-s**) act of yawning > **yawning** *adj*
yawned *v* ▷ **yawn**
yawning ▷ **yawn**
yawns *v, n* ▷ **yawn**
yaws *v* ▷ **yaw**
ye [**yee**] *pron* (*Obs*) you
year *n* (*pl* **-s**) time taken for the earth to make

one revolution around the sun, about 365 days
yearling *n* (*pl* **-s**) animal between one and two years old
yearlings *n* ▷ **yearling**
yearly *adj, adv* (happening) every year or once a year
yearn *v* (**-s, -ing, -ed**) want (something) very much > **yearning** *n* (*pl* **-s**) *adj*
yearned *v* ▷ **yearn**
yearning *v, n* ▷ **yearn**
yearnings *n* ▷ **yearn**
yearns *v* ▷ **yearn**
years *n* ▷ **year**
yeast *n* (*pl* **-s**) fungus used to make bread rise and to ferment alcoholic drinks > **yeasty** *adj*
yeasts *n* ▷ **yeast**
yebo *interj* (S AFR) (*Informal*) yes
yell *v* (**-s, -ing, -ed**) shout or scream in a loud or piercing way ▶ *n* (*pl* **-s**) loud cry of pain, anger, or fear
yelled *v* ▷ **yell**
yelling *v* ▷ **yell**
yellow *n* (*pl* **-s**) the colour of gold, a lemon, etc. ▶ *adj* (**-er, -est**) of this colour ▶ *v* (**-s, -ing, -ed**) make or become yellow
yellowed *v* ▷ **yellow**
yellower *adj* ▷ **yellow**
yellowest *adj* ▷ **yellow**
yellowhammer *n* (*pl* **-s**) European songbird with a yellow head and body
yellowhammers *n* ▷ **yellowhammer**
yellowing *v* ▷ **yellow**
yellows *n, v* ▷ **yellow**
yells *v, n* ▷ **yell**
yelp *v* (**-s, -ing, -ed**) ▶ *n* (*pl* **-s**) (give) a short sudden cry
yelped *v* ▷ **yelp**
yelping *v* ▷ **yelp**
yelps *v, n* ▷ **yelp**
yen[1] *n* (*pl* **yen**) monetary unit of Japan
yen[2] *n* (*pl* **yen**) (*Informal*) longing or desire
yeoman [**yo**-man] *n* (*pl* **-men**) (HIST) farmer owning and farming his own land
yeomen *n* ▷ **yeoman**
yes *interj* expresses consent, agreement, or approval
yesterday *adv, n* (*pl* **-s**) (on) the day before today
yesterdays *n* ▷ **yesterday**
yet *conj* nevertheless, still ▶ *adv* up until then or now
yeti *n* (*pl* **yetis**) large apelike creature said to live in the Himalayas
yetis *n* ▷ **yeti**
yew *n* (*pl* **-s**) evergreen tree with needle-like leaves and red berries
yews *n* ▷ **yew**

> **yex** *v* (**yexes, yexing, yexed**). Yex is a Scots word that means to hiccup or cough. This word gives you a good score, and the verb forms offer the chance to expand it if someone else plays it, or if you get the chance later on. Yex scores 13 points.

yield *v* (**-s, -ing, -ed**) produce or bear ▶ *n* (*pl* **-s**)
yielded *v* ▷ **yield**
yielding *adj* submissive ▶ *v* ▷ **yield**
yields *v, n* ▷ **yield**

> **yo** *interj*. Yo is an informal greeting. This is useful for connecting words ending in Y with ones beginning in O. Yo scores 5 points.

yob *n* (*pl* **-s**) (*Slang*) bad-mannered aggressive youth
yobbo *n* (*pl* **-bboes** *or* **-bbos**) yob
yobboes *n* ▷ **yobbo**
yobbos *n* ▷ **yobbo**
yobs *n* ▷ **yob**
yodel *v* (**-s, -lling, -lled**) sing with abrupt changes between a normal and a falsetto voice
yodelled *v* ▷ **yodel**
yodelling *v* ▷ **yodel**
yodels *v* ▷ **yodel**
yoga *n* (*pl* **-s**) Hindu method of exercise and discipline aiming at spiritual, mental, and physical wellbeing
yogas *n* ▷ **yoga**
yoghurt *n* ▷ **yogurt**
yoghurts *n* ▷ **yogurt**
yogi *n* (*pl* **-s**) person who practises yoga
yogis *n* ▷ **yogi**
yogurt, yoghurt *n* (*pl* **-s**) slightly sour custard-like food made from milk that has had bacteria added to it, often sweetened and flavoured with fruit
yogurts *n* ▷ **yogurt**

> **yok** *n* (**yoks**). A yok is a noisy laugh. This unusual word is useful if there isn't much space on the board, as there's likely to be an O available to form it around. Yok scores 10 points.

yoke *n* (*pl* **-s**) wooden bar put across the necks of two animals to hold them together (*Lit*) ▶ *v* (**-kes, -king, -ked**) put a yoke on
yoked *v* ▷ **yoke**
yokel *n* (*pl* **yokels**) (*Offens*) person who lives in the country and is usu. simple and old-fashioned

yokels *n* ▷ **yokel**
yokes *n*, *v* ▷ **yoke**
yoking *v* ▷ **yoke**
yolk *n* (*pl* **-s**) yellow part of an egg that provides food for the developing embryo
yolks *n* ▷ **yolk**
yonder *adj*, *adv* (situated) over there
yonks *pl n* (*Informal*) very long time
yore *n* (*pl* **-s**) (*Lit*) a long time ago
yores *n* ▷ **yore**
you *pron* refers to: the person or people addressed
young *adj* in an early stage of life or growth ▶ *pl n* young people in general
youngster *n* (*pl* **-s**) young person
youngsters *n* ▷ **youngster**
your *adj* of, belonging to, or associated with you > **yourself** *pron*
yours *pron* something belonging to you
yourself *pron* ▷ **your**
youth *n* (*pl* **-s**) time of being young > **youthful** *adj* > **youthfulness** *n* (*pl* **-es**)
youthful *adj* ▷ **youth**
youthfulness *adj* ▷ **youth**
youthfulnesses *adj* ▷ **youth**
youths *n* ▷ **youth**
yowl *v*, *n* (*pl* **-s**) (produce) a loud mournful cry
yowls *n* ▷ **yowl**
yttrium [**it**-ree-um] *n* (*pl* **-s**) (CHEM) silvery metallic element used in various alloys
yttriums *n* ▷ **yttrium**

> **yu** *n* (**yus**). Yu is a Chinese word that means precious jade. This word is good for connecting words ending in Y with ones beginning in U. Yu scores 5 points.

yucca *n* (*pl* **-s**) tropical plant with spikes of white leaves
yuccas *n* ▷ **yucca**
yuckier *adj* ▷ **yucky**
yuckiest *adj* ▷ **yucky**
yucky *adj* (**-ckier, -ckiest**) (*Slang*) disgusting, nasty

> **yuk** *interj*. Yuk is a noise people make to express disgust or dislike. This funny little word is worth remembering as it give a good score and uses an unpromising combination of letters. Yuk scores 10 points.

yuppie *n* (*pl* **-s**) young highly-paid professional person, esp. one who has a materialistic way of life ▶ *adj* typical of or reflecting the values of yuppies
yuppies *n* ▷ **yuppie**

Zz

Scoring the same as Q but easier to use, Z is the most valuable tile in Scrabble. There is only one two-letter word beginning with Z, **zo** (11 points), but remembering this will save you wasting time looking for others. There some very good three-letter words starting with Z, however. These include another variant of **zo, zho** (15), as well as **zax** and **zex** (19 each), **zap** (14), **zip** (14) and **zoo** (12).

zanier *adj* ▷ **zany**
zaniest ▷ **zany**

zanja *n* **(zanjas)**. A zanja is an irrigation canal. This unusual word is very useful because of its combination of J and Z. As there are many As in the game, if you are lucky enough to get J and Z together, you may well be able to play this somewhere. Zanja scores 21 points.

zanjero *n* **(zanjeros)**. A zanjero is a supervisor of irrigation canals. If you can use all your tiles to play zanjero, you'll earn a 50-point bonus. Zanjero scores 23 points.

zany [**zane**-ee] *adj* **(-nier, -niest)** comical in an endearing way
zap *v* **(-s, -pping, -pped)** (*Slang*) kill (by shooting)
zapped *v* ▷ **zap**
zapping *v* ▷ **zap**
zaps *v* ▷ **zap**

zax *n* **(zaxes)**. A zax a small axe for cutting slates. This is great word combining X and Z. If you get a Z late in the game, check if X has already been played, and whether there is an opportunity to form zax or **zex**. Zax scores 19 points.

zeal *n* (*pl* **-s**) great enthusiasm or eagerness
zealot [**zel**-lot] *n* (*pl* **-s**) fanatic or extreme enthusiast
zealots *n* ▷ **zealot**
zealous [**zel**-luss] *adj* extremely eager or enthusiastic > **zealously** *adv*
zealously *adv* ▷ **zealous**
zeals *n* ▷ **zeal**
zebra *n* (*pl* **-s**) black-and-white striped African animal of the horse family
zebras *n* ▷ **zebra**
zebu [**zee**-boo] *n* (*pl* **-s**) Asian ox with a humped back and long horns
zebus *n* ▷ **zebu**

zed *n* **(zeds)**. Zed is the letter Z. This is a handy word when you have a Z but no space or letters for a longer word. Zed scores 13 points.

zee *n* **(zees)**. Zee is the American pronunciation of the letter Z. This word can be very useful because E is the most common tile in Scrabble, so keep it in mind if you draw a Z. Zee scores 12 points.

zenith *n* (*pl* **-s**) highest point of success or power
zeniths *n* ▷ **zenith**
zephyr [**zef**-fer] *n* (*pl* **-s**) soft gentle breeze
zephyrs *n* ▷ **zephyr**
zeppelin *n* (*pl* **-s**) (HIST) large cylindrical airship
zeppelins *n* ▷ **zeppelin**
zero *n* (*pl* **-ros, -roes**) (symbol representing) the number 0 ▶ *adj* having no measurable quantity or size
zeroes *n* ▷ **zero**
zeros *n* ▷ **zero**
zest *n* (*pl* **-s**) enjoyment or excitement
zests *n* ▷ **zest**

zeuxite *n* **(zeuxites)**. Zeuxite is a mineral. This unusual word is great if you have the letters for it. If you can use all of your tiles to play zeuxite, you'll get a 50-point bonus. Zeuxite scores 23 points.

zex *n* **(zexes)**. Zex means the same as **zax.** If you get a Z late in the game, check if X has already been played, and whether there is an opportunity to form zax. Zex scores 19 points.

zho *n* (**zhos**) Zho is one of several spelling for a Tibetan animal bred from yaks and cattle. The other forms are **dso, dzo** and **zo,** and it's worth remembering all of them. Zho scores 15 points.

zigzag *n* (*pl* **-s**) line or course having sharp turns in alternating directions ▸ *v* (**-zags, -zagging, -zagged**) move in a zigzag ▸ *adj* formed in or proceeding in a zigzag
zigzagged *v* ▷ **zigzag**
zigzagging *v* ▷ **zigzag**
zigzags *n, v* ▷ **zigzag**
zinc *n* (*pl* **-s**) (CHEM) bluish-white metallic element used in alloys and to coat metal
zincs *n* ▷ **zinc**
zing *n* (*pl* **-s**) (*Informal*) quality in something that makes it lively or interesting
zings *n* ▷ **zing**
zip *n* (*pl* **-s**) fastener with two rows of teeth that are closed or opened by a small clip pulled between them ▸ *v* (**-s, -pping, -pped**) fasten with a zip
zipped *v* ▷ **zip**
zipping *v* ▷ **zip**
zips *n, v* ▷ **zip**
zircon *n* (*pl* **-s**) mineral used as a gemstone and in industry
zirconium *n* (*pl* **-s**) (CHEM) greyish-white metallic element that is resistant to corrosion
zirconiums *n* ▷ **zirconium**
zircons *n* ▷ **zircon**

zit *n* (**zits**). A zit is a pimple. This nasty little word can be very useful during a game, especially when there's not much space left on the board. Zit scores 12 points.

zither *n* (*pl* **-s**) musical instrument consisting of strings stretched over a flat box and plucked to produce musical notes
zithers *n* ▷ **zither**

zo *n* (**zos**). Zo is one of several spelling for a Tibetan animal bred from yaks and cattle. The other forms are **dso, dzo** and **zho,** and it's worth remembering all of them. If someone plays zo and you have a D, remember that you can form dzo from it. Zo is the only two-letter word beginning with Z, and scores 11 points.

zodiac *n* (*pl* **-s**) imaginary belt in the sky within which the sun, moon, and planets appear to move, divided into twelve equal areas, called signs of the zodiac, each named after a constellation
zodiacs *n* ▷ **zodiac**
zombi *n* ▷ **zombie**
zombie, zombi *n* (*pl* **-s**) person who appears to be lifeless, apathetic, or totally lacking in independent judgment
zombies *n* ▷ **zombie**
zombis *n* ▷ **zombie**
zonal *adj* ▷ **zone**
zone *n* (*pl* **-s**) area with particular features or properties ▸ *v* (**-nes, -ning, -ned**) divide into zones > **zonal** *adj*
zoned *v* ▷ **zone**
zones *n, v* ▷ **zone**
zoning *v* ▷ **zone**
zoo *n* (*pl* **-s**) place where live animals are kept for show
zoological *adj* ▷ **zoology**
zoologies *n* ▷ **zoology**
zoologist *n* ▷ **zoology**
zoologists *n* ▷ **zoology**
zoology *n* (*pl* **-gies**) study of animals > **zoologist** *n* (*pl* **-s**) > **zoological** *adj*
zoom *v* (**-s, -ing, -ed**) move or rise very rapidly
zoomed *v* ▷ **zoom**
zooming *v* ▷ **zoom**
zooms *v* ▷ **zoom**
zoos *n* ▷ **zoo**

zootaxy *n* (**zootaxies**). Zootaxy is the scientific classification of animals. If you're lucky enough to have the letters for this word, you can earn a 50-point bonus by using all of your tiles to form it. Zootaxy scores 26 points.

zucchini [zoo-**keen**-ee] *n* (*pl* **-ni, -nis**) (US & AUST) courgette
zucchinis *n* ▷ **zucchini**
zulu *n* (*pl* **-s**) member of a tall Black people of southern Africa
zulus *n* ▷ **zulu**
zygote *n* (*pl* **-s**) fertilized egg cell
zygotes *n* ▷ **zygote**

NOTES

NOTES

NOTES

NOTES

NOTES